The ALMANAC *of* AMERICAN POLITICS

The Senators, the Representatives —
their records, states and districts. *1974*

Michael Barone
Grant Ujifusa
Douglas Matthews

GAMBIT
Boston

ACKNOWLEDGMENTS

The authors gratefully acknowledge the assistance of Pat Biondo, Carolyn Carr, Patricia Chock, Rob de Meyer, Stephen and Susan Diamond, Alan C. Feuer, Patricia Francois, Albert Frank III, Fred Frank, Kathy Alessandro Frank, Gail Glick, John and Ruth Glover, Cathy Healy, Dan Healy, Susan Healy, Kate Heath, Debby Hellerstein, Linda Katz, Pamala Koch, Bonnie Olasky, Eric Reuther, Cynthia Shaler, Janet Slavin, Richard Sorensen, Beth Tondreau, Sarah Trott, Tom and Mary Ujifusa, and Sue Wymelenberg.

The authors also thank the people at Inforonics, Inc., who applied their Text Processing System to the composition of the *Almanac*: Nancy Brown, Larry Buckland, Paul Cesario, Joe Dupre, Miriam Johnson, Robert Nerker, Stephen Redmond, and Candy Verhulst; at Cambridge Editorial & Production Service: Sid and Ann Seamans; and to the people at Gambit, who have endured more than publishers should from anxious authors: Gary Cooper, Jill Danzig, Craig Richardson, Morgan Smith, Lovell Thompson, and Norman Wells. We further want to acknowledge Martha Ayres, Al Bachand and The Colonial Press, and Bob Wallingford for their help. Photo credits belong to Dev O'Neill.

Special thanks go to Kathy Glover Ujifusa, Rob and Scheine Lacy, Stewart Mott, and Tim Horan.

None of these people should be held responsible for the errors of fact and judgement contained in the book.

CONTENTS

90986

This book is dedicated to the people of the United States of America.

INTRODUCTION—THE SECOND TIME AROUND

This is the second biennial edition of a single-volume guide to national elections and politics. It goes to press when the public is more profoundly disillusioned with American politics and politicians than at any time since Gallup started polling, but also when the potential for political change and renewal is greater than at any point since the early days of the New Deal. We hope that the new *Almanac* can contribute to that change and renewal.

A plethora of politically significant events has occurred since the appearance of first *Almanac* two years ago. Among them:

—Sam Ervin has become a household word (see North Carolina).

—Various Europeans, the Japanese, and the Arabs seem to prefer the solidity of gold to glut of American paper money funneled abroad to wage a disastrous war and to buy crude oil and color television sets.

—The flip side of Game Plan politics has come out in the White House Enemies List (see Michigan 1).

—Several dynamic women have been elected to Congress, a harbinger of things to come (see, for example, California 37, Colorado 1, and New York 16).

—The idea has begun to perculate in Congress that for the public good, there is perhaps a better way to finance campaigns than having politicians mortgage their attention, energy, and influence to individual fatcats and special interest groups.

—The House of Representatives voted to end the bombing of Cambodia.

—Almost every member of Congress has developed a new self-consciousness of his special responsibilities during this period of constitutional crisis, one that may well last until November 1976; there are even signs of a present willingness to shelve partisan and parochial interests to help see the country through.

But nothing illustrates the potential for change more than the recent careers of Richard M. Nixon and Spiro T. Agnew. When the first edition of the the *Almanac* appeared in December 1971, it looked like Nixon might have trouble winning reelection, and it appeared almost certain that the Democrats would nominate Sen. Edmund Muskie of Maine to oppose him. Vice President Agnew seemed firmly ensconced in the hearts of a large number of his countrymen as the foremost apostle of law and order and the scourge of effete liberal snobs.

No one was sure then—least of all, it seems, the people running the Committee to Reelect the President—that the Nixon-Agnew ticket would be returned to office by a record margin over George McGovern and Sargent Shriver. And no one foresaw the disasters that would befall our President and Vice President only a few months later.

Just as this is written, Vice President Agnew has resigned his office and pleaded guilty to income tax evasion–a development that came too late to be reflected in the Political Background sections of the 1974 *Almanac*. President Nixon has nominated Gerald Ford as Agnew's successor, and now it is the duty of the 535 men and women who make up the Congress to decide whether he will be our next Vice President—and, quite possibly, our next President.

For Richard Nixon, less than twelve months after his record victory, finds himself in more trouble than any President since Andrew Johnson. The breaking open of the Watergate scandal plunged his ratings in the polls from record highs to record lows. Now serious commentators are talking about impeachment of the President. And public attention again must focus on the 535 men and women who alone have the power to impeach and remove from office the most powerful Chief Executive in our history.

Lately, observers have downgraded the Congress to the status of a moribund institution, all too ready to hand over whatever is left of its powers to the Executive Branch. But the possibility of impeachment and the power to approve or disapprove a Vice Presidential nomination show how great the powers of Congress can be, and how much can hinge on the politics, the beliefs, and the idiosyncracies of 535 people. Even more important, talk of impeachment shows how important the individual voter still is, regardless of how unimportant he or she may feel, for more than a few members of Congress owe their office to a pitifully small number of votes. Many, like George McGovern or Carl Albert, were first elected by less than 1,000 votes. So however disillusioned the American people may be with the politicians of our time, they retain the periodic right and power to keep in office the 535 men and women described and analyzed in the *Almanac*—and the power to throw them out.

To exercise their political prerogatives intelligently, people need information. That belief is the basic justification for chopping down the trees necessary to produce the *Almanac*. Moreover, we are impelled by the notion (perhaps a vain one) that the politics of the American nation is a colossally entertaining spectator sport. In these days of zone defenses and running backs, politics is probably more entertaining than professional football, assuming one knows the basic purposes of the politicians involved and the rules of the game. So we have come to think of the *Almanac* as a rough political equivalent of the *Baseball Encyclopedia,* or the *Field Guide to the Birds,* or the *Consumer's Report Buying Guide,* or even the *Guinness Book of World Records.*

From those with a professional interest in politics, the response to the first *Almanac* was gratifying. But we still want to judge our efforts by the extent to which we can turn on and tune in the American people to the spectacle, excitement, and the grave importance of national politics. As we said two years ago, we hope our vision continues to improve with practice.

So much for ultimate purposes. What about the nuts and bolts of the enterprise? The *Almanac* attempts to set forth what each Congressman and each Senator is up to and all about. To do this, it is necessary to understand something of the politics of every state and each of the 435 congressional districts, plus the District of Columbia, which may get home rule and full-fledged congressional representation by 1974 (see the first item in the Appendix). If we have done our job well, a flip through the pages of the *Almanac* is the best way to understand what we have produced. Nevertheless, some background information about the book is necessary.

I. THE LEGISLATOR

This section tries to help you develop an insight into the politician's background, position, ideology, and voting record. It is composed of the following five parts.

A. Biography and Career

Here, the following items of data are provided: date first elected; when seat is up (for Senators); date and place of birth; residence; educational and military background; family and children; religion. Also listed is a brief outline of the legislator's career and his or her Washington and home office addresses and telephone numbers, along with the name of his or her administrative assistant.

B. Committees

Lawyers and pollsters know that the power to shape the question is, to a considerable extent, the power to determine the answer. Congressional committees, as they hammer out the bills that Congress at large passes or rejects, do just that. Although bills in most cases may be amended on the floor, the version that emerges from committee remains the point of departure. Moreover, there remains a reluctance among Senators and Congressmen to alienate powerful committee and subcommittee chairmen by voting against their wishes any more than necessary, either in the smaller units or on the floor. In the words of the late House Speaker Sam Rayburn, "To get along, you have to go along."

Committee chambers, then, are literally the back rooms in which the decisions of Congress are shaped. So crucial are they to the real effectiveness of a legislator—particularly a Congressman —that it might be more useful to think of your vote as electing somebody to a committee rather than to the Congress at large.

The entire workings of the committee system have lately come under attack and scrutiny, and steps have been taken in the direction of loosening the hold that more senior members of Congress have on the entire committee system, from the basic power assignments to the holding of chairmanships. In an important but little-heralded move of 1973, the House organized and funded a select committee, chaired by Richard Bolling (see Missouri 5), to examine the entire committee set-up and make recommendations for its improvement. It remains to be seen what will emerge from the effort, but at least a hard look at the committee system is being taken under the aegis of a man who has been critical of traditional methods of doing things on the Hill.

A number of specific reforms in the system were also instituted in early 1973. In order to understand them, it is useful to review the mechanics of the arrangement.

First of all, some committee assignments are more desirable than others, either objectively because they have more power, or subjectively because one or the other happens to fit the preferences of a certain member. Parceling out assignments, then, is a delicate and highly political task. Technically, committee assignments are made by the entire Senate and House. In fact, they are determined by each party's Committee on Committes, which are dominated by more senior and orthodox members. The major criticism of the system has not revolved so much around the problem of allocating committee choices as around the so-called seniority system and the role it plays in the choice of the powerful committee and subcommittee chairmen.

These committee leadership posts are prized in proportion to their power, which can be great indeed. Chairmen schedule meetings at opportune or inopportune times and draw up agendas that may or may not have one's pet bill listed. They decide which bills deserve hearings—a valuable source of pubilicity for politicians who, after the phrase of the late Earl Long, love publicity like pigs love slop. On another level, the chairmen have a say in who gets to go on the juicy junkets, and they generally do the staff hiring—an important source of patronage and power.

All committee and subcommittee chairmanships go to members of the party that holds a majority in each chamber. Currently, therefore, all committee chairmen are Democrats, both in the House and in the Senate, which makes reforms among the Democrats the more important.

Hitherto, the sole criterion for choosing a committee chairman has been "seniority," time served on that committee. The results of this policy—which was solely a matter of tradition—have been to make of Congress a gerontocracy, where the old hum the tune, and the young—that is, those in their 40s, 50s, and even 60s—dance and undergo various rites of passage. In early 1973, at long last, the House Democratic Caucus instituted a new rule that all committee chairmen may now be elected—or defeated—by majority vote of the full party caucus. Although no chairmen was in fact ousted, notice has been served that seniority, while it will continue as an important criterion of leadership, will not be binding.

The other important set of reforms instituted in 1973 concerned the opening up of secret committee sessions. Now, in the House, all committee hearings are open unless they deal with national security or personal character; and other committee meetings and drafting sessions can be closed only by majority vote of the committee members. In the Senate, a weaker reform proposal was passed allowing each committee to set its own rules.

So, although it's too early to say how much, things are changing in the much criticized area of committees. In the committee section, we have listed each member's committee assignments and in parenthesis his seniority on the committee. Seniority is calculated solely with reference to other members of the same party. For Democrats, the first-ranking member is the chairman, the second one is "2nd," and so on. (This is a slight variation from the Congress' own method, which denominates the second man as "ranking member," but we feel our way is clearer to those unfamiliar with these matters.) For the Republicans, the most senior member is called the ranking member, the next one "2nd," and so on. In the appendix we have indicated the full membership of all standing committees and subcommittees.

The following is a list of the committees of both branches, with a short description of the types of bills each considers. Jurisdictional boundaries are often fuzzy, so there will be occasional overlapping. More complete descriptions of important committees' ways of doing business are provided in the Political Background sections under the districts of committee chairmen and, sometimes, under those of ranking minority members.

Standing Committees of the Senate

Aeronautical and Space Sciences—aerospace activities and science (except military), NASA.

Agriculture and Forestry—agriculture, meat inspection, forestry, nutrition and antihunger programs, rural electrification.

Appropriations—all federal appropriations. Since the Appropriations Committee passes on federal spending for all departments and agencies, its subcommittees with jurisdiction over a given segment of the federal government are often as important in making policy as the standing committee with power over the same agency.

Armed Services—defense, naval petroleum reserves.

Banking, Housing, and Urban Affairs—banking and currency, public and private housing, controls or prices, of commodities, rents, and services, financial aid to industry except when under another committee's jurisdiction.

Commerce—interstate and foreign commerce, including transportation (railroads, buses, trucks, gas pipelines), communications (telephone, telegraph, radio, television), civil aeronautics, merchant marine and navigation, Coast Guard, fisheries and wildlife, Bureau of Standards.

District of Columbia—all lawmaking for the District of Columbia except appropriations.

Finance—taxation, including customs, tariffs, and import quotas, reciprocal trade agreements, social security, veterans' pensions and compensation.

Foreign Relations—foreign affairs, including consideration of all treaties.

Government Operations—structure of the federal government, including reorganizations, the budgetary process, and intergovernmental relations. The main function of the committee and its subcommittees is to investigate the efficiency of federal agencies; this has on occasion involved searing scrutiny of federal policies and operations in varied areas, as the decision surrounding the TFX, corruption in labor unions, and drug prices.

Interior and Insular Affairs—public lands and the minerals thereon, forest reserves and national parks, island possessions of the U.S., irrigation and reclamation, mining, oil conservation, Indians.

Judiciary—the federal judiciary and prison system, constitutional amendments and revision of statutes, antitrust, immigration and naturalization, bankruptcy, espionage, counterfeit, patent, copyright, and trademark law.

Labor and Public Welfare—education, labor, including the various antipoverty programs.

Post Office and Civil Service—civil service and post office, Census Bureau, National Archives.

Public Works—rivers and harbors, bridges and dams, navigation (on internal waterways) and flood control, water power, water pollution, federal buildings, highways.

Rules and Administration—credentials and election of Senators, corrupt practices, internal housekeeping matters.

The Select Committees on Small Business, Aging, and Nutrition and Human Needs do not report legislation; they simply study the problems in their jurisdiction and make reports of their findings to the Senate and appropriate standing committees.

Standing Committees of the House

Agriculture—agriculture, meat inspection, forestry, nutrition and antihunger programs, rural electrification.

Appropriations—all federal appropriations. Since the Appropriations Committee passes on federal spending for all departments and agencies, its subcommittees with jurisdiction over a given segment of the federal government are often as important in making policy as the standing committee with power over the same agency.

Armed Services—defense, naval petroleum reserves.

Banking and Currency—banking and currency, public and private housing, controls of prices and commodities, rents and services, and financial aid to industry except when under another committee's jurisdiction.

District of Columbia—all lawmaking for the District of Columbia except for appropriations.

Education and Labor—education, labor, welfare, including the various antipoverty programs.

Foreign Affairs—foreign affairs. The House Committee on Foreign Affairs is generally considered less important than the Senate Committee on Foreign Relations because, *inter alia,* the Senate but not the House has the responsibility of approving or disapproving treaties and appointments to ambassadorships and other foreign-policy posts.

Government Operations—structure of the federal government, including reorganizations and the budgetary process, and intergovernmental relations. The main function of the committee and its subcommittees is to investigate the efficiency of federal agencies; this can involve close scrutiny of federal policies and operations in many areas. Until recently the House Committee (in contrast to its Senate counterpart) has been considered moribund.

House Administration—internal housekeeping matters.

Interior and Insular Affairs—public lands and the minerals thereon, forest reserves and national parks, island possessions of the U.S., irrigation and reclamation, mining, oil conservation, Indians.

Internal Security—legislation and investigations pertaining to communists and other subversives. Formerly the House Un-American Affairs Committee (HUAC), this body has been attacked by House liberals for reporting out precious little legislation and for conducting McCarthy-like investigations. The liberals, however, have been unsuccessful in trying to cut its appropriations or rescind its status as a standing committee.

Interstate and Foreign Commerce—interstate and foreign commerce, including transportation (railroads, buses, trucks, gas pipelines), communications (telephone, telegraph, radio, television), civil aeronautics, securities and power regulation, railroad labor and retirement, inland waterways, public health.

Judiciary—federal judiciary and prison system, constitutional amendments and revision of statutes, antitrust, immigration and naturalization, bankruptcy, espionage, counterfeit, patent, copyright, and trademark law.

Merchant Marine and Fisheries—merchant marine, navigation, water-borne common carriers except those under the jurisdiction of the Interstate Commerce Commission, Coast Guard, fisheries, and wildlife.

Post Office and Civil Service—civil service and Post Office, Census Bureau, National Archives.

Public Works—rivers and harbors, bridges and dams, navigation (on internal waterways) and flood control, water power, water pollution, federal buildings, highways.

Rules—conduct of House business. The Rules Committee is responsible for setting a "rule" for each bill that comes before the entire House. The "rule" sets the terms of debate and amendment; accordingly a Rules Committee hostile to a particular piece of legislation can often prevent its passage by granting an unfavorable "rule" or, on occasion, no "rule" at all. This power was used with great skill by ultraconservative Chairman Howard W. Smith of Virginia until his defeat in a Democratic primary in 1966.

Science and Astronautics—NASA, National Science Foundation, space research and development, and science scholarships.

Ways and Means—taxation, including customs, tariffs, and import quotas, reciprocal trade agreements, Social Security. The constitutional provision requiring all revenue bills to originate in the House and the canny leadership of Ways and Means Chairman (since 1958) Wilbur Mills have made Ways and Means one of the most important committees in either legislative branch. The Democratic members of Ways and Means also determine committee assignments for all House Democrats.

Joint Committees are made up of members from both houses, with the chairmanship rotating between senior House and Senate members of the majority party (since 1954, the Democrats). The Joint Committees on Congressional Operations, Defense Production, the Library, Navaho-Hopi Indian administration, Printing, and Reduction of Federal Expenditures handle their indicated subject matter without appreciable controversy. The Joint Committee on Internal Revenue Taxation is made up of members of the House Ways and Means and the Senate Finance committees: since these bodies do the actual legislating on tax matters, we also pass over this Joint Committee. That leaves two Joint Committees worthy of special attention.

Joint Committee on Atomic Energy—all matters relating to atomic energy and the Atomic Energy Commission. This committee by common consent has a very high degree of expertise in its field, and it is allowed access to internal (and often classified) information in a manner highly unusual for a congressional committee. It works very closely with the AEC.

Joint Economic Committee—set up under the Full Employment Act of 1946, it reviews the Economic Report of the President and makes recommendations and studies concerning the national economy.

C. Group Ratings

You can tell a lot about a person from knowing who his friends and enemies are. Legislators are no exception, which is why we have compiled this section. The "rating groups," abbreviated ADA, ACA, COPE, and so forth, are all political interest groups of one kind or another. Some base their judgements on general ideology, liberal or conservative; others focus on the economic and political interests of the particular group they represent, such as farmers or small businessmen; still others are concerned with a single issue, such as environment or consumer protection. In most cases, the groups engage in various Washington lobbying activities for the causes they champion.

What they all have in common is sufficient interest in how Congressmen and Senators vote on certain issues to "grade" them on their performance. These ratings as a collection constitute an extremely informative legislative reportcard on each man in Congress. In terms of getting a fix on an unfamiliar legislator, a glance at this section (perhaps followed by a brief perusal of the "Key Votes" section which follows) is as fast and effective a way of getting a statistically valid shorthand composite of his ideology and concerns as we know. To aid quick comprehension, we have arranged our various groups in a rough spectrum—"liberals" on the left and "conservatives" on the right, with single-issue groups in the middle.

Each group has rated legislators by singling out a number of votes it deemed crucial. The legislator's "score" for the year is simply calculated by dividing the number of "correct" votes by the total number of votes chosen, ignoring absences. In some cases, the groups themselves publish the ratings as a percentage, and we have transcribed them directly; in others, only the "rights" and "wrongs" are indicated, in which case we have calculated the percentages ourselves with the permission of the group. Under certain groups, there are blanks for 1971. This is because not all of the groups issue ratings every year. Some do so only at the end of each full session of Congress, which lasts two years.

To interpret these ratings, of course, it is necessary to have a general idea of the groups, their orientation, and what issues and votes the ratings are based upon. Here, then, is a descriptive list of the rating groups and what they stand for. The "ORIENTATION" list is a partial and impressionistic listing derived from the votes chosen by the groups.

1) ADA—Americans for Democratic Action, 1424 16th St. NW, Washington, D.C. 20036, 202-265-5771.

ADA is synonomous with a certain brand of liberalism deemed at once too radical for conservatives and too conservative for radicals (although ADA credentials might be considered blue-chip references for the White House Enemies List). ADA activists include such figures as Allard Lowenstein, John Kenneth Galbraith, Arthur Schlesinger, Jr., and Minnesota's Donald Fraser. ADA members continue to push for New Dealish legislation and against rising defense spending and encroachments on civil liberties.

Orientation. FOR: Busing, $2 minimum wage, Rhodesia sanctions, easy federal voter registration, busting the Highway Trust Fund, no-fault auto insurance, gun control. AGAINST: B-1 bomber, Trident missile, Cambodia bombing, House Internal Security Committee funding, Subversive Activities Control Board funding.

2) COPE—AFL-CIO Committee on Political Education, 815 16th St. NW, Washington, D.C. 20006, 202-637-5000.

As the powerful political arm of the AFL-CIO, COPE keeps an alert eye on who is working for what it perceives to be the interests of the unionized working man.

Orientation. FOR: SST, Lockheed loans, day care, stronger meat inspection, no-fault auto insurance, easy federal voter registration.

AGAINST: Rehnquist and Butz nominations, filibusters, compulsory arbitration.

3) LWV—League of Women Voters, 1730 M Street, N.W., Washington, D.C. 20036, 202-296-1770.

The League of Women Voters needs little introduction to anyone with the mildest interest in politics. It has long been known as one of the most energetic, well-informed, and competent groups operating in the pursuit of better government.

Orientation. FOR: Foreign Aid, more OEO funding, busing, United Nations funding, busting the Highway Trust Fund, day care, D.C. home rule.

AGAINST: Strip mining, freedom-of-choice school plans, social welfare cuts.

4) Ripon—The Ripon Society, 509 C Street NE, Washington, D.C. 20002, 202-546-211.

Founded in 1962 by a group of youthful Republicans, the Ripon Society has developed into the main injector of progressivism into the GOP, having pumped for such notions as revenue sharing, the negative income tax, a new China policy, and the volunteer army. Once termed "juvenile delinquents" by John Mitchell, the organization continues its lively commentary on politics and does battle with the conservatives for the soul of the GOP.

According to the society, "the values underlying the Ripon ratings are intensely libertarian and opposed to the arbitrary exercise of power by government at any level or by extraordinarily powerful private institutions. This approach contrasts sharply with the bureaucratic liberalism of most Northern Democrats and the hostility towards individual liberties and free market mechanisms held by most Southern Democrats. It also constrasts with the excess statism now supported by much of the Republican right wing and the policies of economic cartelization and an excessively powerful executive that have unfortunately characterized the Nixon Administration despite its persistent limited government and free market rhetoric."

Orientation. FOR: Equal Rights Amendment, limiting war powers, busing, legal services for poor, farm subsidy limit, no-fault auto insurance, busting the Highway Trust Fund, equal time rule.

AGAINST: Subversive Activities Control Board, the draft, strip mining, SST.

5) NFU—National Farmers Union, 1012 14th Street NW, Washington, D.C. 20005, 202-628-9774.

NFU represents the interest of small- to medium-sized farmers. Its rating vote selections are about equally divided between farm and nonfarm issues, and reflect a 1970s version of the organization's heritage of Midwestern agrarian populism.

Orientation. FOR: Rural development, price controls, cutting defense spending, day care, no-fault auto insurance, easy voter registration, stronger consumer protection agency.

AGAINST: SST, cattle hide export control, Indochina War, Butz nomination.

6) LCV—League of Conservation Voters, 324 C Street SE, Washington, D.C. 20003, 202-547-7200.

LCV is a campaign committee that solicits money from those interested in conservation issues and channels it to candidates they consider friends of the environment.

Orientation. FOR: Family planning, busting Highway Trust Fund, campaign financing disclosure, clean water and air funds, wilderness areas, strict auto pollution standards, sea mammal protection.

AGAINST: SST, pesticide spraying, Amchitka nuclear blast, Butz nomination, Project Sanguine, timbering in national forests, canal construction, Dickey Dam.

7) CFA—Consumer Federation of America, 1012 14th Street NW, Washington, D.C. 20005, 202-737-3732.

CFA is a group spawned in the mid-1960s as a pro-consumer counterweight to various business-oriented lobbies felt to be all too successful in their efforts to load the market odds. The group presses for various pro-consumer activities and attempts to perform a clearinghouse function for various consumer allies.

Orientation. FOR: independent consumer agency, product safety, public television money, legal services, no-fault auto insurance, meat inspection, strict gas pipeline standards.

AGAINST: SST, newspaper antitrust exemption, high interest charges.

8) NAB—National Association of Businessmen, Inc., 1000 Connecticut Avenue NW, Washington, D.C. 20036, 202-296-5773.

Each year, NAB presents to high-NAB-vote-scoring members of Congress a small golden bulldog, its "Watchdog of the Treasury Award," a symbol that accurately summarizes the philosophy reflected in its ratings. NAB has been preaching against the evils of inflationary government practices for many years. Its "economy voting record" measures a legislator's espousal of economy in government as reflected in his votes against funding for many types of legislation involving spending, which NAB feels often has less long-run beneficial effects than would cuts in spending.

Orientation. FOR: spending ceiling, farm subsidy limit, cuts in a variety of programs, from
      military spending to public works to day care.
      AGAINST: funding increases for a wide variety of causes, from congressional
      staffing to school desegregation.

9) NSI—National Security Index of the American Security Council, 1101 17th Street NW, Washington, D.C. 20036, 202-296-4587.

Founded in 1955, the Council feels that American security is best served by vigorous support for anti-Communist countries around the world and continued large financial outlays for the maintenance and development of large weapons systems. The Council enjoys the support of a number of individuals prominent in the military and in business, as well as from private companies.

In 1972, the Council instituted an interesting innovation in its rating procedure. Instead of rating the rightness or wrongness of a vote on the basis of organizational policy, the group undertook to compile a rating based on "a comparison of key national security votes with majority public opinion. "This complex match was achieved by a combination of unspecified relative weights of a poll of 56,282 opinion-leader-members of the Council's National Advisory Board, a mail poll of 95,504 members of various leadership lists, including "Who's Who" directories, and an Opinion Research Corporation study with a scientifically selected sample of voting-age American. Other poll results were also included in the analysis, and "where no poll was available to clearly establish public opinion on a key vote, the rating on that vote was determined by the votes of members of Congress who had consistently voted with public opinion on other issues."

The results show a complex of attitudes on the part of the American public that is remarkably similar to those one would expect to be held by principals of an organization such as the Council.

Orientation. FOR: House Internal Security Committee, B-1 bomber, Trident missile, nuclear
      carrier, Subversive Activities Control Board, ABM, aid to South Korea and
      Taiwan.
      AGAINST: cutting defense budget, Pentagon picketing right, Pentagon Papers
      revelation, ending Indochina war activities, European troop reduction.

10) ACA—Americans for Constitutional Action, 955 L'Enfant Plaza North SW, Suite 1000, Washington, D.C. 20024, 202-484-5525.

ACA is "firmly convinced that if a significant number of dedicated and determined constitutional conservatives are elected to the Congress of the United States they will retard, and eventually reverse, the current massive movement of our Nation into Socialism and a regimented society," and rates legislators accordingly. ACA describes its rating system as being for individual rights, sound money, fiscal integrity, the private market, local self-government, and strengthening of national sovereignity, while being against group morality, a socialized economy, inflation, price controls, central-government intervention in local affairs, coercion of individuals through government regulation, and any surrender of control of foreign or domestic affairs to any other nation or to any international organization.

Orientation. For: F-14 fighter, B-1 bomber, nuclear carrier, military aid abroad, lower debt ceiling,
      freedom-of-choice desegregation plans.
      AGAINST: Busing, no-fault insurance, campaign subsidies, farm subsidy limits,
      Indochina withdrawal, public service employment, Lockheed loan, United
      Nations contribution, 18-year-old vote.

D. Key Votes

The question this section attempts to answer for you is which side of an important or revealing issue a legislator chose when presented with a clear choice for or against it. In other words, what did he or she do when the chips were down?

It is, of course, a matter of considerable responsibility—and temerity—to condense the substance of a vote into a little headline squib as we have done and then to translate a "yea" or "nay" on the vote into a "for" or "against" what is sometimes a broader issue. Almost every vote on the floor of either branch reflects a complicated tug-of-war among some combination of the myriad interests trying to pry a goodie out of Congress. The process of condensing months of debate, amendment, pressure, persuasion, and compromise into a 15-letter description tends to lose detail, to say the least.

Nor are oversimplification and author prejudice the only sources of possible distortion. How a Congressman or Senator votes on the floor is only one of the many components of his complex and endless job. Unfortunately, the others tend to be nonquantifiable or invisible. Indeed, a recorded vote may be positively misleading. Many are the stories of a legislator eviscerating some bill in the privacy (now disappearing) of committee chambers and then trumpeting glowing support for the subsequently hollow measure in public. A legislator might also promise some lobbyist his vote on an issue if the vote is close, abstain on the first role call, and then vote the opposite way if the bill's fate does not hinge on a few votes. Luckily these craven practices are the exception rather than the rule. But in cases like them, the only comfort to the concerned citizen is belief in eternal damnation.

Despite these and other imperfections, a legislator's voting record remains the best single objective indicator of his position on a specific issue and of his general ideological persuasion. And most of the headlines in the Key Votes section are straightforward, noninterpretive descriptions of the issue. You are either for or against gun control, revenue sharing, or the Equal Rights Amendment. In other cases, we feel justified in generalizing a legislator's position on a broad issue from a relatively narrow but carefully selected vote.

A good example of the latter is Senate Vote 13, labeled "consumer protection." Every politician is going to try to wrap himself in the flag of consumerism. What sane politician is going to describe himself as against consumer protection? This is why the Consumer Product Act of 1972 passed overwhelmingly. But before it did, several watering-down amendments were considered. One of them, which we have chosen for vote 13, would have deleted the provisions of the act which established criminal penalties for violation of regulations and standards for consumer products which the bill established. Perhaps there are good reasons for voting for such a provision, but they are not, in our opinion, pro-consumer reasons. Therefore, we feel that those who voted to delete the protection provisions voted against consumer protection.

To summarize our methodology, we have tried to choose closely contested, revealing, key votes on important and illustrative issues of 1971, 1972, and 1973 that demonstrate what decision a legislator made when the chips were down. And we have tried to present these choices in a convenient shorthand that minimizes the distortion of condensation.

Three technical points: first, the FOR and AGAINST notation we have adopted conveys the legislator's relationship to the basic concept of the bill. Depending on how the legislation is phrased, he can be for the bill and against the concept or vice-versa. For example, a "yes" vote on House vote *2, a strip mining measure, is a vote *against* strip mining, so our notation for this "yes" vote is AGAINST. Second, the notation NE means simply that the Senator or Congressman was not yet elected when the vote was taken. A third detail is our interpretation of paired votes. When a legislator wants to vote on a bill but finds it inconvenient or impossible to attend the vote, he will sometimes call up a colleague taking an opposite position and ask him to refrain from voting. Thus they form a "pair" with each on record, but with zero net result. These pairs are recorded, but only some specify which way each man stood on the issue. In the case of specified pairs, we have listed the result just like a regular "for" or "against" vote. When the pairs are unspecified, we have listed the legislators "absent."

Here are the vital statistics on and a brief explanation of each of the 21 Senate and 15 House key votes:

SENATE

1) Busing—Use of federal funds to force school districts to transport students to different schools if necessary to achieve racial balance, S 659, Omnibus Education Amendments of 1972, Congressional Record Vote 61, February 24, 1972.

This was an anti-busing amendment barring federal courts from ordering busing of schoolchildren on the basis of race, color, religion, or national origin, and forbidding the withholding of federal aid to induce the implementation of busing plans. Amendment passed, 43–40. Yea = AGAINST busing, Nay = FOR busing.

2) Alas P-Line—Construction of oil pipeline across Alaska, S 1081, Alaska Pipeline, Congressional Record Vote 297, July 17, 1973.

This was the Gravel Amendment to bar judicial review of the environmental aspects of the pipeline and to direct the Secretary of the Interior to issue permits for the construction of the project—the major environmental Congressional confrontation of 1973, in the eyes of many. Despite vehement opposition by environmentalists, fear of dependency on foreign (i.e., Arab) oil was apparently the overshadowing consideration in the minds of many legislators. Passed, 49–48. Yea = FOR Alaska Pipeline, Nay = AGAINST Alaska Pipeline.

3) Gun Cntrl—Prohibition of sale or distribution of hand guns, S 2507, Hand Guns, Congressional Roll Call Vote 363, August 9, 1972.

This was a bill outlawing the sale and distribution of cheap domestically produced handguns, commonly known as "Saturday night specials." The bill passed 68–25. Yea = FOR gun control, Nay = AGAINST gun control.

4) Rehnquist—Supreme Court nomination confirmation, Exec Rept 92-16, December 10, 1971.

This was the vote on the confirmation of William H. Rehnquist as an Associate Justice of the Supreme Court. Rehnquist was known for his sun-belt conservative point of view. Confirmed, 68–26. Yea = FOR Rehnquist, Nay = AGAINST Rehnquist.

5) Pub TV $—Public television financing, HR 13918 Corporation for Public Broadcasting, Roll Call Vote 238, June 22, 1972.

This was an amendment that would have provided for a one-year rather than two-year authorization of appropriations for the Corporation for Public Broadcasting, thus keeping public television on a short financial leash. The amendment was rejected, 26–58. Although the amendment, technically, merely provided for a one-year rather than two-year authorization, we feel that a Senator's position on this amendment accurately reflects his attitude toward public television financing. Amendment rejected, 26–58. Yea = AGAINST public TV money, Nay = FOR public TV money.

6) EZ Votr Reg—Simplified national voter registration, S 2574, National Voter Registration Act, Congressional Record Vote 109, March 15, 1972.

The voter registration battles of the sixties in the South and elsewhere did not die with that decade. The proposed National Voter Registration Act would have established a nationwide voter registration by mail for all federal elections, thus enormously facilitating voter registration and encouraging further registration among now-unregistered potential voters, usually poor people. This was a vote on an amendment to table the bill. Motion to kill bill passed, 46–42. Later, after an attempted filibuster, the bill passed the Senate. Yea = AGAINST easy voter registration, Nay = FOR easy voter registration.

7) No-Fault—Automobile insurance reform, S 945, No-Fault Auto Insurance, Congressional Record Vote 358, August 8, 1972.

The necessity of litigating liabilities for small fender-benders provides much employment for attorneys, keeps the courts clogged, and keeps auto insurance rates substantially higher than they would be under a system of insurance providing compensation for injuries, regardless of who caused the accident (at least judging by the Massachusetts experience, where a new no-fault system has substantially lowered auto insurance rates). This was a motion to kill a bill that would have required nationwide adoption of the no-fault system. Motion to kill adopted, 49–46. Yea = AGAINST no-fault, Nay = FOR no-fault.

8) Sea Life Prot—Prohibition of killing marine mammals such as seals, S 2871, Marine Mammals, Congressional Record Vote 316, July 26, 1972.

A number of votes were taken on amendments that weakened the bill establishing a moratorium on the killing of most species of marine mammals, which passed, 88–2. The amendment chosen would have given the states exclusive authority to allow or prohibit such killing unless the Secretary of the Interior made an official determination that the species might be endangered, in which case federal law would apply. It was an obvious weakening of the bill, which probably would have prolonged the killing of such animals. Weakening amendment rejected, 26–63. Yea = AGAINST sea animal protection, Nay = FOR sea animal protection.

9) Campaign Subs—Public assumption of campaign expenditures, HR 10947, Rev Act of 1921, Congressional Record Vote 385, November 22, 1971.

One of the great eternal verities is that there is no such thing as free lunch. As a corollary, there is no such thing as a stringless campaign contribution, particularly when the amount reaches four or more figures. It pays to invest in politicians, or at least people seem to think it does. A politician's need of large amounts of money to get elected has led to a system where almost all nonindependendependently wealthy political figures must pawn a little piece of their souls to campaign contributors. This central fact, more than any other, is responsible for the dismal ethical tenor of public life in this country. One solution is public financing of legitimate candidates. This amendment was designed as a first step. It allowed each taxpayer to designate one dollar of his annual tax payment for a contribution to a campaign of an eligible presidential candidate, or to a public campaign fund to be shared by such candidates. Since the Republicans were afraid they wouldn't get as much money, and the Democrats thought they'd get more, the fors and againsts broke down largely by party. Nevertheless, there were some exceptions, and principle as well as party loyalty was at issue. Amendment adopted, 52–47. Yea = FOR campaign subsidies, Nay = AGAINST campaign subsidies.

10) Cmbodia Bmbg—Prohibition against funds being used to support combat activities in

Cambodia or Laos, HR 7447, Second Supplemental Appropriation Fiscal 1973, Congressional Record Vote 162, May 31, 1973.

This was one of the important votes leading up to the eventual August 15 cut-off date agreement. (See House Vote 6.) Prohibition adopted, 63–19. Yea = AGAINST Cambodia bombing, Nay = FOR Cambodia bombing.

11) Legal Srvices—Independent national legal Services corporation, S 3010, Equal Opportunity Amendments of 1972, Congressional Record Vote no.247, June 26, 1972.

The Office of Economic Opportunity has been a controversial entity ever since its establishment, and no agency within it has generated more debate than the Legal Services Program, whose aggressive litigation, often against state and local governments on behalf of the rights of indigents, has been a thorn in the side of a number of vested interests. Those who would like to see such aggressiveness continue proposed to insulate the program against local political pressure by transforming it into an independent national legal services coporation. This vote was on an amendment designed to block such a move. Amendment rejected, 37–46. Yea = AGAINST legal services, Nay = FOR legal services.

12) Rev Sharing—Direct payment of money to state and local governments, HR 14370, General Revenue Sharing, Congressional Record Vote 419, September 12, 1972.

This was the vote on the bill establishing a five-year program to share some $29.5 billion of federal revenues with state and local governments. (See House Vote 4.) Passed, 64–20. Yea = FOR revenue sharing, Nay = AGAINST revenue sharing.

13) Cnsumr Prot—Consumer protection, S 3419, Food, Drug and Consumer Product Act of 1972, Congressional Record Vote 234, June 21, 1972.

This was a vote on an amendment that would have deleted the provisions of the Consumer Product Act establishing criminal penalties for violation of regulations and standards established for consumer products by the bill. This amendment would have taken much of the bite out of the bill. Amendment rejected, 39–41. Yea = AGAINST consumer protection, Nay = FOR consumer protection.

14) Eq Rts Amend—Equal rights amendment, HJ Res 208, Equal Rights Amendment, Roll Call Vote 110, March 22, 1972.

This was the passage of the resolution containing a constitutional amendment guaranteeing equal rights of women. A two-thirds majority vote (62 in this case) was required since the motion was on a constitutional amendment. Motion passed, 84–8. Yea = FOR Equal Rights Amendment, Nay = AGAINST Equal Rights Amendment.

15) Tax Singls Less—Equalization of tax rates between single and married people, HR 10947, Revenue Act of 1971, Congressional Record Vote *386, November 22, 1971.

This was an amendment by Senator Packwood of Oregon that would have extended to single persons the tax rates applicable to married persons. Amendment rejected, 41–55. Yea = FOR taxing singles less, Nay = AGAINST taxing singles less.

16) Min Tax for Rich—Modification to increase existing minimum tax on income given preferential tax treatment, HR 14370, General Revenue Sharing, Congressional Roll Call 411, September 11, 1972.

A combination of the taxpayer revolt of the late 1960s and the revelation that 155 people making more than $200,000 had not paid any income tax in 1969 led to the imposition of the so-called minimum tax on those who would otherwise owe little or nothing. It is basically a tax on loopholes, that is, on what the Internal Revenue Code terms "income preferences." This was the vote on an amendment that would have modified the existing minimum tax on income given preferential tax treatment to reduce the exemption from $30,000 to $12,000 on income gained through stock options, bad debt reserves, depletion allowances and capital gains, and to increase the tax rate on such income. From the point of view of the authors of this book, people who take advantage of such provisions of the tax code are rich. Therefore we have denominated the vote on this amendment, which failed, 60–23, through a motion to table, Min Tax for Rich. Yea = AGAINST minimum tax for rich, Nay = FOR minimum tax for rich.

17) Euro Troop Rdctn—Reduction of armed forces in Europe, HR 11731, Defense Appropriations Fiscal 1972, Congressional Record Roll Call Vote 392, November 23, 1971.

One of the major causes of the epidemic of dollar devaluations is our military spending abroad. The amendment under consideration would have prohibited the use of funds after June 15, 1972, for the support of U.S. military personnel in Europe in excess of 250,000 men. The then-current strength was 300,000 men. Amendment rejected, 39–54. Yea = FOR European troop reduction, Nay = AGAINST European troop reduction.

18) Bust Hwy Trust—Optional use of highway trust funds for mass transit, S 502, Highway Authorization, Congressional Record Roll Call Vote 37, March 14, 1973.

This amendment gave states and cities the option of using $850 million a year from the Federal Urban Highway Trust Fund for buses and rail transit construction, as well as for highways, which use of the Fund was then limited to. Amendment adopted, 49–44. Yea = FOR busting Highway

Trust Fund, Nay = AGAINST busting Highway Trust Fund.

19) Maid Min Wage—Extension of minimum wage to domestic household employees, S 1861, Minimum Wage Increase, Congressional Record Vote 285, July 20, 1972.

This was an amendment deleting from the committee bill a provision that extended minimum wage coverage to approximately 1.2 million domestic household employees. Amendment rejected, 40–52. Yea = AGAINST maid minimum wage, Nay = FOR maid minimum wage.

20) Farm Sub Limit—Reduction of maximum per-farmer crop subsidy payments, HR 15690, Agriculture, Environment and Consumer Protection Appropriation Fiscal 1973, July 27, 1972.

Amendment to reduce from $55,000 to $20,000 the maximum amount a farmer could receive in annual crop subsidy payments. Amendment rejected, 23–46. Yea = FOR farm subsidy limits, Nay = AGAINST farm subsidy limits.

21) Highr Credt Chgs—Interest calculation practices, S 652, Unfair Billing Practices, Congressional Record Vote *144, April 27, 1972.

This was an amendment that prohibited credit arrangements where a consumer is charged interest against the original balance in his account, rather than the balance remaining after partial payment. No longer would creditors be able to charge you interest on $300 even after you had paid $299 of it. Amendment rejected, 38–38. (In the case of tie, an amendment fails.) Yea = AGAINST higher credit charges, Nay = FOR higher credit charges.

HOUSE

1) Busing—Use of federal funds to force school districts to transport students to different schools if necessary to achieve racial balance, S 659, Omnibus Education Amendments of 1972, Congressional Record Vote 66, March 8, 1972.

A number of anti-busing amendments passed the House in 1972. This particular vote was on a motion instructing those members of the House who were to work out in conference with their Senate counterparts any conflicts between the House-passed and Senate-passed legislation not to compromise on the already approved anti-busing busing amendments. These new bills, among other things, barred the use of federal funds for busing, barred federal pressure for use of state or local funds for busing, and postponed the effective date of court-ordered busing plans. This motion passed, 273–140. Yea = AGAINST busing, Nay = FOR busing.

2) Strip Mines—Surface mining of coal with concomitant destruction of vegetation and landscape, HR 6482, Congressional Record Vote 428, October 11, 1972.

This was a motion to suspend the rules and pass the bill which provided for federal regulation of strip coal mining and required reclamation of strip-mined land. Passed, 265–75. Yea = AGAINST strip mining, Nay = FOR strip mining.

3) Cut Mil $—Amendment to reduce Defense Department appropriations by 5% across the board, HR 16593, Defense Department Appropriation, Congressional Record Vote 367(T), September 14, 1972.

This amendment to the Defense Department appropriations bill would have simply and straightforwardly cut 5% from the money that the Defense Department expected to spend during fiscal 1973. Rejected by recorded teller vote, 98–256. Yea = FOR cutting military funds, Nay = AGAINST cutting military funds.

4) Rev Shrg—Revenue sharing with the states, HR 14370, Revenue Sharing with the States, Congressional Record Vote 220, June 22, 1972.

Motion to pass the bill providing direct and relatively string-free payments totaling $29.6 bill over five years to state and local governments for high-priority expenditures. Passed, 279–122. Yea = FOR revenue sharing, Nay = AGAINST revenue sharing.

5) Pub TV $—Funds for the support of the public television network, HR 13918, Public Broadcating Authorization, Congressional Record Vote 178(T) June 1, 1972.

This was a vote on an amendment that would have reduced the $65 million authorization for the fiscal 1973 Corporation for Public Broadcasting budget to $40 million. The bill would have also deleted the entire fiscal 1974 authorization. This bill was introduced during a time of substantial controversy over the role of public television, which according to many conservatives was placing too much emphasis on public affairs (translation: investigative political reporting and critical commentary). Conservatives also felt that news programs exhibited a liberal bias. The conflict surrounding public TV came to a head in this vote, in which those unhappy with public TV as it stood tried to shorten its financial leash considerably. Defeated by recorded teller vote, 166–183. Yea = AGAINST public TV money, Nay = FOR public TV money.

6) Cmbodia Bmbg—Funds to support the bombing of Cambodia, HR 7447, Second Supplemental Appropriations, Fiscal 1973, Congressional Record Vote 138(T), May 10, 1973.

There were a number of votes in the House and the Senate on the question of ending money for Cambodia bombing, a movement that ultimately culminated in the agreement to stop the bombing by August 15, 1973, unless Congress specifically authorized continued bombing. We've chosen a vote in the middle of the series, and before the bandwagon effect completely determined the issue. This was a mid-May amendment to prohibit the use of funds for financing any combat activities in Cambodia. Passed by recorded teller vote, 224–172. Yea = AGAINST Cambodia bombing, Nay = FOR Cambodia bombing.

7) Bust Hwy Trust—Amend the Highway Trust Fund so as to allow money to be used for mass transit, S 502, Federal-Aid Highway Program, Congressional Record Vote 110(T), April 19, 1972.

For several years, advocates of mass transit eyed the bulging Highway Trust Fund, where all of those gasoline tax dollars go, as a source of financing for inner-city rail development. For just as long, the oil, cement, and road construction lobbies fought to keep Trust Fund money limited exclusively to highways. This was a vote on an amendment to permit urban areas to use a modest $700 million per year from the Highway Trust Fund, from 1974 to 1976, for mass transit projects. A similar amendment passed later in the session, but this one failed by recorded teller vote, 190–215. Yea = FOR busting highway trust, Nay = AGAINST busting highway trust.

8) Farm Sub Lmt—Farm subsidies limit, HR 15690, Agriculture, Environment and Consumer Protection Appropriations, Fiscal 1973, Congressional Record Vote 246(T), June 29, 1972.

This was an amendment to the Department of Agriculture appropriations bill, which would reduce from $55,000 to $20,000 the amount an individual farmer could receive in annual crop subsidy payments, excluding sugar and wool. Rejected by recorded teller vote, 189–193. Even though there is already a farm subsidy limit, the necessity for condensation has led us to denominate this vote as for or against a limit. Yea = FOR farm subsidy limit, Nay = AGAINST farm subsidy limit.

9) School Prayr—School prayer, the permitting of voluntary prayer in public schools by the adoption of a constitutional amendment, HJ Res 191, School Prayer Amendment, Congressional Record Vote 366, November 8, 1971.

This was a vote on the adoption of the proposed constitutional amendment that would have made it constitutionally permissible for persons in public buildings (i.e., schools) to participate in voluntary prayer. Rejected, 240–163. Yea = FOR school prayer, Nay = AGAINST school prayer.

10) Cnsumr Prot—Consumer protection, HR 10835, Consumer Protection Agency, Congressional Record Vote 298(T), October 14, 1971.

Although the bill to establish a Consumer Protection Agency passed easily, 345–44, the House considered several amendments to weaken it. The most important of these would have severely limited the new consumer agency's authority to intervene on behalf of consumers in the proceedings of other federal agencies or in court suits, a provision that would have substantially weakened the practical powers of the agency. It was rejected by recorded teller vote, 149–240, with over 100 of those who voted for the agency also voting for this disemboweling amendment. Thus we have denominated votes on this amendment as follows: Yea = AGAINST consumer protection, Nay = FOR consumer protection.

11) Chkg Acct Intrst—Checking account interest, HR 6370, Interest Payments on Time and Savings Deposits, Congressional Record Vote 132 (T), May 9, 1973.

In 1972, citizens of Massachusetts were greeted with the pleaseant offer from certain savings banks of checking accounts that paid interest. This idea, which would eliminate consumer subsidization of banks' shareholders, but also upset the delicate balance of noncompetion between different types of lending institutions, caused a great consternation among banking interests, who promptly moved to prevent the practice from spreading. Those representatives who were in favor of allowing their constituents to receive interest on checking accounts had an opportunity to demonstrate this support by voting for an amendment to delete from a technical banking bill a provision that forbade mutual savings banks to maintain interest-bearing accounts. The amendment failed by recorded teller vote, 98–264. Yea = FOR checking account interest, Nay = AGAINST checking account interest.

12) End HISC (HUAC)—Abolition of House Internal Security Committee, H Res 308, Internal Security Committee Funding, Congressional Record Vote 56, March 22, 1973.

The House Internal Secutiry Committee, formerly known as the House Un-American Activities Committee, has long been a bugaboo of liberals who believe that it is little more than a paranoid witch-and-headline-hunting committee that does more harm to national security than good. Enemies of the committee attempted to strangle it to death by mobilizing support against the resolution, which provided $475,000 to fund the body during the first session of the 93rd Congress. The resolution passed, 289–101. Yea = AGAINST ending HISC, Nay = FOR ending HICS.

13) Nixon Sewer Veto—HR 3298, Rural Water and Sewer Grants Congressional Record Vote 82, April 10, 1973.

This was a motion to override President Nixon's April 5 veto of a bill requiring the Secretary of Agriculture to spend the entire amount appropriated by Congress each fiscal year for water and sewer grants in rural communities. A two-thirds vote was needed to override the veto. Although nominally concerned with ecology, this vote as much as any other in Congress represented a battle in the Congress' fight to regain control over the budget. The anti-veto vote failed, 225–189. (Because of the two-thirds requirement, 276 would have been needed to override the veto.) Yea = AGAINST Nixon sewer veto, Nay = FOR Nixon sewer veto.

14) Corp Cmpaign $—Corporate campaign contributions, HR 15276, Federal Election Campaign Act, Congressional Roll Call 396, October 2, 1972.

In 1971, the House passed a law prohibiting corporations and labor unions from making political contributions directly to candidates for President, Vice-President, the Senate or the House. Certain exceptions were made for voluntary contributions in the case of corporations that had no government contracts. Corporations and labor organizations having government contracts were not permitted to take advantage of these loopholes. This particular bill, which was reported out of the House Administration Committee without hearings, extended the protection of these loopholes to corporations and unions with government contracts, thus largely sabotaging the purposes of the Federal Election Campaign Act. In view of the controversy over questionable contributions to the 1972 campaign and the fact that this gutting amendment passed by a hair, we find this to be one of the most revealing votes of the session. Amendment passed, 249–124. (Since the vote was taken under suspension of the rules, a two-thirds majority, exactly 249, was needed.) Yea = FOR corporate campaign contributions, Nay = AGAINST corporate campaign contributions.

15) Pol $ Disclosr—Political contributions disclosure, HR 11060, Federal Election Campaign Practices Act, Congressional Record Vote 417 (T) November 30, 1971.

This was an amendment to eliminate provisions of the Federal Election Campaign Practices Act, which would have required that copies of reports of campaign contributions and expenditures be sent to the clerks of the federal district courts of the districts and states in which the election was being held, in addition to merely being filed in Washington. Such provision would have facilitated citizen research into candidates' financial contributions, and the record on this particular amendment is far more revealing than the lopsided passage of the actual act. Amendment passed, 229–155. Yea = AGAINST political finance disclosure, Nay = FOR political finance disclosure.

E. Election Results

A politician can do little without first getting elected. And in Congress one can't accomplish much without getting elected and reelected and reelected—thereby accumulating seniority. This section gives you the raw facts on how many votes each Senator and Representative received and how soundly (or narrowly) he beat his opponents. We have included not only general-election results, but also the results of primary elections. Most constituencies are considered one-party states or districts; winning the Democratic or Republican primary is thus tantamount to victory in the general election. In 1970 and 1972, for example, almost as many House incumbents were beaten in their party's primary as in the general election.

Also included are the 1972 and 1968 presidential election results for each state and congressional district. These give you a chance to measure the reaction of every constituency to the same set of choices. (In some cases we have calculated these figures ourselves, but in most instances we have relied on the excellent work of Dr. Pierre Purves and the National Republican Congressional Campaign Committee, to whom the entire political community owes a debt of gratitude.) Also worth noting is whether the incumbent member of Congress is running far ahead of his party (most are these days) or is coming in on other candidates' coattails. In the political background sections we draw heavily on these and other election statistics to analyze just how each member gets elected and reelected. But we have also provided the raw data, so you can draw your own conclusions.

Obviously, a Senator or a Congressman from a "safe" state or district will behave somewhat differently on Capitol Hill from one who must scramble to win reelection every two or six years. Traditionally, a "safe" seat has been defined as one in which the incumbent won 55% or more of the votes in the past election. Inspection of the figures will show that the vast majority of Congressmen and Senators have safe seats under this definition. In fact, in recent elections, particularly for the House, incumbency has proved to be an almost overwhelming advantage. However, sometimes a "safe" margin really only indicates that the incumbent has not received a serious challenge; he or she may in fact be vulnerable in the next general election or in the primary. We have tried to spot such situations and point them out in the political background sections.

You will find that many incumbents have constituencies which, on paper, would seem implacably hostile, yet they go on winning by comfortable margins year after year. Numerous Democratic members of Congress, for example, managed to win easily in 1972 in constituencies where George McGovern got clobbered, though their positions on issues differed little from

McGovern's. Probably the basic explanation for this phenomenon lies in the advertising benefits of the congressional franking privilege (see Arizona 2) and the good will built up by the ombudsman role of the Congressman (see Virginia 10). Most members of Congress make generous use of the frank—Congress' free mailing privilege—to send their constituents thousands of polls, pamphlets, and flags that have flown over the Capitol. It has been estimated that diligent and astute use of congressional frank allows a Congressman to send out about $100,000 worth of "nonpolitical" material—most with his name and face prominently displayed. Consequently, anyone running against an incumbent starts off at a huge disadvantage.

Most members of Congress also spend much of their time interceding with the federal and other bureaucracies on behalf of their constituents. Helping farmers with hassles at the Department of Agriculture, old people with delayed Social Security checks, veterans with the VA, and so on, not only lends an element of humanity to the massive government machine, it also produces grateful votes and easy reelection.

II. THE DISTRICT

Talking about a member of Congress without taking his or her state or district into account is like talking about Roosevelt without mentioning the Depression, or Lincoln without the Civil War. A vital dimension is lost. To understand the behavior of the political animal, you must understand his habitat. The political, economic, and social demography of the legislator's home base is his political reality principle.

A. Census Data

Along with voting figures, census results are perhaps the hardest kind of data available for analysis of states and congressional districts. Fortunately, the 1970 census results are in—and, with population growth slowing down, they remain relatively fresh. Figures presented here show the population of the state and district and the percentage of population change during the 1960s. The percentage of the population contained in Census Bureau-designated standard metropolitan statistical areas (SMSAs) and central cities is indicated—a fairly good indication of the urban-suburban-rural breakdown of the constituency. In addition, the number of House seats alloted to each state—its apportionment—has been determined by a mathematical formula from the census results.

Important changes can result. California, which elected 38 Congressmen in 1970, elected 43 in 1972; while New York was reduced from 41 to 39 and North Dakota from two to one. The 1972 *Almanac* was printed before most of the states were redistricted from the 1970 census returns, and accordingly we had to predict the likely result of the redistricting process. In some cases (e.g., Wisconsin) we were right on target; in others, especially where courts intervened (e.g., Illinois), we missed the mark. For 1974, this problem has just about vanished. For 1974, the district lines will be changed in at most two states. In California, it seems almost certain that a Special Masters' plan will be adopted that will straighten out the most grotesque of the boundaries, but will have significant effect on the incumbency of only a few Congressmen (see California). In Texas, minor tinkering, at most, is expected, with the exception of one district currently represented by a young Republican (see Texas 5).

The census data also includes the state's percentage of total U.S. population—a useful figure for comparison with its share of the tax burden and federal expenditures. We also show the state's median family income, and the percentage of families making under $3,000 and $15,000 per year. Here too is the category "median years education," which takes in all people 25 years old and older. The ranking of the states includes the 50 states only, and excludes the District of Columbia. Similar figures are included for each congressional district.

B. Federal Outlays and Tax Burden

Politicians like to boast about how much money they can bring into their states or districts. For example, the late Mendel River claimed, with apparent justice, that he was responsible, as Chairman of the House Armed Services Committee, for 35% of the payrolls in his district. He was reelected automatically, usually without opposition (see South Carolina 1). But politicians' claims are not always known for their reliability, and so we have attempted to ascertain just how much federal money goes into each state and district. Outlays listed usually remain fairly stable from year to year.

The 1972 share of the federal tax burden is derived from figures provided by the Tax Foundation, Inc., of New York, a nonprofit, nonpartisan agency whose credentials are beyond reproach. The fiscal 1972 shares of federal outlays were derived from the *Federal Outlays* volumes published annually by the Office of Economic Opportunity. This report shows more than 1,000 expenditure items by agency, program, and appropriation, broken down by individual counties and by cities with populations over 25,000.

Although a rough comparison of federal tax burden and outlay is permissible, a simple input-output relationship should not be forced upon the data. An overly simple reading here would violate many complex accounting problems involved in collating the data—some so complex that nobody in government seems to know how to explain them. An additional caveat: many congressional districts cut across the county lines within which the outlays are compiled. Prompted by a suggestion from Congressman William Hungate of Missouri, we have employed a new formula to allocate the county-calculated spending by congressional district. Each congressional district is credited with the same proportion of the county's spending as its proportion of the county's population—on the assumption that the benefits of federal spending in a single county will be pretty well evenly distributed throughout the county. In the case of counties and congressional districts which are parts of Census Bureau-defined SMSAs, we have credited each district with the same proportion of spending as its percentage of the total SMSA population. However, where SMSAs cross state lines, we have made these calculations only within one state and exclude the other.

Unfortunately, limitations on space have forced us to use the barbaric acronyms that pass for English in official Washington to indicate the outlays for each department. The key is as follows:

DOD	Department of Defense
AEC	Atomic Energy Commission
NASA	National Aeronautic and Space Administration
DOT	Department of Transportation
DOC	Department of Commerce
DOI	Department of the Interior
DOJ	Department of Justice
HEW	Department of Health, Education, and Welfare
HUD	Department of Housing and Urban Development
VA	Veterans' Administration
USDA	Department of Agriculture
CSC	Civil Service Commission
TD	Treasury Department

For each state, we have indicated the percentage of total U.S. outlays for each department and its rank order of money received. The "other" category includes money spent by all departments and agencies in the state or district not specifically listed. The Appendix contains the national summary of total federal outlays by department and agency for fiscal years 1970, 1971, and 1972. The percentages of the total given to the statistical sections of the states were computed from the totals for fiscal year 1972. The percentages were calculated from totals somewhat lower than the ones found in the Appendix because the outlays for our trust territories, territories, and other possessions were excluded.

Obviously, the lion's share of the money goes to the Defense Department. Accordingly, we have tried to indicate just how that money is spent. For each congressional district, we have listed the Major Defense Installations and Leading Defense contractors; also listed are NASA and AEC installations. CIA data we have found impossible to obtain; impressionistic evidence suggests that the Agency spends money through offices around the United States, as well as abroad, and at its large headquarters in Langley, Virginia. Under Leading Defense Contractors we list by congressional district all firms that received over $5 million in prime contract awards from DOD, NASA, and AEC for materials, services, and research and development for fiscal year 1972. The specific amount awarded to a particular firm in a given fiscal year is, we feel, an interesting piece of information in itself; the information takes on greater significance if it is remembered that these amounts remain remarkably stable from year to ficsal year.

Only DOD contractors doing military work are listed here. Those providing goods or services for the civilian functions of the Army Corps of Engineers, for example, are not included. There are also, of course, thousands of contractors doing less than $5 million worth of work for the military. For the names of these concerns, we refer you to the Controller's Office at the Pentagon. Following the amount awarded to the firm, we have given a brief description of what the money paid for. And in the Appendix, we have listed the names of the 100 largest defense contractors for fiscal 1972.

C. Economic Base

Throughout the nineteenth century and well into the twentieth, a major issue in American politics was the tariff, and an observer could predict how most members of Congress would vote by examining the economic underpinnings of their constituencies. Today, it is still so; the tariff remains a major, if unreported, issue, and Congressmen from textile-, or steel-, or shoe-producing districts are generally working for trade restrictions of some kind. But the basis of the economy of a state or district illuminates much more than its politicians' positions on trade restriction issues. It tells us something about the constituency's economic health, its prospects for growth, the jobs its citizens and voters hold, and the sources of wealth of its big money men.

In this section, we list the most important manufacturing, agricultural, mining, finance, insurance, and real estate activities of the state and district, along with tourism. The classifications are derived from the Census Bureau's Standard Industrial Code. Wholesaling, retailing, transportation, construction and other service industries are not included in the book. Such concerns are pretty much spread evenly across the nation; there is, for example, no constituency with a wildly disportionate share of the country's truck drivers. Also, any university or college with a student enrollment greater than 7,500 is listed here under "higher education."

Production activities are classified according to the SIC and the sectors indicated in the *SIC Manual*. An effort has been made to be as specific as possible and to indicate by "esp." cases where one type of production is important but not all-dominant. Production activity is ranked in importance according to the number of people employed. We chose to use this criterion—rather than value of plant, value added, total value of goods and services—since the employment figure seems most likely to be directly related to political activity and voting behavior. Thus the large number of people employed—or formerly employed—by a major business dependent on government contracts can be a major factor in a member of Congress' actions; witness the fact that Henry Jackson of Washington is sometimes referred to as the Senator from Boeing.

No state, let alone a congressional district, exists as an isolated unit in the complex economy of our nation. Geographical divisions are necessarily artificial, and never more so than in the metropolitan areas where so many congressional districts are situated. A person living in one congressional district may well work in another that is 20 miles away; and so we have compiled the economic-base sections in metropolitan districts according to individual formulas that seem most appropriate to the area.

D. Political Lineup

This is very simple—the Governor, the Senators, the House delegation, and the state legislatures, by party.

E. The Voters

You don't really know why candidates get elected until you know who votes—and why. We like to think of the American voter as a one-person civics class, gravely weighing the issues and measuring the mettle of competing candidates. But we know this is not so. Voters like to talk about being for the man, not the party; but there are still plenty who agree with the sentiment ascribed to Harry Truman: "I vote for the better man. He is the Democrat." And when people actually do "vote for the man," it is often just for the only man in the race they've heard of, which in congressional races usually means the incumbent.

Political scientists have shown that more often than not people inherit their political preferences, and that in most elections they remain the same. Accordingly, it makes sense to analyze the electorate by blocs. One source of differentiation is by economic status. We have provided an "employment profile," showing the breakdown in each district of the employed work force by white-collar, blue-collar, service, and farm jobs; in addition, we have shown the "median family income" of each state and district. This gives you a capsule picture of the economic and perhaps the social status of the constituency. But we should add that we do not regard economics as the basic determinant of political preference in America. For example, the richest congressional district in the country in terms of median family income, Maryland 8, voted several percentage points *more* Democratic than the nation as a whole in the 1968 and 1972 presidential elections. The poorest district, Kentucky 5, gave Richard Nixon substantially higher percentages than the nation in both those contests. The conventional wisdom that rich people vote Republican and poor people vote Democratic does not get you very close to an understanding of American political preferences.

To understand current trends the more useful way to divide the electorate, we think, is along ethnic lines. Our preference in this regard may be due to our consciousness of our own varied ethnic heritages; our own ancestors, going back one or more generations, came from Sicily, Ireland, Scotland, Japan, the Portuguese Azores, and both French- and English-speaking Canada. But our considerable research into American voting patterns—both current and historical—seems to force the conclusion that political attitudes and tendencies correlate well with ethnic origin. We are past the day now when Polish-American voters, for example, will automatically vote for a Polish-American candidate (see Wisconsin 4 on Edmund Muskie's experiences on the south side of Milwaukee). But it is clear that even in the 1972 elections, voters' responses to the choices before them varied sharply on ethnic lines. Catholic voters shifted sharply from Hubert Humphrey in 1968 to Richard Nixon in 1972, and Southern whites for George Wallace in 1968 went heavily for Nixon four years later. But Protestants of Scandinavian background voted about as much for McGovern as they had for Humphrey, and black voters stayed almost entirely within the Democratic fold in the presidential contest.

It might be argued that in these days of massive ticket-splitting, an ethnic-based analysis is no longer very useful. We disagree. It is true, certainly, that the days of coattails are over. Richard Nixon carried 377 of the nation's 435 congressional districts in 1972, and won more than 55% of the votes in 348 of them. But the same 435 districts elected only 192 Republican Congressmen; of the districts carried by Nixon, 188—just one less than a majority—elected Democrats to the House. At the same time, George McGovern actually ran ahead of dozens of Democratic House candidates. But if ticket-splitting has become the norm, we still believe that the ways in which people tend to split their tickets can be explained best by focusing on ethnic differences. People of the same ethnic origin tend, statistically, to share the same kind of background, a set of shared attitudes and political ideas, enough so that their ethnic origin provides a useful predictor of electoral preferences and trends.

So for each state and district, we have provided racial and ethnic percentages calculated from the 1970 census. For the most part, these remain pretty accurate, although there are a few glaring exceptions, like the 2nd district of Illinois, where the black percentage rose sharply in the 1960s and has continued to do so, as indicated by the 1972 presidential election results. The census figures represent people who either were born, or one of whose parents were born, in another country (the Census Bureau calls such people "of foreign stock"). Ethnic consciousness, however, often lingers beyond two generations, and so the percentages underrepresent the Irishness of Boston (see Massachusetts 9) or the Polishness of Buffalo (see New York 37). At the same time, there are some ethnic categories—like "British"—which do not represent groups with much ethnic consciousness at all. The category "Spanish heritage" represents a variety of different groups: Mexican-Americans in California, Texas, and Illinois; Puerto Ricans in New York and New Jersey; and the ancient Spanish-speaking community in New Mexico, which antedates Plymouth Rock. We have also included the category "French native tongue" in Maine, New Hampshire, Vermont, Massachusetts, Rhode Island, and upstate New York, to indicate people of French Canadian stock, and in Louisiana to indicate the so-called Cajuns; in both cases, these groups have shown distinctive voting patterns over the years. No group is shown unless it represents 1% or more of the state or district's total population.

One division of an ethnic nature the census does not reveal, but which remains of substantial political importance, is the divide that runs roughly across the middle of the country between people who sympathized with the Union in the Civil War and those who were Copperheads or Rebels. Much of rural Southern Ohio, Indiana, and Illinois, and a large portion of Missouri, retains a Democratic preferences from those days, although it is more likely to come out in local contests than in presidential or even congressional elections these days. In a similar manner, the hill counties of eastern Tennessee, western North Carolina, and the Cumberland Plateau in Kentucky remain some of the strongest Republican territory in the nation. In many ways, these cleavages—between Southern drawls and Northern accents, hill farmers and lowland planters, Methodists and Baptists and Lutherans—are "ethnic," and correlate well with political choices in elections. They are not quantifiable, however, and so are discussed, when relevant, in the political background sections.

III. POLITICAL BACKGROUND

This is the guts of the book—our interpretation of how the pieces fit together. What kind of men and women are your Senators and Representatives? What do they accomplish on the Hill? How do they get elected, and what are their prospects for reelection—or defeat? What are the local issues, and local attitudes on national issues?

These are the questions the political background sections seek to answer. They form a kind of mosaic, we think, a picture of political leanings and trends throughout the nation and what they mean for our federal government and federal elections. Read them all, and we think you will get a pretty accurate picture of what is going on politically around the country and on Capitol Hill. But the *Almanac* is designed to be read and used piecemeal; you might want to begin with your home state, or with the member of a committee whose subject matter interests you, or with those members of Congress considered possible presidential prospects for 1976. We have tried to design the *Almanac* to make it easy to use, whatever your interest.

A. Statewide

American politics, for better or worse, is still the politics of the 50 states. There are signs that the national media have begun to homogenize our politics, to eliminate local peculiarities and to replicate conflicts along the same ideological lines throughout the nation. But even the most contemporary politics is the outgrowth of history, and for 180 years American politics has been a thing of unmatched diversity. Each state has been a little political arena all its own. The Electoral College system—whereby the winner takes all a state's electoral votes—has strengthened this tendency, even in national contests; in most presidential elections, about half the states are not seriously contested by one candidate or the other. Most states have well-developed traditions of political conflict: New York City vs. upstate, Chicago vs. downstate Illinois, east Tennessee vs. middle Tennessee vs. west Tennessee. Some of these are changing; others remain rigidly the same. We have tried to present them in their historical contexts and to explain what, if anything, these regional conflicts mean today.

Each state also has its own political flavor, an ambiance about its politicians and its voting behavior that is not found elsewhere. Connecticut, with its still strong tradition of straight tickets, lies right next to Massachusetts, where voters have been splitting their tickets on a massive scale for years. Illinois is a land of fabled political corruption and cronyism; Wisconsin just to the north, is as clean as a hound's tooth and has nothing resembling Richard J. Daley's machine. These political patterns have grown up in response to local ground-rules, pressures, and personal initiatives; the voting public responds in various ways, and a political culture grows. We have attempted to impart the ambiance of the 50 political cultures which make up our Republic.

B. Congressional Districts

There has been a great deal of writing on the politics of the various states, but very little on the politics of individual congressional districts (CDs). One reason for the dearth of information about CDs is that they, unlike the states, usually do not have a political culture of their own. Each one is just a piece of a culture that exists on a statewide basis, and each is often made up of disparate elements of that culture. The trend toward heterogeneity has been increased by the Supreme Court's one-man-one-vote decision, *Wesberry* v. *Sanders*. Today, the districts are pretty much equal in population, at least according to the 1970 census; but the equal-population requirement makes for some odd political combinations. For example, the 200,000-population, old 4th Texas district, represented for nearly 50 years by Sam Rayburn, was a compact, homogeneous unit; so was the 900,000-population district that existed at the time of Rayburn's death, including all of Dallas County. Now Rayburn's successor has some of Dallas County in his district, and while that is clearly fairer, it makes a description of the current 4th district a more complicated affair. Nevertheless, we have tried to describe and analyze the politics of each district, and to indicate the impact its Congressman makes on Capitol Hill.

What were our sources? Just about everything: interviews with members of Congress and their aides, and with local politicians and political observers in Washington and around the country; newspapers, magazines, books; publicly available data, including the *Congressional Record*; and a lifelong collection of political and historical miscellany. We have paid particular attention to what we consider the hardest of data, the election returns; we taxpayers, after all, spend millions of dollars to get those figures, and political adversaries have the strongest incentives to make sure they are accurate. We have examined in detail returns going back at least to 1964, and we believe that, intelligently read, the election returns give as good an insight as can be had into what Americans think and believe about the issues of the day. They also provide clues for what we imagine must be the major interest of many of our readers: whether Senator X or Congressman Y can be beaten in the next election.

Two apologies-in-advance should be entered. First, we have used the terms "liberal," "conservative," and "moderate" more than we would have liked. They are intended to mean what they in fact mean to most ordinary intelligent observers of American politics today. Thus George McGovern is a "liberal" and Richard Nixon a "conservative." Second, our references to ethnic groups are sometimes made in shorthand. "Italian" in the *Almanac* means "Italian-American";

"black" means the same as "Negro" or "Afro-American." We have tried to use terms that will cause the least possible offense, and if we have failed to do so, we are sorry. By noting ethnic differences we certainly do not intend to imply than any group is monolithic, or in any way inferior or superior to any other group.

Our intention in compiling and writing the *Almanac* was to create something the American public will find useful. To judge from the reception of the 1972 edition, we have had some success. We again ask our readers for their suggestions, criticisms, and comments, and thank those whose ideas have, we hope, improved the book.

Michael Barone
Grant Ujifusa
Douglas Matthews

ABBREVIATIONS

ABS	Absent *or* Abstain
ACA	Americans for Constitutional Action
ADA	Americans for Democratic Action
AEC	Atomic Energy Commission
AIP	American Independent party
CFA	Consumer Federation of America
CG	Coast Guard
CHOB	Cannon House Office Building
Co.	County, Company
Com.	committee
Const.	Constitutional party
COPE	Committee on Political Education
CSC	Civil Service Commission
D	Democrat
DFL	Democrat-Farmer-Labor party
DOC	Department of Commerce
DOD	Department of Defense
DOI	Department of the Interior
DOJ	Department of Justice
DOT	Department of Transportation
HEW	Department of Health, Education, and Welfare
HUD	Department of Housing and Urban Development
Ind.	Independent
Jt. Com.	Joint Committee
LCV	League of Conservation Voters
LHOB	Longworth House Office Building
Lib.	Liberal party
LWV	League of Women Voters
NAB	National Association of Businessmen
NASA	National Aeronautics and Space Agency
NE	Not [yet] Elected
NFU	National Farmers' Union
NSI	National Security Index of the American Security Council
NSOB	New Senate Office Building
OEO	Office of Economic Opportunity
OSOB	Old Senate Office Building
PF	Peace and Freedom party
P.O.	Post Office
R	Republican
Rank. Mbr.	Ranking Member
RHOB	Rayburn House Office Building
Sel. Com.	Select Committee
Sp. Com.	Special Committee
Sub.	Subcommittee
SW	Socialist Worker party
TD	Treasury Department
USAF	United States Air Force
USAFR	United States Air Force Reserve
USDA	United States Department of Agriculture
USMC	United Stated Marine Corps
USMCR	United States Marine Corps Reserve
VA	Veterans Administration

ALABAMA

Political Background

Alabama is George C. Wallace country. After young county judge Wallace lost the 1958 gubernatorial primary, the defeated candidate vowed that he would never again be "out-segged." Wallace has now dominated the state's politics for more than a decade. First elected Governor in 1962, Wallace was succeeded by his wife Lurleen in 1966, and was reelected in 1970, after winning a close primary over Albert Brewer, who had become Governor upon the death of Mrs. Wallace. Brewer's campaign received heavy financial backing from Nixon's White House. Other Southern politicians have enjoyed a long-time dominance in their bailiwicks—Harry Byrd in Virginia and Orval Faubus in Arkansas—but only George Wallace and the legendary Huey Long of Louisiana have become figures of consequence in national politics.

Wallace has shown greater staying power than the Kingfish. Long was murdered before he could run for President—FDR, for one, thought Huey P. would run—but Wallace has already attempted three presidential bids, each time with phenomenal impact on our national politics. In 1964, after just two years as Governor of Alabama, he ran close races against Johnson surrogates in Wisconsin, Indiana, and Maryland; Wallace was the first national politician to demonstrate the potency of the backlash vote in the North. In 1968, his third-party candidacy prevented both Nixon and Humphrey from getting anything like a popular-vote majority. In fact, with rather small shifts in the returns, the Governor would have commanded a king-making bloc of votes in the electoral college. His candidacy was the strongest third-party effort—he won more than 13% of nation's ballots—since Robert La Follette's Progressive party try in 1924.

In 1972, Wallace once again decided to go the route of the Democratic presidential primaries, and he exceeded his 1964 showings. Not only did Wallace win primaries in Southern states like Florida, Tennessee, and North Carolina, but his "send 'em a message" campaign took Northern contests in busing-obsessed Michigan and Maryland. The man from Alabama also finished a strong second in Wisconsin and Pennsylvania. But like his previous national campaigns, his 1972 effort was disorganized and lacked depth. Out in the hustings, the candidate made only a few appearances—usually before friendly, cheering crowds—gave a set speech, and then retired to watch the votes pile up, as if by magic, on election night. The Wallace organization made no effort to win real live delegates to the Convention, which seemed to indicate that much as Wallace wanted to be President, the candidate knew the Democratic party would never give him its nomination. Even if it had, the outlook beyond the primaries was bleak. The man possessed a fanatical hard core of support, but the polls showed that Wallace, even with a respectability bestowed by a national party, could win only about 20% of the vote.

Just at the peak of his national political career, the day before his smashing victories in the Michigan and Maryland primaries, George Wallace was shot. A bullet fired in a Laurel, Maryland shopping center has left the Governor paralyzed below the waist, and complications have sent him into the operating room several times. Wallace is a very game man, as his appearance at the Democratic Convention showed, but it now seems, for better or worse, that his presidential campaign days may well be over. George Wallace, like Huey Long, is an irreplaceable political personality. No one around can display the combination of spunk, wit, and hostility that constitutes his appeal, as John Schmitz, American party presidential candidate in 1972, well knows.

Ironically, just as his name recognition and popularity have grown throughout the country since the mid-sixties, Wallace's dominance back home in Alabama has waned. As Governor, he has been beset by a series of obdurate state legislatures. As state Democratic party leader, Wallace has been successfully challenged by State Chairman Robert Vance and his loyalists, who in 1968 insisted that the Democratic electors support the party's national ticket and forced Wallace to run on his own ticket, denying him use of the traditional rooster symbol of Alabama Democrats.

As a political candidate in the state, Wallace has been opposed, of course, by the blacks. They have, since the passage of the 1965 Voting Rights Act, become a major Alabama electoral force. Of equal significance, Wallace has won the enmity of Alabama businessmen and urban voters generally, people who know that the state's metropolitan areas have suffered economic stagnation during Wallace's tenure as George Wallace is not fully in charge of matters, and that his brother Gerald—once under investigation by the IRS—and staffers control the governorship. The Montgomery *Advertiser*, never a pro-Wallace paper, even dared to suggest in early 1973 that Wallace resign. As if to reply, the Governor stood for a full 30 minutes while addressing the legislature. His appearance with Edward Kennedy on the Fourth of July, 1973, indicates that Wallace still retains an interest in national affairs. And at home, he is the first Alabama Governor eligible for reelection, and there is little doubt that he will be reelected as long as he wants.

The single greatest source of Wallace's national political appeal has been his opposition to most of the things blacks have wanted and have been denied; in short, an appeal to racism. But another theme has been a verbal commitment, at least, to a form of populism—heavy government spending on public works and services for the little man. This kind of Wallace language was picked up by George McGovern and others during the 1972 primaries in the vain hope that not all of the spellbinder's support was tied to race, but some to "alienation" and therefore transferable to competitors in the field. Alabama populism, however, has deeper roots, and it has formed the basis of a successful political tradition going back at least as far as 1926. This was when the late Hugo Black was elected to the U.S. Senate over the opposition of Alabama banks, railroads, and power companies. For 40 years, New Deal-style populists dominated the Alabama congressional delegation; members of it took the obligatory stands against civil rights, but devoted most of their energy to housing, hospital, and highway programs.

Today only two of this breed, Sen. John Sparkman and Rep. Bob Jones, remain in Congress. Most of the rest were beaten by Republicans in the state's 1964 Goldwater landslide (in which Alabama lost 87 years of House seniority). But Sparkman's populist credentials seem a little less solid now than in 1952 when he was Adlai Stevenson's running-mate. In Sparkman's campaign for reelection in 1972, the veteran Senator—he's been on the Hill since 1936 and will be 75 in 1974—reportedly received massive financial support from banking interests throughout the nation. It's not hard to see why: Sparkman is Chairman of the Senate Banking, Housing, and Urban Affairs Committee, a unit which handles banking and housing legislation. Banking and housing, of course, are two of the most heavily regulated sectors of American private enterprise. Right behind Sparkman in seniority on the committee is Wisconsin's William Proxmire, not known for his friends among big bankers.

Sparkman coasted to a surprisingly easy victory in the 1972 general election. His Republican opponent, former Postmaster Winton Blount, was quite incapable of tagging Sparkman a McGovernite, and equally incapable of seizing hold of Nixon's coattails. For all the money the rich man Blount spent (his construction firm built most of the Kennedy Space Center), he managed to carry only one small county. But the primary for Sparkman, back in May, was more of a problem. Sparkman was pressed hard by a large field of challengers, in particular by State Auditor Melba Till Allen. Mrs. Allen campaigned as a consumer advocate and, like the other challengers, criticized Sparkman for being too close to the bankers. The primary returns, however, showed that the real difference in the minds of the voters was her support of Wallace over Brewer in 1970. Mrs. Allen ran strongest where Wallace did, in Mobile and in the nonmetropolitan, piney woods areas in the southern portion of the state. Sparkman won a bare 50% of the votes, and so avoided a runoff election. The veteran Senator was spared the embarrassment only by piling up a large majority in his old congressional district, along the Tennessee River in northern Alabama.

The close primary suggests that this will be Sparkman's last Senate term; but barring mischance or a Republican Senate majority, he will continue to chair the Banking Committee. The state's other Senator, James B. Allen, is up for reelection in 1974. Allen was Lieutenant Governor during Wallace's first term and served as state Senator afterwards—remaining always a loyal Wallace supporter. His reward was nomination to the U.S. Senate in 1968, upon the retirement of aging populist Sen. (1938–69) Lister Hill. Allen won the seat after a close race with Congressman Armistead Selden (now a Pentagon official). Allen has distinguished himself in an old Southern senatorial tradition by becoming a master of parliamentary procedure. The high point of his first term came during the fall of 1972 when he managed to steer an antibusing measure directly to the floor of the Senate after it left the House. Ordinarily the bill would have been referred to committee, where it would have died. The bill died anyway on the floor, succumbing to a desultory filibuster and the general call for adjournment in the face of sundry campaign pressures.

In 1973, Allen led a filibuster against a bill to allow voter registration by post card—a move that was also unsuccessful. Nevertheless, these maneuvers will be worth points in Alabama, as Allen campaigns for reelection in 1974. No one expects that he will be seriously challenged. So the only obstacle in this Southern Senator's road to more seniority is his age, 62 in 1974.

The current Alabama House delegation is composed of four Democrats and three Republicans. All of the Republicans were beneficiaries of the 1964 Goldwater landslide, and all have since strengthened their hold on office; the Democrats are even more entrenched than the Republicans. Alabama's large black minority, which has managed to elect a record number of local officials, is carved up among the state's seven congressional districts, so thoroughly gerrymandered that there is little likelihood that blacks will play any important role in Alabama House elections. The high point of black influence so far in statewide contests came in the 1972 Senate primary when most black voters went for Sparkman and helped him avoid a runoff.

Census Data Pop. 3,444,165; 1.70% of U.S. total, 21st largest; change 1960–70, 5.4%. Central city, 26%; suburban, 27%. Median family income, $7,263; 48th highest; families above $15,000: 11%; families below $3,000: 19%. Median years education, 10.8.

1972 Share of Federal Tax Burden $2,361,910,000; 1.13% of U.S. total, 25th largest.

1972 Share of Federal Outlays $3,489,644,995; 1.61% of U.S. total, 20th largest. Per capita federal spending, $1,013.

DOD	$938,529,000	18th (1.50%)	HEW	$1,165,844,763	21st (1.63%)
AEC	$68,072	41st (—)	HUD	$56,683,585	20th (1.85%)
NASA	$239,250,495	5th (8.00%)	VA	$225,341,751	18th (1.97%)
DOT	$143,579,877	21st (1.82%)	USDA	$238,055,737	25th (1.55%)
DOC	$19,741,859	14th (1.52%)	CSC	$68,472,644	17th (1.66%)
DOI	$8,351,479	41st (0.39%)	TD	$85,342,526	28th (0.52%)
DOJ	$20,003,684	15th (2.04%)	Other	$280,379,523	

Economic Base Agriculture, notably broilers, cattle, cotton lint and eggs; primary metal industries, especially blast furnaces and basic steel products, and iron and steel foundries; finance, insurance and real estate; apparel and other textile products, especially men's and boys' furnishings; textile mill products, especially cotton weaving mills; food and kindred products, especially meat products; lumber and wood products, especially sawmills and planing mills.

Political Line-up Governor, George C. Wallace (D); seat up, 1974. Senators, John J. Sparkman (D) and James B. Allen (D). Representatives, 7 (4 D and 3 R). State Senate (35 D and 0 R); State House (105 D and 2 R).

The Voters

Registration No party registration; no accurate total registration figures available.
Median voting age 42.8
Employment profile White collar, 41%. Blue collar, 43%. Service, 13%. Farm, 3%.
Ethnic groups Black, 26%. Total foreign stock, 2%.

Presidential vote

1972	Nixon (R)	728,701	(74%)
	McGovern (D)	256,923	(26%)
1968	Nixon (R)	146,923	(14%)
	Humphrey (D)	196,579	(19%)
	Wallace (AI)	691,425	(67%)
1964	Johnson (D)	*	
	Goldwater (R)	479,085	(70%)

*210,733 votes were cast for Democratic electors not pledged to Johnson.

Senator

John J. Sparkman (D) Elected 1946, seat up 1978; b. Dec. 20, 1899, near Hartselle; home, Huntsville; U. of Ala., B.A., 1921, LL.B., 1923, M.A., 1924; Student Army Training Corps, 1918; Colonel USAR (Ret.); married, one child, Methodist.

Career Practicing atty., 1925–36; U.S. House of Reps., 1937–46; Majority Whip; Dem. candidate for V.P., 1952; Instructor, Huntsville Col., 1925–28.

Offices 3203 NSOB, 202-225-4124. Also P.O. Bldg., Huntsville 35801, and 1800 Fifth Ave. N., Rm. 208, Birmingham 35203, 205-325-3883.

Administrative Assistant Robert Locklin

Committees

Banking, Housing and Urban Affairs (Chm.); Subs: Financial Institutions; Housing and Urban Affairs (Chm.); Small Business; Consumer Credit.

Foreign Relations (2nd]); Subs: European Affairs (Chm.); Far-Eastern Affairs; Western Hemisphere Affairs; U.S. Security Agreements and Commitments Abroad.

Sel. Com. on Small Business (2nd); Subs: Financing and Investment (Chm.); Government Procurement.

Joint Com. on Defense Production (Chm.).

Joint Economic Com. (2nd); Subs: Priorities and Economy in Government; Inter-American Economic Relationships (Chm.); International Economics.

Group Ratings

	ADA	COPE	LWV	RIPON	NFU	LCV	CFA	NAB	NSI	ACA
1972	0	10	38	24	50	19	40	38	100	80
1971	19	82	80	13	55	–	75	–	–	37
1970	13	25	–	4	43	10	–	57	100	80

Key Votes

1) Busing	ABS	8) Sea Life Prot	FOR	15) Tax Singls Less	AGN
2) Alas P-line	FOR	9) Campaign Subs	FOR	16) Min Tax for Rich	ABS
3) Gun Cntrl	FOR	10) Cmbodia Bmbg	FOR	17) Euro Troop Rdctn	AGN
4) Rehnquist	FOR	11) Legal Srvices	AGN	18) Bust Hwy Trust	AGN
5) Pub TV $	AGN	12) Rev Sharing	ABS	19) Maid Min Wage	AGN
6) EZ Votr Reg	AGN	13) Cnsumr Prot	FOR	20) Farm Sub Limit	AGN
7) No-Fault	AGN	14) Eq Rts Amend	FOR	21) Highr Credt Chgs	ABS

Election Results

1972 general:	John Sparkman (D)	654,491	(62%)
	Winton M. Blount (R)	347,523	(33%)
	John L. LeFlore (NDPA)	31,421	(3%)
	Jerome B. Couch (AI)	10,826	(1%)
	Herbert W. Stone (Con.)	6,838	(1%)
1972 primary:	John Sparkman (D)	331,838	(50%)
	Melba Till Allen (D)	194,690	(29%)
	Lambert C. Mims (D)	87,461	(13%)
	Robert Edington (D)	22,145	(3%)
	Charles Sullins (D)	12,164	(2%)
	Jimmy Harper (D)	7,523	(1%)
	Sam L. Chestnut, Jr. (D)	4,519	(1%)
1966 general:	John Sparkman (D)	482,138	(61%)
	John Grenier (R)	313,018	(39%)

Senator

James Browning Allen (D) Elected 1968, seat up 1974; b. Dec. 28, 1912, Gadsden; home, Gadsden; U. of Ala., U. of Ala. Law School; Navy, WWII; married, four children; Church of Christ.

Career Practicing atty., 1935–68; Lt. Gov. of Ala., 1951–55, 1963–67; Ala. State Senate, 1946–50; Ala. House of Reps., 1938–42.

Offices 6313 NSOB, 202-225-5744. Also 227 Broad St., Gadsden 35902, 202-546-4258; 414 Van Antwerp Bldg., Mobile 36602, 205-438-2635; and Frank Nelson Bldg., Birmingham 35203, 205-251-1874.

Administrative Assistant Tom Coker

Committees

Agriculture and Forestry (4th); Subs: Environment, Soil Conservation and Forestry; Agricultural Credit and Rural Electrification; Agricultural Research and General Legislation (Chm.); Rural Development.

Government Operations (7th); Subs: Permanent Investigations; Reorganization, Research, and International Organizations.

Rules and Administration (4th); Subs: Printing; Restaurant (Chm.).

Joint Com. on Printing (2nd).

Group Ratings

	ADA	COPE	LWV	RIPON	NFU	LCV	CFA	NAB	NSI	ACA
1972	0	30	9	17	50	32	18	58	100	86
1971	15	25	8	12	36	–	14	–	–	75
1970	16	18	–	16	36	40	–	60	100	83

Key Votes

1) Busing	AGN	8) Sea Life Prot	FOR	15) Tax Singls Less	AGN
2) Alas P-line	FOR	9) Campaign Subs	FOR	16) Min Tax for Rich	AGN
3) Gun Cntrl	AGN	10) Cmbodia Bmbg	ABS	17) Euro Troop Rdctn	AGN
4) Rehnquist	FOR	11) Legal Srvices	AGN	18) Bust Hwy Trust	AGN
5) Pub TV $	FOR	12) Rev Sharing	FOR	19) Maid Min Wage	AGN
6) EZ Votr Reg	AGN	13) Cnsumr Prot	AGN	20) Farm Sub Limit	AGN
7) No-Fault	AGN	14) Eq Rts Amend	FOR	21) Highr Credt Chgs	FOR

Election Results

1968 general:	Jim Allen (D)	638,774	(70%)
	Perry Hooper (R)	201,227	(22%)
	Robert P. Schwenn (NDPA)	72,699	(8%)
1968 runoff:	Jim Allen (D)	196,511	(51%)
	Armistead Selden (D)	192,446	(49%)
1968 primary:	Jim Allen (D)	224,483	(40%)
	John Crommelin (D)	10,926	(2%)
	Jim Folsom (D)	32,004	(6%)
	Armistead Selden (D)	190,283	(34%)
	Mrs. Frank Stewart (D)	5,368	(1%)
	Bob Smith (D)	92,928	(17%)

FIRST DISTRICT Political Background

The Tombigbee and Alabama rivers flow south from the Alabama Black Belt—named for the black fertility of its cotton-growing soil—to the port of Mobile and the Gulf of Mexico. Mobile (pop. 190,000) is Alabama's second largest city, and the largest port on the Gulf between New Orleans and Tampa. Dominated by sluggish industries—shipping, shipbuilding, and paper (although paper has done well lately)—Mobile has had no population growth since the 1950s.

Although 35% of its residents are black, Mobile is the most pro-Wallace of Alabama's large cities. It gave the Governor an overwhelming majority in his 1968 presidential bid, and was the only metropolitan area to back him in the crucial 1970 gubernatorial primary. Not coincidentally, Mobile is the most blue-collar of the state's cities. The only discordant place in the Mobile metropolitan area is the suburb of Prichard (pop. 41,000), which elected Jay Cooper, a black man, Mayor in the fall of 1972.

Alabama's 1st congressional district stretches from Mobile and the Gulf north to the Black Belt, and includes one black-majority county (Wilcox). But most of the population lives around Mobile, with Mobile County casting almost 80% of the district's votes. The 1st's feeling toward national issues can be found in Nixon's smashing 76% of the vote in 1972, which matched a similar preference for Republican Barry Goldwater in 1964.

That 1964 election pretty well determined the results of the next four House races in the 1st, as Barry Goldwater helped Republican W. Jack Edwards sweep into office. Edwards shares many of Goldwater's political views. The Congressman had not previously held public office, but in the House he has become well-respected, as witnessed by his winning a seat on the Appropriations Committee and his narrow defeat (85–82) in a 1970 bid bo become Vice-Chairman of the House Republican Conference; today Edwards holds the post of Secretary of the Conference.

Edwards is even more popular in the 1st than among fellow Republican Congressmen. He has beaten various Democrats with ease every two years. Last time out, he even ran ahead of Richard Nixon in Alabama's 1st congressional district; very few Southern Republicans proved to be more popular than the President in the fall of 1972. Edwards can be expected to remain in the House as one of its more important Southern Republicans for some time.

Census Data Pop. 491,747. Central city, 39%; suburban, 38%. Median family income, $7,305; families above $15,000: 11%; families below $3,000: 18%. Median years education, 10.8.

1972 Share of Federal Outlays $328,392,389

DOD	$43,291,000	HEW	$137,417,868
AEC	–	HUD	$306,000
NASA	$20,000	DOI	$1,563,876
DOT	$27,749,243	USDA	$28,858,786
		Other	$89,185,616

Federal Military-Industrial Commitments

DOD Contractors Alabama Refining Company (Theodore), $5.168m: petroleum products.

Economic Base Paper and allied products, especially paper mill products, except building paper; finance, insurance and real estate; agriculture, notably grains, cattle, nursery and greenhouse products, and dairy products; lumber and wood products, especially sawmill and planing mill products; and apparel and other textile products, especially women's and children's underwear.

The Voters

Registration No party registration; no accurate total registration figures available.
Median voting age 42.7
Employment profile White collar, 41%. Blue collar, 42%. Service, 14%. Farm, 3%.
Ethnic groups Black, 33%. Total foreign stock, 2%.

Presidential vote

1972	Nixon (R)	103,842	(76%)
	McGovern (D)	33,276	(24%)
1968	Nixon (R)	14,643	(19%)
	Humphrey (D)	27,878	(10%)
	Wallace (AI)	102,755	(70%)

an. This area is one of the few in the state to show a significant population
sixties; in fact, virtually all Deep South counties with substantial population
blessed with military installations.

lack Belt counties in the south, the 3rd district is mostly white, and the whites
mall towns and hilly farm country comprise George Wallace's kind of people.
ssman, Bill Nichols, was a Wallace floor leader in the Alabama Senate, and his
d is what one might expect from that affiliation. In 1966, Nichols was the only
anaged to unseat a Republican elected in the 1964 Alabama Goldwater
n he has each time been sent back to Washington with more than 75% of the
or position on the Armed Services Committee, Nichols has made little
tol Hill, except perhaps to contribute yet another vote to the already lopsided
the committee's Southern Democrat-Republican majority.

493,588. Central city, 0%; suburban, 16%. Median family income, $6,817;
,000: 8%; families below $3,000: 19%. Median years education, 10.2.

ral Outlays $430,832,295

DOD	$144,411,000	HEW	$160,794,654
AEC	$41,072	HUD	$3,001,957
NASA	$627,070	DOI	$841,491
DOT	$15,902,752	USDA	$26,046,234
		Other	$79,136,065

ustrial Commitments

Golden Industries (Sylacauga), $23.063m: 155mm projectiles.
Anniston Army Depot (Anniston). Fort McClellan AB (Anniston).

le mill products, especially cotton weaving mill products; apparel and other
culture, notably poultry and cattle; primary metal industries, especially iron
d finance, insurance and real estate. Also higher education (Auburn Univ.).

arty registration; no accurate total registration figures available.
42.0
White collar, 34%. Blue collar, 50%. Service, 14%. Farm, 2%.
ck, 31%. Total foreign stock, 1%.

Nixon (R)	98,640	(75%)
McGovern (D)	33,480	(25%)
Nixon (R)	14,611	(11%)
Humphrey (D)	26,024	(19%)
Wallace (AI)	98,246	(71%)

William Nichols (D) Elected 1966; b. Oct. 16, 1918, near Becker, Miss.;
home, Sylacauga; Auburn U., B.S., 1939, M.S., 1941; Army, WWII;
married, three children; Methodist.

Career Ala. House of Reps., 1959; Ala. State Senate, 1963; V.P. Parker
Fertilizer Co., Pres. Parker Gin Co., 1947–66.

Offices 1037 LHOB, 202-225-3261. Also Fed. Bldg. P.O. Box 2042,
Anniston 36201, 205-236-5655.

Administrative Assistant Thomas L. Foster

Representative

W. Jack Edwards (R) Elected 1964; b. Sept. 20, 1928, Birmingham;
home, Mobile; U. of Ala., B.S., 1952, LL.B., 1954; USMC, 1946–48,
1950–51; married, two children; Presbyterian.

Career Practicing atty., 1954–64.

Offices 2439 RHOB, 202-225-4931. Also Suite 806, First Federal Tower,
Mobile 36606, 205-471-1851.

Administrative Assistant David C. Pruitt III

Committees

Appropriations (14th); Subs: Transportation; Treasury-Postal Service-General Government.

Group Ratings

	ADA	COPE	LWV	RIPON	NFU	LCV	CFA	NAB	NSI	ACA
1972	0	10	11	54	50	18	50	88	100	78
1971	8	17	38	35	27	–	0	–	–	81
1970	4	0	–	41	31	0	44	90	100	83

Key Votes

1) Busing	AGN	6) Cmbodia Bmbg	FOR	11) Chkg Acct Intrst	ABS
2) Strip Mines	AGN	7) Bust Hwy Trust	FOR	12) End HISC (HUAC)	AGN
3) Cut Mil $	AGN	8) Farm Sub Lmt	AGN	13) Nixon Sewer Veto	FOR
4) Rev Shrg	FOR	9) School Prayr	FOR	14) Corp Cmpaign $	FOR
5) Pub TV $	AGN	10) Cnsumr Prot	AGN	15) Pol $ Disclosr	AGN

Election Results

1972 general:	Jack Edwards (R)	104,606	(77%)
	D. W. McCrory (D)	24,357	(18%)
	Thomas McAboy, Jr. (NDPA)	7,747	(6%)
1972 primary:	Jack Edwards (R), unopposed		
1970 general:	Jack Edwards (R)	63,457	(61%)
	John Tyson (D)	27,457	(26%)
	Noble Beasley (NDPA)	13,789	(13%)

SECOND DISTRICT   **Political Background**

Alabama's Black Belt was first named for the fertility and color of the region's topsoil. For all of
the nineteenth and most of the twentieth century, the economics of cotton-making required
abundant, cheap labor. For many years after the Civil War the majority of the Black Belt's
citizens were descendants of the slaves brought here to chop and pick cotton. But black migration
to the North so reduced the black percentage in this part of Alabama that when the 1965 Voting
Rights Act finally gave blacks the ballot, only a handful of small, predominantly rural counties
were left with black majorities.

On a map, Alabama's congressional-district lines look perfectly regular. Closer inspection,
however, shows them to have been carefully crafted to divide the black-majority counties among
several districts; this, of course, was intended to prevent blacks from exerting a major influence in
any congressional election. The 2nd district, for example, contains only one black-majority county
(Bullock), but just outside district lines are three others (Macon, Lowndes, and Wilcox).

So the blacks in the 2nd are heavily outnumbered by the whites in Montgomery, the state's
capital, and by those in the "piney woods" counties to the south of the Black Belt. The whites here
are no doubt pleased to remind visitors that Montgomery was the Cradle of the Confederacy, the
rebels' capital before Richmond. Local boosters are less likely to talk about the 1956 Montgomery
bus boycott, which gave national prominence to a young black minister, Martin Luther King, Jr.

The 2nd is basically an amalgam of the old 2nd and 3rd districts, a conjunction rendered necessary by the results of the 1970 census, which cost Alabama a congressional seat. The state's Democratic legislature drew the lines of the new 2nd with the probable hope that Democratic Congressman George W. Andrews, a 28-year House veteran and third ranking member of the Appropriations Committee, would knock off the old 2nd's Republican Congressman William L. Dickinson. But Andrews died in the winter of 1971, after which it was decided more or less by common consent that his widow serve out the term and retire.

At that, the 2nd was still the most hotly-contested Alabama congressional race in 1972. Five Democrats wanted the seat; the winner, after the first primary and the runoff, was Ben C. Reeves, a young state legislator. About 44% of the districts population is in the old 3rd, an area where Dickinson was an unknown, and as a Montgomery Republican, perhaps even a citified alien. In the general election, Reeves carried the old 3rd part of the district by 6,000, certainly an achievement against an incumbent. But Dickinson won just as big in the rural counties of the old 2nd, and swept Montgomery County better than two-to-one. As in many other parts of the South, the urban area of the 2nd provided the Republican with his most commanding margins.

Dickinson's win leaves him in good shape for the rest of the seventies. Because he can now cover with franked mail parts of the district he lost, the Congressman will probably have little trouble winning in the foreseeable future. To the national press, Dickinson is still best known for his charge in 1965 that the Selma marchers—who passed through part of his district—engaged in obscenities; though he promised to document the accusation, he never did.

In the House Dickinson is the second ranking Republican on the House Administration Committee and also sits on Armed Services—a position that enables him to look after Montgomery's two Air Force bases and the Army's giant Fort Rucker near Dothan. On Armed Services, he is known to pepper military officials with critical questions, but in the end the Congressman usually votes with the committee's pro-Pentagon majority.

Census Data Pop. 491,676. Central city, 27%; suburban, 7%. Median family income, $6,749; families above $15,000: 10%; families below $3,000: 21%. Median years education, 11.0.

1972 Share of Federal Outlays $700,875,788

DOD	$300,133,000	HEW	$183,270,275
AEC	–	HUD	$7,238,397
NASA	$78,748	DOI	$1,812,170
DOT	$19,180,371	USDA	$74,416,034
		Other	$114,746,793

Federal Military-Industrial Commitments

DOD Contractors Worthrop Worldwide ADCT Services (Fort Rucker), $21.041m: aircraft maintenance. Hayes International Corp. (Dothan), $9.825m: aircraft maintenance.
DOD Installations Fort Rucker AB (Ozark). Gunter AFB (Montgomery). Maxwell AFB (Montgomery).

Economic Base Agriculture, notably poultry, cattle, dairy products, and hogs and sheep; apparel and other textile products, especially men's and boy's furnishings; finance, insurance and real estate; lumber and wood products, especially sawmill and planing mill products; and food and kindred products.

The Voters

Registration No party registration; no accurate total registration figures available.
Median voting age 42.5
Employment profile White collar, 42%. Blue collar, 39%. Service, 14%. Farm, 5%.
Ethnic groups Black, 30%. Total foreign stock, 2%.

Presidential vote

1972	Nixon (R)	107,702	(78%)
	McGovern (D)	31,190	(22%)

1968	Nixon (R)	
	Humphrey (D)	
	Wallace (AI)	

Representative

William L. Dickinson (R) El
Montgomery; U. of Ala., B.
four children; Methodist.

Career Practicing atty., 1
County Ct. of Common Pl
Ala., 4 yrs.; Asst. V.P. Sc

Offices 339 CHOB, 202-2
36104, 205-265-5611, ext.
205-937-8818.

Administrative Assistant J

Committees

Armed Services (6th); Subs: No. 1; No. 2 (Ran

Sp. Sub. on Armed Services Investigation.

House Administration (Ranking Mbr.).

Joint Com. on Printing (Ranking House Mbr.)

Group Ratings

	ADA	COPE	LWV	RIPON	
1972	0	0	20	46	
1971	3	17	22	31	
1970	4	0	–	35	

Key Votes

1) Busing	AGN	6) Cmbodia Br
2) Strip Mines	AGN	7) Bust Hwy T
3) Cut Mil $	AGN	8) Farm Sub L
4) Rev Shrg	FOR	9) School Pray
5) Pub TV $	AGN	10) Cnsumr Pro

Election Results

1972 general:	William L. Dickinson (R) ..	
	Ben C. Reeves (D)	
	Richard Boone (NDPA) ...	
1972 primary:	William L. Dickinson (R),	
1970 general:	William L. Dickinson (R) .	
	Jack Winfield (D)	
	Percy Smith, Jr. (NDPA) .	

THIRD DISTRICT Political Background

The 3rd district extends from the cotto
clay hills of the north. To the south is Tusk
and the home of Booker T. Washington's
one-time Alabama "sin city" across the Cl
A mid-fifties clean-up of Phenix City pr
Governor's chair; he beat George Walla
Alabama. To the north is the small indus

city, Fort McClell
growth during the
increases are thos

Outside of the B
living in the 3rd's s
The current Congre
House voting recor
Democrat who m
landslide. Since the
votes. With a jun
impression on Capi
margins enjoyed b

Census Data Pop.
families above $15

1972 Share of Fede

Federal Military-Ind

DOD Contractors
DOD Installations

Economic Base Text
textile products; agri
and steel foundries; a

The Voters

Registration No
Median voting age
Employment profil
Ethnic groups Bla

Presidential vote

1972

1968

Representative

Committees

Armed Services (14th); Sub: No. 4.

Group Ratings

	ADA	COPE	LWV	RIPON	NFU	LCV	CFA	NAB	NSI	ACA
1972	0	17	13	27	50	13	100	71	100	92
1971	3	33	13	25	57	–	40	–	–	72
1970	8	34	–	18	33	40	63	50	100	73

Key Votes

1) Busing	AGN	6) Cmbodia Bmbg	FOR	11) Chkg Acct Intrst	ABS
2) Strip Mines	ABS	7) Bust Hwy Trust	AGN	12) End HISC (HUAC)	AGN
3) Cut Mil $	ABS	8) Farm Sub Lmt	AGN	13) Nixon Sewer Veto	AGN
4) Rev Shrg	FOR	9) School Prayr	FOR	14) Corp Cmpaign $	ABS
5) Pub TV $	FOR	10) Cnsumr Prot	AGN	15) Pol $ Disclosr	AGN

Election Results

1972 general:	Bill Nichols (D)	100,045	(76%)
	Robert M. Kerr (R)	27,253	(21%)
	John Ford (NDPA)	3,392	(3%)
	James R. Connell (AI)	1,693	(1%)
1972 primary:	Bill Nichols (D), unopposed		
1970 general:	Bill Nichols (D)	77,701	(84%)
	Glenn Andrews (R)	13,217	(14%)
	Wilpha Harrel, Jr. (NDPA)	1,903	(2%)

FOURTH DISTRICT Political Background

Nowhere is the counterrevolution in Southern white politics—a movement sparked by the civil rights revolution of the sixties—more clearly evident than in the 4th district of Alabama. As recently as 10 years ago, this part of northern Alabama, which is situated between Birmingham on the south and the Tennessee River valley on the north, was a populist stronghold. The local Congressman, Carl Elliott, was considered reliable enough by the Kennedy Administration and the AFL-CIO to be chosen one of the two members added to the House Rules Committee when it was enlarged (or packed) in 1961. Unlike most of the rest of the South, organized labor was strong enough here to play some part in the district's politics. The workingmen from industrial towns like Gadsden, Jasper, and Cullman, and the leather-handed farmers of the north Alabama hills, consistently supported economic liberals like Sens. Lister Hill, John Sparkman, and ex-Gov. "Kissin' Jim" Folsom against the more business-oriented candidates from the Black Belt.

In those days, race was not a big thing in the politics of the 4th. Elliott, Sparkman, and Hill all of course voted and filibustered against civil rights measures; but this kind of activity was not the main reason the men went to Washington, nor was it why most people in the 4th voted to send them there.

But with the onset of the national Democratic party's commitment to civil rights, attitudes in the 4th changed. In 1964, Goldwater Republicans swept the district; Carl Elliott was out, replaced by Republican Jim Martin. Martin was the man who nearly defeated Sen. Lister Hill in 1962, and the fact that the Alabama Republican ran 1% ahead of Goldwater indicated that there was a strong trend toward Martin's kind of politics in the 4th.

Before 1964, the most important political fact about the voters of the district was that they were predominantly blue-collar; from then on, it was that they were predominantly white. Only 9% of the 4th's residents are black, the lowest percentage among Alabama districts—lower, in fact, than the national average. From the late sixties to the present, the only cleavages that have mattered here have been racial ones.

Martin retired from the House after one term, and left Washington for a tempestuous career in statewide politics. He was trounced by Mrs. Lurleen Wallace in the 1966 gubernatorial race, and his poor showing in the 1972 Republican senatorial primary indicates that his political career is over.

Tom Bevill, a Wallace floor leader in the Alabama House, replaced Martin, and in succeeding elections has won by overwhelming margins. Even on economic issues, Bevill more often votes with the Republicans than with Northern Democrats. So the counterrevolution among voters of the 4th has now given them representation that favors business interests they once considered antithetical to their own.

Census Data Pop. 492,196. Central city, 11%; suburban, 21%. Median family income, $6,350; families above $15,000: 7%; families below $3,000: 22%. Median years education, 9.9.

1972 Share of Federal Outlays $349,559,159

DOD	$58,231,884	HEW	$167,117,612
AEC	–	HUD	$10,249,744
NASA	$64,515	DOI	$422,320
DOT	$9,956,272	USDA	$32,331,885
		Other	$71,184,811

Federal Military-Industrial Commitments

DOD Contractors Etowah Manufacturing (Gadsden), $20.374m: rocket components. Wing Manufacturing (Winfield), $7,961m: unspecified. Lanson Industries (Cullman), $5.756m: bomb dispensers.

Economic Base Apparel and other textile products, especially men's and boys' furnishings; agriculture, notably poultry, cattle, dairy products and cotton; food and kindred products, especially poultry dressing plant products; finance, insurance and real estate; and transportation equipment, especially trailer coaches.

The Voters

Registration No party registration; no accurate total registration figures available.
Median voting age 44.9
Employment profile White collar, 31%. Blue collar, 53%. Service, 11%. Farm, 5%.
Ethnic groups Black, 9%.

Presidential vote

1972	Nixon (R)	117,823	(78%)
	McGovern (D)	34,059	(22%)
1968	Nixon (R)	32,027	(19%)
	Humphrey (D)	15,710	(10%)
	Wallace (AI)	117,428	(71%)

Representative

Tom Bevill (D) Elected 1966; b. March 27, 1921, Townley; home, Jasper; U. of Ala., B.S., 1943, LL.B., 1948; Army, WWII, Lt. Col. USAR; married, three children; Baptist.

Career Practicing atty., 1949–67; Ala. House of Reps., 1958–66.

Offices 1126 LHOB, 202-225-4876. Also 600 Broad St., Gadsden 35901, 205-546-0201; 104 Cullman County Courthouse, Cullman 35055, 205-734-6043; and 1312 Highway 78 East, Jasper 35501, 205-387-7213.

Administrative Assistant Hank Sweitzer

Committees

Appropriations (29th); Subs: Foreign Operations; Treasury-Postal Service-General Government.

Group Ratings

	ADA	COPE	LWV	RIPON	NFU	LCV	CFA	NAB	NSI	ACA
1972	19	82	9	17	50	5	100	46	100	65
1971	16	55	22	38	79	–	25	–	–	61
1970	20	42	–	24	46	25	50	56	100	56

Key Votes

1) Busing	AGN	6) Cmbodia Bmbg	FOR	11) Chkg Acct Intrst	AGN
2) Strip Mines	AGN	7) Bust Hwy Trust	AGN	12) End HISC (HUAC)	AGN
3) Cut Mil $	ABS	8) Farm Sub Lmt	AGN	13) Nixon Sewer Veto	AGN
4) Rev Shrg	FOR	9) School Prayr	FOR	14) Corp Cmpaign $	ABS
5) Pub TV $	FOR	10) Cnsumr Prot	ABS	15) Pol $ Disclosr	AGN

Election Results

1972 general:	Tom Bevill (D)	108,039	(70%)
	Ed Nelson (R)	46,551	(30%)
1972 primary:	Tom Bevill (D), unopposed		
1970 general:	Tom Bevill (D), unopposed		

FIFTH DISTRICT Political Background

The booming northernmost part of Alabama owes most of its prosperity and growth to that behemoth whose presence George Wallace says he hates in a bad way: the federal government. Fifty years ago the Tennessee River coursed through the state's northern counties—untamed, every spring flooding the farm country and small towns. Then the Tennessee Valley Authority came in, dammed the wild river for most of its length, produced cheap public power, and controlled the flooding. This part of Alabama was always populistic, and with the coming of TVA felt desposed to send New Dealers like John J. Sparkman to Congress. Sparkman served in the House for ten years prior to his election to the Senate in 1946.

The federal government's largesse, however, was not limited to TVA. In 1950, Huntsville, though one of the area's largest cities, was still just a sleepy hill town of 14,000 souls. Today it has 137,000 inhabitants. The principal agent of change has been the Redstone Missile Arsenal, the home of hundreds of NASA and Army rocket engineers and technicians. In recent years, the Pentagon and NASA have poured into the seven counties that make up Alabama's 5th more than a half a billion dollars a year, most of it going to Huntsville.

Although the Huntsville boom produced an influx of Northern and European rocket people, the politics of the 5th have remained substantially the same. The populist strain in Alabama politics, always strong here, quieted itself during the sixties, as it did elsewhere in the state, when racial issues became the main feature of election contests. But there are signs that the 5th is reverting, slowly, to its populist ways, or it is at least reacting to political choices in ways significantly different from southern and central Alabama. The TVA city of Decatur (pop. 38,000), the district's second largest, is where George Wallace and Ted Kennedy made a joint platform appearance on July 4, 1973.

In the close 1970 gubernatorial primary, George Wallace did worse here in the 5th than in any other part of the state except Birmingham. In 1972, Sen. John Sparkman, a native son, ran much better in the 5th than anywhere else in Alabama, taking 61% of the 5th's votes in the multi-candidate primary and 69% in the general election against Winton Blount. Even George McGovern, though he lost the district by an overwhelming margin, more than doubled Hubert Humphrey's 1968 percentage. McGovern appears to have received about 20% of the whites' votes; while Humphrey got only about 5%. This is not to say that candidates like McGovern are about to carry the 5th. But it is clear that the voters here find liberals and their programs more attractive than they did a few years ago.

The career of Sparkman's successor in the House has been, at least up to now, something of a mirror of the changing attitudes in the district. For many years, Northern Democrats could count on the support of Robert E. Jones, one of the Hill's leading TVA-oriented Southerners. As late as 1961, the Congressman was an important Southern backer of the Kennedy Administration's move to "pack" the House Rules Committee in order to allow Kennedy-backed legislation onto the floor of the House. Since the rise of Wallace, Jones has voted less often with the Northerners; his ratings with organizations like COPE and ADA, accordingly, have dropped. But in the recent fights over impoundment of federal funds, Jones, like many Southerners, has placed himself solidly with the majority of the Democratic caucus in opposition to the Nixon Administration.

As number-two man on the House Public Works Committee, Jones has an important voice in many environmental matters. For the most part, his views have displeased the ecology lobbyists. The nature of his district and his long-time commitment to New Deal-style public works programs doubtless moves him to support massive dam- and road-building projects. The same background allows him to dismiss rather quickly allegations that efforts of this sort can easily damage the environment. Jones' 1972 primary opponent tried to take him to task on the ecology issue, but made little headway. It is unlikely that environmentalists or anyone else will unseat Congressman Jones.

Census Data Pop. 489,771. Central city, 28%; suburban, 18%. Median family income, $8,271; families above $15,000: 17%; families below $3,000: 15%. Median years education, 11.8.

1972 Share of Federal Outlays $864,858,332

DOD	$271,316,000	HEW	$126,462,529
AEC	–	HUD	$4,266,000
NASA	$238,018,962	DOI	$1,031,735
DOT	$26,173,300	USDA	$32,232,286
		Other	$165,357,520

Federal Military-Industrial Commitments

DOD Contractors Thiokol Chemical (Huntsville), $11.595m: propellants for ABM Spartan missile. Genesco (Huntsville), $9.850m: men's shoes. IBM (Huntsville), $7.706m: modification of B-52 bomb navigation system; engineering support for SAM-D missile; training services for Air Force.
DOD Installations Redstone Army Arsenal (Huntsville).
NASA Contractors IBM (Huntsville), $32.737m: computer support for Saturn project. General Electric (Huntsville), $14.061m: electrical support for Saturn and Apollo projects. Sperry Rand (Huntsville), $10.815m: engineering support for Saturn V. Brown Engineering (Huntsville), $8.959m: engineering support for Saturn V. Computer Sciences (Huntsville), $6.211m: computation support services for Saturn V.
NASA Installations Marshall Space Flight Center (Huntsville).

Economic Base Primary metal industries; agriculture, notably poultry, cotton, cattle and grains; finance, insurance and real estate; electrical equipment and supplies, especially communication equipment; and food and kindred products.

The Voters

Registration No party registration; no accurate total registration figures available.
Median voting age 40.4
Employment profile White collar, 47%. Blue collar, 38%. Service, 12%. Farm, 3%.
Ethnic groups Black, 13%. Total foreign stock, 2%.

Presidential vote

1972	Nixon (R)	98,504	(75%)
	McGovern (D)	33,603	(25%)
1968	Nixon (R)	23,576	(17%)
	Humphrey (D)	16,900	(13%)
	Wallace (AI)	94,659	(70%)

Representative

Robert E. Jones (D) Elected 1946; b. June 12, 1912, Scottsboro; home, Scottsboro; U. of Ala., LL.B., 1937; Navy, WWII; married, one child; Methodist.

Career Practicing atty., 1937–40; Judge, Jackson County Ct., 1940–43.

Offices 2426 RHOB, 202-225-4801. Also P.O. Bldg., Scottsboro 35768, 205-574-2618.

Administrative Assistant George L. Milstead

Committees

Government Operations (4th); Subs: Government Activities; Legislation and Military Operations.

Public Works (2nd); Subs: Economic Development (Chm.); Energy; Investigations and Review; Transportation; Public Buildings and Grounds.

Group Ratings

	ADA	COPE	LWV	RIPON	NFU	LCV	CFA	NAB	NSI	ACA
1972	25	70	50	43	71	0	0	20	89	52
1971	19	50	44	40	69	–	63	–	–	43
1970	24	50	–	19	67	56	89	17	70	26

Key Votes

1) Busing	AGN	6) Cmbodia Bmbg	FOR	11) Chkg Acct Intrst	AGN
2) Strip Mines	AGN	7) Bust Hwy Trust	ABS	12) End HISC (HUAC)	ABS
3) Cut Mil $	ABS	8) Farm Sub Lmt	AGN	13) Nixon Sewer Veto	AGN
4) Rev Shrg	AGN	9) School Prayr	AGN	14) Corp Cmpaign $	FOR
5) Pub TV $	FOR	10) Cnsumr Prot	AGN	15) Pol $ Disclosr	ABS

Election Results

1972 general:	Robert E. Jones (D)	101,303	(74%)
	Dieter J. Schrader (R)	33,352	(24%)
	Shirley Irwin (NDPA)	1,898	(1%)
1972 primary:	Robert E. Jones (D)	67,440	(72%)
	Mary Texas Garner (D)	18,756	(28%)
1970 general:	Robert E. Jones (D)	76,413	(85%)
	Ken Hearn (C)	7,599	(8%)
	Thorton Stanley (NDPA)	4,846	(5%)
	Thomas Lee Harris (Ind.)	1,200	(1%)

SIXTH DISTRICT   Political Background

Birmingham is one of the few major Southern cities that was not on the map during the time of the Civil War. It was founded a few years later and named, in hopes of a great industrial future, for the giant English manufacturing center. The hopes of the founders have been realized all too well. Birmingham is, and has been for many years, the major steel center in the South. But American steel is hardly a dynamic industry, and Birmingham, once nearly as large as Atlanta, has been left far behind its booming Georgia neighbor these last 20 years. To make matters worse, in 1972 the steel mills of Birmingham, set in valleys between high ridges, succeeded in so fouling the city's air that the federal government ordered them shut down for several days.

The city's reputation has not aided its economy. Most Alabamans, if not most Americans, still associate the city's name with the events of 1963. That was when the late Eugene "Bull" Connor, then police commissioner, set dogs and firehoses against peaceful civil rights demonstrators.

Shortly thereafter, Connor seemed nonplussed when somebody set off a bomb in a black church and killed three little girls.

Birmingham, however, has long since repudiated Bull Connor. In the 1970 gubernatorial primary—the only time in the last 10 years that Governor Wallace has faced a serious challenge—the city cast the heaviest anti-Wallace vote in the state. Commotion of any kind, of course, deters investment, and businessmen in the area probably noticed the results of the 1970 census: as metropolitan Atlanta's population shot up 37% during the sixties, Birmingham's rose less than 3%.

The 6th district takes in virtually all of the city of Birmingham and most of its suburbs, including Mountain Brook and Vestavia Hills, where most of the city's white establishment lives. Its Congressman is John H. Buchanan, Jr., a Republican who rode in on the 1964 Goldwater wave and who has managed to stay in office with little difficulty since. Buchanan is a Baptist minister, and from his record in the House it seems safe to say that he prefers fundamentalist preaching. At one point in his political career, while serving on the House Un-American Activities Committee (since renamed the House Internal Security Committee), the Congressman surprised some observers by denouncing the Ku Klux Klan. But the KKK was never really very strong in urban areas like Birmingham.

Census Data Pop. 493,045. Central city, 61%; suburban, 39%. Median family income, $8,683; families above $15,000: 16%; families below $3,000: 13%. Median years education, 11.9.

1972 Share of Federal Outlays $413,271,763

DOD	$47,572,576	HEW	$205,311,293
AEC	–	HUD	$21,771,967
NASA	$201,167	DOI	$797,087
DOT	$22,294,364	USDA	$14,115,549
		Other	$101,207,760

Federal Military-Industrial Commitments

DOD Contractors Xerox (Birmingham), $39.879m: unspecified. Hayes International (Birmingham), $32.527m: aircraft modification and repair; management of the Air Force publications center.

Economic Base Primary metal industries, especially blast furnace and steel mill products; finance, insurance and real estate; fabricated metal products, especially fabricated structural metal products; transportation equipment; and food and kindred products, especially bakery products and meat products.

The Voters

Registration No party registration; no accurate total registration figures available.
Median voting age 44.0
Employment profile White collar, 52%. Blue collar, 34%. Service, 14%. Farm, –%.
Ethnic groups Black, 30%. Total foreign stock, 3%.

Presidential vote

1972	Nixon (R)	108,102	(72%)
	McGovern (D)	41,625	(28%)
1968	Nixon (R)	34,505	(23%)
	Humphrey (D)	40,290	(26%)
	Wallace (AI)	78,464	(51%)

Representative

John Hall Buchanan (R) Elected 1964; b. March 19, 1928, Paris, Tenn.; home, Birmingham; Southern Theological Sem. Samford U. (formerly Howard U.) 1949; LL.D., 1967; Navy WWII; married, two children; Baptist.

Career Pastor, 1953–62; Finance Dir., Ala. Repub. Party, 1962–64.

Offices 1212 LHOB, 202-225-4921. Also 113 Fed. Bldg., 1800 Fifth Ave. N., Birmingham 35203, 205-325-3861.

Administrative Assistant Thomas O. Kay

Committees

Foreign Affairs (8th); Subs: Europe; Near East and South Asia State Department Organization and Foreign Operations (Ranking Mbr.).

Government Operations (8th); Subs: Government Activities (Ranking Mbr.); Intergovernmental Relations.

Group Ratings

	ADA	COPE	LWV	RIPON	NFU	LCV	CFA	NAB	NSI	ACA
1972	6	18	42	69	57	54	50	73	100	73
1971	11	17	13	35	27	–	13	–	–	89
1970	4	9	–	41	62	0	43	90	100	79

Key Votes

1) Busing	AGN	6) Cmbodia Bmbg	FOR	11) Chkg Acct Intrst	ABS
2) Strip Mines	FOR	7) Bust Hwy Trust	FOR	12) End HISC (HUAC)	AGN
3) Cut Mil $	AGN	8) Farm Sub Lmt	FOR	13) Nixon Sewer Veto	FOR
4) Rev Shrg	FOR	9) School Prayr	FOR	14) Corp Cmpaign $	AGN
5) Pub TV $	AGN	10) Cnsumr Prot	AGN	15) Pol $ Disclosr	AGN

Election Results

1972 general:	John H. Buchanan, Jr. (R)	91,499	(60%)
	Ben Erdreich (D)	54,497	(36%)
	Al Thomas (NDPA)	3,887	(3%)
	Edna L. Bowling (AI)	1,838	(1%)
	Dan Scott (C)	1,412	(1%)
1972 primary:	John H. Buchanan, Jr. (R), unopposed		
1970 general:	John H. Buchanan, Jr. (R)	50,060	(60%)
	John C. Schmarkey (D)	31,378	(38%)
	Dan Moore (C)	1,900	(2%)

SEVENTH DISTRICT Political Background

Alabama's 7th district provides an observer with some insights into why blacks, except for those in a few urban areas, are not a major factor in Southern congressional politics. On paper, the district has the state's largest black population (38%), but closer inspections show that only 33% of the potential electorate is black, whose birth and mortality rates are higher than those for whites. And that 38% continues to decline, as blacks move North or to the urban South. Add to this the traditional obstacles to black registration and voting—threats of economic reprisal and even of violence—and the picture becomes clear: blacks will never dominate congressional politics here in the 7th.

Not that these obstacles are insurmountable. In Greene County, for example, blacks have taken over all county offices; it was a protracted struggle in which a white probate judge refused to put the names of black candidates on the ballot. But in population, Greene County is the smallest in the state, and the five black-majority counties in the 7th, taken together, have less than a quarter of the district's people.

Most of the district's voters live in and around the city of Tuscaloosa (home of Bear Bryant and the University of Alabama) and in the industrial suburbs of Birmingham, like Bessemer and Fairfield. Overall, the 7th is one of the least pro-Wallace districts in the state, and in 1972 the least pro-Nixon. But this state of affairs has not prevented the election and reelection of Congressman Walter Flowers, whose voting record tends to reflect the views of Wallace and Nixon.

Flowers' position in the district has been enhanced by the split between the National Democratic Party of Alabama (NDPA) and the state's regular Democrats, whose state organization is controlled by Wallace opponents. The NDPA is a nearly all-black party, whose strongest adherents sometimes boycott Democratic primaries, and which in 1972 ran a separate slate of McGovern electors. Also in 1972, when Flowers had strenuous primary competition from Alberta Murphy, a white candidate with significant black support, NDPA adherents in counties like Greene and Hale simply stayed at home or voted in the NDPA primary. In November, the NDPA candidate was there on the ballot as a receptacle for votes cast by people of this inclination. The NDPA man in the general election took 14% of the total.

In other words, it is possible that a Congressman somewhat to the left of Flowers could come out of the 7th sometime. Certainly there are more of the ingredients for change here than in any other Alabama House district.

Census Data   Pop. 492,142. Central city, 14%; suburban, 47%. Median family income, $6,806; families above $15,000: 10%; families below $3,000: 22%. Median years education, 10.4.

1972 Share of Federal Outlays $401,855,268

DOD	$68,019,811	HEW	$185,470,631
AEC	$27,000	HUD	$4,849,519
NASA	$390,667	DOI	$1,882,801
DOT	$22,323,574	USDA	$30,054,962
		Other	$83,836,214

Federal Military-Industrial Commitments

DOD Installations   Craig AFB (Selma).

Economic Base   Primary metal industries, especially blast furnace and steel mill products; agriculture, notably cattle, dairy products and cotton; finance, insurance and real estate; fabricated metal products, especially fabricated structural metal products; and lumber and wood products. Also higher education (Univ. of Alabama).

The Voters

Registration   No party registration; no accurate total registration figures available.
Median voting age   43.4
Employment profile   White collar, 38%. Blue collar, 43%. Service, 15%. Farm, 4%.
Ethnic groups   Black, 38%. Total foreign stock, 1%.

Presidential vote

1972	Nixon (R)	92,421	(66%)
	McGovern (D)	47,536	(34%)
1968	Nixon (R)	14,585	(10%)
	Humphrey (D)	43,408	(29%)
	Wallace (AI)	89,956	(61%)

Representative

Walter W. Flowers (D) Elected 1968; b. April 12, 1933, Greenville; home, Tuscaloosa; U. of Ala., B.A., 1955, LL.B., 1957; Army 1958–59, USAR 1959–64; married, three children; Episcopalian.

Career Practicing atty., 1959–69.

Offices 439 CHOB, 202-225-2665. Also 204 Fed. Bldg., Tuscaloosa 35401, 205-752-3578, and Bessemer Ct. House, Bessemer 35020, 205-425-5031, and Fed. Bldg., Selma 36701, 205-872-2684.

Administrative Assistant Mandeville Christian

Committees

Judiciary (10th); Subs: No. 1 (Immigration and Nationality); No. 5 (Antitrust Matters).

Science and Astronautics (8th); Subs: Manned Space; Science, Research and Development.

Group Ratings

	ADA	COPE	LWV	RIPON	NFU	LCV	CFA	NAB	NSI	ACA
1972	6	18	20	46	67	18	0	64	100	68
1971	5	36	22	41	57	–	29	–	–	74
1970	8	28	–	25	31	0	71	44	100	75

Key Votes

1) Busing	AGN	6) Cmbodia Bmbg	FOR	11) Chkg Acct Intrst	AGN
2) Strip Mines	AGN	7) Bust Hwy Trust	AGN	12) End HISC (HUAC)	AGN
3) Cut Mil $	AGN	8) Farm Sub Lmt	AGN	13) Nixon Sewer Veto	AGN
4) Rev Shrg	FOR	9) School Prayr	FOR	14) Corp Cmpaign $	AGN
5) Pub TV $	FOR	10) Cnsumr Prot	FOR	15) Pol $ Disclosr	FOR

Election Results

1972 general:	Walter Flowers (D)	95,060	(85%)
	Lewis Black (NDPA)	15,703	(14%)
	Hal Radue (C)	1,278	(1%)
1972 primary:	Walter Flowers (D)	35,375	(62%)
	Alberta Murphy (D)	21,870	(38%)
1970 general:	Walter Flowers (D)	78,368	(76%)
	T. Y. Rogers (NDPA)	24,863	(24%)

ALASKA

Political Background

Alaska is the nation's largest state (586,000 square miles) and also its smallest (300,000 people). Alaskans live in the land of the midnight sun and of darkness at noon; of winter wind-chill factors that reach astounding proportions and of muggy, mosquito-filled summers; of the tallest mountains in North America and of thousands of miles of rugged seacoast. Here also is the Texas boomer at the giant North Slope oil strike, the man being none too fond of the desperately poor, often alcoholic, Eskimo and Indian, whose average life span is well under 40 years.

Alaska is more than twice the size of Texas. And like the continental United States, Alaska spans four time zones as the state arcs from a point some 550 miles north and west of Seattle to the Aleutian Island of Attu, not far from the International Dateline and USSR Standard Time. But for all its size and expanse, Alaska has only one railroad (Anchorage to Fairbanks) and few highways—the airplane is the only way one can really get around. Even the most tiny and isolated village in the interior has a place cleared on a frozen river or in the bush for an airstrip. Otherwise the village is cut off completely.

Alaska, our last frontier, reminded us of her still grim character when in October 1972, the small plane carrying Nick Begich, the state's Congressman, and House Majority Leader Hale Boggs disappeared. Both are now presumed dead. The frontier is there, and the caribou and Eskimo hunters range across it. But most of the people in the state are concentrated in a couple of urban areas, more than 40% in greater Anchorage alone. And though dreams of sudden riches still draw men to the Alaskan wilderness, the livelihood of most of the citizens here depends, directly or indirectly, on that most prosaic of employers, the federal government.

For years, Alaskans yearned for statehood, for control of their own affairs, for economic independence from exploitative Seattle. But in many ways, Alaska is still a political dependent; decisions continue to be made in far away Washington, D.C. that will shape her future much as the Northwest Ordinance did to Ohio's or the Homestead Act did to Nebraska's. For example, it was only in 1971, when Congress passed the Alaska Native Claims Act, that the most basic issue—ownership of the land—was settled, or at least the machinery of settlement put into action. Neither the Russians, who, after decimating the Aleutian seal population and committing atrocities upon the natives, sold Alaska in 1867, nor the Americans, who bought it (Seward's Folly), ever gave the territory's natives—Eskimos, Aleuts, and Indians—a thin dime for the real estate itself. The natives never gave either the Russians or Americans title to the land. No agreement similar to the one in which the Indians signed away Manhattan Island for $24 or California for $23 million existed: no lawyer could look it up.

Under the new law passed in 1971, Congress gave the natives $962 million and 40 million acres of land—the money to be administered and the precise acreage chosen by 12 regional native corporations. The legislation also ended the freeze on federal lands imposed in 1966 by then-Interior Secretary Stewart Udall. This means that Alaska can once again go about selecting the 103 million acres promised to it by the Statehood Act. The men in charge will surely choose the lands with the most mineral potential. The state has already laid claim to the North Slope, for which various oil companies paid Alaskans $900 million to lease. But as yet not a drop of the 10 billion barrels of oil under the North Slope (east Texas, 5 billion; Kuwait, 62 billion) has found its way to market. There has been no way to get it there.

In 1972, the Interior Department gave its final approval to a proposal made by a consortium of oil companies to build a 48-inch hot-oil pipeline from the Arctic wells 789 miles across the breadth of Alaska to the warm-water port of Valdez. Earlier, environmentalists had objected to the plan, arguing (1) that the pipeline would melt the permafrost (permanently frozen subsoil) that lies just beneath a cover of Arctic vegetation—with the vegetation gone, summer rains might bring on erosion that could go on forever; (2) that a disastrous pipeline break could easily occur in earthquake-prone Alaska; and (3) that the treacherous waters around Valdez make an oil spill almost certain.

Just after the strike was made, the oil companies miscalculated. Accustomed to the politics of Texas, Oklahoma, and Louisiana, the companies figured that their low-profile, well-heeled operatives could handle any problems. These operatives underestimated the scope, fervor, and sophistication of the nation's environmentalists, whose approach to politics, unlike those of oilmen, consists of publicity and outrage. So now a roughneck is forbidden by his oil company boss to drop so much as a candy wrapper on the lonely Alaskan tundra.

In its 1972 approval, Interior conceded some of the objections raised by the environmentalists, but said that the nation's need for domestic oil was pressing enough to override the concerns. In addition, Alaskans pointed to the state's chronic unemployment, which often exceeds 10%. This, they argued, could be alleviated, at least temporarily, by the jobs the building of the pipeline would produce. Moreover, the state is fast depleting the $900 million lease money, and needs that promised by royalties on actual production.

So the environmentalists took Interior to court, and won a decision in the District of Columbia Circuit. The court refused to rule on the environmental questions involved, and instead based its decision to block construction on the grounds that no federal statute permits Interior to grant as wide a right-of-way across public lands as it allowed the pipeline consortium. In matters of great import, it seems, the government feels free to overlook the letter of the law. An expedited appeal is, at this writing, before the Supreme Court. But the obstacle that the Circuit Court interposed was one Congress took action to remove.

Nobody worked harder at this than the two Senators from Alaska, Democrat Mike Gravel and Republican Ted Stevens. Like almost all Alaskan politicians, these men are pipeline boosters. Gravel, before a group of New Jersey environmentalists, taking a leaf perhaps from slavers of the Old South, went so far as to say that the pipeline was ecologically a "positive good." Among skeptical colleagues on the Hill, both men argued that construction should begin as soon as possible. To that end, they backed legislation sponsored by Interior Committee Chairman Henry Jackson that revised entirely the regulations under which the government can lease its lands to private utilities; and in the event environmentalists continue to battle the pipeline in court, they introduced a measure that would, *post facto*, approve the decision of the Department of Interior. The Gravel-Stevens proposal passed the Senate, 50-49, in July 1973. Opposition to the Alaskan pipeline came not merely from environmentalists but from Midwestern and Eastern members of Congress who wanted a Canadian route, to feed oil directly into their energy-poor parts of the country.

The popularity of the project in Alaska may be gauged by the role it played in the March 1973 special election to replace Congressman Begich, who had been reelected, despite his disappearance, the previous November. Both candidates, state Sen. Don Young and Alaskan Native Federation president Emil Notti, were pipeline advocates. But Democrat Notti made the mistake of featuring Sen. Edward Kennedy, a pipeline foe, on his TV ads; the Republicans, including ex-Gov. (1967–69) and Interior Secretary (1969–70) Walter Hickel, counterattacked fiercely. Another major factor in the outcome—Young won by a small but comfortable margin—was Notti's Indian ancestry. Many Alaskan whites resent the generous terms of the natives' land claims settlement.

Senate passage of the pipeline measure no doubt helps Mike Gravel's electoral chances when his Senate seat comes up in 1974. The word most often used to describe Gravel is "erratic." In 1968, he beat one of the Senate's original doves, Sen. Ernest Gruening, one of the two men to vote against the Gulf of Tonkin resolution in 1964. Gravel's victory was largely the result of a TV blitz engineered by campaign consultant Joe Napolitan the weekend before the decisive Democratic primary. But in a few short years, Gravel himself became one of the Senate's most impassioned foes of the war and of the draft.

In 1971, at the height of the controversy over the publication of the Pentagon Papers, Gravel took the floor of the Senate intending to read into the record massive excerpts from the copy he had obtained. Sen. Robert Griffin of Michigan, a Nixon Administration loyalist, promptly stopped the Alaskan with a little parliamentary legerdemain. And so Gravel called an evening session of a subcommittee he chaired (Public Buildings and Grounds) and read from the papers until he collapsed in tears. Later he apologized to a horrified Senate, which, whatever the carnage in the world outside, cherishes decorum within its chambers. At the 1972 Miami Democratic Convention, Gravel once again demonstrated his impulsive character. As a candidate for Vice-President, he mounted the podium and made the nominating speech for himself—an unprecedented act, but coming at prime time only in Hawaii and Alaska.

Gravel is in some trouble in Alaska because of his behavior. Many people here feel that Alaskan members of Congress, given the state's great dependence on the federal government, should devote their complete energies to the interests of Alaska. Furthermore, the feeling is that, however well Gravel may tend state matters, he loses clout in the Senate because of his non-Alaskan activities. One man who could certainly give Gravel trouble in 1974 is the Alaskan best known to the rest of the country, Walter Hickel. As Interior Secretary, Hickel at first horrified environmentalists by coming out against "conservation for conservation's sake," and then delighted them by, among other things, stopping oil-drilling in the Santa Barbara Channel. Although he was fired from his Cabinet post after the 1970 elections, he was back in Miami Beach in 1972 praising President Nixon. He remains one of the leaders of Alaska'a Republican party. Hickel has said that he would never succumb to Potomac fever, and odds are that he will run for Governor rather than Senator in 1974. Whatever happens, the Republicans can be expected to put up a strong fight for Gravel's seat.

Sen. Stevens is a less tempestuous figure than either Gravel or Hickel. A Republican with a fairly independent voting record, he tends, in the crunch, to come down on the side of the Nixon Administration. After a few years in the Alaska House and a short career as a prosperous Anchorage lawyer and in the Eisenhower Interior Department, Stevens was suddenly elevated to the Senate after the December 1968 death of Sen. Bob Bartlett—the man probably most responsible for Alaskan statehood. Because Bartlett had won reelection in 1966, by an overwhelming majority, Stevens had to face the voters in 1970 to win the remainder of the term and then again in 1972 to win a full term of his own. He won both races easily, the second by a margin approaching those Bartlett used to enjoy. Like Gravel, Stevens left the Interior Committee in 1973 after the native claims issue was settled. He is now a member of the Appropriations Committee and a ranking member of its Interior Subcommittee.

Census Data Pop. 302,173; 0.15% of U.S. total, 50th largest; change 1960–70, 33.6%. Central city, 0%; suburban, 0%. Median family income, $12,441; 1st highest; families above $15,000: 38%; families below $3,000: 7%. Median years education, 12.5.

1972 Share of Federal Tax Burden $355,330,000; 0.17% of U.S. total, 49th largest.

1972 Share of Federal Outlays $966,603,393; 0.45% of U.S. total, 41st largest. Per capita federal spending, $3,199.

DOD	$426,716,000	34th (0.68%)	HEW	$116,912,172	49th (0.16%)
AEC	$20,552,149	19th (0.78%)	HUD	$3,742,290	50th (0.12%)
NASA	$1,396,695	32nd (0.69%)	VA	$9,425,972	50th (0.08%)
DOT	$189,517,856	13th (2.40%)	USDA	$26,687,002	45th (0.17%)
DOC	$18,287,734	15th (1.41%)	CSC	$7,450,745	46th (0.18%)
DOI	$78,221,221	7th (3.69%)	TD	$11,121,972	50th (0.07%)
DOJ	$2,858,056	47th (1.13%)	Other	$53,513,529	

Federal Military-Industrial Commitments

DOD Contractors ITT Artic Serverices (Anchorage), $16.147m: unspecified communication services. Christenson Raber Kief and Associates, Inc. (Adak), $15,589m: unspecified. Tensoro-Alaskan Petroleum Corp. (Kenai Village), $11,455m: petroleum products. General Electric (Shemya Air Force Station), $10,318m: support of military space satellites.
DOD Installations Fort Greely AB (Big Delta). Fort Richardson AB (Anchorage). Fort Wainwright (Fairbanks). Naval Communication Station (Adak). Naval Station (Adak). Eielson AFB (Fairbanks). Elmendorf AFB (Anchorage). Galena Airport, AF (Galena). King Salmon, AF (King Salmon). Shemya AF Station (Shemya).
AEC Operations Holmes & Narver, Inc. (Amchitka), $18,431m: engineering services at Nuclear Test Site.

Economic Base Finance, insurance and real estate; food and kindred products, especially canned and cured sea foods; agriculture and fishing, notably fish, dairy products, eggs, potatoes and cattle; oil and gas field services, and other oil and gas extraction activity; paper pulp, and other paper and allied products.

Political Line-up Governor, William A. Egan (D); seat up, 1974. Senators, Mike Gravel (D) and Ted Stevens (R). Representatives, 1 R, At Large. State Senate (11 R and 9 D); State House (20 D, 19 R, and 1 Ind.).

The Voters

Registration 148,930 Total. 43,076 D (29%); 24,581 R (17%); 79,129 non-partisan (53%); 2,174 other (1%).
Median voting age 34.0
Employment profile White collar, 55%. Blue collar, 30%. Service, 15%. Farm, 4%.
Ethnic groups Black, 3%. Indian, 16%. Total foreign stock, 11%.

Presidential vote

1972	Nixon (R)	55,349	(63%)
	McGovern (D)	32,967	(37%)
1968	Nixon (R)	37,600	(45%)
	Humphrey (D)	35,411	(43%)
	Wallace (AI)	10,024	(12%)
1964	Johnson (D)	44,329	(66%)
	Goldwater (R)	22,930	(34%)

Senator

Mike Gravel (D) Elected 1968, seat up 1974; b. May 13, 1930, Springfield, Mass.; home, Anchorage; Columbia U., B.S., 1956; married, two children; Unitarian.

Career Real estate developer; Alaska House of Reps., 1962–66; Speaker, 1965.

Offices 1251 NSOB, 202-225-6665. Also P.O. Box 2283, Anchorage 99501, 907-272-0713.

Administrative Assistant Martin J. Wolff

Committees

Finance (9th); Subs: Foundations; International Finance and Resources.

Public Works (4th); Subs:

Water Resources (Chm.); Economic Development; Public Buildings and Grounds; Roads.

Joint Com. on Congressional Operations (2nd).

Sp. Com. to Study Questions Related to Secret and Confidential Government Documents (5th).

Group Ratings

	ADA	COPE	LWV	RIPON	NFU	LCV	CFA	NAB	NSI	ACA
1972	75	100	100	71	100	53	100	11	20	0
1971	81	89	100	52	90	–	75	–	–	0
1970	72	83	–	80	94	27	–	14	10	0

Key Votes

1) Busing	FOR	8) Sea Life Prot	AGN	15) Tax Singls Less	FOR
2) Alas P-line	FOR	9) Campaign Subs	FOR	16) Min Tax for Rich	FOR
3) Gun Cntrl	AGN	10) Cmbodia Bmbg	AGN	17) Euro Troop Rdctn	FOR
4) Rehnquist	AGN	11) Legal Srvices	FOR	18) Bust Hwy Trust	AGN
5) Pub TV $	ABS	12) Rev Sharing	FOR	19) Maid Min Wage	FOR
6) EZ Votr Reg	FOR	13) Cnsumr Prot	ABS	20) Farm Sub Limit	AGN
7) No-Fault	FOR	14) Eq Rts Amend	FOR	21) Highr Credt Chgs	ABS

Election Results

1968 general:	Mike Gravel (D)	36,527	(45%)
	Elmer Rasmuson (R)	30,286	(37%)
	Ernest Gruening (write-in)	14,188	(18%)
1968 primary:	Mike Gravel (D)	17,971	(53%)
	Ernest Gruening (D)	16,015	(47%)

Senator

Theodore F. Stevens (R) Elected Appointed 1968, Elected 1970, seat up 1978; b. Nov. 18, 1923, Indianapolis, Ind.; home, Anchorage; Oreg. State Col., Mont. State Col., UCLA, B.A., 1947; Harvard, LL.B., 1950; Army Air Corps, WWII; married, five children; Episcopalian.

Career Practicing atty., 1950–53, 1961–68; U.S. Attorney, 1953–56; U.S. Dept. of Interior, 1956–61, Solicitor, 1960; Alaska House of Reps., 1964–68.

Offices 411 OSOB, 202-225-3004. Also 215 Fed. Bldg., Anchorage 99501, 907-272-9561.

Administrative Assistant None

Committees

Appropriations (8th); Subs: Housing and Urban Development, Space, Science, Veterans; Interior and Related Agencies (Ranking Mbr.); Labor and Health, Education and Welfare, and Related Agencies; Public Works, AEC; Transportation and Related Agencies.

Commerce (6th); Subs: Aviation; Communications; Consumer; Merchant Marine; Oceans and Atmosphere (Ranking Mbr.); Foreign Commerce and Tourism.

Post Office and Civil Service (2nd); Subs: Compensation and Employment Benefits (Ranking Mbr.); Postal Operations.

Group Ratings

	ADA	COPE	LWV	RIPON	NFU	LCV	CFA	NAB	NSI	ACA
1972	35	86	82	68	67	32	73	36	80	38
1971	48	60	69	48	55	–	57	–	–	36
1970	25	64	–	57	67	0	–	38	89	19

Key Votes

1) Busing	FOR	8) Sea Life Prot	AGN	15) Tax Singls Less	FOR
2) Alas P-line	FOR	9) Campaign Subs	AGN	16) Min Tax for Rich	AGN
3) Gun Cntrl	AGN	10) Cmbodia Bmbg	AGN	17) Euro Troop Rdctn	AGN
4) Rehnquist	FOR	11) Legal Srvices	FOR	18) Bust Hwy Trust	AGN
5) Pub TV $	AGN	12) Rev Sharing	FOR	19) Maid Min Wage	FOR
6) EZ Votr Reg	AGN	13) Cnsumr Prot	AGN	20) Farm Sub Limit	AGN
7) No-Fault	FOR	14) Eq Rts Amend	FOR	21) Highr Credt Chgs	ABS

Election Results

1972 general:	Ted Stevens (R)	74,216	(77%)
	Gene Guess (D)	21,791	(23%)
1972 primary:	Ted Stevens (R), unopposed		
1970 general:	Ted Stevens (R)	47,908	(59%)
	Wendell P. Kay (D)	32,636	(41%)

Representative

Donald E. Young (R) Elected March 6, 1973; b. June 9, 1933, Meridian, Calif.; home, Fort Yukon; Chico State Col., B.A., 1956; married, two children; Episcopalian.

Career Riverboat capt.; educator, 9 yrs.; Fort Yukon City Council, 6 yrs., Mayor, 4 yrs.; State House, 1966–70; State Senate, 1970–73.

Offices 1210 LHOB, 202-225-5765.

Administrative Assistant Erol Stone

Committees

Interior and Insular Affairs (18th); Subs: No. 5 (Mines and Mining); No. 6 (Indian Affairs); No. 7 (Public Lands).

Merchant Marine and Fisheries (16th); Subs: Coast Guard and Navigation; Panama Canal.

Group Ratings: Newly Elected

Key Votes

1) Busing	NE	6) Cmbodia Bmbg	FOR	11) Chkg Acct Intrst	AGN
2) Strip Mines	NE	7) Bust Hwy Trust	AGN	12) End HISC (HUAC)	AGN
3) Cut Mil $	NE	8) Farm Sub Lmt	NE	13) Nixon Sewer Veto	FOR
4) Rev Shrg	NE	9) School Prayr	NE	14) Corp Cmpaign $	NE
5) Pub TV $	NE	10) Cnsumr Prot	NE	15) Pol $ Disclosr	NE

Election Results

1973 special: Don Young (R)   35,123   (52%)
                 Emil Notti (D)   33,044   (48%)
1973 primary: Don Young (R), unopposed

ARIZONA

Political Background

To most Americans, Arizona brings to mind the Grand Canyon, Navajo hogans, Tombstone and Wyatt Earp, or maybe even London Bridge, which thanks to a developer now sits proudly in a patch of Arizona desert. But the attention of a political analyst is focused almost entirely on Phoenix and Tucson. Some 55% of the state's voters live in greater Phoenix, and another 21% in and around Tucson. In 1940 the state had a population of 550,000; by 1970, it was 1,772,000, and still growing. A quite literal new majority has completely transformed the politics of Arizona in the last 25 years.

The change here is best illustrated by the contrasting careers of the state's two best-known politicians: Rep. (1912–27) and Sen. (1927–69) Carl Hayden, and Sen. (1953–65, 1969–) Barry Goldwater. Hayden began his political career as a councilman in Tempe (formerly Hayden's Crossing) in 1902, when Phoenix was just a hot, sleepy depot-station on the Southern Pacific Railroad. Hayden was a Democrat, and a fairly conservative one—as was every successful Arizona politician until the 1950s. The state had a Democratic heritage that came out of the Southern origin of most of its early settlers, and the Mexican background of many of the rest. Although Arizona occasionally went Republican in national elections (it never supported a losing presidential candidate until 1960), Hayden and his fellow Democrats rarely had any difficulty with the voters. The basic Hayden success formula was to see that federal money was pumped into the state. Hayden was particularly interested in highways, but his last great legacy to his constituents was the Central Arizona Project, pushed through in 1968 during his last full year in Congress. This will presumably provide all the water that thirsty agricultural Arizona and urban Phoenix will ever need.

The birth of Arizona's now dominant conservative Republicanism can be dated with some accuracy to the year 1949, when Barry Goldwater, then proprietor of his family's Phoenix department store, was elected to the Phoenix City Council. The next year Goldwater helped Republican Howard Pyle win the governorship, and in 1952 the Republicans swept the state: Eisenhower won its electoral votes, Pyle was reelected, and Goldwater went to the United States Senate. (The man he beat, Sen. Ernest MacFarland, was then Senate Majority Leader, whose political demise set the stage for Lyndon Johnson's ascent to the Senate Democratic leadership.) Goldwater won reelection by a large margin in 1958, again against MacFarland; but the Republican directed the brunt of his rhetoric against national union leaders like the late Walter Reuther—labor leaders who then had, and still have, few members and little clout in Arizona.

The year 1958 was a bad one for conservative Republicans in most states. So Goldwater's victory elevated him to national prominence. His frank, often blunt and impolitic articulation of his beliefs brought him such devotion and volunteer support all over the country that he won the 1964 Republican presidential nomination without having to push himself too hard.

Since 1958, things have been very good for Arizona Republicans. They have lost only one major statewide race in the last 12 years, the governorship in 1964, and that was regained two years later. The loser in 1964 was Richard Kleindienst. Some of the bright young men who supported Goldwater during the fifties went on to serve in the Nixon Administration—Kleindienst himself as Attorney General, William Rehnquist as Associate Justice of the Supreme Court, and Dean Burch of the FCC.

Migration patterns promise more of the same kind of politics for the state. The big influx, as Neil Peirce points out in *The Mountain States of America*, consists of white-collar technicians from the South, Midwest, and southern California—the kind of people who made metropolitan Phoenix more Republican in the 1972 presidential race than Orange County, California.

The long-range outlook for the Democrats looks bad. But in the short-run past, the Democrats proved feisty in 1970 and 1972. The combativeness has not come from the so-called "pinto" Democrats, who still dominate the courthouses in the small counties and whose politics are similar to those of Carl Hayden's. Instead, the surprisingly aggressive races have been run by urban Democratic candidates, mainly from Phoenix. These men have not held local office (because the Republicans win everything), and they have usually followed the trends established by the national party, with some concessions to local conservatism.

None of the urban Democrats has yet won a race, but some have come surprisingly close. Perhaps the most successful was Raul Castro (no relation to Fidel), a former judge and Ambassador to Bolivia and El Salvador. He just missed upsetting Gov. (and ex-TV newsman) Jack Williams in 1970. Castro is considered to have an excellent chance of winning the Governorship in 1972. Castro's 1970 ticket-mate, Sam Grossman, a shopping center magnate from California, also managed to scare Sen. Paul Fannin, until certain questions arose about the legitimacy of Grossman's Arizona residency. There were no major statewide races in 1972. But in two congressional districts Democrats put on strong campaigns, and in one of them—the newly created 4th district—came close to scoring an upset.

Meanwhile, Arizona has, in Goldwater and Fannin, about as conservative a Senate delegation as there is. Goldwater, who was once a Brigadier General in the Air Force Reserves, has always sustained a great interest in military policy, and, of course, in high defense spending. He is currently the ranking minority member of the Aeronautics and Space Sciences Committee and also serves on Armed Services. By now he would have been the ranking Republican on Armed Services, had he not given up his Senate seat to run for the presidency. That decision—to give up a safe Senate seat for a presidential effort he never believed he could win—is typical of Barry Goldwater. He is among the most principled and least ambitious politicians in Washington. And his principles sometimes lead him in directions that run contrary to his political loyalties. Goldwater, for example, was one of the Senate's leading opponents of the draft, on libertarian philosophical grounds. He also voted against the Nixon Administration's proposal to bail out Lockheed. Here he cited a basic assumption of free enterprise; if a company cannot operate profitably, it deserves to go under.

As the 93rd Congress convened, there was talk that Goldwater might choose to retire in 1974, when he will be 65. At that time, it appeared as though he could have returned to his mountaintop home near Phoenix with the satisfaction that he had accomplished most of what he set out to do 25 years earlier; with Nixon's 1972 landslide victory, the American people, it seemed, had vindicated the positions the Arizonan took in the 1964 campaign. Then the full Watergate story broke. Goldwater was clearly appalled. He spoke out early and on frequent occasions thereafter; despite his previous strong support of Nixon, Goldwater said that the President should resign if he had lied about the break-in or the cover-up. Goldwater's statements cued responses from many other conservatives, who then began to criticize harshly the tactics of the Committee to Reelect the President. Goldwater himself would never tolerate unseemly political behavior; no hint of scandal ever touched his 1964 campaign or his Arizona Senate races. At this writing, it appears Watergate has so stung Goldwater that he has decided to stay in the 1974 contest, which means staying in the Senate. Democratic Congressman Morris Udall has reportedly considered making the race, but everyone expects Goldwater, if he runs, to win easily, especially after his reaction to Watergate.

Fannin, who easily won the seat Goldwater relinquished in 1964, makes less of a splash in the Senate. He serves quietly on the Finance and Interior committees. In late 1971 and early 1972, however, he did win some headlines in Phoenix, when he was arrested on a drunk-driving charge. According to columnist Jack Anderson, local authorities purposely blew the prosecution to let Fannin off; later, Fannin was convicted. It is generally expected that Fannin will retire in 1976 when his seat comes up and when he will be 69.

Arizona has gained one congressional seat in each of the last three censuses, and all three of the new seats have eventually been captured by the Republicans. The heavily Republican legislature split Phoenix and surrounding Maricopa County among three districts, thereby insuring Phoenix—and Republican—domination of each. The remaining seat is held in secure fashion by Democrat Morris Udall, but if Udall runs for the Senate, as he is expected to do in 1976, the district could go either way.

Census Data Pop. 1,772,482; 0.88% of U.S. total, 33rd largest; change 1960–70, 36.1%. Central city, 27%; suburban, 48%. Median family income, $9,186; 24th highest; families above $15,000: 19%; families below $3,000: 11%. Median years education, 12.3.

1972 Share of Federal Tax Burden $1,630,340,000; 0.78% of U.S. total, 31st largest.

1972 Share of Federal Outlays $2,320,091,012; 1.07% of U.S. total, 30th largest. Per capita federal spending, $1,309.

DOD	$884,370,000	20th	(1.41%)	HEW	$623,441,050	34th (0.87%)
AEC	$366,978	36th	(0.01%)	HUD	$22,584,011	34th (0.74%)
NASA	$6,208,036	23rd	(0.21%)	VA	$135,959,106	32nd (1.19%)
DOT	$89,625,388	30th	(1.14%)	USDA	$125,062,983	37th (0.81%)
DOC	$5,530,303	36th	(0.43%)	CSC	$54,116,995	21st (1.31%)
DOI	$184,517,748	3rd	(8.70%)	TD	$57,459,256	34th (0.35%)
DOJ	$14,571,635	24th	(1.48%)	Other	$116,277,523	

Economic Base Finance, insurance and real estate; electrical equipment and supplies, especially electronic components and accessories; agriculture, notably cattle, cotton lint, lettuce and dairy products; metal mining, especially copper ores; machinery, especially office and computing machines; food and kindred products; tourism.

Political Line-up Governor, Jack Williams (R); seat up, 1974. Senators, Paul J. Fannin (R) and Barry M. Goldwater (R). Representatives, 4 (3 R and 1 D). State Senate (18 R and 12 D); State House (38 R and 22 D).

The Voters

Registration 861,812 Total. 455,985 D (53%); 362,196 R (42%); 43,631 other (5%).
Median voting age 42.0
Employment profile White collar, 51%. Blue collar, 32%. Service, 14%. Farm, 3%.
Ethnic groups Black, 3%. Indian, 5%. Spanish, 19%. Total foreign stock, 17%. Canada, Germany, 1% each.

Presidential vote

1972	Nixon (R)	402,812	(67%)
	McGovern (D)	198,540	(33%)
1968	Nixon (R)	266,721	(55%)
	Humphrey (D)	170,514	(35%)
	Wallace (AI)	46,573	(10%)
1964	Johnson (D)	237,753	(50%)
	Goldwater (R)	242,535	(50%)

Senator

Paul Jones Fannin (R) Elected 1964, seat up 1976; b. Jan. 29, 1907, Ashland, Ky.; home, Phoenix; U. of Ariz., Stanford, B.A., 1930; Gov. of Ariz. 1959–64; married, four children; Methodist.

Career Former partner in Fannin Brothers, industrial firm marketing petroleum; three-term Gov. of Ariz.

Offices 140 OSOB, 202-225-4521. Also 3417 Fed. Bldg., Phoenix 85025, 602-261-4486, and 326 Fed. Bldg., Tucson 85702, 602-792-6336.

Administrative Assistant Joseph Jenckes

Committees

Finance (3rd); Subs: International Trade (Ranking Mbr.); Foundations.

Interior and Insular Affairs (Ranking Mbr.); Subs; Indian Affairs (Ranking Mbr.); Water and Power Resources; Sp. Sub. on Legislative Oversight (Ranking Mbr.).

Joint Com. on Navajo-Hopi Indian Administration.

Joint Study Com. on Budget Control.

Group Ratings

	ADA	COPE	LWV	RIPON	NFU	LCV	CFA	NAB	NSI	ACA
1972	5	0	20	41	22	4	0	91	100	95
1971	0	25	8	14	9	–	17	–	–	95
1970	3	8	–	32	30	0	–	75	100	90

Key Votes

1) Busing	AGN	8) Sea Life Prot	AGN	15) Tax Singls Less	AGN
2) Alas P-line	FOR	9) Campaign Subs	AGN	16) Min Tax for Rich	AGN
3) Gun Cntrl	AGN	10) Cmbodia Bmbg	FOR	17) Euro Troop Rdctn	AGN
4) Rehnquist	FOR	11) Legal Srvices	AGN	18) Bust Hwy Trust	AGN
5) Pub TV $	FOR	12) Rev Sharing	ABS	19) Maid Min Wage	AGN
6) EZ Votr Reg	AGN	13) Cnsumr Prot	AGN	20) Farm Sub Limit	AGN
7) No-Fault	AGN	14) Eq Rts Amend	AGN	21) Highr Credt Chgs	FOR

Election Results

1970 general:	Paul Fannin (R)	228,284	(56%)
	Sam Grossman (D)	179,512	(44%)
1970 primary:	Paul Fannin (R), unopposed		
1964 general:	Paul Fannin (R)	241,089	(51%)
	Roy Elson (D)	227,712	(49%)

Senator

Barry M. Goldwater (R) Elected 1968, seat up 1974; b. Jan. 1, 1909, Phoenix; home, Phoenix; U. of Ariz., 1928; Army Air Corps, WWII; married, four children; Episcopalian.

Career Major Gen. USAFER (Ret.), 1937–67; Pres., Goldwater's Inc., 1929; Chm. Bd., 1937–53; Phoenix City Council, 1949–51; U.S. Senate, 1952–64; Repub. candidate for Pres. 1964.

Offices 440 OSOB, 202-225-2235. Also 5420 Fed. Bldg., Phoenix 85025, 602-261-4086, and P.O. Bldg., Scott and Broadway, Tucson 85701, 602-792-6334.

Administrative Assistant Terry Emerson (L.A.)

Committees

Aeronautical and Space Sciences (Ranking Mbr.).

Armed Services (4th); Subs: Research and Development; National Stockpile and Naval Petroleum Reserves; Preparedness Investigating; Tactical Air Power (Ranking Mbr.); Arms Control (Ranking Mbr.).

Group Ratings

	ADA	COPE	LWV	RIPON	NFU	LCV	CFA	NAB	NSI	ACA
1972	5	0	0	36	20	0	0	100	90	87
1971	4	10	0	33	14	–	0	–	–	100
1970	3	9	–	25	18	1	–	71	100	92

Key Votes

1) Busing	AGN	8) Sea Life Prot	AGN	15) Tax Singls Less	ABS
2) Alas P-line	FOR	9) Campaign Subs	AGN	16) Min Tax for Rich	ABS
3) Gun Cntrl	AGN	10) Cmbodia Bmbg	FOR	17) Euro Troop Rdctn	AGN

4) Rehnquist	FOR	11) Legal Srvices	AGN	18) Bust Hwy Trust	AGN
5) Pub TV $	ABS	12) Rev Sharing	AGN	19) Maid Min Wage	ABS
6) EZ Votr Reg	AGN	13) Cnsumr Prot	ABS	20) Farm Sub Limit	AGN
7) No-Fault	AGN	14) Eq Rts Amend	AGN	21) Highr Credt Chgs	ABS

Election Results

1968 general:	Barry Goldwater (R)	274,607	(57%)
	Roy Elson (D)	205,338	(43%)
1968 primary:	Barry Goldwater (R), unopposed		

FIRST DISTRICT   Political Background

Phoenix is one of those instant cities that lie in what Kevin Phillips calls the Sun Belt. These places are almost totally a creation of the air-conditioned years after World War II. In 1940, Phoenix had 65,000 citizens; by 1970, 581,000. Even in the years before the war, Phoenix was considered Arizona's Republican city; with Tucson, more Spanish, more Southern, and more Democratic. But from the election returns, it seems that virtually all of the hundreds of thousands who flocked to Phoenix in the postwar period were, or quickly became, Goldwater Republicans. No other major metropolitan area—and Phoenix certainly qualifies as one, with close to a million residents—has consistently voted as heavily Republican as the Arizona capital.

Why? Retirees, for one thing. Older people with enough money to afford living in a place like Del Webb's Sun City (nobody under 50, nobody with school children, and effectively no blacks) usually cast huge Republican majorities. But more important, most of the jobs that buttress the boom in Phoenix lie in the defense, electronics, and other technical industries. These are not people who, having moved West, miss the *New York Times*; they have been quite content with Eugene Pulliam's militantly conservative *Arizona Republic*. Finally, there is the state's political culture. The rising Goldwater movement, consisting mostly of clean-cut, talented, hardworking young men from Phoenix (often themselves immigrants from the Midwest) hit it off well with the influx of newcomers. The Democrats, most of them cigar-chewing oldtimers from dusty county seats, did not.

One of the crew-cut young men from the early days of the Goldwater movement—he recently let his hair grow out—is 1st district Congressman John Rhodes. In 1952, when Goldwater was first elected to the Senate, Rhodes became the first Republican Arizona ever sent to the U.S. House of Representatives. At that time, Rhodes' seat was all of Maricopa County, including Phoenix and all of its suburbs. But in the last eight years, the district has been pruned down by successive redistrictings, leaving Rhodes in 1972 with the bulk of the city's black and Chicano populations, as well as with the 30,000 students at Arizona State University in Tempe (pronounced Tem-PEE).

The districting change stimulated Democratic candidate Gerald Pollack into a campaign much more aggressive than the one he waged in 1970, when Rhodes beat him better than 2–1. Rhodes was thrown on the defensive rather badly on environmental issues—on which the Congressman has considerable say in Washington as the ranking Republican on the Appropriations Public Works Subcommittee. Predictably, Rhodes won, but only by a 57–43 margin, far from what he has grown accustomed to. Rhodes now occupies positions of genuine influence on the Hill: Chairman of the House Republican Policy Committee and number two Republican on the vital Appropriations Committee. But his relatively narrow 1972 margin and the fact that, allowing even for redistricting, Rhodes ran worse in the year of Nixon than in 1970, suggest that he will have to spend more time tending his district. His erstwhile opponent Pollock went on to wage a quixotic crusade to recall Gov. Jack Williams, which foundered when its main supporters, Cesar Chavez's United Farm Workers, became preoccupied with a serious challenge to their interests in California. The demography of the new 1st district indicates, however, that if the newly pesky Democrats are going to make any gains in Phoenix, it will be here in the 1st.

Census Data   Pop. 442,589. Central city, 52%; suburban, 48%. Median family income, $9,126; families above $15,000: 18%; families below $3,000: 10.1%. Median years education, 12.2.

1972 Share of Federal Outlays $460,081,276

DOD	$158,801,559	HEW	$152,352,100
AEC	$34,366	HUD	$4,153,995
NASA	$1,792,291	DOI	$14,093,752
DOT	$18,404,900	USDA	$18,658,570
		Other	$$91,789,743

Federal Military-Industrial Commitments

DOD Contractors Garrett Corporation (Phoenix), $48.484m: aircraft engines and parts. Motorola (Phoenix), $43.384m: targeting devices and other electronic ware. Lockheed Aircraft (Phoenix), $14.969m: aircraft maintenance. Talley Industries (Mesa), $7.360m: aircraft ejector seats; bomb racks; grenades.
DOD Installations Williams AFB (Chandler).

Economic Base Electrical equipment and supplies, especially electronic equipment and accessories; finance, insurance and real estate; machinery; agriculture, notably cattle, cotton, vegetables and dairy products; and food and kindred products. Also, higher education (Arizona State Univ.).

The Voters

Registration 210,676 total. 106,405 D (51%); 95,197 R (45%); 9,074 other (4%).
Median voting age 42.0
Employment profile White collar, 52%. Blue collar, 32%. Service, 14%. Farm, 2%.
Ethnic groups Black, 6%. Indian, 1%. Spanish, 17%. Total foreign stock, 16%. Canada, Germany, 2% each.

Presidential vote

1972	Nixon (R)	98,436	(68%)
	McGovern (D)	46,573	(32%)
1968	Nixon (R)	67,853	(56%)
	Humphrey (D)	41,889	(35%)
	Wallace (AI)	11,012	(9%)

Representative

John J. Rhodes (R) Elected 1952; b. Sept. 18, 1916, Council Grove, Kans.; home, Mesa; Kans. State Col., B.S., 1938; Harvard Law School, LL.B., 1941; Army Air Corps, WWII; married, four children; Methodist.

Career Practicing atty., 1946–53; V.P. Farm & Home Life Ins. Co.; V. Chm. Ariz. Pub. Welfare Bd., 1951–52.

Offices 2310 RHOB, 202-225-2635. Also 6081 Fed. Bldg., Phoenix 85025, 602-261-3181.

Administrative Assistant Alma A. Alkire

Committees

Appropriations (2nd); Subs: Legislative; Public Works-AEC (Ranking Mbr.).

Group Ratings

	ADA	COPE	LWV	RIPON	NFU	LCV	CFA	NAB	NSI	ACA
1972	6	30	27	54	50	25	0	89	100	67
1971	11	9	38	56	38	–	20	–	–	92
1970	24	91	–	75	50	6	53	100	100	72

Key Votes

1) Busing	AGN	6) Cmbodia Bmbg	FOR	11) Chkg Acct Intrst	AGN
2) Strip Mines	AGN	7) Bust Hwy Trust	AGN	12) End HISC (HUAC)	AGN
3) Cut Mil $	AGN	8) Farm Sub Lmt	AGN	13) Nixon Sewer Veto	FOR
4) Rev Shrg	FOR	9) School Prayr	FOR	14) Corp Cmpaign $	FOR
5) Pub TV $	AGN	10) Cnsumr Prot	ABS	15) Pol $ Disclosr	ABS

Election Results

1972 general:	John J. Rhodes (R)	80,453	(57%)
	Gerald A. Pollock (D)	59,900	(43%)
1972 primary:	John J. Rhodes (R)	31,838	(88%)
	Marvin L. Cooley (R)	4,265	(12%)
1970 general:	John J. Rhodes (R)	99,706	(68%)
	Gerald A. Pollock (D)	45,870	(32%)

SECOND DISTRICT Political Background

Tucson is Arizona's second city, not an inconsiderable place (pop. 262,000), but still a decided second to Phoenix. Although Tucson has experienced the kind of explosive growth that has characterized most cities in the Southwest, it has not had the benefits, or griefs, that have attended the monumental growth in Phoenix. One can still see Tucson's Spanish heritage in its buildings and its large Mexican-American community. With that heritage goes a Democratic voting preference, but it has been one attenuated by the tides of migration and by the changing attitudes among the Southwests's native Anglos toward party positions of the 1960s.

Tucson and its suburbs are the heart of the 2nd district, with more than half its voters. The remainder, physically, is mostly desert, with a sprinkling of military installations, Indian reservations, and old mining towns like Tombstone and Bisbee.

Udall is an old, respected name in Arizona. It belongs to a large Mormon clan, which since statehood in 1912 has usually had a member on the state Supreme Court, and often in other offices as well. The current Congressman from the 2nd, Morris Udall, succeeded his brother Stewart when the latter became Secretary of the Interior under Kennedy in 1961. Since then, Congressman Udall has become one of the leaders of the antitraditional bloc of Northern Democrats in the House. During 1969, in the Democratic Caucus, Udall went so far as to overstep the bounds of what many considered political decency by challenging old John McCormack for the Speaker's post. Udall lost, of course.

The Arizonan's challenge was probably responsible for getting him into the hot race for the House Majority Leadership in 1971—and for him losing it. Udall had the support of many of the members of the Democratic Study Group, but also had the implacable opposition of the House traditionalists. The latter group generally favored the late Hale Boggs, who, as Whip, might have been expected to move up automatically in easier times. (Boggs was chosen Whip by then Speaker McCormack and then Majority Leader Carl Albert in 1962, and the idea that a decision made by two men should bind the entire body of House Democrats nine years later struck many traditionalists as quite acceptable.) After a strenuous campaign, Udall again lost, but managed to prolong the fight to a second ballot and to win 88 votes. His boldness certainly cost him any chance for a leadership post from then on. After Boggs disappeared in an Alaskan airplane presumed crashed in October 1972, Whip Tip O'Neill of Massachusetts moved up to Majority Leader and John McFall of California became Whip.

So now Udall's chief field of legislative activity is the Post Office and Civil Service Committee, where he ranks third in seniority and chairs a subcommittee. In 1969, before the onset of the Majority Leader fracas, Udall steered an important federal salary bill through the House. The bill set up a commission to set pay levels for civil servants and Congressmen. This went over especially well among Udall's colleagues, as it led to the 1969 pay raise (Congressmen now get $42,500 a year, the same as Senators).

Udall also steered through the House a bill regulating the use of the congressional frank—the free mailing privilege that has helped so many Congressmen turn marginal districts into safe seats. Udall's bill set definitions of frankable and nonfrankable material (franked mail is supposed to be nonpolitical) and provided that aggrieved persons (that is, opponents of Congressmen) can get a decision from a bipartisan House committee within 30 days as to whether a Congressman had abused the frank. Politically useful, if not blatantly political mailings, are still possible, however. Congressmen can write constituents urging them to exercise their right to vote; moreover, the House excised a Udall provision that prohibited franked mailing within 60 days of an election. But at least some standards have now been established, with the bill going about as far as Congress ever will in limiting the use of one of its greatest political assets. At this writing, the legislation is before the Senate.

Udall has few worries at the polls. Despite the Nixon landslide—and it was stronger, of course, in Arizona than in the nation as a whole—Udall won a larger percentage of the votes in 1972 than any of his Arizona Republican counterparts. Recent trends—notably the increased Mexican-American vote and the effect of the 18-year-old vote at the University of Arizona in Tucson—indicate that even if Udall were not on the ballot, the Democrats would have a better than even chance of holding the seat.

Census Data Pop. 443,117. Central city, 59%; suburban, 20%. Median family income, $8,832; families above $15,000: 17%; families below $3,000: 11%. Median years education, 12.3.

1972 Share of Federal Outlays $801,087,503

DOD	$488,445,635	HEW	$155,122,139
AEC	$291,890	HUD	$10,525,186
NASA	$1,862,058	DOI	$9,244,149
DOT	$9,466,824	USDA	$23,649,454
		Other	$102,480,168

Federal Military-Industrial Commitments

DOD Contractors Hughes Aircraft (Tucson), $228.374m: modification of Phoenix missile; production of Maverick missile; production of TOW missile; production of weapons system for F-14 aircraft.
DOD Installations Fort Huachuca AB (Douglas). Davis-Monthan AFB (Tucson).

Economic Base Copper ore mining and other metal mining; finance, insurance and real estate; agriculture, notably cattle, cotton, vegetables and grains; printing and publishing, especially newspapers; and tourism. Also, higher education (Univ. of Arizona).

The Voters

Registration 217,118 total. 125,082 D (58%); 75,058 R (35%); 16,978 other (8%).
Median voting age 42.0
Employment profile White collar, 51%. Blue collar, 32%. Service, 15%. Farm, 2%.
Ethnic groups Black, 3%. Indian, 2%. Spanish, 27%. Total foreign stock, 23%. Canada, Germany, 2% each.

Presidential vote

1972	Nixon (R)	89,052	(57%)
	McGovern (D)	65,926	(43%)
1968	Nixon (R)	59,753	(50%)
	Humphrey (D)	49,567	(41%)
	Wallace (AI)	10,152	(8%)

Representative

Morris K. Udall (D) Elected May 2, 1961; b. June 15, 1922, St. Johns; home, Tucson; U. of Ariz., LL.B., 1949; Army Air Corps, WWII; six children; Church of Jesus Christ of Latter Day Saints.

Career Practicing atty., 1949–61; county atty. Pima County (Tucson), 1952–54; Co-founder and former Dir. of Bank of Tucson and Catalina Savings and Loan Assn.

Offices 1424 LHOB, 202-225-4065. Also 232 Fed. Bldg., Tucson 85702, 602-792-6404.

Administrative Assistant Roger K. Lewis

Committees

Interior and Insular Affairs (4th); Subs: Environment (Chm.); Public Lands; Water and Power Resources; Mines and Mining.

Post Office and Civil Service (3rd); Subs: Census and Statistics; Postal Service.

Joint Com. on Navajo-Hopi Indian Administration.

Group Ratings

	ADA	COPE	LWV	RIPON	NFU	LCV	CFA	NAB	NSI	ACA
1972	100	100	100	77	86	80	100	0	0	0
1971	81	82	100	79	100	–	88	–	–	4
1970	76	82	–	82	100	76	94	9	44	0

Key Votes

1) Busing	FOR	6) Cmbodia Bmbg	AGN	11) Chkg Acct Intrst	AGN
2) Strip Mines	AGN	7) Bust Hwy Trust	FOR	12) End HISC (HUAC)	AGN
3) Cut Mil $	FOR	8) Farm Sub Lmt	AGN	13) Nixon Sewer Veto	AGN
4) Rev Shrg	FOR	9) School Prayr	AGN	14) Corp Cmpaign $	FOR
5) Pub TV $	FOR	10) Cnsumr Prot	FOR	15) Pol $ Disclosr	FOR

Election Results

1972 general:	Morris K. Udall (D)	97,616	(63%)
	Gene Savoie (R)	56,188	(37%)
1972 primary:	Morris K. Udall (D), unopposed		
1970 general:	Morris K. Udall (D)	86,760	(69%)
	Morris Herring (R)	37,561	(30%)
	Cliff Thomallo (AI)	1,357	(1%)

THIRD DISTRICT Political Background

Arizona's 3rd and 4th congressional districts are both hybrids: combinations of large parts of heavily Republican Phoenix and of the sparsely populated, traditionally Democratic northern counties of the state. Geographically, the 3rd spans the desert expanse from Yuma (pop. 29,000), on the hot Colorado River just north of the Mexican border, past the town of Flagstaff (pop. 30,000)—known for Northern Arizona University and as one of the last places in the United States where one can find clean air—up to Glen Canyon Dam and the Navajo and Hopi Indian Reservations near the Utah state line.

Traditionally, this is "pinto" Democrat country; closer in spirit, let's say, to Arkansas than to Pennsylvania. Exceptions are the town of Prescott (pop. 23,000), long a Republican stronghold, where Barry Goldwater has begun all his Senate campaigns, and Mohave County, where in 1972 newcomers ousted Democratic county officials for Republican ones.

But most of the votes in the 3rd—56% in 1972—are cast in the heavily Republican Phoenix area. The district includes the west side of Phoenix, just winging the city's small black and

Mexican-American ghettos. Phoenix is a new city; here on the west side the vacant lots between the small stucco houses and the gaudy roadside businesses easily grow back into small patches of Arizona desert. Sparkling subdivisions can be found all over, each with a street network as rectangular and regular as any in the Midwest. The 3rd does not take in the richest parts of Phoenix. There is less grass here (it's expensive to water the stuff) and fewer palm trees. Yet there is little political difference between the people who live here and their richer neighbors in the eastern and northern parts of the city. Every white Anglo section in Phoenix votes overwhelmingly Republican.

The Congressman from this hybrid district is something of a hybrid himself. Sam Steiger, a Jew from New York, lists his occupation as a Prescott rancher; in Washington, he lives in distant Fauquier County, Virginia, and so probably has the longest commute of anybody on the Hill. Steiger is not the most tactful man: early in his House career, he intimated on a talk show that many of his colleagues were drunks. This comment cost the 3rd district at least one project that would have ordinarily gone through routinely. And Steiger in 1972 pointedly refused to endorse John Conlan, the Republican nominee for the House seat in the adjacent 4th district. Conlan was elected anyway, leaving the small Arizona congressional delegation less than close-knit.

Steiger's unorthodox politics has shown itself in other affairs. In June 1973, it was revealed that one of Steiger's top aides had placed an illegal listening device in a San Diego hotel room to gain information for a Select Committee on Crime investigation. Steiger admitted knowing about the bug after the fact, and added that he may have known about it before the fact. Whether his admission, coming as it did in the wake of the Watergate scandal, will hurt him with his constitutents is unclear. Steiger has easily won reelection in the past, always with more than 60% of the vote.

Census Data Pop. 443,201. Central city, 36%; suburban, 26%. Median family income, $8,964; families above $15,000: 16%; families below $3,000: 10%. Median years education, 12.2.

1972 Share of Federal Outlays $542,881,415

DOD	$142,003,857	HEW	$153,553,504
AEC	$21,071	HUD	$2,557,585
NASA	$1,528,903	DOI	$73,813,710
DOT	$39,657,437	USDA	$36,335,073
		Other	$93,410,275

Federal Military-Industrial Commitments

DOD Installations Navajo Army Depot, reserve status (Flagstaff). Yuma Army Proving Ground (Yuma). Marine Corps Air Station (Yuma). Gila Bend AF Auxiliary Field (Gila Bend). Luke AFB (Phoenix).

Economic Base Agriculture, notably cattle, vegetables and fruits; finance, insurance and real estate; electrical equipment and supplies, especially electronic components and accessories; machinery; men's and boys' furnishings, and other apparel and other textile products; and food and kindred products. Also higher education (Northern Arizona Univ.).

The Voters

Registration 208,537 total. 107,792 D (52%); 92,190 R (44%); 8,555 other (4%).
Median voting age 41.5
Employment profile White collar, 46%. Blue collar, 36%. Service, 13%. Farm, 5%.
Ethnic groups Black, 2%. Indian, 4%. Spanish, 19%. Total foreign stock, 15%. Canada, Germany, 1% each.

Presidential vote

1972	Nixon (R)	104,197	(72%)
	McGovern (D)	41,012	(28%)
1968	Nixon (R)	61,182	(55%)
	Humphrey (D)	37,291	(33%)
	Wallace (AI)	12,937	(12%)

Representative

Sam Steiger (R) Elected 1966; b. March 10, 1929, New York City; home, Prescott; Cornell U., 1946–48; Colorado A & M, B.S., 1950; Army, 1951–53; married, three children; Jewish.

Career Rancher and horse breeder.

Offices 126 CHOB, 202-225-4576. Also 5015 Fed. Bldg., Phoenix 85025, 602-261-4041.

Administrative Assistant Frederick Alderson

Committees

Government Operations (9th); Subs: Legal and Monetary Affairs (Ranking Mbr.).

Interior and Insular Affairs (4th); Subs: Environment; Indian Affairs; Mines and Mining; Public Lands (Ranking Mbr.).

Joint Com. on Navajo-Hopi Indian Administration.

Sel. Com. on Crime (2nd).

Group Ratings

	ADA	COPE	LWV	RIPON	NFU	LCV	CFA	NAB	NSI	ACA
1972	6	10	20	42	57	33	0	91	100	96
1971	8	0	13	44	29	–	0	–	–	96
1970	12	0	–	50	31	0	35	100	100	94

Key Votes

1) Busing	AGN	6) Cmbodia Bmbg	FOR	11) Chkg Acct Intrst	AGN
2) Strip Mines	ABS	7) Bust Hwy Trust	AGN	12) End HISC (HUAC)	AGN
3) Cut Mil $	AGN	8) Farm Sub Lmt	AGN	13) Nixon Sewer Veto	FOR
4) Rev Shrg	FOR	9) School Prayr	FOR	14) Corp Cmpaign $	FOR
5) Pub TV $	AGN	10) Cnsumr Prot	AGN	15) Pol $ Disclosr	FOR

Election Results

1972 general:	Sam Steiger (R)	90,710	(63%)
	Ted Wyckoff (D)	53,220	(37%)
1972 primary:	Sam Steiger (R), unopposed		
1970 general:	Sam Steiger (R)	81,239	(62%)
	Orren Beaty (D)	49,626	(38%)

FOURTH DISTRICT Political Background

Every ten years, the United States census reports shifts of population among and within the states. This requires the creation of perhaps a dozen or two dozen new congressional districts, political units having no previous separate existence and having no incumbent Congressmen. Such districts are often scenes of spirited contests, for the winner of the new seat is an excellent bet to keep the job for at least ten years, and more than likely for longer. The unsuccessful aspirants usually make a quick return to the obscurity of law practices, a business or two, and local political activities.

Of the dozen or so new districts created by the 1970 census, the most fiercely contested race occurred in a rather unlikely spot: the 4th district of Arizona. The 4th's lines were drawn by the state's Republican legislature and approved by a Republican Governor. Although the lines encompassed some Democratic territory—notably old mining towns like Globe and Morenci and the Navajo Indian Reservation in northeast Arizona—the new district without a doubt would be dominated by its share of Maricopa County, which cast 67% of its vote total.

Moreover, this part of Maricopa includes almost all of the most Republican areas of heavily

Republican metropolitan Phoenix: the posh suburbs of Scottsdale and Paradise Valley, and the hilltop homes near the mountains that bisect the northern part of Phoenix itself. This is the part of the 4th where Barry Goldwater lives, and also the part of the district that gave Richard Nixon a whopping 76% in 1972.

So it might be expected that a Republican in the Goldwater mold would win the House election here—which is what, after a bitter struggle, eventually happened. But the fact that there was such a struggle and that the winner's margin was so much smaller than might have been expected is an index of the ferment in Arizona politics today.

First there were the primaries, in which the candidates who seemed the favorites on the basis of past performance lost. Republicans Bill Baker and state Treasurer Ernest Garfield finished behind state Sen. John Conlan, son of ex-major league umpire Jocko Conlan. The younger Conlan carried the Maricopa part of the district by a hair and piled up good margins among the few votes cast in the outer counties. Among the Democrats the most notable primary loser was Sam Grossman, the party's 1970 nominee for U.S. Senator. In 1970, Grossman's big media campaign appeared for a while to have put him on the verge of upsetting Sen. Paul Fannin. In the 1972 House race, Grossman, like many media-oriented candidates, found his support with more breadth than depth, and he fell before another media candidate, millionaire lawyer Jack Brown.

The bitter primaries turned up as a factor in the general election. All of the above-named losing candidates refused to support their party's nominee. Brown began the campaign, asserting, in this heavily pro-Nixon district, that he, the Democratic candidate, supported Nixon's positions on major issues—revenue sharing, welfare reform, trade with Russia and China—much more enthusiastically than did his Republican opponent. Brown also made an issue of Republican Congressman Sam Steiger's comment that John Conlan was unfit for public office. These efforts won Democrat Brown support from a number of prominent Republicans.

Conlan countered with a list of Democrats who supported his candidacy, including some "pintos" from the outlying counties and multimillionaire developer (and former New York Yankees owner) Del Webb. Conlan hit Brown especially hard for his early support of George McGovern, and on the issues of amnesty and the de-criminalization of marijuana. In the last days of the campaign, Conlan trotted out endorsements from President Nixon, Vice-President Agnew, and Sens. Goldwater and Fannin—all of them heavy favorites among the district's majority.

It was probably the most expensive congressional campaign in the state's history, and in 1972 probably one of the most expensive in the nation. Big metropolitan areas like New York or Los Angeles contain so many House seats that few congressional candidates can afford TV time. But in Phoenix both candidates laid out big money for time on the tube. Brown ended up spending more than $200,000 altogether, most of it his own money; Conlan spent over $100,000. The net result was a 53–47 win for Conlan. In the early going, Brown built up a 5,000-vote margin in the outer counties, running far ahead of the Democratic candidates of the national party. Conlan, however, carried the Maricopa portion of the district by more than 14,000—a figure than means he ran about 19% behind Nixon here.

Despite Brown's campaign charges, Conlan has so far emerged as one of the more dependable supporters of the Nixon Administration in Congress. Conlan's support probably is more a result of the changing content of the Administration's legislative program than anything else. Nixon has dropped the welfare reform proposal, which Conlan opposed, and the President has also asked Congress to limit spending on most domestic programs, a position that Conlan endorses heartily.

If it is too early to predict with complete confidence that the Congressman will be easily reelected, it is only because such unlikely pitched battles have been so closely fought on Arizona political turf in past years. By most traditional indicators, Conlan looks like he has an utterly safe seat.

Census Data Pop. 443,575. Central city, 48%; suburban, 9%. Median family income, $9,886; families above $15,000: 23%; families below $3,000: 11%. Median years education, 12.3.

1972 Share of Federal Outlays $516,040,808

DOD	$95,118,948	HEW	$162,413,296
AEC	$19,649	HUD	$5,347,243
NASA	$1,024,782	DOI	$87,366,134
DOT	$22,096,224	USDA	$46,419,883
		Other	$96,234,649

Federal Military-Industrial Commitments

No installations or contractors receiving prime awards greater than $5,000,000.

Economic Base Finance, insurance and real estate; electrical equipment and supplies, especially electronic components and accessories; agriculture, notably cattle, cotton and vegetables; copper ore mining, and other metal mining; primary metal industries, especially primary copper; and machinery.

The Voters

Registration 221,940 total. 114,482 D (52%); 98,349 R (44%); 9,109 other (4%).
Median voting age 42.6
Employment profile White collar, 56%. Blue collar, 29%. Service, 12%. Farm, 3%.
Ethnic groups Black, 1%. Indian, 14%. Spanish, 13%. Total foreign stock, 13%. Canada, Germany, 1% each.

Presidential vote

1972	Nixon (R)	111,127	(71%)
	McGovern (D)	45,029	(29%)
1968	Nixon (R)	74,171	(59%)
	Humphrey (D)	40,592	(32%)
	Wallace (AI)	11,872	(9%)

Representative

John B. Conlan (R) Elected 1972; b. Sept. 17, 1930, Oak Park, Ill.; home, Phoenix; Northwestern U., B.S., 1951; Harvard Law School, LL.B., 1954; Army, 1956–61; married, two children.

Career Partner, law firm of Hughes, Hughes and Conlan; Instructor, U. of Md. and Ariz. State U.; State Senate, 1965–72.

Offices 429 CHOB, 202-225-3361. Also Fed. Bldg., Phoenix 85025, 602-261-3071.

Administrative Assistant Richard Dingman

Committees

Banking and Currency (14th); Subs; Domestic Finance; International Finance; International Trade.

Science and Astronautics (9th); Subs: Aeronautics and Space Technology; Energy; Science, Research, and Development.

Group Ratings: Newly Elected

Key Votes

1) Busing	NE	6) Cmbodia Bmbg	FOR	11) Chkg Acct Intrst	AGN
2) Strip Mines	NE	7) Bust Hwy Trust	AGN	12) End HISC (HUAC)	AGN
3) Cut Mil $	NE	8) Farm Sub Lmt	NE	13) Nixon Sewer Veto	FOR
4) Rev Shrg	NE	9) School Prayr	NE	14) Corp Cmpaign $	NE
5) Pub TV $	NE	10) Cnsumr Prot	NE	15) Pol $ Disclosr	NE

Election Results

1972 general:	John B. Conlan (R)	82,511	(53%)
	Jack E. Brown (D)	73,309	(47%)
1972 primary:	John B. Conlan (R)	18,075	(42%)
	Bill Baker (R)	15,023	(35%)
	Ernest Garfield (R)	10,439	(24%)

ARKANSAS

Political Background

Fifteen years ago, the outlook for Arkansas was pretty bleak. It had been losing population for 20 years, as young people left looking for jobs. And the state's reputation for relatively good race relations was shattered by the shenanigans of Gov. Orval Faubus. In 1957, the Governor's activities pushed President Eisenhower into sending federal troops to Little Rock to enforce a federal court desegregation order. (The Little Rock episode, however, meant personal political success for Faubus, as he was able to break the state's two-term tradition for the governorship and remain in office through 1966.)

Today, the picture has changed dramatically, and largely through the agency of one man, ex-Gov. (1966–70) Winthrop Rockefeller, who died in early 1973. Rockefeller had helped Faubus recruit industry for Arkansas, and when the scion himself became Governor, pushed the program even harder. Aided by a powerful congressional delegation, particularly by Sen. John McClellan, Rockefeller concentrated his efforts on getting small, nondefense industries whose plants could be located out in the country, near the people who needed jobs.

Whereupon the state's dogpatch reputation changed. Moreover, retirees and others seeking a life of greater tranquillity began to move in large numbers to the hills around and north and west of Little Rock. The 1970 census tells the story pretty well: central and northwest Arkansas were among the very few nonmetropolitan areas to score substantial population increases during the sixties.

Rockefeller also managed to effect a total change in the political tone of the state, something Faubus could never have done. Unusual among Southern Republicans for his commitment to civil rights and appointment of blacks to high government positions, Rockefeller managed to beat an outright segregationist in the 1966 gubernatorial race, and a Faubus protégé in 1968. And when he was finally beaten, it was by a young, previously unknown Democrat named Dale Bumpers, who has forthrightly declared that segregation is "immoral." Bumpers, for his part, was free to admit that a candidate like himself could not have won except for the example set by Rockefeller.

This political and sociological transformation has had a less obvious effect on Arkansas' congressional delegation. Its two Senators, John McClellan and J. William Fulbright, have held office since the 1940s. The best known of these is Fulbright, who remains the state's junior Senator though first elected in 1944. Fulbright's chief interest is foreign policy, having chaired the Senate Foreign Relations Committee since the 1950s. Under his leadership, the committee became the nation's leading forum for opposition to the Vietnam war and for a reduction of American commitments—and foreign aid—abroad. Fulbright, who was once president of the University of Arkansas, is a contemplative man, seemingly out of time with the temper of his state. It is hard to see how a man like Fulbright can appreciate the more arcane points of a fiddlin' contest or the fine, sing-song whine of a steel guitar out of Nashville.

But Fulbright does know how to mend Arkansas political fences; in 1968, for example, he won reelection by a very comfortable margin. In the Democratic primary of the same year, Fulbright beat an arch-segregationist—the same man Rockefeller licked in 1966—by a better than 2–1 margin. Arkansans seem to take a certain pride in the respect Fulbright commands among fancy intellectuals and Washington pundits. In turn, he has, over the years, obliged his constituency by quietly voting against civil rights measures, though he was one of four Southern Senators to vote against the Carswell nomination in 1970. Fulbright will be 69 in 1974, and there is talk now that he may not seek reelection. If he does, he seems likely to win another term, despite the sometimes vocal opposition of a former Arkansas resident, Martha Mitchell.

Arkansas' senior Senator is John McClellan, a stern and austere conservative, first elected to the Senate in 1942. On the death of Sen. Allen Ellender, McClellan became Chairman of the Senate Appropriations Committee; he also holds second-ranking status on both Government Operations and Judiciary. The veteran Senator won most of his national recognition as an investigator. He led widely publicized inquiries into such varied matters as labor-union corruption in the 1950s (the subcommittee's counsel being young Robert F. Kennedy) and the TFX (F-111) contract in the 1960s. Also known as a backer of hard-line anti-crime legislation, McClellan has usually voted with Chairman James Eastland on matters before the Judiciary Committee. But McClellan's seat on Appropriations has meant more to Arkansas, for he has managed to funnel large amounts of public works money into the state. His role here is memorialized, even while he continues to serve in the Senate, in the naming of the recently opened McClellan-Kerr Arkansas River Navigation System. It was a hugely expensive project that has opened Little Rock, Arkansas, and Tulsa, Oklahoma to the sea.

Such visible evidence of clout was undoubtedly an asset to the 76-year-old McClellan in 1972, when he was challenged in the Democratic primary by 37-year-old Rep. David Pryor. Pryor was not the kind of Congressman you might expect to represent the Deep South 4th district, just above the Louisiana state line. He captured the seat in 1966, and quickly won a place on the vital Appropriations Committee, with a little help from his fellow Arkansan, Wilbur Mills. But instead of waiting for seniority to elevate him to a position of power, Pryor began, quietly at first, to transgress the usual rules and customs by which young Southern Congressmen are governed. Disturbed about treatment of the elderly, Pryor worked anonymously for several weeks in a nursing home. Denied a subcommittee to investigate these institutions—which have been thriving on money pumped in by Medicare—he rented three trailers and set up a volunteer staff on a vacant lot near Capitol Hill. At the same time, the Congressman began to vote more and more often with young Northern Democrats. Furthermore, as a member of the Credentials Committee at the 1968 Democratic National Convention, he voted against seating the regular all-white Mississippi delegation.

That such apostasy did not automatically bar him from a serious try at statewide office is evidence of the transformation of Arkansas politics during the late 1960s. In Pryor's 1972 campaign, the challenger took aim at McClellan's voting record, which, on most issues, was very, very conservative. Hitting hard on economic issues, Pryor managed to prevent McClellan from winning 50% of the votes in the first primary, and thus forced a runoff.

McClellan then took off the gloves. Early on, to demonstrate his fitness at age 76, the Senator campaigned vigorously, shaking thousands of hands and talking of all the federal money he had brought into Arkansas. But after the first primary, he began to attack Pryor for the support he was getting from national labor leaders; moreover, McClellan's literature hinted that Pryor favored busing and gun control and opposed school prayers. Pryor, thrown on the defensive, in the end lost by the same narrow margin by which he trailed McClellan in the initial primary. Analysis of the returns indicates that the incumbent Senator made significant gains between the first primary and the runoff in Pryor's home district, a generally conservative area that had earlier supported its native son. The elderly politician held his own in the eastern part of the state, along the Mississippi River, where he piled up big majorities in both primaries.

The general election campaign was desultory; McClellan, as usual, won easily. But this will be his last term. During the campaign he promised that he would not run again, which carries some credibility if only because he will be 82 when his current term expires. Pryor plans to run again, and may now be consoled by a bit of precedent. Some 30 years ago, another young Congressman from the southern part of the state ran for an Arkansas Senate seat and lost, but he came back again a few years later and won. That Congressman was John McClellan. Pryor's toughest competition in any Senate race would come from Gov. Dale Bumpers. But with Arkansas having two Senators, each with 30 years' experience, one suspects that within a few years both Pryor and Bumpers will find their way to the U.S. Senate.

Not so many years ago, the Arkansas House delegation had what its Senate contingent still has, the highest average seniority of any state in the nation. In 1966, its four members had served a total of 104 years in the House, with each holding an important committee post. Since then, one,

James Trimble of the 3rd district, member of Rules, was defeated by a Republican; another, Oren Harris of the 4th, Chairman of Commerce, resigned to become a federal judge (in which capacity he has sternly enforced school desegreation orders); and a third, E.C. Gathings of the 1st, Chairman of Agriculture's Cotton Subcommittee, retired.

There remains one Wilbur Mills, of the 2nd district, Chairman of the House Ways and Means Committee, probably the best-known member of the House, and in many ways its most powerful member. Because the Democratic members of Ways and Means decide who gets what committee assignments among the party's Congressmen, Mills has been in an excellent position to see that Arkansas' interests are nicely protected, despite the poverty of seniority in its current House delegation. This he has done. Back home, none of the state's Congressmen faces any conceivable trouble at the polls.

Census Data Pop. 1,923,295; 0.95% of U.S. total, 32nd largest; change 1960–70, 7.7%. Central city, 17%; suburban, 14%. Median family income, $6,271; 49th highest; families above $15,000: 8%; families below $3,000: 22%. Median years education, 10.5.

1972 Share of Federal Tax Burden $1,254,110,000; 0.60% of U.S. total, 34th largest.

1972 Share of Federal Outlays $1,827,462,169; 0.84% of U.S. total, 33rd largest. Per capita federal spending, $950.

DOD	$291,448,000	38th (0.47%)	HEW	$683,658,817	32nd (0.96%)
AEC	$640,415	35th (0.02%)	HUD	$34,009,657	26th (1.11%)
NASA	$94,261	45th (—)	VA	$167,775,679	25th (1.47%)
DOT	$50,981,837	39th (0.65%)	USDA	$344,133,910	14th (2.24%)
DOC	$12,550,491	24th (0.97%)	CSC	$33,409,250	33rd (0.81%)
DOI	$8,533,926	40th (0.40%)	TD	$77,540,994	29th (0.47%)
DOJ	$6,062,679	35th (0.62%)	Other	$116,622,253	

Economic Base Agriculture, notably soybeans, broilers, cattle and cotton lint; food and kindred products, especially meat products; finance, insurance and real estate; lumber and wood products, especially sawmills and planing mills; electrical equipment and supplies, especially electrical industrial apparatus; apparel and other textile products, especially men's and boys' furnishings; furniture and fixtures, especially household furniture.

Political Line-up Governor, Dale Bumpers (D); seat up, 1974. Senators, John L. McClellan (D) and J. William Fulbright (D). Representatives, 4 (3 D and 1 R). State Senate (34 D and 1 R); State House (99 D and 1 R).

The Voters

Registration No party registration; no accurate total registration figures available.
Median voting age 45.6
Employment profile White collar, 39%. Blue collar, 41%. Service, 13%. Farm, 7%.
Ethnic groups Black, 18%. Total foreign stock, 2%.

Presidential vote

1972	Nixon (R)	448,541	(69%)
	McGovern (D)	199,892	(31%)
1968	Nixon (R)	190,759	(31%)
	Humphrey (D)	188,228	(30%)
	Wallace (AI)	240,982	(39%)
1964	Johnson (D)	314,197	(56%)
	Goldwater (R)	243,264	(44%)

Senator

J. William Fulbright (D) Elected 1944, seat up 1974; b. April 9, 1905, Summer, Mo.; home, Fayetteville; U. of Ark., B.A., 1925; Oxford U., Rhodes Scholar, B.A., 1928, M.A., 1931; George Washington U., LL.B., 1934; married, two children; Disciples of Christ Church.

Career Atty., Dept. of Justice, 1934–35; Instructor in law, George Washington U., 1935–36, Lecturer in law, 1936–39; Pres., U. of Ark., 1939–41; Delegate 9th General Assembly of U.N., 1954; U.S. House of Reps., 1943–45.

Offices 1215 NSOB, 202-225-4843. Also 2331 New Fed. Bldg., Little Rock 72203, 501-372-4361, ext. 5503.

Administrative Assistant Lee Williams

Committees

Finance (4th); Subs: Health; Foundations.

Foreign Relations (Chm.); Subs: Near-Eastern Affairs (Chm.); U.S. Agreements and Commitments Abroad.

Joint Economic Com. (2nd); Subs: Economic Progress; Inter-American Economic Relationships; International Economics; Priorities and Economy in Government.

Joint Study Com. on Budget Control.

Group Ratings

	ADA	COPE	LWV	RIPON	NFU	LCV	CFA	NAB	NSI	ACA
1972	50	25	56	41	89	61	50	18	0	22
1971	85	25	64	61	100	–	100	–	–	14
1970	66	36	–	64	75	47	–	20	0	22

Key Votes

1) Busing	AGN	8) Sea Life Prot	FOR	15) Tax Singls Less	AGN
2) Alas P-line	AGN	9) Campaign Subs	FOR	16) Min Tax for Rich	AGN
3) Gun Cntrl	FOR	10) Cmbodia Bmbg	AGN	17) Euro Troop Rdctn	FOR
4) Rehnquist	AGN	11) Legal Srvices	FOR	18) Bust Hwy Trust	AGN
5) Pub TV $	AGN	12) Rev Sharing	FOR	19) Maid Min Wage	ABS
6) EZ Votr Reg	ABS	13) Cnsumr Prot	FOR	20) Farm Sub Limit	AGN
7) No-Fault	AGN	14) Eq Rts Amend	FOR	21) Highr Credt Chgs	FOR

Election Results

1968 general:	J. William Fulbright (D)	349,965	(59%)
	Charles T. Bernard (R)	241,731	(41%)
1968 primary:	J. William Fulbright (D)	220,684	(53%)
	Bob Hayes (D)	52,906	(13%)
	Jim Johnson (D)	132,038	(32%)
	Foster Johnson (D)	11,395	(3%)
1962 general:	J. William Fulbright (D)	214,867	(69%)
	Kenneth Jones (R)	98,013	(31%)

FIRST DISTRICT Political Background

Eastern Arkansas—the flat, fertile, cotton-growing plains that line the west bank of the Mississippi River—is in its economic life more tied to the state of Mississippi or Memphis, Tennessee, than to the hilly regions of central Arkansas or the Ozark Mountains. Like the Delta in Mississippi, eastern Arkansas is occupied by large farms and even plantations, where, if one is enamored with the tradition of the Old South, the black folks do the cotton-picking and the white folks do the voting and the money-making. This part of the state has never been much for country populism, though it does retain at least a nominal Democratic allegiance. In 1972, it

Senator

John L. McClellan (D) Elected 1942, seat up 1978; b. Feb. 25, 1896, Sheridan; home, Little Rock; admitted to Ark. bar by special act of legislature in 1913 after studying law in father's office; Army, WWII; married; Baptist.

Career Practicing atty., 1913–17, 1919–35, 1939–42; Prosecuting Atty., 7th Jud. Dist. of Ark., 1927–30; U.S. House of Reps. 1935–39.

Offices 3241 NSOB, 202-225-2353. Also 3030 Fed. Bldg., Little Rock 72201, 501-372-4361, ext. 5705.

Administrative Assistant Wallace P. Whiteaker

Committees

Appropriations (Chm.); Subs: Defense (Chm.); Foreign Operations; Interior; Public Works; State, Justice, and Commerce, the Judiciary, and Related Agencies; Intelligence Operations (Chm.).

Government Operations (2nd); Subs: Intergovernmental Relations; Permanent Investigations; Budgeting, Management, and Expenditures.

Judiciary (2nd); Subs: Antitrust and Monopoly; Constitutional Rights; Criminal Laws and Procedures (Chm.): Federal Charters; Holidays and Celebrations; Immigration and Naturalization; Improvements in Judiciary Machinery; Internal Security; Refugees and Escapees; Separation of Powers; Patents, Trade-marks, and Copyrights (Chm.).

Joint Study Com. on Budget Control (V-Chm.).

Joint Com. on Reduction of Federal Expenditures (2nd).

Group Ratings

	ADA	COPE	LWV	RIPON	NFU	LCV	CFA	NAB	NSI	ACA
1972	10	0	44	25	75	0	18	60	90	69
1971	30	45	23	20	45	–	57	–	–	64
1970	0	18	–	12	33	27	–	64	100	89

Key Votes

1) Busing	AGN	8) Sea Life Prot	FOR	15) Tax Singls Less	FOR
2) Alas P-line	FOR	9) Campaign Subs	AGN	16) Min Tax for Rich	AGN
3) Gun Cntrl	AGN	10) Cmbodia Bmbg	AGN	17) Euro Troop Rdctn	FOR
4) Rehnquist	FOR	11) Legal Srvices	FOR	18) Bust Hwy Trust	AGN
5) Pub TV $	ABS	12) Rev Sharing	FOR	19) Maid Min Wage	AGN
6) EZ Votr Reg	ABS	13) Cnsumr Prot	ABS	20) Farm Sub Limit	AGN
7) No-Fault	AGN	14) Eq Rts Amend	FOR	21) Highr Credt Chgs	ABS

Election Results

1972 general:	John L. McClellan (D)	386,398	(61%)
	Wayne H. Babbitt (R)	248,238	(39%)
1972 primary:	John L. McClellan (D)	220,588	(45%)
	David Pryor (D)	204,058	(41%
	Ted Boswell (D)	62,496	('
	Foster Johnson (D)	6,358	
1966 general:	John L. McClellan (D), unopposed		

provided almost all of the narrow margin by which Sen. John McClellan retained his seat against the challenge of young Rep. David Pryor.

Eastern Arkansas comprises the heart of the 1st district. Although population-mandated redistricting has forced the inclusion of several hill counties, the flatlands along the great unpredictable Mississippi still dominate the district's balloting. For 30 years, the 1st's Congressman was Ezekiel C. Gathings, who never won much national recognition, but rose diligently on the seniority ladder to become Chairman of Agriculture's Cotton Subcommittee. Gathings retired in 1968, and his successor, Bill Alexander, is a politician in much the same mold. He sought and received a seat on Agriculture, where he already ranks eighth among Democrats; he also sits on Government Operations. Alexander's voting record is not as conservative as his predecessor's, but like Gathings his main interests appear to be local: farm programs and river improvements.

For many years, Southern power in the House was maintained by the tradition among rural districts to elect a young Congressman and then to keep him in office for 20 or 30 years. Southern power was, of course, seniority power. Recently, the one-man-one-vote ruling has cut the number of rural districts in Dixie, and sharp Republican challenges have unseated some Democrats. But here in the 1st district, the old political tradition continues to be a strong one. Gathings was 35 when he first won election in 1938, and Alexander was 34 when he won the seat in 1968. That same year was the last time Alexander had opposition in either the primary or the general election. Odds are that he will continue to serve the 1st district in the House for a long, long time.

Census Data Pop. 479,893. Central city, 0%; suburban, 10%. Median family income, $5,381; families above $15,000: 7%; families below $3,000: 29%. Median years education, 8.8.

1972 Share of Federal Outlays $434,950,875

DOD	$79,193,000	HEW	$168,545,565
AEC	–	HUD	$1,322,512
NASA	–	DOI	$1,143,911
DOT	$8,226,664	USDA	$103,571,573
		Other	$72,947,650

Federal Military-Industrial Commitments

Defense Contractors Aerojet General (Batesville), $15.746m: bomb fuzes. Addison Shoe (Wynne), $5.507m: leather goods.
Defense Installations Blytheville AFB (Blytheville).

Economic Base Agriculture, notably grains, cotton and cattle; shoes, except rubber, and other leather and leather products; finance, insurance and real estate; food and kindred products; and electrical equipment and supplies.

The Voters

Registration No party registration; no accurate total registration figures available.
Median voting age 45.9
Employment profile White collar, 34%. Blue collar, 40%. Service, 13%. Farm, 13%.
Ethnic groups Black, 23%. Total foreign stock, 1%.

Presidential vote

1972	Nixon (R)	98,979	(69%)
	McGovern (D)	45,355	(31%)
1968	Nixon (R)	39,137	(27%)
	Humphrey (D)	44,963	(31%)
	Wallace (AI)	60,971	(42%)

Representative

William Vollie (Bill) **Alexander** (D) Elected 1968; b. Jan. 16, 1934, Memphis, Tenn.; home, Osceola; U. of Ark., Southwestern at Memphis, Tenn., B.A., 1957; Vanderbilt U., LL.B., 1960; Army, Korean War; married, one child; Espiscopalian.

Career Practicing atty., 1960–69.

Offices 116 CHOB, 202-225-4076. Also Drawer FFF, Ark. State U., Jonesboro 72467, 501-972-2135.

Administrative Assistant Dorothy L. Thomas (L.A.)

Committees

Agriculture (8th). Subs; Oilseeds and Rice; Conservation and Credit; Family Farms and Rural Development (Chm).

Government Operations (18th); Subs: Foreign Operations and Government Information; Intergovernmental Relations.

Group Ratings

	ADA	COPE	LWV	RIPON	NFU	LCV	CFA	NAB	NSI	ACA
1972	19	40	60	42	86	24	0	22	80	44
1971	27	75	71	41	92	–	71	–	–	42
1970	20	40	–	40	73	0	67	13	100	50

Key Votes

1) Busing	AGN	6) Cmbodia Bmbg	AGN	11) Chkg Acct Intrst	AGN
2) Strip Mines	AGN	7) Bust Hwy Trust	AGN	12) End HISC (HUAC)	AGN
3) Cut Mil $	AGN	8) Farm Sub Lmt	AGN	13) Nixon Sewer Veto	AGN
4) Rev Shrg	AGN	9) School Prayr	FOR	14) Corp Cmpaign $	FOR
5) Pub TV $	FOR	10) Cnsumr Prot	FOR	15) Pol $ Disclosr	AGN

Election Results

1972 general: Bill Alexander (D), unopposed
1972 primary: Bill Alexander (D), unopposed
1970 general: Bill Alexander (D), unopposed

SECOND DISTRICT Political Background

Almost daily, it seems, the columns of the major newspapers have something to say about a lawyer from Kensett, Arkansas. In the first half of 1973, there was intense speculation around Washington about this man's possible support of a total wage-price freeze; about his feeling toward major tax reform this year; about his support for the President's program to discourage foreign imports; about his belief that no trade agreement was possible with the Soviet Union without a relaxation of its curbs on immigration; and, perhaps most important, about the condition of his aching back.

The lawyer from Kensett is, of course, Wilbur Mills, Congressman from the 2nd district of Arkansas and Chairman of the House Ways and Means Committee. He is probably the best-known, and in many ways the most powerful, member of the House of Representatives. Mills is respected on Wall Street and revered in many precincts of Washington, while his public pronouncements and private hints are assiduously reported by the press. Though the man likes the music of Lawrence Welk and has never traveled abroad, finance ministers and business tycoons in Paris, Tokyo, London, and Bonn keep close tabs on his positions, and sometimes seek audiences with him in Washington. This is what you call power and respect for a country boy.

How does Mills do it? By his seniority, competence, and hard work. Back in the early 1940s, as a young Arkansas Congressman, Mills caught the eye of Sam Rayburn, and unusually early in his career won a seat on the Ways and Means Committee. By 1958 he was Chairman of the committee, and has remained very much the Chairman ever since. Ways and Means has jurisdiction over all tax matters, over Social Security and Medicare (because they are both financed by the payroll tax), over revenue sharing and welfare, and international trade restrictions. The Democratic members of Ways and Means also serve as their party's Committee on Committees—a matter of particular importance to junior Congressmen who believe that their political future could well depend on whether they get the committee assignment of their choice.

It is universally agreed that Wilbur Mills has had about as tight a control over Ways and Means as any committee chairman has had over any committee. It is not just that he has never lost a vote in Ways and Means; in the matters of great complexity over which it has jurisdiction, Mills shapes its decisions according to his own will. For the Chairman, in the first place, is extremely knowledgeable about his committee's work; he can make the most complicated tax problem clear to his colleagues. Second, the committee has a gifted and competent staff, well up to matching the caliber of the Treasury Department's top experts. Third, that staff reports to Mills, and Mills alone; if another member of the committee wants staff help, he must ask for it through the Chairman. Fourth, there are no subcommittees, and therefore no subcommittee staff on which other members of Ways and Means might rely should they want the kind of detailed information needed to oppose positions taken by Mills. Fifth, Mills has cultivated a close working relationship with the leading Republicans on the committee. He and John Byrnes, the ranking minority member who retired in 1972, often worked out compromises together which then won unanimous committee support. The current ranking Republican, Herman Schneebeli of Pennsylvania, is not considered as knowledgeable as Byrnes; Capitol Hill observers therefore believe that Mills, more than ever, will get his way with the committee's Republicans.

Given all this, Mills has usually been able to bring major legislation to the House floor with unanimous committee backing, and all the facts at his ready command. Moreover, bills from Ways and Means have historically been considered under a "closed rule," which means that they cannot be amended on the floor, and must be voted, in their entirety, either up or down.

This means that Mills' personal clout is often enough to insure House passage of controversial, complex, major legislation. His support, for example, was more responsible than anything else for the fact that the House twice passed President Nixon's Family Assistance Program—a measure that never made it out of committee on the Senate side. No one expects that any major trade or health-care legislation will emerge from the 93rd Congress without Mills' approval. Neither will tax reform occur, whatever the feelings of the country at large, until Wilbur Mills decides it should.

Yet it would be unfair to conclude from this that Mills is a dictator, imposing his will against that of the entire Congress and the whole country. Congressmen defer, often with good reason, to colleagues they respect on matters where they have no expertise or detailed knowledge. Few committee chairmen command the kind of confidence and hence deference that Mills does. In turn, Mills defers to what he believes is the will of the House. In fact, the criticism is heard that he blows too easily with the wind; that he is so proud of his record of having never been beaten on the floor on a major issue that he will not take any real risk of losing there.

Certainly such motives seemed to play a part in his 1965 shift on Medicare, for it was clear that the Congress, swept in by the 1964 LBJ landslide, wanted Medicare. Perhaps a similar set of motives played a role in Mills' downplaying, after 1972, of two issues he talked so much about during the previous year: tax reform and health care legislation. The Chairman of Ways and Means, like the Justices of the Supreme Court, reads the election returns.

It should be added that the Chairman's authority has been diminished, if ever so slightly, by the slow tide of change in the House. The "closed rule" will no longer be automatic for bills coming from Ways and Means. Mills opposed the reform, arguing that tax bills will get loaded down with momentarily popular but irresponsible amendments from the floor. This being his forecast, Mills predicted that the House will return, just as it did after the enactment of the disastrous Smoot-Hawley tariff of 1930, to the closed rule. Also, because the House leadership has begun to make efforts to have more say in committee assignments, Mills' control here has slackened. Finally, if the House should ever get down to a unified consideration of taxes and spending, it appears that the Chairman's power over taxation will have to be shared a little more widely.

The one embarrassing episode in Mills' recent career was his presidential run in 1972. Like the Lyndon Johnson of 1960, who mistook congressional clout for popular appeal, Mills launched a well-financed campaign only to see it fall completely flat. For some reason, his strategists figured that his best chance was in the Massachusetts primary, where he won a dismal 2% of the vote. The Washington rumors of a Kennedy-Mills ticket persisted into the Miami Beach Convention; only later did it become clear that Mills, for all his mastery of the House, possessed very little idea of how presidential nominations are won these days.

Mills' failure as a vote-getting politician may stem from inexperience. He has had little occasion to go out after votes these last 20 or 30 years. In Arkansas he has had opposition in the Democratic primary or the general election only once in the last 10 years—the 1966 primary, when he won 73% of the votes. The citizens of the 2nd district of Arkansas—most of them in and around Little Rock, with the rest scattered in a few hill and lowland counties—seem proud of their Congressman. They are certain to continue to reelect him as long as he wants to run. Because of a back ailment, Mills may choose to retire sometime soon, but chances are he will run in 1974. Mills' July 1973 announcement that he was considering retirement because of his back stunned official Washington; if he does refuse to run in 1974, he will leave quite a power vacuum in the House. In the 2nd district, if Mills is not a candidate, prime contenders include former Congressman David Pryor, who just barely lost the Senate primary to John McClellan in 1972, and state Attorney General Jim Guy Tucker. Both are young Democrats inclined to the liberalism of their national party.

Census Data Pop. 481,120. Central city, 40%; suburban, 27%. Median family income, $7,484; families above $15,000: 12%; families below $3,000: 16%. Median years education, 12.0.

1972 Share of Federal Outlays $641,382,007

DOD	$112,633,000	HEW	$162,362,781
AEC	–	HUD	$17,764,176
NASA	$90,061	DOI	$2,649,078
DOT	$26,951,259	USDA	$146,205,675
		Other	$172,725,977

Federal Military-Industrial Commitments

DOD Installations Little Rock AFB (Jacksonville).

Economic Base Finance, insurance and real estate; agriculture, notably grains, poultry and cattle; food and kindred products; electrical equipment and supplies; and chemicals and allied products, especially inorganic chemicals not otherwise classified.

The Voters

Registration No party registration; no accurate total registration figures available.
Median voting age 43.0
Employment profile White collar, 46%. Blue collar, 37%. Service, 13%. Farm, 4%.
Ethnic groups Black, 16%. Total foreign stock, 3%.

Presidential vote

1972	Nixon (R)	100,761	(64%)
	McGovern (D)	56,514	(36%)
1968	Nixon (R)	43,451	(30%)
	Humphrey (D)	46,332	(32%)
	Wallace (AI)	54,248	(38%)

Representative

Wilbur D. Mills (D) Elected 1938; b. May 24, 1909, Kensett; home, Kensett; Hendrix Col., A.B., 1930; Harvard Law School, LL.B., 1933; married, two children; Methodist.

Career County and Probate Judge of White County, Ark., 1934–38.

Offices 1136 LHOB, 202-225-2506. Also 1527 New Fed. Bldg., Little Rock 72201, 501-372-4361, ext. 5522, and P.O. Bldg., Searcy 72143, 501-268-3989.

Administrative Assistant Gene Goss

Committees

Ways and Means (Chm).

Joint Com. on Internal Revenue Taxation (Chm.).

Joint Com. on Reduction of Federal Expenditures (2nd).

Group Ratings

	ADA	COPE	LWV	RIPON	NFU	LCV	CFA	NAB	NSI	ACA
1972	19	63	40	55	43	0	0	22	100	44
1971	22	90	100	63	62	–	50	–	–	33
1970	12	42	–	31	50	20	43	60	84	59

Key Votes

1) Busing	AGN	6) Cmbodia Bmbg	AGN	11) Chkg Acct Intrst	AGN
2) Strip Mines	AGN	7) Bust Hwy Trust	AGN	12) End HISC (HUAC)	AGN
3) Cut Mil $	AGN	8) Farm Sub Lmt	AGN	13) Nixon Sewer Veto	FOR
4) Rev Shrg	FOR	9) School Prayr	AGN	14) Corp Cmpaign $	FOR
5) Pub TV $	ABS	10) Cnsumr Prot	ABS	15) Pol $ Disclosr	FOR

Election Results

1972 general:	Wilbur Mills (D), unopposed
1972 primary:	Wilbur Mills (D), unopposed
1970 general:	Wilbur Mills (D), unopposed

THIRD DISTRICT Political Background

The 3rd district of Arkansas is the northwest quarter of the state. It is a region of green hills rising to mountains, of historic poverty, but recently of relative prosperity. The new wealth comes from retirees and younger people attracted to the area's mild climate, its scenic mountains and reservoirs, by jobs in its small industries, and by the low-keyed pace of life here. The cities of the 3rd are medium-sized, and the tempo of life in them is that which many Americans seem to consider most desirable. Among such places in the district are Fort Smith (pop. 62,000), on the Oklahoma border and Arkansas' second largest city; Fayetteville (pop. 30,000), site of the University of Arkansas and home of its former president, J. William Fulbright; and Hot Springs (pop. 35,000), the one-time gambling center and still a popular resort town. The district also contains the state's most reliably Republican territory, the mountain counties in the north, which never backed the Confederacy and have remained faithful to the party of Union, the Republican party, ever since.

In this century, this is the only Arkansas district to have been the site of real two-party political contests, and it is the only one today that elects a Republican Congressman. In 1966, the 3rd surprised practically everyone when it ousted long-time Rep. James W. Trimble, then 72 and a member of the House Rules Committee, and elected in his place state Republican Chairman John Paul Hammerschmidt. The new Congressman carried the Republican counties in the north by a large margin, and generally profited from Winthrop Rockefeller's strong win in the gubernatorial contest of that year.

Since then Hammerschmidt has had little trouble winning reelection. The lone Republican has apparently gotten on well with the other members of the state's delegation, having received public praise from some of them. Although Democratic candidates keep appearing on the ballot against him, Hammerschmidt wins by overwhelming margins. He will almost certainly continue to do so in the future.

Census Data Pop. 481,106. Central city, 13%; suburban, 9%. Median family income, $6,057; families above $15,000: 7%; families below $3,000: 20%. Median years education, 10.8.

1972 Share of Federal Outlays $374,379,877

DOD	$40,700,000	HEW	$184,509,320
AEC	$640,415	HUD	$4,221,761
NASA	$4,200	DOI	$2,660,208
DOT	$6,468,321	USDA	$42,620,701
		Other	$92,554,951

Federal Military-Industrial Commitments

No installations or contractors receiving prime awards greater than $5,000,000.

Economic Base Agriculture, notably poultry, cattle and dairy products; food and kindred products, especially meat products; furniture and fixtures, especially wood household furniture; finance, insurance and real estate; and electrical equipment and supplies. Also higher education (Univ. of Arkansas).

The Voters

Registration No party registration; no accurate party registration figures available.
Median voting age 46.9
Employment profile White collar, 38%. Blue collar, 42%. Service, 13%. Farm, 7%.
Ethnic groups Black, 3%. Total foreign stock, 3%.

Presidential vote

1972	Nixon (R)	138,541	(74%)
	McGovern (D)	47,922	(26%)
1968	Nixon (R)	73,001	(43%)
	Humphrey (D)	45,627	(27%)
	Wallace (AI)	51,343	(30%)

Representative

John Paul Hammerschmidt (R) Elected 1966; b. May 4, 1922, Harrison; home, Harrison; The Citadel; Oklahoma A & M Col.; U. of Ark.; Army Air Corps, WWII; Major, USAFR; married, one child; Presbyterian.

Career Bd. Chm., Hammerschmidt Lumber Co., Pres., Construction Products Co., Dir., First Natl. Bank and Harrison Fed. Savings and Loan Assn.; Chm., Ark. Repub. State Central Com.; Rep. Natl. Finance Com., 1962–63.

Offices 409 CHOB, 202-225-4301. Also Rm. 209 Main P.O. Bldg., Harrison 72601, 501-365-6900, and Fed. Bldg., Hot Springs 72901, 501-623-4537.

Administrative Assistant Mrs. Nancy Rohr (L.A.)

Committees

Public Works (7th); Subs: Economic Development (Ranking Mbr.); Investigations and Review; Transportation; Water Resources.

Veterans' Affairs (Ranking Mbr.); Subs: Compensation and Pension (Ranking Mbr.).

Group Ratings

	ADA	COPE	LWV	RIPON	NFU	LCV	CFA	NAB	NSI	ACA
1972	6	9	25	38	71	26	0	67	100	74
1971	14	17	33	50	47	–	25	–	–	79
1970	16	17	–	41	38	0	43	82	100	84

Key Votes

1) Busing	AGN	6) Cmbodia Bmbg	FOR	11) Chkg Acct Intrst	AGN
2) Strip Mines	AGN	7) Bust Hwy Trust	AGN	12) End HISC (HUAC)	AGN
3) Cut Mil $	AGN	8) Farm Sub Lmt	AGN	13) Nixon Sewer Veto	FOR
4) Rev Shrg	FOR	9) School Prayr	FOR	14) Corp Cmpaign $	FOR
5) Pub TV $	AGN	10) Cnsumr Prot	AGN	15) Pol $ Disclosr	AGN

Election Results

1972 general:	John Paul Hammerschmidt (R)	144,571	(77%)
	Guy W. Hatfield (D)	42,481	(23%)
1972 primary:	John Paul Hammerschmidt (R), unopposed		
1970 general:	John Paul Hammerschmidt (R)	115,532	(67%)
	Donald Poe (D)	57,679	(33%)

FOURTH DISTRICT   Political Background

The 4th district of Arkansas takes in roughly the southern half of the state geographically. It stretches from the flat delta lands along the Mississippi River, and west across rolling hills to Texarkana, situated so squarely on the Arkansas-Texas boundary that the state line runs right through City Hall. The principal towns in the district are quiet places like El Dorado (pop. 25,000), Camden (pop. 15,000), and Arkadelphia (pop. 9,000). The 4th's largest urban center is Pine Bluff (pop. 57,000), girlhood home of Martha Mitchell.

By a number of indexes, the 4th is more like neighboring northern Louisiana and Mississippi than the rest of Arkansas. It has the largest black population in the state, 31%, and produced the state's largest vote for George Wallace in 1968, 46%. But the measurable resemblances to the Deep South vanish when one looks at the kind of Congressmen the 4th has sent to Washington.

Its most recent ex-Representative (1966–73), David Pryor, achieved distinction not for his opposition to civil rights legislation, but for working incognito in a nursing home, discovering terrible abuses, and then sponsoring federal legislation to reform the industry. In the 1972 Democratic primary, Pryor nearly captured John McClellan's Senate seat, and will probably try for the Senate again. Or conceivably he may return to the House if Wilbur Mills retires, since he has moved his residence out of the 4th to Little Rock.

The present incumbent, former state Attorney General Ray Thornton, comes from a well-connected and influential Arkansas family. The Congressman's uncle, W. R. Stephens, president of the Arkansas Louisiana Gas Company, has for some time been considered a behind-the-throne political power. Thornton won the 1972 Democratic nomination in the four-candidate initial primary, barely avoiding a runoff by winning 50.78% of the votes. The Congressman is one of the founders of the Rural Caucus, a group started by freshmen, mostly from the South and border states, who on most issues are likely to stand somewhere between urban Northern Democrats and the dwindling number of conservative Democrats from the Deep South. In the polarized state of affairs of early 1973, Thornton stood with the vast majority of Democrats against the Nixon Administration.

Census Data   Pop. 481,176. Central city, 16%; suburban, 8%. Median family income, $6,191; families above $15,000: 7%; families below $3,000: 23%. Median years education, 10.4.

1972 Share of Federal Outlays $376,749,410

DOD	$58,922,000	HEW	$168,241,151
AEC	–	HUD	$10,701,208
NASA	–	DOI	$2,080,729
DOT	$9,335,593	USDA	$51,735,961
		Other	$75,732,768

Federal Military-Industrial Commitments

DOD Contractors Ambac Industries (Camden), $8.121m: parachute illumination flares.
DOD Installations Pine Bluff Army Arsenal (Pine Bluff).

Economic Base Agriculture, notably poultry, grains, cotton and cattle; lumber and wood products, especially sawmill and planing mill products; paper and allied products; finance, insurance and real estate; and food and kindred products.

The Voters

Registration No party registration; no accurate total registration figures available.
Median voting age 46.7
Employment profile White collar, 36%. Blue collar, 44%. Service, 14%. Farm, 6%.
Ethnic groups Black, 31%. Total foreign stock, 1%.

Presidential vote

1972	Nixon (R)	107,470	(69%)
	McGovern (D)	49,108	(31%)
1968	Nixon (R)	35,170	(22%)
	Humphrey (D)	51,306	(32%)
	Wallace (AI)	74,420	(46%)

Representative

Ray Thornton (D) Elected 1972; b. July 16, 1928, Conway; home, Sheridan; State College of Ark.; U. of Ark.; Yale U., B.A., 1950; U. of Texas; U. of Ark., J.D., 1956; Navy, Korean War; married; three children.

Career Private law practice, 1957–70; Chairman, State Board of Law Examiners, 1968–70; Deputy prosecuting atty., Sixth Judicial Circuit, 1956–57; Delegate, Seventh Constitutional Convention of Ark., 1969–70; State Atty. Gen., 1970–72.

Offices 1109 LHOB, 202-225-3772.

Administrative Assistant Kay G. Collett (L.A.)

Committees

Judiciary (18th); Subs: No. 2 (Claims); No. 6 (Revision of the Laws).

Science and Astronautics (16th); Subs: Aeronautics and Space Technology; Energy; Science, Research, and Development.

Group Ratings: Newly Elected

Key Votes

1) Busing	NE	6) Cmbodia Bmbg	AGN	11) Chkg Acct Intrst	AGN
2) Strip Mines	NE	7) Bust Hwy Trust	AGN	12) End HISC (HUAC)	AGN
3) Cut Mil $	NE	8) Farm Sub Lmt	NE	13) Nixon Sewer Veto	AGN
4) Rev Shrg	NE	9) School Prayr	NE	14) Corp Cmpaign $	NE
5) Pub TV $	NE	10) Cnsumr Prot	NE	15) Pol $ Disclosr	NE

Election Results

1972 general:	Ray Thornton (D), unopposed		
1972 primary:	Ray Thornton (D)	67,321	(51%)
	Richard Arnold (D)	39,421	(30%)
	Richard H. Mays (D)	18,854	(14%)
	Jack Coleman (D)	6,972	(5%)

CALIFORNIA

Political Background

The 1970 census established California as undisputed number one—the nation's largest state, with nearly 20 million people, and a growth rate, though slackening lately, that leaves it unlikely ever to be surpassed. People have said that California is the one state that could exist as a separate nation unto itself; yet like many not-so-rich states and unlike those in the not-so-fashionable upper Middle West, California gets back much more in federal money than it sends out in taxes. California is a maze of contradictions: one of the nation's most urbanized, yet the home of vast agribusiness conglomerates; one of the most inspiring and scenic states, yet the most smoggy and pollution-ridden; the place where the peace movement first made an impact, yet a state whose economy would collapse the moment the Pentagon stopped sending checks to its giant defense firms and installations. The state is the nation's most auto-dependent; no one knows what will happen if gasoline rationing is begun as recommended recently by the Environmental Protection Agency.

California is thousands of miles away from other heavily populated regions of the country. Still, the state has been a national trend-setter—in suburbanization, in what a few years ago were considered bizarre lifestyles, and in politics. The standard reputation of California politics is zaniness; the country having once tilted, somebody said, with all the loose nuts sliding westward. Scammon and Wattenberg maintain another view in *The Real Majority,* saying that California is "psephologically normal"—and it would be most improbable for a state that casts 10% of the nation's vote to deviate very much from the national average.

There is some truth in both notions; you can see the state as both zany and normal. But in the national politics of the last 15 or 20 years, California's real and most significant role has been, just as it's been in areas of fashion, that of a trend-setter. Currents of public opinion that have swept the country and affected the course of history have surfaced first in California. The gist of the state's political trends: candidates here, both left and right, espousing views considered far out or extremist by the conventionally wise, have been winning elections with increasing frequency. In the process, these men and issues have made obsolete the more moderate, middle-of-the-road politics personified by California's most durable Governor (1943–54) Earl Warren.

The rise of the far out candidate has occurred in a state where political machines, which are still of some importance in places like Chicago and Philadelphia, were wiped out in a series of reforms enacted by California Progressives in 1911. California is a state where the most sophisticated techniques of modern electioneering—sensitive polling, adept use of TV and other media, and pinpointed direct mail—are most advanced. It is also where the efforts of people who are essentially volunteers, with nothing to gain from political participation but the promulgation of their often "extreme" views, are crucial. The volunteers form not only the cadres of door-to-door campaigners, but also raise the money to pay for all the sophisticated electioneering. California is rapidly replacing New York as the political money center of the country. Men like Humphrey Democrat Eugene Wyman, and the conservative Republicans of Orange County's Lincoln Club, were among the biggest givers and money-raisers in the 1972 presidential campaign.

To understand just how California has presaged national trends, it is necessary to go back to what is fast becoming history, the early 1960s. Democrats were in control of things: in the White House, in the California Governor's mansion, and in the state legislature, where the legendary Jess Unruh had just begun his career as Speaker of the Assembly. Across the land, conventional wisdom had it that for Republicans to win elections they had to support many Democratic programs, to be moderate and even liberal. A sizable number of California Republicans did not agree. They noted that Richard Nixon, making concessions to such a strategy, did not become President in 1960, though he did carry California by a hair; moreover in 1962, the same Nixon couldn't even beat Gov. Pat Brown. These California Republicans believed very deeply that the country under the Kennedy-Johnson Administration was moving the wrong way. They were determined to do something about it, and they did. They elected Ronald Reagan Governor of California in 1966 by a margin that approached a million votes.

Reagan's victory, coming just two years after the smashing defeat of another right-winger, Barry

Goldwater, shocked and surprised Eastern pundits. They would have been less surprised had they looked closer at California election results in the years preceding 1966. For one thing, Max Rafferty, running on a platform that looked fundamentalist, was elected State Superintendent of Public Instruction in 1962. For another thing, two decidedly conservative Republicans won off-year congressional races in 1963, both in districts that had been held by Democrats. Significantly, one of these victories came in a white working-class district southeast of Los Angeles, one that sat next to the simmering, but then still quiet, Watts ghetto.

Another sign, generally unnoticed, of the California conservative swing, was the election of 1964. Republicans actually made gains in the congressional races, even though the Democrats had drawn new district lines a few years before. Three of the four non-Southern House districts that elected Democrats in 1962 and Republicans in the Democratic year 1964 were in California. And Barry Goldwater, though he lost the state by more than a million votes, did better here than in most large industrial states. In fact, in southern California, he had a quite respectable 46% of the votes—not much less than the 52% Richard Nixon had won there four years earlier.

So the Reagan victory should not have come as a big surprise. When Watts in 1964 and Berkeley in 1965 brought out the festering resentments of California homeowners and taxpayers, Reagan, promising crackdowns on rioters and stern budget cuts, played on these resentments skillfully. Commentators may have called Reagan's programs simplistic and extreme, but his homey, reasonable manner belied that characterization. When he told the unpoor, unblack, and unrebellious that their basic impulses and fears were well-founded, that their way of life—whatever hippies and academics might think—was fundamentally *right,* the homeowners and taxpayers responded with millions of votes. Reagan was thereby able to revolutionize California state politics, successfully putting to the fore those issues where his positions commanded majority support. It was a masterful political achievement, one that would produce echoes nationally in the Nixon campaigns of 1968 and 1972.

But whatever the successes of Reagan-Nixon politics nationally, it reached its high point in California in 1968, the year Richard Nixon won the presidency and elevated a number of Teutono-Californian advertising men to positions of very great power. That same year, 1968, the Republicans here finally retook control of the state legislature, having painstakingly picked off Democratic incumbents during the course of the last three elections. With the 1970 census coming up, the Republicans were ready to redraw the state's congressional and legislative district lines and thus, they thought, to sew up political control of California for another 10 years.

But the expected didn't happen. Instead, the Democrats won back both houses of the legislature in 1970. They also won a Senate seat and the office of the Secretary of State, both previously held by Republicans. A black educator, Wilson Riles, beat Max Rafferty. And Jess Unruh, a politician by this time several shades to the left of the 1966 Pat Brown, and with much less money, managed to cut Ronald Reagan's margin in half.

The Democrats who won in 1970, or ran far better than expected, were almost without exception politicians who backed the bulk of the "extremist" platform espoused by George McGovern two years later, with such ill consequences nationally. Just as Reagan—the Republican "extremist"—ran better in 1966 than Nixon—the Republican "centrist"—did in 1962, so Unruh—the Democratic "extremist"—ran better in 1970 than Brown—the "centrist"—did in 1966. So there were already signs that the Reagan philosophy was in trouble with the voters, even before the 1970 turning-point election.

The most notable sign was the election of liberal Democrat Alan Cranston to the Senate two years before, in 1968, even as Reaganites took control of the legislature. In early 1968, Cranston looked like a political has-been. The former newspaperman had gone into the California real estate business after World War II, and later helped to found the California Democratic Council (CDC); this was a volunteer group that supported liberal politicians, particularly in primary elections. His CDC credentials helped him to win the Democratic nomination for Controller in 1958, and he swept into office on the strength of the Pat Brown landslide. In 1962, he was reelected with the largest majority of any statewide politician. Then, in 1966, Cranston was unseated by a narrow margin in the Reagan landslide. And finally, in 1968, he prepared himself to run against Sen. Thomas Kuchel, a Republican who had followed the traditional counsel of moderation and liberalism.

Kuchel looked unbeatable, but first had to win renomination in the Republican primary. The Senator was, in fact, the last vestige of Earl Warren's regime, having been appointed to the Senate by Warren after Richard Nixon resigned to become Vice-President. Never badgered by significant primary opposition, Kuchel had brushed aside Democratic opponents with ease in 1954, 1956, and 1962; and had become Republican Whip, the number-two leadership position in the Senate. If he had been reelected, as he doubtless expected to be, he would have probabtly succeeded the late Everett Dirksen as Minority Leader in 1969.

Kuchel's liberal record, however, was far out of line with the preferences of California's registered Republicans. Heavily outnumbered by Democrats, these voters were, and are, concentrated in southern California, with more than half of them living in Los Angeles, Orange, and San Diego counties. Outside these three counties, Kuchel led Rafferty 57–43, but he lost the big three in the south by a solid 60–40 margin. The fervor of the Rafferty supporters was so great that the noise of their victory-night celebration scarcely abated when they heard that Robert Kennedy, who had just won the state's Democratic presidential primary, had been shot.

By all conventional standards, Rafferty should have been a pushover, with Cranston transformed overnight by the conservative's primary victory from sure loser to sure winner. But in California in 1968 things were not so easy. Rafferty did well in the polls, and Cranston's biggest break probably came when a Long Beach newsman, noting Rafferty's harsh condemnation of draft resisters, checked out the candidate's own war record. It appeared that Rafferty sat out World War II with an alleged injury; following that, there was evidence that on VJ Day, Rafferty threw away his crutches. It was a measure of the strength of the state's conservative tide that even with all this, Cranston managed to win only 52% of the votes. Rafferty, defeated two years later for reelection as Superintendent, left California and now teaches at Troy State College in Alabama.

Reagan Republicans succeeded in losing the state's other Senate Seat in 1970. Early that year, Sen. George Murphy, the old song-and-dance man, seemed in pretty good political shape, though his voice had been reduced to a whisper by throat surgery. His election in 1964, over interim appointee Pierre Salinger, was something of a surprise—and a harbinger of conservative victories to come. Murphy won in large part because he, unlike Salinger, refused to oppose anti-open-housing Proposition 14.

But later in 1970 came the news that Technicolor, Inc., headed by a supporter of various Republican and right-wing causes, was paying the Senator $20,000 a year and supplying him with a Washington apartment and use of a credit card. Suddenly Murphy was in political trouble—and he never got out. He was beaten by a 54–44 margin. Today he is sometimes seen in Washington, a forlorn figure eking out a living as a lobbyist. It appears that Murphy, unlike Reagan, never got all that rich in the movies.

The man who beat Murphy and became for two years the Senate's youngest member is a politician even luckier than Cranston. His name is John V. Tunney, whose career, some say, was the model for The Candidate, yet another movie. Son of the heavyweight boxer who unhinged Jack Dempsey, and law school roommate of Sen. Edward Kennedy, Tunney moved to California in 1960 when he was assigned, as an Air Force JAG officer, to March Air Force Base near Riverside. He liked the area, he said, and decided to stay. In the election that followed his exit from the Air Force, Tunney ran for Congress. This was 1964, when the Republican incumbent was a weak candidate who had barely unseated a gravely ill Democrat two years before. Tunney won.

The district he represented (then the 38th, now the 43rd) included not only the fast-growing, onetime citrus center of Riverside, but also the heavily irrigated Imperial Valley, a hot region of huge farms that require the attendance of vast numbers of farm laborers, now predominantly Mexican-American. While supporting the programs of the Johnson Administration generally, Tunney was not inattentive to the problems of his big farming constituents—heavily subsidized, as it happens, by water provided by the federal Bureau of Reclamation. Tunney thereby caught the eye of many of the state's leading political contributors. With Murphy increasingly vulnerable, Tunney accumulated massive financial backing and managed a convincing, though by no means large, primary victory over peacenik Congressman George Brown. (Brown, oddly enough, is now back in the House representing a new district which includes some of Tunney's old one.) The general election in 1970 was easier for the Democrats than in 1968. Tunney fairly coasted to victory. In fact, his margin was greater than Ronald Reagan's.

This last fact, little noted in the national press, is symptomatic of the leftward trend of California public opinion. The trend shows up repeatedly in the returns from the 1970 and 1972 elections. As noted, the Democrats came back in 1970 to win control of the state legislature, which prevented Republican line-drawing of congressional districts. Republican control would have almost certainly given Gov. Reagan's party 10 to 15 new Congressmen. Instead, a compromise redistricting plan was adopted. This safeguarded all of the state's incumbents, with the exception of renegade Republican Pete McCloskey; it then split the five additional seats the state won in 1970, 2–2, with one seat up for grabs, which the Republicans eventually won.

The California Supreme Court has since ruled that the compromise plan could stand only for the 1972 elections. At this writing, it appears almost certain that another redistricting scheme submitted to the court by the Special Masters will be adopted for 1974. The new plan would maintain roughly the same political balance in the California House delegation, but it would smooth out the tortuous boundaries that applied in 1972. One Congressman especially hurt is the 43rd's Victor Veysey, whose constituency was carved up among several districts. Three Democratic incumbents from Los Angeles County also face potential trouble. The 19th's veteran Congressman Chet Holifield and the 29th's George Danielson will probably have to run in heavily Mexican-American districts, and the 31st's Charles Wilson will probably encounter stiff black primary opposition. An additional note: the Masters have renumbered the districts in a manner too complex to relate here.

In 1972, the Democrats increased their margin in the state Assembly to near 2–1 proportions, but because they lost a couple of very close contests, they had to settle for an even split in the state Senate. Significantly, where Democratic incumbent Congressmen were hard pressed to win in 1968, it was Republican incumbents who were in trouble in 1972; the Democrats percentage of the state congressional vote rose to its highest level since 1964. Moreover, George McGovern, like Barry Goldwater before him, did better in California, as compared to his party's previous presidential showing, than in any of the other 10 large states. While McGovern ran eight to nine percentage points behind Humphrey in Pennsylvania and New York, his California showing was within two percentage points of Humphrey. These figures indicate that Californians, unlike voters in other large states, did not find McGovern's "extremist" stance significantly less palatable than the "centrist" position of other Democrats.

An incident that occurred just after the 1970 elections gives a clue as to why the decline in the appeal of Reagan's politics and the state's shift toward the left is occurring. Since coming to office, the Governor strongly opposed withholding of state income taxes; as a believer in tax reduction, he wanted California taxpayers to feel the pinch when they had to scrape together the whole damn thing each April. (In fact, withholding was finally enacted, because Republican legislators, as well as Democratic, became convinced that the state was losing too much revenue without it.) Anyway, taxes, Reagan was fond of saying, should hurt.

A newspaperwoman then discovered that Reagan himself had paid no state income tax during the preceding year. When the issue surfaced, the Governor tensed up and refused to talk about it, apparently unwilling to admit that he, like most wealthy men, arranged his affairs to minimize his tax burden. Although no one suggested that he did anything illegal, Reagan's popularity immediately plummeted in the polls, and he has not wholly recovered. What must have gone through the voters' minds is the idea, doubtless true, that the driving force behind many of Reagan's backers, if not behind Reagan himself, was not their love of Middle American moral values so much as a desire to protect their own rather sizable pocketbooks from the depredations of the tax collector.

But many of Reagan's later problems were the almost inevitable price of his early success. If he had convinced Californians in 1966 that he would reassert and reestablish the values of the middle class against those who disdained them—hippies, blacks, and university professors—it became painfully apparent by the early 1970s that he just couldn't do it. For every long-haired freak thumbing a ride on the Big Sur highway in 1966, there were a dozen by 1970; for every black who actually went looting in Watts in 1966, there were a dozen blacks in sleek Afros wearing dashikis a few years later. Reagan may have won at the polls, but California, before the rest of America caught on, was greening anyway.

It would have been unthinkable back in 1966, for example, that a referendum to legalize marijuana would outpoll a referendum out to clamp limits on obscene movies. Yet exactly that happened in 1972. In a performance that surely no other state but Massachusetts could duplicate, some 33% of the voters in California approved legal pot; the proposition carried six of the state's eighty Assembly districts, and even got 187,000 votes in ultraconservative Orange County.

Demographic change—not so much in the population as a whole, but in the electorate—is responsible for much of the change here. Much of the support for Reagan and Reaganites—it is impossible to say precisely how much—came from immigrants to the state. These were Midwesterners and Southerners who expected to find the kind of order and serenity they had just left behind (or escaped) in hometown USA. But since the salad days of the 1950s, immigration has diminished, and now a new generation of Californians has grown into voting age. Some 18% of California's potential voters are between 18 and 24—a significantly larger percentage than in the country as a whole. Some 7% of the potential electorate attends college, not to mention graduate school. It turned out that the dormitories and communities around California's vast system of higher education produced huge majorities against candidates like Richard Nixon and Ronald Reagan following passage of the 18-year-old vote in time for the 1972 elections.

It is true, as Nixon supporters claim, that students and young voters in the nation as a whole did not favor McGovern and McGovernite candidates nearly as much as had been predicted. But in California, where the Republican party under Reagan has conducted what seems to most young people as a crusade against their very way of life, and where both Berkeley student and gas station attendant smoke grass regularly, the young vote went—and will almost certainly continue to go—heavily against the Republicans.

It is not without significance, then, that Ronald Reagan announced he will not run either for Governor or Senator in 1974. Reagan has done a little better lately in the polls, due mainly to a tax cut he sponsored. But it is entirely possible, as it was not a few years ago, that he could lose either one of these upcoming California contests. Reagan now plans to hit the mashed-potato circuit—that is, deliver banquet speeches—across the country, in what everybody but the man himself concedes is an effort to win the 1976 Republican presidential nomination. Because the nation seems to lag somewhat behind the California scene, he might just win it. After all, the Peter Principle has worked for at least one California politician who managed to win high national office after having been rejected by the voters of his home state.

One of the main reasons Reagan has decided to shun the 1974 Senate race is the popularity of incumbent Sen. Cranston. Early 1973 polls showed Cranston far ahead of Reagan and also showed that far fewer California voters harbored strong negative feelings toward him. Cranston's apparent strength testifies both to the leftward trend in the state's politics and to his own hard work. Holder of the world 100-yard dash record for people in his age group, Cranston displays much the same energy in the Senate, where he sponsors hundreds of bills and becomes involved in many issues. As his first term progressed, he earned a reputation for being "prepared" and "effective." As a former newspaperman, one of the Senator's pet causes is the enactment of a privilege for newsmen, one which would allow them to protect the confidentiality of their sources from judicial inquiry. Cranston favors an unqualified privilege—a position to which other Senators like Sam Ervin have moved as the difficulties of limiting the privilege have become clear.

No doubt Cranston's best-known fight—and one of his biggest political assets—was his leadership in the 1971 struggle to get a $250 million government loan guarantee to the ailing Lockheed corporation, the nation's largest defense contractor. Although Cranston consistently voted to end the Vietnam war and usually supported moves to cut the Pentagon budget, he supported the loan; he was no doubt influenced by Lockheed's status as one of California's largest employers. It can seldom be documented that one Senator swung the decisive vote; but on this issue, Cranston, in fact, did it. As the roll was being called, he managed to convince Montana Sen. Lee Metcalf to vote for the bill, and the measure passed by that single vote.

Cranston's role in the Lockheed matter has been criticized as being out of line with his record on similar issues. It shows, certainly, that though he usually lines up with the Senate's liberal bloc, his approach to things is at least as pragmatic as it is ideological. The same can be said of his junior colleague, John Tunney, who for two years after his election was the youngest member of the Senate. Tunney serves with his law-school roommate, Ted Kennedy, on the Judiciary Committee. Tunney probably achieved his greatest national notice during the Richard Kleindienst confirmation hearings after the Arizonan was nominated for Attorney General. Here the Senator sharply questioned the nominee and others on ITT's campaign contribution, which was allegedly designed to bring the 1972 Republican National Convention to San Diego. Almost singlehandedly Tunney has also focused attention on a fragrant scandal in the San Diego U.S. Attorney's Office.

The campaign organization and network of big contributors Tunney built up during his 1970 runaway victory gave him the reputation, for a while at least, of being the strongest Democratic power in traditionally nonorganization California. His support was much sought after by candidates for the 1972 Democratic presidential nomination. When he came out for Sen. Edmund

Muskie in December 1971, it was taken as a sign that his friend, Ted Kennedy, would not be running. As things worked out, Tunney's blessing made little difference, and today the state party organization, for what it's worth, is in the hands of Assemblyman John Burton, an early McGovern supporter and brother of Congressman Phillip Burton. But at this writing, no one expects Tunney to be in much trouble for 1976. It should be noted that Cranston's and Tunney's good prospects for reelection are a sharp break from recent California tradition; the state has not reelected a Senator since 1962.

In 1974, the main event in California politics will be the Governor's race. There is already a plethora of talented candidates. Among the Democrats are San Francisco Mayor Joseph Alioto, a leading Humphrey supporter in 1968 and 1972, who urges his party to return to the "center" and who seems unhurt by charges of scandal and an unsuccessful Justice Department prosecution; Secretary of State Edmund G. (Jerry) Brown, son of the former Governor; Assembly Speaker Bob Moretti; state Sen. George Moscone; and Congressman Jerome Waldie. Republican speculation centers on Lt. Gov. Ed Reinecke, picked for the post by Reagan when Robert Finch went off to Washington in 1969. But other possibilities include Finch himself, though he has been damaged by an inept performance as HEW Secretary; State Controller Houston Flournoy, considered the best hope of his party's moderates; and Atty. Gen. Evelle Younger, former Los Angeles County District Attorney. Some big contributors, fearing Reinecke's weakness—he was tied into the ITT affair, and several of his staffers have quit, denouncing him—are trying to draft former (1969–73) Undersecretary of Defense David Packard for the slot.

It is possible that the 1974 gubernatorial race will give us another entry in the presidential sweepstakes. In any case, it will tell us a lot about the mood, not only of California, but of the nation. The 1958 Democratic and 1966 Republican gubernatorial landslides preceded each party's presidential victories two years later, and it is entirely possible that California will in 1974 once again prove to be the setter of the national trend.

Census Data Pop. 19,953,134; 9.86% of U.S. total, 1st largest; change 1960–70, 27.0%. Central city, 36%; suburban, 56%. Median family income, $10,729; 9th highest; families above $15,000: 27%; families below $3,000: 8%. Median years education, 12.4.

1972 Share of Federal Tax Burden $23,493,670,000; 11.24% of U.S. total, 1st largest.

1972 Share of Federal Outlays $25,616,884,544; 11.82% of U.S. total, 2nd largest.   Per capita federal spending, $1,284.

DOD	$10,672,252,000	1st (17.08%)	HEW	$7,564,657,586	2nd (10.60%)
AEC	$304,612,975	3rd (11.62%)	HUD	$254,937,803	2nd (8.31%)
NASA	$785,253,158	1st (26.25%)	VA	$1,212,672,920	1st (10.59%)
DOT	$766,385,452	1st (9.72%)	USDA	$843,603,380	3rd (5.48%)
DOC	$156,155,271	2nd (12.06%)	CSC	$462,610,761	2nd (11.22%)
DOI	$231,339,364	1st (10.91%)	TD	$719,245,012	3rd (4.35%)
DOJ	$114,797,654	1st (11.69%)	Other	$1,528,179,208	

Economic Base Finance, insurance and real estate; agriculture, notably cattle, dairy products, grapes and hay; transportation equipment, especially aircraft and parts; electrical equipment and supplies, especially radio and television communication equipment; food and kindred products; machinery, especially office and computing machines; tourism; ordnance and accessories.

Political Line-up Governor, Ronald Reagan (R); seat up, 1974. Senators, Alan Cranston (D) and John V. Tunney (D). Representatives, 43 (23 D and 20 R). State Senate (19 D, 19 R, and 2 vac.); State Assembly (51 D and 29 R).

The Voters

Registration 10,466,215 Total. 5,864,745 D (56%); 3,840,620 R (37%); 615,817 declined to state (6%); 145,033 other (1%).
Median voting age 41.6
Employment profile White collar, 54%. Blue collar, 36%. Service, 13%. Farm, 2%.
Ethnic groups Black, 7%. Japanese, 1%. Spanish, 16%. Total foreign stock, 25%. Canada, UK, Germany, Italy, 2% each; USSR, 1%.

Presidential vote

1972	Nixon (R)	4,602,096	(57%)
	McGovern (D)	3,475,847	(43%)
1968	Nixon (R)	3,467,664	(48%)
	Humphrey (D)	3,244,318	(45%)
	Wallace (AI)	487,270	(7%)
1964	Johnson (D)	4,171,877	(59%)
	Goldwater (R)	2,879,108	(41%)

Senator

Alan Cranston (D) Elected 1968, seat up 1974; b. June 19, 1914, Palo Alto; home, Los Angeles; Pomona Col., 1932–33; U. of Mexico, summer 1935; Stanford U., B.A., 1936; Army, WWII; married, two children; Protestant.

Career Newspaperman, Int. News Svc., 1937–38; Chief Foreign Language Div., Office War Info., 1940–44; businessman, land investment and home construction; Founder, Pres., Calif. Dem. Council, 1953–58; Controller, State of Calif., 1958–66.

Offices 452 CHOB, 202-225-3553. Also 13220 Fed. Bldg., 11000 Wilshire Blvd., Los Angeles 90024, 213-824-7641, and 450 Golden Gate, San Francisco 94102, 415-556-8441.

Administrative Assistant Roy F. Greenaway

Committees

Banking, Housing and Urban Affairs (5th); Subs: Housing and Urban Affairs; International Finance; Small Business (Chm.).

Labor and Public Welfare (8th); Subs: Handicapped; Education; Health; Employment, Poverty, and Migratory Labor; Children and Youth; Aging; Alocholism and Narcotics; Human Resources (Chm.); National Science Foundation.

Veterans' Affairs (5th); Subs: Housing and Insurance; Health and Hospitals (Chm.); Readjustment, Education, and Employment.

Sel. Com. on Nutrition and Human Needs (7th).

Sp. Com. to Study Questions Related to Secret and Confidential Government Documents (4th).

Group Ratings

	ADA	COPE	LWV	RIPON	NFU	LCV	CFA	NAB	NSI	ACA
1972	90	100	100	67	90	92	100	8	0	5
1971	89	92	92	71	100	–	100	–	–	0
1970	91	100	–	81	100	97	–	11	10	0

Key Votes

1) Busing	FOR	8) Sea Life Prot	FOR	15) Tax Singls Less	FOR
2) Alas P-line	AGN	9) Campaign Subs	FOR	16) Min Tax for Rich	ABS
3) Gun Cntrl	FOR	10) Cmbodia Bmbg	AGN	17) Euro Troop Rdctn	FOR
4) Rehnquist	AGN	11) Legal Srvices	FOR	18) Bust Hwy Trust	FOR
5) Pub TV $	AGN	12) Rev Sharing	FOR	19) Maid Min Wage	FOR
6) EZ Votr Reg	FOR	13) Cnsumr Prot	FOR	20) Farm Sub Limit	AGN
7) No-Fault	FOR	14) Eq Rts Amend	FOR	21) Highr Credt Chgs	FOR

Election Results

1968 general:	Alan Cranston (D)	3,680,352	(52%)
	Max Rafferty (R)	3,329,148	(47%)

Paul Jacobs (PF)	91,254	(1%)
1968 primary: Alan Cranston (D)	1,681,825	(59%)
Anthony C. Beilenson (D)	644,844	(23%)
Walter R. Buchanan (D)	227,798	(8%)
William M. Bennett (D)	207,720	(7%)
Charles Crail (D)	89,023	(3%)

Senator

John Varick Tunney (D) Elected 1970, seat up 1976; b. June 26, 1934, New York City; home, Riverside; Yale U., B.A., 1956; Academy in Intl. Law at The Hague, Netherlands, 1957; U. of Va., LL.B., 1959; USAF, 1960–63; divorced, three children; Catholic.

Career Practicing atty., 1959–70; Business Law Lecturer, U. of Calif., 1961–62.

Offices 1415 NSOB, 202-225-3841. Also 4080 Lemon St., Riverside 92501, 714-682-0232, and 11000 Wilshire Blvd., Rm. 14223, Los Angeles 90024, 213-824-7344, and 450 Golden Gate Ave., Rm. 17432, San Francisco, 415-556-4000.

Administrative Assistant Hadley R. Roff

Committees

Commerce (10th); Subs: Aviation; Consumer; Environment; Merchant Marine; Oceans and Atmosphere; Science and Technology (Chm.).

District of Columbia (4th); Subs: Business, Commerce and Judiciary; Public Health, Education, Welfare and Safety (Chm).

Judiciary (9th); Subs: Administrative Practice and Procedure; Antitrust and Monopoly; Constitutional Amendments; Constitutional Rights; Representation of Citizen Rights (Chm.).

Sp. Com. on Aging (12th); Subs: Housing for the Elderly; Federal, State, and Community Services; Health of the Elderly; Long-term Care.

Group Ratings

	ADA	COPE	LWV	RIPON	NFU	LCV	CFA	NAB	NSI	ACA
1972	90	100	100	75	90	90	100	25	10	5
1971	96	91	92	68	100	–	100	–	–	5

Key Votes

1) Busing	ABS	8) Sea Life Prot	FOR	15) Tax Singls Less	AGN
2) Alas P-line	AGN	9) Campaign Subs	FOR	16) Min Tax for Rich	FOR
3) Gun Cntrl	FOR	10) Cmbodia Bmbg	AGN	17) Euro Troop Rdctn	AGN
4) Rehnquist	AGN	11) Legal Srvices	FOR	18) Bust Hwy Trust	FOR
5) Pub TV $	AGN	12) Rev Sharing	FOR	19) Maid Min Wage	FOR
6) EZ Votr Reg	FOR	13) Cnsumr Prot	ABS	20) Farm Sub Limit	AGN
7) No-Fault	FOR	14) Eq Rts Amend	FOR	21) Highr Credt Chgs	AGN

Election Results

1970 general:	John Tunney (D)	3,496,558	(54%)
	George Murphy (R)	2,877,617	(44%)
	Charles Ripley (AI)	61,251	(1%)
	Robert Scheer (PF)	56,731	(1%)
1970 primary:	John Tunney (D)	1,010,812	(42%)
	George Brown, Jr. (D)	812,463	(33%)
	Kenneth Hahn (D)	417,970	(17%)
	Eileen Anderson (D)	60,977	(2%)

Arthur Bell, Jr. (D)	48,878	(2%)
Leonard Kurland (D)	43,923	(2%)
Louis Di Salvo (D)	35,829	(1%)

FIRST DISTRICT Political Background

For 300 miles north out of San Francisco, the California coast extends in massive grandeur. Cut off by the Coast Range from the interior, this region is covered with Douglas fir and redwoods. The first white settlers here were Russians, but little evidence remains of their activities here except for a number of place names. More enduring is the rocky, foggy coastline and the redwoods. The new Redwoods National Park, a subject of controversy a few years back, attracts many tourists. This was lumbering country in the late nineteenth century, and the Victorian mansions in towns like Eureka and Mendocino testify to the richness of the harvest. But today it is not an area of great prosperity; the bulk of the recent population increase seems to be composed of veterans of the counterculture seeking a quiet, rural life in the hills of Mendocino and Sonoma counties.

This is the 1st district of California, one that stretches from the Marin County line, just a few miles north of the Golden Gate, to the Oregon border. Metropolitan growth intrudes only in the southern part of Sonoma County, just over the Marin line, around Santa Rosa. Most of this coastal area is politically marginal; the district having consistently voted for the winners of statewide races by something very close to the statewide percentage.

In congressional races, the 1st has followed the pattern of most California districts: regularly reelecting its Representative, regardless of party. In 1958, on the retirement of a five-term Republican incumbent, it sent Democrat Clement Miller to Washington. Miller, killed in a plane crash during the 1962 campaign, was the author of *Member of the House*, a collection of letters to friends which is probably the most sensitive account extant of the House in the late 1950s and early 1960s. Miller was reelected posthumously in 1962, but the winner of the special election to fill the vacancy in early 1963 was his 1962 opponent, Republican Don Clausen. With a voting record quite different from Miller's, Clausen has been winning just as solidly ever since. It is a measure of his popularity that he ran a full 9% ahead of Richard Nixon in 1972.

Clausen sits on the Interior and Public Works Committees—important assignments to this coastal district, where much of the land is still owned by the federal government. The Congressman maintains a low profile in Washington, voting most of the time with the well-disciplined Republican bloc. With seats on the two committees most closely concerned with ecological issues, Clausen has more often sided with believers in more highways and dams than with the new breed of environmentalists.

Census Data Pop. 468,022. Central city, 18%; suburban, 42%. Median family income, $9,473; families above $15,000: 19%; families below $3,000: 11%. Median years education, 12.3.

1972 Share of Federal Outlays $429,406,003

DOD	$39,388,000	HEW	$252,063,491
AEC	–	HUD	$7,180,050
NASA	–	DOI	$6,739,396
DOT	$25,161,434	USDA	$23,401,553
		Other	$75,472,079

Federal Military-Industrial Commitments

DOD Installations Naval Security Group Activity, Skaggs Island (Sonoma). Klamath AF Station (Requa). Point Arena AF Station (Point Arena).

Economic Base Lumber and wood products, especially general sawmill and planing mill products; agriculture, notably fruits, dairy products, poultry and cattle; finance, insurance and real estate; food and kindred products, especially canned, cured and frozen foods; and tourism.

The Voters

Registration 279,368 total. 155,487 D (56%); 104,064 R (37%); 15,142 declined to state (5%); 4,175 other (1%).
Median voting age 45.3
Employment profile White collar, 47%. Blue collar, 34%. Service, 15%. Farm, 4%.
Ethnic groups Indian, 2%. Spanish, 6%. Total foreign stock, 18%. Italy, Canada, Germany, UK, 2% each.

Presidential vote

1972	Nixon (R)	123,735	(56%)
	McGovern (D)	95,522	(44%)
1968	Nixon (R)	77,855	(47%)
	Humphrey (D)	75,033	(45%)
	Wallace (AI)	14,002	(8%)

Representative

Don H. Clausen (R) Elected 1962; b. April 27, 1923, Ferndale; home, Crescent City; San Jose State Col., Calif. Polytechnic, Weber Col., St. Mary's Col.; Navy, WWII; married, two children; Lutheran.

Career Businesses: Clausen Flying Service, Air Ambulance Service, and Clausen Assoc. (insurance).

Offices 2433 RHOB 202-225-3311. Also 475 H St., Crescent City 95531, 707-464-3241, and 206 Rosenberg Bldg., Santa Rosa 95401, 707-545-8844.

Administrative Assistant William E. Stodart

Committees

Interior and Insular Affairs (5th); Subs: Public Lands; National Parks and Recreation; Water and Power Resources; Territorial and Insular Affairs (Ranking Mbr.).

Public Works (4th); Subs: Economic Development; Investigations and Review; Transportation; Water Resources (Ranking Mbr.).

Group Ratings

	ADA	COPE	LWV	RIPON	NFU	LCV	CFA	NAB	NSI	ACA
1972	0	27	40	44	83	27	0	73	100	75
1971	3	33	33	47	23	–	20	–	–	85
1970	16	17	–	44	54	7	43	75	100	72

Key Votes

1) Busing	AGN	6) Cmbodia Bmbg	FOR	11) Chkg Acct Intrst	AGN
2) Strip Mines	AGN	7) Bust Hwy Trust	AGN	12) End HISC (HUAC)	AGN
3) Cut Mil $	AGN	8) Farm Sub Lmt	AGN	13) Nixon Sewer Veto	FOR
4) Rev Shrg	FOR	9) School Prayr	FOR	14) Corp Cmpaign $	FOR
5) Pub TV $	ABS	10) Cnsumr Prot	ABS	15) Pol $ Disclosr	AGN

Election Results

1972 general:	Don H. Clausen (R)	141,226	(62%)
	William A. Nighswonger (D)	77,610	(34%)
	Jonathan T. Ames (PF)	7,922	(4%)
1972 primary:	Don H. Clausen (R), unopposed		
1970 general:	Don H. Clausen (R)	108,358	(63%)
	William Kortum (D)	62,688	(37%)

SECOND DISTRICT Political Background

The 2nd is physically the largest of California's congressional districts. It extends from the Coast Range and the Oregon border to the Sierra Nevada south of Lake Tahoe. With 2% of the state's population, the district covers 22% of its terrain. Some of the county names here—Placer, El Dorado—recall the Gold Rush of 1849; many of the streams coursing down from the Sierra to the Central Valley probably look little different from the days when the first prospectors began panning for gold in them more than 120 years ago.

But geography, of course, is an imprecise guide to political reality, and most of the voters in the 2nd are concentrated in two small, and totally separate, corners of the district. Almost 40% of the 2nd's residents live in a series of towns and farms along the upper Sacramento River. The northern towns, Redding and Red Bluff, are traditionally Democratic; the southern ones, Chico and Oroville, traditionally Republican. The presence of a state college in Chico, however, put the town in the Democratic column in 1972. The other major concentration of people—about 20% of the total—is located in the northwest suburbs of Sacramento; like all the capital city's metropolitan area, this is usually a Democratic stronghold.

All of this adds up to a district that has been regarded, over the years, as safely Democratic. In fact, the 2nd has not sent a Republican to Congress since 1942. The current Representative, Harold T. (Bizz) Johnson, was first elected in 1958 when his predecessor, Clair Engle, went to the Senate. Since then, Johnson has been winning reelection by overwhelming margins; in 1972, he won 70% of the votes, while George McGovern could only manage 45% in the district.

Johnson is one of those northern Democrats more comfortable with the traditional to-get-along-youhave-to-go-along philosophy of the House Democratic leadership than with the younger, more ideologically-oriented Democrats; the latter are rapidly becoming a majority in the party caucus. Johnson, for example, has not challenged high military spending, nor, as Chairman of various Interior subcommittees, has he opposed the time-honored policy that building more dams and irrigating more land is an unalloyed good. At the same time, he has just about a perfect voting record as far as organized labor and Democratic-oriented farm groups are concerned. With long experience in government—he was a state Senator for 10 years before his election to Congress—he has been effective in getting public works projects and federal money generally for his district. As the third-ranking Democrat on the Interior Committee, he has a good shot at being Chairman some day; only his advancing age (67 in 1974) would seem to be an obstacle.

Census Data Pop. 462,979. Central city, 0%; suburban, 23%. Median family income, $9,035; families above $15,000: 17%; families below $3,000: 11%. Median years education, 12.3.

1972 Share of Federal Outlays $579,380,671

DOD	$104,732,000	HEW	$228,405,901
AEC	$264,108	HUD	$4,072,359
NASA	$2,603,018	DOI	$27,837,298
DOT	$22,650,937	USDA	$79,540,988
		Other	$$109,276,062

Federal Military-Industrial Commitments

DOD Installations Sierra Army Depot (Herlong).

Economic Base Agriculture, notably cattle, fruits and grains; lumber and wood products; finance, insurance and real estate; and tourism. Also higher education (Chico State).

The Voters

Registration 270,105 total. 154,179 D (57%); 100,694 R (37%); 12,742 declined to state (4%); 2,490 other (1%).
Median voting age 45.0
Employment profile White collar, 47%. Blue collar, 32%. Service, 16%. Farm, 5%.
Ethnic groups Black, 1%. Indian, 1%. Spanish, 6%. Total foreign stock, 13%. Canada, UK, Germany, 2% each; Italy, 1%.

Presidential vote

1972	Nixon (R)	115,742	(55%)
	McGovern (D)	94,060	(45%)
1968	Nixon (R)	79,418	(47%)
	Humphrey (D)	74,035	(44%)
	Wallace (AI)	16,342	(10%)

Representative

Harold T. (Bizz) **Johnson** (D) Elected 1958; b. Dec. 2, 1907, Yolo County; home, Roseville; U. of Nev.; married, two children; Presbyterian.

Career Suprv., Pacific Fruit Express Co.; Dist. Chm., Brotherhood of Railway Clerks; Mayor of Roseville, 1941–49; Calif. State Senate, 1948–58.

Offices 2347 RHOB, 202-225-3076. Also U.S. P.O. Bldg., Roseville 95678, 916-782-4411.

Administrative Assistant Dwight H. Barnes

Committees

Interior and Insular Affairs (3rd); Subs: National Parks and Recreation; Water and Power Resources (Chm.); Public Lands.

Public Works (7th); Subs: Economic Development; Energy; Water Resources; Transportation.

Group Ratings

	ADA	COPE	LWV	RIPON	NFU	LCV	CFA	NAB	NSI	ACA
1972	44	82	58	50	100	13	0	17	90	30
1971	35	100	100	47	60	–	75	–	–	33
1970	56	100	–	53	100	39	78	0	70	6

Key Votes

1) Busing	AGN	6) Cmbodia Bmbg	AGN	11) Chkg Acct Intrst	AGN
2) Strip Mines	AGN	7) Bust Hwy Trust	AGN	12) End HISC (HUAC)	AGN
3) Cut Mil $	AGN	8) Farm Sub Lmt	AGN	13) Nixon Sewer Veto	AGN
4) Rev Shrg	FOR	9) School Prayr	AGN	14) Corp Cmpaign $	FOR
5) Pub TV $	FOR	10) Cnsumr Prot	FOR	15) Pol $ Disclosr	AGN

Election Results

1972 general:	Bizz Johnson (D)	149,590	(68%)
	Francis X. Callahan (R)	62,727	(29%)
	Dorothy D. Paradis (AI)	6,431	(3%)
1972 primary:	Bizz Johnson (D), unopposed		
1970 general:	Bizz Johnson (D)	151,070	(78%)
	Lloyd Gilbert (R)	37,223	(19%)
	Jack Carrigg (AI)	5,681	(3%)

THIRD DISTRICT Political Background

The 3rd district of California comprises the city of Sacramento, the state capital, and some of its suburbs. The site of Sutter's Fort, Sacramento has been an important city since the Gold Rush of forty-nine; today it is the largest city in the Central Valley, the much-irrigated and incalculably rich farmland north along the Sacramento River and south along the San Joaquin. Ever since the Gold Rush, Sacramento has been a Democratic stronghold. These days this preference can be explained in part by the city's large number of public employees—federal and local as well as state— people usually happy with the idea of big government. In fact, the 3d district has a higher proportion of public employees than all but four others: three suburban Washington, D. C.

districts and the state of Alaska. Moreover, Sacramento is one of the few American cities with staunchly Democratic newspapers—part of the McClatchy chain that also dominates journalism in Modesto and Fresno farther south in the Valley. So strong are Sacramento's Democratic voting habits that the 3rd was one of eight California districts to go for George McGovern in 1972.

Naturally, the 3rd sends a Democrat to Congress, and for the last 20 years he has been John E. Moss. A serious-minded liberal Democrat, Moss is probably best-known for sponsoring the Freedom of Information Act (FOIA), a measure that inspired much hostility among federal personnel eager to keep their work secret. But for Moss' perseverance the bill would never have passed. The law has been something of a disappointment to Moss and some of its backers, in large part because the courts have widened some of its exceptions into gaping loopholes. The press generally has taken little advantage of the FOIA, its main beneficiary so far being Ralph Nader and his raiders. Still, the measure makes at least a start toward open government, and Moss has shown some interest in revising it.

Currently, Moss' chief legislative interests lie in the Commerce Committee, where he is Chairman of the Commerce and Finance Subcommittee. He was forced to give up the Government Information chairmanship because of the rule that prohibits any Congressman from heading two subcommittees. In the Commerce Subcommittee, Moss will have a major say over legislation, expected to be enacted in the 93rd Congress, reforming the securities industry. Complex questions of great financial importance are involved—whether brokers' fees should be fixed or negotiated, whether financial institutions should be able to become members of stock exchanges, and if so, under what conditions, and so on. Given Moss' record, his aim will be to protect small investors and to eliminate quasi-monopolistic advantages currently enjoyed by various financial institutions.

In the fall of 1972, Moss steered a bill through the House setting up an independent agency to set mandatory safety standards for consumer products; the Nixon Administration wanted the FDA, long sympathetic to the industries it presumably regulates, to do the standard-setting. The Congressman's success on this measure, as well as on the FOIA, is evidence that he is a hard-working, persuasive manager of legislation.

As Moss' record shows, the Congressman is an individualist. But his unwillingness to observe the get-along-go-along traditions of the House has put off many of his colleagues and has prevented him from rising in the House leadership. In 1969, he was passed over for the position of Deputy Whip in favor of his fellow Californian, John McFall; and McFall moved up to the Whip post after the death of Majority Leader Hale Boggs. But at the 93rd Congress, Moss was elected to the Democratic Steering and Policy Committee—a sign that his colleagues from California have respect, if not affection, for him.

It is typical of Moss' blunt style that he was the first member of Congress to suggest, shortly after the Watergate mess broke, that the House set up a procedure to pass on the question, should it come up, of the impeachment of the President. The Congressman's style, however, seems to sit well with the voters of the 3rd district. Although Moss received as little as 56% of the votes in 1968 at the height of Ronald Reagan's popularity, he won a commanding 70% in 1972, and appears to have few worries at home.

Census Data Pop. 463,681. Central city, 47%; suburban, 53%. Median family income, $10,588; families above $15,000: 26%; families below $3,000: 8%. Median years education, 12.5.

1972 Share of Federal Outlays $922,661,095

DOD	$325,435,104	HEW	$249,172,419
AEC	$1,157,122	HUD	$8,000,025
NASA	$10,435,875	DOI	$33,581,805
DOT	$28,237,999	USDA	$36,844,556
		Other	$229,796,190

Federal Military-Industrial Commitments

DOD Contractors Aerojet General (Sacramento), $58.429m: development and production of rocket motors and propellants.
DOD Installations Sacramento Army Depot (Sacramento). McClellan AFB (Sacramento).

NASA Contractors Aerojet General (Sacramento), $18,427m: development of nuclear state regulators and shutoff valves.

Economic Base Finance, insurance and real estate; food and kindred products, especially canned specialties; agriculture, notably cattle, fruits, grains and dairy products; tourism; chemicals and allied products, especially industrial organic chemicals not otherwise classified; and transportation equipment, especially aircraft engines and engine parts. Also higher education (Cal State, Hayward; and Sacramento State).

The Voters

Registration 271,037 total. 168,238 D (62%); 86,443 R (32%); 12,827 declined to state (5%); 3,419 other (1%).
Median voting age 42.0
Employment profile White collar, 61%. Blue collar, 25%. Service, 13%. Farm, 1%.
Ethnic groups Black, 7%. Japanese, Chinese, 2% each. Spanish, 10%. Total foreign stock, 20%. Canada, Germany, 2% each; UK, Italy, 1% each.

Presidential vote

1972	Nixon (R)		104,534	(49%)
	McGovern (D)		107,849	(51%)
1968	Nixon (R)		68,958	(41%)
	Humphrey (D)		90,232	(53%)
	Wallace (AI)		10,769	(6%)

Representative

John Emerson Moss (D) Elected 1952; b. April 13, 1915, Carbon County, Utah; home, Sacramento; Sacramento City Col., 1931–33; Navy, WWII; married, two children; Protestant.

Career Businessman and real estate broker; Calif. Assembly, 1948–52; Asst. Dem. Floor Leader of Assembly, 1949–52.

Offices 2185 RHOB, 202-225-7163. Also 8058 Fed. Bldg., 650 Capitol Mall, Sacramento 95814, 916-449-3543.

Administrative Assistant Jack Matteson

Committees

Government Operations (5th); Subs: Conservation and Natural Resources; Foreign Operations and Government Information.

Interstate and Foreign Commerce (4th); Subs: Commerce and Finance (Chm).

Group Ratings

	ADA	COPE	LWV	RIPON	NFU	LCV	CFA	NAB	NSI	ACA
1972	94	100	92	78	50	86	0	20	0	6
1971	81	82	86	88	93	–	80	–	–	8
1970	72	91	–	82	91	80	100	0	20	7

Key Votes

1) Busing	FOR	6) Cmbodia Bmbg	AGN	11) Chkg Acct Intrst	AGN
2) Strip Mines	FOR	7) Bust Hwy Trust	FOR	12) End HISC (HUAC)	FOR
3) Cut Mil $	FOR	8) Farm Sub Lmt	ABS	13) Nixon Sewer Veto	AGN
4) Rev Shrg	AGN	9) School Prayr	AGN	14) Corp Cmpaign $	FOR
5) Pub TV $	FOR	10) Cnsumr Prot	FOR	15) Pol $ Disclosr	FOR

Election Results

1972 general:	John E. Moss (D)	151,706	(70%)
	John Rakus (R)	65,298	(30%)
1972 primary:	John E. Moss (D), unopposed		
1970 general:	John E. Moss (D)	117,496	(62%)
	Elmore Duffy (R)	69,811	(37%)
	Allen Priest (AI)	3,554	(2%)

FOURTH DISTRICT Political Background

The low, flat delta lands where the Sacramento and San Joaquin rivers empty into San Francisco Bay, the rich fruit-growing land of the lower Sacramento River valley, and the fast-growing suburbs of Sacramento itself make up California's 4th congressional district. The southern part of the 4th—Vallejo and surrounding Solano County—has long been industrial and Democratic. That same political inclination is shared by the Sacramento suburbs in Yolo and Sacramento counties. Only the more sparsely populated northern counties regularly turn in Republican majorities, and these are balanced by a new center of Democratic strength, the town of Davis, site of a medium-sized (13,000 students) branch of the University of California. Davis, not coincidentally, is the American city with what looks like the nation's most well-developed system of bicycle paths.

The 4th district was created by the California legislature after the 1960 census. It is not entirely by accident that its first and only Congressman has been a former state Assemblyman, Robert Leggett. Like many Congressmen, Leggett is a member of committees that are important to his district—Armed Services (the 4th contains three Air Force bases and a Naval shipyard) and Merchant Marine and Fisheries (Vallejo can accommodate ocean-going vessels).

Leggett, however, does not quite fit the usual mold. He is one of the maverick antiwar Democrats on Armed Services, having opposed the Vietnam war and many defense-spending programs. But he does lobby hard for the giant Mare Island Naval Shipyard in Vallejo. Not known for his tact or even temperament, Leggett so incensed the late Mendel Rivers that the Chairman took to the floor and vowed vengeance on the 4th. That never came to pass, and the district, despite Leggett's anti-Administration voting record, emerged from the Pentagon's 1973 base cutbacks with an additional 1,500 defense jobs to show for it.

For 10 years Leggett labored in the House without the reward of a subcommittee chairmanship. In 1973, it finally came—in the form of the Merchant Marine and Fisheries' Panama Canal Subcommittee. Though far from Leggett's normal interests—he is a strong proponent of generous federal maritime subsidies—it may occupy much of his time, since the Panamanians are now trying to get control of the Canal Zone. As befits a Congressman who has more or less designed his own district, Leggett has few worries about reelection.

Census Data Pop. 466,428. Central city, 16%; suburban, 59%. Median family income, $9,473; families above $15,000: 20%; families below $3,000: 9%. Median years education, 12.3.

1972 Share of Federal Outlays $926,322,601

DOD	$520,532,945	HEW	$190,391,989
AEC	$446,507	HUD	$3,235,994
NASA	$4,026,965	DOI	$15,961,813
DOT	$30,795,981	USDA	$34,422,015
		Other	$126,508,337

Federal Military-Industrial Commitments

DOD Installations Naval Schools Command (Vallejo). Mare Island Naval Shipyard (Vallejo). Beale AFB (Marysville). Mather AFB (Sacramento). Travis AFB (Fairfield).

Economic Base Agriculture, notably grains, fruits and vegetables; finance, insurance and real estate; food and kindred products, especially canned, cured and frozen foods; printing and publishing, especially newspapers; and tourism. Also higher education (Univ. of California, Davis).

The Voters

Registration 217,508 total. 134,365 D (62%); 71,274 R (33%); 9,264 declined to state (4%); 2,505 other (1%).
Median voting age 38.7
Employment profile White collar, 49%. Blue collar, 29%. Service, 14%. Farm, 8%.
Ethnic groups Black, 5%. Filipino, 1%. Spanish, 11%. Total foreign stock, 19%. Germany, UK, Canada, 2% each; Italy, 1%.

Presidential vote

1972	Nixon (R)	91,739	(54%)
	McGovern (D)	77,896	(46%)
1968	Nixon (R)	54,046	(42%)
	Humphrey (D)	62,628	(49%)
	Wallace (AI)	12,009	(9%)

Representative

Robert L. Leggett (D) Elected 1962; b. July 26, 1926, Richmond; home, Vallejo; U. of Calif., B.A., 1947, LL.B., 1950; Navy, WWII; married, three children; Catholic.

Career Practicing atty., 1952–64; Calif. State Assembly, 1960–62.

Offices 2263 RHOB, 202-225-5716. Also 1520 Tenn. St., Vallejo 94590, 707-691-0720; 540 Second St., Yuba City 95991, 916-673-3515; and 650 Capitol Mall, Sacramento 95814, 916-449-3535.

Administrative Assistant Owen R. Chaffee

Committees

Armed Forces (11th); Subs: No. 1; No. 4.

Merchant Marine and Fisheries (10th); Subs: Fisheries, Wildlife Conservation and the Environment; Oceanography; Panama Canal (Chm.).

Group Ratings

	ADA	COPE	LWV	RIPON	NFU	LCV	CFA	NAB	NSI	ACA
1972	88	70	100	67	80	40	0	0	11	10
1971	73	100	89	65	85	–	86	–	–	12
1970	84	91	–	56	83	73	100	9	30	17

Key Votes

1) Busing	FOR	6) Cmbodia Bmbg	AGN	11) Chkg Acct Intrst	AGN
2) Strip Mines	AGN	7) Bust Hwy Trust	AGN	12) End HISC (HUAC)	FOR
3) Cut Mil $	FOR	8) Farm Sub Lmt	AGN	13) Nixon Sewer Veto	AGN
4) Rev Shrg	FOR	9) School Prayr	AGN	14) Corp Cmpaign $	FOR
5) Pub TV $	ABS	10) Cnsumr Prot	FOR	15) Pol $ Disclosr	AGN

Election Results

1972 general:	Robert L. Leggett (D)	115,038	(67%)
	Benjamin Chang (R)	55,540	(33%)
1972 primary:	Robert L. Leggett (D), unopposed		
1970 general:	Robert L. Leggett (D)	103,485	(68%)
	Andrew Gyorke (R)	48,783	(32%)

FIFTH DISTRICT Political Background

Surveys show that San Francisco remains the city, among all cities, where Americans would most like to live and work. Each year thousands of tourists come to San Francisco and are captivated by the foggy mornings and sunny afternoons, the vistas from the city's steep hills, the Union Square flower vendors, teeming Chinatown, and of course the cable cars. It is a place with a definite *esprit*: the first American city to rebel against freeways and proud of its newly operational rapid transit system (BART). And many people here are upset with the gleaming Montgomery Street high-rises that now threaten to obstruct the traditional San Francisco view. But the tourist can still savor the old San Francisco ambience in a host of famous restaurants or one of the streets of North Beach—there is a near-European atmosphere on these streets possessing such resolutely American names.

Of the things that touch the tourist about San Francisco, the most notable for political analysts is the city's worldliness; its unself-conscious toleration of topless dancers, hippies, blacks, Mexicans, Chinese, and even homosexuals. Proud of its mélange, the city also seems to remember its more radical past—not just the wild days of the Gold Rush, but the times in the early twentieth century when the radical Longshoremen's Union organized the docks and San Francisco became the most militant union town in the country. Today, a great many of the city's residents are either single or not living within traditional family units—there is little of that horror of heterogeneity that seems so much a part of parenthood in most of the nation. The poor, single, and wealthy people of San Francisco combine to produce a rare degree of toleration. It is certainly the only major city in the U.S.A. that could, as it did in 1972, vote to legalize marijauna. And it is the only city in the country where the Sheriff, an elected official, could conduct a voter registration drive among the inmates of the county jail.

The tourist does not see all of San Francisco, but one can say that all over the city the same *esprit* is found. It is most pronounced in the eastern half of the city, the part that comprises California's 5th congressional district. The 5th does include many of the tourist sights —Chinatown, Telegraph Hill and North Beach, Nob Hill and Union Square, the ornate Opera House and the now almost deserted Haight-Ashbury. But most of the district's residents live in less picturesque settings: the Fillmore black ghetto, the Mexican Mission district, the quiet streets near the Cow Palace, and the Hunters Point housing project. This is perhaps the most polyglot congressional district in the nation: 18% black, 17% Spanish-speaking, 10% Chinese, 4% Italian and Filipino, and even a few Samoans. Only around a quarter of the 5th's residents are white, English-speaking, third-generation Americans.

This, of course, is a very Democratic district, having turned in almost as large a majority for George McGovern in 1972 as for Hubert Humphrey in 1968. Its Congressman, Phillip Burton, is one of the most politically savvy of the House's ultraliberals. It is tempting to describe him as a radical ward-heeler, though he is not quite a radical and not really a ward-heeler. Burton almost always stands on the left of issues, but he is willing to make deals to get results. In the early days of the 93rd Congress, for example, Burton took to the floor and demanded that urban liberals support a popular agricultural program, funds for which had been impounded by President Nixon. But Burton made it very clear that he expected *quid pro quo* from rural Congressmen like Texan Bob Poage, Chairman of Agriculture, on other impoundment issues *he* (Burton) supported. Considered especially knowledgeable about welfare matters, Burton's two proudest legislative accomplishments are a bill that raised the minimum wage and broadened its coverage and one that provides benefits for coal miners suffering from black lung disease.

As Chairman of the Democratic Study Group in 1971 and 1972, Burton worked hard to make the Democratic Caucus both more effective and more liberal. The results are clear in the relatively small number of Democrats deserting positions taken by the party on many important issues that confronted the 93rd Congress in early 1973. The Democrats have a long way to go before they can match the discipline of the House Republicans; that they have gone as far as they have is due in large part to Congressmen like Burton. The kind of politics these men practice has more in common with the tough radicals who organized the San Francisco docks than with, let's say, professors at a Berkeley faculty meeting.

Burton also keeps a political hand in things at home. His brother John is Chairman of the California Democratic party and of the California Assembly Rules Committee. Two of the Congressman's allies include state Sen. George Moscone and Assemblyman Willie Brown. Remembered for his stirring speech before the 1972 Democratic Convention, Brown is Chairman of the Assembly Ways and Means Committee and may become Speaker after the 1974 elections. So national press, after a busy day interviewing the radical politicians in Berkeley and Oakland, might take a look across the Bay at the Burton-Moscone-Brown combine.

Census Data Pop. 460,624. Central city, 100%; suburban, 0%. Median family income, $9,079; families above $15,000: 20%; families below $3,000: 13%. Median years education, 12.2.

1972 Share of Federal Outlays $587,989,739

DOD	$182,078,319	HEW	$188,144,127
AEC	$36,247,810	HUD	$10,458,499
NASA	$1,428,088	DOI	$5,656,710
DOT	$24,801,325	USDA	$22,037,494
		Other	$117,137,686

Federal Military-Industrial Commitments

DOD Contractors Standard Oil of California (San Francisco), $24.512m: petroleum products. Pacific Far East Lines (San Francisco), $13.429m: transportation services. States Steamship (San Francisco), $13.195m: transportation services. American President Lines (San Francisco), $10.852m: transportation services. Rothschild and Raffin (San Francisco), $7.545m: unspecified.

DOD Installations Naval Air Rework Facility (San Francisco). Naval Schools Command, Treasure Island (San Francisco). Naval Station, Treasure Island (San Francisco). Hunters Point Naval Shipyard (San Francisco); closed,1974.

Economic Base Finance, insurance and real estate; printing and publishing, especially commercial printing and newspapers; food and kindred products; apparel and other textile products, especially women's and misses' outerwear; fabricated metal products, especially fabricated structural metal products; and tourism.

The Voters

Registration 238,086 total. 170,055 D (71%); 44,271 R (19%); 20,159 declined to state (8%); 3,601 other (2%).
Median voting age 41.9
Employment profile White collar, 56%. Blue collar, 26%. Service, 18%. Farm, –%.
Ethnic groups Black, 18%. Japanese, 1%. Chinese, 10%. Filipino, 4%. Spanish, 17%. Total foreign stock, 43%. Italy, 4%; Germany, Ireland, UK, 2% each; Canada, USSR, 1% each.

Presidential vote

1972	Nixon (R)	60,503	(36%)
	McGovern (D)	107,755	(64%)
1968	Nixon (R)	41,019	(27%)
	Humphrey (D)	100,917	(66%)
	Wallace (AI)	9,906	(7%)

Representative

Phillip Burton (D) Elected Feb., 1964; b. June 2, 1927, Cincinnati, Ohio; home, San Francisco; U. of So. Calif., B.A., 1947; Golden Gate Law School, LL.B., 1952; Navy, WWII and Korean War; married, one child; Unitarian.

Career Practicing atty., 1952–64; Calif. Assembly, 1956–64.

Offices 2450 RHOB, 202-225-4965. Also Rm. 11152 Fed. Ofc. Bldg., 450 Golden Gate Ave., San Francisco 94102, 415-556-4862.

Administrative Assistant Adrian P. Winkel

Committees

Education and Labor (11th); Subs: No. 3 (Gen. Sub. on Labor); No. 4 (Labor); No. 6 (Education).

Interior and Insular Affairs (5th); Subs: Mines and Mining; Public Lands; Territorial and Insular Affairs (Chm.).

Group Ratings

	ADA	COPE	LWV	RIPON	NFU	LCV	CFA	NAB	NSI	ACA
1972	100	100	100	64	86	74	50	8	0	5
1971	92	91	89	87	100	–	100	–	–	7
1970	96	100	–	59	91	95	100	0	10	6

Key Votes

1) Busing	FOR	6) Cmbodia Bmbg	AGN	11) Chkg Acct Intrst	FOR
2) Strip Mines	FOR	7) Bust Hwy Trust	FOR	12) End HISC (HUAC)	FOR
3) Cut Mil $	FOR	8) Farm Sub Lmt	AGN	13) Nixon Sewer Veto	AGN
4) Rev Shrg	AGN	9) School Prayr	AGN	14) Corp Cmpaign $	FOR
5) Pub TV $	ABS	10) Cnsumr Prot	FOR	15) Pol $ Disclosr	ABS

Election Results

1972 general:	Philip Burton (D)		124,164	(82%)
	Edlo E. Powell (R)		27,474	(18%)
1972 primary:	Philip Burton (D)		54,398	(67%)
	Robert E. Gonzales (D)		27,017	(33%)
1970 general:	Philip Burton (D)		76,567	(71%)
	John Parks (R)		31,570	(29%)

SIXTH DISTRICT Political Background

The 6th district of California takes in the western half of San Francisco and all of Marin County, two rather different parts of the cosmopolitan San Francisco metropolitan area. The San Francisco portion of the district includes the wealthiest parts of the city, the Marina district, Pacific Heights, and Russian Hill. But most of this portion is middle-class residential: the Richmond and Sunset districts, and the Ingleside neighborhood around the once troubled San Francisco State College. The tolerant ambience of San Francisco exists here, but to an extent not as noticeable as in the adjacent 5th district. Many of the residents are second- and third-generation Americans, not long-removed from the poverty of their forebears. But the San Francisco tradition of sophistication and tolerance does affect the voting habits of these middle-class people; unlike their cousins on the East Coast, they have not swung heavily over to the party of Richard Nixon.

The Marin portion of the 6th lies just across the Golden Gate Bridge. A series of suburbs nestled between rugged mountains and the Bay, this is the land of radical chic—the kind of suburbs where women wearing $80 sweaters go shopping in bare feet. Marin is one of the last places in California where there is a significant number of liberal registered Republicans, but the lifestyle of these people—the marijuana referendum got 49% of the votes here—has led them to vote increasingly Democratic.

Since 1952, the 6th's Congressman has been Republican William S. Mailliard, a wealthy member of a patrician San Francisco family. For many years Mailliard had a fairly liberal voting record and little trouble winning reelection. With the rise of Ronald Reagan, he began moving to the right. As a high seniority member, now the ranking Republican, on House Foreign Affairs, he dutifully supported the Nixon Administration's Vietnam policy. This was far from popular in the district, and suddenly his apparently safe seat looked threatened. From 73% of the votes in 1968, Mailliard fell to 53% in 1970, even though his opponent was a political unknown. The 1972 Democratic candidate promised to be even stronger. He was Roger Boas, a San Francisco County Supervisor and former state Democratic Chairman. Boas hired political consultant Sanford Weiner, and waged a tough campaign.

But for Mailliard, jarred by the closeness of the 1970 contest, the advantages of incumbency proved enough to eke out a 52–48 win. Mailliard lost nominally Republican Marin County, which he had represented only since the 1968 redistricting, by 2,000 votes. But in the San Francisco portion of the 6th, the portion of the district that had sent him to Washington for 20 years, the incumbent Congressman piled up an 11,000-vote margin.

The race here in 1974 promises to be another close one; the district is moving left fast enough to insure at least one strong Democratic challenger, and Boas appears likely to run again. As ranking minority member of the Merchant Marine Subcommittee, where he supports the heavy federal subsidy program to the shipping industry, Mailliard can count on solid financial support. Money will also come from wealthy San Francisco Republicans. The Congressman is certainly aware of a tough race to come, and he can be expected to prepare for it accordingly.

Census Data Pop. 461,088. Central city, 56%; suburban, 44%. Median family income, $13,221; families above $15,000: 40%; families below $3,000: 5%. Median years education, 12.8.

1972 Share of Federal Outlays $588,791,361

DOD	$182,327,000	HEW	$188,400,629
AEC	$36,297,238	HUD	$10,472,757
NASA	$1,430,035	DOI	$5,664,422
DOT	$24,835,137	USDA	$22,067,538
		Other	$117,296,596

Federal Military-Industrial Commitments

DOD Installations Presidio of San Francisco (San Francisco). Hamilton AFB (San Rafael); closed, 1973. Mill Valley AF Station (Mill Valley).

Economic Base Finance, insurance and real estate; printing and publishing, especially commercial printing and newspapers; food and kindred products; apparel and other textile products, especially women's and misses' outerwear; and tourism.

The Voters

Registration 309,862 total. 175,275 D (57%); 109,967 R (36%); 22,296 declined to state (7%); 2,324 other (1%).
Median voting age 45.0
Employment profile White collar, 71%. Blue collar, 17%. Service, 12%. Farm, –%.
Ethnic groups Black, 4%. Japanese, 2%. Chinese, 3%. Filipino, 1%. Spanish, 7%. Total foreign stock, 37%. Germany, Italy, 4% each; UK, 3%; Canada, Ireland, USSR, 2% each.

Presidential vote

1972	Nixon (R)	....	121,081	(52%)
	McGovern (D)	....	110,541	(48%)
1968	Nixon (R)	....	88,295	(45%)
	Humphrey (D)	....	99,614	(50%)
	Wallace (AI)	....	9,585	(5%)

Representative

William S. Mailliard (R) Elected 1952; b. June 10, 1917, Belvedere; home, San Francisco; Yale U., B.A., 1939; Navy, WWII; Rear Admiral, USNR; married, seven children; Protestant.

Career With American Trust Co. of S.F., 1940–41, 1946; Asst. to Dir., Calif. Academy of Sciences, 1951–52; Asst. to Dir. Calif. Youth Authority, 1947; Sec. to Gov. Earl Warren, 1949–51; Del., 18th Session UN General Assembly, 1963.

Offices 2336 RHOB 202-225-5161. Also Rm. 11104 New Fed. Bldg., 450 Golden Gate Ave., San Francisco 94102, 415-556-1333.

Administrative Assistant Christian R. Holmes IV

Committees

Foreign Affairs (Ranking Mbr.); Subs: Sp. Sub. for Review of Foreign Aid Programs (Ranking Mbr.).

Merchant Marine and Fisheries (2nd); Subs: Fisheries and Wildlife Conservation and the Environment; Merchant Marine (Ranking Mbr.); Oceanography; Panama Canal.

Group Ratings

	ADA	COPE	LWV	RIPON	NFU	LCV	CFA	NAB	NSI	ACA
1972	38	56	91	100	57	54	100	64	100	40
1971	32	55	63	65	27	–	40	–	–	52
1970	32	64	–	69	82	39	53	60	100	47

Key Votes

1) Busing	FOR	6) Cmbodia Bmbg	FOR	11) Chkg Acct Intrst	ABS
2) Strip Mines	AGN	7) Bust Hwy Trust	FOR	12) End HISC (HUAC)	AGN
3) Cut Mil $	AGN	8) Farm Sub Lmt	FOR	13) Nixon Sewer Veto	FOR
4) Rev Shrg	ABS	9) School Prayr	AGN	14) Corp Cmpaign $	AGN
5) Pub TV $	FOR	10) Cnsumr Prot	ABS	15) Pol $ Disclosr	FOR

Election Results

1972 general:	William S. Mailliard (R)	119,704	(52%)
	Roger Boas (D)	110,144	(48%)
1972 primary:	William S. Mailliard (R), unopposed		
1970 general:	William S. Mailliard (R)	96,393	(53%)
	Russell Miller (D)	84,255	(47%)

SEVENTH DISTRICT Political Background

The most self-consciously radical congressional district in the country is the 7th of California. This is where the first of the great student rebellions broke out, the Free Speech Movement of 1964 at the University of California–Berkeley campus. The 7th also includes Oakland's black ghetto, the birthplace of the Black Panthers. In Berkeley, a self-styled radical slate nearly took control of city government in 1971; since then, the radicals have split into factions, and in 1973, a moderate majority, with a politics roughly McGovernite, won out. Meanwhile in Oakland, Panther leader Bobby Seale managed to win 36% in the city's mayoral election. His showing was testimony to a solid, grass-roots campaign, as well as to changes in the Panther movement.

It is fitting, then, that the 7th sends to Congress one of its few self-proclaimed radicals, Ronald Dellums. Dellums, a former social worker and Berkeley Councilman, defeated 12-year incumbent Jeffrey Cohelan, 55–45, in the 1970 Democratic primary. Organized labor had always backed Cohelan; Dellums' main bases of support were blacks (22% of the district's voting population) and students (now, with the 18-year-old-vote, between 15 and 20% of the potential electorate). Dellums also did well among the districts's high-income voters, many of them strongly antiwar, who live in the hills above Berkeley and Oakland.

Dellums' stands on issues—he readily admits sympathizing with some Panther ideas and he protested illegal treatment of student protesters—have infuriated California Republicans. In both 1970 and 1972, conservatives poured considerable sums of money into Republican campaign coffers in an attempt to beat Dellums. Both times they failed; in 1972, the Congressman increased his percentage within the boundaries of the old 1970 district and held his own in the predominantly working-class Contra Costa suburbs added by the 1972 redistricting. Dellums' outspoken stands do cost him some votes, particularly in white working-class communities, but not too many and in the present 7th he can still win comfortably.

In the House, though not exactly a power, Dellums has done pretty well for a far-out sophomore. He is now Chairman of the District of Columbia Education Subcommittee—thanks to the fact that Michigan's Charles Diggs succeeded South Carolina's defeated John McMillan as Chairman of the full committee. And against the wishes of Chairman F. Edward Hebert, Dellums won a seat on the Armed Services Committee. The black Congressman, a Marine veteran, has held unofficial hearings on racism in the military and has visited military bases and rapped with enlisted men—sometimes to the distress of their officers. Now, as a member of Armed Services, he has a chance to rap with the generals and admirals, too. On the committee, Dellums is presently part of a small minority that believes the defense budget is a bloated one, but the number of such dissenters is increasing. It has only been in the last two Congresses that members of his kind of political persuasion have stopped seeking seats on committees like Education and Labor—where they are, if anything, overrepresented—and taken the harder path of advancing their views in a more hostile environment like Armed Services.

Census Data   Pop. 462,753. Central city, 53%; suburban, 47%. Median family income, $10,591; families above $15,000: 29%; families below $3,000: 10%. Median years education, 12.6.

1972 Share of Federal Outlays $590,795,416

DOD	$182,947,131	HEW	$189,041,883
AEC	$36,420,782	HUD	$10,508,403
NASA	$1,434,902	DOI	$5,683,701
DOT	$24,919,667	USDA	$22,142,649
		Other	$117,696,298

Federal Military-Industrial Commitments

DOD Contractors University of California (Berkeley), $5.363m: various research projects.
DOD Installations Oakland Army Base (Oakland). Naval Supply Center (Oakland).
AEC Operations University of California (Berkeley), $42.223m: operation of Lawerence Radiation Laboratories.

Economic Base   Finance, insurance and real estate; food and kindred products; fabricated metal products, especially fabricated structural metal products; machinery, especially office and computing machines; and transportation equipment, especially motor vehicles and equipment. Also higher education (Univ. of California, Berkeley).

The Voters

Registration 297,828 total. 194,044 D (65%); 77,686 R (26%); 21,132 declined to state (7%); 4,964 other (2%).
Median voting age 42.1
Employment profile White collar, 63%. Blue collar, 24%. Service, 13%. Farm, –%.
Ethnic groups Black, 26%. Japanese, 1%. Chinese, 3%. Spanish, 8%. Total foreign stock, 26%. UK, Canada, Germany, Italy, 2% each.

Presidential vote

1972	Nixon (R)	75,856	(35%)
	McGovern (D)	139,721	(65%)
1968	Nixon (R)	24,422	(30%)
	Humphrey (D)	47,385	(59%)
	Wallace (AI)	7,465	(9%)

Representative

Ronald V. Dellums (D) Elected 1970; b. Nov. 24, 1935, Oakland; home, Oakland; San Francisco State Col., B.A., 1961; U. of Calif., M.A., 1962; Marine Corps, 1954–56; married, five children; Protestant.

Career Psychiatric Social Worker, Dept. Mental Hygiene, 1962–64; Program Dir. Bayview Community Center, 1964–65; Assoc. Dir. and Dir., Hunter's Point Bayview Youth Opportunity Center, 1965–66; Dir., Concentrated Empl. Program, 1967–68; Berkeley City Council, 1967– ; Sr. Counsultant, Social Dynamics, 1968– .

Offices 1417 LHOB, 202-225-2661. Also P.O. Bldg., Civic Center Div., 13th and Alice Streets, Oakland 94607, 415-763-0370.

Administrative Assistant Charles Ward

Committees

Armed Services (21st); Subs: No. 4; Sp. Sub. on Human Relations.

District of Columbia (4th); Subs: Education (Chm.); Revenue and Financial Affairs.

Group Ratings

	ADA	COPE	LWV	RIPON	NFU	LCV	CFA	NAB	NSI	ACA
1972	88	100	91	77	71	93	100	8	0	9
1971	97	83	63	76	86	–	100	–	–	11

Key Votes

1) Busing	FOR	6) Cmbodia Bmbg	AGN	11) Chkg Acct Intrst	FOR
2) Strip Mines	FOR	7) Bust Hwy Trust	FOR	12) End HISC (HUAC)	FOR
3) Cut Mil $	FOR	8) Farm Sub Lmt	FOR	13) Nixon Sewer Veto	AGN
4) Rev Shrg	FOR	9) School Prayr	AGN	14) Corp Cmpaign $	AGN
5) Pub TV $	FOR	10) Cnsumr Prot	FOR	15) Pol $ Disclosr	FOR

Election Results

1972 general:	Ronald V. Dellums (D)	126,913	(56%)
	Peter Hannaford (R)	86,587	(38%)
	Frank V. Cortese (AI)	13,550	(6%)
1972 primary:	Ronald V. Dellums (D)	84,929	(73%)
	Stephen N. Sestanovich (D)	31,188	(27%)
1970 general:	Ronald V. Dellums (D)	89,784	(57%)
	John Healy (R)	64,691	(41%)
	Sarah Scahill (PF)	2,156	(1%)

EIGHTH DISTRICT Political Background

Not all of the East Bay across from San Francisco is a hotbed of political radicalism, Berkeley-style. The suburbs south of Oakland—places like San Leandro, Hayward, Castro Valley—are something like outposts of Middle America on San Francisco Bay. They are places where the people who work in the East Bay's factories live in comfortable, well-tended neighborhoods. These suburbs, together with the southern part of Oakland, which is about half black, and portions of eastern Alameda County, form the bulk of California's 8th congressional district.

More of the people who live here consider themselves Democrats than Republicans, and they usually contribute Democratic margins. But because they have been disturbed, though not as much as southern Californians, by the countercultural trends so close at hand, there is a sizable number of swing voters who have twice put the 8th in Ronald Reagan's electoral column. An important 8th district influence is the Oakland *Tribune*, owned by ex-Sen. (1946–59) William Knowland; he is a man who has modulated his stands on racial issues but is still, as he was in the Senate, a bulwark of conservative Republicanism.

For some 28 years the 8th routinely sent Democrat George Miller to the House of Representatives. There he quietly accumulated seniority and became Chairman of the Science and Astronautics Committee. An unabashed booster of the space program, Miller had little in common with the new breed of Democrats who questioned large appropriations for space and the military. For years, he seemed to have reflected the wishes of his district pretty accurately, and was reelected without any trouble.

But not in 1972. Miller was 81 when it came primary time in the district. His previous primary showings were, it appears in retrospect, more the result of his opponents' weakness than of his own strength. This time the main challenger was Fortney (Pete) Stark, a rather unusual banker and former board member of Common Cause. Stark, a strong opponent of the Vietnam war, attracted attention in the Bay Area some years earlier by erecting a large peace symbol atop a small bank he owned in Walnut Creek. Many peace activists took the trouble to cross the mountains to open accounts, and the bank—which Stark no longer owns—prospered.

But Stark was already wealthy, and he poured much of his own money into the campaign. Stark offices opened throughout the district, volunteers were enlisted and sent out to canvass door-to-door, and the candidate was busy speaking wherever he could find an audience. Meanwhile, Chairman Miller stayed in Washington; he was past the time that he could come on as an impressive candidate.

The result was an almost unprecedented rout. Stark won 56% of the votes, incumbent Miller only 21%, with the remaining 23% split among five minor candidates. Next to this, the general election was almost anticlimactic, though Stark had to hustle in the end as it became clear that George McGovern was not going to carry the district. In the House, Stark is part of the pro-home-rule majority amassed by new Chairman Charles Diggs of the District of Columbia Committee. The Californian also serves on Banking and Currency, where he is more likely than some senior Democrats to support the populistic ideas of Chairman Wright Patman.

Technically, any freshman who wins with less than 55% of the votes, as Stark did, is considered vulnerable in the next election. In practice, the advantages enjoyed by incumbents are such that if they have a modicum of sense they are almost certain to do far better the second time out. Stark's primary campaign shows that kind of acumen, and he can be expected to remain in the House for some time.

Census Data Pop. 462,814. Central city, 25%; suburban, 75%. Median family income, $11,554; families above $15,000: 30%; families below $3,000: 7%. Median years education, 12.4.

1972 Share of Federal Outlays $590,795,416

DOD	$182,947,131	HEW	$189,041,883
AEC	$36,420,782	HUD	$10,508,403
NASA	$1,434,902	DOI	$5,683,701
DOT	$29,919,667	USDA	$22,142,649
		Other	$117,696,298

Federal Military-Industrial Commitments

DOD Contractors World Airways (Oakland), $27.884m: transportation services. Trans International Airlines (Oakland), $22.574m: transportation services. Universal Airlines (Oakland), $22.165m: transportation services. Saturn Airways (Oakland), $17.422m: transportations services. Physics International (San Leandro), $8.388m: research into effects of radiation on propellent components. California Stevedore and Ballast (Oakland), $7.466m: transportation services. MB Associates (San Ramon), $7.042m: design and production of various aircraft munitions components. Sauk Valley MFGG (Oakland), $6.762m: unspecified.
DOD Installations Naval Air Station (Alameda). Naval Hospital (Oakland).
AEC Operations University of California (Livermore), $103,958m: operation of the Lawrence Livermore Laboratory. Sandia Corporation (Livermore), $30.335m: design of nuclear systems meeting DOD requirements. EG&G (San Ramon), $6.893m: various technical services.

Economic Base Finance, insurance and real estate; food and kindred products; fabricated metal products, especially fabricated structural metal products; transportation equipment, especially motor vehicles and equipment; and machinery, especially office and computing machines.

The Voters

Registration 241,440 total. 147,404 D (61%); 78,456 R (32%); 13,780 declined to state (6%); 1,800 other (1%).
Median voting age 41.7
Employment profile White collar, 53%. Blue collar, 34%. Service, 12%. Farm, 1%.
Ethnic groups Black, 13%. Spanish, 13%. Total foreign stock, 22%. Italy, Portugal, UK, Canada, Germany, 2% each.

Presidential vote

	1972	Nixon (R)	97,446	(52%)
		McGovern (D)	89,062	(48%)
	1968	Nixon (R)	65,676	(41%)
		Humphrey (D)	81,816	(51%)
		Wallace (AI)	13,331	(8%)

It was an almost unprecedented rout. Stark won 56% of the votes, incumbent Miller with the remaining 23% split among five minor candidates. Next to this, the general as almost anticlimactic, though Stark had to hustle in the end as it became clear that cGovern was not going to carry the district. In the House, Stark is part of the ule majority amassed by new Chairman Charles Diggs of the District of Columbia . The Californian also serves on Banking and Currency, where he is more likely than r Democrats to support the populistic ideas of Chairman Wright Patman.

lly, any freshman who wins with less than 55% of the votes, as Stark did, is considered in the next election. In practice, the advantages enjoyed by incumbents are such that if modicum of sense they are almost certain to do far better the second time out. Stark's mpaign shows that kind of acumen, and he can be expected to remain in the House for

a Pop. 462,814. Central city, 25%; suburban, 75%. Median family income, $11,554; ove $15,000: 30%; families below $3,000: 7%. Median years education, 12.4.

of Federal Outlays $590,795,416

DOD	$182,947,131	HEW	$189,041,883
AEC	$36,420,782	HUD	$10,508,403
NASA	$1,434,902	DOI	$5,683,701
DOT	$29,919,667	USDA	$22,142,649
		Other	$117,696,298

litary-Industrial Commitments

ontractors World Airways (Oakland), $27.884m: transportation services. Trans al Airlines (Oakland), $22.574m: transportation services. Universal Airlines (Oakland), ransportation services. Saturn Airways (Oakland), $17.422m: transportations services. ernational (San Leandro), $8.388m: research into effects of radiation on propellent s. California Stevedore and Ballast (Oakland), $7.466m: transportation services. MB (San Ramon), $7.042m: design and production of various aircraft munitions s. Sauk Valley MFGG (Oakland), $6.762m: unspecified. tallations Naval Air Station (Alameda). Naval Hospital (Oakland). erations University of California (Livermore), $103.958m: operation of the Lawrence Laboratory. Sandia Corporation (Livermore), $30.335m: design of nuclear systems OD requirements. EG&G (San Ramon), $6.893m: various technical services.

ase Finance, insurance and real estate; food and kindred products; fabricated metal pecially fabricated structural metal products; transportation equipment, especially cles and equipment; and machinery, especially office and computing machines.

tion 241,440 total. 147,404 D (61%); 78,456 R (32%); 13,780 declined to state (6%); her (1%). voting age 41.7 nent profile White collar, 53%. Blue collar, 34%. Service, 12%. Farm, 1%. groups Black, 13%. Spanish, 13%. Total foreign stock, 22%. Italy, Portugal, UK, Germany, 2% each.

vote

1972	Nixon (R)	97,446	(52%)
	McGovern (D)	89,062	(48%)
1968	Nixon (R)	65,676	(41%)
	Humphrey (D)	81,816	(51%)
	Wallace (AI)	13,331	(8%)

Merchant Marine and Fisheries (2nd); Subs: Fisheries and Wildlife Conservation and the Environment; Merchant Marine (Ranking Mbr.); Oceanography; Panama Canal.

Group Ratings

	ADA	COPE	LWV	RIPON	NFU	LCV	CFA	NAB	NSI	ACA
1972	38	56	91	100	57	54	100	64	100	40
1971	32	55	63	65	27	–	40	–	–	52
1970	32	64	–	69	82	39	53	60	100	47

Key Votes

1) Busing	FOR	6) Cmbodia Bmbg	FOR	11) Chkg Acct Intrst	ABS
2) Strip Mines	AGN	7) Bust Hwy Trust	FOR	12) End HISC (HUAC)	AGN
3) Cut Mil $	AGN	8) Farm Sub Lmt	FOR	13) Nixon Sewer Veto	FOR
4) Rev Shrg	ABS	9) School Prayr	AGN	14) Corp Cmpaign $	AGN
5) Pub TV $	FOR	10) Cnsumr Prot	ABS	15) Pol $ Disclosr	FOR

Election Results

1972 general:	William S. Mailliard (R)	119,704	(52%)
	Roger Boas (D)	110,144	(48%)
1972 primary:	William S. Mailliard (R), unopposed		
1970 general:	William S. Mailliard (R)	96,393	(53%)
	Russell Miller (D)	84,255	(47%)

SEVENTH DISTRICT Political Background

The most self-consciously radical congressional district in the country is the 7th of California. This is where the first of the great student rebellions broke out, the Free Speech Movement of 1964 at the University of California–Berkeley campus. The 7th also includes Oakland's black ghetto, the birthplace of the Black Panthers. In Berkeley, a self-styled radical slate nearly took control of city government in 1971; since then, the radicals have split into factions, and in 1973, a moderate majority, with a politics roughly McGovernite, won out. Meanwhile in Oakland, Panther leader Bobby Seale managed to win 36% in the city's mayoral election. His showing was testimony to a solid, grass-roots campaign, as well as to changes in the Panther movement.

It is fitting, then, that the 7th sends to Congress one of its few self-proclaimed radicals, Ronald Dellums. Dellums, a former social worker and Berkeley Councilman, defeated 12-year incumbent Jeffrey Cohelan, 55–45, in the 1970 Democratic primary. Organized labor had always backed Cohelan; Dellums' main bases of support were blacks (22% of the district's voting population) and students (now, with the 18-year-old-vote, between 15 and 20% of the potential electorate). Dellums also did well among the districts's high-income voters, many of them strongly antiwar, who live in the hills above Berkeley and Oakland.

Dellums' stands on issues—he readily admits sympathizing with some Panther ideas and he protested illegal treatment of student protesters—have infuriated California Republicans. In both 1970 and 1972, conservatives poured considerable sums of money into Republican campaign coffers in an attempt to beat Dellums. Both times they failed; in 1972, the Congressman increased his percentage within the boundaries of the old 1970 district and held his own in the predominantly working-class Contra Costa suburbs added by the 1972 redistricting. Dellums' outspoken stands do cost him some votes, particularly in white working-class communities, but not too many and in the present 7th he can still win comfortably.

In the House, though not exactly a power, Dellums has done pretty well for a far-out sophomore. He is now Chairman of the District of Columbia Education Subcommittee—thanks to the fact that Michigan's Charles Diggs succeeded South Carolina's defeated John McMillan as Chairman of the full committee. And against the wishes of Chairman F. Edward Hebert, Dellums won a seat on the Armed Services Committee. The black Congressman, a Marine veteran, has held unofficial hearings on racism in the military and has visited military bases and rapped with enlisted men—sometimes to the distress of their officers. Now, as a member of Armed Services, he has a chance to rap with the generals and admirals, too. On the committee, Dellums is presently part of a small minority that believes the defense budget is a bloated one, but the number of such dissenters is increasing. It has only been in the last two Congresses that members of his kind of political persuasion have stopped seeking seats on committees like Education and Labor—where they are, if anything, overrepresented—and taken the harder path of advancing their views in a more hostile environment like Armed Services.

Census Data Pop. 462,753. Central city, 53%; suburban, 47%. Median family income, $10,591; families above $15,000: 29%; families below $3,000: 10%. Median years education, 12.6.

1972 Share of Federal Outlays $590,795,416

DOD	$182,947,131	HEW	$189,041,883
AEC	$36,420,782	HUD	$10,508,403
NASA	$1,434,902	DOI	$5,683,701
DOT	$24,919,667	USDA	$22,142,649
		Other	$117,696,298

Federal Military-Industrial Commitments

DOD Contractors University of California (Berkeley), $5.363m: various research projects.
DOD Installations Oakland Army Base (Oakland). Naval Supply Center (Oakland).
AEC Operations University of California (Berkeley), $42.223m: operation of Lawerence Radiation Laboratories.

Economic Base Finance, insurance and real estate; food and kindred products; fabricated metal products, especially fabricated structural metal products; machinery, especially office and computing machines; and transportation equipment, especially motor vehicles and equipment. Also higher education (Univ. of California, Berkeley).

The Voters

Registration 297,828 total. 194,044 D (65%); 77,686 R (26%); 21,132 declined to state (7%); 4,964 other (2%).
Median voting age 42.1
Employment profile White collar, 63%. Blue collar, 24%. Service, 13%. Farm, –%.
Ethnic groups Black, 26%. Japanese, 1%. Chinese, 3%. Spanish, 8%. Total foreign stock, 26%. UK, Canada, Germany, Italy, 2% each.

Presidential vote

1972	Nixon (R)	75,856	(35%)
	McGovern (D)	139,721	(65%)
1968	Nixon (R)	24,422	(30%)
	Humphrey (D)	47,385	(59%)
	Wallace (AI)	7,465	(9%)

Representative

Ronald V. Dellums (D) Elected 1970; b. Nov. 24, 1935, Oakland; home, Oakland; San Francisco State Col., B.A., 1961; U. of Calif., M.A., 1962; Marine Corps, 1954–56; married, five children; Protestant.

Career Psychiatric Social Worker, Dept. Mental Hygiene, 1962–64; Program Dir. Bayview Community Center, 1964–65; Assoc. Dir. and Dir., Hunter's Point Bayview Youth Opportunity Center, 1965–66; Dir., Concentrated Empl. Program, 1967–68; Berkeley City Council, 1967– ; Sr. Counsultant, Social Dynamics, 1968– .

Offices 1417 LHOB, 202-225-2661. Also P.O. Bldg., Civic Center Div., 13th and Alice Streets, Oakland 94607, 415-763-0370.

Administrative Assistant Charles Ward

Committees

Armed Services (21st); Subs: No. 4; Sp. Sub. on Human Relations.

District of Columbia (4th); Subs: Education (Chm.); Revenue and

Group Ratings

	ADA	COPE	LWV	RIPON	NFU	LCV	CFA
1972	88	100	91	77	71	93	100
1971	97	83	63	76	86	–	100

Key Votes

1) Busing	FOR				
2) Strip Mines	FOR	6) Cmbodia Bmbg	AGN	11) C	
3) Cut Mil $	FOR	7) Bust Hwy Trust	FOR	12) E	
4) Rev Shrg	FOR	8) Farm Sub Lmt	FOR	13) N	
5) Pub TV $	FOR	9) School Prayr	AGN	14) C	
		10) Cnsumr Prot	FOR	15) P	

Election Results

1972 general:	Ronald V. Dellums (D)	
	Peter Hannaford (R)	
	Frank V. Cortese (AI)	
1972 primary:	Ronald V. Dellums (D)	
	Stephen N. Sestanovich (D)	
1970 general:	Ronald V. Dellums (D)	
	John Healy (R)	
	Sarah Scahill (PF)	

EIGHTH DISTRICT Political Background

Not all of the East Bay across from San Francisco is a hotl Berkeley-style. The suburbs south of Oakland—places like San Valley—are something like outposts of Middle America on San Fra where the people who work in the East Bay's factories live i neighborhoods. These suburbs, together with the southern part of C black, and portions of eastern Alameda County, form the bulk of C district.

More of the people who live here consider themselves Democrats usually contribute Democratic margins. But because they have be much as southern Californians, by the countercultural trends so clos number of swing voters who have twice put the 8th in Ronald Re important 8th district influence is the Oakland *Tribune*, owned by Knowland; he is a man who has modulated his stands on racial issue Senate, a bulwark of conservative Republicanism.

For some 28 years the 8th routinely sent Democrat Georg Representatives. There he quietly accumulated seniority and became Astronautics Committee. An unabashed booster of the space pr common with the new breed of Democrats who questioned large app military. For years, he seemed to have reflected the wishes of his d was reelected without any trouble.

But not in 1972. Miller was 81 when it came primary time in the c showings were, it appears in retrospect, more the result of his oppone strength. This time the main challenger was Fortney (Pete) Stark, a former board member of Common Cause. Stark, a strong opponent c attention in the Bay Area some years earlier by erecting a large peace owned in Walnut Creek. Many peace activists took the trouble to accounts, and the bank—which Stark no longer owns—prospered

But Stark was already wealthy, and he poured much of his own mc offices opened throughout the district, volunteers were enlisted door-to-door, and the candidate was busy speaking wherever I Meanwhile, Chairman Miller stayed in Washington; he was past th as an impressive candidate.

The res only 21%, election w George M pro-home- Committe some seni

Technic vulnerable they have primary ca some time

Census Da families a

1972 Shar

Federal M

DOD C Internation $22.165m: Physics Int component Associates component *DOD In* *AEC Op* Livermore meeting D

Economic E products, e motor vehi

The Voters

Registr 1,800 o *Median* *Employ* *Ethnic* Canada

Presidential

Representative

Fortney H. (Pete) Stark, Jr. (D) Elected 1972; b. Nov. 11, 1931, Milwaukee, Wis.; home, Danville; Mass. Inst. Tech., B.S., 1953; U. Calif., M.B.A., 1960; USAF, 1955–57; married, four children; Unitarian.

Career Founder and Pres., Security Natl. Bank, Walnut Creek, 1963–72; Dir., Common Cause, 1971–72.

Offices 1043 LHOB, 202-225-5065. Also 7 Eastmont Mall, Oakland 94605, 415-635-1092.

Administrative Assistant James M. Copeland, Jr.

Committees

Banking and Currency (23rd); Subs: Consumer Affairs; Domestic Finance; International Finance; Urban Mass Transportation.

District of Columbia (14th); Subs: Business, Commerce, and Taxation; Education; Labor, Social Services, and the International Community.

Group Ratings: Newly Elected

Key Votes

1) Busing	NE	6) Cmbodia Bmbg	AGN	11) Chkg Acct Intrst	FOR
2) Strip Mines	NE	7) Bust Hwy Trust	FOR	12) End HISC (HUAC)	FOR
3) Cut Mil $	NE	8) Farm Sub Lmt	NE	13) Nixon Sewer Veto	AGN
4) Rev Shrg	NE	9) School Prayr	NE	14) Corp Cmpaign $	NE
5) Pub TV $	NE	10) Cnsumr Prot	NE	15) Pol $ Disclosr	NE

Election Results

1972 general:	Fortney Stark (D)	102,153	(53%)
	Lew M. Warden, Jr. (R)	90,970	(47%)
1972 primary:	Fortney Star (D)	50,881	(56%)
	George P. Miller (D)	19,630	(22%)
	Edward W. Vogt (D)	8,402	(9%)
	Clarence L. Davis, Jr. (D)	4,811	(5%)
	Hal Michaels (D)	3,503	(4%)
	Adam W. Nordwall (D)	3,012	(3%)
	John Hancock Abbott (D)	1,199	(1%)

NINTH DISTRICT Political Background

During the recent past, population growth in the San Francisco metropolitan area has been most spectacular around the southern end of San Francisco Bay. The growth has centered around the old farm market town of San Jose. Located in the area is much of northern California's defense business, notably the huge Lockheed plant in Sunnyvale. The many migrants to the area have come from the Southwest and points east, but most of them are natives of some other part of the Bay Area. The migrants are white working-class people, many of whom grew up in neighborhoods that are now dominated by blacks in Oakland or by freaks in San Francisco. Also here are the Mexican-Americans of San Jose; these are people who have moved up from farm labor camps to live in lower-middle-class respectability.

The working-class whites and the Mexican-Americans are the two groups that control the politics of the 9th congressional district. Its terrain spans the southern edge of the Bay from Hayward in Alameda County to Mountain View in Santa Clara County. The district lines in the San Jose area are jagged and eccentric, though not without political design. The result is a congressional district that constitutes no kind of community; it is instead a lumping together of people who for the most part vote the same way.

With one of the largest Mexican-American populations of any California district, the 9th was intended to go Democratic, and it has. Since they were first drawn in 1962, district lines have shifted twice; the 9th, however, has continued to send Democrat Don Edwards, a wealthy title company owner, to the House. The Congressman is an outspoken liberal, an early opponent of the Vietnam war, and former national chairman of the Americans for Democratic Action. Edwards is also a member of an informal group of extremely liberal Congressmen who often act jointly on a wide range of matters and who pool research efforts.

For the most part, Edwards has had little trouble at the polls, though he did slip to 57% in 1968 at the height of Ronald Reagan's popularity. After that election, Edwards considered retiring. But his term as ADA Chairman expired, and the Congressman decided to run again; he then apparently expended a good deal of effort cultivating the district. His 1970 and 1972 showings—69% and 76%—indicate that Edwards is once again in solid political shape. The Californian is a subcommittee Chairman on Judiciary (Civil Liberties and Constitutional Rights) and the number five Democrat on the full committee. One of Edwards' major legislative triumphs occurred when he served as floor manager for the Equal Rights Amendment.

Census Data Pop. 465,966. Central city, 28%; suburban, 72%. Median family income, $11,073; families above $15,000: 24%; families below $3,000: 7%. Median years education, 12.2.

1972 Share of Federal Outlays $666.863,098

DOD	$299,459,000	HEW	$167,873,423
AEC	$23,370,954	HUD	$7,358,328
NASA	$19,626,192	DOI	$5,104,859
DOT	$21,170,246	USDA	$19,290,920
		Other	$103,609,176

Federal Military-Industrial Commitments

DOD Contractors Lockheed (Sunnyvale), $481.449m: research, development, and production of Poseidon and ULMS missile system; ABM and other ballistic missile research and development. FMC Corporation (San Jose), $102.836m: armored personell carriers; Chaparral missile carriers; various armament engineering services. ESL Inc. (Sunnyvale), $9.909m: development and production of various naval radar systems. Durham Meat (San Jose), $6.370m: foodstuffs.
DOD Installations Naval Air Station (Moffett Field, Mountain View).
NASA Contractors Lockheed (Sunnyvale), $6.900m: work on Centaur project.
NASA Installations Ames Research Center (Moffett Field, Mountain View).
AEC Operations General Electric (San Jose), $6.093m: operations of facilities.

Economic Base Electrical equipment and supplies, especially electronic components and accessories; finance, insurance and real estate; machinery, especially office and computing machines; food and kindred products, especially canned, cured and frozen foods; and transportation equipment. Also higher education (Cal State, San Jose).

The Voters

Registration 220,091 total. 140,940 D (64%); 58,818 R (27%); 15,316 declined to state (7%); 5,017 other (2%).
Median voting age 37.8
Employment profile White collar, 47%. Blue collar, 40%. Service, 12%. Farm, 1%.
Ethnic groups Black, 2%. Japanese, 1%. Spanish, 25%. Total foreign stock, 26%. Italy, Portugal, Canada, 2% each; Germany, UK, 1% each.

Presidential vote

1972	Nixon (R)	80,269	(48%)
	McGovern (D)	88,293	(52%)
1968	Nixon (R)	52,587	(37%)
	Humphrey (D)	78,193	(55%)
	Wallace (AI)	11,513	(8%)

Representative

Don Edwards (D) Elected 1962; b. Jan. 6, 1915, San Jose; home, San Jose; Stanford U., Stanford U. Law School, 1936–38; Navy, WWII; unmarried; Unitarian.

Career Sp. Agent, FBI, 1940–41; Pres., Valley Title Co.

Offices 2240 RHOB, 202-225-3072. Also 1961 The Alameda, San Jose 95126, 408-296-7456, and 40979 Fremont Blvd., Fremont 94538, 415-656-5337.

Administrative Assistant Ailsa J. Stickney

Committees

Judiciary (5th); Subs: Civil Rights and Constitutional Rights (Chm.); Criminal Justice.

Veterans' Affairs (8th); Subs: Education and Training; Hospitals; Housing.

Group Ratings

	ADA	COPE	LWV	RIPON	NFU	LCV	CFA	NAB	NSI	ACA
1972	100	100	100	75	71	80	50	8	0	9
1971	95	92	78	72	87	–	100	–	–	4
1970	88	100	–	69	91	65	100	0	0	12

Key Votes

1) Busing	FOR	6) Cmbodia Bmbg	AGN	11) Chkg Acct Intrst	FOR
2) Strip Mines	FOR	7) Bust Hwy Trust	FOR	12) End HISC (HUAC)	FOR
3) Cut Mil $	FOR	8) Farm Sub Lmt	AGN	13) Nixon Sewer Veto	AGN
4) Rev Shrg	FOR	9) School Prayr	AGN	14) Corp Cmpaign $	AGN
5) Pub TV $	ABS	10) Cnsumr Prot	ABS	15) Pol $ Disclosr	AGN

Election Results

1972 general:	Don Edwards (D)	123,994	(72%)
	Herb Smith (R)	43,140	(25%)
	Edmond Kaiser (AI)	4,419	(3%)
1972 primary:	Don Edwards (D)	65,630	(87%)
	Willie Ervin (D)	9,480	(13%)
1970 general:	Don Edwards (D)	120,041	(69%)
	Mark Guerra (R)	49,556	(29%)
	Edmond Kaiser (AI)	4,009	(2%)

TENTH DISTRICT Political Background

Twenty years ago, what is now the 10th district of California consisted, for the most part, of acres of vineyards and fruit orchards below the mountains of the Coast Range near San Jose. This was one of the richest agricultural areas of the country, but it was also directly in the path of some of the most explosive suburban growth the nation has ever seen. Santa Clara County, which includes San Jose and the 10th district, grew from 290,000 in 1950 to 1,064,000 in 1970. In the 1960s alone, the 10th just about doubled in population—a rate of growth exceeded by only four other districts in the country.

Today, the vineyards are almost all gone, their owners having prudently recultivated the grapes in more remote places before selling the land to developers. There is still some agriculture in the southern part of the district, but the 10th is almost entirely suburban in character. Only after the publication of the 1970 census figures have residents here had some second thoughts about the area's growth. In the next few years, it is expected to grow at a much slower rate.

In California, as Lew Archer reminds us, the general rule is that the more desirable subdivisions are those higher up the side of the mountain. This is true in Santa Clara County, at least, and the 10th, which was designed to be firmly Republican, hugs the mountains that form the western border of the county. The foothill suburbs of Los Altos, Los Gatos, and Saratoga are the most Republican parts of the district; the towns lower down, like Mountain View and Sunnyvale, are more marginal. The 10th includes about half of San Jose, but few of its many Mexican-Americans.

Santa Clara County first got its own Congressman after the 1950 census. Since that time, all or part of the county has been represented by Republican Charles S. Gubser. Unlike most Congressmen with equivalent seniority, Gubser serves on only one committee, Armed Services, where he is the fourth-ranking Republican. Considering the number of big defense contractors in the immediate area—recent cutbacks have hurt San Jose—one might suppose that Gubser's support of high military spending and the Nixon Administration's foreign policy is purely expediential. But that would be as unfair as supposing that neighboring Democratic Congressman Don Edwards' opposition to military spending is just a tactic to win himself friends in Georgetown. Because Gubser is deeply committed to the policies he and a solid majority on Armed Services defend, the Congressman becomes incensed when he feels his sincerity is challenged. Gubser's contentiousness has not, however, got him in trouble at home, where he always wins by wide margins.

Census Data Pop. 464,670. Central city, 52%; suburban, 48%. Median family income, $13,977; families above $15,000: 44%; families below $3,000: 4%. Median years education, 12.8.

1972 Share of Federal Outlays $764,148,074

DOD	$457,939,831	HEW	$136,164,566
AEC	$4,874,092	HUD	$2,870,884
NASA	$44,725,818	DOI	$4,231,047
DOT	$15,666,206	USDA	$15,062,834
		Other	$82,612,796

Federal Military-Industrial Commitments

DOD Installations Almaden AF Station (Almaden).

Economic Base Electrical equipment and supplies, especially electronic components and accessories; ordnance and accessories; finance, insurance and real estate; machinery, especially electronic computing equipment; and food and kindred products, especially canned, cured and frozen foods.

The Voters

Registration 260,120 total. 127,736 D (49%); 113,706 R (44%); 16,446 declined to state (6%); 2,232 other (1%).
Median voting age 39.5
Employment profile White collar, 65%. Blue collar, 24%. Service, 10%. Farm, 1%.
Ethnic groups Japanese, 2%. Spanish, 10%. Total foreign stock, 22%. Italy, 3%; Canada, UK, Germany, 2% each.

Presidential vote

1972	Nixon (R)	129,770	(61%)
	McGovern (D)	84,716	(39%)
1968	Nixon (R)	83,762	(51%)
	Humphrey (D)	71,141	(44%)
	Wallace (AI)	8,090	(5%)

Representative

Charles S. Gubser (R) Elected 1952; b. Feb. 1, 1916, Gilroy; home, Gilroy; U. of Calif., B.A., 1937; married, one child; Episcopalian.

Career High school teacher; farmer; Calif. State Assembly, 1950–52.

Offices 2373 RHOB, 202-225-2631. Also 361 Town and Country Village, San Jose 95128, 408-246-1122.

Administrative Assistant Madeleine M. Marceau

Committees

Armed Services (4th); Subs: No. 1 (Ranking Mbr.); Sp. Sub. on Armed Services Investigating.

Group Ratings

	ADA	COPE	LWV	RIPON	NFU	LCV	CFA	NAB	NSI	ACA
1972	13	18	67	56	67	19	0	71	100	55
1971	3	38	75	46	33	–	0	–	–	69
1970	20	25	–	60	70	15	44	64	100	50

Key Votes

1) Busing	AGN	6) Cmbodia Bmbg	FOR	11) Chkg Acct Intrst	AGN
2) Strip Mines	AGN	7) Bust Hwy Trust	FOR	12) End HISC (HUAC)	AGN
3) Cut Mil $	AGN	8) Farm Sub Lmt	AGN	13) Nixon Sewer Veto	FOR
4) Rev Shrg	FOR	9) School Prayr	ABS	14) Corp Cmpaign $	FOR
5) Pub TV $	AGN	10) Cnsumr Prot	ABS	15) Pol $ Disclosr	ABS

Election Results

1972 general:	Charles S. Gubser (R)	140,342	(65%)
	B. Frank Gillette (D)	76,839	(35%)
1972 primary:	Charles S. Gubser (R), unopposed		
1970 general:	Charles S. Gubser (R)	135,864	(62%)
	Stuart McLean (D)	80,530	(37%)
	Joyce Stancliffe (AI)	2,651	(1%)

ELEVENTH DISTRICT Political Background

The Peninsula is the bony finger of land south of San Francisco. Almost down the Peninsula's middle runs the San Andreas Fault, which many experts believe will shift again in the next 20 years or so, producing an earthquake like the one that devastated San Francisco in 1906. To the west of the Fault, the land is mountainous enough to discourage heavy settlement, except in the suburbs of Daly City and Pacifica immediately south of San Francisco itself. Most of the Peninsula's population is packed into neat little suburbs between the Fault and the salt flats and industrial areas created by land fill being dumped into San Francisco Bay. The Bay has begun to disappear in the process.

The Peninsula suburbs are occupied by white-collar people who commute to San Francisco or, more often lately, work near San Jose or on the Peninsula itself. Politically, these towns behave more like Eastern upper-middle-income suburbs than like the arch-conservative towns around Los Angeles. Although the people here tend to register Republican, they are often repelled by the conservatism of some California Republican candidates, and vote for Democrats instead.

The 11th congressional district includes the bulk of the Peninsula suburbs—places like South San Francisco, San Bruno, Millbrae, Burlingame, San Mateo, Belmont, and Redwood City. Formerly, the entire Peninsula comprised a single congressional district. The new boundaries make less geographical than political sense; they exclude from the 11th and include in the 17th district the area's most Republican communities. The 11th, as a result, comes out something like a safe Democratic district. This inclination is undoubtedly one reason maverick Republican Pete McCloskey decided to run in the 17th, rather than the 11th, in 1972, although most of his old district lies in the 11th.

This district fell rather easily into Democratic hands. Leo J. Ryan, who as an Assemblyman presumably had something to do with the 11th's shape, had been winning elections in the northern part of the Peninsula with hugh majorities. He was unchallenged in the Democratic primary, and won the general election with the kind of margin congressional veterans usually enjoy. It is worth noting that California Assemblymen, unlike all other state legislators, have full-time staff and an office in their districts. This means that the Assemblyman can more easily become familiar to his constituents, and helpful as well; it also means an election-time payoff in the voting booth.

The ease with which Ryan won is not only a tribute to his record of service as an Assemblyman. It is also evidence of a leftward trend notable in many election returns on the Peninsula. The key issue has been not so much the Vietnam war as ecology. If you live in the hilly affluence of the Peninsula, you cannot avoid seeing how fast the available land is being occupied; nor can you help noticing, as you drive on the Bayshore Freeway, how the ugly industrial fill gradually eats away at the expanse of San Francisco Bay. "Save the Bay" bumper stickers are common on Peninsula cars, and Sierra Club members abound.

In such circumstances, the politics of Reagan Republicanism are not too popular, for the Governor and his supporters are more likely than Democrats to resolve conflicts between business interests and the environment in favor of business. In 1970, Democrat Arlen Gregorio, an ecology buff, won an upset victory to become state Senator from the Peninsula—an upset that prevented the Reagan forces from controlling the Senate. It should be added that the same impulses that lead Peninsulans to vote for liberal Democratic congressional and legislative candidates lead them to vote for city council candidates opposed to low-income apartments and high-rise developments. These of course at once despoil the environment and attract lower-income residents.

Census Data Pop. 464,324. Central city, 0%; suburban, 100%. Median family income, $12,741; families above $15,000: 35%; families below $3,000: 5%. Median years education, 12.5.

1972 Share of Federal Outlays $592,799,471

DOD	$183,567,712	HEW	$189,683,139
AEC	$36,544,326	HUD	$10,544,049
NASA	$1,439,769	DOI	$5,702,981
DOT	$25,004,199	USDA	$22,217,760
		Other	$118,095,248

Federal Military-Industrial Commitments

DOD Contractors Ampex Corporation (Redwood City), $7.848m: tape recording devices. Varian Associates (San Carlos), $5.550m: various types of electron tubes. Textron (Belmont), $5.509m: development and production of various components for electronic warfare systems.

Economic Base Finance, insurance and real estate; electrical equipment and supplies, especially radio and television communication equipment; machinery; primary metal industries, especially nonferrous rolling and drawing; agriculture, notably nursery and greenhouse products, cattle and vegetables; and tourism.

The Voters

Registration 247,876 total. 146,085 D (59%); 83,819 R (34%); 15,979 declined to state (6%); 1,993 other (1%).
Median voting age 41.5
Employment profile White collar, 57%. Blue collar, 30%. Service, 12%. Farm, 1%.
Ethnic groups Black 5%. Japanese, 1%. Filipino, 1%. Spanish, 12%. Total foreign stock, 31%. Italy, 4%; Germany, Canada, 3% each; UK, 2%; Ireland, USSR, 1% each.

Presidential vote

1972	Nixon (R)		103,931	(53%)
	McGovern (D)		90,388	(47%)
1968	Nixon (R)		64,463	(41%)
	Humphrey (D)		81,881	(52%)
	Wallace (AI)		11,923	(8%)

Representative

Leo J. **Ryan** (D) Elected 1972; b. May 5, 1925, Lincoln, Neb.; Home, South San Francisco; Creighton U., B.S., 1949, M.S., 1951; Navy, WWII; five children.

Career High school teacher; school administrator; South San Francisco City Council, 1956–62; Mayor, South San Francisco, 1962; Calif. State Assembly, 1962–71; Author of "Understanding California Government and Politics," 1966; "USA/From Where We Stand," 1970.

Offices 1113 LHOB, 202-225-3531. Also 210 S. Ellsworth Ave., San Mateo 94401, 415-343-5677.

Administrative Assistant Richard Wolff (L.A.)

Committees

Foreign Affairs (20th); Subs: Asian and Pacific Affairs; Foreign Economic Policy.

Government Operations (22nd); Subs: Legal and Monetary Affairs; Conservation and Natural Resources.

Group Ratings: Newly Elected

Key Votes

1) Busing	NE	6) Cmbodia Bmbg	AGN	11) Chkg Acct Intrst	AGN
2) Strip Mines	NE	7) Bust Hwy Trust	ABS	12) End HISC (HUAC)	FOR
3) Cut Mil $	NE	8) Farm Sub Lmt	NE	13) Nixon Sewer Veto	AGN
4) Rev Shrg	NE	9) School Prayr	NE	14) Corp Cmpaign $	NE
5) Pub TV $	NE	10) Cnsumr Prot	NE	15) Pol $ Disclosr	NE

Election Results

1972 general:	Leo J. Ryan (D)	114,134	(61%)
	Charles E. Chase (R)	69,632	(37%)
	Nicholas Kudrovzeff (AI)	4,881	(3%)
1972 primary:	Leo J. Ryan (D), unopposed		

TWELFTH DISTRICT Political Background

The 12th district of California contains some of the most spectacular scenery in the nation, from the Monterey cypresses at Carmel's Pebble Beach, through the mountainous wild Big Sur coast, to William Randolph Hearst's San Simeon. The 12th also includes some of our richest farmland: the lettuce fields of the Salinas Valley (where Cesar Chavez's troubled United Farm Workers have been struggling to organize the workers) and the artichoke fields around Watsonville. This is John Steinbeck's home country. He grew up in Salinas, and the Cannery Row of Monterey that he described still exists, if only as a tourist attraction.

The coastal counties here have long been politically marginal. Landowners around Salinas and retirees in Santa Cruz and the Monterey Peninsula tend to vote conservative; the district's Mexican-Americans and its sprinkling of artists and writers, liberal. But the 12th is today shifting sharply, though not yet decisively, to the left. Part of the reason is the impact of environmental issues, which have led many erstwhile upper- and middle-income Republicans to vote Democratic. But an even more important cause is the sudden addition in 1972 of a large new bloc in the electorate—students.

In this respect, the 12th is typical of many California districts. We have a tendency to think that the student vote in California is concentrated in Berkeley; it does in fact have plenty of clout there, but nothing like a majority of California students live in Berkeley. Some 8% of the eligible electorate here in the 12th is made up of college students; most of them are enrolled at either

California State Polytechnic in San Luis Obispo or the University of California–Santa Cruz campus, the latter being a highly experimental and unstructured school.

In 1972, Democratic percentages for President rose sharply in both college towns, reflecting the students' affection for George McGovern and their hostility toward the politics of Richard Nixon and Ronald Reagan (see state write-up). The Democratic percentage for Congress rose even more sharply. Republican Burt Talcott, elected in 1968 without Democratic opposition and in 1970 with 64% of the vote, got only 54% of the vote in 1972. And this against a Mexican-American opponent, Julian Camacho, in a district where, in the farm towns, there is still plenty of prejudice against Chicanos among Anglo voters.

It is easy to see why the students did not consider Talcott simpatico. Talcott is one of the most strait-laced members of Congress, having once chided his colleagues for wearing sports coats on the floor. As a middle-seniority member of the Appropriations Committee, he makes little news, and his voting record indicates that he is more a Ronald Reagan than an Earl Warren California Republican. Odds are that Camacho will give Talcott another close race in the 12th in 1974.

Census Data Pop. 465,325. Central city, 18%; suburban, 36%. Median family income, $9,387; families above $15,000: 20%; families below $3,000: 10%. Median years education, 12.4.

1972 Share of Federal Outlays $638,944,647

DOD	$374,209,000	HEW	$175,889,193
AEC	$510,040	HUD	$1,771,559
NASA	$3,548,576	DOI	$1,726,121
DOT	$6,613,552	USDA	$12,756,196
		Other	$61,920,410

Federal Military-Industrial Commitments

DOD Contractors Cochran Western (Salinas), $6.774m: design and production of air cargo loaders.
DOD Installations Presidio of Monterey (Monterey). Fort Ord AB (Monterey). Naval Postgraduate School (Monterey).

Economic Base Agriculture, notably cattle, vegetables and fruits; finance, insurance and real estate; food and kindred products, especially frozen fruits and vegetables; and tourism. Also higher education (Cal State Polytechnic, San Luis Obispo).

The Voters

Registration 241,409 total. 128,847 D (53%); 93,035 R (39%); 15,803 declined to state (7%); 3,724 other (2%).
Median voting age 40.3
Employment profile White collar, 47%. Blue collar, 28%. Service, 16%. Farm, 9%.
Ethnic groups Black, 3%. Japanese, 1%. Filipino, 2%. Spanish, 18%. Total foreign stock, 26%. Germany, Canada, UK, Italy, 2% each.

Presidential vote

1972	Nixon (R)	....	106,577	(56%)
	McGovern (D)	....	83,510	(44%)
1968	Nixon (R)	....	74,667	(49%)
	Humphrey (D)	....	68,937	(45%)
	Wallace (AI)	....	10,335	(7%)

Representative

Burt L. Talcott (R) Elected 1962; b. Feb. 22, 1920, Billings, Mont.; home, Salinas; Stanford U., B.A., 1942, LL.B., 1946; Army Air Corps, WWII; married, one child; Methodist.

Career Atty.; Commissioner of Athletics, Coast Counties Athletic League, 1954–58; Monterey County Supervisor, 1954–62.

Offices 1524 LHOB, 202-225-2861. Also U.S. P.O. Bldg., Salinas 93901, 408-424-6447; Monterey City, 408-373-5402; Hanford, 109-582-3626; Lemoore, 209-924-5926; Paso Robles, 805-238-5447; San Luis Obispo, 805-543-1619; Watsonville, 408-722-6557.

Administrative Assistant William J. MacNelis

Committees

Appropriations. (12th); Subs: Housing and Urban Development, Space, Science, Veterans (Ranking Mbr.); Military Construction.

Group Ratings

	ADA	COPE	LWV	RIPON	NFU	LCV	CFA	NAB	NSI	ACA
1972	0	33	38	75	71	40	0	89	100	59
1971	8	0	44	65	31	–	14	–	–	93
1970	24	25	–	65	38	0	42	82	22	74

Key Votes

1) Busing	AGN	6) Cmbodia Bmbg	FOR	11) Chkg Acct Intrst	AGN
2) Strip Mines	AGN	7) Bust Hwy Trust	ABS	12) End HISC (HUAC)	ABS
3) Cut Mil $	ABS	8) Farm Sub Lmt	AGN	13) Nixon Sewer Veto	FOR
4) Rev Shrg	FOR	9) School Prayr	FOR	14) Corp Cmpaign $	ABS
5) Pub TV $	AGN	10) Cnsumr Prot	AGN	15) Pol $ Disclosr	FOR

Election Results

1972 general:	Burt L. Talcott (R)	105,556	(54%)
	Julian Camacho (D)	84,174	(43%)
	Stanley K. Monteith (AI)	5,752	(3%)
1972 primary:	Burt L. Talcott (R), unopposed		
1970 general:	Burt L. Talcott (R)	95,549	(64%)
	O'Brien Riordan (D)	50,942	(34%)
	Herbert Foster, Jr. (PF)	3,682	(2%)

THIRTEENTH DISTRICT Political Background

There are still some parts of California that are reminiscent of the California that brought so many retirees out here 30 and 40 years ago: the soft climate, the mountains rolling into the sea, the small towns, and smogless cities. One such area is the 13th congressional district, which, on the map, consists of the major portions of Santa Barbara and Ventura counties. But most of the people in the district live in a series of small cities along the Santa Barbara Channel—from Santa Barbara itself through Montecito and Carpinteria to Ventura—and in the foothills above.

It was the Santa Barbara Channel, of course, that was fouled by the gigantic oil spill of 1969. That incident brought the Santa Barbara community together and, for a while at least, came close to radicalizing what had been regarded as a colony of wealthy retirees. But this leftward shift has been countervailed by adroit redistricting, to protect incumbent Republican Congressman Charles Teague. After the 1970 census—and the 1970 election, when Teague was given a hard race by a young teacher—the legislature pared off the University of California–Santa Barbara campus and the Mexican-American community of Oxnard from the district. Left in the 13th were the fast-growing suburbs of Thousand Oaks and Simi Valley, in eastern Ventura County, where thousands of conservative voters are settling, fleeing from the smog of Los Angeles' San Fernando Valley just over the Conejo grade. Also left in the 13th was the town of Lompoc, an ultraconservative community sitting next to Vandenberg Air Force Base.

Congressman Teague is now one of the more senior Republicans. At the beginning of the 93rd Congress, he had the choice of either remaining as ranking minority member of the Veterans' Affairs Committee or assuming the same position on Agriculture. Teague, whose father became the largest lemon grower in the country and head of the Sunkist combine, naturally chose Agriculture. As a long-time opponent of farm subsidies, he can be counted on to back the Nixon Administration's subsidy phase-out when the farm bill comes up for renewal.

Census Data Pop. 465,155. Central city, 27%; suburban, 73%. Median family income, $11,188; families above $15,000: 28%; families below $3,000: 7%. Median years education, 12.6.

1972 Share of Federal Outlays $464,497,254

DOD	$271,239,000	HEW	$114,540,770
AEC	$1,880,024	HUD	$3,714,763
NASA	$4,666,188	DOI	$932,223
DOT	$7,295,512	USDA	$8,630,709
		Other	$51,598,065

Federal Military-Industrial Commitments

DOD Contractors Federal Electric (Lompoc), $24.873m: operation of AF Western Test Range technical facilities. Northrop (Newbury Park), $19.623m: target drones. IBM (Thousand Oaks), $16.106m: computer maintenance. Bunker Ramo (Westlake Village), $9.304m: design and production of various electronic warfare equipment. General Research Corp. (Sanata Barbara), $9.093m: various strategic studies. Lockheed (Lompoc), $5,815m: unspecified. McDonnell Douglas (Lompoc), $5.711m: unspecified.

Economic Base Agriculture, notably cattle, fruits, vegetables and poultry; finance, insurance and real estate; electrical equipment and supplies; tourism; and food and kindred products, especially frozen fruits and vegetables.

The Voters

Registration 255,691 total. 124,619 D (49%); 112,429 R (44%); 15,529 declined to state (6%); 3,114 other (1%).
Median voting age 41.3
Employment profile White collar, 54%. Blue collar, 29%. Service, 13%. Farm, 4%.
Ethnic groups Black, 1%. Spanish, 16%. Total foreign stock, 22%. Canada, 3%; UK, Germany, 2% each; Italy, 1%.

Presidential vote

1972	Nixon (R)	130,134	(64%)
	McGovern (D)	72,367	(36%)
1968	Nixon (R)	75,779	(54%)
	Humphrey (D)	56,359	(40%)
	Wallace (AI)	8,349	(6%)

Representative

Charles M. Teague (R) Elected 1954; b. Sept. 18, 1909, Santa Paula; home, Ojai; Stanford U., B.A., 1931, LL.B., 1934; Army Air Corps, WWII; married, three children; Protestant.

Career Practicing atty., 1934–54.

Offices 1414 LHOB, 202-225-3601. Also 616 E. Main St., P.O. Box 1785, Ventura 93001, 805-643-5401.

Administrative Assistant Montgomery K. Winkler

Committees

Agriculture (Ranking Mbr.).

Veterans' Affairs (3rd). Sub: Hospitals.

Group Ratings

	ADA	COPE	LWV	RIPON	NFU	LCV	CFA	NAB	NSI	ACA
1972	6	20	45	73	67	26	0	82	100	82
1971	14	33	44	44	23	–	25	–	–	79
1970	8	11	–	73	63	0	42	91	100	62

Key Votes

1) Busing	AGN	6) Cmbodia Bmbg	FOR	11) Chkg Acct Intrst	ABS
2) Strip Mines	AGN	7) Bust Hwy Trust	FOR	12) End HISC (HUAC)	AGN
3) Cut Mil $	AGN	8) Farm Sub Lmt	FOR	13) Nixon Sewer Veto	FOR
4) Rev Shrg	FOR	9) School Prayr	FOR	14) Corp Cmpaign $	ABS
5) Pub TV $	AGN	10) Cnsumr Prot	AGN	15) Pol $ Disclosr	AGN

Election Results

1972 general:	Charles M. Teague (R)	153,877	(74%)
	Lester Dean Cleveland (D)	54,299	(26%)
1972 primary:	Charles M. Teague (R), unopposed		
1970 general:	Charles M. Teague (R)	127,507	(59%)
	Gary Hart (D)	87,980	(40%)
	Maude Jordet (AI)	2,339	(1%)

FOURTEENTH DISTRICT   Political Background

Outside of the 14th district of California, which he represents, Jerome R. Waldie is not a household word. On Capitol Hill, Waldie has a reputation for hard work and intelligence. Federal employees who follow such things are familiar with his work as Chairman of the Retirements and Employees Benefits Subcommittee of the Post Office and Civil Service Committee. Close observers of the Judiciary Committee know that the fairly high-ranking liberal Congressman is almost always well-prepared.

It is generally agreed, however, that Waldie will never be much of a power in the House, though he served as Jess Unruh's Majority Leader for five years in the California Assembly. For back in 1969, as he started his second full term, Waldie said the unsayable, and suggested that it was time for Speaker John McCormack to step down. It helps Waldie not at all that McCormack, his office tainted with scandal, announced he would do just that before Congress adjourned.

But Waldie could, just possibly, become a household word before long. Stymied by the slow pace of the House and his meager chances for a leadership post, he has been planning for a long time to run for Governor of California in 1974. He is highly regarded by big Democratic contributors, organized labor, and by the kind of ultraliberal Democrats who watch closely men in the U.S. Congress and the California Assembly. Waldie's main problem is name identification, which is a must in a statewide race in California, and which is low outside his district. It is not clear whether he can raise the money needed to change that. In August 1973, to increase his name identification in southern California, he staged a well-organized walk from San Ysidro on the Mexican border to Los Angeles. But as of now, he is moving up slowly in the polls, gaining on the leading Democratic candidates, San Francisco Mayor Joseph Alioto and Secretary of State and son of the former Governor, Edmund G. (Jerry) Brown.

If Waldie can win the nomination, he will have at least an even chance at the governorship itself. In fact, because our survey of California state politics shows a leftward trend, we feel that the Democratic candidate will have to be considered the favorite. And from there, it is enough to say that anyone who becomes Governor of California also becomes a possible presidential candidate. And so on election night 1974, a heretofore obscure California Congressman might enter the American household-word vocabulary.

The 14th district, which Waldie has represented since a 1965 special election, is politically marginal, usually voting a couple of percent more Democratic than the state as a whole. Although of rather regular shape, and lying wholly within Contra Costa County, the 14th is really a collection of heterogeneous industrial and suburban communities separated by high mountains. Richmond, a working-class city facing San Francisco Bay, is the anchor to the west; the city supplies large Democratic margins, even though redistricting transferred much of the city's black population to Ronald Dellums' 7th district. Along the bay that leads to the Sacramento and San Joaquin River estuaries are the industrial towns of Martinez, Pittsburg, and Antioch—more Democratic bastions. Republican margins come from the more prosperous, faster-growing inland suburbs like Concord (the 14th's largest city with 85,000 people) and Lafayette. It was to protect the estuaries and the fresh water of the Bay that Waldie opposed the Peripheral Canal, part of the California State Water Plan to divert water from the north to the south. The Congressman takes the position, less risky than it used to be for a gubernatorial candidate, that the Los Angeles area has all the water it needs already and should get no more.

With Waldie bowing out of the 1974 House race, the congressional seat here could go either way. The strongest Republican candidate is probably state Sen. John Nejedly, who won a four-year term in 1972 and will be able to run without leaving his current office. Democrats hold both of Contra Costa's Assembly seats, as well as most county offices; any number of these politicians could emerge as strong candidates. If Waldie decides to remain in the House, he will be reelected, as his 1972 performace (78%) indicates.

Census Data   Pop. 464,754. Central city, 0%; suburban, 100%. Median family income, $12,036; families above $15,000: 32%; families below $3,000: 6%. Median years education, 12.5.

1972 Share of Federal Outlays $593,601,093

DOD	$183,815,944	HEW	$189,939,641
AEC	$36,593,744	HUD	$10,558,307
NASA	$1,441,716	DOI	$5,710,693
DOT	$25,038,011	USDA	$22,247,804
		Other	$118,255,233

Federal Military-Industrial Commitments

DOD Contractors Phillips Petroleum (Avon), $9.000m: petroleum products. Standard Oil of California (Richmond), $8.598m: petroleum products. Willamette Iron and Steel (Richmond), $5,080m: ship overhaul.
DOD Installations Naval Weapons Station (Concord).

Economic Base   Finance, insurance and real estate; petroleum and coal products, especially petroleum refining products; agriculture, notably cattle, fruits, vegetables, and nursery and greenhouse products; chemicals and allied products, especially industrial chemicals; and primary metal industries, especially blast furnace and steel mill products.

The Voters

Registration 250,636 total. 149,918 D (60%); 86,983 R (35%); 11,633 declined to state (5%); 2,102 other (1%).
Median voting age 42.0
Employment profile White collar, 53%. Blue collar, 34%. Service, 12%. Farm, 1%.
Ethnic groups Black, 5%. Spanish, 10%. Total foreign stock, 20%. Italy, Canada, UK, Germany, 2% each.

Presidential vote

1972	Nixon (R)	110,079	(55%)
	McGovern (D)	90,872	(45%)
1968	Nixon (R)	71,194	(42%)
	Humphrey (D)	81,124	(48%)
	Wallace (AI)	15,933	(9%)

Representative

Jerome R. Waldie (D) Elected June 20, 1966; b. Feb. 15, 1925, Antioch; home, Antioch; U. of Calif., B.A., 1950, LL.B., 1953; Army, WWII; married, three children; religion unspecified.

Career Practicing atty., 1953–66; Calif. Assembly, 1955–66; Majority Leader, 1961–66.

Offices 408 CHOB, 202-225-5511. Also 805 Las Juntas St., Martinez 94553, 415-687-1200, and 3915 Macdonald Ave., Richmond 94805, 415-233-4425.

Administrative Assistant Robert Neuman (L.A.)

Committees

Judiciary (9th); Subs: No. 1 (Immigration and Nationality); No. 4 (Bankruptcy and Civil Rights Oversight).

Post Office and Civil Service (8th); Subs: Postal Facilities, Mail, and Labor Management; Retirement and Employee Benefits (Chm.).

Sel. Com. on Crime (2nd).

Group Ratings

	ADA	COPE	LWV	RIPON	NFU	LCV	CFA	NAB	NSI	ACA
1972	81	100	100	82	50	93	50	11	0	12
1971	89	91	89	83	79	–	80	–	–	12
1970	96	91	–	71	75	100	100	0	0	19

Key Votes

1) Busing	FOR	6) Cmbodia Bmbg	AGN	11) Chkg Acct Intrst	ABS
2) Strip Mines	AGN	7) Bust Hwy Trust	FOR	12) End HISC (HUAC)	FOR
3) Cut Mil $	ABS	8) Farm Sub Lmt	FOR	13) Nixon Sewer Veto	AGN
4) Rev Shrg	FOR	9) School Prayr	AGN	14) Corp Cmpaign $	ABS
5) Pub TV $	FOR	10) Cnsumr Prot	ABS	15) Pol $ Disclosr	FOR

Election Results

1972 general:	Jerome R. Waldie (D)	159,335	(78%)
	Floyd E. Sims (R)	46,082	(22%)
1972 primary:	Jerome R. Waldie (D), unopposed		
1970 general:	Jerome R. Waldie (D)	148,655	(75%)
	Byron Athan (R)	50,750	(25%)

FIFTEENTH DISTRICT Political Background

The 15th district of California occupies a middle portion of the state's Central Valley, probably the world's richest farmland. Only 50 miles from San Francisco Bay, the 15th is cut off from cosmopolitan influence by the peaks of the Coast Range, and politically at least, the district is almost part of another world. The prosperity of the cities here, the most notable of which is Stockton (pop. 107,000), is rooted firmly in agriculture. The farms of the area—the district goes up as far as the suburbs of Sacramento—are not as often in the hands of huge conglomerates as in the southern reaches of the Valley. Many rather small, family-owned farms still exist in the 15th, as do a whole string of medium-sized cities along the Route 99 freeway. The district has a fair amount of industry, but agriculture is king.

The political traditions of the Valley are Democratic—the result of the politics of its initial settlers, many from the South, and, to an unknown extent, of the assiduously Democratic editorials of the McClatchy papers that dominate the Valley's journalism from Sacramento to Fresno, just as William Loeb's *Manchester Union Leader* dominates New Hampshire. But there is little here of the "new politics," as practiced by the Democrats of the San Francisco Bay suburbs. Social attitudes—measured with nice precision by the plethora of referenda on the California ballot—show the Valley to be decidedly conservative. The 1972 marijuana referendum, for example, ran just about as well as George McGovern in some upper-income San Francisco suburban districts. In the 15th, marijuana ran 20% behind McGovern.

The 15th's Congressman, John J. McFall, is one of an older breed of Democrat, a man who surely feels more comfortable in a party caucus or a union meeting than before a college audience. Organized labor can count on the Congressman just about every time, but he is far less likely to support measures wanted by environmentalists or opponents of high military spending. In Congress since 1957, McFall has risen slowly and almost silently, attaining the chairmanship of the Appropriations Transportation Subcommittee. It was in this capacity that he emerged as the floor manager of the proposal to extend government support to Boeing for development of the SST—a measure that passed the House but died in the Senate in 1971. On the full Appropriations Committee, McFall usually follows the leadership of Chairman George Mahon, a Texan who tends toward lower spending on all programs except defense. McFall is a member of the Defense Subcommittee, which of course has jurisdiction over a very large share of the federal budget.

McFall has also moved quietly up the leadership ladder. After the apparent death of Hale Boggs in an October 1972 plane crash, Whip Tip O'Neill of Massachusetts moved up to Bogg's Majority Leader post. McFall then moved up from one of the two Deputy Whip posts (the other was and is held by John Brademas of Indiana) to Whip. The California Congressman can now walk the streets of downtown Washington unrecognized, but he may some day fairly soon succeed to the Speakership. McFall is 56 in 1974, while Speaker Albert is 66, and Majority Leader O'Neill, 62.

For some reason, McFall has not always run as strongly in his home district as most Congressmen with comparable seniority and high position. In 1968, at the height of Ronald Reagan's popularity, he won with only 54% of the votes. But the strength of California Republicans has been ebbing, and in 1972 McFall went unopposed in the general election. If McFall ever decides not to run, the successor could be one of the two talented Republican ex-state legislators from the area: John Veneman (who went on to be HEW Undersecretary in the first Nixon Administration), or Robert Monagan, who was Speaker of the Republican-controlled state Assembly of 1969 and 1970 and is now Undersecretary of Transportation.

Census Data Pop. 468,000. Central city, 33%; suburban, 67%. Median family income, $9,325; families above $15,000: 18%; families below $3,000: 11%. Median years education, 12.0.

1972 Share of Federal Outlays $507,969,254

DOD	$151,816,000	HEW	$216,486,878
AEC	$130,056	HUD	$2,496,733
NASA	$1,173,176	DOI	$7,254,786
DOT	$6,859,777	USDA	$23,881,157
		Other	$97,870,691

Federal Military-Industrial Commitments

DOD Contractors Norris Industries (Riverbank), $11.624m: production of 105mm and 81mm projectiles. Rudnick and Silva (Stockton), $5.801m: unspecified.
DOD Installations Sharpe Army Depot (Lathrop). Naval Communication Station (Stockton).

Economic Base Agriculture, notably fruits, poultry, dairy products and vegetables; food and kindred products, especially canned, cured and frozen foods; finance, insurance and real estate; and stone, clay and glass products.

The Voters

Registration 223,249 total. 135,410 D (61%); 75,211 R (34%); 10,443 declined to state (5%); 2,175 other (1%).
Median voting age 43.5
Employment profile White collar, 44%. Blue collar, 35%. Service, 13%. Farm, 8%.
Ethnic groups Black, 4%. Filipino, 2%. Spanish, 16%. Total foreign stock, 22%. Italy, 2%; Germany, USSR, Canada, 1% each.

Presidential vote

1972	Nixon (R)	93,600	(56%)
	McGovern (D)	75,020	(44%)
1968	Nixon (R)	72,777	(46%)
	Humphrey (D)	72,828	(46%)
	Wallace (AI)	13,311	(8%)

Representative

John J. McFall (D) Elected 1956; b. Feb. 20, 1918, Buffalo, N.Y.; home, Manteca; Modesto Jr. Col., A.A., 1936; U. of Calif., B.A., 1938, LL.B., 1941; Army, WWII; married, three children; Episcopalian.

Career Practicing atty., 1948–56; Mayor of Manteca, 1948–50; Calif. Assembly, 1951–56; House Majority Whip.

Offices 2346 RHOB, 202-225-2511. Also 146 N. Grant, Manteca 95336, 209-823-1112.

Administrative Assistant Raymond F. Barnes

Committees

Appropriations (18th); Subs: Defense; Transportation (Chm.).

Group Ratings

	ADA	COPE	LWV	RIPON	NFU	LCV	CFA	NAB	NSI	ACA
1972	44	91	83	56	71	0	0	9	100	32
1971	46	100	100	47	64	–	80	–	–	29
1970	52	92	–	56	92	50	89	0	50	12

Key Votes

1) Busing	FOR	6) Cmbodia Bmbg	FOR	11) Chkg Acct Intrst	AGN
2) Strip Mines	AGN	7) Bust Hwy Trust	AGN	12) End HISC (HUAC)	AGN
3) Cut Mil $	AGN	8) Farm Sub Lmt	AGN	13) Nixon Sewer Veto	AGN
4) Rev Shrg	AGN	9) School Prayr	AGN	14) Corp Cmpaign $	FOR
5) Pub TV $	FOR	10) Cnsumr Prot	FOR	15) Pol $ Disclosr	ABS

Election Results

1972 general:	John J. McFall (D), unopposed		
1972 primary:	John J. McFall (D), unopposed		
1970 general:	John J. McFall (D)	98,442	(63%)
	Sam Van Dyken (R)	55,546	(36%)
	Frances Gillings (AI)	1,994	(1%)

SIXTEENTH DISTRICT Political Background

The 16th district of California is another Central Valley district, dominated by the city of Fresno (pop. 165,000). Except for liberal Sacramento, this is the part of the Valley that has maintained most steadily its traditional Democratic leanings. One reason is its large (almost 25%) Mexican-American population, the largest in the Valley. The Chicanos here are not only migrants who pass through; they are often middle-class citizens with roots in their communities. And they vote. Moreover, the Fresno area has a more heterogeneous population than most of the rest of the Valley. There are especially large numbers of Armenian-Americans, like novelist William Saroyan, who is from Fresno. But the largest group no doubt is made up of the descendants of the original Okies, the people who left the dried-out fields of Oklahoma, Kansas, and Texas during the 1930s in search of the promised land of California. Here, as John Steinbeck chronicled in *The Grapes of Wrath*, these poor white people did backbreaking work in the steamy-hot fields for next to nothing and lived in miserable labor camps. Ironically, though perhaps not surprisingly, their sons and daughters are not sympathetic—often even hostile—to the very similar plight of Mexican-Americans in those same fields today.

The Congressman for the 16th district is himself a transplant from the Dust Bowl. B. F. (Bernie) Sisk grew up on the dusty plains of central Texas and moved to the Valley in 1937. Some 17 years later, he upset a Republican Congressman, and ever since his ingratiating personality has helped him to win reelection. He has also mirrored some of the changes in attitude of the people who have shared the man's odyssey. For his first 10 years in the House, he was regarded as a typical Northern liberal Democrat. But in the mid-1960s, as the Reagan tide began to roll in, he became noticeably more conservative. In 1966 his vote in the House Rules Committee—to which he had been elevated to provide liberal votes—killed home rule for the District of Columbia. Apparently, though, he has high regard for the people of Washington, having spent considerable time in the 92nd Congress trying to get a major-league baseball team back into the city.

Sisk's conservative record—and, perhaps, his Texas twang—commended him to some of the more conservative Southern Democrats. In late 1970, he became a candidate for Majority Leader, reportedly at the behest of men like William Colmer of Mississippi, Omar Burleson of Texas, and Bob Sikes of Florida. For a while, Sisk's candidacy made inroads among members of the California and some Southern delegations, but it soon foundered. Organized labor found him unacceptable, and the Southerners returned to one of their own, the late Hale Boggs of Louisiana. Though Sisk will never get a leadership position, his seat on Rules—and his capable management of a congressional reorganization bill a few years back—give him important leverage. He is not a man to be ignored in the House.

Sisk's main legislative interest, according to the Nader Congress report, is agriculture. Sisk has sponsored major water projects which are of benefit to, among others, J. G. Boswell, a cotton farmer in western Fresno County who has received more than $4 million a year in federal subsidy payments—the number one recipient of farm subsidies in the nation. The legislator's attitude toward farm workers is somewhat less enthusiastic. He has sponsored a bill to put them under the National Labor Relations Act; this, however, is opposed by Cesar Chavez since it would deny his union its major weapon, the boycott.

Back home, as one might expect, Sisk is reelected more or less automatically.

Census Data Pop. 470,794. Central city, 35%; suburban, 53%. Median family income, $8,531; families above $15,000: 17%; families below $3,000: 12%. Median years education, 12.1.

1972 Share of Federal Outlays $457,280,236

DOD	$54,420,000	HEW	$203,724,014
AEC	–	HUD	$10,278,169
NASA	–	DOI	$24,086,336
DOT	$10,709,523	USDA	$66,357,551
		Other	$87,704,643

Federal Military-Industrial Commitments

No installations or contractors receiving prime awards greater than $5,000,000.

Economic Base Agriculture, notably fruits, cattle, cotton and poultry; finance, insurance and real estate; and food and kindred products, especially canned, cured and frozen foods. Also higher education (Fresno State).

The Voters

Registration 221,089 total. 141,218 D (64%); 69,057 R (31%); 8,078 declined to state (4%); 2,736 other (1%).
Median voting age 41.8
Employment profile White collar, 47%. Blue collar, 29%. Service, 13%. Farm, 11%.
Ethnic groups Black, 5%. Japanese, 1%. Spanish, 25%. Total foreign stock, 25%. USSR, 2%; Italy, Canada, 1% each.

Presidential vote

1972	Nixon (R)	87,864	(52%)
	McGovern (D)	79,980	(48%)

1968 Nixon (R)	40,925	(40%)
Humphrey (D)	51,627	(51%)
Wallace (AI)	7,281	(7%)

Representative

B. F. Sisk (D) Elected 1954; b. Dec. 14, 1910, Montague, Texas; home, Fresno; Abilene Christian Col., 1929–31; married, two children; Church of Christ.

Career Day laborer, refrigerator salesman, orchard worker, 1937–45; tire company shipping clerk, service mgr., dept. mgr., asst. gen. mgr., 1946–54.

Offices 2313 RHOB, 202-225-6131. Also 1130 O St., Fresno 93721, 209-485-5000, ext. 261.

Administrative Assistant Tony Coelho

Committees

Agriculture (7th); Subs: Cotton (Chm.); Domestic Marketing and Consumer Relations; Livestock and Grains.

Rules (4th).

Sel. Com. on Parking (Chm.).

Group Ratings

	ADA	COPE	LWV	RIPON	NFU	LCV	CFA	NAB	NSI	ACA
1972	50	90	73	60	71	26	0	10	100	32
1971	38	89	100	53	75	–	80	–	–	29
1970	44	89	–	44	92	51	94	0	90	7

Key Votes

1) Busing	FOR	6) Cmbodia Bmbg	AGN	11) Chkg Acct Intrst	AGN
2) Strip Mines	AGN	7) Bust Hwy Trust	AGN	12) End HISC (HUAC)	AGN
3) Cut Mil $	AGN	8) Farm Sub Lmt	AGN	13) Nixon Sewer Veto	AGN
4) Rev Shrg	AGN	9) School Prayr	AGN	14) Corp Cmpaign $	FOR
5) Pub TV $	ABS	10) Cnsumr Prot	FOR	15) Pol $ Disclosr	ABS

Election Results

1972 general:	B. F. Sisk (D)	134,132	(79%)
	Carol D. Harner (R)	35,385	(21%)
1972 primary:	B. F. Sisk (D), unopposed		
1970 general:	B. F. Sisk (D)	95,118	(66%)
	Phillip Sanchez (R)	43,843	(31%)
	James Scott (AI)	4,237	(3%)

SEVENTEENTH DISTRICT Political Background

Pete McCloskey is an unusual Congressman. He is a Republican who challenged his party's President in the primaries and then maintained a tight-lipped silence on whether he would support the nominee in November. He is a man who professes a strong belief in progressive Republicanism, and has refused to leave the party like his friend Don Riegle of Michigan; yet after the 1972 election, McCloskey changed his registration to the category "decline to state." He is a successful California politician who talks publicly about chucking it all and going back to law practice. He is a man whose revulsion against the Vietnam war stemmed not only from his horror of the bombing, but also from his disgust with what the war did to the Marine Corps, in which he saw combat during the Korean war. McCloskey is an ecology buff who . . . and there is more.

But it is better to start at the (political) beginning. For Paul N. (Pete) McCloskey, Jr., that was in 1967. He was practicing law in Menlo Park, home of the *Whole Earth Catalog* and a comfortable suburb on the Peninsula south of San Francisco, when Congressman J. Arthur Younger, a conservative Republican, died. Though McCloskey was active in community affairs and environmental causes, he had never been in politics. Nevertheless, he entered the race to succeed Younger. The candidate who was getting all the national publicity was Shirley Temple Black. But McCloskey had friends and supporters all over the district. As a liberal Republican, he appealed to the district's moderates—more numerous here than in most parts of California—who were dismayed by the recent takeover of Earl Warren's old party by Ronald Reagan and his allies. Through good precinct work, McCloskey won the primary handily, and the general election even more easily, to become Congressman for the 11th district of California.

At first, McCloskey was not so controversial. He stuck with the Republican leadership on many votes and compiled a middle-of-the-road record. But the conservatives back home would not forgive him for sinking the good ship Lollipop. McCloskey won only 53% of the vote in 1968 and 60% in 1970 against conservative primary opponents—very low figures for an incumbent Congressman. General elections were easier. Republicans, having no place else to go, voted for him, and so did a great many Democrats attracted by his liberal record.

McCloskey, however, was not content to take the safe political route, which means sending out tons of franked mail to deter primary opposition. The Vietnam war rubbed his emotions raw. He sought out other Republicans, urging them to run against Nixon. When he could find no one, he did so himself. In New Hampshire, he nearly made the 20% mark he set for his candidacy, and toyed with the idea of staying in the race. But the money was running out, and he had a decision to make back home.

The problem facing McCloskey, if he wanted to return to Congress, was redistricting. The filing deadline was just a few days after New Hampshire. His old 11th district had been split up. The greater portion of it was in a new, more Democratic 11th—basically the old district with the most Republican cities detached. Running in the new 11th was Assemblyman Leo Ryan, a Democrat who ran as well as McCloskey did in general elections, and who, unlike McCloskey, had no worries in his primary. McCloskey's alternative was the new 17th district; this is about one-quarter of his old territory in San Mateo County, with the remainder a tortuous, snake-like portion winding through San Jose and Santa Clara counties. At one point, the snake is only three blocks wide. The 17th was the more Republican of the two. It included his home in the woodsy mountain suburb of Portola Valley and his old law office in Menlo Park; it also included his alma mater, Stanford University. McCloskey chose the 17th as the place to run, and filed.

Just as in the old 11th, McCloskey encountered primary conservative opposition. This time his own initial polls showed that he had only 30% to 40% of the registered Republicans with him. The race against Nixon alienated many Republicans who had earlier supported him. Moreover, he had never represented or campaigned among two-thirds of the registered Republicans who lived in Santa Clara County. Fortunately for McCloskey, the opposition was split. A conservative Republican screening committee had chosen Royce Cole, a Menlo Park physician, to unseat the maverick. Then Robert R. Barry entered the race. Barry was a New York Congressman from 1959 to 1965, who has since run in three different California districts—including a race against John Tunney in 1966 and one against McCloskey in 1968. In 1972 neither candidate could match McCloskey on the platform. But Barry proved capable of spending a fair share of his considerable fortune, and Cole was able to organize a corps of volunteer supporters to match McCloskey's students and ecology-minded housewives. The result was predictable: "those two turkeys," as McCloskey called them, split the anti-McCloskey vote and the Congressman was renominated with 44% to Barry's 31% and Cole's 25%.

But unlike his years in the old 11th, McCloskey had no free ride in the general election. His Democratic opponent, a young attorney named James Stewart, won a tough primary campaign and would have had an excellent chance against either Barry or Cole. Stewart attacked McCloskey for being too much of a Republican, and managed to hold down the incumbent's margin to 13% in the three-quarters of the district lying in Santa Clara County. But in San Mateo County, the Republican cities that had been excised from the old 11th, came through with large McCloskey majorities.

Since the election, McCloskey has talked about returning to law practice. After Watergate, his differences with President Nixon handicap him less; McCloskey was one of the very few Republicans who spoke out on the scandal before the election. But the Congressman can still count on a hard-core of McCloskey-haters who will give him another difficult primary race. His minority victory in 1972—and the fact that a conservative Republican write-in won an amazing 10% of the votes in the 1972 general election—do not augur well for future McCloskey primaries.

If McCloskey does not run, it is hard to say just what will happen. The Democrats will have a good shot at the district, but the Republicans will probably be favored on the basis of past electoral performances. There is no dearth of talented politicians who live within the boundaries of the attenuated 17th. McCloskey, who is one of the least malleable of politicians, will probably again keep us ignorant of his plans until the filing date in March 1974. For the 1974 elections, the Special Masters' redistricting plan (see state write-up) has eliminated the district's present tortuous boundaries, but retains essentially the same territory and the same political balance of the present 17th district.

Census Data Pop. 461,211. Central city, 20%; suburban, 80%. Median family income, $12,894; families above $15,000: 38%; families below $3,000: 5%. Median years education, 12.8.

1972 Share of Federal Outlays $724,868,803

DOD	$400,388,017	HEW	$145,816,498
AEC	$11,114,179	HUD	$4,370,951
NASA	$35,838,358	DOI	$4,493,113
DOT	$17,406,772	USDA	$16,375,131
		Other	$89,065,784

Federal Military-Industrial Commitments

DOD Contractors Philco Ford (Palo Alto), $69.642m: operation of military space satellite program; support services for ABM. GTE Sylvania (Mountain View), $46.478m: design and production of electronic warfare systems. Itek (Sunnyvale), $37.709m: production of electronic warfare systems. Westinghouse (Sunnyvale), $25.552m: ship engines; support for ABM and Poseidon missile systems. Stanford Research Institute (Menlo Park), $24.621m: various strategic and biochemical studies. Watkins Johnson (Palo Alto), $22.499m: design and production of various electronic ware. Hewlett Packard (Palo Alto), $15.378m: design and production of various electronic ware. Lockheed (Palo Alto), $14.256m: laser research. Varian Associates (Palo Alto), $13.211m: production and repair of various electronic tubes. United Aircraft (Sunnyvale), $8.728m: design and production of various rocket motors and propellants. Itek (Palo Alto), $6.881m: production of electronic warfare units. United Technology (Sunnyvale), $6.881m: production of antenna systems. United Aerial Mapping (Sunnyvale), $5.455m: mapping services.
NASA Contractors Philco Ford (Palo Alto), $12.914m: support of weather satellite system.
AEC Operations Stanford University (Menlo Park), $28.793m: research and operation of Stanford Linear Accelerator Center.

Economic Base Electrical equipment and supplies, especially electronic components and accessories; finance, insurance and real estate; machinery, especially electronic computing equipment; ordnance and accessories; and food and kindred products, especially canned, cured and frozen foods. Also higher education (Stanford Univ.).

The Voters

Registration 255,363 total. 135,833 D (53%); 97,572 R (38%); 18,629 declined to state (7%); 3,329 other (1%).
Median voting age 38.8
Employment profile White collar, 63%. Blue collar, 26%. Service, 10%. Farm, 1%.
Ethnic groups Black, 2%. Japanese, 1%. Chinese, 1%. Spanish, 16%. Total foreign stock, 27%. Canada, 3%; UK, Germany, Italy, 2% each.

Presidential vote

1972	Nixon (R)	106,566	(52%)
	McGovern (D)	97,748	(48%)
1968	Nixon (R)	70,673	(47%)
	Humphrey (D)	71,681	(48%)
	Wallace (AI)	6,840	(5%)

Representative

Paul N. (Pete) **McCloskey,** Jr. (R) Elected 1966; b. Sept. 29, 1927, San Bernardino; home, Portola Valley; Occidental Col. and Calif. Inst. of Tech., 1945–46; Stanford U., B.A., 1950, LL.B., 1953; Navy, 1945–47; USMC, Korean War; USMCR, 1952–72; married, four children; Presbyterian.

Career Practicing atty., 1953–67; Deputy Dist. Atty., Alameda County, 1953–54; Lecturer, Santa Clara and Stanford Law Schools, 1964-67.

Offices 205 CHOB, 202-225-5411. Also 900 Welch Rd., Palo Alto 94304, 415-326-7383.

Administrative Assistant Mrs. Celia MacFarland

Committees

Government Operations (7th); Subs: Conservation and Natural Resources; Foreign Operations and Government Information.

Merchant Marine and Fisheries (6th); Subs: Merchant Marine; Fisheries and Wildlife Conservation and the Environment; Oceanography.

Group Ratings

	ADA	COPE	LWV	RIPON	NFU	LCV	CFA	NAB	NSI	ACA
1972	50	72	100	100	67	85	100	50	11	8
1971	65	63	100	100	64	–	50	–	–	23
1970	64	42	–	100	62	95	82	70	22	59

Key Votes

1) Busing	FOR	6) Cmbodia Bmbg	AGN	11) Chkg Acct Intrst	AGN
2) Strip Mines	AGN	7) Bust Hwy Trust	FOR	12) End HISC (HUAC)	FOR
3) Cut Mil $	FOR	8) Farm Sub Lmt	FOR	13) Nixon Sewer Veto	AGN
4) Rev Shrg	FOR	9) School Prayr	AGN	14) Corp Cmpaign $	AGN
5) Pub TV $	ABS	10) Cnsumr Prot	ABS	15) Pol $ Disclosr	FOR

Election Results

1972 general:	Paul N. McCloskey (R)	110,988	(55%)
	James G. Knapp (R, write-in)	19,377	(10%)
	James Stewart (D)	73,123	(36%)
1972 primary:	Paul N. McCloskey (R)	28,564	(44%)
	Robert Barry (R)	20,548	(31%)
	Royce M. Cole (R)	16,138	(25%)
1970 general:	Paul N. McCloskey (R)	144,500	(77%)
	Robert Gomperts (D)	39,188	(21%)
	Jack Wilson (Ind.)	2,786	(1%)

EIGHTEENTH DISTRICT Political Background

Between California's Coast Range and the Sierra Nevada are vast, flat, heavily irrigated plains that lie in almost constant sunshine and often oppressive heat. This is California's Central Valley, probably the world's richest agricultural land. On a relief map, the Valley manifests itself clearly from the surrounding mountains; the flatlands start far north of Sacramento near the Oregon border and extend as far south as the Tehachapi Mountains less than 100 miles from Los Angeles. The region is one of huge farms, particularly in the western part of the Valley where virtually all the land is in the hands of agribusiness conglomerates.

The prosperity of the Central Valley has been built upon the fanatical drive of agricultural entrepreneurs and the backs of migrant laborers. In the 1930s, the laborers were the Okies forced off their land in the Dust Bowl by swirling storms. Today, they are mainly Mexican-Americans. Both groups brought Democratic voting habits with them—to the extent that migrant workers can and do vote. But underlying the common Democratic registration of the thirties migrants and the Chicanos is basic economic conflict: Who shall reap what share of the profits off the land? The descendants of the Okies, and other people here whose ancestors were more fortunate, believe that the demands of the farm workers, especially those led by Cesar Chavez, will affect the white person's share of the economic pie. For everybody in the Valley partakes of the profits of big farming, and nobody in the Valley thinks that the big companies that dominate the farming business will absorb any losses brought on by higher wages and better working conditions for the Chicanos. So the politics in much of the Central Valley has come down to a conflict between the growers and the farm laborers, with the vast majority of the voters on the side of the growers.

The conflict is especially intense in the oddly shaped piece of California called the 18th congressional district. Technically, the 18th does not lie wholly within the Central Valley, since the district spans the Sierra Nevada and includes places like Mount Whitney (the highest point in the continental United States) and, less than 100 miles away, Death Valley (the lowest). But the Sierra and the vast desertlands to the east are virtually uninhabited, leaving the overwhelming bulk of the 18th's population in two otherwise unconnected sections of the Valley.

For 14 years, the 18th (with a different set of boundaries) was represented by Harlen Hagen, a Democrat who generally favored the interests of the growers and served on the House Agriculture Committee. But in 1966, the Republicans made a major assault on Hagen's seat in the person of Bob Mathias, twice Olympic decathlon champion and a local boy. That was the year Ronald Reagan scored a smashing victory over two-term Gov. Pat Brown, with the Republican conservative making especially big gains among the registered Democrats in the southern part of the Valley. Meanwhile, Mathias carried the district with a margin unusually large for a neophyte taking on a six-term veteran.

In the House, Mathias is a four-square conservative, unobtrusive in the well-disciplined Republican ranks. He of course strenuously backs the interests of the big growers. Since his election to the House, Mathias has been joined on the Republican side of the aisle by other former sports heroes like Jackie Kemp of New York (Buffalo Bisons quarterback) and Wilmer "Vinegar Bend" Mizell of North Carolina (major league baseball pitcher). The redistricting that produced the grotesque contours of the current 18th was designed to enhance the reelection prospects of the state's incumbents, which in Mathias' case were already very good. For 1974, the Special Masters' redistricting plan (see state write-up) has placed Mathias' district entirely within the Central Valley, a move that will not affect the incumbent's continued tenure.

Census Data Pop. 460,665. Central city, 4%; suburban, 20%. Median family income, $8,236; families above $15,000: 15%; families below $3,000: 12%. Median years education, 11.8.

1972 Share of Federal Outlays $451,904,892

DOD	$81,158,000	HEW	$214,784,723
AEC	–	HUD	$407,206
NASA	$2,282,243	DOI	$17,559,231
DOT	$3,578,729	USDA	$72,497,500
		Other	$59,637,260

Federal Military-Industrial Commitments

DOD Installations Castle AFB (Merced).

Economic Base Agriculture, notably fruits, cattle and dairy products; finance, insurance and real estate; food and kindred products, especially canned, cured and frozen foods, lumber and wood products, especially general sawmill and planing mill products; and printing and publishing.

The Voters

Registration 215,857 total. 124,362 D (58%); 81,998 R (38%); 7,429 declined to state (3%); 2,068 other (1%).
Median voting age 44.4
Employment profile White collar, 40%. Blue collar, 30%. Service, 14%. Farm, 16%.
Ethnic groups Black, 2%. Spanish, 20%. Total foreign stock, 20%. Canada, 1%.

Presidential vote

1972	Nixon (R)		100,122	(60%)
	McGovern (D)		65,449	(40%)
1968	Nixon (R)		64,071	(49%)
	Humphrey (D)		54,098	(42%)
	Wallace (AI)		11,343	(9%)

Representative

Robert B. Mathias (R) Elected 1966; b. Nov. 17, 1930, Tulare; home, Tulare; Stanford U., B.S., 1953; USMC, 1954–56; Capt. USMCR (Ret.); married, three children; First Methodist Church.

Career Olympic Decathlon winner, 1948 and 1952; Pres. Eisenhower's Rep. to 1956 Olympics; covered 1964 Olympics for *Sports Illustrated;* Sports Advisory Com., Sears Roebuck & Co.

Offices 1114 LHOB, 202-225-3341. Also 1724 M St., Merced 95340, 209-723-0466.

Administrative Assistant Phil Pendergrass

Committees

Agriculture (4th); Subs: Cotton (Ranking Mbr.); Departmental Operations.

Foreign Affairs (14th); Subs: International Organizations and Movements; Near East and South Asia.

Group Ratings

	ADA	COPE	LWV	RIPON	NFU	LCV	CFA	NAB	NSI	ACA
1972	0	18	56	67	75	13	0	91	100	71
1971	8	17	33	40	45	–	17	–	–	86
1970	20	42	–	59	77	0	56	64	100	61

Key Votes

1) Busing	AGN	6) Cmbodia Bmbg	FOR	11) Chkg Acct Intrst	AGN
2) Strip Mines	AGN	7) Bust Hwy Trust	ABS	12) End HISC (HUAC)	AGN
3) Cut Mil $	AGN	8) Farm Sub Lmt	AGN	13) Nixon Sewer Veto	FOR
4) Rev Shrg	FOR	9) School Prayr	FOR	14) Corp Cmpaign $	FOR
5) Pub TV $	AGN	10) Cnsumr Prot	AGN	15) Pol $ Disclosr	AGN

Election Results

1972 general:	Bob Mathias (R)	110,153	(66%)
	Vincent J. Lavery (D)	55,829	(34%)
1972 primary:	Bob Mathias (R), unopposed		
1970 general:	Bob Mathias (R)	86,071	(63%)
	Milton Miller (D)	48,415	(36%)
	Nora Hensley (AI)	1,709	(1%)

NINETEENTH DISTRICT Political Background

Congressman Chet Holifield—now dean of the California congressional delegation, the nation's largest—exemplifies the strengths, and the weaknesses, of the seniority system. Back in 1942, Holifield was first elected to the House from a brand-new district that now lies in the smoggy southeast suburbs of Los Angeles. At that time, Holifield was one of the few Californians with the guts to protest the determined intent of state Attorney General Earl Warren and others to force 110,000 Japanese-Americans off the West Coast and into concentration camps further inland; most politicians could not resist scoring a few points amidst the general hysteria and greed of the period. Later, during the 1950s, Holifield was one of a group of liberal Democrats, along with Gene McCarthy and Lee Metcalf, who helped to start the Democratic Study Group. This was when about half of the Democrats in the House were Southerners, most of them conservatives; many of the rest were the products of big-city machines, content to go-along-toget-along.

So, earlier in his career, Holifield was something of a liberal gadfly; today, most House liberals consider him a brake on reform and progress. In part, the switch reflects a change in context, specifically in the composition of the House. Currently only 31% of the House Democratic membership comes from the Deep South, and many of the Northern machine men have been replaced by ideological liberals. But the idea of Holifield as brake also reflects changes in Holifield himself.

During the 1950s, Holifield was making his way to the top of the seniority ladder in a unique congressional body, the Joint Committee on Atomic Energy. The Joint Committee has members from both the House and the Senate, with the chairmanship alternating between the two senior Democrats from each house. So Holifield has held the chairmanship on and off since the early 1960s. Under his leadership and that of Sen. John Pastore, the Joint Committee became involved far more deeply in the administrative workings of the Atomic Energy Commission (AEC) than other congressional committees charged with oversight. Together the AEC and the Joint Committee have worked to develop atomic energy as a source of cheap power, and have also worked to promote its use. Despite his lack of formal education (like Harry Truman, he has been in the men's clothing business, but with more success), Holifield mastered the complexities of the atomic energy field. Even his detractors say he ran the Joint Committee skillfully. Like other committee members, he believes deeply in the necessity of developing atomic power. Unlike his friends from the early days of the Democratic Study Group, Holifield has in no way questioned the need to pour vast sums of money into the Pentagon and quasi-military agencies like NASA and the AEC.

Near the end of 1970, the California Congressman succeeded to the chairmanship of the Government Operations Committee. Long moribund under the leadership of aged Rep. William Dawson of Chicago, Government Operations has, technically at least, the duty to oversee all federal agencies. Younger members of the committee hoped that Holifield would invigorate it, sparking multiple investigations of the federal bureaucracies. They were disappointed. Under Holifield, some claim, the committee has done even less than it did before. Holifield consolidated two subcommittees under his own leadership; he then proceeded to do very little with it, though the new subcommittee, Legislative and Military Operations, had jurisdiction over programs that spent more than half of our federal dollars.

With such complaints, Benjamin Rosenthal of New York challenged Holifield for the chairmanship at the opening of the 93rd Congress. The new procedures in the Democratic Caucus allow any chairmanship to be put up to a vote if 10 Democrats sign a petition. Under this, 38 votes were cast against the Chairman in the caucus—far from enough to win, but enough to signal Holifield that there was dissatisfaction with his performance.

The tragedy is that at this late hour Holifield, who will be 71 in 1974, cannot be expected to bring to Government Operations the kind of energy and thoughtful attention to detail he brought to the chairmanship of the Joint Committee a dozen years ago. It is more a matter of age than of ideology. But this, sadly, is not the first time a Congressman has reached a chairmanship long after his most active years. Holifield's career—a distinguished one by most standards—unhappily seems to be ending under a cloud of criticism.

Back home in the 19th district, however, the Congressman has had no great difficulties. He wins general elections with ease (71% in 1972). But lately he has had a little more trouble in the Democratic primary. In 1972, he won just 52% of the vote against two opponents: Philip Medgal, a dentist, and Tony Sanchez, who did well among the district's large (35%) Mexican-American minority. Because California's Mexican-Americans have long complained that they have been denied representation in favor of Democratic veterans like Holifield, Republicans like Gov. Reagan have fastened onto the grievances to attack the Democrats. When Holifield retires—or, if he is beaten—his successor will probably be either a Chicano Democrat, or a Republican who is able to win because of anti-Chicano sentiment among the district's Anglo working-class majority. For 1974, the Special Masters' redistricting plan (see state write-up) has given Holifield a heavily Mexican-American constituency. So the incumbent faces potential trouble.

Census Data Pop. 464,323. Central city, 0%; suburban, 100%. Median family income, $10,930; families above $15,000: 24%; families below $3,000: 6%. Median years education, 12.1.

1972 Share of Federal Outlays $593,282,332

DOD	$244,212,735	HEW	$172,946,488
AEC	$2,132,355	HUD	$7,079,516
NASA	$35,784,518	DOI	$778,324
DOT	$17,167,254	USDA	$9,755,104
		Other	$103,425,773

Federal Military-Industrial Commitments

DOD Contractors Norris Industries (Pico Rivera), $38.054m: metal parts for 105mm cartridge cases; motor tubes for 2.75 inch rockets. Powerline Oil Company (Santa Fe Springs), $7.539m: petroleum products. Rocking K Food (Santa Fe Springs), $6.287m: foodstuffs.

Economic Base Transportation equipment, especially aircraft; finance, insurance and real estate; electrical equipment and supplies, especially radio and television communication equipment, and electronic components and acessories, machinery, especially electronic computing equipment; and fabricated metal products, especially fabricated structural metal products.

The Voters

Registration 294,415 total. 128,737 D (63%); 60,256 R (29%); 9,550 declined to state (5%); 5,872 other (3%).
Median voting age 40.3
Employment profile White collar, 44%. Blue collar, 46%. Service, 10%. Farm, –%.
Ethnic groups Spanish, 35%. Total foreign stock, 28%. Canada, 2%; Italy, Germany, UK, USSR, 1% each.

Presidential vote

1972	Nixon (R)	91,302	(59%)
	McGovern (D)	63,474	(41%)
1968	Nixon (R)	67,390	(45%)
	Humphrey (D)	69,517	(47%)
	Wallace (AI)	11,446	(8%)

Representative

Chet Holifield (D) Elected 1942; b. Dec. 3, 1903, Mayfield, Ky.; home, Montebello; married, four children.

Career Mfg., selling men's apparel 38 yrs.; Mbr. Hoover Commission; V. Chm., President's Commission on Gov. Procurement; Rep. at Intl. Atomic Energy Meeting, Vienna, 1967; Cong. Advisor, U.S. Delegations, Int. Conf. on Peaceful Uses of Atomic Energy, Geneva, 1955; Conf. on Discontinuance of Nuclear Weapons Tests, Geneva, 1959; Genl. Conf. of Intl. Atomic Energy Agcy., 1959–63–65–68–69; Disarmament Conf., Geneva, 1967–70.

Offices 2469 RHOB, 202-225-3976. Also 9125 E. Whittier Blvd., Pico-Rivera 90660, 213-723-6561, 213-692-2242.

Administrative Assistant Adam J. Klein

Committees

Government Operations (Chm.); Subs: Legislation and Military Operations (Chm.).

Standards of Official Conduct (4th).

Joint Com. on Atomic Energy (2nd); Subs: Legislation; Military Applications; Raw Materials; Research, Development and Radiation; Energy; Licensing and Regulation (Chm.).

Group Ratings

	ADA	COPE	LWV	RIPON	NFU	LCV	CFA	NAB	NSI	ACA
1972	50	100	80	62	50	5	0	10	50	20
1971	46	100	100	47	67	–	71	–	–	28
1970	60	100	–	59	100	42	94	–	50	0

Key Votes

1) Busing	FOR	6) Cmbodia Bmbg	AGN	11) Chkg Acct Intrst	AGN
2) Strip Mines	AGN	7) Bust Hwy Trust	ABS	12) End HISC (HUAC)	AGN
3) Cut Mil $	AGN	8) Farm Sub Lmt	AGN	13) Nixon Sewer Veto	AGN
4) Rev Shrg	AGN	9) School Prayr	AGN	14) Corp Cmpaign $	FOR
5) Pub TV $	ABS	10) Cnsumr Prot	FOR	15) Pol $ Disclosr	ABS

Election Results

1972 general:	Chet Holifield (D)	105,699	(67%)
	Kenneth M. Fisher (R)	43,792	(28%)
	Joe Harris (PF)	7,745	(5%)
1972 primary:	Chet Holifield (D)	37,413	(52%)
	Anthony M. Sanchez (D)	22,858	(32%)
	Philip Megdal (D)	11,660	(16%)
1970 general:	Chet Holifield (D)	98,578	(70%)
	Bill Jones (R)	41,462	(30%)

TWENTIETH DISTRICT Political Background

Pasadena (pop. 113,000) and Glendale (pop. 132,000) are two Los Angeles-area towns with quite well-established images in the national mind. From sources as diverse as the mid-sixties rock-and-roll song "The Little Old Lady of Pasadena" to Raymond Chandler's description of the massive homes of wealthy recluses, one gets a picture that is still substantially accurate. These are towns of large old houses, of tree-shaded streets, of older, upper-income people whose basic instincts are profoundly conservative. This is also a fairly accurate picture of the 20th congressional district, which includes both Glendale and Pasadena, several adjacent suburbs, and a small part of the city of Los Angeles.

But there is at least one discordant note here today, mentioned neither by Jan and Dean nor by Mr. Chandler. That is the large and growing black population in Pasadena. Because the city's school system has been under a federal court busing order, an anti-busing majority was elected to the school board in early 1973. As in many large cities, the results of the election stemmed mainly from a discrepancy between the school population and the electorate. The schools are 40% black and 12% Chicano, figures that reflect the proportions among the city's younger adults; the voting population, however, remains overwhelmingly white, weighted to the age brackets of the upper range.

This age structure is typical of many older, well-to-do suburbs across the country. As the older and deeply conservative people, who have dominated them for years, slowly die off, they are replaced by younger, more liberal residents. Often these liberals are black, or white faculty members (Pasadena is the home of Caltech), who are notably more flexible in their political attitudes than their neighbors. Twenty-five years ago, this kind of liberal (or at least the whites among them) would have probably moved to the tract houses at the farther edge of suburbia. Today they seem to prefer the older, better-established suburbs, having their well-built, spacious houses with their surrounding trees fully grown.

The political result of such preferences is that communities like Pasadena and Glendale are moving slightly to the left. They still continue to give Republican candidates huge majorities. But it is worth noting that the 20th district gave George McGovern the same percentage of its votes as it did Hubert Humphrey four years earlier—a result far enough out of line with the rest of the country to indicate a significant leftward shift.

Congressman H. Allen Smith, a 16-year Republican veteran, picked 1972 to retire. At 63 he had become ranking minority member on the House Rules Committee. He apparently felt—and quite rightly so—that there was little chance the Republicans would get a majority in the House, and that he would therefore never become Chairman. Smith's successor is Carlos Moorhead, a former Assemblyman and staunch conservative. What is interesting about Moorhead's victory is that it came by somewhat smaller margins than might have been expected.

Moorhead was not closely pressed in the 10-man Republican primary, but he still had only 51% of the vote. His chief competitor, moderate Bill McColl, had 23%; in 1970, McColl ran a closer race in the neighboring 24th district against John Rousselot. In the general election Moorhead won with 57%—far lower than the usual Republican showing in the 20th. The new Congressman's majority probably does not mean that he will face trouble in the future—the advantages of incumbency are enough to avoid that—but it does show a significant erosion of conservative Republican strength in one of its historic strongholds.

Census Data Pop. 463,092. Central city, 18%; suburban, 82%. Median family income, $11,843; families above $15,000: 35%; families below $3,000: 6%. Median years education, 12.6.

1972 Share of Federal Outlays $591,492,642

DOD	$243,476,000	HEW	$172,424,779
AEC	$2,125,923	HUD	$7,058,160
NASA	$35,676,569	DOI	$775,976
DOT	$17,115,466	USDA	$9,725,678
		Other	$103,114,041

Federal Military-Industrial Commitments

DOD Contractors Singer (Glendale), $28.814m: design and production of firing system for MK 48 torpedo and other torpedo systems. Robert E. McKee, Inc. (Long Beach), $12.563m: unspecified. Xerox (Pasadena), $5.733m: development of electro-optical systems.
NASA Contractors California Institute of Technology (Pasadena), $208.793m: research and operation of Jet Propulsion Laboratory.
NASA Installations Jet Propulsion Laboratory.

Economic Base Finance, insurance and real estate; transportation equipment, especially aircraft; electrical equipment and supplies, especially radio and television communication equipment, and electronic components and accessories; machinery, especially electronic computing equipment; fabricated metal products, especially fabricated structural metal products; and tourism.

The Voters

Registration 272,836 total. 113,772 D (42%); 141,485 R (52%); 14,466 declined to state (5%); 3,113 other (1%).
Median voting age 47.1
Employment profile White collar, 65%. Blue collar, 24%. Service, 11%. Farm, –%.
Ethnic groups Black, 7%. Japanese, 1%. Spanish, 11%. Total foreign stock, 29%. Canada, UK, Germany, 3% each; Italy, 2%; USSR, 1%.

Presidential vote

1972	Nixon (R)	144,889	(68%)
	McGovern (D)	68,650	(32%)
1968	Nixon (R)	130,001	(63%)
	Humphrey (D)	66,020	(32%)
	Wallace (AI)	9,560	(5%)

Representative

Carlos John Moorhead (R) Elected 1972; b. May 5, 1922, Long Beach; home, Glendale; U. of Calif. (Los Angeles), B.A., 1943; U. of So. Calif., School of Law, J.D., 1949; Army, 1945–46; married, five children; Presbyterian.

Career Practicing atty.; Dir., Glendale Legal Aid and Lawyer's Reference Service, 16 years; Pres., Glendale Bar Assn.; State Assembly, 1966–72.

Offices 1208 LHOB, 202-225-4176. Also 420 N. Brand Blvd., Glendale 91203, 213-247-8445, and 125 S. Grand Ave., Pasadena 91105, 213-792-6168.

Administrative Assistant Alice Andersen

Committees

Judiciary (16th); Sub: Claims.

Group Ratings: Newly Elected

Key Votes

1) Busing	NE	6) Cmbodia Bmbg	FOR	11) Chkg Acct Intrst	AGN
2) Strip Mines	NE	7) Bust Hwy Trust	FOR	12) End HISC (HUAC)	AGN
3) Cut Mil $	NE	8) Farm Sub Lmt	NE	13) Nixon Sewer Veto	FOR
4) Rev Shrg	NE	9) School Prayr	NE	14) Corp Cmpaign $	NE
5) Pub TV $	NE	10) Cnsumr Prot	NE	15) Pol $ Disclosr	NE

Election Results

1972 general:	Carlos J. Moorhead (R)	122,309	(57%)
	John Binkley (D)	90,842	(43%)
1972 primary:	Carlos J. Moorhead (R)	46,607	(51%)
	Bill McColl (R)	21,025	(23%)
	Eric Stattin (R)	10,365	(11%)
	J. DeWitt Fox (R)	5,053	(6%)
	Patrick Coleman (R)	2,232	(2%)
	Samuel M. Cavnar (R)	1,551	(2%)
	Bryson M. Kratz (R)	1,477	(2%)
	Carl Chandler (R)	1,314	(1%)
	Lewis L. Mathe (R)	869	(1%)
	Kenneth Lackey (R)	608	(1%)

TWENTY-FIRST DISTRICT Political Background

Watts has been a familiar American place-name since the 1965 riot there put it in national headlines. Watts is the heart of Los Angeles black community, directly south of the city's downtown. As those who read newspapers carefully know, Watts, despite its near central location, is isolated from the mainstream of Los Angeles—off the principal bus lines, with no hospitals, few parks, and fewer municipal facilities. The area's most distinctive feature is the Watts Tower, a weird sculpture of bits of broken glass and scrap metal, assembled over some 30 years by Italian immigrant Simon Rodia.

New York journalists sent to Watts in the wake of the riot were quick to write that the place didn't look like a ghetto. Actually, more black Americans live in areas like Watts—small, frame, single- or double-family homes along quiet streets—than in areas like Harlem. But what is more important here is the persistence of hard-and-fast racial borders. In Los Angeles, blacks are moving north, west, and south of Watts, but to the east they still find an impenetrable barrier in Alameda Street. Across Alameda are white working-class suburbs that on first glance look little different from Watts—places like Huntington Park, Lynwood, and South Gate. This, however, is California backlash country, where politicians like Ronald Reagan picked up vast numbers of erstwhile white Democratic votes following the Watts riot.

The 21st congressional district spans Alameda Street. When it was first created in 1961, the 21st was almost entirely black, with Alameda as its eastern border. But, as in most all-black areas, the population, so the Census Bureau said, declined during the 1960s, and the state legislature, eager to create another black district (the 37th), had to tack on additional territory to the 21st. The white working-class people east of Alameda probably do not feel entirely at home in the 21st, and their votes have perceptibly lowered its Democratic majorities. But the 21st remains a black-dominated district, with no doubt as to which party will carry it.

Augustus Hawkins, a Democrat who has represented the 21st since its creation, is probably the most experienced black legislator in the United States. For 28 years, from 1934 to 1962, he served in the California Assembly, for most of that time the only black there; in 1959, he was nearly elected Speaker. Such experience does not usually produce verbal militance, and Hawkins is known as one of the quieter members of the Congressional Black Caucus. Nevertheless, he is capable of sounding off when moved to do so, working well with the younger, more flamboyant members of the caucus. In 1970, Hawkins was one of the Congressmen who discovered the infamous tiger-cage prisons in South Vietnam; in typical fashion, he allowed a junior colleague, William Anderson of Tennessee (since defeated) to get most of the publicity.

After 10 years in the House, the Congressman has attained a chairmanship—Education and Labor's Equal Opportunities Subcommittee. But at his age (67 in 1974), he is unlikely to ever become a committee chairman, and it could well be that like Satchel Paige, Hawkins' race has denied him the opportunity to demonstrate just how talented a man he really is.

Census Data Pop. 464,852. Central city, 50%; suburban, 50%. Median family income, $7,060; families above $15,000: 10%; families below $3,000: 18%. Median years education, 10.8.

1972 Share of Federal Outlays $594,177,177

DOD	$244,581,080	HEW	$173,207,343
AEC	$2,135,571	HUD	$7,090,194
NASA	$35,838,491	DOI	$779,498
DOT	$17,193,147	USDA	$9,769,818
		Other	$103,582,115

Federal Military-Industrial Commitments

DOD Contractors Norris Industries (Vernon), $33.535m: production of bomb bodies, rockets, and other munitions.

Economic Base Transportation equipment, especially aircraft; finance, insurance and real estate; electrical equipment and supplies, especially radio and television communication equipment, and electronic components and accessories; machinery, especially electronic computing equipment; and fabricated metal products, especially fabricated structural metal products. Also higher education (Univ. of Southern California).

The Voters

Registration 178,965 total. 145,647 D (81%); 23,983 R (13%); 6,901 declined to state (4%); 2,434 other (1%).
Median voting age 41.7
Employment profile White collar, 35%. Blue collar, 47%. Service, 18%. Farm, –%.
Ethnic groups Black, 54%. Japanese, 1%. Spanish, 21%. Total foreign stock, 22%.

Presidential vote

1972	Nixon (R)	31,413	(26%)
	McGovern (D)	91,077	(74%)
1968	Nixon (R)	25,630	(19%)
	Humphrey (D)	102,981	(76%)
	Wallace (AI)	5,479	(4%)

Representative

Augustus F. Hawkins (D) Elected 1962; b. Aug. 31, 1907, Shreveport, La.; home, Los Angeles; UCLA, B.A., 1931; widowed; Methodist.

Career Instr. of Gov., U. of So. Calif.; Real estate business, 1945– ; Calif. Assembly, 1935–62; founding member, Southeast Los Angeles Improvement Action Council.

Offices 2350 RHOB 202-225-2201. Also 8563 S. Broadway, Suite 206, Los Angeles 90003, 213-750-0260.

Administrative Assistant Mattie Maynard

Committees

Education and Labor (7th); Subs: No. 1 (Education); No. 7 (Equal Opportunities) (Chm.); No. 8 (Agricultural Labor).

House Administration (7th); Subs: Accounts; Electrical and Mechanical Office Equipment (Chm.); Police.

Group Ratings

	ADA	COPE	LWV	RIPON	NFU	LCV	CFA	NAB	NSI	ACA
1972	81	90	100	63	71	63	0	10	0	6
1971	81	100	75	56	70	–	80	–	–	5
1970	84	100	–	65	73	65	94	0	0	0

Key Votes

1) Busing	FOR	6) Cmbodia Bmbg	AGN	11) Chkg Acct Intrst	AGN
2) Strip Mines	ABS	7) Bust Hwy Trust	FOR	12) End HISC (HUAC)	FOR
3) Cut Mil $	ABS	8) Farm Sub Lmt	AGN	13) Nixon Sewer Veto	AGN
4) Rev Shrg	FOR	9) School Prayr	AGN	14) Corp Cmpaign $	FOR
5) Pub TV $	ABS	10) Cnsumr Prot	ABS	15) Pol $ Disclosr	AGN

Election Results

1972 general:	Augustus F. Hawkins (D)	95,050	(83%)
	Rayfield Lundy (R)	19,569	(17%)
1972 primary:	Augustus F. Hawkins (D), unopposed		
1970 general:	Augustus F. Hawkins (D)	75,127	(95%)
	Southey Johnson (R)	4,344	(5%)

TWENTY-SECOND DISTRICT Political Background

California's 22nd district is the heart of the San Fernando Valley. This vast expanse of land, surrounded on all sides by mountains, is almost entirely part of Los Angeles. Annexed long ago, when it consisted mainly of dusty fields and movie ranches, the Valley is now thoroughly filled up—but still suburban in character. The straight streets go on mile after mile, lined by neat stucco houses or by low-rise commercial clutter. At major intersections are great shopping centers. Hanging over all is the Los Angeles smog, a little less here than in downtown L.A., but still a depressing part of life to those who came here in search of the Golden West.

The Valley has seen southern California's boom industries rise and fall—first the movie business, and now aerospace. With major cutbacks in both government and airline orders, the giant aircraft plants here have laid off thousands of workers. The earthquake of 1971, which did its greatest damage at the northern end of the Valley, occurred just as the layoffs were announced. For secure San Fernando Valley residents, both were shocks: their jobs were at stake, and the Van Norman Dam—which nearly broke and whose reservoir would have destroyed tens of thousands of homes—meant that even their very lives and possessions were endangered. Lately people have been leaving the Valley for points east (or for the new Ventura County suburbs, west over the mountains), and the boom here is now a matter of history.

The 22nd district includes most of the interior parts of the Valley, and touches the rim of the mountains only occasionally. The district lines were designed for the benefit of Democratic Congressman James Corman, who was first elected in 1960 and came close to losing in 1964 and 1966. The largest neighborhood areas (the district lies almost entirely within the L.A. city limits) include North Hollywood, with its large Jewish and Democratic population, middle-class Van Nuys to the west, and the small black ghetto of Pacoima to the north. Pacoima is one of the few areas where there are any black people living in the Valley.

The almost lily-white composition of the 22nd caused particular problems for Corman during the mid-1960s. Strongly committed to civil rights, he struggled to get on the Judiciary Committee, and once there played an active role in the civil rights laws of 1964, 1965, and 1968. The Congressman has also led fights against proposed constitutional amendments to overturn the Supreme Court's decision barring prayer in public schools. None of these stands was particularly popular with his constituency, a more conservative one because of the district lines then in force.

Following the 1968 election, Corman gained a seat on the Ways and Means Committee. Although the newer breed of Democrats who dominate the liberal Democratic Study Group are rapidly becoming a majority in their party's caucus, they are still underrepresented on Wilbur Mills' committee. Corman is one of the very few Ways and Means members who has sponsored comprehensive tax-reform legislation. He is also one of the co-sponsors of the Kennedy-Griffiths-Corman health-care bill; the legislation would create a system of federal health insurance financed in part by a tax similar to Social Security and in part from general revenues. Neither the tax-reform nor health-care measure is likely to come out of Ways and Means with Wilbur Mills' imprimatur during the life of this Congress. But Corman will be in there plugging for both of them. And it is possible that when and if there is a significant shift of opinion on the House floor, these bills, or something very close to them, will become law.

Census Data Pop. 464,780. Central city, 96%; suburban, 4%. Median family income, $11,117; families above $15,000: 27%; families below $3,000: 7%. Median years education, 12.4.

1972 Share of Federal Outlays $594,177,177

DOD	$244,581,000	HEW	$173,207,343
AEC	$2,135,571	HUD	$7,090,194
NASA	$35,838,491	DOI	$779,498
DOT	$17,193,147	USDA	$9,769,818
		Other	$103,582,115

Federal Military-Industrial Commitments

DOD Contractors Lockheed (Van Nuys), $73.158m: development of Cheyenne helicopter. ITT Gilfillan (Van Nuys), $33.314m: design and production of various radar systems. Litton Systems (Van Nuys), $25.589m: design and production of various aircraft electronic systems. CCI (Van Nuys), $20.505m: production of Rockeye cluster bombs. Bendix (North Hollywood), $15.298m: production of sonar systems and other electronic ware. RCA (Van Nuys), $11.457m: research into lasers and other electronic systems.

Economic Base Finance, insurance and real estate; transportaion equipment, especially aircraft; tourism; electrical equipment and supplies, especially radio and television communication equipment, and electronic components and accessories; and machinery, especially electronic computing equipment.

The Voters

Registration 239,126 total. 143,361 D (60%); 76,814 R (32%); 12,898 declined to state (5%); 6,053 other (3%).
Median voting age 41.0
Employment profile White collar, 53%. Blue collar, 36%. Service, 11%. Farm, –%.
Ethnic groups Black, 4%. Spanish, 17%. Total foreign stock, 30%. Canada, USSR, 3% each; Italy, UK, Germany, 2% each; Poland, 1%.

Presidential vote

1972	Nixon (R)		101,594	(56%)
	McGovern (D)		79,296	(44%)
1968	Nixon (R)		76,161	(46%)
	Humphrey (D)		79,583	(48%)
	Wallace (AI)		9,634	(6%)

Representative

James C. Corman (D) Elected 1960; b. Oct. 20, 1920, Galena, Kans.; home, Van Nuys; UCLA, B.A., 1942; U. of So. Calif., LL.B., 1948; USMC, WWII and Korean War; two children; Methodist.

Career Practicing atty., 1949– ; Los Angeles City Council, 1957–61; Natl. Advisory Commission on Civil Disorders, 1967.

Offices 2252 RHOB, 202-225-5811. Also 14545 Friar St., Van Nuys 91401, 213-787-1766.

Administrative Assistant Robert C. Ruben

Committees

Ways and Means (10th).

Sel. Com. on Small Business (6th); Subs: Government Procurement and International Trade (Chm.); Small Business Problems in Smaller Towns and Urban Areas; Minority Small Business Enterprise and Franchising.

Group Ratings

	ADA	COPE	LWV	RIPON	NFU	LCV	CFA	NAB	NSI	ACA
1972	94	100	90	73	71	47	50	8	14	12
1971	76	100	100	60	87	–	75	–	–	4
1970	88	92	–	76	100	20	92	0	22	7

Key Votes

1) Busing	FOR	6) Cmbodia Bmbg	AGN	11) Chkg Acct Intrst	FOR
2) Strip Mines	AGN	7) Bust Hwy Trust	AGN	12) End HISC (HUAC)	FOR
3) Cut Mil $	FOR	8) Farm Sub Lmt	FOR	13) Nixon Sewer Veto	AGN
4) Rev Shrg	AGN	9) School Prayr	AGN	14) Corp Cmpaign $	FOR
5) Pub TV $	ABS	10) Cnsumr Prot	FOR	15) Pol $ Disclosr	AGN

Election Results

1972 general:	James C. Corman (D)	123,863	(68%)
	Bruce P. Wolfe (R)	53,603	(29%)
	Ralph L. Shroyer (PF)	5,705	(3%)
1972 primary:	James C. Corman (D)	62,547	(85%)
	Ernest Cortes (D)	10,673	(15%)
1970 general:	James C. Corman (D)	95,256	(59%)
	Tom Hayden (R)	63,297	(39%)
	Callis Johnson (AI)	1,880	(1%)

TWENTY-THIRD DISTRICT Political Background

The 23rd district of California is a nice example of why party registration figures—so often used by political analysts—are meaningless and sometimes downright misleading. On paper, the 23rd is a Democratic district. Leaving aside minor parties, 53% of its voters are registered Democrats. Yet the areas contained within the current boundaries of the 23rd have never come even close to going Democratic, even when Lyndon Johnson thrashed Barry Goldwater in 1964.

The 23rd is also one of the nation's odder-shaped districts—the explanation, of course, being political. Until the 1971 redistricting, the 23rd consisted of the white, working-class suburbs just east of the Watts ghetto (see California 21). Today, almost all that territory has been added to other districts. The new 23rd shares with its predecessor only the two cities of Downey (pop. 88,000) and Bellflower (pop. 51,000). From the two cities the district winds its way into the heart of ultraconservative Orange County (see California 39). Roughly speaking, the 23rd follows the route of the Santa Ana Freeway, which has also been the path of outmigration taken by many former residents of the old 23rd, fleeing the proximity of Watts.

Who are these people? Mainly blue-collar workers, a large percentage from the South and Southwest. They have been moving into the Los Angeles area since the beginning of World War II, and finding work in many of the huge defense factories not far away. And they settled down in the small frame and stucco houses in the towns southeast of Los Angeles. As they paid off their mortgages, they began to worry about the blacks and whether they might begin to move across Alameda Street into their neighborhoods.

Sometime in the early 1960s things began turning sour for many of these people. The smog grew more overpowering—it is probably worse here than anywhere in the Los Angeles Basin—and defense work grew more precarious. As the blue-collar people struggled to raise their families and pay their taxes, they began to resent the welfare mother whom they believed their money was supporting. They were horrified by the Berkeley riots as shown on television and the Watts riots only a few miles away. And as their values came under heavy attack, they began to look for reassurance. They found it in the politics of Ronald Reagan.

As early as 1963—when Reagan was still host of *Death Valley Days*—these feelings began to show up in the election returns. At that time, the 23rd, with its strong Democratic registration edge, sent conservative Democrat Clyde Doyle (briefly Chairman of the House Un-American Activities Committee) to the House. When he died, a special election was called for June 1963.

This was just after the church bombing and police-dog incidents in Birmingham, and just as President Kennedy was preparing to submit a civil rights bill to Congress. Martin Luther King, Jr., was then beginning to plan the great march on Washington. Several locally prominent Democrats decided to run, while the only Republican candidate was Del Clawson, then Mayor of Compton. (Compton was then a sharply divided city racially; it is now heavily black and no longer in the 23rd.) After an energetic campaign and a respectable primary turnout, Clawson won 53% of the total votes cast. Under a unique California law, he was thereby elected Congressman without having won a general election.

Clawson's conservatism—opposition to civil-rights legislation, hawkish support of the Vietnam war, and stern disapproval of black and student rioters—has won him thousands of votes from registered Democrats, as it has for Ronald Reagan. Since 1963, the Congressman has had no trouble winning reelection. The current redistricting reduced Democratic registration by 10%, making Clawson's reelection even more certain.

In Washington, Clawson cuts an anonymous figure. He is, however, in a position of significant power. Holder of a seat on the Appropriations Committee until 1973, he switched to the Rules Committee, replacing fellow Californian H. Allen Smith, who retired. Like three of Rules' other four Republicans, Clawson can be expected to form part of a rock-hard conservative bloc. But with changes in the Democratic membership on the committee, it is unlikely that these minority members can muster enough votes to block pending liberal legislation—as used to happen when Mississippi's William Colmer and Virginia's Howard Smith were Rules Chairmen.

For 1974, the Special Masters' redistricting plan (see state write-up) has placed Clawson's district entirely within Los Angeles County, a move that will not affect his reelection chances.

Census Data Pop. 462,131. Central city, 37%; suburban, 63%. Median family income, $11,778; families above $15,000: 31%; families below $3,000: 5%. Median years education, 12.4.

1972 Share of Federal Outlays $499,450,983

DOD	$249,203,404	HEW	$134,880,218
AEC	$940,371	HUD	$3,246,665
NASA	$18,876,014	DOI	$930,187
DOT	$8,037,989	USDA	$6,735,528
		Other	$76,598,607

Federal Military-Industrial Commitments

DOD Contractors Hughes Aircraft (Fullerton), $98.976m: design and production of electronic ware. Aerojet General (Downey), $38.518m: bombs and munitions research. Northrop Corp. (Anaheim), $29.017m: production of warheads for 2.75 rockets; design and production of electronic ware. Lear Siegler (Anaheim), $18.885m: production of emergency escape breathing device; production of electronic ware.
NASA Contractors North American Rockwell (Downey), $81.280m: design, develop, and test Apollo command and service module, and S-11 state of the Saturn V; space shuttle system.

Economic Base Electrical equipment and supplies; finance, insurance and real estate; transportation equipment, especially aircraft and parts; ordnance and accessories; and machinery, especially electronic computing equipment. Also higher education (Cal State, Fullerton).

The Voters

Registration 247,211 total. 121,883 D (49%); 107,026 R (43%); 15,249 declined to state (6%); 3,053 other (1%).
Median voting age 40.2
Employment profile White collar, 55%. Blue collar, 34%. Service, 11%. Farm, –%.
Ethnic groups Spanish, 11%. Total foreign stock, 20%. Canada, 3%; UK, Germany, Italy, 2% each; Netherlands 1%.

Presidential vote

1972	Nixon (R)	....	135,119	(70%)
	McGovern (D)	....	57,301	(30%)
1968	Nixon (R)	....	96,967	(59%)
	Humphrey (D)	....	54,518	(33%)
	Wallace (AI)	....	12,788	(8%)

Representative

Delwin (Del) **Morgan Clawson** (R) Elected 1962; b. Jan. 11, 1914, Thatcher, Ariz.; home, Downey; Ariz. Gila Col.; married, one child; Church of Jesus Christ of Latter Day Saints.

Career Salesman and bookkeeper, 1934–41; U.S. Employment Svc., Fed. Pub. Housing Auth., 1941–47; Mgr., Mutual Housing Assn. of Compton, 1947–63; Compton City Council, 1953–57; Mayor of Compton, 1957–63; Dir., Los Angeles County Sanitation Dists. 1, 2, 8, 1957–63.

Offices 2349 RHOB 202-225-3576. Also 11600 S. Paramount Blvd., Downey 90240, 213-923-9206, and 905 S. Euclid, Fullerton 92632.

Administrative Assistant Anita Charles

Committees

Rules (5th).

Group Ratings

	ADA	COPE	LWV	RIPON	NFU	LCV	CFA	NAB	NSI	ACA
1972	0	13	11	23	29	0	50	100	100	100
1971	5	9	28	47	0	–	0	–	–	100
1970	8	34	–	33	91	7	29	90	100	89

Key Votes

1) Busing	AGN	6) Cmbodia Bmbg	FOR	11) Chkg Acct Intrst	ABS
2) Strip Mines	FOR	7) Bust Hwy Trust	AGN	12) End HISC (HUAC)	AGN
3) Cut Mil $	AGN	8) Farm Sub Lmt	ABS	13) Nixon Sewer Veto	FOR
4) Rev Shrg	AGN	9) School Prayr	FOR	14) Corp Cmpaign $	FOR
5) Pub TV $	ABS	10) Cnsumr Prot	AGN	15) Pol $ Disclosr	AGN

Election Results

1972 general:	Del Clawson (R)	120,313	(61%)
	Conrad G. Tuohey (D)	75,546	(39%)
1972 primary:	Del Clawson (R)	57,954	(63%)
	Conrad G. Tuohey (R)	34,273	(37%)
1970 general:	Del Clawson (R)	77,346	(63%)
	G. L. Chapman (D)	44,767	(37%)

TWENTY-FOURTH DISTRICT Political Background

The mountains that encircle the Los Angeles Basin are responsible for the city's mild climate; the desert to the north and east is usually 20 to 30 degrees hotter. But the mountains also bottle up the Basin's air, allowing the sun to interact with auto emissions to produce Los Angeles' choking smog. The same mountains form a neat topographical barrier to dense settlement. North of the mountains, there are 133,000 people in Los Angeles County; to the south, nearly 7,000,000.

These same mountains form the spine of the 24th congressional district. Its geographic outline is rather misleading, containing, as it does, the sparsely populated part of Los Angeles County north of the mountains. To the south, the district includes at least four distinct areas, separated from each other by as much as 60 miles and connected only by the uninhabited mountains. What the areas have in common is a strong conservative Republicanism.

The most conservative and most Republican part of the 24th is the small, wealthy suburb of San Marino, the home of Congressman John Rousselot. Rousselot is not only a conservative Republican, he is also a proud member of that old liberal bugbear, the John Birch Society. In San Marino, where the Republican percentage seldom falls below 88%, Birch membership is not as frightening to voters as it may be elsewhere.

Nonetheless, Rousselot has had some trouble making it to Congress. He was first elected to the House in 1960, but was beaten in 1962, after the Democratic legislature went to great pains to draw him a district he couldn't win. Rousselot then went back to the obscurity of the public relations business. But in 1970 Rep. Glenard P. Lipscomb died. Rousselot entered the primary, beat moderate Republican Bill McColl by 127 votes out of 87,000 cast, and in the general election defeated Myrlie Evers, widow of the slain Mississippi civil rights leader, by better than a two-to-one margin.

Many people may picture Rousselot as a hard-eyed fanatic. He is, to be sure, a man with fierce drive and energy which may derive a la Theodore Roosevelt from having been crippled in childhood. But he is also one of the more personable members of the House, with a ready sense of humor, always prepared to trade quips with colleagues with whom he shares nothing in common politically. Ten years ago, his Birch membership made him a target for both Democrats and moderate Republicans. But in 1972 he had no primary opposition and won the general election by a margin larger than he won in 1970. Rousselot seems likely to be around the House for some time.

Census Data Pop. 463,856. Central city, 14%; suburban, 86%. Median family income, $11,954; families above $15,000: 33%; families below $3,000: 6%. Median years education, 12.5.

1972 Share of Federal Outlays $592,387,487

DOD	$243,844,390	HEW	$172,685,634
AEC	$2,129,139	HUD	$7,068,838
NASA	$35,730,544	DOI	$777,150
DOT	$1,704,190	USDA	$9,740,391
		Other	$118,697,211

Federal Military-Industrial Commitments

DOD Contractors Lockheed (Burbank), $437.567m: production, maintenance, and repair of various aircraft and aircraft weapons systems. McDonnell Douglas (Palmdale), $62.099m: production of A-4 aircraft. Hoffman Electronics (El Monte), $30.498m: aircraft navigation sets

and fin and nozzle fin assemblies for 2.75 inch rockets. Tasker Industries (Saugus), $6.966m: unspecified.
DOD Installations Air Force Plant 42 (Palmdale).

Economic Base Tourism; finance, insurance and real estate; transportation equipment, especially aircraft; electrical equipment and supplies, especially radio and television communication equipment, and electronic components and accessories; and machinery, especially electronic computing equipment.

The Voters

Registration 261,520 total. 114,181 D (44%); 131,068 R (50%); 13,079 declined to state (5%); 3,192 other (1%).
Median voting age 44.0
Employment profile White collar, 58%. Blue collar, 31%. Service, 10%. Farm, 1%.
Ethnic groups Black, 2%. Spanish, 10%. Total foreign stock, 21%. Canada, 3%; UK, Germany, Italy, 2% each.

Presidential vote

	1972	Nixon (R)	148,177	(73%)
		McGovern (D)	55,323	(27%)
	1968	Nixon (R)	116,179	(62%)
		Humphrey (D)	56,120	(30%)
		Wallace (AI)	13,470	(7%)

Representative

John Harbin Rousselot (R) Elected July 1, 1970; b. Nov. 1, 1927, Los Angeles; home, San Marino; Principia Col., B.A., 1949; married, three children; Christian Scientist.

Career Pres. and owner, John H. Rousselot & Assoc., public relations consultants, 1954–58; Dir. Pub. Info., Fed. Housing Admin., 1958–60; Rep. Calif. 25th Congressional Dist., 1961–63; Management consultant, 1967–70.

Offices 1706 LHOB, 202-225-4206. Also 735 West Duarte Road, Arcadia 91006, 213-447-8125, and 567 W. Lancaster Blvd., Lancaster 93534, 805-948-8116, and 23610 San Fernando Rd., Newhall 91321, 805-255-6595.

Administrative Assistant Yvonne Le Masters

Committees

Banking and Currency (10th); Subs: Bank Supervision and Insurance (Ranking Mbr.); Housing; Small Business.

Post Office and Civil Service (5th); Subs: Census and Statistics (Ranking Mbr.); Postal Facilities, Mail, and Labor Management.

Group Ratings

	ADA	COPE	LWV	RIPON	NFU	LCV	CFA	NAB	NSI	ACA
1972	0	38	17	20	40	18	50	100	86	94
1971	8	17	0	18	7	–	0	–	–	96

Key Votes

1) Busing	AGN	6) Cmbodia Bmbg	FOR	11) Chkg Acct Intrst	FOR
2) Strip Mines	FOR	7) Bust Hwy Trust	AGN	12) End HISC (HUAC)	AGN
3) Cut Mil $	AGN	8) Farm Sub Lmt	FOR	13) Nixon Sewer Veto	FOR
4) Rev Shrg	AGN	9) School Prayr	FOR	14) Corp Cmpaign $	FOR
5) Pub TV $	AGN	10) Cnsumr Prot	AGN	15) Pol $ Disclosr	AGN

Election Results

1972 general:	John Rousselot (R)	144,057	(70%)
	Luther Mandell (D)	61,326	(30%)
1972 primary:	John Rousselot (R), unopposed		
1970 general:	John Rousselot (R)	124,071	(65%)
	Myrlie Evers (D)	61,777	(32%)
	Brian Sconlon (AI)	3,018	(2%)
	Harold Kaplan (PF)	1,858	(1%)

TWENTY-FIFTH DISTRICT   Political Background

The 25th congressional district is the lineal descendant of that part of California once (1947–50) represented by a young Navy veteran named Richard M. Nixon. In the days when Alger Hiss made headlines, it was a larger district with fewer people. But the basic terrain is much the same: a string of suburbs east of Los Angeles. The district, as now constituted, also contains part of Whittier, where Nixon grew up and went to college. In California, many fundamental social distinctions rest on topography: whether you live in the valley or up the hill. The latter, of course, is preferable—initially because you had a view, now because you breathe less smog. The 25th today is mainly a hill district, with most of its voters in higher-altitude suburbs like Azusa, Glendora, or San Dimas, just below the towering San Gabriel Mountains; or Whittier, next to the La Puente Hills; or La Habra, at the northern edge of Orange County.

This district was the 12th in Nixon's day, and the rise in numerical designation reflects both the explosive postwar growth of California and the number of times the state's congressional districts have been redrawn. There is a lesson to be learned here for future redistricters: one can get too cute and excessively piggish trying to achieve political advantage. The Democrats who redrew the congressional boundaries in 1961 wanted very much to oust Republican Rep. John Rousselot, a member of the John Birch Society (see California 24). By adroit craftsmanship, they managed to do so, but only by a hair. Then, in 1966, the Reagan tide came in, and the Democratic incumbent was easily unseated. Democratic territory that would have been useful in other districts was now stuck in the safely Republican 25th, while Republican territory left out of the 25th lay in neighboring districts, endangering the chances of Democratic incumbents.

Ironically, Congressman Charles Wiggins' old home town of El Monte, where he was Mayor before winning his first House election in 1966, is no longer in the district. Wiggins is one of those anonymous and at the same time competent members of Congress who seldom receives national publicity, but still maintains his popularity at home at a high level. He is ranking minority member on the Judiciary Subcommittee, with oversight of civil-rights matters; here Wiggins works with Chairman Don Edwards, a fellow Californian. Wiggins holds the same position on the House Select Committee on Crime. The estimate of this body, chaired by Florida's Claude Pepper, is in some dispute. Some think it is just a traveling road show intended to bolster reelection prospects; hearings have been held across the country, often in members' districts. Others think that it has come up with some of Washington's most competent work on crime. At the beginning of the 93rd Congress, the House voted to allow the committee just six more months to prepare its recommendations. It was never intended to be a permanent operation, but Chairman Pepper, for one, indicated he hoped it would have a longer life.

Wiggins' biggest moment in the national spotlight came in 1970, when he proposed that the Equal Rights Amendment (ERA) not strike down laws that, for purposes of public health and safety, distinguish between the sexes. Proponents of ERA argued that this would gut the amendment. Wiggins said that it would preserve laws that discriminate legitimately because of the physical differences between male and female. Despite the quality of Wiggins' advocacy, his amendment was defeated by a large margin in what was the key congressional vote on the ERA.

Census Data Pop. 463,077. Central city, 0%; suburban, 100%. Median family income, $12,549; families above $15,000: 34%; families below $3,000: 4%. Median years education, 12.5.

1972 Share of Federal Outlays $576,924,109

DOD	$244,661,000	HEW	$166,414,064
AEC	$1,932,840	HUD	$6,437,626
NASA	$32,945,856	DOI	$802,132
DOT	$15,637,902	USDA	$9,243,006
		Other	$98,849,683

Federal Military-Industrial Commitments

DOD Contractors. Aerojet General (Azusa), $71.729m: repair of Vietnam damaged helicopter weapons system. Honeywell (West Covina), $20.844m: design and production of radar and sonar devices. Ajax Hardware (City of Industry), $5.912m: design and production of gear and pinion assemblies.

Economic Base Finance, insurance and real estate; transportation equipment, especially aircraft; electrical equipment and supplies, especially radio and television communication equipment, and electronic components and accessories; machinery, especially electronic computing equipment; and fabricated metal products, especially fabricated structural metal products.

The Voters

Registration 228,327 total. 110,375 D (48%); 102,639 R (45%); 12,430 declined to state (5%); 2,883 other (1%).
Median voting age 39.7
Employment profile White collar, 55%. Blue collar, 34%. Service, 11%. Farm, –%.
Ethnic groups Black, 1%. Spanish, 17%. Total foreign stock, 21% Canada, 3%; UK, Italy, Germany, 2% each.

Presidential vote

1972	Nixon (R)	126,156	(70%)
	McGovern (D)	53,059	(30%)
1968	Nixon (R)	94,681	(59%)
	Humphrey (D)	54,939	(34%)
	Wallace (AI)	11,204	(7%)

Representative

Charles E. **Wiggins** (R) Elected 1966; b. Dec. 3, 1927, El Monte; home, El Monte; U. of So. Calif., B.A., 1953, LL.B., 1956; Army, WWII and Korean War; married, two children; Methodist.

Career Practicing atty., 1957–66; Chm., El Monte Planning Commission, 1954–60; Councilman, Mayor, El Monte, 1960–66.

Offices 229 CHOB, 202-225-4111. Also Suite 301, U.S. Life Bldg., 225 N. Barranca, West Covina 91791, 213-332-4025.

Administrative Assistant Patrick Rowland

Committees

House Administration (9th); Subs: Police; Printing.

Judiciary (6th); Subs: No. 1 (Immigration and Nationality); No. 4 (Bankruptcy and Civil Rights Oversight) (Ranking Mbr.).

Sel. Com. on Committees (3rd).

Sel. Com. on Crime (Ranking Mbr.).

Group Ratings

	ADA	COPE	LWV	RIPON	NFU	LCV	CFA	NAB	NSI	ACA
1972	6	13	56	60	29	40	50	100	100	63
1971	14	20	60	56	8	–	20	–	–	83
1970	16	0	–	53	27	0	35	80	90	71

Key Votes

1) Busing	AGN	6) Cmbodia Bmbg	FOR	11) Chkg Acct Intrst	AGN
2) Strip Mines	AGN	7) Bust Hwy Trust	FOR	12) End HISC (HUAC)	AGN
3) Cut Mil $	AGN	8) Farm Sub Lmt	AGN	13) Nixon Sewer Veto	FOR
4) Rev Shrg	FOR	9) School Prayr	AGN	14) Corp Cmpaign $	FOR
5) Pub TV $	AGN	10) Cnsumr Prot	AGN	15) Pol $ Disclosr	FOR

Election Results

1972 general:	Charles E. Wiggins (R)	118,631	(65%)
	Leslie W. Craven (D)	58,323	(32%)
	Alfred Ramirez (AI)	5,697	(3%)
1972 primary:	Charles E. Wiggins (R), unopposed		
1970 general:	Charles E. Wiggins (R)	116,169	(63%)
	Leslie W. Craven (D)	64,386	(35%)
	Kevin Scanlon (AI)	2,994	(2%)

TWENTY-SIXTH DISTRICT Political Background

Hollywood, everybody tells us, is dying. The great movie studios auction off old props, films are shot in Spain or New Mexico where costs are lower, and the great moguls of the studios are now dead, with their successors having a fraction of the old tyrants' power. All true. But there is still plenty of Show Biz in western Los Angeles. If some movie studios have shut down, Universal is still booming and Paramount is prospering, having produced The Godfather. And if there is less work around Los Angeles in the movies, there is more in television, an industry where California has supplanted New York. Though actors, technicians, and writers often complain that they are underpaid, there is work in television. And if TV is a less-than-satisfying medium artistically, the same criticism was made of the movies during their heyday in the 1930s and 1940s.

California Show Biz is still centralized on the west side of Los Angeles and almost entirely within the confines of the 26th congressional district. Here you will find much of Hollywood itself—with a rather disappointing Hollywood Boulevard and tawdry stucco side streets—and, farther west, the gaudy Sunset Strip. To the south and west is Beverly Hills and the new office center of Century City (built on the site of the Fox studios). To the north, their precipitous rise dominating the few smogless days, are the Santa Monica Mountains, among which are picturesque houses built along steep canyons or on flat-topped hills. North of the mountains, the 26th extends to downtown Burbank and, in the other direction, to comfortable Sherman Oaks. Here in the 26th are most of the old movie and new TV studios, almost all the agents and production companies, and the homes of the actors, extras, and cameramen.

Show Biz is in many ways a Jewish industry, and the 26th has the largest Jewish population of any congressional district west of the Hudson River. Not everyone here lives on well-manicured streets and in the spacious houses of Beverly Hills; there are also the neat middle-class streets of the Fairfax district, an older Jewish neighborhood, and the somewhat newer, but otherwise similar precinct of North Hollywood on the other side of the mountains.

Except for the 1972 presidential race, the 26th has been one of the most dependably liberal and Democratic districts in the country. It is one of especial import to national politicians. Within the district's boundaries, or within a mile or so of them, a huge percentage of national campaign funds—particularly for Democrats, but also for Republicans—are raised. In this respect, as in others, California seems to be supplanting New York. The political preferences of the late Eugene Wyman, a successful Beverly Hills lawyer and legendary Democratic fund-raiser, were watched closely by the national press in 1970 and 1972. Following his death at 49 in early 1973, his work is being carried on by his widow, herself an accomplished politico having served on the Los Angeles City Council while still in her twenties.

Curiously, the 26th has never had a Jewish Congressman, though it has been represented by a string of famous people. For one, James Roosevelt (1955–65), son of FDR; the younger Roosevelt's endorsement of Richard Nixon in 1972 coincided with the legal troubles of Investors Overseas Services (IOS), of which he had been Vice-President. For another, Sam Yorty (1951–55), a three-term Mayor of Los Angeles and a hawkishly conservative Democrat (turned Republican after his 1973 defeat) with a lefty political past. And finally, Helen Gahagan Douglas (1945–51), wife of actor Melvyn Douglas and once an actress herself. Loser to Richard Nixon in the 1950 Senate race, Mrs. Douglas was the one smeared as the "Pink Lady" in the campaign.

The district's current Congressman, Thomas M. Rees, has so far had a more conventional, less theatrical political career. When he went to Congress after winning a 1965 special election, Rees was a 10-year veteran of the California legislature. Back in those days, before one-man-one-vote, he was the sole state Senator from Los Angeles County (1970 pop. 7,032,000), representing more people than any other state legislator in American history. Rees has usually voted with the liberal, antiwar bloc of Democrats; he is particularly interested in mass-transit legislation and congressional reform and is known for his puckish sense of humor. But Rees has had a hard time on the Banking and Currency Committee. According to the Nader Congress Project Report, Rees thinks that populistic Chairman Wright Patman runs the committee poorly.

Patman, in turn, seems to doubt Rees' commitment to issues, and it is true that the Californian, like many members of the Banking Committee, owns bank stock. Patman's suspicions seem to have been justified by an incident in early 1973. Rees strongly supported a rent-control measure in committee and on the floor. But when in conference to iron out differences between the House and Senate versions of the bill, Rees voted against rent control. He later justified his action by saying that the measure was rejected overwhelmingly in the House. Conferees are supposed to represent the views of their house of Congress, even when that view conflicts with their own personal one. But this rule is honored mainly in the breach.

Rees' other committee assignment is District of Columbia—one he sought, without initial success, in 1972. At that time, Chairman John McMillan of South Carolina tried to keep him off, but could find no Southerner willing to take the post. Now that McMillan has left the Congress involuntarily (see South Carolina 6), Rees serves as Chairman of the Revenue and Financial Affairs Subcommittee. Here he will probably play a role in deciding the tough financial questions—for example, how much money the federal government will give the District in lieu of property taxes—before home rule can be enacted.

Census Data Pop. 463,630. Central city, 81%; suburban, 19%. Median family income, $12,281; families above $15,000: 38%; families below $3,000: 7%. Median years education, 12.7.

1972 Share of Federal Outlays $592,387,487

DOD	$243,844,390	HEW	$172,685,643
AEC	$2,129,139	HUD	$7,068,838
NASA	$35,730,544	DOI	$777,150
DOT	$1,714,190	USDA	$9,740,391
		Other	$118,697,211

Federal Military-Industrial Commitments

NASA Contractors Litton Systems (Los Angeles), $5.065m: spectrometry and gas chromatography studies.

Economic Base Finance, insurance and real estate; tourism; transportation equipment, especially aircraft; electrical equipment and supplies, especially radio and television communication equipment, and electronic components and accessories; and machinery, especially electronic computing equipment.

The Voters

Registration 315,743 total. 200,070 D (63%); 92,129 R (29%); 19,978 declined to state (6%); 3,566 other (1%).
Median voting age 49.0
Employment profile White collar, 74%. Blue collar, 16%. Service, 10%. Farm, –%.
Ethnic groups Black, 10%. Japanese, 1%. Spanish, 7%. Total foreign stock, 44%. USSR, 10%; Poland, 5%; Canada, UK, Germany, 3% each; Austria, Hungary, Italy, 2% each.

Presidential vote

1972	Nixon (R)	111,555	(45%)
	McGovern (D)	135,535	(55%)
1968	Nixon (R)	85,809	(37%)
	Humphrey (D)	139,458	(60%)
	Wallace (AI)	5,070	(2%)

Representative

Thomas M. Rees (D) Elected 1965; b. Mar. 26, 1925, Los Angeles; home, Los Angeles; Occidental Col., B.A., 1950; Army, WWII; married, two children; Episcopal.

Career Calif. Assembly, 1954–62; Calif. Senate, 1962–65.

Offices 1112 LHOB, 202-225-5911. Also 816 S. Robertson Blvd., Los Angeles 90035, 213-652-4000, and 13535 Ventura Blvd., Sherman Oaks, 213-990-2370.

Administrative Assistant Janes Faulstich

Committees

Banking and Currency (14th); Subs: Domestic Finance; International Finance; International Trade.

District of Columbia (5th); Subs: Judiciary; Revenue and Financial Affairs (Chm.).

Group Ratings

	ADA	COPE	LWV	RIPON	NFU	LCV	CFA	NAB	NSI	ACA
1972	88	73	100	64	71	79	100	9	11	4
1971	84	91	100	82	93	–	100	–	–	0
1970	88	100	–	76	100	85	100	8	0	0

Key Votes

1) Busing	FOR	6) Cmbodia Bmbg	AGN	11) Chkg Acct Intrst	FOR
2) Strip Mines	AGN	7) Bust Hwy Trust	FOR	12) End HISC (HUAC)	FOR
3) Cut Mil $	ABS	8) Farm Sub Lmt	AGN	13) Nixon Sewer Veto	AGN
4) Rev Shrg	AGN	9) School Prayr	AGN	14) Corp Cmpaign $	ABS
5) Pub TV $	FOR	10) Cnsumr Prot	FOR	15) Pol $ Disclosr	FOR

Election Results

1972 general:	Thomas M. Rees (D)	164,351	(69%)
	Philip Robert Rutta	66,731	(28%)
	Mike Timko (PF)	8,313	(3%)
1972 primary:	Thomas M. Rees (D)	97,637	(86%)
	Alan Albert Snow (D)	5,675	(5%)
	Evelyn Elledge (D)	5,578	(5%)
	Eileen Anderson (D)	4,498	(4%)
1970 general:	Thomas M. Rees (D)	130,499	(71%)
	Nathaniel Friedman (R)	47,260	(26%)
	Lewis McCammon (PF)	3,677	(2%)
	Howard E. Hallinan (AI)	1,639	(1%)

TWENTY-SEVENTH DISTRICT Political Background

California's 27th congressional district is the western half of the San Fernando Valley, the southern portion of Ventura County, and a sparsely populated strip connecting the two, comprised of the Santa Monica Mountains and part of Malibu Beach. The district has been done over completely since its first creation in 1961, and today contains none of the same territory as its lineal predecessor. The explanation, as usual, is political. The 27th was first set up to defeat Republican Rep. Edgar Hiestand, who was a member of the John Birch Society. It succeeded in doing that, but the Democrat who won, a veteran of the well-organized and efficient California Assembly, became so disgusted with the trudging, slow pace of the House that he quit after one term. This left the race in 1964 without an incumbent, with the eventual winner being Ed Reinecke, a genial Republican campaigner who had seized the pornography issue. Reinecke is conservative enough to have been chosen Lieutenant Governor by Ronald Reagan when Robert Finch left Sacramento for his ill-starred stint in the Nixon Administration. And the next winner of a district originally designed to oust a Bircher was Barry Goldwater, Jr.

The current district lines make good sense given the rationale behind the most recent redistricting plan adopted: protect all incumbents. The western half of the San Fernando Valley is a prosperous, solidly Republican area. The Ventura County portion includes the city of Oxnard, with its large Mexican-American population, and leans Democratic. Redistricters included Oxnard, not to help Goldwater (who doesn't need it), but to remove Democratic votes from the 13th district of Republican Charles Teague, who was pressed more closely than usual in 1970. In 1972, Goldwater's percentage was reduced sharply; he carried the Ventura portion by only 46 votes and his overall margin was only 57–43. That is still enough, however, to suggest future wins.

Goldwater does not cut a particularly notable figure in the House, although he is ranking Republican on a subcommittee with jurisdiction over an area much in the headlines, Science and Astronautics' Energy Subcommittee. It has been noted that he lacks his father's fervor and sense of humor. Shortly after his first election, young Barry was once seen dozing in the Senate gallery as his father delivered a speech. But the Congressman is still young (36 in 1974), and at his age, Goldwater, Sr., was still running the family department store in Phoenix. The Californian's voting record is of course staunchly conservative.

Census Data Pop. 464,135. Central city, 88%; suburban, 12%. Median family income, $13,811; families above $15,000: 44%; families below $3,000: 5%. Median years education, 12.7.

1972 Share of Federal Outlays $567,389,403

DOD	$262,693,000	HEW	$158,327,488
AEC	$1,516,432	HUD	$7,406,112
NASA	$25,235,947	DOI	$747,172
DOT	$13,547,067	USDA	$8,187,677
		Other	$89,728,508

Federal Military-Industrial Commitments

DOD Contractors Litton Systems (Woodland Hills), $52.941m: various inertial navigation systems; other electronic ware. Hughes Aircraft (Canoga Park), $24.648m: various electronic research projects; redesign of fire control system of F-106 aircraft.
DOD Installations Naval Air Station (Point Mugu). Naval Construction Battalion Center (Port Hueneme). Navy Pacific Missile Range (Point Mugu); closed, 1974.
NASA Contractors North American Rockwell (Canoga Park), $35.649m: support for Saturn engines; design for space shuttle engine.
AEC Operations North American Rockwell (Canoga Park), $15.264m: support for Breeder Reactor Program.

Economic Base Finance, insurance and real estate; transportation equipment, especially aircraft; agriculture, notably fruits, vegetables, cattle and poultry; tourism; and electrical equipment and supplies.

The Voters

Registration 258,183 total. 131,865 D (51%); 107,673 R (42%); 14,768 declined to state (6%); 3,877 other (2%).
Median voting age 40.1
Employment profile White collar, 64%. Blue collar, 24%. Service, 10%. Farm, 2%.
Ethnic groups Black, 1%. Spanish, 13%. Total foreign stock, 26%. Canada, 3%; USSR, UK, Germany, Italy, 2% each; Poland, 1%.

Presidential vote

1972	Nixon (R)	129,909	(64%)
	McGovern (D)	74,361	(36%)
1968	Nixon (R)	89,544	(55%)
	Humphrey (D)	66,422	(41%)
	Wallace (AI)	7,959	(5%)

Representative

Barry M. Goldwater, Jr. (R) Elected 1968; b. July 15, 1938, Los Angeles; home, Burbank; Staunton Military Acad., U. of Colo., 1957–60; Ariz. State U., B.A., 1962; married; Episcopalian.

Career Stock brokerage firm, 1962–69, partner, 1968–69.

Offices 1423 LHOB, 202-225-4461. Also Suite 200, 18751 Ventura Blvd., Tarzana 91356, 213-345-2345.

Administrative Assistant William McClain

Committees

Interstate and Foreign Commerce (15th); Subs: Communications and Power.

Science and Astronautics (6th); Subs: Aeronautics and Space Technology; Energy (Ranking Mbr.); Space Science and Applications.

Group Ratings

	ADA	COPE	LWV	RIPON	NFU	LCV	CFA	NAB	NSI	ACA
1972	0	10	20	38	50	32	0	91	100	86
1971	14	5	25	43	10	–	33	–	–	96
1970	0	9	–	27	25	45	50	91	100	88

Key Votes

1) Busing	AGN	6) Cmbodia Bmbg	FOR	11) Chkg Acct Intrst	FOR
2) Strip Mines	FOR	7) Bust Hwy Trust	FOR	12) End HISC (HUAC)	AGN
3) Cut Mil $	AGN	8) Farm Sub Lmt	AGN	13) Nixon Sewer Veto	FOR
4) Rev Shrg	AGN	9) School Prayr	FOR	14) Corp Cmpaign $	FOR
5) Pub TV $	ABS	10) Cnsumr Prot	AGN	15) Pol $ Disclosr	AGN

Election Results

1972 general:	Barry Goldwater, Jr. (R)	119,475	(43%)
	Mark S. Novak (D)	88,548	(57%)
1972 primary:	Barry Goldwater, Jr. (R), unopposed		
1970 general:	Barry Goldwater, Jr. (R)	139,326	(67%)
	N. Toni Kimmel (D)	63,652	(30%)
	Edward Richer (PF)	3,306	(2%)
	John Hind (AI)	2,642	(1%)

TWENTY-EIGHTH DISTRICT **Political Background**

The 28th California district is surely a finalist in the nation's most grotesquely shaped congressional district contest. The bulk of the district's land area lies in the Santa Monica Mountains, a rugged range that contains, in its canyons and on its hilltops, some of the most elegant and expensive housing in Los Angeles: Bel Air, Brentwood, Benedict Canyon, among others. From here, the district proceeds southward along the Pacific Ocean, except for a wierd bulge inward allowing the 28th to take in the upper-middle-income and Republican Palms district, and Culver City, home of MGM. At its southern tip, some 50 miles from Malibu, there is the Palos Verdes peninsula, a high-income clump of mountainous subdivisions that stick out into the ocean from the flat Los Angeles Basin plain.

Connecting Palos Verdes to the distant mountains is a narrow strip of beach towns, only a block wide at one point. Historically, the beach area has been heavily Republican, the voting habits of its towns—Santa Monica, Venice (actually part of L.A.), and Manhattan, Hermosa, and Redondo Beaches—dominated by the conservatism of elderly Midwestern migrants. Yet mortality and mobility have produced a sharp leftward trend in recent years. The beach towns are now filling up with young people—singles, freaks, surfers, whatever—whose political instincts lead them to oppose the politics and social values of Ronald Reagan and Richard Nixon. Another factor in the 28th's Democratic surge is the presence of UCLA within its borders. It is less important, however, than other University of California campuses; the NCAA basketball champions attend what is mainly a commuter school. Because housing in the immediate area is too expensive for most students, the hottest campus issue is demand for more parking space.

The 28th is a district that went for Barry Goldwater in 1964, but in 1972 showed a swing toward the Democratic ticket despite the McGovern debacle. The swing should, one might suppose, cause some problems for Republican Congressman Alphonzo Bell, but it hasn't yet. Bell is heir to an oil and aircraft fortune (his family name memorialized in the suburbs of Bell and Bell Gardens) who has a reputation as a political moderate. It is not that he has a voting record like a Massachusetts Republican; against the California setting, however, he contrasts sharply with Reagan and Reaganites. In 1969, he ran for Mayor of Los Angeles, making a respectable showing even while being eliminated in the primary. He then enraged big Reagan backers like oilman Henry Salvatori by supporting black Councilman Thomas Bradley over Mayor Sam Yorty. Yorty won in 1969, but in a 1973 rerun Bradley trounced the flamboyant incumbent.

In 1970, as a result of Bell's 1969 support of Bradley, the Congressman faced well-financed conservative opposition in the Republican primary, which Bell won by only a 56–44 margin. It is a measure of the Democratic trend in California generally and the 28th in particular that in 1972 Bell had no primary opponent, while five Democrats took the trouble to seek the nomination to oppose him.

After a dozen years in the House, Bell enjoys high-ranking positions on both the Science and Astronautics and Education and Labor Committees. The former is of importance to the district, which depends heavily on the aerospace industry. On the latter, Bell's primary interest is education, and he has often teamed with 21st-district Democrat Augustus Hawkins in proposing legislation.

Census Data   Pop. 460,679. Central city, 47%; suburban, 53%. Median family income, $13,756; families above $15,000: 45%; families below $3,000: 5%. Median years education, 12.9.

1972 Share of Federal Outlays $588,808,107

DOD	$242,371,010	HEW	$171,642,215
AEC	$2,116,274	HUD	$7,026,126
NASA	$35,514,649	DOI	$772,454
DOT	$17,037,787	USDA	$9,681,537
		Other	$102,646,055

Federal Military-Industrial Commitments

DOD Contractors Western Electric (Santa Monica), $127.778m: support for ABM system. Systems Development Corp. (Santa Monica), $22.470m: various computer software services. McDonnell Douglas Corp. (Santa Monica), $19.850m: research and development for the ABM system. Rand Corp. (Santa Monica), $16.907m: various strategic studies. Lear Siegler (Santa Monica), $14.104m: design and production of various aircraft electronic ware. Northrop (Palos Verde), $9.161m: design and production of aircraft cockpit display units.
DOD Installations Los Angeles AF Station (Los Angeles).
NASA Contractors McDonnell Douglas (Santa Monica), $68.402m: Delta space research vehicle; Thor space boosters; support for Appollo, Skylab, Saturn vehicles.

Economic Base Finance, insurance and real estate; transportation equipment, especially aircraft; tourism; electrical equipment and supplies, especially radio and television communication equipment, and electronic components and accessories; and machinery, especially electronic computing equipment. Also higher education (Univ. of California, Los Angeles).

The Voters

Registration 307,488 total. 156,338 D (51%); 123,091 R (40%); 23,070 declined to state (8%); 4,989 other (2%).
Median voting age 41.6
Employment profile White collar, 71%. Blue collar, 19%. Service, 10%. Farm, –%.
Ethnic groups Black, 1%. Japanese, 2%. Spanish, 10%. Total foreign stock, 33%. Canada, 4%; UK, USSR, Germany, 3% each; Poland, 2%; Italy, 1%.

Presidential vote

1972	Nixon (R)	133,911	(56%)
	McGovern (D)	104,629	(44%)
1968	Nixon (R)	106,142	(53%)
	Humphrey (D)	84,366	(43%)
	Wallace (AI)	7,917	(4%)

Representative

Alphonzo Bell (R) Elected 1960; b. Sept. 19, 1914, Los Angeles; home, Los Angeles; Occidental Col., B.A., 1938; Army Air Corps, WWII; married, nine children; Presbyterian.

Career Pres., Chm., Bell Petroleum Co., 1938– ; Chm., Calif. Repub. Central Com., 1956–58; Chm., Repub. Central Com. of Los Angeles County, 1958–60.

Offices 113 CHOB, 202-225-6451. Also Rm. 14220, New Fed. Bldg., 11000 Wilshire Blvd., Los Angeles 90024, 213-478-0111.

Administrative Assistant Janet Kuhn (L.A.)

Committees

Education and Labor (3rd); Subs: No. 1 (Education) (Ranking Mbr.); No. 7 (Equal Opportunities).

Science and Astronautics (2nd); Subs: International Cooperation in Science and Space; Manned Space Flight; Science, Research, and Development (Ranking Mbr.).

Group Ratings

	ADA	COPE	LWV	RIPON	NFU	LCV	CFA	NAB	NSI	ACA
1972	31	67	100	50	17	15	100	50	100	33
1971	24	60	75	60	21	–	63	–	–	62
1970	28	50	–	83	56	17	63	78	100	62

Key Votes

1) Busing	ABS	6) Cmbodia Bmbg	FOR	11) Chkg Acct Intrst	AGN
2) Strip Mines	ABS	7) Bust Hwy Trust	FOR	12) End HISC (HUAC)	ABS
3) Cut Mil $	ABS	8) Farm Sub Lmt	ABS	13) Nixon Sewer Veto	FOR
4) Rev Shrg	FOR	9) School Prayr	ABS	14) Corp Cmpaign $	ABS
5) Pub TV $	ABS	10) Cnsumr Prot	FOR	15) Pol $ Disclsr	ABS

Election Results

1972 general:	Alphonzo Bell (R)	144,815	(61%)
	Michael Shapiro (D)	89,517	(38%)
	Jack Hampton (PF)	4,297	(2%)
1972 primary:	Alphonzo Bell (R), unopposed		
1970 general:	Alphonzo Bell (R)	154,691	(69%)
	Don McLaughlin (D)	57,882	(26%)
	Derek Gordon (AI)	5,759	(3%)
	Jane Gordon (PF)	4,971	(2%)

TWENTY-NINTH DISTRICT Political Background

Part of Los Angeles and a string of suburbs to the east make up the 29th district of California. It begins just north of downtown L.A., in the Silver Lake and Highland Park districts—once middle-class residential areas, now predominantly Mexican-American. From the Los Angeles city limits, the 29th heads east along the San Bernardino Freeway, encompassing Alhambra, Monterey Park, San Gabriel, Rosemead, El Monte, and Baldwin Park. These are mainly valley, lower-middle-class suburbs; richer people live in the shadows of the San Gabriel Mountains to the north. These suburbs are also among the area's heaviest hit by the Los Angeles smog.

The 29th was intended to be a Democratic district, and, except for a few lapses, still is. Unlike some other blue-collar districts nearby (e.g., the old 23rd), it has not shifted sharply to the Republicans. But the difference lies not so much in the attitude of its white residents as in a substantial population increase of Mexican-Americans here. Los Angeles' large Chicano community has not, as some might suppose, followed the migration patterns of the city's blacks. Rather, as they attain middle-class incomes and status, they have moved southeast and east from the East Los Angeles barrio into what has been white working-class territory.

For eight years after its creation, the 29th was represented by Democrat George Brown. In 1970, he ran for the Senate and lost to John Tunney in the Democratic primary; he currently represents another district in the House (see California 38). Brown was one of the foremost peace advocates in the House. His successor is a man of less controversial views, George Danielson. The new Congressman won a close primary against a Mexican-American in 1970; Danielson was then a state Senator—a nice launching pad for a congressional candidacy, since California state Senate constituencies are now larger than U.S. House districts. In 1972, Danielson had no primary opposition and won the general election by a near two-to-one margin. All of this indicates a long career ahead, assuming that a Chicano is not able to spring a surprise in some future primary, for some 39% of the district's people are now of Spanish heritage. For 1974, the Special Masters' redistricting plan (see state write-up) has given Danielson an even more heavily Mexican-American district. So potential trouble for the incumbent lies ahead.

Census Data Pop. 463,773. Central city, 41%; suburban, 59%. Median family income, $9,534; families above $15,000: 19%; families below $3,000: 9%. Median years education, 12.1.

1972 Share of Federal Outlays $592,387,487

DOD	$243,844,390	HEW	$172,685,634
AEC	$2,129,139	HUD	$7,068,838
NASA	$35,730,544	DOI	$777,150
DOT	$1,714,190	USDA	$9,740,391
		Other	$118,697,211

Federal Military-Industrial Commitments

DOD Contractors Aerojet General (El Monte), $5.785m: various electronic ware.

Economic Base Finance, insurance and real estate; transportation equipment, especially aircraft; electrical equipment and supplies, especially radio and television communication equipment, and electronic components and accessories; machinery, especially electronic computing equipment; and fabricated metal products, especially fabricated structural metal products. Also higher education (Cal State, Los Angeles).

The Voters

Registration 198,022 total. 121,497 D (61%); 57,675 R (29%); 12,168 declined to state (6%); 6,682 other (3%).
Median voting age 42.0
Employment profile White collar, 49%. Blue collar, 40%. Service, 11%. Farm, –%.
Ethnic groups Japanese, 3%. Chinese, 2%. Spanish, 39%. Total foreign stock, 41%. Italy, 3%; Canada, Germany, UK, 2% each.

Presidential vote

1972	Nixon (R)	80,484	(54%)
	McGovern (D)	67,490	(46%)
1968	Nixon (R)	66,536	(44%)
	Humphrey (D)	74,066	(49%)
	Wallace (AI)	9,797	(7%)

Representative

George E. Danielson (D) Elected 1970; b. Feb. 20, 1915, Wausa, Nebr.; home, Los Angeles; U. of Nebr., B.A., 1937, J.D., 1939; Navy, WWII; Lt. USNR; married; Protestant.

Career Lawyer; Sp. agent, FBI; Asst. U.S. Atty. in So. Dist. of Calif., 1949–51; Assemblyman, 1962–66; State Senator, 1966–70.

Offices 318 CHOB, 202-225-5464. Also 312 N. Spring St., Los Angeles 90012, 213-688-3454, and 11001 Valley Mall, El Monte 91731, 213-444-9503.

Administrative Assistant Ray Sebens

Committees

Judiciary (14th); Subs: No. 2 (Claims); No. 3 (Patents, Trademarks and Copyrights).

Veterans' Affairs (11th); Subs: Education and Training; Hospitals; Insurance.

Group Ratings

	ADA	COPE	LWV	RIPON	NFU	LCV	CFA	NAB	NSI	ACA
1972	75	91	64	75	83	82	50	8	40	29
1971	73	92	100	69	87	–	75	–	–	15

Key Votes

1) Busing	AGN	6) Cmbodia Bmbg	AGN	11) Chkg Acct Intrst	AGN
2) Strip Mines	AGN	7) Bust Hwy Trust	FOR	12) End HISC (HUAC)	FOR
3) Cut Mil $	FOR	8) Farm Sub Lmt	AGN	13) Nixon Sewer Veto	AGN
4) Rev Shrg	FOR	9) School Prayr	AGN	14) Corp Cmpaign $	FOR
5) Pub TV $	FOR	10) Cnsumr Prot	FOR	15) Pol $ Disclosr	AGN

Election Results

1972 general:	George E. Danielson (D)	92,856	(63%)
	Richard E. Ferraro (R)	49,590	(34%)
	John W. Blaine (PF)	5,552	(4%)
1972 primary:	George E. Danielson (D), unopposed		
1970 general:	George E. Danielson (D)	71,308	(63%)
	Tom McMann (R)	42,620	(37%)

THIRTIETH DISTRICT Political Background

The 1970 census tells us that almost 16% of all Californians are of "Spanish heritage." The vast majority of these people, of course, are Mexican-Americans, who constitute the largest and, in many respects, the most hidden ethnic group in the state. California blacks live in well-defined areas in a few cities, but Mexican-Americans can be found all over the state; no congressional district has less than 5% "Spanish heritage." Certainly there are large predominantly Mexican-American areas, most notably on the east side of Los Angeles and in several adjacent suburbs. But in general Chicanos seem to blend in more easily with working-class whites than do blacks.

Politically, the Mexican-Americans are the most underrepresented group in the state. California sends three blacks to the House, but only one of its forty-three Congressmen is of Spanish origin. There are no Mexican-American state Senators, and only six (out of eighty) Assemblymen. The situation stems more from design than accident. The Republicans, led by Gov. Ronald Reagan, have charged, with considerable justification, that Democratic redistricters tend to divide up the Mexican-American population among several districts—thereby increasing Democratic margins in each—rather than consolidating the group's voting strength. The Republicans would like to consolidate the Mexican-Americans, which would probably increase the number of Chicano legislators and decrease the number of Democratic ones.

The only California congressional district with anything like a majority of Mexican-Americans is the 30th. It centers on downtown Los Angeles, and reaches westward across MacArthur Park to Hollywood. The bulk of the Spanish-speaking population is toward the east, in the Boyle Heights district of Los Angeles, and in the unincorporated suburb of East Los Angeles. The district, to meet the population standard, also includes a couple of white working-class suburbs to the south.

The 30th is one of the poorest and most Democratic districts in California. Every two years since it was created following the 1960 census, the 30th has routinely returned Congressman Edward Roybal to the House. Roybal, though of Spanish descent, is hardly out of the barrio; instead, he is out of a well-to-do family from Albuquerque, New Mexico, where the Spanish-speaking community antedates Plymouth Rock. Immediately prior to his election to Congress, Roybal served as president pro tem of the Los Angeles City Council.

It has taken Roybal a while to find a comfortable committee niche in the Congress. Assigned at first to Foreign Affairs, he found himself frustrated by the committee's leadership, inclined as it was to follow the Johnson and Nixon administrations wherever they might lead. After building up some seniority, he switched in 1971 to Appropriations. There he has yet to rise to a subcommittee chairmanship. But as one of the still small number of liberals on the committee, he may hope to play some part in the struggles of Congress with the executive for control of the federal budget.

Census Data Pop. 466,629. Central city, 70%; suburban, 30%. Median family income, $7,768; families above $15,000: 14%; families below $3,000: 13%. Median years education, 11.5.

1972 Share of Federal Outlays $595,966,868

DOD	$245,317,770	HEW	$173,729,051
AEC	$2,142,004	HUD	$7,111,550
NASA	$35,946,439	DOI	$781,846
DOT	$17,244,933	USDA	$9,799,246
		Other	$103,893,599

Federal Military-Industrial Commitments

DOD Contractors Norris Industries (Maywood), $12.328m: Mark 82 bomb bodies. Gold Pak Meat (Los Angeles), $10.292m: foodstuffs. Union Oil (Los Angeles), $6.540m: petroleum products. Ralph M. Parsons, Inc. (Los Angeles), $5.958m: engineering services for Minuteman missile. Salem Packing (Los Angeles), $5.958m: foodstuffs. IBM (Los Angeles), $5.076m: engineering services for various missile systems.

Economic Base Finance, insurance and real estate; transportation equipment, especially aircraft; electrical equipment and supplies, especially radio and television communication equipment, and electronic components and accessories; machinery, especially electronic computing equipment; and fabricated metal products, especially fabricated structural metal products.

The Voters

Registration 167,423 total. 102,967 D (62%); 45,055 R (27%); 11,566 declined to state (7%); 7,835 other (5%).
Median voting age 43.1
Employment profile White collar, 48%. Blue collar, 39%. Service, 13%. Farm, –%.
Ethnic groups Black, 4%. Japanese, 3%. Chinese, 2%. Filipino, 1%. Spanish, 50%. Total foreign stock, 55%. USSR, Canada, Germany, 2% each; UK, Italy, 1% each.

Presidential vote

1972	Nixon (R)	55,563	(48%)
	McGovern (D)	60,305	(52%)
1968	Nixon (R)	48,034	(39%)
	Humphrey (D)	69,489	(56%)
	Wallace (AI)	6,484	(5%)

Representative

Edward R. Roybal (D) Elected 1962; b. Feb. 10, 1916, Albuquerque, N. Mex.; home, Los Angeles; UCLA; Southwestern U.; Army, 1944–45; married, three children; Catholic.

Career Social worker, pub. health educator, Calif. Tuberculosis Assn., 1942–49; Dir. Health Ed., Los Angeles County T.B. and Health Assn., 1945–49; L.A. City Council, 1949–62; Pres. Pro-Tempore, 1961–62; Chm. of Bd., Eastland Savings & Loan Assn.

Offices 2404 RHOB, 202-225-6235. Also Rm. 7110 New Fed. Bldg., N. Los Angeles St., Los Angeles 90012, 213-688-4870.

Administrative Assistant Dan Maldonado

Committees

Appropriations (25th); Subs: Foreign Operations; Legislative; Treasury, Postal Service, General Government.

Group Ratings

	ADA	COPE	LWV	RIPON	NFU	LCV	CFA	NAB	NSI	ACA
1972	100	100	100	56	83	79	100	9	0	10
1971	92	90	88	81	100	–	100	–	–	8
1970	100	100	–	80	92	81	100	0	0	6

Key Votes

1) Busing	FOR	6) Cmbodia Bmbg	AGN	11) Chkg Acct Intrst	FOR
2) Strip Mines	AGN	7) Bust Hwy Trust	FOR	12) End HISC (HUAC)	FOR
3) Cut Mil $	FOR	8) Farm Sub Lmt	AGN	13) Nixon Sewer Veto	AGN
4) Rev Shrg	AGN	9) School Prayr	AGN	14) Corp Cmpaign $	FOR
5) Pub TV $	ABS	10) Cnsumr Prot	FOR	15) Pol $ Disclosr	ABS

Election Results

1972 general:	Edward R. Roybal (D)	78,193	(68%)
	Bill Brophy (R)	32,717	(29%)
	Lewis McCammon (PF)	3,427	(3%)
1972 primary:	Edward R. Roybal (D)	42,176	(86%)
	Imogene Scott (D)	3,694	(8%)
	Walter R. Buchanan (D)	3,367	(7%)
1970 general:	Edward R. Roybal (D)	63,903	(68%)
	Samuel Cavnar (R)	28,038	(30%)
	Boris Belousov (AI)	1,681	(2%)

THIRTY-FIRST DISTRICT Political Background

The 31st district of California is a patch of fairly typical Los Angeles suburbia. Most of it is made up of neat single-family pastel stucco homes, often with a cheap backyard swimming pool and some slightly shabby lawn furniture. There are parcels of still-vacant land here and there alongside newly laid out subdivisions. The 31st also contains gaudy boulevards with strip commercial development and sixties-style shopping centers. Undergirding the economy of the district are huge defense plants like those of North American Rockwell in El Segundo and TRW in Redondo Beach.

Lying between the beach and Watts, the 31st has a pretty wide range of suburbs, from well-to-do Torrance to the predominantly black Hyde Park section of Los Angeles. The most notable fact about this middle-class, politically middle-of-the-road area is that it lies directly in the path of black population movement. In 1970, some 17% of the district's residents were black, with the percentage likely to rise significantly during the decade. But the uptightness that one finds in the more blue-collar area to the east of Watts (see California 23) is not found as much here. The suburb of Inglewood, for example, seems comfortably integrated, and to the south, Gardena has long had a large Japanese-American population. This part of California, one of the spiritual homes of America's drag-race culture, produced Jesse M. Unruh, probably the most talented state legislator of the postwar era and Speaker of the California Assembly from 1961 to 1968.

Among Unruh's many Assembly friends and allies who have gone on to the House of Representatives is Congressman Charles H. Wilson of the 31st. His service in Washington has gone without much notice. An assignment to the Post Office and Civil Service Committee produces few headlines, and the positions he has taken as a member of Armed Services have made it difficult to class him either with its pro-military majority or with its small group of antiwar liberals.

After the 1970 census, redistricting posed some difficult problems for the Democratic state legislature, which wanted to keep Wilson in office. His former district had been much more heavily black; the legislature's goal this time was to keep enough blacks in the district to produce good-sized Democratic majorities in November, but not enough to fuel substantial primary opposition from a black challenger in June. From the looks of the 1972 returns, the legislature managed to achieve both goals. But the Special Masters' redistricting plan (see state write-up) indicates that Wilson will encounter stiff black primary opposition in 1974.

Census Data Pop. 464,595. Central city, 12%; suburban, 88%. Median family income, $11,226; families above $15,000: 27%; families below $3,000: 6%. Median years education, 12.4.

1972 Share of Federal Outlays $593,282,332

DOD	$244,213,000	HEW	$172,946,488
AEC	$2,132,355	HUD	$7,079,516
NASA	$35,784,518	DOI	$778,324
DOT	$17,167,254	USDA	$9,755,104
		Other	$103,425,773

Federal Military-Industrial Commitments

DOD Contractors North American Rockwell (Los Angeles), $284.063m: production and services for various aircraft and missile systems. Northrop (Hawthorne), $266.499m: production of F-5 aircraft; other services for various aircraft. Hughes Aircraft (El Segundo), $195.399m: production of F-14 aircraft weapons system and TOW missile launchers. TRW (Redondo Beach), $131.329m: computer program for targeting Minuteman missile; other design and production of aircraft navigation systems. Aerospace Corp (El Segundo), $70.486m: engineering support for space and missile systems organization. Flying Tiger Corp. (Los Angeles), $284.063m: transportation services. Continental Airlines (Los Angeles), $27.317m: transportation services. Garrett Corp. (Torrance), $15.160m: engines and parts for various aircraft. Teledyne (Hawthorne), $14.336m: various electronic components. Mobil Oil (Torrance), $12.213m: petroleum products. Magnavox (Torrance), $9.104m: various navigation and communication components. Logicon (Torrance), $6.951m: support for various missile and aircraft weapons systems. Xerox (El Segundo), $6.794m: telemetry processing systems.
NASA Contractors TRW (Redondo Beach), $24.332m: various trajectory control programs. Hughes Aircraft (El Segundo), $16.785m: orbiting solar observatories; multi-spectral scanner.

Economic Base Finance, insurance and real estate; transportation equipment, especially aircraft; electrical equipment and supplies, especially radio and television communication equipment, and electronic components and accessories; machinery, especially electronic computing equipment; and fabricated metal products, especially fabricated structural metal products.

The Voters

Registration 225,590 total. 138,400 D (61%); 70,339 R (31%); 13,677 declined to state (6%); 3,174 other (1%).
Median voting age 39.4
Employment profile White collar, 51%. Blue collar, 37%. Service, 12%. Farm, –%.
Ethnic groups Black, 17%. Japanese, 3%. Spanish, 12%. Total foreign stock, 22%. Canada, UK, Germany, 2% each; Italy, 1%.

Presidential vote

1972	Nixon (R)	96,740	(57%)
	McGovern (D)	72,054	(43%)
1968	Nixon (R)	71,664	(45%)
	Humphrey (D)	72,662	(46%)
	Wallace (AI)	13,480	(9%)

Representative

Charles H. **Wilson** (D) Elected 1962; b. Feb. 15, 1917, Magna, Utah; home, Torrance; Army, WWII; married, four children.

Career Founded Charles H. Wilson Insurance Co., 1945; Calif. Assembly, 1954–62.

Offices 2335 RHOB, 202-225-5425. Also 15305 S. Normandie Ave., Gardena 90247, and Rm. 2W30, 150000 Aviation Blvd., Lawndale 90261.

Administrative Assistant John Pontius (L.A.)

Committees

Armed Services (10th); Subs: No. 2; No. 5.

Post Office and Civil Service (7th); Subs: Census and Statistics; Postal Facilities, Mail, and Labor Management (Chm.); Retirement and Employee Benefits.

Group Ratings

	ADA	COPE	LWV	RIPON	NFU	LCV	CFA	NAB	NSI	ACA
1972	38	90	55	60	50	26	50	11	75	44
1971	54	100	66	77	75	–	83	–	–	30
1970	68	100	–	71	100	65	86	0	66	13

Key Votes

1) Busing	AGN	6) Cmbodia Bmbg	AGN	11) Chkg Acct Intrst	AGN
2) Strip Mines	AGN	7) Bust Hwy Trust	FOR	12) End HISC (HUAC)	FOR
3) Cut Mil $	AGN	8) Farm Sub Lmt	FOR	13) Nixon Sewer Veto	FOR
4) Rev Shrg	FOR	9) School Prayr	FOR	14) Corp Cmpaign $	FOR
5) Pub TV $	ABS	10) Cnsumr Prot	FOR	15) Pol $ Disclosr	ABS

Election Results

1972 general:	Charles H. Wilson (D)	87,975	(52%)
	Ben Valentine (R)	71,395	(43%)
	Roberta Lynn Wood (PF)	8,788	(5%)
1972 primary:	Charles H. Wilson (D)	38,295	(51%)
	Jack Shaffer (D)	27,176	(36%)
	Gregory P. Page (D)	9,796	(13%)
1970 general:	Charles H. Wilson (D)	102,071	(73%)
	Fred Casmir (R)	37,416	(27%)

THIRTY-SECOND DISTRICT Political Background

Long Beach (pop. 358,000) is one of the few Los Angeles area suburbs with an urban character of its own. Long Beach has long had a man-made harbor competitive with L.A.'s San Pedro next door; and endowed with a beach that gave the city its name, Long Beach drew thousands of Midwestern migrants during the 1920s and 1930s. Whereupon the place built its own little downtown and boardwalk-cum-amusement park. Back in the thirties, the large number of retirees here contributed to California's zany political reputation, its attachment to welfare schemes like the Townsend Plan and the Ham 'n' Eggs movement (which incidentally helped give Earl Warren the governorship in 1942). Oldtimers can still recall the Iowa picnics of the same period, ones that drew more than 50,000 people to Long Beach.

Today, the atmosphere in Long Beach is different. Most of the town is filled with ordinary middle-class people with families. And retirees are as likely to live in developments like the self-contained Rossmoor Leisure World (just across the line in Orange County) as in the stucco walk-up apartments a couple of blocks from the ocean. Suburbia has grown out to Long Beach and absorbed it.

This newer Long Beach is still the center, despite some boundary changes, of the 32nd congressional district. Under the current redistricting, the 32nd extends far into Orange County, and includes most of Huntington Beach (pop. 115,000) and Fountain Valley. The territory appended here is like the older part of the district in at least one important respect—voting behavior that is solidly Republican and conservative.

And so is its Congressman, Craig Hosmer. A House member since 1952, Hosmer is number-two Republican on the Interior Committee. But he devotes most of his time and thought to the field of atomic energy policy, as the ranking minority member on the Joint Committee on Atomic Energy (JCAE). The Joint Committee is probably involved more closely with the agency it regulates, the AEC, than any other congressional body in Washington; because it is, the committee makes stern demands on its members. Hosmer, who has always been interested in the subject, does his homework ably. Together with ex-JCAE Chairman Chet Holifield, Hosmer is a strong backer of the controversial breeder reactor and generally supports the AEC's point of view on things.

When Hosmer strays from the field where he has undeniable expertise, he can come up with some excentric ideas. Several years ago, convinced that victory in Vietnam was possible, he proposed that the Air Force drop the Vietnamese equivalent of voodoo dolls on the Viet Cong; these, he felt, would scare them into surrendering. The Pentagon, so far as we know, never acted on the Congressman's suggestion, but it might have been as effective, and certainly would have been more humane, than what the Pentagon did do.

As for the latest bee in Hosmer's bonnet: the Congressman is chief sponsor of a bill allowing people to buy as many vitamins as they want. Which sounds like apple pie—indeed the bill has a large number of co-sponsors—until one hears what the Food and Drug Administration has declared potentially very harmful, that being high dosages of vitamins A and D. The urgings of the Hosmer's retired constituents prompted the Congressman to introduce the legislation. Hosmer is likely to be reelected until he himself retires.

Census Data Pop. 463,546. Central city, 55%; suburban, 45%. Median family income, $11,851; families above $15,000: 33%; families below $3,000: 7%. Median years education, 12.6.

1972 Share of Federal Outlays $532,323,665

DOD	$247,844,000	HEW	$148,121,070
AEC	$1,350,373	HUD	$4,565,348
NASA	$24,699,742	DOI	$879,427
DOT	$11,179,318	USDA	$7,780,278
		Other	$85,904,109

Federal Military-Industrial Commitments

DOD Contractors McDonnell Douglas (Long Beach), $51,948m: various systems used on A-4 aircraft; research and development on various aircraft components. Atlantic Richfield (Long Beach), $13.295m: petroleum products. Argo Construction (Long Beach), $5.733m: unspecified.
DOD Installations Naval Shipyard (Long Beach). Naval Station (Long Beach); closed, 1974. Naval Supply Center (Long Beach). Naval Weapons Station (Seal Beach).

Economic Base Finance, insurance and real estate; electrical equipment and supplies; transportation equipment, especially aircraft; machinery, especially electronic computing equipment; and ordnance and accessories. Also higher education (Cal State, Long Beach).

The Voters

Registration 288,076 total. 136,588 D (47%); 130,018 R (45%); 18,232 declined to state (6%); 3,238 other (1%).
Median voting age 43.0

Employment profile White collar, 62%. Blue collar, 26%. Service, 12%. Farm, –%.
Ethnic groups Black, 1%. Spanish, 7%. Total foreign stock, 20%. Canada, UK, 3% each;
Germany, 2%; Italy, 1%.

Presidential vote

1972	Nixon (R)	149,953	(67%)
	McGovern (D)	73,970	(33%)
1968	Nixon (R)	106,608	(58%)
	Humphrey (D)	63,883	(35%)
	Wallace (AI)	11,083	(6%)

Representative

Craig Hosmer (R) Elected 1952; b. May 6, 1915, Brea; home, Long Beach; U. of Calif., B.A., 1937; U. of Mich. Law School; U. of So. Calif. Law School, J.D., 1940; U.S. Naval Acad., 1941; Navy, WWII; Rear Adm., USNR; married, three children; Episcopalian.

Career Practicing atty., 1946–48; 1949– ; Atty. for Atomic Energy Commission, 1948; Sp. Asst. U.S. Dist. Atty. at Los Alamos, N. Mex., 1948.

Offices 2217 RHOB, 202-225-2415. Also 620 Security Bldg., Long Beach 90802, 213-436-4865, 213-436-4294.

Administrative Assistant Louis Kriser

Committees

Interior and Insular Affairs (2nd); Subs: No. 2 (Water and Power Resources) (Ranking Mbr.); No. 3 (Environment); No. 4 (Territorial and Insular Affairs); No. 5 (Mines and Mining).

Joint Committee on Atomic Energy Subs: Energy (Ranking House Mbr.); Legislation (Ranking House Mbr.); Military Applications (Ranking House Mbr.); Research, Development, and Radiation (Ranking House Mbr.).

Group Ratings

	ADA	COPE	LWV	RIPON	NFU	LCV	CFA	NAB	NSI	ACA
1972	13	22	55	73	29	16	0	100	100	62
1971	19	25	66	53	14	–	38	–	–	85
1970	24	27	–	53	64	0	38	91	100	76

Key Votes

1) Busing	AGN	6) Cmbodia Bmbg	FOR	11) Chkg Acct Intrst	AGN
2) Strip Mines	AGN	7) Bust Hwy Trust	AGN	12) End HISC (HUAC)	ABS
3) Cut Mil $	AGN	8) Farm Sub Lmt	FOR	13) Nixon Sewer Veto	FOR
4) Rev Shrg	FOR	9) School Prayr	FOR	14) Corp Cmpaign $	FOR
5) Pub TV $	AGN	10) Cnsumr Prot	AGN	15) Pol $ Disclosr	FOR

Election Results

1972 general:	Craig Hosmer (R)	149,514	(66%)
	Dennis Murray (D)	72,481	(32%)
	John S. Donohue (PF)	4,888	(2%)
1972 primary:	Craig Hosmer (R), unopposed		
1970 general:	Craig Hosmer (R)	119,340	(72%)
	Walter Mallonee (D)	44,228	(27%)
	John S. Donohue (PF)	3,227	(2%)

THIRTY-THIRD DISTRICT Political Background

At 20,000 square miles, San Bernardino County is the largest county in the United States—about the size of West Virginia. Most of the county is uninhabitable desert, making up four of the five hours of driving time on any spin from Los Angeles to Las Vegas. But geographically the county makes a nice rectangular package, as does the 33rd congressional district, which includes most of the land area of San Bernardino and a small chunk of eastern Los Angeles County. Only when one gives the map a closer look does one realize that 82% of San Bernardino County's population is tucked away in its southeastern corner, part of the Los Angeles Basin separated from the desert by the San Gabriel Mountains. And within that corner, the congressional district boundary lines are very tortuous indeed—reflecting, as usual in California, political considerations.

In this case, the aim was to provide a safe seat for Republican Congressman Jerry Pettis. As a result, he got the upper-income suburbs of Upland and Redlands and the more prosperous part of San Bernardino—leaving the city's Mexican-American population to the newly-created, Democratic 38th district. The new 33rd also includes parts of Claremont and Pomona in Los Angeles County, including the Claremont, Pomona, Harvey Mudd, and Scripps Colleges. The small enrollments at these private schools pose little threat to Pettis.

Of more significance for the Congressman is the inclusion of Loma Linda University, a Seventh-Day Adventist institution. Pettis, self-made millionaire and former professor at Loma Linda, is the only Adventist member of Congress. He is also a conservative—dependable enough to have been selected by the Republican Committee on Committees for a spot on the House Ways and Means Committee, although from time to time Pettis surprises people and takes liberal positions on issues. There is only an outside chance that the Californian will ever become Chairman of this body. There are younger minority members with more seniority, and when the Republicans will get a majority in the House nobody knows. But Pettis should go on winning reelection back home for some time.

Census Data Pop. 462,827. Central city, 15%; suburban, 85%. Median family income, $10,402; families above $15,000: 25%; families below $3,000: 8%. Median years education, 12.5.

1972 Share of Federal Outlays $499,292,524

DOD	$187,228,036	HEW	$189,918,521
AEC	$575,758	HUD	$9,392,738
NASA	$8,359,603	DOI	$4,194,430
DOT	$13,925,186	USDA	$10,430,729
		Other	$80,267,523

Federal Military-Industrial Commitments

DOD Contractors General Dynamics (Pomona), $85.493m: development projects for terrier, Tartar, and Standard missile systems.
DOD Installations Marine Corps Base (Twenty-Nine Palms). Marine Corps Supply Center (Barstow). George AFB (Muroc).

Economic Base Finance, insurance and real estate; primary metal industries, especially blast furnace and steel mill products; agriculture, notably dairy products, poultry, cattle and fruits; and transportation equipment, especially trailer coaches. Also higher education (Cal State Polytechnic, Pomona).

The Voters

Registration 237,044 total. 112,179 D (47%); 110,837 R (47%); 11,716 declined to state (5%); 2,312 other (1%).
Median voting age 42.9
Employment profile White collar, 57%. Blue collar, 29%. Service, 13%. Farm, –%.
Ethnic groups Black, 3%. Spanish, 10%. Total foreign stock, 17%. Canada, Germany, UK, 2% each; Italy, 1%.

Presidential vote

1972	Nixon (R)	123,412	(67%)
	McGovern (D)	59,603	(33%)
1968	Nixon (R)	85,395	(57%)
	Humphrey (D)	51,293	(34%)
	Wallace (AI)	12,373	(8%)

Representative

Jerry L. Pettis (R) Elected 1966; b. July 18, 1916, Phoenix, Ariz.; home, Loma Linda; Pacific Union Col., B.A., 1938; Air Transport Command pilot, WWII; married, three children; Seventh-Day Adventist Church.

Career Rancher (citrus-avocado); Sp. Asst. to Pres. United Air Lines, 1946–50; Founder, Magnetic Tape Duplicators, Audio-Digest Foundation; Professor of economics, 1948–64, Chm. Bd. of Councilors, 1960–67, V.P. for Development, 1960–64, Loma-Linda U.

Offices 341 CHOB, 202-225-5861. Also Rm. 1A, 242 N. Arrowhead Ave., San Bernadino, 714-884-8818, and 114F Indian Hill Blvd., Claremont, 714-624-5091, and 220 E. Mt. View, Barstow, 714-256-4913.

Administrative Assistant Gerald N. Giovaniello

Committees

Ways and Means (6th).

Group Ratings

	ADA	COPE	LWV	RIPON	NFU	LCV	CFA	NAB	NSI	ACA
1972	13	27	64	78	86	17	0	100	100	80
1971	11	30	44	50	20	–	25	–	–	85
1970	28	42	–	65	73	40	56	67	100	59

Key Votes

1) Busing	AGN	6) Cmbodia Bmbg	AGN	11) Chkg Acct Intrst	AGN
2) Strip Mines	AGN	7) Bust Hwy Trust	FOR	12) End HISC (HUAC)	AGN
3) Cut Mil $	AGN	8) Farm Sub Lmt	AGN	13) Nixon Sewer Veto	FOR
4) Rev Shrg	ABS	9) School Prayr	FOR	14) Corp Cmpaign $	FOR
5) Pub TV $	AGN	10) Cnsumr Prot	AGN	15) Pol $ Disclosr	AGN

Election Results

1972 general:	Jerry L. Pettis (R)	140,868	(75%)
	Ken Thompson (D)	46,911	(25%)
1972 primary:	Jerry L. Pettis (R), unopposed		
1970 general:	Jerry L. Pettis (R)	116,093	(72%)
	Chester Wright (D)	44,764	(28%)

THIRTY-FOURTH DISTRICT   Political Background

"Orange County" are two words that have come to mean "conservative" in this country. Twenty years ago, Orange County, California had all the notoriety that usually comes to a few thousand acres of citrus trees; its 1950 population was 216,000. By 1970, that figure had grown to 1,420,000. During this period of turbulent growth, Orange County has consistently turned in some of the highest Republican percentages in the country (for further discussion, see California 39). And for that reason, when redistricting time came, Orange County was sliced into several odd-shaped strips. By population, it was entitled to almost three full districts; it ended up with only one completely within its borders, and portions of five others. One of these is the 34th.

So what is a Democrat doing representing a major portion of Orange County? This is the question you have to ask about Congressman Richard T. Hanna, who has been winning elections in Orange County since 1956 despite his party affiliation—and who, in the year of Richard Nixon's landslide, won 70% of the 34th district's votes.

The first answer is redistricting, very careful redistricting. Hanna was a member of the California Assembly when it first created the 34th in 1961, and he assured himself of the highest possible Democratic registration within Orange County. Over the years, he and the Democratic redistricters have gotten even more sophisticated. In 1968, they tacked onto the district a small portion of Los Angeles County, which later provided three-quarters of the Democrat's majority in that very Republican year in California. And for 1972, Hanna was made even safer. You can bet there are good reasons for all those twists and turns the district lines make as they pass from Lakewood, a middle-class suburb north of Long Beach, to the Mexican-American community in Santa Ana, the only significant minority concentration in Orange County. For 1974, the Special Masters' redistricting plan (see state write-up) has placed Hanna's district entirely within Los Angeles County, a move that will not affect his reelection prospects.

A second reason for Hanna's political survival is the kind of sophisticated political campaigning typical of California's Democrats as well as Republicans. There are no strong party organizations in the state, which saves people like Hanna the trouble of visiting cigar-chewing potentates who can't deliver votes anyway. Instead, using a computer, Hanna has the district targeted voter-by-voter. Because most of the voters have been interviewed and their responses punched on to computer cards, Hanna can produce thousands of letters keyed to specific voters' interests. He also maintains a list of 90,000 pro-Hanna voters, who are not, of course, necessarily the same people who register Democratic.

The third reason for Hanna's popularity is that he keeps attuned to the attitudes of his district. Not among the farther-out liberals on the California delegation, Hanna has usually supported high defense spending—important in a county like Orange which depends heavily on defense industries and military payrolls. Moreover, as a member of the Banking and Currency Committee, the Congressman has a say over a highly regulated industry entrenched in Orange County: the savings and loan business. California's savings and loan institutions are by far the nation's largest, this being one of the few states where S&Ls can be profit-making, stock-owned companies, rather than mutual associations. These last 20 years, you could have gotten fearsomely rich had you owned an S&L in Orange County, and many people did. The S&Ls, of course, provided most of the financing for the homes that now accommodate the 1.2 million people who have moved to Orange County since 1950.

Congressman Hanna is not unsympathetic to the interests of the S&Ls, having had some pretty profitable investments himself. On the Banking Committee, he has often declined to go along with populistic Chairman Wright Patman and has instead voted more in line with the wishes of big-money people back in Orange County. Incidentally, Hanna was also one of the committee's Democrats who voted not to investigate the Watergate matter prior to the 1972 election.

A final word. Hanna—a Kemmerer, Wyoming native—is an accomplished teller of funny stories and a tireless campaigner with an informal, ingratiating style. Any Democrat and a Mormon to boot who has grown a beard, as Hanna has, must have some kind of personal magic to win elections by two-to-one margins in Orange County, California.

Census Data Pop. 465,762. Central city, 43%; suburban, 57%. Median family income, $11,458; families above $15,000: 26%; families below $3,000: 5%. Median years education, 12.3.

1972 Share of Federal Outlays $484,824,595

DOD	$252,023,000	HEW	$128,445,572
AEC	$714,605	HUD	$2,522,357
NASA	$15,714,422	DOI	$1,159,241
DOT	$6,315,054	USDA	$6,195,797
		Other	$71,734,547

Federal Military-Industrial Commitments

DOD Contractors McDonnell Douglas (Huntington Beach), $46.293m: work on ABM missile. Atlas Fabricators (Long Beach), $12.393m: warheads for 2.75 inch rockets.
DOD Installations Naval Hospital (Long Beach).

, *NASA Contractors* McDonnell Douglas (Huntington Beach), $17.160m: production of Delta research vehicles.

Economic Base Electrical equipment and supplies, especially communication equipment; finance, insurance and real estate; ordnance and accessories; agriculture, notably fruits, poultry, vegetables, and nursery and greenhouse products; and tourism.

The Voters

> *Registration* 216,054 total. 121,067 D (56%); 78,328 R (36%); 13,637 declined to state (6%); 3,022 other (1%).
> *Median voting age* 38.3
> *Employment profile* White collar, 47%. Blue collar, 40%. Service, 12%. Farm, 1%.
> *Ethnic groups* Black, 1%. Spanish, 15%. Total foreign stock, 20%. Canada, UK, 2% each; Germany, Italy, 1% each.

Presidential vote

	1972	Nixon (R)	110,310	(66%)
		McGovern (D)	56,370	(34%)
	1968	Nixon (R)	72,423	(52%)
		Humphrey (D)	55,479	(40%)
		Wallace (AI)	12,531	(9%)

Representative

Richard T. Hanna (D) Elected 1962; b. June 9, 1914, Kemmerer, Wyo.; home, Anaheim; Pasadena Jr. Col., A.A., U. of Calif., B.A., 1937; UCLA Law School, LL.B., 1952; Navy Air Corps, WWII; married, three children; Church of Jesus Christ of Latter Day Saints.

Career Practicing atty., 1952– ; Calif. Assembly, 1957–62.

Offices 2432 RHOB, 202-225-2965. Also Suite 654, 1695 W. Crescent, Anaheim 92801, 714-776-6850.

Administrative Assistant James H. Cousins

Committees

Banking and Currency (11th); Subs: International Finance; International Trade; Housing.

Science and Astronautics (7th); Subs: Science, Research and Development; Energy; International Cooperation in Science and Space (Chm.).

Group Ratings

	ADA	COPE	LWV	RIPON	NFU	LCV	CFA	NAB	NSI	ACA
1972	81	82	73	93	83	49	0	13	25	14
1971	49	100	86	64	70	–	7ᶜ	–	–	24
1970	72	90	–	65	92	66	93	20	78	35

Key Votes

1) Busing	AGN	6) Cmbodia Bmbg	AGN	11) Chkg Acct Intrst	AGN
2) Strip Mines	AGN	7) Bust Hwy Trust	ABS	12) End HISC (HUAC)	FOR
3) Cut Mil $	FOR	8) Farm Sub Lmt	FOR	13) Nixon Sewer Veto	AGN
4) Rev Shrg	FOR	9) School Prayr	AGN	14) Corp Cmpaign $	ABS
5) Pub TV $	ABS	10) Cnsumr Prot	FOR	15) Pol $ Disclosr	ABS

Election Results

1972 general:	Richard T. Hanna (D)	115,880	(67%)
	John D. Ratterree (R)	49,971	(29%)
	Lee R. Rayburn (AI)	6,732	(4%)

1972 primary:	Richard T. Hanna (D), unopposed		
1970 general:	Richard T. Hanna (D)	101,664	(54%)
	William Teague (R)	82,167	(44%)
	Lee Rayburn (AI)	2,843	(2%)

THIRTY-FIFTH DISTRICT Political Background

California 35 is one of the 15 congressional districts wholly or primarily within Los Angeles County. The focus of the 35th is the busy port area of Los Angeles—San Pedro and Wilmington—and in the nearby blue-collar suburbs of Carson, Paramount, Compton, and Lynwood. This is one of the most working-class districts in Los Angeles; people here tend to work on the docks, in one of the area's huge aircraft plants, or in the factories located in the industrial corridor to the northeast. An increasing percentage of the district's residents are black people; they are found in the greatest proportions in the town of Compton, now with a black majority, and in Carson, just to the south. The district also includes the small black ghetto in Long Beach, and, near the port area, a sizable Yugoslav-American community—proof that L.A. is not entirely without ethnic variety.

Most of the residents of the 35th are traditional Democrats, union members who supported the programs of Franklin D. Roosevelt and John F. Kennedy, but who feel threatened by social trends not to their liking. On a few occasions the district has even gone Republican—for Ronald Reagan in 1966 and Richard Nixon in 1972.

For many years the 35th—which before the 1971 redistricting was the 17th—routinely reelected Democratic Congressman Cecil King, the co-sponsor of the original Medicare Act. When King retired in 1968, a real battle developed between Democrat Glenn Anderson and Republican Joseph Blatchford. Anderson was Lieutenant Governor for eight years under Pat Brown and was unlucky enough to have been acting chief executive when the Watts riot broke out. Afterwards some people accused Anderson of having waited too long before dispatching the National Guard. In the 1966 election, he was beaten badly by Robert Finch.

Two years later, Anderson just managed to squeek by Blatchford—who later became head of the Peace Corps. In the House, Anderson, always strongly supported by labor, received the kind of mundane committee assignments that tend to accrue to representatives of port areas—Public Works and Merchant Marine and Fisheries. On both, the Californian has moved up rapidly in seniority, though he has yet to achieve a subcommittee chairmanship. His first moment in the spotlight came in 1973 when he was floor manager for the effort to crack the highway trust fund just a bit for mass transit. The move lost initially in the House, but the fund was partially busted through a conference committee compromise.

Anderson's district is a poignant example of the need for more and better mass transit. Today the 35th is girded by freeways, but those without cars must depend on an indifferent bus system. Some 40 years ago, however, this area had the most highly developed inter-urban rail system in the country; you could get from San Pedro to downtown L.A. in just about the same time as it now takes on the clogged Harbor Freeway. And in those days there was no smog.

Census Data Pop. 465,392. Central city, 44%; suburban, 56%. Median family income, $10,050; families above $15,000: 22%; families below $3,000: 9%. Median years education, 12.1.

1972 Share of Federal Outlays $595,072,022

DOD	$244,284,425	HEW	$173,468,197
AEC	$2,138,787	HUD	$7,100,872
NASA	$35,892,465	DOI	$780,672
DOT	$17,219,039	USDA	$9,784,532
		Other	$104,403,033

Federal Military-Industrial Commitments

DOD Contractors Carson Oil (Carson), $17.232m: petroleum products. Martin Marietta Aluminum (Torrance), $6.049m: extruded components for aircraft launching systems. U.S. Borax (Wilmington), $5.824m: unspecified.

DOD Installations Fort MacArthur AB (San Pedro). Navy Fuel Depot (San Pedro).

Economic Base Transportation equipment, especially aircraft; finance, insurance and real estate; electrical equipment and supplies, especially radio and television communication equipment, and electronic components and accessories; machinery, especially electronic computing equipment; and fabricated metal products, especially fabricated structural metal products.

The Voters

Registration 195,936 total. 126,382 D (65%); 54,889 R (28%); 11,315 declined to state (6%); 3,350 other (2%).
Median voting age 40.0
Employment profile White collar, 43%. Blue collar, 44%. Service, 12%. Farm, 1%.
Ethnic groups Black, 10%. Japanese, Filipino, 2% each. Spanish, 20%. Total foreign stock, 25%. Canada, Italy, UK, 2% each; Germany, Yugoslavia, 1% each.

Presidential vote

1972	Nixon (R)	76,784	(54%)
	McGovern (D)	65,870	(46%)
1968	Nixon (R)	56,088	(42%)
	Humphrey (D)	63,789	(48%)
	Wallace (AI)	12,124	(9%)

Representative

Glenn M. Anderson (D) Elected 1968; b. Feb. 21, 1913, Hawthorne; home, Harbor City; UCLA, B.A., 1936; Army, WWII; married, three children; Protestant.

Career Mayor of Hawthorne, 1940–43; Calif. Assembly, 1943–51; Lt. Governor Calif., 1959–67; Regent, U. of Calif., 1959–66; Trustee, Calif. State Colleges, 1961–66.

Offices 1132 LHOB, 202-225-6676. Also 255 W. 5th St., San Pedro, 213-831-9281 ext. 558.

Administrative Assistant Harry R. Anderson

Committees

Merchant Marine and Fisheries (12th); Subs: Fisheries and Wildlife Conservation and the Environment; Oceanography; Merchant Marine.

Public Works (12th); Subs: Public Buildings and Grounds; Energy; Transportation; Water Resources.

Group Ratings

	ADA	COPE	LWV	RIPON	NFU	LCV	CFA	NAB	NSI	ACA
1972	75	91	75	69	57	68	100	8	10	10
1971	89	100	89	75	87	–	100	–	–	14
1970	84	100	–	59	92	67	86	0	38	12

Key Votes

1) Busing	AGN	6) Cmbodia Bmbg	AGN	11) Chkg Acct Intrst	FOR
2) Strip Mines	AGN	7) Bust Hwy Trust	FOR	12) End HISC (HUAC)	FOR
3) Cut Mil $	FOR	8) Farm Sub Lmt	FOR	13) Nixon Sewer Veto	AGN
4) Rev Shrg	FOR	9) School Prayr	AGN	14) Corp Cmpaign $	AGN
5) Pub TV $	FOR	10) Cnsumr Prot	FOR	15) Pol $ Disclosr	FOR

Election Results

1972 general:	Glenn M. Anderson (D)	105,667	(75%)
	Vernon E. Brown (R)	35,614	(25%)
1972 primary:	Glenn M. Anderson (D), unopposed		
1970 general:	Glenn M. Anderson (D)	183,739	(62%)
	Michael Donaldson (R)	47,778	(36%)
	Robert Copeland (AI)	1,724	(1%)
	Thomas Mathews (PF)	1,292	(1%)

THIRTY-SIXTH DISTRICT Political Background

The 36th congressional district of California has no *raison d'etre* but California politics. The state gained five seats as a result of the 1970 census. The Democratic legislature and Republican Gov. Ronald Reagan had, to put it mildly, differences as to how the new district lines were to be drawn. After a while, the California House delegation, led by San Francisco Democrat Phil Burton, came forward with a bipartisan compromise with the happy effect of strengthening all of the 38 incumbents, regardless of party. The plan also created two new seats that were pretty certain to go Republican (the 17th on the Peninsula and around San Jose, and the 42nd in Orange and San Diego counties), and two that were certain to go Democratic (the 37th, a predominantly black part of Los Angeles County, and the 38th, centering on San Bernardino and Riverside). What was left over became the 36th district, the fifth new seat and a political toss-up.

A leftover is what it looks like on the map. The 36th includes most of Kern and all of Kings counties; these comprise the southern and most conservative part of the Central Valley. It then skips over the mountains—formidable enough that no road traverses the district across them—to the coast. A narrow strip along the coast extends south to include the University of California at Santa Barbara, the district's most Democratic territory, and Vandenberg Air Force Base, where most servicemen who bother to vote do so elsewhere by absentee ballot. The result is a district Democratic by registration, Republican by recent voting habits, and utterly devoid of *any* sense of community.

In the 1972 election, the Republicans took the seat. The winner was Kern County Assemblyman William Ketchum, who in the legislature usually followed the lead of the Reagan Administration. Ketchum now sits on the Interior Committee, and also on District of Columbia, where he is likely to be a little more dubious about home rule than most of the committee's members. His relatively small 1972 margin will probably broaden in successive elections, as he sends out large quantities of franked mail to his widely scattered constituents. For 1974, the Special Masters' redistricting plan (see state write-up) has placed Ketchum's district entirely within the Central Valley, a move that will not affect his reelection chances.

Census Data Pop. 457,890. Central city, 15%; suburban, 63%. Median family income, $8,981; families above $15,000: 18%; families below $3,000: 11%. Median years education, 12.2.

1972 Share of Federal Outlays $607,914,185

DOD	$244,933,000	HEW	$176,052,803
AEC	$312,276	HUD	$1,336,132
NASA	$16,400,051	DOI	$7,557,600
DOT	$15,399,241	USDA	$85,860,753
		Other	$60,062,329

Federal Military-Industrial Commitments

DOD Contractors Ratheon (Goleta), $21.733m: aircraft electronic warfare equipment. General Motors (Goleta), $7.228m: various electronic ware; support for MK 48 torpedo.
DOD Installations Naval Air Station (Lemoore). Naval Weapons Center (China Lake). Boron AF Station (Boron). Vandenberg AFB (Lompoc).
NASA Installations Flight Research Center (Edwards).

Economic Base Agriculture, notably cattle, fruits, vegetables and cotton; finance, insurance and real estate; oil and gas extraction, especially crude petroleum and natural gas, and oil and gas field services; food and kindred products; and nonmetallic minerals, except fuels, especially potash, soda and borate minerals. Also higher education (Univ. of California, Santa Barbara).

The Voters

Registration 209,987 total. 122,075 D (58%); 75,149 R (36%); 10,133 declined to state (5%); 2,630 other (1%).
Median voting age 39.7
Employment profile White collar, 46%. Blue collar, 30%. Service, 14%. Farm, 10%.
Ethnic groups Black, 5%. Spanish, 17%. Total foreign stock, 16%. Canada, UK, 1% each.

Presidential vote

1972	Nixon (R)	95,059	(59%)
	McGovern (D)	64,929	(41%)
1968	Nixon (R)	55,618	(47%)
	Humphrey (D)	50,475	(43%)
	Wallace (AI)	12,335	(10%)

Representative

William M. Ketchum (R) Elected 1972; b. Sept. 2, 1921, Los Angeles; home, Paso Robles; Colo. School of Mines; U. of So. Calif., B.S.; Army, WWII and Korea; married, two children; Episcopalian.

Career Calif. Legislature, 1966; formerly engaged in cattle raising and farming; past Pres., San Luis Obispo County Farm Bureau.

Offices 413 CHOB, 202-225-2915. Also 800 Truxtun Ave., Rm. 302, Bakersfield 93301, 805-323-8322.

Administrative Assistant Chris Seeger

Committees

District of Columbia (9th); Subs: Judiciary; Revenue and Financial Affairs.

Interior and Insular Affairs (16th); Subs: No. 1 (National Parks and Recreation); No. 2 (Water and Power Resources); No. 5 (Mines and Mining).

Group Ratings: Newly Elected

Key Votes

1) Busing	NE	6) Cmbodia Bmbg	ABS	11) Chkg Acct Intrst	ABS
2) Strip Mines	NE	7) Bust Hwy Trust	AGN	12) End HISC (HUAC)	AGN
3) Cut Mil $	NE	8) Farm Sub Lmt	NE	13) Nixon Sewer Veto	AGN
4) Rev Shrg	NE	9) School Prayr	NE	14) Corp Cmpaign $	NE
5) Pub TV $	NE	10) Cnsumr Prot	NE	15) Pol $ Disclosr	NE

Election Results

1972 general:	William M. Ketchum (R)	88,071	(53%)
	Timothy Lemucchi (D)	72,623	(43%)
	William M. Armour (AI)	6,323	(4%)
1972 primary:	William M. Ketchum (R)	37,657	(81%)
	Melville Stephens (R)	8,862	(19%)

THIRTY-SEVENTH DISTRICT Political Background

The 37th is one of the five new congressional districts drawn by the California legislature in 1971. Like the other four, its shape is highly peculiar. From a large central body, the 37th projects two long tentacles at right angles to each other, one south and one west. The central body of the district is part of southern Los Angeles, a black and integrated area that extends from the old Los Angeles Coliseum to the gleaming new Inglewood Forum. For want of something better, this part of L.A. is referred to by the name of one of its major streets, Crenshaw. Crenshaw is a middle- to upper-middle-class area into which blacks have been moving in large numbers since the 1960s. It is notable for several pockets of more or less stable and amiable residential integration; Crenshaw is also where Mayor Tom Bradley lives.

The tentacles of the 37th are a little different. To the south, the district cuts a jagged path through part of Watts and south along the Harbor Freeway; this is really part of the Los Angeles ghetto. To the west, another tentacle extends almost (but not quite—it would sever the attenuated 28th district) to the ocean, taking in the counterculture beach town of Venice and the middle-class, fifties-style Westchester subdivision. The legislature intended to create California's second black-majority congressional district. And it succeeded in fact, if not precisely in theory. In the 1970 census, voting-age blacks in the 37th were slightly outnumbered by whites, but with neighborhood changes occurring since, blacks are now probably in the majority.

The beneficiary of the plan is Yvonne Brathwaite Burke, who will be remembered by television viewers as the charming and competent vice-chairperson of the 1972 Democratic National Convention. Mrs. Burke (she got married just after the June 1972 primary and is scheduled to be the first member of Congress to give birth, some time in 1974) is another product of the California Assembly. She was first elected not so long ago in 1966, but in a legislative body that values seniority less than the Congress, she soon gained favorable attention. In 1972 she won the five-candidate Democratic congressional primary with an absolute majority. Her articulate manner and rhetorical modesty—she prefers to be known as liberal rather than radical—has made her highly popular with white, as well as with black, voters.

In the House, Mrs. Burke serves on two committees with jurisdiction over most environmental issues: Interior, and Public Works. A few years ago, most blacks newly elected to Congress sought service on Education and Labor, which has jurisdiction over social and antipoverty legislation. If anything, blacks have been overrepresented on that committee. Newcomers like Mrs. Burke, by taking seats on committees where their points of view have traditionally been underrepresented, have helped to make the committees more what they should be—that is, a group of people with special expertise, but representing in some reasonable fashion the sentiments of the entire House.

Census Data Pop. 463,155. Central city, 75%; suburban, 25%. Median family income, $9,640; families above $15,000: 23%; families below $3,000: 11%. Median years education, 12.3.

1972 Share of Federal Outlays $591,492,642

DOD	$243,476,000	HEW	$172,424,779
AEC	$2,125,923	HUD	$7,058,160
NASA	$35,676,569	DOI	$775,976
DOT	$17,115,466	USDA	$9,725,678
		Other	$103,114,091

Federal Military-Industrial Commitments

DOD Contractors Hughes Aircraft (Culver City), $109.183m: design and production of various aircraft and missile electronic ware; production of various aircraft and missile hardware. Hughes Aircraft (Los Angeles), $19.486m: training devices for F-14 missile control officer. Hughes Tool (Culver City), $13.039m: various aircraft gun systems; repair of helicopters.

Economic Base Finance, insurance and real estate; transportation equipment, especially aircraft; electrical equipment and supplies, especially radio and television communication equipment, and electronic components and accessories; machinery, especially electronic computing equipment; and fabricated metal products, especially fabricated structural metal products.

The Voters

Registration 234,481 total. 168,788 D (72%); 52,278 R (22%); 10,879 declined to state (5%); 2,536 other (1%).
Median voting age 42.0
Employment profile White collar, 51%. Blue collar, 33%. Service, 16%. Farm, –%.
Ethnic groups Black, 51%. Japanese, 3%. Chinese, 1%. Spanish, 9%. Total foreign stock, 19%. Canada, Germany, UK, 1% each.

Presidential vote

1972	Nixon (R)	62,666	(36%)
	McGovern (D)	109,673	(64%)
1968	Nixon (R)	53,192	(32%)
	Humphrey (D)	108,862	(65%)
	Wallace (AI)	5,911	(4%)

Representative

Yvonne Brathwaite Burke (D) Elected 1966; b. Oct. 5, 1932, Los Angeles; home, Los Angeles; U. of Calif. (Los Angeles), B.A.; U. of So. Calif. School of Law, J.D., 1956; married, one child; Methodist.

Career Practicing atty.; State Assembly, 1966–72; Deputy Corporation Commissioner, L.A.

Offices 1027 LHOB, 202-225-7084. Also 4041 Marlton Ave., L.A., 213-295-5424.

Administrative Assistant Mrs. Valerie Pinson

Committees

Interior and Insular Affairs (19th); Subs: No. 2 (Water and Power Resources); No. 3 (Environment); No. 4 (Territorial and Insular Affairs); No. 6 (Indian Affairs).

Public Works (20th); Subs: Economic Development; Energy; Public Buildings and Grounds; Transportation.

Group Ratings: Newly Elected

Key Votes

1) Busing	NE	6) Cmbodia Bmbg	AGN	11) Chkg Acct Intrst	FOR
2) Strip Mines	NE	7) Bust Hwy Trust	FOR	12) End HISC (HUAC)	FOR
3) Cut Mil $	NE	8) Farm Sub Lmt	NE	13) Nixon Sewer Veto	ABS
4) Rev Shrg	NE	9) School Prayr	NE	14) Corp Cmpaign $	NE
5) Pub TV $	NE	10) Cnsumr Prot	NE	15) Pol $ Disclosr	NE

Election Results

1972 general:	Yvonne W. Brathwaite (D)	123,468	(73%)
	Gregg Tria (R)	41,562	(25%)
	John Haag (PF)	3,612	(2%)
1972 primary:	Yvonne W. Brathwaite (D)	51,831	(54%)
	Billy G. Mills (D)	33,371	(34%)
	John Carl Brogdon (D)	6,935	(7%)
	Al Smith (D)	2,569	(3%)
	Hank Sands (D)	2,156	(2%)

THIRTY-EIGHTH DISTRICT Political Background

Whatever sociologists may say about the diminution, if not the death, of social mobility in our society, there are still plenty of honest-to-God Horatio Alger stories in the U.S. Congress. One of them belongs to George E. Brown, Jr. In the early 1950s, Brown was an industrial physicist living in Monterey Park, a middle-class suburb just east of Los Angeles. In many ways, Brown, then sporting a crew-cut, was scarcely distinguishable from the tens of thousands of Los Angeles-area scientists and engineers—but for his Quaker upbringing, a strong belief in disarmament and peace, and nascent political yearnings. In 1954, he ran for and won a seat on the Monterey Park City Council. His interest in government whetted, he tried for the state legislature, and in the very Democratic year of 1958, he won. There he found himself on the committee in charge of drawing the state's congressional district lines and allotting the eight new districts the state gained in the 1960 census. One of the new seats came to be centered on Monterey Park, and so George Brown became a Congressman in 1962.

uipment, especially trailer coaches; stone, clay and glass products; and food and ts, especially canned, cured and frozen foods.

on 183,220 total. 117,688 D (64%); 54,360 R (30%); 8,585 declined to state (5%); her (1%).

voting age 39.6

ment profile White collar, 39%. Blue collar, 43%. Service, 15%. Farm, 3%.

groups Black, 7%. Spanish, 22%. Total foreign stock 20%. Canada, 2%; Germany, UK, ch.

tial vote

1972	Nixon (R)		71,319	(52%)
	McGovern (D)		64,824	(48%)
1968	Nixon (R)		57,469	(42%)
	Humphrey (D)		66,343	(48%)
	Wallace (AI)		13,245	(10%)

epresentative

George E. Brown, Jr. (D) Elected 1972; b. March 6, 1920, Holtville; home, Colton; U. of Calif. (Los Angeles), B.A., 1946; Army, WWII; married, four children.

Career City councilman, Mayor, Monterey Park, 1954–58; consultant in Engineering and Personnel, City of Los Angeles, 1957–61; State Assembly, 1959–62; U.S. House, 1963–71.

Offices 301 LHOB, 202-225-6161.

Administrative Assistant Terry Goggin

Committees

Agriculture (16th); Subs: Dairy and Poultry; Family Farms and Rural Development

Science and Astronautics (14th); Subs: Energy; Science, Research, and Development; Space Science and Applications.

Group Ratings: Newly Elected

ey Votes

Busing	NE	6) Cmbodia Bmbg	AGN	11) Chkg Acct Intrst	FOR
trip Mines	NE	7) Bust Hwy Trust	FOR	12) End HISC (HUAC)	FOR
ut Mil $	NE	8) Farm Sub Lmt	NE	13) Nixon Sewer Veto	AGN
ev Shrg	NE	9) School Prayr	NE	14) Corp Cmpaign $	NE
b TV $	NE	10) Cnsumr Prot	NE	15) Pol $ Disclosr	NE

Results

neral:	George E. Brown, Jr. (D)	77,922	(56%)
	Howard J. Snider (R)	60,459	(43%)
	Roger Granados (LRU)	1,009	(1%)
ary:	George E. Brown, Jr. (D)	19,504	(29%)
	Ruben S. Ayala (D)	18,307	(27%)
	David A. Tunno (D)	15,299	(23%)
	Terry Goggin (D)	11,235	(17%)
	John C. McCarthy (D)	1,999	(3%)
	Edison P. McDaniel (D)	968	(1%)
	Lee Green (D)	659	(1%)

The story doesn't end here. In the House, Brown w
the big escalation of the Vietnam war in 1965. Becau
positions on issues far out, he had to fight hard each tw
and in 1970 he decided to make a try for the Senate. It
Republican Sen. George Murphy got in serious trouble w
Inc., was paying him $20,000 a year while he was serving in t
the primary, President Nixon invaded Cambodia, and a stron
Brown upward in the polls. But these days Horatio Alger himseh
the June primary, Brown finished 9% behind the well-financed fav
of 99,000 votes out of the 2.4 million cast would have given
and—judging from the size of Tunney's subsequent victory—the

There is more. Relatively few ex-Congressmen make it back to Washi.
too wrenching to return without all that seniority you once had. But Brow.
deep antiwar convictions, decided to try anyway. Once again, redistricting ga
1971, the legislature created a new 38th district in the eastern end of the Los A.
intersection of Los Angeles, San Bernardino, and Riverside counties. The distric
most Democratic parts of San Bernardino and Riverside—the Mexican-American b.
University of California campus, and the working-class subdivisions around the giant
plant in Fontana. Everyone assumed that it would go Democratic in November. But t.
field was crowded, with no less than eight Democrats and three Republicans.

Brown, having moved to the town of Colton in the district, was the favorite and mana
squeak out a win with 28% of the votes. He beat not only San Bernardino County Super
Rueben Ayala, but also—and this must have been especially sweet—David Tunno, a former a
of now-Sen. Tunney. The Republicans, in the person of nominee Howard Snider, hoped
capture the seat; they had Tunno's support and the benefit of a last-minute appearance by
Richard Nixon. But Brown managed a convincing 56–44 win, even while Nixon carried the
district.

Back in the House, Brown is serving on his old committee, Science and Astronautics, with his
former tenure giving him a seniority edge only over other freshmen. He also has the distinction of
being one of the few Congressmen from a predominantly urban district who is on the Agriculture
Committee.

Smog and subdivisions have pretty well wiped out the once-thriving citrus industry in the 38th.
But Brown on Agriculture is not as silly as it sounds. The committee has jurisdiction over food
stamps, food inspection and grading, and commodity prices—all matters of strong interest to city
and suburban dwellers in these days of high food prices. Brown's chances of political survival ar
as good as ever; which is to say, that he takes more political risks to advance his beliefs than m
Congressmen do. Observers expect to see him continue in the House, unless the Congress
once again gets the bug to run for higher office.

Census Data Pop. 465,825. Central city, 31%; suburban, 69%. Median family incom
families above $15,000: 15%; families below $3,000: 11%. Median years educa

1972 Share of Federal Outlays $483,748,817

DOD	$176,810,000	HEW	$195,135,646
AEC	$252,125	HUD	$3,863,381
NASA	$2,642,328	DOI	$4,951,645
DOT	$13,360,648	USDA	$10,663,116
		Other	$76,069,928

Federal Military-Industrial Commitments

DOD Contractors Lockheed Aircraft (Ontario), $23.342m: aircraf
Coast Guard. General Electric (Norton AFB), $5.497m: mainte
DOD Installations Norton AFB (San Bernardino).

Economic Base Agriculture, notably dairy products, poultry, f
and real estate; primary metal industries, especially blast

THIRTY-NINTH DISTRICT Political Background

Only four congressional districts in the country more than doubled their population during the decade of the 1960s. The one with by far the biggest growth—its population up 130% in ten years—was the 39th of California, the one district in the state located entirely within the boundaries of Richard Nixon's birthplace and home turf: Orange County. Orange County is the site of Nixon's estate in San Clemente, and of the estates of many of his financial backers. The anonymous campaign contributions of some of these big-money men were funnelled through Nixon's former personal attorney and another Orange Countian, Herbert Kalmbach. The Watergate may be a building in Washington, but the scandal it has come to represent has many of its roots in Orange County, California—pure Kevin Phillips Sun Belt country.

Long before Watergate, Orange County entered our political vocabulary as a synonym for conservative. The county's population grew at an astronomical rate—from 216,000 in 1950, to 703,000 in 1960, and to 1,420,000 in 1970. Its Republican margins, however, grew even faster. And the kind of Republicans elected were of the rightish variety. The Santa Ana *Register,* the paper with the largest circulation in the county, considers local boy Nixon a dangerous leftist; it was the *Register* which first printed stories about the unusual financing of San Clemente.

Why is Orange County so very conservative? There is a working assumption among political sociologists that wealth produces conservatism. But that simple relationship does not explain the situation here. The median income of the 39th district, to be sure, is high, but it is exceeded by that of five other California districts, none of which produces Republican percentages like the 39th. There is wealth in Orange County, but most of the millionaires of greater Los Angeles live elsewhere, around Beverly Hills or Pasadena; and eight other California districts have a higher proportion of families with incomes over $25,000. But, and now we come to it, some 73% of the families in the 39th have incomes between $7,000 and $25,000. This is an unusually high percentage, and it indicates a homogenous, white, middle-class society. And that is what one might have expected: similar-minded people with similar backgrounds moving into similar kinds of subdivisions, all of which sprang up within a few years of each other.

Undergirding the economy of the 39th district is the defense industry. The people who attend the industry are engineers, technicians, and draftsmen. Such people are usually more comfortable tinkering with machines than dealing with their fellow men, and also people comfortable with order and apprehensive about change. Like most Californians, residents of the 39th are transient, but an even higher percentage of the citizens here are newcomers to California—immigrants within the last five years from the South, Midwest, and sometimes even the East. In fact, the migration rate in the county is exceeded only in retirement- and military-oriented San Diego, the barrio of East Los Angeles, and cosmopolitan San Francisco.

In this context, the conservatism of Orange County is best explained as a response to a sense of rootlessness and a simultaneous yearning for stability and order. The fantastic growth that has made Orange County possible has also produced in the new surroundings little that conveys permanence. The 39th district is full of shopping centers and subdivisions which did not exist ten years ago and which in another ten will be decaying.

Suburban Orange County has not been able to restore the old values of the Midwest or the South, or produce anything satisfactory to take the place of them. Orange Countians wanted to find the simple, orderly life, but instead find themselves baffled by the habits of their own rebellious children, many of whom prefer marijuana to beer. And when the 18-year-old vote came to Orange County, the children registered two-to-one Democratic. The problems of the world outside Orange County and the churnings of twentieth-century L.A. affect the lives of the people here more than they wanted or expected: despite the election of Ronald Reagan, taxes are still high, and the smog simply won't stop at the Los Angeles County line. Moreover, open space in the county continues to be gobbled up. Only a few miles of vacant land remain between the subdivisions and the mountains. And most of that is part of the 80,000-acre Irvine Ranch, the most valuable piece of undeveloped property in the world. This is scheduled to become home for yet another 430,000 more Orange Countians.

The beleaguered residents of Orange County and others like them are the bedrock of southern California conservatism. They are men and women who have achieved modest success by most standards. When that success and their values were sneered at by outsiders and sometimes by their own children, they sought comfort in politics. And they found it, for a while at least, in the rhetoric of Ronald Reagan and Richard Nixon.

But it was a rhetoric that promised more than it could deliver and a politics that could not succeed. A politics based on economics, on who gets what share of the pie, can work; it can make the rich or poor, perhaps both, richer. But a politics based on the notion of reestablishing an imagined home-town moral order could not wash in the long run. Reagan and Nixon could tell the people of Orange County that their basic impulses were right (even if they included racial discrimination) and that there was nothing really wrong with America and Orange County except their detractors. But neither Reagan nor Nixon could produce victory in a war most Americans believed was stupid. Nor could they stop the growth of the counterculture, or still the voices of angry blacks. And despite Reagan and Nixon, even homosexual bars could not be kept out of Orange County shopping centers.

The Watergate must be the final irony. The very men who worked so hard to convince Americans that our government and our leaders were fundamentally decent and fundamentally right have managed to demonstrate the opposite. Even Barry Goldwater said so. So it is not surprising, and is completely within character, that Reagan, whose law-and-order rhetoric won so many votes in Orange County, said that the people who planned and then covered up Watergate were not "criminals at heart."

The election figures tell the story. The right-wing tide in Orange County has crested and now seems about to ebb. One sign of this was the 39th district's 1972 congressional race. For a little over two years, the district was represented by John Schmitz, former state Senator and proud member of the John Birch Society. To the general public he was best known as the American Independent party's candidate for President in 1972. He could not of course replace George Wallace; and his hopeless campaign was distinguished more by the candidate's sprightly sense of humor than by his denunciation of Nixon's trip to China.

But many people did not know that long before Schmitz's presidential nonsense, he was already a lame duck Congressman. He was beaten in the June 1972 Republican primary by Andrew J. Hinshaw, for eight years Orange County Assessor (an elective position). Before that, Hinshaw, a respected professional in his field, served in the Los Angeles County Assessor's office. It goes without saying that there is a lot of work for an Assessor in a county that doubles its population in ten years; while serving in that post Hinshaw is credited with doing an honest, solid job, although some have questioned the valuation of the San Clemente compound.

It is interesting, we think, that Orange County should at this point in its history choose a cool professional over a witty ideologue; at this point in its history, layoffs in the defense and aircraft industries have slowed the county's growth to a near halt. Hinshaw's election suggests that the Orange County politics of the future will be more sober, a more realistic politics having more concrete and attainable goals. Orange Countians may henceforth renounce a politics that seeks to impose a system of morals, a realm of endeavor better suited to the activities of theologians, churches, and religion generally.

Census Data Pop. 465,007. Central city, 23%; suburban, 77%. Median family income, $12,675; families above $15,000: 37%; families below $3,000: –%. Median years education, 12.7.

1972 Share of Federal Outlays $448,295,231

DOD	$254,088,592	HEW	$113,596,058
AEC	$248,163	HUD	$1,022,598
NASA	$9,100,298	DOI	$1,026,605
DOT	$2,742,991	USDA	$5,016,116
		Other	$61,453,402

Federal Military-Industrial Commitments

DOD Contractors Philco Ford (Newport Beach), $64.577m: design and production of various missile systems. Interstate Electronics (Anaheim), $12.634m: design and production of electronic ware for Polaris and Poseidon missile systems. Susquehanna Corp. (Costa Mesa), $11.889m: TOW and Nike missiles support. Wells Marine (Costa Mesa), $7.015m: 20mm projectiles and 30 caliber ammunition. Babcock Electronics (Costa Mesa), $6.815m: various bomb fuzes. Zurn Engineers (Santa Ana), $6.069m: unspecified. Parker Hannifin (Irvine), $5.149m: aircraft engine assemblies.
DOD Installations Marine Corps Air Facility (Santa Ana). Marine Corps Air Station, El Toro (Santa Ana).

Economic Base Finance, insurance and real estate; electrical equipment and supplies, especially communication equipment; ordnance and accessories; machinery, especially electronic computing equipment; and tourism.

The Voters

Registration 280,531 total. 102,400 D (37%); 155,458 R (55%); 19,768 declined to state (7%); 2,905 other (1%).
Median voting age 40.0
Employment profile White collar, 62%. Blue collar, 26%. Service, 11%. Farm, 1%.
Ethnic groups Spanish, 10%. Total foreign stock, 20%. Canada, 3%; UK, Germany, 2% each; Italy, 1%.

Presidential vote

1972	Nixon (R)	164,958	(75%)
	McGovern (D)	56,293	(25%)
1968	Nixon (R)	103,237	(68%)
	Humphrey (D)	39,419	(26%)
	Wallace (AI)	8,471	(6%)

Representative

Andrew J. Hinshaw (R) Elected 1972; b. August 4, 1923, Dexter, Mo.; home, Newport Beach; U. of So. Calif., B.S., 1950; U.S.C. School of Law. 1953–54, Amer. Institute of Real Estate Appraisers, 1961; Navy, WWII; married, two children.

Career Appraiser, Los Angeles County Assessor's Office, 1949–54; Appraiser, Calif. State Board of Equalization, 1954–1964; Assessor, Orange County, 1965–72.

Offices 1128 LHOB, 202-225-5611.

Administrative Assistant Paul M. Stewart

Committees

Government Operations (15th); Subs: Government Activities; Legal and Monetary Affairs.

Post Office and Civil Service (9th); Subs: Census and Statistics; Investigations.

Group Ratings: Newly Elected

Key Votes

1) Busing	NE	6) Cmbodia Bmbg	FOR	11) Chkg Acct Intrst	AGN
2) Strip Mines	NE	7) Bust Hwy Trust	FOR	12) End HISC (HUAC)	AGN
3) Cut Mil $	NE	8) Farm Sub Lmt	NE	13) Nixon Sewer Veto	FOR
4) Rev Shrg	NE	9) School Prayr	NE	14) Corp Cmpaign $	NE
5) Pub TV $	NE	10) Cnsumr Prot	NE	15) Pol $ Disclosr	NE

Election Results

1972 general:	Andrew J. Hinshaw (R)	149,081	(66%)
	John W. Black (D)	77,817	(34%)
1972 primary:	Andrew J. Hinshaw (R)	42,782	(46%)
	John G. Schmitz (R)	40,261	(43%)
	Earl H. Carraway (R)	9,116	(10%)
	Larry Denna (R)	1,597	(2%)

FORTIETH DISTRICT Political Background

San Diego is Navy country: Navy ships, Navy air stations, Navy training centers, Navy wives, Navy widows, Navy retirees, and Navy officers who vote by absentee ballot. San Diego is the home of the U.S. Navy's West Coast headquarters. Not only does the city have a great natural harbor, it has the sun year round and, blessedly, still no smog. Back before World War II, San Diego was still a small, backward city, with a pronounced Mexican flavor. It is now a booming, heavily WASPy, and conservative metropolis of 696,000 people.

At least until 1972, San Diego's profound Republicanism made it Richard Nixon's "lucky city." The city always turned in a large Nixon majority on election day. And it was the San Diego *Union*, the flagship paper of the right-wing Copley chain, that harbored Nixon press man Herb Klein between Nixon's assignments. It was also San Diego, just a few miles down the sunny coast from San Clemente, that was about to host the 1972 Republican Convention and thereby triumphantly renominate Richard Nixon.

Richard Nixon was indeed triumphantly renominated, but on the other side of the country in Miami Beach. The Republican Convention was hastily removed from San Diego when it was revealed that ITT had put up a $400,000 guarantee to the Convention's sponsors, and when it was also revealed that about the same time a nasty antitrust case was settled on terms acceptable to ITT by Richard Nixon's and John Mitchell's Justice Department. Though no one knew it then, Nixon's insistence on having the Convention in his lucky city came just at the end of this string of good luck, which ran out after November 1972 when Watergate became a household word.

There are black and Mexican-American slums in San Diego, of course, but they are not in the city's 40th congressional district. The 40th—roughly similar to the pre-1972 36th—contains most of the city's high-income residential areas: La Jolla, on the cliffs overlooking the Pacific; Mission Bay; and the quaint old island of Coronado, across the Bay from downtown San Diego. The conservative instincts of the Navy have long set the political tone of the 40th—if there is a China lobby vote still about anywhere, it is here. Lately a few discordant elements have surfaced, mostly out of the district's large campuses. Herbert Marcuse used to teach at the La Jolla campus of the University of California, much to the horror of the locals; some of them considered vigilante action against the radical professor, absent denial of tenure. And in 1972, the students started to vote, decreasing the district's usual Republican margins enough to elect a Democratic Assemblyman from a district that occupies part of the 40th.

The dissidence has not meant trouble, at least not yet, for the Congressman from the 40th, Bob Wilson. As the third-ranking Republican on the House Armed Services Committee, he is well-placed to assure continued military spending, both in San Diego and around the world. And Wilson believes fervently that the spending is needed in both places.

Wilson was tangentially involved in the ITT scandal; he was, of course, trying to promote having the Convention in San Diego. But like most Congressmen, Wilson was untouched by the Watergate; as Chairman of the House Republican Congressional Campaign Committee until 1973, he was one of the many Republican political pros whom Nixon and his strategists at the Committee to Reelect were busily ignoring. The men around Nixon, apparently dissatisfied with Wilson's performance (as they were of National Chairman Bob Dole's), sought to depose him shortly after the election. Defiantly, Wilson stayed on for a while, until the House Republicans chose a new campaign chief—one without White House approval.

Perhaps the Nixon people blamed Wilson for the party's failure to capture the House during the 10 years he chaired the Campaign Committee. If so, it was a bum rap. The facts of life these days are that incumbents—like Wilson himself in the 40th—are reelected with near inevitable certainty, and most of the incumbents are Democrats. Under Wilson, the Campaign Committee raised and spent larger sums of money, more intelligently, than any other congressional campaign committee. Finally, political analysts owe Wilson and his staff a special debt, for they are the only group in the country which takes on the onerous task of calculating the presidential, senatorial, and gubernatorial vote within each congressional district.

Census Data Pop. 467,664. Central city, 93%; suburban, 7%. Median family income, $11,400; families above $15,000: 31%; families below $3,000: 7%. Median years education, 12.7.

1972 Share of Federal Outlays $738,236,475

DOD	$413,634,000	HEW	$158,595,689
AEC	$3,023,704	HUD	$4,059,895
NASA	$21,627,051	DOI	$3,484,412
DOT	$32,728,117	USDA	$3,152,388
		Other	$97,931,219

Federal Military-Industrial Commitments

DOD Contractors General Dynamics (San Diego), $3.907m: design and production of various aircraft electronic ware. Stromberg Datagraphix (San Diego), $8.572m: ocean research data processing. Control Data (La Jolla), $6.305m: computer components.

DOD Installations Fleet Anti-Submarine Warfare School (San Diego). Fleet Anti-Air Warfare Training Center (San Diego). Marine Corps Recruit Depot (San Diego) Naval Air Rework Facility (San Diego). Naval Air Station (Miramar). Naval Air Station, North Island (San Diego). Naval Amphibious Base; Coronado (San Diego). Naval Undersea Warfare Center (San Diego). Naval Communication Station (San Diego). Naval Amphibious School (San Diego). Naval Training Center (San Diego). Naval Recruit Training Command (San Diego). Navy Electronics Laboratory (San Diego).

NASA Contractors General Dynamics (San Diego), Centaur procurement and support.

Economic Base Finance, insurance and real estate; ordnance and accessories; transportation equipment, especially aircraft equipment not otherwise classified; machinery, especially office and computing machines; and electrical equipment and supplies, especially radio and television communication equipment. Also higher education (Cal State Univ., San Diego).

The Voters

Registration 275,909 total. 125,262 D (45%); 125,242 R (45%); 22,636 declined to state (8%); 2,769 other (1%).
Median voting age 38.1
Employment profile White collar, 65%. Blue collar, 22%. Service, 13%. Farm, –%.
Ethnic groups Black, 1%. Spanish, 8%. Total foreign stock, 21%. Canada, 3%; UK, Germany, 2% each; Italy, 1%.

Presidential vote

1972	Nixon (R)	144,144	(64%)
	McGovern (D)	80,734	(36%)
1968	Nixon (R)	97,836	(61%)
	Humphrey (D)	53,993	(34%)
	Wallace (AI)	9,045	(6%)

Representative

Bob Wilson (R) Elected 1952; b. April 5, 1916, Calexico; home, San Diego; San Diego State Col., 1933–35; Otis Art Inst.; Army, WWII; Lt. Col., USMCR; three children; Presbyterian.

Career Adv. and pub. relations.

Offices 2307 RHOB, 202-225-3201. Also Suite E285, 123 Camino de la Reina, San Diego 92110, 714-299-2444.

Administrative Assistant Paul Tsompanas

Committees

Armed Services (3rd); Subs: No. 3 (Ranking Mbr.); Intelligence.

Group Ratings

	ADA	COPE	LWV	RIPON	NFU	LCV	CFA	NAB	NSI	ACA
1972	6	18	30	67	17	4	0	91	100	68
1971	3	30	57	63	75	–	20	–	–	82
1970	20	17	–	59	42	0	44	89	100	67

Key Votes

1) Busing	AGN	6) Cmbodia Bmbg	FOR	11) Chkg Acct Intrst	AGN
2) Strip Mines	FOR	7) Bust Hwy Trust	ABS	12) End HISC (HUAC)	AGN
3) Cut Mil $	ABS	8) Farm Sub Lmt	AGN	13) Nixon Sewer Veto	FOR
4) Rev Shrg	FOR	9) School Prayr	FOR	14) Corp Cmpaign $	FOR
5) Pub TV $	AGN	10) Cnsumr Prot	ABS	15) Pol $ Disclosr	FOR

Election Results

1972 general:	Bob Wilson (R)	155,269	(68%)
	Frank Caprio (D)	69,377	(30%)
	Fritjof P. Thygeson (PF)	4,352	(2%)
1972 primary:	Bob Wilson (R), unopposed		
1970 general:	Bob Wilson (R)	132,446	(72%)
	Daniel Hostetter (D)	44,841	(24%)
	Walter Koppelman (PF)	5,139	(3%)
	Orville Davis (AI)	2,723	(1%)

FORTY-FIRST DISTRICT Political Background

To many Americans, San Diego evokes images of La Jolla, its quaint streets lined with boutiques and stockbrokers' offices, or perhaps images of the magnificent Balboa Park Zoo. But there is another way of life in San Diego, down by the docks and on the flat, dusty land going down toward Tijuana. It is here where most of the city's blacks and Mexican-Americans reside, on the south side of San Diego and in the working-class suburbs of Chula Vista and National City. Most of this poorer, blacker, browner part of San Diego County lies in the 41st congressional district, the only San Diego House seat held by a Democrat.

The Democrat is Lionel Van Deerlin, a former TV newscaster, who was a state Assemblyman at the time that this district's predecessor (then numbered the 37th) was drawn up. Van Deerlin has managed to build up a personal following on top of the normal Democratic vote in his constituency, and so to win elections in bad Democratic years as well as good.

In the House, the Congressman is a member of the usually outmaneuvered pro-consumer bloc on the Interstate and Foreign Commerce Committee; after 10 years of service, Van Deerlin has yet to attain a subcommittee chairmanship, though he is the next member in line for one. His greatest notice in the House came in 1967, when he became the first Congressman to urge the ouster of Harlem's Adam Clayton Powell.

Almost immediately a kind of hysteria swept the House, where Republicans had just made big gains in the 1966 off-year elections. For a while, it seemed that an even greater hysteria swept the country. People who might grumble a bit if an ordinary committee chairman abused his powers started screaming when a black committee chairman did the same thing—then flaunted it. Van Deerlin soon lost control of the oust-Powell movement, and so, it seems in retrospect, did everyone else. The ouster action of the House membership was later declared unconstitutional by the Supreme Court: it had excluded Powell without letting him take office, though he met the constitutional requirements. The Court did say that Powell could have been expelled legally once he had been seated. But the House, in its vigilante mood of 1967, had not taken the time to seat the hated Powell.

Census Data Pop. 460,748. Central city, 55%; suburban, 45%. Median family income, $8,945; families above $15,000: 16%; families below $3,000: 11%. Median years education, 12.2.

1972 Share of Federal Outlays $727,304,403

DOD	$407,508,461	HEW	$156,247,146
AEC	$2,978,928	HUD	$3,999,775
NASA	$21,306,790	DOI	$3,432,813
DOT	$32,243,467	USDA	$3,105,706
		Other	$96,481,317

Federal Military-Industrial Commitments

DOD Contractors National Steel and Shipbuilding (San Diego), $17.529m: ship repair. Hunt and Zurn JV (San Diego), $16.614m: unspecified. Christenson Raber Kiel (San Diego), $12.825m: unspecified. International Harvester (San Diego), $10.111m: design and production of various electrical generators.

DOD Installations Naval Air Station (Imperial Beach); closed, 1975. Naval Hospital (San Diego). Naval Public Works Center (San Diego). Naval Station (San Diego). Naval Supply Center (San Diego).

Economic Base Finance, insurance and real estate; ordnance and accessories; transportation equipment, especially aircraft equipment not otherwise classified; machinery, especially office and computing machines; and electrical equipment and supplies, especially radio and television communication equipment.

The Voters

Registration 200,438 total. 117,701 D (59%); 64,919 R (32%); 14,066 declined to state (7%); 3,752 other (2%).
Median voting age 37.0
Employment profile White collar, 47%. Blue collar, 36%. Service, 16%. Farm, 1%.
Ethnic groups Black, 11%. Filipino, 2%. Spanish, 19%. Total foreign stock, 24%. Canada, 2%; UK, Germany, Italy, 1% each.

Presidential vote

1972	Nixon (R)		86,387	(57%)
	McGovern (D)		66,009	(43%)
1968	Nixon (R)		61,818	(45%)
	Humphrey (D)		63,109	(46%)
	Wallace (AI)		11,218	(8%)

Representative

Lionel Van Deerlin (D) Elected 1962; b. July 25, 1914, Los Angeles; home, San Diego; U. of So. Calif., B.A., 1937; Army, WWII; married, six children; Episcopalian.

Career Newspaperman, radio and tv news editor, analyst.

Offices 2427 RHOB, 202-225-5672. Also 205 P.O. Bldg., San Diego 92112, 714-233-8950.

Administrative Assistant Siegmund W. Smith

Committees

Interstate and Foreign Commerce (7th); Subs: Communications and Power.

Group Ratings

	ADA	COPE	LWV	RIPON	NFU	LCV	CFA	NAB	NSI	ACA
1972	88	100	100	87	71	74	0	11	30	14
1971	76	100	89	82	69	–	88	–	–	15
1970	84	92	–	71	85	81	95	8	33	13

Key Votes

1) Busing	FOR	6) Cmbodia Bmbg	AGN	11) Chkg Acct Intrst	FOR
2) Strip Mines	AGN	7) Bust Hwy Trust	FOR	12) End HISC (HUAC)	FOR
3) Cut Mil $	FOR	8) Farm Sub Lmt	FOR	13) Nixon Sewer Veto	AGN
4) Rev Shrg	AGN	9) School Prayr	AGN	14) Corp Cmpaign $	ABS
5) Pub TV $	FOR	10) Cnsumr Prot	FOR	15) Pol $ Disclosr	FOR

Election Results

1972 general:	Lionel Van Deerlin (D)	116,980	(74%)
	D. Richard Kau (R)	40,997	(26%)
1972 primary:	Lionel Van Deerlin (D), unopposed		
1970 general:	Lionel Van Deerlin (D)	93,952	(72%)
	James Kuhn (R)	31,968	(25%)
	Faye Brice (AI)	2,962	(2%)
	Fritjof Thygeson (PF)	1,386	(1%)

FORTY-SECOND DISTRICT   Political Background

The 42nd district was one of the five new seats created by the California legislature after the 1970 census. Like the other new ones, the 42nd has a peculiar shape; it is, in fact, a collection of seemingly random communities that share a common political allegiance. In this case, the communities lie in San Diego and Orange counties, and the allegiance is Republican. The district skirts the fashionable areas of San Diego but takes in the solid middle-class suburbs east of the city and the ocean-side retirement communities to the north. From there it extends across the Marine Corps' Camp Pendleton to Orange County. Here it encompasses Richard Nixon's estate in San Clemente and the Newport Beach homes of Nixon cronies Murray Chotiner and Herbert Kalmbach. This is an affluent, deeply conservative district.

Like four of the five new California districts, the 42nd was captured in 1972 by a member of the state legislature. (The other was won by an ex-Congressman.) It could be that San Clemente's inclusion in the new 42nd was done to remove an embarrassing burden from the President; Nixon's old home district Congressman was John Schmitz, a John Bircher. As it happened, the voters of Orange County turned Schmitz aside anyway (see California 39).

As soon as the 42nd's district lines were set, Republican state Sen. Clair Burgener was regarded widely as a shoo-in. In the state legislature he was respected on both sides of the aisle, especially for his work in welfare legislation. The new Congressman is particularly interested in the problems of handicapped and retarded children. A former real estate man, he was assigned to the Banking and Currency Committee, which has jurisdiction over housing programs, the FHA, and so on. Burgener is expected to win reelection without much difficulty.

Census Data Pop. 463,726. Central city, 2%; suburban, 98%. Median family income, $10,701; families above $15,000: 27%; families below $3,000: 7%. Median years education, 12.6.

1972 Share of Federal Outlays $687,214,356

DOD	$385,503,000	HEW	$150,354,076
AEC	$2,564,935	HUD	$3,552,353
NASA	$19,497,976	DOI	$3,072,243
DOT	$27,771,423	USDA	$3,442,432
		Other	$91,475,918

Federal Military-Industrial Commitments

DOD Contractors RIHA Construction (San Diego), $8.778m: unspecified.
DOD Installations Marine Corps Base (Camp Pendleton). Naval Hospital (Camp Pendleton, Oceanside).

Economic Base Finance, insurance and real estate; ordnance and accessories; transportation equipment, especially aicraft equipment not otherwise classified; agriculture, notably poultry, vegetables and fruits; and machinery, especially office and computing machines.

The Voters

Registration 284,476 total. 113,701 D (40%); 147,716 R (52%); 20,310 declined to state (7%); 2,749 other (1%).
Median voting age 41.2
Employment profile White collar, 58%. Blue collar, 27%. Service, 13%. Farm, 2%.
Ethnic groups Black, 1%. Spanish, 10%. Total foreign stock, 18%. Canada, 3%; UK, Germany, 2% each.

Presidential vote

1972	Nixon (R)	160,940	(70%)
	McGovern (D)	68,162	(30%)
1968	Nixon (R)	96,815	(63%)
	Humphrey (D)	46,112	(30%)
	Wallace (AI)	10,171	(7%)

Representative

Clair W. Burgener (R) Elected 1972; b. Dec. 5, 1921, Vernal, Utah; home, Rancho Santa Fe; San Diego State Col., A.B., 1950; Army, WWII and Korea; married, three children; Mormon.

Career Pres. and owner, Clair W. Burgener Co., Realtors; Vice Mayor and Councilman, San Diego, 1953–57; Calif. Legislature, 1963–1967; Calif. State Senate, 1967–1972.

Offices 1504 LHOB, 202-225-3906. Also 7860 Mission Center Court, #107, San Diego 92108, 714-299-4042.

Administrative Assistant Harry D. Compton

Committees

Banking and Currency (15th); Subs: Consumer Affairs; International Finance; Small Business.

Group Ratings: Newly Elected

Key Votes

1) Busing	NE	6) Cmbodia Bmbg	FOR	11) Chkg Acct Intrst	FOR
2) Strip Mines	NE	7) Bust Hwy Trust	FOR	12) End HISC (HUAC)	AGN
3) Cut Mil $	NE	8) Farm Sub Lmt	NE	13) Nixon Sewer Veto	FOR
4) Rev Shrg	NE	9) School Prayr	NE	14) Corp Cmpaign $	NE
5) Pub TV $	NE	10) Cnsumr Prot	NE	15) Pol $ Disclosr	NE

Election Results

1972 general:	Clair W. Burgener (R)	158,475	(68%)
	Bob Lowe (D)	68,381	(29%)
	Armin R. Moths (AI)	7,902	(3%)
1972 primary:	Clair W. Burgener (R)	68,496	(78%)
	Fred Gage (R)	7,923	(9%)
	Norman J. Ream (R)	7,896	(9%)
	Gay Lewis (R)	3,065	(4%)

FORTY-THIRD DISTRICT Political Background

In the last few years, the Los Angeles smog has been seen making its way through the narrow San Gorgonio Pass into the pristine air of the California desert. Smog has already laid waste to the citrus industry around Riverside, at the far eastern end of the Los Angeles Basin, where the air-pollution levels are above the danger level more often than not. Now the smog is even threatening Palm Springs, the desert oasis of those wealthy enough to live wherever they want (like

Frank Sinatra and Bob Hope, to name two). Some days the smog has been seen floating out over the Joshua trees to the Colorado River, 200 miles away.

Such is the sad story in the 43rd congressional district of California. Most of its land is part of the Mohave Desert, which is virtually uninhabited outside oases like Palm Springs. Most of the district's people live in or near Riverside, which is where Richard Nixon and Patricia Ryan were married in 1940 and which some consider the smog capital of California. But the most interesting part of the 43rd is the Imperial Valley.

This is a desert—or was one until 40 years ago when canals were built and water brought in from the Hoover and Parker Dams on the Colorado River. Poetry has been written about making the desert bloom, but the story of the Imperial Valley is mostly a matter of money out-and-out. Irrigated, the Imperial Valley is immensely rich farmland, said to be worth some $700 million today. Without water, the land would be worth nothing, except perhaps to a few desert freaks.

The Reclamation Act purports to impose a 160-acre limit on farms receiving diverted water made possible by the federal government. But most of the Imperial Valley is owned in huge tracts. A local gadfly named Ben Yellen has filed suit to enforce the 160-acre regulation and won a favorable decision; the case is now on appeal. Obviously the big landowners have much at stake, and they have friends in most of the area's politicians. They argue, with some force, that a limitation not enforced for 40 years has grown inoperative. They also say that it would be impossible to farm the land economically if it were divided into small tracts—the 160-acre limit being a legacy of the Homestead Act of the 1860s. The big landowners neglect to mention, however, that they receive their government-transported water at rates far below what homeowners in Los Angeles pay. The Imperial Valley presents a nice example of welfare statism for the rich—cheap water—and *laissez faire* for the poor—the miserable living conditions of the MexicanAmericans who work the fields.

The Congressman from the 43rd district, Republican Victory Veysey, sides with the big landowners of the Imperial Irrigation District; so did his predecessor Democrat (and now Senator) John Tunney. The district boundaries were redrawn to safeguard Veysey, who managed only a narrow victory in 1970 when Tunney ran for the Senate. The tortuous boundary through the city of Riverside, for example, is designed to put the maximum number of Republican votes in the 43rd and the maximum number of Democratic votes in the adjoining 38th. Confusion may arise from the fact that most of what is now the 43rd was, until 1972, part of the old 38th. The new 38th is represented by liberal Democrat George Brown. Even more confusion has resulted from the redistricting plan submitted by the Special Masters (see state write-up). For 1974, the plan carves up Veysey's constituency among several other districts. His reelection chances, therefore, appear damaged at this writing.

Census Data Pop. 462,787. Central city, 21%; suburban, 63%. Median family income, $8,785; families above $15,000: 19%; families below $3,000: 12%. Median years education, 12.3.

1972 Share of Federal Outlays $1,061,570,819

DOD	$485,363,000	HEW	$310,341,896
AEC	$2,617,194	HUD	$6,121,841
NASA	$18,324,327	DOI	$8,854,447
DOT	$46,360,082	USDA	$26,709,736
		Other	$156,878,296

Federal Military-Industrial Commitments

DOD Installations Naval Air Facility (El Centro). March AFB (Riverside). Mt. Laguna AF Station (Mt. Laguna).

Economic Base Agriculture, notably cattle, vegetables and poultry; finance, insurance and real estate; transportation equipment, especially trailer coaches; tourism; and stone, clay and glass products.

The Voters

Registration 238,599 total. 117,186 D (49%); 106,610 R (45%); 12,111 declined to state (5%); 2,692 other (1%).
Median voting age 46.5
Employment profile White collar, 48%. Blue collar, 29%. Service, 15%. Farm, 8%.
Ethnic groups Black, 4%. Spanish, 21%. Total foreign stock, 25%. Canada, Germany, UK, 2% each.

Presidential vote

1972	Nixon (R)	117,994	(64%)
	McGovern (D)	66,770	(36%)
1968	Nixon (R)	85,708	(55%)
	Humphrey (D)	56,492	(37%)
	Wallace (AI)	12,264	(8%)

Representative

Victor Vincent Veysey (R) Elected 1970; b. April 14, 1915, Los Angeles; home, Brawley; Calif. Inst. of Tech., B.S., 1936; Harvard U., M.B.A., 1938; married, four children; Presbyterian.

Career Rancher; Instr. in industrial relations and industrial management, Caltech, Stanford U.; Calif. State Assembly, 1962–70.

Offices 1227 LHOB, 202-225-2305.

Administrative Assistant Robert A. Geier

Committees

Appropriations (21st); Subs: District of Columbia; Interior.

Group Ratings

	ADA	COPE	LWV	RIPON	NFU	LCV	CFA	NAB	NSI	ACA
1972	6	44	25	67	50	36	0	88	100	67
1971	5	30	44	53	15	–	13	–	–	79

Key Votes

1) Busing	AGN	6) Cmbodia Bmbg	ABS	11) Chkg Acct Intrst	ABS
2) Strip Mines	FOR	7) Bust Hwy Trust	AGN	12) End HISC (HUAC)	AGN
3) Cut Mil $	AGN	8) Farm Sub Lmt	AGN	13) Nixon Sewer Veto	FOR
4) Rev Shrg	FOR	9) School Prayr	FOR	14) Corp Cmpaign $	FOR
5) Pub TV $	ABS	10) Cnsumr Prot	AGN	15) Pol $ Disclosr	FOR

Election Results

1972 general:	Victor V. Veysey (R)	118,536	(63%)
	Ernest Z. Robles (D)	70,455	(37%)
1972 primary:	Victor V. Veysey (R), unopposed		
1970 general:	Victor V. Veysey (R)	87,479	(50%)
	David Tunno (D)	85,648	(49%)
	William Pasley (AI)	2,481	(1%)

COLORADO

Political Background

To outsiders, Colorado means backpacking in the Rockies, skiing at Aspen, or wandering through old mining towns like Central City. But the part of Colorado that matters most politically is the thin strip of land at the base of the Rockies' Eastern Slope, where the arid plateau of eastern Colorado suddenly yields to the mountains. Two-thirds of Colorado's voters live on this sliver of land running up and down the state, and the proportion is growing—Eastern Slope population was up 33% during the sixties, as compared with 10% for the rest of the state. Attracted by the temperate climate, the proximity of winter and summer recreation, and a booming local economy, newcomers continue to arrive, particularly in metropolitan Denver (which has 56% of the state's population) and other Eastern Slope cities like Colorado Springs, Greeley, and Fort Collins.

With one major exception—the large Mexican-American population in Denver, Pueblo, and the southern part of the state—Colorado is a remarkably homogeneous place. It has no readily identifiable voting blocs traditionally pitted against each other. No part of the state is an overwhelmingly Democratic or Republican stronghold. Republicans here have won the lion's share of recent elections, but they do not constitute an overpowering political force.

In the days when the Eastern Slope did not so dominate Colorado, the state had a politics of bipartisan conservatism. Conservative Republicans from the ranching and farming interests of the eastern plains vied against conservative Democrats from the mountainous Western Slope (all the territory west of the first ridge of the Rockies). But in the last dozen years, two political movements have taken over the two parties; first the Republican, then the Democratic. Both movements are rooted in the concerns of the people of the Eastern Slope; they rely heavily on volunteer activity by suburban housewives and, in some cases, high school students; and they reflect the changing concerns of the majority of Coloradoans. One hard on the heels of the other, each movement has overturned—or seems about to overturn—the state's established political order.

First came the Republicans. In 1962, a group of young, personable Republicans from the Eastern Slope got together and planned to unseat the state's Democratic Governor and its senior Democratic Senator, both aging and unpopular at the time. These Republicans put up John Love of Broadmoor (a suburb of Colorado Springs), for Governor, and Peter Dominick of Englewood (a Denver suburb), for Senator. Both men won substantial victories. And both have won succeeding elections—Gov. Love in 1966 and 1970 and Sen. Dominick in 1968—by solid margins. In the summer of 1973, Love resigned to become Nixon's new energy boss, and was succeeded by Lt. Gov. John Vanderhoof. Dominick's success came in spite of, or maybe even because of, his ardent conservatism; one of the things the Senator will be remembered for was his fervent endorsement of Barry Goldwater at the 1964 Republican Convention.

The politics of Love and Dominick has had its strongest appeal in middle-class suburban neighborhoods. The two Republicans made their entry during the Kennedy years and told affluent suburbanites that the federal government was overextending itself—and using their money paid in high taxes to do it. Today this kind of Colorado Republicanism is under an attack led by a new breed of Democrats. These are the politicians who in 1970 started beating the establishment men in primaries, and in 1972 started winning the general election races as well. The source of the new Democrats' fervor and energy was opposition to the Vietnam war; this is what got them together and organized. But the source of their voter appeal is probably something else: a strong insistence on reforming political procedures (Common Cause has one of its strongest local chapters in Denver) and the ecology issue.

In Colorado, as throughout the West, ecology-related issues are fast becoming strong vote-getters for Democrats. You only have to visit a place like Denver, not to mention Los Angeles, to see every day how metropolitan concentrations are shaping the face of the land. In Eastern cities, the suburbs shade gently into farmland; but beyond the last sidewalk of a new Denver suburban development, there is little but arid, virgin land or the side of a giant mountain. Ecology issues almost inevitably involve a trade-off between somebody's economic gain and the general public's interest in environmental purity. Conservative Republicans in Colorado are inclined to sympathize with the affected business people; the antiwar Democrats, by temperament, are biased the other way, and the way that is usually more popular politically.

A prime example of an issue affecting the Colorado environment was the state's 1972 referendum on the Winter Olympics. A group of civic boosters had gotten together and sold the International Olympic Committee on the idea of holding the Winter Games in Denver. Only after the promoters got the nod from the IOC did some problems come to light. For one thing, many of the events would have to be held more than 100 miles away, over mountains with no good highways; for another, the public would have to foot the bill for many new Olympic facilities, the primary beneficiaries of which would be hotel owners, real estate developers, and others on the make. Republicans like the state's senior Senator, Gordon Allott, were strong Olympic boosters. Democrats, like Allott's little-known opponent, Floyd Haskell, supported the referendum that would prohibit the state from spending any money on the Olympics—a referendum put on the ballot through the efforts of activists in the Denver and Boulder areas.

Much to the chagrin of the people who have traditionally attempted (and with much previous success) to promote and sell Colorado, the referendum to stop the Olympics won by a 61% margin. In the process, Sen. Allott, first elected in 1954, was upset by almost 10,000 votes. It would be inaccurate, however, to ascribe Haskell's victory solely to the Olympics issue. A former Republican state Representative from suburban Englewood, Haskell switched parties out of opposition to the Nixon Administration's Vietnam policies. Haskell's campaign consisted primarily of a half-hour television ad, which tried to tell the voters who he was and concluded with clips from statements made by Sen. Allott.

The clips apparently devastated the incumbent. Allott's name was well known in Colorado, but many of his views apparently were not. In Washington, Allott took particular delight in attacking what he considered the shibboleths of liberals; he believed that the liberals and their slogans endangered the pace of scientific development and unnecessarily jeopardized needed economic growth. From his more acerbic comments, it was easy for the Democrat's film-maker to cull some that would go against the grain of most Coloradoans' feelings.

For men of such divergent views, Haskell and his Senior colleague, Sen. Peter Dominick, have remarkably similar backgrounds. They live in adjacent, wealthy Denver suburbs; they were both successful lawyers and served in the Colorado House; both are from the East and went to Ivy League schools. Dominick's background, in fact, is impeccable. His family founded one of the large Wall Street brokerage houses, and his handsome good looks are what one would expect from someone who went to Yale after St. Mark's. The rumor is that he forsook the East expressly to become a U.S. Senator from Colorado.

Dominick's seat is up in 1974, and for the first time in his career, he appears to be in some political trouble. He seems to have recovered completely from a heart attack of several years ago, but as Chairman of the Senate Republican Campaign Committee, remains particularly galled by Allott's surprise defeat. He has made public his displeasure with President Nixon's refusal to help Allott and other Republican candidates who lost in 1972. And as the senior conservative Republican on the Senate Labor and Public Welfare Committee, Dominick has often been called upon to introduce Administration bills. But as of 1973, he began to perform the function with a disclaimer, which was that his action represented only a courtesy, because he had not been consulted on the content of the legislation. It is no wonder then that the Nixon Administration met an almost uniformly hostile Congress when the Watergate broke; if it had alienated so conservative a Senator as Dominick, who could the Administration call a friend?

Colorado has no stable of prominent Democratic officeholders from which a Dominick opponent might emerge. The only Democrat with longish tenure and high visibility, Rep. Frank Evans, turned down the chance to go for the Senate in 1972 and will probably do so again in 1974. Most prominent among the possibilities mentioned are Gary Hart, a Denver lawyer both before and after he served as George McGovern's 1972 campaign manager; and Joseph Dolan, a former top aide to Robert Kennedy, who for the last four years has been one of the top men in the Denver-based Shakey's Pizza empire. All signs today point to a close election, perhaps as close as the one in 1972; these kind of Senate races Colorado has not seen in a long time. With the governorship also up in 1974, Vanderhoof can expect a spirited fight from any one of a number of young Democrats. Most prominently mentioned are ex-Lt. Gov. Mark Hogan and Richard Lamm, minority leader in the state House and one of the leaders in the anti-Olympics campaign.

Census Data Pop. 2,207,259; 1.09% of U.S. total, 30th largest; change 1960–70, 25.8%. Central city, 34%; suburban, 38%. Median family income, $9,553; 21st highest; families above $15,000: 20%; families below $3,000: 9%. Median years education, 12.4.

1972 Share of Federal Tax Burden $2,152,890,000; 1.03% of U.S. total, 26th largest.

1972 Share of Federal Outlays $2,938,637,516; 1.36% of U.S. total, 25th largest. Per capita federal spending, $1,331.

DOD	$856,327,000	22nd (1.37%)		HEW	$725,803,991	32nd (1.02%)
AEC	$88,634,225	15th (3.38%)		HUD	$42,104,884	25th (1.37%)
NASA	$214,160,602	7th (7.16%)		VA	$145,166,146	27th (1.27%)
DOT	$135,884,547	26th (1.72%)		USDA	$179,976,105	31st (1.17%)
DOC	$36,841,229	8th (2.85%)		CSC	$58,619,884	18th (1.42%)
DOI	$135,190,810	4th (6.37%)		TD	$110,633,794	22nd (0.67%)
DOJ	$13,367,145	28th (1.36%)		Other	$195,927,154	

Economic Base Finance, insurance and real estate; agriculture, notably cattle, wheat, dairy products and corn; food and kindred products; machinery, especially electronic computing equipment; electrical equipment and supplies, especially electronic measuring instruments; printing and publishing, especially newspapers; tourism.

Political Line-up Governor, John A. Love (R); seat up, 1974. Senators, Peter H. Dominick (R) and Floyd K. Haskell (D). Representatives, 5 (3 R and 2 D). State Senate (22 R and 13 D); State House (37 R and 28 D).

The Voters

Registration 1,219,591 Total. 413,539 D (34%); 343,193 R (28%); 462,859 other (38%). *Median voting age* 40.4
Employment profile White collar, 54%. Blue collar, 28%. Service, 14%. Farm, 4%.
Ethnic groups Black, 3%. Spanish, 13%. Total foreign stock, 13%. Germany, 2%, UK, USSR, 1% each.

Presidential vote

1972	Nixon (R)	597,189	(64%)
	McGovern (D)	329,980	(36%)
1968	Nixon (R)	409,345	(51%)
	Humphrey (D)	335,174	(42%)
	Wallace (AI)	60,813	(8%)
1964	Johnson (D)	476,024	(62%)
	Goldwater (R)	296,767	(38%)

Senator

Peter H. Dominick (R) Elected 1962, seat up 1974; b. July 7, 1915, Stamford, Conn.; home, Englewood; Yale U., B.A., 1937, LL.B., 1940; Army Air Corps, WWII; Col. USAFR; married, four children; Episcopalian.

Career Practicing atty., 1946–61; Colo. House of Reps., 1956–60; U.S. House of Reps., 1961–63.

Offices 4213 NSOB, 202-225-5852. Also Suite 15030 New Fed. Bldg., Denver 80202, 303-297-3195, and 104 Cascade Plaza Ofc. Bldg., Colorado Springs, 303-471-9096, and 215 Fed. Bldg., Grand Junction, 303-243-5600.

Administrative Assistant James Robb

Committees

Armed Services (3rd); Subs: Central Intelligence (Ranking Mbr.); Preparedness Investigating;

Bomber Defense; National Stockpile and Naval Petroleum Reserves; Military Construction Authorization; Research and Development (Ranking Mbr.); Drug Abuse in the Military (Ranking Mbr.).

Labor and Public Welfare (2nd); Subs: Education (Ranking Mbr.); Health; Employment, Poverty, and Migratory Labor; Alcoholism and Narcotics; Sp. Subcom. on National Science Foundation.

Sel. Com. on Small Business (2nd); Subs: Environmental, Rural, and Urban Economic Development; Financing and Investment; Government Regulation (Ranking Mbr.).

Joint Com. on Atomic Energy (3rd); Subs: Agreements for Cooperation; Raw Material; Research, Development, and Radiation.

Group Ratings

	ADA	COPE	LWV	RIPON	NFU	LCV	CFA	NAB	NSI	ACA
1972	5	0	50	52	44	11	0	90	88	76
1971	7	17	42	46	10	–	0	–	–	96
1970	13	15	–	50	38	6	–	73	90	76

Key Votes

1) Busing	AGN	8) Sea Life Prot	AGN	15) Tax Singls Less	AGN
2) Alas P-line	FOR	9) Campaign Subs	AGN	16) Min Tax for Rich	AGN
3) Gun Cntrl	AGN	10) Cmbodia Bmbg	ABS	17) Euro Troop Rdctn	AGN
4) Rehnquist	FOR	11) Legal Srvices	AGN	18) Bust Hwy Trust	FOR
5) Pub TV $	FOR	12) Rev Sharing	FOR	19) Maid Min Wage	AGN
6) EZ Votr Reg	AGN	13) Cnsumr Prot	AGN	20) Farm Sub Limit	AGN
7) No-Fault	AGN	14) Eq Rts Amend	FOR	21) Highr Credt Chgs	FOR

Election Results

1968 general:	Peter H. Dominick (R)	459,952	(59%)
	Stephen McNichols (D)	325,584	(41%)
1968 primary:	Peter H. Dominick (R), unopposed		
1962 general:	Peter H. Dominick (R)	328,655	(54%)
	John A. Carroll (D)	279,586	(46%)
	Charlotte Benson (SL)	3,546	(1%)

Senator

Floyd K. Haskell (D) Elected 1972; seat up 1978; b. Feb. 7, 1916, Morristown, N.J.; home, Littleton; Harvard U., A.B., 1937, LL.B., 1941; Army, 1941–45; married, three children.

Career Practicing atty., 1941, 1946–72; State Senate, 1964–68 (elected as Repub.); State Coordinator, Rockefeller for Pres., 1968; switched to Dem. Party, 1970.

Offices 204 OSOB, 202-225-5941.

Administrative Assistant James Idena

Committees

Aeronautical and Space Sciences (7th).

Interior and Insular Affairs (7th); Subs: Indian Affairs; Public Lands (Chm.); Water and Power Resources.

Sel. Com. on Small Business (9th); Subs: Environmental, Rural, and Urban Economic Development; Financing and Investment; Retailing, Distribution, and Marketing Practices.

Group Ratings: Newly Elected

Election Results

1972 general:	Floyd K. Haskell (D)	457,545	(49%)
	Gordon Allott (R)	447,957	(48%)
	Secundo Salazar (LRU)	13,228	(1%)
	Henry John Olshaw (AI)	7,353	(1%)
1972 primary:	Floyd K. Haskell (D)	77,574	(59%)
	Anthony F. Vollack (D)	54,298	(41%)

FIRST DISTRICT Political Background

Within sight—except on days when smog obscures—of the Front Range of the Rockies lies the mile-high city of Denver. Denver got its start servicing the needs of local gold miners and cattle ranchers. It is today the service and distribution center for the entire Rocky Mountain region, which has led the city's detractors to call it just a salesman town. Nevertheless, greater Denver comprises the largest metropolitan area in the Rocky Mountain states; in fact, the largest one, but for those in Texas, between the Missouri River and the West Coast. But even what the Census Bureau defines as the central city of Denver does not fit an Easterner's idea of what a city is. Never having had an extensive manufacturing base, most of central city Denver looks like a suburb. The homes and the lawns of Denverites, prosperous and not-so-prosperous, all have a resolute middle-class order about them.

There are, of course, some less respectable, more rundown neighborhoods on the west side where the Chicanos live and the north side where the black reside. In Denver, these two communities are of roughly equal size, but show little bond of common feeling; Denver is rare for a place in the West or Southwest in that it regards its blacks with greater esteem than its Chicanos. However that may be, members of both minority groups seem to live more comfortably here than in most American cities. Denver's many migrants from the small towns of Colorado, Kansas, Nebraska, and Wyoming have helped to keep the city's ambience folksy.

Not that Denver is immune to the nation's urban ills. A couple of years ago, the city's school board was swept out of office because it had transferred students among schools to eliminate segregation. The anti-busing board voted in was then forced to continue the program by court order. And like many large American cities, Denver, almost everybody here says, is in bad need of an effective system of mass transit.

These two issues—busing and mass transit—have been important factors in the last two congressional elections in the 1st district. In 1970, when the 1st included the entire city, veteran (1951–71) Rep. Byron Rogers was defeated by just 30 votes in the Democratic primary by a young lawyer named Craig Barnes. Barnes was one of the lawyers who got an injunction against the anti-busing school board. In the general election, busing seemed to have played a major role, as Barnes lost, 52–45, to Republican (and then District Attorney) Mike McKevitt.

Ordinarily when a new Congressman is elected, he can use the advantages of his office, if not just his name recognition, to win by larger margins in subsequent years. The advantages of incumbency are underscored when, as in the case of the 1st, a friendly legislature removes opposition territory from the district; in this case, some Chicano precincts on the west side and a heavily Democratic portion at the northern edge of the city. But McKevitt, unlike most of his freshman colleagues, was clearly facing a tough race when he went home to campaign in 1972.

One reason was the rise of a young, liberal activist element within the local Democratic party. Symbolic of this was the Democratic primary victory, by a 55–45 margin, of 32-year-old Patricia Schroeder over an 18-year veteran of the state Senate. Ms. Schroeder drew much of her support from the same kind of people who were backing the ultimately successful referendum to ban use of state money on the 1976 Winter Olympics, and from those who had supported Craig Barnes two years before. But she managed to project an image less far-out than Barnes; Ms. Schroeder was opposed, she said, to busing, though she did not make it a major issue.

One issue the candidate did emphasize was mass transit. In Congress, McKevitt had voted against diverting money from the highway trust fund for mass transit; Schroeder took the opposite view. This issue was a factor in the outcome. But most important to Schroeder's victory was a large, well-organized, intensive volunteer effort—something that is seldom seen anywhere in the country for House contests.

If Schroeder's victory represented a departure from the ordinary, so did her actions upon coming to Washington. She sought and, over the objections of Chairman F. Edward Hebert, obtained a seat on the House Armed Services Committee. It was the first time in some years that a woman has sat on this panel, and the first time in memory that a woman who takes a strong stance for cutting the military budget has been here. Chairman Hebert, a courtly man from New Orleans, has come to treat the new member of his committee with Southern gallantry. But he was no doubt displeased when Ms. Schroeder voted, along with a majority of Armed Services' Democrats, to stop the Nixon Administration's bombing of Cambodia.

Census Data Pop. 441,881. Central city, 99%; suburban, 1%. Median family income, $9,977; families above $15,000: 24%; families below $3,000: 9%. Median years education, 12.5.

1972 Share of Federal Outlays $603,390,060

DOD	$141,694,560	HEW	$143,781,832
AEC	$30,478,121	HUD	$11,323,696
NASA	$76,776,570	DOI	$28,552,214
DOT	$17,035,701	USDA	$13,275,794
		Other	$140,471,572

Federal Military-Industrial Commitments

DOD Installations AF Accounting and Finance Center (Denver). Lowry AFB (Denver).

Economic Base Finance, insurance and real estate; food and kindred products, especially cookies and crackers, and meat packing plant products; printing and publishing, especially newspapers; electrical equipment and supplies, especially electric measuring instruments, and telephone and telegraph apparatus; and machinery, especially construction and related machinery. Also higher education (Univ. of Denver).

The Voters

Registration 270,948 total. 117,744 D (43%); 73,892 R (27%); 79,312 unaffiliated (29%).
Median voting age 42.6
Employment profile White collar, 61%. Blue collar, 24%. Service, 15%. Farm, –%.
Ethnic groups Black, 10%. Spanish, 14%. Total foreign stock, 17%. Germany, USSR, UK, 2% each.

Presidential vote

1972	Nixon (R)	101,950	(55%)
	McGovern (D)	82,403	(45%)
1968	Nixon (R)	79,091	(45%)
	Humphrey (D)	86,119	(49%)
	Wallace (AI)	8,813	(5%)

Representative

Patricia Schroeder (D) Elected 1972; b. July 30, 1940, Portland, Oregon; home, Denver; U. of Minn., B.S., 1961; Harvard Law School, J.D., 1964; married, two children.

Career Hearing Officer, NLRB, Colo., Wy., Utah, 1964–66; Lecturer and Law Instructor, 1969–72; Hearing Officer, Colo. Dept. of Personnel, 1971–72; Legal Counsel, Planned Parenthood of Colorado.

Offices 1313 LHOB, 202-225-4431. Also Denver Fed. Bldg., 1961 Stout St., Denver, 303-837-2354.

Administrative Assistant Michael Cheroutes

COLORADO

Committees

Armed Services (24th). Subs: No. 3.

Post Office and Civil Service (13th). Subs: Investigations; Postal Facilities, Mail, and Labor Management.

Group Ratings: Newly Elected

Key Votes

1) Busing	NE	6) Cmbodia Bmbg	AGN	11) Chkg Acct Intrst	FOR
2) Strip Mines	NE	7) Bust Hwy Trust	FOR	12) End HISC (HUAC)	AGN
3) Cut Mil $	NE	8) Farm Sub Lmt	NE	13) Nixon Sewer Veto	AGN
4) Rev Shrg	NE	9) School Prayr	NE	14) Corp Cmpaign $	NE
5) Pub TV $	NE	10) Cnsumr Prot	NE	15) Pol $ Disclosr	NE

Election Results

1972 general:	Patricia Schroeder (D)	101,832	(52%)
	James D. McKevitt (R)	93,733	(48%)
	Marie Pauline Serna (LRU)	1,629	(1%)
1972 primary:	Patricia Schroeder (D)	24,885	(55%)
	Clarence Decker (D)	20,549	(45%)

SECOND DISTRICT Political Background

Between the city of Denver and the Front Range of the Rockies some 20 miles west lies the fastest growing part of Colorado. Just west of the city is Jefferson County, whose population almost doubled during the 1960s. To the immediate north is Boulder County, dominated by its namesake city and home of the University of Colorado. These two counties, plus a predominantly Mexican-American chunk of the west side of Denver, make up the 2nd congressional district.

Like many other booming suburban areas in the West, the economy of the 2nd district has been fueled by electronic and other high-technology industries. And as in many other such areas, the people brought in by this kind of growth have proved to be profoundly conservative politically. But here in the Denver suburbs election results have not been as heavily Republican as in Phoenix or Orange County, California. An older, non-boom-wrought political tradition still has influence, and the growing appeal of ecology-related issues—like the 1972 Olympics referendum—has moved some voters here over to the Democrats.

Nor can one ignore the presence of the University of Colorado in Boulder. The coming of the 18-year-old vote precipitated a mini-revolution; Boulder County's Republican District Attorney was turned out for a Democrat, and, of more significance, Boulder County alone contributed more than half of Sen. Floyd Haskell's 1972 statewide margin.

The Congressman from the 2nd is Donald G. Brotzman, a generally reliable supporter of the Nixon Administration. Brotzman first won the seat in 1962, when then-Rep. Peter Dominick ran for the Senate. Brotzman lost it again in the 1964 Johnson landslide and won it back handily in 1966. His vote-getting ability recently has been solid. In 1970 and 1972 against Democrats who made pitches for the University vote, Brotzman won easily and even held his own on campus—unlike all other major Republican candidates. Brotzman is a junior member of the House Ways and Means Committee. So placed, he gets little publicity, but does have great power, when he chooses to use it, on issues like tax reform, health care, and Social Security. In 1973, Brotzman's voting record suddenly became more liberal on most—though not all—issues. Apparently, he noticed the Haskell and Schroeder victories in Colorado in 1972, and is preparing for a similar challenge in 1974.

Census Data Pop. 439,399. Central city, 17%; suburban, 83%. Median family income, $11,201; families above $15,000: 26%; families below $3,000: 6%. Median years education, 12.6.

1972 Share of Federal Outlays $600,037,893

DOD	$140,907,368	HEW	$142,983,044
AEC	$30,308,798	HUD	$11,260,787
NASA	$76,350,033	DOI	$28,393,591
DOT	$16,941,058	USDA	$13,202,039
		Other	$$139,691,175

Federal Military-Industrial Commitments

DOD Contractors Beech Aircraft (Boulder), $6.676m: unspecified research.
AEC Operations Dow Chemical (Rocky Flats), $69.304m: operation of Rocky Flats plant and design and production of nuclear weapons components.

Economic Base Finance, insurance and real estate; machinery, especially electronic computing equipment; agriculture, notably cattle, nursery and greenhouse products, and dairy products; tourism; and food and kindred products. Also higher education (Univ. of Colorado).

The Voters

Registration 263,937 total. 73,950 D (28%); 72,167 R (27%); 117,820 unaffiliated (45%).
Median voting age 38.7
Employment profile White collar, 60%. Blue collar, 28%. Service, 11%. Farm, 1%.
Ethnic groups Spanish, 10%. Total foreign stock, 12%. Germany, 2%; UK, USSR, 1% each.

Presidential vote

1972	Nixon (R)	142,326	(65%)
	McGovern (D)	76,789	(35%)
1968	Nixon (R)	86,156	(53%)
	Humphrey (D)	63,901	(40%)
	Wallace (AI)	11,277	(7%)

Representative

Donald G. Brotzman (R) Elected 1962–64 and 1966–present; b. June 28, 1922, Logan County; home, Boulder; Colo. U. Law and Business schools; Army, WWII; married, two children; Methodist.

Career Practicing atty., 1949–59; Colo. House of Reps., 1950–52, Senate, 1952–56; Repub. Caucus leader in Colo. Senate, 1956; Repub. candidate for govenor of Colo., 1954, 1956; U.S. Atty. for Colo., 1959–60.

Offices 403 CHOB, 202-225-2161. Also Room 202 Bldg. 40, Denver Fed. Ctr., Denver 80225, 303-234-4222.

Administrative Assistant David W. Delcour

Committees

Ways and Means (8th).

Group Ratings

	ADA	COPE	LWV	RIPON	NFU	LCV	CFA	NAB	NSI	ACA
1972	6	20	50	75	71	33	50	100	100	68
1971	16	0	44	67	40	–	50	–	–	86
1970	24	34	–	82	62	50	58	75	100	67

Key Votes

1) Busing	AGN	6) Cmbodia Bmbg	AGN	11) Chkg Acct Intrst	AGN
2) Strip Mines	AGN	7) Bust Hwy Trust	FOR	12) End HISC (HUAC)	AGN
3) Cut Mil $	ABS	8) Farm Sub Lmt	FOR	13) Nixon Sewer Veto	FOR
4) Rev Shrg	FOR	9) School Prayr	FOR	14) Corp Cmpaign $	AGN
5) Pub TV $	AGN	10) Cnsumr Prot	FOR	15) Pol $ Disclosr	FOR

Election Results

1972 general:	Donald G. Brotzman (R)	132,562	(66%)
	Frances W. Brush (D)	66,817	(34%)
1972 primary:	Donald G. Brotzman (R), unopposed		
1970 general:	Donald G. Brotzman (R)	152.153	(63%)
	Roy H. McVicker	89,917	(37%)

THIRD DISTRICT Political Background

Ordinarily, when the power over redistricting—control of the legislature and the governor's office—is in the hands of one party, the process goes smoothly. Not so in Colorado in 1972. Not until the last days of the legislative session was agreement reached on a major reshaping of the state's congressional district lines. One reason was that the state got a new district as a result of the 1970 census, which meant that various ambitious legislators had more than the usual interest in the way lines were drawn (see Colorado 5). Another reason was Democratic Congressman Frank Evans.

One might suppose that a Republican legislature would try to make things as uncomfortable as possible for a Democratic Congressman. But not in Evans' case. The legislature's aim was to draw him a district that would be as attractive as possible; that is, as Democratic as possible. The Republican state legislators knew that Evans was unbeatable, no matter how they drew the lines. But they also knew that the more difficult they made it for him, the more likely he was to run for the Senate against three-term Republican incumbent Gordon Allott. The assumption at the time—it proved quite inaccurate—was that Evans was the only Democrat who could give Allot trouble.

How does a Congressman get into a position so enviable that the opposition sweats to make things easy for him? Evans was one of the forty-odd Congressmen carried into office by the Johnson landslide of 1964—to judge from the 1972 results, apparently the last presidential landslide in our history with significant coattails. In 1964, Evans beat an aging, veteran incumbent by a narrow margin, and by all political lore should have been eminently unseatable in 1966. The district, as it then stood, was the southeastern quarter of Colorado, which had two major urban centers, Colorado Springs (Republican) and Pueblo (Democratic). But the demography of the old district favored the Republicans, since Colorado Springs was growing rapidly, and Pueblo, a steel-mill town, scarcely at all.

During his first term, Evans, like many of the Democrats elected in 1964, made skillful use of the congressional frank (the free mailing privilege), and attended carefully to his constituents' problems. He compiled what was considered a middle-of-the-road record for a Northern Democrat. In 1966, he won by a reasonable margin, and he kept increasing it in subsequent elections. In 1970, he even managed to carry staunchly Republican Colorado Springs. Meanwhile, he won a seat on the Appropriations Committee.

This was the Evans situation confronting the Republican redistricters in the spring of 1972. Their response was to take most of Colorado Springs out of the 3rd district and place it into a new, heavily Republican 5th district. To make up for the loss of population, redistricters extended the 3rd district across the Rockies, all the way to the Utah line to take in the southern half of the Western Slope. The new 3rd would have been a tough district for most Democrats, but everybody knew it would be easy for Evans, which it was.

Census Data Pop. 442,217. Central city, 28%; suburban, 17%. Median family income, $7,578; families above $15,000: 10%; families below $3,000: 13%. Median years education, 12.1.

1972 Share of Federal Outlays $528,098,816

DOD	$182,006,700	HEW	$163,703,867
AEC	–	HUD	$6,614,348
NASA	$72,526	DOI	$17,642,744
DOT	$17,862,153	USDA	$54,863,188
		Other	$85,333,290

Federal Military-Industrial Commitments

DOD Installations Fort Carson AB (Colorado Springs). Pueblo Army Depot (Pueblo). Peterson Field (Colorado Springs).

Economic Base Agriculture, notably cattle and grains; finance, insurance and real estate; food and kindred products; and metal mining.

The Voters

Registration 213,352 total. 89,970 D (42%); 53,929 R (25%); 69,453 unaffiliated (33%). *Median voting age* 41.5
Employment profile White collar, 43%. Blue collar, 33%. Service, 16%. Farm, 8%.
Ethnic groups Black, 2%. Spanish, 23%. Total foreign stock, 11%. Germany, 2%.

Presidential vote

1972	Nixon (R)		102,569	(64%)
	McGovern (D)		57,152	(36%)
1968	Nixon (R)		71,578	(46%)
	Humphrey (D)		71,673	(46%)
	Wallace (AI)		13,923	(9%)

Representative

Frank Edwards Evans (D) Elected 1964; b. Sept. 8, 1923, Pueblo; home, Pueblo; Pomona Col., 1941–43; U. of Denver, B.A., 1947, LL.B., 1949; Navy, WWII; married, four children; Presbyterian.

Career Practicing atty., 1950–64; Colo. House of Reps., 1961–65; Dem. Whip, 1963–65.

Offices 2443 RHOB, 202-225-4761. Also Fed. Bldg., Pueblo 81002, 303-544-5277 ext. 313, and Rm. 418, 2860 S. Circle Dr., Colorado Springs 80020, 303-576-5596.

Administrative Assistant R. Dale Hulshizer

Committees

Appropriations (23rd); Subs: Agriculture, Environmental and Consumer Protection; Interior; Legislative.

Group Ratings

	ADA	COPE	LWV	RIPON	NFU	LCV	CFA	NAB	NSI	ACA
1972	75	82	89	67	86	40	100	33	22	10
1971	76	73	100	78	87	–	63	–	–	11
1970	84	92	–	88	91	40	90	9	30	21

Key Votes

1) Busing	FOR	6) Cmbodia Bmbg	AGN	11) Chkg Acct Intrst	AGN
2) Strip Mines	ABS	7) Bust Hwy Trust	FOR	12) End HISC (HUAC)	FOR
3) Cut Mil $	AGN	8) Farm Sub Lmt	FOR	13) Nixon Sewer Veto	AGN
4) Rev Shrg	AGN	9) School Prayr	AGN	14) Corp Cmpaign $	ABS
5) Pub TV $	FOR	10) Cnsumr Prot	FOR	15) Pol $ Disclosr	FOR

Election Results

1972 general:	Frank E. Evans (D)	107,511	(66%)
	Chuck Brady (R)	54,556	(34%)
1972 primary:	Frank E. Evans (D), unopposed		
1970 general:	Frank E. Evans (D)	87,000	(64%)
	John C. Mitchell, Jr. (R)	45,610	(34%)
	Martin P. Serna (LRU)	1,828	(1%)
	Walter N. Cranson (Peace)	1,598	(1%)

FOURTH DISTRICT Political Background

It is in the nature of our political system that an obscure primary election in some far corner of the nation can have a substantial impact on the way the federal government does business. This statement is really just a corollary of the seniority system: what power years of service can confer, the voters can quickly revoke. One such primary was the 1966 contest in Virginia, where Howard W. Smith, Chairman of the House Rules Committee, was defeated. Another was the 1972 primary race in the 4th district of Colorado, where Wayne N. Aspinall, Chairman of the House Interior and Insular Affairs Committee and *bete noir* of a host of conservationists and environmental activists, was beaten.

Back in 1948, Aspinall, then an attorney and sometime state Representative, was elected to the first of his twelve terms in the House. He was already 58 years old. The district from which he was elected consisted of all the Western Slope counties of Colorado, an area of rugged mountains and very few people (less than 200,000). Like many Western Congressman, Aspinall wanted to get on the Interior Committee, which has jurisdiction over federal lands, reclamation, and water. He made it and, through good luck, became Chairman after the 1958 elections.

From his position as Chairman, Aspinall could and did extract federal goodies—dams, roads, reclamation projects, and more—for his district. The Western Slope, unlike most of the West, is water-rich, and when Senators from Arizona or California or even Congressmen from Denver wanted to tap the waters of the upper Colorado, they had to give Aspinall what he wanted—or their bills would never come out of committee. But it would be unfair to portray Aspinall as simply a man out for his district's enrichment—the man who wanted to "Californicate" Colorado. Aspinall mastered the Interior Committee's subject matter thoroughly, and if he worked to bring home the bacon, that bacon was only consistent with his general philosophy of favoring maximum use of government lands and the resources on them.

The ecology movement, age, and redistricting finally caught up with Aspinall—in reverse order. In 1964, Colorado had to add Eastern Slope counties to his constituency in order to bring the 4th's population up to the state average. The largest two of these counties, Weld and Larimer, ordinarily cast heavy Republican margins, and Aspinall never ran particularly well in them. Environmentalists had long spotted Aspinall as their most powerful and resourceful adversary in the Congress, and were prepared to work for and contribute to anyone who might run against him in the Democratic primary. In 1970, the 74-year-old Aspinall had his first primary opposition in 22 years, and later got only 55% of the vote in the general election.

Then in 1972 the Republican legislature hastened the end. Its redistricting plan divided the Western Slope, Aspinall's home base, between his district and that of fellow Democrat Frank Evans (see Colorado 3). On the Eastern Slope, the legislature added a piece of Adams County, which contains a number of Democratic suburbs of Denver—Westminster, North Glenn, and Brighton. Only 26% of the new 4th's population lived in the Western Slope counties.

Aspinall's primary opponent was Alan Merson, a 38-year-old law professor and Brooklyn native. Merson campaigned hard, at a pace the 76-year-old Aspinall could not match. The professor won 63% of the votes on the Eastern Slope, with his greatest majorities coming from the ·district's two major college towns, Fort Collins in Larimer County (Colorado State University) and Greeley in Weld County (Colorado State College). But Merson also made inroads on the Western Slope. Here the most striking result came in Aspen, where radical chic socialites, street ·· people, and *Rolling Stone* National Affairs Editor Dr. Hunter Thompson mingle at the famous ski resort. Both groups apparently preferred Merson's stands on the environment to Aspinall's: the county came in with 1,158 votes for the challenger and 99 for the incumbent.

The district's Republican leanings, however, proved disastrous for Merson in the general ·election. The Republican candidate, attorney James Johnson—considered a party moderate —campaigned as hard on environmental issues as Merson. Despite the student vote, which went for Merson, Johnson carried both Weld and Larimer and won 53% of the votes in the Eastern Slope counties. That Merson was able to carry the Western Slope—and run far, far ahead of George McGovern—is a tribute to his campaigning abilities. But the bulk of the 4th votes were cast in Republican territory east of the mountains. To the environmentalists, Merson's loss was not really crushing; the main point was to get rid of the Chairman of the Interior Committee, and that was accomplished.

Census Data Pop. 442,024. Central city, 0%; suburban, 20%. Median family income, $8,992; families above $15,000: 15%; families below $3,000: 10%. Median years education, 12.4.

1972 Share of Federal Outlays $481,027,947

DOD	$38,025,237	HEW	$150,038,712
AEC	$9,958,341	HUD	$2,546,158
NASA	$15,758,657	DOI	$42,833,365
DOT	$63,676,205	USDA	$69,905,781
		Other	$88,285,491

Federal Military-Industrial Commitments

No installations or contractors receiving prime awards greater than $5,000,000.

Economic Base Agriculture, notably cattle, grains, and hogs and sheep; finance, insurance and real estate; food and kindred products, especially meat packing plant products, and beet sugar; tourism; and electrical equipment and supplies. Also higher education (Colorado State Univ.).

The Voters

Registration 268,311 total. 80,281 D (30%); 80,980 R (30%). 107,050 unaffiliated (40%). *Median voting age* 40.2
Employment profile White collar, 47%. Blue collar, 30%. Service, 14%. Farm, 9%.
Ethnic groups Spanish, 10%. Total foreign stock, 12%. USSR, 3%; Germany, 2%.

Presidential vote

1972	Nixon (R)	129,253	(67%)
	McGovern (D)	63,181	(33%)
1968	Nixon (R)	87,571	(55%)
	Humphrey (D)	57,216	(36%)
	Wallace (AI)	13,584	(9%)

Representative

James P. Johnson (R) Elected 1972; b. June 2, 1930, Yankton, South Dakota; home, Fort Collins; Northwestern U., B.A., 1952; U. of Colo., LL.B., 1959; USMC, 1952–56; married, three children; Presbyterian.

Career Municipal Judge, Ault and Fort Collins, Colo.; Poudre R-1 School Board, Fort Collins, 1969–71; Board of Trustees, San Francisco Theological Seminary, presently; Bd. of Dir., Fort Collins Chamber of Commerce, 1968–70.

Offices 514 CHOB, 202-225-4676. Also Fed. Office Bldg., Grand Junction 81501, 303-243-1736, and Fed. Office Bldg., Fort Collins 80521, 303-493-9132.

Administrative Assistant William Cleary

Committees

Agriculture (15th); Subs: Livestock and Grains; Oilseeds and Rice; Domestic Marketing and Consumer Relations.

Group Ratings: Newly Elected

Key Votes

1) Busing	NE	6) Cmbodia Bmbg	AGN	11) Chkg Acct Intrst	AGN
2) Strip Mines	NE	7) Bust Hwy Trust	AGN	12) End HISC (HUAC)	FOR
3) Cut Mil $	NE	8) Farm Sub Lmt	NE	13) Nixon Sewer Veto	FOR
4) Rev Shrg	NE	9) School Prayr	NE	14) Corp Cmpaign $	NE
5) Pub TV $	NE	10) Cnsumr Prot	NE	15) Pol $ Disclosr	NE

Election Results

1972 general:	James T. Johnson (R)	94,994	(51%)
	Alan Merson (D)	91,151	(49%)
1972 primary:	James T. Johnson (R)	16,045	(60%)
	Dal Berg (R)	10,566	(40%)

FIFTH DISTRICT Political Background

It is not often that a state as small as Colorado gains a congressional seat. Sixty years passed between the time Colorado got its fourth seat in the 1910 census and its fifth in the 1970. Naturally, a lot of politicians eyed the new district longingly, and redistricting—even though the legislature and the governorship were both safely in Republican hands—took months of wrangling (see Colorado 3). Given the political situation, it was assumed that in the end the new district would be solidly Republican, as indeed it turned out to be.

The new 5th, like so many congressional districts born of political hassling, looks fairly regular on the map; but when one looks more closely, it becomes clear that the 5th by no means encompasses any kind of cohesive community. The bulk of the district's people live in the Denver suburbs, north, east, and south of the city. As one proceeds around the clock in this manner, one goes from the more Democratic suburbs (Commerce City and a chunk of Denver itself) to middle-of-the-road (Aurora) to Republican (Englewood, Littleton). The latter two are the home of many of Colorado's richest and most prominent citizens, including both the state's U.S. Senators. Englewood and Littleton, developed in the 1950s, have that comfortable, leafy, lived-in look; those suburbs developed in the 1960s and 1970s, of course, do not.

To the south, after traveling Interstate 25 through some residential sprawl and arid, mile-high plateau, lies Colorado Springs. This is a wealthy, fast-growing community, known for its military installations (the Air Force Academy, Fort Carson) and tourist attractions (Pike's Peak, the

Garden of the Gods). Politically, Colorado Springs is a sort of Rocky Mountain San Diego, conservative and Republican—though it should be added that like the Denver suburbs, the city has proved susceptible to Democrats like Floyd Haskell who stress ecology issues.

The 5th also moves east to the Kansas border. It was out in this country, Dee Brown writes, that the first Colorado boomers, in the wake of the Gold Rush of 1858, set some Colorado cavalry on defenseless Cheyenne men, women, and children. What happened, according to Brown, was very bad, full of atrocities. Today this portion of the 5th district of Colorado is virtually uninhabited, a region of large cattle ranches, tumbleweed, and gas-station-stop towns along Interstate 70. It casts only 10% of the district's votes.

It is no surprise that the new Congressman from the 5th had been a major power in the state legislature that drew the new district's lines. William Armstrong, the state Senate Majority Leader from 1969 to 1972, was so clearly in line for the seat that he faced no opposition in the Republican primary. His Democratic opponent Byron Johnson was a former Congressman (1959–61), but in a Republican district like this one, he had no chance. The high point of the campaign was when Armstrong poo-pooed Johnson's charges that the Nixon Administration was corrupt. Given Armstrong's age—only 37 in 1974—and the leanings of the district, he is likely to remain in Congress for a long time, barring a Watergate backlash stronger than most people expect.

Census Data Pop. 441,738. Central city, 26%; suburban, 68%. Median family income, $10,278; families above $15,000: 23%; families below $3,000: 7%. Median years education, 12.5.

1972 Share of Federal Outlays $726,250,371

DOD	$353,732,494	HEW	$125,336,465
AEC	$17,897,430	HUD	$10,363,038
NASA	$45,224,138	DOI	$17,956,834
DOT	$20,374,160	USDA	$28,732,988
		Other	$106,632,824

Federal Military-Industrial Commitments

DOD Contractors Santa Fe Engineers (Colorado Springs), $12.116m: unspecified. Kaman Corp. (Colorado Springs), $6.864m: ABM studies. Cardinal Meat (Denver), $6.814m: foodstuffs.
DOD Installations Fitzsimmons General Army Hospital (Denver). Rocky Mountain Arsenal (Denver). Air Force Academy (Colorado Springs). Ent AFB (Colorado Springs).
NASA Contractors Martin Marietta (Denver), $134.824m: Viking lander system; payload integration for Skylab.

Economic Base Finance, insurance and real estate; agriculture, notably cattle and grains; electrical equipment and supplies; machinery, especially mining machinery; stone, clay and glass products, especially concrete, gypsum and plaster products; and fabricated metal products.

The Voters

Registration 221,725 total. 57,913 D (26%); 66,647 R (30%); 97,165 unaffiliated (44%).
Median voting age 39.2
Employment profile White collar, 55%. Blue collar, 29%. Service, 13%. Farm, 3%.
Ethnic groups Black, 2%. Spanish, 9%. Total foreign stock, 11%. Germany, 2%; UK, 1%.

Presidential vote

1972	Nixon (R)	121,492	(71%)
	McGovern (D)	50,546	(29%)
1968	Nixon (R)	72,124	(55%)
	Humphrey (D)	48,187	(37%)
	Wallace (AI)	11,676	(9%)

Representative

William L. Armstrong (R) Elected 1972; b. Mar. 16, 1937, Fremont, Neb.; home, Aurora; married, two children; Lutheran.

Career Pres. KOSI, AM-FM Radio, Aurora; Bd. of Dir., Peoples Bank & Trust Co.; Board of Directors, Peoples Bank of Arapahoe County; State Rep., 1963–64; State Senate, 1965–72.

Offices 513 CHOB, 202-225-4422. Also Suite #5, 2522 Hanover St., Aurora, 303-837-2655.

Administrative Assistant Frank R. Lee

Committees

Armed Services (14th); Subs: No. 3.

Group Ratings: Newly Elected

Key Votes

1) Busing	NE	6) Cmbodia Bmbg	FOR	11) Chkg Acct Intrst	ABS
2) Strip Mines	NE	7) Bust Hwy Trust	AGN	12) End HISC (HUAC)	AGN
3) Cut Mil $	NE	8) Farm Sub Lmt	NE	13) Nixon Sewer Veto	FOR
4) Rev Shrg	NE	9) School Prayr	NE	14) Corp Cmpaign $	NE
5) Pub TV $	NE	10) Cnsumr Prot	NE	15) Pol $ Disclosr	NE

Election Results

1972 general:	William L. Armstrong (R)	104,214	(62%)
	Byron L. Johnson (D)	60,948	(36%)
	Pipp Boyls (Libertarian)	2,028	(1%)
1972 primary:	William L. Armstrong (R), unopposed		

CONNECTICUT

Political Background

Until quite recently, Connecticut probably had the strongest political parties of any state in the country. The two party organizations were run by a long line of strong leaders: a series of chiefs for the Republicans and, since 1946, John Bailey for the Democrats. These men could manipulate their party's delegations in Hartford and also commanded overwhelming majorities at the state party conventions that chose nominees for major offices. One mainstay of the strong party system was the straight-ticket lever. For years, Connecticut citizens could activate their voting machines only by voting a straight ticket; after doing this, they could, if they wished, split their tickets—but few took the trouble to do so. Consequently, the strength of the candidate at the top of the ticket determined the outcome of races for numerous lesser offices. In the 1956 Eisenhower landslide, for example, the state elected six Republican Congressmen and no Democrats. Two years later, when Abe Ribicoff was reelected Governor by a record margin, the state elected six Democrats and no Republicans.

During the 1960s, some of the rules changed, and the party organizations gradually grew weaker. The straight-ticket lever is no longer mandatory, and the nominees of the party conventions can be challenged by any candidate who gets 20% of the convention votes. But habits linger on. It was not until 1970 that a party convention choice was forced into a primary and beaten. And with the exception of the three-candidate Senate race in 1970, it was not until 1972 that Connecticut voters began to split their tickets to the extent common in almost all the other states. The mores of the state's political culture have thus produced voting behavior that goes against the teachings of political scientists; for Connecticut voters are more affluent, better educated, and more suburban—and hence, one would think, more likely to split tickets—than voters in the nation as a whole. But this is changing now, and it is symbolic that the Connecticut politician best known nationally today, Sen. Lowell Weicker, is not a product of one of the traditional Connecticut machines.

But even as these habits change, one tradition of Connecticut politics will surely remain: the ethnically balanced ticket. Connecticut is one of the most polyglot of states. The public may still cherish the image of the Connecticut Yankee, but the average resident of the state is more likely to be of Irish, Polish, French-Canadian, Jewish, or—most numerous of all—Italian descent. About half the state's population is Roman Catholic.

This ethnic background is essential to an understanding of the state's recent, and not so recent, politics. Until the 1930s, Connecticut was politically still Yankee Republican, going for Hoover in 1932. Only with the Depression and the New Deal did the ethnics begin to vote—in most cases, for Democrats. But the real ascendency of the Democratic party in Connecticut did not begin until John M. Bailey became its State Chairman in 1946. Bailey saw to it that his party's tickets were carefully balanced, groomed strong candidates like Ribicoff, and kept his organization well-fed by controlling the governorship most of the time—for 16 straight years from 1954 to 1970.

But today the Bailey organization is in sad shape, plagued by aging leadership, the great schisms that split the Democratic party during the sixties, and the changing mood of the predominantly Catholic, middle-class voters who were an essential part of its majorities. The Republicans now hold the governorship, one of the two Senate seats, three of the six congressional districts, and majorities in both houses of the state legislature. The margin that Connecticut Democrats used to assume they had by God-given right is pretty much gone.

This decline became most obvious in 1970 when Sen. Thomas J. Dodd, censured by the Senate for unethical practices and seriously ill, announced that he would not seek the Democratic nomination, and was retiring. Bailey's candidate was Adolphus J. Donahue, a wealthy Catholic businessman. Donahue won at the state convention, and in more ordinary times could have been expected to win rather easily in the fall. But instead, he was challenged in a primary—and in an even bigger surprise, beaten—by Rev. Joseph Duffey. Duffey, then national chairman of Americans for Democratic Action, was a leading supporter of Sen. Eugene McCarthy in the 1968 presidential primaries. The upset victor's candidacy represented a revolt by Democrats who were opposed to Bailey's steadfast support of Lyndon Johnson and Hubert Humphrey. Then Dodd, perhaps to avoid a possible income tax indictment, reentered the Senate race. Dodd was never a Bailey favorite, but the veteran Senator's fervent anticommunism made him popular with many of the state's Catholic voters. And as an independent, Dodd managed to win 24% of the vote and carry several blue-collar cities. With the Democrats thus split, the Republican candidate, one-term Congressman Lowell Weicker, was able to win a Senate seat with just 42% of the vote. Meanwhile, Republican Congressman Thomas J. Meskill won the governorship by a 54-46 margin.

Weicker is one of those politicians who rises to high office with comparative ease, aided by feuds and squabbles among his opponents. An heir to the Squibb drug fortune, he was First Selectman (the equivalent of Mayor) of Greenwich when he was elected to the House in 1968 with 51% of the vote. An independent peace candidate in that election took some votes and also helped to put the hawkish Democratic incumbent on the defensive. In 1970, Weicker won the Senate seat with far less than a majority. Nevertheless, the Connecticut politician appears on the way to more solid ground.

During his first years in Congress, Weicker showed an independence of the Nixon Administration. He voted against the ABM, SST, and the Administration's views on the Vietnam war. More recently, he has served on the Watergate Select Committee with special vigor, having conducted his own investigation and becoming the first member of Congress to call for the resignation of top aide, H. R. Haldeman. Weicker's exasperated denunciations of Nixon Administration figures like John Mitchell, John Ehrlichman, and H. R. Haldeman have made him a national figure himself—and have made him so popular in Connecticut that he is just about certain of reelection when his seat comes up in 1976.

One of the most illustrious people to come out of Connecticut politics is Abraham Ribicoff, who has served as Congressman, Governor, and, since 1962, Senator. An early supporter of John F. Kennedy's candidacy, Ribicoff became Secretary of Health, Education, and Welfare for the first two years of the Kennedy Administration. And it is in matters relating to HEW programs that Ribicoff has made his greatest mark in the Senate. As a senior member of the Finance Committee, the Senator was responsible for keeping the Nixon Family Assistance Plan alive as long as possible before it died, beset by attacks from both left and right. At some points during the controversy, it seemed that Ribicoff was fighting harder for the bill than the Administration; and once, in 1972, by threatening to withdraw his support, the Senator got HEW officials to agree on a compromise, which Nixon later repudiated. The man from Connecticut has also distinguished himself as one of the few Northern Democrats to urge imposition of the same desegregation requirements in the North as in the South. His move gets most of its support from erstwhile Southern segregationists, but Ribicoff's idea certainly has an undeniable integrationist logic behind it.

In a heavily suburban state like Connecticut, with its share of racial problems, such stands may be unpopular. But Ribicoff, a man of great intensity and pride, seems more concerned about following his principles than with scoring quick points with the voters. In 1968, for example, while nominating George McGovern at the 1968 Democratic Convention, Ribicoff looked down from the podium, stared directly at Mayor Richard Daley, and accused him of Gestapo-like tactics. Waving his fists, Daley responded with some unprintables. The actions of the Chicago police force no doubt proved popular with many hippie-hating Connecticut voters. Nevertheless, Ribicoff won reelection that year by a solid margin, with only a few defections in blue-collar areas.

In 1974, Ribicoff may face greater difficulty at the polls. In early 1973, he began to speak more often throughout the state, meeting with Democrats of all stripes and trying to restore some of the unity that vanished in the wake of the Vietnam war. Recent election figures do indicate that he may have more trouble than in the past; in 1972, for the first time in nearly 20 years, Democratic candidates for Congress in Connecticut got fewer votes than Republican ones. A particularly strong Republican Senate contender would be Congressman Robert Steele, who won his second term by a near two-to-one margin in 1972.

Another factor affecting Ribicoff's chances will be the 1974 gubernatorial race. Although Connecticut voters abandoned their straight party habits in a big way in 1970—Steele, for example, ran 9% ahead of Nixon in his district, and Democratic Rep. Ella Grasso 21% ahead of McGovern in hers—a strong reelection victory by Gov. Thomas Meskill could hurt Ribicoff. At this writing, however, this possibility seems unlikely. Meskill, who was Mayor of New Britain (pop. 83,000) before he went to Congress, has staffed his administration and the state Republican party with home-town cronies. Moreover, he has promoted a potentially popular conservative program (a kind of East Coast Reaganism) in a hamhanded way. In his first year in office, for example, he refused to either sign or veto an unpopular income tax bill, then forced the legislature into session and won its repeal. Erratic behavior of this sort has apparently upset the voters; in recent polls, Meskill ran far behind Congresswoman Grasso.

The state's House delegation is now split evenly, but there could be some changes in 1974. All but two of the state's six districts are potentially marginal, and the two most popular incumbents, Steele and Grasso, could conceivably seek statewide office.

Census Data Pop. 3,032,217; 1.50% of U.S. total, 24th largest; change 1960–70, 19.6%. Central city, 35%; suburban, 47%. Median family income, $11,808; 2nd highest; families above $15,000: 31%; families below $3,000: 5%. Median years education, 12.2.

1972 Share of Federal Tax Burden $4,473,000,000; 2.14% of U.S. total, 14th largest.

1972 Share of Federal Outlays $3,443,222,538; 1.59% of U.S. total, 21st largest. Per capita federal spending, $1,136.

DOD	$1,396,444,000	16th	(2.23%)	HEW	$1,025,085,090	24th	(1.44%)
AEC	$6,663,595	22nd	(0.25%)	HUD	$69,309,524	15th	(2.26%)
NASA	$18,961,347	16th	(0.63%)	VA	$135,644,140	33rd	(1.18%)
DOT	$110,876,748	29th	(1.41%)	USDA	$38,497,304	42nd	(0.25%)
DOC	$5,960,204	35th	(0.46%)	CSC	$24,209,790	36th	(0.59%)
DOI	$1,661,779	49th	(0.08%)	TD	$384,539,690	8th	(2.33%)
DOJ	$19,209,076	16th	(1.96%)	Other	$206,160,251		

Economic Base Transportation equipment, especially aircraft and parts; finance, insurance and real estate; machinery, especially general industrial machinery; fabricated metal products, especially cutlery, hand tools and hardware; electrical equipment and supplies; primary metal industries, especially nonferrous rolling and drawing; printing and publishing, especially newspapers and commercial publishing.

Political Line-up Governor, Thomas J. Meskill (R); seat up, 1974. Senators, Abraham A. Ribicoff (D) and Lowell P. Weicker, Jr. (R). Representatives, 6 (3 D and 3 R). State Senate (23 R and 13 D); State House (93 R and 58 D).

The Voters

Registration 1,507,000 Total. 554,111 D (37%); 420,210 R (28%); 532,679 unaffiliated (35%).
Median voting age 43.6
Employment profile White collar, 52%. Blue collar, 36%. Service, 11%. Farm, 1%.
Ethnic groups Black, 6%. Spanish, 2%. Total foreign stock, 32%. Italy, 8%, Canada, 4%, Poland, 3%, UK, Ireland, Germany, USSR, 2% each.

Presidential vote

1972	Nixon (R)		810,763	(59%)
	McGovern (D)		555,498	(41%)
1968	Nixon (R)		556,721	(44%)
	Humphrey (D)		621,561	(50%)
	Wallace (AI)		76,650	(6%)
1964	Johnson (D)		826,629	(68%)
	Goldwater (R)		390,996	(32%)

Senator

Abraham A. Ribicoff (D) Elected 1962, seat up 1974; b. April 9, 1910, New Britain; home, Hartford; New York U., U. of Chicago, LL.B., 1933; married, two children; Jewish.

Career Conn. General Assembly, 1938–42; Municipal Judge, Hartford, 1941–43, 1945–47; U.S. House of Reps., 1948–52; Gov. of Conn., 1954–1961; Secy., Dept. of Health, Ed., and Welfare, 1961–62.

Offices 321 OSOB, 202-225-2823. Also 707 New Fed. Bldg., 450 Main St., Hartford 06103, 203-244-3713.

Administrative Assistant John A. Koskinen

Committees

Finance (5th); Subs: International Trade (Chm.); Health; Private Pension Plans.

Government Operations (5th); Subs: Permanent Investigations; Reorganization, Research, and International Organizations (Chm.).

Joint Economic Com. (4th); Subs: Inter-American Economic Relationships; Consumer Economics; Fiscal Policy; International Economics; Urban Affairs.

Group Ratings

	ADA	COPE	LWV	RIPON	NFU	LCV	CFA	NAB	NSI	ACA
1972	80	86	100	78	80	87	100	10	22	18
1971	93	75	100	79	100	–	100	–	–	5
1970	94	100	–	91	81	82	–	20	100	0

Key Votes

1) Busing	FOR	8) Sea Life Prot	FOR	15) Tax Singls Less	FOR
2) Alas P-line	AGN	9) Campaign Subs	FOR	16) Min Tax for Rich	AGN
3) Gun Cntrl	FOR	10) Cmbodia Bmbg	AGN	17) Euro Troop Rdctn	FOR
4) Rehnquist	AGN	11) Legal Srvices	FOR	18) Bust Hwy Trust	FOR
5) Pub TV $	FOR	12) Rev Sharing	FOR	19) Maid Min Wage	FOR
6) EZ Votr Reg	ABS	13) Cnsumr Prot	FOR	20) Farm Sub Limit	FOR
7) No-Fault	FOR	14) Eq Rts Amend	FOR	21) Highr Credit Chgs	AGN

Election Results

1968 general:	Abraham A. Ribiroff (D)	655,043	(54%)
	Edwin H. May, Jr. (R)	551,455	(46%)
1968 primary:	Abraham A. Ribicoff (D), unopposed		
1962 general:	Abraham A. Ribicoff (D)	527,522	(51%)
	Horace Seely-Brown, Jr. (R)	501,694	(49%)

Senator

Lowell P. Weicker, Jr. (R) Elected 1970, seat up 1976; b. May 16, 1931, Paris, France; home, Greenwich; Yale U., B.A., 1953; U. of Va., LL.B., 1958; Army, Korean War; Capt. USAR, 1959–64; married, two children; Episcopalian.

Career Atty.; Conn. Assembly, 1962–68; First Selectman, Greenwich, 1963–68; Legislative Consultant, Conn. Transport Auth., 1965; Secy., Conn. Tax Study Commission, 1966–67.

Offices 342 OSOB, 202-225-4041. Also 1 Bank St., Stamford 06902, 203-325-3866, and Rm. 11-C Fed. Ct. Bldg., Lafayette Plaza, Bridgeport 06603, 203-335-0195.

Administrative Assistant Robert L. Herrema

Committees

Aeronautical and Space Sciences (3rd).

Banking, Housing and Urban Affairs (7th); Subs: Securities; Production and Stabilization; Small Business (Ranking Mbr.).

Sel. Com. on Presidential Campaign Activities (3rd).

Group Ratings

	ADA	COPE	LWV	RIPON	NFU	LCV	CFA	NAB	NSI	ACA
1972	30	50	78	90	38	43	56	50	78	42
1971	30	18	77	55	63	–	25	–	–	57

Key Votes

1) Busing	FOR	8) Sea Life Prot	FOR	15) Tax Singls Less	FOR
2) Alas P-line	FOR	9) Campaign Subs	AGN	16) Min Tax for Rich	AGN
3) Gun Cntrl	AGN	10) Cmbodia Bmbg	AGN	17) Euro Troop Rdctn	AGN
4) Rehnquist	FOR	11) Legal Srvices	FOR	18) Bust Hwy Trust	FOR
5) Pub TV $	FOR	12) Rev Sharing	FOR	19) Maid Min Wage	AGN
6) EZ Votr Reg	AGN	13) Cnsumr Prot	ABS	20) Farm Sub Limit	ABS
7) No-Fault	FOR	14) Eq Rts Amend	FOR	21) Highr Credt Chgs	FOR

Election Results

1970 general:	Lowell P. Weicker, Jr. (R)	443,008	(42%)
	Joseph P. Duffey (D)	360,094	(34%)
	Thomas J. Dodd (Ind.)	260,264	(24%)
1970 primary:	Lowell P. Weicker, Jr. (R), unopposed		

FIRST DISTRICT Political Background

Hartford is Connecticut's largest city, the state capital, and the headquarters of many of the nation's largest insurance companies. Hartford and its suburbs also contain much of Connecticut's defense industry—most notably, United Aircraft, producers of airplane engines. As with most of Connecticut's larger cities, people have long since spread out from Hartford into a series of comfortable suburbs. These range from working-class areas like East Hartford and

Windsor on the Connecticut River to the high-income WASP and Jewish precincts of West Hartford and Bloomfield. Hartford itself, with the bulk of the area's poor and black residents, has many of the typical urban problems. But here in this small city, with its gleaming new office buildings, its ornate old state Capitol, and with its white-collar employment running high, urban problems do not seem as overwhelming as they do in New York or Philadelphia. In fact, optimistic city fathers have launched an ambitious and expensive regional development program for Hartford and environs.

Hartford, and the 1st congressional district, which includes the city and most of its suburbs, has long been the Democratic stronghold of Connecticut. This can be attributed in part to the efforts of John M. Bailey, state and formerly national Democratic Chairman. Analysis of election returns indicates that a higher percentage of low-income, Democratic electors vote here than in other parts of Connecticut—or, for that matter, other parts of the country. Given the traditional strength of the Democratic party here, the present Congressman from the 1st district, William Cotter, came to office in a rather unusual fashion. He challenged an organization candidate in the primary, won, and then went on to win the general election by a paper-thin margin. Cotter was probably hurt by the poor showing of the Democratic gubernatorial candidate, his predecessor Emilio Daddario, and by the strong campaign waged by his Republican opponent, then Hartford Mayor Ann Uccello. Another factor was the independent candidacy of one Edward Coll. Lovers of the best in political humor will recall his later performance: as a putative presidential candidate in the 1972 New Hampshire primary, he hoisted a rubber rat into the air by its tail, so demonstrating to the TV audience and the other solemn candidates on the panel the real issue of the campaign.

Reelection, as it usually does these days, came more easily to Cotter. In the first months of the 93rd Congress, he made some national headlines as the first Representative to endorse the April 1973 meat boycott—a movement that probably attracted more participants than all the 1972 presidential campaigns put together. Cotter has also been one of the few Democrats to break party lines on agricultural programs, voting with the Nixon Administration to cut authorizations for the Department of Agriculture.

Despite his pro-consumer record in Washington, Cotter, in his previous job as Connecticut Insurance Commissioner, won the ire of Ralph Nader. Under state law, any insurance company proposal must be approved by the Commissioner. And for some months in 1969, Cotter refused to permit the acquisition of the Hartford—one of the state's insurance giants—by ITT. Then, after considerable pressure, Commissioner Cotter relented and approved the deal. The Nixon Administration later brought an antitrust suit against ITT, but then allowed the conglomerate to keep the Hartford—allegedly in return for a $400,000 guarantee toward the holding of the Republican National Convention in San Diego. Cotter was in no way connected to the San Diego aspect of the case, but he was the target of an unsuccessful suit by Nader challenging his acts as Insurance Commissioner.

None of the controversy seems to have had an effect on the Congressman's political fortunes. He won 58% of the district's votes in 1972, and has reason to look forward to near automatic reelection.

Census Data Pop. 505,418. Central city, 35%; suburban, 47%. Median family income, $12,031; families above $15,000: 32%; families below $3,000: 6%. Median years education, 12.2.

1972 Share of Federal Outlays $724,405,713

DOD	$370,000,000	HEW	$183,951,106
AEC	$2,201,647	HUD	$18,797,405
NASA	$6,694,241	DOI	$541,002
DOT	$19,463,153	USDA	$4,714,461
		Other	$118,012,698

Federal Military-Industrial Commitments

DOD Contractors United Aircraft (East Hartford), $450.106m: aircraft engines and components. Colt Industries (Hartford), $21.838m: bomb fuzes. Kaman Corp. (Bloomfield), $20.430m: helicopter components. Kaman Aerospace (Bloomfield), $9.071m: aircraft components. Chandler Evans (West Hartford), $7.808m: aircraft engine accessories.

Economic Base Transportation equipment, especially aircraft engines and engine parts; finance, insurance and real estate; machinery, especially ball and roller bearings; fabricated metal products, especially hardware not otherwise classified; and electrical equipment and supplies, especially switchgear and switchboard apparatus. Also higher education (Univ. of Hartford).

The Voters

Registration 259,279 total. 122,197 D (47%); 69,729 R (27%); 67,353 unaffiliated (26%).
Median voting age 44.4
Employment profile White collar, 58%. Blue collar, 31%. Service, 11%. Farm, –%.
Ethnic groups Black, 10%. Spanish, 3%. Total foreign stock, 34%. Italy, 7%; Canada, 6%; Poland, 4%; Ireland, 3%; USSR, UK, Germany, 2% each.

Presidential vote

1972	Nixon (R)	121,196	(51%)
	McGovern (D)	114,473	(49%)
1968	Nixon (R)	85,854	(39%)
	Humphrey (D)	125,090	(56%)
	Wallace (AI)	10,692	(5%)

Representative

William R. Cotter (D) Elected 1970; b. July 18, 1926, Hartford; home, Hartford; Trinity Col., B.A., 1949; unmarried; Catholic.

Career Mbr., Ct. of Common Council, Hartford, 1953; Aide to Governor Abraham A. Ribicoff, 1955–57; Deputy Insurance Commissioner, 1957–64; Insurance Commissioner, 1964–70.

Offices 330 CHOB, 202-225-2265. Also 450 Main St., Hartford 06114, 203-244-2383.

Administrative Assistant Malcolm O. Campbell, Jr.

Committees

Banking and Currency (18th); Subs: Bank Supervision and Insurance; Small Business; Urban Mass Transportation.

Science and Astronautics (10th); Subs: Aeronautics and Space Technology; Manned Space Flight; Science, Research, and Development.

Group Ratings

	ADA	COPE	LWV	RIPON	NFU	LCV	CFA	NAB	NSI	ACA
1972	63	91	75	71	71	51	100	17	25	18
1971	70	91	75	75	67	–	100	–	–	19

Key Votes

1) Busing	AGN	6) Cmbodia Bmbg	AGN	11) Chkg Acct Intrst	AGN
2) Strip Mines	AGN	7) Bust Hwy Trust	FOR	12) End HISC (HUAC)	FOR
3) Cut Mil $	AGN	8) Farm Sub Lmt	FOR	13) Nixon Sewer Veto	AGN
4) Rev Shrg	FOR	9) School Prayr	AGN	14) Corp Cmpaign $	FOR
5) Pub TV $	FOR	10) Cnsumr Prot	FOR	15) Pol $ Disclosr	FOR

Election Results

1972 general:	William R. Cotter (D)	130,701	(57%)
	Richard M. Rittenband (R)	96,188	(42%)
	Charlie A. Burke (AI)	2,778	(1%)
1972 primary:	William R. Cotter (D), unopposed		

1970 general:	William R. Cotter (D)	88,374	(49%)
	Antonio P. Uccello (R)	87,209	(48%)
	Edward T. Coll (Public Party)	5,774	(3%)

SECOND DISTRICT Political Background

The 2nd district comprises the eastern half of Connecticut. The district has Yankee villages and high-income summer and retirement colonies having names like Old Saybrook and Old Lyme; the 2nd also has small and medium-sized industrial mill towns like Norwich, Danielson, and Putnam. Traditional Yankee Republicanism still has some strength here, but the political balance lies in the hands of second- and third-generation ethnics in places like New London and Middletown.

The mix here makes the 2nd a middle-of-the-road, bellwether district, at least when no incumbent is running. During the 1950s, when the straight-party-lever was still mandatory and few tickets were split, congressional elections were usually close in the district, with party control shifting a couple of times. More recent elections have shown a shift to the more common national trend: the election of a Congressman by close margin and his reelection by much larger margins as long as he keeps running.

Thus Democrat William St. Onge, at the time of his death in 1970, was entrenched in the 2nd and would have been very difficult to unseat. And his successor, Robert Steele, judging from his solid reelection majority in 1972, now occupies that same enviable position.

Steele, a former employee of the CIA, won with only 53% of the vote in 1970. He immediately proceeded to an energetic cultivation of this variegated district. For one thing, Steele claims credit for bringing a Coast Guard research and development center to New London; and for another, he has been particularly sympathetic to positions taken by environmentalists—important in a district that still retains much of the beauty and quaintness of old New England. The Congressman attracted some headlines with a 1971 tour of Vietnam to investigate drug abuse among GIs—the first time this matter got national exposure.

In 1972, Steele's Democratic opponent was Roger Hilsman, former summertime-only resident of the 2nd and also Assistant Secretary of State for Far Eastern Affairs in the early days of the Johnson Administration. As it turned out, Hilsman seems to have known less about congressional campaigns than Far Eastern affairs. Like Steele, the Democrat had CIA experience. So this became the first congressional race in American history pitting two CIA veterans against each other. Steele won the contest with a solid 66%, running 6% ahead of Nixon in the district.

There is now speculation that Steele may try for statewide office. If he does, it will be risky. Sen. Abraham Ribicoff will be hard to beat. And it is unlikely that Steele will challenge fellow Republican Gov. Thomas Meskill. Since the other Senate seat is also held by a Republican, Lowell Weicker, that leaves Steele with the choice of a risky race or waiting six more years for a better shot at the Ribicoff seat. Should he choose to wait the six years, the size of his 1972 majority indicates that he will have little trouble remaining in the House.

Census Data Pop. 505,493. Central city, 33%; suburban, 66%. Median family income, $10,885; families above $15,000: 24%; families below $3,000: 7%. Median years education, 12.1.

1972 Share of Federal Outlays $722,417,680

DOD	$453,960,000	HEW	$144,821,572
AEC	$86,297	HUD	$9,983,072
NASA	$438,476	DOI	$347,878
DOT	$41,058,560	USDA	$8,591,375
		Other	$63,130,450

Federal Military-Industrial Commitments

DOD Contractors General Dynamics (Groton), $359.568m: support of Poseidon missile system. Sydney Construction (New London), $6.428m: unspecified. Raymond Engineering (Middletown), $5.268m: bomb fuzes.

Economic Base Textile mill products; finance, insurance and real estate; agriculture, notably poultry, dairy products, and nursery and greenhouse products; fabricated metal products; machinery; and transportation equipment, especially aircraft and parts. Also higher education (Univ. of Connecticut).

The Voters

Registration 236,395 total. 83,380 D (35%); 62,195 R (26%); 90,820 unaffiliated (38%).
Median voting age 40.8
Employment profile White collar, 48%. Blue collar, 39%. Service, 12%. Farm, 1%.
Ethnic groups Black, 2%. Spanish, 1%. Total foreign stock, 26%. Canada, 6%; Italy, 4%; Poland, 3%; UK, Germany, 2% each; USSR, Ireland, 1% each.

Presidential vote

1972	Nixon (R)	127,923	(60%)
	McGovern (D)	85,382	(40%)
1968	Nixon (R)	82,739	(44%)
	Humphrey (D)	95,604	(51%)
	Wallace (AI)	10,025	(5%)

Representative

Robert H. Steele (R) Elected 1970; b. Nov. 3, 1938, Hartford; home, Vernon; Amherst Col., B.A., 1960; Columbia U., M.A., Cert. of Russian Inst., 1963; married, three children; Episcopalian.

Career Soviet Specialist for the Central Intelligence Agency, Latin America, 1963–68; securities analyst, The Travelers Insurance Company, 1968– .

Offices 227 CHOB, 202-225-2076. Also Mail Box 1970, Vernon 06086, 203-872-9183.

Administrative Assistant E. H. Steven Berg

Committees

Foreign Affairs (11th); Subs: Foreign Economic Policy; Inter-American Affairs (Ranking Mbr.).

Merchant Marine and Fisheries (8th); Subs: Coast Guard and Navigation; Fisheries and Wildlife Conservation and the Environment; Oceanography.

Group Ratings

	ADA	COPE	LWV	RIPON	NFU	LCV	CFA	NAB	NSI	ACA
1972	56	90	83	73	71	93	100	33	70	30
1971	51	70	75	88	53	–	75	–	–	44

Key Votes

1) Busing	AGN	6) Cmbodia Bmbg	AGN	11) Chkg Acct Intrst	AGN
2) Strip Mines	AGN	7) Bust Hwy Trust	FOR	12) End HISC (HUAC)	AGN
3) Cut Mil $	AGN	8) Farm Sub Lmt	FOR	13) Nixon Sewer Veto	FOR
4) Rev Shrg	FOR	9) School Prayr	FOR	14) Corp Cmpaign $	AGN
5) Pub TV $	FOR	10) Cnsumr Prot	FOR	15) Pol $ Disclosr	FOR

Election Results

1972 general:	Robert H. Steele (R)	142,094	(66%)
	Roger Hilsman, Jr. (D)	73,400	(34%)
1972 primary:	Robert H. Steele (R), unopposed		
1970 general:	Robert H. Steele (R)	92,846	(53%)
	John F. Pickett (D)	81,492	(47%)

THIRD DISTRICT **Political Background**

The Italian-American has long been the forgotten man in American politics. He is too far up the ladder of economic security and social status to engage the sympathies of foundation heads and affluent academics; yet in ways that still hurt, the society at large discriminates against him. And more often than not, the Italian-American is deprived of those advantages of background most WASPs take for granted. In the years of radical chic and of electoral alliances best exemplified by New York Mayor John Lindsay's winning coalitions (white rich, and the black and brown poor), the ethnic Italian-American felt left out completely. Liberal activists and their friends in the media took little interest in the hum-drum New Deal type programs that benefited the forgotten man and his family. And the same people felt free to condemn the Italian-American as bigot—not knowing or unwilling to learn that most Italian-Americans never possessed those advantages which make enlightenment on race come so painlessly to upper-income liberals.

There are more Italian-Americans, as the census defines them, in the 3rd district of Connecticut, centering on New Haven, than in all but 13 of the nation's 435 congressional districts. They settled here, mostly in the late nineteenth and early twentieth centuries, and found jobs in the factories of New Haven. There are still old, cohesive Italian-American communities in the city, but most of the descendants of the original immigrants have moved out to suburbs like West Haven, East Haven, and Hamden. Unlike most immigrant groups, the Italians of southern Connecticut gravitated to the Republican party, because the Irish seemed to dominate the Democrats. To a surprising extent, the Italians retained their Republican allegiance through the New Deal years; and today, probably a majority of the 3rd district's Italian-Americans have a clear preference for the Republican party of Richard Nixon over the Democratic party of George McGovern or even Abraham Ribicoff.

Most readers, when thinking of the 3rd district and New Haven, think of Yale, and perhaps of the famous urban renewal program of ex-Mayor (1953–69) Richard Lee. But Yale, which has fewer students (8,800) than Southern Connecticut State College, plays little part in the politics of the 3rd, except maybe as something the rest of the district can dislike together. These are the people living in neat New England suburban houses, whose parents lived in what are now black ghettos, and whose sons don't play lacrosse for Yale varsity. And Lee is no longer Mayor; he has been succeeded by an ally of Democratic Town Chairman Arthur Barbieri, a longtime antagonist of State Chairman John Bailey.

The Congressman from the 3rd district, Robert Giaimo (pronounced JYE-moh), is a Barbieri ally and a town rather than gown Democrat. A middle-seniority member of Appropriations, Giaimo's thinking on issues is more in line with that of traditional big-city Democrats than with the liberal Democratic Study Group. In the late 1960s, for example, he vociferously attacked the conduct of New Haven's antipoverty program. In early 1973, area Democrats chose Giaimo to serve on the House Democratic Steering and Policy Committee, which may, or may not, provide some leadership and discipline for the usually badly split majority party. About the only blotches on Giaimo's congressional career were charges of dubious conduct; notably, that he had arranged a Caribbean cruise at government expense for a constituent who turned out to be a racketeer.

This sort of thing has had little noticeable effect on elections in the 3rd district. And Giaimo's increasingly conservative voting record in the late sixties was probably an accurate reflection of his constituency's disenchantment with the programs of the Great Society. His more recent shift to an anti-Nixon position—most notably on Cambodia, where he was one of the leaders of the successful move to stop the bombing in 1973—may signal a corresponding change in mood in his constituency. Nevertheless, the Congressman has not been winning elections in particularly impressive style. With left- and right-wing third-party opponents in 1968 and 1970, Giaimo won with about 55% of the vote. In 1972 he won only 53%. Such performances indicate that the incumbent may be in for trouble in future elections.

Census Data Pop. 505,293. Central city, 27%; suburban, 62%. Median family income, $11,463; families above $15,000: 29%; families below $3,000: 6%. Median years education, 12.2.

1972 Share of Federal Outlays $359,406,125

DOD	$42,050,000	HEW	$194,791,199
AEC	$1,726,893	HUD	$11,342,497
NASA	$834,551	DOI	$84,948
DOT	$7,643,634	USDA	$5,359,272
		Other	$95,563,131

Federal Military-Industrial Commitments

DOD Contractors United Aircraft (Stratford), $119.490m: research, design, and maintenance of aircraft engines. Avco Corp. (Stratford), $68.783m: aircraft engines and components.

Economic Base Finance, insurance and real estate; fabricated metal products, especially cutlery, hand tools and hardware, and metal stampings; primary metal industries, especially copper rolling and drawing; machinery, especially metalworking machinery and general industrial machinery; and rubber and plastics products. Also higher education (Southern Connecticut Univ. and Yale Univ.).

The Voters

Registration 259,270 total. 83,310 D (32%); 52,058 R (20%); 123,902 unaffiliated (48%).
Median voting age 43.8
Employment profile White collar, 53%. Blue collar, 35%. Service, 11%. Farm, 1%.
Ethnic groups Black, 9%. Spanish, 2%. Total foreign stock, 31%. Italy, 10%; Poland, Ireland, UK, Canada, USSR, Germany, 2% each.

Presidential vote

1972	Nixon (R)	142,569	(62%)
	McGovern (D)	87,766	(38%)
1968	Nixon (R)	96,553	(45%)
	Humphrey (D)	102,907	(48%)
	Wallace (AI)	16,308	(8%)

Representative

Robert N. Giaimo (D) Elected 1958; b. Oct. 15, 1919, New Haven; home, North Haven; Fordham Col., B.A., 1941; U. of Conn., LL.B., 1943; Army, WWII; Capt. USAR; married, one child; Catholic.

Career Chm., Conn. Personnel Appeals Bd., 1955–58; Third Selectman of North Haven, 1955–57; Bd. of Ed., 1949–55; Bd. of Finance, 1952–55.

Offices 2265 RHOB, 202-225-3661. Also 301 P.O. Bldg., New Haven 06510, 203-624-1308, 203-772-0800, ext. 6361, and P.O. Bldg., Stratford 06497, 203-378-8410.

Administrative Assistant D. Eileen Nixon

Committees

Appropriations (15th); Subs: Defense; Housing and Urban Development, Space, Science, Veterans; Legislative.

Joint Com. on Congressional Operations (2nd).

Group Ratings

	ADA	COPE	LWV	RIPON	NFU	LCV	CFA	NAB	NSI	ACA
1972	31	70	45	69	57	47	0	40	20	45
1971	38	78	56	47	71	–	71	–	–	50
1970	56	80	–	56	83	73	65	0	70	19

Key Votes

1) Busing	AGN	6) Cmbodia Bmbg	AGN	11) Chkg Acct Intrst	FOR
2) Strip Mines	AGN	7) Bust Hwy Trust	FOR	12) End HISC (HUAC)	FOR
3) Cut Mil $	ABS	8) Farm Sub Lmt	ABS	13) Nixon Sewer Veto	FOR
4) Rev Shrg	AGN	9) School Prayr	FOR	14) Corp Cmpaign $	FOR
5) Pub TV $	FOR	10) Cnsumr Prot	FOR	15) Pol $ Disclosr	AGN

Election Results

1972 general:	Robert Giaimo (D)	121,217	(53%)
	Henry A. Povinelli (R)	106,313	(47%)
1972 primary:	Robert Giaimo (D), unopposed		
1970 general:	Robert Giaimo (D)	89,042	(55%)
	Robert J. Dunn (R)	69,048	(42%)
	Richard P. Antonetti (Dodd Ind.)	5,062	(3%)

FOURTH DISTRICT Political Background

If Hartford County has been the traditional home of Connecticut's Democrats, Fairfield County has been the bedrock of the state's Republicans. Fairfield County is one of the richest in the nation, a land of broad, well-manicured lawns sweeping down to Long Island Sound, of woodsy New Canaan and artsy-craftsy Westport, of commuters driving to the station to take the bedraggled New Haven Railroad into Manhattan. Unlike the rest of Connecticut, Fairfield County is an extension of New York City, economically and otherwise. People watch New York's numerous TV stations rather than Connecticut's two VHF outlets—it's Mets, not Red Sox, territory.

This is the 4th congressional district—a string of high-income, traditionally Republican towns along Long Island Sound: Greenwich, Stamford, Darien, Norwalk, Westport, Fairfield. But it would be inaccurate to imply that the harried advertising executive on an hour commute is the typical 4th-district voter. There is more to the district than the cliche. The 4th takes in the industrial town of Bridgeport as well as the commuter towns; and even in the fancy towns, below the railroad station or around the old downtown, you can see the slightly rundown small houses where the district's poorer voters live. Some 10% of the 4th's residents are black, and it has a higher percentage of foreign-stock residents than any other in the state.

The 4th has been the scene of two countervailing political trends. Its richer residents, moved by the Vietnam war and, often, by the strange new habits of their children, have been edging slightly to the left and toward the Democrats. At the same time, the district's traditional Democrats, particularly blue-collar, Catholic ethnics, have been moving steadily to the right, giving most of their votes to candidates like Richard Nixon and Gov. Thomas Meskill. The result: in 1972, wealthy Westport and industrial Bridgeport gave George McGovern about the same percentage of their votes—41% and 45%. Compare that with 1960, when Westport went 36% and Bridgeport 61% for John F. Kennedy.

These two trends have left the 4th, on balance, more Republican than before, which is good news for its Congressman, Stewart McKinney. For some years the district was considered marginal, with Democrat Donald Irwin actually winning in 1958, 1964, and 1966. But McKinney, who first won in 1970, was reelected easily last time, and probably has no political worries for the future. Despite his lack of seniority, he is ranking minority member of the District of Columbia Education Subcommittee.

Census Data Pop. 505,366. Central city, 68%; suburban, 32%. Median family income, $12,692; families above $15,000: 38%; families below $3,000: 5%. Median years education, 12.3.

1972 Share of Federal Outlays $607,918,843

DOD	$177,954,000	HEW	$147,847,347
AEC	$26,771	HUD	$6,292,206
NASA	$4,261,312	DOI	$65,882
DOT	$17,438,929	USDA	$8,762,554
		Other	$245,269,842

Federal Military-Industrial Commitments

DOD Contractors United Aircraft (Norwalk), $21.947m: aircraft engines and components. United Aircraft (Bridgeport), $8.435m: helicopter maintenance.

Economic Base Finance, insurance and real estate; electrical equipment and supplies, especially communication equipment; transportation equipment, especially aircraft and parts; machinery, especially office and computing machines; and fabricated metal products. Also higher education (Univ. of Bridgeport).

The Voters

Registration 245,710 total. 81,367 D (33%); 83,679 R (34%); 80,664 unaffiliated (33%).
Median voting age 45.1
Employment profile White collar, 56%. Blue collar, 33%. Service, 11%. Farm, –%.
Ethnic groups Black, 10%. Spanish, 5%. Total foreign stock, 35%. Italy, 8%; Poland, UK, 3% each; Canada, Ireland, Germany, USSR, 2% each.

Presidential vote

1972	Nixon (R)	138,496	(63%)
	McGovern (D)	81,802	(37%)
1968	Nixon (R)	105,455	(50%)
	Humphrey (D)	92,922	(44%)
	Wallace (AI)	13,159	(6%)

Representative

Stewart B. McKinney (R) Elected 1970; b. Jan. 30, 1931, Pittsburgh, Pa.; home, Fairfield; Princeton U., 1949–51; Yale U., B.A., 1958; USAF, 1951–55; married, five children; Episcopalian.

Career Former Pres., CMF Tires; operates Lantern Point Real Estate Dev.; Conn. House of Reps., 1967–70; Minority Leader, 1969–70.

Offices 504 CHOB, 202-225-5541. Also P.O. Box 543, Fairfield 06430, 203-259-7802; Fed. Bldg., LaFayette Blvd., Bridgeport 06603, 203-384-2286; and 1116 Summer St., Stamford 06905, 203-259-7802.

Administrative Assistant Joseph McGee (L.A.)

Committees

Banking and Currency (11th); Subs: Consumer Affairs; International Trade; Urban Mass Transportation.

District of Columbia (7th); Subs: Education (Ranking Mbr.); Revenue and Financial Affairs.

Group Ratings

	ADA	COPE	LWV	RIPON	NFU	LCV	CFA	NAB	NSI	ACA
1972	63	60	75	75	50	73	100	67	25	28
1971	49	50	75	78	33	–	75	–	–	54

Key Votes

1) Busing	AGN	6) Cmbodia Bmbg	AGN	11) Chkg Acct Intrst	FOR
2) Strip Mines	AGN	7) Bust Hwy Trust	FOR	12) End HISC (HUAC)	AGN
3) Cut Mil $	FOR	8) Farm Sub Lmt	ABS	13) Nixon Sewer Veto	FOR
4) Rev Shrg	ABS	9) School Prayr	FOR	14) Corp Cmpaign $	AGN
5) Pub TV $	FOR	10) Cnsumr Prot	FOR	15) Pol $ Disclosr	FOR

Election Results

1972 general:	Stewart B. McKinney (R)	135,883	(63%)
	James P. McLoughlin (D)	79,515	(37%)
1972 primary:	Stewart B. McKinney (R), unopposed		
1970 general:	Stewart B. McKinney (R)	104,494	(57%)
	T. F. Gilroy Daly (D)	78,699	(43%)
	Eileen M. Emard (AI)	1,428	(1%)

FIFTH DISTRICT Political Background

The 5th district is an amalgam of Connecticut's lesser-known cities and towns which are spread out over the hills just north of Long Island Sound. The district includes the industrial city of Waterbury and the decaying mill towns of the Naugatuck Valley; the relatively prosperous working-class town of Meriden to the east; and Danbury, onetime hat-manufacturing center, in the west. Danbury is also known for its federal prison that has accommodated such malefactors as the Berrigan brothers and one G. Gordon Liddy. These industrial cities and towns are all traditionally Democratic; found in between are smaller, Republican towns that are more Yankee.

But the most important part of the 5th, politically, in 1972, was a small portion that had been added in the redistricting following the 1970 census. With the Democrats then in control of the state legislature, a plan was passed and ultimately approved by the courts which added to the old, seemingly safe Democratic 5th, the heavily Republican towns of New Canaan, Wilton, and Weston. The idea was to remove Republican votes from the adjacent 4th district, and put that district, on paper at least, within the reach of a Democratic challenger. But, as often happens, the redistricters miscalculated. The 4th was never going to go Democratic. And the reconstituted 5th, as it worked out, retired a veteran Democratic incumbent and elected his Republican challenger.

The Democratic incumbent was John Monagan, who had held office since the Connecticut Democratic sweep of 1958. As Chairman of a subcommittee, Monagan spent much of what turned out to be his last term investigating fraud and incompetence in the administration of an FHA low-income housing program. This seems not to have helped him much in the 5th—nor did a trip that he took to Europe at government expense during the 1972 campaign.

Meanwhile, Republican challenger Ronald Sarasin worked hard all over the district. The younger (45 vs. 60) man must have made a particularly good impression on the district's new residents; while Monagan's style, redolent of an older, Irish tradition, did not seem to go over well with the WASP suburbanites of new Republican towns. Despite a brief campaign, Monagan managed to carry that portion of the district which he had previously represented by about 1,000 votes—a somewhat smaller margin than he had enjoyed in the past. But he lost the new part of the 5th by 6,400 votes. The Connecticut Democrats tried to win both the 4th and 5th districts, and ended up losing both.

On the face of it, Sarasin might seem in precarious shape for 1974, having won by a slim 51–49 margin. But if he attends to his constituents as vigorously as he campaigned, which he seems to be doing, he will probably have little trouble winning. The 5th has a record, going back almost 30 years, of keeping its Representative in office from 12 to 14 years, and it may be on another such string now.

Census Data Pop. 505,316. Central city, 42%; suburban, 39%. Median family income, $12,200; families above $15,000: 33%; families below $3,000: 5%. Median years education, 12.2.

1972 Share of Federal Outlays $450,902,120

DOD	$91,625,000	HEW	$178,070,762
AEC	$1,121,700	HUD	$9,597,763
NASA	$2,082,238	DOI	$75,472
DOT	$11,292,993	USDA	$6,559,161
		Other	$150,477,031

Federal Military-Industrial Commitments

No installations or contractors receiving prime awards greater than $5,000,000.

Economic Base Electrical equipment and supplies, especially communication equipment; machinery, especially office and computing machines; transportation equipment, especially aircraft and parts; finance, insurance and real estate; and fabricated metal products.

The Voters

Registration 254,015 total. 85,890 D (34%); 71,435 R (28%); 96,600 unaffiliated (39%). *Median voting age* 44.4

Employment profile White collar, 51%. Blue collar, 39%. Service, 10%. Farm, –%.
Ethnic groups Black, 4%. Spanish, 2%. Total foreign stock, 34%. Italy, 9%; Canada, 4%; Poland, 3%; UK, Ireland, Germany, 2% each; USSR, 1%.

Presidential vote

1972	Nixon (R)		144,149	(62%)
	McGovern (D)		87,747	(38%)
1968	Nixon (R)		96,604	(45%)
	Humphrey (D)		100,828	(47%)
	Wallace (AI)		15,503	(7%)

Representative

Ronald A. Sarasin (R) Elected 1972; b. Dec. 31, 1934, Fall River, Mass.; home, Beacon Falls; U. of Conn., B.S., 1960; U. Conn. School of Law, J.D., 1963; married, one child; Catholic.

Career State House, 1968–72, Asst. Minority Leader, 1970–72; Town Counsel, Beacon Falls, 1963–72; Asst. Prof. of Law, New Haven Col., 1963–66; Pres., Naugatuck Valley Bar Assn., 1972.

Offices 511 CHOB, 202-225-3822. Also Fed. Bldg., 135 Grand St., Waterbury 06701, 203-573-1418.

Administrative Assistant Marc G. Stanley

Committees

Education and Labor (15th); Subs: No. 3 (Gen. Sub. on Labor); No. 4 (Sel. Sub. on Labor); No. 5 (Education).

Group Ratings: Newly Elected

Key Votes

1) Busing	NE	6) Cmbodia Bmbg	AGN	11) Chkg Acct Intrst	AGN
2) Strip Mines	NE	7) Bust Hwy Trust	FOR	12) End HISC (HUAC)	AGN
3) Cut Mil $	NE	8) Farm Sub Lmt	NE	13) Nixon Sewer Veto	FOR
4) Rev Shrg	NE	9) School Prayr	NE	14) Corp Cmpaign $	NE
5) Pub TV $	NE	10) Cnsumr Prot	NE	15) Pol $ Disclosr	NE

Election Results

1972 general:	Ronald A. Sarasin (R)	117,578	(51%)
	John S. Monagan (D)	112,142	(49%)
1972 primary:	Ronald A. Sarasin (R), unopposed		

SIXTH DISTRICT Political Background

Some congressional districts seem to be made up of territory left over after everyone else has constructed his own constituency. Such a district is the 6th of Connecticut. Its population centers are widely dispersed, usually at the edges of other districts. Enfield and Windsor Locks, in the far northeast corner, are both predominantly Italian and part of the Hartford-to-Springfield (Massachusetts) industrial corridor. In the southeast corner of the 6th are Bristol and New Britain, the latter the home of Gov. (and ex-Rep.) Thomas Meskill and the city with the state's largest concentration of Polish-Americans. In the north-central part of the district, amid the gentle mountains, are the mill towns of Torrington and Winsted, the latter Ralph Nader's home town.

The 1964 legislature, which drew the district's lines (they have been altered only slightly since), expected the 6th to elect a Democrat, and these towns do in fact provide the Democratic majorities. In between are Yankee towns (like Sharon, the home of the Buckley clan) and some posh and Republican Hartford suburbs like Farmington, Avon, and Simsbury.

In its relatively brief history, the 6th has had three Representatives. The first, Bernard Grabowski, was a beneficiary of the tradition that the state's Congressman-at-Large be of Polish descent; he was slated in 1962 when the incumbent rebelled against the leadership of Democratic State Chairman John Bailey. Grabowski did fine while riding the coattails of the state ticket in 1962 and LBJ in 1964; left to his own devices in this rather disparate constituency in 1966, he lost. The winner was Thomas Meskill, the brash, politically conservative Mayor of New Britain, who went on to the governorship in 1970.

Meskill's successor is Democrat Ella Grasso, formerly Connecticut Secretary of State. She has often been considered a bridge between the Bailey and the intellectual wing of her party. Mrs. Grasso's 1970 race was closer than expected, due in large part to a weak state Democratic ticket. She had to run 11% ahead of her party's candidate for Governor to win. In 1972, she did even better, running a full 21% ahead of George McGovern, and in the process winning by a larger margin than any other member of the state's delegation.

At this writing, Mrs. Grasso is being mentioned as a candidate for Governor in 1974. She has led her congressional predecessor Meskill by wide margins in recent polls, and is one of the relatively few Democrats who is trusted and respected by both wings of her party. In a state where Italian-Americans are by far the largest ethnic group, her Italian ancestry is no political handicap. And so it is possible that Ella Grasso will become the nation's first woman Governor since the late Lurleen Wallace of Alabama—and first ever to win the office on her own merits, rather than as some kind of stand-in for, or successor to, her husband.

Census Data Pop. 505,331. Central city, 26%; suburban, 51%. Median family income, $11,898; families above $15,000: 30%; families below $3,000: 5%. Median years education, 12.2.

1972 Share of Federal Outlays $578,123,838

DOD	$260,790,000	HEW	$175,683,513
AEC	$1,500,000	HUD	$13,324,802
NASA	$4,650,461	DOI	$546,582
DOT	$13,897,042	USDA	$4,509,756
		Other	$103,221,682

Federal Military-Industrial Commitments

DOD Contractors United Aircraft (Windsor Locks), $36.716m: aircraft engine components. McGraw Edison (Bristol), $13.165m: bomb fuzes.

Economic Base Transportation equipment, especially aircraft engines and engine parts; finance, insurance and real estate; machinery, especially general industrial machinery; fabricated metal products, especially hardware not otherwise classified; and electrical equipment and supplies. Also higher education (Central Connecticut State).

The Voters

Registration 252,331 total. 97,877 D (39%); 81,113 R (32%); 73,340 unaffiliated (29%).
Median voting age 43.3
Employment profile White collar, 50%. Blue collar, 40%. Service, 9%. Farm, 1%.
Ethnic groups Black, 1%. Spanish, 1%. Total foreign stock, 32%. Italy, 6%; Canada, Poland, 5% each; Germany, UK, 2% each; Ireland, 1%.

Presidential vote

1972	Nixon (R)	136,430	(58%)
	McGovern (D)	98,328	(42%)
1968	Nixon (R)	89,516	(44%)
	Humphrey (D)	104,210	(51%)
	Wallace (AI)	10,963	(5%)

Representative

Ella T. Grasso (D) Elected 1970; b. May 10, 1919, Windsor Locks; home, Windsor Locks; Mount Holyoke Col., B.A., 1940, M.A., 1942; married, two children; Catholic.

Career War Manpower Commission of Conn., WWII; Conn. House of Reps., 1953–58; first woman Floor Leader, 1955–57; Conn. Sec. of State, 1958–70; Dem. State Platform Com., 1956–68; Platform Drafting Com., Dem. Natl. Convention, 1960.

Offices 431 CHOB, 202-225-4476. Also Court House Bldg., New Britain 06051, 203-223-3646.

Administrative Assistant Nancy Lewinsohn

Committees

Education and Labor (16th); Subs: No. 4 (Labor); No. 5 (Education); No. 8 (Agricultural Labor).

Veterans Affairs (12th); Subs: Hospitals; Insurance; Education and Training.

Group Ratings

	ADA	COPE	LWV	RIPON	NFU	LCV	CFA	NAB	NSI	ACA
1972	56	91	73	67	86	93	100	18	43	17
1971	78	91	75	76	100	–	100	–	–	13

Key Votes

1) Busing	AGN	6) Cmbodia Bmbg	AGN	11) Chkg Acct Intrst	FOR
2) Strip Mines	AGN	7) Bust Hwy Trust	FOR	12) End HISC (HUAC)	AGN
3) Cut Mil $	AGN	8) Farm Sub Lmt	FOR	13) Nixon Sewer Veto	AGN
4) Rev Shrg	FOR	9) School Prayr	AGN	14) Corp Cmpaign $	AGN
5) Pub TV $	FOR	10) Cnsumr Prot	FOR	15) Pol $ Disclosr	FOR

Election Results

1972 general:	Ella T. Grasso (D)	140,290	(60%)
	John F. Walsh (R)	92,783	(40%)
1972 primary:	Ella T. Grasso (D), unopposed		
1970 general:	Ella T. Grasso (D)	96,969	(51%)
	Richard C. Kilbourn (R)	92,906	(49%)

DELAWARE

Political Background

Delaware's proudest boast is that it was the first ex-colony to ratify the U.S. Constitution. But since 1787, because of its liberal incorporation laws, the state has become more famous as the technical home of most of the nation's leading corporations. Delaware is also known as the real home of the duPont Company, a firm that dominates the state. In and near Wilmington, the firm has its headquarters, its leading executives and stockholders, and most of its bureaucracy. duPont has annual revenues of about $4 billion, while the state of Delaware brings in only about $300 million. A Ralph Nader report calls Delaware "the Company State."

The politics of this little state (second smallest in area) has seldom engaged the attention of commentators. But it has had as much clout—often more, because of its seniority—in the United States Senate as the giant states of California and New York. Historically, Delaware has wavered between the Democrats and Republicans, with duPont family members, corporation officers, and other retainers (the firm owns the state's most important bank and the Wilmington newspapers, although it is trying to sell the papers) entrenched in both political parties. In the 1960s, the Republicans seemed to have gained the decisive edge, in large part because of the population growth in prosperous suburban New Castle County (Wilmington), which in 1972 cast 61% of the state's vote. Another factor has been the increasing attachment of the duPont establishment to the Republican party. A sizeable percentage of top officials, most of them Republicans, hold public office while on leave from jobs at the corporation or its subsidiaries.

This being the state's background, most observers expected easy reelection for two of the state's top Republicans in 1972: Gov. Russell Peterson and Sen. J. Caleb Boggs. Boggs had held statewide office since 1946 without ever having alienated any substantial segment of the electorate. Peterson had stirred more controversy; he was known best as the sponsor of a law to prevent industrial development—particularly of oil refineries—on Delaware's coastline. He faced substantial opposition from ex-Atty. Gen. David Buckson in the Republican primary and won by only a small margin.

Amid the turmoil generated by Peterson, Republican leaders wanted to avoid a divisive Senate primary. The Republicans knew that Rep. Pierre S. duPont IV and Wilmington Mayor Henry Haskell (both young and both with large duPont fortunes) each wanted to become a U.S. Senator. So the GOP leaders very much encouraged Sen. Boggs to run for reelection. At 63, Boggs was reportedly eager to retire, and stayed in the race only at the urging of President Nixon.

The denouement furnished further proof of the dangers inherent in imposing campaign strategies from Washington. The Democratic nomination for the Senate went without contest to 29-year-old New Castle County Councilman Joseph Biden. While campaigning, the young man was forced to explain again and again that he would reach the minimum age of 30 required by the Constitution before the Senate term for which he was running would begin. Biden took himself all over Delaware, lavishing special care on the state's two southern counties with their south-of-the-Mason-Dixon-line traditions. He assembled a large number of volunteers to augment the efforts of his large family; his 27-year-old sister was his campaign manager. Biden bought no television time (Delaware has no VHF stations), and to save mailing costs had volunteers hand-deliver campaign literature to every house in the state. The Democratic candidate did not attack his opponent ("he's really a nice guy"), but he stressed his opposition to the Vietnam war and his conviction that people had lost confidence in public institutions.

As the fall progressed, it became clear that Biden posed a genuine threat to his veteran rival. And on election night he won, 51–49. Biden's youth, success, and large family pitching in reminded many people of the Kennedys. Then, as with the Kennedys, tragedy struck. Biden's wife and infant daughter were killed in an automobile accident shortly after the election. As his Senate term began, he was commuting each night to Wilmington to be with his two surviving sons; Biden said that if he could not devote enough attention to them he would resign.

At this writing, it appears that Biden will stay in the Senate. He has already attracted notice, joining the relatively small number of liberal Democrats who voted against the confirmation of some members of the Nixon Cabinet.

Delaware's senior Senator, William V. Roth, had almost as quick a political rise as Biden. In 1966, Roth won the state's only House seat; in 1970, he got the Republican nomination to succeed Sen. John Williams, who was so tenacious in his pursuit of wrongdoers like Bobby Baker that he became known as the "conscience of the Senate." Roth then easily won the 1970 general election. The Delaware Senator may be categorized as a conservative on substantive issues and a reformer on procedural matters. He was the leading sponsor, for example, of a successful amendment to shelve the Nixon Administration's welfare reform plan in late 1972. On procedural issues, he has led moves to give the Congress more access to computers; Roth also cosponsored a move to require all Senate committee meetings to be open to the public, unless a committee—in public—voted to hold it in secret. Although a similar reform passed the House in 1973, Roth's proposal lost in the Senate by nine votes. The split was more along lines of seniority than the usual ideological schisms.

Roth's seat will be up in 1976, as will the term of Democratic Gov. Sherman Tribbett, who narrowly defeated Gov. Peterson in 1972. Before 1972, it was safe to predict that no Republican Senator from Delaware could be in any political danger. Now it is harder to make such predictions. One thing seems fairly sure: the state's sole Congressman, Pierre—or, as he prefers to be known, Pete—duPont, will win reelection as long as he seeks it. In 1970, duPont's family ties were thought to be a political disadvantage in his first statewide race, but he overcame whatever problem that this may have posed by speaking out against corporate polluters. And in Delaware, that has to mean the duPont interests. The Congressman apparently wants higher office; he seems, however, to have missed his best chance for a Senate seat in 1972.

Census Data Pop. 302,173; 0.15% of U.S. total, 46th largest; change 1960–70, 33.6%. Central city, 15%; suburban, 56%. Median family income, $12,441; 14th highest; families above $15,000: 22%; families below $3,000: 8%. Median years education, 12.5.

1972 Share of Federal Tax Burden $710,660,000; 0.34% of U.S. total, 42nd largest.

1972 Share of Federal Outlays $475,600,827; 0.22% of U.S. total, 49th largest. Per capita federal spending, $1,574.

DOD	$121,914,000	46th (0.20%)	HEW	$174,702,818	47th (0.24%)
AEC	$13,276	49th (—)	HUD	$8,050,387	44th (0.26%)
NASA	$9,136,626	20th (0.31%)	VA	$29,568,884	46th (0.26%)
DOT	$27,475,873	50th (0.35%)	USDA	$9,018,135	50th (0.06%)
DOC	$996,798	50th (0.08%)	CSC	$6,540,081	49th (0.16%)
DOI	$2,188,491	47th (0.10%)	TD	$25,665,558	44th (0.16%)
DOJ	$3,202,896	46th (0.33%)	Other	$57,128,004	

Federal Military-Industrial Commitments

DOD Installations Naval Facility (Lewes). Dover AFB (Dover).
NASA Contractors ILC Industries, Inc. (Dover), $8.873m: Apollo space suit assemblies.

Economic Base Finance, insurance and real estate; chemicals and allied products, especially plastics materials and synthetics; food and kindred products, especially poultry dressing and canned fruits and vegetables; agriculture, notably broilers, corn, dairy products and soybeans; apparel and other textile products.

Political Line-up Governor, Sherman W. Tribbitt (D); seat up, 1976. Senators, William V. Roth, Jr. (R) and Joseph R. Biden, Jr. (D). Representatives, 1 R, At Large. State Senate (11 R and 10 D); State House (21 R and 20 D).

The Voters

Registration 293,078 Total. 120,770 D (41%); 102,351 R (35%); 69,957 other (24%).
Median voting age 41.3
Employment profile White collar, 51%. Blue collar, 34%. Service, 13%. Farm, 2%.
Ethnic groups Black, 14%. Total foreign stock, 12%.

Presidential vote

1972	Nixon (R)	140,357	(60%)
	McGovern (D)	92,283	(40%)
1968	Nixon (R)	96,714	(45%)
	Humphrey (D)	89,194	(42%)
	Wallace (AI)	28,459	(13%)
1964	Johnson (D)	122,704	(61%)
	Goldwater (R)	78,078	(38%)

Senator

William V. Roth, Jr. (R) Elected 1970, seat up 1976; b. July 22, 1921 Great Falls, Mont.; home, Wilmington; U. of Oregon, B.A., 1944; Harvard, M.B.A., 1947; Harvard Law School, LL.B., 1947; Army, WWII; married, two children; Episcopalian.

Career Chm., Del. Repub. State Com., 1961–64; Repub. Natl. Com., 1961–64; U.S. House of Reps., 1967–71.

Offices 4327 NSOB, 202-225-2441. Also 304 Fed. Bldg., Wilmington 19801, 203-658-6911, ext. 543, and 200 U.S. P.O. Bldg., Georgetown 19947, 302-856-7690.

Administrative Assistant W. Neal Moerschel

Committees

Finance (7th); Subs: Health, Private Pension Plans; International Finance and Resources.

Government Operations (5th); Subs: Intergovernmental Relations; Budgeting, Management, and Expenditures; Reorganization, Research, and International Organizations.

Joint Study Com. on Budget Control.

Group Ratings

	ADA	COPE	LWV	RIPON	NFU	LCV	CFA	NAB	NSI	ACA
1972	25	10	36	68	30	54	64	100	80	73
1971	19	8	54	64	27	–	29	–	–	67

Key Votes

1) Busing	AGN	8) Sea Life Prot	FOR	15) Tax Singls Less	AGN
2) Alas P-line	AGN	9) Campaign Subs	AGN	16) Min Tax for Rich	AGN
3) Gun Cntrl	FOR	10) Cmbodia Bmbg	FOR	17) Euro Troop Rdctn	AGN
4) Rehnquist	FOR	11) Legal Srvices	AGN	18) Bust Hwy Trust	FOR
5) Pub TV $	AGN	12) Rev Sharing	FOR	19) Maid Min Wage	AGN
6) EZ Votr Reg	AGN	13) Cnsumr Prot	AGN	20) Farm Sub Limit	FOR
7) No-Fault	FOR	14) Eq Rts Amend	FOR	21) Highr Credt Chgs	FOR

Election Results

1970 general:	William V. Roth (R)	96,021	(59%)
	Jacob W. Zimmerman (D)	64,835	(40%)
	Donald G. Gies (AI)	2,183	(1%)
1970 primary:	Nominated at state convention		

Senator

Joseph Robinette Biden, Jr. (D) Elected 1972, seat up 1978; b. Nov. 20, 1942, Scranton, Pa.; home, Newark; U. of Del., B.A., 1965; Syracuse U. College of Law, J.D., 1968; widowed, two children; Catholic.

Career Sr. Partner, Biden & Walsh; New Castle County Council, 1970–72.

Offices 5221 NSOB, 202-225-5042. Also 522 Market Tower, Wilmington, 302-656-9495.

Administrative Assistant Wes Barthelmes

Committees

Banking, Housing and Urban Affairs (9th); Subs: International Finance; Production and Stabilization; Securities.

Public Works (8th); Subs: Water and Air Pollution; Disaster Relief; Water Resouces; Public Buildings and Grounds; Panel on Environmental Science and Technology (Chm.).

Group Ratings: Newly Elected

Election Results

1972 general:	Joseph R. Biden, Jr. (D)	116,006	(51%)
	J. Caleb Boggs (R)	112,844	(49%)
1972 primary:	Joseph R. Biden, Jr. (D), unopposed		

Representative

Pierre S. duPont IV (R) Elected 1970; b. Jan. 22, 1935, Wilmington; home, Rockland; Princeton U., B.S., 1956; Harvard Law School, LL.B., 1963; USNR, 1957–60; married, four children; Episcopalian.

Career Atty., marketing and plant control, duPont Co., 1963–70; Del. House of Reps., 1968–70.

Offices 127 CHOB, 202-225-4165. Also 506 Goldsborough Bldg., 1102 West Street, Wilmington 19801, 302-652-3933.

Administrative Assistant Richard H. Evans

Committees

Foreign Affairs (12th); Subs: Asian and Pacific Affairs; National Security Policy and Scientific Developments.

Merchant Marine (10th); Subs: Merchant Marine; Oceanography; Fisheries and Wildlife Conservation and the Environment.

Group Ratings

	ADA	COPE	LWV	RIPON	NFU	LCV	CFA	NAB	NSI	ACA
1972	50	36	83	75	57	71	50	58	89	39
1971	41	0	44	89	40	–	63	–	–	82

Key Votes

1) Busing	AGN	6) Cmbodia Bmbg	AGN	11) Chkg Acct Intrst	AGN
2) Strip Mines	AGN	7) Bust Hwy Trust	FOR	12) End HISC (HUAC)	AGN
3) Cut Mil $	FOR	8) Farm Sub Lmt	FOR	13) Nixon Sewer Veto	FOR
4) Rev Shrg	FOR	9) School Prayr	FOR	14) Corp Cmpaign $	AGN
5) Pub TV $	AGN	10) Cnsumr Prot	FOR	15) Pol $ Disclosr	FOR

Election Results

1972 general:	Pierre S. du Pont IV (R)	141,237	(63%)
	Norma B. Handloff (D)	83,230	(37%)
1972 primary:	Pierre S. du Pont IV (R), unopposed		
1970 general:	Pierre S. du Pont IV (R)	86,125	(54%)
	John D. Daniello (D)	71,429	(45%)
	Walter J. Hoey (AI)	2,459	(2%)

FLORIDA

Political Background

The state of Florida has changed dramatically since 1949, the year the late V. O. Key published his seminal *Southern Politics*. But some 25 years later his capsule description of Florida politics still holds: "every man for himself." When Key wrote those words, the state had only 2.5 million residents; today, it has more than 7 million, with no end of growth in sight. So many have come that most Floridians are immigrants; a mark of this is that only five of the seventeen-member congressional delegation are natives of the state.

The spectacular growth—exceeded in numbers only by California—has made any analysis of Florida politics more tangled than the one Key set forth. The northern panhandle of Florida remains a part of the Old South, much like the adjacent regions of Alabama and Georgia. But at the same time, the panhandle contains university communities that exhibit some of the same lifestyles and political leanings as thier counterparts in the Midwest or California. The southern sections of the state tend to reflect the various Northern origins of their inhabitants. Miami, for one, is well-known for its large Jewish population, but Miami contains an even larger number of people of other ethnic origins from New York and other Eastern cities. Altogether, Miami's voting habits resemble those of New York City.

Just to the north, Fort Lauderdale and Broward County tend to vote like the very conservative suburbs of Chicago, from which many of their residents moved. So do the Gulf Coast cities of Sarasota and Fort Myers. St. Petersburg's Republicanism, likewise, reflects the political preferences of its large number of Northern retirees. The Spanish-speaking people of Tampa—longtime residents here—tend to vote Democratic; but the Cuban emigrees of Miami, once they gain citizenship, seem to be part of whatever is left of Richard Nixon's New Majority. Orlando, near the new Disney World, is booming and even more conservative than the home of Disneyland in California; both Disney operations lie in counties named Orange. Florida does not have as large a proportion of black voters as most other Southern states. There are enough, however, to form an important bloc; and in 1970, a black candidate for Lieutenant Governor was able to win a respectable number of white votes.

The Florida climate, warm and wet, proves hospitable to various forms of exotic plant and animal life. The same climate also fosters varying kinds of human corruption. In a boom economy, there is, of course, plenty of money to be made. And doubtless there are untold stories of bribery behind many of the proud high-rises that line the Atlantic, one after another, from Miami Beach to Palm Beach. Organized crime is supposed to be entrenched in Miami; the Mayor of Miami has been indicted; and county sheriffs in Florida have been removed from office.

Over all of the turbulence presides a man of a very different spirit, Gov. Rubin Askew, a nonsmoker and a nondrinker. Young (45 in 1974), Askew has the demeanor of a Southern Sunday-school teacher. The man also possesses a kind of unswerving determination. Before 1970, Rubin Askew was an unknown state Senator from Pensacola, a small panhandle city 1,000 miles from Miami; he was running for Governor and talked about the need for a corporate tax on Florida industries. In 1970, he became Governor, beating incumbent Republican Claude Kirk. Kirk was the politician whose flamboyance had, in the opinion of most voters, degenerated into asininity. Askew surprised everyone, not just by winning, but by effecting his platform into law. In the first two years of his administration, the Governor got the legislature and the voters to approve a corporate income tax and to make an overall revision of the state's regressive tax structure. A statewide land-use bill was also enacted. His only major defeat—his inability to persuade the voters to reject an anti-busing referendum—has apparently only increased most Floridians' respect for him, much as they may disagree with his stand on this one issue.

By 1972, Askew's stature was such that he was considered—until he ruled it out—a possible Democratic candidate for Vice-President. In 1972, the Governor did suffer some setbacks. Nixon took 72% of the state's votes; Askew's candidate for a seat on the state Public Service Commission was narrowly beaten by a Republican; and the Republicans picked up a couple of seats in the state legislature. But most observers expect him to bounce back strongly in 1974 when he is up for reelection. And perhaps again in 1976, the national spotlight will find its way to him.

Another major Florida officeholder whose seat comes up in 1974 is Republican Sen. Edward J. Gurney. The way he first won the seat—and the way he got into some political trouble after winning—gives a succinct history of recent Florida politics. A New Englander by birth, Gurney was practicing law in the Orlando area when the legislature created a new congressional district centering on Orlando and Cape Kennedy after the 1960 census. This part of Florida is heavily Republican, and as the Republican nominee, Gurney easily became the second Florida Republican elected to Congress since Reconstruction. (The first was St. Petersburg's William Cramer, who held his seat from 1955 to 1971.) In 1968, Gurney, a handsome man with impressively deliberate habits of speech, won the Republican U.S. Senate nomination virtually without contest.

That year, 1968, was a good one for Florida Republican, in fact, their best yet. Sen. George Smathers, a Democrat, was retiring in order to make gobs of money as a Washington wheeler-dealer. At the same time, most Floridians were fed up with the Johnson Administration, and its domestic programs, and the war. Because the Democratic Senate nominee, ex-Gov. Le Roy Collins, had served in the Johnson Administration briefly, it was simple enough for Gurney to hang the "liberal" tag on him. Using the same tactic two years earlier, Gurney's fellow Republican Kirk defeated Miami Mayor Robert High for the governorship. A politician wearing the liberal label does not sit well with most Florida voters. So Gurney carried every county in the state except those containing Miami, Key West, Tampa, and the University of Florida.

But Gurney's political honeymoon lasted not much longer than a happy vacationer's Florida tan. In 1970, he and Kirk got together to engineer the Senate candidacy of one G. Harrold Carswell, just rejected by the Senate for a seat on the Supreme Court. Such a candidacy presented only one problem: there was already a Republican in the race, somebody who had won the encouragement of Richard Nixon himself, Congressman William Cramer. Cramer no doubt kicked himself for not running for the seat Gurney took in 1968, which he surely would have won. And he was not about to be maneuvered out of the race this time. Demography favored Cramer. A quarter of Florida's registered Republicans lived in his own congressional district, with a vast majority of the rest in a few urban counties. By and large, these registered Republicans were Northern emigrees, who would not be impressed by Judge Carswell's heavy accent or the wrapping of himself in the Stars and Bars. Where Carswell was strong—in northern Old South Florida—virtually every voter registered Democratic. Conservatives, yes, but people who never voted in any Republican primary.

So nobody was surprised except Kirk and Gurney when Cramer beat Carswell by a solid two-to-one margin. What did surprise everybody was the man the Democrats chose as their nominee. He was expected to be ex-Gov. Farris Bryant, who could be tarred as plausibly as Collins with the LBJ brush. Instead, the Democratic primary was won by state Sen. Lawton Chiles (about whom more below), who proceeded to whip Cramer in the general election.

This hassle left Florida with the most divided and tattered Republican party in the South. What had looked like a solid Republican state now had room for only one top Republican officeholder. Soon after 1970, rumors of future opposition to Gurney started to appear. The Senator, as his inept try at slate-making showed, was not in touch with what was happening in Florida. Moreover, some charged that he was not particularly effective in the Senate, there being little behind the handsome facade. Rumors circulated that Rep. Louis Frey, Gurney's old law partner, was thinking about running against the Senator; at this writing, however, it looks like Frey would rather try his luck against Gov. Askew. More solid opposition could come from Cramer, who is said to remain bitter about 1970. Gurney is the only member of the Watergate Committee who expects a tough fight in 1974. On the Senate panel, the Florida politician became, as Bob Haldeman predicted, the Nixon Administration's most sympathetic investigator. Though Gurney felt the White House should furnish the committee with the Presidential tapes, he earlier was proud to announce that he had "pierced" John Dean's testimony.

If one can say that Gurney walked into his Senate seat, the same can be said of the state's junior Senator, Lawton Chiles. But with a difference. In early 1970, Chiles was a state Senator, as unknown to Florida voters as Askew. Chiles had few political assets but the good will and endorsement of retiring conservative Democratic Sen. Spessard Holland—a fellow resident of citrus-rich Polk County. So Chiles started walking across the state, all 1,003 miles of it, from Pensacola to Miami. Along the way, he stopped and talked to people about what was bothering them. The talking changed Chiles' mind on the war issue from hawk to dove; and the walking and the talking made the Senate candidate many friends, especially after TV camera crews began to follow him around to film his travels. Chiles started a trend—state-length walks have been taken by the present Governor of Illinois, a Senator from Iowa, and a Congressman from Utah, among others—and Chiles also won the Democratic nomination. Combined with Askew's victory, the nomination changed the image of the Democratic party in Florida from a group dominated by old, not entirely reliable pols, to a party now controlled by young, honest, and idealistic candidates. On election day, all of Bill Cramer's impassioned advocacy of capital punishment and opposition to busing could bring him nowhere near "Walkin' Lawton."

In Washington, Chiles has sometimes disappointed those who thought Florida had elected a liberal Democratic Senator. Unlike Askew, for example, the new Senator took a stand against busing. But on most issues, Chiles has made common cause far more often with Northern Democrats than Southern Senators of the past. Whether Chiles' politics is viable in Florida is something that won't be tested until 1976, when his seat comes up.

There was a lot of talk, before George Wallace took the 1972 Florida presidential primary, that Florida was now more a Northern than Southern state. After the primary, the talk said that Florida was always a Southern state. Both lines of analysis miss the point. Florida, after all, produced a smaller 1972 Wallace primary percentage than Michigan; the point being that the state's reaction to the busing issue was not atypical of the nation as a whole. Florida is some kind of North-South hybrid, but so is the nation as a whole. It is a fact that the politics of the nation are becoming more homogeneous; there was, for example, a smaller difference between regional preferences in the 1972 presidential election than the one in 1968. Amid this growing homogeneity, Florida emerges as an interesting example, if not a model, of how American politics now work: its arena is unstructured and turbulent, where various interests and people with very different backgrounds clash and clang. A state that can, within two years, elect a Gurney and a Chiles to the Senate, demonstrates, even in the face of Watergate, just how much potential exists for the different kinds of officeholders chosen by the same voters.

Census Data Pop. 6,789,443; 3.35% of U.S. total, 9th largest; change 1960–70, 37.1%. Central city, 29%; suburban, 35%. Median family income, $8,261; 35th highest; families above $15,000: 17%; families below $3,000: 13%. Median years education, 12.1.

1972 Share of Federal Tax Burden $6,688,590,000; 3.20% of U.S. total, 10th largest.

1972 Share of Federal Outlays $7,574,362,585; 3.49% of U.S. total, 8th largest. Per capita federal spending, $1,116.

DOD	$2,483,149,000	5th	(3.97%)	HEW	$2,962,229,376	8th	(4.15%)
AEC	$22,335,213	18th	(0.86%)	HUD	$69,799,538	14th	(2.27%)
NASA	$272,611,294	4th	(9.11%)	VA	$501,231,577	6th	(4.38%)
DOT	$301,705,173	6th	(3.83%)	USDA	$173,278,526	33rd	(1.13%)
DOC	$28,216,670	11th	(2.18%)	CSC	$253,088,351	3rd	(6.14%)
DOI	$17,060,487	27th	(0.80%)	TD	$182,074,163	14th	(1.10%)
DOJ	$50,639.756	4th	(5.16%)	Other	$256,943,461		

Economic Base Finance, insurance and real estate; agriculture, notably oranges, cattle, dairy products and grapefruit; food and kindred products, especially canned, cured and frozen foods; tourism; transportation equipment, especially aircraft and parts, and ship and boat building and repairing; electrical equipment and supplies, especially communication equipment.

Political Line-up Governor, Reubin Askew (D); seat up, 1974. Senators, Edward J. Gurney (R) and Lawton Chiles (D). Representatives, 15 (11 D and 4 R). State Senate (25 D, 14 R, and 1 Ind.); State House (77 D and 43 R).

The Voters

Registration 3,487,458 Total. 2,394,604 D (69%); 974,999 R (28%); 117,855 other (4%). *Median voting age* 46.6
Employment profile White collar, 50%. Blue collar, 32%. Service, 15%. Farm, 3%.
Ethnic groups Black, 15%. Spanish, 7%. Total foreign stock, 18%. Germany, UK, Canada, 2% each; Italy, USSR, 1% each.

Presidential vote

1972	Nixon (R)	1,857,759	(72%)

	McGovern (D)	718,117	(28%)
1968	Nixon (R)	886,804	(41%)
	Humphrey (D)	676,794	(31%)
	Wallace (AI)	624,207	(29%)
1964	Johnson (D)	948,540	(51%)
	Goldwater (R)	905,941	(49%)

Senator

Edward John Gurney (R) Elected 1968, seat up 1974; b. Jan. 12, 1914, Portland, Maine; home, Winter Park; Colby Col., B.S., 1935; Harvard Law School, LL.B., 1938; Duke U., LL.M., 1948; Army, WWII; married, two children; Congregational Christian.

Career City Commissioner, Winter Park, 1952–58; Mayor, Winter Park, 1961–62; U.S. House of Reps., 1963–69.

Offices 5107 NSOB, 202-225-3041. Also P.O. Box 1179, Winter Park 32789, 305-647-3525, and 33 Fourth St. North, St. Petersburg 33701, 813-893-3405, and Rm. 93, 51 S.W. First Ave., Miami 33130, 305-350-5727, and 2520 N. Monroe St., Rm. 112, Tallahassee 32303, 904-385-5136.

Administrative Assistant Jim Groot

Committees

Government Operations (3rd); Subs: Permanent Investigations; Intergovernmental Relations.

Judiciary (7th); Subs: Administrative Practice and Procedure; Antitrust and Monopoly; Improvements in Judicial Machinery; Internal Security; Separation of Powers; Constitutional Rights (Ranking Mbr.).

Sp. Com. on Aging (3rd); Subs; Housing for the Elderly (Ranking Mbr.); Employment and Retirement Incomes; Consumer Interests of the Elderly; Retirement and the Individual; Long-Term Care.

Sel. Com. on Presidential Campaign Activities (2nd).

Sp. Com. to Study Questions Related to Secret and Confidential Government Documents (4th).

Sel. Com. on Small Business (4th); Subs: Government Procurement; Monopoly; Environmental, Rural, and Urban Economic Development.

Group Ratings

	ADA	COPE	LWV	RIPON	NFU	LCV	CFA	NAB	NSI	ACA
1972	5	10	30	36	40	15	0	82	100	86
1971	4	36	25	32	20	–	20	–	–	95
1970	6	9	–	16	30	0	–	80	100	85

Key Votes

1) Busing	AGN	8) Sea Life Prot	FOR	15) Tax Singls Less	AGN
2) Alas P-line	AGN	9) Campaign Subs	AGN	16) Min Tax for Rich	AGN
3) Gun Cntrl	FOR	10) Cmbodia Bmbg	AGN	17) Euro Troop Rdctn	AGN
4) Rehnquist	FOR	11) Legal Srvices	AGN	18) Bust Hwy Trust	AGN
5) Pub TV $	AGN	12) Rev Sharing	FOR	19) Maid Min Wage	AGN
6) EZ Votr Reg	AGN	13) Cnsumr Prot	AGN	20) Farm Sub Limit	AGN
7) No-Fault	AGN	14) Eq Rts Amend	FOR	21) Highr Credt Chgs	FOR

Election Results

1968 general:	Edward J. Gurney (R)	1,131,499 (56%)
	LeRoy Collins (D)	892,637 (44%)

1968 primary: Edward J. Gurney (R)   169,805   (80%)
                Herman W. Goldner (R)   42,347   (20%)

Senator

Lawton Mainor Chiles (D) Elected 1970, seat up 1976; b. April 3, 1930, Lakeland; home, Lakeland; U. of Fla., B.S., 1952, LL.B., 1955; Army, Korean War; married, four children; Presbyterian.

Career Practicing atty., 1955– ; Fla. House of Reps., 1958–66; Fla. Senate, 1966–70.

Offices 2107 NSOB, 202-225-5274; Fed. Bldg., Lakeland 33901, 813–688–6681.

Administrative Assistant Dale Marler

Committees

Appropriations (15th); Subs: District of Columbia; Foreign Operations; Housing and Urban Development, Space, Science, and Veterans; Interior; Treasury, U.S. Postal Service, and General Government.

Government Operations (8th); Subs: Intergovernmental Relations; Reorganization, Research, and International Organizations.

Sp. Com. on Aging (13th); Subs: Housing for the Elderly; Consumer Interests of the Elderly; Health of the Elderly; Retirement and the Individual.

Joint Com. on Congressional Operations (3rd).

Group Ratings

	ADA	COPE	LWV	RIPON	NFU	LCV	CFA	NAB	NSI	ACA
1972	35	11	73	58	90	50	83	40	50	45
1971	56	50	55	62	75	–	40	–	–	37

Key Votes

1) Busing	AGN	8) Sea Life Prot	FOR	15) Tax Singls Less	FOR
2) Alas P-line	AGN	9) Campaign Subs	FOR	16) Min Tax for Rich	FOR
3) Gun Cntrl	FOR	10) Cmbodia Bmbg	AGN	17) Euro Troop Rdctn	AGN
4) Rehnquist	FOR	11) Legal Srvices	ABS	18) Bust Hwy Trust	FOR
5) Pub TV $	ABS	12) Rev Sharing	AGN	19) Maid Min Wage	FOR
6) EZ Votr Reg	ABS	13) Cnsumr Prot	ABS	20) Farm Sub Limit	FOR
7) No-Fault	AGN	14) Eq Rts Amend	FOR	21) Highr Credt Chgs	AGN

Election Results

1970 general:	Lawton Chiles (D)	902,438	(54%)
	William C. Cramer (R)	772,817	(46%)
1970 run-off:	Lawton Chiles (D)	474,420	(66%)
	Ferris Bryant (D)	247,211	(34%)
1970 primary:	Lawton Chiles (D)	188,300	(26%)
	Ferris Bryant (D)	240,222	(33%)
	Fred Schultz (D)	175,745	(24%)
	Al Hastings (D)	91,948	(13%)
	Jeel T. Daves III (D)	33,939	(5%)

FIRST DISTRICT Political Background

Does some relationship exist between the site location of military installations and the politics of members of Congress? Evidence from the 1st district of Florida indicates that the answer is yes. This area—basically the northwestern panhandle of Florida—has more huge military bases than almost any other in the nation. Eglin Air Force Base, for one, spreads out over a great portion of three counties. And the man those three counties and the 1st district sends to Congress is Democrat Bob Sikes, Chairman of the House Appropriations Subcommittee on Military Construction.

It would be wrong, however, to suppose that all the military bases in the district are the results of Sikes' efforts. The naval station at Pensacola, for example, antedates his tenure considerably. Moreover, the 1st makes good sense as a place for Navy and Air Force bases; it has a mild climate and lots of coastline, not to mention the Gulf of Mexico itself. But it would also be wrong to conclude that Bob Sikes has nothing to do with the nearly $500 million that comes into the 1st from the Pentagon each year. Sikes has diligently protected his bases from periodic military cutbacks, and his clout with the military is unquestioned.

Beyond this, Sikes' political philosophy and the interests of his district happily coincide. First elected to the House in 1940, Sikes was one of a group of Southern Democrats who stood solidly with Franklin D. Roosevelt when he proposed the draft and Lend-Lease. Since then, the Congressman has been firmly convinced that the nation should be militarily strong, and that it is better to have spent too much on arms than to risk spending too little. And those feelings closely reflect those of the majority of his constituents. Florida's 1st district, to judge from recent presidential voting patterns, is one of the ten most conservative congressional districts in the nation. In the coastal cities of Pensacola and Panama City and in the Piney Woods along the Alabama border, the vast majority of voters here are white and determined backers of the philosophy of George Wallace.

The voters are even more enthusiastic in their support of Congressman Sikes. At 69, he is still a young man for a veteran of 30-plus years in the House. It is not inconceivable that he may wind up, one of these days, as Chairman of the House Appropriations Committee, now being 4th in seniority. What is utterly inconceivable is a Sikes defeat in any 1st-district election.

Census Data Pop. 452,562. Central city, 41%; suburban, 13%. Median family income, $7,621; families above $15,000: 12%; families below $3,000: 15%. Median years education, 12.1.

1972 Share of Federal Outlays $764,601,453

DOD	$540,238,340	HEW	$119,185,355
AEC	–	HUD	–
NASA	$528,690	DOI	$624,235
DOT	$28,080,347	USDA	$12,822,179
		Other	$63,122,307

Federal Military-Industrial Commitments

DOD Contractors Vitro Corp. of America (Valparaiso), $11.922m: operation of Armament Development Test Center. Dyson and Company (Pensacola), $8.796m: construction services.
DOD Installations Naval Air Station (Pensacola). Naval Air Rework Facility (Pensacola). Naval Air Station, Saufley Field (Pensacola). Naval Air Station, Whiting Field (Milton). Naval Aerospace Medical Center (Pensacola). Naval Communications Training Center (Pensacola). Naval Air Station, Ellyson Field (Pensacola). Naval Coastal Systems Laboratory (Panama City). Naval Public Work Center (Pensacola). Elgin AF Auxiliary Field 2 (Niceville). Elgin AF Auxiliary Field 3 (Crestview). Elgin AF Auxiliary Field 9 (Fort Walton Beach). Elgin AFB (Valparaiso). Tyndall AFB (Springfield).

Economic Base Finance, insurance and real estate; agriculture, notably grains, cattle and dairy products; paper and allied products; chemicals and allied products, especially plastics materials and synthetics; lumber and wood products; and electrical equipment and supplies.

The Voters

Registration 218,275 total. 189,218 D (87%); 24,413 R (11%); 4,644 other (2%).
Median voting age 38.7
Employment profile White collar, 48%. Blue collar, 36%. Service, 15%. Farm, 1%.
Ethnic groups Black, 14%. Spanish, 2%. Total foreign stock, 5%.

Presidential vote

1972	Nixon (R)	127,607	(84%)
	McGovern (D)	24,860	(16%)
1968	Nixon (R)	30,438	(21%)
	Humphrey (D)	27,707	(19%)
	Wallace (AI)	87,844	(60%)

Representative

Robert L. F. Sikes (D) Elected 1940; b. June 3, 1906, Isabella, Ga.; home, Crestview; U. of Ga., B.S., 1927; U. of Fla., M.S., 1929; Army, WWII; married, two children; Methodist.

Career Newspaper publisher; Chm., County Dem. Exec. Com., 1934; Fla. Legislature, 1936–38; Asst. to Treas., Dem. Natl. Com., 1936–40–44.

Offices 2269 RHOB, 202-225-4136. Also County Court House, Crestview 32536, 904-682-3132.

Administrative Assistant Alma D. Butler

Committees

Appropriations (4th); Subs: Defense; Military Construction (Chm.); State, Justice, Commerce and Judiciary.

Joint Study Com. on Budget Control.

Group Ratings

	ADA	COPE	LWV	RIPON	NFU	LCV	CFA	NAB	NSI	ACA
1972	13	20	27	60	50	6	0	82	100	94
1971	5	27	0	40	62	–	50	–	–	76
1970	12	17	–	20	25	17	67	46	100	59

Key Votes

1) Busing	AGN	6) Cmbodia Bmbg	FOR	11) Chkg Acct Intrst	AGN
2) Strip Mines	ABS	7) Bust Hwy Trust	AGN	12) End HISC (HUAC)	AGN
3) Cut Mil $	AGN	8) Farm Sub Lmt	ABS	13) Nixon Sewer Veto	AGN
4) Rev Shrg	AGN	9) School Prayr	FOR	14) Corp Cmpaign $	FOR
5) Pub TV $	AGN	10) Cnsumr Prot	ABS	15) Pol $ Disclosr	ABS

Election Results

1972 general:	Robert L. F. Sikes (D), unopposed		
1972 primary:	Robert L. F. Sikes (D)	93,064	(81%)
	Harvie J. Belser (D)	16,016	(14%)
	Amos Brannon (D)	6,206	(5%)
1970 general:	Robert L. F. Sikes (D)	88,744	(80%)
	H. D. Shumake (R)	21,952	(20%)

SECOND DISTRICT Political Background

Like the 1st, the 2nd district is part of the Dixie belt of northern Florida—a region sociologically and politically little different from neighboring south Georgia. For years this area's affection for racial segregation dominated its politics. Its greatest clout was in the hands of a group of north Florida state legislators who, before the one-man-one-vote ruling, dominated the state's politics. For some years, this part of Florida was also overrepresented in the U.S. House of

Representatives. The current 2nd is, for the most part, a result of the consolidation of two congressional districts in 1966.

There are, however, two significant differences between the 1st and 2nd districts—differences that have not yet been decisive in congressional races, but may be in the future. For one, the 2nd is Florida's blackest district; some 28% of its residents, and 20% of its registered voters, are black. For the other, the 2nd's two largest cities, Gainesville and Tallahassee, contain the state's two largest universities, the University of Florida and Florida State. Both of these draw most of their enrollment from south Florida, and they are far more likely to vote for liberal candidates than students in most Southern institutions of higher learning. Some 13% of the 2nd district's eligible voters are students.

Thus the 2nd contains two sizeable voting blocs inclined to oppose the generally conservative politics of the district's Congressman, Don Fuqua. Since he was elected to the House in 1962, Fuqua has usually voted with the dwindling number of conservative Southern Democrats in Washington. With two exceptions, Fuqua has had little trouble at the polls. In 1966, he beat the more senior and slightly more liberal Rep. D. R. (Billy) Matthews, when their districts were combined by redistricting.

The other exception occurred in 1972. In the Democratic primary of that year, Fuqua got by an opponent who won most of his support from blacks and students. Nonetheless, an impact was made in Fuqua's voting record; in 1973, for instance, he said no to the bombing in Cambodia. The various ups and downs of the Florida Republican party have showed little impact in the 2nd. Statewide Republican candidates have done well here on occasion, but few Republican local or legislative candidates have been able to win.

Census Data Pop. 452,633. Central city, 16%; suburban, 30%. Median family income, $7,071; families above $15,000: 13%; families below $3,000: 19%. Median years education, 11.3.

1972 Share of Federal Outlays $522,222,809

DOD	$43,298,884	HEW	$222,156,434
AEC	$1,454,703	HUD	$365,896
NASA	$456,802	DOI	$1,244,870
DOT	$47,268,831	USDA	$49,306,410
		Other	$156,669,979

Federal Military-Industrial Commitments

DOD Contractors Aero Corp. (Lake City), $11.350m: aircraft repair.

Economic Base Agriculture, notably poultry, cattle and dairy products; finance, insurance and real estate; lumber and wood products; and food and kindred products. Also higher education (Florida State Univ. and Univ. of Florida).

The Voters

Registration 241,072 total. 212,081 D (88%); 22,682 R (9%); 5,589 other (2%).
Median voting age 39.0
Employment profile White collar, 49%. Blue collar, 28%. Service, 16%. Farm, 7%.
Ethnic groups Black, 28%. Spanish, 1%. Total foreign stock, 4%.

Presidential vote

1972	Nixon (R)	111,042	(69%)
	McGovern (D)	50,861	(31%)
1968	Nixon (R)	30,161	(21%)
	Humphrey (D)	39,071	(28%)
	Wallace (AI)	72,755	(51%)

Representative

Donald Fuqua (D) Elected 1962; b. Aug. 20, 1933, Jacksonville; U. of Fla., B.S., 1957; Army, Korean War; married, two children; Presbyterian.

Career Fla. House of Reps., 1958–62.

Offices 2266 RHOB, 202-225-5235. Also 308 P.O. Bldg., Tallahassee 32302, 904-224-7510, and 314 Fed. Bldg., Gainesville 32601, 904-376-4215.

Administrative Assistant Herb Wadsworth

Committees

Government Operations (16th); Subs: Intergovernmental Relations; Legislation and Military Operations.

Science and Astronautics (5th); Subs: Manned Space Flight (Chm.); Energy; Science, Research, and Development.

Group Ratings

	ADA	COPE	LWV	RIPON	NFU	LCV	CFA	NAB	NSI	ACA
1972	13	22	36	50	57	40	0	36	100	68
1971	19	56	44	41	71	–	50	–	–	58
1970	16	27	–	12	31	24	55	46	100	63

Key Votes

1) Busing	AGN	6) Cmbodia Bmbg	ABS	11) Chkg Acct Intrst	AGN
2) Strip Mines	AGN	7) Bust Hwy Trust	AGN	12) End HISC (HUAC)	AGN
3) Cut Mil $	AGN	8) Farm Sub Lmt	AGN	13) Nixon Sewer Veto	AGN
4) Rev Shrg	AGN	9) School Prayr	FOR	14) Corp Cmpaign $	AGN
5) Pub TV $	FOR	10) Cnsumr Prot	AGN	15) Pol $ Disclosr	AGN

Election Results

1972 general:	Don Fuqua (D), unopposed		
1972 primary:	Don Fuqua (D)	84,270	(74%)
	Nathan Skinner (R)	29,972	(26%)
1970 general:	Don Fuqua (D), unopposed		

THIRD DISTRICT Political Background

Jacksonville is a border city—on the border between the Old South and the new boom lands of south Florida. It was long Florida's largest city and, on paper, it regained that status by annexing most of surrounding Duval County. But in metropolitan population, Jacksonville has long since been eclipsed by Miami, Tampa, St. Petersburg, and even by Fort Lauderdale. Jacksonville remains an important port, paper manufacturer, and banking and insurance center. The big-money man in Jacksonville is aging Edward Ball—duPont heir, banker, paper magnate, real estate operator, and boss of the Florida East Coast Railroad Co. Because of its coolish wintertime climate, Jacksonville has not attracted the retirees or Northern migrants who flocked to Florida cities farther south. But it does have the largest black percentage of any major Florida city and also the largest percentage of people who voted for George Wallace in 1968.

The 3rd congressional district includes most of Jacksonville and one small county to the north. Its Congressman since 1948, Charles E. Bennett, enjoys a reputation for probity and attention to duty which is second to none in the House. He was stricken by polio in the Army during World War II, and in his first campaign it was suggested that Bennett was incapable of properly representing the district. Perhaps to gainsay that suggestion, Bennett has not missed a roll-call vote since 1951—giving him, as of 1972, the congressional record of 3,428 consecutive votes.

Bennett, a senior member of the Armed Services Committee, over the years usually supported the committee's hawkish majority. But in 1971, he voted for the Nedzi-Whalen amendment to end the Vietnam war. And in 1973, the Congressman introduced a motion in the Democratic Caucus to require the end of all American military action in Southeast Asia in the absence of congressional authorization. The motion passed overwhelmingly, 125–10, a measure of the changes that have occurred in the attitudes of House Democrats. Bennett's own shift on Indochina issues is at least as significant as the general movement in the House, having come earlier in a Congressman scarcely subject to pressures from a dovish constituency. Switches on the part of usually quiet Congressmen—many of them Southern Democrats—are the major reason why the long-hawkish House voted again and again against the bombing of Cambodia and Laos in 1973.

Census Data   Pop. 452,841. Central city, 0%; suburban, 95%. Median family income, $8,252; families above $15,000: 14%; families below $3,000: 14%. Median years education, 11.8.

1972 Share of Federal Outlays $480,845,100

DOD	$191,658,168	HEW	$143,933,387
AEC	–	HUD	$20,778,957
NASA	–	DOI	$389,383
DOT	$29,598,334	USDA	$8,231,194
		Other	$86,255,677

Federal Military-Industrial Commitments

DOD Contractors Jacksonville Shipyards (Mayport), $11.630m: ship repair.
DOD Installations Naval Air Station (Cecil Field, Jacksonville). Naval Air Station (Jacksonville). Naval Air Rework Facility (Jacksonville). Naval Hospital Jacksonville). Naval Station (Mayport). Navy Fuel Depot (Jacksonville). Naval Air Technical Training Unit (Jacksonville).

Economic Base   Finance, insurance and real estate; paper and allied products; agriculture, notably dairy products and poultry; ship and boat building and repairing, and other transportation equipment; printing and publishing, especially newspapers; and fabricated metal products, especially fabricated structural metal products.

The Voters

Registration   204,441 total. Party registration not available.
Median voting age 40.1
Employment profile White collar, 50%. Blue collar, 34%. Service, 15%. Farm, 1%.
Ethnic groups Black, 26%. Spanish, 1%. Total foreign stock, 6%.

Presidential vote

1972	Nixon (R)	96,783	(70%)
	McGovern (D)	41,880	(30%)
1968	Nixon (R)	34,808	(26%)
	Humphrey (D)	47,330	(36%)
	Wallace (AI)	51,138	(38%)

Representative

Charles E. Bennett (D) Elected 1948; b. Dec. 2, 1910, Canton, N.Y.; home, Jacksonville; U. of Fla., B.A., 1934, J.D.; Army, WWII; married, four children; Disciples of Christ Church.

Career Practicing atty., 1934–48; Fla. House of Reps., 1941.

Offices 2113 RHOB, 202-225-2501. Also Suite 352 Fed. Office Bldg., 400 W. Bay St., Jacksonville 32202, 904-791-2587.

Administrative Assistant Nicholas Van Nelson

Committees

Armed Services (4th); Subs: No. 3 (Chm.); No. 5.

Group Ratings

	ADA	COPE	LWV	RIPON	NFU	LCV	CFA	NAB	NSI	ACA
1972	13	45	42	56	71	67	50	58	80	78
1971	32	42	33	61	80	–	88	–	–	59
1970	24	47	–	47	54	70	76	75	100	68

Key Votes

1) Busing	AGN	6) Cmbodia Bmbg	AGN	11) Chkg Acct Intrst	FOR
2) Strip Mines	AGN	7) Bust Hwy Trust	AGN	12) End HISC (HUAC)	AGN
3) Cut Mil $	AGN	8) Farm Sub Lmt	FOR	13) Nixon Sewer Veto	FOR
4) Rev Shrg	AGN	9) School Prayr	FOR	14) Corp Cmpaign $	AGN
5) Pub TV $	FOR	10) Cnsumr Prot	FOR	15) Pol $ Disclosr	FOR

Election Results

1972 general:	Charles E. Bennett (D)	101,441	(82%)
	John F. Bowen (R)	22,219	(18%)
1972 primary:	Charles E. Bennett (D), unopposed		
1970 general:	Charles E. Bennett (D), unopposed		

FOURTH DISTRICT Political Background

The 4th district comprises part of transitional Florida. Occupying territory south of Jacksonville and including some 100,000 residents of the city itself, the 4th sits at the divide of Old Dixie—northern Florida—and the boom land of the south. The territory here lies just beyond the pale of wintertime frost. This feature of the 4th is important not just for the tourist trade, but for the district's big orange crop. A couple of nights of frost can destroy a grower's entire year.

The 4th also contains transitional Florida in politics. In 1968, the district's northern counties went for George Wallace, and would probably do so again if he were to be a third-party presidential candidate. But the southern counties of Lake and Seminole (only parts of which now lie in the 4th), near Orlando, are solidly Republican. In the middle of the district, both geographically and politically, is Daytona Beach, famous for its rock-hard sand beach. The city recently elected a black councilman; it is also the home of Bill France, a racetrack owner and the man who led Florida's Wallace delegation to the 1972 Democratic Convention.

The 4th's Congressman, William V. Chappell, may also be described as a transitional figure. Chappell is a Democrat who was Speaker of the Florida House back in the early 1960s when the legislature was still dominated by Old South conservatives from the northern part of the state. From what appears to be the right approach—a Democrat with a mostly Republican voting record—Chappell has fared surprisingly poorly in 4th-district elections. He first came to the House in 1968 with only 53% of the votes; he then increased his margin to 58% in 1970, and fell to 56% in 1972, having encountered a spirited Republican campaign. His last time out Chappell actually lost Volusia County (Daytona), and came close to losing the 4th's part of Jacksonville.

Chappell's problem was not just the dismal showing of George McGovern. Other Florida

Democrats ran much farther ahead of the national ticket than Chappell did. In 1969, Chappell was charged with diverting the salary of one of his employees to a third person—which is illegal. Although Chappell was never prosecuted in what was, if proved, potentially a criminal offense, the affairs of the Congressman received a great deal of coverage in local papers. The *Washington Monthly*, which keeps tabs on things like this, noted in 1973 that Chappell was one of the Democrats on the House Banking and Currency Committee who voted against holding a Watergate investigation before the 1972 election. The magazine went on to suggest that Chappell's vote was not unrelated to the government's refusal to prosecute the Congressman. Such malodorous situations are now more common in Florida politics than they used to be, and they have been hurting incumbents at the polls. Chappell could find himself in some trouble come 1974.

Census Data Pop. 452,076. Central city, 21%; suburban, 2%. Median family income, $7,719; families above $15,000: 15%; families below $3,000: 15%. Median years education, 12.1.

1972 Share of Federal Outlays $433,098,387

DOD	$100,611,241	HEW	$212,473,532
AEC	–	HUD	$9,018,181
NASA	$1,420,366	DOI	$2,850,490
DOT	$12,088,269	USDA	$13,497,804
		Other	$81,138,504

Federal Military-Industrial Commitments

DOD Contractors Sparton Corp. (DeLeon Springs), $21.523m: sonobuoys.
DOD Installations Jacksonville AF Station (Orange Park).

Economic Base Finance, insurance and real estate; agriculture, notably fruits, cattle and dairy products; paper and allied products; food and kindred products; and tourism.

The Voters

Registration 240,647 total. Party registration not available.
Median voting age 47.7
Employment profile White collar, 51%. Blue collar, 30%. Service, 15%. Farm, 4%.
Ethnic groups Black, 15%. Spanish, 1%. Total foreign stock, 11%. UK, Germany, Canada, 2% each.

Presidential vote

1972	Nixon (R)	135,945	(77%)
	McGovern (D)	41,660	(23%)
1968	Nixon (R)	60,666	(38%)
	Humphrey (D)	46,713	(29%)
	Wallace (AI)	53,340	(33%)

Representative

William V. Chappell, Jr. (D) Elected 1968; b. Feb. 3, 1922, Kendrick; home, Ocala; U. of Fla., B.A., 1947, LL.B., 1949, J.D., 1967; Navy, WWII; Capt., USNR; married, four children; Methodist.

Career Marion County Prosecuting Atty., 1950–54; Fla. House of Reps., 1955–64, 1967–68; Speaker Fla. House of Reps., 1961–63.

Offices 1124 LHOB, 202-225-4035. Also Rm. 258 Fed. Bldg., Ocala 32670, 904-629-0039, and 523 N. Halifax Ave., Daytona Beach 32016, 904-253-7632, and P.O. Box 35086, 727 Fed. Bldg., Jacksonville 32202, 904-791-3675.

Administrative Assistant Thomas E. Hooker

Committees

Appropriations (32nd); Subs: District of Columbia; HUD, Space, Science, Veterans; Foreign Operations.

Group Ratings

	ADA	COPE	LWV	RIPON	NFU	LCV	CFA	NAB	NSI	ACA
1972	0	10	18	43	57	0	50	75	100	95
1971	8	50	11	12	57	–	17	–	–	73
1970	8	25	–	18	23	33	57	67	100	83

Key Votes

1) Busing	AGN	6) Cmbodia Bmbg	FOR	11) Chkg Acct Intrst	AGN
2) Strip Mines	AGN	7) Bust Hwy Trust	AGN	12) End HISC (HUAC)	AGN
3) Cut Mil $	AGN	8) Farm Sub Lmt	AGN	13) Nixon Sewer Veto	FOR
4) Rev Shrg	AGN	9) School Prayr	FOR	14) Corp Cmpaign $	FOR
5) Pub TV $	AGN	10) Cnsumr Prot	AGN	15) Pol $ Disclosr	AGN

Election Results

1972 general:	Bill Chappell, Jr. (D)	92,541	(56%)
	P. T. Fleuchaus (R)	72,960	(44%)
1972 primary:	Bill Chappell, Jr. (D), unopposed		
1970 general:	Bill Chappell, Jr. (D)	75,673	(58%)
	Leonard V. Wood (R)	55,311	(42%)

FIFTH DISTRICT Political Background

How does a nonincumbent Democrat win an election against a vigorous Republican candidate in a congressional district that gave 76% of its votes to Republican presidential nominee Richard Nixon? This is the question posed by the 5th district of Florida, and the 1972 victory here of Democratic Congressman Bill Gunter. Gunter's triumph is made more remarkable because the 5th is not Dixiecrat country. In 1968, the district gave Richard Nixon substantially more of its votes than to George Wallace; moreover, Republican candidates for Congress have carried the area within the current boundaries of the 5th for the last 10 years. And Orlando, the largest city in the 5th, has been casting hefty Republican margins since the days of Dwight D. Eisenhower. There are apparently two reasons behind Democrat Gunter's victory.

First, local popularity. An accomplished orator and expert on citrus agriculture, 32-year-old Bill Gunter managed to win 55% of the votes in the 1966 race for the state Senate in greater Orlando (Orange and Seminole counties). Two years later, after serving as Chairman of the Citrus Committee and following a redistricting that left him with the most Democratic parts of the Republican Orlando area, Gunter won 62% of the votes. He did not have to stand for reelection in 1970.

Second, redistricting. Just as redistricting helped Gunter to keep his state Senate seat, so did it help him make it to the U.S. Congress. As an acknowledged power in the legislature, Gunter got himself on the state Senate Reapportionment and Redistricting Committee in 1972. The 1970 census had given Florida three additional congressional seats. The population figures made it clear that one of the seats had to go to the greater Miami area, one to another part of south Florida, and the third to the central portion of the state. Gunter made sure that the third one included much of his old bailiwick.

The resulting district, particularly at its edges, is of rather odd configuration. It includes part of Orlando and part of Sanford in nearby Seminole County; it then sweeps across to the Gulf of Mexico and down the coast, includes part of the city of Clearwater, and terminates at a point near St. Petersburg. These parts of places are crucial, for Gunter saw to it that he got 70% of the blacks of Orlando, Sanford, and Clearwater into the 5th. He of course knew that most blacks vote Democratic.

The wisdom of the redistricting becomes apparent on inspecting the election returns. Although Gunter's home territory—Orange and Seminole counties—cast only 34% of the district's votes, they provided the Democrat with 90% of his 19,000-vote majority. The almost entirely black precincts in Orlando, Sanford, and Clearwater went more than 90% for Gunter and provided him a 4,000vote edge. And it must be assumed that he got at least as large a margin from black voters in mixed black-and-white precincts.

That, more or less, is the way one Bill Gunter made it to the House. Now there is talk that the Congressman is interested in statewide office. With his proven voter appeal in one of Florida's staunchest Republican areas, he could well make a formidable candidate. At this writing, speculation is that he might become Reubin Askew's running mate as a candidate for Lieutenant Governor, or, perhaps, take on incumbent Edward Gurney for a seat in the U.S. Senate.

Census Data Pop. 452,965. Central city, 52%; suburban, 6%. Median family income, $6,910; families above $15,000: 12%; families below $3,000: 16%. Median years education, 11.7.

1972 Share of Federal Outlays $528,215,376

DOD	$221,267,565	HEW	$209,771,757
AEC	$1,414,909	HUD	$1,659,255
NASA	$923,730	DOI	$353,675
DOT	$9,954,153	USDA	$13,394,415
		Other	$69,475,917

Federal Military-Industrial Commitments

No installations or contractors receiving prime awards greater than $5,000,000.

Economic Base Agriculture, notably fruits, vegetables, poultry and cattle; finance, insurance and real estate; food and kindred products, especially canned, cured and frozen foods; and tourism.

The Voters

Registration 256,373 total. 155,968 D (61%); 92,183 R (36%); 8,222 other (3%).
Median voting age 50.9
Employment profile White collar, 44%. Blue collar, 35%. Service, 14%. Farm, 7%.
Ethnic groups Black, 16%. Spanish, 1%. Total foreign stock, 12%. Germany, UK, Canada, 2% each.

Presidential vote

1972	Nixon (R)	143,766	(76%)
	McGovern (D)	44,600	(24%)
1968	Nixon (R)	57,450	(43%)
	Humphrey (D)	34,194	(26%)
	Wallace (AI)	42,394	(32%)

Representative

Bill Gunter (D) Elected 1972; b. July 16, 1934, Jacksonville; home, Orlando; U. of Fla., B.S.A., 1956; U. of Ga., Grad. work; married, two children; Baptist.

Career Affiliated with State Farm Insurance Co., 1959; State Senator, 1966–72; veteran; teacher.

Offices 423 CHOB, 202-225-2176. Also P.O. Box 386, Orlando 32802, 305-298-1660.

Administrative Assistant Ted Phelps

Committees

Agriculture (20th); Subs: Forests; Livestock and Grains.

Science and Astronautics (17th); Subs: Energy; Manned Space Flight.

Group Ratings: Newly Elected

Key Votes

1) Busing	NE	6) Cmbodia Bmbg	AGN	11) Chkg Acct Intrst	AGN
2) Strip Mines	NE	7) Bust Hwy Trust	ABS	12) End HISC (HUAC)	AGN
3) Cut Mil $	NE	8) Farm Sub Lmt	NE	13) Nixon Sewer Veto	AGN
4) Rev Shrg	NE	9) School Prayr	NE	14) Corp Cmpaign $	NE
5) Pub TV $	NE	10) Cnsumr Prot	NE	15) Pol $ Disclosr	NE

Election Results

1972 general:	William D. Gunter, Jr. (D)	97,902	(56%)
	Jack Insco (R)	78,468	(44%)
1972 primary:	William D. Gunter, Jr. (D)	42,240	(83%)
	Miller Newton (D)	8,690	(17%)

SIXTH DISTRICT Political Background

When somebody says St. Petersburg, almost everybody sees an image of elderly retirees sitting on park benches in the Florida sun. But it would be misleading to imply that everybody in this large and growing city of 216,000 is over 65. St. Petersburg does have some light manufacturing, and also a large number of young families raising children either here or, more likely, in the booming suburbs north of the city. Nevertheless, the median age in the 6th congressional district, which includes all of St. Petersburg and most of suburban Pinellas County, is the highest of any district in the nation. Some 50% of the 6th's eligible voters are over 58 years old and some 39% are 65 or older.

Most of these people, of course, were not born in St. Pete or anywhere else in Florida. They are emigrants from some other part of the South or, more likely, the North. The large Yankee concentration here produced the state's first center of Republican strength. The Republicans first won big in 1954, when William Cramer was elected to the U.S. House. Cramer, a tireless and effective partisan, built up Florida's Republican party at home and rose to become the ranking Republican on the pork-barreling Public Works Committee in Washington. In 1970, Cramer made a move for the Senate. Campaigning vigorously around the state, the Congressman stressed his support of President Nixon, of capital punishment, and his sponsorship of the Rap Brown law that prohibits interstate travel to incite a riot.

But 1970 was not Bill Cramer's year. The founding father of Florida Republicanism still had to face ex-Judge G. Harrold Carswell in what became a bitter primary. In a stupid move, Sen. Edward Gurney and then-Gov. Claude Kirk engineered the hapless judge into the race. Cramer disposed of Carswell neatly, but he could never catch up with the surprise winner of the Democratic nomination, "Walkin' Lawton" Chiles. The ex-Congressman now has a bustling law practice in Washington and Florida, and rumors are that he is itching to oppose Gurney in the 1974 Republican primary.

Despite the general 1970 Republican debacle in Florida, state Sen. Bill Young easily stepped into Cramer's House seat. Young is a usually reliable supporter of the House Republican leadership and sits on the Armed Services Committee. He also has a seat on the Select Committee on Committees, which is supposed to draw up a plan that will permit the House to exert reasoned control over the budgetary process.

Census Data Pop. 452,615. Central city, 52%; suburban, 48%. Median family income, $7,657; families above $15,000: 14%; families below $3,000: 12%. Median years education, 12.1.

1972 Share of Federal Outlays $504,051,861

DOD	$119,804,046	HEW	$248,399,200
AEC	$9,192,801	HUD	$5,762,210
NASA	$3,032,290	DOI	$272,528
DOT	$15,577,098	USDA	$2,901,796
		Other	$9,109,892

Federal Military-Industrial Commitments

DOD Contractors Honeywell (St. Petersburg), $47.272m: guidance units for Minuteman missile. Electronic Communications, Inc. (St. Petersburg), $15.700m: aircraft and shipboard communications equipment. *AEC Operations* General Electric (Clearwater), $19.848m: operation of Pinellas Plant.

Economic Base Finance, insurance and real estate; electrical equipment and supplies; printing and publishing, especially newspapers; transportation equipment; and agriculture, notably fruits, dairy products, and nursery and greenhouse products.

The Voters

> *Registration* 282,350 total. 134,884 D (48%); 137,543 R (49%); 9,923 other (4%).
> *Median voting age* 58.6
> *Employment profile* White collar, 55%. Blue collar, 28%. Service, 17%. Farm, –%.
> *Ethnic groups* Black, 8%. Spanish, 1%. Total foreign stock, 22%. Germany, UK, 4% each; Canada, 3%; Italy, Ireland, Sweden, 1% each

Presidential vote

	1972	Nixon (R)	154,765	(69%)
		McGovern (D)	68,214	(31%)
	1968	Nixon (R)	87,839	(51%)
		Humphrey (D)	57,450	(33%)
		Wallace (AI)	26,711	(16%)

Representative

C. W. Bill Young (R) Elected 1970; b. Dec. 16, 1930, Harmarville, Pa.; home, Seminole; Fla. Natl. Guard, 1948–57; married, three children; Methodist.

Career Dist. asst., Rep. William C. Cramer, 1957–60; Fla. Senate, 1960–70; Minority Leader, 1966; Chm., Southern Highway Policy Com., 1966–68; Eighth Congressional Dist. Campaign Chm. for Nixon-Agnew.

Offices 426 CHOB, 202-225-5961. Also 627 Fed. Bldg., 144 First Ave. South, St. Petersburg 33701, 813-393-3191.

Administrative Assistant Douglas Gregory

Committees

Armed Services (9th); Subs: No. 1; No. 4; Special Subcommittee on Human Relations.

Sel. Com. on Committess (5th).

Group Ratings

	ADA	COPE	LWV	RIPON	NFU	LCV	CFA	NAB	NSI	ACA
1972	13	18	45	69	14	43	100	100	100	87
1971	5	8	22	44	20	–	25	–	–	97

Key Votes

1) Busing	AGN	6) Cmbodia Bmbg	FOR	11) Chkg Acct Intrst	ABS
2) Strip Mines	AGN	7) Bust Hwy Trust	FOR	12) End HISC (HUAC)	AGN
3) Cut Mil $	AGN	8) Farm Sub Lmt	FOR	13) Nixon Sewer Veto	FOR
4) Rev Shrg	AGN	9) School Prayr	FOR	14) Corp Cmpaign $	AGN
5) Pub TV $	AGN	10) Cnsumr Prot	AGN	15) Pol $ Disclosr	FOR

Election Results

1972 general:	C. W. Bill Young (R)	156,150	(76%)
	Michael D. Plunkett (D)	49,399	(24%)
1972 primary:	C. W. Bill Young (R), unopposed		
1970 general:	C. W. Bill Young (R)	120,466	(67%)
	Ted A. Bailey (D)	58,904	(33%)

SEVENTH DISTRICT Political Background

Tampa—population 277,000—dominates the 7th congressional district of Florida. This city is a very different one from St. Petersburg just across Tampa Bay. If St. Petersburg is known for its many retirees, Tampa is almost as well known for its large and long-established Cuban-American community, and for being the nation's leading manufacturer of cigars. Tampa's Cuban community, however, has not grown nearly as fast as Miami's, the latter having absorbed most of the emigration from Castro's island. As a whole, Tampa is as much a white working-class (and union labor) city as there is in Florida. The 1968 presidential returns suggest the divisions in Tampa society. The 7th district split almost equally three ways: 35% for Nixon, 34% for Humphrey, and 32% for Wallace. These figures reflect the approximate split among three groups: (1) Northern migrants; (2) Cubans, blacks, and white labor-union members; and (3) Southern-origin whites.

Until 1960, Tampa lay in the same district as St. Petersburg. After the 1960 census, a Tampa-centered district was created, and its Congressman since that time—the district has been numbered variously the 10th, 6th, and now the 7th—has been Democrat Sam Gibbons. The Floridian has been active among the younger Democrats in the House who have sought to reform its procedures and revamp its leadership. Unlike most Florida Congressmen, Gibbons has supported civil-rights legislation, and he has voted more often than not with the bulk of Northern Democrats. He served for several terms on the Education and Labor Committee and now sits on Ways and Means. On that committee, Gibbons is one of the more assiduous champions of major tax reform (see Arkansas 2).

Gibbons has had little trouble winning reelection, except in 1968 when a conservative primary opponent held him down to 60% of the vote. After the 1972 election, Gibbons made a move to run for the position of Majority Leader after Hale Boggs' apparent death in an Alaskan plane crash. The insurgent wanted to amass a coalition of Southerners and younger Northern liberals, but it soon became clear that Whip Tip O'Neill had the job sewed up, and Gibbons withdrew before the new Congress convened in January.

Census Data Pop. 452,820. Central city, 39%; suburban, 61%. Median family income, $8,256; families above $15,000: 14%; families below $3,000: 12%. Median years education, 12.

1972 Share of Federal Outlays $504,277,388

DOD	$119,857,649	HEW	$248,510,341
AEC	$9,196,914	HUD	$5,764,789
NASA	$3,033,647	DOI	$272,650
DOT	$15,584,068	USDA	$2,903,094
		Other	$99,154,236

Federal Military-Industrial Commitments

DOD Contractors Honeyweell (Tampa), $13.727m: aircraft communications equipment.
DOD Installations MacDill AFB (Tampa).

Economic Base Finance, insurance and real estate; food and kindred products; agriculture, notably fruits, dairy products and poultry; fabricated metal products, especially fabricated structural metal products and metal cans; and chemical and allied products, especially agricultural chemicals. Also higher education (Univ. of South Florida).

The Voters

Registration 201,297 total. 156,483 D (78%); 37,753 R (19%); 7,061 other (4%).

Median voting age 43.0
Employment profile White collar, 49%. Blue collar, 36%. Service, 13%. Farm, 2%.
Ethnic groups Black, 13%. Spanish, 12%. Total foreign stock, 14%. Italy, 2%; Germany, Canada, UK, 1% each.

Presidential vote

1972	Nixon (R)	99,739	(70%)
	McGovern (D)	43,347	(30%)
1968	Nixon (R)	43,565	(35%)
	Humphrey (D)	41,876	(34%)
	Wallace (AI)	39,555	(32%)

Representative

Sam M. Gibbons (D) Elected 1962; b. Jan. 20, 1920, Tampa; home, Tampa; U. of Fla., LL.B., 1947; Army, WWII; married, two children; Presbyterian.

Career Practicing atty., 1947–62; Fla. House of Reps., 1952–58; Fla. Senate, 1958–62.

Offices 2161 RHOB, 202-225-3376. Also 510 Fed. Bldg., 500 Zack St., Tampa 33602, 913-228-7711, ext. 336.

Administrative Assistant Hector Alcalde

Committees

Ways and Means (12th).

Group Ratings

	ADA	COPE	LWV	RIPON	NFU	LCV	CFA	NAB	NSI	ACA
1972	44	60	70	50	100	67	50	18	11	39
1971	65	50	67	76	80	–	100	–	–	39
1970	60	91	–	81	100	66	100	0	89	39

Key Votes

1) Busing	AGN	6) Cmbodia Bmbg	AGN	11) Chkg Acct Intrst	ABS
2) Strip Mines	AGN	7) Bust Hwy Trust	ABS	12) End HISC (HUAC)	AGN
3) Cut Mil $	AGN	8) Farm Sub Lmt	AGN	13) Nixon Sewer Veto	AGN
4) Rev Shrg	AGN	9) School Prayr	FOR	14) Corp Cmpaign $	FOR
5) Pub TV $	ABS	10) Cnsumr Prot	FOR	15) Pol $ Disclosr	FOR

Election Results

1972 general:	Sam Gibbons (D)	91,931	(68%)
	Robert A. Carter (R)	43,343	(32%)
1972 primary:	Sam Gibbons (D), unopposed		
1970 general:	Sam Gibbons (D)	78,832	(72%)
	Robert A. Carter (R)	30,252	(28%)

EIGHTH DISTRICT Political Background

Florida's 8th district is made up of two distinct areas. Somewhat less than half its population lives along the Gulf Coast in towns like Bradenton and Sarasota. These are relatively well-off, sun-baked communities with lots of migrants and retirees from the North; the voters here are very conservative and very Republican. Separated from the Gulf Coast by miles of swampland is the citrus-growing country in and around Polk County. Here the towns are smaller and have fewer of the glittering new high rises that tower along the coast. The interior economy is more attuned to agriculture than to winter tourists.

Incongrously set amidst the boom cities of central Florida, Polk County remains a part of Old Dixie politically. In 1968, Polk preferred George Wallace to Richard Nixon, and in general, the county will give local—but not national—Democratic candidates better vote totals than they get on the Gulf Coast. For almost 30 years, Polk County has been the home of at least one of the state's U.S. Senators; Bartow native Spessard Holland, long unbeatable, gave some valuable help to Lakeland lawyer Lawton Chiles in his upset victory in 1970.

The 8th must be one of the districts national Republican strategists have eyed for 1974. For one thing, the 8th has not gone for a Democratic presidential candidate since the 1940s; for another, the strong Republican voting base in Sarasota and Bradenton should overmatch any Democratic edge in Polk County. Up to now, however, the 8th has continued to reelect Democrat James A. Haley for years on end. Haley, well-established locally, is a former owner, through marriage, of the Ringling Brothers Barnum and Bailey Circus, which is headquartered in Sarasota. The Congressman's local connections, plus 20 years of service, are the principal reasons behind his continued reelection. In recent years, his margins have slipped—down to 53% in 1970. But with redistricting help in 1972, Haley became the only Florida Democrat to run ahead of his 1970 showing. It may have also helped that Haley, who was 73 in 1972, was about to become a Committee Chairman. Wayne Aspinall of Colorado had lost his primary, and thus Haley, by the inexorable workings of the seniority system, would if reelected succeed to the chairmanship of the Interior Committee.

Most of the Congressmen who seek service on Interior are from the Western states, where there is strong local interest in the decisions of the committee. Aspinall had been particularly adept at getting what he considered benefits for his Western constituency in Colorado; at the same time, he became a master of Interior's subject matter. Farmers wanting more reclamation projects, and mining interests eager to work public lands, were two groups most often looking over Interior's shoulder. Today there is another—the ecology activists. This group was in large part responsible for the demise of Aspinall, whose policies environmentalists detested and whose iron control of the committee frustrated them at every turn. Besides Aspinall, the activists had previously zeroed in on other powerful Congressmen they disliked, funnelling money into obscure primaries and winning several of them.

So the environmentalists have become another constituency that an Interior Chairman has to consider, and it appears that Haley is doing just that. His initial speech upon taking the committee's chair was larded with ecological catchwords. The new Chairman is considered less expert than Aspinall, and more open to persuasion. Haley is also far more likely to give Interior's Subcommittees much more discretion than his predecessor. The speculation now is whether Haley, after two years as Chairman, will decide to retire; he will be 76 in 1974. Moreover, with the number of Republicans in his district, any general election for him becomes an uncertain affair. Finally, all things being equal, the 8th likely as not would go Republican should Haley decide to return to Sarasota and the circus for good.

Census Data Pop. 451,776. Central city, 0%; suburban, 8%. Median family income, $7,341; families above $15,000: 13%; families below $3,000: 16%. Median years education, 12.0.

1972 Share of Federal Outlays $346,170,699

DOD	$25,287,888	HEW	$225,898,683
AEC	$760,925	HUD	$1,221,963
NASA	$1,068,728	DOI	$144,653
DOT	$8,664,463	USDA	$8,409,838
		Other	$74,713,558

Federal Military-Industrial Commitments

No installations or contractors receiving prime awards greater than $5,000,000.

Economic Base Agriculture, notably fruits, dairy products, poultry and vegetables; food and kindred products, especially canned, cured and frozen foods; finance, insurance and real estate; chemicals and allied products, especially agricultural chemicals; and stone, clay and glass products.

The Voters

Registration 223,259 total. 147,095 D (66%); 70,638 R (32%); 5,526 other (2%).
Median voting age 50.5
Employment profile White collar, 43%. Blue collar, 35%. Service, 14%. Farm, 8%.
Ethnic groups Black, 14%. Spanish 2%. Total foreign stock 10%. Germany, Canada, 2% each;
UK, 1%.

Presidential vote

1972	Nixon (R)	134,071	(79%)
	McGovern (D)	34,768	(21%)
1968	Nixon (R)	67,444	(44%)
	Humphrey (D)	33,031	(22%)
	Wallace (AI)	51,638	(34%)

Representative

James Andrew Haley (D) Elected 1952; b. Jan. 4, 1899, Jackson, Ala.;
home, Sarasota; U. of Ala., 1919–22; Army, WWI; married; Methodist.

Career Accountant 1922–33; Genl. Mgr., John Ringling estate, 1933–43;
V.P. Ringling Circus, 1943–45, Pres. and Dir. Ringling Bros. Barnum &
Bailey Circus, 1946–48; Fla. House of Reps., 1948 and 1950; Delegate to
Natl. Convention, 1952 and 1960.

Offices 1236 LHOB, 202-225-5015. Also 529 13th St. W., Bradenton
33505, 813-742-4041, and 113 East Main, Bartow 33803, 813-533-2881.

Administrative Assistant Alice V. Myers

Committees

Interior and Insular Affairs (Chm.).

Veterans' Affairs (3rd); Sub: Hospitals.

Joint Com. on Navajo-Hopi Indian Administration.

Group Ratings

	ADA	COPE	LWV	RIPON	NFU	LCV	CFA	NAB	NSI	ACA
1972	0	9	10	23	43	20	50	100	100	100
1971	8	0	0	41	15	–	13	–	–	92
1970	8	25	–	24	23	6	45	73	100	83

Key Votes

1) Busing	AGN	6) Cmbodia Bmbg	FOR	11) Chkg Acct Intrst	AGN
2) Strip Mines	ABS	7) Bust Hwy Trust	AGN	12) End HISC (HUAC)	AGN
3) Cut Mil $	AGN	8) Farm Sub Lmt	FOR	13) Nixon Sewer Veto	FOR
4) Rev Shrg	AGN	9) School Prayr	FOR	14) Corp Cmpaign $	FOR
5) Pub TV $	AGN	10) Cnsumr Prot	AGN	15) Pol $ Disclosr	AGN

Election Results

1972 general:	James A. Haley (D)	89,068	(58%)
	Roy Thompson (R)	64,920	(42%)
1972 primary:	James A. Haley (D), unopposed		
1970 general:	James A. Haley (D)	78,535	(53%)
	Joe Z. Lovingood (R)	68,646	(47%)

NINTH DISTRICT Political Background

Everyone knows about Orange County, California, with its San Clemente estate and its fabled conservative politics. More esoteric is Orange County, Florida, of which Orlando is the county seat. If you use the 1968 or 1972 presidential returns as a benchmark, Orange County, Florida is at least a couple of shades more conservative than its California counterpart. The larger part of Orange County, along with Brevard County of Kennedy Space Center fame, makes up Florida's 9th congressional district. In 1972, the 9th produced Richard Nixon's sixth highest percentage among the 435 House constituencies.

This is a growth area, with plenty of Yankee migrants moving in and bringing their conservative Republicanism along. Historically, the economic base here was the orange crop, but as in the case of Orange County, California, oranges have been supplanted as the chief engine of growth by the Department of Defense and the National Aeronautics and Space Administration. Orlando has the bulk of the area's defense plants, with more than $200 million in contracts, while the NASA money goes to Brevard County on the coast. With the coming of the seventies, the space budget was cut, leaving Brevard in an economic funk. In 1972, a program very much favored here was the space shuttle, which, like busing, proved to be a stumbling block for most Democratic presidential candidates in the primary of that year. Though Richard Nixon wants a shuttle, the program faces some trouble in Congress.

But if NASA became a little less generous, the 9th got a boost from the same organization that sparked much of the growth in Orange County, California. The giant Disney World complex outside Orlando—it will eventually be a city in itself—has set attendance records, triggered a real estate boom, and created traffic jams of monumental proportions. Tourists coming to Florida used to ignore Orlando; now they flock here by the hundreds of thousands, staying as long as a week to catch both Disney World and the Kennedy Space Center.

The 9th district's Congressman is a conservative Republican. When the Orange-Brevard area first got its own congressional seat in 1962, the voters elected Republican Edward Gurney to fill it; he moved up to the Senate in 1968. His successor is his former law partner, Louis Frey, Jr., like the current Senator a migrant from the Northeast. And also like Gurney, Frey has compiled a solidly conservative voting record, wins elections easily, and has ambitions for higher office. At one point, rumors had it that Frey wanted to take on his old legal colleague in the 1974 Republican Senate primary; the better bet, at this writing, is that he will challenge Democratic Gov. Reubin Askew in 1974. If Frey does, it will mean a new, and certainly conservative Republican, Congressman for the 9th.

Census Data Pop. 452,923. Central city, 16%; suburban, 34%. Median family income, $10,267; families above $15,000: 24%; families below $3,000: 8%. Median years education, 12.5.

1972 Share of Federal Outlays $973,129,929

DOD	$502,983,732	HEW	$12,714,328
AEC	–	HUD	$1,443,678
NASA	$256,665,170	DOI	$810,000
DOT	$12,016,721	USDA	$6,908,116
		Other	$69,588,184

Federal Military-Industrial Commitments

DOD Contractors Western Electric (Orlando), $142.288m: research and development of ABM system. Martin Marietta (Orlando), $105.009m: Pershing, Walleye, and Sam-D missile systems; fragmentation bombs. Pan American Airways (Cocoa Beach), $75.377m: operation and maintenance of Eastern Test Range. McDonnell Douglas (Titusville), $5.942m: Dragon missile system. Radiation, Inc. (Melbourne), $19.783m: classified electronic ware. Radiation, Inc. (Palm Bay), $11.008m: shipboard electronic ware. Amron Orlando (Orlando), $7.800m: mine fuzes. General Dynamics (Orlando), $7.472m: communication equipment.
DOD Installations Naval Training Device Center (Orlando). Naval Training Center (Orlando). McCoy AFB (Orlando); closed, 1974. Patrick AFB (Cocoa Beach).
NASA Contractors Boeing (Kennedy Space Center), $38.282m: Saturn V and Skylab launch support. North American Rockwell (Kennedy Space Center), $23.947m: Apollo and Skylab support. McDonnell Douglas (Kennedy Space Center), $21.873m: Skylab support. Bendix

(Kennedy Space Center), $21.405m: launch support for Apollo and Saturn. Federal Electric (Kennedy Space Center), $18.434m: communication support for Apollo. Grumman Aerospace (Kennedy Space Center), $13.701m: Apollo lunar module support. Chrysler (Cape Kennedy), $6.004m: unspecified. Fairchild Industries (Cape Kennedy), $5.430m: Centaur launch support. *NASA Installations* Kennedy Space Center (Space Center).

Economic Base Finance, insurance and real estate; agriculture, notably fruits, nursery and greenhouse products, and cattle; electrical equipment and supplies; food and kindred products, especially canned, cured and frozen foods; tourism; and printing and publishing, especially newspapers.

The Voters

Registration 222,214 total. 128,336 D (58%); 84,555 R (38%); 9,323 other (4%).
Median voting age 41.3
Employment profile White collar, 60%. Blue collar, 27%. Service, 12%. Farm, 1%.
Ethnic groups Black, 8%. Spanish, 2%. Total foreign stock, 11%. UK, Germany, Canada, 2% each.

Presidential vote

1972	Nixon (R)	132,323	(81%)
	McGovern (D)	32,041	(19%)
1968	Nixon (R)	71,359	(51%)
	Humphrey (D)	31,586	(23%)
	Wallace (AI)	37,097	(26%)

Representative

Louis Frey, Jr. (R) Elected 1968; b. Jan. 11, 1934, Rutherford, N.J.; home, Winter Park; Colgate U., B.A., 1955; U. of Mich., J.D., 1961; Navy, 1955–58, Cdr., USNR; married, five children; Lutheran.

Career Practicing atty., 1961–68; Asst. County Solicitor, 1963; Acting General Counsel, Fla. Turnpike Auth., 1966–67; Treas. Fla. Repub. Party, 1966–67.

Offices 214 LHOB, 202-225-3671. Also Rm. 222, 1040 Woodcock Rd., Orlando 32803, 305-843-2210, and 210 Brevard Ave., Cocoa 32922, 305-636-8307, and 504 N. Harbor City Blvd., Melbourne.

Administrative Assistant Oscar Juárez

Committees

Interstate and Foreign Commerce (11th); Sub: Communications and Power.

Science and Astronautics (5th); Subs: Manned Space Flight; Cooperation in Science and Space (Ranking Mbr.).

Group Ratings

	ADA	COPE	LWV	RIPON	NFU	LCV	CFA	NAB	NSI	ACA
1972	13	9	45	57	43	53	0	92	100	91
1971	14	17	33	56	27	–	14	–	–	84
1970	4	0	–	53	17	0	43	100	90	88

Key Votes

1) Busing	AGN	6) Cmbodia Bmbg	FOR
2) Strip Mines	AGN	7) Bust Hwy Trust	FOR
3) Cut Mil $	ABS	8) Farm Sub Lmt	FOR
4) Rev Shrg	AGN	9) School Prayr	FOR
5) Pub TV $	FOR	10) Cnsumr Prot	AGN

11) Chkg Acct Intrst	AGN
12) End HISC (HUAC)	ABS
13) Nixon Sewer Veto	FOR
14) Corp Cmpaign $	FOR
15) Pol $ Disclosr	FOR

Election Results

1972 general:	Louis Frey (R), unopposed		
1972 primary:	Louis Frey (R), unopposed		
1970 general:	Louis Frey (R)	110,841	(76%)
	Roy Girod (D)	35,398	(24%)

TENTH DISTRICT Political Background

The 10th is one of three new congressional districts acquired by Florida in the 1970 census. It is also the only one of the three that the state's Democratic legislature conceded to the opposition. The shape of the 10th makes little sense except as an agglomeration of all the Republican-leaning territory that south Florida's Democratic Congressmen didn't much want. The district sweeps across the Florida peninsula, fronting on the Atlantic north of Palm Beach and on the Gulf of Mexico south of Sarasota. Accordingly, its population centers are widely dispersed; it goes as far north as the Disney World area near Orlando; it takes in some of the fast-growing suburban territory west of West Palm Beach; it includes the largest town on the Gulf Coast south of Sarasota, Fort Myers. In between, there is mostly the remarkable swamp of the Everglades, Lake Okeechobee, the Sebring Grand Prix course, and numerous orange groves.

The beneficiary of this district, conceived by Democratic politicians, is Republican L.A. (Skip) Bafalis, Jr. For Bafalis, the creation of the 10th provided the opportunity for a political comeback. After six years in the Florida legislature, he ran for Governor in 1970. Despite a campaign that attracted some attention, the candidate got caught in a roaring feud between Gov. Claude Kirk and drugstore millionaire Jack Eckerd, with Bafalis winning only 13% of the vote.

In 1972, Bafalis had it easier. He won the Republican nomination without much fuss, and got a landslide 62% in the general election, despite a vigorous campaign by his young Democratic opponent. That percentage is probably a good prognosticator of elections to come in the new 10th.

Census Data Pop. 452,848. Central city, 0%; suburban, 6%. Median family income, $7,323; families above $15,000: 14%; families below $3,000: 15%. Median years education, 12.1.

1972 Share of Federal Outlays $388,045,606

DOD	$52,194,088	HEW	$242,908,052
AEC	–	HUD	$1,293,251
NASA	$696,031	DOI	$1,606,363
DOT	$8,119,510	USDA	$15,263,516
		Other	$65,964,795

Federal Military-Industrial Commitments

No installations or contractors receiving prime awards greater than $5,000,000.

Economic Base Agriculture, notably fruits, vegetables and cattle; finance, insurance and real estate; food and kindred products, especially canned, cured and frozen foods; tourism; printing and publishing, especially newspapers; and transportation equipment, especially aircraft.

The Voters

Registration 262,645 total. 155,909 D (59%); 97,988 R (37%); 8,748 other (3%).
Median voting age 52.6
Employment profile White collar, 43%. Blue collar, 33%. Service, 15%. Farm, 9%.
Ethnic groups Black, 14%. Spanish, 2%. Total foreign stock, 13%. Germany, UK, Canada, 2% each.

Presidential vote

1972	Nixon (R)	157,854	(79%)
	McGovern (D)	41,504	(21%)
1968	Nixon (R)	71,305	(47%)
	Humphrey (D)	37,224	(25%)
	Wallace (AI)	41,877	(28%)

Representative

Louis Arthur Bafalis (R) Elected 1972; b. Sept. 28, 1929, Boston, Mass.; home, Fort Myers; St. Anselm's Col., A.B., 1952; Army, Korean War; married, two children; Protestant.

Career Partner, investment banking firm, Kirk and Co., West Palm Beach, Fla.; Fla. House, 1964; Fla. Senate, 1966; candidate for Governor, 1970.

Offices 1713 LHOB, 202-225-2536. Also Rm. 106 Federal Bldg., Ft. Myers 33901, 813-334-4424 and 700 Virginia Ave., Suite 105, Ft. Pierce 33450, 305-465-3710.

Administrative Assistant Richard T. Nelson

Committees

Public Works (13th); Subs: Economic Development; Investigations and Review; Public Buildings and Grounds; Transportation; Water Resources.

Post Office and Civil Service (10th; Subs: Census and Statistics; Retirement and Employee Benefits.

Group Ratings: Newly Elected

Key Votes

1) Busing	NE	6) Cmbodia Bmbg	FOR	11) Chkg Acct Intrst	ABS
2) Strip Mines	NE	7) Bust Hwy Trust	AGN	12) End HISC (HUAC)	AGN
3) Cut Mil $	NE	8) Farm Sub Lmt	NE	13) Nixon Sewer Veto	FOR
4) Rev Shrg	NE	9) School Prayr	NE	14) Corp Cmpaign $	NE
5) Pub TV $	NE	10) Cnsumr Prot	NE	15) Pol $ Disclosr	NE

Election Results

1972 general:	L. A. Bafalis (R)	113,461	(62%)
	Bill Sikes (D)	69,502	(38%)
1972 primary:	L. A. Bafalis (R)	28,515	(71%)
	Paul J. Myers (R)	11,482	(29%)

ELEVENTH DISTRICT Political Background

Fifty years ago, Palm Beach was already a fashionable resort for the extremely wealthy. Across Lake Worth, West Palm Beach was a small town, a large percentage of whose residents devoted themselves to ministering to the needs of Palm Beach. Palm Beach has changed little since, but West Palm Beach, and the whole "Gold Coast" all the way south to Miami Beach, has been altered beyond recognition. High-rise apartment houses and condominiums practically form a wall that blocks off the mainland from the Atlantic. *Jai alai frontons* vie with gaudy bars for the tourist's money, and the small motels of the late forties have been replaced with giant motor inns.

The northern end of the Gold Coast—in rough terms from Pompano Beach to West Palm Beach—is the 11th congressional district. Like Fort Lauderdale to the south, the 11th has become ever more Republican as more and more people move here from the well-to-do suburbs of the Midwest and Northeast. But the new people have not been much of a problem for Democratic Congressman Paul Rogers. His margins have been holding up despite the vast changes that have occurred in the district he represents. The 11th district and its predecessors (which only ten years ago included most of south Florida outside Miami) have more or less been the property of the Rogers family. The current Congressman was first elected after the death in 1954 of his father, who had represented the district since its creation in 1944.

During his first years in Congress, Rogers had something of a playboy reputation. He settled down, however, after getting married in the early sixties. Soon after that, he became Chairman of the House Commerce Committee's Subcommittee on Public Health. (Why health should be considered the realm of the Commerce Committee is one of those mysteries of congressional custom better left unexplored.) As Chairman, Rogers has become one of the major powers on health policy in the country. The Congressman assembled a good staff, and personally mastered the committee's subject matter. There are those who think that Rogers has stretched his committee's jurisdiction a little farther than it should go, but he is considered one of the more thoughtful and energetic subcommittee chairmen in the House. It was Rogers who led the fight in September 1973 to override President Nixon's veto of emergency health care legislation—a move that came within five votes, the closest yet, of succeeding, and which forced the Republican leadership to promise to enact much of the bill anyway. It is a fact of life in the House that a member must specialize in order to have any impact. Rogers is one of the better examples of intelligent specialization.

Census Data   Pop. 452,170. Central city, 13%; suburban, 87%. Median family income, $8,995; families above $15,000: 21%; families below $3,000: 11%. Median years education, 12.2.

1972 Share of Federal Outlays $674,038,360

DOD	$341,437,716	HEW	$218,907,045
AEC	–	HUD	$670,181
NASA	$2,679,353	DOI	$1,612,591
DOT	$33,735,988	USDA	$8,416,321
		Other	$66,579,165

Federal Military-Industrial Commitments

DOD Contractors   United Aircraft (West Palm Beach), $338.785m: design of various aircraft engines. Dynamics Corporation of America (Boynton Beach), $7.486m: electronic ware.

Economic Base   Agriculture, notably vegetables, nursery and greenhouse products, dairy products and cattle; finance, insurance and real estate; office and computing machines, and other machinery; tourism; and electrical equipment and supplies.

The Voters

Registration   271,646 total. 142,206 D (52%); 115,884 R (43%); 13,556 other (5%).
Median voting age   51.3
Employment profile   White collar, 49%. Blue collar, 31%. Service, 16%. Farm, 4%.
Ethnic groups   Black, 18%. Spanish, 3%. Total foreign stock, 21%. Germany, UK, Canada, 3% each; Italy, 2%; Ireland, 1%.

Presidential vote

1972	Nixon (R)	146,024	(74%)
	McGovern (D)	50,733	(26%)
1968	Nixon (R)	74,707	(55%)
	Humphrey (D)	37,610	(28%)
	Wallace (AI)	24,016	(18%)

Representative

Paul G. Rogers (D)   Elected 1954; b. June 4, 1921, Ocilla, Ga.; home, West Palm Beach; U. of Fla., B.A., 1942, LL.B., 1948; Army, WWII; married, one child; Methodist.

Career   Practicing atty., 1948–54.

Offices   2417 RHOB, 202-225-3001. Also 321 Fed. Bldg., West Palm Beach 33401, 305-832-6424.

Administrative Assistant   Robert W. Maher

Committees

Interstate and Foreign Commerce (6th); Sub: Public Health and Environment (Chm.).

Merchant Marine and Fisheries (6th); Subs: Coast Guard and Navigation; Fisheries and Wildlife Conservation and the Environment; Oceanography.

Group Ratings

	ADA	COPE	LWV	RIPON	NFU	LCV	CFA	NAB	NSI	ACA
1972	6	18	42	53	33	53	100	58	90	87
1971	19	42	33	50	53	–	50	–	–	68
1970	24	17	–	29	38	50	83	67	100	68

Key Votes

1) Busing	AGN	6) Cmbodia Bmbg	AGN	11) Chkg Acct Intrst	AGN
2) Strip Mines	AGN	7) Bust Hwy Trust	FOR	12) End HISC (HUAC)	AGN
3) Cut Mil $	AGN	8) Farm Sub Lmt	FOR	13) Nixon Sewer Veto	FOR
4) Rev Shrg	AGN	9) School Prayr	FOR	14) Corp Cmpaign $	FOR
5) Pub TV $	FOR	10) Cnsumr Prot	FOR	15) Pol $ Disclosr	AGN

Election Results

1972 general:	Paul G. Rogers (D)	116,157	(60%)
	Joel Karl Gustafson (R)	76,739	(40%)
1972 primary:	Paul G. Rogers (D), unopposed		
1970 general:	Paul G. Rogers (D)	120,565	(71%)
	Emil D. Danciu (R)	50,146	(29%)

TWELFTH DISTRICT Political Background

For some, Fort Lauderdale evokes memories of college sand-and-beer vacations in the spring, or maybe scenes from an Annette Funicello movie about life and love on the city's commodious public beach. With a reputation like this the town fathers have not been pleased; the college spring visitors of the sixties brought little money and scared away some people who did. Naturally the Fort Lauderdale people most emphatically do not want to engender any more of these happy memories, and with stern law enforcement have tried to fob the collegians off on some other town like Daytona Beach.

Fort Lauderdale lies in the heart of Florida's Gold Coast. The Fort Lauderdale establishment dredged and filled the swampy coast here and then criss-crossed the result with canals; the fruits of the labor soon became some of the most valuable real estate in the country. The city's canals and its ocean frontage are now lined with the high rises that have made millionaires out of a great many Florida real estate men. Fort Lauderdale's modest population of 172,000 conceals the reality of its importance. The city is the center of Broward County, which has 620,000 people, and it has the wherewithall to entertain and lodge many more affluent tourists than one might guess from its size. There are probably more yacht-like boats (not to mention *jai alai frontons*) per capita here than anywhere else in the country.

The permanent—and therefore voting—population of Fort Lauderdale and Broward County has moved here mostly from the upper-income suburbs of the East and Midwest. The new residents have tripled Broward's population in the last 20 years; back home, these people were Republicans, and they have now made this area one of the leading Republican strongholds in the state. It is convenient, though not completely accurate, to think of Broward and Fort Lauderdale as Chicago suburb-Chicago *Tribune*-Protestant-Republican and to think of Miami and Dade County as New York City-New York *Times*-Jewish-Democratic. So it is fitting that the 12th congressional district, which includes most of Broward County and all of its two largest cities—Fort Lauderdale and Hollywood—elects a Republican Congressman who was brought up in Chicago.

The Congressman is J. Herbert Burke. He was first elected in 1966 when the Democratic Florida legislature could no longer forestall the one-man-one-vote ruling, and was forced to give Broward its own congressional district. In 1972 Burke was aided by a subsequent redistricting that removed from the 12th a strip of northern Dade County and southern Broward, into which an increasing number of Jewish Democrats had been moving. Burke's convincing margin in 1972 indicates that the 12th will continue to send a Republican to the House indefinitely, whatever the turnarounds and upheavals of Florida politics generally.

Census Data Pop. 453,053. Central city, 54%; suburban, 46%. Median family income, $9,717; families above $15,000: 22%; families below $3,000: 9%. Median years education, 12.2.

1972 Share of Federal Outlays $340,215,243

DOD	$21,705,395	HEW	$220,463,620
AEC	–	HUD	$344,934
NASA	$661,331	DOI	$1,156,270
DOT	$27,919,954	USDA	$2,584,734
		Other	$65,379,005

Federal Military-Industrial Commitments

No installations or contractors receiving prime awards greater than $5,000,000.

Economic Base Finance, insurance and real estate; agriculture, notably vegetables, dairy products, and nursery and greenhouse products; tourism; electrical equipment and supplies, especially radio and television communication equipment; and machinery, especially office and computing machines.

The Voters

Registration 244,296 total. 136,741 D (56%); 97,154 R (40%); 10,401 other (4%).
Median voting age 48.8
Employment profile White collar, 53%. Blue collar, 31%. Service, 15%. Farm, 1%.
Ethnic groups Black, 12%. Spanish, 3%. Total foreign stock, 25%. Italy, 4%; Germany, Canada, UK, 3% each; USSR, 2% Poland, Ireland, 1% each.

Presidential vote

1972	Nixon (R)	140,157	(72%)
	McGovern (D)	54,394	(28%)
1968	Nixon (R)	73,128	(53%)
	Humphrey (D)	41,686	(30%)
	Wallace (AI)	23,490	(17%)

Representative

J. Herbert Burke (R) Elected 1966; b. Jan. 14, 1913, Chicago, Ill.; home, Hollywood; Chicago YMCA Col., A.A., 1936; Northwestern U. and Chicago Kent Col. of Law, LL.B., 1940; J.D., 1969; Army, WWII; married, two children; Catholic.

Career Practicing atty., 1940– ; Mgr. Broward County Com., 1952–68; Mbr. Fla. State Repub. Com., 1954–59; Delegate Repub. Natl. Com., 1968; Mbr., Repub. Platform Com., 1968.

Offices 1125 LHOB, 202-225-3026. Also 440 S. Andrews Ave., West Palm Beach 33401.

Administrative Assistant J. Gene Curella

Committees

Foreign Affairs (9th); Subs: Asian and Pacific Affairs; Europe.

Internal Security (3rd).

Group Ratings

	ADA	COPE	LWV	RIPON	NFU	LCV	CFA	NAB	NSI	ACA
1972	13	20	36	45	17	41	50	92	100	100
1971	11	8	14	40	33	–	14	–	–	96
1970	8	17	–	53	15	29	39	91	100	93

Key Votes

1) Busing	AGN	6) Cmbodia Bmbg	FOR	11) Chkg Acct Intrst	AGN
2) Strip Mines	AGN	7) Bust Hwy Trust	FOR	12) End HISC (HUAC)	AGN
3) Cut Mil $	FOR	8) Farm Sub Lmt	ABS	13) Nixon Sewer Veto	FOR
4) Rev Shrg	ABS	9) School Prayr	FOR	14) Corp Cmpaign $	FOR
5) Pub TV $	AGN	10) Cnsumr Prot	AGN	15) Pol $ Disclosr	AGN

Election Results

1972 general:	J. Herbert Burke (R)	110,750	(63%)
	James T. Stephanis (D)	65,526	(37%)
1972 primary:	J. Herbert Burke (R), unopposed		
1970 general:	J. Herbert Burke (R)	81,170	(54%)
	James J. Ward, Jr. (D)	68,847	(46%)

THIRTEENTH DISTRICT Political Background

The 13th is the third Florida district newly conferred on the state by the 1970 census (see Florida 5 and 10). Population growth dictated that a new congressional district be drawn in the Miami area—the most important feature of that growth being the approximately 300,000 Cubans who since 1960 have left Castro's island and come to Miami. Ironically, the new 13th does not contain that many Cubans; most of them live next door in Claude Pepper's 14th district. If there is a single ethnic group that dominates the 13th, it is the Jewish one.

A critic of the 1972 *Almanac* claimed it overestimated the electoral clout of the Jewish voters in the Miami area. The book did not, and a discussion of the 13th gives a good chance to show why. To be sure, the 13th is by no means a majority Jewish— there are no precise figures available, but probably only two districts in the country, both in Brooklyn, are more than 50% Jewish. There are pockets of affluent WASPs living in Fort Lauderdale style in Miami Shores. There are also large numbers of black people residing on the north side of Miami, in adjacent unincorporated Dade County, and in Opa-locka, north of Miami. Then there is Hialeah, which is packed with blue-collar Wallace voters estranged from the Metro Dade County government. One way the people here can thumb their noses is by using its own street-number grid rather than adopting Miami's the way all the other suburbs around here do.

All in all, probably only about 15% of the 13th's residents are Jewish by religion, origin, or marriage. But a breakdown of the entire population is not the same as a breakdown of the electorate. Miami's Jewish community is heavily weighted toward the elderly end of the age scale; a typical Jewish resident of the district is a retired New York couple living in a North Miami Beach condominium. Because so many of the 13th's Jews are over 18, the Jewish proportion of the 13th's potential electorate is about 20%. And because Jewish citizens are more likely to go to the polls than others, the actual percentage of the Jewish vote in general elections here approaches 25%. This is about the same percentage, incidentally, as one finds in New York City. And because few Jewish people are registered Republicans, the percentage voting in Democratic primaries gets even higher.

This last percentage still does not constitute a majority. But it is worth noting that the three leading candidates in the 13th's 1972 Democratic primary—which most thought would be tantamount to election—were all Jewish: William Lehman (who eventually won), state Sen. Lee Weissenborn, and state Rep. Louis Wolfson II. So with the exception of a couple of seats in New York City and one in Los Angeles, the 13th is about as close to being a "Jewish district" as there is in the United States.

William Lehman, the 13th's new Congressman, has had an interesting career. Calling himself "Alabama Bill," Lehman got himself a start in the used-car business. He reportedly developed the reputation, unusual in the trade, of being reliable and strictly honest. Having mastered what is rated the least esteemed profession, he moved up to what is considered the second-least esteemed, politics. (Watergate, however, may have changed the rankings.) In the maelstrom of Dade County politics, Lehman, who now has a Buick dealership, got elected to the County School Board, and, just before his run for Congress, became its Chairman.

Lehman demonstrated his political acumen by defeating two strong candidates in the Democratic primary, and by winning, 62–38, over a hard-campaigning Republican in the general election. In the House, he generally agrees with and supports the more liberal members of the Democratic Caucus.

Census Data Pop. 452,817. Central city, 9%; suburban, 91%. Median family income, $9,411; families above $15,000: 20%; families below $3,000: 9%. Median years education, 12.0.

1972 Share of Federal Outlays $361,594,379

DOD	$52,892,517	HEW	$180,528,425
AEC	$103,117	HUD	$5,049,681
NASA	$510,218	DOI	$1,111,706
DOT	$17,804,071	USDA	$9,428,010
		Other	$94,166,634

Federal Military-Industrial Commitments

No installations or contractors receiving prime awards greater than $5,000,000.

Economic Base Finance, insurance and real estate; apparel and other textile products, especially women's and misses' outerwear; tourism; fabricated metal products, especially fabricated structural metal products; and food and kindred products.

The Voters

Registration 235,284 total. 186,223 D (79%); 40,654 R (17%); 8,407 other (4%).
Median voting age 46.1
Employment profile White collar, 49%. Blue collar, 34%. Service, 16%. Farm, 1%.
Ethnic groups Black, 18%. Spanish, 13%. Total foreign stock, 32%. USSR, 4%; Italy, 3%; Canada, Germany, Poland, UK, 2% each; Austria, 1%.

Presidential vote

1972	Nixon (R)	90,997	(56%)
	McGovern (D)	72,957	(44%)
1968	Nixon (R)	46,377	(35%)
	Humphrey (D)	64,160	(48%)
	Wallace (AI)	22,923	(17%)

Representative

William Lehman (D) Elected 1972; b. Oct. 5, 1913, Selma, Ala.; home, Miami; U. of Ala., 1934; U. of Miami, Teaching Certificate; studied at Barry Col., Oxford U., Kings Col. at Cambridge, and Harvard U.; married, three children; Jewish.

Career Auto sales and finance, 1936–62; G.E. Appliance Co., Miami, 1963; Teacher, Miami Public Schools, 1963; Teacher, Miami Dade Jr. Col.; Dade County School Board, 1964–70, Chm., 1971.

Offices 502 CHOB, 202-225-4211. Also 1110 N.E. 163rd St., Suite 337, N. Miami Beach, 305-945-7518.

Administrative Assistant Joan Kunkel

Committees

Education and Labor (20th); Subs: No. 1 (Education); No. 5 (Sel. Sub. on Education); No. 6 (Sp. Sub. on Education); No. 8 (Agricultural Labor).

Post Office and Civil Service (15th); Subs: Census and Statistics; Manpower and Civil Service.

Group Ratings: Newly Elected

Key Votes

1) Busing	NE	6) Cmbodia Bmbg	FOR	11) Chkg Acct Intrst	ABS
2) Strip Mines	NE	7) Bust Hwy Trust	FOR	12) End HISC (HUAC)	AGN
3) Cut Mil $	NE	8) Farm Sub Lmt	NE	13) Nixon Sewer Veto	FOR
4) Rev Shrg	NE	9) School Prayr	NE	14) Corp Cmpaign $	NE
5) Pub TV $	NE	10) Cnsumr Prot	NE	15) Pol $ Disclosr	NE

Election Results

1972 general:	William Lehman (D)	92,258	(62%)
	Paul D. Bethel (R)	57,418	(38%)
1972 run-off:	William Lehman (D)	26,261	(57%)
	Lee Weissenborn (d)	19,699	(43%)
1972 primary:	William Lehman (D)	10,023	(20%)
	Lee Weissenborn (D)	13,500	(27%)
	Louis Wolfson III (D)	8,795	(18%)
	Jay Kislak (D)	7,868	(16%)
	George Balmer (D)	3,241	(7%)
	Johnson E. Davis (D)	3,189	(6%)
	Betty Page (D)	2,777	(6%)
	Lee Weissenborn (D)	19,699	(43%)

FOURTEENTH DISTRICT Political Background

Claude Pepper is the grand old man of Florida politics. Back in 1936, he first went to Capitol Hill as a 36-year-old United States Senator. A gift for old-fashioned Southern oratory was one of the things that got him to Washington, but once in the Senate he never became a member in good standing of the Southern establishment. When other Senators from Dixie began to sour on the New Deal, Pepper remained as loyal to FDR's domestic policies as he did to FDR's conviction that the United States be fully prepared for another war in Europe. For these stands and for his devotion to civil liberties, the young Senator came to be called "Red Pepper." In 1950, during the era of the first Senator McCarthy, Pepper was defeated in a bitter Senate primary by Rep. George Smathers, and he retired to a lucrative Miami law practice.

Today, Smathers has himself retired (1968) to a lucrative job as a Washington lobbyist, and Claude Pepper is back in Congress. After the 1960 census, when the Florida legislature was compelled to create an additional Miami House seat, Pepper was the logical choice to fill it. He won an absolute majority in the 1962 Democratic primary and has since retained the seat without great difficulty. The Congressman's oratorical style is still out of Dixie, but his record is such that he is a particular favorite of his black and Jewish constituents.

If Pepper had won the 1950 race against Smathers, he would have become Chairman of the Senate Foreign Relations Committee. As things are, Congressman Pepper cuts a figure of less importance. But his years of experience on the Hill count for something—only one Senator (Randolph of West Virginia) and three Representatives preceded Pepper to Congress. Besides serving as a member of the House Rules Committee, where he usually votes in line with the House leadership, Pepper also serves on the Internal Security Committee. Most members of Rules do not have other standing committee assignments. In addition, Pepper has been Chairman of the Select Committee on Crime, which investigated drug abuse, horse racing establishments, and organized crime. The Select Committee has had some accomplishments—getting controls imposed on amphetamines, for example—and has treated its controversial subject of concern with more seriousness and less demagoguery than might be expected from a congressional committee. But because the House is suspicious of specially created committees, it voted, over Pepper's objections, to end the activities of the Select Committee on June 30, 1973.

When Pepper was first elected to the House, the district's most important voting bloc was Jewish. Today, because of the Cuban influx to the Miami area and because of redistricting, things are changing. More than 300,000 Cubans now live in Miami—and most reside in Pepper's district. The Cubans here comprise a diverse group politically and represent all kinds of opposition to Fidel Castro's regime: from right-wingers who supported the Batista dictatorship to liberal democrats and mild socialists who oppose Castro's eradication of civil liberties.

Thus the four Cuban-Americans who broke into the Watergate offices of Larry O'Brien represent only one segment within a range of feeling in the Miami Cuban community. In a significant sense, however, the four are typical of the Latins here. Coming largely out of Cuba's middle class, the migrants eagerly accepted menial jobs upon arrival in Miami and then rapidly worked themselves back up to an American version of middle-class status. Like Cuban society, the Miami Cuban-American community is comprised of many ethnic strains—the color of the people ranging from black to blond. Cuban-Americans, therefore, are less identifiable as a racial group than American blacks. The Latins, however, do speak English with a muted accent, or what is becoming more common, use Spanish.

"Latins are too busy making money to think about politics," one local offical told the *New York Times.* But even as the Cuban-Americans are making themselves successful, they are as well embracing the politics of Richard Nixon. As Cubans obtained citizenship and the franchise, they supported the Vietnam war and tended to favor politicians like Nixon who pay lip service to Cuban liberation. But no sophisticated Cuban expects Nixon or anybody else to make good his threats on the Castro regime. Still, if there is no longer much of a China lobby around in American politics, there is a Cuba lobby vote that grows stronger by the day in Miami.

In 1972, Cuban-Americans gave Richard Nixon an overwhelming majority of their votes, which is why normally Democratic Dade County went Republican by a 59–41 majority. With more and more Cubans beginning to vote, the outlook is for more Republican votes coming out of the Latin community. This is not especially good news for Miami Democrats or for Congressman Pepper, who beat a Cuban-American Republican by a 63–37 margin even as Nixon carried the 14th district. But Pepper will surely survive. He has been a long-time advocate of increased trade and better relations with Latin America, as well as being an oratorical opponent of the Castro government. And one of his major projects is Interama, an exposition park designed to promote U.S.–Latin-American ties. The park, perhaps by a sentimental fillip of redistricting, is included in the Congressman's 14th district.

When Pepper retires, it is conceivable that the 14th could change partisan hands. And in any case, it is fairly likely that Pepper's successor will be a Cuban-American.

Census Data Pop. 452,633. Central city, 58%; suburban, 42%. Median family income, $8,203; families above $15,000: 18%; families below $3,000: 13%. Median years education, 11.4.

1972 Share of Federal Outlays $363,362,918

DOD	$55,701,639	HEW	$176,811,422
AEC	$112,440	HUD	$5,474,868
NASA	$496,237	DOI	$1,107,119
DOT	$16,876,016	USDA	$10,045,458
		Other	$96,737,719

Federal Military-Industrial Commitments

DOD Contractors Airlift International (Miami), $21.702m: transportation services.

Economic Base Finance, insurance and real estate; apparel and other textile products, especially women's and misses' outerwear; tourism; fabricated metal products, especially fabricated structural metal products; and food and kindred products.

The Voters

Registration 172,050 total. 133,394 D (78%); 32,474 R (19%); 6,182 other (4%).
Median voting age 48.5
Employment profile White collar, 46%. Blue collar, 37%. Service, 17%. Farm, –%.
Ethnic groups Black, 15%. Spanish, 41%. Total foreign stock, 56%. USSR, 4%; Poland, 2%; Germany, Canada, Italy, Austria, UK, 1% each.

Presidential vote

1972	Nixon (R)	70,005	(58%)
	McGovern (D)	50,458	(42%)

1968	Nixon (R)	37,739	(34%)
	Humphrey (D)	59,206	(53%)
	Wallace (AI)	13,831	(12%)

Representative

Claude Denson Pepper (D) Elected 1962; b. Sept. 8, 1900, Dudleyville, Ala.; U. of Ala., B.A., 1921; Harvard Law School, LL.B., 1924; married; Baptist.

Career Instr. in law, U. of Ark., 1924–25; practicing atty., 1925–37–1951– ; Fla. House of Reps., 1929; State Bd. of Pub. Welfare, 1931–32; State Bd. of Law Examiners, 1933; U.S. Senate, 1937–51.

Offices 432 CHOB, 202-225-3931. Also 823 Fed. Bldg., Miami 33310, 305-350-5565.

Administrative Assistant James F. Southerland

Committees

Internal Security (2nd).

Rules (6th).

Sel. Com. on Crime (Chm.).

Group Ratings

	ADA	COPE	LWV	RIPON	NFU	LCV	CFA	NAB	NSI	ACA
1972	50	89	90	64	100	26	100	0	60	30
1971	57	100	100	47	77	–	71	–	–	8
1970	56	78	–	56	100	42	87	14	88	13

Key Votes

1) Busing	FOR	6) Cmbodia Bmbg	AGN	11) Chkg Acct Intrst	AGN
2) Strip Mines	AGN	7) Bust Hwy Trust	FOR	12) End HISC (HUAC)	AGN
3) Cut Mil $	AGN	8) Farm Sub Lmt	FOR	13) Nixon Sewer Veto	AGN
4) Rev Shrg	FOR	9) School Prayr	AGN	14) Corp Cmpaign $	FOR
5) Pub TV $	FOR	10) Cnsumr Prot	FOR	15) Pol $ Disclosr	AGN

Election Results

1972 general:	Claude Pepper (D)	75,131	(68%)
	Evelio S. Estrella (R)	35,935	(32%)
1972 primary:	Claude Pepper (D)	25,842	(63%)
	Jay Dermer (D)	15,104	(37%)
1970 general:	Claude Pepper (D), unopposed		

FIFTEENTH DISTRICT Political Background

The suburbs of south Dade County constitute the fastest-growing part of the Miami metropolitan area. Having few Latins, Jews, or blacks, these places lack the special ethnic character of Miami, with the area's physical ambience resembling that of Orange County, California. But while the people of California are bounded by an ocean and mountains, the people here are surrounded mainly by a giant swamp, the Everglades, from which their property was reclaimed. South Dade County is middle-class, middle- to upper-income territory that stretches out on both sides of U.S. Route 1, as it heads toward the Florida Keys.

The bulk of Florida's 15th congressional district lies in the southwest suburbs of Miami. Also in the district are the Keys (Monroe County), and some other territory here for political reasons. The 15th, for example, includes the University of Miami in Coral Gables and the nearby Coconut Grove section of Miami, which is the closest thing in south Florida to a student–street-people community. The district also takes in a couple of blocks of downtown Miami, which connect the mainland 15th to its share of Miami Beach.

The part of Miami Beach in the district includes the older, poorer, and almost entirely Jewish South Beach section, as well as the hall where both 1972 political conventions were held. Those who think that the "Jewish vote" is not an important aspect of Miami politics are invited to look at the statistics. In 1972, Miami Beach (pop. 87,000) cast almost precisely half as many votes as the city of Miami (pop. 334,000). And with only 7% of Dade County's population, Miami Beach cast 9% of the county's votes and 13% of its McGovern votes. This high-turnout, heavily Democratic pattern is a typically Jewish one, and one that is particularly important in the 15th district.

In 1972, the South Beach, with about 10% of the 15th's population, produced 25% of its McGovern votes—meaning that the South Beach was not put here by accident. For Democratic Congressman Dante Fascell did far better here than George McGovern. In 1972, with the southwest suburbs going heavily for Nixon, and an active, Jewish Republican candidate in the race, Fascell was held down to 57% of the votes. Without the South Beach, Fascell would have been in real trouble. Since he was first elected in 1954, the Congressman has usually won with no fuss whatever.

Fascell has developed a middle-of-the-road reputation over the years. Less notably liberal than Claude Pepper of the neighboring 14th, Fascell still votes more often with Northern Democrats than with Southern. One source of his local strength has been his long interest in Latin America. He is Chairman of the Foreign Affairs subcommittee on that area of the world and has devoted considerable attention to it.

Census Data Pop. 452,681. Central city, 8%; suburban, 81%. Median family income, $9,909; families above $15,000: 26%; families below $3,000: 11%. Median years education, 12.3.

1972 Share of Federal Outlays $390,492,745

DOD	$94,210,121	HEW	$169,567,083
AEC	$99,401	HUD	$4,839,967
NASA	$438,690	DOI	$978,730
DOT	$18,417,336	USDA	$9,162,629
		Other	$92,778,778

Federal Military-Industrial Commitments

DOD Installations Fleet Sonar School (Key West); closed, 1974. Naval Security Group Activities (Homestead). Naval Hospital (Key West). Naval Station (Key West); closed, 1974. Homestead AFB (Homestead). Richmond AF Station (Perrine).

Economic Base Finance, insurance and real estate; apparel and other textile products, especially women's and misses' outerwear; agriculture, notably vegetables, fruits, and nursery and greenhouse products; fabricated metal products, especially fabricated structural metal products; and tourism. Also higher education (Univ. of Miami).

The Voters

Registration 235,960 total. 173,270 D (73%); 51,718 R (22%); 10,972 other (5%).
Median voting age 43.7
Employment profile White collar, 60%. Blue collar, 24%. Service, 14%. Farm, 2%.
Ethnic groups Black, 11%. Spanish, 14%. Total foreign stock, 31%. USSR, 5%; Poland, UK, Germany, Canada, 2% each; Italy, Austria, 1% each.

Presidential vote

1972	Nixon (R)	104,864	(63%)
	McGovern (D)	60,483	(37%)
1968	Nixon (R)	52,286	(40%)
	Humphrey (D)	56,927	(44%)
	Wallace (AI)	20,469	(16%)

Representative

Dante B. Fascell (D) Elected 1954; b. March 9, 1917, Bridgehampton, L.I., N.Y.; home, Miami; U. of Miami, J.D., 1938; Army, WWII; married, three children; Protestant.

Career Practicing atty., 1938–54; Legal Attaché Dade County Legis. Delegation, 1947–50; Fla. House of Reps., 1950–54; Mbr. U.S. Delegation 24th General Assembly, UN.

Offices 2160 RHOB, 202-225-4506. Also 920 Fed. Bldg., 51 S.W. First Ave., Miami 33130, 305-350-5301.

Administrative Assistant John R. Buckley

Committees

Foreign Affairs (5th); Subs: Inter-American Affairs (Chm.); International Organizations and Movements; State Department Organization and Foreign Operations; Special Subcommittee for Review of Foreign Aid Programs.

Government Operations (6th); Subs: Conservation and Natural Resources; Legal and Monetary Affairs.

Group Ratings

	ADA	COPE	LWV	RIPON	NFU	LCV	CFA	NAB	NSI	ACA
1972	81	91	92	67	86	80	100	8	40	17
1971	81	82	100	78	80	–	100	–	–	8
1970	56	82	–	75	100	78	100	20	58	17

Key Votes

1) Busing	FOR	6) Cmbodia Bmbg	AGN	11) Chkg Acct Intrst	AGN
2) Strip Mines	AGN	7) Bust Hwy Trust	FOR	12) End HISC (HUAC)	AGN
3) Cut Mil $	AGN	8) Farm Sub Lmt	FOR	13) Nixon Sewer Veto	AGN
4) Rev Shrg	FOR	9) School Prayr	AGN	14) Corp Cmpaign $	FOR
5) Pub TV $	FOR	10) Cnsumr Prot	FOR	15) Pol $ Disclosr	FOR

Election Results

1972 general:	Dante B. Fascell (D)	89,961	(57%)
	Ellis S. Rubin (R)	68,320	(43%)
1972 primary:	Dante B. Fascell (D), unopposed		
1970 general:	Dante B. Fascell (D)	75,895	(72%)
	Robert A. Zinxell (R)	29,935	(28%)

GEORGIA

Political Background

One way to define the Deep South these days is to call it that part of the country where political alignments are simply a matter of black vs. white. In Georgia, politics is a little more complicated than this. The basic division here is between the Atlanta metropolitan area and the rest of the state—mainly small cities and rural farm county.

Atlanta—a bustling, sophisticated metropolis—likes to call itself "the world's next great city." It won its progressive reputation during the 1950s and 1960s under Mayors William Hartsfield and Ivan Allen. Backed by Ralph McGill's Atlanta *Constitution* and the city's business community, Hartsfield and Allen led the white South in a plea for black equal rights and racial harmony.

Among other things, Atlanta's position on race proved to be good business; in the last 20 years Atlanta has become the number one business city in the South.

At the same time, it is possible to overstate the liberalism of metropolitan Atlanta. Though the city itself—which now has a black majority—went for Democratic presidential candidates in 1968 and 1972, the metropolitan area went solidly for Richard Nixon in 1968; and in 1972 it gave Nixon more than 70% of its votes, as Reg Murphy, Ralph McGill's successor, swung the support of the *Constitution* behind the Republican presidential candidate. As for George Wallace, the affluent suburbanites of fast-growing DeKalb County have scorned his politics. But they are no more likely—probably somewhat less so—than their counterparts in the suburbs of Chicago or Los Angeles to embrace the politics of Hubert Humphrey or George McGovern.

The Atlanta metropolitan area is the fastest-growing part of Georgia. In 1970, it contained 30% of the state's residents, and in 1972, it cast 35% of the state's votes. But in political contests between Atlanta and the rest of Georgia, Atlanta has invariably lost.

The closest the city came to victory was in 1966, when Republican Cong. Howard Callaway, with a 63–37 edge in metropolitan Atlanta, managed to win more votes for Governor than Democrat Lester Maddox. But both candidates were anathema to the state's blacks and white liberals. Callaway had been a strong Goldwater supporter in 1964, and Maddox, of course, entered the pages of American history brandishing the axe handles that he thought would keep blacks out of his chicken restaurant. There was a third man in the 1966 race, Ellis Arnall, the state's only notably liberal Governor (1943–47),Maddox beat him in the Democratic primary, but Arnall as write-in candidate in the general election got 51,000 votes, enough to prevent either Callaway or Maddox from getting an absolute majority. Under the Georgia Constitution, the contest was then thrown into the heavily Democratic state legislature, which of course picked Maddox. Today, Lester Maddox looks unbeatable in Georgia. Politicians eagerly seek his endorsement, and it is generally assumed that he will be back in the Governor's chair in 1974. Because Georgia Governors cannot succeed themselves, he was elected Lieutenant Governor in 1970. During his first term as Governor, Maddox was able to increase his popularity. If he was not particularly adept at getting his programs enacted, he was not quite the buffoon his adversaries thought. Maddox more or less let the state government run itself, sometimes in ways that appeared totally contrary to his professed ideology. But what his supporters wanted was not so much action as rhetorical assurance—the lesson statewide politicians drew from Maddox's success was that support in Atlanta is the kiss of death. (Ironically, Maddox himself lives in the big city—the only Governor or Senator elected for years who has.)

So the victories in recent years have gone to politicians who paint themselves as aw-shucks country boys, a little wary of the Atlanta city slickers. Actually, these politicians are about as unsophisticated as famed country boy Wendell Wilkie, the barefoot boy from Wall Street. An example of a good ol' Georgia bumpkin is Gov. Jimmy Carter, who was elected in 1970. During his campaign, Carter liked to describe himself as a peanut farmer from Plains, Georgia. Carter placed somewhat less emphasis on the fact that he had served as a top aide to Admiral Hyman Rickover's in the nuclear submarine program, and that his peanut farm was less a farm than a well-managed, thriving business. Carter lost the Atlanta metropolitan area in both the primary and the general elections, but he was elected Governor by winning overwhelming margins in rural and small-town Georgia.

Once in office, Carter modulated his rhetoric. He asked Georgia citizens to stop resisting desegregation, and installed sophisticated management techniques into the machinery of state government. And only Lt. Gov. Maddox's control of the state Senate foiled Carter's program for a progressive property-tax refund. Carter's ability and charm made him the object of vice-presidential speculation in 1972. In 1974, Carter must leave office, but he will probably not fall into the political oblivion common to most former Georgia Governors.

Another sophisticated country boy who has made it big is U.S. Sen. Sam Nunn. Early in 1972, the 34-year-old state Representative from Perry, Georgia, was unknown statewide. About the only thing the Senate candidate could say about himself was that he was a grandnephew of ex-Rep. (1914–65) Carl Vinson, the long-time Chairman of the House Armed Services Committee. The sitting Senator was then David H. Gambrell, a Harvard-educated Atlanta lawyer. Gambrell was finance chairman of Carter's campaign and was appointed to the Senate by Carter when the venerable Sen. (since 1933) Richard Russell died in 1971. Gambrell's chief primary opponent was expected to be ex-Gov. (1959–63) S. Ernest Vandiver, Russell's nephew by marriage.

Instead, Nunn, with a big media campaign centered on the slogan "Get Tough in Washington," edged Vandiver out of second place in the primary and then whipped Gambrell in the runoff. Gambrell attributed his defeat to the voters' disenchantment with incumbents in a turbulent political year, but it might as well be ascribed to the yoke of Atlanta hanging around his urban neck. Although Gambrell carried the Atlanta metropolitan area, he lost the rest of the state by a 56–44 margin. Nunn was certainly helped in rural Georgia by a last-minute Maddox endorsement. In Atlanta, Nunn shaved Gambrell's margin, getting two more last-minute endorsements from black leaders like state Sen. Leroy Johnson and state Rep. Julian Bond. These black leaders showed sophistication. Their endorsements came in a mass mailing to black voters that arrived the morning of the election; Atlanta's black politicians can deliver votes, but they know that when their endorsements are widely publicized they become counterproductive in Georgia outside Atlanta.

The general election contest between Nunn and Republican Rep. Fletcher Thompson produced more or less the same story. Nunn ran a campaign heavily geared to the nonmetropolitan part of the state. He attacked busing and welfare chislers, and promised to write in George Wallace rather than vote for George McGovern. Moreover, the Democrat won the black vote by default, for Thompson, whose congressional district was 40% black, admitted that he hadn't talked to any black group for four years. Thompson also got into some trouble for having sent a flood of franked mail all over Georgia, though of course as Congressman his constituency made up only 10% of the state's population. Nevertheless, Thompson did manage to carry the Atlanta area by racking up huge majorities in the white suburbs. But he lost the rest of the state by a 58–42 margin, a respectable showing for a candidate coming out of the party of Lincoln, but not enough to win.

Because Nunn was elected to fill the remaining months of Russell's unexpired term, as well as the six-year term following, the young Democrat was sworn in almost immediately after his election. He thereby got a seniority edge on the other 12 freshman Senators. His earlier presence helped him win back Russell's old seat on the Senate Armed Services Committee, but Russell's seniority was something that could not be passed on.

With Nunn's election, the Georgia Republican party remains an urban- (or, rather, suburban-) based minority group—its most faithful voters living in the DeKalb County suburbs. But the strength of local Republicans here has very strongly affected Democratic candidates running statewide. Because of heavy Republican primary voting in DeKalb County, Democratic candidates who attune themselves to rural Georgia win Democratic primaries. Until the early 1960s, a county-unit system determined Democratic primary winners. Under the system, each county had between two and six votes. Naturally, the five counties of the Atlanta metropolitan area were swamped by the 154 counties of the rest of the state. But now, with no county-unit system and with the increasing Republicanism of the Atlanta suburbs, fewer and fewer of the votes cast in statewide Democratic primaries came from the Atlanta area. In the 1972 Senate runoff, metropolitan Atlanta accounted for only 18% of the votes, though it had 30% of the state's population—that 18% being one reason why Gambrell lost to Nunn. If this trend continues, rural Georgia Democrats will continue to dominate statewide elections.

But no trend mattered much in some contests. The late Sen. Russell, for example, faced his last serious opposition in 1936. Among other things, Georgians appreciated Russell's aristocratic bearing and his dignified but unyielding opposition to civil rights legislation. Nor did it hurt Russell that he was for many years Chairman of the Senate Armed Services Committee. Working with Vinson, the Senator helped see that Georgia got far more than its aliquot share of large defense installations.

In a political position like Russell's is the state's current senior Senator, Herman Talmadge. It was his father, Eugene Talmadge, a quasi-populist race-baiter and sometime Governor who gave Russell his big test in 1936. The political career of Herman Talmadge began as turbulently as his father's had always been. When Eugene died in 1946, having just been elected Governor for the fourth time, the state legislature chose young (33) Herman to succeed him. Talmadge held the Governor's office for 67 days against the claims of the duly elected Lieutenant Governor, until the state Supreme Court declared the legislative election illegal. Herman then won the office on his own in 1948 and got a full four-year term in 1950. Two years after leaving the Governor's chair,

Talmadge won election to the Senate, easing aside veteran (1923–57) Walter George, then Chairman of the Foreign Relations Committee.

Since coming to the Senate, Talmadge has gained a polish and respectability his father never enjoyed. The Senator's conservative stands on most issues have won the support of Atlanta's financial establishment, and among rural Georgians, Talmadge, like his father, has complete trust. Talmadge is reputed to be one of the brightest members of the Senate. Like Russell, however, he usually remains closed-mouth and uncommunicative in public, saving his insights for closed committee meetings and the cloakrooms. His incisive, to-the-heart-of-the-matter questioning as a member of the Watergate Committee gave the general public its first real chance to see how the man's mind works.

As Chairman of the Agriculture Committee, Talmadge has a big say in one of the federal government's least understood policy areas. The basic farm programs came up for renewal in 1973. The Nixon Administration wanted to phase out subsidy programs, and Talmadge wants to continue the basic thrust of existing policy. What eventually happened was that the crop price-subsidy programs were changed, in Talmadge's committee, to income-support programs; the former had been designed to control surpluses, the latter to encourage production.

In early 1973, Talmadge appeared to be tutoring his junior colleague Sam Nunn. For example, they cast two of the five Democratic votes against overriding President Nixon's veto of a vocational rehabilitation bill. But whatever the appearances, Nunn must be grateful to Talmadge, who spoke on his behalf in the 1972 campaign and whose seniority provided a solid argument for the election of a Democratic Senator. Talmadge himself comes up for reelection in 1974. There are rumors that he finds the work of the Senate boring, but little doubt exists that he will be returned without significant opposition.

Census Data Pop. 4,589,575; 2.27% of U.S. total, 15th largest; change 1960–70, 16.4%. Central city, 22%; suburban, 27%. Median family income, $8,165; 37th highest; families above $15,000: 15%; families below $3,000: 15%. Median years education, 10.8.

1972 Share of Federal Tax Burden $3,804,140,000; 1.82% of U.S. total, 18th largest.

1972 Share of Federal Outlays $4,780,206,733; 2.21% of U.S. total, 15th largest. Per capita federal spending, $1,042.

DOD	$1,799,287,000	13th	(2.88%)	HEW	$1,409,425,079	16th	(1.97%)
AEC	$1,059,701	31st	(0.04%)	HUD	$76,170,662	12th	(2.48%)
NASA	$5,266,066	24th	(0.18%)	VA	$267,410,801	13th	(2.34%)
DOT	$224,706,407	11th	(2.85%)	USDA	$393,123,574	12th	(2.56%)
DOC	$9,538,390	26th	(0.74%)	CSC	$84,473,598	14th	(2.05%)
DOI	$17,725,057	26th	(0.88%)	TD	$145,435,804	18th	(0.88%)
DOJ	$25,631,037	10th	(2.61%)	Other	$320,953,557		

Economic Base Textile mill products, especially cotton textile mills and floor covering mills; finance, insurance and real estate; agriculture, notably broilers, peanuts, eggs and cattle; apparel and other textile mill products, especially men's and boys' furnishings; food and kindred products; transportation equipment, especially motor vehicles and equipment.

Political Line-up Governor, Jimmy Carter (D); seat up, 1974. Senators, Herman E. Talmadge (D) and Sam Nunn (D). Representatives, 10 (9 D and 1 R). State Senate (48 D and 8 R); State House (152 D and 28 R).

The Voters

Registration 2,167,888 Total. No party registration.

Median voting age 40.5
Employment profile White collar, 44%. Blue collar, 40%. Service, 13%. Farm, 3%.
Ethnic groups Black, 26%. Total foreign stock, 2%.

Presidential vote

1972	Nixon (R)	881,490	(75%)
	McGovern (D)	289,529	(25%)
1968	Nixon (R)	380,111	(30%)
	Humphrey (D)	334,439	(27%)
	Wallace (AI)	535,550	(43%)
1964	Johnson (D)	522,577	(46%)
	Goldwater (R)	616,600	(54%)

Senator

Herman Eugene Talmadge (D) Elected 1956, seat up 1974; b. Aug. 9, 1913, McRae; home, Lovejoy; U. of Ga., 1936; Northwestern U., LL.B., 1942; Navy, WWII; married, two children; Baptist.

Career Atty., Gov. of Ga., 1949–55; owns and operates two farms.

Offices 109 OSOB, 202-225-3643. Also Rm. 430, 275 Peachtree St., N.E., Atlanta 30303; 404-524-7738.

Administrative Assistant Daniel Minchew

Committees

Agriculture and Forestry (Chm.): ex officio member of all subcommittees.

Finance (2nd); Subs: International Trade; Health (Chm.).

Veterans' Affairs (2nd); Subs: Compensation and Pensions (Chm.); Housing and Insurance; Readjustment, Education, and Employment.

Sel. Com. on Standards and Conduct (2nd).

Sel. Com. on Presidential Campaign Activities (2nd).

Joint Study Com. on Budget Control.

Group Ratings

	ADA	COPE	LWV	RIPON	NFU	LCV	CFA	NAB	NSI	ACA
1972	10	10	30	25	60	10	27	58	80	68
1971	22	70	15	12	36	–	50	–	–	70
1970	3	25	–	8	38	24	–	73	100	86

Key Votes

1) Busing	AGN	8) Sea Life Prot	FOR	15) Tax Singls Less	AGN
2) Alas P-line	FOR	9) Campaign Subs	FOR	16) Min Tax for Rich	AGN
3) Gun Cntrl	FOR	10) Cmbodia Bmbg	AGN	17) Euro Troop Rdctn	FOR
4) Rehnquist	FOR	11) Legal Srvices	AGN	18) Bust Hwy Trust	AGN
5) Pub TV $	FOR	12) Rev Sharing	FOR	19) Maid Min Wage	AGN
6) EZ Votr Reg	AGN	13) Cnsumr Prot	AGN	20) Farm Sub Limit	AGN
7) No-Fault	AGN	14) Eq Rts Amend	FOR	21) Highr Credt Chgs	AGN

Election Results

1968 general:	Herman E. Talmadge (D)	885,093	(78%)
	E. Earl Patton, Jr. (R)	256,793	(22%)
1968 primary:	Herman E. Talmadge (D)	627,915	(75%)

Maynard Jackson (D)	207,171	(25%)

1962 general: Herman E. Talmadge (D), unopposed

Senator

Sam Nunn (D) Elected 1942, seat up 1978; b. Sept. 8, 1938, Perry; home, Perry; Emory U., A.B., 1960; Emory Law School, LL.B., 1962; married, two children; Methodist.

Career Cattle farmer; Pres., Perry Chamber of Commerce, 1964; State House of Reps., 1968–72.

Offices 110 OSOB, 202-225-3521.

Administrative Assistant Richard Ray

Committees

Armed Services (9th); Subs: National Stockpile and Naval Petroleum Reserves; Status of Forces; Tactical Air Power; General Legislation; Drug Abuse in the Military.

Government Operations (9th); Subs: Reorganization, Research, and International Organizations; Budgeting, Management, and Expenditures.

Sel. Com. on Small Business (5th); Subs: Environmental, Rural, and Urban Economic Development (Chm.); Government Regulation.

Group Ratings: Newly Elected

Election Results

1972 general:	Sam Nunn (D)	635,970	(54%)
	Fletcher Thompson (R)	542,331	(46%)
1972 run-off:	Sam Nunn (D)	326,186	(52%)
	David H. Gambrell (D)	299,919	(48%)
1972 primary:	Sam Nunn (D)	166,035	(23%)
	David H. Gambrell (D)	225,470	(31%)
	S. Ernest Vandiver (D)	147,135	(21%)
	Hosea Williams (D)	46,153	(6%)
	J. B. Stoner (D)	40,675	(6%)
	Bill Burson (D)	28,566	(4%)
	Jack Dorsey (D)	14,934	(2%)
	Wyman C. Lowe (D)	8,685	(1%)
	Lloyd Russell (D)	8,667	(1%)
	William I. Aynes (D)	7,072	(1%)
	W. M. Wheeler (D)	6,922	(1%)
	Thomas J. Irwin (D)	5,329	(1%)
	Austin D. Graham (D)	4,066	(1%)
	Darrel W. Runyan (D)	3,827	(1%)
	Gerry C. Dokka (D)	3,105	(–)

FIRST DISTRICT Political Background

It's like something out of *All The King's Men.* A young assistant helps an older man win a seat in Congress after several unsuccessful tries. The young man goes to Washington and serves loyally for a couple of years as the Congressman's aide. Then the assistant takes another job, and the Congressman finds himself in some political trouble back home. The big city in the district, with its large number of black voters, keeps supporting his opponents. His vote in the rural areas is not as strong as it should be. Then the Congressman's former assistant decides to run against his old boss, and wins.

The loser in this tale is G. Elliott Hagan, Congressman from the 1st district of Georgia from 1961 to 1973. The assistant, and now Congressman, is Ronald (Bo) Ginn, who worked in Hagan's office for five years before a similar stint with Sen. Herman Talmadge—and before his successful race against Hagan in 1972. The large city is Savannah (pop. 118,000), with its graceful antebellum tree-shaded streets. The rural territory is the cotton, peanut, and pine lands of the southeast corner of the state of Georgia.

The scenario should have come as no surprise to readers of the 1972 edition of the *Almanac*, which described Hagan's vulnerability. As the 1972 edition foresaw, redistricting played some role in the 1972 race. Three new counties, including the city of Brunswick and the posh resort of Sea Island, were added to the 1st. Here Ginn, the challenger, won better than two-to-one margins over the incumbent. And Hagan never did manage to carry Savannah, though he had represented it for 12 years. In the initial primary, Hagan lost the city to Tom Taggart, a young attorney who had strong support in the black community; in the runoff, he lost it to Ginn. Black voters in Savannah shifted heavily from Taggart to Ginn in the runoff, and were as responsible as any identifiable bloc for the result—proof that blacks in Georgia, even outside Atlanta, can make the difference in congressional elections.

Beyond this, Ginn was able to beat Hagan on what was the home turf of both candidates: the rural counties north and west of Savannah where about 60% of the district's votes are cast. Ginn's victory is a striking example—unusual in these days of automatic reelection of incumbent Congressmen—of a hungry challenger defeating an older, lazier incumbent.

In the House, Ginn is one of several Southern Democratic freshmen. More than most of them, he takes notably more conservative stands on issues than those of his Northern brethren. But currently, when the main issues before Congress often come down to a conflict between a Republican President and a Democratic Congress, Ginn has stood with his fellow Democrats far more often than he would have had he been a Congressman a few years ago.

Census Data   Pop. 456,354. Central city, 26%; suburban, 15%. Median family income, $7,102; families above $15,000: 11%; families below $3,000: 19%. Median years education, 10.6.

1972 Share of Federal Outlays $437,452,141

DOD	$145,004,000	HEW	$136,151,768
AEC	$76,788	HUD	$861,680
NASA	–	DOI	$707,621
DOT	$41,344,608	USDA	$49,966,243
		Other	$63,339,433

Federal Military-Industrial Commitments

DOD Contractors Altama Delta Corp. (Darien), $7.753m: unspecified.
DOD Installations Fort Stewart AB (Savannah). Naval Air Station (Glynco). Naval Air Technical Training Center (Glynco); closed, 1974.

Economic Base   Agriculture, notably hogs and sheep, cattle, poultry, and tobacco; paper and allied products, especially paperboard mill products and bags other than textile bags; finance, insurance and real estate; apparel and other textile products; and food and kindred products.

The Voters

Registration 213,250 total. No party registration.
Median voting age 41.6
Employment profile White collar, 39%. Blue collar, 40%. Service, 15%. Farm, 6%.
Ethnic groups Black, 34%. Total foreign stock, 3%.

Presidential vote

1972	Nixon (R)	90,218	(75%)
	McGovern (D)	29,768	(25%)
1968	Nixon (R)	35,520	(27%)
	Humphrey (D)	38,301	(29%)
	Wallace (AI)	58,480	(44%)

Representative

Ronald (Bo) Ginn (D) Elected 1972; b. May 31, 1933, Morgan; home, Millen; Abraham Baldwin Agric. Col., 1953; Georgia Southern Col., B.S., 1955; married, three children; Baptist.

Career Admin. Asst. to Sen. Herman E. Talmadge; teacher; farmer; asst. manager to local corporation.

Offices 508 CHOB, 202-225-5831. Also 304 Fed. 'Bldg., Gloucester St., Brunswick 31520, 912-264-4040, and 405 E. Cotton, Millen 30442, 912-982-2525, and 240 Old Post Office, Wright Sq., Savannah 31401, 912-232-2414.

Administrative Assistant Charles Holm

Committees

Merchant Marine and Fisheries (20th); Subs: Merchant Marine; Oceanography; Panama Canal.

Public Works (21st); Subs: Economic Development; Energy; Investigations and Review; Public Buildings and Grounds; Water Resources.

Group Ratings: Newly Elected

Key Votes

1) Busing	NE	6) Cmbodia Bmbg	AGN	11) Chkg Acct Intrst	AGN
2) Strip Mines	NE	7) Bust Hwy Trust	AGN	12) End HISC (HUAC)	AGN
3) Cut Mil $	NE	8) Farm Sub Lmt	NE	13) Nixon Sewer Veto	AGN
4) Rev Shrg	NE	9) School Prayr	NE	14) Corp Cmpaign $	NE
5) Pub TV $	NE	10) Cnsumr Prot	NE	15) Pol $ Disclosr	NE

Election Results

1972 general:	Ronald B. Ginn (D), unopposed		
1972 run-off:	Ronald B. Ginn (D)	43,120	(55%)
	G. Elliott Hagan (D)	35,569	(45%)
1972 primary:	Ronald B. Ginn (D)	34,536	(39%)
	G. Elliott Hagan (D)	37,968	(43%)
	Tom Taggart (D)	15,023	(17%)

SECOND DISTRICT Political Background

The 2nd district is the southwest corner of Georgia. It is the most agricultural, the poorest, and with the exception of Atlanta's 5th, the blackest congressional district in the state. The 2nd is part of the still unreconstructed, economically underdeveloped Old South. The only areas of the district that experienced population growth during the 1960s were those around its military installations. Blacks still count for far less in elections than their numbers warrant—they don't vote that much because of unspoken local pressures. This was one of George Wallace's banner congressional districts in 1968, and despite Richard Nixon's strength here in 1972, it will undoubtedly be Wallace's once more should he ever run for President again.

The young, sophomore Congressman from the 2nd, Dawson Mathis, is worthy of some note if only because of his previous occupation: a TV newscaster. There are dozens of former TV newsmen (even one TV weatherman, Dale Milford of Texas) in Congress today. Some of them, of course, took to the tube as a kind of moonlighting that would confer some political advantage. Others, like Mathis, earned their livelihood laying on good microphone voices and camera presence. After six years as the nightly newsman on an Albany, Georgia TV station that reaches most of the 2nd district, Mathis, still under 30, was probably better known than any of the district's politicians. This is the best explanation of how he won the Democratic primary and the general election of 1970 when the 2nd's incumbent Congressman retired.

Mathis embodies the traditional Southern Democrat's view of politics. When asked about his goals in Congress, he replied, "To represent the 2nd district as long as I can." As a junior member of the Agriculture Committee, he does not yet have much clout on the Hill. But given the average life expectancy in the United States and the unchanging character of the 2nd's political preferences—the area has gone for conservative Democrats since before the Civil War—Mathis can anticipate a House career of some 40 years, if he does not succumb to the temptation to run for statewide office. If he does end up as a committee chairman, Mathis will differ from the many other Southern chairmen only because he began as a newscaster rather than as a county judge or state representative. The McLuhan revolution has made that much difference, and not much more, in southwestern Georgia.

Census Data Pop. 460,450. Central city, 16%; suburban, 4%. Median family income, $6,238; families above $15,000: 9%; families below $3,000: 23%. Median years education, 9.9.

1972 Share of Federal Outlays $414,227,045

DOD	$103,251,000	HEW	$146,828,700
AEC	–	HUD	$827,220
NASA	–	DOI	$196,256
DOT	$6,536,083	USDA	$108,862,724
		Other	$47,725,062

Federal Military-Industrial Commitments

DOD Installations Marine Corps Supply Center (Albany). Naval Air Station (Albany); closed, 1974. Moody AFB (Valdosta).

Economic Base Agriculture, notably peanuts, hogs and sheep, cattle and tobacco; food and kindred products; apparel and other textile products; finance, insurance and real estate; and lumber and wood products.

The Voters

Registration 198,776 total. No party registration.
Median voting age 42.5
Employment profile White collar, 36%. Blue collar, 38%. Service, 14%. Farm, 12%.
Ethnic groups Black, 37%. Total foreign stock, 1%.

Presidential vote

1972	Nixon (R)	80,769	(80%)
	McGovern (D)	20,745	(20%)
1968	Nixon (R)	23,508	(19%)
	Humphrey (D)	26,693	(21%)
	Wallace (AI)	74,740	(60%)

Representative

M. Dawson Mathis (D) Elected 1970; b. Nov. 30, 1940, Nashville; home, Albany; So. Ga. Col.; married, four children; Baptist.

Career News Director WALB-TV, Albany, Ga.

Offices 236 CHOB, 202-225-3631. Also City-County Govt. Bldg., 225 Pine Ave., Albany 31705, 912-439-8067.

Administrative Assistant W. Julian Holland (L.A.)

Committees

Agriculture (12th); Subs: Oilseeds and Rice; Tobacco; Family Farms and Rural Development.

House Administration (15th); Subs: Elections; Police.

Group Ratings

	ADA	COPE	LWV	RIPON	NFU	LCV	CFA	NAB	NSI	ACA
1972	0	27	25	25	71	12	50	46	100	91
1971	16	55	33	29	54	–	0	–	–	63

Key Votes

1) Busing	AGN	6) Cmbodia Bmbg	FOR	11) Chkg Acct Intrst	AGN
2) Strip Mines	AGN	7) Bust Hwy Trust	AGN	12) End HISC (HUAC)	AGN
3) Cut Mil $	AGN	8) Farm Sub Lmt	AGN	13) Nixon Sewer Veto	AGN
4) Rev Shrg	AGN	9) School Prayr	FOR	14) Corp Cmpaign $	FOR
5) Pub TV $	AGN	10) Cnsumr Prot	AGN	15) Pol $ Disclosr	AGN

Election Results

1972 general:	Dawson Mathis (D), unopposed		
1972 primary:	Dawson Mathis (D), unopposed		
1970 general:	Dawson Mathis (D)	59,994	(92%)
	Thomas Ragdale (R)	5,376	(8%)

THIRD DISTRICT Political Background

The 3rd district of Georgia is one of the state's several rural and small-town congressional districts. The 3rd has one good-sized city, Columbus (pop. 154,000), which in turn is dominated by one good-sized military installation, Fort Benning (pop. 27,000). Columbus is very much an Army town; girls grow up here aspiring to marry young officers. And a local hero is Lt. William Calley, now confined at Fort Benning awaiting amnesty from President Nixon. Fort Benning enjoys a notable chapter in military history: it was here in the 1930s that then Col. George C. Marshall staged the maneuvers that anticipated so much of the kind of fighting that occurred in World War II.

Benning is also of substantial economic importance to the 3rd district. It may have been first sited here on the theory that the excruciatingly hot, humid Georgia climate would best condition soldiers for the rigors of combat. But students of the relationship between the Pentagon and the congressional Armed Services Committees can think of other reasons.

The 3rd has the distinction, unusual for Georgia districts, of having once elected a Republican Congressman. The circumstances were unusual. It was 1964; the incumbent Democrat was retiring; and the Republican candidate, Howard Callaway, had good local connections—he was the scion of a textile family fortune. Callaway was an important Goldwater backer and, as might be expected, the district went heavily for the Arizonan. After only two years in office, Callaway decided to run for Governor in 1966; he won a plurality of the votes but lost the election (see Georgia state write-up). In 1968, Callaway served as Richard Nixon's Southern campaign coordinator, but managed to secure a job in the Administration (Secretary of the Army) only after the Nixon regime came under the cloud of Watergate.

The current Congressman, Democrat Jack Brinkley, was first elected in 1966. He is, not surprisingly, a member of the House Armed Services Committee, which may or may not explain why Fort Benning emerged unscathed from the Pentagon's 1973 base cutbacks. So far as election returns can disclose, Brinkley is popular at home. The Congressman has not had opposition in either primaries or general elections since he was first elected.

Census Data Pop. 460,749. Central city, 33%; suburban, 22%. Median family income, $7,550; families above $15,000: 12%; families below $3,000: 16%. Median years education, 10.9.

1972 Share of Federal Outlays $581,615,318

DOD	$349,390,010	HEW	$134,578,497
AEC	–	HUD	$982,571
NASA	–	DOI	$580,276
DOT	$7,752,099	USDA	$35,885,276
		Other	$52,446,589

Federal Military-Industrial Commitments

DOD Contractors Blair Algernon (Robins AFB), $5.377m: construction services.
DOD Installations Fort Benning AB (Columbus). Robins AFB (Macon).

Economic Base Textile mill products, especially cotton weaving mill products; agriculture, notably cattle, dairy products, poultry and peanuts; finance, insurance and real estate; food and kindred products; and apparel and other textile products.

The Voters

Registration 177,476 total. No party registration.
Median voting age 38.9
Employment profile White collar, 41%. Blue collar, 40%. Service, 15%. Farm, 4%.
Ethnic groups Black, 32%. Spanish, 1%. Total foreign stock, 4%.

Presidential vote

1972	Nixon (R)	81,300	(78%)
	McGovern (D)	23,534	(22%)
1968	Nixon (R)	27,837	(26%)
	Humphrey (D)	25,948	(24%)
	Wallace (AI)	52,278	(49%)

Representative

Jack Thomas Brinkley (D) Elected 1966; b. Dec. 22, 1930, Faceville; home, Columbus; U. of Ga. Law School, LL.B., 1959; USAF, 1951–56; married, two children; Baptist.

Career Teacher, Ga. public schools, 1949–51; practicing atty., 1958–65; Ga. House of Reps., 1965–66.

Offices 407 CHOB, 202-225-5901. Also P.O. Bldg., Americus 31709, 912-222-2054, and P.O. Bldg., Columbus 31902, 404-324-3091.

Administrative Assistant Larry M. Wheeler

Committees

Armed Services (15th); Sub: No. 5.

Veterans Affairs (14th); Subs: Compensation and Pension; Education and Training; Hospitals.

Group Ratings

	ADA	COPE	LWV	RIPON	NFU	LCV	CFA	NAB	NSI	ACA
1972	19	18	33	31	43	20	0	42	100	77
1971	16	42	22	33	60	–	38	–	–	62
1970	4	25	–	24	31	0	55	83	100	74

Key Votes

1) Busing	AGN	6) Cmbodia Bmbg	FOR	11) Chkg Acct Intrst	AGN
2) Strip Mines	AGN	7) Bust Hwy Trust	AGN	12) End HISC (HUAC)	AGN
3) Cut Mil $	AGN	8) Farm Sub Lmt	AGN	13) Nixon Sewer Veto	AGN
4) Rev Shrg	FOR	9) School Prayr	FOR	14) Corp Cmpaign $	AGN
5) Pub TV $	AGN	10) Cnsumr Prot	AGN	15) Pol $ Disclosr	AGN

Election Results

1972 general: Jack Brinkley (D), unopposed
1972 primary: Jack Brinkley (D), unopposed
1970 general: Jack Brinkley (D), unopposed

FOURTH DISTRICT Political Background

Stuck smack in the middle of Old South Georgia is the booming metropolis of Atlanta—"the city," it likes to say, "too busy to hate." The slogan grew out of Atlanta's reputation for racial tolerance and moderation, which it earned back in the 1950s. But if Atlanta practices little overt segregation and possesses the sophistication of Northern cities, it has had of late some of the racial problems common to big cities up North. Most notable among them is a white exodus from the central city. During the 1960s, Atlanta became the first major city in the South to become more than half black.

At the same time, the Atlanta suburbs grew at a pace seen in Houston or Los Angeles. The 4th congressional district, which includes all of suburban DeKalb County and a small part of the city itself, grew by nearly 60% between 1960 and 1970. And most of the newcomers here left the central city. By 1972, it appeared that metropolitan integration of the schools might become necessary (see Georgia 5). This heated up the busing issue in the 4th, much as it did in the suburbs of Detroit or Richmond.

The busing issue, of course, redounded to the benefit of Richard Nixon in 1972. But Republicans have been popular in the 4th for some years; it is the only part of the state that sends majority-Republican delegations to both houses of the state legislature. For the upwardly-mobile people of the 4th, the Republican party presents a patina of respectibility and modernity. The voters here prefer the GOP's sleek, neutral-accented candidates to the rural-oriented, Southern-accented nominees usually chosen by the Democrats. Thus the 4th gave overwhelming majorities to textile heir Bo Callaway over chicken restauranteur Lester Maddox in 1966, and to suburban Congressman Fletcher Thompson over Houston County state Rep. Sam Nunn in 1972. The difference between the Republican and Democratic candidates is not so much a matter of stands on issues as of style and tone. But when the suburbanites of the 4th make their choice, the rest of Georgia almost invariably chooses the opposite.

The 4th was created in 1964 as the direct result of a landmark Supreme Court redistricting decision. Before that, the entire Atlanta area, with a population approaching a million people, had just one Congressman. In 1964, the voters of the 4th elected moderate Democrat James Mackay, though Barry Goldwater carried the district that same year. Two years later, Mackay was defeated by Republican Ben Blackburn, who has been in office ever since. The general disillusionment and unhappiness with the social policies of the Johnson Administration probably explains the Republican's victory. Blackburn has won succeeding elections easily, running just about even with Nixon in 1972. The only possible threat to Blackburn's tenure—and it a remote one—is Watergate. As a member of the Banking and Currency Committee, the Congressman voted to block an investigation of the scandal in October 1972.

Census Data Pop. 459,335. Central city, 16%; suburban, 80%. Median family income, $11,750; families above $15,000: 31%; families below $3,000: 5%. Median years education, 12.4.

1972 Share of Federal Outlays $620,055,863

DOD	$256,651,058	HEW	$148,383,253
AEC	$144,476	HUD	$17,709,485
NASA	$1,621,423	DOI	$3,930,241
DOT	$32,282,458	USDA	$16,974,145
		Other	$142,359,324

Federal Military-Industrial Commitments

No installations or contractors receiving prime awards greater than $5,000,000.

Economic Base Finance, insurance and real estate; food and kindred products, especially natural and processed cheese; electrical equipment and supplies; tourism; and chemicals and allied products, especially polishes and sanitation goods.

The Voters

Registration 223,827 total. No party registration.
Median voting age 38.3

Employment profile White collar, 66%. Blue collar, 25%. Service, 9%. Farm, –%.
Ethnic groups Black, 15%. Spanish, 1%. Total foreign stock, 5%.

Presidential vote

1972	Nixon (R)	110,574	(77%)
	McGovern (D)	33,043	(23%)
1968	Nixon (R)	54,869	(48%)
	Humphrey (D)	31,233	(27%)
	Wallace (AI)	28,216	(25%)

Representative

Ben B. Blackburn (R) Elected 1966; b. Feb. 14, 1927, Atlanta; home, Atlanta; U. of N.C., B.A., 1947; Emory U., LL.B., 1954; Navy, 1944–46, Korean War; Lt. Cdr. USNR, 1952–54; married, four children; Episcopal.

Career Ga. Atty. General's Office, 1952–54; practicing atty., 1954–66.

Offices 1024 LHOB, 202-225-4272. Also New Fed. Bldg., 141 Trinty Place, Decatur 30030, 404-377-7461.

Administrative Assistant Drew V. Tidwell

Committees

Banking and Currency (4th); Subs: Domestic Finance; Housing; International Trade (Ranking Mbr.).

Joint Economic Com. (4th); Subs: Economic Progress; Inter-American Economic Relationships; Priority and Economy in Government; Urban Affairs.

Group Ratings

	ADA	COPE	LWV	RIPON	NFU	LCV	CFA	NAB	NSI	ACA
1972	0	18	11	33	43	15	0	80	100	100
1971	11	18	11	29	18	–	0	–	–	87
1970	0	9	–	29	17	0	36	92	100	87

Key Votes

1) Busing	AGN	6) Cmbodia Bmbg	ABS	11) Chkg Acct Intrst	FOR
2) Strip Mines	ABS	7) Bust Hwy Trust	AGN	12) End HISC (HUAC)	AGN
3) Cut Mil $	ABS	8) Farm Sub Lmt	AGN	13) Nixon Sewer Veto	FOR
4) Rev Shrg	AGN	9) School Prayr	FOR	14) Corp Cmpaign $	FOR
5) Pub TV $	AGN	10) Cnsumr Prot	AGN	15) Pol $ Disclosr	AGN

Election Results

1972 general:	Ben B. Blackburn (R)	103,155	(76%)
	F. Odell Welborn (D)	32,731	(24%)
1972 primary:	Ben B. Blackburn (R), unopposed		
1970 general:	Ben B. Blackburn (R)	85,848	(65%)
	Franklin Shumake (D)	45,908	(35%)

FIFTH DISTRICT Political Background

In 1972, the 5th district of Georgia became the first Deep South congressional district since 1898 to elect a black man to Congress. The 5th, of course, is not a typical district of the Deep South. The bulk of it consists of most of the city of Atlanta, which is now majority black, and a few affluent suburbs, notably Sandy Spring, in northern Fulton County. So constituted, the territory has had a continuing tradition of liberal politics. Atlanta, after all, has had moderate-to-liberal Mayors since the 1940s, and in 1969 elected a Jewish Mayor (Sam Massell) and a black Vice-Mayor (Maynard Jackson). The present 5th district was 44% black in 1970, and in 1972, some 38% of its registered voters were black. Despite all of these favorable circumstances, the election of Andrew Young, a minister and former executive director of Martin Luther King's Southern Christian Leadership Conference, was a formidable political achievement.

Only two years earlier, Young was defeated soundly—57–43—by Republican Fletcher Thompson. Thompson's rapport with the district's large black minority was so bad that he admitted in 1972 that he had not met with a single black group since 1968. Thompson had been a little lucky to win the seat in the first place. He was the Republican nominee in 1966 when Democratic incumbent Charles Weltner withdrew from the race, saying that with Lester Maddox on the ticket he would not sign the oath of loyalty to the Democratic party. Against Young in 1970, Thompson showed film clips which, he said, suggested that the black minister did not favor the continuation of Western civilization; Thompson wound up with more than 80% of the white votes.

In 1972, a court-ordered redistricting changed the make-up of the 5th, a factor in Thompson's decision to run for the Senate. The southern Fulton County suburbs, including Thompson's home town, were removed from the district. The middle-income areas here, insecure about racial change, are prone to backlash. Left in the 5th were Sandy Spring and the affluent northern section of the city ifself, where citizens were more accustomed to voting for black and pro-civil rights candidates in city and state elections. These changes—and Thompson's decision to leave the seat—gave Young a significantly better chance in 1972 than in 1970, and he made the most of it.

Young won the Democratic primary easily, as his campaign concentrated on turning out black voters. His opponent in the general election was Rodney Cook, a moderate Republican who had backed civil rights measures in the past and had run a creditable race for Mayor in 1969. But under the pressure of the campaign and after a court decision in October, Cook began to take a hard anti-busing line. Young, with his black support solid, spent much time in the white community, opposing construction of a freeway there and also promising a clean-up of the Chattahoochee River. On election day, Young won 53% of the vote—including something like 23% of the white vote. He ran as far ahead of McGovern in the white community as he did in the black precincts. In Washington, Young sits on the Banking and Currency Committee, which has jurisdiction over most housing programs.

Since the election, the busing issue has taken a new turn. Although Young, as a Congressman, has not gotten heavily involved in the issue, the current situation deserves comment. Toward the end of 1972 and the beginning of 1973, the Atlanta chapter of the NAACP decided to try to settle the case with the Atlanta school board. Rather than to push for a massive busing plan, the local NAACP moved to get a larger number of black administrators into the present system, and the school board agreed. In Atlanta, as in many Northern school districts, the vast majority of the students are black. So even massive busing, if confined to the city, would probably produce only more white flight to the suburbs and an all-black city school system. The alternative of metropolitan consolidation of school systems and busing across city lines is still favored by the national NAACP, and could produce integration. But Atlanta blacks contend that in a metropolitan district they would become a permanent minority, just when they are about to gain political control of the Atlanta city system. At this writing, the Atlanta NAACP–Atlanta school board settlement is still before the courts, and the Atlanta NAACP has been disowned by the national organization.

Census Data   Pop. 460,589. Central city, 87%; suburban, 13%. Median family income, $9,050; families above $15,000: 24%; families below $3,000: 3%. Median years education, 12.1.

1972 Share of Federal Outlays $640,385,937

DOD	$267,769,580	HEW	$150,616,275
AEC	$150,804	HUD	$18,485,042
NASA	$1,692,431	DOI	$3,943,758
DOT	$33,532,271	USDA	$17,135,312
		Other	$147,060,464

Federal Military-Industrial Commitments

DOD Installations Fort McPherson AB (Atlanta).

Economic Base Finance, insurance and real estate; transportation equipment, especially motor vehicles and equipment; food and kindred products, especially bakery products; printing and publishing, especially commerical printing; and apparel and other textile products, especially men's and boys' shirts and nightwear. Also higher education (Georgia State Univ.).

The Voters

Registration 231,476 total. No party registration.
Median voting age 40.8
Employment profile White collar, 55%. Blue collar, 28%. Service, 17%. Farm, –%.
Ethnic groups Black, 44%. Spanish, 1%. Total foreign stock, 4%.

Presidential vote

1972	Nixon (R)	69,088	(52%)
	McGovern (D)	63,405	(48%)
1968	Nixon (R)	48,876	(35%)
	Humphrey (D)	66,131	(48%)
	Wallace (AI)	22,995	(17%)

Representative

Andrew Young (D) Elected 1972; b. March 12, 1932, New Orleans, La.; home, Atlanta; Howard U., B.S., 1951; Hartford Theological Seminary, B.D., 1955; married, four children; Congregational.

Career Ordained Minister, United Church of Christ; Exec. Committees: Natl. Urban Coalition, Common Cause, Commission on the Cities in the '70s, Citizens Committee for Government Reorganization.

Offices 1533 LHOB, 202-225-3801. Also 327 Old Post Office Bldg., Atlanta 30303, 404-688-8208.

Administrative Assistant Stoney Cooks

Committees

Banking and Currency (21st); Subs: Consumer Affairs; International Finance; International Trade; Urban Mass Transportation.

Group Ratings: Newly Elected

Key Votes

1) Busing	NE	6) Cmbodia Bmbg	AGN	11) Chkg Acct Intrst	FOR
2) Strip Mines	NE	7) Bust Hwy Trust	FOR	12) End HISC (HUAC)	FOR
3) Cut Mil $	NE	8) Farm Sub Lmt	NE	13) Nixon Sewer Veto	AGN
4) Rev Shrg	NE	9) School Prayr	NE	14) Corp Cmpaign $	NE
5) Pub TV $	NE	10) Cnsumr Prot	NE	15) Pol $ Disclosr	NE

Election Results

1972 general:	Andrew Young (D)	72,289	(53%)
	Rodney M. Cook (R)	64,495	(47%)
1972 primary:	Andrew Young (D)	35,926	(60%)
	Wyche Fowler (D)	19,549	(33%)
	H. D. Dodson (D)	3,053	(5%)
	Howell Smith (D)	1,008	(2%)
1970 general:	Fletcher Thompson (R)	78,540	(57%)
	Andrew Young (D)	58,394	(43%)

SIXTH DISTRICT Political Background

The 6th district of Georgia presents a nice example of demographic change in the South. Eight years ago, the dominant city in the district was Macon (1970 pop. 122,000); the Atlanta metropolitan area at the northern boundary of the 6th had only 10% of the district's population. But redistricting removed Macon and added several south Fulton County suburbs of Atlanta. Today, 48% of the district's population lies in metropolitan Atlanta.

These suburbs of Atlanta—particulary East Point, College Park, and Forest Park just south of the city—do not behave politically in quite the manner of the solidly Republican suburbs of Atlanta in the 4th district. South Fulton and Clayton counties have generally given Republican candidates majorities, but not as large as those in the 4th's higher-income DeKalb County. There is still a lingering preference for Southern Democrats of the George Wallace stripe here. It is the only part of the Atlanta metropolitan area where Wallace ran even close to Nixon and Humphrey in 1968.

This should be good news for Rep. John J. Flynt, Jr., a Democrat who has held office with little opposition since 1954. As a high-ranking member of the Appropriations Committee, Flynt is one of those powerful, usually silent Southern Democrat members of the House who still have influence beyond their numbers. A fiscal conservative, Flynt usually votes to hold down government spending. As a politician of this sort, Flynt surprised a lot of people in 1971 when he and fellow Georgia Cong. Phil Landrum—senior members of the state delegation—came out against the Nixon Administration's policies on Vietnam. What may be even more surprising is that Flynt claimed that his stand was very popular in what many observers thought was one of the nation's most hawkish constituencies.

John Flynt has not had much trouble winning reelection, not having had opposition of any kind in recent years. The 6th's shift to the Atlanta suburbs could change things. The district now includes the home of ex-Rep. (1967–71) Fletcher Thompson, the Republican nominee for the U.S. Senate in 1972. Though Thompson lost statewide, he carried the 6th, 55–45, with the help of big margins in south Fulton and Clayton counties. Thompson, who will be 49 in 1974, is rumored to be contemplating a return to the House in 1974, and he could give Flynt, who will then be 60, a very tough race. This would be the first for Flynt in a long, long time. Because Lt. Gov. Lester Maddox is expected to be reelected Governor easily, and Sen. Herman Talmadge will probably draw only nominal opposition, a Flynt-Thompson contest could be the state's hottest political race in 1974.

Census Data Pop. 455,810. Central city, 5%; suburban, 43%. Median family income, $9,284; families above $15,000: 16%; families below $3,000: 10%. Median years education, 10.9.

1972 Share of Federal Outlays $441,423,915

DOD	$130,384,290	HEW	$142,463,061
AEC	$71,783	HUD	$9,390,449
NASA	$805,603	DOI	$2,447,785
DOT	$44,615,394	USDA	$18,447,260
		Other	$92,798,290

Federal Military-Industrial Commitments

DOD Installations Atlanta Army Depot (Forest Park).

Economic Base Apparel and other textile products; textile mill products, especially cotton weaving mill products; finance, insurance and real estate; agriculture, notably poultry, dairy products and cattle; and food and kindred products, especially bakery products.

The Voters

Registration 225,572 total. No party registration.
Median voting age 39.5
Employment profile White collar, 44%. Blue collar, 44%. Service, 11%. Farm, 1%.
Ethnic groups Black, 19%. Total foreign stock, 2%.

Presidential vote

1972	Nixon (R)	96,213	(80%)
	McGovern (D)	24,717	(20%)

1968	Nixon (R)	38,996	(31%)
	Humphrey (D)	27,733	(22%)
	Wallace (AI)	58,042	(47%)

Representative

John James Flynt, Jr. (D) Elected 1954; b. Nov. 8, 1914, Griffin; home, Griffin; U. of Ga., B.A., 1936; Emory U. Law School, 1937–38; George Washington U. Law School, LL.B., 1940; Army, WWII; married, three children; Methodist.

Career Ga. House of Reps., 1947–48; Solicitor Gen., Griffin Judicial Circuit, 1949–54; Pres., Solicitors Gen. Assn. of Ga., 1950–51.

Offices 2187 RHOB, 202-225-4501. Also P.O. Box 103, Griffin 30227, 404-227-1621.

Administrative Assistant Charles L. Redman

Committees

Appropriations (13th); Subs: Defense; Legislative; State, Justice, Commerce, and Judiciary.

Standards of Official Conduct (5th).

Group Ratings

	ADA	COPE	LWV	RIPON	NFU	LCV	CFA	NAB	NSI	ACA
1972	6	10	0	13	33	17	0	86	86	100
1971	14	25	25	24	58	–	0	–	–	67
1970	4	25	–	7	15	42	56	80	100	88

Key Votes

1) Busing	AGN	6) Cmbodia Bmbg	AGN	11) Chkg Acct Intrst	AGN
2) Strip Mines	FOR	7) Bust Hwy Trust	AGN	12) End HISC (HUAC)	AGN
3) Cut Mil $	AGN	8) Farm Sub Lmt	AGN	13) Nixon Sewer Veto	FOR
4) Rev Shrg	AGN	9) School Prayr	FOR	14) Corp Cmpaign $	ABS
5) Pub TV $	ABS	10) Cnsumr Prot	AGN	15) Pol $ Disclosr	AGN

Election Results

1972 general:	John J. Flynt, Jr. (D), unopposed		
1972 primary:	John J. Flynt, Jr. (D)	54,943	(77%)
	Ray Gurley (D)	16,237	(23%)
1970 general:	John J. Flynt, Jr. (D), unopposed		

SEVENTH DISTRICT Political Background

The 7th district of Georgia covers the northwest corner of the state. On the southeast, the district skirts the Atlanta city limits; on the northwest, it does the same to the city limits of Chattanooga, Tennessee. (There is dispute here about the state line—some Georgians insist that the Lookout Mountain home of Tennessee Sen. William Brock actually lies in Georgia.) Most of the 7th's population growth during the 1960s occurred in Cobb County, outside Atlanta, and in the Georgia suburbs of Chattanooga. Because there are few blacks here, about 5% of the electorate, racial politics have never been as big in the district as in south Georgia. For many years the economic mainstay of this area was textiles, but today its largest employer—and most significant politically—is the ailing Lockheed Corporation. Lockheed's hugh plant at Marietta, in Cobb County some 30 miles from downtown Atlanta, is where the C-5As were built and the cost overruns incurred.

If Lockheed has a loyal following in sunny California, it commands more allegiance than Jefferson Davis, CSA, here in the 7th district of Georgia. A Lockheed employee who knew something funny was going on and then testified before Sen. Proxmire's committee on cost overruns now can find virtually no one in Marietta who will speak to him or his family. In California, Pete McCloskey, though he voted against a loan for Lockheed, could get reelected in a district having many Lockheed employees. In the Georgia 7th, any candidate against the loan or the Lockheed Corporation might just as well forget about politics.

Congressman John W. Davis of the 7th district, a high-ranking member of the Science and Astronautics Committee, backed the Lockheed bail-out. Even so, he is the member of the Georgia congressional delegation in the deepest political trouble. Some of his woes have come from a drinking problem, which he acknowledges and says he has licked. Davis also appears to have failed to use the advantages of incumbency—free mailing privileges and taking care of constituents' problems with the federal bureaucracies—as vigorously as most Congressmen. Davis was nearly beaten by a John Bircher in the 1972 Democratic primary, and a Republican took 40% in November. In both elections, Davis ran worst in the fastest-growing parts of the district: Cobb County and the Chattanooga suburbs.

When an incumbent begins to run poorly in the traditional one-party politics of the South, that incumbent is a marked man. He continues to attract strong opposition until, nearly always, he is defeated in due course. In the two-party politics that is slowly emerging in the South, the incumbent has worries not just in the Democratic primary, but in the general election as well. Many aspiring politicians are right now eyeing John Davis' seat in Congress.

Census Data Pop. 460,095. Central city, 0%; suburban, 54%. Median family income, $9,223; families above $15,000: 16%; families below $3,000: 10%. Median years education, 10.6.

1972 Share of Federal Outlays $398,502,654

DOD	$117,899,184	HEW	$141,852,801
AEC	$64,454	HUD	$9,954,468
NASA	$789,357	DOI	$2,610,708
DOT	$16,790,816	USDA	$15,260,016
		Other	$93,280,850

Federal Military-Industrial Commitments

DOD Contractors Lockheed (Marietta), $582.073m: C-5A aircraft.
DOD Installations Naval Air Station, Atlanta (Marietta). Dobbins AFB (Marietta).

Economic Base Textile mill products; finance, insurance and real estate; apparel and other textile products; agriculture, notably poultry, cattle and dairy products; and food and kindred products.

The Voters

Registration 216,181 total. No party registration.
Median voting age 40.1
Employment profile White collar, 43%. Blue collar, 47%. Service, 9%. Farm, 1%.
Ethnic groups Black, 7%. Total foreign stock, 2%.

Presidential vote

1972	Nixon (R)	91,477	(83%)
	McGovern (D)	18,726	(17%)
1968	Nixon (R)	38,976	(33%)
	Humphrey (D)	23,143	(19%)
	Wallace (AI)	57,155	(48%)

Representative

John William Davis (D) Elected 1960; b. Sept. 12, 1916, Rome; home, Summerville; U. of Ga., B.A., 1937, LL.B., 1939; Army, WWII; married, three children; Presbyterian.

Career Practicing atty., 1939–49; Solicitor Gen., Rome Circuit, 1950–53; Judge, Lookout Mt. Judicial Circuit, 1955–60.

Offices 2342 RHOB, 202-225-2931. Also Fed. Bldg., Rome 30161, 404-235-0127, and 25 Atlanta St., Suite 216, Marietta 30062, 404-428-5549, 428-5951.

Administrative Assistant Robert S. Richard

Committees

Foreign Affairs (17th); Subs: Asian and Pacific Affairs; Foreign Economic Policy; National Security Policy and Scientific Developments.

Science and Astronautics (3rd); Subs: Aeronautics and Space Technology; International Cooperation in Science and Space; Science, Research, and Development (Chm.).

Group Ratings

	ADA	COPE	LWV	RIPON	NFU	LCV	CFA	NAB	NSI	ACA
1972	6	56	20	50	67	9	0	56	88	65
1971	16	40	60	56	79	–	50	–	–	48
1970	4	56	–	24	50	13	80	44	100	60

Key Votes

1) Busing	AGN	6) Cmbodia Bmbg	FOR	11) Chkg Acct Intrst	AGN
2) Strip Mines	ABS	7) Bust Hwy Trust	ABS	12) End HISC (HUAC)	AGN
3) Cut Mil $	AGN	8) Farm Sub Lmt	AGN	13) Nixon Sewer Veto	AGN
4) Rev Shrg	FOR	9) School Prayr	AGN	14) Corp Cmpaign $	FOR
5) Pub TV $	AGN	10) Cnsumr Prot	FOR	15) Pol $ Disclosr	AGN

Election Results

1972 general:	John W. Davis (D)	59,031	(58%)
	Charlie Sherrill (R)	42,265	(42%)
1972 primary:	John W. Davis (D)	38,602	(52%)
	Larry P. McDonald (D)	35,594	(48%)
1970 general:	John W. Davis (D)	80,149	(73%)
	Dick Fullerton (R)	30,392	(27%)

EIGHTH DISTRICT Political Background

The 8th district comprises an elongated section of central and southern Georgia. With the major exception of Macon (pop. 122,000), this is mostly a rural area that was once devoted to cotton, but now mainly to peanuts and tobacco. Years ago, the fertile soil of the 8th was worn down by too many crops of cotton. No economic boom exists here. Most of this district, in fact, is a part of the Deep South which people, both black and white, have been leaving; they go to Northern cities and, lately, Atlanta.

Some 31% of the district's residents are black, but black voters here rarely influence the outcome of elections in any significant way. Black turnout is substantially lower here than in

Atlanta. And in the rural counties of Georgia, there are few black political organizers. Moreover, fears of retribution for casting a ballot still exist among potential black voters.

Because few blacks vote in the 8th, the district has delivered overwhelming majorities to candidates like Barry Goldwater, George Wallace, and the Richard Nixon of 1972. In congressional politics, however, the 8th has been rather less predictable. In 1966, that still relatively rare event occurred—an incumbent Southern Congressman was beaten by a young challenger. The winner was Williamson S. (Bill) Stuckey, a member of the family that put up pecan candy and gift shops at hundreds of the nation's freeway interchanges. In Washington, Stuckey is a member of the Commerce Committee. This body oversees most federal regulatory agencies; it has great potential for, but little interest in, consumer legislation. Stuckey is one of leaders of the pro-business, anti-regulation bloc on the committee.

In early 1972, it looked as though Stuckey might have some problems at home. Because the legislature had substantially altered his district, some 56% of it, including Macon, was new territory for Stuckey. But he won his three-way primary easily, and almost as easily beat his Republican opponent, Macon Mayor Ronnie Thompson. In the general election, Stuckey ran nearly as well in the unfamilar new part of the district as he did in the smaller portion where he was the obvious incumbent. A performance of this sort indicates a bright electoral future in the 8th district for Congressman Stuckey.

Census Data Pop. 458,097. Central city, 27%; suburban, 5%. Median family income, $6,836; families above $15,000: 11%; families below $3,000: 20%. Median years education, 9.8.

1972 Share of Federal Outlays $524,960,168

DOD	$238,370,990	HEW	$137,665,167
AEC	–	HUD	$5,911,800
NASA	–	DOI	$1,231,638
DOT	$14,855,748	USDA	$59,601,369
		Other	$67,323,456

Federal Military-Industrial Commitments

DOD Contractors Maxson Electronics (Macon), $11.200m: illuminating cartridges, 60mm. Dell Industries (Waycross), $8.159m: practice bombs. Standard Container (Homerville), $6.367m: ammunition packing boxes.

Economic Base Agriculture, notably poultry, hogs and sheep, and tobacco; finance, insurance and real estate; apparel and other textile products, especially men's and boys' furnishings; textile mill products; and food and kindred products.

The Voters

Registration 239,129 total. No party registration.
Median voting age 43.9
Employment profile White collar, 37%. Blue collar, 42%. Service, 15%. Farm, 6%.
Ethnic groups Black, 31%.

Presidential vote

1972	Nixon (R)	91,338	(78%)
	McGovern (D)	26,033	(22%)
1968	Nixon (R)	33,603	(24%)
	Humphrey (D)	32,588	(23%)
	Wallace (AI)	75,777	(53%)

Representative

Williamson Sylvester Stuckey, Jr. (D) Elected 1966; b. May 25, 1935, Dodge County; home, Eastman; U. of Ga., B.A., LL.B., 1956; married, five children; Episcopalian.

Career Pres., Stuckey's Timberland, Inc.; formerly Exec. V.P., Advisor, Stuckey's Inc., div. of Pet Milk Co.

Offices 223 CHOB, 202-225-6531. Also P.O. Box 310, Old Eastman Bank Bldg., Eastman 31023, 912-374-4366.

Administrative Assistant Gene Bishop

Committees

District of Columbia (3rd); Subs: Business, Commerce, and Taxation (Chm.); Labor, Social Services, and the International Community.

Interstate and Foreign Commerce (13th); Sub: Commerce and Finance.

Group Ratings

	ADA	COPE	LWV	RIPON	NFU	LCV	CFA	NAB	NSI	ACA
1972	0	30	25	38	67	5	0	44	88	90
1971	14	57	40	43	58	–	25	–	–	44
1970	8	36	–	13	50	0	50	50	100	56

Key Votes

1) Busing	AGN	6) Cmbodia Bmbg	AGN	11) Chkg Acct Intrst	AGN
2) Strip Mines	AGN	7) Bust Hwy Trust	AGN	12) End HISC (HUAC)	AGN
3) Cut Mil $	AGN	8) Farm Sub Lmt	AGN	13) Nixon Sewer Veto	AGN
4) Rev Shrg	AGN	9) School Prayr	FOR	14) Corp Cmpaign $	FOR
5) Pub TV $	FOR	10) Cnsumr Prot	AGN	15) Pol $ Disclosr	AGN

Election Results

1972 general:	W. S. Stuckey, Jr. (D)	71,283	(62%)
	Ronnie Thompson (R)	42,986	(38%)
1972 primary:	W. S. Stuckey, Jr. (D)	66,104	(66%)
	Mitch Miller (D)	18,519	(18%)
	Harry Powell (D)	14,863	(15%)
1970 general:	W. S. Stuckey, Jr. (D), unopposed		

NINTH DISTRICT Political Background

The northeastern corner of Georgia is hundreds of miles from the cotton, peanut, and tobacco farmlands of Confederate south Georgia. The northeastern corner is really part of Appalachia, and the part of Georgia that it covers is more or less coextensive with the physical expanse of the 9th congressional district. Most of the upcontry people here live on small farms or in the little towns that dot the hills. There are few blacks—only 6% of the 9th's total population—and a few big landowners. In the mountain counties of northern Georgia, a Republican tradition lives from the days of the Civil War when this area opposed slavery and secession. Other mountain county traditions are also alive. The red clay hills of the 9th district are reputed to contain more moonshine stills than any other place in the United States.

But the 9th is not all hill country. Metropolitan Atlanta has advanced into its southwest corner, and the redistricting of 1970 brought in some outlying suburbs of Chattanooga, Tennessee. So most of the people of the district, like most of Georgia, have always voted Democratic, not Republican like the hill counties.

Phil Landrum has represented his part of Georgia in the House since 1952. Back in 1959, Landrum co-sponsored the House version of the Labor Management Reporting and Disclosure Act, often known as Landrum-Griffin; it is the only piece of labor legislation passed since the

Taft-Hartley Act of 1947. Later, Landrum became a member of the House Ways and Means Committee, where he is a dependable supporter of import restriction on textiles—one of the district's few industries.

Landrum is one of the leaders of moderate-to-conservative Southern Democrats and a spokesman for the group on Ways and Means. The Congressman attracted some attention in 1971 when he came out against the Nixon Administration's Vietnam policies. His break was one of the first in the solid wall of Southern hawkishness. As it has turned out, Landrum's position was a harbinger of the stand later taken by a large number of Southern Democrats who opposed Nixon's bombing of Cambodia. And Southern Democrats made up the group that swung the House against the bombing in 1973.

Census Data Pop. 457,247. Central city, 0%; suburban, 16%. Median family income, $7,657; families above $15,000: 10%; families below $3,000: 14%. Median years education, 9.6.

1972 Share of Federal Outlays $304,674,053

DOD	$63,544,885	HEW	$128,595,523
AEC	$23,669	HUD	$4,218,371
NASA	$265,639	DOI	$1,169,784
DOT	$18,287,836	USDA	$23,326,918
		Other	$65,241,428

Federal Military-Industrial Commitments

No installation or contractors receiving prime awards greater than $5,000,000.

Economic Base Textile mill products, especially floor covering mill products; apparel and other textile products, especially men's and boys' furnishings; agriculture, notably poultry, cattle and dairy products; food and kindred products, especially poultry dressing plant products; and finance, insurance and real estate.

The Voters

Registration 232,611 total. No party registration.
Median voting age 41.0
Employment profile White collar, 34%. Blue collar, 53%. Service, 9%. Farm, 4%.
Ethnic groups Black, 6%.

Presidential vote

1972	Nixon (R)	89,299	(82%)
	McGovern (D)	19,544	(18%)
1968	Nixon (R)	40,908	(32%)
	Humphrey (D)	25,000	(18%)
	Wallace (AI)	60,612	(48%)

Representative

Phillip Mitchell Landrum (D) Elected 1952; b. Sept. 10, 1909, Martin; home, Jasper; Mercer U., 1926–27; La. State U., 1932; Piedmont Col., B.A., 1939; Atlanta Law School, LL.B., 1941; Army Air Corps, WWII; married, two children; Baptist.

Career Practicing atty., 1949–52; Supt. Pub. Schools, Nelson, 1937–41; Asst. Atty. Gen., 1946–47; Exec. Sec., Gov. of Ga., 1947–48.

Offices 2308 RHOB, 202-225-5211. Also Jasper 30143, 404-692-2022.

Administrative Assistant None

Committees

Ways and Means (6th).

Group Ratings

	ADA	COPE	LWV	RIPON	NFU	LCV	CFA	NAB	NSI	ACA
1972	0	0	27	50	50	0	0	75	83	83
1971	22	38	43	58	62	–	14	–	–	43
1970	8	45	–	31	33	0	72	82	100	82

Key Votes

1) Busing	AGN	6) Cmbodia Bmbg	AGN	11) Chkg Acct Intrst	AGN
2) Strip Mines	AGN	7) Bust Hwy Trust	AGN	12) End HISC (HUAC)	AGN
3) Cut Mil $	AGN	8) Farm Sub Lmt	AGN	13) Nixon Sewer Veto	FOR
4) Rev Shrg	FOR	9) School Prayr	AGN	14) Corp Cmpaign $	ABS
5) Pub TV $	ABS	10) Cnsumr Prot	AGN	15) Pol $ Disclosr	ABS

Election Results

1972 general:	Phil M. Landrum (D), unopposed		
1972 primary:	Phil M. Landrum (D), unopposed		
1972 general:	Phil M. Landrum (D)	64,603	(72%)
	Bob Cooper (R)	25,476	(28%)

TENTH DISTRICT Political Background

Georgia 10 comprises a group of counties in the central part of the state. The district is anchored by the cities of Athens (pop. 44,000) in the north and Augusta (pop. 59,000) in the east. Athens, site of the University of Georgia (now home to Dean Rusk), and Augusta, site of the still all-white Masters Golf Tournament, both tend to vote like metropolitan Atlanta. In 1968, Athens and Augusta gave sizeable numbers of votes to Richard Nixon and Hubert Humphrey, and in statewide elections they have often given majorities to the more urban-oriented candidates of the state Republican party. Because Augusta has one of Georgia's best-organized black communities outside Atlanta, black voters here can provide a solid base of support for moderate-to-liberal candidates whenever they appear on the ballot.

The rest of the 10th district—primarily rural and small-town counties—has voting patterns that are entirely different. Out here Republicans get few votes, and national Democrats get virtually all of theirs from black voters. There are a couple of counties with black majorities, and one with a black-controlled county government. But like most rural Southern areas were blacks are still in the majority, these counties are poor and their population declining. The big new crop in these parts is catfish, the cotton fields having been mostly exhausted.

The bulk of the 10th's votes are cast by Civil War Democrats, Southern conservatives who have been drawn away from their party's national ticket first by Goldwater, then by Wallace, and most recently by Richard Nixon. Since 1960, the local Congressman has been Democrat Robert G. Stephens, bearer of a proud antebellum name. Stephens is one of the more powerful members of the House Banking Committee. Banking's Chairman Wright Patman is widely known for his populistic, anti-big bank views, but he can seldom muster a majority on his committee. One of the main reasons for this is Stephens, who can usually swing a couple of other Southern votes in favor of measures more palatable to the financial community.

Stephens was also one of the leaders of the October 1972 move that squelched Patman's plans to investigate the Watergate affair before the election. But no one thinks that Stephens' role will cause much of a fuss in the 10th district. In recent years, congressional politics in the district has been moribund, with Stephens usually opposed for reelection.

Census Data Pop. 460,829. Central city, 13%; suburban, 22%. Median family income, $7,307; families above $15,000: 11%; families below $3,000: 17%. Median years education, 10.5.

1972 Share of Federal Outlays $416,909,612

DOD	$127,022,000	HEW	$142,290,028
AEC	$527,724	HUD	$7,829,571
NASA	$91,611	DOI	$906,986
DOT	$8,709,089	USDA	$47,614,295
		Other	$81,918,308

Federal Military-Industrial Commitments

DOD Installations Fort Gordon (Augusta). Navy Supply Corps School (Athens).

Economic Base Apparel and other textile products; agriculture, notably poultry, cattle and dairy products; textile mill products, especially cotton weaving mill products; finance, insurance and real estate; and food and kindred products. Also higher education (Univ. of Georgia).

The Voters

Registration 208,123 total. No party registration.
Median voting age 38.8
Employment profile White collar, 39%. Blue collar, 43%. Service, 15%. Farm, 3%.
Ethnic groups Black, 33%. Total foreign stock, 3%.

Presidential vote

1972	Nixon (R)	81,220	(73%)
	McGovern (D)	30,014	(27%)
1968	Nixon (R)	36,243	(30%)
	Humphrey (D)	37,329	(31%)
	Wallace (AI)	46,908	(39%)

Representative

Robert Grier Stephens, Jr. (D) Elected 1960; b. Aug. 14, 1913, Atlanta; home, Athens; U. of Ga., B.A., 1935, M.A., 1937, LL.B., 1941; U. of Hamburg, 1935–36; Army, WWII; married, four children; Presbyterian.

Career Legal staff, Nuremberg trials, 1945; Staff, Dept. Pol. Sci. and History, U. of Ga., 1936–41, 1946; practicing atty., 1946–61; City Atty., Athens, 1947–50; Ga. Senate, 1951–53; Ga. House of Reps., 1953–59.

Offices 2410 RHOB, 202-225-4101. Also Southern Mutual Bldg., Athens 30601, 404-549-1421.

Administrative Assistant David Mayne Elder

Committees

Banking and Currency (7th); Subs: Housing; Small Business (Chm.); Domestic Finance; International Finance.

Interior and Insular Affairs (12th); Subs: Indian Affairs; National Parks and Recreation; Territorial and Insular Affairs; Water and Power Resources.

Sel. Com. on Committees (2nd).

Group Ratings

	ADA	COPE	LWV	RIPON	NFU	LCV	CFA	NAB	NSI	ACA
1972	6	11	36	60	83	9	0	46	100	61
1971	19	67	60	50	64	–	50	–	–	52
1970	8	36	–	31	38	13	37	60	100	63

Key Votes

1) Busing	AGN	6) Cmbodia Bmbg	FOR	11) Chkg Acct Intrst	AGN
2) Strip Mines	AGN	7) Bust Hwy Trust	AGN	12) End HISC (HUAC)	AGN
3) Cut Mil $	AGN	8) Farm Sub Lmt	AGN	13) Nixon Sewer Veto	AGN
4) Rev Shrg	FOR	9) School Prayr	AGN	14) Corp Cmpaign $	FOR
5) Pub TV $	ABS	10) Cnsumr Prot	ABS	15) Pol $ Disclosr	AGN

Election Results

1972 general:	Robert G. Stephens, Jr. (D), unopposed		
1972 primary:	Robert G. Stephens, Jr. (D)	59,714	(84%)
	Charles G. Ruark (D)	10,997	(16%)
1970 general:	Robert G. Stephens, Jr. (D), unopposed		

HAWAII

Political Background

Several thousand miles of Pacific Ocean separate Hawaii from the rest of the United States. So as one might expect, Hawaiian politics differs from that of the mainland. The ethnic composition of the Islands accounts for much of the difference. The native Polynesians, the people Captain Cook found here in 1778 and whose royal family ruled Hawaii until 1898, are now a small minority, often mixed racially with Oriental and Caucasian stock. The Japanese-Americans, who first came Hawaii to labor in the pineapple dominions, currently make up almost one-third of the state's population. There are also large numbers of Chinese- and Filipino-Americans living here. Hawaii is the only state among the 50 where Caucasians—or haoles, as they are called here—are a distinct minority.

For the first couple of years after statehood, Hawaii voted Republican; Hawaii had become a state in 1959 during Eisenhower's second term, over the opposition of Southern Democrats. Soon, however, a remarkable Democratic organization took control of Hawaiian politics. One of its leaders was John A. Burns, who was elected Governor in 1962 and has held office ever since. Another was Daniel K. Inouye, the state's first Congressman. Inouye was a distinguished member of an equally distinguished group of Japanese-Americans who fought in the Nisei 442nd Infantry Regimental Combat Team, the most decorated (and most casualty-ridden) American unit of World War II. (Nisei means second generation.) Inouye himself lost his right arm in combat. Coming back to Hawaii after the war, Inouye and others moved into the Democratic party, and soon into high office. The same year Burns was elected Governor, Inouye was elected to the Senate, and Spark Matsunaga, another 442nd veteran, was elected to the House. Inouye, a member of the Senate Watergate Committee, is up for reelection in 1974. His chances can be gauged by noting his percentage of votes in 1968, 83%, and the fact that he ranks highest of all Watergate Committee members in the Gallup poll.

The other major component of the Hawaiian Democratic organization is the International Longshoremen's and Warehousemen's Union (ILWU). This is the largest union in ocean-commerce-dependent Hawaii, and a union with a stormy radical past—its president remains the now not-so-radical Harry Bridges. The ILWU's clout at the polls is so phenomenal that certain areas are referred to matter-of-factly as "ILWU precincts." From statehood until 1972, no major statewide candidate endorsed by the ILWU has lost.

The ILWU is probably why Republican Sen. Hiram Fong is still in the Senate. A wealthy businessman of Chinese descent, Fong wore the tag of a Republican liberal during the late 1950s and 1960s. But in recent years, he has lined up with increasing regularity behind the Nixon Administration. That support, at least in 1970, proved fairly unpopular with the voters, and Democrat Cecil Heftel, who had lived in the state for only three years, almost scored an upset over Fong. The ILWU undoubtedly delivered more votes to the incumbent Senator than the slim majority by which he won the 1970 election.

If an analysis of the state's politics were written during the 1970 campaign, little really important could be said beyond noting the Democratic-ILWU dominance of Hawaiian political life. But party dominance preceding party disintegration is an old pattern in American politics, and Hawaii appears to be running true to form. The first sign of a major split in the dominant coalition came in 1970, when Lt. Gov. Thomas Gill opposed Gov. Burns in the Democratic primary. Gill attacked what he considered the too-rapid development of the state, particularly on tourist-filled Oahu, which contains 82% of the state's population. Gill apparently struck a chord with the voters, winning 40% of the primary votes. He is expected to run again in 1974, whatever Burns decides to do; at this point it is unclear whether the Governor will seek a fourth term.

The next sign of Democratic decline occurred in the 1972 election. Richard Nixon carried the state—the first time a Republican ever has—by a huge 63–37 margin. The ILWU endorsed McGovern, but most of the state's Democrats were lukewarm about their party's presidential nominee. Democrats here are notably progressive when it comes to domestic issues—Hawaii has statewide financing of public schools and one of the nations's most liberalized abortion laws—but they tend toward the hawk's view of things abroad. Sen. Inouye, for example, was one of LBJ's steadiest supporters on Vietnam.

Neal Peirce, in *The Pacific States of America*, theorizes that the various ethnic groups in Hawaii, particularly the Japanese-Americans, feel uneasy unless they support American military power with the standard patriotic fervor of white Americans. After all, it has not been 30 years since their loyalty was severely questioned; Japanese-Americans here, however, were not put in camps like their cousins on the West Coast. In any case, the 442nd soon demonstrated Japanese-American loyalty in dazzling fashion. But the acceptance so won, according to some Sansei (third generation), came at the cost of too many yellow American men too willing to take too many combat risks. Too many died.

Hawaii is also dependent on heavy spending for the military. The Army, Navy, and Air Force have huge bases in Pearl Harbor. And the tourist business, another of the Islands' economic mainstays, was given a solid boost by American soldiers, their wives and girl friends spending R&R periods away from Vietnam in Honolulu. (The slack caused by the loss of this business has been taken up by growing numbers of Japanese tourists.) Finally, Nixon's pre-election confab here with Japanese Prime Minister Tanaka did him no harm in Hawaiian polling booths.

But whatever the explanations, McGovern ran very poorly here. The drop in Democratic presidential percentage between 1968 and 1972 in Hawaii was the nations's largest. Moreover, Republican candidates for Congress and the state legislature ran better in 1972 than they have for a decade. It is no wonder, then, that the Republicans are seriously eyeing the governorship, and even giving some thought towards waging strong campaigns in the state's two congressional districts.

For the 1970 elections, Hawaii was divided for the first time into two separate districts, the city of Honolulu (the 1st) and the rest of Oahu and the Neighbor (i.e., other) Islands. The political differences between the two seats are slight. Voters on the Neighbor Islands have always resented the political and economic influence of Oahu, but even in the 2nd district, Oahu voters predominate. It can also be said that the Neighbor Islands and Honolulu have somewhat smaller percentages of haoles than Windward and Leeward Oahu, which means that they tend to vote marginally more Democratic.

The 1972 Republican tide, which gave Richard Nixon an easy victory in the state and which nearly unseated Honolulu Mayor Frank Fasi (an adversary and possible 1974 primary opponent of Gov. Burns), also sharply reduced the margins usually won by the state's two Democratic members of the House. Spark Matsunaga, a member of the Rules Committee, had been accustomed to showings like the 73% he received in 1970. Two years later, the Congressman was held down to 55% by Republican Fred Rohlfing, another possible gubernatorial candidate. Congresswoman Patsy Mink—who waged a quixotic presidential campaign in the Oregon primary where she won less than 2% of the vote—got almost as nasty a scare from state Rep. Diana Hansen. Rep. Hansen had planned the race for two years. Mrs. Mink is the most unconventional member of the state's congressional delegation. Less close to the leadership than Matsunaga and Inouye, she was an earlier opponent of both Johnson and Nixon on Southeast Asia.

So for the first time in years, it just could be that Hawaii will have close, hotly contested congressional races in 1974. Although Sen. Inouye will win reelection easily, there is sure to be a fierce battle for the governorship, featuring either an insurgent Democrat or a Republican. An upset here is quite possibly in the works.

Census Data Pop. 769,913; 0.38% of U.S. total, 40th largest; change 1960–70, 21.7%. Central city, 42%; suburban, 40%. Median family income, $11,552; 3rd highest; families above $15,000: 33%; families below $3,000: 7%. Median years education, 12.3.

1972 Share of Federal Tax Burden $877,880,000; 0.42% of U.S. total, 37th largest.

1972 Share of Federal Outlays $1,173,339,871; 0.54% of U.S. total, 38th largest. Per capita federal spending, $1,524.

DOD	$669,999,000	28th (1.07%)	HEW	$212,825,973	45th (0.30%)
AEC	$1,245,598	30th (0.05%)	HUD	$18,153,776	36th (0.59%)
NASA	$2,903,625	27th (0.97%)	VA	$29,739.005	45th (0.26%)
DOT	$77,585,688	34th (0.98%)	USDA	$35,929,094	43rd (0.23%)
DOC	$6,023,545	34th (0.47%)	CSC	$35,228,118	30th (0.85%)
DOI	$6,633,815	42nd (0.31%)	TD	$28,290,212	43rd (0.17%)
DOJ	$3,917,510	42nd (0.40%)	Other	$44,864,912	

Economic Base Finance, insurance and real estate; agriculture, notably sugarcane, pineapples, cattle and dairy products; food and kindred products; tourism; apparel and other textile products, especially women's and misses' outerwear; printing and publishing, especially newspapers; stone, clay and glass products, especially concrete, gypsum and plaster products.

Political Line-up Governor, John A. Burns (D); seat up, 1974. Senators, Hiram L. Fong (R) and Daniel K. Inouye (D). Representatives, 2 D. State Senate (17 D and 8 R); State House (35 D and 16 R).

The Voters

Registration 337,837 Total. 171,374 D (51%); 46,890 R (14%); 119,573 other (35%). *Median voting age* 38.3
Employment profile White collar, 50%. Blue collar, 31%. Service, 16%. Farm, 3%.
Ethnic groups Japanese, 28%. Chinese, 7%. Filipino, 12%. Total foreign stock, 33%.

Presidential vote

1972	Nixon (R)	168,865	(62%)
	McGovern (D)	101,409	(38%)
1968	Nixon (R)	91,425	(39%)
	Humphrey (D)	141,324	(60%)
	Wallace (AI)	3,469	(1%)
1964	Johnson (D)	163,249	(79%)
	Goldwater (R)	44,022	(21%)

Senator

Hiram Leong Fong (R) Elected (Elected Aug. 21, 1959); seat up 1976; b. Oct. 1, 1907, Honolulu; home, Honolulu; U. of Hawaii, B.A., 1930; Harvard Law School, LL.B., 1935; Army Air Corps, WWII; Col. (Ret.) USAF; married, four children; Congregational Christian.

Career Atty. and businessman; Corp. Pres. of Finance Factors, Grand Pacific Life Insurance, Finance Realty, Finance Home Builders, Finance Investment, Finance Factors Bldg., Finance Factors Found., Market City; operates banana farm in Honolulu; Legislature of Territory of Hawaii, 1938–54; Speaker, 6 yrs., V. Speaker, 4 yrs.; Delegate, Repub. Natl. Conventions, 1952, '56, '60, '64, '68; V.P., Territorial Constitutional Convention, 1950.

Offices 1313 NSOB, 202-225-6361. Also 702 Finance Factors Bldg., 195 S. King St., Honolulu 96813, 808-533-44441.

Administrative Assistant Mrs. Alyce Thompson

Committees

Appropriations (5th); Subs: Agriculture, Environmental and Consumer Protection (Ranking Mbr.); Defense; HUD, Space, Science, Veterans; State, Justice, Commerce, the Judiciary and Related Agencies; Labor and Health, Education, and Welfare and Related Agencies.

Judiciary (2nd); Subs: Antitrust and Monopoly; Constitutional Amendments (Ranking Mbr.); Consitutional Rights; Immigration and Naturalization (Ranking Mbr.); Juvenile Delinquency; Patents, Trademarks and Copyrights; Refugees and Escapees (Ranking Mbr.).

Post Office and Civil Service (Ranking Mbr.).

Sp. Com. on Aging (Ranking Mbr.); Subs: Consumer Interests of the Elderly; Health of the Elderly; Retirement and the Individual.

Group Ratings

	ADA	COPE	LWV	RIPON	NFU	LCV	CFA	NAB	NSI	ACA
1972	10	10	70	68	40	20	18	55	100	73
1971	19	50	83	38	45	–	40	–	–	50
1970	38	77	–	54	77	18	–	46	100	39

Key Votes

1) Busing	AGN	8) Sea Life Prot	FOR	15) Tax Singls Less	FOR
2) Alas P-line	FOR	9) Campaign Subs	AGN	16) Min Tax for Rich	AGN
3) Gun Cntrl	FOR	10) Cmbodia Bmbg	ABS	17) Euro Troop Rdctn	AGN
4) Rehnquist	FOR	11) Legal Srvices	AGN	18) Bust Hwy Trust	FOR
5) Pub TV $	FOR	12) Rev Sharing	FOR	19) Maid Min Wage	AGN
6) EZ Votr Reg	AGN	13) Cnsumr Prot	AGN	20) Farm Sub Limit	AGN
7) No-Fault	AGN	14) Eq Rts Amend	FOR	21) Highr Credt Chgs	FOR

Election Results

1970 general:	Hiram L. Fong (R)	124,163	(52%)
	Cecil Heftel (D)	116,597	(48%)
1970 primary:	Hiram L. Fong (R), unopposed		
1964 general:	Hiram L. Fong (R)	110,747	(53%)
	Thomas P. Gill (D)	96,789	(46%)
	Lawrence Domine (Ind.)	1,278	(1%)

Senator

Daniel Ken Inouye (D) Elected 1962, seat up 1974; b. Sept. 7, 1924, Honolulu; home, Honolulu; U. of Hawaii, B.A., 1950; George Washington U., J.D., 1952; Army, WWII; married, one child; Methodist.

Career Asst. Pub. Prosecutor, Honolulu, 1953–54; practicing atty., 1954–59; Majority Leader, Territorial House of Reps., 1954–58; Territorial Senate, 1958–59.

Offices 442 OSOB, 202-225-3934. Also 602 Capitol Investment Bldg., Honolulu 96813, 808-533-441.

Administrative Assistant Eiler C. Ravnholt

Committees

Appropriations (11th); Subs: Agriculture, Environmental and Consumer Protection; District of Columbia; Interior; Foreign Operations (Chm.); HUD, Space, Science, Veterans.

District of Columbia (2nd); Sub: Fiscal Affairs.

Commerce (9th); Subs: Aviation; Consumer; Merchant Marine; Oceans and Atmosphere; Foreign Commerce and Tourism (Chm.); Communications.

Sel. Com. on Presidential Campaign Activities (3rd).

Group Ratings

	ADA	COPE	LWV	RIPON	NFU	LCV	CFA	NAB	NSI	ACA
1972	65	100	78	55	100	33	100	0	22	6
1971	63	100	100	50	91	–	100	–	–	0
1970	72	91	–	69	100	76	–	18	14	0

Key Votes

1) Busing	ABS	8) Sea Life Prot	FOR	15) Tax Singls Less	FOR
2) Alas P-line	FOR	9) Campaign Subs	FOR	16) Min Tax for Rich	AGN
3) Gun Cntrl	FOR	10) Cmbodia Bmbg	AGN	17) Euro Troop Rdctn	FOR
4) Rehnquist	AGN	11) Legal Srvices	FOR	18) Bust Hwy Trust	FOR
5) Pub TV $	ABS	12) Rev Sharing	FOR	19) Maid Min Wage	FOR
6) EZ Votr Reg	FOR	13) Cnsumr Prot	ABS	20) Farm Sub Limit	AGN
7) No-Fault	FOR	14) Eq Rts Amend	FOR	21) Highr Credt Chgs	AGN

Election Results

1968 general:	Daniel K. Inouye (D)	189,248	(83%)
	Wayne L. Thiessen (R)	34,008	(15%)
	Oliver M. Lee (PF)	3,671	(2%)
1968 primary:	Daniel K. Inouye (D)	82,319	(83%)
	William Lampard (D)	12,122	(12%)
	J. P. P. Petrowski (D)	982	(1%)
1962 general:	Daniel K. Inouye (D)	136,294	(69%)
	Ben F. Dillingham (R)	60,067	(31%)

FIRST DISTRICT

Census Data Pop. 362,119. Central city, 90%; suburban, 10%. Median family income, $12,491; families above $15,000: 38%; families below $3,000: 6%. Median years education, 12.5.

1972 Share of Federal Outlays $605,381,571

DOD	$372,575,823	HEW	$94,799,905
AEC	$716,842	HUD	$5,710,318
NASA	$1,582,007	DOI	$1,341,638
DOT	$39,368,808	USDA	$14,172,270
		Other	$75,113,960

Federal Military-Industrial Commitments

DOD Contractors Hawaiian Telephone (Honolulu), $7.714m: unspecified.
DOD Installations Fort Shafter Army Military Reservation (Honolulu). Schofield Army Barracks (Honolulu). Tripler Army Hospital (Honolulu). Marine Corps Camp H. M. Smith (Honolulu). Naval Air Station, Barbers Point (Honolulu). Hickam AFB (Honolulu.

Economic Base Finance, insurance and real estate; food and kindred products, especially canned, cured and frozen foods; tourism; apparel and other textile products, especially women's and misses' outerwear; and agriculture, notably sugarcane, pineapples, cattle and dairy products. Also higher education (Univ. of Hawaii).

The Voters

Registration 165,562 total. 79,781 D (48%); 24,533 R (15%); 61,248 other (37%).
Median voting age 38.1
Employment profile White collar, 55%. Blue collar, 29%. Service, 16%. Farm, –%.
Ethnic groups Japanese, 31%. Chinese, 10%. Filipino, 9%. Total foreign stock, 35%.

Presidential vote

1972	Nixon (R)	82,729	(62%)
	McGovern (D)	49,994	(38%)

1968	Nixon (R)	46,842	(40%)
	Humphrey (D)	69,715	(59%)
	Wallace (AI)	1,460	(1%)

Representative

Spark Masayuki Matsunaga (D) Elected 1962; b. Oct. 8, 1916, Kukuiula; home, Honolulu; U. of Hawaii, B.Ed., 1941; Harvard Law School, LL.B., 1951; Army, WWII; Lt. Col. (Ret.) JAGC-USAR; married, five children; Episcopalian.

Career Vets. Counsellor, Dept. of Interior, 1945–47; Chief, Priority Div., War Assets Admin., 1947–48; Asst. Pub. Prosecutor, City and County of Honolulu, 1952–54; practicing atty., 1954–63; Hawaii House of Reps., 1954–59, Majority Leader, 1959.

Offices 442 CHOB, 202-225-2726. Also Rm. 218 Fed. Bldg., Honolulu 96813, 808-531-6407.

Administrative Assistant David S. Nahm

Committees

Agriculture (15th); Subs: Domestic Marketing and Consumer Relations; Department Operations; Livestock and Grains.

Rules (7th).

Group Ratings

	ADA	COPE	LWV	RIPON	NFU	LCV	CFA	NAB	NSI	ACA
1972	75	82	90	84	100	67	0	0	30	9
1971	59	91	78	76	93	–	100	–	–	16
1970	88	100	–	76	100	73	100	0	50	0

Key Votes

1) Busing	FOR	6) Cmbodia Bmbg	AGN	11) Chkg Acct Intrst	FOR
2) Strip Mines	ABS	7) Bust Hwy Trust	FOR	12) End HISC (HUAC)	AGN
3) Cut Mil $	AGN	8) Farm Sub Lmt	AGN	13) Nixon Sewer Veto	AGN
4) Rev Shrg	FOR	9) School Prayr	AGN	14) Corp Cmpaign $	FOR
5) Pub TV $	FOR	10) Cnsumr Prot	FOR	15) Pol $ Disclosr	AGN

Election Results

1972 general:	Spark M. Matsunaga (D)	73,826	(55%)
	Fred W. Rohlging (R)	61,138	(45%)
1972 primary:	Spark M. Matsunaga (D), unopposed		
1970 general:	Spark M. Matsunaga (D)	85,411	(73%)
	Richard K. Kockey (R)	31,764	(27%)

SECOND DISTRICT

Census Data Pop. 407,794. Central city, 0%; suburban, 66%. Median family income, $10,848; families above $15,000: 28%; families below $3,000: 7%. Median years education, 12.2.

1972 Share of Federal Outlays $567,958,300

DOD	$297,423,177	HEW	$118,026,068
AEC	$528,756	HUD	$12,443,458
NASA	$1,321,618	DOI	$5,292,177
DOT	$38,216,880	USDA	$21,756,824
		Other	$72,949,312

Federal Military-Industrial Commitments

DOD Contractors Dynalectron Corp. (Barking Sands), $7.643m: operation of Pacific Missile Range. Genco Industries (Pearl Harbor), $5.516m: unspecified.
DOD Installations Fleet Operations Control Center (Kunia). Marine Barracks (Pearl Harbor). Marine Corps Air Station, Kaneohe Bay (Kailua). Naval Communication Station (Wahiawa). Naval Ammunition Depot (Lualualei); closed, 1974. Naval Station (Pearl Harbor). Naval Submarine Base (Pearl Harbor). Navy Public Works Center (Pearl Harbor). Pearl Harbor Naval Shipyard (Pearl Harbor). Wheeler AFB (Wahiawa).

Economic Base Agriculture, notably sugarcane, pineapples, cattle and dairy products; food and kindred products, especially raw cane sugar and canned, cured and frozen foods; finance, insurance and real estate; tourism; and apparel and other textile products, especially women's and misses' outerwear.

The Voters

Registration 172,275 total. 91,593 D (53%); 22,357 R (13%); 58,325 other (34%).
Median voting age 38.4
Employment profile White collar, 44%. Blue collar, 35%. Service, 15%. Farm, 6%.
Ethnic groups Japanese, 25%. Chinese, 4%. Filipino, 16%. Total foreign stock, 32%.

Presidential vote

1972	Nixon (R)	....	86,136	(63%)
	McGovern (D)	....	51,415	(37%)
1968	Nixon (R)	....	42,770	(37%)
	Humphrey (D)	....	70,345	(61%)
	Wallace (AI)	....	1,648	(1%)

Representative

Patsy Takemoto Mink (D) Elected 1964; b. Dec. 6, 1927, Paia; home, Waipahu; Wilson Col., 1946; U. of Neb., 1947; U. of Hawaii, B.A., 1948; U. of Chicago, J.D., 1951; married, one child; Protestant.

Career Atty., 1953–64; Lecturer, U. of Hawaii, 1952–56, 1959–62; atty., Territorial Legislature, 1955; Hawaii House of Reps., 1956, 1958; Hawaii Senate, 1958–59, 1962–64; Charter Pres., Young Democrats of Oahu, 1954; Pres., Hawaii Young Democrats; Delegate to Natl. Dem. Convention and Platform Com., 1960 and 1972.

Offices 2338 RHOB, 202-225-4906. Also 346 Fed. Office Bldg., Honolulu 96813, 808-531-4602, and 94-801 Farrington Hwy., Waipahu 96797, 808-671-0170.

Administrative Assistant Oscar Johnson

Committees

Education and Labor (9th); Subs: No. 1 (Gen. Sub. on Education); No. 5 (Sel. Sub. on Education); No. 7 (Equal Opportunities).

Interior and Insular Affairs (9th); Subs: National Parks and Recreation; Territorial and Insular Affairs; Mines and Mining (Chm.).

Group Ratings

	ADA	COPE	LWV	RIPON	NFU	LCV	CFA	NAB	NSI	ACA
1972	100	91	100	80	86	80	0	0	0	0
1971	92	90	89	71	100	–	100	–	–	0
1970	96	100	–	65	92	100	100	0	33	5

Key Votes

1) Busing	FOR	6) Cmbodia Bmbg	AGN	11) Chkg Acct Intrst	FOR
2) Strip Mines	AGN	7) Bust Hwy Trust	FOR	12) End HISC (HUAC)	FOR
3) Cut Mil $	FOR	8) Farm Sub Lmt	ABS	13) Nixon Sewer Veto	AGN
4) Rev Shrg	FOR	9) School Prayr	AGN	14) Corp Cmpaign $	ABS
5) Pub TV $	FOR	10) Cnsumr Prot	FOR	15) Pol $ Disclosr	FOR

Election Results

1972 general:	Patsy T. Mink (D)	79,856	(57%)
	Diana Hansen (D)	60,043	(43%)
1972 primary:	Patsy T. Mink (D)	60,729	(75%)
	John W. Goemans (D)	14,164	(17%)
	George B. Carter (D)	6,266	(8%)
1970 general:	Patsy T. Mink (D), unopposed		

IDAHO

Political Background

Back in the 1890s, when populist William Jennings Bryan was urging Americans to abandon the gold standard for the unlimited coinage of that people's metal, silver, Idaho's silver interests dominated the state's politics. Although silver is still mined in places like Sunshine Mine near Kellogg, Idaho's principal economic concern today is agriculture. Potatoes, for which Idaho is famous, are grown in the rich farmlands in the panhandle region just east of Spokane, Washington, and along the Snake River valley in the southern part of the state. Because Idaho is mostly farmland, its population is not concentrated in large urban areas as in other Rocky Mountain and Pacific Coast states. Idaho's largest city is Boise (pop. 74,000)—like many Western cities, a conservative stronghold. The liberal voting base, if it can be called that, lies in the northern panhandle counties. But the sentiments up here are buried by the conservatism of the state's large Mormon community—the largest outside Utah—in the Snake River valley.

In the recent past, the politics in Idaho appear to have travelled full circle. The pattern here, however, has often differed from the one found in the country at large. During the Eisenhower years, a controversy over the construction of Hell's Canyon Dam on the Snake River redounded to the benefit of the Democrats, who have traditionally favored the development of public power over private. During the late 1950s, Idaho Democrats won most of the Senate and House races. In 1960, John F. Kennedy, though a Catholic and an Easterner, got 46% of the state's votes—one of his better showings in the mountain states. But during the 1960s, the people in Idaho became increasingly upset with what they saw as a Democratic Administration dominated by an alien East Coast establishment.

In 1964, a strong conservative push—one especially strong in the southern Mormon counties—resulted in 49% of the state's vote going to Barry Goldwater. In the same year, the state's 2nd congressional district ousted its Democratic Representative for a conservative Republican—the only district outside the South to do so in the year of the LBJ landslide. In 1968, Hubert Humphrey was down to 31%, and in 1972, George McGovern did even worse. Meanwhile, George Wallace in 1968 got 13% of the votes here, his strongest showing west of Texas; and even John Schmitz, the American party candidate in 1972, got 9% of Idaho's votes. Schmitz's totals were generally so poor that they are not listed in our data sections.

But if Idaho has been moving ever rightward in national politics, it has been shifting notably to the left in local races during the last four years. As Idahoans overwhelmingly rejected the candidacy of Hubert Humphrey, they reelected liberal Sen. Frank Church with a resounding 60% of the votes. And in 1972, as McGovern got buried worse here than all but seven other states, the Democrats came within 3% of electing their man to the state's other Senate seat.

Church came to the Senate in 1956 when he was just 32, having beaten an erratic Republican candidate. Church soon got a geat on the Senate Foreign Relations Committee, and then became one of the first in the Senate to take a stand against the Vietnam war. Something of an orator, Church is found of making scholarly speeches (which he writes himself). Ordinarily, doves and scholars are not very popular in rough-and-ready Idaho. But Church has also catered to opinion at home. He has opposed federal gun control legislation and has kept careful watch over the state's water needs. Moreover, his harsh attacks on foreign-aid programs are surely popular in Idaho. Finally, to counter any remaining Republican criticism, Church can invoke the memory of a famous Republican Senator: William E. Borah. Borah was a progressive and an isolationist, who served in the Senate from 1907 until his death in 1940. Fiercely independent and scholarly, Borah was a respected man, and therby—so some have said—elevated the nation's estimate of the state of Idaho. Church partisans claim the same stature for the present Senator.

The evidence certainly is that Church will remain in the Senate as long as Borah and will become Chairman of the Foreign Relations Committee. But in the years before the 1968 election, Idaho Republicans, well aware of the state's rightward shift, were convinced they could defeat Frank Church. So certain was their conviction that some of the more conservative among them supported a recall drive initiated by a right-wing California industrialist. But outside intervention is not the sort of thing appreciated in the mountain states, if anywhere. So Church, as a result of the recall drive, began to receive more sympathy than censure, and by 1968 was once again a shoo-in.

The Senator's seat is up in 1974. At this writing, there is no talk of a strong campaign planned against him. Church, of course, must hustle in a state as conservative as Idaho, but the betting is that he will win again. Moreover, the Foreign Relations chairmanship appears ever nearer. The three Democratic Senators ahead of Church on Foreign Relations will all be at least 69 in 1974, when Church will turn 50.

Idaho's junior Senator, elected in 1972, is Republican James McClure. A three-term Congressman and a member of his party's conservative wing, McClure won a hotly contested four-candidate Republican primary with 36% of the votes. Among the losers in the primary was ex-Gov. (1955–71) Robert Smylie. As Governor, Smylie had gotten too liberal for the tastes of Idaho Republicans and lost a bid for renomination in 1970. Another loser was ex-Rep. (1965–69) George Hansen, Church's 1968 opponent. After the primary, Hansen reported that the agents of four big Idaho corporations had tried to talk him out of the race. Talk of such big-money backing hurt McClure's campaign. Environmental issues presented another problem for McClure. His record on the environment was even more conservative than the conservative records compiled by the other Republican members of the state's congressional delegation.

All this was grist for the mill of Democratic nominee, Bud Davis, former president of Idaho State University. Davis won his four-man primary with a percentage about like McClure's. Another issue then came into play. Davis had announced earlier that he would observe the United Farm Workers' lettuce boycott. McClure charged that the UFW's next goal was the Idaho potato—a plan otherwise never reported— and insinuated that Davis was a potato-boycotter. McClure's charge may have been enough to make the difference, though as Davis tried to point out, any Idaho politician would have to be crazy to come out against the potato.

When McClure went to the Senate, he left vacant the 1st district congressional seat. This is traditionally the more Democratic of Idaho's two districts. The panhandle is almost completely separated from the rest of the state by the Salmon River Mountains; it is economically and sociologically part of the "Inland Empire" centering on Spokane, Washington. With a large labor vote in Lewiston and the new 18-year-old-vote coming to the University of Idaho in Moscow, the panhandle often produces Democratic majorities.

But 1st-district politics these days, the panhandle is outvoted by Boise and nearby Nampa, both heavily consevative. Those conservative votes were more than enought to produce a victory for Republican nominee Steven Symms, a fruit rancher and a businessman who was only 34 as he campaigned for the seat. Symms managed to beat the state Senate Majority Leader in the primary and won the general election with 56% of the vote—a percentage as large as the ones McClure once got. The new Congressman is regarded as something of a conservative-libertarian; he has criticized the Nixon Administration policies as too much big government.

The state's 2nd district is more of a unit. Most of the district's people live within a dozen or so miles of the Snake River. They have taken up residence in the small cities or in farm homes lying among irrigation canals that divert water to the potato fields. The district also includes Sun Valley, the Craters of the Moon National Monument, and Idaho's small slice of Yellowstone National Park. The 2nd district is Mormon country, and except for Pocatello (pop. 40,000), it is rock-hard conservative. In some of the 2nd's counties along the Snake, George Wallace almost equalled Hubert Humphrey's totals in 1968; and in 1972, John Schmitz actually ran ahead of George McGovern in four counties. Nixon, of course, carried all of them by heavy margins.

The Congressman from the 2nd, Orval Hansen, is a member of the Church of Jesus Christ of Latter Day Saints. He is, however, not as conservative as many Idaho Republicans. Orval Hansen was first elected in 1968 when his predecessor, George Hansen (no relation, but like many Mormons also of Danish descent) stepped aside to run for the Senate. But the current Congressman has more going for him than easy name familiarity; he is generally considered an effective and thoughtful legislator. Hansen serves on the Education and Labor Committee and because of the extensive Arco AEC installations in his district, on the Joint Committee on Atomic Energy.

Assuming there is no strong challenge to Frank Church, the main event in Idaho politics during 1974 will be the Governor's race. The current incumbent, Democrat Cecil Andrus, won in 1970 in large part because of the environmental stands taken by his predecessor, crew-cut ultra-conservative Don Samuelson. Samuelson had beaten liberal three-term incumbent Robert Smylie in the 1966 Republican primary and won the general election that year by a narrow margin. While in office, the Gov. Samuelson supported a mining company's proposal to extract molybdenum (a metal in excess supply)from the White Clouds area, one of the scenic wondersof the Salmon River Mountains. Andrus attacked the proposal and won the 1970 election by a narrow margin. In 1972, his party did not do so well. So the question posed by the 1974 campaign will be whether Idaho's slight leftward movement in statewide politics will continue.

Census Data Pop. 713,008; 0.35% of U.S. total, 42nd largest; change 1960–70, 6.9%. Central city, 11%; suburban, 5%. Median family income, $8,381; 34th highest; families above $15,000: 13%; families below $3,000: 11%. Median years education, 12.3.

1972 Share of Federal Tax Burden $564,350,000; 0.27% of U.S. total, 45th largest.

1972 Share of Federal Outlays $826,822,241; 0.38% of U.S. total, 45th largest. Per capita federal spending, $1,160.

DOD	$115,881,000	47th	(0.19%)	HEW	$222,736,928	43rd	(0.31%)
AEC	$95,601,825	12th	(3.65%)	HUD	$16,925,582	43rd	(0.55%)
NASA	—		(—)	VA	$48,060,998	41st	(0.42%)
DOT	$43,797,631	46th	(0.56%)	USDA	$158,932,406	34th	(1.03%)
DOC	$3,055,679	43rd	(0.24%)	CSC	$12,994,138	43rd	(0.32%)
DOI	$36,156,331	18th	(1.70%)	TD	$23,050,186	46th	(0.14%)
DOJ	$3,817,200	43rd	(0.39%)	Other	$45,812,337		

Economic Base Agriculture, notably cattle, potatoes, dairy products and wheat; food and kindred products, especially canned, cured and frozen foods; lumber and wood products, especially general sawmills and planing mills; finance, insurance and real estate; chemicals and allied products, especially industrial chemicals; trailor coaches and other transportation equipment.

Political Line-up Governor, Cecil D. Andrus (D); seat up, 1974. Senators, Frank Church (D) and James A. McClure (R). Representatives, 2 R. State Senate (23 R and 12 D); State House (51 R and 19 D).

The Voters

Registration 397,019 Total. No party registration.
Median voting age 43.3

Employment profile White collar, 43%. Blue collar, 33%. Service, 13%. Farm, 11%.
Ethnic groups Total foreign stock, 10%.

Presidential vote

1972	Nixon (R)	199,384	(71%)
	McGovern (D)	80,826	(29%)
1968	Nixon (R)	165,369	(57%)
	Humphrey (D)	89,273	(31%)
	Wallace (AI)	36,541	(12%)
1964	Johnson (D)	148,920	(51%)
	Goldwater (R)	143,557	(49%)

Senator

Frank Church (D) Elected 1956, seat up 1974; b. July 25, 1924, Boise; home, Boise; Stanford U., B.A., 1947, LL.B., 1950; Harvard, 1948; Army, WWII; married, two children; Presbyterian.

Career Practicing atty., 1950–56; State Chm., Idaho Young Democrats, 1952–54; Keynoter, Dem. Natl. Convention, 1960; U.S. delegate to 21st UN General Assembly; Bd. of Gov., Col. of the Virgin Islands, 1968.

Offices 245 OSOB 202-225-6142. Also Rm. 304 Fed. Office Bldg., Boise 83702, 208-342-2711, ext. 363.

Administrative Assistant Verda Barnes

Committees

Foreign Relations (4th); Subs: Oceans and International Environment; Arms Control, International Law and Organization; Western Hemisphere Affairs; Multinational Corporations (Chm.).

Interior and Insular Affairs (3rd); Subs: Parks and Recreation; Public Lands; Water and Power Resources (Chm.).

Sp. Com. on Aging (Chm.); Subs: Housing for the Elderly; Employment and Retirement Incomes; Consumer Interests of the Elderly (Chm.); Long-Term Care.

Group Ratings

	ADA	COPE	LWV	RIPON	NFU	LCV	CFA	NAB	NSI	ACA
1972	70	80	90	72	88	78	90	33	0	17
1971	93	83	83	71	100	–	100	–	–	17
1970	75	91	–	73	100	73	–	30	0	11

Key Votes

1) Busing	FOR	8) Sea Life Prot	FOR	15) Tax Singls Less	AGN
2) Alas P-line	AGN	9) Campaign Subs	FOR	16) Min Tax for Rich	FOR
3) Gun Cntrl	AGN	10) Cmbodia Bmbg	ABS	17) Euro Troop Rdctn	ABS
4) Rehnquist	AGN	11) Legal Srvices	FOR	18) Bust Hwy Trust	FOR
5) Pub TV $	FOR	12) Rev Sharing	AGN	19) Maid Min Wage	FOR
6) EZ Votr Reg	FOR	13) Cnsumr Prot	FOR	20) Farm Sub Limit	ABS
7) No-Fault	AGN	14) Eq Rts Amend	FOR	21) Highr Credt Chgs	AGN

Election Results

1968 general:	Frank Church (D)	173,482	(60%)
	George V. Hansen (R)	114,394	(40%)
1968 primary:	Frank Church (D), unopposed		
1962 general:	Frank Church (D)	141,657	(55%)
	Jack Hawley (R)	117,129	(45%)

Senator

James A. McClure (R) Elected 1972, seat up 1978; b. Dec. 27, 1924, Payette; home, Payette; U. of Idaho, College of Law, LL.B., 1950; married, three children; Methodist.

Career Practicing atty., Payette, 1950–66; Prosecuting Atty., Payette County, 1950–56; Payette City Atty., 1953–66; Idaho Senate, 1960–66; U.S. House of Reps., 1967–73.

Offices 2106 NSOB, 202-225-2752. Also 304 N. 8th St., Rm. 434, Boise, 208-343-1421 and Federal Bldg., Rm. 305, Coeur d'Alene 83814, 208-664-4086.

Administrative Assistant Richard K. Thompson

Committees

Interior and Insular Affairs (5th); Subs: Indian Affairs; Parks and Recreation; Public Lands (Ranking Mbr.).

Public Works (5th); Subs: Air and Water Pollution; Water Resources; Economic Development (Ranking Mbr.).

Veterans' Affairs (4th); Subs: Housing and Insurance, (Ranking Mbr.); Readjustment, Education, and Employment.

Group Ratings

	ADA	COPE	LWV	RIPON	NFU	LCV	CFA	NAB	NSI	ACA
1972	0	20	17	40	0	0	—	86	100	94
1971	5	13	0	46	54	–	0	–	–	81
1970	12	9	–	29	31	28	33	100	100	83

Key Votes

1) Busing	AGN	8) Sea Life Prot	MOS	15) Tax Singls Less	MOS
2) Alas P-line	ABS	9) Campaign Subs	MOS	16) Min Tax for Rich	MOS
3) Gun Cntrl	ABS	10) Cmbodia Bmbg	AGN	17) Euro Troop Rdctn	MOS
4) Rehnquist	ABS	11) Legal Srvices	FOR	18) Bust Hwy Trust	ABS
5) Pub TV $	AGN	12) Rev Sharing	ABS	19) Maid Min Wage	FOR

Election Results

1972 general:	James A. McClure (R)	161,804	(52%)
	William E. Davis (D)	140,913	(46%)
	Jean Stoddard (AI)	6,885	(2%)
1972 primary:	James A. McClure (R)	46,522	(36%)
	George Hansen (R)	35,412	(27%)
	Glen Wegner (R)	24,582	(19%)
	Robert E. Smylie (R)	22,497	(17%)

FIRST DISTRICT

Census Data Pop. 356,859. Central city, 15%; suburban, 10%. Median family income, $8,466; families above $15,000: 13%; families below $3,000: 11%. Median years education, 12.2.

1972 Share of Federal Outlays $418,116,968

DOD	$53,274,033	HEW	$141,904,090
AEC	–	HUD	$10,598,586
NASA	–	DOI	$18,846,921
DOT	$17,571,750	USDA	$81,543,314
		Other	$64,378,274

Federal Military-Industrial Commitments

No installations or contractors receiving prime awards greater than $5,000,000.

Economic Base Agriculture, notably cattle and grains; lumber and wood products, especially sawmill and planing mill products; finance, insurance and real estate; food and kindred products; and trailer coaches, and other transportation equipment.

The Voters

> *Registration* 201,149 total. No party registration.
> *Median voting age* 44.1
> *Employment profile* White collar, 43%. Blue collar, 34%. Service, 14%. Farm, 9%.
> *Ethnic groups* Total foreign stock, 11%.

Presidential vote

1972	Nixon (R)	99,087	(69%)
	McGovern (D)	45,309	(31%)
1968	Nixon (R)	78,242	(54%)
	Humphrey (D)	49,194	(34%)
	Wallace (AI)	17,250	(12%)

Representative

Steven Darwin Symms (R) Elected 1972; b. April 23, 1938, Caldwell; home, Caldwell; U. of Idaho, B.S., 1960; Marines, 1960–63; married, four children; Protestant.

Career V.P., Symms Fruit Ranch, Inc., 1963–72; operator, Elaine Powers Figure Salon, 1969–72; Boise Chamber of Commerce; Chm., Vallivue School Bond Referendum.

Offices 1410 LHOB, 202-225-6611. Also Box 1638, Boise 83791, 208-336-1492.

Administrative Assistant Bob Smith

Committees

Agriculture (13th); Subs: Forests; Livestock and Grains; Domestic Marketing and Consumer Relations.

District of Columbia (8th); Subs: Government Operations; Labor, Social Services, and the International Community.

Group Ratings: Newly Elected

Key Votes

1) Busing	NE	6) Cmbodia Bmbg	ABS	11) Chkg Acct Intrst	AGN
2) Strip Mines	NE	7) Bust Hwy Trust	AGN	12) End HISC (HUAC)	AGN
3) Cut Mil $	NE	8) Farm Sub Lmt	NE	13) Nixon Sewer Veto	FOR
4) Rev Shrg	NE	9) School Prayr	NE	14) Corp Cmpaign $	NE
5) Pub TV $	NE	10) Cnsumr Prot	NE	15) Pol $ Disclosr	NE

Election Results

1972 general:	Steven D. Symms (R)	85,270	(56%)
	Edward V. Williams (D)	68,106	(44%)
1972 primary:	Steven D. Symms (R)	28,422	(45%)
	Wayne L. Kidwell (R)	22,445	(36%)
	Robert B. Purcell (R)	11,926	(19%)

SECOND DISTRICT

Census Data Pop. 356,149. Central city, 6%; suburban, 1%. Median family income, $8,280; families above $15,000: 13%; families below $3,000: 11%. Median years education, 12.3.

1972 Share of Federal Outlays $408,705,273

DOD	$62,606,967	HEW	$80,832,838
AEC	$95,601,825	HUD	$6,326,996
NASA	–	DOI	$17,309,410
DOT	$26,225,881	USDA	$77,389,092
		Other	$42,412,264

Federal Military-Industrial Commitments

DOD Installations Naval Nuclear Training Unit (Idaho Falls). Mountain Home AFB (Mountain Home).
AEC Opeations Aerojet Nuclear (Idaho Falls), $41.668m: operation of test reactors. Westinghouse (Idaho Falls), $17.283m: operation of test reactors. University of Chicago (Idaho Falls), $15.947m: reactor development technology.

Economic Base Agriculture, notably cattle, potatoes, grains, and hogs and sheep; food and kindred products, especially canned, cured and frozen foods; finance, insurance and real estate; and chemicals and allied products, especially industrial chemicals. Also higher education (Idaho State Univ.).

The Voters

Registration 195,870 total. No party registration.
Median voting age 42.4
Employment profile White collar, 43%. Blue collar, 31%. Service, 12%. Farm, 14%.
Ethnic groups Total foreign stock, 10%.

Presidential vote

1972	Nixon (R)	100,297	(74%)
	McGovern (D)	35,517	(26%)
1968	Nixon (R)	87,160	(59%)
	Humphrey (D)	40,079	(27%)
	Wallace (AI)	19,291	(13%)

Representative

Orval Hansen (R) Elected 1968; b. Aug. 3, 1926, Firth; home, Idaho Falls; U. of Idaho, B.A., 1950; George Washington U., J.D., 1954; U. of London, 1954–55; George Washington U., LL.M., 1973; Navy, WWII; Major USAFR; married, seven children; Church of Latter Day Saints.

Career Practicing atty., 1956–68; Idaho House of Reps., 1956–62, 1964–66, House Majority Leader, 1961–62; Idaho Senate, 1966–68; Chm., Idaho Manpower Advisory Com., 1963–68; Idaho Legis. Council, 1965–67.

Offices 312 CHOB, 202-225-5531. Also First Security Bank Bldg., P.O. Box 396, Idaho Falls 83401, 208-523-1000, and Twin Falls Bank & Trust Bldg., P.O. Box 362, Twin Falls 83301, 208-734-2020, and Fed. Bldg., P.O. Box 2793, Boise 83701, 208-345-2866.

Administrative Assistant Louise Shadduck

Committees

Education and Labor (10th); Subs: No. 3 (Labor); No. 5 (Education).

House Administration (5th); Sub: Printing.

Joint Com. on Atomic Energy (3rd); Subs: Communities (Ranking Mbr.); Licensing and Regulation; Research, Development and Radiation; Security (Ranking Mbr.).

Joint Com. on the Library (2nd).

Group Ratings

	ADA	COPE	LWV	RIPON	NFU	LCV	CFA	NAB	NSI	ACA
1972	38	27	75	57	57	33	0	80	100	60
1971	24	27	40	67	36	–	40	–	–	65
1970	32	60	–	69	83	0	60	75	89	47

Key Votes

1) Busing	FOR	6) Cmbodia Bmbg	AGN	11) Chkg Acct Intrst	FOR
2) Strip Mines	AGN	7) Bust Hwy Trust	AGN	12) End HISC (HUAC)	AGN
3) Cut Mil $	AGN	8) Farm Sub Lmt	AGN	13) Nixon Sewer Veto	ABS
4) Rev Shrg	AGN	9) School Prayr	AGN	14) Corp Cmpaign $	FOR
5) Pub TV $	FOR	10) Cnsumr Prot	FOR	15) Pol $ Disclosr	FOR

Election Results

1972 general:	Orval Hansen (R)	102,537	(69%)
	Willis H. Ludlow (D)	40,081	(27%)
	John Thiebert (AI)	5,560	(4%)
1972 primary:	Orval Hansen (R), unopposed		
1970 general:	Orval Hansen (R)	66,428	(66%)
	Marden Wells (D)	31,872	(32%)
	Joel Anderson (AI)	2,625	(3%)

ILLINOIS

Political Background

As any reader of license-plate slogans knows, Illinois is the "Land of Lincoln." The slogan says nothing, however, about Illinois as the land of tough, patronage-minded politicians—best exemplified by Richard J. Daley—or anything about the land of hard-nosed, party politics generally, which features Daley's Democratic machine and the equally fearsome apparatus of the state's conservative Republicans. At the same time, both parties have traditionally slated blue-chip candidates at the top of tickets. Such slate-making gave the nation Abraham Lincoln and Stephen Douglas in 1858, and more recently, Adlai Stevenson and Paul Douglas in 1948 and Charles Percy and Adlai Stevenson III in 1966 and 1970.

The eminence and probity of these Illinois leading lights is beyond dispute. But the best-known feature of Illinois day-to-day politics is corruption. Among most state politicians, patronage is a way of life, and between elections the leaders of both parties live together quite nicely, sharing the spoils. The most picaresque tales of official misconduct come out of Springfield: in the 1950s, a Republican State Auditor went to jail for stealing $150,000, and in 1970, a Democratic Secretary of State died, leaving some $800,000 in cash in shoeboxes in his hotel room.

But most of Illinois' less colorful and more pervasive corruption occurs in Chicago and Cook County. In the last few years, aggressive Republican prosecutors have indicted five Chicago Aldermen, including Thomas Keane, generally considered Mayor Daley's top lieutenant, on conflict of interest, bribery, and thievery charges. Cook County Assessor P. J. Cullerton has been accused of granting exceedingly low assessments to big landowners (and campaign contributors), and County Clerk Edward J. Barrett was convicted of taking bribes from a voting-machine company. Cook County State's Attorney Edward Hanrahan, considered by many to be Daley's likely heir, was indicted for obstruction of justice in connection with the death of two Black Panther leaders; he was acquitted, but amid the turmoil lost a 1972 reelection bid. Hanrahan's defeat left both the federal and Cook County prosecutors' offices in Republican hands for the first time since the late 1950s. Forty indictments for vote fraud in the March 1972 primary and intensive poll-watching have just about eliminated what Republicans claim was a pattern of massive vote fraud, especially in the West Side Chicago wards. But now even the Mayor's reputation for personal honesty has been questioned; Daley has admitted that he channelled $3 million in city and county insurance contracts to a firm that employs his 26-year-old son.

In short, Mayor Daley's machine—the last major patronage-oriented, old-fashioned ward-based political organization in the country—is in bad shape. There are many people in Chicago, and around the country, who think Daley is one of the few big-city mayors able to handle his job intelligently. And there are still plenty of Chicago voters, probably more than half, who feel a loyalty to the machine and will vote for its slate except in extraordinary circumstances. The problem is, those extraordinary circumstances seem to crop up with unwonted frequency these days.

In the March 1972 primary, for example, the Daley machine suffered two severe defeats. First, black politicians (see Illinois 1) forced Daley to bump Edward Hanrahan from the machine's slate for State's Attorney. Off the slate and no longer with Daley's official blessing, Hanrahan won anyway—only to lose to Republican Bernard Carey in November. Also in the primary, the machine's candidate for Governor, Lt. Gov. Paul Simon, was beaten by insurgent Democrat Daniel Walker.

There are several ironies here. For one, Simon, who had been a downstate legislator, was really a reformer, and only his strong backing from organized labor and his name recognition finally persuaded the machine to endorse him. But Walker was an out-and-out rebel, and he campaigned openly against the machine. Earlier, he had authored a report charging a "police riot" at the 1968 Democratic Convention. A former $100,000 plus Montgomery Ward executive, Walker became a familiar figure by walking 1,000 miles across the state. Meanwhile the less colorful Lt. Gov. Simon worked on legislation in Springfield. Walker's opposition to Daley automatically got the insurgent the liberal vote. But the issue that attracted enough votes for Walker to win both the primary and the general election was outspoken opposition to high taxes. As Governor, Republican Richard Ogilvie pushed through a state income tax, with Simon supporting it over more regressive measures. Most people in Illinois hated the idea of a state income tax. Even at that, Simon would have beaten Walker had not a federal court struck down the state's party registration laws. The court's ruling allowed registered Republicans and independents to vote in the Democratic primary. As a result, Walker got a 2–1 edge in the normally Republican Chicago suburbs and a small edge downstate—margins large enough to overcome Simon's smaller-than-expected lead in Chicago.

The 1972 general election produced some of the most unusual voting patterns ever recorded in Illinois—and also produced further proof of the machine's dilapidation. Illinois elections are usually depicted as contests between Democratic Cook County and Republican downstate. But it makes more sense to divide the state into three parts: Democratic Chicago, the heavily Republican suburbs, and marginal-to-Republican downstate. Each casts roughly a third of the state vote: Chicago (with declining turnout) about 5% less than a third, and downstate about 5% more. With its strong political machines, Illinois has been traditionally regarded as a straight-ticket state. In every presidential election since 1944, the same party carried the state's electoral votes, the governorship, and the Senate race. Not so in 1972—far from it. As Richard Nixon carried the state by a solid 49–41 margin, his fellow Republican, Sen. Charles Percy, did even better against his opponent, Democratic Congressman Roman Pucinski, 62–38. But in the face of these heavy Republican margins, Dan Walker squeaked out a 51–49 win over incumbent Republican Richard Ogilvie, considered by many the nation's most able state Governor.

Though he had the nominal support of the machine, Walker did not run well in Chicago, only 3% better than McGovern. Nor did Walker have much luck in Ogilvie's (and his own) home territory, the suburbs. Where Walker won was downstate, which he carried 52–48. Here his anti-tax stand and 1,000-mile walk were probably decisive. Percy's bulge over Nixon came almost entirely from an area never before know for ticket-splitting: the black South Side of Chicago. Percy actually carried the South Side, the first Republican to do so since the 1930s, before ex-Rep. (1943–72) William Dawson switched to the party of Franklin D. Roosevelt.

The machine's impotence was thus demonstrated in two ways: it could not prevent its heretofore most loyal Democrats from voting for a Republican Senator, nor could it prevent the voters from electing that anathema to the organization, an insurgent Democratic Governor.

The peculiar voting patterns of 1972 in Illinois were to some extent anticipated by Sen. Adlai Stevenson's victory in 1970. Stevenson did run better than Walker in Chicago; after all, before entering the race Stevenson had made a highly publicized accommodation with the Mayor, with whom he had not previously been on the best of terms. But Stevenson scored strongly in the suburbs—where he got 47% of the votes—and like Walker two years later, Stevenson carried downstate, 52–48. The late Sen. Ralph Tyler Smith, appointed to fill the vacancy created by the the death of veteran Sen. Everett Dirksen, mounted a harsh law-and-order campaign. Smith's tactic of tying Adlai Stevenson III to Jerry Rubin and the critics of the Chicago police did not go over with most Illinois voters. Stevenson's statewide margin was a very comfortable 58–42.

Because Dirksen was last elected in 1968, Stevenson must stand for reelection in 1974. In Washington, the Senator has usually been one of the quieter voices on the liberal side of issues. He does not possess the eloquence of his late father, but the man from Illinois has still been on occasion one of the most outraged critics of the Nixon Administration scandals and some of its policy positions. In spite of the Senator's wide popularity and the luster of his name, it appears that Stevenson will face strong opposition in 1974. State Atty. Gen. William Scott, Illinois' politically most successful conservative Republican, may run; and so may Congressman John Anderson, a sometime maverick Republican and the most interesting member of the state's House delegation (see Illinois 16). Both challengers will have to make their decisions early. Illinois' primary comes in March, and candidates must file by December—the earliest filing deadline in the country.

Illinois' senior Senator, Charles Percy, demonstrated the strength of his position in his home state in 1972, winning in a big way. Percy managed to obtain the Republican gubernatorial nomination in 1964, largely because the leading conservative in the field died; but he then lost the general election to Democrat Otto Kerner, later of Kerner Commission and race-track scandal fame. Percy has come a long way since 1964. He is now considered the leading candidate of the Republican party's liberal wing for the presidency in 1976, and in nationwide polls, he runs ahead of Edward Kennedy and other Democrats in trial heats for the presidency. The Senator has opposed Nixon Administration policies on Vietnam and civil rights, and he reportedly infuriated the President in early 1973 by calling for a special prosecutor in the Watergate scandal. In this case, Percy anticipated the clear sentiment of a vast majority of the Congress. But on most issues, he is regarded as something of a loner, without close personal ties in the Senate. Perhaps this is because ambition is written all over the man. Percy was president of Bell and Howell at 30, Senator at 47, and still looks far younger than the 55 he is (in 1974). Moreover, in 1966, he was quite willing to run against—and beat—his old economics professor, the liberal Paul Douglas. Percy now seems equally willing to whip whomever he must to win the presidency in 1976; his campaign consultants have reportedly told him that new delegate-selection rules will enable him to win the nomination without the support of Republican party organizations—which he assuredly does not have.

When Percy called for a special prosecutor, Richard Nixon reportedly said that he would do whatever he could to keep the Senator from Illinois out of the White House. Because of Watergate, it is unclear how much Nixon himself can do. But the great numbers of deeply conservative Republicans who have dominated the GOP conventions since 1964 may be able to do much more. Percy was surely one of the most unpopular figures at the 1972 Reelect-the-President conclave. So Percy will simply have to win a lot of primaries before he can ever hope to win a majority at the 1976 Republican Convention.

Illinois is one of our foremost bellwether states. It has gone for every winning presidential candidate since it mistakenly went for Charles Evans Hughes by a narrow margin in 1916. But with the exception of Gov. Adlai Stevenson and maybe Percy, the state has not produced many strong presidential contenders since Gov. Frank Lowden of the 1920s. Such paucity can be explained by the nature of state politics in Illinois. To win statewide, Democrats have had to be acceptable to the Chicago machine; and the Republicans must appeal to orthodox Illinois conservatives. Passing tests like these has usually meant the candidates are unsuitable to the national electorate.

The new ticket-splitting politics of Illinois, which came into its own in 1972, appears to be producing politicians who, if not of instant presidential caliber, are at least politicians of some national importance—something one would expect from a large and pivotal state. These include Charles Percy, Adlai Stevenson III, Dan Walker, and John Anderson. None of them is closely tied to either the Daley machine or the conservative Republicans whose proudest contribution to the nation was the late Everett Dirksen. Aside from Dirksen, no conservative has won a major Republican nomination since 1960, and there is even talk now of Richard Daley getting a tough challenge in the 1975 mayoralty. For so long, Illinois politics had its own peculiar redolence. It now appears that the state is falling into patterns that are more commonly found throughout the nation. Illinois politics is becoming less predictable and therefore more exciting.

At this writing, the 1974 Illinois Senate race has yet to arouse much interest. Most eyes are on the 1975 Mayor's race. Daley will be 73 in 1975, in office for 20 years; he may retire. If he does, the machine will probably run Lt. Gov. Neil Hartigan, a young (37 in 1974) personable ward committeeman with an unblemished record. But any machine candidate may face trouble from defeated State's Attorney Hanrahan or from a reform candidate supported by Gov. Walker. Moreover, Rep. Ralph Metcalfe and Rev. Jesse Jackson of PUSH will probably play decisive roles in how Chicago's huge and increasingly independent black vote will go. From all appearances, it won't be Chicago-politics-as-usual in 1975. The most successful political machine left in America is in the throes of major change.

A word is in order about the state's 24 congressional districts. The 1972 edition of the *Almanac* predicted that Daley Democrats and the state's Republicans would cut a deal on new district boundaries, one that would preserve the incumbency of all but one or two Congressmen. It is perhaps a sign of the Daley machine's increasing age and debility that such a deal never went through. Instead, the issue went to court, and the court, by a two-to-one margin (two Republican appointees vs. one Democratic), adopted a plan passed in the Illinois House. This was odd because the redistricting plan was accepted there only because it was presented as a step in the bargaining process. In any case, the court-approved redistricting placed two Democratic Congressmen into the same district with two other Democrats (see Illinois 2 and 7), and then deprived 38-year House veteran Leslie Arends, Republican, of virtually all of his old territory (see Illinois 15). The plan thereby gave the Republicans solid advantage in three new, no-incumbent districts (Illinois 3, 10, and 17)—advantages that held up in the year of the Nixon landslide. So the Illinois congressional delegation, deadlocked at 12–12 since 1966, now has 14 Republicans and 10 Democrats. The departure from the cozy Illinois tradition of bipartisan deals was striking. As one Republican Congressman put it, "I could have drawn a 14–10 plan, too, but I sure as hell wouldn't have done it that way."

Census Data Pop. 11,113,976; 5.49% of U.S. total, 5th largest; change 1960–70, 10.2%. Central city, 37%; suburban, 43%. Median family income, $10,957; 7th highest; families above $15,000: 26%; families below $3,000: 8%. Median years education, 12.1.

1972 Share of Federal Tax Burden $13,753,410,000; 6.58% of U.S. total, 3rd largest.

1972 Share of Federal Outlays $9,030,425,280; 4.17% of U.S. total, 5th largest. Per capita federal spending, $813.

DOD	$1,472,505,000	14th (2.36%)	HEW	$3,824,535,678	4th	(5.36%)
AEC	$180,723,089	5th (6.90%)	HUD	$111,863,539	10th	(3.64%)
NASA	$7,457,168	21st (0.25%)	VA	$503,641,338	5th	(4.40%)
DOT	$387,500,414	3rd (4.91%)	USDA	$781,853,356	6th	(5.08%)
DOC	$15,772,544	20th (1.22%)	CSC	$128,271,128	8th	(3.11%)
DOI	$25,856,133	21st (1.22%)	TD	$655,884,314	4th	(3.97%)
DOJ	$49,731,015	5th (5.07%)	Other	$884,830,564		

Economic Base Finance, insurance and real estate; machinery, especially construction and related machinery; electrical equipment and supplies, especially communication equipment; fabricated metal products; agriculture, notably corn, soybeans, hogs and cattle; food and kindred products; printing and publishing, especially commercial printing; primary metal industries, especially blast furnaces and basic steel products.

Political Line-up Governor, Daniel Walker (D); seat up, 1976. Senators, Charles H. Percy (R) and Adlai E. Stevenson III (D). Representatives, 24 (14 R and 10 D). State Senate (30 R and 29 D); State House (89 R, 87 D, and 1 Ind.).

The Voters

Registration No party registration; no accurate total registration figures available.
Median voting age 43.3
Employment profile White collar, 49%. Blue collar, 37%. Service, 12%. Farm, 2%.
Ethnic groups Black, 13%. Spanish, 3%. Total foreign stock, 20%. Germany, Poland, 3% each;
Italy, 2%; UK, 1%.

Presidential vote

1972	Nixon (R)	2,788,179	(59%)
	McGovern (D)	1,913,472	(41%)
1968	Nixon (R)	2,174,774	(47%)
	Humphrey (D)	2,039,814	(44%)
	Wallace (AI)	390,958	(8%)
1964	Johnson (D)	2,796,833	(60%)
	Goldwater (R)	1,905,946	(41%)

Senator

Charles Harting Percy (R) Elected 1966, seat up 1978; b. Sept. 27, 1919,
Pensacola, Fla.; home, Wilmette, U. of Chicago, B.A., 1941; Navy,
WWII; married, four children; Christian Scientist.

Career Pres., Bell & Howell Co., 1949–61; Chief Exec. Office, 1961–63;
Chm. of Bd., 1961–66; Pres., United Repub. Fund of Ill., 1955; Pres.
Eisenhower's Rep. to pres. inaugurations in Peru and Bolivia, 1959;
Head of Repub. Com. on Programs and Progress, 1960: Repub.
candidate for governor, 1964.

Offices 4321 NSOB, 202-225-2152. Also Suite 1860, 219 S. Dearborn,
Chicago 60604, 312-353-4952, and Rm 117, Old P.O. Bldg., Springfield
62706, 217-525-4442.

Administrative Assistant Joseph A. Farrell

Committees

Foreign Relations (6th); Subs: European Affairs; Multinational Corporations; Far-Eastern
Affairs; NearEastern Affairs; South Asian Affairs (Ranking Mbr.).

Government Operations (Ranking Mbr.); Subs: Executive Reorganization and Government
Research; Permanent Investigations (Ranking Mbr.); Budgeting, Management, and Expenditures; Reorganization, Research, and International Organizations.

Sp. Com. on Aging (6th); Subs: Employment and Retirement Incomes; Federal, State, and
Community Services; Consumer Interests of the Elderly; Health of the Elderly; Long-Term Care
(Ranking Mbr.).

Joint Economic Com. (2nd); Subs: Consumer Economics; International Economics; Priorities and
Economy in Government (Ranking Senate Mbr.); Urban Affairs.

Sel. Com. on Nutrition and Human Needs (Ranking Mbr.).

Group Ratings

	ADA	COPE	LWV	RIPON	NFU	LCV	CFA	NAB	NSI	ACA
1972	60	88	100	100	89	57	100	55	44	41
1971	56	27	100	96	70	–	71	–	–	41
1970	18	91	–	73	73	61	–	43	60	31

Key Votes

1) Busing	FOR	8) Sea Life Prot	ABS	15) Tax Singls Less	AGN
2) Alas P-line	AGN	9) Campaign Subs	AGN	16) Min Tax for Rich	AGN
3) Gun Cntrl	FOR	10) Cmbodia Bmbg	AGN	17) Euro Troop Rdctn	AGN
4) Rehnquist	FOR	11) Legal Srvices	FOR	18) Bust Hwy Trust	FOR
5) Pub TV $	FOR	12) Rev Sharing	AGN	19) Maid Min Wage	FOR
6) EZ Votr Reg	ABS	13) Cnsumr Prot	FOR	20) Farm Sub Limit	FOR
7) No-Fault	FOR	14) Eq Rts Amend	FOR	21) Highr Credt Chgs	FOR

Election Results

1972 general:	Charles H. Percy (R)	2,867,078	(62%)
	Roman Pucinski (D)	1,721,031	(38%)
1972 primary:	Charles H. Percy (R), unopposed		
1966 general:	Charles H. Percy (R)	2,100,449	(55%)
	Paul H. Douglas (D)	1,678,147	(44%)
	Robert Sabonjian (write-in)	41,965	(1%)

Senator

Adlai E. Stevenson III (D) Elected 1970, seat up 1974; b. Oct. 10, 1930; home, Chicago; Harvard Col., B.A., 1952; Harvard Law School, LL.B., 1957; USMC, Korean War; married, four children; Unitarian.

Career Atty., Law Clerk to Ill. Supreme Ct. Justice, 1957–58; Past Dir., Com. on Ill. Gov., Chicago Crime Commission; Ill. Rep., 1965–67; Ill. State Treas., 1967–70.

Offices 456 OSOB, 202-225-2854. Also Rm. 1758, Fed. Bldg., 219 S. Dearborn St., Chicago 60603, 312-525-5420, and Rm. 14, P.O. Bldg., 6th and Monroe Sts., Springfield, 217-525-4126.

Administrative Assistant Thomas J. Wagner

Committees

Banking, Housing and Urban Affairs (6th); Subs: Housing and Urban Affairs; International Finance (Chm.); Production and Stabilization.

Commerce (11th); Subs: Aviation; Consumer; Environment; Foreign Commerce and Tourism; Surface Transportation.

the District of Columbia (3rd); Subs: Business, Commerce and Judiciary (Chm.); Public Health, Education, Welfare and Safety.

Sp. Com. on the Termination of the National Emergency (3rd).

Group Ratings

	ADA	COPE	LWV	RIPON	NFU	LCV	CFA	NAB	NSI	ACA
1972	80	89	100	80	100	96	100	27	20	10
1971	100	75	100	76	100	–	100	–	–	14

Key Votes

1) Busing	FOR	8) Sea Life Prot	FOR	15) Tax Singls Less	FOR
2) Alas P-line	AGN	9) Campaign Subs	FOR	16) Min Tax for Rich	FOR
3) Gun Cntrl	FOR	10) Cmbodia Bmbg	AGN	17) Euro Troop Rdctn	AGN
4) Rehnquist	FOR	11) Legal Srvices	FOR	18) Bust Hwy Trust	FOR
5) Pub TV $	FOR	12) Rev Sharing	AGN	19) Maid Min Wage	FOR
6) EZ Votr Reg	FOR	13) Cnsumr Prot	FOR	20) Farm Sub Limit	FOR
7) No-Fault	FOR	14) Eq Rts Amend	FOR	21) Highr Credt Chgs	AGN

Election Results

1970 general:	Adlai E. Stevenson III (D)	2,065,054	(58%)
	Ralph Tyler Smith (R)	1,519,718	(42%)
1970 primary:	Adlai E. Stevenson III (D), unopposed		

FIRST DISTRICT Political Background

In the spring of 1972, the Chicago police beat up two black men. It was not the first time the police had beaten up blacks without justification, nor, assuredly, would it be the last. But this particular gratuitous act would turn out to be one with major consequences for Chicago politics, more profound perhaps than those which flowed from the police riot on the streets outside the Conrad Hilton in August 1968. For the two black men roughed up were well-to-do dentists, prominent in the community. They complained to an old friend, Congressman Ralph H. Metcalfe of the 1st district—the most heavily black and most heavily Democratic congresssional district in the nation.

Metcalfe was appalled. In his 16 years on the City Council, he had always been a loyal follower of the Daley machine; and as such he had been the logical choice to follow veteran Rep. (1943–72) William Dawson to Congress. At 62, Metcalfe was by no stretch of the imagination a black militant; his real moment of glory came in the 1930s as an Olympic sprinter. But these beatings were too much for Metcalfe to stomach. He knew that such abuses were common, though their victims were ordinarily of less repute in the community. Metcalfe demanded a meeting with Mayor Richard J. Daley—at his, Metcalfe's, office. The Mayor refused to come. And so began Metcalfe's break with the Daley machine.

It is not Richard J. Daley's habit to comply with the summonses of other men. But Metcalfe, as the clear political leader of the South Side, holds a position of key importance to the Chicago machine. The South Side is the largest black ghetto in the United States, larger than Harlem or Bedford-Stuyvesant. The Chicago ghetto also comes out and votes in higher proportions. Until 1972, the votes here had been solidly with the machine; Metcalfe himself, challenged by an insurgent black Alderman, won 71% of the votes in his 1970 primary and 91% in the ensuring general election. In 1963, when Mayor Daley lost most of the city's white wards to Benjamin Adamowski, Daley was rescued by huge majorities out of the South Side.

But even before the dentists were beaten up, the South Side—and Metcalfe—were growing restive with the machine. In 1972, Daley had first endorsed State's Attorney Edward Hanrahan for renomination. The black community hated Hanrahan for his role in a raid that left two Chicago Black Panther leaders dead. Metcalfe balked at Hanrahan, and Daley—fearful of losing his black majorities—withdrew the endorsement. Hanrahan won the primary anyway. But in the general election he lost most of the South Side wards to the winner, Republican Bernard Carey.

The same wards also went for Republican Sen. Charles Percy over his challenger Democratic Rep. Roman Pucinski, whose campaign catered to the backlash, anti-busing vote. Jesse Jackson of Operation Push conducted a massive ticket-splitting campaign. And Metcalfe pointedly refused to endorse Hanrahan—a break with the machine discipline that would have been unthinkable two years before. At the same time, the blacks of the South Side showed great ticket-splitting sophistication; the 1st district of Illinois cast the highest percentage and the biggest majority of votes for George McGovern of any congressional district in the United States.

For many years Metcalfe, as a member in good standing of the machine, had opposition from black insurgents and white liberals in the Hyde Park area around the University of Chicago (added to the 1st by redistricting in 1972). Today the Congressman commands virtually undivided support in the district. Even more important, he will be, like Jackson, a key black political figure in the 1975 mayoral election. Blacks are still far from a majority in Chicago, but united black support could make the difference in a race for Mayor, especially if Daley retires and the field is left open.

Census Data Pop. 462,434. Central city, 100%; suburban, 0%. Median family income, $8,373; families above $15,000: 17%; families below $3,000: 14%. Median years education, 11.5.

1972 Share of Federal Outlays $359,541,299

DOD	$57,374,296	HEW	$152,200,302
AEC	$11,721,220	HUD	$5,833,010
NASA	$398,290	DOI	$1,023,453
DOT	$10,246,901	USDA	$17,713,144
		Other	$103,030,683

Federal Military-Industrial Commitments

No installations or contractors receiving prime awards greater than $5,000,000.

Economic Base Electrical equipment and supplies, especially telephone and telegraph apparatus; fabricated metal products, especially metal stampings; finance, insurance and real estate; printing and publishing, especially commercial printing; and machinery, especially metalworking machinery. Also higher education (Univ. of Chicago).

The Voters

Registration No party registration; no accurate total registration figures available.
Median voting age 42.1
Employment profile White collar, 46%. Blue collar, 35%. Service, 19%. Farm, –%.
Ethnic groups Black, 89%. Spanish, 1%. Total foreign stock, 5%.

Presidential vote

1972	Nixon (R)		16,998	(10%)
	McGovern (D)		145,003	(90%)
1968	Nixon (R)		16,308	(9%)
	Humphrey (D)		168,445	(89%)
	Wallace (AI)		3,249	(2%)

Representative

Ralph H. Metcalfe (D) Elected 1970; b. May 29, 1910, Atlanta, Ga.; home, Chicago; Marquette U., B.A., 1936; U. of So. Calif., M.A., 1939; Army, 1942–45; married, one child; Catholic.

Career Coach, Instr., Xavier U., New Orleans; Dir., Dept. of Civil Rights for Commission on Human Relations, 1945; Ill. Athletic Commissioner, 1949–52; Chicago Third Ward Committeeman, 1952– ; Alderman, 1955–70; Chicago City Council, 1955–70; Pres. Pro Tempore of Chicago City Council, 1969–70; Natl. A.A.U. and N.C.A.A. Sports Arbitration Bd.; Dir., U.S. Olympics Com.; Dir., Ill. Fed. Savings & Loan Assn.

Offices 322 CHOB, 202-225-4372. Also 219 S. Dearborn St., Chicago 60604, 313-353-4105.

Administrative Assistant Melvin Turner

Committees

Interstate and Foreign Commerce (21st); Sub: Transportation and Aeronautics.

Merchant Marine and Fisheries (15th); Subs: Fisheries and Wildlife Conservation and the Environment; Oceanography; Panama Canal.

Group Ratings

	ADA	COPE	LWV	RIPON	NFU	LCV	CFA	NAB	NSI	ACA
1972	31	100	90	60	86	52	—	10	0	7
1971	68	88	100	64	86	–	100	–	–	0

Key Votes

1) Busing	FOR	6) Cmbodia Bmbg	ABS	11) Chkg Acct Intrst	AGN
2) Strip Mines	AGN	7) Bust Hwy Trust	FOR	12) End HISC (HUAC)	FOR
3) Cut Mil $	ABS	8) Farm Sub Lmt	AGN	13) Nixon Sewer Veto	AGN
4) Rev Shrg	FOR	9) School Prayr	AGN	14) Corp Cmpaign $	ABS
5) Pub TV $	ABS	10) Cnsumr Prot	FOR	15) Pol $ Disclosr	AGN

Election Results

1972 general:	Ralph H. Metcalfe (D)	136,755	(91%)
	Louis H. Coggs (R)	12,877	(9%)
1972 primary:	Ralph H. Metcalfe (D), unopposed		
1970 general:	Ralph H. Metcalfe (D)	43,272	(91%)
	Janet R. Jennings (R)	9,267	(9%)

SECOND DISTRICT Political Background

On the far South Side of Chicago, where the Calumet River has been deepened to accommodate the huge freighters of the Great Lakes, are the city's giant steel mills, ones that rival those of nearby Gary in size and capacity. This part of Chicago is the heart of the city's heavy industry and has been since the Industrial Revolution first came to the Midwest; this same area was the site of the famous Pullman strike, during which the laissez-faire President Cleveland sent in federal troops. The Calumet steel mills neatly separate the 2nd congressional district of Illinois into two parts. To the east, along the lakefront, are large apartment buildings in a predominantly Jewish neighborhood; behind them are blocks and blocks of the South Side black ghetto. To the west of the steel mills are middle- and upper-middle-income neighborhoods which are inhabited by prosperous whites and by the various ethnic groups that have for so long been part of the steel mill work force.

Both parts of the 2nd district hold one thing in common: they have been the site of Chicago's—and the nation's—most rapid neighborhood racial change. Today more than 40% of the residents of the 2nd are black; ten years ago the figure was under 20%. Blockbusting techniques became a feature of life here. (These are efforts by real estate operators to scare white homeowners into selling at low prices when the first black family moves, or seems about to move, onto the block.) The vast social change has of course affected the district's congressional politics. Twice, in 1966 and 1968, Republican candidates, working the fears of white voters, nearly captured the old 3rd district, which included most of the territory now within the 2nd. By 1970, however, enough blacks had moved in, and begun to vote, to return the Democratic percentage back up to what it was before the years of turbulence. The pace of racial change here continues. In 1972, George McGovern won 66% of the votes here, compared to Hubert Humphrey's 56% in 1968. This sharp jump in Democratic percentage is entirely a result of blacks moving into, and whites moving out of, the district.

The current Congressman from the 2nd is Democrat Morgan F. Murphy, who won the old 3rd in 1970. Before his election, Murphy, the son of the former head of Chicago's Commonwealth Edison, held a number of offices considered within the purview of Mayor Daley's machine. As a machine loyalist, he beat a black candidate in the 1970 primary and then won the general election easily. During his first years in the House, Murphy attracted attention mainly for exposing the wide extent of heroin addiction among American servicemen in Vietnam.

There is a threat to Murphy's tenure, if only a distant one at present. Some time before 1980 the 2nd will probably have a black majority. Yet in 1970 Murphy, with machine support, was able to win half of the black votes in his primary against a black candidate. Nevertheless, Chicago's black voters are no longer completely enchanted with the machine (see Illinois 1). So if Murphy plans to duplicate such electoral performances in the future, he will do so only because of his personal popularity and his attention to the needs and desires of his black constituents.

Census Data Pop. 464,792. Central city, 100%; suburban, 0%. Median family income, $11,147; families above $15,000: 26%; families below $3,000: 7%. Median years education, 11.8.

1972 Share of Federal Outlays $361,168,183

DOD	$57,633,908	HEW	$152,888,991
AEC	$11,774,257	HUD	$5,859,404
NASA	$400,092	DOI	$1,028,084
DOT	$10,293,267	USDA	$17,793,294
		Other	$103,496,886

Federal Military-Industrial Commitments

No installations or contractors receiving prime awards greater than $5,000,000.

Economic Base Finance, insurance and real estate; electrical equipment and supplies, especially telephone and telegraph apparatus; fabricated metal products, especially metal stampings; printing and publishing, especially commercial printing; and machinery, especially metalworking machinery.

The Voters

Registration No party registration; no accurate total registration figures available.
Median voting age 43.8
Employment profile White collar, 48%. Blue collar, 39%. Service, 13%. Farm, –%.
Ethnic groups Black, 40%. Spanish, 5%. Total foreign stock, 25%. Poland, 4%; Italy, Ireland, Germany, 2% each; Yugoslavia, Sweden, 1% each.

Presidential vote

	1972	Nixon (R)	60,220	(34%)
		McGovern (D)	116,534	(66%)
	1968	Nixon (R)	66,747	(34%)
		Humphrey (D)	109,468	(55%)
		Wallace (AI)	20,658	(10%)

Representative

Morgan Francis Murphy (D) Elected 1970; b. April 16, 1932, Chicago; home, Chicago; Northwestern U., B.S., 1955; DePaul U. School of Law, LL.B., 1962; USMC, 1955–58; married, three children; Catholic.

Career Practicing atty., 1962–70; Admin. Asst. to Clerk, Circuit Ct., 1958–61; Hearing Officer, Local Liquor Control Commission, 1969–70; Chm., Gov. Div. Crusade of Mercy, 1967– ; Mbr., Bd. of Assn. of Mercy Hospital.

Offices 1108 LHOB, 202-225-3406. Also Rm. 1640, Dirksen Bldg., 219 S. Dearborn St., Chicago 60604, 312-353-5390.

Administrative Assistant Eugene Callahan

Committees

Rules (8th).

Sel. Com. on Crime (5th).

Group Ratings

	ADA	COPE	LWV	RIPON	NFU	LCV	CFA	NAB	NSI	ACA
1972	63	90	80	50	86	57	0	18	60	22
1971	57	78	88	59	85	–	100	–	–	24
1970	52	92	–	50	100	0	89	9	80	16

Key Votes

1) Busing	AGN	6) Cmbodia Bmbg	AGN	11) Chkg Acct Intrst	AGN
2) Strip Mines	ABS	7) Bust Hwy Trust	FOR	12) End HISC (HUAC)	FOR
3) Cut Mil $	AGN	8) Farm Sub Lmt	FOR	13) Nixon Sewer Veto	AGN
4) Rev Shrg	FOR	9) School Prayr	FOR	14) Corp Cmpaign $	FOR
5) Pub TV $	FOR	10) Cnsumr Prot	FOR	15) Pol $ Disclosr	AGN

Election Results

1972 general:	Morgan F. Murphy (D)	115,306	(75%)
	James E. Doyle (R)	38,391	(25%)
1972 primary:	Morgan F. Murphy (D), unopposed		
1970 general:	Morgan F. Murphy (D)	97,693	(69%)
	Robert P. Rowan (R)	44,013	(31%)

THIRD DISTRICT Political Background

The 3rd district of Illinois is one of three new seats granted the Chicago suburbs by the redistricting plan laid down by the federal court (see Illinois state write-up). For those familiar with the old Illinois congressional districts, the present 3rd can best be described as the portion of the old 4th district nearer the city of Chicago, plus about two wards' worth of the city itself. For those unfamiliar with the old lines, the 3rd comprises the near southwest suburbs of Chicago.

If one phrase could describe the sociological make-up of this patch of suburban Chicago, it would probably be "lace-curtain Irish." Not that the district is all white. There are small black ghettos in the towns of Markham and Harvey. And by no means are all the people here of Irish descent. The area is an ethnic melting pot with Polish-, Italian-, Lithuanian-, German-, Dutch-, Swedish-, and Czech-Americans represented in significant numbers. But the Irish were always the dominant group in southwest Chicago, and that is where most of the people now in the 3rd come from. They moved here during the rush to the suburbs after World War II, or during the 1960s and early 1970s in the panicky days of blockbusting on the Southwest Side. The present-day Irish in the 3rd are much more likely to hold white-collar rather than blue-collar jobs, though one suspects the situation for their parents was just the reverse. So these are people whose hold on middle-class status is a little precarious, their current prosperity notwithstanding.

The Chicago city limits have appeared to constitute a neat divide between Democratic and Republican territory, and in the past the boundaries have done exactly that. Today it is a little different. The Chicago precincts in the 3rd district, for example, have been going Republican for some years in most elections. The city precincts did go for Mayor Daley when he last ran in 1969. But they were probably more taken by the performance of his Chicago police in August 1968, than by any lingering attachment to the welfare and big-government programs Daley also supports. At present, city voters in the outlying wards appear to share the some political concerns and social attitudes of their suburban neighbors. And Chicago, next to Los Angeles, has the most conservative Republican suburbs of any major American city.

The new Congressman from the 3rd is Robert P. Hanrahan, a Republican. He was undoubtedly helped in 1972 by the candidacy of Democratic State's Attorney Edward V. Hanrahan (no relation). The latter Hanrahan ran ahead of his party's slate in areas like the 3rd for pretty much the same reasons he ran behind other Democrats on the black South Side. In any case, Congressman Hanrahan came into the race with a name and a political record of his own. In 1966, a good Republican year, Robert P. Hanrahan was elected Cook County Superintendent of Schools. Even when he lost the job in 1970, he carried the areas now included in the 3rd district.

Census Data Pop. 461,180. Central city, 27%; suburban, 73%. Median family income, $12,762; families above $15,000: 34%; families below $3,000: 4%. Median years education, 12.2.

1972 Share of Federal Outlays $358,456,710

DOD	$57,201,221	HEW	$151,741,176
AEC	$11,685,861	HUD	$5,815,414
NASA	$397,088	DOI	$1,020,366
DOT	$10,215,990	USDA	$17,659,711
		Other	$102,719,883

Federal Military-Industrial Commitments

No installations or contractors receiving prime awards greater than $5,000,000.

Economic Base Finance, insurance and real estate; electrical equipment and supplies, especially telephone and telegraph apparatus; fabricated metal products, especially metal stampings; printing and publishing, especially commercial printing; and machinery, especially metalworking machinery.

The Voters

Registration No party registration; no accurate total registration figures available.
Median voting age 44.8
Employment profile White collar, 53%. Blue collar, 37%. Service, 10%. Farm, –%.
Ethnic groups Black, 5%. Spanish, 2%. Total foreign stock, 28%. Poland, 4%; Ireland, Germany, Italy, 3% each; Lithuania, UK, 2% each; Netherlands, Sweden, Czechoslovakia, 1% each.

Presidential vote

1972	Nixon (R)	155,092	(70%)
	McGovern (D)	65,226	(30%)
1968	Nixon (R)	105,041	(51%)
	Humphrey (D)	69,085	(34%)
	Wallace (AI)	28,019	(14%)

Representative

Robert Paul Hanrahan (R) Elected 1972; b. Feb. 25, 1934, Chicago Heights; home, Homewood; Thornton Community Col., 1954; Bowling Green State U., B.S., 1956, M. Ed., 1959, Honorary Doctor of Pedagogy, 1971; married, three children.

Career Teacher and Guidance Counselor, 1957–64; Admin. Asst. to Superintendent, Thornton Township H.S., 1964–67; Bloom Township Auditor, 1965–67; Cook County Superintendent of Schools, 1967–71; Midwest Regional Commissioner of Ed.

Offices 1229 LHOB, 202-225-5736. Also Dirksen Fed. Office Bldg., Chicago, 312-353-8093, and 333 East 162nd, S. Holland, 312-425-5884, and 5700 W. 95th, Oak Lawn, 312-596-1990.

Administrative Assistant Bruce Brizzolara

Committees

Government Operations (18th); Sub: Government Activities.

Public Works (15th); Subs: Energy; Investigations and Review; Public Buildings and Grounds; Transportation; Water Resources.

Group Ratings: Newly Elected

Key Votes

1) Busing	NE	6) Cmbodia Bmbg	FOR	11) Chkg Acct Intrst	AGN
2) Strip Mines	NE	7) Bust Hwy Trust	FOR	12) End HISC (HUAC)	AGN
3) Cut Mil $	NE	8) Farm Sub Lmt	NE	13) Nixon Sewer Veto	FOR
4) Rev Shrg	NE	9) School Prayr	NE	14) Corp Cmpaign $	NE
5) Pub TV $	NE	10) Cnsumr Prot	NE	15) Pol $ Disclosr	NE

Election Results

1972 general:	Robert P. Hanrahan (R)	128,329	(62%)
	Daniel P. Coman (D)	77,814	(38%)

1972 primary:	Robert P. Hanrahan (R)	14,176	(72%)
	Edward J. Roche (R)	5,445	(28%)

FOURTH DISTRICT Political Background

The 4th district of Illinois takes in the southwest corner of Cook County. The district comprises the most Republican part of what is thought to be one of the nation's prime Democratic counties. It really isn't, especially since the Cook County suburbs began to cast an increasingly large percentage of the county's votes. Chicago's suburbs radiate from the city like spokes on a wheel, and the 4th contains two widely spaced thickly populated areas, one of which stretches almost due south from the city, and other directly west. Nevertheless, the 4th is an area of rather homogeneous political complexion. By most social and economic indicators, it resembles the neighboring 3rd district, the 4th being a shade richer and a shade less ethnic. This last feature probably just means that the 4th has more people of third-generation foreign stock than the 3rd; third-generation Americans are not counted as ethnics by the census.

The 4th is a very Republican district; in fact, one of about sixty-five current districts (figures for some are unobtainable) that went for Barry Goldwater in 1964. Its Congressman since 1958, Edward J. Derwinski, is a conservative proudly in the Goldwater mold. He sports one of the last crew-cuts on Capitol Hill.

Derwinski came to the House as a very young man indeed, when he was 32. He is now the number-two-ranking Republican on the Post Office and Civil Service Committee. Because the only minority member who outranks him, H. R. Gross of Iowa, will be 75 in 1974, Derwinski will probably succeed to the ranking position in a few years. And he will assume the chairmanship if the Republicans ever win control of the House. Although the pay of federal workers has skyrocketed in recent years, no one knows for sure whether the quality of their work has matched salary increases. Gross, as a consistent foe of almost any kind of federal spending, has set himself against the trend for higher government pay, and Derwinski can be expected to do so as well. Though no one can quite fill the shoes of the cantankerous Congressman Gross, Derwinski is as good an understudy as one can hope for.

Census Data Pop. 464,452. Central city, 0%; suburban, 100%. Median family income, $13,451; families above $15,000: 39%; families below $3,000: 3%. Median years education, 12.4.

1972 Share of Federal Outlays $361,168,183

DOD	$57,633,908	HEW	$152,888,991
AEC	$11,774,257	HUD	$5,859,404
NASA	$400,092	DOI	$1,028,084
DOT	$10,293,267	USDA	$17,793,294
		Other	$103,496,886

Federal Military-Industrial Commitments

No installations or contractors receiving prime awards greater than $5,000,000.

Economic Base Electrical equipment and supplies, especially telephone and telegraph apparatus; finance, insurance and real estate; fabricated metal products, especially metal stampings; printing and publishing, especially commercial printing; and machinery, especially metalworking machinery.

The Voters

Registration No party registration; no accurate total registration figures available.
Median voting age 42.0
Employment profile White collar, 56%. Blue collar, 35%. Service, 9%. Farm, –%.
Ethnic groups Black, 4%. Spanish, 2%. Total foreign stock, 23%. Poland, Germany, Italy, 3% each; Czechoslovakia, 2%; UK, Ireland, Canada, 1% each.

Presidential vote

1972	Nixon (R)	142,635	(71%)
	McGovern (D)	57,082	(29%)
1968	Nixon (R)	104,716	(56%)
	Humphrey (D)	59,200	(32%)
	Wallace (AI)	22,737	(12%)

Representative

Edward J. Derwinski (R) Elected 1958; b. Sept. 15, 1926, Chicago; home, South Holland; Loyola U., B.S., 1951; Army, WWII; Major USAR; married, one child; Catholic.

Career Ill. House of Reps., 1957–58; Pres., West Pullman Savings & Loan Assn.

Offices 1401 LHOB, 202-225-3961. Also P.O. Bldg., 2441 Vermont St., Blue Island 60406, 312-389-2440.

Administrative Assistant Mrs. Ann D. Bolton

Committees

Foreign Affairs (2nd); Subs: Africa; Foreign Economic Policy; International Organizations and Movements.

Post Office and Civil Service (2nd); Subs: Manpower and Civil Service (Ranking Mbr.); Postal Service.

Group Ratings

	ADA	COPE	LWV	RIPON	NFU	LCV	CFA	NAB	NSI	ACA
1972	6	27	33	64	33	0	0	100	100	80
1971	11	11	33	55	9	–	50	–	–	100
1970	20	0	–	29	23	28	42	100	90	89

Key Votes

1) Busing	AGN	6) Cmbodia Bmbg	FOR	11) Chkg Acct Intrst	FOR
2) Strip Mines	AGN	7) Bust Hwy Trust	FOR	12) End HISC (HUAC)	AGN
3) Cut Mil $	AGN	8) Farm Sub Lmt	FOR	13) Nixon Sewer Veto	FOR
4) Rev Shrg	FOR	9) School Prayr	ABS	14) Corp Cmpaign $	AGN
5) Pub TV $	AGN	10) Cnsumr Prot	ABS	15) Pol $ Disclosr	ABS

Election Results

1972 general:	Edward J. Derwinski (R)	141,402	(71%)
	C. F. Dore (D)	59,057	(29%)
1972 primary:	Edward J. Derwinski (R), unopposed		
1970 general:	Edward J. Derwinski (R)	117,590	(68%)
	Melvin W. Morgan (D)	55,328	(32%)

FIFTH DISTRICT Political Background

In an unpretentious but reportedly comfortable house on the 3500 block of South Lowe Avenue in the 11th ward of the 5th congressional district in Chicago, Illinois, lives the most powerful ward committeeman in the United States. He is a man whose advice is routinely sought by Presidents and lesser figures like Senators and Governors. Besides being 11th ward committeeman, he has for some years held offices like Chairman of the Cook County Democratic Committee and Mayor of the City of Chicago. The man's name is Richard J. Daley. And no matter how he may be scorned or ridiculed or hated anywhere else, Richard J. Daley is loved and admired in the 11th ward and the 5th congressional district of Illinois.

Both the politics and the physical aspect of Daley's home neighborhood, Bridgeport, are typical of the 5th. Some 31% of the residents of the district are black, but these people live mostly at the 5th's outer edges in the South Side or West Side ghettos, and whites cast the vast majority of the district's votes. They live, as Daley has all his life (Chicago has no official Mayor's residence), in all-white, ethnic neighborhoods like Bridgeport. The people here, unlike so many white city-dwellers, have not fled to the suburbs. So on a nice day a visitor driving down South Lowe Avenue will see dozens of children with Irish faces, playing on sidewalks that are spotlessly clean and lawns that look manicured. Blacks moving out from the center of the city have not found neighborhoods like Bridgeport hospitable (to say the least), and have avoided them. This choice urban property, therefore, not far from the Loop, remains the province of the tightly knit white communities which, it seems, have always lived here. If there is something insular about these neighborhoods and something intolerant, there is also a vitality and rootedness unknown in shopping-center-land America.

Very early in life, children in Bridgeport are taught their basic loyalties: to the United States of America, to the Roman Catholic Church, and to the Democratic party. But old loyalties are disappearing, even in neighborhoods like Bridgeport. The national Democratic party has moved in directions the people of Bridgeport do not like. The party has appeared to them too sympathetic to demonstrators who do not properly respect the flag, and to blacks who do not respect established traditions. In 1968, only 60% of the 5th district's votes went to Hubert Humphrey, as 11% of the voters shifted to George Wallace and the rest to the pre-Watergate, law-and-order Richard Nixon. And in 1972, George McGovern could carry only 53% of the votes in the 5th, though he had Richard J. Daley's support. Whatever may have happened elsewhere, the McGovernites' refusal to seat the Daley delegation at the Miami Beach convention surely hurt McGovern here. After all, Daley and his delegates had been elected by large margins in a perfectly fair and free election in the 5th congressional district.

One of the problems of the Daley machine is that so many of its chief officeholders are past 70. The machine is just not getting—or taking kindly to—the injections of youth it used to receive. One example of age is Daley's own Congressman, John C. Kluczynski, who will be 78 in 1974. Known as Johnny Klu (in part to distinguish him from his brother, Illinois Supreme Court Justice Thomas C. Kluczynski, known as Tommy Klu), he has risen to a position of importance as Chairman of the Roads Subcommittee of the House Public Works Committee. For many years Kluczynski was a favorite of the highway lobby, a strong believer in the need for more and more highway spending and in the sanctity of the highway trust fund. At the beginning of 1973, however, Johnny Klu changed his mind and supported an amendment that would allow cities and states to tap the trust fund for mass-transit projects. His conversion, everybody agrees, was prompted by one of his constituents, Mayor Daley. The Chicago Transit Authority, which probably runs the best-integrated mass-transit system in the nation, is nevertheless in bad financial shape. So the Mayor has been looking for money wherever he can find it. Daley, for example, got the Illinois legislature to override an economy-minded veto by Gov. Daniel Walker concerning the issue. Kluczynski's switch proved fruitless in the House, where the mass-transit proposal failed by 25 votes in early 1973; but the proposal ultimately had some success in conference committee.

One expects that at 78 Kluczynski is contemplating retirement. Possible successors include a number of young men from the 3500 block of South Lowe, notably state Sen. Richard M. Daley. But columnist Mike Royko, no friend of the Mayor, says that the young legislator may be in for bigger things. Royko notes that all the street and traffic signs in Chicago have "Richard J. Daley, Mayor" printed on them. With that, the columnist suggests that the city could save a pot of money if the name of the next Mayor were such that sign painters only had to change one initial.

Census Data Pop. 465,990. Central city, 100%; suburban, 0%. Median family income, $9,881; families above $15,000: 20%; families below $3,000: 10%. Median years education, 10.2.

1972 Share of Federal Outlays $362,252,772

DOD	$57,806,983	HEW	$153,348,117
AEC	$11,809,615	HUD	$5,876,999
NASA	$401,294	DOI	$1,031,171
DOT	$10,324,178	USDA	$17,846,728
		Other	$103,807,687

Federal Military-Industrial Commitments

No installations or contractors receiving prime awards greater than $5,000,000.

Economic Base Electrical equipment and supplies, especially telephone and telegraph apparatus; finance, insurance and real estate; fabricated metal products, especially metal stampings; printing and publishing, especially commercial printing; and machinery, especially metalworking machinery.

The Voters

Registration No party registration; no accurate total registration figures available.
Median voting age 44.3
Employment profile White collar, 40%. Blue collar, 47%. Service, 13%. Farm, –%.
Ethnic groups Black, 31%. Spanish, 6%. Total foreign stock, 30%. Poland, 10%; Italy, Czechoslovakia, Lithuania, Germany, Ireland, 2% each; Yugoslavia, 1%.

Presidential vote

1972	Nixon (R)	86,644	(47%)
	McGovern (D)	96,012	(53%)
1968	Nixon (R)	55,992	(28%)
	Humphrey (D)	119,512	(60%)
	Wallace (AI)	21,366	(11%)

Representative

John C. Kluczynski (D) Elected 1950; b. Feb. 15, 1896, Chicago; home, Chicago; Army, WWI; married; Catholic.

Career Ill. House of Reps., 1933–50; owner, Syrena Restaurant, Chicago.

Offices 2302 RHOB, 202-225-5701. Also Rm. 1730, 219 S. Dearborn St., Chicago 60604, 312-353-7251, and 4270 Archer Ave., Chicago 60632, 312-927-0606.

Administrative Assistant Beverly Pearson

Committees

Public Works (3rd); Subs: Investigations and Review; Public Buildings and Grounds; Economic Development; Transportation (Chm.).

Sel. Com. on Small Business (2nd); Subs: Small Business Problems in Smaller Towns and Urban Areas (Chm.); Taxation and Oil Imports.

Sel. Com. on the House Restaurant (Chm.).

Group Ratings

	ADA	COPE	LWV	RIPON	NFU	LCV	CFA	NAB	NSI	ACA
1972	31	82	58	58	67	32	50	0	100	33
1971	49	100	71	50	77	–	83	–	–	27
1970	40	90	–	53	100	62	87	9	75	13

Key Votes

1) Busing	AGN	6) Cmbodia Bmbg	ABS	11) Chkg Acct Intrst	AGN
2) Strip Mines	AGN	7) Bust Hwy Trust	FOR	12) End HISC (HUAC)	AGN
3) Cut Mil $	ABS	8) Farm Sub Lmt	AGN	13) Nixon Sewer Veto	AGN
4) Rev Shrg	FOR	9) School Prayr	AGN	14) Corp Cmpaign $	FOR
5) Pub TV $	FOR	10) Cnsumr Prot	FOR	15) Pol $ Disclosr	AGN

Election Results

1972 general:	John C. Kluczynski (D)	121,278	(73%)
	Leonard C. Jarzab (R)	45,264	(27%)
1972 primary:	John C. Kluczynski (D)	72,531	(87%)
	Donald J. Lazo (D)	11,129	(13%)
1970 general:	John C. Kluczynski (D)	97,278	(69%)
	Edmund W. Ochenkowski (R)	44,049	(31%)

SIXTH DISTRICT Political Background

One problem with the federal court's Illinois redistricting plan (see Illinois state write-up) is that it needlessly changed the number designation of some districts. The current 6th district, for example, is for all intents and purposed the old 10th. This is a suburban district, but the houses here were not thrown up during the 1950s and 1960s; they have instead an older, more established character. Oak Park for one, was the boyhood home of Ernest Hemingway; it is still a quiet middle-class community lying just over the Chicago city limits. To the south, Cicero is very different. But neither has it changed much since the 1930s, when it was a Syndicate stronghold and a bedroom community for Czech and other Eastern European factory workers. In the mid-1960s, Cicero made headlines and TV footage when its citizens resisted the efforts of Martin Luther King to integrate the city. An anachronism from the 1920s dominates the politics of Cicero: a working-class, ethnic-based Republican machine. In most salient respects, Cicero resembles Chicago neighborhoods like Bridgeport (see Illinois 5), but its voting patterns are just the reverse.

On a map, the 6th looks like a string of towns whose names are various combinations of the words "Park," "River," and "Forest," sometimes appended to more distinctive names. But most of these communities can claim some special quality. Maywood, for example, has a large black community, and Melrose Park is predominantly Italian-American. In fact, the 6th as a whole has more Italian-Americans than any other Illinois district. In most Eastern cities, Italians, so far as the data indicates, have tended to remain in the old neighborhoods. But in Chicago, they have long since moved out to the suburbs. One other feature of the 6th district: here one finds O'Hare International Airport, the nation's busiest. Around it a booming community of motels, restaurants, and office buildings has sprung. Businessmen from around the country have begun flying into O'Hare, meeting in conference rooms near the airport, staying overnight, and then flying out, never bothering to see the Loop.

The 6th is one of 25 congressional districts whose Representative is a member of the House Ways and Means Committee. Republican Harold R. Collier, first elected in 1956, is now the committee's second-ranking Republican. Collier has not made any great waves on Ways and Means, and his membership is more a tribute to his conservative orthodoxy and the security of his tenure than to anything else.

Census Data Pop. 461,360. Central city, 0%; suburban, 100%. Median family income, $12,700; families above $15,000: 35%; families below $3,000: 4%. Median years education, 12.2.

1972 Share of Federal Outlays $358,456,710

DOD	$57,201,221	HEW	$151,741,176
AEC	$11,685,861	HUD	$5,815,414
NASA	$397,088	DOI	$1,020,366
DOT	$10,215,990	USDA	$17,659,711
		Other	$102,719,883

Federal Military-Industrial Commitments

DOD Installations Use of O'Hare Airport (Chicago), contracted by the Air Force.

Economic Base Finance, insurance and real estate; electrical equipment and supplies, especially telephone and telegraph apparatus; fabricated metal products, especially metal stampings; printing and publishing, especially commercial printing; and machinery, especially metalworking machinery.

The Voters

Registration No party registration; no accurate total registration figures available.
Median voting age 45.3
Employment profile White collar, 55%. Blue collar, 36%. Service, 9%. Farm, –%.
Ethnic groups Black, 3%. Spanish, 2%. Total foreign stock, 34%. Italy, 7%; Poland, Germany, Czechoslovakia, 4% each; Ireland, 2%; UK, Canada, Austria, 1% each.

Presidential vote

1972	Nixon (R)	147,633	(69%)
	McGovern (D)	66,815	(31%)
1968	Nixon (R)	119,634	(55%)
	Humphrey (D)	73,583	(34%)
	Wallace (AI)	23,249	(11%)

Representative

Harold R. **Collier** (R) Elected 1956; b. Dec. 12, 1915, Lansing, Mich.; home, Riverside; Morton Jr. Col., 1932–33; Lake Forest Col., 1933–34, 1935–37; married, three children; Methodist.

Career Editor, Berwyn *Beacon,* 1938; columnist, Berwyn *Life,* 1938–40; Personnel Mgr., Match Corp. of America, 1940–52; Alderman, City of Berwyn, 1950–52; Sec.-Treas., Cook County Supervisors Assn., 1953–56; Chm.; First Senatorial Dist. Repub. Com.; Sec., Third Legislative Dist. Repub. Com.

Offices 1436 LHOB, 202-225-4561. Also 8909 Cermak Rd., North Riverside 60546, 312-447-2746.

Administrative Assistant Mrs. Jane K. Ward (L.A.)

Committees

Ways and Means (2nd).

Joint Com. on Internal Revenue Taxation (2nd).

Joint Com. on Reduction of Federal Expenditures (2nd).

Joint Study Com. on Budget Control.

Group Ratings

	ADA	COPE	LWV	RIPON	NFU	LCV	CFA	NAB	NSI	ACA
1972	6	9	33	57	17	61	100	91	100	86
1971	8	8	38	53	33	–	0	–	–	88
1970	16	9	–	50	23	17	50	100	100	89

Key Votes

1) Busing	ABS	6) Cmbodia Bmbg	FOR	11) Chkg Acct Intrst	ABS
2) Strip Mines	ABS	7) Bust Hwy Trust	FOR	12) End HISC (HUAC)	AGN
3) Cut Mil $	AGN	8) Farm Sub Lmt	AGN	13) Nixon Sewer Veto	FOR
4) Rev Shrg	FOR	9) School Prayr	FOR	14) Corp Cmpaign $	FOR
5) Pub TV $	AGN	10) Cnsumr Prot	ABS	15) Pol $ Disclosr	FOR

Election Results

1972 general:	Harold R. Collier (R)	124,486	(61%)
	Michael R. Galasso (D)	79,002	(39%)
1972 primary:	Harold R. Collier (R), unopposed		
1970 general:	Harold R. Collier (R)	107,416	(62%)
	R. G. Patrick Logan (D)	65,170	(38%)

SEVENTH DISTRICT Political Background

The Loop is what one thinks of first when one thinks of Chicago. Here, where high-rise construction was pioneered, stand the city's giant skyscrapers, including the new Sears and Roebuck building—the world's tallest. All this steel, glass, and bustle is girded by a circle of elevated mass-transit lines. Chicago also means the Near North Side, with its huge, well-designed high-rise apartment buildings along Lake Michigan, and behind them, alternately smart and raunchy shopping streets. This part of the 7th congressional district is the glamorous part, best known to the outside world. But beyond the Chicago River and the miles of railroad track—Chicago is still the nation's biggest rail center—lies the grim West Side ghetto. As one goes west from the lakeshore, the territory is at first a potpourri: the nation's largest skid-row district on West Madison, followed by odd settlements of American Indians and Appalachians. Then comes the West Side ghetto, which casts the bulk of the votes in the 7th district.

The West Side is machine country. The black community here is more newly arrived and less well-organized than the one on the South Side (see Illinois 1). So some wards that are virtually 100% black still elect Jewish or Italian ward committeemen—the last vestige of their onetime ethnic composition. When the South Side wards broke ranks and voted for Republicans Charles Percy for Senate and Bernard Carey for State's Attorney, the West Side stayed true to the machine, casting large Democratic majorities for all offices.

Of all of Chicago's 50 wards, ward 24 on the far West Side usually turns in the highest Democratic percentages—sometimes as high as 98%. Ward 24 is the home ward of the district's last two Representatives. In 1970, George W. Collins, then 24th ward Alderman, became Chicago's second black Congressman. In December 1972, Collins was killed in an airplane crash that also took the life of Dorothy Hunt, wife of one of the convicted Watergate conspirators. Collins' successor was his widow, Cardiss Collins, who became Capitol Hill's fifteenth Congresswoman when she won a special election in June 1973. Her margin was so large and her opposition so negligible that it appears that machine control of the West Side is still pretty solid. The Congresswoman's Republican opponent was Lar Daly, who likes to show up on TV talk shows wearing an Uncle Sam suit.

The current 7th district is an amalgam of two old seats, the 6th and the 7th—evidence of population decline in the inner sections of Chicago. Because the current 7th has a black majority, Collins was slated here in 1972, and former 7th district Rep. Frank Annunzio migrated to the 11th district, where he won reelection. The Democratic machine in both old districts had the reputation of being associated with elements of organized crime, especially in some wards along the Chicago River (the "River Wards") and on the West Side. It is also here that vote-stealing and ballot-box-stuffing charges have most often been leveled against the machine. Most recently, some 40 indictments were handed down for ballot-box offenses in the March 1972 primaries.

No one, however, has ever accused Annunzio or either of the Collinses of dealings with criminal elements. The sins of these Congressmen, if any, have been to coexist with the kind of political culture that has had a home in the area for a long time. One form this culture has taken can be seen in the so-called West Side bloc in the Illinois House. State law provides that each state representative district elects three candidates, with each party allowed to put up only two people. The law sounds like an admirable way to make for minority representation. But in the West Side wards, where few if any genuine Republicans can be found, the machine controls the Republican primary. So the machine's bloc of West Side Republicans will vote with Chicago Democrats whenever needed. Once, in the early 1960s, the West Side bloc of Republicans simply vanished when it came time to organize the House, allowing the election of a Democratic Speaker, the late Paul Powell. Powell, who later became Illinois Secretary of State, is the man mentioned in the state write-up who died and left $800,000 in cash stuffed in shoeboxes.

Census Data Pop. 464,283. Central city, 100%; suburban, 0%. Median family income, $7,536; families above $15,000: 13%; families below $3,000: 16%. Median years education, 9.7.

1972 Share of Federal Outlays $360,625,889

DOD	$57,547,371	HEW	$152,659,428
AEC	$11,756,578	HUD	$5,850,606
NASA	$399,491	DOI	$1,026,540
DOT	$10,277,812	USDA	$17,766,578
		Other	$103,341,485

Federal Military-Industrial Commitments

DOD Contrators American Oil (Chicago), $45.602m: petroleum products. Rulon Company (Chicago), $7.184m: artillery fuzes. IIT Research Institute (Chicago), $6.834m: ammunition and explosives research.

Economic Base Electrical equipment and supplies, especially telephone and telegraph apparatus; fabricated metal products, especially metal stampings; printing and publishing, especially commercial printing; machinery, especially metalworking machinery; and food and kindred products, especially bakery products, and confectionery and related products. Also higher education (Univ. of Illinois, Chicago Circle).

The Voters

Registration No party registration; no accurate total registration figures available.
Median voting age 39.3
Employment profile White collar, 35%. Blue collar, 49%. Service, 16%. Farm, –%.
Ethnic groups Black, 55%. Spanish, 17%. Total foreign stock, 22%. Poland, 4%; Italy, 2%; USSR, 1%.

Presidential vote

1972	Nixon (R)	33,266	(26%)
	McGovern (D)	93,318	(74%)
1968	Nixon (R)	22,768	(15%)
	Humphrey (D)	126,222	(81%)
	Wallace (AI)	6,271	(4%)

Representative

Cardiss (Mrs. George W.) Collins (D) Elected June 5, 1973; b. Sept. 24, 1931, St. Louis, Mo.; home, Chicago; Northwestern U., Business Certificate, 1966; Professional Accounting Diploma, 1967; widowed, one child; Baptist.

Career Stenographer, Illinois State Employment Service; Sec., Accountant, Revenue Auditor, Ill. Dept. of Revenue; Accountant, Ill. Dept. of Revenue; Revenue Auditor.

Offices 1610 LHOB, 202-225-5007. Also 219 S. Dearborn, Chicago, 312-353-5754.

Administrative Assistant Vacant

Committees

Government Operations (23rd); Subs: Government Activities; Legal and Monetary Affairs.

Group Ratings: Newly Elected

Key Votes

1) Busing	NE	6) Cmbodia Bmbg	NE	11) Chkg Acct Intrst	AGN
2) Strip Mines	NE	7) Bust Hwy Trust	NE	12) End HISC (HUAC)	NE
3) Cut Mil $	NE	8) Farm Sub Lmt	NE	13) Nixon Sewer Veto	NE
4) Rev Shrg	NE	9) School Prayr	NE	14) Corp Cmpaign $	NE
5) Pub TV $	NE	10) Cnsumr Prot	NE	15) Pol $ Disclosr	NE

Election Results

1973 special:	Cardiss Collins (D)	33,875	(93%)
	Angel Moreno (Ind.)	1,429	(4%)
	Lar Daly (R)	1,311	(4%)

1973 primary: Cardiss Collins (D)   31,849   (85%)
                Otis G. Collins (D)   3,369   (9%)
                Milton Gardner (D)   2,100   (6%)

EIGHTH DISTRICT Political Background

Of Chicago's eight Congressmen, all Democrats, the undoubted leader of the Daley bloc in Washington is 8th district Rep. Daniel Rostenkowski. For a long time he was the youngest member of the city's delegation (only 46 in 1974), but he was, and is, the one to get Chicago's word out. Proof of Rostenkowski's eminence is his membership on the House Ways and Means Committee.

Yet on occasion Rostenkowski's political antenna has not functioned well. From 1967 to 1970, he was Chairman of the House Democratic Caucus, not a really important position, but one which could conceivably lead to a higher leadership post. In late 1970, Rostenkowski flirted briefly with the idea of running for House Majority Leader, but never did. Then, in a real surprise, Olin "Tiger" Teague of Texas unseated him as Democratic Cuacus Chairman. Teague had locked up the votes quietly, and Rostenkowski apparently lost the post because he never realized a serious challenge was in the offing.

Rostenkowski's district is part of the North and Northwest Sides of Chicago. This is middle- and lower-middle-class country in decline, with strip commercial developments and neigh- borhoods of neat one- and two-family houses. Most of the district is resolutely all-white, though the 1972 redistricting did add a substantial chunk of the West Side black ghetto. For the most part, the 8th is the kind of urban area that many young middle-Americans, in a rush to the curved streets and shopping centers of the suburbs, are leaving behind. But the atmosphere here is still ethnic, the 8th being the most Polish and most German of all Chicago congressional districts. Its residents, less prosperous than their cousins in the adjoining 11th, are closer to the old country and more dependent on their ward organizations. Consequently, the voters of the 8th have not deserted the Democratic party to an extent as great as those in the 11th or the 2nd districts—where racial neighborhood change has been much more rapid. Rostenkowski's 8th stood by the Democratic party even in the Republican years of 1966, 1968, and 1972.

Census Data   Pop. 459,902. Central city, 100%; suburban, 0%. Median family income, $9,867; families above $15,000: 20%; families below $3,000: 9%.   Median years education, 10.1.

1972 Share of Federal Outlays $357,372,121

DOD	$57,028,146	HEW	$151,282,049
AEC	$11,650,503	HUD	$5,797,818
NASA	$395,887	DOI	$1,017,278
DOT	$100,185,080	USDA	$17,606,278
		Other	$102,409,082

Federal Military-Industrial Commitments

DOD Contractors Stewart Warner Corp. (Chicago), $11.428m: instruments and laboratory equipment.

Economic Base   Electrical equipment and supplies, especially telephone and telegraph apparatus; finance, insurance and real estate; fabricated metal products, especially metal stampings; printing and publishing, especially commerical printing; and machinery, especially metalworking machinery. Also higher education (Depaul Univ.).

The Voters

Registration   No party registration; no accurate total registration figures available.
Median voting age 42.8
Employment profile   White collar, 39%. Blue collar, 49%. Service, 12%. Farm, –%.
Ethnic groups   Black, 18%. Spanish, 13%. Total foreign stock, 35%. Poland, 9%; Italy, 6%; Germany, 3%; Ireland, 2%; Greece, 1%.

Presidential vote

1972	Nixon (R)	71,343	(44%)
	McGovern (D)	90,093	(56%)
1968	Nixon (R)	65,086	(36%)
	Humphrey (D)	101,161	(55%)
	Wallace (AI)	16,056	(9%)

Representative

Dan Rostenkowski (D) Elected 1958; b. Jan. 2, 1928, Chicago; home, Chicago; Loyola U., 1948–51; Army, 1946–48; married, four children; Catholic.

Career Ill. House of Reps., 1952–54; Ill. Senate, 1954–56.

Offices 2348 RHOB, 202-225-4061. Also 2148 N. Damen Ave., Chicago 60647, 312-341-0330.

Administrative Assistant James C. Healey, Jr.

Committees

Ways and Means (5th).

Joint Study Com. on Budget Control.

Group Ratings

	ADA	COPE	LWV	RIPON	NFU	LCV	CFA	NAB	NSI	ACA
1972	38	90	60	62	86	56	–	0	78	18
1971	62	80	89	50	82	–	60	–	–	23
1970	52	75	–	56	92	40	88	11	78	14

Key Votes

1) Busing	AGN	6) Cmbodia Bmbg	AGN	11) Chkg Acct Intrst	AGN
2) Strip Mines	FOR	7) Bust Hwy Trust	FOR	12) End HISC (HUAC)	AGN
3) Cut Mil $	AGN	8) Farm Sub Lmt	FOR	13) Nixon Sewer Veto	AGN
4) Rev Shrg	FOR	9) School Prayr	FOR	14) Corp Cmpaign $	FOR
5) Pub TV $	FOR	10) Cnsumr Prot	FOR	15) Pol $ Disclosr	AGN

Election Results

1972 general:	Dan Rostenkowski (D)	110,457	(74%)
	Edward Stepnowski (R)	38,758	(26%)
1972 primary:	Dan Rostenkowski (D), unopposed		
1970 general:	Dan Rostenkowski (D)	98,453	(74%)
	Henry S. Kaplinski (R)	34,841	(26%)

NINTH DISTRICT Political Background

Along Chicago's Lake Shore Drive, overlooking Lake Michigan, are a great number of the nation's architecturally most distinguished high-rise apartment buildings. They stand, one hard on the heels of the next; there are more of the distinguished buildings on Lake Shore Drive, probably, than anywhere else in the country. This is the face the nation's second city likes to show to the world: affluent, elegant, massive. Behind the apartment towers, however, lies another Chicago—an incredibly varied, sometimes ramshackled, sometimes posh city. There are Appalachians, Italians, Mexicans, American Indians, and blacks. At the northern end of the city's lakefront is its largest Jewish community, living just south of the suburbs of Evanston and Skokie. The lakefront, and the territory a mile or two behind it, forms Illinois' 9th congressional district, which stretches from the Near North Side to the northern city limits.

The 9th district comprises that part of Chicago which—along with the Hyde Park ward around the University of Chicago—has voted most steadily against the Daley machine. William Singer, the young lawyer who led the anti-Daley delegation seated at the 1972 Democratic National Convention, is an Alderman from one of these wards. The 9th district has also produced the most independent member of the city's congressional delegation, Sidney R. Yates.

Yates has represented the Lake Shore area in Congress since 1948, when Richard Daley was not yet Cook County Clerk. But the Congressman's tenure has not been continuous. Yates spent two years in enforced political retirement following an unsuccessful, but impressive, attempt to unseat Sen. Everett Dirksen in 1962. With his solid base of support in the liberal community here, Yates had no trouble winning back his House seat in 1964. The machine appears to treat the liberal community like any other ethnic group, entitled to representation in rough proportion to its numbers. So the city of Chicago presently has a House delegation composed of two Poles, two blacks, one Irishman, one Italian, and one Jewish liberal.

Yates serves on the Appropriations Committee. But because his current tenure dates from 1964 only, he cannot be found at the top of Appropriations' seniority list. He would have been the sixth-ranking Democrat, if he had not made the Senate try in 1962. In any case, Yates has been heard from. In 1970 and 1971, Yates was the leader of the movement in the House to stop funding the SST; and in 1973, he was one of the leaders in a move to stop appropriations for the bombing of Cambodia.

Census Data Pop. 463,991. Central city, 100%; suburban, 0%. Median family income, $10,966; families above $15,000: 29%; families below $3,000: 8%. Median years education, 12.3.

1972 Share of Federal Outlays $360,625,889

DOD	$57,547,371	HEW	$152,659,428
AEC	$11,756,578	HUD	$5,850,606
NASA	$399,491	DOI	$1,026,540
DOT	$10,277,812	USDA	$17,766,578
		Other	$103,341,485

Federal Military-Industrial Commitments

No installations or contractors receiving prime awards greater than $5,000,000.

Economic Base Finance, insurance and real estate; electrical equipment and supplies, especially telephone and telegraph apparatus; fabricated metal products, especially metal stampings; printing and publishing, especially commercial printing; and machinery, especially metalworking machinery. Also higher education (Loyola Univ.).

The Voters

Registration No party registration; no accurate total registration figures available.
Median voting age 44.7
Employment profile White collar, 64%. Blue collar, 25%. Service, 11%. Farm, –%.
Ethnic groups Black, 5%. Spanish, 9%. Total foreign stock, 41%. USSR, 6%; Germany, 5%; Poland, 3%; Ireland, Sweden, Italy, UK, 2% each; Austria, Canada, Yugoslavia, Greece, 1% each.

Presidential vote

1972	Nixon (R)	79,997	(42%)
	McGovern (D)	111,512	(58%)
1968	Nixon (R)	79,631	(38%)
	Humphrey (D)	118,287	(56%)
	Wallace (AI)	10,547	(5%)

Representative

Sidney Richard Yates (D) Elected 1948; b. Aug. 27, 1909, Chicago; home, Chicago; U. of Chicago, Ph.B., 1931; J.D., 1933; Navy, WWII; married, one child; Jewish.

Career Asst. Atty. Gen. attached to Ill. Commerce Commission as traction atty., 1937–40; U.S. Rep. to Trusteeship Council of UN, 1963–64.

Offices 2234 RHOB, 202-225-2111. Also 1826 Fed. Bldg., 219 S. Dearborn St., Chicago 60604, 312-353-4596.

Administrative Assistant Mary Anderson Bain

Committees

Appropriations (21st); Subs: Foreign Operations; Interior; Transportation.

Group Ratings

	ADA	COPE	LWV	RIPON	NFU	LCV	CFA	NAB	NSI	ACA
1972	94	100	100	78	100	80	100	8	0	0
1971	100	83	89	78	73	–	88	–	–	7
1970	96	100	–	71	91	78	100	8	0	17

Key Votes

1) Busing	FOR	6) Cmbodia Bmbg	AGN	11) Chkg Acct Intrst	FOR
2) Strip Mines	AGN	7) Bust Hwy Trust	FOR	12) End HISC (HUAC)	FOR
3) Cut Mil $	FOR	8) Farm Sub Lmt	FOR	13) Nixon Sewer Veto	AGN
4) Rev Shrg	FOR	9) School Prayr	AGN	14) Corp Cmpaign $	AGN
5) Pub TV $	FOR	10) Cnsumr Prot	FOR	15) Pol $ Disclosr	AGN

Election Results

1972 general:	Sidney R. Yates (D)	131,777	(68%)
	Clark W. Fetridge (R)	61,083	(32%)
1972 primary:	Sidney R. Yates (D), unopposed		
1970 general:	Sidney R. Yates (D)	111,955	(76%)
	Edward Wolbank (R)	35,795	(24%)

TENTH DISTRICT Political Background

The 10th of Illinois is one of the two new Chicago suburban congressional districts created by a federal court order in 1971. As drawn, it had no incumbent for the 1972 election. The 10th is about as compact and contiguous an area possible, and one of substantial social homogeneity. The nature of the homogeneity can, in fact, be summed up in one word: rich. According to the 1970 census, this was the second wealthiest congressional district in the United States, with a median family income of over $16,000—a figure exceeded only by the 8th district of Maryland in the Washington suburbs. And here, of course, there are no hordes of high-salaried GS-16s inflating income data. People of the 10th district make their money producing goods and services other people buy voluntarily.

The 10th could easily be called the North Shore district. Its best-known towns include Evanston, site of Northwestern University and for many years the home of the WCTU, along with Winnetka, Wilmette, and Glencoe, whose New Trier Township High School might well be the best public secondary school in the country. All of these suburbs along Lake Michigan were settled long ago, pioneered by commuters using Chicago's efficient railroad lines. The large houses and shady streets of the 10th have a comfortable, lived-in look—and not the slightest trace of shabbiness.

Behind the Lake Shore and to the west are newer, faster-growing communities: the predominantly Jewish suburb of Skokie, which really grew in the 1950s; and farther inland, Des Plaines, on the northwest rail lines and freeways, which boomed in the 1960s.

Conventional wisdom has it that the richer people are, the more Republican they vote. The 10th district nicely refutes this proposition. Though it is the richest of the Chicago suburban districts, it was the only one that did not go for Barry Goldwater in 1964. Even in 1972, the 10th gave George McGovern just about the same percentage of votes he received nationally; in other words, the liberal South Dakotan did as well in the rich 10th as he did in the nation's 433 poorer districts combined. There are several explanations for McGovern's showing here. First, the district's Jewish population, which produces Democratic majorities, is large and growing. Second, in 1972 the Northwestern University campus finally managed to overmatch Evanston's ancestral Republicans. This happened in part because more and more academics have moved into Evanston's large and comfortable houses—many book-oriented people deserting the racially troubled area around the University of Chicago. Third, there is a small black community in Evanston that gets out and votes. Finally, there is the leftward movement among high-income WASPs, one which conservative political analyst Kevin Phillips has acknowledged disparagingly.

All of this made the district attractive to Congressman Abner J. Mikva. After compiling a staunchly liberal record in the Illinois House, Mikva ran for Congress in the old 2nd district, which took in both the Hyde Park area and the Calumet steel mills. He was beaten in the 1966 primary by the 84-year-old incumbent, Barratt O'Hara, the last member of Congress to have served in the Spanish-American War. But Mikva's 40% of the primary vote was so high that in 1968 he won the machine endorsement and the election. He won reelection in 1970.

A federal-court-ordered redistricting plan, however, wiped out Mikva's old 2nd in 1971, an action which probably led to very little gnashing of teeth in Mayor Daley's office. In any case, Mikva decided to move up Lake Michigan to the 10th. He actually bought a house and moved his family to Evanston; doing this, to paraphrase a Mikva supporter, if only because all our people are moving up there anyway. With no incumbent, Mikva appeared to have a solid chance to win. The Republican nominee, Samuel Young, showed his political stuff by winning his primary over the organization choice. Young was a personable and intelligent candidate, but could not match Mikva's level of sophistication.

This was a race run not so much with money— neither candidate spent more than $100,000, Chicago TV time being prohibitively expensive for area congressional candidates—nor with patronage. There are few city and county employees living above the city limits from which to build patronage armies, and Mikva's longstanding coolness toward Mayor Daley didn't hurt him. The real instruments of electioneering were volunteers, thousands of them. These people registered voters, interviewed them, and identified their sympathies for an election day get-out-the-vote effort. Volunteers also organized speeches and debates by the candidates and their supporters before large audiences and small coffee clatches. The politics of the volunteer, the so-called "new politics," is the trend in the affluent society of the American suburbs. And this species of political activity is probably more in line with what the Founding Fathers expected than patronage armies of $6,500-a-year city workers. Besides, as noted, anybody making $6,500 a year is pretty scarce in the 10th district.

Young, of course, tried to tie Mikva to McGovern, who, it was clear, was not going to carry the district. Mikva did not try to hide his liberal credentials—he was Vice-Chairman of the national ADA, a leading opponent of the Vietnam war, and an advocate of tax reform. It is tempting to say that presidential coattails made the difference in Young's 52–48, 7,000-vote win—tempting but most probably inaccurate. After all, in other congressional races Democrats won by running further ahead of the national ticket than Mikva. Rather, it is better to say that the result indicates that a slight majority of the 10th's 1972 voters preferred Young's views on the issues to Mikva's. Whether this will be true in 1974 is hard to say. Because Mikva is already running again, Young knows he may encounter another hotly contested election. In 1972, a slight change in turnout could have made the difference. If, for example, those Republicans now turned off by Watergate had stayed home in 1972, the election would have probably gone to Mikva.

Census Data Pop. 462,121. Central city, 0%; suburban, 100%. Median family income, $16,576; families above $15,000: 55%; families below $3,000: 3%. Median years education, 12.9.

1972 Share of Federal Outlays $358,999,005

DOD	$57,287,758	HEW	$151,790,739
AEC	$11,703,541	HUD	$5,824,212
NASA	$397,689	DOI	$1,021,909
DOT	$10,231,446	USDA	$17,686,428
		Other	$102,875,283

Federal Military-Industrial Commitments

DOD Contractors Teletype Corp. (Skokie), $8.111m: teletypewriters.
DOD Installations Naval Air Station (Glenview).

Economic Base Finance, insurance and real estate; electrical equipment and supplies, especially telephone and telegraph apparatus; fabricated metal products, especially metal stampings; printing and publishing, especially commercial printing; and machinery, especially metalworking machinery. Also higher education (Northwestern Univ.).

The Voters

Registration No party registration; no accurate total registration figures available.
Median voting age 44.1
Employment profile White collar, 74%. Blue collar, 18%. Service, 8%. Farm, –%.
Ethnic groups Black, 3%. Spanish, 1%. Total foreign stock, 31%. USSR, Germany, Poland, 4% each; Italy, UK, Sweden, Canada, 2% each; Austria, 1%.

Presidential vote

1972	Nixon (R)	147,305	(62%)
	McGovern (D)	89,630	(38%)
1968	Nixon (R)	123,878	(56%)
	Humphrey (D)	89,114	(41%)
	Wallace (AI)	6,786	(3%)

Representative

Samuel Hollingsworth Young (R) Elected 1972; b. Dec. 26, 1922, Casey; home, Glenview; U. of Ill., LL.B., 1947; U. of Ill. Law School. J.D., 1948; Army 1943–46; married, three chldren; Methodist.

Career Practicing atty., 1948–; Instructor, U. of Ill., 1947–48; Instructor, Northwestern U., 1950–51; Atty., U.S. Securities and Exchange Commission, 1948–49; Securities Commissioner, Ill., 1953–55; Asst. Sec. of State, Ill., 1955–58; financial V.P., Treas., American Hospital Supply Corporation., 1965–66; Sr. partner, Samuel H. Young Professional Corp.

Offices 226 CHOB, 202-225-4835. Also, 9701 N. Kenton, Skokie 60076, 312-677-2850, and 770 Lee St., Des Plaines.

Administrative Assistant William Kling

Committees

Interstate and Foreign Commerce (19th); Sub: Commerce and Finance.

Group Ratings: Newly Elected

Key Votes

1) Busing	NE	6) Cmbodia Bmbg	FOR	11) Chkg Acct Intrst	AGN
2) Strip Mines	NE	7) Bust Hwy Trust	ABS	12) End HISC (HUAC)	FOR
3) Cut Mil $	NE	8) Farm Sub Lmt	NE	13) Nixon Sewer Veto	FOR
4) Rev Shrg	NE	9) School Prayr	NE	14) Corp Cmpaign $	NE
5) Pub TV $	NE	10) Cnsumr Prot	NE	15) Pol $ Disclosr	NE

Election Results

1972 general:	Samuel H. Young (R)	120,681	(52%)
	Abner J. Mikva (D)	113,222	(48%)
1972 primary:	Samuel H. Young (R)	19,831	(60%)
	Floyd T. Fulle (R)	13,168	(40%)

ELEVENTH DISTRICT Political Background

The 11th district of Illinois is the northwest corner of the city of Chicago. The 11th, made up largely of comfortable middle-class homes, is one of the richest districts within the city, having the highest percentage of families with incomes over $15,000. It is also the Chicago district with the lowest percentage of blacks and the highest proportion of foreign stock—that is, people who were born in another country or whose parents were. When second- and third-generation ethnics can afford to leave the old neighborhoods, or feel they must because blacks are moving in, they tend to move here to the 11th. The ethnics believe that they would feel less comfortable in the usually WASP-dominated suburbs. Almost all of Chicago's major ethnic groups are well represented in the district, especially Poles, Germans, Italians, Jews, Irish, and Greeks.

For the past seven years or so, the people of the 11th have been caught in something called "the social issue," that not-too-catchy phrase. The people here are by training and inclination Democrats. Their neighborhoods, however, are all white, and they want them to stay that way. They remember with affection and reforms of the New Deal. But because these days they think of themselves first as taxpayers, they do not want their tax money spent on foolish schemes designed to help those too lazy to help themselves.

Such attitudes were reflected in the career of the district's former Congressman, Roman C. Pucinski. They continue to have some bearing on the conduct of its new Congressman, Frank Annunzio, who represented the 7th district for eight years until he was elected here in 1972. In the early 1960s, Pucinski, a member of the House Education and Labor Committee, supported all the social programs of the Kennedy and Johnson Administrations. But as the civil rights revolution ebbed and flowed, and as the urban riots began, the programs over which Pucinski's committee presided, particularly the war on poverty, grew distinctly unpopular in the 11th district.

Sometime in 1966, Pucinski assumed a new role, that of gadfly to antipoverty administrators. The Congressman opposed the community-action programs and voted to hold down their authorizations. At the same time, back in the district, veteran conservative Alderman John J. Hoellen initiated a vigorous campaign to unseat Pucinski. In the 1966 elections, Hoellen got 49% of the vote, as the Republicans captured several of the area's seats in the state legislature. The results must have scared Pucinski and the Daley Organization: no Republican had won a congressional election in a Chicago district since 1946. Hoellen tried again in 1968, but this time Pucinski, who had backed the Mayor and the Chicago police during the Democratic Convention that year, took 56% of the vote.

After an easy victory over an unknown in 1970, Pucinski decided to run against Sen. Charles Percy in 1972. Just why was unclear to many observers. Pucinski had high seniority (fifth) on the Education and Labor Committee, and a subcommittee chairmanship. But there were reports that Pucinski was tired of the grind in the House and wanted either the prestige of the Senate or the relaxed pace of private life (the Congressman's wife owns and manages a Polish radio station and is considered financially comfortable). But there may have been another reason behind the Congressman's decision. The federal-court-ordered redistricting plan that eliminated two Chicago districts sorely hurt the machine. Rep. Abner Mikva of the old 2nd, a liberal reformer, was no problem; he could take care of himself. But the new 7th threw together two incumbents loyal to the machine, Frank Annunzio and George Collins. Even with something close to a black voting majority in the new seat, the Italian Annunzio might have beaten the black Collins. The machine, however, was having troubles with its erstwhile black supporters (see Illinois 1) and could not afford to antagonize them further.

So Annunzio had to move, and with Pucinski stepping aside, he could run in the 11th. There were some problems with positions Annunzio had previously taken. In his old district, which had large black and brown majorities, he had opposed anti-busing legislation; just as soon as he decided to move to the 11th, he unashamedly adopted the opposite view. And then Annunzio started flooding the new district, in which he was still only a candidate and a private citizen, with franked mail. Alderman Hoellen, who was running again, spotted an opening. He went into federal court, where he sought and got an injunction barring Annunzio from sending franked mail into the 11th—the grounds being that such mail could have only political purposes. This was the first time a court ever put limits on the franking privilege, which is theoretically confined to nonpolitical matters but which has obvious political uses. The issue stimulated a number of Congressmen (see Arizona 2) to spell out limitations on the use of the frank—and of courts to interfere with it.

On election day is was once again close-but-no-cigar for Alderman Hoellen. Richard Nixon swept the district, as did Charles Percy against its old Congressman, Pucinski. But Annunzio, taking 53% of the votes, squeaked to victory in his new seat. When Annunzio switched districts, it did not cost him any seniority. In fact, he became Chairman of a House Administration subcommittee. And with the cooperation of Wayne Hays, Chairman of the full committee, he cut the bloated payroll—a move beneficial to the taxpayers but in defiance of hoary House tradition. The outlook for 1974 is a little cloudy. Pucinski, elected a Chicago Alderman in 1973, might like to return to Washington, but it is unthinkable for two machine men to run against each other. Whether the 1974 general election here is close probably depends on whether Hoellen decides to try once more.

Census Data Pop. 461,079. Central city, 100%; suburban, 0%. Median family income, $12,005; families above $15,000: 31%; families below $3,000: 5%. Median years education, 11.5.

1972 Share of Federal Outlays $358,456,710

	DOD	$57,201,221	HEW	$151,741,176
	AEC	$11,685,861	HUD	$5,815,414
	NASA	$397,088	DOI	$1,020,366
	DOT	$10,215,990	USDA	$17,659,711
			Other	$102,719,883

Federal Military-Industrial Commitments

DOD Contractors ASC Systems Corp. (Chicago), $7.227m: aircraft communication units.

Economic Base Finance, insurance and real estate; electrical equipment and supplies, especially telephone and telegraph apparatus; fabricated metal products, especially metal stampings; printing and publishing, especially commercial printing; and machinery, especially metalworking machinery.

The Voters

Registration No party registration; no accurate total registration figures available.
Median voting age 48.7
Employment profile White collar, 53%. Blue collar, 37%. Service, 10%. Farm, –%.
Ethnic groups Spanish, 2%. Total foreign stock, 47%. Poland, 10%; Germany, 7%; Italy, 5%; USSR, 3%; Ireland, Greece, Sweden, Austria, 2% each; UK, Yugoslavia, Czechoslovakia, Hungary, 1% each.

Presidential vote

1972	Nixon (R)	144,169	(63%)
	McGovern (D)	85,928	(37%)
1968	Nixon (R)	112,602	(47%)
	Humphrey (D)	105,630	(44%)
	Wallace (AI)	19,285	(8%)

Representative

Frank Annunzio (D) Elected 1964; b. Jan. 12, 1915, Chicago; home, Chicago; DePaul U., B.S., 1940; married, three children; Catholic.

Career Taught civics and history, Chicago Public Schools, 1940–42; legislative and ed. rep., United Steelworkers of America, 1943–48; Dir. of Labor, Ill., 1948–52; businessman, 1954–64.

Offices 1224 LHOB, 202-225-6661. Also Rm. 1626, U.S. Court House, 219 S. Dearborn St., Chicago 60604, 312-353-4618, and Rm. 201, 4747 W. Peterson Ave., Chicago 60646, 312-736-0700.

Administrative Assistant Anna Azhderian

Committees

Banking and Currency (13th); Subs: Bank Supervision and Insurance; Consumer Affairs; Domestic Finance; Small Business.

House Administration (10th); Subs: Accounts; Personnel (Chm.); Police.

Group Ratings

	ADA	COPE	LWV	RIPON	NFU	LCV	CFA	NAB	NSI	ACA
1972	63	91	73	78	86	33	100	11	50	26
1971	68	100	100	47	71	–	88	–	–	12
1970	60	92	–	59	100	63	94	8	60	14

Key Votes

1) Busing	AGN	6) Cmbodia Bmbg	AGN	11) Chkg Acct Intrst	AGN
2) Strip Mines	ABS	7) Bust Hwy Trust	FOR	12) End HISC (HUAC)	FOR
3) Cut Mil $	AGN	8) Farm Sub Lmt	FOR	13) Nixon Sewer Veto	AGN
4) Rev Shrg	FOR	9) School Prayr	AGN	14) Corp Cmpaign $	FOR
5) Pub TV $	FOR	10) Cnsumr Prot	FOR	15) Pol $ Disclosr	AGN

Election Results

1972 general:	Frank Annunzio (D)	118,637	(53%)
	John J. Hoellen (R)	103,773	(47%)
1972 primary:	Frank Annunzio (D), unopposed		
1970 general:	Frank Annunzio (D)	70,112	(87%)
	Thomas J. Lento (R)	10,235	(13%)

TWELFTH DISTRICT Political Background

Only four congressional districts in the nation more than doubled their population during the 1960s. One of them was the 12th district of Illinois. This is not a particularly neatly shaped district: it includes the six northwest townships of Cook County and, just to the north, the southern portion of Lake County. This territory includes the extremely wealthy North Shore suburbs of Highland Park and Lake Forest, which are, interestingly enough, the richest and least Republican parts of the district. But it is the suburbs farther west, near booming O'Hare Airport, that have been growing most rapidly. One of these places is Arlington Heights, which more than doubled its population, to 62,000, during the single decade of the 1960s.

What sort of people have been moving here with such haste? Politically, they can be summed up in two words: overwhelmingly Republican. They are, more often than not, people in their 30s and 40s who have purchased their first large home in an expensive subdivision and expect to raise families here, outside Chicago. But there are also younger people, with incomes higher than they ever dreamed they'd have, moving into large and luxurious singles apartment complexes. There are fewer old people here, and more children, than in any other Illinois congressional district.

The 12th is more or less a descendant of the old 13th district, which also included all of what is now the 10th. For six years, until the Nixon Administration first assumed power, the old 13th was represented by Donald Rumsfeld. He is a still-young (42 in 1974) Princeton graduate who has since held several top jobs in Washington, including director of OEO and head of the Cost of Living Council. More recently, Rumsfeld has been shunted to Europe as NATO Ambassador, in the Nixon years a kind of convenient dumping ground for men the President or his aides don't know what else to do with. As Illinois Congressman, Rumsfeld had a reputation in his district for being a species of liberal Republican, though his voting record was close to that of an orthodox conservative. He is mentioned here in some detail only because he is considered a possible candidate against Sen. Adlai Stevenson in 1974. It remains to be seen whether the obscurity of his post will hurt or help, because of its obvious remoteness from the Watergate.

Rumsfeld's successor, first elected in a 1969 special election, is Republican Philip Crane. He is a former professor of history at Peoria's Bradley University and an early supporter of presidential candidates Goldwater in 1964 and Reagan in 1968. Crane is a conservative intellectual, a type that has become an increasingly familar figure in American politics. (Two other examples include Sen. John Tower of Texas and former USIA advisor William F. Buckley, Jr.) Crane's conservatism is so principled that he sometimes casts lone dissenting votes against big-spending measures sure to go through.

Crane's militant conservatism weakened him in the old 13th district, particularly in the North Shore suburbs of Evanston, Winnetka, Wilmette, and Glencoe, all now in the 10th district. Here the extremely wealthy elite of Chicago flirted with liberal politics and voted for Crane's Democratic opponents, as did the predominantly Jewish suburb of Skokie. But none of that territory need concern Crane any longer, for with redistricting, the Congressman won his first really solid majority in 1972: 74%. There is no real reason to suppose that a margin like this will be unusual in the years ahead.

Census Data Pop. 461,054. Central city, 0%; suburban, 100%. Median family income, $15,173; families above $15,000: 51%; families below $3,000: 2%. Median years education, 12.7.

1972 Share of Federal Outlays $358,456,710

DOD	$57,201,221	HEW	$151,741,176
AEC	$11,685,861	HUD	$5,815,414
NASA	$397,088	DOI	$1,020,366
DOT	$10,215,990	USDA	$17,659,711
		Other	$102,719,883

Federal Military-Industrial Commitments

DOD Contractors United Airlines (Chicago), $17.045m: transportation services. E. Walters and Co. (Elk Grove Village), $12.483m: detonating fuzes. Bourns, Inc. (Barrington), $5.572m: airborne camera units.
DOD Installations Fort Sheridan AB (Highwood).

Economic Base Finance, insurance and real estate; electrical equipment and supplies, especially telephone and telegraph apparatus; machinery; chemicals and allied products; printing and publishing, especially commercial printing; and fabricated metal products, especially metal stampings.

The Voters

Registration No party registration; no accurate total registration figures available.
Median voting age 39.1
Employment profile White collar, 67%. Blue collar, 25%. Service, 8%. Farm, –%.
Ethnic groups Spanish, 2%. Total foreign stock, 20%. Germany, 4%; Italy, Poland, 2% each; Canada, UK, Sweden, USSR, 1% each.

Presidential vote

1972	Nixon (R)	136,343	(71%)
	McGovern (D)	56,896	(29%)
1968	Nixon (R)	104,981	(64%)
	Humphrey (D)	48,572	(30%)
	Wallace (AI)	8,142	(5%)

Representative

Philip M. Crane (R) Elected Dec. 1969; b. Nov. 3, 1930, Chicago; home, Mt. Prospect; Ind. U., M.A., Ph.D., U. of Mich., U. of Vienna, Hillsdale Col., DePauw U.; Army, 1954–56; married, eight children; unspecified Protestant.

Career Teaching, Indiana U., Asst. Prof. of history, Bradley U.; author, *Democrat's Dilemma,* 1964; employed by Repub. party as public relations expert, 1964; Dir. of Research, Ill. Goldwater Organ., Advisor to Richard Nixon, 1964–68.

Offices 1407 LHOB, 202-225-3711. Also Suite 101, 1450 S. New Withe Rd., Arlington Heights, Ill. 60005, 312-394-0790.

Administrative Assistant Edwin J. Feulner, Jr.

Committees

Banking and Currency (9th); Subs: Bank Supervision and Insurance; Domestic Finance; International Finance; Urban Mass Transportation (Ranking Mbr.).

House Administration (6th); Subs: Accounts; Electrical and Mechanical Equipment; Personnel (Ranking Mbr.).

Group Ratings

	ADA	COPE	LWV	RIPON	NFU	LCV	CFA	NAB	NSI	ACA
1972	0	18	20	38	14	5	0	100	100	100
1971	14	0	0	50	13	–	13	–	–	96
1970	8	0	–	36	15	100	50	100	100	100

Key Votes

1) Busing	AGN	6) Cmbodia Bmbg	ABS	11) Chkg Acct Intrst	AGN
2) Strip Mines	ABS	7) Bust Hwy Trust	AGN	12) End HISC (HUAC)	AGN
3) Cut Mil $	AGN	8) Farm Sub Lmt	FOR	13) Nixon Sewer Veto	FOR
4) Rev Shrg	AGN	9) School Prayr	ABS	14) Corp Cmpaign $	AGN
5) Pub TV $	AGN	10) Cnsumr Prot	AGN	15) Pol $ Disclosr	AGN

Election Results

1972 general:	Philip M. Crane (R)	152,938	(74%)
	E. L. Frank (D)	53,055	(26%)
1972 primary:	Philip M. Crane (R), unopposed		
1970 general:	Philip M. Crane (R)	124,649	(58%)
	Edward A. Warman (D)	90,364	(42%)

THIRTEENTH DISTRICT Political Background

The 13th district of Illinois is a part of the Chicago metropolitan area far beyond the power of Mayor Daley's machine, but well within the reach of the Chicago *Tribune*. The district forms a kind of cordon around the northern and western portions of the metropolitan area, as it stretches from the industrial town of Waukegan on Lake Michigan to a point below the German-Catholic town of Aurora. This area, not quite as prosperous as the suburbs closer to Chicago, contains pockets of poverty, as well as some working-class neighborhoods and towns. The suburban building boom invaded the district's cornfields with real force in the late 1960s, but the growth here has not yet been as explosive as in the neighboring 12th.

In 1964, the 13th (then numbered the 12th) was part of a group of Chicago suburbs and exurbs that went for Barry Goldwater. These places extend all the way around the city at a radius of 20 to

60 miles from the Loop, and constitute what might be called the Chicago *Tribune* belt. It is a measure of the conservatism of the Chicago suburbs that none of the other metropolises of the Great Lakes having similar belts—Detroit, Milwaukee, Cleveland, and Buffalo—plunked for Goldwater; these other suburban belts, along with their respective central cities, all went for Johnson.

Robert McClory, a moderately conservative Illinois Republican, has been the 13th's Congressman for more than 10 years. and barring retirement in 1974 when he will be 66, McClory will continue to serve for some time. He is currently the second-ranking Republican on the House Judiciary Committee, but by odd circumstance does not have the status and perquisites of ranking minority member on any of its subcommittees. The problem may be a conflict with Judiciary's ranking Republican, Edward Hutchinson of Michigan. Congressman Hutchinson is an undynamic conservative who has, inter alia, opposed all civil rights legislation. McClory supported such laws, generally taking more moderate positions on the issues. In the event Hutchinson loses a Michigan primary (he turned aside a serious challenge in 1970), McClory will become ranking minority member, with all the increase in status and leverage a position of the sort entails.

Census Data Pop. 463,096. Central city, 0%; suburban, 100%. Median family income, $11,994; families above $15,000: 31%; families below $3,000: 5%. Median years education, 12.2.

1972 Share of Federal Outlays $360,083,594

DOD	$57,460,833	HEW	$152,429,865
AEC	$11,738,899	HUD	$5,841,808
NASA	$398,891	DOI	$1,024,997
DOT	$10,262,357	USDA	$17,739,861
		Other	$103,186,083

Federal Military-Industrial Commitments

DOD Contractors Corbetta Construction (Great Lakes), $5.696m: construction services.
DOD Installations Navy Electronics Supply Office (Great Lakes); closed, 1974. Naval Hospital (Great Lakes). Naval Training Center (Great Lakes). Naval Public Works Center (Great Lakes). Naval Recruit Training Command (Great Lakes).

Economic Base Machinery; electrical equipment and supplies; finance, insurance and real estate; chemicals and allied products, especially drugs; fabricated metal products; and agriculture, notably grains, cattle and dairy products.

The Voters

Registration No party registration; no accurate total registration figures available.
Median voting age 39.6
Employment profile White collar, 47%. Blue collar, 40%. Service, 12%. Farm, 1%.
Ethnic groups Black, 5%. Spanish, 3%. Total foreign stock, 18%. Germany, 4%; Poland, UK, Sweden, Canada, 1% each.

Presidential vote

1972	Nixon (R)	112,900	(70%)
	McGovern (D)	49,217	(30%)
1968	Nixon (R)	88,969	(61%)
	Humphrey (D)	46,166	(31%)
	Wallace (AI)	11,895	(8%)

Representative

Robert McClory (R) Elected 1962; b. Jan. 31, 1908, Riverside; home, Lake Bluff; Dartmouth Col., 1926–28; Chicago-Kent Col. of Law, LL.B., 1932; USMCR, 1933–37; widowed, remarried, three children; Protestant.

Career Practicing atty., 1932–62; Ill. House of Reps., 1951–53; Ill. Senate, 1953–62.

Offices 2452 RHOB, 202-225-5221. Also 326 N. Genesee St., Waukegan 60085, 312-336-4554.

Administrative Assistant Robert Davenport

Committees

Judiciary (2nd); Subs: No. 4 (Bankruptcy and Civil Rights Oversight); No. 5 (Antitrust Matters).

Group Ratings

	ADA	COPE	LWV	RIPON	NFU	LCV	CFA	NAB	NSI	ACA
1972	38	18	73	69	43	25	0	73	78	45
1971	38	27	78	56	21	–	50	–	–	67
1970	24	50	–	71	69	52	47	58	100	58

Key Votes

1) Busing	FOR	6) Cmbodia Bmbg	ABS	11) Chkg Acct Intrst	FOR
2) Strip Mines	AGN	7) Bust Hwy Trust	FOR	12) End HISC (HUAC)	AGN
3) Cut Mil $	FOR	8) Farm Sub Lmt	AGN	13) Nixon Sewer Veto	FOR
4) Rev Shrg	FOR	9) School Prayr	FOR	14) Corp Cmpaign $	FOR
5) Pub TV $	AGN	10) Cnsumr Prot	FOR	15) Pol $ Disclosr	ABS

Election Results

1972 general:	Robert McClory (R)	98,201	(61%)
	Stanley W. Beetham (D)	61,537	(39%)
1972 primary:	Robert McClory (R), unopposed		
1970 general:	Robert McClory (R)	84,356	(62%)
	James J. Cone (D)	51,499	(38%)

FOURTEENTH DISTRICT Political Background

If one uses median family income as a standard, three of the nation's five richest congressional districts lie in the suburbs of Chicago, Illinois. The 14th is one of them. And of all of these five richest districts, the 14th is the most politically conservative. The district includes almost all of DuPage County, a wealthy, fast-growing area just west of Chicago's Cook County. DuPage is so conservative, in fact, that it regularly produces larger percentages for Republican candidates than Orange County, California.

Long before its current boom, DuPage County contained the palatial estate of Col. Robert R. McCormick, longtime publisher of the Chicago *Tribune*. The *Tribune* today is not what it once was: its news columns are now objective and thorough and its editorial pages include liberal columnists as well as the paper's favorite conservative ones. But for nearly 50 years, the *Tribune* was the militant, biased voice of Midwestern isolationism and conservative Republicanism. The paper's vitriolic loathing of Democrats, including the machine minions who controlled Chicago, must have influenced the thinking of hundreds of thousands of Chicago suburbanites. The fact that the Chicago suburbs, together with those of Los Angeles, are the most conservative in the country must be ascribed not simply to their wealth, but also to the pervasive, still lingering influence of the old *Tribune*.

The *Tribune's* impact on DuPage County is certainly perceptible. In 1964, for example, it gave 60% of its votes to the paper's candidate, Barry Goldwater, and in 1972, 75% for Richard Nixon. It is no wonder that the Chicago suburbs—including suburban Cook, Lake, McHenry, Kane, Will, and DuPage counties—are now the heartland of Illinois Republican vote. This suburban territory has supplanted the relatively marginal downstate area as the place where Republicans run best.

The 14th's Congressman is John Erlenborn, a conservative who usually fits in well with the rest of the state's Republican delegation. Erlenborn is one of the leading conservatives on the liberal-dominated Education and Labor Committee, and also serves as second-ranking Republican on Government Operations. It is on the latter committee that Erlenborn has taken his most interesting positions; which is to say, those that we would not ordinarily expect from a man of his background. He has sponsored bills to limit executive privilege and proposed amendments to strengthen the Freedom of Information Act (see California 3), legislation that on paper gives citizens access to most government documents. Erlenborn appears fast emerging as a leader of young conservative Republicans, having some ideas that go beyond the accepted orthodox conservative agenda.

Census Data Pop. 464,029. Central city, 0%; suburban, 100%. Median family income, $14,527; families above $15,000: 47%; families below $3,000: 2%. Median years education, 12.6.

1972 Share of Federal Outlays $360,625,889

DOD	$57,547,371	HEW	$152,659,428
AEC	$11,756,578	HUD	$5,850,606
NASA	$399,491	DOI	$1,026,540
DOT	$10,277,812	USDA	$17,766,578
		Other	$103,341,485

Federal Military-Industrial Commitments

AEC Operations University Research Association, Inc. (Batavia), $68.963m: construction and operation and research studies on the 200 BEV accelerator. University of Chicago (Argonne), $38.618m: operation of the Argonne National Laboratory.

Economic Base Finance, insurance and real estate; electrical equipment and supplies, especially electronic components and accessories; fabricated metal products, especially fabricated structural metal products; machinery, especially metalworking machinery and general industrial machinery; and printing and publishing, especially commercial printing.

The Voters

Registration No party registration; no accurate total registration available.
Median voting age 40.8
Employment profile White collar, 65%. Blue collar, 27%. Service, 8%. Farm, –%.
Ethnic groups Spanish, 2%. Total foreign stock, 21%. Germany, 4%; Italy, Poland, UK, 2% each; Czechoslovakia, Canada, Sweden, 1% each.

Presidential vote

1972	Nixon (R)	163,652	(75%)
	McGovern (D)	53,631	(25%)
1968	Nixon (R)	118,955	(66%)
	Humphrey (D)	45,922	(26%)
	Wallace (AI)	13,082	(7%)

Representative

John N. Erlenborn (R) Elected 1964; b. Feb. 8, 1927, Chicago; home, Glen Ellyn; U. of Notre Dame, 1944; Indiana State Teachers Col., 1944–45; U. of Ill., 1945–46; Loyola U., LL.B., 1949; Navy, WWII; USNR; married, three children; Catholic.

Career Practicing atty., 1949–64. Asst. State's Atty., 1950–52; Ill. House of Reps., 1956–64.

Offices 2430 RHOB, 202-225-3515. Also 108 N. Main St., Wheaton 60187, 312-668-1417.

Administrative Assistant Finley McGrew

Committees

Education and Labor (4th); Subs: No. 3 (Labor) (Ranking Mbr.); No. 6 (Education).

Government Operations (2nd); Subs: Foreign Operations and Government Information (Ranking Mbr.); Legislation and Military Operations.

Group Ratings

	ADA	COPE	LWV	RIPON	NFU	LCV	CFA	NAB	NSI	ACA
1972	19	25	73	82	17	47	100	100	100	67
1971	22	9	56	62	14	–	38	–	–	88
1970	24	10	–	71	55	13	28	100	90	69

Key Votes

1) Busing	FOR	6) Cmbodia Bmbg	FOR	11) Chkg Acct Intrst	AGN
2) Strip Mines	AGN	7) Bust Hwy Trust	FOR	12) End HISC (HUAC)	AGN
3) Cut Mil $	AGN	8) Farm Sub Lmt	ABS	13) Nixon Sewer Veto	FOR
4) Rev Shrg	FOR	9) School Prayr	ABS	14) Corp Cmpaign $	FOR
5) Pub TV $	AGN	10) Cnsumr Prot	AGN	15) Pol $ Disclosr	FOR

Election Results

1972 general:	John N. Erlenborn (R)	154,794	(73%)
	James M. Wall (D)	57,874	(27%)
1972 primary:	John N. Erlenborn (R), unopposed		
1970 general:	John N. Erlenborn (R)	122,115	(66%)
	William J. Adelman (D)	64,231	(34%)

FIFTEENTH DISTRICT Political Background

Leslie C. Arends of Illinois has been a member of Congress longer than any other Republican now serving. It is nigh on to 40 years since he was first elected, in 1934, when he unseated a Democrat swept into office two years earlier on Franklin D. Roosevelt's coattails. And it has been more than 30 years since Arends first became Republican Whip. Arends has held that position continuously since 1943, which must be some kind of record. He has never moved up to a higher leadership post; but then he has never been seriously challenged as Whip, though he has seen two Republican Minority Leaders ousted in his time. Now close to 80, Arends can still be seen on the floor of the House almost every day, his long white mane of hair turned up in a slight curl at the back.

But the Whip post has not been Arend's only source of power. Until he stepped aside for Indiana's William Bray in 1973, Arends for many years was the ranking minority member of the Armed Services Committee. In that capacity, he served as a stalwart of Armed Services' pro-military majority.

Coming from one of the most Republican areas of downstate Illinois, Arends has seldom had to worry about reelection during his 40-year career. But 1972 was an exception of sorts. The redistricting plan adopted by the federal court eliminated two Democratic seats in Chicago and then put Arends' home county into an almost entirely unfamiliar, new 15th district. The court plan passed the Illinois House, but not its Senate, with most of Arends' old territory placed in a district apparently intended for the House Speaker, W. Robert Blair. In any case, the new lines put Arends into a potential conflict with another Republican incumbent, Charlotte T. Reid, former vocalist with Don McNeil's Breakfast Club. But the conflict was averted because Congresswoman Reid was about to take (and soon did take) a seat on the Federal Communications Commission. In the spring of 1972, there was an election to fill the vacancy left by Reid, but the winner, Republican Cliffard Carlson, announced he would not run against the veteran Arends, though he might run again if and when Arends retires.

The narrowness of Carlson's margin and of Arends' own victory must have come as a shock to the longtime Congressman. Arends had become accustomed to some of the most Republican territory in the country—the fertile Illinois farmlands that are enclosed, roughly speaking, by a line drawn around the cities of Bloomington, Danville, and Kankakee. The Congressman's new district stretched northward, toward exurban Chicago. Here it takes in the German Catholic city of Aurora and DeKalb County, which is normally Republican, but which contains the large and Democratic campus of Northern Illinois University. In the primary, a local mayor from up north held Arends down to 54% in the new part of the district. In the general election, Arends did scarcely better, winning just 56% of the vote in the new counties against an active Democratic opponent. For the new territory of the district, the two percentages are far from the normal percentages given to Republican candidates. Arends maintained something like his usual district-wide percentage in both the primary and general elections only by taking large majorities in the two counties he retained from his old district.

Most veteran Congressmen would take such showings—or would have taken such drastic redistricting—as a clear signal to retire. Arends, however, apparently still loves the clash of political battle on the House floor and wants to miss none of it. The legislator's main campaign assets are his Whip post, his geniality, and his great vigor. And unlike most Congressmen, Arends holds sending out huge batches of franked mail beneath his dignity.

Census Data Pop. 462,969. Central city, 0%; suburban, 33%. Median family income, $10,619; families above $15,000: 22%; families below $3,000: 6%. Median years education, 12.2.

1972 Share of Federal Outlays $326,808,177

DOD	$40,704,663	HEW	$138,462,306
AEC	$3,129,194	HUD	$1,557,229
NASA	$109,328	DOI	$310,037
DOT	$12,245,073	USDA	$57,285,001
		Other	$73,005,346

Federal Military-Industrial Commitments

DOD Contractors General Time Corp. (Peru), $13.193m: bomb and rocket fuzes.

Economic Base Agriculture, notably grains, cattle, and hogs and sheep; electrical equipment and supplies, machinery, especially construction and related machinery; finance, insurance and real estate; and fabricated metal products. Also higher education (Northern Illinois Univ.).

The Voters

Registration No party registration; no accurate total registration figures available.
Median voting age 42.5
Employment profile White collar, 41%. Blue collar, 42%. Service, 12%. Farm, 5%.
Ethnic groups Black, 2%, Spanish, 2%. Total foreign stock, 14%. Germany, 3%; Italy, UK, Sweden, 1% each.

Presidential vote

1972	Nixon (R)	133,061	(66%)
	McGovern (D)	68,288	(34%)

1968	Nixon (R)	110,036	(59%)
	Humphrey (D)	64,529	(35%)
	Wallace (AI)	11,832	(6%)

Representative

Leslie C. Arends (R) Elected 1934; b. Sept. 27, 1895, Melvin; home, Melvin; Oberlin Col., Ill. Wesleyan U., LL.D.; Navy, WWI; married, one child; Methodist.

Career Farming and banking, 1920– ; Minority Whip, 1943–47, 1949–53, 1955– ; Majority Whip, 1947–49, 1953–55; U.S. Delegate to NATO Parliamentarians' Conference (North Atlantic Assembly), 1961–71; Trustee, Ill. Wesleyan U.

Offices 2306 RHOB, 202-225-2976.

Administrative Assistant Joseph H. Macaulay

Committees

Armed Services (2nd); Subs: Armed Services Investigating (Ranking Mbr.); Intelligence.

Group Ratings

	ADA	COPE	LWV	RIPON	NFU	LCV	CFA	NAB	NSI	ACA
1972	6	18	36	57	33	0	0	92	100	70
1971	3	18	44	50	38	–	38	–	–	85
1970	20	9	–	59	54	0	45	100	100	68

Key Votes

1) Busing	AGN	6) Cmbodia Bmbg	FOR	11) Chkg Acct Intrst	AGN
2) Strip Mines	FOR	7) Bust Hwy Trust	AGN	12) End HISC (HUAC)	AGN
3) Cut Mil $	AGN	8) Farm Sub Lmt	AGN	13) Nixon Sewer Veto	FOR
4) Rev Shrg	FOR	9) School Prayr	FOR	14) Corp Cmpaign $	FOR
5) Pub TV $	AGN	10) Cnsumr Prot	FOR	15) Pol $ Disclosr	ABS

Election Results

1972 general:	Leslie C. Arends (R)	111,022	(57%)
	Tim L. Hall (D)	82,925	(43%)
1972 primary:	Leslie C. Arends (R)	27,012	(59%)
	John A. Cunningham (R)	19,107	(41%)
1970 general:	Leslie C. Arends (R)	92,917	(62%)
	Lester A. Hawthorne (D)	56,340	(38%)

SIXTEENTH DISTRICT Political Background

The northwest corner of Illinois is a little different, politically, from the rest of the state. A little like Wisconsin or Iowa, this part of Illinois has larger numbers of Scandinavian-Americans and a stronger good-government tradition. The tradition, of course, contrasts with the patronage-ridden politics of both Chicago and most of downstate Illinois. The largest city here is Rockford, which is actually the state's second largest; but the metropolitan population here is only 272,000. The rest of the 16th is primarily agricultural. Points of interest include Freeport, site of the most famous Lincoln-Douglas debate; and the home of President Ulysses S. Grant—Galena—once a thriving commercial center and mining town, but now a Mississippi River backwater.

John B. Anderson has been the 16th's Congressman since the 1960 election. He began his House career in a fashion more or less indistinguishable from other Illinois conservative Republicans. But as time went on, Anderson strayed occasionally from orthodoxy. At the same time, his parliamentary talents won him a seat on the House Rules Committee and in 1969 the position of Chairman of the House Republican Conference.

Anderson's apostasy, however, angered a number of more conservative Republicans. Samuel Devine of Ohio, chairman of a group called the Regular Republicans, challenged Anderson for the Conference chairmanship (once held by Melvin Laird) at the beginning of the 92nd Congress in 1971. The vote was close. Anderson won by a thin 89–81 margin—a reflection of the deep conservatism of most House Republicans. Two years later, though, there was no further challenge; even Republicans in the House were irritated by the high-handed tactics of the Nixon Administration.

Anderson has probably been foremost among the irritated. When then Atty. Gen. Richard Kleindienst expounded a very broad view of executive privilege before a Senate committee in the spring of 1972, just before the Watergate broke, Anderson insisted on taking the witness stand in response almost immediately, saying that Kleindienst's statement "borders on contempt for the established law of the land." The Congressman has also led a group of Midwestern Congressmen opposing construction of the Alaskan pipeline. These men argue that the pipeline should be built through Canada to terminate in the oil-hungry Midwest. Farmers in Illinois have complained about not enough tractor fuel.

Anderson also opposed the bombing in Cambodia, though on all but one occasion he had previously voted against end-the-war legislation. Even when he has backed Administration measures, he has chosen those with lukewarm and nominal White House support; namely, the family assistance plan and the move to allow local governments to tap the highway trust fund.

By 1973, Anderson had emerged as an important Congressman, not just because of his leadership post, but also because of the strength with which he articulated his obviously sincere and—for an Illinois Republican—unorthodox views. At this writing, Anderson is considering a bid for the Senate in 1974. The main problem is the sitting Senator: Adlai Stevenson III. Though the incumbent is not an especially inspirational campaigner, he is the bearer of one of Illinois' proudest names and a solid 58% winner last time. Another problem is the Republican primary. State Attorney General William Scott, far more conservative than Anderson, is also eyeing the 1974 race. And the body of registered Republicans in Illinois leans heavily toward the conservative side. A 1972 court decision struck down Illinois' closed primary, which could benefit Anderson; but the legislature still has time to remedy the situation.

So a Senate race would be anything but easy for Anderson, though everyone concedes that he would be an attractive candidate. He can choose, of course, to remain in the House, to which the 16th district will reelect him indefinitely. But here he is unlikely to advance in the leadership beyond his present station. And his role will continue to be, as it is now, an articulate Republican who sometimes disagrees with important members of his own party. Partially because of his role, the Congressman is one of the few in the House who has little trouble getting on "Face the Nation." But that, if he wants bigger and better things in Illinois politics, is not enough.

Census Data   Pop. 461,719. Central city, 32%; suburban, 36%. Median family income, $10,668; families above $15,000: 21%; families below $3,000: 7%. Median years education, 12.1.

1972 Share of Federal Outlays $286,116,144

DOD	$49,486,228	HEW	$131,530,562
AEC	$1,096,102	HUD	$545,470
NASA	$175,529	DOI	$1,196,366
DOT	$6,232,195	USDA	$30,877,422
		Other	$64,976,270

Federal Military-Industrial Commitments

DOD Contractors   Sundstrand Corp. (Rockford), $24.151m: aircraft components and accessories.

Economic Base   Machinery, especially metalworking machinery; fabricated metal products, especially screw machine products, bolts, nuts, rivets and washers; agriculture, notably grains, cattle, dairy products, and hogs and sheep; electrical equipment and supplies; and finance, insurance and real estate.

The Voters

Registration No party registration; no accurate total registration figures available.
Median voting age 43.1
Employment profile White collar, 41%. Blue collar, 43%. Service, 11%. Farm, 5%.
Ethnic groups Black, 4%. Spanish, 1%. Total foreign stock, 14%. Germany, Sweden, 3% each;
Italy, 2%; UK, 1%.

Presidential vote

1972	Nixon (R)	120,432	(66%)
	McGovern (D)	62,339	(34%)
1968	Nixon (R)	102,066	(57%)
	Humphrey (D)	62,663	(36%)
	Wallace (AI)	11,524	(7%)

Representative

John B. Anderson (R) Elected 1960; b. Feb. 15, 1922, Rockford; home, Rockford; U. of Ill., B.A., J.D.; Harvard Law School, LL.M.; Army, WWII; married, five children; First Evangelical Free Church.

Career Practicing atty., 1946–60; U.S. State Dept.'s Diplomatic Svc., 1952; Advisor, U.S. High Commissioner for Germany, 1952–55; State's Atty., Winnebago County, 1956–60.

Offices 1101 LHOB, 202-225-5676. Also Rock River Savings Bldg., 401 State St., Rockford 61101, 815-962-8807.

Administrative Assistant Donald R. Wolfensberger (L.A.)

Committees

Rules (2nd).

Joint Com. on Atomic Energy (2nd); Subs: Agreements for Cooperation (Ranking House Mbr.); Legislation; Military Applications; Licensing and Regulation (Ranking House Mbr.).

Group Ratings

	ADA	COPE	LWV	RIPON	NFU	LCV	CFA	NAB	NSI	ACA
1972	44	36	91	100	50	6	0	89	89	43
1971	32	36	78	71	14	–	57	–	–	63
1970	28	34	–	75	62	15	55	91	80	67

Key Votes

1) Busing	FOR	6) Cmbodia Bmbg	AGN	11) Chkg Acct Intrst	AGN
2) Strip Mines	AGN	7) Bust Hwy Trust	FOR	12) End HISC (HUAC)	AGN
3) Cut Mil $	AGN	8) Farm Sub Lmt	FOR	13) Nixon Sewer Veto	FOR
4) Rev Shrg	FOR	9) School Prayr	AGN	14) Corp Cmpaign $	AGN
5) Pub TV $	AGN	10) Cnsumr Prot	FOR	15) Pol $ Disclosr	FOR

Election Results

1972 general:	John B. Anderson (R)	129,640	(72%)
	John E. Devine, Jr. (D)	50,649	(28%)
1972 primary:	John B. Anderson (R), unopposed		
1970 general:	John B. Anderson (R)	83,296	(67%)
	John E. Devine, Jr. (D)	41,459	(33%)

SEVENTEENTH DISTRICT Political Background

The 17th is one of Illinois' new congressional districts, created by a redistricting order issued out of a federal court in 1971. For the 1972 election, it had no incumbent. As drawn, the 17th combines the southern edge of the Chicago metropolitan area with the fertile Illinois farmland and the small city of Kankakee immediately to the south. The district's largest city is Joliet (pop. 78,000), an economically healthy and growing manufacturing center 50 miles from Chicago. It also includes the suburbs of Chicago Heights and Park Forest, the latter a sort of planned town dating from the 1950s.

Taken together, this territory can be considered politically marginal, normally running about 5% more Republican than the state as a whole. The biggest Republican margins here often come out of the district's smallest county, Iroquois, an almost entirely agricultural area that previously lay in Les Arends' bailiwick (see Illinois 15).

When the redistricting plan passed the Illinois House and was then approved by the court, the boundaries of the new 17th were believed to have been especially sculpted for incumbent Illinois House Speaker, W. Robert Blair. Considerable criticism ensued, and Blair never ran. Instead, the Republican nomination went to Joliet state Rep. George M. O'Brien, a veteran of local government. O'Brien's 56-44 victory in the general election over Democrat John J. Houlihan followed, in rough form, the established party preferences in the district. O'Brien got his biggest percentage margins in Kankakee and Iroquois counties, and received smaller advantages in Will County (Joliet) and the Cook County suburbs.

In the old days, a relatively close margin in a House election with no incumbent meant another close race in two years. These days it does not. Once a candidate becomes an incumbent, he has access to the frank (the congressional free mailing privilege) and can literally flood his newly acquired constituency with helpful mail; he can concentrate on servicing the inevitable tussles his constituency will have with the federal bureaucracy; and he can appear at weddings and high school commencements as the genial, smiling Congressman and local VIP.

Some have suggested that the Watergate and the pall that it cast over any and all politicians will alter the advantages held by incumbents, that the public will be in a mood to throw the bums out. Don't count on it. Polls that show the public disenchanted with Congress and Congressmen generally—and they have been coming out for years—do not show that interviewees are upset with their own Congressman. In local polls, some incumbents come out better than Walter Cronkite, whom pollsters say is the most trusted man in the country. Having said this, it must be concluded that George M. O'Brien will be the solid favorite to win reelection as the 17th's Congressman in 1974.

Census Data Pop. 462,943. Central city, 0%; suburban, 72%. Median family income, $11,286; families above $15,000: 26%; families below $3,000: 6%. Median years education, 12.0.

1972 Share of Federal Outlays $356,931,462

DOD	$49,109,802	HEW	$156,387,936
AEC	$8,415,234	HUD	$4,187,802
NASA	$285,952	DOI	$1,393,737
DOT	$7,607,195	USDA	$38,840,809
		Other	$90,702,995

Federal Military-Industrial Commitments

DOD Contractors Uniroyal (Joliet), $69.482m: operation and maintenance of the Army ammunition plant. General Energy Systems Corp. (Joliet), $25.777m: unspecified. Chemical Construction Corp. (Joliet), $7.040m: unspecified. Gould, Inc. (Kankakee), $5.772m: submarine batteries.

Economic Base Agriculture, notably grains, cattle, hogs and sheep, and poultry; finance, insurance and real estate; electrical equipment and supplies; chemicals and allied products; and food and kindred products, especially grain mill products.

The Voters

Registration No party registration; no accurate total registration figures available.
Median voting age 41.7
Employment profile White collar, 42%. Blue collar, 43%. Service, 12%. Farm, 3%.

Ethnic groups Black, 9%. Spanish, 3%. Total foreign stock, 16%. Germany, Italy, 2% each; Poland, 1%.

Presidential vote

1972	Nixon (R)	122,873	(66%)
	McGovern (D)	62,394	(34%)
1968	Nixon (R)	89,060	(52%)
	Humphrey (D)	61,674	(36%)
	Wallace (AI)	20,349	(12%)

Representative

George M. O'Brien (R) Elected 1972; b. June 17, 1917, Chicago; Northwestern U., A.B., 1939; Yale Law School, J.D., 1947; married, two children; Catholic.

Career Illinois State Rep., 1970; Will County Bd. of Supervisors, 1956–64; Law Firm, Sr. partner, O'Brien, Garrison, Berard & Kusta.

Offices 422 CHOB, 202-225-3635. Also 57 N. Ottawa St., Joliet 60431, 815-727-4718.

Administrative Assistant Mr. Marion Burson

Committees

Armed Services (15th); Subs: No. 5; Sp. Sub. on Human Relations.

Group Ratings: Newly Elected

Key Votes

1) Busing	NE	6) Cmbodia Bmbg	FOR	11) Chkg Acct Intrst	ABS
2) Strip Mines	NE	7) Bust Hwy Trust	FOR	12) End HISC (HUAC)	AGN
3) Cut Mil $	NE	8) Farm Sub Lmt	NE	13) Nixon Sewer Veto	FOR
4) Rev Shrg	NE	9) School Prayr	NE	14) Corp Cmpaign $	NE
5) Pub TV $	NE	10) Cnsumr Prot	NE	15) Pol $ Disclosr	NE

Election Results

1972 general:	George M. O'Brien (R)	100,175	(56%)
	John J. Houlihan (D)	79,840	(44%)
1972 primary:	George M. O'Brien (R), unopposed		

EIGHTEENTH DISTRICT Political Background

In the pre-Watergate Nixon Administration, chief domestic advisor John Ehrlichman handled the complaints of Washington liberals by asking a single rhetorical question: How will it play in Peoria? This city (pop. 127,000) constitutes the heart of Illinois' 18th congressional district. Peoria, for a set of reasons buried in American lore, has long epitomized Middle America—both its virtue and vanity. The Caterpillar tractor concern and other heavy industrial employers have kept the town humming; its residents therefore are fairly prosperous and insulated against all but the most serious recessions. This part of the Midwest was the girlhood home of Betty Friedan, one of the nation's most remarkable citizens. Just down the Illinois River is Pekin, home town of the late Sen. Everett McKinley Dirksen, another remarkable citizen and surely a spokesman for Middle America. Dirksen's sonorous voice and his high-minded patriotism produced the hit record, "Gallant Men." But he obviously had other talents, for his Pekin law office somehow obtained large retainers from some of the nation's largest corporations.

If everybody knows that the morality of Middle America is often suspect, the Nixon strategists appear to understand the purely political habits of Peoria a little less thoroughly than they sometimes think. To be sure, Nixon carried Peoria and the 18th district by overwhelming margins in 1972; he also had a solid win here in 1968. But in 1970, the law-and-order campaign of Sen.

Ralph Tyler Smith, the interim appointee to Dirksen's seat, bombed in Peoria. Sen. Adlai Stevenson III, though attacked as a radical liberal, carried the city and the entire district.

The 18th district has produced a steadier record of support for its Republican Congressman, Robert Michel, first elected in 1956. His electoral margins have not shown the ups and downs of the Republican state ticket, moving from 54% in 1964 to a comfortable 65% in 1972. Michel's familiarity in and with his constituency is substantial. A native of Peoria, he served as administrative assistent to his predecessor, Rep. (1949–57) Harold H. Velde, who was famed mostly for his work on the old House Un-American Activities Committee. Before that, the seat was held for 14 years by Dirksen himself, who retired in 1948 when he thought he was going blind. He recovered, ran for the Senate in 1950, and beat then Senate Majority Leader Scott Lucas.

Michel is now the fourth ranking Republican on the House Appropriations Committee, and ranking minority member on the Labor-HEW subcommittee. With such status, he obviously has a lot to say about the social programs the Nixon budget seeks to cut back. Judging from the Congressman's record, he is in basic sympathy with the Administration's aims, if not with some of its methods. But Michel's most important role in the 93rd Congress is probably that of Chairman of the Republican Congressional Campaign Committee. The post was held for 12 years by Bob Wilson of California, who was unceremoniously dumped by White House aides in early 1973. The aides' choice to succeed Wilson was Clarence J. (Bud) Brown of Ohio. But—and this happened before the full Watergate story broke—the approval of Haldeman and Ehrlichman was the kiss of death in the House Republican Caucus. Michel mounted his own candidacy, and won by a margin so large that it was left unannounced lest it embarrass Congressman Brown.

As Chairman of the Campaign Committee, Michel's major responsibility is the election of a Republican Congress in 1974. Before the Watergate, Republican strategists were optimistic. They believed that the Nixon campaign managers had simply failed—or refused—to extend the popularity of Nixon's programs to Republican congressional candidates. If that popularity were properly extended, so the reasoning went, the Republicans in 1974 could win the 26 seats needed to control the House. But after the worst of the Watergate scandal came to light, it became clear that the Nixon imprimatur would hardly help anybody, and that, if anything, the Republican label itself might hurt, all other things being equal. In the coming mid-term elections, the Republicans can look to make some gains, especially in the South, by running young, vigorous candidates against aged Democratic incumbents. The Democrats, however, can play the same game against aged Republicans. The last time the Republicans won control of the House was in 1952. Chances are that Michel will not preside over a Republican victory in House during the 1974 elections.

Census Data Pop. 463,155. Central city, 27%; suburban, 40%. Median family income, $10,096; families above $15,000: 20%; families below $3,000: 7%. Median years education, 12.1.

1972 Share of Federal Outlays $361,628,026

DOD	$52,175,191	HEW	$151,455,346
AEC	–	HUD	–
NASA	$33,607	DOI	$220,648
DOT	$8,205,088	USDA	$55,468,862
		Other	$94,069,284

Federal Military-Industrial Commitments

DOD Contractors Caterpillar Tractor (Peoria), $18.154m: tractors and tractor components. Caterpillar Tractor (East Peoria), $5.436m: tractors and tractor components.

Economic Base Agriculture, notably grains, hogs and sheep, and cattle; machinery, especially construction and related machinery; finance, insurance and real estate; food and kindred products; and fabricated metal products, especially fabricated structural metal products.

The Voters

Registration No party registration; no accurate total registration figures available.
Median voting age 44.7
Employment profile White collar, 44%. Blue collar, 38%. Service, 13%. Farm, 5%.
Ethnic groups Black, 4%. Total foreign stock, 9%. Germany, 2%; UK, 1%.

Presidential vote

1972	Nixon (R)	128,747	(66%)
	McGovern (D)	67,503	(34%)
1968	Nixon (R)	98,747	(51%)
	Humphrey (D)	77,938	(41%)
	Wallace (AI)	15,667	(8%)

Representative

Robert H. Michel (R) Elected 1956; b. March 2, 1923, Peoria; home, Peoria; Bradley U., B.S., 1948; Army, WWII; married, four children; Apostolic Christian.

Career Admin. Asst., Rep. Harold Velde, 1949–56; past Pres., Ill. State Society.

Offices 2112 RHOB, 202-225-6201. 1007 First Natl. Bank, Peoria 61602, 309-673-6358.

Administrative Assistant Ralph Vinovich

Committees

Appropriations (4th); Subs: Agriculture, Environmental and Consumer Protection; Labor, Health, Education, and Welfare (Ranking Mbr.).

Group Ratings

	ADA	COPE	LWV	RIPON	NFU	LCV	CFA	NAB	NSI	ACA
1972	6	30	22	33	33	15	50	89	100	94
1971	3	0	33	43	20	–	29	–	–	96
1970	20	34	–	53	23	15	39	92	100	82

Key Votes

1) Busing	AGN	6) Cmbodia Bmbg	FOR	11) Chkg Acct Intrst	AGN
2) Strip Mines	AGN	7) Bust Hwy Trust	AGN	12) End HISC (HUAC)	AGN
3) Cut Mil $	AGN	8) Farm Sub Lmt	AGN	13) Nixon Sewer Veto	FOR
4) Rev Shrg	AGN	9) School Prayr	FOR	14) Corp Cmpaign $	AGN
5) Pub TV $	ABS	10) Cnsumr Prot	FOR	15) Pol $ Disclosr	ABS

Election Results

1972 general:	Robert H. Michel (R)	124,407	(65%)
	Stephen L. Nordvall (D)	67,514	(35%)
1972 primary:	Robert H. Michel (R), unopposed		
1970 general:	Robert H. Michel (R)	84,864	(66%)
	Rosa Lee Fox (D)	43,601	(34%)

NINETEENTH DISTRICT   Political Background

The 19th district of Illinois is centered on the Rock Island-Moline-Davenport, Iowa metropolitan area—the largest between Chicago and Omaha. Rock Island County contains nearly one-half of the district's population, with the rest in several rural small-city counties. Rock Island, one of the nation's foremost manufacturers of farm machinery, has a large force of blue-collar workers and tends to vote Democratic; so occasionally does Fulton County, situated on the Illinois River below Peoria. The rest of the counties are staunchly Republican, leaving the parties closely divided in the district.

This is the only Illinois district to have changed partisan hands since 1958—an index of the close party split in the 19th. In 1964, an LBJ Democrat upset the incumbent Republican; two years later the Democrat was defeated and was later elected to the state legislature. The Republican winner in 1966 was Tom Railsback, then only 34, who now serves on the House Judiciary Committee. From time to time, Railsback dissents from the orthodox party line. He was, for example, a strong proponent of the 18-year-old vote; he objected to delegate allocations for the 1972 and 1976 Republican National Conventions; and he favors a limited confidentiality for newsmen on their sources. Nevertheless, Railsback remains in good favor with the Republican leadership, and is regarded as a comer in the party. He has also done his homework in the 19th district. In 1972, the Congressman faced no Democratic opposition.

Census Data   Pop. 462,085. Central city, 27%; suburban, 40%. Median family income, $9,579; families above $15,000: 17%; families below $3,000: 9%. Median years education, 12.1.

1972 Share of Federal Outlays $394,921,452

DOD	$112,159,487	HEW	$148,858,226
AEC	–	HUD	$1,575,592
NASA	–	DOI	$309,022
DOT	$15,732,115	USDA	$56,148,947
		Other	$60,138,063

Federal Military-Industrial Commitments

DOD Installations   Rock Island Army Arsenal (Rock Island). Savanna Army Dept (Savanna).

Economic Base   Machinery, espically farm machinery; agriculture, notably cattle, hogs and sheep, and grains; finance, insurance and real estate; fabricated metal products; and primary metal industries. Also higher education (Western Illinois Univ.).

The Voters

Registration   No party registration; no accurate total registration figures available.
Median voting age 44.6
Employment profile   White collar, 39%. Blue collar, 39%. Service, 14%. Farm, 8%.
Ethnic groups   Black, 2%. Spanish, 2%. Total foreign stock, 11%. Germany, Sweden, 2% each.

Presidential vote

1972	Nixon (R)	124,549	(62%)
	McGovern (D)	77,194	(38%)
1968	Nixon (R)	104,149	(52%)
	Humphrey (D)	80,058	(41%)
	Wallace (AI)	13,167	(7%)

Representative

Thomas F. Railsback (R)   Elected 1966; b. Jan. 22, 1932, Moline; home, Moline; Grinnell Col., B.A., 1954; Northwestern U., J.D., 1957; Army, 1957–59; married, four children; First Congregational Church.

Career   Practicing atty., 1957– ; Ill. State Legislature, 1962–66.

Offices   218 CHOB, 202-225-5905, Also Fed. Bldg., 211 19th St., Rock Island 61201, 309-794-9701, ext. 285.

Administrative Assistant   William M. Hermelin

Committees

Judiciary (5th); Subs: No. 1 (Immigration and Nationality); No. 3 (Patents, Trademarks, Copyrights) (Ranking Mbr.).

Group Ratings

	ADA	COPE	LWV	RIPON	NFU	LCV	CFA	NAB	NSI	ACA
1972	44	22	100	100	67	42	0	60	89	47
1971	46	36	83	77	53	–	50	–	–	54
1970	48	60	–	88	83	62	41	75	100	53

Key Votes

1) Busing	FOR	6) Cmbodia Bmbg	AGN	11) Chkg Acct Intrst	AGN
2) Strip Mines	AGN	7) Bust Hwy Trust	AGN	12) End HISC (HUAC)	AGN
3) Cut Mil $	FOR	8) Farm Sub Lmt	ABS	13) Nixon Sewer Veto	AGN
4) Rev Shrg	FOR	9) School Prayr	AGN	14) Corp Cmpaign $	FOR
5) Pub TV $	AGN	10) Cnsumr Prot	FOR	15) Pol $ Disclosr	ABS

Election Results

1972 general:	Thomas F. Railsback (R), unopposed		
1972 primary:	Thomas F. Railsback (R), unopposed		
1970 general:	Thomas F. Railsback (R)	92,247	(68%)
	James L. Shaw (D)	43,094	(32%)

TWENTIETH DISTRICT Political Background

The 20th district of Illinois is a descendant of the district that sent Abraham Lincoln, a young lawyer and local Whig politician, to the House of Representatives in 1846. The western part of the district, at least, has changed little since the nineteenth century. It remains a land of fertile prairies, the bottomland of the Mississippi and Illinois Rivers, farm-marketing towns, and courthouse villages. The river port of Quincy on the Mississippi has not grown much since the turn of the century, now has the little town of Nauvoo, from which the Mormons were expelled back in the 1840s and led by Brigham Young to what is now their promised land in Utah.

The largest city in the 20th is Springfield (pop. 90,000). It must have been a bustling, perhaps even a gracious small town in Abe Lincoln's and Mary Todd's time. Today it is a typical state capital: a middle-sized city with an old capitol building, several not-so-elegant hotels, a small black ghetto, a little bit of industry, and a few shopping centers at the edge of town. The Lincoln tourist business, next to state government, looks like the city's economic mainstay.

On paper, the 20th is a marginal district. It sits right on the traditional boundary separating the Democratic counties to the south and the Republican ones to the north—a division that played a role in the politics of the Republican Abraham Lincoln and the Democrat Stephen Douglas. These same partisan affiliations are still reflected in local elections, though the district has increasingly listed to the Republican side in national contests.

The 1960 census cost Illinois one congressional seat. Two incumbents—a Republican freshman and a Democratic veteran—were forced to fight it out in the 20th. Paul Findley, the Republican, won the 1962 election and continues to represent the district today. Findley is a middle-ranking Republican on the Foreign Affairs Committee, where he is considered a maverick not identified with any of the usual schools of thought. He has taken a particular interest in the affairs of NATO—an unusual concern for a Congressman from an area that has been traditionally isolationist. In the House generally, Findley is something of a loner, making his positions known in crisply articulated speeches, but never gathering a bloc of votes around him. His approach to issues appears popular back home; he has won every election since 1964 with more than 60% of the vote. In 1972, Findley's percentage went up as high as 69%, despite the addition of some Democratic territory by redistricting.

Census Data Pop. 464,551. Central city, 20%; suburban, 31%. Median family income, $9,269; families above $15,000: 17%; families below $3,000: 10%. Median years education, 17.0.

1972 Share of Federal Outlays $530,943,167

DOD	$37,077,105	HEW	$248,037,091
AEC	–	HUD	$14,092,229
NASA	$50,283	DOI	$1,967,357
DOT	$45,893,496	USDA	$61,334,732
		Other	$122,490,874

Federal Military-Industrial Commitments

No installations or contractors receiving prime awards greater than $5,000,000.

Economic Base Agriculture, notably grains, hogs and sheep, and cattle; finance, insurance and real estate; machinery, especially general industrial machinery; primary metal industries, especially blast furnace and steel mill products; food and kindred products, especially grain mill products; and electrical equipment and supplies.

The Voters

Registration No party registration; no accurate total registration figures available.
Median voting age 46.8
Employment profile White collar, 46%. Blue collar, 33%. Service, 14%. Farm, 7%.
Ethnic groups Black, 4%. Total foreign stock, 8%. Germany, 2%; Italy, UK, 1% each.

Presidential vote

1972	Nixon (R)	137,414	(64%)
	McGovern (D)	78,281	(36%)
1968	Nixon (R)	106,487	(49%)
	Humphrey (D)	87,504	(41%)
	Wallace (AI)	20,215	(9%)

Representative

Paul Findley (R) Elected 1960; b. June 23, 1921, Jacksonville; home, Pittsfield; Ill. Col., B.A., 1943; Lindenwood Col., D.H.L., 1969; Navy, WWII; married, two children; Congregational Church.

Career Publisher, Pike Press, Inc., 1947– ; author.

Offices 2133 RHOB, 202-225-5271. Also Rm. 205, Fed. Ct. Bldg., Springfield 62701, 217-525-4062, and 400 WCU Bldg., Quincy 62301, 217-223-5917, and 501 Belle St., Alton 62006, 618-463-0799.

Administrative Assistant Robert J. Wichser

Committees

Agriculture (10th); Subs: Livestock and Grains; Domestic Marketing and Consumer Relations; Dairy and Poultry.

Foreign Affairs (7th); Subs: Europe; International Organizations and Movements; National Security Policy and Scientific Developments.

Group Ratings

	ADA	COPE	LWV	RIPON	NFU	LCV	CFA	NAB	NSI	ACA
1972	25	18	64	78	29	47	100	92	71	70
1971	41	8	50	82	33	–	50	–	–	63
1970	28	27	–	87	58	3	44	90	89	54

Key Votes

1) Busing	FOR	6) Cmbodia Bmbg	AGN	11) Chkg Acct Intrst	AGN
2) Strip Mines	AGN	7) Bust Hwy Trust	AGN	12) End HISC (HUAC)	AGN
3) Cut Mil $	ABS	8) Farm Sub Lmt	FOR	13) Nixon Sewer Veto	FOR
4) Rev Shrg	AGN	9) School Prayr	AGN	14) Corp Cmpaign $	AGN
5) Pub TV $	ABS	10) Cnsumr Prot	FOR	15) Pol $ Disclosr	FOR

Election Results

1972 general:	Paul Findley (R)	148,419	(69%)
	Robert S. O'Shea (D)	67,445	(31%)
1972 primary:	Paul Findley (R), unopposed		
1970 general:	Paul Findley (R)	103,485	(68%)
	Billie M. Cox (D)	49,727	(32%)

TWENTY-FIRST DISTRICT Political Background

Downstate Illinois has always been regarded as overwhelmingly Republican. Such has never really been the case. The largest Republican margins in Illinois come out of the Chicago suburbs. And except for the fertile farmlands in the north central part of Illinois, downstate might more accurately be described as marginally Republican. Take, for example, the 21st congressional district (known before the 1972 redistricting as the 22nd). The 21st lies in flat, central Illinois farm country, but most of its population is concentrated in three urban centers: Decatur (pop. 90,000), a factory town; Champaign-Urbana (total pop. 89,000), site of the University of Illinois; and Bloomington (pop. 66,000 with the suburb of Normal), an insurance town and the ancestral home of the Stevenson family. These places are listed in the order in which they have traditionally shown Democratic inclinations; but lately there have been changes. Most important is the enfranchisement of the 18-year-olds, for the 21st has by far the largest number of college students of any Illinois district: 46,000 or 15% of the eligible electorate. Most of them live in Champaign-Urbana, but a sizable number of students can also be found at Illinois State University in Normal.

The sudden increase in student—and, presumably, Democratic—votes may have contributed to the retirement in 1972 of 11-term Representative William L. Springer. A knowledgeable conservative Republican, Springer was the ranking Republican and often the dominant voice on the House Commerce Committee. With his retirement, President Nixon appointed Springer to the Federal Power Commission, an important post given the controversy surrounding the nation's energy crisis. It was a measure of congressional dissatisfaction with the pro-industry appointment and with the Administration generally that confirmation was held up for several weeks—the opposition being led by Sens. Frank Moss and Philip Hart. Ordinarily, however, a former member of Congress whose technical competence is respected, as Springer's is, could expect speedy and automatic confirmation.

With no incumbent running in the district, the race in the 21st was the closest since 1964, year of the Johnson landslide. The Democratic candidate tried to put together student votes in Champaign-Urbana with blue-collar votes in Decatur. The Democrat did manage to carry Champaign County 52–48, but lost Macon County (Decatur) by 372 votes. The Republican nominee, state Rep. Edward R. Madigan, ran far behind Richard Nixon's showing in the 21st but still managed a convincing 55–45 win. Madigan now sits on the Agriculture Committee. This committee is important not only to the district's many farmers but to a major industry here, farm machinery manufacture. The industry has been booming of late, what with prices on the farm so high; the farmers around here are also pleased with the prices, but wet weather prevented many of them from properly harvesting the 1972 crop and planting the 1973 crop.

Normally, one would expect an incumbent like Madigan to coast to reelection in the years to come. But the new Congressman may encounter trouble from the extraordinarily large number of students here, many of whom will not take kindly to any support Madigan gives the Watergate-besmirched Nixon Administration.

Census Data Pop. 464,693. Central city, 53%; suburban, 31%. Median family income, $10,043; families above $15,000: 21%; families below $3,000: 7%. Median years education, 12.3.

1972 Share of Federal Outlays $463,893,985

DOD	$146,439,356	HEW	$136,633,500
AEC	$3,658,366	HUD	$247,589
NASA	$1,110,645	DOI	$1,255,368
DOT	$24,820,830	USDA	$73,351,757
		Other	$76,376,574

Federal Military-Industrial Commitments

DOD Contractors University of Illinois (Urbana), $5.831m: research in electronic and computer ware.
DOD Installations Chanute AFB (Rantoul).

Economic Base Finance, insurance and real estate; agriculture, notably grains, cattle, and hogs and sheep; food and kindred products; machinery; electrical equipment and supplies; and fabricated metal products. Also higher education (Eastern Illinois Univ., and Illinois State Univ., and Univ. of Illinois).

The Voters

Registration No party registration; no accurate total registration available.
Median voting age 38.3
Employment profile White collar, 51%. Blue collar, 29%. Service, 15%. Farm, 5%.
Ethnic groups Black, 5%. Total foreign stock, 7%. Germany, 2%.

Presidential vote

1972	Nixon (R)	117,230	(62%)
	McGovern (D)	70,380	(38%)
1968	Nixon (R)	88,585	(53%)
	Humphrey (D)	65,529	(39%)
	Wallace (AI)	14,063	(8%)

Representative

Edward R. Madigan (R) Elected 1972; b. Jan. 13, 1936, Lincoln; home, Lincoln; Lincoln Col.; married, three children; Catholic.

Career Lincoln Board of Zoning Appeals, four years; Owner, Yellow-Lincoln Cab Co. and Car Leasing; Ill. State House, 1966–72.

Offices 1238 LHOB, 202-225-2371. Also 501 W. Church St., Champaign, 217-356-8633, and P.O. Bldg., Decatur.

Administrative Assistant Gary Madson

Committees

Agriculture (16th); Subs: Oilseeds and Rice; Tobacco; Conservation and Credit.

Group Ratings: Newly Elected

Key Votes

1) Busing	NE	6) Cmbodia Bmbg	AGN	11) Chkg Acct Intrst	AGN
2) Strip Mines	NE	7) Bust Hwy Trust	FOR	12) End HISC (HUAC)	AGN
3) Cut Mil $	NE	8) Farm Sub Lmt	NE	13) Nixon Sewer Veto	FOR
4) Rev Shrg	NE	9) School Prayr	NE	14) Corp Cmpaign $	NE
5) Pub TV $	NE	10) Cnsumr Prot	NE	15) Pol $ Disclosr	NE

Election Results

1972 general:	Edward R. Madigan (R)	99,966	(55%)
	Lawrence E. Johnson (D)	82,523	(45%)
1972 primary:	Edward R. Madigan (R)	26,242	(69%)
	Elbert S. Smith (R)	10,721	(28%)
	O. George Ryan (R)	984	(3%)

TWENTY-SECOND DISTRICT Political Background

One of the expected casualties of Illinois' court-ordered redistricting plan was Democratic Congressman George Shipley. The Congressman's small margins of victory—never above 56%—have kept him on Republican lists of target seats ever since he unseated a 16-year Republican incumbent by 187 votes in 1958. In an era when Democrats are presumed to draw most of their allegiance from urban areas, Shipley's district has always been predominantly rural and small-town. In a time when Congressmen reap their greatest electoral advantage from representing—writing to and servicing—the same constituency in the same geographical territory, Shipley's district boundaries have shifted beneath him constantly, and never more so than in 1972.

So why has Shipley kept winning reelection? Part of the reason lies in the history of the region. Settled largely by Southerners, the 22nd was Democratic territory during the nineteenth century, and voting habits have a way of being passed from generation to generation—particularly in rural areas—regardless of what may happen to the stated aims of the political parties. Yet the people of the 22nd have responded negatively to the increasingly liberal, pro-civil rights, and antiwar positions of the national Democratic party. As a result, local voters usually give Republican candidates comfortable margins in statewide races. But the trend has not hurt Shipley. Among the district's traditional Democrats, the controversy surrounding the unseating of the regular Illinois delegation, which Shipley led, may have helped.

Shipley's electoral success has been based on his genial, folksy personality, assiduous campaigning, and attention to the problems of his constituents. It has been a winning formula for many years. But, as noted, not by much. So the 1972 election was supposed to give him real trouble. Only 47% of the votes cast in his new 22nd district were from his previous constituency (though he had represented some of the new counties before, under even older redistrictings). Included in the 22nd was the staunchly Republican city of Danville. And finally, the Republicans planned to run a vigorous and well-financed campaign against him. In the face of these pressures, Shipley came through again—and with a larger percentage of the votes, 58%, than he had ever won before. In the part of the district he retained from 1970, he got a startling 64%, and carried the remainder by a solid 53–47.

It appears now that Shipley finally has something most Congressmen take for granted: a safe seat. While he was winning all the close elections, Shipley was also inching up the seniority ladder of the Appropriations Committee. He is now the eleventh ranking Democrat, though he is not yet a subcommittee chairman. Shipley serves on a unit with jurisdiction over HUD and the space program and, of more concern to his district, a unit overseeing agriculture and the environment.

Census Data Pop. 464,121. Central city, 0%; suburban, 1%. Median family income, $8,350; families above $15,000: 13%; families below $3,000: 12%. Median years education, 11.4.

1972 Share of Federal Outlays $393,814,193

DOD	$13,050,376	HEW	$172,976,389
AEC	–	HUD	$269,074
NASA	–	DOI	$1,001,702
DOT	$35,855,904	USDA	$94,023,136
		Other	$76,637,612

Federal Military-Industrial Commitments

No installations or contractors receiving prime awards greater than $5,000,000.

Economic Base Agriculture, notably grains, hogs and sheep, and cattle; finance, insurance and real estate; machinery; electrical equipment and supplies, especially electrical test and distributing equipment; and food and kindred products.

The Voters

Registration No party registration; no accurate total registration figures available.
Median voting age 47.4
Employment profile White collar, 37%. Blue collar, 40%. Service, 13%. Farm, 10%.
Ethnic groups Black, 1%. Total foreign stock, 4%. Germany, 1%.

Presidential vote

1972	Nixon (R)	141,820	(64%)
	McGovern (D)	80,804	(36%)
1968	Nixon (R)	117,778	(52%)
	Humphrey (D)	83,137	(37%)
	Wallace (AI)	22,977	(10%)

Representative

George Edward Shipley (D) Elected 1958; b. April 21, 1927, Olney; home, Olney; USMC, WWII; married, five children; Baptist.

Career Deputy Sheriff, 1950–54; Sheriff, 1954–58, Richland County.

Offices 237 CHOB, 202-225-5001. Also 111 S. Boone St., Olney 62450, 618-395-2171.

Administrative Assistant Goldie M. Eckl

Committees

Appropriations (11th); Subs: Agriculture, Environmental and Consumer Protection; Housing and Urban Development, Space, Veterans; Treasury, Postal Service, General Government.

Group Ratings

	ADA	COPE	LWV	RIPON	NFU	LCV	CFA	NAB	NSI	ACA
1972	25	67	27	31	83	25	100	30	67	57
1971	46	70	75	47	79	–	100	–	–	38
1970	64	67	–	31	77	40	72	25	89	44

Key Votes

1) Busing	AGN	6) Cmbodia Bmbg	AGN	11) Chkg Acct Intrst	AGN
2) Strip Mines	FOR	7) Bust Hwy Trust	FOR	12) End HISC (HUAC)	AGN
3) Cut Mil $	AGN	8) Farm Sub Lmt	ABS	13) Nixon Sewer Veto	AGN
4) Rev Shrg	FOR	9) School Prayr	FOR	14) Corp Cmpaign $	ABS
5) Pub TV $	FOR	10) Cnsumr Prot	FOR	15) Pol $ Disclosr	AGN

Election Results

1972 general:	George E. Shipley (D)	124,589	(57%)
	Robert B. Lamkin (R)	90,390	(41%)
	Cleo A. Duzan (Ind.)	5,389	(2%)
1972 primary:	George E. Shipley (D), unopposed		
1970 general:	George E. Shipley (D)	91,158	(54%)
	Phyllis Schlafly (R)	77,762	(44%)

TWENTY-THIRD DISTRICT Political Background

The 23rd district of Illinois comprises the area around East St. Louis—St. Clair and most of Madison County. From St. Louis' Gateway Arch, one can see East St. Louis, Belleville, and

Granite City through the smog across the Mississippi River. These places are not verdant St. Louis suburbs, but grimy industrial towns crisscrossed by miles of railroad track. They have all the problems usually associated with core-city areas: air pollution, poor housing, crime, and a declining tax base. During the 1960s, East St. Louis became a black-majority city; but when the blacks came into political control, they found the city treasury virtually bare. The Illinois side of the St. Louis metropolitan area has a disproportionate share of its poor and low-income working-class residents. The rich stay well on the St. Louis side of the Mississippi.

The 23rd is by far the most Democratic of all the downstate Illinois congressional districts. In presidential elections, however, Democratic majorities have disappeared. Humphrey won the district by only a plurality when George Wallace took 16% of the vote; McGovern lost the district altogether by a small margin. But in local elections, the 23rd is as Democratic as it ever was. Melvin Price, who served as secretary to the district's Congressman from 1933 to 1943, has represented the district since the 1944 election. He has won reelection easily, since 1962 by margins in excess of two-to-one.

In Congress, Price holds two key positions within units that possess jurisdiction over a great share of the federal budget. He now serves the 93rd Congress as Chairman of the Joint Committee on Atomic Energy, a congressional body that has worked very closely with the agency it administers. Price has been a member of the Joint Committee since its inception just after World War II; the Illinois Congressman has enjoyed an excellent working relationship with Chet Holifield of California, who served as Chairman for many years. (The chairmanship of the committee rotates between senior members from the House and the Senate.)

Price is also the number-two Democrat on the House Armed Services Committee, and as next in line, he would step into the chairmanship should F. Edward Hebert leave Congress. On Armed Services, Price has been a member of the bipartisan coalition that has supported the war in Indochina and the current high levels of military spending. In 1973, however, in what was a significant break with his past positions, Price opposed the bombing of Cambodia after the signing of the Vietnam cease-fire. As a logical exercise, it is possible to reconcile all of Price's stands on the war. But his break in alignment, along with those of other senior Democrats, probably made the difference when the House went on record against further American military involvement in Cambodia.

On paper, Price has yet another important position: Chairman of the House Committee on Standards and Official Conduct. This body has been largely quiescent. No one accuses Price of tolerating corruption, but in 1972 his committee did little when Rep. John Dowdy was convicted on bribery and perjury charges. Dowdy agreed not to cast his vote, and was then allowed to continue to collect his salary. When it became clear that the misdeeds of Congressmen were nothing compared to those of the Committee to Reelect the President, nobody much cared what Price's House Committee was or was not doing.

Census Data Pop. 462,960. Central city, 0%; suburban, 100%. Median family income, $9,872; families above $15,000: 18%; families below $3,000: 10%. Median years education, 11.1.

1972 Share of Federal Outlays $411,112,410

DOD	$123,525,026	HEW	$168,674,647
AEC	–	HUD	$6,405,012
NASA	–	DOI	$1,908,600
DOT	$32,039,429	USDA	$15,864,851
		Other	$62,694,845

Federal Military-Industrial Commitments

DOD Contractors Shell Oil (Wood River), $6.447m: petroleum products. Olin Corp. (East Alton), $10.169m: various types of ammunition and rockets.
DOD Installations Scott AFB (Belleville).

Economic Base Primary metal industries, especially blast furnace and steel mill products; finance, insurance and real estate; food and kindred products, especially meat products; chemicals and allied products, especially cyclic intermediates and crudes; and agriculture, notably grains, hogs and sheep, cattle and dairy products.

The Voters

Registration No party registration; no accurate total registration figures available.
Median voting age 43.1
Employment profile White collar, 45%. Blue collar, 41%. Service, 13%. Farm, 1%.
Ethnic groups Black, 15%. Spanish, 1%. Total foreign stock, 8%. Germany, 2%.

Presidential vote

1972	Nixon (R)	87,654	(53%)
	McGovern (D)	76,971	(47%)
1968	Nixon (R)	59,899	(35%)
	Humphrey (D)	83,886	(49%)
	Wallace (AI)	26,675	(16%)

Representative

Melvin Price (D) Elected 1944; b. Jan. 1, 1905, East St. Louis; home, East St. Louis; St. Louis U., 1923–25; Army, WWII; married, one child; Catholic.

Career Newspaper correspondent, E. St. Louis *Journal,* St. Louis *Globe Democrat,* S. St. Louis *News-Review;* St. Clair County Bd. Supervisors, 1929–31; Sec., Rep. Edwin M. Schaefer, 1933–43.

Offices 2468 RHOB, 202-225-5661. Also Fed. Bldg., 604 Missouri Ave., East St. Louis 62201, 618-397-0500.

Administrative Assistant Peter C. Scrivner

Committees

Armed Services (2nd); Subs: No. 1 (Chm.); Sp. Sub. on Intelligence.

Standards of Official Conduct (Chm.).

Joint Com. on Atomic Energy (Chm.); Subs: Agreements for Cooperation; Legislation (Chm.); Research, Development, and Radiation (Chm.); Energy; Licensing and Regulation.

Group Ratings

	ADA	COPE	LWV	RIPON	NFU	LCV	CFA	NAB	NSI	ACA
1972	69	91	92	76	71	47	100	9	90	17
1971	59	100	100	40	80	–	100	–	–	23
1970	56	100	–	59	100	70	90	0	80	17

Key Votes

1) Busing	FOR	6) Cmbodia Bmbg	AGN	11) Chkg Acct Intrst	AGN
2) Strip Mines	AGN	7) Bust Hwy Trust	FOR	12) End HISC (HUAC)	AGN
3) Cut Mil $	AGN	8) Farm Sub Lmt	FOR	13) Nixon Sewer Veto	AGN
4) Rev Shrg	FOR	9) School Prayr	FOR	14) Corp Cmpaign $	FOR
5) Pub TV $	FOR	10) Cnsumr Prot	FOR	15) Pol $ Disclosr	ABS

Election Results

1972 general:	Melvin Price (D)	121,682	(75%)
	Robert Mays (R)	40,428	(25%)
1972 primary:	Melvin Price (D), unopposed		
1970 general:	Melvin Price (D)	88,637	(74%)
	Scott R. Randolph (R)	30,784	(26%)

TWENTY-FOURTH DISTRICT Political Background

Egypt is the name applied to the southernmost part of Illinois—the flat, fertile farmland where the Ohio River joins the Mississippi. This is low, alluvial land protected from floods—and not always very well, as the heavy spring rains of 1973 showed—by giant levees: hence the name. There is more than a touch of the South here. The southern tip of Illinois is closer to Jackson, Mississippi than Chicago. The unofficial capital of Egypt is Cairo (pronounced KAYro), a declining town at the exact confluence of the two rivers. In recent years, Cairo has been the scene of a virtual war between its white majority and its black minority of nearly equal size.

There are no official boundaries to Egypt, but it is safe to say that the 24th congressional district (formerly numbered the 21st) goes north considerably beyond them. The district takes in the coal-mining country around West Frankfort and proceeds to a point near the suburbs of St. Louis. The fastest-growing part of the 24th lies around Carbondale, the site of Southern Illinois University. In an area with a traditional allegiance to the Democratic party, Carbondale is just about the only part of the district that remains attracted to the party's national candidates. In 1972, the student vote carried Jackson County, around Carbondale, for McGovern; it was the only one of Illinois' 102 counties the Democrat won.

If the politics of the 24th has a definite Southern character, its Congressman defies any pat characterization. Kenneth J. Gray, a Democrat, has represented the district since the 1954 election, which he won just before he turned 30. Before that, Gray had has an interesting career: he flew airplanes and helicopters, and owned an airport. He was also a licenced auctioneer and a talented amateur magician. These latter talents have come in handy in Washington. During a speech on the floor of the House, he once pulled a bouquet of red roses from his sleeve to illustrate the bounteous effects a proposed dam would have on his district. Gray is also in considerable demand to serve as auctioneer at charitable functions in the capital.

Gray's voting record, as might be expected, is somewhat more conservative than those of most Northern Democrats. He serves on Wayne Hays' House Administration Committee. But he is more interested in his seat on Public Works. Here he has used more than magician's tricks to get several dams and flood-control projects for his district. Gray is one of those Congressmen who still believes in the pork barrel. Bacon from the barrel not only helps to tame the wild furies of nature but also keeps the voters of the 24th district happy with its Congressman.

Census Data Pop. 465,018. Central city, 0%; suburban, 0%. Median family income, $7,501; families above $15,000: 11%; families below $3,000: 17%. Median years education, 10.1.

1972 Share of Federal Outlays $469,051,111

DOD	$45,278,000	HEW	$240,026,657
AEC	–	HUD	$1,295,000
NASA	–	DOI	$1,960,310
DOT	$55,366,088	USDA	$50,593,621
		Other	$74,531,435

Federal Military-Industrial Commitments

DOD Contractors Olin Corp. (Marion), $10.451m: 81mm illuminating cartridges.

Economic Base Agriculture, notably grains, hogs and sheep, dairy products and cattle; finance, insurance and real estate; bituminous coal mining; food and kindred products; and shoes, except rubber, and other leather and leather products. Also higher education (Southern Illinois Univ.).

The Voters

Registration No party registration; no accurate total registration available.
Median voting age 47.2
Employment profile White collar, 38%. Blue collar, 40%. Service, 15%. Farm, 7%.
Ethnic groups Black, 4%. Total foreign stock, 5%. Germany, 1%.

Presidential vote

1972	Nixon (R)	138,435	(60%)
	McGovern (D)	92,910	(40%)
1968	Nixon (R)	112,667	(49%)
	Humphrey (D)	92.479	(41%)
	Wallace (AI)	23,147	(10%)

Representative

Kenneth J. Gray (D) Elected 1954; b. Nov. 14, 1924, West Frankfort; home, West Frankfort; Army, Air Force, WWII; married, three children; Baptist.

Career Owner, Gray Motors, 1942–54; licenced auctioneer, airplane and helicopter pilot, formerly airport operator; founder, Walking Dog Foundation for the Blind.

Offices 2372 RHOB, 202-225-5201. Also 212 W. Main St., West Frankfort 62896, 618-932-2560.

Administrative Assistant Margaret J. Bergin

Committees

House Administration (6th); Subs: Elections; Library and Memorials; Electrical and Mechanical Office Equipment; Police (Chm.).

Public Works (5th); Subs: Public Buildings and Grounds (Chm.); Investigations and Review; Transportation; Water Resources.

Group Ratings

	ADA	COPE	LWV	RIPON	NFU	LCV	CFA	NAB	NSI	ACA
1972	31	80	56	70	100	0	0	0	67	16
1971	38	100	87	56	85	–	100	–	–	25
1970	40	92	–	40	100	53	68	8	100	18

Key Votes

1) Busing	AGN	6) Cmbodia Bmbg	AGN	11) Chkg Acct Intrst	AGN
2) Strip Mines	ABS	7) Bust Hwy Trust	AGN	12) End HISC (HUAC)	ABS
3) Cut Mil $	AGN	8) Farm Sub Lmt	ABS	13) Nixon Sewer Veto	AGN
4) Rev Shrg	FOR	9) School Prayr	FOR	14) Corp Cmpaign $	FOR
5) Pub TV $	FOR	10) Cnsumr Prot	FOR	15) Pol $ Disclosr	AGN

Election Results

1972 general:	Kenneth J. Gray (D)	138,867	(94%)
	Hugh Muldoon (Ind.)	9,398	(6%)
1972 primary:	Kenneth J. Gray (D), unopposed		
1970 general:	Kenneth J. Gray (D)	110,374	(62%)
	Fred Evans (R)	66,273	(38%)

INDIANA

Political Background

The most powerful political machines still at work in the country cannot be found in any of the big cities along the East Coast, but in the heart of Middle America: one in the city of Chicago and the other in the state of Indiana. Mayor Daley's machine is famous, the subject of books that sell everywhere. But the Indiana machines, if less well known, are probably in better shape, as they hum away in Indianapolis and in practically every one of the state's 92 courthouse towns. Almost all public offices in Indiana, including the judgeships and clerks of court, are partisan; and nearly every Indiana partisan official and each of his patronage employees must kick in 2% of his salary to party coffers. In few other parts of the nation is this practice, redolent of the politics of the 1880s, so stringently enforced. And because Indiana has about as many patronage jobs as any state in the country, these 2% "donations" keep both parties rolling in money.

The kickback system does not ordinarily produce gross discrepancies in the financial status of the two parties. Indiana has, in fact, been overwhelmingly Republican in its presidential politics; the only Democratic candidate to carry the state since 1936 was Lyndon Johnson with 56%, well below his national average. But in state and local contests, Indiana's voting patterns are usually nicely balanced. While the state has moved to national Republicans over the years, partisan preferences in state and local contests, particularly in rural areas, have changed very little since the Civil War. Thus the Democrats, as well as the Republicans, are guaranteed a sizable number of courthouses and the patronage that comes with them. Many of Indiana's cities are overwhelmingly Republican, notably Indianapolis. And at present, the Republicans have a definite edge, holding both the governorship and City Hall in Indianapolis. But the Democrats control several patronage-rich statewide offices and most of the other large cities and counties.

Another factor contributes to the strength of party machines here. Candidates for statewide office are not chosen in primaries, but by party convention. Primaries are used to select nominees for the U.S. House, but because local party organizations have a lot to say about who gets these nominations, they are seldom seriously contested. Once nominated, the party's candidate usually gets along in fine fashion with the well-oiled party machinery. As a result, unorthodox candidates rarely surface in Indiana politics. There is, for example, no Indiana Republican equivalent of Illinois' Sen. Charles Percy.

Indiana party bosses try hard to slate candidates congenial to the state's Hoosier mores. Elections in Indiana are therefore often very close. Sen. Vance Hartke, for example, won his third term in 1970 by just over 4,000 votes out of 1,700,000 cast. Sen. Birch Bayh, first elected in 1962 over four-term veteran Homer Capehart, won by less than 11,000 votes. And despite his subsequent emergence as a national political figure, Bayh did not win by any convincing margin in 1968; he gained a second term by a 52–48 margin over William Ruckelshaus.

Both Bayh and Ruckelshaus have become much more familiar to national television audiences since the 1968 contest. Ruckelshaus became Nixon's chief pollution fighter as head of the Environmental Protection Agency; here he has often taken positions independent of the Administration. When the Watergate scandal broke open, Ruckelshaus was made interim head of the FBI. Upon receiving the latter post, he announced he would forego the 1974 Senate race in Indiana—a decision that produced a sigh of relief among Bayh forces. Currently he is serving as Deputy Attorney General.

Bayh has also compiled an interesting record in public life. While still in his twenties, he won a seat and a leadership position in the Indiana House, and became Speaker of the House at the age of 30. In 1962, Bayh decided to try for the Senate nomination. By crisscrossing the state and collecting political debts owed in scores of courthouses, he managed to win the convention's nomination against the early favorite. His 1962 victory in the general election was one of the nation's closest and most surprising.

The same kind of hustle shown in the campaign has characterized his Senate career. Bayh took a hitherto unimportant subcommittee chairmanship, Constitutional Amendments, and became a well-known national figure. He steered to passage three constitutional amendments. The 25th, on presidential succession, and 26th, establishing the 18-year-old vote, were quickly ratified by the states; the other, the Equal Rights Amendment, is at this writing still a subject of controversy in various state legislatures. When civil rights and labor groups were looking for a Senator to lead the confirmation fights against Judges Carswell and Haynsworth, Bayh volunteered and succeeded in handing the Nixon Administration two of its most wincing defeats.

With this kind of record, Bayh launched a presidential candidacy in 1971. He went about it in much the same manner he had gone about seeking the Senate nomination in Indiana ten years before. Bayh assembled a talented staff and solid initial financing; he trekked to political dinners and gatherings all over the country. But in a crowded field of candidates, progress was hard to discern, and when the Senator learned that Mrs. Bayh required breast surgery, he left the race.

Bayh's seat is up in 1974. This race will probably be his easiest yet, if only because the two strongest potential candidates—Ruckelshaus and Indianapolis Mayor Richard Lugar—will not be there to run against him. Nevertheless, Democrat Bayh will have to work hard to win in Indiana. Working hard has been no problem for the Senator.

One reason that big Republican names are passing up the 1974 Senate race is that Vance Hartke's seat will be up in 1976. Hartke's margin in 1970 was small enough to make a race against him attractive. Indiana, with its strong party machines, is the closest thing left in the United States to a straight-ticket state; and in 1976 everyone expects the Republican presidential nominee—whoever he might be and whatever he might do elsewhere—to win here. Besides, there are smudges on Hartke's record, notably his acceptance in 1964 of a $30,000 campaign contribution from the Spiegel mail-order house.

Hartke's victory in 1970 came after one of the most acrimonious and bitterly fought Senate campaigns in recent American history. Because Hartke had supported trade with Eastern Europe, Rep. Richard Roudebush, the Republican candidate, ran TV ads that accused Hartke of supplying arms to the North Vietnamese to kill our boys. Meanwhile, Hartke supporters whispered that Roudebush had been married four times and had not fully recovered from head injuries sustained in a plane crash. Hartke's win represented a failure of the Nixon "Law and order" strategy in Hoosier Middle America. Law and order was fine with the voters, but more important was the shaky state of the 1970 economy and the GM strike that had idled thousands of Indiana workers.

Despite Hartke's rather tenuous base in Indiana, he emerged briefly as a presidential candidate in 1972. Some observers felt that his bid in the New Hampshire primary was made to draw votes away from Edmund Muskie to aid Hubert Humphrey. Not much of this happened, but soon afterwards Hartke became Humphrey's campaign chairman.

Hartke's own campaign was financed, so far as can be determined (it occurred before the April 7 deadline after which contributions had to be disclosed), by the railroads, railroad unions, and other interests that favored major pieces of legislation Hartke was—and is—sponsoring as a member of the Senate Commerce and Finance committees. The first measure is the so-called Surface Transportation Act, crafted by the railroads and their unions in cooperation with other transportation interests. A Nader's Raiders unit has charged that Hartke's proposal would pour subsidies into the faltering railroads, and at the same time maintain government subsidies to other modes of transportation. These include interstate highways for the trucking industry, rivers and harbors projects for internal shipping interests, and continued subsidy payments for the maritime industry.

The other major Hartke-sponsored bill, one that has won him wide support in several quarters, is the Burke-Hartke Act. Although the Senator does not like it so characterized, the bill is basically a protectionist measure. It sets mandatory import quotas on items that foreign producers can make more cheaply than American ones. Among Burke-Hartke's biggest proponents are the steel companies and the United Steel Workers, both of which have been battered by foreign competition.

Neither the Surface Transportation Act nor Burke-Hartke is expected to become law in its present form. But in both cases, by presenting carefully drafted legislation and by using his high positions on key committees to push the legislation, Hartke has helped to generate a demand for something like what he has proposed. The Nixon Administration has promised vetoes for both measures if passed as they now stand, but it too is sponsoring aid-to-railroads and trade-restriction bills. These are issues that will be settled in closed-door sessions of the Commerce and Finance committees. The outcomes will be heavily affected by the pressures of the major industrial and financial interests involved. In both cases, Hartke, whatever his electoral chances in 1976, will play a leading legislative role.

Some mention should be made of Indianapolis Mayor Lugar. He is a young (42 in 1974), talented, and ambitious Republican. The quipsters say he won't run for the Senate, but go for the White House directly from City Hall. Lugar pushed through a metropolitan consolidation of the city of Indianapolis and the surrounding suburbs of Marion County. The conjunction, which streamlined the operations of local government, will effectively prevent blacks and Democrats from ever again exerting real influence in local elections. Lugar is a great admirer of Richard Nixon, and when the Hoosier upset New York's John Lindsay to become president of the National League of Cities in 1971, many observers felt that small-city mayors, if not mayors of the big ones, were disposed to go long with the Nixon Administration's domestic policies. It remains to be seen whether Lugar's first exposure to the national public will boost his political ambitions; that exposure came in an unduly cloying speech before TV cameras at the unduly cloying 1972 Republican Convention.

Although a few have become leaders in the House, Indiana Congressmen generally have a hard time accumulating the seniority required to become shakers and movers in Washington. The state's House delegation experiences a great deal of turnover; in this respect it resembles that of Connecticut, until recently the only other major straight-ticket state left in the country. In the Democratic year of 1958, for example, Indiana sent nine Democrats and two Republicans to the House. Two years later, only four Democrats remained, one of them reelected by a mere 99-vote plurality. To make things worse for incumbents, the state has been redistricted no less than four times in the last 12 years, with the 1961, 1968, and 1972 plans favoring the Republicans and the 1965 boundaries favoring the Democrats.

In most states, Congressmen are routinely reelected. In Indiana, both party organizations usually target several seats and work hard to pick them off. Such is the case for 1974, when tough races can be expected in at least four of the state's eleven congressional districts. With one exception (the 1st), there is very little political variation among Indiana House seats, at least with respect to how presidential and statewide candidates run within them. So on paper, a close race is always possible in any Indiana district. This possibility is enhanced, of course, in no-incumbent seats.

Census Data Pop. 5,193,669; 2.57% of U.S. total, 11th largest; change 1960–70, 11.4%. Central city, 34%; suburban, 27%. Median family income, $9,966; 19th highest; families above $15,000: 19%; families below $3,000: 8%. Median years education, 12.1.

1972 Share of Federal Tax Burden $4,995,540,000; 2.39% of U.S. total, 11th largest.

1972 Share of Federal Outlays $4,094,425,585; 1.89% of U.S. total, 17th largest. Per capita federal spending, $788.

DOD	$1,166,272,000	17th (1.87%)		HEW	$1,489,155,199	14th (2.09%)
AEC	$2,520,940	26th (0.10%)		HUD	$148,121,301	6th (4.83%)
NASA	$4,565,021	26th (0.15%)		VA	$222,316,831	19th (1.94%)
DOT	$137,573,077	24th (1.74%)		USDA	$288,388,236	20th (1.87%)
DOC	$16,897,344	18th (1.31%)		CSC	$48,934,003	23rd (1.19%)
DOI	$14,397,193	34th (0.68%)		TD	$285,551,184	10th (1.73%)
DOJ	$21,574,142	14th (2.20%)		Other	$248,159,114	

Economic Base Primary metal industries, especially blast furnaces and steel mills; electrical equipment and supplies, radio and television receiving equipment; finance, insurance and real estate; transportation equipment, especially motor vehicles and equipment; agriculture, notably hogs, corn, soybeans and cattle; machinery, especially general industrial machinery; fabricated metal products, especially fabricated structural metal products.

Political Line-up Governor, Otis R. Bowen (R); seat up, 1976. Senators, Vance Hartke (D) and Birch Bayh (D). Representatives, 11 (7 R and 4 D). State Senate (29 R and 21 D); State House (73 R and 27 D).

The Voters

Registration No statewide registration.
Median voting age 42.5
Employment profile White collar, 42%. Blue collar, 43%. Service, 12%. Farm, 3%.
Ethnic groups Black, 7%. Spanish, 1%. Total foreign stock, 7%. Germany, 1%.
Presidential vote

1972	Nixon (R)	1,405,154	(66%)
	McGovern (D)	708,568	(34%)
1968	Nixon (R)	1,067,885	(50%)
	Humphrey (D)	806,659	(38%)
	Wallace (AI)	243,108	(11%)
1964	Johnson (D)	1,170,848	(56%)
	Goldwater (R)	911,118	(44%)

Senator

Vance Hartke (D) Elected 1958, seat up 1976; b. May 31, 1919, Stendal; home, Evansville; Evansville Col., B.A., 1941; Ind. U. School of Law, J.D., 1948; Navy, WWII; USCGR; USNR; married, seven children; Lutheran.

Career Practicing atty., 1948–56; Deputy Prosecuting Atty., Vanderburgh County, 1950–51; Mayor, Evansville, 1956–58; Chm., Dem. Senatorial Campaign Com., 1961–63; V.P., Natl. Capital Dem. Club, 1960–62; Bd. Mbr., 1963–66.

Offices 313 OSOB, 202-225-4814. Also Rm. 447 Fed. Bldg., Indianapolis 46204, 317-633-7066, and 417 Fed. Bldg., Hammond 46320, 219-932-5500 ext. 281.

Administrative Assistant Dr. Jacques Le Roy

Committees

Commerce (3rd); Subs: Aviation; Communications; Consumer; Surface Transportation (Chm.); Foreign Commerce and Tourism, Sp. Sub. on Freight Car Shortage (Chm.).

Finance (3rd); Subs: Health; Foundations (Ranking Mbr.); International Finance and Resources. *Veterans' Affairs (Chm.); Sub: Readjustment, Education, and Employment (Chm.). Sp. Com. on Aging* (9th); Subs: Employment and Retirement Incomes; Federal, State and Community Services; Consumer Interests of the Elderly; Retirement and the Individual; Health of the Elderly.

Joint Com. on Reduction of Federal Expenditures (4th).

Joint Study Com. on Budget Control.

Joint Com. on Internal Revenue Taxation (3rd).

Group Ratings

	ADA	COPE	LWV	RIPON	NFU	LCV	CFA	NAB	NSI	ACA
1972	65	100	83	65	100	72	100	33	0	6
1971	81	82	86	68	100	–	100	–	–	13
1970	72	100	–	57	100	50	–	33	10	21

Key Votes

1) Busing	ABS	8) Sea Life Prot	FOR	15) Tax Singls Less	FOR
2) Alas P-line	FOR	9) Campaign Subs	FOR	16) Min Tax for Rich	AGN
3) Gun Cntrl	FOR	10) Cmbodia Bmbg	AGN	17) Euro Troop Rdctn	ABS
4) Rehnquist	AGN	11) Legal Srvices	FOR	18) Bust Hwy Trust	AGN
5) Pub TV $	FOR	12) Rev Sharing	FOR	19) Maid Min Wage	FOR
6) EZ Votr Reg	FOR	13) Cnsumr Prot	FOR	20) Farm Sub Limit	AGN
7) No-Fault	FOR	14) Eq Rts Amend	FOR	21) Highr Credt Chgs	AGN

Election Results

1970 general:	R. Vance Hartke (D)	870,990	(50%)
	Richard L. Roudebush (R)	866,707	(50%)
1970 primary:	R. Vance Hartke (D) nominated at convention		
1964 general:	R. Vance Hartke (D)	1,128,505	(55%)
	D. Russell Bontrager (R)	941,519	(45%)

Senator

Birch Bayh (D) Elected 1962, seat up 1974; b. Jan. 22, 1928, Terre Haute; home, Terre Haute; Purdue U., B.S., 1951; Ind. State Col., 1953–60; Ind. U. School of Law, J.D., 1960; Army, 1945–46; married, one child; Lutheran.

Career Farming, 1952–57; Ind. House of Reps., 1954–62; Minority Leader, 1957–58, 1961–62, Speaker, 1959–60.

Offices 363 OSOB, 202-225-5623. Also Rm. 610, 320 N. Meridian Ave., Indianapolis 46204, 317-633-8640.

Administrative Assistant Jason Berman

Committees

Appropriations (13th); Subs: Agriculture,Environmental and Consumer Protection; HUD, Space, Science, Veterans; Legislative; District of Columbia (Chm.); Treasury, U.S. Postal Service, and General Government.

Judiciary (6th); Subs: Administrative Practice and Procedure; Consitutional Amendments (Chm.); Constitutional Rights; Internal Security; Juvenile Delinquency (Chm.); Penitentiaries.

Group Ratings

	ADA	COPE	LWV	RIPON	NFU	LCV	CFA	NAB	NSI	ACA
1972	80	88	89	81	100	52	100	10	10	6
1971	96	80	92	83	90	–	100	–	–	14
1970	72	100	–	62	100	58	–	10	22	11

Key Votes

1) Busing	ABS	8) Sea Life Prot	FOR	15) Tax Singls Less	FOR
2) Alas P-line	AGN	9) Campaign Subs	FOR	16) Min Tax for Rich	FOR
3) Gun Cntrl	FOR	10) Cmbodia Bmbg	AGN	17) Euro Troop Rdctn	FOR
4) Rehnquist	AGN	11) Legal Srvices	FOR	18) Bust Hwy Trust	AGN
5) Pub TV $	FOR	12) Rev Sharing	FOR	19) Maid Min Wage	FOR
6) EZ Votr Reg	FOR	13) Cnsumr Prot	FOR	20) Farm Sub Limit	FOR
7) No-Fault	FOR	14) Eq Rts Amend	FOR	21) Highr Credt Chgs	FOR

Election Results

1968 general:	Birch E. Bayh, Jr. (D)	1,060,456	(52%)
	William D. Ruckelshaus (R)	988,571	(48%)
1968 primary:	Birch E. Bayh, Jr. (D) nominated at convention		
1962 general:	Birch E. Bayh, Jr. (D)	905,491	(50%)
	Homer E. Capehart (R)	894,547	(50%)

FIRST DISTRICT Political Background

Anybody who has driven west on the Indiana Turnpike towards Chicago has seen it. Between the Turnpike and the shores of Lake Michigan is some of the most impressive and most polluted industrial landscape in the country. Here stand several of the nation's largest steel mills. From their chimneys and smokestacks come sulphurous fumes by day and the flare of flame by night. This is the heart of the 1st district of Indiana, the northwest corner of Hoosier America.

Without the giant mills, there would be no 1st district as we know it. The district's largest city, Gary, was founded in 1906 by J. Pierpont Morgan's colossal U.S. Steel Corporation and named after one of Morgan's partners, Chicago lawyer Elbert Gary. The site chosen for the activities of the industry was ideal. Iron ore from the Lake Superior ranges could be carried by Great Lakes barges into the huge man-made port at the southern tip of Lake Michigan. And coal from the interior could be transported to the mills on the great east-west rail lines, as they pass through Gary, Hammond, and East Chicago on their way to Chicago, Illinois. So now no less than five of the great steel manufacturers have mills here.

In the last 60 years, the operations of steel have attracted thousands of immigrants to Gary and vicinity—Irish, Poles, Czechs, Ukrainians, and, most recently, blacks from the American South. These groups, as even casual newspaper readers know, live in uneasy proximity. Hostility between the Eastern European ethnic groups and the blacks has produced turmoil in Gary and Lake County politics. In 1967, Richard Hatcher, a black, won the Democratic nomination and was elected Mayor of Gary, now 53% black. In 1971, he was reelected by a large margin. But meanwhile, the Lake County Democratic machinery, as well as all of the county offices, have remained in control of whites profoundly hostile to Hatcher. To make matters worse, there is garden-variety corruption, which has always been a problem in Lake County; the steel companies have traditionally determined the assessed valuation of their own mills.

There have been efforts to unite the ethnics and blacks around common problems and grievances. The results, however, have been disappointing. In the meantime the continued friction between the two groups has cut into the onetime heavy Democratic majorities of Lake County and the 1st congressional district. Election results suggest that many white voters have identified the Democratic party with the blacks, and have therefore switched support to Richard Nixon's Republicans. In 1972 Nixon carried Lake County and the 1st, both for the first time. But as long ago as 1964, George Wallace carried Lake County in the Democratic presidential primary, and four years later won 16% of the 1st district's votes—his best showing in Indiana. The only major political figure who could command the allegiance of both groups was the late Sen. Robert Kennedy, who won large majorities in both black and ethnic precincts in the 1968 presidential primary.

This is the district that sends to Washington the current Chairman of the House Rules Committee, Ray J. Madden, who will be 82 years old in 1974. For a long, long time Rules was dominated by a conservative coalition of Southern Democrats and Northern Republicans, who were led first by Chairman Howard Smith of Virginia and then by Chairman William Colmer of Mississippi. Smith lost a primary in 1966, and Colmer retired in 1972. But even before the departure of these men, the House leadership was able to appoint members to Rules more congenial to the leadership's interests than Smith or Colmer. The breakthrough came in 1961, when the late Speaker Sam Rayburn led and won, 217–212, a fight to increase the size of the committee. Even so, Rules could, and sometimes did, manage to kill legislation it didn't like by not allowing it to proceed to the House floor. And a body intended to function as a traffic cop became instead a roadblock.

For years, liberal, labor, and civil-rights groups have waited for Madden to become Chairman. It finally happened, but just barely. The problem was not in Washington, but in the 1st district. As he neared 80, Madden's majorities in general elections began to fall toward the danger point, and this of course attracted competition in the primaries. In the 1970 primary, against an undistinguished field, Madden won only 36% of the votes—enough to win, but a showing that guaranteed strong opposition in 1972.

That opposition came from a 36-year-old state Senator named Adam Benjamin. An unlikely coalition then formed around Madden. The Lake County Democratic machine pooled its efforts not just with organized labor but with its bitter enemy, Mayor Hatcher. Labor and Hatcher were less concerned about local feuds than about preserving Madden's clout in Washington. When he became Chairman of the Rules Committee, it was the first time that a liberal-labor man had chaired the unit since the death of Chicago's Adolph Sabath in 1952, a man who never had a majority on the Committee. In 1972, Benjamin cut into the constituencies of all three groups supporting Madden and wound up losing the primary by less than 5,000 votes.

It is hard to see how Madden can go on winning the 1st much longer, regardless how much some national groups want him to stay Chairman. Although healthy for his age, Madden is not the campaigner he once was. His stories of investigating the Katyn Forest massacre of World War II no longer captivate Polish-American audiences; they have other concerns. With Benjamin's strong showing, Madden's 1972 challenger appears the most likely successor, but anything can happen these days in Lake County—maybe even a Republican victory. Republican have run well in the suburbs south of Gary and Hammond, and in 1972 went so far as to win several state legislative seats there. The split between the ethnics and the blacks gives Nixon's party its chance.

Census Data Pop. 471,761. Central city, 70%; suburban, 30%. Median family income, $10,706; families above $15,000: 22%; families below $3,000: 8%. Median years education, 11.6.

1972 Share of Federal Outlays $248,861,644

DOD	$15,959,000	HEW	$117,105,587
AEC	–	HUD	$21,701,601
NASA	–	DOI	$5,706,941
DOT	$3,466,428	USDA	$14,631,960
		Other	$70,290,127

Federal Military-Industrial Commitments

DOD Contractors American Oil (Whiting), $14.417m: petroleum products.

Economic Base Blast furnace and basic steel mill products, and other primary metal industries; finance, insurance and real estate; fabricated metal products, especially fabricated structural metal products; petroleum refining products, and other petroleum and coal products; and food and kindred products.

The Voters

Registration No district-wide registration.
Median voting age 42.2
Employment profile White collar, 37%. Blue collar, 50%. Service, 13%. Farm, –%.
Ethnic groups Black, 24%. Spanish, 7%. Total foreign stock, 20%. Poland, 3%; Germany, 2%.

Presidential vote

1972	Nixon (R)	91,218	(53%)
	McGovern (D)	82,173	(47%)
1968	Nixon (R)	62,439	(34%)
	Humphrey (D)	92,640	(50%)
	Wallace (AI)	29,311	(16%)

Represenatative

Ray J. Madden (D) Elected 1942; b. Feb. 25, 1892, Waseca, Minn.; home, Gary; Creighton U., LL.B., 1913; Navy, WWI; unmarried; Catholic.

Career Practicing atty., 1913–42; Municipal Judge, Omaha, Nebr., 1916; City Comptroller, Gary, 1935–58; Lake County Treas., 1938–42; V. Chm. Dem. Congressional Campaign Com.

Offices 2409 RHOB, 202-225-2461. Also Rm. 310, New P.O. Bldg., Hammond 46320, 219-931-8280, and Fed. Bldg., Gary 46402, 219-886-2411.

Administrative Assistant Virginia P. Turner

Committees

Rules (Chm.).

Group Ratings

	ADA	COPE	LWV	RIPON	NFU	LCV	CFA	NAB	NSI	ACA
1972	81	91	100	62	86	61	100	0	22	9
1971	78	82	89	71	73	–	88	–	–	7
1970	72	100	–	76	100	84	47	0	56	18

Key Votes

1) Busing	FOR	6) Cmbodia Bmbg	AGN	11) Chkg Acct Intrst	ABS
2) Strip Mines	ABS	7) Bust Hwy Trust	FOR	12) End HISC (HUAC)	FOR
3) Cut Mil $	FOR	8) Farm Sub Lmt	FOR	13) Nixon Sewer Veto	AGN
4) Rev Shrg	FOR	9) School Prayr	AGN	14) Corp Cmpaign $	FOR
5) Pub TV $	FOR	10) Cnsumr Prot	FOR	15) Pol $ Disclosr	AGN

Election Results

1972 general:	Ray J. Madden (D)	95,873	(57%)
	Bruce R. Haller (R)	72,662	(43%)
1972 primary:	Ray J. Madden (D)	48,559	(46%)
	Adam Benjamin, Jr. (D)	43,784	(42%)
	Pete Thompson (D)	3,000	(3%)
	Damian J. Santay (D)	2,772	(3%)
	Henry T. Morgan (D)	1,921	(2%)
	James L. Bell (D)	1,286	(1%)
	Claudia Nava-McCain (D)	1,220	(1%)
	Vaughan Barker (D)	1,053	(1%)
	Michael P. Rogan (D)	892	(1%)
1970 general:	Ray J. Madden (D)	73,145	(66%)
	Eugene M. Kirtland (R)	38,294	(34%)

SECOND DISTRICT Political Background

Outside of the industrial complex in Gary and other towns along Lake Michigan, northwest Indiana is vintage Republican territory. The farmers working the fertile land here have never had cause to revolt in the unseemly manner that characterized their cousins living in drier, less productive terrain farther west; William Jennings Bryan never ran well in the eastern sections of the Midwest. The 2nd congressional district includes most of northwest, back-home-in-Indiana, Indiana. Except for the city of Lafayette, which contains Purdue University, and the suburban sprawl out of Gary and Chicago, the district is mostly rural and small-town. The only sizable parcel of Democratic land here, Michigan City on Lake Michigan, was obligingly removed from the 2nd by the Republican legislature before the 1972 election.

Even so, the 2nd district has not been the scene of overwhelming Republican victories in the last three congressional elections—a departure from normal, to say the least. For 34 years, from 1934 to 1968, this district was represented by none other than Charles A. Halleck, the conservative Repbulican "gut fighter" who was House Minority Leader from 1959 to 1965. With the exception of 1964, Halleck always won reelection easily. But his successor, Republican Earl Landgrebe, has had serious trouble in both the Republican primary and the general election.

Landgrebe's difficulties are generally ascribed to his conservatism, which is pronounced even against the background of other Indiana Republicans. He is one of those Congressmen prone to cast a solitary negative vote, out of conservative principle, on legislation clearly going through. Landgrebe is also the only member of the House District of Columbia Committee openly dead set against home rule for the nation's capital. The Congressman has had an especially hard time of it in Tippecanoe County (Lafayette), the district's largest; he has not carried it since the 1970 primary, when he faced two opponents.

In 1972, Landgrebe got very strong primary opposition from state legislator Russell Boehning, who had the support of many organization Republicans—and the backing of Landgrebe's predecessor, Charles Halleck. (Halleck's son is a judge in Washington who is likely to give police who abuse suspects' rights as much flak as his father used to give big spenders; the son, who wears a beard, may have moved his father a little to the left.) Whatever the case, Boehning, despite a vigorous campaign, fell slightly short with 46% of the vote. In the general election, farmer-professor Floyd Fithian, the Democratic candidate, got 45% aginst Landgrebe. Fithian ran 20% of McGovern in what is still a straight-ticket state.

Apparently, local Republicans oppose Landgrebe largely because they fear that his weakness could lead to a Democratic win. The numbers indicate that such fears are well-founded. Fithian is already planning to run again, and Landgrebe will probably encounter another strong primary challenge. So the prospect is for a fourth consecutive close race in what should be one of the safest Republican districts in the nation.

Census Data Pop. 472,460. Central city, 14%; suburban, 51%. Median family income, $10,377; families above $15,000: 21%; families below $3,000: 7%. Median years education, 12.2.

1972 Share of Federal Outlays $326,244,790

DOD	$48,441,000	HEW	$129,174,219
AEC	$1,297,117	HUD	$8,376,874
NASA	$1,455,247	DOI	$3,099,287
DOT	$5,111,603	USDA	$60,387,431
		Other	$68,902,015

Federal Military-Industrial Commitments

No installations or contractors receiving prime awards greater than $5,000,000.

Economic Base Primary metal industries, especially blast furnace and basic steel products; agriculture, notably grains, hogs and sheep, cattle and poultry; finance, insurance and real estate; fabricated metal products; and electrical equipment and supplies. Also higher education (Purdue Univ.).

The Voters

Registration No district-wide registration.
Median voting age 40.3
Employment profile White collar, 42%. Blue collar, 41%. Service, 12%. Farm, 5%.
Ethnic groups Spanish, 1%. Total foreign stock, 9%. Germany, 2%.

Presidential vote

1972	Nixon (R)	149,099	(74%)
	McGovern (D)	53,463	(26%)
1968	Nixon (R)	109,841	(57%)
	Humphrey (D)	58,461	(31%)
	Wallace (AI)	22,705	(12%)

Representative

Earl F. Landgrebe (R) Elected 1968; b. Jan. 21, 1916, Porter County; home, Valparaiso; married, two children; Lutheran.

Career Owns International Harvester Agency and Landgrebe Motor Transport, Inc.; Ind. Senate, 1958–68; past Dir., Porter County Guidance Clinic; United Cerebral Palsy of Northwest Indiana.

Offices 1203 LHOB, 202-225-5777. Also 451 Lincolnway, Box 323, Valparaiso 46383, 219-462-8750, and 3637 Beaumont Ct., Lafayette 47905, 317-447-3070, and 1100 N. Ninth, Lafayette 47904, 317-742-1131.

Administrative Assistant Ken MacKenzie (L.A.)

Committees

Education and Labor (9th); Subs: No. 5 (Education); No. 8 (Agricultural Labor) (Ranking Mbr.).
District of Columbia (6th); Subs: Education; Government Operations (Ranking Mbr.).

Group Ratings

	ADA	COPE	LWV	RIPON	NFU	LCV	CFA	NAB	NSI	ACA
1972	0	18	0	14	29	0	100	91	100	100
1971	0	17	0	6	23	–	0	–	–	96
1970	12	9	–	31	17	33	40	100	100	100

Key Votes

1) Busing	AGN	6) Cmbodia Bmbg	FOR	11) Chkg Acct Intrst	AGN
2) Strip Mines	FOR	7) Bust Hwy Trust	AGN	12) End HISC (HUAC)	AGN
3) Cut Mil $	AGN	8) Farm Sub Lmt	AGN	13) Nixon Sewer Veto	FOR
4) Rev Shrg	AGN	9) School Prayr	FOR	14) Corp Cmpaign $	FOR
5) Pub TV $	AGN	10) Cnsumr Prot	AGN	15) Pol $ Disclosr	AGN

Election Results

1972 general:	Earl F. Landgrebe (R)	110,406	(55%)
	Floyd Fithian (D)	91,533	(45%)
1972 primary:	Earl F. Landgrebe (R), unopposed		
1970 general:	Earl F. Landgrebe (R)	79,163	(50%)
	Philip A. Sprague (D)	77,959	(50%)

THIRD DISTRICT Political Background

"Supercongressman" was the word used by *Washington Monthly* writer Marjorie Boyd to describe John Brademas, Democratic Representative from the 3rd district of Indiana. In many ways, Brademas cuts an anomalous figure. He is a Methodist of mixed Greek descent whose district includes Notre Dame University; he is a bachelor in a Washington that has become, for Congressmen at least, a family town; and he is a Rhodes Scholar and a Harvard College graduate who has succeeded in the rough-hewn fields of Hoosier politics. After 15 years in the House, Brademas has risen to a high seniority position (fifth) on the House Education and Labor Committee. And as a subcommittee chairman, he drafted one of the few pieces of major legislation initiated in the Congress and not in the White House, the Higher Education Act of 1972.

Brademas can be best categorized as a liberal Democrat, one of the generation of younger members who have so changed the complexion of the party's caucus in the last 10 years. But unlike many others who fit the category, Brademas has worked inside the system. He has not sought positions of authority within the Democratic Study Group, but rather within the House as a whole. Currently, he is a Deputy Whip—a position to which he was appointed by the leadership. At the beginning of the 93rd Congress, Brademas was passed over for promotion to the Whip post; it went instead to John McFall of California, who is somewhat more conservative and more disposed to go along with things as they are. Nevertheless, the Indiana Congressman continues to possess an important role: he is one of the main links between Speaker Albert and Majority Leader O'Neill and the younger, more dissatisfied, and increasingly numerous liberal rank and file of the Democratic membership. Brademas may have played a vital role in persuading the leadership to support the limited, but still substantial, internal reforms passed by the Democratic Caucus in early 1973.

Though Brademas was first elected to the House in 1958, he will be only 47 in 1974. With his seniority, he might become Chairman of the Education and Labor Committee; all the more-senior Democrats are at least nine years older. Or Brademas could perhaps advance into one of the top leadership posts, even the Speakership; he has a similar age advantage on Albert, O'Neill, and McFall. But there is of course the problem of winning reelection, which in straight-ticket, Republican-leaning Indiana is not always easy. The heart of Brademas' district is the industrial town of South Bend, a marginally Democratic town. The territory to the west, around Michigan City, is roughly of the same political complexion, but Elkhart, to the east, is decidedly Republican. Brademas had lower percentages than might have been expected in the presidential years when Indiana and the 3rd district went solidly Republican; he took 52% in 1968 and 55% in 1972. Unlike most members with comparable status in committee and leadership, Brademas must spend considerable time cultivating his district.

Census Data Pop. 471,849. Central city, 27%; suburban, 25%. Median family income, $10,606; families above $15,000: 22%; families below $3,000: 6%. Median years education, 12.1.

1972 Share of Federal Outlays $434,047,308

DOD	$196,477,000	HEW	$131,239,842
AEC	$1,046,942	HUD	$7,399,959
NASA	$120,605	DOI	$124,521
DOT	$10,867,631	USDA	$16,396,372
		Other	$70,374,436

Federal Military-Industrial Commitments

DOD Contractors American Motors (South Bend), $171.727m: jeeps, trucks, and spare parts. Bendix Corp. (Mishawaka), $16.178m; electronics support for Talos missile. Bendix Corp. (South Bend), $9.972m: aircraft components.

Economic Base Transportation equipment, especially trailer coaches; lumber and wood products, especially millwork, plywood and related products; machinery; fabricated metal products; and finance, insurance and real estate. Also higher education (Univ. of Notre Dame).

The Voters

Registration No district-wide registration.
Median voting age 43.0
Employment profile White collar, 44%. Blue collar, 43%. Service, 12%. Farm, 1%.
Ethnic groups Black, 6%. Total foreign stock, 13%. Poland, 3%; Germany, 2%.

Presidential vote

1972	Nixon (R)	120,430	(64%)
	McGovern (D)	66,985	(36%)
1968	Nixon (R)	90,557	(48%)
	Humphrey (D)	76,833	(41%)
	Wallace (AI)	19,716	(11%)

Representative

John Brademas (D) Elected 1958; b. March 2, 1927, Mishawaka; home, South Bend; Harvard, B.A., 1949; Oxford U., D. Phil., 1954; Navy, WWII; unmarried; Methodist.

Career Asst. Prof. political science, St. Mary's Col., Notre Dame, Ind., 1945–46; Exec. Asst. to Adlai E. Stevenson, 1955–56; Legislative Asst. to Sen. Pat McNamara of Mich., 1955; Admin. Asst. to Rep. Thomas L. Ashley of Ohio, 1955; Chief Deputy Majority Whip, 1973–.

Offices 2134 RHOB, 202-225-3915. Also 301 Fed. Bldg., South Bend 46601, 219-234-8111.

Administrative Assistant James P. Mooney

Committees

Education and Labor (5th); Subs: No. 2 (Labor); No. 5 (Education)(Chm.); No. 6 (Education).

House Administration (5th); Subs: Library and Memorials; Printing (Chm.); Electrical and Mechanical Office Equipment.

Joint Com. on the Library (3rd).

Joint Com. on Printing (2nd).

Group Ratings

	ADA	COPE	LWV	RIPON	NFU	LCV	CFA	NAB	NSI	ACA
1972	100	100	100	71	86	93	50	8	0	4
1971	97	83	89	89	87	–	88	–	–	3
1970	92	100	–	82	92	84	100	0	33	22

Key Votes

1) Busing	FOR	6) Cmbodia Bmbg	AGN	11) Chkg Acct Intrst	AGN
2) Strip Mines	AGN	7) Bust Hwy Trust	FOR	12) End HISC (HUAC)	FOR
3) Cut Mil $	FOR	8) Farm Sub Lmt	FOR	13) Nixon Sewer Veto	AGN
4) Rev Shrg	AGN	9) School Prayr	AGN	14) Corp Cmpaign $	FOR
5) Pub TV $	FOR	10) Cnsumr Prot	FOR	15) Pol $ Disclosr	FOR

Election Results

1972 general:	John Brademas (D)	103,949	(55%)
	Don M. Newman (R)	81,369	(43%)
	Helen M. Calvin (Ind.)	2,884	(2%)
1972 primary:	John Brademas (D), unopposed		
1970 general:	John Brademas (D)	87,064	(58%)
	Don M. Newman (R)	64,249	(42%)

FOURTH DISTRICT Political Background

The 4th district of Indiana centers on Fort Wayne, the state's second largest city. More than half the district's votes are cast here and in surrounding Allen County. Fort Wayne is a medium-sized Midwestern industrial city (pop. 178,000). It has a small black ghetto, many nondescript frame houses that belong to people who work in factories, and a small neighborhood of imposing houses that belong to the people who own the factories.

The counties lying around Fort Wayne in the district are mostly agricultural flatland. Those to the south and west of the city have a Democratic tradition, while those to the north are heavily Republican. Any sophisticated poll of the two blocks of rural counties would probably show no major dissimilarities on major issues. Their political disagreements are largely a matter of upbringing and tradition, traceable ultimately to differences in ethnic settlement patterns and attitudes toward the Civil War. Returns from the 1868 presidential election—when Republican Ulysses S. Grant beat Democrat Horatio Seymour by a small margin—show configurations differing little from the closely contested 1962, 1968, and 1970 Indiana Senate races. Altogether, the district is politically marginal, and as this district goes, so usually does Indiana.

The 4th is one of those districts that was created for the benefit of one party and wound up in the hands of the other. The race in 1968 pitted two incumbents against each other. E. Ross Adair, ranking Republican on the House Foreign Affairs Committee, had the clear advantage; most of the new 4th's counties, including Allen, had been part of his old district. Democrat J. Edward Roush, on the other hand, lost most of his old constituency to the newly drawn 5th district. Adair, who won in 1968 with 51% of the votes, probably figured he had locked himself in for a long spell.

But Roush decided to run again in 1970, and this time improved his showing enough to win. The big difference was Allen County, where Roush turned a 5,000-vote deficit into a 4,000-vote plurality. High unemployment, much of it due to the GM strike, helped Roush, as did the settling of a decades-old feud within the Allen County Democratic organization.

The 1972 *Almanac* predicted that the race in the once-again new 4th (redistricted by the Republicans once more) would be close, with Roush having the edge. It turned out to be one of the book's best predictions. As Richard Nixon swept the district, Roush squeaked through with a 51–49 victory over state Sen. Allan Bloom, winner of a closely contested Republican primary. The prediction here for 1974 is another close race, with Roush the winner again by a slightly larger margin.

Census Data Pop. 472,678. Central city, 38%; suburban, 22%. Median family income, $10,443; families above $15,000: 20%; families below $3,000: 7%. Median years education, 12.2.

1972 Share of Federal Outlays $408,104,770

DOD	$189,284,000	HEW	$119,906,900
AEC	–	HUD	$1,669,154
NASA	$1,809,474	DOI	$204,011
DOT	$1,808,840	USDA	$22,575,545
		Other	$70,846,846

Federal Military-Industrial Commitments

DOD Contractors Magnavox (Ft. Wayne), $115.457m: aircraft and missile electronic ware. E Systems (Huntington), $24.830m: electronic ware. ITT (Ft. Wayne), $17.418m: electronic ware. International Harvester (Ft. Wayne), $11.837m: tractor-trucks.

Economic Base Electrical equipment and supplies; motor vehicles and equipment, and other transportation equipment; finance, insurance and real estate; agriculture, notably grains, hogs and sheep, dairy products and cattle; and machinery.

The Voters

Registration No district-wide registration.
Median voting age 42.3
Employment profile White collar, 44%. Blue collar, 42%. Service, 11%. Farm, 3%.
Ethnic groups Black, 4%. Total foreign stock, 6%. Germany, 2%.

Presidential vote

1972	Nixon (R)	130,321	(67%)
	McGovern (D)	63,938	(33%)
1968	Nixon (R)	103,502	(55%)
	Humphrey (D)	68,571	(37%)
	Wallace (AI)	15,511	(8%)

Representative

J. Edward Roush (D) Elected 1970; b. Sept. 12, 1920, Barnsdall, Okla.; home, Huntington; Huntington Col., B.A., 1938; Ind. U. Law School, J.D., 1949; Army, 1942–46, 1950; married, four children; United Brethren in Christ.

Career Atty., Indiana Gen. Assembly, 1949–50; Huntington County Prosecuting Atty., 1955–59; U.S. House of Reps., 1959–69.

Offices 2400 RHOB, 202-225-4436. Also 326 Fed. Bldg., Fort Wayne 46802, 219-742-6250, and 212 S. Main St., Kendallville 46755, 219-347-1179.

Administrative Assistant Phyllis O'Callaghan (L.A.)

Committees

Appropriations (27th); Subs: District of Columbia; Foreign Operations; HUD, Space, Science, Veterans.

Group Ratings

	ADA	COPE	LWV	RIPON	NFU	LCV	CFA	NAB	NSI	ACA
1972	50	91	67	69	100	64	100	17	40	30
1971	70	82	67	82	100	–	100	–	–	25

Key Votes

1) Busing	AGN	6) Cmbodia Bmbg	AGN	11) Chkg Acct Intrst	AGN
2) Strip Mines	AGN	7) Bust Hwy Trust	FOR	12) End HISC (HUAC)	AGN
3) Cut Mil $	FOR	8) Farm Sub Lmt	FOR	13) Nixon Sewer Veto	AGN
4) Rev Shrg	FOR	9) School Prayr	FOR	14) Corp Cmpaign $	ABS
5) Pub TV $	FOR	10) Cnsumr Prot	FOR	15) Pol $ Disclosr	FOR

Election Results

1972 general:	J. Edward Roush (D)	100,327	(51%)
	Allan Bloom (R)	94,492	(49%)
1972 primary:	J. Edward Roush (D), unopposed		
1970 general:	J. Edward Roush (D)	86,582	(52%)
	E. Ross Adair (R)	80,326	(48%)

FIFTH DISTRICT Political Background

The 5th congressional district lies smack in the middle of Indiana, which means the middle of the entire Great Lakes region. Here there is rich Hoosier farmland and three small factory towns: Anderson, Kokomo, and Marion. The district also dips down to take a small portion of the recently expanded city of Indianapolis. Just to the north of the city are the political poles of the 5th: Hamilton County, which is high-income, exurban Indianapolis, and very heavily Republican; and Anderson, which has a GM plant, a large number of UAW members, and usually solidly Democratic.

That Anderson was included in this district by a Republican legislature is testimony to the 5th's heavy Republican margins and the confidence the legislators placed in the political durability of Rep. Elwood Hillis. The Congressman is a relative newcomer to the House, having succeeded Richard Roudebush who ran for the Senate in 1970. Roudebush won the Senate nomination at the state convention, having already won the 1970 Republican primary nomination in the 5th; Hillis was selected as the new Republican candidate by a party convention.

Hillis apparently did his homework well during his first term. He increased his 1970 margin of 56-44 to a solid 64-36 over the same candidate in 1972. Indiana Democrats are unlikely to target the 5th for the 1974 elections.

Census Data Pop. 471,921. Central city, 25%; suburban, 17%. Median family income, $10,314; families above $15,000: 22%; families below $3,000: 7%. Median years education, 12.2.

1972 Share of Federal Outlays $341,510,405

DOD	$91,352,000	HEW	$124,762,929
AEC	–	HUD	$9,844,496
NASA	$57,006	DOI	$227,036
DOT	$13,858,215	USDA	$21,265,019
		Other	$80,143,710

Federal Military-Industrial Commitments

DOD Installations Grissom AFB (Peru).

Economic Base Primary metal industries; finance, insurance and real estate; agriculture, notably grains, hogs and sheep, and cattle; electrical equipment and supplies; and fabricated metal products.

The Voters

Registration No district-wide registration.
Median voting age 42.6
Employment profile White collar, 41%. Blue collar, 44%. Service, 12%. Farm, 3%.
Ethnic groups Black, 6%. Total foreign stock, 4%.

Presidential vote

1972	Nixon (R)	135,915	(70%)
	McGovern (D)	58,893	(30%)
1968	Nixon (R)	102,153	(53%)
	Humphrey (D)	70,682	(37%)
	Wallace (AI)	19,443	(10%)

Representative

Elwood Haynes Hillis (R) Elected 1970; b. March 6, 1926, Kokomo; home, Kokomo; Ind. U., B.S., 1949; Ind. U. Law School, J.D., 1952; Army, 1944–46; married, three children; Presbyterian.

Career Practicing atty., 1952– ; Indiana House of Reps., 1966–70; Kokomo Housing Authority Bd.

Offices 1721 LHOB, 202-225-5037. Also 504 Union Bank Bldg., Kokomo 46901, 317-457-4411.

Administrative Assistant Donald W. Ruby

Committees

Post Office and Civil Service (6th); Subs: Postal Facilities, Mail, and Labor Management (Ranking Mbr.); Retirement and Employee Benefits.

Veterans' Affairs (7th); Subs: Hospitals; Housing (Ranking Mbr.); Insurance.

Group Ratings

	ADA	COPE	LWV	RIPON	NFU	LCV	CFA	NAB	NSI	ACA
1972	19	50	44	78	67	27	0	63	100	50
1971	11	33	44	53	36	–	57	–	–	76

Key Votes

1) Busing	AGN	6) Cmbodia Bmbg	AGN	11) Chkg Acct Intrst	ABS
2) Strip Mines	AGN	7) Bust Hwy Trust	AGN	12) End HISC (HUAC)	AGN
3) Cut Mil $	AGN	8) Farm Sub Lmt	AGN	13) Nixon Sewer Veto	FOR
4) Rev Shrg	FOR	9) School Prayr	FOR	14) Corp Cmpaign $	ABS
5) Pub TV $	AGN	10) Cnsumr Prot	FOR	15) Pol $ Disclosr	FOR

Election Results

1972 general:	Elwood H. Hillis (R)	124,692	(64%)
	Kathleen Z. Williams (D)	69,746	(36%)
1972 primary:	Elwood H. Hillis (R)	36,270	(86%)
	Alenzo Harris (R)	5,705	(14%)
1970 general:	Elwood H. Hillis (R)	86,199	(56%)
	Kathleen Z. Williams (D)	67,740	(44%)

SIXTH DISTRICT Political Background

Indianapolis is one of the most conservative and Republican of the nation's major cities. Another such city is Columbus, Ohio, with which Indianapolis can be compared in a number of instructive ways. Both are mainly white-collar cities, much more white-collar than the smaller cities of Indiana or Ohio; both Indianapolis and Columbus have many people employed in banking and insurance as well as state government. Both cities never experienced the tide of immigrants from Eastern and Southern Europe that swept into most factory towns of the Great Lakes area; these immigrants of course soon became Democratic voters. The immigrants Indianapolis and Columbus took were largely from the adjacent rural countryside and from the American South. Both cities have newspapers dominated by conservative voices; the Indianapolis

Star not only refuses to run the syndicated columns of liberal journalists, it also blatantly slants front-page news coverage when it feels strongly about something. And there is a last, curious similarity: for many years, both capital cities elected conservative Democrats Mayor—in Indianapolis until 1967 and in Columbus until 1971.

The current version of the 6th congressional district takes in about a third of the recently expanded city of Indianapolis, four suburban counties, and a couple of townships in a sixth county. Recent changes in the district's boundaries were designed to defeat Democrat Andrew Jacobs in the adjacent 11th district—something Republican state legislators finally accomplished after repeated attempts in 1972. Accordingly, placed here so they could not vote for Jacobs were a fair number of blacks and working-class whites on the west side of Indianapolis. Otherwise, the 6th is all of a piece, heavily conservative and overwhelmingly Republican. The current 6th was the only Indiana district that went for Goldwater in 1964. The candidate's showing was a measure of the district's conservatism and the influence of the *Star*, which endorsed the Arizonan.

The 6th has proved to be a safe district for Republican Congressman William G. Bray, first elected in 1950. Since then, he has represented a variety of Indiana congressional districts—the result of a variety of Indiana redistricting measures. In fact, at one point, Bray's district stretched clear to Terre Haute, some 150 miles away. The Congressman is now the ranking minority member on the House Armed Services Committee, where he steadily supports the bipartisan, pro-military consensus led by Chairman F. Edward Hebert. Reelection should be no problem for him, but there is the possibility of retirement in 1974, when he will be 71.

Census Data Pop. 471,595. Central city, 54%; suburban, 46%. Median family income, $10,497; families above $15,000: 20%; families below $3,000: 6%. Median years education, 12.0.

1972 Share of Federal Outlays $494,142,634

DOD	$157,653,000	HEW	$146,623,323
AEC	–	HUD	$45,825,808
NASA	$276,833	DOI	$508,126
DOT	$20,809,591	USDA	$15,271,302
		Other	$107,174,651

Federal Military-Industrial Commitments

No installations or contractors receiving prime awards greater than $5,000,000. (See Indiana 11).

Economic Base Transportation equipment, especially motor vehicles and equipment; finance, insurance and real estate; electrical equipment and supplies; machinery, especially general industrial machinery; and agriculture, notably grains, hogs and sheep, cattle and dairy products.

The Voters

Registration No district-wide registration.
Median voting age 41.1
Employment profile White collar, 45%. Blue collar, 42%. Service, 11%. Farm, 2%.
Ethnic groups Black, 4%. Total foreign stock, 4%.

Presidential vote

1972	Nixon (R)	127,566	(74%)
	McGovern (D)	45,691	(26%)
1968	Nixon (R)	98,265	(54%)
	Humphrey (D)	55,664	(31%)
	Wallace (AI)	27,095	(15%)

Represenatative

William Gilmer Bray (R) Elected 1950; b. June 17, 1903, Mooresville; home, Martinsville; Ind. U., LL.B., 1927; Army, WWII; Col. (Ret.) USAR, married, one child; Society of Friends.

Career Prosecuting Atty., 1926–30; practicing atty., 1927–51.

Offices 2204 RHOB, 202-225-2276. Also 3901 N. Meridian St., Indianapolis 46208, 317-633-7277.

Administrative Assistant Bruce Merkle

Committees

Armed Services (Ranking Mbr.); Sp. Sub. on Intelligence.

Group Ratings

	ADA	COPE	LWV	RIPON	NFU	LCV	CFA	NAB	NSI	ACA
1972	0	14	40	44	50	9	0	75	100	100
1971	3	8	22	36	27	–	33	–	–	85
1970	0	0	–	20	31	3	37	100	100	86

Key Votes

1) Busing	AGN	6) Cmbodia Bmbg	FOR	11) Chkg Acct Intrst	AGN
2) Strip Mines	AGN	7) Bust Hwy Trust	AGN	12) End HISC (HUAC)	AGN
3) Cut Mil $	AGN	8) Farm Sub Lmt	AGN	13) Nixon Sewer Veto	FOR
4) Rev Shrg	AGN	9) School Prayr	FOR	14) Corp Cmpaign $	FOR
5) Pub TV $	AGN	10) Cnsumr Prot	AGN	15) Pol $ Disclosr	AGN

Election Results

1972 general:	William G. Bray (R)	112,525	(65%)
	David W. Evans (D)	61,070	(35%)
1972 primary:	William G. Bray (R), unopposed		
1970 general:	William G. Bray (R)	115,113	(61%)
	Terrence D. Straub (D)	74,599	(39%)

SEVENTH DISTRICT Political Background

Like the old Cannonball named after it, the Wabash River flows across the rolling farmland of western Indiana on its way to meet the Ohio. And in a near straight line from Indianapolis to St. Louis runs the old National Road (now U.S. 40). The river and the road intersect in Terre Haute (pop. 70,000), the largest city in the 7th congressional district of Indiana. Terre Haute is a rough and rude factory town, once known for its gambling and vice activities; it is known today as the home town of Sen. Birch Bayh. Terre Haute has always had a Democratic machine, which more often than not has controlled the Vigo County Courthouse. Besides that, the machine often produces margins big enough to carry the surrounding territory.

That presumed margin inspired the Democratic redistricting plan of 1965. It created the 7th more or less as it exists today, but with no incumbent Congressman. The best-laid plans of redistricters, of course, often go awry. So with 1966 being a good Republican year, John Myers, an attractive young Republican candidate, won the election in the 7th district by a convincing margin. He has remained in the House ever since. The Democrats, bogged down in various local problems, have never made a concerted effort to capture the district drawn for them.

Things might be different in 1974. Myers has been mentioned as a possible Republican candidate to oppose Sen. Birch Bayh. If Myers stays in the 7th, two important bases of opposition exist, Terre Haute and Bloomington. The latter is the home of Indiana University. Though its student body is not as Democratic as those in state universities of Michigan or Wisconsin (where McGovern trounced Nixon), Bloomington still supplied a Democratic margin of significant size in what was once a solidly Republican town. With the district's farm population dwindling and Terre Haute's population at a standstill, Bloomington—enjoying a university-based local boom—has become an increasingly important city in the 7th. It is just one more example of how the 18-year-old vote has begun to change the face of politics in the Midwest.

Census Data Pop. 472,041. Central city, 15%; suburban, 29%. Median family income, $8,808; families above $15,000: 15%; families below $3,000: 10%. Median years education, 12.1.

1972 Share of Federal Outlays $371,324,258

DOD	$55,909,000	HEW	$176,790,018
AEC	$157,105	HUD	$3,479,533
NASA	$458,279	DOI	$322,167
DOT	$12,644,407	USDA	$46,301,950
		Other	$75,261,799

Federal Military-Industrial Commitments

DOD Contractors Dupont (Newport), $17.313m: operation of Newport Army Ammunition plant.

Economic Base Electrical equipment and supplies; agriculture, notably grains, hogs and sheep, and cattle; finance, insurance and real estate; machinery; and fabricated metal products. Also higher education (Indiana State Univ., and Indiana Univ.).

The Voters

Registration No district-wide registration.
Median voting age 42.3
Employment profile White collar, 42%. Blue collar, 39%. Service, 14%. Farm, 5%.
Ethnic groups Black, 2%. Total foreign stock, 4%.

Presidential vote

1972	Nixon (R)		135,270	(65%)
	McGovern (D)		72,718	(35%)
1968	Nixon (R)		98,751	(51%)
	Humphrey (D)		74,574	(38%)
	Wallace (AI)		21,677	(11%)

Representative

John Thomas Myers (R) Elected 1966; b. Feb. 8, 1927, Covington; home, Covington; Ind. State U., B.S., 1951; Army, WWII; married, two children; Episcopalian.

Career Cashier, trust officer, Foundation Trust Co., 1954–66.

Offices 103 CHOB, 202-225-5805. Also 107 Fed. Bldg., Terre Haute 47808, 812-238-1619.

Administrative Assistant Ronald Hardman

Committees

Appropriations (15th); Subs: District of Columbia; Treasury, Postal Service, General Government.

Group Ratings

	ADA	COPE	LWV	RIPON	NFU	LCV	CFA	NAB	NSI	ACA
1972	0	27	20	38	50	20	50	73	100	86
1971	11	0	33	35	29	–	29	–	–	92
1970	12	9	–	41	55	0	42	92	100	83

Key Votes

1) Busing	AGN	6) Cmbodia Bmbg	FOR	11) Chkg Acct Intrst	ABS
2) Strip Mines	FOR	7) Bust Hwy Trust	AGN	12) End HISC (HUAC)	AGN
3) Cut Mil $	AGN	8) Farm Sub Lmt	AGN	13) Nixon Sewer Veto	AGN
4) Rev Shrg	AGN	9) School Prayr	FOR	14) Corp Cmpaign $	FOR
5) Pub TV $	FOR	10) Cnsumr Prot	AGN	15) Pol $ Disclosr	AGN

Election Results

1972 general:	John T. Myers (R)	128,688	(62%)
	Warren Henegar (D)	80,145	(38%)
1972 primary:	John T. Myers (R), unopposed		
1970 general:	John T. Myers (R)	97,152	(57%)
	William D. Roach (D)	73,042	(43%)

EIGHTH DISTRICT Political Background

The 8th district of Indiana comprises the southwest corner of the state. The district contains the city of Evansville (pop. 138,000) on the Ohio River and several river counties that are hilly or even mountainous by Midwestern standards. This part of Indiana was the first to attract white men. Vincennes, now a small town on the Wabash River, was once the metropolis of Indiana. Today Evansville is a reasonably prosperous city (fourth largest in the state), but most of the rest of the district has suffered ever since railroads took the traffic away from Ohio River steamboats.

Southwest Indiana was settled in large part by German Catholics, who have traditionally voted Democratic. During the Civil War, most of what is now the 8th was Copperhead country, friendly to the South and hostile to Mr. Lincoln's war and the Republican party. Today, though the issues have changed, the 8th remains generally Democratic—except in presidential contests when the Southern-accented Hoosiers here dislike the kind of liberal candidates nominated by the Democratic party. But Sens. Bayh and Hartke have always carried the district. Hartke is a native son, having been Mayor of Evansville when he was first elected Senator.

For many years the 8th belonged to Rep. Winfield K. Denton, middle-of-the-road Democrat. Apparently thinking that Denton was invulnerable, the 1965 redistricters transferred heavily Democratic Clark County (across the Ohio from Louisville, Kentucky) to the 9th district. The change was designed to help then-freshman Democrat Lee Hamilton of the 9th. The result was not anticipated: in 1966 Hamilton won by a surprisingly large margin, while the veteran Denton was swept out of office by 4,000 votes. Figures show that Denton could have won in his old district, and that Hamilton, as it turned out, didn't neet Clark County to win.

A couple of redistrictings later, the man who beat Denton, Republican Roger Zion, continues to hold the seat. In 1970, the Democrats targeted the district and cut Zion's margin, but they were unable to dent his strength in his home town of Evansville, which casts about a third of the district's votes. Zion carried Evansville's Vanderburgh County by a solid 9,000 votes, even as the other native son, Hartke, won by 3,000. The discrepancy showed an amount of ticket-splitting unusual in Indiana. In 1972, the Democrats made little effort here, and Zion won with a whopping 63% of the votes. Barring a strong push by Democrats and an unusual shift of public opinion, Zion would appear to have made his seat safe.

Census Data Pop. 472,175. Central city, 29%; suburban, 12%. Median family income, $8,557; families above $15,000: 13%; families below $3,000: 11%. Median years education, 11.8.

1972 Share of Federal Outlays $394,120,587

DOD	$113,347,000	HEW	$155,352,296
AEC	–	HUD	$869,153
NASA	$20,500	DOI	$3,141,036
DOT	$30,356,375	USDA	$30,576,196
		Other	$60,458,031

Federal Military-Industrial Commitments

DOD Installations Naval Ammunition Depot (Crane).

Economic Base Agriculture, notably grains, hogs and sheep, cattle and poultry; furniture and fixtures, especially household furniture; finance, insurance and real estate; food and kindred products; and machinery.

The Voters

Registration No district-wide registration.
Median voting age 45.4
Employment profile White collar, 38%. Blue collar, 44%. Service, 13%. Farm, 5%.
Ethnic groups Black, 3%. Total foreign stock, 2%. Germany, 1%.

Presidential vote

1972	Nixon (R)	138,545	(65%)
	McGovern (D)	73,835	(35%)
1968	Nixon (R)	108,377	(49%)
	Humphrey (D)	88,442	(40%)
	Wallace (AI)	22,330	(10%)

Representative

Roger H. Zion (R) Elected 1966; b. Sept. 17, 1921, Escanaba, Mich.; home, Evansville; U. of Wis., B.A., 1943; Harvard Graduate School of Business Admin., 1944–45; Navy, WWII; married, three children; Congregationalist.

Career Sales rep., sales training mgr., dir. of training and professional relations, Mead & Johnson Co., 1946–65; author.

Offices 1226 LHOB, 202-225-4636. Also Rm. 128, U.S. Courthouse & Fed. Bldg., Evansville 47708, 812-423-6871.

Administrative Assistant Robert C. Junk

Committees

Internal Security (2nd).

Public Works (6th); Subs: Energy; Investigations and Review; Transportation; Water Resources.

Group Ratings

	ADA	COPE	LWV	RIPON	NFU	LCV	CFA	NAB	NSI	ACA
1972	0	0	33	50	57	20	0	92	100	91
1971	3	9	33	38	33	–	25	–	–	88
1970	12	18	–	47	31	50	45	91	100	89

Key Votes

1) Busing	AGN	6) Cmbodia Bmbg	ABS	11) Chkg Acct Intrst	AGN
2) Strip Mines	AGN	7) Bust Hwy Trust	AGN	12) End HISC (HUAC)	AGN
3) Cut Mil $	AGN	8) Farm Sub Lmt	FOR	13) Nixon Sewer Veto	FOR
4) Rev Shrg	FOR	9) School Prayr	FOR	14) Corp Cmpaign $	FOR
5) Pub TV $	AGN	10) Cnsumr Prot	AGN	15) Pol $ Disclosr	AGN

Election Results

1972 general:	Roger H. Zion (R)	133,850	(63%)
	Richard L. Deen (D)	77,371	(37%)
1972 primary:	Roger H. Zion (R), unopposed		
1970 general:	Roger H. Zion (R)	93,088	(53%)
	J. David Huber (D)	83,911	(47%)

NINTH DISTRICT Political Background

What happens to Congressmen carried into office on the strength of a presidential landslide? Traditionally, they have been swept out when there were no more coattails to ride. But this has not happened in recent years. Of the Democratic Congressmen elected in 1964 in districts previously represented by Republicans, half survived the 1966 elections, and nearly half either still serve in the House or retired voluntarily. One of the former is Lee Hamilton of Indiana's 9th district, and his case is instructive.

In 1964, Hamilton, then president of the Bartholomew County Young Democrats, won a surprisingly big 12,000-vote victory over veteran Republican Congressman Earl Wilson. This was the year Lyndon Johnson became the first Democratic presidential candidate since Franklin D. Roosevelt to carry the 9th—in rough terms, the southeast corner of Indiana. The district is basically Republican territory, from the hills along the Ohio River to the neat small city of Columbus. Columbus, Indiana is the home of Cummins Engine and its scholarly president, J. Irwin Miller. *Esquire* magazine once put Miller—a liberal Republican active in many causes and who showed up on the White House enemies list—on its cover, and suggested that he should be President of the United States—an idea, of course, that has come to look better and better all the time.

In 1966, Hamilton's sharp campaigning and intelligent use of the resources available to incumbents helped him to win reelection over a determined Republican bid to retake the seat. Congressman Hamilton was especially successful in getting post offices and public works projects for his district, which, outside Columbus, is far from prosperous.

By 1970, Hamilton was home free, running far ahead of his party's ticket. And in 1972, he took 63% of the vote—the best showing of any Indiana Democratic Congressman. True, he had help from redistricters along the way. A 1965 Democratic plan added a Democratic county, and by 1972 the Republicans placed all the available Democratic territory in the 9th, knowing that he could not be beaten whatever their efforts. But Hamilton would have won all his races without the help of redistricting.

In the House, Hamilton has generally voted with the other younger Northern Democrats. As a member of the Foreign Affairs Committee, he had supported the Johnson Administration's Vietnam policies, but by the time of the 1970 Cambodia invasion, he switched to the dovish side. The Congressman is Chairman of the Near East and South Asia Subcommittee which has jurisdiction over a politically sensitive area of policy. It is not one, however, of major political importance in the 9th district, which contains few Jewish people and even fewer Arabs.

Census Data Pop. 472,321. Central city, 0%; suburban, 34%. Median family income, $9,001; families above $15,000: 14%; families below $3,000: 9%. Median years education, 11.4.

1972 Share of Federal Outlays $370,393,326

DOD	$116,034,000	HEW	$130,474,204
AEC	$19,894	HUD	$2,795,554
NASA	$54,897	DOI	$390,700
DOT	$13,736,307	USDA	$25,267,318
		Other	$81,620,452

Federal Military-Industrial Commitments

DOD Contractors ICI America (Charlestown), $70.818m: operation of Indiana Army Ammunition plant. Olin Corp. (Charlestown), $12.887m: operation of Indiana Army Ammunition plant.
DOD Installations Jefferson Army Proving Ground (Madison).

Economic Base Agriculture, notably hogs and sheep, cattle and grains; finance, insurance and real estate; machinery, especially general industrial machinery; food and kindred products; and household furniture, and other furniture and fixtures.

The Voters

Registration No district-wide registration.
Median voting age 43.1
Employment profile White collar, 37%. Blue collar, 47%. Service, 11%. Farm, 5%.
Ethnic groups Black, 2%. Total foreign stock, 2%.

Presidential vote

1972	Nixon (R)	123,569	(64%)
	McGovern (D)	70,613	(36%)
1968	Nixon (R)	94,673	(48%)
	Humphrey (D)	76,980	(39%)
	Wallace (AI)	26,178	(13%)

Representative

Lee Herbert Hamilton (D) Elected 1964; b. April 20, 1931, Daytona Beach, Fla.; home, Columbus; DePauw U., B.A., 1952; Goethe U., Germany, 1952–53; Ind. U. School of Law, J.D., 1956; married, three children; Methodist.

Career Practicing atty., 1956–64; instructor in contracts and negotiables at American Banking Inst.; Treas., Bartholomew County Young Democrats, 1960–63, Pres., 1963–64.

Offices 2344 RHOB, 202-225-5315. Also U.S. P.O., Columbus 47201, 812-372-2571, and 1201 E. 10th St., Jeffersonville 47274, 812-283-1261.

Administrative Assistant David McFall

Committees

Foreign Affairs (11th); Subs: Asian and Pacific Affairs; Europe; Near East and South Asia (Chm.).

Group Ratings

	ADA	COPE	LWV	RIPON	NFU	LCV	CFA	NAB	NSI	ACA
1972	50	82	75	80	86	73	50	17	50	26
1971	89	75	83	88	100	–	88	–	–	7
1970	80	73	–	82	100	81	90	11	78	13

Key Votes

1) Busing	AGN	6) Cmbodia Bmbg	AGN	11) Chkg Acct Intrst	AGN
2) Strip Mines	AGN	7) Bust Hwy Trust	AGN	12) End HISC (HUAC)	AGN
3) Cut Mil $	FOR	8) Farm Sub Lmt	FOR	13) Nixon Sewer Veto	AGN
4) Rev Shrg	FOR	9) School Prayr	AGN	14) Corp Cmpaign $	AGN
5) Pub TV $	FOR	10) Cnsumr Prot	FOR	15) Pol $ Disclosr	FOR

Election Results

1972 general:	Lee Hamilton (D)	122,698	(63%)
	William A. Johnson (R)	72,325	(37%)
1972 primary:	Lee Hamilton (D)	51,683	(85%)
	Albert Sheets (D)	8,807	(15%)
1970 general:	Lee Hamilton (D)	104,599	(62%)
	Richard B. Wathen (R)	62,772	(38%)

TENTH DISTRICT Political Background

Muncie, Indiana, was the subject of *Middletown*, a pioneering sociological study done in the 1930s by Robert and Helen Lynd. Before the Lynds published their findings, most educated laymen imagined small Midwestern cities like Muncie were tightly knit, homogeneous communities. But the Lynds discovered a factory town sharply divided along class lines, with local affairs firmly in the hands of a small business elite. Since the 1930s, the GM plants and others around Muncie have been unionized, blue-collar wages have risen greatly, and the power of the local elite has been reduced.

But class divisions remain. A recent *New York Times* article quoted a member of the Muncie elite expressing the belief that everyone in town was a Republican. In his part of town, perhaps; but Muncie, as often as not, gives most of its votes to Democrats. Life-and-death economic power remains in the hands of businessmen; in Muncie today, however, that power can be found in the board room of some far-away conglomerate, not in operations controlled by local families, like the notable Ball family. Ball State University in Muncie owes much to the charitable instincts of the Balls.

Muncie lies roughly in the middle of the 10th congressional district. At 69,000, it is the largest city in the 10th. The only other sizable city here, Richmond (pop. 44,000), is a quite different kind of place. It has a long-standing Quaker tradition, and is the site of the Friend's Earlham College. But the Quakerism of this part of Indiana is closer to that of Richard Nixon than to that of the American Friends Service Committee. Richmond has retained strong Republican voting habits from its antislavery days before the Civil War.

The 10th was a creation of the 1968 Republican redistricting, though its boundaries have been altered significantly since. It is no surprise that the district's first—and so far only—Congressman is a conservative Republican, David Dennis. But Dennis has not gone unchallenged. In 1970, a 28-year-old Ball State professor, Philip Sharp, came within 2,500 votes of upsetting Dennis. Sharp had the strong backing of not only students, but of Democratic organizations and organized labor, especially the UAW. The auto union was striking GM at the time.

In 1972 Sharp tried again, this time falling far short of success. Several reasons account for the Democrat's poorer showing. First, frightened by his near-defeat in 1970, Dennis worked harder on constituency matters. Second, in a state that still has straight-ticket voting habits, the Nixon landslide helped Republican incumbents. Third, redistricting removed the city of Anderson, where a large union vote usually produces Democratic majorities. The Republican legislature substituted the heavily Republican Indianapolis suburbs in Hancock County, which gave 67% of its votes to Dennis.

Dennis is now a middle-seniority member of the Judiciary Committee. He also seems to be working as a kind of understudy for H. R. Gross, the conservative Iowa curmudgeon (see Iowa 3), though he lacks Gross's panache.

Census Data Pop. 472,335. Central city, 15%; suburban, 27%. Median family income, $9,635; families above $15,000: 17%; families below $3,000: 8%. Median years education, 12.1.

1972 Share of Federal Outlays $244,108,681

DOD	$24,890,000	HEW	$129,755,961
AEC	–	HUD	$293,308
NASA	$35,107	DOI	$164,795
DOT	$5,076,858	USDA	$23,386,946
		Other	$60,505,706

Federal Military-Industrial Commitments

DOD Contractors Avco Corp. (Richmond), $13.201m: 25mm, 40mm, and 155mm projectiles.

Economic Base Motor vehicles and equipment, and other transportation equipment; agriculture, notably grains, hogs and sheep, cattle and dairy products; machinery; primary metal industries; and finance, insurance and real estate. Also higher education (Ball State Univ.).

The Voters

Registration No district-wide registration.
Median voting age 42.3
Employment profile White collar, 37%. Blue collar, 47%. Service, 12%. Farm, 4%.
Ethnic groups Black, 3%. Total foreign stock, 3%.

Presidential vote

1972	Nixon (R)	129,455	(69%)
	McGovern (D)	57,073	(31%)
1968	Nixon (R)	99,345	(52%)
	Humphrey (D)	69,746	(36%)
	Wallace (AI)	22,440	(12%)

Representative

David Worth Dennis (R) Elected 1968; b. June 7, 1912, Washington, D.C.; home, Richmond; Earlham Col., B.A., 1933; Harvard Law School, LL.B., 1936; Army, WWII; married, two children; Society of Friends.

Career Practicing atty., 1936– ; Prosecuting Atty., Wayne County, 1939–43; Ind. House of Reps., 1947–49, 1953–59.

Offices 1535 LHOB, 202-225-3021. Also 111 Westcott Hotel Bldg., Richmond 47374, 317-966-6125, and 201 Fed. Bldg., Anderson 46016, 317-642-1777.

Administrative Assistant Dick Powell

Committees

Judiciary (7th); Subs: No. 1 (Immigration and Nationality); No. 5 (Antitrust Matters); Sp. Sub. on Reform of Federal Criminal Laws.

Group Ratings

	ADA	COPE	LWV	RIPON	NFU	LCV	CFA	NAB	NSI	ACA
1972	0	9	36	67	33	53	50	92	100	96
1971	14	0	17	53	20	–	0	–	–	96
1970	12	9	–	63	31	45	43	100	90	84

Key Votes

1) Busing	AGN	6) Cmbodia Bmbg	FOR	11) Chkg Acct Intrst	AGN
2) Strip Mines	AGN	7) Bust Hwy Trust	AGN	12) End HISC (HUAC)	AGN
3) Cut Mil $	AGN	8) Farm Sub Lmt	FOR	13) Nixon Sewer Veto	FOR
4) Rev Shrg	AGN	9) School Prayr	FOR	14) Corp Cmpaign $	AGN
5) Pub TV $	AGN	10) Cnsumr Prot	AGN	15) Pol $ Disclosr	FOR

Election Results

1972 general:	David W. Dennis (R)	106,798	(57%)
	Philip R. Sharp (D)	79,756	(43%)
1972 primary:	David W. Dennis (R), unopposed		
1970 general:	David W. Dennis (R)	81,439	(51%)
	Philip R. Sharp (D)	78,871	(49%)

ELEVENTH DISTRICT Political Background

The 11th district is a portion of the recently expanded city of Indianapolis (see also Indiana 6). It is an apt illustration of how seemingly small changes in district boundaries can make a crucial political difference come election day. Before the 1972 redistricting, the 11th included virtually all of Indianapolis' black community and most of its solidly blue-collar Democratic precincts. For the 1972 election, the Republican legislature added 52,000 whites and subtracted 5,000 blacks. Moreover, whites from integrated working-class neighborhoods were removed and replaced with arch-conservative suburbanites.

The purpose was, of course, political: to defeat Democratic Congressman Andrew Jacobs, Jr. But it almost didn't work. Jacobs, whose father represented the district for two years following the surprise Truman victory of 1948, first won the seat in 1964. That year, Jacobs had the good fortune to be running when Barry Goldwater was the Republican presidential nominee and the 11th district incumbent was not seeking reelection. Even so, Jacobs managed to carry the district, which then included all of Marion County, by only 3,000 votes. In 1966, redistricting pared the district down to one-man-one-vote size by removing suburban areas, which helped Jacobs to win again in 1966. He survived a Republican redistricting to win once more in 1968. In 1970, he accumulated his largest margin, 58–42, against ultraconservative state Sen. Danny Burton.

Burton was a candidate again in the redrawn 11th in 1972. There was, of course, strong competition in the Republican primary—Democratic congressional candidates had not carried the territory within the district's boundaries since 1964. Unfortunately for Jacobs, Burton lost the Republican primary to William H. Hudnut III by a scant 81 votes out of 47,000 cast. Hudnut, a minister considered a moderate, pretty much backed the policies of the Nixon Administration down the line. The candidate's most powerful political support came from Indianapolis Mayor Richard Lugar and Republican National Committeeman L. Keith Bulen.

Hudnut also won the general election by a small margin, 51–49, over Jacobs. One thing helped Hudnut appreciably, and that was the mandatory straight-party lever, which must be pulled to activate the voting machine. The device is still used in some parts of Indiana, including Marion County; in the Goldwater year, however, election officials did not employ its use when it looked like the Republican at the top of the ticket would not carry Indianapolis.

The prospect here for 1974 is for another close race, if Jacobs tries a comeback as expected. In 1974, Sen. Birch Bayh will be at the top of the Indiana Democratic ticket. And if Bayh runs as well in Indianapolis as in the past, Jacobs will not have to run 15% ahead of his ticket to win.

Census Data Pop. 472,533. Central city, 93%; suburban, 7%. Median family income, $10,785; families above $15,000: 26%; families below $3,000: 7%. Median years education, 12.2.

1972 Share of Federal Outlays $472,092,758

DOD	$157,144,379	HEW	$133,578,775
AEC	–	HUD	$45,867,562
NASA	$276,822	DOI	$508,589
DOT	$19,965,272	USDA	$13,917,125
		Other	$100,834,234

Federal Military-Industrial Commitments

DOD Contractors General Motors (Indianapolis), $163.213m: engines, turbines, and components; vehicular equipment components; aircraft components; aircraft launching and ground handling equipment. Engineering Research, Inc. (Indianapolis), $11.617m: 750-pount bomb components.
DOD Installations Fort Benjamin Harrison AB (Indianapolis). Naval Avionics Facility (Indianapolis).

Economic Base Finance, insurance and real estate; electrical equipment and supplies; transportation equipment, especially motor vehicles and equipment, and aircraft and parts; machinery, especially general industrial machinery; and chemicals and allied products, especially drugs.

The Voters

Registration No district-wide registration.
Median voting age 42.6
Employment profile White collar, 53%. Blue collar, 34%. Service, 13%. Farm, –%.
Ethnic groups Black, 2%. Total foreign stock, 6%. Germany, 1%.

Presidential vote

1972	Nixon (R)	125,009	(66%)
	McGovern (D)	63,456	(34%)
1968	Nixon (R)	99,982	(52%)
	Humphrey (D)	74,066	(39%)
	Wallace (AI)	16,702	(9%)

Representative

William Herbert Hudnut III (R) Elected 1972; b. Oct. 17, 1932, Cincinnati, Ohio; home, Indianapolis; Princeton U., B.A., 1954; Union Theological Seminary, B.D., 1957; Hanover Col., honorary D.D., 1967; Wabash College, honorary D.D., 1969; married, five children; Presbyterian.

Career Asst. Minister, Westminster Presbyterian Church, Buffalo, N.Y., 1957–60; Sr. Minister, First Presbyterian Church, Annapolis, Md., 1960–63; Sr. Minister, Second Presbyterian Church, Indianapolis, 1963–72; Pres., Bd. of Trustees, Darrow School, New Lebanon, N.Y.; Bd. Mb., Marion County Mental Health Assoc.

Offices 1004 LHOB, 202-225-4011. Also 441A Fed. Bldg., 46 E. Ohio St.,, Indianapolis 46204, 317-633-7331.

Administrative Assistant Bruce Melchert

Committees

Interstate and Foreign Commerce (18th); Sub: Public Health and Environment.

Group Ratings: Newly Elected

Key Votes

1) Busing	NE	6) Cmbodia Bmbg	FOR	11) Chkg Acct Intrst	AGN
2) Strip Mines	NE	7) Bust Hwy Trust	AGN	12) End HISC (HUAC)	AGN
3) Cut Mil $	NE	8) Farm Sub Lmt	NE	13) Nixon Sewer Veto	FOR
4) Rev Shrg	NE	9) School Prayr	NE	14) Corp Cmpaign $	NE
5) Pub TV $	NE	10) Cnsumr Prot	NE	15) Pol $ Disclosr	NE

Election Results

1972 general:	William H. Hudnut III (R)	95,839	(51%)
	Andrew Jacobs, Jr. (D)	91,238	(49%)
1972 primary:	William H. Hudnut III (R)	21,825	(46%)
	Danny L. Burton (R)	21,744	(46%
	Edmund J. Aocker (R)	3,136	(7%)
	Jimmy L. Kirby (R)	641	(1%)

IOWA

Political Background

Iowa brings to mind the America of the nineteenth century: Grant Wood's American Gothic, Main Street, county fair time, and acres upon acres of fields where the tall corn grows. Indeed, to this day, many aspects of life in Iowa have not been affected by the twentieth century. Most

Iowans, 99% of whom are white, still live on farms or in small towns, not in large cities and surrounding suburbs. Iowa has no military installations and very little defense industry. And Iowa politics have not been afflicted with ills often associated with too much or too rapid urbanization: the state has no equivalent of the Chicago machine or the right-wing movement once so prominent in southern California.

The economic base of Iowa remains pretty much as it was at the turn of the century. It is the nation's largest state of those in which agriculture is the major industry. There are fewer Iowa farmers in the field than ever, but the livelihood of most Iowans still depends, directly or indirectly, on the economics of corn, hogs, and beef cattle. This means that the state is, as it was in the past, an economic colony. The welfare of the people here depends largely on what happens to the price of commodities on the Chicago Board of Trade, the price of hogs and beef on the livestock market, and upon the decisions made by the Department of Agriculture and the congressional committees with which the Washington bureaucracy works.

Because Iowa is an agricultural state, it has not been growing recently. Almost all of the state's counties lost population during the 1960s. Iowa's comparatively small urban areas—where the principal industries include agricultural implements, meat packing, and home appliances —accounted for all of the state's 2% population increase. So with many young people leaving Iowa, the state's median age is one of the highest in the nation. Yet, though there are pockets of poverty, this is not a poor, decrepit state. Iowa has attained a comfortable level of prosperity, the basis of which are industries that are simply not growing much.

Iowa's first white residents were WASPs—part of the migration of Protestants from New England and upstate New York across northern Ohio, Indiana, and Illinois. To this day, that initial migratory stream remains the dominant ethnic group in the state. There are some people of Scandinavian descent in the northern counties; some originally from the American South towards the Missouri border; and pockets of German Catholics in places like Dubuque. But the WASPs dominate, and because they have, Iowa has a reputation for staunch Republicanism. The state has gone for only one Democratic presidential candidate in the last 20 years—Lyndon Johnson. But during the same span, the Republicans held the governorship for only eight years. And today Iowa's Democrats appear to be doing better than ever; they hold both of the state's Senate seats and three of its six congressional districts.

If there has been any pattern in Iowa's response to national issues, it is the Farm Belt's tendency to revolt against the Administration in Washington, of either party. It may be, as John Kenneth Galbraith says, that very few people actually understand the economics of the nation's farm programs. But the residents of Iowa apparently feel that they do and that various national Administrations have not. In the 1950s, for example, the name of Ezra Taft Benson, Eisenhower's ultraconservative Secretary of Agriculture, came up repeatedly in Democratic oratory. Benson's policies helped to elect Democrat Hershel Loveless to the governorship three times (1954–60). Moreover, Iowa, like most of the Farm Belt (and California), and unlike the rest of the country, cast a decidedly smaller percentage of its vote for Ike in 1956 than in 1952.

The pattern recurred in 1972. Iowa was one of four non-Southern states (the others were Wisconsin, South Dakota, and Oregon) that gave George McGovern a higher percentage of its votes than it gave Hubert Humphrey in 1968. This was not a freak happening. During the same election, Iowa voters unseated a Republican Senator and a Republican Congressman. What may have been at work is a revulsion at the incipient scandals in the Nixon Administration, even before the Watergate mess fully came to light. No doubt some of the austere New England morality of the American Gothic couple has come down to latter-day Yankees in Iowa. No one can imagine a honest-to-God Yankee putting up with high campaign officials burglarizing the opposition or laundering secret contributions in Mexican banks.

Perhaps a reaction typical of Iowans to the Watergate scandal belongs to Clark Mollenhoff —Washington bureau chief of the Des Moines *Register*, a newspaper with statewide circulation. The journalist was a White House aide in the early years of the Nixon Administration and a stern conservative who has always been outraged by corruption in government. During the course of the Watergate revelations, Mollenhoff charged up to Press Secretary Ron Ziegler and demanded that he for once tell the truth. Intimidated maybe by the furious newsman, Ziegler almost broke down. During the same period of time, Mollenhoff, by the sheer force of his will and the power of his vocal chords, forced a federal hearing examiner to accept his testimony in the Ernest Fitzgerald case when he accused White House aides and the Pentagon of lying. Fitzgerald is the man who blew the whistle on the Lockheed C5-A scandal. There are many Iowans, like

Mollenhoff life-long Republicans, who cannot tolerate the Nixon Administration's inclination to play fast and loose with the facts.

With prices good on the farm, something like moral outrage must account for the surprise victory of Democrat Dick Clark over two-term Republican Sen. Jack Miller. The Democratic Senate nomination had appeared so worthless that Clark got it by default. The man Clark worked for as administrative assistant, Congressman John Culver, decided not to seek the nomination because the odds against Miller looked too long. But the handsome Clark ran a vigorous campaign, walking, Lawton Chiles-style, across the state, shaking hands and listening to people's problems. He also built a superb organization—a task for which he had plenty of training, having run Culver's impressive congressional races and having plotted a possible Culver Senate bid.

The incumbent Miller had all the charisma one would expect from a onetime Sioux City tax lawyer. Apparently overconfident, the incumbent Senator ignored Clark's charges that as a member of the Finance Committee he pushed through bills for special interests. He presumably expected to be swept in by the Nixon tide. Instead, he was swept out by Clark. The Democrat won a solid 56% of the votes and carried most of the state's counties and all six of its congressional districts.

Clark's appeal was almost uniformly strong all over the state, but his vigor and comparative youth gave him a particular advantage over the stodgy Miller on Iowa's large campuses. In Johnson County, which contains the State University of Iowa, Clark took an astounding 71% of the votes—which must be a record for a Democratic Iowa Senate candidate. In Washington, Clark has shown the same brashness that won him a Senate seat. He has voted against confirmation of numerous Nixon appointees, and has loudly criticized many Administration proposals.

Clark's smashing success has almost pulled the public's attention away from Democrat Harold Hughes, now Iowa's senior Senator. As Governor for six years (1962–68), it was Hughes who really built the Iowa Democratic party. And it was only because of Hughes' earlier efforts that the party was able to score the victories it did in 1972. The Senator's career has a Horatio Alger touch. A reformed alcoholic and truck driver, Hughes founded his own trucking firm, became dissatisfied with the way the state regulated the trucking business, ran as a Democrat for the appropriate commission, and won. Soon, to most people's surprise, he was Governor, and a very popular one. In his second race in 1964, Hughes won 68% of the state's votes, running ahead of Lyndon Johnson. And in 1966, he won a third term when most of the state Democratic ticket went under. In 1968, Hughes replaced retiring Bourke Hickenlooper in the Senate. His election was more difficult than expected because his Republican opponent, David Stanley, spent huge sums (by Iowa standards) on television and other media advertising.

Hughes' popularity is due in part to his unusual frankness. He has never tried to cover up his bout with alcoholism, and, despite his own strong feelings on the subject, he supported liquor-by-the-glass—a hot issue in Iowa during the early 1960s. A man with a massive physical presence and a strong, deep voice, Hughes was one the first major political figures—and probably the first Governor—to say that he opposed Johnson's Vietnam policies. Moreover, unlike many politicians, Hughes was entirely willing to tell Johnson so to his face. The Senator possesses a remarkable evangelical speaking style, which is derived, one suspects, from his deep if not mystical religious faith.

In 1968 the Iowa Senator gained national attention when he nominated Eugene McCarthy at the Democratic National Convention. At the same convention, Hughes pushed through a proposal—the only insurgent move that got past the LBJ convention managers—to reform the delegate-selection process. He was passed over for the chairmanship of the party reform committee in favor of George McGovern, but the Iowan was an important participant in its workings. In 1971, Hughes flirted for a while with the idea of a presidential candidacy, then decided against it. For one thing, the intensity of his fervor unsettled many politicians, and for another, there were just too many antiwar candidates getting into the race.

Hughes is something of a loner in the Senate, not part of any clique. He has been especially interested in the problems of alcoholism and drug abuse—one of the reasons he dropped his presidential bid—and has sponsored legislation to deal with them. Lately, he has been particularly active on the Armed Services Committee. It was through Hughes' efforts that the secret bombing of Cambodia in 1969 and 1970 was exposed in 1970. And he has sternly threatened to cut off all aid to South Vietnam if it is channeled to continue the Cambodia bombing in 1973 or 1974. There are some who still see Hughes as a possible dark-horse candidate for 1976, or perhaps as a vice-presidential nominee. As a former truck driver and a dove, he neatly spans the blue-collar vs. intellectual chasm deep in the Democratic party.

But for now, Hughes must think more about the 1974 Iowa Senate race. Despite the notable Democratic trend in the State, reelection may not come easy. Some Iowans are a little uncomfortable having two Democrats in the Senate. Hughes's toughest opponent would be Republican Gov. Robert Ray, a moderate who won his third term by a 59–41 margin in 1972—running just ahead of Richard Nixon. But other Republicans are queuing up, and Hughes will have to hustle if he wants to win by an impressive margin.

As noted, the state's House delegation is now split evenly between the parties. But Democrats made percentage gains in all but one district, and they have hopes of picking up another seat or two in 1974. As predicted in the 1972 edition of the *Almanac*, Democratic Rep. Neal Smith was the easy victor when redistricting placed him and Republican Rep. John Kyl in the same district.

Census Data Pop. 2,825,041; 1.40% of U.S. total, 25th largest; change 1960–70, 2.4%. Central city, 22%; suburban, 13%. Median family income, $9,017; 26th highest; families above $15,000: 16%; families below $3,000: 10%. Median years education, 12.2.

1972 Share of Federal Tax Burden $2,529,120,000; 1.21% of U.S. total, 23rd largest.

1972 Share of Federal Outlays $2,583,075,856; 1.19% of U.S. total, 27th largest. Per capita federal spending, $914.

DOD	$226,188,000	40th (0.36%)	HEW	$935,688,855	26th (1.31%)
AEC	$25,579,260	17th (0.98%)	HUD	$26,819,939	32nd (0.87%)
NASA	$2,037,288	30th (0.07%)	VA	$156,131,079	26th (1.36%)
DOT	$78,413,511	33rd (0.99%)	USDA	$805,260,465	4th (5.24%)
DOC	$1,161,657	49th (0.09%)	CSC	$34,609,014	31st (0.84%)
DOI	$5,832,488	43rd (0.27%)	TD	$161,880,002	16th (0.98%)
DOJ	$9,233,223	32nd (0.94%)	Other	$114,241,075	

Economic Base Agriculture, notably cattle, hogs, corn and soybeans; food and kindred products, especially meat products; finance, insurance and real estate; machinery, especially farm machinery; electrical equipment and supplies, especially household appliances; printing and publishing, especially newspapers; fabricated metal products, especially fabricated structural metal products.

Political Line-up Governor, Robert D. Ray (R); seat up, 1974. Senators, Harold E. Hughes (D) and Richard Clark (D). Representatives, 6 (3 D and 3 R). State Senate (27 R, 22 D, and 1 vac.); State House (58 R and 42 D).

The Voters

Registration No statewide registration.
Median voting age 45.2
Employment profile White collar, 43%. Blue collar, 31%. Service, 14%. Farm, 12%.
Ethnic groups Black, 1%. Total foreign stock, 11%. Germany, 4%.

Presidential vote

1972	Nixon (R)	706,207	(59%)
	McGovern (D)	496,206	(41%)
1968	Nixon (R)	619,106	(53%)
	Humphrey (D)	476,699	(41%)
	Wallace (AI)	66,422	(6%)
1964	Johnson (D)	733,030	(62%)
	Goldwater (R)	449,148	(38%)

Senator

Harold Everett Hughes (D) Elected 1968, seat up 1974; b. Feb. 10, 1922, near Ida Grove; home, Ida Grove; U. of Iowa, 1940–41; Army, WWII; married, three children; Methodist.

Career Motor transportation business; Iowa State Commerce Commission, 1959–63, Chm., 1959–60, 1961–62; Gov. of Iowa, 1962–68; Mbr., Natl. Governors' Conference Exec. Com., 1965–67; Chm., Dem. Governors' Conference, 1966–68; Asst. Majority Whip, 1969– .

Offices 1327 NSOB, 202-225-3744. Also 721 Fed. Bldg., Des Moines 50309, 515-284-4056, and 1333 Fed. Bldg., Davenport 52801, 319-326-6259, and 228 Fed. Bldg., Sioux City 51102, 712-252-4161 ext. 331.

Administrative Assistant Park Rinard

Committees

Armed Services (8th); Subs: General Legislation; Drug Abuse in the Armed Services (Chm.); Arms Control; Research and Development.

Labor and Public Welfare (9th); Subs: Health; Railroad Retirement; Alcoholism and Narcotics (Chm.); Aging; Labor; Employment, Poverty, and Migratory Labor.

Veterans' Affairs (4th); Subs: Housing and Insurance (Chm.); Health and Hospitals; Compensation and Pensions.

Sp. Com. to Study Questions Related to Secret and Confidential Government Documents (3rd).

Group Ratings

	ADA	COPE	LWV	RIPON	NFU	LCV	CFA	NAB	NSI	ACA
1972	80	100	100	76	100	85	100	8	0	5
1971	96	73	100	73	100	–	86	–	–	9
1970	97	100	–	77	100	100	–	22	0	10

Key Votes

1) Busing	FOR	8) Sea Life Prot	FOR	15) Tax Singls Less	FOR
2) Alas P-line	AGN	9) Campaign Subs	FOR	16) Min Tax for Rich	FOR
3) Gun Cntrl	FOR	10) Cmbodia Bmbg	AGN	17) Euro Troop Rdctn	FOR
4) Rehnquist	AGN	11) Legal Srvices	FOR	18) Bust Hwy Trust	AGN
5) Pub TV $	ABS	12) Rev Sharing	FOR	19) Maid Min Wage	FOR
6) EZ Votr Reg	FOR	13) Cnsumr Prot	FOR	20) Farm Sub Limit	FOR
7) No-Fault	FOR	14) Eq Rts Amend	FOR	21) Highr Credt Chgs	AGN

Election Results

1968 general:	Harold E. Hughes (D)	574,884	(50%)
	David M. Stanley (R)	568,469	(50%)
1968 primary:	Harold E. Hughes (D)	103,936	(86%)
	Robert L. Neveim (D)	15,772	(14%)

Senator

Richard C. Clark (D) Elected 1972, seat up 1978; b. Sept. 14, 1929, Paris; home, Marion; U. of Maryland, Wiesbaden, Germany, 1950–52; U. of Frankfurt, Ger., 1950–52; Upper Iowa U., B.A., 1953; U. of Iowa, M.A., 1956; Army, 1950–1952; married, two children.

Career Asst. Professor, Upper Iowa U.; Admin. Asst. to Congressman John C. Culver, 1965–72.

Offices 404 OSOB, 202-225-3254. Also 214 Fed. Bldg., Council Bluffs, 712-323-3944, and B-2 Fed. Bldg., Cedar Rapids, 319-366-2411 ext. 522, and 733 Fed. Bldg., Des Moines 50309, 515-284-4721.

Administrative Assistant Bob Miller

Committees

Agriculture and Forestry (7th); Subs: Agricultural Production, Marketing, and Stabilization of Prices; Agricultural Research and General Legislation; Rural Development (Chm.); Foreign Agricultural Policy.

Public Works (7th); Subs: Air and Water Pollution; Disaster Relief; Water Resources; Public Buildings and Grounds (Chm.); Panel on Environmental Science and Technology.

Sel. Com. on Small Business (10th); Subs: Government Procurement; Government Regulation.

Group Ratings: Newly Elected

Election Results

1972 general:	Dick Clark (D)	662,637	(55%)
	Jack Miller (R)	530,525	(44%)
	William Rocap (AI)	8,954	(1%)
1972 primary:	Dick Clark (D), unopposed		

FIRST DISTRICT Political Background

Of the nation's 435 congressional districts, the one that has had the closest elections in the last decade, not only in November but also in primaries, is the 1st district of Iowa. To visitors from New York or Los Angeles, the southeast corner of Iowa along the Mississippi River must look like a rather ordinary place in the Midwest. The district has a lot of farmland and some small manufacturing cities. But the 1st does have some distinctive features. The little city of Burlington (pop. 32,000) has a Pulitzer Prize winning journalist, John McCormally of the *Hawkeye*. Davenport (pop. 98,000) is the largest city in the 1st and the home of the Palmer Chiropractic School. Davenport is a marginally Republican city with a Democratic Mayor, Kathryn Kirschbaum. Iowa City (pop. 47,000 and up 40% during the 1960s) is the site of the University of Iowa, the largest institution of higher education in the state, with 19,000 students.

But listing these features is not enough to explain why this district has been one of the most consistently marginal in the nation. Any explanation has to take into account ex-Rep. Fred Schwengel, a generally liberal Republican. A man with a wide range of interests, Schwengel has been president of the National Capital Historical Society. Schwengel was first elected in 1954 and gained the reputation on the Hill as something of a loner. For some time, the Congressman had an easy time winning reelection. But in 1964, Schwengel was beaten by college professor John Schmidhauser, from whom he recaptured the seat in 1966 and defeated once more in 1968. In 1970, Schwengel's electoral troubles began anew, as he faced a primary challenge from the David Stanley who nearly upset Sen. Harold Hughes in 1968. Stanley spent more than $100,000 on the 1st-district campaign and got 44% of the vote. (In 1972, Stanley set his sights lower and finally won an election, a seat in the Iowa House of Representatives.) Then in the 1970 general election, antiwar Democrat Edward Mezvinsky came even closer than Stanley, losing to Schwengel by a slim 765 votes.

From that time on, the Republican was in Congress on borrowed time. Mezvinsky planned another race in 1972, and in the primary of that year he easily disposed of former Congressman

Schmidhauser. The general election campaign was not so much a matter of attack and counter-attack as a contrast in attitudes and styles. Schwengel, the genial 65-year-old incumbent, was middle-of-the-road on most issues; on the other hand, Mezvinsky, the 35-year-old challenger, strongly opposed the Nixon Administration's Vietnam and domestic policies. It may be difficult for the visitors from New York or Los Angeles to understand, but in 1972 in the 1st district of Iowa, Mezvinsky's stance was more popular with the electorate. He won a comparatively easy 54–46 victory, with a 15,000-vote margin.

Once in the House, Mezvinsky was elected Chairman of the Freshman Democratic Caucus. This is a group composed of newly elected Democrats from the North and the South who appear to possess more common feeling and rapport than many of their counterparts of the past. Vice-chairman of the caucus is John Breaux from Louisiana. In the past, most groups of this sort have been mainly social clubs, but the freshman Democrats of the 93rd Congress have gone so far as to consider hiring a staff.

As a member of the Judiciary Committee, Mezvinsky is in the middle of the debate concerning the confidentiality of a newsman's sources. The Congressman is a firm believer in the right of a reporter to keep his sources secret. He has argued therefore that no law should be enacted in this area, saying that protection by statute—unlike a constitutional guarantee—can be revoked at some later time.

The 1974 election should not prove too difficult for Mezvinsky. His rising percentage of the vote in the last two elections and the general Democratic trend in Iowa augur well for the Congressman's chances. Tough opponents would be Stanley, who is also reportedly considering another race against Hughes, or ex-Lt. Gov. Roger Jepsen, a conservative. But in 1972 Mezvinsky got a 61%, 8,000-vote margin in Johnson County (Iowa City and the University), and carried Davenport, Schwengel's home town. The freshman Congressman appears to be in solid shape in a state rapidly shifting to the Democrats.

Census Data Pop. 471,260. Central city, 21%; suburban, 9%. Median family income, $9,594; families above $15,000: 18%; families below $3,000: 9%. Median years education, 12.3.

1972 Share of Federal Outlays $419,929,308

DOD	$65,708,000	HEW	$154,636,097
AEC	$17,866,656	HUD	$3,201,088
NASA	$1,975,404	DOI	$943,347
DOT	$13,936,968	USDA	$80,238,539
		Other	$81,423,209

Federal Military-Industrial Commitments

DOD Contractors Mason & Hanger-Silas Mason Co. (Burlington), $33.788m: operation of Iowa Army Ammunition plant. Bendix (Davenport), $8.534m: aircraft components. J. I. Case (Bettendorf), $6.203m: unspecified.
AEC Operations Mason & Hanger-Silas Mason (Burlington), $15.095m: fabrication of weapons components.

Economic Base Agriculture, notably cattle, hogs and sheep, and grains; food and kindred products; finance, insurance and real estate; machinery; and primary metal industries. Also higher education (Univ. of Iowa).

The Voters

Registration No district-wide registration.
Median voting age 42.7
Employment profile White collar, 45%. Blue collar, 33%. Service, 14%. Farm, 8%.
Ethnic groups Black, 1%. Total foreign stock, 9%. Germany, 3%.

Presidential vote

1972	Nixon (R)	111,577	(56%)
	McGovern (D)	87,448	(44%)

1968	Nixon (R)	93,947	(50%)
	Humphrey (D)	81,468	(44%)
	Wallace (AI)	11,007	(6%)

Representative

Edward Mezvinsky (D) Elected 1972; b. Jan. 17, 1937, Ames; home, Iowa City; U. of Iowa, B.A., 1960; U. of Calif. (Berkeley), M.A., J.D.; married, four children; Jewish.

Career Practicing atty.; Legis. Asst. to Rep. Neal Smith, 1965–67: State Legislature, 1969–71; Law firm, Shulman, Phelan, Tucker, Boyle and Mullen, Iowa City.

Offices 1404 LHOB, 202-225-6576. Also 115 Fed. Bldg., Davenport 52801, 319-326-4088, and 222 Dey Bldg., Iowa City 52240, 319-351-0062, and 210 Fed. Bldg., Burlington 52601, 319-752-4584.

Administrative Assistant Patrick O'Connor and Jonathan H. Kent

Committees

Judiciary (21st); Subs: Patents, Trademarks, Copyrights; Antitrust Matters.

Group Ratings: Newly Elected

Key Votes

1) Busing	NE	6) Cmbodia Bmbg	AGN	11) Chkg Acct Intrst	AGN
2) Strip Mines	NE	7) Bust Hwy Trust	FOR	12) End HISC (HUAC)	FOR
3) Cut Mil $	NE	8) Farm Sub Lmt	NE	13) Nixon Sewer Veto	AGN
4) Rev Shrg	NE	9) School Prayr	NE	14) Corp Cmpaign $	NE
5) Pub TV $	NE	10) Cnsumr Prot	NE	15) Pol $ Disclosr	NE

Election Results

1972 general:	Edward Mezvinsky (D)	107,099	(53%)
	Fred Schwengel (R)	91,609	(46%)
	Lee E. Foster (AI)	1,916	(1%)
1972 primary:	Edward Mezvinsky (D)	15,985	(64%)
	John R. Schmidhauser (D)	9,088	(36%)

SECOND DISTRICT Political Background

The 2nd district of Iowa comprises the northeast corner of the state. The district is dominated by Cedar Rapids (pop. 163,000), Iowa's second largest city, and by two aging Mississippi River towns about half that size, Dubuque and Clinton. Cedar Rapids is politically marginal—a little more Democratic, usually, than the state as a whole. Clinton is heavily Republican. Dubuque, a place that has taken too much flippant abuse from folks back East, actually went for George McGovern in 1972, and by a margin larger than the one the liberal candidate received in New York City. Most of the residents of Dubuque are German Catholics who have always voted Democratic. Agriculture is not quite as important here as in some other Iowa districts. The knobby hills that flank the Mississippi are less suitable for corn, hogs, and wheat than the rolling plains farther west.

In 1962, Republicans won all but one of Iowa's congressional districts, which then totaled seven. But in 1964, Iowans did not receive the Goldwater nomination happily and all but one district elected Democrats. In 1966, things returned to what people then considered normal when only one of the Democratic class of '64 won reelection. That one was Rep. John Culver of the 2nd district. Culver has an unusual background for an Iowa Congressman. He was a college roommate of Sen. Edward Kennedy and a slam-bang Harvard fullback in the early 1950s. He attended the Law School, served in administrative capacities at Harvard, and then worked on Kennedy's staff. Sensing a Democratic year in 1964, Culver returned home to Cedar Rapids, campaigned hard, and unseated the Republican incumbent with 51% of the vote.

Two men behind the success of Iowa's Democratic party in the early 1970s are Culver and Dick Clark, a former member of Culver's staff and now U.S. Senator. They possess great organizational skills. Culver and Clark put together the apparatus that kept Culver in Congress in 1966 and won 60% of the vote for him in 1970—despite a campaign appearance on behalf of his opponent by none other than Vice-President Spiro Agnew. In 1972, Culver considered taking on Jack Miller in the Senate race, but for once in his life Culver was bearish and judged it just too tough. Clark ran instead and won handily.

The organization that Culver and Clark built has also been put to good use by other Iowa Democrats—a reason why Iowa was one of the few states in which Democrats made significant gains in the state legislature in 1972. Today, Culver heads another organization, the Democratic Study Group (DSG). This was started in the late 1950s by a group of liberal Congressmen unhappy with the get-along-go-along leadership of the House at the time. By the early 1970s DSG membership had expanded to include a majority of House Democrats. At the beginning of the 93rd Congress DSG programs for internal House reform were for the most part embraced by the leadership and adopted by the Democratic Caucus. As DSG Chairman, Culver plays an important role in rounding up liberal votes, usually while cooperating with the leadership, but when necessary working against it. So despite his relatively low seniority in committee, Culver has become a substantial power in the House.

Census Data Pop. 471,933. Central city, 37%; suburban, 17%. Median family income, $9,511; families above $15,000: 17%; families below $3,000: 9%. Median years education, 12.2.

1972 Share of Federal Outlays $360,821,434

DOD	$63,625,000	HEW	$130,575,317
AEC	–	HUD	$2,250,646
NASA	$1,946	DOI	$867,637
DOT	$25,417,561	USDA	$67,673,809
		Other	$70,409,518

Federal Military-Industrial Commitments

DOD Contractors Collins Radio (Cedar Rapids), $47.281m: electronic communications equipment used on various aircraft.

Economic Base Agriculture, notably hogs and sheep, cattle, dairy products and grains; food and kindred products, especially grain mill products; electrical equipment and supplies; finance, insurance and real estate; and machinery, especially construction and related machinery.

The Voters

Registration No district-wide registration.
Median voting age 43.8
Employment profile White collar, 41%. Blue collar, 34%. Service, 13%. Farm, 12%.
Ethnic groups Total foreign stock, 10%. Germany, 4%.

Presidential vote

1972	Nixon (R)	108,517	(56%)
	McGovern (D)	86,714	(44%)
1968	Nixon (R)	96,936	(51%)
	Humphrey (D)	83,215	(44%)
	Wallace (AI)	9,684	(5%)

Representative

John C. Culver (D) Elected 1964; b. Aug. 8, 1932, Rochester, Minn.; home, Cedar Rapids; Harvard, B.A., 1954, LL.B., 1962; Cambridge U., Harvard Scholar, 1954–55; USMC, 1955–58; married, four children; Presbyterian.

Career Dean of Men, Harvard U. Summer School, 1960; Legis. Asst. to Sen. Edward M. Kennedy, 1962–63.

Offices 104 CHOB, 202-225-2911. Also 205 Fed. Bldg., Cedar Rapids 52401, 319-366-2411.

Administrative Assistant Bob Power.

Committees

Foreign Affairs (10th); Subs: Africa; Foreign Economic Policy (Chm.); State Department Organization and Foreign Operations.

Government Operations (14th); Subs: Government Activities; Intergovernmental Relations.

Sel. Com. on Committees (3rd).

Group Ratings

	ADA	COPE	LWV	RIPON	NFU	LCV	CFA	NAB	NSI	ACA
1972	88	82	91	77	100	83	100	10	0	0
1971	89	82	83	76	100	–	100	–	–	8
1970	96	100	–	88	92	73	100	0	20	0

Key Votes

1) Busing	FOR	6) Cmbodia Bmbg	AGN	11) Chkg Acct Intrst	AGN
2) Strip Mines	AGN	7) Bust Hwy Trust	FOR	12) End HISC (HUAC)	FOR
3) Cut Mil $	FOR	8) Farm Sub Lmt	FOR	13) Nixon Sewer Veto	AGN
4) Rev Shrg	FOR	9) School Prayr	AGN	14) Corp Cmpaign $	ABS
5) Pub TV $	FOR	10) Cnsumr Prot	FOR	15) Pol $ Disclosr	FOR

Election Results

1972 general:	John C. Culver (D)	115,489	(59%)
	Theodore R. Ellsworth (R)	79,667	(41%)
1972 primary:	John C. Culver (D), unopposed		
1970 general:	John C. Culver (D)	84,049	(60%)
	Cole McMartin (R)	54,932	(40%)

THIRD DISTRICT Political Background

There is no other Congressman quite like H. R. Gross of the 3rd district of Iowa. After more than a quarter century of service, Gross has become the House's reigning curmudgeon. The Iowan spends far more time on the House floor than most members, objecting to what he considers improper procedure. He reads every bill than comes to the floor—a staggering task—trying to spot some new outrage perpetrated on the taxpayers. With a booming voice and a sour face, Gross is inclined to ask for quorum calls, which according to the rules and regulations, assure that the majority required to do business is on hand. These calls force a majority of the House members to rush to the chamber and answer present. Actually, most Congressmen spend most of their time in their offices or in committee rooms; they come to the floor only when important business or a pet bill is scheduled. When another Congressman once rose to attack what he considered the time-wasting practice of quorum calls, Gross' reply was worthy of Calvin Coolidge: he asked for a quorum call.

Gross' political ideology is also reminiscent of Coolidge. The Congressman believes that the federal government wastes far too much money, and he sees himself, often with complete justification, as the only member willing to object to some excesses. As ranking member of the

Post Office and Civil Service Committee, Gross ferreted out some interesting information from the management-technique-obsessed Postal Service executives. E. T. Klassen, the head of the newly organized and financially troubled Postal Service, admitted that the high salaries he decided to pay administrators, allegedly to lure them away from well-compensated jobs in private industry, actually represented raises for a majority of the new public servants. Many Congressmen consider Gross a nit-picking pain in the neck, a man who is penny wise and dollar foolish, especially when it comes to the defense budget. (Gross, however, voted against the bombing in Cambodia; it's too expensive.) Yet some Congressmen will admit that Gross' caustic questioning on the floor has forced them to be better prepared to justify new programs and expenditures.

Oddly enough, Gross, a man who personifies American Gothic virtues—thriftiness, attention to detail, orneriness—came to politics from the news media. For 13 years before his first election to the House in 1948, he was a radio news commentator. Since then, Gross has won consistently without trouble, except for 1964 when he squeaked by with a 419-vote margin. But last time out, Gross' share of the vote was down to 56%. There are indications he may retire in 1974, when he will be 75. That may please some House members, but habitúes of the House galleries will be sad.

Gross' 3rd congressional district, appropriately, is almost precisely square, with a few odd corners when counties were added or removed by redistricting. The 3rd comprises the north central portion of the state. Its largest city is a meat-packing center, Waterloo—scene of some racial disturbances which are unusual for Iowa. Like most of Iowa, the 3rd has been moving in a Democratic direction during the Nixon years. Sen. Dick Clark, a native of the district, got a solid 54% of the votes here, though Harold Hughes four years earlier did not carry it. And George McGovern received 40% of the vote in the 3rd—better than Hubert Humphrey's showing in 1968 and far better than the South Dakotan's finish in other districts around the country considered safely Democratic. Iowa's exultant Democrats hope to capture the 3rd in 1974, even if Gross decides to run again. The betting here is that they will.

Census Data Pop. 471,866. Central city, 16%; suburban, 12%. Median family income, $8,911; families above $15,000: 15%; families below $3,000: 10%. Median years education, 12.2.

1972 Share of Federal Outlays $428,069,835

DOD	$28,886,000	HEW	$150,462,440
AEC	–	HUD	$2,107,476
NASA	–	DOI	$148,468
DOT	$8,160,923	USDA	$174,251,353
		Other	$64,053,175

Federal Military-Industrial Commitments

DOD Contractors Chamberlain Manufacturing (Waterloo), $22.443m: 105mm rockets; other munitions research.

Economic Base Agriculture, notably hogs and sheep, cattle and grains; machinery; food and kindred products, especially meat products; finance, insurance and real estate; and fabricated metal products. Also higher education (Univ. of Northern Iowa.).

The Voters

Registration No district-wide registration.
Median voting age 46.0
Employment profile White collar, 40%. Blue collar, 32%. Service, 14%. Farm, 14%.
Ethnic groups Black, 2%. Total foreign stock, 12%. Germany, 5%.

Presidential vote

1972	Nixon (R)	119,372	(60%)
	McGovern (D)	78,687	(40%)
1968	Nixon (R)	108,995	(56%)
	Humphrey (D)	74,716	(39%)
	Wallace (AI)	9,169	(5%)

Representative

H. R. Gross (R) Elected 1948; b. June 30, 1899, Arispe; home, Waterloo; U. of Mo. School of Journalism; American Expeditionary Forces, WWI; married, two children; Presbyterian.

Career Newspaper reporter, editor, 1921–35; radio news commentator, 1935–48.

Offices 2368 RHOB, 202-225-3301.

Administrative Assistant Julian Morrison

Committees

Foreign Affairs (4th); Subs: Near East; Inter-American Affairs; International Organizations and Movements (Ranking Mbr.); Near East and South Asia; Sp. Sub. for Review of Foreign Aid Programs.

Post Office and Civil Service (Ranking Mbr.).

Sel. Com. on Parking (Ranking Mbr.).

Group Ratings

	ADA	COPE	LWV	RIPON	NFU	LCV	CFA	NAB	NSI	ACA
1972	6	9	0	25	29	33	100	83	80	100
1971	16	0	0	39	13	–	13	–	–	97
1970	20	25	–	29	15	28	35	83	89	89

Key Votes

1) Busing	AGN	6) Cmbodia Bmbg	AGN	11) Chkg Acct Intrst	AGN
2) Strip Mines	ABS	7) Bust Hwy Trust	AGN	12) End HISC (HUAC)	AGN
3) Cut Mil $	FOR	8) Farm Sub Lmt	FOR	13) Nixon Sewer Veto	FOR
4) Rev Shrg	AGN	9) School Prayr	FOR	14) Corp Cmpaign $	ABS
5) Pub TV $	AGN	10) Cnsumr Prot	AGN	15) Pol $ Disclosr	AGN

Election Results

1972 general:	H. R. Gross (R)	109,113	(56%)
	Lyle Taylor (D)	86,848	(46%)
1972 primary:	H. R. Gross (R), unopposed		
1970 general:	H. R. Gross (R)	66,087	(59%)
	Lyle D. Taylor (D)	45,958	(41%)

FOURTH DISTRICT Political Background

Because Iowa registered a very small population gain in the 1970 census, the state lost one of its seven congressional districts. So what had been the 4th and 5th districts were combined into a new 4th. The lion's share of the population came from the old 5th: Polk County, which includes the city of Des Moines, the state's capital and largest city (pop. 200,000). The remaining counties came from the old 4th, the population-losing south central part of Iowa. The largest city here is Ottumwa (pop. 29,000).

The political effect of the consolidation was not too hard to predict. The incumbent from the old 5th, Democrat Neal Smith, had a definite advantage over the incumbent from the old 4th, Republican John Kyl. Smith had previously represented 60% of the new 4th's residents. Moreover, Des Moines, after Dubuque, is Iowa's most Democratic city, and Smith was accustomed for years to racking up better-than-normal Democratic majorities. Meanshile, John Kyl had not run very far ahead of his party in the past; in fact, he lost to a Democrat in 1964. And Kyl was a virtual unknown in the new 4th. So as the 1972 edition of the *Almanac* predicted, Smith won an easy victory in the 1972 two-incumbent contest, with 60% of the votes.

Thus, even with the added difficulty of facing another incumbent, Smith held on to his record of never having won less than 60% of the votes in any election since 1964. Smith first came to the

House in the very Democratic year of 1958. He has stayed on since to climb more than halfway up the seniority ladder of the Appropriations Committee. The Congressman is now in 14th position and within easy sight of a subcommittee chairmanship. Most members of Appropriations remain relatively unknown until they achieve such a position. Here they can set departmental budget levels which, until recently at least, have been binding on the Executive Branch. Smith is no exception. He is little known outside his district and the world of the House. Still, as a member of the Labor-HEW and State-Commerce-Judiciary subcommittees, he has important leverage over important areas of federal policy and federal spending.

Census Data   Pop. 468,881. Central city, 43%; suburban, 18%. Median family income, $9,589; families above $15,000: 19%; families below $3,000: 9%. Median years education, 12.3.

1972 Share of Federal Outlays $440,161,658

DOD	$25,638,000	HEW	$186,377,577
AEC	–	HUD	$16,823,977
NASA	–	DOI	$1,812,645
DOT	$9,437,969	USDA	$66,086,918
		Other	$133,984,572

Federal Military-Industrial Commitments

No installation or contractors receiving prime awards greater than $5,000,000.

Economic Base   Finance, insurance and real estate; agriculture, notably hogs and sheep, cattle and grains; machinery, especially farm machinery; food and kindred products; and printing and publishing, especially newspapers and periodicals.

The Voters

Registration   No district-wide registration.
Median voting age 44.8
Employment profile   White collar, 51%. Blue collar, 30%. Service, 14%. Farm, 5%.
Ethnic groups   Black, 3%. Total foreign stock, 9%. Germany, 1%.

Presidential vote

1972	Nixon (R)	117,283	(56%)
	McGovern (D)	92,752	(44%)
1968	Nixon (R)	92,788	(47%)
	Humphrey (D)	88,899	(45%)
	Wallace (AI)	14,467	(7%)

Represenatative

Neal Smith (D)   Elected 1958; b. March 23, 1920, Hedrick; home, Altoona; U. of Mo., 1945–46; Syracuse U., 1946–47; Drake U. Law School, LL.B., 1950; Army Air Corps, WWII; married, two children; Methodist.

Career   Farm operator, 1937– ; practicing atty., 1950–58, Pres., Natl. Young Democrats, 1953–55; Chm., Polk County Bd. of Social Welfare; Asst. County Atty., Polk County, 1951.

Offices   2458 RHOB, 202-225-4426. Also 544 Insurance Exchange Bldg., Des Moines 50309, 515-284-4634.

Administrative Assistant Tom Dawson

Committees

Appropriations (14th); Subs: Agriculture, Environmental and Consumer Protection; Labor, Health, Education, and Welfare; State, Justice, Commerce, and Judiciary.

Sel. Com. on Small Business (5th); Subs: Business Problems (Chm.); Environmental Problems Affecting Small Business; Government Procurement and International Trade.

Group Ratings

	ADA	COPE	LWV	RIPON	NFU	LCV	CFA	NAB	NSI	ACA
1972	50	90	75	82	100	27	50	17	44	22
1971	62	75	100	71	93	–	100	–	–	19
1970	48	82	–	63	85	62	94	11	100	13

Key Votes

1) Busing	FOR	6) Cmbodia Bmbg	AGN	11) Chkg Acct Intrst	AGN
2) Strip Mines	AGN	7) Bust Hwy Trust	AGN	12) End HISC (HUAC)	AGN
3) Cut Mil $	AGN	8) Farm Sub Lmt	AGN	13) Nixon Sewer Veto	AGN
4) Rev Shrg	FOR	9) School Prayr	AGN	14) Corp Cmpaign $	AGN
5) Pub TV $	ABS	10) Cnsumr Prot	FOR	15) Pol $ Disclosr	AGN

Election Results

1972 general:	Neal Smith (D)	125,431	(60%)
	John Kyl (R)	85,156	(40%)
1972 primary:	Neal Smith (D), unopposed		
1970 general:	Neal Smith (D)	73,820	(65%)
	Don Mahon (R)	37,374	(33%)
	John H. Grant (AI)	1,297	(1%)
	Roy E. Berger (Iowa New Party)	1,262	(1%)

FIFTH DISTRICT Political Background

On paper, the southwestern corner of Iowa—its 5th congressional district—is the most Republican part of the state. In fact, there is little regional variation in the state; in even-tempered Iowa, no congressional district goes more than 5 or 6% more Republican or Democratic than any other in statewide elections. Nevertheless, if there is a "Republican section" of the state it is here, where the plains, as they roll towards the Missouri River, are a little less verdant than they are farther east. The district's largest city, Council Bluffs (pop. 61,000), lies just across the Missouri from Omaha, Nebraska. The city appears to lean more towards the conservatism of Nebraska than towards the middle-of-the-road politics of Iowa. Whatever the case, Council Bluffs was the only sizable population center in the state that produced a majority for ex-Sen. Jack Miller over his successful Democratic challenger, Dick Clark.

Nevertheless, Clark carried the district. One of the reasons behind the Democrat's showing was the addition to the 5th of the city of Ames (pop. 40,000 and up 46% in the 1960s) by the 1971 redistricting. Iowa State University (17,000 students) is in Ames, and that same city was responsible for the unusually close call that Republican William Scherle had here in 1972.

Ever since Scherle recaptured the seat for the Republicans from a class of '64 Democrat, he had become accustomed to majorities of more than 60%. A big, bluff man, with no trace of subtlety, Scherle managed to attract his constituents with his conservative philosophy and his outgoing personality. But in 1972, Scherle suddenly dropped to only 55% of the vote. The main reason was redistricting. The Congressman won 60% in the part of the district he had previously represented—a slight dropoff from past performances. In the new areas, however, Democratic challenger Tom Harkin beat Scherle 55–45. Can Scherle do better in the future? One would expect the answer to be yes. But if Iowa is in the midst of Democratic gains, as the 1972 results indicate, Scherle might be in trouble. Moreover, Scherle's demeanor is not one that appeals to students at Iowa State. His chances for reelection in the 5th aside, Scherle is known to be contemplating a race against Sen. Harold Hughes in 1974.

In the House, the Iowa Congressman has received the most attention for his scathing denunciations of the District of Columbia government while serving on the D.C. Subcommittee of the Appropriations Committee. He is also known for a two-word comment issued upon the resignations of presidential aides, H. R. Haldeman and John Ehrlichman: "Good riddance," a sentiment widely held on both sides of the House aisle. More important in any Iowa race, however, is Scherle's record on Appropriations' Agriculture Subcommittee. As a poor boy who became a wealthy farmer through marriage, Scherle opposed a $20,000 ceiling on farm subsidy payments, and he supported an act to drop the requirement that certain government loans in rural areas be made only to family farmers.

Census Data Pop. 470,214. Central city, 0%; suburban, 19%. Median family income, $8,338; families above $15,000: 14%; families below $3,000: 12%. Median years education, 12.2.

1972 Share of Federal Outlays $454,339,406

DOD	$13,763,000	HEW	$155,439,703
AEC	$7,712,604	HUD	$1,061,852
NASA	$59,938	DOI	$1,087,786
DOT	$16,223,555	USDA	$192,833,474
		Other	$66,157,494

Federal Military-Industrial Commitments

AEC Operations Ames Laboratory, Iowa State University (Ames), $7.314m: operation of Ames Laboratory; research in physical and life sciences.

Economic Base Agriculture, notably cattle, hogs and sheep, and grains; finance, insurance and real estate; and food and kindred products, especially canned, cured and frozen foods. Also higher education (Iowa State Univ.).

The Voters

Registration No district-wide registration.
Median voting age 46.2
Employment profile White collar, 40%. Blue collar, 28%. Service, 14%. Farm, 18%.
Ethnic groups Total foreign stock, 9%. Germany, 3%.

Presidential vote

1972	Nixon (R)	125,720	(63%)
	McGovern (D)	74,495	(37%)
1968	Nixon (R)	110,002	(56%)
	Humphrey (D)	73,320	(37%)
	Wallace (AI)	12,741	(6%)

Representative

William J. Scherle (R) Elected 1966; b. March 14, 1923, Little Falls, N.Y.; home, Henderson; So. Methodist U.; USNR, WWII; married, two children; Catholic.

Career Grain and livestock farmer; Asst. Div. Mgr., George D. Barnard Co., Dallas, Tex.; Iowa House of Reps., 1960–66.

Offices 512 CHOB, 202-225-3806. Also Fed. Bldg., P.O. Box S, Council Bluffs 51501, 712-323-3577, and 413 Kellogg, Ames 50010, 515-232-3668.

Administrative Assistant Dan Passick

Committees

Appropriations (15th); Subs: Agriculture, Environmental and Consumer Protection; HUD, Space, Science, Veterans.

Group Ratings

	ADA	COPE	LWV	RIPON	NFU	LCV	CFA	NAB	NSI	ACA
1972	0	10	30	25	43	27	100	82	100	95
1971	5	0	11	29	43	–	0	–	–	89
1970	8	27	–	13	38	40	21	80	100	88

I O W A   *3 5 0*

Key Votes

1) Busing	AGN	6) Cmbodia Bmbg	FOR	11) Chkg Acct Intrst	AGN
2) Strip Mines	AGN	7) Bust Hwy Trust	AGN	12) End HISC (HUAC)	AGN
3) Cut Mil $	ABS	8) Farm Sub Lmt	AGN	13) Nixon Sewer Veto	AGN
4) Rev Shrg	AGN	9) School Prayr	FOR	14) Corp Cmpaign $	FOR
5) Pub TV $	AGN	10) Cnsumr Prot	AGN	15) Pol $ Disclosr	AGN

Election Results

1972 general:	William J. Scherle (R)	108,596	(55%)
	Tom Harkin (D)	87,937	(45%)
1972 primary:	William J. Scherle (R), unopposed		
1970 general:	William J. Scherle (R)	53,084	(63%)
	Lou Guletich (D)	31,552	(37%)

SIXTH DISTRICT Political Background

The 6th district of Iowa lies in the northwest corner of the state, where water and trees begin to get scarcer and the sky seems to get bigger. Except for Sioux City (pop. 85,000), the 6th is almost entirely rural, with small farm-market towns and towering grain elevators here and there in the landscape. The district is traditionally Iowa Republican, but with some exceptions. Politically deviant counties dot the maps of all the states in the Great Plains. The deviance from the dominant political mores usually stems from the counties having been settled by a particular ethnic group. A colony of German Catholics or Norwegians, to name two groups, would send an encouraging word back to the home country, telling of their own community in Iowa, Kansas, or the Dakotas.

Upon arriving in some East Coast city, the new immigrants would find train fare waiting for them, often a gift of the railroads eager to sell land they had been granted back in the 1870s. Once the immigrant bought the land and raised a crop, he would have to use the same railroad to get it to market. During the 1890s, of course, railroads out here took a lot of Populist flak from outraged farmers, both old stock WASP and immigrant. In any case, the political inclinations of many rural Iowa counties that are heavily Republican (e.g., Sioux County) or more Democratic than one would expect (e.g., Palo Alto County) can be explained by patterns of immigrant settlement.

Palo Alto County in the 6th is particularly interesting for another reason. For as long as anyone can remember, the county has supported the winning presidential candidate. In the recent close elections of 1960 and 1968, Palo Alto sustained its record by going for John F. Kennedy and Richard Nixon respectively. In 1972, the county gave George McGovern a higher percentage of its votes than it gave Hubert Humphrey in 1968, but again came out on the winning side, producing a 52–48 margin for Richard Nixon.

It may be of some significance, then, that 6th-district Congressman Wiley Mayne did not carry Palo Alto in either the 1970 or 1972 elections. Mayne, a mild-mannered, moderate-to-conservative Republican, had been a pretty solid vote-getter since he was first elected in 1966, when he unseated Iowa class of 1964 Democrat, Stanley Greigg. Greigg was later Deputy Chairman of the Democratic National Committee when its Watergate offices were bugged by the Committee to Reelect the President. Since the Nixon Administration assumed office, Congressman Mayne's majorities have been dropping. In 1970, Palo Alto was the only county in the district he failed to carry. But in 1972, he lost 8 of 22 counties, including the largest, Woodbury (Sioux City), to the Democratic challenger, a self-made fishing tackle millionaire from Spirit Lake named Berkley Bedell.

Mayne's decreasing percentages run counter to the usual pattern found in the nation. Ordinarily, incumbents increase their margins year after year, whatever the fortunes of their party at large. The Republican's showings here is certainly more evidence of a strong Democratic trend in Iowa—one that could spell defeat for the Congressman in 1974. Bedell will be running again, and seems to have at least an even chance to win.

Census Data Pop. 470,867. Central city, 18%; suburban, 4%. Median family income, $8,314; families above $15,000: 14%; families below $3,000: 11%. Median years education, 12.2.

1972 Share of Federal Outlays $479,754,215

DOD	$28,568,000	HEW	$158,197,716
AEC	–	HUD	$1,374,900
NASA	–	DOI	$972,605
DOT	$5,236,535	USDA	$224,176,372
		Other	$61,228,087

Federal Military-Industrial Commitments

No installations or contractors receiving prime awards greater than $5,000,000.

Economic Base Agriculture, notably cattle, grains, and hogs and sheep; food and kindred products, especially meat packing plant products; finance, insurance and real estate; transportation equipment, especially motor vehicles and equipment; and machinery.

The Voters

Registration No district-wide registration.
Median voting age 47.4
Employment profile White collar, 40%. Blue collar, 28%. Service, 14%. Farm, 18%.
Ethnic groups Total foreign stock, 16%. Germany, 5%.

Presidential vote

1972	Nixon (R)	123,738	(62%)
	McGovern (D)	76,110	(38%)
1968	Nixon (R)	116,438	(57%)
	Humphrey (D)	75,081	(37%)
	Wallace (AI)	9,354	(5%)

Representative

Wiley Mayne (R) Elected 1966; b. Jan. 18, 1917, Sanborn; home, Sioux City; Harvard Col., B.S., 1938; Iowa Law School, J.D., 1941; USN, 1943–45; married, three children; Presbyterian.

Career Special agent, FBI, 1941–43; trial lawyer, 1946–67; Pres., Iowa State Bar Assn., 1963–64; Chm., Grievance Commission of Iowa Supreme Ct., 1964–66; Commissioner of Uniform State Laws, 1956–60.

Offices 107 CHOB, 202-225-5476. Also 318 Fed. Bldg., Sioux City 51101, 712-252-4161, ext. 281, and 404 Fed. Bldg., Fort Dodge 50501, 515-573-8101.

Administrative Assistant Donald D. Sillivan

Committees

Agriculture (5th); Subs: Livestock and Grains (Ranking Mbr.); Conservation and Credit; Department Operations.

Judiciary (9th); Sp. Sub. on Criminal Justice.

Group Ratings

	ADA	COPE	LWV	RIPON	NFU	LCV	CFA	NAB	NSI	ACA
1972	19	9	64	73	33	24	0	100	100	61
1971	24	8	67	82	33	–	13	–	–	68
1970	24	9	–	71	46	25	57	100	89	38

Key Votes

1) Busing	FOR	6) Cmbodia Bmbg	FOR	11) Chkg Acct Intrst	AGN
2) Strip Mines	AGN	7) Bust Hwy Trust	AGN	12) End HISC (HUAC)	AGN
3) Cut Mil $	AGN	8) Farm Sub Lmt	FOR	13) Nixon Sewer Veto	FOR
4) Rev Shrg	FOR	9) School Prayr	AGN	14) Corp Cmpaign $	AGN
5) Pub TV $	AGN	10) Cnsumr Prot	AGN	15) Pol $ Disclosr	FOR

Election Results

1972 general:	Wiley Mayne (R)	103,284	(52%)
	Berkley Bedell (D)	93,574	(48%)
1972 primary:	Wiley Mayne (R), unopposed		
1970 general:	Wiley Mayne (R)	57,285	(57%)
	Fred H. Moore (D)	43,257	(43%)

KANSAS

Political Background

The political history of Kansas began in the late 1850s. After the passage of the Kansas-Nebraska act of 1854, the question of whether a newly organized state would permit slavery within its borders was to be resolved by "squatter sovereignty," a not-so-enlightened principle developed by Stephen Douglas. Kansas free or slave became a matter of plebiscite. So the idea among both pro- and antislavery partisans was to encourage as much light-footed immigration to Kansas Territory as possible, and thereby win control of the territorial government. Slaveholders from the South were at a disadvantage. They could not very well bring their slaves into Kansas only to risk possible loss of their chattel property should the "squatters" reject the peculiar institution. The cause of slavery in Kansas therefore came to depend not on the physical immigration of slaveholders, but upon Missouri border raiders, who sought to establish slavery by election fraud and violence.

Meanwhile, the actual immigration of antislavery people from the upper Midwest and New England proceeded apace, aided notably by the New England Emigration Aid Society funded by Massachusetts philanthropist Amos A. Lawrence. Up to 1856, most of the outrages were committed by proslavery elements—they sacked the town of Lawrence in that year. Following this, John Brown, later to become a martyr at Harper's Ferry, West Virginia, murdered five proslavery men at Pottawatomie Creek. Then all hell broke loose, as Democratic "bushwhackers" and free-soil and abolitionist "jayhawkers" shot and killed each other with abandon. "Bleeding Kansas" made headlines everywhere. President James Buchanan tried to stop the violence, but misread the situation and bungled matters completely. The killing in the territory so inflamed the nation's sectional animosities that "Bleeding Kansas" became the proximate cause of the Civil War. The struggle out here helped to destroy one national party, the Whigs; helped to split another North and South, the Democrats; and helped to establish a Northern sectional party, the Republicans. When the South seceded, Kansas was admitted to the Union as a free state with the Republican party in solid control. And there the party has remained, with few exceptions, ever since.

The major exception to Republican domination of the state occurred during the depression of the 1890s with the populist revolt. During the 10 or 15 years previous, years of unusually high rainfall on the High Plains, Kansas had attracted thousands of new settlers. Most of them were Republicans from the upper Midwest. But the rainfall soon returned to normal levels—contrary to the slogan, the rain did not follow the plow. The climatic change, coupled with a worldwide drop in wheat prices, showed that the new Kansas farmland could not support all the migrants who had come to live on it. The state's boom had gone bust, and many of those busted went home and are now forgotten by local historical societies. Some Kansas counties have never again reached populations recorded in the 1890 census.

The economic crisis produced Kansas political leaders who spurned the state's Republicanism. Among them were Mrs. Mary Ellen Lease ("What you farmers need to do is raise less corn and more hell") and "Sockless Jerry" Simpson, who served as a Populist Kansas Congressman in Washington for several years. Lease, Simpson, and the simple farmers of the Populist party became advocates of complex doctrines of free silver and commodity credit programs. William Jennings Bryan, the lion of the prairies, was their man, and he swept the state in 1896.

The period of Populist dominance—colorful, revivalistic, desperate—was soon over. Around 1900 the nation began to enjoy a decade or so of agricultural prosperity, one so great that parity prices are still based on these years before World War I. The prosperity, along with the jingoism of the Spanish-American War and the Alaskan gold that loosened up the money market, seemed to satisfy the farmers and killed their interest in Populistic radicalism and free silver. With the small-town Republicans back in control, Bryan failed to carry Kansas in 1900 or 1908. William Allen White, the progressive Republican editor of the Emporia *Gazette*, became the state's resident radical. Few other Kansans showed much enthusiasm for the reforms of the Progressive era.

But echoes of the farm revolt can still sometimes be heard in Kansas politics. As in most of the Great Plains states, fewer and fewer Kansans can make a living as honest-to-God farmers. The state's economy, however, still depends heavily on the money generated by agriculture. Kansas farmers, like farmers everywhere, have a tendency to complain a lot. In fact, they seldom have it very good, and when they do, the American consumers complain bitterly about high food prices. So regardless of how good the market may look at the moment or how supportive the programs of the Department of Agriculture may be, there is usually discontent on the farm with the farm programs of any Administration in Washington. That Administration suffers at least a little whenever Kansans go to the polls.

It is not too surprising, therefore, that in 1972 Kansas voters reelected Democratic Gov. Robert Docking to an unprecedented fourth term, and reelected their Democratic Attorney General Vern Miller. To be sure, neither of these two Democrats could pass muster among liberals of the upper West Side of New York. Docking's proudest accomplishment was to hold down both state spending and taxes; and Miller, former Sedgwick County (Wichita) Sheriff, campaigned as a law-and-order man and a stern foe of student dissidents. The University of Kansas at Lawrence has seen quite a number of these unhappy students.

What was most interesting about the races Docking and Miller ran were the margins they received. It was no surprise that Richard Nixon carried 70% of the vote and all of the state's 105 counties in 1972. Kansas is one of the nation's most Republican states in presidential contests, with Nixon losing only two counties in 1960 and one in 1968. But here one finds a fierce amount of ticket-splitting. Docking won 62% of the vote and lost only nine small counties. Miller did even better, taking 68%, and like Nixon carried all 105 counties.

Yet the biggest percentage—a whopping 71%—belonged to an officeholder who had been considered in severe trouble just a year or two before, Republican Sen. James Pearson. A political moderate from the Kansas City suburbs, Pearson did not have a strong electoral base in the state. While in the Senate, he alienated conservative Kansas Republicans by voting against the Nixon Administration on issues like the ABM and a date-certain withdrawal from Vietnam. There were rumblings that Pearson would get conservative opposition in the 1972 Republican primary. And beyond that, almost everyone thought that Gov. Docking would run and make a very difficult candidate to beat in the general election.

But a heavy Pearson speaking schedule and an early start organizing his campaign in 1971 shored up the Senator's position within the party. Moreover, the Senator's much more conservative colleague and then-Republican National Chairman, Robert Dole, scotched the idea of primary opposition. Pearson began to show well in the polls, and in the spring of 1972, first Gov. Docking and then Atty. Gen. Miller declined to make the race. That left Pearson home free, with only nominal opposition. The Kansas politician was one of several Republican moderate Senators, including Percy of Illinois, Brooke of Massachusetts, and Case of New Jersey, to run ahead of President Nixon's record majorities.

Now the outlook is trouble for Sen. Dole, who is up for reelection in 1974. In 1968, Dole, a firm and unyielding supporter of the Nixon Administration, entered the Senate, straight from eight years in the House. Though only a freshman, he became a spirited and self-appointed defender of Nixon policies. So great was his enthusiasm for the President that Mr. Nixon himself tapped the

Kansan for the position of Republican National Chairman in 1971. Throughout the 1972 campaign, Dole remained a faithful partisan of Richard Nixon. At one point he went so far as to say that the McGovern forees were using Watergate to divert attention from other, more important issues. At the same time, however, it was apparent that Dole was given no real influence in the Nixon reelection effort.

After the election, Dole abandoned his unveering support of the Administration. Republicans all over the nation were unhappy, first because no effort was made to extend the President's coattails, and second because the party had lost, rather than gained, seats in the Senate. The White House made it clear that Dole was through as National Chairman. Dole fought back, though in the end of course he lost his job. When the Watergate scandal finally broke, Dole moved from a previous poo-pooing of the matter to stern denunciation. He pointed out with apparent justification that neither he nor the Republican National Committee had any part in the mess.

Dole faces an unusual problem for a Kansas Republican. In 1974, he has two popular, well-known potential opponents. Gov. Docking, who declined a race against Pearson in 1972, is thinking again about the Senate. The Governor could also run for Kansas' first four-year gubernatorial term in 1974. But, though he has reportedly been less eager to leave his home state for Washington than many other American politicians, at this writing he appears to have decided to make the race—and is ahead of Dole in the polls. If Docking does run for the Senate, Miller is the odds-on favorite for the governorship.

Another possible Democratic nominee is Congressman William Roy, who won an amazing upset victory in 1972 in the 2nd congressional district. Roy upped his percentage in the face of an aggressive Republican campaign in 1972. Roy has been traveling around Kansas, seeking political support, and sounding out Dole's popularity. But Roy will not run if Docking goes for Dole's seat.

Census Data Pop. 2,249,071; 1.11% of U.S. total, 28th largest; change 1960–70, 3.2%. Central city, 18%; suburban, 24%. Median family income, $8,690; 30th highest; families above $15,000: 16%; families below $3,000: 11%. Median years education, 12.3.

1972 Share of Federal Tax Burden $2,069,280,000; 0.99% of U.S. total, 28th largest.

1972 Share of Federal Outlays $2,544,929,596; 1.17% of U.S. total, 29th largest. Per capita federal spending, $1,132.

DOD	$734,845,000	25th	(1.18%)	HEW	$733,820,716	29th	(1.03%)
AEC	$871,865	32nd	(0.03%)	HUD	$30,377,784	29th	(0.99%)
NASA	$2,112,012	29th	(0.07%)	VA	$138,355,836	30th	(1.21%)
DOT	$87,387,245	31st	(1.11%)	USDA	$500,305,709	8th	(3.25%)
DOC	$4,154,953	40th	(0.32%)	CSC	$36,376,608	29th	(0.88%)
DOI	$16,919,640	28th	(0.80%)	TD	$108,563,443	23rd	(0.66%)
DOJ	$13,400,717	27th	(1.36%)	Other	$137,438,068		

Economic Base Agriculture, especially cattle, wheat, hogs and sorghum grain; finance, insurance and real estate; transportation equipment, especially aircraft and parts; food and kindred products; machinery; printing and publishing, especially newspapers; oil and gas extraction, especially crude petroleum and natural gas.

Political Line-up Governor, Robert B. Docking (D); seat up, 1974. Senators, James B. Pearson (R) and Robert Dole (R). Representatives, 5 (4 R and 1 D). State Senate (27 R and 13 D); State House (80 R and 45 D).

The Voters

Registration No figures available.
Median voting age 44.0
Employment profile White collar, 48%. Blue collar, 31%. Service, 13%. Farm, 8%.
Ethnic groups Black, 5%. Spanish, 2%. Total foreign stock, 8%. Germany, 2%.

Presidential vote

1972	Nixon (R)	619,812	(70%)
	McGovern (D)	270,287	(30%)
1968	Nixon (R)	478,674	(55%)
	Humphrey (D)	302,996	(35%)
	Wallace (AI)	88,921	(10%)
1964	Johnson (D)	464,028	(55%)
	Goldwater (R)	386,579	(45%)

Senator

James Blackwood Pearson (R) Elected Appointed Feb. 5, 1962, Elected 1962; seat up 1978; b. May 7, 1920, Nashville, Tenn.; home, Prairie Village; Duke U., 1940–42; U. of Va. Law School, LL.B., 1950; Navy, WWII; married, four children; Presbyterian.

Career Practicing atty., 1950–62; Probate Judge, Johnson County, 1954–66; Kans. Senate, 1956–60; State Repub. Chm., 1960–61; Campaign Mgr. for Gov. Anderson, 1960.

Offices 5313 NSOB, 202-225-4774. Also 600 Merchants' Natl. Bank Bldg., Topeka 66612, 913-357-4312, and 617 First Natl. Bank Bldg., Wichita 67202, 316-262-0021.

Administrative Assistant Jerry B. Waters

Committees

Commerce (2nd); Subs: Aviation; Communications; Environment; Consumer; Surface Transportation; Foreign Commerce and Tourism; Sp. Sub. on Technology and Science.

Foreign Relations (5th); Subs: European Affairs; Africian Affairs; Arms Control, International Law and Organization; Far-Eastern Affairs.

Joint Economic Com. (2nd); Subs: Economic Progress; Priorities and Economy in Government; Inter-American Economic Relationships; International Economies.

Sp. Com. on the Termination of the National Emergency. (3rd).

Group Ratings

	ADA	COPE	LWV	RIPON	NFU	LCV	CFA	NAB	NSI	ACA
1972	45	40	80	88	70	26	100	58	78	35
1971	37	36	85	58	45	–	71	–	–	50
1970	28	46	–	54	60	14	–	80	80	56

Key Votes

1) Busing	FOR	8) Sea Life Prot	AGN	15) Tax Singls Less	FOR
2) Alas P-line	AGN	9) Campaign Subs	AGN	16) Min Tax for Rich	AGN
3) Gun Cntrl	FOR	10) Cmbodia Bmbg	AGN	17) Euro Troop Rdctn	AGN
4) Rehnquist	FOR	11) Legal Srvices	ABS	18) Bust Hwy Trust	FOR
5) Pub TV $	FOR	12) Rev Sharing	FOR	19) Maid Min Wage	AGN
6) EZ Votr Reg	AGN	13) Cnsumr Prot	FOR	20) Farm Sub Limit	AGN
7) No-Fault	FOR	14) Eq Rts Amend	FOR	21) Highr Credt Chgs	AGN

Election Results

1972 general:	James B. Pearson (R)	622,591	(71%)
	Arch O. Tetzlaff (D)	200,764	(23%)
	Gene F. Miller (Con.)	35,510	(4%)
	Howard Hadin (Prohib.)	12,857	(1%)
1972 primary:	James B. Pearson (R)	229,908	(82%)
	Harlan Dale House (R)	49,825	(18%)

1966 general:	James B. Pearson (R)	350,077	(52%)
	J. Floyd Breeding (D)	303,223	(45%)
	Earl F. Dodge (Prohib.)	9,364	(1%)
	George W. Snell (Cons.)	7,103	(1%)

Senator

Robert J. Dole (R) Elected 1968, seat up 1974; b. July 22, 1923, Russell; home, Russell; U. of Kans., 1941–43; Washburn Municipal U., B.A., 1952, LL.B., 1952; Army, 1943–48; married, one child; Methodist.

Career Kans. House of Reps., 1951–53; Russell County Atty., 1953–61; U.S. House of Reps., 1960–68; Repub. Natl. Com. Chm., 1971– .

Offices 2327 NSOB, 202-225-6521. Also 708 Central St., Dodge City 67801, 316-225-4322.

Administrative Assistant Michael Barody

Committees

Agriculture and Forestory (4th); Subs: Agricultural Credit and Rural Electrification; Agricultural Production, Marketing and Stabilization of Prices; Agricultural Research and General Legislation (Ranking Mbr.); Rural Development; Foreign Agricultural Policy.

Finance (5th); Subs: Health; Private Pension Plans; International Finance and Resources (Ranking Mbr.).

Sel. Com. on Nutrition and Human Needs (3rd).

Sel. Com. on Small Business (3rd); Subs: Government Procurement; Monopoly; Environmental, Rural, and Urban Economic Development (Ranking Mbr.).

Group Ratings

	ADA	COPE	LWV	RIPON	NFU	LCV	CFA	NAB	NSI	ACA
1972	0	10	33	54	56	11	0	80	100	84
1971	4	17	54	38	33	–	20	–	–	71
1970	13	15	–	50	43	20	–	91	89	76

Key Votes

1) Busing	AGN	8) Sea Life Prot	AGN	15) Tax Singls Less	FOR
2) Alas P-line	AGN	9) Campaign Subs	AGN	16) Min Tax for Rich	AGN
3) Gun Cntrl	FOR	10) Cmbodia Bmbg	FOR	17) Euro Troop Rdctn	AGN
4) Rehnquist	FOR	11) Legal Srvices	AGN	18) Bust Hwy Trust	AGN
5) Pub TV $	AGN	12) Rev Sharing	FOR	19) Maid Min Wage	AGN
6) EZ Votr Reg	AGN	13) Cnsumr Prot	AGN	20) Farm Sub Limit	AGN
7) No-Fault	AGN	14) Eq Rts Amend	FOR	21) Highr Credt Chgs	ABS

Election Results

1968 general:	Bob Dole (R)	490,911	(60%)
	William I. Robinson (D)	315,911	(39%)
	Joseph F. Hyskell (Prohib.)	10,262	(1%)
1968 primary:	Bob Dole (R)	190,782	(68%)
	William H. Avery (R)	87,801	(32%)

FIRST DISTRICT Political Background

The 1st district of Kansas covers more than half of the state's land area. It contains more counties, 57, than any other congressional district in the United States, save the state of North Dakota which elects one Congressman-at-Large. This fact is not a bit of irrelevant trivia; it tells us a good deal about the expectations of the people who first settled this part of Kansas. Most of them came here in the late nineteenth century from states like Illinois and Iowa. When they organized counties, they made them 36 miles square, just as they were in the upper Midwest. Deceived by a few years of unusually high rainfall, the settlers expected that the new counties would eventually contain as many people as those back home; hence the counties were made conveniently small. Not just the size of the units, but the grandiosity of area place names (Sylvan Grove, Concordia, Minneapolis, Montezuma), testify to the settlers' hopes, dreams, and ambitions.

But these were never realized. Out here past the 98th meridian, rainfall is normally half that in Illinois. In the early years of the nineteenth century, this part of Kansas was considered part of the Great American Desert—a howling wilderness of aridity. The early settlers worked hard to change the image, but never really succeeded. So the thousands more who were expected to come never came. Land prices here began to climb only after great corporations decided to get into the farming business. But the average population of the 1st's 57 counties remains a scant 7,800 souls.

Most are far less populous than 7,800. The county average is inflated by the district's urban aggregations. At 37,000, Salina is the 1st's largest city; Dodge City, terminus of the old cattle drives, has 14,000 people; Holcomb, made famous by Truman Capote, has less than 10,000. Hays, a German-Catholic enclave of 16,000, is a place that generally goes Democratic—an unusual tendency in these parts.

The real 1st district cannot be found in its cities. This is livestock and wheat country, one of the most agricultural districts in the nation. For miles on end, one can see nothing but rolling brown fields, sectioned off here and there by barbed-wire fence, along with the inevitable grain elevator towering over all.

The 1st is predominantly Republican, but discontent among the area's farmers has sometimes put it in the Democratic column. From 1956 to 1960, the western half of the present district elected Democrat J. Floyd Breeding to the House; Kansas then had six congressional districts, though it now has only five. After the 1960 census, Breeding's district was combined with that of then-Rep. Bob Dole. Dole, as Republican legislators expected, beat Breeding in 1962. After surviving a close election in 1964, the Republican scored a runaway victory in 1966.

When Dole moved up to the Senate in 1968, he was succeeded by a like-minded, but less flamboyant Republican, Keith Sebelius. After comparatively close contests in 1968 and 1970, Sebelius in 1972 polled the kind of vote Republicans like in western Kansas, 77%. The Congressman, like Dole, has been a loyal supporter of the Nixon Administration. When he voted to override a Nixon veto of a rural water and sewer bill—a matter of some importance to the 1st district—he announced that he voted to override only with the greatest reluctance. In 1970 and 1972, the northern states of the Farm Belt showed much of its traditional resentment of the Administration in power, but no such thing happened in Kansas. Unless the farmers of the 1st get mad, this is one of the safest Republican seats in the country.

Census Data Pop. 447,787. Central city, 0%; suburban, 0%. Median family income, $7,820; families above $15,000: 12%; families below $3,000: 12%. Median years education, 12.2.

1972 Share of Federal Outlays $505,493,211

DOD	$11,329,000	HEW	$145,592,301
AEC	$242,465	HUD	$678,998
NASA	$106,673	DOI	$2,312,164
DOT	$9,604,876	USDA	$278,048,938
		Other	$57,577,796

Federal Military-Industrial Commitments

No installations or contractors receiving prime awards greater $5,000,000.

Economic Base Agriculture, notably cattle, grains, and hogs and sheep; finance, insurance and real estate; oil and gas extraction, especially oil and gas field services, and crude petroleum and natural gas; food and kindred products; and machinery.

The Voters

Registration Not available.
Median voting age 47.7
Employment profile White collar, 40%. Blue collar, 27%. Service, 14%. Farm, 19%.
Ethnic groups Black, 1%. Spanish, 2%. Total foreign stock, 9%. Germany, 3%.

Presidential vote

1972	Nixon (R)	135,605	(72%)
	McGovern (D)	52,842	(28%)
1968	Nixon (R)	114,688	(59%)
	Humphrey (D)	60,939	(32%)
	Wallace (AI)	16,375	(9%)

Representative

Keith G. Sebelius (R) Elected 1968; b. Sept. 10, 1916, Almena; home, Norton; Fort Hays Kans. State Col., B.A.; George Washington U. Law School, J.D., 1939; Army, WWII and Korean War; married, two children; Methodist.

Career Practicing atty., City Councilman, Mayor, City Atty., County Atty., Norton; Kans. State Senate, 1962–68; Legislative Council, 4 yrs.

Offices 1225 LHOB, 202-225-2715. Also P.O. Box 40, Hays 67601, 913-628-1313.

Administrative Assistant Charles P. Roberts

Committees

Agriculture (8th); Subs: Livestock and Grains; Department Operations; Family Farms and Rural Development (Ranking Mbr.).

Interior and Insular Affairs (10th); Subs: Environment; National Parks and Recreation; Territorial and Insular Affairs.

Group Ratings

	ADA	COPE	LWV	RIPON	NFU	LCV	CFA	NAB	NSI	ACA
1972	0	18	18	44	43	20	0	83	88	95
1971	11	30	20	41	47	–	13	–	–	80
1970	8	9	–	47	25	0	50	92	100	82

Key Votes

1) Busing	AGN	6) Cmbodia Bmbg	FOR	11) Chkg Acct Intrst	AGN
2) Strip Mines	FOR	7) Bust Hwy Trust	AGN	12) End HISC (HUAC)	AGN
3) Cut Mil $	ABS	8) Farm Sub Lmt	AGN	13) Nixon Sewer Veto	AGN
4) Rev Shrg	AGN	9) School Prayr	FOR	14) Corp Cmpaign $	AGN
5) Pub TV $	ABS	10) Cnsumr Prot	AGN	15) Pol $ Disclosr	AGN

Election Results

1972 general:	Keith G. Sebelius (R)	145,712	(77%)
	Morris Coover (D)	40,678	(22%)
	Daniel Scoggin (Prohib.)	2,267	(1%)
1972 primary:	Keith G. Sebelius (R), unopposed		
1970 general:	Keith G. Sebelius (R)	83,923	(57%)
	Billy D. Jellison (D)	63,791	(43%)

SECOND DISTRICT Political Background

In 1970, the 2nd district of Kansas produced one of the most surprising congressional upsets of recent years. This was the defeat of Republican Congressman Chester Mize by Democrat William Roy. No district in Kansas had elected a Democratic Congressman for ten yers, and no one, except Roy and his staff, expected the 2nd to do so in 1970, Mize least of all. He had won reelection with 68% of the votes two years before in what everyone considered a solidly Republican district.

True, the 2nd included a small portion of Wyandot County and Kansas City—just about the only part of the state that normally gives Democrats majorities. But Topeka, the state capital and largest city in the district, regularly votes Republican; Topeka with its suburbs cast about a third of the 2nd's ballots. It is a clean-cut American city and the home town of that man and symbol, Alf Landon, the still vigorous and active progressive Republican who was clobbered in the Roosevelt landslide of 1936.

How did Roy win? In the first place, he was not a run-of-the-mill Democratic candidate. Roy was a lifelong Republican until he filed for Congress; he is also both a physician and a lawyer. As a practicing obstetrician, Dr. Roy had delivered more than 5,000 babies in the Topeka area. Because he had done this sort of thing for only 17 years, none of his deliveries could vote for him, but the parents of the children could and apparently did in great numbers. Morever, Roy organized a highly visible, credible campaign, spending about $100,000—an unusually high amount for Kansas. Given his newsworthiness, he managed to overcome the initial obstacle that does in almost all challengers of incumbent Congressmen: anonymity.

With an effective media and direct-mail campaign, Roy won 52% of the votes to Mize's 45%. Roy got 58% in his home county of Shawnee (Topeka). The challenger's victory must have shocked Kansas Republicans; it was the first time in 63 years that the district had elected a Democratic Congressman. The Republicans were of course determined to reverse what they considered a fluke. They put on a heavy campaign in 1972, attacking Roy for the high ratings organizations like the ADA and COPE gave him. But the incumbent, who returned to the district almost every weekend of his first term, was able to defend his positions, and won reelection with a solid 61% over his Republican opponent's 37%.

In the House, Roy sits on the Public Health Subcommittee, for which as a physician and attorney he is uniquely qualified. At this writing, Congressman Roy is seriously considering a bid for Republican Bob Dole's Senate seat; he will not, however, run if Gov. Robert Docking decides to take on Dole. A run against Dole would be a tough one, but from the looks of the returns, Roy can win reelection in the 2nd easily if he decides he wants to run.

Census Data Pop. 454,028. Central city, 28%; suburban, 14%. Median family income, $8,680; families above $15,000: 15%; families below $3,000: 11%. Median years education, 12.3.

1972 Share of Federal Outlays $686,550,768

DOD	$313,714,394	HEW	$152,278,249
AEC	$471,889	HUD	$10,616,015
NASA	$21,035	DOI	$1,454,678
DOT	$10,390,050	USDA	$62,541,630
		Other	$135,062,828

Federal Military-Industrial Commitments

DOD Installations Fort Leavenworth AB (Leavenworth). Fort Riley AB (Junction City).

Economic Base Agriculture, notably cattle, grains, and hogs and sheep; finance, insurance and real estate; printing and publishing; food and kindred products, especially meat products; and stone, clay and glass products, especially mineral wool. Also higher education (Kansas State Univ., and Wichita State Univ.).

The Voters

Registration Not available.
Median voting age 40.7
Employment profile White collar, 49%. Blue collar, 30%. Service, 14%. Farm, 7%.
Ethnic groups Black, 6%. Spanish, 3%. Total foreign stock, 9%. Germany, 3%.

Presidential vote

1972	Nixon (R)	119,234	(70%)
	McGovern (D)	51,093	(30%)
1968	Nixon (R)	87,812	(54%)
	Humphrey (D)	55,430	(34%)
	Wallace (AI)	18,748	(12%)

Representative

William R. Roy, Sr. (D) Elected 1970; b. Feb. 23, 1926, Bloomington, Ill.; home, Topeka; Ill. Wesleyan U., B.S., 1945; Northwestern U., M.D., 1948; Washburn U. School of Law, J.D., 1970; USAF, 1953–55; married, six children; United Methodist Church.

Career Practicing physician, 1953–70; Delegate, White House Conference on Children and Youth, 1960; Pres., Shawnee County Medical Society, 1967; Delegate, five times, Kans. Med. Soc.; V. Speaker, Kans. Med. Soc. House of Delegates, 1969.

Offices 1110 LHOB, 202-225-6601. Also 909 Topeka Ave., Topeka 66612, 913-233-8951.

Administrative Assistant Paul E. Pendergast

Committees

Interstate and Foreign Commerce (23rd); Sub: Public Health and Environment.

Group Ratings

	ADA	COPE	LWV	RIPON	NFU	LCV	CFA	NAB	NSI	ACA
1972	44	73	64	53	86	57	50	17	11	33
1971	78	83	78	76	100	–	100	–	–	19

Key Votes

1) Busing	AGN	6) Cmbodia Bmbg	AGN	11) Chkg Acct Intrst	AGN
2) Strip Mines	AGN	7) Bust Hwy Trust	AGN	12) End HISC (HUAC)	AGN
3) Cut Mil $	AGN	8) Farm Sub Lmt	AGN	13) Nixon Sewer Veto	AGN
4) Rev Shrg	AGN	9) School Prayr	AGN	14) Corp Cmpaign $	AGN
5) Pub TV $	FOR	10) Cnsumr Prot	FOR	15) Pol $ Disclosr	FOR

Election Results

1972 general:	William R. Roy (D)	106,276	(61%)
	Charles D. McAtee (R)	65,071	(37%)
	Bert Falley (C)	3,107	(2%)
1972 primary:	William R. Roy (D), unopposed		
1970 general:	William R. Roy (D)	80,161	(52%)
	Chester L. Mize (R)	68,843	(45%)
	Fred Kilian (C)	4,145	(3%)

THIRD DISTRICT Political Background

The 3rd congressional district is a not very typical hunk of Kansas. It lies almost entirely within the Kansas City metropolitan area, and contains the state's most Democratic and most

Republican territory. More than 80% of the district's residents live in either heavily Democratic Wyandot County—Kansas City, much smaller than its Missouri neighbor; or in heavily Republican Johnson County—prosperous Kansas City suburbs, including Overland Park, Prairie Village, and Shawnee Mission. A single street separates the Johnson County suburbs from Kansas City, Missouri. On the Kansas side of the line live a disproportionate number of the metropolitan area's wealthy and conservative citizens. Liquor-by-the-glass is the only political issue that Wyandot and Johnson Counties can agree on; both gave the 1970 referendum heavy support, though it lost statewide.

Also included in the 3rd is one small agricultural county and the city of Lawrence, home of the University of Kansas. The institution may be regarded by many Kansans as an alien presence in the state. But the bearded and blue-jeaned students involved in some police-student confrontations are in fact children of Kansas. Lawrence has also developed something of a street-people culture. One of the attractions of River City, as Lawrence is called, is the marijuana that grows in wild profusion in the surrounding farmland.

As noted, the 3rd is not a typical Kansas district. In 1968, both Hubert Humphrey and George Wallace made their best Kansas showings here; in 1972, so did George McGovern. None of these men, of course, came close to carrying the district. The 3rd's Congressman, Larry Winn, Jr., has had some political ups and downs since first being elected in 1966. The strongest showing against him came in 1970 when the Democrats put on a strong effort for then-Lt. Gov. James DeCoursey. The last redistricting helped Winn marginally. But the redrawn lines hardly explain the huge surge in his vote totals in 1972, when he carried the Wyandot portion of the district for the first time. Winn appears to have a safe seat, and is probably more vulnerable to feuding within the local Republican party than to a Democratic challenge.

Census Data Pop. 449,743. Central city, 0%; suburban, 83%. Median family income, $10,928; families above $15,000: 27%; families below $3,000: 7%. Median years education, 12.5.

1972 Share of Federal Outlays $303,370,889

DOD	$43,307,605	HEW	$121,787,919
AEC	$142,510	HUD	$5,690,694
NASA	$804,428	DOI	$10,639,991
DOT	$30,176,698	USDA	$9,446,777
		Other	$81,374,267

Federal Military-Industrial Commitments

DOD Contractors Hercules, Inc. (Lawrence), $9.099m: operation, modernization, and layaway activities at the Sunflower Army Ammunition plant.

Economic Base Finance, insurance and real estate; printing and publishing; food and kindred products, especially meat products; stone, clay and glass products, especially mineral wool; machinery; and electrical equipment and supplies, especially communication equipment. Also higher education (Univ. of Kansas).

The Voters

Registration Not available.
Median voting age 40.5
Employment profile White collar, 58%. Blue collar, 29%. Service, 11%. Farm, 2%.
Ethnic groups Black, 8%. Spanish, 2%. Total foreign stock, 8%. Germany, 1%.

Presidential vote

1972	Nixon (R)	122,474	(67%)
	McGovern (D)	61,367	(33%)
1968	Nixon (R)	87,226	(52%)
	Humphrey (D)	63,698	(38%)
	Wallace (AI)	18,237	(11%)

Representative

Larry Winn, Jr. (R) Elected 1966; b. Aug. 22, 1919, Kansas City Mo.; home, Overland Park; U. of Kans., B.A., 1941; married, five children; Protestant.

Career Radio announcer, WHB; builder; Pub. Relations Dir., American Red Cross; V.P., Winn-Rau Corp., 1950– ; Natl. Dir., Home Builders Assn.; Past GOP Chm., 3rd Dist. Kan.; Mbr., Repub. State Exec. Com. of Kans.; Mbr., Kans. U. Development Com.; Dir., Southgate State Bank.

Offices 434 CHOB, 202-225-2865. Also 204 Fed. Bldg., Kansas City 66101, 913-621-0832.

Administrative Assistant Richard Bond

Committees

Science and Astronautics (4th); Subs: International Cooperation in Science and Space; Manned Space Flight (Ranking Mbr.); Space Science and Applications.

Foreign Affairs (16th); Subs: Africa; International Organizations and Movements.

Group Ratings

	ADA	COPE	LWV	RIPON	NFU	LCV	CFA	NAB	NSI	ACA
1972	0	10	36	64	71	33	50	82	88	76
1971	11	27	33	33	43	–	43	–	–	81
1970	4	17	–	53	25	0	33	75	100	72

Key Votes

1) Busing	AGN	6) Cmbodia Bmbg	FOR	11) Chkg Acct Intrst	ABS
2) Strip Mines	AGN	7) Bust Hwy Trust	AGN	12) End HISC (HUAC)	AGN
3) Cut Mil $	AGN	8) Farm Sub Lmt	AGN	13) Nixon Sewer Veto	FOR
4) Rev Shrg	FOR	9) School Prayr	FOR	14) Corp Cmpaign $	FOR
5) Pub TV $	AGN	10) Cnsumr Prot	AGN	15) Pol $ Disclosr	FOR

Election Results

1972 general:	Larry Winn, Jr. (R)	122,358	(71%)
	Charles Barsotti (D)	43,777	(25%)
	Warren E. Redding (C)	6,258	(4%)
1972 primary:	Larry Winn, Jr. (R), unopposed		
1970 general:	Larry Winn, Jr. (R)	74,603	(53%)
	James H. DeCoursey, Jr. (D)	63,344	(46%)
	Warren E. Redding (C)	1,820	(1%)

FOURTH DISTRICT Political Background

Ever since the 1950 census, Wichita (current pop. 277,000) has been the largest city in Kansas. Before World War II, Wichita, like most Kansas cities, was primarily a trading center in agricultural products, dependent on the prosperity of surrounding farmland. But during the war and the immediate postwar years, Wichita experienced a boom of sorts, sparked by the aviation industry. Boeing has a big plant here, as does Cessna, one of the nation's leading manufacturers of small private aircraft. When the demand for both military and civilian airplanes was high, Wichita did very well. But during the 1960s the boom tapered off. The military aircraft business is, of course, one of the nation's most unstable, with Boeing one of the nation's most troubled companies in this industry group. And even with the demand for private airplanes high, Wichita was unable to generate many jobs from the boom. So today the area around the city is one of stable population, which means that people are leaving for better opportunities.

Because much of Wichita's work force came from the hills of Arkansas and Oklahoma, the city's voting habits have a tinge of the South in them. Though a heavily Republican city in national elections, it has delivered large margins for Democratic candidates in statewide contests. Two beneficiaries of this pattern have been Gov. Robert Docking, who is from nearby Arkansas City (pronounced ar-KAN-sas here), and Atty. Gen. Vern Miller, a law-and-order man who was once Sheriff of Wichita's Sedgwick County.

The 4th congressional district covers all of Wichita and most of its suburbs, plus some farming territory and the small city of Hutchinson, to the north. In congressional elections, this part of Kansas has been Republican for as long as anyone can remember. The 4th's current Representative, first elected in 1960, is Garner E. Shriver (no relation to R. Sargent Shriver). The Kansan is a moderate-to-conservative Congressman inclined not to rock the boat. Shriver has now reached a relatively high rank among Republicans on the House Appropriations Committee (eighth), and the status of ranking minority member on the Foreign Operations Subcommittee, a unit on Appropriations that has been the longtime scourge of the foreign-aid program. Shriver has been a solid vote-getter, in 1972 winning with a little higher than usual share of the votes, 73%.

Census Data Pop. 450,487. Central city, 61%; suburban, 8%. Median family income, $9,097; families above $15,000: 17%; families below $3,000: 9%. Median years education, 12.3.

1972 Share of Federal Outlays $566,966,169

DOD	$244,355,727	HEW	$131,941,252
AEC	$12,130	HUD	$7,888,585
NASA	$931,631	DOI	$1,325,433
DOT	$15,461,312	USDA	$77,364,559
		Other	$87,685,540

Federal Military-Industrial Commitments

DOD Contractors Boeing (Wichita), $190.157m: aircraft and airframe structural components. Cessna Aircraft (Wichita), $9.880m: T-37 aircraft.
DOD Installations McConnell AFB (Wichita).

Economic Base Transportation equipment, especially aircraft and parts; finance, insurance and real estate; agriculture, notably grains, cattle, and hogs and sheep; food and kindred products, especially meat products; and machinery.

The Voters

Registration Not available.
Median voting age 42.8
Employment profile White collar, 51%. Blue collar, 32%. Service, 14%. Farm, 3%.
Ethnic groups Black, 7%. Spanish, 2%. Total foreign stock, 7%. Germany, 2%.

Presidential vote

1972	Nixon (R)	110,805	(68%)
	McGovern (D)	52,191	(32%)
1968	Nixon (R)	84,517	(54%)
	Humphrey (D)	58,290	(37%)
	Wallace (AI)	13,892	(9%)

Representative

Garner E. Shriver (R) Elected 1960; b. July 6, 1912, Towanda; home, Wichita; U. of Wichita, B.A., 1934; U. of So. Calif., 1936; Washburn U. Law School, J.D., 1940; Navy, WWII; married, three children; Methodist.

Career English Speech Instr., 1936–37; practicing atty., 1940–60; Kans. House of Reps., 1947–51; Kans. Senate, 1953–60.

Offices 2209 RHOB, 202-225-6216. Also 830 N. Main, Wichita 62703, 316-265-7111, and 210 P.O. Bldg., Hutchinson 67501, 316-662-0737.

Administrative Assistant Lester Rosen

Committees

Appropriations (8th); Subs: Foreign Operations (Ranking Mbr.); Labor, Health, Education and Welfare.

Group Ratings

	ADA	COPE	LWV	RIPON	NFU	LCV	CFA	NAB	NSI	ACA
1972	0	18	42	64	57	33	50	83	100	74
1971	5	45	44	35	47	–	38	–	–	71
1970	12	34	–	69	54	0	41	83	100	67

Key Votes

1) Busing	AGN	6) Cmbodia Bmbg	FOR	11) Chkg Acct Intrst	AGN
2) Strip Mines	AGN	7) Bust Hwy Trust	AGN	12) End HISC (HUAC)	AGN
3) Cut Mil $	AGN	8) Farm Sub Lmt	AGN	13) Nixon Sewer Veto	FOR
4) Rev Shrg	FOR	9) School Prayr	FOR	14) Corp Cmpaign $	AGN
5) Pub TV $	FOR	10) Cnsumr Prot	FOR	15) Pol $ Disclosr	AGN

Election Results

1972 general:	Garner E. Shriver (R)	120,120	(73%)
	John S. Stevens (D)	40,753	(25%)
	Wayne Nobbs, Jr. (Prohib.)	3,241	(2%)
1972 primary:	Garner E. Shriver (R), unopposed		
1970 general:	Garner E. Shriver (R)	85,058	(63%)
	James C. Juhnke (D)	47,004	(35%)
	George W. Snell (C)	2,452	(2%)

FIFTH DISTRICT Political Background

The southeast corner of Kansas was nicknamed "The Balkans." This is a reference to the Eastern European ancestry of many of the area's residents and to its low hill country, which constitutes the outer fringes of the Ozark Mountains in Arkansas. The hills contain some coal mines. The main town here was named Pittsburg—yet another indication of just how bullish the nineteenth-century Kansas pioneers were (see Kansas 1). This part of Kansas never became a notable coal or manufacturing center, and today, like most of rural America, it is in unmistakable economic decline. The southeast corner of the state is the heartland of the 5th district of Kansas; it stretches north to a point near Kansas City and west toward the Wichita suburbs and beyond.

Emporia (pop. 23,000) is one of the larger towns that dot the district. Emporia was the home of William Allen White, the newspaper editor whose name was a household word a generation ago but one that draws a blank today. White was the voice of progressive Kansas Republicanism. Horrified by the Populists in his youth, White later became enchanted with Theodore Roosevelt, and came to understand the plight of those less fortunate than he. And though a native of one of the nation's most isolationist regions, White was a leading spokesman for American aid to Britain during the ominous days before the German invasion of Poland and Pearl Harbor.

White has been dead now for almost 30 years. And in the years since his death, his spirit has seldom had a place in Kansas Republicanism. It is not particularly evident in the record of 5th-district Congressman Joe Skubitz. The Congressman, a fairly conservative Republican, depends more on personal popularity than articulated issue positions for the large majorities he wins every two years. By the workings of the rules of seniority, Skubitz, from a part of the country with scarcely a scenic mile, is the ranking Republican on the National Parks and Recreation Subcommittee of the Interior Committee. Skubitz has never had much trouble winning reelection. But he has never faced a really serious challenge, either; if he ever does, he might be vulnerable.

Census Data Pop. 447,026. Central city, 0%; suburban, 17%. Median family income, $7,450; families above $15,000: 10%; families below $3,000: 15%. Median years education, 12.1.

1972 Share of Federal Outlays $482,548,549

DOD	$122,138,273	HEW	$182,220,983
AEC	$2,869	HUD	$5,503,490
NASA	$248,243	DOI	$1,187,372
DOT	$21,754,307	USDA	$72,903,803
		Other	$76,589,209

Federal Military-Industrial Commitments

DOD Contractors Day & Zimmerman (Parsons), $28.848m: operation of Kansas Army Ammunition plant. General Electric (Arkansas City), $10.246m: overhaul and modification of J85 aircraft engine. General Aircraft (Pittsburg), $5.381m: short take-off aircraft.

Economic Base Agriculture, notably cattle, grains, hogs and sheep, and dairy products; transportation equipment, especially aircraft and parts; finance, insurance and real estate; food and kindred products, especially meat products; machinery; and fabricated metal products, especially nonelectrical plumbing and heating products.

The Voters

Registration Not available.
Median voting age 48.5
Employment profile White collar, 40%. Blue collar, 36%. Service, 14%. Farm, 10%.
Ethnic groups Black, 2%. Spanish, 1%. Total foreign stock, 6%. Germany, 1%.

Presidential vote

1972	Nixon (R)	124,835	(71%)
	McGovern (D)	50,528	(29%)
1968	Nixon (R)	100,825	(54%)
	Humphrey (D)	62,536	(34%)
	Wallace (AI)	20,869	(12%)

Representative

Joe Skubitz (R) Elected 1962; b. May 6, 1906, Frontenac; home, Pittsburg; Kans. State Col., B.S., 1929, M.S., 1934; Washburn U. Law School, 1938; George Washington U. Law School, LL.B., 1946; married, one child; Methodist.

Career Admin. Asst. to senators Clyde M. Reed and Andrew F. Schoeppel, 1952–62.

Offices 2447 RHOB, 202-225-3911. Also Pittsburg 66762, 316-231-6200; 206 E. 9th, Winfield 67156, 316-221-2020; and Post Ofc. Bldg., Emporia 66801, 316-342-6464.

Administrative Assistant Edward Cooper

Committees

Interior and Insular Affairs (3rd); Subs: Mines and Mining; National Parks and Recreation (Ranking Mbr.); Territorial and Insular Affairs.

Interstate and Foreign Commerce (8th); Sub: Transportation and Aeronautics.

Group Ratings

	ADA	COPE	LWV	RIPON	NFU	LCV	CFA	NAB	NSI	ACA
1972	6	30	36	43	71	16	50	91	100	82
1971	8	33	66	40	50	–	38	–	–	74
1970	4	25	–	36	38	25	50	83	89	67

Key Votes

1) Busing	AGN	6) Cmbodia Bmbg	FOR	11) Chkg Acct Intrst	AGN
2) Strip Mines	AGN	7) Bust Hwy Trust	AGN	12) End HISC (HUAC)	AGN
3) Cut Mil $	FOR	8) Farm Sub Lmt	ABS	13) Nixon Sewer Veto	AGN
4) Rev Shrg	FOR	9) School Prayr	FOR	14) Corp Cmpaign $	AGN
5) Pub TV $	AGN	10) Cnsumr Prot	FOR	15) Pol $ Disclosr	AGN

Election Results

1972 general:	Joe Skubitz (R)	128,639	(72%)
	Lloyd L. Kitch (D)	49,169	(28%)
1972 primary:	Joe Skubitz (R), unopposed		
1970 general:	Joe Skubitz (R)	94,837	(66%)
	T. D. Saar, Jr. (D)	48,688	(34%)

KENTUCKY

Political Background

In 1775, Daniel Boone made his way through the Cumberland Gap in the Appalachian Mountains and came upon what we know today as Kentucky—a fertile, virgin land of gently rolling hills. After the Revolutionary War, streams of people from Virginia traveled Boone's Wilderness Road and settled in the hills and countryside around Lexington. The celebrated exodus was the nation's first frontier boom and, up to that time, one of the most extensive mass migrations in human history. The census of 1790 recorded 73,000 Kentuckians; by 1820, there were 564,000, making this the sixth largest state in the nation. In those days, Kentucky was a frontier, its communities full of opportunity and unburdened by the hierarchies that structured the societies of coastal America. Henry Clay, to take the most famous example, came to Kentucky from Virginia as a penniless young man. By the time he was 30 he had done well enough in the law to build a mansion with silver doorknobs, and well enough in politics to become a United States Senator.

In many respects Kentucky hasn't changed much since Clay's time. Much of the state appears to have remained in the nineteenth century. Kentucky is still largely rural; less than 25% of the state's residents live in greater Louisville and only 8% in the suburbs of Cincinnati, Ohio—the only two large metropolitan areas in the state. During the last few decades, population growth here has been sluggish. Looking for jobs, many Kentuckians have moved out of the hills to the industrial cities of the Midwest, California, or Texas. The tobacco fields and thoroughbred horse farms in the Bluegrass region around Lexington look pretty much today as they always did. Toward the west along the cotton farms of the Mississippi, the landscape is also largely unchanged. The mining of coal, however, has left the once-green mountains and hillsides of eastern Kentucky barren and erose. After a steady 30-year decline, the industry has lately been rejuvenated by the strip-mining technique. Some jobs have resulted, but these have come at the cost of the Kentucky mountains that the people have for so long cherished.

As in many border-state rural areas, political divisions in Kentucky are still based on the splits produced by the Civil War. In general, the hill country was pro-Union and Republican. Some changes took place in this part of Kentucky when miners became union members and began voting Democratic. But the Cumberland Plateau of south central Kentucky remains as heavily Republican as any region in the country. Western Kentucky, which in appearance and economy is part of the South, retains its nineteenth century allegiance to the Democratic party, though not of late to its presidential candidates.

Up through the 1950s, the Democratic counties almost always outvoted the Republican ones. Kentucky politics, therefore, was like that of most Southern states, with the real battles occurring in the Democratic primary. The most famous figure to come out of this era was Alben W. Barkley, who was Congressman from Paducah (1913–27), U.S. Senator (1927–49) and Majority Leader for 10 years after 1937, Vice-President under Harry Truman, and Senator again until his death in 1956.

But time has changed Kentucky's political patterns. Barkley's Democrats have not carried the state in five of the last six presidential elections, while the Republicans here have become solid contenders for the state's top offices. For a four-year period from 1967 to 1971, the Republicans held both Kentucky Senate seats as well as the governorship. To some extent, Republican dominance was a response to a shift within the state's parties, each of which began to assume stands on issues more in line with the image projected by the national party. Since the administration of Gov. Bert Combs (1959–63), the Democratic party has been notably more liberal than was traditional in Kentucky. And the Republicans, with Gov. Louie Nunn (1967–71) leading the way, have become notably more conservative.

The finest example of the traditional old Kentucky Republicanism is ex-Sen. John Sherman Cooper. In and out of the Senate since the 1940s, Cooper was elected to fill unexpired terms in 1946, 1952, and 1956, finally winning a six-year term in 1960. Thereafter, he was reelected by large majorities. Cooper's major interest was foreign affairs. His expertise in the field was recognized by both parties; he received appointments by Democratic and Republican administrations. During the 1950s, the Kentuckian was our Ambassador to India. Cooper was also one of the Senate's most respected men. He co-sponsored the Cooper-Church Amendment, which prohibits the use of American ground troops in Cambodia and Laos. It was the first successful limitation on presidential war-making powers. At age 71, Cooper decided to retire in 1972, and his departure sparked Kentucky's hottest Senate race in some time.

To understand that race, however, we must back up one year to 1971. Kentucky, like Virginia and New Jersey, holds its state elections in off years. The year 1971 marked the end of a long period of Republican success. Not since 1954 had the party lost a Senate race, and Louie Nunn, after a close miss in 1963, captured the Governor's chair in 1967. But as in much of the South, Kentucky Governors cannot succeed themselves. So Nunn ran a young protegé, Tom Emberton, in his place. Meanwhile, the Democrats had a fierce primary between ex-Gov. Combs and Lt. Gov. Wendell Ford, which Ford won. The Democrats, despite wounds inflicted during the primary, put together a winning campaign to defeat Emberton.

The powers of a Kentucky Governor are about as broad as those of any Governor in the union, as are the powers of the Kentuckian over his party's activities. So Ford's win gave the Democrats a big psychological boost; the state's Democrats held most small offices, but had consistently lost the big elections. The party's control of the governorship also showed that the state's movement toward the Republicans had been arrested. When Cooper decided not to run, Ford and State Chairman J. R. Miller slated state Senate Majority Leader Walter "Dee" Huddleston, who, as expected, won his primary with ease.

Things on the Republican side, however, were full of acrimony. Robert Gable, a young former Nunn appointee and friend of Tennessee Sen. Howard Baker, entered the Republican primary and mounted a strong campaign. But with 28 minutes left until a midnight filing deadline, ex-Gov. Nunn entered the race. It was well known at the time that Nunn had little desire to go to Washington, and that he wanted to run for Governor again in 1975. But President Nixon, it appears, decided that Nunn would make the strongest candidate and persuaded him to run. The White House, as the state write-up shows, also miscalculated along similar lines in Delaware.

Nunn won his primary rather easily, but not before absorbing some bitter, well-publicized attacks from Gable. The state of affairs among the Republicans presented a sharp contrast to the harmony among the Democrats. In the general election, Nunn could think of little other than an attempt to link Dee Huddleston, a small-town radio station owner, to George McGovern. The link must have appeared implausible to most Kentuckians; more to the point was Huddleston's main issue: that he had pushed through repeal of a 5% sales tax on food raised during Nunn's administration. Huddleston won by a small margin, one that paralleled Ford's victory the year before. Both men are from western Kentucky, where both ran especially well—far ahead of the national ticket.

Once in the Senate, Huddleston was expected to become one of the more conservative members of the Democratic Caucus. But as of this writing, the issues that have come before the 93rd Congress have united practically all of the Democrats, Northern and Southern, as well as some Republicans, against the Nixon Administration. Within this context, Huddleston has almost always voted with the vast majority of the Democrats in the Senate.

A bit more of a maverick is Kentucky's senior Senator, Marlow Cook. He is both a builder and a beneficiary of the state's most successful Republican organization, put together during the 1960s in Louisville and surrounding Jefferson County. Before his election to the Senate in 1968, Cook served for several years as Jefferson County Judge—the administrative head of the county government. In the Senate, Cook has been as vehement and forceful when opposing the Administration (he cast the deciding vote against the Carswell nomination) as when supporting it (he served as the Administration's floor leader in the Haynsworth nomination). He has also taken a variety of positions on national security issues, opposing the ABM as well as the Cooper-Church and other antiwar amendments. Just as the Watergate scandal broke, Cook was part of the solid Republican front (save Mathias of Maryland) on the Senate Judiciary Committee supporting the nomination of L. Patrick Gray as permanent FBI Director.

Cook seems like an unlikely man for high Kentucky office. He is a Roman Catholic who grew up in Akron, New York, a small town outside Buffalo. But his opponent in 1968 was also something of an outsider, Katherine Peden, then state commerce commissioner and a member of the Kerner Commission on Civil Disorders. Cook won a 37,000-vote victory in an election that fell out pretty much along traditional party allegiances in Kentucky.

The big question for 1974 is whether Cook will inherit Cooper's august, olympian mantle and win reelection easily, or whether the voters will perceive him a more partisan Republican figure at a time when the party's fortunes in the state have been sagging. A number of Democrats appear betting on the latter possibility. Among those interested in the 1974 race is John Y. Brown, Jr. The young man is a Kentucky Fried Chicken millionaire, having furnished the entrepreneurial fanaticism behind the success of Col. Sander's now famous recipe. Brown's talents—and money—were behind the 1972 Democratic telethon. Another Democratic contender is ex-Gov. Edward Breathitt, who succeeded Combs and who is most noted for his opposition to the many tactics of the state's coal mining interests. But Gov. Ford and State Chairman Miller will probably make the final decision; there is talk now that Ford himself might enter the race. As in 1972, Kentucky could again become the arena of one of the more interesting Senate campaigns of 1974.

Census Data Pop. 3,219,311; 1.59% of U.S. total, 23rd largest; change 1960–70, 6.0%. Central city, 17%; suburban, 23%. Median family income, $7,439; 46th highest; families above $15,000: 12%; families below $3,000: 18%. Median years education, 9.9.

1972 Share of Federal Tax Burden $2,403,710,000; 1.15% of U.S. total, 24th largest.

1972 Share of Federal Outlays $2,931,044,550; 1.35% of U.S. total, 26th largest. Per capita federal spending, $910.

DOD	$639,933,000	29th (1.02%)	HEW	$1,082,357,392	22nd (1.52%)
AEC	$91,385,054	14th (3.49%)	HUD	$45,216,407	22nd (1.47%)
NASA	$349,732	39th (0.01%)	VA	$194,806,479	23rd (1.70%)
DOT	$174,550,472	16th (2.21%)	USDA	$228,020,117	27th (1.48%)
DOC	$9,110,844	27th (0.70%)	CSC	$42,548,306	25th (1.03%)
DOI	$15,257,380	32nd (0.72%)	TD	$150,647,400	17th (0.91%)
DOJ	$14,574,346	23rd (1.48%)	Other	$242,287,621	

Economic Base Agriculture, notably tobacco, cattle, dairy products, and hogs; finance, insurance and real estate; electrical equipment and supplies, especially household appliances; machinery; bituminous coal mining; apparel and other textile products, especially men's and boys' furnishings; food and kindred products, especially distilled liquor and other beverages.

Political Line-up Governor, Wendell H. Ford (D); seat up, 1975. Senators, Marlow W. Cook (R) and Walter Huddleston (D). Representatives, 7 (5 D and 2 R). State Senate (63 D and 27 R); State House (27 D and 10 R).

The Voters

Registration 1,454,575 Total. 946,169 D (65%); 475,764 R (33%); 32,642 other (2%).
Median voting age 43.1
Employment profile White collar, 40%. Blue collar, 41%. Service, 13%. Farm, 6%.
Ethnic groups Black, 7%. Total foreign stock, 2%.

Presidential vote

1972	Nixon (R)	676,446	(65%)
	McGovern (D)	371,159	(35%)
1968	Nixon (R)	462,411	(44%)
	Humphrey (D)	397,541	(38%)
	Wallace (AI)	193,098	(18%)
1964	Johnson (D)	669,659	(64%)
	Goldwater (R)	372,977	(36%)

Senator

Marlow W. Cook (R) Elected 1968, seat up 1974; b. July 27, 1926, Akron, N.Y.; home, Louisville; U. of Louisville Law School, LL.B., 1950; Navy, WWII; married, five children; Catholic.

Career Ky. House of Reps., 1957–61; Judge, Jefferson County, 1961–68.

Offices 347 OSOB, 202-225-4343. Also Rm. 172-C New Fed. Office Bldg., 600 Fed. Place, Louisville 40202, 502-582-5986.

Administrative Assistant Richard Greer

Committees

Commerce (5th); Subs: Aviation; Communications; Oceans and Atmosphere; Consumer (Ranking Mbr.); Foreign Commerce and Tourism; Environment (Ranking Mbr.); Sp. Sub. on Freight Car Shortage.

Judiciary (5th); Subs: Constitutional Amendments; Criminal Laws and Procedures; Immigration and Naturalization; Internal Security; Juvenile Delinquency (Ranking Mbr.); Penitentiaries (Ranking Mbr.); Representation of Citizen Interests (Ranking Mbr.).

Rules and Administration (Ranking Mbr.); Subs: Smithsonian Institution (Ranking Mbr.); Restaurant (Ranking Mbr.).

Sp. Com. to Study Questions Related to Secret and Confidential Government Documents.

Sel. Com. on Nutrition and Human Needs (2nd).

Joint Com. on the Library (Ranking Senate Mbr.).

Group Ratings

	ADA	COPE	LWV	RIPON	NFU	LCV	CFA	NAB	NSI	ACA
1972	10	10	60	50	50	31	73	60	90	52
1971	33	42	55	32	55	–	0	–	–	70
1970	41	75	–	63	79	47	–	38	70	67

Key Votes

1) Busing	AGN	8) Sea Life Prot	AGN	15) Tax Singls Less	AGN
2) Alas P-line	AGN	9) Campaign Subs	AGN	16) Min Tax for Rich	FOR
3) Gun Cntrl	FOR	10) Cmbodia Bmbg	AGN	17) Euro Troop Rdctn	AGN
4) Rehnquist	FOR	11) Legal Srvices	AGN	18) Bust Hwy Trust	AGN
5) Pub TV $	FOR	12) Rev Sharing	FOR	19) Maid Min Wage	FOR
6) EZ Votr Reg	AGN	13) Cnsumr Prot	FOR	20) Farm Sub Limit	AGN
7) No-Fault	AGN	14) Eq Rts Amend	FOR	21) Highr Credt Chgs	FOR

Election Results

1968 general:	Marlow W. Cook (R)	484,260	(51%)
	Katherine Peden (D)	448,960	(48%)
	Duane F. Olsen (AI)	9,645	(1%)
1968 primary:	Marlow W. Cook (R)	73,171	(62%)
	Eugene Siler (R)	39,743	(34%)
	E. W. Kemp (R)	3,104	(3%)
	Thurman J. Hamlin (R)	2,015	(2%)

Senator

Walter (Dee) **Huddleston** (D) Elected 1972, seat up 1978; b. April 15, 1926, Cumberland County; home, Elizabethtown; U. of K., B.A., 1949; Army, WWII; married, two children; Methodist.

Career Gen. Mgr., WIEL, Elizabethtown, 1952; Pres., Kentucky Broadcasting Assoc., State Senate, 1966–72; State Chairman, Wendell Ford's gubernatorial campaign, 1971.

Offices 3327 NSOB, 202-225-2542. Also New Fed. Bldg., Louisville, 502-582-6304.

Administrative Assistant Philip L. Swift

Committees

Agriculture and Forestry (6th); Subs: Environment, Soil Conservation and Forestry; Agricultural Credit and Rural Electrification; Agricultural Production, Marketing and Stabilization of Prices (Chm.); Foreign Agricultural Policy.

Government Operations (10th); Subs: Permanent Investigations; Budgeting, Management, and Expenditures.

Group Ratings: Newly Elected

Election Results

1972 general:	Walter "Dee" Huddleston (D)	528,550	(51%)
	Louie B. Nunn (R)	494,337	(48%)
	Helen Breeden (AI)	8,707	(1%)
	William E. Bartley, Jr. (People's Party)	6,267	(1%)
1972 primary:	Walter "Dee" Huddleston (D)	106,144	(72%)
	Sandy Hockensmith (D)	14,786	(10%)
	James E. Wallace (D)	11,290	(8%)
	Willis V. Johnson (D)	8,727	(6%)
	Charles Van Winkle (D)	7,306	(5%)

FIRST DISTRICT Political Background

Western Kentucky—the area that comprises the state's 1st congressional district—is very much part of the great Mississippi Valley. The district is bounded by the Mississippi and Ohio rivers and bisected by the Tennessee and Cumberland rivers. The land here is low and the rivers lined with high levees; the winters are sometimes harsh and the summers steaming hot. There is a fair amount of coal mining here, but the economy is primarily agricultural. This region of the state resembles the Deep South. In 1968, George Wallace carried five Kentucky counties: all but one of them were in the 1st, with the Alabaman running much stronger here than anywhere else in Kentucky. In state elections, the area's Democratic allegiance remains solid.

Because tobacco is the district's principal crop, its Congressman, Democrat Frank Stubblefield, has risen to become Chairman of Agriculture's Tobacco Subcommittee. In Congress since 1959, Stubblefield is also the second-ranking Democrat on the full Agriculture Committee. He is in direct line to succeed 74-year-old Chairman W. R. Poage of Texas. On the committee, the Kentuckian has consistently supported the existing farm programs, including the price-support system. Stubblefield has had little opposition since he won the seat by beating an incumbent. But because the Congressman is not an effective speaker or a diligent campaigner, he might well be unseated himself in a future Democratic primary.

Census Data Pop. 460,754. Central city, 0%; suburban, 8%. Median family income, $6,788; families above $15,000: 8%; families below $3,000: 20%. Median years education, 9.9.

1972 Share of Federal Outlays $592,023,336

DOD	$170,489,255	HEW	$164,810,544
AEC	$91,370,375	HUD	$2,765,946
NASA	–	DOI	$1,547,854
DOT	$32,980,027	USDA	$35,185,268
		Other	$92,874,067

Federal Military-Industrial Commitments

DOD Contractors Blair Algernon, Inc. (Fort Campbell), $7.688m: construction services.
DOD Installations Fort Campbell (Hopkinsville).
AEC Operations Union Carbide (Paducah), $90.383m: operation of gaseous diffusion plants and production and research facilities.

Economic Base Agriculture, notably cattle, grains and tobacco; bituminous coal mining; finance, insurance and real estate; apparel and other textile products, especially men's and boys' furnishings; electrical equipment and supplies; and chemicals and allied products, especially industrial chemicals.

The Voters

Registration 213,956 total. 178,012 D (83%); 34,180 R (16%); 1,764 other (1%).
Median voting age 45.7
Employment profile White collar, 33%. Blue collar, 46%. Service, 13%. Farm, 8%.
Ethnic groups Black, 9%. Total foreign stock, 1%.

Presidential vote

1972	Nixon (R)	87,072	(63%)
	McGovern (D)	51,802	(37%)
1968	Nixon (R)	52,385	(33%)
	Humphrey (D)	61,978	(39%)
	Wallace (AI)	45,478	(28%)

Represenatative

Frank A. Stubblefield (D) Elected 1958; b. April 5, 1907, Murray; home, Murray; U. of Ariz., 1927; U. of Ky., B.S., 1930; USNR, WWII; married, three children; Methodist.

Career Retail druggist, 1933–58; City Council, Murray, 1939–43; Railroad Commission, 1951–58.

Offices 2228 RHOB, 202-225-3115. Also 203 S. Fifth St., Murray 42071, 502-753-7102.

Administrative Assistant Mrs. Marty Harding

Committees

Agriculture (2nd); Subs: Diary and Poultry; Tobacco (Chm.); Conservation and Credit.

Merchant Marine and Fisheries (7th); Subs: Merchant Marine; Panama Canal.

Group Ratings

	ADA	COPE	LWV	RIPON	NFU	LCV	CFA	NAB	NSI	ACA
1972	13	56	44	42	83	13	50	22	100	61
1971	16	67	44	38	67	–	75	–	–	46
1970	20	50	–	24	69	51	75	36	90	44

Key Votes

1) Busing	AGN	6) Cmbodia Bmbg	ABS	11) Chkg Acct Intrst	AGN
2) Strip Mines	AGN	7) Bust Hwy Trust	AGN	12) End HISC (HUAC)	AGN
3) Cut Mil $	AGN	8) Farm Sub Lmt	AGN	13) Nixon Sewer Veto	AGN
4) Rev Shrg	FOR	9) School Prayr	FOR	14) Corp Cmpaign $	FOR
5) Pub TV $	ABS	10) Cnsumr Prot	ABS	15) Pol $ Disclosr	AGN

Election Results

1972 general:	Frank A. Stubblefield (D)	81,459	(65%)
	Charles T. Banken, Jr. (R)	42,286	(34%)
	John M. Katterjohn (Less Federal Taxes)	1,920	(2%)
1972 primary:	Frank A. Stubblefield (D)	26,859	(73%)
	Kenneth A. Burkhardt (D)	8,582	(23%)
	Charles Tandy (D)	1,365	(4%)
1970 general:	Frank A. Stubblefield (D), unopposed		

SECOND DISTRICT Political Background

The 2nd district of Kentucky is a sprawling, largely rural area without a fixed identity. The district extends from the Blue Grass country near Lexington southwest toward the Deep South ambience of Bowling Green and west toward the prosperous manufacturing city of Owensboro on the Ohio River. The best-known features of the 2nd are Fort Knox, where gold is kept, and Bardstown, where one can find Stephen Foster's original "Old Kentucky Home." Also in the district is the birthplace of Abraham Lincoln.

Kentucky was a slave state that did not secede from the Union during the Civil War. If a brother killed a brother during the bloody conflict, they were probably from Kentucky. Much of the current 2nd district is sympathetic to the South, and most of it still votes Democratic today. An exception to the pattern is a group of Republican-leaning counties in the center of this T-shaped district. Lately, the fortunes of national Democratic candidates have been bad in the district; in 1968 and 1972, they appeared to have hit rock-bottom when Humphrey and McGovern got almost identical percentages here.

William H. Natcher, a conservative Democrat, has represented the 2nd in the House since 1953. He now enjoys the status of eighth-ranking Democrat on the House Appropriations Committee.

In Washington, he is known mainly for serving as Chairman of the District of Columbia Subcommittee, in which capacity he effectively controls the D.C. budget.

Over the years, Natcher has worked in tandem with the conservative Southern Democrats who, to the distress of most of Washington's residents, ran the House District of Columbia Committee. They lost control in 1973. An example of Natcher's power was his insistence that an unwanted freeway and bridge be built before any money would be appropriated for the Washington metropolitan mass-transit system. Natcher's position was rejected on the House floor.

The Congressman's defeat on this issue was unusual. Because he is a well-prepared and punctilious Chairman, Natcher's decisions are ordinarily adopted by the full House. By common consensus, the District government is inefficient and poorly organized—a state of affairs that that goes back long before black appointees were placed in charge during the 1960s. Natcher's relations with the new D.C. Committee Chairman, black Congressman Charles Diggs of Michigan, are a little strained, but not as badly as their differences on most issues would suggest. Home rule for the District would cost Natcher much of his power, at least if an elected District government were given the power to tax and a federal payment, in lieu of taxes, of an appropriate amount. If home rule does come in such a form, the Appropriations D.C. Subcommittee would lose its *raison d'etre*.

Census Data Pop. 459,416. Central city, 11%; suburban, 6%. Median family income, $7,042; families above $15,000: 9%; families below $3,000: 18%. Median years education, 9.8.

1972 Share of Federal Outlays $457,754,056

DOD	$262,875,744	HEW	$116,463,527
AEC	–	HUD	$2,713,955
NASA	–	DOI	$4,275,872
DOT	$9,486,478	USDA	$31,099,085
		Other	$30,839,395

Federal Military-Industrial Commitments

DOD Installations Fort Knox (Louisville).

Economic Base Agriculture, notably tobacco, dairy products and cattle; finance, insurance and real estate; electrical equipment and supplies; food and kindred products, especially beverages; and machinery. Also higher education (Western Kentucky Univ.).

The Voters

Registration 201,044 total. 145,129 D (72%); 53,133 R (26%); 2,782 (1%).
Median voting age 39.7
Employment profile White collar, 35%. Blue collar, 42%. Service, 12%. Farm, 11%.
Ethnic groups Black, 6%. Total foreign stock, 2%.

Presidential vote

1972		Nixon (R)	88,384	(65%)
		McGovern (D)	46,922	(35%)
1968		Nixon (R)	59,449	(44%)
		Humphrey (D)	47,859	(35%)
		Wallace (AI)	28,221	(21%)

Representative

William Huston Natcher (D) Elected Aug. 1, 1953; b. Sept. 11, 1909, Bowling Green; home, Bowling Green; Western Ky. State Col., B.A., 1930; Ohio State U., LL.B., 1933; Navy, WWII; married, two children; Baptist.

Career Practicing atty., 1934– ; Fed. Conciliation Commissioner, Western Dist. of Ky., 1936–37; County Atty., Warren County, 1937–49; Commonwealth Atty., 8th Jud. Dist., 1951–53.

Offices 2333 RHOB, 202-225-3501. Also 414 E. 10th St., Bowling Green 42101, 502-842-7376, and 50 Public Square, Elizabethtown 42701, 502-765-4360.

Administrative Assistant None

Committees

Appropriations (8th); Subs: Agriculture, Environmental and Consumer Protection; District of Columbia (Chm.); Labor, Health, Education and Welfare.

Group Ratings

	ADA	COPE	LWV	RIPON	NFU	LCV	CFA	NAB	NSI	ACA
1972	31	64	50	38	86	13	50	25	60	57
1971	30	75	44	50	73	–	63	–	–	48
1970	28	60	–	18	69	50	76	33	100	42

Key Votes

1) Busing	AGN	6) Cmbodia Bmbg	AGN	11) Chkg Acct Intrst	AGN
2) Strip Mines	AGN	7) Bust Hwy Trust	AGN	12) End HISC (HUAC)	AGN
3) Cut Mil $	AGN	8) Farm Sub Lmt	AGN	13) Nixon Sewer Veto	AGN
4) Rev Shrg	FOR	9) School Prayr	FOR	14) Corp Cmpaign $	FOR
5) Pub TV $	FOR	10) Cnsumr Prot	FOR	15) Pol $ Disclosr	AGN

Election Results

1972 general:	William H. Natcher (D)	75,871	(62%)
	J. C. Carter (R)	47,436	(38%)
1972 primary:	William H. Natcher (D), unopposed		
1970 general:	William H. Natcher (D), unopposed		

THIRD DISTRICT Political Background

The 3rd district of Kentucky comprises the city of Louisville and a few of its suburbs to the west and south. Louisville, despite the local pronunciation (LOO-uh-vul), is not really a Southern town, but an old river port, like Cincinnati or St. Louis. All three cities, particularly the large German-American communities within them, were hostile to the slave-holding politics of their Southern-leaning rural neighbors at the time of the Civil War. Hence Louisville's Republican tradition—one that persisted into the 1960s among both the city's whites and blacks. According to reliable estimates, Richard Nixon got 30% of the black vote here—his largest such percentage in the country.

The decade of the 1960s was an especially good one for Louisville Republicans. They built a tightly knit, well-financed organization and elected both a Mayor and a Jefferson County Judge (an administrative position) in 1961. Mayor William Cowger was elected Congressman in 1966 and County Judge Marlow Cook became U.S. Senator in 1968.

But the Jefferson County Republican organization soon found itself in trouble. Political success, as it often does, split the winners and made losers of them once again. In 1969, Democratic ex-Rep. Frank Burke (1959–63) was elected Mayor, while another Democrat won Cook's old post. And as the Nixon Administration took power, Congressman Cowger found himself feuding with Gov. Louie Nunn, and discovered his Republican support among black voters slipping.

In 1970, the Democratic candidate, state Sen. Romano Mazzoli, waged an effective antiwar-oriented campaign. Meanwhile incumbent Cowger, who was seriously ill, adopted an Agnewesque line that alienated many of his longtime supporters in the black community. The result was the closest congressional election of the 1970 general elections. Mazzoli won by 211 votes out of more than 100,000. Cowger died in 1971.

On paper, the narrow victory made Mazzoli's seat marginal. Moreover, at redistricting time, the legislature added suburban territory to the 3rd that presumably created a more Republican district. But Mazzoli won in 1970, though a more conservative Democrat had lost two years earlier, and Mazzoli had no trouble whatever in 1972. It was a stunning example of the strength that a congressional incumbent can develop: the nation's most marginal winner in 1970 became a 62% winner in 1972.

Cities like Boston and Philadelphia, which have large numbers of Italian-American citizens, have never had a Congressman of Italian descent. But Louisville—where cannelloni will never replace fried chicken—now does, and apparently will for some time.

Census Data Pop. 460,340. Central city, 79%; suburban, 21%. Median family income, $8,902; families above $15,000: 15%; families below $3,000: 11%. Median years education, 10.9.

1972 Share of Federal Outlays $343,838,992

DOD	$69,494,476	HEW	$130,995,932
AEC	–	HUD	$19,567,315
NASA	$12,365	DOI	$977,073
DOT	$4,523,734	USDA	$12,061,653
		Other	$106,206,444

Federal Military-Industrial Commitments

DOD Contractors Brown & Williamson Tobacco (Louisville), $8.186m: unspecified.
DOD Installations Naval Ordnance Station (Louisville).

Economic Base Finance, insurance and real estate; electrical equipment and supplies, especially household appliances; machinery, especially service industry machines; food and kindred products, especially beverages; chemicals and allied products, especially plastics materials and synthetics; and tobacco manufactures, especially cigarettes. Also higher education (Univ. of Louisville).

The Voters

Registration Not available.
Median voting age 44.0
Employment profile White collar, 44%. Blue collar, 42%. Service, 14%. Farm, –%.
Ethnic groups Black, 20%. Total foreign stock, 4%.

Presidential vote

1972	Nixon (R)	78,143	(55%)
	McGovern (D)	63,796	(45%)
1968	Nixon (R)	55,549	(38%)
	Humphrey (D)	66,483	(46%)
	Wallace (AI)	22,262	(15%)

Representative

Romano L. Mazzoli (D) Elected 1970; b. Nov. 2, 1932, Louisville; home, Louisville; Notre Dame U., B.S., 1954; U. of Louisville Law School, J.D., 1960; Army, 1954–56; married, two children; Catholic.

Career Practicing atty., 1960–70; Law Dept., Louisville and Nashville Railroad Co., 1960–62; Lecturer, Bellarmine-Ursuline Col., 1963–67; Ky. Senate, 1967–70.

Offices 1017 LHOB, 202-225-5401. Also 551-A Fed. Bldg., 600 Federal Pl., Louisville 40202, 502-582-5129.

Administrative Assistant Robert J. Baughman

Committees

District of Columbia (10th); Subs: Labor, Social Services, and the International Community (Chm.); Revenue and Financial Affairs.

Education and Labor (17th); Subs: No. 3 (Labor); No. 1 (Education); No. 5 (Sel. Sub. on Education).

Group Ratings

	ADA	COPE	LWV	RIPON	NFU	LCV	CFA	NAB	NSI	ACA
1972	63	91	83	69	86	71	100	25	20	26
1971	65	58	44	76	87	–	100	–	–	25

Key Votes

1) Busing	FOR	6) Cmbodia Bmbg	AGN	11) Chkg Acct Intrst	FOR
2) Strip Mines	AGN	7) Bust Hwy Trust	FOR	12) End HISC (HUAC)	AGN
3) Cut Mil $	AGN	8) Farm Sub Lmt	FOR	13) Nixon Sewer Veto	FOR
4) Rev Shrg	FOR	9) School Prayr	AGN	14) Corp Cmpaign $	AGN
5) Pub TV $	FOR	10) Cnsumr Prot	FOR	15) Pol $ Disclosr	FOR

Election Results

1972 general:	Romano L. Mazzoli (D)	86,810	(62%)
	Phil Kaelin, Jr. (R)	51,634	(37%)
	William P. Chambers (AI)	1,227	(1%)
1972 primary:	Romano L. Mazzoli (D)	15,200	(94%)
	Philip Vernon Baker (D)	993	(6%)
1970 general:	Romano L. Mazzoli (D)	50,102	(49%)
	William O. Cowager (R)	49,891	(48%)
	Ronald W. Watson (AI)	3,265	(3%)

FOURTH DISTRICT Political Background

The 4th district of Kentucky is a geographical oddity—the proximate result of the state's loss of a congressional seat in the 1960 census and three subsequent redistrictings. The 4th today consists of two nearly equal-sized suburban areas connected by a strip of rural counties along the Ohio River. The first and larger of the suburban areas is Jefferson County, excluding the city of Louisville and the few suburbs that comprise the 3rd district. This part of the 4th is both prosperous and growing rapidly and, like most such places, votes heavily Republican. The other suburban part of the district lies just across the Ohio River from Cincinnati. About half the voters here live in the old, decaying cities of Covington and Newport on the river, and these, like Cincinnati, go heavily Republican.

The connecting counties along the river are part of an older Kentucky. By-passed by Interstate 71, the little tobacco towns retain a nineteenth-century atmosphere. They also retain nineteenth-century Democratic voting habits, though the few ballots cast here become lost in district-wide totals.

Since 1966, when the district took its present shape, the Congressman from the 4th has been Republican M. G. (Gene) Snyder. He also represented the old 3rd district from 1963 to 1964, when he was swept out of office in the LBJ landslide. In his first election in the 4th, Snyder, whose political base was in Jefferson County, faced strong opposition in the primary from Campbell County (Newport) reform Sheriff George Ratterman (onetime Cleveland Browns quarterback), and in the general election from then-Rep. Frank Chelf. Chelf intended to retire in 1966 but was called back to run after the October death of the Democratic nominee.

Since his first election, Snyder has not had a serious challenge. He has been mentioned as a possible candidate for statewide office, but he pointedly declined to run for the Senate in 1972. That race would have been onerous and risky, while his House seat was utterly safe. Snyder's Goldwaterite views hurt him in 1964, and his way of looking at things has undergone no basic revision. But for some reason, he has supported all the end-the-war amendments for several years, and in 1973 voted against the bombing in Cambodia, despite the tight Republican discipline in the House.

Census Data   Pop. 458,896. Central city, 0%; suburban, 93%. Median family income, $10,359; families above $15,000: 21%; families below $3,000: 7%. Median years education, 12.0.

1972 Share of Federal Outlays $335,266,653

DOD	$38,591,855	HEW	$123,267,617
AEC	–	HUD	$11,747,856
NASA	$6,304	DOI	$607,786
DOT	$42,456,748	USDA	$12,129,725
		Other	$106,458,762

Federal Military-Industrial Commitments

No installation or contractors receiving prime awards greater than $5,000,000.

Economic Base   Finance, insurance and real estate; electrical equipment and supplies, especially household appliances; machinery, especially service industry machines; food and kindred products, especially beverages; and fabricated metal products.

The Voters

Registration   No district-wide registration.
Median voting age   41.7
Employment profile   White collar, 51%. Blue collar, 37%. Service, 10%. Farm, 2%.
Ethnic groups   Black, 2%. Total foreign stock, 5%.

Presidential vote

1972	Nixon (R)	112,607	(70%)
	McGovern (D)	47,238	(30%)
1968	Nixon (R)	66,185	(47%)
	Humphrey (D)	48,000	(34%)
	Wallace (AI)	25,364	(18%)

Representative

Marion Gene Snyder (R) Elected 1962–64, 1966; b. Jan. 26, 1928, Louisville; home, Louisville; Jefferson School of Law, LL.B., 1951; U. of Louisville, J.D., 1969; married, one child; Protestant.

Career Practicing atty., 1950– ; City Atty., 1953–57; Magistrate, 1957–61; farmer, 1957– ; realtor, 1955–; builder, 1958–62.

Offices 306 CHOB, 202-225-3465. Also 140 Chenoweth Lane, St. Matthews 40207, 502-582-5985, and 310 Fed. Bldg., Covington 41011, 513-684-2154.

Administrative Assistant William E. Tanner

Committees

Public Works (5th); Subs: Energy (Ranking Mbr.); Public Buildings and Grounds; Transportation; Water Resources.

Merchant Marine and Fisheries (7th); Subs: Coast Guard and Navigation; Panama Canal; Merchant Marine.

Group Ratings

	ADA	COPE	LWV	RIPON	NFU	LCV	CFA	NAB	NSI	ACA
1972	6	27	18	43	57	40	100	91	56	91
1971	24	18	11	53	53	–	25	–	–	86
1970	8	27	–	27	46	28	38	64	100	76

Key Votes

1) Busing	AGN	6) Cmbodia Bmbg	AGN	11) Chkg Acct Intrst	AGN
2) Strip Mines	AGN	7) Bust Hwy Trust	AGN	12) End HISC (HUAC)	AGN
3) Cut Mil $	AGN	8) Farm Sub Lmt	FOR	13) Nixon Sewer Veto	FOR
4) Rev Shrg	AGN	9) School Prayr	FOR	14) Corp Cmpaign $	AGN
5) Pub TV $	AGN	10) Cnsumr Prot	AGN	15) Pol $ Disclosr	AGN

Election Results

1972 general:	M. Gene Snyder (R)	110,902	(74%)
	James W. Rogers (D)	39,332	(26%)
1972 primary:	M. Gene Snyder (R), unopposed		
1970 general:	M. Gene Snyder (R)	83,037	(67%)
	Charles W. Webster (D)	41,659	(33%)

FIFTH DISTRICT Political Background

If one wants still further proof that political preference in the United States is not simply a function of wealth—the rich voting Republican and the poor, Democratic—consider some election results from the close 1968 presidential race. Two of the wealthiest suburbs in America—Beverly Hills, California, and Scarsdale, New York—went for the Democratic candidate Hubert Humphrey. In the same year, the 5th congressional district of Kentucky, with a median income several notches lower than any other district in the nation, gave 59% of the its votes to Richard Nixon. Only 20 of the country's 435 districts topped the 5th's margin for the Republican candidate.

Nixon's performance here was, if anything, a little below the usual Republican levels of support. The hills and hollows of the Cumberland Plateau in south central Kentucky have consistently delivered some of the largest Republican majorities in the nation for more than a century. The small farmers here were hostile to the slave-holding South and to the uppity slave-holding Blue Grass region in northern Kentucky up to and during the Civil War. And living in one of the most isolated and provincial areas of the United States, the farm folk have remained staunchly Republican ever since.

Only in places where the United Mine Workers organized heavily in the 1930s have the mountain people switched to the Democrats. But there are far fewer mines and miners here than in the adjacent 7th district; about the only Democratic county in the 5th is "Bloody Harlan," where in the 1930s the mine owners' men and members of the United Mine Workers shot and killed each other in pitched battles. But the population of Harlan declined as the mines played out—the 1930 census recorded 64,000 residents; the 1970 census, 36,000.

The Republican counties here have also been losing population, but not so rapidly. So in the 5th, the Republican primary is tantamount to the general election. When Rep. Eugene Siler retired in 1964, the Republican primary attracted no fewer than 15 entrants; by comparison, the Democratic primary had 2. The Republican winner was Dr. Tim Lee Carter, who got a remarkable 45% of the votes. One reason was that 13 of the 14 other candidates were from the western end of the district, while Carter shared the eastern counties with one other, less formidable Republican aspirant. Goldwater's poor showing held Carter to a modest 53% victory in the 1964 general election, but he has won by solid margins ever since. A longtime practicing physician, Carter serves on Commerce's Public Health Subcommittee, one chaired and dominated by Paul Rogers of Florida.

Census Data Pop. 459,586. Central city, 0%; suburban, 0%. Median family income, $4,669; families above $15,000: 6%; families below $3,000: 33%. Median years education, 8.5.

1972 Share of Federal Outlays $351,627,742

DOD	$21,698,361	HEW	$184,080,300
AEC	–	HUD	$1,068,467
NASA	–	DOI	$2,608,259
DOT	$18,706,797	USDA	$62,138,998
		Other	$61,326,560

Federal Military-Industrial Commitments

No installations or contractors receiving prime awards greater than $5,000,000.

Economic Base Agriculture, notably tobacco, cattle and dairy products; apparel and other textile products; finance, insurance and real estate; and bituminous coal mining. Also higher education (Eastern Kentucky Univ.).

The Voters

Registration 269,590 total. No district-wide party registration.
Median voting age 45.0
Employment profile White collar, 33%. Blue collar, 43%. Service, 12%. Farm, 12%.
Ethnic groups Black, 3%.

Presidential vote

1972	Nixon (R)	117,821	(73%)
	McGovern (D)	44,287	(27%)
1968	Nixon (R)	95,407	(59%)
	Humphrey (D)	42,927	(26%)
	Wallace (AI)	23,681	(15%)

Representative

Tim Lee Carter (R) Elected 1964; b. Sept. 2, 1910, Tompkinsville, W.
Ky.; W. Ky. U., B.A., 1934; U. of Tenn., M.D., 1937; Army, WWII;
married, one child; Baptist.

Career Practicing physician, 1937– .

Offices 2441 RHOB, 202-225-4601. Also Hotel Beecher, Somerset 42501,
606-679-2544, and 805 N. Main St., Tompkinsville 42167, 502-487-6121.

Administrative Assistant Douglas L. Francisco

Committees

Interstate and Foreign Commerce (5th); Sub: Public Health and Environment.

Group Ratings

	ADA	COPE	LWV	RIPON	NFU	LCV	CFA	NAB	NSI	ACA
1972	6	10	50	50	50	17	50	56	100	69
1971	8	25	44	53	43	–	38	–	–	70
1970	16	25	–	35	31	9	63	91	90	72

Key Votes

1) Busing	AGN	6) Cmbodia Bmbg	ABS	11) Chkg Acct Intrst	ABS
2) Strip Mines	AGN	7) Bust Hwy Trust	AGN	12) End HISC (HUAC)	AGN
3) Cut Mil $	AGN	8) Farm Sub Lmt	AGN	13) Nixon Sewer Veto	AGN
4) Rev Shrg	FOR	9) School Prayr	FOR	14) Corp Cmpaign $	FOR
5) Pub TV $	AGN	10) Cnsumr Prot	AGN	15) Pol $ Disclosr	FOR

Election Results

1972 general:	Tim Lee Carter (R)	109,264	(74%)
	Lyle Leonard Willis (D)	39,301	(26%)
1972 primary:	Tim Lee Carter (R), unopposed		
1970 general:	Tim Lee Carter (R)	49,266	(80%)
	Lyle Leonard Willis (D)	11,977	(20%)

SIXTH DISTRICT Political Background

Nobody, not even former U.S. Senator Henry Clay, is a more famous Kentuckian than Colonel
Harlan Sanders. If you really wanted to "visit the Colonel," you would have to travel all the way
to Shelby County in the 6th congressional district of Kentucky. Outside of Lexington is the
Colonel's plantation home—a Blue Grass horse farm with the white wood fences and all the
trimmings. Maybe like Henry Clay, who took his cues from the Virginia aristocracy, the Colonel
enjoys a late afternoon sit on the verandah. Here he could savor a mint julep and contemplate the
pleasures of a fried chicken dinner to come. The Colonel lives in fine fashion these days, but he
was a poor man until age 65. This was when young John Y. Brown walked into Sanders'
roadhouse, ate some of his fried chicken, asked about its recipe, and decided on a franchise
operation with a Colonel Sanders up front. The lucky Colonel made a lot of money, but Brown
made a lot more.

Col. Sanders, like most residents of the 6th, is a Democrat. Or at least this is the way John Y.
Brown set him up at the 1972 Democratic Convention. Here the genial man distributed boxes of
chicken to the delegates, mostly McGovernites; waved to the television cameras and received
many dollars in free publicity; and then reserved his warmest personal greeting for Mrs. Cornelia
Wallace, who responded in turn. The old Civil War Democrats of the current 6th district have
never been of the liberal sort.

Moreover, the strength of the Democratic party in the 6th is waning. The party's appeal is
concentrated in the region's rural counties, which are losing population. The political pivot of the
district is Fayette County (Lexington)—the fastest-growing area in the state outside of the
Louisville suburbs. Fayette County has become increasingly more Republican in both national

and statewide elections. The 1972 redistricting also helped the Republicans here when it added parts of Republican Campbell and Kenton counties (suburban Cincinnati).

For years, the growing Republican strength in the district cut into the majorities of its Democratic Congressman, John C. Watts. But Watts turned aside the challenges without too much trouble. During his 20 years in the House, the Congressman rose to the number-two position on the House Ways and Means Committee. Behind Chairman Wilbur Mills, Watts retained an anonymous status. The Kentucky Congressman died in the spring of 1971. In the special election that followed, a young Democratic state legislator, William P. Curlin, was elected to fill the seat. Upon coming to the House, Curlin decided that he did not want to raise his family in Washington and declined to run for reelection. The decision left the seat up for grabs once again.

The mystery is why the Republicans couldn't take the seat, in either the 1971 special or 1972 general election. The Republican candidate in 1972, Laban Jackson, waged a fairly strong campaign; his credentials were attractive, having served as a conservation commissioner in a Democratic state administration. But Jackson was defeated by conservative Democrat John Breckinridge, Attorney General of the state from 1960 to 1964 and again from 1968 to 1972. Breckinridge is, of course, one of the commonwealth's oldest and proudest political names. (Kentucky, like Virginia, Pennsylvania, and Massachusetts, is officially a commonwealth, not a state.)

Breckinridge was 59 when he was elected, making him the oldest freshman in the House. This means, barring the improbable, that he will not accumulate the kind of seniority Watts piled up. But because Breckinridge won in a good Republican year and carried Fayette County to boot, he will probably remain in the House for the immediate future.

Census Data   Pop. 460,521. Central city, 24%; suburban, 27%. Median family income, $8,678; families above $15,000: 16%; families below $3,000: 12%. Median years education, 11.7.

1972 Share of Federal Outlays $444,622,541

DOD	$58,895,803	HEW	$181,250,387
AEC	$11,560	HUD	$3,955,791
NASA	$305,118	DOI	$2,486,236
DOT	$30,523,945	USDA	$34,904,884
		Other	$132,288,817

Federal Military-Industrial Commitments

  DOD Installation Lexington-Blue Grass Army Depot (Lexington)

Economic Base Agriculture, notably tobacco, cattle and dairy products; finance, insurance and real estate; fabricated metal products; food and kindred products; apparel and other textile products; and printing and publishing. Also higher education (Univ. of Kentucky).

The Voters

  Registration No district-wide registration.
  Median voting age 41.4
  Employment profile White collar, 46%. Blue collar, 34%. Service, 13%. Farm, 7%.
  Ethnic groups Black, 9%. Total foreign stock, 2%.

Presidential vote

1972	Nixon (R)		101,147	(67%)
	McGovern (D)		50,777	(33%)
1968	Nixon (R)		61,072	(43%)
	Humphrey (D)		53,844	(38%)
	Wallace (AI)		28,328	(20%)

Representative

John Bayne Breckinridge (D) Elected 1972; b. Nov. 29, 1913, Washington, D.C.; home, Lexington; U. of Ky., A.B., 1937, LL.B., 1939; Army, WWII; Army Reserve, 1950–1967; married, two children; Presbyterian.

Career Practicing atty.; State Rep., 1956–1960; Atty. Gen. of Ky., 1960–1964, 1968–1972.

Offices 125 CHOB, 202-225-4706. Also 401 Security Trust, Lexington.

Administrative Assistant Vince Clephas, Jerry Lundergan.

Committees

District of Columbia (13th); Subs: Education; Government Operations; Judiciary.

Interstate and Foreign Commerce (24th); Sub: Commerce and Finance.

Group Ratings: Newly Elected

Key Votes

1) Busing	NE	6) Cmbodia Bmbg	FOR	11) Chkg Acct Intrst	AGN	
2) Strip Mines	NE	7) Bust Hwy Trust	AGN	12) End HISC (HUAC)	AGN	
3) Cut Mil $	NE	8) Farm Sub Lmt	NE	13) Nixon Sewer Veto	AGN	
4) Rev Shrg	NE	9) School Prayr	NE	14) Corp Cmpaign $	NE	
5) Pub TV $	NE	10) Cnsumr Prot	NE	15) Pol $ Disclosr	NE	

Election Results

1972 general:	John Breckinridge (D)	76,185	(52%)
	Laban P. Jackson (R)	68,012	(47%)
	Thomas F. Lundeen (People's Party)	1,215	(1%)
1972 primary:	John Breckinridge (D)	18,537	(57%)
	Tom Ward (D)	10,330	(32%)
	Phillip E. King (D)	3,433	(11%)

SEVENTH DISTRICT Political Background

The 7th district of Kentucky comprises part of Appalachia. Though the 5th district is the state's poorest, the 7th district is still one of the most poverty-stricken in the entire country. The only city here of any size is Ashland (pop. 29,000) on the Ohio River near Huntington, West Virginia. The rural hills and hollows of the district, however, are thickly populated. Coal has been the region's mainstay. But since the economic collapse of the deep mines in the 1930s, the 7th has exported its young men and women to the industrial cities of the North. Most of them continue to think of eastern Kentucky as "home." On holiday weekends, I-75 is jammed as literally thousands of people return from Appalachian communities in Detroit, Toledo, and Flint to see the old folks and the mountains, and to do the kind of singing and hear the kind of preaching they love best.

During the 1930s, the 7th was the scene of many bitter struggles between the United Mine Workers and mine owners. Today the bitterness lingers and extends to other issues. Strip mining is a cause célèbre here. Some defend it, saying that it produces jobs (though not nearly as many as the deep mines used to). Other mountaineers strongly oppose the practice, as the strippers cut ugly gouges into the beauty of east Kentucky.

The struggles of the 1930s ended much of old Civil War Republican allegiance here. Today, the 7th, as a whole, is staunchly Democratic but there are pockets of Republican sentiment still. Contrasting election results testify to the long isolation of mountain counties. Knott County, for example, cast 65% of its votes for George McGovern, while Jackson County, 20 miles away and quite similar in physical appearance, went 92% for Richard Nixon in 1972.

The voters of the 7th have been especially fond of Democratic Congressman Carl Perkins, who has won recent elections by near two-to-one margins. First elected in 1948, he is currently senior member of the Kentucky delegation. Since the ouster of Adam Clayton Powell in 1967, Perkins has been Chairman of the House Education and Labor Committee. The House panel has jurisdiction over education and labor legislation, as well as over the anti-poverty program, and its Chairman has firmly supported the kind of bills inspired by Lyndon Johnson's Great Society. Perkins is not known as a particularly strong House Committee Chairman, but neither is he known as a particularly weak one. Because Education and Labor has many (some say too many) young liberal members eager to shape social policy, Perkins can usually command a majority in his committee.

In 1973, Nixon appointee Howard Phillips began to dismantle the Office of Economic Opportunity, which ran LBJ's War on Poverty. The Administration figured to drop the agency from the budget for fiscal year 1974. Though Perkins and the Committee were furious, there was little they could do. It took a lawsuit to stop Phillips; because his name had not been submitted to the Senate for confirmation, a judge ruled that Phillips did not hold his job legally.

Even if Education and Labor can write and pass legislation to continue OEO, it is difficult to see how the Committee or Congress can get the Administration to run the operation if it doesn't want to. Circumstances such as this and the wide-spread impoundments of appropriated funds have alienated Perkins and other usually quiet men like him from the Nixon Administration. The OEO and the impoundment issues also demonstrate just how difficult it is for the legislative branch of government to implement its will.

Census Data Pop. 459,798. Central city, 6%; suburban, 5%. Median family income, $5,528; families above $15,000: 6%; families below $3,000: 28%. Median years education, 8.7.

1972 Share of Federal Outlays $378,911,215

DOD	$17,887,502	HEW	$181,489,076
AEC	$3,119	HUD	$3,397,072
NASA	$25,944	DOI	$2,754,296
DOT	$35,872,738	USDA	$40,500,499
		Other	$96,980,969

Federal Military-Industrial Commitments

DOD Contractors Ashland Oil (Ashland), $5.529m: petroleum products.

Economic Base Bituminous coal mining; agriculture, notably tobacco, poultry, dairy products and cattle; finance, insurance and real estate; electrical equipment and supplies; and primary metal industries.

The Voters

Registration 267,074 total. 184,211 D (69%); 79,972 R (30%); 2,891 other (1%).
Median voting age 44.1
Employment profile White collar, 34%. Blue collar, 47%. Service, 12%. Farm, 7%.
Ethnic groups Black, 1%.

Presidential vote

1972	Nixon (R)	93,088	(58%)
	McGovern (D)	67,062	(42%)
1968	Nixon (R)	67,997	(42%)
	Humphrey (D)	74,283	(46%)
	Wallace (AI)	18,913	(12%)

Representative

Carl D. Perkins (D) Elected 1948; b. Oct. 15, 1912, Hindman; home, Hindman; Caney Jr. Col., Jefferson School of Law, LL.B., 1935; Army, WWII; married, one child; Baptist.

Career Practicing atty., 1935–48; Commonwealth Atty., 1939; Ky. House of Reps., 1940; Knott County Atty., 1941–48; Counsel, Ky. Dept. of Highways, 1948.

Offices 2365 RHOB, 202-225-4935.

Administrative Assistant Miss Lucille Blake

Committees

Education and Labor (Chm.); Sub: No. 1 (Education) (Chm.).

Group Ratings

	ADA	COPE	LWV	RIPON	NFU	LCV	CFA	NAB	NSI	ACA
1972	38	100	75	63	86	20	100	9	70	24
1971	57	92	78	56	87	–	88	–	–	28
1970	40	75	–	41	92	60	71	0	80	21

Key Votes

1) Busing	FOR	6) Cmbodia Bmbg	AGN	11) Chkg Acct Intrst	AGN
2) Strip Mines	AGN	7) Bust Hwy Trust	AGN	12) End HISC (HUAC)	AGN
3) Cut Mil $	AGN	8) Farm Sub Lmt	AGN	13) Nixon Sewer Veto	AGN
4) Rev Shrg	FOR	9) School Prayr	FOR	14) Corp Cmpaign $	AGN
5) Pub TV $	FOR	10) Cnsumr Prot	FOR	15) Pol $ Disclosr	AGN

Election Results

1972 general:	Carl D. Perkins (D)	94,840	(62%)
	Robert Holcomb (R)	58,286	(38%)
1972 primary:	Carl D. Perkins (D)	26,047	(93%)
	Bessie Smith (D)	1,815	(7%)
1970 general:	Carl D. Perkins (D)	50,672	(75%)
	Herbert E. Myers (R)	16,648	(25%)

LOUISIANA

Political Background

In 1935, almost 40 years ago, Huey P. Long was shot down and killed in Baton Rouge, Louisiana. But the Kingfish still exerts an important influence in Louisiana politics. When he was murdered, he had been a U.S. Senator for less than six years, and before that served as Governor for less than a full term. In that short span, however, Huey built monuments to himself and to the people of Louisiana: among other things, the state Capitol Building, Louisiana State University, and a system of badly needed concrete roads. When Huey was boss, he dominated the politics of his state as no other man has done in American history; beyond that, his slogans—"Share the Wealth" and "Every Man a King"—were significant factors in Franklin D. Roosevelt's decision to move left as he contemplated his reelection bid of 1936. After Huey's death, there has usually been a Long in either the Governor's chair or in one of the state's Senate seats. From 1937 until his death in the summer of 1972, Allen J. Ellender, who was Huey's Speaker of the Louisiana House, held the Kingfish's old seat in the United States Senate. And since 1948, the state's other Senate seat has been held by the great man's son, Russell Long, who was first elected at age 30.

If Louisiana politics is remarkable for the influence still held by a man long dead, the kind of politics here is equally remarkable for being conducted in two languages, French and English. New Orleans, of course, retains a French and Creole ambience from the days preceding the Louisiana Purchase. The city has the Vieux Carre (the French Quarter), as well as a very un-Southern urbanity and sophistication. The people of New Orleans have traditionally demonstrated more racial tolerance than than other natives of the American South. Furthermore the nation's second busiest seaport has lived rather comfortably with political machines; blacks have long voted in New Orleans, though for most of that time in strict accordance with machine dictates. No other Southern city has a liberal Mayor like Moon Landrieu, or a Mafia organization like that headed by Carlos Marcello, or has had the likes of flamboyant Jim Garrison for a district attorney.

An even more pronounced French influence can be found to the outside of New Orleans in the bayou country south of Alexandria and west of the Mississippi River. This is Cajun country. Here live the descendants of the some 4,000 Acadians who were expelled by the British from Nova Scotia in 1755; knowledge of their lamentable fate was imparted to generations of school children by an equally lamentable poem, Longfellow's "Evangeline." In present-day Cajun Louisiana, almost everyone is a Roman Catholic who speaks a unique dialect of French. The 1970 census reports that 16% of the people in Louisiana consider French their native language. Not many blacks live this far south, and so perhaps the Cajuns are less likely to cast votes solely on the basis of racial issues, unlike the Baptist Louisianans in the northern part of the state.

Huey Long was one of the few Louisiana politicians able to run as well in the Baptist, prohibitionist north as in the joie de vivre Cajun south. And Huey did it without demagoguing the race issue. Long's program was a strictly economic one; he fought big-money interests and spent lots of state money on projects designed to help little people. Since Long's day, the north has dominated Louisiana politics with few exceptions. In 1964 and 1968, the northern parishes (the Louisiana French-derived name for counties) put the state's electoral votes in the Goldwater and Wallace columns, even though Johnson ran well among the Cajuns and Humphrey carried New Orleans. Only when the Cajun Catholics provided huge margins for Eisenhower and Kennedy in 1956 and 1960 did southern Louisiana prevail in presidential contests.

In state elections, the Governor has traditionally come out of the Protestant north. Long himself was from the scrubby hills of Baptist Winn Parish. But tradition was shattered in late 1971 and early 1972. Congressman Edwin W. Edwards—a Cajun and proud of it despite his Welsh name—won the governorship. Edwards' inauguration provided an occasion to celebrate a Cajun revival. As among French-Canadians, the Cajuns insist upon the preservation of French language and of other traditions. The revival here is just another example of Americans grown tired of homogenization—the one imposed by the single, slick, neutral accent used by television announcers and marketing men trying to sell a single, slick, neutral product.

Ironically, just as Louisiana got its first Cajun Governor in decades, the southern, Catholic area lost its traditional hold on one of the state's Senate seats. Since 1936, Sen. Allen J. Ellender had been reelected virtually without opposition. He became the Senate's most senior member, and Chairman of the Appropriations Committee. He made many trips abroad, and also made pungent, often sagacious reports on them. For guests invited to his Senate hideaway, the Senator sometimes concocted a magnificent Creole sauce. In 1972, at age 82, Ellender got formidable opposition in a Democratic primary campaign from ex-state Sen. J. Bennett Johnston. The challenger was 40 and just barely lost the gubernatorial primary to Edwards in 1971. Then, after the filing deadline but before primary election day, Sen. Ellender suddenly died.

The Senator's death left the field pretty much to Johnston, a conservative from Shreveport. He has a charm that so many Southern politicians appear to possess by inheritance. After learning of Ellender's passing, ex-Gov. (1964–72) John McKeithen tried to get the primary reopened, but failed. So Johnston won easily. McKeithen then entered the general election as an independent. He attacked Johnston for being a member of a country-club elite and for being a supporter of George McGovern, which Johnston clearly was not. But because some of McKeithen's top aides had been accused of corruption during the Governor's last year in office, the independent only managed to split the anti-Johnston vote with a hapless Republican nominee.

In the Senate, Johnston has come out as one of the more conservative Southern Democrats. He voted in 1973, for example, to sustain the President's veto of a vocational rehabilitation program—one that many felt was an apple pie issue. Chances are that the much older Ellender would have voted the other way.

The state's other Senator, Russell Long, holds about as safe a seat as there is in Congress. In 1974 when he has to run again, Long will have accumulated 26 years of seniority and he will be only 56 years old. Louisiana voters will almost surely reelect an unopposed Russell Long. From 1965 to 1969, the Senator served as Majority Whip, but he was unseated from the post in 1969 by Edward Kennedy. The loss produced some bad press for Long, some observers calling him an erratic politician. Kennedy in turn lost the job to Robert Byrd of West Virginia two years later.

Today Long's chief source of power is the chairmanship of the Senate Finance Committee. The committee's jurisdiction runs a rough parallel to the Ways and Means Committee on the House side. But because the the Constitution stipulates that revenue measure must originate in the House, Russell Long's bailiwick is inherently less powerful than Wilbur Mills'. Like Mills of Ways and Means, Long tries to dominate his committee; he appoints all staff, and until 1973 there were no standing subcommittees from which other members might build bases of power. But Mills converts his ideas into legislation more often than Long. Long simply does not command the kind of respect in the Senate that Mills does in the House.

In many policy areas, Russell Long is very much the son of Huey Long. Thanks in part to Russell, the Senate invariably votes for higher social security payments than the House; when the differences are reconciled in conference, Long and Mills dominate. And back in the mid-1960s, Long pushed for a $1 checkoff on income tax forms to finance federal elections—a measure enacted in the Tax Reform Act of 1969. But unlike his father Russell is quite solicitous of the oil industry—one of Huey's favorite political targets. Russell, as he freely admits, has made hundreds of thousands of dollars investing in oil. Louisiana is the nation's number-two oil state, much of the stuff coming from offshore operations.

The Senator plays a crucial role in another issue, welfare. He shares with conservative Republican members of Finance a fierce antipathy toward so-called welfare chiselers. He has, as a result, strenuously backed various programs designed to force the mothers on welfare to work and the fathers to return to support deserted families. Not once but twice, Senate Finance was the burial ground of the Nixon Administration's Family Assistance Plan (FAP). So while Huey promised to make every man a king, Russell so loaded the measure with crackdown-on-welfare-chiseler amendments that FAP became unpalatable to its logical supporters.

Over the years, Louisiana's House delegation, like those of most Southern states, specialized in the accumulation of seniority. But also like many other Southern states, Louisiana was hard hit by retirements in 1972. Edwin Edwards left the House to become Governor. Two other Congressmen simply retired, and House Majority Leader Hale Boggs was lost in an October 1972 plane crash. Turnover like this is highly unusual in Louisiana politics. Even more unusual, however, was the election of a Republican Congressman, David Treen. Louisiana was—and still is despite Nixon's 1972 triumph here—the most resolutely one-party state in the nation. Treen lost close races to Boggs in 1964 and 1968 and made a good run for Governor in early 1972. With the creation of a district dominated by Jefferson Parish, suburban New Orleans, he finally won an election in 1972. But aside from Treen, traces of Republican activity in Louisiana are hard to find.

Census Data Pop. 3,643,180; 1.80% of U.S. total, 20th largest; change 1960–70, 11.9%. Central city, 31%; suburban, 23%. Median family income, $7,527; 43rd highest; families above $15,000: 13%; families below $3,000: 19%. Median years education, 10.8.

1972 Share of Federal Tax Burden $2,738,140,000; 1.31% of U.S. total, 22nd largest.

1972 Share of Federal Outlays $2,985,502,861; 1.38% of U.S. total, 23rd largest. Per capita federal spending, $819.

DOD	$722,615,000	26th (1.16%)		HEW	$1,072,665,803	23rd (1.50%)
AEC	$230,300	37th (0.01%)		HUD	$42,532,860	24th (1.39%)
NASA	$58,640,416	12th (1.96%)		VA	$209,570,889	21st (1.83%)
DOT	$136,513,357	25th (1.73%)		USDA	$312,558,650	18th (2.03%)
DOC	$85,817,078	4th (6.63%)		CSC	$38,719,772	28th (0.94%)
DOI	$10,235,231	36th (0.48%)		TD	$97,832,821	26th (0.59%)
DOJ	$16,506,850	19th (1.68%)		Other	$181,063,834	

Economic Base Finance, insurance and real estate; agriculture, notably cattle, soybeans, rice and dairy products; oil and gas extraction, especially oil and gas field services; food and kindred products; chemicals and allied products, especially industrial chemicals; transportation equipment, especially ship building and repairing.

Political Line-up Governor, Edwin W. Edwards (D); seat up, 1976. Senators, Russell B. Long (D) and J. Bennett Johnston, Jr. (D). Representatives, 8 (7 D and 1 R). State Senate (39 D and 0 R); State House (101 D and 4 R).

The Voters

> *Registration* 1,698,165 Total. White 1,322,597 (78%); black 375,568 (22%). 1,627,203 D (96%); 48,277 R (3%); 22,735 other (1%).
> *Median voting age* 41.5
> *Employment profile* White collar, 45%. Blue collar, 36%. Service, 16%. Farm, 3%.
> *Ethnic groups* Black, 30%. Spanish, 2%. Total foreign stock, 4%. French speaking, 16%.

Presidential vote

1972	Nixon (R)		686,852	(70%)
	McGovern (D)		298,142	(30%)
1968	Nixon (R)		257,535	(24%)
	Humphrey (D)		309,615	(28%)
	Wallace (AI)		530,300	(48%)
1964	Johnson (D)		387,068	(43%)
	Goldwater (R)		509,225	(57%)

Senator

Russell B. Long (D) Elected 1948, seat up 1974; b. Nov. 3, 1918, Shreveport; home, Baton Rouge; La. State U., B.A., 1941, LL.B. 1942; Navy, WWII; Lt. USNR; married, two children; Methodist.

Career Practicing atty., 1945–47; U.S. Senate, Asst. Majority Leader, 1965–69.

Offices 217 OSOB, 202-225-4623. Also 502 Union Fed. Bldg., Baton Rouge 70801, 504-343-7696.

Administrative Assistant R. E. Hunter

Committees

Commerce (6th); Subs: Communications; Environment; Merchant Marine (Chm.); Foreign Commerce and Tourism; Surface Transportation; Oceans and Atmosphere.

Finance (Chm.).

Joint Com. on Internal Revenue Taxation (V. Chm.).

Joint Com. on Reduction of Federal Expenditures (2nd).

Joint Study Com. on Budget Control (V. Chm.).

Group Ratings

	ADA	COPE	LWV	RIPON	NFU	LCV	CFA	NAB	NSI	ACA
1972	15	43	50	27	44	5	45	46	89	45
1971	19	60	27	11	50	–	80	–	–	61
1970	13	20	–	13	36	27	–	50	100	67

Key Votes

1) Busing	FOR	8) Sea Life Prot	FOR	15) Tax Singls Less	AGN
2) Alas P-line	FOR	9) Campaign Subs	FOR	16) Min Tax for Rich	AGN
3) Gun Cntrl	FOR	10) Cmbodia Bmbg	FOR	17) Euro Troop Rdctn	AGN
4) Rehnquist	FOR	11) Legal Srvices	AGN	18) Bust Hwy Trust	AGN
5) Pub TV $	FOR	12) Rev Sharing	FOR	19) Maid Min Wage	AGN
6) EZ Votr Reg	FOR	13) Cnsumr Prot	FOR	20) Farm Sub Limit	AGN
7) No-Fault	FOR	14) Eq Rts Amend	FOR	21) Highr Credt Chgs	AGN

Election Results

1968 general:	Russell B. Long (D), unopposed		
1968 primary:	Russell B. Long (D)	494,467	(87%)
	Maurice P. Blache (D)	73,791	(13%)
1962 general:	Russell B. Long (D)	318,838	(76%)
	Taylors Walters O'Hearn (R)	103,066	(24%)

Senator

J. Bennett Johnston, Jr. (D) Elected Appt., Nov. 14–Jan. 3, completion of term of U.S. Senator Allen J. Ellender; 1972; seat up 1975; b. June 10, 1932, Shreveport; home, Shreveport; Washington and Lee U.; La. State U. Law School, 1956, LL.B.; Army 1956–59; married, four children.

Career Practicing atty., Judge Advocate, Army General Corps, 1956–59; State House, 1964–68, Floor Leader; State Senate, 1968–72; atty., Johnston, Johnston and

Offices Thornton. 254 OSOB, 202-225-5824.

Administrative Assistant Charles McBride

Committees

Banking, Housing and Urban Affairs (7th); Subs: Consumer Credit; Production and Stabilization (Chm.); Small Business.

Interior and Insular Affairs (5th); Subs: Minerals, Materials and Fuels; Parks and Recreation; Territories and Insular Affairs (Chm.).

Sel. Com. on Small Business (6th); Subs: Environmental, Rural, and Urban Economic Development; Government Procurement; Retailing, Distribution, and Marketing Practices (Chm.).

Group Ratings: Newly Elected

Election Results

1972 general:	J. Bennett Johnston, Jr. (D)	598,987	(55%)
	John J. McKeithen (Ind.)	250,161	(23%)
	Ben C. Toledano (R)	206,846	(19%)
	Hall M. Lyons (AI)	28,910	(3%)
1972 primary:	J. Bennett Johnston (D)	623,076	(79%)
	Frank Tunney Allen (D)	88,198	(11%)
	Allen J. Ellender (D)	73,088	(9%)

FIRST DISTRICT Political Background

The state's 1st congressional district, the northern and eastern half of New Orleans, does not include the city's most glamorous section. For the most part, this is white middle-class territory filled with neighborhoods laid out on flat, swampy land reclaimed by the city of New Orleans. Farther east, but still within the city limits, lies an unreclaimed swamp that stretches to the Mississippi border. The district has a large black population, but the white vote, which went heavily for Wallace in 1968 and Nixon in 1972, dominates.

A more famous part of the 1st are two small parishes, Plaquemines and St. Bernard, lying in the delta of the Mississippi River. Here an insular community of river pilots and shrimp fishermen has lived for years; the politics of the community were controlled by men like the late Leander Perez of Plaquemines. Perez, a onetime Huey Long ally, was an arch-segregationist. So ardent were his beliefs on race that the Catholic Church excommunicated Perez for them. But he could still deliver the vote in Plaquemines, virtually to the man. Today, his son continues machine control with only slightly reduced effectiveness. Evidence of control appears in the results of the 1972 Senate election, as Plaquemines was one of only three parishes in the state that went for ex-Gov. John McKeithen (see Louisiana).

The political habits of the two small parishes, however, have little significance in the 1st's congressional elections. These have been won without fail since 1940 by Congressman F. Edward Hebert (pronounced AY-bear). After 30 years in Congress, Hebert, at age 70, became the Chairman of the House Armed Services Committee, following the death of Mendel Rivers of South Carolina and the primary defeat of Philip J. Philbin of Massachusetts. Hebert first came to Washington when the draft and Lend-Lease were subjects of heated controversy. He was then, and remains now, a man firmly convinced that military preparedness is an absolute necessity. The Congressman believes the notion—often promulgated when defense spending is debated—that it is much better to have too much defense than to risk not having enough. Hebert has, therefore, offered unyielding support to the demands of the Pentagon, even going so far as to back some military projects not in favor at the White House.

In his hawkish, pro-military sympathies, Hebert differs little from Mendel Rivers and Georgia's Carl Vinson, predecessors in the chairmanship. And like his predecessors, the current Chairman commands a solid majority on Armed Services. But there are differences. Rivers was a flamboyant autocrat, and until he quit the bottle, frequently drunk. Hebert is a canny politician, sober and circumspect. He allows some of the younger members of the committee at least a chance to air their views, little as he likes to hear them. He has also appointed Michigan's Lucien Nedzi, one of the committee's ranking doves, to chair the subcommittee on Intelligence. And unlike his predecessor, the current Chairman has not channeled countless military bases into his home district.

Hebert has suffered some disappointments in the 93rd Congress. Over his expressed objections, the House leadership insisted upon placing Ron Dellums of California and Patricia Schroeder of Colorado on Armed Services. Then in the spring of 1973, the House voted to stop the bombing of Cambodia, against the Chairman's stern warning. A majority of the Democrats on the committee and half of the delegation from his own Louisiana failed to support him. This must have been particularly upsetting. Later in 1973, a coalition of fiscal conservatives and antiwar liberals pushed through the Aspin ceiling amendment, slashing $950 million from the Pentagon budget, over Hebert's objections. These actions were less a repudiation of Hebert personally than a reflection of changing times. Hebert simply became Chairman just as the tides of opinion finally began to shift in the House. Hebert may choose to retire in 1974 when he will be 73; For the last couple of years, his health has been poor.

Census Data Pop. 454,873. Central city, 69%; suburban, 25%. Median family income, $8,655; families above $15,000: 18%; families below $3,000: 14%. Median years education, 11.3.

1972 Share of Federal Outlays $444,956,502

DOD	$103,957,021	HEW	$134,121,137
AEC	$7,920	HUD	$10,603,803
NASA	$23,804,897	DOI	$1,567,192
DOT	$19,590,673	USDA	$35,034,390
		Other	$116,269,470

Federal Military-Industrial Commitments

DOD Installations Naval Air Station (New Orleans). Naval Support Activity (New Orleans). *NASA Contractors* Boeing (New Orleans), $29.580m: S-IC state of the Saturn V. Chrysler (New Orleans), $17.183m: support of Saturn S-IB. Mason-Rust (New Orleans), $6.329m: various support services.

Economic Base Finance, insurance and real estate; food and kindred products; oil and gas extraction, especially crude petroleum and natural gas; apparel and other textile products; and transportation equipment, especially ship building and repairing. Also higher education (Louisiana State Univ., New Orleans).

The Voters

Registration 211,929 total. 203,152 D (96%); 5,997 R (3%); 2,780 other (1%). White 164,069 (77%); black 47,860 (23%).
Median voting age 42.1
Employment profile White collar, 52%. Blue collar, 34%. Service, 14%. Farm, –%.
Ethnic groups Black, 31%. Spanish, 4%. Total foreign stock, 7%. Italy, 2%; French-speaking, 8%.

Presidential vote

1972	Nixon (R)	91,347	(70%)
	McGovern (D)	37,676	(29%)
1968	Nixon (R)	36,495	(25%)
	Humphrey (D)	41,953	(29%)
	Wallace (AI)	66,056	(46%)

Representative

F. Edward Hebert (D) Elected 1940; b. Oct. 12, 1901, New Orleans; home, New Orleans; Tulane U., 1920–24; married, one child; Catholic.

Career Newspaperman, 1917–40; City Editor, 1937–40.

Offices 2340 RHOB, 202-225-3015. Also 642 Fed. Bldg.-South, New Orleans 70130, 504-527-2279.

Administrative Assistant Mary V. Swann

Committees

Standards of Official Conduct (3rd).

Armed Services (Chm.); Subs: Armed Services Investigating (Chm.); Intelligence.

Group Ratings

	ADA	COPE	LWV	RIPON	NFU	LCV	CFA	NAB	NSI	ACA
1972	0	17	13	38	0	0	—	50	100	63
1971	0	50	0	20	50	–	20	–	–	71
1970	4	18	–	17	33	0	60	50	100	64

Key Votes

1) Busing	AGN	6) Cmbodia Bmbg	FOR	11) Chkg Acct Intrst	FOR
2) Strip Mines	FOR	7) Bust Hwy Trust	AGN	12) End HISC (HUAC)	AGN
3) Cut Mil $	AGN	8) Farm Sub Lmt	ABS	13) Nixon Sewer Veto	FOR
4) Rev Shrg	FOR	9) School Prayr	FOR	14) Corp Cmpaign $	FOR
5) Pub TV $	ABS	10) Cnsumr Prot	AGN	15) Pol $ Disclosr	ABS

Election Results

1972 general: F. Edward Hebert (D), unopposed
1972 primary: F. Edward Hebert (D), unopposed
1970 general: F. Edward Hebert (D) 66,284 (87%)
Luke J. Fontana (Ind.) 9,602 (13%)

SECOND DISTRICT Political Background

New Orleans, long recognized as the key to fortunes of the entire Mississippi River Valley, fell into American hands with the Louisiana Purchase of 1803. Since that time, she has been one of the nation's most cosmopolitan cities. The heritage of the European continent can still be seen in the French Quarter, where carefully preserved old houses exist amid the swelter of tourist-packed bars and restaurants. New Orleans, the nation's second busiest port, has always experienced more contact with, and immigration from, the outside world than any other city in the South. There is, for example, a large Italian-American community here.

It is the older, more distinctive part of New Orleans that comprises most of Louisiana's 2nd congressional district. The 2nd takes in not only the French Quarter and Canal Street, but the integrated Garden District, as well as Tulane, Loyola, and Xavier universities. America's last trolleys still run on the narrow streets and wide boulevards of this part of the city. More than half of this section of New Orleans is black, and the blacks here, unlike many in rural Louisiana, have a long, steady tradition of voting on election day.

Besides New Orleans, the district takes in a portion of suburban Jefferson Parish. The parish extends south from the city to Barataria Bay, a place made famous by the exploits of pirate Jean Lafitte during the War of 1812. The 2nd, however, does not include the conservative, upper-income suburb of Metairie in the parish east of New Orleans. The 2nd's portion of Jefferson includes lower-middle-income towns that hug the levees on the banks of the Mississippi.

From 1941 to 1943 and 1947 to 1972—28 years altogether—the 2nd district was represented by Hale Boggs. He won his first race as a rebel running against the local machine, and after a spirited struggle in 1971, became Majority Leader—second highest leadership position in the House. Boggs' career ended suddenly in October 1972, when he was lost in a plane crash while campaigning for freshman Congressman Nick Begich of Alaska; Boggs had often campaigned for junior Democrats. Boggs was a mercurial man: a stirring old-time orator, a gifted trader of votes, and a Southerner who voted liberal on most economic issues and even dared to support the Civil Rights Acts of 1965 and 1968. But some felt that he was abrasive and aloof; though in line for the position, he had to fight and fight hard for the Majority Leadership.

It is ironic that Boggs died just at the time the Louisiana legislature finally drew an utterly safe district for him. In 1964 and 1968, he survived strong challenges from Republican David Treen; in the latter year, Boggs won by a scant 51-49 margin, as his pro-civil rights positions hurt him in the white wards of New Orleans and in Jefferson Parish. But in the current 2nd, which is 40% black, Boggs was easily reelected posthumously in 1972.

The Majority Leader's successor in the 2nd is his wife, Lindy Boggs, who won a March 1973 special election with 81% of the vote. When a Congressman dies, his widow is often elected to fill his seat as a kind of temporary expedient. This is decidedly not the case with Lindy Boggs. For many years, Mrs. Boggs was rated one of the most knowledgeable and active of congressional wives; so even before her election—which was taken for granted in Washington and New Orleans—she enjoyed wide respect. No one has a bad word to say about Lindy Boggs, except perhaps to say that she is a little too nice to people. She has the manners of a girl raised on a plantation (which she was) and the political savvy of one who has campaigned in Louisiana and lived in Washington for 30 years (which she has).

Upon her election, Lindy Boggs expressed qualms about the life of a politician only because she would have to take sides on thorny issues. In her first such test, the issue of bombing in Cambodia, she voted with Speaker Carl Albert against the bombing. In the process, she disregarded the advice of Armed Services Chairman and New Orleans' other Congressman, Edward Hebert.

Census Data Pop. 454,772. Central city, 61%; suburban, 39%. Median family income, $7,611; families above $15,000: 14%; families below $3,000: 18%. Median years education, 10.5.

1972 Share of Federal Outlays $452,630,462

DOD	$99,655,844	HEW	$138,080,338
AEC	$8,389	HUD	$11,231,660
NASA	$25,214,397	DOI	$1,548,949
DOT	$19,921,024	USDA	$36,596,214
		Other	$120,373,647

Federal Military-Industrial Commitments

DOD Contractors Avondale Shipyards (New Orleans), $27.169m: ship repair. Lykes Brothers Steamship (New Orleans), $19.637m: transportation services. Central Gulf Steamship (New Orleans), $13.563m: transportation services.

Economic Base Finance, insurance and real estate; food and kindred products, especially beverages; oil and gas extraction, especially crude petroleum and natural gas; fabricated metal products, especially fabricated structural metal products; and transportation equipment, especially ship building and repairing. Also higher education (Tulane).

The Voters

Registration 184,920 total. 174,928 D (95%); 5,717 R (3%); 4,275 other (2%). White 129,690 (70%); black 55,230 (30%).
Median voting age 42.7
Employment profile White collar, 47%. Blue collar, 35%. Service, 18%. Farm, –%.
Ethnic groups Black, 40%. Spanish, 4%. Total foreign stock, 8%. Italy, 1%; French-speaking, 11%.

Presidential vote

1972	Nixon (R)	65,036	(60%)
	McGovern (D)	43,702	(40%)
1968	Nixon (R)	31,993	(25%)
	Humphrey (D)	51,221	(40%)
	Wallace (AI)	45,894	(36%)

Representative

Corinne "Lindy" (Mrs. Hale) Boggs (D) Elected March 20, 1973; b. March 13, 1916, Pointe Coupee Parish; home, New Orleans; Sophie Newcomb Col. of Tulane U., B.A., 1935; widow, three children; Catholic.

Career Teacher, St. James Parish; active participant, gen. mgr. in her husband's (Hale Boggs) campaign; co-chm., Operations Crossroads, 1956 campaign of Adlai Stevenson; mbr., advance team of 1960 vice presidential southern train tour; co-chm., "Lady Bird Special" train tour, 1964; co-chairman, Inaugural Balls, 1961 and 1965; Past. Pres., Women's Natl. Dem. Club; Pres. Congressional Club, 1971–72.

Offices 1507 LHOB, 202-225-6636. Also 638 Fed. Bldg.-South, New Orleans 70130, 504-527-2274.

Administrative Assistant Barbara Rathe

Committees

Banking and Currency (24th).

Group Ratings: Newly Elected

Key Votes

1) Busing	NE	6) Cmbodia Bmbg	AGN	11) Chkg Acct Intrst	AGN
2) Strip Mines	NE	7) Bust Hwy Trust	AGN	12) End HISC (HUAC)	ABS
3) Cut Mil $	NE	8) Farm Sub Lmt	NE	13) Nixon Sewer Veto	FOR
4) Rev Shrg	NE	9) School Prayr	NE	14) Corp Cmpaign $	NE
5) Pub TV $	NE	10) Cnsumr Prot	NE	15) Pol $ Disclosr	NE

Election Results

1973 special:	Mrs. Hale "Lindy" Boggs (D)	43,255	(81%)
	Robert E. Lee (R)	10,315	(19%)
1973 primary:	Mrs. Hale "Lindy" Boggs (D)	41,520	(73%)
	Harwood Koppel (D)	12,208	(21%)
	Joseph B. Smith (D)	1,345	(2%)
	Jules W. Hillery (D)	999	(2%)
	Rodney Fertel	781	(1%)

THIRD DISTRICT Political Background

Question: how does one go about becoming the first Republican member of Congress from Louisiana in years and years? Answer: by trying, and trying, and trying again. That's how David C. Treen did it. He is now a freshman Republican Congressman from Louisiana. Back in 1964, when Barry Goldwater swept the state, Treen ran against Hale Boggs and got 45% of the vote. Four years later, he tried again and did even better with 49%. Both times Treen emphasized his opposition to the civil rights legislation Boggs had supported.

Those two races occurred in the old 2nd district, whose boundaries have since been redrawn considerably. After a 1971 gubernatorial race in which he got a respectable 43% of the vote, Treen decided to run for Congress again in 1972. This time he picked the redistricted 3rd. On first glance, the 3rd looks like rather unlikely territory for a candidate who achieved a Republican major breakthrough among white urban voters in New Orleans. Most of the physical expanse of the 3rd is Cajun country—miles of bayou and swamp giving way from time to time to sugar cane and rice fields and to little towns where French remains the first language.

But 36% of the 3rd's population is in suburban Jefferson Parish, just east of New Orleans. Moreover, most of the people here live in the suburb of Metairie. Here the lowlands between the levees of the Mississippi River and Lake Pontchartrain were drained and subdivided. Expensive houses were then built within easy commuting distance of downtown New Orleans. Treen, who is from Metairie, had carried the Jefferson Parish portions of the 3rd by big margins in his previous tries for Congress and the governorship. In 1972, the same territory produced Richard Nixon's largest margins in Louisiana.

Treen had other things going for him in the 1972 congressional contest. Incumbent Congressman Patrick Caffery, though only 40, decided against seeking reelection. Moreover, the winner of the Democratic primary was a man whose only electoral strength lay in his home parish of Terrebone, down in the bayou country that no longer controlled things in the redrawn 3rd. So Treen managed to win majorities in both Jefferson Parish, which carried 73–27, and in New Iberia Parish at the far western edge of the district.

Even so, Treen's overall percentage was only 54%—an indication of the difficulties the strongest Republican in Louisiana faces in the most propitious circumstances. If current patterns in congressional elections hold up, Treen will probably find the going easier in 1974. The next time out, he will have all the advantages of incumbency and probably no tough opposition.

Census Data Pop. 455,575. Central city, 0%; suburban, 35%. Median family income, $9,146; families above $15,000: 16%; families below $3,000: 11%. Median years education, 11.3.

1972 Share of Federal Outlays $278,494,782

DOD	$45,102,872	HEW	$109,484,566
AEC	$2,989	HUD	$4,013,951
NASA	$8,984,840	DOI	$1,321,612
DOT	$7,888,631	USDA	$29,556,568
		Other	$72,138,753

Federal Military-Industrial Commitments

No installations or contractors receiving prime awards greater than $5,000,000.

Economic Base Oil and gas extraction, especially oil and gas field services, and crude petroleum and natural gas; finance, insurance and real estate; agriculture, notably grains, cattle and dairy products; food and kindred products; and chemicals and allied products, especially industrial chemicals.

The Voters

Registration 221,761 total. 211,341 D (95%); 6,877 R (3%); 3,543 other (2%). White 196,253 (88%); black 25,508 (12%).
Median voting age 38.9
Employment profile White collar, 50%. Blue collar, 37%. Service, 11%. Farm, 2%.
Ethnic groups Black, 15%. Spanish, 2%. Total foreign stock, 5%. Italy, 1%; French-speaking, 29%.

Presidential vote

1972	Nixon (R)	102,047	(76%)
	McGovern (D)	31,647	(24%)
1968	Nixon (R)	40,392	(31%)
	Humphrey (D)	31,815	(24%)
	Wallace (AI)	58,934	(45%)

Represenatative

David Conner Treen (R) Elected 1972; b. July 16, 1928, Baton Rouge; home, Metairie; Tulane U., B.A., 1948, LL.B., 1950; Air Force, 1950–52; married, three children; Methodist.

Career Assoc., Deutsch, Kerrigan, and Stiles, New Orleans, 1950–51; V.P., Simplex Mfg. Corp., New Orleans; Assoc. and Partner, Beard, Blue, Schmitt and Treen, 1957–72.

Offices 1408 LHOB, 202-225-4031.

Administrative Assistant John S. Rivers

Committees

Armed Services (13th); Sub: No. 2.

Merchant Marine and Fisheries (14th); Subs: Coast Guard and Navigation; Merchant Marine; Oceanography.

Group Ratings: Newly Elected

Key Votes

1) Busing	NE	6) Cmbodia Bmbg	FOR	11) Chkg Acct Intrst	AGN
2) Strip Mines	NE	7) Bust Hwy Trust	AGN	12) End HISC (HUAC)	AGN
3) Cut Mil $	NE	8) Farm Sub Lmt	NE	13) Nixon Sewer Veto	FOR
4) Rev Shrg	NE	9) School Prayr	NE	14) Corp Cmpaign $	NE
5) Pub TV $	NE	10) Cnsumr Prot	NE	15) Pol $ Disclosr	NE

Election Results

1972 general:	David C. Teeen (R)	71,090	(54%)
	J. Louis Watkins (D)	60,521	(46%)
1972 primary:	David C. Treen (R), unopposed		

FOURTH DISTRICT Political Background

Northern Louisiana is part of the Deep South, having none of the Creole ambience of New Orleans or the French influence of the Cajun country. For 150 years, Baptist farmers have inhabited the upcountry hills around Shreveport, the commercial center and the largest city (pop.

182,000) of the 4th congressional district. Shreveport itself was a town built by the descendants of the original Baptist settlers; with the discovery of oil some 30 years ago, the old farm market town boomed. Only 15 miles from the Texas border, Shreveport is very close in spirit to the ultraconservative oil cities of east Texas.

The old-time political tradition in the 4th is populist. But recently, the district has stacked up as solidly conservative; or at least this is the way the overwhelming majority of the white voters here regard themselves. Solidly conservative is also the best description of the district's Congressman, Joe D. Waggoner, Jr., from the town of Plain Dealing. After winning a special election in 1961, Waggoner soon gained the reputation of a segregationist firebrand in the House of Representatives, though lately his temperament seems to have mellowed. Now with a seat on the Ways and Means Committee, the Congressman has become one of the leading strategists of the conservative Southern Democratic bloc.

Waggoner and some of his friends in the House apparently want to organize a body like the Democratic Study Group. Such an organization would focus the interests of conservative Southerners; it would also hire a staff to do research for them. Waggoner's plans for a conservative equivalent of the Democratic Study Group is yet another indication of the change, however glacial, that has occurred in the House over the past decade or so. The Southern conservatives had no such need for something like this before, said one wag, because they simply controlled the whole House of Representatives. This was pretty near the truth. Twenty-five years ago, virtually every one of the 100-odd Southern House seats was held by a conservative Democrat. Today, less than half are. Moreover, retirements and deaths have decimated Dixiecrat seniority. Waggoner is a competent tactician, and because he will be only 56 in 1974, he will probably have many years of service ahead of him. But the question is, how many troops will he have to lead as the House moves into the rest of the 1970s?

Census Data   Pop. 455,272. Central city, 40%; suburban, 25%. Median family income, $7,336; families above $15,000: 11%; families below $3,000: 19%. Median years education, 11.5.

1972 Share of Federal Outlays $572,063,758

DOD	$334,464,000	HEW	$131,041,287
AEC	–	HUD	$1,529,706
NASA	$6,000	DOI	$838,652
DOT	$15,314,176	USDA	$21,814,536
		Other	$67,055,401

Federal Military-Industrial Commitments

DOD Contractors Sperry Rand (Shreveport), $49.913m: operation of Louisiana Army Ammunition plant; 155mm projectile components. Sperry Rand (Doyline), $22.656m: unspecified. Austin Jack and Associates (Fort Polk), $5.747m: construction services.
DOD Installations Fort Polk AB (Leesville). Barksdale AFB (Shreveport).

Economic Base Finance, insurance and real estate; lumber and wood products; agriculture, notably dairy products, poultry and cattle; oil and gas extraction, especially oil and gas field services, and crude petroleum and natural gas; and fabricated structural metal products, and other fabricated metal products.

The Voters

Registration 194,471 total. 181,585 D (93%); 10,519 R (5%); 2,367 other (1%). White 150,729 (78%); black 43,742 (22%).
Median voting age 41.2
Employment profile White collar, 44%. Blue collar, 37%. Service, 17%. Farm, 2%.
Ethnic groups Black, 31%. Spanish, 1%. Total foreign stock, 3%.

Presidential vote

1972	Nixon (R)	89,754	(75%)
	McGovern (D)	29,203	(25%)

1968	Nixon (R)	32,635	(25%)
	Humphrey (D)	31,842	(24%)
	Wallace (AI)	66,398	(51%)

Representative

Joe D. Waggonner, Jr. (D) Elected Dec. 19, 1961; b. Sept. 7, 1918, Plain Dealing; home, Plain Dealing; La. Polytechnic Inst., B.A., 1941; Navy, WWII and Korean War; married, two children; Methodist.

Career Operator, petroleum distributor, 1952– ; Bossier Parish School Bd., 1954–61, Pres., 1956–57; La. Bd. of Ed., 1960–61; Pres., United School Commission of La., 1961.

Offices 221 CHOB, 202-225-2777. Also 210 P.O. Bldg., Shreveport 71101, 318-424-5379.

Administrative Assistant David L. Batt

Committees

Ways and Means (14th).

Group Ratings

	ADA	COPE	LWV	RIPON	NFU	LCV	CFA	NAB	NSI	ACA
1972	0	27	10	29	57	11	0	73	100	86
1971	0	36	22	18	53	–	0	–	–	72
1970	4	25	–	24	15	11	58	67	100	78

Key Votes

1) Busing	AGN	6) Cmbodia Bmbg	FOR
2) Strip Mines	FOR	7) Bust Hwy Trust	AGN
3) Cut Mil $	AGN	8) Farm Sub Lmt	AGN
4) Rev Shrg	AGN	9) School Prayr	FOR
5) Pub TV $	AGN	10) Cnsumr Prot	AGN

11) Chkg Acct Intrst	AGN
12) End HISC (HUAC)	AGN
13) Nixon Sewer Veto	FOR
14) Corp Cmpaign $	FOR
15) Pol $ Disclosr	AGN

Election Results

1972 general:	Joe D. Waggoner, Jr. (D), unopposed
1972 primary:	Joe D. Waggoner, Jr. (D), unopposed
1970 general:	Joe D. Waggoner, Jr. (D), unopposed

FIFTH DISTRICT Political Background

The upcountry 5th congressional district, the state's most rural, is part of the Deep South. Aside from the city of Monroe (pop. 56,000), the 5th has no urban center of any consequence. The agricultural endeavors in the cotton and piney woods country range from large plantations along the Mississippi River to small, poor hill farms in places like Winn Parish, the boyhood home of Huey P. Long. The 5th has the third highest black population (35% in 1970) among Louisiana congressional districts. But here, unlike the 2nd district in New Orleans, blacks have little political leverage; the white vote is usually monolithic.

Since 1946, the 5th has been represented by Otto E. Passman, a forthright conservative and stern critic of government spending. Passman is now the fifth-ranking Democrat on the House Appropriations Committee and Chairman of its Foreign Operations Subcommittee. As Chairman, Passman has gained some recognition as the scourge of the foreign-aid appropriation. But Passman's role in the matter became less pivotal, as foreign aid grew less and less popular generally. Moreover, the subcommittee's current membership will not give the Louisiana Congressman carte blanche on the issue.

For many years, Passman won reelection virtually without opposition. But he was challenged in the last two primaries; age has crept up on him—he will be 74 in 1974. In 1970, Passman was held to 62% of the primary vote by two challengers who split the rest almost equally. Two years later, Charles M. Brown took 30% to the incumbent's 61%. Brown did especially well among black voters, even though Passman promised some local black students scholarships at a university in Mexico. The challenger also ran pretty well in the white parishes of the district.

Passman's performance in 1972 hardly represents an overwhelming margin for a veteran of his stature. In fact, 61% is uncomfortably close to the figure of 50% (or one vote less than that) which would force Passman into a runoff. When that happens in Southern politics, it usually signals vulnerability and defeat next time, even when the incumbent survives the initial indignity of a runoff. Passman may decide that 1974 is the year to retire. If he does, the 5th will experience a free-for-all primary from which his successor will be chosen.

Census Data Pop. 455,205. Central city, 12%; suburban, 13%. Median family income, $5,762; families above $15,000: 8%; families below $3,000: 27%. Median years education, 10.1.

1972 Share of Federal Outlays $305,770,122

DOD	$19,419,115	HEW	$158,413,249
AEC	$24,000	HUD	$901,711
NASA	$51,099	DOI	$822,392
DOT	$7,450,629	USDA	$69,782,715
		Other	$48,905,212

Federal Military-Industrial Commitments

No installations or contractors receiving prime awards greater than $5,000,000.

Economic Base Agriculture, notably grains, cotton and cattle; finance, insurance and real estate; paper and allied products, especially miscellaneous converted paper products; lumber and wood products; and men's and boys' furnishings, and other apparel and other textile products.

The Voters

Registration 222,575 total. 216,017 D (97%); 4,349 R (2%); 2,209 other (1%). White 168,754 (76%); black 53,821 (24%).
Median voting age 44.2
Employment profile White collar, 40%. Blue collar, 37%. Service, 16%. Farm, 7%.
Ethnic groups Black, 35%. Total foreign stock, 1%.

Presidential vote

1972	Nixon (R)	97,039	(73%)
	McGovern (D)	35,213	(27%)
1968	Nixon (R)	30,367	(21%)
	Humphrey (D)	33,068	(23%)
	Wallace (AI)	82,988	(57%)

Representative

Otto Ernest Passman (D) Elected 1946; b. June 27, 1900, near Franklinton; home, Monroe; Navy, WWII; married; Baptist.

Career Owner, Passman Investment Co.

Offices 2108 RHOB, 202-225-2376. Also P.O. Box 6000, New P.O. Bldg., Monroe 71201, 318-387-1800, and U.S. P.O. Bldg., P.O. Box 138, Clinton 70722, 318-683-8666.

Administrative Assistant Martha K. Williams

Committees

Appropriations (5th); Subs: Foreign Operations (Chm.); Public Works, AEC.

Group Ratings

	ADA	COPE	LWV	RIPON	NFU	LCV	CFA	NAB	NSI	ACA
1972	6	43	17	38	40	7	0	86	100	80
1971	5	17	14	33	50	–	0	–	–	76
1970	0	27	–	38	23	9	40	50	100	71

Key Votes

1) Busing	AGN	6) Cmbodia Bmbg	FOR	11) Chkg Acct Intrst	AGN
2) Strip Mines	AGN	7) Bust Hwy Trust	ABS	12) End HISC (HUAC)	AGN
3) Cut Mil $	AGN	8) Farm Sub Lmt	AGN	13) Nixon Sewer Veto	FOR
4) Rev Shrg	AGN	9) School Prayr	AGN	14) Corp Cmpaign $	FOR
5) Pub TV $	ABS	10) Cnsumr Prot	AGN	15) Pol $ Disclosr	AGN

Election Results

1972 general:	Otto E. Passman (D), unopposed		
1972 primary:	Otto E. Passman (D)	67,976	(61%)
	Charles M. Brown (D)	34,314	(31%)
	David I. Patten (D)	9,299	(8%)
1970 general:	Otto E. Passman (D), unopposed		

SIXTH DISTRICT Political Background

When Governor-elect Huey P. Long traveled to Baton Rouge in 1928, the Louisiana state capital was a small, sleepy, Southern town (1930 pop. 30,000). Today, Baton Rouge is a bustling, growing city of 165,000—the boom here produced by the Kingfish and some of his bitterest political enemies. It was Long who built a major university in Baton Rouge (Louisiana State), as well as increasing the size and scope of state government generally. And it was his old enemies, the oil companies, who built the big refineries and the petrochemical plants—these being the other basis of Baton Rouge's current prosperity. Baton Rouge and its suburban fringe make up roughly half of the state's 6th congressional district. To the east is farming and piney woods country. The most notable city out here is Bogalusa, a lumber mill town on the Mississippi line and the scene of some Ku Klux Klan activity.

Petrochemicals and hooded robes have made for a volatile political mix in the 6th district, which in recent years has experienced feverish contests in its Democratic primary. The Republicans here, meanwhile, have remained totally unorganized. For 28 years, from 1939 to 1967, the district was represented by Jimmy Morrison, a battle-scarred Louisiana politician. In 1940, Morrison once challenged Earl Long, Huey's brother, for the governorship. By Louisiana standards, the Congressman compiled a liberal voting record, though he never of course voted for a civil rights bill.

In 1964, as the district moved toward Barry Goldwater, Morrison learned that his end was in sight. The Congressman barely avoided a runoff primary after getting 52% of the votes against a field of nine challengers. The close shave attracted more opposition two years later. Conservative Judge John Rarick of Baton Rouge resigned his post in order to take on Morrison. In the first primary, Rarick ran a hot second behind the incumbent. But Morrison would have again avoided a runoff were it not for a third candidate, one James E. Morrison, whose 6,562 votes were probably meant for the Congressman. In the runoff, Rarick forged through and squeaked by. The challenger beat the incumbent by 3,876 votes in East Baton Rouge Parish and 124 votes in the rest of the district, for a margin of an even 4,000.

A Yankee from Indiana, Rarick is the most rabidly right-wing member of Congress. The ex-judge, who some claim was once associated with the Ku Klux Klan, regularly inserts the most vitriolic kind of far-right, sometimes anti-Semitic, propaganda into the Congressional Record. Even his fellow Southern conservatives don't take him very seriously. Back home, his strident, voluble conservatism appears to have induced similar misgivings in his home town, Baton Rouge, a place not known for its liberalism. Rarick's strength lies in the rural and small-town parishes of the 6th district.

In 1968, Rarick was forced into a runoff primary when he got only 36% of the votes in his home parish. In a 1970 two-man race, the incumbent again lost his home parish and carried the primary with 59% district-wide. In 1972, Rarick did little better. Against three weak opponents, he took 56% of the East Baton Rouge Parish vote, and 61% overall. Once in office, most Congressmen rapidly move to a position of political invulnerability. To judge from the election results, Rarick has not, and it is possible that he could lose his job in some future primary.

Census Data Pop. 456,178. Central city, 36%; suburban, 26%. Median family income, $8,230; families above $15,000: 16%; families below $3,000: 17%. Median years education, 12.0.

1972 Share of Federal Outlays $327,034,515

DOD	$27,128,570	HEW	$153,401,469
AEC	$187,000	HUD	$11,650,448
NASA	$435,730	DOI	$2,729,400
DOT	$14,843,644	USDA	$25,246,536
		Other	$91,411,718

Federal Military-Industrial Commitments

DOD Contractors Humble Oil (Baton Rouge), $14.709m: petroleum products.

Economic Base Chemicals and allied products, especially industrial chemicals; finance, insurance and real estate; agriculture, notably dairy products, poultry and cattle; paper and allied products; and food and kindred products. Also higher education (Louisiana State Univ., and Southern Univ.).

The Voters

Registration 229,222 total. 217,989 D (95%); 6,939 R (3%); 4,294 other (2%). White 180,256 (79%); black 48,966 (21%).
Median voting age 39.6
Employment profile White collar, 48%. Blue collar, 34%. Service, 15%. Farm, 3%.
Ethnic groups Black, 30%. Spanish, 1%. Total foreign stock, 3%. French-speaking 4%.

Presidential vote

1972	Nixon (R)	83,246	(70%)
	McGovern (D)	36,240	(30%)
1968	Nixon (R)	27,875	(21%)
	Humphrey (D)	33,967	(25%)
	Wallace (AI)	72,966	(54%)

Representative

John R. Rarick (D) Elected 1966; b. Jan. 29, 1924, Waterford, Ind.; home, Baton Rouge; Ball State Teachers Col., 1942, 1945; La. State U., 1943–44; Tulane U. Law School, J.D., 1949; Army, WWII; married, three children; Baptist.

Career Atty., Judge, 20th Judicial Dist., 1961–66.

Offices 1525 LHOB, 202-225-3901. Also Rm. 236 New Fed. Bldg., Baton Rouge 70801, 504-344-7679.

Administrative Assistant Lee Brooks

Committees

Agriculture (9th); Subs: Livestock and Grains; Oilseeds and Rice; Forests (Chm.).

Group Ratings

	ADA	COPE	LWV	RIPON	NFU	LCV	CFA	NAB	NSI	ACA
1972	0	50	0	13	0	7	0	89	100	88
1971	3	8	11	12	20	–	38	–	–	96
1970	4	25	–	18	8	0	24	80	100	75

Key Votes

1) Busing	AGN	6) Cmbodia Bmbg	AGN	11) Chkg Acct Intrst	FOR
2) Strip Mines	FOR	7) Bust Hwy Trust	AGN	12) End HISC (HUAC)	ABS
3) Cut Mil $	AGN	8) Farm Sub Lmt	AGN	13) Nixon Sewer Veto	AGN
4) Rev Shrg	AGN	9) School Prayr	FOR	14) Corp Cmpaign $	AGN
5) Pub TV $	AGN	10) Cnsumr Prot	FOR	15) Pol $ Disclosr	AGN

Election Results

1972 general:	John R. Rarick (D), unopposed		
1972 primary:	John R. Rarick (D)	69,274	(61%)
	Lamar Gibson (D)	25,267	(22%)
	James J. Bardon (D)	13,733	(12%)
	James A. Edwards (D)	5,306	(5%)
1970 general:	John R. Rarick (D), unopposed		

SEVENTH DISTRICT Political Background

The nation has few congressional districts which can report that nearly half the people living in them grew up speaking a language other than English. Such a district is the 7th of Louisiana, the heart of the state's Cajun country. The mother tongue of 44% of its residents is Cajun French. The district hugs the Gulf Coast of Louisiana, as it moves east to west from the swamps of the Atchafalaya River, through Lafayette (pop. 69,000), across to Lake Charles (pop. 78,000) and the Texas border. To the west, the flat coastal lands teem with oil derricks.

A Cajun revival has begun to show life in Louisiana. Cajuns have taken increasing pride in south Louisiana's distinctive heritage, making them determined to preserve the French tongue against encroachments engendered by the English media. Cajun pride was bolstered when the 7th's Congressman, Edwin W. Edwards, was elected Governor in 1972. Despite his Welsh name, Edwards is very much a Cajun and the state's first French-background Governor in decades.

Edwards' successor in Congress is a former member of his staff, John B. Breaux. The new Congressman, also of French origin, has deep roots in the 7th district. His election, however, was by no means automatic. Breaux led a six-man Democratic primary, but his 42% of the votes was not enough to avoid a runoff. The second race was fundamentally a contest between Breaux's dominance of the eastern, more Cajun half of the district and his opponent's strength in his home area around Lake Charles. Breaux won with 55% of the votes. He did it by piling up bigger margins in the Cajun east than his opponent could in the west.

Because no Republican opposition existed in the general election and because Edwards had already vacated the seat when he became Governor, Breaux took office immediately after his primary victory. The 93rd Congress still considered Breaux a freshman when it convened; shortly thereafter, he was elected Vice-Chairman of the Freshman Democratic Caucus. Edwards compiled the voting record of a moderate; his successor appears to lean a little more to the liberal side, though the same could be said of many Southern Democrats in the 93rd Congress. Breaux has voted to override several of President Nixon's vetoes and also supported the successful move to stop the bombing of Cambodia. Assuming he can turn an initial narrow win into continuing electoral success, the Louisianan appears likely to become a fairly important Congressman.

When J. Bennett Johnston succeeded the late Allen Ellender, the state's tradition of having one Catholic Senator was broken. Although there are no openings now—Johnston was just elected and Russell Long is unbeatable—it is possible that Breaux may someday run for statewide office.

Census Data Pop. 455,014. Central city, 32%; suburban, 24%. Median family income, $7,197; families above $15,000: 11%; families below $3,000: 19%. Median years education, 10.2.

1972 Share of Federal Outlays $240,356,636

DOD	$23,620,278	HEW	$111,926,781
AEC	–	HUD	$641,792
NASA	$143,452	DOI	$881,574
DOT	$12,097,213	USDA	$40,431,469
		Other	$50,614,077

Federal Military-Industrial Commitments

No installations or contractors receiving prime awards greater $5,000,000.

Economic Base Agriculture, notably grains, cattle and dairy products; oil and gas extraction, especially oil and gas field services; finance, insurance and real estate; food and kindred products; and chemicals and allied products, especially industrial chemicals.

The Voters

Registration 236,058 total. 229,028 D (97%); 5,037 R (2%); 1,993 other (1%). White 195,897 (83%); black 40,161 (17%).
Median voting age 41.2
Employment profile White collar, 42%. Blue collar, 38%. Service, 15%. Farm, 5%.
Ethnic groups Black, 21%. Total foreign stock, 2%. French-speaking, 44%.

Presidential vote

1972	Nixon (R)	85,502	(68%)
	McGovern (D)	41,032	(32%)
1968	Nixon (R)	32,953	(24%)
	Humphrey (D)	39,560	(28%)
	Wallace (AI)	67,241	(48%)

Representative

John B. Breaux (D) Elected Sept. 30, 1972; b. March 1, 1944, Crowley; home, Crowley; U. of Southwestern La., B.A., 1965; La. State U., J.D., 1967; married, three children; Catholic.

Career Law partner, Brown, McKernan, Ingram and Breaux, 1967–68; legis. asst. to Congressman Edwards, 1968–69, dist. asst., 1969–72.

Offices 319 CHOB, 202-225-2031. Also 2530 P.O. and Fed. Bldg., Lake Charles 70601, 318-433-1122, and 301 Fed. Bldg., Lafayette 70501, 318-232-2081.

Administrative Assistant Charlotte Wilmer

Committees

Merchant Marine and Fisheries (16th); Subs: Coast Guard and Navigation; Fisheries and Wildlife Conservation and the Environment; Oceanography.

Public Works (18th); Subs: Economic Development; Energy; Investigations and Review; Public Buildings and Grounds; Water Resources.

Group Ratings: Newly Elected

Key Votes

1) Busing	NE	6) Cmbodia Bmbg	AGN	11) Chkg Acct Intrst	AGN
2) Strip Mines	NE	7) Bust Hwy Trust	AGN	12) End HISC (HUAC)	FOR
3) Cut Mil $	NE	8) Farm Sub Lmt	NE	13) Nixon Sewer Veto	AGN
4) Rev Shrg	NE	9) School Prayr	NE	14) Corp Cmpaign $	NE
5) Pub TV $	NE	10) Cnsumr Prot	NE	15) Pol $ Disclosr	NE

Election Results

1972 general:	John B. Breaux (D), unopposed		
1972 run-off:	John B. Breaux (D)	64,021	(55%)
	Gary Tyler (D)	51,656	(45%)
1972 primary:	John B. Breaux (D)	48,615	(47%)
	Gary Tyler (D)	25,262	(24%)
	D. H. de la Houssave (D)	11,051	(11%)
	Basile Miller (D)	6,870	(7%)
	Eddie Ackal (D)	6,649	(6%)
	William S. Boyd (D)	5,966	(6%)

EIGHTH DISTRICT Political Background

After the lines for seven of the state's eight congressional districts were drawn, the territory remaining became the steam-shovel-shaped 8th district. On the east is Lake Pontchartrain; the 8th then moves up along the Mississippi and Red rivers to a point within 30 miles of the Texas border. Several redistrictings and a variety of political considerations explain the configuration. The net result is a district sharing certain common characteristics, but having little sense of common identity.

First of all, the 8th is notable for its large black population, which comes to 36%, the state's second highest after New Orlean's 2nd district. In the days before the Civil War, the old sugar and cotton plantations along the Mississippi required a good deal of slave labor. Today, in parishes like Pointe Coupee and West Feliciana, blacks comprise the major voting bloc. The district also has a large Cajun population; they are found at the southern edges of the 8th, particularly in St. Landry and Evangeline Parishes. Beyond the influence of the blacks and Cajuns, there is the legacy of the Long family. Ten years ago, the 8th included Huey Long's home parish, Winn; though Winn now lies in the 5th, the northern part of the current 8th is still pretty strong Kingfish territory. So taken together, the politics of the district are relatively liberal. In 1972, the 8th cast 37% of its votes for George McGovern—the best vote the Democrat received in any non-urban Southern district.

An understanding of the last six congressional elections here requires some knowledge of the Long family tree. Since 1960, one or another Long has won every primary election. In 1960, Earl Long, the Kingfish's brother, won the Democratic primary after just having left the Governor's office. In a blow to House gallery-watchers, the colorful Earl Long (see A. J. Liebling's classic *The Earl of Louisiana*) died and never made it to Washington. But the man he beat, Harold B. McSween, did for one more term.

In 1962, McSween was unceremoniously beaten by Gillis Long, who in turn lost two years later, again in the Democratic primary, to Speedy O. Long. These two Longs, both cousins of the great man, are of very different political breeds. Speedy, a member of the Armed Services Committee, is a hard-line conservative. Gillis is quite liberal; after his defeat in 1964, he served inter alia as an assistant director of OEO. In 1972, after an uneventful eight years in the House, Speedy retired. He was succeeded of course by none other than Gillis.

Gillis Long's return to Congress marks a significant shift in the politics of the South these last ten years. The year Gillis lost, 1964, was the year the civil rights revolution pushed most white Southern voters into the arms of arch-conservative candidates. The 8th district went only for Speedy, but repudiated 100 years of history and voted Republican in 1964 for President. For some years thereafter, in national elections and in congressional elections where a candidate got tagged a liberal, Southern politics was polarized. Virtually all of the blacks voted one way and virtually all of the more numerous whites voted the other way.

In 1972, from the looks of things in the 8th district, those days are gone. Against four opponents, Gillis Long won his primary without a runoff. He took the general election with a solid 69% against both Republican and American party candidates. At the same time, McGovern's showing demonstrated a sharp improvement in the fortunes of Democratic presidential aspirants. In the 8th, thousands of whites decided to cast ballots on issues other than just race. As for Gillis Long's political future, his 1972 showing indicates that he can probably count on reelection—a statement that could not be made during the mid-1960s.

In the House, Congressman Long is a member of the Rules Committee—one of the three new members put there by the Democratic leadership. One expects that Long's behavior on the committee, one that controls the flow of legislation onto the House floor, will be responsive to the wishes of the leadership.

Census Data Pop. 456,291. Central city, 0%; suburban, 0%. Median family income, $6,092; families above $15,000: 8%; families below $3,000: 26%. Median years education, 9.2.

1972 Share of Federal Outlays $364,196,060

DOD	$69,267,295	HEW	$136,196,965
AEC	–	HUD	$1,959,786
NASA	–	DOI	$525,449
DOT	$39,407,361	USDA	$54,096,215
		Other	$62,742,989

Federal Military-Industrial Commitments

DOD Installations England AFB (Alexandria).

Economic Base Agriculture, notably grains, cattle and dairy products; chemicals and allied products, especially industrial chemicals; finance, insurance and real estate; food and kindred products; and lubmer and wood products.

The Voters

Registration 233,231 total. 228,392 D (98%); 3,177 R (1%); 1,662 other (1%). White 164,873 (71%); black 68,358 (29%).
Median voting age 42.6
Employment profile White collar, 36%. Blue collar, 39%. Service, 17%. Farm, 8%.
Ethnic groups Black, 36%. Total foreign stock, 2%. French-speaking, 28%.

Presidential vote

1972	Nixon (R)	73,297	(63%)
	McGovern (D)	43,429	(37%)
1968	Nixon (R)	25,451	(18%)
	Humphrey (D)	46,398	(33%)
	Wallace (AI)	70,218	(49%)

Representative

Gillis William Long (D) Elected 1972; b. May 4, 1923, Winnfield; home, Alexandria; La. State U., B.A., 1949, J.D., 1951; Army, WWII; married, two children; Baptist.

Career Legal counsel, U.S. Senate Committee on Small Business, 1951; Chief Counsel, Sp. Com. on Campaign Expenditures; Ass't. Dir., U.S.O.E.O., 1965; lawyer, Long and Hamm, 1970–72; U.S. House, 1962–64.

Offices 215 CHOB, 202-225-4926. Also P.O. Box 410, Alexandria 71301, 318-487-4595.

Administrative Assistant Leah Schroeder

Committees

Rules (9th).

Group Ratings: Newly Elected

Key Votes

1) Busing	NE	6) Cmbodia Bmbg	AGN	11) Chkg Acct Intrst	AGN
2) Strip Mines	NE	7) Bust Hwy Trust	AGN	12) End HISC (HUAC)	AGN
3) Cut Mil $	NE	8) Farm Sub Lmt	NE	13) Nixon Sewer Veto	AGN
4) Rev Shrg	NE	9) School Prayr	NE	14) Corp Cmpaign $	NE
5) Pub TV $	NE	10) Cnsumr Prot	NE	15) Pol $ Disclosr	NE

Election Results

1972 general:	Gillis W. Long (D)	72,607	(69%)
	S. R. Abramson (AI)	17,844	(15%)
	Roy C. Strickland (R)	15,517	(17%)
1972 primary:	Gillis W. Long (D)	61,452	(54%)
	Armand J. Brinkhaus (D)	31,934	(28%)
	J. E. Jumonville (D)	13,995	(12%)
	Huey P. Coleman (D)	3,690	(3%)
	Phillip Pecouci (D)	2,287	(2%)

MAINE

Political Background

The slogan "As Maine goes, so goes the nation" was not intended to imply that Maine was a bellwether state; it never was. The origin of the political cliche stemmed rather from the state holding early general elections, which as recently as 1958 came in September, rather than November. Up north in Maine, it's already cold and snowing by November.

In 1958, however, Maine did accurately forecast the election of a Democratic President in 1960. The voters here unseated one of its Republican Senators and elected in his place the state's young Democratic Governor, Edmund Muskie, who garnered an astounding 61% of the vote. Muskie won the governorship in a 1954 upset, and then in 1956 was reelected with a solid 59%. During his four years as Governor, Muskie built the Maine Democratic party, an organization that has come to dominate the politics of the state. In 1958, when Muskie won a Senate seat, Maine voters chose another Democratic Governor and elected Democrats as Congressmen in two of the state's three House districts. Muskie was reelected to the Senate in 1964, winning an impressive 67%. And by 1966—a Republican year in most parts of the country—the political transformation of the state became nearly complete. Democrat Kenneth Curtis upset the Republican incumbent for the governorship. At the same time, Maine, after losing one of its congressional districts in the 1960 census, sent two Democrats to the House of Representatives. In 1972, the Democrats captured the state's other Senate seat, though the party lost a House seat to an aggressive young Republican.

How did the Democratic party take over Maine, a state known far and wide for its rock-ribbed Republicanism since the time of the Civil War? Principal factors included intelligent organization, attractive candidates, and the carelessness of Maine Republicans, who had enjoyed too much easy success. Muskie played a key role. His serene and plain manner, coupled with his clearly honest idealism, persuaded many Yankee Republicans that not all Democrats were big-city hacks, and that some like Muskie were decent men who could be trusted with government. During the 1950s, Maine was not the only state in the far northern reaches of the country where a popular leader and competent followers built a strong Democratic party within a state previously considered Republican. There was also the Minnesota of Hubert Humphrey, the Wisconsin of William Proxmire and Gaylord Nelson, the Michigan of G. Mennen Williams, and the South Dakota of George McGovern. During the 1960s and 1970s, a half-dozen presidential candidates emerged from these movements, evidence of their quality.

Democrats in Maine benefited from the state's changing demography. As young people left the economically depressed state, the proportion of its traditionally Democratic ethnic voters increased—particularly those of French-Canadian descent. Though a taciturn Yankee is the standard image of a Maine resident, one out of seven people here grew up speaking French. French-Canadian and other Catholic voters in mill towns like Lewiston, the state's secondlargest city, or in the potato country of Aroostook County, have produced lopsided margins for Democratic candidates. Muskie, for example, took 88% of Lewiston's ballots in 1970. These same ethnic voters were responsible for Richard Nixon's easy 1972 Maine triumph, after the solid Humphrey-Muskie win four years earlier. When compared to previous Democratic showings, McGovern totals dropped most dramatically in heavily Catholic, small mill and factory towns—the bedrock of Maine's Democratic majority.

Muskie became a presidential contender the moment Humphrey selected him as the 1968 Democratic vice-presidential nominee. Muskie's Yankee style, his willingness to allow political opponents to speak their piece, impressed voters all over the country. And had it been possible, the country would have probably elected him Vice-President, even while choosing Nixon President. Muskie's impressive performance on national television on the eve of the 1970 elections assured him the position of Democratic front-runner in 1972. During that performance, Muskie answered with typical calm determination Nixon's hysterical law-and-order harangues of the 1970 campaign.

But in the spring of 1972, Muskie's presidential campaign fell to pieces. There were too many advisers, too many prominent endorsements, and not enough first-choice votes. Muskie was probably the solid number-two choice of Democratic primary voters in states like Wisconsin, Pennsylvania, and Massachusetts. But because they could vote for just one candidate, few voted for Muskie.

From the evidence available at this writing, it appears that Muskie's campaign was systematically sabotaged by Nixon operatives. Like many Democrats, the Nixon people believed that Muskie would make the Democrats' strongest choice. No one can say what would have happened in New Hampshire and in the primaries that followed had there been no "Canuck" letter sent to the rabidly anti-Muskie Manchester *Union Leader*. A White House staff member apparently dirty-tricked Muskie, accusing him of using the epithet. Without the trick, the famous crying incident in the New Hampshire snow might never have occurred.

Even so, another weakness of the Senator's candidacy was evident. For some reason, Muskie did not possess the driving ambition usually necessary to win the presidency. Many leading Democrats persuaded him that he had the best chance to win, and therefore had a responsibility to run. But within Muskie himself, there was none of that steely ambition that kept George McGovern in the race when it looked hopeless. Nor did Muskie have what Hubert Humphrey had when the Minnesotan took the gloves off in California, just when it appeared that he had no chance.

Back in Washington and off the campaign trail, Muskie again is one of the Senate's most active members. After his first election, he was given a seat on the Public Works Committee—then regarded as a dreary assignment. But by plodding, little-publicized hard work, Muskie turned his seat on the Committee into an asset: he discovered the issue of the environment and labored over it long before it became fashionable. The Maine Senator is the major congressional force behind air- and water-pollution legislation. He is also an authority on the relationship between the federal government and state and local authorities.

The post-1968 Muskie broadened his interests. He got on the Foreign Relations Committee and there strongly backed end-the-war legislation, though before 1968 the Senator was a hawk. His roots in Maine, however, continue to influence his work on pollution measures. Maine typifies the environmental quandary. It is a poor state in desperate need of jobs; at the same time, it is a place of great natural beauty, which state-of-Mainers want preserved. Muskie has tried to reconcile both felt needs, as can be seen in both his major legislative efforts and in his attitude toward local issues. One such local issue is the controversy surrounding a proposed quota-free oil refinery in Machiasport. Though Nader's raiders have criticized some of the Senator's decisions, Muskie remains the leading anti-pollution authority in Congress and the environment's most capable advocate. With co-sponsor Howard Baker, Muskie led the successful drive in 1973 to open up the highway trust fund for spending on mass transit projects.

Muskie has also played forceful leadership roles in other issues. The Senator has been one of the chief opponents of the Nixon Administration's various notions of executive privilege, and he has also pushed for a rational system of classification—and declassification—of secret government documents. As a member of the Government Operations Committee, Muskie and North

Carolina's Sam Ervin co-sponsored a package of measures in 1973 that set a ceiling on the federal budget and also set limits on the President's authority to impound funds appropriated by Congress. From Muskie's work on these matters, it is clear that he is appalled by the attitudes shown by Nixon's operatives. There is some talk now that the Senator wants another crack at the White House; in this, he is little different from other who have been once around the track. If Muskie does try again, the betting is he will shun the tag of front-runner.

In 1972, Maine surprised most everybody when it ousted its veteran Senator, Margaret Chase Smith, and elected Democratic Congressman William Hathaway in her place. Mrs. Smith had been a fixture in the state's politics since 1939, when she succeeded her husband in the House; in 1948, she won an upset primary victory and went on to the Senate. In 1964, Mrs. Smith waged a hopeless, but still dignified, campaign for the Republican presidential nomination—the first such candidacy by a woman.

But by 1972, Margaret Chase Smith was vulnerable back in Maine. Though she had recovered from a hip operation, the lady was 74 years old. Moreover, she seldom traveled back to Maine, not even maintaining an office in the state. In Washington, the Senator usually refused to announce her position on important issues until her name was called in the roll. She also enjoyed a reputation for political independence, breaking ranks from other Republicans on the ABM, SST, Carswell, and Haynsworth. By and large, however, she supported the Nixon Administration, which moved labor and liberal groups to support Hathaway. No believer in elaborate campaigns, Mrs. Smith did little to respond. She would simply hold receptions where the voters could come and shake her hand if they wished. As always, she hired no campaign staff, bought no advertising, and even refused to appear in the state except on weekends.

The Smith approach to Maine politics had always been enough for easy victories in the past, and it was enough to produce a solid primary win over challenger Robert Monks. Monks is a wealthy businessman and newcomer to Maine who spent some $200,000 making his bid. The challenger forfeited much potential support by backing Nixon on Vietnam, just as Mrs. Smith did. In the primary, elderly Maine voters turned out in huge numbers to renominate their heroine.

But in the general election, Mrs. Smith's support from elderly WASPs was not nearly enough. Hathaway possessed a solid following of his own; in his 2nd congressional district, he had run ahead of Edmund Muskie in 1970. During the 1972 campaign, Hathaway visited every one of the state's 495 cities, towns, and plantations, and it paid off. Using the advantages of House incumbency, the challenger built a personal constituency in his 2nd district, which he carried 57–43 over Mrs. Smith. The two split the first district just about equally. The contest was one between a young, energetic Congressman and an aging incumbent Senator. Mrs. Smith appears to be a Yankee politician in the tradition of John Quincy Adams, who after his presidency accepted election to the House only upon the understanding that he would never deign to go out on the hustings to protect his seat. Adams kept his seat till he died, but that kind of politics is no longer successful, even in New England.

In the Senate, Hathaway emerged as one of the Democratic freshmen most fervently opposed to the Nixon Administration. He has voted against confirmation of Nixon appointees. By adroit maneuvering, the Senator pushed through an amendment to the basic wage-price legislation requiring corporations that raised prices by more than 1.5% a year to disclose cost and profit information. No doubt more will be heard from this talented freshman in the years to come.

But as Hathaway captured a Senate seat for the Democrats, the party lost his old House seat to William S. Cohen, a young Republican. Democratic state Sen. Elmer Violette was the favorite over Cohen, the 32-year-old Mayor of Bangor, in the 2nd district contest. This district is marginally more Democratic than the 1st, largely because of its high percentage of French-Canadian voters. Cohen campaigned hard along the southern edge of this heavily forested, paper-mill-dominated district; his moderate Republicanism made sufficient inroads among normally Democratic areas to win.

The state's 1st district includes Portland and Augusta, the beaches near the New Hampshire border, and the rocky coast between Portland and Mount Desert Island. It rests securely in the hands of Democratic Congressman Peter Kyros. First elected in 1966, when liberal Republican Stanley Tupper retired, Kyros has since won routine reelection with slowly increasing margins.

Like all the members of Maine's congressional delegation, Kyros has felt aggrieved at several decisions made by the federal government that have done nothing for the state's stagnant economy. The Department of Defense, for example, selected Litton Industries' new shipyard in Pascagoula, Mississippi, to build some destroyers costing billions; in so doing, it passed over Maine's more experienced Bath Iron Works. With some asperity, state-of-Mainers have noted that Litton has performed very badly, and that Litton's former president, Roy Ash, is now head of Nixon's Office of Management and Budget. There is the perpetual fight for the Lincoln-Dickey power project, which, like the Machiasport refinery, would serve to reduce power rates in New England—highest in the nation. So because the Nixon Administration has favored the interests of the Sun Belt at the expense of Maine, it is no surprise that the state has become politically hospitable to Democrats and anti-Nixon Republicans.

Census Data Pop. 993,663; 0.49% of U.S. total, 38th largest; change 1960–70, 2.5%. Central city, 13%; suburban, 8%. Median family income, $8,205; 36th highest; families above $15,000: 11%; families below $3,000: 10%. Median years education, 12.1.

1972 Share of Federal Tax Burden $815,170,000; 0.39% of U.S. total, 39th largest.

1972 Share of Federal Outlays $847,064,762; 0.39% of U.S. total, 44th largest. Per capita federal spending, $852.

DOD	$148,351,000	44th (0.24%)	HEW	$370,993,746	36th (0.52%)
AEC	$114,092	39th (—)	HUD	$12,130,975	40th (0.40%)
NASA	—	— (—)	VA	$68,793,681	37th (0.60%)
DOT	$39,508,895	47th (0.50%)	USDA	$34,534,457	44th (0.22%)
DOC	$37,661,254	7th (2.91%)	CSC	$22,062,539	38th (0.54%)
DOI	$4,443,067	45th (0.21%)	TD	$37,015,786	38th (0.22%)
DOJ	$5,963,763	36th (0.61%)	Other	$65,491,507	

Economic Base Leather footwear, and other leather and leather products; paper and allied products, especially paper mills other than building paper; agriculture, notably potatoes, eggs, broilers and dairy products; finance, insurance and real estate; food and kindred products; lumber and wood products.

Political Line-up Governor, Kenneth M. Curtis (D); seat up, 1974. Senators, Edmund S. Muskie (D) and William D. Hathaway (D). Representatives, 2 (1 D and 1 R). State Senate (22 R and 11 D); State House (79 R, 71 D, and 1 vac.).

The Voters

Registration 576,915 Total. 190,831 D (33%); 239,534 R (42%); 146,550 other (25%).
Median voting age 44.6
Employment profile White collar, 41%. Blue collar, 44%. Service, 12%. Farm, 3%.
Ethnic groups Total foreign stock, 19%. Canada, 14%.

Presidential vote

1972	Nixon (R)	256,458	(61%)
	McGovern (D)	160,584	(39%)
1968	Nixon (R)	169,254	(43%)
	Humphrey (D)	217,312	(55%)
	Wallace (AI)	6,370	(2%)
1964	Johnson (D)	262,264	(69%)
	Goldwater (R)	118,701	(31%)

Senator

Edmund S. Muskie (D) Elected 1958, seat up 1976; b. March 28, 1914, Rumford; home, Waterville; Bates Col., B.A., 1936; Cornell U., LL.B., 1939; USNR, WWII; married, five children; Catholic.

Career Practicing atty., Waterville; Maine House of Reps., 1947–51; Floor Leader, 1949–51; Gov. of Maine, 1955–59; Dem. V.P. candidate, 1968.

Offices 115 OSOB, 202-225-5344. Also 112 Main St., Waterville 04901, 207-873-3361.

Administrative Assistant Maynard J. Toll, Jr.

Committees

Foreign Relations (8th); Subs: Arms Control, International Law and Organization (Chm.); Oceans and International Environment; Western Hemisphere Affairs; Multinational Corporations.

Government Operations (4th); Subs: Intergovernmental Relations (Chm.); Budgeting, Management, and Expenditures.

Public Works (2nd); Subs: Consumer Interests of the Elderly; Health of the Elderly (Chm.); Housing for the Elderly; Long-term Care.

Group Ratings

	ADA	COPE	LWV	RIPON	NFU	LCV	CFA	NAB	NSI	ACA
1972	70	86	100	64	80	85	100	0	11	0
1971	85	83	100	58	100	–	100	–	–	7
1970	91	100	–	71	100	73	–	18	10	10

Key Votes

1) Busing	ABS	8) Sea Life Prot	FOR	15) Tax Singls Less	ABS
2) Alas P-line	AGN	9) Campaign Subs	FOR	16) Min Tax for Rich	ABS
3) Gun Cntrl	FOR	10) Cmbodia Bmbg	ABS	17) Euro Troop Rdctn	ABS
4) Rehnquist	AGN	11) Legal Srvices	ABS	18) Bust Hwy Trust	FOR
5) Pub TV $	ABS	12) Rev Sharing	FOR	19) Maid Min Wage	FOR
6) EZ Votr Reg	ABS	13) Cnsumr Prot	ABS	20) Farm Sub Limit	ABS
7) No-Fault	FOR	14) Eq Rts Amend	FOR	21) Highr Credt Chgs	ABS

Election Results

1970 general:	Edmund S. Muskie (D)	199,954	(62%)
	Neil S. Bishop (R)	123,906	(38%)
1970 primary:	Edmund S. Muskie (D), unopposed		
1964 general:	Edmund S. Muskie (D)	253,511	(67%)
	Clifford G. McIntire (R)	127,040	(33%)

Senator

William Dodd Hathaway (D) Elected 1972; seat up 1978; b. Feb. 21, 1924, Cambridge, Mass.; home, Auburn; Harvard U., B.A., LL.B., 1953; Air Force Capt., 1942–46; married, two children; Episcopalian.

Career Practicing atty., 1953–64; Asst. Atty., Androscoggin County, 1955–75; Hearing examiner, State Liquor Comm., 1957–61; U.S. House of Reps., 1964–72.

Offices 248 OSOB, 202-225-2523. Also 235 New Fed. Office Bldg., Bangor 04401, 207-942-8271 ext. 310.

Administrative Assistant Albert P. Gamache

Committees

Banking, Housing and Urban Affairs (8th); Subs: Consumer Credit; International Finance; Production and Stabilization.

Labor and Public Welfare (10th); Subs: Labor; Handicapped; Education; Employment, Poverty, and Migratory Labor; Children and Youth; Railroad Retirement (Chm.).

Sel. Com. on Small Business (7th); Subs: Financing and Investment; Government Procurement (Chm.); Monopoly.

Group Ratings

	ADA	COPE	LWV	RIPON	NFU	LCV	CFA	NAB	NSI	ACA
1972	81	100	90	69	86	67	50	8	0	4
1971	89	83	88	76	100	–	100	–	–	4
1970	88	100	–	65	92	88	100	0	22	0

Key Votes

1) Busing	FOR	8) Sea Life Prot	MOS	15) Tax Singls Less	MOS
2) Alas P-line	ABS	9) Campaign Subs	MOS	16) Min Tax for Rich	MOS
3) Gun Cntrl	FOR	10) Cmbodia Bmbg	AGN	17) Euro Troop Rdctn	MOS
4) Rehnquist	FOR	11) Legal Srvices	AGN	18) Bust Hwy Trust	AGN
5) Pub TV $	FOR	12) Rev Sharing	FOR	19) Maid Min Wage	AGN

Election Results

1972 general:	William D. Hathaway (D)	224,270	(53%)
	Margaret Chase Smith (R)	197,040	(47%)
1972 primary:	William D. Hathaway (D)	61,921	(91%)
	Jack Louis Smith (D)	6,263	(9%)

FIRST DISTRICT

Census Data Pop. 495,681. Central city, 13%; suburban, 15%. Median family income, $8,688; families above $15,000: 13%; families below $3,000: 9%. Median years education, 12.2.

1972 Share of Federal Outlays $460,389,782

DOD	$68,263,000	HEW	$191,322,008
AEC	–	HUD	$7,723,245
NASA	–	DOI	$1,228,966
DOT	$29,015,799	USDA	$11,356,035
		Other	$151,480,729

Federal Military-Industrial Commitments

DOD Contractors Bath Industries (Bath), $12.240m: engineering services and communication equipment. Sanders Associates (South Portland), $10.501m: sonobuoys. Maremont Corp. (Saco), $10.399m: 7.63mm machine guns.

DOD Installations Naval Air Station (Burnswick). Buck Harbor AF Station (Bucks Harbor).

Economic Base Shoes, except rubber, and other leather and leather products; finance, insurance and real estate; agriculture, notably poultry, dairy products and fruits; food and kindred products, especially canned, cured and frozen foods, and meat products; textile mill products; and paper and allied products, especially miscellaneous converted paper products. Also higher education (Univ. of Maine).

The Voters

Registration 298,834 total. 88,902 D (30%); 127,796 R (43%); 82,136 other (27%)
Median voting age 45.2
Employment profile White collar, 44%. Blue collar, 42%. Service, 12%. Farm, 2%.
Ethnic groups Total foreign stock, 18%. Canada, 11%.

Presidential vote

1972	Nixon (R)	135,388	(61%)
	McGovern (D)	85,028	(39%)
1968	Nixon (R)	88,406	(43%)
	Humphrey (D)	112,843	(55%)
	Wallace (AI)	3,390	(2%)

Representative

Peter N. Kyros (D) Elected 1966; b. July 11, 1925, Portland; home, Portland; M.I.T., 1943–44; U.S. Naval Academy, B.S., 1947; Harvard Law School, L.L.B., 1957; Navy, 1944–53; married, two children; Greek Orthodox.

Career Practicing atty., 1957–66; Counsel, Maine Pub. Utilities Commission, 1957–59.

Offices 228 CHOB, 202-225-6116. Also 151 Forest Ave., Portland 04104, 207-775-3131, ext. 561.

Administrative Assistant Alyce D. Canaday

Committees

Interstate and Foreign Commerce (14th); Sub: Public Health and Environment.

Merchant Marine and Fisheries (14th); Subs: Fisheries and Wildlife Conservation and the Environment; Oceanography; Merchant Marine.

Group Ratings

	ADA	COPE	LWV	RIPON	NFU	LCV	CFA	NAB	NSI	ACA
1972	63	89	91	69	86	80	100	10	0	7
1971	86	83	89	72	93	–	88	–	–	7
1970	72	100	–	65	92	100	100	0	78	26

Key Votes

1) Busing	FOR	6) Cmbodia Bmbg	AGN	11) Chkg Acct Intrst	FOR
2) Strip Mines	AGN	7) Bust Hwy Trust	FOR	12) End HISC (HUAC)	FOR
3) Cut Mil $	FOR	8) Farm Sub Lmt	FOR	13) Nixon Sewer Veto	AGN
4) Rev Shrg	FOR	9) School Prayr	AGN	14) Corp Cmpaign $	FOR
5) Pub TV $	ABS	10) Cnsumr Prot	FOR	15) Pol $ Disclosr	AGN

Election Results

1972 general:	Peter N. Kyros (D)	129,408	(59%)
	L. Robert Porteous, Jr. (R)	88,588	(41%)
1972 primary:	Peter N. Kyros (D)	23,357	(67%)
	Everett B. Carson (D)	11,711	(33%)
1970 general:	Peter N. Kyros (D)	99,483	(59%)
	Ronald T. Speers (R)	68,671	(41%)

SECOND DISTRICT

Census Data Pop. 497,982. Central city, 13%; suburban, 1%. Median family income, $7,733; families above $15,000: 9%; families below $3,000: 11%. Median years education, 12.0.

1972 Share of Federal Outlays $386,674,980

DOD	$80,088,000	HEW	$179,671,738
AEC	$114,092	HUD	$4,407,730
NASA	–	DOI	$3,214,101
DOT	$10,493,096	USDA	$23,178,422
		Other	$85,507,801

Federal Military-Industrial Commitments

DOD Installations Naval Radio Station, Cutler (East Machias). Naval Security Group Activity (Winter Harbor). Caswell AF Station (Caswell). Charlestown AF Station (Charleston). Loring AFB (Limestone).

Economic Base Shoes, except rubber, and other leather and leather products; lumber and wood products; agriculture, notably poultry, dairy products and potatoes; paper mill products, except building paper, and other paper and allied products; and finance, insurance and real estate.

The Voters

Registration 278,081 total. 101,929 D (37%); 111,738 R (40%); 64,424 other (23%).
Median voting age 43.9
Employment profile White collar, 37%. Blue collar, 47%. Service, 12%. Farm, 4%.
Ethnic groups Total foreign stock, 20%. Canada, 16%.

Presidential vote

1972	Nixon (R)	121,120	(62%)
	McGovern (D)	75,556	(38%)
1968	Nixon (R)	80,848	(43%)
	Humphrey (D)	104,469	(55%)
	Wallace (AI)	2,980	(2%)

Representative

William S. Cohen (R) Elected 1972; b. Aug. 28, 1940, Bangor; home, Bangor; Bowdoin College, B.A., 1962; Boston U. Law School, LL.B., 1965; married, two children; Unitarian.

Career Asst. editor-chief, Journal of Amer. Trial Lawyers Assn., 1965–66; Law partner, Paine, Cohen, Lynch, Weatherbee and Kobritz, since 1965; instructor, U. of Me.; County Atty., Penobscot, 1968–70; V.P., Maine Trial Lawyers Assn., 1970–72; School Bd., 1971–72, Bd. of Zoning Appeals, City Council, 1969–72, Mayor, 1971–72, Bangor.

Offices 1223 LHOB, 202-225-6306.

Administrative Assistant Michael Harkins

Committees

Judiciary (13th); Subs: No. 3 (Patents, Trademarks, Copyrights); No. 6 (Revision of the Laws).

Merchant Marine and Fisheries (11th); Subs: Fisheries and Wildlife Conservation and the Environment; Merchant Marine; Oceanography.

Group Ratings: Newly Elected

Key Votes

1) Busing	NE	6) Cmbodia Bmbg	AGN	11) Chkg Acct Intrst	FOR
2) Strip Mines	NE	7) Bust Hwy Trust	AGN	12) End HISC (HUAC)	FOR
3) Cut Mil $	NE	8) Farm Sub Lmt	NE	13) Nixon Sewer Veto	AGN
4) Rev Shrg	NE	9) School Prayr	NE	14) Corp Cmpaign $	NE
5) Pub TV $	NE	10) Cnsumr Prot	NE	15) Pol $ Disclosr	NE

Election Results

1972 general:	William S. Cohen (R)	106,280	(54%)
	Elmer H. Violette (D)	89,135	(46%)
1972 primary:	William S. Cohen (R)	28,955	(61%)
	Abbott O. Greene (R)	18,463	(39%)

MARYLAND

Political Background

Maryland is one of the most diverse states. Its attenuated shape reflects this; although only eight other states are smaller in area, you must drive 350 miles entirely within the state to get from one end of it to the other. In that distance you will move from the south-of-the-Mason-Dixon-Line Eastern Shore, through the booming suburbs of Washington and Baltimore, past the industrial and multiethnic city of Baltimore, and up into the Appalachian Mountains. In the last few presidential elections, Maryland's demographic mix has made it the best statistical mirror of the nation's total voting patterns. The nuts and bolts of Maryland politics, however, are anything but typical.

The Maryland-Pennsylvania border constituted the original Mason-Dixon line. And up through World War II, conservative Democratic and Dixie-oriented rural Maryland, where one still finds an indigenous Southern accent, dominated the state's politics. Its only competition came from the old-fashioned machine in Baltimore. Today, Baltimore—now almost half black but still controlled by remnants of the old machine—casts less than 20% of Maryland's votes. The rural areas cast only another 20%. The remaining 60% of the voters are to be found split about equally between suburban Baltimore and suburban Washington, D.C.

Just 40 miles apart, the two metropolitan areas could hardly be more different. A major port, Baltimore has big shipbuilding concerns and huge steel mills. The heavy industries attracted the kind of ethnic migration common to the cities of the East Coast, as well as a large black migration from the South. Of late, metropolitan Baltimore's growth has been rather sluggish; its politics—traditionally Democratic as seen in registration figures—has swung heavily to the Republicans, at least in presidential and senatorial contests.

Washington, of course, is a one-company town—the federal government, probably the nation's most impressive growth industry today. Accordingly, metropolitan Washington is booming. Of all the major urban agglomerations over one million in the country, only Houston has exceeded Washington's rate of growth during the 1960s. And most of the growth took place in the Maryland suburbs, where high-rise office buildings and apartment complexes stand in what was pasture land a few short years ago. So great is the boom here that the cost of homes in suburban Montgomery County, which enjoys the nation's highest family income, currently is rising at the rate of 20% annually.

The Maryland suburbs of Washington have none of the ethnic-industrial history of metropolitan Baltimore, nor have they been part of the conservative Republican trend found in other major urban areas along the East Coast. Montgomery County is especially liberal in its politics. Its favorite kind of candidate is a maverick Republican like Charles Mathias. With no such name appearing on the ballot, the county will usually go solidly Democratic. Prince Georges, the other Washington suburban county, is more blue-collar and more likely to give a large percentage of its votes to candidates like George Wallace. In 1972 and 1973, Prince Georges has experienced a lively controversy over busing. But the county has also taken a large influx of middle-class blacks from Washington; the black population rose here from 31,000 in 1960 (9%) to 92,000 in 1970 (14%). And since 1970, the influx has proceeded at an even faster rate. As a result, the percentage of black voters in Maryland is probably rising more rapidly than in any other state in the country.

Six years ago, Maryland had two Democratic Senators; now it has two Republicans. The man most responsible for the switch is not Maryland's best-known politician, Spiro Agnew, but the man who made Agnew's political career possible. He is George Mahoney, a 70-year-old contractor who has run for Governor and Senator eight times and never won a general election. During the 1950s, Mahoney's independent candidacies helped to produce victories for Republican Senators J. Glenn Beall, Sr. (1952) and John Marshall Butler (1956). In 1966, Mahoney decided to run for Governor in the Democratic primary on the slogan "Your home is your castle"—a message designed to convey the candidate's opposition to open-housing legislation. Mahoney squeaked out a win over liberal Congressman-at-Large Carlton Sickles. In the general election that followed, blacks and liberals deserted Mahoney in droves, as they supported the unknown Republican nominee, Baltimore County Executive Spiro Agnew. If Sickles had gotten just 1,940 more votes in the primary, Agnew would almost certainly have remained a prosperous lawyer in suburban Baltimore, expounding his curious political theories around the country-club swimming pool. Today, Agnew keeps fancier company on the Palm Springs golf links, and his alliterative rhetoric has become a national staple; a few hundred votes can make a lot of difference in American politics. But just as this book is written, a new and even more amazing phase of Agnew's public life has begun. In August 1973, it was revealed that the Vice-President was under federal investigation in Baltimore on bribery and extortion charges, for allegedly taking kickbacks while Baltimore County Executive, Governor, and Vice-President. At this writing, it appears entirely possible that an indictment will be handed down. Just what will happen, no one can say. The possibilities range from total vindication and a successful run for the White House in 1976, to total disgrace, impeachment, and a jail term. With all that at stake, Agnew has handled questions with the cool aplomb that is perhaps his greatest asset in public life.

Mahoney also played a part in the 1968 and 1970 Senate races. In 1968, he ran as an independent and took 13% of the votes, enough to allow Rep. Charles Mathias to win easily with 48%. Mathias, a liberal Republican, beat his old law school roommate, Sen. Daniel Brewster, a horsey-set millionaire, who a few years earlier appeared to have a safe seat. But Brewster's political vulnerability became glaringly evident when in the 1964 presidential primary he ran as an LBJ stand-in against George Wallace. During the next few years, his problem with alcohol spun completely out of control; in 1972, the ex-Senator was convicted on federal bribery charges.

During his first term, Mathias became one of the Senate's most respected men. In 1968, he campaigned as something of a dove on Vietnam (Brewster supported LBJ down the line), and since then the Senator has opposed many of the policies of the Nixon Administration. Mathias' special interest is the political process: he has introduced a bill for public financing of presidential campaigns; another to require the executive branch to provide Congress with more information and data; and a third to end the vast state-of-emergency powers still available to Presidents under Harry Truman's Korean War proclamation of 1950. In the spring of 1972, just as Watergate broke, Mathias delivered a major speech in which he argued that no public official should subordinate loyalty to the Constitution to an allegiance to a particular political officeholder. In the Senate Judiciary Committee, Mathias cast the vote that denied acting FBI Director L. Patrick Gray a permanent job. The Senator's decision has come to look like a good one. According to many sources, Gray apparently destroyed some of E. Howard Hunt's files and in other ways helped to obstruct the Watergate investigation.

Mathias has never been in high favor at the Nixon White House. For a while, some observers felt that he was to be singled out for political extinction in the same manner New York's Charles Goodell was in 1970. But Watergate ended all such speculation. Besides, Mathias has kept his local political fences in good order. The Senator has not supported the anti-busing outcries in Prince Georges County, managing at the same time to avoid unduly irritating Maryland busing foes. And though he is a strong proponent of home rule for the District of Columbia, Mathias, as the ranking Republican on the District Committee, has insisted that Congress prohibit the new D.C. government from taxing commuters who live in the suburbs. So when the politician Mathias had a big fundraiser in May of 1973, Barry Goldwater and Charles Percy were both there, and Spiro Agnew sent warm greetings. In 1974, the Maryland Senator's likely opponent is state House of Delegates Speaker, Thomas Hunter Lowe, a conservative Democrat from the Eastern Shore. If the busing issue stays hot, Lowe might do well in Prince Georges; otherwise Mathias should win easily.

George Mahoney played another important role in the Senate race of 1970. This time he ran in the Democratic primary against incumbent Sen. Joseph Tydings. Tydings was in trouble with the right for his support of gun-control legislation and with the left for his support of the no-knock District of Columbia crime bill. Other, less ideological Maryland voters found him cold and aloof. The kind of people who would vote in a Republican primary in other places participate in Maryland's Democratic primary. Some 71% of the voters are registered Democrats, a vestige of the state's Southern tradition. Given such circumstances, Mahoney held Tydings down to 53% of the primary vote.

In the general election, Tydings' trouble was so bad that his opponent, Rep. J. Glenn Beall, Jr., son of the man Tydings beat easily six years before, ran a quiet, relaxed campaign. The gun lobby took aim at Tydings, pouring in money and thousands of brochures. But the White House delivered the coup de grace. Nixon aide Charles Colson, whose role in the Watergate is unclear at this writing, had charges leaked to *Life* magazine that Tydings used his influence to benefit a Florida company in which he was a large stockholder. Beall won the election by a 24,000-vote, 51–48 margin. A week after the election, John Mitchell's Justice Department cleared Tydings of any conflict of interest.

In Washington, Beall has been a much quieter Senator than his colleague Mathias, and also more amenable to the wishes of the Nixon Administration. This is no surprise, considering how Beall won his seat. When he comes up for reelection in 1976, many Democrats will probably want a serious crack at him.

When Spiro Agnew resigned the governorship to become Vice-President, Marvin Mandel was Speaker of the Maryland House of Delegates. As a Jewish representative of a small portion of Baltimore, Mandel could hardly have hoped to win the governorship in a general election. But under the antiquated Maryland Constitution as it then stood, Agnew's successor was chosen by the legislature—where Mandel's influence and adroitness proved decisive. To some outsiders, Mandel looked vulnerable in 1970. Sargent Shriver, recently returned from a stint as Ambassador to France, made plans for a campaign that year. But Mandel amassed a bulging campaign chest, put on a big advertising campaign, and literally bluffed Shriver out of the race. Mandel's undoubted competence as Governor, coupled with his ability to placate the state's diverse voting blocs on various issues, produced an easy 65–35 general election victory over C. Stanley Blair, a protégé of the Vice-President.

As 1973 opened, Mandel seemed in even better shape for 1974. He had already raised $1 million for his 1974 campaign, preempting virtually all the big financial support in the state. Then, over the Fourth of July weekend, Mandel announced that he wanted to divorce his wife and marry a younger Catholic divorcee. But Mrs. Mandel did not go along with the game plan. She announced her adamant determination to keep both her husband and her address in the Governor's mansion; at this writing, she is living in the Mansion in Annapolis and the Governor is staying at a hotel. As interest in this imbroglio soared, the Governor's political fortunes sagged, and two Republican Congressmen, Gilbert Gude and Lawrence Hogan, hinted at their availability for the 1974 Republican nomination—an honor that would have gone begging a few months before. Meanwhile, Maryland's Republican party was split by Watergate-related charges—its Chairman borrowed $50,000 from Maurice Stans and the Committee to Reelect the President to make a Salute-to-Agnew fundraiser look like a roaring success. Maryland Republicans were presumably not helped either by the Agnew developments or the suicide earlier in the year of 1st-district Congressman William Mills. Maryland politics promises to be anything but boring in 1974; as one Hill aide said, "it's all so sordid that the voters may just decide to vote against all incumbents."

Census Data Pop. 3,922,399; 1.94% of U.S. total, 18th largest; change 1960–70, 26.5%. Central city, 23%; suburban, 61%. Median family income, $11,057; 5th highest; families above $15,000: 29%; families below $3,000: 7%. Median years education, 12.1.

1972 Share of Federal Tax Burden $4,640,210,000; 2.22% of U.S. total, 12th largest.

1972 Share of Federal Outlays $5,490,049,336; 2.53% of U.S. total, 13th largest. Per capita federal spending, $1,400.

DOD	$1,846,438,000	11th (2.95%)	HEW	$1,785,643,962	11th	(2.50%)
AEC	$93,139,160	13th (3.55%)	HUD	$60,775,165	20th	(1.98%)
NASA	$275,281,253	3rd (9.20%)	VA	$178,942,288	24th	(1.56%)
DOT	$161,436,480	19th (2.05%)	USDA	$151,760,878	35th	(0.99%)
DOC	$293,495,900	1st (22.67%)	CSC	$244,439,408	5th	(5.93%)
DOI	$24,705,409	22nd (1.16%)	TD	$91,693,865	27th	(0.56%)
DOJ	$17,564,999	17th (1.79%)	Other	$264,732,569		

Economic Base Finance, insurance and real estate; primary metal industries, especially blast furnaces and steel mills; food and kindred products, agriculture, notably dairy products, broilers, cattle and corn; electrical equipment and supplies, especially communication equipment; transportation equipment, especially motor vehicles and equipment and ship building and repairing; apparel and other textile products.

Political Line-up Governor, Marvin Mandel (D); seat up, 1974. Senators, Charles McC. Mathias, Jr. (R) and J. Glenn Beall, Jr. (R). Representatives, 8 (4 D and 4 R). State Senate (33 D and 10 R); House of Delegates (121 D and 21 R).

The Voters

Registration 1,815,784 Total. 1,260,477 D (69%); 483,623 R (27%); 71,684 other (4%).
Median voting age 41.2
Employment profile White collar, 56%. Blue collar, 31%. Service, 12%. Farm, 1%.
Ethnic groups Black, 18%. Spanish, 1%. Total foreign stock, 12%, Germany, 2%, Italy, USSR, UK, Poland, 1% each.

Presidential vote

1972	Nixon (R)	829,305	(62%)
	McGovern (D)	505,781	(38%)
1968	Nixon (R)	517,995	(42%)
	Humphrey (D)	538,310	(43%)
	Wallace (AI)	178,734	(15%)
1964	Johnson (D)	730,912	(66%)
	Goldwater (R)	385,495	(34%)

Senator

Charles McC. Mathias, Jr. (R) Elected 1968, seat up 1974; b. July 24, 1922, Frederick; home, Frederick; Haverford College, B.A., 1944; Yale, 1943–44; U. of Md., LL.B., 1949; USNR, WWII; married, two children; Episcopalian.

Career Asst. Atty. Gen., 1953–54; City Atty., Frederick, 1954–59; Md. House of Delegates, 1958–60; U.S. House of Reps., 1961–69.

Offices 460 OSOB, 202-225-4654. Also Fed. Office Bldg., Baltimore 21201, 301-962-4850, and P.O. Bldg., Hagerstown 21740,301-733-2710.

Administrative Assistant Samuel Goldberg

Committees

Appropriations (9th); Subs: District of Columbia (Ranking Mbr.); Foreign Operations; Housing and Urban Development, Space, Science and Veterans (Ranking Mbr.); Military Construction; Transportation.

District of Columbia (Ranking Mbr.); Sub: Health, Education, Welfare, and Safety.

Judiciary (6th); Subs: Administrative Practice and Procedure; Juvenile Delinquency; Penitentiaries; Refugees and Escapees; Separation of Powers (Ranking Mbr.).

Sp. Com. on the Termination of the National Emergency (Co-Chm.).

Group Ratings

	ADA	COPE	LWV	RIPON	NFU	LCV	CFA	NAB	NSI	ACA
1972	60	80	100	87	67	57	82	60	38	32
1971	63	58	100	79	60	–	60	–	–	21
1970	78	83	–	87	69	0	–	33	0	15

Key Votes

1) Busing	FOR	8) Sea Life Prot	FOR	15) Tax Singls Less	AGN
2) Alas P-line	AGN	9) Campaign Subs	FOR	16) Min Tax for Rich	AGN
3) Gun Cntrl	FOR	10) Cmbodia Bmbg	AGN	17) Euro Troop Rdctn	AGN
4) Rehnquist	FOR	11) Legal Srvices	FOR	18) Bust Hwy Trust	FOR
5) Pub TV $	FOR	12) Rev Sharing	FOR	19) Maid Min Wage	FOR
6) EZ Votr Reg	FOR	13) Cnsumr Prot	FOR	20) Farm Sub Limit	FOR
7) No-Fault	AGN	14) Eq Rts Amend	FOR	21) Highr Credt Chgs	AGN

Election Results

1968 general:	Charles McC. Mathias, Jr. (R)	541,893	(48%)
	Daniel B. Brewster (D)	443,667	(39%)
	George P. Mahoney (Ind.)	148,467	(13%)
1968 primary:	Charles McC. Mathias, Jr. (R)	66,777	(80%)
	Frederick Harry Lee Simms (R)	11,927	(14%)
	Paul Wattay (R)	4,790	(6%)

Senator

J. Glenn Beall, Jr. (R) Elected 1970; b. June 19, 1927, Cumberland; home, Frostburg; Yale U., A.B., 1950; USN 1945–46; married, one child; Episcopalian.

Career Partner, Beall, Garner and Geare, Inc., Insurance, 1952; Md. House, of Delegates, 1962–68; U.S. House, 1968–70.

Offices 362 OSOB, 202-225-4524. Also 1518 Fed. Bldg., Baltimore 21201, 301-962-3920, and P.O. Bldg., Cumberland 21502, 301-722-4535.

Administrative Assistant David J. Markey

Committees

Commerce (7th); Subs: Aviation; Consumer; Merchant Marine; Surface Transportation; Oceans and Atmosphere; Communications.

Labor and Public Welfare (5th); Subs: Education; Health; Children and Youth; Aging (Ranking Mbr.); Railroad Retirement; Handicapped; Employment, Poverty, and Migratory Labor; Alcoholism and Narcotics; Sp. Sub. on Human Resources (Ranking Mbr.).

Sp. Com. on Aging (8th); Subs: Housing for the Elderly; Employment and Retirement Incomes; Federal, State and Community Services (Ranking Mbr.); Long-Term Care; Retirement and the Individual.

Sel. Com. on Small Business (5th); Subs: Government Regulation; Monopoly (Ranking Mbr.); Retailing, Distribution, and Marketing Practices.

Group Ratings

	ADA	COPE	LWV	RIPON	NFU	LCV	CFA	NAB	NSI	ACA
1972	20	50	73	58	50	20	36	58	100	65
1971	22	25	92	71	36	–	17	–	–	57

Key Votes

1) Busing	AGN		8) Sea Life Prot	FOR		15) Tax Singls Less	AGN
2) Alas P-line	FOR		9) Campaign Subs	AGN		16) Min Tax for Rich	AGN
3) Gun Cntrl	FOR		10) Cmbodia Bmbg	FOR		17) Euro Troop Rdctn	AGN
4) Rehnquist	FOR		11) Legal Srvices	AGN		18) Bust Hwy Trust	FOR
5) Pub TV $	AGN		12) Rev Sharing	FOR		19) Maid Min Wage	AGN
6) EZ Votr Reg	AGN		13) Cnsumr Prot	AGN		20) Farm Sub Limit	FOR
7) No-Fault	FOR		14) Eq Rts Amend	FOR		21) Highr Credt Chgs	FOR

Election Results

1970 general:	J. Glenn Beall, Jr. (R)	484,960	(51%)
	Joseph D. Tydings (D)	460,422	(48%)
	Harvey Wilder (AI)	10,988	(1%)
1970 primary:	J. Glenn Beall, Jr. (R)	99,687	(83%)
	Wainwright Dawson, Jr. (R)	9,786	(8%)
	Frederick Harry Lee Simms (R)	9,927	(8%)

FIRST DISTRICT Political Background

Until the completion of the Bay Bridge in 1952, the Eastern Shore of Maryland was virtually cut off from access to the outside world. "Eastern" means the east side of Chesapeake Bay; it is a part of Maryland that remains almost a world unto itself—a region of Southern drowsiness, chicken farms, and crab fishermen. Before the Civil War, the Eastern Shore was very much slaveholding territory. Up through the 1960s, its attachment to the mores of the South persisted; the town of Cambridge here reacted to civil rights activity just as if it lay in the nation's Deep South. Mostly rural, the economy of the region is buoyed by the dollars spent by tourists and summer people.

The Eastern Shore still bulks large in Maryland politics. It has produced the current Speaker of the House of Delegates and ex-Gov. (1959–67) Millard Tawes. But because its population has not been growing significantly, the Eastern Shore has become increasingly less important psephologically. The 1st congressional district is by reputation an Eastern Shore district; however, only 53% of its residents live east of Chesapeake Bay. The rest can be found in two separate enclaves. The first is Harford County, a northern extension of the Baltimore metropolitan area; and the second is Charles, St. Mary's, and Culvert counties, south of Annapolis and the suburbs of Washington, D.C. Here in these three counties, new residents moving into neat subdivisions and sparkling new apartment complexes have changed an ages-old way of life.

The Eastern Shore and the two enclaves of the 1st share the same basic political inclinations: high Democratic registration (68%) and high conservative voting habits (63% for Wallace in the 1972 primary and 72% for Nixon in the general election). Some 19% of the district's people are black. But as in the congressional districts of the rural South, black voters have little political leverage in either primaries or general elections of the 1st. White opinion is arrayed with near unanimity against them.

Through a variety of circumstances, the 1st district has had four congressional elections in the last four years—more than any other district in the country. Rogers C. B. Morton, who won the seat in 1962 from an indicted Democratic incumbent, resigned after the 1970 election to become Secretary of the Interior. Morton had once served as Republican National Chairman; he is also the brother of ex-Sen. (1957–69) Thruston Morton of Kentucky. An imposing 6′7″ aristocrat, Congressman Morton won reelection easily and managed to pass the seat on to his administrative assistant, William O. Mills, a native Eastern Shoreman. But in the special 1971 election Mills won, Morton arranged a $25,000 loan for him from the Committee to Reelect the President. The loan was apparently never reported as required by Maryland law. When the story appeared in the press, just as the Watergate scandal broke in the spring of 1973, Mills committed suicide.

The August 1973 special election to succeed Mills shaped up as a contest between two conservative state Senators, Republican Robert Bauman and Democrat Frederick Malkus. Their main difference was not so much policy as age. The 60-year-old Malkus argued that "experience counts"; the hard campaigning of the 35-year-old Bauman was clear evidence of his vitality. The winner, by a narrow margin, was Bauman. The contest was cracked up as something of an Administration victory. Vice-President Agnew had appeared on Bauman's behalf the Sunday before the election and had received a warm Eastern Shore reception. And of course the commentators liked to compare the high Democratic registration percentage with the comparatively low Democratic vote. But the 1st district has not voted as Democratic as it registers for many, many years, and Bauman is the third straight Republican to win here. In the House, he is likely to stick with the more ideological conservatives; he is a former activist in the Young Americans for Freedom.

Census Data Pop. 489,455. Central city, 0%; suburban, 34%. Median family income, $8,925; families above $15,000: 17%; families below $3,000: 11%. Median years education, 11.1.

1972 Share of Federal Outlays $531,614,303

DOD	$223,073,464	HEW	$167,099,015
AEC	$273,091	HUD	$3,684,171
NASA	$4,550,501	DOI	$2,582,205
DOT	$13,681,570	USDA	$25,215,433
		Other	$91,454,853

Federal Military-Industrial Commitments

DOD Contractors Bata Shoe Co. (Belcamp), $7.801m: unspecified.
DOD Installations Aberdeen Proving Ground/Edgewood Arsenal (Aberdeen). Naval Air Test Center (Patuxent River). Naval Ordnance Station (Indian Head).

Economic Base Agriculture, notably poultry, grains and tobacco; food and kindred products, especially canned, cured and frozen foods; finance, insurance and real estate; apparel and other textile products, especially men's and boys' furnishings; and lumber and wood products.

The Voters

Registration 212,200 total. 140,315 D (66%); 65,430 R (31%); 6,455 other (3%).
Median voting age 41.4
Employment profile White collar, 42%. Blue collar, 40%. Service, 13%. Farm, 5%.
Ethnic groups Black, 19%. Total foreign stock, 5%. Germany, 1%.

Presidential vote

	1972	Nixon (R)	106,539	(72%)
		McGovern (D)	42,257	(28%)
	1968	Nixon (R)	65,316	(46%)
		Humphrey (D)	44,979	(32%)
		Wallace (AI)	31,977	(22%)

Representative

Robert E. Bauman Elected 1973; b. April 4, 1937; home, Easton; Georgetown U., B.S., 1959; Georgetown Law, J.D., 1964; four children; Roman Catholic.

Career Practicing atty.; executive committee, national Young Republicans, 1965–67; chief, Republican legislative staff, 1965–68; minority staff, House Judiciary Committee, 1955–59.

Offices 1039 LHOB, 202-225-5313. Also Loyola Federal Bank Bldg., Harrison Street, Easton 21601, 301-822-4300.

Administrative Assistant Ross Whealton

Committees

Interior and Insular Affairs (19th); Subs: Environment; Mines and Mining; National Parks and Recreation; Territorial and Insular Affairs.

Merchant Marine and Fisheries (17th); Subs: Coast Guard; Oceanography; Panama Canal.

Group Ratings: Newly Elected

Key Votes

1) Busing	NE	6) Cmbodia Bmbg	FOR	11) Chkg Acct Intrst	AGN
2) Strip Mines	NE	7) Bust Hwy Trust	AGN	12) End HISC (HUAC)	AGN
3) Cut Mil $	NE	8) Farm Sub Lmt	NE	13) Nixon Sewer Veto	FOR
4) Rev Shrg	NE	9) School Prayr	NE	14) Corp Cmpaign $	NE
5) Pub TV $	NE	10) Cnsumr Prot	NE	15) Pol $ Disclosr	NE

Election Results

1973 special:	Robert E. Bauman (R)	27,248	(51%)
	Frederick Malkus (D)	26,001	(49%)
1973 primary:	Robert E. Bauman (R)	5,651	(59%)
	John W. Hardwicker (R)	3,093	(33%)
	Donaldson Cole (R)	613	(6%)
	Charles Grace (R)	141	(1%)

SECOND DISTRICT Political Background

Baltimore County is, as anyone there will tell you, entirely separate from the city of Baltimore. By the definition used by the Census Bureau, Baltimore County, Maryland, is totally suburban. It is, however, far from homogeneous. To the north of the county lie horse farms; just northwest of Baltimore City are Jewish suburbs like Pikesville; northeast of the city are WASPy, high-income suburbs like Towson; and east of Baltimore are the working-class suburbs of Dundalk and Sparrow's Point. In Sparrow's Point is the nation's largest steel mill. So despite its suburban epithet, Baltimore County is as diverse as any of the nation's strictly urban areas, but with one major exception: there are virtually no blacks in the county.

It was out of this political crucible that Spiro Agnew emerged. Like most of Maryland, Baltimore County registers Democratic out of custom, and out of the same custom, usually votes Democratic in local elections. So the Democratic machine here has traditionally controlled the post of Baltimore County Executive. But in 1962, with an odor of scandal about, the Republican candidate for the job, attorney Agnew, won it. Doubtful of reelection, he secured his party's nomination for Governor, which suddenly became worth something when the Democrats chose George Mahoney as their nominee (see Maryland). Today, Agnew is under scrutiny himself for alleged corruption while County Executive, and his successor, Democrat Dale Anderson, has been indicted for bribery.

In 1962, the 2nd congressional district, which then included all of Baltimore County and two other counties besides, elected a new Democratic Congressman. Perhaps to avoid any association with scandal, Democratic candidates running in the 2nd were of the blue-ribbon variety. The retiring Congressman was aristocratic Daniel Brewster, who was elected to the Senate that year; and the new Congressman was Clarence D. Long, Ph.D., a professor of economics at Johns Hopkins University.

Since Long's first election, the district's boundaries have been altered a couple of times. The current 2nd includes the major portion of Baltimore County, including Dundalk, Towson, and Pikesville, plus a small portion of Baltimore City. All along, the Congressman has continued to win reelection by overwhelming margins. Long's principal trade secret is close attention to the needs of his constituency. He returns from Washington every night to his home in the district, and throughout the entire year, Long rides around in a trailer to meet constituents and handle the problems they put to him.

In Washington, people who regard themselves as political pros view the Congressman with the suspicion usually reserved for professors. Everybody calls him "Doc" Long. Nevertheless, he has won a seat on the Appropriations Committee. As one of the few members of Congress whose son actually went to Vietnam in the military, Long strongly supported the war policies of Johnson and Nixon. But he became a dove during the Cambodian invasion of 1970, and in 1973, Long introduced a successful amendment cutting off all American military spending in Cambodia.

Census Data Pop. 491,331. Central city, 5%; suburban, 95%. Median family income, $12,140; families above $15,000: 33%; families below $3,000: 4%. Median years education, 12.1.

1972 Share of Federal Outlays $635,143,812

DOD	$220,807,686	HEW	$221,684,891
AEC	$1,161,987	HUD	$11,573,216
NASA	$14,898,384	DOI	$1,819,660
DOT	$26,060,723	USDA	$11,187,569
		Other	$125,949,696

Federal Military-Industrial Commitments

DOD Contractors Westinghouse (Baltimore), $175.259m: aircraft electronic communication equipment. Bendix (Baltimore), $19.100m: missile and aircraft radar components. AAI Corp. (Cockeysville), $15.671m: small arms and other weapons research. AAI Corp. (Baltimore), $6.112m: munitions research. Martin Marietta (Baltimore), $5.109m: aircraft metals research.

Economic Base Finance, insurance and real estate; transportation equipment; electrical equipment and supplies; machinery, especially special industry machinery; food and kindred products, especially beverages; and paperboard containers and boxes, and other paper and allied products.

The Voters

Registration 260,442 total. 202,071 D (78%); 51,797 R (20%); 6,574 other (3%).
Median voting age 42.6
Employment profile White collar, 59%. Blue collar, 32%. Service, 8%. Farm, 1%.
Ethnic groups Black, 3%. Total foreign stock, 17%. USSR, 4%; Poland, Germany, Italy, 2% each; UK, 1%.

Presidential vote

1972	Nixon (R)	135,329	(68%)
	McGovern (D)	62,755	(32%)
1968	Nixon (R)	76,774	(45%)
	Humphrey (D)	72,706	(42%)
	Wallace (AI)	22,311	(13%)

Representative

Clarence D. Long (D) Elected 1962; b. Dec. 11, 1908, South Bend, Ind.; home, Ruxton; Washington and Jefferson College, B.A.; Princeton, Ph.D.; USN, WWII; married, two children; Presbyterian.

Career Prof., Johns Hopkins U., 1946–63; Assoc. Task Force Dir., Hoover Commission, 1948; Sr. Staff Mbr., Council of Econ. Advisers, 1953–54, 1956–57; Acting Chm., Md. Dem. Central Com., 1961–62.

Offices 2421 RHOB 202-225-3061. Also Rm. 200, P.O. Bldg., Towson 21204, 301-828-6616.

Administrative Assistant Mrs. Kathryn Tollerton (L.A.)

Committees

Appropriations (20th); Subs: Foreign Operations; Interior; Military Construction.

Group Ratings

	ADA	COPE	LWV	RIPON	NFU	LCV	CFA	NAB	NSI	ACA
1972	56	82	58	47	57	0	100	27	22	33
1971	70	82	44	78	67	–	75	–	–	26
1970	64	73	–	53	64	23	73	13	79	56

Key Votes

1) Busing	AGN	6) Cmbodia Bmbg	AGN	11) Chkg Acct Intrst	AGN
2) Strip Mines	AGN	7) Bust Hwy Trust	FOR	12) End HISC (HUAC)	ABS
3) Cut Mil $	AGN	8) Farm Sub Lmt	FOR	13) Nixon Sewer Veto	AGN
4) Rev Shrg	AGN	9) School Prayr	AGN	14) Corp Cmpaign $	FOR
5) Pub TV $	FOR	10) Cnsumr Prot	FOR	15) Pol $ Disclosr	AGN

Election Results

1972 general:	Clarence D. Long (D)	123,346	(66%)
	John J. Bishop, Jr. (R)	64,119	(34%)
1972 primary:	Clarence D. Long (D)	57,048	(72%)
	Rosalie Silber Abrams (D)	22,702	(28%)
1970 general:	Clarence D. Long (D)	87,224	(68%)
	Ross Z. Pierpont (R)	40,177	(32%)

THIRD DISTRICT   Political Background

East Baltimore is a favorite of political sociologists. It is composed of white ethnic communities of Irish-, Italian-, German-, and especially Polish-American descent. These appear to have changed little since the 1930s. The uniquely Baltimore row houses stand here as carefully maintained as ever, and the streets are spotless and teeming with children. But the politics of East Baltimore have experienced some change. The old machine that once dominated Baltimore has now splintered into a dozen different factions. A newer breed of politician has begun to win elections here by use of assiduous door-to-door campaigning and close cultivation of neighborhood groups. One such politician is Barbara Mikulski, City Councilwoman and head of the national Democratic party's committee on delegate selection.

East Baltimore lies at the center of Maryland's 3rd congressional district. The 3rd can be best described as the white-majority parts of Baltimore City and some adjacent suburbs. The district proceeds west from East Baltimore to the city's revitalized downtown area and the old neighborhoods near the harbor. Still farther west are the middle-class suburbs of Catonsville and Arbutus. The 3rd also includes Johns Hopkins University and the northeast corner of Baltimore, along with a small portion of suburban Towson in Baltimore County.

Much has been said about the shift of ethnic, lower-middle-class voters from their traditional Democratic allegiance to the Republicanism of Richard Nixon and Spiro Agnew. The 3rd district, and East Baltimore in particular, is a good place for sociologists to investigate the causes of the political phenomenon. This is an area that went for John F. Kennedy in 1960, but one that gave only 41% to Hubert Humphrey in 1968 and a scant 33% to George McGovern in 1972. The people of the 3rd report little real affection for Nixon or his policies. The shift appears to reflect a feeling that the national Democratic party is no longer concerned with the problems of people who live in ethnic neighborhoods of the district. They are well enough off that the old economic programs of the Democrats seem irrelevant. They remain poor enough, however, to resent the attention paid by fashionable liberals to those who are not doing as well, especially the blacks.

The current 3rd district represents an amalgam of the old 3rd and 4th. The Maryland legislature finally admitted that, under the one-man-one-vote ruling, the city of Baltimore could no longer dominate three congressional districts. The 3rd's boundaries for 1972 were probably drawn for the benefit of Rep. Edward Garmatz, a party regular and Chairman of the Merchant Marine and Fisheries Committee. But Garmatz retired and left the seat to Rep. Paul Sarbanes—an insurgent who had beaten another Committee Chairman from Baltimore City, George Fallon of Public Works, in the 1970 Democratic primary.

Sarbanes (whose ties to Baltimore's Greek-American community are considerably closer than Agnew's) was a four-year veteran of the state House of Delegates when he challenged Chairman Fallon. Earlier he was a classmate and friend of Ralph Nader at Princeton and a Rhodes Scholar. In the 1970 primary, Sarbanes had the support of Nader and peace and ecology groups. More important, and a mark of his political savvy, Sarbanes gained the endorsements of the AFL-CIO, the UAW, and the Teamsters—quite an accomplishment, since organized labor seldom buck big-city regulars like Fallon. Sarbanes won the primary by a 2,000-vote margin, and then took the general election easily.

For the 1972 elections, redistricters had so changed Sarbanes' constituency that he drew two formidable opponents, both old-line state Senators—Harry J. "Softshoes" McGuirk and Frank X. Gallagher. Sarbanes compiled solid majorities over both, but managed to win only a bit more than 50% of the total votes cast. Despite gains made by the party's national candidates, the Republicans put up only token opposition in the general election, as is usually the case in congressional and local elections here. So Sarbanes again won the general election easily.

Census Data Pop. 490,851. Central city, 80%; suburban, 20%. Median family income, $10,022; families above $15,000: 21%; families below $3,000: 9%. Median years education, 10.6.

1972 Share of Federal Outlays $634,607,826

DOD	$220,621,350	HEW	$221,497,815
AEC	$1,616,007	HUD	$11,563,449
NASA	$14,885,811	DOI	$1,818,125
DOT	$26,038,731	USDA	$11,178,128
		Other	$125,843,410

Federal Military-Industrial Commitments

NASA Contractors RCA (Baltimore), $7.560m: logistics support for Apollo.

Economic Base Finance, insurance and real estate; food and kindred products; transportation equipment; apparel and other textile products, especially men's and boys' suits and coats; and printing and publishing. Also higher education (Johns Hopkins Univ., and Towson State).

The Voters

Registration 243,447 total. 196,622 D (81%); 41,122 R (17%); 5,703 other (2%).
Median voting age 45.6
Employment profile White collar, 54%. Blue collar, 35%. Service, 11%. Farm, –%.
Ethnic groups Black, 13%. Spanish, 1%. Total foreign stock, 15%. Germany, 3%; Italy, Poland, 2% each.

Presidential vote

1972	Nixon (R)	111,007	(67%)
	McGovern (D)	53,981	(33%)
1968	Nixon (R)	74,644	(44%)
	Humphrey (D)	69,694	(41%)
	Wallace (AI)	26,406	(15%)

Representative

Paul Spyros Sarbanes (D) Elected 1970; b. Feb. 3, 1933, Salisbury; home, Baltimore; Princeton, A.B., 1954; Oxford, B.A., 1957; Harvard, LL.B., 1960; married, three children; Greek Orthodox.

Career Asst. to Walt W. Heller, Chm. of Council of Economic Advisors, 1962–63; Md. House of Delegates, 1966–70.

Offices 317 CHOB, 202-225-4016. Also 1414 Fed. Office Bldg., Baltimore 21201, 301-962-4436.

Administrative Assistant Judith Davison

Committees

Judiciary (12th); Subs: No. 4 (Bankruptcy and (Civil Rights Oversight); No. 6 (Revision of the Laws).

Merchant Marine and Fisheries (19th). Subs: Coast Guard and Navigation; Merchant Marine; Panama Canal.

Sel. Com. on Committees of the House (5th).

Group Ratings

	ADA	COPE	LWV	RIPON	NFU	LCV	CFA	NAB	NSI	ACA
1972	88	91	82	67	86	93	100	8	0	9
1971	81	82	63	67	85	–	100	–	–	17

Key Votes

1) Busing	AGN	6) Cmbodia Bmbg	AGN	11) Chkg Acct Intrst	FOR
2) Strip Mines	AGN	7) Bust Hwy Trust	FOR	12) End HISC (HUAC)	FOR
3) Cut Mil $	FOR	8) Farm Sub Lmt	FOR	13) Nixon Sewer Veto	AGN
4) Rev Shrg	FOR	9) School Prayr	FOR	14) Corp Cmpaign $	AGN
5) Pub TV $	FOR	10) Cnsumr Prot	FOR	15) Pol $ Disclosr	FOR

Election Results

1972 general:	Paul S. Sarbanes (D)	93,093	(70%)
	Robert D. Morrow (R)	40,442	(30%)
1972 primary:	Paul S. Sarbanes (D)	43,558	(54%)
	Harry J. McQuirk (D)	19,543	(24%)
	Frank X. Gallagher (D)	16,490	(20%)
	Walter T. Dixon (D)	1,297	(2%)
1970 general:	Paul S. Sarbanes (D)	54,936	(70%)
	David Fentress (R)	23,491	(30%)

FOURTH DISTRICT Political Background

Maryland's new 4th congressional district runs from the Baltimore city limits to the District of Columbia line. It is anchored on the north by the suburbs of Baltimore and on the south by those of Washington, D.C. In between is mostly vacant rural land, just waiting for the kind of rapid development that increased the 4th's population by 66% during the 1960s. Lying in the middle of the district is Annapolis (pop. 29,000), a quaint eighteenth-century town that contains Maryland's State House—the oldest in the nation—and the United States Naval Academy. The suburbs of the 4th are the not-so-fashionable ones south of Baltimore (Linthicum, Glen Burnie, Severna Park) and southeast of Washington (Suitland, Camp Springs, Oxon Hill). Lately a great number of lower-middle-class people have been moving into these places.

Anne Arundel County politicians greeted the creation of the 4th with cheers. The county, which has nearly 300,000 residents, had never before had its own Congressman, and by containing 60% of the new district's population, it was sure to dominate its politics. After an easy primary win, County Clerk Marjorie Holt became the Republican nominee. The quiet, non-women's lib moderate was one of Anne Arundel's most popular local officials.

The Democratic primary, by contrast, was a hectic one. On paper, the 4th, like all Maryland congressional districts, is Democratic. Some 70% of the district's voters are registered Democrats. One suspects, however, that most registered in the party only to participate in Democratic primaries, which are inevitably hotter affairs than their Republican counterparts. Whatever the case, the registrants certainly do not support Democratic presidential or senatorial candidates in any great numbers. With no incumbent running, the 1972 congressional primary here attracted no less than 12 Democrats, several others having withdrawn. Three of them were from the Prince Georges minority of the district and the rest from Anne Arundel. The winner was an Anne Arundel man, Werner Fornos, former head of the state social services department and an outspoken liberal. Given a fundamentally conservative constituency, some Democrats felt that a more effective candidate would have been Arthur Marshall, Prince Georges County District Attorney. But he lost by 2,600 votes, apparently because of the ballots siphoned off by Sue Mills, an anti-busing member of the Prince Georges school board.

A Marshall victory, however, would probably have made little difference. Even while losing, Fornos ran well for a liberal; moreover, Marshall's origins in Prince Georges would have counted against him in Anne Arundel. Like all Washington-area Representatives, Mrs. Holt's political future depends on the efficiency with which she copes with her constituents' problems with the federal government. And her constituents are sure to have problems, since 22% of the employed persons here work for some branch of the federal government. Only four other districts in the nation—all in the Washington suburbs—have a greater percentage of federal employees living in them.

Census Data Pop. 495,249. Central city, 0%; suburban, 100%. Median family income, $11,892; families above $15,000: 32%; families below $3,000: 5%. Median years education, 12.3.

1972 Share of Federal Outlays $747,999,238

DOD	$244,052,566	HEW	$241,834,338
AEC	$15,433,802	HUD	$8,820,192
NASA	$44,318,931	DOI	$3,333,671
DOT	$18,553,367	USDA	$19,183,660
		Other	$152,468,711

Federal Military-Industrial Commitments

DOD Contractors Chesapeake Instrument (Shady Side), $13,766m: Sonar systems. Westinghouse (Annapolis), $10.182m: unspecified. IIT Research Institute (Annapolis), $6.690m: operation of electromagnetic compatibility analysis center.
DOD Installations Fort Meade AB (Odenton). Naval Academy (Annapolis). Reconnaissance Technical Support Center (Suitland). Naval Air Facility, Andrews AFB (Camp Springs). Naval Hospital (Annapolis). Navy National Security Agency (Odenton). Naval Station (Annapolis). Naval Oceanographic Office (Suitland). Naval Ship Research and Development Center (Annapolis). Andrews AFB (Camp Springs).

Economic Base Finance, insurance and real estate; electrical equipment and supplies, especially radio and television communication equipment; agriculture, notably tobacco and cattle; printing and publishing, especially commercial printing; and tourism.

The Voters

Registration 192,735 total. 129,196 D (67%); 55,289 R (29%); 8,250 other (4%).
Median voting age 37.7
Employment profile White collar, 60%. Blue collar, 28%. Service, 11%. Farm, 1%.
Ethnic groups Black, 10%. Spanish, 2%. Total foreign stock, 10%. Germany, 2%; Italy, UK, 1% each.

Presidential vote

1972	Nixon (R)		107,379	(70%)
	McGovern (D)		44,937	(30%)
1968	Nixon (R)		55,177	(45%)
	Humphrey (D)		40,163	(33%)
	Wallace (AI)		26,609	(22%)

Representative

Marjorie S. Holt (R) Elected 1972; b. Sept. 17, 1920, Birmingham, Ala.; home, Severna Park; Jacksonville U., B.A., 1946; U. of Fla., J.D., 1949; married, three children; Presbyterian.

Career Practicing atty.; Supervisor of Elections, Anne Arundel County, 1963–65; Clerk of the Circuit Court, Anne Arundel County, 1966–70.

Offices 1510 LHOB, 202-225-8090. Also 5418 Oxon Hill Rd., Oxon Hill 20021, 301-567-9212, and 95 Aquahart Rd., Glen Burnie 21061, 301-768-8050 and 202-261-2008.

Administrative Assistant Pat M. LoCascio

Committees

Armed Services (18th); Subs: No. 2; Sp. Sub. on Human Relations.

Group Ratings: Newly Elected

Key Votes

1) Busing	NE	6) Cmbodia Bmbg	FOR	11) Chkg Acct Intrst	AGN
2) Strip Mines	NE	7) Bust Hwy Trust	AGN	12) End HISC (HUAC)	AGN
3) Cut Mil $	NE	8) Farm Sub Lmt	NE	13) Nixon Sewer Veto	FOR
4) Rev Shrg	NE	9) School Prayr	NE	14) Corp Cmpaign $	NE
5) Pub TV $	NE	10) Cnsumr Prot	NE	15) Pol $ Disclosr	NE

Election Results

1972 general:	Marjorie S. Holt (R)	87,534	(59%)
	Werner Fornos (D)	59,877	(41%)
1972 primary:	Marjorie S. Holt (R)	9,389	(71%)
	Frederick C. Taylor (R)	2,385	(18%)
	Marvin D. Morris (R)	1,431	(11%)

FIFTH DISTRICT Political Background

The 5th district of Maryland comprises most of Prince Georges County, the largest suburban county in the state. Lying north and east of Washington, D.C., Prince Georges is a little less white-collar and less affluent than adjacent Montgomery County. Against national averages, however, Prince Georges ranks very high in both white-collar and income categories; it contains an extremely large proportion of people whose boss is the federal government—some 38% of the employed work force. Yet the towns of the 5th district clearly enjoy less status than those in Montgomery. Rarely does anyone from Hyattsville, College Park, or Bowie make the social chatter of Maxine Cheshire's column. The people living here are the bureaucrats who keep official Washington plugging along day after day, come Johnson or Nixon, Vietnam or Watergate.

The 5th's population shot up 69% during the 1960s, making it one of the fastest-growing congressional districts in the nation. The rapid growth here started in the 1950s; as the Washington schools were integrated, the city's white working class, who had once lived in the now all-black northeast and southeast sections of D.C., moved to Prince Georges County. Today the pace of the growth continues, its only brake being a scarcity of sewer permits. But the exodus to the suburban county has a new kind of participant. These are middle-class blacks—families of teachers, policemen, and government workers. So great is the black exodus that in 1970 some 16% of the 5th's population was black, and that percentage continues to rise rapidly. The percentage of black students in the county school system—now the nation's tenth largest school district—has skyrocketed. A group of black parents instituted a desegregation suit, and a busing order is now in effect.

The busing order, of course, became a hot political issue. In all of Prince Georges County, there was no more vehement or vocal opponent of busing than 5th district Congressman Lawrence J. Hogan. Hogan, a Republican and a former FBI agent, upset a complacent conservative Democrat in 1968 to win his seat, and then retained it in 1970 when he whipped a liberal Democrat. Hogan's performance on election day depends upon services rendered for his constituents, who, unlike the average American, live entwined with the workings of the federal bureaucracies. Adjustments of pension benefits, vacation time, promotions—these are the staples of a suburban Washington Congressman's job, and Hogan, like conservative Republican Joel Broyhill of Virginia and liberal Republican Gilbert Gude of Montgomery County, sees that his constituents are satisfied.

Constituent case work and the anti-busing stand help to explain Hogan's solid 63–27 reelection margin over conservative Democrat and state Sen. Edward Conroy in 1972. Unlike the liberal Democrat who ran here in 1970, Conroy felt that a Democrat holding views closer to Hogan himself would have a good chance to win in the 5th. But as it turned out, Conroy ran significantly behind George McGovern in the district. In fact, the 5th was the only district in the nation's Northeast in which McGovern did better in 1972 than Humphrey in 1968—one index of the size of the middle-class black migration here. (Hogan's conservative stands are not popular with his black constituents.) So as the black migration continues, the Congressman may some day be vulnerable, although for the foreseeable future, he will surely be reelected—if he runs. Because of a local feud, he is reportedly considering a race against Prince Georges County Executive William Gullett, a fellow Republican, in 1974. Hogan might conceivably enter the gubernatorial race then.

Hogan must find his seat on the House Judiciary Committee less rewarding than the campaign hustings in Prince Georges. As a busing foe, he has tried without success to get the committee to approve an anti-busing constitutional amendment. He has had no better luck getting the committee to consider, much less pass, an amendment that would overturn the Supreme Court's decision on abortion. Both of Hogan's causes, if brought to the floor, would probably pass; in the case of an anti-abortion amendment, by a large margin. But as things now stand on the Judiciary Committee, there are enough votes to assure that neither of the two proposed amendments ever sees the light of day.

Census Data Pop. 482,721. Central city, 0%; suburban, 100%. Median family income, $12,286; families above $15,000: 33%; families below $3,000: 4%. Median years education, 12.5.

1972 Share of Federal Outlays $887,245,627

DOD	$269,415,906	HEW	$262,703,839
AEC	$35,961,181	HUD	$4,425,576
NASA	$86,174,060	DOI	$5,448,762
DOT	$6,772,177	USDA	$30,296,143
		Other	$186,047,983

Federal Military-Industrial Commitments

DOD Contractors Litton Industries (College Park), $8.841m: aircraft radar and reconnaissance electronic ware. IBM (Riverdale), $6.966m: classified.
NASA Contractors Computing and software (Greenbelt), $6.479m: various data processing services.

Economic Base Finance, insurance and real estate; tourism; agriculture, notably tobacco, and nursery and greenhouse products; printing and publishing, especially commercial printing; and electrical equipment and supplies, especially radio and television communication equipment. Also higher education (Univ. of Maryland).

The Voters

Registration 179,267 total. 118,415 D (66%); 49,639 R (28%); 11,213 other (6%).
Median voting age 34.9
Employment profile White collar, 67%. Blue collar, 23%. Service, 10%. Farm, –%.
Ethnic groups Black, 16%. Spanish, 2%. Total foreign stock, 13%. Italy, 2%; Germany, UK, 1% each.

Presidential vote

1972	Nixon (R)	83,579	(57%)
	McGovern (D)	63,821	(43%)
1968	Nixon (R)	54,084	(41%)
	Humphrey (D)	55,619	(42%)
	Wallace (AI)	21,733	(17%)

Representative

Lawrence J. Hogan (R) Elected 1968; b. Sept. 30, 1928, Boston, Mass.; home, Landover; Georgetown U., B.A., 1949, J.D., 1954; American U., A.M., 1965; San Francisco State Col., 1956–57; U. of Md., 1966–67.

Career Atty., pub. rel. executive; teacher, U. of Md., 1960–68; FBI, 1948–58; member Governor's Commission on Law Enforcement and the Administration of Justice (Md.), 1967–68.

Offices 1204 LHOB, 202-225-4131. Also Promenade 3, Landover Mall, Landover 20785, 301-763-7480.

Administrative Assistant Jean M. Sparks

Committees

Judiciary (10th); Sp. Sub. on Reform of Federal Criminal Laws.

Post Office and Civil Service (4th); Subs: Retirement and Employee Benefits (Ranking Mbr.).

Group Ratings

	ADA	COPE	LWV	RIPON	NFU	LCV	CFA	NAB	NSI	ACA
1972	0	36	36	50	83	40	50	58	100	61
1971	19	45	44	57	29	–	25	–	–	74
1970	24	25	–	75	77	95	67	58	90	47

Key Votes

1) Busing	AGN	6) Cmbodia Bmbg	FOR	11) Chkg Acct Intrst	ABS
2) Strip Mines	AGN	7) Bust Hwy Trust	AGN	12) End HISC (HUAC)	AGN
3) Cut Mil $	AGN	8) Farm Sub Lmt	FOR	13) Nixon Sewer Veto	AGN
4) Rev Shrg	FOR	9) School Prayr	FOR	14) Corp Cmpaign $	FOR
5) Pub TV $	AGN	10) Cnsumr Prot	AGN	15) Pol $ Disclosr	ABS

Election Results

1972 general:	Lawrence J. Hogan (R)	90,016	(63%)
	Edward T. Conroy (D)	53,049	(37%)
1972 primary:	Lawrence J. Hogan (R)	11,629	(93%)
	William S. Muscovich (R)	817	(7%)
1970 general:	Lawrence J. Hogan (R)	84,314	(61%)
	Royal Hart (D)	52,979	(39%)

SIXTH DISTRICT Political Background

West of Baltimore and Washington, a series of gentle Maryland hills rise to the low mountains of the Catoctins and the Appalachian ridges. Here is a land known for its fertile valleys and its antique cities, one of which is Frederick (1970 pop. 24,000), where Barbara Fritchie reared her old gray head. Also here are the small industrial cities of Hagerstown (pop. 36,000) and, high in the hills, Cumberland (pop. 30,000). The mountain folk and the Pennsylvania Dutch who settled western Maryland left behind a Republican heritage, unusual in a state that is Democratic by tradition and custom. Nevertheless, a majority of the region's voters today, like those in the rest of Maryland, are registered Democrats. Come election time, though, these same Democrats usually vote Republican in the big races.

The 6th congressional district includes all of western Maryland and a portion of suburban Baltimore County. The only part of the 6th that is markedly out of step with the conservative, rural mores of the district is the much-heralded "new town" of Columbia in Howard County. It is a planned, integrated development that had 8,000 people in 1970 and will house some 110,000 by 1982. Columbia's new-town status appears to have attracted a disproportionate number of suburban liberals from the Baltimore area.

The dominant mores of the 6th have been faithfully reflected in the attitudes held by the district's last two Congressmen, Republican J. Glenn Beall, Jr., and Democrat Goodloe Byron. Beall served two years after winning the seat in 1968, and then became a U.S. Senator in 1970. Byron won a narrow victory in 1970 and resounding reelection in 1972. Byron is about as conservative a congressional Democrat as there is from outside the South, and his constituents seem to like that just fine.

Byron and Beall illustrate dynastic lines that sometimes come to dominate Maryland politics. Byron's father and mother served in the House between 1938 and 1942, when Beall's father succeeded to the seat. Beall, Sr., was reelected from the 6th until 1952, when he won election to the Senate. He retired involuntarily when he lost to young Joseph Tydings, himself the son of the Senator. Tydings, in turn, was beaten in 1970 by Beall, Jr. Lineage still matters in Maryland.

Census Data Pop. 491,839. Central city, 0%; suburban, 40%. Median family income, $9,749; families above $15,000: 20%; families below $3,000: 8%. Median years education, 11.6.

1972 Share of Federal Outlays $516,286,136

DOD	$166,908,911	HEW	$182,252,399
AEC	$1,225,309	HUD	$4,692,371
NASA	$7,618,972	DOI	$2,329,235
DOT	$37,526,764	USDA	$12,637,828
		Other	$101,094,347

Federal Military-Industrial Commitments

DOD Contractors Johns Hopkins University (Scaggsville), $88.011m: research into weapons systems development. Martin Marietta (Cumberland), $12.700m: unspecified. Fairchild Camera (Hagerstown), $5.705m: unspecified.
NASA Contractors Bendix Corp. (Columbia), $44.077m: operation of manned space flight tracking network; other SRT services.

Economic Base Agriculture, notably dairy products, cattle, and dairy cattle; finance, insurance and real estate; apparel and other textile products; stone, clay and glass products; and food and kindred products.

The Voters

Registration 232,861 total. 131,268 D (56%); 93,649 R (49%); 7,944 other (3%).
Median voting age 42.9
Employment profile White collar, 46%. Blue collar, 39%. Service, 11%. Farm, 4%.
Ethnic groups Black, 4%. Total foreign stock, 5%.

Presidential vote

1972	Nixon (R)	125,878	(71%)
	McGovern (D)	52,346	(29%)
1968	Nixon (R)	80,752	(51%)
	Humphrey (D)	51,456	(33%)
	Wallace (AI)	25,528	(16%)

Representative

Goodloe E. Byron (D) Elected 1970; b. June 22, 1929, Williamsport; home, Frederick; U. of Va., B.A., 1951; George Washington U., J.D., 1954; Army, 1955–58; married, three children; Episcopalian.

Career Atty., Md. House of Delegates, 1962–66; Md. Senate, 1966–70.

Offices 1730 LHOB, 202-225-2721. Also P.O. Bldg., Hagerstown 21740, 301-797-6043.

Administrative Assistant Doris Solomon

Committees

Interstate and Foreign Commerce (22nd); Sub: Communications and Power.

Group Ratings

	ADA	COPE	LWV	RIPON	NFU	LCV	CFA	NAB	NSI	ACA
1972	6	18	17	27	67	43	100	50	100	83
1971	19	50	33	39	21	–	50	–	–	69

Key Votes

1) Busing	AGN	6) Cmbodia Bmbg	FOR	11) Chkg Acct Intrst	AGN
2) Strip Mines	FOR	7) Bust Hwy Trust	AGN	12) End HISC (HUAC)	AGN
3) Cut Mil $	AGN	8) Farm Sub Lmt	FOR	13) Nixon Sewer Veto	FOR
4) Rev Shrg	AGN	9) School Prayr	FOR	14) Corp Cmpaign $	FOR
5) Pub TV $	FOR	10) Cnsumr Prot	AGN	15) Pol $ Disclosr	FOR

Election Results

1972 general:	Goodloe E. Byron (D)	107,283	(65%)
	Edward J. Mason (R)	58,259	(35%)
1972 primary:	Goodloe E. Byron (D)	25,996	(65%)
	Hugh Burgess (D)	4,704	(12%)
	Thomas F. Conlon (D)	4,011	(10%)
	James R. Madgett (D)	3,434	(9%)
	Edward Hendrickson (D)	1,665	(4%)
1970 general:	Goodloe E. Byron (D)	59,267	(51%)
	George R. Hughes, Jr. (R)	55,511	(48%)
	Audrey B. Carroll (AI)	1,873	(2%)

SEVENTH DISTRICT Political Background

In 1960, 35% of the residents of Baltimore were black—by 1970, 46% were. The blacks, however, do not now dominate Baltimore City politics; the current Mayor, elected in 1971, is Thomas D. Schaefer, a white man. But black voters do control increasingly large sections of the west side of the city, including most of the area that makes up Maryland's 7th congressional district. The 7th's lines were artfully enough drawn to enclose 86% of Baltimore's blacks and only 29% of its whites. This takes in almost the entire west side of the city, plus a predominantly black salient on the east side, lying north of downtown and the docks.

The 7th was not always so constituted. Before the 1972 elections, the 7th was designed to be a heavily Jewish district. It extended from the old Jewish neighborhoods in the city—many now inhabited by blacks—to Jewish suburbs like Pikesville, north of Baltimore. Such an arrangement was much to the liking of then Rep. Samuel Friedel, an old-line Democrat who had accumulated enough seniority to have become Chairman of the House Administration Committee. But in 1970, Friedel got caught in a tough primary. He split the Jewish vote with a candidate named Friedler, as most of the black vote went to challenger Parren J. Mitchell, a political novice and a professor at Baltimore's black Morgan State College. Mitchell won the primary by a paper-thin 38 votes. In the general election, the black candidate ran behind normal Democratic showings, losing the suburbs, but still managing a comfortable win.

The Congressman is out of a prominent Baltimore family. His brother, Clarence Mitchell, is the canny Washington lobbyist for the NAACP, and his nephew, Clarence Mitchell, III, is a Maryland state Senator. But Parren's family connections may have hurt more than helped in 1972. Legislative redistricters placed the 7th entirely within the city of Baltimore, making the district overwhelmingly black. About such an arrangement, Congressman Mitchell voiced no complaints. But nephew Clarence Mitchell ran for Mayor in 1971; the bid angered another black candidate, George Russell, who had connections with remnants of the Baltimore machine. The incensed Russell ran in the 1972 congressional primary against Parren Mitchell, and very nearly won. Russell got 46% of the votes, compared to the incumbent's 50%, with the rest going to two minor candidates.

The primary performance was not a particularly impressive one for an incumbent. And Mitchell may have more trouble in the future. It must be at least a little embarrassing to him that his nephew, state Senator Clarence, has been indicted on federal income tax charges. In 1970, insurgents Parren Mitchell and Paul Sarbanes had an *annus mirabilis*, when both of them toppled House Committee Chairmen in Democratic primaries (and Baltimore's third Committee Chairman, Edward Garmatz, retired in 1972). But from the looks of the 1972 primaries, neither Mitchell nor Sarbanes (see Maryland 3) can expect the old-line Democrats to roll over and concede things.

Census Data Pop. 487,832. Central city, 100%; suburban, 0%. Median family income, $7,841; families above $15,000: 13%; families below $3,000: 16%. Median years education, 9.8.

1972 Share of Federal Outlays $630,587,929

DOD	$219,223,833	HEW	$220,094,746
AEC	$1,153,652	HUD	$11,490,201
NASA	$14,791,518	DOI	$1,806,608
DOT	$25,873,790	USDA	$11,107,321
		Other	$125,046,270

Federal Military-Industrial Commitments

No installations or contractors receiving prime awards greater than $5,000,000.

Economic Base Food and kindred products; finance, insurance and real estate; transportation equipment; apparel and other textile products, especially men's and boys' suits and coats; and printing and publishing.

The Voters

Registration 213,697 total. 176,401 D (83%); 33,268 R (16%); 4,028 other (2%).
Median voting age 42.7
Employment profile White collar, 37%. Blue collar, 40%. Service, 23%. Farm, –%.
Ethnic groups Black, 74%. Total foreign stock, 5%.

Presidential vote

1972	Nixon (R)	32,369	(27%)
	McGovern (D)	89,041	(73%)
1968	Nixon (R)	22,429	(16%)
	Humphrey (D)	106,998	(77%)
	Wallace (AI)	9,066	(7%)

Representative

Parren J. Mitchell (D) Elected 1970; b. April 29, 1922, Baltimore; home, Baltimore; Morgan State Col., B.A., 1950; U. of Md., M.S., 1952; doctoral studies, U. of Conn., 1960; Army 1942–46; unmarried; Episcopalian.

Career Sociology prof., Morgan State; Exec. Sec. Md. Commission on Interracial Problems and Relations, 1963–65; Dir., Baltimore Community Action Agency, 1965–68.

Offices 414 CHOB, 202-225-4741. Also 1018 Fed. Bldg., 31 Hopkins Plaza, Baltimore 21201, 301-962-4436.

Administrative Assistant George M. Minor

Committees

Banking and Currency (18th); Subs: Consumer Affairs; International Trade; Small Business.

Sel. Com. on Small Business (11th); Subs: Government Procurement and International Trade; Minority Small Business Enterprise and Franchising.

Group Ratings

	ADA	COPE	LWV	RIPON	NFU	LCV	CFA	NAB	NSI	ACA
1972	88	100	100	73	86	86	100	8	0	10
1971	100	82	67	81	93	–	100	–	–	11

Key Votes

1) Busing	FOR	6) Cmbodia Bmbg	AGN	11) Chkg Acct Intrst	FOR
2) Strip Mines	AGN	7) Bust Hwy Trust	FOR	12) End HISC (HUAC)	FOR
3) Cut Mil $	FOR	8) Farm Sub Lmt	FOR	13) Nixon Sewer Veto	AGN
4) Rev Shrg	FOR	9) School Prayr	AGN	14) Corp Cmpaign $	AGN
5) Pub TV $	FOR	10) Cnsumr Prot	FOR	15) Pol $ Disclosr	FOR

Election Results

1972 general:	Parren J. Mitchell (D)	83,749	(80%)
	Verdell Adair (R)	20,876	(20%)
1972 primary:	Parren J. Mitchell (D)	32,946	(50%)
	Georgè L. Russell, Jr. (D)	30,202	(46%)
	Richard C. Manning (D)	1,847	(3%)
	John G. Grinage (D)	853	(1%)
1970 general:	Parren J. Mitchell (D)	60,390	(59%)
	Peter Parker (R)	42,566	(41%)

EIGHTH DISTRICT Political Background

By virtually any measure the Census Bureau cares to use, the 8th district of Maryland is the richest congressional district in the country. It comprises virtually all of Montgomery County—a hunk of extremely valuable suburban and exurban real estate lying adjacent to northwest Washington, D.C. Like Prince Georges County to the east, Montgomery County experienced a vast population increase during the 1950s and 1960s. The migrants here, however, are of a little different sort: they have higher incomes, are better educated, and more white-collar. The typical resident of the 8th district is a high-ranking G-15 civil servant or perhaps a lawyer in private practice; the man or woman likely as not has a graduate degree, and professes vaguely liberal politics. Though the Montgomery County voter's favorite kind of politician is a liberal Republican like Sen. Charles Mathias, he usually plunks for Democratic candidates. Even in 1972, not very many 8th district people abandoned the Democratic ticket to vote for Richard Nixon.

The 8th is a rich district for which the term radical chic is inappropriate—League-of-Women-Voters liberal is better. Both the local Democratic and Republican parties here are the most liberal in the state. Since 1966, the 8th's Congressman has been Gilbert Gude, an antiwar

Republican with an ADA rating higher than those compiled by traditional Maryland Democrats. Gude had a tough fight in his first race when he won only 54% of the vote. But since then he has been unbeatable, winning in 1972 with 64% of the votes.

Like all Washington-area Congressmen, Gude pays close attention to the hassles and complaints of his constituents. He is perhaps as much an ombudsman as a legislator. As a member of the House District of Columbia Committee, Gude has taken a position similar to that of Sen. Mathias: the Congressman strongly backs home rule for the district, but opposes even more firmly any measure that would give D.C. the right to tax suburbanites who work there. The liberal politics of the 8th district goes only so far. Gude is sure of reelection if he runs again, but—after Gov. Marvin Mandel announced he was filing for divorce—there began to be talk Gude might run for Governor. He might very well be his party's strongest candidate and give Mandel quite a race. If that does happen, the 8th district contest will probably be a close one between a liberal Republican and a liberal Democrat.

Census Data Pop. 493,121. Central city, 0%; suburban, 100%. Median family income, $17,102; families above $15,000: 58%; families below $3,000: 3%. Median years education, 13.2.

1972 Share of Federal Outlays $906,178,758

DOD	$275,165,032	HEW	$268,309,738
AEC	$36,728,565	HUD	$4,520,015
NASA	$88,012,948	DOI	$5,565,034
DOT	$6,916,690	USDA	$30,942,640
		Other	$190,018,096

Federal Military-Industrial Commitments

DOD Contractors Automation Industries (Silver Spring), $54.489m: technical and engineering support for a variety of missile and shipboard weapons systems. IBM (Bethesda), $21.251m: data processing equipment and engineering services. Johns Hopkins University (Silver Spring), $17.703m: research work for various phases of weapons systems development and other related areas. IBM (Gaithersburg), $12.449m: various data processing services. Singer Co. (Silver Spring), $11.344m: P-3 weapons system trainer. Control Data (Rockville), $6.236m: computer services. Control Data (Bethesda), $6.233m: computer services for ABM.
NASA Contractors Fairchild Industries (Germantown), $40.450m: support of applications technology satellites. Computer Sciences (Silver Spring), $6.929m: tracking and data acquisition.
AEC Operations AEC Headquarters (Germantown), $57.877. Joint AEC-NASA Space Nuclear Systems Office, (Germantown).

Economic Base Finance, insurance and real estate; electrical equipment and supplies, especially electronic components and accessories; tourism; agriculture, notably dairy products, nursery and greenhouse products, and cattle; and printing and publishing, especially book printing.

The Voters

Registration 281,135 total. 166,189 D (59%); 93,429 R (33%); 21,517 other (8%).
Median voting age 41.9
Employment profile White collar, 79%. Blue collar, 13%. Service, 7%. Farm, 1%.
Ethnic groups Black, 4%. Spanish, 3%. Total foreign stock, 21%. USSR, 3%; Germany, UK, 2% each; Canada, Poland, Italy, 1% each.

Presidential vote

1972	Nixon (R)	127,225	(57%)
	McGovern (D)	96,643	(43%)
1968	Nixon (R)	77,821	(44%)
	Humphrey (D)	85,063	(48%)
	Wallace (AI)	13,324	(8%)

Representative

Gilbert Gude (R) Elected 1966; b. March 9, 1923, Washington, D.C.; home, Bethesda; U. of Md.; Cornell U., B.S., 1948; George Washington U., M.A., 1958; Army, WWII; married, five children; Catholic.

Career House of Delegates, Md., 1952–62; Senate 1962–66.

Offices 332 CHOB, 202-225-5341. Also 11141 Georgia Ave., Wheaton 20902, 301-933-3340, and 10227 Wincopin Cir., Columbia 21043, 301-737-6088.

Administrative Assistant Gordon L. Hawk

Committees

District of Columbia (4th); Subs: Business, Commerce, and Taxation; Labor, Social Services, and the International Community.

Government Operations (6th); Subs: Conservation and Natural Resources; Foreign Operations and Government Information.

Group Ratings

	ADA	COPE	LWV	RIPON	NFU	LCV	CFA	NAB	NSI	ACA
1972	81	73	92	100	86	93	100	25	10	18
1971	89	64	100	94	57	–	75	–	–	21
1970	80	82	–	100	92	75	67	18	60	33

Key Votes

1) Busing	FOR	6) Cmbodia Bmbg	AGN	11) Chkg Acct Intrst	FOR
2) Strip Mines	AGN	7) Bust Hwy Trust	FOR	12) End HISC (HUAC)	FOR
3) Cut Mil $	AGN	8) Farm Sub Lmt	FOR	13) Nixon Sewer Veto	FOR
4) Rev Shrg	FOR	9) School Prayr	AGN	14) Corp Cmpaign $	AGN
5) Pub TV $	FOR	10) Cnsumr Prot	FOR	15) Pol $ Disclosr	FOR

Election Results

1972 general:	Gilbert Gude (R)	137,287	(64%)
	Joseph G. Anastasi (D)	77,551	(36%)
1972 primary:	Gilbert Gude (R), unopposed		
1970 general:	Gilbert Gude (R)	104,647	(63%)
	Thomas Hale Boggs, Jr. (D)	60,453	(37%)

MASSACHUSETTS

Political Background

"Massachusetts—the one and only." was a bumper-sticker slogan that began to appear shortly after the November 1972 election. And in the cold, wet New England spring of 1973, more and better slogans adorned the VWs, Volvos, Toyotas, and even Oldsmobiles of the Bay State, as the full Watergate storm broke. "Don't blame me—I'm from Massachusetts," read one; another asked the reader to "Honk if you think he's guilty." The 1972 *Almanac* called Massachusetts "the most liberal large state in the nation," and if "liberal" means a willingness to vote for a candidate like George McGovern, Massachusetts in 1972 was the nation's *only* liberal state. Along with the District of Columbia, the voters here accounted for all of McGovern's 17 electoral votes. It was just the second time in the history of twentieth-century presidential landslides that one of the ten largest states went for the losing candidate. The other instance occurred in 1928, when Massachusetts and its tiny neighbor, Rhode Island, alone among the northern states, plunked for Al Smith over Herbert Hoover.

Except for the Eisenhower years, Massachusetts since 1928 has remained in the Democratic presidential column by large margins. In the politics of 1972, many Bay Staters insist that the behavior of Massachusetts was in no way aberrant: what really needs explainingis why the rest of the country went the other way. Nevertheless, political analysts cannot help asking the question: Why Massachusetts?

The first and easiest explanation is that Massachusetts is a very heavily Democratic state, even though liberal Republicans like Sen. Edward Brooke and Gov. Francis Sargent win easily. In 1964, for example, Massachusetts presented Lyndon Johnson with 76% of its votes; in 1968, 63% went to Hubert Humphrey. In the Great and General Court, as the commonwealth's legislature is called, Republicans are outnumbered 3–1 by Democrats. So even as McGovern carried the state, his 55% represents a significant drop in usual Democratic percentages.

The second explanation was formulated in its most picturesque terms by former Nixon aide Charles Colson, himself a Massachusetts native: the state has just too many kooks. If Colson meant students, he has something; around 6.6% of the eligible voters here are enrolled in colleges, a figure exceeded only in Utah, Colorado, and California. The student vote here went heavily for McGovern and against Nixon. But McGovern would still have carried Massachusetts, though by a narrow margin, even if every one of its students had failed to show up at the polls.

For a sufficient explanation of the political behavior of Massachusetts, we must go back further—to the origins of the state's peculiar political culture. The traumatic event that structured Massachusetts politics was not, as in most of the rest of the country, the Civil War. The event was instead the Irish potato famine of the 1840s. The devastating blight spurred a massive Irish migration to the United States, and nowhere did the new Americans make a greater proportionate impact than in Boston. In response, the established Yankees of the Commonwealth—still only a few years removed from a diehard allegiance to the uptight Federalist party—hung out "No Irish Need Apply" signs. But by the 1880s, an Irishman was elected Mayor of Boston, and from 1906 to this day, none but an Irish Catholic has held the job.

Statewide elections furnished the real political battleground between Yankee Republicans and Irish Democrats. After the turn of the century, the arrival of sizable blocs of Italian, French-Canadian, Portuguese, Jewish, Polish, and even some black voters complicated the struggle between the two principal adversary groups. But in Massachusetts, as nowhere else in the country, the Irish remain *the* ethnic group with clout. Census figures understate the proportion of Irish here; the figures report only those born in Ireland or those whose parents were. Around Boston, anyway, people retain an "Irish" identity for at least six generations.

One classic Yankee-Irish confrontation was the 1918 Senate race between Republican Henry Cabot Lodge and Democrat John F. (Honey Fitz) Fitzgerald. Lodge won, and as Chairman of the Senate Foreign Relations Committee went on to win another struggle—this time against Woodrow Wilson—to keep the United States out of the League of Nations. But 34 years later, Honey Fitz' grandson, John F. Kennedy, evened the score in Massachusetts when he upset Lodge's grandson, another famous Henry Cabot Lodge, in the 1952 Senate race.

The Kennedy influence has played a crucial role in the formation of the state's current political attitudes. For some time now, Massachusetts voters have shied away from entrusting the Governor's office to the Irish; it was 1952 when the Commonwealth's last Irish Catholic Governor, Paul Dever, lost a reelection bid. But the Harvard-educated, aristocratic, even Anglophilic Kennedys are so clearly removed from the corruption and seamy deal-making which has characterized the lower levels of Massachusetts politics that they have become almost as acceptable among old-line Yankees as among the adoring Irish and Italians.

During the last dozen years, Massachusetts Yankees, influenced perhaps by their children at Harvard, Smith, and Andover, have moved steadily left. After all, these are descendants of the Adamses who firebranded the Revolution of 1776; who opposed (along with bachelor Henry David Thoreau) the Mexican War of 1846; who supported abolitionists like William Lloyd

Garrison, though slaveholders provided cotton for New England mills; and who fiercely opposed the "imperialist" foreign policies of William McKinley and Theodore Roosevelt. So one strain (the other belongs to the likes of the late George Apley) of the Massachusetts Puritan heritage of "plain living and high thinking" led to Yankee denunciations of the Vietnam war and to deep distrust of the Johnson and Nixon administrations that promulgated it. In 1966, Thomas Boylston Adams, of the main line and a member of all the right clubs, was a peace candidate for the Senate; in 1968, Adams was a fervent backer of Robert F. Kennedy. Meanwhile, the equally aristocratic historian Samuel Eliot Morison has nothing but kind words for the administration of John F. Kennedy.

In Massachusetts, the upper-class WASP movement to the left has not stirred a corresponding Archie Bunker reaction among middle-class ethnics. In New York, the personification of antiwar liberalism was Mayor John Lindsay, who for a number of reasons—the least of which was his stand-offish, almost self-conscious Yale manner—was hated by the Catholic middle-class. But here in the Bay State, the personification of antiwar liberalism is Sen. Edward M. Kennedy, who—as the reaction to Chappaquiddick showed—can do no wrong in the eyes of hundreds of thousands of Catholic middle-class voters. When John Lindsay ordered the flag flown at half-mast on Moratorium Day, New York hard-hats screamed in wrath. When Ted Kennedy took a strong position on amnesty for war resisters, Massachusetts ethnic voters paused, and mulled the idea over. And it was a state legislature full of local Irish and Italian pols that passed the Shea Act, one which sought to exempt the young men of Massachusetts from military service in the Vietnam war.

Unlike New York, Massachusetts has no kind of undeclared war between students and hard-hats, between rich liberals and Bunkers. The folks in Massachusetts who've got it, don't flaunt it. None of the electric tension, if not open hatred, exists on the streets of Boston—the kind one feels in New York City. While New York produced the hard-line Cardinal Spellman, Boston gave us the ecumenical Cardinal Cushing.

In Massachusetts, there is common agreement that liberal Democrat Kennedy and liberal Republican Brooke should be Senators, the liberal Republican Sargent (except for his handling of prison reform and busing issues) should be Governor, and liberal Democrat Kevin White, Mayor of Boston. Around Boston, which could be described as the world's largest college town (or college metropolitan area), students and factory workers live in the same neighborhoods. Both groups have learned that they have problems in common: getting the garbage picked up, stopping the junkyard down the block, and keeping rents down. In fact, rent control ordinances in Boston and Cambridge are the toughest in the country—an issue that brought town and gown together. Finally, Boston has the nation's best and most prosperous "underground" newspapers, the *Phoenix* and the *Real Paper*. These are read widely, not just by students and street people; the highly influential and liberal Boston *Globe* considers the *Phoenix* and the *Real Paper* honest-to-God competition.

It is, therefore, with good reason that Massachusetts alone among the states voted not to reelect the President. Not just student-dominated Cambridge, but lower-income, Irish Somerville and upper-crust Yankee Lincoln all voted for McGovern over Nixon in 1972.

Things were not always so harmonious here. In 1962, Edward Kennedy, then 30 and an assistant District Attorney in Boston, ran for the Senate. His lack of experience generated a great deal of resentment among Yankee voters, as did his rather blatant "He can do more for Massachusetts" slogan. Meanwhile, a good proportion of the state's academics voted for Harvard professor H. Stuart Hughes, an anti-Cold War candidate and an early 1960s equivalent of a peace candidate; he won only 2% statewide. Once in the Senate, Kennedy impressed senior colleagues by his willingness to do the hum-drum chores of a junior Senator and also impressed home-state voters by his attention to the needs of Massachusetts. After the death of President Kennedy, the youngest Kennedy began to involve himself in more substantive issues. He became the Senator best versed in the problems of Vietnamese refugees and, by the late 1960s, the driving force behind legislation to provide federal financing for comprehensive medical care.

Kennedy also played a major role in a substantial revision of the nation's immigration laws in 1965, one which eliminated the quota system and allowed thousands of people from southern Europe and the Mediterranean to come to the United States. Moreover, Kennedy worked hard to eliminate the poll tax, and later to bring about the 18-year-old vote. So by the late 1960s, hardly anyone, including his detractors of 1962, considered the Senator just a lightweight capitalizing on his name. He earned respect as a politician who studied hard, mastered issues, and steered complex legislation through the Senate. Having so established himself, Kennedy mounted a surprise campaign in early 1969 and won the post of Majority Whip away from Russell Long of Louisiana.

Then, in July 1969, the Chappaquiddick tragedy happened. This ruled out Kennedy, then the frontrunner, as a presidential candidate, and also damaged his standing in the Senate. In 1971, he lost the Whip's post, much as he had won it, to a lightning-fast effort launched by the better-prepared Robert Byrd of West Virginia. Nevertheless, by early 1972, Kennedy again emerged as an important legislator, especially in the field of health care; and in the eyes of the national press at least, he was also a presidential possibility. Though Kennedy later made numerous campaign appearances for McGovern, he spent the week of the Miami convention in Hyannisport, repeatedly turning away McGovern's offer of second spot on the ticket. In 1973, he added to his workload two unusual personal appearances: the first arguing his own case, successfully, in federal court to establish as illegal President Nixon's use of a pocket veto; the second, to appear on July 4, 1973, at Decatur, Alabama, with Gov. George Wallace.

Today, Kennedy once again appears a frontrunner for the presidency, a status he has had, as often as not, since he was 36. Political commentators weigh Chappaquiddick against Watergate; but it is perhaps more important to note that the greatest defections among usually Democratic voters all over the country in 1972 came among Roman Catholics—among whom Kennedy stirs truly strong positive feelings. Still, as Kennedy knows as well as anyone, a lot can happen between now and 1976. If he does make a serious run for the presidency in 1976, as most people in Washington expect, he will have to relinquish his Senate seat. Likely contenders in that event: 6th district Democratic Congressman Michael Harrington; Gov. Francis Sargent; and U. S. Attorney General Elliot Richardson. There is one local problem for Richardson, however; in his brief tenure at the Pentagon, he closed down the bulk of Massachusetts' military installations.

Edward Brooke, the state's junior Senator, is the first black member of the Senate since Blanche K. Bruce was denied reelection by the Mississippi "home rule" legislature in 1881. A native of Washington, D.C., Brooke rose steadily in the Massachusetts Republican party (probably the nation's most liberal) from appointive positions to the Attorney General's office. On his way to becoming Attorney General in 1962, Brooke beat Elliot Richardson in an unusual Republican primary. In 1966, Brooke's election to replace Leverett Saltonstall, the state's most durable Yankee Republican (and also loved among the Irish), surprised no one. Brooke combines liberal stands on issues with a deep devotion to the Republican party. After voting against the Nixon Administration on many crucial matters, the Massachusetts Senator seconded Richard Nixon's nomination in Miami Beach. Brooke praised Nixon for ending the war in Vietnam and for his policy toward China and Russia.

Neither abrasive nor militant, Brooke has never regarded himself a special representative of the black community. With only 3% of the state's population black, Brooke has always won elections in an overwhelmingly white Massachusetts electorate. He has not been asked, nor is he seeking, membership in the congressional Black Caucus, which is made up of black members of the House, most of whom represent black-majority districts. But it should be noted that Brooke has reserved some of his most deeply felt criticism of the Nixon Administration for its record in civil rights and for its nominations of Judges Carswell and Haynsworth to the Supreme Court.

While John McCormack served as House Majority Leader and then as Speaker, the Massachusetts House delegation possessed a remarkable stability. Rumors had it that McCormack took great pains to insure the incumbency of the state's Congressmen of both parties. But in 1970, after 45 years in the House, the Speaker retired, and in 1972 no less than four of the state's twelve House seats were seriously—and closely—contested. Currently the Democrats have a solid 9–3 edge in the delegation—reflecting, as it happens, the party's proportion of the state legislative seats. The three Republican members of the House are among the party's most liberal. The prospects in 1974 are for some more tough races in several districts. Coattails are never a factor in Massachusetts. There is no straight party lever, with well over half the electorate known to split tickets.

Census Data Pop. 5,689,170; 2.81% of U.S. total, 10th largest; change 1960–70, 10.5%. Central city, 30%; suburban, 54%. Median family income, $10,833; 8th highest; families above $15,000: 25%; families below $3,000: 6%. Median years education, 12.3.

1972 Share of Federal Tax Burden $6,751,290,000; 3.23% of U.S. total, 9th largest.

1972 Share of Federal Outlays $5,991,804,889; 2.76% of U.S. total, 12th largest.   Per capita federal spending, $1,053.

DOD	$1,961,143,000	8th	(3.14%)	HEW	$2,350,206,938	9th	(3.29%)
AEC	$15,311,272	20th	(0.58%)	HUD	$157,678,764	5th	(5.14%)
NASA	$62,732,045	11th	(2.10%)	VA	$372,684,596	9th	(3.26%)
DOT	$184,134,036	15th	(2.33%)	USDA	$47,978,589	40th	(0.31%)
DOC	$20,400,234	13th	(1.58%)	CSC	$112,809,550	11th	(2.74%)
DOI	$15,777,398	30th	(0.74%)	TD	$251,545,850	11th	(1.52%)
DOJ	$5,815,579	39th	(0.59%)	Other	$433,587,038		

Economic Base   Finance, insurance and real estate; electrical equipment and supplies, especially communication equipment; machinery, especially special industry machinery; apparel and other textile products, especially women's and misses' outerwear; printing and publishing, especially newspapers and commercial printing; fabricated metal products; food and kindred products.

Political Line-up   Governor, Francis W. Sargent (R); seat up, 1974. Senators, Edward M. Kennedy (D) and Edward W. Brooke (R). Representatives, 12 (9 D and 3 R). State Senate (33 D and 7 R); State House (186 D, 52 R, and 2 Ind.).

The Voters

Registration   2,775,538 total. 1,184,623 D (43%); 527,631 R (19%); 1,063,284 Ind. (38%).
Median voting age 44.2
Employment profile   White collar, 53%. Blue collar, 34%. Service, 13%. Farm, 0%.
Ethnic groups   Black, 3%. Spanish, 1%. Total foreign stock, 33%. Canada, 8%; Italy, 5%; Ireland, 4%; UK, 3%; Poland, USSR, 2% each; Portugal, 1%.

Presidential vote

1972	Nixon (R)	1,112,078	(45%)
	McGovern (D)	1,332,540	(55%)
1968	Nixon (R)	766,844	(33%)
	Humphrey (D)	1,469,218	(63%)
	Wallace (AI)	87,088	(4%)
1964	Johnson (D)	1,786,422	(76%)
	Goldwater (R)	549,727	(24%)

Senator

Edward M. Kennedy (D)   Elected 1962, seat up, 1976; b. Feb. 22, 1932, Boston; home, Boston; Milton Academy; Harvard, B.A., 1956; International Law School, The Hague, Holland, 1958; U. of Va., LL.B., 1959; Army, 1951–53; married, three children; Catholic.

Career   Asst. District Atty., Suffolk Co., 1961–62; Asst. Senate Majority Leader, 1969–71.

Offices   431 OSOB, 202-225-4543. Also Rm. 2400A, Kennedy Fed. Bldg., Boston 02203, 617-223-2826.

Administrative Assistant   Edward T. Martin

Committees

Judiciary (5th); Subs: Administrative Practice and Procedure (Chm.); Antitrust and Monopoly; Constitutional Rights; Criminal Laws and Procedures; Immigration and Naturalization; Juvenile Delinquency; Refugees and Escapees (Chm.).

Labor and Public Welfare (4th); Subs: Education; Aging; Employment, Poverty, and Migratory Labor; Health (Chm.); Alcoholism and Narcotics; Handicapped; Children and Youth; Spec. Sub. on National Science Foundation (Chm.).

Sel. Com. Nutrition and Human Needs (5th).

Spec. Com. Aging (7th); Subs: Housing for the Elderly; Federal, State, and Community Services (Chm.); Consumer Interests of the Elderly; Health of the Elderly; Long-Term Care; Retirement and the Individual.

Group Ratings

	ADA	COPE	LWV	RIPON	NFU	LCV	CFA	NAB	NSI	ACA
1972	90	89	100	79	90	92	100	9	0	5
1971	100	83	100	78	100	–	100	–	–	5
1970	84	100	–	78	100	71	–	18	0	5

Key Votes

1) Busing	FOR	8) Sea Life Prot	FOR	15) Tax Singls Less	AGN
2) Alas P-line	AGN	9) Campaign Subs	FOR	16) Min Tax for Rich	ABS
3) Gun Cntrl	FOR	10) Cmbodia Bmbg	AGN	17) Euro Troop Rdctn	FOR
4) Rehnquist	AGN	11) Legal Srvices	FOR	18) Bust Hwy Trust	FOR
5) Pub TV $	FOR	12) Rev Sharing	ABS	19) Maid Min Wage	FOR
6) EZ Votr Reg	FOR	13) Cnsumr Prot	FOR	20) Farm Sub Limit	FOR
7) No-Fault	FOR	14) Eq Rts Amend	FOR	21) Highr Credt Chgs	AGN

Election Results

1970 general:	Edward M. Kennedy (D)	1,202,856	(63%)
	Josiah Spaulding (R)	715,978	(37%)
1970 primary:	Edward M. Kennedy (D) unopposed		
1964 general:	Edward M. Kennedy (D)	1,716,907	(75%)
	Howard Whitmore, Jr. (R)	587,663	(25%)
1962 special:	Edward M. Kennedy (D)	1,162,611	(56%)
	George C. Lodge (R)	877,669	(42%)
	H. Stuart Hughes (Ind.)	50,013	(2%)

Senator

Edward W. Brooke (R) Elected 1966, seat up, 1978; b. Oct. 26, 1919, Washington, D.C.; home, Newton Centre; Howard U., B.S., 1940; Boston U., LL.B., 1948, LL.M., 1949; Army, WWII; married, two children; Episcopalian.

Career Chm., Boston Finance Commission, 1961–62; Atty. Gen. Mass., 1963–66.

Offices 421 OSOB, 202-225-2742. Also Rm. 2003H, Kennedy Fed. Bldg., Boston 02203, 617-223-7420, and 1421 Main St., Springfield 01103, 413-781-6700.

Administrative Assistant Stephen Hand

Committees

Appropriations (6th); Subs: Defense; Foreign Operations (Ranking Mbr.); Housing and Urban Development, Space, Science, and Veterans; Labor, and Health, Education, and Welfare, and Related Agencies; State, Justice, and Commerce, the Judiciary, and Related Agencies.

Banking, Housing and Urban Affairs (3rd); Subs: Consumer Credit; Securities (Ranking Mbr.); Housing and Urban Affairs.

Sel. Com. on Standards and Conduct (2nd).

Spec. Com. on Aging (5th); Subs: Housing for the Elderly; Federal, State, and Community Services; Consumer Interests of the Elderly (Ranking Mbr.); Health of the Elderly; Long-Term Care.

Group Ratings

	ADA	COPE	LWV	RIPON	NFU	LCV	CFA	NAB	NSI	ACA
1972	80	90	100	96	80	77	100	33	33	19
1971	78	60	100	96	67	–	86	–	–	24
1970	88	92	–	88	93	83	–	18	20	9

Key Votes

1) Busing	FOR	8) Sea Life Prot	FOR	15) Tax Singls Less	FOR
2) Alas P-line	FOR	9) Campaign Subs	AGN	16) Min Tax for Rich	AGN
3) Gun Cntrl	FOR	10) Cmbodia Bmbg	AGN	17) Euro Troop Rdctn	AGN
4) Rehnquist	AGN	11) Legal Srvices	FOR	18) Bust Hwy Trust	FOR
5) Pub TV $	FOR	12) Rev Sharing	FOR	19) Maid Min Wage	FOR
6) EZ Votr Reg	FOR	13) Cnsumr Prot	FOR	20) Farm Sub Limit	FOR
7) No-Fault	FOR	14) Eq Rts Amend	FOR	21) Highr Credt Chgs	AGN

Election Results

1972 general:	Edward W. Brooke (R)	823,278	(35%)
	John J. Droney (D)	1,505,932	(64%)
	Donald Gurewitz (SW)	41,369	(2%)
1972 primary:	Edward W. Brooke (R), unopposed		
1966 general:	Edward W. Brooke (R)	1,213,472	(61%)
	Endicott Peabody (D)	774,761	(39%)

FIRST DISTRICT Political Background

The 1st district of Massachusetts comprises the western part of the state: the Berkshire Mountains and most of the state's portion of the Connecticut River Valley. The Berkshires are famous as a summer resort area and for picturesque towns like Stockbridge, site of Alice's Restaurant, and Lenox, home of the Tanglewood music festival. More important politically are the old mill and manufacturing centers nestled in the mountains, especially Pittsfield, the district's largest city (pop. 57,000), and North Adams (pop. 19,000). Residents of the mill towns, Democrats of ethnic stock, outvote the small-town Republican Yankees by substantial margins.

The Connecticut Valley is a similar kind of place politically: small Republican villages offset by occasional Democratic mill towns. In the middle of the valley are the college towns of Amherst (pop. 18,000), with Amherst College and the University of Massachusetts, and Northampton (pop. 30,000), home of Calvin Coolidge and Smith College. Northampton, despite the presence of Julie and David Eisenhower, went heavily Democratic in 1968; it did the same in 1972. To the south are the industrial and residential suburbs of Springfield: Holyoke (pop. 50,000), Westfield (pop. 31,000), and West Springfield.

In national elections, the 1st votes Democratic. Like 11 of the 12 Massachusetts districts, it went for McGovern in 1972. But in congressional races, the 1st is firmly committed to Republican Silvio Conte. Before he was first elected to the House, Conte was a state Senator from Berkshire County for eight years. He has now become so entrenched that he seldom attracts opposition. Conte's most notable challenge occurred in 1958, his first House race, from Williams College political scientist James MacGregor Burns. The professor got some national publicity, but Conte got the local votes. So Burns went on to finish his Roosevelt biography, while Conte went down to Washington to become, in time, one of the few liberal Republicans on the House Appropriations Committee.

Conte has been unafraid of bucking the Nixon Administration and the Republican leadership on important issues. One such issue was the SST. As ranking Republican member of the Transportation Appropriations Subcommittee, Conte was one of the leading opponents of government funding of the big Boeing project. A perennial Conte project is to place a ceiling on farm subsidy payments to any one farmowner. Though he succeeded in getting a $20,000 limit imposed in the 92nd Congress, Conte has often been frustrated by the power of the farm bloc and the willingness of labor-oriented liberals to barter away their support of this issue for concessions they care more about.

Census Data Pop. 469,438. Central city, 23%; suburban, 38%. Median family income, $10,311; families above $15,000: 20%; families below $3,000: 7%. Median years education, 12.2.

1972 Share of Federal Outlays $441,665,886

DOD	$151,896,912	HEW	$180,387,556
AEC	$227,332	HUD	$8,783,450
NASA	$310,866	DOI	$1,168,470
DOT	$1,919,684	USDA	$6,098,768
		Other	$90,872,848

Federal Military-Industrial Commitments

DOD Contractors General Electric (Pittsfield), $106.945m: design and production of Poseidon missile firing system. Kollmorgen Corp. (Northampton), $10.600m: shipboard electo-optical equipment.

Economic Base Electrical equipment and supplies; paper and allied products, especially miscellaneous converted paper products; finance, insurance and real estate; machinery; and printing and publishing. Also higher education (Univ. of Massachusetts).

The Voters

Registration 228,106 total. 82,747 D (36%); 42,976 R (19%); 102,383 Ind. (45%).
Median voting age 44.1
Employment profile White collar, 49%. Blue collar, 36%. Service, 14%. Farm, 1%.
Ethnic groups Spanish, 1%. Total foreign stock, 27%. Canada, 7%; Poland, 5%; Italy, 3%; Ireland, UK, Germany, 2% each.

Presidential vote

1972	Nixon (R)	....	102,513	(49%)
	McGovern (D)	....	107,528	(51%)
1968	Nixon (R)	....	69,299	(37%)
	Humphrey (D)	....	111,303	(58%)
	Wallace (AI)	....	8,812	(5%)

Representative

Silvio O. Conte (R) Elected 1958; b. Nov. 9, 1921, Pittsfield; home, Pittsfield; Boston Col. and Boston Col. Law School, LL.B., 1949; married, four children; Catholic.

Career Practicing atty., 1949–58; State Senator, 1950–58.

Offices 239 CHOB, 202-225-5335. Also North St., Pittsfield 01201, 413-442-0946.

Administrative Assistant Sally S. Donner

Committees

Appropriations (5th); Subs: Labor, Health, Education, and Welfare; Transportation (Ranking Mbr.); Foreign Operations.

Sel. Com. Small Business (Ranking Mbr.); Subs: Activities of Regulatory Agencies; Special Small Business Problems; Government Procurement and International Trade (Ranking Mbr.).

Group Ratings

	ADA	COPE	LWV	RIPON	NFU	LCV	CFA	NAB	NSI	ACA
1972	63	60	100	93	50	93	100	33	44	22
1971	78	50	100	94	60	–	88	–	–	38
1970	72	75	–	94	92	65	80	42	44	28

Key Votes

1) Busing	FOR	6) Cmbodia Bmbg	AGN	11) Chkg Acct Intrst	FOR
2) Strip Mines	AGN	7) Bust Hwy Trust	FOR	12) End HISC (HUAC)	FOR
3) Cut Mil $	AGN	8) Farm Sub Lmt	FOR	13) Nixon Sewer Veto	FOR
4) Rev Shrg	FOR	9) School Prayr	FOR	14) Corp Cmpaign $	AGN
5) Pub TV $	FOR	10) Cnsumr Prot	FOR	15) Pol $ Disclosr	FOR

Election Results

1972 general:	Silvio O. Conte (R), unopposed
1972 primary:	Silvio O. Conte (R), unopposed
1970 general:	Silvio O. Conte (R), unopposed

SECOND DISTRICT Political Background

The 2nd district of Massachusetts comprises the city of Springfield, many of its suburbs, and a collection of rural and small industrial towns to the east. Springfield (pop. 163,000) and Chicopee (pop. 66,000) are Democratic bastions of the district, though most of the rest of the 2nd usually produces Democratic margins as well. The image of the small New England town is a place inhabited by taciturn Yankees. But to a large extent the WASPs have either died out or have long since moved west, their descendants now populating much of the Midwest. In their place are people of immigrant stock, Irish-, Italian-, and even Polish-Americans. The storefronts here may have a New England Yankee fascade, but hanging from it are signs often sporting the name of an Italian or Polish proprietor.

Springfield is the home town of several famous political pros—Lawrence O'Brien, the Democratic National Chairman who was the target of Watergate buggers; Joseph Napolitan, the well-known campaign consultant; and Alaska Sen. Mike Gravel, of French-Canadian descent—all grew up in the city and learned their first political lessons in its wards and precincts. Another such pro is Congressman Edward P. Boland, a Democrat who has now had more than 20 years of service in the House. For many years, Boland was a bachelor and roomed with Tip O'Neill of Cambridge; Boland got married in August 1973. The 2nd-district Congressman is a politician who bridges some of the gaps between old-line, big-city Democrats and the younger, more ideological liberals who have come to dominate the party caucus. In 1971, the highly regarded Boland was mentioned as a candidate for House Majority Leader, but he instead supported the late Hale Boggs. Boggs then appointed O'Neill Majority Whip, and in 1973, O'Neill succeeded to the Majority Leadership.

Boland himself holds a powerful position in the House as Chairman of the Appropriations Committee's HUD-Space-Science-Veterans Subcommittee. As the seventh-ranking Democrat on the full Appropriations Committee and as a comparatively youthful 63 (in 1974) for a man in that position, Boland has an outside chance to become Chairman. Reelection is no problem. During the last ten years, the Republicans have fielded a candidate in the 2nd district only once, a man who won 26% of the votes.

Census Data Pop. 472,270. Central city, 49%; suburban, 28%. Median family income, $10,268; families above $15,000: 20%; families below $3,000: 7%. Median years education, 12.1.

1972 Share of Federal Outlays $339,491,666

DOD	$68,688,178	HEW	$178,213,444
AEC	$30,678	HUD	$11,905,022
NASA	$117,622	DOI	$457,540
DOT	$2,921,701	USDA	$2,777,630
		Other	$74,379,851

Federal Military-Industrial Commitments

DOD Installations Westover AFB (Chicopee Falls); closed, 1974.

Economic Base Finance, insurance and real estate; machinery, especially metalworking machinery; fabricated metal products; paper and allied products, especially miscellaneous converted paper products; and printing and publishing.

The Voters

Registration 221,264 total. 96,277 D (44%); 40,666 R (18%); 84,321 Ind. (38%).
Median voting age 45.1
Employment profile White collar, 45%. Blue collar, 42%. Service, 12%. Farm, 1%.
Ethnic groups Black, 5%. Spanish, 2%. Total foreign stock, 31%. Canada, 9%; Poland, 5%;
Italy, 3%; Ireland, UK, 2% each; USSR, Germany, 1% each.

Presidential vote

1972	Nixon (R)	88,652	(48%)
	McGovern (D)	95,348	(52%)
1968	Nixon (R)	62,441	(34%)
	Humphrey (D)	114,197	(61%)
	Wallace (AI)	8,787	(5%)

Representative

Edward P. Boland (D) Elected 1952; b. Oct. 1, 1911, Springfield; home,
Springfield; Boston Col. Law School; Army, WWII; unmarried;
Catholic.

Career State Rep., 1935–40; Register of Deeds, Hampden County,
1941–52.

Offices 2111 RHOB, 202-225-5601. Also 1883 Main St., Rm. 100,
Springfield 01103, 413-733-4127.

Administrative Assistant P. Joseph Donoghue

Committees

Appropriations (7th); Subs: Housing and Urban Development, Space, Science, Veterans (Chm.);
Public Works, AEC; Transportation.

Group Ratings

	ADA	COPE	LWV	RIPON	NFU	LCV	CFA	NAB	NSI	ACA
1972	69	91	75	87	86	60	100	17	22	17
1971	86	92	89	83	71	–	86	–	–	14
1970	76	83	–	73	100	80	95	17	40	12

Key Votes

1) Busing	FOR	6) Cmbodia Bmbg	AGN	11) Chkg Acct Intrst	AGN
2) Strip Mines	AGN	7) Bust Hwy Trust	FOR	12) End HISC (HUAC)	FOR
3) Cut Mil $	AGN	8) Farm Sub Lmt	FOR	13) Nixon Sewer Veto	FOR
4) Rev Shrg	FOR	9) School Prayr	AGN	14) Corp Cmpaign $	FOR
5) Pub TV $	FOR	10) Cnsumr Prot	FOR	15) Pol $ Disclosr	FOR

Election Results

1972 general: Edward P. Boland (D), unopposed
1972 primary: Edward P. Boland (D), unopposed
1970 general: Edward P. Boland (D), unopposed

THIRD DISTRICT Political Background

Worcester (pop. 176,000), the second-largest city in Massachusetts, is a manufacturing town
that lies in the rough geographical center of the state. Worcester is surrounded by a number of mill

towns and comfortable suburbs, situated in the craggy New England hills. Though there are a number of colleges and universities about (Sigmund Freud's first American appearance was before a polite but skeptical audience at Clark University here), they do not, as in the Boston area, constitute a major presence in the community. Nor is there as strong a movement here among upper-income Yankees toward antiwar political positions (see state write-up). This is nitty-gritty New England, where the Democratic majorities result almost entirely from the all but genetically ingrained voting habits of middle- and lower-middle-class voters of various ethnic groups.

In congressional elections, the Worcester-based district (it used to be numbered the 4th) has been strongly Democratic for about as long as anyone can remember. Since 1946, it has regularly returned Democrat Harold Donohue to Congress with strong majorities. Donohue is an aging (73 in 1974) bachelor who is the second-ranking Democrat on the House Judiciary Committee. In many ways, he is the last of the get-along-to-go-along Irish politicians who dominated Massachusetts Democratic politics for so many years.

For a couple of years, rumors have been out that Donohue will soon retire. After the 1970 elections, two of his closest friends left the House: John McCormack retired and the late Philip J. Philbin suffered a primary defeat in an adjacent district (then called the 3rd, now the 4th). Donohue still spends long afternoons on the floor of the House; some gallery denizens claim to have caught him napping quietly. A number of young, ambitious politicians are said to be interested—or in the case of John Kerry, to have been interested (see Massachusetts 5)—in the the seat. Even if Donohue decides to run again in 1974, he may find—for a change—substantial opposition in the district.

Census Data Pop. 469,443. Central city, 38%; suburban, 36%. Median family income, $10,863; families above $15,000: 23%; families below $3,000: 6%. Median years education, 12.2.

1972 Share of Federal Outlays $373,712,161

DOD	$80,357,227	HEW	$184,611,594
AEC	$548,878	HUD	$9,496,525
NASA	$2,238,267	DOI	$657,839
DOT	$8,953,675	USDA	$2,804,438
		Other	$8,403,718

Federal Military-Industrial Commitments

No installations or contractors receiving prime awards greater than $5,000,000.

Economic Base Finance, insurance and real estate; machinery, especially metalworking machinery; fabricated metal products, especially cutlery, hand tools and hardware; primary metal industries; and rubber and plastics products, especially miscellaneous plastics products.

The Voters

Registration 227,854 total. 90,855 D (40%); 41,614 R (18%); 95,385 Ind. (42%).
Median voting age 44.5
Employment profile White collar, 49%. Blue collar, 38%. Service, 13%. Farm, –%.
Ethnic groups Total foreign stock, 32%. Canada, 8%; Italy, 5%; Ireland, 3%; UK, Poland, Sweden, 2% each; USSR, Lithuania, 1% each.

Presidential vote

1972	Nixon (R)	83,423	(46%)
	McGovern (D)	98,449	(54%)
1968	Nixon (R)	62,260	(32%)
	Humphrey (D)	125,551	(64%)
	Wallace (AI)	5,810	(3%)

Representative

Harold D. Donohue (D) Elected 1946; b. June 18, 1901, Worcester; home, Worcester; Northeastern U., 1925; Navy, WWII; unmarried; Catholic.

Career Atty., 1926- ; Alderman, acting Mayor, Worcester.

Offices 2206 RHOB, 202-225-6101. Also 390 Main St., Worcester 01608, 617-754-7264.

Administrative Assistant William A. Rourke

Committees

Government Operations (20th); Subs: Government Activities; Special Studies.

Judiciary (2nd); Sub: No. 2 (Claims) (Chm.).

Group Ratings

	ADA	COPE	LWV	RIPON	NFU	LCV	CFA	NAB	NSI	ACA
1972	81	91	91	81	86	82	100	10	14	5
1971	62	90	100	58	100	–	88	–	–	5
1970	72	100	–	56	92	90	80	0	90	17

Key Votes

1) Busing	FOR	6) Cmbodia Bmbg	AGN	11) Chkg Acct Intrst	AGN
2) Strip Mines	AGN	7) Bust Hwy Trust	FOR	12) End HISC (HUAC)	FOR
3) Cut Mil $	FOR	8) Farm Sub Lmt	FOR	13) Nixon Sewer Veto	AGN
4) Rev Shrg	FOR	9) School Prayr	FOR	14) Corp Cmpaign $	FOR
5) Pub TV $	FOR	10) Cnsumr Prot	FOR	15) Pol $ Disclosr	AGN

Election Results

1972 general:	Harold D. Donahue (D), unopposed		
1972 primary:	Harold D. Donahue (D), unopposed		
1970 general:	Harold D. Donahue (D)	95,016	(54%)
	Howard A. Miller (R)	79,870	(46%)

FOURTH DISTRICT Political Background

Dozens of Protestant clergymen have served in the House of Representatives, but only one Roman Catholic priest has ever been elected a voting Congressman: Father Robert F. Drinan of the 4th district of Massachusetts. By any reckoning, he is an unusual political figure. With no political experience, Drinan beat an incumbent Congressman not once but twice in 1970, and then in 1972 won a close contest over a rare kind of Republican challenger. Drinan has yet to win a large majority in a district that McGovern carried easily, but the Congressman appears in good shape for reelection in 1974.

The story began in 1970, when Drinan was, as he had been for 14 years, the highly respected Dean of the Boston College Law School. Living near the school, the scholar-priest was a resident of the old 3rd district—a geographic monstrosity that stretched from suburban Newton, just outside Boston, some 100 miles out in a narrow corridor past the factory city of Fitchburg in central Massachusetts. Congressman Philip J. Philbin, who had represented the 3rd for 28 years, was under attack for his hawkish stands as the second-ranking Democrat on the House Armed Services Committee. In 1968, after redistricting added Newton and several other Boston suburbs to the district, Philbin won only 49% of the votes in a four-candidate Democratic primary, and only 48% in the general election where an independent peace candidate finished second.

This was obviously a constituency waiting for a candidate. About half of the district's population had not been represented by Philbin before 1968, and these people felt little rapport with the old-line politician. The problem was to put together a majority composed of upper-middle-class Newton, with its large Jewish population; Waltham, a Catholic working-class suburb; and the upper-income, woodsy, WASP towns of Weston, Lincoln, and Wayland. The majority here had to be enough to overcome Philbin's strength as a long-time incumbent in the western end of the district. First the liberals of the old 3rd got together in caucus to avoid splitting their efforts; they chose Father Drinan to be their man, with John Kerry bowing out (see Massachusetts 5). Then with the help of campaign consultant John Marttila and hundreds of volunteers, Drinan accumulated the majority he needed in the Democratic primary, edging Philbin. The old regular, refusing to accept defeat, entered the general election as an independent. There was also a strong Republican candidate in the field. Drinan finished just enough votes ahead to win a plurality.

The Republicans eyed the district in 1972 for a number of reasons. In 1970, Drinan won only 38% of the votes; many Catholics opposed the idea of a priest in politics; and Drinan lost the heavily Catholic, mill-town western end of the district. Redistricting complicated the picture, adding the prosperous Boston suburban enclave of Brookline. Though the home of Brahmins like Elliot Richardson, Brookline is important politically for its large and elderly Jewish community. (In 1917, John F. Kennedy was born here in what was then and remains today a Jewish neighborhood.) Finally, the Republicans possessed a strong candidate in personable and popular state Rep. Martin Linsky of Brookline, who is Jewish and a favorite of the liberal Ripon Society. Linsky lost the 1970 Republican nomination for Lieutenant Governor when Frances Sargent bumped him off the ticket after an alleged scandal involving Linsky and a prostitute, but that played no part in the 1972 House contest.

Meanwhile, Drinan had prepared himself. The incumbent set up an impressive constituent service organization in the Fitchburg area and also developed good contacts among local Democrats. Drinan's fervent stands against the Vietnam war made him popular in most of Newton as well as in the WASPy suburbs. Moreover, in the span of two years the Congressman had even become something of a national figure. Unlike most prominent Massachusetts Democrats, he did no early jumping on the putative Muskie bandwagon. Instead, Drinan backed the long-shot, George McGovern, and after the South Dakotan's sweep of the Massachusetts primary—his best primary showing—Drinan became Chairman of the Massachusetts delegation in Miami Beach.

Nevertheless, Linsky proved to be a tough candidate. He spent a lot of money on TV advertising, and charging that Drinan was insufficiently pro-Israel, Linsky got a majority in Brookline. Drinan won by almost 11,000 votes out of 204,000 cast, with an independent-conservative candidate nearly draining off enough votes to prevent Drinan from getting an absolute majority. Linsky's showing was a tribute to his own record and to the importance of the Jewish vote in the state's most Jewish district. Against any other candidate, Drinan would have surely won a large majority in Brookline (McGovern did) and won reelection by a margin closer to that enjoyed by most incumbents. But Drinan did carry the western part of the district, which he had lost two years earlier.

In the House, Drinan, as befits a law-school dean who brought his school to a position of considerable prestige, sits on the Judiciary Committee. He is also a member of the House Internal Security Committee, formerly the House Un-American Activities Committee. The Congressman must see his assignment on Internal Security as some kind of hair shirt. Drinan believes the committee simply wastes the taxpayer's money; he is the only member of the panel who believes it should be abolished. He attracted national attention in July 1973 by offering— but not pressing— a resolution to impeach President Nixon; he has also attracted attention as the only Congressman denied entry to Russia because of his outspoken defense of the rights of Soviet Jews.

Census Data Pop. 476,130. Central city, 16%; suburban, 71%. Median family income, $12,409; families above $15,000: 36%; families below $3,000: 5%. Median years education, 12.5.

1972 Share of Federal Outlays $522,214,590

DOD	$174,737,040	HEW	$200,032,213
AEC	$1,519,573	HUD	$14,060,859
NASA	$6,405,988	DOI	$1,223,848
DOT	$17,482,365	USDA	$3,824,201
		Other	$102,928,503

Federal Military-Industrial Commitments

DOD Contractors Raytheon (Waltham), $37.928m: various electron tubes. Raytheon (Wayland), $15.069m: various radar systems. General Electric (Fitchburg), $14.664m: electrical generating turbines. Raytheon (Sudbury), $13.255m: various electronics research. *DOD Installations* Ft. Devens AB (Ayer).

Economic Base Finance, insurance and real estate; machinery; electrical equipment and supplies, especially communication equipment, and electronic components and accessories; instruments and related products; and fabricated metal products. Also higher education (Boston College).

The Voters

Registration 224,327 total. 85,292 D (38%); 42,948 R (19%); 96,087 Ind. (43%).
Median voting age 42.9
Employment profile White collar, 62%. Blue collar, 27%. Service, 11%. Farm, –%.
Ethnic groups Black, 1%. Spanish, 1%. Total foreign stock, 37%. Canada, 11%; Italy, USSR, 5% each; Ireland, 3%; UK, Poland, 2% each; Germany, 1%.

Presidential vote

1972	Nixon (R)	92,341	(44%)
	McGovern (D)	116,100	(56%)
1968	Nixon (R)	63,795	(33%)
	Humphrey (D)	124,055	(64%)
	Wallace (AI)	4,202	(2%)

Representative

Robert F. Drinan (D) Elected 1970; b. Nov. 15, 1920, Boston; home, Newton; Boston Col., B.A., 1942, M.A., 1947; Georgetown U. Law Center, LL.B., 1949, LL.M., 1950; Catholic.

Career Jesuit Priest; Dean of Boston Col. Law School, 1956–70.

Offices 224 CHOB, 202-225-5931. Also 76 Summer St., Fitchburg 01420, 617-342-8722, and 400 Totten Pond Rd., Waltham 02154, 617-890-9455.

Administrative Assistant William G. Flynn

Committees

Internal Security (4th).

Judiciary (15th); Subs: No. 4 (Civil Rights and Constitutional Rights); No. 3 (Courts, Civil Liberties and the Administration of Justice).

Group Ratings

	ADA	COPE	LWV	RIPON	NFU	LCV	CFA	NAB	NSI	ACA
1972	100	100	100	73	86	86	100	8	0	9
1971	100	83	100	83	80	–	100	–	–	14

Key Votes

1) Busing	FOR	6) Cmbodia Bmbg	AGN	11) Chkg Acct Intrst	FOR
2) Strip Mines	ABS	7) Bust Hwy Trust	FOR	12) End HISC (HUAC)	FOR
3) Cut Mil $	FOR	8) Farm Sub Lmt	FOR	13) Nixon Sewer Veto	AGN
4) Rev Shrg	FOR	9) School Prayr	AGN	14) Corp Cmpaign $	AGN
5) Pub TV $	FOR	10) Cnsumr Prot	FOR	15) Pol $ Disclosr	FOR

Election Results

1972 general: Robert F. Drinan (D) 99,977 (49%)

	Martin A. Linsky (R)	93,927	(46%)
	John T. Collins (C)	11,141	(5%)
1972 primary:	Robert F. Drinan (D), unopposed		
1970 general:	Robert F. Drinan (D)	63,942	(38%)
	John McGlennon (R)	60,575	(36%)
	Philip J. Philbin (Ind.)	45,278	(27%)

FIFTH DISTRICT Political Background

The 5th congressional district of Massachusetts centers on two transportation arteries that have been vital to the state's economic development. The first is the Merrimack River, whose falls provided the power for the great textile mills built by famed Brahmins in the company towns they named after themselves, Lowell and Lawrence. Back in the mid-nineteenth century, the New England textile business was a boom industry that first employed local farm girls and then moved on to hire hundreds of thousands of immigrants from Ireland and French Canada. The New England textile firms have, of course, long since moved to the South, where lower wages prevail (and even there the industry suffers from Japanese competition). With the mills of Lowell and Lawrence quiet, the cities have languished in economic stagnation for some time.

Today, both places have perked up just a little, if only because of the peripheral influence of the state's industrial artery, Route 128, a circumferential superhighway around greater Boston. Many of the nation's leading electronic and defense contracting firms, drawing brain-power from area universities, have located along both sides of the roadway. Route 128 just skirts the bottom of the 5th district, but its influence extends up through the leafy suburbs to the north. As the 1970s opened, Defense Department cutbacks made for gloomy faces on 128. Things are going better now, provided the Nixon Administration does not decide to channel government money, like the outlays planned for the space shuttle, to the politically more congenial climates of Texas, California, and Florida. The Administration apparently did retaliate on Massachusetts, "the one and only," when the state absorbed nearly a quarter of the Defense Department installation cutbacks announced in the spring of 1973.

Like all but one of Massachusetts' congressional districts, the 5th went for George McGovern in 1972. Yet for as long as anyone can remember, the district has been represented by Republican Congressmen. From 1924 to 1960, the 5th elected Edith Nourse Rogers, a genteel Republican who always ran ahead of her party. Her successor was F. Bradford Morse, a generally liberal Republican. Morse surprised a number of observers when he supported the Nixon candidacy before the 1968 Republican convention. One explanation was that he was persuaded to do so by Charles Colson, an old friend from the days when both men worked on Sen. Leverett Saltonstall's staff. Colson may have also had something to do with the way Morse left Congress. In 1972, Nixon nominated him to replace the late Ralph Bunche as Undersecretary of the United Nations—a choice job which Morse, always interested in foreign policy, promptly took.

That left the seat in the 5th up for grabs, and the candidate who did the most visible kind of grabbing was a 28-year-old Yale graduate, John Kerry. For a couple of years, Kerry had made headlines as the national leader of the Vietnam Veterans Against the War (VVAW). Moreover, the Massachusetts native made it known to all that he was shopping around for a congressional district from which to run (see Massachusetts 4). In order to challenge veteran Democrat Harold Donohue (see Massachusetts 3) in the 1972 primary, Kerry and his wife purchased a home in Worcester. Then he learned of Morse's appointment, moved to Lowell, and started to run in the 5th.

Kerry's light-footedness was the first of the several things that hurt his campaign. The eventual Republican nominee, former state Rep. Paul Cronin of Andover, who had been an aide to Morse, was well-known locally and made the most of Kerry's district-hopping. Then, on the night before the primary, Kerry's brother was caught in the adjacent basement of a rival candidate's headquarters; he was, he said, searching for a possible disruption of Kerry telephone banks. Besides Kerry and Cronin, there was another candidate in the general election, independent Roger Durkin, who put out literature and ads accusing Kerry of radicalism. Just before the election, Durkin withdrew in favor of Cronin. All this time, the Lowell *Sun* waged a vigorous anti-Kerry campaign that featured a book-jacket photo of Kerry and other VVAW members demonstrating with an upside-down American flag. The *Sun* also complained about the scads of money poured into the Kerry campaign from New York radical chic sources. The Kerry campaign itself stressed opposition to the war in the suburbs and economic issues in Lowell and Lawrence.

Cronin campaigned quietly, and on election night scored a solid victory. Outpolling Nixon in the district, Cronin even managed to carry Lowell and Lawrence, both heavily Democratic by tradition. But there may have been more to Cronin's victory than was at first apparent, and more than Cronin himself could gauge. Charles Colson was known to have taken an especially close interest in the 5th district and in John Kerry. The ambitiousness of the young man disturbed even some of his supporters, and Colson, who was in charge of veterans' affairs for the White House, did not want to see the Vietnam war's first veteran in Congress one strongly opposed to Mr. Nixon's policies (there are still no Vietnam veterans of any kind in Congress). As the campaign opened, independent candidate Durkin, it appears, was in considerable trouble with the Securities and Exchange Commission—trouble that never resulted in prosecution after Durkin mounted his campaign against Kerry. Durkin has never revealed the sources of his considerable campaign funds.

So in 1972, the 5th district may have had a mini-Watergate working beneath the surface. No one believes that Cronin, a moderate respected by both local Democrats and Republicans, had any knowledge of any dirty tricks played. But it is entirely possible that Kerry, who talked after his upset defeat about running for the Lowell City Council, may run for Congress again in 1974 on a Watergate scandal platform. At this writing, the picture in the 5th is not clear enough to make intelligent prediction.

In the meantime, Cronin has been compiling an interesting record on his own behalf. Like all the members of the Massachusetts delegation, the Congressman has steadily voted against the bombing in Cambodia. He has also obtained committee assignments far different from those usually sought by Massachusetts Congressmen: the Interior Committee and Science and Astronautics. Moreover, Cronin has become something of an expert on the energy crisis; he spoke out early in his term, predicting gasoline shortages and rationing—predictions that looked good in the summer of 1973. The Congressman is promoting construction of an oil refinery in Lowell, which would be the first in Massachusetts, an energy-poor state for many years. So if there is to be a rematch in 1974, Cronin will make a very strong incumbent, even if he never falls heir to the kind of national publicity Kerry once enjoyed.

Census Data   Pop. 473,154. Central city, 34%; suburban, 57%. Median family income, $11,532; families above $15,000: 29%; families below $3,000: 6%. Median years education, 12.3.

1972 Share of Federal Outlays $596,501,640

DOD	$224,116,008	HEW	$205,736,387
AEC	$2,031,262	HUD	$16,371,557
NASA	$8,604,577	DOI	$1,517,556
DOT	$21,921,201	USDA	$4,331,046
		Other	$111,772,046

Federal Military-Industrial Commitments

DOD Contractors Raytheon (Bedford), $112.512m: SAM-D missile guidance and control; Sparrow missile guidance and control; various other electronic research and development. Raytheon (Lowell), $100.196m: guidance and control for Sparrow, Chaparral, Sidewinder missile systems. Raytheon (Andover), $94.657m: Sparrow missile guidance and control; Sam-D missile guidance and control. Western Electric (Bedford), $86.461m: research and development of ABM. MIT (Lexington), $78.709m: various electronics research. Avco (Wilmington), $27.968m: various electronics and ballistics research. Sanders Associates (Bedford), $15.631m: design and production of anti-aircraft radar system. Mitre Corp. (Bedford), $13.977m: design of information and communications systems. Honeywell (Lexington), $10.894m: various electronics research. Avco (Lowell), $5.809m: research and production of various structural components of ballistic weapons.
DOD Installations Hanscom Field, AF (Bedford).

Economic Base Electrical equipment and supplies, especially communication equipment, and electronic components and accessories; finance, insurance and real estate; machinery, especially office and computing machines; instruments and related products; and food and kindred products. Also higher education (Lowell Technological Inst.).

The Voters

Registration 226,785 total. 96,821 D (43%); 45,187 R (20%); 84,777 Ind. (37%).
Median voting age 43.1
Employment profile White collar, 52%. Blue collar, 36%. Service, 11%. Farm, 1%.
Ethnic groups Spanish, 1%. Total foreign stock, 31%. Canada, 10%; Italy, 4%; UK, Ireland, 3%
each; Poland, Greece, Germany, 1% each.

Presidential vote

1972	Nixon (R)	106,658	(47%)
	McGovern (D)	120,470	(53%)
1968	Nixon (R)	64,516	(34%)
	Humphrey (D)	118,447	(62%)
	Wallace (AI)	5,958	(3%)

Representative

Paul W. Cronin (R) Elected 1972; b. March 14, 1938, Boston; home, Andover; Boston U., B.A.; Harvard U., Kennedy School of Government, M.A.; married, two children.

Career Andover Selectman; State Rep., two terms; Chief Asst. to Rep. Bradford Morse.

Offices 1019 LHOB, 202-225-3411. Also 9 Central St., Lowell 01852, 617-459-3321.

Administrative Assistant S. Steven Karalekas

Committees

Interior and Insular Affairs (17th); Subs: No. 1 (National Parks and Recreation); No. 3 (Environment); No. 5 (Mines and Mining).

Science and Astronautics (11th); Subs: Energy; Science, Research, and Development.

Group Ratings: Newly Elected

Key Votes

1) Busing	NE	6) Cmbodia Bmbg	AGN	11) Chkg Acct Intrst	FOR
2) Strip Mines	NE	7) Bust Hwy Trust	FOR	12) End HISC (HUAC)	AGN
3) Cut Mil $	NE	8) Farm Sub Lmt	NE	13) Nixon Sewer Veto	FOR
4) Rev Shrg	NE	9) School Prayr	NE	14) Corp Cmpaign $	NE
5) Pub TV $	NE	10) Cnsumr Prot	NE	15) Pol $ Disclosr	NE

Election Results

1972 general:	Paul W. Cronin (R)	110,970	(45%)
	John F. Kerry (D)	92,847	(53%)
	Roger P. Durkin (Ind.)	3,803	(2%)
1972 primary:	Paul W. Cronin (R)	10,812	(59%)
	Ellen A. Sampson (R)	4,330	(24%)
	Armand Morissette (R)	2,486	(13%)
	George P. Macheras (R)	790	(4%)

SIXTH DISTRICT Political Background

The 6th of Massachusetts is the Nawth Shoah (a stab at the local accent) district. Along and just back of the rocky coast north of Boston are the estates of some of the Commonwealth's oldest families, including, to name some still important politically, the Lodges and the Saltonstalls. Only a few miles away are the fishermen of Gloucester, who suffer badly these days because of an inability to match the technologically superior Russian trawlers. Here also are the textile-mill workers of Haverhill and Newburyport on the Merrimack River, and the artists and summer people in Rockport. To the south is Salem, where 20 witches were once hanged and pressed to death and where Nathaniel Hawthorne's House of Seven Gables still stands. Also to the south is the boating suburb of Marblehead, which Jews now share with WASPs, and Lynn, whose troubled shoe industry is part of the movement within organized labor and some sectors of the business community pushing protectionist trade legislation.

The rich towns of the North Shore have given the district a reputation for Republicanism, one that is not really accurate. Democratic presidential candidates, including McGovern in 1972, have carried the 6th easily. But for many years the district elected Republican Congressmen with big majorities,: this is how William H. Bates won from 1950 to 1968 and his father before him from 1936 to 1950.

Bates died unexpectedly in 1969. In the special election to fill the vacancy, state Rep. Michael Harrington, a Democrat, waged a vigorous and sophisticated campaign to beat state Sen. William Saltonstall. The race tested the popularity of the Nixon Administration's foreign policy and spending priorities. Harrington fervently opposed the Vietnam war and the ABM, while Saltonstall, son of the former Senator Leverett Saltonstall, supported Nixon on both issues. Harrington won by a 52-48 margin. In 1970, Harrington won reelection with 61% of the votes over a Republican who would later become one of the political heavies of early 1973—Howard Phillips. He was the young conservative Nixon appointed to dismantle the Office of Economic Opportunity and the War on Poverty. The courts ruled that his appointment was illegal since it was not submitted to the Senate.

Harrington does not seem entirely happy with the pace of life in the House or with his position as one of its junior members. In the 92nd Congress, Harrington was a member of the Armed Services Committee, and as an outspoken dove, he tangled in one especially bitter session with the contentious hawk, Charles Gubser of California. In 1973, the Massachusetts Congressman switched to Foreign Affairs, in part to open a seat on Armed Services for Ronald Dellums of California. He is interested in running for statewide office someday, and considered running— and then decided not to— for Attorney General of Massachusetts in 1974. But with the asssets of an Irish heritage and a Harvard education, Harrington could be a formidable statewide contender, and if Edward Kennedy relinquishes his Senate seat in 1976, Harrington might well seek— and win— it.

Census Data Pop. 475,885. Central city, 10%; suburban, 72%. Median family income, $10,904; families above $15,000: 25%; families below $3,000: 6%. Median years education, 12.3.

1972 Share of Federal Outlays $599,907,788

DOD	$225,395,757	HEW	$206,911,185
AEC	$2,042,861	HUD	$16,465,042
NASA	$8,653,711	DOI	$1,526,222
DOT	$22,046,376	USDA	$4,355,777
		Other	$112,510,857

Federal Military-Industrial Commitments

DOD Contractors General Electric (Lynn and West Lynn), $221.554m: various aircraft engines and parts. Varian Associates (Beverly), $8.709m: design and production of various electronic ware.

Economic Base Electrical equipment and supplies, especially communication equipment; machinery; leather and leather products, especially shoes, except rubber; finance, insurance and real estate; and rubber and plastics products, especially miscellaneous plastics products.

The Voters

Registration 248,574 total. 85,513 D (34%); 61, 408 R (25%); 101,653 Ind. (41%).
Median voting age 45.5
Employment profile White collar, 52%. Blue collar, 36%. Service, 12%. Farm, –%.
Ethnic groups Total foreign stock, 31%. Canada, 10%; Italy, 4%; Ireland, UK, 3% each; USSR, Poland, Greece, 2% each.

Presidential vote

1972	Nixon (R)	104,027	(47%)
	McGovern (D)	116,157	(53%)
1968	Nixon (R)	76,125	(36%)
	Humphrey (D)	125,950	(60%)
	Wallace (AI)	6,588	(3%)

Represenatative

Michael J. Harrington (D) Elected Sept. 1969; b. Sept. 2, 1936, Salem; home, Beverly; Harvard Col., A.B., 1958; Harvard Law School, LL.B., 1961; Harvard Grad. School of Pub. Admin., 1962–63; married, five children; Catholic.

Career Salem City Council, 1960–63; State Rep., 1964–69; partner atty., Ronan and Harrington, Salem, Mass., 1962– .

Offices 435 CHOB, 202-225-8020. Also Salem P.O. Bldg., Salem 01970, 617-745-5800; and P.O. Bldg., Lynn 617-599-7105.

Administrative Assistant Christine B. Sullivan

Committees

Foreign Affairs (19th); Subs: Africa; Foreign Economic Policy; Inter-American Affairs.

Group Ratings

	ADA	COPE	LWV	RIPON	NFU	LCV	CFA	NAB	NSI	ACA
1972	94	90	100	73	83	80	—	10	0	10
1971	97	83	89	83	85	–	100	–	–	11
1970	88	100	–	87	92	100	100	0	13	18

Key Votes

1) Busing	FOR	6) Cmbodia Bmbg	AGN	11) Chkg Acct Intrst	AGN
2) Strip Mines	ABS	7) Bust Hwy Trust	FOR	12) End HISC (HUAC)	FOR
3) Cut Mil $	FOR	8) Farm Sub Lmt	FOR	13) Nixon Sewer Veto	AGN
4) Rev Shrg	FOR	9) School Prayr	AGN	14) Corp Cmpaign $	AGN
5) Pub TV $	FOR	10) Cnsumr Prot	FOR	15) Pol $ Disclosr	AGN

Election Results

1972 general:	Michael Harrington (D)	139,697	(64%)
	James Brady Mosely (R)	78,381	(36%)
1972 primary:	Michael Harrington (D)	30,769	(74%)
	Ronald E. Kowalski (D)	10,684	(26%)
1970 general:	Michael Harrington (D)	60,372	(61%)
	Howard Phillips (R)	38,179	(39%)

SEVENTH DISTRICT Political Background

The 7th district of Massachusetts is a collection of suburbs just north of Boston. The district's sociological range extends from working-class Chelsea, where Jewish immigrants first disembarked, to Melrose, a comfortable and still distinctly Yankee town. Most of the communities here lie somewhere between the two extremes and contain many descendants of Irish and Italian immigrants who have reached some degree of financial security, if not affluence. The trend in the 7th illustrates the liberalization of Massachusetts politics during the past dozen years. In the 1950s, the 7th was considered a Republican district, and in 1960, John F. Kennedy was thought to have made an unusually strong showing here when he got 57% of the vote. But in 1968, the Minnesotan Hubert Humphrey won 66% of the vote, and George McGovern in 1972 got the same 57% native son Kennedy did. Nationally, there are only a handful of congressional districts where McGovern ran as well or better than Kennedy.

Obviously, the trend in the 7th represents a considerable shift of opinion. It reflects a growing belief that voting for a Republican like Richard Nixon is somehow no longer respectable. To a considerable extent, the man responsible for the shift is Sen. Edward Kennedy, whose positions on the issues—no matter how "radical" some might consider them—can hardly be attacked here as un-American. So the voters living north of Boston, many of whom supported Joe McCarthy passionately during the 1950s, have for several years believed that American involvement in Southeast Asia was a big mistake right from the start.

One of the beneficiaries of the liberal trend is Congressman Torbert H. Macdonald, a college roommate of John F. Kennedy. Macdonald is generally considered a liberal, though he did have primary opposition from a peace candidate in 1968. The Congressman is currently number-two man on the House Interstate and Foreign Commerce Committee, and stands a good chance of becoming its Chairman. He is 10 years younger than the present Chairman, Harley Staggers of West Virginia. The Commerce Committee has jurisdiction over almost all the federal regulatory agencies, and like so many of the agencies, the Committee is usually sympathetic to the interests of those it is supposed to oversee. Macdonald, who is Chairman of the Communications and Power Subcommittee, has the clout and policy inclinations to lead the committee toward greater concern for consumer legislation.

As Chairman of the subcommittee, Macdonald is especially interested in the regulation of the electronic media. The Congressman was the major force in the House behind the enactment of media spending limits for the 1972 campaign. He also consistently locks horns with the big power companies—a popular stand in the district, since power rates are higher in New England than anywhere else in the country. In 1973, Macdonald sponsored a bill to set up mandatory quotas to force big oil companies to distribute gasoline to independents as well as their own dealers. As for his reelection chances, the rumors that Macdonald might encounter tough primary opposition have never materialized.

Census Data Pop. 476,565. Central city, 0%; suburban, 100%. Median family income, $11,406; families above $15,000: 28%; families below $3,000: 5%. Median years education, 12.3.

1972 Share of Federal Outlays $600,759,325

DOD	$225,715,694	HEW	$207,204,884
AEC	$2,045,761	HUD	$16,488,414
NASA	$8,665,994	DOI	$1,528,388
DOT	$22,077,670	USDA	$4,361,960
		Other	$112,670,560

Federal Military-Industrial Commitments

DOD Contractors Avco (Everett), $16.086m: laser and ABM research; RCA (Burlington), $15.411m: support of automated missile testing unit.
DOD Installations Naval Hospital (Chelsea); closed, 1974.

Economic Base Finance, insurance and real estate; electrical equipment and supplies, especially communication equipment, and electronic components and accessories; machinery, especially office and computing machines; printing and publishing, especially commercial printing and newspapers; and food and kindred products.

The Voters

Registration 251,449 total. 110,771 D (44%); 41,153 R (16%); 99,525 Ind. (40%).
Median voting age 45.3
Employment profile White collar, 57%. Blue collar, 32%. Service, 11%. Farm, –%.
Ethnic groups Total foreign stock, 37%. Italy, 12%; Canada, 9%; Ireland, 4%; USSR, UK, 3% each; Poland, 1%.

Presidential vote

1972	Nixon (R)	91,607	(43%)
	McGovern (D)	122,026	(57%)

1968	Nixon (R)	64,760	(31%)
	Humphrey (D)	137,995	(65%)
	Wallace (AI)	7,053	(3%)

Representative

Torbert H. Macdonald (D) Elected 1954; b. June 6, 1917, Boston; home, Malden; Harvard Col., A.B., 1940; Harvard Law School, LL.B., 1946; Navy, WWII; married, four children; Catholic.

Career Practicing atty., 1946– .

Offices 2470 RHOB, 202-225-2836. Also Rm. 2100A, Kennedy Fed. Bldg., Boston 02203, 617-223-2781.

Administrative Assistant Harry M. Shooshan III

Committees

Government Operations (8th); Subs: Foreign Operations and Government Information; Intergovernmental Relations.

Interstate and Foreign Commerce (2nd); Subs: Communications and Power (Chm.).

Group Ratings

	ADA	COPE	LWV	RIPON	NFU	LCV	CFA	NAB	NSI	ACA
1972	56	89	70	71	86	74	100	22	14	11
1971	65	78	89	69	69	–	88	–	–	32
1970	80	83	–	57	77	90	100	9	0	16

Key Votes

1) Busing	FOR	6) Cmbodia Bmbg	AGN	11) Chkg Acct Intrst	FOR
2) Strip Mines	FOR	7) Bust Hwy Trust	FOR	12) End HISC (HUAC)	FOR
3) Cut Mil $	FOR	8) Farm Sub Lmt	FOR	13) Nixon Sewer Veto	AGN
4) Rev Shrg	FOR	9) School Prayr	AGN	14) Corp Cmpaign $	AGN
5) Pub TV $	FOR	10) Cnsumr Prot	FOR	15) Pol $ Disclosr	FOR

Election Results

1972 general:	Torbert H. Macdonald (D)	135,193	(68%)
	Joan M. Aliberti (R)	64,357	(32%)
1972 primary:	Torbert H. Macdonald (D)	38,648	(83%)
	R. John Waka (D)	8,171	(17%)
1970 general:	Torbert H. Macdonald (D)	107,770	(67%)
	Gordon F. Hughes (R)	52,290	(33%)

EIGHTH DISTRICT Political Background

The 8th of Massachusetts is a congressional district with a number of distinctive features. It is home to no less than four major universities—Harvard, MIT, Boston University, and Tufts—along with a myriad of small colleges. In all, the 8th has the second highest proportion of college students, 14.9%, of any congressional district in the country. And over the years, the district has also had unusually distinctive representation in the House. From 1943 to 1947, its Congressman was James Michael Curley, a roguish Irish politician and model for the hero of the novel *The Last Hurrah*. Curley was also Governor once and Mayor of Boston five times—elected, the last time, while serving a jail sentence.

The politician who succeeded Curley was a very different kind of Boston Irishman, a young Harvard graduate and former gunboat commander named John F. Kennedy. From all accounts, Kennedy knew little about politics when he first ran in 1946, and won largely because of his father's political acumen—and money. Nor was the young Kennedy a particularly enthusiastic junior member of the House, but he did go on to bigger things. Kennedy's successor was Thomas P. "Tip" O'Neill, Jr., who had made a mark as a state legislator. He was the first Democratic Speaker of the Massachusetts General Court (state House of Representatives) in years. Today, after 20 years in Congress, O'Neill is Majority Leader of the U.S. House of Representatives, and next in line for the Speakership.

O'Neill is a man out of town, not gown, politics. Until the early 1970s, the university community in the district was not an especially important factor in congressional politics. The 8th has at least a dozen or so major neighborhood areas, each with its own political traditions and local alliances. These include five wards in the city of Boston: East Boston, an Italian enclave separated from the rest of the city by the harbor; Charlestown, the insular (and now redeveloped) Irish community centered on Bunker Hill; the Back Bay, once the home of elderly Brahmin ladies, now largely given over to students; and Allston and Brighton, lower-middle-class communities having a significant Jewish population. Then there are the Irish and Italian communities in Cambridge and Somerville (plus some Portuguese-Americans in East Cambridge); the middle-class suburbs of Arlington and Watertown; and finally Belmont, the upper-income suburban home of many Harvard academics and of Robert Welch—head of the John Birch Society.

O'Neill has served as an excellent bridge between various parts of his district and its large student and street-people community. But by temperament and background, O'Neill is most comfortable among experienced Irish pols. In the House, he was a man who got along with the leadership (obtaining a seat on the Rules Committee) by going along. In 1967, however, he took the step—rare at the time—of coming out publicly against Johnson's policy in Vietnam. O'Neill did this long before the student vote in his district could have posed any serious threat to him in the district. More important, he said, were the arguments of his own children, who were passionately against the war. (One of them, Thomas P. O'Neill III, now represents his father in the General Court.)

O'Neill was appointed Majority Whip in 1971, when he supported Hale Boggs' candidacy for Majority Leader and brought a number of Eastern votes along with him. In 1973, after Boggs was lost in a plane crash, O'Neill was elected Majority Leader without opposition. Others, like Sam Gibbons of Florida, had tested the water and found House members unwilling to support any challenge of the popular Massachusetts Congressman. Upon assuming the job O'Neill became the first dove in a major position within the Democratic leadership; in 1973, he played an important role in getting various reforms passed by the Democratic Caucus and the House. O'Neill's support was as responsible as anything else for the House's decision to open all committee meetings to the public unless the committee voted in public to close them. This is a reform measure the Senate has refused to adopt. O'Neill's efforts also secured a timely compromise that allowed House Democrats to vote by secret ballot on committee chairmanships.

So it is easy to see why the increased student vote in the 8th has not given O'Neill any problems. For some years now, he has had no primary or general election opposition. The students and peace activists apparently realize that O'Neill is vastly more effective in behalf of, if not quite as strongly committed to, their political causes than any insurgent they might care to support.

Census Data   Pop. 474,090. Central city, 35%; suburban, 65%. Median family income, $10,317; families above $15,000: 24%; families below $3,000: 7%. Median years education, 12.3.

1972 Share of Federal Outlays $597,778,945

DOD	$224,595,914	HEW	$206,176,936
AEC	$2,035,612	HUD	$16,406,614
NASA	$8,623,002	DOI	$1,520,806
DOT	$21,968,142	USDA	$4,340,320
		Other	$112,111,599

Federal Military-Industrial Commitments

DOD Contractors MIT (Cambridge), $48.641m: various missile guidance and other electronics research. Bolt Beranek and Newman (Cambridge), $8.559m: various computer services.
DOD Installations Army Materiel and Mechanical Research Center (Watertown). Boston Naval Shipyard (Boston); closed, 1974.
NASA Contractors MIT (Cambridge), $5.741m: Apollo and Skylab support.

Economic Base Finance, insurance and real estate; electrical equipment and supplies, especially communication equipment, and electronic components and accessories; machinery, especially office and computing machines; food and kindred products; and instruments and related products. Also higher education (Boston Univ., and Harvard Univ., and MIT).

The Voters

Registration 224,006 total. 126,829 D (57%); 26,107 R (12%); 71,070 Ind. (32%).
Median voting age 39.4
Employment profile White collar, 63%. Blue collar, 24%. Service, 13%. Farm, –%.
Ethnic groups Black, 2%. Spanish, 1%. Total foreign stock, 41%. Italy, 10%; Canada, 8%; Ireland, 6%. UK, USSR, 2% each; Portugal, Greece, Germany, Poland, 1% each.

Presidential vote

1972	Nixon (R)	65,660	(34%)
	McGovern (D)	127,868	(66%)
1968	Nixon (R)	45,580	(24%)
	Humphrey (D)	136,775	(72%)
	Wallace (AI)	6,881	(4%)

Representative

Thomas P. O'Neill, Jr. (D) Elected 1952; b. Dec. 9, 1912, Cambridge; home, Cambridge; Boston Col., A.B., 1936; married, five children; Catholic.

Career Insurance; Cambridge School Com., 1946–47; State Rep., 1936–52; Minority Leader, 1947–48; Speaker, 1948–52; U.S. House Dem. Whip, 1971–72; U.S. House Dem. Majority Leader, 1973– .

Offices 2231 RHOB, 202-225-5111. Also 2200 Kennedy Fed. Bldg., Boston 02203, 617-223-2784.

Administrative Assistant Leo Diehl

Committees

None (Majority Whip)

Group Ratings

	ADA	COPE	LWV	RIPON	NFU	LCV	CFA	NAB	NSI	ACA
1972	69	90	100	64	80	53	100	10	33	5
1971	78	91	100	72	93	–	100	–	–	11
1970	76	100	–	69	92	71	79	0	30	6

Key Votes

1) Busing	FOR	6) Cmbodia Bmbg	AGN	11) Chkg Acct Intrst	FOR
2) Strip Mines	AGN	7) Bust Hwy Trust	FOR	12) End HISC (HUAC)	AGN
3) Cut Mil $	ABS	8) Farm Sub Lmt	AGN	13) Nixon Sewer Veto	AGN
4) Rev Shrg	FOR	9) School Prayr	AGN	14) Corp Cmpaign $	FOR
5) Pub TV $	FOR	10) Cnsumr Prot	FOR	15) Pol $ Disclosr	AGN

Election Results

1972 general:	Thomas P. O'Neill, Jr. (D)	142,470	(99%)
	John E. Powers, Jr. (SW)	18,169	(11%)
1972 primary:	Thomas P. O'Neill, Jr. (D), unopposed		
1970 general:	Thomas P. O'Neill, Jr. (D), unopposed		

NINTH DISTRICT Political Background

An index of recent changes in Massachusetts congressional elections is what has occurred to the politics of the state's 9th district. For 45 years, the 9th was represented by John W. McCormack, who for his last nine years in Congress was Speaker of the House. All this time, McCormack was reelected either without opposition of by overwhelming majorities. Then in the two elections since the Speaker's retirement, the district has elected two different Representatives, each winning with less than a majority of the vote in three-candidate races. Not coincidentally, the 9th, which before 1972 consisted of several wards in the central part of Boston, was substantially redistricted. So great was the change that almost 40% of the 9th's votes are now cast in the suburbs.

The recent turbulence here has long been common in the local politics of the state, as readers of political novels can attest. But turmoil was never a tradition in the state's congressional races. McCormack is an austere man who was devoted to his wife and the House of Representatives. He was venerated in many of the neighborhoods of three-decker houses in South Boston and Dorchester, where generations of Irish have lived and died. (The 9th is surely the most Irish district in the nation.) McCormack, a beneficiary of this kind of loyalty and rootedness at home, possessed a similar kind of feeling toward his Democratic colleagues and the traditions of the House. So the Speaker was more inclined to temper his actions to the wishes of his conservative Southern and old-line big-city Democratic colleagues than to the concerns of the young, more ideological liberals who were coming to dominate the Democratic Caucus. McCormack simply seemed unable to understand the language used by young Democratic liberals. During his last years in the House, this Irish Puritan of Boston learned the sad news that his aide Martin Sweig and lobbyist Nathan Voloshen had used his office to solicit favors for well-paying clients. Few people, except the author of *The Washington Payoff,* believes McCormack knew anything about the matter, but it may well have been the major factor in his decision to retire in 1970.

McCormack's departure left the seat to a very different kind of Boston Irish politician, Mrs. Louise Day Hicks. Daughter of a South Boston politico, Mrs. Hicks had made a career out of opposing changes in school district lines designed to promote integration. From her seat on the Boston School Committee, she ran for Mayor in 1967 and came within a few thousand votes of beating liberal Democrat Kevin White. In 1970 she ran for Congress, won the primary with a plurality of 39%, and then captured the general election with 59% against split opposition. In 1971, Hicks ran for Mayor again, this time running much further behind White.

Mrs. Hicks' political strength lies with the undying devotion of thousands of voters in the Irish wards of South Boston and Dorchester. But she is quite unpopular elsewhere, not just among the blacks, but among the younger voters who have come to represent an increasing share of the Boston electorate. Nor is she liked in the suburbs, where busing is not a big issue; here her wooden speaking style and her South Boston accent turn off voters accustomed to thinking of themselves as moderate and up-to-date.

Mrs. Hicks' attempts to become Mayor showed that she could not command a majority in the city as a whole and that her bedrock support was slowly eroding away. In 1971, the Massachusetts legislature, which never had much use for her, began to draw the state's new district lines; when the redistricters finished, the composition of the 9th was drastically altered—to the obvious disadvantage of Mrs. Hicks. The legislature devised a plan that eliminated four all-white wards in the Dorchester and Hyde Park sections of Boston, while it retained virtually all of the city's still comparatively small black population. The lines of the district were then extended to the southwest to include seven anti-Hicks suburban towns. There remained enough bedrock Hicks support to give her 38% of the votes in the 1972 Democratic primary—enough to win because five other candidates had filed to run against her. In the general election, however, Boston City Councilman J. Joseph Moakley was determined to beat her. Previously, Moakley had served for 19 years in the Great and General Court (the Commonwealth's 340-year-old name for its legislature) and made an unsuccessful bid against Hicks in 1970. In that year, Moakley shared with a black candidate an almost equal number of the anti-Hicks votes.

As the 1972 primary began to heat up, it was clear that the plethora of candidates would so split the anti-Hicks votes that Mrs. Hicks could win with her devoted minority. So Moakley, though he had always been a Democrat, decided to run in the general election as an independent. It turned out to be a good strategy. No black candidates entered to split the anti-Hicks votes, while the Republican party here has been insignificant since the 1880s when the Irish began to dominate Boston politics. After a spirited campaign, Moakley won 43%, Hicks took 41%, with 14% going to the Republican nominee. With solid support in the black wards, Moakley lost the city of Boston portion of the 9th by just 208 votes and carried the suburbs by 3,600. He accumulated his largest margin in Needham, home of the Republican candidate, who probably siphoned off a lot of votes that would otherwise have gone to Hicks.

With a history of this sort, what is likely to happen here in 1974? Moakley, who voted with the Democrats to organize the House, is probably committed to run in the Democratic primary. But since he is now an incumbent and acceptable to all the anti-Hicks groups, there will probably be no crush of anti-Hicks candidates—the kind that allowed her to win the 1970 and 1972 primaries—filing for the seat. Hicks herself is currently running for the Boston City Council once again, perhaps eyeing still another shot at Mayor Kevin White. At any rate, given her bedrock support, she will almost surely win a seat on the council; several members are elected at large, which means that a majority is not needed and seldom attained. But an issue that has cost Mrs. Hicks support is the charge of office-hopping. She ran for Mayor in 1967 from her seat on the School Committee, for Congress in 1970 while serving on the City Council, and for Mayor again in 1974 while a member of the council, Moakley will use it against her. If she runs for Mayor from the council, both Moakley and White will be delighted. In any case, even her staunchest supporters no doubt would like her to settle down in one office and do her anti-busing thing. In the spring of 1973, the legislature, under intense pressure, repealed the nation's first school racial imbalance law; but Gov. Sargent vetoed it. Because busing remains an issue in Boston politics, Hicks can continue to get a hearing. But the likelihood is that the voters of the 9th district will reelect their Congressman in 1974 for the first time since 1968.

Census Data Pop. 473,680. Central city, 70%; suburban, 30%. Median family income, $10,144; families above $15,000: 25%; families below $3,000: 9%. Median years education, 12.2.

1972 Share of Federal Outlays $597,353,177

DOD	$224,435,945	HEW	$206,030,087
AEC	$2,034,162	HUD	$16,394,929
NASA	$8,616,860	DOI	$1,519,722
DOT	$21,952,495	USDA	$4,337,229
		Other	$112,031,748

Federal Military-Industrial Commitments

DOD Contractors GTE Sylvania (Needham Heights), $56.464m: maintenance of Minuteman ground electronics system. Central Beef (Boston), $11.117m: foodstuffs. Keystone Micro Scan (Boston), $10.970m: bomb fuzes. Northrop (Norwood), $7.066m: design and production of missile and aircraft gyrocompass systems. North American Packing (Boston), $5.351m: foodstuffs. *DOD Installations* Naval Station (Boston); closed, 1975.

Economic Base Finance, insurance and real estate; printing and publishing, especially newspapers and commercial printing; food and kindred products; apparel and other textile products, especially women's and misses' outerwear; and electrical equipment and supplies. Also higher education (Northeastern Univ.).

The Voters

Registration 210,972 total. 118,411 D (56%); 29,760 R (14%); 62,801 Ind. (30%).
Median voting age 43.5
Employment profile White collar, 55%. Blue collar, 28%. Service, 17%. Farm, –%.
Ethnic groups Black, 20%. Spanish, 3%. Total foreign stock, 34%. Ireland, 7%; Italy, Canada, 5% each; UK, USSR, 2% each; Poland, Germany, 1% each.

Presidential vote

1972	Nixon (R)	68,748	(41%)
	McGovern (D)	100,720	(59%)
1968	Nixon (R)	46,437	(26%)
	Humphrey (D)	121,436	(68%)
	Wallace (AI)	8,478	(5%)

Representative

John Joseph Moakley (D) Elected 1972; b. April 27, Boston; home, Boston; U. of Miami, B.A.; Suffolk Law School, LL.B.; Navy, WWII; married; Catholic.

Career Practicing atty.; State Senate; Boston City Councilor.

Offices 238 CHOB, 202-225-8273. Also Rm. 1907A, JFK Bldg., Gov. Ctr., Boston 02203, 617-223-5715, and Warren St., Roxbury 02119, and 11 Walpole St., Norwood 02062, and 472 W. Broadway, So. Boston 02127.

Administrative Assistant Patrick McCarthy

Committees

Banking and Currency (22nd); Subs: Bank Supervision and Insurance; Consumer Affairs; International Trade; Urban Mass Transportation.

Post Office and Civil Service (14th); Subs: Investigations; Retirement and Employee Benefits.

Group Ratings: Newly Elected

Key Votes

1) Busing	NE	6) Cmbodia Bmbg	AGN	11) Chkg Acct Intrst	FOR
2) Strip Mines	NE	7) Bust Hwy Trust	FOR	12) End HISC (HUAC)	FOR
3) Cut Mil $	NE	8) Farm Sub Lmt	NE	13) Nixon Sewer Veto	AGN
4) Rev Shrg	NE	9) School Prayr	NE	14) Corp Cmpaign $	NE
5) Pub TV $	NE	10) Cnsumr Prot	NE	15) Pol $ Disclosr	NE

Election Results

1972 general:	John Joseph Moakley (Ind.)	70,571	(43%)
	Louise Day Hicks (D)	67,143	(41%)
	Howard M. Miller (R)	23,177	(14%)
	Jeanne Lafferty (SW)	2,397	(1%)
1972 primary:	John Joseph Moakley (Ind.), unopposed		

TENTH DISTRICT Political Background

The 10th district of Massachusetts is one example of a grotesquely shaped monstrosity, drawn to suit the political needs of one longtime incumbent, and eventually serving the needs of another in equally fine fashion. The 10th is really two districts. In the north are the Boston suburbs: posh, WASPy Wellesley and a little less prosperous Natick next door. In the south is the city of Fall River (pop. 119,000 in 1910; 96,000 in 1970) the district's largest; it is an aging mill town that never really recovered from the southward migration of its 101 cotton mills. The huge granite structures are now filled typically with marginal dress and curtain sweatshops which pay the French Canadian and Portuguese workers minimum wage rates. This end of the 10th is dominated by ethnics of Portuguese, French Canadian, and Italian descent, who ordinarily vote Democratic. The middle of the district is composed of sparsely populated towns spread out over the rolling hills between Boston and Providence, Rhode Island. These include places like Foxboro, home of the beleaguered New England Patriots, and North Attleboro, home of the 10th's longtime (1925–67) Congressman Joseph W. Martin, Jr.

For many years the district's boundaries were drawn to provide a safe seat for Martin, best known to historians of the New Deal as a member of FDR's famous Republican trio of Martin, Barton, and Fish. Beginning in 1939, Martin was a Republican leader in the House, serving as Speaker twice, from 1947 to 1949 and from 1953 to 1955, when the Republicans gained the necessary majorities. But as Martin aged, he became more and more congenial with Speaker Sam Rayburn, much to the disgust of many aggressive Republican Congressmen. After the Democrats' big win in the 1958 elections, Martin was ousted from the Minority Leadership; he soon became a melancholy and forlorn old man. In 1966, Martin was beaten in the Republican primary—he was 82 and long past the time when he could cut an impressive figure out on the hustings.

The winner of the primary was Margaret Heckler, a Wellesley attorney, who was then the only Republican member of the Governor's Council—an antique institution that passes on some of the executive's appointments. It survives from colonial days only in Massachusetts, New Hampshire, and Maine. The general election that followed also presented Mrs. Heckler with the toughest one she has had so far. In national terms, the 10th is a solidly liberal district; it gave Hubert Humphrey a large majority in 1968 and went for George McGovern in 1972. But Heckler's generally liberal record helped her to relatively easy wins in 1968 and 1970. She held her own in the southern, ethnic part of the district and piled up big margins in the towns north of Fall River. In 1972, the Congresswoman was unopposed in both the primary and the general election.

There is a slight possibility that Heckler will have more trouble in 1974. She has opposed the Nixon Administration on some foreign and domestic issues. She is, however, no firebrand, but rather likes to stay within the dictates of the Republican Caucus and the Administration whenever her own public stands on issues and her district will let her. One instance of Republican loyalty could haunt her in 1974. She voted, along with all the other Republicans and several Democrats on the Banking and Currency Committee, against holding an investigation of the Watergate affair in October 1972—a move that delayed any congressional probe of Watergate until well after the 1972 election. The vote will hurt her only if an impressive Democratic candidate emerges with strength in both ends of the district. This is something that has not happened in the past and, according to local observers, is an unlikely prospect in 1974.

Census Data Pop. 477,054. Central city, 20%; suburban, 55%. Median family income, $10,747; families above $15,000: 24%; families below $3,000: 6%. Median years education, 12.1.

1972 Share of Federal Outlays $388,139,247

DOD	$86,145,379	HEW	$176,762,836
AEC	$591,951	HUD	$11,128,262
NASA	$2,299,383	DOI	$834,867
DOT	$11,714,087	USDA	$2,750,888
		Other	$80,538,743

Federal Military-Industrial Commitments

DOD Contractors Raytheon (North Dighton), $11.536m: missile fire control systems.
DOD Installations Natick Army Laboratories (Natick).

Economic Base Apparel and other textile products, especially women's and misses' outerwear; miscellaneous manufacturing industries, especially jewelry, silverware and plated ware; finance, insurance and real estate; textile mill products, especially textile finishing, except wool; and rubber and plastics products, especially miscellaneous plastics products.

The Voters

Registration 232,598 total. 78,805 D (34%); 51,908 R (22%); 101,885 Ind. (44%).
Median voting age 44.1
Employment profile White collar, 46%. Blue collar, 41%. Service, 12%. Farm, 1%.
Ethnic groups Total foreign stock, 32%. Canada, 8%; Portugal, 6%; UK, 3%; Italy, Ireland, Poland, 2% each; USSR, 1%.

Presidential vote

1972	Nixon (R)	100,844	(50%)
	McGovern (D)	102,368	(50%)
1968	Nixon (R)	70,773	(37%)
	Humphrey (D)	114,410	(59%)
	Wallace (AI)	6,842	(4%)

Representative

Margaret M. Heckler (R) Elected 1966; b. June 21, 1931, Flushing, N.Y.; home, Wellesley; Albertus Magnus Col., A.B., 1953; Boston Col. Law Sch., LL.B., 1956; married, three children; Catholic.

Career Governor's Council, 1962–66.

Offices 303 CHOB, 202-225-4335. Also 217 P.O. Bldg., Fall River 02722, and 1 Washington St., Wellesley Hills 02162, 617-235-3350, and P.O. Bldg., Taunton 02780.

Administrative Assistant Christopher Knapton

Committees

Banking and Currency (8th); Subs: Consumer Affairs; Housing; Small Business.

Veterans' Affairs (4th); Subs: Education and Training (Ranking Mbr.); Hospitals; Housing.

Sel. Com. on House Beauty Shop (Ranking Mbr.).

Group Ratings

	ADA	COPE	LWV	RIPON	NFU	LCV	CFA	NAB	NSI	ACA
1972	63	56	100	100	67	79	50	44	29	12
1971	73	73	100	88	67	–	88	–	–	33
1970	72	70	–	94	85	100	76	40	50	38

Key Votes

1) Busing	FOR	6) Cmbodia Bmbg	AGN	11) Chkg Acct Intrst	FOR
2) Strip Mines	AGN	7) Bust Hwy Trust	FOR	12) End HISC (HUAC)	AGN
3) Cut Mil $	ABS	8) Farm Sub Lmt	FOR	13) Nixon Sewer Veto	FOR
4) Rev Shrg	FOR	9) School Prayr	FOR	14) Corp Cmpaign $	AGN
5) Pub TV $	FOR	10) Cnsumr Prot	FOR	15) Pol $ Disclosr	FOR

Election Results

1972 general:	Margaret M. Heckler (R), unopposed		
1972 primary:	Margaret M. Heckler (R), unopposed		
1970 general:	Margaret M. Heckler (R)	102,895	(57%)
	Bertram A. Yaffe (D)	77,497	(43%)

ELEVENTH DISTRICT Political Background

The 11th district of Massachusetts comprises the southern third of Boston, most of the city's South Shore suburbs, and more suburban territory stretching south to include the shoe-manufacturing town of Brockton. With few exceptions, the 11th's Dorchester and Hyde Park wards of Boston and its suburban towns—like the older Quincy and Braintree, and the newer Canton, Stoughton, and Randolph, away from the coast—are filled with the sons and daughters and grandsons and granddaughters of Irish, Italian, and Jewish immigrants. Because most the district's residents have remained loyal to their forebears' Democratic voting habits, the 11th as a whole is heavily Democratic. Its Yankee minority, whose ancestors sent John Quincy Adams to the House for the last 16 years of his life (1831–48), has been steadily abandoning the Republican party, thereby adding to the election majorities received by Democratic candidates.

The succession of Congressmen from the district points up changes that have occurred in Massachusetts politics. For 30 years, from 1929 to 1959, the district's Congressman was Republican Richard B. Wigglesworth, bearer of a fine old Brahmin name. When Wigglesworth retired in 1958, his successor was Democrat James A. Burke, who has held the seat ever since. Before going to Congress, Burke had held a leadership position in the Massachusetts legislature. Once in Washington, he won a seat on the House Ways and Means Committee early in his congressional career, doubtless with John McCormack's sponsorhip. Burke is now the third-ranking Democrat on that crucial body and, perhaps not coincidentally, was an enthusiastic backer of Wilbur Mills in the 1972 presidential primary season. The Congressman is a man from the older, Irish tradition of Massachusetts politics, by temperament attuned to the traditional ways of doing things in the House. Nevertheless, he has accommodated himself to some changes. As a Democrat on Ways and Means, he has used his power to give some of the younger, more liberal Democrats choice committee assignments, in line with the wishes of Speaker Carl Albert and Majority Leader Tip O'Neill.

Like most northern Democrats, Burke has always supported liberal domestic legislation. And in the past few years, he has joined most Democrats in opposing Administration policies in Southeast Asia. Recently, the Congressman's major legislative initiative has taken place in an area under the jurisdiction of the Ways and Means Committee. He is the co-sponsor of the Burke-Hartke bill, one which would restrict importation of many goods that compete with the efforts of American industry and workers. Though Burke's measure has the support of the AFL-CIO, it is not expected to emerge from Ways and Means in its present form. The committee's Democrats in general, and Chairman Wilbur Mills in particular, have always been inclined toward free trade. Nevertheless, there is substantial pressure coming from hard-pressed industries and labor unions for legislation along the lines of Burke-Hartke. No little pressure stems from the beleaguered electronics and shoe industries, both of which are of major importance to the 11th district. Foreign-trade legislation will probably be an area of major controversy in 1974, and Burke, as a senior member of Ways and Means and co-sponsor of an important bill, will probably play a major role in working out the specifics of the matter.

Census Data Pop. 475,789. Central city, 49%; suburban, 51%. Median family income, $11,052; families above $15,000: 25%; families below $3,000: 6%. Median years education, 12.3.

1972 Share of Federal Outlays $520,539,089

DOD	$177,208,114	HEW	$192,632,729
AEC	$1,555,706	HUD	$13,536,556
NASA	$6,622,239	DOI	$1,179,348
DOT	$17,348,457	USDA	$4,122,874
		Other	$106,333,070

Federal Military-Industrial Commitments

DOD Contractors General Dynamics (Quincy), $5.335m: various engineering services for ships.

Economic Base Finance, insurance and real estate; printing and publishing; food and kindred products; apparel and other textile products, especially women's and misses' outerwear; and machinery.

The Voters

Registration 243,206 total. 134,821 D (55%); 35,885 R (15%); 72,500 Ind. (30%).
Median voting age 45.5
Employment profile White collar, 54%. Blue collar, 33%. Service, 13%. Farm, –%.
Ethnic groups Black, 2%. Total foreign stock, 35%. Ireland, Canada, 7% each; Italy, 6%; UK, USSR, 3% each; Poland, Lithuania, 1% each.

Presidential vote

1972	Nixon (R)	86,139	(43%)
	McGovern (D)	112,397	(57%)
1968	Nixon (R)	56,259	(28%)
	Humphrey (D)	132,497	(66%)
	Wallace (AI)	10,262	(5%)

Representative

James A. Burke (D) Elected 1958; b. March 30, 1910, Boston; home, Milton; Suffolk U.; Army, WWII; married; Catholic.

Career State Rep., 1947–54; Asst. Majority Leader, 1949–52; Vice-Chm. Mass. Dem. State Com., 4 yrs.

Offices 241 CHOB, 202-225-3215. Also Rm. 203, P.O. Bldg., 47 Washington St., Quincy 02169, 617-472-1314.

Administrative Assistant Edward J. Moore

Committees

Ways and Means (3rd).

Jt. Com. Internal Revenue Taxation (3rd).

Sel. Com. on the House Restaurant (3rd).

Joint Study Com. on Budget Control.

Group Ratings

	ADA	COPE	LWV	RIPON	NFU	LCV	CFA	NAB	NSI	ACA
1972	94	91	92	81	86	53	100	17	10	0
1971	86	92	100	67	100	–	100	–	–	7
1970	64	86	–	50	92	90	76	8	80	11

Key Votes

1) Busing	FOR	6) Cmbodia Bmbg	AGN	11) Chkg Acct Intrst	FOR
2) Strip Mines	AGN	7) Bust Hwy Trust	FOR	12) End HISC (HUAC)	FOR
3) Cut Mil $	AGN	8) Farm Sub Lmt	FOR	13) Nixon Sewer Veto	AGN
4) Rev Shrg	FOR	9) School Prayr	FOR	14) Corp Cmpaign $	FOR
5) Pub TV $	FOR	10) Cnsumr Prot	FOR	15) Pol $ Disclosr	AGN

Election Results

1972 general: James A. Burke (D), unopposed
1972 primary: James A. Burke (D), unopposed
1970 general: James A. Burke (D), unopposed

TWELFTH DISTRICT Political Background

The 12th congressional district of Massachusetts is the state's most Republican—the only one of twelve to deliver a majority, though a very small one, to Richard Nixon in the 1972 presidential election. Like the 10th, the 12th was long ago designed to return a Republican Congressman. The heavily Democratic city of New Bedford (pop. 101,000), an old whaling port where the hard-pressed fishing industry is still important, was combined with predominantly Republican territory. This includes the South Shore suburbs of Boston, Plymouth County, Cape Cod, and the two resort islands of Martha's Vineyard and Nantucket. The last was the whaling port from which Herman Melville sailed in pursuit of Moby Dick and the ultimate Void; today, like the Vineyard, Nantucket is a place for summer people, quaint New England seashore houses, and touristy shops.

The move to the left in Massachusetts has shown itself in recent congressional elections held in the 12th district. Republican Hastings Keith represented the district for 12 years after first winning the seat in 1958. Despite his gray personality and solidly conservative voting record, Keith scarcely attracted any opposition as he won reelection. But in 1970, things changed. In the primary, the Congressman encountered a strong and well-financed challenge from state Sen. William Weeks, son of Eisenhower's Commerce Secretary Sinclair Weeks. And in the general election, Gerry (with a hard "g") Studds, a former presidential campaign aide to Sen. Eugene McCarthy, nearly upset the incumbent.

Neither Studds nor Weeks—both of whom come from the picturesque South Shore town of Cohasset—quit campaigning after losing in 1970. In 1971, the Democratic legislature eliminated several Republican towns in Plymouth County from the district. Faced with a close call in 1970 and the redistricting of 1971, Keith decided to retire. There were no primaries in the race for succession, but there was a very spirited general election. Weeks spent in the six figures and campaigned hard, while Studds, who was not poorly financed also campaigned assiduously. After the 1970 election, Studds took the time to learn Portuguese, a language spoken by immigrants in the New Bedford area. (The 12th and the neighboring 10th have more Portuguese-Americans than any other district in the country.) Studds' skill as a student of Portuguese, as much as anything else, may well have made the difference. The results of the 1972 election was even closer than those of 1970: Studds won by 1,118 votes.

Much of the fervor behind Studds' campaigns came from his opposition to the American war in Southeast Asia. But his committee assignments—Merchant Marine and Fisheries along with Public Works—suggest a close concern with the nitty-gritty economic problems of the district. There could be another close race here in 1974. Weeks is rumored to be willing to spend yet another hunk of his substantial fortune to make a race of it once more. But the advantages of incumbency make Studds the favorite in any rematch.

Census Data Pop. 475,672. Central city, 21%; suburban, 47%. Median family income, $10,132; families above $15,000: 22%; families below $3,000: 8%. Median years education, 12.2.

1972 Share of Federal Outlays $414,204,583

DOD	$98,010,797	HEW	$195,211,000
AEC	$718,941	HUD	$6,653,207
NASA	$1,549,668	DOI	$2,643,408
DOT	$13,843,821	USDA	$3,876,542
		Other	$91,697,199

Federal Military-Industrial Commitments

DOD Contractors Woods Hole Oceanographic Institute (Woods Hole), $7.585m: oceanographic and anti-submarine research.
DOD Installations Naval Air Station (South Weymouth). Naval Facility (Nantucket). North Truro AF Station (North Truro).

Economic Base Finance, insurance and real estate; agriculture, notably fruits, dairy products and poultry; leather and leather products, especially shoes, except rubber; printing and publishing; and tourism.

The Voters

Registration 253,301 total. 76,589 D (30%); 68,546 R (27%); 107,896 Ind. (43%).
Median voting age 46.0
Employment profile White collar, 48%. Blue collar, 38%. Service, 13%. Farm, 1%.
Ethnic groups Black, 2%. Total foreign stock, 31%. Canada, 7%; Portugal, 5%; UK, 4%; Italy, Ireland, 2% each; Poland, 1%.

Presidential vote

1972	Nixon (R)	121,406	(52%)
	McGovern (D)	113,109	(48%)
1968	Nixon (R)	84,470	(43%)
	Humphrey (D)	106,256	(53%)
	Wallace (AI)	7,406	(4%)

Representative

Gerry Eastman Studds (D) Elected 1972; b. May 12, 1937, Mineola, N.Y.; home, Cohasset; Yale U., B.A., 1959, M.A.T., 1961; unmarried.

Career Foreign Service Officer, U.S. State Dept., 1961–63; Exec. asst., Domestic Peace Corps Task Force; legis. asst., N.J. U.S. Senator Williams; Teacher, St. Paul's School, Concord, N.H., 1965–69.

Offices 1511 LHOB, 202-225-3111. Also P.O. Bldg., New Bedford 02740, 617-999-1251, and 1143 Washington St., Hanover 02601, 617-826-3866, and P.O. Bldg., Hyannis 02601, 617-771-0666.

Administrative Assistant Robert T. Francis II

Committees

Merchant Marine and Fisheries (21st); Subs: Fisheries and Wildlife Conservation and the Environment; Merchant Marine; Oceanography.

Public Works (19th); Subs: Economic Development; Energy; Investigations and Review; Public Buildings and Grounds; Water Resources.

Group Ratings: Newly Elected

Key Votes

1) Busing	NE	6) Cmbodia Bmbg	AGN	11) Chkg Acct Intrst	FOR
2) Strip Mines	NE	7) Bust Hwy Trust	FOR	12) End HISC (HUAC)	FOR
3) Cut Mil $	NE	8) Farm Sub Lmt	NE	13) Nixon Sewer Veto	AGN
4) Rev Shrg	NE	9) School Prayr	NE	14) Corp Cmpaign $	NE
5) Pub TV $	NE	10) Cnsumr Prot	NE	15) Pol $ Disclosr	NE

Election Results

1972 general:	Gerry E. Studds (D)	117,710	(50%)
	William D. Weeks (R)	116,592	(50%)
1972 primary:	Gerry E. Studds (D), unopposed		

MICHIGAN

Political Background

A six-letter word (some spell it with seven) dominated Michigan politics in 1972: b-u-s-i-n-g. Michigan, which has been regarded a Democratic state, went Republican in November. Moreover, in the Democratic primary held earlier in the year, the voters here gave 51% of their ballots to George Wallace, much to the chagrin of the Michigan Democratic party. And because both parties in the state like to overstate their commitment to liberal political ideals, even the state Republican party in Michigan was disappointed by the showing Wallace made. To some observers, it appeared that the Northern state fell into the throes of a political reaction—the kind that hit the Deep South during the 1950s and early 1960s, when hundreds of thousands of people changed lifetime voting habits and supported the loudest demagogue in sight.

But it must be remembered that the Wallace primary victory—the one the Governor seems most delighted to recount—came at the very height of the 1972 Michigan busing furor. And because Wallace had been shot just a day before the election, the determination among his supporters to get out the vote was definitely heightened; this clearly pushed the Governor's expected number of percentage points up several notches. The results show that Wallace carried all but the state's two black-majority congressional districts, but he made his strongest showing in the Detroit suburbs. These suburbs are where the busing issue had its most pronounced impact, for obvious reasons. A federal judge had ordered a metropolitan busing plan; he ruled that the Detroit schools, which are two-thirds black, could not be desegregated without busing across city limits. Whites, who had moved to the suburbs expecting to send their children to all-white schools, were stunned by the decision of the court and reacted furiously.

But even though Wallace swept the state in the primary, by November the strength of the Michigan anti-busing reaction was limited to the Detroit suburbs.

Meanwhile, George McGovern, who was seen by the voters as a pro-buser (or an anti-antibuser), took 43% of the state's votes—down 5% from Hubert Humphrey's total in 1968. McGovern ran 11% behind Humphrey in the Detroit metropolitan area and more than 20% off Humphrey's totals in suburban Macomb County, where anti-busing sentiment was its most fervent (see Michigan 12, 14, and 18). By contrast, however, McGovern actually ran fractionally ahead of Humphrey in outstate Michigan, just as he did in other states of the Upper Midwest, like Wisconsin and Iowa. McGovern improved on Humphrey's showing even as busing orders were in effect or pending in outstate cities like Grand Rapids, Lansing, and Kalamazoo.

The higher McGovern vote is part of a current trend in Michigan politics. For the last five years, voters in the Detroit metropolitan area, heavily Democratic by tradition, have been swinging toward Republican candidates. Meanwhile, in traditionally Republican outstate Michigan, which casts between 52% and 55% of the state's ballots, Democratic candidates are running much better than in the past. The result is that the Republicans now win all the closely contested statewide races, just as they have for more than a dozen years. So the conventional wisdom of Michigan as a Democratic state has to undergo revision.

The major factor behind Republican success here is a sophisticated use of the media and of public-opinion polling. Michigan Republicans have hired nationally known experts like Walter deVries, co-author of *The Ticket Splitter*, and Frederick Currier of Market Opinion Research, a Detroit firm and the principal pollster in the 1972 Nixon campaign. Michigan Democrats distrust fancy politicking; they still like to think of themselves as the vanguard of the working class, though union members here make far more money than the average American wage-earner. In the crunch, the Democrats appeal to old-time party loyalties—always a losing tactic in these ticket-splitting times.

Both Michigan political parties are the products of remarkable organizations assembled around a single charismatic figure, and both of these men rode high for about ten years before being soundly repudiated by the voters. In one way or another, both men—Democrat G. Mennen Williams and Republican George Romney—have origins in the industry that dominates Michigan as no other one industry dominates any other major state: automobiles. The volatility of the car manufacturing business remains a major economic fact of life in Michigan. As somebody said, when the national economy sneezes, Michigan gets pneumonia. The sluggish growth of the state's economy is due mainly to the below-average growth rate of the American auto industry, though it did enjoy record profits in 1972 and 1973. Detroit car makers have shown themselves far less capable of technological innovation or market adaptability than foreign competitors. Until recently, Detroit has done little about the emissions-control problem, and now with the gasoline shortage and the trend toward smaller cars, the entire industry may be headed toward real trouble.

But it was the once-booming automobile business that brought the immigrants to Michigan. People came to man the assembly lines from such diverse points as Canada, Poland, and the Appalachians, and the various Black Belts of the South. These immigrants constituted the voting base for the Democratic organization assembled around G. Mennen Williams, Governor from 1949 to 1960. And it was the large suburban middle class created by the auto prosperity of the 1950s and 1960s that produced the votes behind the election triumphs of George Romney, the former president of American Motors. Romney won the governorship in 1962, 1964, and 1966.

Curious parallels exists between Williams and Romney. Both politicians assembled talented organizations. Williams picked men from the United Auto Workers, and New Deal liberals like longtime Democratic State Chairman Neil Stabler. Romney chose from academic people like deVries, and from a corps of business and advertising men. Both Williams and Romney developed presidential ambitions, and both were thwarted by events for which they received undue censure. Because a Republican legislature refused to compromise on any tax plan, the state government went on "payless paydays" for a few weeks; Williams was then charged with allowing the state to go bankrupt. Later, Romney's presidential hopes crumbled under the impact of an offhand remark that he had been "brainwashed" on a trip to Vietnam— a common enough experience in our times. In 1960, Williams never mounted a presidential campaign and instead endorsed John F. Kennedy. And in 1968, Romney withdrew from the New Hampshire primary when polls showed that he would receive something like 10% of the vote against Richard Nixon.

After these disappointments, both Williams and Romney went on to further humiliation. They got administration jobs that did not match their expectations. Williams became Kennedy's Assistant Secretary of State for African Affairs, and Romney, Nixon's Secretary of Housing and Urban Development. Both left their posts while notably out of favor with their respective bosses. And finally, both were crushed—Williams in person and Romney by proxy—by the Michigan voters who had once given them large majorities. In 1966, Williams returned from Washington to Michigan to run for Democrat Pat McNamara's Senate seat. Detroit Mayor Jerome Cavanagh, then 38, opposed Williams in the Democratic primary and ran virtually even with the former Governor, getting a respectable 40% of the vote. Then Williams ignored the portent of the Cavanagh showing and vastly underestimated his Republican opponent in the general election, 10-year House veteran Robert Griffin. In May 1966, Gov. Romney had appointed Griffin to fill the seat upon Sen. McNamara's death. Griffin—well-financed, shrewdly advertised, and canny though hardly charismatic—won a 56–44 margin over Williams, a margin larger than any Williams had won in six successful races for Governor. Today Williams sits on the Michigan Supreme Court, after winning election to it in 1970. But among many Michigan voters he remains an unpopular political figure; in 1970 Williams ran considerably behind ex-Gov. (1961–62) and now Michigan Supreme Court Justice John Swainson, the man who had succeeded Williams when he left for the Kennedy Administration job.

Romney's humiliation came in 1970, when he ran his wife Lenore for the U.S. Senate against two-term Democratic incumbent Philip Hart. In the eyes of many voters, Mrs. Romney's candidacy was simply a ploy to keep George's options open. It rapidly turned into a textbook example of how not to run a campaign. Mrs. Romney on the stump proved to be even less fortunate in her choice of words than her husband. Almost simultaneously, she managed to alienate the black community and white suburban voters. She lost by a 67–33 margin—a sure sign that Michigan voters had had enough of the Romneys. At this writing, the former Governor, whose resignation as HUD Secretary was readily accepted by the Nixon White House, is testing the political waters in Utah, where he apparently plans to run to represent his fellow Mormons in the Senate in 1974 (see Utah state write-up).

Since the defeats of Williams and Romney, Michigan has not produced a dominant politician figuring in any kind of presidential speculation. In fact, Michigan is the largest state in the nation never to have produced a President. Current Gov. William Milliken, a generally liberal Republican, inspires no strong feelings. He is regarded as a pleasant, well-intentioned man. However, recent minor scandals in his office and his failure over the course of five years to work out a reform to finance state education have not helped his reelection chances in 1974. Even in 1970, Milliken was nearly beaten by state Sen. Sander Levin; the major issue in the campaign was "parochiaid," state aid to parochial schools. Milliken's support of parochiaid helped him make inroads in traditionally Democratic areas of Detroit and its suburbs. At the same time, Levin won an unusually high 45% of the outstate vote. Milliken is expected to seek reelection in 1974, his opponent being either Levin or former Mayor Cavanagh—a man whose public standing appears to have recovered significantly from the effects of the 1967 Detroit riot.

As predicted in the 1972 edition of the *Almanac*, Sen. Robert Griffin won reelection in 1972. Griffin, the Republican Whip, is one of the Senate's shrewdest partisan operators. Back in the 1950s, Griffin, as a member of the House, helped to put together the Landrum-Griffin Act—the only piece of labor legislation enacted since Taft-Hartley. Organized labor disliked some of the provisions of Landrum-Griffin, mainly those added by Griffin and others to the bill sponsored by then Sen. John F. Kennedy. But Griffin has been able to win in Michigan, though the state has one of the highest percentages of unionization in the country. In 1966, Griffin beat the state's best-known Democrat, G. Mennen Williams, by a solid 56–44 margin. And during his first term as Senator, the Republican built a record of occasional but well-publicized dissents from the Nixon Administration—notably on the Haynsworth nomination and the SST. These dissents served him well at election time. Most of the time, however, Griffin fights like a tiger for partisan Republican causes.

Griffin seized the busing issue in 1971. In spite of his previous record of support for civil rights legislation, Griffin was able to convince white suburban voters that he was a more dependable anti-buser than state Attorney General Frank Kelley, the Democratic candidate for Senator, who was also opposed to busing. But in an age of growing suspicion of all politicians, cynical white voters apparently concluded that the most reliable anti-buser was the Republican. Since Williams' day, Michigan Democrats have had a reputation for supporting black causes; one mark of this cropped up in 1960, when John F. Kennedy carried a larger percentage of the black vote here than in any other large state.

Would Griffin have won without busing? Probably. The Senator has convinced a far greater number of voters in Michigan than observers in Washington that he is an independent thinker. He also brought other assets to the campaign, like sponsoring the repeal of the auto excise tax. And in the crunch, Michigan's Republicans— the Romneys not withstanding— are notably more accomplished campaigners than the state's Democrats. Evidence of this was Kelley's decision to concentrate on the busing issue, though he couldn't possibly out-antibus Griffin.

Michigan's senior Senator, Democrat Philip Hart, is a very different sort—where Griffin is an indefatigable partisan fighter, Hart has little of the ambition and drive customarily associated with politicians. Hart won his seat in 1958, when he was serving as Lieutenant Governor under G. Mennen Williams. Since then, the Senator has kept his seat by overwhelming margins against minimal opposition. Hart's major area of legislative activity lies in consumer affairs antitrust; as Chairman of the Judiciary Antitrust Subcommittee, the Michigan Senator has crusaded against the evils of monopoly and oligopoly. He has also concentrated his efforts on particular problems in the field—whether, for example, the major oil companies conspired to contrive the "energy crisis." He is one of the leading pro-consumer voices on the Commerce Committee, and the Senate's leading champion of national no-fault auto insurance. Hart, as the ranking liberal on the full Judiciary Committee, has played an important, though quiet, role opposing various Nixon nominations, like that of L. Patrick Gray's designation to become head of the FBI.

Any contentiousness, however, goes against Hart's grain. The Senator is the kind of man who tries to see merit in the positions taken by his adversaries, even when he considers the consequences of their views horrifying. But his gentle nature is admixed with some steel. He was the only Senator to vote against the nomination of James O. Eastland for Senate President pro tem. The office is of only formal importance, except that its holder is fourth in line for the presidency. Hart's action was particularly audacious since Eastland is Chairman of the full Judiciary Committee. Neither is Hart afraid to court political trouble back home if he feels the cause is right. He has opposed anti-busing legislation; in fact, he was one of the leaders in the Senate fight that prevented its enactment in the fall of 1972.

There is talk in Michigan that Hart will retire when his seat comes up in 1976. But there was similar talk in 1970, when he ran. If Hart does leave the Senate, possible replacements include Flint Congressman Donald Riegle, a Republican who became a Democrat in the spring of 1973; ex-Gov. John Swainson, currently state Supreme Court Justice; and Republican Gov. William Milliken, provided he wins in 1974.

Census Data Pop. 8,875,083; 4.38% of U.S. total, 7th largest; change 1960–70, 13.4%. Central city, 28%; suburban, 49%. Median family income, $11,029; 6th highest; families above $15,000: 27%; families below $3,000: 7%. Median years education, 12.1.

1972 Share of Federal Tax Burden $9,656,650,000; 4.62% of U.S. total, 7th largest.

1972 Share of Federal Outlays $6,119,580,884; 2.82% of U.S. total, 11th largest. Per capita federal spending, $690.

DOD	$837,139,000	23rd (1.34%)	HEW	$2,968,508,035	7th (4.16%)
AEC	$4,099,238	24th (0.16%)	HUD	$120,261,010	9th (3.92%)
NASA	$22,787,576	15th (0.76%)	VA	$393,281,734	8th (3.44%)
DOT	$270,399,745	9th (3.43%)	USDA	$246,894,293	23rd (1.61%)
DOC	$16,937,040	17th (1.31%)	CSC	$58,903,505	17th (1.43%)
DOI	$15,399,150	31st (0.73%)	TD	$530,567,534	5th (3.21%)
DOJ	$38,010,819	6th (3.87%)	Other	$596,392,205	

Economic Base Motor vehicles and equipment, and other transportation equipment; machinery, especially metalworking machinery; finance, insurance and real estate; fabricated metal products, especially metal stampings; primary metal industries, especially iron and steel foundries; agriculture, notably dairy products, cattle, dry beans and corn; food and kindred products.

Political Line-up Governor, William G. Milliken (R); seat up, 1974. Senators, Philip A. Hart (D) and Robert R. Griffin (R). Representatives, 19 (11 R and 8 D). State Senate (19 D and 19 R); State House (60 D and 50 R).

The Voters

Registration 4,711,855 total. No party registration.
Median voting age 40.1
Employment profile White collar, 45%. Blue collar, 41%. Service, 13%. Farm, 1%.
Ethnic groups Black, 11%. Spanish, 1%. Total foreign stock, 19%. Canada, 4%; Poland, Germany, UK, 2% each; Italy, 1%.

Presidential vote

1972	Nixon (R)	1,961,721	(57%)
	McGovern (D)	1,459,435	(43%)
1968	Nixon (R)	1,370,665	(42%)
	Humphrey (D)	1,593,082	(48%)
	Wallace (AI)	331,968	(10%)
1964	Johnson (D)	2,136,615	(67%)
	Goldwater (R)	1,060,152	(33%)

Senator

Philip A. Hart (D) Elected 1958, seat up 1976; b. Dec. 10, 1912, Bryn Mawr, Pa.; home, Mackinac Island; Georgetown U., B.A., 1934; U. of Mich., J.D., 1937; Army, WWII; married, eight children; Catholic.

Career Mich. Corp. and Securities Comm., 1949–50; Dir. Office of Price Stabilization, 1951; U.S. Atty., E. Mich., 1952–53; legal adviser to Gov. Williams, 1953–54; Lt. Gov., 1955–58; Asst. Majority Whip, 1966–67.

Offices 253 OSOB, 202-225-4822. Also 438 Fed. Bldg., Detroit 48226, 313-226-3188.

Administrative Assistant Sidney H. Woolner

Committees

Commerce (4th); Subs: Aviation; Communications; Consumer (Vice Chm.); Environment (Chm.); Oceans and Atmosphere.

Judiciary (4th); Subs: Administrative Practice and Procedure; Antitrust and Monopoly (Chm.); Criminal Laws and Procedures; Immigration and Naturalization; Improvements in Judicial Machinery; Juvenile Delinquency; Patents, Trademarks, and Copyrights; Revision and Codification; Refugees and Escapees; Penitentiaries.

Sel. Com. on Nutrition and Human Needs (3rd).

Sp. Com. on Termination of the National Emergency (2nd).

Group Ratings

	ADA	COPE	LWV	RIPON	NFU	LCV	CFA	NAB	NSI	ACA
1972	95	100	100	74	90	84	100	0	0	5
1971	96	75	100	80	82	–	100	–	–	4
1970	87	100	–	81	100	60	–	8	0	9

Key Votes

1) Busing	FOR	8) Sea Life Prot	FOR	15) Tax Singls Less	FOR
2) Alas P-line	AGN	9) Campaign Subs	FOR	16) Min Tax for Rich	FOR
3) Gun Cntrl	FOR	10) Cmbodia Bmbg	AGN	17) Euro Troop Rdctn	FOR
4) Rehnquist	AGN	11) Legal Srvices	FOR	18) Bust Hwy Trust	FOR
5) Pub TV $	FOR	12) Rev Sharing	FOR	19) Maid Min Wage	FOR
6) EZ Votr Reg	FOR	13) Cnsumr Prot	FOR	20) Farm Sub Limit	FOR
7) No-Fault	FOR	14) Eq Rts Amend	FOR	21) Highr Credt Chgs	ABS

Election Results

1970 general:	Philip A. Hart (D)	1,744,672	(67%)
	Lenore Romney (R)	858,438	(33%)
1970 primary:	Philip A. Hart (D), unopposed		
1964 general:	Philip A. Hart (D)	1,996,912	(64%)
	Elly M. Peterson (R)	1,096,272	(35%)

Senator

Robert P. Griffin (R) Elected 1966, seat up 1978; b. Nov. 6, 1923, Detroit; home, Traverse City; Central Mich. U., A.B., B.S., 1947; U. of Mich., J.D., 1950; Army, WWII; married, four children; United Church of Christ.

Career Practicing atty., 1950–56; U.S. House of Reps., 1957–66; Minority Whip, 1969– .

Offices 353 OSOB, 202-225-6221. Also 1039 Fed. Bldg., 231 W. Lafayette, Detroit 48226, 313-226-6020.

Administrative Assistant C. William Cardin

Committees

Commerce (3rd); Subs: Aviation; Communications; Merchant Marine; Oceans and Atmosphere; Foreign Commerce and Tourism (Ranking Mbr.).

Foreign Relations (7th); Subs: European Affairs; Oceans and International Environment; Western Hemisphere Affairs; South Asian Affairs

Rules and Administration (3rd); Subs: Standing Rules of the Senate (Ranking Mbr.); Privileges and Elections (Ranking Mbr.).

Group Ratings

	ADA	COPE	LWV	RIPON	NFU	LCV	CFA	NAB	NSI	ACA
1972	15	10	60	74	63	59	67	70	88	74
1971	33	8	92	80	33	–	0	–	–	63
1970	28	40	–	65	38	24	–	78	100	74

Key Votes

1) Busing	AGN	8) Sea Life Prot	FOR	15) Tax Singls Less	FOR
2) Alas P-line	FOR	9) Campaign Subs	AGN	16) Min Tax for Rich	FOR
3) Gun Cntrl	FOR	10) Cmbodia Bmbg	FOR	17) Euro Troop Rdctn	AGN
4) Rehnquist	FOR	11) Legal Srvices	AGN	18) Bust Hwy Trust	FOR
5) Pub TV $	AGN	12) Rev Sharing	FOR	19) Maid Min Wage	AGN
6) EZ Votr Reg	AGN	13) Cnsumr Prot	ABS	20) Farm Sub Limit	FOR
7) No-Fault	FOR	14) Eq Rts Amend	FOR	21) Highr Credt Chgs	FOR

Election Results

1972 general:	Robert P. Griffin (R)	1,781,065	(52%)
	Frank J. Kelley (D)	1,577,178	(46%)
	Patrick V. Dillinger (AI)	23,121	(1%)
	Barbara Halpert (Human Rights)	19,118	(1%)
1972 primary:	Robert P. Griffin (R), unopposed		
1966 general:	Robert P. Griffin (R)	1,363,808	(56%)
	G. Mennen Williams (D)	1,070,484	(44%)

FIRST DISTRICT Political Background

The 1st district of Michigan includes the north and near-northwest sides of Detroit, plus the enclave of Highland Park enclosed by the city. The 1st presents a nice example of the pace of neighborhood change in twentieth-century urban America. Sixty-odd years ago, the land here was given over completely to Michigan farms; at that time, Detroit's growth had not yet reached the southern boundary of the current 1st district, which is some five miles from the Detroit River. Whereupon Henry Ford built his first big auto plant in Highland Park. Then, as now, manufacturers located factories at the edges of urban settlements, where a labor force is at hand, land prices are cheap, and room to expand is available. In the years that followed, mile after mile of closely spaced one- and two-family houses were built here—this part of America owing its existence to the Model T Ford. Ethnic neighborhood patterns emerged: Polish in the eastern and southern parts of the current 1st, Jewish in the middle, and a rich WASP region just north of Highland Park. The growth during the 1910s and 1920s was explosive, with most of the district's current housing having been built during those two decades.

In the years following World War II, another kind of change took place here. At the war's end, few black enclaves could be found within the current lines of the 1st; even by 1950, less than 5% of the residents of this area were black. But by 1970, the figure was 70%. The first exodus occurred in the late 1940s and early 1950s. Thousands of blacks who had come to Detroit during the war left the small ghettos in which they had been confined, while whites fled to the outer edges of the city or to the FHA-financed suburbs. Whole square miles of Detroit changed racial complexion within a year or two. Then in the wake of the 1967 Detroit riot, another particularly rapid racial transformation took place. What was previously Detroit's primary Jewish neighborhood along Seven Mile Road soon became heavily black. Around the same time, the city's most affluent areas opened up to blacks; today parts of northwest Detroit contain elegant black or integrated neighborhoods, as posh as any black or integrated community in the country.

There are still pockets of all-white territory in the 1st, particularly in the Polish neighborhoods that resist change of every sort. Generally speaking, the blacks living in the 1st are more affluent and better educated than those in the neighboring 13th district; most here own their own homes. They are also far more likely to vote. Some analysts have speculated that blacks, as they grow more affluent, will, like members of other ethnic groups, grow more conservative and Republican. Maybe so, but little confirmation for the theory exists in the voting habits of the 1st district. This is one of the nation's two or three most heavily Democratic congressional districts.

It should therefore come as no surprise that the 1st's Congressman ended up on one of the Nixon "enemies lists." In fact, Rep. John Conyers—described as "coming on fast. Emerging as a leading black anti-Nixon spokesman"—was the only black Congressman singled out for special mention, with the entire House Black Caucus being placed on another list without specifics. It is rather fitting that Conyers made the list. He was the first of the new breed of outspoken black Congressmen who organized and now dominate the Black Caucus. When Conyers was first elected in 1964, only four other blacks served in the House. Adam Clayton Powell was Chairman of the Education and Labor Committee, but was already headed for trouble. The senior black Congressman, William Dawson of Chicago, was an aging politician who very rarely rocked the boat. From the start, Conyers was different: energetic, ambitious, and unwilling to kowtow to the powers or the traditions of the House of Representatives. The Detroit Congressman was the first black member of the Judiciary Committee, a unit with jurisdiction over civil rights legislation. And Conyers was also one of the first members of the House to oppose the Vietnam war, as he worked closely with antiwar white Representatives.

Like most Congressmen, Conyers' first race was his toughest. In the 1964 Democratic primary, Conyers beat Richard Austin, the other principal contender in the race, by a scant 108 votes out of 60,000 cast. (In 1970, Austin became Michigan Secretary of State after a narrow defeat in the 1969

Detroit mayoralty election; both times Austin had Conyers' support.) Since his first election, Conyers has won all the elections in which he has had opposition, including primaries, by percentages ranging from 85 to 90%. As predicted in the 1972 *Almanac*, redistricting here added much of northwest Detroit to the 1st. But the additional territory has no effect on the 1972 House contest here; it simply returned to Conyers many of his former constituents.

Census Data Pop. 467,636. Central city, 92%; suburban, 8%. Median family income, $9,997; families above $15,000: 23%; families below $3,000: 10%. Median years education, 11.5.

1972 Share of Federal Outlays $316,398,241

DOD	$45,509,011	HEW	$146,473,927
AEC	$21,369	HUD	$8,469,947
NASA	$85,830	DOI	$375,209
DOT	$15,258,545	USDA	$5,711,757
		Other	$94,492,646

Federal Military-Industrial Commitments

No installations or contractors receiving prime awards greater than $5,000,000.

Economic Base Transportation equipment, especially motor vehicles and equipment; finance, insurance and real estate; fabricated metal products, especially metal stampings; machinery; and primary metal industries, especially blast furnace and basic steel products. Also higher education (Univ. of Detroit).

The Voters

Registration 278,351 total. No party registration.
Median voting age 43.0
Employment profile White collar, 41%. Blue collar, 42%. Service, 17%. Farm, –%.
Ethnic groups Black, 70%. Total foreign stock, 15%. Canada, Poland, 2% each; USSR, UK, Germany, 1% each.

Presidential vote

1972	Nixon (R)	22,815	(14%)
	McGovern (D)	137,732	(86%)
1968	Nixon (R)	25,093	(13%)
	Humphrey (D)	157,660	(83%)
	Wallace (AI)	8,241	(4%)

Representative

John Conyers, Jr. (D) Elected 1964; b. May 16, 1929, Detroit; home, Detroit; Wayne State U., B.A., 1957, LL.B., 1958; Army, Korean War; unmarried; Baptist.

Career Legis. Asst., Rep. John Dingell, 1958–61; Mich. Workingmen's Compensation Referee, 1961–63.

Offices 2444 RHOB, 202-225-5126. Also 307 Fed. Bldg., 231 Lafayette St., Detroit 48226, 313-226-7022.

Administrative Assistant Heidi Napper

Committees

Judiciary (7th); Sub: Revision of the Laws (Chm.).

Committee on Government Operations (17th); Subs: Legal and Monetary Affairs; Special Studies.

Group Ratings

	ADA	COPE	LWV	RIPON	NFU	LCV	CFA	NAB	NSI	ACA
1972	88	91	91	69	83	60	100	13	0	6
1971	76	78	78	71	67	–	100	–	–	17
1970	92	100	–	67	82	90	100	0	0	21

Key Votes

1) Busing	FOR	6) Cmbodia Bmbg	AGN	11) Chkg Acct Intrst	FOR
2) Strip Mines	AGN	7) Bust Hwy Trust	FOR	12) End HISC (HUAC)	FOR
3) Cut Mil $	FOR	8) Farm Sub Lmt	FOR	13) Nixon Sewer Veto	AGN
4) Rev Shrg	FOR	9) School Prayr	AGN	14) Corp Cmpaign $	AGN
5) Pub TV $	ABS	10) Cnsumr Prot	FOR	15) Pol $ Disclosr	AGN

Election Results

1972 general:	John Conyers, Jr. (D)	131,353	(88%)
	Walter F. Girardot (R)	16,096	(11%)
	Nina J. Hubbard (AI)	817	(1%)
1972 primary:	John Conyers, Jr. (D), unopposed		
1970 general:	John Conyers, Jr. (D)	93,075	(88%)
	Howard L. Johnson (R)	11,876	(11%)
	Jacqueline Rice (SW)	617	(1%)

SECOND DISTRICT   Political Background

The 2nd district of Michigan is an odd amalgam: an admixture of university campuses, burgeoning suburbs, and aging factories. In rough terms, the district takes in the western and southern edges of the Detroit metropolitan area and lies entirely within the Detroit TV media market. But the 2nd's most important city, Ann Arbor, thinks itself no part of what it considers a grimy and industrial Detroit. Ann Arbor (pop. 99,000) is the home of the University of Michigan (40,000 students), one of the nation's largest and most prestigious state universities. This institution, along with Eastern Michigan University (18,000 students) in nearby Ypsilanti, gives the 2nd district the largest proportion of college students in the eligible electorate—15.2%—of any district in the nation. In Ann Arbor, the student vote has produced a left-wing third party with some vitality. In the 1973 city elections, however, the Human Rights candidates split the student vote with local liberal Democrats, and in so doing, handed control of the city government to Ann Arbor's Republicans, a rather conservative set.

In fact, until the late 1960s, Ann Arbor was a conservative Republican town. Its heritage stemmed from its large German-American population, many of whom are descended from immigrants who fled after the failure of the revolutions of 1848. So until the coming of the student vote, the Democratic strength here lay in the working-class wards of Ypsilanti, near the giant Willow Run plant, and in Monroe County to the south along Lake Erie. For the 1972 election, the shape of the 2nd was altered to include the Detroit suburb of Livonia (pop. 110,000), which, despite the presence of a couple of large GM plants, is middle- to upper-middle-income, and, more often than not, Republican in its politics. Livonia is a place that bloomed with instant subdivisions—its population in 1950 was just 17,000. But its demographic make-up, top-heavy with schoolchildren, means that it is outvoted by the less populous Ann Arbor in 2nd-district elections. Like virtually all of the Detroit suburbs, Livonia has been in the grips of an anti-busing fever ever since a federal judge ruled in favor of a plan that would bus children in and out of Detroit. The decision, however, is not yet in force, as it is currently on appeal to the U.S. Supreme Court.

The current district was largely the design of ex-state Rep. Marvin Stempien of Livonia. He apparently figured that he could carry his home city, sweep the student and blue-collar vote, and unseat Republican Congressman Marvin Esch. Stempien could not have been more wrong; he failed to carry any of these communities. The challenger's strong anti-busing stance did nothing for him in Livonia, which was content with Esch's position on the matter. But Stempien's rhetoric did antagonize student voters, who were happy with Esch's votes against the war. Esch, a native of Ann Arbor, ran far ahead of Richard Nixon in the university town, while the blue-collar vote went Republican in the congressional race, as it has increasingly for other offices as well.

As his ratings by various groups indicate, Esch is a Congressman who has something in his record for everyone. He has always had some difficulty retaining his seat, ever since he beat a beneficiary of the LBJ landslide, Democrat Weston Vivian, in 1966. But each time out Esch has come through nicely. Yet because of the 2nd's heavy student population, the Congressman remains potentially vulnerable. He is in real trouble if the Democrats can ever nominate a candidate who can win ballots in Livonia and among the working-class voters, while at the same time commanding solid support in the student wards of Ann Arbor and Ypsilanti. Such a candidate could be John Reuther, a young member of the UAW family, who was the McGovern state coordinator in the Massachusetts primary and held the same position in Minnesota for the November general election of 1972.

Census Data Pop. 466,852. Central city, 21%; suburban, 79%. Median family income, $12,908; families above $15,000: 37%; families below $3,000: 4%. Median years education, 12.4.

1972 Share of Federal Outlays $333,876,365

DOD	$32,420,515	HEW	$151,375,713
AEC	$1,894,382	HUD	$3,424,113
NASA	$17,580,131	DOI	$2,589,497
DOT	$14,781,630	USDA	$9,115,440
		Other	$100,694,944

Federal Military-Industrial Commitments

DOD Contractors University of Michigan (Ann Arbor), $7.109m: various electronic, medical, and psychological research projects. Bendix (Ann Arbor), $5.271m: mini-telemetry systems.
NASA Contractors Bendix (Ann Arbor), $13.081m: development program for Apollo space craft.

Economic Base Motor vehicles and equipment, and other transportation equipment; finance, insurance and real estate; agriculture, notably cattle, vegetables and diary products; paper and allied products, especially paperboard mill products; and fabricated metal products. Also higher education (Eastern Michigan Univ., and Univ. of Michigan).

The Voters

Registration 257,981 total. No party registration.
Median voting age 36.5
Employment profile White collar, 53%. Blue collar, 33%. Service, 13%. Farm, 1%.
Ethnic groups Black, 5%. Spanish, 1%. Total foreign stock, 17%. Canada, 4%; Germany, UK, 2% each; Poland, Italy, 1% each.

Presidential vote

1972	Nixon (R)	106,155	(56%)
	McGovern (D)	85,093	(44%)
1968	Nixon (R)	69,610	(45%)
	Humphrey (D)	70,528	(45%)
	Wallace (AI)	15,950	(10%)

Representative

Marvin L. Esch (R) Elected 1966; b. Aug. 4, 1927, Flinton, Pa.; home, Ann Arbor; U. of Mich., A.B., 1950, M.A., 1951, Ph.D., 1957; Maritime and Army, WWII; married, three children; Presbyterian.

Career Asst. prof. Wayne State U., 1953–55; lecturer, Inst. of Labor and Industrial Relations, Wayne State U., 1955–64; State Rep., 1965–66.

Offices 412 CHOB, 202-225-4401. Also 200 E. Huron, Ann Arbor 48108, 313-665-0618.

Administrative Assistant George W. Stevens

Committees

Education and Labor (6th); Subs: No. 2 (Sp. Sub. on Labor); No. 41 (Sel. Sub.. on Labor) (Ranking Mbr.); No. 6 (Sp. Sub. on Education).

Science and Astronautics (7th); Subs: Science, Research and Development; Energy; Space Science and Applications (Ranking Mbr.).

Group Ratings

	ADA	COPE	LWV	RIPON	NFU	LCV	CFA	NAB	NSI	ACA
1972	56	30	75	84	100	63	50	44	60	39
1971	54	30	67	94	57	–	86	–	–	52
1970	52	60	–	94	70	95	70	63	77	38

Key Votes

1) Busing	AGN	6) Cmbodia Bmbg	AGN	11) Chkg Acct Intrst	AGN
2) Strip Mines	AGN	7) Bust Hwy Trust	FOR	12) End HISC (HUAC)	AGN
3) Cut Mil $	FOR	8) Farm Sub Lmt	FOR	13) Nixon Sewer Veto	FOR
4) Rev Shrg	ABS	9) School Prayr	FOR	14) Corp Cmpaign $	AGN
5) Pub TV $	ABS	10) Cnsumr Prot	FOR	15) Pol $ Disclosr	FOR

Election Results

1972 general:	Marvin L. Esch (R)	103,321	(56%)
	Marvin R. Stempien (D)	79,762	(43%)
	Henry W. Kroes, Jr. (AI)	1,313	(1%)
1972 primary:	Marvin L. Esch (R), unopposed		
1970 general:	Marvin L. Esch (R)	88,071	(63%)
	R. Michael Stillwagon (D)	52,782	(37%)

THIRD DISTRICT Political Background

Many pundits have speculated upon Watergate's impact on the country's 1974 congressional elections. A way to get a handle on the matter is to look at a district, the 3rd of Michigan, where the scandal may well have a direct and specific impact. For this district's Congressman went to bat for the Nixon Administration and the Committee to Reelect the President (CREEP) at a critical moment, and almost singlehandedly managed to delay any investigation of Watergate until after the 1972 elections. Moreover, despite an impeccably Republican past, the 3rd is a district that has shown in its recent behavior at the polls signs of disenchantment with the Nixon Administration and some of its seamier practices.

Part of southwestern Michigan, the 3rd district centers on the cities of Kalamazoo (pop. 86,000) and Battle Creek (pop. 39,000), though it does reach north to include some of the suburbs of Lansing. The district's Congressman is Garry Brown, a feisty, hard-working Republican, and a member of the House Banking and Currency Committee. Brown's moment in the Watergate limelight occurred in the fall of 1972. At that time, as Chairman Wright Patman prepared an investigation to look into the scandal, White House press secretary Ron Ziegler issued periodic blasts at the shoddy journalism of the stories appearing in the *Washington Post*—stories that later turned out to be true. As one of the most active Republicans on Banking and Currency, Brown opposed Patman's pre-election probe of Watergate. Convinced that any investigation might infringe on the rights of potential defendants then before the grand jury—and might decrease the likelihood of successful prosecution—Brown prodded the Justice Department to send a letter to the Banking Committee opposing the issuance of subpoenas, a necessary preliminary to the Patman investigation. Brown also helped line up the Committee's Republicans solidly against the probe, and every one of them, plus six Democrats, voted against the subpoenas— thus killing the investigation. Former White House Counsel John Dean testified before the Ervin Committee that Brown's involvement was even deeper, but Brown denies these charges with considerable vehemence, and it is difficult to believe that he would consciously be involved in a cover-up operation. Nevertheless, it remains a fact that Brown was in large part responsible for the suppression of an investigation which, if launched, might have informed the voters about the Watergate crimes when they could have done something about them—before the 1972 election.

Brown's activities in this affair typifies the Congressman: aggressive, partisan, unyielding, and also lawyerlike. Earlier, Brown took up a similar kind of aggressive bat in behalf of Upjohn, a drug company based in Kalamazoo, when the FDA wanted to take the firm's very profitable Panalba drug off the market. He has also argued that the manufacturers of Checker cabs, whose plant is here in the 3rd, should be exempted from certain safety standards. And no doubt, if Kellogg's and Post—cereal companies with big plants in Battle Creek—ever have trouble in Washington, they would have no trouble enlisting the aid of Congressman Brown. He has certainly supported modular housing programs (Banking and Currency has jurisdiction over housing) and George Romney's Operation Breakthrough, and it doesn't hurt that some of the nation's biggest manufacturers of the modules work out of Brown's district.

Many members of the Banking and Currency Committee own banks or bank stock, and may therefore be accused of voting their own interest. Not Brown. He has no such interests and clearly acts from personal conviction. If he lines up behind the big banks or the district's major industries, he does so because his own analysis as a lawyer has convinced him that their stands have merit—independent of any regard for political consequences.

But so far at least, the political consequences have been quite beneficial. Brown first won the seat in 1966, after spending four years in the state Senate, where he was one of then Gov. George Romney's major backers. Since Brown's first election, he has encountered serious opposition only once, in 1970, from a popular former judge and liberal Democrat Richard Enslen. But recent political trends in the 3rd have not been especially favorable to the kind of Republicanism practiced by Richard Nixon and usually supported by Garry Brown.

The 3rd district of Michigan is one of the few districts in the country where George McGovern ran stronger in 1972 than Hubert Humphrey did in 1968. One factor behind McGovern's showing is the presence of Western Michigan University (20,000 students) in Kalamazoo. Even five years ago, the university, which draws most of its students from comfortable suburban homes, would have been a Republican stronghold. The school's move to the left is a typical, if somewhat exaggerated, aspect of a trend in the 3rd district and outstate Michigan generally. For years people in neat, well-ordered cities like Kalamazoo have voted Republican. They did so out of a reaction to what they saw as a Democratic party dominated by Detroit and the labor unions. But today, to judge from the returns, the voters of outstate Michigan consider almost equally obnoxious the domination of Richard Nixon's Republican party by big money from southern California, Texas, and Florida. These Michigan people take the old Protestant-Republican virtues—honesty, thrift, and abstention from foreign wars—a good deal more seriously than does, it appears, the Nixon Administration.

So the 3rd district might have a pitched battle for its congressional seat in 1974. But Brown, a tireless defender of his conduct in the Watergate matter, has always worked in behalf of his constituents, and so far anyway, no strong Democratic candidate has emerged to challenge the incumbent.

Census Data Pop. 467,546. Central city, 19%; suburban, 44%. Median family income, $10,913; families above $15,000: 25%; families below $3,000: 7%. Median years education, 12.2.

1972 Share of Federal Outlays $346,649,812

DOD	$56,173,345	HEW	$164,202,353
AEC	$70,491	HUD	$3,771,139
NASA	$440,470	DOI	–
DOT	$6,640,151	USDA	$16,906,284
		Other	$97,797,175

Federal Military-Industrial Commitments

No installations or contractors receiving prime awards greater than $5,000,000.

Economic Base Machinery; paper and allied products, especially paper mill products, except building paper, and paperboard containers and boxes; finance, insurance and real estate; food and kindred products, especially grain mill products; and fabricated metal products. Also higher education (Western Michigan Univ.).

The Voters

Registration 248,799 total. No party registration.
Median voting age 40.6
Employment profile White collar, 46%. Blue collar, 39%. Service, 13%. Farm, 2%.
Ethnic groups Black, 5%. Total foreign stock; 10%. Netherlands, Canada, 2% each; Germany, UK, 1% each.

Presidential vote

1972	Nixon (R)	118,023	(62%)
	McGovern (D)	71,608	(38%)
1968	Nixon (R)	91,974	(53%)
	Humphrey (D)	64,544	(37%)
	Wallace (AI)	17,857	(10%)

Representative

Garry Brown (R) Elected 1966; b. Aug. 12, 1923, Schoolcraft; home, Schoolcraft; Mich. State U. (Kalamazoo Col.), B.A., 1951; George Washington U. Law School, LL.B., 1954; Army, 1946–47; married, four children; Presbyterian.

Career Atty., partner, Ford, Kriekard, Brown and Staton, 1954–67; Com. U.S. Dist. Court, Western Mich., 1957–62; State Sen., 1962–66; Minority Floor Leader.

Offices 404 CHOB, 202-225-5011. Also Rm. 2-1-36 Fed. Center, 74 N. Washington St., Battle Creek 49017, 616-962-1551, and Rm. 112, Fed. Bldg., Kalamazoo 49006, 616-381-8290.

Administrative Assistant John W. Lampmann

Committees

Banking and Currency (5th); Subs: Housing; International Trade; Urban Mass Transportation (Ranking Mbr.).

Government Operations (10th); Subs: Intergovernmental Relations; Legal and Monetary Affairs.

Joint Com. on Defense Production (2nd).

Group Ratings

	ADA	COPE	LWV	RIPON	NFU	LCV	CFA	NAB	NSI	ACA
1972	13	9	60	88	50	56	0	100	100	64
1971	30	30	44	67	27	–	38	–	–	81
1970	24	42	–	71	55	28	41	67	77	71

Key Votes

1) Busing	AGN	6) Cmbodia Bmbg	FOR	11) Chkg Acct Intrst	AGN
2) Strip Mines	AGN	7) Bust Hwy Trust	FOR	12) End HISC (HUAC)	AGN
3) Cut Mil $	AGN	8) Farm Sub Lmt	FOR	13) Nixon Sewer Veto	FOR
4) Rev Shrg	FOR	9) School Prayr	FOR	14) Corp Cmpaign $	FOR
5) Pub TV $	AGN	10) Cnsumr Prot	AGN	15) Pol $ Disclosr	FOR

Election Results

1972 general:	Garry Brown (R)	110,082	(59%)
	James T. Brignall (D)	74,114	(40%)
	Marvin P. Lightvoet (AI)	1,741	(1%)
1972 primary:	Garry Brown (R), unopposed		
1970 general:	Garry Brown (R)	80,447	(56%)
	Richard A. Enslen (D)	62,530	(44%)

FOURTH DISTRICT Political Background

The 4th district of Michigan is L shaped. It comprises Michigan's southwest corner, plus a string of counties along the state's border with Indiana and Ohio. The district's urban concentration lies in the Benton Harbor–St. Joseph area on Lake Michigan—two cities quite dissimilar from each other. Benton Harbor (pop. 16,000) is industrial and majority black, while St. Joseph (pop. 11,000) is residential and well-to-do. There is also a community of black people in and around Cassopolis and Dowagiac—descendants of slaves who found their way to these stations on the underground railway. For the most part, the 4th is agricultural and small town, with rolling hills, occasional lakes, and many dairy farms. The district has large number of German-Americans; in ethnic composition, therefore, it is more like northern Ohio and Indiana than the rest of outstate Michigan. The 4th is also disconnected from the rest of Michigan in that much of it is part of the South Bend, Indiana, or Toledo, Ohio media markets.

This is one of the state's most conservative and Republican districts. For the last 40 years, the 4th has elected some of the nation's most conservative Republican Congressmen. For 28 years it was represented by Clare E. Hoffman, an irascible money-saver who made H. R. Gross of Iowa (see Iowa 3) look like a free-spending New Dealer. The 4th's current Representative, elected in 1962 and returned with much difficulty since, is Republican Edward Hutchinson.

The seniority system in the House sometimes produces strange results. One Congressman can serve for 30 years and never get beyond the number-three notch on a committee; another can become his party's top member in the space of just 10 years. Hutchinson has been one of the lucky Congressmen. When Ohio's William McCulloch retired in 1972, Hutchinson became ranking minority member—Chairman if the Republicans ever get a majority in the House—of the Judiciary Committee. McCulloch, generally conservative on issues, was an effective and tireless supporter of civil rights legislation, having led the committee's Republicans on such legislation in 1964, 1965, and 1968. Hutchinson is one member who did not follow McCulloch's lead; the Michigan Congressman voted against all three civil rights bills.

With Hutchinson as the top Republican on the committee, one expects a hostile environment for civil rights legislation. But none is now pending. Moreover, Hutchinson does not cut an important figure in the House. In fact, after 10 years of service, he remains quiet and anonymous; the Congressman is scarcely know even by people interested in the areas where he has enormous potential—and so far unused—power.

Hutchinson's relative anonymity may have been the thing that inspired a primary challenge in 1972 for state Sen. Charles Zollar, a man nearly as conservative politically as Hutchinson, though more flamboyant in personal style. Zollar spent freely of his large fortune and had high hopes of winning, but he got only 34% of the Republican votes against Hutchinson's 61%. The incumbent's margin in the primary indicates that he is safely ensconced. There is no chance that a Democrat will ever win a general election in the 4th of Michigan.

Census Data Pop. 467,140. Central city, 0%; suburban, 0%. Median family income, $9,693; families above $15,000: 18%; families below $3,000: 10%. Median years education, 12.1.

1972 Share of Federal Outlays $277,770,531

DOD	$7,921,182	HEW	$164,649,201
AEC	–	HUD	$2,041,016
NASA	$1,096,104	DOI	$347,204
DOT	$3,380,467	USDA	$37,418,340
		Other	$60,917,017

Federal Military-Industrial Commitments

No installations or contractors receiving prime awards greater than $5,000,000.

Economic Base Machinery; primary metal industries, especially iron and steel foundries; agriculture, notably fruits, hogs and sheep, and vegetables; fabricated metal products; and finance, insurance and real estate.

The Voters

Registration 232,512 total. No party registration.
Median voting age 43.6
Employment profile White collar, 37%. Blue collar, 47%. Service, 12%. Farm, 4%.
Ethnic groups Black, 6%. Spanish, 1%. Total foreign stock, 10%. Germany, 3%; Canada, 1%.

Presidential vote

1972	Nixon (R)		116,712	(68%)
	McGovern (D)		55,846	(32%)
1968	Nixon (R)		91,836	(54%)
	Humphrey (D)		58,484	(34%)
	Wallace (AI)		20,275	(12%)

Representative

Edward Hutchinson (R) Elected 1962; b. Oct. 13, 1914, Fennville; home, Fennville; U. of Mich., A.B., 1936, LL.B. and J.D., 1938; Army, WWII; married; Christian Scientist.

Career State Rep., 1946–50; State Sen., 1951–60; Delegate, Vice-Pres., Mich. Constitutional Convention of 1961–62.

Offices 2436 RHOB, 202-225-3761. Also 201 Fed. Bldg., Benton Harbor 49022, 616-925-7962.

Administrative Assistant Mrs. A. G. Schultz

Committees

Judiciary (Ranking Mbr.); Sub: No. 5 (Antitrust Matters) (Ranking Mbr.).

Standards of Official Conduct (3rd).

Group Ratings

	ADA	COPE	LWV	RIPON	NFU	LCV	CFA	NAB	NSI	ACA
1972	0	27	27	44	20	32	0	92	100	91
1971	8	8	11	39	20	–	0	–	–	93
1970	12	0	–	53	23	25	45	100	90	100

Key Votes

1) Busing	AGN	6) Cmbodia Bmbg	FOR	11) Chkg Acct Intrst	AGN
2) Strip Mines	AGN	7) Bust Hwy Trust	AGN	12) End HISC (HUAC)	AGN
3) Cut Mil $	AGN	8) Farm Sub Lmt	FOR	13) Nixon Sewer Veto	FOR
4) Rev Shrg	AGN	9) School Prayr	FOR	14) Corp Cmpaign $	AGN
5) Pub TV $	AGN	10) Cnsumr Prot	AGN	15) Pol $ Disclosr	AGN

Election Results

1972 general:	Edward Hutchinson (R)	111,185	(67%)
	Charles W. Jameson (D)	54,141	(33%)
1972 primary:	Edward Hutchinson (R)	34,549	(61%)
	Charles Zollar (R)	19,304	(34%)
	Thomas J. Wich (R)	2,444	(4%)
1970 general:	Edward Hutchinson (R)	74,471	(62%)
	David R. McCormack (D)	45,838	(38%)

FIFTH DISTRICT Political Background

What sort of district returns the House Minority Leader to Congress? The easy answers are "Grand Rapids" and "Dutch." Grand Rapids (pop. 197,000), located at the falls of the Grand River, is the state's second largest city. It is best known for its furniture manufacturing, a business that got a start here because of the city's proximity to the state's once-thriving lumber industry. Today, Grand Rapids is more diversified; it is also healthy economically, as witnessed by its metropolitan growth rate which, like that of most outstate Michigan cities, was higher than Detroit's during the 1960s.

The nation's largest concentration of Dutch-Americans can be found living in and around Grand Rapids. Fully 7% of the 5th's residents were either born in the Netherlands or had parents who were. And many more than 7% here have Dutch names, as a glance at the city phone book's listing of Vander . . . s will show. Visitors to present-day Amsterdam know that the European Dutch are highly tolerant of diverse life styles. But when these people emigrate, it seems, they become less tolerant and sternly conservative. Such is clear from the political attitudes held by the Boers of South Africa and from the Dutch of Grand Rapids. The Michigan Calvinists of the Christian Reform Church frown on sinful activities like drinking, smoking, and dancing.

The Grand Rapids Dutch produced Michigan's best-known Senator, Arthur H. Vandenberg, who served from 1929 until his death in 1951. Born and bred an isolationist, the Senator went to his grave a deep-dyed conservative. But Vandenberg cooperated with the Roosevelt and Truman administrations when it came to the issues of the United Nations, the Marshall Plan, and the Truman Doctrine. Sen. Vandenberg is the man whose name crops up immediately when mention is made of a "bipartisan foreign policy." When Vandenberg was serving as Chairman of the Senate Foreign Relations Committee, he was embarrassed by Grand Rapid's local Congressman, Bartel J. Jonkman—a man who in the years just after World War II was as fully isolationist as he was before Pearl Harbor. So in 1948 Vandenberg and other Republican internationalists supported the challenge of a young lawyer and ex-University of Michigan football star in a primary campaign against Jonkman. The challenger was Gerald R. Ford, Jr., who won that primary and today is the Minority Leader in the House.

Ford became the House's top Republican in 1965, when he was a comparatively junior member of the body with only 16 years of service, by unseating Indiana's Charles Halleck. The dump-Halleck movement was one led by the likes of Robert Griffin, Melvin Laird, and Charles Goodell, now all gone on to other things. In the face of the Republican debacle of 1964, Ford promised new, constructive programs, as opposed to the purely negative stance assumed by Halleck. But the obstruction of Democratic proposals has also come to be the present Minority Leader's forte.

Gerald Ford is a deeply conservative man, one who fervently believes in the programs and the leadership of the Nixon Administration. He is anything but charismatic; since 1965, Ford lost the golden locks that journalists liked to contrast with Charlie Halleck's bald pate. Nor does Ford get high marks for erudition. But he works hard, grinding out, one could say, the necessary four yards at a crack. His Republican Caucus is far more disciplined and cohesive than its Democratic counterpart. When an important roll call begins, most of Ford's Republicans are firmly in their seats, and when it is over, they usually prevail with some help from some Southern Democrats.

The strength of Ford's leadership received a stiff test in early 1973. The Nixon Administration supported opening the highway trust fund for mass transit; Ford opposed it. A vast majority of the House Republicans went along with the Minority Leader, not the White House.

When the House has gone in ways opposed by Ford—notably on the issue of the bombing in Cambodia—switches among House Democratic members accounted for the final majority. Only about a dozen of Ford's Republicans changed their minds and voted to stop the bombing. Ford may be a plodder, but he is nevertheless an effective, competent Minority Leader.

Back home in Grand Rapids, Ford is a household word. But reelection time for the Congressman is not as routine as it once was. In 1970 and 1972, attorney Jean McKee has held him to 61%—a figure he has often exceeded in the past. No one expects Ford to lose an election in the 5th district, but unlike his Democratic counterpart, Speaker Carl Albert, Ford has to campaign to win.

Census Data Pop. 467,543. Central city, 42%; suburban, 46%. Median family income, $10,550; families above $15,000: 22%; families below $3,000: 7%. Median years education, 12.1.

1972 Share of Federal Outlays $285,005,338

DOD	$30,487,955	HEW	$144,978,104
AEC	$3,831	HUD	$4,163,903
NASA	$45,030	DOI	$324,358
DOT	$24,276,915	USDA	$10,442,120
		Other	$70,283,140

Federal Military-Industrial Commitments

DOD Contractors Lear Siegler (Grand Rapids), $21.718m: aircraft navigation sets.

Economic Base Fabricated metal products, especially metal stampings, and cutlery, hand tools and hardware; finance, insurance and real estate; machinery; furniture and fixtures; apparel and other textile products; and agriculture, notably dairy products, fruits and cattle.

The Voters

Registration 255,091 total. No party registration.
Median voting age 42.2
Employment profile White collar, 46%. Blue collar, 40%. Service, 12%. Farm, 2%.
Ethnic groups Black, 5%. Spanish, 1%. Total foreign stock, 17%. Netherlands, 7%; Poland, Canada, Germany, 2% each.

Presidential vote

	1972	Nixon (R)	117,832	(61%)
		McGovern (D)	75,224	(39%)
	1968	Nixon (R)	96,621	(54%)
		Humphrey (D)	69,234	(39%)
		Wallace (AI)	13,226	(7%)

Representative

Gerald R. Ford (R) Elected 1948; b. July 14, 1913, Omaha, Neb.; home, Grand Rapids; U. of Mich., B.A., 1935; Yale U., LL.B., 1941; Navy, WWII; married, four children; Episcopalian.

Career Practicing atty., 1941–48; House Minority Leader, 1965– .

Offices H-230, Capitol, 202-225-3831. Also 720 Fed. Bldg., 110 Michigan Ave., Grand Rapids 49502, 616-456-9607.

Administrative Assistant Mildred Leonard

Committees

None (Minority Leader).

Group Ratings

	ADA	COPE	LWV	RIPON	NFU	LCV	CFA	NAB	NSI	ACA
1972	6	11	40	62	20	17	50	92	100	68
1971	8	25	44	56	27	–	50	–	–	79
1970	12	9	–	59	54	10	50	83	100	68

Key Votes

1) Busing	AGN	6) Cmbodia Bmbg	FOR	11) Chkg Acct Intrst	FOR
2) Strip Mines	ABS	7) Bust Hwy Trust	AGN	12) End HISC (HUAC)	AGN
3) Cut Mil $	AGN	8) Farm Sub Lmt	ABS	13) Nixon Sewer Veto	FOR
4) Rev Shrg	FOR	9) School Prayr	FOR	14) Corp Cmpaign $	AGN
5) Pub TV $	AGN	10) Cnsumr Prot	FOR	15) Pol $ Disclosr	FOR

Election Results

1972 general:	Gerald Ford (R)	118,027	(61%)
	Jean McKee (D)	72,782	(37%)
	Dwight W. Johnson (AI)	2,045	(1%)
1972 primary:	Gerald Ford (R), unopposed		
1970 general:	Gerald Ford (R)	88,208	(61%)
	Jean McKee (D)	55,337	(39%)

SIXTH DISTRICT Political Background

The 6th district of Michigan comprises one of the best places in the country to examine the impact of college students on congressional politics, and to take a look at the changes that have occurred in the political attitudes of students during the recent past. Among the nation's 435 districts, the 6th is one with the fourth highest student percentage of the eligible electorate, 14.7%. Since the 1950s, the 6th has been safely Republican; until then, it included the industrial and Democratic city of Flint. Yet the 6th is a district that nearly elected a Democratic Congressman in 1972, and will very likely do so in 1974.

Before the advent of the student vote, the 6th was a fairly typical outstate Michigan district. The largest city in the area, Lansing (pop. 130,000), is one dominated by State government (it is the Michigan capital) and the auto industry (Oldsmobile). Also here is Jackson (pop. 45,000), an older industrial city and site of the state prison—one of the nation's largest. Lansing and Jackson generally gave Republican candidates small majorities. When these were added to the lopsided Republican majorities reported from the district's rural areas and small towns, the 6th emerged a solidly Republican district.

Within a setting of this sort, East Lansing was a small, well-to-do, heavily Republican suburb that happened to be the site of Michigan State University. Until recently, of course, the institution's 42,000 students could not vote; moreover, had they been able to, they would have probably voted pretty much as their parents did back home in the comfortable suburbs or in the middle-class neighborhoods of various Michigan cities. Michigan State was founded as an agricultural college and remained one until the 1930s, when it acquired the services of an empire-building president named John Hannah. A Republican who cultivated relationships with key legislators, Hannah proceeded to build a giant university. In many areas, Michigan State has developed a distinguished faculty and also has one of the nation's largest contingents of National Merit Scholars. Hannah left Michigan State to head AID in the Nixon Administration. As he left the campus, Hannah could see that the university had become a place where students showed less concern about the school's traditionally powerful football team than about the evils of war, poverty, and racism. Journalists have ground out reams of copy about the thinking of a small number of articulate student radicals. But the greening of middle-class kids at places like Michigan State—the quantum jump from fraternity beer parties to McGovern rallies—is a much bigger, and probably more important story.

With the coming of the student vote, university-based candidates took over the East Lansing City Council in 1971 and then poised themselves for the congressional race in 1972. The incumbent was Charles Chamberlain, a conservative member of the Ways and Means Committee and a Republican who dutifully toes any mark drawn by Minority Leader Gerald Ford. Chamberlain has also had problems among the voters with his short temper, which has gotten him into some bad scenes. One such was a nasty altercation with a Washington traffic patrolman into whose car, witnesses said, Chamberlain had driven. In the 1972 Republican primary, Chamberlain encountered significant opposition from moderate Jim Brown, a state Representative who probably expected to lose his East Lansing seat to a Democrat (it did go Democratic in November). Brown held Chamberlain to 59% of the vote—a poor percentage for a 16-year incumbent.

The Democratic nominee gave Chamberlain an even tougher fight. The challenger was 29-year-old Robert Carr, a neatly mustached former assistant Attorney General. The young man was able to pacify both wings of the feuding local Democratic party (labor vs. East Lansing liberals) and won an overwhelming majority of the student vote. But Carr also did well elsewhere in the district. He carried 57% in the city of Lansing, which has precious few students, and 48% in Jackson, which has virtually none. Unlike many areas of the country, the student vote in outstate Michigan does not appear to be bucking a rightward trend in the rest of the constituency; all of the voters here are trending the same way. In any case, the student votes of the 6th were enough to make the 1972 election a close one, with gains in other parts of the district nearly putting Carr over the top. The Democrat took 49.4% of the vote.

The day after the election, Carr announced his 1974 candidacy. Three months later, Chamberlain announced his retirement—an odd move and a virtual admission of impending defeat. Carr has not stopped running and continues to attract favorable local attention. In 1972, he proved unusually adept for a Michigan Democrat at raising and spending campaign money. Local Republicans are expected to field a candidate younger and more attractive than Chamberlain, but at this point the odds clearly favor Carr.

Census Data Pop. 467,536. Central city, 38%; suburban, 54%. Median family income, $11,105; families above $15,000: 27%; families below $3,000: 6%. Median years education, 12.3.

1972 Share of Federal Outlays $430,268,922

DOD	$70,575,891	HEW	$197,531,699
AEC	$483,693	HUD	$10,885,581
NASA	$3,550,416	DOI	$2,150,461
DOT	$14,573,884	USDA	$22,923,890
		Other	$107,593,407

Federal Military-Industrial Commitments

DOD Contractors Diamond Reo Trucks (Lansing), $52.195m: 2 ½-ton trucks and various truck engines and parts. Sparton Corp. (Jackson), $12.015m: sonobuoys. AM General Corp. (Lansing), $8.329m: unspecified.

Economic Base Motor vehicles and equipment, and other transportation equipment; machinery; finance, insurance and real estate; fabricated metal products; and agriculture, notably dairy products, cattle and grains. Also higher education (Michigan State Univ.).

The Voters

Registration 259,120 total. No party registration.
Median voting age 37.8
Employment profile White collar, 50%. Blue collar, 34%. Service, 14%. Farm, 2%.
Ethnic groups Black, 5%. Spanish, 2%. Total foreign stock, 12%. Canada, Germany, 2% each; UK, Poland, 1% each.

Presidential vote

1972	Nixon (R)	115,810	(59%)
	McGovern (D)	80,875	(41%)

1968	Nixon (R)	86,772	(53%)
	Humphrey (D)	63,306	(38%)
	Wallace (AI)	14,901	(9%)

Representative

Charles E. Chamberlain (R) Elected 1956; b. July 22, 1917, Ingham County; home, East Lansing; U. of Va., B.S., 1941, LL.B., 1949; USCG, WWII; married, three children.

Career Atty., 1950–56; Counsel, Mich. Senate Judiciary Com., 1953–54; Pros. Atty., Ingham Co., 1955–56.

Offices 2211 RHOB, 202-225-4872. Also 245 Fed. Bldg., Lansing 48933, 517-489-6517

Administrative Assistant J. R. Schuck

Committees

Ways and Means (5th).

Group Ratings

	ADA	COPE	LWV	RIPON	NFU	LCV	CFA	NAB	NSI	ACA
1972	13	40	50	75	80	27	0	90	100	52
1971	11	25	44	61	29	–	38	–	–	82
1970	12	8	–	59	54	6	48	91	100	78

Key Votes

1) Busing	AGN	6) Cmbodia Bmbg	FOR	11) Chkg Acct Intrst	AGN
2) Strip Mines	AGN	7) Bust Hwy Trust	AGN	12) End HISC (HUAC)	AGN
3) Cut Mil $	AGN	8) Farm Sub Lmt	FOR	13) Nixon Sewer Veto	FOR
4) Rev Shrg	FOR	9) School Prayr	FOR	14) Corp Cmpaign $	FOR
5) Pub TV $	AGN	10) Cnsumr Prot	FOR	15) Pol $ Disclosr	FOR

Election Results

1972 general:	Charles E. Chamberlain (R)	97,666	(51%)
	M. Robert Carr (D)	95,209	(49%)
1972 primary:	Charles E. Chamberlain (R)	26,199	(92%)
	Glenn E. Miller (R)	2,306	(8%)
1970 general:	Charles E. Chamberlain (R)	84,276	(60%)
	John A. Cihon (D)	55,591	(40%)

SEVENTH DISTRICT Political Background

With five major General Motors plants, Flint (pop. 193,000) is probably the nation's largest company town. Some 60% of Flint's wage earners are on the GM payroll. Though there is some GM white-collar employment here, this is mainly a Chevrolet and Buick factory town. Flint has no five o'clock rush hour; all the traffic jams pile up just after three-thirty when the shifts break. Even those who have profited most handsomely from the auto industry have not taken themselves out of Flint: the plushest residential district here has a panoramic view of a Chevrolet plant. Charles Stewart Mott, a GM pioneer and one of the nation's richest men, lived in Flint and ran the Mott Foundation out of the city; he died recently at age 97.

Flint owes its present existence to the boom years of the auto industry, the two decades between 1910 and 1930 and the early 1940s of World War II. During both periods, Flint attracted thousands of immigrants from the rural South—whites from the hills of Kentucky and Tennessee and blacks from Alabama and Mississippi. The politics of the migrants has usually been Democratic: old-timers can still remember the sit-down strikes of the 1930s. These started in Flint, organized by three young unionists named Roy, Victor, and Walter Reuther. Recently, however, racial friction has split Flint's working-class whites and blacks. In 1968, George Wallace had the support of many white UAW members and a few UAW locals. Only a concerted union effort held Wallace's share of the ballots down to 15%. But unlike Detroit, Flint has experienced no busing crisis; so in the Flint area, McGovern actually ran better in 1972 than Humphrey did in 1968.

Flint comprises the nucleus of Michigan's 7th district. The city's metropolitan area (and media market) coincides almost perfectly with the district lines of the 7th. Over the years, the district has usually gone Democratic in statewide contests—blue-collar Democrats here, of course, outnumber management Republicans. But the manner in which the district acquired its current Democratic Congressman, Donald W. Riegle, Jr., is a little odd. For Riegle spent his first six years in the House as a Republican, each year growing increasingly more uncomfortable in the party of Richard Nixon.

The year 1966 marked the beginning of Riegle's political career. Democrat John Mackie, former state Highway Commissioner (the last elected in the country), was the Congressman from Flint, having won 66% of the votes in 1964. It appeared that he was on his way to more seniority in the House. As the election of 1966 approached, Riegle, a Flint native, was working on a doctorate at the Harvard Business School. Because the Republicans back home were looking for a congressional candidate, someone suggested to Riegle that he return and run, which he did. After hiring the California firm of Spencer-Roberts, Riegle waged a vigorous and well-financed campaign. Meanwhile, incumbent Mackie relaxed on his Virginia farm. In an upset, Riegle won with 54% of the votes; he ran almost as well in the district as Romney in what was the Governor's best year.

Riegle's book, *O Congress!*, contains material for anyone who wants to learn more about the Michigan politician's first six years in the House. The only other book written by a Congressman that is as frank and informative is the late Clem Miller's *Member of the House*. But it is worth noting that Riegle began his House career distinguished more by his youth (28 when first elected) and his ambitiousness (he talked openly about running someday for President—a real taboo in the House) than by his maverick political stands. Riegle won a seat on the House Appropriations Committee with the help of Minority Leader Gerald Ford, and Riegle stayed on friendly terms with Ford even while he became increasingly disenchanted with the policies laid down by the Republican House leadership.

It must be said, however, that there were signs of apostasy during Riegle's first two years. He dissented with some frequency from orthodox Republican positions and he made a point of paying special attention to the complaints and needs of his black constituents; as a result, Riegle ran better in black areas than any Republican before him. During the Congressman's second term, his ADA and COPE ratings continued to climb toward 100, and by 1970 he won the endorsement of the UAW—a real coup for a Republican in Flint.

It was the war in Vietnam that produced Riegle's most emphatic dissent. Like John Lindsay and Ogden Reid of New York and Pete McCloskey of California—other liberal Republicans—Riegle opposed the war policy of both Johnson and Nixon. (Presently, all of these men are now Democrats, except McCloskey who registered independent in California but retains membership in the House Republican Caucus.) When Riegle supported McCloskey's presidential candidacy in 1972, his break with the Nixon Administration became complete. The Michigan Congressman was the only Republican member of the House to back McCloskey.

Unlike McCloskey, Riegle never faced the problem of conservative primary opposition at home. And general elections were no trouble whatever for either Republican politican. But as the 93rd Congress convened, Riegle finally decided to switch to the Democratic party, doing so late in the winter of 1973 shortly before the full Watergate story broke. The Congressman thereby lost his seat and seniority on the Appropriations Committee; he now serves as the junior Democrat on the Foreign Affairs Committee. Despite his loss of status, Riegle is undeniably more comfortable in the Democratic Caucus than he ever was in its Republican counterpart. Here he is far less often forced to choose between his conscience and the desires of the leadership.

Now that he is a Democrat, no one expects Riegle will have any more trouble than before in winning reelection. But neither does anyone expect him to remain in the House indefinitely. Because he would make an attractive statewide candidate, he might very well run for the Senate if Philip Hart decides to retire in 1976; or the Congressman may take on Republican Sen. Robert Griffin in 1978. As for 1974, Riegle will probably concentrate on winning his spurs as a Democrat (though there is some talk he may run for Governor). This he does by working for liberal Democratic candidates in Michigan and around the country.

Census Data Pop. 466,287. Central city, 41%; suburban, 57%. Median family income, $11,207; families above $15,000: 27%; families below $3,000: 6%. Median years education, 12.1.

1972 Share of Federal Outlays $236,873,973

DOD	$7,074,651	HEW	$133,832,028
AEC	–	HUD	$9,286,653
NASA	$6,114	DOI	$773,874
DOT	$6,582,703	USDA	$10,006,258
		Other	$69,331,692

Federal Military-Industrial Commitments

No installations or contractors receiving prime awards greater than $5,000,000.

Economic Base Motor vehicles and equipment, and other transportation equipment; fabricated metal products, especially metal stampings and cutlery, hand tools and hardware; and finance, insurance and real estate.

The Voters

Registration 236,063 total. No party registration.
Median voting age 40.1
Employment profile White collar, 37%. Blue collar, 50%. Service, 12%. Farm, 1%.
Ethnic groups Black, 13%. Spanish, 1%. Total foreign stock, 12%. Canada, 3%; UK, 2%; Germany, 1%.

Presidential vote

1972	Nixon (R)	90,776	(54%)
	McGovern (D)	76,745	(46%)
1968	Nixon (R)	67,184	(39%)
	Humphrey (D)	77,858	(46%)
	Wallace (AI)	25,630	(15%)

Representative

Donald W. Riegle, Jr. (D) Elected 1966; b. Feb. 4, 1938, Flint; home, Flint; Flint Jr. Col.; Western Mich. U.; U. of Mich., B.A., 1960; Mich. State U., M.B.A., 1961; married, three children; Methodist.

Career IBM Corp., 1961–64, consultant; Harvard-MIT Joint Center on Urban Studies; faculty Mich. State U., Boston U., Harvard U; author, *O Congress.*

Offices 438 CHOB, 202-225-3611.

Administrative Assistant Carl Blake

Committees

Foreign Affairs (22nd); Subs: Asian and Pacific Affairs; Europe.

Group Ratings

	ADA	COPE	LWV	RIPON	NFU	LCV	CFA	NAB	NSI	ACA
1972	94	90	100	84	83	83	100	20	0	5
1971	84	64	89	88	69	–	83	–	–	19
1970	80	82	–	100	75	40	68	44	63	35

Key Votes

1) Busing	ABS	6) Cmbodia Bmbg	ABS	11) Chkg Acct Intrst	AGN
2) Strip Mines	AGN	7) Bust Hwy Trust	FOR	12) End HISC (HUAC)	FOR
3) Cut Mil $	FOR	8) Farm Sub Lmt	FOR	13) Nixon Sewer Veto	AGN
4) Rev Shrg	FOR	9) School Prayr	AGN	14) Corp Cmpaign $	AGN
5) Pub TV $	FOR	10) Cnsumr Prot	FOR	15) Pol $ Disclosr	FOR

Election Results

1972 general:	Donald W. Riegle (R)	114,656	(70%)
	Eugene L. Mattison (D)	48,883	(30%)
1972 primary:	Donald W. Riegle (R), unopposed		
1970 general:	Donald W. Riegle (R)	97,683	(69%)
	Richard J. Ruhala (D)	41,235	(29%)
	Eugene L. Mattison (AI)	2,194	(2%)

EIGHTH DISTRICT Political Background

The Lower Peninsula of Michigan is shaped like a mittened hand, and the state's 8th congressional district comprises the Thumb (as it is called locally) and a bottom part of the index finger. The Thumb is almost entirely agricultural, tilled by descendants of the sturdy German and Canadian farmers who first came here a century ago. As ever, the Thumb remains vintage Republican country. Much of Saginaw (pop. 92,000) and Bay City (pop. 49,000), the urban centers of the 8th district, also seem to come out of the nineteenth century. Both places got started as lumber towns, being at one time among the state's largest cities. Today Saginaw and Bay City have fewer people than many Detroit suburbs; they are sustained in large part by auto plants, notably GM's Saginaw Steering, which makes all of the company's power-steering apparatus. Unlike most of the rest of outstate Michigan, the 8th district has few institutions of higher learning and relatively little economic growth.

A Democratic redistricting adopted by a federal court gave the district its current shape. Placed in the same district for the first time were Saginaw, with its large black population (one that dates from the turn of the century), and Bay City, with its many Polish-Americans. The blacks and the Poles constitute the bedrock of the 8th's Democratic strength. That combined strength, however, is usually not enough to carry the district for the Democrats, and it was certainly not enough to elect the 8th's 1972 Democratic candidate for Congress, state Sen. Jerome Hart.

Hart's 1972 bid and 1964 have been the closest calls for the district's current Congressman, Republican James Harvey. A moderate, Harvey is inclined by temperament to support the House leadership and fellow Michigander Gerald Ford; Harvey has, however, dissented from time to time on issues like the SST and the bombing of Cambodia. As the fourth-ranking Republican on the Commerce Committee, Congressman Harvey makes few waves, but he is a little more likely than his minority colleagues on Commerce to vote for measures pushed by consumer groups. As one might expect from a politician whose district includes a major GM plant, however, Harvey always goes to bat for the auto industry in the Commerce Committee and the House at large.

But the 8th may see a closer race in the end of 1973 or the beginning of 1974—one that could be a significant test of post-Watergate partisan sentiment. At this writing, Congressman Harvey has been recommended for a federal judgeship by Sen. Robert Griffin, and though his appointment is not final, it is expected to go through without controversy. A special election is expected some time in the snow-covered winter months. Among the possible candidates: Republican state Sens. Robert Richardson and Alvin DeGrow and Harvey's administrative assistant, James Sparling; and Democratic state Rep. Bob Traxler and state Sen. Jerome Hart, the 1972 nominee. Normally the winner of the Republican primary would have a solid edge here. But Democrats hope to build on their minority strength and what they hope will be a sharp drop in Republican allegiance in the wake of Watergate. However, the Democratic trend visible in much of outstate Michigan has been relatively weak both in the Thumb and in Saginaw and Bay City.

Census Data Pop. 467,206. Central city, 30%; suburban, 45%. Median family income, $10,270; families above $15,000: 21%; families below $3,000: 9%. Median years education, 11.9.

1972 Share of Federal Outlays $263,781,284

DOD	$19,029,346	HEW	$148,714,171
AEC	–	HUD	$3,368,188
NASA	$90,126	DOI	$412,614
DOT	$4,408,901	USDA	$23,589,291
		Other	$64,168,647

Federal Military-Industrial Commitments

DOD Installations Port Austin AF Station (Port Austin).

Economic Base Transportation equipment, especially motor vehicles and equipment; agriculture, notably grains, dairy products and cattle; finance, insurance and real estate; machinery; and fabricated metal products.

The Voters

Registration 227,842 total. No party registration.
Median voting age 42.6
Employment profile White collar, 38%. Blue collar, 45%. Service, 13%. Farm, 4%.
Ethnic groups Black, 6%. Spanish, 3%. Total foreign stock, 16%. Canada, 4%; Germany, 3%; Poland, 2%; UK, 1%.

Presidential vote

1972	Nixon (R)	106,524	(64%)
	McGovern (D)	65,422	(38%)
1968	Nixon (R)	87,500	(52%)
	Humphrey (D)	65,863	(39%)
	Wallace (AI)	14,012	(8%)

Representative

James Harvey (R) Elected 1960; b. July 4, 1922, Iron Mountain; home, Saginaw; U. of Mich., LL.B., 1948; USAF, WWII; married, two children; Presbyterian.

Career Atty., 1949–61; Asst. City Atty., 1949–53; City Councilman, 1955–57; County Supervisor, 1955–57; Mayor, 1957–59.

Offices 2352 RHOB, 202-225-2806. Also 2700 W. Genesee Ave., Saginaw 48602, 517-799-0336.

Administrative Assistant Vacant

Committees

House Administration (4th); Subs: Elections (Ranking Mbr.); Library and Memorials (Ranking Mbr.); Electrical and Mechanical Office Equipment (Ranking Mbr.).

Interstate and Foreign Commerce (4th); Sub: Transportation and Aeronautics (Ranking Mbr.).

Group Ratings

	ADA	COPE	LWV	RIPON	NFU	LCV	CFA	NAB	NSI	ACA
1972	25	33	55	62	83	47	50	75	90	50
1971	27	18	44	76	40	–	38	–	–	83
1970	20	34	–	83	50	15	53	91	89	78

Key Votes

1) Busing	AGN	6) Cmbodia Bmbg	AGN	11) Chkg Acct Intrst	AGN
2) Strip Mines	AGN	7) Bust Hwy Trust	ABS	12) End HISC (HUAC)	AGN
3) Cut Mil $	AGN	8) Farm Sub Lmt	FOR	13) Nixon Sewer Veto	ABS
4) Rev Shrg	FOR	9) School Prayr	ABS	14) Corp Cmpaign $	ABS
5) Pub TV $	AGN	10) Cnsumr Prot	AGN	15) Pol $ Disclosr	FOR

Election Results

1972 general:	James Harvey (R)	100,597	(59%)
	Jerome Hart (D)	66,873	(39%)
	John B. Lipinski (AI)	2,280	(1%)
1972 primary:	James Harvey (R), unopposed		
1970 general:	James Harvey (R)	85,634	(66%)
	Richard E. Davies (D)	44,400	(34%)

NINTH DISTRICT Political Background

From Gary, Indiana, up through Chicago and Milwaukee, north to towns like Sheboygan and Manitowoc, Wisconsin, the west shore of Lake Michigan is heavily industrial. Behind the giant sand dunes that line the east shore of the lake, there are a few grimy industrial towns like Muskegon and old lumber ports like Ludington. But most of the east side of Lake Michigan is given over to farming; despite the cold weather, fruits and vegetables of various kinds do well here.

Michigan's 9th congressional district contains most of the east shore of the lake. The 9th extends from Allegan County in the south to Leelenau in the north, the latter the little finger of the state's mitten-shaped Lower Peninsula. Along with Grand Rapids, the southern portion of the district has the nation's largest concentration of Dutch-Americans; one of the cities here, Holland, holds a tulip festival every year, complete with people walking around in wooden shoes. The Dutch (see Michigan 5) are probably the most conservative and Republican of all identifiable American ethnic groups; they are responsible in large part for the heavy Republican margins invariably turned in by the voters of the 9th. An oddity here is tiny Lake County, a large number of whose residents are black and which always goes Democratic. It contains one of the country's first black resort areas, formed at the turn of the century by members of the Chicago black bourgeoisie.

Though it no longer includes his home town of Traverse City, the 9th is Sen. Robert Griffin's old congressional district. He relinquished the 9th's seat for the risks of a Senate race in 1966. Griffin always won elections in the 9th with big majorities, his closest call being 57% in 1964 when his opponent was a man named Griffen. After the passage of the Landrum-Griffin Act in 1959, organized labor would have dearly loved to beat Griffin, but the Republican incumbent always carried even Muskegon County, which has a large union membership. Griffin's successor in the House, Guy Vander Jagt, has done at least as well, winning every general election by two-to-one margins. In his most difficult test, the 1966 Republican primary, Vander Jagt managed to cover both bases: he represented the northern half of the district in the state senate, while his Dutch ancestry was an obvious and considerable asset in the southern portion of the 9th.

Vander Jagt is one of an increasing number of former TV newscasters in Congress. He also has other talents, holding a law degree and a bachelor of divinity. As ranking minority member on the Conservation and Natural Resources Subcommittee of the Government Operations Committee, the Congressman has shown considerable interest in environmental issues. Government Operations, in fact, is one of the most ecology-oriented congressional committees with jurisdiction over that area of concern. Vander Jagt was largely responsible for the Sleeping Bear Dunes National Lakeshore, the creation of which Congressman Griffin had held up. On major issues, Vander Jagt dissents occasionally from Republican positions laid down by the leadership; this has appeared to enhance his standing among the voters in the Congressman's solidly Republican district.

Census Data Pop. 467,245. Central city, 13%; suburban, 48%. Median family income, $9,474; families above $15,000: 16%; families below $3,000: 9%. Median years education, 11.8.

1972 Share of Federal Outlays $310,041,086

DOD	$41,921,080	HEW	$166,170,178
AEC	–	HUD	$2,147,596
NASA	$385,239	DOI	$533,050
DOT	$15,319,459	USDA	$15,680,783
		Other	$67,883,701

Federal Military-Industrial Commitments

DOD Contractors Teledyne Industries (Muskegon), $26.499m: tank engines and components.
DOD Installations Empire AF Station (Empire).

Economic Base Machinery; primary metal industries, especially iron and steel foundries; agriculture, notably fruits, dairy products, vegetables and poultry; fabricated metal products; and finance, insurance and real estate.

The Voters

Registration 247,070 total. No party registration.
Median voting age 43.6
Employment profile White collar, 37%. Blue collar, 46%. Service, 13%. Farm, 4%.
Ethnic groups Black, 4%. Spanish, 2%. Total foreign stock, 15%. Netherlands, 4%; Germany, Canada, 2% each; Poland, 1%.

Presidential vote

1972	Nixon (R)	130,463	(67%)
	McGovern (D)	64,561	(33%)
1968	Nixon (R)	102,528	(57%)
	Humphrey (D)	61,457	(34%)
	Wallace (AI)	15,814	(9%)

Representative

Guy Adrian Vander Jagt (R) Elected 1966; b. Aug. 26, 1931, Cadillac; home, Cadillac; Hope Col., B.A., 1953; Yale U., B.D., 1955; Bonn U., 1956; U. of Mich., LL.B., 1960; married, one child; Presbyterian.

Career Atty., 1960–64; State Sen., 1965–66.

Offices 1211 LHOB, 202-225-3511. Also 408 W. Western, Muskegon 49411, 616-722-3741.

Administrative Assistant Bernard Nagelvoort

Committees

Foreign Affairs (10th); Subs: Africa; Europe; Foreign Economic Policy.

Government Operations (5th); Subs: Conservation and Natural Resources (Ranking Mbr.); Intergovernmental Relations.

Group Ratings

	ADA	COPE	LWV	RIPON	NFU	LCV	CFA	NAB	NSI	ACA
1972	25	27	70	87	67	73	0	100	100	64
1971	24	20	43	67	43	–	50	–	–	72
1970	48	42	–	88	58	75	63	83	75	69

Key Votes

1) Busing	AGN	6) Cmbodia Bmbg	ABS	11) Chkg Acct Intrst	ABS
2) Strip Mines	AGN	7) Bust Hwy Trust	AGN	12) End HISC (HUAC)	ABS
3) Cut Mil $	ABS	8) Farm Sub Lmt	FOR	13) Nixon Sewer Veto	AGN
4) Rev Shrg	FOR	9) School Prayr	FOR	14) Corp Cmpaign $	AGN
5) Pub TV $	AGN	10) Cnsumr Prot	AGN	15) Pol $ Disclosr	FOR

Election Results

1972 general:	Guy A. Vander Jagt (R)	132,268	(69%)
	Larry H. Olson (D)	56,236	(30%)
	DeLloyd G. Hesselink (AI)	2,110	(1%)
1972 primary:	Guy A. Vander Jagt (R), unopposed		
1970 general:	Guy A. Vander Jagt (R)	94,027	(64%)
	Charles A. Rogers (D)	51,223	(35%)
	Patrick V. Dillinger (AI)	811	(1%)

TENTH DISTRICT Political Background

Draw a line on a map across Michigan's Lower Peninsula from Bay City to Muskegon. South of the line live 91% of the state's people, half in the Detroit metropolitan area and the other half mostly in and around the state's smaller industrial cities. North of the line, most of Michigan is covered by forests, ravaged by the lumber barons at the turn of the century and just now coming back. Today, this sparsely populated area of the state depends mainly on the tourist and recreation business. Every weekend in the summer, cars jam I-75, as city people flee to cottages on Michigan lakes—not just the Great Lakes, but thousands of inland lakes as well. There is also some great fishing to be done on the rivers of northern Michigan; as a boy, Ernest Hemingway fished one of them and later wrote a remarkable short story, "Big Two-Hearted River." During the winter, people come here to ski, while snowmobilers insist upon disturbing the quiet of cold Michigan woods.

The 10th congressional district spans this line across Lower Michigan. The 10th dips down to touch the Lansing city limits; around here, the small towns and farms are rather frequent, with many residents commuting to jobs in Lansing and Flint. Up north, there are only a few concentrations of people. One of them, Traverse City (pop. 18,000), has produced both Gov. William Milliken and Sen. Robert Griffin. Two others are Mount Pleasant (pop. 20,000), site of Central Michigan University (13,000 students), and Midland (pop. 35,000), the district's largest and most distinctive city. Midland contains the home of the Dow Chemical Company, whose giant plants once produced napalm used in the Vietnam war; it also contains prosperous residential streets having the ambience and the voting habits of an upper-income suburb.

The 10th was designed to be, and is, a Republican district—before the 1972 election, the 10th included Democratic Bay City, now in the 8th. But like most outstate Michigan districts, the 10th is trending Democratic. The movement shows itself not just in presidential contests (McGovern bested Humphrey's 1968 totals here), but to an even greater extent in statewide races. Nevertheless, the 10th's long-standing Republican inclinations will almost surely be enough to keep it in the Republican column for the foreseeable future.

The 10th is the district that sends to Congress the current ranking minority member of the House Appropriations Committee, Rep. Elford Cederberg. First elected in the Eisenhower year of 1952, Cederberg climbed the seniority ladder slowly and attained his position on the committee when two senior Republicans retired in 1972. Like most senior members of Appropriations, Cederberg is disposed to be parsimonious with the federal purse—Senate Appropriations invariably votes to spend more money than its House counterpart. Cederberg, however, does not extend his concern for thrift to the budget requests of the Defense Department; he is, in fact, quite sympathetic to the money needs of the Pentagon brass. The Congressman is also the ranking minority member of the Appropriations Subcommittee on State, Commerce, and the Judiciary, for years run with an iron hand by Brooklyn's John J. Rooney. But lately, Rooney has been unwell, leaving Cederberg and other members of the subcommittee with more leverage.

Michigan's House Republicans enjoy a disproportionate share of powerful positions. Besides Cederberg, there is Gerald Ford, Minority Leader; Edward Hutchinson, ranking Republican on Judiciary; and Charles Chamberlain, member of Ways and Means. Chamberlain plans to retire in

1974; Cederberg may also do the same, if not in 1974, when he will be just 56, then in some election year soon thereafter. In his book *O Congress!*, Donald Riegle, a Michigan Republican Congressman turned Democrat, quotes Cederberg as saying: "It's not as much fun here as it used to be." Such is a common sentiment among senior and usually conservative Congressmen. These are politicians who can remember the days when the House was not in session year round; they can also remember when Congressmen were not besieged by ecology activists, peace enthusiasts, and ingenuous interviewers from Nader's Congress Project.

Census Data Pop. 467,547. Central city, 0%; suburban, 11%. Median family income, $9,299; families above $15,000: 17%; families below $3,000: 11%. Median years education, 12.1.

1972 Share of Federal Outlays $319,226,771

DOD	$21,908,912	HEW	$176,214,852
AEC	$22,819	HUD	$1,881,070
NASA	$124,772	DOI	$773,154
DOT	$28,244,071	USDA	$25,116,623
		Other	$64,940,498

Federal Military-Industrial Commitments

No installations or contractors receiving prime awards greater than $5,000,000.

Economic Base Chemicals and allied products; agriculture, notably dairy products, grains and cattle; finance, insurance and real estate; electrical equipment and supplies; and transportation equipment, especially motor vehicles and equipment. Also higher education (Central Michigan Univ., and Ferris State).

The Voters

Registration 247,484 total. No party registration.
Median voting age 41.9
Employment profile White collar, 41%. Blue collar, 41%. Service, 14%. Farm, 4%.
Ethnic groups Spanish, 1%. Total foreign stock, 11%. Canada, 3%; Germany, 2%.

Presidential vote

1972	Nixon (R)	119,706	(64%)
	McGovern (D)	66,980	(36%)
1968	Nixon (R)	96,386	(58%)
	Humphrey (D)	55,600	(34%)
	Wallace (AI)	13,974	(8%)

Representative

Elford Cederberg (R) Elected 1953; b. March 6, 1918, Midland; home, Midland; Bay City Col.; Army, WWII; married; Evangelical church.

Career Mgr. Nelson Mfg. Company; Mayor, Bay City, 1949–52.

Offices 2303 RHOB, 202-225-3561. Also 624 E. Superior, Alma 48801, 517-463-3010.

Administrative Assistant Michael A. Forgash

Committees

Appropriations (Ranking Mbr.); Subs: Legislative; State, Justice, Commerce, and Judiciary (Ranking Mbr.).

Joint Com. on Reduction of Federal Expenditures (Ranking House Mbr.).

Joint Study Com. on Budget Control.

Group Ratings

	ADA	COPE	LWV	RIPON	NFU	LCV	CFA	NAB	NSI	ACA
1972	0	18	27	57	29	20	0	92	100	68
1971	8	25	38	50	33	–	25	–	–	89
1970	16	18	–	69	54	15	67	100	100	65

Key Votes

1) Busing	AGN	6) Cmbodia Bmbg	FOR	11) Chkg Acct Intrst	AGN
2) Strip Mines	AGN	7) Bust Hwy Trust	AGN	12) End HISC (HUAC)	AGN
3) Cut Mil $	AGN	8) Farm Sub Lmt	AGN	13) Nixon Sewer Veto	FOR
4) Rev Shrg	FOR	9) School Prayr	FOR	14) Corp Cmpaign $	FOR
5) Pub TV $	ABS	10) Cnsumr Prot	AGN	15) Pol $ Disclosr	AGN

Election Results

1972 general:	Elford A. Cederberg (R)	121,368	(67%)
	Bennie D. Graves (D)	56,149	(31%)
	Richard Friske (AI)	4,369	(2%)
1972 primary:	Elford A. Cederberg (R)	41,859	(82%)
	Felice Brunett (R)	9,417	(18%)
1970 general:	Elford A. Cederberg (R)	82,528	(59%)
	Gerald J. Parent (D)	57,031	(41%)

ELEVENTH DISTRICT Political Background

Michigan's Upper Peninsula (or the U.P., as it is called) constitutes a world unto itself. It is isolated most of the year from the rest of the state by the elements, and any travel during whatever is left of the year is discouraged by the exorbitant tolls extracted by people manning the booths on the Mackinac Straits Bridge. The U.P. was settled around the turn of the century; at that time, its copper and iron mines boomed and the place had a Wild West air about it. The Upper Peninsula population influx was polyglot: Irish, Italians, Swedes, Norwegian, and Finns, who remain the largest single ethnic group here. While working in the mines, the immigrants picked up radical social ideas and Democratic voting habits, the latter of which most of their descendants still retain. Some time ago, however, the mines petered out, leaving the U.P.'s stagnant economy dependent on summer tourists and fall hunters. Not much farming is done here, since it has been known to snow in July. After World War II, the young people of the Upper Peninsula began to move to Detroit, Chicago, and the West Cost. Since the 1940 census, its population has hovered around 300,000. Today the only prosperous locale here lies in and around its largest city, Marquette (pop. 22,000).

The Upper Peninsula forms the larger part of Michigan's 11th congressional district. The 11th, a vast expanse, includes 40% of the state's land area, but holds only 5% of its population. It is the second largest congressional district east of the Mississippi. From Tawas City, in the southern end of the 11th, to Ironwood, in the extreme west, is a distance of 477 miles. Obviously any serious district-wide campaigner must have an airplane.

The Lower Peninsula portion of the district has neither the tradition of the mines nor the Democratic voting habits of the U.P. It is a more prosperous area, having a booming trade in summer and winter tourists. As a whole, the 11th is politically marginal, though oddly it has elected a Democrat to Congress only once in the last 20 years. Before the 1964 redistricting, what is now the 11th contained two full districts and part of a third—a vestige of the days when the Upper Peninsula had a far higher percentage of the state's population than it does today. In 1964, two incumbents, both Republicans, prepared to square off in a primary when the more liberal of the two, Rep. John Bennett, died suddenly, leaving Rep. Victor Knox the winner by default. In 1964, however, the Republican nominee having, as Democrat Raymond Clevenger won the general election with 53% of the votes.

At least three Michigan Democrats elected in the LBJ landslide failed to cultivate their constituencies with sufficient care and were defeated in 1966. Clevenger was one of them. The winner of the 11th's seat in 1966 was Republican Philip Ruppe, scion of a wealthy Houghton brewing family. As befits a Republican from a marginal district, Ruppe has compiled a moderate-to-liberal voting record in the House. And now that Don Riegle has become a

Democrat, Ruppe is probably the least likely of the state's Republican Congressmen to follow the lead of Majority Leader Gerald Ford. Ruppe appears to have a very solid hold on the 11th district—one that is unlikely to be broken if only because of the sheer physical effort required by a possible campaign in this vast district.

Census Data Pop. 467,547. Central city, 0%; suburban, 0%. Median family income, $7,884; families above $15,000: 10%; families below $3,000: 14%. Median years education, 12.0.

1972 Share of Federal Outlays $474,085,438

DOD	$149,380,070	HEW	$204,086,508
AEC	$164,556	HUD	$843,000
NASA	–	DOI	$3,096,628
DOT	$18,782,983	USDA	$23,037,014
		Other	$74,694,679

Federal Military-Industrial Commitments

DOD Installations Sawyer AFB (Marquette). Saulte Ste. Marie AF Station (Sault Ste. Marie). Wurtsmith AFB (Oscoda).

Economic Base Agriculture, notably dairy products, cattle and fruits; finance, insurance and real estate; metal mining, especially iron ores; lumber and wood products; and machinery. Also higher education (Northern Michigan Univ.).

The Voters

Registration 260,151 total. No party registration.
Median voting age 45.8
Employment profile White collar, 41%. Blue collar, 40%. Service, 16%. Farm, 3%.
Ethnic groups Total foreign stock, 23%. Canada, Finland, 5% each; Germany, Sweden, UK, 2% each; Italy, Poland, 1% each.

Presidential vote

1972	Nixon (R)	117,006	(57%)
	McGovern (D)	86,548	(43%)
1968	Nixon (R)	88,694	(48%)
	Humphrey (D)	85,510	(46%)
	Wallace (AI)	10,940	(6%)

Representative

Philip E. Ruppe (R) Elected 1966; b. Sept. 29, 1926, Laurium; home, Houghton; Yale U., B.A., 1948; Navy, Korean War; married, five children; Catholic.

Career Pres., Bosch Brewing Co., 1955–1965; Dir. Houghton Natl. Bank and Commercial Natl. Bank of L'Anse.

Offices 203 CHOB, 202-225-4735. Also West Memorial Rd., Houghton 49931, 906-482-4041.

Administrative Assistant Chirstopher Farrand

Committees

Interior and Insular Affairs (6th); Subs: Environment (Ranking Mbr.); National Parks and Recreation; Mines and Mining; Territorial and Insular Affairs.

Merchant Marine and Fisheries (4th); Subs: Coast Guard and Navigation (Ranking Mbr.); Fisheries and Wildlife Conservation and the Environment; Merchant Marine.

Group Ratings

	ADA	COPE	LWV	RIPON	NFU	LCV	CFA	NAB	NSI	ACA
1972	44	40	82	78	80	54	0	80	63	29
1971	32	36	50	85	50	–	50	–	–	52
1970	56	60	–	80	85	28	63	75	89	53

Key Votes

1) Busing	FOR	6) Cmbodia Bmbg	AGN	11) Chkg Acct Intrst	ABS
2) Strip Mines	AGN	7) Bust Hwy Trust	AGN	12) End HISC (HUAC)	AGN
3) Cut Mil $	AGN	8) Farm Sub Lmt	ABS	13) Nixon Sewer Veto	AGN
4) Rev Shrg	FOR	9) School Prayr	FOR	14) Corp Cmpaign $	AGN
5) Pub TV $	AGN	10) Cnsumr Prot	FOR	15) Pol $ Disclosr	FOR

Election Results

1972 general:	Philip E. Ruppe (R)	135,786	(69%)
	James E. McNamara (D)	58,334	(30%)
	James P. Hoy (AI)	1,489	(1%)
1972 primary:	Philip E. Ruppe (R), unopposed		
1970 general:	Philip E. Ruppe (R)	85,323	(62%)
	Nino Green (D)	53,146	(38%)

TWELFTH DISTRICT Political Background

Macomb County, adjoining Detroit to the city's northeast, is an area of incredibly fast-growing suburban sprawl commonly found in many of the nation's metropolitan areas. In 1950, Macomb had a population of 184,000 people; by 1970, 625,000—having more than tripled in size within 20 years. The northern reaches of the county are still rural, but for 20 miles beyond Eight Mile Road, the Detroit city limit, Macomb is an agglomeration of neat subdivisions, winding streets, modern thin-walled apartment complexes, and gleaming new shopping centers. But unlike the new suburban residents of southern California, the people living in Macomb have roots, and these lie in the East Side of Detroit. Census figures show that the descendants of the Polish and Italian immigrants who came to man the East Side auto plants have beelined out to suburbs like Warren (pop. 179,000), East Detroit, Roseville, St. Clair Shores, and Sterling Heights.

Though filled with suburbs, Macomb remains blue-collar territory, with most people here earning livelihoods in factory or service jobs. But thanks to high UAW wages, Macomb is also one of the most prosperous suburban counties in the nation; its median family income is over $12,000 annually. Yet the upward mobility has meant more in dollars than in social status: people here can buy a $55,000 home, but the head of the household still works on an assembly line. Having absorbed a monumental population influx in the past twenty years, Macomb County has written its politics on a virtual tabula rasa: its native aristocracy were too few in number to quiet and modulate changes in local political opinion.

Aside from a small ghetto in the old county seat town of Mount Clemens, Macomb is virtually all white and intends to stay that way. Because of the sheer pressure of numbers, most of the population growth here was inevitable; but one factor behind the exodus to Macomb has been racial: a desire to escape the city of Detroit, which is 42% black. This became clear—if it was ever in doubt—in 1970, when Warren voted down an urban renewal scheme proposed by HUD Secretary George Romney. The former Michigan Governor talked about making Warren a kind of national laboratory for suburban integration. Romney's plans for Warren hardly helped his wife Lenore's Senate candidacy in 1970. The people in Macomb County wanted to know why the Romneys didn't want to integrate their own Bloomfield Hills, a posh suburb in adjacent Oakland County.

But the real depth of Macomb's racial feelings became manifest in 1972, when federal judge Stephen Roth ordered a metropolitan busing plan to cure segregation in Detroit schools. If the plan were ever enforced (at this writing the case is on appeal to the Supreme Court), Eight Mile Road would no longer serve as an impenetrable racial barrier. The reaction in Macomb to the prospect was outrage. Nowhere in the Detroit was anti-busing fervor as intense as in Macomb County, and this is clear from the results of local elections.

For a time, the new residents of Macomb County voted Democratic, just as they had in Detroit. In 1960, for example, John F. Kennedy got 63% of the votes here—his best showing in any of the nation's all-suburban counties. But in the 1972 Michigan presidential primary, George Wallace took 67% of the votes; George McGovern won 19%, leaving only 14% to Hubert Humphrey, the supposed champion of the working man. Earlier, in the 1968 presidential contest, Wallace managed 14%, while Humphrey took a solid 55%, and Nixon 31%. With the coming of the busing issue, however, Nixon more than doubled his total in 1972 to 64%; McGovern, meanwhile, had only 36%—just over half of what Kennedy had won 12 years before. The switch away from the national Democratic party was almost as extensive here as it was in the Deep South following the civil rights revolution of the 1960s.

Nor was McGovern's showing an isolated phenomenon. Frank Kelley, the 1972 Democratic Senate candidate, lost Macomb to Republican Sen. Robert Griffin, though both came out loud and strong against busing. Moreover, Republicans picked up several Macomb County seats in the state legislature and performed far better than usual in county-wide contests. And in the congressional race, Republicans had never shown more strength since the early days of the great migration from the East Side of Detroit.

From 1964 to 1970, Macomb County constituted a congressional district by itself. With the population increase recorded in the 1970 census, the county was split, with half of Warren and East Detroit going to the 14th district, and the other half of Warren and Sterling Heights to the 18th. The redistricting left most of the county's area in the 12th district. Also part of the district is the aging city of Port Huron (pop. 36,000) and surrounding St. Clair County, which is marginally Republican.

Up until 1972, the 12th looked like a safe district for Democratic Congressman James O'Hara, who was first elected from Macomb in 1958. Because O'Hara had grown accustomed to margins as great as 75% of the vote, he turned much of his attention to national matters. The Congressman is Chairman of an Education and Labor subcommittee, and as the sixth-ranking member on the full committee, he is a major spokesman on matters pertaining to education and labor. With strong backing from much of organized labor, O'Hara made a bid for House Majority Leader in 1971, but he was humiliated, finishing last with just 25 votes. He was whipsawed between the regulars, who supported Hale Boggs, the eventual winner, and the antiwar liberals (O'Hara was a late convert to the cause), who went mostly for Arizona's Morris Udall.

O'Hara's biggest moment in the national spotlight came during the summer of 1972. As parliamentarian of the Democratic National Convention, he was asked to make crucial rulings on the delegate challenge procedures. The decisions that O'Hara made in concert with then National Chairman Larry O'Brien have been generally conceded to be fair ones. They also paved the way for the nomination of George McGovern, who was not O'Hara's own first choice.

But back home trouble was brewing. Anti-busing fervor had made political activists out of many formerly apathetic housewives, few of them kindly disposed toward O'Hara. The Congressman had taken an anti-busing position before the Roth decision was announced; moreover, he was working on a constitutional amendment to reverse court-ordered busing. But O'Hara's reputation as a liberal and civil rights proponent led many of his anti-busing constituents to conclude that the Congressman's heart was not with them. These voters placed greater confidence in the views of the Republican candidate, state Rep. David Serotkin, who ran an aggressive, well-financed campaign grounded on the busing issue. In the end, O'Hara squeaked through mainly because he ran far ahead of usual Democratic showings in St. Clair county, though he failed to carry it. The Congressman had previously represented the county prior to 1964. Meanwhile, O'Hara's customary 3–1 and 2–1 margins in Macomb were reduced to a near 1–1 level. O'Hara, who most observers felt had a safe district, won with just under 51% of the vote—his closest margin since his first election in 1958.

So in the 93rd Congress, O'Hara has been paying more attention to his district and less to national issues. Accordingly, he has not cut the figure of as major a force in the House as in the past. Whether O'Hara will face another close election in 1974 depends on the efforts the Republicans (and Serotkin) decide to put into the race.

Census Data Pop. 467,543. Central city, 0%; suburban, 74%. Median family income, $12,003; families above $15,000: 31%; families below $3,000: 6%. Median years education, 12.1.

1972 Share of Federal Outlays $322,494,345

DOD	$39,262,009	HEW	$148,921,246
AEC	$15,724	HUD	$11,058,525
NASA	$63,158	DOI	$681,397
DOT	$12,063,809	USDA	$7,581,493
		Other	$102,846,984

Federal Military-Industrial Commitments

No installations or contractors receiving prime awards greater than $5,000,000.

Economic Base Motor vehicles and equipment, and other transportation equipment; machinery, especially metalworking machinery; fabricated metal products, especially metal stampings; finance, insurance and real estate; and primary metal industries.

The Voters

Registration 227,284 total. No party registration.
Median voting age 40.8
Employment profile White collar, 46%. Blue collar, 42%. Service, 11%. Farm, 1%.
Ethnic groups Black, 2%. Total foreign stock, 24%. Canada, 7%; Germany, Italy, 3% each; Poland, UK, 2% each.

Presidential vote

1972	Nixon (R)		112,291	(65%)
	McGovern (D)		61,288	(35%)
1968	Nixon (R)		61,859	(39%)
	Humphrey (D)		75,674	(48%)
	Wallace (AI)		20,093	(13%)

Representative

James G. O'Hara (D) Elected 1958; b. Nov. 8, 1925, Washington, D.C.; home, Utica; U. of Mich., B.A., 1954, LL.B., 1955; Army, WWII; married, seven children; Catholic.

Career Atty., 1955–58.

Offices 2241 RHOB, 202-225-2106. Also 215 S. Gratiot, Mt. Clemens 48043, 313-465-0911, and 102A Fed. Bldg., 536 Water St., Port Huron 48060, 313-987-3117.

Administrative Assistant Eugene C. Zack

Committees

Education and Labor (6th); Subs: Sel. Sub. on Labor; Sp. Sub. on Labor; Sp. Sub. on Education (Chm.).

Interior and Insular Affairs (8th); Subs: Environment; Mines and Mining; National Parks and Recreation.

Joint Com. on Congressional Operations (3rd).

Group Ratings

	ADA	COPE	LWV	RIPON	NFU	LCV	CFA	NAB	NSI	ACA
1972	75	100	83	62	100	60	100	0	11	10
1971	73	83	67	71	100	–	88	–	–	11
1970	92	92	–	71	92	84	100	10	38	17

Key Votes

1) Busing	AGN	6) Cmbodia Bmbg	AGN	11) Chkg Acct Intrst	AGN
2) Strip Mines	AGN	7) Bust Hwy Trust	AGN	12) End HISC (HUAC)	FOR
3) Cut Mil $	ABS	8) Farm Sub Lmt	AGN	13) Nixon Sewer Veto	AGN
4) Rev Shrg	FOR	9) School Prayr	AGN	14) Corp Cmpaign $	FOR
5) Pub TV $	FOR	10) Cnsumr Prot	FOR	15) Pol $ Disclosr	FOR

Election Results

1972 general:	James G. O'Hara (D)	83,351	(51%)
	David M. Serotkin (R)	80,667	(49%)
1972 primary:	James G. O'Hara (D), unopposed		
1970 general:	James G. O'Hara (D)	129,287	(76%)
	Patrick Driscoll (R)	38,946	(23%)
	Milton E. Deschaine (AI)	1,562	(1%)

THIRTEENTH DISTRICT Political Background

The 13th congressional district of Michigan comprises Detroit's inner city, the only district completely contained within the Detroit city limits. Like the 1st, the 13th has a majority black population (66%), but also has fewer middle-class blacks. During the 1960s, the 13th suffered the largest population loss, 19%, of any congressional district in the country. Many of the buildings here were bulldozed to make way for urban renewal projects and giant freeways, most of which are named for Motown auto magnates: Edsel B. Ford, Walter P. Chrysler, and the Fisher brothers of General Motors. An even more important factor in the district's population loss was the voluntary exodus of the black community itself. After the 1967 riot, many residents of this part of Detroit moved to the more middle-class surroundings of the 1st district. The migrants left many neighborhoods utterly deserted and others pocked with vacant homes. The problem was compounded by the operations of the FHA program here, which became a scandal of national proportions and did nothing to enhance the battered reputation of ex-Gov. and HUD Secretary George Romney.

The 13th has always contained some old ethnic, especially Polish, neighborhoods that remain remarkably resistant to racial, or any kind of, change. After the 1970 census, the boundaries of the district were expanded to include some white middle-class areas. The rest of the district is a collection of poor black neighborhoods, plus a couple of high-income apartment complexes and the skyscrapers of downtown Detroit.

With the death of William Dawson of South Side Chicago and the electoral defeat of the late Adam Clayton Powell in 1970, the Congressman from the 13th, Charles C. Diggs, Jr., became at age 48 the dean of the black delegation in the House and Chairman for a term of the increasingly militant Black Caucus. By trade, Diggs is a mortician like his late father, who 20 years ago was the leading politician and one of the wealthiest men in the Detroit black community. Diggs, Sr. masterminded his son's first congressional race in 1954, when he surprised an aging white incumbent in the Democratic primary, winning by a margin in excess of two-to-one. Ever since, Diggs, Jr. has been unbeatable in the district. Some blacks feel that the Congressman is insufficiently militant. Though his voting record is solidly liberal and antiwar, Diggs is a cautious man, less given to au courant rhetoric than some of his colleagues in the Black Caucus. Serious opposition, however, has never materialized in the 13th and probably never will, now that he has 20 years of seniority and a committee chairmanship.

Two years ago it seemed highly unlikely that Diggs would soon become Chairman of the District of Columbia Committee. He was the fourth-ranking Democrat on the panel, and its most senior member supporting home rule for the District. As the 92nd Congress convened, Diggs ran in the Democratic Caucus for the chairmanship against South Carolina's John McMillan, and lost. Whereupon McMillan, in typically vindictive and autocratic fashion, refused to assign Diggs to any subcommittee. But in 1972, things changed suddenly. John Dowdy of Texas, the committee's third-ranking Democrat, was convicted on federal bribery and perjury charges and left the House; Thomas Abernethy, the number-two man, decided at age 64 to return to Mississippi and retire; and McMillan himself was defeated in a South Carolina primary. Other resignations, retirements, and defeats gave virtually all of the Democratic seats on the District Committee to pro-home-rule Congressmen. Diggs was then quickly elevated from limbo to the chairmanship as the 93rd Congress convened.

The main item, of course, on the committee's agenda is home rule. Diggs moved cautiously at first, generating fears among some Washington blacks that Diggs, now with power over the District, would not want to relinquish it. But progress toward home rule went on steadily, with a bill reported out of subcommittee by the summer of 1973. The main problems facing the committee include: first, the size of the federal payment, to which the Congress will be irrevocably committed, to compensate the District for property taxes the federal government would pay if it were not exempt; second, what to do with the recommendations for District government reorganization made by a commission headed by Ancher Nelsen, the ranking Republican on the committee; and third, how much organizational detail of the new home-rule District government should be prescribed by the bill and how much left to the voters of the District and their elected representatives. Aside from solutions to these problems, the committee must fend off an attempt to grant statehood to the District. The move is lead by, of all people, anti-home-rule committee member Joel Broyhill of suburban Virginia. His idea is to report out a bill giving the District so much that the full House will vote it down. The whole business is tricky and complex, and will occupy most of Diggs' attention during the first session of the 93rd Congress.

Before 1973, Diggs devoted most of his time to African matters. As Chairman of the Foreign Affairs Africa Subcommittee, he travels frequently to Africa; he is thereby the most knowledgeable expert in the House on issues pertaining to the often ignored continent. Diggs has been especially forceful in his opposition to the apartheid policies of South Africa and in his urging continued economic sanctions against the Ian Smith regime in Rhodesia.

For all of his experience in the House, Diggs still makes an occasional misstep. Some felt that the elaborate ceremony held by Diggs upon assuming the chairmanship was a little gauche. Soon thereafter, the Chairman requested funds for District Committee members to travel to Europe, there to see how other capitals are governed. He was voted down by the full House—a rebuff that would have probably been spared a white committee chairman. The seniority system impartially elevates both black and white Congressmen. But it appears that some committee chairmen are still, in Orwell's words, more equal than others.

Census Data Pop. 465,076. Central city, 100%; suburban, 0%. Median family income, $7,770; families above $15,000: 13%; families below $3,000: 19%. Median years education, 10.0.

1972 Share of Federal Outlays $314,692,591

DOD	$45,263,680	HEW	$145,684,310
AEC	$21,253	HUD	$8,424,287
NASA	$85,367	DOI	$373,187
DOT	$15,176,289	USDA	$5,680,966
		Other	$93,983,252

Federal Military-Industrial Commitments

DOD Contractors General Motors (Detroit), $6.460m: diesel engines.

Economic Base Transportation equipment, especially motor vehicles and equipment; fabricated metal products, especially metal stampings; machinery, especially metalworking machinery; primary metal industries, especially blast furnace and basic steel products; and finance, insurance and real estate. Also higher education (Wayne State Univ.).

The Voters

Registration 239,204 total. No party registration.
Median voting age 44.6
Employment profile White collar, 32%. Blue collar, 48%. Service, 20%. Farm, –%.
Ethnic groups Black, 66%. Spanish, 2%. Total foreign stock, 12%. Canada, Poland, 2% each; Germany, 1%.

Presidential vote

1972	Nixon (R)	20,561	(16%)
	McGovern (D)	104,556	(84%)

1968	Nixon (R)	18,192	(12%)
	Humphrey (D)	127,178	(82%)
	Wallace (AI)	9,780	(6%)

Representative

Charles C. Diggs, Jr. (D) Elected 1954; b. Dec. 2, 1922, Detroit; home, Detroit; U. of Mich., 1940–42; Fisk U., 1942–43; Wayne U. Mortuary Sch., 1945–46; Detroit Col. of Law, 1950–51; Army, WWII; married, five children; Baptist.

Career State Sen., 1951–54.

Offices 2208 RHOB, 202-225-2261. Also, 4825 Woodward Ave., Detroit 48201, 313-832-6700.

Administrative Assistant Dorothy Quarker

Committees

District of Columbia (Chm.).

Foreign Affairs (6th); Subs: Africa (Chm.); State Department Organization and Foreign Operations.

Group Ratings

	ADA	COPE	LWV	RIPON	NFU	LCV	CFA	NAB	NSI	ACA
1972	88	89	100	67	86	70	100	14	14	5
1971	54	83	60	75	67	–	100	–	–	0
1970	80	100	–	53	82	80	100	0	11	6

Key Votes

1) Busing	FOR	6) Cmbodia Bmbg	AGN	11) Chkg Acct Intrst	ABS
2) Strip Mines	AGN	7) Bust Hwy Trust	FOR	12) End HISC (HUAC)	FOR
3) Cut Mil $	FOR	8) Farm Sub Lmt	FOR	13) Nixon Sewer Veto	AGN
4) Rev Shrg	FOR	9) School Prayr	AGN	14) Corp Cmpaign $	FOR
5) Pub TV $	FOR	10) Cnsumr Prot	ABS	15) Pol $ Disclosr	ABS

Election Results

1972 general:	Charles C. Diggs, Jr. (D)	97,562	(86%)
	Leonard T. Edwards (R)	15,180	(13%)
	Raymond D. Moon (AI)	685	(1%)
1972 primary:	Charles C. Diggs, Jr. (D), unopposed		
1970 general:	Charles C. Diggs, Jr. (D)	56,872	(86%)
	Fred W. Engel (R)	9,141	(14%)

FOURTEENTH DISTRICT Political Background

The East Side of Detroit forms the heart of Michigan's 14th congressional district. It is composed of a series of residential neighborhoods that are nearly all-white and heavily Catholic. Suburban territory nicely defines and brackets the East Side. To the east are the five Grosse Pointes: wealthy, conservative, and snobbish. But the Grosse Pointes include not only many of Detroit's leading families like the Fords, but also upwardly mobile and well-to-do Irish and Italian Catholics. Those of immigrant descent here live in the smaller houses set on the smaller lots; politically, they are if anything more conservative than their WASP neighbors.

In the district's southwest corner lies the enclave of Hamtramck, a predominantly Polish-American city surrounded by Detroit. It was here that thousands of immigrants flocked to get jobs in the Dodge Main, Plymouth, and Packard auto plants. In fact, during the 1910s, Hamtramck was the fastest-growing city in the country. In 1930, as many as 56,000 people lived in the city; today, the population is down to 27,000, most of whom are old people. Hamtramck has been the butt of thousands of Polish jokes, but anybody who takes the trouble to visit the city will find freshly painted houses and carefully tended lawns—evidence of the pride of ownership found in so many Polish-American neighborhoods.

The people who were brought up in Hamtramck have moved by the thousands to the East Side of Detroit and increasingly of late to the Macomb County suburb of Warren. For the 1972 election, half of Warren and the Italian- and Polish-American suburb of East Detroit, both in Macomb, were added to the 14th district for the first time. The inclusion of the two places was appropriate, for most of the people now living in them moved there from the confines of the old 14th. But the new parts of the district also created something of a political upheaval in the 14th's politics. In 1972, Warren and Macomb County lay in the midst of a furor over busing —specifically over a federal court order that required busing between Detroit and its suburbs (see also Michigan 12). Ironically, white parents on the East Side of Detroit forced the entire issue; they did not want a busing order confined to the city alone, because it would mean their children would attend schools two-thirds black. Such was the local scene confronting Democratic Congressman Lucien Nedzi when he sought reelection in 1972.

Nedzi had first captured the seat in a 1961 special election, and won a tough primary against another incumbent after the 1964 redistricting. After that, he never had much trouble at the polls, though the Republican vote in the Grosse Pointes and in some of the more prosperous East Side neighborhoods kept his majorities slightly below those of other white Detroit-area Democrats. Even when the Republicans targeted the district in 1968, Nedzi won reelection easily.

In recent years, therefore, the Congressman had not found it necessary to campaign particularly hard, devoting most of his time to duties on the House Armed Services Committee. Moreover, he was unfamiliar to many voters in the new, Macomb County portion of the 14th. Some time before the onset of the 1972 campaign, Nedzi had of course stated an opposition to busing, but one that did not seem to satisfy his consituents. His leading opponent in the primary, Warren Councilman Howard Austin, left absolutely no doubt where he stood on the matter; in fact, Austin steadfastly refused to discuss any issue except busing. In the South, voters no longer take kindly to such racial singlemindedness, but the citizens of south Warren loved it. The challenger carried the Macomb portion of the district by an overwhelming margin, and in a four-way race, finished with 39% district-wide. Nedzi, who is of Polish descent, just squeaked by with 43%, though he had 11 years of experience and had earned the respect of many area newspaper editorialists. The incumbent had an easier time in the general election, with the Republican opposition less formidable. Even so, the Congressman took only 55% of the vote—a sign of possible trouble ahead. The Republicans may well contest the district vigorously in 1974, and could conceivably win it.

Some years before it became popular among House liberals, Nedzi got a seat on Mendel Rivers' Armed Services Committee. There he and a few Northern Democrats waged hopeless struggles against the Southern Democratic-Republican coalition that possessed absolute control of the committee. The coalition, of course, usually went along with the desires of the Pentagon. For his efforts, Nedzi is now the eighth-ranking Democrat and first-ranking dove on Armed Services. In 1971, Nedzi co-sponsored the Nedzi-Whalen amendment, the principal piece of end-the-war legislation of that session of the House. And so after plugging on for many lonely years, Nedzi must have taken great satisfaction when a majority of the Democrats on Armed Services voted to stop the bombing of Cambodia in 1973.

For the 93rd Congress, thanks to Chairman Edward Hebert's sense of fairness, Nedzi is Chairman of the Special Subcommittee on Intelligence, otherwise made up of the senior members of the full committee. Nedzi's panel was much in the news during 1973; it investigated charges that the Nixon Administration used CIA help to burglarize the office of Daniel Ellsberg's psychiatrist and that the White House attempted to get top CIA officials to cover up the Watergate scandal. Nedzi conducted the hearings in executive session and the briefed the press in the corridors. The Congressman appeared to have deliberately eschewed controversy, refusing to take political advantage of an opportunity for wide publicity.

Census Data Pop. 467,603. Central city, 47%; suburban, 53%. Median family income, $12,394; families above $15,000: 34%; families below $3,000: 5%. Median years education, 11.9.

1972 Share of Federal Outlays $316,398,241

DOD	$45,509,011	HEW	$146,473,927
AEC	$21,369	HUD	$8,469,947
NASA	$85,830	DOI	$375,209
DOT	$15,258,545	USDA	$5,711,757
		Other	$94,492,646

Federal Military-Industrial Commitments

DOD Installations Detroit Arsenal (Warren).

Economic Base Transportation equipment, especially motor vehicles and equipment; finance, insurance and real estate; fabricated metal products, especially metal stampings; machinery, especially metalworking machinery; and primary metal industries, especially blast furnace and basic steel products.

The Voters

Registration 275,655 total. No party registration.
Median voting age 47.2
Employment profile White collar, 50%. Blue collar, 39%. Service, 11%. Farm, –%.
Ethnic groups Black, 3%. Total foreign stock, 37%. Poland, 9%; Italy, Canada, 6% each; Germany, 4%; UK, 2%; Austria, Yugoslavia, 1% each.

Presidential vote

1972	Nixon (R)	85,618	(60%)
	McGovern (D)	57,045	(40%)
1968	Nixon (R)	69,970	(33%)
	Humphrey (D)	117,906	(55%)
	Wallace (AI)	27,116	(13%)

Representative

Lucien N. Nedzi (D) Elected Nov. 1961; b. May 28, 1925, Hamtramck; home, Detroit; U. of Mich., B.A., 1948, LL.B., 1951; WWII and Korea; married, five children; Catholic.

Career Atty., 1952–60; Wayne County Public Admin., 1955.

Offices 2418 RHOB, 202-225-6276. Also 11498 Portlance, Detroit 48205, 313-521-4880.

Administrative Assistant James G. Pyrros

Committees

Armed Services (8th); Subs: No. 2; Sp. Sub. on Intelligence (Chm.).

House Administration (4th); Subs: Library and Memorials (Chm.); Electrical and Mechanical Office Equipment.

Joint Com. on the Library (Chm.).

Group Ratings

	ADA	COPE	LWV	RIPON	NFU	LCV	CFA	NAB	NSI	ACA
1972	75	91	82	69	100	67	100	8	0	9
1971	84	82	67	76	87	–	88	–	–	14
1970	92	100	–	60	100	76	94	0	20	13

Key Votes

1) Busing	AGN	6) Cmbodia Bmbg	AGN	11) Chkg Acct Intrst	FOR
2) Strip Mines	AGN	7) Bust Hwy Trust	FOR	12) End HISC (HUAC)	FOR
3) Cut Mil $	AGN	8) Farm Sub Lmt	FOR	13) Nixon Sewer Veto	AGN
4) Rev Shrg	FOR	9) School Prayr	AGN	14) Corp Cmpaign $	FOR
5) Pub TV $	FOR	10) Cnsumr Prot	FOR	15) Pol $ Disclosr	AGN

Election Results

1972 general:	Lucien N. Nedzi (D)	93,923	(55%)
	Robert V. McGrath (R)	77,273	(45%)
1972 primary:	Lucien N. Nedzi (D)	21,377	(43%)
	Howard D. Austin (D)	19,511	(39%)
	Don D. Cramer (D)	5,563	(11%)
	Walter Bezz (D)	2,999	(6%)
1970 general:	Lucien N. Nedzi (D)	91,111	(70%)
	John L. Owen (R)	38,956	(30%)

FIFTEENTH DISTRICT Political Background

The 15th district of Michigan takes in the suburbs lying southwest of Detroit. No high-income WASPy havens, these suburbs are bedroom communities occupied by people who keep the paperwork and assembly lines of Detroit auto companies moving. The various towns here possess the ambience of the decade during which they experienced the most growth: for the 1940s, Lincoln Park; for the 1950s, Dearborn Heights; and for the 1960s, Westland, a suburb distinguished for having been named after a shopping center. Most of the suburbs of the district are predominantly blue-collar, though only one of them, Inkster, has a significant number of black people, 44%. Many of the citizens here grew up in the immigrant neighborhoods of southwest Detroit; many others, in the mountains of Kentucky and Tennessee.

The suburbs of most American cities usually vote Republican. Those of Detroit generally go Democratic. Over the years, places like the state's 15th district have turned in Democratic majorities of two-to-one or better more often than not; as recently as 1968, the Detroit suburbs produced most of the state's Democratic majority. But the metropolitan busing order (see Michigan 12) has produced a notable Republican surge in the Detroit suburbs. In 1968, the 15th presaged the trend when it gave George Wallace 16% of its votes—more than in all but 16 other non-Southern congressional district.

The district's largest employer is the Ford Motor Company, and its Congressman, William D. Ford, is a Democrat but no relation to the auto barons. When the state legislature split the old 16th district in 1964, Ford, a young attorney active in local politics, jumped from the state Senate to the U.S. House. In Washington, Ford serves on the Education and Labor Committee, along with James O'Hara of Michigan's 12th district. It is no surprise that Ford has a 100% rating from COPE of the AFL-CIO, coming as he does from a district where most wage earners are union members. But like other Detroit-area Congressmen with suburban constituencies, Ford's reputation as a liberal helped him not at all during the 1972 campaign in which busing was the biggest issue. Though Ford opposed cross-district busing, he received unusually low totals against undistinguished opposition in both the Democratic primary and the general election.

Census Data Pop. 466,608. Central city, 0%; suburban, 100%. Median family income, $12,460; families above $15,000: 32%; families below $3,000: 4%. Median years education, 12.1.

1972 Share of Federal Outlays $315,006,132

DOD	$44,997,233	HEW	$145,983,484
AEC	$21,100	HUD	$8,383,546
NASA	$84,750	DOI	$372,788
DOT	$15,298,604	USDA	$5,843,880
		Other	$94,020,747

Federal Military-Industrial Commitments

No installations or contractors receiving prime awards greater than $5,000,000.

Economic Base Transportation equipment, especially motor vehicles and equipment; fabricated metal products, especially metal stampings; machinery, especially metalworking machinery; finance, insurance and real estate; and primary metal industries, especially blast furnace and basic steel products.

The Voters

Registration 233,179 total. No party registration.
Median voting age 38.4
Employment profile White collar, 42%. Blue collar, 47%. Service, 11%. Farm, –%.
Ethnic groups Black, 5%. Spanish, 1%. Total foreign stock, 19%. Canada, 5%; Poland, 3%; UK, Germany, Italy, 2% each.

Presidential vote

1972	Nixon (R)	94,812	(61%)
	McGovern (D)	61,803	(39%)
1968	Nixon (R)	41,959	(29%)
	Humphrey (D)	79,439	(55%)
	Wallace (AI)	23,973	(16%)

Representative

William David Ford (D) Elected 1964; b. Aug. 6, 1927, Detroit; home, Taylor; Neb. Teachers Col., 1946; Wayne State U., 1947–48; U. of Denver, B.S., 1949, LL.B., 1951; USNR, WWII; Lt., USAF, 1950–58; married, three children; United Church of Christ.

Career Atty., 1951– ; J.P. of Taylor Township, 1955–57; city atty., Melvindale, 1957–59; State Senator, 1962–64; Delegate, Mich. Const. Conv., 1961–62.

Offices 343 CHOB, 202-225-6261. Also, Wayne Fed. Bldg., Wayne 48184, 313-722-1411.

Administrative Assistant Frank H. Rathbun

Committees

Education and Labor (8th); Subs: Agricultural Labor (Chm.); Education; Labor.

Post Office and Civil Service (10th); Subs: Manpower and Civil Service; Postal Service.

Group Ratings

	ADA	COPE	LWV	RIPON	NFU	LCV	CFA	NAB	NSI	ACA
1972	75	88	75	62	100	90	100	9	0	12
1971	78	82	67	79	86	–	100	–	–	8
1970	92	100	–	63	100	95	100	0	11	6

Key Votes

1) Busing	AGN	6) Cmbodia Bmbg	AGN	11) Chkg Acct Intrst	AGN
2) Strip Mines	ABS	7) Bust Hwy Trust	FOR	12) End HISC (HUAC)	FOR
3) Cut Mil $	ABS	8) Farm Sub Lmt	ABS	13) Nixon Sewer Veto	AGN
4) Rev Shrg	FOR	9) School Prayr	AGN	14) Corp Cmpaign $	FOR
5) Pub TV $	FOR	10) Cnsumr Prot	FOR	15) Pol $ Disclosr	ABS

Election Results

1972 general:	William D. Ford (D)	97,054	(66%)
	Ernest C. Fackler (R)	48,504	(33%)
	Aldi C. Fuhrman (AI)	1,972	(1%)
1972 primary:	William D. Ford (D)	21,374	(62%)
	Frank E. Lubinski (D)	13,091	(38%)
1970 general:	William D. Ford (D)	101,018	(80%)
	Ernest C. Fackler (R)	25,340	(20%)

SIXTEENTH DISTRICT Political Background

Michigan's 16th is an industrial district made up of three areas of nearly equal size: the Delray section of Detroit, the Downriver suburbs, and the city of Dearborn. Delray, the southwest corner of Detroit, is an old ethnic neighborhood that exists much like it did 50 years ago. The Downriver suburbs grow more prosperous and modern as one proceeds south along the Detroit River, though an insular quality remains in places like River Rouge and Ecorse, divided neatly into ethnic and black sections by railroad tracks. Dearborn (pop. 104,000) is the district's most famous suburb; here the Ford Motor Company has its headquarters and its giant Rouge plant. Dearborn is also rather famous for Orville Hubbard, Mayor since 1942. Hubbard has plastered the city with signs reading "Keep Dearborn Clean," a slogan that some say is an euphemism for his primary concern: keeping Dearborn white. Though Dearborn lies adjacent to part of Detroit's ghetto, and though thousands of blacks work at the Rouge, no blacks live in Dearborn and no one expects any to move in. Oddly enough, Hubbard was as vigorous an opponent of the Vietnam war as he is of suburban integration. He realized early on that a disproportionate number of his working-class constituents were being drafted—and killed—in the war. The Mayor put an antiwar referendum on the city ballot and got it approved as long ago as 1968.

The 16th is one of the nation's most heavily industrial districts. From the I-75 bridge over the Rouge River, one can see the Ford Rouge plant and a couple of oil refineries on one side, and the huge steel mills of the Downriver communities on the other. For the distinction of the premier industrial landscape in America, the scene here competes with the view of Gary from the Indiana Turnpike and the spectacle of northern New Jersey from the Pulaski Skyway. Almost flush up against the industrial plants and well within the range of their sulphurous odors are the neat, tightly-packed houses of the old ethnic neighborhoods, still mostly Polish, Hungarian, and Italian—but some now with considerable numbers of Arabs and Mexican-Americans. The 16th does contain a few high-income WASP enclaves in the western part of Dearborn and on the island of Grosse Ile in the Detroit River. Most of the district, however, is vintage Democratic country.

It is perhaps fitting that the Congressman from this pollution-ridden district is one of the leading conservationists in the House of Representatives. John D. Dingell, Jr., comes by his interest not from reading the coffee table books of the Sierra Club, but from a long-time love of hunting. Because of this, he is as well an impassioned foe of gun controls. As Chairman of the Fisheries and Wildlife Conservation Subcommittee of the Merchant Marine and Fisheries Committee, Dingell has been responsible for many conservationist measures. And on such issues outside the committee's jurisdiction, he is an authority who wields clout.

On other issues, Dingell is less likely to line up with the ideological liberals of the House. He was, for example, a latecomer to the ranks of the Vietnam doves. Alone of Detroit-area Democrats with suburban constituents, Dingell did not face electoral trouble on the busing controversy in 1972; he won both the primary and the general election by customarily large margins. Dingell has had only one tough election, in 1964, when redistricting forced him into the same district with Rep. John Lesinski, Jr. Both were Democrats of Polish descent and both had succeeded their fathers, who had both been first elected to Congress in 1932. But in pre-backlash days Lesinski had voted against the Civil Rights Act of 1964—the only Northern Democrat to do so—while Dingell had vigorous support from labor in the primary. Though Lesinski enjoyed the status of incumbent in most of the district, Dingell won and has had no difficulties since.

Census Data Pop. 467,168. Central city, 29%; suburban, 71%. Median family income, $11,800; families above $15,000: 31%; families below $3,000: 6%. Median years education, 11.4.

1972 Share of Federal Outlays $316,113,966

DOD	$45,468,123	HEW	$146,342,324
AEC	$21,349	HUD	$8,462,337
NASA	$85,753	DOI	$374,872
DOT	$15,244,836	USDA	$5,706,625
		Other	$94,407,747

Federal Military-Industrial Commitments

DOD Contractors Ford Motor (Dearborn), $7.644m: research in high temperature gas turbine engines.

Economic Base Transportation equipment, especially motor vehicles and equipment; finance, insurance and real estate; fabricated metal products, especially metal stampings; machinery, especially metalworking machinery; and primary metal industries, especially blast furnace and basic steel products.

The Voters

Registration 257,732 total. No party registration.
Median voting age 45.1
Employment profile White collar, 43%. Blue collar, 45%. Service, 12%. Farm, –%.
Ethnic groups Black, 8%. Spanish, 3%. Total foreign stock, 31%. Poland, 7%; Canada, 5%; Italy, 3%; UK, Germany, Hungary, 2% each.

Presidential vote

1972	Nixon (R)	95,564	(54%)
	McGovern (D)	82,219	(46%)
1968	Nixon (R)	49,774	(27%)
	Humphrey (D)	110,387	(60%)
	Wallace (AI)	23,555	(13%)

Representative

John D. Dingell (D) Elected 1954; b. July 8, 1926, Colorado Springs, Colo.; home, Trenton; Georgetown U., B.S., 1949, LL.B., 1952; Army, WWII; Catholic.

Career Atty., 1952– ; Res. Asst. U.S. Dist. Judge Levin, 1952–53; Asst. Pros. Atty., Wayne County, 1953–55.

Offices 2210 RHOB, 202-225-4071. Also 4917 Schaefer, Deaborn 48126, 313-846-1276.

Administrative Assistant Margaret A. Matus

Committees

Interstate and Foreign Commerce (5th); Sub: Transportation and Aeronautics.

Merchant Marine and Fisheries (4th); Subs: Fisheries and Wildlife—Conservation and the Environment (Chm.); Merchant Marine.

Sel. Com. on Small Business (4th); Subs: Activities of Regulatory Agencies (Chm.); Taxation and Oil Imports.

Group Ratings

	ADA	COPE	LWV	RIPON	NFU	LCV	CFA	NAB	NSI	ACA
1972	63	89	83	73	100	90	100	20	30	15
1971	76	83	67	65	86	–	88	–	–	22
1970	68	100	–	50	91	80	100	0	44	12

Key Votes

1) Busing	AGN	6) Cmbodia Bmbg	AGN	11) Chkg Acct Intrst	FOR
2) Strip Mines	AGN	7) Bust Hwy Trust	FOR	12) End HISC (HUAC)	FOR
3) Cut Mil $	AGN	8) Farm Sub Lmt	FOR	13) Nixon Sewer Veto	AGN
4) Rev Shrg	FOR	9) School Prayr	AGN	14) Corp Cmpaign $	ABS
5) Pub TV $	FOR	10) Cnsumr Prot	FOR	15) Pol $ Disclosr	AGN

Election Results

1972 general:	John D. Dingell (D)	110,715	(68%)
	William E. Rostron (R)	48,414	(30%)
	Peter P. Gayner (AI)	3,554	(2%)
1972 primary:	John D. Dingell (D)	30,972	(86%)
	Zigmund Niparko (D)	5,095	(14%)
1970 general:	John D. Dingell (D)	90,540	(79%)
	William E. Rostron (R)	23,867	(21%)

SEVENTEENTH DISTRICT Political Background

Northwest Detroit is the most white middle-class and white-collar part of the city. For mile after mile, the straight streets here are lined with single-family homes, with the factories responsible for making household ends meet far away. Northwest Detroit comprises the political fulcrum of Michigan politics. During the early 1950s, this part of the city was, as it had been for years, pretty solidly Republican. But in 1954, it went in a big way for Democratic Gov. G. Mennen Williams and retired many Republican legislators—including its Congressman—in favor of Democratic politicians. Since then, northwest Detroit goes Democratic more often than not, though it has delivered majorities for Republicans like ex-Gov. George Romney and Sen. Robert Griffin.

One reason the 17th is more Democratic than most white middle-class areas in other major cities is the presence of a large number of Canadian immigrants. For some reason, Canadian-Americans are far less likely to vote Republican than their WASP counterparts raised in the United States. And attracted by jobs in the auto industry, more immigrants from Canada live in the Detroit area than in any other part of the country except northern New England. (A survey taken north of the border suggests that Canadians, like residents of Massachusetts and the District of Columbia, preferred McGovern to Nixon in 1972.) Over the years, Detroit has generally been the nation's second most Democratic large metropolitan area, after Boston.

For the 1972 elections, redistricting forced a major reshaping of the 17th congressional district. It used to take in just about all of northwest Detroit, including areas that had gone from white to black majorities during the 1960s. The redistricters decided to give most of the black neighborhoods to the 1st district and John Conyers, and added to the 17th several suburbs to the west. One of them, Redford Township, is politically and otherwise indistinguishable from northwest Detroit, which it adjoins. Southfield, just to the north, is the site of dozens of new high-rise office buildings; it is also growing rapidly and contains a large percentage of the Detroit area's Jewish community. Farmington, to the west of Southfield, is more WASPish and the only heavily Republican part of the district.

The boundary changes did not pose many problems for Rep. Martha W. Griffiths, the Democrat who has represented the 17th since 1954. Mrs. Griffiths has enjoyed phenomenal popularity in her district, winning as much as 80% of the votes in 1970; she was also well-known outside of what was the old 17th district. As a member of the House Ways and Means Committee, she has great potential clout over much important legislation and over Democratic committee assignments. The Congresswoman used the clout to play a major role in the repeal of the auto excise tax, a popular cause in the Motor City. She is also the chief House sponsor of the Kennedy-Griffiths comprehensive health-care bill, which, as of this writing, has not gotten far in Ways and Means as Chairman Wilbur Mills recovers from a back operation. There is also a side of Griffiths' record that is clearly conservative, particularly on issues like criminal procedures. This, too, is popular in the outer reaches of Detroit, which possesses one of the nation's highest murder rates.

The Congresswoman's most outstanding achievement, however, was the passage of the Equal Rights Amendment. For years, she introduced the measure to guarantee equal rights for women, only to see it bottled up in Emanuel Celler's Judiciary Committee. But in 1971, enough House members were persuaded to sign a discharge petition to force the ERA to the floor of the House, where Mrs. Griffiths was its floor manager. She succeeded in defeating a crippling amendment offered by Charles Wiggins of California. The ERA passed the House and the Senate and, at this writing, it has been ratified by many of the states. But because a strong anti-ERA campaign is going on in various state legislatures where it has not yet been approved, it is unclear whether the few states necessary to assure ratification will vote to make it part of the Constitution. Mrs. Griffiths is presently working toward that end.

Census Data Pop. 467,544. Central city, 56%; suburban, 44%. Median family income, $13,449; families above $15,000: 41%; families below $3,000: 4%. Median years education, 12.3.

1972 Share of Federal Outlays $316,398,241

DOD	$45,509,011	HEW	$146,473,927
AEC	$21,369	HUD	$8,469,947
NASA	$85,830	DOI	$375,209
DOT	$15,258,545	USDA	$5,711,757
		Other	$94,492,646

Federal Military-Industrial Commitments

No installations or contractors receiving prime awards greater than $5,000,000.

Economic Base Transportation equipment, especially motor vehicles and equipment; machinery, especially metalworking machinery; finance, insurance and real estate; fabricated metal products, especially metal stampings; and primary metal industries, especially blast furnace and basic steel products.

The Voters

Registration 285,339 total. No party registration.
Median voting age 45.7
Employment profile White collar, 58%. Blue collar, 31%. Service, 11%. Farm, –%.
Ethnic groups Black, 2%. Spanish, 1%. Total foreign stock, 34%. Canada, 8%; Poland, UK, 4% each; Germany, USSR, 3% each; Italy, 2%.

Presidential vote

1972	Nixon (R)	118,347	(60%)
	McGovern (D)	77,659	(40%)
1968	Nixon (R)	79,749	(39%)
	Humphrey (D)	101,819	(50%)
	Wallace (AI)	21,458	(11%)

Representative

Martha W. Griffiths (D) Elected 1954; b. Jan. 29, 1912, Pierce City, Mo.; home, Detroit; U. of Mo., B.A., 1934; U. of Mich., LL.B., 1940; married; Protestant.

Career State Rep., 1949–52; Judge and Recorder of Recorder's Court of Detroit, 1953.

Offices 1536 LHOB, 202-225-4961. Also 26547 Grand River, Detroit 48240, 313-537-1400.

Administrative Assistant Marilynne Mikulich

Committees

Ways and Means (4th).

Sel. Com. on the House Beauty Shop (Chm.).

Joint Economic Com. (4th); Subs: Economic Progress; Fiscal Policy (Chm.); Urban Affairs; Consumer Economics; Inter-American Economic Relationships; Priorities and Economy in Government.

Joint Study Com. on Budget Control.

Group Ratings

	ADA	COPE	LWV	RIPON	NFU	LCV	CFA	NAB	NSI	ACA
1972	31	78	82	46	71	54	—	13	25	13
1971	49	80	100	75	92	–	50	–	–	18
1970	64	82	–	63	91	71	72	13	63	0

Key Votes

1) Busing	AGN	6) Cmbodia Bmbg	ABS	11) Chkg Acct Intrst	FOR
2) Strip Mines	AGN	7) Bust Hwy Trust	ABS	12) End HISC (HUAC)	AGN
3) Cut Mil $	FOR	8) Farm Sub Lmt	FOR	13) Nixon Sewer Veto	FOR
4) Rev Shrg	FOR	9) School Prayr	AGN	14) Corp Cmpaign $	FOR
5) Pub TV $	FOR	10) Cnsumr Prot	FOR	15) Pol $ Disclosr	AGN

Election Results

1972 general:	Martha W. Griffiths (D)	123,331	(66%)
	Ralph E. Judd (R)	60,337	(33%)
	Hector M. McGregor (AI)	1,480	(1%)
1972 primary:	Martha W. Griffiths (D), unopposed		
1970 general:	Martha W. Griffiths (D)	108,176	(80%)
	Thomas E. Klunzinger (R)	27,608	(20%)

EIGHTEENTH DISTRICT Political Background

The 1972 redistricting created the 18th district, a congressional seat without an incumbent. It was apparently designed to send a Democrat to Washington, but in the year busing was the major issue in the Detroit suburbs, the 18th elected an arch-conservative Republican Congressman. The new constituency combined two areas that have little in common and that had never before been part of the same congressional district. One-third of the 18th's residents live in fast-growing Macomb County—Sterling Heights and Warren—the hottest anti-busing part of the Detroit metropolitan area (see Michigan 12). Macomb had always been Democratic, but in 1972 Warren and Sterling Heights went for Republican candidates— not just for Richard Nixon, but all the way down the line.

The other two-thirds of the 18th is the southeast corner of Oakland County—higher income, much more white-collar, and by tradition more Republican than Macomb. The district's portion of Oakland includes a pastiche of suburbs: Oak Park, which is mostly Jewish; Hazel Park and Madison Heights, which contain many residents who are natives of the Kentucky and Tennessee mountains; Royal Oak, which is middle-class residential; and Troy, a rapidly growing place where a Saks Fifth Avenue shopping center was built on land that was formerly a Michigan farm.

The diverse district possesses suburban territory of almost every kind, from a tiny black ghetto to neighborhoods composed of $100,000 homes. In 1972, the 18th was the scene of spirited primary and general election contests; as in most 1972 political campaigns held in the Detroit suburbs, the only issue here was busing. Of course, all of the candidates were against it, with the voters gauging the depth of opposition by the decibel count that accompanied the candidates' statements. The opponents who met in the general election were two veterans of the state Senate whose opinions on most everything except busing differed greatly. Daniel Cooper, state Senator from the southern, more Democratic half of Oakland County, easily won a seven-candidate Democratic primary. He had compiled a liberal record over the years, and in 1972 opposed most of the positions taken by the Nixon Administration, the notable exception being busing.

The Republican nominee, ex-state Sen. (1965–70) Robert J. Huber, had the reputation of a militant conservative on just about everything. In 1970, Huber gave up an utterly safe seat in the state Senate to challenge Lenore Romney in the Republican U.S. Senate primary and came close to pulling off an upset. Shunned by most Michigan Republicans, he organized his own Conservative party. But when the 18th was created just at the time the busing controversy began to heat up, Huber decided to return to the Republican fold and entered the district's congressional primary. Among his supporters was Irene McCabe, the T-shirted Pontiac housewife who led an anti-busing walk from Michigan to Washington, D.C.; since then, Mrs. McCabe's appetite for publicity has alienated most of her followers.

Huber, the owner of a chrome company, waged an energetic, well-financed campaign. He charged Cooper with having engaged in various forms of liberal political behavior. The implication was that Cooper's heart was not really in the anti-busing cause. Despite his solid anti-busing record in the legislature, most of the voters apparently shared Huber's analysis. In a notable reversal of political form, the Republican carried the Macomb County portion of the 18th and made heavy inroads into the normally Democratic areas of Madison Heights and Hazel Park. Huber's margins were enough to give him a 53–47 victory. Cooper's greatest strength lay in his home town of Oak Park. It is worth noting that Southfield, like Oak Park, has a large Jewish population; if the redistricters had included Southfield, rather than Sterling Heights (of nearly equal size), the results in the 18th would probably have gone to Democrat Cooper.

At this writing, the outlook for 1974 is for another vigorous campaign, if not an upset of incumbent Congressman Huber. As a state Senator, Huber demonstrated a great talent for keeping in touch with his constituents, a talent that he no doubt retains in his present office. Huber won elections to the state Senate easily, even though most regular Republicans regarded him as something of a nut. Meanwhile, Cooper wants to run again. Another possible candidate is Annetta Miller, a member of the state Board of Education; in 1970, she nearly defeated the then state AFL-CIO president in a Democratic primary conducted in the old 18th. The outcome here in the 1974 election will probably depend on the Supreme Court's decision in the Detroit busing case, one expected sometime in the spring of 1974. If the Court rules in favor of busing between Detroit and its suburbs, Huber will run as the heavy favorite; if the Court does not so rule, other issues may emerge, leading to a possible change in the district's representation Then too, there is always the possibility that Huber will run for statewide office, which is what he did in 1970; he may try for Governor in 1974 or, what is more likely, for Philip Hart's Senate seat in 1976.

Census Data Pop. 465,916. Central city, 0%; suburban, 100%. Median family income, $13,627; families above $15,000: 40%; families below $3,000: 3%. Median years education, 12.3.

1972 Share of Federal Outlays $315,261,141

DOD	$45,345,457	HEW	$145,947,516
AEC	$21,292	HUD	$8,439,507
NASA	$85,521	DOI	$373,861
DOT	$15,203,707	USDA	$5,691,229
		Other	$94,153,051

Federal Military-Industrial Commitments

DOD Contractors Chrysler Corp. (Detroit), $78.156m: trucks, tanks, and component parts. LTV Aerospace (Warren), $60.336m: engineering services for Lance missile system. General Motors (Warren), $18.675m: design of new tank system.

Economic Base Motor vehicles and equipment, and other transportation equipment; machinery, especially metalworking machinery; finance, insurance and real estate; and fabricated metal products, especially metal stampings and fabricated structural metal products.

The Voters

Registration 238,542 total. No party registration.
Median voting age 39.9
Employment profile White collar, 57%. Blue collar, 34%. Service, 9%. Farm, –%.
Ethnic groups Total foreign stock, 29%. Canada, 7%; Poland, 4%; UK, 3%; Italy, Germany, USSR, 2%.

Presidential vote

1972	Nixon (R)	115,552	(63%)
	McGovern (D)	68,193	(37%)
1968	Nixon (R)	58,586	(35%)
	Humphrey (D)	89,485	(54%)
	Wallace (AI)	17,245	(10%)

Representative

Robert J. Huber (R) Elected 1972; b. Aug. 29, 1922, Detroit; home, Troy; Culver Military Academy; Ford School in Detroit; Sheffield Scientific School; Yale U., B.S., 1943; married; Catholic.

Career Pres., Michigan Chrome and Chemical Co., Detroit; Pres., Tolber Corp., Hope, Ark.; Dir., Troy National Bank, Troy; Dir., Alloy Steels, Inc., Detroit; Michigan State Senate, 1964–1970; Mayor of Troy, 1959–1964; Mbr. Oakland County Bd. of Sups., 1959–64.

Offices 419 CHOB, 202-225-2101. Also 710 W. Eleven Mile Rd., Royal Oak, 48067, 313-399-0960.

Administrative Assistant Frederic N. Smith

Committees

Education and Labor (16th); Subs: No. 3 (Labor); No. 6 (Education).

Veterans' Affairs (10th); Subs: Education and Training; Hospitals; Housing.

Group Ratings: Newly Elected

Key Votes

1) Busing	NE	6) Cmbodia Bmbg	FOR	11) Chkg Acct Intrst	ABS
2) Strip Mines	NE	7) Bust Hwy Trust	AGN	12) End HISC (HUAC)	AGN
3) Cut Mil $	NE	8) Farm Sub Lmt	NE	13) Nixon Sewer Veto	FOR
4) Rev Shrg	NE	9) School Prayr	NE	14) Corp Cmpaign $	NE
5) Pub TV $	NE	10) Cnsumr Prot	NE	15) Pol $ Disclosr	NE

Election Results

1972 general:	Robert J. Huber (R)	95,053	(53%)
	Daniel S. Cooper (D)	85,580	(47%)
1972 primary:	Robert J. Huber (R)	13,426	(84%)
	Harriet Rotter (R)	1,872	(12%)
	Ronald Y. Gutman (R)	698	(4%)

NINETEENTH DISTRICT Political Background

Just under half of Oakland County, the second largest county in Michigan, lies in the 19th congressional district. The 19th also contains 22,000 residents living in a small slice of adjacent Livingston County, to the west. Technically, almost all of the territory of the 19th is considered part of the Detroit metropolitan area, but beyond the district's southern rim the influence of Detroit wanes. The northern part of Oakland County is still rural, having summer cottages that line Michigan lakes, and ski resorts that rest on man-made Michigan hills. The 19th's principal city is Pontiac (pop. 85,000), for which the car was named and where it is still manufactured. Like Flint, Pontiac is a one-company—GM—town; most of its residents are natives of the Appalachian Mountains or of the Black Belts of the Deep South. Pontiac became the scene of a busing controversy in 1971, when a federal court ordered the implementation of a desegregation plan. Boycotts followed, private academies established, and chesty, T-shirted Irene McCabe led a Pontiac-to-Washington anti-busing march. But by 1972, Pontiac, where the busing plan was working reasonably well, had less anti-busing sentiment than the Detroit suburbs farther south, where residents lived in fearful anticipation of a busing order not yet implemented.

Just to the south of Pontiac, but separated from it by years of social conditioning, are the Detroit suburbs of Birmingham and Bloomfield Hills. These, along with the Grosse Pointes, are Detroit's richest suburbs. Birmingham and Bloomfield Hills, however, are less snobbish and exclusive, with many Jews living in them; Birmingham even has an open-housing ordinance. The busing controversy did not produce the political upheaval here that it did in other Detroit suburbs (see Michigan 12); the voters in 1972 simply went to the polls and cast their customary 75% to 80% Republican majorities.

The 19th was intended to be a Republican district, which it is. For the 1972 general election, Pontiac, the only part of the district with Democratic voting habits, went more Republican because of the busing controversy; and this was doubly true of its adjacent suburb of Waterford Township, where George Wallace had taken 18% of the votes in 1968. The real race took place in the Republican primary, and because it pitted two incumbent Republican Congressmen against each other, the primary was a hot one.

It need not have been. Jack McDonald, who had defeated an LBJ Democrat in 1966 in the old 19th, appeared to have clear title to the new district. He had previously represented some 68% of its constituents. But William Broomfield, of the old 18th, was unwilling to run in the newly created 18th, figuring it for a Democratic district (see Michigan 18). And because he had represented all of Oakland County before 1964, Broomfield decided to run in the 19th. In the primary, both candidates of course condemned busing. Broomfield got the best of the issue, having authored an anti-busing amendment that became law in the spring of 1972, though it ultimately had little effect on the courts. Broomfield was particularly popular in the Birmingham-Bloomfield area, part of his old 18th district and one that turned out on election day and gave its incumbent Congressman huge majorities. McDonald was unable to match these margins in his old district, where people are more likely to vote in the Democratic primary. Also, because of gobs of franked mail that got here prior to 1964, Broomfield's name recognition was still strong. In the end, Broomfield won the primary 59–41, and went on to win the anticlimactic general election easily.

In the House, Broomfield is the third-ranking Republican on the Foreign Affairs Committee and ranking minority member of its Asian and Pacific Affairs Subcommittee. On the subcommittee, he has firmly supported the policies of the Nixon Administration in Indochina; the Congressman has also given equally enthusiastic support to most other programs of the Administration. In the past, one of his political trump cards was heavy support of Israel, which was appreciated in the Jewish neighborhoods of Oak Park and Southfield. Such support will be less important in the future, as the current 19th has no large Jewish population. In the years to come, Broomfield will probably win reelection easily.

Census Data   Pop. 467,540. Central city, 0%; suburban, 95%. Median family income, $13,405; families above $15,000: 41%; families below $3,000: 5%. Median years education, 12.4.

1972 Share of Federal Outlays $309,123,423

DOD	$43,407,972	HEW	$144,436,229
AEC	$20,351	HUD	$8,066,617
NASA	$81,743	DOI	$398,580
DOT	$14,577,479	USDA	$6,026,021
		Other	$92,108,431

Federal Military-Industrial Commitments

DOD Contractors Williams Research Corp. (Walled Lake), $7.010m: turbojet aircraft engines.

Economic Base Motor vehicles and equipment, and other transportation equipment; machinery, especially metalworking machinery; finance, insurance and real estate; and fabricated metal products, especially fabricated structural metal products and metal stampings.

The Voters

Registration 264,456 total. No party registration.
Median voting age 41.3

Employment profile White collar, 53%. Blue collar, 35%. Service, 11%. Farm, 1%.
Ethnic groups Black, 5%. Spanish, 2%. Total foreign stock, 17%. Canada, 5%; UK, Germany, 2% each; Poland, 1%.

Presidential vote

1972	Nixon (R)	122,205	(68%)
	McGovern (D)	57,144	(32%)
1968	Nixon (R)	86,378	(52%)
	Humphrey (D)	61,150	(37%)
	Wallace (AI)	17,928	(11%)

Representative

William S. Broomfield (R) Elected 1957; b. April 28, 1922, Royal Oak; home, Royal Oak; Mich. State U., B.A., 1951; married, three children; Presbyterian.

Career State Rep., 1948–54; State Sen., 1954–56; U.S. Delegate to 22nd UN General Assembly.

Offices 2435 RHOB, 202-225-6135. Also 1029 S. Washington, Royal Oak, 313-543-2400.

Administrative Assistant John R. Sinclair

Committees

Foreign Affairs (3rd); Subs: National Security Policy and Scientific Developments; Near East and South Asia; Asian and Pacific Affairs; Review of Foreign Aid Programs.

Group Ratings

	ADA	COPE	LWV	RIPON	NFU	LCV	CFA	NAB	NSI	ACA
1972	6	33	44	69	33	47	0	80	100	54
1971	22	17	56	65	27	–	63	–	–	82
1970	32	36	–	76	67	53	44	73	100	50

Key Votes

1) Busing	AGN	6) Cmbodia Bmbg	FOR	11) Chkg Acct Intrst	FOR
2) Strip Mines	AGN	7) Bust Hwy Trust	FOR	12) End HISC (HUAC)	AGN
3) Cut Mil $	AGN	8) Farm Sub Lmt	ABS	13) Nixon Sewer Veto	FOR
4) Rev Shrg	FOR	9) School Prayr	FOR	14) Corp Cmpaign $	FOR
5) Pub TV $	ABS	10) Cnsumr Prot	FOR	15) Pol $ Disclosr	AGN

Election Results

1972 general:	William S. Broomfield (R)	123,697	(70%)
	George F. Montgomery (D)	50,355	(29%)
	Henry Lloyd George (AI)	1,737	(1%)
1972 primary:	William S. Broomfield (R)	26,720	(59%)
	Jack McDonald (R)	18,796	(41%)
1970 general:	William S. Broomfield (R)	113,309	(65%)
	August Scholle (D)	62,081	(35%)

MINNESOTA

Political Background

Minnesota has supplied the nation with iron ore, flour, and political talent. In the recent past, Senators Hubert Humphrey, Eugene McCarthy, and Walter Mondale, along with Supreme Court Justices Warren Burger and Harry Blackmun (the so-called Minnesota Twins), have all come out of the state. And to go back a few years, there was ex-Gov. (1939–43) Harold Stassen, the one-time *wunderkind* of American politics and a figure of national consequence. No other state of this size—or any size—has produced so many serious presidential candidates in recent years, and few have maintained congressional delegations of similar distinction. Is it simply the work of the crisp northern air, or is it something unique in the politics of this state?

Minnesota lay far to the north of the nation's great paths of east-west migration, with Minneapolis and St. Paul sharing a line of latitude with Portland, Maine. So placed, Minnesota developed into the hub of a northern agricultural empire. Both of the Dakotas, eastern Montana, along with the prairies and lakes of Minnesota itself, grew into economic tributaries of the grain-milling and railroad centers of Minneapolis and St. Paul. Meanwhile, the Yankee and Midwestern immigrants who streamed into Iowa, Nebraska, and Kansas left Minnesota to the Norwegians, Swedes, and Germans.

Minnesota's ethnic history has given its politics a liberal, almost Scandinavian ambience. As in neighboring Wisconsin and North Dakota, a strong third party developed here after the Populist era, and that organization, the Farmer-Labor party, dominated Minnesota politics during the 1930s. The great Farmer-Labor Governor of the period, Floyd B. Olson, might well have become a presidential candidate had he not died of cancer in 1936. During the 1940s, after Harold Stassen swept the Republicans back into power in the state, the Farmer-Labor party fell upon hard times. The party eventually joined forces with the heavily outnumbered Democrats to form the Democratic-Farmer-Labor party (DFL), and this group, under the leadership of young Minneapolis Mayor Hubert Humphrey, triumphed in the elections in 1948. The DFL—and Humphrey—have dominated the state's politics ever since. Other Democratic organizations that emerged during the immediate post-war years have floundered of late (the one in Michigan, for example), but the DFL in Minnesota prospers and continues to flourish.

Because an ethnic map of the state is also a political one, the ancestral origin of any community usually determines its political allegiance. One key to the map is that Norwegians, for some reason, are more Republican than Swedes; for example, the state's most heavily Norwegian county, Otter Tail, remained loyal to the Republicans in 1964 and went for Goldwater. The pattern in the state's southern counties resembles the one in Iowa: WASP and German rural counties voting Republican, with some of the cities like Austin and Albert Lea casting strong Democratic margins. The city of St. Paul, settled by Irish and German Catholics, has always been Democratic, while Minneapolis, settled by Swedes, is somewhat less so. But the Twin Cities, which now contain 48% of the state's population, do not constitute the most Democratic part of Minnesota. Instead, that distinction goes to the north country around Duluth and the iron-bearing Mesabi Range. Here in the early days of settlement, the Swedes—joined by Finns, Poles, and other Eastern European ethnics—developed an attachment to the programs of the Democratic party, an attachment that continues to this day. In 1972, not a good Democratic year, the Duluth metropolitan area cast 59% of its votes for George McGovern; the showing was his best among the nation's metropolitan areas.

In fact, McGovern, with 47% of the votes, ran better in Minnesota than anywhere else but Massachusetts and the District of Columbia. And his candidacy seems not to have hurt—indeed may have helped—the DFL to one of its best years. The DFL easily held on to a congressional seat won by a narrow margin in 1970, and almost captured another held by a Republican. Moreover, for the first time in history, the DFL won majorities in both houses of the state's technically nonpartisan legislature, which was a triumph of good organization and youthful candidates over aged veterans. By all odds, the DFL ought to have been long since splintered by feuds between Humphreyites and labor on the one side and McCarthyites and middle-class liberals on the other. Instead, the party came out of both the 1970 and in particular the 1972 elections as one of the strongest political organizations to be found anywhere in the country.

One 1972 contest was never in doubt: the 57% reelection victory of the state's senior Senator, Walter F. Mondale. While serving as the youngest state Attorney General ever elected in Minnesota history, Mondale was appointed to fill Hubert Humphrey's seat in 1964. The incumbent then won a full term in 1966. Mondale is one of the most active members of the Labor and Public Welfare and of the Banking, Housing, and Urban Affairs committees. One of his greatest legislative achievements so far came in 1972, when Congress passed a comprehensive child-care program, one that included voluntary day-care. But because President Nixon vetoed the bill, Mondale's effort never became law. The Senator's opposition to the Administration has not been limited to his child-care measure. On a whole range of social issues, Mondale has often led the marshaling of liberal forces in Congress. This he has done not simply to pass legislation, but also to monitor and influence the manner in which laws are administered. A good deal of Mondale's work goes unnoticed; but without it, thousands of poor and middle-class people who have virtually no impact in our political system would have even less.

Though Mondale is an adept political operator, his motivations are clearly those of an old-fashioned idealist concerned for the poor and disadvantaged. In no other way can one explain the Senator's staunch opposition to anti-busing legislation or the time the man has devoted to the problem of child abuse. Some, including the state's junior Senator, Hubert Humphrey, have suggested that Mondale is a politician of presidential caliber. And it does appear that Mondale is someone acceptable to the national Democratic party. McGovernites like his committed liberalism, and the regulars remember that Mondale, co-chairman of Humphrey's 1968 campaign, did not speak out against the Vietnam war too early—that is, while a Democrat occupied the White House. Though his concern for the poor might come over as cloying to some, Mondale articulates his views in a clear and matter-of-fact way, and can hold his own on any platform. At this writing, Edward Kennedy seems to have a lock on the 1976 Democratic nomination, but if he chooses not to run, Mondale is as likely as anyone to emerge the favorite. And head-to-head the Minnesotan could give Kennedy a real contest in the primaries. There is no question, of course, that Mondale would make an excellent vice-presidential nominee.

The number-two spot, however, has not been such a lucky one for Hubert Humphrey, the state's other Senator. He is a man who worked in his father's Huron, South Dakota drugstore during the Depression, was forced to delay getting a college degree until he was 28, and was then elected Mayor of Minneapolis at 34. In the meantime, he helped to organize the DFL party, and, as its Senate nominee in 1948, easily unseated a Republican incumbent.

Memories of Humphrey's civil rights speech at the 1948 Democratic National Convention still linger in the nation's black communities and account for a lot of Humphrey votes among black people. And older liberals still remember how Humphrey, virtually alone, carried their torch in the Senate during the 1950s. But also a team player, Humphrey learned to play ball with Majority Leader Lyndon Johnson. In 1960, he was forced to drop out of the presidential running; his reputation was that of a far-out liberal, and he was unable to raise the kind of money necessary to challenge efforts of John F. Kennedy in the crucial West Virginia primary. But Humphrey went on in the Senate to become Majority Whip and the floor manager of the Civil Rights Act of 1964. That same year his old friend Lyndon Johnson awarded him the vice-presidency.

The office was both an opportunity and a burden. To the disgust of many of his partisans, Humphrey became the head cheerleader for LBJ's policies in Vietnam. This he did with his customary ebullience. In 1968, LBJ designated Humphrey his successor. After staying away from all the primaries, the Minnesotan won the nomination, thanks to the party's big power brokers. Upon winning the prize, Humphrey kissed his TV set, while Chicago police beat up and gassed hundreds of convention demonstrators. After the horror of Chicago, 1968, the real surprise: Humphrey came very close to winning the biggest prize of all. Humphrey's campaign against Nixon testifies to HHH's unflagging spirit and always-abounding energy and the political acumen of Richard Nixon's 1968 campaign manager, John Mitchell.

In 1970, Humphrey made a comeback in Minnesota, winning the seat relinquished by his 1968 rival, Eugene McCarthy. Humphrey took 58% of the vote, as he defeated a formidable Republican opponent, Rep. Clark MacGregor, later head of the Committee to Reelect the President. Once again, in 1972, Humphrey decided to make a bid for the White House. This time he entered the primaries and for the first time actually won a couple, in Pennsylvania and Ohio; he remained George McGovern's chief competitor until the credentials challenges were settled in Miami Beach. All along, Humphrey's campaign had something desperate about it, in the California debates when Humphrey did little but carp at McGovern, and during the July 1972 convention when he made a last-ditch effort to undermine the conditions under which the California primary was conducted. Before he lost the primary, Humphrey himself renounced such a move. Today, there is talk that the thrice-rejected Humphrey may try it again in 1976, when he will be 65. If he does, it will be his fourth try in five elections, and probably no more successful than the others.

Nevertheless, it is unwise to underestimate the ability of Hubert Humphrey to pick himself up off the mat. His speechifying still bubbles with new ideas, slogans of the past, inspirational rhetoric, and shameless clichés. And he remains, as he has been for the last quarter-century, one of the most active and productive members of the Senate. Most of his colleagues tend to specialize in one or two policy area. Not Humphrey, who has his hand in everything: disarmament, poverty, agriculture, civil rights, foreign policy, Social Security, and so on and on. Though he does not possess a major committee assignment or an especially important subcommittee chairmanship, Humphrey—by the sheer energy of the man—still constitutes an important force within the Senate. Two existing Senate office buildings have been named for two recently deceased conservatives, Richard Russell and Everett Dirksen. The Senate should wait before naming the third, which is now under construction, until Humphrey retires—a date probably still far in the future.

The main political event for 1974 in Minnesota will be the Governor's race. Incumbent DFL Gov. Wendell Anderson, elected in 1970 at age 38, is a heavy favorite to win reelection. In 1973, Anderson was featured in a *Time* cover story on the glories of Minnesota—and the success of his legislative program. In recent years, Minnesota Republicans have fielded strong candidates, but as Republicans won big in most of the country, the Republicans here have had little luck. The DFL has just been too tough.

Census Data   Pop. 3,805,069; 1.88% of U.S. total, 19th largest; change 1960–70, 11.5%. Central city, 24%; suburban, 33%. Median family income, $9,928; 16th highest; families above $15,000: 20%; families below $3,000: 9%. Median years education, 12.2.

1972 Share of Federal Tax Burden $3,636,920,000; 1.74% of U.S. total, 19th largest.

1972 Share of Federal Outlays $3,608,937,376; 1.67% of U.S. total, 19th largest.   Per capita federal spending, $948.

DOD	$590,588,000	30th (0.94%)	HEW	$1,302,690,191	17th (1.82%)
AEC	$3,627,639	25th (0.14%)	HUD	$52,892,591	21st (1.72%)
NASA	$12,954,305	18th (0.43%)	VA	$239,339,188	16th (2.09%)
DOT	$130,006,564	27th (1.65%)	USDA	$789,717,344	5th (5.13%)
DOC	$6,708,276	32nd (0.52%)	CSC	$46,953,177	24th (1.14%)
DOI	$33,648,023	19th (1.59%)	TD	$186,329,860	14th (1.13%)
DOJ	$16,915,687	18th (1.72%)	Other	$196,566,531	

Economic Base   Agriculture, notably cattle, dairy products, corn and hogs; finance, insurance and real estate; machinery, especially electronic computing equipment; food and kindred products, especially meat products; printing and publishing, especially commercial printing; electrical equipment and supplies; fabricated metal products, especially fabricated structural metal products.

Political Line-up   Governor, Wendell R. Anderson (D); seat up, 1974. Senators, Walter F. Mondale (D) and Hubert H. Humphrey (D). Representatives, 8 (4 D and 4 R). State Senate (37 Liberals and 30 Conservatives); State House (77 Liberals and 57 Conservatives).

The Voters

Registration   No statewide registration.
Median voting age 43.2
Employment profile   White collar, 49%. Blue collar, 31%. Service, 13%. Farm, 7%.
Ethnic groups   Total foreign stock, 19%. Germany, 4%; Sweden, Norway, 3%; Canada, 2%.

Presidential vote

1972	Nixon (R)	898,269	(53%)
	McGovern (D)	802,346	(47%)

1968	Nixon (R)	658,643	(42%)
	Humphrey (D)	857,738	(54%)
	Wallace (AI)	68,931	(4%)
1964	Johnson (D)	991,117	(64%)
	Goldwater (R)	559,624	(36%)

Senator

Walter F. Mondale (D) Elected Appointed Dec. 1964, elected 1966, seat up 1978; b. Jan. 5, 1928, Ceylon, Minn.; home, Minneapolis; Macalester Col., U. of Minn., B.A., 1951, LL.B., 1956; Army, 1951–53; married, three children; Presbyterian.

Career Practicing atty., 1956–60; Minn. Atty. Gen., 1960–64.

Offices 443 OSOB, 202-225-5641. Also 170 Fed. Ctr. Bldg., Minneapolis 55401, 612-725-2041.

Administrative Assistant Richard Moe

Committees

Finance (8th); Subs: International Trade; Health; State Taxation of Interstate Commerce (Chm.).

Labor and Public Welfare (6th); Subs: Alcoholism and Narcotics; Children and Youth (Chm.); Education; Employment, Poverty, and Migratory Labor; Health; Railroad Retirement; Sp. Sub. on Arts and Humanities; National Science Foundation.

Sp. Com. on Aging (8th); Subs: Housing for the Elderly; Employment and Retirement Incomes; Consumer Interests of the Elderly; Health of the Elderly; Retirement and the Individual (Chm.).

Sel. Com. on Nutrition and Human Needs (4th).

Group Ratings

	ADA	COPE	LWV	RIPON	NFU	LCV	CFA	NAB	NSI	ACA
1972	95	90	100	76	100	92	100	0	0	0
1971	100	83	100	74	100	–	100	–	–	9
1970	97	100	–	80	100	80	–	20	0	5

Key Votes

1) Busing	FOR	8) Sea Life Prot	FOR	15) Tax Singls Less	FOR
2) Alas P-line	AGN	9) Campaign Subs	FOR	16) Min Tax for Rich	FOR
3) Gun Cntrl	FOR	10) Cmbodia Bmbg	AGN	17) Euro Troop Rdctn	FOR
4) Rehnquist	AGN	11) Legal Srvices	FOR	18) Bust Hwy Trust	FOR
5) Pub TV $	FOR	12) Rev Sharing	FOR	19) Maid Min Wage	FOR
6) EZ Votr Reg	FOR	13) Cnsumr Prot	FOR	20) Farm Sub Limit	FOR
7) No-Fault	FOR	14) Eq Rts Amend	FOR	21) Highr Credt Chgs	AGN

Election Results

1972 general:	Walter F. Mondale (DFL)	981,320	(57%)
	Phil Hansen (R)	742,121	(43%)
1972 primary:	Walter F. Mondale (DFL)	230,679	(90%)
	Tom Griffin (DFL)	11,266	(4%)
	Richard Leaf (DFL)	7,750	(3%)
	Ralph E. Franklin (DFL)	6,946	(3%)
1966 general:	Walter F. Mondale (DFL)	685,840	(54%)
	Robert A. Forsythe (R)	574,868	(46%)

Senator

Hubert Horatio Humphrey, Jr. (D) Elected 1970 (previously U.S. Senator, 1948–64); seat up 1976; b. May 27, 1911, Wallace, S.D.; home, Minneapolis; Denver Col. of Pharmacy, 1932–33; U. of Minn., A.B., 1939; U. La., A.M., 1940; U. Minn. graduate studies, 1940–41; married, four children; Protestant.

Career Adm. Staff, WPA; Asst. State Supervisor, adult education, Minn.; war services div. chief, 1941–43; Asst. Dir. War Manpower Commission, 1943; vis. prof. of pol. science, Macalester Col., 1943–44; state campaign manager, Roosevelt-Truman campaign; Mayor, Minneapolis, 1945–48; U.S. Senate, 1949–64, Majority Whip, 1961–64; Vice Pres., 1965–69.

Offices 232 OSOB, 202-225-3244. Also 176 Fed. Bldg., Minneapolis 55401, 612-725-2533.

Administrative Assistant Kenneth E. Gray

Committees

Agriculture and Forestry (5th); Subs: Agricultural Credit and Rural Electrification; Agricultural Production, Marketing and Stabilization of Prices; Foreign Agricultural Policy (Chm.); Rural Development.

Foreign Relations (10th); Subs: Near-Eastern Affairs; Western Hemisphere Affairs; Arms Control, International Law and Organization; African Affairs (Chm.).

Joint Economic Com. (5th); Subs: Priorities and Economy in Government; Urban Affairs; International Economics; Consumer Economics (Chm.).

Sel. Com. on Nutrition and Human Needs (8th).

Group Ratings

	ADA	COPE	LWV	RIPON	NFU	LCV	CFA	NAB	NSI	ACA
1972	60	100	100	75	100	73	100	17	11	0
1971	89	91	100	70	100	–	100	–	–	3

Key Votes

1) Busing	AGN	8) Sea Life Prot	FOR	15) Tax Singls Less	FOR
2) Alas P-line	AGN	9) Campaign Subs	FOR	16) Min Tax for Rich	FOR
3) Gun Cntrl	FOR	10) Cmbodia Bmbg	AGN	17) Euro Troop Rdctn	AGN
4) Rehnquist	AGN	11) Legal Srvices	FOR	18) Bust Hwy Trust	AGN
5) Pub TV $	FOR	12) Rev Sharing	FOR	19) Maid Min Wage	FOR
6) EZ Votr Reg	ABS	13) Cnsumr Prot	FOR	20) Farm Sub Limit	FOR
7) No-Fault	FOR	14) Eq Rts Amend	FOR	21) Highr Credt Chgs	ABS

Election Results

1970 general:	Hubert H. Humphrey (DFL)	788,256	(58%)
	Clark MacGregor (R)	568,025	(42%)
1970 primary:	Hubert H. Humphrey (DFL)	388,705	(79%)
	Earl D. Craig, Jr. (DFL)	88,709	(21%)

FIRST DISTRICT Political Background

The 1st district of Minnesota, the southeast corner of the state, is a region of farms, grain elevators, and small industrial cities. This is the Minnesota district having the most in common with the rest of the rural Midwest farther south; in its ethnic and political traditions, it is much like Iowa—that is, WASPier and more Republican than Minnesota as a whole. The district's largest city, Rochester (pop. 53,000), is the home of the Mayo Clinic and until a few years ago of its onetime counsel and now Supreme Court Justice, Harry Blackmun. Rochester is a comparatively wealthy, idyllic, white-collar town. Olmsted County, of which it is a part, is the largest Minnesota county that failed to appear in the winning columns of either Hubert Humphrey or Walter Mondale, Senate candidates who otherwise won big in 1970 and 1972.

The only discordant political notes sounded in the 1st come out of the Minneapolis-St. Paul metropolitan area, parts of which were added to the district to meet the equal population standard. Here one finds the working-class suburbs of St. Paul, with the newly laid out subdivisions thinning out into Minnesota farmland. Though the suburbanites living in this part of the 1st vote DFL, its Republican Congressman, Albert Quie (pronounced *kwee*), has no trouble whatever district-wide.

In fact, Quie, who has served in the House since capturing a 1958 special election, wins every two years by the biggest margins of any Minnesota Republican. Early in his congressional career, Quie gave up a seat on the Agriculture Committee—a plum, it would seem, for any Congressman from this part of Minnesota—and moved to Education and Labor. Now, after a dozen years, the Congressman is the ranking minority member of the committee and an important shaper of legislation on a unit that possesses broad jurisdiction.

Quie's position on most educational and social issues appears to lie somewhere between those held by the committee's liberal Democrats and conservative Republicans. During the spate of Great Society legislation coming out of the Johnson Administration, House Republicans, under Gerald Ford, promised a series of alternatives to Democratic proposals; but the Republicans on Education and Labor, under Quie, were the only ones to have delivered very many alternatives. The Congressman has often mustered a committee majority by getting the votes of some of the more conservative Democrats on Education and Labor, especially the one belonging to Edith Green, but this high-ranking Democrat moved to the Appropriations Committee in 1971.

Typical of Quie's role in the legislative process was his fight for the Older Americans bill of 1973. The measure, which provides a variety of programs for senior citizens, enjoyed the Congressman's particular favor. It got through the committee, the House, and the Senate, only to be vetoed by President Nixon. Quie, who very much wanted some kind of bill, went to work on a compromise. He was able to produce a bill that the Democrats would support and that also won the approval of the usually intransigent Nixon White House.

Census Data Pop. 473,918. Central city, 11%; suburban, 43%. Median family income, $10,272; families above $15,000: 20%; families below $3,000: 8%. Median years education, 12.3.

1972 Share of Federal Outlays $372,512,281

DOD	$54,670,610	HEW	$158,408,941
AEC	$165,318	HUD	$4,231,789
NASA	$1,292,549	DOI	$3,106,891
DOT	$13,458,214	USDA	$61,815,187
		Other	$75,362,782

Federal Military-Industrial Commitments

No installations or contractors receiving prime awards greater than $5,000,000.

Economic Base Agriculture, notably dairy products, cattle, hogs and sheep, and grains; finance, insurance and real estate; food and kindred products; machinery; and fabricated metal products.

The Voters

Registration No district-wide registration.
Median voting age 42.1
Employment profile White collar, 46%. Blue collar, 30%. Service, 15%. Farm, 9%.
Ethnic groups Total foreign stock, 14%. Germany, 4%; Norway, 2%; Sweden, Canada, 1% each.

Presidential vote

1972	Nixon (R)	122,634	(60%)
	McGovern (D)	82,155	(40%)

1968	Nixon (R)	87,825	(47%)
	Humphrey (D)	91,415	(49%)
	Wallace (AI)	7,645	(4%)

Represenatative

Albert Harold Quie (R) Elected Feb. 1958; b. Sept. 18, 1923, Dennison; home, Dennison; St. Olaf Col., B.A., 1950; USN, WWII; married, five children; Lutheran.

Career Dairy farmer; State Senator, 1954–58; Sec., Board of Supv. of Rice County Soil Conservation Dist.

Offices 2182 RHOB, 202-225-2271; Also Rm. 436, First Natl. Bank Bldg., Rochester 55901, 507-288-2384, and 520 Fed. Bldg., Ft. Snelling, St. Paul 55111, 612-725-3680.

Administrative Assistant Vernon C. Loen

Committees

Education and Labor (Ranking Mbr.).

Group Ratings

	ADA	COPE	LWV	RIPON	NFU	LCV	CFA	NAB	NSI	ACA
1972	13	18	67	86	57	67	0	100	90	65
1971	35	17	56	83	53	–	38	–	–	69
1970	40	34	–	76	67	42	62	73	90	53

Key Votes

1) Busing	FOR	6) Cmbodia Bmbg	FOR	11) Chkg Acct Intrst	AGN
2) Strip Mines	AGN	7) Bust Hwy Trust	AGN	12) End HISC (HUAC)	ABS
3) Cut Mil $	AGN	8) Farm Sub Lmt	FOR	13) Nixon Sewer Veto	FOR
4) Rev Shrg	FOR	9) School Prayr	FOR	14) Corp Cmpaign $	FOR
5) Pub TV $	AGN	10) Cnsumr Prot	AGN	15) Pol $ Disclosr	FOR

Election Results

1972 general:	Albert H. Quie (R)	142,698	(71%)
	Charles S. Thompson (DFL)	59,106	(29%)
1972 primary:	Albert H. Quie (R), unopposed		
1970 general:	Albert H. Quie (R)	121,802	(69%)
	B. A. Lundeen (DFL)	53,995	(31%)

SECOND DISTRICT Political Background

South central Minnesota, most of which is included in the 2nd congressional district, is the most Republican part of the state. A majority of the people of the district live in the valley of the Minnesota River, where it flows into the Mississippi. The towns along the banks of the river, like New Ulm, Mankato, and St. Peter, are old, and their political allegiences are usually deeply rooted and Republican. To the southeast, the district includes the small industrial and usually Democratic city of Austin, on the Iowa border. Finally, as a result of the 1971 redistricting, the 2nd moves into the Twin Cities metropolitan area to take in the heavily Republican high-income territory around Lake Minnetonka and a politically marginal section of Dakota County, south of St. Paul.

Ancher Nelsen, the Congressman from the 2nd district, is the most conservative member of the Minnesota delegation. After a long career in state politics and a post in the Eisenhower Administration, Nelsen entered the House after the 1958 election. The Congressman is currently the second-ranking Republican on the Interstate and Foreign Commerce Committee, and the ranking minority member of its Public Health and Environment Subcommittee dominated by its Chairman, Paul Rogers of Florida.

But Nelsen's busiest area of legislative concern is the District of Columbia. As the ranking Republican on the District Committee, the Congressman is, at this writing, playing a critical role in whether the 93rd Congress will give the District home rule. In a sharp break from the past, the committee's Democrats are almost solidly for some kind of home rule legislation and have the votes to push a measure through the committee. But Nelsen, more than anyone, will determine whether the bill reported will get the necessary Republican support on the floor to pass. The Minnesotan is Chairman of the Nelsen Commission, which, upon an investigation of the District's government, made a number of recommendations for its reorganization. Accordingly, Nelsen has argued that any home rule measure should contain provisions for reorganization. Currently, the committee's Democrats are working closely with Nelsen, hoping to come up with a bill that will meet his approval.

Though Nelsen has predicted that there will be no home rule in 1973, chances are that some sort of bill will become law before the end of the 93rd Congress—thereby diminishing the power of the District Committee and its ranking minority member. This probability has fed speculation that Nelsen will reitre in 1974, when he will be 70. Up to now, he has regularly won reelection by solid margins, though his percentage was down notably in 1972. If he does not run, the district will be in for a hot succession fight. Like most of Minnesota, the 2nd has been trending toward the DFL.

Census Data Pop. 476,647. Central city, 0%; suburban, 19%. Median family income, $9,703; families above $15,000: 19%; families below $3,000: 9%. Median years education, 12.2.

1972 Share of Federal Outlays $463,981,765

DOD	$45,181,291	HEW	$153,189,326
AEC	$84,747	HUD	$4,617,615
NASA	$624,869	DOI	$1,823,045
DOT	$26,621,827	USDA	$164,155,372
		Other	$67,683,673

Federal Military-Industrial Commitments

DOD Contractors Downs Foods (Madelia), $8.922m: foodstuffs.

Economic Base Agriculture, notably grains, cattle, hogs and sheep, and dairy products; food and kindred products; finance, insurance and real estate; electrical equipment and supplies; and machinery. Also higher education (Mankato State).

The Voters

Registration No district-wide registration.
Median voting age 43.2
Employment profile White collar, 43%. Blue collar, 33%. Service, 12%. Farm, 12%.
Ethnic groups Total foreign stock, 14%. Germany, 5%; Norway, 2%; Sweden, 1%.

Presidential vote

1972	Nixon (R)	129,432	(59%)
	McGovern (D)	88,633	(41%)
1968	Nixon (R)	98,724	(50%)
	Humphrey (D)	90,522	(46%)
	Wallace (AI)	7,917	(4%)

Representative

Ancher Nelsen (R) Elected 1958; b. Oct. 11, 1904, Renville County; home, Hutchinson; married, three children; Lutheran.

Career State Senator, 1935–48; Lt. Gov., 1952; State Repub. Chm.

Offices 2329 RHOB, 202-225-2472. Also Citizens Bank Bldg., Hutchinson 55350, 612-879-2002.

Administrative Assistant Donald W. Olson

Committees

District of Columbia (Ranking Mbr.).

Interstate and Foreign Commerce (2nd); Sub: Public Health and Environment (Ranking Mbr.).

Group Ratings

	ADA	COPE	LWV	RIPON	NFU	LCV	CFA	NAB	NSI	ACA
1972	0	18	45	86	50	6	0	89	100	68
1971	11	9	33	40	43	–	29	–	–	85
1970	16	0	–	76	46	6	44	90	100	72

Key Votes

1) Busing	AGN	6) Cmbodia Bmbg	FOR	11) Chkg Acct Intrst	AGN
2) Strip Mines	AGN	7) Bust Hwy Trust	AGN	12) End HISC (HUAC)	AGN
3) Cut Mil $	AGN	8) Farm Sub Lmt	FOR	13) Nixon Sewer Veto	FOR
4) Rev Shrg	FOR	9) School Prayr	FOR	14) Corp Cmpaign $	AGN
5) Pub TV $	AGN	10) Cnsumr Prot	ABS	15) Pol $ Disclosr	AGN

Election Results

1972 general:	Ancher Nelson (R)	124,350	(57%)
	Charlie Turnbull (DFL)	93,433	(43%)
1972 primary:	Ancher Nelson (R), unopposed		
1970 general:	Ancher Nelson (R)	94,080	(63%)
	Clifford R. Adams (DFL)	54,498	(37%)

THIRD DISTRICT Political Background

The Minneapolis suburbs constitute the fastest-growing part of Minnesota. The gravity of metropolitan development appears to be pulling people to territory west of Minneapolis, with much of the magnetism supplied by the booming white-collar industries of the Minneapolis area. Companies like Honeywell, 3M, General Mills, Control Data, and Investors Diversified Services are based in the Twin Cities. Most of the suburban growth has occurred in a string of cities and townships lying west and southwest of Minneapolis; these, along with 18,000 residents of the city itself, make up the 3rd congressional district.

Like most suburban districts, the 3rd is not a sociological monolith. At the northern edge of the district, along the Mississippi as it flows into Minneapolis, are blue-collar suburbs like Brooklyn Park (pop. 26,000) and Brooklyn Center (pop. 35,000). At the far southern end are upper-middle-income Richfield (pop. 47,000) and Bloomington (pop. 82,000), the latter the state's fourth largest city and site of the stadium where the Twins and Vikings play baseball and football. Lying in the middle of the district are high-income WASP retreats like Plymouth, Golden Valley, and Minnetonka, along with Edina (pop. 44,000) at the southwest corner of Minneapolis. Edina is one of the state's highest-income and most Republican towns. Just north of Edina is the predominantly Jewish suburb of St. Louis Park (pop. 49,000), which as much as any place holds the political balance in the 3rd.

Despite the wealth in the district, it is by no means heavily Republican. By most standards, the 3rd must be considered marginal. It has, however, elected only Republican Congressmen in the past dozen years. From 1961 to 1971, the district sent Clark MacGregor, then one of the most competent Republicans on the Hill, to Washington. In 1970, he sacrificed himself and ran against Hubert Humphrey for the senate; for this, he was rewarded by the Nixon Administration with the post of chief congressional lobbyist. And when John Mitchell left the Committee to Reelect the President just after the Watergate break-in, MacGregor succeeded him. According to Robert Mardian, a Mitchell aide, the ex-Congressman took the job only after assurances from the White House that nobody from Nixon's staff or CREEP was involved in the burglary. Mardian also said before the Ervin Committee that he tried to tell MacGregor differently, but that MacGregor insisted upon standing by his assurances and wanted to hear no more. But immediately after the election, the Minnesotan resigned to take a job in the private sector as a Washington lobbyist.

When MacGregor ran for the Senate in 1970, there was an exceedingly close race to succeed him in the 3rd district, which then encompassed a bit more terrain. The winner, by a 3,000-vote margin, was Bill Frenzel, a moderate-to-liberal Republican who had been a member of the Minnesota House since 1962. A well-publicized Frenzel trip to Israel may have accounted for the margin: a Minneapolis *Tribune* survey showed the candidate running 30% ahead of the Republican ticket in selected St. Louis Park precincts.

In the House, Frenzel often votes like a liberal, though he did go along with other House Republicans on the Banking Committee and voted thumbs down on a Watergate investigation in October 1972. Back home, he appears to have tended district matters to the satisfaction of his constituents. After a 51% victory in 1970, he got 63% of the votes in 1972—some 4% better than Nixon's showing in the 3rd of Minnesota.

Census Data Pop. 472,662. Central city, 4%; suburban, 96%. Median family income, $13,248; families above $15,000: 38%; families below $3,000: 3%. Median years education, 12.7.

1972 Share of Federal Outlays $484,981,030

DOD	$133,228,623	HEW	$152,361,020
AEC	$453,494	HUD	$11,608,464
NASA	$3,343,755	DOI	$6,612,846
DOT	$16,878,903	USDA	$57,751,730
		Other	$102,742,195

Federal Military-Industrial Commitments

DOD Contractors Honeywell (Hopkins), $36.560m: bombs, mines, grenades, mortars, and various detonating devices. Honeywell (St. Louis Park, $36.096m: anti-personnel bombs.

Economic Base Finance, insurance and real estate; machinery; instruments and related products; printing and publishing, especially commercial printing; and tourism.

The Voters

Registration No district-wide registration.
Median voting age 39.1
Employment profile White collar, 64%. Blue collar, 26%. Service, 10%. Farm, –%.
Ethnic groups Total foreign stock, 16%. Sweden, 3%; Norway, Germany, Canada, 2% each.

Presidential vote

1972	Nixon (R)	129,587	(59%)
	McGovern (D)	89,281	(41%)
1968	Nixon (R)	89,127	(46%)
	Humphrey (D)	98,643	(51%)
	Wallace (AI)	6,572	(3%)

Representative

Bill Frenzel (R) Elected 1970; b. July 31, 1929, St. Paul; home, Golden Valley; Dartmouth Col., B.A., 1950, M.B.A., 1951; USNR 1951–54; married, three children.

Career Minneapolis Terminal Warehouse Co., 1954–62, Pres., 1960–70; State Rep., 1962–70.

Offices 1026 LHOB, 202-225-2871. Also 120 U.S. Courthouse, Minneapolis 55401, 612-725-2173, and 3601 Park Ctr. Blvd., St. Louis Park 55416, 612-925-4540.

Administrative Assistant Richard Willow

Committees

Banking and Currency (12th); Subs: Domestic Finance; International Finance; International Trade.

House Administration (8th); Subs: Elections; Library and Memorials.

Group Ratings

	ADA	COPE	LWV	RIPON	NFU	LCV	CFA	NAB	NSI	ACA
1972	63	18	92	100	57	79	100	90	50	32
1971	65	25	75	100	43	–	40	–	–	50

Key Votes

1) Busing	FOR	6) Cmbodia Bmbg	AGN	11) Chkg Acct Intrst	FOR
2) Strip Mines	AGN	7) Bust Hwy Trust	FOR	12) End HISC (HUAC)	FOR
3) Cut Mil $	FOR	8) Farm Sub Lmt	FOR	13) Nixon Sewer Veto	FOR
4) Rev Shrg	FOR	9) School Prayr	AGN	14) Corp Cmpaign $	AGN
5) Pub TV $	FOR	10) Cnsumr Prot	FOR	15) Pol $ Disclosr	FOR

Election Results

1972 general:	Bill Frenzel (R)	132,638	(63%)
	Jim Bell (DFL)	66,070	(31%)
	Donald Wright (Minnesota Taxpayers Party)	12,234	(6%)
1972 primary:	Bill Frenzel (R)	20,278	(93%)
	William Schnase (R)	1,498	(7%)
1970 general:	Bill Frenzel (R)	110,921	(51%)
	George Rice (DFL)	108,141	(49%)

FOURTH DISTRICT Political Background

St. Paul, the smaller of the Twin Cities, is an old river town with a history much like that of St. Louis, Missouri, farther down the Mississippi. Settled before Minneapolis, St. Paul was for some years the larger of the two, as the state's capital city attracted great numbers of Irish and German-Catholic immigrants. St. Paul got its start as a transportation hub—a railroad center and river port; Minneapolis, on the other hand, was from the beginning a grain-milling center and remains the nation's largest such center to this day. Long before the DFL was organized, St. Paul's early immigrants gave the place a Democratic stamp, one that the city and its suburbs have retained ever since.

In these one-man-one-vote times, the 4th district of Minnesota is the closest thing to a congressional district totally coincident with a single county. The 4th includes all but the tiniest smidgin of Ramsey County, of which St. Paul is the county seat. A solidly Democratic district, the 4th was represented for 10 years, from 1949 to 1959, by Eugene J. McCarthy. As a young politician, McCarthy was not one to dabble in poetry, but a team player, one of the founders of the liberal Democratic Study Group; he busied himself doing all the tiresome chores politicians feel they must perform to survive.

McCarthy won election to the Senate in 1958. His successor and present 4th district Congressman is a rather different sort: Democrat Joseph E. Karth, a former union negogiator and state legislator. More interested in the nuts and bolts of legislation, Karth served for many years on committees with important economic impact on his district, but with little national éclat. These were Science and Astronautics, and Merchant Marine and Fisheries. At the beginning of the 93rd Congress, however, he switched to Wilbur Mills' Ways and Means Committee, giving up valuable seniority to take a seat on the tax-writing panel. Over the years, Karth has won 100% ratings from COPE, and as an old labor man, the Congressman will make sure that the counsels of organized labor are not totally ignored in Mills' committee room.

Reelection is usually no problem for Karth, though he was held down to 53% of the vote in 1966, a good Republican year. In 1972, he received 72%, and appears assured of a long and continuing career in the House.

Census Data Pop. 473,902. Central city, 65%; suburban, 35%. Median family income, $11,306; families above $15,000: 26%; families below $3,000: 6%. Median years education, 12.4.

1972 Share of Federal Outlays $486,283,742

DOD	$133,586,489	HEW	$152,770,278
AEC	$454,712	HUD	$11,639,646
NASA	$3,352,737	DOI	$6,630,609
DOT	$16,924,242	USDA	$57,906,858
		Other	$103,081,171

Federal Military-Industrial Commitments

DOD Contractors Sperry Rand (St. Paul), $87.417m: various computers and computer services. Northwest Airlines (St. Paul), $23.395m: transportation services. Honeywell (New Brighton), $20.934m: bombs and grenade fuzes.

Economic Base Machinery, especially electronic computing equipment; finance, insurance and real estate; printing and publishing, especially commercial printing; food and kindred products; and fabricated metal products, especially fabricated structural metal products.

The Voters

Registration No district-wide registration.
Median voting age 41.5
Employment profile White collar, 56%. Blue collar, 31%. Service, 13%. Farm, –%.
Ethnic groups Black, 2%. Total foreign stock, 19%. Germany, 3%; Sweden, Canada, 2% each; Norway, 1%.

Presidential vote

1972	Nixon (R)	95,201	(47%)
	McGovern (D)	107,924	(53%)
1968	Nixon (R)	63,721	(33%)
	Humphrey (D)	122,174	(62%)
	Wallace (AI)	8,517	(4%)

Representative

Joseph E. Karth (D) Elected 1958; b. Aug. 26, 1922, New Brighton; home, St. Paul; U. of Neb.; Army, WWII; married, three children; Presbyterian.

Career Labor-management relations for Oil, Chemical and Atomic Workers, 1947–58; State Rep., 1950–58.

Offices 2408 RHOB, 202-225-6631. Also 544 Fed. Cts. Bldg., St. Paul 55101, 202-225-6631.

Administrative Assistant Robert E. Hess

Committees

Ways and Means (15th).

Group Ratings

	ADA	COPE	LWV	RIPON	NFU	LCV	CFA	NAB	NSI	ACA
1972	88	89	100	73	86	68	50	0	0	0
1971	86	83	100	78	100	–	100	–	–	12
1970	88	100	–	60	92	71	82	0	22	12

Key Votes

1) Busing	FOR	6) Cmbodia Bmbg	AGN	11) Chkg Acct Intrst	FOR
2) Strip Mines	AGN	7) Bust Hwy Trust	FOR	12) End HISC (HUAC)	FOR
3) Cut Mil $	ABS	8) Farm Sub Lmt	ABS	13) Nixon Sewer Veto	AGN
4) Rev Shrg	FOR	9) School Prayr	AGN	14) Corp Cmpaign $	FOR
5) Pub TV $	FOR	10) Cnsumr Prot	FOR	15) Pol $ Disclosr	AGN

Election Results

1972 general:	Joseph E. Karth (DFL)	138,292	(72%)
	Steve Thompson (R)	52,786	(28%)
1972 primary:	Joseph E. Karth (DFL), unopposed		
1970 general:	Joseph E. Karth (DFL)	131,263	(74%)
	Frank L. Loss (R)	45,680	(26%)

FIFTH DISTRICT Political Background

The 5th district of Minnesota comprises virtually all of the city of Minneapolis and a couple of blue-collar suburbs in Anoka County just to the north. Minneapolis, the nation's premier grain-milling center, is the final destination of all the grain stored in the giant elevators of the northern prairies. The now high-priced wheat, oats, and barley comes to Minneapolis to be turned into Pillsbury flour, Bisquick, Cream of Wheat, and hundreds of other similarly packaged items. Minneapolis also contains several large, growing, and technologically sophisticated industries (see Minnesota 3) that have made the city and its metropolitan area one of the healthiest to be found on the Great Plains.

But the great business firms of Minneapolis do not account for the city's distinctive political tradition. This comes instead from the Swedish and other Scandinavian immigrants who have lived in Minneapolis since the 1880s. The Scandinavians were probably attracted to Minnesota for two reasons: first, the resemblance of the American north country, with its hilly countryside, thousands of glacier-carved lakes, and long cold winters, to the Europe of Scandinavia; and second, economic opportunities were to be found in Minnesota which native-stock Americans, eager to head straight west out of Illinois and Missouri, failed to pursue. The Scandinavians have given Minneapolis, which is still practically all white (96%), a liberal political tradition, hospitable to the Harold Stassens of the Republican party and the Hubert Humphreys of the DFL. Humphrey, in fact, was Mayor here from 1943 to 1948.

It was therefore a surprise when liberal academic Arthur Naftalin was succeeded as Mayor of Minneapolis in 1969 by a law- and-order man, ex-police detective Charles Stenvig. By big-city standards, Minneapolis is relatively placid; but Stenvig, a quasi-populist, apparently reached something in the make-up of the older, lower-income whites left behind in the city, as others made the great exodus to the suburbs during the 1960s. These whites supplied Stenvig with many votes, which could not be countered by any coming from blacks—Minneapolis simply has no large black community. Another factor behind Stenvig's victory was a split between labor and the peace-oriented elements of the DFL. The McCarthy people took over the party apparatus here in 1968, but efforts to deliver votes for their candidates have failed dismally. By 1971 the more disciplined labor troops, once opposed to Stenvig, wound up supporting him.

One politician left uncomfortable by the local labor-McCarthy split is Congressman Donald M. Fraser, a vigorous opponent of the war with longtime ties to the Humphrey and labor wings of the DFL. Fraser won his seat from veteran (1943–63) Rep. Walter Judd, keynoter at the 1960 Republican Convention and unofficial head of the old China Lobby. Fraser achieved his first victory in 1962 with some redistricting help and a tough campaign, and for the next few elections, the incumbent had little trouble. But after the Stenvig victory, Fraser began to draw opposition from law-and-order Republicans, and in 1972 from a candidate of the Minnesota Taxpayers party, who got 8% of the votes. Nevertheless, Fraser occupies what must be considered a safe seat.

In the past few years, Fraser has devoted a great deal of time to extracurricular activities. Aside from membership on the Foreign Affairs and District of Columbia committees, he served as Chairman of the liberal Democratic Study Group during the 91st Congress (1969–71). Then in 1971 and 1972, he led the Democratic party's commission that reformed the delegation selection procedures to the national convention. Finally, in the spring of 1973, Fraser was elected national Chairman of the Americans for Democratic Action. Were he from virtually any other state, the Congressman would have long since run for the Senate. But Minnesota and the DFL are top-heavy with political talent. Moreover, Fraser would never challenge two old friends, Hubert Humphrey and Walter Mondale.

Census Data Pop. 479,280. Central city, 87%; suburban, 13%. Median family income, $10,323; families above $15,000: 22%; families below $3,000: 8%. Median years education, 12.3.

1972 Share of Federal Outlays $491,680,691

DOD	$135,069,080	HEW	$154,465,777
AEC	$459,759	HUD	$11,768,827
NASA	$3,389,947	DOI	$6,704,198
DOT	$17,112,073	USDA	$58,549,528
		Other	$104,161,602

Federal Military-Industrial Commitments

DOD Contractors Honeywell (Minneapolis), $71.483m: aircraft navigation and target acquisition systems. Federal Cartridge Corp. (Minneapolis), $55.700m: operation of Twin Cities Army Ammunition plant. FMC Corp. (Fridley), $53.337m: gun mounts; guided missile launching systems. Control Data (Minneapolis), $16.798m: lease and maintenance of data processing equipment. FMC Corp. (Minneapolis), $15.924m: gun mounts and guided missile launching systems.

Economic Base Finance, insurance and real estate; machinery; instruments and related products; printing and publishing, especially commercial printing; fabricated metal products; and food and kindred products, especially beverages. Also higher education (Univ. of Minnesota).

The Voters

Registration No district-wide registration.
Median voting age 42.3

Employment profile White collar, 55%. Blue collar, 30%. Service, 15%. Farm, –%.
Ethnic groups Black, 4%. Total foreign stock, 23%. Sweden, 5%; Norway, 4%; Germany, 3%; Canada, 2%; Poland, 1%.

Presidential vote

1972	Nixon (R)	92,951	(44%)
	McGovern (D)	116,090	(56%)
1968	Nixon (R)	75,684	(36%)
	Humphrey (D)	123,092	(59%)
	Wallace (AI)	9,161	(4%)

Representative

Donald M. Fraser (D) Elected 1962; b. Feb. 20, 1924, Minneapolis; home, Minneapolis; U. of Minn., B.A., 1944, LL.B., 1948; USNR, WWII; married, six children.

Career Atty., 1948–62; State Senator, 1954–62.

Offices 1111 Cannon House Bldg., 202-225-4755. Also 180 Fed. Cts. Bldg., Minneapolis 55401, 612-725-2081.

Administrative Assistant Dale MacIver

Committees

District of Columbia (2nd); Subs: Government Operations; Labor, Social Services, and the International Community.

Foreign Affairs (8th); Subs: International Organizations and Movements (Chm.); National Security Policy and Scientific Developments; State Department Organization and Foreign Operations.

Group Ratings

	ADA	COPE	LWV	RIPON	NFU	LCV	CFA	NAB	NSI	ACA
1972	94	90	100	75	100	80	100	9	0	5
1971	100	83	89	83	92	–	86	–	–	7
1970	96	100	–	82	85	100	100	0	0	12

Key Votes

1) Busing	FOR	6) Cmbodia Bmbg	AGN	11) Chkg Acct Intrst	ABS
2) Strip Mines	AGN	7) Bust Hwy Trust	FOR	12) End HISC (HUAC)	FOR
3) Cut Mil $	FOR	8) Farm Sub Lmt	AGN	13) Nixon Sewer Veto	AGN
4) Rev Shrg	FOR	9) School Prayr	AGN	14) Corp Cmpaign $	AGN
5) Pub TV $	ABS	10) Cnsumr Prot	FOR	15) Pol $ Disclosr	FOR

Election Results

1972 general:	Donald M. Fraser (DFL)	135,108	(66%)
	Allan Davisson (R)	50,014	(24%)
	Norm Selby (Minnesota Taxpayers Party)	15,845	(8%)
	William E. Peterson (SW)	4,233	(2%)
1972 primary:	Donald M. Fraser (DFL), unopposed		
1970 general:	Donald M. Fraser (DFL)	82,307	(57%)
	Dick Enroth (R)	61,682	(43%)
	Derrel Myers (SW)	783	(1%)

SIXTH DISTRICT Political Background

The 6th district of Minnesota is farm country, the beginnings of the great wheat fields that sweep across Minnesota into the Dakotas and Montana. Long freight trains move through the landscape—part of the empire of immigrant James J. Hill, the "Empire Builder," and the Great Northern Railway. The groaning, though still magnificent, diesel engines pull cars west to the Pacific or east to St. Paul and Chicago; engines and cars whiz through dozens of little crossroads towns, each with a grain elevator and a depot. The voting patterns of the 6th, the state's most marginal district, record the ethnic groups James J. Hill himself induced to settle this part of Minnesota: Republican Norwegians and WASPs, Democratic Swedes, and ticket-switching German Catholics.

The German population here is most heavily concentrated in Stearns County, which contains St. Cloud (pop. 39,000) and Sauk Centre (pop. 3,000). The latter was the boyhood home of Sinclair Lewis and the fictional home of many of the author's ugly Americans. Up until the outbreak of World War I, the nineteenth-century German immigrants who settled in places like St. Louis, Milwaukee, and the 6th district of Minnesota came to be regarded as the nation's "best" immigrants: thrifty and hardworking, just like the Yankee old stock. So thrifty and hardworking, one imagines, that a German-American could easily come to inhabit the *Main Street* of Sinclair Lewis.

Politically, the German of Stearns are Democrats by tradition, but they have often supported Republican candidates. As Samuel Lubell says in *The Future of American Politics*, German-Americans were the nation's prototypical isolationists—against intervention in the days before World War I and II not so much for abstract reasons as out of a desire to avoid war with the old homeland. Though the Germans were the most intense isolationsists, they were often joined by Scandinavians. This ethnic combination produced the country's most powerful isolationist voting bloc in Minnesota and its neighbors, Wisconsin and the Dakotas.

Stearns County, by far the largest in the district, has played a pivotal role in the last two congressional elections. Contests are usually close; only once in the last 12 years has any candidate won with as much as 56% of the votes. The current incumbent, Republican John Zwach, was first elected in 1966, after spending twenty years in the legislature, including eight as state Senate Majority Leader. In 1966, he edged DFL incumbent Alec Olson and won reelection in 1968 with 56%.

That 56% was Zwach's best performance. In 1970, his margin was only 7,000 votes, with a 4,000-vote Republican bulge in Stearns County. And in 1972 the race was even closer. Zwach edged out 28-year-old state Rep. Richard Nolan by only 4,500 votes—even though redistricting had helped Republicans—and in the summer of 1973, the 66-year-old incumbent announced that he would not run again in 1974.

The closeness of the 1972 result is symptomatic of recent shifts in opinion in the Upper Midwest. Nolan campaigned strongly in favor of public financing of elections and opening up the legislative process; he scored points by disclosing all his campaign contributions and his personal finances. The voters here were obviously not pleased with Zwach's refusal to do so—and this was well before Watergate became a household word. In addition, Nolan was helped by the 18-year-old vote; with the help of the 9,000 student votes at St. Cloud State College, he was able to carry Stearns County this time.

As for 1974, Nolan was hitting the factory gates and announcing his candidacy the morning after the 1972 results came in, and, despite the rumors around at this writing, Nolan appears a clear favorite. He appears to have a solid hold on the DFL endorsement—politicians in Minnesota usually defer to the party conventions and avoid primaries—and Zwach's retirement simply underlines the fact that it looks like a DFL year in the 6th district in 1974.

Census Data   Pop. 476,748. Central city, 0%; suburban, 6%. Median family income, $7,984; families above $15,000: 12%; families below $3,000: 13%. Median years education, 11.5.

1972 Share of Federal Outlays $455,550,325

DOD	$,075,322	HEW	$161,870,278
AEC	$1,913,202	HUD	$2,248,229
NASA	$189,899	DOI	$1,410,996
DOT	$15,376,343	USDA	$182,840,962
		Other	$75,625,094

Federal Military-Industrial Commitments

No installations or contractors receiving prime awards greater than $5,000,000.

Economic Base Agriculture, notably grains, cattle, hogs and sheep, and dairy products; food and kindred products; machinery; finance, insurance and real estate; and instruments and related products. Also higher education (St. Cloud State).

The Voters

> *Registration* No district-wide registration.
> *Median voting age* 46.0
> *Employment profile* White collar, 38%. Blue collar, 30%. Service, 13%. Farm, 19%.
> *Ethnic groups* Total foreign stock, 18%. Germany, 6%; Norway, Sweden, 3% each.

Presidential vote

1972	Nixon (R)	114,196	(53%)
	McGovern (D)	102,231	(47%)
1968	Nixon (R)	90,969	(45%)
	Humphrey (D)	98,899	(49%)
	Wallace (AI)	10,101	(5%)

Representative

John M. Zwach (R) Elected 1966; b. Feb. 8, 1907, Gales Township; home, Walnut Grove; U. of Minn., B.S., 1933; married, five children; Catholic.

Career State Rep., 1934–46; State Senator, 1946–66; Majority Leader, 1959–66.

Offices 1502 LHOB, 202-225-2331. Also 216 Fed. Bldg., St. Cloud 56301, 612-251-2120.

Administrative Assistant Arthur A. Graf, Jr.

Committees

Agriculture (6th); Subs: Dairy and Poulty; Livestock and Grains; Conservation and Credit (Ranking Mbr.).

Veterans' Affairs (5th); Subs: Education and Training; Hospitals; Insurance (Ranking Mbr.).

Group Ratings

	ADA	COPE	LWV	RIPON	NFU	LCV	CFA	NAB	NSI	ACA
1972	38	55	75	78	83	40	50	73	78	27
1971	41	25	67	76	73	–	75	–	–	64
1970	44	50	–	73	82	61	68	64	89	56

Key Votes

1) Busing	FOR	6) Cmbodia Bmbg	AGN	11) Chkg Acct Intrst	AGN
2) Strip Mines	AGN	7) Bust Hwy Trust	AGN	12) End HISC (HUAC)	AGN
3) Cut Mil $	ABS	8) Farm Sub Lmt	FOR	13) Nixon Sewer Veto	FOR
4) Rev Shrg	FOR	9) School Prayr	FOR	14) Corp Cmpaign $	AGN
5) Pub TV $	AGN	10) Cnsumr Prot	FOR	15) Pol $ Disclosr	FOR

Election Results

1972 general:	John M. Zwach (R)	114,537	(51%)
	Richard M. Nolan (DFL)	109,955	(49%)
1972 primary:	John M. Zwach (R), unopposed		

1970 general: John M. Zwach (R) 88,753   (52%)
                 Terry Montgomery (DFL) 81,004   (47%)
                 Richard Martin (Ind.) 1,625   (1%)

SEVENTH DISTRICT   Political Background

The 7th district of Minnesota lies to the north and west in the state. This is the most sparsely populated part of Minnesota, containing some 39% of its land area, though only 12% of its people. Along the Red River Valley of the north are wheat fields, while the rest of the 7th is composed of lakes, forests, and resorts. This is the legendary country of Paul Bunyan and his blue ox Babe, whose statues stand together in Bemidji, a small town on the shores of one of Minnesota's 10,000 lakes. Another one of these is Lake Itasca, the headwaters of the Mississippi River.

The district was settled by hardy Swedish and Norwegian lumberjacks and farmers. It is today one of the state's more marginal districts; like the 6th, the 7th usually votes for winners in statewide contests, with its congressional races traditionally close. Only twice in the last 15 years has the victor here won more than 55% of the votes. The Republican stronghold in the 7th is heavily Norwegian Otter Tail County, near the southern end of the district; the strongest DFL territory is to the north, where the farmers of the once radical prairies constituted the backbone of the state's old Farmer-Labor party.

During the 1950s, DFL Rep. Coya Knutson of the 7th made newspapers all over the country. Her husband issued a public statement urging her to come home and mind housewifely duties. This act of male chauvinism apparently produced what Mr. Knutson wanted; Ms. Knutson lost her job in the otherwise big Democratic year of 1958. (The Knutsons were divorced in 1962, but Coya never returned to Congress.) The winner in 1958 was state legislator Odin Langen, who eventually spent six terms in the House; but apart from the Republican year of 1966, he barely managed to hold on each time out. And each time, Langen, one of Minnesota's most conservative Republicans, was a prime DFL target. In 1968, despite 10 years of incumbency, challenger Bob Bergland came within 4,000 votes of unseating Langen. In 1970, Bergland decided to try again.

Bergland possessed good credentials. He had worked in the Department of Agriculture in Washington, then returned to his farm in Roseau County on the Manitoba border. (Only Congressman Don Young of Alaska has a residence farther north.) Because districts in the farm belt tend to vote against the party of the national administration in power, Bergland in 1970 cultivated an advantage. He was an outspoken critic of Nixon Administration farm policies, objecting to them in one of the nation's most agricultural House districts. Langen bravely, though perhaps unwisely, defended the Administration. In 1970, Langen's task was as thankless as it had been in the days of Ezra Taft Benson, a demon among farmers whose name still crops up in Hubert Humphrey's oratory. With Humphrey at the top of the ticket, the DFL in 1970 was organized as never before; and in the 7th, the party conducted an elaborate get-out-the-vote campaign with help of computers. Voter turnout dropped only 9% from the presidential year of 1968—the smallest such dip among Minnesota districts—which probably accounted for the difference. Bergland won by a 54–46 margin, one of the best showings made against an incumbent Congressman in recent years anywhere in the nation.

After going to Washington, Bergland of course wanted and got a seat on the Agriculture Committee, where he is a vehement critic of Nixon Administration plans to end farm subsidies. Wheat, the main crop in the 7th, has over the years been supported by public money whenever the price per bushel fell below a specified level. But thanks to the Russian wheat deal, the commodity of late has been doing very nicely, and in 1973, Congress shifted to a policy of supporting farmers' income, rather than commodity prices. Bergland's performance in Congress has apparently satisfied constituents back home. In 1972, he carried 25 of the district's 28 counties, taking 59% of the votes—the biggest margin the 7th has given any congressional candidate in a long, long time. All indications are that Bergland has converted the chronically marginal 7th into a safe DFL seat.

Census Data   Pop. 472,753. Central city, 6%; suburban, 4%. Median family income, $7,089; families above $15,000: 10%; families below $3,000: 17%. Median years education, 10.9.

1972 Share of Federal Outlays $470,165,623

DOD	$13,581,000	HEW	$196,869,686
AEC	–	HUD	$1,501,373
NASA	–	DOI	$4,572,896
DOT	$7,353,067	USDA	$175,595,275
		Other	$70,692,326

Federal Military-Industrial Commitments

DOD Installations Baudette AF Station (Baudette).

Economic Base Agriculture, notably grains, dairy products, cattle and poultry; finance, insurance and real estate; food and kindred products; transportation equipment, especially boat building and repairing; and lumber and wood products.

The Voters

Registration No district-wide registration.
Median voting age 48.4
Employment profile White collar, 39%. Blue collar, 28%. Service, 15%. Farm, 18%.
Ethnic groups Total foreign stock, 21%. Norway, 7%; Germany, Sweden, 4% each; Canada, 2%.

Presidential vote

1972	Nixon (R)	118,727	(54%)
	McGovern (D)	100,410	(46%)
1968	Nixon (R)	94,790	(46%)
	Humphrey (D)	100,375	(48%)
	Wallace (AI)	10,253	(5%)

Representative

Bob Bergland (D) Elected 1970; b. July 22, 1925, Roseau; home, Roseau; U. of Minn., 1946–48; married, seven children; Lutheran.

Career Farmer, Midwest area Dir. of Agric. Stabilization and Conservation Service, 1961–68; Sec. and Chm., Roseau County Democratic Farmer Labor Party of Minn., 1951–54.

Offices 1008 LHOB, 202-225-2165. Also 920 28th Ave. South, Moorehead 56560, 218-236-5050.

Administrative Assistant Ron Schrader

Committees

Agriculture (13th); Subs: Livestock and Grains; Conservation and Credit; Dairy and Poultry.

Science and Astronautics (12th); Subs: Energy; Manned Space Flight; Space Science and Applications.

Sel. Com. on Small Business (12th); Subs: Environmental Problems Affecting Small Busines; Minority Small Business Enterprise and Franchising.

Group Ratings

	ADA	COPE	LWV	RIPON	NFU	LCV	CFA	NAB	NSI	ACA
1972	75	82	91	81	100	50	0	0	10	0
1971	86	83	100	83	100	–	88	–	–	3

Key Votes

1) Busing	FOR	6) Cmbodia Bmbg	AGN	11) Chkg Acct Intrst	AGN
2) Strip Mines	AGN	7) Bust Hwy Trust	AGN	12) End HISC (HUAC)	ABS
3) Cut Mil $	FOR	8) Farm Sub Lmt	AGN	13) Nixon Sewer Veto	AGN
4) Rev Shrg	FOR	9) School Prayr	AGN	14) Corp Cmpaign $	FOR
5) Pub TV $	FOR	10) Cnsumr Prot	FOR	15) Pol $ Disclosr	FOR

Election Results

1972 general:	Bob Bergland (DFL)	133,067	(59%)
	Jon Haaven (R)	92,283	(41%)
1972 primary:	Bob Bergland (DFL), unopposed		
1970 general:	Bob Bergland (DFL)	79,378	(54%)
	Odin Langen (R)	67,296	(46%)

EIGHTH DISTRICT Political Background

The 8th district of Minnesota comprises the northeast corner of the state. Like the 7th, most of the district is composed of lakes and forests, but the 8th has fewer farmers, with most of the people here concentrated in a few urban areas. Because of redistricting, the 8th currently reaches south to Anoka County—Democratic suburban territory that is part of the Minneapolis-St. Paul metropolitan area. But the focus of the district is still St. Louis County, in the Lake Superior port of Duluth (pop. 101,000) and the towns of the Mesabi Range. This part of Minnesota, of course, has long been the nation's leading source of iron ore, which is dug out of the Mesabi, sent by rail to Duluth, loaded on giant freighters plying the Great Lakes, and headed toward Chicago, Gary, Detroit, Cleveland, and Pittsburgh.

The men who came to work the mines and the Duluth docks were mostly Swedes, Finns, Norwegians, Italians, Poles, and Yugoslavs. Their ethnic background and difficult economic lot disposed them toward the Democratic-Farmer-Labor party. That DFL loyalty has been intensified now that the region has fallen into economic decline—both Duluth and the Mesabi towns are losing population. The 8th is the number-one DFL congressional district in Minnesota.

It is a measure of DFL strength here that DFL Congressman John Blatnik was first elected to Congress in 1946, one of the best Republican years of the century. Blatnik, who won 76% in 1972, has never had to worry about reelection and probably never will. In 1970, with the primary defeat of Baltimore's George Fallon, Blatnik became Chairman of the House Public Works Committee.

Because the Minnesotan had compiled a solidly liberal voting record, environmentalists hoped that the pork-barreling committee, under Blatnik's chairmanship, would undergo a change in orientation. But Blatnik went along with the committee's majority when it refused to crack the highway trust for mass transit needs. In general, the Congressman has not pushed environmental legislation as actively as many had wanted. Blatnik, who will be 63 in 1974, belongs to the generation for which the Depression was the single most traumatic event. During the Depression, building roads and canals and reclaiming land did not mean despoiling the earth, but creating jobs for people who would otherwise go hungry. But if Blatnik has disappointed ecology activists, he has not, as others before him, used the power of the Public Works Committee to allocate projects for short-term political advantage or to enhance his personal leverage within the House.

Census Data Pop. 479,159. Central city, 21%; suburban, 46%. Median family income, $9,393; families above $15,000: 14%; families below $3,000: 9%. Median years education, 12.1.

1972 Share of Federal Outlays $383,781,589

DOD	$61,195,585	HEW	$172,755,335
AEC	$96,407	HUD	$5,232,103
NASA	$710,837	DOI	$2,786,541
DOT	$16,281,894	USDA	$31,802,432
		Other	$92,920,455

Federal Military-Industrial Commitments

DOD Installations Finland AF Station (Finland).

Economic Base Iron ore mining; agriculture, notably dairy products, dairy cattle, cattle and poultry; finance, insurance and real estate; primary metal industries, especially blast furnace and steel mill products; and machinery.

The Voters

> *Registration* No district-wide registration.
> *Median voting age* 44.0
> *Employment profile* White collar, 41%. Blue collar, 42%. Service, 14%. Farm, 3%.
> *Ethnic groups* Total foreign stock, 24%. Sweden, 5%; Finland, 4%; Norway, 3%; Canada, Germany, 2% each.

Presidential vote

1972	Nixon (R)	95,536	(45%)
	McGovern (D)	115,622	(55%)
1968	Nixon (R)	57,803	(29%)
	Humphrey (D)	132,618	(66%)
	Wallace (AI)	8,765	(4%)

Representative

John A. Blatnik (D) Elected 1947; b. Aug. 17, 1911, Chisholm; home, Chisholm; Winona State Col., B.E., 1935; U. of Chicago; U. of Minn., 1941–42; Army Air Corps., WWII; married, three children; Catholic.

Career Teacher, school administration, 1932–40; State Senator, 1941–46.

Offices 2449 RHOB, 202-225-6211. Also 412 Fed. Bldg., Duluth 55802, 218-727-7474.

Administrative Assistant James L. Oberstar

Committees

Public Works (Chm.).

Group Ratings

	ADA	COPE	LWV	RIPON	NFU	LCV	CFA	NAB	NSI	ACA
1972	50	91	78	69	100	47	50	0	17	7
1971	65	88	86	79	100	–	83	–	–	5
1970	76	92	–	69	91	78	100	0	44	7

Key Votes

1) Busing	FOR	6) Cmbodia Bmbg	AGN	11) Chkg Acct Intrst	AGN
2) Strip Mines	AGN	7) Bust Hwy Trust	AGN	12) End HISC (HUAC)	FOR
3) Cut Mil $	ABS	8) Farm Sub Lmt	AGN	13) Nixon Sewer Veto	AGN
4) Rev Shrg	FOR	9) School Prayr	AGN	14) Corp Cmpaign $	FOR
5) Pub TV $	FOR	10) Cnsumr Prot	FOR	15) Pol $ Disclosr	ABS

Election Results

1972 general:	John A. Blatnik (DFL)	161,823	(76%)
	Edward Johnson (R)	51,314	(24%)
1972 primary:	John A. Blatnik (DFL)	39,798	(76%)
	Ray Murdock (DFL)	9,141	(17%)
	James R. Miller (DFL)	2,035	(4%)
	John J. Perko (DFL)	1,666	(3%)
1970 general:	John A. Blatnik (DFL)	118,149	(75%)
	Paul Reed (R)	38,369	(25%)

MISSISSIPPI

Political Background

Mississippi, a land of gentle hills and fertile river bottoms, was once the booming frontier of the American South. In the late 1820s, land-hungry Jacksonian farmers poured in from Tennessee after the Chickasaws and Choctaws were driven out of the northern and central parts of the state. The farmers and would-be planters (Faulkner's Thomas Sutpen was a farm boy who made it) eventually took away control of the state from a group of already-established Whig planter-aristocrats who had settled around Natchez, to the south, at the turn of the nineteenth century. King Cotton brought both groups to Mississippi, and because cotton was then a labor-intensive crop, slaves bred in Virginia and the Carolinas were purchased and brought in by the thousands. In 1940, some 75 years after the Civil War, over 49% of the state's population was black, and today, after decades of black migration to Northern cities, Mississippi still has the largest black percentage of any state, 37%.

The place of the slave and the ex-slave has always been the central issue in the politics of Mississippi. From the end of Reconstruction in the 1880s to the mid-1960s, the franchise was a prerogative of whites only. But for some 20 years after the Civil War, the black man was not totally shut out of the political process. He was a ward of the rich Delta planters, so-called Bourbons, who had "redeemed" Mississippi from the control of Northern carpetbaggers and black Republicans. With slavery gone, blacks became the planters' cheapest source of tenant labor. The planter, therefore, often defended his new economic interest, the ex-slave; and in so doing, the planter demonstrated his sense of *noblesse oblige*. Shortly after the turn of the century, the poor white farmers of the eastern hill country—descendants of the old Jacksonian boomers who failed to make good—worked another revolution in Mississippi politics and wrested control away from the Bourbons. The political style of the poor whites, often called "rednecks," was a strange mix of buffoonery (the politician was first of all a yarn-swapper), of populistic humanitarianism (a poor white Governor abolished the state's infamous convict-labor system), and of the most extreme form of race-baiting demogoguery imaginable.

The poor whites feared and resented the wealth of the Bourbons; unlike the favored of Mississippi, the poor whites were in no way dependent on the blacks. In fact, redneck and black competed for the right to lease the Bourbon landlord's cotton acreage, creating a seller's market. Faced with a new kind of Mississippi politics, the planter class tried to "out-nigger" the upcountry politicians, but they never enjoyed much success against the masters of the demogogic art, men like Gov. (1904–08) and Sen. (1913–19) James K. Vardaman and Sen. (1934–47) Theodore Bilbo.

Throughout its history, Mississippi has had little of the moderating influence that could have come from urban life or the economic interests of large business firms. Even today, it remains a rural and small-town state; Jackson, the state capital and largest city in Mississippi, has just 153,000 residents and no suburbs of any size. For the most part, the state is still an economic colony of the cotton exchanges and banks of Memphis and New Orleans.

During the 1960s, the *sine qua non* of Mississippi politics—the exclusion of the black man—was challenged for the first time since Yankee farm boys came South to fight the Civil War. Hundreds of civil rights activists descended upon the state and organized black voter-registration drives. Out of the movement, local leaders began to emerge—Charles Evers, Aaron Henry, Fannie Lou Hamer. So by the time the federal registrars were sent into the state under the Voting Rights Act of 1965, Mississippi blacks were ready to register, and they did so by the thousands. Even so, the classic sanctions against black political participation—economic reprisals and physical violence—still obtain in many areas of the state. Moreover, in 1970 the state legislature set up a series of requirements designed to cut down on black registration; then-Attorney General John Mitchell could have vetoed the moves, but approved them, presumably with one eye on the 1972 election.

Nevertheless, blacks have won election to the legislature and control of several units of local government, the most notable example being Charles Evers' mayoral triumph in the town of Fayette. It is, however, easy to overstate the degree of progress made by blacks here; most of it has occurred in small, population-losing rural enclaves that still have black majorities. Fewer than 2,000 souls live in Fayette.

Until 1972, black voters had little effect on the outcome of elections conducted in Mississippi, because white people here voted with near monolithic unanimity. In 1968, for example, George Wallace took 63% of the state's votes; and in state contests Democratic candidates never faced serious challenges. The same white unanimity showed itself in the statewide races of 1972: Richard Nixon won with 80% of the votes—his best margin in any of the 50 states—and Sen. James Eastland came away with a solid 60% in his reelection bid. But as the state's 1972 Senate and House races demonstrated, opportunity for significant black leverage does exist. In the House contests, the Republicans waged tough races in three of the state's five districts, and actually won two of them. So if a competitive two-party system opens up in local races, the chance for increased black political influence is strengthened.

Meanwhile, the decibel level of Mississippi politics has subsided. In 1972, the governorship passed from John Bell Williams, a former Congressman inclined to use oldtime rhetoric, to William Waller, a Democrat who has attacked the interests of big business and called for racial harmony. In the contested House races of 1972, the nominees of both parties were young and forward-looking, unlike the back-slapping, hell-of-a-fellow, rural orators of the past.

Both of the state's Senators, however, have served since the 1940s. Both chair important committees, and both will no doubt be reelected as long as they care to run. The senior Senator, James Eastland, has been Chairman of the Judiciary Committee since the 1950s. There was a time when Eastland could—and did—bottle up civil rights legislation singlehandedly. But those days are gone. Most of the Democrats and some of the Republicans now on Judiciary are Northern liberals. Eastland, however, can still use the chairman's power to schedule and delay, as he did on occasion during the Kleindienst nomination-ITT hearings in 1972. For Eastland's help here and for his aid in matters like the Haynsworth and Carswell nominations, the White House was reportedly grateful; in fact, Eastland's entire voting record has been pretty solidly pro-Nixon.

The Administration reciprocated in 1972. The Democratic Senator was up for reelection, and it was clear that Nixon would sweep Mississippi. Though local Republicans had nominated a businessman named Gil Carmichael to challenge Eastland, word went out from Nixon operatives that Eastland was the one. As it happened, Carmichael, underfinanced and ignored, got 39% of the votes against Eastland's 58%—figures that indicate Eastland might have been vulnerable. When the Watergate story broke, however, Eastland hardly rushed to aid the Administration. As Chairman of Judiciary, he could have entered the breach and helped the Administration in its efforts to avoid the naming of a special prosecutor; instead, Eastland chomped his usual cigar placidly, as the committee's liberals grilled Attorney General designate Elliot Richardson until they extracted a promise from him to appoint Archibald Cox. Eastland does not face the voters again until 1978, when he will be 74 and when Nixon will no longer be President.

A footnote: Eastland is the President Pro Tempore of the Senate, a title traditionally reserved for the senior member of the majority party. Though it is a purely formal post, the office does put Eastland fourth in line for the presidency. So if Richard Nixon, Spiro Agnew, and House Speaker Carl Albert go down in a plane crash, James Eastland goes to the White House.

Mississippi's junior Senator, John C. Stennis, is Chairman of the Armed Services Committee. As Chairman, Stennis has usually supported the budget requests of the military and the war policies of the Johnson and Nixon administrations. The Senator was the floor leader in the fight for the ABM, one the Administration just barely won; moreover, Nixon himself credited Stennis for playing a major role in the defeat of end-the-war legislation. Yet Stennis is no unabashed partisan of Nixon and Thieu; indeed Stennis may have shared a Vietnam opinion ascribed to the late Richard Russell, who told Johnson that he opposed American involvement in Southeast Asia but would support the flag once the troops were in. In any case, Stennis, along with Jacob Javits and Thomas Eagleton, has co-sponsored the Senate version of the war powers bill. The legislation, which Nixon says he will veto, purports to set limits on the power of the President to commit American troops to warfare overseas, and provides a means allowing Congress to call a halt to the activities unless it declares war. Some observers have criticized the Senate version for having too many loopholes. And if the legislation goes through, it will need reconciling with a House version of the same bill—the failure to get agreement scuttled a war powers measure in the 92nd Congress.

In January 1973, Stennis was shot by muggers outside his Washington home. His condition at first appeared grave, but he rallied and recovered. The 71-year-old man was obviously in excellent physical shape. Just after he was shot, and seriously wounded, he walked up the steps into his house, sat down, and told his wife to call the hospital. Back in Mississippi, Stennis wins elections easily and if he wants another term in 1976 he will surely get it.

Because Stennis has a reputation in the Senate for fairness and rectitude, he is the Chairman of the Select Committee on Standards and Conduct. Recently, his Select Committee has had considerably less business to transact than Sam Ervin's Select Committee on Presidential Campaign Activities.

Like most Southern states, Mississippi has been happy to reelect its Congressmen time and time again. Such reelection is the only way politicians can accumulate seniority. But three retirements in 1972 have reduced the state's seniority in the House to an unprecedented low. Only 1st district Congressman Jamie Whitten has more than 10 years in the House, with three of the state's Representatives being freshmen. Even more surprising is that two of the freshmen are Republicans, elected in the Nixon landslide. The big question in 1974 is whether the two Republicans can hold on. The betting here is that they will continue to win by larger and larger margins, just like most of the Alabama Republican Congressmen swept in by the local Goldwater landslide of 1964.

Mississippi congressional races were a bit harder to follow in 1972 than in the past. Though the seats underwent only slight change in redistricting, the state legislature decided to renumber them. What was the 1st district is now the 2nd; and the 3rd, the 4th; and vice versa all around. Nobody knows why any legislatures insist on doing this kind of thing.

Census Data Pop. 2,216,912; 1.10% of U.S. total, 29th largest; change 1960–70, 1.8%. Central city, 11%; suburban, 7%. Median family income, $6,068; 50th highest; families above $15,000: 8%; families below $3,000: 25%. Median years education, 10.7.

1972 Share of Federal Tax Burden $1,233,210,000; 0.59% of U.S. total, 35th largest.

1972 Share of Federal Outlays $2,567,206,420; 1.18% of U.S. total, 28th largest. Per capita federal spending, $1,158.

DOD	$930,707,000	19th (1.49%)	HEW	$768,394,573	27th (1.08%)
AEC	$65,850	42nd (—)	HUD	$32,646,782	27th (1.06%)
NASA	$14,125,478	17th (0.05%)	VA	$142,319,422	28th (1.24%)
DOT	$46,223,009	42nd (0.59%)	USDA	$352,286,797	13th (2.29%)
DOC	$28,873,143	10th (2.23%)	CSC	$32,023,645	34th (0.78%)
DOI	$14,542,388	33rd (0.69%)	TD	$67,835,084	32nd (0.41%)
DOJ	$7,949,306	33rd (0.81%)	Other	$129,213,943	

Economic Base Agriculture, notably cattle, cotton lint, soybeans and broilers; apparel and other textile products, especially men's and boys' furnishings; finance, insurance and real estate; lumber and wood products, especially sawmills and planing mills; transportation equipment, especially motor vehicles and equipment and ship building and repairing; food and kindred products.

Political Line-up Governor, William L. Waller (D); seat up, 1975. Senators, James O. Eastland (D) and John C. Stennis (D). Representatives, 5 (3 D and 2 R). State Senate (50 D and 2 R); State House (119 D, 2 R, and 1 Ind.).

The Voters

Registration Not available.
Median voting age 43.3
Employment profile White collar, 39%. Blue collar, 41%. Service, 14%. Farm, 6%.
Ethnic groups Black, 37%. Total foreign stock, 1%.

Presidential vote

1972	Nixon (R)	505,125	(80%)
	McGovern (D)	126,782	(20%)

1968	Nixon (R)	88,516	(14%)
	Humphrey (D)	150,644	(23%)
	Wallace (AI)	415,349	(63%)
1964	Johnson (D)	52,618	(13%)
	Goldwater (R)	356,528	(87%)

Senator

James O. Eastland (D) Elected 1942, seat up 1978; b. Nov. 28, 1904, Doddsville; home, Doddsville; U. of Miss.; Vanderbilt U.; U. of Ala.; married, four children; Methodist.

Career State Rep., 1928–32; practicing atty., 1932–41; U.S. Senate, 1941.

Offices 2241 NSOB, 202-225-5054. Also P.O. Bldg., Jackson 39205, 601-352-6298, and Ruleville 38771, 601-756-4766.

Administrative Assistant Courtney C. Pace

Committees

Agriculture and Forestry (2nd); Subs: Agricultural Production, Marketing and Stabilization of Prices; Agricultural Research and General Legislation; Environment, Soil Conservation and Forestry (Chm.); Rural Development.

Judiciary (Chm.); Subs: Constitutional Amendments; Criminal Laws and Procedures; Immigration and Naturalization (Chm.); Internal Security (Chm.).

(*Ex officio member of Appropriations Subcommittee on Agriculture and Related Agencies.*)

Group Ratings

	ADA	COPE	LWV	RIPON	NFU	LCV	CFA	NAB	NSI	ACA
1972	5	0	20	13	40	2	11	50	100	81
1971	7	33	9	0	27	–	40	–	–	74
1970	3	18	–	4	22	3	–	56	100	80

Key Votes

1) Busing	AGN	8) Sea Life Prot	FOR	15) Tax Singls Less	AGN
2) Alas P-line	FOR	9) Campaign Subs	AGN	16) Min Tax for Rich	AGN
3) Gun Cntrl	ABS	10) Cmbodia Bmbg	FOR	17) Euro Troop Rdctn	AGN
4) Rehnquist	FOR	11) Legal Srvices	AGN	18) Bust Hwy Trust	AGN
5) Pub TV $	FOR	12) Rev Sharing	FOR	19) Maid Min Wage	AGN
6) EZ Votr Reg	AGN	13) Cnsumr Prot	AGN	20) Farm Sub Limit	AGN
7) No-Fault	AGN	14) Eq Rts Amend	AGN	21) Highr Credt Chgs	FOR

Election Results

1972 general:	James O. Eastland (D)	375,102	(58%)
	Gil Carmichael (R)	249,779	(39%)
	Prentiss Walker (Ind.)	14,662	(2%)
	C. L. McKinley (Ind.)	6,203	(1%)
1972 primary:	James O. Eastland (D)	203,847	(70%)
	Taylor Webb (D)	67,656	(23%)
	Louis Fondren (D)	18,753	(6%)
1966 general:	James O. Eastland (D)	258,248	(66%)
	Prentiss Walker (R)	105,150	(27%)
	Clifton R. Whitley (Ind.)	30,502	(8%)

Senator

John C. **Stennis** (D) Elected 1947, seat up 1976; b. Aug. 3, 1901, Kemper County; home, De Kalb; Miss. State U., B.S., 1923; U. of Va., LL.B., 1928; married, two children; Presbyterian.

Career State Rep., 1928–32; Dist. Atty., 16th Judicial Dist., 1931–37; circuit judge, 1937–47.

Offices 205 OSOB, 202-225-6253. Also 303 P.O. Bldg., Jackson 39201, 601-353-5494.

Administrative Assistant William E. Cresswell

Committees

Aeronautical, and Space Sciences (4th).

Appropriations (3rd); Subs: Agriculture Environmental and Consumer Protection; Defense; Labor, and Health Education, and Welfare, and Related Agencies; Public Works (Chm.); Transportation; Housing and Urban Development, Space, Science, and Veterans; Intelligence Operations.

Armed Services (Chm.); Subs: Central Intelligence (Chm.); Preparedness Investigating (Chm.); Bomber Defense (Chm.); Arms Control; Reprograming of Funds (Chm.).

Sel. Com. on Standards and Conduct (Chm.).

Joint Study Com. on Budget Control.

Joint Com. on Reduction of Federal Expenditures (3rd).

Group Ratings

	ADA	COPE	LWV	RIPON	NFU	LCV	CFA	NAB	NSI	ACA
1972	0	0	20	20	50	0	9	55	100	77
1971	7	42	22	5	18	–	33	–	–	77
1970	9	17	–	8	29	22	–	70	100	80

Key Votes

1) Busing	AGN	8) Sea Life Prot	FOR	15) Tax Singls Less	AGN
2) Alas P-line	ABS	9) Campaign Subs	AGN	16) Min Tax for Rich	AGN
3) Gun Cntrl	AGN	10) Cmbodia Bmbg	ABS	17) Euro Troop Rdctn	AGN
4) Rehnquist	FOR	11) Legal Srvices	AGN	18) Bust Hwy Trust	AGN
5) Pub TV $	FOR	12) Rev Sharing	AGN	19) Maid Min Wage	AGN
6) EZ Votr Reg	AGN	13) Cnsumr Prot	AGN	20) Farm Sub Limit	AGN
7) No-Fault	AGN	14) Eq Rts Amend	AGN	21) Highr Credt Chgs	FOR

Election Results

1970 general:	John C. Stennis (D)	286,622	(88%)
	William R. Thompson (Ind.)	37,593	(12%)
1970 primary:	Results not consolidated by the Mississippi Secretary of State		
1964 general:	John C. Stennis (D), unopposed		

FIRST DISTRICT Political Background

The 1st district of Mississippi occupies the northernmost section of the state. The 1st spans the gamut of Mississippi's geopolitical terrain, from the cotton-rich Delta to Tishomingo County on the Tennessee River in the state's northeast corner. The black majority in some of the Delta counties has become more and more active politically, though Mississippi blacks have been hobbled by changes in registration laws sanctioned by the Nixon Administration. There are fewer and fewer blacks as one moves east into the hill country, where poor white farmers have worked the hardscrabble land for more than a century without much luck. In the middle of the district lies

Oxford, site of Ole Miss and of racial disorders accompanying the enrollment of James Meredith in 1962. Oxford was also the lifelong home of William Faulkner, one of the most remarkably gifted and visionary men who ever drew breath on American soil.

Since winning a special election a month before Pearl Harbor, Jamie Whitten has represented the 1st district and its predecessors. There were many such predecessors in the 1960s, as Mississippi redistricters drew a series of lines to prevent any district from having a black voting majority. Before a mid-1960s redistricting, Whitten's constituency consisted of nearly all the Delta, which then had a voteless 59% black majority.

In Washington, where he has more seniority than all but six other Congressmen, Whitten is Chairman of the Agriculture Subcommittee of the Appropriations Committee. So ensconced, Whitten can do plenty for the rich Delta planters who have always supported him politically. Whitten takes the position, popular in Mississippi, of backing large government agricultural subsidies for owners of big cotton plantations, and opposing government programs to feed the poor. Just outside the 1st in Sunflower County, Sen. James Eastland has received about $160,000 annually for not growing cotton on his plantation. According to the Joint Economic Committee, only 7% of the benefits issuing from farm programs go to the poorest 41% of the nation's farms, while 32% of the help goes to the richest 7%.

Because Whitten controls the pursestrings of the Department of Agriculture—the government's fourth largest writer of checks—the Congressman can promote his views within that bureaucracy regardless of the party that happens to control the White House. Whitten is known to use his power shrewdly. Moreover, he has friends not just at the USDA in Washington, but in state agriculture departments, which are important in the South, and among county agents all over the nation. In 1974, Whitten will be 64 years old, quite young for a man with 33 years of seniority. This means that he will probably succeed George Mahon of Texas, who will be 74 in 1974, as Chairman of the full Appropriations Committee. So barring an audacious move by House liberals, Whitten will someday enjoy vast power over the entire federal budget.

At the beginning of the 92nd Congress, Whitten's subcommittee was given jurisdiction over environmental programs, which horrified ecology activists. Though these activists were surprisingly successful in targeting and unseating Congressmen not to their liking in 1970 and 1972, they can do very little about Whitten. Blacks now make up just 29% of the potential electorate in the 1st; moreover, ecology has yet to dislodge race as the major concern of the district's white voters.

Census Data   Pop. 433,825. Central city, 0%; suburban, 0%. Median family income, $5,577; families above $15,000: 6%; families below $3,000: 28%. Median years education, 9.7.

1972 Share of Federal Outlays $328,418,805

DOD	$13,387,000	HEW	$147,183,711
AEC	$65,850	HUD	$3,277,565
NASA	–	DOI	$3,934,020
DOT	$6,385,134	USDA	$89,674,822
		Other	$64,510,703

Federal Military-Industrial Commitments

No installations or contractors receiving prime awards greater than $5,000,000.

Economic Base   Agriculture, notably cotton, grains and dairy products; apparel and other textile products, especially men's and boys' furnishings; furniture and fixtures, especially household furniture; finance, insurance and real estate; and food and kindred products, especially meat products.

The Voters

Registration   Not available.
Median voting age   44.4
Employment profile   White collar, 34%. Blue collar, 45%. Service, 12%. Farm, 9%.
Ethnic groups   Black, 35%.

Presidential vote

1972	Nixon (R)	92,680	(80%)
	McGovern (D)	23,058	(20%)
1968	Nixon (R)	17,832	(14%)
	Humphrey (D)	29,660	(23%)
	Wallace (AI)	82,062	(63%)

Representative

Jamie L. Whitten (D) Elected 1940; b. April 18, 1910, Cascilla; home, Charleston; U. of Miss.; married, two children; Presbyterian.

Career State Rep., 1931; Dist Atty., 1933.

Offices 2413 RHOB, 202-225-4306. Also P.O. Bldg., Charleston 38921, 601-647-2413.

Administrative Assistant Marion F. Bishop

Committees

Appropriations (2nd); Subs: Agriculture, Environmental and Consumer Protection (Chm.); Defense; Public Works, AEC.

Joint Com. on Reduction of Federal Expenditures (3rd).

Joint Study Com. on Budget Control (Co-Chm.).

Group Ratings

	ADA	COPE	LWV	RIPON	NFU	LCV	CFA	NAB	NSI	ACA
1972	6	30	17	6	57	6	100	78	100	91
1971	8	33	11	25	62	–	25	–	–	80
1970	4	25	–	6	23	13	67	64	100	71

Key Votes

1) Busing	AGN	6) Cmbodia Bmbg	FOR	11) Chkg Acct Intrst	AGN
2) Strip Mines	FOR	7) Bust Hwy Trust	AGN	12) End HISC (HUAC)	AGN
3) Cut Mil $	AGN	8) Farm Sub Lmt	AGN	13) Nixon Sewer Veto	AGN
4) Rev Shrg	AGN	9) School Prayr	FOR	14) Corp Cmpaign $	FOR
5) Pub TV $	AGN	10) Cnsumr Prot	AGN	15) Pol $ Disclosr	AGN

Election Results

1972 general:	Jamie L. Whitten (D), unopposed		
1972 primary:	Jamie L. Whitten (D)	34,829	(87%)
	Jimmie Richardson (D)	5,206	(13%)
1970 general:	Jamie L. Whitten (D)	51,689	(86%)
	Eugene Carter (Ind.)	8,092	(14%)

SECOND DISTRICT Political Background

The 2nd district, a belt of counties lying in north-central Mississippi, stretches from the Mississippi River to the hill country along the Alabama border. The flat fertile land along the river is the Delta, an area not fully developed until after the Civil War. But soon enough the swampy land was drained, the great river lined with levees, and the Illinois Central track laid out of Memphis for New Orleans. It was discovered that the topsoil here, thanks to the deposits laid down by countless centuries of the Mississippi running wild, often reached depths of 25 feet. So the Delta wilderness in northern Mississippi, the destruction of which Faulkner lamented in stories like "The Bear," became the region of the state's largest and most productive cotton plantations.

The Delta, therefore, became the part of Mississippi with the greatest concentration of black people, who still constitute a majority in many counties along the river. The threat of black voting strength under the Voting Rights Act of 1965 led white Mississippians to do some redistricting. Because the rich Delta counties and the poor hill country of the east had been political enemies since before the Civil War, they were never found in the same congressional district. But lines had to be redrawn to make sure that blacks could not seize control of an old Delta district. Three districts were made to stretch across across the entire expanse of the state from west to east. The resulting constituencies united the whites of the Delta and the upcountry.

In 1960, some 51% of the current 2nd district's population was black. In 1970, after another decade of out-migration, the figure fell to 46%, with only 39% of the population over 18. But until 1972, the large black minority had virtually no chance to flex political muscle in the congressional politics of the district. The local Congressman, Democrat Thomas G. Abernethy, was first elected in 1942 and seldom faced opposition.

Abernethy decided to retire in 1972, having served 30 years without attaining a committee chairmanship. As it happened, he would have, had he stayed on; South Carolina's John McMillan, Chairman of the District of Columbia Committee on which Abernethy stood next in line, lost a primary in 1972. Abernethy's retirement triggered some political fireworks back home: a nine-candidate Democratic primary and a strong Republican aspirant to boot. After all, in these parts, the ambitious get only one chance in thirty years to win a seat in Congress, which means they better run when the incumbent retires.

The eventual outcome was something of a surprise. The new Congressman, David R. Bowen, a former assistant professor at Millsaps College, received only 15% of the votes in the first primary, edging ex-Rep. (1951–63) Frank Smith for second place. Smith lost his seat when he was placed in the same district with Jamie Whitten in 1962; Smith later wrote a book in which he lamented the hypocritical stance that he, as an elective official from Mississippi, was forced to adopt on civil rights. Bowen is also a moderate by Mississippi standards; in the runoff he apparently captured majorities in black areas, margins that may have produced his win.

Bowen had a somewhat easier time of it in the general election. He defeated Republican Carl Butler, also a man with a background in the academy, by a solid 62–35 margin. In 1972, the Democrats withstood the 1972 Republican challenge better in northern Mississippi than in southern; Bowen ran almost even with James Eastland, who got 64% of the votes in the 2nd, his home district. In the House, Bowen won a seat on the Agriculture Committee; he also took one on Merchant Marine and Fisheries, a unit of considerable importance to a Congressman out of a district laced with rivers.

Census Data Pop. 440,689. Central city, 0%; suburban, 0%. Median family income, $5,446; families above $15,000: 7%; families below $3,000: 29%. Median years education, 9.9.

1972 Share of Federal Outlays $420,801,538

DOD	$72,209,000	HEW	$152,422,744
AEC	$131,864	HUD	$3,544,056
NASA	–	DOI	$744,177
DOT	$5,174,897	USDA	$118,232,485
		Other	$68,342,315

Federal Military-Industrial Commitments

DOD Installations Columbus AFB (Columbus).

Economic Base Agriculture, notably cattle, dairy products, cotton and grains; apparel and other textile products; finance, insurance and real estate; transportation equipment, especially motor vehicles and equipment; and lumber and wood products. Also higher education (Mississippi State Univ.).

The Voters

Registration Not available.
Median voting age 43.8

Employment profile White collar, 37%. Blue collar, 39%. Service, 15%. Farm, 9%.
Ethnic groups Black, 46%. Total foreign stock, 1%.

Presidential vote

1972	Nixon (R)	84,346	(77%)
	McGovern (D)	24,633	(23%)
1968	Nixon (R)	15,781	(13%)
	Humphrey (D)	30,303	(26%)
	Wallace (AI)	72,655	(61%)

Representative

David Reece Bowen (D) Elected 1972; b. Oct. 21, 1932, Houston; home, Cleveland; Harvard, A.B., 1954; Oxford, M.A.; single; Protestant.

Career Political science professor, Mississippi College, 1958–59; Political science professor, Millsaps College, 1959–64; OEO, 1966–67; U.S. Chamber of Commerce, 1967–68; Special Asst. to the Gov. and Coordinator of State-Federal Programs, Mississippi, 1968–1972.

Offices 1207 LHOB, 202-225-5876, Also 101 S. Court St., Cleveland 38732, and Golden Triangle Regional Airport, Columbus 29701.

Administrative Assistant Nicholas B. Roberts, Jr.

Committees

Agriculture (17th); Subs: Cotton; Dairy and Poultry.

Merchant Marine and Fisheries (22nd); Subs: Coast Guiard and Navigation; Fisheries and Wildlife Conservation and the Environment; Panama Canal.

Group Ratings: Newly Elected

Key Votes

1) Busing	NE	6) Cmbodia Bmbg	FOR	11) Chkg Acct Intrst	AGN
2) Strip Mines	NE	7) Bust Hwy Trust	AGN	12) End HISC (HUAC)	AGN
3) Cut Mil $	NE	8) Farm Sub Lmt	NE	13) Nixon Sewer Veto	AGN
4) Rev Shrg	NE	9) School Prayr	NE	14) Corp Cmpaign $	NE
5) Pub TV $	NE	10) Cnsumr Prot	NE	15) Pol $ Disclosr	NE

Election Results

1972 general:	David Bowen (D)	69,892	(62%)
	Carl Butler (R)	39,117	(35%)
	Robert Coleman (Ind.)	2,801	(2%)
	Norman Smith (Ind.)	1,027	(1%)
1972 run-off:	David Bowen (D)	28,091	(57%)
	Tom Cook (D)	21,315	(43%)
1972 primary:	David Bowen (D)	8,733	(15%)
	Tom Cook (D)	13,881	(23%)
	Frank Smith (D)	7,188	(12%)
	Hugh Potts (D)	6,587	(11%)
	Clant Seay (D)	6,189	(10%)
	Corbet Patridge (D)	6,158	(10%)
	Pat Dunne (D)	4,013	(7%)
	Hainon Miller (D)	3,610	(6%)
	Wallace Dabbs (D)	2,863	(5%)

THIRD DISTRICT Political Background

The 3rd is one of three Mississippi districts that stretch from the heavily black Delta across the hills of central Mississippi to the Alabama border. Like the others, the 3rd was designed to prevent blacks from controlling or influencing in any significant way the outcome of congressional elections held here. The 3rd is predominantly agricultural with most of its voters living in or near little crossroads towns. Meridian (pop. 45,000) is the district's largest city, and its most famous is Philadelphia, where three civil rights workers were found murdered in 1964.

The longtime (since 1942) Congressman from the 3rd, Philadelphia native W. Arthur Winstead, suffered a rude surprise in 1964: he was beaten by a Republican named Prentiss Walker. That year, as Barry Goldwater carried the state by a 7–1 margin, the unfortunate Winstead was the only Mississippi Congressman with a Republican opponent. If Republicans had run in other districts, they too would probably have won, thereby disposing of some 95 years of accumulated seniority. Walker's later ventures in politics showed that his victory was simply the function of Goldwater coattails. Walker won just 27% of the votes against James Eastland in 1966, 39% in a 1968 congressional race, and a pathetic 2% as an independent candidate against Eastland in 1972.

When Walker ran for the Senate in 1966, the Democrats promptly recaptured the seat in the person of state Sen. G. V. (Sonny) Montgomery, who has won since without trouble and usually without opposition. His conservative voting record no doubt please the white majority in the district. A veteran of both World War II and Korea, Montgomery serves on the Armed Services and Veterans Affairs Committee; on the former he is an unabashed hawk and enthusiast for things military. As Republicans and middle-of-the-road Democrats capture more and more seats in the House, deep-dyed conservative Southern Democrats like Montgomery are becoming increasingly rare. Even in Mississippi Republicans and more moderate Democrats appear to have a majority between them. But Montgomery shows every sign of staying around for at least another decade or so.

Census Data Pop. 445,713. Central city, 0%; suburban, 10%. Median family income, $5,320; families above $15,000: 6%; families below $3,000: 30%. Median years education, 10.2.

1972 Share of Federal Outlays $389,611,298

DOD	$53,208,109	HEW	$166,645,505
AEC	–	HUD	$2,140,444
NASA	$7,893	DOI	$5,828,947
DOT	$11,273,078	USDA	$81,753,640
		Other	$68,753,682

Federal Military-Industrial Commitments

DOD Contractors Pioneer Recovery System (Columbia), $6.601m: 26-foot canopy cargo parachutes.
DOD Installations Naval Air Station (Meridian).

Economic Base Agriculture, notably poultry, cattle and cotton; food and kindred products; finance, insurance and real estate; lumber and wood products, especially sawmill and planing mill products; and apparel and other textile products, especially men's and boys' furnishings.

The Voters

Registration Not available.
Median voting age 45.5
Employment profile White collar, 33%. Blue collar, 44%. Service, 13%. Farm, 10%.
Ethnic groups Black, 40%.

Presidential vote

1972	Nixon (R)	110,710	(79%)
	McGovern (D)	28,941	(21%)
1968	Nixon (R)	12,703	(9%)
	Humphrey (D)	32,431	(23%)
	Wallace (AI)	97,866	(68%)

Representative

Gillespie V. (Sonny) **Montgomery** (D) Elected 1966; b. Meridian; home, Meridian; Miss. State U., B.S.; Army, WWII, Korea; Episcopalian.

Career Miss. Senate, 1956–66.

Offices 208 CHOB, 202-225-5031. Also Meridian 39301, 601-693-6681.

Administrative Assistant Jack Vance

Committees

Armed Services (18th); Sub: No. 2.

Veterans' Affairs (9th); Subs: Compensation and Pension; Hospitals; Insurance (Chm.).

Group Ratings

	ADA	COPE	LWV	RIPON	NFU	LCV	CFA	NAB	NSI	ACA
1972	0	11	8	20	43	0	100	90	100	100
1971	0	27	13	22	50	–	38	–	–	78
1970	0	20	–	24	9	0	43	88	100	87

Key Votes

1) Busing	AGN	6) Cmbodia Bmbg	FOR	11) Chkg Acct Intrst	AGN
2) Strip Mines	FOR	7) Bust Hwy Trust	AGN	12) End HISC (HUAC)	AGN
3) Cut Mil $	AGN	8) Farm Sub Lmt	AGN	13) Nixon Sewer Veto	FOR
4) Rev Shrg	AGN	9) School Prayr	FOR	14) Corp Cmpaign $	FOR
5) Pub TV $	ABS	10) Cnsumr Prot	FOR	15) Pol $ Disclosr	AGN

Election Results

1972 general: G. V. Montgomery (D), unopposed
1972 primary: G. V. Montgomery (D), unopposed
1970 general: G. V. Montgomery (D), unopposed

FOURTH DISTRICT Political Background

Jackson, the state capital, is the center of the state's only significant urban concentration. Jackson (pop. 153,000) has experienced substantial growth in the last 20 years—aside from the state's Gulf Coast, just about the only part of Mississippi to have any. Like most Southern cities, Jackson has shown itself to be more Republican than the surrounding countryside, at least in contests featuring a serious Republican aspirant. As in the rest of the Deep South, Mississippi Republicans put up candidates who are younger and more urban-oriented than those run by Democrats. These Republicans have been especially successful in attracting the votes of the younger, better-educated, and upwardly mobile residents of metropolitan areas. Around Jackson, one prominent Republican figure has been Frederick LaRue, a Watergate defendant.

So it is no real surprise that the 4th district elected a Republican Congressman in 1972. Though the 4th comprises 12 counties in the lower reaches of the Mississippi, Jackson and surrounding Hinds County contain 48% of the district's population. The seat here has changed hands a couple of times in recent years. Congressman John Bell Williams was stripped of his seniority after openly supporting Barry Goldwater in 1964; the defiant Democrat was then elected Governor of the state in 1967. Williams was succeeded by his administrative assistant, Charles Griffin, who won a much-publicized contest over Charles Evers, the black Mayor of Fayette in Jefferson County.

Jefferson is one of three small counties in the 4th which are majority black. All of them abut the Mississippi River, with their black residents being descendants of the slaves who worked the large plantations of the Delta. The 4th also contains the old river cities of Natchez (pop. 20,000), famous for its antebellum mansions, and Vicksburg (pop. 26,000), site of a great battle of the Civil War. Both places have significant numbers of black people, but the whites retain a substantial majority, just as they do in the district as a whole. Though blacks are more likely to register here than elsewhere in Mississippi, they make up only 37% of the eligible electorate in the 4th district.

So black candidates attracted little attention when Congressman Griffin announced a decision to retire in 1972 because of illness. Six candidates entered the Democratic primary, and the winner, after a runoff, was state legislator Ellis Bodron. But the Democratic nomination is no longer tantamount to victory in Mississippi. The Republican nominee, young, 35-year-old Jackson attorney Thad Cochran, waged a strong, well-financed campaign; he attempted to grasp the coattails of Richard Nixon as firmly as he could. Cochran's success was only partial; Nixon took 76% of the votes in the district, as Cochran won only 48%. More than half of Cochran's votes came from Jackson and Hinds County; in fact, so urban-based was his support that he carried only two of the district's other 11 counties. But 48% was enough for a victory, because an independent black candidate won 8% of the votes, leaving Bodron, the Democrat, with a losing 44%.

Will Cochran be able to hold on in 1974? Nixon, of course, will not appear on the ballot, but neither will any major statewide Democratic candidates, there being no race for Senator or Governor. Cochran will have the advantages of incumbency, which are usually enough to lift a narrowly elected freshman's percentage five to ten points. So his prospects are good.

There is another, more important, aspect of the election here in 1974: it was the first congressional contest in Mississippi where black voters clearly played a critical role in the outcome. By withholding votes from Bodron, the Democrat, they insured the victory of Cochran, the Republican. To be sure, the 4th is the part of Mississippi were blacks are best organized, the most likely to register and vote. But because of the Cochran victory, Mississippi Democrats may conclude that they had best pay a little more attention to black voters and to court them a bit more. Of course limits exist on how much solicitude Democratic politicians can show towards Mississippi blacks; too much will lose them all the white votes. Another conclusion aspiring politicos here may draw: why go through the hassle of a Democratic primary and a runoff when you can have the Republican nomination for the asking and then win the election?

Census Data Pop. 444,704. Central city, 35%; suburban, 14%. Median family income, $6,802; families above $15,000: 12%; families below $3,000: 21%. Median years education, 11.8.

1972 Share of Federal Outlays $419,746,408

DOD	$59,902,890	HEW	$183,033,553
AEC	–	HUD	$12,810,383
NASA	$38,621	DOI	$2,686,480
DOT	$7,114,228	USDA	$39,224,299
		Other	$114,935,954

Federal Military-Industrial Commitments

No installations or contractors receiving prime awards greater than $5,000,000.

Economic Base Finance, insurance and real estate; agriculture, notably cattle, dairy products and poultry; lumber and wood products; food and kindred products, especially meat products; and apparel and other textile products, especially men's and boys' furnishings.

The Voters

Registration Not available.
Median voting age 43.3
Employment profile White collar, 47%. Blue collar, 35%. Service, 15%. Farm, 3%.
Ethnic groups Black, 43%. Total foreign stock, 1%.

Presidential vote

1972	Nixon (R)	101,007	(76%)
	McGovern (D)	32,496	(24%)
1968	Nixon (R)	22,236	(16%)
	Humphrey (D)	41,696	(30%)
	Wallace (AI)	77,047	(55%)

Representative

William Thad Cochran (R) Elected 1972; b. Dec. 7, 1937, Pontotoc; home, Jackson; U. of Miss., B.A., 1959; J.D., 1965; Trinity Col., Dublin, 1963–64; Navy, 1959–61; married, two children; Baptist.

Career Pres., Young Lawyers Section, Miss. State Bar, 1972–73; Bd. of Dirs., Jackson Rotary Club 1970–71; Chm. Miss. Law Institute.

Offices LHOB 1609, 202-225-5865. Also Box 22581, Jackson 39205, 601-355-4242, and Box 1411, Natchez 39120, 601-442-9188.

Administrative Assistant Jon Hinson

Committees

Public Works (12th); Subs: Economic Development; Energy; Investigations and Review; Public Buildings and Grounds.

Group Ratings: Newly Elected

Key Votes

1) Busing	NE	6) Cmbodia Bmbg	FOR	11) Chkg Acct Intrst	AGN
2) Strip Mines	NE	7) Bust Hwy Trust	AGN	12) End HISC (HUAC)	AGN
3) Cut Mil $	NE	8) Farm Sub Lmt	NE	13) Nixon Sewer Veto	FOR
4) Rev Shrg	NE	9) School Prayr	NE	14) Corp Cmpaign $	NE
5) Pub TV $	NE	10) Cnsumr Prot	NE	15) Pol $ Disclosr	NE

Election Results

1972 general:	Thad Cochran (R)	67,655	(48%)
	Ellis B. Bodron (D)	62,148	(44%)
	Eddie L. McBride (Ind.)	11,571	(8%)
1972 primary:	Thad Cochran (R), unopposed		

FIFTH DISTRICT Political Background

The 5th of Mississippi is the state's Gulf Coast district. About half its population lives in and around the Gulf cities of Biloxi, Gulfport, and Pascagoula. The remainder live inland on farms or in the middle-sized cities of Hattiesburg and Laurel. This region of Mississippi is unlike the rest of the state in a number of ways. First, there was never an extensive plantation culture here of the kind that dominated the Delta; second, there are far fewer blacks here, only 19% of the total population, than in the state's four other congressional districts; third, there was significant population growth here during the 1950s and 1960s, unlike most other areas of the state. The second of these differences, the low black population, accounts for one distinction enjoyed by the 5th: in 1972, it produced the largest percentage for Richard Nixon of any congressional district in the country, 87%. In Mississippi, where almost all blacks voted for McGovern and almost as high a percentage of whites for Nixon, presidential vote totals remain a function of race.

The vast majority of 5th-district residents would surely be disgusted at any notion that suggested their local economy is subsidized by the federal government. After all, the 5th of Mississippi is one part of the country fiercely opposed to heavy federal spending and government dole. But hardly anybody here objects to the annual $500 million the Defense Department pours into the Litton Shipbuilding yards in Pascagoula. Litton is the California-based conglomerate whose former president, Roy Ash, now serves as Richard Nixon's director of the Office of Management and Budget. Litton, though it had previously done no shipbuilding, won the contract over the experienced Bath Iron Works in Maine. Litton's performance, to say the least, has been disappointing—the project is poorly organized, qualified labor is not available, and completion times are not being met. No one down here, however, dares to suggest the obvious: the government money wasted on the Litton project is really a subsidy to the now-prosperous Pascagoula area.

Some observers speculated that the Nixon Administration awarded the destroyer contract to Litton to please Sen. John Stennis, Chairman of the Armed Services Committee, and Sen. James

Eastland, Chairman of Judiciary. But there was another member of Congress the Administration probably wanted to accomodate, Rep. William M. Colmer of the 5th district. Since 1932, the voters of the district had returned Colmer to office, and 35 years later, in 1967, their man became Chairman of the House Rules Committee. Colmer, however, was a good deal less popular among many House Democrats than he was back home in Mississippi. Rules, under Colmer's predecessor Howard Smith of Virginia, used its power to control the flow of legislation to the House floor to block measures the committee's bipartisan conservative majority found distasteful. When the Kennedy Administration assumed office, House liberals plotted to undermine Rules; they wanted to deny Colmer his seat because the Congressman had not supported Kennedy. Instead, Speaker Sam Rayburn persuaded the liberals to support an enlargement (to its opponents, packing) of the committee—a measure that passed by an extremely narrow margin, 217–212. The significance of this victory may be gauged by the fact that some commentators have referred to it as the single most important House vote of the 1960s. That left Smith, and later Colmer, without a sure majority on Rules; nevertheless, both chairmen still had room to maneuver and to pigeonhole liberal legislation from time to time.

Traditionally, old Southern conservatives like Colmer are seldom defeated and even less often do they retire voluntarily. But Colmer surprised everybody when he announced that he would not seek reelection in 1972. It is a measure of how the seniority system works that the 82-year-old Colmer of Mississippi was succeeded as Chairman of Rules by 80-year-old Ray Madden of Indiana.

For men like Colmer, the label "Democrat" had long since become a convenience, accouterment needed to maintain his seniority. Colmer had no more in common with the national nominees of his party than did the most conservative Republican. So it is fitting that his successor is his protégé and a declared Republican. Trent Lott spent four years as Colmer's administrative assistant, with both he and Colmer spending their boyhood days in Pascagoula. At age 31, Lott filed for the 1972 election in the party of Richard Nixon. As a Republican, he faced only desultory primary competition, while 10 Democratic candidates carved each other up, with everybody trying to make the runoff. In the general election, Lott scored a relatively easy triumph over the winner of the Democratic runoff, state Sen. Ben Stone. The new Republican took a solid 55% of the vote district-wide—a figure that would have been higher but for Stone's home-town strength in the district's largest county, Harrison (Biloxi and Gulfport).

Lott's totals were the best accumulated by a Mississippi Republican in 1972. And with a clear majority in his initial try, he looks like a good bet for reelection in 1974. When Lott took the oath of office, he was 11 years younger than Colmer was when he took the same oath 40 years earlier. It could turn out that Lott will serve his constituents as long as his predecessor. Whether the young man ever becomes a committee chairman depends on whether the Republicans ever regain a majority in the House.

Census Data Pop. 451,981. Central city, 20%; suburban, 10%. Median family income, $7,053; families above $15,000: 9%; families below $3,000: 18%. Median years education, 11.9.

1972 Share of Federal Outlays $1,008,808,362

DOD	$732,000,000	HEW	$119,112,058
AEC	–	HUD	$10,874,333
NASA	$13,947,099	DOI	$1,348,763
DOT	$16,275,771	USDA	$23,351,550
		Other	$91,898,788

Federal Military-Industrial Commitments

DOD Contractors Litton Industries (Pascagoula), $492.861m: construction of DD-963 class destroyers; ship and submarine overhaul and repair. Chevron Oil (Pascagoula), $15.271m: petroleum products.
DOD Installations Naval Construction Battalion Center (Gulfport). Keesler AFB.
NASA Contractors Global Associates (Bay St. Louis), $6.941m: services for Mississippi Test Facility.
NASA Installations Mississippi Test Facility (Bay St. Louis).

Economic Base Lumber and wood products; finance, insurance and real estate; agriculture, notably poultry, cattle and dairy products; food and kindred products; and apparel and other textile products, especially women's and children's underwear. Also higher education (Univ. of Southern Mississippi).

The Voters

Registration Not available.
Median voting age 40.0
Employment profile White collar, 42%. Blue collar, 43%. Service, 13%. Farm, 2%.
Ethnic groups Black, 19%. Total foreign stock, 3%.

Presidential vote

1972	Nixon (R)	116,382	(87%)
	McGovern (D)	17,654	(13%)
1968	Nixon (R)	19,964	(16%)
	Humphrey (D)	16,554	(14%)
	Wallace (AI)	85,719	(70%)

Representative

Chester Trent Lott (R) Elected 1972; b. Oct. 9, 1941, Grenada; home, Pascagoula; U. of Miss., B.A., 1963; U. of Miss. School of Law, 1967; married, two children; Southern Baptist.

Career Bryan, Gordon, Nelson & Allen Law firm, Pascagoula, 1967–68. Admin. Asst. to Congressman William M. Colmer, 1968–72.

Offices 1712 LHOB, 202-225-5772. Also P.O. Box 1557, P.O. Bldg., Gulfport 39501, 601-864-7670, and P.O. Box 83, Fed. Bldg., Laurel 39440, 601-649-1231.

Administrative Assistant Tom H. Anderson, Jr.

Committees

Judiciary (14th); Sub: Bankruptcy and Civil Rights Oversight.

Merchant Marine and Fisheries (13th); Subs: Coast Guard and Navigation; Merchant Marine; Wildlife and Fisheries.

Group Ratings: Newly Elected

Key Votes

1) Busing	NE	6) Cmbodia Bmbg	FOR	11) Chkg Acct Intrst	AGN
2) Strip Mines	NE	7) Bust Hwy Trust	AGN	12) End HISC (HUAC)	AGN
3) Cut Mil $	NE	8) Farm Sub Lmt	NE	13) Nixon Sewer Veto	FOR
4) Rev Shrg	NE	9) School Prayr	NE	14) Corp Cmpaign $	NE
5) Pub TV $	NE	10) Cnsumr Prot	NE	15) Pol $ Disclosr	NE

Election Results

1972 general:	Trent Lott (R)	77,826	(55%)
	Ben Stone (D)	62,101	(45%)
1972 primary:	Trent Lott (R)	5,038	(70%)
	Paul E. Grady (R)	1,192	(17%)
	Charles E. Klumb (R)	578	(8%)
	Karl C. Mertz (R)	348	(5%)

MISSOURI

Political Background

Missouri no doubt has a larger percentage of voters who consider themselves Democrats than any of the nation's other large states. But at the polls, Missouri is politically marginal, and in recent statewide elections, trending Republican. The discrepancy between partisan identification and voter behavior is rooted in the state's history. Missouri entered the Union in 1821 as a slave state, and its residents, both urban and rural, have been, out of tradition, members of the Southern wing of the Democratic party. Though this border state decided against secession in 1861, many Missourians, including the uncle of Missouri's most famous citizen, Harry S. Truman, fought in the Confederate Army.

So it was hardly surprising that the great man himself, after going broke in the haberdashery business, became active in Democratic politics. The late President's background—Southern rural and Kansas City urban—exemplifies the tensions found within the Missouri Democratic party and also explains why Truman, who integrated the armed forces as President, later reacted negatively to the sit-in demonstrations of the early 1960s. Truman's combination of liberalism on economic issues, a mixed response on social questions, and an affection for old political friends still characterizes the leaders of the Missouri Democrats.

Over the years, this combination produced many election-day victories for Truman and the Democrats—though not many recently. Since Truman's win, presidential elections here have usually been close; except for the landslides of 1964 and 1972, no candidate has carried the state by more than 30,000 votes. Moreover, in the last five years, Republicans have also run well in statewide elections. The first major Republican breakthrough came in 1968 with the election of John Danforth as state Attorney General. Danforth, a young heir to the Ralston Purina fortune, ran against Sen. Stuart Symington two years later and took 49% of the votes. As Danforth pulled the near upset, another young Republican, Christopher Bond, unseated a longtime state Treasurer. In 1972, Bond ran for Governor and won by a solid 55–45 margin. At the same time, Atty. Gen. Danforth garnered 63% of the votes, doing better among Missouri voters than Richard Nixon.

Bond and Danforth have a number of things in common. Both are young, Bond 35 in 1974 and Danforth 38. Both are rich and went to Ivy League schools. Both have hired staffs exhibiting a range of expertise not ordinarily found in Jefferson City, Missouri's sleepy state capital town. Finally, both men fashioned careers out of attacking the cronyism and the old-fashion politicking of the once-entrenched Missouri Democrats.

Danforth's near win in the 1970 Senate race surprised many of the nation's political pundits. It also surprised incumbent Sen. Stuart Symington. Symington, then 69, had served three terms in the Senate after holding a number of high posts in the Truman Administration, including Secretary of the Air Force. During the 1950s, Symington became a nationally known advocate of military preparedness in general and the big bomber in particular. His status led him to make an unsuccessful bid for the Democratic presidential nomination in 1960. Symington wanted a deadlocked convention that would turn to him. But young Senator John F. Kennedy had a majority locked up before the gavel fell in Los Angeles.

During the course of the Vietnam war, Symington, the onetime big bomber man, became a committed dove, convinced that the war was futile and wrong. Because he sat on the Foreign Relations and Armed Services committees—the only Senator to sit on both—Symington was nicely placed to lobby for end-the-war legislation and against weapons systems like the ABM. In early 1973, when Mississippi's John Stennis was shot and hospitalized, Symington became acting Chairman of Armed Services, and conducted hearings into the apparent involvement of the CIA in the Watergate scandal.

During his heyday, Symington was quite a vote-getter in Missouri, running 3% ahead of Lyndon Johnson in 1964. But the close call in 1970, and his age—75 in 1976 when his seat is up—leads most observers to conclude that Symington will retire after serving out his present term. Leading

Republican contenders for the seat include Danforth and Bond; the best bet among Democratic possibilities is the Senator's son, Rep. James W. Symington of the 2nd district.

By his own admission, Missouri's other Senator is a man whose name was no household word—until July 1972, that is. When Thomas F. Eagleton was nominated for Vice President in Miami Beach, he was scarecely known outside Missouri. But in Missouri his career had been meteoric: circuit attorney in St. Louis at 27, state Attorney General at 31, Lieutenant Governor at 35, and U.S. Senator at 39. The race to become Senator was his toughest. In the primary, Eagleton had to beat incumbent Democrat Edward V. Long, who according to *Life* magazine received large retainers from one of Jimmy Hoffa's attorneys. In the general election, Eagleton had to beat suburban St. Louis Congressman Thomas B. Curtis, a respected moderate. Eagleton did both, but by only narrow margins—and, in early July 1972, he expected vigorous opposition from John Danforth in 1974.

But whatever 1974 may bring, Eagleton of course already has a place in American history. Everyone knows that George McGovern made a last-minute call and asked Eagleton to become his vice-presidential running mate. Ten days later, it came out that Eagleton had twice received electro-shock therapy for depression. The response to the news was mixed. Many felt compassion, while others did not want a possibly unbalanced man Vice-President of the United States. For his part, Eagleton happily beamed and took his case to the public as McGovern announced he was 1000% behind him. A few days later, however, Eagleton was dropped from the ticket.

Public reaction to McGovern's decision was unmistakable: for Eagleton and against McGovern. The episode probably destroyed whatever chances the McGovern candidacy had of getting off the ground. Young voters in particular—the people McGovern needed for any chance at all—apparently felt that the jettisoning of Eagleton was something straight out of the old politics, a concession to the unenlightened fear of mental illness. To be sure, Eagleton's career in the Senate has been in no way affected by what he admits were bouts of severe depression (all of which occurred before 1968). He quickly became Chairman of the District of Columbia Committee. In 1973, Eagleton steered a home rule bill to Senate passage (the real fight on the issue will come in the House). The Senator is also a co-sponsor of the Javits-Stennis-Eagleton bill to limit the capacity of the President to wage war unilaterally, and Eagleton was the chief sponsor of the Senate measure to stop the bombing of Cambodia immediately. After compromise with the White House, Eagleton's bill resulted in a cut-off date of August 15, 1973. But for some reason, Eagleton has yet to reveal his medical records, as he promised to do back in August 1972, nor has he given a completely satisfying explanation of why he did not mention the fact of his hospitalization to McGovern and his staff.

In early 1973, it looked like Eagleton would easily win in 1974. The sympathy he garnered nationally was especially intense in Missouri. But it is still possible that Eagleton may have a real fight on his hands. Much depends on whether Danforth decides to run. The two make for a nice contrast. Eagleton is an extremely fluent, often witty politician; Danforth, an ordained Episcopal priest, inclines toward a preaching tone. In his 1970 Senate campaign, Danforth solemnly spoke about the country's need to back the President and to unify itself; after Watergate, however, the young man may have to rework some of his material. An Eagleton-Danforth confrontation should produce two of the best-run and heavily financed campaigns of 1974.

Missouri politics has changed since Harry Truman's time. A onetime haberdasher has little chance these days, as rich young men with Ivy League educations seem to win everything in sight. But the same kind of young men win just about everywhere else, too.

Missouri is different, though, in the lopsided composition of its House delegation. Nine of the state's ten Congressmen are Democrats, even though Richard Nixon carried nine of its ten congressional districts in 1972. This odd state of affairs reflects past political tradition more than present partisan preference. Most of the Congressmen win out of personal popularity, and in most cases, their seats could go Republican if the incumbents retired. In the meantime, the state's young and aggressive Republicans appear to be concentrating on state offices to the exclusion of seats in Congress. They won 19 new seats in the state legislature, enough to prevent the Democrats from mustering any two-third majority necessary to override a veto from Gov. Bond. The same Republicans, however, missed an excellent opportunity to capture the 6th congressional district.

Census Data Pop. 4,677,399; 2.31% of U.S. total, 13th largest; change 1960–70, 8.3%. Central city, 30%; suburban, 35%. Median family income, $8,908; 29th highest; families above $15,000: 17%; families below $3,000: 12%. Median years education, 11.8.

1972 Share of Federal Tax Burden $4,514,800,000; 2.16% of U.S. total, 13th largest.

1972 Share of Federal Outlays $6,167,973,446; 2.85% of U.S. total, 10th largest. Per capita federal spending, $1,319.

DOD	$2,336,144,000	7th	(3.74%)	HEW	$1,687,660,942	12th	(2.36%)
AEC	$100,980,464	11th	(3.85%)	HUD	$64,728,919	17th	(2.11%)
NASA	$227,033,918	6th	(7.59%)	VA	$277,189,611	12th	(2.42%)
DOT	$169,478,263	11th	(2.15%)	USDA	$510,995,497	7th	(3.32%)
DOC	$12,804,730	22nd	(0.99%)	CSC	$86,741,989	13th	(2.10%)
DOI	$58,955,053	12th	(2.78%)	TD	$225,691,691	13th	(1.37%)
DOJ	$27,271,300	8th	(2.78%)	Other	$382,297,169		

Economic Base Agriculture, notably cattle, hogs, soybeans and dairy products; finance, insurance and real estate; transportation equipment, especially motor vehicles and equipment; food and kindred products; printing and publishing; electrical equipment and supplies; apparel and other textile products, especially men's and boys' furnishings, and women's and misses' outerwear.

Political Line-up Governor, Christopher S. Bond (R); seat up, 1976. Senators, Stuart Symington (D) and Thomas F. Eagleton (D). Representatives, 10 (9 D and 1 R). State Senate (21 D and 13 R); State House (97 D and 66 R).

The Voters

Registration No statewide registration.
Median voting age 44.7
Employment profile White collar, 47%. Blue collar, 36%. Service, 13%. Farm, 4%.
Ethnic groups Black, 10%. Total foreign stock, 7%, Germany, 2%.

Presidential vote

1972	Nixon (R)	1,153,852	(62%)
	McGovern (D)	697,147	(38%)
1968	Nixon (R)	811,932	(45%)
	Humphrey (D)	791,444	(44%)
	Wallace (AI)	206,126	(11%)
1964	Johnson (D)	1,164,344	(64%)
	Goldwater (R)	653,535	(36%)

Senator

Stuart Symington (D) Elected 1952, seat up 1976; b. June 26, 1901, Amherst, Mass.; home, St. Louis; Yale, A.B., 1923; Army, WWI; widower, two children; Episcopalian.

Career Asst. Sec. of War for Air, 1946–47; Sec. of the AF, 1947–50; Chm., Natl. Security Resources Bd., 1950–51; Reconstruction Finance Corp. Admin., 1951–52.

Offices 229 OSOB 202-225-6154. Also 7730 Carondelet, Clayton 63105, 314-725-5860, and U.S. Courthouse, Kansas City 64106, 816-374-3068.

Administrative Assistant Stanley R. Fike

Committees

Aeronautical and Space Sciences (3rd).

Armed Services (2nd); Subs: Central Intelligence; National Stockpile and Naval Petroleum Reserves; Preparedness Investigating; Military Construction Authorization (Chm.); Arms Control; Nuclear Test Ban Treaty Safeguards; Tactical Air Power.

Foreign Relations (5th); Subs: European Affairs; Near-Eastern Affairs; U.S. Security Agreement and Commitments Abroad (Chm.); Multinational Corporations.

Joint Com. on Atomic Energy (3rd); Subs: Military Applications (Chm.); Security; Energy.

Group Ratings

	ADA	COPE	LWV	RIPON	NFU	LCV	CFA	NAB	NSI	ACA
1972	70	90	82	52	70	58	100	73	10	23
1971	85	83	75	33	91	–	100	–	–	25
1970	69	100	–	61	100	34	–	11	25	6

Key Votes

1) Busing	FOR	8) Sea Life Prot	FOR	15) Tax Singls Less	FOR
2) Alas P-line	AGN	9) Campaign Subs	FOR	16) Min Tax for Rich	FOR
3) Gun Cntrl	FOR	10) Cmbodia Bmbg	AGN	17) Euro Troop Rdctn	FOR
4) Rehnquist	FOR	11) Legal Srvices	FOR	18) Bust Hwy Trust	FOR
5) Pub TV $	FOR	12) Rev Sharing	AGN	19) Maid Min Wage	FOR
6) EZ Votr Reg	FOR	13) Cnsumr Prot	FOR	20) Farm Sub Limit	AGN
7) No-Fault	FOR	14) Eq Rts Amend	FOR	21) Highr Credt Chgs	AGN

Election Results

1970 general:	Stuart Symington (D)	654,831	(51%)
	John C. Danforth (R)	617,903	(48%)
	Gene Chapman (AI)	10,065	(1%)
1970 primary:	Stuart Symington (D)	392,670	(89%)
	Douglas V. White (D)	15,187	(3%)
	William M. Thomas (D)	13,018	(3%)
	Lee C. Sutton (D)	11,105	(3%)
	Hershel V. Page (D)	7,843	(2%)
1964 general:	Stuart Symington (D)	1,186,666	(67%)
	Jean Paul Bradshaw	596,377	(33%)

Senator

Thomas F. Eagleton (D) Elected 1968, seat up 1974; b. Sept. 4, 1929, St. Louis; home, St. Louis; Amherst College, B.A. cum laude, 1950; Harvard, LL.B., 1953; USN, 1948–49; married, two children; Catholic.

Career St. Louis Circuit atty., 1956–60; Mo. Atty. Gen., 1960–64; Mo. Lt. Gov., 1964–68.

Offices 6235 NSOB, 202-225-5721. Also 4039 Fed. Bldg., St. Louis, and Rm. 911, 811 Grand, Kansas City.

Administrative Assistant Gene E. Godley

Committees

Appropriations (14th); Subs: Agriculture, Environmental and Consumer Protection; Labor and Health, Education, and Welfare, and Related Agencies; State, Justice, and Commerce, the Judiciary and Related Agencies; Legislative; Treasury, U.S. Postal Service, and General Government.

District of Columbia (Chm.).

Labor and Public Welfare (7th); Subs: Education; Health; Labor; Aging (Chm.); Special Subcommittees on Arts and Humanities; National Science Foundation.

Sp. Com. on Aging (11th); Subs: Federal, State and Community Services; Consumer Interests of the Elderly; Health of the Elderly; Long-Term Care; Retirement and the Individual.

Group Ratings

	ADA	COPE	LWV	RIPON	NFU	LCV	CFA	NAB	NSI	ACA
1972	70	90	100	60	67	75	89	50	0	21
1971	89	73	82	50	100	–	100	–	–	24
1970	91	100	–	63	100	80	–	18	0	4

Key Votes

1) Busing	FOR	8) Sea Life Prot	ABS	15) Tax Singls Less	FOR
2) Alas P-line	AGN	9) Campaign Subs	FOR	16) Min Tax for Rich	FOR
3) Gun Cntrl	FOR	10) Cmbodia Bmbg	AGN	17) Euro Troop Rdctn	FOR
4) Rehnquist	FOR	11) Legal Srvices	FOR	18) Bust Hwy Trust	ABS
5) Pub TV $	FOR	12) Rev Sharing	AGN	19) Maid Min Wage	FOR
6) EZ Votr Reg	FOR	13) Cnsumr Prot	FOR	20) Farm Sub Limit	ABS
7) No-Fault	AGN	14) Eq Rts Amend	FOR	21) Highr Credt Chgs	AGN

Election Results

1968 general:	Thomas F. Eagleton (D)	880,113	(51%)
	Thomas R. Curtis (R)	845,144	(49%)
1968 primary:	Thomas F. Eagleton (D)	224,017	(37%)
	Edward V. Long (D)	198,901	(33%)
	True Davis (D)	178,961	(29%)
	William M. Thomas (D)	4,879	(1%)

FIRST DISTRICT Political Background

The 1st district of Missouri is the north side of the city of St. Louis and a slice of the separate, totally suburban St. Louis County to the west. Because of black migration and the transformation of neighborhood patterns within the city of St. Louis, the north side is predominantly black, and in 1968 the fourth Missouri redistricting of the decade made blacks a majority district-wide. Boundary adjustments in 1972 left a smaller black percentage in the 1st, though still a majority. The suburban part of the district hugs the western city limits of St. Louis, and is mostly white; there are, however, significant numbers of blacks here in University City, Richmond Heights, and Webster Groves. The socioeconomic makeup of the suburbs ranges from blue collar in the north (Normandy, Bel-Ridge) to white collar in the south (Webster Groves, Brentwood). Lying in the middle is Clayton, which is developing into a center of large high-rise office buildings, and which is also the home of Washington University and its adjacent liberal-academic community.

The 1st, the most heavily Democratic district in Missouri, is the only one of the state's ten to give a majority to George McGovern, even though the South Dakotan had dropped St. Louis' own Tom Eagleton. For years, the 1st was represented by Democrat Frank Karsten, but after the 1968 redistricting, he lost a primary to then-Alderman and erstwhile civil rights activist William Clay. Clay had spurned the traditional political machines of St. Louis, and built up a following of his own in the black wards of the north side.

Clay is one of the more militant and outspoken and at the same politically savvy members of the Congressional Black Caucus. Back in 1963, he spent 105 days in jail for participating in a civil rights demonstration. Having a background of this sort, the Congressman has not run especially well in the predominantly white suburbs; in 1972, he ran 9% behind George McGovern in the St. Louis County portion of the 1st. Nevertheless, Clay is comfortably ensconced within the 1st's current borders, which were drawn to his specifications after rival politicians in the Missouri legislature threatened to create a white-majority 1st district.

In Washington, Clay sits on the House Education and Labor Committee, a body whose Democratic members are mostly solid liberals. At the beginning of the 93rd Congress, Clay picked up another committee assignment, Post Office and Civil Service. Back home, the Congressman has few reelection worries.

Census Data Pop. 468,056. Central city, 66%; suburban, 34%. Median family income, $8,485; families above $15,000: 17%; families below $3,000: 3%. Median years education, 10.7.

1972 Share of Federal Outlays $775,173,534

DOD	$443,116,008	HEW	$141,399,238
AEC	$67,558	HUD	$8,223,771
NASA	$55,222,450	DOI	$1,305,731
DOT	$7,636,540	USDA	$13,912,908
		Other	$104,289,330

Federal Military-Industrial Commitments

DOD Contractors Donovan Construction Co. (St. Louis), $16.307m: maintenance and work at St. Louis Army Ammunition plant. General Motors (St. Louis), $12.018m: operation of St. Louis Army Ammunition plant. Emerson Electric (St. Louis), $11.470m: launcher equipment for TOW missiles. Kisco Co. (St. Louis), $8.920m: 105mm cartridge cases.

Economic Base Finance, insurance and real estate; transportation equipment; fabricated metal products, especially fabricated structural metal products; food and kindred products; and printing and publishing, especially commercial printing. Also higher education (Univ. of Missouri, St. Louis).

The Voters

Registration No district-wide registration.
Median voting age 45.5
Employment profile White collar, 46%. Blue collar, 33%. Service, 21%. Farm, –%.
Ethnic groups Black, 54%. Total foreign stock, 8%. Germany, 2%.

Presidential vote

1972	Nixon (R)	45,765	(31%)
	McGovern (D)	101,307	(69%)
1968	Nixon (R)	41,869	(26%)
	Humphrey (D)	110,310	(68%)
	Wallace (AI)	9,671	(6%)

Representative

William L. Clay (D) Elected 1968; b. April 30, 1931, St. Louis; home, St. Louis; St. Louis U., B.S., 1953; married, three children; Catholic.

Career Alderman, 26th Ward, St. Louis, 1959–64; business rep., city employees union, 1961–64; education coordinator, Steamfitters Local No. 562, 1966–67.

Offices 328 CHOB, 202-225-2406. Also 515A Delmar, St. Louis 63108, 314-367-0930.

Administrative Assistant Michael C. McPherson

Committees

Education and Labor (13th); No. 2 (Sp. Sub. on Labor); No. 3 (Gen. Sub. on Labor); No. 7 (Equal Opportunities).

Post Office and Civil Service (12th); Subs: Manpower and Civil Service; Postal Facilities, Mail, and Labor Management.

Group Ratings

	ADA	COPE	LWV	RIPON	NFU	LCV	CFA	NAB	NSI	ACA
1972	81	88	100	75	100	54	—	0	0	7
1971	78	75	67	67	73	–	100	–	–	0
1970	84	100	–	69	82	100	100	0	0	7

Key Votes

1) Busing	FOR	6) Cmbodia Bmbg	AGN	11) Chkg Acct Intrst	FOR
2) Strip Mines	ABS	7) Bust Hwy Trust	FOR	12) End HISC (HUAC)	FOR
3) Cut Mil $	FOR	8) Farm Sub Lmt	ABS	13) Nixon Sewer Veto	AGN
4) Rev Shrg	FOR	9) School Prayr	AGN	14) Corp Cmpaign $	ABS
5) Pub TV $	ABS	10) Cnsumr Prot	FOR	15) Pol $ Disclosr	AGN

Election Results

1972 general:	William Clay (D)	95,098	(64%)
	Richard O. Funsch (R)	53,596	(36%)
1972 primary:	William Clay (D)	44,081	(76%)
	Tom Fitzgerald (D)	13,826	(24%)
1970 general:	William Clay (D)	58,082	(91%)
	Gerald G. Fischer (AI)	6,078	(9%)

SECOND DISTRICT Political Background

The 2nd district of Missouri is the heart of St. Louis County, one that lies adjacent to, but includes no part of, the city of St. Louis. The county is one of the largest and fastest-growing in the state. The 2nd is a totally suburban district, and like most such areas has considerably more social diversity than many people might think. To the north of the district, along Interstate 70, are blue-collar communities like Jennings, Ferguson, Berkley, and Airport Township. Most of the people living here grew up on the north side of St. Louis, which is now predominantly black; many work in the giant McDonnell-Douglas plants located on the north side of St. Louis County. To the south of the district are WASPy, traditionally Republican suburbs like Kirkwood and Webster Groves, fully occupied by the 1950s and placid in their conservatism. To the west, the 2nd has the bulk of the Jewish population of metropolitan St. Louis in University City and in the towns lying north of the Daniel Boone Expressway. Here too is the ultra-posh city of Ladue, home of the St. Louis Establishment (median family income: $32,000).

Altogether, the political makeup of the district produces election results that are exceedingly close to those produced by the state as a whole, and indeed, by the nation as a whole. This made the 2nd, for 1972 at least, a pretty solidly Republican district. In congressional elections, however, it has provided a safe seat for either one party or the other for the last 20 years. Until 1968, the 2nd was represented by Republican Thomas B. Curtis, who rose to become a senior member of the House Ways and Means Committee. In Washington circles, Curtis was regarded as one of the leading Republican experts on economics and tax issues in the House. After taking a commanding 66% in the 1966 congressional election, Curtis decided to run for Edward Long's Senate seat in 1968. If Long, who was the target of sensational charges in *Life* magazine, had won the Democratic primary, Curtis would probably have become Senator. But his general election opponent turned out to be 39-year-old Lt. Gov. Thomas F. Eagleton, who beat Curtis by 35,000 votes. One mark of Eagleton's strength was that he held the popular Curtis down to 52% in his own congressional district.

Curtis' successor is Democrat James W. Symington, son of Sen. Stuart Symington. Like his father, Rep. Symington held a number of important positions in a Democratic national administration before returning to Missouri to run for Congress. Prior to winning the seat in the 2nd district—something he did easily—Symington was Deputy Director of the Food for Peace program under George McGovern, an administrative assistant to then-Attorney General Robert Kennedy, Director of the President's Commission on Juvenile Delinquency (an RFK program used as a model for much of the antipoverty program), and Chief of Protocol in the State Department.

Despite a wide range of administrative experience, Symington chose to play the role of a typically unobtrusive junior Congressman, rising, in 1973, to the chairmanship of the Space Sciences and Applications Subcommittee. He is best known, at least in the Washington social circuit, as the Congressman who plays the guitar and sings songs of his own composition. A strong vote-getter, Symington can stay in the House as long as he likes; in 1972, for example, the Congressman ran 26% ahead of his old boss McGovern in the 2nd district. But it is possible that he will run for the Senate in 1976, when his father's current term expires. If Symington does win a seat in the Senate, he will continue the service thereof not only his father, but also his maternal grandfather and namesake, James W. Wadsworth, a Republican Senator from New York from 1915 to 1927.

Census Data Pop. 468,808. Central city, 0%; suburban, 100%. Median family income, $12,597; families above $15,000: 35%; families below $3,000: 4%. Median years education, 12.4.

1972 Share of Federal Outlays $776,445,352

DOD	$443,843,023	HEW	$141,631,230
AEC	$67,669	HUD	$8,237,264
NASA	$55,313,053	DOI	$1,307,873
DOT	$7,649,070	USDA	$13,935,734
		Other	$104,460,436

Federal Military-Industrial Commitments

DOD Contractors McDonnell Douglas (St. Louis), $1,464.831m: F-4 series aircraft and components; Harpoon anti-ship missile development. American Air Filter Co. (St. Louis), $10.385m: portable heating units and air conditioning equipment. Meyer Labs Maryland Heights), $10.011m: F-111 maintenance equipment.
DOD Installations Aeronautical Chart and Information Center (St. Louis).
NASA Contractors McDonnell Douglas (St. Louis), $221.360m: orbital workshops and airblock modules for Skylab program; space shuttle support.

Economic Base Transportation equipment, especially motor vehicles and equipment; finance, insurance and real estate; machinery; electrical equipment and supplies, especially electrical industrial apparatus; and fabricated metal products.

The Voters

Registration No district-wide registration.
Median voting age 42.3
Employment profile White collar, 63%. Blue collar, 28%. Service, 9%. Farm, –%.
Ethnic groups Black, 4%. Total foreign stock, 12%. Germany, 2%; Italy, 1%.

Presidential vote

1972	Nixon (R)	127,123	(63%)
	McGovern (D)	75,564	(37%)
1968	Nixon (R)	85,185	(46%)
	Humphrey (D)	79,326	(43%)
	Wallace (AI)	18,994	(10%)

Representative

James W. Symington (D) Elected 1968; b. Sept. 28, 1927, Rochester, N.Y.; home, Ladue; Yale, A.B., 1950; Columbia U., LL.B., 1954; USMCR, 1945–46; married, two children; Episcopalian.

Career Asst. city counselor, St. Louis, 1954–55; atty., 1955–58, 1960–61; U.S. Foreign Service, London, 1958–60; Deputy Dir., Food for Peace, 1961–62; Adm. Asst., Atty. Gen. Robert F. Kennedy, 1962–63; Dir., Pres. Comm. on Juv. Del., 1965–66; Consultant, Pres. Comm. on Law Enforcement, 1965–66; Chief of Protocol, Dept. of State, 1966–68.

Offices 307 CHOB, 202-225-2561. Also 10 S. Brentwood, Clayton 63105, 314-726-1410.

Administrative Assistant Charles G. Houghton III

Committees

Interstate and Foreign Commerce (19th); Sub: Public Health and Environment.

Science and Astronautics (6th); Subs: International Cooperation in Science and Space; Science, Research, and Development; Space Science and Applications (Chm.); Energy.

Group Ratings

	ADA	COPE	LWV	RIPON	NFU	LCV	CFA	NAB	NSI	ACA
1972	81	91	90	64	71	66	100	18	33	0
1971	73	67	78	81	100	–	88	–	–	25
1970	72	92	–	53	90	95	100	0	78	24

Key Votes

1) Busing	FOR	6) Cmbodia Bmbg	AGN	11) Chkg Acct Intrst	FOR
2) Strip Mines	ABS	7) Bust Hwy Trust	FOR	12) End HISC (HUAC)	AGN
3) Cut Mil $	ABS	8) Farm Sub Lmt	AGN	13) Nixon Sewer Veto	AGN
4) Rev Shrg	FOR	9) School Prayr	AGN	14) Corp Cmpaign $	FOR
5) Pub TV $	FOR	10) Cnsumr Prot	FOR	15) Pol $ Disclosr	AGN

Election Results

1972 general:	James W. Symington (D)	134,332	(64%)
	John W. Cooper, Jr. (R)	77,192	(36%)
1972 primary:	James W. Symington (D), unopposed		
1970 general:	James W. Symington (D)	93,294	(58%)
	Phil R. Hoffman (R)	66,503	(41%)
	Sterling E. Lacy (AI)	2,206	(1%)

THIRD DISTRICT Political Background

Missouri's 3rd district consists of the south side of the city of St. Louis and an adjacent portion of suburban St. Louis County. The line drawn through the middle of St. Louis to separate the 1st from the 3rd district also neatly separates the predominantly black part of the city from that which remains overwhelmingly (92%) white. Here on the south side, there are still signs of the German immigrants who made St. Louis one of the nation's gemutlichkeit cities of the nineteenth and early twentieth centuries. The immigrant Carl Schurz, the first great German-American, was a friend of President Lincoln, a Northern officer in the Civil War, and later a U.S. Senator from Missouri. Today, an Altenheim (old folks' home) still sits on the banks of the Mississippi. In the ethnic and elderly neighborhoods of south side St. Louis (median voting age is 50), people have stayed with their historic Democratic preferences or, in the case of the well-to-do neighborhoods in the southwest corner of the city, with their Republican ones.

The suburban portion of the district is a natural extension of the city. Most of the people now living here moved out along the radial avenues extending out of St. Louis. The suburban voters tend to be somewhat more conservative and more Republican than their counterparts in the city, though the parents of these people probably voted for Roosevelt and Truman.

Like many women elected to Congress, the Representative from the 3rd district, Leonor K. Sullivan, won her seat following the death of her husband, Rep. John B. Sullivan, who served intermittently during the 1940s and early 1950s. A Republican captured the seat in a 1951 special election called to fill the vacancy caused by Congressman Sullivan's death, but in 1952, Mrs. Sullivan ousted the Republican easily. Since then, the Congresswoman has had no trouble winning reelection, and no doubt can continue to do so for as long as she wishes.

Mrs. Sullivan is currently the third-ranking Democrat on the Banking and Currency Committee, and for some years, the Chairman of its subcommittee on Consumer Affairs. In that capacity, she led the fight for the Truth-in-Lending bill, her major congressional achievement, over the opposition of the banking lobby and general apathy. She was also one of the chief supporters of the Truth-in-Packaging Act. At the beginning of the 93rd Congress, Mrs. Sullivan succeeded to the chairmanship of the Merchant Marine and Fisheries Committee. Like most members of that body, she has backed the continuation of heavy government subsidies to the American shipping and shipbuilding industries. These subsidies are acclaimed by the companies and union involved, both of which maintain an unstinting interest in the workings of this otherwise little-known committee.

Mrs. Sullivan has enjoyed a solidly respectable 20 years in Congress. She is not, however, one of the heroines of the women's liberation movement. The lady from Missouri was the only female member of Congress to vote against the Equal Rights Amendment, saying that it would wipe out certain legal advantages currently held by women. Of trivial interest, she insists upon keeping her age secret, a traditional feminine prerogative, and after years of widowhood prefers to be called Mrs. John B. Sullivan. There is some speculation that Mrs. Sullivan, having achieved a chairmanship, may decide to retire soon—in which case, an interesting fight for her seat will develop in the 3rd district.

Census Data Pop. 467,544. Central city, 67%; suburban, 33%. Median family income, $10,199; families above $15,000: 20%; families below $3,000: 8%. Median years education, 10.6.

1972 Share of Federal Outlays $774,219,670

DOD	$442,570,746	HEW	$141,225,244
AEC	$67,475	HUD	$8,213,651
NASA	$55,154,498	DOI	$1,304,124
DOT	$7,627,143	USDA	$13,895,787
		Other	$104,161,002

Federal Military-Industrial Commitments

DOD Contractors Honeywell (St. Louis), $24.621m: unspecified.

Economic Base Finance, insurance and real estate; transportation equipment; fabricated metal products, especially fabricated structural metal products; food and kindred products; and printing and publishing, especially commercial printing. Also higher education (St. Louis Univ.).

The Voters

Registration No district-wide registration.
Median voting age 47.3
Employment profile White collar, 52%. Blue collar, 36%. Service, 12%. Farm, –%.
Ethnic groups Black, 6%. Spanish, 1%. Total foreign stock, 15%. Germany, 4%; Italy, 2%.

Presidential vote

1972	Nixon (R)	102,959	(58%)
	McGovern (D)	73,362	(42%)
1968	Nixon (R)	70,887	(40%)
	Humphrey (D)	85,327	(48%)
	Wallace (AI)	21,754	(12%)

Representative

Leonor K. (Mrs. John B.) **Sullivan** (D) Elected Nov. 7, 1952; b. St. Louis; home, St. Louis; Washington U.; widowed; Catholic.

Career Teacher and Dir., St. Louis Comptometer Sch.; Adm. Asst., U.S. Rep. John B. Sullivan, 1941–51.

Offices 2221 RHOB, 202-225-2671. Also 2918 Fed. Bldg., 1520 Market St., St. Louis 63103, 314-622-4500.

Administrative Assistant Irene M. Peterson

Committees

Banking and Currency (3rd); Subs: Consumer Affairs (Chm.); Housing; International Trade.

Merchant Marine and Fisheries (Chm.).

Joint Com. on Defense Production (3rd).

Group Ratings

	ADA	COPE	LWV	RIPON	NFU	LCV	CFA	NAB	NSI	ACA
1972	38	100	80	40	86	67	100	22	56	25
1971	65	67	43	38	92	–	88	–	–	25
1970	68	92	–	64	92	95	95	17	70	22

Key Votes

1) Busing	AGN	6) Cmbodia Bmbg	AGN	11) Chkg Acct Intrst	FOR
2) Strip Mines	ABS	7) Bust Hwy Trust	FOR	12) End HISC (HUAC)	AGN
3) Cut Mil $	AGN	8) Farm Sub Lmt	AGN	13) Nixon Sewer Veto	AGN
4) Rev Shrg	FOR	9) School Prayr	FOR	14) Corp Cmpaign $	FOR
5) Pub TV $	FOR	10) Cnsumr Prot	FOR	15) Pol $ Disclosr	AGN

Election Results

1972 general:	Leonor K. Sullivan (D)	124,365	(69%)
	Albert Holst (R)	54,523	(31%)
1972 primary:	Leonor K. Sullivan (D)	63,129	(94%)
	Al Deutsch (D)	3,934	(6%)
1970 general:	Leonor K. Sullivan (D)	73,021	(75%)
	Dale F. Troske (R)	24,651	(25%)

FOURTH DISTRICT Political Background

The home district of the late Harry S. Truman was the 4th congressional district of Missouri. Though Truman never represented the district in the House, he did serve the state as a U.S. Senator from 1935 to 1945. Truman was born in Lamar, Missouri, at the southern end of the 4th, near the Oklahoma and Arkansas borders. The largest city in the district is Independence (pop. 111,000), and old courthouse town, where Truman lived on Truman Road in an old Victorian house belonging to his wife's family. Just a few blocks from the house is the Jackson County Courthouse where the late President was County Judge, an administrative post, before his election to the Senate. In those days, Independence was a small town, the incongruous seat of political business for a metropolitan county that included Kansas City. Today, the suburban growth around Kansas City has so increased the size of Independence that it has engulfed the old Victorian center of town.

The 4th district is a combination of rural Missouri counties and part of the Kansas City metropolitan area. It was from the rural counties that pro-slavery Missouri men crossed into Kansas during the 1850s to battle abolitionist Republicans for control of the territorial government (see Kansas state write-up). The rural counties possess an old Democratic tradition, but in recent years, they have more often than not produced Republican majorities. Kansas City also has a Democratic tradition—one from the days of Tom Pendergast, the political boss who gave Harry Truman a start and later ended up in jail. (Truman himself had no part in any graft.) But in recent years, the Kansas City metropolitan area has been trending Republican, much like the rest of the country. In fact, results from the metropolitan area (including the two counties in Kansas) in the last few presidential elections have run a close parallel to those turned in by the nation as a whole.

The trend has made the 4th district a little less safe for Democratic Congressman William Randall. Like Truman, the Congressman served as Jackson County Judge, in Randall's case from 1946 to 1959. He then went to the House after a special election held in 1959, and has remained there ever since, accumulating seniority on the Armed Services and Government Operations committees. Particularly on Armed Services, Randall has aligned himself with the committee's more conservative Democrats; which is to say, when he is in doubt, the Congressman supports the position taken by the military. On domestic issues, Randall is also more conservative than most Northern Democrats.

Randall's approach looks like a formula tailor-made for the 4th district of Missouri. But for a longtime incumbent, Randall has not done especially well at the polls. In 1972, for example, he took only 57% of the vote—enough for a solid victory, but small enough conceivably to tempt a well-financed, hard-campaigning Republican into a 1974 effort. Randall, who will be 65 in 1974, could retire; in that case, there will certainly be a hard-fought and quite possibly close race in Harry Truman's old Democratic district.

Census Data Pop. 466,940. Central city, 2%; suburban, 47%. Median family income, $8,740; families above $15,000: 15%; families below $3,000: 12%. Median years education, 12.1.

1972 Share of Federal Outlays $529,192,172

DOD	$114,356,152	HEW	$172,312,467
AEC	$26,791,110	HUD	$4,913,985
NASA	$35,965	DOI	$9,960,430
DOT	$22,439,470	USDA	$75,393,123
		Other	$102,989,470

Federal Military-Industrial Commitments

DOD Contractors Remington Arms (Independence), $80.002m: operation of Lake City Army Ammunition plant.
DOD Installations Whitman AFB (Knobnoster).

Economic Base Agriculture, notably cattle, hogs and sheep, and grains; finance, insurance and real estate; printing and publishing, especially greeting card publishing; electrical equipment and supplies; and apparel and other textile products. Also higher education (Central Missouri State).

The Voters

Registration No district-wide registration.
Median voting age 44.6
Employment profile White collar, 42%. Blue collar, 38%. Service, 12%. Farm, 8%.
Ethnic groups Black, 2%. Total foreign stock, 4%. Germany, 1%.

Presidential vote

1972	Nixon (R)	131,874	(69%)
	McGovern (D)	60,472	(31%)
1968	Nixon (R)	85,872	(48%)
	Humphrey (D)	70,811	(40%)
	Wallace (AI)	22,118	(12%)

Representative

William J. Randall (D) Elected 1958; b. July 16, 1909, Independence; home, Independence; U. of Mo., A.B., 1931; U. of Kansas City, LL.B., 1936; Army, WWII; married, one child; Methodist.

Career Judge, Jackson County Ct., 1946–58.

Offices 2431 RHOB, 202-225-2876. Also 219 Fed. Bldg., 301 W. Lexington, Independence 64050, 816-252-7171.

Administrative Assistant Mrs. Mary Bly

Committees

Armed Services (9th); Subs: No. 2; No. 3; Sp. Sub. on Armed Services Investigating.

Government Operations (10th); Subs: Legal and Monetary Affairs (Chm.); Special Studies.

Group Ratings

	ADA	COPE	LWV	RIPON	NFU	LCV	CFA	NAB	NSI	ACA
1972	13	67	40	64	83	27	50	36	100	62
1971	32	82	25	41	67	–	50	–	–	62
1970	32	64	–	29	62	67	65	50	100	53

Key Votes

1) Busing	AGN	6) Cmbodia Bmbg	AGN	11) Chkg Acct Intrst	AGN
2) Strip Mines	AGN	7) Bust Hwy Trust	AGN	12) End HISC (HUAC)	AGN
3) Cut Mil $	AGN	8) Farm Sub Lmt	FOR	13) Nixon Sewer Veto	AGN
4) Rev Shrg	FOR	9) School Prayr	FOR	14) Corp Cmpaign $	FOR
5) Pub TV $	AGN	10) Cnsumr Prot	FOR	15) Pol $ Disclosr	AGN

Election Results

1972 general:	William J. Randall (D)	108,131	(57%)
	Raymond E. Barrows (R)	80,228	(43%)
1972 primary:	William J. Randall (D), unopposed		
1970 general:	William J. Randall (D)	80,153	(60%)
	Leslie O. Olson (R)	53,204	(40%)

FIFTH DISTRICT Political Background

The 5th district of Missouri comprises the bulk of Kansas City—the central portion of the city, though little of the territory recently acquired through annexation. The 5th takes in the core of the Kansas City metropolitan area, which is an important manufacturing center and commercial hub for most of the farmlands of Missouri and Kansas. The 5th includes the downtown skyscrapers of Kansas City that sit up on the bluffs above the Missouri River and the Kansas City stockyards; all of the city's large black ghetto and many of its white working-class neighborhoods; and the upper-income areas in the southwest portion of the city, just across the state line from the high-income suburbs of Johnson County, Kansas.

In 1948, a young, 32-year-old World War II veteran named Richard Bolling was elected Congressman from the 5th. Democrat Bolling soon became one of Speaker Sam Rayburn's protégés, and the old Texan schooled him in the ways of the House. In those days, Bolling was a favorite of the House establishment, and at the same time, as a Congressman from urban Kansas City, maintained a solidly liberal voting record. The Congressman won a seat on the crucial Rules Committee; to many, he appeared destined to be Speaker one day. But after Rayburn's death in 1961, Bolling veered off the track leading to the top. House Democrats, following the seniority principle, elevated Majority Leader John McCormack to the Speaker's chair, just as they would elevate Majority Leader Carl Albert 11 years later. Whereupon Bolling, one might say, resigned from the get-along-go-along ambience of the House, writing two books, *House out of Order* and *Power in the House*, that attacked the traditional ways of doing things in that body. To some, it seemed Bolling simply lost interest in the House; in 1970, for example, he missed an important vote in the Rules Committee when he refused to fly back from a Caribbean vacation to cast it.

But in the last two Congresses, Bolling has experienced a resurgence of interest—and power. When Carl Albert became Speaker, one of the Congressmen on whose advice he came to rely was Richard Bolling. When, in 1973, the leadership decided it needed a special committee to study how the House could more intelligently deal with the budgetary process, Bolling was named Chairman. And on the Rules Committee, Bolling has inched toward the top of the seniority ladder. At age 82, Chairman William Colmer of Mississippi chose to retire in 1972. The only other Rules Democrats senior to Bolling—Colmer's successor, 82-year-old Ray J. Madden of Indiana, and 73-year-old James Delaney of New York—have both had trouble in recent primary outings and could conceivably retire, or be defeated, soon.

Bolling's counsel is already important on the committee and in the House generally. Bolling believes in strong leadership, one that is responsive to the Democratic Caucus and at the same time capable of cracking the party whip when necessary. Few observers think that the Democratic leadership teams of the recent past have met the standards laid out in Bolling's books, but the current leadership has taken at least a few faltering steps toward them.

Census Data Pop. 467,457. Central city, 93%; suburban, 7%. Median family income, $9,727; families above $15,000: 20%; families below $3,000: 9%. Median years education, 12.2.

1972 Share of Federal Outlays $597,990,869

DOD	$118,370,630	HEW	$155,728,439
AEC	$55,383,727	HUD	$9,762,538
NASA	$74,348	DOI	$19,996,779
DOT	$25,568,572	USDA	$67,333,343
		Other	$145,772,493

Federal Military-Industrial Commitments

DOD Contractors Libby Welding (Kansas City), $17.942m: 30 kw generating sets.
DOD Installations Richards-Bebaur AFB (Grandview).
AEC Operations Bendix (Kansas City), $94.830m: operation of Kansas City plant and the fabrication and assembly of components for atomic weapons.

Economic Base Finance, insurance and real estate; printing and publishing, especially greeting card publishing; electrical equipment and supplies; transportation equipment, especially motor vehicles and equipment; machinery; and primary metal industries, especially blast furnace and steel mill products. Also higher education (Univ. of Missouri, Kansas City).

The Voters

Registration No district-wide registration.
Median voting age 44.7
Employment profile White collar, 53%. Blue collar, 32%. Service, 15%. Farm, –%.
Ethnic groups Black, 24%. Spanish, 3%. Total foreign stock, 9%. Germany, Italy, 1% each.

Presidential vote

	1972	Nixon (R)	80,553	(69%)
		McGovern (D)	71,527	(47%)
	1968	Nixon (R)	57,971	(37%)
		Humphrey (D)	83,098	(52%)
		Wallace (AI)	17,562	(11%)

Representative

Richard Bolling (D) Elected 1948; b. May 17, 1916. New York; home, Kansas City; U. of the South, B.A., 1937, M.A., 1939; Vanderbilt U., 1939–40; Army, WWII; married, one child; Episcopalian.

Career Dir. student activities and vet. affairs, U. of Kansas City, 1946–47; Midwest Dir. Americans for Democratic Action, 1947; Natl. Vice-Chm. Am. Vets. Comm., 1947–48.

Offices 2465 RHOB, 202-225-4535. Also 935 Fed. Ct. Bldg., 811 Grand Ave., Kansas City 64106, 816-842-4798.

Administrative Assistant Mrs. Gladys Uhl

Committees

Rules (3rd).

Joint Economic Com. (2nd); Subs: Fiscal Policy; Urban Affairs.

Sel. Com. on Committees of the House (Chm.).

Group Ratings

	ADA	COPE	LWV	RIPON	NFU	LCV	CFA	NAB	NSI	ACA
1972	75	90	90	73	86	66	100	0	44	17
1971	5	90	89	63	86	–	88	–	–	11
1970	52	82	–	65	100	55	100	9	22	6

Key Votes

1) Busing	FOR	6) Cmbodia Bmbg	AGN	11) Chkg Acct Intrst	FOR
2) Strip Mines	AGN	7) Bust Hwy Trust	FOR	12) End HISC (HUAC)	FOR
3) Cut Mil $	AGN	8) Farm Sub Lmt	AGN	13) Nixon Sewer Veto	AGN
4) Rev Shrg	AGN	9) School Prayr	AGN	14) Corp Cmpaign $	ABS
5) Pub TV $	FOR	10) Cnsumr Prot	FOR	15) Pol $ Disclsr	ABS

Election Results

1972 general:	Richard Bolling (D)	93,812	(63%)
	Vernon E. Rice (R)	53,257	(36%)
	Stella Sollars (Ind.)	2,381	(2%)
1972 primary:	Richard Bolling (D), unopposed		
1970 general:	Richard Bolling (D)	51,668	(61%)
	Randall Vanet (R)	31,806	(38%)
	Jim E. Kernodle (AI)	778	(1%)

SIXTH DISTRICT Political Background

Northwest Missouri is taken up by farmland, gentle hill country rolling down to the Missouri River and its tributaries. In many ways, this region is one left behind by the twentieth century. With the mechanization of the labor required to maintain a farm, people here have been moving away. All of the counties in northwest Missouri—except those lying in the Kansas City metropolitan area—contained more people at the turn of the nineteenth century than they do today. Perhaps the most melancholy story belongs to St. Joseph, one of the leading points of entry to the great American West. It was here that Pony Express riders saddled up for the transcontinental sprint to Sacramento. The transcontinental railroad, however, soon put the Pony Express out of business. As late as 1900, St. Joseph was still a solid commercial competitor of Kansas City, having a population of 102,000, compared to Kansas City's 163,000. Today, Kansas City contains over 507,000 people, while St. Joseph has dwindled to 72,000 and is becoming still smaller.

The 6th congressional district coincides almost precisely with what is called northwest Missouri: north and east of the Missouri River and west of a line drawn north and south through the middle of the state. Though most of the physical expanse of the 6th is given over to agriculture, more than half its residents live in two metropolitan areas. One such area lies in and around St. Joseph, but by far the larger and faster growing area lies in Clay and Platte counties. To give itself space to grow, Kansas City has annexed vacant land in the two counties for the last dozen years. The land has been subdivided for new homes and bulldozed to accommodate Kansas City's giant new airport. The Census Bureau considers most of Clay and Platte counties part of central city, but their character, by any measure, is really suburban.

For 18 years, the 6th was represented by W. R. Hull, the kind of conservative Democrat rural Missourians have traditionally found congenial. But in recent years, Hull's margins began to slip, and he decided to retire in 1972. That left the Republicans with a good chance to win the district, but, in customary fashion, most of the action occurred in the Democratic primary. The principal contenders in the contest were state Rep. Charles Broomfield of suburban Kansas City, and Jerry Litton, a 35-year-old successful farmer out of Livingston County. Broomfield carried Clay and Platte counties, but Litton swamped him in the rural counties; a third candidate deflected enough votes in Buchanan County (St. Joseph) to allow Litton to win with 36% of the votes. Missouri has no primary runoffs.

By all odds, Republican nominee Russell Sloan came into the general election as the favorite. But Litton campaigned vigorously, especially in the Kansas City area where he had done poorly in the primary. So while George McGovern took just 34% of the votes in the 6th district, Litton won, 55–45, over the Republican Sloan. Litton asked for and got a seat on the Agriculture Committee. He has emerged as a vigorous advocate of the family farmer and a leader in the nascent Rural Caucus. From the looks of his showing in 1972, the new Congressman has a safer seat than his veteran predecessor.

Census Data Pop. 469,642. Central city, 30%; suburban, 22%. Median family income, $8,507; families above $15,000: 14%; families below $3,000: 12%. Median years education, 12.1.

1972 Share of Federal Outlays $473,349,986

DOD	$49,369,706	HEW	$181,407,925
AEC	$18,457,887	HUD	$4,767,112
NASA	$24,778	DOI	$7,082,428
DOT	$24,491,914	USDA	$96,376,825
		Other	$91,344,411

Federal Military-Industrial Commitments

No installation or contractors receiving prime awards greater than $5,000,000.

Economic Base Agriculture, notably cattle, grains, and hogs and sheep; food and kindred products, especially meat products; finance, insurance and real estate; fabricated metal products; and paper and allied products.

The Voters

Registration No district-wide registration.
Median voting age 45.9
Employment profile White collar, 43%. Blue collar, 35%. Service, 12%. Farm, 10%.
Ethnic groups Black, 1%. Total foreign stock, 5%. Germany, 1%.

Presidential vote

1972	Nixon (R)	134,977	(67%)
	McGovern (D)	65,754	(33%)
1968	Nixon (R)	96,811	(49%)
	Humphrey (D)	82,503	(41%)
	Wallace (AI)	20,275	(10%)

Representative

Jerry Litton (D) Elected 1972; b. May 12, 1937, Lock Springs; home, Chillicothe; U. Mo., B.S., 1961; National Guard, 1950–62; married, two children; Protestant.

Career Part owner, Charolais Ranch; State Pres., Future Farmers of America; Mo. Gov.'s Advisory Council on Agric.; Mo. State Council on Education.

Offices 1005 LHOB, 202-225-7041. Also Royal Inn, 11828 Plaza Circle, Kansas City 64153, 816-243-5977.

Administrative Assistant Ed Turner

Committees

Agriculture (19th); Subs: Livestock and Grains; Tobacco; Department Operations.

Group Ratings: Newly Elected

Key Votes

1) Busing	NE	6) Cmbodia Bmbg	AGN	11) Chkg Acct Intrst	AGN
2) Strip Mines	NE	7) Bust Hwy Trust	AGN	12) End HISC (HUAC)	AGN
3) Cut Mil $	NE	8) Farm Sub Lmt	NE	13) Nixon Sewer Veto	AGN
4) Rev Shrg	NE	9) School Prayr	NE	14) Corp Cmpaign $	NE
5) Pub TV $	NE	10) Cnsumr Prot	NE	15) Pol $ Disclosr	NE

Election Results

1972 general:	Jerry Litton (D)	110,047	(55%)
	Russell Sloan (R)	91,610	(45%)

1972 primary:	Jerry Litton (D)	26,257	(36%)
	Charles S. Broomfield (D)	24,682	(34%)
	Truman E. Wilson (D)	12,372	(17%)
	Dexter Davis (D)	6,734	(9%)
	Robert V. Williams (D)	1,812	(2%)
	R. D. Hines (D)	1,130	(2%)

SEVENTH DISTRICT Political Background

Mention of the Ozarks sets up an image of rural poverty: people with quaint accents living in hillside shacks, cut off from the currents of twentieth-century America—a kind of Dogpatch. But for the Ozark Mountains region of southwest Missouri, the Dogpatch image is far from accurate, and growing more and more inaccurate every year. Southwest Missouri comprises an area roughly coincident with the state's 7th congressional district. Here one finds sizable and reasonably prosperous cities—Springfield (pop. 120,000), the state's third largest, and Joplin (pop. 39,000). Outside the cities, the Ozarks region has taken substantial growth in recent years, as people look for vacation homes or year-round residences in the pleasant green hills and along large man-made lakes.

In many mountain areas—eastern Tennessee and central Kentucky, to take two examples—political preferences have undergone little change in over a century. The Ozarks present a third example. Because the people here did not share the Confederate sympathies of many central Missourians, they became staunch Republicans and stayed that way. The Republican inclination has been strengthened of late by two things: first, a distaste for the social programs pushed by the Democrats of the 1960s, and second, the urban-bred conservatism of many of the area's recent arrivals. In the close Missouri Senate elections of 1968 and 1970, every county in the 7th district went for the Republican nominees.

The 7th is the only Missouri district to send a Republican to Congress. For 12 years, before his voluntary retirement in 1972, its Representative was Dr. Durward G. Hall, a physician. Doc Hall, as he was of course called, was one of the sternest watchdogs of the federal treasury sitting in Congress, often working in tandem with H. G. Gross of Iowa. Like Gross (see Iowa 3), Hall spent a good deal of time on the House floor fighting programs he thought smelled a little funny; occasionally, Hall would score a point and come out on top. Hall was more generous, however, on the Armed Services Committee; here he went along with a philosophy shared by the committee's majority that it was better to err by spending too much rather than too little on national defense. Hall's retirement, like those of so many other senior members in 1972, came as something of a surprise.

Back in the 7th, winning the Republican primary is tantamount to election. The principal contender in the primary was Gene Taylor, an auto dealer from Sarcoxie who was also Missouri's Republican National Committeeman. Taylor encountered a little more trouble in the contest than expected from Springfield-based John Ashcroft, now State Auditor. But in the general election, of course, Taylor won with ease. In the House, he has been voting a solid conservative line, as Hall always did. The new Congressman, however, has not yet developed a personal style to match old Doc's.

Census Data Pop. 466,699. Central city, 26%; suburban, 7%. Median family income, $6,832; families above $15,000: 9%; families below $3,000: 18%. Median years education, 11.7.

1972 Share of Federal Outlays $353,866,223

DOD	$27,269,000	HEW	$180,241,617
AEC	–	HUD	$1,722,739
NASA	$102,492	DOI	$1,605,304
DOT	$24,483,052	USDA	$43,662,499
		Other	$74,779,520

Federal Military-Industrial Commitments

No installations or contractors receiving prime awards greater than $5,000,000.

Economic Base Agriculture, notably dairy products, cattle, hogs and sheep, and poultry; food and kindred products; finance, insurance and real estate; apparel and other textile products, especially men's and boys' furnishings; and machinery. Also higher education (Southwest Missouri State).

The Voters

Registration No district-wide registration.
Median voting age 47.0
Employment profile White collar, 41%. Blue collar, 39%. Service, 13%. Farm, 7%.
Ethnic groups Total foreign stock, 3%.

Presidential vote

1972	Nixon (R)	153,239	(73%)
	McGovern (D)	57,616	(27%)
1968	Nixon (R)	112,012	(57%)
	Humphrey (D)	62,783	(32%)
	Wallace (AI)	19,718	(10%)

Representative

Gene Taylor (R) Elected 1972; b. Feb. 10, 1928, Sarcoxie; home, Sarcoxie; Southwest Mo. State Col.; married, two children; Methodist.

Career Teacher, three years; Mayor of Sarcoxie, three terms; owner-manager automobile dealership; trustee, Mo. Southern Col.; past Pres. Sarcoxie Bd. of Ed.

Offices 1221 LHOB, 202-225-6536. Also Springfield, Joplin, and Kinberling City, 417-862-4317.

Administrative Assistant Gerald L. Henson

Committees

Public Works (16th); Subs: Economic Development; Energy; Public Buildings and Grounds; Water Resources.

District of Columbia (10th); Subs: Business, Commerce, and Taxation; Education.

Group Ratings: Newly Elected

Key Votes

1) Busing	NE	6) Cmbodia Bmbg	FOR	11) Chkg Acct Intrst	AGN
2) Strip Mines	NE	7) Bust Hwy Trust	AGN	12) End HISC (HUAC)	ABS
3) Cut Mil $	NE	8) Farm Sub Lmt	NE	13) Nixon Sewer Veto	FOR
4) Rev Shrg	NE	9) School Prayr	NE	14) Corp Cmpaign $	NE
5) Pub TV $	NE	10) Cnsumr Prot	NE	15) Pol $ Disclosr	NE

Election Results

1972 general:	Gene Taylor (R)	132,780	(64%)
	William Thomas (D)	75,613	(36%)
1972 primary:	Gene Taylor (R)	71,756	(50%)
	John Ashcroft (R)	37,283	(45%)
	Don Glenn (R)	2,681	(3%)
	Lawrence C. Smith (R)	1,759	(2%)

EIGHTH DISTRICT Political Background

After five redistrictings in the last dozen years, the 8th congressional district of Missouri has at last gotten a fairly regular shape (see map in appendix). In the 1972 *Almanac*, the 8th, as it was then constituted, was said to look like a slingshot; today, after the latest redistricting, it looks more like a rooster. Its head includes Columbia, home of the University of Missouri; the tail feathers take in the western end of suburban St. Louis County; at the base of the neck lies Jefferson City, Missouri's small state capital. These are areas of diverse political tendencies. Columbia, having an old-line Democratic tradition, now provides additional support to Democrats with the coming of the 18-year-old vote. The St. Louis County suburbs are heavily Republican. Perhaps the most interesting parts of the district politically are Jefferson City and the counties to the east, which have been strongly Republican ever since they were settled by antislavery German '48ers in the mid-nineteenth century. Though the southernmost counties in the 8th—the feet of the rooster—dip into the Republican Ozarks, most of the rural counties are traditional Missouri Democratic. The most notable feature down here is Fort Leonard Wood in Pulaski County, long one of the Army's centers for basic training.

People living in this diverse district seem pretty well agreed on the merits of Congressman Richard H. Ichord. He has carried every county in the last few elections, and has had little trouble winning the Democratic primary. In Congress since 1960, Ichord is a high-ranking member of the Armed Services Committee, where he dependably supports its pro-military bipartisan majority.

But Ichord is best known as the Chairman of the House Internal Security Committee (HISC), better known by its previous name and acronym: House Un-American Activities Committee (HUAC). The panel is an anomaly among House committees, one that over its 30 years of existence has seldom reported out legislation. It has, however, launched the political careers of several notable men—Richard M. Nixon being the most notable among them. HUAC, or HISC, concentrates on making investigations—less frequent and less publicized these past few years—of subversives who are purportedly out to undermine our society and government.

In 1969, Ichord took over what looked like the jinxed chairmanship of the committee. One HUAC Chairman from the 1940s went to jail, and during the 1960s, three Chairmen, Francis Walter of Pennsylvania, Clyde Doyle of California, and Joe Pool of Texas, died in rapid succession. Another, Edwin Willis of Louisiana, was unseated in a Democratic primary. But it appears that Ichord has broken the jinx. Perhaps the innovations he wrought—a new committee name and a toning down of the circus atmosphere at hearings—have been responsible.

Nevertheless, Ichord and a majority of the committee remain convinced that the campus disorders of the late 1960s were organized by a nationwide conspiracy. Chairman Ichord once circulated a list of 65 alleged subversives who spoke at various universities in defiance of a court order. For the last 10 years, there has been a movement in the House to abolish HISC's status as a standing committee, or if not that, to cut its budget. One of the main proponents of abolition is HISC member Robert Drinan of Massachusetts, who wants to do away with a committee on which he sits. The anti-HISC movement has been gaining votes over the years, though still far from a majority. But opponents of HISC apparently convinced Wayne Hays' House Administration Committee to make substantial cuts in HISC's budget. After all, considerable evidence exists in these Nixon days that the committee had looked for conspiracies in the wrong places.

Census Data Pop. 467,532. Central city, 13%; suburban, 24%. Median family income, $7,743; families above $15,000: 14%; families below $3,000: 15%. Median years education, 11.2.

1972 Share of Federal Outlays $878,246,402

DOD	$365,881,466	HEW	$221,807,426
AEC	$86,968	HUD	$7,765,461
NASA	$21,875,268	DOI	$13,607,526
DOT	$15,330,330	USDA	$51,200,435
		Other	$180,691,522

Federal Military-Industrial Commitments

DOD Installations Fort Leonard Wood AB (Waynesville).

Economic Base Agriculture, notably cattle, hogs and sheep, and dairy products; finance, insurance and real estate; shoes, except rubber, and other leather and leather products; and apparel and other textile products. Also higher education (Univ. of Missouri, Columbia).

The Voters

Registration No district-wide registration.
Median voting age 40.0
Employment profile White collar, 46%. Blue collar, 37%. Service, 12%. Farm, 5%.
Ethnic groups Black, 3%. Total foreign stock, 5%. Germany, 2%.

Presidential vote

1972	Nixon (R)	124,585	(68%)
	McGovern (D)	58,036	(32%)
1968	Nixon (R)	88,961	(54%)
	Humphrey (D)	59,344	(36%)
	Wallace (AI)	17,822	(11%)

Representative

Richard H. Ichord (D) Elected 1960; b. June 27, 1926, Licking; home, Houston; U. of Mo., B.S., 1949, LL.B., 1952; married, three children; Baptist.

Career State Rep., 1952–60, Speaker, 1959.

Offices 2402 RHOB, 202-225-5155. Also Houston 65483, 417-967-2270.

Administrative Assistant None

Committees

Armed Services (7th); Subs: No. 1; Sp. Sub. on Human Relations. *Internal Security* (Chm.).

Group Ratings

	ADA	COPE	LWV	RIPON	NFU	LCV	CFA	NAB	NSI	ACA
1972	19	73	44	46	83	11	50	63	100	71
1971	8	44	33	31	58	–	38	–	–	71
1970	12	45	–	31	64	40	53	46	100	63

Key Votes

1) Busing	AGN	6) Cmbodia Bmbg	FOR	11) Chkg Acct Intrst	AGN
2) Strip Mines	AGN	7) Bust Hwy Trust	AGN	12) End HISC (HUAC)	AGN
3) Cut Mil $	ABS	8) Farm Sub Lmt	FOR	13) Nixon Sewer Veto	FOR
4) Rev Shrg	FOR	9) School Prayr	FOR	14) Corp Cmpaign $	AGN
5) Pub TV $	AGN	10) Cnsumr Prot	AGN	15) Pol $ Disclosr	AGN

Election Results

1972 general:	Richard H. Ichord (D)	112,556	(62%)
	David R. Countie (R)	68,580	(38%)
1972 primary:	Richard H. Ichord (D), unopposed		
1970 general:	Richard H. Ichord (D)	97,560	(64%)
	John L. Caskanett (R)	53,181	(35%)
	Charles H. Byford (Ind.)	879	(1%)

NINTH DISTRICT Political Background

The part of rural Missouri that has most faithfully sustained the Southern Democratic tradition cannot be found along the state's common border with Arkansas. It lies instead in the Little Dixie section, north of the Missouri River and across the Mississippi River from Illinois. The territory here was settled early in the nineteenth century, mainly by migrants from Kentucky and Tennessee. During the Civil War, some of the citizens of Little Dixie fought in the Confederate

Army. Since then, not much urbanization has come to this part of Missouri; so little that Mark Twain would probably still recognize Hannibal and the surrounding countryside, except for the tourist traps laid using Twain himself for bait. Meanwhile, the Democratic tradition has been so well preserved that even a candidate like George McGovern carried a county in Little Dixie.

Little Dixie was once a congressional district unto itself. Now, because of the one-man-one-vote decision, the region comprises just 51% of the 9th district. The rest of the current 9th lies in fast-growing and conservative-trending St. Charles County and a northern chunk of suburban St. Louis County—including Black Jack, a newly incorporated city that was sued by HUD for excluding blacks. The St. Louis County portion of the district is predominantly blue-collar Democratic.

For some 40 years until his death in 1964, Clarence Cannon, Chairman of the House Appropriations Committee for more than 20 years, was the Congressman from Missouri's 9th district. Cannon had been Parliamentarian of the House before he was elected Congressman: he was a crusty, fiercely independent conservative Democrat. The Chairman often refused to appropriate money for programs wanted by the Kennedy and Johnson Administrations, thereby killing them. During the Chairman's last year, Cannon and the late Carl Hayden, Chairman of the Senate Appropriations Committee, got into a monumental battle over which side of the Capitol building a House-Senate conference committee meeting should take place. For several months, there was a stalemate in this battle of octogenarians—and no federal budget.

Cannon's successor, William Hungate, votes with Northern liberals on most issues. In 1971, he resigned as Chairman of a District of Columbia subcommittee, saying that its staff, under the control of the Chairman of the full committee, John McMillan, was influenced by special interests. Hungate is now Chairman of a Judiciary subcommittee. In this capacity, he delayed the approval, pending congressional revision, of a new set of court rules promulgated by the Burger Court; many observers felt that these changed substantive areas in the law.

In such matters, Hungate has considerable expertise. He also speaks with a pronounced Missouri accent and possesses a down-home sense of humor. He wrote and recorded a little ditty called "The Ballad of the Watergate," which could be heard in the spring of 1973 over the phone lines of the Democratic National Committee. Back in Little Dixie, the Congressman is a solid vote-getter, having won all of his elections but one by large margins. This is a case where the exception proves the rule, for the Republican who held Hungate to 52% of the vote in 1972 was Christopher (Kit) Bond, who has since gone on to election as Auditor and Governor of Missouri by landslide margins.

Census Data Pop. 467,990. Central city, 0%; suburban, 49%. Median family income, $9,573; families above $15,000: 18%; families below $3,000: 11%. Median years education, 12.1.

1972 Share of Federal Outlays $564,701,791

DOD	$220,401,109	HEW	$164,510,402
AEC	$32,753	HUD	$4,317,172
NASA	$26,773,148	DOI	$710,122
DOT	$5,863,960	USDA	$61,408,857
		Other	$80,684,268

Federal Military-Industrial Commitments

No installations or contractors receiving prime awards greater than $5,000,000. (See Missouri 2)

Economic Base Agriculture, notably hogs and sheep, cattle and grains; finance, insurance and real estate; stone, clay and glass products, especially clay refractories; industrial chemicals and other chemicals and allied products; and printing and publishing.

The Voters

Registration No district-wide registration.
Median voting age 43.6
Employment profile White collar, 45%. Blue collar, 36%. Service, 11%. Farm, 8%.
Ethnic groups Black, 3%. Total foreign stock, 5%. Germany, 2%.

Presidential vote

1972	Nixon (R)	129,159	(65%)
	McGovern (D)	69,218	(35%)
1968	Nixon (R)	81,840	(45%)
	Humphrey (D)	75,883	(42%)
	Wallace (AI)	23,189	(13%)

Representative

William L. Hungate (D) Elected 1964; b. Dec. 14, 1922, Benton, Ill.; home, Troy; Mo. U., A.B., 1943; Harvard, LL.B., 1948; Army, WWII; married, two children; First Christian Church.

Career Practicing atty.; Prosecuting Atty. of Lincoln County; Sp. Asst. Atty. Gen. of Mo., 1958–64.

Offices 2437 RHOB, 202-225-2956. Also 219 W. College St., Troy 63379, 314-528-7533.

Administrative Assistant Marion C. Ross

Committees

Judiciary (6th); Sub: Reform of Federal Criminal Laws (Chm.).

Sel. Com. on Small Business (8th); Subs: Environmental Problems Affecting Small Business (Chm.); Activities of Regulatory Agencies; Special Small Business Problems.

Group Ratings

	ADA	COPE	LWV	RIPON	NFU	LCV	CFA	NAB	NSI	ACA
1972	50	82	44	64	100	40	50	20	30	18
1971	59	80	33	59	77	–	63	–	–	38
1970	60	83	–	47	67	81	79	17	70	32

Key Votes

1) Busing	AGN	6) Cmbodia Bmbg	AGN	11) Chkg Acct Intrst	AGN
2) Strip Mines	ABS	7) Bust Hwy Trust	FOR	12) End HISC (HUAC)	AGN
3) Cut Mil $	FOR	8) Farm Sub Lmt	AGN	13) Nixon Sewer Veto	AGN
4) Rev Shrg	FOR	9) School Prayr	AGN	14) Corp Cmpaign $	FOR
5) Pub TV $	FOR	10) Cnsumr Prot	FOR	15) Pol $ Disclosr	AGN

Election Results

1972 general:	William L. Hungate (D)	132,150	(67%)
	Robert L. Prange (R)	66,528	(33%)
1972 primary:	William L. Hungate (D), unopposed		
1970 general:	William L. Hungate (D)	100,988	(63%)
	Anthony C. Schroeder (R)	58,103	(36%)
	Orvil C. Hale (AI)	1,198	(1%)

TENTH DISTRICT Political Background

The 10th district of Missouri, the southeast corner of the state known as the Boot-heel, was first settled by Southerners coming up the Mississippi River looking for more cotton land. Because the Boot-heel could sustain the crop, the area has more of a Deep South feel to it than any other part of Missouri. One gauge of this is the 19% of the votes won here by George Wallace in 1968—a showing far better than the Alabaman made in any other Missouri congressional district. Generally speaking, the voting patterns of the 10th resemble those found in adjacent areas of Arkansas, Tennessee, Kentucky, and Illinois.

Bill Burlison was first elected Congressman from the district in 1968. He was formerly prosecutor in Cape Girardeau, the district's large urban concentration at 31,000. Compiling a middle-of-the-road voting record, Burlison has kept the low profile traditionally expected of junior House members. His committee choices have obviously been made with an eye to district matters. In 1973, the politician representing a rural, farming district switched out of two committees —Agriculture and Interior—to Appropriations. Here in his new committee, the Congressman's major subcommittee assignment is Agriculture, a panel that also handles appropriations having to do with the environment and consumer protection.

Burlison exemplifies a Congressman who pays close attention to his district and builds up a personal following far beyond the customary strength enjoyed by his party. Though Republicans have made a number of concerted attempts to defeat him, Burlison continues to increase his margins each time out. He is now so entrenched that ex-Gov. Warren Hearnes was reportedly persuaded not to make a race against the incumbent Congressman. Hearnes, who is from the Boot-heel, was prohibited from running for a third term as Governor in 1972 by the Missouri constitution.

Census Data Pop. 466,731. Central city, 0%; suburban, 23%. Median family income, $7,048; families above $15,000: 9%; families below $3,000: 20%. Median years education, 9.4.

1972 Share of Federal Outlays $494,678,678

DOD	$110,917,645	HEW	$187,368,639
AEC	$15,240	HUD	$6,686,448
NASA	$12,457,894	DOI	$2,071,097
DOT	$28,383,561	USDA	$73,863,741
		Other	$72,914,413

Federal Military-Industrial Commitments

No installations or contractors receiving prime awards greater than $5,000,000. (See Missouri 2).

Economic Base Agriculture, notably cattle, grains, and hogs and sheep; shoes, except rubber, and other leather and leather products; finance, insurance and real estate; apparel and other textile products; and stone, clay and glass products.

The Voters

Registration No district-wide registration.
Median voting age 45.7
Employment profile White collar, 36%. Blue collar, 44%. Service, 13%. Farm, 7%.
Ethnic groups Black, 5%. Total foreign stock, 2%.

Presidential vote

1972	Nixon (R)	111,777	(66%)
	McGovern (D)	57,754	(34%)
1968	Nixon (R)	71,624	(42%)
	Humphrey (D)	66,638	(39%)
	Wallace (AI)	32,365	(19%)

Representative

Bill D. Burlison (D) Elected 1968; b. March 15, 1935, Wardell; home, Cape Girardeau; Mo. State Col., B.A., 1953, B.S., 1959; U. of Mo., LL.B., 1956; M. Ed., 1964; USMC, 1956–59; married, three children; Baptist.

Career Atty., 1956–59; real estate broker, 1960–62; Pres., Cape Girardeau County Bd. of Ed., 1966; Asst. Atty. Gen. Mo., 1959–62; Pros. Atty. Cape Girardeau County, 1962–68.

Offices 1338 LHOB, 202-225-4404. Also New Fed. Bldg., Cape Girardeau 63701, 314-335-0101.

Administrative Assistant Miss Michal Sue Prossea

Committees

Appropriations (33rd); Subs: Agriculture—Environmental and Consumer Protection; District of Columbia.

Group Ratings

	ADA	COPE	LWV	RIPON	NFU	LCV	CFA	NAB	NSI	ACA
1972	44	73	55	40	86	27	50	18	60	48
1971	49	83	67	50	93	–	88	–	–	32
1970	48	60	–	53	67	67	75	59	80	53

Key Votes

1) Busing	AGN	6) Cmbodia Bmbg	FOR	11) Chkg Acct Intrst	FOR
2) Strip Mines	AGN	7) Bust Hwy Trust	AGN	12) End HISC (HUAC)	AGN
3) Cut Mil $	AGN	8) Farm Sub Lmt	AGN	13) Nixon Sewer Veto	AGN
4) Rev Shrg	FOR	9) School Prayr	AGN	14) Corp Cmpaign $	FOR
5) Pub TV $	AGN	10) Cnsumr Prot	FOR	15) Pol $ Disclosr	AGN

Election Results

1972 general:	Bill D. Burlison (D)	106,301	(64%)
	M. Francis Svendrowski (R)	59,083	(36%)
1972 primary:	Bill D. Burlison (D)	56,894	(76%)
	Ed Faulkenbery (D)	17,839	(24%)
1970 general:	Bill D. Burlison (D)	62,764	(56%)
	Gary Rust (R)	49,355	(44%)

MONTANA

Political Background

Montana is the nation's fourth largest state in area, but only forty-third in population. To the west, in Big Sky country, are rugged mountains, and to the east, barren plains. Montanans can often drive 40 miles down a highway without seeing another car. The people here like life under the Big Sky and prefer weekends of fishing, hunting, or boating to the headier attractions available in urban America. The state's largest urban centers are Billings and Great Falls, each with less than 90,000 people. All Montanans were sickened by the massive forest fires that hit the state in August 1973.

Montana's first white settlers were miners, some of whom found large deposits of gold, silver, and copper in the Rocky Mountains to the west. Later, cattlemen and dry-land wheat farmers moved onto the plains and river valleys of the state. All over the country, miners gravitated toward the Democratic party, and Montana miners were no exception. Butte and Anaconda, copper and gold towns, still cast 3–1 Democratic majorities in nearly every election, though both are losing population as the profitable ores peter out. To the east, around Billings, the state's fastest growing area, voters lean toward conservative Republicanism.

Montana politics has featured a long-standing hostility between mine owners, power companies, and cattlemen on one side—mainly Republicans—and labor unions and miners on the other—mainly Democrats. Traditionally, the split has meant that the state's eastern plains go Republican, while the western mountains vote Democratic. But Montana voters are quite unpredictable. Often a county here will switch parties to vote for losing candidates in successive elections—a form of political behavior rare in other states.

The senior Senator from Montana is Mike Mansfield, the Senate Majority Leader. Born in Manhattan in 1903, Mansfield was sent by his Irish immigrant parents to live with relatives in Montana. At age 14, he enlisted in the Navy, and later served in the Army and the Marine Corps. After a few years of working in the mines, Mansfield went back to school, at his wife's insistence, and earned two degrees. During the 1930s, he was a professor of Latin American and Far Eastern history at Montana University in Missoula. In 1942, the professor was elected to the House, replacing Jeanette Rankin, the first woman to serve in Congress. (In her two widely separated terms in the House, Rankin voted against American entry into both Wold War I and World War II.) Ten years later, Mansfield beat incumbent Zales N. Ecton in a Senate race, and since has never received less than 60% of the votes in Montana.

Mansfield has been Senate Majority Leader since 1961—far longer than anyone else in history. Some observers have criticized him for being too gentle and timid, and Mansfield himself prefers to be called a "coordinator" rather than a leader. Whatever the case, it is not at all clear that the highly ideological and individualistic Democratic Senate members of today could be led around in the manner Lyndon Johnson manipulated the very different Senate of the mid-1950s.

With a seat on the Foreign Relations Committee, Mansfield maintains a good feel for, and a strong interest in, foreign policy. He is one of a few Senators who was always skeptical about American involvement in Indochina, and most Americans probably wish that Kennedy and Johnson had taken the Senator's advice and withdrawn. Though Johnson was the man who promoted Mansfield to Whip, the Montanan was one of the few men in public life with the nerve to disagree with LBJ about Vietnam to the President's face. As Mansfield grew increasingly disgusted with the war, he pushed for, and got, Senate passage of various end-the-war amendments. Later he was a quiet force behind the successful congressional moves to stop the American bombing of Cambodia.

Mansfield has also crusaded for a reduction of American forces in Europe. Though no one claims they constitute a credible deterrent to a conventional attack, they do serve as a major drain on American balance of payments. Once again, Mansfield persuaded the majority of the Senate that he was right, but the House refused to go along, preferring to leave the matter to negotiations being conducted by the Nixon Administration.

Though Mansfield is not a dynamic leader, his fairmindedness and humility are universally respected in the Senate. His regard for the rights of his opponents is matched only by an unflagging determination to make his own point. But Mansfield is also a tiger when it comes to protecting the interests of his constituency. When Amtrak threatened to cut off rail passenger service in Montana, the Majority Leader made certain that it was not. In Montana, Mansfield has been an unbeatable politician. In 1970, however, a Republican opponent, a sporting-goods dealer, cut into the Senator's customary margins by attacking Mansfield's support of gun-control legislation. The issue was a potent one in Montana, where the attitudes of firearm buffs approach the intense devotion of car buffs in other places. Mansfield will probably retire when his seat comes up in 1976, when he will be 73. Possible Democratic successors include 2nd district Rep. John Melcher and Gov. Thomas Judge; the Republicans, who currently hold few high offices in the state, are expected to make a determined effort to win their first Montana Senate race since 1946.

Democrat Lee Metcalf won Montana's western (1st district) House seat in 1952 and became the state's junior Senator in 1960. Like many western politicians, Metcalf is especially interested in power issues; he is a strong proponent of public power development and a vigorous critic of private utilities. Organized labor has given Metcalf its staunch backing. The unions appreciate not just his 100% rating from COPE, but in particular his vote in favor of the Lockheed loan—he changed his mind at the last minute and cast the decisive vote in the matter. Metcalf is not the vote-getter that his colleague Mansfield is. The junior Senator won a second term in 1966 by a 53–47 margin over then-Gov. Tim Babcock; and then won reelection in 1972 over state Sen. Henry Hibbard by an even narrower margin. Metcalf will be 67 in 1978, when his present term expires, and like Mansfield he may choose to retire.

Montana's two congressional districts roughly match the two halves of the state. Oddly enough, however, the western (1st district) elects a Republican Congressman, and the 2nd, situated almost entirely on the plains, returns a Democrat. Over the last dozen years, the 1st has been one of the nation's most marginal congressional districts in the nation, though it sent nobody but Democrats to Congress from 1942 to 1968. Both Mansfield and Metcalf represented the district, followed by Arnold Olsen in 1960. In 1970, after winning five straight elections with less than 55% of the vote, Olsen finally lost to Dick Shoup, the Republican Mayor of Missoula, by 1,300 votes.

Shoup beat Olsen more convincingly in 1972, winning 54–46. Population shifts and the advantages of incumbency helped Shoup in both elections. The Democratic towns of Butte and Anaconda once dominated the district, but both have lost population. By 1970, the more marginal town of Missoula became the largest in the district. For 1972, the students at the University of Montana at Missoula got the vote and cut Shoup's margin in his home town. After two years of incumbency, however, Shoup ran significantly better in the rest of the 1st district.

The 2nd district, by contrast, has seldom been the site of close elections. This is a vast expanse—in area the fourth largest district in the nation. Here are cattle ranges stretching as far as the eye can see, towering buttes and magnificently eroded high plains country, the huge earthen Fort Peck Dam on the Missouri, and the battlefield where the Sioux feel they gave Custer only what he deserved. Politically, the 2nd is dominated by two urban concentrations, Great Falls and Billings, which cast almost half of the district's votes. Great Falls is usually Democratic, and Billings Republican. The district as a whole, however, is more Republican than otherwise, and for many years provided comfortable margins for Republican Congressmen.

The most recent of these Republican House members, James Battin, resigned in 1969 to accept a federal judgeship. In the special election that followed, a Democrat captured what was formerly a Republican seat, as was the case in several other such contests held that year (Massachusetts 6 and Wisconsin 7). Democratic state Sen. John Melcher forced his Republican opponent to the defensive by attacking the economic policies of the Nixon Administration, in particular its farm programs. Melcher also offered a mild criticism of Nixon's ABM program—but voted for ABM appropriations once in office. One of the nation's two ABM sites is located at Malstrom Air Force Base near Great Falls.

Melcher won the 1969 special election by a 51–49 margin. He has since become phenomenally popular in the 2nd district. In 1972, hardly a vintage Democratic year, Melcher took 76% of the votes, more than Mike Mansfield ever won. Melcher has committee assignments of special interest to his constituents: Interior and Agriculture. On the latter, Melcher became a leading critic of the 1972 Soviet grain deal and the profits made by big grain dealers. The men who run the elevators allegedly used inside information provided by men in the Administration's Agriculture Department. Melcher's ability to win House elections is no longer in doubt; the question is whether he will succeed to one of the state's Senate seats in 1976 or 1978.

Census Data Pop. 694,409; 0.34% of U.S. total, 43rd largest; change 1960–70, 2.9%. Central city, 18%; suburban, 7%. Median family income, $8,510; 32nd highest; families above $15,000: 14%; families below $3,000: 11%. Median years education, 12.3.

1972 Share of Federal Tax Burden $606,150,000; 0.29% of U.S. total, 44th largest.

1972 Share of Federal Outlays $1,092,313,219; 0.50% of U.S. total, 39th largest. Per capita federal spending, $1,573.

DOD	$336,135,000	36th (0.54%)	HEW	$245,498,483	40th (0.34%)
AEC	$60,016	43rd (—)	HUD	$8,981,802	43rd (0.29%)
NASA	$94,888	44th (—)	VA	$41,693,377	43rd (0.36%)
DOT	$67,864,441	36th (0.86%)	USDA	$222,911,374	29th (1.45%)
DOC	$6,756,374	31st (0.52%)	CSC	$14,096,990	42nd (0.34%)
DOI	$58,417,410	13th (2.75%)	TD	$33,867,385	40th (0.21%)
DOJ	$4,626,822	39th (0.47%)	Other	$53,308,857	

Economic Base Agriculture, notably cattle, wheat, barley and dairy products; finance, insurance and real estate; lumber and wood products, especially sawmills and planing mills; primary nonferrous metals, and other primary metal industries; food and kindred products; metal mining.

Political Line-up Governor, Thomas L. Judge (D); seat up, 1976. Senators, Mike Mansfield (D) and Lee Metcalf (D). Representatives, 2 (1 D and 1 R). State Senate (27 D and 23 R); State House (54 D and 46 R).

The Voters

Registration 386,867 Total. No party registration.
Median voting age 43.6
Employment profile White collar, 45%. Blue collar, 28%. Service, 15%. Farm, 12%.
Ethnic groups Indian, 4%. Total foreign stock, 17%.

Presidential vote

1972	Nixon (R)	183,976	(60%)
	McGovern (D)	120,197	(40%)
1968	Nixon (R)	138,835	(51%)
	Humphrey (D)	114,117	(42%)
	Wallace (AI)	20,015	(7%)
1964	Johnson (D)	164,246	(59%)
	Goldwater (R)	113,032	(41%)

Senator

Michael J. Mansfield (D) Elected 1952, seat up 1976; b. March 16, 1903, New York City; home, Missoula; Mont. School of Mines, 1927–28; Mont. State U., B.A., 1933, M.A., 1934; U. of Calif., 1936–37; Navy 1918–19; Army, 1919–20; USMC, 1920–22; married, one child; Catholic.

Career Miner, mining engineer, 1922–31; Prof., Mont. U., 1933–43; U.S. House of Reps., 1943–53; Asst. Majority Leader, U.S. Senate, 1957–61, Majority Leader, 1961– .

Offices 133 OSOB, 202-225-2644.

Administrative Assistant Mrs. Margaret DeMichele

Committees

Appropriations (8th); Subs: Defense; Housing and Urban Development, Space, Science, and Veterans; Military Construction (Chm.); State, Justice, and Commerce, the Judiciary, and Related Agencies; Transportation.

Foreign Relations (3rd); Subs: Far-Eastern Affairs (Chm.); Near-Eastern Affairs; U.S. Security Agreements and Commitments Abroad; Western Hemisphere Affairs.

Sp. Com. to Study Questions Related to Secret and Confidential Government Documents (Co-Chm.).

Group Ratings

	ADA	COPE	LWV	RIPON	NFU	LCV	CFA	NAB	NSI	ACA
1972	80	88	70	57	100	63	100	0	10	5
1971	78	75	73	48	91	–	100	–	–	11
1970	75	83	–	65	94	27	–	20	20	29

Key Votes

1) Busing	FOR	8) Sea Life Prot	FOR	15) Tax Singls Less	AGN
2) Alas P-line	AGN	9) Campaign Subs	FOR	16) Min Tax for Rich	FOR
3) Gun Cntrl	AGN	10) Cmbodia Bmbg	AGN	17) Euro Troop Rdctn	FOR
4) Rehnquist	AGN	11) Legal Srvices	ABS	18) Bust Hwy Trust	AGN
5) Pub TV $	ABS	12) Rev Sharing	AGN	19) Maid Min Wage	FOR
6) EZ Votr Reg	FOR	13) Cnsumr Prot	ABS	20) Farm Sub Limit	AGN
7) No-Fault	FOR	14) Eq Rts Amend	FOR	21) Highr Credt Chgs	ABS

Election Results

1970 general:	Mike Mansfield (D)	150,060	(61%)
	Harold E. Wallace (R)	97,809	(39%)
1970 primary:	Mike Mansfield (D)	68,146	(77%)
	Tom McDonald (D)	10,733	(12%)
	John W. Lawlor (D)	9,384	(11%)
1964 general:	Mike Mansfield (D)	180,643	(65%)
	Alex Blewett (R)	99,367	(35%)

Senator

Lee Metcalf (D) Elected 1960, seat up 1978; b. Jan. 28, 1911, Stevensville; home, Helena; Stanford U., B.A., 1936; Mont. State U., LL.B., 1936; Army, WWII; married, one child; Methodist.

Career Practicing atty., 1936–53; Mont. House of Reps., 1937; Asst. Atty. Gen., Mont., 1937–41; Assoc. Justice, Mont. Supreme Ct., 1946; U.S. House of Reps., 1953–61.

Offices 427 OSOB, 202-225-2651. Also Lalonde Bldg., 41½ N. Main St., Helena 59601, 406-442-4361, and 4439 Fed. Bldg., Billings 59101, 406-259-5966.

Administrative Assistant Merrill Englund

Committees

Government Operations (6th); Subs: Intergovernmental Relations; Budgeting, Management, and Expenditures (Chm.).

Interior and Insular Affairs (4th); Subs: Indian Affairs; Minerals, Materials and Fuels (Chm.); Territories and Insular Affairs; Water and Power Resources.

Joint Com. on Congressional Operations (Chm.).

Group Ratings

	ADA	COPE	LWV	RIPON	NFU	LCV	CFA	NAB	NSI	ACA
1972	40	100	100	76	100	57	100	10	0	6
1971	74	92	90	68	100	–	86	–	–	14
1970	72	100	–	61	100	63	–	0	13	0

Key Votes

1) Busing	FOR	8) Sea Life Prot	AGN	15) Tax Singls Less	FOR
2) Alas P-line	AGN	9) Campaign Subs	FOR	16) Min Tax for Rich	FOR
3) Gun Cntrl	AGN	10) Cmbodia Bmbg	AGN	17) Euro Troop Rdctn	FOR
4) Rehnquist	AGN	11) Legal Srvices	FOR	18) Bust Hwy Trust	FOR
5) Pub TV $	ABS	12) Rev Sharing	FOR	19) Maid Min Wage	FOR
6) EZ Votr Reg	ABS	13) Cnsumr Prot	ABS	20) Farm Sub Limit	AGN
7) No-Fault	FOR	14) Eq Rts Amend	FOR	21) Highr Credt Chgs	AGN

Election Results

1972 general:	Lee Metcalf (D)	163,609	(52%)
	Henry S. Hibbard (R)	151,316	(48%)
1972 primary:	Lee Metcalf (D)	106,491	(86%)
	Jerome Peters (D)	16,729	(14%)
1966 general:	Lee Metcalf (D)	138,166	(53%)
	Tim Babcock (R)	121,697	(47%)

FIRST DISTRICT

Census Data Pop. 347,447. Central city, 0%; suburban, 0%. Median family income, $8,576; families above $15,000: 13%; families below $3,000: 10%. Median years education, 12.3.

1972 Share of Federal Outlays $580,329,836

DOD	$223,412,000	HEW	$117,328,151
AEC	$60,016	HUD	$7,779,900
NASA	$94,888	DOI	$24,841,234
DOT	$39,183,119	USDA	$85,227,748
		Other	$82,402,780

Federal Military-Industrial Commitments

DOD Contractors Kiewit Morrison Fischback JV (Conrad), $160.928m: construction of ABM missile launching site. Smith Boeing (Conrad), $17.731m: unspecified. Berg Chris (Conrad), $10.717m: unspecified.
DOD Installations Kalispell AF Station (Kalispell).

Economic Base Agriculture, notably cattle, grains, and hogs and sheep; lumber and wood products, especially general sawmill and planing mill products; finance, insurance and real estate; and primary metal industries, especially primary nonferrous metals. Also higher education (Montana State Univ., and Univ. of Montana).

The Voters

Registration 199,079 total. No party registration.
Median voting age 43.6
Employment profile White collar, 46%. Blue collar, 31%. Service, 15%. Farm, 8%.
Ethnic groups Indian, 3%. Total foreign stock, 16%.

Presidential vote

1972	Nixon (R)	92,166	(58%)
	McGovern (D)	65,384	(42%)
1968	Nixon (R)	65,689	(48%)
	Humphrey (D)	59,110	(43%)
	Wallace (AI)	11,227	(8%)

Representative

Richard G. Shoup (R) Elected 1970; B. Nov. 29, 1923, Salmon, Idaho; home, Missoula; U. of Mont., B.S., 1950; Army, WWII and Korean War; married, three children; Disciples of Christ.

Career Alderman; Missoula City Council, 1963–67, Pres., 1965–67; Mayor, Missoula, 1967–70; owner-operator, laundry and drycleaning business.

Offices 1127 LHOB, 202-225-3211. Also P.O. Box 1509, Missoula 59801, 406-543-7882, and 528 Sanders, Helena 59601, 406-442-9040.

Administrative Assistant Roy Julian

Committees

Interstate and Foreign Commerce (14th); Sub: Transportation and Aeronautics.

Group Ratings

	ADA	COPE	LWV	RIPON	NFU	LCV	CFA	NAB	NSI	ACA
1972	6	30	33	57	57	27	0	75	100	77
1971	8	8	25	41	57	–	33	–	–	78

Key Votes

1) Busing	AGN	6) Cmbodia Bmbg	AGN	11) Chkg Acct Intrst	FOR
2) Strip Mines	AGN	7) Bust Hwy Trust	AGN	12) End HISC (HUAC)	AGN
3) Cut Mil $	ABS	8) Farm Sub Lmt	ABS	13) Nixon Sewer Veto	FOR
4) Rev Shrg	AGN	9) School Prayr	FOR	14) Corp Cmpaign $	FOR
5) Pub TV $	AGN	10) Cnsumr Prot	AGN	15) Pol $ Disclosr	AGN

Election Results

1972 general:	Richard G. Shoup (R)	88,373	(54%)
	Arnold Olsen (D)	76,073	(46%)
1972 Primary:	Richard G. Shoup (R)	41,234	(90%)
	Kay M. Thompson (R)	4,504	(10%)
1970 general:	Richard G. Shoup (R)	64,388	(50%)
	Arnold Olsen (D)	63,175	(50%)

SECOND DISTRICT

Census Data Pop. 346,962. Central city, 35%; suburban, 14%. Median family income, $8,436; families above $15,000: 14%; families below $3,000: 11%. Median years education, 12.3.

1972 Share of Federal Outlays $511,983,383

DOD	$112,723,000	HEW	$128,170,332
AEC	–	HUD	$1,201,902
NASA	–	DOI	$33,576,176
DOT	$28,681,322	USDA	$137,683,626
		Other	$69,947,025

Federal Military-Industrial Commitments

DOD Contractors Tumpane Co. (Glasgow), $5.609m: unspecified.
DOD Installations Malstrom AFB (Great Falls). Havre AF Station (Havre). Opheim AF Station (Opheim).

Economic Base Agriculture, notably cattle, grains, and hogs and sheep; finance, insurance and real estate; food and kindred products; and primary metal industries, especially primary nonferrous metals.

The Voters

Registration 187,788 total. No party registration.
Median voting age 43.6
Employment profile White collar, 45%. Blue collar, 25%. Service, 14%. Farm, 16%.
Ethnic groups Indian, 5%. Total foreign stock, 19%.

Presidential vote

1972	Nixon (R)	91,810	(63%)
	McGovern (D)	54,813	(37%)

1968	Nixon (R)	73,146	(53%)
	Humphrey (D)	55,007	(40%)
	Wallace (AI)	8,788	(6%)

Representative

John Melcher (D) Elected 1969; b. Sept. 6, 1924, Sioux City, Iowa; home, Forsyth; U. of Minn., 1942–43; Iowa State U., D.V.M., 1950; Army, WWII; married, five children; Catholic.

Career Veterinarian; Alderman, Forsyth, 1953; Mayor, Forsyth, 1955–61; Mont. House of Reps., 1961–62, 1969; Mont. Senate, 1963–67.

Offices 1641 LHOB, 202-225-1555. Also 1016 Fed. Bldg., Billings 59102, 406-245-6644, and 9 Sixth St. N., Great Falls 59401, 406-761-3365.

Administrative Assistant Benton J. Stong

Committees

Agriculture (11th); Subs: Livestock and Grains; Family Farms and Rural Development; Forests.

Interior and Insular Affairs (14th); Subs: Environment; Indian Affairs; Mines and Mining; Public Lands (Chm.).

Group Ratings

	ADA	COPE	LWV	RIPON	NFU	LCV	CFA	NAB	NSI	ACA
1972	50	82	88	71	100	53	100	8	50	20
1971	78	83	100	71	100	–	100	–	–	19
1970	68	75	–	56	92	100	100	36	75	35

Key Votes

1) Busing	FOR	6) Cmbodia Bmbg	AGN	11) Chkg Acct Intrst	ABS
2) Strip Mines	AGN	7) Bust Hwy Trust	AGN	12) End HISC (HUAC)	AGN
3) Cut Mil $	FOR	8) Farm Sub Lmt	AGN	13) Nixon Sewer Veto	AGN
4) Rev Shrg	FOR	9) School Prayr	FOR	14) Corp Cmpaign $	FOR
5) Pub TV $	ABS	10) Cnsumr Prot	FOR	15) Pol $ Disclosr	AGN

Election Results

1972 general:	John Melcher (D)	114,524	(76%)
	Richard Forester (R)	36,063	(24%)
1972 primary:	John Melcher (D), unopposed		
1970 general:	John Melcher (D)	78,082	(64%)
	Jack Rehberg (R)	43,752	(36%)

NEBRASKA

Political Background

Nebraska is the nation's most consistently Republican state. Richard Nixon got his best percentages here in both 1960 and 1968, and only a few Southern states did better for him in 1972. Moreover, Nebraska voters have usually sent all-Republican congressional delegations to Washington. The origin of the state's Republicanism lies in the great land rush of the 1880s, one that brought some half million new residents to Nebraska, mainly from the Republican Midwest. In 1880, Nebraska had a population of 452,000; ten years later, it reached 1,062,000—not far below the 1970 figure of 1,483,000.

During the depression of the 1890s, Nebraska produced the populist prairie radicalism of William Jennings Bryan, the "Silver-Tongued Orator of the Platte," and one of a long line of American disparagers of the effete snobs of the East. But the state quickly reverted to its Republican voting habits, supporting McKinley over Bryan in 1900. Since then, Nebraska's only notable lapse from conservative Republicanism lay in the long career of George W. Norris (Congressman, 1903–13 and Senator, 1913–43). During the Progressive era, Norris led the House rebellion against Speaker Cannon in 1911, and during the 1930s, the Nebraskan fathered the TVA and the Norris-LaGuardia Anti-Injunction Act.

Since 1900, most of Nebraska's growth has occurred in and around the state's major cities—Omaha (pop. 347,000) and Lincoln (pop. 150,000)—which between them contain about 40% of the state's people. Most of the immigrants to Omaha, a railroad, meat-packing, and manufacturing center, and Lincoln, the state capital and home of the University of Nebraska, come from the rural, Republican hinterlands. There is a sizable Eastern European, especially Czech, community on the south side of Omaha, which, like the city's small black ghetto, votes Democratic as do a few isolated German-Catholic rural counties. But as a whole the Nebraska political picture is solidly Republican. In the close presidential elections of 1960 and 1968, Richard Nixon carried both Omaha and Lincoln and all but three or four rural Nebraska counties.

Yet if the state is overwhelmingly Republican in national and congressional elections, it has achieved a kind of equilibrium in state political contests. As in a number of Midwestern states, Nebraska's minority Democratic party has made especially strong efforts to win state elections—feeling free to outflank the majority Republicans on the right. Since 1960, Democrats have held the governorship for all but four years. In 1970, Democratic gubernatorial candidate J. J. Exon won a 55% victory with a classic Republican platform—lower taxes and less government spending. That same year the Democratic surge in the state was also seen in the senatorial and congressional races, and produced some near upsets.

One near-upset in 1972 that produced some eyebrow-raising in Washington was the narrow victory of Carl Curtis, an 18-year veteran of the Senate and one of its most conservative members. In 1964, he was an especially enthusiastic pre-convention booster of Barry Goldwater, and in 1973, during the darkest days of Watergate for Richard Nixon, Curtis led a delegation of 10 conservative Senators to the White House, assuring the President of their full confidence. Up until 1972, Curtis was thought to have one of the Senate's safest seats. But state Sen. Terry Carpenter held him down to 53% of the votes—a career low and probably an indication that the 69-year-old (in 1974) legislator will choose to retire when his seat comes up in 1978.

Carpenter is one of the authentic zanies in American politics—a gas station operator from Scottsbluff and a Democrat-turned-Republican-turned-Democrat. In 1932, Carpenter was elected to Congress in the Roosevelt landslide; since then, he has sought the governorship three times and a U.S. Senate seat at least four times. His latest try against Curtis, made when he was 72, was the closest he has come to success. But Carpenter's big moment in American history occurred in 1956 when he was delegate to the Republican National Convention. He stood up and nominated Joe Smith for Vice-President. No such person existed, he later admitted; he was merely objecting to the renomination of Richard Nixon. All along, the man's switching of party affiliation has not hurt him in state legislative races, because the unicameral Nebraska House is elected on a non-partisan basis—the most lasting of the Norris reforms.

As a matter of tradition, Nebraska has chosen one Senator from Omaha and one from the rural part of the state. Since 1954, Roman L. Hruska, the state's senior Senator by a few months, has held the Omaha seat. In 1970, Hruska was challenged by another veteran campaigner, Democrat Frank B. Morrison, who served as Governor from 1961 to 1966. Morrison had run unsuccessfully against Hruska once before in 1958, and against Curtis in 1966. In 1968, the only election year since 1956 in which Morrison was not a candidate for statewide office, his wife ran for Congress in the 2nd district. In 1972, Morrison was not on the hustings, but served as chairman of Nebraska's McGovern delegation at the Democratic National Convention.

In the 1970 Senate campaign, Hruska positioned himself as a staunch and conservative supporter of the Nixon Administration—a position to which he was fully entitled. Meanwhile, Morrison projected a middle-of-the-road image and contrasted his record as Governor with that of his unpopular successor, who had pushed a state income tax, the issue responsible for his 1970 defeat. But the most highly charged issue in the campaign was Morrison's charge that a chain of drive-in theaters, of which Hruska was an owner and officer, showed movies like "The Blood

Drinker" and "Girl on a Chain Gang," and "Catch-22." No doubt Hruska was embarrassed, since he was an outspoken critic of pornography and stern dissenter from a report on the subject submitted by a presidential commission some months before. The Senator countered with an "I-didn't-do-it-but-if-I-did-it-wasn't-so-bad" defense, saying that he did not run the firm, but claiming credit for the firm's being one the few chains that refused to show X-rated films. The drive-in movie issue was a major factor in Morrison's 47% showing—Hruska's poorest outing in 16 years and the closest the Democrats have come to electing a Senator for a long time.

Hruska, like Curtis, is getting on in years. The senior Senator will be 72 when his seat comes up in 1976. Also like Curtis, Hruska may well retire. Putative successors: to Hruska's Omaha seat, 2nd district Rep. John McCollister; to Curtis' outstate seat, 1st district Rep. Charles Thone. Such would be the normal order of succession, as both Hruska and Curtis ascended to the Senate from the House. But there have been enough surprises, or near-surprises, in Nebraska politics of the last few years to create at least some uncertainty about matters like these.

Census Data Pop. 1,483,791; 0.73% of U.S. total, 35th largest; change 1960–70, 5.1%. Central city, 34%; suburban, 9%. Median family income, $8,562; 31st highest; families above $15,000: 15%; families below $3,000: 11%. Median years education, 12.3.

1972 Share of Federal Tax Burden $1,379,520,000; 0.66% of U.S. total, 32nd largest.

1972 Share of Federal Outlays $1,617,993,269; 0.75% of U.S. total, 35th largest. Per capita federal spending, $1,090.

DOD	$287,420,000	39th (0.46%)	HEW	$497,771,803	35th (0.70%)
AEC	$48,000	44th (—)	HUD	$12,033,924	41st (0.39%)
NASA	$642,436	37th (0.02%)	VA	$84,914,393	35th (0.74%)
DOT	$50,837,259	40th (0.64%)	USDA	$491,178,751	10th (3.19%)
DOC	$1,551,866	46th (0.12%)	CSC	$24,108,180	37th (0.58%)
DOI	$12,585,259	35th (0.59%)	TD	$70,728,974	30th (0.43%)
DOJ	$5,840,392	37th (0.59%)	Other	$78,332,032	

Economic Base Agriculture, notably cattle, corn, hogs and wheat; finance, insurance and real estate; food and kindred products, especially meat products; electrical equipment and supplies; machinery, especially farm machinery; printing and publishing, especially newspapers; fabricated metal products, especially fabricated structural metal products.

Political Line-up Governor, J. James Exon (D); seat up, 1974. Senators, Roman L. Hruska (R) and Carl T. Curtis (R). Representatives, 3 R. Unicameral Legislature (49 non-partisan Senators).

The Voters

Registration 807,267 Total. 370,993 D (46%); 401,409 R (50%); 34,865 Ind. (4%).
Median voting age 44.5
Employment profile White collar, 45%. Blue collar, 28%. Service, 14%. Farm, 13%.
Ethnic groups Black, 3%. Total foreign stock, 14%. Germany, 4%.

Presidential vote

1972	Nixon (R)	406,298	(71%)
	McGovern (D)	169,991	(29%)
1968	Nixon (R)	321,163	(60%)
	Humphrey (D)	170,784	(32%)
	Wallace (AI)	44,904	(8%)
1964	Johnson (D)	307,307	(53%)
	Goldwater (R)	276,847	(47%)

Senator

Roman Lee Hruska (R) Elected 1954, seat up 1976; b. Aug. 16, 1904, David City; home, Omaha; U. of Omaha, 1923–25; U. of Chicago, 1927–28; Creighton U., J.D., 1929; married, three children; Unitarian.

Career Practicing atty., 1929–53; Commissioner, Douglas County, 1944–52; Regent, U. of Omaha, 1950–57; U.S. House, 1953–54.

Offices 209 OSOB, 202-225-6551. Also 8424 Fed. Office Bldg., 215 N. 17th St., Omaha 68102, 402-221-4791.

Administrative Assistant David J. Tishendorf

Committees

Appropriations (2nd); Subs: Agriculture, Environmental and Consumer Protection; Interior; Public Works, AEC; State, Justice, and Commerce, the Judiciary, and Related Agencies (Ranking Mbr.); Intelligence Operations; Defense.

Judiciary (Ranking Mbr.); Subs: Antitrust and Monopoly (Ranking Mbr.); Constitutional Amendments; Constitutional Rights; Criminal Laws and Procedures (Ranking Mbr.); Federal Charters, Holidays and Celebrations (Chm.); Improvements in Judicial Machinery (Ranking Mbr.); Juvenile Delinquency.

Joint Com. on Reduction of Federal Expenditures (Ranking Senate Mbr.).

Joint Study Com. on Budget Control.

Group Ratings

	ADA	COPE	LWV	RIPON	NFU	LCV	CFA	NAB	NSI	ACA
1972	5	0	27	46	44	4	0	91	100	95
1971	0	25	17	18	9	–	20	–	–	91
1970	0	0	–	23	20	0	–	83	100	87

Key Votes

1) Busing	AGN	8) Sea Life Prot	AGN	15) Tax Singls Less	AGN
2) Alas P-line	FOR	9) Campaign Subs	AGN	16) Min Tax for Rich	AGN
3) Gun Cntrl	FOR	10) Cmbodia Bmbg	FOR	17) Euro Troop Rdctn	AGN
4) Rehnquist	FOR	11) Legal Srvices	AGN	18) Bust Hwy Trust	AGN
5) Pub TV $	AGN	12) Rev Sharing	FOR	19) Maid Min Wage	AGN
6) EZ Votr Reg	AGN	13) Cnsumr Prot	AGN	20) Farm Sub Limit	AGN
7) No-Fault	AGN	14) Eq Rts Amend	FOR	21) Highr Credt Chgs	FOR

Election Results

1970 general:	Roman L. Hruska (R)	240,894	(53%)
	Frank B. Morrison (D)	217,681	(47%)
1970 primary:	Roman L. Hruska (R)	159,059	(86%)
	Otis Glebe (R)	26,627	(14%)
1964 general:	Roman L. Hruska (R)	345,772	(61%)
	Raymond Arnt (D)	217,605	(39%)

Senator

Carl T. Curtis (R) Elected 1954, seat up 1978; b. March 15, 1905, Minden; home, Minden; Neb. Wesleyan U., LL.D., 1958; married, one child; Presbyterian.

Career Practicing atty., 1931–35; Kearney County Atty., 1931–35; U.S. House, 1939–55; Repub. Natl. Convention, 1964, Chm., Neb. Delegation, Floor Manager for Sen. Barry M. Goldwater.

Offices 2213 NSOB, 202-225-4224. Also Masonic Bldg., Minden 68959, 308-832-2670.

Administrative Assistant Doris M. Rook

Committees

Aeronautical and Space Science (2nd).

Agriculture and Forestry (Ranking Mbr.); Sub: Rural Development (Ranking Mbr.).

Finance (2nd); Subs: International Trade; Private Pension Plans (Ranking Mbr.); Foundations (Ranking Mbr.).

Sel. Com. on Standards and Conduct (Ranking Mbr.).

Joint Com. on Internal Revenue Taxation (2nd).

Joint Study Com. on Budget Control.

Group Ratings

	ADA	COPE	LWV	RIPON	NFU	LCV	CFA	NAB	NSI	ACA
1972	0	0	18	46	30	0	18	90	100	100
1971	4	9	17	27	9	–	0	–	–	100
1970	0	0	–	19	21	3	–	100	100	95

Key Votes

1) Busing	AGN	8) Sea Life Prot	AGN	15) Tax Singls Less	AGN
2) Alas P-line	FOR	9) Campaign Subs	AGN	16) Min Tax for Rich	AGN
3) Gun Cntrl	FOR	10) Cmbodia Bmbg	FOR	17) Euro Troop Rdctn	AGN
4) Rehnquist	FOR	11) Legal Srvices	AGN	18) Bust Hwy Trust	AGN
5) Pub TV $	FOR	12) Rev Sharing	AGN	19) Maid Min Wage	AGN
6) EZ Votr Reg	AGN	13) Cnsumr Prot	AGN	20) Farm Sub Limit	AGN
7) No-Fault	AGN	14) Eq Rts Amend	FOR	21) Highr Credt Chgs	FOR

Election Results

1972 general:	Carl T. Curtis (R)	301,841	(53%)
	Terry Carpenter (D)	265,922	(47%)
1972 primary:	Carl T. Curtis (R)	141,213	(74%)
	Ronald L. Bauvelt (R)	30,138	(16%)
	Christine M. Kneifl (R)	10,941	(6%)
	Otis Glebe (R)	8,143	(4%)
1966 general:	Carl T. Curtis (R)	296,116	(61%)
	Frank B. Morrison (D)	187,950	(39%)

FIRST DISTRICT Political Background

The 1st district is a band of 27 counties in eastern Nebraska. Outside of Lincoln, the district's largest city (pop. 150,000), the economy of the 1st is based on agriculture. The political inclination of the region is Republican, of course, but there are some rural counties with large German-Catholic communities in the middle of the district near the Platte River that are either Democratic or marginal. Lincoln, the state capital and the home of Bob Devaney's University of

Nebraska Cornhuskers, is traditionally Republican. But the city's large numbers of state employees have sometimes joined members of the university community to swing Lincoln into the Democratic column. That vote can also work in favor of moderate Republican aspirants. In 1970, for example, Democratic gubernatorial candidate J. J. Exon ran an anti-tax, anti-spending campaign. Exon carried most of the state, including Omaha, but lost badly in Lincoln. State employees and academics are not fond of politicians eager to slash the state budget.

For the past 10 years, the 1st has been the state's most closely contested congressional district. In 1964, it went Democratic, electing Clair Callan to the House with 51% of the votes. Callan took Lancaster County (Lincoln) by a 3–2 margin, and just missed carrying the rest of the district. In 1966 and 1968, Callan lost close elections to conservative Republican Robert V. Denney. Because Denney knew he was to be appointed a federal judge, he did not run in 1970, and there developed a curious three-way race to succeed him. This time Callan, who had been the Democratic nominee in the district since 1962, failed to win his party's endorsement, but ran anyway as an independent. As it turned out, Callan beat his Democratic rival; in the process, however, he split the vote and allowed Republican Charles Thone to win by a large plurality, though his percentage district-wide was just 51%.

Thone ran as a supporter of the Nixon Administration and with the backing of his mentor and the man he reportedly hopes to succeed, Sen. Carl Curtis. Withal, Thone's 51% was a rather poor performance. No Republican has been able to carry Lancaster County since Callan started running, but Thone polled just 52% in the remainder of the district. This was the weakest Republican showing in that part of Nebraska since 1964 and an indication of the trouble Republicans had in the Farm Belt during 1970.

The story in 1972 was, of course, a different one. Thone won easily, compiling a near 2–1 majority; Callan for the first time in 10 years was not a candidate. So for once it looks like it may be clear sailing for Thone until his expected try for Curtis' Senate seat in 1978.

Census Data Pop. 494,335. Central city, 30%; suburban, 6%. Median family income, $8,203; families above $15,000: 13%; families below $3,000: 12%. Median years education, 12.2.

1972 Share of Federal Outlays $518,513,347

DOD	$41,143,000	HEW	$189,418,465
AEC	$48,000	HUD	$8,393,136
NASA	$199,191	DOI	$4,341,365
DOT	$15,053,700	USDA	$176,705,971
		Other	$83,210,519

Federal Military-Industrial Commitments

DOD Contractors Iowa Beef Processors (Dakota City), $12.227m: foodstuffs.

Economic Base Agriculture, notably cattle, grains, and hogs and sheep; finance, insurance and real estate; food and kindred products, especially meat products; and printing and publishing. Also higher education (Univ. of Nebraska, Lincoln).

The Voters

Registration 196,275 total. 87,213 D (44%); 105,150 R (54%); 3,912 Ind. (4%).
Median voting age 45.2
Employment profile White collar, 43%. Blue collar, 27%. Service, 15%. Farm, 15%.
Ethnic groups Total foreign stock, 14%. Germany, 6%.

Presidential vote

1972	Nixon (R)	133,282	(67%)
	McGovern (D)	66,001	(33%)
1968	Nixon (R)	110,909	(60%)
	Humphrey (D)	61,274	(33%)
	Wallace (AI)	11,633	(6%)

Representative

Charles Thone (R) Elected 1970; b. Jan. 4, 1925, Hartington; home, Lincoln; U. of Neb. Law School, J.D., 1950; Army, WWII; married, three children; Presbyterian.

Career Deputy Neb. Sec. of State, 1950–51; Asst. State Atty. Gen., 1951–52; Asst. U.S. Dist. Atty., 1952–54; Admin. Asst. to Sen. Roman L. Hruska, 1954–59; practicing atty., 1959–70.

Offices 1531 LHOB, 202-225-2806. Also 120 Anderson Bldg., Lincoln 68501, 402-432-8541.

Administrative Assistant William H. Palmer

Committees

Government Operations (11th); Subs: Special Studies; Foreign Operations and Government Information.

Agriculture (12th); Subs: Dairy and Poultry; Forests; Livestock and Grains.

Group Ratings

	ADA	COPE	LWV	RIPON	NFU	LCV	CFA	NAB	NSI	ACA
1972	6	18	36	71	50	50	50	67	89	59
1971	11	0	44	71	53	–	38	–	–	83

Key Votes

1) Busing	AGN	6) Cmbodia Bmbg	AGN	11) Chkg Acct Intrst	AGN
2) Strip Mines	AGN	7) Bust Hwy Trust	AGN	12) End HISC (HUAC)	AGN
3) Cut Mil $	AGN	8) Farm Sub Lmt	FOR	13) Nixon Sewer Veto	AGN
4) Rev Shrg	FOR	9) School Prayr	FOR	14) Corp Cmpaign $	AGN
5) Pub TV $	FOR	10) Cnsumr Prot	AGN	15) Pol $ Disclosr	FOR

Election Results

1972 general:	Charles Thone (R)	126,789	(64%)
	Darrel E. Berg (D)	70,570	(36%)
1972 primary:	Charles Thone (R), unopposed		
1970 general:	Charles Thone (R)	79,131	(51%)
	Clair A. Callan (Ind.)	40,919	(26%)
	George B. Borrows (D)	36,240	(23%)

SECOND DISTRICT Political Background

The 2nd district of Nebraska is metropolitan Omaha. The rest of the district is politically negligible, because Omaha and its suburbs cast three-quarters of the 2nd's votes and inevitably determine the winner of the House seat. Both of the industries for which the city is famous—meat-packing and railroading—have until recently experienced some difficult years. Omaha, as a result, has shown very little growth in recent years; less, in fact, than Lincoln, which is blessed with the boom industries of state government and higher education. But Omaha is still the commercial and industrial center for much of the Great Plains—the largest city on the Union Pacific and Interstate 80 between Chicago and Denver. Though Omaha contains significant numbers of Democratic Czechs and blacks, it tends to vote Republican, turning margins almost as great as those compiled in the Republican rural Nebraska.

Until 1970, the 2nd was represented by Republican Glenn Cunningham, who left his mark in Washington as the sponsor of the law requiring any person receiving mail from a Communist country to register with the post office. The legislation was designed to pinpoint subversives getting written instructions from the Kremlin; in practice, however, it simply irritates scholars and people with relatives in Eastern Europe. Cunningham was never especially popular with the voters of the 2nd; in 1968, he was nearly beaten by Mrs. Frank Morrison (see Nebraska state write-up) in the general election. Then, in 1970, he was upset in a Republican primary. For some months Cunningham held a sinecure post in the Nixon Administration. Today, sadly, he is looking for a job as an appliance salesman.

The Republican primary winner in 1970 was John McCollister. In the general election that followed, he encountered a tougher race than most Nebraska Republicans face. His Democratic opponent, former TV newsman John Hlavacek, was well-known and had a Czech name. The contest was probably decided by a state issue, Amendment 12, a referendum that aimed to permit state aid to private and parochial schools. Though defeated statewide, Amendment 12 carried Douglas County (Omaha), being especially popular in the heavily Catholic precincts of the city. Hlavacek came out against the amendment, while McCollister took no position. Hlavacek still managed to run ahead of the Republican in Catholic neighborhoods, but by less than he expected and needed. McCollister slipped by with a 52% win. Ironically, Amendment 12, had it passed, was doomed; the Supreme Court, led by Nixon nominees, has declared unconstitutional any direct or indirect aid to church-related schools.

As predicted in the 1972 Almanac, McCollister had an easier time of it last time out, and will probably go on winning as long as he likes. He is, however, expected to go after the Senate seat traditionally reserved for an Omaha native and currently held by Roman Hruska when it comes up in 1976.

Census Data Pop. 495,095. Central city, 70%; suburban, 21%. Median family income, $10,163; families above $15,000: 21%; families below $3,000: 7%. Median years education, 12.4.

1972 Share of Federal Outlays $539,625,245

DOD	$212,862,000	HEW	$140,667,055
AEC	–	HUD	$9,038,588
NASA	–	DOI	$2,547,788
DOT	$16,818,661	USDA	$51,181,887
		Other	$106,509,266

Federal Military-Industrial Commitments

DOD Contractors Wilkinson Manufacturing (Fort Calhoun), $8.972m: detonating fuzes and fin assemblies for 60mm and 81mm mortars.
DOD Installations Offutt AFB (Omaha).

Economic Base Finance, insurance and real estate; food and kindred products, especially meat products; agriculture, notably cattle, grains, and hogs and sheep; machinery; printing and publishing, especially commercial printing; and primary metal industries. Also higher education (Univ. of Nebraska, Omaha).

The Voters

Registration 244,672 total. 130,489 D (53%); 100,958 R (41%); 13,225 Ind. (5%).
Median voting age 40.8
Employment profile White collar, 53%. Blue collar, 31%. Service, 14%. Farm, 2%.
Ethnic groups Black, 7%. Total foreign stock, 14%. Germany, 3%.

Presidential vote

1972	Nixon (R)	124,791	(69%)
	McGovern (D)	56,204	(31%)
1968	Nixon (R)	84,690	(52%)
	Humphrey (D)	59,078	(36%)
	Wallace (AI)	19,044	(12%)

Representative

John Y. McCollister (R) Elected 1970; b. June 19, 1921, Iowa City, Iowa; home, Omaha; U. of Iowa, B.S., 1943; USNR, WWII; married, three children; Presbyterian.

Career IBM salesman; Pres., McCollister and Co., selling lubricants; Commissioner, Douglas County, 1964–68.

Offices 217 CHOB, 202-225-4155. Also 2313 Fed. Bldg., 215 N. 15th St., Omaha 68102, 402-221-3251.

Administrative Assistant Charles T. Hagel

Committees

Interstate and Foreign Commerce (13th); Sub: Commerce and Finance.

Sel. Com. on Small Business (7th); Subs: Environmental Problems Affecting Small Business; Minority Small Business Enterprise and Franchising (Ranking Mbr.); Special Small Business Problems.

Group Ratings

	ADA	COPE	LWV	RIPON	NFU	LCV	CFA	NAB	NSI	ACA
1972	0	9	33	50	57	29	0	83	100	83
1971	11	8	22	56	50	–	13	–	–	79

Key Votes

1) Busing	AGN	6) Cmbodia Bmbg	FOR	11) Chkg Acct Intrst	AGN
2) Strip Mines	AGN	7) Bust Hwy Trust	AGN	12) End HISC (HUAC)	AGN
3) Cut Mil $	AGN	8) Farm Sub Lmt	AGN	13) Nixon Sewer Veto	FOR
4) Rev Shrg	FOR	9) School Prayr	FOR	14) Corp Cmpaign $	FOR
5) Pub TV $	AGN	10) Cnsumr Prot	AGN	15) Pol $ Disclosr	FOR

Election Results

1972 general:	John Y. McCollister (R)	114,669	(64%)
	Patrick L. Cooney (D)	64,696	(36%)
1972 primary:	John Y. McCollister (R), unopposed		
1970 general:	John Y. McCollister (R)	69,671	(52%)
	John Hlavacek (D)	64,520	(48%)

THIRD DISTRICT Political Background

One third of Nebraska's population is spread out over the western three-quarters of its land area—the state's 3rd congressional district. As one drives west through the district, the rolling cornfields and wheatlands give way to sand hills and cattle country, much of it devoid of human habitation for miles on end. This is the part of Nebraska to which settlers thronged during the 1880s and which their descendants have been leaving, often reluctantly, ever since. Today most of the people here live along the Platte River in and near towns like Grand Island (pop. 31,000), Hastings (pop. 23,000), Kearney (pop. 19,000), and Scottsbluff (pop. 14,000).

The 3rd is conservative on most issues, and except for a few counties with large ethnic populations, like Greeley and Sherman, the district is solidly Republican by long-standing tradition. But the 3rd stands ready to vote against whatever party occupies the White House whenever commodity or cattle prices drop. As recently as 1958, it elected a Democratic Congressman—two of them, in fact, since Nebraska at the time had four congressional districts. And during the early 1960s, the current Republican incumbent, David Martin, won by only small majorities. Recently, Martin has won with much greater ease, though his percentage did dip in the mini farm-revolt year of 1970.

Martin is the only one of Nebraska's three Congressmen to enjoy significant seniority. He is one of five Republicans on the House Rules Committee. The unit controls the flow of legislation, and the terms under which it may be considered, on the House floor. In the past, Rules power has often frustrated the movement of liberal bills; Martin and the other Republicans on the committee often joined conservative Democratic chairmen Howard Smith and William Colmer to pigeonhole any legislation not to their liking. But Smith and Colmer are no longer in Congress, and one Republican on Rules, John Anderson of Illinois, sometimes strays from the Republican party line. The Democratic leadership now has pretty solid control of its party's members on the committee. Accordingly, Martin and the other minority members on Rules have less influence and leverage than they once had.

Moreover, Martin has been in poor health recently, and may well retire in 1974, when he will be 67. Normally, it would be easy to predict a Republican victory in the 3rd of Nebraska. But in 1974, what with a volatile market for commodities produced on the farm and the impact of Watergate on the strait-laced morality of old-line Protestant Nebraska, betting on the Republican is no sure thing. If Martin retires, a pretty wide-open race for succession may ensue.

Census Data Pop. 494,361. Central city, 0%; suburban, 0%. Median family income, $7,549; families above $15,000: 11%; families below $3,000: 13%. Median years education, 12.2.

1972 Share of Federal Outlays $559,854,677

DOD	$33,415,000	HEW	$167,686,283
AEC	–	HUD	$1,093,000
NASA	$443,245	DOI	$5,696,106
DOT	$18,964,898	USDA	$263,290,901
		Other	$69,265,244

Federal Military-Industrial Commitments

DOD Contractors Mason and Hanger-Silas Mason (Grand Island), $21.447m: operation of the Cornhusker Army Ammunition plant.

Economic Base Agriculture, notably cattle, grains, and hogs and sheep; finance, insurance and real estate; food and kindred products; and machinery, especially farm machinery.

The Voters

Registration 366,320 total. 153,291 D (42%); 195,301 R (53%); 17,728 Ind. (5%).
Median voting age 47.7
Employment profile White collar, 38%. Blue collar, 27%. Service, 14%. Farm, 21%.
Ethnic groups Total foreign stock, 13%. Germany, 4%.

Presidential vote

1972	Nixon (R)	148,142	(76%)
	McGovern (D)	47,750	(24%)
1968	Nixon (R)	125,564	(66%)
	Humphrey (D)	50,432	(27%)
	Wallace (AI)	14,227	(7%)

Representative

David Thomas Martin (R) Elected 1960; b. July 9, 1907, Kearney; home, Kearney; Dartmouth Col., 1925–28; married, three children; Presbyterian.

Career Retail lumber business; Chm., Neb. State Repub. Com., 1949–54; Rebpub. Natl. Com., 1952–54.

Offices 2227 RHOB, 202-225-6435. Also Kearney 68847, 308-237-2155.

Administrative Assistant Jack Odgaard

Committees

Rules (Ranking Mbr.).

Sel. Com. on Committees of the House (Vice-Chm.).

Group Ratings

	ADA	COPE	LWV	RIPON	NFU	LCV	CFA	NAB	NSI	ACA
1972	0	9	18	38	33	27	0	91	100	100
1971	5	18	0	41	40	–	14	–	–	92
1970	8	10	–	33	23	0	44	90	89	89

Key Votes

1) Busing	AGN	6) Cmbodia Bmbg	FOR
2) Strip Mines	ABS	7) Bust Hwy Trust	AGN
3) Cut Mil $	AGN	8) Farm Sub Lmt	AGN
4) Rev Shrg	AGN	9) School Prayr	FOR
5) Pub TV $	AGN	10) Cnsumr Prot	AGN

11) Chkg Acct Intrst	FOR
12) End HISC (HUAC)	AGN
13) Nixon Sewer Veto	FOR
14) Corp Cmpaign $	FOR
15) Pol $ Disclosr	AGN

Election Results

1972 general:	Dave Martin (R)	133,607	(70%)
	Warren Fitzgerald (D)	58,378	(30%)
	1972 primary:		
	Dave Martin (R), unopposed		
1970 general:	Dave Martin (R)	93,705	(60%)
	Donald Searcy (D)	63,698	(40%)

NEVADA

Political Background

After the discovery of the Comstock Lode in 1859, thousands of miners and other fortune-seekers poured into the deserts of the Great Basin. The region was quickly organized as the state of Nevada, one of the first out West to be admitted to the Union in 1864. Thereupon, as expected, the new state cast three electoral votes toward the reelection of President Abraham Lincoln. Soon enough the veins of silver and gold petered out, leaving the state in economic doldrums for decades. During the Depression of the 1930s, the state of Nevada was on the verge of complete collapse. So the state legalized gambling and liberalized its divorce laws; meanwhile, the federal government opened Hoover Dam near Las Vegas in 1936. These events brought in tourists, six-week residents, water, and eventually big (and some said, tainted) money.

The single most important event in modern Nevada history occurred in 1947 when Bugsy Siegel opened the Flamingo, the first big casino-hotel on the Las Vegas Strip. At the same time, just outside the city, the Atomic Energy Commission, now the state's third largest employer, established the Nevada Proving Grounds. Since 1947, Las Vegas has grown from a small desert crossroads town into a major urban center. Clark County, which contains Las Vegas, the Strip, and Hoover Dam, now has 56% of the state's rapidly growing population. Washoe County and Reno, to the north and west, have another 23%, leaving just 21% of the state's people in its so-called "cow counties."

As it stands now, Nevada constitutes part of the American Sun Belt, a swath of states comprising the nation's southern rim. Drawing people wanting to escape cold weather, companies fleeing unions, and defense industry dollars that like neither the cold nor unions, the urban centers of the Sun Belt have been the most rapidly growing part of the country. At the same time, Nevada has little rural settlement for one very good reason: no water. Because of the economic foundations of the Sun Belt and the habits of mind the immigrants have brought to it, the region is the bed-rock of support for the politics of Richard Nixon and other conservatives of similar bent.

In Nevada, however, the influx of conservative Republican voters has not worked wholesale change in the political habits of the state. Nevada's early settlers, like those in Arizona and New Mexico, were natives of the South, and therefore conservative Democrats by tradition and upbringing. So, as is the tradition in the South, Nevada has elected conservative Democrats to the Senate and kept them there to accumulate seniority. One such man was Sen. Key Pittman, Chairman of the Senate Foreign Relations Committee during the 1930s; another during the 1950s was the influential Sen. Pat McCarran, sponsor of the McCarran-Walter Act—legislation designed to curb the activities of subversives, most of which turned out to be unconstitutional.

Today, the state's Senators are more moderate men out of the same tradition. Alan Bible, first elected in 1954, is Chairman of the Select Committee on Small Business, and a senior member of Appropriations, Interior, and the Joint Committee on Atomic Energy. As Chairman of Appropriations' Interior Subcommittee, Bible has much to say over the department that controls the lion's share of the state's land, and therefore the economic health of many of his constituents. In the tradition of Nevada Democrats, Bible has put state issues first, while maintaining a moderate and sometimes conservative stance on other matters. Over the years, Nevada Senators have been among the staunchest defenders of the filibuster, in as much as it gives the state's two Senators leverage all out of proportion to the number of people they represent, although Nevada contains only 0.24% of the nation's population.

Most observers expected that Bible would be reelected easily in 1974. But in August 1973, he startled everyone by announcing that he would not run again. He cited his health and his age; he will be 65 just a few weeks after the 1974 election. Just about everyone in Nevada politics was immediately mentioned as a possible successor, and at this writing the field has not been narrowed down enough to make any hard predictions possible. But one of the strongest candidates, if he chooses to make the race, would be Democratic Gov. Mike O'Callaghan, whose popularity has increased during his four years in office.

The state's junior Senator, Howard W. Cannon, has had a somewhat tougher time at the polls than Bible. In 1964, when Goldwater hurt many Republican candidates, the Democratic Senator barely managed a 48-vote win over then Lt. Gov. Paul Laxalt. In 1970, Nevada Republicans and Richard Nixon hoped for a rematch. In 1966, Laxalt had been elected Governor and became a popular one, in large part because of his relationship with Howard Hughes; the billionaire's period of residence in the state coincided almost precisely with Laxalt's term as Governor. But the Republicans were disappointed, as Laxalt announced that he was retiring from politics and then surprised most observers by doing just that. The former Governor, a descendant of Basque sheepherders, is an enigmatic man. He could conceivably be a factor in some future Nevada election, like the contest for Bible's seat in 1974, though no one right now is betting on it.

Cannon had two strokes of good fortune as he campaigned for reelection in 1970: Laxalt's retirement and the Senator's opponent, one hand-picked by Spiro Agnew. A phone call from Agnew got Washoe County (Reno) District Attorney William Raggio into the race against Cannon. In the manner of White House-backed candidates of that year, Raggio stressed "law and order" issues—probably not the wisest strategy in Las Vegas and Reno, which thrive on legalized gambling and girlie shows, or in many of the "cow counties," which have legalized prostitution. Moreover, Bible and the state's sole Congressman at the time were, like Raggio, from Reno, while

Cannon was from Las Vegas. Clark County apparently wanted to keep its own man in Congress and gave Cannon 68% of its votes, enough to produce a solid statewide Cannon win.

Despite its record-breaking population growth—up 71% during the 1960s, the highest rate in the nation—Nevada still elects only one Congressman. For 20 years (1949–53 and 1957–73), that Congressman was Walter S. Baring, who described himself as a "states' rights Democrat." Since the early 1960s, Baring compiled an unvaryingly conservative voting record; he was easily the most conservative Democrat in Congress outside the South. Efforts to unseat him were concentrated in the Democratic primary, since in general elections he received the votes of most Republicans and thereby won reelection with virtual unanimity. Finally, in 1972, Baring lost a primary election. Over time, the incumbent incurred the ire—and fears—of environmentalists who had noted his creep toward the top of the seniority ladder on the House Interior Committee. The successful primary challenger was James Billray, a wealthy Las Vegas businessman, who spent something like $100,000 to win the primary.

But in 1972, the Democratic primary was by no means tantamount to victory in Nevada, as was the case in the 4th district of Colorado and several other places where insurgents knocked off conservative incumbents in Democratic primaries. The 35-year-old Republican nominee and real estate man, David Towell, won better than 60% of the votes in Washoe and the cow counties, which was enough to overcome Billbray's lead in Las Vegas and Clark County. So, for the first time in nearly 20 years, Nevada is represented by a Republican in Congress.

Census Data Pop. 488,738; 0.24% of U.S. total, 47th largest; change 1960–70, 71.3%. Central city, 41%; suburban, 40%. Median family income, $10,687; 10th highest; families above $15,000: 25%; families below $3,000: 7%. Median years education, 12.4.

1972 Share of Federal Tax Burden $668,860,000; 0.32% of U.S. total, 43rd largest.

1972 Share of Federal Outlays $629,730,057; 0.29% of U.S. total, 47th largest. Per capita federal spending, $1,288.

DOD	$150,620,000	43rd (0.24%)	HEW	$125,946,978	48th (0.18%)
AEC	$129,488,069	7th (4.94%)	HUD	$5,108,425	48th (0.17%)
NASA	$584,756	38th (0.02%)	VA	$26,681,824	49th (0.23%)
DOT	$59,189,949	38th (0.75%)	USDA	$24,077,446	48th (0.16%)
DOC	$3,091,252	42nd (0.24%)	CSC	$11,754,267	44th (0.29%)
DOI	$33,029,461	20th (1.56%)	TD	$18,344,570	47th (0.11%)
DOJ	$1,902,429	49th (0.19%)	Other	$39,910,631	

Federal Military-Industrial Commitments

DOD Installations Naval Ammunition Depot (Hawthorne). Naval Auxiliary Air Station (Fallon). Fallon AF Station (Fallon). Indian Springs Auxiliary Air Field (Indian Springs). Nellis AFB (Las Vegas).

AEC Operations Reynolds Electrical and Engineering (Mercury), $67.484m: Design, construction, maintenance, services, and operation of Nevada Nuclear Test Site. EG & G, Inc. (Mercury), $16.455m: technical services. AEC Western Headquarters (Las Vegas), $6.179m: administrative.

Economic Base Tourism (Las Vegas, Reno, Tahoe); finance, insurance and real estate; agriculture, notably cattle, dairy products, hay and sheep; metal mining, especially copper ores; paper and allied products; primary metal industries, especially nonferrous rolling and drawing.

Political Line-up Govenor, Mike O'Callaghan (D); seat up, 1974. Senators, Alan Bible (D) and Howard W. Cannon (D). Representatives, 1 R At Large. State Senate (14 D and 6 R); State Assembly (25 D and 15 R).

The Voters

Registration 205,220 Total. 120,446 D (59%); 70,649 R (34%); 14,125 other (7%).
Median voting age 40.5
Employment profile White collar, 47%. Blue collar, 26%. Service, 25%. Farm, 2%.
Ethnic groups Black, 6%. Spanish, 6%. Total foreign stock, 14%.

Presidential vote

1972	Nixon (R)	115,750	(64%)
	McGovern (D)	66,016	(36%)
1968	Nixon (R)	73,188	(48%)
	Humphrey (D)	60,598	(39%)
	Wallace (AI)	20,432	(13%)
1964	Johnson (D)	79,339	(59%)
	Goldwater (R)	56,094	(41%)

Senator

Alan Bible (D) Elected 1954, seat up 1974; b. Nov. 20, 1909, Lovelock; home, Reno; U. of Nev., B.A., 1930; Georgetown U. School of Law, LL.B., 1934; married, four children; Methodist.

Career Practicing atty., 1934–54; Dist. Atty., Storey County, 1935–37; Atty. Gen., Nev., 1942–50; Pres., Natl. Assn. of Attys. Gen., 1950.

Offices 145 OSOB, 202-225-3542. Also 2014 Fed. Bldg., Reno 89502, 702-784-5568, and 4626 Fed. Bldg., Las Vegas 89101, 702-385-6341.

Administrative Assistant Jack M. Carpenter

Committees

Appropriations (5th); Subs: Defense; Interior (Chm.); Labor, and Health, Education, and Welfare, and Related Agencies; Public Works, AEC; Transporattion.

Interior and Insular Affairs (2nd); Subs: Minerals, Materials and Fuels; Parks and Recreation (Chm.); Special Subcommittee on Legislative Oversight.

Sel. Com. on Small Business (Chm.).

Sp. Com. on Aging (3rd); Sub: Employment and Retirement Incomes; Federal, State and Community Services; Retirement and the Individual.

Joint Study Com. on Budget Control.

Joint Com. on Atomic Energy (4th); Subs: Agreements for Cooperation; Legislation; Licensing and Regulation, Raw Materials (Chm.); Research, Development, and Radiation; Military Applications.

Group Ratings

	ADA	COPE	LWV	RIPON	NFU	LCV	CFA	NAB	NSI	ACA
1972	35	60	55	24	80	16	70	64	80	36
1971	33	75	42	8	69	–	80	–	–	42
1970	9	62	–	15	64	41	–	33	90	59

Key Votes

1) Busing	AGN	8) Sea Life Prot	FOR	15) Tax Singls Less	AGN
2) Alas P-line	FOR	9) Campaign Subs	FOR	16) Min Tax for Rich	AGN
3) Gun Cntrl	AGN	10) Cmbodia Bmbg	ABS	17) Euro Troop Rdctn	FOR
4) Rehnquist	FOR	11) Legal Srvices	FOR	18) Bust Hwy Trust	AGN
5) Pub TV $	FOR	12) Rev Sharing	AGN	19) Maid Min Wage	FOR
6) EZ Votr Reg	FOR	13) Cnsumr Prot	FOR	20) Farm Sub Limit	AGN
7) No-Fault	AGN	14) Eq Rts Amend	FOR	21) Highr Credt Chgs	ABS

Election Results

1968 general:	Alan Bible (D)	83,622	(55%)
	Ed Firke (R)	69,083	(45%)

1968 primary:	Alan Bible (D), unopposed		
1962 general:	Alan Bible (D)	63,443	(65%)
	William B. Wright (R)	33,749	(35%)

Senator

Howard Walter Cannon (D) Elected 1958, seat up 1976; b. Jan. 26, 1912, St. George, Utah; home, Las Vegas; Ariz. State Teachers Col., B.E., 1933; U. of Ariz., LL.B., 1937; Army Air Corps, WWII; Maj. Gen., USAAFR; married, two children; Church of Latter Day Saints.

Career Practicing atty., 1938– ; Atty., Utah Senate, 1939; Washington County Atty., 1940–41; City Atty., Las Vegas, 1949–58.

Offices 259 OSOB, 202-225-6244. Also 4602 Fed. Bldg., Las Vegas 89101, 702-385-6278, and 4024 Fed. Bldg., 300 Booth St., Reno 89502, 702-784-5544.

Administrative Assistant Chester B. Sobsey

Committees

Aeronautical and Space Sciences (5th).

Armed Services (5th); Subs: Ad hoc sub. on Tactical Air Power (Chm.); Military Construction Authorization; National Stockpile and Naval Petroleum Reserves (Chm.); Preparedness Investigation.

Commerce (5th); Subs: Aviation (Chm.); Consumer; Communications; Surface Transporattion; Foreign Commerce and Tourism.

Rules and Administration (Chm.); Subs: Standing Rules of the Senate; Computer Services (Chm.); Library (Chm.); Printing (Chm.).

Joint Com. on the Library (Vice-Chm.).

Joint Com. on Printing (Chm.).

Group Ratings

	ADA	COPE	LWV	RIPON	NFU	LCV	CFA	NAB	NSI	ACA
1972	25	44	45	48	70	11	88	50	75	45
1971	41	75	70	16	82	–	71	–	–	39
1970	19	73	–	26	85	21	–	27	78	50

Key Votes

1) Busing	AGN	8) Sea Life Prot	ABS	15) Tax Singls Less	AGN
2) Alas P-line	FOR	9) Campaign Subs	FOR	16) Min Tax for Rich	FOR
3) Gun Cntrl	AGN	10) Cmbodia Bmbg	ABS	17) Euro Troop Rdctn	AGN
4) Rehnquist	FOR	11) Legal Srvices	FOR	18) Bust Hwy Trust	AGN
5) Pub TV $	FOR	12) Rev Sharing	FOR	19) Maid Min Wage	AGN
6) EZ Votr Reg	FOR	13) Cnsumr Prot	FOR	20) Farm Sub Limit	AGN
7) No-Fault	AGN	14) Eq Rts Amend	FOR	21) Highr Credt Chgs	AGN

Election Results

1970 general:	Howard W. Cannon (D)	85,187	(58%)
	William J. Raggio (R)	60,838	(41%)
	Harold G. De Sellem (AI)	1,743	(1%)
1970 primary:	Howard W. Cannon (D)	54,320	(89%)
	Walter D. Dvesenberg (D)	4,350	(7%)
	George R. Lill (D)	2,160	(4%)

1964 general: Howard W. Cannon (D) 67,336 (50%)
Paul Laxalt (R) 67,288 (50%)

Representative

David G. Towell (R) Elected 1972; b. June 9, 1937, Bronxville, N.Y.; home, Gardnerville; U. of Pacific, B.A., 1960; married, two children; Episcopalian.

Career Independent real estate broker; Nevada Air National Guard, 1960–66; Chm. Douglas County Repub. Central Com., 1970.

Offices 1206 LHOB, 202-225-5965. Also Fed. Bldg., 300 Las Vegas Blvd. South, Las Vegas, 702-385-6530, and 300 Booth St., Reno, 702-784-5507.

Administrative Assistant Tony Payton

Committees

Interior and Insular Affairs (13th); Subs: No. 2 (Water and Power Resources); No. 3 (Environment); No. 6 (Indian Affairs); No. 7 (Public Lands).

Education and Labor (14th); Subs: No. 1 (Gen. Sub. on Education); No. 8 (Agricultural Labor).

Group Ratings: Newly Elected

Key Votes

1) Busing	NE	6) Cmbodia Bmbg	FOR	11) Chkg Acct Intrst	AGN
2) Strip Mines	NE	7) Bust Hwy Trust	AGN	12) End HISC (HUAC)	AGN
3) Cut Mil $	NE	8) Farm Sub Lmt	NE	13) Nixon Sewer Veto	FOR
4) Rev Shrg	NE	9) School Prayr	NE	14) Corp Cmpaign $	NE
5) Pub TV $	NE	10) Cnsumr Prot	NE	15) Pol $ Disclosr	NE

Election Results

1972 general:	David Towell (R)	94,113	(52%)
	James H. Bilbray (D)	86,349	(48%)
1972 primary:	David Towell (R)	13,453	(41%)
	William T. Byrnes (R)	11,764	(36%)
	Robert J. Edwards (R)	2,764	(9%)
	Wayne Goodin (R)	2,411	(7%)
	V. M. Markoff (R)	2,029	(6%)

NEW HAMPSHIRE

Political Background

Once every four years New Hampshire becomes the center of the nation's political attention. Presidential candidates trudge through the melting snow and the gooey mud of the state's industrial cities and small New England towns, wooing the votes of less than 100,000 people. New Hampshire's presidential primary, the first in the country and often the most influential, draws politicians, volunteers, TV crews, and newspapermen to the state. And the local voters have had a habit of surprising the outsiders. In 1964, for example, New Hampshire Republicans rejected the candidacies of Nelson Rockefeller and Barry Goldwater, both of whom spent lots of money and time campaigning here, and produced a write-in victory for Henry Cabot Lodge, who at that time was the nation's Ambassador in Saigon. Four years later, Eugene McCarthy's 42% showing against Lyndon Johnson destroyed the myth of an incumbent President's invulnerability. Most recently, in 1972, George McGovern's surprisingly high 37% confounded everyone's prediction that Edmund Muskie of neighboring Maine would sweep the primary—and got McGovern's primary campaign off to a sprinting start.

Whatever the presidential year, the various political aspirants are out of New Hampshire by the second week in March, and because the state casts only four electoral votes, the important men usually never return. Politics in the state then returns to normal, dominated as it is by fractious local politicians and by William Loeb, owner of the *Manchester Union Leader*. The newspaper reaches about a quarter of the state's households with Loeb's ardent conservatism, his opposition to pornography, civil rights legislation, and taxes of all kinds. The *Union Leader* is outspoken about its political likes and dislikes, and those whom it dislikes claim that Loeb slants not just the paper's lengthy front-page editorials, but also its news columns, against them.

During the 1972 campaign, it became fashionable to say that the *Union Leader's* political clout was overstated. Loeb had backed a string of losers—Mrs. Styles Bridges, the late Senator's widow (1962 Senate), Barry Goldwater (1964 presidential primary), General Harrison Thyng (1966 Senate), and Emil Bussiere and Roger Crowley (1968 and 1970 Governor race, respectively). No Loeb-backed candidate had won a major statewide race since Norris Cotton was reelected to the Senate in 1968, and Cotton would have won even if Loeb had opposed him. Finally, Loeb's 1972 presidential primary choice, then Los Angeles Mayor Sam Yorty, finished with a dismal 6% of the votes in the Democratic contest.

But the influence of the *Union Leader* can just as easily be underestimated. It was Loeb's newspaper that published the letter, apparently written by a White House staffer, which accused Muskie of using the term "Canuck" to mean French-Canadian, an important New Hampshire voting bloc. The letter led more or less directly to the scene in which Muskie was moved to tears while the New Hampshire snow fell around him. The resulting media coverage of the event perhaps destroyed Muskie's presidential chances once and for all. And if Loeb ran into a bad streak in recent New Hampshire elections, he more than recouped his fortunes in the September 1972 state primaries, as *Union Leader*-backed candidates won both the Republican and Democratic gubernatorial nominations. The winner in November, a transplanted Southerner named Meldrin Thompson, has since stirred up quite a fuss by perusing confidential tax and criminal intelligence data on political figures. Because Thompson is a stern opponent of higher taxes, however, the Governor retains the vigorous support of Loeb. Local politicians think that the newspaper owner can swing 25,000 votes—quite a few in a state that casts only 200,000 votes in off-year elections. The figure 25,000 is probably on the high side; yet a look at the returns indicates that Loeb is especially influential in the city of Manchester, a Democratic city by tradition, but one having many conservatively inclined blue-collar workers.

One politician the *Union Leader* has endorsed over the years is the state's senior Senator Norris Cotton. First elected in 1954, Cotton serves on the Appropriations and Commerce committees, and on Commerce is the ranking minority member. Cotton has compiled the record of a conservative Republican, and it was therefore a measure of Nixon's Watergate trouble in the spring of 1973 that Cotton vigorously opposed the Administration's bombing of Cambodia. The Senator also held up an important Nixon appointment in the Commerce Committee.

Cotton will retire in 1974, when he will be 74. The main Republican contender for his seat is 1st district Rep. Louis Wyman, a staunch conservative. For a while, Eugene J. McCarthy, ex-Senator from Minnesota and now unhappy with his job as a book editor in New York City, considered making a Democratic Senate bid in New Hampshire. After looking the situation over, McCarthy decided against it, saying that "New Hampshire can provide its own candidates." So it looks like Wyman is the odds-on favorite to succeed Cotton. The New Hampshire Congressman has been a longtime crusader against domestic subversives; as state Attorney General in the 1950s, he pushed for the adoption of some anti-subversive legislation that was ultimately found defective by the Supreme Court. Once in Congress, Wyman became a leader in the movement on Capitol Hill to impeach Justice William Douglas. Also a no-nonsense man at home, Wyman posted bail for his 19-year-old son, arrested on a marijuana charge, only on the condition that the young man adopt conventional dress and get a haircut every ten days.

In 1972, New Hampshire voters gave Nixon almost twice as many votes as McGovern. At the same time, however, they provided Democratic Sen. Thomas McIntyre with an easy reelection win. A dozen years ago in this reputedly solid Republican state, the odds that the Democrats could win a statewide election, not to speak of three of them, were very long indeed. But dominant parties have a way of splitting into warring factions, thereby giving nice openings to the otherwise hapless candidates of the minority party. And that is exactly what happened when Sen. Styles Bridges, the grand old man of New Hampshire conservative Republicanism, died in 1961.

News of the death reached McIntyre in Laconia, where he was living the comfortable life of a successful lawyer. He dabbled in Democratic politics, having once lost a race for Congress in 1954. Meanwhile the fight for the Republican nomination in the 1962 special election included Mrs. Bridges, both of the state's Congressmen, Chester Merrow and Perkins Bass, and the interim Senate appointee, Maurice Murphy. The primary was so bitter that when Bass finally won it, he was beaten in the general election by McIntyre, who was also helped by the coattails of John W. King, Democratic gubernatorial candidate. King won the first of his three two-year terms as Governor. In 1966, when McIntyre's seat was up, the Republicans expected to recapture it, but the Senator rather easily took care of Loeb-backed General Thyng.

The story in 1972 was pretty much the same. The Republican nominee endorsed by Loeb was ex-Gov. Wesley Powell. The candidate waged a hard-line conservative campaign, but was unable to make many of his charges against McIntyre stick. Though McIntyre hired McGovern pollster Pat Caddell for the reelection effort, the Senator is no McGovernite. He is by instinct a cautious man, and by no stretch of the imagination any kind of radical. In fact, during the LBJ years, McIntyre supported the Administration's policies, both foreign and domestic; he also campaigned for Johnson in the disastrous 1968 primary.

As a member of the Armed Services Committee, McIntyre has been more reluctant than many Northern Democrats to oppose the Pentagon. But when he does, he has considerable effect. In 1969, he possessed a crucial undecided vote on the ABM; he came out against it, though the measure passed by Vice-President Agnew's tie-breaking ballot. In 1973, as an Armed Services subcommittee chairman, the Senator cut in half the Administration's request for the Trident nuclear submarine program, one that critics say merely duplicates the already operational Polaris-Poseidon system. In late September 1973, the issue went to the floor, where the Trident and the Nixon Administration were sustained by a 49–47 vote. Had McIntyre's move succeeded, it would have effected a major revision in Defense Department outlays, saving the taxpayers some $1 billion annually.

With only the slightest changes, New Hampshire's two congressional districts have had the same boundaries since 1881. The lines neatly divide the cities of Manchester (pop. 87,000) and Nashua (pop. 55,000), mill towns on the Merrimack River. In both places the sons and daughters of Irish, Italian, and French-Canadian immigrants (the last the most numerous) usually vote Democratic. The purpose of the 1881 districting was to put both districts permanently out of the reach of New Hampshire Democrats, and with few exceptions—the most recent being the 1st district in 1964—it has done just that.

The 1st district is dominated by Manchester, the state's largest city. There are also significant concentrations of people in the Portsmouth area and along the Massachusetts border, where Boston-area commuters, in search of life in the country and lower taxes, have come in great numbers. The 1st's Congressman, Louis Wyman, will run for the Senate in 1974. The outlook in the race for succession is unclear. It can be said, however, that the 1st is where the *Union Leader* has the bulk of its influence. So if the winner is not a conservative Republican, it will likely as not be an equally conservative Democrat.

The 2nd district is slightly less urban than its counterpart and, in recent elections at least, slightly less conservative. As is the case throughout the Northeast, Catholic city-dwellers trend Republican, while suburban and small-town WASPs become more Democratic. But none of that has had much effect on congressional elections in the 2nd, which have been won without difficulty (except in 1964 when the race was close) by Republican James C. Cleveland. Though Cleveland supports the Nixon Administration with nearly the same enthusiasm as Wyman, the 2nd-district Congressman is considered a shade more moderate. He is also considered a little less aggressive. When Wyman jumped right into the 1974 Senate race the moment Norris Cotton announced his retirement, Cleveland bided his time. Most likely he will run for reelection to the House and win.

Census Data Pop. 737,681; 0.36% of U.S. total, 41st largest; change 1960–70, 21.5%. Central city, 19%; suburban, 8%. Median family income, $9,682; 18th highest; families above $15,000: 17%; families below $3,000: 7%. Median years education, 12.2.

1972 Share of Federal Tax Burden $710,660,000; 0.34% of U.S. total, 41st largest.

1972 Share of Federal Outlays $775,919,927; 0.36% of U.S. total, 46th largest. Per capita federal spending, $1,052.

DOD	$301,464,000	37th (0.48%)	HEW	$245,303,301	41st	(0.34%)
AEC	$47,041	45th (—)	HUD	$24,995,954	33rd	(0.81%)
NASA	$990,726	35th (0.03%)	VA	$43,136,261	42nd	(0.38%)
DOT	$45,859,906	44th (0.58%)	USDA	$25,452,930	46th	(0.17%)
DOC	$3,784,030	40th (0.29%)	CSC	$19,715,220	39th	(0.48%)
DOI	$1,343,795	50th (0.06%)	TD	$25,610,766	45th	(0.16%)
DOJ	$3,246,439	45th (0.33%)	Other	$34,969,558		

Economic Base Leather footwear, and other leather and leather products; tourism; electrical equipment and supplies; finance, insurance and real estate; machinery; textile mill products; rubber and plastics products not otherwise classified, especially miscellaneous plastics products.

Political Line-up Governor, Meldrim Thomson, Jr. (R); seat up, 1974. Senators, Norris Cotton (R) and Thomas J. McIntyre (D). Representatives, 2 R. State Senate (14 R and 10 D); State House (262 R, 137 D, and 1 vac.).

The Voters

Registration 292,915 Total. 123,514 D (42%); 169,401 R (58%).
Median voting age 43.2
Employment profile White collar, 45%. Blue collar, 42%. Service, 12%. Farm, 1%.
Ethnic groups Total foreign stock, 23%. Canada, 13%.

Presidential vote

1972	Nixon (R)	213,724	(65%)
	McGovern (D)	116,435	(35%)
1968	Nixon (R)	154,903	(52%)
	Humphrey (D)	130,589	(44%)
	Wallace (AI)	11,173	(4%)
1964	Johnson (D)	184,064	(64%)
	Goldwater (R)	104,029	(36%)

Senator

Norris Cotton (R) Elected 1954, seat up 1974; b. May 11, 1900, Warren; home, Lebanon; Wesleyan U., 1919–21; Georgetown U. Law School, 1927; married; United Church of Christ.

Career Sec., Senator George Moses, 1924–28; Grafton County Atty., 1933–39; Justice, Lebanon Municipal Ct., 1939–44; N.H. House of Reps., 1923, 1943–46, Speaker, 1945; U.S. House of Reps., 1947–55.

Offices 4121 NSOB, 202-225-3324. Also Fed. Bldg., Concord 03301, 603-224-4321.

Administrative Assistant John Ahlers

Committees

Appropriations (3rd); Subs: Defense; Labor, and Health, Education, and Welfare, and Related Agencies (Ranking Mbr.); Legislative (Ranking Mbr.); State, Justice and Commerce, the Judiciary, and Related Agencies; Transportation.

Commerce (Ranking Mbr.); Sub: Aviation (Ranking Mbr.).

Joint Study Com. on Budget Control.

Group Ratings

	ADA	COPE	LWV	RIPON	NFU	LCV	CFA	NAB	NSI	ACA
1972	0	0	20	36	22	0	0	88	100	76
1971	0	17	9	35	20	–	0	–	–	96
1970	0	8	–	15	42	34	–	73	100	85

Key Votes

1) Busing	AGN	8) Sea Life Prot	AGN	15) Tax Singls Less	AGN
2) Alas P-line	FOR	9) Campaign Subs	AGN	16) Min Tax for Rich	AGN
3) Gun Cntrl	FOR	10) Cmbodia Bmbg	ABS	17) Euro Troop Rdctn	ABS
4) Rehnquist	FOR	11) Legal Srvices	AGN	18) Bust Hwy Trust	AGN
5) Pub TV $	AGN	12) Rev Sharing	FOR	19) Maid Min Wage	AGN
6) EZ Votr Reg	AGN	13) Cnsumr Prot	AGN	20) Farm Sub Limit	FOR
7) No-Fault	AGN	14) Eq Rts Amend	AGN	21) Highr Credt Chgs	FOR

Election Results

1968 general:	Norris Cotton (R)	170,163	(59%)
	John W. King (D)	116,816	(41%)
1968 primary:	Norris Cotton (R)	78,053	(93%)
	John Mongan (R)	6,279	(7%)
1962 general:	Norris Cotton (R)	190,444	(60%)
	Alfred Catalfa, Jr. (D)	134,035	(40%)

Senator

Thomas James McIntyre (D) Elected 1962, seat up 1978; b. Feb. 20, 1915, Laconia; home, Laconia; Dartmouth Col., A.B., 1937; Boston U. Law School, LL.B., 1940; Army, WWII; married, one child; Catholic.

Career Practicing atty., 1940– ; Mayor of Laconia, 1949–51; City Solicitor, 1953; Dir., Laconia Industrial Dev. Corp., 1962.

Offices 405 OSOB, 202-225-2841. Also 208 Fed. Bldg., Manchester 03103, 603-669-1232, and Fed. Bldg., Portsmouth 03001, 603-436-7720.

Administrative Assistant Larry K. Smith

Committees

Armed Services (6th); Subs: Preparedness Investigating; Status of Forces; Research and Development (Chm.); General Legislation; Drug Abuse in the Military; Bomber Defense.

Banking, Housing, and Urban Affairs (4th); Subs: Financial Institutions (Chm.); Small Business; Securities.

Sel. Com. on Small Business (4th); Subs: Financing and Investment; Government Regulation (Chm.); Monopoly.

Group Ratings

	ADA	COPE	LWV	RIPON	NFU	LCV	CFA	NAB	NSI	ACA
1972	35	88	100	80	78	76	100	50	78	33
1971	67	83	85	54	100	–	100	–	–	29
1970	50	100	–	46	100	54	–	10	60	39

Key Votes

1) Busing	FOR	8) Sea Life Prot	FOR	15) Tax Singls Less	FOR
2) Alas P-line	AGN	9) Campaign Subs	FOR	16) Min Tax for Rich	FOR
3) Gun Cntrl	FOR	10) Cmbodia Bmbg	AGN	17) Euro Troop Rdctn	FOR
4) Rehnquist	FOR	11) Legal Srvices	FOR	18) Bust Hwy Trust	ABS
5) Pub TV $	ABS	12) Rev Sharing	ABS	19) Maid Min Wage	FOR
6) EZ Votr Reg	ABS	13) Cnsumr Prot	ABS	20) Farm Sub Limit	FOR
7) No-Fault	FOR	14) Eq Rts Amend	ABS	21) Highr Credt Chgs	AGN

Election Results

1972 general:	Thomas J. McIntyre (D)	184,495	(57%)
	Wesley Powell (R)	139,852	(43%)
1972 primary:	Thomas J. McIntyre (D), unopposed		
1966 general:	Thomas J. McIntyre (D)	123,888	(54%)
	Harrison R. Thyng (R)	105,241	(46%)

FIRST DISTRICT

Census Data Pop. 367,075. Central city, 24%; suburban, 8%. Median family income, $9,631; families above $15,000: 17%; families below $3,000: 7%. Median years education, 12.2.

1972 Share of Federal Outlays $415,311,737

DOD	$201,231,000	HEW	$112,122,105
AEC	–	HUD	$13,016,876
NASA	$610,024	DOI	$427,732
DOT	$12,778,424	USDA	$13,300,307
		Other	$61,825,269

Federal Military-Industrial Commitments

DOD Contractors Simplex Wire and Cable (Newington), $19.706m: oceanographic cable for Project Caesar, a submarine detection system.
DOD Installations Naval Disciplinary Command (Portsmouth). Naval Hospital (Portsmouth); closed, 1974. Portsmouth Naval Shipyard (Portsmouth). Pease AFB (Portsmouth).

Economic Base Footwear, except rubber, and other leather and leather products; tourism; electrical equipment and supplies; finance, insurance and real estate; rubber and plastics products, especially miscellaneous plastics products; and machinery, especially special industry machinery. Also higher education (Univ. of New Hampshire).

The Voters

Registration 155,251 total. 68,583 D (44%); 87,668 R (56%).
Median voting age 43.2
Employment profile White collar, 45%. Blue collar, 42%. Service, 12%. Farm, 1%.
Ethnic groups Total foreign stock, 23%. Canada, 13%.

Presidential vote

	1972	Nixon (R)	111,167	(67%)
		McGovern (D)	54,375	(33%)
	1968	Nixon (R)	78,662	(53%)
		Humphrey (D)	64,045	(43%)
		Wallace (AI)	6,347	(4%)

Representative

Louis Crosby Wyman (R) Elected 1962; b. March 16, 1917, Manchester; home, Manchester; U. of N.H., B.S., 1938; Harvard Law School, LL.B., 1941; USNR, WWII; married, two children; United Church of Christ.

Career Gen. Counsel, Senate Com. on Campaign Expenditures, 1946; Secy., Sen. Styles Bridges, 1947; Atty. Gen. N.H., 1953–61: Pres., Natl. Assn. of Atty. Gen., 1957; Legislative Council, Gov. of N.H., 1961; Chm., N.H. Commission on Interstate Cooperation. 1953–61; Commissioner, Uniform State for N.H., 1953–61.

Offices 410 CHOB, 202-225-5456. Also Rm. 217, P.O. Bldg., Manchester 03104, 603-669-7011, and Rm. 209, Fed. Bldg., Portsmouth 03801, 603-436-7720.

Administrative Assistant Jerry Schiappa

Committees

Appropriations (11th); Subs: Defense; Legislative (Ranking Mbr.).

Group Ratings

	ADA	COPE	LWV	RIPON	NFU	LCV	CFA	NAB	NSI	ACA
1972	0	27	36	56	57	33	100	92	100	83
1971	11	9	11	44	33	–	17	–	–	88
1970	8	9	–	53	38	50	67	82	100	84

Key Votes

1) Busing	AGN	6) Cmbodia Bmbg	FOR	11) Chkg Acct Intrst	ABS
2) Strip Mines	AGN	7) Bust Hwy Trust	AGN	12) End HISC (HUAC)	AGN
3) Cut Mil $	AGN	8) Farm Sub Lmt	FOR	13) Nixon Sewer Veto	FOR
4) Rev Shrg	FOR	9) School Prayr	FOR	14) Corp Cmpaign $	FOR
5) Pub TV $	AGN	10) Cnsumr Prot	AGN	15) Pol $ Disclosr	FOR

Election Results

1972 general:	Louis C. Wyman (R)	115,732	(73%)
	Chester E. Merrow (D)	42,996	(27%)
1972 primary:	Louis C. Wyman (R), unopposed		
1970 general:	Louis C. Wyman (R)	72,170	(67%)
	Chester E. Merrow (D)	34,882	(33%)

SECOND DISTRICT

Census Data Pop. 370,606. Central city, 15%; suburban, 8%. Median family income, $9,736; families above $15,000: 18%; families below $3,000: 7%. Median years education, 12.2.

1972 Share of Federal Outlays $360,608,190

DOD	$100,233,000	HEW	$133,181,196
AEC	$47,041	HUD	$11,979,078
NASA	$308,702	DOI	$916,063
DOT	$33,081,482	USDA	$12,152,623
		Other	$68,709,005

Federal Military-Industrial Commitments

DOD Contractors Sanders Associates (Nashua), $105.579m: aircraft transmitter-receiver sets; various radar and navigational devices; electronic warfare units.

Economic Base Tourism; electrical equipment and supplies; finance, insurance and real estate; leather and leather products, especially shoes, except rubber; and machinery.

The Voters

> *Registration* 137,664 total. 55,931 D (41%); 81,733 R (59%).
> *Median voting age* 43.3
> *Employment profile* White collar, 45%. Blue collar, 42%. Service, 12%. Farm, 1%.
> *Ethnic groups* Total foreign stock, 23%. Canada, 13%.

Presidential vote

	1972	Nixon (R)	102,557	(62%)
		McGovern (D)	62,060	(38%)
	1968	Nixon (R)	76,241	(52%)
		Humphrey (D)	66,544	(45%)
		Wallace (AI)	4,826	(3%)

Representative

James C. Cleveland (R) Elected 1962; b. June 13, 1920, Montclair, N.J.; home, New London; Colgate U., B.A., 1941; Yale Law School, LL.B., 1948; Army, WWII and Korean War; married, five children; unspecified Protestant.

Career Practicing atty., 1949–62; N.H. Senate, 1950–62, Majority Floor Leader, 1952–55.

Offices 2236 RHOB, 202-225-5206. Also Fed. Bldg., 55 Pleasant St., Concord 03301, 603-224-4187, and 23 Temple St., Nashua 03060, 603-883-4225.

Administrative Assistant William R. Joslin

Committees

House Administration (3rd); Subs: Accounts; Printing (Ranking Mbr.); Contracts.

Public Works (3rd); Subs: Investigations and Review (Ranking Mbr.); Economic Development; Transportation; Energy.

Joint Com. on Congressional Operations (Ranking House Mbr.).

Group Ratings

	ADA	COPE	LWV	RIPON	NFU	LCV	CFA	NAB	NSI	ACA
1972	19	36	50	47	43	60	100	75	100	65
1971	30	9	22	61	53	–	83	–	–	86
1970	44	34	–	59	46	63	67	83	90	84

Key Votes

1) Busing	AGN	6) Cmbodia Bmbg	FOR	11) Chkg Acct Intrst	ABS
2) Strip Mines	AGN	7) Bust Hwy Trust	AGN	12) End HISC (HUAC)	AGN
3) Cut Mil $	AGN	8) Farm Sub Lmt	FOR	13) Nixon Sewer Veto	FOR
4) Rev Shrg	FOR	9) School Prayr	FOR	14) Corp Cmpaign $	AGN
5) Pub TV $	AGN	10) Cnsumr Prot	FOR	15) Pol $ Disclosr	AGN

Election Results

1972 general:	James C. Cleveland (R)	105,915	(68%)
	Charles B. Officer (D)	50,066	(32%)
1972 primary:	James C. Cleveland (R), unopposed		
1970 general:	James C. Cleveland (R)	74,219	(70%)
	Eugene S. Daniell, Jr. (D)	32,374	(30%)

NEW JERSEY

Political Background

After years of obscurity, New Jersey has at last found a political identity: the nation's most corrupt state. Though it is the eighth largest state in the country, New Jersey long languished in national inattention. Sandwiched between New York City and Philadelphia, some 78% of the state's residents live within the metropolitan areas of the two giant cities. The people here read out-of-state newspapers, watch out-of-state television stations, and follow out-of-state political contests. In fact, aside from Delaware, New Jersey is the only state in the country without a VHF television station of its own. New Jersey residents are among the nation's best educated and most affluent voters, but they have appeared content over the years to leave politics to local political bosses. And the bosses, it turns out, have been the most venal and corrupt political manipulators outside, perhaps, the 1600 and 1700 blocks of Pennsylvania Avenue.

At this writing, the list of New Jersey politicians convicted of crimes or under indictment reads like a Who's Who of state politics. Among those convicted: ex-Newark Mayor (1963–71) and Congressman (1949–63) Hugh Addonizio; former Congressman (1959–73) Cornelius Gallagher; former New Jersey Secretary of State (1962–70) Robert Burkhardt; former Assembly Speaker Peter Moraites; former Mayor Thomas Whelan of Jersey City; and former Hudson County (Jersey City) Democratic boss John V. Kenny. Among those indicted: former state Secretary of State (1970–72) Paul Sherwin; former Bergen County Republican boss Walter Jones; former State Treasurer (1970–73) Joseph McCrane; and former Republican State Chairman and 1970 Senate candidate Nelson Gross. The list, by the way, is a thoroughly bipartisan one. It includes top appointees of the state's last two Governors, Democrat Richard Hughes (1962–70) and Republican William Cahill (1970–74). Though neither of these two men is himself suspected of wrongdoing, the corruption issue clearly contributed to the 1973 primary defeat of Gov. Cahill by ultraconservative Congressman Charles Sandman.

Why so much corruption in New Jersey, and why has it been exposed and prosecuted only in recent years? The answer to the first question lies in the power of the county bosses of both parties, and the answer to the second is a peculiar combination of political circumstances. The county machines have traditionally selected candidates not only for local offices, but also for the state legislature, Congress, and the governorship. The last is of critical importance, because the Governor appoints the state Attorney General and all the county prosecutors. By calling in their political chips, the county bosses have been able to control state and local law enforcement—or nonenforcement.

But the appointment of the federal prosecutor, the United States Attorney, is the prerogative of the senior U.S. Senator of the President's political party. Since the Nixon Administration assumed office, the prerogative has belonged to Sen. Clifford Case, a liberal Republican, with few, if any, debts to local Republican organizations. The Senator's appointees, Frederick Lacey (now a federal judge) and Herbert Stern, have been responsible for virtually all of the prosecutions of major political figures here in the last four years. The two men have just about destroyed the old-line Hudson County Democratic machine, and have wounded, with no concern for partisan interests, almost every other political organization in New Jersey.

The boom-lowering has not made Sen. Case especially popular among old-guard Republicans, but he never was. Case first won a Senate seat in 1954 by a narrow margin, after a career as a Wall Street lawyer, nine years in the House, and a stint with the Fund for the Republic. The politician has always compiled a solidly liberal and independent voting record. In the Senate, Case serves on the Foreign Relations Committee, where he has long opposed American involvement in Southeast Asia. In 1972, he co-sponsored the Case-Church amendment to end the war, and in 1973 played an important role in ending American bombing in Cambodia.

The Senator's record has won Case very solid support in New Jersey general elections. In 1972, for example, he ran ahead of Nixon's very strong showing in the state. Conceivably, Case is vulnerable in a Republican primary. In 1972, an unknown conservative running against him took 30% of the primary votes. So a concerted effort—like the one in New York of Conservative James Buckley against liberal Republican Charles Goodell in 1970—might produce an upset. But in

1972, the Nixon Administration was not willing to wage such a campaign, and Case, should he chose to run again when his seat comes up in 1978 (when he will be 74), should win easily.

Another term also appears the likely prospect for New Jersey's junior Senator, Democrat Harrison Williams. Back in 1970, as Williams completed his second term, he looked extremely vulnerable. He was an admitted alcoholic not long off the wagon, and he was once censured by the state NAACP for showing up drunk at a breakfast speaking appearance. Moreover, Harrison's major legislative accomplishment, a mass-transit bill, was enacted during the mid-1960s and had little impact on the mostly suburban voters of New Jersey.

To add to the Senator's troubles, the state's Republicans were then riding a solid winning streak. The had won four straight statewide elections—1966 Senate, 1967 legislature, 1968 President, and 1969 Governor—all but the one in 1968 by big margins. But Richard Nixon was still happy to carry the state by 61,000 votes; he had lost it by 22,000 votes in 1960. New Jersey was Nixon's only major Eastern state win in 1968. Williams' 1970 opponent was state Republican chairman Nelson Gross, who at the 1968 National Convention swung vital votes to Nixon, much to the displeasure of favorite-son Clifford Case. Gross waged an aggressive law-and-order campaign, complete with references to Williams' radical-liberalism.

Williams choose to ignore Gross, speaking instead of the serious unemployment in the state and the value of his seniority. In the spring of 1970, Ralph Yarborough was beaten in the Texas Democratic primary, which meant that Williams, if reelected, would become Chairman of the Senate Labor and Public Welfare Committee. Organized labor then began to support the incumbent in a big way. In the end, Williams won a solid 54% of the votes, making up for marginal losses in blue-collar areas with gains in white-collar suburbs. Gross' law-and-order campaign backfired, like so many others that year. The Republican has since been indicted for tax fraud, ostruction of justice, and subornation of perjury.

Williams' third term promises to be more productive than his first two. As Chairman of the Labor Committee, he and Jacob Javits of New York have co-sponsored the principal pension fund reform bill in Congress, which, at this writing, has just passed the Senate by a 93–0 vote. Also, as Chairman of the Banking Committee's Securities Subcommittee, Williams has played a major role in the overhaul of the nation's stock exchange regulation laws.

It is something of an anomaly that a liberal Senate delegation comes out of New Jersey, which after trending conservative in recent years is now a classically marginal state. Its key electoral votes went to the winners by narrow margins in the close presidential elections of 1960 and 1968. New Jersey also gave a greater than average percentage of its votes to landslide winners Lyndon Johnson in 1964 and Richard Nixon in 1972. It will likely be a crucial state again in 1976.

New Jersey is more suburban than most states. Sometimes, in fact, it seems that the whole state is a suburb, aside from decaying central cities like Newark and Jersey City, which by themselves, of course, would have never generated the state's huge suburban population. Every kind of suburb is found here, from the posh horse-farm country in parts of Morris and Somerset counties, to the grim two-family houses in the towns on the ridge just north of Jersey City. New Jersey has become the final destination of many of the successful or at least comfortable children of the immigrants who poured into New York or Philadelphia at the turn of the century. It is a place where the shopping center rather than downtown is the focal point of commerce, and where the size of one's lawn and the shade cast by one's trees is a measure of success in life.

It is clear that the biggest political gains made by the politics of Richard Nixon's Republicanism occurred in the ethnic middle-class neighborhoods and suburbs of the East Coast. Italian-Americans—a larger proportion of whom live here than anywhere else but Rhode Island, Connecticut, and New York—have been especially prone to switch to the Republicans. In 1960, the Italians of the state gave John F. Kennedy some 69% of their votes; and 12 years later, in 1972, they cast about the same percentage for Richard M. Nixon.

The Italian homeowners who overwhelmingly supported the first Roman Catholic President remained basically conservative on many issues—ones that rightly or wrongly played a key role in the 1968 and 1972 elections. Moreover, the Democrats to whom the Italians gave heavy support seemed not to remember their old friends. Instead of promoting Italian politicians, the fashionable Democrats doted on blacks and Puerto Ricans, the very people who, in the minds of many Italian voters, were out to destroy their old ethnic neighborhoods. Finally, it was no help that at least a proportionate number of the Jersey politicians indicted and sent to jail in the last four years were of Italian descent. The Italian-American desire for respectability and an affirmation of old values persisted, and translated into votes for Republican politicians.

Currently, five of New Jersey's fifteen Congressmen are Italian-Americans—a higher percentage than in any other state except Wyoming, whose single House member is of Italian descent. But no one with an Italian surname has come even close to the governorship, the office that is, after all, the most important political post in the state. At this writing, the 1973 contest is one between Republican Congressman Charles Sandman, who defeated incumbent William Cahill in the primary, and Democrat Brendan T. Byrne. (New Jersey is one of three states that continues to elect state officials in odd-numbered years.) Sandman's victory over Cahill resulted largely from scandals involving some of Cahill's top appointees. The incumbent Governor also antagonized voters when he asked for a state income tax to ease the state's steep property-tax rates. Sandman's campaign is managed by F. Clifton White, the conservative strategist who put together Barry Goldwater's 1964 bid for the Republican presidential nomination and masterminded the successful Senate campaigns of James Buckley of New York in 1970 and Jesse Helms of North Carolina in 1972.

The favorite, however, is the Democratic nominee, Byrne. The former judge and Essex County (Newark) prosecutor's strongest political asset came out of the work of federal wiretappers, who recorded for posterity a statement by a Mafioso who said that Byrne was too honest to be bought. Byrne won the Democratic primary easily, and appears, at this writing, headed toward a general election victory, although his campaign is far less well-run than Clifton White's Sandman operation. But whatever happens, it seems likely that the power of the old-line county bosses—even those not sent to jail—is on the wane. What will replace the county organizations as *the* political force in apathetic, identity-less, and unloved New Jersey is less clear.

Census Data Pop. 7,168,164; 3.54% of U.S. total, 8th largest; change 1960–70, 18.2%. Central city, 16%; suburban, 61%. Median family income, $11,403; 4th highest; families above $15,000: 30%; families below $3,000: 6%. Median years education, 12.1.

1972 Share of Federal Tax Burden $9,050,500,000; 4.33% of U.S. total, 8th largest.

1972 Share of Federal Outlays $7,911,708,229; 3.65% of U.S. total, 6th largest. Per capita federal spending, $1,104.

DOD	$1,912,124,000	10th (3.06%)	HEW	$2,341,428,789	10th (3.28%)
AEC	$11,974,727	21st (0.46%)	HUD	$125,142,099	8th (4.08%)
NASA	$58,129,680	13th (1.94%)	VA	$304,822,297	10th (2.66%)
DOT	$171,340,992	17th (2.17%)	USDA	$176,607,418	32nd (1.15%)
DOC	$38,494,094	6th (2.97%)	CSC	$100,292,809	12th (2.43%)
DOI	$17,869,082	25th (0.84%)	TD	$2,090,601,521	2nd (12.66%)
DOJ	$26,397,812	9th (2.69%)	Other	$536,482,909	

Economic Base Finance, insurance and real estate; chemicals and allied products, especially industrial chemicals and drugs; electrical equipment and supplies, especially communication equipment; apparel and other textile products, especially women's and misses' outerwear; machinery; fabricated metal products; food and kindred products.

Political Line-up Governor, William T. Cahill (R); seat up, 1973. Senators, Clifford P. Case (R) and Harrison A. Williams, Jr. (D). Representatives, 15 (8 D and 7 R). State Senate (22 R, 16 D, and 2 vac.); General Assembly (40 D, 38 R, 1 Ind., and 1 vac.).

The Voters

Registration 3,672,606 total. No party registration.
Median voting age 44.1
Employment profile White collar, 53%. Blue collar, 36%. Service, 11%. Farm, 0%.
Ethnic groups Black, 11%. Spanish, 2%. Total foreign stock, 30%. Italy, 7%; Germany, Poland, 3% each; UK, USSR, Ireland, 2% each; Austria, 1%.

Presidential vote

1972	Nixon (R)	1,845,502	(63%)
	McGovern (D)	1,102,211	(37%)

1968	Nixon (R)	1,325,467	(46%)
	Humphrey (D)	1,264,206	(44%)
	Wallace (AI)	262,187	(9%)
1964	Johnson (D)	1,867,671	(66%)
	Goldwater (R)	963,843	(34%)

Senator

Clifford P. Case (R) Elected 1954, seat up 1978; b. April 16, 1904, Franklin Park; home, Rahway; Rutgers U., B.A., 1925; Columbia U., LL.B. 1928; married, three children; Presbyterian.

Career Practicing atty., N.Y.C., 1928–53; Rahway Common Council, 1938–42; N.J. House of Assembly, 1943–44; U.S. Delegate to 21st Gen. Assembly of UN; U.S. House of Reps., 1945–53.

Offices 315 OSOB, 202-225-3224.

Administrative Assistant Frances Henderson

Committees

Appropriations (4th); Subs: Labor, and Health, Education, and Welfare, and Related Agencies; Public Works-AEC; Defense; Housing and Urban Development, Space, Science, and Veterans; Transportation (Ranking Mbr.).

Foreign Relations (2nd); Subs: European Affairs (Ranking Mbr.); Oceans and International Environment; Arms Control, International Law and Organization (Ranking Mbr.); U.S. Security Agreements and Commitments Abroad; Western Hemisphere Affairs; Multinational Corporations (Ranking Mbr.).

Sp. Com. on the Termination of the National Emergency (2nd).

Group Ratings

	ADA	COPE	LWV	RIPON	NFU	LCV	CFA	NAB	NSI	ACA
1972	80	100	100	88	70	95	100	36	22	14
1971	81	83	100	92	82	–	100	–	–	0
1970	88	92	–	92	87	81	–	10	0	4

Key Votes

1) Busing	FOR	8) Sea Life Prot	FOR	15) Tax Singls Less	AGN
2) Alas P-line	AGN	9) Campaign Subs	FOR	16) Min Tax for Rich	AGN
3) Gun Cntrl	FOR	10) Cmbodia Bmbg	AGN	17) Euro Troop Rdctn	AGN
4) Rehnquist	AGN	11) Legal Srvices	FOR	18) Bust Hwy Trust	FOR
5) Pub TV $	FOR	12) Rev Sharing	FOR	19) Maid Min Wage	FOR
6) EZ Votr Reg	FOR	13) Cnsumr Prot	FOR	20) Farm Sub Limit	AGN
7) No-Fault	FOR	14) Eq Rts Amend	FOR	21) Highr Credt Chgs	AGN

Election Results

1972 general:	Clifford P. Case (R)	1,743,854	(63%)
	Paul J. Krebs (D)	963,573	(35%)
	A. Howard Freund (AI)	40,980	(1%)
	Charles W. Wiley (Concerned Voter's Voice)	33,442	(1%)
1972 primary:	Clifford P. Case (R)	187,268	(70%)
	James Walter Ralph (R)	79,766	(30%)
1966 general:	Clifford P. Case (R)	1,278,843	(60%)
	Warren W. Wilentz (D)	788,021	(37%)
	Robert Lee Schlachter (Con.)	53,606	(3%)

Senator

Harrison Arlington Williams, Jr. (D) Elected 1958, seat up 1976; b. Dec. 10, 1919, Plainfield; home, Westfield; Oberlin Col., B.A., 1941; Columbia Law School, LL.B., 1948; Georgetown Foreign Service School; USN, WWII; Presbyterian

Career Practicing atty., 1951– ; U.S. House, 1953–57.

Offices 352 OSOB, 202-225-4744. Also Rm. 939A, Fed. Bldg., 970 Broad St., Newark 07102, 201-645-3030.

Administrative Assistant Benjamin L. Palumbo

Committees

Banking, Housing and Urban Affairs (3rd); Subs: Financial Institutions; Housing and Urban Affairs; Securities (Chm.).

Labor and Public Welfare (Chm.); Subs: Education; Aging; Alcoholism and Narcotics; Children and Youth; Handicapped; Health; Labor (Chm.).

Rules and Administration (5th); Subs: Smithsonian Institution; Restaurant; Computer Services.

Sp. Com. on Aging (2nd); Subs: Housing for the Elderly (Chm.); Consumer Interests of the Elderly; Health of the Elderly; Long-Term Care.

Joint Com. on Defense Production (3rd).

Joint Com. on the Library (3rd).

Group Ratings

	ADA	COPE	LWV	RIPON	NFU	LCV	CFA	NAB	NSI	ACA
1972	85	100	100	82	90	87	100	8	0	5
1971	93	92	100	65	91	–	100	–	–	5
1970	94	100	–	74	94	68	–	10	0	5

Key Votes

1) Busing	FOR	8) Sea Life Prot	ABS	15) Tax Singls Less	FOR
2) Alas P-line	AGN	9) Campaign Subs	FOR	16) Min Tax for Rich	AGN
3) Gun Cntrl	FOR	10) Cmbodia Bmbg	AGN	17) Euro Troop Rdctn	FOR
4) Rehnquist	AGN	11) Legal Srvices	FOR	18) Bust Hwy Trust	FOR
5) Pub TV $	ABS	12) Rev Sharing	FOR	19) Maid Min Wage	FOR
6) EZ Votr Reg	FOR	13) Cnsumr Prot	FOR	20) Farm Sub Limit	FOR
7) No-Fault	FOR	14) Eq Rts Amend	FOR	21) Highr Credt Chgs	AGN

Election Results

1970 general:	Harrison A. Williams, Jr. (D)	1,157,074	(55%)
	Nelson G. Gross (R)	903,026	(43%)
	Four others	54,291	(3%)
1970 primary:	Harrison A. Williams, Jr. (D)	190,692	(66%)
	Frank J. Guarini (D)	100,045	(34%)
1964 general:	Harrison A. Williams, Jr. (D)	1,677,515	(62%)
	Bernard M. Shanley (R)	1,011,280	(38%)

FIRST DISTRICT Political Background

The 1st district of New Jersey is part of suburban Philadelphia, a region of the state more attuned to the city across the Delaware River than to Trenton. The 1st takes in a nice cross-section of suburban America. Along the banks of the Delaware are the factories and oil-tank farms of industrial cities like Camden (pop. 103,000), places that are declining in population and suffering from many of the same ills afflicting much larger central cities. To the east, on the flat plains of south Jersey, are the subdivisions laid out during the 1940s, 1950s, and 1960s, covering what was once truck-farming country. In general, the suburbs along the river vote Democratic, while the newer, higher-income suburbs farther inland go Republican.

On paper, the 1st is a Democratic district. In 1968, it gave Hubert Humphrey a solid margin, and even in 1972, the district compiled a respectable total for George McGovern. Nevertheless, the 1st and its predecessor districts have sent only Republicans to Congress since 1883. Liberal Republican William Cahill represented the district from 1959 to 1967, before leaving to capture the seat in the newly created 6th district and then the governorship in 1969. One reason Cahill left the 1st for the 6th was a feeling that the Democratic legislature of the day designed the 1st to go Democratic in 1966, one that turned out to be a Republican year. So conservative John Hunt, then a state Senator and formerly Gloucester County Sheriff, won the seat and has held it ever since.

Hunt, whose career was in law enforcement, is one of the most outspoken conservatives in the House. The Congressman is an ardent admirer of both Richard Nixon and Frank Rizzo, the former police chief and now the nominally Democratic Mayor of Philadelphia. The Watergate affair has not dimmed Hunt's respect for Nixon; indeed, he is as pugnacious as ever when declaring his support for the man he, like so many Republicans, refers to as The President. Hunt's political style also makes him one of the most outspoken hawks on the hawkish Armed Services Committee. Accordingly, he had little use for demonstrators or peace advocates of any kind. After the Cambodian invasion of 1970, Hunt was the only Congressman on the Hill to throw lobbying students out of his office.

Hunt's constituents, many of them Italian immigrants who had to work their way out of the South Philadelphia slums, approved of the Congressman's performance during his first few years in office. He won steadily increasing percentages of the vote up through the 1970 election. But in 1972, a strange thing happened. As Hunt's man Richard Nixon swept the nation and 1st district of New Jersey, the Congressman's own percentage dropped sharply. He came close to losing to Democrat James Florio. Redistricting, which made only slight adjustments in district lines, accounted for little of the result. Hunt's problem came, rather, from a Democratic campaign more vigorous than those that had been waged in the past. The prospect for 1974 is for an even tougher campaign and another close result. Next time out, Hunt will be 66, and it is quite possible that his ringing endorsement of the post-Watergate Nixon will not be shared by his constituents.

Census Data Pop. 478,002. Central city, 0%; suburban, 100%. Median family income, $10,314; families above $15,000: 20%; families below $3,000: 7%. Median years education, 11.3.

1972 Share of Federal Outlays $510,696,447

DOD	$284,393,040	HEW	$127,562,863
AEC	–	HUD	$2,569,484
NASA	$12,239,616	DOI	$187,149
DOT	$5,001,342	USDA	$5,498,131
		Other	$73,244,822

Federal Military-Industrial Commitments

DOD Contractors RCA (Camden), $56.256m: various airborne and shipboard communications equipment.
DOD Installations Gibbsboro AF Station (Gibbsboro).
NASA Contractors RCA (Camden), $19.264m: Tiros M and TOS spacecraft.

Economic Base Finance, insurance and real estate; electrical equipment and supplies, especially communication equipment; food and kindred products; chemicals and allied products; and fabricated metal products, especially fabricated structural metal products. Also higher education (Glassboro State).

The Voters

Registration Not available.
Median voting age 43.2

Employment profile White collar, 46%. Blue collar, 42%. Service, 11%. Farm, 1%.
Ethnic groups Black, 13%. Spanish, 2%. Total foreign stock, 18%. Italy, 5%; UK, Germany, Poland, 2% each; Ireland, 1%

Presidential vote

1972	Nixon (R)	112,632	(60%)
	McGovern (D)	74,821	(40%)
1968	Nixon (R)	75,624	(40%)
	Humphrey (D)	87,392	(46%)
	Wallace (AI)	27,954	(15%)

Representative

John E. Hunt (R) Elected 1966; b. Nov. 25, 1908, Lambertville; home, Pitman; Newark Business School; N.J. State Police Academy; FBI National Academy; Harvard School of Police Science; U.S. Army Intelligence School; Army, WWII; Lt. Col. USAR; married, one child; Baptist.

Career Criminology Consultant, N.J. State Police, 1930–59; Sheriff, Gloucester County, 1960–64; N.J. Senate, 1964–66.

Offices 1440 LHOB, 202-225-6501. Also 114 N. 7th St., Camden 08102, 609-365-4442, and 67 Cooper St., Woodbury 08096, 609-845-0200.

Administrative Assistant Mrs. Nancy Sohl

Committees

Armed Services (7th); Subs: No. 4 (Ranking Mbr.); Sp. Sub. on Armed Services Investigating; Human Relations (Ranking Mbr.).

Standards of Official Conduct (6th).

Group Ratings

	ADA	COPE	LWV	RIPON	NFU	LCV	CFA	NAB	NSI	ACA
1972	0	20	33	64	43	18	0	100	100	90
1971	5	27	11	39	27	–	20	–	–	86
1970	8	17	–	50	31	50	50	82	100	89

Key Votes

1) Busing	AGN	6) Cmbodia Bmbg	ABS	11) Chkg Acct Intrst	ABS
2) Strip Mines	AGN	7) Bust Hwy Trust	AGN	12) End HISC (HUAC)	AGN
3) Cut Mil $	AGN	8) Farm Sub Lmt	FOR	13) Nixon Sewer Veto	FOR
4) Rev Shrg	FOR	9) School Prayr	FOR	14) Corp Cmpaign $	FOR
5) Pub TV $	AGN	10) Cnsumr Prot	AGN	15) Pol $ Disclosr	AGN

Election Results

1972 general:	John E. Hunt (R)	97,650	(53%)
	James J. Florio (D)	87,492	(47%)
1972 primary:	John E. Hunt (R), unopposed		
1970 general:	John E. Hunt (R)	83,726	(77%)
	Salvatore T. Mansi (D)	25,567	(23%)

SECOND DISTRICT Political Background

The 2nd district of New Jersey takes in Atlantic, Cape May, Cumberland, and Salem counties, along with parts of Ocean and Burlington counties. The 2nd spreads out across the flat, often swampy coastal plain of south Jersey. Along the ocean are the great, aging beach resorts of Atlantic City, Wildwood, and Cape May. Cumberland and Salem counties are filled with vegetable farms, and the conditions in the migrant camps here have prompted some controversy. Like the neighboring state of Delaware, Cumberland and Salem have a Southern ambiance about them, and the voting patterns are traditionally Democratic. Cape May is a Republican bastion. Atlantic City, where most of the district's large black population lives, sometimes goes Democratic; but it is also the home of ex-state Sen. Frank (Hap) Farley, long one of New Jersey's most powerful and effective Republican county bosses. The fastest-growing part of the district lies in Ocean County, north of Atlantic City. Here many of the 2nd's new residents are New York and Philadelphia retirees in search of sandy beaches and clean air.

The district's conservative Republican Congressman, Charles W. Sandman, Jr., first won the seat in 1966, when he defeated a Democrat elected on the strength of the 1964 LBJ landslide. But Sandman's principal interest has always been state government. During the mid-1960s, he was the Republican leader in the state Senate, and since then, he has tried for the governorship no less than three times. In 1965 and 1969, Sandman lost Republican primary bids to more moderate candidates. But in 1973, the south Jersey Congressman got a little sweet revenge, beating the incumbent Governor, William Cahill, the same man who had licked him four years earlier. So for the first time, Sandman made it to the general election.

The decisive issue in Sandman's primary victory over Cahill was corruption. Two of Cahill's appointees, Secretary of State Paul Sherwin and State Treasurer Joseph McCrane, were indicted on federal election law and tax fraud charges, respectively. Sandman, meanwhile, is apparently clean as a whistle. But there was more to the primary victory than public wrongdoing. The Congressman's long record of opposition to a state income tax probably helped him among the conservatively inclined Republican primary voters, especially since Cahill as Governor had tried, unsuccessfully, to get one enacted.

Sandman's chief campaign advisor was F. Clifton White, one of the shrewdest campaign managers around. He concentrated the Sandman efforts on what White likes to call the peripheral urban ethnics—that is, Italian-, Polish-, and even Jewish-Americans who have moved from what they consider crime-ridden cities to the sprawling subdivision or spanking new retirement colonies of small Jersey towns. At this writing, the odds heavily favor Sandman's Democratic opponent, former Judge Brendan Byrne (see New Jersey state write-up). But Sandman's chances—and White's strategy—should not be discounted. If Sandman does win, his House seat will be up for grabs in a special election. Past voting history indicates that either party could win it, with the Democrats strengthened by the eclipse of the Atlantic City Republican machine. In fact, Sandman himself, if he loses the gubernatorial race, could conceivably be in trouble anyway in 1974. Conservative Democratic candidates have run close races against him as recently as 1970.

Census Data Pop. 478,126. Central city, 29%; suburban, 47%. Median family income, $9,039; families above $15,000: 17%; families below $3,000: 9%. Median years education, 11.1.

1972 Share of Federal Outlays $417,791,363

DOD	$57,841,686	HEW	$223,446,395
AEC	–	HUD	$8,921,042
NASA	$98,788	DOI	$1,008,027
DOT	$52,340,891	USDA	$9,195,234
		Other	$64,939,300

Federal Military-Industrial Commitments

DOD Installations Naval Air Station (Lakehurst); reduced substantially by 1974.

Economic Base Stone, clay and glass products, especially pressed or blown glass and glassware; finance, insurance and real estate; apparel and other textile products, especially men's and boys' suits and coats; agriculture, notably vegetables and poultry; and food and kindred products, especially canned, cured and frozen foods. Also higher education (Trenton State).

The Voters

Registration Not available.
Median voting age 48.2
Employment profile White collar, 42%. Blue collar, 41%. Service, 15%. Farm, 2%.

Ethnic groups Black, 13%. Spanish, 2%. Total foreign stock, 20%. Italy, 5%; Germany, 3%; UK, USSR, 2% each; Poland, Ireland, 1% each.

Presidential vote

1972	Nixon (R)	138,957	(66%)
	McGovern (D)	73,018	(34%)
1968	Nixon (R)	91,726	(46%)
	Humphrey (D)	85,603	(43%)
	Wallace (AI)	23,194	(12%)

Representative

Charles W. Sandman, Jr. (R) Elected 1966; b. Oct. 23, 1921, Philadelphia, Pa.; home, Cape May; Temple U., 1940–42; Rutgers U., 1946–48; USAAF, WWII; married, six children; Catholic.

Career N.J. Senate, 1956–66, Majority Leader, 1962–63, Pres., 1964–65; Acting Governor, 1964–65.

Offices 115 CHOB, 202-225-6572. Also 421 Washington St., Cape May 08204, 608-884-8492, and Landis Ave., Vineland 08360.

Administrative Assistant Mrs. Dorothy Vagnozzi

Committees

Judiciary (4th); Subs: No. 3 (Patents, Trademarks, Copyrights); No. 5 (Antitrust Matters).

Sel. Com. on Crime (4th).

Group Ratings

	ADA	COPE	LWV	RIPON	NFU	LCV	CFA	NAB	NSI	ACA
1972	0	11	30	43	29	11	100	92	100	96
1971	5	25	38	41	27	–	25	–	–	86
1970	16	25	–	65	46	25	58	75	100	63

Key Votes

1) Busing	AGN	6) Cmbodia Bmbg	ABS	11) Chkg Acct Intrst	AGN
2) Strip Mines	ABS	7) Bust Hwy Trust	AGN	12) End HISC (HUAC)	AGN
3) Cut Mil $	AGN	8) Farm Sub Lmt	FOR	13) Nixon Sewer Veto	FOR
4) Rev Shrg	AGN	9) School Prayr	FOR	14) Corp Cmpaign $	FOR
5) Pub TV $	AGN	10) Cnsumr Prot	AGN	15) Pol $ Disclosr	AGN

Election Results

1972 general:	Charles W. Sandman, Jr. (R)	133,096	(66%)
	John D. Rose (D)	69,374	(34%)
1972 primary:	Charles W. Sandman, Jr. (R), unopposed		
1970 general:	Charles W. Sandman, Jr. (R)	69,392	(52%)
	William J. Hughes (D)	64,882	(48%)

THIRD DISTRICT   Political Background

Monmouth County, one that bears a name made famous by a Revolutionary War battle and a present-day race track, takes up the northernmost part of the Jersey Shore. Here, around the turn of the century, some of America's first beach resorts were created, to cater to the increasing number of people with the time and money for summer sojourns to the seashore. Beach manners have changed a lot from the days of full-length swimsuits, but the Monmouth County shore still attracts hundreds of thousands of bathers each year. Its summer home areas, with houses ranging from shacks to mansions, have increasingly become year-round communities, with many residents commuting to jobs in north Jersey or even Manhattan. The flatlands behind the beaches have been the area of greatest recent growth; here retirement villages and subdivisions attract people from the outer Jersey reaches of the New York metropolitan area.

Virtually all of Monmouth County, plus Lakewood township and Point Pleasant in Ocean County just to the south, make up New Jersey's 3rd congressional district. By tradition, Monmouth is a Republican bastion, but its voting patterns have become less predictable with the recent growth. Nevertheless, the 3rd would surely elect a Republican Congressman were it not for the presence of Democrat James Howard. Howard was lucky enough to have been the Democratic candidate in the LBJ year of 1964, when at the same time the district's Republican James Auchincloss was retiring after 24 years in the House. Howard won by a scant majority of 1,740 votes, and he has since worked to strengthen his position. For the most part, he has succeeded in that, even though his record in Congress is a fairly liberal one.

In the last couple of elections, however, Howard's percentages—unlike those of most Congressmen with comparable seniority—has been on the decline. The aggressive campaigning of 1970 and 1972 Republican nominee William Dowd accounts for Howard's recent troubles. Returning to the district after a stint in the Nixon White House, Dowd got 44% of the votes in 1970 and 47% in 1972. But 1972 was the Nixon Administration's most potent political year. So should he run again in 1974, Dowd's association with the White House will probably be less an asset than in the past. Accordingly, Howard's chances look far better now than they did just after the 1972 election.

Census Data Pop. 475,599. Central city, 0%; suburban, 0%. Median family income, $11,291; families above $15,000: 30%; families below $3,000: 7%. Median years education, 12.3.

1972 Share of Federal Outlays $616,135,812

DOD	$229,156,084	HEW	$163,552,738
AEC	$50,341	HUD	$3,108,735
NASA	$2,687,773	DOI	$601,182
DOT	$5,031,171	USDA	$6,390,579
		Other	$205,557,209

Federal Military-Industrial Commitments

DOD Contractors Harvard Industries (Farmingdale), $18.902m: shipboard and aircraft communications equipment. Bendix (Eatontown), $6.586m: various electric generators and parts.
DOD Installations Fort Monmouth AB (Oceanport). Naval Ammunition Depot (Earle).

Economic Base Finance, insurance and real estate; electrical equipment and supplies, especially communication equipment; apparel and other textile products, especially women's and misses' outerwear; agriculture, notably nursery and greenhouse products, poultry and vegetables; and stone, clay and glass products, especially glass containers.

The Voters

Registration Not available.
Median voting age 43.9
Employment profile White collar, 56%. Blue collar, 31%. Service, 12%. Farm, 1%.
Ethnic groups Black, 8%. Spanish, 1%. Total foreign stock, 25%. Italy, 5%; Germany, UK, 3% each; USSR, Poland, Ireland, 2% each.

Presidential vote

1972	Nixon (R)	133,272	(67%)
	McGovern (D)	65,028	(33%)
1968	Nixon (R)	90,913	(51%)
	Humphrey (D)	72,420	(41%)
	Wallace (AI)	13,260	(8%)

Representative

James J. Howard (D) Elected 1964; b. July 24, 1927, Irvington; home, Spring Lake Heights; St. Bonaventure U., B.A., 1952; Rutgers U., M.Ed., 1958; Navy, WWII; married, three children; Catholic.

Career Teacher, principal, Wall Township, N.J., 1952–64; Pres., Monmouth County Ed. Assn., Mbr. Delegate Assembly of N.J. Ed. Assn.

Offices 131 CHOB, 202-225-4671. Also P.O. Bldg., 501 Main St., Asbury Park 07712, 201-774-1600.

Administrative Assistant Timothy F. Sullivan

Committees

District of Columbia (8th); Subs: Education; Government Operations.

Public Works (11th); Subs: Investigations and Review; Economic Development; Energy (Chm.); Water Resources.

Group Ratings

	ADA	COPE	LWV	RIPON	NFU	LCV	CFA	NAB	NSI	ACA
1972	75	91	83	80	86	68	50	9	13	5
1971	86	82	88	82	93	–	100	–	–	4
1970	76	92	–	76	92	85	100	0	33	11

Key Votes

1) Busing	FOR	6) Cmbodia Bmbg	AGN	11) Chkg Acct Intrst	FOR
2) Strip Mines	AGN	7) Bust Hwy Trust	AGN	12) End HISC (HUAC)	FOR
3) Cut Mil $	AGN	8) Farm Sub Lmt	FOR	13) Nixon Sewer Veto	AGN
4) Rev Shrg	FOR	9) School Prayr	AGN	14) Corp Cmpaign $	FOR
5) Pub TV $	FOR	10) Cnsumr Prot	FOR	15) Pol $ Disclosr	AGN

Election Results

1972 general:	James J. Howard (D)	103,893	(53%)
	William F. Dowd (R)	92,285	(47%)
1972 primary:	James J. Howard (D), unopposed		
1970 general:	James J. Howard (D)	87,937	(56%)
	William F. Dowd (R)	68,675	(44%)

FOURTH DISTRICT Political Background

The 4th congressional district of New Jersey is one whose shape has undergone almost complete transformation not once, but twice, within the past six years. The one constant geographical feature of the 4th is the city of Trenton (pop. 104,000), the state capital, which, with surrounding Mercer County, is a Democratic stronghold. Under the current, court-imposed redistricting plan, the 4th extends south from Trenton into Burlington County, to a point almost directly across the Delaware River from Philadelphia. To the north and east, the 4th stretches in a narrow corridor toward Raritan Bay, which separates the district from Staten Island. The district lines, of course, encompass no coherent community; instead, the 4th is a collection of older central cities, booming suburbs, and rolling farmlands. Its most marked political characteristic is a mild proclivity toward the Democratic party.

During the transmogrifications of the 4th, the district sustained another constant: the continued incumbency of Rep. Frank Thompson, Jr. The Congressman is currently the second-ranking Democrat on the House Education and Labor Committee, just one slot below Chairman Carl Perkins of Kentucky. Because he is several years younger than Perkins, Thompson stands a good chance of someday becoming Chairman of the committee. Thompson was helped along when Oregon's Edith Green, who outranked him, switched to the Appropriations Committee at the beginning of the 93rd Congress, reportedly because she couldn't get along with other Democrats on the committee.

Back in the 1950s, Education and Labor reported out legislation that ultimately became the Landrum-Griffin Act, several sections of which were vehemently opposed by organized labor. That kind of bill is unlikely to come out of the committee ever again. Today, the Democratic members of Education and Labor are almost all Northern liberals, with a number of its Republicans falling into the same category. One of the committee's most faithful friends of liberal causes in general and the positions espoused by organized labor in particular is Frank Thompson. For years, Thompson has compiled a 100% COPE rating, while at the same time establishing an antiwar voting record. Because both big labor and big management have learned to live with the country's basic labor legislation, Thompson's name has not appeared on any major bill. But he is active legislatively. In 1973, for instance, Thompson was the driving force behind the act permitting labor unions to bargain for group legal services—a move that could vastly change the structure of the legal profession.

The New Jersey Congressman is one of the more veteran House liberals. Back during the mid-1950s, he helped to found the Democratic Study Group; he is now one of the few original members still in the House, many others having been elected to the Senate. In 1960, Thompson headed the voter registration drive in John F. Kennedy's presidential campaign, the last time the Democrats have conducted a really successful registration effort on a nationwide basis. Thompson agreed to head a similar effort for McGovern in 1972, but quit during the campaign after a falling out with campaign manager Gary Hart. Back home in New Jersey, whatever the boundaries set down for him, Thompson has always won more or less routine reelection. When the district's contours were changed drastically, as in 1966 and 1972, Thompson did not run especially well in areas appended that are traditionally Republican. In later elections, however, he has increased his percentages in such territory. Barring unforeseen circumstances, Thompson is likely to do so again in 1974.

Census Data   Pop. 478,045. Central city, 22%; suburban, 45%. Median family income, $11,086; families above $15,000: 25%; families below $3,000: 6%. Median years education, 12.1.

1972 Share of Federal Outlays $644,503,411

DOD	$158,576,161	HEW	$195,293,519
AEC	$7,666,753	HUD	$9,004,780
NASA	$18,904,711	DOI	$4,820,265
DOT	$32,276,946	USDA	$8,704,233
		Other	$209,256,043

Federal Military-Industrial Commitments

DOD Contractors DeLaval Turbine, Inc. (Trenton), $12.281m: component parts for ship turbine engines. Chamberlain Manufacturing (Burlington), $5.981m: metal parts for 81mm projectiles. DeLaval Turbine, Inc. (Florence), $5.048m: shipsets for main condensers.

DOD Installations Fort Dix AB (Wrightstown). McGuire AFB (Wrightstown). Naval Air Propulsion Test Center (Trenton).

Economic Base   Chemicals and allied products, especially drugs; finance, insurance and real estate; electrical equipment and supplies; machinery; fabricated metal products; and primary metal industries.

The Voters

    Registration Not available.
    Median voting age 40.1
    Employment profile White collar, 49%. Blue collar, 38%. Service, 12%. Farm, 1%.
    Ethnic groups Black, 13%. Spanish, 1%. Total foreign stock, 25%. Poland, 4%; Germany, 3%; UK, Hungary, USSR, 2% each; Ireland, Austria, 1% each.

Presidential vote

1972	Nixon (R)	102,645	(58%)
	McGovern (D)	74,902	(42%)
1968	Nixon (R)	64,841	(39%)
	Humphrey (D)	81,145	(48%)
	Wallace (AI)	22,228	(13%)

Representative

Frank Thompson, Jr. (D) Elected 1954; b. July 20, 1918, Trenton; home, Trenton; Wake Forest Col., LL.B., 1941; Navy, WWII; Cdr. USNR; married, two children; Catholic.

Career Practicing atty., 1948– ; N.J. Gen. Assembly, 1949–54, Asst. Minority Leader, 1950, Minority Leader, 1954; Chm., Natl. Voters Registration Com. for 1960 Pres. Campaign.

Offices 2246 RHOB, 202-225-3765. Also 10 Rutgers Pl., Trenton 08618, 609-599-1619.

Administrative Assistant William T. Deitz

Committees

Education and Labor (2nd); Subs: No. 2 (Labor) (Chm.); No. 8 (Agricultural Labor).

House Administration (2nd); Subs: Accounts (Chm.); Library and Memorials.

Group Ratings

	ADA	COPE	LWV	RIPON	NFU	LCV	CFA	NAB	NSI	ACA
1972	75	88	91	60	100	76	100	11	0	6
1971	86	82	89	83	69	–	80	–	–	10
1970	92	100	–	76	92	80	100	0	0	0

Key Votes

1) Busing	FOR	6) Cmbodia Bmbg	AGN	11) Chkg Acct Intrst	ABS
2) Strip Mines	ABS	7) Bust Hwy Trust	FOR	12) End HISC (HUAC)	FOR
3) Cut Mil $	FOR	8) Farm Sub Lmt	AGN	13) Nixon Sewer Veto	AGN
4) Rev Shrg	FOR	9) School Prayr	AGN	14) Corp Cmpaign $	FOR
5) Pub TV $	FOR	10) Cnsumr Prot	ABS	15) Pol $ Disclosr	AGN

Election Results

1972 general:	Frank Thompson, Jr. (D)	98,206	(58%)
	Peter P. Garibaldi (R)	71,030	(42%)
1972 primary:	Frank Thompson, Jr. (D), unopposed		
1970 general:	Frank Thompson, Jr. (D)	91,670	(59%)
	Edward A. Costigan (R)	65,030	(41%)

FIFTH DISTRICT Political Background

Most people's image of the essential New Jersey is the one gotten on the drive from the Newark Airport to Manhattan: factories belching smoke into the already smoggy air, swampland, grim lines of Jersey City row houses, and finally the docks on the Hudson River. But there is another New Jersey—one which begins some 40 to 50 miles out of Manhattan, just past the first ridge west of Newark. Such is the area that makes up the 5th congressional district. Out here the high-income suburbs fade into horse-farm country near Far Hills and Peapack. The 5th also includes middle-income suburbs, places like fast-growing Parsippany-Troy Hills, where subdivisions of tightly grouped houses sell for prices deemed moderate these days. But most of the 5th district, from the country around Morristown down through Somerset County to the elegant university town of Princetown, is high-income territory. The 5th, in fact, ranks eleventh in the nation in median family income among the 435 congressional districts.

The 5th is appropriately represented in the House by Peter H. B. Frelinghuysen, a member of an old aristocratic family which has produced three New Jersey Senators and a Secretary of State in the Arthur Administration. The current Frelinghuysen is a wealthy man with a 200-acre estate near Morristown. A moderate Republican, Frelinghuysen is not as conservative as most Midwestern and New Jersey Republicans, and not as liberal as some of his New York GOP colleagues. In 1965, he was the liberals' candidate for Chairman of the Republican Policy Committee and nearly defeated Melvin Laird for the post. Since then, Frelinghuysen has not sought other leadership positions, and now sits as the second-ranking minority member of the House Foreign Affairs Committee.

Because the Congressman has supported the Nixon Administration policy in Southeast Asia, he has encountered opposition from Democratic peace candidates—in the 5th, like most high-income areas, peace activists tend to dominate the Democratic party. Recently, Democrats have whittled down Frelinghuysen's margins, but not enough to create doubts about his continued incumbency. It is worth noting, however, that as the country moved to the right, very rich areas like the 5th shifted at least a little to the left. In 1972, the year of the Nixon landslide, Frelinghuysen received a smaller percentage of the votes (62%) than he got in 1964 with Barry Goldwater at the top of the ticket (64%).

One reason for the drop was the addition of Princeton to the district. It must have saddened Frelinghuysen—a mark of the direction in which his kind of people are going politically—to see his alma mater vote heavily against him, with Princeton as a whole casting a 2–1 margin for his Democratic opponent. Because of Watergate, a possibility exists that a strong Democratic effort will be made here in 1974, either in behalf of the 1972 candidate, Frederick Bohen, or maybe for ex-Assemblywoman Anne Klein, who ran a surprisingly strong second in the 1973 Democratic gubernatorial primary. Odds, however, favor the reelection of Frelinghuysen.

Census Data   Pop. 478,007. Central city, 0%; suburban, 54%. Median family income, $14,218; families above $15,000: 46%; families below $3,000: 3%. Median years education, 12.6.

1972 Share of Federal Outlays $540,145,842

DOD	$98,872,520	HEW	$153,235,573
AEC	$1,254,656	HUD	$10,440,911
NASA	$3,197,473	DOI	$1,392,589
DOT	$9,870,665	USDA	$13,762,839
		Other	$248,118,616

Federal Military-Industrial Commitments

DOD Contractors Western Electric (Whippany), $120.356m: ABM research and development. Western Electric (Morris Plains), $30.000m: ABM research and development. RCA (Princeton), $29.285m: various electronics research.
NASA Contractors RCA (Princeton), $8.843m: Tiros M and TOS spacecraft.
AEC Operations Princeton University (Princeton), $18.461m: research and development at Princeton Plasma Physics Laboratory.

Economic Base   Finance, insurance and real estate; chemicals and allied products, especially drugs; electrical equipment and supplies; stone, clay and glass products, especially gaskets and insulations; machinery; and fabricated metal products.

The Voters

Registration Not available.
Median voting age 42.6
Employment profile White collar, 65%. Blue collar, 26%. Service, 9%. Farm, –%.
Ethnic groups Black, 3%. Total foreign stock, 29%. Italy, 6%; Germany, UK, Poland, 3% each; USSR, Ireland, 2% each; Austria, Canada, Hungary, 1% each.

Presidential vote

1972	Nixon (R)	139,407	(66%)
	McGovern (D)	73,268	(34%)
1968	Nixon (R)	103,944	(53%)
	Humphrey (D)	77,217	(40%)
	Wallace (AI)	13,176	(7%)

Representative

Peter H. B. Frelinghuysen (R) Elected 1952; b. Jan. 17, 1916, New York City; home, Morristown; Princeton, B.A., 1938; Yale Law School, LL.B., 1941; USNR, WWII; married, five children; Episcopalian.

Career Business—investments; Dir., American Natl. Bank and Trust, Morristown; Bd. of Managers, Howard Savings Institution, Newark; Bd. of Trustees, John F. Kennedy Center for the Performing Arts and Metropolitan Museum of Art; Bd. of Directors, United Nations Assn. of the U.S.A.

Offices 2110 RHOB, 202-225-7300. Also 3 Schuyler Place, Morristown 07960, 201-538-7267.

Administrative Assistant William T. Kendall

Committees

Foreign Affairs (2nd); Subs: Europe (Ranking Mbr.); Inter-American Affairs; State Department Organization and Foreign Operations; Review of Foreign Aid Programs.

Sel. Com. on Committees of the House (2nd).

Group Ratings

	ADA	COPE	LWV	RIPON	NFU	LCV	CFA	NAB	NSI	ACA
1972	13	22	60	86	17	41	50	75	100	53
1971	32	18	50	63	29	–	40	–	–	73
1970	40	34	–	76	69	28	61	80	55	53

Key Votes

1) Busing	AGN	6) Cmbodia Bmbg	ABS	11) Chkg Acct Intrst	ABS
2) Strip Mines	AGN	7) Bust Hwy Trust	FOR	12) End HISC (HUAC)	AGN
3) Cut Mil $	AGN	8) Farm Sub Lmt	FOR	13) Nixon Sewer Veto	FOR
4) Rev Shrg	FOR	9) School Prayr	AGN	14) Corp Cmpaign $	FOR
5) Pub TV $	FOR	10) Cnsumr Prot	FOR	15) Pol $ Disclosr	AGN

Election Results

1972 general:	Peter H. B. Frelinghuysen (R)	127,310	(62%)
	Frederick M. Bohen (D)	78,076	(38%)
1972 primary:	Peter H. B. Frelinghuysen (R), unopposed		
1970 general:	Peter H. B. Frelinghuysen (R)	111,553	(68%)
	Ronald C. Eisele (D)	53,436	(32%)

SIXTH DISTRICT Political Background

The 6th district of New Jersey, like the 4th, is a weirdly shaped district, spanning the entire state. The 6th brings together in a constituency people from sociologically diverse and geographically disparate communities. More than 60% of these people live in the Philadelphia suburbs of Burlington and Camden counties. Important towns here include Cherry Hills (home of Muhammed Ali along with many more conventional folks) and Willingboro (formerly Levittown), both of which more than doubled in population during the 1960s. About another 20% live in an another, even faster-growing area on the Jersey Shore. Connecting the two regions—which have little in common except growth rates and Republican political preferences—are the flatlands of south Jersey and a hunk of Fort Dix.

The 6th was created in something like its present form by the 1966 redistricting, one that recognized that south Jersey was growing faster than north Jersey. Its first Congressman was liberal Republican William Cahill, who had formerly represented the more marginal 1st district. Cahill was then elected Governor in 1969, but has since fallen on sadder, scandal-ridden times; as a candidate for reelection, he was defeated in the 1973 Republican primary.

In 1970, the 6th was the scene of a vigorous contest, as Democrat Charles Yates, a wealthy young businessman, tried to buck the political odds. He managed to carry the Burlington County suburbs, but the margins here were not enough to beat Republican state Sen. Edwin Forsythe, who won big majorities in Camden and Ocean counties. The Congressman sports one of the last crewcuts seen in the House; he is, however, not as reliably conservative as most Republicans. In 1973, he supported the successful effort to halt the bombing of Cambodia. The 1972 election appears to show that he will have no future trouble at the polls; Forsythe won a resounding 63% of the votes.

Census Data Pop. 478,137. Central city, 0%; suburban, 78%. Median family income, $11,689; families above $15,000: 30%; families below $3,000: 5%. Median years education, 12.3.

1972 Share of Federal Outlays $493,245,555

DOD	$246,297,999	HEW		$155,721,474
AEC	–	HUD		$2,010,545
NASA	$9,577,134	DOI		$241,451
DOT	$4,942,089	USDA		$5,616,996
		Other		$68,837,867

Federal Military-Industrial Commitments

DOD Contractors RCA (Moorestown), $108.920m: missile radar systems; other electronic ware. Alcotronics Corp. (Mount Laurel), $11.255m: rocket fuzes and detonators.

Economic Base Finance, insurance and real estate; electrical equipment and supplies, especially radio and television communication equipment; agriculture, notably fruits, dairy products, vegetables and poultry; primary metal industries; and tourism.

The Voters

Registration Not available.
Median voting age 42.8
Employment profile White collar, 59%. Blue collar, 31%. Service, 9%. Farm, 1%.
Ethnic groups Black, 5%. Total foreign stock, 21%. Italy, 5%; Germany, UK, 3% each; Poland, USSR, 2% each; Ireland 1%.

Presidential vote

1972	Nixon (R)	130,276	(66%)
	McGovern (D)	67,191	(34%)
1968	Nixon (R)	88,880	(50%)
	Humphrey (D)	70,760	(40%)
	Wallace (AI)	18,361	(10%)

Representative

Edwin B. Forsythe (R) Elected 1970; b. Jan. 17, 1916, Westtown, Pa.; home, Moorestown; married, one child; Society of Friends.

Career Sec., Moorestown Bd. of Adjustment, 1948–52; Mayor of Moorestown, 1957–62; Moorestown Township Com., 1953–62; Chm., Moorestown Planning Bd., 1962–63; N.J. State Senate, 1964–70, Asst. Minority Leader, 1966, Minority Leader, 1967, Pres., 1968; acting Governor, 1968; Senate Pres. Pro Tem., 1969.

Offices 331 CHOB, 202-225-4765. Also Third and Mill Streets, Moorestown 08057, 609-235-6622.

Administrative Assistant Robert Gatty

Committees

Education and Labor (11th); Subs: No. 1 (Gen. Sub. on Education); No. 4 (Sel. Sub. on Labor).

Merchant Marine and Fisheries (9th); Subs: Oceanography; Panama Canal; Fisheries and Wildlife Conservation and the Environment.

Group Ratings

	ADA	COPE	LWV	RIPON	NFU	LCV	CFA	NAB	NSI	ACA
1972	50	30	75	80	57	53	0	67	60	36
1971	43	45	50	72	53	–	63	–	–	57

Key Votes

1) Busing	AGN	6) Cmbodia Bmbg	AGN	11) Chkg Acct Intrst	FOR
2) Strip Mines	AGN	7) Bust Hwy Trust	FOR	12) End HISC (HUAC)	FOR
3) Cut Mil $	ABS	8) Farm Sub Lmt	FOR	13) Nixon Sewer Veto	FOR
4) Rev Shrg	FOR	9) School Prayr	FOR	14) Corp Cmpaign $	FOR
5) Pub TV $	AGN	10) Cnsumr Prot	FOR	15) Pol $ Disclosr	FOR

Election Results

1972 general:	Edwin B. Forsythe (R)	123,610	(63%)
	Francis P. Brennan (D)	71,113	(36%)
	Ida Ebert (Ind.)	1,147	(1%)
1972 primary:	Edwin B. Forsythe (R), unopposed		
1970 general:	Edwin B. Forsythe (R)	88,051	(55%)
	Charles B. Yates (D)	72,347	(45%)

SEVENTH DISTRICT Political Background

Bergen County comprises New Jersey's northeast corner. Behind the Palisades that line the Hudson River, the county includes some of the state's richest suburbs: sparsely settled (because of minimum-acreage zoning), hilly, and tree-shaded. Along the Passaic and Hackensack rivers are some out-of-gas industrial towns like East Paterson and Hackensack. But for the most part Bergen county constitutes a near bucolic retreat from New York City or Newark, and shopping centers here are Bergen's most notable local landmarks. In fact, the town of Paramus probably has more shopping-center parking places than people.

Bergen County is divided into two congressional districts, of which, roughly speaking, the 7th occupies the western half. Republicans drew the slightly irregular boundary lines to spread the county's Democratic minority evenly between the two districts. Accordingly, the 7th bulges southward to take in industrial Hackensack and predominantly Jewish Teaneck, leaving most of the district Republican. Ever since a special election held in 1950, Republican William Widnall has represented this locale in Congress. For several years, Widnall has served as the senior Republican on the Banking and Currency Committee, where he has generally taken positions sympathetic to the banking industry. But the bulk of his legislative effort has gone into the field of housing.

Serving as the ranking minority member on the Housing Subcommittee, the Congressman has worked closely with Chairman William Barrett to develop low- and moderate-income housing programs. Widnall has consistently favored spending more money on housing than has the Nixon Administration. He and Barrett have also worked to establish oversight over the administration of housing programs already enacted. Moreover, Widnall strongly supports federal aid to mass transit, assiduously pushing such legislation since the mid-1960s. It might be added that neither of the Congressman's concerns seems to mean much to his constituents, most of whom live in expensive single-family homes and drive to work on the freeways and toll roads that crisscross the 7th district. His is a case of a Congressman who has come to take positions out of conviction and experience dealing with these problems.

Widnall's margins of victory have been cut, to a degree, in recent years, largely because of the strenuous efforts of young (40 in 1972) Arthur Lesemann, the Democratic nominee in 1970 and 1972. Lesemann stressed the peace issue, one on which Widnall's record is mixed. He opposed the Cambodian invasion of 1970, but has otherwise usually supported the Nixon Administration. In 1972, despite the Nixon landslide, Lesemann carried Hackensack, Fair Lawn (a "new town" of the 1940s), and Teaneck, the three largest communities in the district. Widnall, however, carried everything else, and won by a 3–2 margin.

Census Data Pop. 479,999. Central city, 0%; suburban, 100%. Median family income, $14,257; families above $15,000: 46%; families below $3,000: 3%. Median years education, 12.4.

1972 Share of Federal Outlays $525,239,456

DOD	$97,084,263	HEW	$146,147,381
AEC	$165,754	HUD	$10,384,115
NASA	$955,972	DOI	$794,331
DOT	$6,064,004	USDA	$14,289,925
		Other	$249,354,611

Federal Military-Industrial Commitments

DOD Contractors Curtis Wright Corp. (Wood-Ridge), $46.989m: various aircraft engines and components.

Economic Base Finance, insurance and real estate; electrical equipment and supplies, especially radio and television communication equipment; chemicals and allied products, especially soap, cleaners and toilet goods; printing and publishing; and machinery.

The Voters

Registration Not available.
Median voting age 45.0
Employment profile White collar, 65%. Blue collar, 27%. Service, 8%. Farm, –%.
Ethnic groups Black, 3%. Total foreign stock, 36%. Italy, 9%; Germany, 5%; Poland, UK, 3% each; USSR, Ireland, 2% each; Austria, Canada, Netherlands, 1% each.

Presidential vote

1972	Nixon (R)	150,619	(66%)
	McGovern (D)	76,583	(34%)
1968	Nixon (R)	121,037	(56%)
	Humphrey (D)	82,220	(38%)
	Wallace (AI)	11,103	(5%)

Representative

William Beck Widnall (R) Elected 1950; b. March 17, 1906, Hackensack; home, Saddle River; Brown U., Ph.B., 1926; N.J. Law School (now Rutgers), LL.B., 1931; married, two children; Episcopalian.

Career Practicing atty., 1932– ; N.J. Legislature, 1946–50.

Offices 2309 RHOB, 202-225-4465. Also 97 Farview Ave., Paramus 07652, 201-265-3550.

Administrative Assistant Mrs. Beverly Shay

Committees

Banking and Currency (Ranking Mbr.); Subs: Domestic Finance; Housing (Ranking Mbr.); Urban Mass Transportation.

Joint Com. on Defense Production (Ranking House Mbr.).

Joint Economic Com. (Ranking House Mbr.); Subs: Fiscal Policy (Ranking House Mbr.); Urban Affairs (Ranking House Mbr.); Consumer Economics (Ranking House Mbr.); International Economics (Ranking House Mbr.).

Group Ratings

	ADA	COPE	LWV	RIPON	NFU	LCV	CFA	NAB	NSI	ACA
1972	19	36	67	86	86	53	100	100	78	59
1971	32	55	63	69	40	–	43	–	–	52
1970	40	36	–	88	69	53	92	82	100	47

Key Votes

1) Busing	AGN	6) Cmbodia Bmbg	AGN	11) Chkg Acct Intrst	AGN
2) Strip Mines	AGN	7) Bust Hwy Trust	FOR	12) End HISC (HUAC)	AGN
3) Cut Mil $	AGN	8) Farm Sub Lmt	FOR	13) Nixon Sewer Veto	FOR
4) Rev Shrg	FOR	9) School Prayr	FOR	14) Corp Cmpaign $	FOR
5) Pub TV $	AGN	10) Cnsumr Prot	FOR	15) Pol $ Disclosr	FOR

Election Results

1972 general:	William B. Widnall (R)	124,365	(58%)
	Arthur J. Lesemann (D)	85,712	(40%)
	Martin E. Wendelken (Ind.)	4,557	(2%)
1972 primary:	William B. Widnall (R), unopposed		
1970 general:	William B. Widnall (R)	90,410	(59%)
	Arthur J. Lesemann (D)	63,928	(41%)

EIGHTH DISTRICT Political Background

In the late eighteenth century, Alexander Hamilton looked out across the Hudson River from Manhattan and predicted major industrial development around Paterson, New Jersey. Here, the great Federalist said, the falls of the Passaic River would provide the waterpower needed to drive the machines of the period. Hamilton died long before Paterson did in fact become one of the largest industrial centers in northern New Jersey. So great was the impact of industry that home-town poet, William Carlos Williams, using Hamilton's prose for a start, wrote a remarkable poem about not-so-poetic Paterson. Today both Paterson and Passaic, just down the river, are industrial, blue-collar towns, having sizable communities of black, Italian, Polish, and other ethnic groups. All of them, by tradition at least, vote heavily Democratic. Clifton, which lies halfway between Paterson and Passaic, is more middle-class and Republican. These three cities form the heart of New Jersey's 8th congressional district. West of Paterson, before the first mountain ridges, is Wayne Township, a rapidly growing upper-middle-class suburb and usually the source of the 8th district's Republican strength.

Traditional voting patterns, however, have not been decisive in congressional races here, owing to the personal popularity of the district's two most recent Congressmen. Charles Joelson, who represented the 8th from 1961 to 1969, was a liberal whose assiduous cultivation of his constituency brought him more than 60% of the votes in every election. Joelson retired from the House for the quieter life of a judge in 1969, a year when New Jersey Democrats were in trouble. In 1960, John Kennedy had carried Passaic County—which is virtually coextensive with the 8th—by 10,000 votes; eight years later, Humphrey lost it by 6,000, the difference being the 16,000 votes taken by Wallace. The conservative tide was also running in state elections. Republican Congressman William Cahill won the governorship by a record margin in 1969, which hardly hurt the Republican candidate in the simultaneous special election occurring in the 8th. Nevertheless, Robert Roe, the Democratic candidate, bucked the tide and won by a paper-thin margin of 960 votes.

Roe won subsequent elections much more easily. In 1970, he beat an Italian-American Assemblyman with 61% of the votes, and in the year of the Nixon landslide the incumbent Democrat took 63%. As a former Mayor of Wayne Township, Roe has carried his Republican home town almost as convincingly as the industrial cities of Paterson and Passaic—much as Joelson used to. In the House, Roe serves as one of the more environment-conscious members of the Public Works Committee, having served as New Jersey state Conservation Commissioner before his election.

Census Data Pop. 478,369. Central city, 59%; suburban, 41%. Median family income, $10,783; families above $15,000: 25%; families below $3,000: 7%. Median years education, 10.9.

1972 Share of Federal Outlays $523,722,884

DOD	$96,803,943	HEW	$145,725,396
AEC	$165,275	HUD	$10,354,132
NASA	$952,314	DOI	$792,038
DOT	$6,046,495	USDA	$14,248,665
		Other	$248,634,626

Federal Military-Industrial Commitments

DOD Contractors REDM Corp. (Wayne), $7.128m: bomb fuzes. ITT (Clifton), $6.517m: various electronic communications ware.

Economic Base Electrical equipment and supplies, especially communication equipment; apparel and other textile products, especially women's and misses' outerwear; textile mill products, especially textile finishing, except wool; finance, insurance and real estate; and chemicals and allied products, especially soap, cleaners and toilet goods. Also higher education (William Paterson College).

The Voters

Registration Not available.
Median voting age 45.0
Employment profile White collar, 46%. Blue collar, 44%. Service, 10%. Farm, –%.
Ethnic groups Black, 11%. Spanish, 4%. Total foreign stock, 38%. Italy, 10%; Poland, 5%; Germany, 3%; USSR, UK, Netherlands, Austria, Hungary, 2% each; Czechoslovakia, Ireland, 1% each.

Presidential vote

1972	Nixon (R)	111,671	(63%)
	McGovern (D)	65,125	(37%)
1968	Nixon (R)	82,011	(46%)
	Humphrey (D)	77,904	(44%)
	Wallace (AI)	17,639	(10%)

Representative

Robert A. Roe (D) Elected Nov. 4, 1969; b. Feb. 28, 1924, Wayne; home, Wayne; Oregon State U.; Washington State U.,; Army, WWII; unmarried; Catholic.

Career Chm., Bd. of Dir., Morris Canal & Banking Co.; Committeeman, Wayne Township, 1955–56; Mayor of Wayne, 1956–61; Mbr. of Passaic County Bd. of Freeholders, 1959–62, Dir., 1962–63; N.J. Commissioner, Conservation and Econ. Dev., 1963–69.

Offices 1007 LHOB, 202-225-5751. Also U.S. P.O. Bldg., 194 Ward St., Paterson 07510, 201-523-5152.

Administrative Assistant Mrs. Kathryn M. Marazzo

Committees

Public Works (13th); Subs: Investigations and Review; Public Buildings and Grounds; Economic Development; Transportation; Water Resources.

Science and Astronautics (9th); Subs: International Cooperation in Science and Space; Manned Space Flights; Energy.

Group Ratings

	ADA	COPE	LWV	RIPON	NFU	LCV	CFA	NAB	NSI	ACA
1972	63	91	58	56	86	60	100	18	50	48
1971	73	91	75	50	67	–	100	–	–	31
1970	80	78	–	58	75	100	100	0	56	28

Key Votes

1) Busing	AGN	6) Cmbodia Bmbg	AGN	11) Chkg Acct Intrst	AGN
2) Strip Mines	AGN	7) Bust Hwy Trust	AGN	12) End HISC (HUAC)	AGN
3) Cut Mil $	FOR	8) Farm Sub Lmt	FOR	13) Nixon Sewer Veto	AGN
4) Rev Shrg	FOR	9) School Prayr	FOR	14) Corp Cmpaign $	AGN
5) Pub TV $	FOR	10) Cnsumr Prot	FOR	15) Pol $ Disclosr	AGN

Election Results

1972 general:	Robert A. Roe (D)	104,381	(63%)
	Walter E. Johnson (R)	61,073	(37%)
1972 primary:	Robert A. Roe (D), unopposed		
1970 general:	Robert A. Roe (D)	75,056	(61%)
	Alfred E. Fontanella (R)	48,011	(39%)

NINTH DISTRICT Political Background

In rough terms, the 9th district of New Jersey consists of the eastern half of Bergen County and, to bring it up to the equal-population standard, the northern end of Hudson County. North of the George Washington Bridge and west of the Palisades that rise above the Hudson are the wealthy, most heavily Republican parts of the 9th: Tenafly, Dumont, Closter, Old Tappan. Near the Jersey end of the bridge are several predominantly Jewish and liberal Democratic suburbs; the largest of these is Teaneck, which was excised from the neighboring 7th and placed in the 9th for what appear to be political reasons. Atop the Palisades, huge apartment towers overlook New York City, occupied by well-to-do people who wish to escape the city (and its taxes) but retain a view of Manhattan. South of the bridge, toward and into Hudson County, are older, less affluent suburbs, which nevertheless usually vote Republican.

The Jersey Meadows separate the southern portion of the 9th—a section with about a fifth of the district's population—from the rest of the 9th. The Meadows are a swamp for which environmentalists have great love, but for which developers have equally great plans, including a new stadium for the erstwhile New York Giants. Because none of the plans has yet been realized, that part of the Meadows which has taken human habitation consists of gas stations, oil-tank farms, truck terminals, and eight lanes of the Jersey Turnpike. The 9th's southern towns, ones that lie on either side of the Meadows, are dominated by Polish- and Italian-American citizens who are Democrats by tradition. This is the part of the district that produced the 9th's current Congressman, Henry Helstoski.

From 1957 to 1964, Helstoski was the flamboyant Mayor of East Rutherford (pop. 8,500). In 1964, he for some reason decided to challenge the 9th's veteran (1939–43, 1951–65) Republican Congressman, Frank Osmers. And in the Johnson landslide, Helstoski won by a little more than 2,000 votes. As a Congressman, he emerged a liberal who opposed escalation of the Vietnam war as early as 1965; he was not expected to win reelection. In 1965, however, the then Democratic legislature redistricted the 9th to include the working-class towns of Garfield, East Paterson, and Hackensack. So in 1966, Helstoski won again by a margin just slightly smaller than his edge in 1964. As it turned out, the 1965 redistricting failed to meet the approval of the courts; in 1968, the legislature, this time a Republican one, redrew the district's lines for the benefit of House Speaker Peter Moraites, who then ran against Helstoski in 1968. Once again Helstoski won by a little more than 2,000 votes. Moraites, incidentally, has since gone to jail for violating federal banking laws.

By the 1970 and 1972 elections, Helstoski was winning by much more solid margins, despite a court-ordered 1972 redistricting that favored the Republicans. More than anything else, the Congressman's most recent triumphs are a tribute to his assiduous attention to his constituents. Like so many Congressman able to survive in seemingly hostile districts, Helstoski has taken full advantage of the franking privilege—to an extent so great that his 1972 opponent obtained a court decision against him. The incumbent has also showed an ability to solve his constituents' problems with the federal government. The two-part formula appears likely to assure Helstoski's continued reelection for some time.

Census Data Pop. 478,427. Central city, 0%; suburban, 100%. Median family income, $12,428; families above $15,000: 36%; families below $3,000: 5%. Median years education, 12.1.

1972 Share of Federal Outlays $522,711,836

DOD	$96,617,063	HEW	$145,444,073
AEC	$164,956	HUD	$10,334,143
NASA	$950,475	DOI	$790,509
DOT	$6,034,823	USDA	$14,221,158
		Other	$248,154,636

Federal Military-Industrial Commitments

DOD Contractors Bendix Teterboro), $72.087m: various aircraft navigation and missile guidance systems. Seatrain Lines (Edgewater), $5.281m: transportation services.

Economic Base Finance, insurance and real estate; electrical equipment and supplies, especially radio and television communication equipment; chemicals and allied products, especially soap, cleaners and toilet goods; printing and publishing; and machinery. Also higher education (Fairleigh Dickinson Univ.).

The Voters

Registration Not available.
Median voting age 46.0
Employment profile White collar, 58%. Blue collar, 34%. Service, 8%. Farm, –%.
Ethnic groups Black, 2%. Spanish, 1%. Total foreign stock, 44%. Italy, 12%; Germany, 5%; Ireland, Poland, 3% each; UK, USSR, 2% each; Austria, 1%.

Presidential vote

1972	Nixon (R)	146,286	(66%)
	McGovern (D)	74,851	(34%)
1968	Nixon (R)	112,279	(53%)
	Humphrey (D)	86,031	(41%)
	Wallace (AI)	13,160	(6%)

Representative

Henry Helstoski (D) Elected 1964; b. March 21, 1925, Wallington; home, East Rutherford; Paterson State Col., B.A., 1947; Montclair State Col., M.A., 1949; Army Air Corps, WWII; married, two children; Catholic.

Career Teacher; high school principal; Superintendent of Schools, 1949–62; Councilman, E. Rutherford, 1956, Mayor, 1957–64; Chm. Jt. Sewer Authority, 1957–64.

Offices 2445 RHOB, 202-225-5061. Also 666 Paterson Ave., East Rutherford 07073, 201-939-9090.

Administrative Assistant Joseph T. Sullivan

Committees

Interstate and Foreign Commerce (18th); Sub: Commerce and Finance.

Veterans' Affairs (7th); Subs: Education and Training (Chm.); Housing; Hospitals.

Group Ratings

	ADA	COPE	LWV	RIPON	NFU	LCV	CFA	NAB	NSI	ACA
1972	100	91	92	73	86	87	100	8	0	0
1971	95	83	78	71	79	–	100	–	–	7
1970	96	100	–	82	92	88	100	0	0	6

Key Votes

1) Busing	FOR	6) Cmbodia Bmbg	AGN	11) Chkg Acct Intrst	FOR
2) Strip Mines	AGN	7) Bust Hwy Trust	FOR	12) End HISC (HUAC)	FOR
3) Cut Mil $	FOR	8) Farm Sub Lmt	FOR	13) Nixon Sewer Veto	AGN
4) Rev Shrg	FOR	9) School Prayr	AGN	14) Corp Cmpaign $	AGN
5) Pub TV $	FOR	10) Cnsumr Prot	FOR	15) Pol $ Disclosr	AGN

Election Results

1972 general:	Henry Helstoski (D)	119,543	(56%)
	Alfred D. Schiaffo (R)	94,747	(44%)
1972 primary:	Henry Helstoski (D), unopposed		
1970 general:	Henry Helstoski (D)	91,589	(57%)
	Henry L. Hoebel (R)	68,974	(43%)

TENTH DISTRICT Political Background

Some urban experts have predicted that Newark, New Jersey, will be the first American city to die. Twenty years ago, Newark was a fairly prosperous industrial city, having the largest downtown business area in the state, along with tree-shaded middle-class neighborhoods. Today, downtown is still here, even sporting some new buildings put up by companies like Prudential Insurance, which is headquartered in the city. But much of the rest of Newark resembles Berlin after the war. For the most part, the middle class has left in search of the nicer lawns and safer streets of the suburbs. Most of the people remaining are here because they cannot get out. According to the 1970 census, some 54% of Newark's residents are black, a percentage that is considerably higher today. Moreover, like their white counterparts, the more prosperous, middle-class segment of the black community has also exited for suburbs like East Orange, Orange, or for places even more distant.

Then there is the Italian-American community of Newark that has chosen to remain in the city. Sociologists have found that the Italians are often the last ethnic group to leave the central city, which is the case in Newark. The Jews who once lived in Philip Roth's old Weequahic neighborhood have long since taken themselves to places like Maplewood and Short Hills. But many Italians stay. They have an attachment to close-knit neighborhoods where everyone knows everyone else, nobody steals from anyone else, and people speak Italian on the streets and in the shops.

The Italians of Newark fear what they regard as black crime, and resist the movement of blacks into their neighborhoods. Since the 1967 Newark riot, the North Ward of Newark—the city's principal Italian area—has armed itself heavily, with Anthony Imperiale, former City Councilman and now an Assemblyman, organizing neighborhood patrols to guard the streets. Fear in the North Ward intensified when black playwright and Newark political strategist Imamu Baraka spearheaded a drive to build a housing project called Kawaida Towers in the North Ward. Neighborhood people picketed and stopped construction.

Just after the 1970 census figures came out, the political balance in Newark shifted, as black man Kenneth Gibson was elected Mayor of the city. Gibson defeated Hugh Addonizio, the incumbent for eight years, who was then on trial and is now in jail. It was the first time, of course, that Newark had a black Mayor. And though Gibson supporters failed to win a majority on the City Council, they do control the school board and most of the city departments.

As a matter of tradition, Newark was divided between two or more congressional districts—the idea being to dilute the city's Democratic margins. But the redistricting plan ordered into effect by a federal court in 1972 placed all of Newark into the 10th district—one that the city dominates, since it contains 80% of the district's population. Other towns in the 10th are East Orange, which is also approaching a black voting majority, along with Harrison and Glen Ridge. Taken together, the new 10th was 52% black in 1970, and several points more than that today.

The district's new boundaries seemed to assure the election of a black Congressman. But it was not to be, at least in 1972. For one thing, blacks are less likely to be of voting age; in 1970, with the district 52% black, some 54% of the eligible electorate was white. Blacks are also less likely to turn out and vote. And finally, the 10th's incumbent Congressman, Democrat Peter Rodino, was not about to quit. For a while, Rodino flirted with the idea of running in the 11th district against his Democratic colleague Joseph Minish; the 11th contained much of Rodino's old, predominantly suburban constituency. But instead he decided to run in the 10th, and he won.

When two black candidates entered the Democratic primary, Rodino was helped. These were East Orange Mayor William Hart and ex-Assemblyman George Richardson. But Hart cornered most of the black support, including endorsements from Mayor Gibson and Baraka; in the end, Richardson took only 5% of the votes. Meanwhile, Rodino's biggest assets were his record and his seniority on a key committee, Judiciary, a panel that passes on all civil rights legislation. By 1972, the Congressman was the second-ranking Democrat on Judiciary; moreover, he had consistently supported and voted for all civil rights legislation. During the brief campaign, Rodino stressed both assets, along with his work as Chairman of an immigration subcommittee—something of great interest to many Italian constituents. The incumbent won overwhelming majorities in the white areas and enough black votes for a solid 58% plurality.

Rodino reminded his constituents that he stood just one slot under 84-year-old Emanuel Celler, Chairman of the Judiciary Committee. The clear implication was the he, Rodino, might soon succeed Celler—an event that came to pass quicker than anyone expected. Just three weeks after Rodino was renominated (the Democratic nomination here is tantamount to election), Celler lost his Democratic primary in Brooklyn (see New York 16). So at the start of the 93rd Congress, Rodino became a committee chairman. As such, he has been a little less dominating than his predecessor. Rodino has given the subcommittees clearer jurisdiction, not simply assigning bills to them at personal discretion. Rodino himself has assumed the chairmanship of Celler's antitrust subcommittee.

Census Data Pop. 478,217. Central city, 80%; suburban, 20%. Median family income, $8,300; families above $15,000: 15%; families below $3,000: 13%. Median years education, 10.5.

1972 Share of Federal Outlays $522,711,836

DOD	$96,617,063	HEW	$145,444,073
AEC	$164,956	HUD	$10,334,143
NASA	$950,475	DOI	$790,509
DOT	$6,034,823	USDA	$14,221,158
		Other	$248,154,636

Federal Military-Industrial Commitments

No installations or contractors receiving prime awards greater than $5,000,000.

Economic Base Finance, insurance and real estate; chemicals and allied products, especially drugs; electrical equipment and supplies, especially electric and wiring equipment; food and kindred products, especially malt liquors; machinery; and fabricated metal products. Also higher education (Newark State).

The Voters

Registration Not available.
Median voting age 41.7
Employment profile White collar, 39%. Blue collar, 46%. Service, 15%. Farm, –%.
Ethnic groups Black, 52%. Spanish, 6%. Total foreign stock, 23%. Italy, 7%; Poland, 2%; Ireland, USSR, Germany, UK, 1% each.

Presidential vote

1972	Nixon (R)	46,034	(37%)
	McGovern (D)	78,416	(63%)
1968	Nixon (R)	40,030	(28%)
	Humphrey (D)	91,975	(64%)
	Wallace (AI)	12,677	(9%)

Representative

Peter Wallace Rodino, Jr. (D) Elected 1948; b. June 7, 1909, Newark; home, Newark; N.J. Law School (now Rutgers), LL.B., 1937; Army, WWII; married, two children; Catholic.

Career Praticing atty., 1938; Senior Mbr., N.J. Congressional Delegation, 1971.

Offices 2462 RHOB, 202-225-3436. Also Fed. Bldg., 970 Broad St., Newark 07102, 201-645-3213.

Administrative Assistant Merle Baungart

Committees

Judiciary (Chm.); Subs: No. 5 (Antitrust Matters).

Group Ratings

	ADA	COPE	LWV	RIPON	NFU	LCV	CFA	NAB	NSI	ACA
1972	88	91	100	78	86	70	100	9	25	0
1971	86	91	89	86	87	–	100	–	–	7
1970	84	100	–	81	100	84	84	0	60	16

Key Votes

1) Busing	FOR	6) Cmbodia Bmbg	AGN	11) Chkg Acct Intrst	AGN
2) Strip Mines	ABS	7) Bust Hwy Trust	FOR	12) End HISC (HUAC)	FOR
3) Cut Mil $	FOR	8) Farm Sub Lmt	FOR	13) Nixon Sewer Veto	AGN
4) Rev Shrg	FOR	9) School Prayr	AGN	14) Corp Cmpaign $	FOR
5) Pub TV $	ABS	10) Cnsumr Prot	FOR	15) Pol $ Disclosr	ABS

Election Results

1972 general:	Peter W. Rodino, Jr. (D)	94,308	(80%)
	Kenneth C. Miller (R)	23,949	(20%)
1972 primary:	Peter W. Rodino, Jr. (D)	37,650	(57%)
	William S. Hart (D)	24,118	(37%)

	George C. Richardson (D)	3,086	(5%)
	Wilburt Kurnegay, Jr. (D)	718	(1%)
1970 general:	Peter W. Rodino, Jr. (D)	71,003	(70%)
	Griffith H. Jones (R)	30,460	(30%)

ELEVENTH DISTRICT Political Background

The 11th district of New Jersey is the suburbs of Newark, a set of towns stretching west of the state's largest and most troubled city. Though most of these towns lie within what is considered commuting distance of New York City, the basic orientation here is toward Newark and things New Jersey. The district's ethnic patterns appear to follow the radial avenues coming out of Newark. Many Italian-Americans live in the towns of Belleville, Bloomfield, and Nutley, all of which adjoin Newark's heavily Italian North Ward. A large number of Jews reside in South Orange and Maplewood, which are near the once Jewish neighborhoods of Newark. An anomaly is Montclair, situated on a ridge overlooking the Manhattan skyline; half of it is high-income WASP, half middle-income black.

Like the 10th, redistricting substantially altered the 11th. Before 1972, the district included the Central Ward of Newark and East Orange, both of which now possess black majorities. As it stands today, the 11th is considerably less Democratic. But that circumstance posed few problems for Democratic Congressman Joseph Minish in 1972. Ten years earlier, Minish came out of the labor movement to replace Hugh Addonizio, who went on to fame as Mayor of Newark and infamy as a convicted felon. Though the present Congressman is supported by the Essex County Democratic machine, his connections with it are not particularly strong. Minish has never had trouble winning elections. For the 1972 election, about two-thirds of the territory was unfamiliar to the politician, but he retained his seat easily.

In the House, Minish serves on the Banking and Currency Committee. Here he is often part of the minority more concerned about the interests of consumers than those of the big bankers and the savings and loan institutions. According to the Nader Congress Project, the New Jerseyite's biggest legislative achievement was a bill that set up credit unions for servicemen living on bases overseas.

Census Data Pop. 475,297. Central city, 0%; suburban, 100%. Median family income, $12,508; families above $15,000: 36%; families below $3,000: 5%. Median years education, 12.2.

1972 Share of Federal Outlays $523,217,˙˙9

DOD	$96,710,503	HEW	$145,584,735
AEC	$165,116	HUD	$10,344,138
NASA	$951,395	DOI	$791,273
DOT	$6,040,659	USDA	$14,234,911
		Other	$248,394,630

Federal Military-Industrial Commitments

DOD Contractors Singer (Little Falls), $54.751m: A-7 and P-3 aircraft communications equipment. ITT (Nutley), $50.429m: design and fabrication of electronic warfare equipment; other electronic ware. Walter Kidde Co. (Belleville), $9.923m: 105mm projectiles detonating fuzes; aircraft parts and components.

Economic Base Finance, insurance and real estate; chemicals and allied products, especially drugs; electrical equipment and supplies, especially electric and wiring equipment; food and kindred products, especially malt liquors; machinery; and fabricated metal products. Also higher education (Montclair State, and Seton Hall Univ.).

The Voters

Registration Not available.
Median voting age 47.3
Employment profile White collar, 60%. Blue collar, 30%. Service, 10%. Farm, –%.

Ethnic groups Black, 7%. Total foreign stock, 38%. Italy, 11%; Poland, USSR, 4% each; Germany, UK, 3% each; Ireland, Austria, 2% each.

Presidential vote

1972	Nixon (R)	128,378	(60%)
	McGovern (D)	84,859	(40%)
1968	Nixon (R)	100,354	(46%)
	Humphrey (D)	100,188	(46%)
	Wallace (AI)	17,215	(8%)

Representative

Joseph George Minish (D) Elected 1962; b. Sept. 1, 1916, Throop, Pa.; home, West Orange; Army, WWII; married, three children; Catholic.

Career Pres., local 445 I.U.E. AFL-CIO, 1949–53; Political Action Dir., Dist. 4, 1953–54; Exec. Sec., Essex W. Hudson Labor Council, 1954–61, Exec. Sec, and Treas., 1961–62.

Offices 2162 RHOB, 202-225-5035. Also 308 Main St., Orange 07050, 201-676-0827.

Administrative Assistant Margaret M. Sullivan

Committees

Banking and Currency (10th); Subs: Domestic Finance; Urban Mass Transportation (Chm.).

Group Ratings

	ADA	COPE	LWV	RIPON	NFU	LCV	CFA	NAB	NSI	ACA
1972	88	91	92	80	86	80	100	9	50	14
1971	86	82	89	78	71	–	100	–	–	18
1970	84	100	–	94	92	100	84	0	60	21

Key Votes

1) Busing	FOR	6) Cmbodia Bmbg	AGN	11) Chkg Acct Intrst	AGN
2) Strip Mines	AGN	7) Bust Hwy Trust	FOR	12) End HISC (HUAC)	AGN
3) Cut Mil $	FOR	8) Farm Sub Lmt	FOR	13) Nixon Sewer Veto	AGN
4) Rev Shrg	FOR	9) School Prayr	AGN	14) Corp Cmpaign $	AGN
5) Pub TV $	FOR	10) Cnsumr Prot	FOR	15) Pol $ Disclosr	AGN

Election Results

1972 general:	Joseph G. Minish (D)	120,277	(58%)
	Milton A. Waldor (R)	82,957	(40%)
	Philip R. Nicolaus (AI)	3,077	(1%)
	James Klimaski (People's Party)	2,791	(1%)
1972 primary:	Joseph G. Minish (D), unopposed		
1970 general:	Joseph G. Minish (D)	68,075	(68%)
	James W. Shue (R)	31,369	(32%)

TWELFTH DISTRICT Political Background

The 12th district of New Jersey contains all of Union County except for one city (Linden) and two townships (Hillside and Winfield). For the most part, the 12th is classic suburban territory. There are a few stereotypical affluent WASP suburbs like Summit, but more typical of the district are places like Cranford, Westfield, and Union—places dominated by the sons and daughters of Italian, Polish, and German immigrants, whose claim on prosperity is new and sometimes precarious. Union County is not as wealthy as Bergen or as industrial as Passaic; it is, in most respects, middle class. Even its two most industrial cities, Elizabeth and Plainfield, are not afflicted with all of the ills normally associated with central cities. The district is bisected by perhaps the most garish strip of highway in the East, U.S. 22; the frenetic neon signs that line the roadway give evidence perhaps of the human energy to be found in the leafy-green, placid suburbs through which it runs.

Union County politics goes down the middle of the road. In the close elections of 1960 and 1968, this New Jersey seat came within a couple percentage points of duplicating the national figures for the major candidates. It is also a pretty accurate bellwether in state contests. Moreover, in an interesting coincidence, both of New Jersey's Senators spent time representing Union County in the House, Clifford Case from 1945 to 1953 and Harrison Williams from 1955 to 1957.

Congressman Williams was defeated for reelection in 1956 by the woman who represented the district until the last election, Republican Florence Dwyer. Thanks to her liberal voting record and good constituency services, she won subsequent elections by record margins. When she retired in 1972, many observers felt that the district would see its first closely contested election in more than a decade.

Things, however, did not turn out that way. State Sen. Matthew Rinaldo, always a solid vote-getter in the area, won the Republican primary and then easily defeated ex-state Sen. Jerry English in the general election. In the 93rd Congress, Rinaldo had compiled a fairly unorthodox voting record, having opposed the Nixon Administration, for example, on the Cambodia bombing issue. Rinaldo is one of two newly elected New Jersey Congressmen of Italian descent. Italian-Americans, who comprise an ethnic group so important in the state, have finally begun to produce major officeholders in rough proportion to their numbers.

Census Data Pop. 477,887. Central city, 0%; suburban, 100%. Median family income, $12,787; families above $15,000: 37%; families below $3,000: 5%. Median years education, 12.3.

1972 Share of Federal Outlays $523,217,360

DOD	$96,710,503	HEW	$145,584,735
AEC	$165,116	HUD	$10,344,138
NASA	$951,395	DOI	$791,273
DOT	$6,040,659	USDA	$14,234,911
		Other	$248,394,630

Federal Military-Industrial Commitments

DOD Contractors Sea Land Services (Elizabeth), $89.287m: transportation services. Lockheed (Plainfield), $38.211m: MK 86 gun fire control systems.

Economic Base Chemicals and allied products, especially drugs; finance, insurance and real estate; electrical equipment and supplies, especially electric test and distributing equipment; machinery, especially general industrial machinery and metalworking machinery; and fabricated metal products.

The Voters

Registration Not available.
Median voting age 46.0
Employment profile White collar, 56%. Blue collar, 34%. Service, 10%. Farm, –%.
Ethnic groups Black, 12%. Total foreign stock, 35%. Italy, 7%; Poland, Germany, 4% each; USSR, 3%; UK, Ireland, Austria, 2% each; Canada, 1%.

Presidential vote

1972	Nixon (R)	130,187	(63%)
	McGovern (D)	77,367	(37%)
1968	Nixon (R)	100,089	(47%)
	Humphrey (D)	93,199	(45%)
	Wallace (AI)	16,085	(8%)

Representative

Matthew J. Rinaldo (R) Elected 1972; b. Sept. 1, 1931, Elizabeth; home, Union; Rutgers, B.S., 1953; Seton Hall U., M.B.A. 1959; N.Y.U., doctoral work.

Career Rutgers faculty member; Bd. of Dir., Union Center Natl. Bank, 1970–72; N.J. State Senate, 1968–72; Pres., Township of Union Zoning Bd. of Adjustment, 1962–63.

Offices 1513 LHOB, 202-225-5361.

Administrative Assistant Francis J. Keenan

Committees

Banking and Currency (16th); Subs: Supervision Consumer Affairs; Bank Supervision and Insurance; Domestic Finance.

Group Ratings: Newly Elected

Key Votes

1) Busing	NE	6) Cmbodia Bmbg	AGN	11) Chkg Acct Intrst	FOR
2) Strip Mines	NE	7) Bust Hwy Trust	FOR	12) End HISC (HUAC)	AGN
3) Cut Mil $	NE	8) Farm Sub Lmt	NE	13) Nixon Sewer Veto	FOR
4) Rev Shrg	NE	9) School Prayr	NE	14) Corp Cmpaign $	NE
5) Pub TV $	NE	10) Cnsumr Prot	NE	15) Pol $ Disclosr	NE

Election Results

1972 general:	Matthew J. Rinaldo (R)	127,690	(64%)
	Jerry F. English (D)	72,758	(36%)
1972 primary:	Matthew J. Rinaldo (R), unopposed		

THIRTEENTH DISTRICT Political Background

The 13th district of New Jersey is an entirely new seat, created by the Republican-oriented redistricting of 1972. It takes in portions of the old 4th and 5th districts of the state, appearing on the map to constitute New Jersey's northwestern wedge. Some twenty years ago, the region was predominantly agricultural, probably having more dairy cows than people. In the time since, however, adjacent metropolitan areas have steadily invaded old pastureland. To the south, in the Mercer County portion of the district, people have spilled over out of Trenton, but the really massive growth has occurred in Morris County, about half of which lies in the 13th. Unlike the other half of Morris that remains in the 5th, the part in the new district cannot be called posh horse-farm country. Rather, the small communities here are randomly settled townships. They are havens for what conservative political consultant F. Clifton White calls peripheral urban ethnics. These are people, often of Italian or Irish descent, who have moved to the periphery of commuting distance from their jobs; they have left the smoggy and crime-ridden cities where they grew up for the more open, cleaner, and presumably safer precincts of places like Morris County. The ethnics bring with them sternly conservative attitudes on most political issues, ones reinforced by the unhappiness with the changes taking place in the cities left behind.

The 13th, of course, was drawn to produce a Republican Congressman. Indeed, because it was drawn to produce a particular Republican Congressman, the new 13th became known around Trenton as the Maraziti district—after state Sen. Joseph Maraziti, the intended beneficiary. But actually winning the seat proved a bit more difficult than Maraziti and his friends expected. In the Republican primary, the state legislator won by just a hair under 50% of the votes, 49.88% to be precise. Morris County provided its native son Maraziti with a solid 72%, thereby carrying the election for him; but the eventual winner was defeated in the other counties of the district by home-town candidates.

In the general election, Maraziti again encountered more trouble than expected. The Democrats put up Helen Stevenson Meyner, wife of ex-Gov. (1954–62) Robert Meyner and cousin of the late Adlai Stevenson. Though Gov. Meyner was badly beaten in a 1969 gubernatorial comeback try,

Ms. Meyner emerged an attractive and articulate candidate. She ran 13% ahead of George McGovern in the 13th and finished with a respectable 43%. It is unlikely that any candidate will do as well against Maraziti in the future, now that he enjoys the benefits of incumbency.

Census Data Pop. 478,164. Central city, 0%; suburban, 69%. Median family income, $11,731; families above $15,000: 30%; families below $3,000: 5%. Median years education, 12.3.

1972 Share of Federal Outlays $490,742,006

DOD	$60,909,825	HEW	$154,396,352
AEC	$1,678,055	HUD	$5,993,121
NASA	$3,787,598	DOI	$3,269,070
DOT	$13,405,700	USDA	$13,485,164
		Other	$233,817,121

Federal Military-Industrial Commitments

DOD Installations Picatinny Army Arsenal (Dover).

Economic Base Finance, insurance and real estate; machinery; chemicals and allied products; agriculture, notably dairy products and poultry; and fabricated metal products.

The Voters

Registration Not available.
Median voting age 42.9
Employment profile White collar, 51%. Blue collar, 37%. Service, 10%. Farm, 2%.
Ethnic groups Black, 2%. Total foreign stock, 24%. Italy, Germany, 4% each; UK, 3%; Poland, 2%; Hungary, Ireland, USSR, Austria, 1% each.

Presidential vote

1972	Nixon (R)	141,609	(70%)
	McGovern (D)	61,509	(30%)
1968	Nixon (R)	103,051	(55%)
	Humphrey (D)	66,092	(36%)
	Wallace (AI)	16,548	(9%)

Representative

Joseph J. Maraziti (R) Elected 1972; b. June 15, 1912, Boonton; home, Boonton; Fordham U., J.D.; married, seven children; Catholic.

Career Atty.; Sr. Partner, Maraziti and Lynch; Municipal Court Judge; Asst. County Prosecutor; State Assemblyman, 1958–68; State Senate, 1968–72, majority whip, 1972.

Offices 1228 LHOB, 202-225-5801. Also 105 Cornelia St., Boonton 07005, 201-335-1344.

Administrative Assistant James McBain (L.A.)

Committees

Interior and Insular Affairs (13th). Subs: No. 1 (National Parks and Recreation); No. 3 (Environment); No. 4 (Territorial and Insular Affairs); No. 5 (Mines and Mining); No. 6 (Indian Affairs).

Veterans' Affairs (8th). Subs: Education and Training; Hospitals; Insurance.

Group Ratings: Newly Elected

Key Votes

1) Busing	NE	6) Cmbodia Bmbg	FOR	11) Chkg Acct Intrst	AGN
2) Strip Mines	NE	7) Bust Hwy Trust	AGN	12) End HISC (HUAC)	AGN
3) Cut Mil $	NE	8) Farm Sub Lmt	NE	13) Nixon Sewer Veto	FOR
4) Rev Shrg	NE	9) School Prayr	NE	14) Corp Cmpaign $	NE
5) Pub TV $	NE	10) Cnsumr Prot	NE	15) Pol $ Disclosr	NE

Election Results

1972 general:	Joseph J. Maraziti (R)	109,640	(56%)
	Helen S. Meyner (D)	84,492	(43%)
	Samuel Golub (Ind. Con.)	2,826	(1%)
1972 primary:	Joseph J. Maraziti (R)	14,696	(50%)
	Walter C. Keogh-Dwyer (R)	7,491	(25%)
	Karl Weidel (R)	4,930	(17%)
	Delmar D. Miller (R)	2,344	(8%)

FOURTEENTH DISTRICT Political Background

"I am the law," Frank Hague used to say, and in Hudson County, New Jersey, he was. Back in the 1930s, when Hague was at the peak of his powers as boss of the Hudson County Democratic machine, he chose Governors and U.S. Senators, prosecutors and judges, and also possessed influence in the White House of Franklin D. Roosevelt. In Jersey City and the other towns of Hudson County—then and still the most densely populated county in the nation outside of Manhattan—Hague controlled almost every facet of life. He determined who could stay in business and who could not; he controlled tax assessments and the issuance of parking tickets; and he kept the CIO out of town for years. Hague's power was anchored firmly on votes. Jersey City and Hudson County then had huge payrolls, and every jobholder was of course expected to produce a certain number of votes on election day. Democratic candidates could expect a 100,000-vote margin out of Hudson County, usually larger than the ones gotten statewide. No wonder Democratic politicians from Roosevelt on down paid close attention to whatever Hague might have to say.

To the naked eye, Hudson County has changed little since Frank Hague's golden days. It still consists of a series of towns on the Palisades ridge between the New York harbor and the Jersey Meadows: in addition to Jersey City, places like Bayonne, Hoboken, Weehawken, and Union City. To exploit a view of the Manhattan skyline, a few luxury high-rises have gone up in the northern reaches of the county. Most of Hudson's residents, however, still live in the polluted Jersey air, fetid apartments, and grimy two-family houses that were old when the nation fell into the Great Depression. For many years now, the county's population has been declining, as virtually no one chooses to move here. Hudson's population and its electorate remain predominantly Italian, Irish, and Polish, just as they have been since the turn of the century when the county experienced days of impressive growth. Today, in vivid contrast to nearby Newark, which is majority black, less than 13% of the people here are black, with around 6% of Puerto Rican descent.

But if most things have changed little in Hudson County, its politics in the last four years has. To oversimplify a bit, what has happened is that all of the people who have been running the Hague machine since his death have gone to jail. Leading the list are former Democratic County boss John V. Kenny, now in his 80s; ex-Jersey City Mayor Thomas Whelan; and ex-Congressman (1959–73) Cornelius Gallagher. At least 10 other high officials were convicted and most sentenced to prison terms. A new group has moved into the resulting power vacuum, led by reform Jersey City Mayor Paul Jordan, a 32-year-old physician, and Mayor Francis Fitzpatrick of Bayonne. In 1973, Jordan won a full term by a resounding margin over the son of a former mayor (one forced to leave office when it was revealed he was not a U.S. citizen). Some people here are a little suspicious of the reformers, who have joined forces with some holdovers from the old machine; the reformers, in turn, say the holdovers are clean. In any case, the old days of Hudson County politics are gone forever.

In the old days, the Hague machine delivered staggering margins to Democratic presidential candidates. Today, however, the conservatively inclined Catholic voters of the county have shown a growing tendency to support Richard Nixon's Republicans in the big races. In 1968, Hubert Humphrey carried Hudson by only 33,000 votes, and in 1972, George McGovern managed only

39% of the votes here. Moreover, in the 1969 gubernatorial race, the county went Republican, reportedly because the old bosses were unhappy with ex-Gov. (1954–62) Robert Meyner, the Democratic nominee. It also went Republican again in the 1972 Senate race, for incumbent Clifford Case.

In local races, however, Hudson County remains staunchly Democratic, with the machine imprimatur still carrying weight on primary day. In the 14th congressional district, which includes 78% of the county's population, the Democratic primary continues to be tantamount to a general election. As it currently stands, the 14th is an amalgam of two old districts once dominated by Hudson County. It now controls only one—a measure of population decline and the waning clout of the Hudson County machine.

The 1972 amalgamation put two incumbent Democrats, the now-jailed Cornelius Gallagher and Dominick Daniels, together in the same district. The reformers thought the situation set up an opening for them to capture the seat, but it was not to be. Gallagher was seriously weakened by his indictment on income tax and perjury charges (he later pleaded guilty), and wound up winning only 15% of the vote. The real opposition to Daniels, who had the endorsement of the old-line organization, came from reform West New York Mayor Anthony DeFino, who was backed by reform colleagues Jordan in Jersey City and Fitzpatrick in Bayonne. DeFino garnered a respectable 32% of the votes, as Daniels, who had represented most of the district for 14 years, took a mite over 50%. The general election, of course, posed no problems for incumbent Daniels—who, incidentally, was not implicated in any of the Hudson County corruption.

In Washington, Daniels is a quiet Congressman, though he possesses senior status on both the Education and Labor and Post Office and Civil Service committees. The New Jerseyite votes a 100% COPE line. His 1972 showing indicates that he can probably continue to win indefinitely. Daniels may, however, choose to retire because of age (66 in 1974) or if a judicial appointment comes his way.

Census Data Pop. 477,939. Central city, 55%; suburban, 45%. Median family income, $9,607; families above $15,000: 19%; families below $3,000: 9%. Median years education, 10.3.

1972 Share of Federal Outlays $523,217,360

DOD	$96,710,503	HEW	$145,584,735
AEC	$165,116	HUD	$10,344,138
NASA	$951,395	DOI	$791,273
DOT	$6,040,659	USDA	$14,234,911
		Other	$248,394,630

Federal Military-Industrial Commitments

DOD Contractors Seatrain Lines (Weehawken), $5.307m: transportation services.

DOD Installations Army Military Ocean Terminal (Bayonne).

Economic Base Apparel and other textile products, especially women's and misses' outerwear; electrical equipment and supplies; finance, insurance and real estate; food and kindred products; and chemicals and allied products, especially soap, cleaners and toilet goods.

The Voters

Registration Not available.
Median voting age 45.4
Employment profile White collar, 45%. Blue collar, 43%. Service, 12%. Farm, –%.
Ethnic groups Black, 13%. Spanish, 6%. Total foreign stock, 39%. Italy, 10%; Poland, 5%; Ireland, UK, 3% each; Germany, USSR, 2% each; Austria, 1%.

Presidential vote

1972	Nixon (R)	104,907	(60%)
	McGovern (D)	71,098	(40%)
1968	Nixon (R)	70,360	(37%)
	Humphrey (D)	102,257	(53%)
	Wallace (AI)	18,731	(10%)

Representative

Dominick V. Daniels (D) Elected 1958; b. Oct. 18, 1908, Jersey City; home, Jersey City; Fordham U., 1925–26; Rutgers U. Law School, LL.B., 1929; married, two children; Catholic.

Career Practicing atty., 1930– ; Magistrate, Jersey City Municipal Ct., 1952–58.

Offices 2370 RHOB, 202-225-2765. Also 895 Bergen Ave., Jersey City 07306, 201-659-7700, and Kearny P.O., Kearny 07032, 201-991-5100, and P.O. Bldg., Bayonne 07002, 201-823-2900.

Administrative Assistant Gerard F. Devlin

Committees

Education and Labor (4th); No. 4 (Sel. Sub. on Labor) (Chm.); No. 3 (Gen. Sub. on Labor).

Post Office and Civil Service (4th); Subs: Retirement and Employee Benefits; Investigations.

Group Ratings

	ADA	COPE	LWV	RIPON	NFU	LCV	CFA	NAB	NSI	ACA
1972	63	91	89	67	86	47	50	18	63	20
1971	76	100	88	59	67	–	88	–	–	14
1970	72	100	–	53	100	71	95	0	78	20

Key Votes

1) Busing	FOR	6) Cmbodia Bmbg	AGN	11) Chkg Acct Intrst	FOR
2) Strip Mines	ABS	7) Bust Hwy Trust	FOR	12) End HISC (HUAC)	AGN
3) Cut Mil $	AGN	8) Farm Sub Lmt	FOR	13) Nixon Sewer Veto	AGN
4) Rev Shrg	FOR	9) School Prayr	AGN	14) Corp Cmpaign $	FOR
5) Pub TV $	ABS	10) Cnsumr Prot	FOR	15) Pol $ Disclosr	AGN

Election Results

1972 general:	Dominick V. Daniels (D)	103,089	(61%)
	Richard T. Bozzone (R)	57,683	(34%)
	Edward F. Zampella (Concerned and Capable)	5,188	(3%)
	Perfecto Dyola (Protest, Progress, Dignity)	1,556	(1%)
	Vincent J. Carrino (People over Politics)	847	(1%)
1972 primary:	Dominick V. Daniels (D)	34,631	(51%)
	Anthony M. DeFino (D)	21,969	(32%)
	Cornelius E. Gallagher (D)	10,392	(15%)
	Vincent J. Dellay (D)	1,194	(2%)
1970 general:	Dominick V. Daniels (D)	77,771	(71%)
	Carlo N. DeGennaro (R)	31,161	(29%)

FIFTEENTH DISTRICT Political Background

The 15th district of New Jersey takes in most of Middlesex County, the state's fastest-growing traditionally Democratic area. The 15th has the largest concentration of Hungarian-Americans of any district in the nation, centered in New Brunswick. There are also large numbers of Poles living in Woodbridge, and Italians in Perth Amboy. From the substantial ethnic communities in the older cities, the hyphenated Americans have moved out into places like Edison Township, Piscataway Township, North Brunswick Township, and Sayreville. These towns, classic blue-collar suburbs, all had populations over 30,000 in 1970. Here, with the New Jersey countryside developed à la Levittown, the sons and daughters of immigrants have come to live in a setting that is pastoral when compared to the central cities of New Brunswick or Perth Amboy. The suburban voters have not completely forgotten their Democratic heritage, but they are upset with social trends and personal values not consistent with their upbringing. The plurality the voters of Middlesex County gave Hubert Humphrey in 1968 was much smaller than John F. Kennedy got in 1960. And in 1972, Richard Nixon did better than either one of these Democrats.

Middlesex County and the 15th district have long had a successful Democratic machine run by David Willentz, whose Perth Amboy law office somehow attracts clients out of the state's largest business firms. Formerly split between the 3rd and 5th districts, Middlesex acquired its own congressional district in 1962. The Willentz machine than picked Edward J. Patten as its candidate for the seat. At the time, Patten was N.J. Secretary of State—an appointive position usually reserved for the Governor's top political operator. The machine candidate won election and reelection to Congress easily.

On the campaign trail, Patten's greatest asset is a garrulous sense of humor, one that Don Riegle's book, *O Congress*, commemorates in numerous anecdotes. In 1970, Patten got much-heralded primary opposition from a 28-year-old peace candidate, whom he defeated easily even though the primary took place just after the Cambodian invasion. The Willentz machine and Patten's own good humor were largely responsible for the result. As the incumbent's Republican opponent that year put it, "Running against Ed Patten is like running against Santa Claus."

But in 1972, the New Jersey Santa Claus found himself in some trouble. Republican nominee Fuller Brooks, looking for Nixon coattails, waged an effective campaign and wound up with 48% of the votes. One is tempted to ascribe Patten's near loss to George McGovern, but it is a fact that all other incumbent New Jersey Democratic Congressman ran much further ahead of the South Dakotan than Ed Patten. A better explanation of his poor showing is age. In 1974, when Patten turns 69, he will have held public office continuously for 40 years. He is simply not the campaigner he once was. If the Congressman chooses to retire in 1972, recent trends in the district indicate a close race for succession in 1974. A Republican edge, it appears now, will be blunted by Watergate.

Census Data   Pop. 477,949. Central city, 0%; suburban, 9%. Median family income, $11,793; families above $15,000: 29%; families below $3,000: 4%. Median years education, 12.1.

1972 Share of Federal Outlays $523,217,360

DOD	$96,710,503	HEW	$145,584,735
AEC	$165,116	HUD	$10,344,138
NASA	$951,395	DOI	$791,273
DOT	$6,040,659	USDA	$14,234,911
		Other	$248,394,630

Federal Military-Industrial Commitments

DOD Contractors Amerada Hess (Woodbridge), $8.364m: petroleum products.

Economic Base Chemicals and allied products, especially drugs and industrial chemicals; finance, insurance and real estate; primary metal industries, especially primary cooper; electrical equipment and supplies, especially electronic components and accessories; and machinery.

The Voters

Registration Not available.
Median voting age 41.7
Employment profile White collar, 49%. Blue collar, 41%. Service, 10%. Farm, –%.
Ethnic groups Black, 6%. Spanish, 2%. Total foreign stock, 33%. Italy, Poland, 5% each; Hungary, 4%; Germany, 3%; USSR, UK, Czechoslovakia, Austria, 2% each; Ireland, 1%.

Presidential vote

1972	Nixon (R)		118,439	(61%)
	McGovern (D)		74,752	(39%)
1968	Nixon (R)		76,756	(41%)
	Humphrey (D)		90,902	(48%)
	Wallace (AI)		20,591	(11%)

Representative

Edward James Patten (D) Elected 1962; b. Aug. 22, 1905, Perth Amboy; home, Perth Amboy; Newark State Col.; Rutgers Law School, LL.B., 1926; Rutgers U., B.S.Ed., 1928; married, one child; Catholic.

Career Practicing atty., 1927– ; teacher, 1927–34; Mayor, Perth Amboy, 1934–40; Middlesex County Clerk, 1940–54; Campaign Mgr. for Gov. Robert B. Meyner, 1953, 1957; N.J. Sec. of State, 1954–62; Pres., Salvation Army Bd.

Offices 2332 RHOB, 202-225-6301. Also Natl. Bank Bldg., Perth Amboy 08861, 201-826-4610.

Administrative Assistant Stephen G. Callas

Committees

Appropriations (19th); Subs: Labor—Health, Education and Welfare; Military Construction.

Group Ratings

	ADA	COPE	LWV	RIPON	NFU	LCV	CFA	NAB	NSI	ACA
1972	81	82	83	67	86	47	100	25	56	22
1971	70	83	88	67	80	–	75	–	–	7
1970	80	100	–	71	92	81	89	10	70	16

Key Votes

1) Busing	FOR	6) Cmbodia Bmbg	AGN	11) Chkg Acct Intrst	AGN
2) Strip Mines	AGN	7) Bust Hwy Trust	ABS	12) End HISC (HUAC)	FOR
3) Cut Mil $	AGN	8) Farm Sub Lmt	AGN	13) Nixon Sewer Veto	AGN
4) Rev Shrg	FOR	9) School Prayr	AGN	14) Corp Cmpaign $	FOR
5) Pub TV $	FOR	10) Cnsumr Prot	FOR	15) Pol $ Disclosr	AGN

Election Results

1972 general:	Edward J. Patten (D)	98,155	(52%)
	Fuller H. Brooks (R)	89,400	(48%)
1972 primary:	Edward J. Patten (D), unopposed		
1970 general:	Edward J. Patten (D)	94,772	(61%)
	Peter P. Garibaldi (R)	60,450	(39%)

NEW MEXICO

Political Background

The politics of New Mexico demonstrates that the average is not necessarily the typical. Since it was admitted to the Union in 1912, New Mexico has voted for the winner in 16 consecutive presidential elections. Though it is the most reliable bellwether state in the country, New Mexico could hardly be more atypical. For a start, nearly one-third of its people are Spanish-speaking; few of them are recent immigrants from Mexico, most being descendants of Spanish conquistadores and Pueblo Indians. A Hispanic civilization has existed in what is now northern New Mexico around Santa Fe and Taos since 1610, and in the years before World War II the Spanish community made up nearly half of the state's population.

The southeast part of the state is called "Little Texas." With small cities, oil-well activity, and vast cattle ranches, the region is economically and politically similar to the adjacent plains of west Texas. The oil here is important, but more important to the area are its military installations.

These include a number of Air Force bases, along with the Army's White Sands Missile Range, near Alamogordo, where the first atomic bomb was detonated. Little Texas is traditionally Democratic and conservative; in recent years, more conservative than Democratic.

Lying in the middle of the state is Albuquerque, which, with the advent of the air conditioner, grew from a small desert town into a booming Sun Belt city—booming, at least, until recent cutbacks in defense spending. Albuquerque depends heavily on the Pentagon and the Atomic Energy Commission. There are two military bases within the city limits, and its largest employer is the Bell System's Sandia Laboratories, an AEC contractor. Like most Sun Belt cities, greater Albuquerque is more Republican than the territory surrounding it. The voters in the city and its suburbs, often migrants from other places, cast about one-third of the state's votes and often hold the balance of power in New Mexico elections.

For many years, New Mexico politics was a somnolent business. Local bosses—first Republican, then Democratic—controlled the large Hispanic vote, which meant that elections here were often only a ratification of the power brokers' decisions. The most interesting feature of this politics was the balanced ticket: New Mexico usually had one Spanish and one Anglo Senator, with the positions of Governor and Lieutenant Governor alternating between the two groups. Recently, as Albuquerque emerged as a major political force in itself, and as Little Texas grew increasingly conservative, New Mexico elections have tested the skills of political leaders charged with assembling winning coalitions from three roughly equal-sized voting blocs: the Hispanic, Little Texas, and Albuquerque.

In the 1972 Senate election, the state's Republicans were, for once, the clear and undisputed winners in the three-cornered game. Incumbent Democratic Sen. Clinton Anderson was suffering from Parkinson's disease, diabetes, and a heart condition, and in 1972, he decided to retire after spending 24 years in the Senate. Anderson, a South Dakota native, enjoyed a long and colorful career. As a young reporter, he helped to break the Teapot Dome scandal in 1924, and later served in the House and the Truman Cabinet. In the Senate, he was Chairman for many years, on and off, of the Joint Committee on Atomic Energy. So it was not entirely coincidental that the AEC, having installed post-World War II facilities at White Sands and Los Alamos, still spends more money in New Mexico than any other state in the nation. During the 1950s, Anderson led the fight to deny Lewis Strauss, former head of the AEC, confirmation as Commerce Secretary. It was one of the few times in American history that the Senate rejected a Cabinet nominee.

Aside from 1966, when he was 71, Anderson had little trouble winning reelection. In fact, until 1972, New Mexico had not elected a Republican Senator since progressive Bronson Cutting won reelection in 1934. But the year 1972 looked like a Republican one. The GOP sported a tested candidate in Pete Domenici, the 40-year-old former Mayor of Albuquerque, who had just barely lost the Governor's race in 1970. Domenici, a conservative, was strong in Albuquerque and his campaign made a particular effort to win votes in Hispanic areas.

Meanwhile, the Democrats found themselves in the midst of chaos. In April of 1972, a federal court ruled the state's $2,550 filing fee unconstitutional. Thereupon a herd of political hopefuls proceeded to file for the Democratic Senate nomination. Though the court ruling was modified, twenty-five Democrats stayed on the ballot. Leading candidates included Lt. Gov. Robert Mondragon, State Atty. Gen. David Norvell, and ex-Rep. (1959–69) Thomas Morris. These and the others lost, however, to a former state Representative with the arresting name of Jack Daniels, who had spent some of his considerable fortune retaining the services of campaign consultant Joe Napolitan.

But the wizard's ad copy came up short against the well-organized and well-financed Republican campaign in the 1972 general election. Domenici, like Richard Nixon, ran well in Hispanic precincts, carried Albuquerque 57–43, and got a small but sufficient edge in Little Texas and other Anglo areas—all of which was good enough for a 54% victory statewide. In Washington, Domenici serves on the Aeronautics and Space Sciences Committee (of which his predecessor, Anderson, was Chairman) and Public Works. Both units are of bread-and-butter significance to New Mexico.

Some interesting political strategy was also practiced in the 1970 Senate election. Republican politicos considered Democratic Sen. Joseph Montoya vulnerable, even though he had spent 34 successful years in New Mexico politics after first winning a seat in the state legislature at age 21. The campaign forced the Republicans to make a basic decision. There were two ways to go. One was the conservative model provided by Richard Nixon's 1968 victory in the state; the

Republicans carried Little Texas and Albuquerque by margins large enough to overcome Humphrey's edge in the Hispanic counties. The other model was established by then Republican Gov. David Cargo, who won in 1966 and 1968 by making strong inroads into the Spanish vote as well as carrying Albuquerque—but losing conservative Little Texas.

Because Cargo was barred from seeking a third term as Governor, he entered the Senate primary; so did Anderson Carter, a wealthy rancher and backer of Goldwater and Reagan. In 1966, Carter had taken 47% of the votes against Clinton Anderson. The Republican voters had a clear choice, and they picked the conservative Carter by an overwhelming 2–1 margin. Their repudiation of Cargo was made even clearer in 1972, when he ran against Domenici for the Senate nomination and got only 12% of the votes. Few Spanish voters register Republican, and in Albuquerque and Little Texas, the Goldwater conservatives who do vote in Republican primaries preferred a candidate like Carter. It should be noted, however, that not many in New Mexico considered themselves Republican; registered Democrats outnumber registered Republicans in every county.

The conservative strategy chosen by the Republicans was not as successful in 1970 as it would be in 1972. While Carter attacked all federal spending (except by the Pentagon), Montoya talked about how much federal money he was bringing into New Mexico. Montoya wound up winning by a lackluster, but decisive, 53–47 margin. When Anderson retired, Montoya assumed a seat on the Joint Committee on Atomic Energy. The Senator also retains a place on the Appropriations Committee.

To most Americans Montoya is best known today as a member of the Watergate Committee. He was chosen for it, some have said, because of his Hispanic background, to forestall any criticism that the committee, looking into a burglary committed by several Cubans, was anti-Latin. Montoya was not the committee's most effective investigator, and his questioning style seemed to many soporific; reportedly he is a far better orator in Spanish than English. At one point during the hearings, Montoya was accused of irregular reporting practices in his own 1970 campaign, though it appears that he personally complied with all laws applicable at the time. It is too early to predict what effect the TV exposure will have in 1976, when the Senator's seat comes up; most probably, the tube has enhanced Montoya's stature in the state.

Since the 1940 census, New Mexico has elected two Congressmen, but until 1968 both were elected at large. The switch to separate districts in 1968 proved disastrous for the Democrats, who after winning the seats routinely before lost both the 1st and 2nd districts in 1968. The 1st covers the northeastern third of the state, including all of Albuquerque and the vast bulk of the Hispanic areas. Santa Fe, the small state capital city and a place of old-world charm, is included, as is Taos, which has attracted artists and hangers-on ever since D. H. Lawrence did some writing here in the 1920s.

The Democrats' problem in the 1st was a mismatching of the candidate and the district. During the 1960s, the Hispanic voters of northern New Mexico were the state's staunchest Democrats. But by the end of the decade, they felt taken for granted and began to flirt with the Republicans. So when the Democrats ran Anglo Congressman Thomas Morris and the Republicans put up Manuel Lujan, Jr., voters in the Spanish counties split tickets in great numbers and plunked for Lujan, who also did well in his home town of Albuquerque. Like his father, Lujan is a long-established and well-known insurance agent in Albuquerque and had served on a city commission. In 1970, Lujan was reelected easily over erratic ex-Lt. Gov. Fabian Chavez.

In 1972, Manuel Lujan became something of a national figure, as he appeared to get more TV exposure at the Republican National Convention than Richard Nixon. Lujan, as the only national Republican elected official of Spanish descent, was given tube time by Republican strategists who made major efforts to win Spanish-speaking voters—with more success, it turned out, in Texas than in New Mexico. As a delegate, the New Mexico Congressman actually cast the lone convention vote for Paul McCloskey, but the vote was strictly a set-up. By state law, the number-two finisher in the presidential primary gets at least one delegate, no matter how few votes he wins. Those gathered at the state Republican convention chose Lujan to cast it, because they knew he would neither place McCloskey's name in nomination nor make speeches against the war.

Curiously, Lujan's percentage dropped just a little in 1972, mainly because Democratic nominee Eugene Gallegos waged a campaign more creditable than Chavez had two years before. It will be interesting to see whether Lujan's association with Nixon will hurt his chances in 1974.

The state's 2nd district has produced more capricious results. The constituency contains Little Texas, most of the Rio Grande Valley, the Navajo country around Gallup, and the Anglo mining boom town of Farmington in the state's northwest corner. In 1968, the defeat of the Democratic incumbent, E. S. Johnny Walker of Little Texas, was largely the result of an action taken by the Johnson Administration. At that time, Roswell (pop. 39,000) was the largest city in the district and one heavily dependent on Walker Air Force Base. But in 1967, the Pentagon closed the base; within a year, Roswell's population dropped to 32,000, with many unemployed. In 1968, Walker lost Chaves County, which includes Roswell, by more votes than his total deficit district-wide.

The winner of the election was conservative Republican Ed Foreman, who thereby gained the distinction of being the second person in this century to have won election to the House from two different states. In 1962, Foreman captured the adjoining 16th district of Texas (El Paso) in the wake of the Billie Sol Estes scandal. In 1970, Foreman gained the further distinction of being the first person in American political history to have been elected and then at the next election defeated in two different states. The man who beat him was state Sen. Harold Runnels, whose outlook is nearly as conservative as Foreman's. The Democrat serves on the Armed Services Committee, where he finds its hawkish ideology and temperament congenial.

Some observers have described Runnels as a "good old boy from Little Texas," and a good old boy is apparently what voters in the 2nd want. In 1972, Runnels took 72% of the votes. In 1973, Runnels made headlines: he was quoted as charging that he had purchased documents from the Pentagon that he was not able to obtain through ordinary channels as a member of Armed Services Committee. After Runnels denied it, a House investigative subcommittee left the matter hanging. Runnels is said to be contemplating making the Governor's race in 1974. If he does run, local predictions are that another good old boy from Little Texas will win the vacated seat.

Census Data Pop. 1,016,000; 0.50% of U.S. total, 37th largest; change 1960–70, 6.8%. Central city, 24%; suburban, 7%. Median family income, $7,845; 38th highest; families above $15,000: 15%; families below $3,000: 15%. Median years education, 12.2.

1972 Share of Federal Tax Burden $752,470,000; 0.36% of U.S. total, 40th largest.

1972 Share of Federal Outlays $1,721,202,106; 0.79% of U.S. total, 34th largest. Per capita federal spending, $1,694.

DOD	$446,565,000	33rd (0.71%)	HEW	$332,145,996	38th (0.47%)
AEC	$333,372,472	1st (12.72%)	HUD	$19,474,376	35th (0.63%)
NASA	$4,580,730	25th (0.15%)	VA	$79,387,717	36th (0.69%)
DOT	$82,390,364	32nd (1.04%)	USDA	$137,107,523	36th (0.89%)
DOC	$7,300,706	30th (0.56%)	CSC	$30,087,807	35th (0.73%)
DOI	$130,679,192	6th (6.16%)	TD	$39,075,618	37th (0.24%)
DOJ	$7,522,641	34th (0.77%)	Other	$71,511,964	

Economic Base Agriculture, notably cattle, dairy products, hay and cotton lint; finance, insurance and real estate; oil and gas extraction, especially oil and gas field services; metal mining, especially uranium-radium-vanadium ores; food and kindred products; tourism.

Political Line-up Governor, Bruce King (D); seat up, 1974. Senators, Joseph M. Montoya (D) and Pete V. Domenici (R). Representatives, 2 (1 D and 1 R). State Senate (30 D and 12 R); State House (51 D and 19 R).

The Voters

Registration 505,432 Total. 321,513 D (64%); 151,203 R (30%); 32,716 other (6%).
Median voting age 40.3.
Employment profile White collar, 51%. Blue collar, 30%. Service, 15%. Farm, 4%.
Ethnic groups Black, 2%. Indian, 7%. Spanish, 40%. Total foreign stock, 9%.

Presidential vote

1972	Nixon (R)	235,606	(63%)
	McGovern (D)	141,084	(37%)
1968	Nixon (R)	169,692	(52%)
	Humphrey (D)	130,081	(40%)
	Wallace (AI)	25,737	(8%)
1964	Johnson (D)	194,017	(59%)
	Goldwater (R)	131,838	(41%)

Senator

Joseph M. Montoya (D) Elected 1964, seat up 1976; b. Sept. 24, 1915, Pena Blanca; home, Santa Fe; Regis Col., 1931, 1933–34; Georgetown U. Law School, LL.B., 1938; married, three children; Catholic.

Career Practicing atty., 1939– ; N.M. House of Reps., 1936–40, Majority Floor Leader, 1939–40; N.M. Senate, 1940–46, Majority Whip, 1945–46; Lt. Gov., 1946–48, 1954–56; U.S. House, 1957–64.

Offices 4107 NSOB, 202-225-5521. Also New Fed. Bldg., Albuquerque 87101, 505-843-2551, and Rm. 221, Fed. Bldg., Santa Fe 87501, 505-982-3801, ext. 461.

Administrative Assistant Marv J. Sektnan

Committees

Appropriations (10th); Subs: Interior; Labor, and Health, Education, and Welfare, and Related Agencies; Military Construction; Public Works-AEC; Treasury, U.S. Postal Service and General Government (Chm.).

Public Works (3rd); Subs: Air and Water Pollution; Roads; Economic Development (Chm.).

Sel. Com. on Presidential Campaign Activities (4th).

Joint Com. on Atomic Energy (5th); Subs: Agreements for Cooperation (Chm.); Military Applications; Research, Development and Radiation; Raw Materials; Energy.

Group Ratings

	ADA	COPE	LWV	RIPON	NFU	LCV	CFA	NAB	NSI	ACA
1972	45	90	70	35	88	42	90	40	60	24
1971	74	70	69	38	100	–	100	–	–	19
1970	63	100	–	65	93	62	–	11	33	20

Key Votes

1) Busing	FOR	8) Sea Life Prot	FOR	15) Tax Singls Less	AGN
2) Alas P-line	AGN	9) Campaign Subs	FOR	16) Min Tax for Rich	AGN
3) Gun Cntrl	AGN	10) Cmbodia Bmbg	AGN	17) Euro Troop Rdctn	FOR
4) Rehnquist	FOR	11) Legal Srvices	FOR	18) Bust Hwy Trust	AGN
5) Pub TV $	FOR	12) Rev Sharing	FOR	19) Maid Min Wage	FOR
6) EZ Votr Reg	FOR	13) Cnsumr Prot	FOR	20) Farm Sub Limit	AGN
7) No-Fault	AGN	14) Eq Rts Amend	FOR	21) Highr Credt Chgs	FOR

Election Results

1970 general:	Joseph M. Montoya (D)	151,486	(52%)
	Anderson Carter (R)	135,004	(47%)
	William L. Higgs (AI)	3,382	(1%)
1970 primary:	Joseph M. Montoya (D)	85,285	(73%)
	Richard B. Edwards (D)	31,381	(27%)
1964 general:	Joseph M. Montoya (D)	178,209	(55%)
	Edwin L. Mechem (R)	17,562	(45%)

Senator

Pete V. Domenici (R) Elected 1972, seat up 1978; b. May 7, 1932, Albuquerque; home, Albuquerque; U. of N.M., B.S., 1954; Denver U., LL.B., 1958; married, eight children; Catholic.

Career Elected Member, Albuquerque City Commission, 1966–67; Chm. (and ex-officio Mayor), Albuquerque City Comm., 1967–69. lawyer, Domenici and Bonham; Republican gubernatorial nominee, 1970.

Offices 5229 NSOB, 225-6621. Also 10013 New Fed. Bldg., and U.S. Courthouse, Albuquerque 87101, 505-843-3481.

Administrative Assistant Dennis Howe

Committees

Aeronautical and Space Sciences (6th).

Public Works (6th); Subs: Air and Water Pollution; Disaster Relief; Roads; Economic Development.

District of Columbia (3rd); Subs: Business, Commerce, and Judiciary (Ranking Mbr.).

Sp. Com. on Aging (7th); Subs: Housing for the Elderly; Health of the Elderly; Long-Term Care; Retirement and the Individual.

Group Ratings: Newly Elected

Election Results

1972 general:	Pete V. Domenici (R)	204,253	(54%)
	Jack Daniels (R)	173,815	(46%)
1972 primary:	Pete V. Domenici (R)	37,337	(63%)
	David F. Cargo (R)	12,522	(21%)
	E. Lee Francis (R)	4,583	(8%)
	Bennis M. Chavez (R)	1,169	(2%)
	Stella M. Montoya (R)	1,219	(2%)
	William J. Dahnke (R)	1,112	(2%)
	Crisiforo Gallegos (R)	833	(1%)

FIRST DISTRICT

Census Data Pop. 511,135. Central city, 48%; suburban, 14%. Median family income, $8,187; families above $15,000: 18%; families below $3,000: 15%. Median years education, 12.3.

1972 Share of Federal Outlays $1,042,506,241

DOD	$180,231,000	HEW	$187,791,973
AEC	$333,372,472	HUD	$12,587,292
NASA	$731,605	DOI	$50,279,262
DOT	$65,017,231	USDA	$60,464,161
		Other	$152,031,248

Federal Military-Industrial Commitments

DOD Contractors EG&G (Albuquerque), $5.522m: ABM research.

DOD Installations Kirtland AFB/Sandia Base (Albuquerque).
AEC Operations Sandia Corp. (Albuquerque), $169.017m: operation of Sandia Laboratory for design of components that incorporate nuclear systems into weapons meeting DOD requirements. University of California (Los Alamos), $94.908m: operation of Los Alamos Scientific Laboratory.

Economic Base Finance, insurance and real estate; agriculture, notably cattle, dairy products and grains; tourism; food and kindred products; and lumber and wood products, especially millwork, plywood and related products. Also higher education (Univ. of New Mexico).

The Voters

Registration 277,033 total. 165,939 D (60%); 90,388 R (33%); 20,706 other (7%).
Median voting age 40.5
Employment profile White collar, 57%. Blue collar, 26%. Service, 15%. Farm, 2%.
Ethnic groups Black, 1%. Indian, 3%. Spanish, 49%. Total foreign stock, 7%.

Presidential vote

1972	Nixon (R)	125,326	(59%)
	McGovern (D)	85,996	(41%)
1968	Nixon (R)	91,729	(52%)
	Humphrey (D)	75,328	(43%)
	Wallace (AI)	7,850	(5%)

Representative

Manuel Lujan (R) Elected 1968; b. May 12, 1928, San Ildefonso; home, Albuquerque; Col. of Santa Fe, B.S., 1950; married, four children; Catholic.

Career Businessman—insurance; Bernalillo County Crime Commission, 1967–68; Pres., N.M. Assn. Industrial Insurance Agents, 1968; Mbr., State Corp. Commission, Advisory Bd. on Insurance, 1965–68.

Offices 1323 LHOB, 202-225-6316. Also Rm. 1004 Fed. Bldg., 500 Gold Ave., S.W., Albuquerque 87103, 505-843-2538, and San Fidel Hotel, Las Vegas 87701, 505-425-6684.

Administrative Assistant Jack Crandall

Committees

Interior and Insular Affairs (8th); Subs: Indian Affairs (Ranking Mbr.); Territorial and Insular Affairs; Water and Power Resources.

Joint Com. on Atomic Energy (4th); Subs: Communities; Energy; Raw Materials (Ranking House Mbr.); Security.

Group Ratings

	ADA	COPE	LWV	RIPON	NFU	LCV	CFA	NAB	NSI	ACA
1972	13	40	63	67	50	47	100	100	63	50
1971	27	22	0	67	45	–	100	–	–	82
1970	36	30	–	67	25	100	40	100	100	69

Key Votes

1) Busing	AGN	6) Cmbodia Bmbg	AGN	11) Chkg Acct Intrst	AGN
2) Strip Mines	AGN	7) Bust Hwy Trust	AGN	12) End HISC (HUAC)	AGN
3) Cut Mil $	ABS	8) Farm Sub Lmt	FOR	13) Nixon Sewer Veto	FOR
4) Rev Shrg	AGN	9) School Prayr	FOR	14) Corp Cmpaign $	ABS
5) Pub TV $	ABS	10) Cnsumr Prot	ABS	15) Pol $ Disclosr	FOR

Election Results

1972 general:	Manuel Lujan, Jr. (R)	118,403	(56%)
	Eugene Gallegos (D)	94,239	(44%)
1972 primary:	Manuel Lujan, Jr. (R)	32,445	(91%)
	Richard Martinez (R)	3,341	(9%)

1970 general:	Manuel Lujan, Jr. (R)	91,187	(58%)
	Fabian Chavez, Jr. (D)	64,598	(41%)
	Anita Montano (PCP)	1,763	(1%)
	Norbert J. McGovern (INM)	811	(1%)

SECOND DISTRICT

Census Data Pop. 504,865. Central city, 0%; suburban, 0%. Median family income, $7,551; families above $15,000: 12%; families below $3,000: 16%. Median years education, 12.0.

1972 Share of Federal Outlays $678,695,865

DOD	$266,334,000	HEW	$144,354,023
AEC	–	HUD	$6,887,084
NASA	$3,849,125	DOI	$80,399,930
DOT	$17,373,133	USDA	$76,643,362
		Other	$82,855,208

Federal Military-Industrial Commitments

DOD Contractors Sperry Rand (White Sands Missile Range), $14.482m: lease and purchase of Univac computers. Dynalectron (White Sands Missile Range), $6.822m: support services of Missile Range.

DOD Installations Army White Sands Missile Range (Las Cruces). Naval Ordance Missile Test Facility (Las Cruces). Cannon AFB (Clovis). Holloman AFB (Alamagordo).

Economic Base Agriculture, notably cattle, cotton and dairy products; finance, insurance and real estate; metal mining; potash, soda, and borate minerals, and other nonmetallic minerals except fuels; and oil and gas extraction. Also higher education (New Mexico State Univ.).

The Voters

Registration 228,399 total. 155,574 D (68%); 60,815 R (17%); 12,010 other (5%).
Median voting age 40.1
Employment profile White collar, 45%. Blue collar, 35%. Service, 14%. Farm, 6%.
Ethnic groups Black, 2%. Indian, 11%. Spanish, 31%. Total foreign stock, 10%.

Presidential vote

1972	Nixon (R)	110,280	(67%)
	McGovern (D)	55,088	(33%)
1968	Nixon (R)	77,963	(52%)
	Humphrey (D)	54,753	(36%)
	Wallace (AI)	17,887	(12%)

Representative

Harold L. Runnels (D) Elected 1970; b. March 17, 1924, Dallas, Tex.; home, Lovington; Cameron State Agricultural Col., B.S., 1943; USAFR, WWII; married, four children; Baptist.

Career Owner and manager of two oil-drilling equipment companies; N.M. State Senate, 1960–70.

Offices 1728 LHOB, 202-225-2365. Also Suite D, McCrory Bldg., Lovington 88260, 505-396-2252, and Suite 1022, First Natl. Tower, Las Cruces 88001, 505-526-6156, and City Hall, Gallup 87301, 505-863-3400.

Administrative Assistant Richard D. Haptke

Committees

Armed Services (19th); Subs: No. 1; Sp. Sub. on Human Relations.

Interior and Insular Affairs (18th); Subs: No. 2 (Water and Power Resources); No. 5 (Mines and Mining); No. 7 (Public Lands).

Group Ratings

	ADA	COPE	LWV	RIPON	NFU	LCV	CFA	NAB	NSI	ACA
1972	25	55	27	14	71	37	0	88	100	91
1971	16	38	0	31	80	–	50	–	–	65

Key Votes

1) Busing	AGN	6) Cmbodia Bmbg	AGN	11) Chkg Acct Intrst	AGN
2) Strip Mines	AGN	7) Bust Hwy Trust	AGN	12) End HISC (HUAC)	AGN
3) Cut Mil $	ABS	8) Farm Sub Lmt	AGN	13) Nixon Sewer Veto	AGN
4) Rev Shrg	AGN	9) School Prayr	FOR	14) Corp Cmpaign $	ABS
5) Pub TV $	AGN	10) Cnsumr Prot	AGN	15) Pol $ Disclosr	AGN

Election Results

1972 general:	Harold Runnels (D)	116,152	(72%)
	George E. Presson (R)	44,784	(28%)
1972 primary:	Harold Runnels (D), unopposed		
1970 general:	Harold Runnels (D)	64,518	(51%)
	Ed Foreman (R)	61,074	(48%)
	Julian A. Roybal (PCP)	1,388	(1%)

NEW YORK

Political Background

Because so much that is written about New York state or New York City is really about Manhattan, we might for a start consider just how important Manhattan is in statewide politics. Back in 1910, after decades of heavy immigration, some 2,331,000 people lived on the famous island; by 1970, its population had declined to 1,539,000—just 8% of the state's total. And in 1972, Manhattan cast only 7% of the votes in New York state. To a large extent, Manhattan sets cultural patterns picked up by or sold to the rest of the country: book publishers and the *New York Times* determine what people read; Sixth Avenue television executives determine what people watch; and Seventh Avenue businessmen determine what people wear. But Manhattan does not determine how New York, state or city, votes.

Indeed, quite the contrary argument can be advanced; namely, that an endorsement from Gloria Steinem or the *Village Voice* constitutes the kiss of death in New York politics. In this view, the archetypical event of recent times was the fund-raiser hosted by Leonard Bernstein for certain Black Panther defendants—a party memorialized in Tom Wolfe's phrase, "Radical Chic." Not that Bernstein's cause was a bad one; the Panthers were later acquitted by a middle-class jury. The point, as Wolfe's piece makes clear, was the fatuous acceptance by rich intellectuals and assorted hangers-on of anything the Panthers said or did.

Radical chic among privileged Manhattanites produced a negative reaction of considerably greater electoral strength in the state—one personified by Archie Bunker of Queens. As Manhattan has trended left, the rest of New York City, as well the suburbs and upstate, has moved right. It is easy to forget that New York is still essentially a white middle-class city, despite having large and festering black and Puerto Rican ghettos. Some 64% of the city's residents, and a higher percentage of its voters, are neither black nor Spanish-speaking. A dozen years ago, when John F. Kennedy occupied the White House, the white middle-class voters of New York, harboring memories perhaps of their immigrant parents, usually voted for liberal Democratic candidates for public office. Today, even in New York City, these same people do not, at least in statewide or presidential elections, vote that way. In 1972, for example, New York state cast a larger percentage of its votes for Richard Nixon than California or Michigan or even Iowa. And New York City gave Nixon a larger percentage—48%—than Detroit or Chicago or Philadelphia or even Los Angeles.

So much for the idea, still widely believed and nowhere more fervently than in Manhattan, that New York is some kind of liberal bastion. In electoral terms, such is simply not the case; that distinction (or stigma) belongs to Massachusetts. But the liberal bastion notion is just one of the persistent myths that bedevils anyone trying to understand the politics of New York state. Another is the idea that upstate New York, which casts about 40% of the state's votes, is mostly bucolic, Protestant farmland. In fact, upstate—an empire in itself with a population greater than all but nine states—is a collection of aging industrial cities. Probably a majority of upstaters are of Catholic background, most often of Italian, Irish, and Polish descent. There are, of course, pockets of old-line WASPs, but the big metropolitan areaas around Albany, Utica, Syracuse, Rochester, and Buffalo are heavily Catholic. That they are not correspondingly Democratic, like most such Catholic areas in the East, results from a historic suspicion of traditionally Democratic New York City. Nevertheless, some Democrats, notably Robert F. Kennedy when he ran for the Senate in 1964, carried upstate.

Yet another prevalent myth is that New York is a big Democratic state. John F. Kennedy and Hubert Humphrey did carry the state in 1960 and 1968. But to accept the myth, one must overlook the fact that since 1950, Republicans have won all but two races for Senator and Governor—the exceptions being Averell Harriman's paper-thin 1954 margin and Robert Kennedy's victory in 1964. As the 1972 returns indicate, New York is not much more likely to wind up in the Democratic column than other big states like California, Pennsylvania, and Illinois. Humphrey, to take one example, carried the state by 370,000 votes—an impressive margin in raw numbers—but it represents only 50.1% of the total votes cast.

The other buttress for the myth of New York as a solidly Democratic state lies in party registration figures. In this regard, New York continues to be hopelessly Democratic. But the numbers have no relation whatever to the way people actually vote in general elections. Most New Yorkers, especially those in New York City, register Democratic just so they can vote in that party's primary, one more likely to generate excitement. Nonetheless, commentators persist in using as a measure of a Republican candidate's strength how far he or she ran ahead of party registration figures, to which one can only reply that Barry Goldwater ran 4% ahead of Republican registration in New York City.

Closely connected to the myth of the state's awesome Democratic character is the myth of equally awesome New York Democratic machines. To be sure, Democratic organizations do exist in the four big boroughs of New York City—ones to which newspaper reporters pay considerable attention. The machines here have little effect on the kind of elections that concern the *Almanac* (for an exception, see New York 14). Aside from Robert Kennedy, a newcomer to the state, the much-vaunted organizations have failed to support a single winning candidate for Senator, Governor, or Mayor since 1957. Their one recent success—the nomination and, it appears at this writing, almost certain election of Abraham Beame as Mayor in 1973— would almost certainly have happened if there were no bosses at all. Instead, judgeships are the lifeblood of the bosses; from these offices, they derive enough patronage to keep their wheels greased.

The machines control the judgeships because Democratic nominees are chosen in conventions dominated by the bosses, and in the four big boroughs the Democratic nominees for offices like judgeships always win. In places like Chicago, machines have traditionally registered as many minority-group voters as it could; only in this way could they produce the required margins on election day. In New York, the bosses don't need votes to hold the judgeships and don't care much about anything else. So New York City had the lowest level of voter participation among blacks and Spanish-speaking people of any place in the United States—including the Black Belts of the rural South and the Chicano precincts of the Lower Rio Grande Valley in Texas. In 1972, fewer votes for President were cast in New York's 21st district (the south Bronx) than in any other congressional district in the country.

The final myth is the notion that the Liberal party is some kind of force for "good government" and politics of the antiwar variety. In fact, the Liberal party is controlled by a septuagenarian labor leader, Alex Rose, and staffed by hacks heavily into patronage politics. Rose delayed coming out against the Vietnam war as long as he possibly could, supporting the effort until 1968.

In recent years, the party's major achievement was the slating of John Lindsay in 1965 and 1969; the decision in 1969 was especially important since the incumbent mayor had lost the Republican primary. For the decision, the party received ample patronage rewards. More typical of Liberal operations is a series of cozy arrangements, just being revealed at this writing, with the Republicans in the 1972 elections.

If one wants an ideologically committed group in New York politics that can command hundreds of real volunteers and genuine popular enthusiasm, the group is the Conservative party. Organized as recently as 1962, the party has elected a U.S. Senator on its own line, James Buckley in 1970; moreover, its support was decisive for a crucial number of incumbents in the Republican-controlled state legislature. Conservative elan may be waning, however, in the wake of the party's expediential nomination of Democratic Congressman Mario Biaggi for Mayor in 1973; early in the race, he looked like a winner (see New York 10). Later it was revealed that Biaggi had lied about taking the Fifth Amendment before a grand jury, and his candidacy collapsed. Nevertheless, the faction of the Conservatives backing Biaggi stuck with him, though in retrospect they would have done better with state Sen. John Marchi. Marchi, a man with the Republican mayoral nomination, holds positions on issues considerably closer than Biaggi's to the programs of the Conservative party.

The one unchanging feature of the changing politics of New York is the continued tenure of Gov. Nelson Rockefeller. First elected in 1958, Rockefeller is now the nation's most senior Governor; in fact, he has been Governor longer than any American has ever been Governor of any state—runners-up include Thomas E. Dewey, also of New York, Orval Faubus of Arkansas, G. Mennen Williams of Michigan, and William Guy of North Dakota. New York Governors have established a tradition of longevity in office. The state has had only five chief executives in the past 40 years, and one of them served only briefly when Herbert Lehman resigned just before his term expired. Rockefeller, however, has succeeded in turning the governorship into something of a monarchy. He seldom speaks directly to the press or other politicians, but he still does campaign with gusto. Every few years, Rockefeller conducts a series of town meetings across the state, fending off questions and hostile remarks in regal fashion.

For three years, New Yorkers grumble about Rockefeller, but around election time the Governor's ad campaign begins, after which he is reelected—the last time, in 1970, with a record majority. In many respects, Rockefeller has been an outstanding Governor. If he has indulged in huge overruns to build the Albany Mall (a sign of his "edifice complex," critics complain), he has also built the State University system from scratch to one of the largest in the country. If he has been unable to solve some of the state's problems—heroin addiction, for example—his Albany regime is clearly more efficient and apparently more honest than the one in New York City. And of course there is another reason why Rockefeller always wins: cold, hard cash.

Rockefeller's opponents charge that he spends as much as $15 million per campaign, with much of the money going to hire the services of the nation's shrewdest ad agencies and polling firms. Moreover, none of the four Democrats Rockefeller has beaten has really wanted the job in Albany. All four Democrats were slated because they looked like good candidates on paper, but all of them campaigned poorly. The four appear far happier doing what they now do than out on the hustings—Averell Harriman, as elder statesman; Robert Morgenthau, as a racket-busting federal prosecutor (until 1971); Frank O'Connor, as a judge in Queens; and Arthur Goldberg, as a Washington lawyer.

In 1974, Rockefeller will come before the voters once more, with most observers at this point assuming that the man and his money will win routine reelection. But at least one contrary sign has appeared: the two Democrats vying to run against Rockefeller—Howard Samuels, head of the city's successful Off Track Betting operation, and Congressman Ogden Reid, of New York 24—are both ambitious men eager to become Governor.

Rockefeller's political astuteness, however, deserts him when he runs for President, something he seems to do every four years. In 1960, he left the race early in return for policy concessions from Richard Nixon. In 1964, he mounted his most sustained effort for the Republican nomination in a year when no Republican could have won. In 1968, Rockefeller was out of the race, in, out, in, and finally out again at the Miami Beach convention. Rumors say he is eyeing 1976. Recently, Rockefeller has moved to the right, as his refusal to meet with Attica prison rebels and his proposal for mandatory life sentences for heroin pushers demonstrate. Accordingly, the Governor is now somewhat more palatable to conservative Republicans, who remember that he supported Nixon's policies in Vietnam wholeheartedly, as indeed he had Johnson's except during the 1968 campaign.

But the presidential primaries, where most Republican ballot-casters lean right, will still give Rockefeller problems, should he run. These are problems he has never had to face in New York, where he has vetoed primary bills for years, and where even now only a modified primary system is at work. The parties hold conventions to endorse nominees—which means the Democrat is inevitably tagged as the candidate of the bosses—who may then be challenged in the primaries. The Republican endorsee is never so challenged.

The absence of a primary for statewide office has also helped the state's senior Senator, Jacob Javits. If he had been forced to win the Republican nomination by winning a primary against a conservative candidate, Javits might never have made it to Washington. As it is, Javits today is the first New York Senator to accumulate an appreciable amount of seniority since the first Robert Wagner. First elected in 1956 against Wagner's son, then Mayor, Javits won routine reelection in 1962 and 1968.

In the Senate, the New Yorker is probably the leading and certainly the best-known Republican liberal. He has broken with the Nixon Administration on issues like Southeast Asia, social and educational programs, and indeed most other matters of major importance. Currently Javits is the ranking minority member of the Labor and Public Welfare Committee; he is one of its most able and diligent members, striving to influence how social programs enacted actually work in the world outside. His most recent achievement is Senate passage of the Williams-Javits pension regulation bill. Javits is a politically adroit man—a measure of which is his simultaneous and eminent acceptability to both organized labor and Wall Street.

Javits is also good at winning the approval of ordinary New York voters. Though he constantly criticizes Nixon policies, his support of Republican candidates, including Nixon himself, is never in doubt. Moreover, as one of two Jewish Senators in Washington, Javits is especially popular among the state's large number of Jewish voters, of whom there are more here than in Israel. Nonetheless, the last election showed a certain weakness in Javits' appeal; he won with only 49.8% of the votes. But the percentage was good enough for a plurality of more than a million votes over liberal Democrat Paul O'Dwyer (about to become New York City Council President at this writing) and Conservative James Buckley.

The outlook for 1974 is for more of the same good news for Javits. Liberal Democrat and ex-Congressman Allard Lowenstein (see New York 5) has reportedly decided to enter the race; another possible candidate is Bronx Borough President Robert Abrams, a major McGovern backer in 1972. And the Conservative party will no doubt feel bound to field a candidate. If it does, the question will be who Senator Buckley, himself elected on the Conservative ticket, will support. Finally, just after the 1972 election, there was talk that upstate Congressman Jack Kemp (see New York 38), an ardent Nixon loyalist, might force a primary against Javits. But the idea seems to have been dropped when the Watergate story broke.

Just over ten years ago, the Conservative party was organized, and most political pundits laughed—the idea of a conservative party in liberal New York was ridiculous. Eight years later, in 1970, the Conservative candidate, James Buckley, was elected a United States Senator. His slogan—"Isn't time we had a Senator?"—encapsulates many of the changes that have occurred in New York politics during the intervening years, and also summarized the strategy Buckley used to win. Both of his opponents were certified liberals, with scarcely an issue dividing them. The Republican candidate, Sen. Charles Goodell, had been appointed to fill the vacancy left by Robert Kennedy in 1968. Goodell metamorphosed from a middle-of-the-road upstate Congressman to one of the nation's most outspoken opponents of the Vietnam war and the Nixon Administration. Congressman Richard Ottinger, the Democratic nominee, having a similar record and a special interest in environmental matters, won the nomination with a saturation TV ad campaign, financed from his family's plywood fortune.

The election of Buckley, therefore, represented a revolt against the process by which the New York Republican party always slated a liberal candidate. By tradition, the party felt it needed a liberal to win what they considered the votes necessary for victory in general elections. One such candidate, of course, was Charles Goodell, who had little in common with the 45% of the New York electorate that voted for Richard Nixon in 1968. Shrewd Nixon and Rockefeller operatives aided the Buckley candidacy when they passed the word that it was all right to support the

Conservative, Buckley, over Goodell, the Republican. The signal, if any were needed, was flashed by Vice-President Agnew, who attended a Buckley dinner in New York City. Agnew's appearance also created liberal sympathy—and votes—for the spurned Goodell, who if he was an enemy of Agnew was surely a friend of the liberal. But Goodell never had a chance, since he had already lost the bedrock of Republican support necessary to win statewide. As it turned out, enough liberal votes went from Ottinger to Goodell to allow Buckley to slip through with 39% of the votes.

That 39% represents no derogation of Buckley, who was a personable, homey candidate and no right-wing fanatic. Moreover, he was wise enough to engage the services of top conservative campaign consultant F. Clifton White. In the Senate, Buckley, as expected, has shown himself to be a far more reliable supporter of the Nixon Administration than Javits or Goodell. Buckley, however, did oppose certain Nixon ideas, like the now-defunct Family Assistance Plan. The Senator has tried to carve out a reputation as an environmentalist, becoming the first New Yorker to serve on the Interior Committee in some time. Not all of Buckley's stands, though, have won the approval of environmental lobbying groups.

In all, Buckley's greatest achievement was just winning—an event that has begun to change much of the style, tone, and substance of politics in New York. Where did Buckley's votes come from? The Conservative piled up his biggest margins in Suffolk County, one of two where he won an absolute majority. The county comprises the eastern end of Long Island, the fastest-growing part of the state. Here thousands of middle-class families have settled in what are bucolic suburbs by any comparison to the city. Suffolk is also heavily Catholic, with Buckley's support all over the state coming in disproportionate fashion from Catholic voters.

In fact, New York Catholics constitute the group most responsible for the rightward shift in the state's politics. The question is why the shift is much more pronounced here than in Massachusetts. In the Bay State, the leading liberal politician is Sen. Edward M. Kennedy, whose support from Catholic voters is so ardent that Chappaquiddick hardly mattered. Moreover, his late brother's presidential picture adorns the wall of every Irish workingman's bar in Boston. In New York, or at least in metropolitan New York City, the chief liberal officeholder has been John Lindsay, a Wasp and a Republican until he decided to run for President. In the eyes of voters from Queens, Lindsay is a politician who reserves all his sympathies for the blacks and Puerto Ricans and none for the ordinary white workingman and his family.

One of Lindsay's closest advisers now admits that the Mayor of Fun City never "persuaded middle-class New Yorkers that he really cared about them." This insight is hardly one of profound originality. As Lindsay took office, he professed a sympathy for the plight of the city's poor people. Soon thereafter, the Mayor adamantly refused to deal with union leaders in a transit strike, and his posture was one of complete disdain for the subway workers who were then trying to raise families on something like $6,000 a year. Lindsay finally settled the strike, agreeing to terms that any knowledgeable bargainer would have rejected out of hand. The settlement led to exorbitant pay and pension hikes for other city employees, while at the same time alienating the kind of people it actually benefited.

Lindsay was eminently the candidate of the rich and the poor, to the exclusion of others. In both 1965 and 1969, he carried Manhattan, where virtually no middle-income people live, and lost the rest of the city. Both times he was elected with a minority of the vote, with the opposition split between two candidates more congenial to the homeowners of Queens or the Bronx. So it is no surprise that Archie Bunker loathes John Lindsay. Queens homeowners screamed bloody murder when the snow wasn't plowed in 1968, and when the city decided to locate a major low-income housing project in middle-income Forest Hills in 1971.

The Ocean Hill-Brownsville controversy was another Lindsay crisis that alienated many middle-class New Yorkers, and one that shows what has happened to the city's once-liberal electorate. Ocean Hill-Brownsville was an experimental school district in Brooklyn's black ghetto. When a locally elected school board (later thrown out by its constituents) wanted to fire certain teachers, the teacher's union struck. The city's teaching jobs, like most of its civil service positions, are held in disproportionate numbers by Jews who have scored the highest marks on the city's competitive (and critics say outmoded) civil service examinations. Many of these people got their first jobs during the Depression; they were barred from business and the professions, for which they were superbly qualified, by anti-Semitic bias. So the attachment of these people to the exams and their hatred of quotas and other devices to give top jobs in larger proportions to blacks or Puerto Ricans is intense.

The WASP-dominated Ford Foundation first set up the Ocean Hill project, and Lindsay supported it. In the ensuing controversy, Albert Shanker, the head of the union who led the strike, became an important political figure, and Lindsay lost the support of hundreds of thousands of Jewish voters and civil servants all over New York City. Because of changes in the delegate selection process to the Democratic national convention, the quota issue became a part of national politics. The issue explains in part George McGovern's poor showing in the city's Jewish areas (see, for example, New York 13).

Why, then, was John Lindsay, having won 42% of the votes in his last election, considered a creditable presidential candidate? The answer is that New York City is the media capital of the nation; if its sports writers always feel that the Mets, Yanks, or Jets are destined to go all the way, its political writers are no less confident of the city's local entry in the more complex game of national politics. Hip New Yorkers of various kinds held the erroneous belief that the Kennedy appeal was simply one of good looks which could be transferred to a WASP by a skillful media campaign. In the early 1972 presidential primaries, Lindsay spent a lot of money and made a lot of noise; he even gimmicked a night's sleep on a couch in a south side Milwaukee working-class home. But if the media threw up a plentiful supply of Lindsay, the electorate generated little demand. The New York Mayor won less than 10% of the votes in both Florida and Wisconsin.

So New York voters showed little disappointment when Lindsay announced that he would not seek another term as Mayor. Earlier, Nelson Rockefeller went so far as to push through a law requiring a runoff in the Democratic mayoral primary—one designed to keep Lindsay from winning again with less than a majority. Rumors have it that Lindsay is once more thinking about public office, perhaps Governor or Senator in 1974 or Senator in 1976. But he is unlikely to run against his old friend Javits, and unlikely, at this stage, to survive any race against Rockefeller. Reputations of former New York Mayors do tend to grow one they leave office, as witness the flurry of interest when Rockefeller and Liberal party boss Alex Rose announced they would back ex-Mayor (1954–66) Robert Wagner in 1973. Wagner, however, after a few weeks of keeping the political writers busy, decided not to run. So as yet one cannot be completely confident that this is an obituary to Lindsay's political career.

It is significant that none of the Congressmen who ran for Mayor of New York in 1973 came close to winning. The almost certain winner, Abraham Beame, who was twice City Controller, has roots in city government. He beat Congressman Herman Badillo in the Democratic runoff, and, at this writing, seems sure to dispose of Congressman Mario Biaggi, the Conservative nominee; state Senator John Marchi, the Republican; and Assemblyman Albert Blumenthal, the Liberal, in November 1973. Congressmen are not that big a deal in New York, and over the years New York Congressmen have not been that big a deal in Washington. Traditionally, the delegation from New York, particularly from New York City, has developed little seniority, aside from spectacular exceptions like Emanuel Celler, first elected in 1922 and defeated in 1972.

In Texas—a state that does prize seniority—young politicians traditionally move from local judgeships to the House. In New York, the customary progression was reversed, with machine politicians spending a few years in Washington to qualify for a judgeship. In the past dozen years, the turnover has been even greater. Insurgent reformers have unseated regulars and then, because of Republican redistricting plans, fallen to fighting among themselves. The prospect today, however, is for fewer changes in New York ranks, in the city as well as the suburbs and upstate. Redistricting is set for the 1970s, reformers have knocked off most of the regulars in the city, and Republican Congressmen are pretty safely ensconced in most districts upstate.

Census Data Pop. 18,241,266; 9.01% of U.S. total, 2nd largest; change 1960–70, 8.7%. Central city, 51%; suburban, 35%. Median family income, $10,609; 11th highest; families above $15,000: 26%; families below $3,000: 8%. Median years education, 12.1.

1972 Share of Federal Tax Burden $23,221,950,000; 11.11% of U.S. total, 2nd largest.

1972 Share of Federal Outlays $25,968,402,317; 11.98% of U.S. total, 1st largest. Per capita federal spending, $1,424.

DOD	$4,257,639,000	3rd (6.81%)		HEW	$8,504,156,743	1st (11.91%)
AEC	$148,372,599	6th (5.66%)		HUD	$319,473,947	1st (10.41%)
NASA	$48,545,961	14th (1.62%)		VA	$903,404,566	2nd (7.89%)
DOT	$356,573,552	4th (4.52%)		USDA	$1,532,488,215	1st (9.96%)
DOC	$155,053,276	3rd (11.98%)		CSC	$638,672,136	1st (15.50%)
DOI	$19,727,856	23rd (0.93%)		TD	$7,067,640,306	1st (42.79%)
DOJ	$97,837,067	2nd (9.97%)		Other	$1,918,817,093	

Economic Base Finance, insurance and real estate; apparel and other textile products, especially women's and misses' outerwear; electrical equipment and supplies, especially communication equipment; printing and publishing, especially commercial printing and newspapers; machinery, especially office and computing machines; food and kindred products, especially bakery products and beverages; agriculture, especially dairy products, cattle, eggs, and greenhouse products.

Political Line-up Governor, Nelson A. Rockefeller (R); seat up, 1974. Senators, Jacob K. Javits (R) and James L. Buckley (Cons.-R). Representatives, 39 (22 D and 17 R). State Senate (37 R and 23 D); State Assembly (83 R and 67 D).

The Voters

Registration 8,687,414 total. 4,226,604 D (49%); 3,201,059 R (37%); 159,669 L (2%); 147,685 C (2%); 952,397 blank, missing, and void (11%).
Median voting age 44.2
Employment profile White collar, 55%. Blue collar, 31%. Service, 13%. Farm, 1%.
Ethnic groups Black, 12%. Spanish, 5%. Total foreign stock, 33%. Italy, 7%; USSR, Poland, Germany, 3% each; Ireland, UK, Canada, 2% each; Austria, 1%.

Presidential vote

1972	Nixon (R)	4,192,778	(59%)
	McGovern (D)	2,951,084	(41%)
1968	Nixon (R)	3,007,932	(45%)
	Humphrey (D)	3,378,470	(50%)
	Wallace (AI)	358,864	(5%)
1964	Johnson (D)	4,913,156	(69%)
	Goldwater (R)	2,243,559	(31%)

Senator

Jacob K. Javits (R) Elected 1956, seat up 1974; b. May 18, 1904, New York City; home, New York City; N.Y.U. Law School, LL.B., 1926; Army, WWII; married, three children; Jewish.

Career Practicing atty., 1927– ; Sp. Asst. to the Chief of Chemical Warfare Service during WWII; Atty. Gen. N.Y. State, 1955–57.

Offices 326 OSOB, 202-225-6542. Also 110 E. 45th St., New York City 10017, 212-687-7777, and Rm. 414, W.S. Courthouse, Buffalo 14202, 716-842-3690.

Administrative Assistant Jean McKee

Committees

Foreign Relations (3rd); Subs: European Affairs; Western Hemisphere Affairs; U.S. Security Agreements and Commitments Abroad; Arms Control, International Law and Organization.

Government Operations (2nd); Subs: Reorganization, Research, and International Organizations (Ranking Mbr.); Permanent Investigations.

Labor and Public Welfare (Ranking Mbr.); Subs: Alcoholism and Narcotics; Education; Employment, Poverty, and Migratory Labor; Health; Labor (Ranking Mbr.); Sp. Sub. on Arts and Humanities (Ranking Mbr.).

Select Com. on Small Business (Ranking Mbr.).

Sp. Com. to Study Questions Related to Secret and Confidential Government Documents. (2nd).

Joint Economic Committee (Ranking Senate Mbr.); Subs: Urban Affairs (Ranking Senate Mbr.); Fiscal Policy (Ranking Senate Mbr.); Consumer Economics (Ranking Senate Mbr.); International Economics (Ranking Senate Mbr.).

Group Ratings

	ADA	COPE	LWV	RIPON	NFU	LCV	CFA	NAB	NSI	ACA
1972	80	90	100	92	80	72	100	42	20	15
1971	70	64	100	96	73	–	100	–	–	22
1970	75	92	–	85	93	48	–	25	10	0

Key Votes

1) Busing	FOR	8) Sea Life Prot	FOR	15) Tax Singls Less	AGN
2) Alas P-line	AGN	9) Campaign Subs	AGN	16) Min Tax for Rich	AGN
3) Gun Cntrl	FOR	10) Cmbodia Bmbg	AGN	17) Euro Troop Rdctn	AGN
4) Rehnquist	AGN	11) Legal Srvices	FOR	18) Bust Hwy Trust	FOR
5) Pub TV $	FOR	12) Rev Sharing	FOR	19) Maid Min Wage	FOR
6) EZ Votr Reg	FOR	13) Cnsumr Prot	FOR	20) Farm Sub Limit	FOR
7) No-Fault	FOR	14) Eq Rts Amend	FOR	21) Highr Credt Chgs	AGN

Election Results

1968 general:	Jacob K. Javits (R-L)	3,269,772	(50%)
	Paul D. Dwyer (D)	2,150,659	(33%)
	James L. Buckley (C)	1,139,402	(17%)
1968 primary:	Jacob K. Javits (R), unopposed		
1962 general:	Jacob K. Javits (R)	3,272,417	(58%)
	James B. Donovan (D)	2,289,323	(40%)
	Kieran O'Doherty (C)	116,151	(2%)

Senator

James Lane Buckley (Cons.) Elected 1970, seat up 1976; b. March 9, 1923, New York City; home, New York City; Yale, B.A., Oct. 1943, LL.B., 1949; Navy, WWII; married, six children; Catholic.

Career Businessman; Conservative candidate for Senate, 1968.

Offices 5323 NSOB, 202-225-4451. Also 110 E. 45th St., New York City 10022, 212-697-3000.

Administrative Assistant David R. Jones

Committees

Interior and Insular Affairs (4th); Subs: Minerals, Materials and Fuels (Ranking Mbr.); Public Lands; Territories and Insular Affairs.

Public Works (2nd); Subs: Air and Water Pollution (Ranking Mbr.); Water Resources; Roads; Disaster Relief; Panel on Environmental Science and Technology (Ranking Mbr.).

Sel. Com. on Small Business (6th); Subs: Financing and Investment (Ranking Mbr.); Government Regulation; Retailing, Distribution, and Marketing Practices.

Group Ratings

	ADA	COPE	LWV	RIPON	NFU	LCV	CFA	NAB	NSI	ACA
1972	10	0	30	44	30	39	0	91	100	95
1971	4	8	42	52	11	–	20	–	–	87

Key Votes

1) Busing	AGN	8) Sea Life Prot	ABS	15) Tax Singls Less	AGN
2) Alas P-line	AGN	9) Campaign Subs	AGN	16) Min Tax for Rich	AGN
3) Gun Cntrl	FOR	10) Cmbodia Bmbg	FOR	17) Euro Troop Rdctn	AGN
4) Rehnquist	FOR	11) Legal Srvices	AGN	18) Bust Hwy Trust	FOR
5) Pub TV $	AGN	12) Rev Sharing	FOR	19) Maid Min Wage	AGN
6) EZ Votr Reg	AGN	13) Cnsumr Prot	AGN	20) Farm Sub Limit	AGN
7) No-Fault	AGN	14) Eq Rts Amend	AGN	21) Highr Credt Chgs	FOR

Election Results

1970 general:	James L. Buckley (C-Ind. Alliance)	2,288,190	(39%)
	New York City	797,144	
	Outside New York City	1,491,046	
	Richard L. Ottinger (D)	2,171,232	(37%)
	New York City	979,328	
	Outside New York City	1,191,904	
	Charles E. Goodell (R-L)	1,434,472	(24%)
	New York City	439,452	
	Outside New York City	995,020	
1970 primary:	James L. Buckley (C), unopposed		

FIRST DISTRICT Political Background

The 1st district of New York occupies the extreme eastern end of Long Island. The district's western boundary lies some 50 miles from Manhattan Island. The best-known part of the 1st consists of the picturesque eastern tip, which juts out into the Atlantic Ocean. Here rich New Yorkers flock to the elegant beach resorts of Southampton, Easthampton, and Montauk Point, sending the value of Ocean-front real estate ever upward. These folks, however, pay little attention to what happens year round. Chic parties have been thrown in Southampton "cottages" to benefit migrant farm workers in California, though the plight of those working the potato and vegetable farms around nearby Riverhead is equally miserable.

Before World War II, virtually all of the current 1st district was agricultural, little changed from days New Englanders moved across Long Island Sound during the seventeenth century. Today, metropolitan New York has moved inexorably into eastern Suffolk County. The 1st more than doubled in size during the 1960s, showing by far the largest population growth of any East Coast congressional district. Most of the district's people are clustered in middle-class suburbs toward the western end of the 1st: Commack, Smithtown, Setauket, Brookhaven, and Patchogue.

The mood out here is very conservative. A correlation exists, it seems, between political attitudes and the attitudes that impel people to move this far away from New York City—a fear of crime, a dislike of blacks and Puerto Ricans, a desire to escape what is regarded the chaos of the city for the simpler, less hectic pace of life on Long Island. There is also an ethnic basis for the conservatism. Jewish voters, who have provided the bulk of the ideologically committed liberal votes in the city over the years, are not found in Suffolk County or the 1st district in great numbers. Most of the people here are Catholics of Italian, Irish, or German origin—people brought up in a much more conservative tradition. Buttressing the area's political inclinations is the importance of defense-oriented industry to the economy of eastern Long Island. Two of the biggest employers here are the Grumman Aviation plant and the Atomic Energy Commission's Brookhaven National Laboratory.

The presence of the two giants also helps to explain why a Democrat, Congressman Otis Pike, consistently wins reelection in a very conservative district. Pike is the sixth-ranking Democrat on the House Armed Services Committee. The incumbent first won the seat in 1960, when the district extended all the way into Nassau County, and during the 1960s, Pike won elections by 2–1 margins. Lately, however, his margins have decreased with the growth of Conservative party strength in the area; Suffolk was one of two counties where Conservative Sen. James Buckley won an absolute majority in 1970. Pike, still an able campaigner, generates one of the most iconoclastic and witty congressional newsletters in Washington. Nevertheless, in the last two elections, well-financed Republicans have pressed him hard.

The election in 1972 may well have been Pike's toughest test. His Republican opponent, Joseph H. Boyd, Jr., was once a top aide to Gov. Nelson Rockefeller, which meant that big Rockefeller money poured into the challenger's campaign. Moreover, Richard Nixon was on his way to 70% of the ballots in the 1st, doing better in only five other districts in the Eastern states. Yet Pike won by a comfortable 53–37 margin. Because of a feud on Long Island between the Republican and Conservative parties, most of the rest of the votes went to a separate Conservative candidate, Robert D. L. Gardiner, a descendant of one of the original settlers of the Island. Gardiner lives on Gardiner's Island, which he owns in toto, though he has sold off much of his Long Island property to developers of shopping centers and subdivisions.

In Washington, Pike has long been considered a maverick on the Armed Services Committee. The Congressman, however, did not break with the Johnson or Nixon administrations on Indochina until the Cambodia bombing vote in 1973. So his reputation stems not from an opposition to American war policies, but rather from a caustic criticism of what he considers wasteful military spending. In 1973, for example, he helped lead the move to deny flight pay bonuses to deskbound Air Force generals. From time to time, speculation runs that he would be a good candidate for statewide office, occupying a position to snatch away some conservative votes. But it is now obvious to even the most obtuse hacks that Pike would in the process lose thousands of antiwar voters, and would therefore be unable to mount a viable statewide candidacy.

Census Data Pop. 467,742. Central city, 0%; suburban, 100%. Median family income, $11,643; families above $15,000: 30%; families below $3,000: 6%. Median years education, 12.3.

1972 Share of Federal Outlays $721,322,935

DOD	$122,243,289	HEW	$233,424,141
AEC	$2,872,019	HUD	$9,617,686
NASA	$1,398,055	DOI	$303,769
DOT	$9,676,059	USDA	$51,379,591
		Other	$290,408,326

Federal Military-Industrial Commitments

DOD Contractors Grumman Aerospace (Calverton), $12.439m: A-6 aircraft. Comtec Labs (Smithtown), $5.167m: electronic communication equipment.
DOD Installations Montauk AF Station (Montauk).
AEC Operations Associated Universities (Upton), $53.052m: operation and management of Brookhaven National Laboratory.

Economic Base Finance, insurance and real estate; electrical equipment and supplies, especially radio and television communication equipment; agriculture, notably nursery and greenhouse products, poultry and vegetables; aircraft and parts, and other transportation equipment; and apparel and other textile products, especially women's and misses' outerwear. Also higher education (SUNY, Stony Brook).

The Voters

Registration 226,415 total. 62,156 D (27%); 117,205 R (57%); 2,612 L (1%); 8,025 C (4%); 36,417 blank, missing and void (16%).
Median voting age 41.0
Employment profile White collar, 55%. Blue collar, 30%. Service, 14%. Farm, 1%.
Ethnic groups Black, 4%. Spanish, 1%. Total foreign stock, 28%. Italy, 7%; Germany, 4%; UK, Poland, Ireland, 2% each; USSR, 1%.

Presidential vote

1972	Nixon (R)	141,383	(70%)
	McGovern (D)	59,420	(30%)

1968	Nixon (R)	93,472	(59%)
	Humphrey (D)	50,908	(32%)
	Wallace (AI)	15,320	(10%)

Representative

Otis G. Pike (D) Elected 1960; b. Aug. 31, 1921, Riverhead; home, Riverhead; Princeton U., B.A., 1943; Columbia U., J.D., 1948; USMC, WWII; married, three children; Congregationalist.

Career Practicing atty., 1953– ; Justice of Peace and Mbr. Town Bd., Riverhead, 1953–60; V. Pres., Long Island Home, Ltd., Past Dir., Central Suffolk.

Offices 2428 RHOB, 202-225-3826. Also 209 W. Main St., Riverhead 11901, 516-727-2332.

Administrative Assistant Mrs. Robert Gale Woolbert

Committees

Armed Services (6th); Subs: No. 1; No. 5 (Chm.); Sp. Sub. on Armed Services Investigating.

Group Ratings

	ADA	COPE	LWV	RIPON	NFU	LCV	CFA	NAB	NSI	ACA
1972	63	82	83	47	43	87	100	33	50	39
1971	59	58	56	67	47	–	88	–	–	48
1970	84	67	–	76	92	90	74	25	40	37

Key Votes

1) Busing	FOR	6) Cmbodia Bmbg	AGN	11) Chkg Acct Intrst	ABS
2) Strip Mines	AGN	7) Bust Hwy Trust	FOR	12) End HISC (HUAC)	AGN
3) Cut Mil $	AGN	8) Farm Sub Lmt	FOR	13) Nixon Sewer Veto	AGN
4) Rev Shrg	AGN	9) School Prayr	FOR	14) Corp Cmpaign $	FOR
5) Pub TV $	FOR	10) Cnsumr Prot	FOR	15) Pol $ Disclosr	AGN

Election Results

1972 general:	Otis G. Pike (D)	102,628	(53%)
	Joseph H. Boyd, Jr. (R)	72,133	(40%)
	Robert D. L. Gardiner (C)	18,627	(10%)
	Robert P. Samek (L)	2,056	(1%)
1972 primary:	Otis G. Pike (D), unopposed		
1970 general:	Otis G. Pike (D-L)	108,746	(52%)
	Malcolm E. Smith, Jr. (R-C)	99,249	(48%)

SECOND DISTRICT Political Background

The population of Suffolk County, which takes in the eastern two-thirds of Long Island, increased some 69% during the 1960s. Most of the growth occurred near the western end of the county. The immigration of the 1960s possessed a somewhat different character than previous ones to hit Long Island. After World War II, hundreds of thousands of young New Yorkers left Brooklyn and Queens for the Levittowns then replacing the potato fields of Nassau County—which lies between Suffolk and New York City. Taken together, the new suburbanites comprised a proportionate sample of white New Yorkers. The migration to Suffolk County has been different, having a composition that is conservative by self-selection. The county has far more Catholics and fewer Jews than the New York metropolitan area as a whole. As a result, while 26% of Nassau's residents are Jewish, only 4% of Suffolk's belong to that group. Accordingly, while Nassau is marginal-to-Republican, Suffolk is Republican-to-Conservative.

That hyphenated description certainly fits the 2nd congressional district, whose boundaries were redrawn in 1972 to reflect population shifts and now lies wholly within Suffolk County. In rough terms, the district covers the southwestern portion of Suffolk, including all of the town of Islip and most of the town of Babylon. Using the 1972 presidential elections as a benchmark, the 2nd is the second most conservative district in New York state, and as immigration continues, it will probably become even more conservative.

Republican James Grover has represented the 2nd since the district was first created for the 1962 election. It then had rather different boundaries, but similar political inclinations. Reelection for the conservative Congressman has been routine—the only irritant being that the Conservative party nominates a separate candidate. This is because the Suffolk Republican organization, fearing Conservative power, refuses to endorse anyone who runs as a Conservative. Meanwhile, it is unthinkable that a Suffolk Republican would get the Liberal nomination, not that it would be worth much anyway.

Quietly, in the standard House manner, Grover has risen on the seniority ladder to the position of ranking Republican on the House Merchant Marine and Fisheries Committee, and the number-two minority position on Public Works. The two committees have jurisdiction over important areas of public policy. Merchant Marine supervises heavy government subsidization of the shipping industry, and Public Works passes on air and water pollution control, as well as traditional legislation regarding highways and rivers and harbors projects. So Grover has great potential say over matters of this sort. For the most part, he has gone along with the Republican minority on both committees and with existing trends in policy. The Congressman has no inclination to place significant pollution clean-up costs on business.

Census Data Pop. 467,722. Central city, 0%; suburban, 100%. Median family income, $11,938; families above $15,000: 29%; families below $3,000: 4%. Median years education, 12.1.

1972 Share of Federal Outlays $721,322,935

DOD	$122,243,289	HEW	$233,424,141
AEC	$2,872,019	HUD	$9,617,686
NASA	$1,398,055	DOI	$303,769
DOT	$9,676,059	USDA	$51,379,591
		Other	$290,408,326

Federal Military-Industrial Commitments

DOD Contractors Fairchild Camera (Copiague), $15.688m: MK 80 bomb fuzes.

Economic Base Finance, insurance and real estate; electrical equipment and supplies, especially radio and television communication equipment; transportation equipment, especially aircraft and parts; apparel and other textile products, especially women's and misses' outerwear; and agriculture, notably nursery and greenhouse products, poultry and vegetables.

The Voters

Registration 191,706 total. 55,528 D (29%); 99,158 R (52%); 2,228 L (1%); 8,002 C (4%); 26,790 blank, missing and void (14%).
Median voting age 41.2
Employment profile White collar, 49%. Blue collar, 37%. Service, 14%. Farm, –%.
Ethnic groups Black, 4%. Spanish, 2%. Total foreign stock, 28%. Italy, 9%; Germany, 3%; Ireland, UK, 2% each; Canada, Poland, 1% each.

Presidential vote

1972	Nixon (R)	123,030	(72%)
	McGovern (D)	46,695	(28%)
1968	Nixon (R)	84,034	(58%)
	Humphrey (D)	46,141	(32%)
	Wallace (AI)	14,650	(10%)

Representative

James R. Grover, Jr. (R) Elected 1962; b. March 5, 1919, Babylon; Hofstra Col., B.A., 1941; Columbia U., LL.B., 1949; Army Air Corps, WWII; married, four children; Catholic.

Career Practicing atty., 1951–; N.Y. Assembly, 1957–62; Sp. Counsel, Babylon.

Offices 2244 RHOB, 202-225-3335. Also 1801 Argyle Square, Babylon 11702, 516-669-1028.

Administrative Assistant Brenda King

Committees

Merchant Marine and Fisheries (Ranking Mbr.); Sub: Coast Guard and Navigation.

Public Works (2nd); Subs: Investigations and Review; Public Buildings and Grounds (Ranking Mbr.); Energy; Water Resources.

Group Ratings

	ADA	COPE	LWV	RIPON	NFU	LCV	CFA	NAB	NSI	ACA
1972	6	0	42	50	29	20	50	100	100	91
1971	5	27	22	59	13	–	25	–	–	92
1970	12	10	–	41	25	50	60	100	100	75

Key Votes

1) Busing	AGN	6) Cmbodia Bmbg	FOR	11) Chkg Acct Intrst	ABS
2) Strip Mines	AGN	7) Bust Hwy Trust	ABS	12) End HISC (HUAC)	AGN
3) Cut Mil $	AGN	8) Farm Sub Lmt	FOR	13) Nixon Sewer Veto	FOR
4) Rev Shrg	FOR	9) School Prayr	FOR	14) Corp Cmpaign $	FOR
5) Pub TV $	AGN	10) Cnsumr Prot	FOR	15) Pol $ Disclosr	AGN

Election Results

1972 general:	James R. Grover, Jr. (R)	99,348	(66%)
	Fern Coste Dennison (D)	49,454	(33%)
	Robert Atlas (L)	2,213	(1%)
1972 general:	James R. Grover, Jr. (R), unopposed		
1970 general:	James R. Grover, Jr. (R-C)	107,433	(66%)
	Harvey M. Sherman (D-L)	54,996	(34%)

THIRD DISTRICT Political Background

Upon the release of the 1970 census figures, it became clear that Long Island was entitled to an additional seat in Congress. Accordingly, the Republican New York legislature created the 3rd district. Designed carefully, as New York Republicans design all congressional districts, it was intended to produce a Republican Congressman. The new 3rd took in a slice of far western Suffolk County, including the small black ghetto of Wyandanch, and the much larger middle-class suburb of Huntington. But the greater part of the district, about 60%, lies in Nassau County, as it extends from the fashionable and high-income North Shore south to deeply conservative and middle-income Massapequa.

Enough Democratic voters live here, in Wyandanch and places like Syosett that have many Jews, to have stimulated the Democratic candidacy of Carter Bales. The aspirant waged a vigorous campaign and thought he was going to win. But as predicted, victory went to Nassau County Controller Angelo Roncallo.

Roncallo is a product of the Nassau Republican machine, which today is once again riding high. During the early 1960s, Nassau Republicans were afflicted by scandal, allowing Democrat Eugene Nickerson to capture the crucial post of County Executive. Moreover, on the strength of LBJ's 1964 landslide, the Democrats won several Assembly seats. Nickerson wanted bigger things, but he failed to win the Democratic nominations for Governor in 1966 and Senator in 1968. He then gave up the County Executive post and retired from politics in 1970. His successor was Republican Ralph Caso, an ally of astute County Republican Chairman (and Assemblyman) Joseph Margiotta. Through skillful redistricting and campaigns that have taken advantage of the rightward trend in New York politics generally, Nassau Republicans have regained most of the offices they lost during the 1960s. They are very definitely in control of that large suburban county (pop. 1,428,000) once more.

As might be expected from a man who has gained advancement from service to a tightly run Republican organization, Roncallo has usually voted with the Republican organization Roncallo has usually voted with the Republican leadership in the House. He holds a seat on the Banking and Currency Committee, a unit of vital concern to Long Island developers. These people, of course, depend on banks and savings and loan institutions (called savings banks in New York) for mortgage money. All indications are that Roncallo will have little trouble winning reelection.

Census Data Pop. 467,894. Central city, 0%; suburban, 100%. Median family income, $14,396; families above $15,000: 47%; families below $3,000: 4%. Median years education, 12.5.

1972 Share of Federal Outlays $721,322,935

DOD	$122,243,289	HEW	$233,424,141
AEC	$2,872,019	HUD	$9,617,686
NASA	$1,398,055	DOI	$303,769
DOT	$9,676,059	USDA	$51,379,591
		Other	$290,408,326

Federal Military-Industrial Commitments

DOD Contractors Grumman Aerospace (Bethpage), $1,102.979m: F-14, A-6, and E-2 aircraft. PRD Electronics (Syosett), $106.687m: avionics systems for F-14, E-2, and S-3 aircraft. Sperry Rand (Syosett), $47.398m: shipboard navigational equipment. Fairchild Industries (Farmingdale), $39.317m: various aircraft components and engineering services. Cutler Hammer (Deer Park), $23.911m: electronic warfare equipment; other electronic ware for A-6 aircraft. Hazeltine Corp. (Greenlawn), $20.917m: radar and sonar equipment. Dynell Electronics (Melville), $16.443m: radar equipment. Fairchild Camera (Syosett), $8.388m: camera systems and parts for aircraft.
NASA Contractors Grumman Aerospace (Bethpage), $12.314m: orbiting astronomical observatories; study of alternate space shuttle concepts.

Economic Base Finance, insurance and real estate; electrical equipment and supplies, especially radio and television communication equipment; apparel and other textile products, especially women's and misses' outerwear; transportation equipment, especially aircraft and parts; fabricated metal products, especially fabricated structural metal products; and printing and publishing.

The Voters

Registration 226,295 total. 74,378 D (33%); 109,154 R (48%); 3,204 L (1%); 5,941 C (3%); 33,618 blank, missing and void (15%).
Median voting age 42.8
Employment profile White collar, 62%. Blue collar, 27%. Service, 11%. Farm, –%.
Ethnic groups Black, 5%. Total foreign stock, 32%. Italy, 9%; Germany, 4%; USSR, 3%; UK, Poland, Ireland, 2% each; Canada, Austria, 1% each.

Presidential vote

1972	Nixon (R)	137,271	(67%)
	McGovern (D)	68,617	(33%)
1968	Nixon (R)	103,012	(56%)
	Humphrey (D)	70,161	(38%)
	Wallace (AI)	11,195	(6%)

Representative

Angelo D. Roncallo (R) Elected 1972; b. May 28, 1927, Port Chester; home, Massapequa; Manhattan Col., B.A., 1951; Georgetown U. Law School, J.D., 1953; married, five children; Catholic.

Career Nassau County Comptroller, 1967–72; Oyster Bay Town Councilman, 1965–67; Sr. partner, Roncallo, Leff, Weber and Shapiro; partner, Roncallo and Dunn, 1955–67.

Offices 1232 LHOB, 202-225-3865. Also 130 Main St., Cold Spring Harbor, L.I., 516-367-3600.

Administrative Assistant Frances Funk

Committees

Banking and Currency (13th); Subs: Bank Supervision and Insurance; Consumer Affairs; Small Business.

Group Ratings: Newly Elected

Key Votes

1) Busing	NE	6) Cmbodia Bmbg	FOR	11) Chkg Acct Intrst	AGN
2) Strip Mines	NE	7) Bust Hwy Trust	FOR	12) End HISC (HUAC)	AGN
3) Cut Mil $	NE	8) Farm Sub Lmt	NE	13) Nixon Sewer Veto	FOR
4) Rev Shrg	NE	9) School Prayr	NE	14) Corp Cmpaign $	NE
5) Pub TV $	NE	10) Cnsumr Prot	NE	15) Pol $ Disclosr	NE

Election Results

1972 general:	Angelo D. Roncallo (R)	103,620	(53%)
	Carter F. Bales (D)	73,429	(38%)
	Lawrence P. Russo (C)	14,768	(8%)
	Leo E. James (L)	3,343	(2%)
1972 primary:	Angelo D. Roncallo (R), unopposed		

FOURTH DISTRICT Political Background

At the end of World War II, Nassau County on Long Island consisted mostly of potato fields. Here and there, in this flat country 30 or 40 miles east of Manhattan, a few subdivisions were laid out before the war. On the North Shore and in places like Old Westbury sat the palatial estates of some of New York's wealthiest families. But the vast center of Nassau County lay virtually undeveloped. It did not stay that way very long. Just after the war, a young builder named Levitt built an entire town of small tract houses and named it after himself. Levittown came to symbolize Long Island's vast postwar growth. Young marrieds, after years of war and Depression childhoods pent up in the city, flocked out to the Island and created a new life style.

During the late 1940s and 1950s, Nassau County filled up. And during the 1960s, the county grew little, up less than 10%, below the national average. Some twenty years ago, many observers said that Nassau migrants switched from Democrat to Republican when they left New York City. In retrospect, the assessment seems inaccurate. The more affluent, and hence more Republican, people from Queens and Brooklyn left for Nassau, but there were enough Democrats among them to make that party a competitive force in the county's politics up to the mid-1960s.

The 4th congressional district of New York is one of two that lies totally within Nassau County. The 4th includes many areas of the 1950s boom, in particular Levittown and Hicksville. Both of these places, however, have lost population since 1960, as the original settlers aged and their children moved away. The district also encompasses posh Old Westbury and the black ghetto of New Cassel not far away. But the nucleus of the 4th, that part of it which connects the district with its predecessor seats, is a string of towns along the South Shore of Long Island. They include Oceanside, Freeport, and Merrick, which, having large Jewish populations, sustain marginal-to-Democratic voting habits. Also here are Bellmore, Wantagh, and Seaford, which are heavily

Catholic and much more Republican. These towns were all part of the old 5th district, which first elected the 4th's current Congressman, Norman F. Lent.

Lent is the beneficiary of a couple of redistrictings. The first, which took effect in 1970, had as its clear intent the defeat of antiwar Democrat Allard Lowenstein. In 1967, Lowenstein, with his myriad contacts in universities and liberal groups, helped to put together the antiwar campaign that toppled President Johnson from office. The New Yorker first tried to get Robert Kennedy into the race and failed; he then enlisted Eugene McCarthy and supported him. In 1968, after being somewhat disenchanted with McCarthy, Lowenstein, then a Manhattan resident, got into the 5th district race when then-incumbent Herbert Tenzer decided to retire. With the help of student volunteers who canvassed practically the entire district, Lowenstein defeated the organization candidate in the Democratic primary, and then beat Conservative Mason Hampton, who had the Republican nomination, in the general election.

Lowenstein's victory enraged New York Republicans. When it came time for them to redraw the district, Republican state legislators eliminated the Democratic and Jewish "Five Towns" (now in the current 5th) and added heavily conservative Massapequa (now in the 3rd). The new lines were enough to elect Lent, a state Senator who had earlier made a name for himself as an opponent of busing. While losing, Lowenstein actually ran better than he had in his first campaign. The new boundaries drawn for 1972 proved at least as congenial to incumbent Lent, who won much more impressively than in 1970.

Because of the rules of the Nassau County Republican organization, Lent did not have the endorsement of the Conservative party. He has, nevertheless, compiled a fairly conservative record in Congress, where he now sits on the Interstate and Foreign Commerce Committee. But during his first term, he was a member of Banking and Currency—something that could conceivably give him trouble in 1974: all of the Republicans and several of the Democrats on that congressional panel voted in October of 1972 to squelch an investigation of the Watergate affair. The squelching, of course, denied the public evidence of White House complicity in the burglary and the cover-up before people went to the polls in 1972. So it is possible that the reaction of Nassau County voters to the Watergate revelations will have a decisive bearing on the contest in the 4th district, which would otherwise be a Lent shoo-in.

Census Data Pop. 467,610. Central city, 0%; suburban, 100%. Median family income, $14,376; families above $15,000: 46%; families below $3,000: 3%. Median years education, 12.4.

1972 Share of Federal Outlays $721,322,935

DOD	$122,243,289	HEW	$233,424,141
AEC	$2,872,019	HUD	$9,617,686
NASA	$1,398,055	DOI	$303,769
DOT	$9,676,059	USDA	$51,379,591
		Other	$290,408,326

Federal Military-Industrial Commitments

DOD Contractors Lundy Electrics and Systems (Glen Head), $9.967m: components for Mark 12 reentry vehicle.

Economic Base Finance, insurance and real estate; electrical equipment and supplies, especially radio and television communication equipment; printing and publishing; machinery; and fabricated metal products, especially fabricated structural metal products.

The Voters

Registration 236,742 total. 114,118 D (48%); 85,233 R (36%); 2,801 L (1%); 5,461 C (2%); 29,129 blank, missing and void (12%).
Median voting age 43.3
Employment profile White collar, 63%. Blue collar, 26%. Service, 11%. Farm, –%.
Ethnic groups Black, 3%. Total foreign stock, 33%. Italy, 7%; USSR, 5%; Germany, 4%; Poland, Ireland, 3% each; UK, Austria, 2% each; Canada, 1%.

Presidential vote

1972	Nixon (R)	138,983	(64%)
	McGovern (D)	78,124	(36%)
1968	Nixon (R)	108,949	(50%)
	Humphrey (D)	98,158	(45%)
	Wallace (AI)	10,791	(5%)

Representative

Norman Frederick Lent (R) Elected 1970; b. March 23, 1931, Oceanside; home, East Rockaway; Hofstra Col., B.A., 1952; Cornell U. Law School, LL.B., 1957; USNR, 1952–54; married, three children; Methodist.

Career Practicing atty.; Asst. Police Justice, East Rockaway, N.Y., 1960–62; N.Y. State Senate, 1962–70.

Offices 428 CHOB, 202-225-7896. Also County Fed. Savings and Loan Bldg., 53 North Park Ave., Rockville Centre 11572, 516-536-2121.

Administrative Assistant Reed Boatright (L.A.)

Committees

Interstate and Foreign Commerce (16th); Sp. Sub. on Investigations.

Group Ratings

	ADA	COPE	LWV	RIPON	NFU	LCV	CFA	NAB	NSI	ACA
1972	13	44	50	80	17	64	100	70	100	53
1971	22	17	33	56	38	–	43	–	–	81

Key Votes

1) Busing	AGN	6) Cmbodia Bmbg	FOR	11) Chkg Acct Intrst	FOR
2) Strip Mines	AGN	7) Bust Hwy Trust	FOR	12) End HISC (HUAC)	AGN
3) Cut Mil $	ABS	8) Farm Sub Lmt	FOR	13) Nixon Sewer Veto	FOR
4) Rev Shrg	FOR	9) School Prayr	FOR	14) Corp Cmpaign $	AGN
5) Pub TV $	AGN	10) Cnsumr Prot	AGN	15) Pol $ Disclosr	FOR

Election Results

1972 general:	Norman F. Lent (R)	125,422	(62%)
	Elaine B. Horowitz (D)	72,280	(36%)
	Aaron M. Schein (L)	3,332	(2%)
1972 primary:	Norman F. Lent (R), unopposed		
1970 general:	Norman F. Lent (R-C)	93,824	(53%)
	Allard K. Lowenstein (D-L)	84,738	(47%)

FIFTH DISTRICT Political Background

The 5th district of New York, as it currently stands, includes most of the older suburban areas of Long Island. In the northern part of the district is Garden City, a WASPy suburb laid out in the 1920s; it is, as it always has been, heavily Republican. To the south are places like Hempstead, Rockville Centre, and Valley Stream, which were developed somewhat later. These include a fairly good mix of middle-class New Yorkers, who vote marginal-to-Republican. At the southern end of the district, below Kennedy Airport and just north of the Atlantic shore, are Long Beach and the Five Towns—Lawrence, Inwood, Cedarhurst, Hewlett, and Woodmere—all developments begun in the 1920s, all heavily Jewish, and in most elections, solidly Democratic. The 5th as a constituency was tipped towards the Republicans with the inclusion of East Meadow and Uniondale, both heavily Republican, which lie to the east of Garden City and Hempstead.

Like the 4th, the 5th is a district carefully sculpted by the Republican Legislature to preserve the incumbency of a Republican Congressman. In this case, the beneficiary is John Wydler, who first won a congressional seat in 1962 and has since won reelection without much difficulty. Wydler is a Congressman who generates little attention and publicity, but who has climbed the seniority ladder with fair rapidity. He is now the third-ranking Republican on both the Government Operations and the Science and Astronautics committess. To head-counters, Wydler is one of the more reliable votes for the Nixon Administration and the House Republican leadership. The outlook is for his continued reelection.

Census Data Pop. 467,694. Central city, 0%; suburban, 100%. Median family income, $14,102; families above $15,000: 45%; families below $3,000: 5%. Median years education, 12.4.

1972 Share of Federal Outlays $721,322,935

DOD	$122,243,289	HEW	$233,424,141
AEC	$2,872,019	HUD	$9,617,686
NASA	$1,398,055	DOI	$303,769
DOT	$9,676,059	USDA	$51,379,591
		Other	$290,408,326

Federal Military-Industrial Commitments

DOD Contractors AMF Inc. (Garden City), $26.967m: components for 750-pound bombs. Bulova Watch (Valley Stream), $11.060m: detonating fuzes for 81mm projectiles.

Economic Base Finance, insurance and real estate; electrical equipment and supplies, especially radio and television communication equipment; printing and publishing; machinery; and fabricated metal products, especially fabricated structural metal products. Also higher education (Adelphi Univ., and Hofstra Univ.).

The Voters

Registration 246,279 total. 123,057 D (50%); 89,461 R (36%); 2,936 L (1%); 4,103 C (2%); 26,722 blank, missing and void (11%).
Median voting age 46.5
Employment profile White collar, 65%. Blue collar, 24%. Service, 11%. Farm, –%.
Ethnic groups Black, 8%. Total foreign stock, 38%. Italy, 9%; USSR, 5%; Germany, 4%; Poland, Ireland, 3% each; UK, Austria, 2% each.

Presidential vote

1972	Nixon (R)	145,996	(63%)
	McGovern (D)	87,445	(37%)
1968	Nixon (R)	108,949	(50%)
	Humphrey (D)	98,158	(45%)
	Wallace (AI)	10,791	(5%)

Representative

John W. Wydler (R) Elected 1962; b. June 9, 1924, Brooklyn; home, Garden City; Brown U., 1941–42, 1945–47; Harvard Law School, LL.B., 1950; Army, WWII; USAFR; married, three children; Episcopalian.

Career Practicing atty., 1950– ; U.S. Atty's Office, 1953–59; Mbr., N.Y. State Investigation Commission to probe N.Y.C. school construction irregularities, 1959–60.

Offices 2334 RHOB, 202-225-5516. Also 150 Old Country Rd., Mineola, Long Island 11501, 516-248-7676.

Administrative Assistant Elizabeth D. Hoppel

Committees

Government Operations (3rd); Subs: Legislation and Military Operations; Special Studies (Ranking Mbr.).

Science and Aeronautics (3rd); Subs: Aeronautics and Space Technology (Ranking Mbr.); Manned Space Flight; Energy.

Group Ratings

	ADA	COPE	LWV	RIPON	NFU	LCV	CFA	NAB	NSI	ACA
1972	25	20	58	67	29	54	100	83	100	73
1971	24	33	50	65	36	–	50	–	–	71
1970	56	60	–	80	69	66	83	75	89	58

Key Votes

1) Busing	AGN	6) Cmbodia Bmbg	FOR	11) Chkg Acct Intrst	ABS
2) Strip Mines	FOR	7) Bust Hwy Trust	FOR	12) End HISC (HUAC)	AGN
3) Cut Mil $	AGN	8) Farm Sub Lmt	FOR	13) Nixon Sewer Veto	FOR
4) Rev Shrg	FOR	9) School Prayr	FOR	14) Corp Cmpaign $	AGN
5) Pub TV $	AGN	10) Cnsumr Prot	FOR	15) Pol $ Disclosr	AGN

Election Results

1972 general:	John W. Wydler (R)	133,332	(62%)
	Ferne M. Steckler (D)	67,709	(32%)
	Vincent A. Joy (C)	7,676	(4%)
	Paul F. Harper (L)	3,896	(2%)
1972 primary:	John W. Wydler (R), unopposed		
1970 general:	John W. Wydler (R)	91,787	(57%)
	Karen S. Burstein (D-L)	56,411	(35%)
	Donald A. Derham (C)	12,701	(8%)

SIXTH DISTRICT Political Background

New York's 6th congressional district consists of almost equal parts of the North Shore of Long Island in Nassau County and the Borough of Queens in New York City. The North Shore has long been famous for its rich and the powerful like Theodore Roosevelt, 26th President of the United States, and Jay Gatsby, a creation of F. Scott Fitzgerald's imagination. Today, huge WASPy estates still sit on peninsulas jutting out into Long Island Sound, as well as in towns like Sands Point and Port Washington. But politically more significant in the 6th-district portion of the North Shore are the wealthy, predominantly Jewish suburbs like Great Neck. Great Neck and the surrounding towns, despite their wealth, regularly produce large Democratic majorities. They even went for George McGovern in 1972. To the south, in the more middle-class, WASPy suburbs like Mineola and New Hyde Park, one finds the greatest Republican strength.

Another anomaly of the 6th is that its suburban Nassau portion is more liberal and Democratic than the part of it that lies in Queens and New York City. Political district-sculpting explains the phenomenon just as nicely as the indigenous political leanings of western Queens. The 6th's tortuous lines were carefully drawn by the Republican legislature to include neighborhoods of conservative homeowners and to exclude housing projects inhabited mainly by low-income Democrats.

The shape of the district was intended to oust a Democratic incumbent and preserve a Republican seat—in vain, as it turned out. The Democrat was Lester Wolff, an advertising man elected in a surprise from the North Shore 3rd district on the strength of 1964 LBJ landslide. Thereafter, he was reelected with surprisingly large margins. The Republican incumbent, the longtime (since 1958) Congressman from the old 6th district (one entirely within Queens), was Seymour Halpern, whose mildly liberal record helped him to big majorities.

On paper, then, the odds favored Halpern. But there were other factors. Back in 1969, the *Wall Street Journal* charged that Halpern had received loans of $100,000 from various banks, without collateral. The newspaper went on to say that the unusually favorable treatment was perhaps related to the high position Halpern enjoyed on the House Banking and Currency Committee. After the revelation, the Republican Congressman resigned his committee post and paid back the loans. In the 1970 election, Halpern was spared embarrassment when a borough-wide deal was struck, leaving him and other incumbents with the Republican, Conservative, and Democratic nominations. In 1972, however, Wolff let it be known that he would use the issue, whereupon Halpern retired precipitously.

The retirement gave the Republican nomination to conservative Queens Assemblyman John T. Gallagher, a politician who may have tested Wolff more severely than Halpern could have. Though Gallagher carried the Queens portion of the 6th, Wolff won on the basis of his larger margin on the North Shore, which he had represented for eight years. The result was an example, once again, of the advantage of incumbency. It appears likely that the same advantage will benefit Wolff, a man who cultivates his constituency unceasingly, in the Queens portion of the district in future elections.

Census Data   Pop. 467,602. Central city, 54%; suburban, 46%. Median family income, $14,483; families above $15,000: 47%; families below $3,000: 4%. Median years education, 12.4.

1972 Share of Federal Outlays $721,322,935

DOD	$122,243,289	HEW	$233,424,141
AEC	$2,872,019	HUD	$9,617,686
NASA	$1,398,055	DOI	$303,769
DOT	$9,676,059	USDA	$51,379,591
		Other	$290,408,326

Federal Military-Industrial Commitments

DOD Contractors Sperry Rand (Great Neck), $84.238m: various shipboard navigational units; radar and fire control systems. Etechoscope Corp. (Westbury), $13.157m: unspecified.

Economic Base Finance, insurance and real estate; electrical equipment and supplies; tourism; apparel and other textile products, especially women's and misses' outerwear; fabricated metal products, especially fabricated structural metal products; and printing and publishing.

The Voters

Registration 245,082 total. 125,393 D (51%); 79,792 R (33%); 4,049 L (2%); 5,652 C (2%); 30,196 blank, missing and void (12%).
Median voting age 47.1
Employment profile White collar, 68%. Blue collar, 22%. Service, 10%. Farm, –%.
Ethnic groups Black, 2%. Total foreign stock, 45%. Italy, 10%; USSR, Germany, 5% each; Poland, Ireland, 4% each; UK, 3%; Austria, 2%; Canada, Greece, 1% each.

Presidential vote

1972	Nixon (R)	140,072	(62%)
	McGovern (D)	84,480	(38%)
1968	Nixon (R)	108,298	(49%)
	Humphrey (D)	98,431	(45%)
	Wallace (AI)	12,106	(6%)

Representative

Lester Lionel Wolff (D) Elected 1964; b. Jan. 4, 1919, New York City; home, Great Neck; N.Y.U., 1939; Army Air Corps, WWII; married, two children; Jewish.

Career Head, Marketing Dept., Collegiate Inst., 1945–49; Chm. of Bd., Coordinated Marketing Agency, 1945–64; Bd. Mbr., Madison Life Insurance Co.; TV moderator, producer, "Between the Lines," 1948–60; Mbr., U.S. Trade Mission to Philippines, 1962, Malaysia and Hong Kong, 1963.

Offices 2463 RHOB, 202-225-5956. Also 156A Main St., Port Washington 11050, 516-767-4343.

Administrative Assistant Marc E. Miller

Committees

Foreign Affairs (13th); Subs: Asian and Pacific Affairs; Foreign Economic Policy; Near East and South Asia, Sp. Sub. on International Drug Problems (Chm.).

Veterans' Affairs (13th); Subs: Education and Training; Hospitals.

Group Ratings

	ADA	COPE	LWV	RIPON	NFU	LCV	CFA	NAB	NSI	ACA
1972	94	82	92	83	67	76	100	8	0	5
1971	92	82	89	71	80	–	100	–	–	25
1970	84	92	–	80	92	100	69	0	10	27

Key Votes

1) Busing	FOR	6) Cmbodia Bmbg	AGN	11) Chkg Acct Intrst	ABS
2) Strip Mines	AGN	7) Bust Hwy Trust	FOR	12) End HISC (HUAC)	FOR
3) Cut Mil $	FOR	8) Farm Sub Lmt	FOR	13) Nixon Sewer Veto	FOR
4) Rev Shrg	FOR	9) School Prayr	FOR	14) Corp Cmpaign $	FOR
5) Pub TV $	FOR	10) Cnsumr Prot	FOR	15) Pol $ Disclosr	AGN

Election Results

1972 general:	Lester L. Wolff (D-L)	109,620	(52%)
	John T. Gallagher (R-C)	103,038	(48%)
1972 primary:	Lester L. Wolff (D), unopposed		
1970 general:	Lester L. Wolff (D-L)	94,414	(54%)
	Raymond J. Rice (R)	66,196	(38%)
	Lola Carmardi (C)	12,925	(7%)

SEVENTH DISTRICT Political Background

The 7th district of New York in southern Queens takes in a series of middle-class neighborhoods of varying ethnic composition. Just north of Kennedy Airport is the two-family-house neighborhood of Ozone Park, and along Queens Boulevard are the high-rise apartments of Rego Park. But the district's largest ethnic group is black—making up some 37% of the residents of the 7th. The blacks live in the near-slum conditions of South Jamaica and in the middle-class neighborhoods of St. Albans and Springfield Gardens to the east.

The 7th is a heavily Democratic district, largely because of the solidly Democratic allegiance of its black voters. But the 7th is also conservatively inclined, full of homeowners who feel oppressed by New York's high taxes and high cost of living, and who feel neglected by the city administration of Mayor John Lindsay. In 1969, Lindsay ran poorly here, but in 1970, Sen. James Buckley did quite well. In congressional elections, the 7th has backed moderate-to-liberal Democrat Joseph P. Addabbo since the election of 1960. For some years, Addabbo, in the tradition of most New York Congressmen, was a quiet backbencher. He managed to win a seat on the Appropriations Committee and made few waves. But in 1970, he emerged as a relatively vocal and fierce opponent of the SST—a position shared by many of his constituents who are plagued by the noise of airliners taking off, landing, or stacked up over nearby Kennedy Airport.

Addabbo bucked tradition in the House even more strenuously during the first months of the 93rd Congress. The Congressman had for some years opposed the Nixon policies in Indochina, quietly. But as a member, and one with considerable seniority, of the Appropriations Committee, he took up the cause of stopping the Cambodia bombing when the Defense Department requested a supplemental appropriation to finance the affair for the rest of the fiscal year—something usually approved routinely. The move to halt the bombing lost in the Appropriations Committee, whereupon antiwar members—their numbers augmented by recent converts—took the issue to the floor.

Once there, the decisive vote came on Addabbo's own amendment that prohibited the Pentagon from spending any transferred funds on the bombing in Cambodia. It passed, 219–189, carrying an absolute majority of the entire House. The occasion marked the first ever in which the House voted to stop American involvement in the Indochina war. President Nixon vetoed the bill because of Addabbo's amendment, but he subsequently agreed to a compromise that cut off the bombing on August 15, 1973.

Census Data Pop. 467,449. Central city, 100%; suburban, 0%. Median family income, $11,317; families above $15,000: 30%; families below $3,000: 7%. Median years education, 12.1.

1972 Share of Federal Outlays $721,322,935

DOD	$122,243,289	HEW	$233,424,141
AEC	$2,872,019	HUD	$9,617,686
NASA	$1,398,055	DOI	$303,769
DOT	$9,676,059	USDA	$51,379,591
		Other	$290,408,326

Federal Military-Industrial Commitments

DOD Installations Naval Hospital (St. Albans); closed, 1974.

Economic Base Finance, insurance and real estate; electrical equipment and supplies; food and kindred products; apparel and other textile products, especially women's and misses' outerwear; fabricated metal products, especially fabricated structural metal products; and tourism.

The Voters

Registration 187,716 total. 129,826 D (69%); 32,886 R (18%); 5,620 L (3%); 2,814 C (1%); 16,570 blank, missing and void (9%).
Median voting age 45.6
Employment profile White collar, 59%. Blue collar, 27%. Service, 14%. Farm, –%.
Ethnic groups Black, 37%. Spanish, 2%. Total foreign stock, 41%. Italy, 7%; USSR, 5%; Poland, Germany, 4% each; Austria, Ireland, 2% each; UK, 1%.

Presidential vote

1972	Nixon (R)	66,305	(41%)
	McGovern (D)	93,806	(59%)
1968	Nixon (R)	46,602	(29%)
	Humphrey (D)	108,562	(67%)
	Wallace (AI)	7,658	(5%)

Representative

Joseph P. Addabbo (D) Elected 1960; b. March 17, 1925, Queens; home, Ozone Park; City Col. of N.Y., 1942–44; St. John's Law School, LL.B., 1946; married, three children; Catholic.

Career Practicing atty., 1946– .

Offices 2440 RHOB, 202-225-3461. Also 96-11 101st Ave., Ozone Park, 212-849-6625.

Administrative Assistant Mrs. Helen T. MacDonald

Committees

Appropriations (17th); Subs: Defense; Treasury, Postal Service, General Government.

Sel. Com. on Small Business (7th); Subs: Minority Small Business Enterprise and Franchising (Chm.); Government Procurement and International Trade; Special Small Busines Problems.

Group Ratings

	ADA	COPE	LWV	RIPON	NFU	LCV	CFA	NAB	NSI	ACA
1972	94	91	83	78	83	73	100	18	10	4
1971	76	92	78	65	87	–	100	–	–	23
1970	80	92	–	65	100	73	89	8	33	12

Key Votes

1) Busing	FOR	6) Cmbodia Bmbg	AGN	11) Chkg Acct Intrst	FOR
2) Strip Mines	AGN	7) Bust Hwy Trust	FOR	12) End HISC (HUAC)	FOR
3) Cut Mil $	FOR	8) Farm Sub Lmt	ABS	13) Nixon Sewer Veto	AGN
4) Rev Shrg	FOR	9) School Prayr	FOR	14) Corp Cmpaign $	AGN
5) Pub TV $	FOR	10) Cnsumr Prot	FOR	15) Pol $ Disclosr	AGN

Election Results

1972 general:	Joseph P. Addabbo (D-L)	104,110	(75%)
	John E. Hall (R)	28,296	(21%)
	Frank O. Wuertz (C)	6,053	(4%)
1972 primary:	Frank J. Brasco (D)	8,850	(67%)
	Gerald R. Jacobs (D)	4,284	(33%)
1970 general:	Joseph P. Addabbo (D-R-L)	112,983	(91%)
	Christopher T. Acer (C)	11,515	(9%)

EIGHTH DISTRICT Political Background

Roughly speaking, the 8th district of New York encompasses the central part of the borough of Queens. The tortuous boundaries of the district were drawn to keep as many conservative and Republican voters as possible within the confines of the adjacent 6th and 9th districts. In effect, the 8th is a seat Republican redistricters conceded to the Democrats. The district radiates in three directions like spokes from the hub of a wheel. The hub is Flushing Meadow Park, site of the World's Fairs of 1939 and 1964, and today the home of Shea Stadium's Mets and Jets. One of the spokes passes through the middle-class and predominantly Jewish neighborhood of Flushing on its way to Long Island Sound. Another proceeds east through Fresh Meadows and a neighborhood called Utopia, and on towards the Nassau County line. The third spoke moves west from Flushing Meadows to include the high-rise apartment complex of Lefrak City, a small black ghetto, and the two- and four-family houses of Jackson Heights.

These seemingly disparate areas have certain things in common. All have large Jewish populations; it is as if the redistricters had drawn together virtually all the predominantly Jewish neighborhoods in Queens. And writhing about, the district lines manage to corral most of the borough's big high-rise apartment complexes and many of its public-housing projects. The 8th is postwar Queens. Before World War II, most of the borough was given over to neighborhoods of one- and two-family houses, inhabited by Irish, Italian, and many German immigrants. It was a conservative Republican stronghold in a liberal Democratic city. Most of Queens' population growth since has resulted from the construction of high-rises, the majority of whose occupants are Jewish liberal Democrats.

So the district as a whole is overwhelmingly Democratic. But it is worth noting that George McGovern barely managed to carry the 8th—a measure of the disaffection for his candidacy in the Jewish middle-class community. In congressional elections, however, the district happily returns liberal Democrat Benjamin Rosenthal with resounding majorities. The Congressman was apparently not much hurt by the position he took on the Forest Hills controversy. This was one in which local residents fiercely opposed a Lindsay administration proposal to build three 24-story high-rises for lower- and middle-income residents. Rosenthal came out against the specific proposal, but endorsed the idea of scatter-site housing in principle. And Rosenthal favored the compromise finally worked out which reduced the size of the project by one-half.

Rosenthal has become one of the foremost advocates of consumer legislation in Congress, not so much because of actions taken from his committee assignments as from the legislation he sponsors. His most important piece of legislation is one that seeks to establish a federal Consumer

Protection Agency, which would constitute a kind of advocate body, responsible to Congress rather than the executive. It would assert consumer interests before federal regulatory agencies and in departmental rule-making procedures.

In 1970, Rosenthal's measure was killed in the Rules Committee when Richard Bolling refused to interrupt a Caribbean vacation to cast a vote in favor of the idea. Later, in October 1972, the measure died in the Senate during the closing days of the session. But the Consumer Protection Agency issue will likely surface again in the 93rd Congress. Rosenthal has also hired student interns, whom he calls Rosenthal's Roustabouts; the young people have written reports on the Better Business Bureau and prescription drug advertising. The Queens' politician presents one of the few examples of a Congressman who has worked outside the committee structure on major issues.

One reason Rosenthal works outside the structure is that he is forced to. At the beginning of the 93rd Congress, Californian Chet Holifield, Chairman of the full Government Operations Committee, refused to give Rosenthal something he actively sought: namely, the chairmanship of a consumer affairs subcommittee. Disappointed by Holifield's perversity and unhappy with what many regarded as his do-nothing leadership, Rosenthal mounted a campaign to unseat the Chairman—one that the New Yorker of course lost. As a result, Holifield did not even ask Rosenthal whether he wanted an available subcommittee chairmanship, though he was next in line for it. The Queens Congressman, however, continues to chair the Europe Subcommittee of the Foreign Affairs Committee.

Rosenthal's career parallels the metamorphosis experienced by the New York City congressional delegation over the last 10 years. He was first selected to run for the seat by the regular Queens organization. During the politician's first few years in the House, he stayed quiet and went unnoticed. But in the early stages of American involvement in Vietnam, Rosenthal found himself opposed to the war policies of the Johnson Administration. He then began to vote with a small group of antiwar Congressman, most of whom represented constituencies far less middle-class than his own. Unlike traditional New York Congressman, Rosenthal has considered the House a place worthy of a full-time effort, not just somewhere to hang around waiting for a judgeship. Nor does the Congressman harbor ambitions for higher office, endemic among so many New York Representatives. All indications are that Rosenthal will remain in Washington for some years to come.

Census Data   Pop. 467,691. Central city, 100%; suburban, 0%. Median family income, $12,244; families above $15,000: 35%; families below $3,000: 5%. Median years education, 12.3.

1972 Share of Federal Outlays $721,322,935

DOD	$122,243,289	HEW	$233,424,141
AEC	$2,872,019	HUD	$9,617,686
NASA	$1,398,055	DOI	$303,769
DOT	$9,676,059	USDA	$51,379,591
		Other	$290,408,326

Federal Military-Industrial Commitments

DOD Contractors Kollsman Instrument (Elmhurst), $23.495m: aircraft altimeters.

Economic Base Finance, insurance and real estate; electrical equipment and supplies; food and kindred products; apparel and other textile products, especially women's and misses' outerwear; tourism; and fabricated metal products, especially fabricated structural metal products. Also higher education (CUNY, Queens; and St. John's Univ.).

The Voters

Registration 212,267 total. 144,932 D (68%); 37,639 R (18%); 5,769 L (3%); 4,075 C (2%); 19,852 blank, missing and void (9%).
Median voting age 45.5
Employment profile White collar, 68%. Blue collar, 23%. Service, 9%. Farm, –%.
Ethnic groups Black, 4%. Chinese, 1%. Spanish 2%. Total foreign stock, 59%. Italy, USSR, 8% each; Poland, 6%; Ireland, Germany, 4% each; Austria, 3%; UK, Greece, 2% each; Hungary, Rumania, 1% each.

Presidential vote

1972	Nixon (R)	94,222	(50%)
	McGovern (D)	95,212	(50%)
1968	Nixon (R)	61,484	(33%)
	Humphrey (D)	117,111	(63%)
	Wallace (AI)	8,709	(5%)

Representative

Benjamin S. Rosenthal (D) Elected 1962; b. June 8, 1923, New York City; home, Elmhurst, L.I.; Brooklyn Col., LL.B., 1949; New York U., LL.M., 1952; Army, WWII; married, two children; Jewish.

Career Practicing atty., 1949–70.

Offices 2453 RHOB, 202-225-2601. Also GPO Bldg., 41-65 Main St., Flushing, L.I. 11351, 212-939-8200.

Administrative Assistant Mary W. Davis

Committees

Foreign Affairs (9th); Subs: Europe (Chm.); Inter-American Affairs; International Organizations and Movements.

Government Operations (11th); Subs: Intergovernmental Relations; Legislation and Military Operations.

Group Ratings

	ADA	COPE	LWV	RIPON	NFU	LCV	CFA	NAB	NSI	ACA
1972	100	91	100	73	86	87	100	9	0	9
1971	100	82	100	89	73	–	88	–	–	18
1970	96	100	–	75	92	83	100	0	0	17

Key Votes

1) Busing	FOR	6) Cmbodia Bmbg	AGN	11) Chkg Acct Intrst	ABS
2) Strip Mines	AGN	7) Bust Hwy Trust	FOR	12) End HISC (HUAC)	FOR
3) Cut Mil $	FOR	8) Farm Sub Lmt	FOR	13) Nixon Sewer Veto	AGN
4) Rev Shrg	FOR	9) School Prayr	AGN	14) Corp Cmpaign $	AGN
5) Pub TV $	FOR	10) Cnsumr Prot	FOR	15) Pol $ Disclosr	FOR

Election Results

1972 general:	Benjamin S. Rosenthal (D-L)	110,293	(65%)
	Frank A. La Pina (R-C)	60,166	(35%)
1972 primary:	Benjamin S. Rosenthal (D), unopposed		
1970 general:	Benjamin S. Rosenthal (D-L)	93,666	(63%)
	Cosmo J. Di Tucci (R-C)	55,406	(37%)

NINTH DISTRICT Political Background

It can be said with some certainty that Archie Bunker lives in the 9th congressional district of Queens. The aerial shot taken by TV cameramen of Archie's neighborhood shows the kind of aging, though still neatly maintained, one- and two-family homes that line the streets of Jackson Heights, Long Island City, Ridgewood, or Glendale. Moreover, Archie's views are a fairly accurate, if exaggerated, portrayal of what appears from an examination of election returns to be the solid majority opinion in the 9th district. Geographically, the 9th is the Queens district lying nearest Manhattan's chic and liberal Upper East Side—but farthest away in spirit. People in Queens refer to Manhattan as "the City," as if it were some distant and foreign place. And if the residents of Queens seldom sample the cultural attractions of Manhattan, one reason is that they cannot afford most of them.

The district lines of the 9th were carefully drawn to include the middle-class, heavily Catholic Queens neighborhoods of conservative homeowners—people who live on salaries or wages that make middle-class respectability hard to maintain in New York City. It is ironic—or at least a reversal of the conventional wisdom retained from the New Deal—that the people of the wealthy East Side voted 58% for George McGovern, while those across the East River, living amid the factories of Sunnyside and Long Island City, went 73% for Richard Nixon. The 9th district total stems in part from the ethnic composition of its constituency: there are virtually no blacks or Puerto Ricans living within the 9th district, and many of its present homeowners, living in neighborhoods along the Brooklyn line, fear that there soon will be. So the 9th, lying in the heart of supposedly Democratic New York City, produced the largest Nixon percentage in New York state. In fact, Nixon's 73% was exceeded in only two other congressional districts among the Eastern states, both of them in the heavily Republican area of tradition-bound Pennsylvania Dutch country.

This part of Queens was not always so enthusiastically Republican. The historic allegiance of at least a large minority of its residents lies with the Democratic party of Franklin D. Roosevelt and John F. Kennedy. But during the years the Democrats appeared more interested in ending the Vietnam war and advancing the interests of blacks and Puerto Ricans than the welfare of people like Archie Bunker, the 9th shifted solidly to the Republicans.

A similar shift can be discerned in the career of the 9th's Congressman, James J. Delaney. First elected in 1944, Delaney was defeated in the Republican sweep of 1946, then returned to the House in 1948, where he has served to the present day. At one time, the Queens politician was considered a reliable enough supporter of Democratic programs to win a seat on the House Rules Committee, on which Delaney now ranks just behind Ray Madden of Indiana, Rules' 82-year-old Chairman. The New Yorker's most significant legislative achievement is the Delaney Amendment, one that prohibits the sale of any drug known to produce any trace of cancer in animals. The amendment was supported by liberal Democrats and opposed by the drug industry, which maintained that an agent that created a cancer in an animal will not necessarily do the same in a human being.

But Delaney has dissented from Democratic positions on important issues more and more in recent years. Because he had a vote on Rules, the Congressman singlehandedly held up federal aid to education for more than five years. Delaney opposed the legislation because it contained no provision for aid to Catholic schools. By the early 1970s, the Congressman's voting record was almost as Republican as Democratic, and his relationship with most other members of the New York City delegation was practically nonexistent. In 1970, he even endorsed Conservative party Senate candidate James Buckley, and himself obtained the Republican and Conservative nominations in the general election.

Delaney's activities were too much for Queens County Democratic boss Matthew J. Troy, Jr., a picturesque character who deserves much more space than the *Almanac* can give him. The boss has exhibited an interesting combination of views. He raised the flag at City Hall to full mast when Mayor John Lindsay ordered it at half mast on Moratorium Day in 1969; later, in 1971, Troy was an early supporter of George McGovern's presidential candidacy. As Democratic County Leader, Troy was irritated by Delaney's close relationship with the Conservatives, who have been cutting heavily into the Democratic majorities needed by the boss. So in 1972, Troy ran City Councilman Thomas Manton against Delaney in the Democratic primary. Manton, a former policeman whose politics had mellowed, much as Troy's had, waged a vigorous campaign and wound up with 43% of the votes. Even if Manton had won, Delaney might still have prevailed in the general election as the Republican-Conservative nominee. But winning under such a banner could have cost Delaney his seniority and his seat on Rules.

Perhaps because of fears of this sort, or perhaps because of the increasing intransigence of the Nixon Administration, Delaney at the beginning of the 93rd Congress appeared more in line with his Democratic colleagues. He was even elected Chairman of the New York City congressional delegation, a position for which he had no chance a year earlier. Though Delaney will be 73 in 1974, he shows no signs of wanting to retire. But if he does, a possible successor is 33-year-old Patrick Delaney, who managed his father's 1972 primary campaign. It is also entirely possible that if the incumbent is not a candidate, a Republican-Conservative will capture the district. And that is what must have been in the minds of the Republican redistricters who drew the 9th's current boundaries.

Census Data Pop. 467,207. Central city, 100%; suburban, 0%. Median family income, $10,657; families above $15,000: 24%; families below $3,000: 7%. Median years education, 10.8.

1972 Share of Federal Outlays $721,322,935

DOD	$122,243,289	HEW	$233,424,141
AEC	$2,872,019	HUD	$9,617,686
NASA	$1,398,055	DOI	$303,769
DOT	$9,676,059	USDA	$51,379,591
		Other	$290,408,326

Federal Military-Industrial Commitments

No installations or contractors receiving awards greater than $5,000,000.

Economic Base Finance, insurance and real estate; electrical equipment and supplies; food and kindred products; apparel and other textile products, especially women's and misses' outerwear; and fabricated metal products, especially structural metal products.

The Voters

Registration 201,267 total. 118,725 D (59%); 57,131 R (28%); 3,373 L (2%); 7,286 C (4%); 14,752 blank, missing and void (7%).
Median voting age 48.7
Employment profile White collar, 53%. Blue collar, 34%. Service, 13%. Farm, –%.
Ethnic groups Black, 2%. Spanish, 2%. Total foreign stock, 55%. Italy, 14%; Germany, 8%; Poland, USSR, 3% each; Austria, Greece, UK, 2% each; Czechoslovakia, Hungary, 1% each.

Presidential vote

1972	Nixon (R)	128,699	(73%)
	McGovern (D)	46,700	(27%)
1968	Nixon (R)	98,641	(54%)
	Humphrey (D)	68,644	(37%)
	Wallace (AI)	16,997	(9%)

Representative

James J. Delaney (D) Elected 1948; b. March 19, 1901, New York City; home, Long Island City; St. John's U., LL.B., 1932; married, one son; Catholic.

Career Asst. Dist. Atty., Queens County, 1936–44; U.S. House of Reps., 1945–47.

Offices 2267 RHOB, 202-225-3965. Also 100-35 Metropolitan Ave., Forest Hills 11375, 212-793-0729.

Administrative Assistant Dolores Cook

Committees

Rules (2nd).

Group Ratings

	ADA	COPE	LWV	RIPON	NFU	LCV	CFA	NAB	NSI	ACA
1972	31	82	50	62	67	32	100	44	100	55
1971	24	64	25	38	38	–	57	–	–	58
1970	40	75	–	25	85	73	82	27	75	47

Key Votes

1) Busing	AGN	6) Cmbodia Bmbg	ABS	11) Chkg Acct Intrst	ABS
2) Strip Mines	AGN	7) Bust Hwy Trust	FOR	12) End HISC (HUAC)	AGN
3) Cut Mil $	ABS	8) Farm Sub Lmt	FOR	13) Nixon Sewer Veto	AGN
4) Rev Shrg	FOR	9) School Prayr	FOR	14) Corp Cmpaign $	FOR
5) Pub TV $	AGN	10) Cnsumr Prot	FOR	15) Pol $ Disclosr	AGN

Election Results

1972 general:	James J. Delaney (D-R-C)	141,323	(93%)
	Loretta E. Gressey (L)	9,965	(7%)
1972 primary:	James J. Delaney (D)	15,570	(56%)
	Thomas J. Manton (D)	12,405	(46%)
1970 general:	James J. Delaney (D-R-C)	102,205	(92%)
	Rose L. Rubin (L)	9,025	(8%)

TENTH DISTRICT Political Background

In early 1973, Mario Biaggi looked like tha man most likely to become the next Mayor of New York City. For eight years, City Hall was in the hands of John V. Lindsay, an Ivy League WASP who had been elected twice with less than an absolute majority of the vote and who each time had failed to carry the city outside Manhattan. A discussion with any cab driver in Fun City made it abundantly clear that Lindsay was more than a little unpopular in the middle-class residential neighborhoods of the outer boroughs, where a vast majority of New York voters live. Part of the discontent stemmed from a feeling that Lindsay was overly sympathetic to blacks and Puerto Ricans, and to a related fear of increasing crime. Part of it stemmed from a deterioration of city services, most notably in the middle-class areas at the edges of the city. Part of it stemmed from a basic cultural hostility to the kind of effete, snobbish Manhattanites who were perceived as Lindsay's chief backers.

For all of this, 10th district Congressman Mario Biaggi seemed like a campaign consultant's dream. When he retired in 1968, Biaggi was the most decorated member of the New York Police force. He was later elected Congressman three times from a heavily Italian, middle-class district in the Bronx (to which a similar portion of Queens was added in 1972), with the endorsement of both the Democratic and Conservative parties, and his district was formerly represented by a Republican. Biaggi still lived in a small apartment on Mosholu Boulevard in the Bronx, and he spoke the language of middle-class New Yorkers in clear, unmistakable fashion.

The Italian-American mayoral aspirant was against crime and said he knew what to do about it. He was also, of course, for proper city services in middle-class areas. But Biaggi was by no means a knee-jerk conservative. He had worked to expose and improve the conditions of hospitals for retarded children. As a Congressman, he had moved to uphold the basic rights of servicemen. And he had voted for at least some measures to end the Vietnam war. Biaggi was, as the 1972 *Almanac* put it, a kind of urban populist with a law-and-order accent. Accordingly, he represented pretty accurately the views of hundreds of thousands of New Yorkers, and in early 1973, it was plain that Biaggi was the only mayoral candidate who could evoke genuine enthusiasm and massive popular support.

But Biaggi was certainly not getting support from any of what John Lindsay long ago called the City's "power brokers." No Democratic boss backed the Congressman. Neither, of course, did Lindsay, and Gov. Nelson Rockefeller appeared almost as eager to do in Biaggi as he was Lindsay. Biaggi did receive the support of a fraction of the Conservative party, and then its nomination, after giving the party several assurances about his past.

If there was genuine popular enthusiasm for Biaggi, there was also widespread suspicion about his past. The issue was not simply that he was of Italian descent, as Biaggi charged. There were questions about the circumstances under which Biaggi, as an off-duty policeman, had killed a gunman in a car, an act of presumed heroism for which he was decorated. There were questions about who was financing his campaign. And there were questions about what he had said to a grand jury investigating private immigration bills. Both the *New York Times* and the New York *Daily News* assigned reporters to dig out some of the answers. In April of 1973, both papers broke the story on the same day: Biaggi had taken the Fifth Amendment before the grand jury. In itself, perhaps, this was not so bad, but he had denied doing so several times during the campaign—most notably when the Conservative party leaders asked him about it before giving him their party's nomination.

There followed a fracas in which Biaggi attempted to get a federal court to reveal some, but not all, of the grand jury transcripts. The judge (of Italian descent himself) ordered all of the records made public, and they confirmed the newspaper charges. Biaggi did take the Fifth, and then said he didn't. The story almost kept the Watergate revelations—many of them breaking at the same time—out of headlines on New York newspapers. The Biaggi campaign collapsed. In the Democratic primary held in June, the Bronx Congressman took only 21% of the votes and finished third in a field of four. At this writing, Biaggi is still on the November ballot as the Conservative candidate, but no one gives him a chance.

In the June primary, virtually all of Biaggi's support came from heavily Italian, middle-class neighborhoods. Because of his strength in these places, he clearly would have won the primary without a runoff (necessary under New York law when no candidate gets 40% of the vote), if the April charges had not surfaced. In his own district—the east Bronx, and the Whitestone and Astoria sections of Queens—Biaggi ran well enough to expect reelection to Congress. Whether he will continue to get the Conservative nomination, after lying to its leaders, is less clear. The incumbent might encounter strong Republican opposition. One possibility is ex-Rep (1953–68) Paul Fino, who retired to a judgeship but apparently found politics more interesting and left the bench after a few years. Another is state Sen. John Calandra, the Bronx Republican leader, who is feuding with Fino. In any case, the 10th-district race in 1974 will certainly turn out closer than the one held in 1972.

But beyond the 1974 congressional campaign, one has to wonder what might be going on in the minds of the people who have furnished the bedrock of support for politicians like Biaggi. These are the middle-class homeowners of outer New York City—the Archie Bunker people, as they have become known. During the past decade, they have grown profoundly unhappy with the economic and ethnic trends in the City, and long for a reimposition of the kind of moral certainties so many of them learned in Catholic schools. The homeowners supported law-and-order candidate Mario Biaggi only to learn later that he had lied about his own encounter with the law; they abandoned life-long loyalties to the Democratic party to vote for law-and-order candidate Richard Nixon, who then emerged as the politician who presided over the most lawless presidential campaign in American history.

Many middle-class New Yorkers remain defiantly loyal to their heroes. *New York* magazine reporters who canvassed Queens bars on Watergate found dozens of vocal Nixon supporters, and the 1973 mayoral primary showed the tainted Biaggi still able to carry the middle-class Italian neighborhoods easily. Yet behind the show of bravado must lie a deep disillusionment. As the price of food and clothing continues to climb, it has become painfully clear that the politicians who paid the most verbal heed to the problems of these people were really interested in other things—Watergate, if anything, demonstrated that the law-and-order line of recent years was a cynical sham. Out in the 10th district, people by this time may have concluded that nothing in politics is for them, that they have been manipulated back and forth so much that they have nowhere to turn. What the state of affairs means for the future of American politics nobody really knows.

Census Data Pop. 474,745. Central city, 100%; suburban, 0%. Median family income, $9,988; families above $15,000: 22%; families below $3,000: 9%. Median years education, 10.7.

1972 Share of Federal Outlays $732,035,652

DOD	$124,058,784	HEW	$236,890,836
AEC	$2,914,673	HUD	$9,760,523
NASA	$1,418,818	DOI	$308,281
DOT	$9,819,763	USDA	$52,142,654
		Other	$294,721,320

Federal Military-Industrial Commitments

DOD Contractors EDO Corp. (College Point), $21.320m: sonar and minesweeping equipment. Loral Co. (Bronx), $9.256m: aircraft electronic warfare equipment.

Economic Base Finance, insurance and real estate; apparel and other textile products, especially women's and misses' outerwear; food and kindred products; electrical equipment and supplies; and fabricated metal products, especially fabricated structural metal products. Also higher education (Fordham Univ.).

The Voters

Registration 190,204 total. 124,537 D (65%); 42,253 R (22%); 3,983 L (2%); 5,609 C (3%); 13,822 blank, missing and void (7%).
Median voting age 45.8
Employment profile White collar, 52%. Blue collar, 34%. Service, 14%. Farm, –%.
Ethnic groups Black, 13%. Spanish 9%. Total foreign stock, 47%. Italy, 17%; Ireland, 6%; Germany, 3%; USSR, Poland, Greece, UK, 2% each; Austria, 1%.

Presidential vote

1972	Nixon (R)	103,372	(63%)
	McGovern (D)	60,343	(37%)
1968	Nixon (R)	77,684	(46%)
	Humphrey (D)	78,323	(46%)
	Wallace (AI)	13,830	(8%)

Representative

Mario Biaggi (D) Elected 1969; b. Oct. 26, 1917, New York City; home, Bronx; N.Y. Law School, LL.B., 1963; married, four children; Catholic.

Career U.S. Post Office, 1936–42; N.Y. City Police Dept., 1942–65; Community Relations Specialist, N.Y. State Div. of Housing, 1961–63; Asst. to Sec. of State, N.Y., 1961–65; Pres., Natl. Police Officers Assn., 1967; Consultant, Pres., Grand Council of Columbia Assn. in Civil Service; practicing atty., 1966– .

Offices 211 CHOB, 202-225-2464. Also 2004 Williamsbridge Rd., Bronx 10461, 212-931-0100, and 21-77 31st St., Astoria 11102, 212-932-4448.

Administrative Assistant Peter K. Ilchuck

Committees

Education and Labor (15th); Subs: No. 1 (Gen. Sub. on Education); No. 3 (Gen. Sub. on Labor); No. 6 (Sp. Sub. on Education).

Merchant Marine and Fisheries (11th); Subs: Coast Guard and Navigation; Fisheries and Wildlife Conservation and the Environment; Oceanography.

Group Ratings

	ADA	COPE	LWV	RIPON	NFU	LCV	CFA	NAB	NSI	ACA
1972	56	91	75	50	71	40	100	25	50	27
1971	65	83	67	65	60	–	83	–	–	32
1970	52	83	–	59	100	100	50	9	66	37

Key Votes

1) Busing	AGN	6) Cmbodia Bmbg	ABS	11) Chkg Acct Intrst	ABS
2) Strip Mines	AGN	7) Bust Hwy Trust	ABS	12) End HISC (HUAC)	ABS
3) Cut Mil $	ABS	8) Farm Sub Lmt	AGN	13) Nixon Sewer Veto	AGN
4) Rev Shrg	FOR	9) School Prayr	AGN	14) Corp Cmpaign $	FOR
5) Pub TV $	FOR	10) Cnsumr Prot	FOR	15) Pol $ Disclosr	AGN

Election Results

1972 general:	Mario Biaggi (D-R-C)	130,200	(94%)
	Michael S. Bank (L)	8,397	(6%)

1972 primary:	Mario Biaggi (D), unopposed		
1970 general:	Mario Biaggi (D-C)	106,942	(70%)
	Joseph F. Periconi (R)	38,173	(25%)
	John Patrick Hagan (L)	7,970	(5%)

ELEVENTH DISTRICT Political Background

The 11th district of New York is the southeastern corner of Brooklyn, the extreme southern and southeastern edges of Queens, and the Rockaway Peninsula. Also here is Kennedy Airport. Separated from each other by marshy Jamaica Bay, these are geographically disparate areas and the neighborhoods contained within them are diverse. East New York in Brooklyn is an aging Italian community, hard by the black ghetto of Brownsville, which lies in such miserable condition that it is rapidly being abandoned. To the south, Carnarsie and Flatlands are middle-class Italian and Jewish communities. These two places were developed on the swampland along Jamaica Bay some time after the rest of Brooklyn; here, in 1970, the borough's first suburban-style shopping center was opened. The Rockaways are largely Jewish, with a black ghetto at one end. North of Kennedy Airport, entirely cut off from the rest of the district, is the middle-class black neighborhood of Springfield Gardens.

In the face of an increasing conservatism among its voters, the 11th remains heavily Democratic in local elections. Even as it went for Richard Nixon in 1972, the district provided Democratic Congressman Frank Brasco a 2–1 reelection margin. Brasco was first elected in 1966, when Eugene Keogh, then 59, retired after 30 years in the House. When Keogh quit, he was the third-ranking Democrat on the House Ways and Means Committee, but had apparently given up all hope of ever succeeding to Wilbur Mills' chairmanship. Brasco was slated by the Brooklyn Democratic machine, to which he has remained loyal; at the same time, the Congressman has compiled a solidly liberal, antiwar record.

So a rather peculiar event was marked when in October 1972 Brasco joined all of the Republicans on the Banking and Currency Committee along with several of its Southern Democrats and voted against having a Watergate investigation. Writing in the *Washington Monthly*, Marjorie Boyd suggested that Brasco's vote was obtained by Nixon operatives in exchange for the Administration taking no action against Brasco for his intercession on behalf of a reputed Mafia-connected business with a government agency. The Congressman maintains, however, that his vote was based on a concern that the seven Watergate defendants, then under indictment, receive a fair trial. The decision of the committee, of course, resulted in no Watergate investigation before the 1972 election.

What effect, if any, Brasco's nay-saying will have on the 1974 election in the 11th district is unclear. The district being so disparate, many of its residents have little idea who Brasco is and simply vote the Democratic ticket. Moreover, the area encompassed by the 11th has had no history of organized opposition to the machines in either Brooklyn or Queens.

Census Data Pop. 469,790. Central city, 100%; suburban, 0%. Median family income, $10,834; families above $15,000: 26%; families below $3,000: 9%. Median years education, 11.7.

1972 Share of Federal Outlays $724,893,840

DOD	$122,848,454	HEW	$234,579,706
AEC	$2,886,237	HUD	$9,665,298
NASA	$1,404,976	DOI	$305,273
DOT	$9,723,961	USDA	$51,633,945
		Other	$291,845,990

Federal Military-Industrial Commitments

DOD Contractors Pan American Airways (JFK Airport), $56.078m: transportation services. Seaboard World Airlines (Jamaica), $34.457m: transportation services. TWA (JFK Airport), $27.344m: transportation services. Overseas National Airways (Jamaica), $25.973m: transportation services.

DOD Installations Naval Station (Brooklyn; reduced substantially by 1974.)

Economic Base Finance, insurance and real estate; apparel and other textile products, especially women's and misses' outerwear; food and kindred products; fabricated metal products; and textile mill products, especially knitting mill products.

The Voters

Registration 182,108 total. 133,035 D (73%); 27,422 R (15%); 5,038 L (3%); 4,001 C (2%); 12,612 blank, missing and void (7%).
Median voting age 43.7
Employment profile White collar, 58%. Blue collar, 31%. Service, 11%. Farm, –%.
Ethnic groups Black, 17%. Spanish, 6%. Total foreign stock, 41%. Italy, 9%; USSR, 8%; Poland, 6%; Germany, Austria, Ireland, 2% each; UK, 1%.

Presidential vote

1972	Nixon (R)	80,662	(52%)
	McGovern (D)	75,129	(48%)
1968	Nixon (R)	52,709	(33%)
	Humphrey (D)	95,497	(61%)
	Wallace (AI)	9,281	(6%)

Representative

Frank James Brasco (D) Elected 1966; b. Oct., 15, 1932, Brooklyn; home, Brooklyn; Brooklyn Col., B.A., 1955, LL.B., 1957; Capt. USAR; married, four children; Catholic.

Career Staff Atty., Legal Aid Society, 1957–61; Asst. Dist. Atty., Rackets Bureau, Kings County, 1961–66; JAGC; 4th Judge Advocate General Corps; Athletic Director, Brownsville Boys Club.

Offices 405 CHOB, 202-225-5471. Also 1449 Rockaway Parkway, Brooklyn 11236, 212-649-0614, and 18-36 Mott Ave., Far Rockaway 11691, 212-327-1220.

Administrative Assistant Francis X. Kilroy

Committees

Banking and Currency (16th); Subs: Bank Supervision and Insurance; Small Business; Urban Mass Transportation.

Post Office and Civil Service (11th); Subs: Manpower and Civil Service; Retirement and Employee Benefits.

Sel. Com. on Crime (3rd).

Group Ratings

	ADA	COPE	LWV	RIPON	NFU	LCV	CFA	NAB	NSI	ACA
1972	75	91	82	77	86	68	50	18	22	13
1971	78	91	75	71	93	–	100	–	–	8
1970	84	100	–	75	100	75	100	0	0	6

Key Votes

1) Busing	FOR	6) Cmbodia Bmbg	AGN	11) Chkg Acct Intrst	AGN
2) Strip Mines	AGN	7) Bust Hwy Trust	FOR	12) End HISC (HUAC)	FOR
3) Cut Mil $	ABS	8) Farm Sub Lmt	AGN	13) Nixon Sewer Veto	AGN
4) Rev Shrg	FOR	9) School Prayr	AGN	14) Corp Cmpaign $	FOR
5) Pub TV $	FOR	10) Cnsumr Prot	FOR	15) Pol $ Disclosr	AGN

Election Results

1972 general:	Frank J. Brasco (D)	87,869	(64%)
	Melvin Solomon (R-C)	43,105	(31%)
	Jessie I. Levine (L)	6,572	(5%)
1972 primary:	Frank J. Brasco (D), unopposed		
1970 general:	Frank J. Brasco (D)	60,919	(79%)
	William Sampol (C)	9,462	(12%)
	Paul Meyrowitz (L)	7,156	(9%)

TWELFTH DISTRICT Political Background

First created in 1968, the 12th district of New York was designed to be Brooklyn's first black-majority district. The 12th includes the neighborhoods of Bedford-Stuyvesant, Crown Heights, and much of Brownsville. Bedford-Stuyvesant, the main ghetto in Brooklyn, is now more populous than Harlem in Manhattan; previously, Bedford-Stuyvesant was carved up among several districts to provide Democratic votes for Jewish and Irish Congressmen. Like most ghetto areas, this one is not completely homogeneous. There are, of course, blocks of dilapidated tenements that are inhabited *inter alia* by drug addicts; and there are several typical high-rise housing projects. But Bedford-Stuyvesant also has some middle-clsss neighborhoods, many of them occupied by blacks from the West Indies. Finally, some of the old brownstones in the ghetto are being renovated by Robert Kennedy's development corporation and other similar groups.

In 1968, the new seat attracted two major contenders: Assemblywoman Shirley Chisholm, who won the Democratic nomination, and the former director of CORE, James Farmer, who got both the Republican and Liberal nominations. Farmer's campaign, which was well-financed, took a cue from militant rhetoric and stressed black masculine pride. Meanwhile, Ms. Chisholm's efforts relied on her forceful speaking style and on the corps of women volunteers who had helped her to defeat machine-backed candidates in other elections. Farmer's strategy was probably a mistake. According to the 1970 census, some 58% of the district's residents over 18 are women. More important, however, in the 12th district is the Democratic line, which is much more attractive to most voters than the Republican and Liberal levers combined. Accordingly, Chisholm finished with 66% of the votes, and Farmer, only 26%.

Shirley Chisholm, who entitled her autobiography *Unbought and Unbossed*, was given the kind of committee assignment usually reserved for those who seem likely to defy the congressional establishment—a seat on Veterans' Affairs. Nevertheless, her position as the first black woman in Congress and her commanding presence won Ms. Chisholm a national forum and a full schedule on the liberal speech-making circuit—earning more in lecture fees in 1972 than any other House member. In 1971, the Brooklyn Congresswoman was reassigned to Education and Labor, a House unit that handles most social legislation. The reassignment was reportedly a reward for having joined the rest of the Brooklyn delegation to support Hale Boggs for Majority Leader.

But fame and a seat on a good committee were not enough for Ms. Chisholm. In 1972, she became a full-fledged presidential candidate. She ran in most of the primaries and stayed in the race—and joined the stop-McGovern forces—clear through to the Democratic Convention in Miami Beach. Though Ms. Chisholm was unable to carry as much as 10% of the votes, she did manage to get treatment on a par with other candidates when it came to television debates.

During the campaign, Ms. Chisholm often complained that people were not taking her candidacy as seriously as they should, and that she was as qualified for the office as the others. But around Capitol Hill, many people, some of them ideologically sympathetic to her, complained that Ms. Chisholm had done little legislating, preferring, they said, the glamor of the lecture circuit to the drudgery of the committee room. In 1973, Chisholm answered her critics by becoming deeply, though quietly, involved in the legislative process. When the minimum-wage law came before Education and Labor, Ms. Chisholm lobbied on committee and with other women members to extend minimum-wage protection to domestic workers. And she won. So most domestics, who had been earning something like $1.60 an hour, will now receive $2.20 under the terms of the law.

In the early summer of 1973, Ms. Chisholm surprised observers when she announced that she would retire from Congress in 1974, or 1976 at the latest. She said that she wanted to establish a public affairs institute in Washington. Ms. Chisholm could certainly win reelection easily, much as she did in 1972. Many people in Washington think she will change her mind, come election time. For now, however, nobody knows for sure what will happen in the 12th district.

Census Data Pop. 465,195. Central city, 100%; suburban, 0%. Median family income, $6,344; families above $15,000: 8%; families below $3,000: 19%. Median years education, 10.3.

1972 Share of Federal Outlays $717,752,029

DOD	$121,638,124	HEW	$232,268,576
AEC	$2,857,801	HUD	$9,570,073
NASA	$1,391,134	DOI	$302,265
DOT	$9,628,158	USDA	$51,125,236
		Other	$288,970,662

Federal Military-Industrial Commitments

DOD Contractors Pfizer Inc. (Brooklyn), $6.086m: unspecified.

Economic Base Finance, insurance and real estate; apparel and other textile products, especially women's and misses' outerwear; food and kindred products, especially beverages; fabricated metal products; and textile mill products, especially knitting mill products.

The Voters

Registration 103,568 total. 79,960 D (77%); 10,740 R (10%); 3,718 L (4%); 567 C (1%); 8,583 blank, missing and void (8%).
Median voting age 37.9
Employment profile White collar, 41%. Blue collar, 38%. Service, 21%. Farm, –%.
Ethnic groups Black, 77%. Spanish, 13%. Total foreign stock, 16%.

Presidential vote

	1972	Nixon (R)	11,937	(16%)
		McGovern (D)	64,673	(84%)
	1968	Nixon (R)	8,743	(11%)
		Humphrey (D)	66,929	(87%)
		Wallace (AI)	1,578	(2%)

Representative

Shirley Anita Chisholm (D) Elected 1968; b. Nov. 30, 1924, Brooklyn; home, Brooklyn; Brooklyn Col., B.A., 1946; Columbia U., M.A., 1952; married; Methodist.

Career Nursery school teacher and dir., 1946–53; Dir., Hamilton-Madison Child Care Center, N.Y., 1953–59; Educational Consultant, Div. of Day Care, N.Y., 1959–64; N.Y. Legislature, 1964–68.

Offices 123 CHOB, 202-225-6231. Also 1149 Eastern Parkway, Brooklyn 11216, 212-596-3500.

Administrative Assistant Carolyn J. Smith

Committees

Education and Labor (14th); Subs: No. 1 (Gen. Sub. on Education); No. 5 (Sel. Sub. on Education); No. 7 (Equal Opportunities).

Group Ratings

	ADA	COPE	LWV	RIPON	NFU	LCV	CFA	NAB	NSI	ACA
1972	69	100	100	64	83	83	100	9	0	7
1971	97	82	67	76	85	–	100	–	–	8
1970	80	100	–	65	83	90	100	0	0	25

Key Votes

1) Busing	FOR	6) Cmbodia Bmbg	AGN	11) Chkg Acct Intrst	FOR
2) Strip Mines	ABS	7) Bust Hwy Trust	FOR	12) End HISC (HUAC)	FOR
3) Cut Mil $	FOR	8) Farm Sub Lmt	ABS	13) Nixon Sewer Veto	AGN
4) Rev Shrg	FOR	9) School Prayr	AGN	14) Corp Cmpaign $	ABS
5) Pub TV $	ABS	10) Cnsumr Prot	FOR	15) Pol $ Disclosr	FOR

Election Results

1972 general:	Shirley Chisholm (D-L)	57,821	(88%)
	John M. Coleman (R)	6,373	(10%)
	Martin S. Shepherd, Jr. (C)	1,073	(2%)
	John C. Hawkins (SW)	480	(1%)
1972 primary:	Shirley Chisholm (D), unopposed		
1970 general:	Shirley Chisholm (D-L)	31,500	(82%)
	John M. Coleman (R)	5,816	(15%)
	Martin S. Shepherd, Jr. (C)	1,204	(3%)

THIRTEENTH DISTRICT Political Background

The 13th district of New York, in south central Brooklyn, might be called the Ocean Parkway district. The 13th takes in terrain on both sides of the throughfare as it makes its way from Prospect Park to Coney Island. A large number of Italian-Americans live in Bensonhurst and Bath Beach along the district's western boundary; in fact, according to census figures, the 13th is one of the most Italian districts in the entire nation. But most of the neighborhoods, from Midwood in the north, through the streets lined with low-rise apartments along the Parkway, to Sheepshead Bay, Brighton Beach, and Coney Island in the south, are heavily Jewish. With Flatbush, the 13th comprises the heartland of liberal Jewish Brooklyn. Though no reliable figures exist, it is likely that the 13th is the nation's most Jewish district. It is, of course, also overwhelmingly Democratic by tradition. So anyone who refuses to believe that George McGovern lost a large number of the normally Democratic ballots of elderly Jewish voters should take a look at the results in the 13th, where Richard Nixon took 49% of the votes.

The current Congressman from the district is Bertram Podell, a former Assemblyman. He was chosen to replace Rep. Abraham Multer, when Multer became a judge in early 1968. The special election won by Podell was heralded at the time as a Johnson Administration victory, because Podell had the support of the Brooklyn machine and his opponent was an outspoken peace candidate. But such an assessment was not really accurate. Podell did not campaign as a Johnson man, and, in fact, like most Brooklyn organization Democrats, soon started to vote against the war pretty consistently.

Abraham Multer developed a rather bad image for himself. He retired to his judgeship amid charges that he used his position on the Banking and Currency Committee to his own financial advantage. Now his successor is under a similar, and more threatening, cloud. In 1973, Podell was indicted on charges that he received $41,000 for an attempt to get the Civil Aeronautics Board to award a Bahamas route to a Florida airline. Podell charged that the indictment was trumped up by the Nixon Administration—toward which he had directed vigorous attacks—to discredit him and to divert attention away from the Watergate scandal. At this writing, no date for a trial has been set.

Podell's trial, however, may make trouble for him in 1974—assuming he runs again. In 1972, he got well-financed primary opposition from Assemblyman Leonard Simon. Despite the twin handicaps, in this area, of an endorsement from Mayor John Lindsay and his support of Sen. George McGovern, Simon won a respectable percentage of the vote. The likelihood is that various candidates, including Simon, will challenge Podell in 1974, unless he is by then completely cleared of the charges against him.

Census Data Pop. 470,242. Central city, 100%; suburban, 0%. Median family income, $10,368; families above $15,000: 24%; families below $3,000: 9%. Median years education, 11.1.

1972 Share of Federal Outlays $724,893,840

DOD	$122,848,454	HEW	$234,579,706
AEC	$2,886,237	HUD	$9,665,298
NASA	$1,404,976	DOI	$305,273
DOT	$9,723,961	USDA	$51,633,945
		Other	$291,845,990

Federal Military-Industrial Commitments

No installations or contractors receiving prime awards greater than $5,000,000.

Economic Base Finance, insurance and real estate; apparel and other textile products, especially women's and misses' outerwear; food and kindred products, especially beverages; fabricated metal products; and textile mill products, especially knitting mill products.

The Voters

Registration 221,304 total. 169,087 D (76%); 28,093 R (13%); 6,639 L (3%); 3,004 C (1%); 14,481 blank, missing and void (7%).
Median voting age 50.1
Employment profile White collar, 63%. Blue collar, 29%. Service, 8%. Farm, –%.
Ethnic groups Black, 2%. Spanish, 2%. Total foreign stock, 60%. Italy, 18%; USSR, 13%; Poland, 9%; Austria, 4%; Rumania, Germany, UK, Hungary, 1% each.

Presidential vote

1972	Nixon (R)	91,690	(49%)
	McGovern (D)	97,155	(51%)
1968	Nixon (R)	53,713	(27%)
	Humphrey (D)	136,671	(69%)
	Wallace (AI)	7,602	(4%)

Representative

Bertram L. Podell (D) Elected Feb. 20, 1968; b. Dec. 27, 1925, Brooklyn; home, Brooklyn; St. John's U., B.A., 1944; Brooklyn Law School, LL.B., 1950; Navy, WWII; married, three children; Jewish.

Career Atty., N.Y. Assembly, 1954–68.

Offices 204 CHOB, 202-225-2361. Also 1628 Kings Hwy., Brooklyn 11229, 212-336-7575.

Administrative Assistant Peggy Murphy

Committees

House Administration (9th); Subs: Accounts; Electrical and Mechanical Office Equipment.

Interstate and Foreign Commerce (17th); Sub: Transportation and Aeronautics.

Group Ratings

	ADA	COPE	LWV	RIPON	NFU	LCV	CFA	NAB	NSI	ACA
1972	100	91	91	80	83	79	100	11	0	0
1971	86	82	89	76	100	–	100	–	–	8
1970	92	100	–	69	92	62	100	0	0	14

Key Votes

1) Busing	FOR	6) Cmbodia Bmbg	AGN	11) Chkg Acct Intrst	FOR
2) Strip Mines	AGN	7) Bust Hwy Trust	ABS	12) End HISC (HUAC)	FOR
3) Cut Mil $	FOR	8) Farm Sub Lmt	FOR	13) Nixon Sewer Veto	AGN
4) Rev Shrg	FOR	9) School Prayr	AGN	14) Corp Cmpaign $	FOR
5) Pub TV $	FOR	10) Cnsumr Prot	FOR	15) Pol $ Disclosr	FOR

Election Results

1972 general:	Bertram L. Podell (D)	113,294	(65%)
	Joseph F. Marcucci (R)	44,293	(26%)
	Leonard M. Simon (L)	9,173	(4%)
	Michael P. Gioia (C)	7,087	(5%)
1972 primary:	Bertram L. Podell (D)	32,680	(68%)
	Leonard M. Simon (D)	15,725	(32%)
1970 general:	Bertram L. Podell (D)	102,247	(77%)
	Geoge W. McKenzie (R)	20,550	(15%)
	Herbert Dicker (L)	9,925	(7%)

FOURTEENTH   DISTRICT   Political Background

The 14th district of New York, in Brooklyn, is about as polyglot an area as one can find in the United States. The district extends along the Brooklyn waterfront from the Italian neighborhood of South Brooklyn to the Queens border, and along the way drifts inland to varying extents. Just north of South Brooklyn are Brooklyn Heights and Cobble Hill, where young, affluent, and politically liberal New Yorkers have renovated picturesque brownstones. To the east is downtown Brooklyn, which has a skyline that might be called impressive in any city but New York. East of the skyline is the Fort Greene area, in part of a black slum, where a brownstone revival has just begun. North along the waterfront are Greenpoint and Williamsburg, having larger Orthodox and Hasidic Jewish and also Puerto Rican communities that live in uneasy proximity. To the southeast of Williamsburg is Bushwick, added to the 14th by the 1972 redistricting. Bushwick is an old-time Italian neighborhood that is slowly and painfully becoming mostly black. All in all, the 14th is an area where ethnicity is a major fact of life, and where hostilities and fears between and among ethnic groups cannot be ignored in political activity.

First elected on D-Day in 1944, the 14th's Congressman, John J. Rooney, is now the third-ranking Democrat on the House Appropriations Committee. He chairs the subcommittee that determines how much money the State, Commerce, and Justice Departments (and the federal judiciary) will receive to run their affairs. Over the years, Rooney has won a reputation as a penny-pincher, though few persons in the bureaucracies affected will say this publicly, for Rooney's temper and vengefulness are also well-known in Washington. Moreover, he is a man accustomed to getting his way. He managed, for example, to get the federal government to pump large amounts of money into the ailing Brooklyn waterfront after the Brooklyn Navy Yard was closed in 1965.

Rooney's conservative leanings have prompted strong primary opposition in each of the last three elections. In 1968, millionaire Frederick Richmond spent an estimated $200,000 in a campaign to unseat Rooney, only to fall some 3,000 votes short. That margin and more went to a third candidate, Peter Eikenberry, who then emerged as the lone liberal challenger in 1970. Despite a vigorous campaign Eikenberry also fell short. Finally, in 1972, Allard Lowenstein decided to run against Rooney. Lowenstein was the most important figure in the Dump-Johnson movement of 1967 and 1968; he then served as a Long Island Congressman from 1969 to 1971 (see New York 4). With Lowenstein in the race, it looked as though the 68-year-old Rooney was nearing the end of his political career.

But despite lots of money and hundreds of enthusiastic volunteers, Lowenstein's campaign ran into a number of problems. For a start, it was difficult to portray Rooney as a mossback conservative, because he had started to vote against the war in 1970—a matter of pure expediency, to protect himself. Then there was Meade Esposito's Brooklyn machine, unhappy with Lowenstein because he was an outsider, and happy with Rooney because he got money for the waterfront. The machine, therefore, went to work for Rooney. And so, of course, did the Longshoreman's Union, as did George Meany and the AFL-CIO. To Meany and many of his friends, Lowenstein personified the liberal antiwar movement which had given the AFL-CIO so much trouble all over the country. Meany desperately wanted Lowenstein defeated and discredited.

But Lowenstein probably could have overcome all of the difficulties if he had been able to make inroads among the district's ethnics. As an outsider, he just couldn't. For years, Rooney had courted the Orthodox and Hasidic Jews; his fliers characterized Lowenstein as an assimilated Long Island Jew living in a goyish neighborhood (Fort Greene, with blacks yet). Neither did Lowenstein get anywhere in Italian South Brooklyn, even though an insurgent Assembly candidate, who grew up in the neighborhood, was unseating an incumbent. Finally, when Lowenstein supporters attempted to get his backers in Brooklyn Heights and Fort Greene to the polls (during the ridiculous New York primary hours from three in the afternoon to ten at night), they found machines breaking down, poll officials refusing to recognize credentials of qualified voters, and so on and on. The machine had obviously pulled out all stops. The result was an election so fraudulent that William F. Buckley, Jr.—no admirer of Lowenstein's—compared it unfavorably to elections held in South Vietnam.

Lowenstein eventually lost by 890 votes. Even as the votes were counted, he began to prepare a court challenge. Lowenstein argued before the state's highest court that because fraud was so pervasive, a new election was justified. Amazingly enough, the court agreed and ordered a rerun of the primary on September 19. This time, the machine was able to out get-out-the-vote Lowenstein's dispirited organization, and Rooney's plurality reached 2,000 votes. Not surprisingly, Rooney won the general election, with Lowenstein, as the Liberal nominee, getting 18% of the votes.

Ironically, the voters of the 14th went through all this without really electing a Congressman. At this writing, Rooney has yet to appear on Capitol Hill since the opening day of the 93rd Congress. Seriously ill, he is not expected to serve out his term. But a replacement is at hand. After the 1968 election, millionaire insurgent Fred Richmond joined forces with the regulars. Richmond set up a foundation that has distributed thousands of dollars to groups which just happen to exist in the 14th district. So when a City Council vacancy occurred in early 1973, Meade Esposito's machine picked Richmond to fill it. The expectation is that Richmond will move on the House in 1974, if not before. Meanwhile, Lowenstein, apart from all his other activities, is planning to run for the Senate in 1974 against Jacob Javits.

Census Data   Pop. 467,517. Central city, 100%; suburban, 0%. Median family income, $6,959; families above $15,000: 11%; families below $3,000: 17%. Median years education, 9.5.

1972 Share of Federal Outlays $721,322,935

DOD	$122,243,289	HEW	$233,424,141
AEC	$2,872,019	HUD	$9,617,686
NASA	$1,398,055	DOI	$303,769
DOT	$9,676,059	USDA	$51,379,591
		Other	$290,408,326

Federal Military-Industrial Commitments

No installations or contractors receiving prime awards greater than $5,000,000.

Economic Base   Finance, insurance and real estate; apparel and other textile products, especially women's and misses' outerwear; food and kindred products, especially beverages; fabricated metal products; and textile mill products, especially knitting mill products.

The Voters

Registration 111,929 total. 79,935 D (71%); 18,505 R (17%); 3,100 L (3%); 1,637 C (1%); 8,752 blank, missing and void (8%).
Median voting age 39.9
Employment profile White collar, 43%. Blue collar, 43%. Service, 14%. Farm, –%.
Ethnic groups Black, 23%. Spanish, 25%. Total foreign stock, 32%. Italy, 11%; Poland, 3%; Germany, Hungary, USSR, 1% each.

Presidential vote

1972	Nixon (R)	45,586	(48%)
	McGovern (D)	49,825	(52%)
1968	Nixon (R)	30,724	(35%)
	Humphrey (D)	49,998	(57%)
	Wallace (AI)	6,798	(8%)

Representative

John J. Rooney (D) Elected June 6, 1944; b. Nov. 29, 1903, Brooklyn; home, Brooklyn; St. Francis Col., 1920–22; Fordham U., LL.B., 1925; married, five children; Catholic.

Career Practicing atty., 1926–40; Asst. Dist. Atty., 1940–44.

Offices 2268 RHOB, 202-225-5936. Also Suite 276, U.S. Ct. House, 225 Cadman Plaza East, Brooklyn 11201, 212-596-6910.

Administrative Assistant Mrs. Jenalee Nivens

Committees

Appropriations (3rd); Subs: Foreign Operations; State, Justice, Commerce, and Judiciary (Chm.).

Joint Study Com. on Budget Control.

Group Ratings

	ADA	COPE	LWV	RIPON	NFU	LCV	CFA	NAB	NSI	ACA
1972	25	100	78	56	67	4	—	38	100	25
1971	49	100	89	47	58	–	71	–	–	22
1970	60	100	–	53	100	80	88	0	78	6

Key Votes

1) Busing	FOR	6) Cmbodia Bmbg	ABS	11) Chkg Acct Intrst	ABS
2) Strip Mines	ABS	7) Bust Hwy Trust	ABS	12) End HISC (HUAC)	AGN
3) Cut Mil $	ABS	8) Farm Sub Lmt	AGN	13) Nixon Sewer Veto	AGN
4) Rev Shrg	FOR	9) School Prayr	AGN	14) Corp Cmpaign $	ABS
5) Pub TV $	ABS	10) Cnsumr Prot	FOR	15) Pol $ Disclosr	AGN

Election Results

1972 general:	John J. Rooney (D-C)	45,515	(54%)
	Allard K. Lowenstein (L)	23,732	(28%)
	Frances J. Voyticky (R)	14,813	(18%)
1972 primary:	John J. Rooney (D)	15,578	(53%)
	Allard K. Lowenstein (D)	13,206	(45%)
	Irving Gross (D)	485	(2%)
1970 general:	John J. Rooney (D)	31,586	(55%)
	John F. Jacobs (R-C)	15,222	(27%)
	Peter Eikenberry (L)	10,452	(18%)

FIFTEENTH DISTRICT Political Background

To many who have never seen it, Brooklyn means nonstop slums, the tenement apartment of Ralph and Alice Kramden, and the fear of lurking crime. The facts of the matter are a little different. Brooklyn has all of the diversity one might expect in a city of more than 2.5 million nation's most fearsome slums—and it does in Brownsville and Bedford-Stuyvesant—New York's largest borough also has neighborhoods of $60,000 homes. And though the downtown streets are grimy, the parks of Brooklyn are green and its yacht harbors filled with wind-blown sails and spinakers. Nothing is dainty about Brooklyn, but in its pleasant middle-class neighborhoods, the fear of crime is more academic than its residents care to admit—in short, a few trees do grow in Brooklyn.

A disproportionate number of Brooklyn's middle-class neighborhoods lie within the boundaries of the 15th congressional district. The 15th begins amidst the newly renovated brownstones of Park Slope, a neighborhood just off Prospect Park—one laid out by the architects of Central Park, and often considered their masterpiece. To the south is the Sunset Park neighborhood, which has the largest concentration of Norwegian-Americans east of Minnesota and North Dakota. In the same area is Borough Park, a middle-class Italian and Irish area. And below that, where the New York Harbor spills into the Atlantic and the Verrazano Bridge archs over to Staten Island, is Bay Ridge.

Except for parts of renovated Brooklyn Heights, the home of people like millionaire Norman Mailer, Bay Ridge is probably Brooklyn's highest income neighborhood. Well-to-do Brooklyn Irish and Italians have moved here as a matter of tradition. But despite a climb on the social ladder, the residents of Bay Ridge still take political cues from the *Daily News*, not the *New York Times*. The neighborhood is one of the most Republican and conservative (with both capital and small c) in New York. The rest of the 15th has grown increasingly conservative in recent years; most of it now elects Republicans to the New York state legislature.

Until 1960, what is now the 15th was a Republican stronghold in congressional elections. But in 1960, Democrat Hugh Carey, a 39-year-old Irish lawyer, captured the seat from eight-year incumbent Francis E. Dorn. In 1962, despite the efforts of Republican redistricters, Carey won again—by 383 votes. An indefatigable campaigner, the Congressman was reelected by increasing margins in subsequent contests. In 1970, Carey won with 65% of the votes after Republican redistricters virtually conceded the district to him when they placed Bay Ridge in John Murphy's Staten Island district (see New York 17).

In 1972, the Republican legislature decided to target Carey rather than Murphy, and once again placed Bay Ridge in the 15th. The result was a closer race than the one two years before; Carey whipped Republican John Gangemi by a 52–43 margin, with a Conservative and a Liberal candidate splitting the rest. And though no McGovern albatross will hang around his neck in 1974, Carey will probably encounter a tougher fight for reelection than those to which he had grown accustomed.

Nonetheless, Carey is one of the few remaining New York politicians who can win Irish working-class votes and at the same time maintain a generally liberal voting record. He switched from hawk to dove in 1966, reportedly after listening to the arguments of several of his 12 children. From time to time, the Congressman has entertained ambitions for city-wide office. In 1969, he started to run for Mayor, then decided to try for City Council president on ex-Mayor (1954–66) Robert Wagner's ticket. In a crowded field, Carey finished a recount-close second to the candidate slated by mayoral primary winner Mario Proccacino. But since the office of City Council President has precious few powers, it is probably just as well that Carey lost. In 1973, observers again speculated about a possible Carey mayoral bid. Nothing came of it, however, as the Brooklyn machine—with which Carey maintains good relations—supported Abraham Beame, who at this writing looks like the certain eventual winner.

Between bouts of city politics, Carey has become something of a power in the House. In 1971, Carey led the Brooklyn delegation when it supported Hale Boggs for Majority Leader. After Boggs won, Carey moved from Education and Labor, a committee where he had less seniority than some younger liberals, to Ways and Means. Wilbur Mills' House panel, of course, not only handles all tax and social security legislation, but its Democratic members make their party's committee assignments, as well. As a member of Ways and Means, Carey has urged federal tax breaks for parents with children in parochial and private schools—a position strongly supported by many of his constituents but apparently ruled unconstitutional by the Supreme Court in 1973. On the chance that Wilbur Mills retires in 1974, Carey could emerge as one of the movers and shakers on Ways and Means, provided, of course, he wins reelection in a rather ornery 15th district.

Census Data Pop. 467,453. Central city, 100%; suburban, 0%. Median family income, $9,529; families above $15,000: 21%; families below $3,000: 11%. Median years education, 10.5.

1972 Share of Federal Outlays $721,322,935

DOD	$122,243,289	HEW	$233,424,141
AEC	$2,872,019	HUD	$9,617,686
NASA	$1,398,055	DOI	$303,769
DOT	$9,676,059	USDA	$51,379,591
		Other	$290,408,326

Federal Military-Industrial Commitments

DOD Installations Fort Hamilton AB (Brooklyn).

Economic Base Finance, insurance and real estate; apparel and other textile products, especially women's and misses' outerwear; food and kindred products, especially beverages; fabricated metal products; and textile mill products, especially knitting mill products.

The Voters

Registration 211,921 total. 131,473 D (62%); 54,256 R (26%); 4,196 L (2%); 5,499 C (3%); 16,497 blank, missing and void.
Median voting age 47.1
Employment profile White collar, 55%. Blue collar, 34%. Service, 11%. Farm, –%.
Ethnic groups Black, 5%. Spanish, 9%. Total foreign stock, 51%. Italy, 18%; Ireland, Poland, 4% each; USSR, UK, 2% each; Greece, Canada, Austria, 1% each.

Presidential vote

1972	Nixon (R)	107,188	(68%)
	McGovern (D)	51,109	(32%)
1968	Nixon (R)	77,238	(50%)
	Humphrey (D)	66,349	(43%)
	Wallace (AI)	10,574	(7%)

Representative

Hugh L. Carey (D) Elected 1960; b. April 11, 1919, Brooklyn; home, Brooklyn; St. John's Law School, LL.B., 1951; Army, WWII; Lt. Col. USAR; married, twelve children; Catholic.

Career Practicing atty., 1951– ; Bd. of Dir., Gallaudet Col.

Offices 106 CHOB, 202-225-4105. Also Suite 699A Fed. Ct. House, 225 Cadman Plaza East, Brooklyn 11201, 212-596-3839.

Administrative Assistant Albert Caccese

Committees

Ways and Means (13th).

Joint Economic Com. (6th); Subs: Consumer Economics; Fiscal Policy; International Economics; Priorities and Economy In Government; Urban Affairs.

Group Ratings

	ADA	COPE	LWV	RIPON	NFU	LCV	CFA	NAB	NSI	ACA
1972	63	78	82	92	86	56	100	9	0	5
1971	89	90	89	75	79	–	88	–	–	8
1970	84	100	–	67	100	40	100	0	0	18

Key Votes

1) Busing	FOR	6) Cmbodia Bmbg	AGN	11) Chkg Acct Intrst	AGN
2) Strip Mines	AGN	7) Bust Hwy Trust	FOR	12) End HISC (HUAC)	FOR
3) Cut Mil $	AGN	8) Farm Sub Lmt	FOR	13) Nixon Sewer Veto	AGN
4) Rev Shrg	FOR	9) School Prayr	AGN	14) Corp Cmpaign $	FOR
5) Pub TV $	ABS	10) Cnsumr Prot	FOR	15) Pol $ Disclosr	AGN

Election Results

1972 general:	Hugh L. Carey (D)	77,019	(52%)
	John F. Gangemi (R)	63,446	(43%)
	Franklin C. Jones (C)	4,831	(3%)
	Carl Saks (L)	2,333	(2%)
1972 primary:	Hugh L. Carey (D), unopposed		
1970 general:	Hugh L. Carey (D)	50,767	(65%)
	Frank C. Spinner (R)	17,931	(23%)
	Stephen P. Marion (C)	5,307	(7%)
	Carl Saks (L)	4,506	(6%)

SIXTEENTH DISTRICT Political Background

Flatbush is the heart of Brooklyn, lying square at the borough's geographical center. The name Flatbush, in fact, has become practically synonymous in the public mind with that of Brooklyn itself. Many of the people who now live in Queens or Long Island were born and raised in Brooklyn, but a glance at the map shows how these two places differ from Flatbush country. Freeways crisscross the newer suburban terrain; Brooklyn meanwhile, has only one, running along its shore. Proposals for another, cutting across the borough, are apparently dead. Most of Flatbush and Brooklyn was laid out and occupied before the automobile became a necessity: one- and two-family homes, miles of low-rise apartment houses, and clusters of retail stores on main thoroughfares. The last spurt of growth in Brooklyn occurred during the 1920s, and its population has remained relatively stable since the 1930 census.

During the 1910s and 1920s, the new neighborhoods of Flatbush and East Flatbush attracted thousands of newly prosperous Jews who had grown up in Lower East Side of Manhattan. Today, Flatbush remains heavily Jewish, though more and more blacks have been moving in from Crown Heights and Bedford-Stuyvesant to the north. And as many younger people leave for Long Island, Westchester County, or the Upper East Side of Manhattan, the average age of Flatbush residents has risen. Among the older people, there is a good deal of nervous talk about crime. Nevertheless, Flatbush remains solidly Democratic.

In the 1920 landslide for Warren G. Harding, the area that is now the 16th congressional district in Flatbush elected a Republican Congressman. Two years later a 34-year-old Jewish lawyer won the Democratic nomination and unseated the incumbent by a small majority. Since then, the congressional district lines in Brooklyn have been altered many times, but the borough has always retained a district centering on Flatbush, and that district always reelected Emanuel Celler to the House of Representatives. Until 1972, that is.

Nobody thought Celler was in much trouble in 1972. He was 84, to be sure, but Nelson Rockefeller and the Republican legislature made certain Celler got a district to his liking. The new 16th includes most of Flatbush and East Flatbush, part of the black ghetto of Brownsville, and all of Crown Heights, which is integrated but not without problems. The district extends to a point near the ocean at Sheepshead Bay. Overall the new 16th was solidly Jewish, and at one point or another in the preceding 50 years, Celler had carried all of it easily.

Moreover, Celler possessed a record that was likely to commend itself to his constituents. As Chairman of the House Judiciary Committee for 22 years, he was a major force behind all the civil rights legislation enacted in the period. He also worked hard, and with ultimate success, to liberalize the nation's immigration laws—a popular cause among the majority of his constituents who have ties to Eastern or Southern Europe. Furthermore, the Congressman co-authored the Celler-Kefauver Amendment, passed in 1950, to the nation's anti-trust legislation. In most cases, the amendment proved to be a near absolute bar to corporate mergers, at least when the government chose to challenge them. If Celler was not the most adroit legislative parliamentarian, he did come out on the right side of most issues in the eyes of his constituents.

But in 1972, a 30-year-old attorney, Elizabeth Holtzman, decided to make a bid against Celler; her only political experience came after serving on Mayor Lindsay's staff two years before, when she was elected a Democratic district leader. When she filed, the veteran Congressman was perfectly content to say "She doesn't exist, as far as I'm concerned." Indeed, Celler had once told a reporter that his electoral chances were as good as they had been in any year ending in two, four, six, eight, or zero. He had, therefore, long since quit campaigning very much. Meanwhile, Celler's friends in the Brooklyn machine busied themselves saving the seat of John Rooney (see New York 14).

Holtzman, on the other hand, mounted a steady and dogged campaign effort. She attacked Celler for a legal fee accepted from a defense contractor and for an initial opposition, which he later withdrew, to the 18-year-old vote. The challenger also attacked—and this is what got the attention of the press, to the extent it paid the race any mind whatever—Celler's opposition to the Equal Rights Amendment. There was no gainsaying that the Chairman had bottled up the measure for 20 years, until a discharge petition forced it out of the Judiciary Committee.

But most important of all, at least in Holtzman's view, was that she actually got out and campaigned. Spending about $37,000, she enlisted enough volunteers to distribute 200,000 pieces of literature. Holtzman also attended the meetings of community organizations, listened to people's complaints about what seemed an increasingly distant government, and promised to work hard once in office to solve the problems of her constituents. As the campaign progressed, a clear and growing feeling developed that Celler was too old and that Celler paid no attention to the district. Celler's Manhattan law office served as his local district office, and his claim of Brooklyn residence was generally considered apocryphal. So given Holtzman's presence among the voters and Celler's absence, the young woman surprised nearly everyone on primary day when she unseated Manny Celler. His was a classic case of a Congressman hanging on too long. Fifty years in Washington—only months shy of the House longevity record set by Georgia's Carl Vinson—was long enough.

Celler was still on the Liberal line in the general election, but he declined any bid for reelection and left Holtzman with an easy win. In the House, she received Celler's old seat—though not, of course, his seniority—on the Judiciary Committee. As a politician, Elizabeth Holtzman is not as vocal as Bella Abzug. Nevertheless, the freshman made her mark early when she led a move to block implementation of new federal rules of evidence promulgated by the Supreme Court—rules, critics said, that went beyond the scope allowable by changing substantive points of law. The Congresswoman also made some headlines when she sued in a federal court to block the bombing of Cambodia, and winning, at least temporarily, when federal Judge Orrin Judd (a Republican) ruled that the policy of the Nixon Administration in the affair was illegal. The order was stayed by an appeals court, and soon afterwards, on August 15, 1973, a congressional ban on the bombing took effect.

Apologists for big-city political machines have always argued that the organizations serve a useful function, providing services for their constituents and serving as a bridge between the citizenry and an otherwise unresponsive bureaucracy. In the case of Celler and the Brooklyn machine, a justification of this sort had no basis, as Holtzman demonstrated by winning the primary. Using the resources of incumbency and paying close attention to constituency needs, chances are Holtzman will soon have a seat as safe as Celler once did, and should she be favored with longevity, she just might occupy it for just as long.

Census Data Pop. 466,756. Central city, 100%; suburban, 0%. Median family income, $10,504; families above $15,000: 26%; families below $3,000: 9%. Median years education, 12.0.

1972 Share of Federal Outlays $719,537,482

DOD	$121,940,707	HEW	$232,846,359
AEC	$2,864,910	HUD	$9,593,879
NASA	$1,394,595	DOI	$303,017
DOT	$9,652,109	USDA	$51,252,414
		Other	$289,689,492

Federal Military-Industrial Commitments

No installations or contractors receiving awards greater than $5,000,000.

Economic Base Finance, insurance and real estate; apparel and other textile products, especially women's and misses' outerwear; food and kindred products, especially beverages; fabricated metal products; and textile mill products, especially knitting mill products. Also higher education (CUNY, Brooklyn).

The Voters

Registration 197,394 total. 147,710 D (75%); 26,979 R (14%); 5,930 L (3%); 3,259 C (2%); 13,516 blank, missing and void (7%).
Median voting age 46.7
Employment profile White collar, 64%. Blue collar, 25%. Service, 11%. Farm, -%.
Ethnic groups Black, 22%. Spanish, 4%. Total foreign stock, 49%. USSR, 11%; Poland, 7%; Italy, 6%; Austria, Ireland, 3% each; Germany, UK, 2% each; Rumania, 1%.

Presidential vote

1972	Nixon (R)	74,403	(46%)
	McGovern (D)	86,597	(54%)
1968	Nixon (R)	50,182	(28%)
	Humphrey (D)	120,449	(68%)
	Wallace (AI)	6,730	(4%)

Representative

Elizabeth Holtzman (D) Elected 1972; b. Aug. 11, 1941, Brooklyn; home, Brooklyn; Radcliffe Col., B.A., 1962; Harvard Law School, J.D., 1965; single; Jewish.

Career Associate, Paul, Weiss, Rifkind, Wharton and Garrison, 1970–72; Asst. to the Mayor, New York City, 1967–70; Wachtell, Lipton, Rosen and Katz, 1965–67; Dem. State Committeewoman and Dist. Leader, 1970–72; Delegate to Dem. Natl. Convention, 1972.

Offices 1009 LHOB, 202-225-6616. Also 1452 Flatbush Ave., Brooklyn 11210, 212-859-9111.

Administrative Assistant Marilyn Shapiro

Committees

Judiciary (19th); Subs: Immigration Citizenship and International Law; Criminal justice.

Group Ratings: Newly Elected

Key Votes

1) Busing	NE	6) Cmbodia Bmbg	AGN	11) Chkg Acct Intrst	FOR
2) Strip Mines	NE	7) Bust Hwy Trust	FOR	12) End HISC (HUAC)	FOR
3) Cut Mil $	NE	8) Farm Sub Lmt	NE	13) Nixon Sewer Veto	AGN
4) Rev Shrg	NE	9) School Prayr	NE	14) Corp Cmpaign $	NE
5) Pub TV $	NE	10) Cnsumr Prot	NE	15) Pol $ Disclosr	NE

Election Results

1972 general:	Elizabeth Holtzman (D)	96,984	(66%)
	Nicholas R. Macchio, Jr. (R)	33,828	(23%)
	Emanuel Celler (L)	10,337	(4%)
	William Sampol (L)	6,743	(7%)
1972 primary:	Elizabeth Holtzman (D)	15,596	(45%)
	Emanuel Celler (D)	14,986	(43%)
	Robert E. O'Donnell (D)	4,395	(12%)

SEVENTEENTH DISTRICT Political Background

Staten Island is the smallest (pop. 295,000) and least densely populated of the five boroughs of New York City (5,000 per square mile as against 31,000 for the rest of the city). Staten Island differs from the rest of the city in practically every other respect as well. Parts of the borough retain a rural character, even in the wake of the new development spurred by the opening of the Verrazano Narrows Bridge in 1965. Before the completion of the bridge to Brooklyn, the only road route from Staten Island to the rest of New York City passed through New Jersey.

And most Staten Islanders are quite content to keep away from the other side of the water. The people here, to ape a phrase, are more suburban than suburbanites. A large proportion are middle-class Italian Catholics, many of them brought up in Brooklyn and happy to leave the city behind. Politically, Staten Islanders are intensely conservative, with Conservative candidates sometimes receiving more votes than Democratic ones in elections here. Staten Island's most interesting political figure is state Sen. John Marchi. He is an austere, almost Thomistic conservative who was twice the Republican candidate for Mayor of New York. But many Staten Islanders consider even Marchi too liberal, because of his support for a form of planned development for the Island.

Because its population has not merited a full congressional district, Staten Island over the years has been linked with various parts of Brooklyn or Manhattan. During the 1950s and 1960s, the island was joined to several different areas of Brooklyn in what was called the 16th district. Today the number has changed to 17, and the borough has changed to Manhattan. So the conservative homeowners of Staten Island find themselves in the same congressional seat with elderly Jewish people living in housing projects, and well-to-do Greenwich Village liberals. The Manhattan portion of the 17th also contains many other groups, but these do not cast enough votes to assume any significance. The incongruous linking found within the constituency shows up nicely in the 1972 presidential election results. The Manhattan portion of the 17th, which casts 33% of the district's votes, went 63% for McGovern; the district's Staten Island majority, meanwhile, gave 74% of its votes to Nixon.

Because the non-Staten Island part of the district has constantly shifted beneath the feet of Democratic Congressman John Murphy, he has had to hustle to win reelection ever since he first captured the seat in 1962. Murphy had an especially close call in 1970 when Republican Bay Ridge, then in his district (see New York 15), gave his opponent a near 7,000-vote margin and held the incumbent to 52% of the votes. The election two years later promised to be, and indeed turned out to be, decidedly easier.

In 1972, Murphy's Republican-Conservative opponent put on a vigorous campaign, spending much of the money his family made in the wine business. But the challenger could not crack Murphy's hold on Staten Island. Murphy certainly benefitted from the feeling of the Islanders that he was their kind of Democrat; for example, unlike most members of the New York City delegation, the Congressman voted against end-the-war legislation, though he was, at the same time, a critic of the system of military justice. Moreover, Murphy was by no means an enthusiastic partisan of George McGovern's candidacy. The incumbent's record and years of service to his constituency were enough to give Murphy 56% of the Staten Island vote.

In Manhattan, some of Murphy's positions on issues might have given him trouble—if Manhattan had constituted a larger portion of the constituency. But apparently Manhattan politicos concluded, and quite correctly, that Staten Island would never accept anybody more liberal, and that voters in the big borough would be better off with a Democrat and half a loaf than a Republican-Conservative and no bread at all. So in 1972 Murphy got no opposition in the primary—an exceedingly rare happening these last dozen years among Manhattan Congressmen —and then won 72% of Manhattan's votes in the general election. Chances are that a pattern of the same sort will prevail in 17th-district congressional elections for the rest of the 1970s.

Census Data Pop. 467,656. Central city, 100%; suburban, 0%. Median family income, $10,632; families above $15,000: 26%; families below $3,000: 8%. Median years education, 11.8.

1972 Share of Federal Outlays $721,322,935

DOD	$122,243,289	HEW	$233,424,141
AEC	$2,872,019	HUD	$9,617,686
NASA	$1,398,055	DOI	$303,769
DOT	$9,676,059	USDA	$51,379,591
		Other	$290,408,326

Federal Military-Industrial Commitments

DOD Contractors American Tel and Tel (New York), $285.696m: ABM research and development; communications equipment and services. US Lines (New York), $56.700m: transportations services. Waterman Steamship (New York), $24.218m: transportations services. American Export Isbrandsten Lines (New York), $24.185m: transportation services. Seatrain Lines (New York), $20.231m: transportation services. States Marine Lines (New York), transportation services. Hudson Waterways (New York), $10.885m: transportation services. Prudential Grace Lines (New York), $10.077m: transportation services. Moore McCormack Lines (New York), $8.607m: transportation services. Western Tankers Corp. (New York), $6.069m: transportation services. American Foreign Steamship (New York), $5.913m: transportation services.

Economic Base Apparel and other textile products, especially women's and misses' outerwear; printing and publishing; finance, insurance and real estate; miscellaneous manufacturing industries, especially jewelry, silverware and plated ware, and costume jewelry and notions; and leather and leather products, especially handbags and personal leather goods. Also higher education (Pace).

The Voters

Registration 183,542 total. 117,526 D (64%); 42,029 R (23%); 4,434 L (2%); 6,132 C (3%); 13,421 blank, missing and void (7%).
Median voting age 41.9
Employment profile White collar, 57%. Blue collar, 28%. Service, 15%. Farm, –%.
Ethnic groups Black, 6%. Chinese, 6%. Spanish, 7%. Total foreign stock, 40%. Italy, 12%; Poland, Ireland, USSR, Germany, UK, 2% each; Austria, 1%.

Presidential vote

1972	Nixon (R)	....	105,543	(62%)
	McGovern (D)	....	64,601	(38%)
1968	Nixon (R)	....	67,427	(46%)
	Humphrey (D)	....	67,720	(46%)
	Wallace (AI)	....	12,870	(9%)

Representative

John Michael Murphy (D) Elected 1962; b. Aug. 3, 1926, Staten Island; home, Staten Island; Amherst Col., U.S. Military Academy, B.S., 1950; Army, WWII and Korean War; married, three children; Catholic.

Career Mbr., Bd. of Dir., Empire State Highway Transportation Assoc., 1960–67; Pres., Cleveland Gen. Transport Co., Inc., 1957–65; Delegate, N.Y. Constitutional Convention, 1967; Delegate, Dem. Natl. Convention, 1964; Parliamentarian, 1968 Dem. Natl. Convention.

Offices 2235 RHOB, 202-225-3371. Also Gen. P.O. Bldg., 505 Manor Rd., Staten Island 10314, 121-981-9800.

Administrative Assistant Boyd Bashore

Committees

Interstate and Foreign Commerce (10th); Sub: Communications and Power.

Merchant Marine and Fisheries (8th); Subs: Merchant Marine; Panama Canal; Coast Guard and Navigation (Chm.).

Group Ratings

	ADA	COPE	LWV	RIPON	NFU	LCV	CFA	NAB	NSI	ACA
1972	38	89	80	80	86	41	100	13	100	30
1971	43	100	88	39	85	–	60	–	–	23
1970	56	83	–	59	100	75	87	11	70	13

Key Votes

1) Busing	FOR	6) Cmbodia Bmbg	FOR	11) Chkg Acct Intrst	ABS
2) Strip Mines	ABS	7) Bust Hwy Trust	FOR	12) End HISC (HUAC)	AGN
3) Cut Mil $	ABS	8) Farm Sub Lmt	ABS	13) Nixon Sewer Veto	AGN
4) Rev Shrg	FOR	9) School Prayr	FOR	14) Corp Cmpaign $	ABS
5) Pub TV $	FOR	10) Cnsumr Prot	FOR	15) Pol $ Disclosr	AGN

Election Results

1972 general:	John M. Murphy (D)	92,252	(60%)
	Mario D. Belardino (R-C)	60,812	(40%)
1972 primary:	John M. Murphy (D), unopposed		
1970 general:	John M. Murphy (D-Ind. Alliance)	71,550	(52%)
	David D. Smith (R-C)	62,597	(45%)
	George D. McLain (L)	4,415	(3%)

EIGHTEENTH DISTRICT Political Background

The 18th district of New York is the silk stocking district. It is one dominated by the chi chi Upper East Side of New York, which Theodore White, who himself lives in an East 64th Street townhouse, once called the "perfumed stockade." The 18th also includes the skyscrapers of midtown Manhattan and much of Greenwhich Village, which, in spite of its reputed Bohemianism, contains many addresses as fashionable and expensive as any in New York City. By no means is all of the 18th wealthy: the Stuyvesant Town housing development in the south is middle-class, and below that are the part ethnic, part freak slums of the Lower East Side (or the East Village, as it is called today). But taken together, the 18th is a very rich district indeed. It is the most white-collar district in the nation and possesses the country's fourth highest median family income.

Yet at the same time, the 18th is one of the most politically liberal districts in New York state and the nation. In 1972, the 18th gave George McGovern 58% of its votes—more than in all but six New York districts. Such was not always the case. As recently as the 1950s, what is now the 18th—boundaries of course have changed several times—was a stronghold of wealthy conservatives, the kind of Manhattanites who felt that Franklin D. Roosevelt had betrayed his class.

The first indication of the Upper East Side's leftward trend appeared in 1958, when young (then 36) John V. Lindsay won the district's Republican primary and then a seat in Congress. As Lindsay's voting record grew more liberal, his margins also grew larger; in 1964, for example, he won 72% of the votes—one of the best percentages for any Republican Congressman in the year of Goldwater. Congressman Lindsay resigned from the House in 1965 to become Mayor. But he maintained his popularity on the East Side, where he received 80% of the votes in his reelection bid of 1969, even as he took only 42% city-wide. Subsequently, the liberalization of the silk stocking district continued apace. By 1970, a Democrat reprsented the constitutency in Congress and the 18th's last Republican Assemblyman, from a district along posh Fifth and Park avenues, was ousted by a liberal Democrat.

The greening of the Upper East Side represents a significant revolution in New York City politics—one made even more notable by the counter-revolution that has occurred in the rest of the city. Indeed it can be said that greening here set the stage for the making of the Silent Majority in the middle-class neighborhoods of the outer boroughs. For an affluent liberal community resides in the 18th, one that probably has more writers, painters, theater people, TV personalities, book editors, and figures out of the national news media, than any other congressional district in the country. Such people in the last 15 years have moved away from New York *Herald Tribune* RRepublicanism to *Village Voice* liberalism. And for many of these people, at once sobered by the McGovern debacle and elated by the Watergate mess, liberal or even radical politics has become a fashionable, if not mandatory, article of faith.

The term "radical chic' still best sums up the current fashion. The two words were coined by Tom Wolfe in a piece about a cocktail party held to benefit certain Black Panthers and about a Southampton affair for the California grape strikers. "Radical Chic" aroused a chorus of protests from the kind of people it ridiculed. The fashionables ardently defended the sincerity of their beliefs, but in doing so missed the point. For middle-class New Yorkers recognized that silk-stocking liberalism intensifies as the object of concern and sympathy grows more distant. Though a couple of New York policemen and a fireman suddenly came to enjoy "in" status, little sympathy is generated here for the concerns and fears of the people whose tedious work makes life amenable in the apartment houses of the 18th. Middle-class New Yorkers saw that the East Side knew a great deal about the grape fields of California, but knew little and cared less about life in Queens.

It is no surprise that the rest of the city takes visceral offense toward the political preferences of high-living and with-it Manhattanites. The 18th liked Adlai Stevenson better than John F. Kennedy in 1960, Eugene McCarthy over Robert Kennedy in 1968, and George McGovern over Richard Nixon in 1972. All three times the rest of the city reversed the preferences. But the greatest irritant to residents of the outer boroughs was the 18th's former Congressman and the city's ex-Mayor, John Lindsay, a politician who never has carried New York City outside Manhattan.

The current Congressman from the 18th is a man with deep roots in the reform Democratic politics of Greenwich Village. In 1961, Carmine de Sapio was Manhattan's Democratic leader and the foremost political boss in New York state. His power was ultimately based on his ability to win election to the post of assembly district leader in Greenwich Village. But here the affluent liberals were quickly beginning to outnumber residents of the aging Italian community where de Sapio was based. So in 1961, a young lawyer named Edward I. Koch defeated de Sapio for district leader and the boss commenced his fall from political power. De Sapio is now in federal prison, convicted on bribery charges.

Koch went on to serve as Councilman, and in 1968 got the Democratic nomination for Congress. In the general election, he beat Sen. Whitney North Seymour, Jr., a well-known Wall Street lawyer who after his defeat became United States Attorney in Manhattan. In the returns of 1968, Koch received 52% of the votes, hardly an overwhelming endorsement. But his win represented the first time the silk-stocking district had elected a Democratic Congressman in 34 years. Subsequent elections have been far easier for Koch. In 1970 and 1972, he carried all but a handful of the election districts in the 18th.

Once in Washington, Koch immediately became part of the hard-core liberal group that opposed the Vietnam war and supported major procedural reforms. He also worked for more aid to mass transit—obviously a big need in the district, given the dilapidated condition of New York's subway system. Furthermore, the Manhattan Congressman fought for the law to end income provisions that discriminate against unmarried people. Koch, himself a bachelor, represents a district in which 56% of adult residents are single, widowed, or divorced.

In 1973, Koch made moves to run for Mayor. He tried to court non-Manhattan voters by assuring them that he, too, was concerned about crime and the deterioration of residential neighborhoods. But as one of a half-dozen potential contenders based in Manhattan, he made no headway in the outer boroughs, while his anti-crime talk cost him some support in his home area. Wisely, Koch left the mayoralty race early and spent most of his time during the campaign in Washington. He will no doubt continue to spend even more time there for many years to come.

Census Data Pop. 467,533. Central city, 100%; suburban, 0%. Median family income, $14,853; families above $15,000: 50%; families below $3,000: 8%. Median years education, 13.0.

1972 Share of Federal Outlays $721,322,935

DOD	$122,243,289	HEW	$233,424,141
AEC	$2,872,019	HUD	$9,617,686
NASA	$1,398,055	DOI	$303,769
DOT	$9,676,059	USDA	$51,379,591
		Other	$290,408,326

Federal Military-Industrial Commitments

DOD Contractors Pan American Airways (New York), $56.078m: transportation services. American Airlines (New York), $29.578m: transportation services. Mobil Oil (New York), $27.757m: petroleum products. ITT (New York), $12.320m: unspecified. Sperry Rand (New York), $11.192m: unspecified. Riverside Research Institute (New York), $5.243m: missile radar research.

Economic Base Apparel and other textile products, especially women's and misses' outerwear; finance, insurance and real estate; printing and publishing; miscellaneous manufacturing industries, especially jewelry, silverware and plated ware, and costume jewelry and notions; and leather and leather products, especially handbags and personal leather goods. Also higher education (New School for Social Research; CUNY, Bernard M. Baruch; CUNY, Hunter; and New York Univ.).

The Voters

Registration 224,935 total. 121,486 D (54%); 62,910 R (28%); 7,695 L (3%); 2,413 C (1%); 30,431 blank, missing and void (14%).
Median voting age 44.0
Employment profile White collar, 79%. Blue collar, 10%. Service, 11%. Farm, –%.
Ethnic groups Black, 4%. Chinese, 1%. Spanish, 7%. Total foreign stock, 44%. USSR, 7%; Germany, Poland, Italy, 4% each; Ireland, UK, Austria, 3% each; Hungary, 2%; Canada, France, Czechoslovakia, 1% each.

Presidential vote

1972	Nixon (R)	82,516	(42%)
	McGovern (D)	114,237	(58%)
1968	Nixon (R)	69,963	(35%)
	Humphrey (D)	121,186	(61%)
	Wallace (AI)	8,076	(4%)

Representative

Edward I. Koch (D) Elected 1968; b. Dec. 12, 1924, New York City; home, New York City; City Col. of N.Y., 1949; N.Y.U., LL.B., 1948; Army, WWII; unmarried; Jewish.

Career Practicing atty., 1949–68; Dem. Dist. Leader, Greenwich Village, 1963–66; N.Y.C. Council, 1967–68.

Offices 1134 LHOB, 202-225-2436. Also Suite 3139, 26 Fed. Plaza, New York City, 212-264-1066.

Administrative Assistant Ronay Arlt

Committees

Banking and Currency (17th); Subs: Consumer Affairs; International Trade; Small Business; Urban Mass Transportation.

House Administration (14th); Subs: Contracts; Printing.

Group Ratings

	ADA	COPE	LWV	RIPON	NFU	LCV	CFA	NAB	NSI	ACA
1972	100	91	100	75	86	93	100	8	0	4
1971	92	83	100	81	73	–	100	–	–	15
1970	100	100	–	94	92	100	100	0	0	17

Key Votes

1) Busing	FOR	6) Cmbodia Bmbg	AGN	11) Chkg Acct Intrst	FOR
2) Strip Mines	AGN	7) Bust Hwy Trust	FOR	12) End HISC (HUAC)	FOR
3) Cut Mil $	FOR	8) Farm Sub Lmt	FOR	13) Nixon Sewer Veto	AGN
4) Rev Shrg	FOR	9) School Prayr	AGN	14) Corp Cmpaign $	AGN
5) Pub TV $	FOR	10) Cnsumr Prot	FOR	15) Pol $ Disclosr	FOR

Election Results

1972 general:	Edward I. Koch (D-L)	125,117	(70%)
	Jane P. Langley (R-C)	52,379	(29%)
	Rebecca Finch (SW)	1,398	(1%)
1972 primary:	Edward I. Koch (D), unopposed		
1970 general:	Edward I. Koch (D-L)	98,300	(62%)
	Peter J. Sprague (R)	50,647	(32%)
	Richard J. Callahan (C)	9,586	(6%)

NINETEENTH DISTRICT Political Background

In the years after World War I, Harlem, whose tenements were built just two decades earlier for white working-class people, became the relatively prosperous center of American black culture. But the Depression of the 1930s hit Harlem hard, and since then, its name has become synonymous with a festering slum and attendant social ills. A few middle-class pockets are still left here, mostly in apartment projects constructed along the Harlem River. But most of Harlem is very poor, ridden with crime and heroin—making it the kind of place people will leave if they can. And leave they did during the 1960s, when Harlem's population dropped 20%. (Census Bureau figures for population decline are reliable, though its total count of blacks in the past are not.) To compound indigenous social and economic woes, little of the antipoverty money poured into Harlem seems to have gotten to the people who need it. Projects meant to benefit the community have been designed with good intentions, but with little expertise. As a result, the cross-currents of black politics have tossed them to and fro; the construction of a state office building on 125th Street, for example, was held up by protesting militants.

For nearly a quarter of a century, Harlem had one of the best-known Congressmen in the entire nation, the late Adam Clayton Powell, Jr. The politician's career peaked during the early 1960s, when he was Chairman of the House Education and Labor Committee, a congressional unit with jurisdiction over most important social legislation. Then, in 1966, after Powell refused to pay a libel judgement he had called a "bag woman," the Congressman's troubles with the New York courts became a regular feature of national television newscasts. Powell got into more trouble when it was learned that he had diverted staff salaries into his own ample bank account.

It was no more, Powell said in his defense, than what other Congressman also did. He was right. And Powell, knowing that it enhanced his stature in Harlem, loved to thumb his nose at Middle America. But in 1967, as the conservative 90th Congress convened, Middle America struck back. Against the wishes of the House leadership, Powell was forbidden to take the oath of office. The Supreme Court later found the action unconstitutional. By that time, however, Powell had already returned to his district and won glorious reelection to replace himself in the very seat he was denied.

Stripped of his seniority, Powell returned to Capitol Hill in 1969. But in Harlem, "Where's Adam?" became the common question, as he continued to dodge the process-server in New York and missed virtually every roll call in Washington. He was then living on Bimini and allowed himself to be photographed lolling on his boat. Soon thereafter, the romance between the minister of Harlem's largest church, the Abyssinian Baptist, and the voters of Harlem came to an end.

When he first won election to the House in 1944, Powell's district was confined to Harlem. But as its population continued to decline, the one-man-one-vote doctrine required the addition of more territory. So a few blocks of the white Upper West Side were added to Powell's district, something, as it turned out, that undid the black Congressman. The Democratic primary in 1970 attracted four challengers, and one of them, Assemblyman Charles Rangel, beat Powell by 150 votes. Rangel carried the new Upper West Side portion of the district by 1,500 votes—a figure representing 10 times his margin district-wide. But Rangel would have had no chance if Powell had still commanded the practically unanimous support he once enjoyed in Harlem. Instead, the veteran Congressman managed only 40% of the votes in his old bailiwick, a sure sign that his career was finished. In 1972, Powell, a drained man defeated in large part by his own failings, died.

In the House, Powell was always something of a lone wolf, concerned about antipoverty patronage but unable to get along with other black or liberal colleagues. Congressman Rangel works better with both groups. He is not as vocal as some other members of the Black Caucus; he waited a full term, for example, before receiving his preferred committee assignment (Judiciary). Rangel also serves on the District of Columbia Committee as part of its new home-rule majority. The Congressman has voiced his opinion on several matters, notably the issue of heroin maintenance, which he opposes vigorously, saying it would keep down the black community.

For 1972, redistricting added a far larger hunk of the Upper West Side to Rangel's constituency, but he easily disposed of Livingston Wingate, a former protege of Powell, in the Democratic primary. In the general election, Rangel ran on three lines—Democratic, Republican, and Liberal.

Census Data Pop. 466,876. Central city, 100%; suburban, 0%. Median family income, $6,712; families above $15,000: 13%; families below $3,000: 18%. Median years education, 10.6.

1972 Share of Federal Outlays $719,537,482

DOD	$121,940,707	HEW	$232,846,359
AEC	$2,864,910	HUD	$9,593,879
NASA	$1,394,595	DOI	$303,017
DOT	$9,652,109	USDA	$51,252,414
		Other	$289,689,492

Federal Military-Industrial Commitments

No installations or contractors receiving prime awards greater than $5,000,000.

Economic Base Apparel and other textile products, especially women's and misses' outerwear; printing and publishing; finance, insurance and real estate; miscellaneous manufacturing industries, especially jewelry, silverware and plated ware, and costume jewelry and notions; and leather and leather products, especially handbags and personal leather goods.

The Voters

Registration 176,474 total. 134,763 D (76%); 20,074 R (11%); 5,713 L (3%); 904 C (1%); 15,020 blank, missing and void (9%).
Median voting age 43.3
Employment profile White collar, 49%. Blue collar, 27%. Service, 24%. Farm, –%.
Ethnic groups Black, 59%. Spanish, 17%. Total foreign stock, 18%. Italy, 2%; USSR, Germany, 1%.

Presidential vote

1972	Nixon (R)	24,302	(19%)
	McGovern (D)	106,164	(81%)
1968	Nixon (R)	16,073	(13%)
	Humphrey (D)	105,053	(84%)
	Wallace (AI)	3,924	(3%)

Representative

Charles B. Rangel (D) Elected 1970; b. June 11, 1930, New York City; home, New York City; N.Y.U., B.S., 1957; St. John's Law School, LL.B., 1960; Army, 1948–52; married, one child; Catholic.

Career Asst. U.S. Atty., Justice Dept., 1963–64; Asst. Counsel, Speaker Travia of N.Y. Assembly, 1965; Gen. Counsel, Natl. Advisory Commission on Selective Svc., 1966; Bd. Mbr., Harlem Neighborhood Assn.

Offices 230 CHOB, 202-225-4365. Also 144 W. 125th St., New York City 10027, 212-866-8600.

Administrative Assistant George A. Dalley

Committees

Judiciary (16th); Subs: No. 4 (Bankruptcy and Civil Rights Oversight); No. 6 (Revision of the Laws).

District of Columbia (12th); Subs: Business, Commerce and Taxation; Judiciary; Labor, Social Services, and the International Community.

Sel. Com. on Crime (6th).

Group Ratings

	ADA	COPE	LWV	RIPON	NFU	LCV	CFA	NAB	NSI	ACA
1972	94	90	100	60	86	89	100	9	0	4
1971	92	80	67	78	75	–	100	–	–	15

Key Votes

1) Busing	FOR	6) Cmbodia Bmbg	AGN	11) Chkg Acct Intrst	AGN
2) Strip Mines	AGN	7) Bust Hwy Trust	FOR	12) End HISC (HUAC)	FOR
3) Cut Mil $	ABS	8) Farm Sub Lmt	AGN	13) Nixon Sewer Veto	AGN
4) Rev Shrg	FOR	9) School Prayr	AGN	14) Corp Cmpaign $	FOR
5) Pub TV $	FOR	10) Cnsumr Prot	FOR	15) Pol $ Disclosr	FOR

Election Results

1972 general:	Charles Rangel (D-R-L)	104,427	(96%)
	Marshall L. Dodge III (C)	2,517	(2%)
	Bobby R. Washington (SW)	982	(1%)
	Jose Stevens (Communist)	843	(1%)
1972 primary:	Charles Rangel (D)	21,165	(77%)
	Livingston Wingate (D)	6,324	(23%)
1970 general:	Charles Rangel (D-R)	52,851	(89%)
	Charles Taylor (L)	6,385	(11%)
	Jose Stevens (Communist)	374	(1%)

TWENTIETH DISTRICT Political Background

The West Side of Manhattan, the funkiest part of New York City, is a polyglot area so diverse that it defies adequate description. It is not very far from Riverside Park and the Hudson River docks to the invisible line that separates the West Side from midtown or Harlem. But nearly every block on the West Side possesses a character unto itself, and so, it seems, does almost every building on every block. New York's 20th congressional district includes most of the West Side. It begins with a salient into hip, expensive Greenwich Village, then moves up through renovated and raffish Chelsea, past apartment-house complexes and the obscenity palaces of Times Square, north to the Upper West Side. Here, about half of the two-block segment between Amsterdam Avenue and the Hudson lies in the 20th district. In the segment, well-known writers and well-paid professionals live in West End Avenue apartments, Puerto Ricans occupy the side streets, students inhabit seedy high-rises, and old people exist up in Washington Heights.

The 20th goes on to include the expensive apartment units and large single-family homes of the Riverdale section of the Bronx. But because most of the district's votes are cast on the Upper West Side, its politics are worth some examination. For the Upper West Side is the heartland of the reform Democrat movement, so far as it still exists, in Manhattan. The politics here came out of the desires of upper-income professionals—Adlai Stevenson enthusiasts of 1952, 1956, and 1960—to break the hold of the old Tammany machine on Manhattan politics. Demography was with the reformers, at least in their home areas. Aged ethnics whose votes propped up the rotting machine were dying or leaving Manhattan for lower rents elsewhere, and the machine people had no rapport with the growing constituency of the reformers. Blacks and Puerto Ricans do live on the Upper West Side, but because they vote in such small numbers, they constitute no significant political factor.

By the early 1960s, the reformers had captured most assembly district leaderships and other party posts from regulars in the Upper West Side and Greenwich Village. Thereupon, the reformers fell into fighting among themselves—the kind of bitter, acrimonious fighting in which articulate upper-income political activists, having no bread-and-butter stake in the outcome of elections, can afford to indulge themselves.

At the same time, however, the reform movement produced at least one authentic hero, supported by virtually all its West Side factions. He was William F. Ryan. First elected to Congress in 1960 against a Columbia law professor with Tammany support, Ryan was reelected in 1962, after the Republican legislature placed him and another Tammany follower in the same district. When the reformer went to Washington, he was scorned by most Democrats already there, not to speak of Republicans. Nevertheless, the Manhattanite was the first Congressman to condemn American involvement in the Vietnam was and vote against it. He led the biennial fight to abolish the House Un-American Activities Committee, and took on just about every other cause at which the get-along-go-along Congress of the early 1960s scoffed. Ryan's efforts were lonely ones at first, Congress having few likeminded men or women. But as time went on, Ryan gained allies, and his point of view came to be regarded as less extreme. Meanwhile, of course, he was always reelected easily from the Upper West Side.

After Ryan's election, reformers challenged regulars in other New York City districts. In what was then the 19th, for example, there was always a contest against Tammany-backed Leonard Farbstein. Roughly speaking, the old district covered the Lower East Side, most of Greenwich Village, and the southern reaches of the Upper West Side. Every two years, Farbstein proved a little too wily for his challengers. His 1964 opponent, William Haddad, was called an Arab, though like most voters in the district, he was Jewish.

In 1970, however, Farbstein met his match in Bella Abzug, a lawyer long active in civil rights and peace groups. Ms. Abzug's powerful vocal chords, sometimes profane language, and floppy hats are now familiar to almost all who take any interest in American politics. But in 1970, Bella and her ways were a novelty, and when she campaigned on the Lower East Side with Barbra Streisand, the candidate's brassy voice brought Jewish retirees out on their balconies and jarred them out of their allegiance to Farbstein.

Once in Congress, Abzug jarred the sensibilities of aging Congressmen even more than had freshman Ryan ten years earlier. When once requested by House Doorkeeper Fishbait Miller to remove her hat, Bella reportedly told him to perform an impossible act. Some, including the writers of Nader's Congress Project, said that her support of any measure would cost it 20 or 30 votes. This is possible, but the more important feature of her first term was symbolic: a militant, radical Congresswoman. Like Shirley Chisholm of Brooklyn, Bella Abzug hit the lecture circuit; later she was a major figure in the National Women's Political Caucus and in several negotiations that took place at the Democratic National Convention in Miami.

By convention time, however, Bella looked like a lame duck Congresswoman. The New York legislature, controlled by upstate and suburban Republicans, has even less affection for her than most members of Congress. So when it came time to draw new congressional district lines, the Republicans eliminated Ms. Abzug's district. A substantial portion of it was attached to conservative Staten Island to form the new 17th district—clearly a seat far too conservative for Bella. A much smaller portion was placed in Ed Koch's silk-stocking 18th. And the rest went to Bill Ryan's 20th.

Abzug was determined to stay in Congress. The 17th was out, and she soon learned that she couldn't beat Koch in the 18th. Bella's base of support lay in Greenwich Village and the Upper

West Side; besides, the Upper East Side likes its politicians a little more suave than Bella could make herself. There was also the possibility of moving across the East River and taking on John Rooney in Brooklyn's 14th district, but Allard Lowenstein was already there before Bella could do anything. So she decided to run against Ryan in the 20th.

One can only suppose that Abzug reached the conclusion with some reluctance. Upon arriving in Congress, Ryan had helped her out, showing the new legislator the ropes. For 12 years, Ryan had fought for just about all of the things both of them stood for. But the problem—and the factor that made the primary campaign here the nation's most bitter (with California 38 a close second)—was the question of Ryan's health. Neither candidate spoke about it openly. But Ryan, at 49, had undergone throat surgery that reduced his voice to a whisper. Though his doctors said any cancer present was removed, he looked haggard as he put in long hours campaigning.

Because Abzug was far better known nationally, she was the one who attracted the cameras of national television to the race. It soon became apparent, however, that Ryan commanded the deepest loyalties within the district itself. The veteran liberal garnered endorsements from the vast majorities of local political figures and columnists. During the campaign, the *Village Voice* read like a Ryan broadside, though far more vitriolic. It was Ryan's 12 years of service—and his pioneer efforts in reform and antiwar causes—versus Abzug's two years in Congress. Ryan won by better than 2–1.

In September, three months after the primary, Bill Ryan died. Within nine days, his widow Priscilla entered the race, with the Democratic nomination to be determined by committeemen from the district—which meant reformers virtually to a person. But this time, Bella Abzug, still a sitting Congresswoman, had the votes. Ms. Ryan then became a candidate to succeed her husband as the Liberal nominee.

If the primary was bitter, the general election was ten times worse. The unspoken premise of Ms. Ryan's campaign was that Bella—by forcing Bill Ryan through a rough primary—had hastened his death. Meanwhile, for an entirely different set of reasons, political figures like Albert Shanker of the New York teachers' union and Al Barkan of the AFL-CIO poured money into Ms. Ryan's efforts. For them, Abzug, like Allard Lowenstein in the 14th, was a symbol of things they hated about the new people in the Democratic party. As in so many other political struggles on the Upper West Side, symbolism and personal hatred were the issues at stake: everyone knew that not a dime's worth of difference separated the two candidates (the Republican was no serious factor) on matters of political substance.

Ms. Abzug won by a margin approaching 2–1. The Abzug win possessed national symbolic importance of sorts. Had she lost, it would have been taken as a repudiation of her kind of politics—which would have been incorrect, of course, since she and Ms. Ryan felt the same way about virtually every issue. During her second term, Ms. Abzug showed Washington observers that they had missed something: namely, that she is in fact a hard-working legislator, not content with loud rhetoric (though she produces plenty of that), but also capable of plowing through mind-deadening detail to shape legislation.

Take, for example, Bella's service on the House Public Works Committee, hardly a glamor spot for a Manhattan politician. Traditionally, it has been the repository of pork-barreling rivers-and-harbors legislation. But in the post-Earth Day world, the congressional panel clearly has jurisdiction over many matters that affect the environment and the quality of urban life. One such matter is the highway program. A bill came before Public Works with provisions for pushing through the construction of freeways in certain cities where citizens' action groups have blocked them. The committee met in open session to "mark up" or draft the exact language of the bill—it met in public because of an innovation produced by the reform of 1973 which provides that a committee session must be open unless the committee votes in public to close it.

Ms. Abzug, the number 17 Democrat on the committee, made a point of order. House rules, she said, prohibit legislation affecting the construction of specific highway projects in a general highway bill; the provisions, therefore, on the specific projects had to go. The committee's leadership and its majority were stunned. So eager were they to build the roads that they had forgotten about the rule. It was checked, and Abzug was right. She won the point, and then got the committee to make major concessions on other matters, using her point of order as leverage. Sources indicate that Bella would have had no chance, were the committee's meeting closed—an interesting commentary on how powers that be treat the rules of the legislative process.

What are Bella's reelection chances in 1974? By now it would seem that the reformers of the 20th district are tired of bitter primaries, or that might become more interested in the scandalously low number of voters registered in New York City. But neither possibility appears likely. Old West Side hatreds never die; they are just savored for a while between elections. So the prospect is for another primary and, if one may venture to predict the course of politics on the West Side, another Abzug victory.

Census Data Pop. 468,667. Central city, 100%; suburban, 0%. Median family income, $9,743; families above $15,000: 27%; families below $3,000: 9%. Median years education, 12.2.

1972 Share of Federal Outlays $723,108,388

DOD	$122,545,872	HEW	$234,001,924
AEC	$2,879,128	HUD	$9,641,492
NASA	$1,401,516	DOI	$304,521
DOT	$9,700,010	USDA	$51,506,768
		Other	$291,127,157

Federal Military-Industrial Commitments

No installations or contractors receiving prime awards greater than $5,000,000.

Economic Base Apparel and other textile products, especially women's and misses' outerwear; printing and publishing; finance, insurance and real estate; miscellaneous manufacturing industries, especially jewelry, silverware and plated ware, and costume jewelry and notions; and leather and leather products, especially handbags and personal leather goods. Also higher education (Columbia Univ. and CUNY, City).

The Voters

Registration 206,220 total. 145,217 D (70%); 28,316 R (14%); 7,704 L (4%); 2,098 C (1%); 22,885 blank, missing and void (11%).
Median voting age 45.1
Employment profile White collar, 64%. Blue collar, 22%. Service, 14%. Farm, –%.
Ethnic groups Black, 15% Chinese, 1%. Spanish, 9%. Total foreign stock, 52%. USSR, 6%; Germany, 5%; Ireland, 4%; Poland, 3%; Austria, Italy, UK, Greece, 2% each; Hungary, 1%.

Presidential vote

1972	Nixon (R)	57,319	(34%)
	McGovern (D)	109,341	(66%)
1968	Nixon (R)	40,319	(24%)
	Humphrey (D)	122,931	(72%)
	Wallace (AI)	8,273	(5%)

Representative

Bella S. Abzug (D) Elected 1970; b. July 24, 1920, New York City; home, New York City; Hunter Col., B.A., 1942; Columbia U., LL.B., 1945; married, two children; Jewish.

Career Practicing atty., 1947–70; Natl. Legislative Rep. for Women's Strike for Peace Movement.

Offices 1506 LHOB, 202-225-5635. Also 252 7th Ave., New York City 10011, 212-269-8535.

Administrative Assistant Eric Hirschhorn (L.A.)

Committees

Government Operations (19th); Subs: Foreign Operations and Government Information; Special Studies.

Public Works (17th); Subs: Public Buildings and Grounds; Water Resources; Transportation; Energy; Economic Development.

Group Ratings

	ADA	COPE	LWV	RIPON	NFU	LCV	CFA	NAB	NSI	ACA
1972	100	91	100	75	86	93	100	9	0	10
1971	100	82	67	78	69	–	100	–	–	15

Key Votes

1) Busing	FOR	6) Cmbodia Bmbg	AGN	11) Chkg Acct Intrst	FOR
2) Strip Mines	AGN	7) Bust Hwy Trust	FOR	12) End HISC (HUAC)	FOR
3) Cut Mil $	FOR	8) Farm Sub Lmt	FOR	13) Nixon Sewer Veto	AGN
4) Rev Shrg	FOR	9) School Prayr	AGN	14) Corp Cmpaign $	ABS
5) Pub TV $	FOR	10) Cnsumr Prot	FOR	15) Pol $ Disclosr	FOR

Election Results

1972 general:	Bella S. Abzug (D)	85,558	(56%)
	Priscilla M. Ryan (L)	43,045	(28%)
	Annette Flatto Levy (R)	18,024	(11%)
	Harvey J. Michelman (C)	6,253	(4%)
1972 primary:	Bella S. Abzug (D), nominated by county party caucus.		
1970 general:	Bella S. Abzug (D)	46,947	(52%)
	Barry Farber (R-L)	38,460	(43%)
	Salvatore Lodico (C)	4,426	(5%)

TWENTY-FIRST DISTRICT Political Background

The 21st district of New York is the South Bronx—a part of the world a mile or so from Manhattan's Upper East side, but nowhere near it in any other way. For the South Bronx constitutes one of the nation's most desperate slum areas. It is 44% Puerto Rican, 42% black, and just 14% mainland white, with most of that out of immigrant stock. Unlike Harlem or even Bedford-Stuyvesant, the South Bronx is not a ghetto possessing a history of any length or a set of traditional institutions that have served the area. As in most slum areas, a huge percentage (43% here) of its residents are under age 18, with many of them living in large, often fatherless families. And of those who are older, probably more than half lived somewhere other than the South Bronx ten years ago. Most of the older Jewish or Italian people who then lived here have since fled (or died), to escape from what has become the most crime-ridden part of New York City.

By any measure, the South Bronx is full of what urban experts call social disintegration. It is therefore no surprise that most people eligible to vote here do not. But the low level of political participation in the 21st district is worthy of special attention. In 1972, only 28% of those eligible voted; fewer votes were cast here, on both percentage and absolute bases, then in any other congressional district in country, including those in the Deep South where many people are rural blacks, and in south Texas, which contains many Mexican aliens. The conditions of life in the South Bronx offer one explanation. And another, one that New Yorkers like to cite, is the absurd restrictions that are part of the state's registration laws. But the most important factor behind the deplorable situation is that nobody cares. The machines do not want the votes of minorities; they can win judgeships, the source of most of their patronage, without them. The reformers are more interested in hate-fest primaries (see New York 20, for example). And local politicians get along fine, thank you. One reason New York has moved to the right in recent elections is that minority voters—people who would cast ballots for liberal candidates—are less likely to be registered here than anywhere else in the United States.

The situation might now be changing just a little, and if such proves to be the case, the Congressman from the 21st may well be responsible for some of the progress. He is Herman Badillo, the first full-fledged, voting member in Congress of Puerto Rican background. (Puerto Rico sends a Delegate to the House who has a voice but no vote.) Badillo's career, the Congressman likes to say, resembles Horatio Alger's. Born to poverty in Puerto Rico, Badillo moved to New York, worked himself through college, got a C.P.A. certificate and a law degree, and then held a post in the Wagner Administration. In 1965, Badillo was elected Borough President of the Bronx, winning by the barest of margins in both the primary and general election.

It is plain that Badillo's real interest is city government. In 1970, he ran for Congress only after having finished a close third in the 1969 mayoral primary, behind Mario Proccacino and Robert Wagner. In his first election for Congress, the 21st district included parts of Queens and Manhattan, as well as the South Bronx. And Badillo, perhaps overconfident, nearly lost the primary to a candidate supported mainly by conservative Queens homeowners. But of course Badillo won the general election easily in 1970, and both the primary and general, elections easily in 1972. In Washington, he compiled a predictably liberal voting record.

Everyone knew, however, that Badillo's eye was on the 1973 mayoral race. It appeared that Badillo had little chance, Lindsay being as unpopular as he was among the city's white majority for alleged mayoral favoritism toward blacks and Puerto Ricans. Nor did Badillo strengthen his own chances when he lost the endorsement of the New Democratic Coalition, the city's catch-all reform group, or when he later angrily denounced the NDC. There was always talk that Badillo, though able, was arrogant and short-tempered. Nevertheless, the candidate continued to campaign, even as his cause appeared hopeless. Then, just a week before the June 1973 primary, Badillo won the endorsement of the *New York Times.* Liberal votes, once seemingly headed for Assemblyman Albert Blumenthal, the man with the NDC nod, went to Badillo instead, who finished a strong second, 28%, to Controller Abraham Beame, 33%. Under a new primary law designed to prevent John Lindsay from winning the nomination with a minority of the votes—something he did in the 1965 and 1969 general elections—Badillo and Beame faced each other in a runoff.

Beame, of course, had the support of the city machines, and waged an energetic campaign in an attempt to counter complaints about his age, 67. Compared to previous outings, Badillo appeared less fiery on the stump and more concerned about the problems of the middle class. He was attacked for living in affluent Riverdale, out of the district, and for driving a Mercedes. The candidate met that, saying he wanted to help bring the impoverished minorities of New York into the kind of middle-class prosperity he himself enjoyed. It was a plea, of course, for middle-class votes. But after having been twice outfoxed by Lindsay, the city's white middle-class people were not much interested in Badillo. In the runoff, they came out in record numbers and gave Beame 63% of their votes.

The turnout in New York City in 1973 resembled the turnout that sunk Tom Bradley, a black Councilman, and reelected Sam Yorty Mayor of Los Angeles in 1969—a white majority fearing the consequences of a minority member winning control of City Hall. The city's Democratic bosses like to take credit for the turnout, but it was too large to be anything but a spontaneous, voluntary response by hundreds of thousands of voters. But it may not happen that way again. For Bradley in Los Angeles there was a happy sequel when he came back four years later to beat Yorty. In the 1973 California contest, turnout in conservative white areas was lower than in 1969; memories of Watts had dimmed; and fears of blacks and Hispanic-Americans had grown less acute.

The same thing may occur in New York City. Beame, who at this writing seems certain to win the 1973 general election, will be 71 when his term expires. Chances are that, after having achieved his ambition of becoming the first Jewish Mayor of New York, he will retire. Chances are also good that Badillo will get into the race to succeed him. In the first and second primaries of 1973, Badillo managed to pull far larger-than-normal turnouts in Puerto Rican and black neighborhoods in the Bronx and Manhattan, though not in Brooklyn. The minorities even outvoted some middle-class Italian areas. Obviously, there was some kind of grass-roots enthusiasm at work for Badillo, which over the next four years could mean bigger registration rolls in minority areas. Meanwhile, Beame, unlike Lindsay, is likely to cool the antagonisms held by middle-class voters. Badillo will win certain reelection to Congress as long as he wants, but he is probably even now thinking about 1977.

Census Data Pop. 462,030. Central city, 100%; suburban, 0%. Median family income, $5,613; families above $15,000: 5%; families below $3,000: 23%. Median years education, 9.2.

1972 Share of Federal Outlays $712,395,671

DOD	$120,730,377	HEW	$230,535,229
AEC	$2,836,474	HUD	$9,498,655
NASA	$1,380,753	DOI	$300,010
DOT	$9,556,306	USDA	$50,743,705
		Other	$286,814,162

Federal Military-Industrial Commitments

DOD Contractors Texaco (Long Island City), $9.639m: petroleum products.

Economic Base Finance, insurance and real estate; apparel and other textile products, especially women's and misses' outerwear; food and kindred products, especially bakery products; fabricated metal products, especially fabricated structural metal products; and electrical equipment and supplies, especially household appliances.

The Voters

> *Registration* 95,303 total. 75,483 D (79%); 8,934 R (9%); 2,932 L (3%); 567 C (1%); 7,387 blank, missing and void (8%).
> *Median voting age* 37.4
> *Employment profile* White collar, 37%. Blue collar, 42%. Service, 21%. Farm, –%.
> *Ethnic groups* Black, 42%. Spanish, 44%. Total foreign stock, 14%. Italy, USSR, 1% each.

Presidential vote

1972	Nixon (R)	15,293	(20%)
	McGovern (D)	59,375	(80%)
1968	Nixon (R)	10,417	(14%)
	Humphrey (D)	59,363	(83%)
	Wallace (AI)	2,094	(3%)

Representative

Herman Badillo (D) Elected 1970; b. Aug. 21, 1929, Caguas, P.R.; home, Bronx; City Col. of N.Y., B.A., 1951; Brooklyn Law School, LL.B., 1954; married, one child; Protestant.

Career Practicing atty., 1955– ; set up J. F. Kennedy Dem. Club, 1962; Deputy Commissioner for Relocation, N.Y.C., 1962, 1963–66; Bronx Borough Pres., 1966–70; Chm., Com. on Health, Housing and Social Security at State Constitutional Convention, 1967.

Offices 510 CHOB, 202-225-4361. Also 840 Grand Concourse, Bronx 10451, 212-665-9400.

Administrative Assistant Paul A. Schosberg

Committees

Education and Labor (18th); Subs: No. 1 (Gen. Sub. on Education); No. 4 (Sel. Sub. on Labor); No. 5 (Sel. Sub. on Education).

Group Ratings

	ADA	COPE	LWV	RIPON	NFU	LCV	CFA	NAB	NSI	ACA
1972	100	91	100	73	83	86	—	8	0	4
1971	92	83	67	75	93	–	100	–	–	7

Key Votes

1) Busing	FOR	6) Cmbodia Bmbg	AGN	11) Chkg Acct Intrst	ABS
2) Strip Mines	AGN	7) Bust Hwy Trust	FOR	12) End HISC (HUAC)	FOR
3) Cut Mil $	FOR	8) Farm Sub Lmt	FOR	13) Nixon Sewer Veto	AGN
4) Rev Shrg	FOR	9) School Prayr	AGN	14) Corp Cmpaign $	AGN
5) Pub TV $	FOR	10) Cnsumr Prot	FOR	15) Pol $ Disclosr	FOR

Election Results

1972 general:	Herman Badillo (D-L)	48,441	(87%)
	Manuel A. Ramos (R)	6,366	(11%)
	Lillian Immediato (C)	937	(2%)

1972 primary:	Herman Badillo (D)	11,421	(78%)
	Manuel Ramos (D)	3,084	(22%)
1970 general:	Herman Badillo (D)	38,866	(84%)
	George B. Smaragdas (C)	7,561	(16%)

TWENTY-SECOND DISTRICT Political Background

The 22nd congressional district runs from the Grand Concourse to Co-op City. The same route sums up rather nicely the history of the borough of the Bronx. The Bronx was scarcely occupied at the turn of the century. But from 1900 to 1930, its population grew from 200,000 to 1,265,000—a figure near the 1,471,000 of today. Settlement in the borough followed the subway and elevated lines, as Jews, Italians, and Irish left the teeming tenements of Manhattan for the comparatively spacious and comfortable apartments of the Bronx. There are several large parks and two major universities (NYU and Fordham) here, but few other amenities. The Bronx has never had much white-collar office employment, or, for that matter, not many factories either. The borough remains today basically residential.

The Grand Concourse was designed to be the showcase of the Bronx. It extends, past blocks and blocks of apartment buildings, from the Harlem River to Van Cortlandt Park. Lately the advancing slums of the South Bronx have shattered the tranquillity of the Concourse. Consequently, the elderly Jewish people who are the main occupants of the apartment buildings have begun to leave. One of the places to which they have gone, assuming they can get in, is Co-op City—a staggeringly vast complex of towering apartment buildings, financed mainly by an offshoot of the Amalgamated Clothing Workers' Union. Co-op City is unspeakably ugly, situated on a flat swamp and overlooking a couple of freeways. And though it is totally without aesthetic merit and is miles from the nearest subway stop, Co-op City does deliver clean, safe, inexpensive housing—the most many middle-income New Yorkers can hope for.

Politics, of course, explain the oddly shaped boundaries of the 22nd district. In tacit cooperation with the old-line Bronx machine, the Republican legislature decided to place in one district the borough's two reform Democratic Congressmen. In 1964, both Jonathan B. Bingham and James H. Scheuer first won election to the House when they defeated two stalwarts of the old Buckley machine. Bingham surprised most observers by beating the boss himself, Charles A. Buckley, who was then Chairman of the House Public Works Committee. Since then, Bingham has had little trouble winning reelection. In 1969, Scheuer was a disastrous candidate for Mayor, finishing dead last in the Democratic primary, behind Norman Mailer. And in 1970, he had to fight off Jacob Gilbert in another two-incumbent redistricting maneuver.

Both Bingham and Scheuer come from wealthy, non-Bronx backgrounds. Bingham, whose father was a Senator from Connecticut, served as a delegate to the United Nations just before running for Congress. Scheuer made his own fortune as a developer, in the process putting up some of the most imaginative publicly financed housing in the country. When redistricting forced them into the same district, each man clearly did not want to run against the other, but neither had any place else to go. The heavily Puerto Rican 21st district obviously belonged to Herman Badillo, while Mario Biaggi was obviously unbeatable in the heavily Italian and conservative 10th district. And the 23rd district, one partially in the Bronx, was held by a Republican who was being challenged by a former Democratic Congressman.

At first, Bingham and Scheuer tried to work out something that would drop one of them out of the race before the primary. But that fell through, and it was a horserace. Both could afford to spend money and both campaigned vigorously. Because Bingham had represented most of the district's territory previously, he possessed an advantage. But Scheuer was not without one too; like about half the district's residents—no reliable figures exist—he was Jewish. The result was a 55–45 win for Bingham and the elimination of one liberal Democrat from the New York City delegation.

In the House, Bingham serves on the Foreign Affairs Committee, an assignment it took him a long time to get, despite his obvious qualification for it. Though he is still far from a subcommittee chairmanship, the Congressman is able to use the House panel as a forum for his liberal ideas about foreign policy.

Census Data Pop. 466,931. Central city, 100%; suburban, 0%. Median family income, $8,850; families above $15,000: 18%; families below $3,000: 11%. Median years education, 11.1.

1972 Share of Federal Outlays $719,537,482

DOD	$121,940,707	HEW	$232,846,359
AEC	$2,864,910	HUD	$9,593,879
NASA	$1,394,595	DOI	$303,017
DOT	$9,652,109	USDA	$51,252,414
		Other	$289,689,492

Federal Military-Industrial Commitments

No installations or contractors receiving prime awards greater than $5,000,000.

Economic Base Finance, insurance and real estate; apparel and other textile products, especially women's and misses' outerwear; food and kindred products, especially bakery products; fabricated metal products, especially fabricated structural metal products; and tourism. Also higher education (CUNY, Herbert H. Lehman; and New York Univ.).

The Voters

Registration 202,230 total. 151,718 D (75%); 23,997 R (12%); 6,946 L (3%); 3,353 C (2%); 17,216 blank, missing and void (9%).
Median voting age 47.0
Employment profile White collar, 58%. Blue collar, 28%. Service, 14%. Farm, –%.
Ethnic groups Black, 18%. Spanish, 14%. Total foreign stock, 46%. USSR, 9%; Ireland, Poland, 6% each; Italy, 5%; Austria, 3%; Germany, UK, 2% each; Hungary, Rumania, 1% each.

Presidential vote

1972	Nixon (R)	67,371	(40%)
	McGovern (D)	101,683	(60%)
1968	Nixon (R)	45,102	(27%)
	Humphrey (D)	116,715	(69%)
	Wallace (AI)	8,077	(5%)

Representative

Jonathan B. Bingham (D) Elected 1964; b. April 24, 1914, New Haven, Conn.; home, Bronx and Manhattan; Yale U., B.A., 1936, LL.B., 1939; Army, WWII (Capt. Military Intelligence); married, four children; United Church of Christ.

Career Practicing atty., 1940–45, 1951–61; Correspondent, N.Y. *Herald Tribune*, 1935, 1938; Asst. Dir., Office Intl. Security Affairs, 1951; Deputy Admin., Technical Cooperation Admin., 1951–53; Sec., Gov. Averell Harriman, 1955–58; U.S. Rep., UN Econ. and Social Council, Advisor to Ambassador Adlai E. Stevenson, 1961–63; U.S. Delegation to four UN Gen. Assemblies, 1961–63; U.S. Rep. on UN Trusteeship Council, 1961–62; Pres. of Council, 1962.

Offices 133 CHOB, 202-225-4441, Also 1 East Fordham, Bronx 10468, 212-933-2310.

Administrative Assistant Roger Majak

Committees

Foreign Affairs (14th); Subs: International Organizations and Movements; National Security Policy and Scientific Developments; Near East and South Asia.

Interior and Insular Affairs (16th); Subs: No. 1 (National Parks and Recreation); No. 4 (Territorial and Insular Affairs); No. 3 (Environment).

Group Ratings

	ADA	COPE	LWV	RIPON	NFU	LCV	CFA	NAB	NSI	ACA
1972	75	89	100	71	100	93	100	10	0	0
1971	100	83	100	83	79	–	100	–	–	7
1970	100	100	–	82	92	100	100	0	0	16

Key Votes

1) Busing	FOR	6) Cmbodia Bmbg	ABS	11) Chkg Acct Intrst	FOR
2) Strip Mines	AGN	7) Bust Hwy Trust	FOR	12) End HISC (HUAC)	FOR
3) Cut Mil $	FOR	8) Farm Sub Lmt	FOR	13) Nixon Sewer Veto	AGN
4) Rev Shrg	FOR	9) School Prayr	AGN	14) Corp Cmpaign $	AGN
5) Pub TV $	ABS	10) Cnsumr Prot	FOR	15) Pol $ Disclosr	FOR

Election Results

1972 general:	Jonathan B. Bingham (D-L)	107,448	(76%)
	Charles A. Avarello (R-C)	33,045	(24%)
1972 primary:	Jonathan B. Bingham (D)	24,938	(55%)
	James H. Scheuer (D)	20,493	(45%)
1970 general:	Jonathan B. Bingham (D)	78,723	(76%)
	George E. Sweeney	16,172	(16%)
	Nora M. Kardian (C)	8,456	(8%)

TWENTY-THIRD DISTRICT Political Background

The line that separates the Bronx from Westchester County has traditionally marked the end of Democratic New York City and the beginning of the Republican suburbs and upstate. Even in these days of ticket-splitting, a look at the origin of the allegiances, ones that still have some applicability, remains worthwhile. The traditional New York antagonism is most clearly contrasted in the state's 23rd congressional district, two-thirds of which lies in Westchester and one-third in the Bronx.

The Bronx portion of the district, a large middle-class residential area, is totally cut off from the rest of the 23rd by Van Cortlandt Park. Most of its people are of Italian or Jewish descent. As is the case in all the outer boroughs of New York City, far more people here hold jobs in the service-industry or the government than is commonly found in the rest of the country. The Democratic allegiance of the Bronx residents stems from an immigrant heritage—days when the Tammany machine brought by enough coal to last the winter in return for a couple of votes. Though the machine today provides little in the way of services, most voters here still believe that the Democrats are more likely than Republicans to favor their interests as city dwellers.

The tradition in the Westchester portion of the 23rd is quite different. It includes most of Yonkers, the towns of Greensburgh and Mount Pleasant, and the suburbs along the Hudson where Washington Irving once lived. With a few exceptions—one being the current Democratic Mayor of Yonkers—the Republicans have been in control here as long as anyone can remember. Many of the citizens of this part of the 23rd have backgrounds similar to those living in the the Bronx portion. Nevertheless, the Westchester people have come to perceive their interests as suburban and Republican. The perennial struggle in state government over money is one between New York City and the rest of the state. Over the years, the gerrymandered, malapportioned, and Republican legislatures have favored the suburbs and upstate at the expense of the city. So voting Republican has become almost a corollary of living north of the city limits.

In 1972, the 23rd was the scene of the closest congressional race in New York state and one of the closest in the nation. The competitors were a freshman Republican Congressman and a former Democratic Congressman, both from Westchester. The Democrat, Richard Ottinger, first won the district—then entirely in Westchester County and numbered the 25th—in 1964. He spent $200,000 doing it, and routed a conservative Republican named Robert Barry. One of the issues of the campaign was that Barry spent too much time in California; he has since run for Congress in three different California districts, losing each time. Ottinger, meanwhile, provided good constituency service, spent tons of his family's plywood fortune every two years, and concentrated on what are now called environmental issues—one of the first members of Congress to do so. Ottinger paid especially close attention to the Hudson Valley and opposed a freeway planned for its banks by Gov. Nelson Rockefeller, whose vast Pocantico Hills estate, incidentally, lies within the district.

In 1970, Ottinger made an ill-starred try for the Senate. More spending of family money for a saturation TV campaign brought him the Democratic nomination, but after leading in the polls during most of the campaign, he lost by a 39–37 margin to Conservative candidate, James Buckley. Ottinger ran fairly well upstate and in the suburbs, where he targeted much of his effort; the Democrat, however, lost important liberal votes in New York City to Republican incumbent Charles Goodell, who finished a poor third. Ottinger's family spent something like $2 million on the futile attempt.

Meanwhile, Republican Peter Peyser captured the House seat in Ottinger's old district. Peyser, then Mayor of Irvington, won with a minority (43%) of the votes in a four-candidate race. He stressed an opposition to the use of drugs by teenagers, perhaps because he was pressed by a Conservative candidate who eventually took 17% of the ballots. The 1972 redistricting, which kept the most Democratic parts of Yonkers out of the district and added the Bronx portion, was designed to help Peyser. The new lines, however, posed problems for both candidates. For Peyser, the problem was the Democratic tradition of the new Bronx appendage; for Ottinger, it was the same area's conservative stance on issues—along with the traditional Republicanism of the old Westchester constituency. Both candidates had good name identification in Westchester, but neither was especially well-known in the Bronx.

Ottinger, therefore, struck up an alliance with 10th-district Bronx Congressman Mario Biaggi. Elected on the Democratic-Conservative lines—and at the point a leading 1973 mayoral contender (see New York 10)—Biaggi was extremely popular with the 23rd's Italian-American voters. As an ex-policeman, Biaggi professed great expertise on the crime issue, and Ottinger, to capitalize on Biaggi's law-and-order image, offered the voters a detailed anti-crime program. Ottinger's strategy worked well in the Bronx, where he won 58% of the votes.

But the plan did not work quite as well in the district as a whole. Though the Bronx contains a near precise one-third of the 23rd's residents, it casts only one-quarter of the district's votes—another example of low registration and voter participation that characterizes even middle-class areas of New York City. And the turnout factor was enough to make the difference. For Peyser's two years of service made an impression good enough in Westchester to erase memories of Ottinger's six—good enough in this case means a 53–47 Peyser edge in the suburban county. That works out to a 1,402-vote Peyser reelection victory.

The narrow margin coming in a Republican year like 1972 might confront Peyser with another tight race in 1974. But things may not turn out that way, or if they do, someone other than Ottinger might be the challenger. After his 1973 defeat, Ottinger supported Mario Biaggi for Mayor, obviously in return for Biaggi's help in 1972. After it was learned that Biaggi had lied about having taken the Fifth Amendment before a grand jury, his campaign collapsed. Ottinger's support then became much more quiet. Nonetheless, Ottinger's involvement with Biaggi scarcely constitutes an asset, at least north of the city limits, where Watergate seems likely to dominate the 1974 elections. Moreover, Ottinger might still engender some resentment for alleged office-hopping; certainly had he not run for the Senate, he would surely still be in Congress today. Meanwhile, Peyser will continue to use the advantages of incumbency in an attempt to make himself invulnerable in 1974.

Census Data Pop. 467,778. Central city, 34%; suburban, 66%. Median family income, $12,693; families above $15,000: 39%; families below $3,000: 6%. Median years education, 12.3.

1972 Share of Federal Outlays $721,322,935

DOD	$122,243,289	HEW	$233,424,141
AEC	$2,872,019	HUD	$9,617,686
NASA	$1,398,055	DOI	$303,769
DOT	$9,676,059	USDA	$51,379,591
		Other	$290,408,326

Federal Military-Industrial Commitments

No installations or contractors receiving prime awards greater than $5,000,000.

Economic Base Finance, insurance and real estate; apparel and other textile products, especially women's and misses' outerwear; tourism; printing and publishing; and electrical equipment and supplies.

The Voters

Registration 230,807 total. 104,902 D (45%); 88,634 R (38%); 4,063 L (2%); 4,159 C (2%); 29,049 blank, missing and void (13%).
Median voting age 46.0
Employment profile White collar, 62%. Blue collar, 26%. Service, 12%. Farm, –%.
Ethnic groups Black, 13%. Spanish, 2%. Total foreign stock, 42%. Italy, 13%; Ireland, 4%; USSR, Germany, Poland, 3% each; UK, Austria, 2% each; Canada, 1%.

Presidential vote

1972	Nixon (R)	120,690	(61%)
	McGovern (D)	76,152	(39%)
1968	Nixon (R)	99,301	(48%)
	Humphrey (D)	92,265	(45%)
	Wallace (AI)	13,532	(7%)

Representative

Peter A. Peyser (R) Elected 1970; b. Sept. 7, 1921, Cedarhurst; home, Irvington; Colgate U., B.A., 1943; Army, WWII; married, five children; Episcopalian.

Career Insurance; Mgr., Peter A. Peyser Agency of Mutual of N.Y., 1961–70; Mayor of Irvington, 1963–70.

Offices 1133 LHOB, 202-225-5536. Also Rm. 209A, Yonkers General P.O., Yonkers 10701, 914-423-0990, and 655 E. 233rd St., Bronx 10466, 212-324-3387.

Administrative Assistant Lee Greif

Committees

Education and Labor (13th); Subs: No. 1 (Gen. Sub. on Education); No. 4 (Sel. Sub. on Labor); No. 5 (Sel. Sub. on Education).

Group Ratings

	ADA	COPE	LWV	RIPON	NFU	LCV	CFA	NAB	NSI	ACA
1972	44	89	80	90	67	43	100	42	100	33
1971	32	73	78	61	33	–	63	–	–	58

Key Votes

1) Busing	AGN	6) Cmbodia Bmbg	AGN	11) Chkg Acct Intrst	AGN
2) Strip Mines	ABS	7) Bust Hwy Trust	FOR	12) End HISC (HUAC)	AGN
3) Cut Mil $	AGN	8) Farm Sub Lmt	FOR	13) Nixon Sewer Veto	FOR
4) Rev Shrg	FOR	9) School Prayr	AGN	14) Corp Cmpaign $	FOR
5) Pub TV $	FOR	10) Cnsumr Prot	FOR	15) Pol $ Disclosr	AGN

Election Results

1972 general:	Peter A. Peyser (R-C)	99,777	(50%)
	Richard L. Ottinger (D-L)	98,335	(50%)
1972 primary:	Peter A. Peyser (R), unopposed		
1970 general:	Peter A. Peyser (R)	76,611	(43%)
	William Dretzin (D)	66,688	(37%)
	Anthony J. DeVito (C)	31,250	(17%)
	William S. Greenawalt (L)	5,697	(3%)

TWENTY-FOURTH DISTRICT Political Background

In the public mind, Westchester County is *the* suburb for the wealthy: the large, comfortable houses of Scarsdale and White Plains, each of them with a gently sloping lawn shaded by towering trees. Then there are the woodsier hills of Pound Ridge, Armonk, and Briarcliff Manor. All of these places lie in New York's 24th congressional district, the only seat entirely within Westchester County. But the conventional image of Westchester and the 24th is not really accurate. Plenty of rich people of course do live here—the constituency ranks 18th in median family income among the nation's congressional districts. Nevertheless, taken as a whole, the 24th is not homogeneously wealthy. Not far from the posh former home of the John N. Mitchells in Rye are middle-class, predominantly Italian-American neighborhoods, which in many ways are more typical of Westchester than the WASP and Jewish precincts of Scarsdale.

By tradition, Westchester is Republican. In recent years, some of its richer towns have moved to the left politically. Scarsdale, for example, went for Hubert Humphrey in 1968 and nearly went for George McGovern in 1972. But like most middle-income urban areas on the East Coast, the lower-income portions of the county have trended Republican. So as Scarsdale became more Democratic, traditional Democrats found in places like Mount Vernon and Rye began to vote Republican.

Westchester County and the 24th district constitute one of the ancestral homes of liberal Republicanism. Upper-income voters have traditionally set the tone of Westchester Republican politics; among them were some of the chief backers of figures like Thomas Dewey, Dwight Eisenhower, and Nelson Rockefeller. But as upper-income liberal voters switched to Democratic candidates, the less mellowed conservatism of middle-income voters has come to dominate New York Republican politics, even here in Westchester County.

Congressional elections in the 24th have reflected the same pattern. Ogden Reid, heir to the New York *Herald Tribune* fortune and onetime (1959–61) Ambassador to Israel, has represented the district since 1962. Reid himself was once the personification of liberal Republicanism. His grandfather, Whitelaw Reid, was one of the founders and early powers in the nation's Republican party. And though Ogden Reid's voting record in Congress was solidly liberal, he retained Republican allegiances and campaigned for Nelson Rockefeller whenever the Governor decided to run for President.

At general election time, Reid's kind of Republicanism proved extremely popular. He received many normally Democratic votes and regularly won by margins exceeding 2–1. But in the late 1960s, the Republican primary began to give Reid more trouble, as the mood of the district's registered Republicans hardened. In 1970, an unknown conservative challenger got 46% of the votes against Reid. Conservative Republicans in the district had clearly grown unhappy with the incumbent; these people took little satisfaction from having so-called Republican representation when the Congressman himself voted contrary to their convictions on most major issues.

As it turned out, Reid had also grown dissatisfied with the situation. In the years ahead, he could expect nothing but more tough congressional primaries. Moreover, the Republican road to political advancement was shut off. Though New York Republicans are far more adept at winning statewide elections than Democrats, none of the Republicans in the top spots showed any inclination to retire. So in early 1972, Reid decided to become a Democrat, thereby giving up high-ranking positions on both the Education and Labor and Government Operations committees for a junior Democratic slot on Foreign Affairs.

Reid's switch came not long after the same move by John Lindsay, who promptly began to run for President. Reid enraged Republican Nelson Rockefeller, among others. Over the years, Rockefeller had nurtured the Congressman's career; he now sensed a potential rival for the governorship in 1974. So Rockefeller was determined to see Reid lose his seat in 1972. He and Lt. Gov. Malcolm Wilson, an old Westchester politico, picked Reid's opponent, County District Attorney Carl Vergari. He had run well in a recent election, and seemed likely to prove especially popular with the district's large number of conservative-trending Italian-American voters.

On paper, Vergari's candidacy looked strong. Reid, therefore, ran scared—harder, he said, than he had ever run before. But the incumbent possessed a couple of advantages. As the campaign went on, it became clear that Vergari had no burning desire to go to Congress. It also became clear—and Reid stressed this—that Vergari's candidacy was a Rockefeller power play. So after the votes were counted, Reid came away with a 52–48 victory. In so doing, he retained enough of his former support, and even added the votes of a few liberal Democrats who had not supported him as a Republican.

Reid could probably go on winning in the 24th indefinitely. At this writing, however, he appears determined to run for Governor. Traveling around the state, Reid has met with Democratic leaders and spoken at various political gatherings. His chief rival for the nomination is Howard Samuels, currently head of New York City's Off-Track Betting Corporation. Neither man is a particular favorite of the Democratic bosses, the men who control the convention that confers the nomination. But because the decision of the bosses is not binding, the contest will probably be settled in the Democratic primary.

Census Data Pop. 468,148. Central city, 0%; suburban, 100%. Median family income, $13,577; families above $15,000: 44%; families below $3,000: 5%. Median years education, 12.4.

1972 Share of Federal Outlays $721,322,935

DOD	$122,243,289	HEW	$233,424,141
AEC	$2,872,019	HUD	$9,617,686
NASA	$1,398,055	DOI	$303,769
DOT	$9,676,059	USDA	$51,379,591
		Other	$290,408,326

Federal Military-Industrial Commitments

DOD Contractors General Foods (White Plains), $5.548m: foodstuffs. IBM (Armonk), $5.031m: unspecified.

Economic Base Finance, insurance and real estate; electrical equipment and supplies, especially electronic components and accessories; tourism; apparel and other textile products, especially women's and misses' outerwear; and chemicals and allied products, especially pharmaceutical preparations.

The Voters

Registration 229,630 total. 82,056 D (36%); 103,423 R (45%); 3,029 L (1%); 2,947 C (1%); 38,175 blank, missing and void (17%).
Median voting age 46.0
Employment profile White collar, 63%. Blue collar, 24%. Service, 13%. Farm, –%.
Ethnic groups Black, 13%. Total foreign stock, 39%. Italy, 13%; USSR, Germany, Ireland, UK, 3% each; Poland, 2%; Austria, Canada, 1% each.

Presidential vote

1972	Nixon (R)	135,553	(61%)
	McGovern (D)	87,068	(39%)
1968	Nixon (R)	100,797	(48%)
	Humphrey (D)	95,508	(46%)
	Wallace (AI)	12,064	(6%)

Representative

Ogden Rogers Reid (D) Elected 1962; b. June 24, 1925, New York City; home, Purchase; Yale, B.A., 1949; Army, WWII; Capt. USAR; married, six children; Presbyterian.

Career Pres., N.Y. *Herald Tribune,* Societe Anonyme, 1953–58; Pres. and Editor, N.Y. *Herald Tribune,* 1955–59; Dir., Panama Canal Co., 1956–59; U.S. Ambassador to Israel, 1959–61; Gov. Rockefeller's Cabinet, 1961–62; Chm., N.Y. State Commission for Human Rights, 1961–62; Dir., Atlantic Council of U.S.

Offices 240 CHOB, 202-225-6506. Also 371 Mamaroneck Ave., White Plains 10605, 914-428-3040.

Administrative Assistant Lawrence A. Turk

Committees

Foreign Affairs (18th); Subs: Europe; International Organizations and Movements; Near East and South Asia.

Group Ratings

	ADA	COPE	LWV	RIPON	NFU	LCV	CFA	NAB	NSI	ACA
1972	75	90	100	70	100	90	100	8	0	0
1971	89	91	100	94	64	–	88	–	–	7
1970	84	83	–	94	92	90	95	18	0	12

Key Votes

1) Busing	FOR	6) Cmbodia Bmbg	AGN	11) Chkg Acct Intrst	ABS
2) Strip Mines	ABS	7) Bust Hwy Trust	FOR	12) End HISC (HUAC)	FOR
3) Cut Mil $	FOR	8) Farm Sub Lmt	FOR	13) Nixon Sewer Veto	AGN
4) Rev Shrg	FOR	9) School Prayr	AGN	14) Corp Cmpaign $	AGN
5) Pub TV $	FOR	10) Cnsumr Prot	FOR	15) Pol $ Disclosr	FOR

Election Results

1972 general:	Ogden R. Reid (D-L)	107,979	(52%)
	Carl A. Vergari (R-C)	94,224	(48%)
1972 primary:	Ogden R. Reid (D-L), unopposed		
1970 general:	Ogden R. Reid (R-L)	109,783	(66%)
	Michael A. Coffey (C)	29,702	(18%)
	G. Russell James (D)	25,909	(16%)

TWENTY-FIFTH DISTRICT Political Background

The 25th congressional district of New York occupies the heart of the Hudson River Valley. The 25th extends from the Bear Mountain Bridge, some 30 miles north of Manhattan, to a point about half way to Albany. Like most rivers in the country, the Hudson is hideously polluted, but a panoramic view of the river valley remains one of the most breath-taking in America. Within the bounds of the 25th lies the Hyde Park estate of Franklin D. Roosevelt.

The area encompassed by the district is one of the few in upstate New York to have experienced substantial population growth of late. This part of the state is traditionally Republican, a political preference strengthened by the recent arrival of large numbers of conservative-minded middle-class people from New York City. During the 1930s and 1940s, Roosevelt could never carry his home area, and it persisted in reelecting one of FDR's most vituperative adversaries, Congressman Hamilton Fish, an isolationist Republican. Socially prominent Hamilton Fishes have been sent to Congress from the Hudson Valley off and on since 1842. FDR's old enemy was defeated in 1944. He was replaced by a Republican named J. Ernest Wharton, who will probably be best remembered in American history as having attracted writer Gore Vidal as a Democratic opponent in 1960. Vidal lost, but Wharton was defeated in 1964 by Joseph Y. Resnick, a self-made millionaire, domestic liberal, and a Vietnam hawk. Resnick made an unsuccessful bid for the Democratic Senate nomination in 1968 and died shortly thereafter.

In 1968, the Fish dynasty regained control of the Hudson Valley district in the person of 42-year-old Hamilton Fish, Jr. This Fish, like his father, is also a Republican, but a considerably more liberal one. Like his father, who is still living, the Congressman is skeptical about American intervention abroad, having voted for end-the-war measures in the House. Fish, Jr.'s only difficult election occurred in 1968, when he got through a tough primary and faced a vigorous Democratic opponent in the general election. Fish's Republican primary opponent, a Dutchess County Assistant District Attorney, ran in the general election as the Conservative nominee, but campaigned little. When Fish won, he sent a pro forma letter recommending his erstwhile opponent for a position in the Nixon Administration.

The letter would mean little today, except that Fish endorsed a man named G. Gordon Liddy. The Congressman, however, can scarcely be blamed for Liddy's subsequent activities. The now-famous man was fired from a post in the Treasury Department when he spoke out against the Administration's policy towards gun control. So the people who hired him at the White House and the Committee to Reelect the President had every reason to know what kind of nut they signed on. It seems that some people move ever upward, despite one defeat after another. Liddy moved to the highest levels of the White House and the Nixon campaign, while Fish, someone who trounced him in 1968, remains a rather junior Congressman in the House of Representatives.

Census Data Pop. 467,859. Central city, 0%; suburban, 26%. Median family income, $11,885; families above $15,000: 32%; families below $3,000: 6%. Median years education, 12.3.

1972 Share of Federal Outlays $489,910,987

DOD	$51,516,642	HEW	$168,313,961
AEC	$739,331	HUD	$6,227,189
NASA	$2,152,196	DOI	$1,037,397
DOT	$3,660,591	USDA	$16,001,658
		Other	$240,262,022

Federal Military-Industrial Commitments

DOD Contractors IBM (Kingston), $11.789m: electronics research.

Economic Base Machinery; finance, insurance and real estate; printing and publishing; apparel and other textile products, especially women's and misses' outerwear; electrical equipment and supplies, especially electronic components and accessories; and agriculture, notably dairy products, cattle and poutlry.

The Voters

Registration 176,800 total. 49,417 D (28%); 76,659 R (43%); 2,280 L (1%); 4,176 C (2%); 44,268 blank, missing and void (25%).
Median voting age 42.8
Employment profile White collar, 56%. Blue collar, 30%. Service, 13%. Farm, 1%.
Ethnic groups Black, 5%. Total foreign stock, 25%. Italy, 6%; Germany, 4%; UK, Ireland, 2% each; Canada, Poland, USSR, 1% each.

Presidential vote

1972	Nixon (R)	148,003	(70%)
	McGovern (D)	63,536	(30%)
1968	Nixon (R)	102,353	(55%)
	Humphrey (D)	68,225	(37%)
	Wallace (AI)	14,735	(8%)

Representative

Hamilton Fish, Jr. (R) Elected 1968; b. June 3, 1926, Washington, D.C.; home, Millbrook; Harvard Col., B.A., 1949; N.Y.U., LL.B., 1957; USNR, WWII; widower, four children; Episcopalian.

Career Vice Counsel, U.S. Foreign Svc., Ireland, 1951–53; Counsel, N.Y. State Assembly Judicial Com., N.Y. Judiciary Com., 1961; Dir., Dutchess County Civil Defense, 1967–68.

Offices 1534 LHOB, 202-225-5441. Also 509 Warren St., Hudson 12534, 518-828-6960, and 292 Fair St., Kingston 12401, 914-331-4466.

Administrative Assistant John D. Barry

Committees

Judiciary (8th); Subs: No. 2 (Claims); No. 6 (Revision of the Laws) (Ranking Mbr.).

Group Ratings

	ADA	COPE	LWV	RIPON	NFU	LCV	CFA	NAB	NSI	ACA
1972	38	55	89	100	57	80	0	58	100	29
1971	43	42	67	76	43	–	57	–	–	59
1970	48	42	–	94	62	100	86	83	89	68

Key Votes

1) Busing	AGN	6) Cmbodia Bmbg	AGN	11) Chkg Acct Intrst	FOR
2) Strip Mines	ABS	7) Bust Hwy Trust	FOR	12) End HISC (HUAC)	AGN
3) Cut Mil $	AGN	8) Farm Sub Lmt	FOR	13) Nixon Sewer Veto	AGN
4) Rev Shrg	FOR	9) School Prayr	FOR	14) Corp Cmpaign $	AGN
5) Pub TV $	AGN	10) Cnsumr Prot	FOR	15) Pol $ Disclosr	FOR

Election Results

1972 general:	Hamilton Fish, Jr. (R-C)	144,386	(72%)
	John M. Burns III (D)	54,271	(27%)
	Robert P. Falisey (L)	2,879	(1%)
1972 primary:	Hamilton Fish, Jr. (R), unopposed		
1970 general:	Hamilton Fish, Jr. (R)	119,954	(71%)
	John J. Greaney (D)	41,908	(25%)
	Harry S. Hoffman, Jr. (C)	7,606	(4%)

TWENTY-SIXTH DISTRICT Political Background

The 26th district of New York lies just at the margin of the New York City suburbs and the vast expanse of upstate New York. Fast-growing Rockland County, the southern end of the district, is definitely within the city's orbit. Though it almost always goes Republican, Rockland has a Democratic edge in registration and a large Jewish population. Many of the county's residents work in the city, commuting across the Tappan Zee or George Washington bridges. Situated above Rockland County and separated from it by a mountain ridge, lies Orange County, once a largely rural area, with one small, stagnant city on the Hudson, Newburgh. In recent years, Orange County has experienced explosive growth, much of it resulting from the exodus of New York City policemen, firemen, and civil servants. These are people escaping the horrors which they have to deal with from one day to the next. By long-standing tradition, Orange County is Republican; the new migrants have made that political preference as intense and popular as it is in the county's California namesake. James Buckley was a big favorite here in 1970, as was Richard Nixon in 1972.

The 26th, therefore, is a solidly Republican district these days. But in three of the last five elections, the district—one that has undergone several boundary changes and a renumbering—has elected a Democratic Congressman. And that Democrat was scarcely one to concede much to the conservative sensibilities of his constituents. John G. Dow, a beneficiary of the 1964 Johnson landslide, was an outspoken peace advocate and a general all-round liberal during his six years in Congress from 1965 to 1969, and again from 1971 to 1973. He used to do things like vote for bills lifting the penalty for desecrating the flag and against ones increasing criminal penalties for drug use. It was no surprise, then, that Dow was beaten by Republican Martin McKneally, a former national commander of the American Legion, in 1968. A staunch law-and-order man, McKneally looked like a cinch for reelection in 1970. During the course of the campaign, however, it was suddenly revealed that the incumbent had not bothered to file federal income tax returns for several years. The revelation blew the law-and-order issue and the election for McKneally. Dow was returned to office with 52% of the votes.

But 1972 was too much for Dow. As in 1968, Richard Nixon carried a solid majority in the district, and Dow lost again in a presidential election year. The victor this time was liberal Republican Assemblyman Benjamin Gilman, who won a minority victory, as the Conservative nominee took 13% of the votes. Gilman lost Rockland to Dow, but carried his home county of Orange by a solid 16,000 votes. Odds are that Gilman, a member of the Foreign Affairs Committee, will be reelected easily in the years to come.

Census Data Pop. 467,424. Central city, 0%; suburban, 49%. Median family income, $11,632; families above $15,000: 31%; families below $3,000: 6%. Median years education, 12.3.

1972 Share of Federal Outlays $641,637,416

DOD	$143,684,949	HEW	$201,897,662
AEC	$1,414,682	HUD	$6,659,657
NASA	$688,664	DOI	$372,023
DOT	$5,499,433	USDA	$27,496,806
		Other	$253,923,540

Federal Military-Industrial Commitments

DOD Installations West Point Military Academy and Reservation (West Point).

Economic Base Finance, insurance and real estate; chemicals and allied products, especially drugs and soap, cleaners and toilet goods; agriculture, notably dairy products, vegetables and poultry; apparel and other textile products, especially women's and misses' outerwear; textile mill products; and paper and allied products. Also higher education (State Univ. College, Brockport).

The Voters

Registration 223,730 total. 85,947 D (38%); 97,604 R (44%); 3,148 L (1%); 8,899 C (4%); 28,132 blank, missing and void (13%).
Median voting age 42.2
Employment profile White collar, 53%. Blue collar, 32%. Service, 14%. Farm, 1%.
Ethnic groups Black, 6%. Spanish, 2%. Total foreign stock, 28%. Italy, 6%; Germany, USSR, Ireland, 3% each; Poland, UK, 2% each; Austria, Canada, 1% each.

Presidential vote

1972	Nixon (R)	133,873	(68%)
	McGovern (D)	63,450	(32%)
1968	Nixon (R)	89,655	(53%)
	Humphrey (D)	66,783	(39%)
	Wallace (AI)	13,301	(8%)

Representative

Benjamin A. Gilman (R) Elected 1972; b. Dec. 6, 1922, Poughkeepsie; home, Middletown; Wharton School, U. of Pa., B.S.; N.Y. Law School, LL.B.; Army, WWII; married, five children; Jewish.

Career Deputy Asst. Atty. Gen., 1952; Asst. Atty. Gen., 1954; Partner, Gilman & Gilman, 1955; Atty., N.Y. Temp. Comm. on the Courts, 1956–57; State Assembly, 1967–72.

Offices 1723 LHOB, 202-225-3776. Also Newburgh, 914-565-6400, and Nyack, 914-358-6688, and Middletown, 914-343-6666.

Administrative Assistant Kenneth M. Bellis

Committees

Foreign Affairs (17th); Subs: Foreign Economic Policy; Near East and South Asia.

Group Ratings: Newly Elected

Key Votes

1) Busing	NE	6) Cmbodia Bmbg	AGN	11) Chkg Acct Intrst	AGN
2) Strip Mines	NE	7) Bust Hwy Trust	FOR	12) End HISC (HUAC)	AGN
3) Cut Mil $	NE	8) Farm Sub Lmt	NE	13) Nixon Sewer Veto	FOR
4) Rev Shrg	NE	9) School Prayr	NE	14) Corp Cmpaign $	NE
5) Pub TV $	NE	10) Cnsumr Prot	NE	15) Pol $ Disclosr	NE

Election Results

1972 general:	Benjamin A. Gilman (R)	90,922	(48%)
	John G. Dow (D)	74,906	(39%)
	Yale Rapkin (C-Ind.)	24,596	(13%)
1972 primary:	Benjamin A. Gilman (R)	17,677	(58%)
	Yale Rapkin (R)	12,752	(42%)

TWENTY-SEVENTH DISTRICT Political Background

New York's 27th congressional district extends along the state's southern boundary from the Catskills to the Southern Tier. The Catskills are famous for huge Borscht Belt hotels like Grossinger's and the Concord; for Dutch-descended Rip van Winkle; and for the phenomenon of the Woodstock festival. The happening actually took place some 50 miles from Woodstock, which is the Catskills home of people like Bob Dylan. The Catskills make up the eastern portion of the 27th. To the west the mountains subside into the Appalachian plateau and a row of counties along New York's boundary with Pennsylvania, called the Southern Tier. Here is Binghamton, an old manufacturing city that is the largest in the district, and Ithaca, the home of Cornell University.

With the exception of Sullivan County in the Jewish Borscht Belt, most of the territory encompassed by the 27th is ancestrally Republican. Unlike the rest of New York state, however, the district has not shown a rapid shift to the right in recent elections. One reason is that the 27th contains proportionally fewer members of those ethnic groups in which the rightward shift is most pronounced.

The 27th's Congressman, Howard Robison, first went to Congress after a 1958 special election. At that time, conservative Republicans with high seniority dominated the upstate congressional delegation. During the Eisenhower years, upstaters John Taber (Chairman of the Appropriations Committee in 1953–54), Sterling Cole (Chairman of the Joint Committee on Atomic Energy), and Daniel Reed (Chairman of Ways and Means), were all leaders of the Taftish wing of the GOP in Congress. Today, Robison is the dean of the Republican delegation, and the 7th-ranking Republican on the House Appropriations Committee. Here he is the ranking minority member on the treasury, Post Office, General Government Subcommittee, which, among other things, controls the purse-strings for the bloated operations and payroll of the White House. After the Watergate story broke, Robison joined other members of the subcommittee when it supported reductions in the appropriation used to run the White House.

Robison's moderate-to-liberal voting record is a nice illustration of the changes in the upstate delegation since he first came to Washington. In the 93rd Congress, there are no more than half a dozen Upstate Congressmen with solidly conservative voting records, as compared to more than a dozen 15 years ago. Robison has had little trouble winning reelection, though he was reportedly unhappy with the substantial changes made in his district's boundaries for the 1972 election.

Census Data Pop. 467,980. Central city, 14%; suburban, 44%. Median family income, $9,904; families above $15,000: 20%; families below $3,000: 8%. Median years education, 12.3.

1972 Share of Federal Outlays $566,339,878

DOD	$133,978,924	HEW	$179,473,307
AEC	$895,672	HUD	$9,531,792
NASA	$1,077,858	DOI	$866,773
DOT	$3,298,332	USDA	$9,952,980
		Other	$227,264,240

Federal Military-Industrial Commitments

DOD Contractors IBM (Owego), $52.782m: navigation, sonar, weapons delivery electronic systems. Singer (Binghamton), $29.399m: flight trainer devices. General Electric (Binghamton), $17.270m: auto pilots; computers for aircraft weapons delivery systems.

Economic Base Machinery; finance, insurance and real estate; agriculture, notably dairy products and poultry; leather and leather products, especially shoes, except rubber; and electrical equipment and supplies, especially electronic components and accessories. Also higher education (Cornell Univ., and SUNY, Binghamton; and State Univ. College, New Paltz).

The Voters

Registration 224,938 total. 74,585 D (33%); 120,107 R (53%); 2,691 L (1%); 2,522 C (1%); 25,033 blank, missing and void (11%).
Median voting age 42.7
Employment profile White collar, 51%. Blue collar, 32%. Service, 14%. Farm, 3%.
Ethnic groups Black, 2%. Total foreign stock, 19%. Italy, 3%; Germany, UK, Poland, Czechoslovakia, 2% each; USSR, Austria, Canada, 1% each.

Presidential vote

1972	Nixon (R)	141,972	(64%)
	McGovern (D)	81,179	(36%)
1968	Nixon (R)	100,771	(54%)
	Humphrey (D)	73,629	(40%)
	Wallace (AI)	11,771	(6%)

Representative

Howard Winfield Robison (R) Elected Jan. 14, 1958; b. Oct. 30, 1915, Owego; home, Owego; Cornell U., B.A., 1937, LL.B., 1939; Army, WWII; married, two children; Methodist.

Career Practicing atty., 1939–57; County Atty., 1946–58.

Offices 2330 RHOB, 202-225-6335. Also 302 Fed. Bldg., Binghamton 13902, 607-723-4425.

Administrative Assistant Allan Schimmel

Committees

Appropriations (7th); Subs: Public Works, AEC; Treasury, Postal Service, General Government (Ranking Mbr.).

Group Ratings

	ADA	COPE	LWV	RIPON	NFU	LCV	CFA	NAB	NSI	ACA
1972	50	9	83	86	29	47	100	83	50	45
1971	43	18	67	94	33	–	63	–	–	63
1970	64	60	–	94	80	40	47	67	80	56

Key Votes

1) Busing	FOR	6) Cmbodia Bmbg	AGN	11) Chkg Acct Intrst	FOR
2) Strip Mines	AGN	7) Bust Hwy Trust	FOR	12) End HISC (HUAC)	AGN
3) Cut Mil $	ABS	8) Farm Sub Lmt	AGN	13) Nixon Sewer Veto	FOR
4) Rev Shrg	FOR	9) School Prayr	AGN	14) Corp Cmpaign $	AGN
5) Pub TV $	AGN	10) Cnsumr Prot	FOR	15) Pol $ Disclsr	FOR

Election Results

1972 general:	Howard W. Robison (R)	114,902	(62%)
	David H. Blazer (D)	55,076	(30%)
	Patrick M. O'Neil (C)	9,521	(5%)
	William J. Osby (L)	5,329	(3%)
1972 primary:	Howard W. Robison (R), unopposed		
1970 general:	Howard W. Robison (R)	90,196	(67%)
	David Bernstein (D-L)	45,373	(33%)

TWENTY-EIGHTH DISTRICT Political Background

The 28th district of New York is the Albany-Schenectady area, where the Mohawk River flows into the Hudson. The district contains virtually all of Albany and Schenectady counties, along with the aging, carpet-milling town of Amsterdam in Montgomery County. Of these places, the most interesting and politically significant is Albany, where an old-fashioned Democratic machine still holds sway over local politics. Daniel O'Connell, at 87, still runs the machine from his home. To measure the antiquity of the machine, one need only know that O'Connell has been the man to see in Albany for more than 50 years, and his Mayor, a local aristocrat named Erastus Corning II, has held that office since 1942. It remains the practice in Albany, or so a state commission found, for all aspiring city employees to get clearance from their local Democratic ward boss. Moreover, favoritism still exists for the well-connected contractor, as does the no-show job for the ward heeler. Nevertheless, local government in Albany services its citizens poorly, who, however, may know some consolation because so many of them are already on the payroll.

Albany once ground out the largest Democratic majorities between the New York City limits and Buffalo. It is still more Democratic than most of upstate, but often goes Republican. One reason may be the ward heeler's inability to influence people how to vote for President or Senator; another may be their indifference to politics above the county level. Yet another reason, surely, is the political clout of Gov. Nelson Rockefeller. For Albany is the state capital, and Rockefeller has poured something like $1 billion into the construction of the huge Albany Mall, which will undoubtedly be the chief monument to his reign. Albany gratefully voted for Rockefeller in 1970, and the city cast its votes for his current political friend, Richard Nixon, in 1972.

For a while, Albany also had a Republican Congressman—another indication of the machine's ineffectiveness at anything but perpetuating its own existence. When machine man Leo O'Brien retired in 1966, the district was captured by Daniel Button, a newspaperman and TV commentator, whose book, *Lindsay, A Man For Tomorrow*, suggests his politics. Congressman Button compiled a liberal, antiwar record, and won easy reelection in 1968.

But in 1970, the Republican legislature placed Button in the same district with Democratic Samuel Stratton. Stratton also began his local career as a TV commentator. He could be seen on the tube in Schenectady—a town dominated by General Electric and one more amenable than Albany to GE's solidly Republican sentiments. Stratton managed to get himself elected Mayor in 1956, and then went on to become Congressman in the big Democratic year of 1958.

The upstate Republicans who control the New York legislature, outraged by Stratton's political survival in 1960, planned to get rid of him in 1962. They designed him a district that stretched halfway across the state to the Finger Lakes country, leaving out Schenectady. Stratton moved his residence to Amsterdam, campaigned vigorously, and won reelection by a 2-1 margin. So by 1970, the legislature decided to give him Schenectady once more, and Albany to boot. This way they could be sure of doing in either a liberal Republican, Button, or a pesky Democrat, Stratton. They did in Button, whom Stratton beat 66–34. For the 1972 elections, the legislature courteously strengthened Stratton in the 28th, and at the same time, denuded adjoining districts of Democrats who might bother Republican incumbents there.

If New York Republicans consider Stratton pesky, so probably do many members of Congress. As a member of the Armed Services Committee, Stratton has developed the reputation of a maverick—and not because he is some kind of dove. On the contrary, he was always a proponent of American military intervention in Indochina. Instead, it is his irreverent sniping at military shibboleths that irritates the powers that be on Armed Services.

Stratton is also the perennial leader of the fight to prevent extension of the West Front of the Capitol. This is a pet project of the House leadership and its patronage employee, the Architect of the Capitol, who is usually an ex-Congressman, not an architect. The extension is designed to cost some fabulous sum, and like the Rayburn Office Building, will no doubt end up costing far more. The project would also destroy the last remaining visible section of the original Capitol. Stratton has dared to say what is surely the truth, that the real reason behind the scheme is to create more hideaway office space for senior Congressmen. To say so is not the sort of thing that wins friends and influences people on Capitol Hill. But Stratton probably doesn't care. He currently enjoys fifth-ranking Democratic status on the Armed Services Committee, where he is several years younger than more senior members. Back home, he is sure to win indefinite reelection.

Because of his phenomenal vote-getting prowess, Stratton has been mentioned from time to time as a possible candidate for statewide office. Most recently, it was suggested that he run for Governor in 1974. But despite the enthusiasm of some upstate Democrats for the idea, it seems unlikely that the Congressman could win the Democratic primary. Stratton is scarcely known in the New York City metropolitan area, and his hawkish voting record would turn off hundreds of thousands of Democratic primary voters. Even if he got the nomination, Stratton's ideology would also become a problem in the general election. With Stratton the nominee, the Liberal party would likely run a separate candidate like John Lindsay, who would get many usually Democratic votes. So the outlook is for Stratton to remain in the House.

Census Data Pop. 467,219. Central city, 13%; suburban, 47%. Median family income, $10,764; families above $15,000: 25%; families below $3,000: 6%. Median years education, 12.2.

1972 Share of Federal Outlays $928,464,737

DOD	$203,387,452	HEW	$279,556,167
AEC	$42,712,858	HUD	$13,815,957
NASA	$1,857,826	DOI	$1,944,279
DOT	$17,519,880	USDA	$10,726,298
		Other	$356,953,020

Federal Military-Industrial Commitments

DOD Contractors General Electric (Schenectady), $259.136m: research and development on naval nuclear propulsion work; nuclear reactor components; electronic ware. Condec Corp. (Schenectady), $6.325m: trucks with fuel tanks.
DOD Installations Watervliet Army Arsenal (Watervliet).
AEC Operations General Electric (Schenectady), $67.372m: multi-project research and development on nuclear reactors.

Economic Base Finance, insurance and real estate; stone, clay and glass products; food and kindred products; electrical equipment and supplies, especially electrical industrial apparatus; and printing and publishing, especially commercial printing. Also higher education (SUNY, Albany).

The Voters

Registration 176,194 total. 47,386 D (27%); 88,898 R (50%); 1,473 L (1%); 1,147 C (1%); 37,290 blank, missing and void (21%).
Median voting age 46.0
Employment profile White collar, 58%. Blue collar, 29%. Service, 12%. Farm, 1%.
Ethnic groups Black, 4%. Total foreign stock, 27%. Italy, 7%; Poland, 4%; Germany, 3%; Canada, UK, Ireland, 2% each; USSR, 1%.

Presidential vote

1972	Nixon (R)	134,123	(57%)
	McGovern (D)	101,128	(43%)
1968	Nixon (R)	89,880	(41%)
	Humphrey (D)	121,389	(55%)
	Wallace (AI)	9,596	(4%)

Representative

Samuel S. Stratton (D) Elected 1958; b. Sept. 27, 1916, Yonkers; home, Amsterdam; U. of Rochester, B.A., 1937; Haverford Col., M.A., 1938; Harvard U., M.A., 1940; USNR, WWII and Korean War; Capt. USNR; married, five children; Presbyterian.

Career Sec., Rep. Thomas H. Eliot of Mass., 1940–42; Deputy Sec. Gen., Far Eastern Commission, 1946–48; City Councilman, 1950–56; Mayor of Schenectady, 1956–59.

Offices 2466 RHOB, 202-225-5076. Also P.O. Bldg., Schenectady 12304, 518-374-4547, and P.O. Bldg., Amsterdam 12010, 518-843-3400, and 150 State St., Albany,

Administrative Assistant Vacant

Committees

Armed Services (5th); Subs: No. 4 (Chm.); No. 5; Sp. Sub. on Armed Services Investigating.

Group Ratings

	ADA	COPE	LWV	RIPON	NFU	LCV	CFA	NAB	NSI	ACA
1972	38	82	73	78	71	47	50	18	100	22
1971	41	89	67	35	64	–	88	–	–	40
1970	7	80	–	59	90	53	71	30	100	21

Key Votes

1) Busing	AGN	6) Cmbodia Bmbg	FOR	11) Chkg Acct Intrst	FOR
2) Strip Mines	AGN	7) Bust Hwy Trust	FOR	12) End HISC (HUAC)	AGN
3) Cut Mil $	AGN	8) Farm Sub Lmt	FOR	13) Nixon Sewer Veto	AGN
4) Rev Shrg	FOR	9) School Prayr	FOR	14) Corp Cmpaign $	FOR
5) Pub TV $	FOR	10) Cnsumr Prot	FOR	15) Pol $ Disclosr	AGN

Election Results

1972 general:	Samuel S. Stratton (D)	182,395	(80%)
	John F. Ryan, Jr. (R-C)	45,623	(20%)
1972 primary:	Samuel S. Stratton (D), unopposed		
1970 general:	Samuel S. Stratton (D)	128,017	(66%)
	Daniel E. Button (R-L)	65,339	(34%)

TWENTY-NINTH DISTRICT Political Background

The 29th district of New York, once a predominantly rural area, has now become pretty urban. More than half the district's people live within 20 miles of Albany, a city located in the adjacent 28th district. Many of these, some 63,000, reside in the aging, population-losing city of Troy, just across and up the Hudson River from Albany. Saratoga County constitutes the part of the district that has experienced the most growth recently. The county catches the spill-over from the Albany-Schenectady-Troy metropolitan area. To some extent, the shifts in population have also affected the district's politics. Much of it is still very much Yankee Republican, namely, the rolling hills and mountains aroung Lake George and Fort Ticonderoga. Many of the original settlers here came from Vermont, which until 1791 was part of New York. But as the population continues to grow around Saratoga, long known as a fashionable spa and site of an equally fashionable race track, the district assumes more the cast of a conservative Catholic Republican hue.

The trend no doubt sits well with Congressman Carleton J. King, who was first elected in 1960 after a long career as Saratoga County District Attorney. His closest call came in 1964, when he was reelected by a scant 1,109 votes. As far as can be determined, King would have lost the district as presently drawn. Recent large percentages can therefore be taken as an indication of his increasing political strength.

Congressman King is a conservative Republican—on most issues, the most conservative Congressman from New York state. In Washington, he is a middle-ranking member of the House Armed Services Committee, where he rarely dissents from its hawkish, bi-partisan consensus. Barring the unexpected, King will return to Capitol Hill as long as he likes. Only his advancing age (70 in 1974) suggests that he may chose to retire.

Census Data Pop. 467,767. Central city, 13%; suburban, 47%. Median family income, $9,621; families above $15,000: 18%; families below $3,000: 8%. Median years education, 12.1.

1972 Share of Federal Outlays $749,697,471

DOD	$132,648,922	HEW	$249,507,118
AEC	$27,529,523	HUD	$9,180,475
NASA	$1,197,416	DOI	$1,448,076
DOT	$13,283,028	USDA	$9,813,466
		Other	$305,089,447

Federal Military-Industrial Commitments

DOD Installations Saratoga AF Station (Saratoga Springs).

Economic Base Finance, insurance and real estate; paper and allied products; agriculture, notably dairy products, poultry and dairy cattle; apparel and other textile products; chemicals and allied products; and textile mill products, especially knitting mill products.

The Voters

Registration 258,205 total. 56,307 D (22%); 137,925 R (53%); 2,150 L (1%); 2,400 C (1%); 59,423 blank, missing and void (23%).
Median voting age 44.7
Employment profile White collar, 47%. Blue collar, 38%. Service, 12%. Farm, 3%.
Ethnic groups Black, 2%. Total foreign stock, 18%. Italy, Canada, 3% each; Germany, UK, Ireland, 2% each; Poland, 1%.

Presidential vote

1972	Nixon (R)	156,842	(70%)
	McGovern (D)	67,570	(30%)
1968	Nixon (R)	112,265	(56%)
	Humphrey (D)	76,151	(38%)
	Wallace (AI)	11,412	(6%)

Representative

Carleton J. King (R) Elected 1960; b. June 15, 1904, Saratoga Springs; home, Saratoga Springs; Union U., LL.B., 1926; married, two children; Catholic.

Career Practicing atty., 1926–60; Acting City Judge, Saratoga Springs, 1936–41; Asst. Dist. Atty., Saratoga County, 1942–50; Dist. Atty., Saratoga County, 1950–61; Pres., N.Y. State Dist. Attys.' Assn., 1955.

Offices 2245 RHOB, 202-225-5615. Also P.O. Bldg., Troy 12180, 518-274-3121, and 444 Broadway, Saratoga Springs 12866, 518-584-2200.

Administrative Assistant George L. Berg, Jr.

Committees

Armed Services (5th); Sub: No. 5.

Standards of Official Conduct (4th).

Group Ratings

	ADA	COPE	LWV	RIPON	NFU	LCV	CFA	NAB	NSI	ACA
1972	0	9	33	58	57	18	0	82	100	90
1971	6	9	33	47	43	–	13	–	–	92
1970	4	9	–	36	25	14	37	90	100	80

Key Votes

1) Busing	AGN	6) Cmbodia Bmbg	ABS	11) Chkg Acct Intrst	ABS
2) Strip Mines	AGN	7) Bust Hwy Trust	ABS	12) End HISC (HUAC)	ABS
3) Cut Mil $	AGN	8) Farm Sub Lmt	FOR	13) Nixon Sewer Veto	FOR
4) Rev Shrg	FOR	9) School Prayr	FOR	14) Corp Cmpaign $	FOR
5) Pub TV $	AGN	10) Cnsumr Prot	AGN	15) Pol $ Disclosr	AGN

Election Results

1972 general:	Carleton J. King (R-C)	139,270	(70%)
	Harold B. Gordon (D-L)	63,920	(30%)
1972 primary:	Carleton J. King (R), unopposed		
1970 general:	Carleton J. King (R-C)	95,470	(57%)
	Edward W. Pattison (D-L)	71,832	(43%)

THIRTIETH DISTRICT Political Background

The 30th district covers the northernmost reaches of New York state. It includes the counties across from Canada along the St. Lawrence River and the ones at the eastern end of Lake Ontario. The large French-Canadian population in Clinton and Franklin counties, just 100 miles south of Montreal, constitutes the only Democratic voting bloc in the district. As one moves west and south, there are fewer French-Canadians and more Yankees. Here in the farm country between the St. Lawrence and the Adirondacks, where it gets bitterly cold in the winter and not too warm in the summer, the voting patterns are decidedly Republican. This region accounts for the Republican leanings of the district overall. Much of the 30th is taken up by the Adirondack Forest Preserve, a giant state park that the New York Constitution stipulates must remain "forever wild." Some enterprising developers, however, have begun to fight the stipulation. Massena, in St. Lawrence County, contains the administrative headquarters of the St. Lawrence Seaway, and its failure to live up to economic expectations has been a blow to this economically depressed area.

In 1964, the Congressman from the 30th, conservative Republican Clarence E. Kilburn, having just turned 70, announced that he was going to retire because of age. At the time, his was an unusual move for a Congressman with considerable seniority and no reason to expect defeat at the polls. (It is considerably more common today, now that the congressional pension runs as high as $32,000 annually.)

Kilburn's successor was Robert McEwen, a like-minded Republican, who was a state Senator from the area for 10 years. Every two years, McEwen has won reelection with solid majorities, doing particularly well in the usually Democratic portions of the district. As a low-ranking member of the Appropriations Committee, the Congressman makes his biggest policy inputs as the ranking minority member on the District of Columbia Subcommittee. He still has a long climb to the top of the seniority ladder on Appropriations, but because he is only 54 (in 1974), he will presumably have many years to make the effort.

Census Data Pop. 467,920. Central city, 0%; suburban, 20%. Median family income, $8,584; families above $15,000: 14%; families below $3,000: 10%. Median years education, 12.0.

1972 Share of Federal Outlays $535,815,420

DOD	$87,789,581	HEW	$156,350,704
AEC	$98,033	HUD	$2,349,485
NASA	$45,174	DOI	$1,490,337
DOT	$5,734,538	USDA	$12,976,979
		Other	$268,980,589

Federal Military-Industrial Commitments

DOD Installations Plattsburg AFB (Plattsburg). Watertown AF Station (Watertown).

Economic Base Agriculture, notably dairy products, dairy cattle and vegetables; paper and allied products, especially paper mill products other than building paper; primary metal industries; and finance, insurance and real estate. Also higher education (State Univ. College, Oswego).

The Voters

Registration 207,635 total. 70,184 D (34%); 119,231 R (57%); 2,547 L (1%); 1,406 C (1%); 14,267 blank, missing and void (7%).
Median voting age 43.1
Employment profile White collar, 41%. Blue collar, 37%. Service, 16%. Farm, 6%.
Ethnic groups Total foreign stock, 15%. Canada, 7%; Italy, 2%; UK, 1%.

Presidential vote

1972	Nixon (R)	122,127	(67%)
	McGovern (D)	60,180	(33%)
1968	Nixon (R)	93,004	(55%)
	Humphrey (D)	67,935	(40%)
	Wallace (AI)	7,306	(4%)

Representative

Robert Cameron McEwen (R) Elected 1964; b. Jan. 5, 1920, Ogdensburg; home, Ogdensburg; U. of Vt.; U. of Pa., Wharton School of Finance and Commerce; Albany Law School, LL.B., 1947; Army Air Corps, WWII; married, two children; Presbyterian.

Career N.Y. Senate, 1954–64.

Offices 2464 RHOB, 202-225-4611. Also 314 Ford St., Ogdensburg 13669, 315-393-0570.

Administrative Assistant John E. Mellon

Committees

Appropriations (16th); Subs: District of Columbia (Ranking Mbr.); Military Construction.

Group Ratings

	ADA	COPE	LWV	RIPON	NFU	LCV	CFA	NAB	NSI	ACA
1972	0	22	44	69	33	27	0	89	100	67
1971	3	30	13	44	7	–	13	–	–	88
1970	12	18	–	44	46	0	42	82	90	65

Key Votes

1) Busing	AGN	6) Cmbodia Bmbg	FOR	11) Chkg Acct Intrst	AGN
2) Strip Mines	ABS	7) Bust Hwy Trust	AGN	12) End HISC (HUAC)	AGN
3) Cut Mil $	AGN	8) Farm Sub Lmt	FOR	13) Nixon Sewer Veto	AGN
4) Rev Shrg	FOR	9) School Prayr	FOR	14) Corp Cmpaign $	FOR
5) Pub TV $	AGN	10) Cnsumr Prot	AGN	15) Pol $ Disclosr	FOR

Election Results

1972 general:	Robert C. McEwen (R-C)	114,194	(66%)
	Ernest J. Labaff (D-L)	58,788	(34%)
1972 primary:	Robert C. McEwen (R)	14,055	(87%)
	Emerson V. Laughlin (R)	2,063	(13%)
1970 general:	Robert C. McEwen (R-C)	90,585	(72%)
	Erwin L. Bornstein (D)	34,568	(28%)

THIRTY-FIRST DISTRICT Political Background

The 31st district of New York includes most of the Mohawk River Valley, much of the Adirondack Forest Preserve, and a couple of agricultural counties. Most of the population of the 31st is concentrated within 30 miles of the Mohawk. During the Revolutionary War, this part of New York was a frontier, as American colonists fought the British and their Iroquois allies. Both groups wanted to halt further American penetration of the interior, but failed.

In the early years of the nineteenth century, the Mohawk River Valley became the major route west for migrating New Englanders, some of whom stayed to settle the valley. When the Erie Canal, which runs parallel to the river, was opened in 1825, the nation had its first major, and for long its most important, path of east-west commerce. The canal provided the cheapest way to get bulky agricultural products out of the old Northwest Territory (Ohio, Indiana, Michigan, and others) and finished goods back into the interior. At first the canal, and then the New York Central Railroad of the Vanderbilts, accounted for the phenomenal nineteenth-century growth of New York City and its port facilities. Its competitors, Boston and Philadelphia, having no similar access inland, were left far behind.

Also during the nineteenth century, small Mohawk Valley towns with classical names grew into sizable industrial centers like Utica and Rome. First settled by New England Yankees, these places attracted a new wave of immigration from the Atlantic coast in the early twentieth century. Today, they are the most heavily Italian- and Polish-American communities between Albany and Buffalo.

In most parts of the nation, a change in ethnic composition of such magnitude would have moved the area from Republican to Democratic politics. But not in upstate New York, where suspicion of Democratic New York City has worked to the advantage of the Republican party. To be sure, Republican politicians here pay close attention to the pro-union, anti-abortion, and pro-parochiaid wishes of their blue-collar Catholic constituents. Only those Democrats who enjoy the especially strong favor among these people manage to carry the 31st district. One such was Robert F. Kennedy in 1964.

For 14 years, the 31st—for most of that time, numbered the 32nd—was represented by Alexander Pirnie, whose voting record and constituency services were shrewdly designed to win him maximum support at election time. As a member of the Armed Services Committee, Pirnie was a conservative on matters relating to the military and foreign policy. But he compiled a fairly liberal and pro-labor record on domestic issues, winning the endorsement of the Liberal party in 1966, 1968, and 1970. In 1972, at 69, Pirnie decided to retire.

As is usually the case here, the Republican primary determined Pirnie's successor. In it, Herkimer County Assemblyman Donald Mitchell, who already had the Conservative nomination, defeated Oneida County Assemblyman John Buckley, who had the Liberal nomination. Mitchell won, even though Oneida, which contains Utica and Rome, casts just over half the district's votes. Buckley lost his home-town advantage because two other Oneida-based candidates were in the race. The general election produced a similar pattern in its results. Mitchell was held to less than an absolute majority of votes, solely because he was hard-pressed by Democrat Robert Castle of Utica in Oneida County. The Republican-Conservative, however, carried solid majorities elsewhere in the district. Once in the House, Mitchell asked for and got a seat on Armed Services, Pirnie's old committee. Here the new Congressman will protect the interests of the district, which include an Air Force base near Rome and several big General Electric defense contracts in Utica.

Census Data Pop. 467,717. Central city, 30%; suburban, 44%. Median family income, $9,388; families above $15,000: 17%; families below $3,000: 8%. Median years education, 11.9.

1972 Share of Federal Outlays $621,460,533

DOD	$174,604,205	HEW	$191,197,839
AEC	$510,762	HUD	$3,884,952
NASA	$197,476	DOI	$297,741
DOT	$16,180,863	USDA	$8,781,185
		Other	$225,805,510

Federal Military-Industrial Commitments

DOD Contractors General Electric (Utica), $56.628m: various aircraft electronic ware. Oldfield Construction (Rome), $6.289m: unspecified.
DOD Installations Griffis AFB (Rome).

Economic Base Electrical equipment and supplies; agriculture, notably diary products, dairy cattle and vegetables; finance, insurance and real estate; primary metal industries, especially nonferrous rolling and drawing; and leather and leather products.

The Voters

Registration 231,412 total. 85,192 D (37%); 121,203 R (52%); 2,749 L (1%); 1,732 C (1%); 20,536 blank, missing and void (9%).
Median voting age 46.1
Employment profile White collar, 44%. Blue collar, 39%. Service, 13%. Farm, 4%.
Ethnic groups Black, 2%, Total foreign stock, 22%. Italy, 6%; Poland, 3%; Germany, UK, Canada, 2% each.

Presidential vote

1972	Nixon (R)	140,433	(70%)
	McGovern (D)	61,141	(30%)
1968	Nixon (R)	100,614	(54%)
	Humphrey (D)	75,508	(40%)
	Wallace (AI)	10,833	(6%)

Representative

Donald J. Mitchell (R) Elected 1972; b. May 8, 1923, Ilion; home, Herkimer; Hobart Col.; Columbia U., B.S., 1949, M.A., 1950; Navy, WWII and Korea; married, three children; Methodist.

Career Optometrist; Herkimer Town Councilman, 1954–57; Mayor, Herkimer, 1957–61; Pres., Mohawk Valley Conf. of Mayors, 1959; Appt., Herkimer Zoning Bd. of Appeals, 1963; N.Y. State Assembly, 1965–72, Majority Whip, 1969–72.

Offices 1527 LHOB, 202-225-3665. Also 6 Steuben Pk., Utica, 315-724-9302, and 307 N. Prospect St., Herkimer, 315-866-1051.

Administrative Assistant Sherwood L. Boehlert

Committees

Armed Services (17th); Sub: N.Y.

Group Ratings: Newly Elected

Key Votes

1) Busing	NE	6) Cmbodia Bmbg	FOR	11) Chkg Acct Intrst	AGN
2) Strip Mines	NE	7) Bust Hwy Trust	AGN	12) End HISC (HUAC)	AGN
3) Cut Mil $	NE	8) Farm Sub Lmt	NE	13) Nixon Sewer Veto	FOR
4) Rev Shrg	NE	9) School Prayr	NE	14) Corp Cmpaign $	NE
5) Pub TV $	NE	10) Cnsumr Prot	NE	15) Pol $ Disclosr	NE

Election Results

1972 general:	Donald J. Mitchell (R-C)	98,454	(51%)
	Robert Castle (D)	75,513	(39%)
	Frank A. Nichols (Action Party)	12,075	(6%)
	John T. Buckley (L)	7,179	(4%)

1972 primary: Donald J. Mitchell (R)   12,183   (34%)
               John T. Buckley (R)   10,557   (30%)
               Vincent A. DeIorio (R)   7,142   (20%)
               Sherwood L. Boehlert (R)   5,880   (16%)

THIRTY-SECOND DISTRICT Political Background

Since the 1920s, upstate and suburban Republicans have controlled the New York legislature, with few exceptions. And the Republican legislature has always drawn the congressional district lines very carefully. They traditionally divided two large cities in upstate New York—Buffalo and Rochester—into two or more districts, each with plenty of suburban and rural territory to overmatch any possible urban Democratic majority. During the 1960s, the legislators abandoned the ploy in Buffalo, when one city district became overwhelmingly Democratic, though they retained it in Rochester. In 1970, however, redistricters applied the technique in Syracuse.

Until then, Syracuse and surrounding Onondaga County had formed a single district for as long as anyone could remember. Like Rome and Utica (see New York 31), Syracuse is a Republican city by tradition, suspicious of New York City, and vehemently opposed to high taxes and state spending. But Syracuse also has a large Italian-American blue-collar minority—General Electric, as in much of upstate New York, is the major employer here. That minority has shown a willingness to vote for Democrats on occasion.

In fact, Democrats won across the board here in 1964, when both Lyndon Johnson and Robert Kennedy carried Onondaga County by large margins. In the same year, the county dumped a long-time Republican Congressman in favor of Democrat James Hanley. In 1966, Democratic gubernatorial candidate Frank O'Connor beat incumbent Gov. Rockefeller here, as the people felt Rockefeller had raised taxes too much. The voters also reelected Hanley, and did so again in 1968. So for 1970, the legislators removed half of Syracuse and Onondaga County from Hanley's district, and added rural and small-town Madison, Cortland, and Chenango counties. During the 1850s, these places were centers of abolitionist agitation, and since then, they have retained ancestral Republican allegiances, though Yankee names here have grown scarcer and Italian names more common. Nevertheless, Hanley, as an incumbent, was able to roll up a margin big enough in Syracuse and hold down the Republican edge in the outer counties to win convincingly.

For 1972, the legislature took more of Syracuse and Onondaga away from Hanley, and again added more rural territory. Currently, Onondaga casts only 58% of the district's votes; nevertheless, Hanley, after eight years of incumbency, managed to win 65% of the urban county's ballots. And in the smaller counties, he once again ran well, getting at least 40% of the vote in each of them—far, far above George McGovern's performance in the same area. No doubt Hanley will increase his percentages in the rural counties over the years, and so carry the 32nd with larger majorities during the remainder of the 1970s.

Census Data Pop. 467,826. Central city, 22%; suburban, 47%. Median family income, $10,416; families above $15,000: 22%; families below $3,000: 7%. Median years education, 12.3.

1972 Share of Federal Outlays $516,139,303

DOD	$72,728,516	HEW	$68,736,405
AEC	$80,966	HUD	$3,720,609
NASA	$345,620	DOI	$1,123,431
DOT	$11,921,011	USDA	$9,617,090
		Other	$347,865,655

Federal Military-Industrial Commitments

DOD Contractors Western Electric (Syracuse), $45.057m: ABM radar systems. General Electric (Syracuse), $30.999m: various shipboard and aircraft communication equipment.

Economic Base Electrical equipment and supplies; finance, insurance and real estate; leather and leather products, especially footwear, except rubber; agriculture, notably dairy products, dairy cattle and poultry; and machinery. Also higher education (Syracuse Univ.).

The Voters

Registration 220,785 total. 63,426 D (29%); 126,198 R (57%); 2,582 L (1%); 2,988 C (1%); 25,591 blank, missing and void (12%).
Median voting age 41.5
Employment profile White collar, 53%. Blue collar, 32%. Service, 12%. Farm, 3%.
Ethnic groups Black, 2%. Total foreign stock, 18%. Italy, 4%; Canada, Germany, UK, 2% each; Poland, 1%.

Presidential vote

1972	Nixon (R)	138,607	(70%)
	McGovern (D)	60,343	(30%)
1968	Nixon (R)	101,486	(55%)
	Humphrey (D)	72,172	(39%)
	Wallace (AI)	9,516	(5%)

Representative

James Michael Hanley (D) Elected 1964; b. July 19, 1920, Syracuse; home, Syracuse; Army, WWII; married, two children; Catholic.

Career Funeral Dir., Callahan-Hanley-Mooney Funeral Home, 1940–64.

Offices 109 CHOB, 202-225-3701. Also 509 Loew Bldg., Syracuse 13202, 315-422-2751.

Administrative Assistant John F. Mahoney

Committees

Banking and Currency (15th); Subs: Bank Supervision and Insurance; Small Business; Urban Mass Transportation.

Post Office and Civil Service (6th); Subs: Census and Statistics; Postal Service (Chm.).

Group Ratings

	ADA	COPE	LWV	RIPON	NFU	LCV	CFA	NAB	NSI	ACA
1972	50	82	83	73	86	53	—	17	67	26
1971	73	92	89	44	87	–	88	–	–	21
1970	72	100	–	67	100	81	90	9	80	17

Key Votes

1) Busing	FOR	6) Cmbodia Bmbg	AGN	11) Chkg Acct Intrst	AGN
2) Strip Mines	AGN	7) Bust Hwy Trust	FOR	12) End HISC (HUAC)	AGN
3) Cut Mil $	FOR	8) Farm Sub Lmt	FOR	13) Nixon Sewer Veto	AGN
4) Rev Shrg	FOR	9) School Prayr	FOR	14) Corp Cmpaign $	FOR
5) Pub TV $	FOR	10) Cnsumr Prot	FOR	15) Pol $ Disclosr	AGN

Election Results

1972 general:	James M. Hanley (D)	111,481	(57%)
	Leonard C. Koldin (R-C)	83,451	(43%)
	1972 primary:		
	James M. Hanley (D), unopposed		
1970 general:	James M. Hanley (D)	82,425	(52%)
	John F. O'Conner (R-C)	76,381	(48%)

THIRTY-THIRD DISTRICT Political Background

The Finger Lakes of upstate New York are long, narrow bodies of water, surrounded by gentle hills. They lie within a triangle, the apexes of which are Syracuse, Rochester, and Elmira.

Encompassed is an area dotted with small towns to which some early nineteenth-century Yankee, obviously devoted to the classics, gave names: Ovid, Scipio, Romulus, Camillus, Pompey, and many others. The Finger Lakes region is pleasant vacation country, but it is best known for its increasingly respected vineyards and vintners. Just north of the lakes is the line of the Erie Canal, now replaced by one with a less pleasing name—the New York State Barge Canal. Also here are small industrial cities like Auburn, Geneva, and Canandaigua. In contrast to the Finger Lakes countryside, these towns are heavily Catholic and sometimes Democratic. Like most of upstate New York, however, the region as a whole is usually solidly Republican.

The Republican territory described makes up a little more than half of New York's 33rd congressional district. The remainder consists of the west side of Syracuse and surrounding Onondaga County. (For a genesis of the arrangement, see New York 32.) In its short existence as a district—its boundaries were drawn in 1970, and shifted slightly in 1972—the 33rd has elected two Republican Congressmen. John H. Terry, a former New York Assemblyman, was elected in 1970, but decided to retire, though only 48, in 1972; he said he did not want to move his family to Washington. So in 1972, the local Republicans had to find another strong candidate, which they did in former (1962–69) Syracuse Mayor William F. Walsh. The candidate had been succeeded in the mayoralty to a Democrat named Lee Alexander. But Walsh remained popular and well-known locally, something that is critically important in low-visibility House races.

In 1972, therefore, nonincumbent Walsh got 71% of the votes in the 33rd. The figure represents a phenomenal percentage—more than Richard Nixon received in the district. In the House, Walsh was given the kind of committee assignments freshmen usually get: Public Works and Veterans' Affairs. Walsh, who was once a social worker, an unusual background for a Republican politician, may decide to change committee assignments later. All signs but one point to a long House career for Walsh: he was 60 years old when first elected. And with the increasing resistance among voters to elderly candidates, Walsh may last only another 10 years or so on Capitol Hill.

Census Data Pop. 467,610. Central city, 20%; suburban, 27%. Median family income, $9,851; families above $15,000: 19%; families below $3,000: 8%. Median years education, 12.1.

1972 Share of Federal Outlays $512,917,497

DOD	$60,181,183	HEW	$104,080,225
AEC	$52,466	HUD	$3,154,467
NASA	$567,674	DOI	$1,783,020
DOT	$4,048,316	USDA	$14,894,451
		Other	$324,155,697

Federal Military-Industrial Commitments

DOD Installations Seneca Army Depot (Romulus).

Economic Base Electrical equipment and supplies; finance, insurance and real estate; machinery; leather and leather products, especially footwear, except rubber; and agriculture, notably dairy products, grains and poultry.

The Voters

Registration 219,458 total. 66,753 D (30%); 123,735 R (56%); 2,476 L (1%); 3,066 C (1%); 23,428 blank, missing and void (11%).
Median voting age 44.6
Employment profile White collar, 46%. Blue collar, 37%. Service, 14%. Farm, 3%.
Ethnic groups Black, 4%. Total foreign stock, 18%. Italy, 5%; Canada, UK, Germany, Poland, 2% each; Ireland, 1%.

Presidential vote

1972	Nixon (R)	135,504	(70%)
	McGovern (D)	59,196	(30%)
1968	Nixon (R)	97,648	(53%)
	Humphrey (D)	75,964	(41%)
	Wallace (AI)	10,566	(6%)

Representative

William F. Walsh (R) Elected 1972; b. July 11, 1912, Syracuse; home, Syracuse; St. Bonaventure Col., A.B., 1970; U. of Buffalo, M.A.; Syracuse U., Ph.D.; married, seven children; Catholic.

Career Remington Rand Co.; Accountant; social work, 15 yrs.; Dir. of R&D, Onondaga County, 3 yrs.; Instructor, Syracuse U.; Commissioner of Welfare, 1960–62; Mayor, Syracuse, 1962–1970; Mbr., Public Service Comm., 1970.

Offices 1330 LHOB, 202-225-3333. Also Syracuse, 315-473-3333 and Auburn, 315-252-2222.

Administrative Assistant F. Gibson Darrison

Committees

Public Works (11th); Subs: Economic Development; Energy; Investigations and Review; Public Buildings and Grounds.

Veterans' Affairs (11th); Subs: Education and Training; Hospitals; Housing.

Group Ratings: Newly Elected

Key Votes

1) Busing	NE	6) Cmbodia Bmbg	FOR	11) Chkg Acct Intrst		ABS
2) Strip Mines	NE	7) Bust Hwy Trust	AGN	12) End HISC (HUAC)		AGN
3) Cut Mil $	NE	8) Farm Sub Lmt	NE	13) Nixon Sewer Veto		FOR
4) Rev Shrg	NE	9) School Prayr	NE	14) Corp Cmpaign $		NE
5) Pub TV $	NE	10) Cnsumr Prot	NE	15) Pol $ Disclosr		NE

Election Results

1972 general:	William F. Walsh (R-C)	132,139	(71%)
	Clarence Kadys (D)	53,039	(29%)
1972 primary:	William F. Walsh (R), unopposed		

THIRTY-FOURTH DISTRICT Political Background

The 34th district of New York lies along the southern shore of Lake Ontario, and includes the east side of the city of Rochester, eastern Monroe County, and Wayne County. Rochester's economy, unlike those of other upstate New York cities, depends on highly trained labor; major employers here are Eastman Kodak and Xerox. The high-technology industries make the city, New York's third largest, an area of economic growth, in contrast to the economic stagnation of other upstate communities which depend on traditional heavy industry. The city of Rochester is almost large enough in itself to form a congressional district. But because it usually goes Democratic, Republican state legislators have for years divided Rochester between two districts. In both of these, the 34th and 35th, Republican voters in the surrounding suburbs and rural hinterlands of western New York overwhelm the Democratic strength in the city. Accordingly, both districts are safely Republican. Profoundly conservative Wayne County is a particular Republican stronghold and, incidentally, the birthplace of the Mormon religion (see Utah state write-up).

Since 1962, the 34th's Congressman has been Frank Horton, on most issues upstate New York's most liberal Republican. That political coloration is traditional in the district; some years ago (1947–59) its Congressman was Kenneth Keating, a U.S. Senator from 1959 until Robert Kennedy beat him in 1964, and later a judge on New York's highest court and Ambassador to India. Congressman Horton, who currently serves as the ranking Republican on the Government Operations Committee, is phenomenally popular among the district's voters; in 1972, for example, he ran 9% better than Richard Nixon here. The only conceivable threat to his tenure is conservative primary opposition, which is yet to develop, and probably never will.

Census Data Pop. 467,461. Central city, 38%; suburban, 62%. Median family income, $12,082; families above $15,000: 34%; families below $3,000: 6%. Median years education, 12.2.

1972 Share of Federal Outlays $497,951,651

DOD	$30,994,459	HEW	$188,140,537
AEC	$2,450,430	HUD	$5,271,571
NASA	$1,404,174	DOI	$185,983
DOT	$7,682,704	USDA	$8,660,711
		Other	$253,161,082

Federal Military-Industrial Commitments

DOD Contractors General Dynamics (Rochester), $5.634m: telephone switchborads.

Economic Base Instruments and related products, especially photographic equipment and supplies; finance, insurance and real estate; machinery, especially metalworking machinery; electrical equipment and supplies, especially communication equipment; and food and kindred products. Also higher education (Rochester Inst. of Technology).

The Voters

Registration 227,473 total. 68,208 D (30%); 127,847 R (56%); 2,825 L (1%); 2,661 C (1%); 25,932 blank, missing and void (11%).
Median voting age 44.2
Employment profile White collar, 54%. Blue collar, 34%. Service, 11%. Farm, 1%.
Ethnic groups Black, 6%. Spanish, 1%. Total foreign stock, 27%. Italy, 7%; Germany, Canada, 3% each; UK, USSR, Poland, 2% each.

Presidential vote

1972	Nixon (R)		130,757	(63%)
	McGovern (D)		77,699	(37%)
1968	Nixon (R)		98,521	(51%)
	Humphrey (D)		88,744	(46%)
	Wallace (AI)		7,584	(4%)

Representative

Frank J. Horton (R) Elected 1962; b. Dec. 12, 1919, Cuero, Tex.; home, Rochester; La. State U., B.A., 1941; Cornell U., LL.B., 1947; Army, WWII; married, two children; Presbyterian.

Career Practicing atty., 1947–62; Rochester City Council, 1955–61.

Offices 2229 RHOB, 202-225-4916. Also 107 Fed. Bldg., Rochester 14614, 716-546-4900, ext. 1380.

Administrative Assistant David Lovenheim

Committees

Government Operations (Ranking Mbr.); Sub: Legislation and Military Operations (Ranking Mbr.).

Group Ratings

	ADA	COPE	LWV	RIPON	NFU	LCV	CFA	NAB	NSI	ACA
1972	44	73	83	77	43	49	50	42	100	35
1971	51	64	78	80	53	–	63	–	–	46
1970	76	83	–	82	92	75	68	17	44	25

Key Votes

1) Busing	AGN	6) Cmbodia Bmbg	FOR	11) Chkg Acct Intrst	AGN
2) Strip Mines	AGN	7) Bust Hwy Trust	FOR	12) End HISC (HUAC)	AGN
3) Cut Mil $	AGN	8) Farm Sub Lmt	AGN	13) Nixon Sewer Veto	FOR
4) Rev Shrg	FOR	9) School Prayr	AGN	14) Corp Cmpaign $	FOR
5) Pub TV $	FOR	10) Cnsumr Prot	FOR	15) Pol $ Disclosr	ABS

Election Results

1972 general:	Frank Horton (R)	142,803	(72%)
	Jack Rubens (D)	46,509	(23%)
	Richard E. Lusink (C)	5,603	(3%)
	Rafael Martinez (L)	3,088	(2%)
1972 primary:	Frank Horton (R), unopposed		
1970 general:	Frank Horton (R)	123,209	(71%)
	Jordan E. Pappas (D)	38,898	(22%)
	David F. Hampson (C)	10,442	(6%)
	Morley Schloss (L)	2,165	(1%)

THIRTY-FIFTH DISTRICT Political Background

The 35th district of New York comprises the western half of the city of Rochester, the western Monroe County suburbs, and the adjacent western New York countryside of Genesee, Wyoming, Livingston, and part of Ontario counties. The countryside is dominated by small cities like Batavia, locale of novelist John Gardner's *Sunlight Dialogues*, and Attica, site of a September 1971 prison tragedy. Also here is rich farmland. As in the case of the 34th district, Rochester's Democratic majorities are nullified by the Republican votes coming out of the suburbs and smaller counties, which together cast two-thirds of the ballots in the district. Some 400 miles from New York City, this region of upstate New York has a near Midwestern feel to it. Celebrity New York politicians like Nelson Rockefeller, Jacob Javits, and the late Robert Kennedy seem as out of their element campaigning here as they might in Indiana.

In 1964, Congressman Harold Ostertag retired, and was succeeded by Barber Conable, a state Senator from Genesee County. Expected to be another backbench Republican conservative, Conable has distinguished himself. He was chosen to sit on the powerful House Ways and Means Committee, and owing to the retirements of senior members, the New Yorker has enjoyed a rapid rise to the number-four position on the Republican side. Congressman John W. Byrnes of Wisconsin decided not to run in 1972; long the ranking minority member on Ways and Means, Byrnes worked closely with Chairman Wilber Mills. Byrnes' departure left something of a vacuum on the Republican side of the committee, one that Conable appears likely to fill. And with Chairman Mills' bad back forcing him to consider retirement in 1974, Conable's leverage may increase substantially in the 94th Congress.

Reform of House procedure is Conable's other major area of interest. In 1971, he pushed through a proposal that made the position of ranking Republican on all committees subject to a secret-ballot election in which all Republican Congressmen participated. Having adopted the plan, House Republicans were far ahead of more insistent and vocal Democrats, who did not adopt a similar reform until 1973. Conable was also the moving force behind the Legislative Reorganization Act of 1970. He assembled a coalition of moderate Republicans and liberal Democrats to support an agenda of reform, including the recording of teller votes and the disclosure of roll-call votes taken in committee. Both measures have opened important facets of the decision-making process to public view, which has, on occasion, appeared to have changed outcomes.

Census Data Pop. 467,415. Central city, 26%; suburban, 51%. Median family income, $11,528; families above $15,000: 27%; families below $3,000: 5%. Median years education, 12.2.

1972 Share of Federal Outlays $489,828,322

DOD	$24,732,876	HEW	$182,775,633
AEC	$1,896,913	HUD	$6,936,353
NASA	$1,101,666	DOI	$323,973
DOT	$6,220,515	USDA	$12,077,983
		Other	$253,762,410

Federal Military-Industrial Commitments

DOD Contractors Textron Inc. (Wheatfield), \$73.679m: Minuteman missile engines; aircraft design research. Eastman Kodak (Rochester), \$23.776m: photographic equipment.

Economic Base Instruments and related products, especially photographic equipment and supplies; electrical equipment and supplies, machinery, especially metalworking machinery; finance, insurance and real estate; agriculture, notably dairy products, grains and dairy cattle; and food and kindred products. Also higher education (Univ. of Rochester).

The Voters

Registration 221,668 total. 66,297 D (30%); 129,145 R (58%); 2,550 L (1%); 2,636 C (1%); 21,040 blank, missing and void (9%).
Median voting age 41.5
Employment profile White collar, 46%. Blue collar, 40%. Service, 12%. Farm, 2%.
Ethnic groups Black, 6%. Total foreign stock, 20%. Italy, 6%; Canada, Germany, 3% each; UK, 2%; Poland, 1%.

Presidential vote

1972	Nixon (R)	134,216	(66%)
	McGovern (D)	70,126	(34%)
1968	Nixon (R)	94,124	(51%)
	Humphrey (D)	81,707	(44%)
	Wallace (AI)	8,853	(5%)

Representative

Barber B. Conable, Jr. (R) Elected 1964; b. Nov. 2, 1922, Warsaw; home, Alexander; Cornell U., B.A., 1942, LL.B., 1948; USMC, WWII and Korean War; married, four children; Methodist.

Career Practicing atty., 1949–64; N.Y. State Senate, 1963, 1964.

Offices 2429 RHOB, 202-225-3615. Also 311 Fed. Ofc. Bldg., Rochester 14614, 716-263-3156.

Administrative Assistant Harry K. Nicholas

Committees

Ways and Means (4th).

Joint Economic Com. (2nd); Subs: Fiscal Policy; Inter-American Economic Relationships; International Economics; Priorities and Economy in Government (Ranking House Mbr.).

Group Ratings

	ADA	COPE	LWV	RIPON	NFU	LCV	CFA	NAB	NSI	ACA
1972	6	20	50	81	17	48	100	91	100	65
1971	19	17	43	65	20	–	20	–	–	86
1970	28	25	–	76	50	25	63	83	90	79

Key Votes

1) Busing	AGN	6) Cmbodia Bmbg	FOR	11) Chkg Acct Intrst	AGN
2) Strip Mines	AGN	7) Bust Hwy Trust	FOR	12) End HISC (HUAC)	AGN
3) Cut Mil \$	AGN	8) Farm Sub Lmt	FOR	13) Nixon Sewer Veto	FOR
4) Rev Shrg	FOR	9) School Prayr	FOR	14) Corp Cmpaign \$	FOR
5) Pub TV \$	AGN	10) Cnsumr Prot	AGN	15) Pol \$ Disclosr	FOR

Election Results

1972 general:	Barber B. Conable, Jr. (R)	127,298	(68%)
	Terence J. Spencer (D)	53,321	(28%)
	Terence C. Brennan (C)	4,879	(3%)
	Alicia Burgos (L)	2,082	(1%)
1972 primary:	Barber B. Conable, Jr. (R), unopposed		
1970 general:	Barber B. Conable, Jr. (R)	107,677	(66%)
	Richard N. Anderson (D)	48,061	(29%)
	Keith R. Wallis (C)	7,729	(5%)

THIRTY-SIXTH DISTRICT Political Background

The 36th district of New York consists of Niagara County, site of the Falls; part of suburban Erie County (Buffalo); and the southern shore of Lake Ontario extending to a point near Rochester. From the Falls, power lines strung on gigantic pylons hum out to the urban Northeast, the midwest, and southern Canada. The city of Niagara Falls is mostly industrial, with many of its industries having done poorly of late. The city and its suburbs lost population during the 1960s. Though Niagara Falls has large Polish and Italian communities that lean Democratic, the rest of the county subscribes to typical upstate New York Republicanism. The Erie County portion of the district takes in the middle-class and politically marginal suburbs of Tonawanda and Grand Island, as well as a few blocks of the city of Buffalo itself.

On paper, the 36th is politically marginal. In fact, however, its character in congressional elections is Republican. From 1951 to 1965, the district was represented by William E. Miller, a hardshelled partisan who was Republican National Chairman during the early 1960s and Barry Goldwater's running mate in 1964. Miller, who barely won reelection in 1962, had already planned to retire from Congress when Goldwater tapped him for the vice-presidential nomination. As a Catholic, Miller was expected to attract some votes for the Republican ticket in Catholic areas. But he apparently did little of that, or much else either. Then, as now, he remains the least-known major party vice-presidential nominee of the last three or four decades. Unlike most ex-Congressman, Miller chose not to hang around Washington, and is now reported practicing law and living comfortably in his home on Lake Ontario.

Miller's successor in the House, Republican Henry P. Smith III, has run much stronger races in the district. After a 9,000-vote margin in 1964, Smith won more than 60% of the votes in three straight elections. And a favorable redistricting—one that added rural Orleans County and some Rochester suburbs—appeared to make his seat even safer for the rest of the 1970s.

But in 1972, Smith encountered a tough challenge, when Democrat Richard M. "Max" McCarthy, former Congressman from the Buffalo suburban district (then the 39th, now the 38th), decided to run against him. While in Congress, McCarthy had made some headlines—and some alterations in the way the Pentagon does business—when he exposed the Defense Department's stockpile of chemical and biological weapons. McCarthy would probably still be a Congressman, had he not run for the Senate in 1970. During his campaign, he managed to attract some publicity by scuba-diving in the hideously-polluted Hudson River, but never managed to raise much money, and finished a poor fourth statewide.

. In the Senate race, McCarthy showed strength in Erie and Niagara counties, which may explain why he chose to run in the 36th two years later. But he lost. Smith held on to 57% of the votes, and, as it turned out, did not need the help redistricters provided him. The Republican-Conservative margins in Erie and Niagara counties nearly matched the one he received district-wide.

Census Data Pop. 467,761. Central city, 7%; suburban, 93%. Median family income, $10,702; families above $15,000: 23%; families below $3,000: 6%. Median years education, 12.1.

1972 Share of Federal Outlays $534,868,924

DOD	$59,823,037	HEW	$177,519,208
AEC	$379,505	HUD	$4,887,655
NASA	$1,346,962	DOI	$400,912
DOT	$3,702,995	USDA	$45,249,149
		Other	$241,559,501

Federal Military-Industrial Commitments

DOD Contractors GTE Sylvania (Buffalo), $29.077m: radio sets.

Economic Base Electrical equipment and supplies; primary metal industries; chemicals and allied products, especially industrial chemicals; finance, insurance and real estate; and food and kindred products, especially canned, cured and frozen foods.

The Voters

Registration 225,926 total. 90,277 D (40%); 119,911 R (53%); 3,602 L (2%); 2,087 C (1%); 10,049 blank, missing and void (4%).
Median voting age 44.3
Employment profile White collar, 47%. Blue collar, 40%. Service, 12%. Farm, 1%.
Ethnic groups Black, 3%. Total foreign stock, 27%. Canada, 7%; Italy, 5%; Poland, 4%; UK, Germany, 3% each.

Presidential vote

1972	Nixon (R)	119,213	(60%)
	McGovern (D)	78,931	(40%)
1968	Nixon (R)	84,839	(46%)
	Humphrey (D)	86,526	(47%)
	Wallace (AI)	13,219	(7%)

Representative

Henry P. Smith III (R) Elected 1964; b. Sept. 29, 1911, North Tonawanda; home, North Tonawanda; Dartmouth Col., B.A., 1933; Cornell U., LL.B., 1936; married, three children; Presbyterian.

Career Practicing atty., 1936–64; Mayor of N. Tonawanda, 1961–63; Judge, Niagara County, 1963.

Offices 2331 RHOB, 202-225-3231. Also 4 Webster St., N. Tonawanda 14120, 716-695-1577.

Administrative Assistant Russell A. Rourke

Committees

Judiciary (3rd); Subs: No. 3 (Patents, Trademarks, Copyrights); Sp. Sub. on Reform of Federal Criminal Laws (Ranking Mbr.).

District of Columbia (5th); Subs: Judiciary (Ranking Mbr.); Labor, Social Services, and the International Community.

Group Ratings

	ADA	COPE	LWV	RIPON	NFU	LCV	CFA	NAB	NSI	ACA
1972	19	18	73	86	29	68	0	88	89	57
1971	30	27	50	65	31	–	38	–	–	70
1970	20	25	–	79	42	38	53	91	89	78

Key Votes

1) Busing	AGN	6) Cmbodia Bmbg	AGN	11) Chkg Acct Intrst	ABS
2) Strip Mines	AGN	7) Bust Hwy Trust	FOR	12) End HISC (HUAC)	AGN
3) Cut Mil $	AGN	8) Farm Sub Lmt	FOR	13) Nixon Sewer Veto	FOR
4) Rev Shrg	FOR	9) School Prayr	FOR	14) Corp Cmpaign $	AGN
5) Pub TV $	AGN	10) Cnsumr Prot	AGN	15) Pol $ Disclosr	FOR

Election Results

1972 general: Henry P. Smith III (R-C) 110,238 (57%)
                Max McCarthy (D-L) 82,095 (43%)
1972 primary: Henry P. Smith III (R), unopposed
1970 general: Henry P. Smith III (R-C) 87,183 (63%)
                Edward Cuddy (D-L) 50,418 (37%)

THIRTY-SEVENTH DISTRICT Political Background

Buffalo is the second largest city in New York state and one of the most important industrial centers on the Great Lakes. Huge steel mills line the shore of Lake Erie, as the principal east-west rail lines feed into downtown Buffalo and an industrial area to the south. The city is the easternmost American port on the Great Lakes, and here ships unload iron ore from the Mesabi Range and grain from the western prairies. Buffalo is one of the nation's leading steel producers and its number-one miller of grain.

Despite a recent surge, both of these industries are currently in relative decline here, expanding far less rapidly than the economy as a whole. But at the turn of the century, they constituted the fastest-growing, most dynamic sectors of the economy. Accordingly, Buffalo experienced some flush times, as it attracted tens of thousand of Polish and Italian blue-collar workers. Today, the city's steel mills, grain elevators, and docks, along with its downtown and radial avenues, still look like something out of the 1920s, only a little run-down and shabby. Moreover, because the ethnic groups here do not get on with the city's growing black population, any dreams of a melting-pot American city have died. Finally, the big money, and the Buffalo branch of the State University of New York, are moving to the suburbs, leaving the city and its problems behind.

Nearly all of Buffalo, the industrial city of Lackawanna just to the south (home of Bethlehem's giant steel mill), plus a few precincts in the suburban town of Cheektowaga, make up New York's 37th congressional district. This is, of course, a very heavily Democratic district—these days the only one in upstate New York that can be so described. The 37th is also the home of a competent Democratic party organization, led by the present state Democratic Chairman, Joseph Crangle. Unlike the machine's counterparts in New York City, the one in Buffalo is as eager to win congressional and statewide races as it is to control the judgeships.

Among the beneficiaries of the organization is 37th district Congressman Thaddeus J. Dulski. First elected in 1958, Dulski is now Chairman of the Post Office and Civil Service Committee. Hardly the most exciting House panel, the committee once handled matters like federal pay increases (now determined in initial form by an independent commission) and postal patronage (now at the disposal of E. T. Klassen's U.S. Postal Service). Dulski's committee is of course lobbied constantly by government and postal workers' unions, which have little else to do since they are not allowed to strike. Under Dulski's leadership—which is not considered the most astute or influential among committee chairmen—Post Office and Civil Service has generally been receptive to pleas for increased pay and fringe benefits.

Census Data Pop. 467,759. Central city, 92%; suburban, 8%. Median family income, $8,845; families above $15,000: 14%; families below $3,000: 11%. Median years education, 10.6.

1972 Share of Federal Outlays $540,518,509

DOD	$63,861,446	HEW	$176,239,526
AEC	$94,282	HUD	$4,839,805
NASA	$1,340,477	DOI	$430,973
DOT	$3,157,983	USDA	$50,342,583
		Other	$240,211,434

Federal Military-Industrial Commitments

No installations or contractors receiving prime awards greater than $5,000,000.

Economic Base Primary metal industries; motor vehicles and equipment, and other transportation equipment; finance, insurance and real estate; fabricated metal products, especially metal stampings; and machinery, especially general industrial machinery. Also higher education (SUNY, Buffalo; and State Univ. College, Buffalo).

The Voters

Registration 219,251 total. 142,215 D (65%); 62,517 R (29%); 4,574 L (2%); 1,718 C (1%); 8,227 blank, missing and void (4%).
Median voting age 46.0
Employment profile White collar, 43%. Blue collar, 43%. Service, 14%. Farm, –%.
Ethnic groups Black, 21%. Total foreign stock, 28%. Poland, 8%; Italy, 6%; Germany, Canada, 3% each; UK, Ireland, 1% each.

Presidential vote

1972	Nixon (R)	74,998	(43%)
	McGovern (D)	99,509	(57%)
1968	Nixon (R)	47,192	(25%)
	Humphrey (D)	123,678	(67%)
	Wallace (AI)	14,764	(8%)

Representative

Thaddeus J. Dulski (D) Elected 1958; b. Sept. 27, 1915, Buffalo; home, Buffalo; Canisius Col., U. of Buffalo; Navy, WWII; married, five children; Catholic.

Career Accountant and tax consultant, Bureau of Internal Revenue, 1940–47; Sp. Agent, Price Stabilization Admin., 1951–53; Walden Dist. Councilman, 1954–57; Councilman-at-large, 1957.

Offices 2312 RHOB, 202-225-3306. Also 212 U.S. Courthouse, Buffalo 14202, 716-853-4131.

Administrative Assistant Mrs. Helen Burton (L.A.)

Committees

Post Office and Civil Service (Chm.); Sub: Investigations (Chm.).

Veterans' Affairs (4th); Subs: Hospitals; Insurance.

Group Ratings

	ADA	COPE	LWV	RIPON	NFU	LCV	CFA	NAB	NSI	ACA
1972	50	90	50	47	60	54	100	90	70	43
1971	51	80	67	47	57	–	100	–	–	42
1970	80	100	–	76	100	73	100	8	70	22

Key Votes

1) Busing	AGN	6) Cmbodia Bmbg	AGN	11) Chkg Acct Intrst	AGN
2) Strip Mines	FOR	7) Bust Hwy Trust	ABS	12) End HISC (HUAC)	ABS
3) Cut Mil $	AGN	8) Farm Sub Lmt	FOR	13) Nixon Sewer Veto	AGN
4) Rev Shrg	FOR	9) School Prayr	FOR	14) Corp Cmpaign $	AGN
5) Pub TV $	FOR	10) Cnsumr Prot	FOR	15) Pol $ Disclosr	AGN

Election Results

1972 general:	Thaddeus J. Dulski (D-L)	114,605	(72%)
	William F. McLaughlin (R-C)	44,103	(28%)
1972 primary:	Thaddeus J. Dulski (D), unopposed		
1970 general:	Thaddeus J. Dulski (D-L)	79,151	(80%)
	William M. Johns (R-C)	20,108	(20%)

THIRTY-EIGHTH DISTRICT Political Background

The 38th district of New York includes almost all of suburban Erie County, from the Buffalo city limits to the small state Indian reservations at the northern and southern edges of the county. Altogether, the district takes in the most prosperous part of the so-called Niagara Frontier, the heavily industrial Buffalo-Niagara Falls metropolitan area along the Canadian border. The Buffalo and environs constitute the Democratic stronghold of upstate New York. In fact, the region often produces higher Democratic percentages, though not nearly as many votes, as metropolitan New York City. Buffalo is a place much more like Cleveland or Detroit than New York City, and its residents—in large part, Polish, Italian, or black—are not as susceptible to either the fashionable liberalism or the Archie Bunker reaction as people in New York City.

A totally suburban district, the 38th is usually the most Republican part of Erie County, having most of Buffalo's rather scant supply of wealthy suburban enclaves. Much of the district, however, is working-class Democratic, particularly the places lying near the city, like the town of Cheektowaga (pop. 113,000). Here are small tract houses to which the people who grew up in immigrant quarters escaped. Overall, the 38th is probably as politically marginal as any district in New York state.

Such was certainly the case in the district's 1970 congressional race. Three-term incumbent Democrat Richard "Max" McCarthy planned to step down in order to run for the Senate; to succeed him, the Republicans had a hot candidate in Jack Kemp, public relations man for the biggest bank in Buffalo and former quarterback for the Buffalo Bills. Against him, the Democrats slated a lawyer named Thomas Flaherty. After McCarthy lost the Senate primary, he tried to retrieve the House nomination. The attendant feuding may have helped to increase Kemp's narrow 52–48 margin of victory.

A native of California, Kemp has a Ron Ziegleresque look and a solidly Nixonian voting record. After a big reelection win in 1972, there was talk that he might run for the Senate in 1972. That race would presumably mean a primary against liberal Republican Jacob Javits; the idea, apparently, was to convince the generally conservative body of New York registered Republicans that they should vote for a man who would more faithfully support The President. As the Watergate scandal broke, the talk died down, and the outlook now is for Kemp to remain in the House for some years to come.

Census Data Pop. 467,761. Central city, 0%; suburban, 100%. Median family income, $11,583; families above $15,000: 27%; families below $3,000: 4%. Median years education, 12.3.

1972 Share of Federal Outlays $540,986,220

DOD	$63,916,706	HEW	$176,392,026
AEC	$94,364	HUD	$4,843,993
NASA	$1,341,637	DOI	$431,346
DOT	$3,160,715	USDA	$50,386,145
		Other	$240,419,288

Federal Military-Industrial Commitments

DOD Contractors Sierra Research Corp. (Buffalo), $15.196m: components Nike-Hercules missile; aircraft navigation units; radar bomb directing sets. Cornell Aeronautical Lab (Buffalo), $14.729m: various DOD research projects.

Economic Base Primary metal industries; finance, insurance and real estate; motor vehicles and equipment, and other transportation equipment; fabricated metal products, especially metal stampings; machinery, especially general industrial machinery; and food and kindred products.

The Voters

Registration 255,937 total. 102,931 D (40%); 128,609 R (50%); 5,069 L (2%); 2,708 C (1%); 16,620 blank, missing and void (6%).
Median voting age 43.2
Employment profile White collar, 52%. Blue collar, 36%. Service, 11%. Farm, 1%.
Ethnic groups Total foreign stock, 23%. Poland, 5%; Germany, 4%; Italy, Canada, 3% each; UK, 2%.

Presidential vote

1972	Nixon (R)	132,331	(61%)
	McGovern (D)	85,221	(39%)
1968	Nixon (R)	86,360	(45%)
	Humphrey (D)	88,720	(47%)
	Wallace (AI)	15,444	(8%)

Representative

Jack F. Kemp (R) Elected 1970; b. July 13, 1935, Los Angeles, Calif.; home, Hamburg; Occidental Col., B.A., 1957; USAR, 1958–62; married, three children; Presbyterian.

Career Quarterback for Buffalo Bills, professional football team; Player of the Year, 1965; Cofounder, Pres., American Football League Players Assn., 1965–70; Sp. Asst. to Gov. of Calif., 1967; Sp. Asst. to Chm. of Repub. Natl. Com., 1969; television and radio commentator, national networks and local stations; public relations officer, Marine Midland Bank of Buffalo.

Offices 132 CHOB, 202-225-5265. Also 414 U.S. Ct. House, 68 Court Street, Buffalo 14202, 716-854-2155.

Administrative Assistant James Cromwell

Committees

Education and Labor (12th); Subs: No. 3 (Gen. Sub. on Labor); No. 6 (Sp. Sub. on Education).

Sel. Com. on Small Business (6th); Subs: Government Procurement and International Trade; Taxation and Oil Imports (Ranking Mbr.).

Group Ratings

	ADA	COPE	LWV	RIPON	NFU	LCV	CFA	NAB	NSI	ACA
1972	25	36	50	67	43	20	100	92	100	70
1971	16	18	22	47	21	–	29	–	–	85

Key Votes

1) Busing	AGN	6) Cmbodia Bmbg	FOR	11) Chkg Acct Intrst	AGN
2) Strip Mines	AGN	7) Bust Hwy Trust	FOR	12) End HISC (HUAC)	AGN
3) Cut Mil $	FOR	8) Farm Sub Lmt	FOR	13) Nixon Sewer Veto	FOR
4) Rev Shrg	FOR	9) School Prayr	FOR	14) Corp Cmpaign $	AGN
5) Pub TV $	FOR	10) Cnsumr Prot	AGN	15) Pol $ Disclosr	FOR

Election Results

1972 general:	Jack F. Kemp (R-C)	156,967	(73%)
	Anthony P. LoRusso (D-L)	57,585	(27%)
1972 primary:	Jack F. Kemp (R), unopposed		
1970 general:	Jack F. Kemp (R-C)	96,989	(52%)
	Thomas P. Flaherty (D-L)	90,949	(48%)

THIRTY-NINTH DISTRICT Political Background

The 39th district of New York comprises the western half of the Southern Tier—a term used to refer to the group of counties found along New York's border with Pennsylvania. Extending from the small city of Elmira to Lake Erie, the district contains the Corning Glass Works in Steuben County, two state Indian reservations, and a point on the state's western boundary exactly 496 miles from New York City via the Thomas E. Dewey Thruway. The small cities scattered among the district's valleys—Jamestown, Olean, Hornell, Corning, and along Lake Erie—Dunkirk, Fredonia—tend to be Democratic or politically marginal. The status reflects the presence of Irish and Italian Catholics who came to this part of upstate New York after it had been first settled by Yankee migrants. Outside the towns, Yankee Republicans still predominate and, as in most of non-urban upstate, control the district politically.

Before he was appointed to fill the late Robert 'Kennedy's Senate seat, Charles Goodell was Congressman from the district. In the House, Goodell was an innovative conservative, one of the leaders of the group that rebelled against Charlie Halleck in 1965 and installed Gerald Ford as Minority Leader. Once in the Senate, the New Yorker became its most outspoken dove, and so the target of a Nixon-Agnew purge in 1970. Goodell was always popular in his home district, however. In the bad Republican year of 1964, he won with a margin larger than one received by any other New York Republican Congressman, and in 1970, he carried what is now the 39th, even while running a poor third in the rest of the state.

The district's present Congressman, James F. Hastings, is more conservative than Goodell ever was. He is also somewhat more popular, at least when measured by the commanding margins he has received since his first election in 1968. In 1972, despite the addition of a substantial hunk of new territory to the district (mainly Elmira), Hasting won a record 72% of the votes, some 6% better than Richard Nixon's performance in the district.

Census Data Pop. 467,859. Central city, 0%; suburban, 1%. Median family income, $8,936; families above $15,000: 15%; families below $3,000: 9%. Median years education, 12.2.

1972 Share of Federal Outlays $488,423,691

DOD	$19,654,429	HEW	$189,124,846
AEC	$516	HUD	$3,372,704
NASA	$324,594	DOI	$300,252
DOT	$19,414,476	USDA	$12,274,976
		Other	$243,956,898

Federal Military-Industrial Commitments

No installations or contractors receiving prime awards greater than $5,000,000.

Economic Base Machinery; agriculture, notably dairy products, fruits and dairy cattle; fabricated metal products; food and kindred products; and stone, clay and glass products.

The Voters

Registration 212,784 total. 75,165 D (35%); 122,240 R (57%); 2,633 L (1%); 1,763 C (1%); 10,983 blank, missing and void (5%).
Median voting age 45.2
Employment profile White collar, 43%. Blue collar, 39%. Service, 14%. Farm, 4%.
Ethnic groups Black, 1%. Total foreign stock, 14%. Italy, 3%; Sweden, Germany, Poland, 2% each; UK, Canada, 1% each.

Presidential vote

1972	Nixon (R)	101,792	(66%)
	McGovern (D)	51,963	(34%)
1968	Nixon (R)	99,328	(55%)
	Humphrey (D)	71,296	(39%)
	Wallace (AI)	11,290	(6%)

Representative

James F. Hastings (R) Elected 1968; b. April 10, 1926, Olean; home, Rushford Lake; Navy, WWII; married, five children; Methodist.

Career Allegany Town Bd., Allegany Police Justice; N.Y. State Assembly, 1962–65; Bd. of Advisors, N.Y.U. Center for Research and Advanced Training in Deafness Rehab.; Mgr., V. Pres., radio station WHDL, 1952–66; Natl. Advertising Mgr., the *Times Herald*, Olean, 1964–66; Hastings & Jewell, real estate and insurance, 1966–69.

Offices 118 CHOB, 202-225-3161. Also 63 W. Main St., Allegany 14706, 716-373-2234, and Rm. 122, P.O. Bldg., 300 E. 3rd St., Jamestown 14701, 716-484-0252, and 243 Lake St., Elmira 14901, 607-734-0302.

Administrative Assistant Spencer C. Johnson

Committees

House Administration (10th); Subs: Accounts; Electrical and Mechanical Office Equipment.

Interstate and Foreign Commerce (9th); Sub: Public Health and Environment.

Group Ratings

	ADA	COPE	LWV	RIPON	NFU	LCV	CFA	NAB	NSI	ACA
1972	0	0	33	83	29	41	0	91	100	68
1971	16	0	38	60	29	–	43	–	–	88
1970	16	20	–	75	70	0	50	86	100	60

Key Votes

1) Busing	AGN	6) Cmbodia Bmbg	AGN	11) Chkg Acct Intrst	AGN
2) Strip Mines	AGN	7) Bust Hwy Trust	AGN	12) End HISC (HUAC)	AGN
3) Cut Mil $	AGN	8) Farm Sub Lmt	ABS	13) Nixon Sewer Veto	FOR
4) Rev Shrg	FOR	9) School Prayr	FOR	14) Corp Cmpaign $	AGN
5) Pub TV $	FOR	10) Cnsumr Prot	AGN	15) Pol $ Disclosr	FOR

Election Results

1972 general:	James F. Hastings (R-C)	126,147	(72%)
	Wilbur White, Jr. (D)	49,253	(28%)
1972 primary:	James F. Hastings (R), unopposed		
1970 general:	James F. Hastings (R-C)	94,906	(71%)
	James G. Cretekos (D)	37,961	(29%)

NORTH CAROLINA

Political Background

For more than two centuries, the differences between east and west have structured the politics of North Carolina. During the Revolutionary War, the Tidewater region in the east was pro-Tory, while the Piedmont to the west was a hotbed of anti-British radicalism. Likewise, during the Civil War, the east, where most of the slaves in North Carolina could be found, was strongly pro-Confederate, while to the west, particularly in the Appalachians, there was considerable Union sentiment. All in all, North Carolina was rather lukewarm about the Southern cause. The state voted to take leave of the Union only after Virginia decided to secede and thereby cut it off from the rest of the Union.

Today, each of North Carolina's three major topographical regions has distinctive politics. The Tidewater still has a large black population, and its white residents retain Democratic-segregationist voting habits, much like those found in the rest of the Deep South. The people of the Appalachians remain traditional, antiplanter Republicans, and fiercely independent of the rest of the state. The central Piedmont, with textile, tobacco, and furniture manufacturing cities, has become increasingly Republican and conservative, as those terms are commonly understood.

Because of the regional mix, Republicans have always been an important factor, though usually a minority, in North Carolina politics. And because of the relatively small black population found in most of the state (21% overall), North Carolina has been relatively free of the racist demagoguery often practiced in South Carolina, Georgia, Alabama, Mississippi, and elsewhere in the South.

Before the Civil War, North Carolina was an economic backwater, but for a full century after the conflict, industrial development in the state ran ahead of the rest of the South. Recently, other Southern states have been catching up, and some have passed it. None of the cities in North Carolina has managed to take off and become a major regional center like Atlanta or Dallas. So the urban population here remains scattered; there are four metropolitan areas with populations between 200,000 and 350,000—Charlotte, Greensboro, Winston-Salem, and Raleigh—and several other not much smaller. Moreover, much of the state is still rural, with nearly 10% of all North Carolinians living on farms. Tobacco, of course, is very important to the state, both as an agricultural crop and an industry, which means that not too many North Carolina politicians support efforts to discourage its use.

Moderate Republicans have long pointed to the state's relatively calm attitude towards race and its established bases of Republican urban support, and looked for the coming of a new, Republican South. There have been predictions of a GOP takeover since Republican Charles Jonas was first elected to the House in 1952. But the takeover was a long time coming. In 1968, Richard Nixon carried the state with 40% of the ballots—the first time a Republican presidential candidate took North Carolina's electoral votes since Herbert Hoover did it in 1928. Also in 1968, Goldwaterish Republican James Gardner waged a strong but losing race for Governor. It was not until 1972 that the Republicans really won big, and that win was confined to the top of the ticket, where moderate James Holshouser was elected Governor and ultraconservative Jesse Helms, U.S. Senator.

Holshouser's victory over North Carolina moderate and millionaire Democrat Hargrove (Skipper) Bowles followed the traditional lines of partisan division in the state. Holshouser is a native of the western mountains—since the 1860s, the traditional Republican stronghold—and he ran best there, west of Winston-Salem and Charlotte. He also carried the Piedmont cities of Greensboro and Raleigh by smaller margins. But the eastern coastal plain stayed true to its Democratic traditions, as Holshouser lost all four congressional districts nearest the Atlantic Ocean, even as he carried the state's seven others. The same pattern of support obtains in virtually all the state's major electoral contests—like the reelection victory of Sen. Sam Ervin in 1968—except, of course, that in the past Democrats have usually run 10% to 20% better than Bowles all over the state.

So it becomes interesting to compare the traditional pattern of support to the one that elected Sen. Helms over Rep. Nick Galifianakis in an upset. Helms is a former Raleigh TV commentator who accused Richard Nixon of "appeasing Red China" following the President's trip there. Helms won the Republican primary easily against desultory opposition. Galifianakis, the first and so far the only North Carolina Congressman of Greek descent, narrowly edged 73-year-old incumbent Sen. B. Everett Jordan in the Democratic primary.

In the House, Galifianakis compiled a moderate, sometimes liberal record—he supported end-the-war legislation, for example—which Helms of course tried to identify with positions taken by George McGovern. In turn, Galifianakis argued that Helms was far to the right of Richard Nixon. Galifianakis made gains in traditionally Republican areas, carrying all the big cities except Raleigh, Helms' home town. But Helms did far better than the average Republican in rural east North Carolina, most of which lay within the range of his TV broadcasts. He also scored well in the smaller textile-mill towns of the Piedmont. The result was a 54–46 Helms victory and the first Republican Senator from North Carolina since Reconstruction. Helms' campaign, by the way, was run by F. Clinton White, a political consultant who managed Barry Goldwater's pre-nomination effort in 1964 and James Buckley's New York Senate race in 1970.

Political scientist Walter deVries, a former aide to Michigan Gov. George Romney and author of *The Ticket Splitter*, is now a North Carolina resident. He has analyzed the North Carolina returns, discovering, he says, a Republican surge—younger people, in particular, are trending heavily toward the Republicans. That analysis certainly applies to the 1972 gubernatorial race, but a decisive portion of Helms' support appears to have come from the older, rural areas. Nevertheless, the trend could conceivably cause trouble for North Carolina's most famous Senator ever, Sam J. Ervin, Jr., when he comes up for reelection at age 78 in 1974. Numerous candidates, both Democratic and Republican, are jockeying for position, with no one here entirely sure that Senator Sam's new eminence is all that much of a political asset in North Carolina.

"North Carolina," we wrote in the 1972 *Almanac*, "was one of the last of the thirteen ex-colonies to ratify the Constitution. Members of the state legislature of that day balked because the document, as written, did not contain a section guaranteeing fundamental civil rights. That delay was in large part responsible for the first ten amendments to the Constitution known as the Bill of Rights. It is therefore fitting that North Carolina's senior Senator, Sam Ervin, Jr., is a persistent and articulate opponent of federal legislation and administrative action that, in his opinion, violates constitutional freedoms." Today, because of his devotion to the Constitution, the Chairman of the Senate Watergate Committee has become a legendary man. Like the late Justice Hugo Black, Sam Ervin always carries a copy of the Constitution around with him.

At 76, Chairman Sam sometimes tires; he stammers, pauses, stutters—but when he gets the question out or makes the point, it usually goes straight to the heart of the matter. Sam Ervin is not one to read the Constitution (or the Bible) the way most of his North Carolina friends and neighbors do. Or for that matter, does he see the great political document the way sophisticated liberals see it; for Ervin, the Constitution seems not so much an absolute to draw out the happy, progressive nature of man, but one to restrain his ever present, dark instincts. But whatever the case, Sam Ervin shows his Morganton, North Carolina upbringing— and his experience as a Justice of the North Carolina Supreme Court. He comes out of it a wiser man, perhaps, than any high-powered mover in Charlotte, Atlanta, and maybe even New York City. Stripped of its twin evils of sentimentality and fanaticism, the tradition of the American South is a rich one indeed. Anyone who disputes the proposition can turn to the literature of William Faulkner, the history of C. Vann Woodward, or the journalism of Tom Wicker.

Ervin sometimes has difficulty disguising his outrage at the acts and statements of the high Nixon officials who have come before his committee. But it is not the first time he has tangled with them and their interpretation of the Constitution and the law. At the end of his second decade in the Senate, and even before the creation of the Watergate committee, he was investigating Army surveillance of civilians and the abuse of information stored in computers, writing legislation on impoundment, and trying to find his way through the thicket of problems around the effort to establish a newsman's privilege to refuse to testify about confidential sources. As Chairman of the Senate Judiciary Committee's Subcommittee on Constitutional Rights, all these issues came before him, and all of them found him in fundamental opposition to the positions taken by the Nixon Administration.

Ervin likes to say that he is just a country lawyer. Indeed for much of his life he was just that. Years of defending moonshiners in his native Morganton (pop. 13,625) probably helped him to formulate ideas concerning the sanctity of a man's home under the Fourth Amendment. The Senator tried, unsuccessfully, to provide Congress with the fruits of his experience when he led the fight against no-knock legislation. But Ervin's country background has more often led him to stand on the conservative side of many issues. He has opposed all civil rights legislation, arguing that basic freedoms are thereby abridged. Nor has he been an especially keen friend of organized labor—the Carolinas have the nation's lowest level of unionization. Ervin has voted with both the Johnson and Nixon administrations on the war, and yet he is the first to defend the First Amendment rights of war protesters, hardly a popular group among most North Carolina voters. Many in the Senate and elsewhere defend the rights of those with whom they agree. It is a measure of Sam Ervin's devotion to the Constitution that he has spent many of his years in the Senate defending the rights of people whose ideas he does not share.

In the past, Ervin has always campaigned like the country lawyer he is. He drives around the state in his Chrysler, stopping to talk and shake hands with people in the small towns of North Carolina. It is a mode of campaigning not often seen these days, even in North Carolina, where skillful use of the electronic media was a major factor in the Republican gubernatorial and Senate victories of 1972. Because Richard Nixon would like nothing better than to see Sam Ervin defeated in 1974, one can assume that a lot of Nixon money will find its way to North Carolina for that purpose. There are also many younger Democrats, like Attorney General Robert Morgan and former Chicago Board of Trade head Henry Hall Wilson, who long for Ervin's seat. But with all his other activities, Senator Sam has been back in North Carolina almost every weekend, accompanied by his aide, Rufus Edmiston. Ervin swaps country-lawyer stories with the folks and quotes the Bible for college students. It somehow seems impossible that he could lose.

Census Data Pop. 5,082,059; 2.51% of U.S. total, 12th largest; change 1960–70, 11.5%. Central city, 19%; suburban, 19%. Median family income, $7,770; 40th highest; families above $15,000: 12%; families below $3,000: 15%. Median years education, 10.6.

1972 Share of Federal Tax Burden $3,908,640,000; 1.87% of U.S. total, 17th largest.

1972 Share of Federal Outlays $4,141,463,156; 1.91% of U.S. total, 16th largest. Per capita federal spending, $815.

DOD	$1,417,815,000	15th (2.27%)		HEW	$1,449,509,714	15th (2.03%)
AEC	$1,654,965	28th (0.06%)		HUD	$79,556,851	11th (2.59%)
NASA	$2,560,094	28th (0.09%)		VA	$278,126,052	11th (2.43%)
DOT	$139,193,446	23rd (1.76%)		USDA	$334,979,537	16th (2.18%)
DOC	$17,806,737	16th (1.38%)		CSC	$54,165,016	19th (1.31%)
DOI	$18,085,639	24th (0.85%)		TD	$102,091,920	24th (0.62%)
DOJ	$16,104,397	20th (1.64%)		Other	$229,813,788	

Economic Base Textile mill products, especially knitting mills and yarn and thread mills; agriculture, notably tobacco, broilers, hogs and eggs; apparel and other textile products, especially men's and boys' furnishings; finance, insurance and real estate; household furniture, and other furniture and fixtures; food and kindred products, especially meat products; electrical equipment and supplies, especially communication equipment.

Political Line-up Governor, James E. Holshouser, Jr. (R); seat up, 1976. Senators, Sam J. Ervin, Jr. (D) and Jesse A. Helms (R). Representatives, 11 (7 D and 4 R). State Senate (35 D and 15 R); State House (85 D and 35 R).

The Voters

Registration 2,357,645 Total. White 1,970,026 (84%); non-white 387,619 (16%). 1,729,436 D (73%); 541,916 R (23%); 86,293 other (4%).
Median voting age 40.9
Employment profile White collar, 38%. Blue collar, 46%. Service, 11%. Farm, 5%.
Ethnic groups Black, 22%. Total foreign stock, 2%.

Presidential vote

1972	Nixon (R)	1,054,889	(71%)
	McGovern (D)	438,705	(29%)
1968	Nixon (R)	627,192	(40%)
	Humphrey (D)	464,113	(29%)
	Wallace (AI)	496,188	(31%)
1964	Johnson (D)	800,139	(56%)
	Goldwater (R)	624,844	(44%)

Senator

Sam J. Ervin, Jr. (D) Elected Appointed June 5, 1954, seat up 1974; b. Sept. 27, 1896, Morganton; home, Morganton; U. of N.C., B.A., 1917; Harvard U., LL.B., 1922; Army, WWI; married, three children; Presbyterian.

Career Practicing atty., 1922– ; N.C. General Assembly, 1923, 1925, 1931; Judge, Burke County Crimininal Ct., 1935–37; Judge, N.C. Superior Ct., 1937–43; U.S. House of Reps., 1946–47; Assoc. Justice, N.C. Supreme Ct., 1948–54.

Offices 337 OSOB, 202-225-3154. Also Box 69, Morganton 28655, 704-437-5532.

Administrative Assistant Pat Shore

Committees

Armed Services (4th); Subs: Military Construction Authorization; National Stockpile and Naval Petroleum Reserves; Reprograming of Funds; Status of Forces (Chm.).

Government Operations (Chm.); Subs: Permanent Investigations; Intergovernmental Relations.

Judiciary (3rd); Subs: Antitrust and Monopoly; Constitutional Amendments; Constitutional Rights (Chm.); Criminal Laws and Procedures; Immmigration and Naturalization; Improvements in Judicial Machinery; Internal Security; Revision and Codification (Chm.); Separation of Powers (Chm.).

Sel. Com. on Presidential Campaign Activities (Chm.).

Group Ratings

	ADA	COPE	LWV	RIPON	NFU	LCV	CFA	NAB	NSI	ACA
1972	10	10	18	20	40	13	9	73	90	91
1971	30	25	15	17	36	–	67	–	–	87
1970	13	15	–	8	33	34	–	82	100	78

Key Votes

1) Busing	AGN	8) Sea Life Prot	FOR	15) Tax Singls Less	AGN
2) Alas P-line	FOR	9) Campaign Subs	AGN	16) Min Tax for Rich	AGN
3) Gun Cntrl	FOR	10) Cmbodia Bmbg	ABS	17) Euro Troop Rdctn	AGN
4) Rehnquist	FOR	11) Legal Srvices	AGN	18) Bust Hwy Trust	AGN
5) Pub TV $	FOR	12) Rev Sharing	AGN	19) Maid Min Wage	AGN
6) EZ Votr Reg	FOR	13) Cnsumr Prot	AGN	20) Farm Sub Limit	AGN
7) No-Fault	AGN	14) Eq Rts Amend	AGN	21) Highr Credt Chgs	AGN

Election Results

1968 general:	Sam J. Ervin, Jr. (D)	870,406	(61%)
	Robert Vance Somers (R)	566,934	(39%)
1968 primary:	Sam J. Ervin, Jr. (D)	499,392	(78%)
	Charles A. Pratt (D)	60,362	(9%)
	John T. Gathings, Sr. (D)	48,357	(8%)
	Fred G. Brummitt (D)	30,126	(5%)
1962 general:	Sam J. Ervin, Jr. (D)	491,520	(60%)
	Claude L. Greene, Jr. (R)	321,635	(40%)

Senator

Jesse Helms (R) Elected 1972, seat up 1978; b. Oct. 18, 1921, Monroe, home; Raleigh; Wingate Col.; Wake Forest Col.; Navy, 1942–45; married, three children; Baptist.

Career City Editor, *The Raleigh Times*; News Dir. Station WRAL; Admin. Asst. to Sens. Willis Smith and Alton Lennon 1951–53; Exec. Dir., N.C. Bankers Assn.; Raleigh City Council, 1957–1961.

Offices 4104 NSOB, 202-225-6342. Also P.O. Box 28125, Raleigh 27611, 919-755-4630, and P.O. Box 2944, Hickory 28601, 704-322-5170.

Administrative Assistant J. Harold Herring, Jr.

Committees

Aeronautical and Space Sciences (5th).

Agriculture and Forestry (6th); Subs: Environment, Soil Conservation and Forestry (Ranking Mbr.); Agricultural Credit and Rural Electrification; Agricultural Production, Marketing, and Stabilization of Prices; Foreign Agricultural Policy.

Joint Com. on Congressional Operation (2nd).

Group Ratings: Newly Elected

Election Results

1972 general:	Jesse A. Helms (R)	795,248	(54%)
	Nick Galifianakis (D)	677,293	(46%)
1972 primary:	Jesse A. Helms (R)	92,496	(60%)
	James C. Johnson (R)	45,303	(29%)
	William H. Booe (R)	16,032	(10%)

FIRST DISTRICT Political Background

Since the end of the draft, eastern North Carolina has produced a larger percentage of volunteers for the Army than any other part of the country. Aggressive recruiting accounts for some of the enlistments. But the total number signing up tells us a great deal about life on the rolling coastal plain east of Raleigh, a region that has no metropolitan area containing as many as 100,000 people. Plenty of people here still make their living on small tobacco farms, but more of them work in area textile mills, which are located in small towns and, to an increasing extent, simply along rural highways. The textile industry is largely nonunionized, the hours are long, the working conditions poor, and the wages low. Few young men (or young women) from eastern North Carolina go to college; book-learning is not especially prized, and parents cannot afford the luxury of more schooling. So the choice comes down to the mills or the Army, and around here the Army often looks better.

North Carolinas' 1st congressional district lies entirely within the state's eastern coastal zone. It includes the Outer Banks, the string of coastal islands beyond Pamlico and Albemarle Sounds where the Wright brothers first flew; also here is Cape Hatteras where countless ships have sunk. But nearly all of the residents of the 1st live inland, in small cities like New Bern, Elizabeth, and Greenville—at 29,000, the district's largest city. Far more of them live in the countryside, on small farms or in isolated houses or trailers. Some 36% of the residents of the 1st are black, the second largest black population among North Carolina congressional districts.

The white voters of the 1st retain from their slaveholding days a Democratic preference. They steadfastly supported Democratic candidates for President until 1968. In that year, when it looked like the election might be thrown into the House of Representatives, the 1st's Congressman, Walter Jones, was one of several Southern members of the House to announce that he would vote for the candidate who carried his district. That turned out to be George Wallace in the 1st district, as white voters abandoned the Democratic party en masse.

Walter Jones is one of the dwindling number of conservative Southern Democratic Congressmen. He spent a dozen years in the state legislature before winning a 1966 special election to succeed Herbert C. Bonner, who had served in the House since 1940 and was Chairman of the Merchant Marine and Fisheries Committee at the time of his death. Today, Jones also serves on that panel and on the Agriculture Committee, where he is next in line for the chairmanship of the Tobacco Subcommittee. These are all choice positions for a Congressman from the 1st district. Jones has never run into a serious challenge at election time, and appears certain to stay in the House as long as he wants.

Census Data Pop. 459,543. Central city, 0%; suburban, 0%. Median family income, $6,368; families above $15,000: 8%; families below $3,000: 22%. Median years education, 10.2.

1972 Share of Federal Outlays $396,003,680

DOD	$136,275,000	HEW	$134,900,235
AEC	$114,950	HUD	$3,888,172
NASA	–	DOI	$2,327,608
DOT	$11,842,450	USDA	$57,647,267
		Other	$49,007,998

Federal Military-Industrial Commitments

DOD Installations Marine Corps Air Facility (New River). Marine Corps Air Station (Cherry Point). Naval Facility (Buxton). Naval Air Rework Facility (Cherry Point).

Economic Base Agriculture, notably tobacco, grains, and hogs and sheep; apparel and other textile products; finance, insurance and real estate; lumber and wood products; and textile mill products. Also higher education (East Carolina Univ.).

The Voters

Registration 203,288 total. 149,756 white (74%); 53,532 non-white (26%). 177,284 D (87%); 21,933 R (11%); 4,071 other (2%).
Median voting age 42.1
Employment profile White collar, 36%. Blue collar, 40%. Service, 13%. Farm, 11%.
Ethnic groups Black, 36%. Total foreign stock, 1%.

Presidential vote

1972	Nixon (R)	83,557	(70%)
	McGovern (D)	35,333	(30%)
1968	Nixon (R)	31,143	(22%)
	Humphrey (D)	47,780	(34%)
	Wallace (AI)	62,324	(44%)

Representative

Walter B. Jones (D) Elected Feb. 5, 1966; b. Aug. 19, 1913, Fayetteville; home, Farmville; N.C. State U., B.S., 1934; married, two children; Baptist.

Career Businessman, office supplies, 1934–49; Mayor of Farmville, 1949–53; N.C. Gen. Assembly, 1955–59; N.C. Senate, 1965.

Offices 130 CHOB, 202-225-3101. Also Farmville 27828, 919-753-3082.

Administrative Assistant Floyd J. Lupton

Committees

Agriculture (6th); Subs: Livestock and Grains; Oilseeds and Rice (Chm.); Tobacco.

Merchant Marine and Fisheries (9th); Subs: Coast Guard and Navigation; Oceanography; Merchant Marine.

Group Ratings

	ADA	COPE	LWV	RIPON	NFU	LCV	CFA	NAB	NSI	ACA
1972	19	18	25	31	43	2	0	50	89	83
1971	22	36	22	35	71	–	25	–	–	63
1970	12	42	–	18	31	10	40	67	100	79

Key Votes

1) Busing	AGN	6) Cmbodia Bmbg	AGN	11) Chkg Acct Intrst	ABS
2) Strip Mines	AGN	7) Bust Hwy Trust	AGN	12) End HISC (HUAC)	AGN
3) Cut Mil $	AGN	8) Farm Sub Lmt	AGN	13) Nixon Sewer Veto	AGN
4) Rev Shrg	AGN	9) School Prayr	FOR	14) Corp Cmpaign $	FOR
5) Pub TV $	AGN	10) Cnsumr Prot	AGN	15) Pol $ Disclosr	AGN

Election Results

1972 general:	Walter B. Jones (D)	77,438	(69%)
	J. Jordan Bonner (R)	35,063	(31%)
1972 primary:	Walter B. Jones (D), unopposed		
1970 general:	Walter B. Jones (D)	41,674	(70%)
	R. Frank Everett (R)	16,217	(27%)
	Gene Leggett (AI)	1,452	(2%)

SECOND DISTRICT Political Background

North of Raleigh and south of the Virginia line, the 2nd district of North Carolina is situated on an inland portion of the coastal plain where it rises to meet the state's western mountains. The 2nd is a predominantly rural and small-town district; its largest city, Rocky Mount, has only 34,000 residents. And like much of North Carolina, the 2nd's economy depends almost entirely on textiles and the tobacco crop. What makes the 2nd distinctive politically is the size of its black population—some 40% of its residents (though only 34% of those over 18) are black, making both percentages the highest in the state. To stem black outmigration and to encourage black capitalism, former civil rights leader Floyd McKissick has announced plans to build a black "new town" in Warren County. After receiving some federal support, McKissick endorsed Richard Nixon in 1972.

Most 2nd-district black voters, however, refused to go along, as they furnished most of the ballots cast here for George McGovern. The rest of them, to a large extent, came from Orange County, which was added to the district for 1972. The county includes Chapel Hill, home of the University of North Carolina—one of the few Southern universities to produce large numbers of liberal votes in the 1972 elections.

The addition of Orange County also made for the first seriously contested congressional race in the district since 1952, the year the 2nd first elected Democratic Congressman L. H. Fountain. He is a politician who wears white linen suits in the summertime and speaks with gentle Southern courtliness all year around. During his 20 years in Congress, Fountain has compiled a solidly conservative voting record on both economic and racial issues. But the Congressman, a member of the Government Operations Committee, has been something of a crusader in one area. As Chairman of the Intergovernmental Relations Subcommittee, Fountain has conducted thorough investigations of the Food and Drug Administration for more than 10 years. Fountain has argued that the policy of the FDA has been all too liberal in allowing possibly dangerous drugs on the market. He has also worked hard to penetrate the veil of secrecy which this bureaucracy —convinced that mere laymen cannot understand its workings—puts over its affairs.

The workings of the FDA, however, are not a big issue in the 2nd district. The real issue, at least for most voters, in the 1972 Democratic primary between Fountain and Chapel Hill Mayor Howard Lee, was race. Lee, a black who was elected Mayor of a white-majority university town, conducted an energetic campaign, one that registered an estimated 18,000 black voters. The challenger also sought white votes, pleading common economic concerns. Lee was fairly successful among both blacks and whites; Fountain nevertheless managed to win with 59% of the votes.

Lee's showing represents a substantial improvement over the efforts of another black, Eva Clayton, in 1968. But Lee's defeat does point up, once again, how difficult it is for even a large black minority to make its political weight felt in the rural South. Poor whites went overwhelmingly for the conservative Fountain. Meanwhile, blacks are still less likely to register and vote than their white counterparts. Part of the failure of blacks to do so stems, no doubt, from the fear of economic and physical reprisals that have prevailed in the community since the 1900 defeat of 2nd-district Congressman George H. White, the last black to represent any part of the Deep South until the elections of 1972. But part of the failure also stems from the same set of factors that account for low black registration and voter participation in the North—mainly, a simple lack of awareness. The question is whether campaigns like Lee's can make a difference over the long haul.

Census Data Pop. 457,601. Central city, 0%; suburban, 13%. Median family income, $6,550; families above $15,000: 9%; families below $3,000: 20%. Median years education, 9.8.

1972 Share of Federal Outlays $337,233,519

DOD	$16,500,688	HEW	$149,954,406
AEC	$374,527	HUD	$3,691,150
NASA	$334,929	DOI	$177,667
DOT	$8,940,065	USDA	$94,804,484
		Other	$62,455,603

Federal Military-Industrial Commitments

DOD Installations Roanoke Rapids AF Station (Roanoke Rapids).

Economic Base Agriculture, notably tobacco, poultry and grains; textile mill products; apparel and other textile products; finance, insurance and real estate; and lumber and wood products. Also higher education (Univ. of North Carolina).

The Voters

Registration 222,692 total. 158,233 white (71%); 64,459 non-white (29%). 197,158 D (86%); 21,013 R (9%); 4,521 other (2%).
Median voting age 42.0
Employment profile White collar, 36%. Blue collar, 41%. Service, 13%. Farm, 10%.
Ethnic groups Black, 40%. Total foreign stock, 1%.

Presidential vote

1972	Nixon (R)	86,006	(64%)
	McGovern (D)	47,674	(36%)
1968	Nixon (R)	31,392	(22%)
	Humphrey (D)	48,483	(34%)
	Wallace (AI)	60,991	(43%)

Representative

L. H. Fountain (D) Elected 1952; b. April 23, 1913, Leggett; home, Tarboro; U. of N.C., B.A., 1934, LL.B., 1936; Army, WWII; married, one child; Presbyterian.

Career Practicing atty., 1936– ; Reading Clerk, N.C. Senate, 1936–41; N.C. Senate, 1947–52; V.Pres., Plains Broadcasting Co., WCPS Radio, Tarboro, 1949– .

Offices 2188 RHOB, 202-225-4531. Also P.O., Tarboro 27886, 919-823-4200.

Administrative Assistant Walter J. Pittman

Committees

Foreign Affairs (4th); Subs: International Organizations and Movements; National Security Policy and Scientific Developments; Near East and South Asia; Sp. Sub. for Review of Foreign Aid Programs.

Government Operations (3rd); Subs: Intergovernmental Relations (Chm.); Conservation and Natural Resources.

Group Ratings

	ADA	COPE	LWV	RIPON	NFU	LCV	CFA	NAB	NSI	ACA
1972	6	27	25	40	57	20	50	90	100	91
1971	5	18	22	33	50	–	38	–	–	85
1970	4	17	–	18	23	30	46	75	100	79

Key Votes

1) Busing	AGN	6) Cmbodia Bmbg	AGN	11) Chkg Acct Intrst	ABS
2) Strip Mines	AGN	7) Bust Hwy Trust	AGN	12) End HISC (HUAC)	AGN
3) Cut Mil $	AGN	8) Farm Sub Lmt	AGN	13) Nixon Sewer Veto	AGN
4) Rev Shrg	FOR	9) School Prayr	FOR	14) Corp Cmpaign $	AGN
5) Pub TV $	AGN	10) Cnsumr Prot	FOR	15) Pol $ Disclosr	FOR

Election Results

1972 general:	L. H. Fountain (D)	88,798	(72%)
	Erick P. Little (R)	35,193	(28%)
1972 primary:	L. H. Fountain (D)	60,289	(59%)
	Howard N. Lee (D)	42,242	(41%)
1970 general:	L. H. Fountain (D), unopposed		

THIRD DISTRICT Political Background

The 3rd district of North Carolina is one of small farms, small towns, and Atlantic shore seascapes. Lying in the middle of the state's coastal plain, the 3rd runs from a point a few miles south of Raleigh and Durham to the Atlantic Ocean near Wilmington. The district's largest city is Goldsboro (pop. 26,000), but its largest concentration of people live in Camp Lejeune (pop. 34,000), the Marine Corps' giant base at the estuary of the New River. One of the Marines' most important installations, Camp Lejeune looms large in the economy of the district, though its voters have been disturbed by recent racial conflict at the base. Also in the 3rd is an Air Force base near Goldsboro, with Fort Bragg just over the line in the 7th district. The 3rd's dependence on the military and its low (27%) black percentage probably accounts for the very conservative political inclinations. In 1972, despite the Democratic heritage of its residents, the district cast the state's lowest percentage of ballots for Senate candidate Nick Galifianakis, a Congressman who had voted for antiwar measures, and the highest percentage for Republican Jesse Helms, whose ultraconservative commentaries on Raleigh's WRAL-TV were beamed into much of the district for a dozen years.

In 1960, Congressman Graham Barden of the 3rd, then Chairman of the House Education and Labor Committee, retired; he was succeeded in the chairmanship by Harlem's Adam Clayton Powell. Barden was succeeded in the 3rd district by David Henderson, who had served briefly on the committee staff when Barden was Chairman. But like most Southern Democrats these days, Henderson did not obtain a seat on the increasingly liberal House panel. Instead, he sits on Post Office and Civil Service, where he is today the second-ranking Democrat. As a member of the committee, Henderson shares in such unpleasant tasks as determining civil service fringe benefits and staving off strikes by government workers.

Henderson has seldom had any trouble at the polls. In 1968, however, when a conservative Republican ran for Governor, the Congressman's Republican opponent carried a couple of the larger counties in the district. Despite the local Nixon landslide, Henderson had no such problems in 1972, when he was left unopposed.

Census Data Pop. 458,000. Central city, 0%; suburban, 0%. Median family income, $6,193; families above $15,000: 6%; families below $3,000: 21%. Median years education, 10.4.

1972 Share of Federal Outlays $499,593,762

DOD	$313,070,000	HEW	$109,145,918
AEC	–	HUD	$500,000
NASA	–	DOI	$384,000
DOT	$12,628,011	USDA	$31,638,441
		Other	$32,227,392

Federal Military-Industrial Commitments

DOD Installations Marine Corps Base (Camp LeJeune). Naval Hospital (Camp LeJeune). Seymour-Johnson AFB (Goldsboro).

Economic Base Agriculture, notably tobacco, poultry, and hogs and sheep; apparel and other textile products; textile mill products; finance, insurance and real estate; and food and kindred products.

The Voters

Registration 178,515 total. 146,333 white (82%); 32,182 non-white (18%). 145,643 D (82%); 28,886 R (16%); 3,986 other (2%).
Median voting age 37.7
Employment profile White collar, 34%. Blue collar, 43%. Service, 12%. Farm, 11%.
Ethnic groups Black, 27%. Total foreign stock, 2%.

Presidential vote

1972	Nixon (R)		79,431	(74%)
	McGovern (D)		27,878	(26%)
1968	Nixon (R)		35,730	(30%)
	Humphrey (D)		32,586	(27%)
	Wallace (AI)		50,931	(43%)

Representative

David Newton Henderson (D) Elected 1960; b. April 16, 1921, near Hubert; home, Wallace; Davidson Col., B.S., 1942; U. of N.C., LL.B., 1949; Army Air Corps, WWII; married, three children; Presbyterian.

Career Practicing atty., 1949–60; Asst. Gen. Counsel, House Ed. and Labor Com., 1951–52; Solicitor, Duplin County Gen. Ct., 1954–58; Judge, 1957–59.

Offices 235 CHOB, 202-225-3415. Also 110½ E. Main St., Wallace 28466, 919-285-2102, and Fed. Bldg., Goldsboro 27530, 919-736-1844.

Administrative Assistant Charles O. Whitley

Committees

Post Office and Civil Service (2nd); Subs: Manpower and Civil Service (Chm.); Investigations.

Public Works (9th); Subs: Economic Development; Energy; Investigations; Transportation; Water Resources.

Group Ratings

	ADA	COPE	LWV	RIPON	NFU	LCV	CFA	NAB	NSI	ACA
1972	13	27	18	33	57	4	50	50	100	73
1971	11	33	11	33	57	–	38	–	–	76
1970	8	42	–	21	27	39	48	67	100	72

Key Votes

1) Busing	AGN	6) Cmbodia Bmbg	AGN	11) Chkg Acct Intrst	AGN
2) Strip Mines	ABS	7) Bust Hwy Trust	AGN	12) End HISC (HUAC)	AGN
3) Cut Mil $	AGN	8) Farm Sub Lmt	AGN	13) Nixon Sewer Veto	AGN
4) Rev Shrg	AGN	9) School Prayr	FOR	14) Corp Cmpaign $	FOR
5) Pub TV $	AGN	10) Cnsumr Prot	AGN	15) Pol $ Disclosr	AGN

Election Results

1972 general:	David N. Henderson (D), unopposed		
1972 primary:	David N. Henderson (D)	45,616	(79%)
	Joseph Edwards (D)	11,828	(21%)
1970 general:	David N. Henderson (D)	41,065	(60%)
	Herbert H. Howell (R)	27,224	(40%)

FOURTH DISTRICT Political Background

The 4th district of North Carolina consists of four counties in the middle of the state, where the state's coastal plains rise to meet the Piedmont. Raleigh (pop. 121,000) is the state capital and the district's largest city. It is also a tobacco center and the home of North Carolina State University. Durham (pop. 95,000), another tobacco center and home of Duke University (where Richard Nixon got his law degree), has one of North Carolina's largest and politically most sophisticated black communities. The beginnings of a Boston Route 128-style electronics boom is evident in the Research Triangle area between Raleigh and Durham. The two other counties in the district are far smaller. Randolph, in the west, is traditionally Republican; and Chatham, closer to Raleigh and Durham, is traditionally Democratic.

The 4th's strong academic and black communities have made it one of the most liberal districts in North Carolina, and one of the most closely contested in congressional elections. The Democrats here have nominated candidates who have taken liberal positions on many issues, which have come under sharp attack by aggressive Republicans. Until 1972, the Representative from the 4th was Nick Galifianakis, whose issue positions—including opposition to the Vietnam war—made him a prime Republican target in 1970. R. Jack Hawke, the young Republican nominee, had heavy financial support and a last-minute campaign appearance from Vice President Agnew—politics, in this case, being thicker than Greek-American blood. Nonetheless, Galifianakis won reelection with 52% of the votes, just as he did in 1968.

After two close races, Galifianakis toyed with the idea of running for the Senate. His thinking, perhaps, was that his chances of winning were as good in a Senate race as in another House contest, and if he won, reelection time would come up only once every six years. Galifianakis opted for a Senate try when the legislature removed Orange County from his district for the 1972 election. The small county includes Chapel Hill and accounted for more than half of his 1970 margin. As things turned out, the Congressman upset Sen. B. Everett Jordan in the Democratic primary, but then lost the general election to Republican Jesse Helms, himself a resident of the 4th district (see state write-up).

So in 1972, it looked very much like the Republican would pick up the seat in the 4th. Though it was George McGovern's second-best North Carolina district, Nixon still walked away with 69% of the votes. And if the President had any coattails whatever, they should have been enough for Republican Hawke, running a second time, to win. But they were not. After a heated primary, state Rep. Ike F. Andrews won the Democratic nomination. Andrews, whose name is easier to say than Galifianakis, possessed a moderate reputation, having served as state House Majority Leader. In the general election, the Democrat carried his native Chatham County and Durham by enough votes to overcome Hawke's advantage in Randolph County and Raleigh. Andrews won by precisely 1,000 votes.

The new Congressman is now the only Southern Democrat on the House Education and Labor Committee. In these days of confrontation between a Democratic Congress and a Republican President, Andrews appears to line up mostly with his Democratic colleagues. The odds are that this district, having a tradition of close races, will be the scene of another one in 1974, unless Andrews uses the advantages of incumbency to maximum electoral benefit.

Census Data Pop. 467,046. Central city, 46%; suburban, 47%. Median family income, $8,999; families above $15,000: 16%; families below $3,000: 10%. Median years education, 11.5.

1972 Share of Federal Outlays $492,487,609

DOD	$60,576,342	HEW	$214,416,760
AEC	$1,147,798	HUD	$9,715,244
NASA	$1,045,877	DOI	$2,564,234
DOT	$16,849,755	USDA	$37,404,859
		Other	$148,766,740

Federal Military-Industrial Commitments

DOD Contractors Athey Products (Wake Forest), $7.077m: fork lift trucks.

Economic Base Textile mill products, especially knitting mill products; finance, insurance and real estate; agriculture, notably poultry, tobacco and dairy products; machinery; food and kindred products, especially meat products; and electrical equipment and supplies. Also higher education (Duke Univ., and North Carolina State Univ.).

The Voters

Registration 236,811 total. 198,773 white (84%); 65,038 non-white (27%). 173,620 D (73%); 53,179 R (22%); 10,012 other (4%).
Median voting age 39.3
Employment profile White collar, 50%. Blue collar, 35%. Service, 12%. Farm, 3%.
Ethnic groups Black, 23%. Total foreign stock, 3%.

Presidential vote

1972	Nixon (R)	107,283	(69%)
	McGovern (D)	47,343	(31%)
1968	Nixon (R)	58,928	(40%)
	Humphrey (D)	46,425	(32%)
	Wallace (AI)	40,923	(28%)

Representative

Ike F. **Andrews** (D) Elected 1972; b. Sept. 2, 1925, Bonlee; home, Siler City; Fork Union Military Academy; Mars Hill Col.; U. of N.C., B.S., 1950, LL.D., 1952; Army, WWII; married, two children.

Career Assoc. of Andrews and Stone, law firm; State Senate, 1959; State Rep., 1961, 67, 69, 71; Majority Leader and Speaker Pro Tem of N.C. House, 1971.

Offices 501 CHOB, 202-225-1784. Also 220 Fed. Bldg, 310 Newbern Ave., Raleigh, 919-755-4120.

Administrative Assistant G. Eugene Boyce

Committees

Education and Labor (19th); Subs: Gen. Sub. on Education; Sp. Sub. on Education.

Group Ratings: Newly Elected

Key Votes

1) Busing	NE	6) Cmbodia Bmbg	AGN	11) Chkg Acct Intrst	AGN
2) Strip Mines	NE	7) Bust Hwy Trust	AGN	12) End HISC (HUAC)	AGN
3) Cut Mil $	NE	8) Farm Sub Lmt	NE	13) Nixon Sewer Veto	AGN
4) Rev Shrg	NE	9) School Prayr	NE	14) Corp Cmpaign $	NE
5) Pub TV $	NE	10) Cnsumr Prot	NE	15) Pol $ Disclosr	NE

Election Results

1972 general:	Ike F. Andrews (D)	73,072	(50%)
	R. Jack Hawke (R)	71,972	(50%)
1972 run-off:	Ike F. Andrews (D)	35,604	(52%)
	Jyles J. Coggins (D)	32,936	(48%)
1972 primary:	Ike F. Andrews (D)	24,763	(30%)
	Jyles J. Coggins (D)	25,642	(31%)
	William A. Creech (D)	13,214	(16%)
	R. W. Grabarek (D)	10,676	(13%)
	A. A. McMillan (D)	4,248	(5%)
	Charles D. Bullock (D)	3,064	(4%)

FIFTH DISTRICT Political Background

The 5th district of North Carolina is part of western North Carolina's hill country. While the tradition of the state's hot, swampy flatland is Democratic, that of the cool, green mountains has always been Republican. It is, however, a Republicanism more of an insurgent rather than a conservative kind—one that has grown out of a resistance to the domination imposed by the wealthy tobacco planters of the coast. If a respect for "law and order" exists in the mountain country, so also does a distrust of the federal government, whose presence is made clear by men going around smashing distilling apparatus.

The largest city in the 5th is one not quite in the mountains, Winston-Salem (pop. 132,000). The name of the town indicates its dependence on the tobacco industry and the R. J. Reynolds Company in particular. Like the rest of the district, Winston-Salem tends to go Republican more often than not these days. But it sometimes exhibits a twinge of the ornery, populistic streak it shares with the mountain country; in 1972, for example, Winston-Salem went for Democratic Senate candidate Nick Galifianakis over Republican Jesse Helms.

Galifianakis' success here may have come, in part, from local familiarity. He represented Winston-Salem in the House when he was first elected Congressman in 1966, a time congressional district lines looked very different from their appearance today. When the lines were altered for the 1968 elections, a no-incumbent seat resulted and a real fight for it soon developed. The Democratic candidate was Smith Bagley, an heir to the Reynolds tobacco fortune; two years earlier, Bagley had been defeated in the primary by Galifianakis. Bagley's Republican opponent was Wilmer ("Vinegar Bend") Mizell, a pitcher for several major league baseball teams during the 1950s. Mizell settled here after retiring from the game probably because he had been a big local favorite playing for the Winston-Salem club in his minor league days. Mizell was once named the team's "most popular player" and "Mr. Strike-Out King."

Mizell campaigned as a conservative and as a supporter of Richard Nixon, while Bagley took a somewhat more liberal stance. Bagley carried several mountain counties and took Forsyth County (Winston-Salem) by 2,000 votes. But he was unable to overcome Mizell's advantage in textile-milling Davidson (where his wife grew up) and Davie counties; both are no longer in the district. So Mizell joined other ex-athletes in the House—Decatholon champ Bob Mathias of California and Buffalo Bills quarterback Jack Kemp—and became one of Richard Nixon's "team players."

Mizell has now been reelected with 58% and 60% of the votes, both better figures than his won-lost percentage in the big leagues. The campaign in 1972 was the more interesting. In it, the Democratic nominee was ex-Arkansas Congressman (1943–59) Brooks Hays. Back in Arkansas, Hays was unseated by a segregationist write-in candidate in 1958, following the Little Rock school desegration flap. Then after holding several posts in Washington, Hays retired to live in Winston-Salem. Though 74, the ex-Congressman gamely walked through the district and enlisted volunteer supporters. He was no doubt helped when the *Winston-Salem Journal* revealed that Mizell, one prone to the politics of draft-dodger denouncing, had himself skillfully evaded military duty for a time during the Korean war. Nevertheless, Mizell still won, a sign of his popularity and the apparent acceptance of the Nixon Administration in Winston-Salem and the Republicanism of the mountains of the 5th district.

Census Data Pop. 462,401. Central city, 29%; suburban, 18%. Median family income, $8,191; families above $15,000: 12%; families below $3,000: 13%. Median years education, 10.3.

1972 Share of Federal Outlays $290,532,564

DOD	$76,848,081	HEW	$120,536,068
AEC	$7,187	HUD	$11,111,366
NASA	$17,853	DOI	$616,157
DOT	$10,799,213	USDA	$17,909,120
		Other	$52,687,501

Federal Military-Industrial Commitments

DOD Contractors R.J. Reynolds Industries (Winston-Salem), $21.508m: unspecified. Western Electric (Winston Salem), $20.016m: underwater electronic ware.

Economic Base Textile mill products, especially knitting mill products; furniture and fixtures, especially wood household furniture; agriculture, notably tobacco, poultry and cattle; finance, insurance and real estate; and apparel and other textile products.

The Voters

Registration 244,842 total. 213,090 white (87%); 31,752 non-white (13%). 154,404 D (53%); 81,653 R (33%); 8,785 other (4%).
Median voting age 41.6
Employment profile White collar, 38%. Blue collar, 50%. Service, 9%. Farm, 3%.
Ethnic groups Black, 14%. Total foreign stock, 1%.

Presidential vote

1972	Nixon (R)	109,952	(71%)
	McGovern (D)	45,830	(29%)
1968	Nixon (R)	80,504	(49%)
	Humphrey (D)	44,362	(27%)
	Wallace (AI)	39,406	(24%)

Representative

Wilmer David Mizell (R) Elected 1968; b. Aug. 13, 1930, Vinegar Bend, Ala.; home, Winston-Salem; Army, 1953–54; married, two children; Baptist.

Career Baseball pitcher, 1949–63; Natl. League All Star Team, 1959; sales management and public relations, Pepsi-Cola Co., 1963–67; Chm., Bd. of Davidson County Commissioners, 1966.

Offices 225 CHOB, 202-225-2071. Also 2217 Wachovia Bank Bldg., Winson-Salem 27101, 919-723-9211, ext. 348.

Administrative Assistant Willard (Bill) Phillips, Jr.

Committees

Agriculture (9th); Subs: Cotton; Family Farms and Rural Development; Tobacco.

Public Works (8th); Subs: Energy; Transportation; Public Buildings and Grounds; Economic Development; Investigations and Review.

Group Ratings

	ADA	COPE	LWV	RIPON	NFU	LCV	CFA	NAB	NSI	ACA
1972	0	9	18	33	43	20	0	82	100	91
1971	0	17	22	22	33	–	13	–	–	93
1970	0	9	–	31	31	0	43	100	100	94

Key Votes

1) Busing	AGN	6) Cmbodia Bmbg	FOR	11) Chkg Acct Intrst	AGN
2) Strip Mines	FOR	7) Bust Hwy Trust	AGN	12) End HISC (HUAC)	AGN
3) Cut Mil $	AGN	8) Farm Sub Lmt	AGN	13) Nixon Sewer Veto	FOR
4) Rev Shrg	FOR	9) School Prayr	FOR	14) Corp Cmpaign $	FOR
5) Pub TV $	AGN	10) Cnsumr Prot	AGN	15) Pol $ Disclosr	AGN

Election Results

1972 general:	Wilmer D. Mizell (R)	101,375	(65%)
	Brooks Hays (D)	54,986	(35%)
1972 primary:	Wilmer D. Mizell (R), unopposed		
1970 general:	Wilmer D. Mizell (R)	68,937	(58%)
	James G. White (D)	49,663	(42%)

SIXTH DISTRICT Political Background

The 6th district of North Carolina takes in the cities of Greensboro (pop. 144,000), High Point (pop. 63,000), and Burlington (pop. 35,000)—all in the heart of the booming Piedmont region. One of the textile giants, Burlington Industries, is headquartered in the district, and most of the other big textile firms have mills here. But the area is also one of diversification, having moved beyond the traditional North Carolina industries of textiles, tobacco, and furniture. Western Electric, for example, now operates out of both Greensboro and Burlington. The attendant influx of Northern managerial and technical talent is responsible in part for the growing Republican strength in Guilford County (Greensboro and High Point). Since the Eisenhower years, Guilford has trended Republican in national and many statewide elections.

The two other counties in the district retain a Southern Democratic preference. Both of them went for George Wallace in 1968. But because fewer blacks live here (22%) than in the Tidewater districts to the east, campaign time manifests less out-and-out racist politics, though busing is a big issue in Greensboro these days. All in all, the voting patterns in the 6th are somewhat more conservative than those in the otherwise quite similar 4th, which contain larger black and academic communities.

In 1968, Horace Kornegay, a conservative Democrat, decided to retire from the House, perhaps because he had won reelection two years before by a scant 2,000 votes over a Republican challenger. In most Southern districts, the retirement of a veteran Congressman would have triggered a riproaring Democratic primary fight. But the 6th district of North Carolina had no primary. L. Richardson Preyer was nominated without opposition, as if by silent acclamation. The phenomenon was quite remarkable because Preyer is a liberal by North Carolina standards. He does, however, have establishment credentials that are impeccable. Richardson is an heir to the Richardson-Merrell drug fortune (Vicks Vaporub) and a graduate of Princeton and Harvard Law School. He became a judge at age 34, and served in city and state courts until appointed to to the federal bench in 1961. Preyer resigned from the judgeship, a lifetime appointment, to run for Governor in 1964.

Candidate Preyer conducted a campaign in the tradition of moderate Gov. Terry Sanford (president of Duke University and briefly a presidential hopeful in 1972) and Luther Hodges (ex-Secretary of Commerce). But with the conservative tide then sweeping the South in reaction to the civil rights movement, Preyer lost the primary to conservative Dan K. Moore, and returned to legal and business circles in Greensboro.

In 1968, Preyer's local prominence made him the logical successor to Kornegay. And in spite of the strong 1968 Nixon-Wallace showing in the 6th district, he defeated a well-known Republican in the general election. In 1970, he improved on his initial effort, getting 66% of the votes in a three-candidate field. In 1972, Preyer was unopposed.

As a Congressman, Preyer has compiled a moderate-to-liberal voting record. He was one of two North Carolina members of the House to support antiwar legislation. At the same time, however, Preyer has backed military spending projects like the ABM, for which Western Electric, the prime contractor for the system, has more than $100 million in awards for work done in the district. A member of the Commerce Committee, Preyer has spent much of his time working on tobacco legislation; he of course takes a position favorable to the interests of North Carolina tobacco growers and manufacturers. The Congressman also serves on Paul Rogers' prolific Public Health Subcommittee, where he usually finds himself agreeing with Rogers (see Florida 11).

As a former federal judge, Preyer has introduced legislation, written by Yale law professor Alexander Bickel, designed to spur states into solving the problems for which courts have ordered busing schemes. Oddly enough, Preyer is also a member of the House Internal Security Committee; though he is hardly a hunter of subversives, he has worked on employee security legislation. Some speculate that Preyer may eventually run for the Senate. But his first stab at statewide office was an unlucky one. Moreover, the Congressman will not run against Sam Ervin in 1974, and by the time Republican Jesse Helms' seat comes up in 1978, Preyer will be nearing 60.

Census Data Pop. 457,354. Central city, 45%; suburban, 18%. Median family income, $9,300; families above $15,000: 17%; families below $3,000: 9%. Median years education, 11.0.

1972 Share of Federal Outlays $422,102,220

DOD	$211,263,859	HEW	$123,424,700
AEC	$9,677	HUD	$11,300,335
NASA	$24,040	DOI	$766,406
DOT	$3,654,861	USDA	$12,387,572
		Other	$59,270,770

Federal Military-Industrial Commitments

DOD Contractors Western Electric (Greensboro), $142.355m: ABM electronic ware. Western Electric (Burlington), $110.100m: research and development for ABM system.

Economic Base Textile mille products; furniture and fixtures, especially household furniture; apparel and other textile products; finance, insurance and real estate; and agriculture, notably tobacco, dairy products and poultry.

The Voters

Registration 212,466 total. 179,745 white (85%); 32,721 non-white (15%). 153,112 D (72%); 47,332 R (22%); 12,022 other (6%).
Median voting age 41.4
Employment profile White collar, 43%. Blue collar, 45%. Service, 10%. Farm, 2%.
Ethnic groups Black, 21%. Total foreign stock, 2%.

Presidential vote

1972	Nixon (R)	97,946	(72%)
	McGovern (D)	38,163	(28%)
1968	Nixon (R)	59,401	(42%)
	Humphrey (D)	40,619	(29%)
	Wallace (AI)	42,214	(30%)

Represenatative

Lunsford Richardson Preyer (D) Elected 1968; b. Jan. 11, 1919, Greensboro; home, Greensboro; Princeton U., B.A., 1941; Harvard, LL.B., 1949; Navy, WWII; married, five children; Presbyterian.

Career Practicing atty., 1950–56; City Judge, 1953–54; Superior Ct. Judge, 1956–61; U.S. Dist. Judge, 1961–63; Candidate for Gov., 1964; Sr. V.Pres. Trust Officer, N.C. Natl. Bank, Greensboro, 1964–66.

Offices 316 CHOB, 202-225-3065. Also Fed. Bldg., 326 W. Market St., Greensboro 27401, 919-272-3161.

Administrative Assistant Tom W. Lambeth

Committees

Internal Security (3rd).

Interstate and Foreign Commerce (16th); Sub: Public Health and Environment.

Group Ratings

	ADA	COPE	LWV	RIPON	NFU	LCV	CFA	NAB	NSI	ACA
1972	44	40	83	60	86	54	50	17	70	29
1971	51	50	78	72	87	–	75	–	–	31
1970	40	50	–	50	85	100	86	42	90	37

Key Votes

1) Busing	FOR	6) Cmbodia Bmbg	AGN	11) Chkg Acct Intrst	ABS
2) Strip Mines	AGN	7) Bust Hwy Trust	AGN	12) End HISC (HUAC)	AGN
3) Cut Mil $	AGN	8) Farm Sub Lmt	AGN	13) Nixon Sewer Veto	AGN
4) Rev Shrg	FOR	9) School Prayr	AGN	14) Corp Cmpaign $	AGN
5) Pub TV $	FOR	10) Cnsumr Prot	FOR	15) Pol $ Disclosr	FOR

Election Results

1972 general:	L. Richardson Preyer (D)	82,158	(94%)
	Lynwood Bullock (R)	5,331	(6%)
1972 primary:	L. Richardson Preyer (D), unopposed		
1970 general:	L. Richardson Preyer (D)	47,693	(66%)
	Clifton B. Barham (R)	20,739	(29%)
	Lynwood Bullock (AI)	3,849	(5%)

SEVENTH DISTRICT Political Background

The 7th district of North Carolina is a southern portion of the state's Tidewater region. This is a part of North Carolina most like the Deep South. Wilmington (pop. 46,000) is an old Carolina coastal city that never became a major port—a would-be Charleston or Savannah. Fayetteville (pop. 53,000), the district's other population center, lies across the state's rather sparsely settled coastal plain to the west. The city's population only slightly exceeds that of adjacent Fort Bragg, the huge Army base (pop. 47,000) to which Fayetteville owes much of its relatively prosperous status.

The 7th has a fairly large number of blacks (26%), but its most notable minority consists of American Indians (7%). In fact, more Indians live here than in any other congressional district east of the Mississippi. Most of them are the Lumbees of Robeson County, and their place in the traditional caste system of the South has always been somewhat uncertain. From time to time, the Indians have had civil rights demonstrations, but they have also objected to having their children bused to go to school with blacks.

In 1968, the 7th showed a near even split in the presidential contest. Wallace finished first, but Nixon, who finished third, was only 6% behind the Alabaman. Four years later, the district shifted in a big way to Nixon; McGovern apparently lost some Humphrey votes because of his stand on military spending, one that hardly sat well in places like Fayetteville or Fort Bragg. At the same time, however, the voters of the 7th elected a Democrat to the House by a solid margin. The new Congressman, Charles Rose III, is a liberal, at least by standards used in North Carolina. He is one of the young men tutored by ex-Gov. (1961–64) Terry Sanford. Rose once worked in Sanford's law firm and supported him in his 1972 presidential bid; Sanford ran second in the North Carolina primary and remained a candidate at the Miami Beach convention.

After leaving Sanford's firm, Rose, a Fayetteville native, became a prosecutor in his home city. In 1970, he quit to run for Congress. The incumbent was Alton Lennon, age 64 and a former U.S. Senator who was appointed in 1953 and defeated for a full term in 1954. In the House, Lennon was an unyielding conservative and a member of the Armed Services Committee. Apparently, however, he was a poor campaigner, as challenger Rose carried the counties around Fayetteville and wound up with 43% of the votes district-wide. So it was hardly a surprise when Lennon announced a decision to retire in 1972.

Rose did not succeed to the seat without a contest, however. In the initial primary, two opponents held him to just under the 50% required to win the election outright. In the runoff that followed, Rose beat state Rep. Hector McGeachy by a 55–45 margin. The winner carried every county in the district, but got his largest margins in Lumbee Indian country. The general election was easier. Though the people in the Tidewater will vote Republican for President, and in 1972 even for Senator, their Democratic allegiances return to them in House elections. Accordingly, Rose beat a Republican and an American party candidate without fuss.

In the House, Rose serves on the Agriculture Committee. He is also one of the leaders, along with Oklahoma's Clem Rogers McSpadden, of the Rural Caucus, a group composed largely of freshmen. Most members of the caucus would call themselves political moderates. They hope to work for programs that will aid the orderly development of rural areas, and so allow people to stay in places like the 7th district of North Carolina rather than move to the slums of New York or Chicago.

On most major issues, Rose finds himself voting with most of his Democratic colleagues. This phenomenon—in effect, one of Southerners rejoining the Democratic party—is derived from the intransigence of the Nixon Administration. With issues of the mid-1960s like civil rights removed from the legislative agenda, many of the younger House members from the South, like Rose, find that they have a great deal more in common with their Democratic colleagues than with the Administration backers of Gerry Ford's Republicans. Rose himself appears likely to become a leader of the emerging group of moderate-to-liberal Southern and border-state Democrats.

Census Data Pop. 467,476. Central city, 21%; suburban, 47%. Median family income, $6,875; families above $15,000: 9%; families below $3,000: 18%. Median years education, 11.2.

1972 Share of Federal Outlays $682,145,567

DOD	$490,980,000		HEW	$104,524,313
AEC	–		HUD	–
NASA	–		DOI	$1,288,999
DOT	$14,046,802		USDA	$24,101,640
			Other	$47,203,813

Federal Military-Industrial Commitments

DOD Contractors Kings Point Manufacturing (Fayetteville), $11.344m: small arms ammunition; aircraft components. Poole and Kent (Fort Bragg), $11.311m: unspecified. International Terminal Operations (Southport), transportation services. Burlington Industries (Raeford), $7.816m: unspecified. Osterneck Co. (Lumberton), $5.915m: sand bags.
DOD Installations Fort Bragg AB (Fayetteville). Sunny Point Army Ocean Terminal (Southport). Pope AFB (Fayetteville). Fort Fisher AF Station (Kure Beach).

Economic Base Agriculture, notably tobacco, grains, and hogs and sheep; textile mill products; apparel and other textile products; finance, insurance and real state; and chemicals and allied products.

The Voters

Registration 166,530 total. 118,941 white (71%); 47,589 non-white (29%). 138,245 D (83%); 22,801 R (14%); 5,484 other (3%).
Median voting age 35.9
Employment profile White collar, 40%. Blue collar, 40%. Service, 13%. Farm, 7%.
Ethnic groups Black, 26%. Indian, 7%. Total foreign stock, 4%.

Presidential vote

1972	Nixon (R)	71,346	(70%)
	McGovern (D)	30,409	(30%)
1968	Nixon (R)	30,786	(30%)
	Humphrey (D)	35,336	(34%)
	Wallace (AI)	36,867	(36%)

Representative

Charles G. (Charlie) Rose III (D) Elected 1972; b. Aug. 10, 1939, Fayetteville; home, Fayetteville; Davidson College, B.A.; U. of N.C. Law School, LL.D.; married, one child; Presbyterian.

Career Atty.; Chief Dist. Court Prosecutor for 12th Judicial District, N.C., 1967–70.

Offices 1724 LHOB, 202-225-2731. Also Rm. 208, P.O. Bldg., Wilmington 28401.

Administrative Assistant Miss Saith Memory

Committees

Agriculture (18th); Subs: Cotton; Oilseeds and Rice; Tobacco.

Group Ratings: Newly Elected

Key Votes

1) Busing	NE	6) Cmbodia Bmbg	AGN	11) Chkg Acct Intrst	AGN
2) Strip Mines	NE	7) Bust Hwy Trust	AGN	12) End HISC (HUAC)	AGN
3) Cut Mil $	NE	8) Farm Sub Lmt	NE	13) Nixon Sewer Veto	AGN
4) Rev Shrg	NE	9) School Prayr	NE	14) Corp Cmpaign $	NE
5) Pub TV $	NE	10) Cnsumr Prot	NE	15) Pol $ Disclosr	NE

Election Results

1972 general:	Charles Rose (D)	57,348	(60%)
	Jerry C. Scott (R)	36,726	(39%)
	Alvis H. Ballard (AI)	863	(1%)
1972 run-off:	Charles Rose (D)	31,558	(55%)
	Hector McGeachy (D)	25,338	(45%)
1972 primary:	Charles Rose (D)	33,760	(49%)
	Hector McGeachy (D)	17,896	(26%)
	Doran Berry (D)	17,486	(25%)

EIGHTH DISTRICT Political Background

The 8th district of North Carolina consists of two areas: a hunk out of the middle of the Piedmont textile country and the Sand Hills region of the state's coastal plain. The textile counties lie on both sides of Interstate 85 between Charlotte and Greensboro; along the way, the roadway passes through the 8th district towns of Salisbury and Kannapolis (home of giant Cannon Mills). Here the textile magnates reign supreme. There is no nonsense about unions, or workers' rights—the boss calls the shots. He does in the mill anyway, and, it seems, in the voting booth as well. For this area, in election after election, is one of the most Republican and conservative in North Carolina.

The three main textile counties in the district—Rowan, Cabarrus, and Stanly—cast just over half the votes in the 8th. Most of the rest are cast in the more sparsely populated Sand Hills counties to the east. Here the traditional allegiance is strongly Democratic, though of course candidates like George Wallace and the Richard Nixon of 1972 have carried the area.

In 1967, Democratic state legislators drew the lines of the 8th, ones the district retains for the most part today. In 1968, the 8th had no incumbent. The legislators presumably felt that the Democratic votes out of the Sand Hills counties would prevail over the Republican margins cast in the textile counties. It worked, however, just the other way around. The Democratic nominee in 1968 was Voit Gilmore, a liberal of sorts, and head of the U.S. Travei Service in the Johnson Administration—an affiliation that evoked little enthusiasm among 8th-district voters. The Republican candidate was Earl B. Ruth, a conservative ex-Democrat and former athletic director at a small area college. Ruth won 56% of the vote in the textile counties, as Gilmore took 56% in the rest of the district—percentages that work out to a 3,199-vote Ruth victory. It was the closest margin in North Carolina that year.

By 1970, Ruth had established himself as a conservative on questions of fiscal, social, and foreign policy. The Democrats ran a more conservative candidate against him, a former Speaker of the North Carolina House who had nearly won the gubernatorial nomination in 1968. But the ex-Speaker did worse than Gilmore—proof, if more is needed, of the advantages of incumbency. By 1972, Ruth was up to 60% of the votes. He carried the Sand Hills counties, for the first time, with 51% of the votes, while getting a solid 66% in the rest of the district. Ruth is one of the most conservative members of the generally liberal House Education and Labor Committee. He will probably stay on Capitol Hill as long as he wants.

Census Data Pop. 454,275. Central city, 0%; suburban, 17%. Median family income, $7,872; families above $15,000: 9%; families below $3,000: 13%. Median years education, 10.0.

1972 Share of Federal Outlays $247,423,123

DOD	$25,804,643	HEW	$124,582,766
AEC	$824	HUD	$6,727,991
NASA	$2,074	DOI	$298,633
DOT	$5,118,386	USDA	$17,116,894
		Other	$67,770,912

Federal Military-Industrial Commitments

No installations or contractors receiving prime awards greater than $5,000,000.

Economic Base Textile mill products; agriculture, notably poultry, dairy products, grains and tobacco; apparel and other textile products; finance, insurance and real estate; and food and kindred products.

The Voters

Registration 214,029 total. 186,190 white (87%); 27,839 non-white (13%). 146,863 D (69%); 59,776 R (28%); 7,390 other (3%).
Median voting age 43.7
Employment profile White collar, 30%. Blue collar, 56%. Service, 10%. Farm, 4%.
Ethnic groups Black, 20%.

Presidential vote

1972	Nixon (R)	100,830	(73%)
	McGovern (D)	37,880	(27%)
1968	Nixon (R)	67,350	(44%)
	Humphrey (D)	39,820	(26%)
	Wallace (AI)	46,703	(30%)

Representative

Earl B. Ruth (R) Elected 1968; b. Feb. 7, 1916, Spencer; home, Salisbury; U. of N.C., B.A., 1938, M.A., 1942, Ph.D., 1955; Navy, WWII; married, four children; Presbyterian.

Career Teacher-coach 1938–40; Asst. Supt., N.C. State Parks, 1941; Graduate Asst. Phys., Ed. Dept., U. of N.C., 1941–42; Recreation Dir., Kings Mt., 1945; Athletic Dir., Dean of Students, Catawba Col., 1946–68; Mbr., Salisbury City Council, 1963–68; Mayor Pro Tem., 1967–68.

Offices 129 CHOB, 202-225-3715. Also 507 W. Innes St., Salisbury 28144, 704-633-6038.

Administrative Assistant Norman Martin

Committees

Appropriations (20th); Subs: HUD, Space, Science, Veterans; Legislative.

Group Ratings

	ADA	COPE	LWV	RIPON	NFU	LCV	CFA	NAB	NSI	ACA
1972	0	0	17	31	29	20	50	83	100	95
1971	8	0	22	39	33	–	25	–	–	97
1970	0	9	–	33	38	45	57	92	100	89

Key Votes

1) Busing	AGN	6) Cmbodia Bmbg	FOR	11) Chkg Acct Intrst	AGN
2) Strip Mines	FOR	7) Bust Hwy Trust	AGN	12) End HISC (HUAC)	AGN
3) Cut Mil $	AGN	8) Farm Sub Lmt	AGN	13) Nixon Sewer Veto	FOR
4) Rev Shrg	FOR	9) School Prayr	FOR	14) Corp Cmpaign $	FOR
5) Pub TV $	AGN	10) Cnsumr Prot	AGN	15) Pol $ Disclosr	AGN

Election Results

1972 general:	Earl B. Ruth (R)	82,060	(60%)
	Richard Clark (D)	54,198	(40%)
1972 primary:	Earl B. Ruth (R), unopposed		
1970 general:	Earl B. Ruth (R)	51,873	(56%)
	H. Clifton Blue (D)	40,563	(44%)

NINTH DISTRICT Political Background

The name of Charlotte, North Carolina, will no doubt be linked in the minds of future American historians with the political and legal issue that we have come to know as "busing." For it was here that a federal district judge, a Republican appointee not regarded as a liberal, ordered a plan for massive integration between Charlotte and surrounding Mecklenburg County. The district court's decision was reversed on appeal, but it was reinstated by a unanimous Supreme Court, led by Chief Justice Warren Burger. The Nixon jurist declared that transportation—that is, busing—could be ordered when it was necessary to achieve integration of schools.

When the district-court decision was announced, consternation followed in Charlotte. It was never, of course, a city known for its liberal social or political attitudes. In fact, quite the contrary is true. With 241,000 people, Charlotte is the largest city in North Carolina, but by no means a giant by national standards. It is a predominantly white-collar city, having less manufacturing than other Piedmont centers. And that white-collar population was for some time the factor behind the election and reelection of a Republican Congressman, Charles Jonas, and also behind the Republican majorities cast for presidential candidates like Dwight Eisenhower and Richard Nixon.

So it must have come as a shock to the white citizens of Charlotte that an appointee of their choice for President ordered them to bus some of their children so that they could go to school with black children. Richard Nixon, after all, was a politician who had run as an enemy of the Warren Court. But what is interesting, politically, is that the shock and disappointment produced no electoral response among white people in Charlotte. One reason was that the busing plan, once implemented, worked smoothly. Another is that they really had nowhere else to turn; Charlotte voted for those who called themselves anti-busing candidates, and busing came anyway.

Nor did the busing decision result in a more massive than usual rejection of the supposedly pro-busing national Democratic ticket of 1972. In that year, most of the 1968 Wallace votes clearly went to Richard Nixon, thus giving him an overwhelming majority. But even in 1968, the 9th district, which Charlotte dominates, had provided Nixon with an absolute majority—the only one in the state to do so. What is more interesting is that George McGovern received a larger percentage of the votes here than Hubert Humphrey got four years earlier, an indication that white Southerners have begun to vote on the basis of issues other than simply race.

All this leaves Charlotte a Republican-majority, and the 9th district, a Republican-majority district. At least such has been the case in congressional elections since 1952, when Republican Jonas won his first election. The ardent hope among Democrats was that Jonas would be a one-term wonder, just like his father, who was elected in the Hoover landslide of 1928 and defeated in 1930. Accordingly, the Democrats adjusted district lines in an attempt to oust him. But Jonas weathered some close contests and built up his popularity. By 1972, when he decided to retire, he was unbeatable. Also by 1972, he had reached the number-two Republican position on the House Appropriations Committee. But at age 68, after two decades of trying to keep federal spending down, he apparently decided that his party would never win control of the House and that he would therefore never chair the committee. So he retired.

On Jonas' departure, Charlotte Democrats made something more than a halfhearted attempt to capture the district. They put up Jim Beatty, a former Olympic distance runner and young businessman whose name was well-known in the community. But Beatty ran out of gas and lost by a 59–41 margin to Mecklenburg County Commissioner James Martin, a chemistry professor at Davidson College outside Charlotte. Most likely Martin will continue to win reelection without too much trouble in the future.

Census Data Pop. 459,535. Central city, 52%; suburban, 25%. Median family income, $9,594; families above $15,000: 20%; families below $3,000: 9%. Median years education, 11.8.

1972 Share of Federal Outlays $261,236,381

DOD	$39,201,937	HEW	$102,933,024
AEC	–	HUD	$25,060,254
NASA	$175	DOI	$374,791
DOT	$27,759,967	USDA	$9,820,786
		Other	$56,085,447

Federal Military-Industrial Commitments

DOD Contractors Union Carbide Corp. (Charlotte), $10.141m: dry batteries.

Economic Base Textile mill products, especially knitting mill products and synthetics-weaving mill products; finance, insurance and real estate; food and kindred products, especially bakery products; machinery; and apparel and other textile products.

The Voters

Registration 231,214 total. 199,446 white (86%); 31,768 non-white (14%). 156,945 D (68%); 63,571 R (27%); 10,698 other (5%).
Median voting age 40.2
Employment profile White collar, 51%. Blue collar, 37%. Service, 11%. Farm, 1%.
Ethnic groups Black, 22%. Total foreign stock, 3%.

Presidential vote

1972	Nixon (R)	102,879	(70%)
	McGovern (D)	23,918	(30%)
1968	Nixon (R)	73,070	(50%)
	Humphrey (D)	40,024	(28%)
	Wallace (AI)	32,252	(22%)

Representative

James G. Martin (R) Elected 1972; b. Dec. 11, 1935, Savannah, Ga.; home, Davidson; Davidson Col., B.S., 1957; Princeton, Ph.D., 1960; married, three children; Presbyterian.

Career Instructor, Davidson Col., 1960–64; Mbr., Mecklenburg Bd. of County Commissioners, 1966–72, Chm., 1966–68 and 1970–72; Vice-Pres., Natl. Assn. of Regional Councils, 1970–72.

Offices 1021 LHOB, 202-225-3476. Also 1214 American Bldg., Charlotte 28286, 704-376-7489.

Administrative Assistant James Lofton

Committees

Interior and Insular Affairs (15th); Subs: No. 1 (National Parks and Recreation); No. 3 (Environment); No. 4 (Territorial and Insular Affairs); No. 5 (Mines and Mining).

Science and Astronautics (12th; Subs: Energy; Science, Research, and Development.

Group Ratings: Newly Elected

Key Votes

1) Busing	NE	6) Cmbodia Bmbg	FOR	11) Chkg Acct Intrst	AGN
2) Strip Mines	NE	7) Bust Hwy Trust	FOR	12) End HISC (HUAC)	AGN
3) Cut Mil $	NE	8) Farm Sub Lmt	NE	13) Nixon Sewer Veto	FOR
4) Rev Shrg	NE	9) School Prayr	NE	14) Corp Cmpaign $	NE
5) Pub TV $	NE	10) Cnsumr Prot	NE	15) Pol $ Disclosr	NE

Election Results

1972 general:	James G. Martin (R)	80,356	(59%)
	James Beatty (D)	56,171	(41%)
1972 primary:	James G. Martin (R)	15,389	(82%)
	Graem Yates (R)	3,333	(18%)

TENTH DISTRICT Political Background

The 10th district of North Carolina is a collection of seven counties in the western Piedmont and the Appalachian Mountains. The southern part of the district, on the South Carolina border, is dominated by the city of Gastonia (pop. 47,000), a textile-mill town that traditionally votes Democratic. North of Gastonia, the hills rise to mountains around towns like Morganton, the home of Sen. Sam Ervin. This is furniture-manufacturing country, and the farther one gets into the mountains, the more Republican the territory. The political preferences here reflect old Civil War allegiances, ones that have ceased to be of much importance in presidential politics. In local and congressional contest, however, they still matter.

The 10th took its shape in the 1968 redistricting, having had only one minor change since. The 1968 election featured two incumbents thrown into the same district to fight it out. Basil Whitener, a conservative Democrat, came into the fray with 12 years of seniority in the House, and during that time he had represented most of the counties in the new 10th. On the other hand, Republican James Broyhill had only six years of seniority. But the political trends in the district favored the Republican candidate—it was clear that Richard Nixon was to carry the 10th easily in 1968.

The surprising thing was not that Broyhill won, but that his margin was so large. He lost the two counties around Gastonia by a total of 9,000 votes. But Broyhill carried the rest of the district—most of it Whitener's old territory—by 25,000 votes. In 1970, Whitener came back to try again and did worse. This time he even lost the Gastonia area. Against another opponent in 1972, Broyhill won with the biggest percentage of any opposed North Carolina Congressman, Democrat or Republican.

Like other North Carolina Republicans in the House, Broyhill is a solid conservative. Having done well on the seniority ladder, he is now the third-ranking Republican on the Commerce Committee. He is able to look out for the interests of the state's major industries—tobacco, textiles, and furniture. The Broyhill family itself is in the furniture business.

Census Data Pop. 471,777. Central city, 0%; suburban, 0%. Median family income, $8,449; families above $15,000: 11%; families below $3,000: 10%. Median years education, 10.0.

1972 Share of Federal Outlays $196,719,217

DOD	$14,680,000	HEW	$110,715,289
AEC	–	HUD	$4,049,263
NASA	–	DOI	$93,856
DOT	$4,337,537	USDA	$12,595,203
		Other	$50,248,069

Federal Military-Industrial Commitments

No installations or contractors receiving prime awards greater than $5,000,000.

Economic Base Textile mill products, especially yarn and thread mill products, and knitting mill products; furniture and fixtures, especially household furniture; apparel and other textile products; finance, insurance and real estate; and agriculture, notably poultry and dairy products.

The Voters

Registration 215,197 total. 198,340 white (92%); 16,857 non-white (8%). 139,424 D (65%); 63,824 R (30%); 11,949 other (6%).
Median voting age 40.9
Employment profile White collar, 30%. Blue collar, 59%. Service, 9%. Farm, 2%.
Ethnic groups Black, 11%.

Presidential vote

1972	Nixon (R)	105,093	(73%)
	McGovern (D)	38,202	(27%)
1968	Nixon (R)	75,393	(48%)
	Humphrey (D)	37,971	(24%)
	Wallace (AI)	45,157	(28%)

Representative

James Thomas Broyhill (R) Elected 1962; b. Aug. 19, 1927, Lenoir; home, Lenoir; U. of N.C., B.S., 1950; married, three children; Baptist.

Career Sales and admin., Broyhill Furniture Industries, 1945–62.

Offices 2159 RHOB, 202-225-2576. Also 431 Pennton Ave., Lenior 28645, 704-758-4247, and Rm. 304 Commercial Bldg., Gastonia 28052, 704-864-9922.

Administrative Assistant Mrs. Cecile Srodes

Committees

Interstate and Foreign Commerce (3rd); Sub: Commerce and Finance (Ranking Mbr.).

Sel. Com. on Small Business (2nd); Subs: Activities of Regulatory Agencies (Ranking Mbr.); Environmental Problems Affecting Small Business.

Joint Study Com. on Budget Control

Group Ratings

	ADA	COPE	LWV	RIPON	NFU	LCV	CFA	NAB	NSI	ACA
1972	0	9	27	63	29	58	100	100	89	82
1971	14	11	25	47	45	–	13	–	–	84
1970	8	17	–	35	42	0	40	83	90	87

Key Votes

1) Busing	AGN	6) Cmbodia Bmbg	FOR	11) Chkg Acct Intrst	AGN
2) Strip Mines	AGN	7) Bust Hwy Trust	AGN	12) End HISC (HUAC)	AGN
3) Cut Mil $	AGN	8) Farm Sub Lmt	AGN	13) Nixon Sewer Veto	FOR
4) Rev Shrg	FOR	9) School Prayr	FOR	14) Corp Cmpaign $	FOR
5) Pub TV $	AGN	10) Cnsumr Prot	AGN	15) Pol $ Disclosr	FOR

Election Results

1972 general:	James T. Broyhill (R)	103,119	(73%)
	Paul L. Beck (D)	39,025	(27%)

1972 primary:	James T. Broyhill (R), unopposed		
1970 general:	James T. Broyhill (R)	63,936	(57%)
	Basil L. Whitener (D)	48,113	(43%)

ELEVENTH DISTRICT Political Background

The 11th district of North Carolina occupies the western end of the state. Its main features include Asheville (pop. 57,000), the place to which Tom Wolfe could not go home again, and the Great Smoky Mountains National Park. The park is the nation's most heavily visited. Its roads have become so crowded that the Park Service was forced to install a traffic light—the first ever within a national park. During the summer it is 20 degrees cooler in the mountains than in the lowland towns. The climatological endowment and the forested, green mountains, having wisps of fog, attracts some seven million visitors to the Smokies annually. Over the years, the same elements have made the western end of North Carolina a unit rather separate from the rest of the state. During the Civil War, it was the most reluctant part of a state reluctant to secede. Have few slaves, many of the small farmers in the hollows remained loyal to the Union. Today, only 6% of the district's population is black.

So the ancestral political loyalty here is to the Republican party, especially in the most isolated mountain counties. But western North Carolina is not as monolithically Republican as adjacent east Tennessee. People in the Carolina mountains have perhaps reacted against the Republicans of the nearby Piedmont as well as against the Democrats of the faraway Tidewater. In any case, Sen. Jesse Helms, the ultraconservative TV commentator from Raleigh, got only 53% of the votes in the 11th district on his way to becoming the first popularly elected Republican Senator from North Carolina.

Moreover, the 11th has refused to elect Republican Congressmen, unlike other western North Carolina districts. Instead, it has continued to reelect Democrat Roy Taylor by sizable, though not usually overwhelming, margins. First elected in a 1960 special election, Taylor is one of the few Easterners on the House Interior Committee—of its 41 members, only 10 are from states east of the Mississippi River. After 10 years of service and after the defeat of several senior members opposed by environmentalists, Taylor has advanced to the number-two position among Interior's Democrats. He is now directly in line to succeed 75-year-old James Haley of Florida, Chairman of the Committee.

Taylor is considered a middle-of-the road man on most issues that come before Interior, willing to listen to pleas of environmentalist as well as to those of people who seek more intensive use of public lands and resources. As Chairman of the National Parks and Recreation Subcommittee, the Congressman is an enthusiast for creating new parks. Since he became chairman of the unit, some 1.5 million acres of parkland have been added to the national parks system. On Interior, Taylor has also tried to improve the lot of the Cherokee Indians who live near the Smokies Park. These people make up 1% of the district's population.

Census Data Pop. 467,051. Central city, 12%; suburban, 19%. Median family income, $6,857; families above $15,000: 8%; families below $3,000: 18%. Median years education, 10.5.

1972 Share of Federal Outlays $315,915,220

DOD	$32,594,000	HEW	$154,349,540
AEC	–	HUD	$3,511,474
NASA	$1,135,140	DOI	$9,193,087
DOT	$23,203,784	USDA	$19,551,580
		Other	$72,376,615

Federal Military-Industrial Commitments

DOD Contractors Stencel Aero Engineering Corp. (Asheville), $8.161m: parachute assemblies. Mills Manufacturing Corp. (Asheville), $5.484m: parachute assemblies.

Economic Base Textile mill products; agriculture, notably poultry and dairy products; apparel and other textile products; finance, insurance and real estate; and household furniture and other furniture and fixtures.

The Voters

Registration 232,061 total. 221,179 white (95%); 10,882 non-white (5%). 146,738 D (63%); 77,948 R (34%); 7,375 other (3%).
Median voting age 44.8
Employment profile White collar, 35%. Blue collar, 51%. Service, 11%. Farm, 3%.
Ethnic groups Black, 6%. Total foreign stock, 2%.

Presidential vote

1972		Nixon (R)	110,566	(71%)
		McGovern (D)	46,095	(29%)
	1968	Nixon (R)	83,495	(48%)
		Humphrey (D)	50,707	(29%)
		Wallace (AI)	38,420	(22%)

Representative

Roy A. Taylor (D) Elected June 25, 1960; b. Jan. 31, 1910, Vader, Wash.; home, Black Mountain; Maryville Col., B.A., 1931; Asheville U. Law School, admitted to bar, 1936; Navy, WWII; married, two children; Baptist.

Career Practicing atty., 1949–60; N.C. Assembly, 1947–53.

Offices 2233 RHOB, 202-225-6401. Also 1204 Northwestern Bank Bldg., Asheville 28801, 704-254-6526.

Administrative Assistant Luther W. Shaw

Committees

Foreign Affairs (16th); Subs: Europe; Inter-American Affairs; Asian and Pacific Affairs.

Interior and Insular Affairs (2nd); Subs: Indian Affairs; National Parks and Recreation (Chm.); Territorial and Insular Affairs.

Group Ratings

	ADA	COPE	LWV	RIPON	NFU	LCV	CFA	NAB	NSI	ACA
1972	19	36	50	50	71	40	0	50	90	70
1971	24	27	0	53	79	–	38	–	–	65
1970	20	50	–	29	54	62	48	55	100	63

Key Votes

1) Busing	AGN	6) Cmbodia Bmbg	FOR	11) Chkg Acct Intrst	AGN
2) Strip Mines	AGN	7) Bust Hwy Trust	AGN	12) End HISC (HUAC)	AGN
3) Cut Mil $	AGN	8) Farm Sub Lmt	AGN	13) Nixon Sewer Veto	AGN
4) Rev Shrg	FOR	9) School Prayr	FOR	14) Corp Cmpaign $	FOR
5) Pub TV $	AGN	10) Cnsumr Prot	AGN	15) Pol $ Disclosr	FOR

Election Results

1972 general:	Roy A. Taylor (D)	94,465	(60%)
	Jesse I. Ledbetter (R)	64,062	(40%)
1972 primary:	Roy A. Taylor (D), unopposed		
1970 general:	Roy A. Taylor (D)	90,199	(67%)
	Luke Atkinson (R)	44,376	(33%)

NORTH DAKOTA

Political Background

North Dakota occupies the northern section of the Great Plains—one of the world's largest hunks of arable land. Most of North Dakota is wheat country, with the state producing some 17% of the nation's wheat crop; only Kansas grows more. As the North Dakota plains grow more arid towards the west, ranchers and the grazing of livestock predominate. Both varieties of agricultural experience here are demanding and discouraging. North Dakota is a hard, treeless land; its winters are cold, the plains open to Arctic blasts from Canada, and its summers are often too short and too dry. Some 50 years ago, the state had 632,000 people; today, only 617,000. Moreover, for every 10 college graduates the state produces, seven chose to leave it; there are greener pastures elsewhere. North Dakota now has a lower per capita income level than several states in the South.

About 25% of all North Dakotans still live on farms or ranches, the highest such percentage in any state. For the past two years, of course, the prices of wheat and beef have been very good, with wheat reaching an astronomical $5.00 a bushel in August of 1973. But the more common fate of North Dakota farmers and ranchers has been a sad one. Because the economy of the state depends on the agriculturalists and because they, as nonmonopolists or nonoligopolists, exercise little control over the fluctuations of the commodity and livestock markets, North Dakota has seen raging dissatisfaction with the farm programs of the federal government. By tradition, the most common topics of the state's political discourse are the minutiae of wheat and feed-grain legislation. In fact, agricultural discontent was the driving force behind the state's sometimes radical political past, a radicalism that goes back to the years around World War I.

Most of North Dakota's settlement occurred in the years between 1890 and 1910. A large proportion of the settlers were of immigrant stock: Norwegians to the east, Canadians along the northern border, Volga Germans to the west, and native Germans throughout the state. (Volga Germans were people who migrated to Russia during the early 1800s, but who retained their German language and character. They are recorded in U.S. census figures as Russians.) All of the new North Dakotans lived on lonely, often marginal farms, cut off, in many cases, from the wider currents of American culture by the forbidding barrier of language. Their economic fate was at the mercy of the grain millers in Minneapolis, the railroads, the banks, and commodity traders.

These circumstances led A. C. Townley and William Lemke to organize the North Dakota Non-Partisan League (NPL) in 1915. Its program was frankly socialist—government ownership of railroads and grain elevators—and, like many North Dakota ethnics, the League opposed going to war with Germany. The positions taken by the NPL won it many adherents in North Dakota, and the League spread into neighboring states. But North Dakota was its bastion; the NPL often determined the outcome of the usually decisive Republican primary, and sometimes swung its support to the otherwise hopelessly outnumbered Democrats. A particular favorite of the NPL was "Wild Bill" Langer, who served intermittently as Governor during the 1930s. He was elected Senator in 1940, but was allowed to take his seat only after a lengthy investigation of alleged campaign irregularities. His subsequent career was fully as controversial; Langer was the Senate's most unpredictable maverick until his death in 1959.

Another NPL favorite was Congressman Usher Burdick, who served from 1935 to 1945 and then again from 1949 to 1959. Burdick, like Langer, was a nominal Republican, but usually voted with New Deal liberals on economic issues. Burdick's son, Quentin, a Democrat, was a member of the House when Langer died, and won a special election to fill the Senate seat after waging a campaign directed mainly at the allegedly iniquitous policies of Agriculture Secretary Ezra Taft Benson. The Non-Partisan League, of course, supported the younger Burdick. By the 1960s, however, its name had become misleading, since then as now it consistently supports Democratic candidates for office.

North Dakota is ordinarily a Republican state—only a few counties along the Canadian border or one with large Indian populations regularly turn in Democratic majorities. But Democrat Quentin Burdick demonstrated his appeal in 1964 when he equalled Lyndon Johnson's 58% in North Dakota. In 1970, Burdick did even better, winning with 61% of the votes. The North Dakotan's victory illustrates some of the problems faced by Nixon strategists in their attempts to unseat liberal Democrats in 1970, and, for that matter, in 1972. Congressman Thomas Kleppe, millionaire (Gold Seal wax) who had run against Burdick in 1964, was again his opponent in 1970. Kleppe spent about $300,000—a huge sum in a state where $32.50 bought 30 seconds of prime time on its most powerful TV station. Kleppe bombarded North Dakota voters with TV spots that reminded them that Burdick had not voted in line with their presumed views on issues like school prayer, interstate travel to incite riots, and so on.

The feedback from the Kleppe media campaign was bad. North Dakota voters are accustomed to seeing their candidates in person, not hearing an ad man's message over the tube. Moreover, they simply could not believe that rough-hewn Quentin Burdick, Usher's son and their Senator for 10 years, was the awful man Kleppe said he was. Herschel Lashkowitz, the Mayor of Fargo, the state's largest city (pop. 53,000), summed it up: "people looked at those ads and then they thought of Quentin Burdick and they resented it."

Indeed, Burdick's record both on the Senate floor and in the Judiciary Committee was one of a quiet liberal. But he was on the right side of an issue much more important to North Dakotans than any of those issues of style and rhetoric that have won votes for Republicans in industrial cities. Interstate rioters may be bad, but worse was the Nixon Administration's wheat bill, which Burdick opposed. Kleppe, on the other hand, had worked out the compromise measure as a member of the House Agriculture Committee. Farmers felt the legislation would produce a great wheat surplus, the kind that clobbered the price for the commodity during the 1950s. Even the support of the state's senior Senator, Republican Milton Young, could not save Kleppe from the worst defeat ever suffered by a North Dakota Republican.

Over the years, Senator Young has had even less trouble winning reelection than his Democratic colleague. First elected to the Senate in 1945, Young has held elective office continuously since 1924. The Senator likes to say that he is a farmer first and a Republican second. Accordingly, during his years in Congress he has been at odds, more often than not, with Administration farm policy—whatever party the Administration. For many years, Young was the ranking Republican on the Senate Agriculture Committee, and in that capacity fought long and hard for high price supports for agricultural commodities, especially wheat. He gave up his status on the committee, in accordance with a rule of the Senate Republican Caucus, to remain the ranking minority member of the Appropriations Committee, which of course has jurisdiction over the flow of money to the entire federal government.

Though Young is the second most senior Republican in the Senate, he is not well-known nationally; like Burdick, he concentrates largely on issues that can help North Dakota. In these days of high food prices, however, Young got some national attention for being the chief architect for the farm bill of 1973. The bill is designed to help the consumer, the taxpayer, and the farmer. To increase the supply of food, the legislation removes the restrictions of acreage allotments; to help the taxpayer, it does away with most subsidy programs and supplemental payments; and to allay the fears and anxieties of the farmer, it guarantees a base price for his commodites.

Little doubt exists that Young will be reelected in 1974 for his sixth term, but for one factor: age. During the campaign, he will be 76. And though his health is good and his hair scarcely gray, voters in most parts of the country have shown an increasing tendency to vote against septuagenarians in the last few elections. In 1972, only two Senators over 70 were reelected, and both of them—John Sparkman of Alabama and John McClellan of Arkansas—faced far tougher battles than usual. By the summer of 1973, two of the Senate's over-70 Republicans, up for reelection in 1974, had announced intentions to retire. Young is not expected to join them—at least not voluntarily. But William Guy, a Democrat who served as the state's Governor for 12 years (1961–1972), is reportedly in the race; and if he does not run, Lt. Gov. Wayne Sanstead, a Minot teacher, probably will. Either would make as formidable an opponent as Young has faced since he defeated Quentin Burdick back in 1956.

Because the 1970 census showed North Dakota's population down, the state—under the complex formula used for reapportionment—lost one of its two congressional seats. Democratic Congressman Arthur Link, elected by a hair in the western 2nd district in 1970, apparently decided to leave Congress and run for Governor. In a mild surprise, Link won; so Republican North Dakota has not elected a Republican Governor since 1958. The holder of the eastern 1st district seat, Republican Mark Andrews, easily became the state's Congressman-at-Large in 1972, running ten full percentage points ahead of Richard Nixon. Andrews is a member of the Appropriations subcommittee with jurisdiction over farm programs. Like most North Dakota republicans, at least those who win reelection, he has often opposed Administration farm policies. Like Sen. Young, Andrews is himself a farmer.

Census Data Pop. 617,761; 0.31% of U.S. total, 45th largest; change 1960–70, –2.3%. Central city, 9%; suburban, 3%. Median family income, $7,836; 39th highest; families above $15,000: 13%; families below $3,000: 12%. Median years education, 12.0.

1972 Share of Federal Tax Burden $438,940,000; 0.21% of U.S. total, 47th largest.

1972 Share of Federal Outlays $1,088,632,977; 0.50% of U.S. total, 40th largest. Per capita federal spending, $1,762.

DOD	$207,723,000	41st (0.33%)	HEW	$217,090,958	44th (0.30%)
AEC	$31,648	46th (—)	HUD	$12,232,070	39th (0.40%)
NASA	$15,950	47th (—)	VA	$30,609,056	44th (0.27%)
DOT	$45,024,772	45th (0.57%)	USDA	$460,404,397	11th (2.99%)
DOC	$1,860,097	45th (0.14%)	CSC	$7,394,098	47th (0.18%)
DOI	$39,187,719	17th (1.85%)	TD	$31,000,293	42nd (0.19%)
DOJ	$3,648,489	44th (0.37%)	Other	$32,410,430	

Federal Military-Industrial Commitments

DOD Contractors Western Electric, Div. ATT (Nekoma), $9.955m: ABM radar. Morrison Knudson Co and Assoc. JV (Grand Forks), $9.923m: ABM site construction. Woerfel Corp and Towne Realty, Inc. JV (Grand Forks), $7.902m: ABM site construction. Needham Packing Co. (West Fargo), $5.704m: foodstuffs.
DOD Installations Finley AF Station (Finley). Fortuna AF Station (Fortuna). Grand Forks AFB (Grand Forks). Minot AFB (Minot).

Economic Base Agriculture, notably wheat, cattle, barley and dairy products; finance, insurance and real estate; food and kindred products, especially dairy products; printing and publishing, especially newspapers; tourism; machinery, especially farm machinery. Also higher education (Univ. of North Dakota).

Political Line-up Governor, Arthur A. Link (D); seat up, 1976. Senators, Milton R. Young (R) and Quentin N. Burdick (D). Representatives, 1 R At Large. State Senate (41 R and 10 D); State House (79 R and 23 D).

The Voters

Registration No statewide registration.
Median voting age 44.0
Employment profile White collar, 42%. Blue collar, 21%. Service, 16%. Farm, 21%.
Ethnic groups Total foreign stock, 24%. Norway, 6%; USSR, 5%.

Presidential vote

1972	Nixon (R)	174,109	(63%)
	McGovern (D)	100,384	(37%)
1968	Nixon (R)	138,669	(56%)
	Humphrey (D)	94,769	(38%)
	Wallace (AI)	14,244	(6%)
1964	Johnson (D)	149,784	(58%)
	Goldwater (R)	108,207	(42%)

Senator

Milton R. Young (R) Elected Appointed March 12, 1945, seat up 1974; b. Dec. 6, 1897, Berlin; home, La Moure; N.D. Agricultural Col., Graceland Col.; married; Church of Latter Day Saints.

Career Farmer; N.D. State Legislature, 1932; N.D. Senate, 1943–45, Pres. Pro Tem., 1941, Majority Floor Leader, 1943.

Offices 5205 NSOB, 202-225-2043. Also Box 241, La Moure 58102, 701-237-4000, and Fed. Bldg., Bismarck 58501, 701-255-2553.

Administrative Assistant Christopher U. Sylvester

Committees

Agriculture and Forestry (3rd); Subs: Agriculture Production, Marketing, and Stabilization of Prices (Ranking Mbr.); Agricultural Research and General Legislation.

Appropriations (Ranking Mbr.); Subs: Agriculture, Environmental and Consumer Protection; Defense (Ranking Mbr.); Operations (Ranking Mbr.); Public Works, AEC; Interior.

Joint Study Com. on Budget Control.

Group Ratings

	ADA	COPE	LWV	RIPON	NFU	LCV	CFA	NAB	NSI	ACA
1972	5	10	36	57	50	7	10	64	80	82
1971	15	33	50	35	45	–	20	–	–	78
1970	3	23	–	15	43	14	–	75	100	75

Key Votes

1) Busing	AGN	8) Sea Life Prot	AGN	15) Tax Singls Less	FOR
2) Alas P-line	FOR	9) Campaign Subs	AGN	16) Min Tax for Rich	AGN
3) Gun Cntrl	FOR	10) Cmbodia Bmbg	AGN	17) Euro Troop Rdctn	FOR
4) Rehnquist	FOR	11) Legal Srvices	ABS	18) Bust Hwy Trust	AGN
5) Pub TV $	FOR	12) Rev Sharing	AGN	19) Maid Min Wage	AGN
6) EZ Votr Reg	AGN	13) Cnsumr Prot	AGN	20) Farm Sub Limit	AGN
7) No-Fault	AGN	14) Eq Rts Amend	FOR	21) Highr Credt Chgs	FOR

Election Results

1968 general:	Milton R. Young (R)	154,968	(65%)
	Herschel Lashkowitz (D)	80,815	(34%)
	Duane Mutch (Ind.)	3,393	(1%)
1968 primary:	Milton R. Young (R) unopposed		
1962 general:	Milton R. Young (R)	135,705	(61%)
	William Lanier (D)	88,032	(39%)

Senator

Quentin N. Burdick (D) Elected June 28, 1960, seat up 1976; b. June 19, 1908, Munich; home, Fargo; U. of Minn., B.A., 1931, LL.B., 1932; married; Congregationalist.

Career Practicing atty., 1932–58; Candidate for Gov., 1946.

Offices 451 OSOB, 202-225-2551. Also Fed. Bldg., Fargo 58102, 701-237-4000, and Fed. Bldg., Bismarck 58501, 701-255-2553.

Administrative Assistant Hugh Kelly

Committees

Judiciary (7th); Subs: Administrative Practice and Procedure; Improvements in Judicial Machinery (Chm.); Juvenile Delinquency; Patents, Trademarks and Copyrights; Penitentiaries (Chm.); Separation of Powers; Constitutional Amendments.

Post Office and Civil Service (3rd); Subs: Civil Service Policies and Practices; Compensation and Employment Benefits (Chm.).

Public Works (6th); Subs: Disaster Relief (Chm.); Water Resources; Roads; Economic Development.

Group Ratings

	ADA	COPE	LWV	RIPON	NFU	LCV	CFA	NAB	NSI	ACA
1972	75	90	73	56	100	58	100	55	0	14
1971	85	75	67	33	100	–	80	–	–	25
1970	84	100	–	62	87	78	–	18	30	22

Key Votes

1) Busing	FOR	8) Sea Life Prot	AGN	15) Tax Singls Less	FOR
2) Alas P-line	AGN	9) Campaign Subs	FOR	16) Min Tax for Rich	AGN
3) Gun Cntrl	FOR	10) Cmbodia Bmbg	AGN	17) Euro Troop Rdctn	FOR
4) Rehnquist	FOR	11) Legal Srvices	FOR	18) Bust Hwy Trust	AGN
5) Pub TV $	FOR	12) Rev Sharing	AGN	19) Maid Min Wage	AGN
6) EZ Votr Reg	AGN	13) Cnsumr Prot	FOR	20) Farm Sub Limit	AGN
7) No-Fault	FOR	14) Eq Rts Amend	FOR	21) Highr Credt Chgs	AGN

Election Results

1970 general:	Quentin Burdick (D)	134,519	(61%)
	Thomas S. Kleppe (R)	82,996	(38%)
	Russell Kleppe (Ind.)	2,045	(1%)
1970 primary:	Quentin Burdick (D), unopposed		
1964 general:	Quentin Burdick (D)	149,264	(58%)
	Thomas S. Kleppe (R)	109,681	(42%)

Representative

Mark Andrews (R) Elected Oct. 23, 1963; b. May 19, 1926, Fargo; home, Mapleton; N.D. State U., B.S., 1949; U.S. Military Acad., 1944–46; Army, WWII; married, three children; Episcopalian.

Career Farmer, 1949– ; Exec. Commissioner, Garrison Conservancy Dist., admin. irrigation from Garrison Dam, 1955– ; Candidate for Gov., 1962.

Offices 2411 RHOB, 202-225-2611. Also Fed. Bldg., Fargo 58102, 701-232-8030, and Fed. Bldg., Grand Forks 58201, 701-775-9601, and Fed. Bldg., Bismarck 58501, 701-258-4648, and Heritage Pl., Minot 58701, 701-839-5510.

Administrative Assistant Van R. Olsen

Committees

Appropriations (10th); Subs: Agriculture, Environmental and Consumer Protection (Ranking Mbr.); State, Justice, Commerce and Judiciary.

Group Ratings

	ADA	COPE	LWV	RIPON	NFU	LCV	CFA	NAB	NSI	ACA
1972	6	36	36	67	71	47	50	67	88	57
1971	27	33	56	59	67	–	63	–	–	66
1970	24	36	–	71	54	25	61	50	100	36

Key Votes

1) Busing	AGN	6) Cmbodia Bmbg	AGN	11) Chkg Acct Intrst	AGN
2) Strip Mines	AGN	7) Bust Hwy Trust	AGN	12) End HISC (HUAC)	AGN
3) Cut Mil $	AGN	8) Farm Sub Lmt	AGN	13) Nixon Sewer Veto	AGN
4) Rev Shrg	FOR	9) School Prayr	FOR	14) Corp Cmpaign $	AGN
5) Pub TV $	FOR	10) Cnsumr Prot	FOR	15) Pol $ Disclosr	FOR

Election Results

1972 general:	Mark Andrews (R)	195,368	(73%)
	Richard Ista (D)	72,850	(27%)
1972 primary:	Mark Andrews (R), unopposed		
1970 general:	Mark Andrews (R)	72,168	(66%)
	James E. Brooks (D)	37,688	(34%)

OHIO

Political Background

Ohio is the epitome of Middle America: a land of carefully tended farms, God-fearing small towns, and sprawling industrial cities. In 1803, Ohio became the first state from the old Northwest Territory to be admitted to the Union, and within 25 years it was the fourth largest in the nation. Its patterns of settlement were somewhat unusual. The first white people here moved up through Kentucky or down the Ohio River to the southwest corner of the state around Cincinnati. The old-stock Americans were then joined by Germans, who were fleeing the consequences of the failed European revolution of 1848. By the time of the Civil War, Cincinnati was a heavily German and pro-Union city and the fourth largest in the country. Meanwhile, the northeast corner of Ohio remained placid farmland, settled by Yankee migrants from New England and upstate New York. Not until the growth of the steel industry during the late nineteenth century did the huge industrial complexes of Cleveland, Akron, and Youngstown spring into being. By 1910, Cleveland was larger than Cincinnati and was itself the fourth largest city in the country.

In politics, Ohio has a reputation for being a profoundly Republican state. Though its reputation somewhat exaggerates the reality of the matter, Republicans do win more than a random share of elections in Ohio. One reason commonly given is the decentralization of its urban population; Ohio has six metropolitan areas with more than half a million people. Consequently, no one city can provide the state with a strong Democratic base, which historically Chicago has done for Illinois and New York City for New York state. Moreover, some Ohio cities—notably Cincinnati and Columbus—are heavily Republican (see Ohio 1, 2, 12, and 15). In fact, these Ohio cities regularly turn in larger Republican majorities than people living in nonmetropolitan Ohio, which constitutes roughly a quarter of the state.

But much of the credit for the state's Republicanism, at least in the last 20 years or so, belongs to the organization assembled by Ray Bliss, longtime Republican State Chairman. Bliss and his machine made fund-raising a science, pioneered the latest in campaign techniques, and picked candidates with the kind of care and precision that no computer can match. After the dark days of the New Deal, the Bliss organization built solid control of the state's House delegation, district by district, as well as the state legislature and minor statewide offices.

Today, the House delegation shows a 16–7 Republican margin. A few major statewide offices, however, have eluded Bliss' Republicans. One big source of irritation was the electoral success of Democrat Frank J. Lausche, longtime Governor (1945–45 and 1949–56) and Senator (1957–69). But one of the reasons behind Lausche's triumphs was his intense conservativism, one that could match that of any Ohio Republican. The Republicans made their only serious mistake in 1958, when they waged an all-out drive for a state right-to-work law. For once, organized labor, which has a large membership in Ohio, was able to organize its forces. The result was that a Republican Governor and Senator were defeated in reelection bids. The Senate loss was particularly startling. Veteran conservative John W. Bricker—the GOP vice-presidential nominee in 1944—was ousted by 68-year-old Stephen Young, a maverick liberal who had served four terms as Congressman-at-Large during the 1930s and 1940s. The Republicans confidently expected to get rid of Young the next time, but the acerbic incumbent beat Robert Taft, Jr., son of the late Mr. Republican, by 16,000 votes in 1964.

The last few years have produced some notable victories, but also some bad times, for the state's Republicans. After the Goldwater debacle, Bliss moved up to the GOP national chairmanship. Despite general agreement that he had done a good job, he was unceremoniously sacked by Richard Nixon after his 1968 victory. One cannot help wondering who suggested the axing, and also speculating whether a pro like Bliss would have tolerated anything like the Watergate nonsense had he stayed on as National Chairman.

Meanwhile, back in Ohio, Republican party unity lay in tatters. Robert Taft, Jr., who had won a House seat in 1966, decided in 1970 to run for the Senate against Republican Gov. James Rhodes, who was ineligible for a third term. The resulting primary was hard-fought and divisive. The Republicans were then struck by scandal. The organization's candidate for Governor and several other statewide officials were found to have received contributions from a Columbus firm, which had earlier wangled a couple of million dollars of illegal loans from the state treasury. The so-called Crofters scandal was largely responsible for the election in 1970 of Democratic Gov. John Gilligan, along with a Democratic Attorney General, State Treasurer, and State Auditor.

For Gilligan, the election represented quite a comeback. In 1966, he had lost his House seat to Taft, and in 1968, after beating Lausche in the Democratic primary, he lost a bid for a Senate seat in the general election. In 1970, Ohio Democrats controlled redistricting of the state legislature for the first time in memory. A Democratic redistricting was not enough to give them control of the full legislature in the Democratic flop year of 1972, but it may in the future. Much hangs on the popularity of Gilligan, who pushed a large part of his tax-reform program through the Republican legislature. When the governorship comes up in 1974, Gilligan's big asset may once again be disarray among the Republicans. Ex-Gov. Rhodes wants to run again, provided he can get an opinion that he is eligible under the Ohio Constitution. Other possible candidates include conservative ex-Congressman Donald "Buz" Lukens, and Cincinnati Congressman William Keating, who has the tacit support of Sen. Taft. All have weaknesses: Rhodes, at 63, has perhaps been around too long; Lukens is too ideological; and Keating is unknown in most parts of the state.

Ohio Republicans can, however, take some comfort in having captured the state's two Senate seats, both formerly held by Democrats, in 1968 and 1970. In 1968, the Republicans got some help from an unexpected source, John Gilligan. Organized labor backed Gilligan, who defeated incumbent Frank Lausche in the Democratic primary. Lausche was unbeatable in general elections; as a well-known conservative he received hundreds of thousands of ballots cast by usually Republican voters. In the general election that followed Gilligan's primary victory, Attorney General William Saxbe beat the Democrat by a scant 114,000 votes out of nearly four million cast. The Republican attributed his win to discontent with the war policies of the Johnson Administration.

Saxbe had gone into the race expecting to be little more than a sacrificial Republican candidate thrown against Lausche. In the Senate he appears to act like a man whose seat was a windfall. He has robustly criticized, and on occasion robustly defended, the Nixon Administration. One complaint is that the Administration does not seek his advice. Saxbe's other complaints and remarks are often scathing and frank; when Nixon unleashed terror bombing over North Vietnam during the Christmas season of 1972, Saxbe said to the press, "The President left his senses." Later, during the height of the Watergate revelations, Saxbe told Ohio reporters that Nixon saying he didn't know what went on with the Watergate is like a piano player in a whorehouse saying he doesn't know what's going on upstairs. Nor does Saxbe confine his tart forays to the President. Aside from J. William Fulbright, who used considerably more moderate tones, Saxbe was the only Senator who spoke out against the Jackson Amendment, which would deny most-favored-nation status to the Russians until they allowed Jews and others who wished to leave to emigrate freely. Saxbe's stance may not have been an especially prudent one for a politician coming up for reelection in Ohio, where Jewish contributors are important to both political parties.

During 1973, Saxbe's salty tongue produced a guessing game in Washington, the question being whether the Senator would seek reelection in 1974. There was talk that he had bought a ranch in Costa Rica, or that he wanted to go back to Ohio and tend his farm. Capitol Hill observers monitored changes in his staff closely: was he or was he not hiring people who could help him in the upcoming election? Finally, in the fall of 1973, Saxbe announced his retirement, and spoke out once again of his dissatisfaction with the pace and productivity of the Senate. Immediately, a number of candidates surged forward, including Republican Lt. Gov. John W. Brown; other Republican possibilities include Congressmen William Keating, Clarence Brown, and J. William Stanton. But the real fight—and the ultimate winner—may well come from the Democratic side. John Glenn, the onetime astronaut, seems to be running again, but the real favorite is the man who upset him in the 1970 primary, Howard Metzenbaum.

So it seems that the 1974 race may be as exciting as the 1970 contest. In the Republican primary of 1970, Gov. James Rhodes had the support of most local party organizations—Ohio is still a big patronage state. But the support proved not quite enough to beat Robert Taft, Jr. Rhodes may have been hurt by the reaction to the Kent State shootings, which occurred just a few days before the primary; he had sent the National Guard onto the campus. Meanwhile, the 1970 Democratic primary produced a surprise winner in Howard Metzenbaum, a Cleveland businessman (Airport Parking). Earlier, Metzenbaum had masterminded and contributed heavily to Sen. Young's campaigns. Normally, in Ohio, it would have been easy to pick the winner in a contest between a Taft and a Metzenbaum. But with the Republican state ticket in trouble and the economic policies of the Nixon Administration unpopular, Metzenbaum made a game fight of it. He ran far better than most Democrats in Republican strongholds like Cincinnati (Taft's home town), Columbus, and nonmetropolitan areas of the state. Taft, however, made inroads into normally Democratic Cleveland (Metzenbaum's home town) and managed to score a 70,000-vote victory.

For a man whose late father epitomized Republican conservatism, Sen. Taft has compiled a surprisingly moderate record. His father wrote the Taft-Hartley Act, which unions called a slave-labor law, but the younger Taft's votes on the Labor and Public Welfare Committee have often met the approval of labor. And though the younger Taft has supported the Nixon war policies, he is one of the few Senators to advance a proposal for amnesty for those who left the country or the Army in protest against the war. By temperament, Taft is a quiet man, and not as eloquent as his father; in this respect, he resembles his Senate colleague, Adlai Stevenson III of Illinois, another son of a famous man. Nevertheless, Taft will probably encounter few problems when he comes up for reelection in 1976. From time to time, his name has been mentioned as a possible presidential candidate. But he is spending much of his time tending to Republican politics of Ohio; in 1974, he suffered something of a defeat when his candidate for state party chairman was defeated by a man more amenable to ex-Gov. Rhodes.

Census Data Pop. 10,652,017; 5.26% of U.S. total, 6th largest; change 1960–70, 9.7%. Central city, 32%; suburban, 45%. Median family income, $10,309; 13th highest; families above $15,000: 22%; families below $3,000: 8%. Median years education, 12.1.

1972 Share of Federal Tax Burden $11,307,900,000; 5.41% of U.S. total, 5th largest.

1972 Share of Federal Outlays $7,672,373,619; 3.54% of U.S. total, 7th largest. Per capita federal spending, $720.

DOD	$1,957,967,000	9th (3.13%)	HEW	$3,084,099,295	6th (4.32%)
AEC	$121,501,056	9th (4.64%)	HUD	$132,036,687	7th (4.30%)
NASA	$113,153,865	9th (3.78%)	VA	$501,163,040	7th (4.38%)
DOT	$217,844,501	12th (2.76%)	USDA	$336,893,513	15th (2.19%)
DOC	$8,475,069	28th (0.65%)	CSC	$119,706,269	9th (2.90%)
DOI	$8,845,944	39th (0.41%)	TD	$434,903,686	7th (2.63%)
DOJ	$36,341,281	7th (3.70%)	Other	$599,442,413	

Economic Base Machinery, especially metalworking machinery; transportation equipment, especially motor vehicles and equipment; finance, insurance and real estate; primary metal industries, especially blast furnaces and basic steel products; fabricated metal products, especially metal stampings and fabricated structural metal products; electrical equipment and supplies, especially household appliances and electrical industrial apparatus; agriculture, especially dairy products, cattle, soybeans and corn.

Political Line-up Governor, John J. Gilligan (D); seat up, 1974. Senators, William R. Saxbe (R) and Robert Taft, Jr. (R). Representatives, 23 (16 R and 7 D). State Senate (17 D and 16 R); State House (57 D and 42 R).

The Voters

Registration No statewide registration.
Median voting age 42.8
Employment profile White collar, 45%. Blue collar, 41%. Service, 12%. Farm, 2%.
Ethnic groups Black, 9%. Total foreign stock, 12%. Germany, Italy, 2% each; Poland, UK, 1% each.

Presidential vote

1972	Nixon (R)	2,441,827	(63%)
	McGovern (D)	1,558,889	(37%)
1968	Nixon (R)	1,791,014	(45%)
	Humphrey (D)	1,700,586	(43%)
	Wallace (AI)	467,495	(12%)
1964	Johnson (D)	2,498,331	(63%)
	Goldwater (R)	1,470,865	(37%)

Senator

William B. Saxbe (R) Elected 1968, seat up 1974; b. June 24, 1916, Mechanicsburg; home, Mechanicsburg; Ohio State U., B.A., 1940, LL.B., 1948; Army Air Corps, WWII; Ohio Natl. Guard, 1940–45, 1951–52; married, three children; Episcopalian.

Career Ohio House of Reps., 1947–54, Majority Leader, 1951–52; Speaker, 1953–54; Ohio Atty. Gen., 1957–58, 1963–68.

Offices 1203 NSOB, 202-225-3353. Also 2956 Fed. Bldg., 1240 E. 9th St., Cleveland 44114, 216-522-4845, and Fed. Bldg., 85 Marconi Blvd., Columbus 43215, 614-469-6697.

Administrative Assistant William McHenry Hoiles

Committees

Armed Services (5th); Subs: Arms Control; Status of Forces; General Legislation (Ranking Mbr.); Preparedness Investigating.

Government Operations (4th); Subs: Permanent Investigations; Budgeting, Management and Expenditures (Ranking Mbr.).

Post Office and Civil Service (4th); Subs: Civil Service Policies and Practices; Postal Operations (Ranking Mbr.).

Sp. Com. on Aging (4th); Subs: Housing for the Elderly; Consumer Interests of the Elderly; Health of the Elderly (Ranking Mbr.); Long-Term Care.

Group Ratings

	ADA	COPE	LWV	RIPON	NFU	LCV	CFA	NAB	NSI	ACA
1972	15	13	43	81	22	3	50	44	63	58
1971	30	38	78	55	33	–	0	–	–	63
1970	47	56	–	55	64	47	–	50	22	47

Key Votes

1) Busing	ABS	8) Sea Life Prot	AGN	15) Tax Singls Less	AGN
2) Alas P-line	FOR	9) Campaign Subs	AGN	16) Min Tax for Rich	AGN
3) Gun Cntrl	AGN	10) Cmbodia Bmbg	AGN	17) Euro Troop Rdctn	ABS
4) Rehnquist	FOR	11) Legal Srvices	FOR	18) Bust Hwy Trust	ABS
5) Pub TV $	FOR	12) Rev Sharing	AGN	19) Maid Min Wage	AGN
6) EZ Votr Reg	AGN	13) Cnsumr Prot	AGN	20) Farm Sub Limit	FOR
7) No-Fault	AGN	14) Eq Rts Amend	FOR	21) Highr Credt Chgs	AGN

Election Results

1968 general:	William B. Saxbe (R)	1,928,964	(52%)
	John J. Gilligan (D)	1,814,152	(48%)
1968 primary:	William B. Saxbe (R)	575,178	(82%)
	William L. White (R)	71,191	(10%)
	Albert E. Payne (R)	52,393	(7%)

Senator

Robert Taft, Jr. (R) Elected 1970, seat up 1976; b. Feb. 26, 1917, Cincinnati; home, Cincinnati; Yale U., B.A., 1939; Harvard U., LL.B., 1942; Navy, WWII; married, four children; Episcopalian.

Career Practicing atty., 1946–62, 1965–66; Ohio House of Reps., 1955–62, Majority Floor Leader, 1961–62; nominee for Senate, 1964; U.S. House of Reps., 1962–64, 1966–70.

Offices 405 OSOB, 202-225-2315. Also 754 P.O. and Courthouse Bldg., Cincinnati 45202, 513-684-3284, and 523 U.S. Customs and Court House, Cleveland 44114, 216-522-4850, and 121 E. State St., Columbus 43215, 614-469-6774.

Administrative Assistant John R. Gomien

Committees

Banking, Housing and Urban Affairs (6th); Subs: Housing and Urban Affairs; International Finance; Production and Stabilization (Ranking Mbr.).

Labor and Public Welfare (4th); Subs: Labor; Employment, Poverty, and Migratory Labor (Ranking Mbr.); Children and Youth (Ranking Mbr.); Aging; Railroad Retirement; Health; Handicapped; Sp. Sub. on Arts and Humanities.

Joint Com. on Congressional Operation (Ranking Senate Mbr.).

Sel. Com. on Nutrition and Human Needs (6th).

Group Ratings

	ADA	COPE	LWV	RIPON	NFU	LCV	CFA	NAB	NSI	ACA
1972	25	20	70	86	33	26	33	78	100	70
1971	30	17	77	61	9	–	20	–	–	64

Key Votes

1) Busing	ABS	8) Sea Life Prot	FOR	15) Tax Singls Less	AGN
2) Alas P-line	FOR	9) Campaign Subs	AGN	16) Min Tax for Rich	AGN
3) Gun Cntrl	AGN	10) Cmbodia Bmbg	FOR	17) Euro Troop Rdctn	AGN
4) Rehnquist	FOR	11) Legal Srvices	FOR	18) Bust Hwy Trust	FOR
5) Pub TV $	COI	12) Rev Sharing	AGN	19) Maid Min Wage	AGN
6) EZ Votr Reg	AGN	13) Cnsumr Prot	AGN	20) Farm Sub Limit	FOR
7) No-Fault	FOR	14) Eq Rts Amend	FOR	21) Highr Credt Chgs	FOR

Election Results

1970 general:	Robert Taft, Jr. (R)	1,565,682	(50%)
	Howard H. Metzenbaum (D)	1,495,262	(47%)
	Richard B. Kay (AI)	61,261	(2%)
	John O'Neill (SL)	29,069	(1%)
1970 primary:	Robert Taft, Jr. (R)	472,202	(50%)
	James A. Rhodes (R)	466,932	(50%)

FIRST DISTRICT Political Background

The 1st district of Ohio is the eastern half of Cincinnati and suburban Hamilton County. This is, by and large, the more prosperous half of the old river city, which was the cultural and commercial center of the Midwest even before the Tafts arrived. In some neighborhoods within Cincinnati and in the hills beyond the city limits are the fashionable estates of the city's elite. Probably the most prestigious is the suburb of Indian Hill, home of Sen. Robert Taft, Jr. To the north one finds a mix of shopping centers and high-income suburb terrain. Within the city itself are the formerly Jewish sections of Avondale and Walnut Hills, now predominantly black. Many neighborhoods, like Norwood, a suburban enclave surrounded by Cincinnati, are inhabited mainly by migrants from the hills of Kentucky and Tennessee. The 1st also has most of the city's Jewish population; from its early days as a heavily German river town, Cincinnati has had an important German Jewish community. Politically, it is more conservative and Republican than Jewish communities in other major cities. Over the years, many prominent Cincinnati Jews have supported the Tafts.

Cincinnati has a well-deserved reputation for being a Republican city. Of the nation's 25 largest metropolitan areas, only Dallas and San Diego turn in Republican margins with greater regularity. Such has been the case since before the Civil War, when Cincinnati was a German, pro-Union, and Republican island surrounded by a sea of Southern Democratic sentiment. Moreover, Cincinnati has never attracted large numbers of those ethnic groups which have traditionally voted for Democratic politicians. There are fewer blacks here than in Cleveland, Detroit, or Buffalo, and very few people of Eastern or Southern European origin. And many of the city's Appalachians come from solidly Republican mountain counties, bringing both their politics and religion to the big Ohio city.

Out of Cincinnati have come several prominent Republicans, including Chief Justice Salmon P. Chase, President and Chief Justice William Howard Taft, Speaker of the House Nicholas Longworth (whose aged widow, the former Alice Roosevelt, still reigns as one of Washington's social elite), and finally, of course, Sen Robert A. Taft, Mr. Republican. More recently, the 1st has elected a succession of prominent men of both parties to the House. In 1964, the district unseated a conservative Republican in favor of John Gilligan, then a college professor and now Governor of Ohio. Two years later, in a race that attracted national attention, Gilligan was challenged by none other than Robert Taft, Jr., who had lost a Senate bid in 1964. Gilligan demonstrated his vote-getting prowess even while losing; after all, a 7,000-vote defeat in a heavily Republican district, to the son of Mr. Republican, is not bad.

In 1968, Taft won reelection easily and then went on in 1970 to capture Stephen Young's seat in the Senate. Taft's margin of victory, however, was surprisingly small, and he ran behind normal Republican showings in Cincinnati. Taft's successor in the House is William J. Keating, who had been a popular City Councilman. (The Cincinnati City Council seems to be a stepping stone to Congress; Donald Clancy of the 2nd district also served on the body, and so had Gilligan.) Keating's brother Charles, a Nixon appointee to the commission on obscenity, filed a vehement dissent to the group's permissive findings and formed a national citizens' organization to combat pornography. Charles' activities surely did no harm to Williams' campaign efforts. Against a black opponent, Keating took a larger percentage of the votes than Taft had two years before.

For 1972, the redistricting plan of the Republican legislature shifted the 1st's boundaries slightly. Now in the district is the University of Cincinnati, which is not an especially liberal school, but which is nonetheless considerably less Republican than the average Cincinnati suburb. The inclusion did not hurt Keating perceptibly; in fact, he won a higher percentage of the votes in 1972 than in 1970. But Keating is considering, or so it is said, leaving the House to run for Governor or Senator in 1974, with Sen. Taft's support. If he does vacate the seat, the 1st looks a little closer to marginal than it has in the past.

Census Data Pop. 462,725. Central city, 48%; suburban, 52%. Median family income, $10,535; families above $15,000: 26%; families below $3,000: 8%. Median years education, 12.1.

1972 Share of Federal Outlays $404,486,042

DOD	$132,899,221		HEW	$140,504,433
AEC	$4,985,239		HUD	$6,776,191
NASA	$3,327,058		DOI	$131,490
DOT	$10,648,417		USDA	$7,333,895
			Other	$97,880,098

Federal Military-Industrial Commitments

   DOD Contractors General Electric (Cincinnati), $133.119m: aircraft engines and components.
General Electric (Evendale), $92.503m: J-79 aircraft engines. Avco Corp. (Cincinnati), $21.116m:
electronic communications equipment. Procter and Gamble Distributers (Cincinnati), $12.299m:
unspecified.

Economic Base Transportation equipment; finance, insurance and real estate; machinery,
especially metalworking machinery; food and kindred products; printing and publishing,
especially commercial printing; and chemicals and allied products, especially soap, cleaners and
toilet goods. Also higher education (Univ. of Cincinnati).

The Voters

   Registration No district-wide registration.
   Median voting age 43.6
   Employment profile White collar, 53%. Blue collar, 33%. Service, 14%. Farm, –%.
   Ethnic groups Black, 20%. Total foreign stock, 9%. Germany, 2%.

Presidential vote

1972	Nixon (R)	111,925	(66%)
	McGovern (D)	57,516	(34%)
1968	Nixon (R)	88,124	(49%)
	Humphrey (D)	71,824	(40%)
	Wallace (AI)	20,838	(12%)

Representative

William J. Keating (R) Elected 1970; b. March 30, 1927, Cincinnati;
home, Cincinnati; U. of Cincinnati, B.B.A., 1950; U. of Cincinnati Law,
J.D., 1950; Navy, WWII; USAFR; married, seven children; Catholic.

Career Practicing atty., 1954–58, 1967–70; Asst. Atty. Gen., 1957–58;
Cincinnati Municipal Ct. Judge, 1958–63; Judge, Hamilton County
Common Pleas Court, 1965–67; Cincinnati City Council, 1967–70.

Offices 213 RHOB, 202-225-3164. Also 9407 Fed. Bldg., Cincinnati
45202.

Administrative Assistant Thomas A. Hayes

Committees

Judiciary (11th); Subs: No. 1 (Immigration and Nationality): No. 6 (Revision of the Laws).

Sel. Com. on Crime (5th).

Group Ratings

	ADA	COPE	LWV	RIPON	NFU	LCV	CFA	NAB	NSI	ACA
1972	25	36	58	86	57	36	0	100	100	68
1971	14	17	44	72	13	–	80	–	–	90

Key Votes

1) Busing	AGN	6) Cmbodia Bmbg	FOR	11) Chkg Acct Intrst	AGN
2) Strip Mines	AGN	7) Bust Hwy Trust	FOR	12) End HISC (HUAC)	AGN
3) Cut Mil $	AGN	8) Farm Sub Lmt	FOR	13) Nixon Sewer Veto	FOR
4) Rev Shrg	FOR	9) School Prayr	FOR	14) Corp Cmpaign $	AGN
5) Pub TV $	FOR	10) Cnsumr Prot	FOR	15) Pol $ Disclosr	FOR

Election Results

1972 general:	William J. Keating (R)	119,469	(70%)
	Karl F. Heiser (D)	50,575	(30%)
1972 primary:	William J. Keating (R), unopposed		
1970 general:	William J. Keating (R)	89,169	(69%)
	Bailey W. Turner (D)	39,820	(31%)

SECOND DISTRICT Political Background

The 2nd district of Ohio is the western half of Cincinnati and Hamilton County. On the whole, this is the less fashionable half of Cincinnati, though the 2nd does have plenty of comfortable neighborhoods, mostly in the suburbs. For the most part, the district consists of middle- and lower-middle-class areas. They are spread out over Cincinnati's hills, which also separate the neighborhoods from each other. The 2nd also includes some of the older and poorer sections of the city, like the Appalachian Over the Rhine area (a name that recalls Cincinnati's German heritage).

At the eastern end of the district winds Mill Creek, and next to it lies Cincinnati's major industrial corridor. Here are the great Procter and Gamble soap factories and many of the city's machine-tool makers; Cincinnati is a leading producer of both soap and machine tools. Also here is the General Electric plant that was once tooled up to make engines for Boeing's SST.

Like the 1st, the 2nd overall is heavily Republican. In the case of both districts, the suburbs, not the population-losing city of Cincinnati, supply the lion's share of the Republican margin. The line between the districts splits the city's Democratic votes. So if the Democrats ever get control of the Ohio legislature and the governorship at the same time, they would redraw the lines here. The boundaries would make most of the central city of Cincinnati into one, possibly Democratic district, and place virtually all of the hopelessly Republican suburbs in the other.

The current Congressman from the district is Donald Clancy, a former Cincinnati City Councilman who was first elected to the House in 1960. Clancy, a conservative Republican, was a member of the Armed Services Committee until 1973. And not surprisingly, he was one of the leading House proponents of the ill-fated SST. At the beginning of the 93rd Congress, Clancy switched committees. He got the seat (though not, of course, the seniority) on Ways and Means formerly held by Ohio Congressman Jackson Betts, who retired.

Seats on Ways and Means are usually reserved for incumbents with utterly safe districts—a category in which Clancy has usually fit. In 1970, however, a young Democrat named Gerald Springer cut Clancy's majority to 56%—a considerable achievement in this district. Redistricters in the Ohio legislature helped Clancy by putting the University of Cincinnati in the 1st and adding some heavily Republican townships to the 2nd. In the 1st, William Keating is totally entrenched. But here in the 2nd a closer-than-usual race may still be possible.

Census Data Pop. 463,260. Central city, 49%; suburban, 51%. Median family income, $10,439; families above $15,000: 23%; families below $3,000: 8%. Median years education, 11.9.

1972 Share of Federal Outlays $404,969,184

DOD	$133,057,963	HEW	$140,672,260
AEC	$4,991,194	HUD	$6,784,285
NASA	$3,331,032	DOI	$131,647
DOT	$10,661,136	USDA	$7,342,655
		Other	$97,997,912

Federal Military-Industrial Commitments

AEC Operations National Lead Co. (Fernald), $11.493m: operation of feed materials facilities.

Economic Base Transportation equipment; finance, insurance and real estate; machinery, especially metalworking machinery; food and kindred products; printing and publishing, especially commercial printing; and chemicals and allied products, especially soap, cleaners and toilet goods.

The Voters

Registration No district-wide registration.
Median voting age 43.0
Employment profile White collar, 53%. Blue collar, 34%. Service, 13%. Farm, –%.
Ethnic groups Black, 11%. Total foreign stock, 9%. Germany, 3%.

Presidential vote

1972	Nixon (R)	127,655	(67%)
	McGovern (D)	61,676	(33%)
1968	Nixon (R)	96,018	(52%)
	Humphrey (D)	63,535	(34%)
	Wallace (AI)	26,140	(14%)

Representative

Donald D. Clancy (R) Elected 1960; b. July 24, 1921, Cincinnati; home, Cincinnati; Xavier U., 1939–43; U. of Cincinnati Law School, LL.B., 1948; married, three children; Presbyterian.

Career Practicing atty., 1948– ; Cincinnati Council, 1951–57; Mayor of Cincinnati, 1957–60.

Offices 2367 RHOB, 202-225-2216. Also Rm. 430, P.O. and Courthouse Bldg., Cincinnati 45202, 513-684-3738.

Administrative Assistant Arlo T. Wagner

Committees

Ways and Means (9th).

Group Ratings

	ADA	COPE	LWV	RIPON	NFU	LCV	CFA	NAB	NSI	ACA
1972	0	30	36	77	0	8	0	90	100	95
1971	5	9	11	41	21	–	13	–	–	100
1970	0	10	–	41	33	39	42	89	100	88

Key Votes

1) Busing	AGN	6) Cmbodia Bmbg	FOR	11) Chkg Acct Intrst	AGN
2) Strip Mines	AGN	7) Bust Hwy Trust	AGN	12) End HISC (HUAC)	AGN
3) Cut Mil $	ABS	8) Farm Sub Lmt	FOR	13) Nixon Sewer Veto	FOR
4) Rev Shrg	AGN	9) School Prayr	FOR	14) Corp Cmpaign $	FOR
5) Pub TV $	AGN	10) Cnsumr Prot	AGN	15) Pol $ Disclosr	FOR

Election Results

1972 general:	Donald D. Clancy (R)	109,961	(63%)
	Penny Manes (D)	65,237	(37%)
1972 primary:	Donald D. Clancy (R)	30,500	(89%)
	Orville E. Brown (R)	3,746	(11%)
1970 general:	Donald D. Clancy (R)	77,071	(56%)
	Gerald N. Springer (D)	60,860	(44%)

THIRD DISTRICT Political Background

In many way, Dayton, Ohio, is a typical Middle American city. It sits on the old National Road that spans the middle of the Midwest; it is middle-sized (metropolitan pop. 850,000) and predominantly middle-class. Like most central cities, the city of Dayton itself is losing population; it is now about 30% black and even has a black Mayor. As in most metropolitan areas, the most substantial growth here has occurred in the suburbs, like middle-class Kettering just south of the city. Dayton—or one of its suburbs—is the home of Richard Scammon and Ben Wattenberg's typical American voter: a housewife whose husband works in a factory and whose brother-in-law is a policeman. Usually a Democrat, she is, according to the view presented in *The Real Majority*, worried about crime and leaning toward Richard Nixon's kind of Republicanism.

As it turns out, the Scammon and Wattenberg personification presents a fairly accurate summary of the politics of the major portion of the Dayton metropolitan area, if not of the entire nation. This part of Ohio comprises the state's 3rd congressional district, an area which normally delivers small Democratic majorities in statewide elections, but which also votes for popular Republicans in local and national elections. It gave Hubert Humphrey a pretty good margin in 1968, but a better one to Richard Nixon in 1972.

Ohio Republicans have traditionally selected congressional candidates suited to the constituencies of the various districts. Accordingly, the Congressman from the Democratic-leaning 3rd, Charles Whalen, is one of the two most liberal members of the Ohio Republican delegation. In 1966, Whalen was a 12-year veteran of the Ohio legislature when he challenged Democratic Congressman Rodney Love, a beneficiary of the LBJ landslide. Whalen won with 52% of the votes, and has since been reelected by huge margins.

Whalen's liberal record has attracted the support of many staunchly Democratic voters. In the House, he labored for several years as the only dovish Republican on the House Armed Services Committee. The fruits of his labor were the Nedzi-Whalen amendments, of which he was chief co-sponsor. These were the major efforts on the House side to set a deadline to American involvement in the Vietnam war. At the beginning of the 93rd Congress, Whalen quit Armed Services—losing his seniority there—and transferred to the Foreign Affairs Committee.

Census Data Pop. 463,140. Central city, 53%; suburban, 47%. Median family income, $11,481; families above $15,000: 29%; families below $3,000: 7%. Median years education, 12.2.

1972 Share of Federal Outlays $555,989,378

DOD	$324,345,393	HEW	$116,785,407
AEC	$21,457,982	HUD	$5,717,673
NASA	$427,354	DOI	$269,605
DOT	$8,892,544	USDA	$10,935,108
		Other	$67,158,312

Federal Military-Industrial Commitments

DOD Contractors IBM (Dayton), $10.050m: data processing equipment.

Economic Base Machinery; electrical equipment and supplies; transportation equipment; printing and publishing, especially commercial printing; and finance, insurance and real estate. Also higher education (Univ. of Dayton, and Wright State Univ.).

The Voters

Registration No district-wide registration.
Median voting age 41.9
Employment profile White collar, 51%. Blue collar, 37%. Service, 12%. Farm, –%.
Ethnic groups Black, 16%. Total foreign stock, 7%. Germany, 2%.

Presidential vote

1972	Nixon (R)	88,701	(58%)
	McGovern (D)	63,890	(42%)
1968	Nixon (R)	64,092	(40%)
	Humphrey (D)	76,285	(48%)
	Wallace (AI)	17,984	(11%)

Representative

Charles W. Whalen, Jr. (R) Elected 1966; b. July 31, 1920, Dayton; home, Dayton; U. of Dayton, B.S., 1942; Harvard U., M.B.A., 1946; Army, WWII; married, six children; Catholic.

Career Businessman, V. Pres., Dayton Dress Co., 1946–52; Ohio House of Reps., 1955–60; Ohio Senate, 1961–66; Prof. and Head, Dept. of Econ., U. of Dayton, 1962–66.

Offices 1035 LHOB, 202-225-6465. Also 315 Old P.O. Bldg., 118 W. Third, Dayton 45402, 513-461-4830, ext. 5286.

Administrative Assistant Alfred S. Frank, Jr.

Committees

Foreign Affairs (13th); Subs: Foreign Economic Policy; Inter-American Affairs.

Group Ratings

	ADA	COPE	LWV	RIPON	NFU	LCV	CFA	NAB	NSI	ACA
1972	94	100	100	87	100	87	50	25	0	4
1971	84	73	100	94	71	–	75	–	–	15
1970	88	75	–	88	100	50	65	27	10	26

Key Votes

1) Busing	FOR	6) Cmbodia Bmbg	AGN	11) Chkg Acct Intrst	FOR
2) Strip Mines	AGN	7) Bust Hwy Trust	FOR	12) End HISC (HUAC)	FOR
3) Cut Mil $	FOR	8) Farm Sub Lmt	FOR	13) Nixon Sewer Veto	FOR
4) Rev Shrg	FOR	9) School Prayr	AGN	14) Corp Cmpaign $	AGN
5) Pub TV $	AGN	10) Cnsumr Prot	FOR	15) Pol $ Disclosr	FOR

Election Results

1972 general:	Charles W. Whalen, Jr. (R)	111,253	(76%)
	John W. Lelak, Jr. (D)	34,819	(24%)
1972 primary:	Charles W. Whalen, Jr. (R), unopposed		
1970 general:	Charles W. Whalen, Jr. (R)	86,973	(74%)
	Dempsey A. Kerr (D)	26,735	(23%)
	Russell G. Butcke (AI)	3,545	(3%)

FOURTH DISTRICT Political Background

The 4th district of Ohio comprises a group of counties, mostly rural but with some having small cities, in western Ohio. This is a deeply conservative part of the nation, a sort of Grant Woodish enclave set in industrial Middle America. It is therefore fitting that the town of Wapkoneta here in the 4th district produced the first man to walk on the moon—strait-laced and sober Neil Armstrong. The conservatism of the 4th runs so deep that it is often the most Republican district in Ohio, or so it was in the 1972 presidential election. The district's urban centers, to the extent they can be called such, are as heavily Republican as the countryside, if not more so. Findlay (pop. 35,000) is an old Republican town, made newly prosperous as the headquarters of the Marathon Oil concern. Allen County, which contains Lima, the district's largest city (pop. 53,000), was the largest county east of Chicago and north of Richmond, Virginia, to support the candidacy of Barry Goldwater in 1964. Then there are smaller Republican towns like Bucyrus, Piqua, and Upper Sandusky (which is no where near Sandusky).

For 25 years, Republican William McCulloch represented the 4th district. When he retired in 1972, McCulloch was the dean of the Ohio delegation and the ranking Republican on the House Judiciary Committee, which has jurisdiction over civil rights legislation. Because McCulloch usually voted with other Midwestern conservatives, many of whom were leary about civil rights bills, but who trusted him, the Ohioan was able to swing many votes in favor of the Civil Rights Act of 1964. McCulloch was also a major backer of subsequent civil rights legislation, served on the Kerner Commission on Civil Disorders, and the presidential commission on violence chaired by Milton Eisenhower.

By 1972, McCulloch was 71 and seriously ill. He announced his retirement, then said he might run again, and then made his retirement final. One factor producing the unequivocal decision was redistricting. The Ohio legislature had more or less combined McCulloch's district with that of another senior Republican, Jackson Betts, second-ranking minority member of the Ways and Means Committee. As it turned out, Betts, who was 68, decided to retire too. So the redrawn 4th district was left without an incumbent.

No dogfight for the seat, the kind seen in many no-incumbent congressional districts, ensued. Ohio Republicans do not do things that way, except perhaps at the statewide level. State Sen. Tennyson Guyer, a conservative, encountered only weak opposition in the primary, and, of course, won the general election with ease. He will no doubt continue to win reelection in the same fashion.

Census Data Pop. 463,143. Central city, 12%; suburban, 31%. Median family income, $9,710; families above $15,000: 17%; families below $3,000: 8%. Median years education, 12.1.

1972 Share of Federal Outlays $310,098,792

DOD	$81,189,408	HEW	$121,041,348
AEC	$3,887,515	HUD	$1,841,267
NASA	$241,045	DOI	$151,604
DOT	$5,312,847	USDA	$40,130,407
		Other	$56,303,351

Federal Military-Industrial Commitments

DOD Contractors Goodyear Tire (St. Mary's), $8.930m: track assemblies for tanks.

Economic Base Machinery; transportation equipment; agriculture, notably grains, hogs and sheep, and cattle; finance, insurance and real estate; and electrical equipment and supplies.

The Voters

Registration No district-wide registration.
Median voting age 43.6
Employment profile White collar, 38%. Blue collar, 46%. Service, 12%. Farm, 4%.
Ethnic groups Black, 3%. Total foreign stock, 4%. Germany, 1%.

Presidential vote

1972	Nixon (R)	120,089	(71%)
	McGovern (D)	49,780	(29%)
1968	Nixon (R)	99,879	(55%)
	Humphrey (D)	62,741	(35%)
	Wallace (AI)	18,848	(10%)

Representative

Tennyson Guyer (R) Elected 1972; b. Nov. 29, 1913, Findlay; home, Findlay; Findlay Col., B.A., 1934; married, two children; College Church of God.

Career Minister, Mercer County Churches; Public Relations, Cooper Tire & Rubber Co., Findlay, 1950–72; Ohio State Senate, 1961–72; Pres, City Council; Mayor, Celina, 1940–44; Treas. and Pres., International Platform Assn.

Offices 114 CHOB, 202-225-2676. Also 658 W. Market, Lima 45801, 419-223-0903.

Administrative Assistant Marvin E. Monroe

Committees

Foreign Affairs (18th); Subs: Asian and Pacific Affairs; State Department Organization and Foreign Operations.

Internal Security (4th).

Group Ratings: Newly Elected

Key Votes

1) Busing	NE	6) Cmbodia Bmbg	FOR	11) Chkg Acct Intrst	ABS
2) Strip Mines	NE	7) Bust Hwy Trust	AGN	12) End HISC (HUAC)	AGN
3) Cut Mil $	NE	8) Farm Sub Lmt	NE	13) Nixon Sewer Veto	FOR
4) Rev Shrg	NE	9) School Prayr	NE	14) Corp Cmpaign $	NE
5) Pub TV $	NE	10) Cnsumr Prot	NE	15) Pol $ Disclosr	NE

Election Results

1972 general:	Tennyson Guyer (R)	109,612	(63%)
	Dimitri Nicholas (D)	65,216	(37%)
1972 primary:	Tennyson Guyer (R)	34,880	(75%)
	James M. Carpenter (R)	11,372	(25%)

FIFTH DISTRICT   Political Background

Some 150 years ago, New England Yankee farmers settled the flatlands in the northwest corner of Ohio. They were later joined in the agricultural enterprise by German Protestants. The land here is more fertile and easier to work than the hills of southern Ohio; in fact, it begins the great corn-and-hog belt that stretches into Illinois and Iowa. This part of Ohio is one of vintage Republicanism, as it has been since the party was founded in the 1850s.

Unlike so much of rural America, northwest Ohio is not in economic or population decline. The fertility of its soil, the industry of its farmers, and most important, its strategic location account for the happy state of affairs. For this area finds itself encircled by the giant industrial cities of the Midwest, and also lies on both sides of the nation's major east-west rail lines and Interstate highways. To take advantage of the proximity of markets and easy access to them, small factories have sprung up in the towns and countryside of northwest Ohio. These have provided marginal farmers with part-time employment, allowing them to remain on the land and still make a decent living.

The 5th congressional district covers most of northwest Ohio. Not included here is the city of Toledo (and a few of its suburbs) which are in the 9th district. The 5th, of course, has a Republican constituency that has provided predictably steady support for its Republican Congressman, Delbert Latta. He is one of many Congressmen not widely recognized outside of his district. Even his service on the House Rules Committee has not made him anything like a celebrity. On the committee, Latta consistently supports the desires of the Republican leadership. Perhaps typical of his interests is a controversy in which he became involved during 1973. A bill came before Congress to allow unions to bargain for legal services for their members. The issue was whether the unions could bargain for group legal services, or whether any single member could select personal counsel. Latta supported the latter alternative, one that would have effectively precluded the development of group legal services. He was concerned, it appears, about the interests of small-town private lawyers—a formidable group in the 5th congressional district. Though Latta lost his case in Washington, he can count on winning reelection in the 5th as long as he wants.

Census Data Pop. 463,727. Central city, 0%; suburban, 37%. Median family income, $9,945; families above $15,000: 18%; families below $3,000: 8%. Median years education, 12.1.

1972 Share of Federal Outlays $257,499,429

DOD	$33,513,160	HEW	$127,163,089
AEC	–	HUD	$1,220,622
NASA	$221,044	DOI	$386,048
DOT	$2,121,850	USDA	$36,819,500
		Other	$56,054,116

Federal Military-Industrial Commitments

DOD Contractors Standard Products (Port Clinton), $5.232m: track assemblies for tanks.

Economic Base Agriculture, notably grains, cattle, poultry, and hogs and sheep; stone, clay and glass products; electrical equipment and supplies; food and kindred products, especially canned, cured and frozen foods; machinery; and fabricated metal products. Also higher education, (Bowling Green State Univ.).

The Voters

Registration No district-wide registration.
Median voting age 42.4
Employment profile White collar, 37%. Blue collar, 46%. Service, 12%. Farm, 5%.
Ethnic groups Total foreign stock, 7%. Germany, 2%.

Presidential vote

1972	Nixon (R)	118,678	(66%)
	McGovern (D)	62,332	(34%)
1968	Nixon (R)	96,579	(55%)
	Humphrey (D)	61,852	(35%)
	Wallace (AI)	16,031	(9%)

Representative

Delbert L. Latta (R) Elected 1958; b. March 5, 1920, Weston; home, Bowling Green; Ohio Northern U., B.A., LL.B.; married, two children; Church of Christ.

Career Practicing atty.; Ohio Senate.

Offices 2423 RHOB, 202-225-6405. Also 309 Wood County Bank Bldg., Bowling Green 43402, 419-353-8871.

Administrative Assistant Kaye M. Burchell

Committees

Rules (4th).

Group Ratings

	ADA	COPE	LWV	RIPON	NFU	LCV	CFA	NAB	NSI	ACA
1972	0	0	42	60	43	27	100	92	100	91
1971	8	9	13	38	40	–	14	–	–	79
1970	8	36	–	56	38	40	60	82	100	71

Key Votes

1) Busing	AGN	6) Cmbodia Bmbg	FOR	11) Chkg Acct Intrst	AGN
2) Strip Mines	AGN	7) Bust Hwy Trust	AGN	12) End HISC (HUAC)	AGN
3) Cut Mil $	AGN	8) Farm Sub Lmt	FOR	13) Nixon Sewer Veto	AGN
4) Rev Shrg	FOR	9) School Prayr	FOR	14) Corp Cmpaign $	AGN
5) Pub TV $	AGN	10) Cnsumr Prot	AGN	15) Pol $ Disclosr	AGN

Election Results

1972 general:	Delbert L. Latta (R)	132,032	(73%)
	Bruce Edwards (D)	49,465	(27%)
1972 primary:	Delbert L. Latta (R), unopposed		
1970 general:	Delbert L. Latta (R)	92,577	(71%)
	Carl G. Sherer (D)	37,545	(29%)

SIXTH DISTRICT Political Background

The 6th district of Ohio is a rural district in the southern part of the state. Though the 6th touches the metropolitan areas of Cincinnati to the east and Columbus to the north, little in the 6th itself partakes of the metropolitan. From the outer edges of urban Cincinnati and Columbus to the decaying industrial city of Portsmouth on the Ohio River, the district has a Southern-accented, small-town feeling. The rolling hill country of the valley of the Scioto River, which runs through Columbus, Chillicothe, and Portsmouth, was once Democratic terrain, reflecting the Southern origin of the valley's earliest settlers. Lately, like much of the South, this region of Ohio has become more conservative and far less Democratic; only tiny Pike County here delivers Democratic majorities with any regularity in statewide races. In the western part of the district, some Cincinnati exurban growth spilling into Clermont County has contributed to the Republican trend in the 6th.

Until the late 1950s, the district, as a matter of tradition, sent a Democrat to the House. After the incumbent's death in 1959, the Republican organization of Ray Bliss carefully selected the party nominee, William Harsha, who won in 1960 and who has won reelection easily ever since. The former Scioto County (Portsmouth) prosecutor is a reliably conservative member of the reliably conservative Ohio Republican delegation.

During the last two Congresses, Harsha has served as the ranking minority member of the House Public Works Committee. Traditionally, the committee has run a pork barrel operation, conferring federal projects and dollars upon the districts of deserving Congressmen. But in the last few years, Public Works has assumed a new importance—the place where the fate of much legislation concerning the environment is determined. Air- and water-pollution bills, for example, usually lie within the jurisdiction of Public Works.

In the 93rd Congress, the most important piece of Public Works legislation affecting the environment was the highway bill. The big question was whether the highway trust fund, one financed by gasoline taxes, could be used to benefit mass transit. The trust-busters, as their adversaries called them, were convinced that undesirable highways were being built and that desirable mass-transit projects were not. Harsha stood solidly against any efforts to divert money from the trust. Most Republican members of Public Works and the full House followed his lead, though the Nixon Administration was part of the trust-busting coalition. The issue was resolved in conference committee, where a limited diversion of trust moneys was agreed upon—a compromise not at all to Harsha's liking.

Census Data Pop. 463,067. Central city, 0%; suburban, 37%. Median family income, $8,595; families above $15,000: 13%; families below $3,000: 13%. Median years education, 11.2.

1972 Share of Federal Outlays $421,710,671

DOD	$60,996,347	HEW	$155,532,466
AEC	$67,006,901	HUD	$3,328,304
NASA	$1,125,429	DOI	$301,679
DOT	$16,835,325	USDA	$24,980,906
		Other	$91,603,314

Federal Military-Industrial Commitments

AEC Operations Goodyear Atomic Corp. (Piketon), $63.819m: operation of gaseous diffusion plant.

Economic Base Agriculture, notably hogs and sheep, cattle, and grains; finance, insurance and real estate; fabricated metal products; miscellaneous plastics products and other rubber and plastic products; and food and kindred products.

The Voters

Registration No district-wide registration.
Median voting age 43.7
Employment profile White collar, 37%. Blue collar, 46%. Service, 12%. Farm, 5%.
Ethnic groups Black, 2%. Total foreign stock, 2%.

Presidential vote

1972	Nixon (R)	118,484	(70%)
	McGovern (D)	49,892	(30%)
1968	Nixon (R)	86,824	(49%)
	Humphrey (D)	56,809	(32%)
	Wallace (AI)	32,180	(18%)

Representative

William H. Harsha (R) Elected 1960; b. Jan. 1, 1921, Portsmouth; home, Portsmouth; Kenyon Col., B.A., 1943; Western Reserve U., LL.B., 1947; USMCR, WWII; married, four children; Presbyterian.

Career Practicing atty., 1947–61; Asst. City Solicitor, Portsmouth, 1947–51; Scioto County Prosecutor, 1951–55.

Offices 2457 RHOB, 202-225-5705. Also 285 Main St., Batavia 45103, 513-732-2247, and P.O. Bldg., Hillsboro 45133, 513-393-4223.

Administrative Assistant None

Committees

District of Columbia (2nd); Subs: Business, Commerce and Taxation (Ranking Mbr.); Judiciary.

Public Works (Ranking Mbr.); Sub: Transportation (Ranking Mbr.).

Group Ratings

	ADA	COPE	LWV	RIPON	NFU	LCV	CFA	NAB	NSI	ACA
1972	0	18	45	57	71	32	0	73	100	81
1971	8	18	22	47	47	–	29	–	–	89
1970	8	17	–	29	31	40	48	92	100	84

Key Votes

1) Busing	AGN	6) Cmbodia Bmbg	FOR	11) Chkg Acct Intrst	AGN
2) Strip Mines	AGN	7) Bust Hwy Trust	AGN	12) End HISC (HUAC)	ABS
3) Cut Mil $	AGN	8) Farm Sub Lmt	FOR	13) Nixon Sewer Veto	FOR
4) Rev Shrg	FOR	9) School Prayr	FOR	14) Corp Cmpaign $	AGN
5) Pub TV $	AGN	10) Cnsumr Prot	AGN	15) Pol $ Disclosr	AGN

Election Results

1972 general:	William H. Harsha (R), unopposed		
1972 primary:	William H. Harsha (R), unopposed		
1970 general:	William H. Harsha (R)	82,772	(68%)
	Raymond H. Stevens (D)	39,265	(32%)

SEVENTH DISTRICT Political Background

Bellefontaine, Ohio, is the site of the first concrete street in the United States. And despite all the gouges and smotherings that concrete has wreaked upon the American landscape in the last 70 years, the first concrete street in Bellefontaine still lies here, with the old courthouse looming up one side and a row of stores on the other. Bellefontaine is part of Ohio's 7th congressional district, most of which has enjoyed a similarly stable existence. It is true that the suburbs of Dayton have begun to encroach on the southwest corner of the district, where Wright-Patterson Air Force Base was built. But the industrial city of Springfield (pop. 81,000), the district's largest urban concentration, has grown little in the last 50 years. Neither has the city of Marion (pop. 39,000), where young Socialist-to-be Norman Thomas delivered newspapers edited by President-to-be Warren G. Harding.

From 1938 to 1965, the 7th was represented by Clarence J. Brown, a Republican newspaper editor. He was a man who himself seemed out of the era of Harding or McKinley. At the time of his death, Brown was the senior Republican on the House Rules Committee, where he often joined Chairman Howard Smith of Virginia to kill or postpone liberal legislation that they both heartily disdained. In a 1965 special election, the Congressman's son, Clarence J. (Bud) Brown, was chosen to succeed him. The younger Brown, however, did not become a member of Rules. He is already a high-ranking member of the Commerce Committee and the Government Operations Committee, and is ranking minority member on two subcommittes. His father would have probably disapproved of a few of Brown's votes on issues. But on most of them Brown is a good soldier in Gerald Ford's well-disciplined Republican bloc.

At the beginning of the 93rd Congress, Brown was a candidate for the chairmanship of the House Republican Campaign Committee. Bob Wilson of California, apparently under protest, was about to vacate the post by orders from the White house. Unfortunately for Brown, it was known that he was the choice of the White House for the job. Even before the Watergate revelations had reached full tide and even in the House Republican Caucus, the Haldeman-Ehrlichman imprimatur was the kiss of death. Brown lost the election, which was conducted by secret ballot. His successful opponent, Robert Michel of Illinois, refused to release the totals. The contest was apparently so one-sided that knowledge of the magnitude of Brown's defeat would have caused him serious embarrassment. Whether out of disappointment over this defeat or of just a normal desire to move up, Brown is reportedly considering a bid for the Senate seat vacated by William Saxbe in 1974.

Census Data Pop. 463,217. Central city, 18%; suburban, 52%. Median family income, $10,132; families above $15,000: 20%; families below $3,000: 7%. Median years education, 12.1.

1972 Share of Federal Outlays $379,529,351

DOD	$138,877,841	HEW	$121,336,281
AEC	$7,550,977	HUD	$3,054,954
NASA	$204,543	DOI	$94,823
DOT	$4,703,846	USDA	$25,001,124
		Other	$78,704,912

Federal Military-Industrial Commitments

   DOD Contractors Frank Messer and Sons (Wright Patterson AFB), $8.739m: construction services. Ashland Oil (Medway), $5.901m: petroleum products.
   DOD Installations Gentile AF Station (Dayton). Wright-Patterson AFB (Dayton).

Economic Base Machinery; agriculture, notably grains, hogs and sheep, cattle, and dairy products; finance, insurance and real estate; fabricated metal products, especially fabricated structural metal products; and primary metal industries.

The Voters

   Registration No district-wide registration.
   Median voting age 41.0
   Employment profile White collar, 44%. Blue collar, 42%. Service, 11%. Farm, 3%.
   Ethnic groups Black, 6%. Total foreign stock, 5%. Germany, 1%.

Presidential vote

	1972	Nixon (R)	106,807	(67%)
		McGovern (D)	52,240	(33%)
	1968	Nixon (R)	75,960	(48%)
		Humphrey (D)	61,715	(39%)
		Wallace (AI)	21,288	(13%)

Representative

Clarence J. **Brown** (R) Elected Nov. 2, 1965; b. June 18, 1927, Columbus; home, Columbus; Duke U., B.A., 1947; Harvard, M.B.A., 1949; USNR, Korean War; married, three children; Presbyterian.

Career Editor, *Star Republican*, 1949–53; Editor, co-owner, *Franklin Chronicle*, 1953–57; Editor, *Urbana Daily Citizen*, 1957–65, Publisher, 1959– ; Mgr., WCOM-FM, 1965–69; Pres., Brown Publishing Co.; farm owner.

Offices 212 CHOB, 202-225-4324. Also 220 U.S. P.O., 150 N. Limestone St., Springfield 45501, 513-325-0474.

Administrative Assistant Jay T. Scheck (L.A.)

Committees

Government Operations (4th); Subs: Legislation and Military Operations; Intergovernmental Relations (Ranking Mbr.).

Interstate and Foreign Commerce (6th); Sub: Communications and Power (Ranking Mbr.).

Joint Economic Com. (3rd); Subs: Economic Progress; Priorities and Economy in Government; Urban Affairs; Consumer Economics; International Economics.

Group Ratings

	ADA	COPE	LWV	RIPON	NFU	LCV	CFA	NAB	NSI	ACA
1972	19	27	50	73	57	26	50	100	100	57
1971	19	20	67	65	27	–	43	–	–	84
1970	24	36	–	46	67	14	28	82	100	56

Key Votes

1) Busing	FOR	6) Cmbodia Bmbg	ABS	11) Chkg Acct Intrst	AGN
2) Strip Mines	AGN	7) Bust Hwy Trust	AGN	12) End HISC (HUAC)	AGN
3) Cut Mil $	AGN	8) Farm Sub Lmt	AGN	13) Nixon Sewer Veto	FOR
4) Rev Shrg	FOR	9) School Prayr	FOR	14) Corp Cmpaign $	FOR
5) Pub TV $	FOR	10) Cnsumr Prot	AGN	15) Pol $ Disclosr	FOR

Election Results

1972 general:	Clarence J. Brown (R)	112,350	(73%)
	Dorothy Franke (Ind.)	40,945	(27%)
1972 primary:	Clarence J. Brown (R), unopposed		
1970 general:	Clarence J. Brown (R)	84,448	(69%)
	Joseph D. Lewis (D)	37,294	(31%)

EIGHTH DISTRICT Political Background

Along the Indiana border, just north of Cincinnati and just west of Dayton, lies the 8th congressional district of Ohio. Though the suburban sprawl of both Cincinnati and Dayton spill into the 8th, the district is dominated by two aging cities in Butler County: Hamilton (pop. 67,000) and Middletown (pop. 48,000). In the 8th, the hilly Ohio River country slides into the flatter land of the northern part of the state. Over the years, the district has taken most of its settlers from around the Ohio River and farther south, a fact that shows up in election returns. In most elections these days, the 8th is heavily Republican and conservative. But a Southern Democratic heritage does lie hidden here, one that surfaced in the hefty 18% of the vote cast for George Wallace in 1968. This percentage represents the most the Alabamian got in any Ohio district that year, and, outside Oklahoma, the best he did in any district among the states that did not allow slavery at the time of the Civil War.

A redistricting in 1964 created the 8th essentially as it now stands; the district was then numbered the 24th, but in the 1970 census, Ohio lost its 24th House seat. For the first four years of the district's existence, it was represented by Donald E. (Buz) Lukens, a young (35 when first elected) ideological conservative. He was then and remains today a maverick in staid Ohio Republican circles. In 1970, Lukens decided to run for Governor, and in the Republican primary ran a fairly strong second to the establishment's choice, Auditor Roger Cloud. The Republican winner, however, went on to lose by a large margin to Democrat John Gilligan.

Lukens' successor in the House is ex-state Sen. Walter Powell. The crew-cut conservative won a narrow victory over a rather conservative Democrat, James Ruppert, in 1970, and beat Ruppert again by an even smaller margin in 1972. Meanwhile, oddly enough, Lukens won Powell's old state Senate seat, and is reportedly aiming for the governorship again in 1974. The closeness of the 1972 result, particularly when compared to Richard Nixon's massive 69–31 sweep of the 9th, indicates that Powell may be in trouble in 1974, especially if Ruppert runs again.

Census Data Pop. 462,915. Central city, 25%; suburban, 64%. Median family income, $10,455; families above $15,000: 21%; families below $3,000: 7%. Median years education, 11.8.

1972 Share of Federal Outlays $323,178,637

DOD	$117,286,789	HEW	$117,903,260
AEC	$6,898,149	HUD	$2,485,604
NASA	$452,756	DOI	$170,019
DOT	$3,742,840	USDA	$12,021,417
		Other	$62,227,803

Federal Military-Industrial Commitments

AEC Operations Monsanto Research Corp. (Miamisburg), $36.561m: operation of Mound Laboratory and design of weapons and non-weapons components.

Economic Base Machinery; electrical equipment and supplies; fabricated metal products; paper and allied products, especially paper mill products, except building paper, and miscellaneous converted paper products; and primary metal industries, especially blast furnace and steel mill products. Also higher education (Miami Univ.).

The Voters

Registration No district-wide registration.
Median voting age 40.7
Employment profile White collar, 41%. Blue collar, 45%. Service, 11%. Farm, 3%.
Ethnic groups Black, 4%. Total foreign stock, 4%. Germany, 1%.

Presidential vote

1972	Nixon (R)	104,889	(69%)
	McGovern (D)	47,638	(31%)
1968	Nixon (R)	71,399	(48%)
	Humphrey (D)	50,913	(34%)
	Wallace (AI)	26,420	(18%)

Representative

Walter E. Powell (R) Elected 1970; b. April 25, 1931, Hamilton; home, Fairfield; Heidelberg Col., B.A., 1953; Miami U. (Ohio), M.Ed., 1961; married, two children; Presbyterian.

Career Teacher, Fairfield Jr. High School; Principal, Hopewell Elementary and Fairfield West Elementary; Fairfield City Clerk, 1956; Fairfield Councilman, 1957; Ohio Legislature, 1960–66; Ohio Senate, 1966–70.

Offices 1532 LHOB, 202-225-6205.

Administrative Assistant Sam Hale

Committees

Armed Services (11th); Subs: No. 2; No. 4.

Post Office and Civil Service (7th); Subs: Facilities, Mail, and Labor Management; Investigations (Ranking Mbr.).

Group Ratings

	ADA	COPE	LWV	RIPON	NFU	LCV	CFA	NAB	NSI	ACA
1972	6	20	27	33	67	0	0	92	100	95
1971	16	20	25	56	38	–	14	–	–	84

Key Votes

1) Busing	ABS	6) Cmbodia Bmbg	FOR	11) Chkg Acct Intrst	AGN
2) Strip Mines	FOR	7) Bust Hwy Trust	ABS	12) End HISC (HUAC)	AGN
3) Cut Mil $	AGN	8) Farm Sub Lmt	FOR	13) Nixon Sewer Veto	FOR
4) Rev Shrg	AGN	9) School Prayr	FOR	14) Corp Cmpaign $	AGN
5) Pub TV $	AGN	10) Cnsumr Prot	AGN	15) Pol $ Disclosr	AGN

Election Results

1972 general:	Walter E. Powell (R)	80,050	(52%)
	James D. Ruppert (D)	73,344	(48%)
1972 primary:	Walter E. Powell (R)	20,431	(73%)
	Ralph Dull (R)	7,389	(27%)
1970 general:	Walter E. Powell (R)	63,344	(52%)
	James D. Ruppert (D)	55,455	(45%)
	Joseph F. Payton (AI)	4,179	(3%)

NINTH DISTRICT Political Background

The city of Toledo rises in incongruous fashion from the flat plains of northwest Ohio (see Ohio 5). The city differs from the surrounding countryside in many ways. Situated in the middle of rich agricultural territory, Toledo is heavily industrial; set among WASP farmers and small-town residents, Toledo is heavily ethnic (mainly Polish-American); surrounded by one of the nation's most traditionally staunch Republican areas, Toledo is defiantly Democratic. Sitting at the mouth of the Maumee River, Toledo, a major Great Lakes port, handles more tonnage than the much larger city of Detroit, 60 miles away. But like Detroit, Toledo experienced its period of most substantial growth between 1910 and 1930, during the initial expansion of the auto industry. Many of the city's big concerns (Libbey-Owens-Ford, for one) remain heavily dependent on the car business.

Lucas County, which contains Toledo, is one of two in Ohio that went for George McGovern in 1972. Except for a few suburban and rural townships, most of Lucas County makes up Ohio's 9th congressional district. The 9th, of course, is a Democratic stronghold; in fact, it is the only district in northwest Ohio that elects a Democratic Congressman. The current incumbent is Thomas Ludlow Ashley, first elected in 1954. Ashley comes to the seat almost by inheritance. His great-grandfather, a radical Republican, was Toledo's Congressman during the Civil War years, and as a member of the Committee on Territories, he was responsible for choosing names for several Western states.

The present Congressman Ashley serves on committees with jurisdictions more mundane: Merchant Marine and Fisheries (Toledo, as mentioned, is a port), along with Banking and Currency. On the latter, Ashley is Chairman of the International Trade Subcommittee, which does not have all the clout its name might imply, since basic tariff legislation passes through the House Ways and Means Committee. Over the years, Ashley has devoted more energy to housing legislation, over which the often fractious Banking Committee has jurisdiction. The Nader Congress Project says that Ashley is "an unyielding foe of the strongest corporate lobby in the area—the home builders." The Congressman sponsored the section of the 1970 Housing Act that provided for a national urban growth policy. Perhaps not coincidentally, a disproportionately large share of HUD funds have found their way to Toledo. Its central city has a large urban renewel project, and a new town is going up on the outskirts.

"Lud" Ashley has had little trouble winning reelection since he first won the seat, ousting Independent Congressman Frazier Reams. About the only thing likely to cause him trouble in 1974 is a matter that most politicians would have hushed up—or tried to. In the spring of 1973, Ashley was sentenced to three days in jail and a fine for drunk driving in Toledo. In our time—a season in which high-ranking officials hide behind various forms of executive privilege or seek various kinds of immunity—Ashley served his time as, he said, any ordinary citizen would.

Census Data Pop. 463,286. Central city, 83%; suburban, 17%. Median family income, $10,786; families above $15,000: 24%; families below $3,000: 7%. Median years education, 12.1.

1972 Share of Federal Outlays $259,298,945

DOD	$37,485,957	HEW	$126,376,413
AEC	–	HUD	$5,141,141
NASA	$684,361	DOI	$135,754
DOT	$2,893,127	USDA	$12,100,245
		Other	$64,481,447

Federal Military-Industrial Commitments

DOD Contractors Teledyne (Toledo), $27.935m: gas turbine engines.

Economic Base Transportation equipment, especially motor vehicles and equipment; finance, insurance and real estate; machinery; primary metal industries, especially nonferrous foundries; and stone, clay and glass products. Also higher education (Univ. of Toledo).

The Voters

Registration No district-wide registration.
Median voting age 44.4
Employment profile White collar, 48%. Blue collar, 39%. Service, 13%. Farm, –%.
Ethnic groups Black, 12%. Spanish, 2%. Total foreign stock, 15%. Poland, Germany, 3% each; Canada, UK, 1% each.

Presidential vote

1972	Nixon (R)	83,768	(49%)
	McGovern (D)	87,151	(51%)
1968	Nixon (R)	66,329	(39%)
	Humphrey (D)	88,945	(52%)
	Wallace (AI)	16,371	(10%)

Representative

Thomas Ludlow Ashley (D) Elected 1964; b. Jan. 11, 1923, Toledo; home, Waterville; Yale U., B.A., 1948; Ohio State U., LL.B., 1951; Army, WWII; married, one child; Episcopalian.

Career Practicing atty., 1951–52; Gen. Counsel, Formed Steel Products, 1951–52; Co-Dir., Press Sec., Asst. Dir. Spec. Projects, Radio Free Europe, 1952–54.

Offices 2406 RHOB, 202-225-4146. Also 234 Summit St., Toledo 43604, 419-248-5325.

Administrative Assistant Mrs. June Clendening

Committees

Banking and Currency (5th); Subs: Housing; International Trade (Chm.); Domestic Finance; Bank Supervision and Insurance.

Merchant Marine and Fisheries (3rd); Subs: Merchant Marine; Oceanography.

Group Ratings

	ADA	COPE	LWV	RIPON	NFU	LCV	CFA	NAB	NSI	ACA
1972	88	100	92	64	71	66	100	17	60	14
1971	68	78	88	89	64	–	80	–	–	28
1970	100	91	–	82	100	80	100	20	0	11

Key Votes

1) Busing	FOR	6) Cmbodia Bmbg	AGN	11) Chkg Acct Intrst	ABS'
2) Strip Mines	AGN	7) Bust Hwy Trust	FOR	12) End HISC (HUAC)	FOR
3) Cut Mil $	FOR	8) Farm Sub Lmt	FOR	13) Nixon Sewer Veto	AGN
4) Rev Shrg	AGN	9) School Prayr	AGN	14) Corp Cmpaign $	FOR
5) Pub TV $	FOR	10) Cnsumr Prot	FOR	15) Pol $ Disclosr	ABS

Election Results

1972 general:	Thomas L. Ashley (D)	110,450	(69%)
	Joseph C. Richards (R)	49,388	(31%)
1972 primary:	Thomas L. Ashley (D)	40,466	(89%)
	Henry Black (D)	4,937	(11%)
1970 general:	Thomas L. Ashley (D)	82,777	(71%)
	Allen H. Shapiro (R)	33,947	(29%)

TENTH DISTRICT Political Background

The 10th district of Ohio is the state's southeast corner, a hilly, sparsely populated area. Though the district covers 14% of Ohio's land area, it contains only 4% of the state's residents. Marietta, on the Ohio River here, was the site of the first (1788) permanent American settlement in the Northwest Territory, ceded to the new nation by the British following the Revolutionary War. The town's Republican leanings are evidence still of the Yankee origin of its first settlers. Most of the 10th district, however, resembles West Virginia, across the Ohio River. The voters tend to think of themselves as Democrats and plunk for conservatives, which, these days, means almost exclusively for Republicans on the state and national levels. A glaring exception to the pattern is the town of Athens, where the enfranchisement of 18-year-olds at Ohio University has made for a complete turnaround in voting habits. Accordingly, Athens County, which contains Athens, was one of two Ohio counties that refused to give Richard Nixon a majority in 1972 (for the other, see Ohio 9).

The 10th's Democratic-conservative tradition has produced rather frequent changes in the district's congressional representation—an unusual phenomenon in Ohio politics. In 1958, 1960, and 1964, conservative Democrat Walter Moeller was chosen to represent the 10th, when it had rather different boundaries. In 1962, the man was conservative Republican Homer Abele. The most recent change occurred in 1966, when Republican Clarence Miller unseated Moeller by some

4,000 votes (52%). Since then Miller, like most Ohio Republican Congressmen, has worked hard to strengthen his position in the district. His efforts have succeeded, even though the 1968 redistricting added some marginal counties to his constituency. Miller has not missed a House roll call since he was first elected, and his 77% of the votes in 1972 put him up with the top winners among Ohio Congressmen.

After the 1972 victory, Miller decided to make a big committee shift in the House. In the 92nd Congress, Miller enjoyed a high seniority position on the Agriculture Committee, one not especially important to his district. The 10th has as many farmers as any Ohio district, but the farms in hilly, rocky countryside here tend to be small; moreover, they are often not the principal source of the farmers' income. Miller also had a seat on the Public Works Committee, which was considerably more important to the district. But his seat on the committee was not so valuable because the Congressman was bogged down in the middle of the seniority ladder.

In 1973, therefore, Miller became a member of the Appropriations Committee, taking the place of retired (and now deceased) Ohio Republican Frank Bow. Miller's only subcommittee assignments—Foreign Operation and Treasury, Postal Service, General Government—are far removed from his previous areas of specialization. But back in Ohio, 10th-district voters will continue to reelect incumbent Miller.

Census Data Pop. 463,353. Central city, 0%; suburban, 12%. Median family income, $7,894; families above $15,000: 10%; families below $3,000: 14%. Median years education, 11.8.

1972 Share of Federal Outlays $247,396,848

DOD	$12,594,089	HEW	$154,085,474
AEC	$161,965	HUD	$3,206,732
NASA	$75,638	DOI	$3,458
DOT	$2,355,784	USDA	$18,394,372
		Other	$56,519,336

Federal Military-Industrial Commitments

No installations or contractors receiving prime awards greater than $5,000,000.

Economic Base Stone, clay and glass products, especially pressed or blown glass and glassware; agriculture, notably cattle, dairy products, and hogs and sheep; finance, insurance and real estate; and primary metal industries, especially blast furnace and basic steel products. Also higher education (Ohio Univ.).

The Voters

Registration No district-wide registration.
Median voting age 43.2
Employment profile White collar, 39%. Blue collar, 45%. Service, 13%. Farm, 3%.
Ethnic groups Black, 2%. Total foreign stock, 3%.

Presidential vote

1972	Nixon (R)	119,083	(67%)
	McGovern (D)	58,831	(33%)
1968	Nixon (R)	89,759	(52%)
	Humphrey (D)	67,417	(39%)
	Wallace (AI)	15,689	(9%)

Representative

Clarence E. Miller (R) Elected 1966; b. Nov. 1, 1917, Lancaster; home, Lancaster; professional schooling from Intl. Correspondence School, Scranton, Pa.; married, two children; Methodist.

Career Electrical engineer; Lancaster City Council, 1957–63; Mayor of Lancaster, 1964–66.

Offices 128 CHOB, 202-225-5131. Also 212 S. Broad St., Lancaster 43130, 614-654-5149.

Administrative Assistant Robert A. Reintsema

Committees

Appropriations (19th); Subs: Foreign Operations; Treasury, Postal Service, General Government.

Group Ratings

	ADA	COPE	LWV	RIPON	NFU	LCV	CFA	NAB	NSI	ACA
1972	6	0	33	56	43	60	50	100	90	87
1971	22	8	33	56	47	–	13	–	–	79
1970	40	25	–	53	46	50	48	75	80	68

Key Votes

1) Busing	AGN	6) Cmbodia Bmbg	AGN	11) Chkg Acct Intrst	AGN
2) Strip Mines	AGN	7) Bust Hwy Trust	AGN	12) End HISC (HUAC)	AGN
3) Cut Mil $	AGN	8) Farm Sub Lmt	FOR	13) Nixon Sewer Veto	FOR
4) Rev Shrg	FOR	9) School Prayr	FOR	14) Corp Cmpaign $	AGN
5) Pub TV $	AGN	10) Cnsumr Prot	AGN	15) Pol $ Disclosr	FOR

Election Results

1972 general:	Clarence E. Miller (R)	129,683	(73%)
	Robert H. Whealey (D)	47,456	(27%)
1972 primary:	Clarence E. Miller (R)	51,052	(87%)
	Paul M. Brown (R)	7,911	(13%)
1970 general:	Clarence E. Miller (R)	80,838	(67%)
	Doug Arnett (D)	40,699	(33%)

ELEVENTH DISTRICT Political Background

After putting in years of service on Capitol Hill, some Congressmen grow more grouchily conservative. They begin to feel comfortable in the company of their colleagues and resent the demands placed on them by outsiders. The veterans have metamorphosed from young crusaders to defenders of the establishment which they, after all, have become a part. The pattern is a common one, though perhaps not seen as often today as in the past. The opposite pattern also exists. Congressmen come to Washington as believers in political orthodoxy, convinced that whatever is, is probably for the best. Then, after a few years in Congress, they change. They begin to listen to arguments and consider points of view not part of life back home; these politicians soon begin to vote and operate on committees in unorthodox fashion. Such is an increasingly common pattern in the House these days, and one exemplar is Congressman J. William Stanton of the 11th district of Ohio.

This is not what one would have predicted when Stanton first came to Congress. His first election, in 1964, was a considerable achievement. He ran in an 11th district that had rather different boundaries than at present. It included the steel-manufacturing city of Warren (pop. 63,000), no longer in the district, along with the Democratic-leaning Cleveland suburbs of Lake County (Willowick, Wickliffe, and Willoughby), industrial Ashtabula in the far northeast corner of the state, and Kent State University. The University was then less well-known than it is today, and of course it cast far fewer liberal votes. The old 11th was clearly a marginal district, having been won by a Democrat as recently as 1960. But Stanton, who campaigned as a conventional

Ohio Republican conservative, managed to run almost 20% ahead of the Goldwater-Miller ticket and to capture the seat with 55% of the votes.

Stanton's vote-getting prowess has been further demonstrated by his landslide reelection victories in 1968, 1970, and 1972. His success, in part, may come from his liberal position on issues. For example, the Congressman voted for end-the-war legislation and against the SST, and since his first election, his ADA and COPE ratings have risen considerably. A more typical wrench from tradition was his support for allowing states to divert some of their highway trust fund money for mass transit. Stanton voted for the move against the stern opposition of fellow Ohio Republican William Harsha, the ranking Republican on the Public Works Committee.

Stanton's increasing electoral majorities, however, are probably less a response to his voting record than an appreciation of the kind of constituency service that helps so many Congressmen win easy reelection in technically marginal districts. In fact, the 11th, on paper, has become more Republican and conservative in successive redistrictings. It has long since lost Warren, and by 1972, no longer included Kent or the easternmost (and most Democratic) suburbs in Lake County. The line-drawing was as much an accommodation of neighboring Democratic Congressmen as an attempt to aid Stanton, who doesn't need help. But it also might make it easier for the Republican nominee to carry the 11th in the event Stanton vacates the seat. There are rumors that he is interested in statewide office and may run for Sen. William Saxbe's seat in 1974.

Census Data Pop. 462,701. Central city, 0%; suburban, 79%. Median family income, $11,142; families above $15,000: 25%; families below $3,000: 6%. Median years education, 12.2.

1972 Share of Federal Outlays $280,797,388

DOD	$45,408,447	HEW	$128,273,393
AEC	$1,279,160	HUD	$8,061,997
NASA	$7,904,395	DOI	$145,833
DOT	$9,772,724	USDA	$8,262,908
		Other	$71,688,531

Federal Military-Industrial Commitments

DOD Contractors General Motors (Hudson), $6.638m: unspecified.
DOD Installations Use of Youngstown Municipal Airport contracted by the Air Force.

Economic Base Motor vehicles and equipment and other transportation equipment; primary metal industries, especially blast furnace and basic steel products; rubber and plastic products, especially fabricated rubber products not otherwise classified and miscellaneous plastics products; chemicals and allied products; fabricated metal products; and machinery.

The Voters

Registration No district-wide registration.
Median voting age 41.7
Employment profile White collar, 41%. Blue collar, 47%. Service, 10%. Farm, 2%.
Ethnic groups Black, 2%. Total foreign stock, 15%. Italy, UK, 2% each; Germany, Hungary, Czechoslovakia, 1% each.

Presidential vote

1972	Nixon (R)	104,236	(62%)
	McGovern (D)	63,864	(38%)
1968	Nixon (R)	71,395	(47%)
	Humphrey (D)	62,840	(41%)
	Wallace (AI)	17,970	(12%)

Representative

John William Stanton (R) Elected 1964; b. Feb. 20, 1924, Painesville; home, Painesville; Georgetown U., B.S., 1949; Army, WWII; married, one child; Catholic.

Career Lake County Commissioner, 1956–64.

Offices 2448 RHOB, 202-225-5306. Also 170 N. St. Clair St., Painesville 44077, 216-352-6167, and 10748 N. Main, Mantua 44255, 216-274-8444.

Administrative Assistant Shirlee Enders McGloon

Committees

Banking and Currency (3rd); Subs: Housing; International Finance; Small Business (Ranking Mbr.).

Sel. Com. on Small Business (3rd); Subs: Minority Small Business Enterprise and Franchising; Small Business Problems in Smaller Towns and Urban Areas (Ranking Mbr.); Taxation and Oil Imports.

Group Ratings

	ADA	COPE	LWV	RIPON	NFU	LCV	CFA	NAB	NSI	ACA
1972	19	30	70	80	43	52	50	91	100	52
1971	24	50	67	60	33	–	57	–	–	65
1970	52	50	–	94	77	38	45	83	80	41

Key Votes

1) Busing	ABS	6) Cmbodia Bmbg	FOR	11) Chkg Acct Intrst	AGN
2) Strip Mines	AGN	7) Bust Hwy Trust	FOR	12) End HISC (HUAC)	AGN
3) Cut Mil $	AGN	8) Farm Sub Lmt	FOR	13) Nixon Sewer Veto	FOR
4) Rev Shrg	FOR	9) School Prayr	ABS	14) Corp Cmpaign $	FOR
5) Pub TV $	AGN	10) Cnsumr Prot	AGN	15) Pol $ Disclosr	AGN

Election Results

1972 general:	J. William Stanton (R)	106,841	(68%)
	Dennis M. Callahan (D)	49,849	(32%)
1972 primary:	J. William Stanton (R), unopposed		
1970 general:	J. William Stanton (R)	91,437	(68%)
	Ralph Rudd (D)	42,542	(32%)

TWELFTH DISTRICT Political Background

In 1960, while campaigning in Columbus, Ohio, John F. Kennedy was greeted by a tumultuous crowd; he was moved to remark that Columbus was the city where he got the loudest cheers and the fewest votes. He was not far off the mark—at least about the votes. Columbus, like Cincinnati, is an urban Republican stronghold. Of all the urban counties in Ohio, Barry Goldwater, to name one Republican, made his best showing (46%) in Franklin County, which contains Columbus. The city's Republicanism can be explained by many of the factors that produce a similar political inclination in the rather similar city of Indianapolis, Indiana. Like Indianapolis, Columbus does have a significant black population (18%), but it has few residents of Eastern and Southern European ethnic stock. These are people who for years have provided the Democratic-vote base in places like Gary in northwest Indiana, or in Cleveland and Youngstown in northeast Ohio. Like Indianapolis, the economy of Columbus is more white-collar than most cities of the Great Lakes region. Major employers here include state government (with patronage rolls dominated by Republicans and conservative Democrats), Ohio State University, and several big banks and insurance companies.

Columbus is divided into two congressional districts, the 12th and the 15th. The line between them runs right through the middle of the city. It was carefully drawn by the Ohio Republican legislature to keep the city's students and blacks in the district (the 15th) where they can do the least harm. The 12th district takes in the east side of Columbus and its suburbs, along with two heavily Republican rural counties.

The current Congressman from the 12th is former FBI agent, state legislator, and Franklin County prosecutor Samuel Devine. In the 91st Congress, Devine helped to organize a group called the Republican Regulars. This was a hard-shell conservative organization unhappy with some Nixon Administration programs like the Family Assistance Plan. The thrust of the Administration's fiscal 1974 budget was much more welcome among Devine and the Regulars. At the beginning of the 92nd Congress, Devine challenged Illinois' John Anderson, a politician grown increasingly liberal, for the chairmanship of the House Republican Conference. Devine lost, but only by an 88–82 margin, and as consolation prize became Vice-Chairman. Many conservatives voted for Anderson out of personal friendship or Illinois delegation loyalty; so the close contest is a good indicator of the deeply conservative nature of House Republicans.

Despite the loss, Devine continues to hold a position of potential power. In the 92nd Congress, he was the ranking minority member on the House Administration Committee. But that unit is one completely dominated by Chairman Wayne Hays (see Ohio 18). So Devine was surely happy to give up his status on House Administration when he was presented with an opportunity to become the ranking Republican on the Commerce Committee at the beginning of the 93rd Congress. The main area of jurisdiction for Commerce is over federal regulatory agencies. Devine, along with a majority of the committee, usually takes positions favored by the interests that are presumably regulated.

One would suppose that Devine, coming out of heavily Republican Columbus, has no problems at election time. This is not the case. In both 1970 and 1972, Devine was challenged by hard-campaigning Democratic liberal James Goodrich. In 1970, Goodrich surprised observers when he received 42% of the votes in the district. Following the scare, the Republican legislature redrew the lines of the district and placed virtually all Ohio State students and most of the city's black community into the neighboring 15th, where Republican incumbent Chalmer Wylie was having no problems whatever. Despite the move, Goodrich did even better in 1972. So an upset in the 12th is possible in 1974. It is certain, however, that if the Democrats ever gain control of both the legislature and the governorship at the same time—something that hasn't happened since the 1930s—they will draw a marginal-to-Democratic district consisting of most of the central areas of Columbus. In such a district, a candidate like Goodrich would have an excellent chance.

Census Data Pop. 463,120. Central city, 55%; suburban, 41%. Median family income, $10,710; families above $15,000: 23%; families below $3,000: 6%. Median years education, 12.3.

1972 Share of Federal Outlays $505,527,213

DOD	$197,218,512	HEW	$163,239,643
AEC	$1,106,230	HUD	$9,005,911
NASA	$1,771,395	DOI	$1,782,541
DOT	$17,113,553	USDA	$17,418,681
		Other	$96,870,747

Federal Military-Industrial Commitments

DOD Contractors North American Rockwell (Columbus), $137.753m: Condor missile system; T-2 aircraft; OV-10 aircraft; glided bomb system.
DOD Installations Lockbourne AFB (Columbus).

Economic Base Finance, insurance and real estate; machinery, especially service industry machines; electrical equipment and supplies; and fabricated metal products.

The Voters

Registration No district-wide registration.
Median voting age 39.2
Employment profile White collar, 54%. Blue collar, 34%. Service, 11%. Farm, 1%.
Ethnic groups Black, 10%. Total foreign stock, 7%. Germany, Italy, 1% each.

Presidential vote

1972	Nixon (R)		128,129	(68%)
	McGovern (D)		61,644	(32%)
1968	Nixon (R)		81,336	(51%)
	Humphrey (D)		54,511	(34%)
	Wallace (AI)		24,509	(15%)

Representative

Samuel L. Devine (R) Elected 1958; b. Dec. 21, 1915, South Bend, Ind.; home, Columbus; Colgate U., 1933–34; Ohio State U., 1934–37; U. of Notre Dame, LL.B., 1940; married, three children; Methodist.

Career Sp. Agent, FBI, 1940–45; practicing atty., 1945–55; Ohio House of Reps., 1951–55; Pros. Atty., Franklin County, 1955–58.

Offices 2262 RHOB, 202-225-5355. Also 231 New Fed. Bldg., 85 Marconi Blvd., Columbus 43215, 614-221-3533.

Administrative Assistant John S. Hoyt

Committees

House Administration (2nd); Subs: Accounts (Ranking Mbr.); Police (Ranking Mbr.).

Interstate and Foreign Commerce (Ranking Mbr.); Sp. Sub. on Investigations (Ranking Mbr.).

Joint Com. on the Library (Ranking House Mbr.).

Group Ratings

	ADA	COPE	LWV	RIPON	NFU	LCV	CFA	NAB	NSI	ACA
1972	0	20	18	45	0	8	—	100	100	100
1971	8	9	0	35	14	–	0	–	–	100
1970	4	9	–	35	17	6	42	100	100	94

Key Votes

1) Busing	AGN	6) Cmbodia Bmbg	FOR	11) Chkg Acct Intrst	AGN
2) Strip Mines	AGN	7) Bust Hwy Trust	AGN	12) End HISC (HUAC)	AGN
3) Cut Mil $	AGN	8) Farm Sub Lmt	FOR	13) Nixon Sewer Veto	FOR
4) Rev Shrg	AGN	9) School Prayr	FOR	14) Corp Cmpaign $	FOR
5) Pub TV $	AGN	10) Cnsumr Prot	AGN	15) Pol $ Disclosr	AGN

Election Results

1972 general:	Samuel L. Devine (R)	103,655	(56%)
	James W. Goodrich (D)	81,074	(44%)
1972 primary:	Samuel L. Devine (R), unopposed		
1970 general:	Samuel L. Devine (R)	82,486	(58%)
	James W. Goodrich (D)	60,538	(42%)

THIRTEENTH DISTRICT Political Background

The 13th district of Ohio occupies a northern part of the state. It sits between Ohio's industrial, Democratic northeast and its rural, Republican center. The contours of the district have undergone a marked change in the course of redistrictings in 1964, 1968, and 1972. But throughout, the 13th has retained Lorain County, which contains about half the district's population. Most of the county's residents live in or near the industrial cities of Lorain and Elyria. Sherwood Anderson once tried to embody the feelings of Elyria, a small town in the nineteenth century, in his novel and his lament, *Winesburg, Ohio*. Lorain County also contains the little town of Oberlin, home of Oberlin College, founded by abolitionists and the first in the nation to admit both blacks and women (1833).

Before the 1964 redistricting, the 13th was a predominantly rural district that contained several Republican counties now in the 5th and 17th districts. The 13th presently has only one rural, Republican county, Medina, one which is, technically at least, part of the Cleveland metropolitan area. The rest of the district lies west of Lorain (Sandusky in Erie County) or east of Medina (the Akron suburbs of Barberton and Norton).

As it now stands, the 13th often reports Democratic margins in statewide contests. But it continues to reelect Republican Congressman Charles Mosher. Lately, he has won with margins like those he used to get when the district was rural and more Republican. With the possible exception of Dayton's Charles Whalen, Mosher is the most liberal Republican in the Ohio delegation, indeed one of the most liberal Republicans in the House. He has come by this distinction slowly. After first winning the seat in 1960, Mosher usually went along with the desires of the conservative Republican leadership. But his opposition to the Vietnam war—he was one of the first House Republicans to turn firmly against it—has led him to change his mind on other issues during the last few years.

Fortunately for Mosher, his shift of opinion on issues has roughly coincided with similar shifts made in his constituency by redistricting. So he has been reelected with ease. Mosher is now the ranking minority member of the Science and Astronautics Committee and holds the same status on the Oceanography subcommittee of Merchant Marine and Fisheries. The only possible obstacle to continued reelection is his age (68 in 1974).

Census Data Pop. 464,056. Central city, 28%; suburban, 55%. Median family income, $10,795; families above $15,000: 22%; families below $3,000: 6%. Median years education, 12.1.

1972 Share of Federal Outlays $234,074,008

DOD	$24,613,413	HEW	$113,383,068
AEC	$47,201	HUD	$3,378,540
NASA	$6,996,487	DOI	$123,033
DOT	$8,131,187	USDA	$9,015,593
		Other	$68,385,486

Federal Military-Industrial Commitments

No installations or contractors receiving prime awards greater than $5,000,000.

Economic Base Fabricated metal products; primary metal industries, especially blast furnaces and steel mills, and iron and steel foundries; transportation equipment; machinery; and rubber and plastics products.

The Voters

Registration No district-wide registration.
Median voting age 41.7
Employment profile White collar, 40%. Blue collar, 46%. Service, 12%. Farm, 2%.
Ethnic groups Black, 5%. Spanish, 2%. Total foreign stock, 15%. Germany, Hungary, 2% each; Poland, UK, Italy, Czechoslovakia, Yugoslavia, 1% each.

Presidential vote

1972	Nixon (R)	98,505	(59%)
	McGovern (D)	68,481	(41%)
1968	Nixon (R)	67,381	(43%)
	Humphrey (D)	71,992	(46%)
	Wallace (AI)	17,607	(11%)

OHIO 798

Representative

Charles Adams Mosher (R) Elected 1960; b. May 7, 1906, Sandwich, Ill.; home, Oberlin; Oberlin Col., B.A., 1928; married, two children; United Church of Christ.

Career Newsman, Aurora, Ill., 1928–38, Janesville, Wisc., 1938–40; Pres., Oberlin Printing Co.; Editor-Publisher, Oberlin *News-Tribune,* 1940–62; Oberlin City Council, 1945–59; Ohio Senate, 1951–60.

Offices 2442 RHOB, 202-225-3401. Also 517 E. 28th St., Lorain 44055, 216-244-1572.

Administrative Assistant William H. Oliver

Committees

Merchant Marine and Fisheries (3rd); Subs: Merchant Marine; Oceanography (Ranking Mbr.); Panama Canal.

Science and Astronautics (Ranking Mbr.).

Group Ratings

	ADA	COPE	LWV	RIPON	NFU	LCV	CFA	NAB	NSI	ACA
1972	56	50	83	75	67	73	100	44	17	21
1971	81	45	100	100	64	–	71	–	–	32
1970	88	67	–	94	92	60	64	64	10	42

Key Votes

1) Busing	FOR	6) Cmbodia Bmbg	AGN	11) Chkg Acct Intrst	ABS
2) Strip Mines	AGN	7) Bust Hwy Trust	FOR	12) End HISC (HUAC)	FOR
3) Cut Mil $	FOR	8) Farm Sub Lmt	ABS	13) Nixon Sewer Veto	FOR
4) Rev Shrg	ABS	9) School Prayr	AGN	14) Corp Cmpaign $	AGN
5) Pub TV $	AGN	10) Cnsumr Prot	FOR	15) Pol $ Disclosr	FOR

Election Results

1972 general:	Charles A. Mosher (R)	111,242	(68%)
	John Michael Ryan (D)	51,991	(32%)
1972 primary:	Charles A. Mosher (R)	23,456	(81%)
	Daniel E. Kenyon (R)	5,509	(19%)
1970 general:	Charles A. Mosher (R)	85,858	(62%)
	Joseph J. Bartolomeo (D)	53,271	(38%)

FOURTEENTH DISTRICT Political Background

Akron is the rubber capital of America, the city where most of our millions of automobile and truck tires are produced. The rubber industry imparts a peculiar odor to the city and gives its politics an old-time character. Political contests here are still very often what they were in the 1930s and 1940s—classic confrontations between labor and management. Because labor has the numbers, Akron and the surrounding 14th congressional district usually go Democratic in state and national elections. But management spends more money and shows more entrepreneurial skill. Akron is the home town of Ray Bliss, longtime Ohio Republican State Chairman and the man most responsible for the GOP's Ohio victories over the years.

The 1970 collapse of the Republican state ticket was paralleled in Akron by the defeat of Republican Congressman William Ayres, a man out of the Bliss organization, of course. Bliss always prided himself on matching candidates to their districts, and for the 20 years Ayres served in the House, he was perfectly suited to Akron. A plumber by profession, the Congressman was an unabashed gladhander—always ready to show up at Rotary Club luncheons, rubber company picnics, and Akron's now-tainted Soap Box Derby. Here and at other places he mingled among the voters, cracked jokes and pressed the flesh.

Ayres helped Akron's many ethnic residents with ethnic problems and also won the favor of pastors of the largest West Virginia fundamentalist churches. An extraordinary number of Akron voters have roots in West Virginia, having left it to find work in the Goodyear, Goodrich, General Tire, and Firestone tire factories. Country and Western blues, recalling the green grass of home, are often written by, and sold to, homesick people from the Appalachians forced to live in places like Akron, Cincinnati, Detroit, or Flint. There is the story about the Akron judge who sentenced a prisoner to jail or West Virginia; he was promptly defeated at the next election.

In 1970, Ayres still looked like he was riding high. He was the ranking member of the House Education and Labor Committee. Over the years, he tempered his allegiance to the conservative Republican leadership just enough to appease labor voters back in Akron. But during the 1960s, his majorities began to dwindle quietly. Ayres was always a prime Democratic target; in 1968, he won with only 55% of the votes in what was otherwise a pretty good year for Ohio Republicans.

The fact that five Democrats fought for the right to oppose Ayres in 1970 was another sign of his vulnerability. The winner of the primary was John Seiberling, Jr., whose grandfather founded both the Seiberling and Goodyear rubber companies. Though Seiberling was a staff lawyer for Goodyear, his labor credentials were not bad. For example, he had supported the recent strike by the United Rubber Workers. Also an ecology buff, Seiberling worked for some years to keep power lines and highways out of the Cuyahoga River valley. Ayres, on the other hand, was named one of the Dirty Dozen by the Washington-based Environmental Action group. Moreover, Seiberling was a longtime foe of the Vietnam war; Ayres supported the Nixon Administration position.

Many of Ayres' previous Democratic opponents were well-known in the district, but all of them lost to Ayres. Taking a solid 56%, Seiberling won. Why? The answers tell us about changes that have come over politics in Akron, which are apparent not just in Seiberling's victory in 1970, but in the presidential returns in 1972. The key is a slow shift from labor-vs.-management politics to the politics of peace and ecology.

In the congressional campaign, Ayres attacked Seiberling, showing the voters a photo of the challenger speaking before students at the University of Akron just after the Kent State shootings. Seiberling then turned the matter around. He made it clear to the voters that the photo recorded his attempt to convince students to protest peaceably and to work through the system. Later, the Akron *Beacon-Journal*, a newspaper that had supported Ayres for 20 years, backed Seiberling. The *Beacon-Journal* is the flagship paper of the chain owned by John S. Knight (he has others in Philadelphia, Detroit, Miami, and Charlotte). On most issues, Knight is a rather conservative Republican, but he has opposed American involvement in Indochina steadily since the 1950s. The *Beacon-Journal*'s endorsement was Seiberling's seal of respectability. Ayres' other opponents had usually won the bulk of the union vote; but only Seiberling, whose last name is almost as familiar as the name Ford in Detroit, could win the extra 10% of the votes needed for victory.

In 1972, the same issues appear to have affected the Akron area results, with peace and ecology cutting a pattern here different from the one made in most industrial cities. Seiberling was easily reelected with almost 75% of the votes. For the election, the town of Kent and Kent State University were added to the district, but had little impact on Seiberling's whopping margin. In the presidential race, however, the 14th district actually went for peace candidate George McGovern—one of three Ohio districts to do so. Moreover, it gave him a larger percentage of its votes than it had given Hubert Humphrey four years earlier.

The relative performance of these two Democrats here lies in stark contrast to those found in other centers of industry, like those in nearby western Pennsylvania, where the Democratic percentage plummeted more than 10% between the two elections. One reason for Akron's behavior is that it contains fewer ethnic Americans than many other factory towns; ethnics comprise the groups among whom Democratic defections were the most extensive. But another reason, apparently, was the positive appeal in Akron of McGovern's stance on the issues. The South Dakotan was certainly helped here by the support he received from the United Rubber Workers, which like UAW, backed him strongly.

In the House, Seiberling has voted almost invariably with peace and pro-ecology forces. About his only concession to more traditional politics is a sponsorship of a repeal of the excise tax on tires. Seiberling is not an ambitious man, or one particularly enamored with politics, but indications are that he will be reelected for as long as he likes.

Census Data Pop. 464,578. Central city, 59%; suburban, 41%. Median family income, $10,876; families above $15,000: 24%; families below $3,000: 7%. Median years education, 12.2.

1972 Share of Federal Outlays $281,373,034

DOD	$75,750,264	HEW	$124,293,311
AEC	$32,490	HUD	$12,520,110
NASA	$200,991	DOI	$368,950
DOT	$1,948,056	USDA	$6,523,518
		Other	$59,735,344

Federal Military-Industrial Commitments

DOD Contractors Goodyear Aerospace (Akron), $36.704m: engineering services for anti-submarine weapons system. Goodyear Tire and Rubber (Akron), $22.343m: aircraft brakes, wheels, tires; tank tracks. B.F. Goodrich (Akron), $8.477m: aircraft brakes, wheels and tires.

Economic Base Rubber and plastics products, especially tires and inner tubes; fabricated metal products, especially fabricated structural metal products; finance, insurance and real estate; machinery, especially metalworking machinery; and paper and allied products, especially paper coating and glazing. Also higher education (Kent State Univ.).

The Voters

Registration No district-wide registration.
Median voting age 42.4
Employment profile White collar, 49%. Blue collar, 38%. Service, 13%. Farm, –%.
Ethnic groups Black, 11%. Total foreign stock, 14%. Italy, 2%; Germany, UK, Yugoslavia, Hungary, 1% each.

Presidential vote

1972	Nixon (R)	88,384	(48%)
	McGovern (D)	94,320	(52%)
1968	Nixon (R)	67,145	(39%)
	Humphrey (D)	85,837	(49%)
	Wallace (AI)	21,320	(12%)

Representative

John F. Seiberling (D) Elected 1970; b. Sept. 8, 1918, Akron; home, Akron; Harvard Col., B.A., 1941; Columbia U. Law School, LL.B., 1947; Army, WWII; married, three children; Protestant.

Career Practicing atty., 1949–54; legal staff, Goodyear Tire & Rubber Co., 1954–70; Mbr., Tri-County Regional Planning Commission, 1964–70.

Offices 1234 LHOB, 202-225-5231. Also 411 Wolf Ledges, Akron 44322, 216-762-9323.

Administrative Assistant Donald W. Mansfield

Committees

Interior and Insular Affairs (17th); Subs: Environment; Mines and Mining; National Parks and Recreation.

Judiciary (13th); Subs: Immigration, Citizenship and International Law; Monopolies and Commercial Law.

Group Ratings

	ADA	COPE	LWV	RIPON	NFU	LCV	CFA	NAB	NSI	ACA
1972	100	100	100	84	83	86	100	0	0	5
1971	89	82	88	72	92	–	86	–	–	8

Key Votes

1) Busing	FOR	6) Cmbodia Bmbg	AGN	11) Chkg Acct Intrst	FOR
2) Strip Mines	AGN	7) Bust Hwy Trust	FOR	12) End HISC (HUAC)	FOR
3) Cut Mil $	FOR	8) Farm Sub Lmt	FOR	13) Nixon Sewer Veto	AGN
4) Rev Shrg	FOR	9) School Prayr	AGN	14) Corp Cmpaign $	AGN
5) Pub TV $	FOR	10) Cnsumr Prot	FOR	15) Pol $ Disclosr	AGN

Election Results

1972 general:	John F. Seiberling, Jr. (D)	135,068	(74%)
	Norman W. Holt (R)	46,490	(26%)
1972 primary:	John F. Seiberling, Jr. (D)	53,897	(82%)
	William James Lambert, Jr. (D)	11,964	(18%)
1970 general:	John F. Seiberling, Jr. (D)	71,282	(56%)
	William H. Ayres (R)	55,038	(44%)

FIFTEENTH DISTRICT Political Background

The 15th district of Ohio comprises the west side of Columbus, its Franklin County suburbs, and Pickaway County to the west. Next to Cincinnati, Columbus is Ohio's most Republican metropolitan area; it is also the state's fastest-growing one (see Ohio 12). The 15th, as it was first created in the 1964 and 1968 redistrictings, was the more Republican of the two Columbus districts, in large part because of Upper Arlington. This suburb, just across the Scioto River from the Ohio State campus, is the largest in the Columbus area (pop. 38,000) and one of the most Republican (78% for Nixon in 1968, and 81% in 1972).

The first and only Congressman from the 15th has been Chalmers P. Wylie, a former state legislator and Columbus city attorney (an elective post). Wylie has compiled a solidly conservative record in Washington. He is best known among his colleagues for his work on the school prayer issue. Wylie perennially introduces and pushes a constitutional amendment to overturn the Supreme Court decision that prevented state-sponsored prayers in public schools.

Unlike Samuel Devine, who represents the other half of Columbus, Wylie has not attracted vigorous opposition in recent elections. Perhaps for that reason, at redistricting time, the Republican Ohio legislature took some of the more troublesome areas out of Devine's constituency and put them into Wylie's. As a result, Wylie's portion of the city of Columbus is actually Democratic in most elections; he has 17,000 more blacks and about that many more college students (mostly on the Ohio State campus) than he did before 1972. The two groups had already demonstrated their potential clout when they voted solidly against conservative Democratic Mayor Maynard E. Sensenbrenner and installed moderate Republican Tom Moody in 1971. Wylie, however, is not their kind of Republican. His percentage slipped a bit in 1972 despite Richard Nixon's triumph in Columbus. So it is possible that Wylie will attract fromidable opposition in some future election.

Census Data Pop. 462,703. Central city, 52%; suburban, 32%. Median family income, $10,074; families above $15,000: 23%; families below $3,000: 9%. Median years education, 12.3.

1972 Share of Federal Outlays $503,026,651

DOD	$194,172,936	HEW	$163,574,449
AEC	$1,087,647	HUD	$8,854,629
NASA	$1,741,639	DOI	$1,752,598
DOT	$16,407,172	USDA	$19,330,824
		Other	$96,104,757

Federal Military-Industrial Commitments

DOD Contractors Battelle Memorial Institute (Columbus), $10.293m: various technical studies.

Economic Base Finance, insurance and real estate; electrical equipment and supplies; machinery, especially service industry machines; fabricated metal products; and food and kindred products. Also higher education (Ohio State Univ.).

The Voters

>   *Registration* No district-wide registration.
>   *Median voting age* 39.1
>   *Employment profile* White collar, 57%. Blue collar, 29%. Service, 13%. Farm, 1%.
>   *Ethnic groups* Black, 13%. Total foreign stock, 7%. Germany, 1%.

Presidential vote

1972	Nixon (R)	119,846	(65%)
	McGovern (D)	65,381	(35%)
1968	Nixon (R)	87,406	(54%)
	Humphrey (D)	55,970	(35%)
	Wallace (AI)	18,578	(11%)

Representative

Chalmers Pangburn Wylie (R) Elected 1966; b. Nov. 23, 1920, Norwich; home, Columbus; Otterbein Col., Ohio State U., B.A.; Harvard Law School, LL.B.; Army, WWII; Lt. Col. USAR; married, two children; Methodist.

Career Asst. City Atty., Columbus, 1949–50; Asst. Atty. Gen. of Ohio, 1948, 1951–54; City Atty., 1953–56; Admin., Bureau of Workmen's Compensation, 1957; First Asst. to Gov., 1957–58; practicing atty., 1959–66; State Rep., 1961–67; Pres., Ohio Municipal League, 1957.

Offices 137 CHOB, 202-225-2015, Also 404 Fed. Bldg., 85 Marconi Blvd., Columbus 43215, 614-469-5614.

Administrative Assistant Jack M. Foulk

Committees

Banking and Currency (7th); Subs: Bank Supervision and Insurance; Consumer Affairs (Ranking Mbr.); Urban Mass Transportation.

Veterans' Affairs (6th); Subs: Education and Training; Hospitals; Compensation and Pension.

Group Ratings

	ADA	COPE	LWV	RIPON	NFU	LCV	CFA	NAB	NSI	ACA
1972	6	18	45	58	43	40	100	100	100	83
1971	11	8	50	65	20	–	0	–	–	89
1970	24	18	–	53	23	50	50	91	100	89

Key Votes

1) Busing	AGN	6) Cmbodia Bmbg	FOR	11) Chkg Acct Intrst	AGN
2) Strip Mines	ABS	7) Bust Hwy Trust	FOR	12) End HISC (HUAC)	AGN
3) Cut Mil $	AGN	8) Farm Sub Lmt	FOR	13) Nixon Sewer Veto	FOR
4) Rev Shrg	FOR	9) School Prayr	FOR	14) Corp Cmpaign $	AGN
5) Pub TV $	AGN	10) Cnsumr Prot	AGN	15) Pol $ Disclosr	FOR

Election Results

1972 general:	Chalmers P. Wylie (R)	115,779	(66%)
	Manley L. McGee (D)	55,314	(31%)
	Edward Price (AI)	4,820	(3%)
1972 primary:	Chalmers P. Wylie (R), unopposed		
1970 general:	Chalmers P. Wylie (R)	81,536	(71%)
	Manley L. McGee (D)	34,018	(29%)

SIXTEENTH DISTRICT Political Background

Canton, Ohio is the home of the Pro Football Hall of Fame. But to American historians, Canton is most memorable as the home of President William McKinley. It was here that McKinley sat on his famous front porch in 1896 and received the delegations of voters carefully selected by Republican organizations throughout the country. And it was also here that he received the news that he had been elected President over William Jennings Bryan. Some historians of either the progressive or new left inclination still attempt to prop up the notion that factory workers voted for McKinley only because their bosses threatened to fire them if they didn't. What is sometimes forgotten today is that a factor behind McKinley's triumph was his ability to attract the votes of workingmen. No more evidence of coercion exists in the election of 1896 than at any other presidential election; indeed the election of this staid gentleman has less taint to it than other much more recent attempts to elect or reelect a President. According to some, McKinley was only the plaything of Cleveland industrialist Mark Hanna, another all-time heavy in American history. But McKinley was also a man who won the enthusiastic votes of workingmen in Canton, Ohio.

McKinley's big issue was the tariff. During the 1890s, steel was still an "infant industry" in the United States. And in Canton, steelworkers and steel mill owners both believed that the industry needed protection from foreign competition. Then, as now, steel was big in Canton. Today we seem to have come full circle. The steel barons and the United Steel Workers under I. W. Abel are again asking for trade barriers, saying that they cannot compete with the efficiency practiced by German and Japanese makers of the product.

McKinley was elected to the House of Representatives six times from the rough equivalent of what is now Ohio's 16th congressional district: Stark County, which includes Canton and the smaller industrial cities of Massillon and Alliance; Wayne County, a rural and small-town area which takes in John Dean's alma mater of Wooster College; and two rural townships in Medina County. Canton (pop. 100,000) has a habit of going Democratic, but outside the city limits the voting gets much more heavily Republican. Over the years, the Republicans have controlled the district more often than not. In the more volatile nineteenth century, however, Congressman McKinley twice lost his seat to Democratic challengers. At that time, Congress had no seniority rule, and so McKinley became Chairman of the Ways and Means Committee without spending 20 or 30 years in apprenticeship.

More recently, the 16th's Congressman was the late Frank Bow, who was first elected in 1950 and rose to become the ranking Republican on the House Appropriations Committee. After being held to 56% of the votes in 1970, Bow decided to retire in 1972 and did not appear on the ballot. But he was denied retirement and the substantial pension he had earned when he died during the last days of the 92nd Congress, at age 71.

The Republican nominee in 1972 was state Sen. Ralph Regula, considered a moderate in Canton. Regula's opponent was 38-year-old Virgil Musser, who had run a creditable race against Bow two years before. But this time, Musser's performance in Canton and Stark County sagged, though he actually did better in rural Wayne County, probably because of the votes out of Wooster College. In the House, Regula serves on the Government Operations and Interior committees, the latter assignment being an unusual one for a man from this part of the country.

Census Data Pop. 463,699. Central city, 24%; suburban, 57%. Median family income, $10,197; families above $15,000: 19%; families below $3,000: 6%. Median years education, 12.1.

1972 Share of Federal Outlays $221,379,350

DOD	$23,247,488	HEW	$127,042,250
AEC	$2,400	HUD	$3,093,603
NASA	$334,600	DOI	$171,635
DOT	$355,913	USDA	$11,535,713
		Other	$55,595,748

Federal Military-Industrial Commitments

DOD Contractors White Engines (Canton), $16.127m: various truck engine components.

Economic Base Machinery; primary metal industries, especially blast furnace and steel mill products; fabricated metal products; finance, insurance and real estate; and food and kindred products, especially meat products.

The Voters

Registration No district-wide registration.
Median voting age 43.3
Employment profile White collar, 41%. Blue collar, 45%. Service, 12%. Farm, 2%.
Ethnic groups Black, 5%. Total foreign stock, 11%. Italy, 2%; Germany, UK, 1% each.

Presidential vote

1972	Nixon (R)	113,402	(65%)
	McGovern (D)	61,173	(35%)
1968	Nixon (R)	84,405	(50%)
	Humphrey (D)	66,946	(39%)
	Wallace (AI)	18,844	(11%)

Representative

Ralph S. Regula (R) Elected 1972; b. Dec. 3. 1924, Beach City; home, RFD 3, Navarre; Mt. Union Col., B.A., 1948; Wm. McKinley School of Law, LL.B., 1952; married, three children.

Career Practicing atty., 1952–73; Ohio Bd. of Ed., 1960–64; State Rep., 1965–66; State Sen., 1967–72.

Offices 1729 LHOB, 202-225-3876. Also 717 39th St., NE, Canton, 216-456-2869.

Administrative Assistant Robert M. Gants

Committees

Government Operations (14th); Subs: Foreign Operations and Government Information; Special Studies.

Interior and Insular Affairs (11th); Subs: National Parks and Recreation; Territorial and Insular Affairs; Public Lands.

Group Ratings: Newly Elected

Key Votes

1) Busing	NE	6) Cmbodia Bmbg	FOR	11) Chkg Acct Intrst	AGN
2) Strip Mines	NE	7) Bust Hwy Trust	FOR	12) End HISC (HUAC)	AGN
3) Cut Mil $	NE	8) Farm Sub Lmt	NE	13) Nixon Sewer Veto	FOR
4) Rev Shrg	NE	9) School Prayr	NE	14) Corp Cmpaign $	NE
5) Pub TV $	NE	10) Cnsumr Prot	NE	15) Pol $ Disclosr	NE

Election Results

1972 general:	Ralph S. Regula (R)	102,013	(57%)
	Virgil L. Musser (D)	75,929	(43%)
1972 primary:	Ralph S. Regula (R)	40,506	(86%)
	Edward A. Mahoney, Jr. (R)	6,677	(14%)

SEVENTEENTH DISTRICT Political Background

Congressman John Ashbrook of Ohio's 17th district began his 1972 presidential campaign as the least-known major-party candidate. He finished his campaign not much better known. By almost any standard, Ashbrook's candidacy was a flop: he got no more than 10% of the votes in any of the primaries he entered, and he failed to get a single delegate vote at the Republican National Convention. Ashbrook did not, however, run with any hope of winning, but rather out of deeply held principle.

Ashbrook is one of several House Republicans who can be described as an ideological conservative. Accordingly, much of his quarrel with Richard Nixon was over the Administration's policy of rapprochment with what Nixon now calls the People's Republic of China. Ashbrook's other major disagreement with the Administration was the wage-price freeze. Committed to the free market, the Congressman opposes all mandatory controls. Neither issue ever caught on—at least for Ashbrook. Nixon's China policy was probably his biggest vote-getter, and during the campaign at least, his economic policies were widely popular.

Not too long ago, any hint of accommodation with what Nixon used to call Red China would have sparked howls of protest from editorial writers and powerful politicians all over the nation. More important, any move toward mainland China would have angered hundreds of thousands, perhaps millions, of voters brought up on the idea that Chiang Kai-shek had created an American-style democracy in Asia. Ashbrook's campaign showed clearly that those days are gone; the China Lobby can no longer command significant popular support in the United States. His campaign also demonstrated that American voters, even Republican voters, are willing to accept economic controls, so long as they feel that they themselves will not be hurt by the restraints. The reaction to the Administration's Phase III program made plain that the public's enthusiasm for controls quickly wane when its own ox—or beef—is gored. Ashbrook probably took some satisfaction from the public's adverse reaction to Phase III, and he no doubt took even more satisfaction from the rightward-moving spending priorities in the Administration's fiscal 1974 budget.

Ashbrook's unpleasant campaign experience proved conclusively that the American public did not share his most deeply held convictions. Nevertheless, candidate Ashbrook remained dignified and sometimes even quietly humorous throughout the entire affair. The press never paid much attention to him, largely because Ashbrook lacked the fire and intensity of Nixon's other Republican challenger, liberal Peter McCloskey of California.

Nor has Ashbrook attracted much attention in the House. He is ranking minority member of the House Internal Security Committee (formerly the House Un-American Activities Committee). But that congressional panel no longer conducts the chaotic, free-wheeling investigations it did in the days when Richard Nixon, for one, was a member. Ashbrook is also the second-ranking Republican on the Education and Labor Committee. Here, too, he makes little news, although he did play a major—and seemingly uncharacteristic—role in pushing through the bill to allow labor unions to bargain for group legal services. But usually the Congressman's conservative views are so far out of line with those held by the committee's liberal majority that he seldom has any impact on legislation.

One reason Ashbrook felt free to take on a quixotic presidential bid was the apparent safeness of his district. To be sure, he had won it for the first time in 1960 against a Democrat who snuck in by virtue of the 1958 anti-right-to-work landslide in Ohio. But in recent years, the 17th has gone solidly Republican in all statewide and, of course, all congressional elections. The district is composed almost entirely of rural and small-town counties in north-central Ohio; the 17th's largest city is Mansfield (pop. 53,000).

Nevertheless, when Ashbrook got home from his presidential campaigning in 1972, he discovered that his support in the district had eroded somewhat. Though Ashbrook easily defeated a challenger in the May Republican primary, the incumbent was held to 57% in the November general election. That figure is considerably lower than the 62% and the 65% he won in the more Democratic years of 1970 and 1968. Some of the voters here probably resented Ashbrook running against the President; moreover, an American Independent party candidate siphoned off 4% of the vote. The 1972 results in the 17th do not spell problems for Ashbrook in 1974, but they do indicate that he paid some price for acting on his principles.

For all his troubles, Ashbrook is reportedly considering a Senate try in 1974. His chances of winning are very slight, even if Sen. William Saxbe decides to retire (see Ohio state write-up). For Ashbrook's ideological conservativism does not sit well with Ohio's conservative *and* pragmatic Republican party organization.

Census Data Pop. 462,846. Central city, 12%; suburban, 16%. Median family income, $9,460; families above $15,000: 16%; families below $3,000: 9%. Median years education, 12.1.

1972 Share of Federal Outlays $254,621,889

DOD	$56,883,951	HEW	$115,760,435
AEC	–	HUD	$2,626,752
NASA	$53,594	DOI	$396,976
DOT	$4,959,536	USDA	$16,838,302
		Other	$57,102,343

Federal Military-Industrial Commitments

No installations or contractors receiving prime awards greater than $5,000,000.

Economic Base Agriculture, notably dairy products, grains, cattle, and hogs and sheep; electrical equipment and supplies; machinery, especially general industrial machinery; fabricated metal products; and finance, insurance and real estate.

The Voters

Registration No district-wide registration.
Median voting age 42.7
Employment profile White collar, 38%. Blue collar, 46%. Service, 12%. Farm, 4%.
Ethnic groups Black, 3%. Total foreign stock, 6%. Germany, 1%.

Presidential vote

1972	Nixon (R)	111,545	(69%)
	McGovern (D)	50,374	(31%)
1968	Nixon (R)	89,436	(54%)
	Humphrey (D)	58,551	(35%)
	Wallace (AI)	18,828	(11%)

Representative

John Milan Ashbrook (R) Elected 1960; b. Sept. 21, 1928, Johnstown; home, Johnstown; Harvard U., B.A., 1952; Ohio State U., J.D., 1955; Navy, 1946–48; three children; Baptist.

Career Publisher, *Johnstown Independent,* 1953– ; practicing atty., 1955– ; Young Repub. Chm., 1957–59; Ohio House of Reps., 1956–60.

Offices 206 CHOB, 202-225-6431. Also 53 S. Main St., Johnstown 43031, 614-967-5941, and 43 W. Main St., Ashland 44805, 419-322-1732, and 130½ E. Liberty St., Wooster 44691, 216-264-9779.

Administrative Assistant Electra C. Wheatley

Committees

Education and Labor (2nd); Subs: No. 2 (Sp. Sub. on Labor) (Ranking Mbr.); No. 1 (General Sub. on Education).

Internal Security (Ranking Mbr.).

Group Ratings

	ADA	COPE	LWV	RIPON	NFU	LCV	CFA	NAB	NSI	ACA
1972	6	10	9	15	14	9	50	100	100	100
1971	8	10	0	27	8	–	0	–	–	93
1970	4	25	–	18	15	40	33	75	100	93

Key Votes

1) Busing	AGN	6) Cmbodia Bmbg	AGN	11) Chkg Acct Intrst	AGN
2) Strip Mines	FOR	7) Bust Hwy Trust	AGN	12) End HISC (HUAC)	AGN
3) Cut Mil $	FOR	8) Farm Sub Lmt	FOR	13) Nixon Sewer Veto	FOR
4) Rev Shrg	AGN	9) School Prayr	FOR	14) Corp Cmpaign $	FOR
5) Pub TV $	ABS	10) Cnsumr Prot	AGN	15) Pol $ Disclosr	AGN

Election Results

1972 general:	John M. Ashbrook (R)	92,666	(57%)
	Raymond Beck (D)	62,512	(39%)
	Clifford J. Simpson (AI)	6,376	(4%)
1972 primary:	John M. Ashbrook (R)	28,582	(75%)
	William L. White (R)	9,366	(25%)
1970 general:	John M. Ashbrook (R)	79,472	(62%)
	James C. Hood (D)	44,066	(34%)
	Clifford J. Simpson (AI)	4,253	(3%)

EIGHTEENTH DISTRICT **Political Background**

Probably the most hated, and certainly the most feared, man in the House of Representatives today is Congressman Wayne Hays of the 18th district of Ohio. In the last three or four years, he has also become one of the most powerful members of the House. Hays holds several institutional positions of great leverage: the chairmanship of the House Administration Committee, the chairmanship of the Democratic Congressional Campaign Committee, and the number-three spot on the Foreign Affairs Committee, along with the chairmanship of the Foreign Affairs subcommittee that oversees State Department operations. But his clout depends finally on the fact that he is mean.

In the House, where even the most bitter disputes are cloaked in words of elaborate courtesy, Hays is always ready with an insult—not just in the cloakroom, but on the floor. He has lashed out at such powers as Speaker Carl Albert ("everybody thought McCormack was the weakest Speaker in memory, but Albert's beginning to make him look like Superman") and Ways and Means Chairman Wilbur Mills (in the words of writer Marshall Frady, suggesting "that Mills' conversion to revenue sharing had perhaps been prompted by a vertigo lingering from Mills' brief Presidential fancies").

Such incidents have made Hays the subject of recent articles in the *Wall Street Journal*, the *New York Times*, Newsweek, and *Playboy*. But for the first 22 years of his House career (he was first elected in 1948), the press paid little attention to him. And neither did many Congressmen until he became Chairman of the House Administration Committee in 1971. Previously, the chairmanship had been just a housekeeping post. So it was scarcely news when the preceding Chairman, Samuel Friedel of Baltimore, was defeated in a 1970 primary; the Chairman before Friedel, Omar Burleson of Texas, thought so little of the committee's jurisdiction that he gave up the top post for a junior seat on the Ways and Means Committee.

But Hays had other ideas. He set up a computer system, which now leaves other Congressmen drooling for access to it, and he pushed the House into adopting an electronic voting system. Hays also cut costs and raised prices in the House cafeteria, raised the prices charged by House barbers, and took the operator's seats out of the House elevators—all actions designed to give the taxpayer more work for his money. Nor did Hays stop here. The Congressman mercilessly slashed the staff help of House Doorkeeper Fishbait Miller, who has been a fixture on Capitol Hill for almost 30 years. And once, when an aide to Minnesota Rep. Donald Fraser arranged for witnesses to testify before Hays' Foreign Affairs Subcommittee, the Congressman refused to sign the aide's pay voucher; later, in an encore, Hays went back to the 18th district for a while and left dozens of pay vouchers of House employees unsigned. Not many people on the House side of the Hill will say a bad word about Hays for attribution.

The House Administration Committee also affects the outside world, for it has jurisdiction over campaign-spending legislation. Here Hays has been accused of conflict of interest. He steered the 1971 campaign-spending bill to passage, but in the process, or so say many critics, cut out some key provisions. At this writing, it seems certain that Hays will have an important, if not crucial, say on what happens to such legislation in 1973 and 1974. In any case, the accusations of conflict of interest arose because Hays chairs the Democratic Congressional Campaign Committee, and under its current regulations, which it seems to like, the committee can direct money from a certain contributor to a specific congressional candidate without telling anyone that the money was so earmarked. Apparently to keep something of a watch over Hays, House Majority Leader Tip O'Neill has been installed as Vice-Chairman of the Campaign Committee.

Despite the heavy workload carried by Hays in the House Administration Committee, he also remains active on the Foreign Affairs Committee. The Congressman is a veteran participant of NATO parliamentary conferences, and he regularly travels to Europe for meetings with legislators of other countries. In the foreign policy area, Hays is best known as a determined hawk on Vietnam. But his views on this issue, as on so many others, cannot be easily categorized. For years, Hays voted to support the war effort. Yet when President Nixon vetoed the first piece of legislation that banned the bombing in Cambodia, Hays announced that he would offer antiwar amendments to every bill on the floor. In his view, it was a matter of Congress not knuckling under to the executive branch. Hays has also led congressional moves to cut off military aid to Greece, saying he doesn't like dictators who won't hold elections. And, though Hays has sneering contempt for antiwar protestors, he is just as caustic toward the Pentagon brass. Some observers mistakenly view Hays as an unlettered buffoon. He is not. Even his detractors on the Hill—and they are legion, if usually anonymous—concede that he is smart and does his homework. And his insults are almost always directed carefully and shrewdly.

If not many people in Washington like Wayne Hays, his constituents in Ohio do. In the 1972 primary, some 61% of the voters of the 18th district cast their ballots for national convention delegates pledged to Wayne Hays for President. (The other 39% went to delegates for George McGovern, no Hays favorite.) Hays, of course, will never become President, but he will remain the Congressman from the 18th district for as long as he wants. His district consists of the industrial, coal-mining, and marginal farm country across the Ohio River from West Virginia. It is heavily Democratic and Hays wins reelection by overwhelming margins: about 70–30 in 1972, for example.

The small city of Steubenville (pop. 30,000) in the 18th enjoys the distinction of having the dirtiest air in the country. Or so says the National Air Pollution Control Administration. Beyond foul air, much of Belmont County, where Hays himself lives, is given over to the strip mining of coal—an environmental blight that Hays has introduced legislation to put under better regulation. The people of the 18th are the kind of Americans who work hard, get little for it, and pay taxes with few complaints. So Hays is probably speaking for them when he eliminates $33,000 House staff jobs in Washington. However unpleasant Hays may be, he is something of a tribune for a poor and feisty district, and his constituents seem to appreciate his services.

Census Data Pop. 462,797. Central city, 7%; suburban, 32%. Median family income, $8,701; families above $15,000: 11%; families below $3,000: 11%. Median years education, 11.5.

1972 Share of Federal Outlays $240,633,793

DOD	$6,820,793	HEW	$138,985,947
AEC	$15,347,759	HUD	$2,855,908
NASA	$12,487	DOI	$1,758,950
DOT	$2,066,960	USDA	$12,050,839
		Other	$60,734,150

Federal Military-Industrial Commitments

No installations or contractors receiving prime awards greater than $5,000,000.

Economic Base Primary metal industries; stone, clay and glass products, especially pottery and related products and structural clay products; machinery; bituminous coal mining; and agriculture, notably dairy products, cattle and poultry.

The Voters

Registration No district-wide registration.
Median voting age 46.4
Employment profile White collar, 34%. Blue collar, 51%. Service, 12%. Farm, 3%.
Ethnic groups Black, 2%. Total foreign stock, 12%. Italy, 3%; UK, 2%; Poland, Czechoslovakia, Germany, 1% each.

Presidential vote

1972	Nixon (R)	111,800	(61%)
	McGovern (D)	72,581	(39%)
1968	Nixon (R)	78,803	(41%)
	Humphrey (D)	95,894	(50%)
	Wallace (AI)	17,152	(9%)

Representative

Wayne L. Hays (D) Elected 1948; b. May 13, 1911, Bannock; home, Flushing; Ohio State U., B.S., 1933; Duke U., 1935; USAR, WWII; married, one child; Presbyterian.

Career Belmont County Commissioner, 1945–49; owner, Red Gate Farms; Mayor of Flushing, 1939–45; Ohio State Senator, 1941–42; Chm. of Bd., Citizens Natl. Bank; Pres., NATO Parliamentarians' Conference, 1956–57; V.Pres. N. Atlantic Assembly, 1958–60, 1962–68, 1971– .

Offices 2264 RHOB, 202-225-6265. Also Flushing 43977, 614-968-4114, and Columbia 44408, 216-482-3317.

Administrative Assistant H. Elaine Heslin

Committees

Foreign Affairs (3rd); Subs: Europe; National Security Policy and Scientific Developments; State Department Organization and Foreign Operations (Chm.); Sp. Sub. for Review of Foreign Air Programs.

House Administration (Chm.).

Joint Com. on the Library (2nd).

Joint Com. on Printing (Vice-Chm.).

Sel. Com. on Parking.

Group Ratings

	ADA	COPE	LWV	RIPON	NFU	LCV	CFA	NAB	NSI	ACA
1972	38	100	75	40	80	32	100	18	88	41
1971	30	100	67	29	64	–	83	–	–	38
1970	32	82	–	38	91	42	71	10	75	17

Key Votes

1) Busing	AGN	6) Cmbodia Bmbg	FOR	11) Chkg Acct Intrst	AGN
2) Strip Mines	AGN	7) Bust Hwy Trust	AGN	12) End HISC (HUAC)	AGN
3) Cut Mil $	AGN	8) Farm Sub Lmt	AGN	13) Nixon Sewer Veto	AGN
4) Rev Shrg	FOR	9) School Prayr	FOR	14) Corp Cmpaign $	FOR
5) Pub TV $	FOR	10) Cnsumr Prot	FOR	15) Pol $ Disclosr	AGN

Election Results

1972 general:	Wayne L. Hays (D)	128,663	(70%)
	Robert Stewart (R)	54,572	(30%)
1972 primary:	Wayne L. Hays (D)	58,981	(85%)
	Nick B. Karnick (D)	10,007	(15%)
1970 general:	Wayne L. Hays (D)	82,071	(68%)
	Robert Stewart (R)	38,104	(32%)

NINETEENTH DISTRICT Political Background

The 19th district of Ohio is one of the most heavily industrial in the nation. Both Youngstown (pop. 140,000) and Warren (pop. 63,000), the district's two major cities, are important steel towns (Youngstown Sheet and Tube and Republic Steel). Situated about halfway between Cleveland and Pittsburgh, these two cities are also halfway between the docks that unload iron from the Great Lakes ranges and the coal fields of western Pennsylvania and West Virginia. Recently, they have been victims of the declining fortunes of the great steel firms. During the winter of 1969–70, Youngstown simply closed down its school system for a month. There was not enough money to keep it going, and hard-pressed local taxpayers, many of them laid off or unable to get overtime, refused to vote for higher taxes.

Even this somewhat depressed area has seen a flight to the suburbs—not just of people, but of industry. Some 15 miles east of Youngstown, for example, is the Lordstown GM assembly plant, probably the nation's most written-about factory in recent years. Designed as an ultramodern, capital-intensive facility, the operation was to turn out Vegas at the lowest possible cost; and it was located in a field next to the Ohio Turnpike, miles from anybody. The work force at the plant is young, a large percentage under 30. Not long after the factory went into production, the workers began to object to what they considered the inhuman pace of the assembly line. Management, they said, treated the workers like machines. There followed a full-scale strike over working conditions, which was settled, finally, after UAW officials came flying down from Detroit to find out what was going on.

Lordstown has come to represent a new industrial phenomenon, a revolt by young workers against the inhumanity of the work place. Older hands quite rightly point out that auto plants have never been pleasant places to work. But Lordstown has something different from events that occurred in other parts of the 19th district during the 1930s. These were the sit-down strikes in the steel mills of Youngstown and Warren, when the workers held the factories until management agreed to recognize their union. The participants in the sometimes bloody strikes had a specific cause, union recognition, and a general faith that with it, life would become better for them. The writers who flocked to Lordstown to interview the Lordstown personnel found no cause, faith, or sense of directed effort, only cynicism—to put in time and get out of the plant as soon as possible. They are apparently willing to fight management to improve working conditions, but many seem to feel that even if they win once in a while, it doesn't really make much difference. Things are just bad.

The same cynicism and indifference appears to have become a part of the politics of the 19th district. Back in the days of the New Deal and the bloody steel strikes, the majority of Youngstown area voters—whether from West Virginia, Italy, or Czechoslovakia—had few doubts as to who was and who was not a political friend. The district went heavily for Franklin D. Roosevelt, Harry Truman, John F. Kennedy, and Lyndon Johnson. But lately sentiment has shifted. In 1972, Richard Nixon actually carried the 19th, though by a small margin. Moreover, Democratic percentages in other elections here have also declined. Obviously, confidence in the Democrats has eroded, and the indications are that young blue-collar voters are not blindly accepting the voting habits of their parents. Rather, the young appear ready to vote for a candidate like George Wallace was in 1968—or simply not vote at all.

The waning of the New Deal tradition in the 19th district was symbolized by the death in 1970 of its former Congressman, Michael J. Kirwan, at age 83. With a third-grade education and a canny political sense, Kirwan spent 34 years on Capitol Hill and became a power in the House. When he died, Kirwan was the number-two Democrat on the Appropriations Committee and the shameless Chairman of its pork-barreling Public Works Subcommittee. He was also longtime Chairman of the Democratic Congressional Campaign Committee—a post that has devolved to Wayne Hays of the adjacent 18th district. Kirwan ruthlessly pushed his pet projects, including a $10 million aquarium for Washington, D.C., and a proposed Ohio River-Lake Erie Canal, known affectionately as "Mike's ditch." After his death, both projects were abandoned.

Kirwan's successor, Democrat Charles Carney, is a 20-year veteran of the Ohio state Senate and a former staffer with the United Steel Workers and the United Rubber Workers. In 1970, Carney won a 13-candidate Democratic primary—the most crowded field in the country that year—and went on to beat Republican Margaret Dennison, whose husband had represented the neighboring 11th district during the 1950s. In 1972, the man who finished second in the primary two years before, Richard McLaughlin, again challenged Carney; McLaughlin kept the incumbent to 56% of the vote in the high-turnout primary, one held simultaneously with Ohio's presidential primary. Carney won the ensuing general election easily, but the primary result may indicate that Carney has a rather shaky hold on the seat.

Census Data Pop. 463,625. Central city, 44%; suburban, 56%. Median family income, $10,311; families above $15,000: 21%; families below $3,000: 7%. Median years education, 12.1.

1972 Share of Federal Outlays $219,490,554

DOD	$10,324,431	HEW	$126,762,329
AEC	–	HUD	$2,445,485
NASA	$36,686	DOI	–
DOT	$12,385,438	USDA	$7,716,477
		Other	$59,819,208

Federal Military-Industrial Commitments

No installations or contractors receiving prime awards greater than $5,000,000.

Economic Base Primary metal industries, especially blast furnace and basic steel products; transportation equipment, especially motor vehicles and equipment; finance, insurance and real estate; and fabricated metal products, especially fabricated structural metal products. Also higher education (Youngstown State Univ.).

The Voters

Registration No district-wide registration.
Median voting age 44.7
Employment profile White collar, 41%. Blue collar, 46%. Service, 12%. Farm, 1%.
Ethnic groups Black, 11%. Spanish, 1%. Total foreign stock, 23%. Italy, 6%; Czechoxlovakia, 3%; UK, Poland, 2% each; Yugoslavia, Austria, Germany, Hungary, 1% each.

Presidential vote

1972	Nixon (R)	96,607	(52%)
	McGovern (D)	88,500	(48%)
1968	Nixon (R)	65,508	(36%)
	Humphrey (D)	98,277	(54%)
	Wallace (AI)	18,342	(10%)

Representative

Charles J. Carney (D) Elected 1970; b. April 17, 1913, Youngstown; home, Youngstown; Youngstown State U., three years; married, two children; Catholic.

Career Pres., V.Pres., United Rubber Workers Union, 1934; Pres. Dist. Council No. 1, United Rubber Workers Union, 1940–43, Staff Rep., Dist. Dir., 1942–50; Staff Rep., United Steelworkers of America, 1950–68; Ohio State Senate, 1951–70, Dem. Whip, 1959–69, Minority Leader, 1969–70.

Offices 1123 LHOB, 202-225-5261. Also 1108 Wick Bldg., Youngstown 44503.

Administrative Assistant Thomas J. Keyes, Jr.

Committees

Interstate and Foreign Commerce (20th); Sub: Sp. Sub. on Investigations.

Veterans' Affairs (10th); Subs: Hospitals; Housing (Chm.); Insurance.

Sel. Com. on Small Business (10th); Subs: Environmental Problems Affecting Small Business; Small Business Problems in Smaller Towns and Urban Areas.

Group Ratings

	ADA	COPE	LWV	RIPON	NFU	LCV	CFA	NAB	NSI	ACA
1972	75	100	91	46	83	53	100	11	22	11
1971	70	100	100	47	92	–	88	–	–	12

Key Votes

1) Busing	FOR	6) Cmbodia Bmbg	AGN	11) Chkg Acct Intrst	FOR
2) Strip Mines	AGN	7) Bust Hwy Trust	FOR	12) End HISC (HUAC)	FOR
3) Cut Mil $	ABS	8) Farm Sub Lmt	AGN	13) Nixon Sewer Veto	AGN
4) Rev Shrg	FOR	9) School Prayr	FOR	14) Corp Cmpaign $	FOR
5) Pub TV $	FOR	10) Cnsumr Prot	FOR	15) Pol $ Disclosr	AGN

Election Results

1972 general:	Charles J. Carney (D)	109,979	(64%)
	Norman M. Parr (R)	61,934	(36%)
1972 primary:	Charles J. Carney (D)	57,885	(56%)
	Richard P. McLaughlin (D)	44,834	(44%)
1970 general:	Charles J. Carney (D)	73,222	(58%)
	Margaret Dennison (R)	52,057	(42%)

TWENTIETH DISTRICT Political Background

Down the center of Cleveland flows the Cuyahoga River, a waterway so polluted with industrial wastes that it recently caught fire. On both sides of the Cuyahoga are Cleveland's giant steel mills and other factories—many of the same operations that made Cleveland the nation's fourth-largest city in 1910. In the years that followed, Cleveland lost the auto industry to Detroit and otherwise failed to match the growth rate of big-city America; so the Cleveland metropolitan area is now only the twelfth-largest in the nation. Moreover, the central city has more than its share of urban problems. These are symbolized by the Cuyahoga, and not just for its pollution: the river also divides the races in the city of Cleveland.

East of the Cuyahoga, most of Cleveland is black. Here and there are remnants of ethnic neighborhoods, called cosmo wards in Cleveland, which absorbed the Poles, Czechs, Hungarians, and Italians who came over on various grimy boats to work in the equally grimy steel mills along the Cuyahoga. But the vast majority of Clevelanders now living east of the river are black, and many of the black neighborhoods are so forbidding that Carl Stokes, the city's first and so far only black Mayor (1967–71), lived in a Cleveland house that sat on the line separating the city from the posh suburb of Shaker Heights. By glaring contrast, Cleveland west of the Cuyahoga is just about 100% white. Here, in this largely working-class area, are the city's remaining cosmo wards. The population in the wards is tipped towards the elderly end of the age scale, as younger people have moved out to suburbs like Parma (see Ohio 23).

Almost all of the west side of Cleveland, plus a couple of cosmo wards in the east, and a few suburbs to the south (Brook Park, Brooklyn, part of Parma, and Garfield Heights), make up the 20th congressional district of Ohio. A Democratic district by tradition, the people here have been upset for some time with the trends at work in the party of their ancestors. In 1967 and 1969, Carl Stokes' name on the Democratic line got him only around 20% of the votes in the area. The district went for Hubert Humphrey in 1968, but gave George Wallace a whopping 17% at the same time. In 1972, Richard Nixon carried the district.

For nearly 30 years, from 1943 to 1971, the 20th's Congressman was Michael Feighan, a rather conservative Democrat. As Chairman of the Judiciary Subcommittee on Immigration, Feighan managed to block liberalization of the nation's immigration laws for many years. By doing so, Feighan insured that Congressmen who wanted to help constituents with immigration problems—and that meant big-city Democrats especially—were forced to deal with him on a case-by-case basis.

The laws were rewritten in 1965. Thereafter, Feighan seemed to lose his grip on the district. During the late 1960s, he encountered tough primary opposition. Then, in 1970, the 65-year-old Feighan was finally unseated by 38-year-old James Stanton, then President of the Cleveland City Council. In 1968, Stanton had been the Democratic nominee in the much more Republican 23rd district, and had nearly won there. When he moved to the 20th for the 1970 election, Stanton proved so popular that he beat Feighan by 11,000 votes—in percentage terms, a 58–33 margin—with the rest going to a minor candidate. Stanton then won the general election with 81% of the votes, better than Feighan ever did.

Stanton bested his 1970 figure with 84% in 1972, a percentage higher than black Congressman Louis Stokes took in the much more Democratic and heavily black 21st district. In the House, Stanton stands with other urban Democrats on most issues, though he tends to heed his constituency's instincts on matters of law-and-order. With his vote-getting prowess well establish in Cleveland, Ohio's largest city, Stanton must be considered a possibility for statewide office in the years ahead.

Census Data Pop. 462,480. Central city, 65%; suburban, 35%. Median family income, $10,550; families above $15,000: 20%; families below $3,000: 7%. Median years education, 11.1.

1972 Share of Federal Outlays $340,864,361

DOD	$62,452,096	HEW	$133,730,444
AEC	$256,009	HUD	$9,104,258
NASA	$21,431,676	DOI	$131,823
DOT	$19,468,293	USDA	$8,322,823
		Other	$85,966,939

Federal Military-Industrial Commitments

NASA Installations Lewis Research Center (Cleveland).

Economic Base Machinery, especially metalworking machinery; primary metal industries, especially blast furnace and steel mill products; fabricated metal products, especially metal stampings; transportation equipment, especially motor vehicles and equipment; and electrical equipment and supplies, especially electrical industrial apparatus. Also higher education (Cleveland State Univ.).

The Voters

Registration No district-wide registration.
Median voting age 44.4
Employment profile White collar, 41%. Blue collar, 47%. Service, 12%. Farm, –%.

Ethnic groups Black, 3%. Spanish, 2%. Total foreign stock, 32%. Poland, 6%; Czechoslovakia, Italy, 4% each; Germany, 3%; Hungary, Austria, Yugoslavia, 2% each; USSR, UK, Ireland, 1% each.

Presidential vote

1972	Nixon (R)	79,056	(52%)
	McGovern (D)	74,041	(48%)
1968	Nixon (R)	48,106	(29%)
	Humphrey (D)	89,863	(54%)
	Wallace (AI)	27,696	(17%)

Representative

James Vincent Stanton (D) Elected 1970; b. Feb. 27, 1932, Cleveland; home, Cleveland; U. of Dayton, B.A., 1958; Cleveland-Marshall Col., J.D., 1961; USAF, Korean War; married, three children; Catholic.

Career Cleveland City Council, 1959–70; Pres., Cleveland City Council, 1964–70.

Offices 1107 LHOB, 202-225-5871. Also Rm. 116, Fed. Ct. House, Cleveland 44113, 216-522-4927.

Administrative Assistant Sanford Watzman

Committees

Government Operations (21st); Subs: Government Activities; Intergovernmental Relations; Foreign Operations and Government Information.

Public Works (16th); Subs: Water Resources; Transportation; Investigations and Review; Public Buildings and Grounds.

Group Ratings

	ADA	COPE	LWV	RIPON	NFU	LCV	CFA	NAB	NSI	ACA
1972	56	82	75	60	83	51	50	10	11	22
1971	76	80	67	71	93	–	88	–	–	18

Key Votes

1) Busing	AGN	6) Cmbodia Bmbg	AGN	11) Chkg Acct Intrst	AGN
2) Strip Mines	AGN	7) Bust Hwy Trust	FOR	12) End HISC (HUAC)	AGN
3) Cut Mil $	AGN	8) Farm Sub Lmt	AGN	13) Nixon Sewer Veto	AGN
4) Rev Shrg	FOR	9) School Prayr	AGN	14) Corp Cmpaign $	FOR
5) Pub TV $	FOR	10) Cnsumr Prot	FOR	15) Pol $ Disclosr	AGN

Election Results

1972 general:	James V. Stanton (D)	100,678	(84%)
	Thomas E. Vilt (R)	16,624	(12%)
	Richard B. Kay (AI)	5,285	(4%)
1972 primary:	James V. Stanton (D)	48,923	(75%)
	Raymond A. Stachewicz (D)	15,924	(25%)
1970 general:	James V. Stanton (D)	70,140	(81%)
	J. William Petro (R)	16,118	(19%)

TWENTY-FIRST DISTRICT Political Background

The 21st district of Ohio is the east side of Cleveland (see also Ohio 20), plus a couple of adjacent suburbs. This area was once a checkerboard of Polish, Czech, Hungarian, and Italian neighborhoods, but today it is heavily black (66% district-wide). The central part of the 21st includes some of the poorest black ghettos in the nation, while the black neighborhoods to the north and south are more middle-class. There are still a few ethnic ("cosmo" in Cleveland) enclaves left in the 21st, populated mainly by old people who cannot afford to move out of the city; this group has constituted the source of most of the district's Republican votes in the recent past. The suburban cities in the district are either already black (East Cleveland) or in the process of becoming so (Warrensville Heights). Ironically, some of Cleveland's wealthiest suburbs, like Shaker Heights and Cleveland Heights, are no more than a mile or two from some of the big city's most dilapidated slums.

Liberal Democrat Charles Vanik represented the 21st from 1955 until 1969. When the 1968 redistricting made it clear that the new 21st would have a solid black majority, Vanik left to run in the suburban 22nd, where he ousted the Republican incumbent. His successor in the 21st was Louis Stokes, brother of then Cleveland Mayor Carl Stokes. Like his brother, Congressman Stokes grew up in poverty, and was able to attend college and law school only after serving in the Army during World War II.

Stokes' election was a clear reflection of his brother's popularity on the east side. After the congressional victory of 1968, the two Stokes brothers put together their own political machine, knows as the 21st District Caucus. The Caucus endorsed candidates in local elections, not necessarily Democratic ones, and proved it could swing large numbers of votes. But it also had problems. Mayor Stokes decided not to run for reelection in 1971, and the Caucus, after endorsing a white candidate in the Democratic primary who won, then switched to Independent Arnold Pinkney, head of the city school board and a Caucus leader. The move allowed Republican Ralph Perk to win the Mayor's office in the general election with a minority of the votes.

Subsequently, Carl Stokes moved to New York to become a TV newscaster (reversing the usual career progression) and Louis Stokes broke with other 21st-district Caucus leaders. But Congressman Stokes remains the Chairman of the Congressional Black Caucus, considered a happy medium between the newer, more militant black Congressmen (and Congresswomen) and the older, quieter members of the group. Stokes has continued Caucus policy of criticizing the actions of the usually unsympathetic Nixon Administration and trying to mold the Caucus into a power bloc to which the rest of the House will pay heed. Stokes also serves as the first black member of the Appropriations Committee.

Census Data Pop. 462,584. Central city, 87%; suburban, 13%. Median family income, $8,573; families above $15,000: 14%; families below $3,000: 16%. Median years education, 10.9.

1972 Share of Federal Outlays $341,016,533

DOD	$62,479,976	HEW	$133,790,144
AEC	$256,124	HUD	$9,108,323
NASA	$21,441,244	DOI	$131,881
DOT	$19,476,984	USDA	$8,326,539
		Other	$86,005,318

Federal Military-Industrial Commitments

No installations or contractors receiving prime awards greater than $5,000,000.

Economic Base Machinery, especially metalworking machinery; primary metal industries, especially blast furnace and steel mill products; fabricated metal products, especially metal stampings; transportation equipment, especially motor vehicles and equipment; and electrical equipment and supplies, especially electrical industrial apparatus.

The Voters

Registration No district-wide registration.
Median voting age 42.9
Employment profile White collar, 37%. Blue collar, 44%. Service, 19%. Farm, –%.
Ethnic groups Black, 66%. Total foreign stock, 14%. Yugoslavia, Italy, Hungary, 2% each; Czechoslovakia, Poland, Germany, 1% each.

Presidential vote

1972	Nixon (R)		27,661	(21%)
	McGovern (D)		101,276	(79%)
1968	Nixon (R)		23,965	(15%)
	Humphrey (D)		123,971	(77%)
	Wallace (AI)		12,391	(8%)

Representative

Louis Stokes (D) Elected 1968; b. Feb. 23, 1925, Cleveland; home, Cleveland; Western Reserve U., 1946–48; Cleveland-Marshall Law School, J.D., 1953; Army, WWII; married, four children; Methodist.

Career Practicing atty., 1954–68; Chairman, Congressional Black Caucus, Feb. 1972– .

Offices 315 CHOB, 202-225-7032. Also New Fed. Bldg., 1240 E. 9th St., Cleveland 44199, 216-522-4900.

Administrative Assistant James C. Harper

Committees

Appropriations (26th); Subs: District of Columbia; Legislative; Treasury, Postal Service, General Government.

Group Ratings

	ADA	COPE	LWV	RIPON	NFU	LCV	CFA	NAB	NSI	ACA
1972	100	90	100	69	100	83	100	10	0	5
1971	89	80	63	72	78	–	100	–	–	4
1970	96	100	–	76	83	100	100	0	0	18

Key Votes

1) Busing	FOR	6) Cmbodia Bmbg	AGN	11) Chkg Acct Intrst	ABS
2) Strip Mines	ABS	7) Bust Hwy Trust	FOR	12) End HISC (HUAC)	FOR
3) Cut Mil $	FOR	8) Farm Sub Lmt	AGN	13) Nixon Sewer Veto	AGN
4) Rev Shrg	FOR	9) School Prayr	AGN	14) Corp Cmpaign $	FOR
5) Pub TV $	ABS	10) Cnsumr Prot	FOR	15) Pol $ Disclosr	AGN

Election Results

1972 general:	Louis Stokes (D)	99,190	(81%)
	James D. Johnson (R)	13,861	(11%)
	Joseph Pirincin (Socialist Labor)	5,779	(5%)
	Cecil Lampkins (Ind.)	3,509	(3%)
1972 primary:	Louis Stokes (D)	49,595	(83%)
	Thomas M. Shaughnessy (D)	10,240	(17%)
1970 general:	Louis Stokes (D)	74,340	(78%)
	Bill Mack (R)	21,440	(22%)

TWENTY-SECOND DISTRICT Political Background

The 22nd district of Ohio is the eastern half of the ring of suburbs around Cleveland, plus a very small part (12,000 residents) of the city itself. The various suburbs have been settled by people of varying ethnic stock, who have moved here following the radial avenues out of central-city Cleveland. There are suburbs that are predominantly Italian (Mayfield Heights), Servian (Solon), Hungarian (Euclid), Jewish (University Heights, Beachwood), and high-income WASP (Gates Mills, Pepper Pike). The most well-known of the 22nd's communities is also one of its most varied, Shaker Heights. This suburb, hard by the Cleveland city limits, contains the estate-like homes of some of Cleveland's wealthiest WASPs and Jews. Lying next to the Cleveland ghetto, Shaker Heights has been opened up in recent years to affluent blacks, as has Cleveland Heights, just to the north.

Before 1972, the 22nd lay entirely within Cleveland's Cuyahoga County. With redistricting, it has now spread into adjacent Lake, Geauga, and Summit counties. The move has made little difference in the sociological or political composition of the district. The appended territory is part of the Cleveland urban area, and new residents from it are moving out here daily.

On balance the 22nd is a Democratic district, having delivered majorities on the order of 10% to Senate candidates Stephen Young in 1964, John Gilligan in 1968, and Howard Metzenbaum (a resident of Shaker Heights) in 1970. But for 30 years, the district always went Republican in congressional elections, thanks to the vote-getting prowess of Mrs. Frances P. Bolton. A member of a socially prominent Cleveland family, Mrs. Bolton succeeded her late husband in 1940, and was reelected enough times to become the ranking Republican in the House Foreign Affairs Committee. But in 1968, her time was up. Democratic Congressman Charles Vanik, who had represented the 21st district in Cleveland for 14 years, moved into the district after his old seat became majority black. Vanik was almost 30 years younger than Mr. Bolton, and his longtime support of Israel gave him a big edge in the Jerish suburbs.

After defeating Mrs. Bolton in 1968, Vanik has since won reelection easily. Now the seventh-ranking Democrat on Ways and Means, the Congressman is one of the members of the panel pushing hardest for major tax reform. He has also been active on a number of other issues, most notably the Jackson-Vanik Amendment. This is a measure to prohibit the granting of most-favored-nation trade status to countries that refuse to permit free emigration of their citizens. It is aimed at the Soviet Union, which dearly wants trade concessions from the United States, yet refuses to allow the free emigration of Jews to Israel.

Vanik rounded up more than a majority of House members as co-sponsors of the measure, and then enlisted, as a major sponsor, Ways and Means Chairman Wilbur Mills. Because there was even greater support for the amendment in the Senate, Vanik's move presented the Nixon Administration and the Soviets with a *fait accompli*. The move also give Vanik a good issue in the 22nd district, where a large percentage of the residents are Jewish or of Eastern European stock.

Census Data Pop. 462,271. Central city, 3%; suburban, 97%. Median family income, $13,427; families above $15,000: 41%; families below $3,000: 3%. Median years education, 12.5.

1972 Share of Federal Outlays $335,777,768

DOD	$63,490,654	HEW	$132,866,988
AEC	$237,625	HUD	$9,375,956
NASA	$19,687,584	DOI	$151,038
DOT	$18,027,746	USDA	$8,170,391
		Other	$83,769,786

Federal Military-Industrial Commitments

DOD Contractors Gould, Inc. (Cleveland), $156.870m: production of MK48 torpedoes.

Economic Base Finance, insurance and real estate; fabricated metal products; machinery, especially metalworking machinery; rubber and plastics products; and primary metal industries, especially blast furnace and basic steel products.

The Voters

Registration No district-wide registration.
Median voting age 45.2
Employment profile White collar, 63%. Blue collar, 29%. Service, 8%. Farm, –%.
Ethnic groups Black, 2%. Total foreign stock, 32%. Italy, 5%. USSR, Poland, Germany, Yugoslavia, 3% each; Hungary, UK, Czechoslovakia, Austria, 2% each; Canada, 1%.

Presidential vote

1972	Nixon (R)	119,412	(57%)
	McGovern (D)	90,689	(43%)
1968	Nixon (R)	89,300	(44%)
	Humphrey (D)	96,883	(47%)
	Wallace (AI)	18,560	(9%)

Representative

Charles A. Vanik (D) Elected 1954; b. April 7, 1913, Cleveland; home, Cleveland; Western Reserve U., B.A., 1933, LL.B., 1936; USNR, WWII; married, two children; Catholic.

Career Practicing atty., 1936– ; Cleveland City Council, 1938–39; Ohio Senate, 1940–41; Cleveland Bd. of Ed., 1941–42; Assoc. Judge, Cleveland Municipal Ct., 1947–54.

Offices 2371 RHOB, 202-225-6331. Also 107 Old Fed. Bldg., Cleveland 44114, 216-522-4253.

Administrative Assistant Mark Talisman

Committees

Ways and Means (7th).

Group Ratings

	ADA	COPE	LWV	RIPON	NFU	LCV	CFA	NAB	NSI	ACA
1972	94	100	92	73	71	87	100	8	0	4
1971	92	83	89	82	67	–	100	–	–	31
1970	96	100	–	82	92	90	85	0	10	25

Key Votes

1) Busing	FOR	6) Cmbodia Bmbg	AGN	11) Chkg Acct Intrst	AGN
2) Strip Mines	AGN	7) Bust Hwy Trust	FOR	12) End HISC (HUAC)	FOR
3) Cut Mil $	FOR	8) Farm Sub Lmt	FOR	13) Nixon Sewer Veto	AGN
4) Rev Shrg	FOR	9) School Prayr	AGN	14) Corp Cmpaign $	AGN
5) Pub TV $	FOR	10) Cnsumr Prot	FOR	15) Pol $ Disclosr	AGN

Election Results

1972 general:	Charles A. Vanik (D)	126,462	(64%)
	Donald W. Gropp (R)	64,577	(33%)
	Thomas W. Lippitt (AI)	3,463	(2%)
	Caryl L. Loeb (Ind.)	3,342	(2%)
1972 primary:	Charles A. Vanik (D), unopposed		
1970 general:	Charles A. Vanik (D)	114,790	(72%)
	Adrian Fink (R)	45,657	(28%)

TWENTY-THIRD DISTRICT Political Background

In rough terms, the 23rd district of Ohio is the suburbs south and west of Cleveland. These can be divided, and considered, in two parts. The suburbs to the west are upper-middle-income WASPy towns like Lakewood, Rocky River, and Bay Village—all cast heavy Republican margins and front on Lake Erie. As one moves away from the Lake, Republican percentages tend to decline. The 23rd's suburbs to the south are rather different. These were settled more recently in the 1950s and 1960s, generally by people of Slavic and Hungarian descent who grew up in the smoggier, less spacious streets of west-side Cleveland.

The largest and best known of the ethnic suburbs is Parma (pop. 100,000), most of which lies in the 23rd. It is a diffuse town whose bowling alleys are closely monitored by national political reporters for signs of change in public opinion. Parma is heavily Polish, Ukrainian, and Slavic; it is ancestrally Democratic, but a place inclined to switch to Republican politicians in recent years. Parma went for Humphrey in 1968, but only by a plurality, as Wallace took 14% of its votes. Four years later, Nixon carried Parma, 59–41; more recently, however, a reporter from the *New York Times* visiting the suburb found Nixon support evaporating because of the Watergate revelations. The towns around Parma, beginning with Parma Heights, grow less Democratic as one moves away from Brook Park Road, which is the Cleveland city limit.

The 23rd also contains the larger parts of Cleveland's 1st and 4th wards, which are somewhat more Democratic than the district as a whole. The fact that the wards are here would be politically insignificant but for the fact that Cleveland has produced some surprisingly strong opponents for the 23rd's Republican Congressman, William Minshall. He has represented this district, which of course has undergone several redistrictings, since he was elected in 1954. Minshall is now the third-ranking minority member of the House Appropriations Committee, and the ranking Republican on its Defense Subcommittee, which reports out something like half the federal budget. A man enjoying positions of such eminence could normally expect to occupy a safe seat, especially when his district itself appears safely Republican, having gone for Republican candidates in the close Senate elections of 1968 and 1970.

Nevertheless, Minshall has encounted stiff competition two of his last three times out, and local observers would not be surprised to see him retire (he is 63) or even lose in 1974. Minshall's apparent problem is that some very heavy local vote-getters seem to find the Cleveland City Council too small an arena for their ambitions. In 1968, Council President James Stanton got 48% of the votes against Minshall; in 1970, Stanton might well have been able to win here, but instead ran against veteran Democrat Michael Feighan in the 20th district and beat him easily. In that year, Minshall's opponent was Ronald Mottl, a crew-cut state Senator from Parma, who made the mistake of divorcing his wife and marrying an 18-year-old beauty-contest runner-up just before beginning his campaign. Even at that, Minshall only won 60% of the votes.

Then, in 1972, Minshall found himself facing 25-year-old Cleveland Councilman Dennis Kucinich, who had won his seat in the Council a few years before by beating a longtime incumbent. After defeating a McGovern-backing priest in the Democratic congressional primary, Kucinich was determined to unseat Minshall. The challenger's positions on issues were similar to Stanton's: opposition to both busing and the Vietnam war. One observer called him a "combination of Fiorello La Guardia and George Wallace." Kucinich was unable to win a majority of the votes in the year of the Nixon landslide, but neither was Minshall, winner by plurality. The incumbent's final margin was a little over 4,000 votes—hardly a strong showing for an 18-year House veteran having a Republican-leaning district and running in a good Republican year. Kucinich actually did better than the very popular Stanton had done in 1968. So the new challenger can be expected to run, and probably win, in 1974.

Census Data Pop. 462,724. Central city, 9%; suburban, 91%. Median family income, $13,101; families above $15,000: 37%; families below $3,000: 3%. Median years education, 12.4.

1972 Share of Federal Outlays $341,168,704

DOD	$62,507,856	HEW	$133,849,846
AEC	$256,238	HUD	$9,112,387
NASA	$21,450,811	DOI	$131,940
DOT	$19,485,625	USDA	$8,330,254
		Other	$86,043,697

Federal Military-Industrial Commitments

No installations or contractors receiving prime awards greater than $5,000,000.

Economic Base Finance, insurance and real estate; machinery, especially metalworking machinery; primary metal industries, especially blast furnace and steel mill products; fabricated metal products, especially metal stampings; and transportation equipment, especially motor vehicles and equipment.

The Voters

Registration No district-wide registration.
Median voting age 44.4
Employment profile White collar, 61%. Blue collar, 30%. Service, 9%. Farm, –%.
Ethnic groups Total foreign stock, 28%. Czechoslovakia, 4%; Germany, Poland, Italy, 3% each; UK, Hungary, Austria, 2% each; Yugoslavia, Canada, Ireland, 1% each.

Presidential vote

1972	Nixon (R)	131,709	(65%)
	McGovern (D)	71,361	(35%)
1968	Nixon (R)	97,416	(51%)
	Humphrey (D)	74,119	(39%)
	Wallace (AI)	19,802	(10%)

Representative

William E. Minshall (R) Elected 1954; b. Oct. 24, 1911, East Cleveland; home, Lakewood; U. of Va., 1932–34; Cleveland Law School, LL.B., 1940; Army, WWII; Lt. Col. USAR (Ret.); married, three children; Portestant.

Career Ohio House of Reps., 1939–40; Practicing atty., 1940– ; Gen. Counsel, Maritime Admin., 1953–54.

Offices 2243 RHOB, 202-225-5731. Also 2951 New Fed. Office Bldg., 1240 E. 9th St., Cleveland 44199, 216-522-4382.

Administrative Assistant Mrs. Patricia Coombe

Committees

Appropriations (3rd); Subs: Defense (Ranking Mbr.); Transportation.

Group Ratings

	ADA	COPE	LWV	RIPON	NFU	LCV	CFA	NAB	NSI	ACA
1972	13	44	43	70	75	49	50	88	100	70
1971	5	20	0	41	38	–	29	–	–	77
1970	12	27	–	44	50	51	40	75	100	71

Key Votes

1) Busing	AGN	6) Cmbodia Bmbg	FOR	11) Chkg Acct Intrst	ABS
2) Strip Mines	ABS	7) Bust Hwy Trust	FOR	12) End HISC (HUAC)	ABS
3) Cut Mil $	AGN	8) Farm Sub Lmt	FOR	13) Nixon Sewer Veto	FOR
4) Rev Shrg	FOR	9) School Prayr	FOR	14) Corp Cmpaign $	ABS
5) Pub TV $	AGN	10) Cnsumr Prot	FOR	15) Pol $ Disclosr	FOR

Election Results

1972 general:	William E. Minshall (R)	98,594	(49%)
	Dennis J. Kucinich (D)	94,366	(47%)
	John O'Neill (Socialist Labor)	3,615	(2%)
	Frederick D. Lyon (AI)	2,976	(1%)
1972 primary:	William E. Minshall (R)	27,635	(87%)
	Eldon P. Roe (R)	4,004	(13%)
1970 general:	William E. Minshall (R)	111,218	(60%)
	Ronald M. Mottl (D)	73,765	(40%)

OKLAHOMA

Political Background

Somebody said Oklahoma is a little cow, a little dirt, and a little oil. Ninety years ago, it was mostly dirt—impoverished Indian reservations onto which the Cherokees and the other Civilized Tribes had been herded from their ancestral lands in the South and the Midwest. In 1889, the federal government decided to open up what is now Oklahoma to white settlement. On the morning of the great land rush, thousands of would-be homesteaders drove their wagons across the territorial line in a moment that numerous movies have recaptured.

The "Sooners," as they were called (for those who crossed the line sooner than they were supposed to), quickly came to outnumber the Indians. Nonetheless, Oklahoma today has the largest Indian population of any state (97,000); the state, however, has no reservations, because the Indians are pretty well assimilated into the rest of the population. During its first years, Oklahoma held out great promise to the new white settlers, mainly from the South. But for many of them, the promise of Oklahoma turned as sour as it had for the transplanted Indians. The Depression and drought of the 1930s drove thousands of Okies, as they were called, to the greener fields of California. As it stands, the population of Oklahoma is about 2.5 million; at statehood in 1907, the figure was not much lower, at 1.5 million. Today 42 of the state's 77 counties contain fewer people than they did in 1907. Almost all of Oklahoma's recent growth has occurred in and around its two large cities, Oklahoma City and Tulsa.

The changing demography of the state shows up in recent election returns. By tradition, Oklahoma has been a Democratic state, since most of its settlers came from the South; even today, some 76% of its voters still register Democratic. But Oklahoma has also always had a strong Republican minority, especially in the northwest and north-central parts of the state, which were settled largely by people from Republican Kansas. But the fast-growing, oil-rich cities of Oklahoma City and Tulsa are now conservative Republican, urban strongholds, much like Dallas in Texas, and Phoenix in Arizona. In the East and Midwest, the cities usually go Democratic and the countryside, Republican; in Oklahoma and most of the Southwest, the pattern in exactly reversed. And here the urban share of the state's votes and its population is growing. In 1964, both Oklahoma City and Tulsa went for Barry Goldwater, and together they cast 36% of the state's votes. In 1972, both Oklahoma City and Tulsa went even more heavily for Richard Nixon than the rest of the state, and together they cast 40% of the state's votes.

In presidential contests, Oklahoma has long favored the Republicans in a big way. Since 1948, the state has gone Democratic only one time, and that was Lyndon Johnson's narrow victory here in 1964. In 1972, only one state, Mississippi, cast a higher percentage of its votes for Richard Nixon. In statewide races, however, it took Oklahoma Republicans some time to become competitive. Their first breakthrough occurred in 1962, when Henry Bellmon was elected Governor. In 1966, the Republicans elected a second Republican Governor, and a Princeton-educated Catholic at that, Dewey Bartlett. In 1970, Democrat David Hall defeated Bartlett—the first Oklahoma Governor eligible for two consecutive terms—by 2,000 votes. Most of the Democrats' gains came in rural areas, where the farmers' chronic dissatisfaction with the national Administration's farm programs worked against the Republicans. But today both former Governors, Bellmon and Bartlett, sit in the U.S. Senate, with every prospect of staying there if they choose.

Probably the most spectacular Republican victory was Bellmon's in 1968, when he unseated three-term Sen. Mike Monroney. A liberal-leaning Democrat, Monroney was elected to the House in 1938, serving there until going to the Senate in 1950. During his 30 years of service in Washington, Monroney was an effective politician; he was largely responsible, for example, for the Federal Aviation Administration's huge Aeronautical Center in Oklahoma City. But by 1968, Monroney had obviously lost touch with Oklahoma voters, as Bellmon swept the cities (though Monroney was from Oklahoma City) and made solid inroads in the traditionally Democratic rural areas.

In the Senate, Bellmon began as one of Richard Nixon's most fervent supporters; indeed, he had served as Nixon's national Campaign Chairman in 1968 before making the Oklahoma Senate race. But lately, Bellmon's ardor has cooled somewhat; and because he has begun to dissent from the Administration on a number of issues, his vote is no longer an automatic pro-Nixon one. For a long time Bellmon, apparently disenchanted with things in Washington, was considering retirement. But he has decided to run again in 1974, and at this writing, is a solid favorite to win.

From 1949 until his death in 1963, Oklahoma's other Senate seat belonged to Robert Kerr, who made himself one of Washington's most powerful politicians. As Chairman of the Senate committee overseeing the space program in its early years, Kerr channeled many valuable NASA contracts to Oklahoma firms. Moreover, it was not a complete coincidence that James Webb, head of NASA during the Kennedy and Johnson years, had earlier grown rich while working for Kerr's oil conglomerate, Kerr-McGee. As the number-two Democrat on the Senate Finance

Committee behind Virginia's Harry Byrd, Kerr blocked passage of Medicare legislation and also jealously guarded the interest of the oil companies, including, of course, Kerr-McGee. As Kerr himself once put it, "I represent myself first, the state of Oklahoma second, and the people of the United States third—and don't you forget it." Already a wealthy man when he first came to Washington, Kerr was worth something on the order of $40 million when he died. A permanent legacy of Kerr's clout is the McClellan-Kerr Navigation System on the Arkansas River; opened just recently, the project has made Tulsa an ocean port.

Kerr held onto his seat and his power with an iron grip. His successor, after a meteoric rise, relinquished both. On Kerr's death, lame-duck Gov. J. Howard Edmondson appointed himself to the seat—a move always unpopular with voters. Edmondson was defeated in the 1964 Democratic primary by an unknown 34-year-old state Senator named Fred Harris, whom people assumed was the more conservative candidate. Harris was given little chance in the general election, but he managed to beat Bud Wilkinson, the former football coach at the University of Oklahoma.

After his reelection to the Senate in 1966, Harris' Senate career took some interesting turns. He served on the Kerner Commission on Civil Disorders, and came away in full agreement with its basic conclusion, namely, that the black riots were a response to America's "white racism." Harris also deepened his interest in Indian problems; his wife La Donna is a Comanche and a leader among Indian organizations. In 1968, Hubert Humphrey came close to naming Harris his Vice-Presidential running mate; when he picked Edmund Muskie, Harris became Chairman of the Democratic National Committee instead.

After leaving the chairmanship, Harris moved further left, and away from Oklahoma. In 1971, he announced a presidential candidacy on a "new populist" platform, which called for a breakup of major corporations and thoroughgoing tax reform. The platform was not the kind of thing people were used to hearing from an Oklahoma member of the Senate Finance Committee; nor was it anything that appealed to big contributors. So Harris' presidential campaign folded for lack of money before the end of 1971. Moreover, he had already counted himself out of reelection to the Senate from Oklahoma—polls showed he would lose badly if he ran. Today, a former Senator at 44, Harris heads an organization in Washington that is calling for massive reform of the nation's tax structure.

One reason Harris would have failed to run well in 1972 was the Senate candidacy of 2nd-district Congressman Ed Edmondson, brother of the man Harris defeated in 1964. When he first came to Washington 20 years earlier, Edmondson was regarded as a grass-roots liberal. But over the years, his record grew more conservative, to some extent even on economic issues. In 1972, Edmondson scored an easy 56% victory in the 11-candidate Senate Democratic primary. But the general election proved tougher.

The Republican nominee was ex-Gov. Bartlett, fresh from one of the narrowest statewide defeats in Oklahoma history. As he campaigned, Bartlett grasped firmly to Richard Nixon's coattails. Edmondson, meanwhile, spoke of his conservatism, his distaste for McGovern, and his support of economic measures to help the little man. But Edmondson's efforts were only good enough for a bare 52–48 majority in rural Oklahoma, while Bartlett carried Oklahoma City and Tulsa by a 54–41 margin and won the election by almost 30,000 votes. In the Senate, Bartlett has been a reliably conservative Republican, seldom dissenting from the party consensus. Calling himself "an Okie in Washington," Bartlett has yet to show any of the fire of his predecessors, Harris and Kerr.

Census Data Pop. 2,559,253; 1.26% of U.S. total, 27th largest; change 1960–70, 9.9%. Central city, 30%; suburban, 20%. Median family income, $7,720; 41st highest; families above $15,000: 13%; families below $3,000: 16%. Median years education, 12.1.

1972 Share of Federal Tax Burden $2,131,990,000; 1.02% of U.S. total, 27th largest.

1972 Share of Federal Outlays $2,947,632,846; 1.36% of U.S. total, 24th largest. Per capita federal spending, $1,152.

DOD	$880,181,000	21st	(1.41%)	HEW	$973,310,597	25th	(1.36%)
AEC	$207,029	38th	(0.01%)	HUD	$44,125,898	23rd	(1.44%)
NASA	$1,106,917	34th	(0.04%)	VA	$195,643,985	22nd	(1.71%)
DOT	$185,798,072	14th	(2.36%)	USDA	$275,945,841	22nd	(1.79%)
DOC	$6,507,857	33rd	(0.50%)	CSC	$59,488,325	16th	(1.44%)
DOI	$64,407,196	10th	(3.04%)	TD	$116,586,030	20th	(0.71%)
DOJ	$13,159,501	30th	(1.34%)	Other	$131,164,598		

Economic Base Agriculture, notably cattle, wheat, dairy products and peanuts; finance, insurance and real estate; oil and gas extraction, especially oil and gas field services and crude petroleum and natural gas; machinery, especially construction and related machinery; fabricated metal products, especially fabricated structural metal products; food and kindred products; electrical equipment and supplies, especially communication equipment.

Political Line-up Governor, David Hall (D); seat up, 1974. Senators, Henry Bellmon (R) and Dewey F. Bartlett (R). Representatives, 6 (5 D and 1 R). State Senate (26 D and 10 R); State House (75 D and 38 R).

The Voters

Registration 1,247,157 total. 942,188 D (76%); 287,003 R (23%); 17,966 other (1%).
Median voting age 44.2
Employment profile White collar, 48%. Blue collar, 33%. Service, 14%. Farm, 5%.
Ethnic groups Black, 7%. Indian, 4%. Spanish, 1%. Total foreign stock, 4%.

Presidential vote

1972	Nixon (R)	759,025	(75%)
	McGovern (D)	247,147	(25%)
1968	Nixon (R)	449,697	(48%)
	Humphrey (D)	301,658	(32%)
	Wallace (AI)	191,731	(20%)
1964	Johnson (D)	519,834	(56%)
	Goldwater (R)	412,655	(44%)

Senator

Henry L. Bellmon (R) Elected 1968, seat up 1974; b. Sept. 3, 1921, Tonakawa; home, Billings; Okla. State U., B.S., 1942; USMC, WWII; married, three children; Presbyterian.

Career Farming, wheat and cattle, 1946– ; Okla. House of Reps., 1946–48; Okla. Repub. Chm., 1960–62; First Repub. Gov. of Okla., 1963–67; Natl. Chm., Nixon for Pres. Com., 1968.

Offices 4203 NSOB, 202-225-5754. Also 820 Old P.O. Bldg., 215 N.W. Third, Oklahoma City 73102, 405-231-4941, and Suite 3003, 333 W. 4th, Tulsa 74103 74103, 918-581-7651, and 204 Fed. Bldg., Lawton 73501, 405-353-4673, and 205 Fed. Bldg., Ardmore 73401, 405-226-2160, and 223 P.O. Bldg., Enid 73701, 405-233-3914, and 405 Fed. Bldg., McAlester 74501, 918-426-0573.

Administrative Assistant Drew Mason

Committees

Appropriations (11th); Subs: Agriculture, Environmental and Consumer Protection; District of Columbia; Interior; Military Construction; Public Works, AEC; Treasury; U.S. Postal Service, and General Government (Ranking Mbr.).

Agriculture and Forestry (5th); Subs: Agricultural Production, Marketing, and Stabilization of Prices; Agricultural Research and General Legislation; Rural Development; Foreign Agricultural Policy (Ranking Mbr.).

Post Office and Civil Service (3rd); Subs: Civil Service Policies and Practices (Ranking Mbr.); Compensation and Employment Benefits.

Sel. Com. on Nutrition and Human Needs (4th).

Group Ratings

	ADA	COPE	LWV	RIPON	NFU	LCV	CFA	NAB	NSI	ACA
1972	10	22	57	56	70	19	9	38	100	65
1971	11	17	78	32	33	–	33	–	–	63
1970	19	13	–	43	40	0	–	83	100	85

Key Votes

1) Busing	FOR	8) Sea Life Prot	AGN	15) Tax Singls Less	AGN
2) Alas P-line	FOR	9) Campaign Subs	AGN	16) Min Tax for Rich	ABS
3) Gun Cntrl	FOR	10) Cmbodia Bmbg	AGN	17) Euro Troop Rdctn	AGN
4) Rehnquist	FOR	11) Legal Srvices	AGN	18) Bust Hwy Trust	AGN
5) Pub TV $	AGN	12) Rev Sharing	FOR	19) Maid Min Wage	FOR
6) EZ Votr Reg	FOR	13) Cnsumr Prot	AGN	20) Farm Sub Limit	AGN
7) No-Fault	AGN	14) Eq Rts Amend	FOR	21) Highr Credt Chgs	FOR

Election Results

1968 general:	Harry Bellmon (R)	470,120	(52%)
	A. S. Mike Monroney (D)	419,658	(46%)
	George Washington (AI)	19,341	(2%)
1968 primary:	Harry Bellmon (R), unopposed		

Senator

Dewey Follett Bartlett (R) Elected 1972, seat up 1978; b. Mar. 28, 1919, Marietta, Ohio; home, Tulsa; Princeton U., B.S., 1942; Marines, WWII; married, three children; Catholic.

Career Farmer; Rancher; Okla. State Senate, 1963–67; Gov., 1967–71.

Offices 140 OSOB, 202-225-4721. Also 914 Old P.O. Bldg., 215 N.W. 3, Oklahoma City 73102, 405-231-4941, and Rm. 204, Fed. Bldg., 5th and E. Lawton 73501, 405-353-4677, and 405 Fed. Bldg., Ardmore 73401, 405-226-2160, and 223 P.O. Bldg., Enid, 73701, 405-233-3914, and Fed. Bldg., McAlester 74501, 918-426-1414, and Fed. Bldg., 333 W. 4th, Tulsa 74103, 918-581-7191.

Administrative Assistant Don Cogman

Committees

Aeronautical and Space Sciences (4th).

Interior and Insular Affairs (6th); Subs: Indian Affairs (Ranking Mbr.); Minerals, Materials, and Fuels; Territories and Insular Affairs.

District of Columbia (2nd); Sub: Fiscal Affairs.

Group Ratings: Newly Elected

Election Results

1972 general:	Dewey F. Bartlett (R)	516,934	(52%)
	Ed Edmondson (D)	478,212	(48%)

William G. Roach (AI)	5,769	(1%)
Dewey F. Bartlett (R)	94,935	(93%)
C. W. Wood (R)	7,029	(7%)

FIRST DISTRICT Political Background

Tulsa is a city built on oil. Unlike Oklahoma City, however, no oil wells pump away in the middle of town getting at the stuff directly below the place. Tulsa is simply a regional center of the oil industry, which means it is the city where the money comes pouring in. Even today, years after oil was first discovered in these parts, Tulsa is still growing rapidly. Its population rose from 261,000 in 1960 to 331,000 in 1972. Like so many of the oil-boom cities of the Southwest, Tulsa is very deeply conservative; one thinks of Dallas and Houston, but better examples are the smaller Texas cities of Odessa and Midland. The new rich, some observers have noted, are usually the most resentful toward politicians whose programs appear to take from the rich and give to the poor, and they are also the most suspicious of new ideas and stalwart in the defense of old virtues. Tulsa is full of the new rich. And for that and other reasons, Tulsa is one of the most conservative urban centers in the country. In fact, outside of the South, it cast a larger percentage of its votes for Richard Nixon in 1972 (79%) than any other major metropolitan area (200,000 residents and over).

Nonetheless, in local elections Tulsa sometimes goes Democratic. Some 60% of Tulsa County voters register Democratic. Many of them are migrants from the mountains and the countryside of the South, having come to work here in comparatively high-paying blue- and sometimes white-collar jobs. Though the migrants may still think of themselves as Democrats, their idea of the party is way out of line with the kind of national candidates nominated not just in 1972, but for 20 years or more.

Tulsa makes up the bulk of Oklahoma's 1st congressional district. The remainder consists of parts of neighboring counties, and much of that is suburban. The 1st also includes a part of the city of Bartlesville, another smaller, oil-boom town (headquarters of Phillips Petroleum). And because the boundaries of the district were drawn by Democratic legislators, the 1st's portion of Bartlesville contains virtually all of the city's black population.

The legislators took some pains drawing the boundaries. The reason was that in 1972 for the first time in years there promised to be a real contest in the 1st. Page Belcher, a conservative Republican, had been the district's Congressman for 22 years. While in the House, he had succeeded to the position of ranking minority member of the Agriculture Committee—an assignment that was much more attractive and useful back in the early 1960s when the district included much of agricultural northwest Oklahoma. Belcher usually won reelection easily, but in 1970 he ran into a tough Democratic opponent, James Jones. Only 30 at the time, Jones was once an appointments secretary to President Johnson. The candidate, a native of Tulsa, conducted an aggressive campaign which brought him 44% of the votes.

With that, Belcher, at 73, decided to retire in 1972. But the retirement did not leave the field clear for Jones, who was, of course, running again. His Republican opponent was J. M. Hewgley, former Mayor of Tulsa. Nevertheless, Jones captured the seat, getting 55% of the votes in Tulsa County and 54% district-wide. It was a formidable achievement; at the top of the ticket, George McGovern just barely got 20%. In the House, Jones comes over as a moderate-to-conservative Democrat, though he did vote to stop the bombing of Cambodia.

Census Data Pop. 425,620. Central city, 78%; suburban, 18%. Median family income, $7,720; families above $15,000: 13%; families below $3,000: 9%. Median years education, 12.1.

1972 Share of Federal Outlays $322,861,896

DOD	$49,631,662	HEW	$133,021,343
AEC	$130,601	HUD	$5,091,172
NASA	$97,393	DOI	$8,214,169
DOT	$20,811,975	USDA	$5,784,884
		Other	$100,078,697

Federal Military-Industrial Commitments

DOD Contractors North American Rockwell (Tulsa), $8.768m: components and engineering services for AGM-28 missile. LaBarge, Inc. (Tulsa), $5.633m: seismic intrusion devices. Sun Oil (Tulsa), $5.701m: petroleum products.

Economic Base Finance, insurance and real estate; fabricated metal products, especially fabricated structural metal products; machinery, especially construction and related machinery; and transportation equipment, especially aircraft and parts.

The Voters

Registration 208,508 total. 127,025 D (61%); 76,615 R (37%); 4,868 other (2%).
Median voting age 42.3
Employment profile White collar, 55%. Blue collar, 31%. Service, 13%. Farm, 1%.
Ethnic groups Black, 9%. Indian, 3%. Spanish, 1%. Total foreign stock, 4%.

Presidential vote

1972	Nixon (R)	133,381	(79%)
	McGovern (D)	35,199	(21%)
1968	Nixon (R)	86,106	(57%)
	Humphrey (D)	35,522	(23%)
	Wallace (AI)	30,440	(20%)

Representative

James Robert Jones (D) Elected 1972; b. May 5, 1939, Muskogee; home, Tulsa; U. of Okla., B.S.; Georgetown U., LL.D.; married, one child; Catholic.

Career Formerly practicing attorney; owner of business consulting company; Mbr., White House Staff; Asst. to the Pres., 1965–69.

Offices 327 CHOB, 212-225-2211. Also 4536 Fed. Bldg., Tulsa, 918-581-7111.

Administrative Assistant John Lynn

Committees

Armed Services (23rd); Sub: No. 3.

Interior and Insular Affairs (23rd); Subs: No. 2 (Water and Power Resources); No. 3 (Environment); No. 5 (Mines and Mining); No. 6 (Indian Affairs).

Group Ratings: Newly Elected

Key Votes

1) Busing	NE	6) Cmbodia Bmbg	ABS	11) Chkg Acct Intrst	ABS
2) Strip Mines	NE	7) Bust Hwy Trust	AGN	12) End HISC (HUAC)	AGN
3) Cut Mil $	NE	8) Farm Sub Lmt	NE	13) Nixon Sewer Veto	FOR
4) Rev Shrg	NE	9) School Prayr	NE	14) Corp Cmpaign $	NE
5) Pub TV $	NE	10) Cnsumr Prot	NE	15) Pol $ Disclosr	NE

Election Results

1972 general:	James R. Jones (D)	91,864	(54%)
	J. M. Hewgley, Jr. (R)	73,786	(44%)
	Paul W. Polin (Ind.)	3,002	(2%)
1972 primary:	James R. Jones (D)	31,306	(80%)
	Richard W. Ninde (D)	7,679	(20%)

SECOND DISTRICT Political Background

The 2nd district of Oklahoma takes in all of the northeast quarter of the state, except for the Tulsa area that makes up the 1st district. The 2nd is the place where most of Oklahoma's Indians, removed from their ancestral lands in the South and the Midwest, were forcibly relocated. Fully 8% of the population of the 2nd is Indian, and probably a larger percentage can claim Indian blood. The county names echo the Civilized Tribes: Cherokee, Delaware, Ottawa, Osage, Creek. Beginning in 1889 (see Oklahoma state write-up), white settlers from the Democratic Deep South and the Republican Ozarks moved in. As a result, the 2nd district remains to this day something of a political borderland between Republican and Democratic territory. Meanwhile, the Indians here do not vote in any markedly different way from the rest of the population.

The district's largest city is Muskogee (pop. 37,000), a rather run-down Oklahoma rural center. Anyone who has heard Merle Haggard's classic "Okie From Muskogee" has a fair idea of the political leanings of the area; people here have little use for longhairs, peace demonstrators, or intellectuals of any sort. Will Rogers is remembered in these parts with favor; but Woody Guthrie, also a native Oklahoman, is not.

Until Democrat Ed Edmondson ran for the Senate in 1972, he represented the 2nd district in the House for 20 years. His own changing political views pretty well reflect the similarly changing views of his constituency. During the New Frontier, Edmondson was a fairly dependable supporter of the Kennedy Administration, which did not create too many problems for him at home. But during the Johnson and Nixon years, Edmondson grew steadily more conservative. By the time he ran for the Senate, he embraced that label; and the reason he lost was probably only because Oklahoma voters failed to perceive him as conservative enough.

To make a Senate bid, Edmondson gave up a good deal of seniority in the House. In the 92nd Congress, he was the number-three Democrat on the Interior Committee, and held a high position on Public Works. The latter assignment was quite significant to this district, one laced with dams and man-made lakes, and above all, blessed with the McClellan-Kerr Navigation System, which has made the Arkansas River navigable up to the port of Tulsa.

The 2nd district, however, got some compensation for the loss of Edmondson, having elected a new Congressman who clearly has high-placed friends. By 1972, Clem Rogers McSpadden, a grand-nephew of the late Will Rogers, had spent nearly 20 years in the state Senate, and had also run the National Finals Rodeo in Oklahoma City. As such, McSpadden was well known in the district; he therefore easily won both the Democratic primary and the general election—the latter, in fact, by a margin larger than Edmondson's recent ones. In the House, McSpadden was favored with an assignment to the Rules Committee, something not usually given a freshman. But McSpadden clearly had the support of Speaker Carl Albert of Oklahoma's 3rd district. So there is little chance that the new Congressman will cast any votes on Rules that will displease the Speaker.

Census Data Pop. 426,778. Central city, 0%; suburban, 22%. Median family income, $9,527; families above $15,000: 19%; families below $3,000: 21%. Median years education, 12.3.

1972 Share of Federal Outlays $395,327,580

DOD	$35,794,132	HEW	$201,356,294
AEC	$22,214	HUD	$3,463,220
NASA	$16,566	DOI	$16,437,005
DOT	$16,474,996	USDA	$21,410,039
		Other	$100,353,114

Federal Military-Industrial Commitments

DOD Contractors Glen Barry Manufacturing (Commerce), $5.180m: unspecified.

Economic Base Agriculture, notably cattle, dairy products and grains; finance, insurance and real estate; and stone, clay and glass products, especially pressed or blown glass and glassware, and flat glass.

The Voters

Registration 215,929 total. 167,395 D (78%); 46,181 R (21%); 2,353 other (1%).
Median voting age 47.3
Employment profile White collar, 41%. Blue collar, 39%. Service, 15%. Farm, 5%.
Ethnic groups Black, 6%. Indian, 8%. Total foreign stock, 2%.

Presidential vote

1972	Nixon (R)	126,446	(73%)
	McGovern (D)	46,648	(27%)
1968	Nixon (R)	73,878	(45%)
	Humphrey (D)	55,776	(34%)
	Wallace (AI)	35,640	(22%)

Representative

Clem McSpadden (D) Elected 1972; b. Nov. 9, 1925, Bushyhead; home, Chelsea; U. of Redlands; Arlington State; U. of Texas; Okla. State U., B.A.; married, one child; Methodist.

Career Sportscaster, ABC's Wide World of Sports; Okla. State Senate, 1954–72.

Offices 1233 LHOB, 202-225-2701. Also Will Rogers Hotel, Claremore, 918-341-6776.

Administrative Assistant Peggy McBride

Committees

Rules (10th).

Group Ratings: Newly Elected

Key Votes

1) Busing	NE	6) Cmbodia Bmbg	ABS	11) Chkg Acct Intrst	AGN
2) Strip Mines	NE	7) Bust Hwy Trust	AGN	12) End HISC (HUAC)	ABS
3) Cut Mil $	NE	8) Farm Sub Lmt	NE	13) Nixon Sewer Veto	AGN
4) Rev Shrg	NE	9) School Prayr	NE	14) Corp Cmpaign $	NE
5) Pub TV $	NE	10) Cnsumr Prot	NE	15) Pol $ Disclosr	NE

Election Results

1972 general:	Clem R. McSpadden (D)	105,110	(71%)
	Emery H. Toliver (R)	42,632	(29%)
1972 primary:	Clem R. McSpadden (D)	59,063	(62%)
	Robert S. Gee (D)	17,506	(18%)
	Robert Collins (D)	14,691	(15%)
	Davis J. Moore (D)	3,539	(4%)

THIRD DISTRICT Political Background

In 1908, Carl Albert, now Speaker of the House, was born in the village of Bug Tussle, here in the 3d district of Oklahoma. His father was a coal miner in this poor country of red hills. The family never had much money, but young Carl was good at the books and won a scholarship to the University of Oklahoma. There he excelled in his studies and on the debating team, and won a Rhodes scholarship. After military service in World War II, "the little giant from Little Dixie" (he is 5´4˝) ran for Congress in 1946. Albert took the Democratic runoff primary by 330 votes out of 54,000 cast.

Republicans are scarce in the southern Oklahoma counties (Little Dixie) that make up the 3rd congressional district. So Albert easily won the general election and went to Washington, where he quickly caught the eye of Speaker Sam Rayburn, whose Texas district lay just across the Red River from Albert's 3rd. Albert became Majority Whip in 1955 and, on the elevation of John McCormack to the Speakership, Majority Leader in 1962.

Seniority determines almost everything in the House, and so when McCormack retired in 1970, Albert, who was clearly in line, became Speaker. During the many years he put in marshalling votes for the leadership, Albert made few enemies. Moreover, he possessed a solidly liberal record on domestic issues and an even more solid record of support for the foreign and military policies of the Johnson and Nixon Administrations. In 1971, at least, Albert's combination of views were palatable to a majority of the House Democratic Caucus.

Once Albert became Speaker, however, complaints began to accumulate. Democrats of all kinds said that Albert was not leading, that his style was too polite, languid, and do-nothing. By contrast, Albert's critics continued, Gerald Ford exerted tight discipline on House Republicans. And there was some talk about Albert's health, the Speaker having suffered a heart attack in the mid-1950s. In Albert's defense, it must be said that the body of House Democrats is not one prone to discipline or regimentation. Democratic Congressmen tend to be feisty and individualistic, knowing that reelection depends on their own personal popularity and not on what their constituents think of the Democratic party in general. The days when a tightly run Democratic Caucus could automatically work its will in the House are gone; indeed, they have been gone since the second term of Woodrow Wilson.

Nevertheless, Albert has made some moves to make the leadership more effective and responsive. He has tried to revive the Democratic Steering Committee, which has a membership elected by Congressmen representing the various regions. He has called more frequent meetings of the Democratic Caucus; in the most important meeting so far the Caucus voted overwhelmingly in the spring of 1973 to stop the bombing of Cambodia—over the opposition of key committee chairmen. Albert has also worked to wrest for the leadership some of the power held by committee chairmen. For example, the Speaker bucked Chairman Edward Hébert when Albert insisted that California's Ron Dellums and Colorado's Patricia Schroeder, two antiwar liberals, serve on Hébert's Armed Services Committee. And with the retirement of Mississippi's William Colmer, Albert has pretty well gotten control of the Rules Committee, which schedules the flow of legislation onto the floor and sets the rules under which it may be considered.

Albert has also made concessions to Caucus opinion on policy questions. For example, the Speaker himself vigorously backed the move to halt the bombing of Cambodia, which was a sharp break with his previous position on the issue. And though personally unenthusiastic about the measure, he helped clear the bill to crack the highway trust fund through the Rules Committee. The Speaker is not yet in a position to deliver Democratic votes with the reliability Gerald Ford delivers Republican ones, but Albert has made some progress in that direction. The one thing Albert has not done, and surely never will do, is to depose committee chairmen who work against positions taken by Caucus majorities.

While Albert has had troubles in Washington he can do very little wrong back in the 3rd district of Oklahoma. The 3rd is the most Democratic district in the state, even though it delivered a solid majority to Richard Nixon in 1972. The banner Democratic counties are found along the Red River and in Albert's native coal mining counties just to the north. Farther north, the odd excrescence of the district was added to bring the population-losing 3rd up to equal population standards. Albert's district is a hotbed of an old-fashioned kind of populism. But it also has roots in the South, as shown by the 27% George Wallace took here in 1968; that percentage represents Wallace's best in any congressional district outside of the 11 states of the old Confederacy. Nevertheless, since his first election in 1946, the Democratic Albert has not had any trouble winning reelection. The residents of the 3rd seem proud of the native son's success; the main street in McAlester, the Speaker's home town, has been renamed Carl Albert Parkway.

Census Data Pop. 426,596. Central city, 0%; suburban, 8%. Median family income, $6,567; families above $15,000: 9%; families below $3,000: 24%. Median years education, 10.9.

1972 Share of Federal Outlays $392,714,421

DOD	$49,687,859	HEW	$214,040,839
AEC	–	HUD	$3,919,845
NASA	–	DOI	$5,187,114
DOT	$7,002,066	USDA	$43,864,871
		Other	$69,011,827

OKLAHOMA

830

Federal Military-Industrial Commitments

DOD Installations Naval Ammunition Depot (McAlester).

Economic Base Agriculture, notably cattle, poultry, grains and dairy products; oil and gas extraction, especially oil and gas field services and crude petroleum and natural gas; finance, insurance and real estate; and apparel and other textile products, especially men's and boys' furnishings.

The Voters

Registration 229,811 total. 211,895 D (92%); 16,619 R (7%); 1,297 other (1%).
Median voting age 49.8
Employment profile White collar, 39%. Blue collar, 40%. Service, 15%. Farm, 6%.
Ethnic groups Black, 6%. Indian, 5%. Total foreign stock, 2%.

Presidential vote

1972	Nixon (R)	113,281	(70%)
	McGovern (D)	47,962	(30%)
1968	Nixon (R)	57,086	(35%)
	Humphrey (D)	63,021	(39%)
	Wallace (AI)	43,355	(27%)

Representative

Carl Bert Albert (D) Elected 1946; b. May 10, 1908, McAlester; home, McAlester; U. of Okla., B.A., 1931; Rhodes Scholar, Oxford U., B.A., 1933, B.C.L., 1934; Army, WWII; married, two children; Methodist.

Career Legal Clerk, FHA, 1934–37; Atty., Accountant, Sayre Oil Co., 1937–38; Legal Dept., Ohio Oil Co., 1939–40; practicing atty., 1938–39; Majority Whip, 1955–62; Dem. Majority Leader, 1962–1970.

Offices 2205 RHOB, 202-225-4565. Also Fed. Bldg., McAlester 74501, 918-423-7710.

Administrative Assistant Charles Ward

Committees

(Speaker of the House)

Group Ratings and Key Votes: Speaker votes only to break ties.

Election Results

1972 general:	Carl Albert (D)	101,732	(93%)
	Harold J. Marshall (Ind.)	7,242	(7%)
1973 primary:	Carl Albert (D)	100,810	(86%)
	Marvin D. Andrews (D)	16,755	(14%)
1970 general:	Carl Albert (D), unopposed		

FOURTH DISTRICT Political Background

The 4th district of Oklahoma includes most of southwestern Oklahoma and part of metropolitan Oklahoma City. The counties along the Red River, which constitutes the state's southern border, resemble adjacent areas in Texas—cotton-growing Democratic strongholds. But as one moves north, the district becomes politically more marginal. The 4th's portion of Oklahoma City and its suburbs is definitely Republican, and so, more often than not, is Cleveland County, which contains Norman and the University of Oklahoma. The campus here is one where the football program, though tainted by scandal, remains considerably more popular than Herman Hesse, not to speak of McGovernite politics. The 1967 redistricting radically altered the 4th district, and the only county it now has in common with the pre-1967 district is Pottawatomie, the home of Congressman Tom Steed.

First elected in 1948, Steed is a moderate-to-conservative Democrat. Recently, he has experienced some trouble at the polls. In 1966, a good Republican year in Oklahoma, Steed won reelection by a scant 364 votes. And in 1968, Steed was forced to run against another incumbent, Republican James Smith, whose home also lay in the redistricted 4th. The Steed-Smith race possessed national significance that went unnoticed at the time. If Steed had lost, the Oklahoma delegation would have been deadlocked at three Democrats and three Republicans. Then if the presidential election had gone to the House—a real possibility, as George Wallace knew —Oklahoma would have had no vote in an election where each state would have had one vote. The result could have resulted in a complete deadlock over the making of the President in 1968.

The contingency, of course, never arose. And in any case, Steed won the election in 1968, improving on his showing the last time out. But the results failed to prevent the Republicans from making a major effort to win the seat in 1970. Their candidate was Jay Wilkinson, a 28-year-old White House assistant and son of presidential advisor and ex-football coach in Norman, Bud Wilkinson. Young Wilkinson's campaign was an energetic one, with TV and radio ads and visits from Cabinet members. Jay was also the beneficiary of a large contribution from Nixon's favorite financial angel, W. Clement Stone, Chicago insurance millionaire. Nevertheless, Steed again improved on his previous time out, winning 64% of the votes.

It seemed a bit odd to see so much White House involvement with the campaign in the 4th district. Steed, after all, was the Chairman of the Appropriations subcommittee with jurisdiction over the White House budget, and following the revelations about White House spending, it now appears that Steed and his colleagues gave the Nixon operatives a generous purse and a free hand, especially when it came to any question about the President's personal security. Accordingly, the Western White House at San Clemente was the recipient of millions of taxpayer dollars in the name of security, with some of the dollars being spent for such things as a swimming pool heater and pillow cushions.

Steed's subcommittee reacted with some chagrin to the accounting. Written into its new appropriations bill was a provision that made all security improvements subject to subcommittee scrutiny. And the $1.5 million White House "special projects" fund—out of which the plumbers were paid—was eliminated. Even at that, the rebellious House came within a few votes of slashing Steed's subcommittee's bill even further.

Census Data Pop. 426,330. Central city, 20%; suburban, 41%. Median family income, $5,846; families above $15,000: 7%; families below $3,000: 15%. Median years education, 10.2.

1972 Share of Federal Outlays $685,144,302

DOD	$358,408,442	HEW	$138,265,916
AEC	$9,241	HUD	$11,491,458
NASA	$28,588	DOI	$14,877,467
DOT	$34,700,668	USDA	$49,974,054
		Other	$77,388,468

Federal Military-Industrial Commitments

DOD Installations Fort Sill AB (Lawton). Altus AFB (Altus). Oklahoma City AF Station (Midwest City).

Economic Base Agriculture, notably cattle, grains and dairy products; finance, insurance and real estate; food and kindred products; oil and gas extraction, especially crude petroleum and natural gas; and machinery. Also higher education (Univ. of Oklahoma)

The Voters

Registration 170,002 total. 143,241 D (84%); 24,001 R (14%); 2,760 other (2%).
Median voting age 38.8
Employment profile White collar, 49%. Blue collar, 32%. Service, 14%. Farm, 5%.
Ethnic groups Black, 6%. Indian, 3%. Spanish, 3%. Total foreign stock, 5%.

Presidential vote

1972	Nixon (R)	107,548	(74%)
	McGovern (D)	37,542	(26%)
1968	Nixon (R)	60,270	(41%)
	Humphrey (D)	54,299	(37%)
	Wallace (AI)	31,065	(21%)

Representative

Tom Steed (D) Elected 1948; b. March 2, 1904, near Rising Star, Tex.; home, Shawnee; Army, WWII; married, one child; Methodist.

Career Office of War Information, 1944–45; newspaperman on Okla. dailies; Managing Editor, *Shawnee News and Star.*

Offices 2405 RHOB, 202-225-6165. Also P.O. Box 1265, 124 E. Main St., Norman 73069, 405-329-6500.

Administrative Assistant Truman Richardson

Committees

Appropriations (10th); Subs: Transportation; Treasury, Postal Service, General Government (Chm.).

House Restaurant (2nd).

Sel. Com. on Small Business (2nd); Sub: Taxation and Oil Imports (Chm.).

Group Ratings

	ADA	COPE	LWV	RIPON	NFU	LCV	CFA	NAB	NSI	ACA
1972	19	73	44	44	86	11	0	40	100	62
1971	22	100	67	47	71	–	57	–	–	40
1970	24	34	–	47	69	39	69	44	89	42

Key Votes

1) Busing	AGN	6) Cmbodia Bmbg	FOR	11) Chkg Acct Intrst	AGN
2) Strip Mines	AGN	7) Bust Hwy Trust	AGN	12) End HISC (HUAC)	AGN
3) Cut Mil $	AGN	8) Farm Sub Lmt	AGN	13) Nixon Sewer Veto	AGN
4) Rev Shrg	AGN	9) School Prayr	AGN	14) Corp Cmpaign $	FOR
5) Pub TV $	FOR	10) Cnsumr Prot	FOR	15) Pol $ Disclosr	FOR

Election Results

1972 general:	Tom Steed (D)	85,578	(71%)
	William E. Crozier	34,484	(29%)
1972 primary:	Tom Steed (D)	47,970	(88%)
	Owen Trotter (D)	6,768	(12%)
1970 general:	Tom Steed (D)	67,743	(64%)
	Jay G. Wilkinson (R)	37,081	(35%)
	Mary H. Rawls (AI)	1,000	(1%)

FIFTH DISTRICT Political Background

Oklahoma City is the capital of Oklahoma and its largest city (pop. 366,000). During the last ten years, the people here apparently decided that a given set of city limits would not, as it has other central cities, serve as a straitjacket, and thereby cut Oklahoma City off from the prosperity and growth of the surrounding suburbs. Accordingly, Oklahoma City has now annexed so much territory that it spills into five counties and three congressional districts. As it is, Oklahoma City is a sprawling and unplanned metropolis—towering above the plains are a few skyscrapers, at the foot of which are some parking lots. Like Tulsa, the wealth of Oklahoma City is based mainly on oil; even the grounds of the state Capitol building sport a few pumping units. And like most cities in the Southwest, Oklahoma City is conservative and Republican; less so, however, than Tulsa (see Oklahoma 1).

Sitting at just about mid-continent and far enough south to avoid the heaviest winter snows, Oklahoma City has become something of an aviation center—thanks mostly to the federal government. The FAA's Aeronautical Center is located within the city limits, as is an Air Force base. The siting of the FAA installation here was largely due to the efforts of the last two Congressmen from the 5th district, one that contains most of Oklahoma City and a few suburbs. Mike Monroney, who represented the district from 1939 until his election to the Senate in 1950, was Chairman of a committee with jurisdiction over the nation's aviation efforts. And John Jarman, the present Congressman who succeeded Monroney, is Chairman of the Commerce Subcommittee on Transportation and Aeronautics. Jarman is not an especially active legislator. Until 1971, he chaired the Public Health Subcommittee, one that made few waves until his successor, Paul Rogers of Florida, took over (see Florida 11).

Jarman is a fairly conservative Democrat from a district that has trended Republican in most elections for at least a decade. Nonetheless, until 1972, he won reelection by margins on the order of 3–1. One is tempted to ascribe Jarman's rather low 60% showing in 1972 to the Nixon landslide. But the Democratic primary also gave Jarman a little more trouble than usual. Jarman faced five opponents, none of whom came close, but all of whom held him to 65% of the votes—a smaller percentage than is usually won by incumbents of long standing. Whether these showings indicate vulnerability to strong opposition—which Jarman has not faced in some time—will not become clear until 1974, or at some later election. One asset Jarman will continue to enjoy is the solid support of 100-year-old E. K. Gaylord, the still-active and conservative publisher of the two Oklahoma City newspapers.

Census Data Pop. 426,484. Central city, 79%; suburban, 21%. Median family income, $7,569; families above $15,000: 12%; families below $3,000: 9%. Median years education, 12.1.

1972 Share of Federal Outlays $655,259,264

DOD	$283,550,124	HEW	$136,621,831
AEC	$25,834	HUD	$17,526,021
NASA	$79,919	DOI	$11,202,128
DOT	$87,925,045	USDA	$8,927,882
		Other	$109,400,480

Federal Military-Industrial Commitments

DOD Contractors Blair Algernon, Inc. (Tinker AFB), $10.516m: construction services.
DOD Installations Tinker AFB (Oklahoma City).

Economic Base Finance, insurance and real estate; machinery; fabricated metal products, especially fabricated structural metal products; oil and gas extraction, especially crude petroleum and natural gas; and food and kindred products, especially meat products. Also higher education (Central State Univ.).

The Voters

Registration 200,106 total. 144,906 D (72%); 51,044 R (26%); 4,156 other (2%).
Median voting age 42.1
Employment profile White collar, 56%. Blue collar, 30%. Service, 13%. Farm, 1%.
Ethnic groups Black, 11%. Indian, 2%. Spanish, 2%. Total foreign stock, 4%.

Presidential vote

1972	Nixon (R)	126,859	(76%)
	McGovern (D)	39,955	(24%)
1968	Nixon (R)	67,193	(50%)
	Humphrey (D)	42,532	(32%)
	Wallace (AI)	24,428	(18%)

Representative

John Jarman (D) Elected 1950; b. July 17, 1915, Sallisaw; home, Oklahoma City; Westminster Col., 1932–34; Yale U., B.A., 1937; Harvard, LL.B., 1941; Army, WWII; widowed, three children; Presbyterian.

Career Practicing atty; Okla. House of Reps., 1947; Okla. State Senate, 1948.

Offices 2416 RHOB, 202-225-2132. Also 715 Fed. Bldg., Oklahoma City 73102, 405-231-4541, ext. 543.

Administrative Assistant Mrs. Juanita Mosher

Committees

Interstate and Foreign Commerce (3rd); Sub: Transportation and Aeronautics (Chm.).

Group Ratings

	ADA	COPE	LWV	RIPON	NFU	LCV	CFA	NAB	NSI	ACA
1972	6	9	22	47	33	27	100	91	100	80
1971	8	10	0	60	50	–	25	–	–	88
1970	0	20	–	47	17	40	70	89	100	75

Key Votes

1) Busing	AGN	6) Cmbodia Bmbg	FOR	11) Chkg Acct Intrst	AGN
2) Strip Mines	AGN	7) Bust Hwy Trust	AGN	12) End HISC (HUAC)	AGN
3) Cut Mil $	AGN	8) Farm Sub Lmt	FOR	13) Nixon Sewer Veto	FOR
4) Rev Shrg	FOR	9) School Prayr	FOR	14) Corp Cmpaign $	FOR
5) Pub TV $	ABS	10) Cnsumr Prot	FOR	15) Pol $ Disclosr	FOR

Election Results

1972 general:	John Jarman (D)	69,710	(60%)
	Llewellyn L. Keller, Jr. (R)	45,711	(40%)
1972 primary:	John Jarman (D)	28,785	(65%)
	Al E. Engel (D)	9,011	(20%)
	Archibald Hill (D)	3,278	(7%)
	Robert R. Sanders (D)	1,988	(4%)
	Jack K. Gillespie (D)	1,234	(3%)
1970 general:	John Jarman (D)	62,034	(74%)
	Terry L. Campbell (R)	22,301	(26%)

SIXTH DISTRICT Political Background

The 6th district of Oklahoma occupies the northwest and north central part of the state. It includes the thin panhandle that goes west to touch the borders of Colorado and New Mexico. Aside from a small portion of Oklahoma City and its suburbs, the 6th is almost entirely rural. Around the turn of the century, the plains west of Tulsa and Oklahoma City attracted thousands of migrants—probably a majority of them from nearby Kansas. Like so many settlers of the Great Plains, these people mistakenly assumed the land was more fertile and the rain fell more often than was really the case. The Dust Bowl of the 1930s hit already-arid northwest Oklahoma hard, and in many ways it has yet to recover. In 1907, when Oklahoma was admitted to the Union, there were 401,000 people living in the counties now contained in the 6th district. According to the 1970 census, the same territory now has only 390,000 residents.

Due probably to the Kansas origin of its first settlers, the 6th has always been the most Republican part of Oklahoma. Now, with a strong conservative trend running in the state, it has become one of the most Republican regions of the entire nation. In 1972, Richard Nixon won a larger share of the votes in the 6th district (79%) than in any other congressional district outside the Deep South.

For the most part, the radical redistricting of 1967 accounts for the present shape of the district. Before 1967, most of what is now the 6th was in the same district with Tulsa—a convenient way for the Democratic legislature to corral all the most Republican parts of the state into one district. In 1968, the then-new 6th district elected its first and so far only Congressman—a man with the agreeable name of John N. Happy Camp. A staunchly conservative Republican and 20-year veteran of the state Senate, Camp serves on the Interior and the Science and Astronautics committees. The Congressman has won reelection easily, something he will continue to do as long as he runs.

Census Data Pop. 427,445. Central city, 5%; suburban, 10%. Median family income, $9,305; families above $15,000: 19%; families below $3,000: 15%. Median years education, 12.3.

1972 Share of Federal Outlays $522,879,662

DOD	$103,810,034	HEW	$166,698,057
AEC	$19,122	HUD	$3,057,025
NASA	$791,236	DOI	$8,488,420
DOT	$19,987,646	USDA	$147,025,404
		Other	$73,002,718

Federal Military-Industrial Commitments

DOD Contractors Service Air, Inc. (Enid), $10.813m: transportation services.

DOD Installations Vance AFB (Enid).

Economic Base Agriculture, notably cattle, grains and dairy products; finance, insurance and real estate; food and kindred products; and oil and gas extraction. Also higher education (Oklahoma State Univ.).

The Voters

Registration 222,801 total. 147,726 D (66%); 72,543 R (33%); 2,532 other (1%).
Median voting age 45.2
Employment profile White collar, 45%. Blue collar, 29%. Service, 15%. Farm, 11%.
Ethnic groups Black, 2%. Indian, 2%. Spanish, 1%. Total foreign stock, 5%.

Presidential vote

1972	Nixon (R)	150,998	(79%)
	McGovern (D)	39,712	(21%)
1968	Nixon (R)	101,498	(57%)
	Humphrey (D)	49,023	(28%)
	Wallace (AI)	26,737	(15%)

Representative

John N. (Happy) **Camp** (R) Elected 1968; b. May 11, 1908, Enid; home, Waukomis; Phillips U.; married, four children; Disciples of Christ.

Career Pres., Waukomis State Bank; Okla. House of Reps., 1943–62; Chm., Okla. Bd. of Public Affairs, 1967–68.

Offices 1406 LHOB, 202-225-5565. Also 231 Fed. Bldg., Enid 73701, 405-233-1969.

Administrative Assistant Mrs. Joan Southard

Committees

Interior and Insular Affairs (7th); Subs: Mines and Mining (Ranking Mbr.); Indian Affairs; National Parks and Recreation; Water and Power Resources.

Science and Astronautics (8th); Subs: Space Science and Applications; International Cooperation in Science and Space; Manned Space Flight.

Group Ratings

	ADA	COPE	LWV	RIPON	NFU	LCV	CFA	NAB	NSI	ACA
1972	0	0	17	38	43	17	0	92	100	100
1971	5	9	11	38	43	–	0	–	–	85
1970	12	9	–	33	25	0	43	100	100	88

Key Votes

1) Busing	AGN	6) Cmbodia Bmbg	ABS	11) Chkg Acct Intrst	ABS
2) Strip Mines	AGN	7) Bust Hwy Trust	AGN	12) End HISC (HUAC)	AGN
3) Cut Mil $	AGN	8) Farm Sub Lmt	AGN	13) Nixon Sewer Veto	AGN
4) Rev Shrg	AGN	9) School Prayr	FOR	14) Corp Cmpaign $	FOR
5) Pub TV $	ABS	10) Cnsumr Prot	AGN	15) Pol $ Disclosr	FOR

Election Results

1972 general:	John N. (Happy) Camp (R)	113,567	(73%)
	William P. Schmitt (D)	42,663	(27%)
1972 primary:	John N. (Happy) Camp (R), unopposed		
1970 general:	John N. (Happy) Camp (R)	81,959	(64%)
	R. O. (Joe) Cassity, Jr. (D)	45,742	(36%)

OREGON

Political Background

"Come visit Oregon again and again, but for heaven's sakes don't come to live here." Such are not the words of a Portland nature-food freak or Sierra Club activist, but of Tom McCall, Governor of Oregon. The sentiment reflects a growing consensus in this sparsely populated state—one settled by some Yankee farmers who first took the Oregon Trail west in 1848. McCall and the present-day citizens of Oregon—still overwhelmingly white and Protestant—do not advocate a policy of no growth for the state; in fact, during the 1960s its population rose 18%, a figure higher than the national average. But the first priority of Oregonians is a desire to preserve the state's natural environment: the lush hills and mountainsides studded with wildflowers; the long, rocky beaches; and the majestic Columbia River.

Yet for all of the wonders of nature, most of the people of the state live in its urban and suburban areas, with some 80% of its two million plus residents in the Willamette River valley alone. But even here Oregonians have managed to do some good things; for one, they have cleaned up the once-polluted Willamette River over the objections of lumber interests and lumber workers. And statewide, Gov. McCall and the Republican legislature made Oregon the first to ban throwaway beer and soft-drink containers.

What Oregonians fear most is the fate that descended upon its neighbor to the south—California—a fate that some call "Californication." So far, Oregon has escaped it. In the two decades following World War II, both California and Washington to the north boomed, as defense and aerospace industries moved in. But Oregon experienced little of the West Coast post-war boom; in fact, the Defense Department, one of the nation's great agents of change, spends less money per capita here than in any other state except Iowa and West Virginia. The economy of Oregon depends instead upon a rather old-fashioned industry—lumber. The market for lumber, of course, is one subject to ups and downs; presently, it is down as interest rates are high, mortgage money tight, and hence a decline in new home construction and lumber use. But in Oregon, the effects of the building slump have been cushioned by an increasing demand from Japan for lumber. So with lumber prices still high, Oregon has not suffered from the kind of heavy unemployment that has afflicted Los Angeles and Seattle.

If the economy of Oregon demonstrates a certain stability, so, too, does its politics. Unlike most other states, no long-standing political divisions exist between various parts of the state. It is true that the coastal areas and the Columbia River valley are marginally more Democratic than the rest of the state; and that Salem, the state capital, is usually more Republican than Eugene, the site of the University of Oregon. Also, the low-lying, less affluent sections of Portland near the Columbia and Willamette rivers are usually Democratic, while the city neighborhoods and suburbs in the surrounding hills are Republican. But there is no tradition here of regional rivalry—nothing like the difference between arch-conservative Orange County and liberal San Francisco in California.

It is, therefore, no real surprise that Oregon's two Senators hold office by virtue of a combined total of a scant 73,000 votes. The closer of the two Senate races occurred in 1968, when state Rep. Robert Packwood upset incumbent Sen. Wayne Morse by 3,445 votes. A University of Oregon law professor, Morse first won election to the Senate as a Republican in 1944. Later, out of disgust with the Eisenhower Administration, Morse switched to Independent status, and then in 1956 and 1962, he was reelected as a Democrat. Morse was one of the earliest and most vehement opponents of the Vietnam war; he was, in fact, one of the two Senators who voted against the Gulf of Tonkin resolution in 1964. Morse also served as Chairman of the Senate Labor and Public Welfare Committee. All in all, the Oregon Senator's outspoken ways won him many enemies. And in 1968, when he just barely beat hawkish Congressman Robert Duncan in the Democratic primary, everyone knew that Morse was in deep trouble.

Republican Packwood's close victory over Morse than made him the Senate's youngest member, though Packwood has since been supplanted in that position by the even younger Joseph Biden of Delaware. The Oregon politician has rather liberal inclinations, but also an instinctive desire to hold fast to orthodox Republican positions whenever possible. Therefore, his vote was one of several key swing votes in several close issues confronting the Senate during the first Nixon term, and will probably be the same during the second.

Packwood has gained the most recognition as the Senate's leading proponent of the zero population growth idea—a position not unpopular in pollution-conscious, heavily Protestant Oregon. At this writing, his prospects for reelection look good. But because most major races in Oregon are close, no one can say that Packwood is a sure winner.

The state's senior Senator, Mark Hatfield, is a former professor at Willamette College and a man who holds deeply to the convictions of a "born-again" evangelical Christian. In 1958, at age 36, Hatfield was elected Governor of Oregon. He was a popular Governor for two terms, the maximum allowed by the Oregon Constitution. So it was a surprise when he won the 1966 Senate race with only 52% of the votes. His opponent in 1966 was the same Congressman Duncan who eventually ran against Morse in 1968; part of Hatfield's problem was his dovish position on the war—still something of a liability during the early years of heavy American involvement in Indochina. During the campaign, Hatfield had the support of Democratic Sen. Morse, but he undoubtedly lost some conservative Republican votes to Duncan, who was then one of the nation's most vocal supporters of LBJ's war policies.

Hatfield is best known in the Senate for his position on the war. In 1970, he co-sponsored the unsuccessful McGovern-Hatfield amendment to end the war, and consistently voted against both the Johnson and the Nixon administrations on matters concerning military and foreign policy. Hatfield's record must have made him feel a little uncomfortable. Like several other liberal Republicans in the Senate, Hatfield believes very strongly in his party, even when its views are out of line with his own. Back in 1968, he even delivered the speech nominating Richard Nixon at the Republican National Convention. As the Senator's first term neared an end in 1971, Hatfield began to hear from more and more Republicans unhappy with his opposition to Nixon policies. Back home, there were rumors that Gov. McCall, a liberal Republican on most issues but a Nixon backer on the war, was considering a primary bid against the Senator. There was also talk that Congresswoman Edith Green of Portland would run for the Democratic nomination; and the polls indicated that she could beat Hatfield. Confronted with the situation, Hatfield appeared genuinely at sea. So in the summer of 1971, he went on a little-publicized tour of Oregon and talked with voters informally.

What came out of it was a strong, well-organized Hatfield campaign in 1972. McCall soon dropped out of the picture, as did Mrs. Green. Hatfield muted his criticism on Nixon, and talked less and less about the war; meanwhile, the White House mounted no campaign against the Oregon heretic. In the Democratic primary, two old adversaries, ex-Sen. Morse, now 71, and ex-Rep. Duncan, competed for the right to face Hatfield. A third candidate, state Sen. Don Willner, stressed ecology issues, but got lost in the crowd. Morse, with the enthusiastic support of hundreds of students, won the primary easily.

The general election, however, was a different kind of affair. Because both candidates were longtime doves and because Morse himself had supported Hatfield six years earlier, most voters could see little difference between the two candidates. So most of them voted for the younger incumbent, Hatfield. Some differences, of course, did exist. Over the years, Morse had compiled a somewhat stronger labor record, while Hatfield was somewhat more responsive to the interests of lumber companies. But the differences, such as they were, cut many ways. Morse's energetic, spirited campaigning, along with his great familiarity with the state, brought him 46% of the votes. But Hatfield won, by nearly 70,000 votes, with 54%.

During the mid-1960s, Democrats had held both of Oregon's Senate seats and then lost them after bitter primaries in which Vietnam was the main issue. For a while, before Hatfield's campaign coalesced in late 1970, it looked as if the Republicans were in for the same thing. Possibilities of splits still exist. Gov. McCall, unable to run for a third term, once threatened to become a Democrat and run against Packwood. But Republican National Chairman George Bush was right when he said that the threat was only part of the effervescent McCall's rites of spring. McCall soon dropped the idea. The Governor's most likely successor is the Secretary of State, Clay Myers. Myers' job is a kind of stepping stone in Oregon politics; fellow liberal Republicans Hatfield and McCall both ascended to the governorship from the post. Meanwhile, all four of Oregon's House members—the state just missed winning a fifth seat after the 1970 census—appear to have made their seats utterly safe.

A final word on presidential politics here. Oregon has gone Republican in five of the last six presidential elections, but seldom by large margins. During the same period, Democratic registration has risen substantially in Oregon. While the voters here seem to retain a narrow preference for liberal Republicans over liberal Democrats in statewide elections, they seem to be shifting to the left in presidential contests. Oregon is one of the four non-Southern states where George McGovern won a larger percentage of the votes in 1972 than Hubert Humphrey did in 1968. Consequently, though Oregon has plunked for Richard Nixon three times, it might very well find itself in the Democratic column in 1976.

Because the Oregon presidential primary takes place just a few weeks before the big contest in California, Oregon voters have often played a decisive role in national elections. In 1948, Oregon's voters eliminated Harold Stassen from any future serious consideration as a presidential candidate. In 1964, Oregon kept Nelson Rockefeller in the race against Barry Goldwater, whom the New Yorker almost beat in California. In 1968, Oregonians gave Eugene McCarthy a hefty boost when it chose him over Robert Kennedy—the only defeat any of the Kennedy brothers has ever suffered at the polls. Oregon's law, which is now being copied by an increasing number of states, requires all candidates, that are recognized as such by the news media to appear on the ballot. The law virtually guarantees an important test of the strength of all candidates.

Census Data Pop. 2,091,385; 1.03% of U.S. total, 31st largest; change 1960–70, 18.2%. Central city, 25%; suburban, 36%. Median family income, $9,487; 22nd highest; families above $15,000: 18%; families below $3,000: 9%. Median years education, 12.3.

1972 Share of Federal Tax Burden $2,006,580,000; 0.96% of U.S. total, 29th largest.

1972 Share of Federal Outlays $1,995,798,845; 0.92% of U.S. total, 32nd largest. Per capita federal spending, $954.

DOD	$180,928,000	42nd	(0.29%)	HEW	$764,643,677	28th	(1.07%)
AEC	$791,427	33rd	(0.03%)	HUD	$28,495,550	31st	(0.93%)
NASA	$866,272	36th	(0.03%)	VA	$141,901,103	29th	(1.24%)
DOT	$151,942,109	20th	(1.93%)	USDA	$285,002,469	21st	(1.85%)
DOC	$14,805,554	21st	(1.14%)	CSC	$50,556,649	21st	(1.23%)
DOI	$132,777,637	5th	(6.26%)	TD	$70,125,315	31st	(0.42%)
DOJ	$13,847,292	25th	(1.41%)	Other	$159,115,791		

Economic Base Lumber and wood products, especially millwork, plywood and related products, and sawmills and planing mills; agriculture, notably cattle, dairy products, wheat and greenhouse; finance, insurance and real estate; food and kindred products, especially canned, cured and frozen foods; machinery, especially construction and related machinery; paper and allied products, especially paper mills other than building paper; transportation equipment.

Political Line-up Governor, Tom McCall (R); seat up, 1974. Senators, Mark O. Hatfield (R) and Robert W. Packwood (R). Representatives, 4 (2 D and 2 R). State Senate (18 D and 12 R); State House (33 D and 27 R).

The Voters

Registration 1,197,676 Total. 673,710 D (56%); 473,907 R (40%); 50,059 other (4%).
Median voting age 44.1
Employment profile White collar, 48%. Blue collar, 34%. Service, 14%. Farm, 4%.
Ethnic groups Black, 1%. Spanish, 2%. Total foreign stock, 14%. Canada, 3%, Germany, 2%, UK, 1%.

Presidential vote

1972	Nixon (R)	486,686	(55%)
	McGovern (D)	392,760	(45%)
1968	Nixon (R)	408,433	(50%)
	Humphrey (D)	358,866	(44%)
	Wallace (AI)	49,683	(6%)
1964	Johnson (D)	501,017	(64%)
	Goldwater (R)	282,779	(36%)

Senator

Mark O. Hatfield (R) Elected 1966, seat up 1978; b. July 12, 1922, Dallas; home, Salem; Williamette U., B.A., 1943; Stanford U., M.A., 1948; USNR, WWII; married, four children; Baptist.

Career Resident Asst., Stanford U., 1947–49; Instr., Williamette U., 1949, Dean of Students, Assoc. Prof., political science, 1950–56; Oreg. House of Reps., 1951–55; Oreg. Senate, 1955–57; Sec. of State, 1957–59; Gov., 1959–67.

Offices 463 OSOB, 202-225-3753. Also 475 Cottage St. NE, Salem 97301, 503-585-1793, ext. 228, and 520 S.W. Morrison, Portland, 503-221-3386

Administrative Assistant Gerald W. Frank

Committees

Appropriations (7th); Subs: Agriculture, Environmental and Consumer Protection; Foreign Operations; Interior; Public Works; Treasury, U.S. Postal Service, and General Government.

Interior and Insular Affairs (3rd); Subs: Parks and Recreation; Public Lands; Water and Power Resources (Ranking Mbr.).

Rules and Administration (4th); Subs: Library (Ranking Mbr.); Computer Services (Ranking Mbr.).

Joint Com. on the Library (2nd).

Sp. Com. to Study Questions Related to Secret and Confidential Government Documents (3rd).

Group Ratings

	ADA	COPE	LWV	RIPON	NFU	LCV	CFA	NAB	NSI	ACA
1972	55	50	90	88	80	47	83	33	0	29
1971	74	33	91	83	64	–	67	–	–	20
1970	84	92	–	91	94	44	–	18	0	17

Key Votes

1) Busing	FOR	8) Sea Life Prot	AGN	15) Tax Singls Less	FOR
2) Alas P-line	AGN	9) Campaign Subs	AGN	16) Min Tax for Rich	AGN
3) Gun Cntrl	FOR	10) Cmbodia Bmbg	AGN	17) Euro Troop Rdctn	FOR
4) Rehnquist	FOR	11) Legal Srvices	FOR	18) Bust Hwy Trust	FOR
5) Pub TV $	ABS	12) Rev Sharing	AGN	19) Maid Min Wage	AGN
6) EZ Votr Reg	AGN	13) Cnsumr Prot	ABS	20) Farm Sub Limit	ABS
7) No-Fault	AGN	14) Eq Rts Amend	FOR	21) Highr Credt Chgs	AGN

Election Results

1972 general:	Mark O. Hatfield (R)	494,671	(54%)
	Wayne L. Morse (D)	425,036	(46%)
1972 primary:	Mark O. Hatfield (R)	171,594	(61%)
	Lynn Engdahl (R)	63,859	(23%)
	Kenneth A. Brown (R)	30,826	(11%)
	John E. Smets (R)	13,397	(5%)
1966 general:	Mark O. Hatfield (R)	354,391	(52%)
	Robert B. Duncan (D)	330,374	(48%)

Senator

Robert W. Packwood (R) Elected 1968, seat up 1974; b. Sept. 11, 1932, Portland; home, Portland; Williamette U., B.A., 1954; N.Y.U., LL.B., 1957; married, two children; Unitarian.

Career Practicing atty., 1958–68; Oreg. House of Reps., 1963–67.

Offices 6327 NSOB, 202-225-5244. Also 1002 N.E. Holladay St., Portland 97232, 503-233-4471.

Administrative Assistant Alan F. Holmer

Committees

Banking, Housing and Urban Affairs (4th); Subs: Housing and Urban Affairs; International Finance; Small Business.

Finance (6th); Subs: International Trade; Health; State Taxation of Interstate Commerce.

Group Ratings

	ADA	COPE	LWV	RIPON	NFU	LCV	CFA	NAB	NSI	ACA
1972	45	40	80	82	33	58	73	22	70	55
1971	30	20	90	77	44	–	43	–	–	60
1970	50	69	–	88	71	47	–	82	60	50

Key Votes

1) Busing	ABS	8) Sea Life Prot	FOR	15) Tax Singls Less	FOR
2) Alas P-line	AGN	9) Campaign Subs	AGN	16) Min Tax for Rich	AGN
3) Gun Cntrl	AGN	10) Cmbodia Bmbg	AGN	17) Euro Troop Rdctn	FOR
4) Rehnquist	FOR	11) Legal Srvices	AGN	18) Bust Hwy Trust	FOR
5) Pub TV $	AGN	12) Rev Sharing	FOR	19) Maid Min Wage	AGN
6) EZ Votr Reg	AGN	13) Cnsumr Prot	FOR	20) Farm Sub Limit	AGN
7) No-Fault	AGN	14) Eq Rts Amend	ABS	21) Highr Credt Chgs	ABS

Election Results

1968 general:	Robert W. Packwood (R)	408,825	(50%)
	Wayne Morse (D)	405,380	(50%)
1968 primary:	Robert W. Packwood (R)	241,464	(88%)
	John S. Boyd (R)	32,087	(12%)

FIRST DISTRICT Political Background

The 1st district of Oregon occupies the northwest corner of the state. This is the area around the mouth of the Columbia River and the coastal counties of Clatsop, Tillamook, and Lincoln—all marginally Democratic. Most of the 1st's residents, however, live in the Portland metropolitan area. The district includes that part of Portland west of the Willamette—hilly, high-income neighborhoods that overlook the city's downtown and both the Willamette and Columbia rivers. Here, as in most Western cities, more affluent people live on the hills, and poorer people in the flat parts of town. About a quarter of the district's votes are cast in Washington County, the fastest-growing in the state; it is an affluent suburban area where the hills rise to meet the Coast Range west of Portland. The 1st also takes in the bulk of three Republican-leaning counties on the west bank of the Willamette. The Republican tendencies of these counties were somewhat lessened in 1972 by the enfranchisement of most of the 14,000 students at Oregon State University in Corvallis.

The district was created in roughly its present form in 1892. Since then, the 1st district has never elected a Democratic Congressman. In recent years, the success of the Republicans cannot be attributed to the overwhelming Republican character of the district; it gave Hubert Humphrey a respectable 42% of the votes in 1968 and George McGovern 43% in 1972. Instead, Republican Congressmen have won here because of personal popularity. The current Congressman, Wendell Wyatt, was a former FBI agent and state legislator; he was first elected in 1964, and has won reelection by phenomenal margins ever since. In 1968, for example, he took 81% of the votes. Wyatt's margins declined somewhat in 1972, mainly because of the student vote in Corvallis and at Portland State College (12,000 students), which lies on the west side of Portland.

In the House, Wyatt is a middle-ranking member of the Appropriations Committee. Accordingly, he has claimed credit for a number of navigational projects important to the district. By and large, Wyatt's voting record is middle-of-the-road He dissents, however, enough times against the Nixon Administration to win him the votes of some, though not all, of the new antiwar students in the district. The Congressman looks like a sure thing in future elections.

Census Data Pop. 523,428. Central city, 15%; suburban, 48%. Median family income, $10,430; families above $15,000: 24%; families below $3,000: 8%. Median years education, 12.5.

1972 Share of Federal Outlays $479,704,652

DOD	$49,916,489	HEW	$194,184,845
AEC	$471,290	HUD	$7,487,020
NASA	$429,421	DOI	$27,539,642
DOT	$33,629,766	USDA	$54,126,041
		Other	$111,920,141

Federal Military-Industrial Commitments

DOD Contractors Textronix, Inc. (Beaverton), $6.203m: laboratory equipment.

Economic Base Finance, insurance and real estate; agriculture, notably fruits, dairy products and poultry; lumber and wood products, especially millwork, plywood and related products; and paper mill products other than building paper, and other paper and allied products. Also higher education (Oregon State Univ., and Portland State University).

The Voters

Registration 319,818 total. 162,779 D (51%); 142,200 R (44%); 14,839 other (5%).
Median voting age 43.1
Employment profile White collar, 54%. Blue collar, 30%. Service, 13%. Farm, 3%.
Ethnic groups Spanish, 2%. Total foreign stock, 16%. Canada, 3%; Germany, UK, 2% each.

Presidential vote

1972	Nixon (R)	137,345	(57%)
	McGovern (D)	101,616	(43%)

1968	Nixon (R)	112,543	(54%)
	Humphrey (D)	85,679	(41%)
	Wallace (AI)	9,230	(4%)

Representative

Wendell Wyatt (R) Elected Nov. 5, 1964; b. June 15, 1917, Eugene; home, Gearhart; U. of Oreg., LL.B., 1941; USMC, WWII; married, five children; Episcopalian.

Career Sp. Agent, FBI, 1941–42; practicing atty., 1946–64.

Offices 2438 RHOB, 202-225-2206. Also 985 42nd St., Milwaukee 97222, 503-654-8408.

Administrative Assistant L. Stanley Kemp

Committees

Appropriations (13th); Subs: Interior; State, Justice, Commerce, and Judiciary.

Group Ratings

	ADA	COPE	LWV	RIPON	NFU	LCV	CFA	NAB	NSI	ACA
1972	25	60	36	47	50	20	0	58	100	52
1971	16	36	67	60	29	–	63	–	–	75
1970	40	50	–	59	45	7	61	83	89	69

Key Votes

1) Busing	AGN	6) Cmbodia Bmbg	AGN	11) Chkg Acct Intrst	AGN
2) Strip Mines	FOR	7) Bust Hwy Trust	FOR	12) End HISC (HUAC)	AGN
3) Cut Mil $	AGN	8) Farm Sub Lmt	AGN	13) Nixon Sewer Veto	FOR
4) Rev Shrg	FOR	9) School Prayr	FOR	14) Corp Cmpaign $	FOR
5) Pub TV $	AGN	10) Cnsumr Prot	FOR	15) Pol $ Disclosr	FOR

Election Results

1972 general:	Wendell Wyatt (R)	166,476	(69%)
	Ralph E. Bunch (D)	76,307	(31%)
1972 primary:	Wendall Wyatt (R), unopposed		
1970 general:	Wendall Wyatt (R)	147,239	(72%)
	Vern Cook (D)	57,837	(28%)

SECOND DISTRICT Political Background

The 2nd district of Oregon contains 25% of the state's population and 73% of its land area. Most of the land lies east of the Cascade Mountains. To the south, the terrain is desert-like; to the north, where rain falls in more generous amounts, one finds much of Oregon's vast forests and supplies of timber. Oregon east of the Cascades is a sparsely-populated region, having some 270,000 people in an area about the size of New England. Before 1965, the 2nd district lay entirely west of the Cascades; it was therefore far out of line with the requirements of the one-man-one-vote ruling. So the redistricting of 1965 added Marion (Salem) and Linn (Albany) counties west of the mountains. The redistricting of 1971 modified the boundaries still further, moving the 2nd into the Portland suburbs of Milwaukie and Oregon City.

All of this line-drawing failed to change the political complexion of the 2nd very much. East Oregon is marginal political territory, where traditional Rocky Mountain populism on pocketbook issues—the area is especially keen on public power development—has been overmatched lately by the mountain country's dislike for what it perceives as East Coast liberalism. The 2nd's portions west of the Cascades, which now come close to outvoting East Oregon, are traditionally more Republican, but not by any great margin.

The 1965 redistricting was expected to cause problems for Democratic Congressman Al Ullman, but did not. After unseating a Republican in 1956, Ullman has won subsequent elections with larger and larger majorities; in 1972, he was unopposed in both the primary and general elections. Though Ullman is hardly a name widely recognized, it soon may become one. The Oregonian is currently the number-two Democrat on the House Ways and Means Committee; and at this writing, Chairman Wilbur Mills is thinking about retirement if his back ailment fails to clear up. Mills announced his intentions in the summer of 1973. And when he did, a sense of surprise moved through Washington, especially in Ullman's office. For more than 15 years, Mills has ruled Ways and Means with an iron hand, and no one claims that Ullman can in any way match the Chairman's expertise among the intricacies of the tax code or the laws governing Social Security.

During the 93rd Congress, Ullman has served as the co-chairman of the Joint Study Committee. The unit is supposed to come up with some procedures allowing Congress to deal with the entire federal budget—income and expenditure—in a manner more rational than it now does. But liberals have already criticized the direction taken by the committee. The critics argue that the upper levels of the Appropriations and the Ways and Means committees (Finance in the Senate) are considerably more conservative than the membership of the Congress as a whole. Therefore, the argument continues, any proposal that would give them more leverage than they already possess would simply give conservatives even more power to bend the political process to their will.

In their assessment of the upper echelons of Appropriations and Ways and Means, the liberals are certainly correct, and Ullman is proof of it. The Congressman was first elected during a time when Eisenhower Administration opposition to public power development on the Snake River was a raging issue. On that issue, Ullman stood clearly to the left of consensus House sentiment. But on the kind of issues that have come increasingly to the fore during the late 1960s and 1970s, Ullman has often taken a more conservative position. He is less sympathetic, for example, to the pleas of environmentalists than to the arguments of lumber companies that want increased cutting privileges on federal land. Moreover, Ullman has supported existing levels of military spending and projects such as the SST. And in an area where Ways and Means has jurisdiction, the Oregon Congressman is not known as a crusader for progressive tax reform.

Census Data Pop. 522,898. Central city, 12%; suburban, 29%. Median family income, $8,821; families above $15,000: 14%; families below $3,000: 11%. Median years education, 12.2.

1972 Share of Federal Outlays $570,155,600

DOD	$44,925,000	HEW	$199,973,655
AEC	$29,534	HUD	$8,518,549
NASA	$20,982	DOI	$30,235,479
DOT	$44,316,021	USDA	$114,495,863
		Other	$127,640,517

Federal Military-Industrial Commitments

DOD Installations Umatilla Army Depot (Hermiston). Keno AF Station (Keno). Kingsley Field, AF (Klamath Falls).

Economic Base Agriculture, notably cattle and grains; lumber and wood products, especially sawmills and planing mills; finance, insurance and real estate; food and kindred products, especially canned, cured and frozen foods; and paper and allied products, especially paper mill products other than building paper.

The Voters

Registration 285,204 total. 155,237 D (54%); 119,248 R (42%); 10,719 other (4%).
Median voting age 45.1
Employment profile White collar, 43%. Blue collar, 34%. Service, 14%. Farm, 9%.
Ethnic groups Spanish, 2%. Total foreign stock, 12%. Canada, Germany, 2% each; UK, 1%.

1972	Nixon (R)	123,857	(60%)
	McGovern (D)	81,195	(40%)
1968	Nixon (R)	104,600	(53%)
	Humphrey (D)	78,080	(40%)
	Wallace (AI)	13,099	(6%)

Representative

Al Ullman (D) Elected 1956; b. March 9, 1914, Great Falls; home, Baker; Whitman Col., B.A., 1935; Columbia U., M.A., 1939; USNR, WWII; married, four children.

Career Real estate broker, builder, 1945–56.

Offices 2207 RHOB, 202-225-5711. Also Box 247, P.O. Bldg., Salem 97308, 503-585-1793, ext. 220.

Administrative Assistant Loren Cox

Committees

Ways and Means (2nd).

Joint Com. on Internal Revenue Taxation (2nd).

Joint Com. on Reduction of Federal Expenditures (4th).

Joint Study Com. on Budget Control (Co-Chm.).

Group Ratings

	ADA	COPE	LWV	RIPON	NFU	LCV	CFA	NAB	NSI	ACA
1972	38	60	89	73	100	26	50	30	20	18
1971	49	75	50	63	92	–	100	–	–	28
1970	52	67	–	47	69	62	83	8	40	41

Key Votes

1) Busing	FOR	6) Cmbodia Bmbg	AGN	11) Chkg Acct Intrst	AGN
2) Strip Mines	AGN	7) Bust Hwy Trust	AGN	12) End HISC (HUAC)	ABS
3) Cut Mil $	AGN	8) Farm Sub Lmt	AGN	13) Nixon Sewer Veto	AGN
4) Rev Shrg	FOR	9) School Prayr	AGN	14) Corp Cmpaign $	FOR
5) Pub TV $	FOR	10) Cnsumr Prot	ABS	15) Pol $ Disclosr	AGN

Election Results

1972 general:	Al Ullman (D), unopposed		
1972 primary:	Al Ullman (D), unopposed		
1970 general:	Al Ullman (D)	100,943	(71%)
	Everett Thoren (R)	40,620	(29%)

THIRD DISTRICT Political Background

Portland is Oregon's big city. Almost half the people of the state live within its metropolitan area, and far more than half within 60 miles of its downtown. The 3rd district of Oregon takes in most of Portland—the four-fifths of it that lies east of the Willamette River. The district also includes most of the Portland suburbs along the Willamette and Columbia rivers. The 3rd's eastern borders stretch to a point near the snow-covered peak of Mount Hood, which at 11,000 feet looks down on Portland, a city famous for roses.

Portland has few of the problems usually associated with central cities. It has little crime, smog, or dilapidated housing. There is a movement to the suburbs, but the city itself retains a sound tax base. Portland is so idyllic that perhaps only its great distance from other urban centers has kept it from growing much faster than it has. One can understand why Oregon Gov. Tom McCall has asked people not to move here, lest the city's attractions turn it into another Los Angeles.

Since 1954, Edith Green has represented Portland and the 3rd district in the House of Representatives. She came to the House with 12 years of classroom teaching experience and a reputation of a flaming liberal. Upon receiving a seat on the Education and Labor Committee, she became known in some quarters as "Mrs. Education." In her early years of service on the committee, Education and Labor was a far different body than it is today. It was then dominated by an alliance of conservative Southern Democrats and Republicans. Today, it lies firmly in the hands of liberal Democrats and a few like-minded Republicans. During both eras of the committee, Mrs. Green found herself among the panel's unhappy minorities. As the flood of Great Society legislation hit Education and Labor, the Congresswoman grew increasingly conservative. She was especially upset when the committee attempted to bypass established state and local boards of education to stimulate innovation. She then emerged as a leading defender of the educational establishment.

Other issues also found Mrs. Green out of step with her former liberal friends. For example, she voted against antiwar legislation. Symbolic of her transformation (or of those around her) were the candidates she supported in Oregon's often crucial presidential primary. In 1968, she was Oregon's big-name backer of Robert Kennedy; in 1972, she supported Sen. Henry Jackson of neighboring Washington.

It was long known that both personal and ideological relations between Mrs. Green and other Democrats on Education and Labor had been deteriorating. But at the beginning of the 93rd Congress, she surprised just about everybody when she left the committee and moved to Appropriations. A move of this sort, if done at all, is something a Congressman would generally attempt in his second or third term, if he is able to swing the requisite votes. But after 18 years in the House, Mrs. Green was the number-two Democrat on Education and Labor, just behind Chairman Carl Perkins of Kentucky. Veteran observers could not remember the last time a House member switched from a position in line for the chairmanship of a major committee to the number-thirty seniority position on another committee. To be sure, Mrs. Green got a seat on the Appropriations subcommittee that has jurisdiction over education, where she will be listened to. Here she might also be able to foil the plans of some of her old adversaries on Education and Labor. But she can never hope to succeed to the chair of her subcommittee, not to speak of the full committee.

Over the years, Mrs. Green has been a champion vote-getter in the 3rd district. She has won as much as 74% of the votes in Portland, which is only a mildly Democratic city. In recent years, however, her percentages have begun to slip a little; last time out, she got only 62%. At 64 years old, Mrs. Green has said that she has no intention of staying in the House for the rest of her life. Nevertheless, she has yet to show any inclination toward retiring, unless her committee shift is a cue that she is thinking of quitting soon.

Census Data Pop. 522,258. Central city, 59%; suburban, 41%. Median family income, $10,001; families above $15,000: 19%; families below $3,000: 8%. Median years education, 12.3.

1972 Share of Federal Outlays $504,092,558

DOD	$55,092,558	HEW	$188,669,871
AEC	$48,740	HUD	$10,525,971
NASA	$179,456	DOI	$32,665,255
DOT	$41,823,940	USDA	$62,587,787
		Other	$113,289,116

Federal Military-Industrial Commitments

DOD Installations Use of Portland International Airport contracted by the Air Force.

Economic Base Finance, insurance and real estate; food and kindred products; transportation equipment, especially ship building and repairing; machinery, especially construction and related machinery; and fabricated metal products, especially fabricated structural metal products.

The Voters

Registration 299,083 total. 188,394 D (63%); 99,753 R (33%); 10,936 other (4%).
Median voting age 45.0
Employment profile White collar, 51%. Blue collar, 34%. Service, 14%. Farm, 1%.
Ethnic groups Black, 4%. Spanish, 2%. Total foreign stock, 18%. Canada, 3%; Germany, UK,
2% each.

Presidential vote

1972	Nixon (R)	106,955	(48%)
	McGovern (D)	115,283	(52%)
1968	Nixon (R)	93,641	(42%)
	Humphrey (D)	116,136	(52%)
	Wallace (AI)	10,757	(5%)

Representative

Edith Green (D) Elected 1954; b. Jan. 17, 1910, Trent, S.D.; home, Portland; Willamette U., 1927–29; U. of Oreg., B.S., 1939; Stanford U., 1944; married, two children; Disciples of Christ.

Career Teacher, 1930–41; Commentator, KALE Radio, 1944–45; free lance radio work, 1944–48; Dir., Public Relations, Oreg. Ed. Assn., 1952–55.

Offices 1501 LHOB, 202-225-4811. Also 344 U.S. Courthouse, Portland 97205, 503-226-3361, ext. 1028.

Administrative Assistant Marilyn Stapleton

Committees

Appropriations (30th); Subs: Labor, Health, Education, and Welfare; Legislative.

Sel. Com. on the House Beauty Shop (2nd).

Group Ratings

	ADA	COPE	LWV	RIPON	NFU	LCV	CFA	NAB	NSI	ACA
1972	25	64	29	58	57	61	0	22	67	55
1971	38	55	44	46	77	–	50	–	–	48
1970	40	55	–	60	64	56	83	10	63	41

Key Votes

1) Busing	AGN	6) Cmbodia Bmbg	ABS	11) Chkg Acct Intrst	ABS
2) Strip Mines	ABS	7) Bust Hwy Trust	FOR	12) End HISC (HUAC)	AGN
3) Cut Mil $	FOR	8) Farm Sub Lmt	AGN	13) Nixon Sewer Veto	FOR
4) Rev Shrg	AGN	9) School Prayr	ABS	14) Corp Cmpaign $	ABS
5) Pub TV $	AGN	10) Cnsumr Prot	FOR	15) Pol $ Disclosr	FOR

Election Results

1972 general:	Edith Green (D)	141,046	(62%)
	Mike Walsh (R)	84,697	(38%)
1972 primary:	Edith Green (D), unopposed		
1970 general:	Edith Green (D)	118,919	(74%)
	Robert E. Dugdale (R)	42,391	(26%)

FOURTH DISTRICT Political Background

The 4th district of Oregon occupies the southwest corner of the state. Though the district contains about half of Oregon's rocky and picturesque Pacific shoreline, most of its people are found inland, in the southern end of the Willamette River valley between the Coast Range and the Cascades. As in most of the West, few people here actually live on farms, though the area produces much of Oregon's famed fruit crop. Instead, most of the people live in small, well-ordered cities like Medford, Grant's Pass, Roseburg, Coos Bay, and Springfield. The largest city here is Eugene (pop. 76,000), the home of the University of Oregon. The ballots of the university's peace-oriented students showed up clearly in the 1972 election returns.

As is the case throughout Oregon, the 4th district has no sharp extremes of political allegiance. Accordingly, party control of its congressional seat has changed three times since 1956 —something that has not occurred in the state's other three districts. From 1962 to 1966, the 4th's Congressman was Democrat Robert Duncan, a liberal on domestic issues and a hawk on Vietnam. Duncan has since appeared to have burned himself out by running for the Senate in 1966, 1968, and 1972—each time doing worse.

Duncan's successor in the House is moderate-to-liberal Republican John Dellenback, a man with a passion for thin bow ties and 1950s style glasses. Though Dellenback has never won by huge margins, he has always hovered in the comfortable 60% region against a wide variety of Democratic opponents. His most recent challenger was Charles Porter, who had served one House term after the 1958 election and was then beaten in 1960. Even then, Porter was a strong peace advocate, but his stance proved not enough to crack Dellenback's support in the district, as the incumbent even carried Eugene. Dellenback has backed antiwar measures and broken with the Nixon Administration on a number of issues where the standard Republican position is not an especially popular in Eugene or the rest of the 4th.

With less than eight years in Congress, Dellenback has risen to become the number-five Republican on the Education and Labor Committee. Barring unforeseen circumstances, he should continue to climb the panel's seniority ladder. One such circumstance might be a congressional candidacy of ex-Sen. (1945–69) Wayne Morse, who lives on his farm near Eugene. As his 1972 Senate bid demonstrated, Morse is still as active and aggressive as ever, though he may not now be quite so popular statewide.

Census Data Pop. 522,801. Central city, 15%; suburban, 26%. Median family income, $8,854; families above $15,000: 14%; families below $3,000: 10%. Median years education, 12.2.

1972 Share of Federal Outlays $441,055,885

DOD	$30,993,953	HEW	$181,815,297
AEC	$241,860	HUD	$1,964,008
NASA	$236,410	DOI	$42,337,256
DOT	$27,711,153	USDA	$53,792,769
		Other	$101,963,179

Federal Military-Industrial Commitments

DOD Installations Naval Facility (Coos Head). North Bend AF Station (North Bend).

Economic Base Lumber and wood products, especially millwork, plywood and related products, and sawmill and planing mill products; agriculture, notably cattle, fruits and dairy products; finance, insurance and real estate; food and kindred products; and paper and allied products, especially paperboard mill products. Also higher education (Univ. of Oregon).

The Voters

Registration 293,571 total. 167,300 D (57%); 112,706 R (38%); 13,565 other (5%).
Median voting age 43.4
Employment profile White collar, 43%. Blue collar, 40%. Service, 13%. Farm, 4%.
Ethnic groups Spanish, 1%. Total foreign stock, 11%. Canada, Germany, 2% each; UK, 1%.

Presidential vote

1972	Nixon (R)	117,977	(56%)
	McGovern (D)	94,456	(44%)

1968   Nixon (R)   97,649   (51%)

1968   Nixon (R)   97,649   (51%)
      Humphrey (D)   78,971   (41%)
      Wallace (AI)   16,597   (9%)

Representative

John Dellenback (R) Elected 1966; b. Nov. 6, 1918, Chicago, Ill.; home, Medford; Yale U., B.S., 1940; U. of Mich., J.D., 1949; USNR, WWII; Lt. Cdr. USNR; married, three children; Presbyterian.

Career Instr., Oreg. State Col. 1949, Asst. Prof., 1950–51; practicing atty., 1951–66; Oreg. House of Reps., 1960–66.

Offices 1214 LHOB, 202-225-6416. Also 163 E. 12th, Eugene 97501, 503-342-5141.

Administrative Assistant Frederic Hansen

Committees

Education and Labor (5th); Subs: No. 2 (Sp. Sub. on Labor).; No. 6 (Sp. Sub. on Education).

Interior and Insular Affairs (9th); Subs: Environment; Public Lands; Water and Power Resources.

Joint Com. on Congressional Operations (2nd).

Group Ratings

	ADA	COPE	LWV	RIPON	NFU	LCV	CFA	NAB	NSI	ACA
1972	50	30	83	75	29	61	0	91	78	48
1971	43	25	56	93	40	–	50	–	–	57
1970	32	50	–	88	62	25	44	82	80	47

Key Votes

1) Busing	FOR	6) Cmbodia Bmbg	AGN	11) Chkg Acct Intrst	FOR
2) Strip Mines	AGN	7) Bust Hwy Trust	FOR	12) End HISC (HUAC)	AGN
3) Cut Mil $	FOR	8) Farm Sub Lmt	FOR	13) Nixon Sewer Veto	AGN
4) Rev Shrg	FOR	9) School Prayr	AGN	14) Corp Cmpaign $	AGN
5) Pub TV $	AGN	10) Cnsumr Prot	FOR	15) Pol $ Disclosr	FOR

Election Results

1972 general:	John R. Dellenback (R)	138,965	(63%)
	Charles O. Porter (D)	83,134	(27%)
1972 primary:	John R. Dellenback (R)	50,354	(79%)
	William A. Singler (R)	13,517	(21%)
1970 general:	John R. Dellenback (R)	84,474	(58%)
	James H. Weaver (D)	60,299	(42%)

PENNSYLVANIA

Political Background

A look at the map will illustrate how Pennsylvania got its nickname, the Keystone State. Pennsylvania connects New York state and New England with the rest of the country. For many years, the geography of Pennsylvania promised to make it the commercial and transportation hub of the nation, as indeed it was at the time the Constitution was ratified. But things failed to work out that way. The rugged mountains of central Pennsylvania stalled the early development of transportation arteries west. And it was New York City, rather than Philadelphia, that thrived from the building of the Erie Canal and the first water-level railroad line west. In 1776, Philadelphia, home of the remarkable Benjamin Franklin, was the nation's capital and largest city. Within 50 years, it was eclipsed by Washington in the affairs of government and New York City in commerce. And New Englanders will argue that Boston was never surpassed as the nation's center of culture and education.

During the late nineteenth century, however, Pennsylvania experienced a second renaissance based on the then-booming industries of coal and steel. Immigrants poured in to work the mines of Scranton and the steel mills of Pittsburgh—flush towns in those days. The boom ended conclusively with the coming of the Great Depression of the 1930s, and good times have yet to return to much of Pennsylvania. The coal industry collapsed after World War II, and though doing better of late, employs far fewer people than it did in the 1920s. Pennsylvania steel, meanwhile, has long since grown complacent. Because it chose to ignore technological advances following World War II, its ancient mills are today far less efficient than the modern steel plants constructed in bombed-out West Germany and Japan. Indeed, the industry here appears to have thrown in the towel, refusing to compete any longer. Management and the United Steel Workers have mounted a major campaign for steel import quotas. A century ago, steel producers wanted high tariffs, arguing that theirs was an "infant industry" needing protection. Today, they want the same protection, arguing, it seems, that they are a senile one.

These economic developments have left Pennsylvania in rather sorry shape. People growing up here are as likely to leave the state as stay, while out-of-staters show little inclination to move in. In 1930, after its last decade of prosperity, Pennsylvania recorded 9.5 million residents; today, the number stands at 11.5 million. The growth rate represents the smallest among the nation's 10 largest states. So Pennsylvania, once the nation's second-largest state, will, by 1980, slip to forth or perhaps fifth, behind California, New York, Texas, and maybe Illinois. In 1950, Pennsylvania could claim 32 seats in the House of Representatives. Today it has only 25, just one more than Texas or Illinois.

In politics, Pennsylvania is divided into two parts, east and west. East of the Appalachian ranges, the state leans slightly Republican, even though heavy Democratic margins usually come out of Philadelphia and industrial towns like Scranton, Wilkes-Barre, and Reading. The main source of Republican strength in eastern Pennsylvania is found in the suburbs of Philadelphia and the Pennsylvania Dutch country around Lancaster and York. Some 25 years ago, the Republican preferences of eastern Pennsylvania were more pronounced. Philadelphia was then still the stronghold of an aging, old-time Republican city machine. The power of the organization was broken, however, in 1951, when Joseph Clark was elected Mayor. Clark then went on to serve in the U.S. Senate from 1957 to 1969.

Western Pennsylvania leans Democratic. Despite the connecting link of the bankrupt Penn Central (once the thriving and politically powerful Pennsylvania Railroad), the state west of the mountains constitutes an economic unit quite separate from Pennsylvania east of the mountains. Western Pennsylvania is part of the coal-and-steel empire that also encompasses parts of northeast Ohio and northern West Virginia. Like Philadelphia, Pittsburgh casts heavy Democratic margins; unlike its counterpart, however, the Pittsburgh suburbs and the small-town and rural areas beyond the city also go Democratic. Organized labor is especially powerful in western Pennsylvania, which is one of the most unionized regions of the entire country. Pittsburgh's Democratic machine, under mayors Joseph Barr and David Lawrence (Governor from 1959 to 1962), was once the mainstay of the state Democratic party. But in 1969, insurgent reform candidate Peter Flaherty captured the Mayor's office, leaving the Pittsburgh machine in decline.

A similar thing has happened to the governorship. A dozen years ago, the state of Pennsylvania had 50,000 patronage employees, appointed for the most part on the recommendations of local party machines. The number was whittled down by Republican Gov. (1963–66) William Scranton and his successor (1967–70), Raymond Shafer, and cut down even further by the current incumbent, Democrat Milton Shapp. A millionaire businessman, Shapp ran a heavy media campaign in 1966, beat the Democratic organization candidate, and almost defeated Shafer in the general election. Four years later, Shapp beat the organization in the primary once again, and this time pulverized the Republican nominee. Shapp had even less use for patronage jobs than Scranton, another rich man. The Democrat's victory was due largely to campaing consultant Joe Napolitan and middle-class volunteers, none of whom was interested in $8,500 a year sinecures in Harrisburg.

By some accounts, Shapp has served as an effective Governor. He has streamlined the state bureaucracies somewhat and hired an Insurance Commissioner named Herbert Denenberg, a professor at the University of Pennsylvania. Denenberg has since won a great deal of national publicity as the scourge of insurance companies. Shapp, the first Pennsylvania Governor eligible for a second term, will be running again in 1974, perhaps against liberal Republican Congressman John Heinz of suburban Pittsburgh (who is also a prime Senate candidate if Hugh Scott decides to retire in 1976). Another possible candidate is Philadelphia Mayor Frank Rizzo. In mid-1973 he looked like a formidable opponent, whose strength could not be fully gauged. Rizzo still likes being known as the nation's toughest cop, and he stepped into the Mayoralty, with the aid of Peter Camiel's Democratic machine, from his position as Police Commissioner. (See Pennsylvania 3 for more detail.) Rizzo won with the overwhelming percentage of white votes and he did particularly well in the Italian wards; there has never been an Italian-American Mayor or even an Italian-American Congressman from Philadelphia.

But in 1972, Rizzo broke with Camiel, in large part because the Mayor—long before McGovern was nominated—endorsed Richard Nixon for reelection, calling him the greatest President in our history. Then, in 1973, Camiel charged that Rizzo had offered him control over certain city contracts in return for Camiel's support of Rizzo's candidate for District Attorney. Rizzo denied the charges, and when the Philadelphia *Daily News* suggested that he and Camiel both take a lie detector test, they both accepted. Camiel passed; Rizzo flunked. Before the test the Mayor had said, "If this machine says a man lied, he lied."Afterwards, he nonetheless insisted he had been telling the truth. The incident could not help but hurt Rizzo's image, although he, like Mayoral candidate Mario Biaggi in New York, probably retains a great following among Italian-American voters. (See New York 10.) But it is hard to see Rizzo now defeating incumbent Shapp in the Democratic primary, or being welcomed into the Republican party, or running successfully as an Independent. If he does decide to make the race, he will have to resign as Mayor under the terms of Philadelphia's city charter.

From the Civil War until the Great Depression, Pennsylvania was one of the nation's most Republican states, thanks in large part to the clout wielded by the officers of the Pennsylvania Railroad and the owners of various steel mills and coal mines—and a competent old-fashioned Republican machine. The state even went for Hoover in 1932. Though far less conservative than it was in its heyday, the Pennsylvania Republican party remains well organized and tightly controlled. Though the party was unable to carry the state in any of the presidential elections of the 1960s, it was able to unseat the very liberal Sen. Joseph Clark in 1968. The Republican who beat him was Richard Schweiker, then a young (42) and relatively unknown Congressman from the Philadelphia suburbs. In some ways, however, it was Clark who lost, not Schweiker who won the election. In his second term, Clark had antagonized many of the state's large number of Italian-American voters, and his support of gun-control legislation attracted the wrath of the nation's gun lobby.

But today Schweiker is a well-established political figure in his own right. His voting record in the Senate has been markedly more liberal than it was in the House. And though he serves on the Armed Services Committee (as he did in House), Schweiker supported end-the-war legislation and cutbacks in military spending. The Senator looks like he is in fine shape for 1974, when his seat is up. By the spring of 1973, he had already gotten the support of organized labor—he is one of the very few Republican Senators with a 100% rating from COPE—and he enjoys the backing of antiwar liberals as well. Moreover, the state's Republican party is solidly behind him; his dissents from various Nixon positions look far better now than they did before the Watergate scandal. The only question remaining is the identity of the Democrat Schweiker will beat. One possible candidate is acerbic Insurance Commissioner Denenberg, who could at least make the campaign interesting.

Pennsylvania's senior Senator is Hugh Scott, the late Everett Dirksen's successor as Senate Minority Leader. Scott has won a number of elections under unlikely circumstances. From 1943 to 1959, he was a Congressman from Philadelphia, serving as Republican National Chairman of the Dewey campaign in 1948. Scott then chose the Democratic year of 1958 to run for the Senate, perhaps thinking that his House seat would be wiped out after the 1960 census; he got enough voters to split tickets to win. In 1964, the Goldwater candidacy appeared to doom his career, but Senator Scott again squeaked by with a narrow 70,000-vote margin. Scott won all these elections running as a liberal Republican, paying special court to the Jewish and black communities.

The Pennsylvanian is one of the Senate's consummate and suave politicians, able to gloss over inconsistencies and present his side of the story in the strongest possible terms. So despite his reputation as a liberal Republican, he managed to win the post of Majority Leader over the more conservative Howard Baker, then a freshman, by a 24–19 vote. The narrow margin—Baker challenged him again in 1971 with similar results—and the positions taken by the Nixon Administration put Scott in many a nasty bind.

The Senator antagonized the Administration and Senate conservatives when he opposed the Haynsworth nomination and Nixon's proposed changes in the Voting Rights Act. Mostly, however, Scott upset some of his erstwhile backers in Pennsylvania when he supported the Carswell nomination, the ABM, the SST, and opposed a fixed Vietnam withdrawal date. As Nixon stock went rising in the polls during 1971 and 1972, Scott came down on the side of the Administration virtually every time, but he proved adept at slipping out of positions when politically desirable. For example, he voted to install Carswell after the most prolonged and searching Senate debate over a Supreme Court nominee in recent history; after the vote, Scott then blithely turned around and called the judge a racist and admitted to his constituents that he should never have supported him. By early 1973, the Senator had for months supported the Administration's bombing of Cambodia; but after the Senate voted overwhelmingly to stop it, Scott announced that he could support the bombing no longer—starting June 30, then a few weeks off. Scott is a shameless practitioner of such serpentine twisting and turning, a form of political behavior that he justifies with the same urbane aplomb with which he appraises Chinese vases (on which he is an expert).

Because of Scott'e stature in Washington, analysts assumed he would win easy reelection in 1970. As it turned out, the would-be landslide wound up a rather close contest. An obscure state Senator from Erie, a city located in the far northwest corner of the state, managed to hold the Senate Minority Leader down to 52% of the votes. But it was the first time that a Pennsylvania Senator had ever won a third term from the voters, and it occurred just a few days before Scott's 70th birthday. So Scott, a man who does not look his age, will be 76 when his seat comes up in 1976. That year, being the bicentennial in Pennsylvania, Scott might like to cap his career with one final victory. Lately, American voters have not eagerly reelected septuagenarian Senators, but the political graveyards of Pennsylvania are full of people who have underestimated Hugh Scott.

In 1970, for the first time since the days of James Buchanan, Pennsylvania Democrats controlled the governorship and the legislature. But because of feuds between Gov. Shapp and Philadelphia boss Peter Camiel, there was no partisan Democratic gerrymadering effected. Instead, the Democrats retained a one-Congressman edge in the state's House delegation, one that they have held since 1966. In 1972, there were no upsets in House races, despite the big Nixon sweep in the state.

Because of Pennsylvania's small population growth during the 1960s, the state lost two House seats. The two eliminated were easily chosen. Two suburban Pittsburgh districts held by 30-year Republican veterans, Robert Corbett and James Fulton, were combined into a single district. Both men had died in 1971. And in population-losing Philadelphia, the machine decided that the seat held by William J. Green III was the one to get the axe. In 1971, Green had the temerity to run against the organization's choice, Frank Rizzo, in the 1971 mayoral primary. As it turned out, Green retained his House seat despite the enmity of the machine. Otherwise, the redistricting in Pennsylvania worked out as expected.

Census Data Pop. 11,793,909; 5.83% of U.S. total, 3rd largest; change 1960–70, 4.2%. Central city, 29%; suburban, 51%. Median family income, $9,554; 20th highest; families above $15,000: 18%; families below $3,000: 8%. Median years education, 12.0.

1972 Share of Federal Tax Burden $12,227,580,000; 5.85% of U.S. total, 4th largest.

1972 Share of Federal Outlays $9,908,450,054; 4.57% of U.S. total, 4th largest. Per capita federal spending, $840.

DOD	$2,436,185,000	6th (3.90%)		HEW	$4,365,278,855	3rd (6.11%)
AEC	$103,729,027	10th (3.96%)		HUD	$199,422,847	3rd (6.50%)
NASA	$68,096,173	10th (2.28%)		VA	$620,402,299	4th (5.42%)
DOT	$282,796,804	8th (3.59%)		USDA	$224,323,341	28th (1.46%)
DOC	$16,597,227	19th (1.28%)		CSC	$188,966,907	6th (4.59%)
DOI	$70,820,911	8th (3.34%)		TD	$507,062,382	6th (3.07%)
DOJ	$22,726,383	13th (2.31%)		Other	$802,041,898	

Economic Base Primary metal industries, especially blast furnaces and steel mills; finance, insurance and real estate; apparel and other textile products, especially women's and misses' outerwear; machinery; electrical equipment and supplies, especially electronic components and accessories; fabricated metal products, especially fabricated structural metal products; food and kindred products, especially bakery products.

Political Line-up Governor, Milton J. Shapp (D); seat up, 1974. Senators, Hugh Scott (R) and Richard S. Schweiker (R). Representatives, 25 (13 D and 12 R). State Senate (25 D, 24 R, and 1 vac.); State House (105 R, 96 D, and 2 Ind.).

The Voters

Registration 5,849,082 Total. 2,977,631 D (51%); 2,689,620 R (46%); 181,831 other (3%).
Median voting age 45.3
Employment profile White collar, 45%. Blue collar, 42%. Service, 12%. Farm, 1%.
Ethnic groups Black, 9%. Total foreign stock, 18%. Italy, 4%, Poland, Germany, UK, 2% each; USSR, Austria, Czechoslovakia, Ireland, 1% each.

Presidential vote

1972	Nixon (R)	2,714,521	(60%)
	McGovern (D)	1,796,951	(40%)
1968	Nixon (R)	2,090,017	(44%)
	Humphrey (D)	2,259,405	(48%)
	Wallace (AI)	378,582	(8%)
1964	Johnson (D)	3,130,954	(65%)
	Goldwater (R)	1,673,657	(35%)

Senator

Hugh Scott (R) Elected 1958, seat up 1974; b. 1900, Fredericksburg, Va.; home, Philadelphia; Randolph-Macon Col., B.A., 1919; U. of Va., LL.B., 1922; Army, WWII; USNR, WWII; married, one child; Episcopalian.

Career Practicing atty.; author; U.S. House, 1941–45, 1947–59; Natl. Chm., Repub. Party, 1948–49; Chm., Eisenhower Headquarters Com., 1952; Gen. Counsel, Repub. Natl. Com., 1955–60; V. Chm., Senatorial Campaign Com., 1964; Minority Whip, U.S. Senate, 1969; Senate Minority Leader, 1969– .

Offices 260 OSOB, 202-225-6324. Also 4004 U.S. Courthouse, Philadelphia 19107, 215-925-8181, and 434 Fed. Bldg., 1000 Liberty Ave., Pittsburgh 15222, 412-261-3231, and P.O. Box 55, Fed. Bldg., Harrisburg 17108, 717-782-3770.

Administrative Assistant Martin G. Hamberger

Committees

Foreign Relations (4th); Subs: Far-Eastern Affairs; Near-Eastern Affairs; European Affairs; Western Hemisphere Affairs.

Judiciary (3rd); Subs: Criminal Laws and Procedures; Improvements in Judicial Machinery; Patents, Trademarks and Copyrights (Ranking Mbr.); Revision and Codification (Ranking Mbr.); Constitutional Amendments; Administrative Practices and Procedures.

Rules and Administration (2nd); Sub: Printing (Ranking Mbr.).

Joint Com. on Printing (Ranking Senate Mbr.).

Sp. Com. to Study Questions Related to Secret and Confidential Government Documents (Vice-Chm.).

Group Ratings

	ADA	COPE	LWV	RIPON	NFU	LCV	CFA	NAB	NSI	ACA
1972	35	60	80	75	44	26	63	56	89	55
1971	26	50	100	64	27	–	25	–	–	45
1970	31	77	–	58	47	56	–	42	100	60

Key Votes

1) Busing	FOR	8) Sea Life Prot	AGN	15) Tax Singls Less	AGN
2) Alas P-line	FOR	9) Campaign Subs	AGN	16) Min Tax for Rich	AGN
3) Gun Cntrl	FOR	10) Cmbodia Bmbg	FOR	17) Euro Troop Rdctn	AGN
4) Rehnquist	FOR	11) Legal Srvices	FOR	18) Bust Hwy Trust	FOR
5) Pub TV $	AGN	12) Rev Sharing	FOR	19) Maid Min Wage	AGN
6) EZ Votr Reg	AGN	13) Cnsumr Prot	AGN	20) Farm Sub Limit	FOR
7) No-Fault	AGN	14) Eq Rts Amend	FOR	21) Highr Credt Chgs	ABS

Election Results

1970 general:	Hugh Scott (R)	1,874,106	(52%)
	William G. Sesler (D)	1,653,774	(46%)
	Frank W. Gaydosh (Const.)	85,813	(2%)
	W. H. MacFarland (AI)	18,275	(1%)
1970 primary:	Hugh Scott (R), unopposed		
1964 general:	Hugh Scott (R)	2,429,858	(51%)
	Genevieve Blatt (D)	2,359,223	(49%)

Senator

Richard Schultz Schweiker (R) Elected 1968, seat up 1974; b. June 1, 1926, Norristown; home, Worcester; Penn. State U., B.A., 1950; Navy, WWII; married, five children; Central Schwenkfelder Church.

Career Business executive, 1950–60; U.S. House, 1961–69.

Offices 6221 NSOB, 202-225-4254. Also 2001 Fed. Office Bldg., 1000 Liberty Ave., Pittsburgh 15222, 412-644-3400, and 4048 U.S. Courthouse, 9th and Chestnut, Philadelphia 19107, 215-597-7200.

Administrative Assistant David Newhall III

Committees

Appropriations (10th); Subs: Labor, and Health, Education, and Welfare, and Related Agencies; Legislative; Public Works-AEC; Transportation; Military Construction (Ranking Mbr.).

Labor and Public Welfare (3rd); Subs: Education; Labor; Railroad Retirement (Ranking Mbr.); Alcoholism and Narcotics (Ranking Mbr.); Aging; Health (Ranking Mbr.); Employment, Poverty, and Migratory Labor; Handicapped.

Sel. Com. on Nutrition and Human Needs (5th).

Joint Economic Com. (4th); Subs: Economic Progress; Fiscal Policy; Inter-American Economic Relationships; Priorities and Economy in Government.

Group Ratings

	ADA	COPE	LWV	RIPON	NFU	LCV	CFA	NAB	NSI	ACA
1972	60	100	100	88	70	79	100	42	70	27
1971	70	50	100	78	82	–	86	–	–	33
1970	75	100	–	77	81	60	–	25	20	29

Key Votes

1) Busing	FOR	8) Sea Life Prot	FOR	15) Tax Singls Less	FOR
2) Alas P-line	FOR	9) Campaign Subs	AGN	16) Min Tax for Rich	AGN
3) Gun Cntrl	AGN	10) Cmbodia Bmbg	AGN	17) Euro Troop Rdctn	AGN
4) Rehnquist	FOR	11) Legal Srvices	FOR	18) Bust Hwy Trust	FOR
5) Pub TV $	FOR	12) Rev Sharing	FOR	19) Maid Min Wage	FOR
6) EZ Votr Reg	FOR	13) Cnsumr Prot	FOR	20) Farm Sub Limit	FOR
7) No-Fault	FOR	14) Eq Rts Amend	FOR	21) Highr Credt Chgs	AGN

Election Results

1968 general:	Richard S. Schwieker (R)	2,399,762	(52%)
	Joseph S. Clark (D)	2,117,662	(46%)
	Frank W. Gaydosh (Const.)	96,742	(2%)
1968 primary:	Richard S. Schweiker (R), unopposed		

FIRST DISTRICT Political Background

The 1st district of Pennsylvania is the southern end of the city of Philadelphia. The Schuylkill River divides the district into two just about equal parts. On the west bank is the University of Pennsylvania and, beyond the campus, the West Philadelphia black ghetto. On the east side of the river is the heavily Italian-American neighborhood of South Philadelphia. This is a stronghold of Mayor (and former Police Commissioner) Frank Rizzo, who carried the area by margins exceeding 12–1 in both the 1971 primary and general elections held in the city.

Back during the Kennedy years of the early 1960s, both South and West Philadelphia voted overwhelmingly Democratic. But in recent years, as the black areas have voted Democratic with near unanimity, South Philadelphia has shifted toward the Republicans. The shift culminated in 1972 when Richard Nixon carried South Philadelphia. The pattern in 1972, of course, was precisely the opposite of the one in 1971 when Rizzo was the Democratic candidate for Mayor. The case in South Philadelphia presents another example of the inherent conservative nature of ethnic communities on many issues, particularly those involving crime and race. That conservatism—one demonstrated in central cities all along the Eastern seaboard—has produced big dividends for Republican candidates for public office.

William Barrett has represented the 1st district in the House since 1949. Barrett cuts an unobstrusive figure in Washington, though his seniority makes him the second-ranking Democrat on the House Banking and Currency Committee and Chairman of its Housing Committee. The Congressman has supported expanded federal aid and subsidies for housing, having shepherded numerous housing bills to passage. On banking issues, Barrett has been somewhat less hostile to the arguments of banking lobbyists than has 81-year-old committee Chairman Wright Patman. One can only suppose that the American Banking Association looks forward to the day when Barrett succeeds to the chairmanship.

Barrett's real forte, however, is tending his district. Representing a racially divided district like the 1st, another Congressman could expect to find himself in real political trouble. But Barrett stays away from the divisive issues, and instead concentrates on giving his constituents the kind of service they might expect from an old-fashioned machine politician, which Barrett most assuredly is. Every night the Congressman flies home from Washington and holds office hours from 9 until 1. Here, as he told one reporter, he tries to solve problems "on marital matters, child welfare, foreclosures, evictions—everything that affects the human person." There was a time when many political machines provided Barrett's kind of service; today few politicians of any kind do.

Barrett is just about the only Congressman who runs such an operation. It has, of course, paid off at the polls—Barrett consistently runs ahead of the Democratic ticket. Accordingly, though Barrett is neither Italian nor black, he will continue to win in this heavily Italian and black district as long as he wants.

Census Data Pop. 478,310. Central city, 100%; suburban, 0%. Median family income, $8,690; families above $15,000: 15%; families below $3,000: 12%. Median years education, 10.4.

1972 Share of Federal Outlays $496,696,023

DOD	$180,628,285	HEW	$177,621,653
AEC	$968,773	HUD	$12,193,750
NASA	$7,492,181	DOI	$1,742,851
DOT	$12,986,616	USDA	$8,893,952
		Other	$94,167,963

Federal Military-Industrial Commitments

DOD Contractors General Electric (Philadelphia), $222.401m: Mark 12 re-entry systems for Minuteman III missiles; ABM research.
DOD Installations Defense Personnel Support Center (Philadelphia). Naval Air Engineering Center (Philadelphia). Naval Hospital (Philadelphia). Naval Station (Philadelphia). Philadelphia Naval Shipyard (Philadelphia).

Economic Base Finance, insurance and real estate; apparel and other textile products, especially men's and boys' suits and coats; printing and publishing, especially commercial printing; food and kindred products, especially bakery products; electrical equipment and supplies, especially electric test and distributing equipment; and fabricated metal products. Also higher education (Drexel Univ. and Pennsylvania Univ.).

The Voters

Registration 245,023 total. 163,908 D (67%); 74,903 R (31%); 6,212 other (3%).
Median voting age 44.3
Employment profile White collar, 43%. Blue collar, 40%. Service, 17%. Farm, –%.
Ethnic groups Black, 39%. Total foreign stock, 23%. Italy, 13%; USSR, Ireland, 2% each; UK, 1%.

Presidential vote

1972	Nixon (R)	77,078	(42%)
	McGovern (D)	107,549	(58%)
1968	Nixon (R)	58,692	(29%)
	Humphrey (D)	128,387	(62%)
	Wallace (AI)	16,856	(8%)

Representative

William A. Barrett (D) Elected 1948; b. Aug. 14, ca. 1900, Philadelphia; home, Philadelphia; St. Joseph's Col.; married, three children; Catholic.

Career Real estate broker.

Offices 2304 RHOB, 202-225-4731. Also 2401 Wharton St., Philadelphia 19146, 215-389-2822.

Administrative Assistant Michael Corbett

Committees

Banking and Currency (2nd); Subs: Housing (Chm.); Bank Supervision and Insurance; Consumer Affairs.

Joint Com. on Defense Production (2nd).

Group Ratings

	ADA	COPE	LWV	RIPON	NFU	LCV	CFA	NAB	NSI	ACA
1972	81	100	92	64	86	8	100	8	0	5
1971	70	90	80	62	92	–	100	–	–	16
1970	80	100	–	77	100	53	89	8	40	6

Key Votes

1) Busing	FOR	6) Cmbodia Bmbg	ABS	11) Chkg Acct Intrst	FOR
2) Strip Mines	AGN	7) Bust Hwy Trust	FOR	12) End HISC (HUAC)	FOR
3) Cut Mil $	AGN	8) Farm Sub Lmt	FOR	13) Nixon Sewer Veto	AGN
4) Rev Shrg	FOR	9) School Prayr	ABS	14) Corp Cmpaign $	FOR
5) Pub TV $	FOR	10) Cnsumr Prot	FOR	15) Pol $ Disclosr	AGN

Election Results

1972 general:	William A. Barrett (D)	118,953	(66%)
	Gus A. Pedicone (R)	59,807	(33%)
	Nancy Strebe (SW)	1,172	(1%)
1972 primary:	William A. Barrett (D), unopposed		
1970 general:	William A. Barrett (D)	79,425	(69%)
	Joseph S. Ziccardi (R)	34,699	(30%)
	Paul K. Botts (AI)	677	(1%)

SECOND DISTRICT Political Background

The 2nd district of Pennsylvania is an oddly shaped chunk of Philadelphia. Though the 2nd was designed as the city's black district, it does not center on either one of the city's two large black ghettos. Instead, the district takes in part of West Philadelphia and then moves across Fairmount Park and the Schuylkill River to encompass part of the North Philadelphia ghetto. The 2nd proceeds north to include some of the more middle-class black areas of Germantown, which at the time of the Revolution was a settlement separate from Philadelphia. The district then goes all the way out to the WASP upper-income precincts of Chestnut Hill, where some of Philadelphia's richest and most prominent families have lived for generations. Chestnut Hill usually goes Republican, but its votes are swamped by the huge Democratic majorities coming out of the black neighborhoods to the south and east. Altogether, the 2nd consistently reports the largest Democratic percentages in Pennsylvania.

Robert N. C. Nix has represented the 2nd district since a special election held in 1958. He is the state's first, and so far only, black Congressman. In Washington, Nix is now the second most senior member of the Congressional Black Caucus, but he is scarcely the most active. Nix is a man who has the Philadelphia Democratic machine to thank for his political career. Accordingly, he is a politician who makes few waves of any kind. On the Foreign Affairs Committee, Nix generally followed the lead of fellow Pennsylvanian, Chairman Thomas (Doc) Morgan, who for years supported the Vietnam policies of both Johnson and Nixon. Moreover, the Asian and Pacific Affairs Subcommittee, which Nix chairs, has contributed little to the debate on Vietnam, which is both Asian and Pacific.

Back home in the 2nd district, Nix has demonstrated a similar kind of lassitude. He has hardly manifested the concern for his constituents' problems shown by the remarkable William Barrett of the neighboring 1st. In 1972, Nix's inactivity showed up in the election returns, as Nix received only 47% of the votes in the Democratic primary. Because the rest was split among three candidates, the Congressman experienced no near defeat. But the showing could indicate trouble ahead for Nix in 1974.

Census Data Pop. 470,267. Central city, 100%; suburban, 0%. Median family income, $8,670; families above $15,000: 19%; families below $3,000: 14%. Median years education, 11.4.

1972 Share of Federal Outlays $488,270,647

DOD	$177,564,316	HEW	$174,608,685
AEC	$952,340	HUD	$11,986,909
NASA	$7,365,092	DOI	$1,713,287
DOT	$12,766,326	USDA	$8,743,086
		Other	$$92,570,607

Federal Military-Industrial Commitments

DOD Contractors Sun Oil (Philadelphia), $11.706m: petroleum products. IBM (Philadelphia), $5.359m: unspecified.

Economic Base Finance, insurance and real estate; apparel and other textile products, especially men's and boys' suits and coats; printing and publishing, especially commercial printing; food and kindred products, especially bakery products; electrical equipment and supplies, especially electric test and distributing equipment; and fabricated metal products.

The Voters

Registration 224,560 total. 159,197 D (71%); 56,648 R (25%); 8,715 other (4%).
Median voting age 45.4
Employment profile White collar, 49%. Blue collar, 33%. Service, 18%. Farm, –%.
Ethnic groups Black, 65%. Total foreign stock, 15%. USSR, 4%; Italy, 2%; Ireland, UK, Germany, 1% each.

Presidential vote

1972	Nixon (R)	39,889	(25%)
	McGovern (D)	121,786	(75%)
1968	Nixon (R)	39,297	(21%)
	Humphrey (D)	146,658	(76%)
	Wallace (AI)	4,690	(3%)

Representative

Robert N. C. Nix (D) Elected May 20, 1958; b. Aug. 9, 1905, Orangeburg, S.C.; home, Philadelphia; Lincoln U., B.A., 1921; U. of Pa., LL.B., 1924; married, one child; Baptist.

Career Practicing atty., 1925– ; Sp. Deputy Atty. Gen. of Pa., assigned to Escheats Div., State Dept. of Revenue, 1934–38; Ward Com. Chm., 1950–58.

Offices 2201 RHOB, 202-225-4001. Also 2139 N. 22nd St., Philadelphia 19121, 215-236-8341.

Administrative Assistant Cyril Jenious

Committees

Foreign Affairs (7th); Subs: Africa; Asian and Pacific Affairs (Chm.).

Post Office and Civil Service (5th); Subs: Postal Facilities, Mail, and Labor Management; Postal Service.

Group Ratings

	ADA	COPE	LWV	RIPON	NFU	LCV	CFA	NAB	NSI	ACA
1972	88	100	92	53	100	47	100	8	20	17
1971	84	91	89	65	80	–	88	–	–	14
1970	88	100	–	71	92	53	100	0	20	17

Key Votes

1) Busing	FOR	6) Cmbodia Bmbg	AGN	11) Chkg Acct Intrst	FOR
2) Strip Mines	AGN	7) Bust Hwy Trust	FOR	12) End HISC (HUAC)	FOR
3) Cut Mil $	AGN	8) Farm Sub Lmt	FOR	13) Nixon Sewer Veto	AGN
4) Rev Shrg	FOR	9) School Prayr	AGN	14) Corp Cmpaign $	FOR
5) Pub TV $	FOR	10) Cnsumr Prot	FOR	15) Pol $ Disclosr	AGN

Election Results

1972 general:	Robert N. C. Nix (D)	107,509	(70%)
	Frederick D. Bryant (R)	45,753	(30%)
1972 primary:	Robert N. C. Nix (D)	24,473	(47%)
	Peter A. McGrath (D)	11,475	(22%)

	Phillip H. Savage (D)	11,462	(22%)
	Mitchell W. Melton (D)	4,816	(9%)
1970 general:	Robert N. C. Nix (D)	70,530	(68%)
	Edward L. Taylor (R)	32,858	(32%)

THIRD DISTRICT Political Background

Whatever the opinion of W. C. Fields, Center City Philadelphia is one of the more amenable of American downtowns. The height of buildings here has been kept down to a reasonable 38 stories by an old ordinance that allows none to exceed the height of the spire on Philadelphia's ornate City Hall. Moreover, a large new urban renewal project, Penn Center, is going up on the site of the Penn Central tracks—the old "Chinese wall." Hard by the office buildings are the elegant Victorian neighborhoods around Rittenhouse Square and the restored eighteenth-century town houses of Society Hill, near Independence Hall. But as one moves a few blocks north out of Center City, one comes to the nineteenth-century suburbs now long-since become slums. Much of the northern parts of the area described, along with some of Center City itself including Society Hill, lies in Pennsylvania's 3rd congressional district.

At its western fringes, the 3rd also takes in part of the black ghetto of North Philadelphia. But most of the district is made up of white neighborhoods where levels of income and education are little better than they are in the ghetto. An example is Kensington, north of Center City, which seems to have been transported intact straight out of the 1930s. Here, in the red-brick Philadelphia rowhouses, live the Irish and Italians left behind after the postwar exodus to the suburbs. Most of these people own their own houses—Philadelphia is a city of homeowners, not renters. But the value of the real estate is pathetically low, since there is little demand for it. According to the Census Bureau, the median value of a house belonging to its owner is only $7,800 in the 3rd district. Kensington and other neighborhoods like it here are traditionally Democratic, but like other ethnic enclaves all over the East, they have trended Republican and conservative in recent years.

For the most part, the 3rd is an amalgam of two previous congressional districts. Behind its formation is a tale of machine politics and insurgency, reward and punishment. The central figure in the tale is William J. Green III, son of a former Philadelphia Democratic boss and Congressman. Green himself was elected to the House at age 25 after his father's untimely death in 1964. The young man had accumulated all the rewards the machine could bestow: a safe House seat, the Philadelphia Democratic chairmanship, and a possible chance for future state or city-wide office. But in 1968, Green split with then-Mayor James H. J. Tate and the machine. The Congressman favored the candidacy of Robert Kennedy and wanted to open up the party to those previously excluded; Tate and the others preferred Hubert Humphrey's politics of joy and wanted to keep things as they were.

Then, in 1971, Green committed the ultimate apostasy. Mayor Tate and Peter Camiel, Democratic City Chairman, decided to run Police Commissioner Frank Rizzo for Mayor. Rizzo, of course, was a law-and-order hard-liner and popular among the city's whites. Green didn't like Rizzo's ideas, and ran himself. The Congressman waged a well-financed, well-organized campaign, but lost the Democratic primary—partly because of the prowess of the machine, but more because of Rizzo's popularity in white, especially Italian, neighborhoods. Meanwhile, the men of the machine in the legislature presided over the evisceration of Green's old congressional district. He was dumped into the 3rd, most of which had been represented by James (Digger) Byrne, a man once in the funeral-directing business. Byrne had also served as 31st Ward Chairman for 38 years, as had his father for 42 years before that. The younger Byrne was definitely the organization's choice in 1972. The machine knew that within the boundaries of the new 3rd, Green had lost to Rizzo by a margin exceeding 3–2.

So for the second time in two years Green, unaccustomed to trouble at the polls, faced another tough election. This time he won. With an organization staffed by the people who had backed his mayoral bid, Green outcampaigned the complacent Byrne, rolled up huge margins in the black wards, and won over hundreds of Rizzo voters in places like Kensington. Green took a solid 58% of the votes. So, aside from a try for higher office, he will probably not encounter another tough election for many years to come.

The victory made Green, at 36, the eleventh-ranking Democrat on the House Ways and Means Committee, which may not seem like much. But as these things go, position number 11 is very good indeed. Chairman Wilbur Mills has announced that he might retire in 1974 because of back problems. The other more senior members of Ways and Means are considerably older than Green. If they follow Mills' apparent example and retire at 65, Green will become Chairman, assuming the Democrats then have a majority in the House, in 1993.

Census Data Pop. 472,041. Central city, 100%; suburban, 0%. Median family income, $8,368; families above $15,000: 14%; families below $3,000: 13%. Median years education, 9.9.

1972 Share of Federal Outlays $490,276,689

DOD	$178,293,832	HEW	$175,326,058
AEC	$956,253	HUD	$12,036,157
NASA	$7,395,351	DOI	$1,720,326
DOT	$12,818,776	USDA	$8,779,006
		Other	$92,950,930

Federal Military-Industrial Commitments

DOD Contractors N.W. Ayers and Sons (Philadelphia), $25.817m: unspecified. Charles Kurz Co. (Philadelphia), $12.624m: unspecified.
DOD Installations Frankford Arsenal (Philadelphia).

Economic Base Finance, insurance and real estate; apparel and other textile products, especially men's and boys' suits and coats; printing and publishing, especially commercial printing; food and kindred products, especially bakery products; electrical equipment and supplies, especially electric test and distributing equipment; and fabricated metal products. Also higher education (Temple Univ.).

The Voters

Registration 225,455 total. 144,524 D (64%); 74,696 R (33%); 6,235 other (3%).
Median voting age 46.0
Employment profile White collar, 40%. Blue collar, 45%. Service, 15%. Farm, –%.
Ethnic groups Black, 28%. Spanish, 5%. Total foreign stock, 22%. Poland, 4%; Italy, USSR, 3% each; Germany, UK, Ireland, 2% each.

Presidential vote

1972	Nixon (R)	74,829	(46%)
	McGovern (D)	86,379	(54%)
1968	Nixon (R)	57,238	(30%)
	Humphrey (D)	114,922	(60%)
	Wallace (AI)	18,395	(10%)

Representative

William Joseph Green (D) Elected April 28, 1964; b. June 24, 1938, Philadelphia; home, Philadelphia; St. Joseph's Col., B.A., 1960; Villanova Law School, 1961–63; married, three children; Catholic.

Career Elected to fill the vacancy caused by the death of his father, William J. Green.

Offices 2434 RHOB, 202-225-6271. Also 401 Walnut St., Philadelphia 19106, 215-923-9868.

Administrative Assistant Estelle Tyler

Committees

Ways and Means (11th).

Group Ratings

	ADA	COPE	LWV	RIPON	NFU	LCV	CFA	NAB	NSI	ACA
1972	100	89	100	80	86	74	100	9	0	5
1971	86	82	100	64	82	–	100	–	–	4
1970	100	100	–	82	100	73	100	0	0	6

Key Votes

1) Busing	FOR	6) Cmbodia Bmbg	AGN	11) Chkg Acct Intrst	FOR
2) Strip Mines	AGN	7) Bust Hwy Trust	FOR	12) End HISC (HUAC)	FOR
3) Cut Mil $	FOR	8) Farm Sub Lmt	ABS	13) Nixon Sewer Veto	AGN
4) Rev Shrg	FOR	9) School Prayr	AGN	14) Corp Cmpaign $	AGN
5) Pub TV $	FOR	10) Cnsumr Prot	FOR	15) Pol $ Disclosr	AGN

Election Results

1972 general:	William J. Green (D)	101,144	(64%)
	Alfred Marroletti (R)	57,787	(36%)
1972 primary:	William J. Green (D)	32,593	(58%)
	James A. Byrne (D)	22,229	(39%)
	Robert Coyle (D)	1,832	(3%)
1970 general:	William J. Green (D)	80,142	(67%)
	James H. Ring (R)	38,955	(33%)
	John Donahue (AI)	724	(1%)

FOURTH DISTRICT Political Background

The 4th district of Pennsylvania is northeast Philadelphia. It constitutes the most middle-class, prosperous, and indeed a still-growing part of Philadelphia. Geographically, most of the 4th is farther from Center City than the Main Line suburbs. Out here, some 10 to 20 miles from Independence Hall, middle-income suburban tract housing was still going up during the 1960s. In fact, more than half of the housing units in northeast Philadelphia were built after 1950; in the rest of the city, more than 80% of the units went up before 1950. Most of the 4th's residents are migrants from more crowded areas closer to downtown Philadelphia. The district has a fair ethnic mixture, one representing the outward movement of various groups. Of these, the Jews are the most important politically. More than half of the city's Jewish people live within the district.

The 4th is the least Democratic of Philadelphia's four districts, the only one to go for Richard Nixon in 1972. It is also the only district that the city's Republicans have contested seriously in the past several elections. In 1966, after a major redistricting, ailing Congressman Herman Toll retired, and Republican candidate Robert Cohen waged a vigorous campaign to capture the seat. He fell 7,000 votes short. The winner was Joshua Eilberg, then majority leader in the state House of Representatives.

In Washington, Eilberg has compiled a liberal, antiwar record. And back home, he has managed to placate both the machine and the local reformers. After several convincing wins, Eilberg's share of the vote dropped to 56% in 1972. The Congressman was the target of an aggressive campaign waged by Republican William Pfender, a former policeman who ran as an anti-welfare, anti-busing candidate. The result is not necessarily an indication that Eilberg is in any real trouble—he won by 29,000 votes—but it does show that his seat is not quite as safe as he may have once presumed.

Census Data Pop. 474,684. Central city, 100%; suburban, 0%. Median family income, $11,069; families above $15,000: 24%; families below $3,000: 5%. Median years education, 11.9.

1972 Share of Federal Outlays $492,683,939

DOD	$179,169,252	HEW	$176,186,907
AEC	$960,948	HUD	$12,095,255
NASA	$7,431,662	DOI	$1,728,773
DOT	$12,881,716	USDA	$8,822,111
		Other	$93,407,315

Federal Military-Industrial Commitments

DOD Installations Naval Publications and Forms Center (Philadelphia). Marine Corps Supply Activity (Philadelphia); closed, 1976. Naval Supply Office (Philadelphia).

Economic Base Finance, insurance and real estate; apparel and other textile products, especially men's and boys' suits and coats; printing and publishing, especially commercial printing; food and kindred products, especially bakery products; electrical equipment and supplies, especially electric test and distributing equipment; and fabricated metal products.

The Voters

Registration 286,533 total. 160,970 D (56%); 117,682 R (41%); 7,881 other (3%).
Median voting age 45.8
Employment profile White collar, 57%. Blue collar, 33%. Service, 10%. Farm, –%.
Ethnic groups Black, 5%. Total foreign stock, 32%. USSR, 8%; Italy, Germany, 4% each; Poland, Ireland, UK, 3% each; Austria, 1%.

Presidential vote

1972	Nixon (R)	131,066	(56%)
	McGovern (D)	100,940	(44%)
1968	Nixon (R)	87,115	(37%)
	Humphrey (D)	126,215	(53%)
	Wallace (AI)	20,977	(9%)

Representative

Joshua Eilberg (D) Elected 1966; b. Feb. 12, 1921, Philadelphia; home, Philadelphia; U. of Pa., B.S., 1941; Temple U., J.D., 1948; USNR, WWII; married, two children; Jewish.

Career Practicing atty., 1948– ; Asst. Dist. Atty., Philadelphia, 1952–54; Pa. Legislature, 1954–66, Majority Leader, 1965–66.

Offices 1130 LHOB, 202-225-4661. Also 216 First Fed. Savings & Loan Assn. Bldg., 1931 Cottman Ave., Philadelphia 19111, 215-722-1717.

Administrative Assistant Nancy Nelson

Committees

Judiciary (8th); Sub: No. 1 (Immigration and Nationality) (Chm.).

Group Ratings

	ADA	COPE	LWV	RIPON	NFU	LCV	CFA	NAB	NSI	ACA
1972	81	91	73	67	86	43	100	8	0	13
1971	81	90	67	69	80	–	100	–	–	15
1970	84	100	–	63	100	62	100	0	38	11

Key Votes

1) Busing	AGN	6) Cmbodia Bmbg	AGN	11) Chkg Acct Intrst	FOR
2) Strip Mines	ABS	7) Bust Hwy Trust	FOR	12) End HISC (HUAC)	FOR
3) Cut Mil $	FOR	8) Farm Sub Lmt	AGN	13) Nixon Sewer Veto	AGN
4) Rev Shrg	FOR	9) School Prayr	AGN	14) Corp Cmpaign $	FOR
5) Pub TV $	FOR	10) Cnsumr Prot	FOR	15) Pol $ Disclosr	ABS

Election Results

1972 general:	Joshua Eilberg (D)	129,105	(56%)
	William Pfender (R)	102,013	(42%)
1972 primary:	Joshua Eilberg (D), unopposed		

1970 general: Joshua Eilberg (D) 113,920 (59%)
   Charles F. Dougherty (R) 77,817 (41%)

FIFTH DISTRICT Political Background

The 5th district of Pennsylvania can be called an exurban Philadelphia district. It takes in the outer edges of suburban Delaware and Montgomery counties, along with most of Chester County farther out. Though technically all within the Philadelphia metropolitan area, the 5th is really a kind of borderland where the influence of Philadelphia wanes and the Pennsylvania Dutch country (see Pennsylvania 16) begins. In other words, vintage John O'Hara country: grimy small industrial towns surrounded by large suburban estates, and the perfectly tended farms of the Brandywine, where the Wyeth family lives and paints. Not far away is the sleepy town of Oxford, home of Lincoln University, one of the nation's leading black institutions of higher education. The 5th also contains many of the famed Main Line suburbs of Philadelphia, so named because they lay on the main line of the erstwhile Pennsylvania Railroad. The 5th is a Republican district, very Republican. The only time it has been known to go Democratic was in the 1964 presidential election, and then by a very narrow margin.

The district's Congressman, conservative Republican G. Robert Watkins, died in the summer of 1970, after serving three terms in the House. Since the primary had already been held, the 5th's Republican organization named John H. Ware, an Oxford utilities executive and state Senator, as its candidate. Ware won the general election, but by a surprisingly small 59% of the votes. As predicted in the first *Almanac*, Ware did better at the polls after two years of incumbency, taking 65% in 1972.

Nevertheless, it is by no means certain that Ware will remain Congressman much longer. In the 1972 Republican primary, he got barely half the votes, and avoided a close race only because the opposition was divided. And at 66, Ware is hardly the most active member of the Pennsylvania delegation, either in Washington or back home. If Ware loses the seat, the loss will occur in the Republican primary, which in the 5th district is tantamount to election.

Census Data Pop. 474,435. Central city, 0%; suburban, 100%. Median family income, $12,148; families above $15,000: 33%; families below $3,000: 4%. Median years education, 12.4.

1972 Share of Federal Outlays $492,683,939

DOD	$179,169,252	HEW	$176,186,907
AEC	$960,948	HUD	$12,095,255
NASA	$7,431,662	DOI	$1,728,773
DOT	$12,881,716	USDA	$8,822,111
		Other	$93,407,315

Federal Military-Industrial Commitments

DOD Installations Valley Forge Army General Hospital (Phoenixville); closed, 1974.

Economic Base Machinery; blast furnace and basic steel products, and other primary metal industries; finance, insurance and real estate; chemicals and allied products; food and kindred products; and electrical equipment and supplies. Also higher education (West Chester State).

The Voters

Registration 235,633 total. 62,809 D (27%); 160,929 R (68%); 11,895 other (5%).
Median voting age 42.4
Employment profile White collar, 54%. Blue collar, 35%. Service, 9%. Farm, 2%.
Ethnic groups Black, 4%. Total foreign stock, 15%. Italy, 3%; UK, Germany, 2% each; Ireland, 1%.

Presidential vote

1972	Nixon (R)	131,393	(69%)
	McGovern (D)	58,454	(31%)

1968	Nixon (R)	104,074	(58%)
	Humphrey (D)	59,915	(34%)
	Wallace (AI)	13,703	(8%)

Representative

John H. Ware (R) Elected 1970; b. Aug. 29, 1908, Vineland, N.J.; home, Oxford; U. of Pa., B.S., 1930; married, four children; Presbyterian.

Career Chm. of Bd., North Penn Gas Co. and American Water Works Co.; Pres., Penn Fuel Gas Inc. and United Utilities Co.; Dir., Oxford Corp., Pa. Gas Assn.; Mayor, Borough of Oxford, 1956–60; Pa. Senate, 1961–70, Majority Caucus Chm., 1967–70; Chm., Repub. Finance Com. of U.S.

Offices 425 CHOB, 202-225-5761. Also 323 West Front St., Media 19063, 215-566-1734, and 21 S. Church St., West Chester 19380.

Administrative Assistant Sallie Weaver

Committees

House Administration (7th); Subs: Elections; Police.

Interstate and Foreign Commerce (12th); Sub: Commerce and Finance.

Group Ratings

	ADA	COPE	LWV	RIPON	NFU	LCV	CFA	NAB	NSI	ACA
1972	6	20	42	60	29	27	50	100	100	65
1971	5	17	44	56	14	–	38	–	–	93

Key Votes

1) Busing	AGN	6) Cmbodia Bmbg	FOR	11) Chkg Acct Intrst	FOR
2) Strip Mines	FOR	7) Bust Hwy Trust	AGN	12) End HISC (HUAC)	AGN
3) Cut Mil $	AGN	8) Farm Sub Lmt	FOR	13) Nixon Sewer Veto	FOR
4) Rev Shrg	FOR	9) School Prayr	FOR	14) Corp Cmpaign $	FOR
5) Pub TV $	AGN	10) Cnsumr Prot	FOR	15) Pol $ Disclosr	FOR

Election Results

1972 general:	John H. Ware III (R)	121,346	(65%)
	Brower B. Yerger (D)	66,329	(35%)
1972 primary:	John H. Ware III (R)	33,029	(51%)
	Charles C. Holt III (R)	20,296	(31%)
	Boyd Miller (R)	11,573	(18%)
1970 general:	John H. Ware III (R)	76,535	(59%)
	Louis F. Waldmann (D)	52,852	(41%)

SIXTH DISTRICT Political Background

The 6th district of Pennsylvania comprises Berks and Schuylkill counties and a small portion of Northumberland County. The 6th, a region of both industry and agriculture, lies on the margin between two parts of the state that rest on two very different economies. In Schuylkill County, the anthracite coal veins reach down from northern Pennsylvania. Reading, in Berks County, is a factory town, as is Allentown and Bethlehem in the Lehigh Valley to the east. To the south, the district takes in part of the Pennsylvania Dutch county (see Pennsylvania 16). Politically, the 6th is more industrial than Dutch. The factory workers in Reading and the anthracite coal miners—or ex-miners—in Schuylkill County towns like Tamaqua and Mahonoy City vote Democratic in most elections. The blue-collar vote here usually overcomes the Republican margins cast in the southern, agricultural area of the district. The hard-pressed conditions of local industries have intensified the 6th's Democratic leanings.

For 20 years, from 1949 to 1969, the 6th was represented by George Rhodes. The Congressman was a stalwart Democrat, labor leader, and one of the founders of the liberal Democratic Study Group. He decided to retire in 1968 and was succeeded by Gus Yatron, a 12-year veteran of the state legislature and owner of a local ice cream business. Like Rhodes, Yatron usually votes with liberal Democrats. The present Congressman serves on the Foreign Affairs Committee, chaired by fellow Pennsylvanian Thomas (Doc) Morgan. Here Yatron has sometimes voted for antiwar measures, but usually sticks with the committee's prevailing consensus. For example, neither the committee nor Yatron considers it wise to withdraw some American troops from Europe unilaterally. Yatron had to run ahead of the Democratic ticket to win (with 51% of the votes) in 1968, but since then he has won easily and appears entrenched in the 6th district.

Census Data Pop. 473,574. Central city, 19%; suburban, 44%. Median family income, $9,009; families above $15,000: 13%; families below $3,000: 8%. Median years education, 11.0.

1972 Share of Federal Outlays $304,110,751

DOD	$27,289,374	HEW	$186,097,123
AEC	–	HUD	$7,609,593
NASA	$1,089	DOI	$1,714,158
DOT	$3,798,699	USDA	$6,034,685
		Other	$71,566,030

Federal Military-Industrial Commitments

No installations or contractors receiving prime awards greater than $5,000,000.

Economic Base Apparel and other textile products; knitting mill products and other textile mill products; primary metal industries, especially iron and steel foundries; finance, insurance and real estate; electrical equipment and supplies; and food and kindred products.

The Voters

Registration 236,128 total. 119,982 D (51%); 109,439 R (46%); 6,707 other (3%).
Median voting age 47.4
Employment profile White collar, 35%. Blue collar, 53%. Service, 10%. Farm, 2%.
Ethnic groups Black, 1%. Total foreign stock, 14%. Poland, 3%; Italy, Germany, 2% each; Austria, Lithuania, 1% each.

Presidential vote

1972	Nixon (R)	114,537	(63%)
	McGovern (D)	66,807	(37%)
1968	Nixon (R)	90,818	(47%)
	Humphrey (D)	89,782	(46%)
	Wallace (AI)	12,956	(7%)

Representative

Gus Yatron (D) Elected 1968; b. Oct. 16, 1927, Reading; home, Reading; Kutztown State Teachers Col., 1950; married, two children; Greek Orthodox.

Career Businessman, Yatron's Ice Cream, 1950–68; Reading School Bd., 1955–60; Pa. Legislature, 1956–60; Pa. Senate, 1960–68.

Offices 313 CHOB, 202-225-5546. Also 203 P.O. Bldg., 5th and Washington Sts., Reading 19603, 215-375-4573, and 603 American Bank Bldg., Pottsville 17901, 717-622-4212.

Administrative Assistant James Crandall (L.A.)

Committees

Foreign Affairs (15th); Subs: Europe; Africa; Foreign Economic Policy.

Group Ratings

	ADA	COPE	LWV	RIPON	NFU	LCV	CFA	NAB	NSI	ACA
1972	44	100	50	33	83	63	50	30	22	40
1971	68	90	78	63	86	–	88	–	–	33
1970	68	92	–	59	92	100	86	9	66	26

Key Votes

1) Busing	AGN	6) Cmbodia Bmbg	AGN	11) Chkg Acct Intrst	ABS
2) Strip Mines	ABS	7) Bust Hwy Trust	FOR	12) End HISC (HUAC)	AGN
3) Cut Mil $	ABS	8) Farm Sub Lmt	FOR	13) Nixon Sewer Veto	AGN
4) Rev Shrg	ABS	9) School Prayr	FOR	14) Corp Cmpaign $	FOR
5) Pub TV $	FOR	10) Cnsumr Prot	FOR	15) Pol $ Disclosr	AGN

Election Results

1972 general:	Gus Yatron (D)	119,557	(64%)
	Eugene W. Hubler (R)	64,076	(35%)
	Frank E. Huet (Const.)	1,775	(1%)
1972 primary:	Gus Yatron (D), unopposed		
1970 general:	Gus Yatron (D)	96,453	(65%)
	Michael Kitsock (R)	48,397	(33%)
	George T. Atkins (C)	3,469	(2%)

SEVENTH DISTRICT Political Background

The 7th district of Pennsylvania contains the larger part of Delaware County, one that is more populous than the adjacent state of Delaware. The district itself is a suburban area southwest of Philadelphia, though it includes none of the famous Main Line; most of the suburbs in the 7th lie along the less fashionable Penn Central route to Wilmington. Here also is Chester, a declining industrial city with a large black minority. Most of the rest of the district is of similar age, if in better condition. To a large extent, the original WASP inhabitants of these suburbs have been supplanted by people from Philadelphia of Italian and Irish backgrounds. Nevertheless, the area's general allegiance to the Republican party has not abated; in fact it has intensified somewhat in recent years.

The boundaries of the 7th were shifted a bit for the 1972 elections, in the manner predicted by the first *Almanac.* Some of the heavily Republican Main Line suburbs were moved to the 5th district, while Chester and adjacent areas were given to the 7th. The Democratic legislature apparently took aim at the seat held since 1966 by Republican Lawrence Williams, probably the most conservative member of the Pennsylvania delegation. But the legislators failed in their intent. Democratic nominee Stuart Bowie made some efforts to mount an effective campaign, but was smothered in the McGovern debacle. As it turned out, Williams ran stronger in 1972 than he and other Republican candidates had run within the same territory in recent years. The 1972 results do not preclude the emergence of a strong challenger here sometime before the next redistricting, but they do indicate that his (or her) chances are not good.

Census Data Pop. 470,714. Central city, 0%; suburban, 100%. Median family income, $11,383; families above $15,000: 27%; families below $3,000: 5%. Median years education, 12.2.

1972 Share of Federal Outlays $488,671,855

DOD	$177,710,219	HEW	$174,752,160
AEC	$953,123	HUD	$11,996,759
NASA	$7,371,144	DOI	$1,714,695
DOT	$12,776,816	USDA	$8,750,270
		Other	$92,646,669

Federal Military-Industrial Commitments

DOD Contractors Boeing (Philadelphia), $46.264m: helicopter components. Boeing (Morton), $40.467m: helicopter components. Boeing (Ridley), $20.641m: helicopter components.

Economic Base Finance, insurance and real estate; machinery, especially engines and turbines; paper and allied products, especially miscellaneous converted paper products; printing and publishing; and electrical equipment and supplies, especially electrical industrial apparatus.

The Voters

Registration 260,011 total. 62,222 D (24%); 189,038 R (73%); 8,751 other (3%).
Median voting age 45.1
Employment profile White collar, 57%. Blue collar, 33%. Service, 10%. Farm, –%.
Ethnic groups Black, 8%. Total foreign stock, 21%. Italy, 6%; Ireland, UK, 3% each; Germany, Poland, USSR, 1% each.

Presidential vote

1972	Nixon (R)	133,151	(64%)
	McGovern (D)	73,432	(36%)
1968	Nixon (R)	99,692	(48%)
	Humphrey (D)	85,858	(42%)
	Wallace (AI)	21,108	(10%)

Representative

Lawrence G. Williams (R) Elected 1966; b. Sept. 15, 1913, Pittsburgh; home, Springfield; Drexel Inst. of Tech.; Army, Air Corps, WWII; married, two children; Methodist.

Career Exec., Curtis Publishing Co., 1936–66; Rep., Del. County on Penn-Jersey Transportation Study, 1959–66; Del. Valley Reg. Planning Com., 1963–66.

Offices 1503 LHOB, 202-225-2011. Also Township Bldg., 50 Powell Rd., Springfield 19064, 215-543-2082.

Administrative Assistant Mrs. Anita Wiesman

Committees

Banking and Currency (6th); Subs: Small Business; Bank Supervision and Insurance; Urban Mass Transportation.

Standards of Official Conduct (2nd).

Group Ratings

	ADA	COPE	LWV	RIPON	NFU	LCV	CFA	NAB	NSI	ACA
1972	0	27	27	57	14	9	0	91	100	71
1971	5	33	22	33	20	–	38	–	–	86
1970	12	17	–	41	23	25	50	100	90	100

Key Votes

1) Busing	AGN	6) Cmbodia Bmbg	FOR	11) Chkg Acct Intrst	AGN
2) Strip Mines	ABS	7) Bust Hwy Trust	AGN	12) End HISC (HUAC)	AGN
3) Cut Mil $	ABS	8) Farm Sub Lmt	FOR	13) Nixon Sewer Veto	FOR
4) Rev Shrg	FOR	9) School Prayr	FOR	14) Corp Cmpaign $	FOR
5) Pub TV $	AGN	10) Cnsumr Prot	FOR	15) Pol $ Disclosr	AGN

Election Results

1972 general:	Lawrence G. Williams (R)	122,622	(61%)
	Stuart S. Bowie (D)	79,578	(39%)
1972 primary:	Lawrence G. Williams (R), unopposed		
1970 general:	Lawrence G. Williams (R)	91,042	(59%)
	Joseph R. Breslin (D)	62,722	(41%)

EIGHTH DISTRICT Political Background

The 8th district of Pennsylvania is one of four suburban Philadelphia districts. This one, aside from a few WASPy townships lying in Montgomery County, is almost entirely coextensive with Bucks County. The political complexion of Bucks County may have become familiar to some readers through the prose of best-selling author James Michener—one of many writers and artists living in Bucks' more bucolic reaches. Michener wrote a book about his efforts as Democratic County Chairman on behalf of John F. Kennedy in 1960. The author's efforts fell short; Kennedy lost the district, as most Democrats do.

But Kennedy's showing here does not mean that Bucks County has no pockets of Democratic strength. For the county is by no means a complete rich man's retreat. To be sure, northern Bucks is a pastoral place where writers and rentiers live in stone Quaker farmhouses set in rolling hills near villages like New Hope and Doylestown. But the lower end of the county, just beyond northeast Philadelphia, is predominantly industrial, blue-collar, and traditionally Democratic. Here, near the site of U.S. Steel's huge Fairless works, is one of the original Levittowns.

The Congressman from the 8th is Edward (Pete) Biester, a member of Pennsylvania's current good-sized bloc of liberal Republicans. First elected in 1966, Biester has won reelection easily, and should have no future troubles. Were he not the candidate, however, the district might become marginal. In 1973, at the beginning of the 93rd Congress, Biester switched from the Judiciary Committee, where he had considerable seniority, to Foreign Affairs. On his new committee, the Congressman has joined an increasing number of Republicans to oppose American military intervention in Indochina. For many years, Foreign Affairs firmly backed the war policies of the Johnson and Nixon administrations. But with the addition of new members in 1972 and 1973, and with the changes of mind of Chairman Thomas Morgan and second-ranking Democrat Clement Zablocki, Foreign Affairs in 1973 produced a solid majority in opposition to the American bombing of Cambodia.

Census Data Pop. 475,406. Central city, 0%; suburban, 100%. Median family income, $11,807; families above $15,000: 29%; families below $3,000: 4%. Median years education, 12.3.

1972 Share of Federal Outlays $493,486,356

DOD	$179,461,059	HEW	$176,473,856
AEC	$962,513	HUD	$12,114,954
NASA	$7,443,766	DOI	$1,731,589
DOT	$12,902,696	USDA	$8,836,479
		Other	$93,559,444

Federal Military-Industrial Commitments

DOD Installations Naval Air Development Center (Johnsville). Naval Air Station (Willow Grove). Naval Air Facility (Johnsville).

Economic Base Primary metal industries; finance, insurance and real estate; instruments and related products, especially mechanical measuring devices; machinery; and paper and allied products, especially miscellaneous converted paper products.

The Voters

Registration 229,787 total. 93,055 D (40%); 123,523 R (54%); 13,209 other (6%).
Median voting age 41.4
Employment profile White collar, 52%. Blue collar, 38%. Service, 9%. Farm, 1%.
Ethnic groups Black, 2%. Total foreign stock, 18%. Germany, Italy, 3% each; UK, 2%; Poland, Ireland, USSR, 1% each.

Presidential vote

1972	Nixon (R)	118,601	(65%)
	McGovern (D)	64,330	(35%)
1968	Nixon (R)	84,293	(51%)
	Humphrey (D)	65,369	(39%)
	Wallace (AI)	17,107	(10%)

Representative

Edward G. Biester, Jr. (R) Elected 1966; b. Jan. 5, 1931, Trevose; home, Furlong; Wesleyan U., B.A., 1952; Temple U., LL.B., 1955; married, four children; United Church of Christ.

Career Practicing atty., 1956–66; Asst. Dist. Atty., Bucks County, 1958–64.

Offices 325 CHOB, 202-225-4276. Also 68 E. Court St., Doylestown 18901, 215-348-4005, and 7500 Bristol Pike, Rt. 13, P.O. Box 12, Levittown 19059, 215-348-2558.

Administrative Assistant Ronald Strouse

Committees

Foreign Affairs (15th); Subs: Africa; National Security Policy and Scientific Developments.

Group Ratings

	ADA	COPE	LWV	RIPON	NFU	LCV	CFA	NAB	NSI	ACA
1972	75	82	83	94	86	87	100	25	30	9
1971	73	58	78	94	67	–	88	–	–	33
1970	76	75	–	94	100	95	79	58	90	32

Key Votes

1) Busing	AGN	6) Cmbodia Bmbg	AGN	11) Chkg Acct Intrst	FOR
2) Strip Mines	AGN	7) Bust Hwy Trust	FOR	12) End HISC (HUAC)	AGN
3) Cut Mil $	FOR	8) Farm Sub Lmt	FOR	13) Nixon Sewer Veto	FOR
4) Rev Shrg	FOR	9) School Prayr	AGN	14) Corp Cmpaign $	AGN
5) Pub TV $	AGN	10) Cnsumr Prot	FOR	15) Pol $ Disclosr	FOR

Election Results

1972 general:	Edward G. Biester, Jr. (R)	115,799	(64%)
	Alan Williams (D)	64,069	(36%)
1972 primary:	Edward G. Biester, Jr. (R)	25,459	(81%)
	William H. Allen (R)	5,905	(19%)
1970 general:	Edward G. Biester, Jr. (R)	73,041	(56%)
	Arthur Leo Hennessy, Jr. (D)	51,464	(40%)
	Charles B. Moore (C)	5,118	(4%)

NINTH DISTRICT Political Background

The Appalachian Mountain chains run like a series of backbones through central Pennsylvania. Throughout the state's history, the mountains have constituted a formidable barrier, not so much because of their height, which is unimpressive, but because of their persistence: one rugged chain right after another for 50 to 100 miles. During the eighteenth century, the mountains provided eastern Pennsylvania with a kind of rampart against Indian attacks, but in the nineteenth century they proved less useful. The mountains prevented Pennsylvania from ever digging a satisfactory statewide canal system—the boom mode of transportation in the early nineteenth century. They also delayed, until other states had them, the building of an east-west railroad. Only the aggressive policy of the Pennsylvania Railroad, a relative late-comer to the business, saved the state from trunk-line status.

Before the 1972 redistricting, most of what is now the 9th district was part of the old 12th district. As it stands, the 9th is the only Pennsylvania district to lie wholly within the mountains. This part of the Alleghenies (as the Appalachians are often called in Pennsylvania) was first settled by poor Scotch and Ulster Irish farmers just after the Revolutionary War. They were a people of fierce independence and pride, as the Whiskey Rebellion demonstrated. Later, not much coal was found here in the southern half of the state's mountains. So what is now the 9th was spared the boom-then-bust cycle that the coal industry inflicted on places like Scranton and Wilkes-Barre. However, the district's largest city, Altoona (pop. 62,000), has suffered from the decline of its major employer, the Pennsylvania Railroad. Altoona is located near the Horseshoe

Curve, one of the engineering wonders of nineteenth-century railroading, and the city has long been the home of many railroad employees. The city's declining population figures reflect the deterioration, and finally the bankruptcy, of what is now the Penn Central.

In 1972, a combination of redistricting and the journalistic efforts of Jack Anderson made for a change in the 9th's congressional representation. Somerset County, the home of ex-Rep. 1960–69) J. Irving Whalley, was removed from the district by the Democratic state legislature in 1972. With the county gone, Whalley was faced with either running against John Saylor in the new 12th district or moving his residence to the 9th. Anderson effectively eliminated both options when his column revealed that Whalley, a 72-year-old small-town banker, had been demanding—and getting—salary kickbacks from some members of his staff. Whalley promptly decided not to run in 1972, and in 1973, he pleaded guilty to federal criminal charges and was sentenced to jail.

Whalley's demise, it appeared, left the 9th to state Sen. D. Elmer Hawbaker, a seasoned politico from Mercersburg. But in the Republican primary, Hawbaker was upset by E. G. (Bud) Shuster, a 40-year-old entrepreneur who had made a fortune by building up a business and then selling it to IBM. Shuster decided to settle in the southern Pennsylvania mountains, got involved in local affairs, and decided to run for Congress in 1972. His ample fortune allowed him to wage an effective media campaign, mostly radio in these parts. Not only did Shuster upset the favorite in the primary, he also ran better than other Republicans had within the boundaries of the district in previous general elections. His first months in Congress appear to show that Shuster leans to the conservative side on most issues.

Census Data   Pop. 468,008. Central city, 13%; suburban, 26%. Median family income, $8,124; families above $15,000: 10%; families below $3,000: 10%. Median years education, 11.4.

1972 Share of Federal Outlays $444,742,055

DOD	$106,795,378	HEW	$184,497,639
AEC	$2,126	HUD	$7,974,351
NASA	$4,951	DOI	$579,635
DOT	$24,692,774	USDA	$14,193,083
		Other	$$106,002,018

Federal Military-Industrial Commitments

DOD Installations Letterkenny Army Depot (Chambersburg).

Economic Base   Agriculture, notably dairy products, poultry and cattle; apparel and other textile products; machinery; finance, insurance and real estate; and food and kindred products.

The Voters

Registration 197,754 total. 78,105 D (39%); 114,674 R (58%); 5,065 other (3%).
Median voting age 44.7
Employment profile White collar, 34%. Blue collar, 50%. Service, 12%. Farm, 4%.
Ethnic groups Total foreign stock, 4%. Italy, 1%.

Presidential vote

1972	Nixon (R)	114,144	(74%)
	McGovern (D)	40,131	(26%)
1968	Nixon (R)	97,270	(59%)
	Humphrey (D)	51,959	(32%)
	Wallace (AI)	14,836	(9%)

Representative

E. G. (Bud) Shuster (R) Elected 1972; b. Jan. 23, 1932, Glassport; home, Everett; U. of Pittsburgh, B.S., 1954; Duquesne U., M.B.A., 1960; American U., Ph.D., 1967; Army; married, five children.

Career V.Pres., Radio Corporation of America; trustee, U. of Pittsburgh; operator, Shuster Farms.

Offices 1116 LHOB, 202-225-2431.

Administrative Assistant Laurence Fitzgerald

Committees

District of Columbia (11th); Subs: Judiciary; Revenue and Financial Affairs.

Public Works (10th); Subs: Economic Development; Investigations and Review; Public Buildings and Grounds; Transportation; Water Resources.

Group Ratings: Newly Elected

Key Votes

1) Busing	NE	6) Cmbodia Bmbg	FOR	11) Chkg Acct Intrst	AGN
2) Strip Mines	NE	7) Bust Hwy Trust	AGN	12) End HISC (HUAC)	AGN
3) Cut Mil $	NE	8) Farm Sub Lmt	NE	13) Nixon Sewer Veto	AGN
4) Rev Shrg	NE	9) School Prayr	NE	14) Corp Cmpaign $	NE
5) Pub TV $	NE	10) Cnsumr Prot	NE	15) Pol $ Disclosr	NE

Election Results

1972 general:	E. G. Shuster (R)	95,913	(62%)
	Earl P. Collins (D)	59,386	(38%)
1972 primary:	E. G. Shuster (R)	26,899	(52%)
	D. Elmer Hawbaker (R)	19,895	(38%)
	Kenneth W. Ferry (R)	4,944	(10%)

TENTH DISTRICT Political Background

Scranton is the anthracite coal town par excellence. Back around the turn of the century, hard coal was much in demand, as it was used to stoke the nation's home furnaces and pot-bellied stoves. Because the only major deposits of anthracite in the United States lay in the Scranton–Wilkes-Barre area of northeast Pennsylvania, Scranton and Wilkes-Barre fell upon flush times. Immigrants from Italy, Poland, Austria-Hungary, and Ireland poured in to join the Scots and Welsh already here to work the mines. Scranton became the third-largest city in Pennsylvania, its population peaking at 143,000 in 1930.

Soon thereafter, the demand for hard coal began to decline, as oil and gas furnaces grew more popular. Accordingly, since the 1930s, Scranton and the industrial Lackawanna area have experienced a kind of depression. Textile mills have arrived in some numbers, as the family of former Gov. William Scranton—after which the city was named—has made great efforts to attract new industry. But the city of Scranton, isolated in the mountains, can no longer support the numbers it once could. In 1970, the city's population stood at 103,000, which was about the figure of 1900. And Scranton today continues to lose population.

A look at the edges of Scranton shows what happened to it. On one block stand some large houses, maintained with some care, but obviously built in the 1920s—the city's last boom decade. On the next block, one finds no new suburban tract housing or shopping centers, only trees and hills. In few parts of the country is such a sudden halt in urban development so apparent.

Scranton and the industrial towns around it presently make up about half of Pennsylvania's 10th congressional district. The 10th consists of a rather anomalous mix: the heavily ethnic city and surrounding Lackawanna County, combined with several Scots-Irish-Welsh counties in the Pocono Mountains (a favorite resort of many New Yorkers), along with some counties out of the state's northern tier. As the number of votes in traditionally Democratic Scranton declines, the Republican leanings of the rest of the district have come to dominate the 10th more and more. Accordingly, statewide Republican candidates have done better and better here in recent elections.

The district has not elected a Democratic Congressman since the recession year of 1958. Two years after that, William Scranton was elected Congressman from the district—the start of a political career that saw him become Governor of Pennsylvania (1963–66) and the dark-horse presidential candidate of Republican liberals in 1964. Scranton retired from office in 1966, and unlike so many other politicians, he has managed to make his decision to quit stick. He has emerged from his home near Scranton onto the national scene only briefly. One such appearance was when he chaired the presidential commission on the Kent State and Jackson State killings, which produced a report ignored by the Nixon Administration.

Scranton's successor in the House is Joseph McDade, a liberal Republican in the Scranton mold. After close shaves in 1962 and 1964, McDade has gotten a firm hold on the district. In 1972, the Republican Congressman carried Lackawanna County (Scranton) by almost as much, 70%, as he carried the district as whole, 74%. McDade is one of the few liberal Republicans on the House Appropriations Committee; he also serves as the ranking Republican on its Interior Subcommittee run by Julia Hansen of Washington. The subcommittee seat is an unusual one for an Easterner. McDade has made use of it to advance some programs to help the environment.

Census Data Pop. 472,007. Central city, 22%; suburban, 36%. Median family income, $8,318; families above $15,000: 12%; families below $3,000: 10%. Median years education, 12.0.

1972 Share of Federal Outlays $414,740,278

DOD	$113,734,000	HEW	$196,330,277
AEC	–	HUD	$3,324,134
NASA	–	DOI	$2,342,303
DOT	$14,635,392	USDA	$11,313,127
		Other	$73,061,045

Federal Military-Industrial Commitments

DOD Contractors Chamberlain Manufacturing (Scranton), $44.668m: operation of Scranton Army Ammunition plant; production of 155mm projectile components.
DOD Installations Tobyhanna Army Depot (Tobyhanna).

Economic Base Apparel and other textile products, especially women's and misses' outerwear; agriculture, notably dairy products and poultry; electrical equipment and supplies; fabricated metal products; finance, insurance and real estate; and textile mill products.

The Voters

Registration 255,614 total. 130,995 D (51%); 119,558 R (47%); 5,061 other (2%).
Median voting age 46.9
Employment profile White collar, 38%. Blue collar, 47%. Service, 11%. Farm, 4%.
Ethnic groups Total foreign stock, 20%. Italy, Poland, 4% each; UK, Austria, Germany, 2% each; Ireland, 1%.

Presidential vote

1972	Nixon (R)	125,686	(64%)
	McGovern (D)	71,105	(36%)
1968	Nixon (R)	101,917	(49%)
	Humphrey (D)	94,627	(46%)
	Wallace (AI)	9,880	(5%)

Representative

Joseph Michael McDade (R) Elected 1962; b. Sept. 29, 1931, Scranton; home, Scranton; U. of Notre Dame, B.A., 1953; U. of Pa., LL.B., 1956; married, four children; Catholic.

Career Clerk to Fed. Judge, 1956–57 practicing atty., 1957– ; Scranton City Solicitor, 1962.

Offices 2202 RHOB, 202-225-3731. Also 1233 Northeastern Natl. Bank Bldg., Scranton 18503, 717-346-3834.

Administrative Assistant Francis O'Gorman

Committees

Appropriations (9th); Subs: HUD, Space, Science, Veterans; Interior (Ranking Mbr.).

Select Com. on Small Business (4th); Subs: Special Small Business Problems (Ranking Mbr.); Government Procurement and International Trade.

Group Ratings

	ADA	COPE	LWV	RIPON	NFU	LCV	CFA	NAB	NSI	ACA
1972	38	56	75	80	50	32	0	42	100	42
1971	43	73	78	67	57	–	88	–	–	46
1970	56	67	–	76	91	63	76	64	90	39

Key Votes

1) Busing	AGN	6) Cmbodia Bmbg	AGN	11) Chkg Acct Intrst	AGN
2) Strip Mines	AGN	7) Bust Hwy Trust	FOR	12) End HISC (HUAC)	AGN
3) Cut Mil $	AGN	8) Farm Sub Lmt	ABS	13) Nixon Sewer Veto	FOR
4) Rev Shrg	FOR	9) School Prayr	FOR	14) Corp Cmpaign $	AGN
5) Pub TV $	AGN	10) Cnsumr Prot	FOR	15) Pol $ Disclosr	FOR

Election Results

1972 general:	Joseph M. McDade (R)	143,670	(74%)
	Stanley R. Coveleskie (D)	51,550	(26%)
1972 primary:	Joseph M. McDade (R), unopposed		
1970 general:	Joseph M. McDade (R)	102,716	(65%)
	Edward J. Smith (D)	51,506	(33%)
	Stephen P. Depue (C)	2,731	(2%)

ELEVENTH DISTRICT Political Background

In June 1972, Hurricane Agnes dropped torrential rains on much of the East. Flood waters ensued, and the place hardest hit was the Wyoming Valley in and around Wilkes-Barre, Pennsylvania. Here more than 20% of the residents of Luzerne County were displaced from their homes. As writer Sanford Ungar, a native of the area, has pointed out, the Wyoming Valley has long been vulnerable to such disaster; its cities lie in a narrow flood plain on both sides of the mighty Susquehanna River. So located, Wilkes-Barre was one of the first settlements in northeast Pennsylvania. It was named in the late 1770s to commemorate two heroes of the Revolutionary War.

During the nineteenth century, Wilkes-Barre, like Scranton in the 10th district, enjoyed a boom produced by the presence of anthracite coal. The flush times attracted thousands of immigrants to the mines. Like Scranton, Wilkes-Barre reached its peak population (86,000) in 1930, and its waning population—down to 58,000 in 1970—reflects the decline and fall of the anthracite industry. Today, residents of Wilkes-Barre depend mainly on textile mills, which moved into it during the 1950s and 1960s. Many workers here, however, are unemployed.

Luzerne County contains some 73% of the people living in Pennsylvania's 11th congressional district. Outside of Philadelphia and Pittsburgh, the territory encompassed by the 11th is usually the most Democratic region of Pennsylvania. In 1972, however, a heavy switch among ethnic voters put the district in Richard Nixon's Republican column. Nevertheless, the 11th stayed safely Democratic in the House election, thanks to the local popularity of Congressman Daniel J. Flood.

Flood was first elected in 1944, and then defeated in the Republican years of 1946 and 1952—times when such a thing as coattails existed. Flood is now one of the most senior, and most distinctive, members of the House. As Chairman of the Labor-HEW Subcommittee of the Appropriations Committee, the Congressman has as much say as anyone on the hill over the amount of money spent for most of the federal government's social programs, though lately, of course, the Nixon Administration has impounded much of it. Toward social programs, Flood is usually sympathetic, but like most senior members of Appropriations, he works hard to keep the levels of spending down somewhat. Traditionally, Senate Appropriations is more generous with the purse, with the resulting discrepancies resolved in conference committee.

Many senior members of the House cut anonymous figures, so anonymous that few people on the street give them a second look. Flood is not such a man. He keeps his thin mustache carefully waxed, and when he speaks, words flow out in a style he picked up on stage as a Shakespearean actor. In orotund sentences, pointing first with one forefinger and then the other, the Congressman is wont to remind his colleagues of the perils to follow should they ignore the recommendations of the Appropriations Committee; indeed the very evils of Pandora's box, should they begin to amend appropriations bills on the floor of the House. Flood not only defends the actions of the committee where he has expertise, but also the committee's usually permissive attitude toward military expenditures. He was one of those, for example, to vote against cutting off funds for the bombing of Cambodia.

Like the Chairman of the Appropriations Committee, George Mahon of Texas, Flood looks nowhere near his age (74 in 1974). For the past 20 years, Flood has had no problems winning reelection to Congress, and he will probably continue to win reelection until he decides to retire.

Census Data Pop. 470,457. Central city, 19%; suburban, 54%. Median family income, $8,161; families above $15,000: 10%; families below $3,000: 9%. Median years education, 11.6.

1972 Share of Federal Outlays $378,030,209

DOD	$42,364,000	HEW	$233,284,901
AEC	–	HUD	$9,756,283
NASA	–	DOI	$4,312,301
DOT	$3,493,623	USDA	$6,095,976
		Other	$78,723,125

Federal Military-Industrial Commitments

DOD Contractors Kennedy Van Saun Manufacturing (Danville), $11.342m: 81mm and 105mm projectiles. Philco Ford (Willow Grove), $11.101m: telecommunications systems. U.S. Steel (Berwick), $9.007m: unspecified. Medico Industries (Wilkes Barre), $6.449m: 57mm projectiles. *DOD Installations* Benton AF Station (Red Rock).

Economic Base Apparel and other textile products, especially women's and misses' outerwear; textile mill products; finance, insurance and real estate; food and kindred products; and electrical equipment and supplies.

The Voters

Registration 212,767 total. 109,670 D (52%); 99,506 R (47%); 3,591 other (2%).
Median voting age 47.9
Employment profile White collar, 35%. Blue collar, 53%. Service, 11%. Farm, 1%.
Ethnic groups Total foreign stock, 25%. Poland, 6%; Italy, 4%; Austria, 3%; Czechoslovakia, UK, 2% each; Lithuania, Germany, 1% each.

Presidential vote

1972	Nixon (R)	113,556	(62%)
	McGovern (D)	68,764	(38%)

1968	Nixon (R)	84,118	(43%)
	Humphrey (D)	101,135	(51%)
	Wallace (AI)	10,244	(5%)

Representative

Daniel J. Flood (D) Elected 1954; b. Nov. 26, 1903, Hazleton; home, Wilkes-Barre; Syracuse U., B.A., 1924, M.A.; Harvard Law School, 1925–26; Dickinson School of Law, LL.B., 1929; married; Catholic.

Career Practicing atty., 1930– ; Deputy Atty. Gen., Pa., and Counsel for Pa. Liquor Control Bd., 1935–39; Dir., Bureau of Public Assistance Disbursements, State Treas., and Exec. Asst. to State Treas., 1941–44; Sp. Ambassador to Peru, 1945; U.S. House of Reps., 1944–46, 1948–52.

Offices 108 CHOB, 202-225-6511. Also Rm. 1015, United Penn Bank Bldg., Wilkes-Barre 18701, 717-822-2194.

Administrative Assistant Stephen Elko

Committees

Appropriations (9th); Subs: Defense; Labor, Health, Education, and Welfare (Chm.).

Group Ratings

	ADA	COPE	LWV	RIPON	NFU	LCV	CFA	NAB	NSI	ACA
1972	44	91	82	57	71	27	0	25	100	29
1971	35	92	78	24	73	–	88	–	–	41
1970	36	92	–	38	100	62	67	8	89	29

Key Votes

1) Busing	FOR	6) Cmbodia Bmbg	FOR	11) Chkg Acct Intrst	AGN
2) Strip Mines	AGN	7) Bust Hwy Trust	AGN	12) End HISC (HUAC)	AGN
3) Cut Mil $	AGN	8) Farm Sub Lmt	ABS	13) Nixon Sewer Veto	AGN
4) Rev Shrg	FOR	9) School Prayr	FOR	14) Corp Cmpaign $	FOR
5) Pub TV $	FOR	10) Cnsumr Prot	FOR	15) Pol $ Disclosr	AGN

Election Results

1972 general:	Daniel J. Flood (D)	124,336	(68%)
	Donald B. Ayers (R)	57,809	(32%)
1972 primary:	Daniel J. Flood (D)	40,661	(88%)
	Samuel W. Daley (R)	5,560	(12%)
1970 general	Daniel J. Flood (D)	146,789	(97%)
	Alvin J. Balschi (C)	5,123	(3%)

TWELFTH DISTRICT Political Background

The hills of western Pennsylvania, eastern Ohio, and northern West Virginia that encircle the Pittsburgh metropolitan area constitute one of the few parts of the country that is predominantly industrial without having a major city. The easternmost part of these industrial mountains forms Pennsylvania's 12th congressional district: five counties and part of another, the largest city of which is Johnstown (pop. 42,000). More typical of the district are small towns like Kittanning and Puxsutawney, both with less than 10,000 residents. First settled by Scots-Irish, this region of the state became part of the bituminous coal belt boom in the late nineteenth century. Today coal is still important to the district's economy, though the industry employs far fewer people than it did 30 years ago.

In statewide elections the 12th is as marginal as any district in Pennsylvania. It usually comes in a couple of points more Republican than the state as a whole. In congressional elections, however, the results are more one-sided, which pleases the district's Republican Congressman, John Saylor. In the House, Saylor is known for his longtime advocacy of conservation and the protection of the enivironment. As ranking Republican on the Interior Committee, Saylor, along with veteran Chairman Wayne Aspinall (defeated in the 1972 primary), often determined the fate of legislation affecting the environment. Though Saylor and Aspinall did work together, Saylor has been considered far more sympathetic to the ideas advanced by conservationists.

Probably Saylor's major achievement so far was the passage in 1964 of the Wilderness Preservation Act. At Aspinall's insistence, the measure does permit some mining activities in wilderness areas until 1984, but the legislation allows the government to establish wilderness areas, mostly free of any development. Some, like the Nader Congress Project people, have charged that Saylor opposes projects like the SST and the AEC's breeder reactor less out of genuine concern for ecology than a solicitude for the coal interests, which run counter to such projects. Nevertheless, most conservation lobbying groups consider Saylor a true friend and somebody who fought for their cause long before it became popular to do so.

In 1970, Saylor won reelection by a margin not up to his usual ones. And in 1972, he attracted primary opposition. But Saylor disposed of his Republican opponent, Martin Horowitz, by a 72–28 count, even though Horowitz was backed by several important local Republicans. In the general election that followed, Saylor won easily. About the only thing that would end Saylor's House career is retirement; he is 66 in 1974.

Census Data Pop. 469,999. Central city, 9%; suburban, 47%. Median family income, $8,030; families above $15,000: 10%; families below $3,000: 11%. Median years education, 11.2.

1972 Share of Federal Outlays $294,195,547

DOD	$16,995,091	HEW	$193,903,918
AEC	$894,418	HUD	$2,733,870
NASA	–	DOI	$2,876,570
DOT	$1,182,526	USDA	$11,381,822
		Other	$$64,227,332

Federal Military-Industrial Commitments

No installations or contractors receiving prime awards greater than $5,000,000.

Economic Base Agriculture, notably dairy products and poultry; bituminous coal mining; finance, insurance and real estate; and stone, clay and glass products. Also higher education (Indiana Univ. of Pennsylvania).

The Voters

Registration 227,282 total. 114,179 D (50%); 109,173 R (48%); 3,930 other (2%).
Median voting age 46.5
Employment profile White collar, 35%. Blue collar, 50%. Service, 12%. Farm, 3%.
Ethnic groups Black, 1%. Total foreign stock, 15%. Italy, 3%; Czechoslovakia, Poland, Austria, 2% each; UK, Germany, 1% each.

Presidential vote

1972	Nixon (R)	112,694	(64%)
	McGovern (D)	64,049	(36%)
1968	Nixon (R)	91,394	(48%)
	Humphrey (D)	87,198	(46%)
	Wallace (AI)	12,186	(6%)

Representative

John Phillips Saylor (R) Elected Sept. 13, 1949; b. July 23, 1908, Johnstown; home, Johnstown; Mercersburg Acad., Franklin and Marshall Col., B.A., 1929; Dickinson Law School, LL.B., 1933; Navy, WWII; Capt. USNR; married, two children; United Church of Christ.

Career Pres., Bd. of Dir., Johnstown Fed. Savings and Loan Assn.; V. Chm., Rep. Congressional Delegation.

Offices 2354 RHOB, 202-225-2065.

Administrative Assistant Harry M. Fox

Committees

Interior and Insular Affairs (Ranking Mbr.); Subs: Environment; National Parks and Recreation; Water and Power Resources; Territorial and Insular Affairs; Mines and Mining; Indian Affairs; Public Lands.

Veterans' Affairs (2nd); Subs: Compensation and Pension; Hospitals (Ranking Mbr.); Insurance.

Group Ratings

	ADA	COPE	LWV	RIPON	NFU	LCV	CFA	NAB	NSI	ACA
1972	25	70	50	57	43	77	100	82	100	70
1971	22	50	13	38	40	–	0	–	–	74
1970	40	50	–	47	33	90	53	78	100	73

Key Votes

1) Busing	FOR	6) Cmbodia Bmbg	FOR	11) Chkg Acct Intrst	ABS
2) Strip Mines	AGN	7) Bust Hwy Trust	AGN	12) End HISC (HUAC)	AGN
3) Cut Mil $	AGN	8) Farm Sub Lmt	FOR	13) Nixon Sewer Veto	FOR
4) Rev Shrg	AGN	9) School Prayr	FOR	14) Corp Cmpaign $	AGN
5) Pub TV $	AGN	10) Cnsumr Prot	ABS	15) Pol $ Disclosr	AGN

Election Results

1972 general:	John P. Saylor (R)	122,628	(68%)
	Joseph Murphy (D)	57,314	(32%)
1972 primary:	John P. Saylor (R)	35,608	(72%)
	Martin M. Horowitz (R)	13,622	(28%)
1970 general:	John P. Saylor (R)	81,675	(58%)
	Joseph F. O'Kicki (D)	58,720	(41%)
	Ellsworth L. Hahn (AI)	1,213	(1%)

THIRTEENTH DISTRICT Political Background

The 13th district of Pennsylvania, part of Montgomery County, comprises a fair cross-section of upper-income Philadelphia suburbia. The 13th, along with the 5th, contains the posh Main Line suburbs. Here in the 13th are places like Haverford, Byrn Mawr, and Ardmore—some of them with colleges, and all of them with a patina of wealth, social standing, and the dignity of age. An area of similar composition is the 21st ward of Philadelphia, part of the elite Chestnut Hill neighborhood and also part of the 13th district. On the other side of Philadelphia are predominantly Jewish suburbs, in places like Cheltenham township, which are products mostly of the 1950s. As one moves away from the city limits, the land becomes hillier and more sparsely settled, with the exception of the old industrial towns, Norristown and Conshohocken, hard by the banks of the Schuylkill.

The 13th is today, as it alway has been, a solidly Republican district. It is not, however, as adamantly conservative as it was during the New Deal. In fact, the district's last two Congressmen have been liberal Republicans. Richard Schweiker represented the 13th for eight years before his election to the Senate in 1968. And the current Congressman, Lawrence Coughlin, has supported measures such as those to set a deadline on American involvement in Vietnam. The district has some Quaker and pacifist influence.

Until 1972, Coughlin was not as strong at the polls as his predecessor Schweiker. But in the year of the Nixon landslide, the incumbent liberal Republican was reelected with 67% of the votes. At the beginning of the 93rd Congress, Coughlin switched from the Judiciary and the Science committees to Appropriations, where he is currently its lowest ranking Republican. His switch, however, indicates that Coughlin expects to stay in the House for some time to come. There is little doubt that he will.

Census Data Pop. 473,179. Central city, 11%; suburban, 89%. Median family income, $13,251; families above $15,000: 41%; families below $3,000: 4%. Median years education, 12.4.

1972 Share of Federal Outlays $491,079,106

DOD	$178,585,639	HEW	$175,613,008
AEC	$957,818	HUD	$12,055,856
NASA	$7,407,455	DOI	$1,723,142
DOT	$12,839,756	USDA	$8,793,374
		Other	$93,103,058

Federal Military-Industrial Commitments

DOD Contractors Ambac Industries (Fort Washington), $6.335m: telemetry units.
NASA Contractors General Electric (King of Prussia), $46.724m: ground data processing; Nimbus.
AEC Operations General Electric (King of Prussia), $5.704m: research into nuclear reactors.

Economic Base Finance, insurance and real estate; machinery electrical equipment and supplies; fabricated metal products; and chemicals and allied products, especially drugs.

The Voters

Registration 260,171 total. 76,860 D (30%); 171,167 R (66%); 12,144 other (5%).
Median voting age 45.8
Employment profile White collar, 64%. Blue collar, 27%. Service, 9%. Farm, –%.
Ethnic groups Black, 4%. Total foreign stock, 25%. Italy, 6%; USSR, UK, Germany, 3% each; Poland, Ireland, 2% each.

Presidential vote

1972	Nixon (R)	135,464	(64%)
	McGovern (D)	77,715	(36%)
1968	Nixon (R)	110,987	(52%)
	Humphrey (D)	87,709	(42%)
	Wallace (AI)	12,316	(6%)

Representative

R. Lawrence Coughlin (R) Elected 1968; b. April 11, 1929, Wilkes-Barre; home, Villanova; Yale U., B.A., 1950; Harvard, M.B.A., 1954; Temple U. Evening Law School, LL.B., 1958; USMC, Korean War; married, four children; Episcopalian.

Career Practicing atty., 1958–1969; Pa. Legislature, 1965–66; Pa. Senate, 1967–68.

Offices 336 CHOB, 202-225-6111. Also 607 Swede St., Norristown 19401, 215-277-4040.

Administrative Assistant Mitchell Rosenfeld

Committees

Appropriations (22nd); Subs: District of Columbia; Foreign Operations.

Group Ratings

	ADA	COPE	LWV	RIPON	NFU	LCV	CFA	NAB	NSI	ACA
1972	38	36	83	87	71	86	100	67	75	35
1971	49	25	78	83	36	–	71	–	–	67
1970	64	42	–	100	67	100	83	80	80	65

Key Votes

1) Busing	AGN	6) Cmbodia Bmbg	AGN	11) Chkg Acct Intrst	AGN
2) Strip Mines	AGN	7) Bust Hwy Trust	FOR	12) End HISC (HUAC)	AGN
3) Cut Mil $	AGN	8) Farm Sub Lmt	FOR	13) Nixon Sewer Veto	FOR
4) Rev Shrg	FOR	9) School Prayr	FOR	14) Corp Cmpaign $	AGN
5) Pub TV $	AGN	10) Cnsumr Prot	ABS	15) Pol $ Disclosr	FOR

Election Results

1972 general:	Lawrence Coughlin (R)	139,085	(67%)
	Katherine L. Camp (D)	69,728	(33%)
1972 primary:	Lawrence Coughlin (R), unopposed		
1970 general:	Lawrence Coughlin (R)	101,953	(58%)
	Frank R. Romano (D)	68,743	(39%)
	John S. Matthews (C)	3,356	(2%)

FOURTEENTH DISTRICT Political Background

Pittsburgh, Pennsylvania's second largest city, was the first urban center of the American interior. Pittsburgh grew because of its propitious site; here the Allegheny and Monongahela rivers join to form the Ohio. And where that happens—at the Golden Triangle—remains the city's focal point. It is now filled with high-rise buildings, products of a downtown renaissance. When most of the nation's commerce moved over water, Pittsburgh's location was ideal; and when the traffic switched to the railroads, the city adapted nicely. By the turn of the century, Pittsburgh, having large deposits of coal nearby, was the center of the steel industry, then the nation's largest and also one of the fastest-growing sectors of the economy. Today, Pittsburgh remains the headquarters of many of the nation's largest corporations. Here are the corporate offices of U.S. Steel, Jones & Laughlin Steel, along with several other steel companies; also Westinghouse and H. J. Heinz; and the giant concerns associated with the Mellon family: Alcoa, Gulf Oil, and Koppers. The Mellons, of course, have been long the richest family in Pittsburgh and one of the richest in the country.

But in spite of the city's recent progress—its program of downtown renewal and its relatively successful campaign against air pollution—Pittsburgh has been unable to keep pace with other major metropolitan areas. Its major industry, steel, has not shown much dynamism lately. As a result, the population of central city Pittsburgh has declined, and so also has the population of the entire Pittsburgh metropolitan area—the only major metropolitan area in the country to lose population during the 1960s.

The 14th district of Pennsylvania includes most of the city of Pittsburgh, plus a few suburbs. The district takes in most of the city's landmarks: the Golden Triangle, the University of Pittsburgh and its skyscraper campus, and Carnegie Mellon University. Though few of the city's steel mills lie within the 14th, many of the steel workers do live here, mostly in ethnic neighborhoods nestled between the Pittsburgh hills. Only 21% of the people in the district are black—a far smaller figure than in most major industrial cities. Employment opportunities in Pittsburgh peaked before the big waves of black migration from the South. Since the New Deal, the 14th has been solidly Democratic; in 1972, for example, it was one of only four districts in the state (the other three lie entirely within Philadelphia) to give George McGovern a majority of its votes.

The district's Congressman is liberal Democrat William Moorhead. After 15 years in the House, Moorhead is now a senior member of the Banking and the Government Operations committees.

He inherited from John Moss of California the chairmanship of the Government Operations Subcommittee on Foreigh Operations and Government Information. It was from this chairmanship that Moss developed the Freedom of Information Act (see California 5). In the same aggressive manner, Moorehead has uncovered various forms of government deception, especially in foreign and military matters. Moorhead has denounced the government's system of classification and what he regards as unjustified use of the doctrine of executive privilege. The Congressman has investigated the tangled affairs of the Lockheed Corporation, probing not just the massive C5-A cost overruns, but corporate mismanagement and incompetence.

Back home, Moorhead has never encountered a really serious challenge since he was first slated by Gov. David Lawrence's organization in 1958. Some, however, have criticized the Congressman's allegedly close ties to the Mellons; he does own considerable Mellon Bank stock and serves on the Banking and Currency Committee. Nevertheless, Moorhead always wins reelection easily. His 60% of the votes in 1972 was uncommonly low for the veteran incument.

Census Data Pop. 470,537. Central city, 83%; suburban, 17%. Median family income, $8,952; families above $15,000: 18%; families below $3,000: 11%. Median years education, 11.9.

1972 Share of Federal Outlays $362,231,813

DOD	$47,410,346	HEW	$165,720,200
AEC	$18,553,854	HUD	$8,604,779
NASA	$862,946	DOI	$6,859,971
DOT	$13,859,363	USDA	$6,172,675
		Other	$94,187,679

Federal Military-Industrial Commitments

DOD Contractors Westinghouse Electric (Pittsburgh), $136.147m: nuclear reactor components. *AEC Operations* Aerojet General Corp. (Pittsburgh), $8.667m: unspecified.

Economic Base Primary metal industries, especially blast furnace and basic steel products; finance, insurance and real estate; fabricated metal products, especially fabricated structural metal products; machinery; and electrical equipment and supplies, especially electric test and distributing equipment. Also higher education (Duquesne Univ., and Univ. of Pittsburgh).

The Voters

Registration 262,063 total. 186,618 D (71%); 67,237 R (26%); 8,208 other (3%).
Median voting age 47.1
Employment profile White collar, 53%. Blue collar, 29%. Service, 18%. Farm, –%.
Ethnic groups Black, 21%. Total foreign stock, 25%; Italy, 5%; Poland, Germany, 3% each; USSR, UK, Ireland, 2% each; Austria, 1%.

Presidential vote

1972	Nixon (R)	86,912	(48%)
	McGovern (D)	95,687	(52%)
1968	Nixon (R)	60,996	(30%)
	Humphrey (D)	122,887	(60%)
	Wallace (AI)	20,721	(10%)

Representative

William S. Moorhead (D) Elected 1958; b. April 8, 1923, Pittsburgh; home, Pittsburgh; Yale U., B.A., 1944; Harvard Law School, J.D., 1949; Navy, WWII; married, four children; Episcopalian.

Career Practicing atty., 1949– ; Asst. City Solicitor, Pittsburgh, 1954–57; Allegheny County Housing Authority, 1956–58; Art Commission, Pittsburgh, 1958; Co-Chm., Pa. State Dem. Platform Com., 1966, 1970.

Offices 2467 RHOB, 202-225-2301. Also 2005 Fed. Bldg., Pittsburgh 15222, 412-644-2870.

Administrative Assistant Mollie Cohen

Committees

Banking and Currency (6th); Subs: Bank Supervision and Insurance; Housing; International Finance.

Government Operations (9th); Subs: Foreign Operations and Government Information (Chm.); Legislation and Military Operations.

Joint Economic Com. (5th); Subs: Urban Affairs (Chm.); Priorities and Economy in Government; Inter-American Economic Relationships;. Consumer Economics; International Economics.

Group Ratings

	ADA	COPE	LWV	RIPON	NFU	LCV	CFA	NAB	NSI	ACA
1972	94	100	100	78	86	87	100	9	0	0
1971	95	82	100	82	87	–	60	–	–	8
1970	80	92	–	88	100	84	78	20	22	6

Key Votes

1) Busing	FOR	6) Cmbodia Bmbg	AGN	11) Chkg Acct Intrst	FOR
2) Strip Mines	AGN	7) Bust Hwy Trust	FOR	12) End HISC (HUAC)	FOR
3) Cut Mil $	FOR	8) Farm Sub Lmt	FOR	13) Nixon Sewer Veto	AGN
4) Rev Shrg	FOR	9) School Prayr	AGN	14) Corp Cmpaign $	FOR
5) Pub TV $	FOR	10) Cnsumr Prot	FOR	15) Pol $ Disclosr	AGN

Election Results

1972 general:	William S. Moorhead (D)	106,158	(59%)
	Roland S. Catarinella (R)	72,275	(41%)
1972 primary:	William S. Moorhead (D)	58,275	(86%)
	John A. Adams (D)	5,829	(9%)
	William Bouie Haden (D)	3,644	(5%)
1970 general:	William S. Moorhead (D)	72,509	(77%)
	Barry Levine (R)	21,572	(23%)
	Reuben Francis Chaitin (AI)	687	(1%)

FIFTEENTH DISTRICT Political Background

The 15th district comprises the industrial Lehigh Valley in eastern Pennsylvania. It is one of two congressional districts in the country that is made up of two and only two counties (the other is South Carolina 4). Here in Northampton and Lehigh counties are the adjoining cities of Allentown and Bethlehem, the two population centers of the district. Bethlehem is the original home of Bethlehem Steel, the industry's number-two company. The 15th has some rural and Republican areas, especially along the southern edge of Lehigh County, where there is

Pennsylvania Dutch influence. But most of the district's voters are members of families who work in steel or textile mills, and they go Democratic in most elections. Neither of the state's two Republican U.S. Senators has ever carried the 15th.

From 1933 to 1963, Francis E. Walter represented the district in the House. Walter became a power on the Hill, chairing the House Un-American Activities Committee and the Judiciary Subcommittee on Immigration. Because of the nation's restrictive immigration laws—which Walter preserved from reform until his death—Congressmen with ethnic constituencies constantly found themselves seeking private bills for the relief of his constituents' relatives and friends. The situation meant that many Northern big-city Congressman had to curry favor with Francis Walter, who, of course, looked with disfavor on any liberal seeking to abolish the Un-American Activities Committee. Walter was also a co-sponsor of the McCarran-Walter Act, a piece of antisubversive legislation, much of which has turned out to be unconstitutional.

Walter's successor, Fred Rooney, is a very different kind of Congressman. Rather than worry about the enemy within, Rooney has devoted his legislative energies to matters that come before the Communications and Power Subcommittee of the Commerce Committee. On that business-oriented unit, Rooney rates as one of the more consumer-minded members. Back home, Rooney has had little trouble winning reelection. His share of the votes did dip to 52% in the Republican year of 1966, but in the even more Republican year of 1972, Rooney took 61% of the votes—an indication that he has a long congressional career ahead of him.

Census Data Pop. 469,672. Central city, 45%; suburban, 55%. Median family income, $10,171; families above $15,000: 19%; families below $3,000: 6%. Median years education, 11.7.

1972 Share of Federal Outlays $237,966,298

DOD	$17,830,000	HEW	$140,962,389
AEC	$36,000	HUD	$2,618,218
NASA	$2,014,090	DOI	$1,424,270
DOT	$4,910,190	USDA	$6,574,573
		Other	$61,596,568

Federal Military-Industrial Commitments

No installations or contractors receiving prime awards greater than $5,000,000.

Economic Base Apparel and other textile products, especially women's and misses' outerwear; electrical equipment and supplies; finance, insurance and real estate; textile mill products, especially knitting mill products; and food and kindred products.

The Voters

Registration 209,039 total. 117,807 D (56%); 84,682 R (41%); 6,550 other (3%).
Median voting age 45.4
Employment profile White collar, 41%. Blue collar, 47%. Service, 11%. Farm, 1%.
Ethnic groups Black, 1%. Total foreign stock, 19%. Italy, Austria, 3% each; Hungary, Germany, Czechoslovakia, 2% each; Poland, UK, 1% each.

Presidential vote

1972	Nixon (R)	99,664	(60%)
	McGovern (D)	65,557	(40%)
1968	Nixon (R)	79,288	(46%)
	Humphrey (D)	86,587	(50%)
	Wallace (AI)	7,176	(4%)

Representative

Fred B. Rooney (D) Elected Aug. 6, 1963; b. Nov. 6, 1925, Bethlehem; home, Bethlehem; U. of Ga., B.S., 1950; Army, WWII; married, three children; Catholic.

Career Real estate and insurance business.

Offices 2301 RHOB, 202-225-6411. Also 405 E. Fourth St., Bethlehem 18015, 215-866-0916, and P.O. Bldg., Allentown 18101, 215-437-4418.

Administrative Assistant Ray Huber

Committees

Interstate and Foreign Commerce (9th); Sub: Communications and Power.

Merchant Marine and Fisheries (17th); Subs: Coast Guard and Navigation; Fisheries and Wildlife Conservation and the Environment; Merchant Marines.

Group Ratings

	ADA	COPE	LWV	RIPON	NFU	LCV	CFA	NAB	NSI	ACA
1972	56	89	73	60	100	68	50	27	50	15
1971	62	91	63	60	86	–	88	–	–	22
1970	72	83	–	65	92	81	65	18	90	21

Key Votes

1) Busing	AGN	6) Cmbodia Bmbg	AGN	11) Chkg Acct Intrst	FOR
2) Strip Mines	ABS	7) Bust Hwy Trust	AGN	12) End HISC (HUAC)	ABS
3) Cut Mil $	FOR	8) Farm Sub Lmt	FOR	13) Nixon Sewer Veto	AGN
4) Rev Shrg	FOR	9) School Prayr	FOR	14) Corp Cmpaign $	FOR
5) Pub TV $	FOR	10) Cnsumr Prot	FOR	15) Pol $ Disclosr	AGN

Election Results

1972 general:	Fred B. Rooney (D)	99,937	(61%)
	Wardell F. Steigerwalt (R)	64,560	(39%)
1972 primary:	Fred B. Rooney (D)	31,323	(86%)
	Walter J. Tray (D)	4,987	(14%)
1970 general:	Fred B. Rooney (D)	93,169	(67%)
	Charles H. Roberts (R)	44,103	(32%)
	Chester R. Litz (C)	2,093	(2%)

SIXTEENTH DISTRICT Political Background

Millions of Americans know about Pennsylvania Dutch country: farms scrupulously tended and set out among rolling hills, barns decorated with hex signs, and Amish families clad in black, riding along in horse-drawn carriages. Fewer Americans know that use of the word "Dutch" here is a misnomer, or at least a corruption of the word "Deutsch." The Pennsylvania Dutch are actually German in origin. They are descended from members of Amish, Mennonite, and other pietistic sects who left principalities of eighteenth-century Germany for the religious freedom of William Penn's Quaker-dominated colony of Pennsylvania. The Quakers were happy to welcome the German immigrants, but a little leery of how they might get along in Philadelphia. So they were sent to what was then the frontier, the rolling green hills in Lancaster, Lebanon, and York counties. The land was naturally fertile, and careful cultivation by the Dutch increased its productivity. Today, farms in Lancaster County sustain some of the highest per-acre yields of any land on earth.

The Pennsylvania Dutch are perhaps the most conservative people in America. But unlike the residents of a conservative place like Orange County, California, the Dutch make no effort to restore an imagined paradise left behind. Instead, the people here believe that they live in a paradise now, and aside from some unpleasant tourists, much evidence exists to support their belief. Of course, not all of the Pennsylvania Dutch have clung fast to all of the old traditions, but German names are exceedingly common here. Moreover, the farms managed with meticulous care and the factories without unions reflect some of the old Dutch heritage shared by most residents of the Lancaster area. During the early career of James Buchanan, who lived in Lancaster, the politics of Pennsylvania Dutch country was Jeffersonian Democrat. But some years before the Civil War, the Dutch became Republican, a preference that they have retained to this day. The heart of the Dutch country, Lancaster County, regularly returns Republican majorities on the order of 3–1—usually the highest of any area of similar size in the East.

The most Dutch of all the Pennsylvania congressional districts is the 16th, which includes all of Lancaster County and parts of Chester and Lebanon counties. Of all the congressional districts in the East, the 16th cast the highest percentage of votes for Richard Nixon in 1968 (62%) and in 1972 (76%). The district's Congressman is Edwin Eshleman, a rather moderate Republican, given his constituency. Eshleman serves on the Education and Labor Committee, where he is part of the minority that would like to follow the lead of the Nixon Administration—if only Administration officials would bother to send word of their desires. First elected in 1966, Eshleman has no problems in the Republican primary, the only place where he could possibly lose his seat.

Census Data Pop. 467,811. Central city, 12%; suburban, 72%. Median family income, $9,905; families above $15,000: 18%; families below $3,000: 6%. Median years education, 11.4.

1972 Share of Federal Outlays $265,849,750

DOD	$66,874,297	HEW	$129,011,067
AEC	$152,593	HUD	$3,700,609
NASA	$1,291,580	DOI	$501,312
DOT	$4,724,621	USDA	$3,993,933
		Other	$55,599,738

Federal Military-Industrial Commitments

DOD Contractors Hamilton Watch (Lancaster), $16.136m: bomb fuzes and wrist watches; idle factory maintenance. RCA (Lancaster), $8.212m: electron tubes.

Economic Base Agriculture, notably dairy products, cattle and poultry; apparel and other textile products; primary metal industries; fabricated metal products, especially valves and pipe fittings; and food and kindred products.

The Voters

Registration 195,913 total. 58,225 D (30%); 127,160 R (65%); 10,528 other (5%).
Median voting age 43.6
Employment profile White collar, 38%. Blue collar, 46%. Service, 12%. Farm, 4%.
Ethnic groups Black, 3%. Total foreign stock, 7%. Germany, Italy, 1% each.

Presidential vote

1972	Nixon (R)	115,651	(76%)
	McGovern (D)	37,223	(24%)
1968	Nixon (R)	97,356	(62%)
	Humphrey (D)	47,091	(30%)
	Wallace (AI)	13,307	(8%)

Representative

Edwin D. Eshleman (R) Elected 1966; b. Dec. 4, 1920, Lancaster County; home, Lancaster; Franklin and Marshall Col., B.S.; Temple U.; USCG, WWII; married, two children; Lutheran.

Career Public school teacher; Pa. Legislature, 12 years, Majority and Minority Whip; V. Chm., Pa. Higher Ed. Assistance Agency, 1964–67.

Offices 416 CHOB, 202-225-2411. Also Rm. 210, P.O. Bldg., Lancaster 17604, 717-393-0666, and Rm. 16, P.O. Bldg., Coatsville 19320, 215-383-5684.

Administrative Assistant June Burke

Committees

Education and Labor (7th); Subs: No. 5 (Sel. Sub. on Education) (Ranking Mbr.); No. 7 (Equal Opportunities).

Group Ratings

	ADA	COPE	LWV	RIPON	NFU	LCV	CFA	NAB	NSI	ACA
1972	0	18	22	83	17	48	0	100	100	71
1971	14	18	28	44	31	–	40	–	–	78
1970	12	9	–	59	23	75	58	100	100	94

Key Votes

1) Busing	AGN	6) Cmbodia Bmbg	FOR	11) Chkg Acct Intrst	AGN
2) Strip Mines	ABS	7) Bust Hwy Trust	FOR	12) End HISC (HUAC)	AGN
3) Cut Mil $	AGN	8) Farm Sub Lmt	FOR	13) Nixon Sewer Veto	AGN
4) Rev Shrg	FOR	9) School Prayr	FOR	14) Corp Cmpaign $	AGN
5) Pub TV $	ABS	10) Cnsumr Prot	FOR	15) Pol $ Disclosr	FOR

Election Results

1972 general:	Edwin D. Eshleman (R)	112,292	(73%)
	Shirley S. Garrett (D)	40,534	(27%)
1972 primary:	Edwin D. Eshleman (R), unopposed		
1970 general:	Edwin D. Eshleman (R)	74,006	(66%)
	John E. Pflum (D)	33,986	(31%)
	Walter B. Willard III (C)	3,319	(3%)

SEVENTEENTH DISTRICT Political Background

The 17th district of Pennsylvania lies at just about the center of the state. It takes in a collection of counties along the Susquehanna River. The southern end of the district, around Harrisburg, contains more than half (62%) of the 17th's population. The main industry in Harrisburg, the state capital, is state government. In recent years—that is, from 1955 to 1962 and again from 1971 to the present—the Democrats have often controlled the Governor's office, one traditionally rich in patronage. But for about 80 of the last 100 years, the Governor has been a Republican. Harrisburg itself is a heavily Republican city.

Farther up the Susquehanna, there is some Democratic territory in Northumberland County, the waist, as it were, of the district. Here, seams of anthracite once drew ethnics to towns like Sunbury and Shamokin. Right across the river is the Lewisburg federal prison, where people like Jimmy Hoffa and Carmine de Sapio did time. To the north is Williamsport, a small manufacturing town on the upper Susquehanna. Its All-American character makes it an appropriate host for the annual Little League World Series.

Despite Northumberland, the 17th is a heavily Republican district. In fact, it has not elected a Democratic Congressman in the twentieth century. The current incumbent, Herman Schneebeli, first won the seat in a 1960 special election, and has kept it ever since. For 10 years or so, Schneebeli labored in obscurity, little known to the press, and recognized by readers of the

Congressional Directory as a middle-ranking Republican member of the House Ways and Means Committee. Then, in the spring of 1972, the ranking Republican on the Committee, John Byrnes of Wisconsin, though only 59, decided to retire. So did Jackson Betts of Ohio, the number-two Republican. Suddenly Herman Schneebeli found himself Wilbur Mills' Republican counterpart on Ways and Means, thanks to the wonder-working seniority system.

Byrnes had always worked smoothly with Mills. Like the Chairman, he knew the tax code and Social Security laws thoroughly. Moreover, Byrnes and Mills were inclined to give the House just about what it wanted when it came to tax reform and Social Security increases. What Schneebeli will do is not entirely clear. He cannot match Mills' expertise or political acumen, but then few members of Congress can. On most issues, Schneebeli has taken positions favored by business groups. For example, the Congressman, who owns an oil distributorship, has opposed lowering the oil-depletion allowance below 22%.

One way to gauge Schneebeli's activities and preferences in committee is to look at the 17th's politics of 1970. In that year, Schneebeli was opposed by the Dauphin County (Harrisburg) Republican Chairman in the primary, and by a big-spending Democrat in the general election. Schneebeli, who had encountered only desultory opposition in the past, quickly amassed a campaign chest of over $100,000. Most of the money was contributed by large stockholders or top executives of big companies. Schneebeli won both elections, though by margins somewhat smaller than usual. In 1972, the Congressman had no trouble at all winning reelection. The hostility of the Dauphin and Northumberland County Republican organizations toward the Congressman appears to have cooled. Short of a resurgency of ill will, Schneebeli most probably can look forward to easy reelection.

Census Data Pop. 476,141. Central city, 14%; suburban, 33%. Median family income, $8,933; families above $15,000: 14%; families below $3,000: 8%. Median years education, 12.1.

1972 Share of Federal Outlays $535,796,407

DOD	$140,954,967	HEW	$220,257,945
AEC	$9,846	HUD	$3,894,114
NASA	$22,930	DOI	$1,346,098
DOT	$27,100,364	USDA	$9,296,061
		Other	$132,914,082

Federal Military-Industrial Commitments

No installations or contractors receiving prime awards greater than $5,000,000.

Economic Base Food and kindred products; apparel and other textile products; finance, insurance and real estate; primary metal industries, especially blast furnace and basic steel products; and agriculture, notably dairy products, poultry and cattle.

The Voters

Registration 217,804 total. 79,611 D (37%); 131,202 R (60%); 6,991 other (3%).
Median voting age 45.3
Employment profile White collar, 44%. Blue collar, 42%. Service, 12%. Farm, 2%.
Ethnic groups Black, 6%. Total foreign stock, 8%. Italy, 1%.

Presidential vote

1972	Nixon (R)	119,178	(71%)
	McGovern (D)	48,205	(29%)
1968	Nixon (R)	104,128	(59%)
	Humphrey (D)	58,308	(33%)
	Wallace (AI)	13,613	(8%)

Representative

Herman T. Schneebeli (R) Elected April 26, 1960; b. July 7, 1907, Lancaster; home, Williamsport; Dartmouth, B.A., 1930; Amos Tuck School, M.C.S., 1961; Army, WWII; married, two children; Episcopalian.

Career Distributor, Gulf Oil Corp., 1939– ; Delegate German-American Alliance Conference, West Geneva, 1961; U.S.-Japan Parliamentary Conference, Tokyo, Japan, April 1968, 1970, 1973.

Offices 1336 LHOB, 202-225-4315. Also Rm. 408 Fidelity Natl. Bank Bldg., Williamsport 17701, 717-326-2814, and 1146 Fed. Bldg., Harrisburg 17108, 717-238-0395.

Administrative Assistant Mrs. Helen Ward

Committees

Ways and Means (Ranking Mbr.).

Joint Com. on Internal Revenue Taxation (Ranking House Mbr.).

Joint Study Com. on Budget Control (Vice-Chm.).

Group Ratings

	ADA	COPE	LWV	RIPON	NFU	LCV	CFA	NAB	NSI	ACA
1972	0	20	33	60	0	40	0	100	80	79
1971	19	0	44	71	27	–	38	–	–	89
1970	28	10	–	76	55	39	62	100	83	73·

Key Votes

1) Busing	AGN	6) Cmbodia Bmbg	AGN	11) Chkg Acct Intrst	AGN
2) Strip Mines	AGN	7) Bust Hwy Trust	AGN	12) End HISC (HUAC)	AGN
3) Cut Mil $	AGN	8) Farm Sub Lmt	FOR	13) Nixon Sewer Veto	FOR
4) Rev Shrg	AGN	9) School Prayr	FOR	14) Corp Cmpaign $	AGN
5) Pub TV $	AGN	10) Cnsumr Prot	AGN	15) Pol $ Disclosr	FOR

Election Results

1972 general:	Herman T. Schneebeli (R)	120,214	(72%)
	Donald J. Rippon (D)	44,202	(27%)
	Andrew J. Watson (Const.)	2,066	(1%)
1972 primary:	Herman T. Schneebeli (R), unopposed		
1970 general:	Herman T. Schneebeli (R)	88,173	(58%)
	William P. Zurick (D)	60,714	(40%)
	Robert C. Weber (C)	3,342	(2%)

EIGHTEENTH DISTRICT Political Background

The 18th district of Pennsylvania is the Pittsburgh suburban district. As is so often the case with suburban districts, the 18th does not comprise a homogeneous area. The towns along the Allegheny and Ohio rivers, which include some of the Pittsburgh area's smaller steel mills, are industrial, blue-collar, and Democratic. The towns are too numerous to list: by last count Allegheny County contains the city of Pittsburgh, along with 128 other cities, boroughs, and townships, and almost half of these are in the 18th district. In the hills that rise above both rivers and all the smokestacks are the more comfortable, affluent, and Republican neighborhoods where management personnel live. Among these are places like posh Fox Chapel, middle-class Carnegie and Mount Lebanon, along with three Republican-leaning wards of Pittsburgh itself. All in all, the district is about as marginal as possible in statewide elections. In 1968, for example, Richard Nixon won here by the slightest of pluralities, though he did much better, of course, in 1972.

A detailed recounting of the current 18th's redistricting history is too complex for a complete reconstruction here. It is enough to know that before 1972, Allegheny County had two suburban districts, the 18th and the 27th, both of which were held by Republicans Robert Corbett and James Fulton since the 1940s. The two House veterans had long since mastered the art of winning the support of organized labor—always a major political force in Pittsburgh. The art was first perfected by Republican James J. Davis, a union man who was Secretary of Labor during the 1920s and a U.S. Senator from 1930 to 1945. In any case, observers felt that for the 1972 election the Democratic legislature would choose to amalgamate the districts of Fulton and Corbett. Any resistance to such a plan ended when Corbett died in the spring of 1971. Moreover, a possible fight between the winner of the special election to succeed Corbett and Fulton was averted when Fulton died in October 1971.

The winner of the special election to succeed Corbett was H. John Heinz III of the catsup family. Later, in an odd circumstance, the special election to succeed Fulton was held the very day that Heinz was renominated in the primary. Heinz is young (36 in 1974), attractive, rich, and ambitious; and if voting returns are to be trusted in the 18th district, he is also extremely popular. After spending only a year in office, Heinz won reelection to a full term with 73% of the votes, running 10% ahead of Richard Nixon in the district. At this writing, it appears that Heinz wants to run for Governor in 1974. If he does, the race would seem a simple square-off between Heinz and Democratic incumbent Milton Shapp—except for the possible candidacy of Philadelphia Mayor Frank Rizzo, who could run as a Republican, a Democrat, or an independent. Heinz has all the credentials for a successful political career at high levels of influence, including a solidly liberal voting record in the House. But Rizzo presents a wild-card factor, allowing no one to predict with certainty the course of Pennsylvania politics in 1974.

If Heinz vacates the seat in the 18th, the district will have no dearth of candidates having plenty of experience running for Congress. There is William Conover II, a Republican who served in the House briefly as Fulton's successor. Conover ignominiously lost the Republican primary in the neighboring 22nd district the very day he won the special election to succeed Fulton. Another possibility is Douglas Walgren, a Democrat who nearly beat Conover for the Fulton vacancy and then lost to Heinz in November 1972. Doubtless there will be others. The Pittsburgh suburban seats were sewed up for nearly 30 years, so if Heinz tries to step up, the 18th may not be available for another 30 years.

Census Data Pop. 472,074. Central city, 13%; suburban, 87%. Median family income, $10,770; families above $15,000: 25%; families below $3,000: 6%. Median years education, 12.2.

1972 Share of Federal Outlays $363,526,159

DOD	$47,579,755	HEW	$166,312,360
AEC	$18,620,152	HUD	$8,635,526
NASA	$866,029	DOI	$6,884,484
DOT	$13,908,886	USDA	$6,194,732
		Other	$94,524,235

Federal Military-Industrial Commitments

AEC Operations Westinghouse Electric (Pittsburgh), $5.202m: design of Liquid Metal Fast Breeder Reactor Program.

Economic Base Primary metal industries, especially blast furnace and basic steel products; finance, insurance and real estate; fabricated metal products, especially fabricated structural metal products; food and kindred products; and machinery.

The Voters

Registration 276,838 total. 154,919 D (56%); 113,638 R (41%); 8,281 other (3%).
Median voting age 46.6
Employment profile White collar, 57%. Blue collar, 32%. Service, 11%. Farm, –%.
Ethnic groups Black, 2%. Total foreign stock, 24%. Italy, 5%; Germany, Poland, 3% each; UK, Austria, Czechoslovakia, 2% each; Yugoslavia, Ireland, 1% each.

Presidential vote

1972	Nixon (R)	125,938	(63%)
	McGovern (D)	74,949	(27%)
1968	Nixon (R)	92,077	(45%)
	Humphrey (D)	90,621	(44%)
	Wallace (AI)	21,508	(11%)

Representative

H. John Heinz III (R) Elected Nov. 2, 1971; b. Oct. 23, 1938, Pittsburgh; home, Pittsburgh; Yale U., B.A., 1960; Harvard U., M.B.A., 1963; USAF, 1963–69; married, three children, Episcopalian.

Career Marketing, H. J. Heinz Co., Pittsburgh, 1965–70; Sales Rep., Intl. Harvester, Australia; Rep., State Platform Com.; Sp. Asst., Sen. Hugh Scott, 1964; Lecturer, Carnegie-Mellon U., 1970.

Offices 507 CHOB, 202-225-2135. Also 2031 Fed. Bldg., Pittsburgh 15222, 412-562-0533.

Administrative Assistant Warren Eisenberg

Committees

Interstate and Foreign Commerce (17th); Sub: Public Health and Environment.

Group Ratings

	ADA	COPE	LWV	RIPON	NFU	LCV	CFA	NAB	NSI	ACA
1972	63	55	83	93	86	83	100	57	14	9
1971	67	100	50	80	0	–	–	–	–	44

Key Votes

1) Busing	AGN	6) Cmbodia Bmbg	AGN	11) Chkg Acct Intrst	FOR
2) Strip Mines	AGN	7) Bust Hwy Trust	FOR	12) End HISC (HUAC)	FOR
3) Cut Mil $	FOR	8) Farm Sub Lmt	FOR	13) Nixon Sewer Veto	FOR
4) Rev Shrg	FOR	9) School Prayr	AGN	14) Corp Cmpaign $	AGN
5) Pub TV $	AGN	10) Cnsumr Prot	NE	15) Pol $ Disclosr	FOR

Election Results

1972 general:	H. John Heinz III (R)	144,521	(73%)
	Douglas Walgren (D)	53,929	(27%)
1972 primary:	H. John Heinz III (R), unopposed		
1971 special:	H. John Heinz III (R)	104,175	(67%)
	John E. Connelly (D)	49,428	(32%)
	John E. Backman (C)	2,718	(2%)

NINETEENTH DISTRICT Political Background

The 19th district of Pennsylvania—Adams and York counties and most of Cumberland County—sits at the western edge of the deeply conservative Pennsylvania Dutch country (see Pennsylvania 16). This is a land of rolling green farmland extending up to the base of the Appalachian ridges that begin to rise at the district's western boundary. The most famous part of the 19th is also the most sparsely populated by year-round residents: Gettysburg, the tourist-thronged site of the Civil War's northernmost slaughter. Outside the town is the retirement home of the late President Dwight Eisenhower, who was descended from Pennsylvania Dutch stock. In the late nineteenth century, his father had migrated with a group of Mennonite brethren out into Kansas and Texas.

The largest city in the district is York (pop. 50,000), which, from September of 1777 until June 1778, was the capital of a young nation. While the Continental Congress met in York, it passed the

Articles of Confederation, received word from Ben Franklin in Paris that the French would help with money and ships, and issued the first proclamation calling for a national day of thanksgiving. Today, York is less Republican than other cities in the Pennsylvania Dutch area, perhaps because of the lingering influence of the old York *Gazette*, which until a recent change in ownership was one of the most liberal and antiwar newspapers in the United States.

The other large population center in the 19th is the fastest-growing. This is Cumberland County around Camp Hill, Mechanicsburg, and Carlisle—just across the Susquehanna River from Harrisburg. During the last 20 years, Cumberland absorbed most of the white exodus from the small state capital city. The county, already very Republican, is growing even more so.

The 19th is a Republican district that elected Democratic Congressmen in 1954, 1958, and 1964. The current incumbent is Republican George Goodling, one of the most conservative members of the Pennsylvania delegation. Goodling won in 1960 and 1962, lost in 1964, came back to win in 1966, and has served since. But his margins of victory have never been particularly impressive; Goodling has not received as much as 60% of the votes in some time. In 1972, he had Republican primary opposition, and though he won easily, two opponents were able to split 39% of the votes.

The mediocre showings and the Congressman's age (78 in 1974) indicate that he may encounter trouble in the near future. One possible opponent is a summer of 1973 sports columnist for the *Philadelphia Bulletin* who maintains a voting residence in the district: David Eisenhower. A flurry of rumor in 1973 had it that Eisenhower, the grandson of one President and son-in-law of another, would gently push Goodling aside and seek the seat himself in 1974.

Then came Watergate, followed by an announcement that young Eisenhower had gotten a job writing about baseball. Earlier he said that he wanted to write a political column, but his one effort at such commentary was an egregious one: David tried to score a few political points off the suicide of a radical Amherst classmate. In some circles, there was also wonderment when Eisenhower, coming out of a family with one of nation's most illustrious Army traditions, chose to enlist in the Navy—the branch of the military with the lowest Vietnam casualty rates while he campaigned for candidates who urged a continuation of the war. At any rate, Goodling got the word out that retirement was not for him, in favor of Eisenhower or anybody else. So if the society columnists have it straight, David has given up the idea of the House of Representatives for the present.

Census Data Pop. 467,999. Central city, 11%; suburban, 89%. Median family income, $10,107; families above $15,000: 19%; families below $3,000: 6%. Median years education, 12.0.

1972 Share of Federal Outlays $448,165,031

DOD	$163,213,126	HEW	$167,216,841
AEC	$6,091	HUD	$2,500,572
NASA	$41,728	DOI	$1,775,441
DOT	$8,107,346	USDA	$10,612,367
		Other	$94,691,519

Federal Military-Industrial Commitments

DOD Contractors AMF Inc. (York), $49.026m: Mark 82 bomb bodies. Harsco Corp. (York), $10.607m: self-propelled 8-inch howitzers; tank components.
DOD Installations Carlisle Army Barracks (Carlisle). New Cumberland Army Depot (New Cumberland). Naval Ships Parts Control Center (Mechanicsburg).

Economic Base Machinery; finance, insurance and real estate; apparel and other textile products; food and kindred products; and agriculture, notably dairy products, poultry, fruit and cattle.

The Voters

Registration 207,449 total. 92,280 D (44%); 107,116 R (52%); 8,053 other (4%).
Median voting age 43.6
Employment profile White collar, 44%. Blue collar, 43%. Service, 10%. Farm, –%.
Ethnic groups Black, 2%. Total foreign stock, 5%.

Presidential vote

1972	Nixon (R)	115,528	(72%)
	McGovern (D)	45,769	(28%)
1968	Nixon (R)	93,067	(58%)
	Humphrey (D)	53,049	(33%)
	Wallace (AI)	14,010	(9%)

Representative

George A. Goodling (R) Elected 1960–64, 1966; b. Sept. 26, 1896, Loganville; home, Loganville; Penn. State U., B.S.; widowed, seven children; Methodist.

Career Fruit grower; Pa. Legislature, seven terms; Dir. of a bank, motor club, insurance co.; Exec. Sec., Pa. State Horticulture Assn

Offices 1714 LHOB, 202-225-5836. Also Fed. Bldg., York 17403, 717-843-8887.

Administrative Assistant Paul A. Kline

Committees

Agriculture (3rd); Subs: Conservation and Credit; Forests (Ranking Mbr.); Domestic Marketing and Consumer Relations (Ranking Mbr.).

Merchant Marine and Fisheries (5th); Sub: Fisheries and Wildlife Conservation and the Environment (Ranking Mbr.).

Group Ratings

	ADA	COPE	LWV	RIPON	NFU	LCV	CFA	NAB	NSI	ACA
1972	0	18	18	36	14	26	0	90	100	100
1971	11	0	11	50	23	–	0	–	–	100
1970	8	0	–	29	8	50	45	100	89	100

Key Votes

1) Busing	AGN	6) Cmbodia Bmbg	FOR	11) Chkg Acct Intrst	ABS
2) Strip Mines	FOR	7) Bust Hwy Trust	AGN	12) End HISC (HUAC)	AGN
3) Cut Mil $	AGN	8) Farm Sub Lmt	AGN	13) Nixon Sewer Veto	FOR
4) Rev Shrg	AGN	9) School Prayr	FOR	14) Corp Cmpaign $	FOR
5) Pub TV $	AGN	10) Cnsumr Prot	AGN	15) Pol $ Disclosr	AGN

Election Results

1972 general:	George A. Goodling (R)	93,536	(58%)
	Richard P. Noll (D)	67,018	(41%)
	Paul H. Leese (Const.)	2,019	(1%)
1972 primary:	George A. Goodling (R)	23,816	(61%)
	John W. Eden (R)	11,039	(28%)
	E. Mason Biggs (R)	3,957	(10%)
1970 general:	George A. Goodling (R)	71,497	(54%)
	Arthur I. Berger (D)	58,399	(44%)
	Joseph Paul (C)	2,704	(2%)

TWENTIETH DISTRICT Political Background

The 20th district of Pennsylvania could be called the Monongahela district. Most of its residents live in a string of industrial communities along the heavily polluted Monongahela River and a tributary, the Youghiogheny. "Monongahela," Walt Whitman once wrote, "it rolls off the tongue like venison." But during the last 100 years, area residents have sighted few deer and eaten little venison. What is more common is steel. The 20th district probably makes as much steel as any congressional district in the nation. Here are the operations of Jones & Laughlin and no less than four mills of U.S. Steel. They are found along the banks of the Monongahela, which provides just about the only level land available in the Pittsburgh metropolitan area. Most of the mills are ancient and technologically backward; the best-known among them is the Homestead Works, site of a great and bloody strike in 1892 when it was owned by Andrew Carnegie.

Not many blacks live in the district, only 7%, and those are not found in ghettos, but live scattered throughout various Pittsburgh neighborhoods and the smaller towns like McKeesport, Clairton, and Duquesne. Most residents of the 20th are members of the white working class—the children and grandchildren of people who came from Slovakia, southern Italy, Poland, Wales, and the mountains of West Virginia and Pennsylvania to work in the steel mills. Many of them lived through the 1920s, when the prosperity of the great steel corporations failed to trickle down to its sweat-covered workers, through the privations of the 1930s and exhilaration of the United Steel Workers' organizing the mills, and finally through the slow decline of the industry after World War II. Today, the steelworkers and their families live in the same small frame houses found up and down the hills of the Braddock, Swissvale, Homestead, Hazelwood, and St. Clair neighborhoods of Pittsburgh. The air in the neighborhoods, of course, is never entirely free of soot from the mills. For some time, the population of the 20th district has been declining—mute testimony to the condition of the steel industry.

The image of the American melting pot comes to us from the steel-making process. And in one respect, at least, communities of the 20th, though separated from each other by hills, have melted into a unit: their political preference, which is solidly Democratic. The one-man-one-vote ruling has forced the 20th to append some relatively affluent, Republican areas like Bethel Park and Monroeville. Overall, however, the district remains blue-collar and Democratic. Some of the voters here have become dissatisfied with the candidates nominated by the national Democratic party. Pittsburgh people seem to prefer the earthier and socially more conservative candidates, like the kind slated by the Allegheny County Democratic machine. In 1968, George Wallace got 13% of the 20th's votes—his best showing in any Pennsylvania district; and in 1972, the district recorded a 24% shift to Richard Nixon—again the largest such deflection among Pennsylvania districts.

But since the New Deal, the 20th has sent only Democrats to the House of Representatives, and it shows every sign of continuing to do so. The current Congressman is Joseph Gaydos, a former state Senator and attorney for United Mine Workers District 5. Gaydos had Democratic organization and union backing when he first won the seat in 1968. In Washington, his record is as one might expect—liberal on most economic issues and conservative on many social issues. At the same time, Gaydos has supported a number of end-the-war measures, something one might not expect. As a member of the Education and Labor Committee, Gaydos of course backs positions favored by organized labor.

Census Data Pop. 468,959. Central city, 14%; suburban, 86%. Median family income, $9,937; families above $15,000: 19%; families below $3,000: 7%. Median years education, 12.1.

1972 Share of Federal Outlays $361,122,374

DOD	$47,265,138	HEW	$165,212,634
AEC	$18,497,028	HUD	$8,578,424
NASA	$860,303	DOI	$6,838,961
DOT	$13,816,915	USDA	$6,153,770
		Other	$93,899,201

Federal Military-Industrial Commitments

AEC Operations Westinghouse Electric (West Mifflin), $72.129m: operation of Bettis Atomic Power Laboratory.

Economic Base Primary metal industries, especially blast furnace and basic steel products; finance, insurance and real estate; fabricated metal products, especially fabricated structural metal products; food and kindred products; and machinery.

The Voters

Registration 274,137 total. 190,354 D (69%); 77,251 R (28%); 6,532 other (2%).
Median voting age 46.1
Employment profile White collar, 50%. Blue collar, 38%. Service, 12%. Farm, –%.
Ethnic groups Black, 7%. Total foreign stock, 26%. Italy, Czechoslovakia, 4% each; Poland, UK, 3% each; Germany, Austria, Hungary, Yugoslavia, 2% each; Ireland, 1%.

Presidential vote

1972	Nixon (R)	108,506	(56%)
	McGovern (D)	83,576	(44%)
1968	Nixon (R)	66,107	(32%)
	Humphrey (D)	111,159	(54%)
	Wallace (AI)	27,052	(13%)

Representative

Joseph M. Gaydos (D) Elected Nov. 5, 1968; b. July 3, 1926, Braddock; home, McKeesport; Duquesne U.; U. of Notre Dame, LL.B., 1951; USNR, WWII; married, five children; Catholic.

Career Deputy Atty. Gen., Asst. Solicitor, Allegheny County; Gen. Counsel, United Mine Workers of America, District 5; Pa. Senate, 1967–68.

Offices 1033 LHOB, 202-225-4631. Also Rm. 707, New Fed. Office Bldg., Pittsburgh 15222, 412-644-2860, and Rm. 207, 224 Fifth Ave. Bldg., McKeesport 15132, 412-673-3755.

Administrative Assistant Bernard Mandella

Committees

Education and Labor (12th); Subs: No. 3 (Gen. Sub. on Labor); No. 4 (Sel. Sub. on Labor); No. 6 (Sp. Sub. on Education).

House Administration (11th); Subs: Library and Memorials; Printing; Electrical and Mechanical Office Equipment; Accounts.

Group Ratings

	ADA	COPE	LWV	RIPON	NFU	LCV	CFA	NAB	NSI	ACA
1972	63	90	80	33	86	60	100	18	13	41
1971	73	83	88	65	80	–	80	–	–	33
1970	72	100	–	50	75	95	83	22	60	21

Key Votes

1) Busing	ABS	6) Cmbodia Bmbg	AGN	11) Chkg Acct Intrst	FOR
2) Strip Mines	AGN	7) Bust Hwy Trust	FOR	12) End HISC (HUAC)	AGN
3) Cut Mil $	FOR	8) Farm Sub Lmt	FOR	13) Nixon Sewer Veto	AGN
4) Rev Shrg	FOR	9) School Prayr	FOR	14) Corp Cmpaign $	FOR
5) Pub TV $	FOR	10) Cnsumr Prot	FOR	15) Pol $ Disclosr	AGN

Election Results

1972 general:	Joseph M. Gaydos (D)	117,933	(62%)
	William R. Hunt (R)	73,817	(38%)
1972 primary:	Joseph M. Gaydos (D), unopposed		
1970 general:	Joseph M. Gaydos (D)	84,911	(77%)
	Joseph Honeygosky (R)	22,553	(20%)
	Alan Staub (C)	2,840	(3%)

TWENTY-FIRST DISTRICT Political Background

The 21st district is Westmoreland County, just to the east of Pittsburgh, plus a small portion of suburban Allegheny County. It is a mixed area. There are a few wealthy enclaves here, like Arnold Palmer's Latrobe. But most of Westmoreland is industrial—small factory towns that lie between the hills or along the Allegheny and Monongahela rivers at the county's western edge. The district contains an especially large number of Italian-Americans, with other ethnic people present in smaller numbers. The 21st is part of western Pennsylvania's "black country," so named for the region's bituminous coal deposits. Steel is a major industry here, as it is all over western Pennsylvania. Politically, the 21st is traditionally Democratic, and just as heavily Democratic as the anthracite region around Scranton and Wilkes-Barre in eastern Pennsylvania.

The Congressman from the district, Democrat John Dent, served for 19 years as one of his party's floor leaders in the Pennsylvania state Senate. He was first elected to Congress in 1958. Like many Democrats (and Republicans) from safe districts, Dent has been quietly winning reelection by large margins and accumulating seniority. He now enjoys third-ranking Democratic status on the House Education and Labor Committee, and also has a high seniority position on Wayne Hays' House Administration Committee. On Education and Labor, Dent chairs a labor subcommittee. It is, of course, easy to predict the thrust of the Congressman's legislative efforts: he represents a heavily unionized district, and is himself an old union man. In 1973, Dent was the chief sponsor of the bill raising the minimum wage.

The Congressman has made one stab at statewide office. Like many of his constituents, Dent is of Italian descent. In 1968, he challenged Sen. Joseph Clark, who had antagonized many Italian-American voters, in the Democratic primary. Dent did not expect to win (though he got a respectable number of votes); he merely served to focus opposition to Clark for many Pennsylvania backers of the Vietnam war and opponents of gun registration. Such voters played an instrumental role in Clark's general election defeat later. Dent did not have to give up the seat to run in the 1968 Senate primary, and it seems unlikely that the voters of the 21st will want him to leave it, either. In 1972, however, Dent did encounter a primary opponent, whom he beat by less than 2–1—a margin less than one would suppose he would get in the district.

Census Data Pop. 473,040. Central city, 0%; suburban, 100%. Median family income, $9,645; families above $15,000: 16%; families below $3,000: 7%. Median years education, 12.1.

1972 Share of Federal Outlays $364,265,785

DOD	$47,676,561	HEW	$166,650,737
AEC	$18,658,036	HUD	$8,653,096
NASA	$867,791	DOI	$6,898,491
DOT	$13,937,185	USDA	$6,207,336
		Other	$94,716,552

Federal Military-Industrial Commitments

DOD Contractors Alcoa (New Kensington), $5.655m: aluminum alloy research.

Economic Base Primary metal industries, especially blast furnace and steel mill products; finance, insurance and real estate; machinery, especially metalworking machinery; stone, clay and glass products, especially pressed or blown glass not otherwise classified; and electrical equipment and supplies.

The Voters

Registration 231,555 total. 148,039 D (64%); 78,370 R (34%); 5,146 other (2%).
Median voting age 45.0
Employment profile White collar, 45%. Blue collar, 43%. Service, 11%. Farm, 1%.
Ethnic groups Black, 2%. Total foreign stock, 21%. Italy, 6%; Poland, Czechoslovakia, Austria, UK, 2% each; Germany, Yugoslavia, 1% each.

Presidential vote

	1972	Nixon (R)	99,366	(58%)
		McGovern (D)	73,049	(42%)
	1968	Nixon (R)	69,023	(37%)
		Humphrey (D)	98,072	(53%)
		Wallace (AI)	19,543	(10%)

Representative

John H. Dent (D) Elected Jan. 21, 1958; b. March 10, 1908, Johnetta; home, Ligonier; Great Lakes Naval Aviation Acad.; correspondence courses; U.S. Marine Air Corps., 1924–28; married, two children; Catholic.

Career Mbr., Natl. Council of United Rubber Workers, 1923–37, Pres., Local 1875; newspaperman; Pa. Legislature, 1934–36; Pa. Senate, 1936–58, Floor Leader, 1939–58; Exec. with coal and coke co. and building and transportation companies.

Offices 2104 RHOB, 202-225-5631. Also 35 W. Pittsburgh St., Greensburg 15601, 412-837-6420.

Administrative Assistant Rosaline Black (L.A.)

Committees

Education and Labor (3rd); Subs: No. 3 (Gen. Sub. on Labor) (Chm.); No. 4 (Sel. Sub. on Labor).

House Administration (3rd); Subs: Accounts; Elections (Chm.).

Group Ratings

	ADA	COPE	LWV	RIPON	NFU	LCV	CFA	NAB	NSI	ACA
1972	56	78	73	43	80	47	50	25	100	42
1971	51	90	83	50	100	–	100	–	–	16
1970	60	89	–	56	88	56	69	0	63	22

Key Votes

1) Busing	FOR	6) Cmbodia Bmbg	AGN	11) Chkg Acct Intrst	FOR
2) Strip Mines	ABS	7) Bust Hwy Trust	AGN	12) End HISC (HUAC)	AGN
3) Cut Mil $	AGN	8) Farm Sub Lmt	ABS	13) Nixon Sewer Veto	AGN
4) Rev Shrg	FOR	9) School Prayr	FOR	14) Corp Cmpaign $	FOR
5) Pub TV $	AGN	10) Cnsumr Prot	FOR	15) Pol $ Disclosr	AGN

Election Results

1972 general:	John H. Dent (D)	104,203	(62%)
	Thomas H. Young (R)	63,812	(38%)
1972 primary:	John H. Dent (D)	40,195	(64%)
	Eugene F. O'Leary (D)	22,201	(36%)
1970 general:	John H. Dent (D)	76,915	(68%)
	Glenn G. Anderson (R)	33,396	(30%)
	Lloyd G. Cope (C)	1,979	(2%)

TWENTY-SECOND DISTRICT Political Background

The 22nd district of Pennsylvania is the northern tip of Appalachia—the southwest corner of the state between West Virginia and the Pittsburgh suburbs. The region is one of rugged hills and polluted rivers, lined with steel mills and blast furnaces. The operations here are smaller than those in the 20th district, which contains the really big steel mills. But the poverty endemic in West Virginia is also found here. Residents of Italian, Polish, and Czech descent have the same problems as the old-line Scots-Irish of the area. The 22nd district begins in rough, tough coal mining country. It was in a small town here—the district has no large urban center—that Joseph Yablonski, the insurgent candidate for president of the United Mine Workers, was found shot to death with his wife and daughter.

In 1972, for the first time since the New Deal, the 22nd district plunked for a Republican presidential candidate. It remains, however, one of the state's safest Democratic districts in most elections. Since the election of 1944, the 22nd has sent Democrat Thomas Morgan, a physician from tiny Fredricktown (pop. 1,067), to the House of Representatives. Through the inexorable working of the seniority system, Doc Morgan has become Chairman of the Foreign Affairs Committee. Perhaps because of Morgan's influence, Foreign Affairs has a disproportionate number of members from Pennsylvania, along with Wayne Hays of nearby eastern Ohio. The Chairman himself is hardly a scholar in the field, and his committee has regularly suffered adverse comparison with its counterpart in the Senate, the Foreign Relations Committee, chaired by J. William Fulbright. Much of the criticism has stemmed from the long-standing support that Foreign Affairs and Morgan gave to the Vietnam war. Because the committee backed Administration policies in Southeast Asia, it saw no reason to hold hearings on the war until the spring of 1971, while Fulbright, of course, had held hearings as early as 1966.

But since 1971, Morgan's opinions on the war have undergone some alteration. In 1972, when the Democratic Caucus voted to require Foreign Affairs to report out an antiwar amendment, Morgan was willing to comply. And in 1973, the Chairman joined the struggle to end the bombing of Cambodia. It was his vote, and the votes of other like-minded Democratic regulars, that made the difference between this successful challenge to Administration policy and the adverse treatment the House had always given to antiwar measures in the past.

For 1972, redistricting added some Pittsburgh suburbs in Allegheny County to Morgan's bailiwick. In the same year, Morgan almost found himself facing a Republican incumbent in the general election. This most unusual event did not come to pass, but only because William Conover, who won a special election to fill a vacated seat in the old 27th (see Pennsylvania 18), on the same day lost the Republican primary in the new 22nd by some 2,000 votes. As usual, Morgan won the general election. The only obstacle to his continued service is age (68 in 1974).

Census Data Pop. 469,778. Central city, 0%; suburban, 59%. Median family income, $8,396; families above $15,000: 13%; families below $3,000: 12%. Median years education, 11.7.

1972 Share of Federal Outlays $345,798,438

DOD	$32,185,910	HEW	$196,393,352
AEC	$11,005,400	HUD	$5,104,009
NASA	$555,590	DOI	$4,581,040
DOT	$8,245,774	USDA	$9,321,560
		Other	$78,405,803

Federal Military-Industrial Commitments

DOD Installations Use of the Greater Pittsburgh Airport (Coraopolis) contracted by the Air Force.

Economic Base Bituminous coal mining; primary metal industries; finance, insurance and real estate; stone, clay and glass products; and agriculture, notably dairy products and cattle.

The Voters

Registration 226,590 total. 151,418 D (67%); 71,106 R (31%); 4,066 other (2%).
Median voting age 46.2
Employment profile White collar, 40%. Blue collar, 47%. Service, 12%. Farm, 1%.
Ethnic groups Black, 4%. Total foreign stock, 20%. Italy, 5%; Czechoslovakia, 3%; Poland, Austria, UK, 2% each; Germany, Yugoslavia, 1% each.

Presidential vote

1972	Nixon (R)	95,927	(57%)
	McGovern (D)	72,151	(43%)

1968	Nixon (R)	64,570	(35%)
	Humphrey (D)	101,381	(54%)
	Wallace (AI)	18,473	(10%)

Representative

Thomas E. Morgan (D) Elected 1944; b. Oct. 13, 1906, Ellsworth; home, Fredericktown; Waynesburg Col., B.S., 1930; Detroit Col. of Medicine and Surgery, M.D., 1934; married, one child; Methodist.

Career Intern, Grace Hospital, Detroit, Mich., 1933–34; practice of medicine and surgery, 1934– .

Offices 2183 RHOB, 202-225-4665. Also Fed. Bldg, Uniontown 15401, 412-438-9131.

Administrative Assistant Gertrude King

Committees

Foreign Affairs (Chm.); Sub: Sp. Sub. for Review of Foreign Aid Programs (Chm.).

Group Ratings

	ADA	COPE	LWV	RIPON	NFU	LCV	CFA	NAB	NSI	ACA
1972	69	91	91	67	67	33	100	0	100	17
1971	46	100	88	29	75	–	50	–	–	25
1970	56	100	–	59	100	84	78	0	80	18

Key Votes

1) Busing	FOR	6) Cmbodia Bmbg	AGN	11) Chkg Acct Intrst	AGN
2) Strip Mines	AGN	7) Bust Hwy Trust	ABS	12) End HISC (HUAC)	AGN
3) Cut Mil $	AGN	8) Farm Sub Lmt	FOR	13) Nixon Sewer Veto	AGN
4) Rev Shrg	FOR	9) School Prayr	FOR	14) Corp Cmpaign $	FOR
5) Pub TV $	FOR	10) Cnsumr Prot	ABS	15) Pol $ Disclosr	AGN

Election Results

1972 general:	Thomas E. Morgan (D)	100,918	(61%)
	James R. Montgomery (R)	65,005	(39%)
1972 primary:	Thomas E. Morgan (D)	54,063	(71%)
	Theodore J. Kozel (D)	12,107	(16%)
	Charles Gillespie (D)	9,578	(13%)
1970 general:	Thomas E. Morgan (D)	80,734	(68%)
	Domenick A. Cupelli (R)	35,038	(30%)
	Bernard M. Dae Check (C)	2,176	(2%)

TWENTY-THIRD DISTRICT Political Background

The 23rd district of Pennsylvania lies in the rural north central part of the state. The region is not only the most sparsely populated in Pennsylvania, but in the entire East. The district's terrain is mountainous, and its valleys have only a few small towns here and there. The only significant concentrations of people are found in the Nittany Valley to the south of the district, and around Oil City to the extreme west. The Nittany Valley is the home of Pennsylvania State University, commonly called Penn State, long known for its powerful football teams. Another part of the university complex, the Ordnance Research Lab, is busy at work on the Navy's controversial Mark 48 torpedo program. Oil City is the site of the nation's first oil well, which was sunk in 1859. Today, Pennsylvania crude—a relatively scarce, but higher quality oil than found in the Southwest—continues to occupy an important place in the region's economy.

The isolation of this part of Pennsylvania was ended by the recent opening of the Pennsylvania Shortway, a superhighway that has replaced the aging Pennsylvania Turnpike as the main road between New York and Chicago. Some people hoped that the Shortway would bring light industrial development to the area; all it seems to have attracted, however, are gas stations with 60-foot signs and Holiday Inns. So the 23rd remains a rural and small-town district, dominated by old-stock farmers. These people have lived apart from the movements of population and social change that have affected— and afflicted—their neighbors in other parts of the East and Great Lakes region.

The 23rd is, of course, a Republican district. It has a long, long tradition of electing Republican Congressmen. The current Congressman, Albert Johnson, was first elected in 1963, and is now the second-ranking Republican on the House Banking and Currency Committee. With that going for him, one would expect Johnson to win reelection easily. But in the last two elections, the Congressman has faced increasing difficulty. In 1970, he was held to 58% of the votes, the first time his precentage has dipped below 60%. And in 1972, Johnson took only 61% of the votes in a two-candidate Republican primary, and then got only 56% in the general election against Democrat Ernest Kassab.

Kassab charged that Johnson was a tool of big-money interests. In fact, the Congressman's record shows that he has voted against programs that would benefit poor rural areas like the 23rd, while mostly voting for legislation sought by the big banks. Johnson ran especially poorly in the larger counties of the district, including Centre (Penn State). So it appears that Johnson, if he decides to seek reelection, may have even more trouble in November 1974, when he will be 68.

Johnson was a high-ranking member of the Banking and Currency majority that torpedoed a Watergate investigation in October 1972. He is thus one of the few members of Congress with tangible connection with the Watergate business. Polls indicate that Watergate has done the Republicans particular harm in rural, Protestant areas like the 23rd district. So 1974 could produce a race here far closer than any in the past.

Census Data Pop. 469,717. Central city, 0%; suburban, 0%. Median family income, $8,272; families above $15,000: 11%; families below $3,000: 10%. Median years education, 12.1.

1972 Share of Federal Outlays $304,462,738

DOD	$33,103,908	HEW	$166,565,183
AEC	$244,384	HUD	$3,106,002
NASA	$813,371	DOI	$2,077,232
DOT	$7,849,922	USDA	$25,433,411
		Other	$65,269,325

Federal Military-Industrial Commitments

DOD Contractors Visicon, Inc. (State College), $9.865m: data processing equipment. Pennsylvania State University (University Park), $9.620m: research into MK 48 torpedo. Singer (University Park), $9.272m: aircraft communications equipment.

Economic Base Electrical equipment and supplies, especially electronic components and accessories; machinery; stone, clay and glass products, especially pressed or blown glass and glassware; finance, insurance and real estate; and agriculture, notably dairy products, poultry and dairy cattle. Also higher education (Pennsylvania State Univ.).

The Voters

Registration 202,056 total. 86,308 D (43%); 109,155 R (54%); 6,593 other (3%).
Median voting age 42.9
Employment profile White collar, 41%. Blue collar, 44%. Service, 13%. Farm, 2%.
Ethnic groups Total foreign stock, 10%. Italy, 2%; UK, Germany, 1% each.

Presidential vote

1972	Nixon (R)	105,463	(66%)
	McGovern (D)	54,138	(34%)
1968	Nixon (R)	88,223	(54%)
	Humphrey (D)	65,033	(40%)
	Wallace (AI)	9,321	(6%)

Representative

Albert W. Johnson (R) Elected Nov. 5, 1963; b. Apr. 17, 1906, Smethport; home, Smethport; U. of Pa., 1926–27; Stetson U., LL.B., 1938; married, four children; Protestant.

Career Practicing atty.; Pa. Legislature, 1946–62, Majority Whip, 1951, Minority Whip, 1955, Minority Leader, 1959, 1961, Majority Leader, 1953, 1957, 1963.

Offices 2351 RHOB, 202-225-5121. Also 205 Hamlin Bank Bldg., Smethport 16749, 814-887-2225.

Administrative Assistant Jane Dodds (L.A.)

Committees

Banking and Currency (2nd); Subs: Bank Supervision and Insurance; International Finance (Ranking Mbr.); International Trade.

Post Office and Civil Service (3rd); Sub: Postal Service (Ranking Mbr.).

Sel. Com. on the House Restaurant (2nd).

Group Ratings

	ADA	COPE	LWV	RIPON	NFU	LCV	CFA	NAB	NSI	ACA
1972	0	82	42	57	43	17	0	100	100	70
1971	8	17	38	44	33	–	33	–	–	88
1970	4	9	–	44	20	52	47	100	100	89

Key Votes

1) Busing	AGN	6) Cmbodia Bmbg	FOR	11) Chkg Acct Intrst	AGN
2) Strip Mines	FOR	7) Bust Hwy Trust	AGN	12) End HISC (HUAC)	AGN
3) Cut Mil $	AGN	8) Farm Sub Lmt	FOR	13) Nixon Sewer Veto	FOR
4) Rev Shrg	FOR	9) School Prayr	FOR	14) Corp Cmpaign $	FOR
5) Pub TV $	AGN	10) Cnsumr Prot	AGN	15) Pol $ Disclosr	AGN

Election Results

1972 general:	Albert W. Johnson (R)	90,615	(56%)
	Ernest A. Kassab (D)	69,813	(46%)
1972 primary:	Albert W. Johnson (R)	30,365	(61%)
	Richard McCormack (R)	19,020	(39%)
1970 general:	Albert W. Johnson (R)	70,074	(58%)
	Cecil R. Harrington (D)	50,908	(42%)

TWENTY-FOURTH DISTRICT Political Background

Situated in the northwest corner of the state, the 24th district of Pennsylvania is part of the industrial Great Lakes region. It is a long way overland to the East Coast, and the district has none of metropolitan Philadelphia's seaboard ambiance. The city of Erie (pop. 129,000), the state's third largest, dominates the 24th. Like most industrial cities on the nation's most polluted lake of the same name, Erie is a Democratic stronghold. As one goes inland, the territory becomes more Republican. An exception to this pattern is the steel town of Sharon, just a few miles from Youngstown, Ohio; like most towns dependent on steel mills, Sharon votes Democratic. All in all, the political balance in the 24th makes it one of the state's most marginal districts. In 1968, Humphrey edged out Nixon here 49% to 46%, with 5% going to Wallace—a virtual mirror of statewide results. Moreover, the 24th is one of only two Pennsylvania districts to have changed partisan hands in the last decade.

The turnabout occurred in 1964, when Democrat Joseph Vigorito, an academic and a political unknown, defeated Republican Congressman James Weaver by 2,784 votes. Weaver was expected to regain the seat in 1966, but Vigorito, despite lack of experience, emerged a strong campaigner and beat the Republican by a margin much larger than the one he had received two years earlier. Since then, Vigorito's performance at the polls has improved each time out. In 1972, for example, despite the weakness of the McGovern-Shriver ticket, Vigorito took 69% of the votes.

The Congressman is one of the few Northern Democrats on the House Agriculture Committee and one of the few Easterners on the Interior Committee. The assignments are hardly conventional ones for a Representative from a district like the 24th. However, Vigorito's district does have a fair number of dairy farmers, and Interior does have jurisdiction over some items of local interest. But Vigorito is best-known in Congress as an assiduous constituency man, keeping close tabs on the voters of his district and acting as their ombudsman in problems they have with the federal government. The legislative action for which the Congressman received the most attention was his sponsorship of a bill to ban throwaway bottles.

Census Data Pop. 472,171. Central city, 27%; suburban, 28%. Median family income, $9,215; families above $15,000: 15%; families below $3,000: 8%. Median years education, 12.2.

1972 Share of Federal Outlays $290,431,802

DOD	$33,108,000	HEW	$153,563,014
AEC	–	HUD	$12,437,154
NASA	$80,765	DOI	$447,185
DOT	$2,565,909	USDA	$9,927,932
		Other	$78,301,843

Federal Military-Industrial Commitments

DOD Contractors General Electric (Erie), $6.838m: electrical generators.

Economic Base Primary metal industries, especially blast furnace and basic steel products; electrical equipment and supplies, especially electronic components and accessories; fabricated metal products; machinery, especially metalworking machinery; and finance, insurance and real estate.

The Voters

Registration 228,334 total. 117,931 D (52%); 103,992 R (46%); 6,411 other (3%).
Median voting age 44.5
Employment profile White collar, 42%. Blue collar, 45%. Service, 11%. Farm, 2%.
Ethnic groups Black, 3%. Total foreign stock, 16%. Italy, Poland, 3% each; Germany, 2%; UK, Czechoslovakia, 1%.

Presidential vote

1972	Nixon (R)	107,785	(61%)
	McGovern (D)	69,394	(39%)
1968	Nixon (R)	81,256	(46%)
	Humphrey (D)	85,763	(49%)
	Wallace (AI)	9,733	(6%)

Representative

Joseph Phillip Vigorito (D) Elected 1964; b. Nov. 10, 1918, Niles, Ohio; home, Erie; U. of Pa., B.S., 1947; U. of Denver, M.B.A., 1949; Army, WWII; married, three children; religion unspecified.

Career Certified Public Accountant; Asst. Professor, Penn. State U., 1949–64.

Offices 440 CHOB, 202-225-5406.

Administrative Assistant None.

Committees

Agriculture (5th); Subs: Forests; Family Farms and Rural Development; Domestic Marketing and Consumer Relations (Chm.).

Interior and Insular Affairs (13th); Subs: Environment; Mines and Mining; Territorial and Insular Affairs.

Group Ratings

	ADA	COPE	LWV	RIPON	NFU	LCV	CFA	NAB	NSI	ACA
1972	44	100	70	50	86	33	50	10	40	23
1971	57	100	78	53	77	–	100	–	–	15
1970	72	83	–	65	100	75	95	17	80	21

Key Votes

1) Busing	AGN	6) Cmbodia Bmbg	AGN	11) Chkg Acct Intrst	AGN
2) Strip Mines	ABS	7) Bust Hwy Trust	FOR	12) End HISC (HUAC)	AGN
3) Cut Mil $	ABS	8) Farm Sub Lmt	AGN	13) Nixon Sewer Veto	AGN
4) Rev Shrg	AGN	9) School Prayr	ABS	14) Corp Cmpaign $	AGN
5) Pub TV $	FOR	10) Cnsumr Prot	FOR	15) Pol $ Disclosr	AGN

Election Results

1972 general:	Joseph P. Vigorito (D)	122,092	(69%)
	Alvin W. Levenhagen (R)	55,406	(31%)
1972 primary:	Joseph P. Vigorito (D)	42,568	(87%)
	Joseph L. Heimbold, Jr. (D)	4,531	(9%)
	Bobby S. Jancek (D)	1,914	(4%)
1970 general:	Joseph P. Vigorito (D)	94,029	(67%)
	Wayne R. Merrick (R)	44,395	(32%)
	Robert Shilling (AI-C)	2,424	(2%)

TWENTY-FIFTH DISTRICT Political Background

The 25th district is part of industrial western Pennsylvania. The district adjoins Ohio and the tip top of the West Virginia panhandle. Almost half of the people of the 25th live in Beaver County, where the steel mills sit in little grimy towns along the banks of the Ohio and Beaver rivers. The best-known of these towns is Beaver Falls, the boyhood home of White House enemy Joe Namath. Like all of western Pennsylvania within 100 miles of Pittsburgh, Beaver County is rich in ethnic diversity, with especially large numbers of Italian-Americans. The county is ordinarily a Democratic bulwark. It has gone Republican only twice in recent statewide elections—for Richard Schweiker over Joseph Clark in 1968, and for Richard Nixon over George McGovern in 1972. The 25th also includes the northern tier of townships in Pittsburgh's Allegheny County, which usually go Republican.

The other two counties in the district are politically more marginal. Lawrence, dominated by the manufacturing city of New Castle, is Pennsylvania's bellwether county—a pretty reliable indicator of statewide winners. Butler County a few miles distant from the industrial concentrations on the Ohio, Beaver, and Allegheny rivers, is less thickly settled and tends mildly toward Republicanism.

Frank Clark has represented the 25th district in Washington since 1954. The Congressman is a Democrat who usually toes the AFL-CIO line: liberal on domestic issues, conservative on matters of foreign policy and defense spending. Clark is a relatively high-ranking member of the Public Works and the Merchant Marine and Fisheries committees. Like many politicians from coal-producing states, he is a supporter of private power (which mostly burns coal) over public power (usually hydroelectric); for many years, Clark has led the successful battle to prevent construction of the Dickey-Lincoln hydroelectric project in Maine.

Until 1972, Clark had won reelection routinely for many years. But in 1972, he suddenly dropped to 56% of the votes. Given a man with Clark's political inclinations, one is tempted to ascribe the drop to George McGovern's poor showing in the district. But that probably does not account for the phenomenon; other Pennsylvania Democrats ran much further ahead of McGovern than Clark. The Congressman's opponent, Republican Gary Myers, criticized the incumbent for supporting seniority and opposing institutional reforms. Another problem Clark faced was his propensity to travel—he is one of the most assiduous junketeers in the House. The relatively close race in 1972 may point to future close congressional elections in the 25th.

Census Data Pop. 472,929. Central city, 0%; suburban, 50%. Median family income, $9,208; families above $15,000: 14%; families below $3,000: 8%. Median years education, 12.1.

1972 Share of Federal Outlays $314,598,644

DOD	$30,803,287	HEW	$159,145,195
AEC	$9,376,373	HUD	$4,348,510
NASA	$474,686	DOI	$5,657,820
DOT	$13,421,419	USDA	$6,749,947
		Other	$$84,621,407

Federal Military-Industrial Commitments

No installations or contractors receiving prime awards greater than $5,000,000.

Economic Base Primary metal industries, especially blast furnace and steel mill products; fabricated metal products, especially fabricated structural metal products; finance, insurance and real estate; machinery, especially construction and related machinery; and stone, clay and glass products.

The Voters

Registration 219,489 total. 117,045 D (53%); 97,368 R (44%); 5,076 other (2%).
Median voting age 44.8
Employment profile White collar, 39%. Blue collar, 48%. Service, 12%. Farm, 1%.
Ethnic groups Black, 3%. Total foreign stock, 19%. Italy, 5%; Poland, Yugoslavia, 2% each; UK, Germany, Czechoslovakia, Austria, 1% each.

Presidential vote

1972	Nixon (R)	103,715	(60%)
	McGovern (D)	67,926	(40%)
1968	Nixon (R)	73,104	(40%)
	Humphrey (D)	90,833	(50%)
	Wallace (AI)	16,987	(9%)

Representative

Frank M. Clark (D) Elected 1954; b. Dec. 24, 1915, Bessemer; home, Bessemer; USAF, WWII; Major USAFR; maried, two children; Presbyterian.

Career Chief of police, Bessemer, 1945–55; Delegate to NATO Conference 1965, 1960, 1964–70; Delegate, Interparliamentary Conference, 1957; International Christian Leadership Conference for Peace, The Hague, 1958.

Offices 2238 RHOB, 202-225-2565. Also Fed. Bldg., New Castle 16103, 412-654-9176, and Fed. Bldg., Beaver Falls 15010, 412-843-6840, and Fed. Bldg., Butler 16001, 412-287-1865.

Administrative Assistant Mrs. Arlene Farlow

Committees

Merchant Marine and Fisheries (2nd); Subs: Coast Guard and Navigation; Merchant Marine (Chm.); Panama Canal.

Public Works (6th); Subs: Development; Energy; Investigations and Review; Transportation.

Group Ratings

	ADA	COPE	LWV	RIPON	NFU	LCV	CFA	NAB	NSI	ACA
1972	13	88	56	55	83	16	100	22	100	41
1971	24	100	63	31	82	–	100	–	–	43
1970	32	83	–	21	100	78	63	8	100	31

Key Votes

1) Busing	ABS	6) Cmbodia Bmbg	AGN	11) Chkg Acct Intrst	AGN
2) Strip Mines	AGN	7) Bust Hwy Trust	ABS	12) End HISC (HUAC)	AGN
3) Cut Mil $	ABS	8) Farm Sub Lmt	AGN	13) Nixon Sewer Veto	AGN
4) Rev Shrg	FOR	9) School Prayr	FOR	14) Corp Cmpaign $	FOR
5) Pub TV $	FOR	10) Cnsumr Prot	FOR	15) Pol $ Disclosr	AGN

Election Results

1972 general:	Frank M. Clark (D)	97,549	(56%)
	Gary A. Myers (R)	77,123	(46%)
1972 primary:	Frank M. Clark (D), unopposed		
1970 general:	Frank M. Clark (D)	92,638	(70%)
	John Loth (R)	37,355	(28%)
	Albert H. Thorton (C)	2,959	(2%)

RHODE ISLAND

Political Background

The state of Rhode Island and Providence Plantations—the full official name—owes its existence to a religious schism within the Massachusetts Bay Colony. Roger Williams, as most schoolchildren know, founded Providence in 1636 as a haven for dissident Calvinists fleeing the regime to the north. Williams had a profound—and, for that day unusual—belief in religious and political freedom; he was the New World's first civil libertarian. Williams' colony soon attracted a motley gathering of Baptists, Antinomians, and even some Papists (Roman Catholics), along with a few American Indians. Williams, unlike many of his contemporaries and Americans to follow, was kindly disposed to the native Americans and became a scholar of their languages and customs. Perhaps the most famous of Williams' fellow colonists was the Antinomian Anne Hutchinson, who presumed to know which of the male ministers in Boston preached the true word and which did not. She was banished to Rhode Island, but history has done well by her. Mistress Hutchinson became a martyr among Quakers and Hawthorne's model for Hester Prynne of *The Scarlet Letter.*

Rhode Island's later history was almost as idiosyncratic. The descendants of Williams' colonists began to prosper and, as people do, grew more conservative. The "triangle trade" out of Newport—rum, sugar, and slaves—was especially lucrative. After the Revolutionary War, Rhode Island was the last of the 13 colonies to ratify the Constitution. It had declined to send delegates to the Convention for fear that any proposed Union could impose tariffs inamicable to the former colony's ocean-dependent trade. Only after the new nation threatened to sever commercial relations with Rhode Island did it agree to become the thirteenth state. As late as 1840, when most other states had granted the franchise to free white males, Rhode Island still allowed only large property-holders to vote. The situation led to open revolt—the Dorr Rebellion; during the trouble, Rhode Island had two separate state governments, each claiming sovereignty.

In the state's economic history, the key event occurred in 1793, when Samuel Slater, a British emigré, built the nation's first water-powered cotton mill in Pawtucket and launched the nation's Industrial Revolution. During the nineteenth century, the textile industry in Rhode Island boomed, and the tiny state attracted immigrants eager to work the looms and on the cutting floor.

The immigrants came from French Canada, Ireland, and especially from Italy. So by the turn of the nineteenth century, this erstwhile colony of dissident Protestants had become the most heavily Roman Catholic state in the nation. Today, something like two-thirds of its citizens are Catholic.

The Protestants and Catholics did not, of course, get along very well in politics. Long after they had become a minority, the Protestants, through the Republican party, were able to maintain control of Rhode Island. The big switch came in 1928, when thousands of immigrants, especially women, who had never before voted, streamed to the polls and carried the state for Catholic Al Smith. Two years later in 1930, the Republicans were able to elect a Senator, but have never been able to elect one since. The last time any Republican has been sent to Congress from Rhode Island was in 1938. Since 1924, the state has gone Republican in presidential elections only three times, twice for Eisenhower and once for Nixon, and only once by anything like a substantial margin (1956).

The Republicans have done better in gubernatorial elections. They won in 1958, 1962, 1964, and 1966, and have come close in each election since. But for most races, the decisive battle, when there is one to be fought, occurs in the Democratic primary. And the outcome of the contest is almost always determined by the endorsement of the state Democratic machine. Among other things, the endorsee gets the first line on the primary ballot. With the onset of the Democratic hegemony, only twice has the endorsed candidate lost the Democratic primary.

The 1960 Senate race furnished one of the occasions, the winner being something of an anomaly in ethnic Rhode Island. For Claiborne deB. Pell is a blue-blood WASP from Bellevue Avenue in Newport, where one finds the Vanderbilt and Auchincloss "cottages." Pell's father was a Congressman from New York for a term, a friend of Franklin D. Roosevelt, and Minister to Portugal and Hungary during the period just before and after 1939. With a background of this sort, Claiborne Pell served as a Foreign Service officer for several years. But such service hardly explains how he was able to beat ex-Gov. (1950–58) Dennis J. Roberts and ex-Gov. (1941–45), Sen. (1947–49), and U.S. Attorney General (1949–52) J. Howard McGrath in the 1960 Democratic primary. All of them were running for the seat first won by Theodore F. Green in 1936 when he was 69. Green, once Chairman of the Foreign Relations Committee, had decided to retire when he reached 93. An entire generation of Rhode Island politicians had made plans on the assumption that Green's seat would soon become available. Part of the reason for Pell's victory was the odor of scandal that attached itself to both of his rivals. But the win was also attributable to his quiet, aloof, but still vigorous mode of campaigning.

That mode may have been something that Navy Secretary John Chafee failed to recall when he decided to run for Pell's Senate seat in 1972. Chafee was Rhode Island's most successful Republican politician since the crash of 1929. He won the governorship three times during the 1960s, and lost in 1968, by a 51–49 margin, only after he had pushed for a state income tax. Chafee's position of Navy Secretary allowed him to return to Rhode Island often, for the Navy had some of its chief Atlantic fleet facilities in Newport and Quonset Point on Narragansett Bay. Chafee felt that Pell's position in the state was soft and vulnerable. So just as the raids on Haiphong began in May 1972, the Secretary announced that he was leaving the Pentagon to run for the Senate.

As Chafee made the announcement, he enjoyed a solid edge in the polls, and seemed to be one of the Republicans' best chances of picking up a Senate seat. He attacked Pell for an allegedly do-nothing record, citing the incumbent's interest in such esoterica as mass transit, oceanography, conversion to the metric system, and the law of the sea. Chafee proudly pointed to his own record of having attracted industry to Rhode Island, which began to lose its textile mills to the South after World War II. Most observers agreed that Chafee was the more charismatic campaigner.

But Chafee took no measure of the steel backbone which seems to lie beneath Pell's sometimes halting aristocratic demeanor. While Chafee was complaining about Pell's interest in obscure subjects, Pell was steering the higher education bill of 1972 through the Senate. The legislation purported to give every citizen a chance at a higher education for the first time. It was one of the few bills that was developed entirely within the Congress, and it passed with little encouragement from the Executive Branch. Pell was Chairman of the Labor and Public Welfare Subcommittee on Education, and as the campaign wore on, he gained the active support of most of the state's teachers.

Pell also held a seat on the Foreign Relations Committee, where he had spoken out, quietly but firmly, against the Vietnam war since the mid-1960s. Pell's antiwar reputation was probably an asset in heavily Democratic Rhode Island. Meanwhile, Chafee's position—and this may have hurt him more than anything else—was blatantly opportunistic. After three years as one of the highest-ranking officials in Richard Nixon's Pentagon, the ex-Navy Secretary turned around and said he didn't think much of Nixon's war policies either. Pell attacked Chafee's position vigorously. By October, as Pell pulled up even in the polls, Chafee began a series of personal attacks, which, as it turned out, only compounded the challenger's woes. So while Nixon carried the state 53–47 over McGovern, Pell beat Chafee 54–46.

Pell's triumph was not the only disaster that befell Republicans in Rhode Island. They had confidently expected their candidate, former state Attorney General Herbert de Simone, to win the governorship. The incumbent Democrat, Frank Licht, was reelected by a hair in 1970, and had since instituted a state income tax, something he had promised not to do when he upset Chafee in 1968. But Licht decided to retire, and 41-year-old Warwick Mayor Philip Noel got the Democratic nomination. Noel, who is half French Canadian and half Italian in descent, upset de Simone by a narrow margin.

Then more disaster. Just a few months after Richard Nixon's reelection, Elliot Richardson, during his brief tenure as Secretary of Defense, ordered massive base cutbacks—ones that hit Rhode Island especially hard. The entire Atlantic Fleet stationed there was to be moved out of Newport to Norfolk, Charleston, South Carolina, and Mayport, Florida—all locations that the Nixon Administration found politically more congenial than Rhode Island. Moreover, the Quonset Point Naval Air Station and Air Rework Facility were to be shut down completely. By June 1974, Rhode Island will lose 13,000 military personnel and nearly 5,000 civilian jobs, and will have absorbed more than half of the Navy's total cutbacks.

The people of Rhode Island who split tickets for Nixon might have taken the news more equitably, but for some political promises. The Nixon campaign staff in the state ran numerous ads claiming that McGovern, if elected, would close down the bases, and pledging that Nixon would retain them. Moreover, much of Chafee's appeal centered on his Navy connection. Gov. Noel promptly announced a program to attract industry to the sites, but most Rhode Islanders felt that they had been targeted for the cuts because they were not Richard Nixon's kind of people. Only two states, Massachusetts (which absorbed about a quarter of the total cutback) and Minnesota, along with the District of Columbia, gave Nixon lower percentages of their votes. The Pentagon decision, coming just after the statewide Republican losses of 1972, just about wipes out the Rhode Island Republican party. The Democrats now appear in much better shape than they were during the divisive 1960s.

But the Democrats, of course, were never in any danger of losing their other congressional seats. Sen. John Pastore, for example, could not be in better political shape. His career is proof that there is some truth left in Horatio Alger stories, even for boys who grow up in poor Italian neighborhoods. Pastore's father died young, but John stayed with his books, while supporting the family, and ended up with a law degree. Starting out in the state legislature, Pastore put in hard, honest work in the vineyards of local politics. He was rewarded when he was slated for Lieutenant Governor in 1944. Then, after Gov. McGrath resigned in 1945, Pastore was reelected in his own right twice and became the nation's first elected Italian-American Governor. In 1950, Pastore ran for the Senate and won by an overwhelming margin, as he has ever since.

Pastore has now accumulated much valuable seniority. As Chairman of the Commerce Committee's Communications Subcommittee, the Senator is the most influential man on Capitol Hill on matters relating to television and the other media. He has opposed the initiatives of Nixon's media czar Clay Whitehead, and decried the analyses of the media offered by Vice-President Agnew. Pastore was also the chief sponsor of the campaign media spending limit law, one that took effect on April 7, 1972.

The Rhode Island Senator also has another major committee assignment. Pastore alternates as Chairman of the Joint Committee on Atomic Energy, with Congressman Mel Price of Illinois. This body possesses great expertise. It also has, or did have until recently, a very close working relationship with the Atomic Energy Commission. More than any other congressional committee, the Joint Committee tends to get into the actual administration of a program it oversees. Perhaps because of his association with the quasi-military AEC, Pastore was notably more sympathetic to the war policies and military programs of the Johnson and Nixon administrations than his colleague, Sen. Pell. Pastore's term is not up until 1976, when he will be 69; unless he chooses to retire, he will certainly be reelected by a margin exceeding 2–1.

For the last 20-plus years, the Rhode Island delegation has kept the kind of ethnic balance that one expects in a state where a party organization makes most of the political decisions. One Senator is an Italian-American, one a blue-blood WASP. One Congressman, Fernand St Germain of the 1st district, is of French-Canadian descent; the other, Robert Tiernan of the 2nd, sports an Irish name. Appropriately, the 1st is the more French-Canadian of the two districts; French is still spoken in the streets of Woonsocket and Central Falls, two textile-mill towns in the district. The 1st also takes in the wealthier precincts of Providence, including Brown University, all of Pawtucket, and the east side of Narragansett Bay, including Newport. Newport sits on an island and votes Democratic; servants and their descendants outnumber the summertime patricians.

In the 1st, bread and butter issues are the staple of politics. One such issue is a demand here for restrictions on textile imports. Congressman St Germain, first elected in 1960, is less distinguished by his ideological fervor than by a scrupulous attention to district affairs. He is currently the eighth-ranking Democrat on the Banking and Currency Committee. He finds his seniority useful not so much for shaping national housing policy or regulating high finance, as for seeing that the 1st has, as it does, more federally funded senior-citizen housing than any of the other 434 congressional districts. On the issues, St Germain has combined an opposition to the Vietnam war with an opposition to the liberal conclusions of the presidential commission on obscenity. First elected when he was 32, and an easy winner since, St Germain could conceivably become Chairman of the full committee in 15 or 20 years. He is currently Chairman of the subcommittee that oversee the FDIC.

The 2nd district is slightly more Republican. It includes the towns having experienced the greatest suburban growth. This is one of the most heavily Italian-American districts in the nation. Over time, the children of the original immigrants have moved out of Providence (pop. 179,000) to the more middle-class suburbs of Cranston (pop. 73,000) and Warwick (pop. 83,000). From 1941 to 1967, the 2nd was represented by John Fogarty, who was a high-ranking member of the Appropriations Committee when he died at age 53. Had he lived longer, Fogarty might have become Chairman of the full committee; as it was, he was an able Chairman of the HEW subcommittee, which channelled hundreds of millions of dollars to the National Institutes of Health. The special election to fill Fogarty's seat came at the nadir of Johnson Administration popularity in 1967. Fogarty had always won easily, but an Italian-American Republican came within 313 votes of upsetting the slated Democrat, Robert Tiernan.

It was the closest the Republicans had come since 1938 of winning a Rhode Island congressional seat. Tiernan has since won easily. He is slowly climbing the seniority ladder on a couple of committees of economic importance to the district. Tiernan is reportedly interested in statewide office, but there are no openings as yet; the only major Republican officeholder is Attorney General Richard Israel. Besides, the Democratic organization controls the nomination process. In the past, the machine has shown an inclination to elect its Congressmen young and keep them in the House for years to accumulate seniority. That will probably happen with Tiernan.

Census Data Pop. 949,723; 0.47% of U.S. total, 39th largest; change 1960–70, 10.5%. Central city, 36%; suburban, 49%. Median family income, $9,734; 17th highest; families above $15,000: 19%; families below $3,000: 9%. Median years education, 11.5.

1972 Share of Federal Tax Burden $982,390,000; 0.47% of U.S. total, 36th largest.

1972 Share of Federal Outlays $950,606,112; 0.44% of U.S. total, 42nd largest. Per capita federal spending, $1,001.

DOD	$344,164,000	35th (0.55%)		HEW	$360,555,151	37th (0.51%)
AEC	$661,430	34th (0.03%)		HUD	$15,893,115	38th (0.52%)
NASA	$240,897	40th (0.01%)		VA	$59,456,453	39th (0.52%)
DOT	$28,604,550	49th (0.36%)		USDA	$13,577,590	49th (0.09%)
DOC	$3,276,756	41st (0.25%)		CSC	$18,874,433	40th (0.46%)
DOI	$1,782,522	48th (0.08%)		TD	$34,268,723	39th (0.21%)
DOJ	$4,108,925	40th (0.42%)		Other	$65,141,567	

Economic Base Miscellaneous manufacturing industries, especially jewelry, silverware and plated ware; textile mill products, especially narrow fabric mills; finance, insurance and real estate; primary metal industries, especially nonferrous rolling and drawing; fabricated metal products; electrical equipment and supplies; machinery, especially metalworking machinery.

Political Line-up Governor, Philip W. Noel (D); seat up, 1974. Senators, John O. Pastore (D) and Claiborne Pell (D). Representatives, 2 D. State Senate (37 D and 13 R); State House (73 D and 27 R).

The Voters

Registration 510,312 Total. No party registration.
Median voting age 44.0
Employment profile White collar, 45%. Blue collar, 42%. Service, 12%. Farm, 1%.
Ethnic groups Black, 3%. Total foreign stock, 33%. Italy, 8%, Canada, 7%, UK, 4%, Portugal, 3%.

Presidential vote

1972	Nixon (R)	220,383	(53%)
	McGovern (D)	194,645	(47%)
1968	Nixon (R)	122,359	(32%)
	Humphrey (D)	246,518	(64%)
	Wallace (AI)	15,678	(4%)
1964	Johnson (D)	315,463	(81%)
	Goldwater (R)	74,615	(19%)

Senator

John O. Pastore (D) Elected Dec. 19, 1950, seat up 1976; b. March 17, 1907, Cranston; home, Cranston; Northeastern U., LL.B., 1931; married, three children; Catholic.

Career R.I. Legislature, 1935–38; Asst. Atty. Gen., 1940–44; Lt. Gov., 1944–45; Gov. of R.I., 1945–50.

Offices 3215 NSOB, 202-225-2921. Also 301 P.O. Annex, Providence 02903, 401-421-4583.

Administrative Assistant C. J. Maisano

Committees

Appropriations (4th); Subs: Defense; Intelligence Operations; Housing and Urban Development, Space, Science, and Veterans; Public Works, AEC; State, Justice, and Commerce, the Judiciary, and Related Agencies (Chm.); Transportation.

Commerce (2nd); Subs: Communications (Chm.); Consumer; Environment; Merchant Marine; Oceans and Atmosphere.

Joint Com. on Atomic Energy (Vice-Chm.); Subs: Agreements for Cooperation; Legislation; Research, Development, and Radiation; Security (Chm.); Energy; Licensing and Regulation.

Joint Study Com. on Budget Control.

Sp. Com. to Study Questions Related to Secret and Confidential Government Documents (2nd).

Group Ratings

	ADA	COPE	LWV	RIPON	NFU	LCV	CFA	NAB	NSI	ACA
1972	75	90	91	72	80	49	100	40	33	21
1971	74	64	92	60	82	–	83	–	–	17
1970	78	92	–	69	93	66	–	33	40	14

Key Votes

1) Busing	FOR	8) Sea Life Prot	FOR	15) Tax Singls Less	AGN
2) Alas P-line	AGN	9) Campaign Subs	FOR	16) Min Tax for Rich	AGN
3) Gun Cntrl	FOR	10) Cmbodia Bmbg	AGN	17) Euro Troop Rdctn	FOR
4) Rehnquist	FOR	11) Legal Srvices	FOR	18) Bust Hwy Trust	FOR
5) Pub TV $	FOR	12) Rev Sharing	FOR	19) Maid Min Wage	FOR
6) EZ Votr Reg	FOR	13) Cnsumr Prot	FOR	20) Farm Sub Limit	FOR
7) No-Fault	FOR	14) Eq Rts Amend	FOR	21) Highr Credit Chgs	ABS

Election Results

1970 general:	John O. Pastore (D)	230,469	(68%)
	John McLaughlin (R)	107,351	(32%)
1970 primary:	John O. Pastore (D)	54,090	(88%)
	John Quattrocchi, Jr. (D)	7,332	(12%)
1964 general:	John O. Pastore (D)	319,607	(83%)
	Ronald R. Lagueux (R)	66,715	(17%)

Senator

Claiborne Pell (D) Elected 1960, seat up 1978; b. Nov. 22, 1918, New York City; home, Newport; Princeton U., B.A., 1940; Columbia, M.A., 1946; USCG, WWII; Capt. USCGR; married, four children; Episcopalian.

Career Sp. Asst. at San Francisco UN Conference, 1945; State Dept., 1945–46; U.S. Embassy, Czechoslovakia, 1946–47; Consulate Gen., Bratislava, Czech., 1947–48; V. Consul, Genoa, Italy, 1949; State Dept., 1950–52; Director, Intl. Rescue Com.; Asst. to R.I. Dem. State Chm., 1952, 1954; Chief Delegation Tally Clerk, Dem. Natl. Conv., 1956, 1960, 1964, 1968; Natl. Dem. Registration Chm., 1956.

401-528-4547.

Offices 325 OSOB, 202-225-4642. Also 418 Fed. Bldg., Providence 02903,

Administrative Assistant Ray Nelson

Committees

Foreign Relations (6th); Subs: European Affairs; Arms Control, International Law and Organization; Oceans and International Environment (Chm.); NearEastern Affairs.

Labor and Public Welfare (3rd); Subs: Education (Chm.); Handicapped; Health; Aging; Labor; Railroad Retirement; Sp. Sub. on Arts and Humanities (Chm.); National Science Foundation.

Rules and Administration (2nd); Subs: Library; Smithsonian Institution (Chm.); Privileges and Elections (Chm.).

Sp. Com. on the Termination of the National Emergency (3rd).

Sp. Com. on Aging (10th); Subs: Housing for the Elderly; Federal, State and Community Services; Health of the Elderly; Long-Term Care; Retirement and the Individual.

Joint Com. on the Library (2nd).

Group Ratings

	ADA	COPE	LWV	RIPON	NFU	LCV	CFA	NAB	NSI	ACA
1972	75	88	100	77	86	72	100	38	30	16
1971	89	75	91	63	82	–	100	–	–	23
1970	84	100	–	75	92	55	–	17	10	5

Key Votes

1) Busing	FOR	8) Sea Life Prot	FOR	15) Tax Singls Less	FOR
2) Alas P-line	AGN	9) Campaign Subs	FOR	16) Min Tax for Rich	ABS
3) Gun Cntrl	ABS	10) Cmbodia Bmbg	AGN	17) Euro Troop Rdctn	AGN
4) Rehnquist	FOR	11) Legal Srvices	ABS	18) Bust Hwy Trust	FOR
5) Pub TV $	FOR	12) Rev Sharing	FOR	19) Maid Min Wage	FOR
6) EZ Votr Reg	FOR	13) Cnsumr Prot	FOR	20) Farm Sub Limit	FOR
7) No-Fault	FOR	14) Eq Rts Amend	FOR	21) Highr Credt Chgs	AGN

Election Results

1972 general:	Claiborne Pell (D)	221,942	(54%)
	John H. Chafee (R)	188,990	(46%)
1972 primary:	Claiborne Pell (D), unopposed		
1966 general:	Claiborne Pell (D)	219,331	(68%)
	Harriet Briggs (R)	104,838	(32%)

FIRST DISTRICT

Census Data Pop. 475,441. Central city, 28%; suburban, 56%. Median family income, $9,713; families above $15,000: 19%; families below $3,000: 9%. Median years education, 11.4.

1972 Share of Federal Outlays $481,193,539

DOD	$222,385,618	HEW	$178,243,306
AEC	$293,057	HUD	$8,455,456
NASA	$119,292	DOI	$809,910
DOT	$13,666,049	USDA	$6,452,921
		Other	$50,767,940

Federal Military-Industrial Commitments

DOD Contractors Raytheon (Portsmouth), $44.617m: sonar systems. Mine Safety Appliances Co. (Esmond), $8.719m: fire fighting, rescue, and safety equipment.
DOD Installations Naval Communication Station (Newport). Naval Hospital (Newport); closed, 1974. Naval Schools Command (Newport). Naval Station (Newport); closed, 1974. Naval Supply Center (Newport), closed, 1974. Naval Underseas Research and Development Center (Newport). Naval Public Works Center (Newport); closed, 1974.

Economic Base Miscellaneous manufacturing industries, especially jewelry, silverware and plated ware; textile mill products; finance, insurance and real estate; primary metal industries; fabricated metal products; and machinery, especially metalworking machinery.

The Voters

Registration 260,517 total. No party registration.
Median voting age 43.7
Employment profile White collar, 46%. Blue collar, 42%. Service, 12%. Farm, –%.
Ethnic groups Black, 3%. Total foreign stock, 35%. Canada, 9%; Portugal, Italy, 5% each; UK, 4%.

Presidential vote

1972	Nixon (R)	107,156	(52%)
	McGovern (D)	98,881	(48%)
1968	Nixon (R)	58,868	(31%)
	Humphrey (D)	126,226	(65%)
	Wallace (AI)	6,804	(4%)

Representative

Fernand Joseph St. Germain (D) Elected 1960; b. Jan. 9, 1928, Blackstone, Mass.; home, Woonsocket; Providence Col., Ph.B., 1948; Boston U., LL.B., 1955; Army, Korean War; married, two children; Catholic.

Career R.I. Legislature, 1952–60; practicing atty., 1956–.

Offices 2136 RHOB, 202-225-4911. Also 200 John Fogarty Bldg., Providence 02903, 401-528-4323.

Administrative Assistant Joseph Scanlon

Committees

Banking and Currency (8th); Subs: Bank Supervision and Insurance (Chm.); Housing; International Trade.

Government Operations (13th); Subs: Legal and Monetary Affairs; Legislation and Military Operations.

Sel. Com. on Small Business (9th); Subs: Activities of Regulatory Agencies; Special Small Business Problems.

Group Ratings

	ADA	COPE	LWV	RIPON	NFU	LCV	CFA	NAB	NSI	ACA
1972	75	91	70	67	71	61	100	17	33	5
1971	84	82	78	83	67	–	100	–	–	15
1970	72	100	–	69	92	78	94	0	40	17

Key Votes

1) Busing	AGN	6) Cmbodia Bmbg	AGN	11) Chkg Acct Intrst	AGN
2) Strip Mines	AGN	7) Bust Hwy Trust	FOR	12) End HISC (HUAC)	FOR
3) Cut Mil $	AGN	8) Farm Sub Lmt	FOR	13) Nixon Sewer Veto	AGN
4) Rev Shrg	FOR	9) School Prayr	AGN	14) Corp Cmpaign $	FOR
5) Pub TV $	ABS	10) Cnsumr Prot	FOR	15) Pol $ Disclosr	AGN

Election Results

1972 general:	Fernand J. St Germain (D)	120,705	(62%)
	John M. Feeley (R)	67,125	(35%)
	Walter J. Miska (Ind.)	5,762	(3%)
1972 primary:	Fernand J. St Germain (D), unopposed		
1970 general:	Fernand J. St Germain (D)	86,283	(61%)
	Walter J. Miska (R)	52,962	(37%)
	Stephen Bruce Murray (PF)	2,327	(2%)

SECOND DISTRICT

Census Data Pop. 474,282. Central city, 44%; suburban, 42%. Median family income, $9,755; families above $15,000: 19%; families below $3,000: 9%. Median years education, 11.6.

1972 Share of Federal Outlays $469,412,573

DOD	$121,778,392	HEW	$182,311,845
AEC	$368,373	HUD	$7,437,659
NASA	$121,605	DOI	$972,612
DOT	$14,938,501	USDA	$7,124,969
		Other	$134,358,617

Federal Military-Industrial Commitments

DOD Contractors Bulova Watch (Warwick), $9.063m: bomb fuzes.
DOD Installations Naval Air Station (Quonset Point); closed, 1974. Naval Construction Battalion Center (Davisville). Naval Air Rework Facility (Quonset Point); closed, 1974.

Economic Base Miscellaneous manufacturing industries, especially jewelry, silverware and plated ware; finance, insurance and real estate; textile mill products, especially narrow fabric mill products; electrical equipment and supplies; and rubber and plastics products, especially fabricated rubber products not otherwise classified.

The Voters

Registration 258,795 total. No party registration.
Median voting age 44.4
Employment profile White collar, 45%. Blue collar, 42%. Service, 13%. Farm, –%.
Ethnic groups Black, 3%. Total foreign stock, 31%. Italy, 10%; Canada, 5%; UK, 3%; Portugal, 1%.

Presidential vote

1972	Nixon (R)	113,072	(54%)
	McGovern (D)	94,935	(46%)
1968	Nixon (R)	63,491	(33%)
	Humphrey (D)	120,292	(62%)
	Wallace (AI)	8,874	(5%)

Representative

Robert Owens Tiernan (D) Elected March 28, 1967; b. Feb. 24, 1929, Providence; home, Warwick; Providence Col., B.S., 1953; Catholic U., J.D., 1956; unmarried; Catholic.

Career Practicing atty., 1957–67; R.I. Legislature, 1961–67.

Offices 417 CHOB, 202-225-2735. Also 307 P.O. Annex, Providence 02903, 401-528-4561.

Administrative Assistant William Hagan

Committees

Appropriations (31st); Subs: District of Columbia; HUD, Space, Science, Veterans.

Group Ratings

	ADA	COPE	LWV	RIPON	NFU	LCV	CFA	NAB	NSI	ACA
1972	75	91	82	80	83	63	100	9	13	0
1971	81	82	67	78	85	–	88	–	–	15
1970	80	100	–	76	100	100	100	0	50	13

Key Votes

1) Busing	AGN	6) Cmbodia Bmbg	AGN	11) Chkg Acct Intrst	AGN
2) Strip Mines	AGN	7) Bust Hwy Trust	FOR	12) End HISC (HUAC)	FOR
3) Cut Mil $	FOR	8) Farm Sub Lmt	FOR	13) Nixon Sewer Veto	AGN
4) Rev Shrg	FOR	9) School Prayr	AGN	14) Corp Cmpaign $	AGN
5) Pub TV $	FOR	10) Cnsumr Prot	FOR	15) Pol $ Disclosr	AGN

Election Results

1972 general:	Robert O. Tiernan (D)	122,739	(63%)
	Donald P. Ryan (R)	71,661	(37%)
1972 primary:	Robert O. Tiernan (D), unopposed		
1970 general:	Robert O. Tiernan (D)	121,704	(66%)
	William A. Dimitri, Jr. (R)	61,819	(34%)

SOUTH CAROLINA

Political Background

South Carolina is the state that split the Union. Back in 1856, the Democratic Convention made an unfortunate choice and selected Charleston, then the South's second-largest city (behind New Orleans) and a hotbed of secession, as the site for its next national gathering. So in 1860, the Democrats came to Charleston and found themselves split over the platform. The Southerners, in essence, wanted the platform to read that slavery was *right*—no ifs, ands, or buts. The Northerners preferred a more moderate stance and got their way. Thereupon, the Southerners walked out, and the Northerners remaining were unable to generate a two-thirds majority for any nominee. The Convention was adjourned, and later reconvened in Baltimore, where it nominated Stephen Douglas. The seceders then decided to support a third-party candidate in John Breckinridge, who in the November election captured all of the South, plus Delaware and Maryland. Douglas carried only Missouri, which meant that Abraham Lincoln became President of the United States (with only 38% of the votes).

Lincoln probably understood the hotheads of Charleston better than they understood themselves. When he took office, South Carolina had already seceded formally, but the Union garrison of Fort Sumter remained in Charleston harbor. Lincoln's advisors and the South Carolinians agreed: Lincoln would have to fight or quit the harbor. The President did neither. He announced that he would continue to supply Fort Sumter with nonmilitary provisions. For Charlestonians, the prospect of a Union flag flying over the harbor indefinitely was too much, and they opened fire. Fort Sumter surrendered, but not before becoming the Pearl Harbor of the Civil War.

South Carolina was an uncompromising state—one that brooked no talk of reform, let alone abolition. Its quintessential antebellum politician was John C. Calhoun, who was himself an austere man, but who in Washington defended the interests of high-living Charleston planters and merchants. Before the war, the state's economy was based exclusively on the labor-intensive crops of cotton, rice, and indigo; the resulting wealth was, to say the least, maldistributed—at the very top rungs of the social ladder. At the time of the Civil War, the whites of the state were heavily outnumbered by black slaves, about whom the power structure was of two minds. Without the blacks, South Carolina would have no economy, and yet the whites were uneasy about the presence of so many black people among them. In 1822, Denmark Vesey led the nation's first slave rebellion, in Charleston; though the revolt of the "happy slave" of Southern mythology was quickly suppressed, it was never forgotten.

So after the Civil War, it enraged the state's white minority to see blacks take political power. For a time during the 1870s, blacks controlled the South Carolina legislature and the state's congressional delegation. Such "outrages" of Reconstruction were soon ended, and the blacks—and most poor whites—were shorn of the franchise and all political rights. As the nineteenth century proceeded, the once booming port of Charleston settled into economic stagnation, as did the rest of the state. For most of the twentieth century, South Carolina has been among the lowest ranking states in per capita income, education levels, and health services. It has also had one of the lowest levels of political participation: as late as 1948, only 142,000 South Carolinians voted in the presidential election. Politics was still a matter that concerned only a small minority of the people of South Carolina.

Like the other Southern states, South Carolina has long since ceased to have a black majority, as blacks have migrated North and new whites have moved into the state. South Carolina has also long since ceased to be the nation's most Democratic state, which it was as recently as the presidential election of 1944. Since then, it has voted for the regular Democratic nominee only three times, and twice (1952 and 1960) by margins of less than 10,000. In 1964, Barry Goldwater carried the state easily, the first Republican to do so since Reconstruction. South Carolina again went Republican in 1968, but only after a massive shift in traditional voting habits. The Voting Rights Act of 1965 enfranchised thousands of blacks, who voted almost to a man for Hubert Humphrey. The black votes, plus a few white ones (less than 10%) gave the Democrat 30% of the ballots statewide. George Wallace did significantly poorer here than in the other states of the

Deep South, finishing with 32% of the votes. Most of these came from whites who had carried the state for Kennedy in 1960—Democrats turned Dixiecrats. Richard Nixon captured the state's electoral votes with 38%—aside from Tennessee, his lowest winning percentage in any state.

The 1968 Nixon victory in South Carolina, as well as those in several other states, has been properly credited to one man: Strom Thurmond, who has remained a constant amidst the moiling changes in recent South Carolina politics. From 1947 to 1951, Thurmond served as Governor of the state, and in 1948 received 39 electoral votes for President on the States' Rights Democratic ticket. He was elected to the Senate in 1954 in a stunning victory as a write-in candidate. Then, pursuant to a 1954 campaign promise, Thurmond resigned and was returned to office in 1956. In 1964, Thurmond became a Republican out of enthusiasm for Barry Goldwater and a distaste for Lyndon Johnson and his policies. And in 1968, he lobbied effectively among Southern Republican convention delegations for Richard Nixon, preventing any Reagan breakthrough and getting Nixon his majority on the first ballot.

After the Convention, Thurmond took to the stump in the South. He was persuasive because white Southerners knew that for 20 years Strom had stood for what they wanted—segregation and no civil-rights nonsense. By 1968, to be sure, he professed to have modified his views, given the legislation that had already passed. But Southerners, black and white, believed that Thurmond would stand as hard as he could against any changes in what is called the Southern way of life. Thurmond is a man without guile, his beliefs are as sincere as his Southern accent is thick. One verdict, reportedly rendered by a Southern colleague during a Thurmond anti-civil rights tirade, was "The trouble with ol' Strom is that he believes all that shit."

After the Nixon triumph in 1968, Thurmond basked in glory and achievement. His political protégé, Harry Dent, was a ranking White House politico, while other Thurmond men also held high positions in the new Administration. But it suddenly became clear that his own position in South Carolina left something to be desired. Campaigning in 1968 on Nixon's behalf, Thurmond promised freedom-of-choice integration plans for schools and textile import quotas for South Carolina's leading industry. By 1970, the Supreme Court ruled the former unconstitutional, and the Nixon Administration was unable to secure the latter. In the 1970 gubernatorial election, Lt. Gov. John West, considered a moderate, ran against Republican Congressman Albert Watson, and by inference, against Thurmond. West used the slogan "broken promises." Meanwhile, Watson made it known how he felt when he urged a crowd of voters in the town of Lamar to stand up against a desegregation order. A few days later, a Lamar mob attacked and overturned three buses containing black school children. In the end, despite campaign appearances by Thurmond, Vice-President Agnew, and David Eisenhower, Watson lost to West by a 52–46 margin.

Watson's loss suggested possible trouble for Thurmond in 1972. Watson failed to do much better than Nixon's 38% in 1968; obviously many Wallace voters—traditional Democrats— voted for West, who of course finished with virtually 100% of the black votes. In 1966, Thurmond had won with 62% of the votes, but that total was accumulated before the Voting Rights Act had had its maximum effect. It appeared that Thurmond needed more white votes than Watson got to win in 1972, and that Thurmond might have trouble getting them if ex-Gov. (1967–71) Robert McNair were the Democratic candidate.

But Thurmond engineered one of the spriest political recoveries in recent history. He helped secure action limiting textile imports—thus fulfilling one of his 1968 promises—and came out sternly against some Nixon Administration policies on school integration. Then, after hiring blacks for his Washington and South Carolina staff, the Senator started to provide blacks the same services he had been providing whites and helped them take advantage of federal programs. Finally, the elderly (70 in 1972) Thurmond, still in excellent physical shape, married a young South Carolina beauty queen, and for the first time became a father.

As the filing deadline for the 1972 South Carolina elections approached, Thurmond was riding as high as he ever rode in the polls among white voters. And for a Republican and a Thurmond, he was even getting a fair share of the black votes. McNair declined to make the race, leaving it to state Sen. Nick Ziegler, whose platform was more in line with the national Democratic party than with South Carolina tradition. So Thurmond was reelected easily with 63% of the votes, topping his 1966 percentage.

South Carolina's junior Senator, Democrat Ernest (Fritz) Hollings, comes up for reelection in 1974. His political standing appears almost as healthy and substantial as Thurmond's. Elected Governor in 1958, Hollings was defeated for the Senate in 1962 by incumbent Olin Johnston.

After Johnston's death, then-Gov. Donald Russell had himself appointed to the seat—always an unpopular move these days. Hollings then beat Russell in the 1966 Democratic primary, and won a narrow 51% over Republican Marshall Parker in the general, while Thurmond took 62% at the same time. But in 1966, once more against Parker, Hollings won easily, carrying every county in the state.

Like McNair and West, Hollings is considered a moderate. He has voted against civil-rights legislation, but after it is passed the Senator urged compliance with the law. His support of current military and foreign policy is as staunch as Thurmond's, though without Thurmond's vehemence. On domestic issues, however, the junior Senator has often differed with his colleague. A few years ago, Hollings stirred the Senate with a speech concerning the hunger and malnutrition he had found endemic in some parts of South Carolina. During his years in politics, the Senator said, he had not known that such conditions of deprivation existed and, as a South Carolina booster, had not much wanted to know. Hollings is now one of the major proponents of legislation to alleviate hunger in the United States. The South Carolinian has sometimes been mentioned as a possible Democratic vice-presidential nominee. In 1972, he served as Chairman of the Senate Democratic Committee, which, aside from races in North Carolina and Virginia, enjoyed surprising success.

The big South Carolina race in 1974 will be, as it was in 1970, for the governorship. Gov. West is prohibited from seeking a second term. Democratic possibilities include 3rd-district Congressman William Jennings Bryan Dorn, Lt. Gov. Earl Morris, and ex-Gov. Robert McNair. Among the Republican possibilities are longtime Republican leader William Workman and—South Carolina is a very military state—Gen. William Westmoreland.

Census Data Pop. 2,590,516; 1.28% of U.S. total, 26th largest; change 1960–70, 8.7%. Central city, 9%; suburban, 30%. Median family income, $7,620; 42nd highest; families above $15,000: 11%; families below $3,000: 16%. Median years education, 10.5.

1972 Share of Federal Tax Burden $1,708,660,000; 0.85% of U.S. total, 30th largest.

1972 Share of Federal Outlays $2,282,074,507; 1.05% of U.S. total, 31st largest. Per capita federal spending, $881.

DOD	$832,310,000	24th (1.33%)	HEW	$642,152,556	33rd (0.90%)
AEC	$127,729,918	8th (4.87%)	HUD	$30,586,757	28th (1.00%)
NASA	$134,707	41st (—)	VA	$137,433,429	31st (1.20%)
DOT	$64,663,470	37th (0.82%)	USDA	$217,741,282	30th (1.42%)
DOC	$12,624,307	23rd (0.98%)	CSC	$42,379,619	26th (1.03%)
DOI	$5,400,902	44th (0.25%)	TD	$51,493,256	35th (0.31%)
DOJ	$9,563,046	31st (0.97%)	Other	$107,861,258	

Economic Base Textile mill products, especially cotton weaving mills; apparel and other textile products, especially women's and misses' outerwear; agriculture, notably tobacco, soybeans, cattle and cotton lint; finance, insurance and real estate; chemicals and allied products, especially plastics materials and synthetics; machinery, especially special industry machinery; food and kindred products.

Political Line-up Governor, John C. West (D); seat up, 1974. Senators, Strom Thurmond (R) and Ernest F. Hollings (D). Representatives, 6 (4 D and 2 R). State Senate (43 D and 31 R); State House (103 D and 21 R).

The Voters

Registration 1,033,688 total. No party registration. 772,603 white (75%); 260,749 black (25%); 336 other (-).
Median voting age 40.3
Employment profile White collar, 37%. Blue collar, 47%. Service, 12%. Farm, 4%.
Ethnic groups Black, 30%. Total foreign stock, 2%.

Presidential vote

1972	Nixon (R)	477,044	(72%)
	McGovern (D)	186,824	(28%)

1968	Nixon (R)	254,062	(38%)
	Humphrey (D)	197,486	(30%)
	Wallace (AI)	215,430	(32%)
1964	Johnson (D)	215,700	(42%)
	Goldwater (R)	309,048	(59%)

Senator

Strom Thurmund (R) Elected 1956, seat up 1978; b. Dec. 5, 1902, Edgefield; home, Aiken; Clemson U., B.S., 1923; admitted to S.C. bar in 1930 after studying law at night; Army, WWII; Major Gen. USAR; married, two children; Baptist.

Career Farmer; teacher, 1923–29; Edgefield County Supt. of Ed., 1929–33; practicing atty., 1930–38, 1951–55; S.C. Senate, 1933–38; Circuit Judge, 1938–46; States Rights Candidate for Pres., 1948; U.S. Senate, Dec. 24, 1954–April 4, 1956; Gov. of S.C., 1947–51; switched from Dem. to Repub., Sept. 16, 1964.

Offices 4241 NSOB 202-225-5972. Also P.O. Bldg., Aiken 29801, 803-649-2591, and Palmetto State Life Bldg., 1310 Lady St., Columbia 29201, 803-765-5496, and P.O. Drawer O, Charleston, 803-722-3196.

Administrative Assistant Daniel J. Carrison

Committees

Armed Services (Ranking Mbr.); Subs: Military Construction Authorization; Preparedness Investigating (Ranking Mbr.); Tactical Air Power; Bomber Defense (Ranking Mbr.); Central Intelligence; Reprograming of Funds.

Judiciary (4th); Subs: Administrative Practices and Procedure (Ranking Mbr.); Antitrust and Monopoly; Constitutional Amendments; Constitutional Rights; Criminal Laws and Procedures; Immigration and Naturalization; Internal Security.

Veterans' Affairs (2nd); Subs: Compensation and Pensions; Health and Hospitals (Ranking Mbr.).

Group Ratings

	ADA	COPE	LWV	RIPON	NFU	LCV	CFA	NAB	NSI	ACA
1972	0	10	10	25	30	7	0	91	100	95
1971	0	25	8	20	9	–	14	–	–	96
1970	0	0	–	12	13	27	–	91	100	96

Key Votes

1) Busing	AGN	8) Sea Life Prot	FOR	15) Tax Singls Less	FOR
2) Alas P-line	FOR	9) Campaign Subs	AGN	16) Min Tax for Rich	AGN
3) Gun Cntrl	FOR	10) Cmbodia Bmbg	FOR	17) Euro Troop Rdctn	AGN
4) Rehnquist	FOR	11) Legal Srvices	AGN	18) Bust Hwy Trust	AGN
5) Pub TV $	AGN	12) Rev Sharing	FOR	19) Maid Min Wage	AGN
6) EZ Votr Reg	AGN	13) Cnsumr Prot	AGN	20) Farm Sub Limit	AGN
7) No-Fault	AGN	14) Eq Rts Amend	FOR	21) Highr Credt Chgs	FOR

Election Results

1972 general:	Strom Thurmond (R)	415,806	(63%)
	Eugene N. Zeigler (D)	241,056	(37%)
1972 primary:	Thurmond nominated by Republican State Convention		
1966 general:	Strom Thurmond (R)	271,297	(62%)
	Bradley Morrah, Jr. (D)	164,955	(38%)

Senator

Ernest F. Hollings (D) Elected 1966, seat up 1974; b. Jan. 1, 1922, Charleston; home, Charleston; The Citadel, B.A., 1942; U. of S.C., LL.B., 1947; Army, WWII; married, four children; Lutheran.

Career Practicing atty., 1947–58, 1962–66; S.C. House of Reps., 1949–55, Speaker Pro Tem., 1951–55; Lt. Gov., 1955–59; Gov., 1959–63.

Offices 432 OSOB, 202-225-6121. Also 306 Fed. Bldg., Columbia 29201, 803-254-7636, and 323 Fed. Bldg., Spartanburg 29301, 803-585-8272, and 141 E. Bay St., Charleston 29402, 803-254-7636.

Administrative Assistant Michael B. Joy

Committees

Appropriations (12th); Subs: Agriculture, Environmental and Consumer Protection; Labor, and Health, Education, and Welfare, and Related Agencies; Legislative (Chm.); Military Construction; State, Justice, Commerce, the Judiciary, and Related Agencies.

Commerce (8th); Subs: Aviation; Communications; Merchant Marine; Surface Transportation; Oceans and Atmosphere (Chm.).

Post Office and Civil Service (4th); Subs: Compensation and Employment Benefits; Postal Operations (Chm.).

Group Ratings

	ADA	COPE	LWV	RIPON	NFU	LCV	CFA	NAB	NSI	ACA
1972	25	40	45	39	89	42	90	30	67	40
1971	44	75	44	9	73	–	80	–	–	39
1970	22	34	–	8	86	51	–	30	89	55

Key Votes

1) Busing	AGN	8) Sea Life Prot	FOR	15) Tax Singls Less	AGN
2) Alas P-line	FOR	9) Campaign Subs	FOR	16) Min Tax for Rich	FOR
3) Gun Cntrl	FOR	10) Cmbodia Bmbg	AGN	17) Euro Troop Rdctn	FOR
4) Rehnquist	FOR	11) Legal Srvices	FOR	18) Bust Hwy Trust	AGN
5) Pub TV $	FOR	12) Rev Sharing	FOR	19) Maid Min Wage	AGN
6) EZ Votr Reg	FOR	13) Cnsumr Prot	ABS	20) Farm Sub Limit	AGN
7) No-Fault	AGN	14) Eq Rts Amend	FOR	21) Highr Credt Chgs	FOR

Election Results

1968 general:	Ernest F. Hollings (D)	404,060	(62%)
	Marshall Parker (R)	248,780	(38%)
1968 primary:	Ernest F. Hollings (D)	308,016	(78%)
	John Bolt Culbertson (D)	84,913	(22%)
1966 special:	Ernest F. Hollings (D)	223,790	(51%)
	Marshall Parker (R)	212,032	(49%)

FIRST DISTRICT Political Background

In the spring, the pastel row houses of Charleston are wreathed by the flowers of blossoming trees. There are few, if any, more beautiful urban scenes in the United States. Charleston, founded in 1670 and blessed with one of the finest harbors on the Atlantic, was one of the South's leading cities up to the time of the Civil War. Across its docks went cargos of rice, indigo, and cotton—all crops cultivated by black slaves and designed to enrich white planters and merchants, who dominated the state's economy and political life. In the years following the Civil War, Charleston became an economic backwater. Today, the old part of the city, still beautifully preserved, houses fewer people than it did in 1860.

But in the mid-twentieth century, Charleston discovered a benefactor who restored some of its old majesty and much of its old power. His name was L. Mendel Rivers, Congressman from the 1st district of South Carolina for 30 years. He was also Chairman of the House Armed Services Committee from 1965 until his death in December 1970. Rivers was as proud of the Defense Department money he funneled into the Charleston area as he was of his super-patriotism (though he himself never served in the military). It was largely his doing that 35% of the payrolls in the 1st district come either from military installations or defense industries. The 1st district, which includes Charleston and several coastal, heavily black and rural counties, contains no less than 11 major naval installations alone.

With his long flowing white locks and his thick accent, Rivers looked and talked the part of a Southern Congressman. He was bellicose, self-righteous, and, many said, too often drunk. According to all reports, however, he quit drinking completely during his last few years. Rivers, of course, compiled an unflinching pro-Pentagon, conservative record in the House. But the Congressman sometimes supported bread-and-butter economic legislation. He had begun life not as a Charleston aristocrat, but as a poor country boy. Invincible at the polls, Rivers won his last election in 1970 with no opposition in either the primary or general election.

The race to succeed the Chairman illustrates the volatility of South Carolina politics these days. The heir apparent, and eventual winner, was Mendel Davis, Rivers' 28-year-old godson who had served on his staff in Washington. Although Davis easily won the Democratic primary, the Republicans put up a strong effort to capture the district, one that had gone for Nixon in 1968. There was even a Republican primary, where ultraconservative dentist James Edwards defeated Charleston businessman Arthur Ravenel, who tried to attract black support. And there was a third independent candidate, civil-rights activist Victoria deLee, who eventually won 10% of the votes.

Most of the black votes, however, went to Mendel Davis, as they had to Mendel Rivers before him. The Republicans sent in Vice-President Agnew, Sen. James Buckley, Gov. Ronald Reagan, and Sen. Barry Goldwater, which was taken as a sign that they were interested in white votes only. Davis' victory, a narrow one with black voters supplying the decisive ballots, may have changed the Republican strategy for 1972. For example, in 1972, Sen. Strom Thurmond went to some trouble to enlist the support of Mrs. deLee, the independent candidate here in the 1971 special election.

For 1972, the Republicans by no means gave up on the seat in the 1st. State legislator J. Sidi Limehouse won 46% of the votes against Davis in the general election—a fine showing against an incumbent. In 1973, Davis managed to get his mentor's seat, though not, of course, his seniority, on the Armed Services Committee. But he still may have trouble in 1974. There is talk that Mendel Rivers, Jr., who was too young to run when his father died, may challenge Davis. There is also a good possibility that the Republicans will make another strong bid in the 1st district.

Census Data Pop. 442,646. Central city, 15%; suburban, 54%. Median family income, $7,355; families above $15,000: 12%; families below $3,000: 18%. Median years education, 11.4.

1972 Share of Federal Outlays $623,955,321

DOD	$413,355,000	HEW	$95,762,896
AEC	–	HUD	$1,738,593
NASA	–	DOI	$788,922
DOT	$20,649,988	USDA	$30,407,061
		Other	$61,252,861

Federal Military-Industrial Commitments

DOD Installations Charleston Army Depot (North Charleston); closed, 1974. Marine Corps Air Station (Beaufort). Marine Corps Recruit Depot (Parris Island). Charleston Naval Shipyard (Charleston). Naval Hospital (Charleston). Naval Hospital (Beaufort). Naval Station (Charleston). Naval Supply Center (Charleston). Naval Weapons Station (Charleston). Navy Fleet Ballistic Missile, Submarine Training Center (Charleston). Polaris Missile Facility, Atlantic (Charleston). Charleston AFB (Charleston). North Charleston AF Station (North Charleston).

Economic Base Finance, insurance and real estate; agriculture, notably grains, vegetables and poultry; transportation equipment, especially aircraft and parts; lumber and wood products; and apparel and other textile products.

The Voters

Registration 169,894 total. 114,324 white (67%); 55,469 black (25%); 101 other (–). No party registration.
Median voting age 36.9
Employment profile White collar, 34%. Blue collar, 39%. Service, 15%. Farm, 2%.
Ethnic groups Black, 34%. Total foreign stock, 4%.

Presidential vote

1972	Nixon (R)	73,480	(69%)
	McGovern (D)	33,488	(31%)
1968	Nixon (R)	39,768	(38%)
	Humphrey (D)	37,187	(35%)
	Wallace (AI)	28,303	(27%)

Representative

Mendel J. Davis (D) Elected Apr. 28, 1970; b. Oct. 23, 1942, N. Charleston; home, N. Charleston; Col. of Charleston, B.A., 1967; U. of S.C. Law School, LL.B., 1970; married, one child; Protestant.

Career Practicing atty., 1970–71.

Offices 1726 LHOB, 202-225-3176. Also 334 Meeting St., Charleston, 803-577-4171.

Administrative Assistant W. Mullins McLeod

Committees

Armed Services (22nd); Sub: No. 4.

Internal Security (5th).

Group Ratings

	ADA	COPE	LWV	RIPON	NFU	LCV	CFA	NAB	NSI	ACA
1972	13	75	38	50	100	1	0	30	100	53
1971	22	63	56	15	64	–	29	–	–	57

Key Votes

1) Busing	AGN	6) Cmbodia Bmbg	FOR	11) Chkg Acct Intrst	AGN
2) Strip Mines	ABS	7) Bust Hwy Trust	AGN	12) End HISC (HUAC)	AGN
3) Cut Mil $	AGN	8) Farm Sub Lmt	ABS	13) Nixon Sewer Veto	AGN
4) Rev Shrg	AGN	9) School Prayr	FOR	14) Corp Cmpaign $	ABS
5) Pub TV $	FOR	10) Cnsumr Prot	AGN	15) Pol $ Disclosr	ABS

Election Results

1972 general:	Mendel J. Davis (D)	61,625	(54%)
	J. Sidi Limehouse (R)	51,469	(46%)
1972 primary:	Mendel J. Davis (D)	37,493	(72%)
	Benjamin Fraser (D)	11,247	(22%)
	Milton L. Dukes (D)	3,093	(6%)
1971 special:	Mendel J. Davis (D)	38,012	(49%)
	James Edwards (R)	32,227	(41%)
	Victoria DeLee (Ind.)	7,965	(10%)

SECOND DISTRICT Political Background

Between the coastal swamps and the industrialized Piedmont of South Carolina, square in the middle of the state, lies the capital, Columbia. This is South Carolina's largest city (pop. 113,000) and its fastest growing. Like so many comparable cities in the South, Columbia is becoming more and more Republican. In some quarters, the trend is attributed to an influx of Northerners, especially business executives, who presumably bring their Republican politics with them. But such is surely not the case in Columbia, nor with many other Southern cities. The migration to Columbia is mostly from the smaller towns and rural areas of South Carolina, upwardly mobile people taking white-collar jobs in state government, insurance, and banking. Uprooted from their traditionally Democratic, rural environment, and thrust up several notches in social class, the migrants usually find the state's Republicans younger, more modern, and hence more congenial than old-style South Carolina Democrats. So Columbia and its all-white suburbs, particularly those in Lexington County, have become a bastion of South Carolina Republicanism.

Columbia, with its suburbs in Richland and Lexington counties, casts between 70% to 75% of the votes in the state's 2nd congressional district. The remainder comes from an older part of South Carolina: the near black-majority counties closer to the coast. The largest town here is Orangeburg (pop. 13,000), where white highway patrolmen massacred several black students at South Carolina State College in 1968. These lower counties usually go Democratic, but of course are heavily outvoted by Columbia and environs.

For eight years, from 1963 to 1971, the 2nd was represented by Albert Watson, a flamboyant conservative. In 1964, Watson, though a Democrat, openly supported Barry Goldwater for President. As a result, Congressman Watson and Mississippi Congressman John Bell Williams were stripped of their seniority by the Democratic Caucus. As it was, Watson had relatively little seniority, so he resigned his office, campaigned for reelection as an out-and-out Republican, and won. Thereafter he retained his seat until he ran for Governor in 1970—an ill-fated bid that saw him lose to moderate Democrat John West (see statewide write-up).

Watson's successor in the House is the man he beat in the 1962 Democratic primary, Floyd Spence, who, like Watson, is now a Republican. Spence's 1970 victory was a narrow one; he ran not much ahead of Watson and won with only 53% of the votes. But after two years in office and a seat on the Armed Services Committee—a good spot to tend to the needs of Columbia's Fort Jackson—Spence won reelection in 1972 unopposed in either the primary or general election. A genial man with the views of a solid right-winger, Spence should have no trouble winning reelection in the future.

Census Data Pop. 446,267. Central city, 25%; suburban, 47%. Median family income, $7,900; families above $15,000: 14%; families below $3,000: 15%. Median years education, 11.4.

1972 Share of Federal Outlays $525,523,992

DOD	$210,420,000	HEW	$143,946,926
AEC	$82,964	HUD	$10,746,750
NASA	$99,896	DOI	$1,850,523
DOT	$14,962,062	USDA	$44,536,746
		Other	$98,878,125

Federal Military-Industrial Commitments

DOD Installations Fort Jackson AB (Columbia).

Economic Base Finance, insurance and real estate; agriculture, notably poultry, grains and dairy products; textile mill products; and apparel and other textile products. Also higher education (Univ. of South Carolina).

The Voters

Registration 188,995 total. 131,851 white (70%); 81 other (–). No party registration.
Median voting age 37.7
Employment profile White collar, 47%. Blue collar, 36%. Service, 14%. Farm, 3%.
Ethnic groups Black, 34%. Total foreign stock, 3%.

Presidential vote

1972	Nixon (R)	85,637	(69%)
	McGovern (D)	37,756	(31%)
1968	Nixon (R)	48,621	(42%)
	Humphrey (D)	37,542	(33%)
	Wallace (AI)	28,848	(25%)

Representative

Floyd D. Spence (R) Elected 1970; b. April 9, 1928, Columbia; home, Lexington; U. of S.C., B.A., 1952, LL.B., 1956; USNR, Korean War; Cpt. USNR; married, four children; Lutheran.

Career Practicing atty., S.C. House of Reps., 1956–62; S.C. Senate, 1966–68, Minority Leader, 1966–70; Chm., Jt. Senate-House Com. to Investigate Communist Activities in S.C., 1967–70; Sunday school teacher.

Offices 120 CHOB, 202-225-2452. Also 509 Fed. Bldg., Sumpter St., Columbia 29201, 803-765-5871, and 372 St. Paul St. N.E., Orangeburg 29115, 803-536-4641.

Administrative Assistant W. A. Cook

Committees

Armed Services (10th); Subs: No. 1; No. 3.

Standards of Official Conduct (5th).

Group Ratings

	ADA	COPE	LWV	RIPON	NFU	LCV	CFA	NAB	NSI	ACA
1972	0	11	25	38	40	7	50	90	100	95
1971	0	18	11	7	29	–	0	–	–	92

Key Votes

1) Busing	AGN	6) Cmbodia Bmbg	FOR	11) Chkg Acct Intrst	AGN
2) Strip Mines	AGN	7) Bust Hwy Trust	AGN	12) End HISC (HUAC)	AGN
3) Cut Mil $	AGN	8) Farm Sub Lmt	AGN	13) Nixon Sewer Veto	FOR
4) Rev Shrg	FOR	9) School Prayr	FOR	14) Corp Cmpaign $	FOR
5) Pub TV $	AGN	10) Cnsumr Prot	AGN	15) Pol $ Disclosr	AGN

Election Results

1972 general:	Floyd D. Spence (R), unopposed		
1972 primary:	Floyd D. Spence (R), nominated by district convention		
1970 general:	Floyd D. Spence (R)	48,093	(53%)
	Heyward McDonald (D)	42,005	(46%)
	Donald R. Cole (Ind.)	486	(1%)

THIRD DISTRICT Political Background

As one moves inland from the South Carolina coast, one sees fewer and fewer black people. It is a matter of history and agricultural economics. The land along the coast is ideal for growing crops like rice and cotton, which require much labor; so the early planters kept thousands of slaves. Inland, the terrain is hilly, the rainfall less plentiful, and the soil less fertile; the tradition here is of one-family farms, few of which could afford to support slaves. And so, while many of the still-rural counties along the coast are near majority-black, the citizenry of the Piedmont country of the 3rd congressional district is 77% white.

The 3rd is an upcountry district, lying mostly along the Savannah River, the boundary with Georgia. The southern part of the district is Strom Thurmond territory: he grew up in Edgefield and maintains his residence in Aiken, a prosperous AEC city that lies halfway between Columbia and Augusta, Georgia. Like the Senator, Aiken and Edgefield are solidly Republican these days. The counties farther upriver remain traditionally Southern Democratic. George Wallace ran especially well here in 1968. Anderson, a heavily white textile town and the most populous city in the district (pop. 27,000), was the largest South Carolina city Wallace carried in 1968.

William Jennings Bryan Dorn has represented the 3rd district in Congress continuously since the 1950 election. Very early on, Dorn was a politician. He was 23 when he was elected to the state House of Representatives, 25 when first chosen for the state Senate, and 30 when first elected to Congress in 1946. Dorn tried and failed to win a senate seat in 1948, and then returned to the House in 1950. He is now Chairman of the Veteran's Affairs Committee, but only the eighth-ranking Democrat on Public Works, which he joined relatively late in his congressional career.

At 58, Dorn has reportedly decided to end his stay in Congress and run for Governor. He is gambling. Dorn's record resembles that of incumbent Gov. John West: conservative-to-moderate on social issues, sometimes liberal on bread-and-butter economic issues. In 1970, West won with only 52% of the votes. Moreover, Dorn will encounter strenuous opposition in the general election and quite possibly in the Democratic primary. Meanwhile, the seat in the 3rd district is likely to stay in Democratic, and relatively conservative, hands.

Census Data Pop. 434,427. Central city, 0%; suburban, 35%. Median family income, $8,002; families above $15,000: 10%; families below $3,000: 13%. Median years education, 10.1.

1972 Share of Federal Outlays $348,309,426

DOD	$32,918,802	HEW	$109,711,382
AEC	$127,646,954	HUD	$2,130,290
NASA	$6,847	DOI	$1,471,519
DOT	$5,728,286	USDA	$23,310,373
		Other	$45,384,973

Federal Military-Industrial Commitments

DOD Contractors C.M. London Co. (Anderson), $7.429m: unspecified.
AEC Operations Dupont (Aiken), $115.776m: operation of Savannah River plant; design, production of plutonium and tritium for weapons program and operation of nuclear reactors.

Economic Base Textile mill products, especially cotton weaving mill products; apparel and other textile products; agriculture, notably poultry, dairy products and cattle; and finance, insurance and real estate. Also higher education (Clemson Univ.).

The Voters

Registration 169,576 total. 143,001 white (84%); 26,558 black (16%); 17 other. No party registration.
Median voting age 42.1
Employment profile White collar, 32%. Blue collar, 56%. Service, 10%. Farm, 2%.
Ethnic groups Black, 23%. Total foreign stock, 1%.

Presidential vote

1972	Nixon (R)	84,401	(77%)
	McGovern (D)	24,723	(23%)
1968	Nixon (R)	41,678	(36%)
	Humphrey (D)	26,585	(23%)
	Wallace (AI)	47,223	(41%)

Representative

William Jennings Bryan Dorn (D) Elected 1950; b. April 14, 1916, Greenwood; home, Greenwood; Army Air Force, WWII; married, five children; Baptist.

Career S.C. Legislature, 1939–40; S.C. Senate, 1941–42; U.S. House of Reps., 1946–48; Staff of *U.S. News and World Report.*

Offices 2256 RHOB, 202-225-5301. Also 124 Fed. Bldg., Greenwood 29646, 803-223-8251.

Administrative Assistant Edward Poliakoff

Committees

Public Works (8th); Subs: Economic Development; Energy; Transportation; Water Resources.

Veterans' Affairs (Chm.).

Group Ratings

	ADA	COPE	LWV	RIPON	NFU	LCV	CFA	NAB	NSI	ACA
1972	19	27	45	29	67	2	0	36	100	67
1971	22	67	88	39	62	–	0	–	–	46
1970	16	34	–	24	38	3	60	58	100	56

Key Votes

1) Busing	FOR	6) Cmbodia Bmbg	FOR	11) Chkg Acct Intrst	AGN
2) Strip Mines	FOR	7) Bust Hwy Trust	AGN	12) End HISC (HUAC)	AGN
3) Cut Mil $	AGN	8) Farm Sub Lmt	AGN	13) Nixon Sewer Veto	FOR
4) Rev Shrg	FOR	9) School Prayr	AGN	14) Corp Cmpaign $	FOR
5) Pub TV $	AGN	10) Cnsumr Prot	AGN	15) Pol $ Disclosr	AGN

Election Results

1972 general:	W. J. Bryan Dorn (D)	82,579	(75%)
	Roy A. Ethridge (R)	27,173	(25%)
1972 primary:	W. J. Bryan Dorn (D), unopposed		
1970 general:	W. J. Bryan Dorn (D)	60,708	(75%)
	H. Grady Ballard (R)	19,981	(25%)

FOURTH DISTRICT Political Background

The major textile-producing area in the United States is a strip of land lying along Interstate 85 in North and South Carolina. Two of the biggest textile centers here are Greenville and Spartanburg in South Carolina. These two cities, along with the counties that surround them, make up the state's 4th congressional district. There is, in fact, little industry in the hills of the piedmont, aside from textiles. The mills are sited not just in the two cities here, but scattered about in small towns and in the countryside along major highways—near the workers, many of whom still live on small farms. Few blacks reside in the 4th—only 18% district-wide—the lowest percentage in South Carolina. But there are even fewer union members. South Carolina has the least unionized work force of any state in the nation. Conditions in the mills are apparently no source of pride among local residents; according to some reports, mill hands, both men and women, are often the victims of on-the-job alcoholism and pill-popping.

Politically, Greenville and Spartanburg have different traditions. Greenville (pop. 61,000) is South Carolina's premier Republican city. Plenty of textile management personnel live here. The city also sports a local establishment that includes Judge Clement Haynsworth and Donald Russell. Haynsworth still serves on the Fourth Circuit federal court of appeals after his rejection for a seat on the Supreme Court; Russell is an ex-Governor (1963–66) and U.S. Senator (1966–67) and now a federal judge. Spartanburg (pop. 45,000) is a rougher, more blue-collar town, traditionally Democratic. Its most famous citizen was the late Governor (1935–39, 1943–45) and Senator (1945–66) Olin Johnston, who was something of an oldtime Southern populist.

Despite the two traditions, the 4th today is the most Republican district in South Carolina. It manifests its Republicanism not just in presidential elections, where Democratic nominees have received precious few white votes since 1964, but also in statewide contests. Only in House elections do the 4th's voters return to the Democratic column to reelect Congressman James Mann, a charter member of the Greenville establishment. Mann was first elected in 1968 to succeed Robert Ashmore, whom he has also succeeded as Greenville County Solicitor (prosecutor).

In 1971, Congressman Mann, concerned about Japanese textile imports, inserted the lyrics of a folk song called "The Import Blues" into the *Congressional Record*. Written by a constituent, the song contained terms like "Jap," "sleazy," and "slant-eyed." Hawaii's Patsy Mink, a Congresswoman of Japanese decent, confronted Mann on the floor about the insertion. Mann replied that he could not see how any real American could take offense; the song was directed at foreigners. Besides, he continued, any expression of ethnic loyalty was bad for America. Mann later apologized, though nobody back in South Carolina, it seems, heard about it.

The Congressman serves as one of the more conservative members of the House Judiciary Committee. He could conceivably win a judgeship some day. In the meantime, he appears reasonably sure of reelection. Mann had opposition in 1972 for the first time in four years, and won with 66% of the votes against a Republican candidate. The Congressman thus ran a clean 46% ahead of George McGovern in the 4th district of South Carolina.

Census Data Pop. 414,270. Central city, 15%; suburban, 43%. Median family income, $8,416; families above $15,000: 13%; families below $3,000: 11%. Median years education, 10.8.

1972 Share of Federal Outlays $218,443,221

DOD	$32,629,197	HEW	$101,701,498
AEC	–	HUD	$8,505,445
NASA	$27,963	DOI	$490,588
DOT	$3,488,976	USDA	$15,566,362
		Other	$56,033,192

Federal Military-Industrial Commitments

No installations or contractors receiving prime awards greater than $5,000,000.

Economic Base Textile mill products, especially cotton and synthetic weaving mill products; apparel and other textile products; finance, insurance and real estate; machinery, especially special industry machinery; and chemicals and allied products.

The Voters

Registration 154,660 total. 134,370 white (87%); 20,273 black (13%); 17 other. No party registration.
Median voting age 41.5
Employment profile White collar, 39%. Blue collar, 49%. Service, 11%. Farm, 1%.
Ethnic groups Black, 18%. Total foreign stock, 2%.

Presidential vote

1972	Nixon (R)	77,547	(80%)
	McGovern (D)	19,702	(20%)
1968	Nixon (R)	49,835	(47%)
	Humphrey (D)	24,395	(23%)
	Wallace (AI)	32,587	(31%)

Representative

James Robert Mann (D) Elected 1968; b. April 27, 1920, Greenville; home, Greenville; The Citadel, B.A., 1941; U. of S.C., LL.B., 1947; Army, WWII; Col. USAR; married, four children; Baptist.

Career Practicing atty.; S.C. Legislature, 1949–52; Solicitor, 13th Judicial Circuit of S.C., 1953–63.

Offices 1117 LHOB, 202-225-6030. Also P.O. Box 10011, Fed. Station, Greenville 29603, 803-232-1141, and Spartanburg 29301, 803-582-6422.

Administrative Assistant Mrs. Elizabeth Seeley

Committees

District of Columbia (9th); Subs: Business, Commerce, and Taxation; Judiciary.

Judiciary (11th); Subs: No. 2 (Claims); Sp. Sub. on Reform of Federal Criminal Laws.

Select Com. on Crime (4th).

Group Ratings

	ADA	COPE	LWV	RIPON	NFU	LCV	CFA	NAB	NSI	ACA
1972	0	0	36	57	43	11	50	92	100	90
1971	8	17	22	38	33	–	29	–	–	84
1970	4	9	–	27	36	0	71	67	100	75

Key Votes

1) Busing	AGN	6) Cmbodia Bmbg	AGN	11) Chkg Acct Intrst	AGN
2) Strip Mines	AGN	7) Bust Hwy Trust	AGN	12) End HISC (HUAC)	AGN
3) Cut Mil $	AGN	8) Farm Sub Lmt	AGN	13) Nixon Sewer Veto	FOR
4) Rev Shrg	FOR	9) School Prayr	FOR	14) Corp Cmpaign $	FOR
5) Pub TV $	AGN	10) Cnsumr Prot	AGN	15) Pol $ Disclosr	FOR

Election Results

1972 general:	James R. Mann (D)	64,989	(66%)
	Wayne N. Whatley (R)	33,363	(34%)
1972 primary:	James R. Mann (D), unopposed		
1970 general:	James R. Mann (D), unopposed		

FIFTH DISTRICT Political Background

Stock-car racing, one of the nation's most popular spectator sports, thrives best today in places like the 5th district of South Carolina. After World War II, New England textile mills fled to shiny new factories on the outskirts of small towns like Rock Hill and Gaffney in South Carolina. Here plenty of people were eager to work long hours for low wages under poor conditions, and few of them had any funny ideas about joining a union. In the textile towns and their outskirts, whites heavily outnumber blacks, though in some smaller, less developed counties, blacks still constitute a near majority of the population. But the political spirit that prevails in the 5th district is best symbolized by the fan at the stock-car races—the yahooing, white Southerner whom W. J. Cash called a "hell of a fellow." The 5th is a traditionally Democratic district, but it was one of two South Carolina districts to go for George Wallace in 1968, and would again if he were to run.

Democrat Thomas Gettys has been the 5th's Congressman since the 1964 election, when he succeeded Robert Hemphill, who had been appointed a federal judge. Gettys has enjoyed an interesting career, redolent of an earlier era. He even served as Postmaster of Rock Hill for three years and is surely the last Postmaster—now that Postal Service has been depoliticized—to serve in Congress. Around Washington, Gettys is known as the "invisible man," having made little impact on the legislative process. As a member of the Banking and Currency Committee, the Congressman usually supports the positions taken by the big banks. He was also one of the Democrats who cast a decisive vote against holding an investigation of the Watergate business in October 1972.

If Gettys is invisible in Washington, he appears little more than that back home in the 5th. His share of the votes has been dropping steadily, from 75% in 1968, to 66% in 1970, and to 61% in 1972. He has not encountered primary opposition recently, but he might well be vulnerable in such a contest. If Gettys does not choose to retire in 1974 (he is 62), he will probably be the number-two target for the South Carolina Republicans. (The number-one man is Mendel Davis of the 1st district.)

Census Data Pop. 441,907. Central city, 0%; suburban, 0%. Median family income, $7,623; families above $15,000: 9%; families below $3,000: 15%. Median years education, 9.8.

1972 Share of Federal Outlays $277,048,785

DOD	$85,995,000	HEW	$102,567,879
AEC	–	HUD	$2,655,309
NASA	–	DOI	$530,020
DOT	$9,795,982	USDA	$31,815,022
		Other	$43,689,573

Federal Military-Industrial Commitments

DOD Installations Shaw AFB (Sumter).

Economic Base Textile mill products, especially cotton weaving mill products; apparel and other textile products; agriculture, notably poultry and grains; and finance, insurance and real estate.

The Voters

Registration 178,678 total. 134,590 white (75%); 44,005 black (25%); 83 other (–). No party registration.
Median voting age 41.2
Employment profile White collar, 30%. Blue collar, 56%. Service, 12%. Farm, 2%.
Ethnic groups Black, 32%. Total foreign stock, 1%.

Presidential vote

1972	Nixon (R)		78,994	(71%)
	McGovern (D)		32,044	(29%)
1968	Nixon (R)		39,722	(34%)
	Humphrey (D)		33,705	(29%)
	Wallace (AI)		43,635	(37%)

Representative

Thomas Southwick Gettys (D) Elected Nov. 4, 1964; b. June 19, 1912, Rock Hill; home, Rock Hill; Clemson U.; Erskine Col., B.A. 1933; Duke U., Winthrop Col.; Navy, WWII; married, two children; Presbyterian.

Career Teacher, coach, Rock Hill High School, 1933–35; Principal, Rock Hill, 1935–41; Sec. Rep. Richards, 1941–51; Postmaster, Rock Hill, 1951–54; practicing atty., 1954–64.

Offices 2412 RHOB, 202-225-5501. Also Box 707 Fed. Bldg., Rock Hill 29730, 803-327-4729, and Fed. Bldg., Sumter 29150, 803-775-2943.

Administrative Assistant John Bankhead

Committees

Banking and Currency (12th); Subs: Domestic Finance; Small Business; Urban Mass Transportation; Personnel.

House Administration (8th); Subs: Accounts; Printing; Police; Contracts (Chm.); Library and Memorials.

Group Ratings

	ADA	COPE	LWV	RIPON	NFU	LCV	CFA	NAB	NSI	ACA
1972	0	27	11	44	67	20	—	60	100	65
1971	5	42	11	13	57	–	0	–	–	75
1970	8	27	–	12	25	38	69	44	88	62

Key Votes

1) Busing	AGN	6) Cmbodia Bmbg	FOR	11) Chkg Acct Intrst	AGN
2) Strip Mines	FOR	7) Bust Hwy Trust	AGN	12) End HISC (HUAC)	AGN
3) Cut Mil $	AGN	8) Farm Sub Lmt	AGN	13) Nixon Sewer Veto	AGN
4) Rev Shrg	AGN	9) School Prayr	FOR	14) Corp Cmpaign $	FOR
5) Pub TV $	FOR	10) Cnsumr Prot	ABS	15) Pol $ Disclosr	AGN

Election Results

1972 general:	Tom S. Gettys (D)	66,343	(61%)
	B. Leonard Phillips (R)	42,620	(39%)
1972 primary:	Tom S. Gettys (D), unopposed		
1970 general:	Tom S. Gettys (D)	43,742	(67%)
	B. Leonard Phillips (R)	21,911	(33%)

SIXTH DISTRICT Political Background

The 6th district of South Carolina takes in the northeastern corner of the state, where the Pee Dee and Santee rivers flow. It is a region of tobacco farms, textile mills, and ocean beaches. Most of the 6th's residents and voters live in and around textile towns like Florence and Darlington, the latter the site of the Southern 500 stock-car race. But the district is not nearly as white as the state's other textile districts. Some of the lowland counties here have black-majority populations and near black-majorities among its registered voters. Altogether, some 42% of the people of the 6th, and 36% of its over-18 population, are black.

The fact that blacks now comprise, or can comprise if they get out and vote, one-third of the electorate in the district, has made for a kind of minor revolution in the politics of the 6th. It is the only district is South Carolina—indeed, the only predominantly rural district in the entire South—to have gone for Hubert Humphrey in 1968, though by a narrow margin in a very close three-man contest. In 1972, it cast a larger share of its votes for George McGovern the any other South Carolina district. That share came to only 32%, however, an indication that few whites here voted for McGovern and that the black turnout has declined since 1968. And, far more important, in 1972 the 6th district ousted its Congressman of 34 years and allowed a major change in congressional policy toward an area of concern quite removed from local events—the governance of the District of Columbia.

The Congressman ousted was John L. McMillan, first elected in 1938 and, aside from the years the Republicans controlled the House, the Chairman of the House District of Columbia Committee since 1948. More important to the 6th district, McMillan by 1972 had risen to become the number-two Democrat on the House Agriculture Committee. Here he had plenty of power to influence matters of interest regarding the 6th's most important product—tobacco. Marlboro County is part of the 6th district, while Chesterfield is part of the adjoining 5th.

But it was probably McMillan's policy toward the District of Columbia that got his opponents into the race, though once in, they were eager to criticize his record on tobacco. McMillan was one of the classic tyrannical committee chairmen. He called meetings when he wanted to, refused to recognize members who held opposing views, and controlled subcommittee staff so tightly that one subcommittee Chairman, William Hungate of Missouri, resigned from the D.C. Committee in frustration. Though Washington became a black-majority city in the mid-1950s, McMillan was determined to maintain white control. No home-rule bill was ever reported out of his committee. The issue reached the floor in 1965, only to be defeated, after a discharge petition was signed by a majority of the members of the House. In other matters, McMillan was also a thoroughgoing conservative, and unlike many younger Congressmen, did little constituency work. There was even some dispute about his age. For many years, McMillan listed the year of his birth as 1898; then in the 1971 *Congressional Directory*, he reported the proper year as 1902.

McMillan was seriously challenged, for the first time, in 1970. The Congressman encountered three opponents in the Democratic primary, who together held him to just below 50%. The totals meant that he had to face the number-two finisher, Dr. Claude Stephens, in the runoff. The veteran politician was not accustomed to such indignities, but because Dr. Stephens was black, McMillan did not have much trouble winning. In 1972, however, the competition was tougher. Running for a chance to face the incumbent in the runoff were Bill Craig, a lawyer who had just missed second place in 1970, and state Rep. John Jenrette of Horry County (Myrtle Beach). Both men were a good bit more liberal than the average South Carolina Democrat. This time the challengers held McMillan to 44% of the votes, with Jenrette second with 29%. In the runoff, Jenrette won the vast majority of the black votes, and made inroads into McMillan's strength in his heavily white home county of Florence as well as in Darlington County. The combination was enough for an 845-vote Jenrette victory. McMillan muttered about recount, but the result stood.

Meanwhile, South Carolina's canny Republicans were not asleep. For years they had not contested the McMillan seat seriously. The Republicans felt that he was unbeatable, or believed, in any case, that they were poorly positioned to appeal for the black votes needed to win. But in 1972, the Republican nominee, Edward Young—a wealthy farmer from Florence—was prepared to wage a vigorous general election campaign. He attacked Jenrette as a liberal. And of course Young did not need to say to his white audiences that the Democrat had the overwhelming support of black voters.

It is true these days in the South—and Jenrette's primary victory is further evidence for the case—that black support is no longer an automatic kiss of death in a white-majority constituency. But it can still hurt. The result in the 6th was a 10,000-vote, 54–46 Young victory. The South Carolina Republicans elected their third Congressman, and their first outside the 2nd district since Reconstruction. Young is reportedly in good shape for 1974, though both Jenrette and Craig may run again. Apparently John McMillan, whatever his real age, has no desire to return to the House shorn of his seniority.

Census Data Pop. 410,999. Central city, 0%; suburban, 0%. Median family income, $6,203; families above $15,000: 9%; families below $3,000: 23%. Median years education, 9.7.

1972 Share of Federal Outlays $288,790,738

DOD	$56,992,000	HEW	$96,455,664
AEC	–	HUD	$4,790,369
NASA	–	DOI	$141,299
DOT	$9,744,054	USDA	$72,105,717
		Other	$48,561,635

Federal Military-Industrial Commitments

DOD Installations Myrtle Beach AFB (Myrtle Beach).

Economic Base Agriculture, notably tobacco, grains, and hogs and sheep; textile mill products; apparel and other textile products; finance, insurance and real estate; and lumber and wood products.

The Voters

Registration 171,885 total. 114,467 white (67%); 57,381 black (33%); 37 other (–). No party registration.
Median voting age 42.0
Employment profile White collar, 33%. Blue collar, 43%. Service, 13%. Farm, 11%.
Ethnic groups Black, 42%. Total foreign stock, 1%.

Presidential vote

1972	Nixon (R)	76,985	(68%)
	McGovern (D)	36,846	(32%)
1968	Nixon (R)	34,438	(32%)
	Humphrey (D)	38,072	(35%)
	Wallace (AI)	34,834	(32%)

Representative

Edward L. Young (R) Elected 1972; b. Sept. 7, 1920, Florence; home, Florence; Clemson Col., B.S., 1941; Air Force, WWII; married, four children; Protestant.

Career Dairy Farmer, Pres., Cable Dairy; Chm., Pee Dee Production Credit Assn.; Chm., Fed. Land Bank in Florence; Program Host and Director, WBTW-TV; State Rep., 1958–62.

Offices 516 CHOB, 202-225-3315. Also P.O. Drawer 1660, Florence 29501, 803-665-7828, and 210 Elm St., Conway 29569, 803-248-2283.

Administrative Assistant LaRose Smith

Committees

Agriculture (14th); Subs: Cotton; Tobacco; Family Farms and Rural Development.

Merchant Marine and Fisheries (15th); Subs: Coast Guard and Navigation; Oceanography; Merchant Marine.

Group Ratings: Newly Elected

Key Votes

1) Busing	NE	6) Cmbodia Bmbg	FOR	11) Chkg Acct Intrst	AGN
2) Strip Mines	NE	7) Bust Hwy Trust	AGN	12) End HISC (HUAC)	AGN
3) Cut Mil $	NE	8) Farm Sub Lmt	NE	13) Nixon Sewer Veto	AGN
4) Rev Shrg	NE	9) School Prayr	NE	14) Corp Cmpaign $	NE
5) Pub TV $	NE	10) Cnsumr Prot	NE	15) Pol $ Disclosr	NE

Election Results

1972 general:	Edward L. Young (R)	63,527	(54%)
	John W. Jenrette, Jr. (D)	53,324	(46%)
1972 primary:	Edward L. Young (R), nominated by district convention		

SOUTH DAKOTA

Political Background

South Dakota was once the heartland of the Sioux Indians, who roamed the plains hunting buffalo. Then the white man came and exterminated the buffalo and, in places like Wounded Knee, many of the Indians. Those who survived were herded onto reservations. Today, South Dakota has one of the highest Indian populations in the nation; one of twenty South Dakotans is an American Indian. As the Wounded Knee crisis of 1973 showed, proximity does not necessarily produce amity. There is as much anti-Indian feeling among whites in South Dakota as there is anywhere in the United States.

The Black Hills gold rush brought the first white settlers to the state. Men like Wild Bill Hickock, America's first dime-novel hero, made legends in mining towns like Deadwood, Lead, and Spearfish, and then, as the rich veins of ore petered out, moved on. They left behind the plains, which were slowly being peopled by homesteaders. Some of them were of Scandinavian stock, moving over from Minnesota; but most were WASPs from Nebraska, Iowa, and points east. South Dakota experienced most of its population growth during two decades of agricultural prosperity—1880–1890, and 1900–1910; the decade between the two, the 1890s, was a period of drought and depression. By 1910, the population of the state had reached seven-eighths of the current figure.

By 1910, the political character of South Dakota had also been set. During the 1890s, the state flirted briefly with Populism and William Jennings Bryan, but by the turn of the century, South Dakota had become almost as monolithically Republican as Nebraska. So later, South Dakotans never had much use for the radical, socialistic ideas of the Non-Partisan League, which enjoyed considerable success among the immigrant Scandinavians and Volga Germans of North Dakota.

As in other states of the Great Plains, voters in South Dakota have been chronically dissatisfied with the farm programs of national administrations, Republican and Democratic alike. But until very recently, that dissatisfaction seldom dented the state's commitment to Republican politics. Between 1936 and 1970, South Dakota sent only one Democrat—George McGovern—to Congress, and elected only one Democratic Governor, Ralph Herseth, who won a two-year term in 1958.

Then, suddenly, in 1970, there was a startling shift in the state's voting patterns. Democrats were elected to the governorship and both of South Dakota's two congressional seats. The Democratic success was the result of a sharp disillusionment with the farm policies of the Nixon Administration, the unpopularity of the incumbent Governor, and the retirement of both of the state's two Republican Congressmen. But the Democratic trend had been set in motion long before, in 1953, when George McGovern, then a professor at Dakota Wesleyan College, became the operating head of the nearly defunct South Dakota Democratic party.

The McGovern story is doubtless more familiar now than it was to readers of the first *Almanac*: how the preacher's son drove his beat-up car over back roads to set up Democratic county organizations, how he ran for Congress himself in 1956 and upset an overconfident incumbent hurt by the farm policies of Ezra Taft Benson, and how he was reelected in 1958 and then ran a close but losing race against Sen. Karl Mundt in 1960. After the loss, McGovern became head of the Food-for-Peace program in the Kennedy Administration, quit that post following the death of Sen. Francis Case to run for the Senate again in 1962, and beat Gov. Joe Bottum by 597 votes.

McGovern then became known as one of the Senates's leading advocates of peace in Vietnam, the co-sponsor of the McGovern-Hatfield Amendment to end the war, and a peace candidate for President in 1968 and 1972. But back in South Dakota, McGovern was from the start, and is now, best known for his views on agricultural policy.

The economy of the Senator's state is one almost totally dependent on agriculture; in fact, some 24% of its people still live on farms, more than any other state except North Dakota. McGovern has always been an outspoken advocate of the family farm and federal programs to insure an adequate income for the family farmer. He is now the third-ranking Democrat on the Senate Agriculture Committee, and quietly played a role in drafting the new income-maintenance farm program of 1973. That role will help McGovern when he faces the voters of South Dakota again in 1974.

Ironically, the year 1972, the one in which McGovern was a landslide loser nationally, was also the one in which his South Dakota Democratic party had its greatest triumphs. It is true, of course, that McGovern failed to carry his home state, but he did get 46% of the votes here—a performance better than anywhere except the District of Columbia, Massachusetts, Minnesota, and Rhode Island. And the rest of the Democratic ticket did fine in South Dakota. Gov. Richard Kneip was reelected with 60% of the votes, an unprecedented margin for a Democrat here; Kneip is expected to win again in 1974, provided he can get a court ruling allowing him a third term. Lt. Gov. William Dougherty, who spent most of his time with McGovern and the national campaign, was reelected by a margin nearly as large as Kneip's. Democrats also won the offices of Attorney General, Secretary of State, Commissioner of Schools and Public Lands, and Public Utilities Commissioner. Finally, they captured a one-man advantage in the state Senate and an even split of the seats in the South Dakota House.

Nationally, however, the most significant aspect of the Democratic sweep was the Senate victory of Congressman James Abourezk (*AB-or-esk*). Five years ago, Abourezk was an obscure lawyer in Rapid City, the son of an immigrant Lebanese Indian trader and not long out of the University of South Dakota Law School. In 1970, Abourezk secured the Democratic nomination for the 2nd district's seat in Congress. In these parts, that is not usually a great political prize; but to get it Abourezk did have to beat 28-year-old Donald Barnett, who later received some national publicity as Mayor of Rapid City when the disastrous flood of 1972 struck. But Abourezk ran into some good luck in 1970. Republican Congressman E. Y. Berry, a 20-year incumbent, decided to retire. The Republicans then decided to run Fred Brady, whose proposal to set up compulsory youth camps to teach "decency and respect for the law" was too much even for some South Dakota conservatives. Abourezk defeated Brady 52–48.

Ordinarily, election by a skinny margin would have simply positioned Abourezk for a tough reelection struggle two years later. But ordinary was not a word that fit the South Dakota situation in 1972. George McGovern, of course, was busy running for President. Meanwhile, senior Senator Karl Mundt, a conservative Republican, lay incapacitated by a stroke; he failed to appear in the Senate from 1969 until his term expired after the 1972 elections. McGovern's campaigning and Mundt's condition gave Abourezk an opening. Soon the Congressman began to provide South Dakotans the kind of constituency service they had come to expect from their Senators. He made personal appearances all over the state. And through personal contact, which is so important in South Dakota politics, Abourezk's quick and often self-deprecating sense of humor overcame the qualms many voters had about the Congressman's solidly liberal record. As the 1972 Senate campaign began, Abourezk was far ahead in the polls. He easily won the Democratic nomination over a former state party chairman, and then almost as easily defeated the colorless Republican nominee, Robert Hirsch, former state Senate Majority Leader.

Abourezk's election transferred the South Dakota seat from one of the Senate's most conservative members (Mundt) to one of its most liberal. Always a vigorous opponent of the Vietnam war, Abourezk was among the few Senators who voted against virtually all Nixon appointees as the 93rd Congress opened. From McGovern, he took over the chairmanship of the Senate's Indian Affairs Subcommittee, and emerged a stronger advocate of Indian rights than McGovern ever was. Such advocacy, of course, is not the safest political position to assume in South Dakota. Nevertheless, even as Abourezk broke all the traditional customs prescribed for getting along with the South Dakota electorate, he grew ever more popular politically. His main concern sometimes appeared to be insuring the reelection of McGovern, whom he has always warmly supported.

The Senate race will be South Dakota's main political event in 1974. McGovern has never gone into a South Dakota race as the favorite, and in early 1973, it appeared as if he might again have problems. A POW colonel, a recent migrant from Minnesota, began to make anti-McGovern speeches in the state and talked about running. There were also a host of other Republicans interested in a shot at McGovern. Meanwhile, as the Watergate revelations began to get headlines, the Senator said almost nothing. Instead of talking to the national media, he was going back home every weekend to campaign. He also quietly used the mailing lists that had financed his presidential campaign and raised more than $400,000 by the summer of 1973—quite enough for a campaign in South Dakota. As McGovern continued to talk personally to the voters, his position grew more secure. In a small state, one-to-one campaigning is entirely possible, and is also the most effective means of winning votes.

McGovern's comment in 1972 that the Nixon Administration was the most corrupt in history was not one well-received by sophisticated Washington observers. But today everyone, including the people of South Dakota, has second thoughts. At this writing, McGovern's big problem is his attitude toward the Indians of the state. At one point, McGovern and Abourezk met briefly with the occupiers of Wounded Knee; the Senators tried to mediate the differences the Indians had with federal authorities. But many, perhaps most, South Dakotans simply wanted to see the troops go in with guns blazing. Nevertheless, if any sizable number of South Dakota Nixon voters feel that McGovern, though not suitable for the Presidency, is a good Senator, then McGovern is sure to win reelection.

South Dakota still has two congressional districts. But because its population continues to decline, the state will probably lose one of its seats after the 1980 census. The 1st district is the eastern edge of South Dakota and includes its largest city, Sioux Falls (pop. 72,000). The 1st is slightly more urban and also more Democratic than the 2nd. But in both districts, the usual political patterns found in the Northern industrial states are reversed. Here in South Dakota, the towns, not the countryside, provide the bulk of the Republican votes. The small businessmen, salesmen, and bankers in places like Brookings (pop. 13,000) and Watertown (pop. 13,000) are ordinarily more prosperous and more Republican than the farmers they service.

The 1st district was the one that sent George McGovern to the Congress in 1956 and 1958. It then included all of South Dakota east of the Missouri River. When McGovern stepped down to challenge Karl Mundt in 1960, the seat was captured by Republican Ben Reifel, who held it until he retired 10 years later. In the 1970 general election, Democrat Frank Denholm, a Brookings lawyer, upset Republican Dexter Gunderson, former Speaker ot the state House. Congressman

Denholm, an ex-FBI agent, is not as liberal as McGovern nor as flamboyant as Abourezk. During his first term, he quietly tended to the problems of his constituents and to the details of farm policy on the House Agriculture Committee. He was rewarded for his service when he received 60% of the votes and easy reelection in 1972. Denholm appears almost certain to become the first South Dakota Democrat to win a third House term in modern times.

The 2nd congressional district takes in some of the state's most fertile land east of the Missouri River. Here is McGovern's home town of Mitchell, famous also for its Corn Palace. This is a huge and remarkable structure, decorated with corn-cob mosaics; from a distance, it is most properly described as a cross between the Kremlin and the Taj Mahal. West of the Missouri, rainstorms are less common and the soil is more barren. Western South Dakota is more cattle-grazing than corn and hog country. Cattlemen are among the nation's most conservative occupational groups, and the cattlemen here make the 2nd district a bit more conservative then the 1st. The 2nd also includes almost all of South Dakota's Indians, who cast very heavy Democratic margins. The largest city in the district is Rapid City (pop. 43,000), which is not far from the scenic Badlands, the Black Hills, and Mount Rushmore.

From 1971 to 1973, Sen. Abourezk was the 2nd's Congressman. When he vacated the seat to run for the Senate, the district—once considered utterly Republican—was thrown wide open. Unopposed for the Democratic nomination was Pat McKeever, a former McGovern aide. But the race here, along with McGovern's loss of his home state, wound up the major disappointments for South Dakota Democrats in what was otherwise an exhilarating year. The Republican nominee was ex-Lt. Gov. (1969–70) James Abdnor, who had just narrowly missed winning the 1970 Republican primary. If Abdnor, rather than Mr. Brady—the youth-camps man—had won that primary, Abourezk might never have made it to Congress at all.

Abdnor bucked the Democratic tide and won, 55–45, over McKeever. The new Congressman is a conservative. During the Wounded Knee crisis, Abdnor urged that the troops be sent in immediately—an index of his feelings toward issues. It is hard to say whether Abdnor can make the seat safely Republican again. It appears, however, that he is not interested in running for Governor or Senator in 1974. If Abnor stays to protect his seat, his toughest competion would probably come from Rapid City Mayor Donald Barnett.

Census Data Pop. 666,257; 0.33% of U.S. total, 44th largest; change 1960–70, –2.1% Central city, 11%; suburban, 3%. Median family income, $7,490; 44th highest; families above $15,000: 12%; families below $3,000: 15%. Median years education, 12.1.

1972 Share of Federal Tax Burden $480,740,000; 0.23% of U.S. total, 46th largest.

1972 Share of Federal Outlays $854,722,035; 0.39% of U.S. total, 43rd largest. Per capita federal spending, $1,283.

DOD	$128,655,000	45th (0.21%)	HEW	$241,273,256	42nd (0.34%)
AEC	$25,000	47th (—)	HUD	$5,986,002	46th (0.20%)
NASA	$10,600	48th (—)	VA	$53,180,039	40th (0.46%)
DOT	$46,938,816	41st (0.60%)	USDA	$246,496,828	24th (1.60%)
DOC	$2,461,310	44th (0.19%)	CSC	$10,704,389	45th (0.26%)
DOI	$44,798,745	15th (2.11%)	TD	$31,795,542	41st (0.19%)
DOJ	$2,643,361	48th (0.27%)	Other	$39,753,147	

Economic Base Agriculture, notably cattle, hogs, wheat and dairy products; finance, insurance and real estate; food and kindred products, especially meat packing plants; printing and publishing, especially newspapers; metal mining, especially lode gold; tourism.

Political Line-up Governor, Richard F. Kneip (D); seat up, 1974. Senators, George McGovern (D) and James Abourezk (D). Representatives, 2 (1 D and 1 R). State Senate (18 D and 17 R); State House (35 D and 35 R).

The Voters

Registration 392,256 Total. 158,816 D (40%); 195,737 R (50%); 37,703 other (10%).
Median voting age 45.3
Employment profile White collar, 41%. Blue collar, 22%. Service, 15%. Farm, 22%.
Ethnic groups Indian, 5%. Total foreign stock, 16%. Germany, 4%.

Presidential vote

1972	Nixon (R)	166,476	(54%)
	McGovern (D)	139,945	(46%)
1968	Nixon (R)	149,841	(53%)
	Humphrey (D)	118,023	(42%)
	Wallace (AI)	13,400	(5%)
1964	Johnson (D)	163,010	(56%)
	Goldwater (R)	130,108	(44%)

Senator

George McGovern (D) Elected 1962, seat up 1974; b. July 19, 1922, Avon; home, Mitchell; Dakota Wesleyan U., B.A., 1945; Northwestern U., M.A., 1949, Ph.D., 1953; Army Air Corps, WWII; married, five children; Methodist.

Career Professor, Dakota Wesleyan U., 1949–53; Exec. Sec., S.D. Dem. Party, 1953–56; U.S. House of Reps., 1957–61;Sp. Asst. to Pres. Kennedy and Dir. of Food for Peace, 1961–62; Dem. candidate for Pres. 1972.

Offices 2313 NSOB, 202-225-2321. Also 108 E. Third, P.O. Box 1061, Mitchell 57301, 605-996-7563.

Administrative Assistant George V. Cunningham

Committees

Agriculture and Forestry (3rd); Subs: Agricultural Credit and Rural Electrification (Chm.); Agricultural Production, Marketing, and Stabilization of Prices; Agricultural Research and General Legislation; Foreign Agricultural Policy.

Foreign Relations (9th); Subs: European Affairs; Far-Eastern Affairs; South Asian Affairs (Chm.); U.S. Security Agreements and Commitments Abroad.

Sel. Com. on Nutrition and Human Needs (Chm.).

Group Ratings

	ADA	COPE	LWV	RIPON	NFU	LCV	CFA	NAB	NSI	ACA
1972	45	100	100	78	100	74	100	0	0	0
1971	96	75	90	63	100	–	100	–	–	9
1970	84	100	–	75	100	79	–	8	0	5

Key Votes

1) Busing	ABS	8) Sea Life Prot	ABS	15) Tax Singls Less	FOR
2) Alas P-line	AGN	9) Campaign Subs	FOR	16) Min Tax for Rich	ABS
3) Gun Cntrl	FOR	10) Cmbodia Bmbg	AGN	17) Euro Troop Rdctn	ABS
4) Rehnquist	AGN	11) Legal Srvices	ABS	18) Bust Hwy Trust	FOR
5) Pub TV $	FOR	12) Rev Sharing	FOR	19) Maid Min Wage	FOR
6) EZ Votr Reg	FOR	13) Cnsumr Prot	FOR	20) Farm Sub Limit	ABS
7) No-Fault	FOR	14) Eq Rts Amend	ABS	21) Highr Credt Chgs	FOR

Election Results

1968 general:	George S. McGovern (D)	158,961	(57%)
	Archie Gubbrud (R)	120,951	(43%)
1968 primary:	George S. McGovern (D), unopposed		
1962 general:	George S. McGovern (D)	127,458	(50%)
	Joe Bottum (R)	126,861	(50%)

Senator

James G. Abourezk (D) Elected 1972, seat up 1978; b. Feb. 24, 1931, Wood; home, Rapid City; S.D. School of Mines, B.S., 1961, U. of S.D. Law School, J.D., 1966; Navy, 1948–52; married, three children; Syrian Orthodox.

Career Practicing atty.; Partner, LaFleur & Abourezk, Rapid City, 1966–70; Bd. of Dir., West River Mental Health Center; Western S.D. Community Action Agency; Black Hills Consumers League; Rosebud Legal Aid Program; U.S. House, 1971–73.

Offices 1105 NSOB, 202-225-5842. Also P.O. Box 1606, Sioux Falls, 605-339-2880.

Administrative Assistant Peter Stavrianos

Committees

Aeronautical and Space Science (6th).

Interior and Insular Affairs (6th); Subs: Indian Affairs (Chm.); Public Lands; Territories and Insular Affairs.

Sel. Com. on Small Business (8th); Subs: Environmental, Rural, and Urban Economic Development; Monopoly; Retailing, Distribution, and Marketing Practices.

Group Ratings

	ADA	COPE	LWV	RIPON	NFU	LCV	CFA	NAB	NSI	ACA
1972	63	100	90	58	100	71	0	14	0	13
1971	97	82	78	76	100	–	100	–	–	7

Key Votes

1) Busing	FOR	8) Sea Life Prot	MOS	15) Tax Singls Less	MOS
2) Alas P-line	AGN	9) Campaign Subs	MOS	16) Min Tax for Rich	MOS
3) Gun Cntrl	FOR	10) Cmbodia Bmbg	AGN	17) Euro Troop Rdctn	MOS
4) Rehnquist	AGN	11) Legal Srvices	AGN	18) Bust Hwy Trust	FOR
5) Pub TV $	FOR	12) Rev Sharing	FOR	19) Maid Min Wage	FOR

Election Results

1972 general:	James Abourezk (D)	174,773	(57%)
	Robert Hirsch (R)	131,613	(43%)
1972 primary:	James Abourezk (D)	46,931	(79%)
	George Blue (D)	12,163	(21%)

FIRST DISTRICT

Census Data Pop. 333,107. Central city, 22%; suburban, 7%. Median family income, $7,695; families above $15,000: 12%; families below $3,000: 14%. Median years education, 12.1.

1972 Share of Federal Outlays $339,649,160

DOD	$13,299,000	HEW	$117,028,208
AEC	$25,000	HUD	$5,229,002
NASA	$5,000	DOI	$16,386,801
DOT	$20,341,214	USDA	$106,964,956
		Other	$60,369,976

Federal Military-Industrial Commitments

No installations or contractors receiving prime awards greater than $5,000,000.

Economic Base Agriculture, notably cattle, hogs and sheep, and grains; food and kindred products, especially meat products; and finance, insurance and real estate.

The Voters

Registration 200,509 total. 78,651 D (39%); 101,095 R (50%); 20,758 other (10%).
Median voting age 45.5
Employment profile White collar, 42%. Blue collar, 23%. Service, 16%. Farm, 19%.
Ethnic groups Indian, 1%. Total foreign stock, 18%. Germany, 4%.

Presidential vote

1972	Nixon (R)	80,576	(51%)
	McGovern (D)	76,932	(49%)
1968	Nixon (R)	75,400	(53%)
	Humphrey (D)	61,801	(43%)
	Wallace (AI)	5,513	(4%)

Representative

Frank Edward Denholm (D) Elected 1970; b. Nov. 29, 1923, Andover; home, Brookings; S.D. State U., B.S., 1956; U. of S.D. Law School, J.D., 1962; U. of Minn.; married; Catholic.

Career Farmer; auctioneer; interstate truck transportation business, 1945–53; Sheriff, Day County, 1950–52; FBI Agent, U.S. Dept. of Justice, 1956–60; practicing atty., 1962– ; Lecturer in economics, law, pol. sci., S.D. State U., 1962–66; Corporate Counsel for cities of Brookings, Volga, White, 1962–71.

Offices 1321 LHOB, 202-225-2801. Also 418 Fourth St., Brookings 57006, 605-692-2102.

Administrative Assistant Arthur O. Anderson

Committees

Agriculture (14th); Subs: Livestock and Grains; Domestic Marketing and Consumer Relations; Department Operations.

Group Ratings

	ADA	COPE	LWV	RIPON	NFU	LCV	CFA	NAB	NSI	ACA
1972	38	82	60	36	100	36	0	22	40	52
1971	68	82	78	63	93	–	100	–	–	14

Key Votes

1) Busing	AGN	6) Cmbodia Bmbg	FOR	11) Chkg Acct Intrst	AGN
2) Strip Mines	AGN	7) Bust Hwy Trust	AGN	12) End HISC (HUAC)	AGN
3) Cut Mil $	FOR	8) Farm Sub Lmt	AGN	13) Nixon Sewer Veto	AGN
4) Rev Shrg	AGN	9) School Prayr	AGN	14) Corp Cmpaign $	AGN
5) Pub TV $	FOR	10) Cnsumr Prot	FOR	15) Pol $ Disclosr	AGN

Election Results

1972 general:	Frank E. Denholm (D)	94,442	(61%)
	John Vickerman (R)	61,589	(39%)
1972 primary:	Frank E. Denholm (D), unopposed		
1970 general:	Frank E. Denholm (D)	71,636	(56%)
	Dexter H. Gunderson (R)	56,330	(44%)

SECOND DISTRICT

Census Data Pop. 333,150. Central city, 0%; suburban, 0%. Median family income, $7,283; families above $15,000: 11%; families below $3,000: 16%. Median years education, 12.1.

1972 Share of Federal Outlays $515,072,875

DOD	$115,356,000	HEW	$124,245,048
AEC	–	HUD	$757,000
NASA	$5,600	DOI	$28,411,944
DOT	$26,597,602	USDA	$139,531,872
		Other	$80,167,809

Federal Military-Industrial Commitments

DOD Contractors Boeing (Ellsworth AFB), $17.624m: unspecified. Boeing (Rapid City), $9.888m: unspecified.
DOD Installations Ellsworth AFB (Rapid City).

Economic Base Agriculture, notably cattle, grains, and hogs and sheep; finance, insurance and real estate; and food and kindred products, especially meat products.

The Voters

Registration 191,747 total. 80,160 D (42%); 94,642 R (49%); 16,945 other (9%).
Median voting age 45.1
Employment profile White collar, 40%. Blue collar, 21%. Service, 15%. Farm, 24%.
Ethnic groups Indian, 8%. Total foreign stock, 15%. Germany, 4%.

Presidential vote

1972	Nixon (R)	85,900	(58%)
	McGovern (D)	62,013	(42%)
1968	Nixon (R)	74,441	(54%)
	Humphrey (D)	56,222	(41%)
	Wallace (AI)	7,887	(6%)

Representative

James Abdnor (R) Elected 1972; b. Feb. 13, 1923, Kennebec; home, Kennebec; U. of Nebraska, B.A.; single; Methodist.

Career Farmer; former school teacher and coach; State Senator, 1956–69, Pres. Pro Tem., 1967–69; Lt. Gov., S.D., 1969–71.

Offices 1230 LHOB, 202-225-5165. Also Box 151, Mitchell 57301, 605-996-3601, and 439 Fed. Bldg., Pierre 57501, 605-224-2891, and Box 1365, Huron 57350, 605-352-5117, and Box 930, Rapid City 57701, 605-343-5000.

Administrative Assistant Philip N. Hogen

Committees

Public Works (14th); Subs: Economic Development; Energy; Public Buildings and Grounds; Water Resources.

Veterans' Affairs (9th); Subs: Education and Training; Hospitals; Insurance.

Group Ratings: Newly Elected

Key Votes

1) Busing	NE	6) Cmbodia Bmbg	FOR	11) Chkg Acct Intrst	AGN
2) Strip Mines	NE	7) Bust Hwy Trust	AGN	12) End HISC (HUAC)	AGN
3) Cut Mil $	NE	8) Farm Sub Lmt	NE	13) Nixon Sewer Veto	AGN
4) Rev Shrg	NE	9) School Prayr	NE	14) Corp Cmpaign $	NE
5) Pub TV $	NE	10) Cnsumr Prot	NE	15) Pol $ Disclosr	NE

Election Results

1972 general:	James Abdnor (R)	79,546	(55%)
	Patrick McKeever (D)	65,415	(45%)
1972 primary:	James Abdnor (R)	31,780	(65%)
	Mike DeMersseman (R)	17,312	(35%)

TENNESSEE

Political Background

Tennessee currently represents the number-one success story for the Republican party in the South. For the first time in its history, Tennessee has two Republican Senators, a Republican Governor, and a majority-Republican delegation in the House of Representatives. In 1968, Richard Nixon carried the state with just a fraction under 38%, his smallest winning percentage; but in 1972, of course, Nixon triumphed here easily. The Republican upsurge in Tennessee during the 1960s and early 1970s is a story of talented young men overthrowing the remnants of a once-vigorous Democratic hierarchy. It is not yet clear whether the Republican talent in the state possesses the depth its Democratic predecessors lacked, but at the moment, the Republicans are probably in better shape here than in any state in the Union.

Any study of Tennessee politics should begin with topography. The state is divisible into three distinct sections, each with its own history and political inclination. East Tennessee is part of the Appalachian chain, an area populated almost completely by white mountaineers. East Tennessee produced Andrew Johnson, Lincoln's vice-presidential choice and successor. It was against secession in 1861, and has since remained one of the most Republican areas of the entire nation. The Republicanism of the mountaineers has usually been matched by the Democratic leaning of middle Tennessee. This is a region of hilly farmland which, in rough terms, lies between the lower Tennessee River and the Appalachians. Middle Tennessee was the home of Andrew Jackson, the first President to call himself a Democrat, and since Jackson's time, the area has remained Democratic in practically every election. West Tennessee, the flat cotton-lands along the Mississippi River, was the part of the state with the largest slave-tended plantations. Like middle Tennessee, it has been Democratic by tradition. Lately, however, west Tennessee has begun to vote much more like the rest of the Deep South. When middle Tennessee stayed with the national Democratic party in 1964, west Tennessee moved toward the Goldwater candidacy.

Urban-rural differences have not been nearly as important in Tennessee as elsewhere. The state's four large cities vote more like the rural territory around them than like each other. Recently, Memphis, with a large black vote, has been slightly less conservative than the rest of west Tennessee, while Chattanooga, on the Georgia border, is traditionally less Republican than east Tennessee. But the political behavior of Nashville and Knoxville is virtually indistinguishable from the rural counties around them. In general, the cities are gaining more political importance; in 1964, the four major urban counties cast 42% of the states votes; in 1972, 46%.

So long as middle and west Tennessee remained strongly Democratic, the Republicans were unable to win a statewide election, no matter how many votes the party of Lincoln piled up in east Tennessee. Between Reconstruction and the 1960s, the allegiances created by the Civil War were forsaken only twice: once in the 1920 Harding landslide, when a Republican Governor was elected, and again in 1928 when Protestant Tennessee rejected Catholic Al Smith for Calvin Coolidge. Even the initial impact of the civil rights issues failed to shake the old patterns of political preference. The state's two Senators during the 1950s and 1960s, Estes Kefauver and

Albert Gore, had both come to office as liberal reformers. Both of them beat aged veterans supported by the equally aged Crump machine in Memphis. And both Kefauver and Gore supported, or a least failed to oppose very strenuously, civil rights legislation. Moreover, neither of them came close to defeat during this period. The decisive battle, it appears, occurred in the 1960 primary, when Kefauver took an overwhelming 65% against a hard-line, well-financed segregationist opponent.

Kefauver had long since won national fame for his investigations of organized crime—the first nationally televised congressional hearings. Overnight, the Tennessee Senator became a major presidential contender, and won several presidential primaries in 1952. But he could not overcome the support Adlai Stevenson had among the power brokers of the Democratic party. Trying again in 1956, Kefauver left the race and wound up as Stevenson's running mate, after edging out John F. Kennedy in a convention floor free-for-all. The last years of Kefauver's career were devoted to reform of the nation's drug laws. His tough bill, once gutted by lobbyists, was suddenly resurrected and passed in the wake of the publicity given the thalidomide tragedies.

Kefauver died in 1963. For his seat, there followed two spirited battles in the 1964 and 1966 Democratic primaries between Gov. Frank Clement and Rep. Ross Bass. It was like the old days, when winning the Democratic primary was tantamount to victory. But times were changing. The civil rights issues had begun to make conservatives out of many of the state's traditional Democrats—people who used to be more concerned about the TVA and the price of farm commodities than about race. Lyndon Johnson carried the state with just 55% of the votes, while Sen. Albert Gore was reelected with 54%. And in the other Senate race, a young east Tennessee lawyer named Howard Baker, Jr., came within 50,000 votes of upsetting Congressman Bass.

Baker was then only 38, with a prosperous law practice and a fine political pedigree. Both his father (1951–63) and stepmother (1963–65) served as Republican Representatives from the 2nd district; moreover, Baker's father-in-law was none other than Everett McKinley Dirksen. Earlier, Baker passed up a chance to run in his parents' old district; instead, he assembled an able, young organization for the 1964 Senate bid. Baker's campaign used the latest sophisticated techniques. It was not the sort of affair, traditional in Tennessee, of coming around to a town and swapping stories with old courthouse regulars. Unlike so many Southern Republicans, however, Baker did not exploit the civil rights issue. He could easily have done so, because his opponent, Bass, was one of the few Southern Congressmen who had voted for the Civil Rights Act of 1964.

Baker was well prepared for another Senate campaign effort in 1966. Longtime Governor Frank Clement (1953–58 and 1963–66) defeated Bass this time in the Democratic primary. The nominee was still a young man who nonetheless personified the old virtues—and new liabilities—of traditional Tennessee Democrats. It was not so much Clement's moderate liberalism that hurt him, it was his style. Those who can recall his keynote speech at the 1956 Democratic National Convention remember his arm-waving, lecturn-thumping, florid oratorical style. The speech was the kind that used to liven up a hot afternoon on the courthouse square, but in the age of television campaigning, it was obsolete. So, long before commentators began to talk about the youth and peace vote, Howard Baker had sewed up the young vote in Tennessee—not just in the growing cities, but in the countryside as well. Viewers of the Watergate hearings know that Baker's demeanor is not one of an arm-waver. Baker defeated Clement in 1966, with 56% of the votes.

The Watergate hearings have made Baker something of a media star and a possible presidential candidate—a summer 1973 poll showed the Tennessee Senator running ahead of Edward Kennedy, 45–44. The way Baker got where he is tells us something about the way he operates. In early 1973, as the Senate considered ways to set up the Watergate committee, it was Baker who carried the ball for the Republicans. He backed amendments that would provide equal representation for each party on the committee, and tried to stretch the committee's mandate to cover Democratic practices in 1964 and 1968. Running with the Republican ball was not out of the Senator's character. In 1969, Baker, though only a freshman, was considered sufficiently partisan to enjoy the support of most conservative Republican Senators for the post of Minority Leader. He lost to Pennsylvania's supposedly more liberal Hugh Scott, then Whip, by a narrow 24–19 margin. And on most major issues, Baker took a conservative, pro-Nixon approach to things. For example, he consistently supported the Administration policy in Southeast Asia, and he slammed away at the Administration's media critics from his post on the Senate Commerce Committee.

There is, however, another side to Baker, which manifested itself during the Watergate hearings. He likes to reason carefully and speak a solemn lawyer-like language. And Baker is open to persuasion. Back when his father-in-law Everett Dirksen was still Minority Leader, pushing for a constitutional repeal of the one-man-one-vote formula, Baker worked with Edward Kennedy on the opposite side of the issue—and won. In 1973, aside from his Watergate duties, he co-sponsored (with Edmund Muskie, fellow member of the Public Works Committee) a bill to allow states to divert money from the highway trust fund for mass-transit projects. The legislation went through at long last, though it opens only a small crack in the heretofore sacrosanct trust fund.

So if Baker usually takes the positions of a conventional conservative, he does not have a conventional mind. As he questioned Watergate witnesses, he probed constantly at personal motivation. So persistent was his almost philosophical line of inquiry that some found the approach tiresome. Baker worked closely with Chairman Sam Ervin. And though he tried to find areas of accommodation between the committee and the White House, Baker himself moved that the committee take legal action to secure the Nixon tapes.

But perhaps what most impressed TV viewers was Baker's boyish appearance—he kept reminding the audience that he had practiced law for 20 years. What was also most impressive was the clarity and precision with which he ad libbed questions and witty responses. Baker is surely presidential timber. But at this writing, he must, if he is ever to win the nomination, satisfy both the Republicans who believe their President and the general public, which is no longer buying used cars in Nixon's lot. The political pitfalls that Baker and other Watergate committee members face when writing their report are indeed legion. It is so difficult to gauge the effects of the language to be used that one can easily believe Baker when he says he will simply do what he thinks is right, without regard to political consequences.

Four of the members of the Watergate committee are up for reelection in 1974. Only Baker is fresh from a reelection victory in 1972, which was his easiest race. He ran a well-financed and superbly organized campaign, his young campaign group humming. Baker's most serious problem was the race issue. The Democratic challenger, Congressman Ray Blanton, did not criticize Baker's work on the passage of the 1968 fair housing act, but Blanton did come down on busing. In the Senate, Baker had supported anti-busing measures. But Baker, like the Democratic Senators who preceded him, had selected the federal judges who wrote major busing decisions—notably the one for Nashville, the state's second-largest (and most Democratic) city. Blanton's anti-busing strategy—tinged with a little populism—turned out to be a dud. The Democrat, unable to raise much money, lost even Democratic middle Tennessee. Meanwhile, Baker won about 40% of the black votes and picked up many white votes never before received by a Tennessee Republican. The phenomenal 62–38 victory means that Baker will have no more trouble winning elections in Tennessee.

Neither, it seems likely, will junior Senator Bill Brock, the millionaire heir to a candy fortune. In 1962, Brock was elected Congressman in a 3rd-district upset. He held on to his House seat, and then went after Sen. Albert Gore in 1970. The confrontation was a classic one, between Gore, the old-style populistic liberal, and Brock, the sleek, media-created conservative.

Gore—"the old grey fox" one Tennessee Republican called him—had been around a long time. First elected to the House in 1938, he moved up to the Senate in 1952. He was a dirt farmer's son who worked up through county politics and campaigned for Congress by playing a fiddle in country towns. Later, as a member of the Senate Finance Committee, Gore was one of the chief advocates of the little man against the big interests; most notably, the Senator pushed for progressive tax reform and higher Social Security benefits.

But in 1970, Gore was vulnerable. During the mid-1960s, he had become a critic of the Vietnam war—a stand not particularly popular in hell-of-a-fellow Tennessee. Moreover, the Senator had openly proclaimed his support of civil rights legislation, voted against the Haynsworth and Carswell nominations, and cast votes against the ABM and SST. Vice-President Agnew thereupon called Gore the number-one target of the Nixon Administration—a designation Gore acknowledged with pride. The Senator even welcomed Agnew to Tennessee when the Vice-President arrived at the Memphis airport to denounce him. During the campaign, Republican orators were wont to follow Agnew's theme; they liked to call Gore the third Senator from Massachusetts—a reference perhaps to Edward Brooke, the black Senator from the New England state.

A shy man and a poor speaker, Brock hired Kenneth Rietz as his campaign manager; Rietz was out of the Harry (*Selling of the President 1968*) Treleaven political consulting firm. Brock, of course, had plenty of money and a good organization based on the Baker model. Everything looked like a set-up for the challenger. In 1968, Hubert Humphrey—who took roughly the same stands on issues as Gore—won only 28% of Tennessee's votes, as George Wallace carried traditionally Democratic middle and west Tennessee. So Brock's barrage of TV ads attacked Gore as a backer of school busing, an opponent of school prayer, and in general a traitor to the South. But the old grey fox fought back. He cited Brock's votes in the House against Medicare and the Appalachia program, and then boasted of his own record on the issues.

It was a struggle, as Tom Wicker said, between attitudes and interests, and, as usual these days, attitudes won. Gore ran well in east Tennessee, though of course he failed to carry it, and held his own in middle Tennessee. But in west Tennessee, which has the state's largest black population and the most intense racial animosities, Gore ran 8% behind his 1964 showing. All in all, Brock won the election with 51% of the votes. Probably more than any other sitting Senator, Brock owes his place in the Senate to shrewd exploitation of racial fears and prejudices.

That is not, of course, the image Brock likes to project. According to rumors, Brock was a possible presidential candidate for a time in 1972 and 1973. The speculation started when he was appointed head of the Committee to Reelect's youth campaign. In that role, with the aid of his former campaign manager, Rietz, who ran the operation, Brock helped to produce a much higher percentage of the youth vote for Nixon than anyone had expected—most likely an absolute majority of those under 30. Brock's experiences in 1972 led him to buck most other Senate Republicans and to back the 1973 measure to allow the post-card registration of voters. He was convinced—and there is much evidence to support him—that a large percentage of those a little too apathetic to register otherwise would, if they voted, form part of Richard Nixon's New Majority.

After the 1972 election, Brock clearly became a favorite at the Nixon-Haldeman White House. He was named Chairman of the Senate Republican Campaign Committee. Moreover, his protégé Rietz was hired to run the New Majority campaign of the Republican National Committee. The Rietz operation was to recruit young conservative candidates for the 1974 congressional elections. Some muttered that the two groups developed into branches of the Brock-for-President drive.

Nevertheless, Brock began to get favorable notices in the press. As the Watergate cover-up unraveled, Brock came out with a set of compaign reform proposals. These included a ban on large cash contributions and a requirement that all contributions be channeled through a single bank account. Brock's reforms were plausible ones. Then, suddenly, bad publicity engulfed the Brock surge. First, it was reported that Brocks's former campaign manager Rietz was responsible for hiring at least one undercover agent to infiltrate the McGovern campaign. Second, Brock himself was shown to have a financial interest in a land-development scheme that allegedly employed fraudulent advertising. The scheme was the type regulated by HUD, whose affairs Brock supervised as a member of the Senate Banking, Housing, and Urban Affairs Committee.

No one has proven any wrongdoing on Brock's part. He apparently left the details of the Youth for President drive to Rietz, and had nothing to do with the management of the real estate business. Nevertheless, Brock's reputation was tarnished enough to stop all further presidential talk. Moreover, once the cameras closed in on the Watergate hearings, it became clear that if Tennessee was to have a presidential candidate, Howard Baker was the man. At this writing, Brock appears reasonably sure of winning reelection in 1976, but he will have to postpone any plans he may have had for higher office until some more propitious time.

In 1974, the main event in Tennessee politics is the gubernatorial contest. Winfield Dunn is not eligible for reelection; he is the Memphis dentist who became the state's first Republican Governor in 48 years. The list of possible contenders, both Democratic and Republican, is too long to recount here. The important question is whether the Republican party of Howard Baker and Bill Brock will sustain its dominance of the state's politics. Republican margins in Tennessee looked a little shaky in 1970, but 1972 was the party's best year yet. The Republicans not only carried the statewide races, they picked up a congressional seat even as the state lost one in the 1970 census. The taking of an additional seat looks all the more impressive because the redistricting plan was drawn by the Democratic legislature and effected over Gov. Dunn's veto.

To be sure, six of the eight districts as redrawn had shown Democratic margins in the 1970 congressional elections. But those advantages stemmed from popular incumbents running in areas switched to other districts; an unfamilar Democrat running in the same areas could not sustain the margins received by incumbent Democrats. In the end, the Republicans held two seats that looked shaky on paper (the 3rd and the 8th) and captured another held by a Democrat (the 6th). The

1972 elections marked the first time that the Republicans had ever won a majority of the state's House delegation. It was also a classic example of a redistricting plan backfiring on its creators.

The Democratic party of Estes Kefauver and Albert Gore has now virtually disappeared from Tennessee politics. Why? Because of a lack of depth. The brightest people in the party, it seems, went to Washington or became federal judges. Those left were tobacco-chewing old-timers who could not compete for young votes in statewide elections featuring sleek Republicans like Baker, Brock, and Dunn. Do the Republicans have any more depth themselves? The answer, so far, is yes. For example, Robin Beard, the new Congressman from the 6th, is one of the dozens of talented, attractive young men groomed for public office by the Baker-Brock-Dunn organizations. There are plenty of others—people like Fred Thompson, the minority counsel on the Watergate committee. Tennessee Republicans have so far been unable to win control of the state legislature. They have, however, come close, despite Democratic redistricting plans. For the future, one can point to the race run by a state legislator elected from Memphis. He was the president of the Memphis State University student body chosen for the state House with the support of both blacks and students—and a Republican.

Census Data Pop. 3,924,164; 1.94% of U.S. total, 17th largest; change 1960–70, 10.0%. Central city, 35%; suburban, 14%. Median family income, $7,447; 45th highest; families above $15,000: 12%; families below $3,000: 17%. Median years education, 10.7.

1972 Share of Federal Tax Burden $3,051,670,000; 1.46% of U.S. total, 21st largest.

1972 Share of Federal Outlays $3,937,902,212; 1.82% of U.S. total, 18th largest. Per capita federal spending, $1,004.

DOD	$671,953,000	27th (1.08%)	HEW	$1,231,190,187	18th	(1.72%)
AEC	$321,827,413	2nd (12.28%)	HUD	$66,869,927	16th	(2.18%)
NASA	$1,130,567	33rd (0.04%)	VA	$255,931,422	15th	(2.24%)
DOT	$139,643,282	22nd (1.77%)	USDA	$497,899,947	9th	(3.24%)
DOC	$9,863,393	25th (0.76%)	CSC	$50,247,917	22nd	(1.22%)
DOI	$9,239,101	38th (0.44%)	TD	$123,260,419	19th	(0.75%)
DOJ	$13,219,457	29th (1.35%)	Other	$545,626,180		

Economic Base Apparel and other textile products, especially men's and boys' furnishings; agriculture, notably cattle, dairy products, soybeans and tobacco; finance, insurance and real estate; chemicals and allied products, especially plastics materials and synthetics; electrical equipment and supplies, especially household appliances; food and kindred products; textile mill products, especially knitting mills.

Political Line-up Governor, Winfield Dunn (R); seat up, 1974. Senators, Howard H. Baker, Jr. (R) and William E. Brock (R). Representatives, 8 (5 R and 3 D). State Senate (18 D, 13 R, and 1 AI); State House (51 D and 49 R).

The Voters

Registration 1,990,026 Total. No party registration.
Median voting age 42.7
Employment profile White collar, 41%. Blue collar, 42%. Service, 13%. Farm, 4%.
Ethnic groups Black, 16%. Total foreign stock, 2%.

Presidential vote

1972	Nixon (R)	813,147	(69%)
	McGovern (D)	357,293	(31%)
1968	Nixon (R)	472,592	(38%)
	Humphrey (D)	351,233	(28%)
	Wallace (AI)	424,792	(34%)
1964	Johnson (D)	635,047	(55%)
	Goldwater (R)	508,965	(45%)

Senator

Howard H. Baker, Jr. (R) Elected 1966, seat up 1978; b. Nov. 15, 1925, Huntsville; home, Huntsville; Tulane U., U. of the South; U. of Tenn. Law Col., LL.B., 1949; Navy, WWII; Lt. USNR; married, two children; Presbyterian.

Career Practicing atty., 1949–66.

Offices 2107 NSOB, 202-225-4944. Also 1002 P.O. Bldg., Memphis 38101, 901-534-3861, and 313 P.O. Bldg., Knoxville 37901, 615-546-5486, and U.S. Courthouse, 801 Broadway, Nashville 37201, 615-749-5129, and 204 Fed. Bldg., Chattanooga 37402, 615-266-3151, and Tri-Cities Airport, Blountville, 37617, 615-323-6243.

Administrative Assistant Hugh Branson

Committees

Commerce (4th); Subs: Aviation; Communications (Ranking Mbr.); Foreign Commerce and Tourism; Environment; Surface Transportation.

Public Works (Ranking Mbr.); Sub: Air and Water Pollution.

Sel. Com. on Presidential Campaign Activities (Ranking Mbr.).

Joint Com. on Atomic Energy (4th); Subs: Communities; Military Applications; Energy; Licensing and Regulation; Security (Ranking Senate Mbr.).

Group Ratings

	ADA	COPE	LWV	RIPON	NFU	LCV	CFA	NAB	NSI	ACA
1972	0	13	50	40	40	0	0	40	100	71
1971	4	27	50	39	30	–	0	–	–	55
1970	13	18	–	36	45	54	–	78	100	89

Key Votes

1) Busing	AGN	8) Sea Life Prot	ABS	15) Tax Singls Less	FOR
2) Alas P-line	FOR	9) Campaign Subs	AGN	16) Min Tax for Rich	ABS
3) Gun Cntrl	AGN	10) Cmbodia Bmbg	ABS	17) Euro Troop Rdctn	AGN
4) Rehnquist	FOR	11) Legal Srvices	ABS	18) Bust Hwy Trust	FOR
5) Pub TV $	AGN	12) Rev Sharing	FOR	19) Maid Min Wage	ABS
6) EZ Votr Reg	AGN	13) Cnsumr Prot	AGN	20) Farm Sub Limit	AGN
7) No-Fault	AGN	14) Eq Rts Amend	FOR	21) Highr Credt Chgs	FOR

Election Results

1972 general:	Howard H. Baker, Jr. (R)	716,539	(62%)
	Ray Blanton (D)	440,599	(38%)
	Dan East (Ind.)	7,026	(1%)
1972 primary:	Howard H. Baker, Jr. (R)	242,373	(93%)
	Hubert Patly (R)	7,581	(3%)
1966 general:	Howard H. Baker, Jr. (R)	483,063	(56%)
	Frank G. Clement (D)	383,843	(44%)

Senator

William Emerson Brock III (R) Elected 1970, seat up 1976; b. Nov. 23, 1930, Chattanooga; home, Chattanooga; Washington and Lee U., B.S., 1953; Navy, 1953–56; Lt. USNR; married, four children; Presbyterian.

Career V. Pres., Brock Candy Co., 1956–62; Chm., Natl. Teen Com., 1961; U.S. House of Reps., 1963–71.

Offices 254 OSOB, 202-225-3344. Also 230 Fed. Bldg., Chattanooga 37402, 615-266-3151, and Fed. Bldg., Knoxville 37901, 615-749-5176, and Fed. Bldg., Nashville 37201, 615-532-0992, and 102 Jackson State Bank, Jackson, 901-424-8021, and Fed. Bldg., Memphis 38103, 901-534-3686.

Administrative Assistant Robert E. Bradford

Committees

Banking, Housing and Urban Affairs (5th); Subs: Financial Institutions; Consumer Credit (Ranking Mbr.); International Finance.

Government Operations (6th); Subs: Intergovernmental Relations; Budgeting, Management, and Expenditures.

Group Ratings

	ADA	COPE	LWV	RIPON	NFU	LCV	CFA	NAB	NSI	ACA
1972	0	0	14	47	17	11	0	88	100	88
1971	0	17	10	30	11	–	0	–	–	93

Key Votes

1) Busing	AGN	8) Sea Life Prot	AGN	15) Tax Singls Less	AGN
2) Alas P-line	FOR	9) Campaign Subs	AGN	16) Min Tax for Rich	AGN
3) Gun Cntrl	FOR	10) Cmbodia Bmbg	FOR	17) Euro Troop Rdctn	AGN
4) Rehnquist	FOR	11) Legal Srvices	AGN	18) Bust Hwy Trust	FOR
5) Pub TV $	AGN	12) Rev Sharing	FOR	19) Maid Min Wage	AGN
6) EZ Votr Reg	AGN	13) Cnsumr Prot	AGN	20) Farm Sub Limit	AGN
7) No-Fault	ABS	14) Eq Rts Amend	FOR	21) Highr Credt Chgs	FOR

Election Results

1970 general:	William E. Brock III (R)	562,645	(51%)
	Albert Gore (D)	519,858	(47%)
	Cecil R. Pitard (AI)	8,691	(1%)
	Dan R. East (Ind.)	5,845	(1%)
1970 primary:	William E. Brock III (R)	176,703	(75%)
	Tex Ritter (R)	54,401	(23%)
	James Durelle Boles (R)	4,942	(2%)

FIRST DISTRICT Political Background

The 1st district of Tennessee is the far northeast corner of the state. Most of it is an extension of the Shenendoah Valley of Virginia and the Blue Ridge Mountains of the Appalachian chain. In fact, the district is closer to Richmond, Virginia than to Memphis, Tennessee. Though the 1st is part of the Appalachian region, it is better off than most mountain areas of West Virginia and Kentucky. Because coal has never been very important here, the district has never been much affected by the ups or the downs of that industry. In recent years, towns like Johnson City (pop. 33,000), Kingsport (pop. 31,000), and Bristol (pop. 20,000) have attracted new industry. The region has low taxes and its valleys provide reasonably level east-west transportation routes. Interstate 81, which is nearing completion, will also be an economic blessing.

The changing economy of the district has not, however, produced any shift in its political inclinations. For more than 100 years, the 1st has remained solidly Republican, as Republican as any district in Kansas or Nebraska. People up here in the mountains never had many slaves or much use for secession in 1861. They stayed loyal to the Union and to Mr. Lincoln throughout the Civil War. In fact, Lincoln picked a local boy, Andrew Johnson from Greeneville—one of the older and smaller towns in the district—to be his Vice-President in 1864. To this day, the voters of the 1st have continued to support the party of Union. In 1964, for example, the 1st district of Tennessee produced one of the highest Republican percentages of any contested House race in the nation.

For 40 years, the congressional politics of the 1st was dominated by Republican B. Carroll Reece. He represented the district from 1921 to 1931, 1933 to 1947, and again from 1951 until his death in 1961. Reece also served as Republican National Chairman from 1946 to 1948; in 1948, perhaps thinking that another postwar Republican decade like the 1920s was in the offing, he ran for the Senate in still solidly Democratic Tennessee and lost. Reece was succeeded in 1962 by Jimmy Quillen, a Republican conservative of similar bent. Quillen's seat on the House Rules Committee attests to the utter security of his tenure and the orthodoxy of his conservatism.

Census Data Pop. 490,518. Central city, 0%; suburban, 0%. Median family income, $6,820; families above $15,000: 8%; families below $3,000: 18%. Median years education, 9.8.

1972 Share of Federal Outlays $395,262,842

DOD	$106,085,000	HEW	$130,319,648
AEC	–	HUD	$2,278,658
NASA	–	DOI	$1,257,162
DOT	$28,340,672	USDA	$46,272,769
		Other	$80,708,933

Federal Military-Industrial Commitments

DOD Contractors Eastman Kodak (Kingsport), $56.203m: operation of Holston Army Ammunition plant and production of explosives. Metals Engineering Co. (Greeneville), $11.052m: fin assemblies for Mark 80 bombs. Raytheon (Bristol), $9.148m: Sparrow missile test and training components and bomb fuzes. Tennessee Valley Authority (Erwin), $6.206m: unspecified.

Economic Base Chemicals and allied products; agriculture, notably dairy products, cattle and tobacco; furniture and fixtures, especially household furniture; finance, insurance and real estate; and textile mill products. Also higher education (East Tennessee State Univ.).

The Voters

Registration 245,393 total. No party registration.
Median voting age 42.0
Employment profile White collar, 36%. Blue collar, 49%. Service, 10%. Farm, 5%.
Ethnic groups Black, 2%.

Presidential vote

1972	Nixon (R)	113,840	(78%)
	McGovern (D)	31,200	(22%)
1968	Nixon (R)	92,635	(60%)
	Humphrey (D)	30,418	(20%)
	Wallace (AI)	30,619	(20%)

Representative

James H. (Jimmy) **Quillen** (R) Elected 1962; b. Jan. 11, 1916, near Gate City, Va.; home, Kingsport; Navy, WWII; married; Methodist.

Career Former newspaper publisher; Pres., Chm. of Bd., real estate, mortgage loans and insurance business; Tenn. House of Reps., 1954–62, Minority Leader, 1959–60; Tenn. Legislative Council, 1957–59, 1961; Dir., Kingsport Natl. Bank.

Offices 102 CHOB, 202-225-6356. Also Rm. 157, P.O. Bldg., Kingsport 37662, 615-247-8161.

Administrative Assistant Mrs. Frances Light

Committees

Rules (3rd).

Standards of Official Conduct (Ranking Mbr.).

Group Ratings

	ADA	COPE	LWV	RIPON	NFU	LCV	CFA	NAB	NSI	ACA
1972	6	9	27	38	50	0	0	83	100	85
1971	5	20	22	41	29	–	38	–	–	81
1970	4	9	–	29	23	7	41	83	100	94

Key Votes

1) Busing	AGN	6) Cmbodia Bmbg	FOR	11) Chkg Acct Intrst	ABS
2) Strip Mines	FOR	7) Bust Hwy Trust	AGN	12) End HISC (HUAC)	AGN
3) Cut Mil $	AGN	8) Farm Sub Lmt	AGN	13) Nixon Sewer Veto	FOR
4) Rev Shrg	FOR	9) School Prayr	FOR	14) Corp Cmpaign $	FOR
5) Pub TV $	AGN	10) Cnsumr Prot	AGN	15) Pol $ Disclosr	AGN

Election Results

1972 general:	James H. Quillen (R)	110,868	(79%)
	Bernard Cantor (D)	28,736	(21%)
1972 primary:	James H. Quillen (R), unopposed		
1970 general:	James H. Quillen (R)	78,896	(68%)
	David Bruce Shine (D)	37,348	(32%)

SECOND DISTRICT Political Background

John Gunther called Knoxville, the largest city in east Tennessee (pop. 174,000), the "ugliest city I ever saw in America." It is, in fact, an undistinguised-looking industrial city, sitting in a hot valley flanked by the nondescript hills that do not seem to anticipate the beautiful Smokies 40 miles away. A factory town like this one, one would think, is Democratic. Moreover, the thinking would continue, Knoxville is the headquarters of one of the most successful government projects in history, the Tennessee Valley Authority. The TVA has brought low-cost power, recreational lakes, and plenty of jobs to Knoxville and the surrounding area. And the TVA, of course, is identified with the Democrats. But this is east Tennessee, and Knoxville, for all its factories and the TVA, has been one of the most heavily Republican cities in the country. Because the mountain allegiance to the party of Union dies hard, Knoxville, over the years, has seen its interests opposed by the traditionally Democratic majority of the state.

Knoxville is the center of Tennessee's 2nd congressional district, a safe Republican seat if there ever was one. It is also Sen. Howard Baker's home base. His father, Howard Baker, Sr., represented the district from 1951 until his death in 1963; he was succeeded for the remainder of the term by his widow. Baker, Jr., could have had the seat for the asking, but he decided to run for the Senate instead (see Tennessee state write-up).

So the Republican nomination went to then Knoxville Mayor John Duncan. He won by a comfortable margin in the Democratic year of 1964, and has been reelected easily ever since. Duncan does not make much noise around the Capitol, blending quietly into the conservative folds of the Republican Caucus. But he does hold a position of potential power, as one of the middle-ranking members of the House Ways and Means Committee. The Republican Committee on Committees—senior members from each state with Republican representation—has traditionally chosen anonymous, reliably conservative Congressmen like Duncan to serve on important committees like Ways and Means and Appropriations. Senior Republicans know that such men with safe seats are unlikely either to lose an election or spring unpleasant surprises on the leadership. The House Republican tradition has to account for the fact that the major committees are several notches more conservative than the House as a whole.

Census Data Pop. 492,539. Central city, 35%; suburban, 34%. Median family income, $7,285; families above $15,000: 11%; families below $3,000: 17%. Median years education, 10.8.

1972 Share of Federal Outlays $542,083,876

DOD	$29,106,929	HEW	$157,354,929
AEC	$138,740,894	HUD	$11,276,483
NASA	$192,148	DOI	$1,524,446
DOT	$31,035,240	USDA	$21,771,253
		Other	$151,081,554

Federal Military-Industrial Commitments

DOD Installations Richard Wynne Enterprises (Knoxville), $6.394m: unspecified.

Economic Base Apparel and other textile products, especially men's and boys' furnishings; finance, insurance and real estate; agriculture, notably cattle, dairy products and tobacco; food and kindred products; and textile mill products, especially knitting mill products. Also higher education (Univ. of Tennessee).

The Voters

Registration 242,526 total. No party registration.
Median voting age 42.9
Employment profile White collar, 43%. Blue collar, 42%. Service, 13%. Farm, 2%.
Ethnic groups Black, 6%. Total foreign stock, 1%.

Presidential vote

1972	Nixon (R)	112,505	(73%)
	McGovern (D)	40,799	(27%)
1968	Nixon (R)	86,588	(54%)
	Humphrey (D)	42,200	(26%)
	Wallace (AI)	31,762	(20%)

Representative

John James Duncan (R) Elected 1964; b. March 24, 1919, Scott County; home, Knoxville; Army, WWII; married, four children; Presbyterian.

Career Asst. Atty. Gen., Tenn., 1947–56; Law Dir., Knoxville, 1956–59; Mayor, 1959–64.

Offices 117 CHOB, 202-225-5435. Also Rm. 314, P.O. Bldg., Knoxville 37902, 615-546-5686.

Administrative Assistant Pat DeLozier

Committees

Ways and Means (7th).

Group Ratings

	ADA	COPE	LWV	RIPON	NFU	LCV	CFA	NAB	NSI	ACA
1972	0	9	25	44	57	40	0	92	100	91
1971	14	17	22	61	33	–	25	–	–	76
1970	12	25	–	35	54	38	48	83	100	74

Key Votes

1) Busing	AGN	6) Cmbodia Bmbg	FOR	11) Chkg Acct Intrst	AGN
2) Strip Mines	FOR	7) Bust Hwy Trust	AGN	12) End HISC (HUAC)	AGN
3) Cut Mil $	AGN	8) Farm Sub Lmt	AGN	13) Nixon Sewer Veto	FOR
4) Rev Shrg	FOR	9) School Prayr	FOR	14) Corp Cmpaign $	FOR
5) Pub TV $	AGN	10) Cnsumr Prot	AGN	15) Pol $ Disclosr	FOR

Election Results

1972 general:	John Duncan (R), unopposed		
1972 primary:	John Duncan (R), unopposed		
1970 general:	John Duncan (R)	85,849	(73%)
	Roger Cowan (D)	30,146	(26%)
	William E. Butcher (Ind.)	1,116	(1%)

THIRD DISTRICT Political Background

The 3rd district of Tennessee is the state's most marginal. It is dominated by the city of Chattanooga (pop. 119,000). East of the city is the rugged hill country, solidly Republican except for Polk County, where the borders of Tennessee, North Carolina, and Georgia meet. Polk is a Democratic county with a history of violent politics; three people were killed here during the 1948 campaign. The 3rd also includes several counties west of the Tennessee River, which lean Democratic like the rest of middle Tennessee.

Though situated in Republican east Tennessee, Chattanooga itself has never been a consistently Republican city. It lies between the winding Tennessee River and the Georgia line; flanked by steep ridges (one of which is Lookout Mountain of Civil War fame), Chattanooga has voted for many years like a city in the Deep South—somewhat populistic and Democratic. Even today the east Tennessee city shows some signs of its maverick political past. In recent municipal elections, its residents elected a conservative white mayor and a black health and education administrator.

But with the onset of the civil rights revolution and the growth of the state's Republican party, Chattanooga's voting habits have moved steadily to the right. A comparative look at the district's last four Congressmen nicely illustrates the trend. The late Estes Kefauver got his political start here, representing the district from 1938 to 1949. He then went on to the Senate, where he became famous fighting organized crime and the drug industry. He was also famous for wearing a coonskin cap while he campaigned in the presidential primaries of 1952 and 1956. Kefauver was succeeded by a much more conservative Democrat, James Frazier. In 1962, Frazier, then a member of Ways and Means Committee was upset in the Democratic primary by a young liberal—Wilkes Thrasher, Jr.—by 269 votes out of 70,000 cast. Thrasher, in turn, lost the general election by 2,000 votes, out of 93,000 cast, to Republican William E. Brock III. Brock's forces made particularly good use of a photo of Thrasher with then President Kennedy, who was not especially popular around Chattanooga at the time.

Brock was the young (then 32) heir to candy millions, whose belief in free enterprise was so intense that he voted against the Appalachia bill. That vote did not go over too well in the hill country of the 3rd. Nevertheless, his constituents were quite happy with Brock's other positions: he opposed the Civil Rights Act of 1964, as well as virtually all the social legislation of the Kennedy and Johnson years. In 1970 narrowly defeated veteran incumbent Albert Gore in a race for his Senate seat.

Brock's departure set the stage for a close contest here in 1970. The competitors were Republican state Sen. LaMar Baker and Democratic Hamilton County Councilman Richard Winningham. Baker (no relation to Howard Baker) won, 51–46. He carried Hamilton County (Chattanooga) by the same 51–46 margin and won most of the rural counties. But once in office, Baker proved less than an inspiring politician. So, in 1972, the Democratic nominee, Howard

Sompayrac, had high hopes of unseating the incumbent. Two years earlier, Sompayrac had lost his primary by just 573 votes. In the 1972 general election, the Democrat expected to pick up what he needed to win the two counties added to the 3rd by redistricting. These were traditionally Democratic Roane (which he did eventually carry) and Anderson, which includes Oak Ridge, site of the Atomic Energy Commission installation. The scientists of Oak Ridge vote in ways independent of the usual Civil War patterns found in Tennessee. But Sompayrac's hopes failed to pan out. He got only 42% of the votes district-wide, and ran far behind Baker in Chattanooga. The incumbent Republican finished with 55%. Baker's margin, however, is not enough to indicate that he has created a safe seat for himself. He will probably again face substantial opposition in 1974.

Census Data Pop. 486,363. Central city, 25%; suburban, 40%. Median family income, $7,940; families above $15,000: 13%; families below $3,000: 15%. Median years education, 11.2.

1972 Share of Federal Outlays $664,327,975

DOD	$70,425,071	HEW	$155,472,472
AEC	$182,896,353	HUD	$5,415,763
NASA	$78,613	DOI	$907,166
DOT	$20,933,001	USDA	$17,729,141
		Other	$210,470,395

Federal Military-Industrial Commitments

DOD Installations ICI America (Chattanooga), $24.955m: operation of Volunteer Army Ammunition plant. Cal Constructors (Chattanooga), $11.187m: unspecified. Chemical Construction. (Chattanooga), $6.629m: unspecified.

AEC Operations Union Carbide (Oak Ridge), $212.578m: operation of gaseous diffusion plants and production and research facilities at the Oak Ridge National Laboratory. AEC administrative (Oak Ridge), $8.968m.

Economic Base Textile mill products, especially knitting mill products; fabricated metal products; chemicals and allied products; finance, insurance and real estate; and primary metal industries, especially iron and steel foundries.

The Voters

Registration 247,334 total. No party registration.
Median voting age 42.8
Employment profile White collar, 42%. Blue collar, 45%. Service, 12%. Farm, 1%.
Ethnic groups Black, 11%. Total foreign stock, 2%.

Presidential vote

1972	Nixon (R)	108,187	(72%)
	McGovern (D)	41,430	(28%)
1968	Nixon (R)	63,359	(39%)
	Humphrey (D)	44,042	(27%)
	Wallace (AI)	53,448	(33%)

Representative

Lamar Baker (R) Elected 1970; b. Dec. 29, 1915, Chattanooga; home, Chattanooga; Harding Col., B.A., 1940; Army Air Corps, 1941–46; married, two children; Church of Christ.

Career Owner, Commercial Janitors Inc. and Floormaster Rug Cleaning Co.; Tenn. House of Reps., 1966–68; Senate, 1968–70.

Offices 119 CHOB, 202-225-3271. Also 230 Fed. Bldg., Chattanooga 37402, 615-266-3151.

Administrative Assistant Charles Freburg

Committees

Agriculture (11th); Subs: Forests; Oilseed and Rice; Family Farms and Rural Development.

Public Works (9th); Subs: Public Buildings and Grounds; Economic Development; Energy; Transportation; Water Resources.

Group Ratings

	ADA	COPE	LWV	RIPON	NFU	LCV	CFA	NAB	NSI	ACA
1972	0	9	18	14	40	0	50	100	100	100
1971	0	18	17	21	21	–	38	–	–	91

Key Votes

1) Busing	AGN	6) Cmbodia Bmbg	FOR	11) Chkg Acct Intrst	AGN
2) Strip Mines	AGN	7) Bust Hwy Trust	AGN	12) End HISC (HUAC)	AGN
3) Cut Mil $	ABS	8) Farm Sub Lmt	AGN	13) Nixon Sewer Veto	FOR
4) Rev Shrg	AGN	9) School Prayr	FOR	14) Corp Cmpaign $	ABS
5) Pub TV $	AGN	10) Cnsumr Prot	AGN	15) Pol $ Disclosr	AGN

Election Results

1972 general:	LaMar Baker (R)	82,561	(55%)
	Howard Sompayrac (D)	62,536	(42%)
	Sarah Delaney (AI)	4,345	(3%)
1972 primary:	LaMar Baker (R), unopposed		
1970 general:	LaMar Baker (R)	61,527	(51%)
	Richard Winningham (D)	54,662	(45%)
	Robert Shockey (Ind.)	2,124	(2%)
	Frank Massey (Ind.)	1,375	(1%)

FOURTH DISTRICT Political Background

The Tennessee River crosses the state twice. The first time, the river heads south from its headwaters to Chattanooga; the second time, after turning around in Alabama and Mississippi, the river moves lazily north to its confluence with the Ohio River in Kentucky. Along most of its route, the Tennessee is made amenable to the needs of man by the presence of TVA dam sites. Between the two lengths of river lies middle Tennessee, with most of its geographical expanse making up the state's 4th congressional district. To the east, the district is mountain country, but most of the 4th exists as part of the hilly farmlands of the Cumberland Plateau, which is known locally as the "dimple of the universe."

For 150 years, Cumberland Plateau has been a region of small and medium-sized farms and small county-seat towns. The district's largest city is Murfreesboro (pop. 26,000). The first local hero in these parts was Andrew Jackson, victor at the Battle of New Orleans and later President of the United States. With the exception of a couple of mountain counties, the 4th has remained loyal to Jackson's Democratic party ever since. Over the years, the 4th has produced a number of leaders of the national Democratic party, including Rep. (1907–21 and 1923–31), Sen. (1931–33), and Secretary of State (1933–44) Cordell Hull, and Rep. (1939–53) and Sen. (1953–71) Albert Gore.

The race issue in the 4th has seldom been the burning one that it has been in other places in the Deep South. So the district's traditional allegiance to the Democratic party is apparent in even the most recent voting figures. In 1972, the 4th gave George McGovern 35% of its votes, which represents a higher percentage of white support that the South Dakotan won just about anywhere in the South. In the same year, the district gave Republican Sen. Howard Baker, whose home county adjoins the 4th, only 53%, as he otherwise swept to a landslide reelection victory. The percentage here represented the poorest Baker showing in any congressional district in the state.

Gore's successor in the House is Joe L. Evins, a middle-of-the-road Democrat. Having won reelection regularly with more than 70% of the district's votes, Evins has quietly risen to a position of considerable influence in the Congress. He is one of the most senior (sixth-ranking) members of the House Appropriations Committee, and Chairman of its Public Works-AEC Subcommittee.

Evins' chairmanship, which he inherited from the late Mike Kirwan of Ohio, used to be one of the big plums in the House, since it confers power of the purse over all federal pork-barrel projects. It remains a fact that a well-placed dam or federal building will help to sew up a district for a Congressman otherwise in trouble. Accordingly, House members who fit the category dare not irritate Evins. The Congressman himself has demonstrated a willingness to use his leverage for advantage. When he was Chairman of the subcommittee controlling housing appropriations, Evins' home town of Smithville (pop. 2,997) was named as one of the original Model Cities.

Census Data Pop. 492,124. Central city, 0%; suburban, 19%. Median family income, $6,451; families above $15,000: 8%; families below $3,000: 20%. Median years education, 9.2.

1972 Share of Federal Outlays $401,590,960

DOD	$102,306,656	HEW	$156,755,474
AEC	$22,242	HUD	$7,054,500
NASA	$658,209	DOI	$1,232,300
DOT	$11,934,611	USDA	$32,997,593
		Other	$88,629,375

Federal Military-Industrial Commitments

DOD Contractors Aro, Inc. (Arnold), $46.994m: operation of Arnold Air Force Engineering Development Center; laser research. Tennessee Overall Co. (Tullahoma), $5.524m: clothing goods. Capitol Airways (Smyrna), $5.112m: transportations services.
DOD Installations Arnold Air Force Engineering Development Center (Arnold).

Economic Base Apparel and other textile products, especially boys' furnishings and women's and misses' outerwear; agriculture, notably dairy products, cattle, hogs and sheep, and poultry; finance, insurance and real estate; shoes, except rubber, and other leather and leather products; and electrical equipment and supplies, especially electrical industrial apparatus. Also higher education (Middle Tennessee State Univ.).

The Voters

Registration 255,083 total. No party registration.
Median voting age 43.6
Employment profile White collar, 34%. Blue collar, 47%. Service, 11%. Farm, 8%.
Ethnic groups Black, 6%.

Presidential vote

1972	Nixon (R)	82,879	(65%)
	McGovern (D)	44,719	(35%)
1968	Nixon (R)	43,438	(29%)
	Humphrey (D)	42,847	(28%)
	Wallace (AI)	65,592	(43%)

Representative

Joe L. Evins (D) Elected 1946; b. Oct. 24, 1910, DeKalb County; home, Smithville; Vanderbilt U., B.A., 1933; Cumberland U., LL.B., 1934; George Washington U., 1938–40; Army, WWII; married, three children; Church of Christ.

Career Asst. Sec., legal staff, Federal Trade Commission, 1935–41; Chm. of Bd., First Natl. Bank.

Offices 2300 RHOB, 202-225-4231. Also Fed. Bldg., Smithville 37166, 615-597-4099.

Administrative Assistant William A. Keel, Jr.

Committees

Appropriations (6th); Subs: HUD, Space, Science, Veterans; Public Works, AEC (Chm.).

Sel. Com. on Small Business (Chm.).

Group Ratings

	ADA	COPE	LWV	RIPON	NFU	LCV	CFA	NAB	NSI	ACA
1972	19	50	44	56	60	15	–	33	100	53
1971	11	50	43	47	64	–	50	–	–	56
1970	20	30	–	19	75	30	89	43	100	42

Key Votes

1) Busing	AGN	6) Cmbodia Bmbg	AGN	11) Chkg Acct Intrst	ABS
2) Strip Mines	AGN	7) Bust Hwy Trust	ABS	12) End HISC (HUAC)	AGN
3) Cut Mil $	ABS	8) Farm Sub Lmt	AGN	13) Nixon Sewer Veto	AGN
4) Rev Shrg	FOR	9) School Prayr	AGN	14) Corp Cmpaign $	FOR
5) Pub TV $	FOR	10) Cnsumr Prot	AGN	15) Pol $ Disclosr	ABS

Election Results

1972 general:	Joe L. Evins (D)	93,042	(81%)
	Billy Jo Finney (R)	21,689	(19%)
1972 primary:	Joe L. Evins (D), unopposed		
1970 general:	Joe L. Evins (D)	86,437	(83%)
	(Mrs.) J. Durelle Boles (R)	18,180	(17%)

FIFTH DISTRICT Political Background

Nashville is Tennessee's capital and second largest city. After its recent consolidation with surrounding Davidson County, the city now sports an impressive population of 447,000. Because of its location in the center of the state, Nashville is in many ways more important to Tennessee than the larger Memphis. The two newspapers in Nashville neatly reflect the state's two-party politics; the *Banner* is as firmly Republican as the *Tennesseean* is resolutely Democratic. The city is also a major city for the enterprises of printing and insurance. The activity for which Nashville is best known, however, is music—the home of the Grand Ole Opry since the 1920s. And now, with several major recording studios, Nashville is the undisputed country-and-western music capital of the world.

Today country-music millionaires live in suburban mansions that sit uncomfortably close to Nashville's older, established upper class. Country music personalities have even gotten into politics. Tex Ritter, for example, was an unsuccessful candidate for the Republican Senate nomination in 1970. And in the same year, Minnie Pearl indirectly contributed as much as anyone to the defeat of John J. Hooker, the Democratic gubernatorial candidate. Hooker promoted stock in the Minnie Pearl chicken franchise operation (later renamed Performance Systems). It was a bust, and Hooker lost many votes.

Nashville lays claim to ornaments other than country music. The city contains several colleges, including Vanderbilt and Fisk universities. Also here, not far from the old state Capitol, is the famous replica of the Parthenon. But Nashville's favorite shrine—and the one most significant politically—is the Hermitage, home of Andrew Jackson, Old Hickory. Jackson moved to Nashville from the Carolinas when Tennessee was still very much the frontier. He made a small fortune, won election to the House while George Washington was still President, and was then elected to the Senate, where he served briefly just after he turned 30. Jackson, at age 31, began a term of service on the Tennessee Supreme Court that lasted from 1798 to 1804. When the great man moved into the Hermitage in the early 1800s, he had not yet made a national reputation as a merciless Indian fighter, the scourge of the British at New Orleans, and the commoners' candidate for President. But he had already helped to set Nashville's political preferences. Jackson was a Democrat, and Nashville has remained, with only the most occasional exceptions, Democratic ever since.

The 5th congressional district of Tennessee includes Nashville and two small rural counties appended after the 1970 census. With the recent exceptions of the 1968 and 1972 presidential contests and the 1972 Senate election, the 5th always goes Democratic. In congressional elections, the Democratic margins here are almost invariably large. The district's current Congressman, Richard Fulton, is today easily the most liberal member of the Tennessee delegation. He is the only one from the group to have voted to set a definite time limit to American involvement in the Vietnam war. Fulton was first elected in 1962, when he ousted the conservative incumbent, J. Carlton Loser. In the Democratic primary of that year, Loser appeared to have won by 72 votes. But because of allegations of vote fraud, neither candidate was given the Democratic nomination. Instead, both ran as independents in the general election, with Fulton coming out on top by a surprisingly large 17,000-vote margin. After only one term in Congress, Fulton caught the eye of the leadership and received a seat on the House Ways and Means Committee.

In 1968, Fulton had an unexpected close call, winning reelection by just 8,000 votes. Stung by near-defeat, he bounced back with 71% of the votes in the next election against the same opponent. In 1972, when the top of the Republican ticket carried the district, Fulton still took 63%. Incidentally, the liberal Fulton ran just as well—in fact, better—in the two rural counties as in Nashville.

Census Data Pop. 490,178. Central city, 100%; suburban, 0%. Median family income, $9,231; families above $15,000: 18%; families below $3,000: 10%. Median years education, 11.9.

1972 Share of Federal Outlays $420,840,349

DOD	$48,665,344	HEW	$185,210,506
AEC	$106,771	HUD	$3,904,108
NASA	$146,845	DOI	$2,286,485
DOT	$13,603,992	USDA	$15,448,209
		Other	$151,470,089

Federal Military-Industrial Commitments

No installations or contractors receiving prime awards greater than $5,000,000.

Economic Base Finance, insurance and real estate; printing and publishing; transportation equipment; food and kindred products; and chemicals and allied products, especially plastics materials and synthetics.

The Voters

Registration 246,232 total. No party registration.
Median voting age 41.4
Employment profile White collar, 53%. Blue collar, 33%. Service, 13%. Farm, 1%.
Ethnic groups Black, 19%. Total foreign stock, 3%.

Presidential vote

1972	Nixon (R)	89,046	(63%)
	McGovern (D)	53,175	(37%)
1968	Nixon (R)	46,646	(31%)
	Humphrey (D)	47,636	(32%)
	Wallace (AI)	54,290	(37%)

Representative

Richard Harmon Fulton (D) Elected 1962; b. Jan. 27, 1927, Nashville; home, Nashville; U. of Tenn.; Navy, WWII; married, six children; Methodist.

Career Real estate broker; Tenn. Senate, 1959.

Offices 2422 RHOB, 202-225-4311. Also 552 U.S. Court House, Nashville 37203, 615-242-8321, ext. 296.

Administrative Assistant James E. Drake

Committees

Ways and Means (8th).

Group Ratings

	ADA	COPE	LWV	RIPON	NFU	LCV	CFA	NAB	NSI	ACA
1972	38	89	67	69	100	63	100	10	50	27
1971	73	91	67	71	86	–	100	–	–	19
1970	44	82	–	64	100	28	84	0	86	21

Key Votes

1) Busing	AGN	6) Cmbodia Bmbg	AGN	11) Chkg Acct Intrst	AGN
2) Strip Mines	AGN	7) Bust Hwy Trust	AGN	12) End HISC (HUAC)	AGN
3) Cut Mil $	ABS	8) Farm Sub Lmt	ABS	13) Nixon Sewer Veto	AGN
4) Rev Shrg	FOR	9) School Prayr	AGN	14) Corp Cmpaign $	FOR
5) Pub TV $	ABS	10) Cnsumr Prot	ABS	15) Pol $ Disclosr	AGN

Election Results

1972 general:	Richard Fulton (D)	93,555	(63%)
	Alfred Adams (R)	55,067	(37%)
1972 primary:	Richard Fulton (D)	67,483	(73%)
	Casey Jenkins (D)	23,034	(26%)
	Randolph Shannon (D)	1,303	(1%)
1970 general:	Richard Fulton (D)	89,900	(71%)
	George Kelly (R)	37,522	(29%)

SIXTH DISTRICT Political Background

During the 1960s, Tennessee's population growth failed to match that of the national average. As a result, the state lost a congressional seat after the 1970 census. In 1972, the Tennessee legislature, controlled by Democrats, passed a redistricting plan over the veto of Republican Gov. Winfield Dunn. Designed to help the Democrats, the plan failed miserably. In essence, the legislature chose to amalgamate the 6th and the 7th districts into one. In 1970, both of them had Democratic Congressmen; the consolidated territory, the new 6th, elected a want to Congressman in 1970. The 6th and 7th were so chosen because the legislature did not want to place two incumbent Democrats in the same district. Congressman Ray Blanton of the 7th had earlier decided to vacate the seat to run for the Senate (quite unsuccessfully, it turned out, as Howard Baker clobbered him). The new 6th was left to William Anderson. He was a four-term Congressman who had been the commander of the nuclear submarine Nautilus when it first voyaged under the ice cap of the North Pole.

Anderson was not the typical Congressman from rural Tennessee. After compiling a comparatively liberal record on domestic issues, he won a seat on the House Rules Committee. On a 1969 inspection trip of Vietnam, Anderson and two other Congressmen discovered the Con San tiger cages, inhuman contrivances in which the Thieu regime had imprisoned political prisoners. Before the discovery, Anderson has usually gone along with the Vietnam policies of the Johnson and Nixon adminstrations; thereafter, he became a vehement critic. Later, Anderson met the Berrigan brothers, and when J. Edgar Hoover accused the two of plotting to kidnap Henry Kissinger, Anderson demanded that Hoover bring the case to court or retract the charges. The

Justice Department responded by bringing the case to trial, one that resulted, as did virtually all such Nixon Administration prosecutions, in acquittal on the main charges.

Up through 1970, the Congressman's rather unorthodox conduct had not hurt him at home. In the eyes of the voters, Anderson remained a popular native son and a famous Navy commander. Though the shape of his middle Tennessee district was altered grotesquely the constituency contained within the lines stayed so heavily Democratic that the Republicans never put up strong opposition. But the 1972 redistricting changed the picture drastically. Anderson kept only five counties from the old 6th district that had reelected him with 82% of the votes in 1970. Of the 14 new rural counties, a few were traditionally Republican, and several others on the Mississippi border were usually Democratic, but at the same time very conservative. Even that, however, Anderson could manage. What really hurt was the addition of 84,000 people in the city of Memphis and Shelby County. This virtually all-white, adamantly conservative territory was kept out of the Memphis 8th district, which the legislature hoped would go Democratic, but did not (see Tennessee 8).

A look at the percentages won by George McGovern in the three parts of the district measures the severity of Anderson's problems. In the five counties retained from the old 6th, McGovern took 36% of the votes—not bad at all compared to the rest of the South. In these ticket-splitting days, this territory posed no problems for Anderson. In the 14 new rural counties, McGovern won 31%, not much worse. But in the Memphis-Shelby County portion of the new 6th, which cast 27% of the district's ballots, McGovern came away with a rock-bottom 11%. This shows an almost monolithic white support for Nixon in these high-income Memphis and suburban residential areas—one of which bears the appropriate name of Whitehaven.

The strength of Anderson's opposition compounded the incumbent's problems. The Republican nominee, Robin Beard, was typical of the young men that Sens. Baker and Brock and Gov. Dunn have attracted to careers in Tennessee politics. Beard was young (33), articulate, and solidly conservative. He was also experienced, having served for two years as head of the state personnel commission. Moreover, his campaign was both well-financed and well-organized. Beard's identification with the district was tenuous—he was an east Tennessee native and lived in a Nashville suburb just over the Williamson County line. But voters did not seem to mind.

The challenger cut Anderson's majorities sharply in the counties in both rural portions of the district. In Anderson's old rural counties, Beard took 43% of the votes, and carried the 14 new rural counties with 52%. But Beard's attacks on busing and Anderson's antiwar positions really scored in Memphis and Shelby County. Here the challenger clobbered Anderson by a 26,000 to 6,000 margin, which works out to 80% of the votes. The urban votes easily wiped out the 3,000-vote edge Anderson had accumulated in the rural areas.

Since taking office, Beard has returned to the district nearly every weekend and makes the rounds of the rural county seats. No need to worry about Memphis, where he can scarcely improve his showing. According to David Broder of the *Washington Post*, Beard has further ingratiated himself with the voters by concentrating on constituency services. The new Congressman handles Watergate questions by deflection, talking instead about Angela Davis and Daniel Ellsberg—a good tactic, since people in the South are more likely than those in the North to stand behind Nixon. At this writing, Beard appears ready to win reelection in 1974.

Census Data Pop. 472,341. Central city, 15%; suburban, 3%. Median family income, $7,151; families above $15,000: 12%; families below $3,000: 19%. Median years education, 10.3.

1972 Share of Federal Outlays $330,474,426

DOD	$43,239,551	HEW	$139,500,597
AEC	$7,123	HUD	$4,961,566
NASA	–	DOI	$786,636
DOT	$4,852,978	USDA	$65,911,494
		Other	$71,214,481

Federal Military-Industrial Commitments

DOD Contractors Kilgore Corp. (Toone), $8.473m: parachute flare target markers.
DOD Installations Naval Air Technical Training Command (Memphis).

Economic Base Agriculture, notably cattle, and hogs and sheep; apparel and other textile products, especially men's and boys' furnishings; finance, insurance and real estate; shoes, except rubber, and other leather and leather products; and transportation equipment.

The Voters

Registration 226,909 total. No party registration.
Median voting age 42.9
Employment profile White collar, 39%. Blue collar, 45%. Service, 11%. Farm, 5%.
Ethnic groups Black, 14%. Total foreign stock, 2%.

Presidential vote

1972	Nixon (R)	104,742	(72%)
	McGovern (D)	39,799	(28%)
1968	Nixon (R)	52,684	(33%)
	Humphrey (D)	36,380	(23%)
	Wallace (AI)	68,322	(43%)

Representative

Robin Leo Beard, Jr. (R) Elected 1972; b. Aug. 21, 1939, Knoxville; home, Brentwood; Vanderbilt U., B.A., 1961; married, two children; Methodist.

Career Asst. for Development, Vanderbilt U.; Management Trainee, Performance Systems; Field man, Jarman for Governor, Dunn for Governor; Chm., Inaugural Com. for Gov. Dunn; State Commissioner of Personnel, 1970–72.

Offices 124 CHOB, 202-225-2811. Also 710 N. Garden St., Columbia 38401, 615-388-2133; and Suite 226, First Am. Bank. Bldg., 5384 Popular Ave., Memphis, 38117, 901-767-4652.

Administrative Assistant Albert F. Ganier III

Committees

Armed Services (16th); Sub: No. 5.

Group Ratings: Newly Elected

Key Votes

1) Busing	NE	6) Cmbodia Bmbg	FOR	11) Chkg Acct Intrst	AGN
2) Strip Mines	NE	7) Bust Hwy Trust	AGN	12) End HISC (HUAC)	AGN
3) Cut Mil $	NE	8) Farm Sub Lmt	NE	13) Nixon Sewer Veto	FOR
4) Rev Shrg	NE	9) School Prayr	NE	14) Corp Cmpaign $	NE
5) Pub TV $	NE	10) Cnsumr Prot	NE	15) Pol $ Disclosr	NE

Election Results

1972 general:	Robin L. Beard (R)	77,263	(55%)
	William R. Anderson (D)	60,254	(43%)
	W. N. Doss (AI)	2,244	(2%)
1972 primary:	Robin L. Beard (R)	13,499	(77%)
	Edward Lyman (R)	4,063	(23%)

SEVENTH DISTRICT Political Background

The 7th district of Tennessee is the northwest part of the state. The district extends from the TVA lakes of the Tennessee and Cumberland rivers at the Kentucky state line to the city of Memphis. Physically and politically, the 7th resembles the Mississippi Delta or eastern Arkansas: flat cotton lands, occasional small towns, and a fairly large (19%), mostly rural black population.

Outside of Memphis and Shelby County, the district's largest city is Jackson (pop. 39,000), whose political attitudes have much in common with its Mississippi namesake. Most of the counties here are traditionally Democratic, but only those around the Tennessee River have given statewide Democratic candidates significant margins in recent years. Most of the rest have responded favorably to the thinly disguised segregationist appeals of Republican candidates like Sen. Bill Brock or the crisp, modern tones of Sen. Howard Baker. The Shelby County (Memphis) portion of the district, with 124,000 residents (26% of the district total), is 98% white, relatively high-income, and heavily conservative.

Perhaps because of its long-standing Democratic tradition, Tennessee Republicans did not contest the seat in the 7th district for some time. From 1958 to 1969, the district was represented by conservative Democrat Bob Everett, who faced Republican opposition only once during his tenure. In 1969, Everett died, and a special election was called. George Wallace, who had carried nearly 50% of the votes within the district the year before, came in to campaign for American party candidate William Davis, while Sen. Howard Baker and other Republicans stumped for Republican Leonard Dunavant. The race got some attention in the national press as a test of the Wallace and Nixon strategies in the South.

The result made both look rather bad. Davis won 25% of the votes, Dunavant 24%, and the winner, conservative Democrat Ed Jones, took 51%. Jones, former state Commissioner of Agriculture, had not asked outsiders to come in and campaign for him; he wisely relied on the traditional Democratic sentiments of the voters in his district. These people may plunk for Wallace in a presidential election, or go for a Republican like Nixon over a Democrat like McGovern, but most of them preferred to stay with a Tennessee Democrat in what is, after all, a local election. Then, too, against Wallace-backed and Nixon-backed candidates, Jones won the black vote with no effort at all.

In Congress, Jones received a seat on the House Agriculture Committee and on its Cotton Subcommittee. No doubt both assignments pleased him. Back home, the voters are apparently content with his conservative record. He had no opposition whatever in 1970, and won 71% of the votes against a Republican in 1972. The election was close only in Shelby County. Here Jones still beat his opponent by a 54–46 margin—a significant contrast to the showing of more liberal incumbent William Anderson in a similar, though somewhat higher-income, portion of Shelby County in the 6th district. At 60, Jones seems to have an utterly safe district.

Census Data Pop. 487,097. Central city, 10%; suburban, 16%. Median family income, $7,030; families above $15,000: 10%; families below $3,000: 19%. Median years education, 10.2.

1972 Share of Federal Outlays $537,613,224

DOD	$134,145,716	HEW	$163,155,257
AEC	$10,621	HUD	$7,103,258
NASA	–	DOI	$1,016,649
DOT	$14,920,937	USDA	$94,238,821
		Other	$123,021,965

Federal Military-Industrial Commitments

DOD Contractors Martin Marietta (Milan), $64.003m: operation of a government-owned facility. Airport Machining (Union City), $8.717m: 60mm and 2.75-inch rockets. Heckethorn Manufacturing (Dyersburg), $5.437m: 40mm projectiles. Security Signals (Cordova), $5.338m: bomb detonating fuzes. J.M. O'Brien Co. (Millington), $5.261m: unspecified.
DOD Installations Naval Air Station (Memphis). Naval Hospital (Memphis).

Economic Base Agriculture, notably grains, cattle, and hogs and sheep; apparel and other textile products; food and kindred products; finance, insurance and real estate; and electrical equipment and supplies.

The Voters

Registration 238,957 total. No party registration.
Median voting age 43.5
Employment profile White collar, 37%. Blue collar, 44%. Service, 12%. Farm, 7%.
Ethnic groups Black, 19%. Total foreign stock, 2%.

Presidential vote

1972	Nixon (R)	105,072	(75%)
	McGovern (D)	34,241	(25%)
1968	Nixon (R)	42,049	(28%)
	Humphrey (D)	35,390	(23%)
	Wallace (AI)	74,448	(49%)

Representative

Ed Jones (D) Elected March 25, 1969; b. April 20, 1912, Yorkville; home, Yorkville; U. of Tenn., B.S., 1934; married, two children; Presbyterian.

Career Inspector, Div. of Insect and Plant Diseases Control, 1934; Tenn. Dairy Products Assn., 1941–43; Agricultural Agent, Ill. Central Railroad, 1944–69; Tenn. Commissioner of Agriculture, 1949–52; Organizer, Pres., West Tenn. Artificial Breeding Assoc.; Assoc. Farm Dir., radio station WMC, Memphis.

Offices 1315 LHOB, 202-225-4714. Also 3179 N. Watkins, Memphis 38127, 901-358-4094, and Yorkville 38389, 901-643-6123.

Administrative Assistant Ray Lancaster

Committees

Agriculture (10th); Subs: Cotton; Dairy and Poultry (Chm.); Department Operations.

House Administration (12th); Subs: Elections; Printing.

Group Ratings

	ADA	COPE	LWV	RIPON	NFU	LCV	CFA	NAB	NSI	ACA
1972	13	44	25	33	80	4	0	57	100	74
1971	22	45	80	47	79	–	43	–	–	48
1970	24	42	–	13	50	45	80	27	88	60

Key Votes

1) Busing	AGN	6) Cmbodia Bmbg	ABS	11) Chkg Acct Intrst	ABS
2) Strip Mines	AGN	7) Bust Hwy Trust	AGN	12) End HISC (HUAC)	AGN
3) Cut Mil $	AGN	8) Farm Sub Lmt	AGN	13) Nixon Sewer Veto	AGN
4) Rev Shrg	AGN	9) School Prayr	FOR	14) Corp Cmpaign $	FOR
5) Pub TV $	ABS	10) Cnsumr Prot	AGN	15) Pol $ Disclosr	AGN

Election Results

1972 general:	Ed Jones (D)	92,419	(70%)
	Stockton Adkins (R)	38,726	(30%)
1972 primary:	Ed Jones (D), unopposed		
1970 general:	Ed Jones (D), unopposed		

EIGHTH   DISTRICT   Political Background

Memphis, Tennessee's largest city (pop. 623,000), is set in the far southwest corner of the state. The city is the major financial and commercial center for much of the lower Mississippi Valley. As such, Memphis looks as much south to Mississippi and west to Arkansas as it does to the rest of Tennessee. In recent years, Memphis has grown rapidly, having doubled its population since World War II. Most of the newcomers are from the Deep South, especially Mississippi. Blacks have found more economic opportunity here, and more political power; Memphis has elected black state legislators and a black judge—Benjamin Hooks—now on the Federal Communications Commission.

Memphis, however, is still dominated politically by its middle-class whites. These are people, many from rural counties, who are now making more money than they ever imagined they would. They live comfortable lives in the vast suburban tracts that have sprung up around Memphis in the last 20 years. Their political traditions are Democratic, but they now use their ballots to protect a new-found prosperity, which means they vote Republican. Moreover, Memphis is one of the most segregated cities in the South. It has little of the phenomenon, once common in Atlanta and New Orleans, where small white and black neighborhoods sit cheek by jowl. So until 1972, some 88% of the black pupils of Memphis went to virtually all-black schools. Whites responded to a federal court busing order by doing three things: first, organizing a sizable boycott; second, setting up so-called "Christian" private academies; and third, voting for Nixon.

Despite its Southern heritage and folkways, Memphis likes to think of itself as a typically American city. Out in the suburbs, people modulate their accents and vote for politicians like Howard Baker whose drawls cause no embarrassment. And it is true that Memphis is the home of many peculiarly American institutions. Beale Street here gave birth to jazz in the 1920s, and in the 1930s, the first supermarket—a Piggly Wiggly—opened in Memphis. Then in the 1950s, Memphis gave us the Holiday Inn and Elvis Presley. In 1968, Memphis was the scene of Martin Luther King's murder. He had come here to work in behalf of the city's virtually all-black garbage men who were on strike.

Most of Memphis is contained in Tennessee's 8th congressional district. The 8th included 99% of the city's black population, which in turn makes up 47% of the district's citizenry and 41% of those over 18. For 10 years, the Tennessee legislature carved up the black areas of Memphis into two or three districts to forestall the election of a black Congressman. But in 1972, the legislature—or at least its Democratic majority—decided that the only way it could get a Democratic Congressman out of Memphis was to place the maximum possible number of blacks in the 8th district. The legislature miscalculated, at least in the short run. The decision also cost the Democrats the seat in the 6th, where incumbent William Anderson was trounced by votes cast by white suburbanites.

Only 10 or 15 years ago, any Memphis district would have gone Democratic. And 20 or 30 years ago, there was virtually no difference between the voting habits of Memphis whites and blacks. Those were the days of the Crump machine, when boss Ed Crump could deliver virtually 100% of the Memphis vote in the Democratic primary. He thereby dominated the politics of Tennessee. But Estes Kefauver beat a Crump incumbent in the 1948 Senate race, and Crump's power faded from the scene; he died in 1954. Nevertheless, a Crump Congressman, Clifford Davis, kept the Memphis seat for another 10 years, until a more liberal Democrat, George Grider, beat him in the 1964 primary.

Grider managed to win the 1964 election, but was ousted in 1966 by Republican Dan Kuykendall. Kuykendall had come to Memphis 11 years before as a Procter and Gamble regional executive. In 1964, he made a political name for himself when he won 46% of the votes in a Senate race against Albert Gore. After his initial election to the House, Kuykendall paid close attention to the needs of his district; he has thereafter won margins exceeding 2–1 in white neighborhoods.

He needed every vote he could get and more in 1972, and he got them. White voters, now accustomed to voting Republican, failed to turn out in any numbers for the Democratic primary, which was won easily by state Sen. J. O. Patterson, a black. Patterson campaigned hard, but won very few white votes in the general election. The challenger's 44% total—and George McGovern's 43% here—indicate almost completely segregated voting patterns. Something like 90% of the blacks went for Patterson and McGovern, and something like 90% of the whites went for Kuykendall and Nixon. In the Senate race, the configuration of results was different, as Howard Baker received something close to a majority of the black votes and lost some white votes to his anti-busing opponent. Altogether, Baker ran ahead of Nixon in the district with 62%.

In the years ahead, the prospect is for similar races and similar results in the 8th district. Kuykendall will now try to deliver constituency services for blacks as well as whites, hoping to produce votes. But he will likely face black opponents in future elections, and will unlikely make inroads in the black community. Conversely, in polarized Memphis black nominees can expect to win few votes in white neighborhoods. So Kuykendall is likely to continue to win, barring substantial neighborhood change. And change in the magnitude required is not probable until the late 1970s.

Census Data Pop. 513,004. Central city, 99%; suburban, 1%. Median family income, $7,874; families above $15,000: 14%; families below $3,000: 15%. Median years education, 11.4.

1972 Share of Federal Outlays $654,706,530

DOD	$137,978,731	HEW	$142,520,585
AEC	$43,404	HUD	$24,675,587
NASA	–	DOI	$230,638
DOT	$14,021,062	USDA	$209,530,660
		Other	$125,705,863

Federal Military-Industrial Commitments

DOD Contractors Delta Refining Co. (Memphis), $7.819m: petroleum products.
DOD Installations Memphis Army Defense Depot (Memphis).

Economic Base Finance, insurance and real estate; food and kindred products; chemicals and allied products; electrical equipment and supplies; paper and allied products, especially miscellaneous converted paper products; and machinery. Also higher education (Memphis State Univ.).

The Voters

Registration 266,526 total. No party registration.
Median voting age 42.3
Employment profile White collar, 47%. Blue collar, 36%. Service, 17%. Farm, –%.
Ethnic groups Black, 47%. Total foreign stock, 3%.

Presidential vote

1972	Nixon (R)	96,876	(57%)
	McGovern (D)	71,930	(43%)
1968	Nixon (R)	45,193	(28%)
	Humphrey (D)	72,320	(44%)
	Wallace (AI)	46,311	(28%)

Representative

Dan H. Kuykendall (R) Elected 1966; b. July 9, 1924, Cherokee, Tex.; home, Memphis; Tex. A&M U., B.S., 1947; Army Air Corps, WWII; married, four children; Methodist.

Career Mgr., Proctor & Gamble Co., 1947–64; Equitable Life Insurance Society of U.S., 1964– ; Mbr., Bd. of Dir., group drafting charter for Memphis, 1965–66.

Offices 1526 LHOB, 202-225-3265. Also 369 Fed. Bldg., Memphis 38103, 901-534-3319.

Administrative Assistant Michael Dineen

Committees

Interstate and Foreign Commerce (7th); Sub: Transportation and Aeronautics.

Group Ratings

	ADA	COPE	LWV	RIPON	NFU	LCV	CFA	NAB	NSI	ACA
1972	0	11	13	60	17	15	0	89	100	81
1971	0	17	25	44	38	–	25	–	–	88
1970	12	9	–	41	33	0	43	100	100	60

Key Votes

1) Busing	AGN	6) Cmbodia Bmbg	FOR	11) Chkg Acct Intrst	AGN
2) Strip Mines	ABS	7) Bust Hwy Trust	AGN	12) End HISC (HUAC)	AGN
3) Cut Mil $	AGN	8) Farm Sub Lmt	AGN	13) Nixon Sewer Veto	FOR
4) Rev Shrg	FOR	9) School Prayr	FOR	14) Corp Cmpaign $	ABS
5) Pub TV $	FOR	10) Cnsumr Prot	AGN	15) Pol $ Disclosr	FOR

Election Results

1972 general:	Dan Kuykendall (R)	93,173	(55%)
	J. D. Patterson, Jr. (D)	74,240	(45%)
	Louis L. Porter (Ind.)	893	(1%)
1972 primary:	Dan Kuykendall (R), unopposed		
1970 general:	Dan Kuykendall (R)	72,498	(62%)
	Michael Osborn (D)	43,279	(37%)
	Malley Byrd (Ind.)	744	(1%)

TEXAS

Political Background

Everybody's image of Texas and the Texan is pretty much the same. It is something of John Wayne at the Alamo, cowboys and cattle on the Chisholm trail, and happy new oil millionaires riding around in air-conditioned Cadillacs while their wives roll up bills at Neiman Marcus. The stereotype has some truth, but not much. Before the east Texas oil strike of the 1930s, the typical Texan was a poor dirt farmer, and even today the state has many more marginal farmers than oil millionaires. Moreover, the descendants of the white men who came to Texas with Sam Houston and defended the Alamo are greatly outnumbered by the 18% of all Texans who are of Mexican descent. And Neiman Marcus has far fewer people with charge accounts than the number of black Texans, who make up 12% of the state's population.

In one respect, however, the stereotypical picture of Texas is accurate: the state is a vast one. It is farther from El Paso to Texarkana—or from Amarillo to Brownsville—than it is from Chicago to New York. As one drives from east to west across Texas, the scenery shifts from fertile lands that receive ample rain to flat, waterless desert. During the winter, blizzards sweep across the northern panhandle, while the Rio Grande basks in semitropical temperatures. Despite its size, Texas lost its status as the nation's biggest when Alaska became a state in 1959. Nevertheless, during the 1960s, Texas passed both Illinois and Ohio to become the fourth largest in population, and by 1980, Texas will outrank Pennsylvania to occupy the number-three position.

"In no other state," writes Neal Peirce, an expert on all 50 of them, "has the control (of a single moneyed establishment) been so direct, so unambiguous, so commonly accepted." Of course, the biggest money here is in oil. But Texas millionaires are also big in petrochemicals, construction (Brown & Root contractors, an LBJ favorite), insurance, and computers. Ross Perot, an old IBM salesman, made millions when he set up his own company and designed programs for Medicaid administrators; Perot is therefore the first welfare millionaire. Almost without exception, the big-money men are conservative and, bowing to local traditions, they have chosen—at least until very recently—to exert control through the Democratic party. Big money put pressure on congressional powers like Speaker Sam Rayburn and Senate Majority Leader Lyndon Johnson, neither of whom brooked any tampering with the oil depletion allowance. But the rich have devoted their most sustained efforts to statewide politics. Their heroes are Tory Democrats like ex-Gov. (1951–56) Allan Shivers, who broke with the party to support Eisenhower in 1952 and 1956, and of course ex-Gov. (1963–68) John B. Connally. As Governor, Connally permitted some progressive legislation to be enacted, but never anything that would really hurt the state's moneyed establishment. To note just one fact, Connally's home state is the only one of the eight largest with no income tax.

Lately, as Peirce notes, the dominance of the moneyed establishment and the Tory Democrats is on the wane. Which does not mean that conservative Democrats are no longer in power— they are. But it does mean that their success is no longer automatic, and also that changes—in population patterns, in political preference, and in political organization—may greatly alter Texas politics in the next few years. John Connally's switch to Republican status in 1973 symbolizes what has happened here. When Connally, a man who could become President, speaks, everybody in the nation's highest circles of high finance listens. But he no longer has all that much say about how his native Texas is to run its affairs.

Connally could come back in 1974 if he decided to head a major drive for Texas Republicans, or if he ran for Governor, as a Republican, himself. But the latter possibility seems unlikely. Big John on the Republican stump would only rekindle lingering mistrust. For 20 years, Republicans like conservative state Rep. Fred Agnich of Dallas and ultraconservative Harris County (Houston) leader Nancy Palm labored to build an effective Texas Republican party; all the while, their most effective adversary was Tory Democrat John Connally. Moreover, few of Connally's old friends still active in state politics have made the move to the Republican party. So the betting here is that Connally will find little time to help Texas Republicans in 1974, and will instead advise the President from time to time, hit the fried chicken and mashed potatoes circuit around the country, and hop around to homes in Washington and Jamaica.

The issue that shook the Texas Tory Democratic establishment was the same one that has shaken the Nixon Administration: scandal. In Texas, though, the affair was more of the money-grubbing kind. At the center of the scandal was Frank Sharp, a legendary Texas promoter who built the Sharpstown shopping center in Houston. The details are too complex to recount here, but in the end, state House Speaker Gus Mutscher went to jail, Assistant Attorney General Will Wilson was forced to resign from John Mitchell's Justice Department, and Gov. Preston Smith was implicated. The heroes of the moment were a group of 30 state Representatives—liberal Democrats plus a few conservative Republicans—who voted against a banking bill wanted by Sharp. Colleagues of the state legislators, angered by the refusal to go along, dubbed the recalcitrants the "Dirty 30," a name to which they clung proudly.

The scandal of 1971 and 1972 set the stage for one of the wildest gubernatorial campaigns in Texas history. Competitors included wealthy rancher Dolph Briscoe, whose chief asset, aside from a bulging campaign chest, was the fact that he had not held public office since the 1950s; incumbent Gov. Smith; and two extraordinary figures who nicely illustrate the variety of contemporary Texas politics. One was Lt. Gov. Ben Barnes, who was widely touted as the brightest young politician in Texas and the heir to Johnson and Connally. LBJ himself once predicted that Barnes would someday be President. The gubernatorial candidate was elected to the legislature at 21, became Speaker at 25, and Lieutenant Governor at 29. In Texas, the Lieutenant Governorship is a powerful office, since its holder appoints all state Senate committee chairman and members. For the 1972 election, Barnes was considered the front runner. The wunderkind, however, had a whiff of scandal about him. Though not connected with the Sharp mess, Barnes had become quite wealthy for a young man who had never made as much as $10,000 a year during his adult life. It seems that he was loaned a lot of money without collateral, which he steered toward some sure-fire investments.

The fourth major candidate—and it was not until late in the campaign that the Texas papers would admit that she was a major candidate—was state Rep. Frances Farenthold. Sissy, as she is called, was a leader of the Dirty 30 and had been a member of the state legislature since 1968. When Lyndon Johnson returned to Texas, Sissy was the only member of the legislature to vote against a resolution honoring the ex-President, because of her opposition to the Vietnam war. In general, Farenthold was everything that a candidate for public office in Texas was not supposed to be: a Catholic in a Baptist state, a woman in a state full of aspiring football players and oilmen, a proponent of liberalizing abortion laws, and a critic of the Texas Rangers, who often harass Mexican-Americans in south Texas.

Farenthold's main asset was a powerful one in scandal-conscious Texas: honesty. Everyone knew she could not be bought. Out on the stump, Sissy spoke in a flat, calm voice, as if what she was saying was unremarkable. In the initial primary, Smith, after two terms as Governor, won just 9% of the votes; Barnes, the brainy kid bound for the White House, got just 18% and became a political has-been at age 33. Surprising most of the pundits, Farenthold finished second with 28%, as Briscoe finished first with 44%. During the campaign, it was Briscoe's habit to refuse comment on the issues, which led Sissy to call him "a bowl of pablum." Looking at the results, observers predicted an easy Briscoe win in the runoff. But Farenthold campaigned hard; she managed to construct jerry-built, but effective organizations in the large cities; and won 45% of the votes. Briscoe's victory in the general election again ran counter to Texas tradition—the Democrat just barely won. He beat archconservative Republican state Sen. Henry Grover by a scant 100,000 votes. Meanwhile, La Raza Unida party candidate Ramsey Muniz aimed his campaign solely at Mexican-Americans and got 200,000 votes.

So the liberal Democrats and the conservative Republicans almost upset a Democrat who enjoyed all of the traditional Tory support. Shivers and Connally had always stoutly defended the Texas one-party system, one they could control so long as all the voters in the state continued to cast ballots in the Democratic primary and nominate conservative candidates. But Texas has changed, and so has its politics. Its economy has moved from one dominated by farmers to one dominated by oil. Accordingly, Texas politics is now moving from one under the thumb of rural areas—the bastion of conservative Democrats—to one controlled by the big cities, dominated by liberal Democrats and Republicans. In 1960, the 221 Texas counties with fewer than 50,000 people cast 33% of the state's votes; in 1972, they cast only 26%. Meanwhile, the big cities—Houston, Dallas, Fort Worth, and San Antonio—which cast 36% of the state's votes in 1960, accounted for 43% of them in 1972.

Houston and Dallas are reputed to be strongholds of the new rich, which they are to a considerable extent. But the grip of the wealthy has slackened some in the last dozen years. Since 1960, the state's poll tax has been outlawed, and liberal organizations have sprung up, particularly in Houston. The groups have registered blacks, Mexican-Americans, and white working-class people in great numbers. In 1960, 2.2 million people voted in Texas; by 1972, 3.4 million did—the largest percentage rise among the big states. Most of the new voters live in the four major urban centers, and by no means all of the big-city residents are affluent conservatives. As the growing Texas cities shift to the left and the declining rural areas move farther to the right, no one knows for sure what will happen to Texas politics, but everybody does know it will change.

In 1970, however, the Senate race demonstrated that the power of rural Texas was still a factor, for against considerable odds, the Tory Democratic candidate won. He was Lloyd Bentsen, a former Congressman (1949–55), who came out of lucrative political retirement to upset Sen. (1957–71) Ralph Yarborough in the Democratic primary. Yarborough is the patron saint of Texas liberals—the only one of their number to win major office. Over the years, he and John Connally continually feuded; it was to reconcile them that John Kennedy came to Dallas in 1963. In the Senate, Yarborough compiled a near perfect liberal record. As chairman of the Labor and Public Welfare Committee, the Senator received the full support of the state's small but feisty labor movement.

But in 1970, Yarborough was 66 and Bentsen 51. As usual, the incumbent was poorly financed, while Bentsen had tons of money. Yarborough was busy in Washington and badly organized at home; Bentsen of course bought all the campaign support he needed. Throughout the spring of 1970, Bentsen ran TV clips of the riots outside the 1968 Democratic National Convention. These implied that Yarborough—a longtime opponent of the Vietnam war—was somehow responsible for the carnage, as well as for the other riots and scenes of civil disobedience of the 1960s. The Bentsen media campaign foreshadowed the 1970 Nixon-Agnew congressional law-and-order campaign. But unlike the White House no-more-permissiveness effort, Bentsen's strategy worked. Yarborough's east Texas stump oratory failed to bring back the rural votes, and because of local feuds, the Senator also lost many Mexican-American votes. Moreover, Bentsen, a big landowner in the lower Rio Grande Valley, could speak fluent Spanish. The challenger won a solid 53–47 victory.

Soon thereafter, apparently on the advice of Lyndon Johnson, Bentsen swung to the center. Other right-wing Democratic primary winners—the men who ran against Sen. John Tower in 1961 and 1966—suffered severe desertions from white liberals, blacks, and Chicanos in the general election. So Bentsen wanted to avoid the right-wing path to defeat. He cultivated and won the support of liberals like state Sen. (and now Congresswoman) Barbara Jordan, Rep. Henry Gonzalez, and the state AFL-CIO.

In the end, however, Bentsen's salvation was the traditional rural Democratic vote. The Republican nominee, George Bush—then a Houston Congressman and now Republican National Chairman—waged an effective media campaign. He emphasized his good looks and made a clear pitch for liberal votes. National Republicans felt that Bush was one of the strongest, or at least most photogenic, candidates in the country in 1970. There was even talk that if elected to the Senate, Bush might replace Spiro Agnew on the Republican ticket in 1972. The rumors helped

Bush carry the four big cities, 54–46. But he lost the rural counties by an overwhelming margin of 63–37. A liquor-by-the-glass referendum brought out lots of Baptist Democrats, and these people were not about to vote for a man who looked and talked like a product of an Eastern prep school, which Bush was.

In the Senate, Bentsen has continued to move towards his party's center. The confrontation-prone strategies of the Nixon Administration have nudged Bentsen along. As John Connally, Bentsen's old friend and 1970 backer, became a Republican, Bentsen assumed the chairmanship of the Senate Democratic Campaign Committee. And on major issues, the Texan has usually lined up with other Democrats, including opposition to the bombing of Cambodia. For Bentsen, the antiwar stance represents something of a switch; as a young Congressman, he urged that atomic bombs be dropped on North Korea.

If Bentsen's 1970 triumph showed the persistence of the traditional patterns in Texas politics, the 1972 Senate race manifested a significant break with the past that may well become permanent. Once again, Ralph Yarborough ran, this time at 68. When questioned about his age, the still vigorous man said that his father had lived to be 100. In the initial primary, where more than two million ballots were cast, Yarborough came within 268 votes of securing the Democratic nomination outright. So he faced a runoff, which gave the other major contender, Barefoot Sanders, a second chance. The 47-year-old Sanders was an Assistant Attorney General in the Johnson Administration; in 1968, his appointment to a federal judgeship was blocked by Senate inaction. Sanders did not have the money Bentsen had, nor did he wage Bentsen's kind of hard-line compaign. But for money, Sanders substituted a youthful energy, and though he set forth no hard line, he was clearly more conservative than Yarborough. In a mild surprise, Sanders won the runoff by a 53–47 margin, in large part because he broke into Yarborough's support among rural voters. Yarborough's margin dropped 5% in the rural counties between the first primary and the runoff.

The general election was closer than most pundits had predicted. The favorite, of course, was two-term Republican Sen. John Tower, if only because he had a $2.4 million campaign chest. In fact, Tower had more money at his disposal than any 1972 statewide candidate in the country except perhaps Sen. Charles Percy of Illinois. Tower also took advantage of whatever coattails Nixon had to offer, as he cited his support of the President whenever he got the chance. As Tower campaigned, he knew that Texas had twice rejected Nixon's presidential candidacy—in 1960, when LBJ was on the Democratic ticket, and in 1968, when Humphrey took 41% to Nixon's 40%. But 1972 was a Nixon year in Texas, as the incumbent President won a landslide 67% in the state. The number-one Republican scored the greatest gains in the traditionally Democratic and rural central and eastern parts of Texas. To buck the trend, Sanders had little money—some $2 million less than his opponent. But he and his wife managed to shake 100,000 hands, hoping as they did that the traditionally Democratic allegiances in rural Texas would produce an upset win for Sanders.

But Tower hung on to post a 55% victory. The result was not really a matter of coattails—the difference between Tower and Nixon percentages varied widely from place to place in Texas. Rather, Tower's triumph and Sanders' defeat was a matter of the Republican scoring better than he ever had before in the rural counties. Sanders ran just a single point behind Bentsen's showing in the four big cities—45% compared to 46%. But Sanders got only 46% of the votes in the 221 small counties, compared to Bentsen's 63%.

The rural areas of Texas, unlike those in the other 10 states of the old Confederacy, did not move en masse to Barry Goldwater in 1964 or George Wallace in 1968. They stayed with Lyndon Johnson in 1964 and with Johnson's man Humphrey in 1968. But with Johnson effectively removed from the political picture—he died just a few months after the 1972 election—rural Texas shifted to the right just as the rest of rural South had some years earlier. In part, the political behavior of rural Texans was a repudiation of George McGovern. But beyond that, as the Senate race shows, it evidenced a repudiation of a moderate Texas Democrat who enjoyed John Connally's endorsement. The trend has not yet affected congressional contests, though it probably will when aged Democrats retire or lose Democratic primaries. There is no doubt, however, that even moderate Democrats must build on their increasing strength in Texas cities if they plan to win future statewide elections.

Tower is something of an accidental Senator—a beneficiary of good luck and hard work. In 1959, Tower was an unknown professor at Midwestern University in Wichita Falls; his wife, however, had money. So in 1960, he waged a quixotic campaign against Sen. Lyndon Johnson.

Because Johnson had engineered a bill in the state legislature which allowed him to run for the Senate and the vice-presidency simultaneously, his opponent, Tower, was helped to a respectable showing. And in the 1961 special election to fill Johnson's seat after he became Vice-President, the Republican defeated the ultraconservative Democrat appointed to fill the vacancy.

In 1966, Tower won a full term and his largest margin (57%) so far against then Atty. Gen. Waggoner Carr, who has since been implicated in aspects of the Frank Sharp scandal. In both elections, Tower received the votes of many Texas liberals, either because they considered his opponents more conservative or because they figured that the Republican Tower would be easier to dislodge when a more agreeable candidate emerged. In 1972, of course, Tower got little support from the liberals, but won anyway with Republican-trending rural Texas supplying the needed votes.

Tower, one of the more conservative members of the Senate, is the ranking Republican on the Banking, Housing, and Urban Affairs Committee. He also sits as the number-two Republican on the Armed Services Committee. In general, the Texas Senator opposes high levels of federal spending on domestic programs and supports generous outlays for the military and space programs. Tower's position on fiscal matters is quite acceptable in Texas, which receives far more that its proportionate share of Pentagon and NASA dollars. It is, of course, too early to predict how Tower will fare in 1978 when his seat is up. But the first Republican Senator from Texas since Reconstruction has shown himself no duffer when it comes to winning votes from a changing Texas electorate.

The pace of Texas political activity in 1974 will problbly slacken a bit. Neither of the two Senate seats is up, and incumbent Dolph Briscoe appears likely to win what will be the state's first four-year gubernatorial term. But a host of politicians have expressed an interest in higher office, most of them with backgrounds in conservative Democratic politics but with liberal records of late. These include Atty. Gen. John Hill, who wants to be Governor; House Speaker Price Daniel, Jr., who may run against Lt. Gov. Bill Hobby (who would like to be Governor himself); and state Insurance Commissioner Joe Christie. And several Republicans, encouraged by Briscoe's weak 1972 showing, may be tempted to take him on. Then there is always Frances Farenthold, who has moved from Corpus Christi to Houston, and may run for something. These days, nothing is for sure in Texas politics.

Texas gained one congressional seat after the 1950 census, and another after the 1960 count, for a total of 24. Because of vast population movements within the state, the results of congressional redistricting have been grotesque. Most of rural Texas is losing population, while Houston and Dallas are growing as fast as any metropolitan areas in the nation. Back in the time of Sam Rayburn (who died in 1961), the Texas delegation consisted almost exclusively of conservative-leaning Democrats from rural and small-town districts. The one-man-one-vote decisions have required the elimination of some of the old districts, and others, notably the 6th, have taken grafts composed of urban areas to attain the equal population requirement.

The Texas legislature, always dominated by conservative Democrats, has tried to protect the seats of senior, conservative, and rural-oriented Democrats. Some of the old politicians have had to go, and they have been replaced by Congressmen from the cities, where the two-party system of liberal Democrats and conservative Republicans is now almost fully developed. Accordingly, the Texas delegation, once the most cohesive in Washington, is now much more heterogeneous and somewhat less powerful than it used to be. There is a chance that a pending suit before a federal court will require further redistricting for 1974, but at this writing, it appears that the boundaries currently in effect will be only slightly altered except, possibly, in Dallas (see Texas 5).

Census Data Pop. 11,196,730; 5.53% of U.S. total, 4th largest; change 1960–70, 16.9%. Central city, 48%; suburban, 25%. Median family income, $8,486; 33rd highest; families above $15,000: 17%; families below $3,000: 13%. Median years education, 11.7.

1972 Share of Federal Tax Burden $10,283,710,000; 4.92% of U.S. total, 6th largest.

1972 Share of Federal Outlays $12,624,945,465; 5.82% of U.S. total, 3rd largest.   Per capita federal spending, $1,128.

DOD	$5,121,450,000	2nd (8.19%)	HEW	$3,263,353,480	5th (4.57%)
AEC	$27,210,883	16th (1.04%)	HUD	$170,754,840	4th (5.56%)
NASA	$291,506,357	2nd (9.74%)	VA	$713,948,734	3rd (6.24%)
DOT	$463,698,943	2nd (5.88%)	USDA	$1,161,073,938	2nd (7.55%)
DOC	$29,904,407	9th (2.31%)	CSC	$177,535,987	7th (4.31%)
DOI	$59,215,310	11th (2.79%)	TD	$360,075,408	9th (2.18%)
DOJ	$78,082,695	3rd (7.95%)	Other	$707,134,483	

Economic Base Finance, insurance and real estate; agriculture, notably cattle, sorghum grain, cotton lint and dairy products; transportation equipment, especially aircraft; food and kindred products, especially meat products; oil and gas extraction, especially oil and gas field services; apparel and other textile products, especially men's and boys' furnishings; machinery, especially construction and related machinery.

Political Line-up Governor, Dolph Briscoe (D); seat up, 1974. Senators, John G. Tower (R) and Lloyd Bentsen (D). Representatives, 24 (20 D and 4 R). State Senate (28 D and 3 R); State House (133 D and 17 R).

The Voters

Registration 5,212,815 Total. No party registration.
Median voting age 41.5
Employment profile White collar, 49%. Blue collar, 34%. Service, 13%. Farm, 4%.
Ethnic groups Black, 12%. Spanish, 18%. Total foreign stock, 11%.

Presidential vote

1972	Nixon (R)	2,298,896	(67%)
	McGovern (D)	1,154,289	(33%)
1968	Nixon (R)	1,227,844	(40%)
	Humphrey (D)	1,266,804	(41%)
	Wallace (AI)	584,269	(19%)
1964	Johnson (D)	1,663,185	(63%)
	Goldwater (R)	958,566	(37%)

Senator

John Goodwin Tower (R) Elected May 27, 1961, seat up 1978; b. Sept. 29, 1925, Houston; home, Wichita Falls; Southwestern U., B.A., 1948; So. Methodist U., M.A., 1953; U. of London, 1952; Navy, WWII; USNR; married, three children; Methodist.

Career Faculty, Midwestern U., 1951–60; first Repub. to be elected to U.S. Senate from Tex. since 1870, elected to fill vacancy caused by resignation of Sen. Lyndon B. Johnson.

Offices 142 OSOB, 202-225-2934. Also 784 Fed. Office Bldg., 300 E. 8th St., Austin 78701, 512-397-5933, and 1814 Fed. Bldg., 1114 Commerce St., Dallas 75202, 214-749-3441.

Administrative Assistant Elwin Skiles, Jr.

Committees

Armed Services (2nd); Subs: Military Construction Authorization (Ranking Mbr.); Preparedness Investigating; Strategic Arms Limitation Talks; Tactical Air Power; Reprograming of Funds (Ranking Mbr.); General Legislation.

Banking, Housing and Urban Affairs (Ranking Mbr.); Subs: Housing and Urban Affairs (Ranking Mbr.); Financial Institutions; Production and Stabilization; Small Business

Joint Com. on Defense Production (Ranking Senate Mbr.).

Group Ratings

	ADA	COPE	LWV	RIPON	NFU	LCV	CFA	NAB	NSI	ACA
1972	0	0	18	38	40	0	0	80	100	94
1971	0	27	38	20	18	–	17	–	–	88
1970	3	0	–	15	13	8	–	90	100	94

Key Votes

1) Busing	AGN	8) Sea Life Prot	AGN	15) Tax Singls Less	AGN
2) Alas P-line	FOR	9) Campaign Subs	AGN	16) Min Tax for Rich	AGN
3) Gun Cntrl	AGN	10) Cmbodia Bmbg	FOR	17) Euro Troop Rdctn	AGN
4) Rehnquist	FOR	11) Legal Srvices	AGN	18) Bust Hwy Trust	AGN
5) Pub TV $	AGN	12) Rev Sharing	FOR	19) Maid Min Wage	AGN
6) EZ Votr Reg	AGN	13) Cnsumr Prot	AGN	20) Farm Sub Limit	AGN
7) No-Fault	AGN	14) Eq Rts Amend	FOR	21) Highr Credt Chgs	FOR

Election Results

1972 general:	John G. Tower (R)	1,822,877	(54%)
	Barefoot Sanders (D)	1,511,985	(44%)
	Flores Amaya (LRU)	63,543	(2%)
1972 primary:	John G. Tower (R), unopposed		
1966 general:	John G. Tower (R)	841,501	(57%)
	Waggoner Carr (D)	643,855	(43%)

Senator

Lloyd Millard Bentsen, Jr. (D) Elected 1970, seat up 1976; b. Feb. 11, 1921, Mission; home, Houston; U. of Tex., LL.B., 1942; Army, WWII; married, three children; Presbyterian.

Career Practicing atty., County Judge, Hidalgo County, 1946–48; U.S. House, 1948–55.

Offices 240 OSOB, 202-225-5922. Also Fed. Bldg., Houston 77002, 713-226-5496, and Suite 769, Fed. Bldg., Austin 78701, 512-397-5834.

Administrative Assistant Loyd Hackler

Committees

Finance (10th); Subs: Internation Trade; Private Pension Plans; State Taxation of Interstate Commerce.

Public Works (5th); Subs: Water Resources; Air and Water Pollution; Roads (Chm.); Economic Development; Panel on Environmental Science and Technology.

Joint Economic Com. (6th); Subs: Inter-American Economic Relationships; Economic Progress; Fiscal Policy; International Economics; Urban Affairs.

Group Ratings

	ADA	COPE	LWV	RIPON	NFU	LCV	CFA	NAB	NSI	ACA
1972	35	30	50	48	67	26	91	60	70	45
1971	33	55	69	36	73	–	57	–	–	33

Key Votes

1) Busing	AGN	8) Sea Life Prot	FOR	15) Tax Singls Less	AGN
2) Alas P-line	FOR	9) Campaign Subs	FOR	16) Min Tax for Rich	AGN
3) Gun Cntrl	AGN	10) Cmbodia Bmbg	AGN	17) Euro Troop Rdctn	AGN
4) Rehnquist	FOR	11) Legal Srvices	FOR	18) Bust Hwy Trust	AGN
5) Pub TV $	FOR	12) Rev Sharing	AGN	19) Maid Min Wage	FOR
6) EZ Votr Reg	FOR	13) Cnsumr Prot	FOR	20) Farm Sub Limit	AGN
7) No-Fault	AGN	14) Eq Rts Amend	FOR	21) Highr Credt Chgs	FOR

Election Results

1970 general:	Lloyd Bentsen (D)	1,226,568	(53%)
	George Bush (R)	1,071,234	(47%)
1970 primary:	Lloyd Bentsen (D)	841,316	(53%)
	Ralph W. Yarborough (D)	726,477	(47%)

FIRST DISTRICT Political Background

The 1st district of Texas is the northeast corner of the state. Its largest cities are Marshall (pop. 22,000), Paris (pop. 23,000), and the Texas half of Texarkana (pop. 30,000). The character of the district has remained agricultural; in fact, this part of Texas constitutes a rarity: it is one of the few places where the old tradition of Southern populism retains some vitality. Like Jim Hogg, the populist Governor of Texas in the 1890s, the farmers and townspeople of the 1st district are suspicious of bankers, insurance companies, oil men, and Republicans. Neither are they especially fond of race-mixers; in 1968, George Wallace almost carried the 1st, running a close second to Hubert Humphrey.

It is therefore fitting that Wright Patman represents the district in Congress. Born in 1893, Patman first went to Washington in 1929. Those two years were the two in which the greatest financial crashes of American history occurred, and Patman has forgotten neither. He combines the attitudes of a farmer who lost his savings in a failing bank and a shrewd lawyer's understanding of the workings of American financial institutions. In most Congressmen, the existence of such traits would deserve only passing comment. But Wright Patman has been Chairman of the House Banking and Currency Committee for the past dozen years.

Patman was long known for his zealous attacks on the big New York banks and the Federal Reserve Board. The Texan regularly took on former (1951–69) Fed Chairman William McChesney Martin, who was otherwise a species of sacred cow on Capitol Hill and Wall Street. Nor has Patman spared current Fed Chairman Arthur Burns. Patman has also decried the abuses of big foundations, and helped to frame the recent legislation that severely regulates how they operate. And Patman was the man who blew the whistle on the Nixon Administration's plan to bail out the Penn Central Railroad. He deserves much of the credit for stopping any flow of the taxpayer's dollar to what the Penn Central's bankruptcy revealed was a scandalously mismanaged corporate giant.

Patman is not one of the more powerful committee chairmen. He has, however, managed to keep the Democrats on Banking and Currency together on price-control legislation, over which the committee has jurisdiction. Moreover, the Chairman has sustained a reasonable bipartisan cooperation on housing bills; he enjoys good working relationships with the committee's number-two Democrat, William Barrett of Pennsylvania, and its number-one Republican, William Widnall of New Jersey. But on banking issues, Patman steers a rudderless ship. Banking is one of the most closely regulated private industries. Consequently, the banking lobbies seek legislation that is congenial to the way the banks want to do business. The entreaties of lobbyists receive sympathy and respect among the committee's Republicans, as well as among a sizable number of its Democrats, who are often led by Robert Stephens of Georgia. After all, a majority of the Banking Committee's members own bank stock themselves; so it's no surprise that they tend to look at things from a banker's point of view.

With varying success, Patman sets himself against such thinking. The result is a fractious committee. Patman controls the staff, which means that he can draw up legislation the way he wants. Other committee members, however, will often vote down Patman's draft for one written by bank lobbyists. One example that nicely illustrates the rancor on the committee occurred in October 1972. Patman wanted to organize a hearing on the Watergate scandal, the initial focus of which would be possible illegal banking transactions—the laundering of campaign contributions through Mexican banks, for example. But Garry Brown of Michigan lined up the committee's Republicans in solid opposition. And Stephens, along with Nixon operatives, came up with enough Democratic votes to stymie Patman by a 20–15 head count. The efforts of Brown and Stephens kept the Watergate scandal from public view until after the 1972 elections. Some committee members, however, will no doubt face questions about their conduct as they campaign for reelection in 1974.

Patman, of course, is hardly a favorite on Wall Street, where his ideas enjoy no more respect than those of William Jennings Bryan. But back home, at least until 1972, Patman has been a popular politician. His constituents have readily forgiven him for voting for civil rights bills, and have reelected him handily. Redistricting was kind to Patman in 1972, perhaps because the chairman of the Texas legislative committee on redistricting was state Sen. William Patman, the Congressman's son. Nevertheless, Wright Patman does have one problem that may hurt him in future elections: age. Though still hale and active, he was 78 in 1972, when he was held to just 62% of the votes in the Democratic primary; in this part of Texas, the Republican party is still a negligible factor in congressional politics.

Census Data Pop. 461,879. Central city, 7%; suburban, 8%. Median family income, $6,549; families above $15,000: 9%; families below $3,000: 21%. Median years education, 10.6.

1972 Share of Federal Outlays $522,437,309

DOD	$210,303,000	HEW	$209,076,463
AEC	–	HUD	$4,002,838
NASA	–	DOI	$215,574
DOT	$6,122,989	USDA	$27,260,454
		Other	$65,455,691

Federal Military-Industrial Commitments

DOD Contractors Day and Zimmerman, Inc. (Texarkana), $91.484m: operation of Lone Star Army Ammunition plant. Thiokol Chemical Corp. (Marshall), $33.082m: operation of Long Horn Army Ammunition plant. United Ammunition Container Co. (Atlanta), $6.503m: fiber containers.

DOD Installations Red River Army Depot (Texarkana).

Economic Base Agriculture, notably cattle, dairy products and poultry; finance, insurance and real estate; food and kindred products; lumber and wood products; and fabricated metal products.

The Voters

Registration 214,561 total. No party registration.
Median voting age 49.7
Employment profile White collar, 37%. Blue collar, 44%. Service, 13%. Farm, 6%.
Ethnic groups Black, 23%. Total foreign stock, 1%.

Presidential vote

1972	Nixon (R)	99,658	(70%)
	McGovern (D)	41,763	(30%)
1968	Nixon (R)	39,801	(27%)
	Humphrey (D)	56,212	(38%)
	Wallace (AI)	52,639	(35%)

Representative

Wright Patman (D) Elected March 4, 1929; b. Aug. 6, 1893, Patman's Switch; home, Texarkana; Cumberland U., LL.B., 1916; Army, WWII; married, three children; Baptist.

Career Cotton farmer, 1913–14; Asst. County Atty., 1916–17; Tex. House of Reps., 1921–24; Dist. Atty. 5th Judicial Dist., 1924–29.

Offices 2328 RHOB, 202-225-3035. Also P.O. Box 1868, Texarkana 75501, 214-793-2471.

Administrative Assistant Baron Shacklette

Committees

Banking and Currency (Chm.); Sub: Domestic Finance (Chm.).

Joint Com. on Defense Production (Vice-Chm.).

Joint Economic Com. (Chm.); Subs: Economic Progress (Chm.); Priorities and Economy in Government.

Group Ratings

	ADA	COPE	LWV	RIPON	NFU	LCV	CFA	NAB	NSI	ACA
1972	13	72	33	33	86	19	100	29	100	50
1971	24	64	83	47	73	–	75	–	–	48
1970	24	45	–	21	46	39	88	20	86	40

Key Votes

1) Busing	AGN	6) Cmbodia Bmbg	FOR	11) Chkg Acct Intrst	FOR
2) Strip Mines	ABS	7) Bust Hwy Trust	AGN	12) End HISC (HUAC)	AGN
3) Cut Mil $	AGN	8) Farm Sub Lmt	AGN	13) Nixon Sewer Veto	AGN
4) Rev Shrg	AGN	9) School Prayr	AGN	14) Corp Cmpaign $	AGN
5) Pub TV $	ABS	10) Cnsumr Prot	FOR	15) Pol $ Disclosr	AGN

Election Results

1972 general:	Wright Patman (D), unopposed		
1972 primary:	Wright Patman (D)	69,579	(57%)
	Fred Hudson, Jr. (D)	53,255	(43%)
1970 general:	Wright Patman (D)	67,883	(78%)
	James Hogan (R)	18,614	(22%)

SECOND DISTRICT Political Background

How does it happen that a Texas district that went for George Wallace in 1968 ended up four years later electing a liberal Congressman? The answer tells us something about the recent state of affairs in Texas politics and its potential to generate unlikely results. The 2nd district comprises an almost entirely rural area in east Texas; altogether, it includes 20 counties. The largest cities here are Orange (pop. 24,000) and Lufkin (pop. 23,000). More than any other Texas district, the 2nd is an extension of the Deep South. Farmers from the Deep South first settled this none-too-fertile part of the state. Their lot was a hard one, and to this day, the residents of the district retain a streak of populism. During the 1930s, it was here in the 2nd that the richest oil fields were found. But for the most part, the money went elsewhere—to Houston and Dallas, and to smaller towns like Tyler and Longview.

For 20 years, the 2nd district was represented by a man who fit in easily with the older, more conservative Southern Democrats on Capitol Hill. For most of his career, Congressman John Dowdy worked anonymously; he became a high-seniority member of the Judiciary Committee and one of the quiet anti-home-rule powers on the District of Columbia Committee. As often as not, he was unopposed in primaries and general elections.

Then, in 1970, Dowdy was indicted on federal bribery, conspiracy, and perjury charges. In the general election of that year, no opposition appeared on the ballot; nevertheless, some 25% of the voters took the trouble to write in somebody else. Dowdy was, as the 1972 *Almanac* had it, "serving his last term." In 1972, after delays occasioned by his alleged poor health, Dowdy was convicted and sentenced to prison. Earlier, he had decided not to run for reelection, but Dowdy's wife, who was collecting a handsome salary as a member of his staff, did file for the seat. In the meantime, Congressman Dowdy decided not to cast any more votes in the House, lest there be some action—as threatened by the Black Caucus, among others—to oust him from office before his term expired.

Dowdy blamed his conviction on Eastern liberals and homosexuals. Back home, there may have been a time when his presumably conservative constituents would have elected his wife to replace him. But not in Texas in 1972. For scandal was the biggest political issue of the year, and though Dowdy's crimes paled when compared to the Frank Sharp scandal (see Texas state write-up), the Congressman's misdeeds still ruined him politically.

The man who beat Mrs. Dowdy and the three others in the race was state Sen. Charles Wilson. He earned the "liberal" tag in Austin for his support of progressive taxation and his opposition to the kind of Tory cronyism that bred so much corruption. Wilson carried every county in the district, for a total of 64%, in the Democratic primary. Mrs. Dowdy finished with a pathetic 18%. In the general election, Wilson did even better against a Republican opponent. There is every indication that the new Congressman, who just turned 40, will be around for a long time.

Census Data Pop. 466,836. Central city, 5%; suburban, 28%. Median family income, $7,258; families above $15,000: 10%; families below $3,000: 19%. Median years education, 10.5.

1972 Share of Federal Outlays $308,864,433

DOD	$33,500,503	HEW	$164,044,542
AEC	$39,888	HUD	$2,576,724
NASA	$11,124,478	DOI	$1,868,398
DOT	$9,136,045	USDA	$21,654,926
		Other	$64,918,929

Federal Military-Industrial Commitments

No installations or contractors receiving prime awards greater than $5,000,000.

Economic Base Lumber and wood products, especially sawmill and planing mill products; agriculture, notably cattle and poultry; chemicals and allied products; finance, insurance and real estate; and oil and gas extraction, especially oil and gas field services. Also higher education (Sam Houston State Univ. and Stephen F. Austin State Univ.).

The Voters

Registration 223,630 total. No party registration.
Median voting age 44.5
Employment profile White collar, 38%. Blue collar, 44%. Service, 14%. Farm, 4%.
Ethnic groups Black, 20%. Spanish 3%. Total foreign stock, 2%.

Presidential vote

1972	Nixon (R)	98,598	(67%)
	McGovern (D)	47,499	(33%)
1968	Nixon (R)	38,316	(27%)
	Humphrey (D)	50,599	(36%)
	Wallace (AI)	51,017	(36%)

Representative

Charles Wilson (D) Elected 1972; b. June 1933, Trinity; home, Lufkin; Sam Houston State U.; U.S. Naval Academy, Annapolis, B.S.; 1956; married, no children; Methodist.

Career Manager, retail lumber store; State Rep., 1967–70; State Sen., 1970–72.

Offices 2307 RHOB, 202-225-2401. Also Fed. Bldg., Lufkin 75901, 713-632-2434.

Administrative Assistant Charles W. Simpson

Committees

Foreign Affairs (21st); Subs: Near East and South Asia; National Security Policy and Scientific Developments.

Veterans' Affairs (15th); Subs: Education and Training; Hospitals; Housing.

Group Ratings: Newly Elected

Key Votes

1) Busing	NE	6) Cmbodia Bmbg	AGN	11) Chkg Acct Intrst	AGN
2) Strip Mines	NE	7) Bust Hwy Trust	AGN	12) End HISC (HUAC)	AGN
3) Cut Mil $	NE	8) Farm Sub Lmt	NE	13) Nixon Sewer Veto	FOR
4) Rev Shrg	NE	9) School Prayr	NE	14) Corp Cmpaign $	NE
5) Pub TV $	NE	10) Cnsumr Prot	NE	15) Pol $ Disclosr	NE

Election Results

1972 general:	Charles Wilson (D)	100,345	(74%)
	Charles D. Brightwell (R)	35,600	(26%)
1972 primary:	Charles Wilson (D)	85,517	(64%)
	John D. Dowdy (D)	23,808	(18%)
	Norman T. Birdwell (D)	13,398	(10%)
	Louis V. McIntire (D)	9,863	(7%)
	Thomas W. Porter (D)	1,919	(1%)

THIRD DISTRICT Political Background

The rich Texan in all the rich Texan jokes probably lives on the north side of Dallas. This is where right-wing oilman H. L. Hunt resides in his replica of Mount Vernon, and where Jimmy Ling built his huge mansion before he was driven out of the conglomerate he put together. The area is also the fastest-growing around Dallas. Affluence has pushed the boundaries of settlement northward, past the Dallas city limits to suburbs like Irving, Farmers Branch, and Richardson. Along with most of north Dallas, these suburbs form the 3rd congressional district of Texas.

Dallas is the older and more conservative of the state's two great cities. The wealth in Houston is based on oil and chemicals; in Dallas, more on oil and high finance and, lately, computers. Until recently, Dallas, though smaller than Houston, had larger bank deposits. The smaller of the two still ranks as the Southwest's leading financial, banking, and insurance center. Though the big oil companies prefer Houston to Dallas as their headquarters, Dallas has developed a host of computer and electronics firms. All in all, Dallas is more white-collar and more Republican. In fact, Texans in the city were first in the state to send a Republican to Congress since Reconstruction—Bruce Alger in 1952. Today, Dallas and environs sends two Republicans to the House, the only Southern metropolitan area to do so.

The 3rd district, being the richest part of Dallas, is its most conservative and most Republican. In fact, the 3rd's current boundaries were drawn to corral most of the Republican parts of the area in one district. The 3rd was first created in 1965, when the one-man-one-vote ruling forced the Texas legislature to eliminate a rural district and cede it to Dallas. The district's first Congressman was the picturesque sort of conservative Southern Democrat now relatively uncommon—a rotund, garrulous, bibulous man named Joe Pool. He was elected Congressman-at-Large from the state in 1962 and 1964; after the seat was eliminated, he ran in the 3rd and won in 1966. Following a brief term as Chairman of the House Un-American Activities Committee, he died in 1967. Pool was succeeded by Republican James Collins.

Like all the Republicans who represented Texas in Congress during the 1960s, Collins lost a race—to Pool in 1966—before winning his seat. And like most Texas Congressmen, Collins is a wealthy man (insurance and other ventures). In Congress, he has, of course, voted a solid conservative line. What is unusual about Collins is a touch of scandal. His former administrative assistant was convicted and sent to federal prison for exacting kickbacks from members of Collins' staff. Collins himself was accused of involvement in the scheme by Jack Anderson, but was not indicted after a federal investigation. Nonetheless, the Congressman's troubles helped to inspire primary opposition from former Dallas County Republican Chairman Tom Crouch in 1972. In a light turnout, Collins won renomination by a 2–1 margin; most Texas, even Dallasites, still vote in the Democratic primary, where most of the action is. Barring any further whiff of scandal, Collins appears in good shape for reelection.

Census Data Pop. 465,221. Central city, 61%; suburban, 39%. Median family income, $12,437; families above $15,000: 36%; families below $3,000: 6%. Median years education, 12.7.

Economic Base Finance, insurance and real estate; machinery; electrical equipment and supplies, especially communication equipment; transportation equipment, especially aircraft and parts; apparel and other textile products, especially women's and misses' dresses; and food and kindred products.

1972 Share of Federal Outlays $499,428,371

DOD	$266,404,295		HEW	$110,768,658
AEC	$5,765		HUD	$3,398,362
NASA	$6,583,736		DOI	$812,299
DOT	$24,925,035		USDA	$34,804,694
			Other	$51,725,527

Federal Military-Industrial Commitments

DOD Contractors Ling-Tempco-Vought (Dallas), $337.921m: A-7 aircraft; aircraft structural components; aircraft electronic components. Texas Instruments (Dallas), $172.292m: aircraft radar and communication equipment; guided bomb kits; ABM support; other electronic ware. Collins Radio (Richardson), $20.262m: aircraft radar and communications equipment. Braniff Airways (Dallas), $12.731m: transportation services.

The Voters

Registration 238,056 total. No party registration.
Median voting age 38.5
Employment profile White collar, 68%. Blue collar, 23%. Service, 9%. Farm, –%.
Ethnic groups Black, 9%. Spanish, 9%. Total foreign stock, 9%.

Presidential vote

1972	Nixon (R)	136,195	(77%)
	McGovern (D)	39,892	(23%)
1968	Nixon (R)	85,296	(61%)
	Humphrey (D)	38,119	(27%)
	Wallace (AI)	15,879	(11%)

Representative

James M. Collins (R) Elected Aug. 24, 1968; b. April 29, 1916, Hallsville; home, Irving; So. Methodist U., B.S.C., 1937; Northwestern U., M.B.A., 1938; American Col., C.L.U., 1940; Harvard, M.B.A., 1943; Army, WWII; married, three children; Baptist.

Career Pres., Consolidated Industries, Inc., and Intl. Industries, Inc.; Pres., Fidelity Union Life Insurance Co., 1954–65.

Offices 1512 LHOB, 202-225-4201. Also 5C48 Fed. Bldg., 1100 Commerce St., Dallas 75202, 214-749-2453. Bill Andrews

Administrative Assistant Roy Sausset (O.M.)

Committees

Interstate and Foreign Commerce (10th); Sub: Communications and Power.

Group Ratings

	ADA	COPE	LWV	RIPON	NFU	LCV	CFA	NAB	NSI	ACA
1972	6	9	18	21	14	24	50	92	89	91
1971	8	17	0	44	38	–	13	–	–	93
1970	0	9	–	31	23	0	40	91	90	84

Key Votes

1) Busing	AGN	6) Cmbodia Bmbg	FOR	11) Chkg Acct Intrst	AGN
2) Strip Mines	FOR	7) Bust Hwy Trust	AGN	12) End HISC (HUAC)	AGN
3) Cut Mil $	AGN	8) Farm Sub Lmt	AGN	13) Nixon Sewer Veto	FOR
4) Rev Shrg	FOR	9) School Prayr	FOR	14) Corp Cmpaign $	FOR
5) Pub TV $	AGN	10) Cnsumr Prot	AGN	15) Pol $ Disclosr	AGN

Election Results

1972 general:	James Collins (R)	122,984	(73%)
	George A. Hughes, Jr. (D)	44,708	(27%)
1972 primary:	James Collins (R)	13,367	(68%)
	Tom Crouch (R)	6,362	(32%)
1970 general:	James Collins (R)	63,690	(61%)
	John Mead (R)	41,425	(39%)

FOURTH DISTRICT Political Background

The 4th congressional district of Texas is part of the Red River Valley. From the time it was first settled by white men more than a century ago, until the 1972 elections, the valley has remained staunchly Democratic. This is a part of Texas where the Deep South becomes the Southwest. As one moves west, there are fewer and fewer blacks: only 15% here in the 4th as compared to 23% in the 1st district to the east. The 4th, moreover, has virtually no Mexican-Americans. From the early days, the valley has been peopled mostly by poor white farmers and the residents of the small towns where the farm families come to market every Saturday.

Though never rich or cosmopolitan, the Red River Valley can claim a number of famous sons. Dwight Eisenhower was born in Texas just a few miles south of the river, and Carl Albert comes from Bug Tussle, Oklahoma, just north of the river. But the valley's most fabled son is Mister Sam, Speaker Sam Rayburn, who represented the 4th district in Congress from 1913 to 1961. Rayburn's career spans almost all of our modern political history. When the young Texan was first elected, Henry Adams still lived in Lafayette Park across from the White House. Rayburn then saw Washington grow from the provincial outpost, disdained by the Boston Brahmin, into the most powerful city in the world.

Rayburn entered the House just after it had freed itself from the iron rule of Speaker Joe Cannon. In 1961, Rayburn went home to die just a few months after he had led, and won, a struggle to increase the membership of the Rules Committee, which augmented the power of both the Speaker and the Kennedy Administration over Congress. During Rayburn's first term in the House, President Wilson, working with Speaker Champ Clark and Majority Leader Oscar Underwood, enacted the entire Democratic legislative program with automatic votes from the Democratic Caucus. Some half century later, the Rules Committee imbroglio exposed all the cracks and fissures that had developed within the caucus since Wilson's time.

"To get along, you have to go along," Mister Sam often said, and in so saying, he admitted that the Democratic party, split by civil rights and other issues, could no longer operate as a cohesive unit. Members of the party would simply have to take account of the differences among them. Aside from the four years the Republicans controlled the House, Rayburn held the Speakership from 1940 until his death in 1961—for 17 years, a term longer than any man has ever occupied the post. Critics said that he did not exert his power often enough or forcefully enough; Rayburn replied that a heavy hand would only lead to the dissolution of the Democratic party.

Sam Rayburn also witnessed nearly all of the modern political history of Texas. Back in 1912, the big oil strikes lay in the future. So oil was not yet a factor in the state's politics. Fifty years later, oil dominated just about everything in Texas. Rayburn, as much as anyone, built the politics of oil into the congressional establishment. He made certain, for example, that any Congressman who said he wanted to cut the oil depletion allowance never got a seat on the tax-writing Ways and Means Committee. Rayburn was also largely responsible for the cohesiveness of the Texas delegation, whether the issue was oil, cotton, or military installations.

Oil changed Sam Rayburn's Texas, as did shifts in population. In 1912, towns like Rayburn's Bonham (1970 pop. 7,698) were typical of the state—small, dusty agricultural market centers. By 1961, Dallas and Houston had begun to dominate Texas politics, as the state had just elected its first Republican Senator since Reconstruction. Today, Bonham is no longer part of Rayburn's 4th. The town was moved into Wright Patman's 1st district to satisfy the one-man-one-vote requirement. As it stands now, two-thirds of the 4th is classified as metropolitan; most of it is part of the Dallas Standard Metropolitan Statistical Area. Since Rayburn's death, the 4th has also come to include the arch-conservative, heavily Republican oil towns of Tyler and Longview. These are here mainly because populistic Wright Patman wanted no part of them, and his son chaired the redistricting committee of the Texas Senate. Finally, what was the old Rayburn district now takes in a small portion of the city of Dallas itself.

Rayburn's successor in the 4th district is Ray Roberts, who was born some three weeks after Mister Sam was first sworn in. When first elected in 1962, Roberts was a state Senator and, before that, a staff assistant to the Speaker. Roberts is a man out of the Rayburn mold. When Lyndon Johnson was President, the White House could usually count on Roberts to deliver a liberal vote when needed. But lately, the Congressman's record has grown conservative, reflecting the changing attitudes in his constituency. In 1960, Kennedy carried the 4th, but eight years later, Humphrey lost to Nixon within the district's current boundaries. In 1972, McGovern lost the 4th by a margin exceeding 2–1.

Since the last couple of redistrictings, Roberts has never really been tested in the district. He beat ex-Rep. (1939–53, 1957–67) Beckworth in the 1966 primary when Beckworth's district was eliminated. In 1972, the Republicans ran a candidate in the 4th for the first time since 1964. Roberts won with 70% of the votes, but failed to carry the Dallas portion of the district. Because of Republican strength in the Dallas area and in Tyler and Longview, Roberts could face a stiffer Republican challenge some time soon.

Census Data Pop. 463,142. Central city, 24%; suburban, 44%. Median family income, $8,284; families above $15,000: 14%; families below $3,000: 13%. Median years education, 11.6.

1972 Share of Federal Outlays $428,415,100

DOD	$163,455,027	HEW	$148,892,707
AEC	$1,648	HUD	$2,086,253
NASA	$1,925,164	DOI	$668,997
DOT	$18,490,154	USDA	$22,918,694
		Other	$69,976,456

Federal Military-Industrial Commitments

DOD Contractors E Systems, Inc. (Greenville), $52.497m: support for low attitude drone avionics. Marathon Le Tourneau (Longview), $27.585m: metal parts for 750-pound bombs.

Economic Base Finance, insurance and real estate; agriculture, notably cattle, grains, dairy products and poultry; apparel and other textile products; oil and gas extraction, especially crude petroleum and natural gas, and oil and gas field services; and machinery. Also higher education (East Texas State Univ., and Lamar Univ.).

The Voters

Registration 221,991 total. No party registration.
Median voting age 43.9
Employment profile White collar, 44%. Blue collar, 39%. Service, 14%. Farm, 3%.
Ethnic groups Black, 15%. Spanish, 3%. Total foreign stock, 2%.

Presidential vote

1972	Nixon (R)	107,025	(74%)
	McGovern (D)	36,736	(26%)
1968	Nixon (R)	47,966	(37%)
	Humphrey (D)	44,554	(35%)
	Wallace (AI)	36,508	(28%)

Representative

Ray Roberts (D) Elected Jan. 30, 1962; b. March 29, 1913, Collin County; home, McKinney; Tex. A&M; N. Tex. State; Tex. U.; Navy, WWII; Capt. USNR (Ret.); married, one child; Methodist.

Career Dist. Dir., NYA of Texas, 1935–37; Staff of Speaker Sam Rayburn, 1940–42; Tex. Senate, 1955–62.

Offices 2455 RHOB, 202-225-6673. Also Rm. 225 Fed. Bldg., McKinney 75069, 214-542-2617, and 105 Smith County Court House, Tyler 75701, 214-597-3222.

Administrative Assistant A. M. Willis, Jr.

Committees

Public Works (10th); Subs: Public Buildings and Grounds; Energy; Transportation; Water Resources (Chm.).

Veterans' Affairs (5th); Subs: Compensation and Pension; Hospitals; Housing.

Group Ratings

	ADA	COPE	LWV	RIPON	NFU	LCV	CFA	NAB	NSI	ACA
1972	6	27	18	20	50	11	0	64	100	87
1971	3	27	17	13	54	–	14	–	–	77
1970	12	34	–	18	36	28	53	55	100	61

Key Votes

1) Busing	AGN	6) Cmbodia Bmbg	FOR
2) Strip Mines	AGN	7) Bust Hwy Trust	AGN
3) Cut Mil $	AGN	8) Farm Sub Lmt	AGN
4) Rev Shrg	AGN	9) School Prayr	FOR
5) Pub TV $	AGN	10) Cnsumr Prot	AGN

11) Chkg Acct Intrst	AGN
12) End HISC (HUAC)	AGN
13) Nixon Sewer Veto	AGN
14) Corp Cmpaign $	FOR
15) Pol $ Disclosr	AGN

Election Results

1972 general:	Ray Roberts (D)	95,674	(70%)
	James Russell (R)	40,548	(30%)
1972 primary:	Ray Roberts (D), unopposed		
1970 general:	Ray Roberts (D), unopposed		

FIFTH DISTRICT Political Background

The political history of the 5th congressional district of Texas has been shaped in a special way by the event that is perhaps central to the political history of the 1960s: the assassination in Dallas of President Kennedy in November 1963. For the ten years preceding the murder, Dallas was personified in the minds of many by its Congressman, Bruce Alger, a Republican. Alger was a raucous and fiery ideological right-winger, who had won the seat (which then included all of Dallas County) in 1952 and who held it for 12 years. In Washington, he produced little, critics said, aside from an incessant rant at liberals. Alger's moment in American history came in 1960, when he took part in a pushing-and-shoving demonstration against Lyndon and Lady Bird Johnson in a Dallas hotel lobby.

The Kennedy assassination seemed to create a politics of remorse among Texans generally and among Dallas residents in particular. In 1964, LBJ captured his home state by a huge majority, and even carried Dallas County in the process. The Dallas establishment was in a mood to atone for what seemed to be the city's violent predilections, as memories of the assassination lingered. Bruce Alger was through in Dallas politics. Though he had won previous elections easily, Alger managed only 43% of the votes in 1964—less than Barry Goldwater got in the district.

The winner was Earle Cabell, a former Dallas Mayor, and, accordingly, a member in good standing of the city's business and financial elite. Through the Citizens' Charter Association (CCA), the Dallas elite had dominated city elections for the preceding 20 years. During the Johnson years, Cabell compiled a moderate-to-conservative record in Washington. Thereafter, he was mostly conservative—notably as a high-ranking member of the House District of Columbia Committee.

But lately the CCA, which adapted to the shock of the assassination, has been less adept at reading the mood of Dallas. And so, as the 1972 election proved, has Cabell. In 1971, the CCA's candidate for Mayor was defeated by an upstart named Wes Wise, who became so popular that he was reelected with 84% of the votes in 1973. And in 1972, Earle Cabell, considered unbeatable, lost his seat.

Cabell's demise developed in a rather expected way. In 1970, liberal state Sen. Mike McKool challenged Cabell in the Democratic primary. The insurgent surprised the incumbent when McKool came within 4,000 votes of winning. McKool's strength lay for the most part in the district's black community, which then made up about a quarter of the constituency. So when redistricting time rolled around, Cabell made arrangements with friendly members of the legislature to remove many black areas from the 5th and to replace them with white neighborhoods.

The redistricting left Cabell without trouble in the 1972 primary, as McKool ran and lost in the newly created 24th district. But the general election was another matter. The Republican nomination had gone to 30-year-old Alan Steelman, a former director of Nixon's Office of Minority Business Enterprises. He received some hefty financial contributions from certain members of Dallas' business elite. But Steelman's ideas were not always consistent with those of the CCA. One of the main issues was the Trinity River Canal Project—a $1.3 billion program to build a waterway from the Gulf of Mexico to Dallas and Fort Worth. The Dallas establishment enthusiastically embraced the idea; like Houston, Dallas would become a sea port. But Steelman questioned both the cost and the desirability of the project. Endless, uncontrolled growth, he argued, was not necessarily a good thing, even for Dallas; moreover, the benefits would accrue to a well-placed minority, while a majority would bear most of the costs.

In our time, when ecological issues have benefited insurgents throughout the country, Steelman's argument struck a chord, even in Dallas. And as he bought plenty of media time and went door to door, Steelman found increasing support for his position on the canal. When the votes were counted, the Republican scored a 56% victory—a major upset. His stance toward the

Trinity River Canal was later vindicated when voters in a 17-county area including Dallas rejected a proposition that would have levied a tax needed to finance the project.

On other issuses, Steelman usually supports the Nixon Administration. But he does have an eye for ecological concern; he was one of three Texas Congressmen to vote for a proposal to tap the highway trust fund for mass transit systems. Moreover, as a believer in free enterprise, he is skeptical about government aid to mismanaged corporations.

Steelman's prospects for 1974 look good. The redistricting plan which, at this writing, seems likely to be adopted by the federal court, will significantly change the 5th's boundaries —eliminating about 30 heavily Republican, high-income, precincts and adding lower-income, theoretically more Democratic areas. But these areas went pretty heavily Republican in 1972, and will probably do so in the future. Steelman will try to win a larger share of the black vote in the district; most of them last time voted for Cabell, despite his conservative record and opposition to home rule in Washington. Steelman should do well in the white neighborhoods of the 5th. After 1963, the Dallas elite effected some changes from the top. Steelman's election indicates that further change will come from the grassroots and that nothing in Texas politics is as secure as it once was.

Census Data Pop. 465,093. Central city, 68%; suburban, 32%. Median family income, $10,009; families above $15,000: 21%; families below $3,000: 8%. Median years education, 12.1.

1972 Share of Federal Outlays $499,261,338

DOD	$226,328,574	HEW	$110,731,611
AEC	$5,763	HUD	$3,397,226
NASA	$6,581,534	DOI	$812,027
DOT	$24,916,699	USDA	$34,793,053
		Other	$91,694,851

Federal Military-Industrial Commitments

DOD Contractors Collins Radio (Dallas), $20.946m: various electronics communications equipment. Intercontinental Manufacturing (Garland), 414.225m: bomb bodies. TemTex Industries (Garland), $9.970m: bomb fin assemblies and bomb dispensers. U.S. Department of Transportation (Dallas), $6.564m: unspecified. Varo, Inc. (Garland), $5.826m: electronic image intensifiers.

Economic Base Finance, insurance and real estate; machinery; electrical equipment and supplies, especially communication equipment; transportation equipment, especially aircraft and parts; and apparel and other textile products, especially women's and misses' dresses.

The Voters

Registration 209,758 total. No party registration.
Median voting age 40.0
Employment profile White collar, 55%. Blue collar, 32%. Service, 13%. Farm, –%.
Ethnic groups Black, 17%. Spanish, 5%. Total foreign stock, 5%.

Presidential vote

1972	Nixon (R)	98,434	(69%)
	McGovern (D)	43,360	(31%)
1968	Nixon (R)	61,004	(48%)
	Humphrey (D)	45,759	(36%)
	Wallace (AI)	20,970	(16%)

Representative

Alan Watson Steelman (R) Elected 1972; b. Mar. 15, 1942, Little Rock, Ark.; home, Dallas; Baylor U., B.A., 1964; So. Methodist U., M.L.A., 1971; JFK Institute of Politics, Harvard, 1972; married, four children; Baptist.

Career Exec. Dir. Repub. Party of Dallas County, 1966–69; Exec. Dir., President's Advisory Council on Minority Business Enterprise, 1969–72; Mbr., Special White House Speakers Task Force on Phase I, II, of Admin. Econ. Program; Exec. Dir., Sam Wyly Foundation of Dallas, 1969.

Offices 437 CHOB, 202-225-2231. Also 1100 Commerce, Suite 9C60, Fed. Office Bldg., Dallas 75202, 214-749-7277.

Administrative Assistant Marvin Collins

Committees

Government Operations (16th); Subs: Conservation and Natural Resources; Intergovernmental Relations.

Interior and Insular Affairs (12th); Subs: No. 1 (National Parks and Recreation); No. 2 (Water and Power Resources); No. 3 (Environment); No. 5 (Mines and Mining).

Group Ratings: Newly Elected

Key Votes

1) Busing	NE	6) Cmbodia Bmbg	FOR	11) Chkg Acct Intrst	AGN
2) Strip Mines	NE	7) Bust Hwy Trust	FOR	12) End HISC (HUAC)	AGN
3) Cut Mil $	NE	8) Farm Sub Lmt	NE	13) Nixon Sewer Veto	FOR
4) Rev Shrg	NE	9) School Prayr	NE	14) Corp Cmpaign $	NE
5) Pub TV $	NE	10) Cnsumr Prot	NE	15) Pol $ Disclosr	NE

Election Results

1972 general:	Alan Steelman (R)	74,932	(56%)
	Earle Cabell (D)	59,601	(44%)
1972 runoff:	Alan Steelman (R)	2,782	(63%)
	Robert E. Lyle (R)	1,619	(27%)
1972 primary:	Alan Steelman (R)	2,803	(42%)
	Robert E. Lyle (R)	2,058	(31%)
	Gaylord E. Marshall (R)	1,578	(24%)
	Ken Sikorski (R)	256	(4%)

SIXTH DISTRICT Political Background

On the map, the 6th district of Texas looks like a predominantly rural and small-town district. As it stretches south out of Dallas and Fort Worth to a point near Houston, the district moves through Waxahachie and Hillsboro to Bryan and College Station, home of Texas A & M. Some blacks live in the rural counties here (12% district-wide), as do a few Mexican-Americans (5%). But overall, poor white farmers and their children who have moved to town, dominate this part of the 6th. Raised as staunch Democrats, the farmers and their offspring still vote Democratic from Congressman on down. In recent statewide and national elections, however, they have switched in vast numbers to Republicans like Richard Nixon and John Tower; in fact, the shift of allegiance here is as extensive as any place in the country.

The map, however, is misleading. For the majority of the residents of the district reside in metropolitan areas, with 49% of them living in either Dallas or Tarrant (Fort Worth) counties. The shape of the 6th district represents the typical response of the Texas legislature to the one-man-one-vote doctrine: rather than eliminate an underpopulated rural district, tack on enough metropolitan territory to preserve the seat for the incumbent.

The incumbent in this case is Olin. E. (Tiger) Teague, one of the more senior and most personally popular members of the House. Teague first won the seat in a 1946 special election, while still a colonel in the Army. He was a much-decorated and severely wounded combat veteran of World War II. As one of the first World War II veterans elected to Congress, Teague sought and obtained a seat on the Veteran's Affairs Committee; in the November elections of 1946, scads more just out of uniform joined Teague in Congress, including John Kennedy, Richard Nixon, Carl Albert, and so on and on. For Teague, the Veteran's Committee was his chief source of power for many years. He was Chairman of the Veterans' Committee from 1963 to 1973, a period when its major concerns shifted from the problems of the World War II and Korea veterans to those of a rather different sort who served in Vietnam. During most of his tenure, Congressmen generally were pleased with the way Teague balanced the claims of the veterans with fiscal realities. But during his later years in the chair, as both prices and expectations rose, programs under the committee's jurisdiction came under attack from Vietnam veterans who complained about meager G. I. Bill checks.

In early 1973, Teague moved from the chair of Veterans, where he remains the second-ranking member, to the chair of Science and Astronautics, which he had joined when it was formed. The Congressman has always enthusiastically supported manned space flights and high levels of military spending. It is not without coincidence that a disproportionate share of NASA and Pentagon money finds its way to Texas.

Teague's favorite position, however, is probably his chairmanship of the House Democratic Caucus. This he won in a kind of a coup in January 1971. The incumbent, Dan Rostenkowski of Illinois had thoughts about running for Majority Leader; so occupied, Rostenkowski was not aware of Teague's upcoming challenge for the Caucus chairmanship. The Texan quietly assembled a coalition of Southerners, conservatives, and personal friends, and unseated Rostenkowski. Teague, one of the most popular denizens of the paddleball courts, is probably the premier back-slapper in the House.

It appears that the Congressman can keep his seat for as long as he wants. In 1972, the first time he encountered Republican opposition in years, Teague won 83% in the rural counties of his constituency and 63% in the 6th's portion of Dallas and Tarrant counties. The latter territory—relatively affluent suburban fringes of Dallas and Fort Worth—tends to go Republican in other elections. So if Nixon appoints Teague as head of the Veterans' Administration, as rumored, the 6th could conceivably elect a Republican Congressman.

Census Data Pop. 467,913. Central city, 46%; suburban, 36%. Median family income, $9,366; families above $15,000: 20%; families below $3,000: 12%. Median years education, 12.0.

1972 Share of Federal Outlays $602,184,282

DOD	$301,310,080	HEW	$138,415,395
AEC	$806,426	HUD	$4,154,320
NASA	$3,840,728	DOI	$843,710
DOT	$24,243,474	USDA	$46,712,662
		Other	$81,857,487

Federal Military-Industrial Commitments

No installations or contractors receiving prime awards greater than $5,000,000. (See Texas 3 and Texas 5).

Economic Base Finance, insurance and real estate; transportation equipment; agriculture, notably cattle, dairy products and poultry; apparel and other textile products; and food and kindred products. Also higher education Texas A & M).

The Voters

Registration 229,979 total. No party registration.
Median voting age 42.2
Employment profile White collar, 52%. Blue collar, 33%. Service, 11%. Farm, 4%.
Ethnic groups Black, 12%. Spanish, 5%. Total foreign stock, 5%.

Presidential vote

1972	Nixon (R)	107,759	(71%)
	McGovern (D)	43,773	(29%)
1968	Nixon (R)	54,264	(41%)
	Humphrey (D)	52,259	(40%)
	Wallace (AI)	25,107	(19%)

Representative

Olin E. Teague (D) Elected Aug. 24, 1946; b. April 6, 1910, Woodward, Okla.; home, College Station; Tex. A&M, 1928–32; Col. Army, WWII; Tex. Natl. Guard; married, three children; Baptist.

Career Employed by Post Office, Animal Husbandry Dept., railroad; Supt. U.S. Post Office, College Station, 1932–40. Bd. of Visitors, U.S. Military Academy; Chm. Dem. Caucus, 1971 & 1973.

Offices 2311 RHOB, 202-225-2002.

Administrative Assistant George Fisher

Committees

Science and Astronautics (Chm.);

Standards and Official Conduct (2nd).

Veterans' Affairs (2nd). Subs: Compensation and Pension (Chm.); Education and Training; Hospitals.

Group Ratings

	ADA	COPE	LWV	RIPON	NFU	LCV	CFA	NAB	NSI	ACA
1972	6	33	27	29	40	0	50	82	100	90
1971	5	45	33	19	58	–	29	–	–	67
1970	8	0	–	33	40	6	46	50	100	42

Key Votes

1) Busing	AGN	6) Cmbodia Bmbg	ABS	11) Chkg Acct Intrst	ABS
2) Strip Mines	AGN	7) Bust Hwy Trust	ABS	12) End HISC (HUAC)	AGN
3) Cut Mil $	ABS	8) Farm Sub Lmt	AGN	13) Nixon Sewer Veto	ABS
4) Rev Shrg	AGN	9) School Prayr	FOR	14) Corp Cmpaign $	FOR
5) Pub TV $	FOR	10) Cnsumr Prot	FOR	15) Pol $ Disclsr	ABS

Election Results

1972 general:	Olin E. Teague (D)	100,917
	Carl Nigliazzo (R)	38,086
1972 primary:	Olin E. Teague (D), unopposed	
1970 general:	Olin E. Teague (D), unopposed	

SEVENTH DISTRICT Political Background

Houston is the biggest boom city in Texas. In fact, it is the fastest-growing major metropolitan area in the entire nation. New skyscrapers, hotels, apartment buildings, and suburban homes spring up constantly. One after another, the big oil companies move their center of operations to Houston, and these are joined here by giant petrochemical and electronics concerns. Houston today is what Los Angeles was in the 1950s, or Chicago in the 1880s.

The biggest boom in Houston has occurred on the west side. Though it has few of the big new office buildings, those who occupy the most luxurious executive suites in them during the day come home to the west side. The 7th district of Texas includes virtually all of the west side of Houston. The district takes in the rapidly expanding suburbs to the north, moves through the posh

River Oaks section, where many of the state's richest and most powerful people live (John Connally, for one), to the new neighborhood named after the Sharpstown shopping center. It is characteristic of boom towns that a man like Frank Sharp, the developer of Sharpstown, was at the center of the state's most widespread recent scandal.

Fewer blacks (2%) and Mexican-Americans (6%) live in the 7th that in any other Texas district—this richest part of Houston is for Anglo whites only. The district's statistics are spectacular. Its population more than doubled during the 1960s—the third-fastest growth rate of any of the 435 current congressional districts. Only California's 39th in Orange County and New York's 1st at the eastern tip of Long Island grew faster. Some 77% of the employed residents of the 7th hold white-collar jobs—again the third-highest percentage of any congressional district. Only Maryland's 8th in the Washington suburbs and New York's 18th on Manhattan's Upper East Side outrank the Texas district. In median income, the 7th stands not so high—17th in the nation—but the position sets it far ahead of any other Texas district or any in the South aside from the Washington suburbs of Virginia.

The 7th is extraordinary in still another respect: its preference for Republican politics. Of all current congressional districts, only three gave Richard Nixon a higher percentage of their votes in 1968. And in 1972, only a half dozen or so districts in the Deep South recorded larger Nixon percentages. So it is no surprise that the 7th, ever since its creation in something like its present form in 1965, has elected Republican Congressmen.

Its first was George Bush, an oil millionaire with a background unusual for a Texas politician. Bush's father, a partner in Brown Brothers Harriman, was a Connecticut Senator from 1953 to 1963. Bush himself attended fashionable schools back East. He then moved to Texas, made his own fortune in oil, and entered politics.

His first try for public office was unsuccessful; he ran against Sen. Ralph Yarborough in the year of LBJ, and lost. But in 1966 and 1968, he was elected to the House from the 7th. In 1970, Bush again ran for the Senate; he was touted by an admiring Nixon Administration as the nation's most likely challenger to succeed. But he lost again, this time to Lloyd Bentsen, who had earlier defeated Yarborough in the Democratic primary. With the defeat, Bush's electoral career in Texas was pretty much over. Since then, he has served as Ambassador to the United Nations and now as Republican National Chairman. There is talk that he should run for Governor in 1974, but he does not seem interested.

The current Congressman, Bill Archer, comes from a more conventional Texas background. A successful businessman, he was elected to the Texas legislature as a Democrat, then became a Republican. With a safe seat in Congress and a pleasant manner, Archer appears destined to rise in the Republican Caucus. During his first term, he was elected to the Chowder and Marching Society, an unofficial group from whose ranks springs most of the Republican leadership. After two years on the Banking and Currency Committee, he was elevated to Ways and Means in 1973. Here Archer will no doubt labor on behalf of a higher oil depletion allowance. In his official biography, Archer notes with pride that he received the highest percentage—83%—of any opposed Republican House candidate in 1972. The figure is a good indication of just how safe his seat is.

Census Data Pop. 461,704. Central city, 76%; suburban, 24%. Median family income, $13,593; families above $15,000: 42%; families below $3,000: 3%. Median years education, 13.0.

1972 Share of Federal Outlays $350,358,867

DOD	$46,339,735	HEW	$100,966,240
AEC	$223,032	HUD	$10,260,800
NASA	$61,121,988	DOI	$702,866
DOT	$13,867,049	USDA	$26,357,394
		Other	$90,519,763

Federal Military-Industrial Commitments

NASA Contractors Spectrix Corp. (Houston), $5.400m: communications support.

Economic Base Finance, insurance and real estate; fabricated metal products, especially fabricated structural metal products; machinery, especially oil field machinery; chemicals and allied products; and oil and gas extraction.

The Voters

Registration 298,246 total. No party registration.
Median voting age 39.1
Employment profile White collar, 77%. Blue collar, 16%. Service, 6%. Farm, 1%.
Ethnic groups Black, 2%. Spanish, 6%. Total foreign stock, 10%. Germany, UK, 1% each.

Presidential vote

1972	Nixon (R)	107,655	(82%)
	McGovern (D)	24,069,	(18%)
1968	Nixon (R)	89,585	(65%)
	Humphrey (D)	29,323	(21%)
	Wallace (AI)	18,735	(14%)

Representative

William R. Archer (R) Elected 1970; b. March 22, 1928, Houston; home, Houston; Rice U., 1945–46; U. of Tex., B.B.A., LL.B., 1946–51; USAF, Korean War; Capt. USAFR; married, five children; Catholic.

Career Lawyer; Pres. Uncle Johnny Mills, 1953–61; Councilman, Mayor Pro Tem., Hunters Creek Village, 1955–62; Tex. House of Reps., 1966–70.

Offices 1608 LHOB, 202-225-2571. Also 5607 Fed. Bldg., Houston 77002, 713-226-4741.

Administrative Assistant Lloyd O. Pierson

Committees

Ways and Means (10th).

Group Ratings

	ADA	COPE	LWV	RIPON	NFU	LCV	CFA	NAB	NSI	ACA
1972	6	9	18	38	14	21	100	92	100	100
1971	5	8	11	50	7	–	13	–	–	100

Key Votes

1) Busing	AGN	6) Cmbodia Bmbg	AGN	11) Chkg Acct Intrst	AGN
2) Strip Mines	FOR	7) Bust Hwy Trust	AGN	12) End HISC (HUAC)	AGN
3) Cut Mil $	AGN	8) Farm Sub Lmt	FOR	13) Nixon Sewer Veto	FOR
4) Rev Shrg	AGN	9) School Prayr	FOR	14) Corp Cmpaign $	FOR
5) Pub TV $	AGN	10) Cnsumr Prot	AGN	15) Pol $ Disclosr	FOR

Election Results

1972 general:	Bill Archer (R)	171,127	(82%)
	Jim Brady (D)	36,899	(18%)
1972 primary:	Bill Archer (R), unopposed		
1970 general:	Bill Archer (R)	93,457	(65%)
	Jim Greenwood (D)	50,750	(35%)

EIGHTH DISTRICT Political Background

When visitors come to Houston, the home folks like to show the out-of-towners the sights of the city: the gleaming new skyscrapers downtown; the Rivers Oak mansion of Ima Hogg (daughter of

1890s populist Gov. Jim Hogg), Rice University and the expanse of the Texas Medical Center, and, of course, the Astrodome. The drive to see these sights takes one southwest from downtown, away from east and northeast Houston to which visitors are not usually taken. Here lie the industrial and working-class sections of the city that make up the 8th district of Texas. The tremendous growth of Houston's petrochemical and oil industries has produced some of the nation's worst air pollution. From a downtown high-rise, one can look out across the flat Texas plains, but the view of east Houston is obscured by a smoggy haze. Below the smog flows the sluggish Houston Ship Channel, a marvel of engineering that has made this inland city a major American port. Unfortunately, the waterway is so full of sludge and effluent from the chemical plants and refineries that line its base that the Ship Channel is something of a fire hazard.

The 8th is mostly white working-class, though some 22% of its residents are black. This part of Houston has not experienced the kind of growth that has hit the west side of town. And the homes here are far less likely to enjoy the benefits of air conditioning; moreover, they are often within sight (or smell) of chemical plants and refineries. Most people in the 8th are natives of the Texas countryside, or some other place in the rural South. Their politics combines populism and racial fears, as was demonstrated in the results of the 1968 presidential election: 47% for Humphrey, 27% for Wallace, and only 26% for Nixon.

Fifteen years ago, the 8th district included all of Harris County, which in 1970 had a population of 1,741,000. Obviously, the arrangement could not survive the one-man-one-vote doctrine. So the 8th was pared down over time to its present boundaries. Meanwhile, however, the district continued to reelect Albert Thomas, a get-along-go-along Democrat, to the House. Thomas ascended to high rank on the Appropriations Committee. And he, probably more than anyone else, was responsible for bringing the NASA Manned Space Craft Center (since renamed the Johnson Center) to the Houston area (though it is in the 22nd district, not the 8th). Thomas chaired the Appropriations' subcommittee with jurisdiction over the space program. After Thomas died in 1965, he was succeeded for the remainder of his term, in time-honored fashion, by his widow.

Albert Thomas' eventual successor, however, was Bob Eckhardt, who was elected in 1966. The new Congressman's politics are quite different from those of Thomas. Eckhardt is one of that hardy breed, a Texas liberal. Before coming to Washington, he served for eight years in the state legislature, where he fought valiantly, though usually without success, for those things in which he believed. Eckhardt does the same in Congress. Outside of Texas, many liberals become discouraged when they encounter a losing streak, and drop out of politics. But in Texas, where liberals have little reason to expect to win anything, they fight on. Even their sense of humor remains intact. In Washington, Eckhardt is the most outspoken and most scholarly member of the Texas delegation. Traditionally, Texas Congressmen have preferred to work in the cloakrooms, speaking quietly to each other. Eckhardt, sporting a bow tie and a brightly colored shirt, does his work on the floor, where he declaims on some subject that has aroused his attention. He is now a middle-ranking member of the Commerce Committee. Here he is one of the more dependable backers of proconsumer legislation. In 1973, Eckhardt picked up another committee assignment, Merchant Marine and Fisheries.

Eckhardt had little competition in his first election, and he has won reelection in fairly routine fashion ever since. The 1972 redistricting, however, took many of the black neighborhoods from his old district and placed them in the 18th. The move cost him some votes, as he won only 65% in the general election. Eckhardt could conceivably encounter primary opposition from a conservative. Such a candidate would try to mine the racial fears of the 8th's white blue-collar voters. Eckhardt has a liberal record on social issues.

Census Data Pop. 461,216. Central city, 49%; suburban, 51%. Median family income, $9,483; families above $15,000: 15%; families below $3,000: 9%. Median years education, 11.0.

1972 Share of Federal Outlays $349,906,985

DOD	$46,279,967	HEW	$100,836,017
AEC	$222,745	HUD	$10,247,566
NASA	$61,043,155	DOI	$701,960
DOT	$13,849,164	USDA	$26,323,399
		Other	$90,403,012

Federal Military-Industrial Commitments

DOD Contractors Humble Oil (Baytown), $28.698m: petroleum products.
NASA Contractors Bludworth Shipyard (Houston), $7.468m: systems integration and assessment for Apollo program. Spectrix Corp. (Houston), $5.090m: lease and maintenance of Univac ADPE system.

Economic Base Finance, insurance and real estate; fabricated metal products, especially fabricated structural metal products; machinery, especially oil field machinery; chemicals and allied products, especially industrial chemicals; and oil and gas extraction.

The Voters

> *Registration* 188,176 total. No party registration.
> *Median voting age* 38.9
> *Employment profile* White collar, 40%. Blue collar, 46%. Service, 14%. Farm, –%.
> *Ethnic groups* Black, 22%. Spanish, 10%. Total foreign stock, 7%.

Presidential vote

1972	Nixon (R)	63,861	(54%)
	McGovern (D)	53,672	(46%)
1968	Nixon (R)	26,793	(26%)
	Humphrey (D)	49,283	(47%)
	Wallace (AI)	27,990	(27%)

Representative

Bob Eckhardt (D) Elected 1966; b. July 16, 1913, Austin; home, Houston; U. of Tex. B.A., 1935, LL.B., 1939; Army Air Corps, WWII; married, six children; Presbyterian.

Career Practicing atty., 1939–66; Tex. House of Reps., 1958–66.

Offices 1741 LHOB, 202-225-4901. Also Rm. 8632 Fed. Bldg., Houston 77002, 713-226-4931.

Administrative Assistant Charles Holmes

Committees

Interstate and Foreign Commerce (15th); Sub: Commerce and Finance.

Merchant Marine and Fisheries (18th). Subs: Fisheries and Wildlife Conservation and the Environment; Merchant Marine; Oceanography.

Group Ratings

	ADA	COPE	LWV	RIPON	NFU	LCV	CFA	NAB	NSI	ACA
1972	94	90	100	71	100	90	50	0	0	5
1971	94	82	89	88	100	–	88	–	–	7
1970	92	100	–	71	91	100	95	0	10	0

Key Votes

1) Busing	FOR	6) Cmbodia Bmbg	AGN	11) Chkg Acct Intrst	FOR
2) Strip Mines	AGN	7) Bust Hwy Trust	FOR	12) End HISC (HUAC)	FOR
3) Cut Mil $	ABS	8) Farm Sub Lmt	ABS	13) Nixon Sewer Veto	AGN
4) Rev Shrg	FOR	9) School Prayr	AGN	14) Corp Cmpaign $	FOR
5) Pub TV $	FOR	10) Cnsumr Prot	FOR	15) Pol $ Disclosr	FOR

Election Results

1972 general:	Bob Eckhardt (D)	73,909	(64%)
	Lewis Emerich (R)	39,636	(35%)

	Susan Ellis (SW)	847	(1%)
1972 primary:	Bob Eckhardt (D)	37,109	
	David L. Shall (D)	11,022	
1970 general:	Bob Eckhardt (D), unopposed		

NINTH DISTRICT Political Background

The 9th district of Texas is the eastern segment of the state's Gulf Coast—an area of heavy industry. The district has one of the highest concentrations of blue-collar workers in Texas. It is dominated by two urban centers of roughly equal size. On Galveston Bay, which leads into the Houston Ship Channel, are the cities of Galveston (pop. 61,000) and Texas City (pop. 38,000). Galveston, one of the oldest cities in Texas, is situated on a sand bar where the Bay empties into the Gulf of Mexico. It was the state's first port, but now handles far less tonnage than Houston or Texas City. The other major population center in the 9th lies around Beaumont (pop. 115,000) and Port Arthur (pop. 57,000). Like Galveston and Texas City, these are industrial towns dominated by the oil and petrochemical industries. The 9th also includes a small portion (pop. 40,000) of Harris County and Houston.

Most of the residents of the district are migrants from the rural South, and their children. Some 22% of then are black; another 6% are Cajuns from nearby southern Louisiana. To a surprising extent the people here have retained populistic, Democratic beliefs. The political attitudes are sustained in large part by the Texas labor movement, which is stronger in the 9th than in just about any other part of the state. Though plenty of votes were cast here for George Wallace in 1968 (26%), Hubert Humphrey still carried the district. In 1972, George McGovern ran only 2% behind Humphrey's 1968 showing—the closest the South Dakotan came to matching the Minnesotan in any Texas congressional district. Also in 1972, the 9th was one of the few Texas districts to go for Democrat Barefoot Sanders over Republican Sen. John Tower.

Before the 1965 redistricting, Galveston–Texas City and Beaumont–Port Arthur were in two separate districts. Congressman Clark Thompson, who served from 1933 to 1935 and from 1947 to 1967, was a member of the Ways and Means Committee. As the elder of the two incumbents thrown together by the redistricting, Thompson decided to retire. His decision left the seat to Jack Brooks, who continues to occupy it. Brooks is a Texas Congressman in the Rayburn tradition. He often, though not always, takes liberal positions on issues and stays close to the House Democratic leadership. His rather liberal voting record was noteworthy during the early 1960s, when his district included some east Texas rural counties akin to the Deep South. In 1964, Brooks voted for the Civil Rights Act.

Only 30 when first elected in 1952, Brooks is the kind of Congressman who usually becomes part of the leadership. But the surfeit of men from Texas, Oklahoma, and Louisiana in Democratic leadership positions has closed off this avenue of advancement to him, though he does serve as regional Whip. After 20 years, Brooks is yet to attain a chairmanship, though he is likely to get one soon. He is the second-ranking Democrat on the Government Operations Committee behind 70-year-old Chet Holifield of California. As a subcommittee chairman on the panel, Brooks did as much as anyone to ferret out information from the White House regarding government dollars spent to improve Nixon residences in San Clemente and Key Biscayne. Brooks is also the third-ranking Democrat on the Judiciary Committee, just behind 65-year-old Chairman Peter Rodino (whose New Jersey district has a black voting majority) and 73-year-old Harold Donohue of Massachusetts. So it appears that within a few years Brooks will emerge from the media obscurity he now enjoys.

Census Data   Pop. 467,483. Central city, 59%; suburban, 38%. Median family income, $9,341; families above $15,000: 17%; families below $3,000: 11%. Median years education, 11.5.

1972 Share of Federal Outlays $367,143,673

DOD	$87,686,368	HEW	$125,026,505
AEC	$19,656	HUD	$5,840,855
NASA	$5,583,617	DOI	$299,402
DOT	$37,177,036	USDA	$14,059,723
		Other	$91,450,511

Federal Military-Industrial Commitments

DOD Contractors Mobil Oil (Beaumont), $41.289m: petroleum products. Texaco (Port Arthur), $14.284m: petroleum products. Gulf Oil (Port Arthur), $7.742m: petroleum products.

Economic Base Petroleum refining products, and other petroleum and coal products; chemicals and allied products, especially industrial chemicals; finance, insurance and real estate; fabricated metal products; and ship building and repairing, and other transportation equipment.

The Voters

Registration 221,944 total. No party registration.
Median voting age 42.6
Employment profile White collar, 45%. Blue collar, 40%. Service, 14%. Farm, 1%.
Ethnic groups Black, 22%. Spanish, 7%. Total foreign stock, 7%.

Presidential vote

1972	Nixon (R)	84,903	(60%)
	McGovern (D)	57,669	(40%)
1968	Nixon (R)	46,225	(32%)
	Humphrey (D)	61,476	(42%)
	Wallace (AI)	37,879	(26%)

Representative

Jack Brooks (D) Elected 1952; b. Dec. 18, 1922, Crowley, La.; home, Beaumont; Lamar Jr. Col., 1939–41; U. of Tex., B.J., 1943, J.D., 1949; USMC, WWII; married, two children; Methodist.

Career Tex. House of Reps., 1946–50; atty., admitted to bar, 1949; elected by Tex. House Dem. Delegation as Majority Whip, 1964– .

Offices 2239 RHOB, 202-225-6565. Also 230 Fed. Bldg., Beaumont 77701, 713-832-8539, and Rm. 204, Fed. Bldg., Galveston 77550, 713-762-2733.

Administrative Assistant Sharon Matts

Committees

Government Operations (2nd); Subs: Government Activities (Chm.); Conservation and Natural Resources.

Judiciary (3rd); Sub: No. 5 (Antitrust Matters).

Joint Com. on Congressional Operations (Vice-Chm.).

Group Ratings

	ADA	COPE	LWV	RIPON	NFU	LCV	CFA	NAB	NSI	ACA
1972	25	90	64	40	86	25	100	9	100	35
1971	43	80	67	50	86	–	86	–	–	36
1970	36	75	–	43	90	51	76	18	67	29

Key Votes

1) Busing	AGN	6) Cmbodia Bmbg	FOR	11) Chkg Acct Intrst	ABS
2) Strip Mines	AGN	7) Bust Hwy Trust	AGN	12) End HISC (HUAC)	AGN
3) Cut Mil $	AGN	8) Farm Sub Lmt	AGN	13) Nixon Sewer Veto	AGN
4) Rev Shrg	AGN	9) School Prayr	AGN	14) Corp Cmpaign $	FOR
5) Pub TV $	FOR	10) Cnsumr Prot	FOR	15) Pol $ Disclosr	AGN

Election Results

1972 general:	Jack Brooks (D)	89,113	(66%)
	Randolph Reed (R)	45,462	(34%)
1972 primary:	Jack Brooks (D), unopposed		
1970 general:	Jack Brooks (D)	57,180	(64%)
	Henry Pressler (R)	31,483	(36%)

TENTH DISTRICT Political Background

The 10th district of Texas is the LBJ congressional district. Here in central Texas the towns are farther apart and the trees less common than in east Texas, which is more fertile and gets more rain. Lyndon Johnson was born, brought up, and began his political career amid the rolling hills of central Texas, which yielded a living only to those who worked hard. The 10th district left its mark on Johnson. The comparative poverty of its people—especially back in the 1930s, when Johnson was a young man—helped to shape his populistic impulses. And the comparatively good relations here between the Anglo majority and the black (presently 15%) and the Mexican-American (15%) minorities helped prepare Johnson to lead Congress to pass the great civil rights acts of 1964 and 1965.

Johnson, in turn, has certainly left his imprint on the 10th district. Though its boundaries have changed, the district still includes the town of Johnson City and the LBJ Ranch in Blanco County; Southwest Texas State Teachers College in San Marcos, where Johnson got his degree; and Austin, the state capital and site of the Lyndon B. Johnson Library. Also in Austin is television station KTBC (renamed, since Johnson's death, KLBJ)—the cornerstone of the Johnson family fortune.

Austin (pop. 251,000) has grown substantially since Johnson represented the 10th. Today, the city contains half the district's residents. Unlike most Texas cities, Austin is not an oil town, or an industrial town, or even a farm-market town. Instead, it is dominated by growth industries like state government and higher education (the University of Texas). Accordingly, Austin has more than its proportionate share of liberal intellectuals. The city contains not just the headquarters of LBJ's operations, but also of Texas liberalism. That hardy creed is maintained, in the face of all kinds of adversity, by the *Texas Observer*, an irreverent periodical devoted to the shenanigans of Texas politicians.

Austin and surrounding Travis County usually turn in Democratic majorities. But when the Democratic nominee in a major statewide race is a conservative, Austin will sometimes go Republican. For example, it gave 62% of its votes to Sen. John Tower in 1966, many of them in protest against the equally conservative Democratic nominee of that year. In recent years, however, Texas liberals have defected less often, as the Republican party grows stronger in Texas and the Democrats at least marginally more liberal.

Despite the prominence of the local liberal vote—and despite the number of new liberal votes coming out of the University of Texas campus (39,000 students)—the liberals have remained a negligible force in 10th-district congressional races. Johnson was succeeded in the House by Homer Thornberry, a moderate-to-liberal Democrat who was appointed to the federal bench in 1963. Judge Thornberry was Johnson's nominee to fill the Supreme Court vacancy that would have been created had Abe Fortas been confirmed as Chief Justice. No one took exception to Thornberry's performance as a judge, but the nomination did smack of cronyism. Johnson's choice may have therefore contributed to Fortas' rejection by the Senate.

Thornberry's successor in the House is a member in good standing of the state's Tory Democratic establishment. Congressman J. J. (Jake) Pickle, like John Connally and many other Johnson protégés, always backed his mentor's foreign policy. But when left to himself, Pickle almost always takes positions on domestic matters more conservative than Johnson was wont to do. Over the years, the Congressman has demonstrated more concern for the problems of the rural areas of his district that for those of Austin. Pickle may change his tune, however, in light of Austin's sharply increased percentage of district voters. Pickle has not had a primary opponent since 1964, nor faced a Republican contender in the general election since 1968. But since the 1972 election, young liberals have won races in Austin with remarkable frequency. So Pickle might encounter a tough primary if someone like recently elected 26-year-old state Sen. Lloyd Doggett ran against him. With the increased student vote, Travis County cast 76% of the district's votes in 1972.

Census Data Pop. 465,493. Central city, 54%; suburban, 9%. Median family income, $7,839; families above $15,000: 16%; families below $3,000: 15%. Median years education, 11.8.

1972 Share of Federal Outlays $707,173,890

DOD	$140,983,000	HEW	$259,724,061
AEC	$1,092,609	HUD	$20,249,065
NASA	$1,533,032	DOI	$3,760,618
DOT	$30,661,571	USDA	$34,796,344
		Other	$214,373,590

Federal Military-Industrial Commitments

DOD Contractors Texas Instruments (Austin), $14.513m: various electronic communications equipment and research. Tracor, Inc. (Austin), $14.173m: various electronic communications equipment and research. University of Texas (Austin), $5.989m: various research projects. *DOD Installations* Bergstrom AFB (Austin).

Economic Base Agriculture, notably cattle, poultry, and hogs and sheep; finance, insurance and real estate; printing and publishing, especially commercial printing; food and kindred products; and furniture and fixtures, especially household furniture. Also higher education (Southwest Texas State Univ., and Univ. of Texas, Austin).

The Voters

Registration 254,029 total. No party registration.
Median voting age 39.4
Employment profile White collar, 53%. Blue collar, 26%. Service, 16%. Farm, 5%.
Ethnic groups Black, 15%. Spanish, 15%. Total foreign stock, 10%. Germany, 2%.

Presidential vote

1972	Nixon (R)	103,675	(59%)
	McGovern (D)	71,652	(41%)
1968	Nixon (R)	52,588	(40%)
	Humphrey (D)	60,848	(46%)
	Wallace (AI)	17,710	(14%)

Representative

J. J. (Jake) Pickle (D) Elected Dec. 24, 1963; b. Oct. 14, 1913, Roscoe; home, Austin; U. of Tex., B.A., 1938; Navy, WWII; married, three children; Methodist.

Career Area Dir., Natl. Youth Admin., 1939–41; Co-organizer, KVET Radio, Austin; public relations and advertising business; Dir., Texas Dem. Exec. Com., 1957–60; Texas Employment Commission, 1961–63.

Offices 231 CHOB, 202-225-4865. Also 774 Fed. Bldg., Austin 78701, 512-397-5921.

Administrative Assistant Michael Keeling

Committees

Interstate and Foreign Commerce (8th); Sub: Sp. Sub. on Investigations.

Science and Astronautics (13th); Subs: Aeronautics and Space Technology; Energy; Science, Research, and Development.

Group Ratings

	ADA	COPE	LWV	RIPON	NFU	LCV	CFA	NAB	NSI	ACA
1972	13	36	50	31	67	26	50	27	100	65
1971	30	73	44	50	71	–	75	–	–	56
1970	16	50	–	41	62	0	59	73	90	47

Key Votes

1) Busing	AGN	6) Cmbodia Bmbg	AGN	11) Chkg Acct Intrst	AGN
2) Strip Mines	ABS	7) Bust Hwy Trust	AGN	12) End HISC (HUAC)	AGN
3) Cut Mil $	AGN	8) Farm Sub Lmt	AGN	13) Nixon Sewer Veto	AGN
4) Rev Shrg	AGN	9) School Prayr	ABS	14) Corp Cmpaign $	FOR
5) Pub TV $	FOR	10) Cnsumr Prot	FOR	15) Pol $ Disclosr	AGN

Election Results

1972 general:	J. J. Pickle (D)	130,973	(91%)
	Melissa Singler (SW)	12,682	(9%)
1972 primary:	J. J. Pickle (D), unopposed		
1970 general:	J. J. Pickle (D), unopposed		

ELEVENTH DISTRICT Political Background

The 11th congressional district lies deep in the heart of Texas. Made up of 14 counties, the district sits slightly off the geographical center of the state, but just about at its center of population. The 11th includes two good-sized cities, Waco (pop. 95,000) and Temple (pop. 33,000), and a huge Army base, Fort Hood (pop. 33,000). The rest of the district is classic Texas agricultural country, given over to cotton, livestock, and occasional small towns. People here are descended from settlers who came from the Deep South in the nineteenth century. For years, they remained solidly Democratic. But suddenly, in 1972, the political alignments in the 11th district—and in many other parts of non-metropolitan Texas—shifted sharply.

To be sure, the voters of the district had always preferred the more conservative Democrats. In 1966, for example, it was the only district in Texas that voted against Republican Sen. John Tower and for his conservative Democratic opponent. But the 11th was also willing to go along with liberals. In 1968, Hubert Humphrey got just a shade over 50% of the votes here, his best Texas showing outside of three heavily Mexican-American and two inner-city urban districts. Once again, in 1970, the 11th gave Sen. Lloyd Bentsen a solid majority in the primary; Bentsen campaigned as a hard-line conservative.

But in 1972, the 11th went solidly Republican at the top of the ticket. George McGovern received only 31% of the district's votes, which meant that Richard Nixon gained 38% over his first four years in office—the Republican's largest such percentage in any congressional district outside the Deep South. The same pattern held in the 1972 Senate race, even though the Democratic nominee, Barefoot Sanders, had the endorsement of John Connally and the Tory Democratic establishment. Whereas Bentsen took 66% of the votes in 1970, Sanders managed only 45%. The coattail power of the Nixon-Agnew ticket is not enough to explain the phenomenon; Texas voters have frequently demonstrated a capacity to split tickets in great numbers. The big question for 1974 and beyond is whether the move to the Republican party in rural Texas is permanent, or merely an isolated episode. If the trend persists, it could even begin to affect contests farther down the ballot, like the one for Congressman from the 11th district.

"Contest" is hardly the right word, for the 11th district's Congressman, W. R. Poage, has usually been reelected without opposition since he first won the seat in 1936. The last time Poage faced Republican opposition was in 1964, when he took 81% of the votes. But Poage has had some troubles—and the promise of more—in the Democratic primary lately. In 1972, state Sen. Murray Watson won 40% of the votes against Poage, who was then 70. And in 1974, the Congressman may have opposition from state Rep. Lane Denton of Waco, one of the original "Dirty 30" (see Texas state write-up). Denton has captured some recent headlines for an investigation of child-care facilities.

The situation in the 11th is important because Poage, thanks to the inexorable workings of the seniority system, is Chairman of the House Agriculture Committee. The Texan has held the post since Harold Cooley of North Carolina was ousted by a Republican in 1964. On the Committee, Poage lines up with its conservative Southern Democratic-Republican majority. The Chairman dislikes proposals to feed the poor, though he was quite content with the farm programs that gave certain rich farmers tens of thousands of dollars for not planting crops.

Poage has been no innovator in farm policy. The 1973 farm bill moved from subsidies for maintaining proper supplies to a system of income supplements that would come into play should the price for a commodity fall below a specified level. The bill was drafted in the Senate Agriculture Committee. When Poage appeared on the House floor with the legislation, he found himself embarrassed because of a major dispute with the Nixon Administration. Things got so far out of hand that the bill had to be returned to committee—a highly unusual step. Moreover, more votes were cast against Poage in the 1973 Democratic Caucus than against any other chairman. The Texan is not the strongest committee chairman. All things considered, Poage might find himself in electoral trouble in the years ahead. So he may choose to retire in 1974, after 38 years of service, which would entitle him to the maximum pension of $32,000 annually.

Census Data Pop. 468,148. Central city, 20%; suburban, 11%. Median family income, $6,963; families above $15,000: 10%; families below $3,000: 17%. Median years education, 11.2.

1972 Share of Federal Outlays $748,319,140

DOD	$419,566,000	HEW	$156,656,655
AEC	$20,000	HUD	$8,547,718
NASA	$1,637	DOI	$450,559
DOT	$17,844,886	USDA	$41,091,035
		Other	$104,140,650

Federal Military-Industrial Commitments

DOD Contractors Urban Systems Development Corp. (Fort Hood), $17.553m: unspecified. North American Rockwell (McGregor), $6.552m: rocket motors and igniters. *DOD Installations* Fort Hood AB (Killeen).

Economic Base Agriculture, notably cattle, poultry and grains; finance, insurance and real estate; food and kindred products, especially meat products; and furniture and fixtures, especially public building furniture.

The Voters

Registration 206,609 total. No party registration.
Median voting age 42.6
Employment profile White collar, 44%. Blue collar, 33%. Service, 16%. Farm, 7%.
Ethnic groups Black, 12%. Spanish, 8%. Total foreign stock, 8%. Germany, 2%.

Presidential vote

1972	Nixon (R)	90,802	(69%)
	McGovern (D)	40,234	(31%)
1968	Nixon (R)	38,899	(32%)
	Humphrey (D)	61,849	(50%)
	Wallace (AI)	22,672	(18%)

Representative

William Robert (Bob) **Poage** (D) Elected 1936; b. Dec. 28, 1899, Waco; home, Waco; U. of Tex.; U. of Colo.; Baylor U., B.A., 1921, LL.B., 1924, LL.D., 1967; Navy, WWII; married; Universalist.

Career Practicing atty., 1924–36; Tex. House of Reps., 1925–29; Tex. Senate, 1931–37.

Offices 2107 RHOB, 202-225-6105. Also 205 Fed. Bldg., Waco 76701, 817-752-7271.

Administrative Assistant C. Dayle Henington

Committees

Agriculture (Chm.); Sub: Conservation and Credit (Chm.).

Group Ratings

	ADA	COPE	LWV	RIPON	NFU	LCV	CFA	NAB	NSI	ACA
1972	6	33	18	33	43	0	50	67	100	81
1971	5	36	33	14	54	–	13	–	–	71
1970	8	27	–	11	36	28	64	64	100	55

Key Votes

1) Busing	AGN	6) Cmbodia Bmbg	FOR	11) Chkg Acct Intrst	AGN
2) Strip Mines	FOR	7) Bust Hwy Trust	AGN	12) End HISC (HUAC)	AGN
3) Cut Mil $	ABS	8) Farm Sub Lmt	AGN	13) Nixon Sewer Veto	AGN
4) Rev Shrg	AGN	9) School Prayr	FOR	14) Corp Cmpaign $	FOR
5) Pub TV $	AGN	10) Cnsumr Prot	AGN	15) Pol $ Disclosr	AGN

Election Results

1972 general:	W. R. Poage (D), unopposed		
1972 primary:	W. R. Poage (D)	62,410	(60%)
	Murray Watson (D)	40,761	(40%)
1970 general:	W. R. Poage (D), unopposed		

TWELFTH DISTRICT Political Background

"Cowtown" is what Dallasites are inclined to call Fort Worth. Though the two are often considered twin cities, Dallas (pop. 844,000) long ago eclipsed Fort Worth (pop. 393,000) in size and wealth. Other differences also exist. According to the cliché, Dallas is the end of the East and Fort Worth the beginning of the West. And if one examines the economic underpinning of the two cities, the notion has some truth. Fort Worth did, in fact, get its start as a cowtown, a place where cowboys drove longhorns to a railhead and later to local stockyards. After the Texas oil strikes, Dallas became the leading financial center of the Southwest and a white-collar town; Fort Worth remained much more blue collar.

Even the kinds of defense contracts awarded to the two cities illustrate how they differ. Dallas produces radar systems, infrared detecting devices and special communications equipment—all high-technology and high value-added spin-offs of its computer industries. Fort Worth, meanwhile, produces the structural components of the F-111 fighter aircraft. The F-111 contract (the old TFX) is one of the Pentagon's largest and most controversial. It has been alleged, with considerable supporting evidence, that General Dynamics, the city of Fort Worth, and the state of Texas got the F-111 contract through political pull. Also produced here were most of the helicopters used in the Vietnam war.

Given the differences, Fort Worth, as one might expect, is less Republican and less conservative than Dallas. The 12th congressional district, which includes most of Fort Worth and the Tarrant County suburbs to the north, is therefore one of the state's more liberally inclined seats. Since the elections of 1954, the 12th has sent Congressman Jim Wright to Washington. During his first years of service, Wright was the foremost liberal in the Texas delegation. He remains one of its enthusiastic backers of liberal positions on economic issues. But on other issues, he has found that his views have diverged from those held by most House Democrats. For one thing, Wright always supported American military intervention in Southeast Asia; in 1969, he sponsored a resolution that was widely interpreted as an endorsement of Nixon's policies in Vietnam. For another, Wright does not share the enthusiasm exhibited by many younger, less senior Democrats—and some Republicans—for environmental causes.

These days, Wright's clout comes mostly from his seat on the Public Works Committee. Though he is not Chairman of the unit or of its Transportation Subcommittee, he was the member who led the 1973 fight against those who wanted to open the highway trust fund to mass-transit projects. Chairman John Blatnik was ailing, while Transportation Subcommittee Chairman John Kluczynski switched to support the idea, apparently on orders from Chicago Mayor Richard Daley. Wright argued that he was no opponent of mass transit; and he drafted a bill that would provide as much money for such projects from the general fund as would be available from the highway trust fund. Wright's opponents contended that such moneys would be more vulnerable to impoundment by the Nixon Administration. Wright steered his plan through the Public Works Committee and then beat the trust-busters on the floor of the House. But the Senate went the other way on the issue, and in conference committee a compromise was struck that allowed some tapping of the fund for mass transit.

Though the compromise represented a minor setback to the Congressman, Wright nevertheless demonstrated considerable legislative skill even while losing. Back home, his ability once made him a solid candidate for statewide office. Wright has a capacity to speak a folksy-erudite language and to write in a clear style; he also has a lively sense of humor. In 1961, Wright ran for the Senate seat vacated by Lyndon Johnson, running a close third behind Republican John Tower and ultraconservative Democrat William Blakely. In 1966, he wanted another shot at Tower's Senate seat. But the Tory Democrat establishment and Gov. John Connally decided that state Atty. Gen. Waggoner was to be the party's candidate. To make the race, Wright was unable to raise the money needed from friendly sources, and was unwilling to seek contributions from those who have traditionally bankrolled Texas politicians. So Wright appeared on television and asked for $10 contributions. He received a lot of them, but not enough for a Senate race in Texas. Accordingly, Wright decided to stay in the House.

Wright might very well have won the Senate seat had he been able to get into the general elections of either 1961 or 1966. Both times, Tower won largely because Texas liberals supported the Republican over more conservative Democratic candidates. Those liberal votes would have gone to Wright. Moreover, in the 1960s, conservative Texans in rural counties were still plunking for the Democratic ticket.

As the struggle over the highway trust fund showed, Wright is on his way toward becoming a major power in the House. He is currently Whip of the Texas delegation—a more demanding job than it once was, as the diversity of the group has grown. Wright stands a good chance of succeeding to the chair of Public Works within five or ten years. Back in the 12th district, he wins routine reelection, usually without opposition.

Census Data Pop. 465,671. Central city, 59%; suburban, 41%. Median family income, $9,418; families above $15,000: 18%; families below $3,000: 9%. Median years education, 11.6.

1972 Share of Federal Outlays $913,279,602

DOD	$663,184,288	HEW	$110,963,581
AEC	$431,240	HUD	$4,888,736
NASA	$1,771,466	DOI	$509,994
DOT	$39,351,004	USDA	$14,626,693
		Other	$77,552,600

Federal Military-Industrial Commitments

DOD Contractors General Dynamics (Fort Worth), $772.150m: F-111 aircraft and components. Textron (Fort Worth), $129.112m: helicopters and helicopter components. American Manufacturing of Texas (Fort Worth), $23.358m: bomb bodies and rockets.
DOD Installations Carswell AFB (Fort Worth).

Economic Base Transportation equipment; finance, insurance and real estate; food and kindred products; machinery; and printing and publishing.

The Voters

Registration 190,223 total. No party registration.
Median voting age 40.9
Employment profile White collar, 46%. Blue collar, 40%. Service, 14%. Farm, –%.
Ethnic groups Black, 16%. Spanish, 7%. Total foreign stock, 6%.

Presidential vote

1972	Nixon (R)	73,669	(62%)
	McGovern (D)	45,183	(38%)
1968	Nixon (R)	38,162	(36%)
	Humphrey (D)	50,853	(48%)
	Wallace (AI)	16,436	(16%)

Representative

James C. Wright, Jr. (D) Elected 1954; b. Dec. 22, 1922, Fort Worth; home, Fort Worth; Weatherford Col., U. of Tex.; Army, WWII; married, four children; Presbyterian.

Career Partner in trade extension and advertising firm; Tex. House of Reps.; Mayor of Weatherford; Pres., League of Tex. Municipalities, 1953.

Offices 2459 RHOB, 202-225-5071. Also 9A-10 Lanham Fed. Office Bldg., Fort Worth 76102, 817-334-3212.

Administrative Assistant Marshall Lynam

Committees

Government Operations (12th); Subs: Foreign Operations and Government Information; Legislation and Military Operations.

Public Works (4th); Subs: Public Buildings and Grounds; Investigations and Review (Chm.); Transportation; Water Resources.

Group Ratings

	ADA	COPE	LWV	RIPON	NFU	LCV	CFA	NAB	NSI	ACA
1972	19	80	55	58	83	25	50	0	100	41
1971	24	86	83	33	75	–	80	–	–	40
1970	32	67	–	40	92	71	83	18	80	35

Key Votes

1) Busing	AGN	6) Cmbodia Bmbg	FOR	11) Chkg Acct Intrst	AGN
2) Strip Mines	FOR	7) Bust Hwy Trust	AGN	12) End HISC (HUAC)	AGN
3) Cut Mil $	AGN	8) Farm Sub Lmt	AGN	13) Nixon Sewer Veto	AGN
4) Rev Shrg	AGN	9) School Prayr	FOR	14) Corp Cmpaign $	FOR
5) Pub TV $	FOR	10) Cnsumr Prot	FOR	15) Pol $ Disclosr	ABS

Election Results

1972 general: Jim Wright (D), unopposed
1972 primary: Jim Wright (D), unopposed
1970 general: Jim Wright (D), unopposed

THIRTEENTH DISTRICT Political Background

There comes a time in the life of many Congressmen representing rural America when they find themselves forced by redistricting into a race with another incumbent. For Democrat Graham Purcell and Republican Bob Price that time came in 1972. Purcell had represented the 13th district of Texas since a special election held in 1962; Price had represented the 18th district since he had upset a complacent Democrat in 1966. Both men were first elected from north Texas districts that have been losing population. So it was no real surprise when the Texas legislature decided to combine the old 13th and 18th into a new 13th district. The rapidly growing metropolitan areas of Houston and Dallas were each entitled to an additional seat. And shrewd legislators, notably then state Sen. Barbara Jordan (see Texas 18), made sure that both Dallas and Houston got what they deserved.

Though both had the same economic base—cattle, oil, and cotton—the political character of the two districts combined differed greatly. The old 13th on the south side of the Red River Valley, was Democratic by tradition (see Texas 4). Both the rural counties and the major city here, Wichita Falls (pop. 97,000), gave Purcell large majorities. Typical of the rural territory is Archer County, where *The Last Picture Show* was filmed. The only part of the district Purcell could not carry was the north side of Dallas, which was removed by the 1972 redistricting.

Price's old 18th, along with one county that had been in neither of the old districts, contained 61% of the population of the new constituency. Price's old territory—the High Plains of the Texas panhandle—is drier and less fertile than the Red River Valley. West of the 100th meridian, the wind blows as hard and as unremittingly as anywhere in the United States. Over the years, most of panhandle farmers and ranchers have moved into Amarillo (pop. 127,000) and smaller places like Pampa and Borger. First settled mostly by people from neighboring northwest Oklahoma and western Kansas, the panhandle has always been one of the most Republican areas of Texas. In recent years, the heavily conservative leanings of Amarillo have strengthened the region's traditional Republicanism. Since capturing the seat, Price had little trouble retaining it; in fact, he was unopposed for reelection in 1970.

The election in 1972 could have been settled on a number of potential issues. Both Price and Purcell served on the House Agriculture Committee, where they disagreed on some elements of the Nixon farm programs. Moreover, because wheat is an important crop in the panhandle, Purcell, as Chairman of the Livestock and Grains subcommittee, conducted an investigation of the Russian wheat sale. He criticized the Nixon Administration for favoring the interests of the big grain dealers. Other differences existed as well, and overall, Purcell's voting record was a bit less conservative than Price's.

To judge from the returns, however, none of the potential issues played a major role in the election. Instead, each of the old districts simply stayed loyal to its Congressman. In 1968—the last time Price and Purcell both encountered opposition in the general election—the combined Republican-Democratic vote within the confines of the new 13th district gave the Republican a 54–46 edge. The result in 1972: 55% for Price, 45% for Purcell. Price won 67% of the votes in the counties from his old district, down 1% from 1968 when he was not, of course, running against another incumbent. Purcell won 66% of the votes in his old territory, down 4% from his 1968 showing. Because neither man made much of a dent in the other's home turf, the fact that a majority of the new district was drawn from Price's old constituency determined the outcome of the election.

Price's prospects for 1974 look very good indeed. With Purcell no longer in Congress, Price has an opportunity to provide constituency services to the portion of the district taken from the old 13th. With such services, many Congressmen have earned large majorities in theoretically hostile territory. So Price should do considerably better than 54% in 1974.

Census Data Pop. 477,856. Central city, 47%; suburban, 10%. Median family income, $8,120; families above $15,000: 14%; families below $3,000: 12%. Median years education, 12.1.

1972 Share of Federal Outlays $590,631,342

DOD	$187,756,000	HEW	$141,985,606
AEC	$23,469,482	HUD	$1,009,193
NASA	$38,135	DOI	$5,918,612
DOT	$18,923,159	USDA	$139,718,504
		Other	$71,812,651

Federal Military-Industrial Commitments

DOD Contractors Textron (Amarillo), $15.091m: repair of crash-damaged helicopters.
DOD Installations Sheppard AFB (Wichita Falls).
NASA Contractors LTV Aerospace (Dallas), $11.979m: Scout systems management.
AEC Operations Mason & Hanger-Silas Mason (Amarillo), $20.847m: operation of government
facility and fabrication of weapons components.

Economic Base Agriculture, notably cattle and grains; finance, insurance and real estate; oil and
gas extraction, especially crude petroleum and natural gas, and oil and gas field services; and food
and kindred products.

The Voters

Registration 221,266 total. No party registration.
Median voting age 44.0
Employment profile White collar, 45%. Blue collar, 32%. Service, 14%. Farm, 9%.
Ethnic groups Black, 5%. Spanish, 6%. Total foreign stock, 4%.

Presidential vote

1972	Nixon (R)	118,004	(76%)
	McGovern (D)	37,575	(24%)
1968	Nixon (R)	72,843	(45%)
	Humphrey (D)	55,534	(34%)
	Wallace (AI)	32,785	(20%)

Representative

Robert Dale (Bob) Price (R) Elected 1966; b. Sept. 7, 1927, Reading,
Okla.; home, Pampa; Okla. State U., B.S., 1951; USAF, Korean War;
married, three children; Baptist.

Career Rancher.

Offices 430 CHOB, 202-225-3706. Also Box 2476, Pampa 79065,
806-665-2351, and 310 P.O. Bldg., Amarillo 79105, 806-376-5151, ext.
381, and 308 P.O. Bldg., Wichita Falls 76301.

Administrative Assistant Ronald Martinson

Committees

Agriculture (7th); Subs: Cotton; Livestock and Grains; Department Operations (Chm.).

Armed Services (12th); Sub: No. 1.

Group Ratings

	ADA	COPE	LWV	RIPON	NFU	LCV	CFA	NAB	NSI	ACA
1972	0	10	10	14	43	11	0	90	100	100
1971	3	17	22	18	47	–	14	–	–	86
1970	4	0	–	25	8	0	32	89	100	86

Key Votes

1) Busing	AGN	6) Cmbodia Bmbg	ABS	11) Chkg Acct Intrst	ABS
2) Strip Mines	FOR	7) Bust Hwy Trust	AGN	12) End HISC (HUAC)	ABS
3) Cut Mil $	AGN	8) Farm Sub Lmt	AGN	13) Nixon Sewer Veto	AGN
4) Rev Shrg	AGN	9) School Prayr	FOR	14) Corp Cmpaign $	ABS
5) Pub TV $	AGN	10) Cnsumr Prot	AGN	15) Pol $ Disclosr	AGN

Election Results

1972 general:	Bob Price (R)	87,084	(55%)
	Graham Purcell (D)	71,730	(45%)
1972 primary:	Bob Price (R), unopposed		
1970 general	Bob Price (R), unopposed		

FOURTEENTH DISTRICT Political Background

The 14th district of Texas moves along the state's steamy Gulf Coast from the Brazosport area just south of Houston to Padre Island, the National Seashore below Corpus Christi. Behind the sand bars that protect the harbors from the Gulf are some of the largest oil refineries and chemical plants in Texas. The installations are found in places like Brazosport, Port Lavaca, Victoria, and Corpus Christi (pop. 204,000), the district's largest city. There are plans to build an offshore "superport" in Brazosport to accommodate giant oil tankers.

The 14th takes in sweaty, heavy-industry country. It is one of the few parts of Texas where the state's labor unions have much influence. Few blacks live this far south and west in Texas, making up only 7% of the district's population. But the 14th does have a large Mexican-American minority (36%). On economic issues, the district is one of the more liberal in the state. In statewide primaries, it has supported liberal candidates like ex-Sen. Ralph Yarborough and Frances Farenthold, who represented Corpus Christi in the state legislature.

The 14th's current Congressman, John Young, has held office since he knocked off an incumbent in the 1956 primary. Young's votes in the House were often part of the majorities fashioned by Speakers Sam Rayburn and John McCormack behind the passage of liberal legislation. Young, as a result, won a seat on the Rules Committee. Lately, he has voted less frequently with House liberals, a tendency due perhaps to his attitude toward the Vietnam war. During the course of the conflict, Young maintained solid support for the policies of both the Johnson and Nixon administrations. Like many of the dwindling band of economic liberals who share such views, Young appears to have fallen away from antiwar liberals on issues other than the war.

Nevertheless, the Congressman remains responsive to the House leadership. His vote in the Rules Committee is usually cast in favor of allowing liberal legislation onto the floor. He also voted to spring an anti-busing law from the Judiciary Committee; Young's vote might be explained by an acrimonious busing controversy in Corpus Christi. At home, Young's record in the House seems to set pretty well. Since 1964, he has run into only one opponent in either the primary or general election. Yancy White, his primary rival in 1972, attempted to win labor, Mexican-American, and youth support, but wound up with only 34% of the votes. Age does not suggest that Young might retire, or possible lose an election—he is only 58. But the Congressman does have problems with his eyesight, though that is no necessary bar to further service. Thomas P. Gore of Oklahoma (Gore Vidal's grandfather) was a Senator for 18 years, though totally blind.

Census Data Pop. 474,467. Central city, 43%; suburban, 22%. Median family income, $7,869; families above $15,000: 13%; families below $3,000: 15%. Median years education, 11.2.

1972 Share of Federal Outlays $439,522,189

DOD	$157,357,397	HEW	$119,738,540
AEC	$10,643	HUD	$4,129,971
NASA	$2,943,434	DOI	$3,184,964
DOT	$10,062,661	USDA	$55,154,085
		Other	$86,940,494

Federal Military-Industrial Commitments

DOD Contractors Coastal States Marketing, Inc. (Corpus Christi), $21.724m: unspecified.
DOD Installations Naval Air Station (Corpus Christi). Naval Hospital (Corpus Christi).

Economic Base Agriculture, notably grains and cattle; oil and gas extraction, especially crude petroleum and natural gas, and oil and gas field services; finance, insurance and real estate; industrial chemicals and other chemicals and allied products; primary nonferrous metal production, and other primary metal industries.

The Voters

Registration 212,463 total. No party registration.
Median voting age 41.6
Employment profile White collar, 43%. Blue collar, 37%. Service, 15%. Farm, 5%.
Ethnic groups Black, 7%. Spanish, 36%. Total foreign stock, 13%.

Presidential vote

1972	Nixon (R)	83,780	(60%)
	McGovern (D)	55,365	(40%)
1968	Nixon (R)	44,726	(34%)
	Humphrey (D)	68,965	(52%)
	Wallace (AI)	19,194	(14%)

Representative

John Young (D) Elected 1956; b. Nov. 10, 1916, Corpus Christi; home, Corpus Christi; St. Edward's U., B.A., 1937; U. of Tex., 1937–40; married, five children; Catholic.

Career Practicing atty., 1940– ; Asst. County Atty., Nueces County, 1947–50; County Atty., 1951–52; County. Judge, 1953–56.

Offices 2419 RHOB, 202-225-2831. Also 311 Fed. Bldg., Corpus Christi 78401, 512-883-5511, ext. 348.

Administrative Assistant Harry McAdams

Committees

Rules (5th).

Joint Com. on Atomic Energy (3rd); Subs: Communities (Chm.); Energy; Raw Materials; Security.

Group Ratings

	ADA	COPE	LWV	RIPON	NFU	LCV	CFA	NAB	NSI	ACA
1972	19	73	50	38	86	13	0	27	100	55
1971	18	83	44	29	73	–	63	–	–	88
1970	24	64	–	21	69	50	78	18	89	38

Key Votes

1) Busing	AGN	6) Cmbodia Bmbg	FOR	11) Chkg Acct Intrst	AGN
2) Strip Mines	FOR	7) Bust Hwy Trust	AGN	12) End HISC (HUAC)	AGN
3) Cut Mil $	AGN	8) Farm Sub Lmt	AGN	13) Nixon Sewer Veto	AGN
4) Rev Shrg	AGN	9) School Prayr	FOR	14) Corp Cmpaign $	FOR
5) Pub TV $	FOR	10) Cnsumr Prot	FOR	15) Pol $ Disclosr	AGN

Election Results

1972 general:	John Young (D), unopposed		
1972 primary:	John Young (D)	61,118	(66%)
	Yancy White (D)	31,374	(34%)
1970 general:	John Young (D), unopposed		

FIFTEENTH DISTRICT Political Background

South Texas lives closer to the feudal ages than any region in the United States. Here are the fabled Texas ranches: the King Ranch, covering more acreage than Rhode Island, produces an annual income of $25 million—mostly from oil, not cattle. Just down the road (which is to say, in the next county) is a spread, not too much smaller, that belongs to White House Counsellor Anne Armstrong and her husband. Farther south is the Lower Rio Grande Valley. Here, thanks to irrigation water and the semitropical climate, are fields of cotton, fruits, and vegetables tended by

Mexican farm hands. Cesar Chavez tried to do some organizing among the laborers, but without much success.

This is the land of the state's 15th congressional district. It includes not only the Lower Rio Grande, but also some of the interior counties between Corpus Christi and Laredo, though it contains neither of the two cities. Economic and political power is highly concentrated in the 15th. Though 75% of the residents of the district are of Mexican stock, virtually all the important decisions here are made by Anglo ranchers, bankers, lawyers, and farmers. Evidence of Anglo power is rife in the election returns reported by the 15th.

Richard Kleberg, owner of the King Ranch, represented this part of Texas from 1931 to 1945. A young poor boy named Lyndon Johnson from the hills around Austin got his first government job in Kleberg's office. Sen. Lloyd Bentsen is a big landowner in Hidalgo County on the Lower Rio Grande. He was elected County Judge at 25 and Congressman at 27. Bentsen retired from the House in 1955 to make a really big fortune in Houston. He was succeeded by Joe M. Kilgore, a pillar of the Connally Tory Democratic establishment. Kilgore wanted badly to run against liberal Sen. Ralph Yarborough in the 1964 primary. It took Lyndon Johnson himself to deter him from doing so.

In the smaller counties of the district, the voters are easy to manipulate. Almost all of them are cast by Mexican field hands whose jobs depend on a single big landowner. Jim Hogg County, to take one example, went from 82% for Humphrey in 1968 to 47% for Nixon in 1972. Even more interesting is the voting history of Duval County, long the fiefdom of the Parr family. Its most famous performance occurred in the 1948 Senate runoff primary. After some delay, Duval reported 4,622 votes for Lyndon Johnson and 40 for his opponent. "Landslide Lyndon," as he became known, won the runoff by 87 votes statewide. In the last two presidential elections, Duval has been the most Democratic county in the entire nation—George McGovern carried it 3,729 to 623. As an incidental note, George Parr, the so-called "Duke of Duval," was indicted on charges of income tax evasion in April of 1973.

Duval, however, represents an exception among rural Texas counties in its devotion to the Democratic party. In south Texas, both Mexican-American and Anglo voters moved to Nixon and the Republicans in 1972. So great was the rush to Nixon that the incumbent President even carried the 15th district, which is heavily Democratic by tradition. The results reflected the energetic campaign waged in the Mexican-American community by Nixon forces. But because urban Chicano areas in Texas reported much smaller Republican swings, one must ascribe some of the rural shift to the clout wielded by Anglo and Nixonophile *patrons*.

Kilgore's successor in the House was the district's first Mexican-American Congressman, Eligio (Kika) de la Garza. To say the least, de la Garza is not a favorite among militant (but vote-poor) younger generation Chicanos; the Congressman usually votes with the more conservative Texas Democrats. The seniority system has been especially good to de la Garza. Mainly because of the retirement of aging Southern Democrats, he is now the fourth-ranking Democrat on the House Agriculture Committee and Chairman of its Department Operations Subcommittee. Because two of the three Democrats on the committee senior to him are more than 20 years older, de la Garza has a good chance to become Chairman of Agriculture. The few times he has had opposition in the 15th, the Congressman has won easily.

Census Data Pop. 458,581. Central city, 37%; suburban, 33%. Median family income, $5,035; families above $15,000: 8%; families below $3,000: 29%. Median years education, 8.2.

1972 Share of Federal Outlays $385,450,902

DOD	$45,508,000	HEW	$134,915,995
AEC	–	HUD	$6,887,224
NASA	–	DOI	$26,832,435
DOT	$18,487,036	USDA	$56,559,820
		Other	$96,260,392

Federal Military-Industrial Commitments

DOD Installations Naval Air Station (Kingsville).

Economic Base Agriculture, notably cattle, vegetables and cotton; food and kindred products, especially canned, cured and frozen foods; finance, insurance and real estate; and oil and gas extraction, especially oil and gas field services, and crude petroleum and natural gas. Also higher education (Texas A & I).

The Voters

Registration 201,586 total. No party registration.
Median voting age 41.3
Employment profile White collar, 40%. Blue collar, 34%. Service, 13%. Farm, 13%.
Ethnic groups Spanish, 75%. Total foreign stock, 36%.

Presidential vote

1972	Nixon (R)	64,410	(55%)
	McGovern (D)	53,083	(45%)
1968	Nixon (R)	36,946	(35%)
	Humphrey (D)	61,851	(58%)
	Wallace (AI)	7,712	(7%)

Representative

Eligio De La Garza (D) Elected 1964; b. Sept. 22, 1927, Mercedes; home, Mission; Edinburg Jr. Col.; St. Mary's U., LL.B., 1952; Navy, WWII, Korean War; married, three children; Catholic.

Career Practicing atty., 1952–64; Tex. House of Reps., 1952–64.

Offices 1434 LHOB, 202-225-2531. Also 804 Quince, McAllen 78501, 512-682-5545.

Administrative Assistant Celia Hare Martin

Committees

Agriculture (4th); Subs: Cotton; Conservation and Credit; Department Operations (Chm.).

Merchant Marine and Fisheries (13th) Subs: Coast Guard and Navigation; Fisheries and Wildlife Conservation and the Environment; Oceanography.

Group Ratings

	ADA	COPE	LWV	RIPON	NFU	LCV	CFA	NAB	NSI	ACA
1972	13	60	56	54	86	18	50	27	100	55
1971	35	83	88	47	79	–	50	–	–	35
1970	28	70	–	33	69	57	59	38	100	40

Key Votes

1) Busing	AGN	6) Cmbodia Bmbg	ABS	11) Chkg Acct Intrst	AGN
2) Strip Mines	AGN	7) Bust Hwy Trust	AGN	12) End HISC (HUAC)	AGN
3) Cut Mil $	AGN	8) Farm Sub Lmt	AGN	13) Nixon Sewer Veto	AGN
4) Rev Shrg	AGN	9) School Prayr	FOR	14) Corp Cmpaign $	FOR
5) Pub TV $	FOR	10) Cnsumr Prot	ABS	15) Pol $ Disclosr	AGN

Election Results

1972 general:	Eligio de la Garza (D), unopposed		
1972 primary:	Eligio de la Garza (D)	73,101	(84%)
	Ben A. Martinez (D)	14,177	(16%)
1970 general:	Eligio de la Garza (D)	54,498	(76%)
	Ben A. Martinez (R)	17,049	(24%)

SIXTEENTH DISTRICT Political Background

"West of the Pecos" is a phrase associated with Judge Roy Bean. But it is also a pretty fair description of the 16th congressional district of Texas. When Bean held barroom court in the town of Langtry, there was precious little of anything except uninhabited desert west of the Pecos. Today, there is not much more—except for the city of El Paso. With 359,000 residents, El Paso dominates the 16th district. Aside from the little town of Pecos (pop. 12,000) and the district's portion (pop. 49,000) of the oil-rich, ultraconservative city of Odessa, El Paso is the only significant population center in the 16th. More typical of the landscape here is the harsh desert of Loving County, which in 1970 recorded a population of 164 people—the lowest in the nation.

El Paso is a Sun Belt city that mushroomed after World War II. Its economy was fueled by the nearby presence of giant military installations like Fort Bliss and the White Sands Proving Grounds. Across the Rio Grande, whose flow is only a trickle during most of the year, lies the even larger Ciudad Juarez, Mexico. Beneath looming and eroded mountains, the two of them sit huddled together amid a vast expanse of desert. A majority of El Paso's residents are Mexican in origin, though no one can say for sure how many live here. This part of Texas gave the nation the term "wetback." Many Mexican nationals still cross the border every day looking for higher paying jobs in the United States.

Power in El Paso rests firmly in the hands of Anglos, as Mexican-Americans do not cast anything like their proportionate share of votes. The hottest issue in the city is the strike at the Farah plant. Non-unionized El Paso has become the western center of the garment industry, and many of the Farah workers—almost all of them of Mexican origin—are on strike to get a union election. A Lebanese immigrant and self-made millionaire runs the company autocratically. Content to wait out the slow working of the NLRB, the owner points out, with some apparent justification, that wages and working conditions at Farah are better than in most El Paso garment factories. The strike has split both the work force and the community. The local Roman Catholic bishop supports the strikers, while the city's Anglo business establishment is solidly behind Farah. Meanwhile, the plant continues to turn out clothes.

The 16th is one of the few Texas districts to change partisan hands in recent years. The Billie Sol Estes scandal of 1962 fully accounts for the shift. Estes, a businessman from the town of Pecos, was caught defrauding the Department of Agriculture and was eventually sent to prison. Because he had contributed to campaigns of several prominent Texas Democrats, area Republicans smelled a potential issue. One of the recipients of Estes' generosity was the 16th's then-Congressman J. T. (Slick) Rutherford, a moderate Democrat first elected in 1954. Rutherford will be perhaps best remennered in American history for having once employed writer Larry L. King, former editor at _Harper's_ and author of the _Confessions of a White Racist_. During the campaign, Republican candidate Ed Foreman trumpeted the Estes-Rutherford connection up and down the district, and the Goldwaterite won the seat here in 1962.

Foreman's tenure was short-lived. In 1964, he was beaten by Democrat Richard White, the current incumbent. Foreman later moved to New Mexico, got elected to Congress again in 1968, and lost again in 1970—setting a record for himself in the process (see New Mexico 2). White is a Texas moderate. He has compiled a liberal record on several issues, notably on civil rights. He has obviously kept himself in line with the thinking of the 16th's large number of Mexican-American voters. At the same time, White's record shows a kind of innate conservatism, attuned with the desires of the Anglo voting majority. The Congressman is not an especially forceful campaigner. With the inclusion of most of Odessa in his district, he might run into a strong challenge from a Republican candidate. But so far, none has surfaced.

Census Data Pop. 478,087. Central city, 78%; suburban, 10%. Median family income, $7,848; families above $15,000: 14%; families below $3,000: 13%. Median years education, 11.9.

1972 Share of Federal Outlays $467,822,084

DOD	$231,482,307	HEW	$92,392,022
AEC	–	HUD	$2,105,299
NASA	–	DOI	$3,357,141
DOT	$25,071,730	USDA	$33,911,512
		Other	$79,502,073

Federal Military-Industrial Commitments

DOD Contractors Raytheon (Fort Bliss), $6.506m: Hawk missile ground support equipment. Santa Fe Engineers (Fort Bliss), $5.479m: unspecified. Chevron Oil (El Paso), $5.190m: petroleum products.
DOD Installations Fort Bliss (El Paso).

Economic Base Men's and boys' furnishings, and other apparel and other textile products; finance, insurance and real estate; oil and gas extraction, especially oil and gas field services; agriculture, notably cattle and cotton; and food and kindred products. Also higher education (Univ. of Texas, El Paso).

The Voters

Registration 184,160 total. No party registration.
Median voting age 38.8
Employment profile White collar, 48%. Blue collar, 37%. Service, 13%. Farm, 2%.
Ethnic groups Black, 4%. Spanish, 50%. Total foreign stock, 33%. Germany, 2%.

Presidential vote

1972	Nixon (R)	75,221	(64%)
	McGovern (D)	41,962	(36%)
1968	Nixon (R)	41,945	(42%)
	Humphrey (D)	42,764	(43%)
	Wallace (AI)	14,140	(14%)

Representative

Richard Crawford White (D) Elected 1964; b. April 29, 1923, El Paso; home, El Paso; U. of Tex. at El Paso; U. of Tex. at Austin, B.A., 1946, LL.B., 1949; USMC, WWII; married, three children; Episcopalian.

Career Practicing atty., 1949–64; Tex. House of Reps., 1955–58; El Paso County Dem. Chm., 1962–63.

Offices 401 CHOB, 202-225-4831. Also 146 U.S. Courthouse, El Paso 79901, 915-533-9351, ext. 5330.

Administrative Assistant Hawley Richeson

Committees

Armed Services (13th); Subs: No. 3; No. 5.

Post Office and Civil Service (9th); Subs: Census and Statistics (Chm.); Postal Service.

Group Ratings

	ADA	COPE	LWV	RIPON	NFU	LCV	CFA	NAB	NSI	ACA
1972	13	45	42	38	71	27	50	33	100	57
1971	22	50	33	41	67	–	25	–	–	70
1970	32	64	–	47	75	38	70	42	90	47

Key Votes

1) Busing	ABS	6) Cmbodia Bmbg	AGN	11) Chkg Acct Intrst	AGN
2) Strip Mines	AGN	7) Bust Hwy Trust	AGN	12) End HISC (HUAC)	AGN
3) Cut Mil $	ABS	8) Farm Sub Lmt	AGN	13) Nixon Sewer Veto	AGN
4) Rev Shrg	AGN	9) School Prayr	FOR	14) Corp Cmpaign $	AGN
5) Pub TV $	FOR	10) Cnsumr Prot	AGN	15) Pol $ Disclosr	AGN

Election Results

1972 general:	Richard C. White (D), unopposed		
1972 primary:	Richard C. White (D), unopposed		
1970 general:	Richard C. White (D)	54,617	(83%)
	J. R. Provencio (R)	11,420	(17%)

SEVENTEENTH DISTRICT Political Background

Why has the Texas delegation always been so powerful in the House, and the much larger New York delegation so impotent? The answer lies in the seniority system, and the difference between Texas and New York politics. The difference can be summed this way: in Texas, judges become Congressmen, and in New York, Congressmen become judges. New York judgeships pay something more than $30,000 a year; the hours are short, and the working conditions excellent. Besides, most New Yorkers consider Washington scarcely more civilized than Albany. So it is no surprise that in the last 20 years, nine New York City Congressmen have resigned to become judges. Accordingly, New York Democrats from safe seats have spent less time on the seniority ladder than they could have.

In Texas, the story is quite another one. Small county judgeships pay only a pittance. Bright young men often hold them as a political step up. So it is no surprise that six of the current members of the Texas House delegation, plus Sen. Lloyd Bentsen, once served as either a local judge or district attorney. Moreover, only one member of the Texas delegation has resigned or retired to take a judgeship. That member was Rep. (1949–63) Homer Thornberry, who was proferred a seat on the U.S. Court of Appeals by his predecessor in the House, Lyndon Johnson. When Texas Congressmen do quit, they quit like ex-Rep. Frank Ikard, himself an ex-judge. Ikard, now head lobbyist for the American Petroleum Institute, makes $200,000 a year.

One of the ex-county judges who is now a Congressman is Omar Burleson of the 17th district. His career illustrates the value of seniority in Texas politics. Burleson was one of the many World War II veterans elected to the House in 1946, and one of the half dozen who remain there. For a decade or two he rose on the seniority ladder, finally achieving the pinnacle of most Congressmen's dreams: a committee chairmanship. To be sure, it was only the chairmanship of House Administration, then a musty housekeeping body. Later developments, however, have demonstrated its potential for power (see Ohio 18). In any case, the chairmanship was not what Burleson or the powers that be in Texas wanted. In 1966, Congressman Clark Thompson of the state's 9th district decided to retire. Thompson held the Texas seat on the Ways and Means Committee, where he could protect the 27½% oil depletion allowance. So big oil wanted that seat to stay in Texas hands. The industry's candidate was Burleson, who was perfectly willing to surrender his chairmanship for it.

But House liberals had other ideas. They supported Congressman Jacob Gilbert of the Bronx, a machine liberal who might not take so kindly to the politics of oil. After a heated struggle, Gilbert won the seat by one vote in the Democratic Caucus. The liberals would have lost, but for the unavoidable absence of the Mississippi delegation, which had returned to Jackson to watch former colleague John Bell Williams sworn in as Governor.

So Burleson had to bide another two years chairing his committee. He finally won the seat on Ways and Means after the 1968 elections. Ironically, it was only after the Texas seat was reoccupied that Congress cut the depletion allowance in the Tax Reform Act of 1969. But Burleson, the ex-Chairman, remains content today as the ninth-ranking Democrat on Ways and Means. At 68, he is too old to succeed to a chairmanship ever again.

Burleson represents a district that is the geographical heart of Texas: acres and acres of arid farming and grazing land west of Dallas and Fort Worth and north of San Antonio and Austin. The 17th has only two urban centers of any size, Abilene (pop. 89,000) and Big Spring (pop. 28,000)—both profoundly conservative towns. This is traditionally Texas Democratic country. But in 1972, the area, like much of rural Texas, shifted sharply to Nixon's Republicans (see Texas 11 for analysis). Nevertheless, Burleson has not had an opponent since 1964, when the Republicans, apparently anticipating a Goldwater landslide that never developed, ran candidates in every Texas congressional district. Local politicians apparently now assume that any race in the 17th would be futile. These days, however, such assumptions grow increasingly more dubious when it comes to incumbents nearing 70, as Burleson is. If Burleson retires, one intriguing candidate is ex-Lt. Gov. Ben Barnes. He was widely touted as presidential material until he ran a disastrous third in the Democratic primary of 1972, the year of scandal in Texas politics. Barnes is from Brown County in the 17th, and could be ripe for a political comeback in 1974, at the tender age of 35.

Census Data Pop. 467,912. Central city, 19%; suburban, 5%. Median family income, $7,010; families above $15,000: 10%; families below $3,000: 17%. Median years education, 11.2.

1972 Share of Federal Outlays $492,469,076

DOD	$136,435,000	HEW	$181,977,534
AEC	–	HUD	$89,000
NASA	$97,450	DOI	$1,153,016
DOT	$9,161,688	USDA	$95,974,560
		Other	$67,580,828

Federal Military-Industrial Commitments

DOD Contractors Southern Airways (Mineral Wells), $14.769m: helicopter pilot training services. Centron Corp (Mineral Wells), $8.598m: components for 155mm projectiles.
DOD Installations Fort Wolters (Mineral Wells); closed, 1974. Dyess AFB (Abilene). Webb AFB (Big Spring).

Economic Base Agriculture, notably cattle, cotton and grains; oil and gas extraction; finance, insurance and real estate; and food and kindred products.

The Voters

Registration 221,140 total. No party registration.
Median voting age 47.5
Employment profile White collar, 40%. Blue collar, 34%. Service, 15%. Farm, 11%.
Ethnic groups Black, 4%. Spanish, 9%. Total foreign stock, 4%.

Presidential vote

1972	Nixon (R)	104,249	(73%)
	McGovern (D)	37,811	(27%)
1968	Nixon (R)	55,136	(37%)
	Humphrey (D)	64,758	(44%)
	Wallace (AI)	27,958	(19%)

Representative

Omar Burleson (D) Elected 1946; b. March 19, 1906, Anson; home, Anson; Abilene Christian Col., 1924–26; Hardin Simmons U., 1926–27; Cumberland U., 1927–29; Navy, WWII; married; Church of Christ.

Career Atty., Jones County, 1931–35; County Judge, 1935–41; Sp. Agent, FBI, 1940–41; Sec., Rep. Sam Russell, 1941–42; Gen. Counsel, Natl. Capital Housing Auth., 1942.

Offices 2369 RHOB, 202-225-6605. Also New Fed. Bldg., Rm. 2101, 3rd and N. Pine St., Abilene 79601, 915-673-7221.

Administrative Assistant Mrs. Judith Curtis

Committees

Ways and Means (9th).

Group Ratings

	ADA	COPE	LWV	RIPON	NFU	LCV	CFA	NAB	NSI	ACA
1972	0	9	0	31	43	13	50	91	100	90
1971	0	18	0	17	50	–	0	–	–	86
1970	0	17	–	12	42	17	28	83	100	72

Key Votes

1) Busing	AGN	6) Cmbodia Bmbg	FOR	11) Chkg Acct Intrst	AGN
2) Strip Mines	FOR	7) Bust Hwy Trust	AGN	12) End HISC (HUAC)	AGN
3) Cut Mil $	AGN	8) Farm Sub Lmt	AGN	13) Nixon Sewer Veto	AGN
4) Rev Shrg	AGN	9) School Prayr	FOR	14) Corp Cmpaign $	FOR
5) Pub TV $	AGN	10) Cnsumr Prot	AGN	15) Pol $ Disclosr	AGN

Election Results

1972 general:	Omar Burleson (D), unopposed
1972 primary:	Omar Burleson (D), unopposed
1970 general:	Omar Burleson (D), unopposed

EIGHTEENTH DISTRICT Political Background

Texas politics in general and Houston politics in particular are full of anomalies. For example, the liberal candidate for Mayor of Houston in November 1973 was Fred Hofheinz, son of the flamboyant judge who built and runs the Astrodome. The conservative candidate was a Councilman named Dick Gottlieb. Consider another oddity. In this muscular, macho city, the two leading political strategists and personages of power are women. There is Nancy Palm, leader of Houston's Republicans, considered an ultraconservative in conflict with the party's conservative Dallas wing. Lately, Palm has been winning; her candidate, Houston state Sen. Hank Grover, won the Republican gubernatorial nomination. He was helped by an overwhelming margin coming out of Houston's Harris County, which happens to cast almost half of the state's Republican primary votes. (Out in the Texas sticks, people stay in the Democratic primary, however they plan to vote in November.) In the general election, Grover came within 100,000 votes of defeating Democrat Dolph Briscoe and winning the governorship for the Republicans—a formidable achievement.

Quite far to Ms. Palm's left is Billie Carr, head of the Harris County Democrats. Ms. Carr leads a liberal organization that has won primaries and got out the vote in general elections with the same telling effect as Palm's Republicans. In the 1972 gubernatorial runoff, for example, Harris County delivered 60% of its votes to state Rep. Frances (Sissy) Farenthold. And in the 1972 general election, Harris County produced a respectable number of McGovern votes, given its previous performances. In presidential elections, the county has gone Democratic only once since 1948. So even as liberal Democrats lose votes in rural Texas, they have kept abreast statewide or even gained some, by dint of the organization efforts of urban, especially Houston, liberals.

One reason behind the relative success of the liberals is the political sophistication of Houston's black community. According to the Joint Center on Political Studies, the Houston blacks cast Democratic votes in greater proportion than blacks do just about anywhere in the United States; and what is more important, the blacks here turn out in fairly large proportion. By contrast, the Houston Mexican-Americans, scattered throughout the city, are fractious and inclined to conservatisim. Probably the most sophisticated, and certainly the most politically savvy, product of Houston black politics in Congresswoman Barbara Jordan.

Barbara Jordan is one of those people with a long string of firsts: along with Atlanta Andrew Young, the first black elected to Congress from the South in the twentieth century; the first black woman elected to Congress from the South; the first black member of the Texas state Senate, and so on, and on.

But her career is even more remarkable than any list of firsts would imply. It was just six years ago (1967) that she was elected, at age 31, to the Texas Senate—a body with only 31 members, 30 of them men and white. Moreover, most Texas state Senators come from rural areas and most are responsive to the blandishments of big lobbyists. Nevertheless, within four years, Jordan was the president pro tempore of the Senate; so she served as acting Governor (another first) whenever Gov. Preston Smith and Lt. Gov. Ben Barnes were out of the state. How did she achieve such success in a forum like the Texas Senate? First, by hard work and thorough knowledge of the issues; few of her colleagues dared to debate her. Second, by political horse-trading as shrewd as has been seen in Austin for some time.

Those two things also explain how Barbara Jordan got her congressional seat. It was clear from the 1970 census that the Houston area was entitled to another congressional district. The question was where it would go—boundaries, obviously, were crucial. Jordan drew a district that contained most of central Houston, including the black neighborhoods south of Texas Southern University, and north and northeast toward Kashmere Gardens. The new 18th also encompassed the all-white neighborhoods toward the west and northwest, as well as the city's downtown. So drawn, the district was not black majority. A number of the black precincts were retained in the 8th for the benefit of liberal incumbent Bob Eckhardt. Overall, the district was only 42% black and 20% Mexican-American. Both figures, however, somewhat overstate the proportion of those groups eligible to vote (38% and 15% respectively).

Later, the men who had the most to say about the redistricting process, among other things, were brought low by scandal. Both Gov. Smith and Lt. Gov. Barnes were ignominiously defeated in the Democratic gubernatorial primary, and House Speaker Gus Mutscher was sentenced to jail. Meanwhile, Jordan, untouched by scandal, walked away with a House seat. The Democratic primary was touted as a race between Jordan and state Rep. Curtis Graves, a notably more militant representative of Houston's black community. But Jordan won an amazing 81% of the votes, as Curtis took 14%. She carried every neighborhood by overwhelming margins.

The showing testified to Ms. Jordan's willingness to provide services for her constituents, a trait that will help to make her already safe seat even safer in the years ahead. As yet, Jordan has been relatively quiet in the House. But she knows how to work in a legislative area, and she enjoys the reputation of a politician not to be crossed lightly.

Census Data Pop. 462,062. Central city, 100%; suburban, 0%. Median family income, $7,343; families above $15,000: 10%; families below $3,000: 15%. Median years education, 10.4.

1972 Share of Federal Outlays $350,660,121

DOD	$46,379,580	HEW	$101,053,055
AEC	$223,224	HUD	$10,269,622
NASA	$61,174,543	DOI	$703,471
DOT	$13,878,972	USDA	$26,380,057
		Other	$90,597,597

Federal Military-Industrial Commitments

DOD Contractors Humble Oil (Houston), $29.090m: petroleum products. Shell Oil (Houston), $24.049m: petroleum products. Gulf Oil (Houston), $13.206m: petroleum products. *NASA Contractors* SIP, Inc. (Houston), $13.891m: unspecified support services.

Economic Base Finance, insurance and real estate; fabricated metal products, especially fabricated structural metal products; machinery, especially oil field machinery; chemicals and allied products, especially industrial chemicals; and oil and gas extraction. Also higher education (Univ. of Houston).

The Voters

Registration 184,937 total. No party registration.
Median voting age 40.2
Employment profile White collar, 40%. Blue collar, 40%. Service, 20%. Farm, –%.
Ethnic groups Black, 42%. Spanish, 19%. Total foreign stock, 12%.

Presidential vote

1972	Nixon (R)	34,173	(35%)
	McGovern (D)	62,954	(65%)
1968	Nixon (R)	24,896	(25%)
	Humphrey (D)	61,263	(61%)
	Wallace (AI)	14,186	(14%)

Representative

Barbara C. Jordan (D) Elected 1972; b. Feb. 21, 1936, Houston; home, Houston; Tex. So. U., B.A., 1956; Boston U. School of Law, 1959; single; Baptist.

Career Adm. Asst., Judge of Harris County; State Senator; Tex. Legislative Council; Exec. Com. Natl. Dem. Policy Council; D.N.C.

Offices 1725 LHOB, 202-225-3816. Also Fed. Bldg., 515 Rusk St., Houston, 713-226-5724.

Administrative Assistant Rufus (Bud) Myers

Committees

Judiciary (17th). Subs: No. 2 (Claims); No. 5 (Antitrust Matters).

Group Ratings: Newly Elected

Key Votes

1) Busing	NE	6) Cmbodia Bmbg	AGN	11) Chkg Acct Intrst	AGN
2) Strip Mines	NE	7) Bust Hwy Trust	FOR	12) End HISC (HUAC)	AGN
3) Cut Mil $	NE	8) Farm Sub Lmt	NE	13) Nixon Sewer Veto	FOR
4) Rev Shrg	NE	9) School Prayr	NE	14) Corp Cmpaign $	NE
5) Pub TV $	NE	10) Cnsumr Prot	NE	15) Pol $ Disclosr	NE

Election Results

1972 general:	Barbara Jordan (D)	85,672	(81%)
	Paul Merritt (R)	19,355	(18%)
	Manuel Barrera (SW)	1,287	(1%)
1972 primary:	Barbara Jordan (D)	47,713	(81%)
	Curtis M. Graves (D)	8,106	(14%)
	B. T. Bonner (D)	1,777	(3%)
	Milton King (D)	1,573	(3%)

NINETEENTH DISTRICT Political Background

The 19th district of Texas takes in part of the flat, dusty plains and distant, treeless skylines of west Texas. The small towns and ranching communities of the district, which never had many people, are now in general economic and population decline. Two oil cities, Lubbock (pop. 149,000) and Midland (pop. 59,000), plus the smaller portion (pop. 29,000) of another oil city, Odessa, dominate the 19th. Lubbock owes most of its present size to expansion in the decade following World War II. Midland and Odessa are creatures of the Permian Basin oil boom of the 1950s. One of the beneficiaries of the discovery here is George Bush, a former Congressman from Houston and now Republican National Chairman; he made a fortune in Midland. Recently, the aura of boom has worn thin, as the cities of the district have grown little or none. In 1971, a tornado hit downtown Lubbock, as if the elements wanted to reclaim the place from the confident men who had so recently built it up.

The voters of the 19th district have the privilege of sending to the House of Representatives one of its most senior and most powerful members, George Mahon. The congressman was a county district attorney when he was first elected in 1934 (see Texas 17). Since the death of Clarence Cannon of Missouri in 1964, Mahon has been Chairman of the House Appropriations Committee. For some years before he became Chairman of the full committee, Mahon chaired its Defense Subcommittee, a post that he retains. The two positions give him as much influence as anybody in Congress over the federal budget, for by tradition all appropriations bills originate in the House. Moreover, when, as usually happens, the Senate sets different outlay figures, the discrepancies are resolved in conference committee; here the House side is usually more knowledgeable, better prepared, and hence more often gets its way.

Mahon, a tall, slender man whose dark hair belies his age (74), is considered by most a fair-minded, responsible Chairman. Most also feel that he knows his specialty—defense spending—as well as anyone on the Hill. Mahon's general leanings are conservative; the House Apporpriations Committee almost always comes up with lower spending figures that its Senate counterpart. But like most members of his seniority and regional origin, Mahon would rather err by giving the military too much than too little.

Like most other important committee chairmen, Mahon has worked over the years to restrict membership on Appropriations to Congressmen who share his general approach to things. Consequently, the Democrats on the committee are, as a group, considerably more conservative than the Democratic Caucus as a whole. The same is true of the committee's Republicans. In the end, other committees can authorize as much money as they please, but if Mahon's committee fails to appropriate it, the money does not get spent. And under Nixon's impoundment policies, the funds often don't get spent, if Congress does appropriate it. In any case, Mahon and his committee have been a powerful force for conservatism and fiscal restraint over the years—excepting the Pentagon, of course.

Like Wilbur Mills of Ways and Means, Mahon has a fine sense of what the House will and will not accept. So there is seldon a serious floor fight over an appropriations bill. But recent exceptions have shown that Mahon's predispositions are not necessarily those of a majority in the House. The SST was defeated in 1971, despite the support of the Appropriations Committee. And in 1973, the House voted to cut off funds for the bombing of Cambodia, despite Mahon's impassioned pleas; the decisive votes on both issue came on appropriations bills.

Mahon's committee likes to work in quiet, secret surroundings. When the House voted to require all committee hearings open to the public unless the committee determined otherwise, Mahon announced that he expected Appropriations to vote to hold all hearings in executive session. Accordingly, even key members of the important committee are not widely known, though they hold vast power over the budget, and hence policy. Walking down the street, Mahon would not be recognized outside of Washington and the 19th district of Texas.

Back home, the Congressman has, of course, had little trouble winning reelection. The year 1964 marked the last time the Republicans fielded a candidate to run against him, and Mahon took 78% of the votes. But the brute facts of demography have forced the Texas legislature to make the 19th more Republican, at least on paper. It first added Midland and then a part of Odessa. Though it seems inconceivable that Mahon could lose an election, he is 74. The Republicans may therefore try to field a strong candidate who could hold the Chairman's margin down, and so persuade him to retire.

Census Data Pop. 476,986. Central city, 50%; suburban, 8%. Median family income, $8,326; families above $15,000: 17%; families below $3,000: 12%. Median years education, 12.1.

1972 Share of Federal Outlays $507,236,195

DOD	$56,117,692	HEW	$105,637,291
AEC	$9,000	HUD	$14,191,636
NASA	$88,004	DOI	$2,460,990
DOT	$15,584,695	USDA	$247,953,593
		Other	$65,193,294

Federal Military-Industrial Commitments

DOD Contractors Kain Cattle Co. (Lubbock), $5.295m: foodstuffs.
DOD Installations Reese AFB (Lubbock).

Economic Base Agriculture, notably cattle, grains and cotton; oil and gas extraction, especially crude petroleum and natural gas, and oil and gas field services; finance, insurance and real estate; and food and kindred products. Also higher education (Texas Tech.).

The Voters

Registration 219,082 total. No party registration.
Median voting age 40.2
Employment profile White collar, 47%. Blue collar, 29%. Service, 13%. Farm, 11%.
Ethnic groups Black, 6%. Spanish, 19%. Total foreign stock, 7%.

Presidential vote

1972	Nixon (R)	145,504	(76%)
	McGovern (D)	34,307	(24%)
1968	Nixon (R)	67,763	(48%)
	Humphrey (D)	41,821	(30%)
	Wallace (AI)	31,760	(22%)

Representative

George H. Mahon (D) Elected 1934; b. Sept. 22, 1900, Haynesville, La.; home, Lubbock; Simmons U., B.A., 1924; U. of Texas, LL.B., 1925; U. of Minn., 1925; married, one child; Methodist.

Career Practicing atty., 1925– ; County Atty., Mitchell County, 1926; Dist. Atty., 32nd Jud. Dist., 1927–34; Regent, Smithsonian Institution.

Offices 2314 RHOB, 202-225-4005. Also P.O. Bldg., Lubbock 79408, 806-763-1611.

Administrative Assistant None

Committees

Appropriations (Chm.); *Defense* (Chm.).

Joint Com. on Reduction of Federal Expenditures (Chm.).

Joint Study Com. on Budget Control.

Group Ratings

	ADA	COPE	LWV	RIPON	NFU	LCV	CFA	NAB	NSI	ACA
1972	6	30	8	25	43	7	50	80	100	77
1971	5	27	11	39	64	–	13	–	–	79
1970	8	18	–	24	62	20	67	67	90	58

Key Votes

1) Busing	AGN	6) Cmbodia Bmbg	FOR	11) Chkg Acct Intrst	AGN
2) Strip Mines	FOR	7) Bust Hwy Trust	AGN	12) End HISC (HUAC)	AGN
3) Cut Mil $	AGN	8) Farm Sub Lmt	AGN	13) Nixon Sewer Veto	AGN
4) Rev Shrg	AGN	9) School Prayr	FOR	14) Corp Cmpaign $	FOR
5) Pub TV $	AGN	10) Cnsumr Prot	AGN	15) Pol $ Disclosr	AGN

Election Results

1972 general:	George Mahon (D), unopposed
1972 primary:	George Mahon (D), unopposed
1970 general:	George Mahon (D), unopposed

TWENTIETH DISTRICT Political Background

San Antonio was the most important town in Texas when the state was part of Mexico. It was here, of course, that Santa Ana and his troops wiped out Davie Crockett, Jim Bowie, and 184 others at the Alamo. In fact, Crockett was a Tennessee Congressman, serving from 1827 to 1831 and again from 1833 to 1835; if the unlettered man had not lost the 1834 election, he would never have gone to Texas. Today, San Antonio is the state's third-largest city (pop. 654,000). Because it has never been a center of the Texas boom industries of oil, electronics, and high finance, San Antonio has not grown as fast as Houston, Dallas, or even Fort Worth. The city is not a withering one, however, and it has retained a Hispanic ambiance along the San Antonio River that winds through the tree-shaded center of town. The Alamo, of course, is overrun by tourists.

Only 130 miles from the Mexican border, San Antonio is 51% Mexican-American—according to the Census Bureau. The figure makes it the most Mexican-American of any major city in the country. But San Antonio enjoys another distinction, one that accounts for much of the city's economic growth: namely, the presence of a large number of Defense Department installations. There is Fort Sam Houston with 10,000 men; the Brooks Aero Medical Center, the major medical facility of the Air Force; and no less than three Air Force bases either within the city limits or just outside them. Why one city has so many military bases remains a mystery. Some local people figure it might have had something to do with San Antonio's longtime (1939–61) Congressman Paul Kilday, who was a prominent member of the House Armed Services Committee. Kilday was the man who defeated the fabled Texas liberal, Maury Maverick, in the 1938 Democratic primary. Thereafter, Kilday, a staunch conservative, headed a local political machine that dominated San Antonio for most of the Congressman's tenure in the House.

The domination ended in 1961, when Kilday resigned to become a judge of the U.S. Court of Military Appeals. He was succeeded by a young Mexican-American lawyer and state Senator, Henry B. Gonzalez, then 35. Gonzalez was the first Mexican-American Congressman from the district. He campaigned as an outspoken liberal and, with the help of many Anglo as well as Mexican-American votes, Gonzalez in effect reversed the result of the 1938 primary.

Gonzalez is now a high-ranking member of the Banking and Currency Committee and Chairman of its International Finance Subcommittee. Many members of the Banking Committee are known for their solicitude toward the troubles of friendly big bankers. But Gonzalez is a man of stubborn rectitude; unlike many of his colleagues, he has declined lucrative offers of bank stock and directorships. Gonzalez's sense of integrity has also cost him the enthusiasm, if not the support, of many liberals—he was once their favorite Texas politician. Long after it was fashionable among liberals, Gonzalez continued to back Lyndon Johnson's conduct of the Vietnam war. And the Congressman has little but scorn for the younger generation of Chicano militants who preach a kind of political separatism. Gonzalez is convinced that for Mexican-Americans to achieve social and economic goals they must work with others with similar interests. These days, the Congressman finds himself reasonably comfortable at meetings of the Texas delegation, where he was once not altogether welcomed.

When Gonzalez was first elected, all of San Antonio and surrounding Bexar County made up the 20th congressional district. The one-man-one-vote doctrine and shifts of population have pared down the territory. It now includes only the central portion of San Antonio, along with Fort Sam Houston and a little suburban land around Kelly Air Force Base. The Anglo areas of Alamo Heights and Castle Hills and the northern part of the city lie in the 21st district, leaving most of San Antonio's Mexican-American population and virtually all of its small black community in the 20th. The arrangement gives the district a solid 60% Mexican-American majority; accordingly, the 20th is often the most liberal district in Texas. Henry B., as he is often called, has not had trouble in recent elections and expects none in the future, even though some of the younger militants grumble about his performance.

Census Data   Pop. 467,942. Central city, 92%; suburban, 8%. Median family income, $6,567; families above $15,000: 7%; families below $3,000: 18%. Median years education, 9.4.

1972 Share of Federal Outlays $846,004,980

DOD	$606,367,236	HEW	$123,867,039
AEC	$31,759	HUD	$16,300,638
NASA	$449,392	DOI	$660,515
DOT	$5,336,785	USDA	$14,451,030
		Other	$78,540,586

Federal Military-Industrial Commitments

DOD Contractors Lyda, Inc. (San Antonio), $15.696m: unspecified.
DOD Installations Fort Sam Houston AB (San Antonio). Kelly AFB (San Antonio). Lackland AFB (San Antonio).

Economic Base Finance, insurance and real estate; food and kindred products, especially meat products; and apparel and other textile products, especially men's and boys' furnishings.

The Voters

Registration 160,377 total. No party registration.
Median voting age 40.1
Employment profile White collar, 42%. Blue collar, 40%. Service, 18%. Farm, –%.
Ethnic groups Black, 11%. Spanish, 60%. Total foreign stock, 25%. Germany, 1%.

Presidential vote

1972	Nixon (R)	36,907	(39%)
	McGovern (D)	56,713	(61%)
1968	Nixon (R)	22,242	(25%)
	Humphrey (D)	62,211	(69%)
	Wallace (AI)	5,861	(7%)

Representative

Henry B. Gonzalez (D) Elected Jan. 10, 1962; b. May 3, 1916, San Antonio; home, San Antonio; San Antonio Col.; U. of Tex.; St. Mary's U.; Army, WWII; married, eight children; Catholic.

Career Chief Probation Officer, Bexar County, 1946; San Antonio City Council, 1953–56; Mayor Pro Tem, 1955–61; Tex. Senate, 1956–61.

Offices 2446 RHOB, 202-225-3236. Also 203 Fed. Bldg., San Antonio 78205, 512-223-8851 or 512-225-5511, ext. 4389.

Administrative Assistant Gail Beagle

Committees

Banking and Currency (9th); Subs: Consumer Affairs; Housing; International Finance (Chm.); Small Business.

Group Ratings

	ADA	COPE	LWV	RIPON	NFU	LCV	CFA	NAB	NSF	ACA
1972	56	100	83	44	86	40	50	0	67	26
1971	57	92	100	39	73	–	75	–	–	32
1970	64	100	–	47	85	67	86	8	70	11

Key Votes

1) Busing	FOR	6) Cmbodia Bmbg	AGN	11) Chkg Acct Intrst	AGN
2) Strip Mines	AGN	7) Bust Hwy Trust	AGN	12) End HISC (HUAC)	FOR
3) Cut Mil $	AGN	8) Farm Sub Lmt	AGN	13) Nixon Sewer Veto	AGN
4) Rev Shrg	AGN	9) School Prayr	AGN	14) Corp Cmpaign $	AGN
5) Pub TV $	AGN	10) Cnsumr Prot	FOR	15) Pol $ Disclosr	AGN

Election Results

1972 general:	Henry B. Gonzalez (D)	81,443	(97%)
	Steven Wattenmaker (SW)	2,596	(3%)
1972 primary:	Henry B. Gonzalez (D), unopposed		
1970 general:	Henry B. Gonzalez (D), unopposed		

TWENTY-FIRST DISTRICT Political Background

Most of the physical expanse of the 21st district of Texas is unpopulated—a vast near-desert given over to the raising of cattle and cotton, the pumping of oil, and the extraction of natural gas. As a congressional constituency, the 21st combines two disparate urban areas. Though the district contains twenty-nine full counties some 49% of its votes are cast in part of a thirtieth. This is Bexar County, and votes come from the north side of San Antonio and its northern suburbs—the heavily Anglo, conservative, and Republican portion of this predominantly Mexican-American city. The district's other urban center is San Angelo (pop. 65,000). Before the 1965 redistricting, which brought part of Bexar County and San Antonio into the 21st, San Angelo was the largest city in an underpopulated district, and it shares the conservative Democratic inclination of the surrounding rural counties.

Also noteworthy are the Texas German areas around San Antonio, which lie in both the 21st and 23rd districts. Towns like New Braunfels and Fredericksburg (where Lyndon Johnson used to go to church) were founded by '48ers—liberal Germans who left Europe after the failure of the revolutions of 1848 and settled on the frontier of southern Texas. Because the Germans considered slave-holding barbarous, they soon became attracted to the then-radical Republican party, and their opposition to secession solidified an allegiance to the party of Lincoln. To this day, the counties in which the descendants of the '48ers still constitute a majority—Comal, Kendall, Gillespie, and Kerr—cast huge Republican majorities in almost every election.

All in all, the composition of the district has made the 21st pretty solidly Republican in most recent statewide elections. But so far it has remained Democratic in congressional elections. After all, the 21st is the lineal descendant, though one vastly altered, of the district that elected John Nance Garner to the House from 1902 to 1932; Garner was Speaker from 1931 to 1933, and Vice-President under Franklin D. Roosevelt for eight years. Even today, when the district selects House representation, it is as if only the traditionally Democratic counties of the constituency voted—counties that now make up far less that half the district's population. From 1942 until the 1965 redistricting, the 21st elected conservative Democrat O. C. Fisher to Congress. He has since continued to win reelection.

Congressman Fisher has made about as little impression on official Washington as it is possible to make in more than 30 years of service. The extremely reliable conservative has risen silently to occupy the number-three slot on the House Armed Services Committee. Here he is a solid supporter of high defense outlays and a bulwark of the committee's bipartisan, hawkish majority.

There are signs that Fisher is preparing to retire. He will be 69 in 1974, at which time he will have completed 32 years on the Hill—enough to entitle him to the maximum congressional pension of $32,500 annually. And in the last election, Republican candidate Doug Harlan, not yet 30, managed to hold Fisher to just 57% of the votes—the incumbent's poorest showing in years. Harlan carried the Bexar County half of the district 56–44; it was only Fisher's popularity in the other 29 counties that created a margin as comfortable as it was. In 1974, another Democrat is unlikely to match Fisher's performance in the rural counties. Consequently, the 21st of Texas might very well be one of the districts that will chose a Republican Congressman in 1974, despite Watergate, high food prices, or traditional off-year losses.

Census Data Pop. 466,656. Central city, 42%; suburban, 17%. Median family income, $8,787; families above $15,000: 20%; families below $3,000: 11%. Median years education, 12.2.

1972 Share of Federal Outlays $650,224,421

DOD	$337,221,309	HEW	$145,774,502
AEC	$221,527	HUD	$7,933,222
NASA	$195,322	DOI	$1,295,225
DOT	$24,942,763	USDA	$50,502,039
		Other	$82,138,512

Federal Military-Industrial Commitments

DOD Contractors Gary Aircraft Corp. (San Antonio), $7.360m: overhaul of aircraft engines. Southwestern Research Institute (San Antonio), $5.805m: various electronics researches.
DOD Installations Goodfellow AFB (San Angelo). Laughlin AFB (Del Rio).

Economic Base Agriculture, notably cattle, and hogs and sheep; finance, insurance and real estate; oil and gas extraction, especially oil and gas field services; food and kindred products, especially meat products; apparel and other textile products, especially men's and boys' furnishings.

TEXAS

The Voters

Registration 227,911 total. No party registration.
Median voting age 44.0
Employment profile White collar, 57%. Blue collar, 26%. Service, 11%. Farm, 6%.
Ethnic groups Black, 2%. Spanish, 24%. Total foreign stock, 14%. Germany, 2%.

Presidential vote

1972	Nixon (R)	121,423	(76%)
	McGovern (D)	38,093	(24%)
1968	Nixon (R)	71,363	(52%)
	Humphrey (D)	46,119	(34%)
	Wallace (AI)	18,496	(14%)

Representative

O. Clark Fisher (D) Elected 1942; b. Nov. 22, ca. 1905, near Junction; home, San Angelo; U. of Tex.; Baylor U., LL.B., 1929; married, one child; Church of Christ.

Career County Atty., Green County, 1931–35; Tex. House of Reps., 1935–37; Dist. Atty., 51st Jud. Dist., 1937–43.

Offices 2407 RHOB, 202-225-4236. Also Fed. Bldg., P.O. Box 170, San Angelo 76901, 915-653-3971, and 602-03 South Texas Bldg., San Antonio 78205, 512-225-5511, ext. 4787.

Administrative Assistant Mrs. Helen Pauly

Committees

Armed Services (3rd); Subs: No. 2 (Chm.); Sp. Sub. on Intelligence.

Group Ratings

	ADA	COPE	LWV	RIPON	NFU	LCV	CFA	NAB	NSI	ACA
1972	6	9	20	40	43	11	50	82	100	95
1971	0	17	11	24	43	–	0	–	–	89
1970	8	17	–	12	25	3	50	80	100	76

Key Votes

1) Busing	AGN	6) Cmbodia Bmbg	FOR	11) Chkg Acct Intrst	AGN
2) Strip Mines	AGN	7) Bust Hwy Trust	AGN	12) End HISC (HUAC)	AGN
3) Cut Mil $	AGN	8) Farm Sub Lmt	AGN	13) Nixon Sewer Veto	AGN
4) Rev Shrg	AGN	9) School Prayr	FOR	14) Corp Cmpaign $	FOR
5) Pub TV $	ABS	10) Cnsumr Prot	AGN	15) Pol $ Disclosr	AGN

Election Results

1972 general:	O. C. Fisher (D)	91,180	(57%)
	Doug Harlan (R)	69,374	(43%)
1972 primary:	O. C. Fisher (D), unopposed		
1970 general:	O. C. Fisher (D)	76,004	(61%)
	Richardson B. Gill (R)	47,868	(39%)

TWENTY-SECOND DISTRICT Political Background

The 22nd district of Texas moves from the south side of Houston across the coastal plain to the Brazosport area on the Gulf of Mexico. This territory was almost vacant 25 years ago. Like so many other Sun Belt boom areas, its subsequent development would not have occurred but for the existence of the air conditioner. Life here goes on inside: in air conditioned houses, air conditioned shopping malls, and in the air conditioned Houston Astrodome. Outside is the shimmering heat and an almost eerie silence.

The 22nd takes in the prosperous, middle-class, and rapidly growing suburban tracts of south Houston, including the Astrodome and Rice University. Though most of the area's blacks were placed in Barbara Jordan's 18th district, some 13% of the Houston residents in the 22nd are black. The 22nd also includes a substantial population in southeastern Harris County—the middle-income suburb of Pasadena and down around the burgeoning NASA Manned Spacecraft Center between the Gulf Freeway and Galveston Bay. Houston Congressman (1937–65) Albert Thomas, a Democrat, brought the NASA complex to the city, but the technicians and astronauts who live near the facility cast heavy Republican margins.

The 22nd also includes exurban Fort Bend and Brazoria counties, which have just begun to experience the phenomenal growth that has hit the south and west sides of Houston. But 70% of the district's voters live in Houston and Harris County; accordingly, this part of the 22nd is the political focus of the constituency.

The 22nd district was first created in 1957, when the Texas legislature eliminated the state's at-large seat and gave rapidly growing Harris County a second Congressman. The district's first and only Congressman has been Democrat Bob Casey. After 15 years in Congress, Casey now occupies a middle-seniority position on the Appropriations Committee. Upon the death of Alabama's George Andrews in 1971, Casey succeeded to the chairmanship of the Legislative Subcommittee. The unit accounts for only a minuscule segment of the federal budget, but because the subcommittee determines Congress' own budget, it does have clout on Capitol Hill. So far, however, Casey has not used his chairmanship the way Wayne Hays of the House Administration Committee has his (see Ohio 18).

On most issues, Casey is a vocal conservative. He is especially fond of portraying himself as a hardline opponent of crime. Nevertheless, Casey has been unable to create a safe seat in the 22nd. As a Democrat, he is a potential target of Houston's archconservative Republicans, who have otherwise carried the district in presidential, gubernatorial, and senatorial races. And as a conservative, Casey is no favorite of Houston's liberal Democrats. Redistricting, however, reduced the proportion of blacks in the 22nd from 22% to 13%; the reduction has helped to protect the incumbent from a liberal challenge in the Democratic primary. In 1973, there were rumors that liberal Frances (Sissy) Farenthold, fresh from a near-upset in the 1972 gubernatorial primary and a new Houston resident, might take a crack at Casey. But at this writing the possibility appears unlikely. Though the odds in any race are with Casey, he is potentially vulnerable to a challenge from either a conservative Republican or a liberal Democrat.

Census Data Pop. 454,820. Central city, 41%; suburban, 59%. Median family income, $11,092; families above $15,000: 25%; families below $3,000: 6%. Median years education, 12.3.

1972 Share of Federal Outlays $345,086,915

DOD	$45,642,447	HEW	$90,446,971
AEC	$219,676	HUD	$10,106,402
NASA	$60,202,267	DOI	$692,290
DOT	$13,658,387	USDA	$25,960,787
		Other	$98,157,688

Federal Military-Industrial Commitments

DOD Installations Ellington AFB (Houston).
NASA Contractors Philco Ford (Houston), $22.937m: mission control equipment and implementation. Lockheed (Houston), $22.594m: electronics and computing support services for Apollo. General Electric (Houston), $18.528m: Apollo spacecraft checkout. IBM (Houston), $14.187m: computer services for Gemini, Apollo, and Mission Control systems. Brown & Root (Houston), $13.609m: support for Apollo. Singer (Houston), $7.469m: manned space craft simulator complex for Apollo.
NASA Installations Johnson Manned Spacecraft Center.

Economic Base Chemicals and allied products; finance, insurance and real estate; fabricated metal products, especially fabricated structural metal products; machinery, especially oil field machinery; and oil and gas extraction.

The Voters

Registration 221,417 total. No party registration.
Median voting age 38.0
Employment profile White collar, 54%. Blue collar, 34%. Service, 11%. Farm, 1%.
Ethnic groups Black, 13%. Spanish, 10%. Total foreign stock, 8%.

Presidential vote

1972	Nixon (R)	94,187	(64%)
	McGovern (D)	52,395	(36%)
1968	Nixon (R)	51,061	(43%)
	Humphrey (D)	43,903	(37%)
	Wallace (AI)	24,932	(21%)

Representative

Robert (Bob) **Randolph Casey** (D) Elected 1958; b. July 27, 1915, Joplin, Mo.; home, Houston; U. of Houston; S. Tex. School of Law, 1934–40; married, ten children; First Christian Church.

Career Practicing atty., 1941–43, 1947–51; Asst. Dist. Atty., Harris County, 1943–47; County Judge, 1951–58; Tex. House of Reps., 1949–50.

Offices 2353 RHOB, 202-225-5951. Also Rm. 12102, Fed. Bldg., 515 Rusk St., Houston 77002, 713-226-4486.

Administrative Assistant Ingrid Lewis

Committees

Appropriations (22nd); Subs: Agriculture, Environmental, and Consumer Protection; Labor, Health, Education, and Welfare; Legislative (Chm.).

Group Ratings

	ADA	COPE	LWV	RIPON	NFU	LCV	CFA	NAB	NSI	ACA
1972	6	27	25	27	43	7	100	60	100	73
1971	8	33	22	33	57	–	38	–	–	68
1970	16	34	–	36	54	3	50	58	88	56

Key Votes

1) Busing	AGN	6) Cmbodia Bmbg	FOR	11) Chkg Acct Intrst	AGN
2) Strip Mines	FOR	7) Bust Hwy Trust	AGN	12) End HISC (HUAC)	AGN
3) Cut Mil $	AGN	8) Farm Sub Lmt	AGN	13) Nixon Sewer Veto	AGN
4) Rev Shrg	AGN	9) School Prayr	FOR	14) Corp Cmpaign $	FOR
5) Pub TV $	FOR	10) Cnsumr Prot	AGN	15) Pol $ Disclosr	AGN

Election Results

1972 general:	Bob Casey (D)	101,786	(70%)
	James Griffin (R)	42,094	(29%)
	Frank Peto (Ind.)	1,169	(1%)
1972 primary:	Bob Casey (D)	51,040	(68%)
	Johnny Nelms (D)	19,532	(26%)
	Ben G. Levy (D)	4,282	(6%)
1970 general:	Bob Casey (D)	73,514	(56%)
	A. W. Busch (R)	58,598	(44%)

TWENTY-THIRD DISTRICT Political Background

From San Antonio south, Texas is majority Mexican-American. Much of the territory can be called feudal: desert-like rural counties where big landowners effectively run the lives of their

Mexican field hands. Seeds of protest have sprouted against the old order in little towns like Crystal City, Carrizo Springs, and Cotulla. Here, because of "brown power" movements, the Mexican-American majorities have for the first time elected Chicanos, often young militants, as local officials. The area is also where support of the state's La Raza Unida party is strongest, an organization that scorns cooperation with either the Democrats or Republicans. In 1972, La Raza's gubernatorial candidate got 6% of the votes statewide; as a result, ultraconservative Republican Hank Grover nearly upset conservative Democrat Dolph Briscoe for the job. La Raza also refused to endorse George McGovern—one of several reasons why he ran so far behind usual Democratic showings in Mexican-American precincts.

The ferment of Chicano political separatism is as powerful in the 23rd congressional district as anywhere in Texas. Some 51% of the district's residents are of Spanish origin. But "brown power" is still nothing like a major political force. It has had its greatest success in the little towns between San Antonio and Laredo, but in Laredo itself—a heavily Mexican-American town on the Rio Grande—politics goes on much as it always has. The 23rd also includes 92,000 people living on the south and east sides of San Antonio, many of them Mexican-Americans. But this part of the district is middle-class country, where voters have retained traditional Democratic allegiances or have moved quietly to the Republicans. The rest of the district comprises a group of counties east and southeast of San Antonio. The area contains some Texas Germans (see Texas 21) and a fairly large Mexican-American minority; nevertheless, the politics of Texas Tory Democrats is what usually finds favor in these parts. John Connally himself, once the state's dominant Democrat and now a Republican, comes from Wilson County in the 23rd.

The 1965 redistricting created the 23rd in something like its present form. From the large Mexican-American population, it was clear that the 23rd would be one of the state's more liberal congressional districts. And since 1966, it has elected one of the state's more liberal Congressmen, Democrat Abraham (Chick) Kazen. Of Lebanese descent, Kazen spent 20 years in the Texas legislature before winning his House seat. In Washington, the Congressman has compiled the record of an LBJ liberal: pretty close to the AFL-CIO line on domestic issues, cocombined with support of the Vietnam war and high levels of military spending. Back home, Kazen has had little trouble winning reelection. And despite the activities of young Chicano militants and the La Raza Unita party, the Congressman is unlikely to encounter any in the near future.

Census Data Pop. 466,248. Central city, 35%; suburban, 22%. Median family income, $6,482; families above $15,000: 9%; families below $3,000: 20%. Median years education, 9.7.

1972 Share of Federal Outlays $618,253,368

DOD	$337,837,455	HEW	$144,651,629
AEC	$13,076	HUD	$14,005,235
NASA	$185,034	DOI	$595,319
DOT	$18,328,480	USDA	$29,938,092
		Other	$72,699,048

Federal Military-Industrial Commitments

DOD Contractors Chromalloy American Corp. (San Antonio), $14.244m: maintenance of aircraft engines.
DOD Installations Naval Air Station, Chase Field (Beeville). Brooks AFB (San Antonio). Randolph AFB (San Antonio).

Economic Base Agriculture, notably cattle, vegetables and grains; finance, insurance and real estate; food and kindred products; apparel and other textile products, especially men's and boys' furnishings; and oil and gas extraction.

The Voters

Registration 194,432 total. No party registration.
Median voting age 41.9
Employment profile White collar, 43%. Blue collar, 35%. Service, 13%. Farm, 9%.
Ethnic groups Black, 3%. Spanish, 48%. Total foreign stock, 23%. Germany, 2%.

Presidential vote

1972	Nixon (R)	71,812	(62%)
	McGovern (D)	44,358	(38%)
1968	Nixon (R)	33,722	(35%)
	Humphrey (D)	49,618	(52%)
	Wallace (AI)	12,911	(13%)

Representative

Abraham Kazen, Jr. (D) Elected 1966; b. Jan. 17, 1919, Laredo; home, Laredo; U. of Tex., 1937–40; Cumberland U. Law School, 1941; USAF, WWII; married, five children; Catholic.

Career Practicing atty., 1945–66; Tex. House of Reps., 1947–53; Tex. Senate, 1953–66, Pres. Pro Tem, 1959.

Offices 1514 LHOB, 202-225-4511. Also Rm. 201, Fed. Bldg., Laredo 78040, 512-723-4336, and 1818 Tower Life Bldg., San Antonio 78205, 512-225-6276.

Administrative Assistant Robert Fleming

Committees

Foreign Affairs (12th); Subs: Inter-American Affairs; State Department Organization and Foreign Operations; Near East and South Asia.

Interior and Insular Affairs (11th); Subs: Mines and Mining; National Parks and Recreation; Water and Power Resources.

Group Ratings

	ADA	COPE	LWV	RIPON	NFU	LCV	CFA	NAB	NSI	ACA
1972	13	64	44	50	86	13	0	9	100	45
1971	27	91	78	33	73	–	63	–	–	41
1970	28	75	–	29	69	25	86	25	90	39

Key Votes

1) Busing	AGN	6) Cmbodia Bmbg	FOR	11) Chkg Acct Intrst	AGN
2) Strip Mines	FOR	7) Bust Hwy Trust	AGN	12) End HISC (HUAC)	AGN
3) Cut Mil $	AGN	8) Farm Sub Lmt	AGN	13) Nixon Sewer Veto	AGN
4) Rev Shrg	AGN	9) School Prayr	FOR	14) Corp Cmpaign $	FOR
5) Pub TV $	FOR	10) Cnsumr Prot	FOR	15) Pol $ Disclosr	AGN

Election Results

1972 general:	Abraham Kazen, Jr. (D), unopposed		
1972 primary:	Abraham Kazen, Jr. (D)	57,156	(79%)
	Frank Boone (D)	15,514	(21%)
1970 general:	Abraham Kazen, Jr. (D), unopposed		

TWENTY-FOURTH DISTRICT Political Background

The 24th of Texas is known as the Mid-Cities district. It sits between Dallas and Fort Worth and contains parts of both. The 24th is also one of the most grotesquely shaped districts in the United States and the first to elect a TV weatherman to Congress.

The shape of the 24th is a product of the 1972 redistricting, and outdoes in eccentricity even the most inspired previous efforts of the Texas legislature. Geographically, the district has three tentacles that emanate from the Dallas-Fort Worth Regional Airport—soon to be completed and covering more area than Manhattan Island.

As for the first tentacle, about 36% of the district's population lies within the city of Dallas. This does not include the high-rise boom area of downtown or the grandiose mansions of the north side (see Texas 3). Most of the 24th's portion of Dallas is an older part of the city to the south, called Oak Cliff. The neighborhood once boasted some of Dallas' largest mansions, which sat on a bluff overlooking the Trinity River. Today, few of the mansions remain, with much of Oak Cliff a black ghetto. Oak Cliff, incidentally, is the most Democratic and liberal part of the Dallas-Fort Worth metropolitan area.

The second tentacle, with another third of the population, consists of suburban Fort Worth and Dallas, and includes east Fort Worth, Grand Prairie, and Arlington. The last of these is the most interesting, or at least the most flamboyant. Thanks in large part to the promotional activities of Mayor Tom Vandergiff, Arlington has grown from a town of 7,000 in 1950, to a suburb of 44,000 in 1960, to a city of 90,000 in 1970. Situated along the Dallas-Fort Worth Turnpike, Arlington attracts thousands of visitors each year to the Six Flags Over Texas amusement park. It is also the smallest city with a major league baseball franchise, the Texas Rangers, who play at the game in an aptly-named place called Turnpike Stadium.

The third tentacle lies a dozen miles to the north, connected to the rest of the district by a narrow corridor across the airport. This is Denton County, which has undergone some of the more rapid growth and development in the Dallas-Fort Worth metropolitan area. As the growth continues, Denton has moved from a rural-oriented Democratic allegiance to a Dallas-like Republican preference. But the 14,000 students at Texas Northern University and the 5,000 at Texas Women's University have contributed some liberal votes.

All in all, the Mid-Cities district is quite an amalgam. And the 1972 Democratic primary here was quite a free-for-all. One competitor was Dallas Councilman Jesse Price, a hard-line conservative, who finished a poor third. He had the misfortune of being best known in the part of the district—Oak Cliff—where his views were the least popular. Another entrant was state Sen. Mike McKool, a Dallas liberal, who in 1970 primary nearly beat Rep. Earle Cabell in the 5th district, which then included Oak Cliff. In 1972, McKool ran first in the initial primary with 37%, not nearly enough to avoid a runoff. And in the runoff, the winner was Dale Milford, the WFAA-TV weathercaster who quit to run for Congress. Milford presented a more conservative image than McKool, and of course had much better name and face recognition. Aside from Oak Cliff, he carried all of the district by small, but respectable margins. In the general election, Milford benefited from solid Oak Cliff support to beat Republican Courtney Roberts, 65-35.

Milford likes to emphasize that he was not simply an announcer who read the weather report over the air. He was also, he says, a professional meteorologist who, besides being a broadcaster, ran a successful weather forecasting business on the side. In Congress, Milford has generally voted a conservative Democratic line. However, in these days of confrontation between the White House and the Congress, Milford's line differs less than one might expect from the liberal Democratic line. The Texan surprised some observers when he voted against the bombing of Cambodia. Oddly enough, Milford might encounter a primary challenge from another television personality who sports a background in the professions: Martin Frost, an attorney, who was a newscaster on the educational station KERA-TV in Dallas. And, depending on the outcome of the redistricting court case (see Texas 5), Milford might face another challenge from McKool.

Census Data Pop. 465,314. Central city, 42%; suburban, 58%. Median family income, $9,815; families above $15,000: 19%; families below $3,000: 7%. Median years education, 12.1.

1972 Share of Federal Outlays $633,512,332

DOD	$367,974,734	HEW	$110,810,574
AEC	$143,712	HUD	$3,880,921
NASA	$5,022,224	DOI	$714,128
DOT	$29,597,471	USDA	$28,255,843
		Other	$87,112,725

Federal Military-Industrial Commitments

DOD Installations Naval Air Station (Dallas).

TEXAS

Economic Base Transportation equipment; machinery; electrical equipment and supplies, especially communication equipment; finance, insurance and real estate; food and kindred products; and apparel and other textile products. Also higher education (North Texas State Univ., and Univ. of Texas, Arlington).

The Voters

Registration 220,871 total. No party registration.
Median voting age 37.3
Employment profile White collar, 50%. Blue collar, 37%. Service, 12%. Farm, 1%.
Ethnic groups Black, 19%. Spanish, 5%. Total foreign stock, 4%.

Presidential vote

1972	Nixon (R)	54,150	(37%)
	McGovern (D)	91,867	(63%)
1968	Nixon (R)	48,321	(40%)
	Humphrey (D)	50,652	(42%)
	Wallace (AI)	20,424	(17%)

Representative

Dale Milford (D) Elected 1972; b. Feb. 8, 1926, Bug Tussle, Tex.; home, Grand Prairie; Baylor U., B.A., 1957; Army, 1944–53; married, two children; Lutheran.

Career Weather Observer, Civil Aero. Admin., 1942–44; Meteorologist, 1953–57; Aircraft Dealer, 1957–59; Consultant Meteorologist, 1959–64; Consultant, Aviation and Meteorology, 1964–72; wrote and produced documentary: "Tornado," 1964 and "Flight Report," 1960.

Offices 427 CHOB, 202-225-3605. Also P.O. Box 1450, Grand Prairie 75050, 214-263-4736.

Administrative Assistant Richard H. White

Committees

Public Works (22nd); Subs: Economic Development; Energy; Investigations and Review; Public Buildings and Grounds; Transportation.

Science and Astronautics (15th); Subs: Energy; International Cooperation in Science and Space; Space Science and Applications.

Group Ratings: Newly Elected

Key Votes

1) Busing	NE	6) Cmbodia Bmbg	FOR	11) Chkg Acct Intrst	AGN
2) Strip Mines	NE	7) Bust Hwy Trust	AGN	12) End HISC (HUAC)	ABS
3) Cut Mil $	NE	8) Farm Sub Lmt	NE	13) Nixon Sewer Veto	FOR
4) Rev Shrg	NE	9) School Prayr	NE	14) Corp Cmpaign $	NE
5) Pub TV $	NE	10) Cnsumr Prot	NE	15) Pol $ Disclosr	NE

Election Results

1972 general:	Dale Milford (D)	91,054	(65%)
	Courtney Roberts (R)	48,853	(35%)
1972 run-off:	Dale Milford (D)	37,287	(54%)
	Mike McKool (D)	31,595	(46%)
1972 primary:	Dale Milford (D)	21,992	(32%)
	Mike McKool (D)	25,655	(37%)
	Jesse Price (D)	6,646	(10%)
	Jesse A. Coffey (D)	5,570	(8%)

Lee Goodman (D)	5,248	(8%)
Lon Williams (D)	1,620	(2%)
Jim Gilley (D)	1,474	(2%)
Dorothy Bach (D)	934	(1%)

UTAH

Political Background

In 1827, Joseph Smith, a young Palmyra, New York farmer, experienced a vision in which the Angel Moroni appeared to him. Moroni was a prophet of the lost tribe of Israel (the American Indians) which had presumably found its way to the New World some six hundred years before the birth of Christ. Moroni told Smith where to unearth several golden tablets inscribed with hieroglyphical writings. With the help of some magic spectacles, Smith translated the tablets and published them as the Book of Mormon in 1830. He then declared himself a prophet and founded a religious group he called the Church of Jesus Christ of Latter Day Saints.

The group was just one wave in a wash of religious revivalism, prophecy, and utopianism that swept across upstate New York—Palmyra lies just east of Rochester—during the 1820s and 1830s; the region was so alive with religious enthusiasm that it was known as the "burned-over district." Very quickly, the prophet's new sect attracted hundreds of converts. Persecuted for their beliefs, these Mormons, as they were called, moved west to Ohio, Missouri, and then Illinois. In 1844, the Mormon colony at Nauvoo, Illinois contained some 15,000 members, all living under the strict theocratic auspices of Joseph Smith. In secular Illinois politics, Nauvoo—which was then the largest city in the state—often swung the balance of power between the contending Democrats and Whigs. It was also here that Smith received a revelation to begin the practice of polygamy, which led to his death at the hands of a mob in 1844.

After the murder, the new president of the church, the remarkable Brigham Young, decided to move the faithful, "the saints," farther west into territory that was still part of Mexico and far beyond the pale of white settlement. Young led a migration across the Great Plains and into the Rocky Mountains. In 1847, the prophet and his followers stopped along the western slope of the Wasatch Range, and as Brigham Young viewed the valley of the Great Salt Lake spread out below, he uttered the now famous words, "This is the place."

The place was Utah. It is the only state that continues to live by the teachings of the church responsible for its founding. Throughout the nineteenth century, "Zion" attracted thousands of converts from the Midwest, the north of England, and Scandinavia. The object of religious fear, prejudice, and perhaps some envy, Utah was not granted statehood until 1896, when the church renounced polygamy. In fact, only the wealthiest Mormons, those able to afford more than one wife, ever practiced polygamy. The state now has more than a million people, with 88% of them living within 60 miles of the Great Salt Lake; they reside hundreds of miles from other significant concentrations of people. Presently, more than 70% of all Utahans are members of the Church of Jesus Christ of Latter Day Saints (LDS).

The distinctive features of the LDS faith dominates Utah politics. Leaders of the church have always exerted great political influence. For one thing, Utah has sent very few Gentiles (non-Mormons) to Congress during nearly 80 years of statehood. Currently, the church owns one of the two leading Salt Lake City newspapers and an influential television station. It also has holdings in an insurance company, various banks, and real estate, and runs the largest department store in Salt Lake City. The Mormon hierarchy confidently takes stands on secular matters, economic and political. It strongly supports, for example, Utah's right-to-work law.

One church doctrine in particular has embarrassed many Mormons—the faith denies blacks, having been cursed in the Bible, the "priesthood," i.e., full-fledged membership in the church. All Mormons are lay people, as the church does not employ a professional clergy. Revision of the doctrine, if it is to come, awaits a revelation to the LDS President, an office usually held by the most senior of the church's 12 Apostles. President David McKay died in 1970 at age 96, and was succeeded by Joseph Fielding Smith, who was 93 at the time.

In more general terms, the LDS doctrine carries the virtues of nineteenth-century upstate New York Protestantism to a logical end. Even today, Mormons are forbidden to consume alcohol, tobacco, coffee or tea, though dancing at church social events has always been encouraged. Many so-called "Jack Mormons," however, violate doctrine without overly stern reprimand from the community at large. Yet many youths still give two years of their lives on "missions" both at home and overseas, in which they attempt to win new converts to the faith; moreover, members are required to pledge a tithe of 10 percent of their income to the church.

That income is often substantial, as Mormons possess a deserved reputation for hard work and tend to do well in business and the professions. During the 1960s, sometime before Richard Nixon popularized the "work ethic," people in Utah had already reacted negatively to the social policies of the Johnson Administration. Civil rights legislation, in particular, did not sit well here. Accordingly, the economic issues of the 1940s and 1950s that helped Democrats win Utah elections grew less important among the voters during the prosperous 1960s. In 1964, Utah reacted sharply against the national Democrats, as Barry Goldwater collected 45% of its votes. The conservative trend has since grown stronger, as Richard Nixon got 72% in 1972. Even Utah's young people, at least those who stay close to the church, are part of the trend. At Brigham Young University—a Mormon institution known for its conservatism—Nixon took 79%, Schmitz 15%, and McGovern 6% in 1972.

Nevertheless, the Republican surge in national elections has not produced straight-ticket Republican victories in Utah contests. On the contrary, Utah Democrats have run as well as they ever have. The state's most popular politician is Gov. Calvin Rampton, a rather conservatively inclined Democrat. Rampton first won election in 1964, and was reelected to a third term in 1972 with 70% of the votes, as he ran 42% ahead of George McGovern. Rampton appears capable of winning indefinite reelection.

The same assessment holds for the state's junior Senator, Democrat Frank Moss. He was first elected in 1958 because of a split in the Republican party between incumbent Sen. (1947–59) Arthur V. Watkins, chairman of the committee that recommended the censure of Joe McCarthy, and J. Bracken Lee, later Mayor of Salt Lake City. Unhappy because he had failed to win a third gubernatorial term in 1956, Lee jumped into the Senate race as an independent and allowed Moss to capture the seat with just 38% of the votes. Nevertheless, Moss held on nicely in 1964, defeating the ultraconservative president of Brigham Young University, Ernest Wilkinson, by a 57–43 margin.

Moss was supposed to encounter a tougher race in 1970. The Republican candidate, Congressman Laurence Burton of the 1st district, waged a campaign typical of Nixon-backed challengers of that year. He called Moss a radical for opposing the Vietnam war and Nixon's appointments to the Supreme Court. Burton's effort was well-financed. Moreover, both Nixon and Agnew—presumed to be popular figures in Utah—flew in to help out. But Moss led in the polls all the way, and wound up winning by a margin close to the one he got in 1964.

Moss possessed several assets in the campaign that Burton could not match. Utah, like all small states, tends to value the seniority of its congressional delegation. Moss had 12 years of seniority and the chair of the Interior Committee's subcommittee on Minerals, Materials, and Fuels—an important post for a Senator from one of the leading copper-producing states. And as Chairman of the Commerce Committee's Consumer subcommittee, Moss has long been one of the Senate's most active advocates of consumer legislation. But even more important in Utah was the fact that Moss was the sponsor and the driving force behind the law that banned cigarette advertising from television. To Mormons, smoking is a sin. And Moss' victory over the tobacco lobby probably impressed the voters of Utah more than the Senator's ability to defend the state's interest in national parks, Hill Air Force Base, and so on.

In the 93rd Congress, Moss has been especially vigorous on the consumer front. As one of the leading sponsors of the Consumer Product Safety Commission, the Senator has worked to insure the effective administration of the law requiring complete separation of the new agency from the Executive Branch. He is also one of the major sponsors of national no-fault automobile insurance. And along with Michigan's Philip Hart, Moss led the successful fight to block confirmation of Robert Morris, a onetime oil company lawyer, to the Federal Power Commission.

Though both are devout Mormons, few states have Senators with voting records as different as those from Utah. The state's senior Senator, Wallace Bennett, is a former president of the National Association of Manufacturers. One of the Senate's senior Republicans, Bennett seldom strays from the conservative fold. He is the ranking Republican on the tax-writing Senate Finance Committee and the number-two minority member on Banking, Housing, and Urban Affairs. As predicted in the 1972 *Almanac*, Bennett has decided to retire in 1974, when he will be 76. The Senator received only 54% of the votes last time out. Though no wrongdoing was involved, Bennett might have been embarrassed by his son who heads a Washington public relations firm that employed Watergate burglar E. Howard Hunt before he became a White House consultant.

The contest for Bennett's seat promises to be the hottest—and perhaps the closest—race Utah has seen in some years. As Bennett announced his retirement, the likely Republican nominee seemed to be George Romney, though other Republicans, notably popular Attorney General Vernon Romney, George's cousin, wanted to run. Most observers considered George Romney the favorite. He was, after all, high in the councils of the LDS church and the only Mormon ever to make a serious run for the Presidency. If his tenure as Secretary of Housing and Urban Development was not as successful as he might have liked, it was not for lack of trying. And, in these post-Watergate days, it would not have hurt Romney that he was never one to toady to the White House.

Romney, however, also had political liabilities. He has never lived in Utah; moreover, his desire to run here for the Senate followed the apparent failure of his announced plans to organize a citizens' lobby group akin to Common Cause. Finally, Romney will be 67 years old in 1974, not an asset in a state that likes to elect its Senators young and watch them accumulate seniority. And though the ex-Michigan Governor ran slightly ahead of Democratic contenders in the polls, his showing was not impressive for a man whose name identification in Utah approaches 100%. So in the fall of 1973, it was not too surprising when Romney announced he would not run.

That left the identity of the Republican candidate uncertain. The Democratic nominee is likely to be one of the state's two Congressmen, probably Wayne Owens of the 2nd district. To Eastern observers, this relatively liberal freshman Congressman may seem an unlikely candidate in conservative Utah, but he has numerous assets. For one thing, Owens is as devout a Mormon as anyone, and on election day in 1974, the Congressman will be only 37. After serving as an administrative assistant to Sens. Edward Kennedy and Frank Moss, Owens, at 35, set out to win the 2nd district seat from four-term Republican Sherman Lloyd. Though 86% of the 2nd's votes are cast in Salt Lake County (Salt Lake City and suburbs), the district also includes 10 rural counties that extend to the Canyonlands National Park and the Arizona border. Owens demonstrated his stamina to the voters by hiking 689 miles across the rugged hinterlands of the 2nd to Salt Lake City. Along the way, the Democrat attacked Lloyd for trying to force a road through the Escalante wilderness of southern Utah, in particular, and for a bad record on the environment, in general. Lloyd was one of Environmental Action's "Dirty Dozen" and also got poor ratings from *Field and Stream.*

The challenger also hit the incumbent for his opposition to tax reform and his support of the Vietnam war. Despite McGovern's poor showing in the 2nd, Owens' vigorous campaigning gave him a solid 55-45 upset victory. And the publicity generated by Owens' campaign made him a popular, well-konwn figure statewide—the 88% of the state's voters who live along the Wasatch Front all get Salt Lake City television. So if Owens can get the Democratic nomination, he has an excellent chance for another upset.

Another possible contender for the Democratic Senate nomination is 1st-district Congressman K. Gunn McKay. He first won election in the 1st in 1970 when Republican Laurence Burton vacated the seat to run for the Senate. On a map, the district looks compactly shaped. But the distribution of voters within it is rather odd. Though the 1st moves south to the Four Corners region, most of its votes are cast either just north of south of Salt Lake City. To the north is suburban Davis County, which also contains the old Union Pacific town of Ogden (pop. 69,000); to the south, around the shores of Lake Utah, is Provo (pop. 53,000).

The 1st is the more conservative of the state's two districts. In 1972, it gave Richard Nixon 77% of its votes—the Republican's best showing in any Western congressional district. Yet McKay possesses campaign assets, too. He is the nephew of the late LDS president David McKay, and worked as Gov. Rampton's administrative assistant. In 1970, K. Gunn McKay won with 51% of the votes; in 1972, he was reelected with a solid 57%—far, far ahead of the national ticket. McKay, however, is not as magnetic a campaigner as Owens, and for a Northern Democrat, has a notably conservative voting record.

In the event that either (or both) Congressman leaves his seat to run for the Senate, the Republicans have an excellent chance to pick up one or two House seats. But the Republicans should not be regarded as automatic victors. Utah Democrats have managed to win elections, and by large margins, even while the national ticket continues to lose ground in the state. They have succeeded not so much by disassociating themselves from the national candidates (though they do not embrace them), as by stressing local issues and their own personal qualifications. Consequently, one possible Democratic candidate, former Democratic National Chairperson and McGovern-backer Jean Westwood, would have a tough time following suit. In any case, Utah today presents a nice example of the politics of ticket-splitting, a phenomenon that permits a minority party to win elections by fielding strong candidates.

Census Data Pop. 1,059,273; 0.52% of U.S. total, 36th largest; change 1960–70, 18.9%. Central city, 31%; suburban, 47%. Median family income, $9,320; 23rd highest; families above $15,000: 17%; families below $3,000: 9%. Median years education, 12.5.

1972 Share of Federal Tax Burden $815,170,000; 0.39% of U.S. total, 38th largest.

1972 Share of Federal Outlays $1,348,078,794; 0.62% of U.S. total, 37th largest. Per capita federal spending, $1,273.

DOD	$535,367,000	31st	(0.86%)	HEW	$303,324,000	39th	(0.42%)
AEC	$1,789,884	27th	(0.07%)	HUD	$7,761,677	45th	(0.25%)
NASA	$1,680,307	31st	(0.06%)	VA	$65,450,226	38th	(0.57%)
DOT	$95,597,233	29th	(1.21%)	USDA	$79,039,387	39th	(0.51%)
DOC	$4,886,731	38th	(0.38%)	CSC	$34,081,435	32nd	(0.83%)
DOI	$68,197,159	9th	(3.21%)	TD	$61,663,728	33rd	(0.37%)
DOJ	$3,988,930	441st	(0.41%)	Other	$85,251,097		

Economic Base Finance, insurance and real estate; agriculture, notably cattle, dairy products, turkeys and sheep; primary metal industries; metal mining; food and kindred products; transportation equipment, especially aircraft and parts; apparel and other textile products, especially women's and misses' outerwear.

Political Line-up Governor, Calvin L. Rampton (D); seat up, 1976. Senators, Wallace F. Bennett (R) and Frank E. Moss (D). Representatives, 2 D. State Senate (16 R and 13 D); State House (44 R and 31 D).

The Voters

Registration 621,014 Total. No party registration.
Median voting age 39.3
Employment profile White collar, 52%. Blue collar, 32%. Service, 13%. Farm, 3%.
Ethnic groups Spanish, 4%. Total foreign stock, 12%. UK, 3%.

Presidential vote

1972	Nixon (R)	323,643	(72%)
	McGovern (D)	126,284	(28%)
1968	Nixon (R)	238,728	(57%)
	Humphrey (D)	156,665	(37%)
	Wallace (AI)	26,906	(6%)
1964	Johnson (D)	219,628	(55%)
	Goldwater (R)	181,785	(45%)

Senator

Wallace Foster Bennett (R) Elected 1950, seat up 1974; b. Nov. 13, 1898, Salt Lake City; home, Salt Lake City; U. of Utah, B.A., 1919; Army, WWI; married, five children; Church of Latter Day Saints.

Career Principal, San Luis Stake Acad., 1919–20; Bd. Chm., Bennett's; Bd. Chm., Bennett Motor Co., V.Pres., Natl. Paint, Varnish & Lacquer Assn., 1935–36; Pres., Natl. Glass Distributors Assn., 1937; Pres., Natl. Assn. of Manufacturers, 1949; author, "Faith and Freedom," 1950, "Why I Am a Mormon," 1958.

Offices 1121 NSOB, 202-225-5444. Also 4227 Fed. Bldg., Salt Lake City 84111, 801-524-5939, and 1010 Fed. Bldg., Ogden, 801-399-6208.

Administrative Assistant Paul Denham

Committees

Banking, Housing and Urban Affairs (2nd); Subs: Consumer Credit; Financial Institutions (Ranking Mbr.); Finance (Ranking Mbr.).

Select Com. on Standards and Conduct (Vice-Chm.).

Joint Com. on Atomic Energy (2nd); Subs: Agreements for Cooperation (Ranking Senate Mbr.); Military Applications (Ranking Senate Mbr.); Raw Materials (Ranking Senate Mbr.); Research, Development and Radiation.

Joint Com. on Defense Production (2nd).

Joint Com. on Internal Revenue Taxation (Ranking Senate Mbr.).

Joint Com. on Reduction of Federal Expenditures (2nd).

Joint Study Com. on Budget Control.

Group Ratings

	ADA	COPE	LWV	RIPON	NFU	LCV	CFA	NAB	NSI	ACA
1972	5	11	27	44	20	7	0	63	100	90
1971	0	25	55	41	13	–	0	–	–	70
1970	0	0	–	27	33	11	–	83	100	90

Key Votes

1) Busing	AGN	8) Sea Life Prot	AGN	15) Tax Singls Less	AGN
2) Alas P-line	FOR	9) Campaign Subs	AGN	16) Min Tax for Rich	AGN
3) Gun Cntrl	AGN	10) Cmbodia Bmbg	ABS	17) Euro Troop Rdctn	AGN
4) Rehnquist	ABS	11) Legal Srvices	AGN	18) Bust Hwy Trust	FOR
5) Pub TV $	AGN	12) Rev Sharing	FOR	19) Maid Min Wage	AGN
6) EZ Votr Reg	AGN	13) Cnsumr Prot	AGN	20) Farm Sub Limit	AGN
7) No-Fault	AGN	14) Eq Rts Amend	AGN	21) Highr Credt Chgs	FOR

Election Results

1968 general:	Wallace F. Bennett (R)	225,075	(54%)
	Milton Weilenmann (D)	192,168	(46%)
1968 primary:	Wallace F. Bennett (R)	81,945	(61%)
	Mark E. Anderson (R)	52,689	(39%)
1962 general:	Wallace F. Bennett (R)	166,755	(52%)
	David S. King (D)	151,656	(48%)

Senator

Frank Edward Moss (D) Elected 1958, seat up 1976; b. Sept. 23, 1911, Holladay; home, Salt Lake City; U. of Utah, B.A., 1933; George Washington U., J.D., 1937; Army Air Corps, WWII; Col. USAFR; married, four children; Church of Latter Day Saints.

Career Practicing atty.; Atty. for Securities and Exchange Commission, 1937–39; Judge, Salt Lake City, 1941–50; Salt Lake County Atty., 1951–58; Pres., Natl. Assn. of Dist. Attys., 1956–58.

Offices 3121 NSOB, 202-225-5251. Also 5430 New Fed. Bldg., Salt Lake City 84111, 801-524-5935, and Fed. Bldg., Ogden, and Fed. Bldg., Provo.

Administrative Assistant Kem C. Gardner

Committees

Aeronautical and Space Sciences (Chm.).

Commerce (7th); Subs: Aviation; Communications; Consumer (Chm.); Environment (Vice-Chm.); Foreign Commerce and Tourism; Oceans and Atmosphere.

Post Office and Civil Service (5th); Subs: Civil Service Policies and Practices; Compensation and Employment Benefits; Postal Operations.

Sp. Com. on Aging (6th); Subs: Employment and Retirement Incomes; Health of the Elderly; Long-Term Care (Chm.).

Group Ratings

	ADA	COPE	LWV	RIPON	NFU	LCV	CFA	NAB	NSI	ACA
1972	70	90	100	60	100	42	100	10	0	15
1971	81	92	100	57	91	–	80	–	–	5
1970	69	100	–	64	94	29	–	0	10	6

Key Votes

1) Busing	FOR	8) Sea Life Prot	FOR	15) Tax Singls Less	AGN
2) Alas P-line	AGN	9) Campaign Subs	FOR	16) Min Tax for Rich	FOR
3) Gun Cntrl	AGN	10) Cmbodia Bmbg	AGN	17) Euro Troop Rdctn	FOR
4) Rehnquist	AGN	11) Legal Srvices	FOR	18) Bust Hwy Trust	FOR
5) Pub TV $	FOR	12) Rev Sharing	FOR	19) Maid Min Wage	FOR
6) EZ Votr Reg	FOR	13) Cnsumr Prot	FOR	20) Farm Sub Limit	AGN
7) No-Fault	FOR	14) Eq Rts Amend	FOR	21) Highr Credt Chgs	AGN

Election Results

1970 general:	Frank Moss (D)	210,207	(56%)
	Laurence J. Burton (R)	159,004	(42%)
	Clyde B. Freeman (AI)	5,092	(1%)
1970 primary:	Frank Moss (D), unopposed		
1964 general:	Frank Moss (D)	227,822	(57%)
	Ernest L. Wilkinson (R)	169,562	(43%)

FIRST DISTRICT

Census Data Pop. 529,688. Central city, 28%; suburban, 41%. Median family income, $9,080; families above $15,000: 16%; families below $3,000: 9%. Median years education, 12.5.

1972 Share of Federal Outlays $836,936,516

DOD	$381,398,154	HEW	$155,359,833
AEC	$353,559	HUD	$2,237,487
NASA	$690,918	DOI	$45,758,155
DOT	$49,623,537	USDA	$58,956,984
		Other	$142,557,889

Federal Military-Industrial Commitments

DOD Contractors Thiokol Chemical Corp. (Thiokol), $48.977m: Minuteman III rocket engines. Thiokol Chemical Corp. (Brigham City), $16.359m: rocket and projectile propellants. Santa Fe Engineers (Hill AFB), $5.284m: unspecified.
DOD Installations Ogden Defense Depot (Ogden). Hill AFB (Ogden).

Economic Base Agriculture, notably cattle, dairy products and grains; finance, insurance and real estate; primary metal industries, especially blast furnace and steel mill products; and food and kindred products. Also higher education (Brigham Young Univ., and Weber State).

The Voters

Registration 301,371 total. No party registration.
Median voting age 38.5
Employment profile White collar, 50%. Blue collar, 33%. Service, 13%. Farm, 4%.
Ethnic groups Spanish, 4%. Total foreign stock, 10%. UK, 2%.

Presidential vote

1972	Nixon (R)		166,517	(77%)
	McGovern (D)		50,225	(23%)
1968	Nixon (R)		119,524	(58%)
	Humphrey (D)		69,487	(34%)
	Wallace (AI)		14,758	(7%)

Representative

K. Gunn McKay (D) Elected 1970; b. Feb. 23, 1925, Ogden; home, Huntsville; Weber State Col., A.A., 1960; Utah State U., B.S., 1962; USCG, 1943–46; married, nine children; Church of Latter Day Saints.

Career Farmer; businessman; educator; Utah House of Reps., 1962–66; Legislative Council, 1963–66; Administrative Asst. to Gov. Calvin L. Rampton, 1968–70.

Offices 1427 LHOB, 202-225-3171. Also Suite 213, First Security Bank, Provo 84601, 801-373-4150, and Rm. 1424, Fed. Bldg., Ogden 84401, 801-399-6816.

Administrative Assistant Sheldon Vincenti

Committees

Appropriations (28th); Subs: District of Columbia; Interior; Military Construction.

Group Ratings

	ADA	COPE	LWV	RIPON	NFU	LCV	CFA	NAB	NSI	ACA
1972	31	89	44	46	100	21	0	30	80	30
1971	46	91	78	53	71	–	88	–	–	23

Key Votes

1) Busing	AGN	6) Cmbodia Bmbg	ABS	11) Chkg Acct Intrst	ABS
2) Strip Mines	FOR	7) Bust Hwy Trust	AGN	12) End HISC (HUAC)	AGN
3) Cut Mil $	AGN	8) Farm Sub Lmt	AGN	13) Nixon Sewer Veto	AGN
4) Rev Shrg	AGN	9) School Prayr	AGN	14) Corp Cmpaign $	FOR
5) Pub TV $	FOR	10) Cnsumr Prot	FOR	15) Pol $ Disclosr	AGN

Election Results

1972 general:	K. Gunn McKay (D)	127,027	(55%)
	Robert K. Wolthuis (R)	96,296	(42%)
	L. S. Brown (AI)	6,043	(3%)

1972 primary: K. Gunn McKay (D), unopposed
1970 general: K. Gunn McKay (D) 95,499 (51%)
               Richard Richards (R) 89,269 (48%)
               Daniel L. Worthington (AI) 1,489 (1%)

SECOND DISTRICT

Census Data Pop. 529,585. Central city, 33%; suburban, 53%. Median family income, $9,537; families above $15,000: 18%; families below $3,000: 8%. Median years education, 12.5.

1972 Share of Federal Outlays $511,142,278

DOD	$153,968,846	HEW	$147,964,167
AEC	$1,436,325	HUD	$5,524,190
NASA	$989,389	DOI	$22,439,004
DOT	$45,973,696	USDA	$20,082,403
		Other	$112,764,258

Federal Military-Industrial Commitments

DOD Installations Dugway Proving Ground (Dugway). Tooele Army Depot (Tooele).

Economic Base Finance, insurance and real estate; metal mining, especially lead and zinc mining, and copper mining; agriculture, notably cattle, poultry and dairy products; electrical equipment and supplies, especially radio and television communication equipment; and food and kindred products, especially dairy products.

The Voters

Registration 319,643 total. No party registration.
Median voting age 40.1
Employment profile White collar, 53%. Blue collar, 32%. Service, 13%. Farm, 2%.
Ethnic groups Spanish, 5%. Total foreign stock, 14%. UK, 3%.

Presidential vote

1972	Nixon (R)	157,126	(67%)
	McGovern (D)	76,059	(33%)
1968	Nixon (R)	119,204	(54%)
	Humphrey (D)	87,178	(40%)
	Wallace (AI)	12,148	(6%)

Representative

Douglas Wayne Owens (D) Elected 1972; b. May 2, 1937, Panguitch; home, Salt Lake City; U. of Utah, B.S., J.D., 1964; married, five children; Mormon.

Career Church of the Latter Day Saints, mission work, 1957–60; Field man, Sen. Frank E. Moss, 1965–68; law practice, 1965–68; Admin. Asst., R. F. Kennedy for Pres., 1968, and to Edward Kennedy, 1969–70; Admin. Asst. Sen. Moss, 1971–72.

Offices 222 CHOB, 202-225-3011. Also Fed. Bldg., Rm. 2311, Salt Lake City, 801-524-5583.

Administrative Assistant Ted Wilson

Committees

Interior and Insular Affairs (21st); Subs: National Parks and Recreation; Environment; Mines and Mining; Public Lands.

Judiciary (20th); Subs: Patents, Trademarks, Copyrights; Revision of the Laws.

Group Ratings: Newly Elected

Key Votes

1) Busing	NE	6) Cmbodia Bmbg	AGN	11) Chkg Acct Intrst	AGN
2) Strip Mines	NE	7) Bust Hwy Trust	FOR	12) End HISC (HUAC)	FOR
3) Cut Mil $	NE	8) Farm Sub Lmt	NE	13) Nixon Sewer Veto	AGN
4) Rev Shrg	NE	9) School Prayr	NE	14) Corp Cmpaign $	NE
5) Pub TV $	NE	10) Cnsumr Prot	NE	15) Pol $ Disclosr	NE

Election Results

1972 general:	Wayne Owens (D)	132,832	(55%)
	Sherman P. Lloyd (R)	107,185	(44%)
	Bruce R. Bangerter (AI)	3,685	(2%)
1972 primary:	Wayne Owens (D), unopposed		

VERMONT

Political Background

In many ways, Vermont still seems to be in the nineteenth century. The classic New England town squares still stand here; the cows still graze on the hillsides; and the taciturn Yankee farmers still tap the sugar maple trees in the early spring. And in the fall, these same trees still produce the most beautiful, blazing red foliage in the world. According to the Census Bureau, Vermont is the nation's most rural (68%) state. So it is no wonder that Vermont's most famous man of letters, Robert Frost, felt that to understand his poetry "one had to be versed in country things."

But the 1960s did bring change to Vermont. There are now large IBM and GE complexes around Burlington, the state's largest city (pop. 38,000). Moreover, the ski-resort and summer-home industries have so boomed that the price of rural land has skyrocketed, forcing many farmers to sell. From 1850 to 1960, Vermont's population hovered between 300,000 and 400,000, and the year 1963 marked the first time the number of people exceeded the number of cows in the state.

The rapid development—rapid for Vermont at least—has created a new kind of politics in the state. For more than a century, Vermont politics was utterly predictable—the nation's most Republican state. The only areas of Democratic strength lay in the small Irish and French Canadian communities in Burlington and other towns near the Canadian border. But in 1962, Vermont elected Governor Philip Hoff—the first Democrat to hold the office in 109 years—and then reelected him with solid margins in 1964 and 1966. Hoff proved to be a popular Governor; he encouraged economic development and fostered the state's educational system, while at the same time supporting tough environmental legislation. When Hoff retired, he was replaced by a Republican, Dean Davis, who in a surprise, continued programs similar to those of Hoff. As a result, Vermont now has some of the most stringent legislation regarding land use in the nation.

After two years out of office, Hoff decided to run for a Senate seat in 1970. It was held by Republican Winston Prouty. But Hoff fell prey to the same kind of split that sunk Democratic candidates that year in Connecticut and New York—one between ethnic and white-collar Democrats. An opponent of the Vietnam war, Hoff had backed Robert Kennedy in the 1968 presidential campaign; in 1970, Hoff encountered primary opposition—tougher than expected —from a hawkish state Senator. In the general election, Hoff suffered severe defections in the usually Democratic, heavily Catholic precincts of Burlington and the northern part of the state, which resulted in an easy Prouty win.

So as 1972 began, it looked as though the brief Vermont Democratic renaissance had petered out. Yet analysis of that sort overlooked Vermont's growing concern over the costs of growth. Republican gubernatorial candidate Luther Hackett leaned away from limits on development, going so far as to oppose some of Gov. Davis' programs. His opponent, an unknown Democrat named Thomas Salmon, took vigorous exception to Hackett's position and won a surprisingly large 56–44 victory. Though Salmon ran well in traditionally Democratic precincts, he made his largest gains in the WASPy Republican areas that have undergone the least change since the nineteenth century; people in them want no more change. Flinty Vermonters apparently do not want to go plastic.

Prouty died less than a year after his reelection in 1970. The state's present junior Senator is Robert Stafford, a former Governor and Congressman-at-Large. Since 1954, Stafford had won statewide elections easily every two years. He was appointed to fill the Senate vacancy, then had no trouble in a special election to win the remaining five years of Prouty's term. Stafford's appointment was rather hurried. The White House pressured Gov. Davis into quick action because it wanted Stafford's vote on the draft extension issue. Stafford stood with the Administration on the matter, though he has since dissented from Nixon's line from time to time. In the House, Stafford was known as one of the more liberal Republicans.

The state's senior Senator, George Aiken, is currently the most senior member of the Senate. For years, Aiken has been one of the body's most respected members; in Vermont, he is something of a state monument. During the 1930s, he served as one of the state's most progressive Governors; Aiken was particularly strong in opposing the interests of private power companies, which charged Vermonters the nation's highest rates. First elected to the Senate in 1940, Aiken has since been reelected with minimal opposition. In 1968, for example, the Senator won the Democratic nomination on write-in votes, leaving no need for a general election.

Aiken now serves as the ranking Republican on the Senate Foreign Relations Committee. Like most members of the panel, he has been rather skeptical about both Johnson and Nixon administration policies in Southeast Asia. Some time ago, Aiken suggested that the nation announce that it had won and then withdraw, which is what some think Nixon's "peace with honor" really meant. Recently, Aiken has supported the Nixon Administration a bit more frequently than he did in its first years. He likes to support a President, especially one of his own party, whenever he feels he can.

Aiken will be 82 when his seat comes up in 1974. In most states, a Senator that old could not expect to win reelection, given the current mood of the voters toward elderly politicians. But if Aiken runs, he will have very little trouble. Nevertheless, because the Senator is not as hale as he once was, he may choose to retire. Awaiting his decision with intense interest are Congressman-at-Large Richard Mallary and Gov. Salmon. Mallary, a former Speaker of the state House of Representatives, was elected to the House the same day Stafford was elected to the Senate. Like Stafford, the Congressman has compiled a fairly liberal record in the House, and has won reelection without difficulty. A Salmon-Mallary race would likely be close, and as hard-fought as these things are in the still placid Green Mountains of Vermont.

Census Data Pop. 444,732; 0.22% of U.S. total, 48th largest; change 1960–70, 14.1%. Central city, 0%; suburban, 0%. Median family income, $8,928; 28th highest; families above $15,000: 16%; families below $3,000: 9%. Median years education, 12.2.

1972 Share of Federal Tax Burden $397,130,000; 0.19% of U.S. total, 48th largest.

1972 Share of Federal Outlays $408,696,225; 0.19% of U.S. total, 49th largest. Per capita federal spending, $919.

DOD	$54,535,000	50th (0.09%)	HEW	$183,642,705	46th (0.26%)
AEC	$20,377	48th (—)	HUD	$5,452,545	47th (0.18%)
NASA	$125,370	42nd (—)	VA	$27,183,537	48th (0.24%)
DOT	$29,250,007	48th (0.37%)	USDA	$25,035,470	47th (0.16%)
DOC	$1,334,989	48th (0.10%)	CSC	$6,903,952	48th (0.17%)
DOI	$1,999,186	47th (0.09%)	TD	$17,007,843	48th (0.10%)
DOJ	$23,406,847	12th (2.38%)	Other	$32,798,397	

Federal Military-Industrial Commitments

DOD Contractors General Electric (Burlington), $28.854m: production of and parts for 20mm guns.
DOD Installations St. Albans AF Station (St. Albans).

Economic Base Agriculture, notably dairy products, cattle, eggs and forest products; finance, insurance and real estate; electrical equipment and supplies, especially electronic components and accessories; machinery, especially metalworking machinery; printing and publishing, especially book printing; lumber and wood products; cut stone and stone products, and other stone, clay and glass products. Also tourism (Green Mountains).

Political Line-up Governor, Thomas P. Salmon (D); seat up, 1974. Senators, George D. Aiken (R) and Robert T. Stafford (R). Representatives, 1 R At Large. State Senate (23 R and 7 D); State House (87 R, 58 D, 4 R-D, and 1 Ind.).

The Voters

Registration 273,056 Total. No party registration.
Median voting age 42.8
Employment profile White collar, 46%. Blue collar, 35%. Service, 14%. Farm, 5%.
Ethnic groups Total foreign stock, 18%. Canada, 10%.

Presidential vote

1972	Nixon (R)	117,149	(63%)
	McGovern (D)	68,174	(37%)
1968	Nixon (R)	85,142	(53%)
	Humphrey (D)	70,255	(44%)
	Wallace (AI)	5,104	(3%)
1964	Johnson (D)	108,127	(66%)
	Goldwater (R)	54,942	(34%)

Senator

George David Aiken (R) Elected 1940, seat up 1974; b. Aug. 20, 1892, Dummerston; home, Putney; married; Protestant.

Career School Dir., 1920–37; Vt. House of Reps., 1931–35, Speaker, 1933–35; Lt. Gov. of Vt., 1935–37; Gov. of Vt., 1937–39; author, *Pioneering with Wildflowers*, 1933, *Pioneering with Fruits and Berries*, 1936, *Speaking from Vermont*, 1938.

Offices 358 OSOB, 202-225-4242.

Administrative Assistant Mrs. Lola Aiken

Committees

Agriculture and Forestry (2nd); Subs: Environment, Soil Conservation and Forestry; Agricultural Credit and Rural Electrification (Ranking Mbr.).

Foreign Relations (Ranking Mbr.); Subs: U.S. Security Agreements and Commitments Abroad (Ranking Mbr.); FarEastern Affairs (Ranking Mbr.); Western Hemisphere Affairs (Ranking Mbr.); Near-Eastern Affairs (Ranking Mbr.).

Joint Com. on Atomic Energy (Ranking Senate Mbr.); Subs: Communities (Ranking Senate Mbr.); Legislation (Ranking Senate Mbr.); Research, Development and Radiation (Ranking Senate Mbr.); Energy (Ranking Senate Mbr.); Licensing and Regulation (Ranking Senate Mbr.).

Group Ratings

	ADA	COPE	LWV	RIPON	NFU	LCV	CFA	NAB	NSI	ACA
1972	45	50	91	72	40	31	36	36	60	43
1971	41	25	100	70	55	–	60	–	–	43
1970	34	46	–	75	53	41	–	67	44	43

Key Votes

1) Busing	FOR	8) Sea Life Prot	FOR	15) Tax Singls Less	AGN
2) Alas P-line	AGN	9) Campaign Subs	AGN	16) Min Tax for Rich	AGN
3) Gun Cntrl	FOR	10) Cmbodia Bmbg	AGN	17) Euro Troop Rdctn	FOR
4) Rehnquist	FOR	11) Legal Srvices	AGN	18) Bust Hwy Trust	FOR
5) Pub TV $	AGN	12) Rev Sharing	AGN	19) Maid Min Wage	FOR
6) EZ Votr Reg	AGN	13) Cnsumr Prot	FOR	20) Farm Sub Limit	AGN
7) No-Fault	AGN	14) Eq Rts Amend	FOR	21) Highr Credt Chgs	AGN

Election Results

1968 general:	George D. Aiken (R and D), unopposed		
1968 primary:	George D. Aiken (R)	42,318	(73%)
	William K. Tufts (R)	15,786	(27%)
1962 general:	George D. Aiken (R)	81,242	(67%)
	W. Robert Johnson, Sr. (D)	40,134	(33%)

Senator

Robert Theodore Stafford (R) Elected Appointed September 16,1971, seat up 1976; b. Aug. 8, 1913, Rutland; home, Rutland; City; Middlebury Col., B.S., 1935; U. of Mich., Boston U., LL.B., 1938; Navy, WWII, Korean War; Capt. USNR; married, four children; Congregationalist.

Career Rutland City Grand Juror, 1938–42; Rutland County State Atty., 1947–51; Deputy Atty. Gen., 1953–55; Atty. Gen., 1955–57; Lt. Gov. of Vt., 1957–59; Gov. of Vt., 1959–61, U.S. House of Reps., 1961–71.

Offices 5215 NSOB, 202-225-5141. Also 27 S. Main St., Rutland 05701, 802-775-5446.

Administrative Assistant Neal J. Houston

Committees

Labor and Public Welfare (6th); Subs: Labor; Handicapped (Ranking Mbr.); Education; Children and Youth; Aging; Sp. Sub. on National Science Foundation; Human Resources.

Public Works (3rd); Subs: Air and Water Pollution; Water Resources; Roads (Ranking Mbr.); Economic Development; Panel on Environmental Science and Technology.

Veterans' Affairs (3rd); Subs: Housing and Insurance; Readjustment, Education, and Employment (Ranking Mbr.).

Sp. Com. on Aging (7th); Subs: Housing for the Elderly; Employment and Retirement Incomes; Health of the Elderly; Retirement and the Individual (Ranking Mbr.).

Group Ratings

	ADA	COPE	LWV	RIPON	NFU	LCV	CFA	NAB	NSI	ACA
1972	45	70	90	76	33	50	75	25	50	33
1971	46	33	100	75	83	–	50	–	–	33
1970	60	60	–	94	77	–	–	67	80	28

Key Votes

1) Busing	FOR	8) Sea Life Prot	FOR	15) Tax Singls Less	AGN
2) Alas P-line	AGN	9) Campaign Subs	AGN	16) Min Tax for Rich	ABS
3) Gun Cntrl	AGN	10) Cmbodia Bmbg	AGN	17) Euro Troop Rdctn	FOR
4) Rehnquist	FOR	11) Legal Srvices	FOR	18) Bust Hwy Trust	FOR
5) Pub TV $	FOR	12) Rev Sharing	FOR	19) Maid Min Wage	FOR
6) EZ Votr Reg	AGN	13) Cnsumr Prot	AGN	20) Farm Sub Limit	FOR
7) No-Fault	AGN	14) Eq Rts Amend	FOR	21) Highr Credt Chgs	AGN

Election Results

1972 special:	Robert T. Stafford (R)	45,888	(64%)
	Randolph T. Major, Jr. (D)	23,842	(33%)
	Bernard Sanders (Liberty Union)	1,571	(2%)
1972 primary:	Robert T. Stafford (R), unopposed		

Representative

Richard Walker Mallary (R) Elected Jan. 7, 1972; b. Feb. 21, 1929, Springfield, Mass.; home, Fairlee; Dartmouth Col., B.A., 1949; married, four children.

Career Dairy farmer, 1950–71; Chm., Fairlee Bd. of Selectmen, 1951–53; Chm., Vermont Repub. Platform Convention, 1966, 1970; State Rep., 1961–68, Speaker 1966–68; State Sen. 1969–70; Commissioner of Administration, 1971.

Offices 1131 LHOB, 202-225-4115. Also P.O. Box 220, Fed. Bldg., Montpelier 05602, 802-223-5273.

Administrative Assistant B. Waring Partridge

Committees

Government Operations (12th); Sub: Legislation and Military Operations.

Post Office and Civil Service (8th); Subs: Postal Service; Manpower and Civil Service.

Group Ratings

	ADA	COPE	LWV	RIPON	NFU	LCV	CFA	NAB	NSI	ACA
1972	31	27	83	94	57	–	50	100	83	61

Key Votes

1) Busing	FOR	6) Cmbodia Bmbg	AGN	11) Chkg Acct Intrst	AGN
2) Strip Mines	AGN	7) Bust Hwy Trust	FOR	12) End HISC (HUAC)	FOR
3) Cut Mil $	AGN	8) Farm Sub Lmt	FOR	13) Nixon Sewer Veto	FOR
4) Rev Shrg	AGN	9) School Prayr	NE	14) Corp Cmpaign $	AGN
5) Pub TV $	AGN	10) Cnsumr Prot	NE	15) Pol $ Disclosr	NE

Election Results

1972 general:	Richard W. Mallary (R)	120,924	(65%)
	William H. Meyer (D)	65,062	(35%)
1972 primary:	Richard W. Mallary (R), unopposed		
1972 special:	Richard W. Mallary (R)	39,903	(56%)
	J. William O'Brien (D)	26,889	(38%)
	Doris Lake (Liberty Union)	3,362	(5%)
	Anthony N. Doris (Vermont Ind.)	1,353	(2%)

VIRGINIA

Political Background

Ten years ago, any analysis of Virginia politics started and ended with a description of the Byrd machine. This was a unique organization that enjoyed almost complete domination of the state's politics from 1925—the year Harry Flood Byrd was elected Governer—until 1964. Political machines of the common variety are operated by men who can make what they regard as a good living only in politics, and do so by manipulating large blocs of votes in big cities. In contrast, the men of the Byrd machine were usually bankers, established lawyers, wealthy businessmen, and gentlemen farmers—people who dominated life in the small towns of the Shenandoah Valley, Byrd's home bailiwick, or in Southside Virginia, an area that is really part of the Deep South. The key to the machine's success was a small electorate. The state's voting laws, especially the poll tax, kept turnout low and effectively excluded blacks and most poor whites from the ballot box. So the succession of Byrd-machine Governors included personal friends and social equals of those who ran the Virginia Electric and Power Company (VEPCO), the state's largest banks, and the University of Virginia. All were rich, elderly, respected, reserved, and, of course, conservative.

The same set of adjectives certainly applied to Harry Byrd himself. Though he served only one term as Governor, Byrd easily controlled the machine and thus the politics of Virginia from the United States Senate for more than 30 years. Ironically, Byrd's path to the Senate was smoothed by Franklin D. Roosevelt, but the Virginian soon turned against FDR, and Byrd's name came to represent an opposition to government spending and deficit budgets. As Chairman of the Senate Finance Committee and founder and Chairman of the Joint Committee on Reduction of Federal Expenditures, Byrd possessed two forums from which to promulgate his views. The chairmanship of the Finance Committee, of course, was what made the Senator powerful, since the unit must approve all federal taxation; the Joint Committee never did much to reduce expenditures. Despite Byrd's best efforts, the federal budget continued to grow inexorably over the years; in 1965, Byrd resigned from the Senate just as Congress had finished enacting most of Lyndon Johnson's Great Society programs.

During the mid-1950s, the Byrd machine made its only appeal to the mass of public opinion. This was the Massive Resistance Program. For a few years, the Virginia schools under federal court orders to integrate were shut down by the state, as attempts were made to subsidize private, all-white academies. (The state did nothing, however, for the black children out of school.) But the program of defiance collapsed, and the Byrd Governor then in office capitulated and agreed to comply with the law. The style of Massive Resistance was typical of the Byrd machine: its oratory was closer in spirit to John C. Calhoun's stringent interpretation of the Constitution than the standing-in-the-school-house-door bombast of Orval Faubus and George Wallace. But because the Byrd machine in effect chose to rally the great mass of Virginia voters, Massive Resistance stimulated increased electoral participation, particularly among segregationist poor whites, who had never really been the machine's kind of people.

As Byrd left the Senate in 1965 (he died in 1966), his machine was collapsing. Demography accounts for its decline. During the Byrd years, Virginia had undergone a virtually unnoticed change from a predominantly rural state, with only one large urban voting bloc in Richmond (and that solidly conservative), to part of the East Coast megalopolis. In 1960, the rapidly growing Virginia suburbs of Washington constituted 15% of the state's population; in 1970, 20%. And in 1960, the industrial Tidewater area around Norfolk and Newport News accounted for another 19%; in 1970, 21%.

This explosive growth was due mostly to the operations of the federal government, especially the Department of Defense. The Tidewater area is the home of the largest naval installations along the Atlantic Coast, and Arlington, of course, is the site of the Pentagon. When one adds the two areas to the traditionally anti-Byrd mountain counties of Western Virginia, the traditional Byrd strongholds—Richmond, Southside, the Piedmont, the Shenandoah Valley—are left with a minority of the state's votes. The Senator's retirement occurred just after the passage of the Voting Rights Act of 1965—a bill that vastly increased the number of black rural poor white, and industrial blue-collar white votes in Virginia.

Suddenly, after 40 years of unrelieved machine victories, Virginia elections approached the status of wide-open affairs. Though conservative candidates with positions on issues rather similar to those of Byrd have won most elections so far, more potential for change exists now than as recently as eight years ago. Because the array of candidates and issues has varied markedly in each campaign, it is best to examine them one at a time.

The 1966 races. As expected for so many years, state Sen. Harry F. Byrd, Jr., was appointed to fill the vacancy created by his father's retirement. And, as expected, Byrd was reelected to the Senate by the voters. The real surprise occurred in the contest for the state's other Senate seat. The incumbent, A. Willis Robertson, a Byrd man who was Chairman of the Senate Banking Committee, was upset in the Democratic primary by a 46-year-old state Senator from Tidewater region named William Spong. In the general election, Spong, a political moderate who had won the support of black voters in the primary, ran a full 6% ahead of Harry Byrd, Jr., who got only 53% of the votes against an unknown Republican.

The 1969 gubernatorial race. There has always been a Republican party in Virginia, one based in the Blue Ridge and Appalachian mountains; this part of Virginia was always hostile to the Byrd machine. It disliked the machine's absorption with the race issue, particularly during the period of Massive Resistance. Virginia's Republicans also had a populist streak, if only a faint one; after all, the leading economic powers in the state were all Byrd Democrats. Western Virginia is relatively poor, and out of it came A. Linwood Holton, a Roanoke lawyer and a Republican. In 1965, Holton ran a creditable race against Byrd-stalwart Mills Godwin in the gubernatorial election.

Holton was again his party's candidate in 1969, (Virginia, along with New Jersey, Kentucky, and Louisiana, persists in holding state elections in off years.) In his second attempt, Holton benefited from splits among the Democrats. Because the machine no longer controlled the primary, it turned out to be a close contest, among three candidates: moderate liberal William Battle (whose father was a Byrd Governor), populistic Norfolk state Sen. Henry Howell (of whom more later), and Lt. Gov. Fred Pollard of the machine. The candidates finished in that order. In the general election, Holton made inroads among black, Washington suburban, and Richmond voters, which, combined with his base in the mountains, were enough to produce a victory.

Once in office, Holton became one of the most aggressive defenders of the Nixon Administration, particularly on those issues, like revenue sharing, that bore on the states. But one act quickly lost him the favor of Nixon operatives. When Richmond came under a federal court order to bus, Holton escorted his young daughter to the predominantly black school to which she had been assigned. Holton's decision made headlines and news photos all over the country. The Administration, however, wanted to make as much political hay out of the busing issue as possible, and Holton's call for all citizens to comply with court orders was not part of the game plan. So, despite his loyalty to Nixon on other issues, Holton entered the conservatives' doghouse. And despite a good record as Governor, he is at this writing scheduled to retire in January 1974 with no prospects of a future in politics. The Nixonite conservatives who took over the state's Republican party now have little use for their onetime leader.

The 1970 Senate race. Nothing showed the dismantlement of the Byrd machine better than the younger Harry Bryd's decision to run for reelection to the Senate in 1970 as an independent. With the increasing number of black, suburban Washington, and Tidewater voters in the Democratic primary, Byrd apparently figured—and many agreed—that he could easily lose, just as his father's colleague Robertson had lost four years earlier. In the Senate, Byrd was not an especially voluble politician; he made a name for himself chiefly as an advocate of economy in government—his father's old issue. But a Byrd asset did develop as the campaign went on. In Richmond, a federal judge ordered busing between the predominantly black schools in the central city and the virtually all-white suburban counties. The decision raised a storm of antibusing sentiment all over Virginia. Byrd's response was his campaign slogan, "You know what he stands for."

Many Republicans, including key Nixon politicos and 10th-district Rep. Joel Broyhill, wanted to give Byrd the Republican nomination at the state convention. They hoped two things would happen as a result: first that Byrd would vote with the Republicans to organize the Senate; and second that his emergence as a Republican would create solid new Republican strongholds in the old Byrd territory of the Valley, Southside, and the Piedmont. But Gov. Holton balked. He had fought Byrd Democrats all his political life. So Holton engineered the nomination of a Roanoke moderate, Ray Garland, to oppose Byrd. As it turned out, Byrd won the general election by a large margin (54%), though running only 1% above his 1966 showing. Meanwhile, his opponents split the remaining 46%, with liberal Democrat George Rawlings getting 31% and Republican Ray Garland, 15%.

The 1971 Lieutenant Governor race. In 1971, Lt. Gov. J. Sergeant Reynolds, a liberal Democrat and heir to an aluminum fortune, died of a brain tumor. Had he not been stricken, he would have probably been elected Governor in 1973. The vacancy was filled in the 1971 state elections. The winner was another independent, but this time a man very different from Byrd, Jr. This was Henry Howell, who had finished a close second in the 1969 primary, and apparently figured that a populist could play the independent game as effectively as a Byrd. So against a moderate Democrat and a mountain Republican, Howell ran the same kind of campaign he had run two years before. Howell's slogan: "Keep the big boys honest." Using folksy campaign oratory, the candidate lashed out against VEPCO, the big banks, the Byrd machine, and against both Republicans and Democrats. After forging a coalition of working-class whites, well-to-do Washington suburbanites, and blacks, Howell won the election with 41% of the votes.

The 1972 Senate race. This race was supposed to feature relatively easy reelection for Sen. Spong. Elected with 59% of the votes in 1966, he appeared in good political shape for the campaign of 1972. In the Senate, Spong dissented on occasion from the Nixon Administration: for example, on the Carswell nomination. His dissents came often enough to please liberals, but so spaced, it seemed, to avoid unduly irritating conservatives. Moreover, the Senator's cautious, scholarly demeanor created few political enemies. And though Nixon was expected to carry the state by an overwhelming margin (which he did, with 69%), Spong appeared to possess enough ticket-splitting support to win.

But such an assessment failed to account for the aggressive campaign waged by the Republican nominee, William Scott, Congressman from the 8th district. Scott's nomination itself demonstrated that control of the state Republican party had shifted from Holton's moderates to a new breed of Nixon conservatives. To get votes, these politicians were eager to push racial animosities to the limit. In the last months of the campaign, Scott came into large infusions of cash contributed by a little-known millionaire named J. D. Stetson Coleman. With the money, Scott's managers waged a saturation TV ad campaign, which presented Scott as the man more in line with the feelings of most Virginians. Spong, apparently overconfident, did not react until it was too late. The result was a 51–46 upset win for Scott, the first Republican Senator from Virginia since Reconstruction.

Scott was never a highly regarded member of the House of Representatives. His presence there was as much an accident as anything else. In 1966, Scott, perennially unsuccessful Republican office-seeker, received what appeared to be a worthless nomination to oppose Howard W. Smith, Chairman of the House Rules Committee, in the 8th district. But Smith was upset in the primary by a liberal Democrat; so the Chairman's old courthouse supporters switched to back the conservative Scott. The new Senator, an intense, fervent man, is best known for high turnover among his staff; in the Senate, he of course now ranks near the bottom in seniority—and, say his critics, dead last in a number of other respects. His most pressing concern, it seems, is the extension of Interstate 66 from Washington out into Fairfax County, where the Senator resides.

The 1973 Governor race. The embrace of the remnants of the old Byrd machine and the Virginia Republican party was consumated in 1973 when Mills Godwin was nominated for Governor. Godwin, a Byrd man all of his political life, was one of the architects of Massive Resistance and the last Byrd-backed Governor (1962–65). His opponent was Lt. Gov. Henry Howell, once again running as an independent. For the first time in the twentieth century, the Democratic party fielded no gubernatorial candidate. The two contenders were both ex-Democrats, though from very different wings of the party. Godwin ran on much the same platform as Scott—a believer in what the majority of Virginians presumably believe in; he was backed by all the interests that supported him when he ran under the colors of the Byrd machine.

Howell again ran "to keep the big boys honest." His opponent Godwin attacked him for his onetime support of busing; Howell, meantime, said he accepts the decisions of the court, which ruled out cross-district busing in Richmond. Howell also attacked the sales tax on food, which Godwin, as Governor, had imposed. The Independent hoped to combine the vaguely populistic mountain Republicans, who distrust the Byrd machine; the Washington suburbanites; and, in particular, the working-class whites and blacks of his home Tidewater area. Godwin wants to forge a coalition between the traditional Republicans and the old Byrd machine.

As this is written, the outcome is not yet known, but it seems likely to be close. The results will surely set the tone of Virginia politics for years, and perhaps determine the nature of the heretofore shifting coalitions that have held sway in Virginia elections since the retirement of Harry Byrd, Sr.

The Howell-Godwin confrontation is also one with some national significance. Howell has made full financial disclosure of the sources of his campaign funds; he then challenged Godwin to do the same, but without success so far. After Watergate headlines began to hit the papers, Godwin, who was head of a Virginia unit of the Committee to Reelect the President, announced that he did not want President Nixon to campaign for him, but would welcome Vice-President Agnew. Shortly thereafter, the media reported that Agnew was under investigation in Baltimore. In the face of all the conservative victories in Virginia recently, however, Howell would seem to have little chance. But none of those victories was achieved with much more than 50% of the total number of votes cast. Moreover, Howell has demonstrated a capacity to put together the support of disparate groups that few American politicians, at least those of a populistic bent, can match.

Census Data Pop. 4,648,494; 2.30% of U.S. total, 14th largest; change 1960–70, 17.2%. Central city, 24%; suburban, 37%. Median family income, $9,045; 25th highest; families above $15,000: 20%; families below $3,000: 11%. Median years education, 11.7.

1972 Share of Federal Tax Burden $4,284,880,000; 2.05% of U.S. total, 15th largest.

1972 Share of Federal Outlays $6,197,755,523; 2.86% of U.S. total, 9th largest. Per capita federal spending, $1,333.

DOD	$3,289,439,000	4th	(5.26%)	HEW	$1,226,412,598	19th	(1.72%)
AEC	$1,278,750	29th	(0.05%)	HUD	$62,306,500	18th	(2.03%)
NASA	$134,788,409	8th	(4.51%)	VA	$263,026,244	14th	(2.30%)
DOT	$289,886,698	7th	(3.68%)	USDA	$232,227,440	26th	(1.51%)
DOC	$26,482,000	12th	(2.05%)	CSC	$249,074,819	4th	(6.04%)
DOI	$39,340,057	16th	(1.85%)	TD	$100,448,607	25th	(0.61%)
DOJ	$15,200,688	21st	(1.55%)	Other	$267,843,713		

Economic Base Finance, insurance and real estate; agriculture, notably dairy products, tobacco, cattle and broilers; textile mills products, especially cotton weaving mills; apparel and other textile products, especially men's and boys' furnishings, and women's and misses outerwear; chemicals and allied products, especially plastics materials and synthetics; food and kindred products; electrical equipment and supplies.

Political Line-up Governor, Linwood Holton (R); seat up, 1973. Senators, Harry F. Byrd, Jr. (Ind. D) and William Lloyd Scott (R). Representatives, 10 (7 R and 3 D). State Senate (33 D and 7 R); House of Delegates (71 D, 25 R, and 4 Ind.).

The Voters

Registration 2,107,367 Total. No party registration.
Median voting age 40.6
Employment profile White collar, 49%. Blue collar, 36%. Service, 12%. Farm, 3%.
Ethnic groups Black, 19%. Spanish, 1%. Total foreign stock, 5%.

Presidential vote

1972	Nixon (R)	988,493	(69%)
	McGovern (D)	438,887	(31%)
1968	Nixon (R)	590,319	(44%)
	Humphrey (D)	442,387	(33%)
	Wallace (AI)	321,833	(24%)
1964	Johnson (D)	558,038	(54%)
	Goldwater (R)	481,334	(46%)

Senator

Harry Flood Byrd, Jr. (Independent) Elected Appointed Nov. 12, 1965, seat up 1976; b. Dec. 20, 1914, Winchester; home, Winchester; Va. Military Inst., 1931–33; U. of Va., 1933–35; USNR, WWII; married, three children; Episcopalian.

Career Newspaper editor; orchardist; Chm., Va. Advisry Bd. on Industrial Dev., 1962–67; Va. Senate, 1948–65; second person in history of U.S. Senate to be elected as an Independent.

Offices 417 OSOB, 202-225-4024. Also Winchester 22601, 703-662-7745.

Administrative Assistant John T. White

Committees

Armed Services (7th); Subs: Research and Development; Preparedness Investigating; Bomber Defense; Military Construction Authorization; General Legislation (Chm.); Reprograming of Funds; Arms Control.

Finance (6h); Subs: Private Pension Plans; Interantional Finance Resources (Chm.).

Group Ratings

	ADA	COPE	LWV	RIPON	NFU	LCV	CFA	NAB	NSI	ACA
1972	20	10	18	28	30	26	9	100	80	91
1971	15	0	8	32	27	–	14	–	–	87
1970	22	8	–	17	47	47	–	75	90	87

Key Votes

1) Busing	AGN	8) Sea Life Prot	FOR	15) Tax Singls Less	AGN
2) Alas P-line	FOR	9) Campaign Subs	AGN	16) Min Tax for Rich	AGN
3) Gun Cntrl	FOR	10) Cmbodia Bmbg	AGN	17) Euro Troop Rdctn	AGN
4) Rehnquist	FOR	11) Legal Srvices	AGN	18) Bust Hwy Trust	AGN
5) Pub TV $	AGN	12) Rev Sharing	AGN	19) Maid Min Wage	AGN
6) EZ Votr Reg	AGN	13) Cnsumr Prot	AGN	20) Farm Sub Limit	FOR
7) No-Fault	AGN	14) Eq Rts Amend	FOR	21) Highr Credt Chgs	FOR

Election Results

1970 general:	Harry F. Byrd, Jr. (Ind.)	506,327	(54%)
	George C. Rawlings, Jr. (D)	294,582	(31%)
	Ray Garland (R)	144,765	(15%)
1970 primary:	Harry F. Byrd, Jr. (Ind.), unopposed		
1966 special:	Harry F. Byrd, Jr. (D)	389,028	(53%)
	Lawrence M. Traylor (R)	272,804	(37%)
	John W. Carter (Ind)	57,692	(8%)
	J. B. Brayman (Ind.)	10,180	(1%)

William Lloyd Scott (R) Elected 1972, seat up 1978; b. July 1, 1915, Williamsburg; home, Fairfax County; George Washington U., J.D., 1938; married, three children; Methodist.

Career Atty., employed by fed. gov., 1934–61; practicing atty., 1961–66; U.S. House of Reps., 1967–73.

Offices 2121 NSOB, 202-225-2023. Also Fed. Bldg., Rm. 8000, Richmond, 703-649-0049.

Administrative Assistant Donald J. Musch

Committees

Armed Services (6th); Subs: National Stockpile and Naval Petroleum Reserves (Ranking Mbr.); Status of Forces (Ranking Mbr.); Arms Control; General Legislation; Drug Abuse in the Military.

Public Works (4th); Subs: Water Resources (Ranking Mbr.); Public Buildings and Grounds (Ranking Mbr.); Roads; Economic Development.

Sel. Com. on *Small Business* (7th); Subs: Financing and Investment; Government Procurement; Retailing, Distribution, and Marketing Practices (Ranking Mbr.).

Group Ratings

	ADA	COPE	LWV	RIPON	NFU	LCV	CFA	NAB	NSI	ACA
1972	0	9	11	25	43	20	50	56	100	100
1971	3	17	11	44	15	–	13	–	–	93
1970	4	9	–	29	31	13	33	92	100	89

Key Votes

1) Busing	AGN	8) Sea Life Prot	MOS	15) Tax Singls Less	MOS
2) Alas P-line	ABS	9) Campaign Subs	MOS	16) Min Tax for Rich	MOS
3) Gun Cntrl	AGN	10) Cmbodia Bmbg	FOR	17) Euro Troop Rdctn	MOS
4) Rehnquist	AGN	11) Legal Srvices	FOR	18) Bust Hwy Trust	ABS
5) Pub TV $	AGN	12) Rev Sharing	AGN	19) Maid Min Wage	AGN

Election Results

1972 general:	William Lloyd Scott (R)	718,337	(51%)
	William B. Spong, Jr. (D)	643,963	(46%)
	Horace Henderson (Ind.)	33,912	(2%)
1972 primary:	William Lloyd Scott (R), unopposed		

FIRST DISTRICT Political Background

The 1st district is part of Tidewater Virginia, the lowlands by the wide tidal inlets of the Atlantic Ocean and Chesapeake Bay. The district includes the southern tip of the Delmarva peninsula, connected with Norfolk by a 20-mile-long bridge and tunnel complex, and several rural Tidewater counties that have changed little since George Washington's time. In fact, both Washington and Robert E. Lee were born within the confines of the present 1st. Some 62% of the district's population, however, is concentrated in the Hampton Roads area, mostly in Newport News (pop. 138,000) and Hampton (pop. 120,000).

The Hampton Roads area has been growing rapidly, thanks to spending by the federal government. Because this part of the Tidewater contains one of the best natural harbors on the Atlantic seaboard, Hampton Roads is the headquarters for the Atlantic Fleet. Most of the naval bases themselves lie across the bay in Norfolk and Portsmouth, but Newport News absorbs plenty of federal money through the Newport News Shipbuilding and Dry Dock Company, one of the nation's biggest shipbuilders. The firm does hundreds of millions of dollars in military work annually, and any civilian work it performs is heavily subsidized. Next door, Hampton is the site of a major NASA installation.

It does the Tidewater area no harm that the 1st district Congressman, Democrat Thomas Downing, serves on the House Merchant Marine and the Science and Astronautics committee. For many Congressmen, these would be humdrum assignments; for one with a district like Downing's, they are politically invaluable. NASA is unlikely to make any cutbacks at the Hampton facilities while Downing is Chairman of the NASA Oversight Subcommittee, and it is a fair bet that a good bit of federal oceanographic research money will find its way to the 1st district now that Downing is Chairman of the Oceanography Subcommittee.

So it should be no surprise that the 1st is one of the few Virginia congressional districts that has not had a major contest in recent years. It is also one in which the state's Republicans have failed to come even close. Downing has been unopposed in two of the four last general elections, and received well above 70% of the votes in the other two. Without Downing in the race, the district would be a far more marginal one, although Newport News and Hampton—both with large black and white working-class neighborhoods—usually go for liberal Democrats in Virginia state elections.

Census Data Pop. 465,981. Central city, 56%; suburban, 7%. Median family income, $8,490; families above $15,000: 16%; families below $3,000: 13%. Median years education, 11.5.

1972 Share of Federal Outlays $1,176,887,232

DOD	$822,922,000	HEW	$111,797,611
AEC	$105,000	HUD	$2,150,807
NASA	$127,577,635	DOI	$2,245,866
DOT	$15,214,051	USDA	$11,983,151
		Other	$82,891,111

Federal Military-Industrial Commitments

DOD Contractors Newport News Shipbuilding and Dry Dock Co. (Newport News), $485.411m: construction and overhaul of submarines and ships. System Development Corp. (Hampton), $16.868m: computer programing services.
DOD Installations Fort Eustis AB (Newport News). Fort Monroe AB (Hampton). Naval Administrative Command, Armed Forces Staff College (Williamsburg). Naval Weapons Laboratory (Dahlgren). Naval Weapons Station (Yorktown). Naval Weapons Station, Skiffes Creek Annex (Yorktown). Cape Charles AF Station (Kiptopeke). Langley AFB (Hampton).
NASA Installations Langley Research Center (Langley Field).

Economic Base Agriculture, notably vegetables and grains; finance, insurance and real estate; food and kindred products, especially canned, cured and frozen foods; and lumber and wood products.

The Voters

Registration 196,790 total. No party registration.
Median voting age 40.2
Employment profile White collar, 45%. Blue collar, 38%. Service, 14%. Farm, 3%.
Ethnic groups Black, 30%. Spanish, 1%. Total foreign stock, 5%.

Presidential vote

1972	Nixon (R)	95,400	(69%)
	McGovern (D)	43,069	(31%)
1968	Nixon (R)	47,210	(35%)
	Humphrey (D)	45,273	(34%)
	Wallace (AI)	40,601	(31%)

Representative

Thomas N. Downing (D) Elected 1958; b. Feb. 1, 1919, Newport News; home, Newport News; Va. Military Inst., B.S., 1940; U. of Va., LL.B., 1947; Army, WWII; married, two children; Episcopalian.

Career Practicing atty., 1947–58; Substitute Judge, Municipal Ct., City of Warwick (now Newport News), 1953–58.

Offices 2135 RHOB, 202-225-4261. Also 1 Court St., Hampton 23669, 804-723-1885, and P.O. Bldg., Cape Charles 23310, 804-331-3767.

Administrative Assistant E. M. Hutton

Committees

Merchant Marine and Fisheries (5th); Subs: Merchant Marine; Oceanography (Chm.).

Science and Astronautics (4th); Sub: Space Science and Applications.

Group Ratings

	ADA	COPE	LWV	RIPON	NFU	LCV	CFA	NAB	NSI	ACA
1972	0	18	27	38	29	13	0	92	88	95
1971	8	25	22	39	53	–	13	–	–	75
1970	8	25	–	31	46	28	52	67	100	61

Key Votes

1) Busing	AGN	6) Cmbodia Bmbg	AGN	11) Chkg Acct Intrst	AGN
2) Strip Mines	FOR	7) Bust Hwy Trust	AGN	12) End HISC (HUAC)	AGN
3) Cut Mil $	AGN	8) Farm Sub Lmt	AGN	13) Nixon Sewer Veto	AGN
4) Rev Shrg	AGN	9) School Prayr	FOR	14) Corp Cmpaign $	FOR
5) Pub TV $	AGN	10) Cnsumr Prot	AGN	15) Pol $ Disclosr	AGN

Election Results

1972 general:	Thomas N. Downing (D)	100,901	(78%)
	Kenneth D. Wells (R)	28,310	(22%)
1972 primary:	Thomas N. Downing (D), unopposed		
1970 general:	Thomas N. Downing (D), unopposed		

SECOND DISTRICT Political Background

Norfolk, Virginia is the headquarters of the Navy's Atlantic Fleet. Within its city limits is one of the world's largest naval bases and more than a half dozen other naval installations, not to mention the dozen or so other military facilities in nearby Portsmouth, Virginia Beach, or in Hampton and Newport News across Hampton Roads. The naval buildup here during and after World War II is what has made Norfolk what it is today. Before World War II, it was a city of 144,000 with perhaps another 100,000 in adjacent areas; today, Norfolk is the center of an urban agglomeration of nearly a million people. Suburban homes have sprouted in the low-lying land near the wide inlets off the bay, and shopping centers put up at freeway interchanges. During the 1960s, the area of fastest growth shifted east, to the high-income suburb of Virginia Beach.

Norfolk is the home turf of Henry Howell—at this writing, Lieutenant Governor and independent candidate for Governor (see Virginia state write-up). Politically, Norfolk is a working-class town. For the most part, Navy personnel do not vote here, and their absence from the electorate shows up in low turnout figures. So Howell has managed to forge a populist coalition of blue-collar whites and blacks. This is a formidable achievement, for Norfolk maintains a high degree of residential segregation. In national elections, its voters have split almost entirely along racial lines. Norfolk blacks went almost unanimously for Humphrey and McGovern in 1968 and 1972 while whites, in 1968, split their votes almost evenly between Nixon and Wallace, and then came out solidly for Nixon four years later. But Howell has managed to carry the city overwhelmingly, winning large majorities among voters of both races.

But Howell's kind of politics has had little effect on elections in the 2nd congressional district, which includes Norfolk and virtually all of high-income and 91% white Virginia Beach. For 22 years, the district sent a relatively conservative Democrat, Porter Hardy, to the House, and watched him rise to a high seniority position on the House Armed Services Committee. Hardy retired in 1968, and the resulting contest for the seat was a close one. Because a Howell-type Democrat was hampered by intraparty feuding, the Republican nominee, G. William Whitehurst, came away with a 54–46 victory. It probably did not hurt that Whitehurst, a professor at Old Dominion College, was also a local TV commentator.

Since his first election, Whitehurst has won reelection easily. He is one of those Congressmen who return to the district every weekend, and who take care to speak before and attend to the needs of even those whom one would think are not ideologically disposed to support him. These people, in Whitehurst's case, are black. The Congressman's diligence has paid off at the polls, as it usually does for most Congressmen. It also helps that Whitehurst, like his predecessor, is a member of the House Armed Services Committee. In committee and on the floor, Whitehurst usually votes the conservative, Nixon Administration line. With nearly $500 million a year coming into his district from the Pentagon, the Congressman is not one to support major cuts in the defense budget.

Census Data Pop. 464,692. Central city, 66%; suburban, 34%. Median family income, $8,733; families above $15,000: 18%; families below $3,000: 12%. Median years education, 12.1.

1972 Share of Federal Outlays $757,015,102

DOD	$395,754,294	HEW	$106,464,552
AEC	–	HUD	$22,472,599
NASA	$976,789	DOI	$616,274
DOT	$44,903,581	USDA	$10,204,380
		Other	$175,622,633

Federal Military-Industrial Commitments

DOD Contractors Kirkpatrick and Associates (Virginia Beach), $10.587m: unspecified. Norfold Shipbuilding and Dry Dock Co. (Norfolk), $9.569m: submarine and ship overhaul. Automation Terminal Services (Norfolk), $5.762m: transportation serices.

DOD Installations Fleet Anti-Air Warfare Training Center, Dam Neck (Virginia Beach). Operational Control Office, U.S. Atlantic Fleet (Norfolk). Naval Air Station (Norfolk). Naval Air Station, Oceana (Virginia Beach). Naval Weapons Station, St. Juliens Creek Annex (St. Juliens Creek). Naval Amphibious Base, Little Creek (Norfolk). Naval Communication Station (Norfolk). Naval Air Rework Facility (Norfolk). Naval Supply Center (Norfolk). Naval Station (Norfolk). Naval Public Works Center (Norfolk). Naval Degaussing Station (Norfolk).

Economic Base Finance, insurance and real estate; transportation equipment, especially ship and boat building and repairing; food and kindred products; rubber and plastics products; and tourism. Also higher education (Old Dominion Univ.).

The Voters

Registration 177,791 total. No party registration.
Median voting age 34.5
Employment profile White collar, 55%. Blue collar, 30%. Service, 15%. Farm, –%.
Ethnic groups Black, 22%. Spanish, 2%. Total foreign stock, 8%. UK, 1%.

Presidential vote

1972	Nixon (R)	73,728	(68%)
	McGovern (D)	35,107	(32%)
1968	Nixon (R)	37,700	(38%)
	Humphrey (D)	37,647	(38%)
	Wallace (AI)	25,038	(25%)

Representative

G. William Whitehurst (R) Elected 1968; b. March 12, 1925, Norfolk; home, Norfolk; Washington and Lee U., B.A., 1950; U. of Va., M.A., 1951; W.Va. U., Ph.D., 1962; Navy, WWII; married, two children; Methodist.

Career Faculty, hist. dept., Old Dominion Col., 1950–68, Dean of Students, 1963–68; Bd. Chm., Norfolk Forum; Staff of pub. affairs and news dept., WTAR-TV, 1962–68.

Offices 424 CHOB, 202-225-4215. Also 201 Fed. Bldg., Norfolk 23510, 703-627-7471, ext. 7550, and Rm. 216, Fed. Bldg., Portsmouth 23704, 703-441-6763.

Administrative Assistant R. Burnett Thompson

Committees

Armed Services (8th); Sub: No. 5.

Group Ratings

	ADA	COPE	LWV	RIPON	NFU	LCV	CFA	NAB	NSI	ACA
1972	6	0	27	60	29	26	0	78	100	86
1971	17	36	22	44	36	–	13	–	–	79
1970	16	42	–	47	67	45	80	58	100	50

Key Votes

1) Busing	AGN	6) Cmbodia Bmbg	FOR	11) Chkg Acct Intrst	AGN
2) Strip Mines	FOR	7) Bust Hwy Trust	AGN	12) End HISC (HUAC)	AGN
3) Cut Mil $	AGN	8) Farm Sub Lmt	FOR	13) Nixon Sewer Veto	FOR
4) Rev Shrg	FOR	9) School Prayr	FOR	14) Corp Cmpaign $	AGN
5) Pub TV $	AGN	10) Cnsumr Prot	AGN	15) Pol $ Disclosr	AGN

Election Results

1972 general:	G. William Whitehurst (R)	79,672	(73%)
	L. Charles Burlage (D)	28,803	(27%)
1972 primary:	G. William Whitehurst (R), unopposed		
1970 general:	G. William Whitehurst (R)	44,099	(62%)
	Joseph T. Fitzpatrick (D)	27,362	(38%)

THIRD DISTRICT Political Background

Richmond, once the capital of the Confederacy, remains the capital of Virginia and a major tobacco-producing center. In many ways, Richmond is also still the state's most important city, which is rather odd. In the recent past the Virginia suburbs of Washington and the Tidewater complex around Norfolk and Newport News have grown much larger than Richmond; today, only 11% of the state's population resides in the Richmond metropolitan area. Nevertheless, the city still contains the state government and the headquarters of the big statewide banks and the Virginia Electric and Power Company, all of which seem to be run by the same people. In spite of icy winters, Richmond sustains a definite Southern aura, something the Washington suburbs and the Tidewater do not. The city is also one of the most conservative metropolitan areas in the country, an inclination strengthened by the politics of its two major newspapers.

Virginia's 3rd congressional district consists of Richmond and virtually all of its two principal suburban counties, Henrico and Chesterfield. This is the area covered by the Richmond school case, where federal judge Robert Merhige ordered busing across city and county lines. The decision was reversed by the Fourth Circuit Court of Appeals, with the reversal upheld by an evenly divided Supreme Court. (Justice Lewis Powell, a member of the Richmond school board during the days of Massive Resistance, did not participate in the ruling.) Ever since the Merhige decision came down, metropolitan Richmond whites, already conservative, have generated a flurry of anti-busing sentiment. Many moved to Hanover County, farther out.

The politics of the 3rd district nicely illustrates the kind of flux that has characterized Virginia politics since the collapse of the Byrd machine. Richmond was usually a Byrd city, with a small number of dissenting Republican votes, most of them cast by blacks. In 1969, Republican gubernatorial candidate Linwood Holton carried 65% of the votes in the 3rd, as he won heavy majorities among white suburbanites and city blacks. The Crusade for Voters, a Richmond-based black organization, was unhappy enough with the state's Democrats to support the moderate Holton. The Governor's success inspired Holton Republicans to make a fight for the 3rd's House seat in 1970. Their candidate was 26-year-old J. Harvie Wilkinson III, whose father was a Richmond banker well-connected to the city's establishment. The idea was to combine, once again, the white suburban vote with the city's blacks, who were not especially happy with the record of the district's conservative Democratic Congressman, David E. Satterfield III.

Satterfield came to the seat more or less by inheritance. His father was the area's Congressman from 1937 to 1945; he was followed by another Byrd Democrat, J. Vaughn Gary. When Gary decided to retire in 1964, Satterfield III seemed a logical candidate. But Virginia congressional seats were not as easily passed along in the 1960s as they were in the 1950s. In 1964, when Republican Barry Goldwater carried the 3rd, Republican congressional candidate Richard Obenshain (now state Party Chairman) waged a strong campaign. Moreover, independent liberal Edward Haddock won most of the black votes. So the election resulted in that rare political event, a close three-candidate congressional race. Satterfield edged Obenshain by 654 votes and got by Haddock by 4,657 votes.

Once in office, Satterfield had less difficulty. The 1970 Wilkinson challenge, which had seemed so promising to Holton Republicans, fizzled. Reaction to the busing case, along with Holton's acceptance of the court decisions (see Virginia state write-up), torpedoed Wilkinson's support in the suburban counties, where he lost, 2–1. Wilkinson did make some inroads in black precincts, but those gains were not nearly enough to make the election close.

Wilkinson's defeat was another blow to Gov. Holton's brand of Republicanism. It also indicated that a Byrd Democrat was still acceptable to the citizens of Richmond, who have been voting for Republican presidential candidates for 20 years. Satterfield even ran unopposed in 1972.

Census Data Pop. 465,289. Central city, 54%; suburban, 46%. Median family income, $9,945; families above $15,000: 21%; families below $3,000: 8%. Median years education, 11.7.

1972 Share of Federal Outlays $571,256,844

DOD	$139,088,972	HEW	$185,864,971
AEC	$41,925	HUD	$12,145,648
NASA	$119,443	DOI	$2,684,984
DOT	$37,412,844	USDA	$63,788,469
		Other	$130,109,588

Federal Military-Industrial Commitments

DOD Installations Army Defense Supply Center (Richmond).

Economic Base Finance, insurance and real estate; tobacco manufactures, especially cigarettes; chemicals and allied products, especially plastics materials and synthetics; printing and publishing, especially commercial printing; and apparel and other textile products.

The Voters

Registration 233,622 total. No party registration.
Median voting age 42.0
Employment profile White collar, 55%. Blue collar, 32%. Service, 13%. Farm, –%.
Ethnic groups Black, 26%. Total foreign stock, 5%.

Presidential vote

1972	Nixon (R)	117,472	(72%)
	McGovern (D)	44,566	(28%)
1968	Nixon (R)	78,797	(51%)
	Humphrey (D)	46,336	(30%)
	Wallace (AI)	29,265	(19%)

Representative

David Edward Satterfield III (D) Elected 1964; b. Dec. 2, 1920, Richmond; home, Richmond; U. of Richmond; U. of Va.; Navy, WWII; Capt. USNAR; married, two children; Episcopalian.

Career Practicing atty., 1948–50, 1953–65; Asst. U.S. Atty., 1950–53; Richmond Councilman, 1954–56; Va. Legislature, 1960–64; Civilian Adviser to Natl. Health Svc.

Offices 324 CHOB, 202-225-2815. Also Fed. Office Bldg., Richmond 23240, 703-782-2519.

Administrative Assistant Reginald Armistead

Committees

Interstate and Foreign Commerce (11th); Sub: Public Health and Environment.

Veterans' Affairs (6th); Subs: Hospitals (Chm.); Housing; Insurance.

Group Ratings

	ADA	COPE	LWV	RIPON	NFU	LCV	CFA	NAB	NSI	ACA
1972	0	9	18	19	29	13	50	91	100	100
1971	8	8	22	28	40	–	0	–	–	93
1970	4	17	–	29	13	13	45	82	100	79

Key Votes

1) Busing	AGN	6) Cmbodia Bmbg	FOR	11) Chkg Acct Intrst	AGN
2) Strip Mines	FOR	7) Bust Hwy Trust	AGN	12) End HISC (HUAC)	AGN
3) Cut Mil $	AGN	8) Farm Sub Lmt	AGN	13) Nixon Sewer Veto	FOR
4) Rev Shrg	AGN	9) School Prayr	AGN	14) Corp Cmpaign $	FOR
5) Pub TV $	AGN	10) Cnsumr Prot	AGN	15) Pol $ Disclosr	AGN

Election Results

1972 general:	David E. Satterfield III (D), unopposed		
1972 primary:	David E. Satterfield III (D), unopposed		
1970 general:	David E. Satterfield III (D)	73,104	(67%)
	J. Harvie Wilkinson III (R)	35,229	(32%)

FOURTH DISTRICT Political Background

The 4th district of Virginia presents a good example of the changes wrought in congressional districting by the one-man-one-vote rulings. In the past ten years, the 4th has shifted from an almost entirely rural, small-county district to a predominantly urban one. Before the 1965 redistricting, the district took in most of Southside Virginia, tobacco-growing country south of Richmond, which was a prime area for the breeding of slaves before the Civil War. This is the part of Virginia most like the rural Deep South, with small courthouse towns and the continuing dominance of a large black population by white landowners. Today, having been moved far to the east, the district has a majority of its population (56%) living in the Tidewater area. The 4th does not include Norfolk, but it does take in Portsmouth (pop. 110,000 and 40% black), Chesapeake (pop. 89,000 and 23% black), and a small part of Virginia Beach. As in the past, the district also includes the small metropolitan area around Petersburg, site of several major battles of the Civil War, just south of Richmond.

For 1972, the 4th lost eight counties, including Appomattox, where Lee surrendered to Grant. But of more significance for recent congressional politics, Appomattox is the home of Watkins M. Abbitt, ex-Representative from the 4th district. First elected in a 1948 special election, Abbitt was a leading member of the Byrd machine. He served as state Democratic Chairman in 1964—the last year the machine was in really solid control—and also rose to become a high-ranking member of the House Agriculture Committee. Despite a series of challenges from black or black-supported candidates, Abbitt won reelection easily. His chairmanship of the Tobacco Subcommittee was a nice asset during campaign time.

But when redistricting seemed certain to remove Appomattox County from the 4th, Abbitt, who had previously announced his intention to seek reelection, decided to retire. That he would have had to change his formal residence is probably not enough to explain Abbitt's decision; many Congressmen are quite willing to do that when necessary. The changed boundaries, however, would have made it difficult for him to win renomination and possibly reelection. The new district was no more heavily black (37%) than the old one—both were the most heavily black districts in Virginia—but the 4th lost rural blacks and picked up urban blacks, particularly in Portsmouth. Rural blacks are less likely to vote or at least less likely to vote contrary to wishes of important white men than their urban cousins. Earlier, blacks won majorities on the Petersburg City Council and the Surry County Board of Supervisors, auguries of change not to Abbitt's liking. Moreover, Democrat Abbitt wanted to support Nixon's reelection drive openly, and that support might well have cost Abbitt's seniority in the House had he stayed there.

So the 4th district was up for grabs in 1972. The two main contestants were Republican Robert Daniel, a young (36), well-to-do farmer and businessman from the Petersburg area, and Democrat state Delegate Robert Gibson from the Tidewater region. There were also two independents and a write-in candidate, who drew 5% of the votes. The result was a 47–37 victory for Daniel over Gibson. Virtually all of Daniel's margin came from his home Petersburg area, where he won virtually all the white votes and apparently some black votes as well. Meanwhile, Richard Nixon carried the district with 65%—high, but still his second-lowest percentage in a Virginia congressional district. Daniel's win, however, was not a matter of coattails, for he ran ahead of Nixon in some areas and far behind in others.

In the House, Daniel is a conservative member of the almost uniformly conservative Virginia delegation. He has also cultivated his constituency assiduously enough to suggest that he will have no trouble winning reelection. A former employee of the CIA, Daniel serves on the House Armed Services Committee, an assignment that may have something to do with the large naval installations in Portsmouth.

Census Data Pop. 465,738. Central city, 35%; suburban, 39%. Median family income, $8,294; families above $15,000: 13%; families below $3,000: 12%. Median years education, 10.4.

1972 Share of Federal Outlays $604,123,012

DOD	$299,245,706	HEW	$116,905,714
AEC	–	HUD	$14,226,140
NASA	$485,941	DOI	$639,419
DOT	$27,610,265	USDA	$27,992,529
		Other	$117,017,298

Federal Military-Industrial Commitments

DOD Installations Fort Lee AB (Petersburg). Naval Hospital (Portsmouth). Norfolk Naval Shipyard (Portsmouth). Fort Lee AF Station (Petersburg).

Economic Base Agriculture, notably hogs and sheep, and tobacco; finance, insurance and real estate; chemicals and allied products, especially industrial chemicals; paper and allied products; and electrical equipment and supplies, especially communication equipment.

The Voters

Registration 207,490 total. No party registration.
Median voting age 41.2
Employment profile White collar, 39%. Blue collar, 43%. Service, 15%. Farm, 3%.
Ethnic groups Black, 37%. Total foreign stock, 3%.

Presidential vote

1972	Nixon (R)	85,780	(65%)
	McGovern (D)	45,346	(35%)
1968	Nixon (R)	38,500	(28%)
	Humphrey (D)	48,549	(36%)
	Wallace (AI)	49,568	(36%)

Representative

Robert W. Daniel, Jr. (R) Elected 1972; b. Mar. 17, 1936, Richmond; home, Spring Grove; U. of Va., B.A., 1958; Columbia U., M.B.A., 1961; Army, 1959; married, three children; Episcopalian.

Career Financial analyst, 1961–62; Instructor, Economics, U. of Richmond School of Business, 1963; USCIA, 1964–68; Board of Conservation and Economic Development, Va., 1972; Prince George County Planning Commission, 1972; farmer, businessman.

Offices 1331 LHOB, 202-225-6365. Also Rm. 209, P.O. Bldg., Petersburg 23803, 703-732-2544, and Rm. 215, Fed. Bldg., Portsmouth 23704, 703-441-6797.

Administrative Assistant Thad S. Murray

Committees

Armed Services (19th); Sub: No. 3.

Group Ratings: Newly Elected

Key Votes

1) Busing	NE	6) Cmbodia Bmbg	FOR	11) Chkg Acct Intrst	AGN		
2) Strip Mines	NE	7) Bust Hwy Trust	AGN	12) End HISC (HUAC)	AGN		
3) Cut Mil $	NE	8) Farm Sub Lmt	NE	13) Nixon Sewer Veto	FOR		
4) Rev Shrg	NE	9) School Prayr	NE	14) Corp Cmpaign $	NE		
5) Pub TV $	NE	10) Cnsumr Prot	NE	15) Pol $ Disclosr	NE		

Election Results

1972 general:	Robert W. Daniel, Jr. (R)	57,520	(47%)
	Robert E. Gibson (D)	45,796	(38%)
	Robert R. Hardy (Ind.)	8,668	(7%)
	William E. Ward (Write-in)	6,172	(5%)
	John G. Vonetes (Ind.)	4,003	(3%)
1972 primary:	Robert W. Daniel, Jr. (R), unopposed		

FIFTH DISTRICT Political Background

The 5th district of Virginia covers most of Southside Virginia, from the Richmond city limits out to the Blue Ridge near Roanoke. The eastern counties are flat and humid, and the most heavily black part of the district. Slowly, as the land gets hillier, it rises into the Piedmont, and moves past textile and furniture manufacturing cities like Danville (pop. 46,000) and Martinsville (pop. 19,000). As one goes west, there is more livestock and less tobacco, more whites with mountain accents and fewer blacks. Altogether, the 5th is only 29% black—significantly less than the figure for blacks in the 4th district, which takes in the Southside counties just to the east.

Southside Virginia was always a stronghold of Byrd Democrats, with its politics firmly in the hands of prosperous bankers and planters who still remember the Civil War. More recently, Southside has fallen into the racially polarized voting patterns that characterize the Deep South. This is one of the two Virginia districts (the other is the 4th) that went for George Wallace in 1968, and the one where the Alabamian got his highest percentage. And despite Southside's Democratic heritage, the 5th was Republican challenger William Scott's best district in his 1972 race against moderate Democrat Sen. William Spong.

For 15 years, until his retirement in 1968, Congressman William Tuck represented the 5th in the House. A former Governor (1946–50) and Byrd-machine stalwart, Tuck was an ardent segregationist and an equally ardent opponent of the one-man-one-vote doctrine (which, as it happens, hasn't much changed the political balance in his old district). The current incumbent is a more up-to-date conservative Democrat, W. C. (Dan) Daniel, a former executive at Danville's Dan River Mills and a former national commander of the American Legion. In his first election, Daniel got spirited competition from both Republican and independent candidates, who held his share of votes down to 55%. In 1970, the incumbent Congressman rolled up a margin more typical in traditional Southside Virginia—73%; and in 1972, he was unopposed. Daniel is one of three Virginia members of the House Armed Services Committee, where he is a determined and unswerving supporter of the panel's pro-Pentagon majority.

Census Data Pop. 462,807. Central city, 0%; suburban, 13%. Median family income, $7,471; families above $15,000: 10%; families below $3,000: 15%. Median years education, 9.4.

1972 Share of Federal Outlays $265,414,955

DOD	$30,100,097	HEW	$127,740,045
AEC	$161,779	HUD	$2,262,991
NASA	$40,302	DOI	$467,050
DOT	$5,702,023	USDA	$31,187,271
		Other	$67,753,397

Federal Military-Industrial Commitments

No installations or contractors receiving prime awards greater than $5,000,000.

Economic Base Agriculture, notably tobacco, dairy products and cattle; textile mill products; furniture and fixtures; lumber and wood products; and fabricated metal products.

The Voters

Registration 218,947 total. No party registration.
Median voting age 43.2
Employment profile White collar, 32%. Blue collar, 52%. Service, 10%. Farm, 6%.
Ethnic groups Black, 29%. Total foreign stock 1%.

Presidential vote

1972	Nixon (R)	101,546	(72%)
	McGovern (D)	39,194	(28%)
1968	Nixon (R)	54,213	(35%)
	Humphrey (D)	40,770	(26%)
	Wallace (AI)	59,451	(38%)

Representative

W. C. (Dan) **Daniel** (D) Elected 1968; b. May 12, 1914, Chatham; home, Danville; Dan River Textile School; married, one child; Baptist.

Career Various positions including Asst. to Bd. Chm., Dan River Mills, Inc., 1939–68; Va. Legislature, 1959–68.

Offices 1705 LHOB, 202-225-4711. Also 202 P.O. Bldg., Danville 24541, 703-792-1280, and 104-A High St., Farmville, 703-392-6644.

Administrative Assistant W. Fred Fletcher

Committees

Armed Services (17th); Subs: No. 2; Sp. Sub. on Armed Services Investigating; Human Relations.

Group Ratings

	ADA	COPE	LWV	RIPON	NFU	LCV	CFA	NAB	NSI	ACA
1972	0	10	17	31	33	20	0	90	100	100
1971	3	8	22	28	47	–	0	–	–	93
1970	0	17	–	24	31	33	43	75	100	79

Key Votes

1) Busing	AGN	6) Cmbodia Bmbg	FOR	11) Chkg Acct Intrst	AGN
2) Strip Mines	FOR	7) Bust Hwy Trust	AGN	12) End HISC (HUAC)	AGN
3) Cut Mil $	AGN	8) Farm Sub Lmt	AGN	13) Nixon Sewer Veto	FOR
4) Rev Shrg	AGN	9) School Prayr	FOR	14) Corp Cmpaign $	FOR
5) Pub TV $	AGN	10) Cnsumr Prot	AGN	15) Pol $ Disclosr	AGN

Election Results

1972 general:	W. C. Daniel (D), unopposed		
1972 primary:	W. C. Daniel (D), unopposed		
1970 general:	W. C. Daniel (D)	54,261	(73%)
	Allen T. St. Clair, Jr. (R)	20,029	(27%)

SIXTH DISTRICT Political Background

The most Republican part of Virginia is the great valley west of the Blue Ridge around Roanoke (pop. 92,000). Because this fertile land was never given over to slave-tended antebellum plantations, the hardy farmers here were not especially sympathetic to the cause of the Confederacy. In the hundred years following the Civil War, the Roanoke area was usually the most Republican—or least Democratic—region of the state; it was always suspicious of the Byrd machine, and to some extent, of its close alliance with Virginia's largest and most powerful economic interests. Though the boundaries have shifted many times in the last two decades, the district has always centered on Roanoke. Also in the district are much of the valley and the mountains to the north, and the more Democratic Southside city of Lynchburg (pop. 54,000). Ordinarily, the 6th is the state's most Republican district. It was the only one in Virginia to give Richard Nixon an absolute majority on 1968, and in 1972, presented the Republican with his largest Virginia percentage.

Moreover, the 6th has not elected a Democratic Congressman since 1950. In 1952, out of distaste for the national Democratic ticket, Harry Byrd's organization quietly pass the word on the grapevine that people should vote Republican. Byrd's "golden silence" carried the Commonwealth for Eisenhower; it has since gone for every Republican presidential nominee except Barry Goldwater. At the same time, aggressive young Republican candidates ran for Congress in the mountain and suburban Washington districts, and, in those days of long coattails, won.

One of them was Richard H. Poff, a 29-year-old lawyer who unseated a complacent 66-year-old Democratic incumbent in 1952. In the years that followed, Poff began to win reelection by large margins; so the Byrd machine, pleased with his conservative record, abandoned any serious attempt to defeat him. By the early 1970s, before he was 50, Poff was the second-ranking Republican on the House Judiciary Committee. He voted a pretty solid conservative line, including opposition to civil rights legislation. But he also won enough respect for his knowledgeability and fairness to be named Vice-Chairman of the National Commission on Reform of the Federal Criminal Law. Poff helped to select the commission's staff, among whom was an unknown attorney named John Dean III.

In Nixon's first term, Poff's name suddenly appeared in speculative stories about nominations to the Supreme Court. It was widely known that Nixon was seeking an appointee from the South, and one, moreover, with a definite background in the Republican party. Poff, therefore, was apparently given serious consideration. Liberal attacks ensued on a possible Poff nomination, and Poff retreated, withdrawing his name from consideration.

In an even bigger surprise, he soon thereafter announced that he would not seek reelection to Congress. Though the Democratic legislature moved his home town of Radford out of the 6th district, Poff could have easily established residence in Roanoke. There was absolutely no question about his vote-getting credentials; in 1970, he won 75% of the votes. Rumors of a federal judgeship circulated, but as it happened, Poff was appointed instead to the Virginia Court of Appeals—the Commonwealth's highest judicial body—by Gov. Linwood Holton.

Poff's decision to leave Congress left the seat to M. Caldwell Butler, former Republican leader in the Virginia House of Delegates and a former law partner of Linwood Holton. Caldwell, like Holton, is a moderate mountain Republican, loath to exploit the race issue for votes in any way. Otherwise, he usually supports the policies of the Nixon Administration. He won rather easy election in 1972, as he carried all the counties in the district and all but two small independent cities (which have the same status as counties in Virginia). Butler was pressed fairly hard in Roanoke, but in all likelihood, the incumbent will win future elections with less worry.

Census Data Pop. 464,356. Central city, 31%; suburban, 25%. Median family income, $8,594; families above $15,000: 14%; families below $3,000: 10%. Median years education, 11.3.

1972 Share of Federal Outlays $300,384,087

DOD	$29,391,579	HEW	$130,240,927
AEC	$310,512	HUD	$2,130,278
NASA	$107,809	DOI	$3,995,743
DOT	$8,465,207	USDA	$11,989,008
		Other	$113,753,024

Federal Military-Industrial Commitments

DOD Installations Bedford AF Station (Bedford).

Economic Base Finance, insurance and real estate; apparel and other textile products, especially women's and misses' outerwear; agriculture, notably cattle, dairy products and poultry; food and kindred products; and machinery.

The Voters

Registration 201,595 total. No party registration.
Median voting age 43.7
Employment profile White collar, 43%. Blue collar, 42%. Service, 13%. Farm, 2%.
Ethnic groups Black, 12%. Total foreign stock, 2%.

Presidential vote

1972	Nixon (R)	104,443	(74%)
	McGovern (D)	35,356	(25%)
1968	Nixon (R)	74,741	(53%)
	Humphrey (D)	34,679	(24%)
	Wallace (AI)	32,625	(23%)

Representative

M. Caldwell Butler (R) Elected 1972; b. June 22, 1925, Roanoka; home, Roanoke; U. of Richmond, B.A.; U. of Va. Law School, J.D.; married, four children; Episcopalian.

Career Former Minority Leader, Va. Gen. Assembly; Former Leader, Repub. Caucus of Va. Gen. Assembly.

Offices 329 CHOB, 202-225-5431. Also P.O. Bldg., Roanoke, 703-344-3406; and P.O. Bldg., Waynesboro, 703-942-7758; and Fed. Bldg., Lynchburg, 703-845-1378.

Administrative Assistant Charles A. Wilson

Committees

Judiciary (12th); Subs: No. 2 (Claims) (Ranking Mbr.); No. 4 (Bankruptcy and Civil Rights Oversight).

Group Ratings: Newly Elected

Key Votes

1) Busing	NE	6) Cmbodia Bmbg	FOR	11) Chkg Acct Intrst	AGN
2) Strip Mines	NE	7) Bust Hwy Trust	AGN	12) End HISC (HUAC)	AGN
3) Cut Mil $	NE	8) Farm Sub Lmt	NE	13) Nixon Sewer Veto	FOR
4) Rev Shrg	NE	9) School Prayr	NE	14) Corp Cmpaign $	NE
5) Pub TV $	NE	10) Cnsumr Prot	NE	15) Pol $ Disclosr	NE

Election Results

1972 general:	M. Caldwell Butler (R)	75,189	(55%)
	Willis M. Anderson (D)	53,928	(39%)
	Roy R. White (Ind.)	8,531	(6%)
1972 primary:	M. Caldwell Butler (R), unopposed		

SEVENTH DISTRICT Political Background

East and west of the Blue Ridge Mountains in northern Virginia lies some of the most beautiful country in the United States. And according to some reports, this part of America is very good for those worried about their health. The Shenandoah Valley, west of the mountains, also contains some of the nation's most productive farmland, which Union forces took some pains to cut off from the rest of the Confederacy during the Civil War. East of the mountains are the gentle hills of the Piedmont, which contain the headwaters of the Rappahannock and Pamunkey rivers. The megalopolis has yet to reach the 7th district of Virginia. The region's major cities—Winchester (pop. 14,000) and Harrisonburg (pop. 14,000) in the Valley, and Charlottesville (pop. 38,000) and Fredericksburg (pop. 14,000) on the Piedmont— still retain a colonial ambience; or so it is in the narrow streets of the downtowns, though a McDonald's strip culture has begun to develop on the outskirts.

The 7th district of Virginia is the home of three Presidents (Jefferson, Madison, and Monroe) and the scene of more carnage and killing in the Civil War then any other area of comparable size in the nation. The district is also the home turf of the twentieth-century Byrd dynasty. The late Sen. Harry Byrd, Sr., developed one of the world's largest and most productive apple farms in the Shenandoah Valley, and also acquired newspapers in Winchester and Harrisonburg; his son, the current Senator, retains these interests. The 7th district today continues to be a Byrd stronghold—steadily, but never raucously, conservative. The district supported Sen. Byrd with 61% of its votes when he ran for reelection as an independent in 1970. In other races, it has quietly switched from its traditional allegiance of Democratic conservatism to Nixon Republicanism.

The shift is nicely illustrated by recent congressional elections in the 7th. In 1970, when Byrd announced that he was not interested in the Democratic nomination for Senator (see Virginia state write-up), incumbent 7th-district Congressman John Marsh, a Byrd Democrat, made a similar statement. First elected in 1962 by a narrow margin, Marsh won only 54% of the votes in 1964. The speculation was that Marsh wanted to be drafted as the Democratic nominee, or to be launched as an independent candidate for reelection. But neither of these things happened. The local Democrats, with their Byrd ranks depleted and filled with liberal activists, nominated liberal gentleman farmer and former Ambassador to El Salvador, Murat Williams. And the Byrd loyalists preferred, it seemed, to go Republican rather than risk a Williams victory in a three-way race.

The Republican candidate combined impeccable party credentials and a solid Byrd tinge. J. Kenneth Robinson, a Winchester lawyer, was the man who nearly beat Marsh in 1962; three years later, he succeeded Harry Byrd, Jr., in the state Senate. Robinson tagged Williams a liberal, made the label stick, and of course won the election. The interesting thing is that his share of the votes—62%—was an almost exact parallel to Byrd's showing in the district. The Byrd machine, driven out of the Democratic party, seems to have reappeared in Republican guise.

Republicans now hold seven of Virginia's ten congressional seats; twenty-two years ago, the entire delegation was Democratic. Robinson's victory was typical of Republican strategy: running a strong, conservative candidate with good local ties whenever a Democratic incumbent retires or is beaten in a primary. Since 1952, only one of the seven seats now held by Republicans was won by a challenger who defeated a Democratic incumbent. Once in office, Robinson has given the

Nixon Administration solid support. So the Robinson victory and others like it account for the record compiled by the Virginia delegation—in 1973, the highest rate of support for Nixon programs.

Census Data Pop. 465,342. Central city, 0%; suburban, 8%. Median family income, $7,952; families above $15,000: 13%; families below $3,000: 12%. Median years education, 10.5.

1972 Share of Federal Outlays $338,719,255

DOD	$82,656,781	HEW	$141,076,276
AEC	$373,689	HUD	$2,297,844
NASA	$493,737	DOI	$2,944,999
DOT	$13,600,575	USDA	$21,995,698
		Other	$73,279,656

Federal Military-Industrial Commitments

DOD Contractors Sperry Rand (Charlottesville), $8.440m: shipboard navigational equipment. *DOD Installations* Army Vint Hills Farm Station (Warrenton).

Economic Base Agriculture, notably cattle, dairy products and poultry; finance, insurance and real estate; food and kindred products; apparel and other textile products; and lumber and wood products. Also higher education (Univ. of Virginia).

The Voters

Registration 207,073 total. No party registration.
Median voting age 42.4
Employment profile White collar, 40%. Blue collar, 42%. Service, 13%. Farm, 5%.
Ethnic groups Black, 15%. Total foreign stock, 3%.

Presidential vote

1972	Nixon (R)	104,720	(73%)
	McGovern (D)	39,691	(27%)
1968	Nixon (R)	66,452	(50%)
	Humphrey (D)	37,190	(28%)
	Wallace (AI)	29,949	(22%)

Representative

J. Kenneth Robinson (R) Elected 1970; b. May 14, 1916, Winchester; home, Winchester; Va. Polytechnic Inst., B.S., 1937; Army, WWII; married, seven children; Society of Friends.

Career Fruit grower; Dir., Winchester Cold Storage Co.; owner, J. K. Robinson's Orchard; Dir., Winchester Apple Growers Assn., Green Chemical Co.; Sec., Treas., R & T Packing Corp., Inc.; Va. Senate, 1965–70; Chm., Repub. delegation to 1968, 1969 Gen. Assembly.

Offices 418 CHOB, 202-225-6561. Also 36 Rouss Ave., Winchester 22601, 703-667-0990.

Administrative Assistant Chris Mathisen

Committees

Appropriations (18th); Subs: Labor, Health, Education and Welfare; Agriculture, Environmental and Consumer Protection.

Group Ratings

	ADA	COPE	LWV	RIPON	NFU	LCV	CFA	NAB	NSI	ACA
1972	0	9	17	31	29	7	0	92	100	100
1971	5	17	22	50	20	–	13	–	–	93

Key Votes

1) Busing	AGN	6) Cmbodia Bmbg	FOR	11) Chkg Acct Intrst	AGN
2) Strip Mines	FOR	7) Bust Hwy Trust	AGN	12) End HISC (HUAC)	AGN
3) Cut Mil $	AGN	8) Farm Sub Lmt	ABS	13) Nixon Sewer Veto	FOR
4) Rev Shrg	AGN	9) School Prayr	FOR	14) Corp Cmpaign $	FOR
5) Pub TV $	AGN	10) Cnsumr Prot	AGN	15) Pol $ Disclosr	AGN

Election Results

1972 general:	J. Kenneth Robinson (R)	89,120	(66%)
	Murat Willis Williams (D)	45,513	(34%)
1972 primary:	J. Kenneth Robinson (R), unopposed		
1970 general:	J. Kenneth Robinson (R)	52,619	(62%)
	Murat Willis Williams (D)	32,617	(38%)

EIGHTH DISTRICT Political Background

The 8th district is the fastest-growing congressional district in Virginia. Indeed, only 11 other districts in the country experienced faster population growth during the 1960s. In rough terms, the 8th comprises the southern portion of Virginia's share of the Washington suburbs—a portion that grew some 66% between the Census Bureau headcounts of 1960 and 1970. Just across the Potomac from Washington is Alexandria (pop. 110,000); it is a city whose restored section recalls the Potomac tobacco port that George Washington once frequented, and which has a fairly large black community (14%). It also contains huge new high-rise apartment buildings. South of Alexandria is Fairfax County; here the suburban communities of Springfield, Annandale, and Mount Vernon are included in the 8th. The slightly larger remainder of Fairfax lies in the 10th district. Then follows Prince William County, which more than doubled in population during the 1960s. It is here, to suburbs like Dale City, that low-salaried federal workers have been moving; these people cannot afford housing in the more expensive suburbs, closer to Washington. The 8th also contains a small portion of rural Stafford County, south of Prince William.

The growth of the area has been generated, of course, by the principal employer of the district's residents, the federal government. Some 29% of the wage-earners bring home a federal paycheck, and the size of those checks underwent rapid increase during the 1960's.

The area boom has increased suburban Virginia property values, but it has also increased property taxes, with the need for more local services. Recently, the Democrats won control of the Fairfax County Board of Supervisors on a slow-growth platform. The plan was to hold down growth by a leisurely issuance of sewer permits, though, at this writing, the idea has been frustrated by a local court decision. Most of the new suburban homes are going up in less affluent Prince William, where the slow-growth philosophy has not yet taken root.

But no kind of unconventional politics has enjoyed much success in 8th-district congressional elections. The district assumed its current shape in 1972; prior to that, it spread far into the Piedmont countryside. Until 1966, the 8th was represented by Howard W. Smith—known as Judge Smith, since he had once served as a judge in Alexandria. Judge Smith was Chairman of the House Committee on Rules from 1955 to 1967; an unbending conservative, Smith used the power of the committee to schedule bills and restrict amendments to kill legislation not to his liking. The power of the Chairman was to some extent reduced in 1961, when the Kennedy Administration and Speaker Sam Rayburn led the House to enlarge the committee's membership. On occasion, however, the Judge was still able to stop the flow of legislation by repairing to his prosperous dairy farm in northern Virginia; in his absence the committee could not meet.

Judge Smith was caught napping, however, in the 1966 Democratic primary. At age 83, he perhaps failed to notice the sudden enfranchisement of blacks after the passage of the Voting

Rights Act of 1965, or the abolition of the poll tax, or the one-man-one-vote rule that required the attachment of more suburban territory to his constituency. At any rate, Smith was defeated in the 1966 Democratic primary by liberal George Rawlings. The liberal candidate did not fare as well in the general election—the Judge's old friends switched to the Republican nominee and slapped the electoral wrists of the upstart Democrat.

This set of circumstances is how William Lloyd Scott, now a United States Senator, first made it to the Congress. Scott, a longtime government lawyer who practiced briefly in Fairfax, had previously run for office as a Republican, with no success whatever. In 1966, he would have surely lost again had the Judge not chanced to be upset. But such luck is behind many congressional careers; and Scott, a fervent, hard-working, if not sophisticated conservative, managed to win the district's loyalties in the next two elections. He then upset Democratic Sen. William Spong in 1972 (see Virginia state write-up).

Scott's departure left the seat open again. This time there was a plethora of candidates—four men in the Democratic primary, two in the Republican primary, and two independents in the general election. But the race boiled down to a contest between Republican Delegate Stanford Parris and Democratic Fairfax County District Attorney Robert Horan. The Democrat was a law-and-order type and a supporter of Nixon Administration policies in Vietnam. Horan forfeited some liberal votes, while at the same time was unable to recoup enough conservative ballots to beat Parris. For his part, Parris typified the attitudes of many Virginia suburbanites toward central-city Washington; he joked, for example, that the 14th Street bridge between Arlington and Washington was the longest bridge in the world, stretching, as it did, from Virginia to Africa. Parris apparently did not know that a reporter from the *Washington Post* was present when he made his little joke.

But Parris' remark and his solidly conservative voting record may be less important at reelection time than the quality of his constituency service. If they want to survive politically, suburban Washington Congressmen are at least as much ombudsmen as legislators. Congressional offices are only a local call away, and many constituents are federal employees who hold many work-a-day grievances against the policies of the U.S. government. Parris has reportedly performed his casework duties with admirable dispatch; accordingly, he must be considered the favorite for reelection as long as he seeks it.

Census Data Pop. 464,038. Central city, 0%; suburban, 98%. Median family income, $13,146; families above $15,000: 40%; families below $3,000: 4%. Median years education, 12.7.

1972 Share of Federal Outlays $868,240,114

DOD	$615,444,551	HEW	$67,412,695
AEC	$113,810	HUD	$1,199,939
NASA	$2,212,330	DOI	$10,766,979
DOT	$45,630,472	USDA	$12,571,826
		Other	$112,887,512

Federal Military-Industrial Commitments

DOD Contractors Susquehanna Corp. (Alexandria), $6.923m: rocket motors and propellants. RCA (Springfield), $5.610m: technical services for shipboard rocket and gun fire control systems. Beiro AA Development Corp. (Fort Belvoir), $5.124m: unspecified.
DOD Installations Fort Belvoir AB (Alexandria). Cameron Army Station (Alexandria). Marine Corps Air Station (Quantico). Marine Corps Development and Education Command (Quantico). Naval Hospital (Quantico).

Economic Base Finance, insurance and real estate; electrical equipment and supplies; agriculture, notably dairy products and cattle; and tourism.

The Voters

Registration 109,855 total. No party registration.
Median voting age 36.2
Employment profile White collar, 68%. Blue collar, 21%. Service, 10%. Farm, 1%.
Ethnic groups Black, 7%. Spanish, 2%. Total foreign stock, 11%. Germany, UK, 1% each.

Presidential vote

1972	Nixon (R)	94,715	(67%)
	McGovern (D)	46,870	(33%)
1968	Nixon (R)	47,505	(45%)
	Humphrey (D)	39,796	(38%)
	Wallace (AI)	17,375	(17%)

Representative

Stanford E. Parris (R) Elected 1972; b. Sept. 9, 1929, Champaign, Ill.; home, Fairfax Station; U. of Ill., B.S.; George Washington U., J.D.; USAF; married, three children; Episcopalian.

Career Partner, Swayze, Parris, Tydings & Bryant, Fairfax; Pres., Woodbridge Chrysler-Plymouth Corp, Woodbridge; Pres., Flying Circus Aerodrome, Inc., Bealeton; Va. House of Delegates, 1969–72.

Offices 509 CHOB, 202-225-4376. Also 9257 Lee Ave., Manassas 22110, 703-361-8223.

Administrative Assistant Charles G. Drago

Committees

Government Operations (13th). Subs: Government Activities; Legal and Monetary Affairs.

Science and Astronautics (10th); Subs: Aeronautics and Space Technology; Energy; Science, Research, and Development.

Group Ratings: Newly Elected

Key Votes

1) Busing	NE	6) Cmbodia Bmbg	FOR	11) Chkg Acct Intrst	AGN
2) Strip Mines	NE	7) Bust Hwy Trust	AGN	12) End HISC (HUAC)	AGN
3) Cut Mil $	NE	8) Farm Sub Lmt	NE	13) Nixon Sewer Veto	FOR
4) Rev Shrg	NE	9) School Prayr	NE	14) Corp Cmpaign $	NE
5) Pub TV $	NE	10) Cnsumr Prot	NE	15) Pol $ Disclosr	NE

Election Results

1972 general:	Stanford E. Parris (R)	60,446	(44%)
	Robert F. Horan, Jr. (D)	51,444	(38%)
	William R. Durland (Ind.)	18,654	(14%)
	Robert E. Harris (Ind.)	5,553	(4%)
1972 primary:	Stanford E. Parris (R)	7,144	(63%)
	James Tate (R)	4,120	(37%)

NINTH DISTRICT Political Background

The southwest corner of Virginia is perhaps the only part of the nation known in ordinary discourse by the number of its congressional district: the Fighting 9th. Part of the Appalachian mountain country, the 9th probably has more in common with neighboring eastern Kentucky and Tennessee than with the rest of Virginia. It does not, however, constitute one of the poorer regions of Appalachia. The district was never as dependent on coal as southern West Virginia; moreover, it has recently benefited from some economic development in the valley that reaches from the Shenandoah to Knoxville, Tennessee, along Interstate 81. The mountain area of southwest Virginia is a place with its own cultural traditions, where the federal government still means the hated revenuers. And every August it hosts the Galax Old Time Fiddlers' Convention, where fiddlers, and guitar, banjo, and mandolin pickers, from several states around make some of the most exhilarating music ever thought up out of the head of man.

The Fighting 9th never did cotton much to the Byrd organization. In fact, its Republican tradition goes back to the days before the Civil War, when the virtually all-white mountaineers had little use for slavery and the Confederacy. Moreover, the local breed of Democrats date mostly from the Mine Workers' struggles of the 1930s, and therefore have little in common with the Democratic politics practices by the Byrd men. Even as late as 1970, this was the only part of Virginia that Harry Byrd, Jr. could not carry when he ran as an independent for reelection to the Senate. At this writing, it is a prime area of contention in the 1973 gubernatorial race. Independent Lt. Gov. Henry Howell has tried to appeal to the latent populism of the Fighting 9th, and its opposition to the sales tax on food in particular. Meanwhile, ex-Gov. (1962–66) Mills Godwin has tried to underscore the area's current Republican inclinations, now that he is running as a Republican and not, as he did in the past, as a Byrd Democrat.

For 12 years, from 1955 to 1967, the Fighting 9th was represented by Virginia's only recent liberal Democratic Congressman, W. Pat Jennings. In 1966, however, given the negative sentiment that had built up against the Johnson Administration, Jennings was unseated by the man he defeated in 1954 and 1956, William Wampler. Jennings went on to become Clerk of the House of Representatives; his appointment to the post was taken as a form of patronage to the liberal Democratic Study Group, and therefore something of a milepost in the progress made by the reform organization in the House.

Wampler, who was first elected to Congress in 1952 at age 26, reentered the House at age 40. His was a notable political comeback: Wampler was not enticed to stay in the capital by the blandishments of Washington, but went back home to the 9th. It probably did not hurt that he married the sister of Tennessee Sen. Howard Baker, who won his seat the same year Wampler recaptured his.

This time Wampler went about making sure that he would not be defeated again. His previous service gave him a seniority edge over other members newly elected in 1966; he is now the second-ranking Republican on the Agriculture Committee, behind 65-year-old Charles Teague of California. With Jennings happily ensconced in the Clerk's office, Wampler has been able to increase his share of the Fighting 9th's votes in every election since 1966. Redistricting added several cities and counties to Wampler's constituency, but the additions failed to prevent the incumbent—a solid Nixon conservative—from winning 72% of the votes in 1972, a margin 4% better than the President himself.

Census Data Pop. 465,136. Central city, 0%; suburban, 0%. Median family income, $6,608; families above $15,000: 7%; families below $3,000: 19%. Median years education, 8.8.

1972 Share of Federal Outlays $437,881,394

DOD	$116,316,000	HEW	$171,701,920
AEC	$55,973	HUD	$3,242,805
NASA	$518,302	DOI	$4,048,692
DOT	$45,568,211	USDA	$25,194,295
		Other	$71,235,196

Federal Military-Industrial Commitments

DOD Contractors Hercules, Inc. (Radford), $83.710m: operation of Radford Army Ammunition plant.

Economic Base Agriculture, notably cattle, dairy products and tobacco; bituminous coal mining; textile mill products, especially knitting mill products; apparel and other textile products, especially men's and boys' furnishings and women's and misses' outerwear; and finance, insurance and real estate.

The Voters

Registration 233,174 total. No party registration.
Median voting age 42.7
Employment profile White collar, 32%. Blue collar, 52%. Service, 11%. Farm, 5%.
Ethnic groups Black, 2%. Total foreign stock, 1%.

Presidential vote

1972	Nixon (R)	95,065	(68%)
	McGovern (D)	44,540	(32%)
1968	Nixon (R)	75,781	(49%)
	Humphrey (D)	53,436	(35%)
	Wallace (AI)	25,105	(16%)

Representative

William Creed Wampler (R) Elected 1966; b. April 21, 1926, Pennington Gap; home, Bristol; Va. Polytechnic Inst., B.S., 1948; U. of Va., 1949–50; Navy, WWII; married, two children; Presbyterian.

Career Pres., Va. Young Repub.'s Fed., 1950–52; U.S. House of Reps., 1952–54; Chm., Va. 9th Dist. Repub. Com., 1965–66; furniture and carpet business; newspaperman; Sp. Asst. to Gen. Mgr., Atomic Energy Commission; Bristol Redev. and Housing Auth., 1965–66, Bristol Utilities Bd., 1966.

Offices 323 CHOB, 202-225-3861. Also 324 Cumberland St., P.O. Box 890, Bristol 24201, 703-669-9451.

Administrative Assistant J. Ray Dotson

Committees

Agriculture (2nd); Subs: Dairy and Poultry (Ranking Mbr.); Oilseeds and Rice (Ranking Mbr.); Tobacco.

Group Ratings

	ADA	COPE	LWV	RIPON	NFU	LCV	CFA	NAB	NSI	ACA
1972	6	40	27	31	67	40	0	83	100	85
1971	8	17	38	53	43	–	38	–	–	82
1970	16	0	–	41	31	25	55	92	100	84

Key Votes

1) Busing	AGN	6) Cmbodia Bmbg	FOR	11) Chkg Acct Intrst	AGN
2) Strip Mines	FOR	7) Bust Hwy Trust	AGN	12) End HISC (HUAC)	AGN
3) Cut Mil $	FOR	8) Farm Sub Lmt	AGN	13) Nixon Sewer Veto	AGN
4) Rev Shrg	FOR	9) School Prayr	FOR	14) Corp Cmpaign $	FOR
5) Pub TV $	AGN	10) Cnsumr Prot	AGN	15) Pol $ Disclosr	AGN

Election Results

1972 general:	William C. Wampler (R)	98,178	(72%)
	Zane Dale Christian (D)	36,000	(26%)
	Nicholas Ventura (Ind.)	2,292	(2%)
1972 primary:	William C. Wampler (R), unopposed		
1970 general:	William C. Wampler (R)	53,950	(61%)
	Tate C. Buchanan (D)	34,690	(39%)

TENTH DISTRICT Political Background

There are three things to remember about the 10th congressional district of Virginia. First, it contains more federal employees than any other district in the United States—some 31% of its wage-earners and salary-earners are employed by Uncle Sam. Second, in terms of median family income, the 10th is the seventh-richest congressional district in the country—the consequence of the skyrocketing federal salaries of the last decade. Third, the 10th is overwhelmingly white; over 95% of its citizens are so classified.

Those three things tell you most of what there is to know about the 10th district, and about its Congressmen, Joel T. Broyhill. The 10th includes Arlington, a little more than half of Fairfax

County, the small independent cities of Falls Church and Fairfax, and Loudon County. The last is exurban, between 30 and 70 miles from Washington; the green hills of Loudon have just begun to experience the effects of suburbanization. Arlington, of course, is the site of the Pentagon, and also of two booming high-rise office districts, Rosslyn and Crystal City. These have kept Arlington property taxes the lowest in the Washington metropolitan area. Arlington was once Washington's bedroom community; today, more of its residents work in the suburbs than in the District. It has also become age-segregated. Affluent people of child-bearing age have most often chosen to move to Fairfax County—a phenomenon that has made its national and congressional politics steadily more conservative. Arlington, meanwhile, appears to be moving slightly to the left. One discordant note in the Fairfax landscape is the "new town" of Reston, out near Dulles Airport. This planned city seems to attract liberals; it went heavily for McGovern and against Broyhill in 1972. Though it had only 5,000 residents in 1970, it will house 75,000 by 1980.

All in all, the Virginia suburbs of Washington are slightly more conservative and Republican than the District's Maryland environs. One reason may be the differing character of the federal bureaucracies located in each. In Maryland's affluent Montgomery County (see Maryland 8), the biggest local federal employer is the National Institutes of Health, whose employees can be expected to support Democrats or liberal Republicans sympathetic to high health research expenditures. On the other hand, the Pentagon is the largest federal employer in the 10th district of Virginia; employees of the Defense Department can be expected to favor conservatives who back high military budgets.

The 10th district was created for the 1952 elections. It has had one and only one Congressman, Republican Joel Broyhill. In the Eisenhower landslide, Broyhill, a prosperous Arlington real estate developer, won by just 322 votes, and he has hung on since despite spirited opposition; in 1964, he won by just 2,128 votes. Broyhill's main secret of political success is constituency service. The Congressman estimates that he has aided more than 100,000 10th-district residents in his 20-plus years in office. There are few congressional offices in which the demand for services is so high, given the number of federal employees in Broyhill's district; and there are few indeed that take care of constituents' needs and complaints with more efficiency.

Broyhill's other great asset is membership on the House District of Columbia Committee, where he demonstrates an unwavering devotion to the interests of his suburban constituents. Broyhill is a deeply conservative man, an advocate of hard-line crackdowns on crime and alleged welfare chiselers. The Congressman has long been an opponent of home rule for the black-majority District. In 1973, when the District Committee seemed disposed to report a home-rule bill, Broyhill suddenly proposed statehood for Washington—a simple tactic explicitly designed to embarrass home-rule advocates and to defeat them on the floor if possible.

Broyhill also remembers that many of his constituents are auto commuters. He stands firmly for the right of every federal employee to a free, government-subsidized parking place; moreover, he has staunchly backed construction of Interstate 66 from the Capital Beltway through Arlington to the 10th district. Arlington residents in the path of the proposed freeway fiercely oppose the idea, but Fairfax County citizens—considerably more numerous and fed up with traffic jams, and unwilling to use mass transit—support the idea just as strenuously. Broyhill, whose name appears constantly in the Washington press, is the most controversial Washington area Congressman: hated by thousands, and loved, in the 10th district at least, by a few thousand more.

Most Congressmen who are longtime Representatives of marginal districts attempt to modulate positions on issues to keep themselves in the good graces of all their constituents. Broyhill does not bother. When he feels strongly about an issue—and he usually does—he presses ahead aggressively without caring whom he might antagonize. As a result, Broyhill never wins by the giant margins usually enjoyed by Congressmen with comparable seniority. In fact, Broyhill has never received as much as 60% of the vote. In 1972, he got only 56%, while Richard Nixon carried the district with 64%; most Republican Congressmen having similar tenure and operations of constituency service actually ran ahead of the President in 1972. But Broyhill has managed to create a solid block of 35% to 40% of the district's voters who are bitterly opposed to him—along with the 50% or so who will vote for him no matter what. Every two years, the liberal Democrats of the 10th put on a concerted effort to defeat Broyhill, and every two years they fail.

Will it be another story in 1974? As of now, the year looks like a Democratic one. But Broyhill has survived Democratic landslides before, if only by narrow margins. On balance, demographic changes favor Broyhill for 1974, when he will most certainly enter the campaign as the favorite. These 10th district campaigns center on the Congressman's positions on local and District issues, his constituency service, and his generally conservative outlook. What is often overlooked is Broyhill's status as the number-three ranking Republican on the House Ways and Means Committee. It is a measure of his determination and clout—and the importance of the District Committee to his constituents—that Broyhill is the only member of Ways and Means with another committee assignment. Ahead of him on Wilbur Mills' committee are two older Republicans, so it is conceivable that Broyhill may some day become ranking minority member, or even Chairman if the Republicans win control of the House. The Virginia Congressman is assuredly one of the most aggressive and unyielding bargainers in the House. It therefore becomes an interesting exercise to speculate what he might do as the floor manager on a general taxation bill; right now, however, he is more concerned about an effort to forestall a commuter tax on people who work in the District of Columbia and who live in the 10th district of Virginia.

Census Data Pop. 465,115. Central city, 0%; suburban, 100%. Median family income, $14,457; families above $15,000: 47%; families below $3,000: 4%. Median years education, 12.9.

1972 Share of Federal Outlays $878,333,280

DOD	$626,851,022	HEW	$66,206,825
AEC	$116,063	HUD	$1,223,691
NASA	$2,256,121	DOI	$10,980,101
DOT	$45,768,568	USDA	$12,631,632
		Other	$112,299,257

Federal Military-Industrial Commitments

DOD Contractors Mitre Corp. (McLean), $19.589m: transportation systems research. Computer Sciences Corp. (Falls Church), $13.068m: various engineering and technical services. Bendix (McLean), $10.684m: classified electronic equipment. Institute for Defense Analysis (Arlington), $9.852m: various research studies. University of Rochester (Arlington), $9.331m: various anti-submarine studies. E Systems (Falls Church), $8.280m: design of various electronic triggering devices. Research Analysis Corp. (McLean), $8.088m: various computer-based research projects. TRW (McLean), $6.264m: studies of anti-submarine warfare.
DOD Installations The Pentagon (Arlington). Fort Myer AB (Arlington).

Economic Base Finance, insurance and real estate; agriculture, notably cattle and dairy products; and tourism.

The Voters

Registration 240,030 total. No party registration.
Median voting age 40.3
Employment profile White collar, 75%. Blue collar, 15%. Service, 9%. Farm, 1%.
Ethnic groups Black, 5%. Spanish, 3%. Total foreign stock, 15%. UK, Germany, 2% each.

Presidential vote

1972	Nixon (R)	115,664	(64%)
	McGovern (D)	65,148	(36%)
1968	Nixon (R)	69,600	(48%)
	Humphrey (D)	58,661	(40%)
	Wallace (AI)	18,247	(12%)

Representative

Joel T. Broyhill (R) Elected 1952; b. Nov. 4, 1919, Hopewell; home, Arlington; George Washington U., 1939–41; Army, WWII; married, three children; Lutheran.

Career Partner, Gen. Mgr., M. T. Broyhill & Sons, Real Estate, 1945–52.

Offices 2109 RHOB, 202-225-5136.

Administrative Assistant Homer Krout

Committees

District of Columbia (3rd); Subs: Business, Commerce, and Taxation; Revenue and Financial Affairs (Ranking Mbr.); Government Operations.

Ways and Means (3rd).

Joint Study Com. on Budget Control.

Group Ratings

	ADA	COPE	LWV	RIPON	NFU	LCV	CFA	NAB	NSI	ACA
1972	6	27	18	43	43	56	0	78	100	86
1971	16	20	20	36	33	–	14	–	–	77
1970	4	10	–	35	38	28	57	73	100	71

Key Votes

1) Busing	AGN	6) Cmbodia Bmbg	FOR	11) Chkg Acct Intrst	AGN
2) Strip Mines	ABS	7) Bust Hwy Trust	AGN	12) End HISC (HUAC)	AGN
3) Cut Mil $	AGN	8) Farm Sub Lmt	ABS	13) Nixon Sewer Veto	FOR
4) Rev Shrg	AGN	9) School Prayr	FOR	14) Corp Cmpaign $	AGN
5) Pub TV $	AGN	10) Cnsumr Prot	AGN	15) Pol $ Disclosr	ABS

Election Results

1972 general:	Joel T. Broyhill (R)	101,138	(56%)
	Harold O. Miller (D)	78,638	(44%)
1972 primary:	Joel T. Broyhill (R), unopposed		
1970 general:	Joel T. Broyhill (R)	67,468	(55%)
	Harold O. Miller (D)	56,255	(45%)

WASHINGTON

Political Background

In the far northwest corner of the continental United States lies the state of Washington. The massive Cascade Range separates the state into two topographical regions. To the east is the so-called Inland Empire. Here the Columbia River winds its way through plateau country; along the route its waters are backed up into giant reservoirs, the largest of which is Roosevelt Lake behind the Grand Coulee Dam. Except for the cities of Spokane and Yakima, and the urban complex around the AEC's Hanford Works, the Inland Empire is predominantly rural. Wheat is the biggest crop here, though apples and hops are also raised—Washington is the West's largest beer producer. Like most of rural America, this part of Washington experienced little population growth in the last decade. The more populous region of the state is the urban complex west of the Cascades around Puget Sound. The hilly land along the island-studded Sound accounts for 65% of the state's residents; thanks to the Olympic Mountains to the west, the area enjoys a mild, though rainy, climate. Today, there is a continuous strip of urban development for more than 50 miles along the Sound, from Everett south through Seattle and beyond Tacoma.

Scandinavian immigrants from Minnesota, Wisconsin, and the Dakotas bulked large among Washington's first white settlers. They rode the Great Northern and Northern Pacific railroads west, and soon gave the territory a radical political cast. In the years before World War I, the IWW, also known as the "Wobblies," had its largest following in Washington; even today the state ranks third (after West Virginia and Michigan) in the percentage of its wage-earners who are union members. The Scandinavians also help to nurture a political atmosphere hospitable to public power and the development of cooperatives. During the New Deal, the Puget Sound area gave Franklin D. Roosevelt some of his largest majorities anywhere. In recent years, Washington has lost some of its cultural and political distinctiveness, as management personnel from various parts of the country have moved in. (John Ehrlichman, one of Washington's more famous citizens these days, is a native of southern California.) What brought many of them here and what still shapes the politics of the state is the aircraft industry, notably the Boeing concern.

Building airplanes is anything but a stable business enterprise. In the late 1960s it became clear that Boeing, and the state of Washington with it, was in trouble. Though it had, and still has, a reputation as one of the nation's most dependable and honest defense contractors, Boeing lost out on a couple of major awards; the TFX (F-111) went to General Dynamics of Lyndon Johnson's Texas, and the NASA Apollo project went to California's North American Aviation. Moreover, the anticipated demand for the jumbo-jet 747 peaked and declined early. In 1969, Boeing employed 101,000 people in Washington, a figure that represented 8% of the state's total work force; by the end of 1971, Boeing's Washington payrolls had declined to 30,000. Boom became depression, and thousands of white-collar executives and engineers, as well as production workers, found themselves living on unemployment checks.

The two Senators from Washington, Warren Magnuson and Henry Jackson, have often been called "the Senators from Boeing." In 1970 and 1971, the two Democrats allied themselves with the Nixon Administration in a major effort to maintain government support for Boeing's supersonic transport (SST). Few other states—none outside the South—could have called on a pair of Senators with comparable seniority and clout. After spending eight years in the House, Magnuson was first elected to the Senate in 1944; and Jackson, after twelve years in the House, went to the Senate in 1952. Currently, the two have accumulated 72 years on Capitol Hill, and know their way around. Moreover, both have been committee chairmen for several years, Magnuson of Commerce and Jackson of Interior, and both are highly regarded experts in their committees' areas of jurisdiction, as well as in some other fields. Nevertheless, despite a myriad of assets, Magnuson and Jackson were unable to sell the cause of the SST to the Senate; a majority of their colleagues apparently found the environmental and economic objections raised against the project more compelling than the arguments advanced by the two Senators and the Administration. The program has since folded, and Boeing, after trimming its payrolls, has begun to diversify. The worst of the Seattle area depression has passed, but the aura of boom has left it.

Neither of the Senators is likely to suffer at the polls because of the demise of SST. Up for reelection in 1970, Sen. Jackson won a phenomenal 82% of the votes—the best performance that year of any opposed Senator except John Stennis of Mississippi. "Scoop" Jackson, as he is called (there are various stories of the nickname's origin), is one of an increasingly rare breed on Capitol Hill: a solid liberal on most domestic issues, while a supporter of the Nixon Administration's Vietnam and military spending policies. A member of the Senate Armed Services Committee, Jackson enjoys a reputation for expertise in defense matters; he was so well regarded that President-elect Nixon asked him to become Secretary of Defense. On some matters, Jackson actually stands to the right of the Administration. He was, for example, the only Senator who advanced a detailed set of reservations about the results of the SALT disarmament talks.

As Chairman of the Interior Committee, Jackson demonstrated a keen interest in ecological concerns long before they became a matter of popular interest. He is generally regarded as the father of the Environmental Protection Act, which set up the Environmental Protection Agency and required the filing of an environmental impact statement before most government projects could proceed. Jackson's stance on the Alaska pipeline issue in 1973 presents a good example of the Senator's priorities in matters before the Interior Committee. A federal court blocked the pipeline because a law prohibited the government from leasing the amount of land needed for the project's construction. So Jackson then sponsored a major overhaul of the law pertaining to the leasing of federal land—one that for the most part satisfied both the environmentalists and the business interests, and one that would have overcome the court's objections. But Alaska's Sen. Mike Gravel and Ted Stevens wanted to speed the pipeline along, and tried an end run around the provisions of the Environmental Protection Act when they asked Congress to declare that the pipeline, as planned, met environmental standards. Jackson firmly opposed the strategem of the Alaska Senators. But he lost the issue by one vote on the floor—an unusual fate for a Jackson position on an Interior bill.

As much as anyone these days, Scoop Jackson is running for President in 1976. The one stab he made for the nomination in 1972 fizzled rather badly. What he had hoped for was an upset in the Florida primary, in which he campaigned as a vehement critic of busing, despite a long pro-civil rights record. George Wallace's entry into the Florida affair destroyed any chance that Jackson may have had; the Washington Senator finished a poor third, and failed to do any better in later contests. The main impact of his presence in the presidential field was damage to George McGovern's candidacy. It was Jackson, in the Ohio primary campaign, who first started to attack McGovern as the candidate of "amnesty, abortion, and acid."

But this time around, Jackson's chances look considerably better. The Senator has played a major role on several important issues, almost all of which could help his candidacy. For example, it does not hurt Jackson among Jewish voters that he was the principal sponsor of the Jackson-Vanik Amendment. This is a move to deny most-favored-nation status to the Soviet Union unless it ends restrictive emigration policies, which have been used to prohibit Jews from leaving the USSR for Israel. And it does not hurt Jackson, as Chairman of the Government Operations Permanent Investigations Subcommittee, has probed the way in which the big oil companies allegedly engineered the "energy crisis" to fatten profits and squeeze independents out of business. With good cause, Jackson fancies himself as something of an expert on energy; and he brings to this issue, and others as well, a solid command of the facts and a dogged determination to advance his views.

Jackson, however, also has liabilities as a presidential candidate. If he can command the support of big business and George Meany, he will never win over the highly vocal liberal segment of the Democratic party, which in the 1972 presidential primaries, at least, was the dominant segment. Jackson is just too hawkish. Neither are his stolid speaking style and general lack of humor any assets. And in an era when people are increasingly suspicious of big organizations, it is at the top of such organizations that Jackson has his strongest support. So it is not at all clear that the Washington Senator can inspire the number of volunteers that seem necessary to win the Democratic nomination these days.

The state's senior Senator, Warren Magnuson, is less well known than Jackson, though he retains at least as much clout in the Senate. Though Magnuson and Jackson have long worked together on most issues, they parted company several years ago on foreign and military policy. To oversimplify matters a bit, Magnuson now usually votes with the doves while Jackson remains a steadfast hawk. Long before anyone heard of Ralph Nader, Magnuson, as Chairman of the Commerce Committee, fought for consumer legislation, and continues to do so with considerable effectiveness. The Senator combines nicely a dedication to liberal causes and a canny political sense that is second to none.

Magnuson need not remind anyone that he has been on the Hill longer than all but one other Senator and three Congressmen. Nevertheless, he will be only 69 on election day 1974, when his seat comes up. Though Magnuson has never been quite as strong as Jackson at the polls, the senior Senator has done well enough. In 1962, he encounterd an anticipated close call, probably because of overconfidence and perhaps because of his reputation as one of Washington's most socially active bachelors. But Magnuson got married in 1964, and in 1968 won reelection with 65% of the votes. A young professor named Kirk Hart, a liberal Republican, seems Magnuson's most likely opponent in 1974. Hart may simply be aiming to reserve a place for himself in 1976.

For if Jackson does get the Democratic presidential nomination, a clear opening will exist for a Washington Senate seat for the first time in 24 years. Expected candidates include 7th district Rep. Brock Adams and 5th district Rep. Thomas Foley, both Democrats; and possibly Gov. Daniel Evans or Attorney General Slade Gorton, both liberal Republicans. But should the latter two candidacies develop, they would seem to violate Washington's unspoken political nonaggression pact that exists between the dominant forces in each of the two parties. The Jackson-Magnuson Democrats hold a 6–1 edge in the state's House delegation, with the one Republican nearly beaten by a Jackson Democrat in 1972. On the other hand, the state government is dominated by Evans Republicans like Gorton and Secretary of State Ludlow

Kramer. The Jackson Democrats make no special effort to unseat the Evans Republicans, and vice versa.

According to some reports, Evans himself may become a presidential candidate in 1976. By virtually every account, he has compiled a solid record as Governor and is, of course, completely free of Watergate taint. But Evans seems to prefer Washington state to Washington, D. C. And if he did enter the race, it would appear that he would get lost among the other, better-known contenders. Yet it is a tribute to the quality of Washington politics that the state could produce two plausible presidential contenders. The only other small state that has done so in recent times is talent-rich Minnesota in 1968.

Census Data Pop. 3,409,169; 1.68% of U.S. total, 22nd largest; change 1960–70, 19.5%. Central city, 27%; suburban, 39%. Median family income, $10,404; 12th highest; families above $15,000: 23%; families below $3,000: 8%. Median years education, 12.4.

1972 Share of Federal Tax Burden $3,574,210,000; 1.71% of U.S. total, 20th largest.

1972 Share of Federal Outlays $5,100,948,611; 2.35% of U.S. total, 14th largest. Per capita federal spending, $1,496.

DOD	$1,817,377,000	12th (2.91%)		HEW	$1,181,696,028	20th (1.66%)
AEC	$224,229,373	4th (8.56%)		HUD	$70,966,561	13th (2.31%)
NASA	$10,272,576	19th (0.34%)		VA	$221,712,988	20th (1.94%)
DOT	$356,456,418	5th (4.52%)		USDA	$313,833,747	17th (2.04%)
DOC	$54,644,646	5th (4.22%)		CSC	$113,880,778	10th (2.76%)
DOI	$190,359,002	2nd (8.97%)		TD	$114,996,870	21st (0.69%)
DOJ	$25,476,310	11th (2.59%)		Other	$405,046,314	

Economic Base Finance, insurance and real estate; transportation equipment, especially aircraft and parts; agriculture, notably wheat, dairy products, cattle and apples; lumber and wood products, especially sawmills and planing mills; food and kindred products, especially canned, cured and frozen foods; paper and allied products; primary metal industries, especially primary nonferrous metals.

Political Line-up Governor, Daniel J. Evans (R); seat up, 1976. Senators, Warren G. Magnuson (D) and Henry M. Jackson (D). Representatives, 7 (6 D and 1 R). State Senate (30 D and 19 R); State House (57 D and 41 R).

The Voters

Registration 1,973,895 Total. No party registration.
Median voting age 42.3
Employment profile White collar, 51%. Blue collar, 33%. Service, 13%. Farm, 3%.
Ethnic groups Black, 2%. Spanish, 2%. Total foreign stock, 19%. Canada, 4%, Germany, UK, Norway, 2% each; Sweden, 1%.

Presidential vote

1972	Nixon (R)	837,135	(60%)
	McGovern (D)	568,334	(40%)
1968	Nixon (R)	588,510	(45%)
	Humphrey (D)	616,037	(47%)
	Wallace (AI)	96,990	(7%)
1964	Johnson (D)	776,699	(62%)
	Goldwater (R)	470,366	(37%)

Senator

Warren G. Magnuson (D) Elected Appointed Dec. 1944, seat up 1974; b. Apr. 12, 1905, Moorhead, Minn.; home, Seattle; U. of N.D., N.D. State, 1923–24; U. of Wash., LL.B., 1929; USNR, WWII; married; Lutheran.

Career Practicing atty.; sp. prosecutor, King Co., 1931; Wash. Legislature, 1933–34; Asst. U.S. Dist. Atty., 1934; Prosecuting Atty., King County, 1934–36; U.S. House, 1937–44.

Offices 127 OSOB, 202-225-2621. Also 900 U.S. Courthouse, Seattle 98104, 206-583-5545.

Administrative Assistant Stanley H. Barer

Committees

Aeronautical and Space Sciences (2nd).

Appropriations (2nd); Subs: Defense; Labor, Health, Education, and Welfare, and Related Agencies (Chm.); Public Works, AEC; State, Justice, and Commerce, the Judiciary, and Related Agencies.

Commerce (Chm.); Sub: Aviation.

Sel. Com. on Equal Educational Opportunity.

Group Ratings

	ADA	COPE	LWV	RIPON	NFU	LCV	CFA	NAB	NSI	ACA
1972	60	100	91	56	100	42	100	40	50	19
1971	78	92	85	42	91	–	100	–	–	19
1970	72	92	–	48	100	35	–	30	33	21

Key Votes

1) Busing	FOR	8) Sea Life Prot	FOR	15) Tax Singls Less	FOR
2) Alas P-line	ABS	9) Campaign Subs	FOR	16) Min Tax for Rich	FOR
3) Gun Cntrl	FOR	10) Cmbodia Bmbg	AGN	17) Euro Troop Rdctn	FOR
4) Rehnquist	AGN	11) Legal Srvices	FOR	18) Bust Hwy Trust	FOR
5) Pub TV $	FOR	12) Rev Sharing	FOR	19) Maid Min Wage	FOR
6) EZ Votr Reg	FOR	13) Cnsumr Prot	FOR	20) Farm Sub Limit	AGN
7) No-Fault	FOR	14) Eq Rts Amend	FOR	21) Highr Credt Chgs	ABS

Election Results

1968 general:	Warren G. Magnuson (D)	796,183	(65%)
	Jack Metcalf (R)	435,894	(35%)
1968 primary:	Warren G. Magnuson (D)	373,303	(93%)
	Arthur De Witt (R)	28,683	(7%)
1962 general:	Warren G. Magnuson (D)	491,365	(52%)
	Richard G. Christensen (R)	446,204	(48%)

Senator

Henry M. Jackson (D) Elected 1952, seat up 1976; b. May 31, 1912, Everett; home, Everett; U. of Wash., LL.B., 1935; married, two children; Presbyterian.

Career Practicing atty., 1936–38; Prosecuting Atty. Snohomish County, 1938–40; U.S. House of Reps., 1941–53.

Offices 134 OSOB, 202-225-3441. Also Rm. 802 U.S. Courthouse, Seattle 98104, 206-583-7476.

Administrative Assistant S. Sterling Munro, Jr.

Committees

Armed Services (3rd); Subs: Central Intelligence; Military Construction Authorization; Nuclear Test Ban Treaty Safeguards (Chm.); Preparedness Investigating; Tactical Air Power; Arms Control (Chm.).

Government Operations (3rd); Subs: Permanent Investigations (Chm.); Reorganization, Research, and International Organizations.

Interior and Insular Affairs (Chm.); Subs: Indian Affairs; Minerals, Materials, and Fuels; Parks and Recreations; Public Lands; Territories and Insular Affairs; Water and Power Resources; Sp. Sub. on Legislative Oversight (Chm.).

Joint Com. on Atomic Energy (2nd); Subs: Communities; Legislation; Research, Development and Radiation; Security; Energy (Chm.).

Group Ratings

	ADA	COPE	LWV	RIPON	NFU	LCV	CFA	NAB	NSI	ACA
1972	40	100	91	56	90	40	100	11	80	38
1971	56	100	100	48	82	–	100	–	–	27
1970	56	100	–	54	100	53	–	8	80	24

Key Votes

1) Busing	ABS	8) Sea Life Prot	FOR	15) Tax Singls Less	FOR
2) Alas P-line	AGN	9) Campaign Subs	FOR	16) Min Tax for Rich	FOR
3) Gun Cntrl	FOR	10) Cmbodia Bmbg	FOR	17) Euro Troop Rdctn	AGN
4) Rehnquist	AGN	11) Legal Srvices	FOR	18) Bust Hwy Trust	FOR
5) Pub TV $	FOR	12) Rev Sharing	FOR	19) Maid Min Wage	FOR
6) EZ Votr Reg	ABS	13) Cnsumr Prot	FOR	20) Farm Sub Limit	AGN
7) No-Fault	FOR	14) Eq Rts Amend	ABS	21) Highr Credt Chgs	ABS

Election Results

1970 general:	Henry M. Jackson (D)	879,385	(82%)
	Charles W. Elicker (R)	170,790	(16%)
	Bill Massey (SW)	9,255	(1%)
	Edison S. Fisk (Buffalo)	7,377	(1%)
1970 primary:	Henry M. Jackson :D;	497,309	(84%)
	Carl Maxey (D)	79,201	(13%)
	John Patric (D)	7,267	(1%)
	Clarice Privette (D)	6,240	(1%)
1964 general:	Henry M. Jackson (D)	875,950	(72%)
	Lloyd J. Andrews (R)	337,138	(28%)

FIRST DISTRICT Political Background

Every major American city is divided into distinct neighborhoods. There is always a part of town where the wealthier, more white-collar, better-educated people tend to live. In Seattle, this has been on the north side, in the hills between Puget Sound and Lake Washington. Accordingly, the pleasant neighborhoods around the lake and the University of Washington have always been the more Republican part of Seattle, even though many of the younger affluent people have moved out to the suburbs. The north side contains the heart of Washington's 1st congressional district—the only part of the state to send a Republican to Congress.

Before the 1972 redistricting, the 1st district was more Republican than it is now. A redistricting plan concocted by a geography professor sheared off several high-income, heavily Republican areas, and added some Democratic territory—notably Mountlakes Terrace, a blue-collar community just across the line in Snohomish County. But despite the addition and the presence of the university, the north side of the city remains a Republican district; it also retains most of Seattle's largest suburb of Bellevue (pop. 61,000), a Republican area east of Lake Washington. In the old district, the big race, when one took place, occurred in the Republican primary; in the new district, there were real contests in both the primary and general elections.

For 18 years the 1st district saw little electoral turbulence of any kind. Things were quiet from 1952, when Republican Thomas Pelly was first elected, until 1970, when state Sen. Joel Pritchard challenged Pelly in the Republican primary. On the face of it, Pelly seemed to enjoy an overwhelming advantage. With 18 years of service, the incumbent was the ranking Republican on the House Merchant Marine and Fisheries Committee, a unit of obvious importance to the district. Moreover, after compiling a mildly liberal voting record, the Republican even won support from organized labor. But Pelly was 68, and lately had not spent much time in the 1st district; he refused to fly, and so traveled from Capitol Hill to Seattle by train. Pritchard, on the other hand, was 45, well-known in the district, and regarded as a kind of Daniel Evans liberal. In 1970, Pritchard waged a vigorous, well-financed campaign, and received 47% of the primary votes against Pelly.

As predicted in the 1972 *Almanac*, Pelly was prompted to retire. But succession for Pritchard was not automatic in 1972. He first encountered primary opposition from William Boeing, a wealthy, conservative member of the aircraft concern family. Pritchard disposed of Boeing with comparative ease. Thanks to the changed composition of the district, however, it was a different story in the general election. Pritchard, now 47, was suddenly the old man in the race. His opponent was 30-year-old John Hempelmann, a former member of Sen. Henry Jackson's staff; and the young Democrat enjoyed the kind of heavy financial support Jackson can muster. Campaigning as a liberal and avoiding Jackson's hawkish positions on foreign and military policy, Hempelmann carried the university community and the blue-collar Democratic areas. But after the absentee ballots were counted, Pritchard squeezed out enough votes in the district's Republican territory to win by a 2,600-vote margin.

Pritchard will probably have an easier time of it in 1974. He has Pelly's seat, though of course not his seniority, on the Merchant Marine and Fisheries Committee; moreover, because the new Congressman has compiled a liberal voting record on most issues, he will receive support from constituents who usually vote Democratic. And considering the distance, Pritchard has returned to the district relatively often; once back home, he conducts open meetings in every neighborhood of the 1st. If Pritchard can build solid majorities as the incumbent, his tenure in Congress will be fairly easy to predict: with no ambitions for statewide office, the politician is on record that no one should stay in the House for more than 12 years, which means 1984 for Pritchard.

Census Data Pop. 465,810. Central city, 68%; suburban, 32%. Median family income, $12,084; families above $15,000: 33%; families below $3,000: 5%. Median years education, 12.7.

1972 Share of Federal Outlays $785,131,726

DOD	$340,505,839	HEW	$164,225,814
AEC	$775,844	HUD	$14,478,999
NASA	$3,420,194	DOI	$4,876,153
DOT	$79,892,455	USDA	$20,645,375
		Other	$156,311,053

Federal Military-Industrial Commitments

DOD Contractors University of Washington (Seattle), $7.009m: various oceanographic and electronics research studies.
DOD Installations Naval Support Activity (Seattle).

Economic Base Finance, insurance and real estate; transportation equipment, especially aircraft and parts; food and kindred products, especially bakery products; and tourism. Also higher education (Washington Univ.).

The Voters

Registration 327,182 total. No party registration.
Median voting age 42.5
Employment profile White collar, 65%. Blue collar, 23%. Service, 12%. Farm, –%.
Ethnic groups Spanish, 2%. Total foreign stock, 25%. Canada, 6%; Norway, UK, 3% each; Germany, Sweden, 2% each.

Presidential vote

1972	Nixon (R)	137,563	(58%)
	McGovern (D)	97,967	(42%)
1968	Nixon (R)	NA	
	Humphrey (D)	NA	
	Wallace (AI)	NA	

Representative

Joel M. Pritchard (R) Elected 1972; b. May 5, 1925, Seattle; home, Seattle; Marietta Col., 1946–48; Army, 1944–46; married, four children; Presbyterian.

Career Pres., Griffin Envelope Co.; State House, 1958–66; State Senate, 1966–70; Wash. Constitutional Advisory Comm.

Offices 506 CHOB, 202-225-6311.

Administrative Assistant Robert W. Davidson

Committees

Government Operations (17th); Subs: Conservation and Natural Resources; Special Studies.

Merchant Marine and Fisheries (14th); Subs: Fisheries and Wildlife Conservation and the Environment; Merchant Marine; Oceanography.

Group Ratings: Newly Elected

Key Votes

1) Busing	NE	6) Cmbodia Bmbg	AGN	11) Chkg Acct Intrst	AGN
2) Strip Mines	NE	7) Bust Hwy Trust	FOR	12) End HISC (HUAC)	FOR
3) Cut Mil $	NE	8) Farm Sub Lmt	NE	13) Nixon Sewer Veto	FOR
4) Rev Shrg	NE	9) School Prayr	NE	14) Corp Cmpaign $	NE
5) Pub TV $	NE	10) Cnsumr Prot	NE	15) Pol $ Disclosr	NE

Election Results

1972 general:	Joel Pritchard (R)	107,581	(50%)
	John Hempelman (D)	104,959	(49%)
	Craig Honts (SW)	1,401	(1%)
1972 primary:	Joel Pritchard (R)	52,007	(76%)
	C. Y. Jesse Chiang (R)	16,388	(24%)

SECOND DISTRICT Political Background

The 2nd district of Washington constitutes the far northwest corner of the continental United States. This is a region of towering mountains, of heavily wooded inlets, and of gentle rain and fog. The 2nd takes in the sparsely populated islands in Puget Sound and the Straits of Juan de Fuca, along with the counties just east of the sound from Seattle to the Canadian border. Most of the residents of the district are concentrated in a narrow strip of land between the sound and the

Cascade Mountains, in or near cities like Bellingham, Everett, and several northern suburbs of Seattle. Politically, the district is marginal, usually leaning slightly Democratic in national elections.

The 2nd perhaps best illustrates the Washington tradition in congressional politics: it elects a young Congressman in a good year for his party, continues to reelect him, and turns him out only if he gets overconfident in a bad year for his party. From 1941 to 1953, the 2nd was represented by Scoop Jackson. Perhaps anticipating the Eisenhower landslide of 1952, Jackson decided on a Senate try rather than face a House contest that might have been riskier than usual. His successor in the House was Republican Jack Westland, who won routine reelection until 1964 when the Goldwater debacle apparently caught him napping.

The winner that year was Democrat Lloyd Meeds, who, like Jackson 24 years earlier, ran for Congress while serving as Snohomish County (Everett) Prosecutor. Ever since, Meeds has been reelected with near automatic regularity; in 1972, he was anything but napping, as he ran 22% ahead of George McGovern in the district. As a member of the Education and Labor and Interior committees, Meeds usually votes with the liberals. The Congressman's political coloration combines a Jacksonish attitude toward issues with a more dovish strain of liberalism.

Census Data Pop. 472,289. Central city, 11%; suburban, 54%. Median family income, $10,563; families above $15,000: 22%; families below $3,000: 8%. Median years education, 12.4.

1972 Share of Federal Outlays $698,198,942

DOD	$279,537,926	HEW	$165,781,557
AEC	$517,703	HUD	$10,342,592
NASA	$2,267,953	DOI	$7,718,401
DOT	$65,020,985	USDA	$28,228,009
		Other	$138,783,816

Federal Military-Industrial Commitments

DOD Installations Naval Air Station, Whidbey Island (Oak Harbor). Blaine AF Station (Blaine). Makah AF Station (Neah Bay).

Economic Base Finance, insurance and real estate; agriculture, notably dairy products, poultry and vegetables; lumber and wood products, especially millwork, plywood and related products; and paper and allied products. Also higher education (Western Washington State).

The Voters

Registration 271,566 total. No party registration.
Median voting age 41.1
Employment profile White collar, 48%. Blue collar, 37%. Service, 12%. Farm, 3%.
Ethnic groups Spanish, 1%. Total foreign stock, 20%. Canada, 5%; Norway, UK, Germany, Sweden, 2% each.

Presidential vote

1972	Nixon (R)	121,349	(62%)
	McGovern (D)	75,728	(38%)
1968	Nixon (R)	NA	
	Humphrey (D)	NA	
	Wallace (AI)	NA	

Representative

Lloyd Meeds, Jr. (D) Elected 1964; b. Dec. 11, 1927, Dillon, Mont.; home Everett; Everett Community Col., Gonzaga U., LL.B., 1958; USNR, WWII; married, four children; Episcopalian.

Career Deputy Prosecuting Atty., Spokane County, 1958–59, Snohomish County, 1959–61; practicing atty., 1961–62; Prosecuting Atty., Snohomish County, 1962–64.

Offices 308 CHOB, 202-225-2605. Also Fed. Bldg., 3002 Colby Ave., Everett 98201, 206-252-3188.

Administrative Assistant Leonard Saari

Committees

Education and Labor (10th); Subs: No. 1 (Gen. Sub. on Education); No. 5. (Sel. Sub. on Education); No. 4 (Sel. Sub. on Labor).

Interior and Insular Affairs (10th); Subs: Indian Affairs (Chm.); National Parks and Recreation; Territorial and Insular Affairs; Water and Power Resources.

Sel. Com. on Committees of the House (4th).

Group Ratings

	ADA	COPE	LWV	RIPON	NFU	LCV	CFA	NAB	NSI	ACA
1972	75	100	91	64	100	57	50	0	30	13
1971	81	100	89	65	80	–	100	–	–	3
1970	84	100	–	76	92	63	95	0	40	0

Key Votes

1) Busing	FOR	6) Cmbodia Bmbg	AGN	11) Chkg Acct Intrst	AGN
2) Strip Mines	AGN	7) Bust Hwy Trust	FOR	12) End HISC (HUAC)	FOR
3) Cut Mil $	ABS	8) Farm Sub Lmt	AGN	13) Nixon Sewer Veto	AGN
4) Rev Shrg	AGN	9) School Prayr	AGN	14) Corp Cmpaign $	FOR
5) Pub TV $	FOR	10) Cnsumr Prot	FOR	15) Pol $ Disclosr	FOR

Election Results

1972 general:	Lloyd Meeds (D)	114,900 (60%)
	Bill Reams (R)	75,181 (40%)
1972 primary:	Lloyd Meeds (D), unopposed	
1970 general:	Lloyd Meeds (D)	117,562 (73%)
	Edward A. McBride (R)	44,049 (27%)

THIRD DISTRICT Political Background

Lumber is one of Washington's most important industries. And nowhere in the state is lumber a more important part of the economy than in the damp, mountainous region along the Pacific coast and the lower Columbia River. This is the state's 3rd congressional district, which encircles the Seattle and Tacoma metropolitan areas, and just fails to include the industrial town of Vancouver, right across the Columbia from Portland, Oregon. The district is predominantly rural; its biggest cities include Longview (pop. 28,000) and Olympia (pop. 23,000). But the 3rd's largest center of population is the Army's Fort Lewis (pop. 38,000), which sits just at the district's edge, near Tacoma. The atmosphere in most of the 2nd has not really changed much since the turn of the century, when the lumberjacks first attacked the firs and the sawmill towns grew up on the bays off the Pacific and Puget Sound. The politics of the 3rd retains a kind of rough-hewn populist, Democratic aura reminiscent of the region's lumbercamp days.

Since 1960, the 3rd has been represented by Julia Butler Hansen, who is probably one of the most powerful, if not best publicized, women in Congress today. Before coming to the House, Ms.

Hansen served for 22 years in the Washington legislature. By virtue of seniority, she has risen in the House to become Chairman of the Appropriations Interior Subcommittee. This is a unit that controls spending on matters of considerable significance to both the 3rd district and the nation at large. Holding the pursestrings of the Interior Department, Ms. Hansen has impact on policies concerning the private use of public lands, dams and reclamation, American Indians, and a host of ecological issues. More often than not, she comes out on the environmentalists' side of issues; and like Washington's Sen. Henry Jackson, who chairs the Senate Interior Committee, she is knowledgeable, hard-working, and when need be, tough as nails.

Back home in the 3rd district, Ms. Hansen has been a champion vote-getter. Though the Congresswoman has not lately gotten the 70% of the votes she received in 1964, she appears in no danger whatever of losing an election.

Census Data Pop. 506,840. Central city, 0%; suburban, 36%. Median family income, $9,736; families above $15,000: 18%; families below $3,000: 9%. Median years education, 12.2.

1972 Share of Federal Outlays $637,843,481

DOD	$150,871,573	HEW	$211,796,184
AEC	$112,659	HUD	$8,028,762
NASA	$496,641	DOI	$14,001,279
DOT	$40,198,890	USDA	$29,650,277
		Other	$182,687,216

Federal Military-Industrial Commitments

DOD Installations Fort Lewis AB (Tacoma). Naval Facility (Pacific Beach). McChord AFB (Tacoma).

Economic Base Lumber and wood products; transportation equipment, especially aircraft and parts; agriculture, notably dairy products, poultry and cattle; paper and allied products, especially paperboard mill products and paper mill products other than building paper; finance, insurance and real estate; and food and kindred products.

The Voters

Registration 272,250 total. No party registration.
Median voting age 40.9
Employment profile White collar, 42%. Blue collar, 42%. Service, 13%. Farm, 3%.
Ethnic groups Black, 1%. Spanish, 2%. Total foreign stock, 15%. Canada, 3%; Germany, 2%; UK, Norway, Sweden, 1% each.

Presidential vote

1972	Nixon (R)	112,130	(58%)
	McGovern (D)	82,747	(42%)
1968	Nixon (R)	NA	
	Humphrey (D)	NA	
	Wallace (AI)	NA	

Representative

Julia Butler Hansen (D) Elected Nov. 8, 1960; b. June 14, 1907, Portland, Oreg.; home, Cathlamet; U. of Wash., B.A., 1931; married, one child; Christian Scientist.

Career Wash. State Legislature, 1939–60, Minority Leader, 1953–55; Speaker Pro Tem, 1955–60.

Offices 201 CHOB, 202-225-3536. Also Fed. Bldg., Vancouver 98664, 206-695-8291, and P.O. Bldg., Longview 98632, 206-423-5652.

Administrative Assistant Roy Carlson

Committees

Appropriations (16th); Subs: Interior (Chm.); Transportation.

Group Ratings

	ADA	COPE	LWV	RIPON	NFU	LCV	CFA	NAB	NSI	ACA
1972	50	100	75	60	100	24	50	13	62	20
1971	46	100	63	33	77	–	100	–	–	22
1970	68	91	–	67	100	39	80	0	56	0

Key Votes

1) Busing	FOR	6) Cmbodia Bmbg	AGN	11) Chkg Acct Intrst	AGN
2) Strip Mines	ABS	7) Bust Hwy Trust	ABS	12) End HISC (HUAC)	AGN
3) Cut Mil $	ABS	8) Farm Sub Lmt	AGN	13) Nixon Sewer Veto	AGN
4) Rev Shrg	FOR	9) School Prayr	AGN	14) Corp Cmpaign $	FOR
5) Pub TV $	FOR	10) Cnsumr Prot	FOR	15) Pol $ Disclosr	AGN

Election Results

1972 general:	Julia Butler Hansen (D)	122,933	(66%)
	R. C. McConkey (R)	62,564	(34%)
1972 primary:	Julia Butler Hansen (D)	65,726	(64%)
	Robert Corcoran (D)	37,708	(36%)
1970 general:	Julia Butler Hansen (D)	81,892	(59%)
	R. C. McConkey (R)	56,566	(41%)

FOURTH DISTRICT Political Background

For most of its length in Washington, the Columbia River flows either within or along the borders of the 4th congressional district. To the west, the district extends to the city of Vancouver (pop. 42,000), across the Columbia from Portland, Oregon. Up river, the 4th cuts through the Cascade Mountains at the Bonneville Dam, past McNary Dam to the town of Richland near the AEC's Hanford Works, and still farther up river past Wenatchee to the Grand Coulee Dam. In area, the 4th is the state's largest congressional district, and most of the area encompassed is taken up by the Cascades and its ridges, blessed with picturesque names like Horse Heaven Hills. The district's largest center of population does not lie along the Columbia, but instead in the fertile Yakima valley, which contains the district's largest city of Yakima (pop. 45,000). The valley produces a great share of the state's agricultural crops; not just wheat, but also apples, hops, and other vegetables and fruits.

The 1972 redistricting changed the 4th substantially. Its lines were drawn by an academic geographer, not a group of politicians. The old district was the southeast quarter of the state; the redistricting cost it seven southeastern counties and extended its territory all the way up to the Canadian border. The new shape was thought to threaten the seat of freshman Congressman Mike McCormack, inasmuch as it excluded the city of Pasco, where the Democratic challenger had won a large majority in his 1970 upset of Republican incumbent Catherine May; McCormack's home town of Richland lies just across the Columbia from Pasco.

It is fairly unusual these days for a challenger to unseat an incumbent Congressman. It is even more unusual in Washington, where, aside from 1964 when four Republican incumbents lost, only one other incumbent House member besides Mrs. May has been defeated in the last 20 years. Several factors account for McCormack's victory in 1970. As a 14-year veteran of the state legislature, he was well-known and well-liked in the Richland-Pasco area. Mrs. May, on the other hand, had recently been divorced and remarried; more important, she had not returned to the district very often (today, as Catherine May Bedell, she is Chairman of the U.S. Tariff Commission). There was also discontent among the district's farmers; in some farm counties, McCormack equaled Lyndon Johnson's 1964 showings.

But most important was the support of Sen. Henry "Scoop" Jackson, who was up for reelection in 1970 and finished with 82% of the state's votes. Jackson did not confine his efforts for McCormack to a few stump speeches. The Senator raised money (especially through organized labor), appeared constantly on McCormack TV ads, and in general tried to define the race as a referendum on Jackson, rather than Mrs. May. The strategy worked, as McCormack won with 53% of the votes.

Reelection in 1972 was supposed to be tougher for McCormack. Neither Jackson nor Sen. Warren Magnuson was on the ticket, but Richard Nixon and Gov. Daniel Evans, both Republicans who had carried the 4th easily, were. Nevertheless, McCormack capitalized on the traditional Democratic leanings of Vancouver to carry the new counties in the district by a bare margin, and took 60% in the counties retained from the old district, thanks to work done courting the constituency. McCormack's committee assignments proved helpful in his reelection bid. A seat on Public Works obviously confers benefits to a Congressman representing a district on the Columbia River and all its dams; and membership on Science and Astronautics had some value for a district that receives more than $200 million annually from the AEC. After the 1972 election, McCormack won a seat on the Joint Committee on Atomic Energy, which has direct jurisdiction over the AEC. Moreover, from the looks of the Congressman's 1972 margin, he appears in good shape for future elections.

Census Data Pop. 467,171. Central city, 0%; suburban, 25%. Median family income, $9,206; families above $15,000: 17%; families below $3,000: 11%. Median years education, 12.2.

1972 Share of Federal Outlays $694,495,595

DOD	$32,206,391	HEW	$164,162,968
AEC	$221,717,247	HUD	$2,285,249
NASA	$198,095	DOI	$72,019,340
DOT	$36,797,552	USDA	$69,890,706
		Other	$95,218,047

Federal Military-Industrial Commitments

DOD Installations Yakima Army Firing Center (Yakima).
AEC Operations Westinghouse Hanford Co. (Richland), $116.718m: operation of Hanford Engineering Development Laboratory. Atlantic Richfield Hanford Co. (Richland), $39.968m: operation of chemical separation facilities and support services. Douglas United Nuclear (Richland), $23.149m: operation of NPR. Battelle Memorial Institute (Richland), $5.921m: operation of Pacific Northwest Laboratory.

Economic Base Agriculture, notably cattle and fruits; finance, insurance and real estate; food and kindred products, especially canned, cured and frozen foods; lumber and wood products, especially sawmill and planing mill products; and paper and allied products, especially paper mill products other than building paper.

The Voters

Registration 269,836 total. No party registration.
Median voting age 44.1
Employment profile White collar, 44%. Blue collar, 34%. Service, 12%. Farm, 10%.
Ethnic groups Spanish, 4%. Total foreign stock, 14%. Canada, 3%; Germany, 2%. UK, 1%.

Presidential vote

1972	Nixon (R)	112,728	(59%)
	McGovern (D)	77,042	(41%)
1968	Nixon (R)	NA	
	Humphrey (D)	NA	
	Wallace (AI)	NA	

Representative

Mike McCormack (D) Elected 1970; b. Dec. 14, 1921, Basil, Ohio; home, Richland; Wash., U., B.S., 1948, M.S., 1949; Army, WWII; married, three children; religion unspecified.

Career Research scientist; Wash. House, 1956–60, Senate, 1960– .

Offices 1205 LHOB, 202-225-5816. Also Richland 99352, 509-946-4672.

Administrative Assistant John Andelin

Committees

Public Works (15th); Subs: Investigations and Review; Public Buildings and Grounds; Water Resources.

Science and Astronautics (11th); Subs: Science, Research and Development; Energy (Chm.); International Cooperation in Science and Space.

Joint Com. on Atomic Energy (5th); Subs: Energy; Research, Development, and Radiation; Legislation.

Group Ratings

	ADA	COPE	LWV	RIPON	NFU	LCV	CFA	NAB	NSI	ACA
1972	63	90	80	50	100	57	0	9	22	18
1971	78	100	89	67	93	–	100	–	–	7

Key Votes

1) Busing	FOR	6) Cmbodia Bmbg	ABS	11) Chkg Acct Intrst	AGN
2) Strip Mines	FOR	7) Bust Hwy Trust	ABS	12) End HISC (HUAC)	FOR
3) Cut Mil $	FOR	8) Farm Sub Lmt	AGN	13) Nixon Sewer Veto	AGN
4) Rev Shrg	FOR	9) School Prayr	AGN	14) Corp Cmpaign $	ABS
5) Pub TV $	FOR	10) Cnsumr Prot	FOR	15) Pol $ Disclosr	FOR

Election Results

1972 general:	Mike McCormack (D)	97,593	(52%)
	Steward Bledsoe (R)	89,812	(48%)
1972 primary:	Mike McCormack (D), unopposed		
1970 general:	Mike McCormack (D)	70,119	(53%)
	Catherine May (R)	63,244	(47%)

FIFTH DISTRICT Political Background

The 5th district is the western part of Washington state. It is the heart of the Inland Empire, and centers on Spokane (pop. 170,000), the state's second-largest city. Lying between the Cascades and the Rockies, the land here was originally arid plateau; but with the help of irrigation, it has become one of the major wheat-growing regions in the United States. Much of the water is provided by the Grand Coulee Dam, that engineering marvel of the New Deal; the reclamation project also furnishes cheap public hydroelectric power. So enjoying the lowest electric power rates in the country, Washington has always been a big backer of public power development.

In the intermountain West, Spokane is the largest city north of Salt Lake City. Spokane County, which contains the city and its suburbs, has nearly 60% of the 5th district's people and voters.

Because Spokane is somewhat more conservative than the cities on Puget Sound, the 5th district is inclined toward the Republican column in statewide races. This inclination is strengthened by the conservative Republican preference of Walla Walla and the other towns in the southern portion of the district.

For the past 30 years, the 5th district has had only two Congressmen: conservative Republican Walt Horan, who served from 1943 to 1965, and Democrat Thomas Foley, who, after beating Horan in 1964, has won easily ever since. Though Foley has a fairly solid liberal voting record on most issues, he has backed military spending projects like the ABM. Considered a Jackson man, Foley served as a Jackson staffer on the Senate Interior Committee before running for Congress. In the election of 1964, he received a lot of help from Jackson, whose seat was up the same year.

Foley has been especially lucky playing the seniority game. As a freshman, he was assigned to the Agriculture and the Interior committees, both of great interest to the state. On Interior, the Congressman has risen to the 6th-ranking Democratic position—a good climb for less than 10 years of service. His rise on Agriculture has been even more rapid. Over the years, most of the Democrats on the Agriculture Committee have been from the South; relatively few Northern Democrats hail from farming districts, and those who do often have had shaky holds on their seats. Just four years ago, Foley was the 8th-ranking Democrat on Agriculture. But three senior Southern Democrats have retired, and two—John McMillan of South Carolina and Graham Purcell of Texas—have been defeated. That leaves the 45-year-old Foley third in seniority behind 75-year-old Bob Poage of Texas and 67-year-old Frank Stubblefield of Kentucky.

The committee's line-up means that Foley has an excellent chance to become Chairman of Agriculture, and he could hold the post for a long, long time. But there is one caveat. Because Foley has won reelection by such solid margins, he is considered statewide material. As a Jackson protégé, he may be tempted to run for the Senate in 1976, if Jackson seeks and gets the Democratic presidential nomination. Or he might be interested in the state's other Senate seat. Warren Magnuson, assuming he wins reelection in 1974, will be 75 when his seat comes up again in 1980. The year 1976 will probably be the one which will force Foley to make a decision. He must weigh the chances of winning a Senate seat against the likelihood of succeeding to the chairmanship of Agriculture.

Census Data Pop. 471,144. Central city, 35%; suburban, 24%. Median family income, $9,164; families above $15,000: 17%; families below $3,000: 10%. Median years education, 12.4.

1972 Share of Federal Outlays $690,051,558

DOD	$155,479,173	HEW	$173,253,154
AEC	$223,572	HUD	$15,120,375
NASA	–	DOI	$80,081,703
DOT	$31,373,385	USDA	$132,672,569
		Other	$101,847,627

Federal Military-Industrial Commitments

DOD Installations Mica Peak AF Station (Mica). Othello AF Station (Othello).

Economic Base Agriculture, notably grains, cattle and dairy products; finance, insurance and real estate; food and kindred products, especially canned, cured and frozen foods; and lumber and wood products, especially sawmill and planing mill products. Also higher education (Washington State Univ.).

The Voters

Registration 280,809 total. No party registration.
Median voting age 43.7
Employment profile White collar, 49%. Blue collar, 28%. Service, 16%. Farm, 7%.
Ethnic groups Black, 1%. Spanish, 2%. Total foreign stock, 16%. Canada, 4%; Germany, 2%; UK, Norway, Sweden, 1% each.

Presidential vote

1972	Nixon (R)	126,627	(63%)
	McGovern (D)	72,966	(37%)
1968	Nixon (R)	NA	
	Humphrey (D)	NA	
	Wallace (AI)	NA	

Representative

Thomas Stephen Foley (D) Elected 1964; b. March 6, 1929, Spokane; home, Spokane; U. of Wash., B.A., 1951, J.D., 1957; married; Catholic.

Career Practicing atty., 1957: Dep. Prosecuting Atty., Spokane County, 1958–60; instructor, Gonzaga U. Law School, 1958–60; Asst. Atty. Gen., Wash., 1960–61; Asst. Chief Clerk and Counsel, Senate Interior and Insular Affairs Com., 1961–63.

Offices 1201 LHOB, 202-225-2006. Also U.S. Courthouse, Spokane 99201, 509-456-4680.

Administrative Assistant William L. First (L.A.)

Committees

Agriculture (3rd); Subs: Forests; Livestock and Grains (Chm.); Operational Sub. on Domestic Marketing and Consumer Relations.

Interior and Insular Affairs (6th); Subs: Mines and Mining; Territorial and Insular Affairs; Water and Power Resources; Environment.

Standards of Official Conduct (6th).

Group Ratings

	ADA	COPE	LWV	RIPON	NFU	LCV	CFA	NAB	NSI	ACA
1972	69	82	100	81	83	60	50	9	50	9
1971	73	90	89	69	87	–	86	–	–	15
1970	88	83	–	71	92	57	100	25	44	22

Key Votes

1) Busing	FOR	6) Cmbodia Bmbg	AGN	11) Chkg Acct Intrst	FOR
2) Strip Mines	AGN	7) Bust Hwy Trust	FOR	12) End HISC (HUAC)	AGN
3) Cut Mil $	AGN	8) Farm Sub Lmt	AGN	13) Nixon Sewer Veto	AGN
4) Rev Shrg	FOR	9) School Prayr	AGN	14) Corp Cmpaign $	FOR
5) Pub TV $	FOR	10) Cnsumr Prot	FOR	15) Pol $ Disclosr	FOR

Election Results

1972 general:	Thomas S. Foley (D)	150,580	(81%)
	Clarice L. R. Privette (R)		(19%)
1972 primary:	Thomas S. Foley (D), unopposed		
1970 general:	Thomas S. Foley (D)	88,189	(67%)
	George Gamble (R)	43,376	(33%)

SIXTH DISTRICT Political Background

Tacoma (pop. 154,000), the second-largest city on Puget Sound, has always lived in the shadow of its larger neighbor, Seattle. Back in 1900, just before the state's most explosive decade of growth, Tacoma was still a creditable rival—it had 37,000 people to Seattle's 80,000. But in the years that followed, Seattle's growth took off, while Tacoma got itself embroiled in an unsuccessful attempt to rewrite history and change the name of Mount Rainer (which lies in Pierce County like the city) to Mount Tacoma. Subsequently, Seattle grew, diversified, became too dependent on the aircraft industry, and floundered in the early 1970s; Tacoma, meanwhile, remained mostly a lumber town (Weyerhaeuser), with only about a quarter of the metropolitan population of its larger neighbor. Tacoma never experienced the white-collar influx that descended upon Seattle; it stayed a blue-collar, and usually the most Democratic, town in Washington.

Tacoma is the heart of the state's 6th congressional district, which includes the city and virtually all of its suburbs. The 6th also crosses the Puget Sound Narrows (where the Tacoma Straits Bridge collapsed in 1940) to include Kitsap County, which lies directly across the sound from Seattle. Despite Tacoma's Democratic leanings, a Republican Congressman represented the district for 20 years, from 1945 to 1965, a politician with the asset here of an unmistakably Scandinavian name, Thor Tollefson. In the Johnson landslide of 1964, Tollefson was upset by Democrat Floyd Hicks, who resigned a local judgeship to make the race. Hicks has won reelection easily ever since. In Washington, he serves on the House Armed Services Committee; after the 1972 boundary changes, huge Fort Lewis sits just outside Tacoma and over the district line in the 3rd. And there are several naval facilities in and near Bremerton in Kitsap County. Though not a leader of the dovish minority on Armed Services, Hicks usually votes with the outnumbered group.

Census Data Pop. 454,793. Central city, 32%; suburban, 47%. Median family income, $10,481; families above $15,000: 22%; families below $3,000: 8%. Median years education, 12.3.

1972 Share of Federal Outlays $800,133,694

DOD	$516,520,459	HEW	$135,314,483
AEC	$105,589	HUD	$6,657,005
NASA	$465,476	DOI	$4,460,786
DOT	$21,643,227	USDA	$11,696,764
		Other	$103,269,905

Federal Military-Industrial Commitments

DOD Installations Polaris Missile Facility, Pacific (Bremerton). Naval Hospital (Bremerton). Naval Supply Center, Puget Sound (Bremerton). Naval Torpedo Station (Keyport). Puget Sound Naval Shipyard (Bremerton).

Economic Base Finance, insurance and real estate; agriculture, notably poultry, dairy products and nursery and greenhouse products; and lumber and wood products, especially millwork, plywood and related products.

The Voters

Registration 269,665 total. No party registration.
Median voting age 42.2
Employment profile White collar, 50%. Blue collar, 36%. Service, 13%. Farm, 1%.
Ethnic groups Black, 3%. Spanish, 1%. Total foreign stock, 19%. Canada, Germany, 3% each; Norway, UK, 2% each; Sweden, 1%.

Presidential vote

1972	Nixon (R)		115,377	(60%)
	McGovern (D)		75,698	(40%)
1968	Nixon (R)		NA	
	Humphrey (D)		NA	
	Wallace (AI)		NA	

Representative

Floyd V. Hicks (D) Elected 1964; b. May 29, 1915, Prosser; home, Tacoma; Cen. Wash. State Col., B.Ed., 1938; U. of Wash., LL.B., 1948; AAF, WWII; married, two children; religion unspecified.

Career Practicing atty., 1949–60, 1963–64; judge, Pierce County Superior Ct., 1961–63.

Offices 1202 LHOB, 202-225-5916. Also 210 Broadway, Tacome 98402, 206-383-1666.

Administrative Assistant John C. Horsley

Committees

Armed Services (12th); Sub: No. 1; Sp. Sub. on Human Relations (Chm.).

Government Operations (15th); Conservation and Natural Resources; Special Studies (Chm.).

Group Ratings

	ADA	COPE	LWV	RIPON	NFU	LCV	CFA	NAB	NSI	ACA
1972	69	91	92	63	86	33	50	17	56	13
1971	68	90	78	50	86	–	75	–	–	30
1970	68	92	–	63	85	45	86	8	70	24

Key Votes

1) Busing	FOR	6) Cmbodia Bmbg	AGN	11) Chkg Acct Intrst	AGN
2) Strip Mines	AGN	7) Bust Hwy Trust	FOR	12) End HISC (HUAC)	AGN
3) Cut Mil $	AGN	8) Farm Sub Lmt	AGN	13) Nixon Sewer Veto	AGN
4) Rev Shrg	FOR	9) School Prayr	FOR	14) Corp Cmpaign $	FOR
5) Pub TV $	FOR	10) Cnsumr Prot	FOR	15) Pol $ Disclosr	AGN

Election Results

1972 general:	Floyd V. Hicks (D)	126,349	(72%)
	Thomas C. Lowry (R)	48,914	(28%)
1972 primary:	Floyd V. Hicks (D), unopposed		
1970 general:	Floyd V. Hicks (D)	98,282	(69%)
	John Jarstad (R)	42,213	(30%)
	Richard Congress (SW)	1,180	(1%)

SEVENTH DISTRICT Political Background

The 7th district of Washington is the south side of Seattle and its suburbs. Seattle has fewer urban ills than most major cities. The crime rate is relatively low, and the city neighborhoods on the steep hills overlooking Puget Sound or Lake Washington retain a comfortable and forever green look, thanks to the almost constant rain. But as in other major metropolitan areas, the population here has been shifting to the suburbs. Seattle's downtown, which is part of the 7th district, is doing well commercially, but few people live in it any more. To the south is the city's not-so-large black ghetto; nearly half of the state's blacks live in the 7th, but only 7% of the district's residents are black. Though the 7th also contains smaller Mexican-American and Asian communities, most of south side Seattle remains working-class white.

The real heart of the district, however, are the suburbs south of the city. Here the major Boeing plants are located, along with the people who work—or used to work—in them. Though a few wealthy, heavily Republican suburbs—a part of Bellevue and Mercer Island—were added to the district after the 1970 census, most of the subdivisions are places like Renton and Kent, which are occupied by blue-collar and white-collar clerical workers. Up through the 1950s and 1960s, this area of rapid growth exuded the kind of prosperity built on the boom in the aircraft industry and attendant high union wages. But as the 1960s ended, the fortunes of the Boeing Company—then the district's major employer—turned sour, and the 7th, along with the entire Seattle area, was thrown into a kind of depression. White-collar workers found themselves in unemployment lines, and real estate values plummeted as people moved south or east to find work. The affluence of the 7th was based on brittle foundations: the inherently unstable aircraft industry. Like the 1930s, people who had prided themselves on what they had achieved found themselves helpless to preserve it in the face of economic forces beyond their control.

Nevertheless, the Boeing depression has not appeared to have had much of an effect on the political habits of the 7th district. To be sure, Richard Nixon carried this normally Democratic district in 1972, but with only 56% of the votes. This is not an especially large share by national standards, nor is it one that represents a larger than normal drop in Democratic percentages. And the developments in the Seattle economy have not at all hurt Brock Adams, the liberal Democratic Congressman from the 7th.

Like all members of the Washington delegation, Adams was a strong proponent of the unsuccessful move to get the government to loan Boeing the money to build the supersonic transport (SST). But on other issues involving military and defense-related spending, Adams has more often voted with Sen. Warren Magnuson than with the state's other, more hawkish Senator, Henry Jackson. Nevertheless, the Republicans have made no move to attack Adams on these grounds; in 1972, the Congressman won reelection by a margin even bigger than the one he usually gets.

In the House, Adams serves on the Commerce Committee and its subcommittee on Transportation and Aeronautics. He has used his position not only to boost the cause of Boeing, but also to advance proposals for better-integrated rail transportation. In the 93rd Congress, however, Adams has devoted most of his energies to a committee he just recently joined. As Chairman of the Government Operations Subcommittee of the House District of Columbia Committee, Adams has had the task of drawing up home rule legislation for the nation's capital. While doing this, he has had to mollify Republicans by including some of the major recommendations of the Nelsen Commission for streamlining the District government. At this writing, the bill has come out of both Adams' subcommittee and the full committee, and awaits action on the floor. The fate of the legislation is uncertain. But if home rule fails to pass in late 1973, the issue will surely come up again in 1974.

Adams is widely regarded as a possible successor to either Sen. Magnuson or Sen. Jackson. The Congressman is something of a Magnuson protege, having held the office of U.S. Attorney in Seattle—a prerogative of Magnuson—before he went to Congress. An articulate public speaker, Adams is well known in the Seattle media market, which contains two-thirds of the state's voters. He will probably be the favorite should Scoop Jackson pass up sure reelection for the 1976 Democratic presidential nomination.

Census Data Pop. 420,058. Central city, 43%; suburban, 57%. Median family income, $11,706; families above $15,000: 30%; families below $3,000: 6%. Median years education, 12.4.

1972 Share of Federal Outlays $786,285,653

DOD	$341,006,289	HEW	$164,467,180
AEC	$776,984	HUD	$14,500,279
NASA	$3,425,220	DOI	$4,883,319
DOT	$80,009,875	USDA	$20,675,718
		Other	$156,540,789

Federal Military-Industrial Commitments

DOD Contractors Boeing (Seattle), $724.322m: Short Range Attack Missile; Minuteman weapons system; hydrofoil research. Boeing (Kent), $69.461m: Air Force satellite program. Alaska Barge and Transport Co. (Seattle), $13.200m: transportations services.

Economic Base Transportation equipment, especially aircraft and parts; finance, insurance and real estate; food and kindred products, especially bakery products; and printing and publishing, especially newspapers.

The Voters

Registration 282,597 total. No party registration.

Median voting age 41.8
Employment profile White collar, 54%. Blue collar, 33%. Service, 13%. Farm, –%.
Ethnic groups Black, 7%. Spanish, 2%. Total foreign stock, 22%. Canada, 4%; UK, Germany, Norway, 2% each; Sweden, 1%.

Presidential vote

1972	Nixon (R)	111,127	(56%)
	McGovern (D)	85,891	(44%)
1968	Nixon (R)	NA	
	Humphrey (D)	NA	
	Wallace (AI)	NA	

Representative

Brock Adams (D) Elected 1964; b. Jan. 13, 1927, Atlanta, Ga.; home, Seattle; U. of Wash., B.A., 1949; Harvard, LL.B., 1952; Navy, WWII; married, four children; Episcopalian.

Career Practicing atty., 1952–61; U.S. Dist. Atty. for Western Wash., 1961–64.

Offices 436 CHOB, 202-225-3106. Also Rm. 1006, U.S. Courthouse, Seattle 98104, 206-583-7478.

Administrative Assistant Alan Butchman

Committees

District of Columbia (6th). Subs: Government Operations (Chm.); Revenue and Financial Affairs.

Interstate and Foreign Commerce (12th); Sub: Transportation and Aeronautics.

Group Ratings

	ADA	COPE	LWV	RIPON	NFU	LCV	CFA	NAB	NSI	ACA
1972	94	100	100	62	100	48	100	9	22	9
1971	86	100	88	76	87	–	100	–	–	0
1970	88	100	–	92	92	81	94	0	40	6

Key Votes

1) Busing	FOR	6) Cmbodia Bmbg	AGN	11) Chkg Acct Intrst	AGN
2) Strip Mines	AGN	7) Bust Hwy Trust	FOR	12) End HISC (HUAC)	FOR
3) Cut Mil $	FOR	8) Farm Sub Lmt	FOR	13) Nixon Sewer Veto	AGN
4) Rev Shrg	AGN	9) School Prayr	AGN	14) Corp Cmpaign $	FOR
5) Pub TV $	FOR	10) Cnsumr Prot	FOR	15) Pol $ Disclosr	ABS

Election Results

1972 general:	Brock Adams (D)	140,307	(85%)
	J. J. Freeman (R)	19,889	(12%)
	Thomas Forsythe (Write-in)	4,128	(3%)
1972 primary:	Brock Adams (D), unopposed		
1970 general:	Brock Adams (D)	99,308	(67%)
	Brian Lewis (R)	47,426	(32%)
	Russell Block (SW)	2,378	(1%)

WEST VIRGINIA

Political Background

West Virginia lies in the middle of the Appalachian chain that separates the East Coast from the vast Mississippi Valley of Mid-America. Somebody has opined that if all the mountains in the state were smoothed out, West Virginia would cover the entire nation. No one, it seems, would want to demonstrate the truth of the proposition, but the mountains—and the narrow, twisting roads that wind through them—do give West Virginians a sense of isolation and distance from the rest of the country. Residents of the Appalachian heartland do not think of themselves as Easterners, Midwesterners, or to a marked degree as Southerners.

Residents of the mountain counties of old Virginia never kept many slaves, the symbol of wealth and social status among aristocratic Tidewater planters. Accordingly, the mountaineers felt that they always got the short end of the stick at any convocation of state government in Williamsburg or Richmond. In the late 1820s, state legislators from the mountain counties and liberal aristocrats in the tradition of Thomas Jefferson teamed up and almost abolished slavery in Virginia. Because the tobacco lands of the Tidewater were pretty near exhaustion, even the plantation owners flagged in their enthusiasm for the peculiar institution. Soon, however, the market for slaves improved sharply, as new cotton lands opened up in Alabama and Mississippi. As a result, Virginia plantations became breeding grounds for human chattel, and any hopes for voluntary abolition went by the boards. Nevertheless, the mountain counties remained hostile to slavery and secession; when the shots were fired at Fort Sumter, they chose to stay loyal to the Union and Republican President Lincoln. In 1863, the mountain counties were admitted to the Union as the separate state of West Virginia.

The new state included about a quarter of the residents of old Virginia. But in the years following the Civil War, West Virginia grew much faster than its parent. The reason was simple: coal. Under virtually all the mountains here are rich veins of bituminous coal, which was the essential fuel for industry and home heating during the late nineteenth and early twentieth centuries. Men from all over the Appalachian region and even some immigrants from Eastern and Southern Europe came to work the booming mines. Even today, West Virginia still produces more than a quarter of the nation's coal, which means tha coal industry continues to dominate the state's economy.

The working conditions in the mines were never very good, of course. Lovers of country music know something of life in coal company towns and the practices of company stores. During the 1930s, bloody strikes were common, as John L. Lewis' United Mine Workers established itself as the bargaining agent for the miners. But even as unionization proceeded, the coal industry began to decline. Houses built in the 1930s and 1940s were heated by oil, not coal, and the railroads began to switch from the coal-fired steam locomotive to the oil-powered Diesel engine. After World War II, Lewis and the UMW worked with the companies to encourage mechanization of the industry and the reduction of the work force. The program was a remarkable success, but resulted in bad times for West Virginia. In 1950, the state's population exceeded 2,000,000; by 1970, the figure dropped to 1,744,000. The decline represents heavy outmigration of people looking for jobs, for most West Virginians love the mountain country, which they would not leave were it not absolutely necessary.

Recently, the coal industry has come upon better times. As other fuels grow more expensive, coal becomes more attractive. Moreover, there is no shortage of the black commodity—West Virginia alone has enough to supply the country for hundreds of years. But the new prosperity has brought new problems. The practice of strip mining has increased manyfold; and despite company claims about reclamation, it leaves ugly, woeful scars on the once green hills. Moreover, the narrow valleys and hollows of West Virginia now experience serious water and air pollution. Stripping also employs far fewer miners per ton produced than underground mining. Finally, the Buffalo Creek disaster of 1972—where a dam burst and waters inundated and destroyed a small town—points out once again how casual even the largest coal companies are about safety precautions.

Meanwhile, the UMW has undergone a revolution of sorts. Tony Boyle, who succeeded John L. Lewis as the president of the union, seemed to possess all of the great man's vices and none of his virtues. In 1969, Joseph Yablonski challenged Boyle for the office. The election was marked by all manner of irregularities; and several weeks after the contest, Yablonski, his wife, and daughter were found murdered in their Pennsylvania home. A couple of UMW officials have been convicted of the crime, and Boyle himself was indicted in September 1973; shortly thereafter, he tried to kill himself. Meanwhile, after the Labor Department was finally persuaded to interest itself in the conduct of the 1969 election, a rerun was ordered. This time, under strict supervision, Arnold Miller, head of the Miners of Democracy, defeated Boyle soundly; Miller was himself a West Virginia miner forced to leave the pits because of a black-lung condition.

The new Miller leadership has ended the cozy relationship between the UMW and the coal companies—they once jointly opposed antipollution legislation, for instance. Moreover, the union leadership now keeps an open mind about the desirablility of strip mining. Only a few West Virginia politicians have come out against stripping, notably Congressman Ken Hechler and ex-Secretary of State John D. (Jay) Rockefeller, and Hechler was an untiring supporter of the Miners for Democracy movement. But the old Boyle cronies retain power in some West Virginia UMW locals, particularly in the isolated, though densely populated, southern counties. Here politics remains a rough business.

For years after statehood, West Virginia was a Republican state. But with the rise of the coal industry and the UMW, it became solidly Democratic in both registration and elections. Today, the state sends an all-Democratic delegation to Washington. So it was rather surprising, at least to outsiders, when a Republican incumbent, Arch Moore, defeated Democratic challenger Jay Rockefeller for Governor in 1972. A former Congressman from the 1st district, Moore parlayed his folksy manner and scandals among the Democrats into a narrow gubernatorial win in 1968. Two years later, he secured passage of a state constitutional amendment that permitted the incumbent a second consecutive term. Politics in West Virginia is notably patronage-ridden and corrupt; ex-Gov. (1961–64) W. W. Barron, for example, is now in jail. So by comparison with past administrations, at least, Moore's tenure has been honest and efficient. Moore also knows how to use his patronage powers to best political effect, and has aggressively promoted new jobs in the state. As he came up for a third term, Moore won the support of both the coal companies—unhappy with Rockefeller's proposal to abolish strip mining—and the Boyle types in the UMW.

Moore's record and political savvy accounted for his 55–45 victory over Rockefeller. Moore's bumper stickers summed things up nicely: "Reelect a good Governor." But Moore also waged an aggressive, hard-hitting campaign against the challenger. The Governor implied that Rockefeller opposed not just strip mining, but underground mining as well, and that the opposition stemmed from the Rockefeller family interests in oil and natural gas. Nor did it help the political chances of the present John D. Rockefeller that the first John D. Rockefeller resisted the efforts of the United Mine Workers to organize the fields of the Colorado Fuel and Iron Company. The conflict resulted in the "Ludlow Massacre," which occupies a special place in the history of the American miner and the UMW (and about which a young graduate student named George McGovern wrote his doctoral thesis in the 1940's).

In 1964, Jay Rockefeller came to West Virginia to work in the anti-poverty program. He then decided to stay in the state and enter politics, winning election to the state legislature and the office of Secretary of State. But West Virginians are suspicious of outsiders—few people, after all, immigrate here. Accordingly, Moore ran a series of TV ads showing an interviewer asking New Yorkers whether they wanted someone from West Virginia to move in and run for Governor. Nor was Rockefeller liked by many of the traditional Democratic pols, who doubted whether he would deliver the patronage they were used to. In the end, Rockefeller lost every area in the state, even the heavily Democratic southern coal counties. A few months after the election, the defeated candidate became president of West Virginia Wesleyan College in Buckhannon. Rockefeller says his intention to remain a West Virginian has never wavered. So everybody assumes he will run for Governor again in 1976, when Moore will be ineligible for reelection.

The other major race on the 1972 ballot was not much of a contest. Sen. Jennings Randolph was easily reelected with 66% of the votes. Randolph is one of the most experienced war horses on Capitol Hill. He first came to Washington in 1932, at age 30, as a freshman New Deal member of the House. Defeated in the Republican year of 1946, he became a Hill lobbyist, but kept a hand in West Virginia politics. In 1958, he won election to the Senate, and has had little trouble staying there since.

Randolph is now Chairman of the Senate Public Works Committee, the keeper of the traditional pork barrel. But the unit also passes on major legislation concerning air and water pollution. The Chairman remains a kind of old New Dealer, willing and even eager to issue job-creating projects to his Senate colleagues. Moreover, Randolph usually makes sure that West Virginia's interests—which is to say, the interests of coal—are protected when it comes time to consider antipollution legislation. On such measures, however, Randolph takes a back seat to the committee's second-ranking Democrat, Edmund Muskie. Nevertheless, Muskie is careful to touch base with Randolph and gets his support whenever possible.

One issue that split Randolph and Muskie was whether the highway trust fund should be tapped for mass transit projects. Randolph still sees the highway program as a way to create jobs and tie isolated communities together. Though most of the Interstate Highway money scheduled to be spent is earmarked for urban areas, Randolph's vision represents an accurate picture of the situation in West Virginia; much of the Interstate mileage over the mountains remains unfinished. The Muskie forces on the issue prevailed over Randolph. Then, after the House reached a contrary decision, a conference committee reported out a compromise bill, which allowed some limited diversions from the fund. Randolph will probably retire in 1978 when his seat comes up and he will be 76. A possible successor is young (31) state Supreme Court Justice Richard Neely, grandson of longtime Sen. and Gov. Matthew Neely, who served intermittently from 1923 to 1958.

West Virginia's junior Senator is a man who has begun to cut an increasingly important national figure—Senate Majority Whip Robert Byrd. No relation to the Virginia Byrds, Robert Byrd comes from a background of extreme poverty. Though his instincts are basically conservative, Byrd has enjoyed a surprisingly successful ascent in the Senate and in the increasingly liberal Democratic Caucus. He only quit the Ku Klux Klan in 1945, a year before he was elected to the West Virginia House of Delegates. In Congress, he has voted against civil rights legislation and conducted what many considered a vindictive campaign against alleged welfare abuses in the District of Columbia. Byrd moved from the state legislature to the U. S. House in 1952, and on to the Senate in 1958. His success involved no gladhanding, or charm, or even patronage. His secret, rather, was the same one that got him the Whip's job and now makes him a likely successor to Majority Leader Mike Mansfield: hard work.

For Byrd is a charmless, dour man of the grindstone. He courts Senators with the same assiduity that prompts him to keep card files on thousands of West Virginia voters. With these in hand, Byrd writes and telephones the people, asking them their opinions on issues. In 1969 and 1970, while Edward Kennedy was Whip, Byrd was Secretary of the Senate Democratic Conference. On the job, Byrd paid meticulous attention to the petty details that make the lives of Senators easier: keeping them informed of the pace of floor debate and the schedule of upcoming votes, helping them to get amendments before the Senate, arranging pairs, and so forth. Moreover, Byrd has always shown his colleagues elaborate courtesy, writing them thank-you notes on the slightest pretext. It all paid off in 1971, when Byrd suddenly challenged Kennedy for the Whip post. The West Virginian did not announce his candidacy until he was absolutely sure of a majority, which he got by securing Richard Russell's death-bed proxy.

As Whip, Byrd has continued to attend to the smallest details. He assists Majority Leader Mansfield and other Democrats in just about every way possible. But such diligence alone did not move him into contention for the Majority Leadership—his record no longer demonstrates the solid conservatism it once did. Fortunately for Byrd, the kind of issues that have come before the Senate, especially after Nixon's landslide reelection, have taken the shape of a confrontation between the executive and legislative branches. And Byrd has had little trouble supporting the legislative branch nearly every time.

Here, too, the Senator's penchant for hard work has paid off. While L. Patrick Gray testified before the Judiciary Committee during his confirmation hearings, Byrd made a close study of the record. Byrd's scrutiny enabled him to put the question that forced Gray to admit that then White House Counsel John Dean "probably lied" to him about Watergate conspirator E. Howard Hunt. Later, Byrd was ready with proposals to promote the independence of the FBI, and also made a solid case against the Nixon position on executive privilege. Byrd hammered away relentlessly at the facts, and so helped to dissolve the White House cover-up and break the Watergate scandal open.

Byrd has also moved toward the center of his party on other issues. These days, he does not talk very much about welfare chiselers. But he has urged, for example, that the United States resume normal diplomatic relations with Cuba and that we quit the SEATO alliance. And he has come forward with dozens of solid proposals on other matters, notably campaign regulations and disclosure of assets by officeholders. The chances now are that he will become Majority Leader if Mansfield retires in 1976 or otherwise relinquishes the post.

Byrd's rise in West Virginia politics is also attributable to hard work. He was never part of the clubby, good-old-boy atmosphere of West Virginia's Democratic politics, nor was he an important participant in the patronage system. In 1952, cut off from funds by the party for his past membership in the Klan, Byrd financed his own House campaign with contributions of fifty cents and a dollar. He then won reelection to Congress largely because of his careful, meticulous attention to the problems of constituents. The Senator is now, of course, totally invulnerable statewide in West Virginia. In 1970, he whipped a liberal primary challenger with 89% of the votes. In the general election that followed, he became the first candidate in history to carry all of the state's 55 counties, some of them rock-ribbed Republican since the Civil War. His margin was so great that he received at least 61% of the votes in every county. Byrd's seat in the Senate is thus not in doubt; the question is how important a man he will become within the Senate.

Census Data Pop. 1,744,237; 0.86% of U.S. total, 34th largest; change 1960–70, –6.2%. Central city, 13%; suburban, 19%. Median family income, $7,414; 47th highest; families above $15,000: 10%; families below $3,000: 17%. Median years education, 10.6.

1972 Share of Federal Tax Burden $1,337,720,000; 0.64% of U.S. total, 33rd largest.

1972 Share of Federal Outlays $1,536,100,410; 0.71% of U.S. total, 36th largest. Per capita federal spending, $881.

DOD	$99,418,000	48th (0.16%)	HEW	$732,271,120	30th (1.03%)
AEC	—	— (—)	HUD	$9,641,615	42nd (0.31%)
NASA	$50,782	46th (—)	VA	$130,611,898	34th (1.14%)
DOT	$230,195,411	10th (2.92%)	USDA	$101,560,440	38th (0.66%)
DOC	$7,540,383	29th (0.58%)	CSC	$18,550,232	41st (0.45%)
DOI	$16,274,686	29th (0.77%)	TD	$48,235,402	36th (0.29%)
DOJ	$13,505,859	26th (1.38%)	Other	$128,244,582	

Economic Base Bituminous coal mining; chemicals and allied products, especially industrial chemicals; primary metal industries, especially blast furnaces and basic steel products; stone, clay and glass products, especially glassware, pressed or blown; finance, insurance and real estate; agriculture, especially cattle, dairy products, apples and eggs.

Political Line-up Governor, Arch A. Moore, Jr. (R); seat up, 1976. Senators, Jennings Randolph (D) and Robert C. Byrd (D). Representatives, 4 D. State Senate (24 D and 10 R); House of Delegates (57 D and 43 R).

The Voters

Registration 1,062,519 Total. 686,620 D (65%); 359,016 R (34%); 16,883 Ind. (2%).
Median voting age 45.3
Employment profile White collar, 40%. Blue collar, 45%. Service, 13%. Farm, 2%.
Ethnic groups Black, 4%. Total foreign stock, 4%.

Presidential vote

1972	Nixon (R)	484,964	(64%)
	McGovern (D)	277,435	(36%)
1968	Nixon (R)	307,555	(41%)
	Humphrey (D)	374,091	(50%)
	Wallace (AI)	72,560	(10%)
1964	Johnson (D)	538,087	(68%)
	Goldwater (R)	253,953	(32%)

Senator

Jennings Randolph (D) Elected 1958, seat up 1978; b. Mar. 8, 1902, Salem; home, Elkins; Salem Col., B.A., 1924; married, two children; Baptist.

Career U.S. House, 1933–47; newspaper and magazine editor; col. professor; university dean; airline executive.

Offices 5121 NSOB, 202-225-6472. Also 303 New P.O. Bldg., Clarksburg 26301, 304-623-2811.

Administrative Assistant James W. Harris

Committees

Labor and Public Welfare (2nd); Subs: Education; Labor; Handicapped (Chm.); Alcoholism and Narcotics; Aging; Children and Youth; Employment, Poverty, and Migratory Labor; Sp. Com. on Human Resources.

Post Office and Civil Service (2nd); Subs: Civil Service Policies and Practices (Chm.); Postal Operations.

Public Works (Chm.); Sub: Air and Water Pollution.

Veterans' Affairs (3rd); Subs: Compensation and Pensions; Health and Hospitals.

Sp. Com. on Aging (4th); Sub: Employment and Retirement Incomes (Chm.).

Group Ratings

	ADA	COPE	LWV	RIPON	NFU	LCV	CFA	NAB	NSI	ACA
1972	40	70	64	46	80	20	91	50	40	28
1971	67	83	62	32	64	–	100	–	–	25
1970	59	69	–	42	93	21	–	25	40	26

Key Votes

1) Busing	AGN	8) Sea Life Prot	FOR	15) Tax Singls Less	AGN
2) Alas P-line	FOR	9) Campaign Subs	FOR	16) Min Tax for Rich	AGN
3) Gun Cntrl	FOR	10) Cmbodia Bmbg	AGN	17) Euro Troop Rdctn	FOR
4) Rehnquist	FOR	11) Legal Srvices	FOR	18) Bust Hwy Trust	AGN
5) Pub TV $	FOR	12) Rev Sharing	FOR	19) Maid Min Wage	FOR
6) EZ Votr Reg	FOR	13) Cnsumr Prot	FOR	20) Farm Sub Limit	AGN
7) No-Fault	AGN	14) Eq Rts Amend	FOR	21) Highr Credt Chgs	AGN

Election Results

1972 general:	Jennings Randolph (D)	486,310	(66%)
	Louise Leonard (R)	245,531	(34%)
1972 primary:	Jennings Randolph (D), unopposed		
1966 general:	Jennings Randolph (D)	292,325	(60%)
	Francis J. Love (R)	198,891	(40%)

Senator

Robert C. Byrd (D) Elected 1958, seat up 1976; b. Jan. 15, 1918, N. Wilkesboro, N.C.; home, Sophia; Beckley Col., Concord Col., and Morris Harvey Col., 1950–51; American U., J.D., 1963; married, two children; Baptist.

Career W. Va. Legislature, 1946–50, Senate, 1950–52; U.S. House of Reps., 1953–59.

Offices 105 OSOB, 202-225-3954.

Administrative Assistant Virginia M. Yates

Committees

Appropriations (6th); Subs: Agriculture, Environmental and Consumer Protection; Labor and Health, Education, and Welfare, and Related Agencies; Public Works, AEC; Transportation (Chm.); Interior.

Judiciary (8th); Subs: Constitutional Amendments; Constitutional Rights; Criminal Laws and Procedures; Separation of Powers.

Rules and Administration (3rd); Subs: Privileges and Elections; Standing Rules of the Senate (Chm.).

Group Ratings

	ADA	COPE	LWV	RIPON	NFU	LCV	CFA	NAB	NSI	ACA
1972	35	70	45	32	90	20	90	46	70	50
1971	26	58	38	22	45	–	100	–	–	45
1970	3	46	–	19	87	30	–	27	90	50

Key Votes

1) Busing	AGN	8) Sea Life Prot	FOR	15) Tax Singls Less	AGN
2) Alas P-line	FOR	9) Campaign Subs	FOR	16) Min Tax for Rich	AGN
3) Gun Cntrl	FOR	10) Cmbodia Bmbg	AGN	17) Euro Troop Rdctn	FOR
4) Rehnquist	FOR	11) Legal Srvices	AGN	18) Bust Hwy Trust	AGN
5) Pub TV $	FOR	12) Rev Sharing	AGN	19) Maid Min Wage	FOR
6) EZ Votr Reg	FOR	13) Cnsumr Prot	FOR	20) Farm Sub Limit	AGN
7) No-Fault	FOR	14) Eq Rts Amend	FOR	21) Highr Credt Chgs	AGN

Election Results

1970 general:	Robert C. Byrd (D)	345,965	(78%)
	Elmer H. Dodson (R)	99,663	(22%)
1970 primary:	Robert C. Byrd (D)	195,725	(89%)
	John J. McOwen (D)	24,286	(11%)
1964 general:	Robert C. Byrd (D)	515,015	(68%)
	Cooper P. Benedict (R)	246,072	(32%)

FIRST DISTRICT Political Background

West Virginia's northern panhandle is the least isolated part of the state—the terrain here is just hilly, not mountainous. The panhandle is steel country that sits along the Ohio River just west of Pittsburgh and south of Youngstown. Along the river are giant blast furnaces in Wheeling (pop. 48,000) and Weirton (pop. 27,000). With the Pittsburgh area, the panhandle is also one of the leading glassmaking regions of the country. So industrial pollution here is a major problem. The Ohio River Valley around Wheeling has the worst air in the United States, and water pollution is bad in the Ohio River itself and in the Monongahela, which flows through Clarksburg (pop. 24,000) and Fairmont (pop. 25,000).

These two towns in the Monongahela Valley, the panhandle, and the Ohio River counties as far south as Parkersburg (pop. 44,000) make up West Virginia's 1st congressional district. Aside from a few rural counties and Parkersburg, which tend to go Republican, the 1st district is Democratic territory in most elections. But such has not always been the case in congressional elections, thanks to the vote-getting prowess of Arch Moore, former 1st-district Congressman and now Governor. Moore was first elected to the House in 1956, when Eisenhower swept the state and the Republicans won a Senate seat and the governorship. Though the years to come proved less happy for the GOP, Moore, an enthusiastic campaigner and an unabashed booster of West Virginia, won reelection by larger and larger margins. He faced his toughest contest in 1962, when he was thrown into the same district with Democratic incumbent Cleveland Bailey. Moore won a solid 61% of the votes against the 76-year-old Democrat; two years later, despite Barry Goldwater's disastrous showing here, Moore won with 71%.

Electoral achievements of this magnitude are enough to make a man think of bigger things. So Moore decided to run for Governor in 1968. The experts figured his chances were slim; but relying heavily on home-district strength, the Republican defeated ex-Gov. (1957–60) Cecil Underwood in the primary and edged Democratic State Chairman James Sprouse by 12,000 votes in the general election. The victory over Sprouse occurred with the help of a 36,000-vote margin within the boundaries of what was then the 1st district.

Moore's successor in the House, Robert Mollohan, is the Democrat Moore beat back in 1956. A veteran of the West Virginia political wars, Mollohan now serves on the House Armed Services Committee. Here the Congressman usually finds himself agreeing with the unit's hawkish bipartisan majority; in 1973, for example, he was the only member of the West Virginia delegation to vote to continue the bombing of Cambodia. Mollohan's prospects for reelection appear good. In 1970, he beat Sam Huff, former New York Giants star linebacker, in the Democratic primary, and then took 62% of the votes in the general election. The addition of Republican Parkersburg did nothing to prevent Mollohan from winning a significantly larger share of the votes than ever before in the year of the Nixon landslide.

Census Data Pop. 436,337. Central city, 17%; suburban, 22%. Median family income, $8,457; families above $15,000: 12%; families below $3,000: 12%. Median years education, 11.6.

1972 Share of Federal Outlays $321,315,913

DOD	$17,407,000	HEW	$151,950,874
AEC	–	HUD	$1,441,754
NASA	–	DOI	$2,060,692
DOT	$57,621,160	USDA	$14,264,855
		Other	$76,569,578

Federal Military-Industrial Commitments

No installations or contractors receiving prime awards greater than $5,000,000.

Economic Base Stone, clay and glass products; chemicals and allied products, especially plastics materials and synthetics; bituminous coal mining; finance, insurance and real estate; and primary metal industries.

The Voters

Registration 271,481 total. 167,519 D (62%); 99,077 R (36%); 4,885 Ind. (2%).
Median voting age 45.6
Employment profile White collar, 39%. Blue collar, 47%. Service, 13%. Farm, 1%.
Ethnic groups Black, 2%. Total foreign stock, 9%.

Presidential vote

1972	Nixon (R)	126,902	(64%)
	McGovern (D)	70,735	(36%)
1968	Nixon (R)	83,951	(42%)
	Humphrey (D)	99,294	(50%)
	Wallace (AI)	16,366	(8%)

Representative

Robert H. Mollohan (D) Elected 1952–56, 1968; b. Sept. 18, 1909, Grantsville; home, Fairmont; Shepherd Col.; married, three children; Baptist.

Career Chief, tax div. and cashier, IRS in W.Va., 1933–36; Dist. Mgr. and State Pers. Dir., WPA, 1937–40; supt., W.Va. Industrial School for Boys, 1945–49; U.S. Marshal, 1949–51; clerk, U.S. Senate Com. on District of Columbia.

Offices 314 CHOB, 202-225-4172. Also Rm. 603, Deveny Bldg., Fairmont 26554, 304-363-3356.

Administrative Assistant Patricia Muncy

Committees

Armed Services (16th); Subs: No. 3; Sp. Sub. on Armed Services Investigating; Human Relations.

House Administration (13th); Subs: Elections; Electrical and Mechanical Office Equipment.

Group Ratings

	ADA	COPE	LWV	RIPON	NFU	LCV	CFA	NAB	NSI	ACA
1972	19	90	33	46	100	33	50	10	100	26
1971	27	100	63	35	79	–	86	–	–	42
1970	36	100	–	36	82	67	67	0	88	18

Key Votes

1) Busing	AGN	6) Cmbodia Bmbg	ABS	11) Chkg Acct Intrst	FOR
2) Strip Mines	FOR	7) Bust Hwy Trust	AGN	12) End HISC (HUAC)	AGN
3) Cut Mil $	AGN	8) Farm Sub Lmt	FOR	13) Nixon Sewer Veto	AGN
4) Rev Shrg	FOR	9) School Prayr	FOR	14) Corp Cmpaign $	ABS
5) Pub TV $	FOR	10) Cnsumr Prot	FOR	15) Pol $ Disclosr	AGN

Election Results

1972 general:	Robert H. Mollohan (D)	130,062	(69%)
	George E. Kapnicky (R)	57,274	(31%)
1972 primary:	Robert H. Mollohan (D), unopposed		
1970 general:	Robert H. Mollohan (D)	61,296	(62%)
	Ken Doll (R)	38,327	(38%)

SECOND DISTRICT Political Background

The 2nd district of West Virginia occupies the eastern part of the state, and contains the most mountainous and sparsely populated counties of West Virginia. The district extends from Harper's Ferry, not far from Washington, D.C., where John Brown's raiders seized the arsenal in 1859, south and west to Fayette County, near the state capital of Charleston, and to Monroe County, not far from the Kentucky line. In the northwest part of the district, not far from Pittsburgh, is the 2nd's only significant city, Morgantown (pop. 29,000)—part of the industrial Monongahela River Valley and home of West Virginia University.

The problems of the 2nd district are typical of the entire Appalachian region. For one thing, there are virtually no four-lane highways in the district, and the existing roads, twisting around the mountains effectively make the rural coal towns here more remote from the East Coast than the geographically more distant cities of the Great Lakes. For another thing, the beauty of the West Virginia hills is often despoiled by emissions from coal mines and paper mills, and by the ugly scars left by strip miners. And what is even worse for the people who want to stay here, many of the industries have been gradually leaving.

The political map of the 2nd district is an odd-looking patchwork of Democratic industrial and mining areas and Republican mountain strongholds. In most statewide elections, the district is marginal; but in congressional contests, it is solidly Democratic. Congressman Harley Staggers has represented the 2nd in the House since the 1948 election; recently, he has grown accustomed to winning with percentages approaching 70%. For the past seven years, Staggers has served as Chairman of the House Interstate and Foreign Commerce Committee. His unit has jurisdiction over most of the federal regulatory agencies, and passes on consumer legislation. Some have criticized the Commerce Committee for being overly attentive to the lobbyists representing the industries it is supposed to regulate. And indeed, the full committee can usually marshal a solid majority against pro-consumer legislation. Though now known as an especially active Chairman, Staggers does see that the full committee and his own Subcommittee on Investigations get most of the staff budget. Very little money goes to active subcommittee chairmen like Paul Rogers of Florida or John Moss of California.

In 1971, Staggers found himself in the headlines resulting from an imbroglio with CBS. Staggers sought a contempt citation against the network's president for his refusal to provide "outtakes"—edited pieces of film—from the controversial documentary "The Selling of the Pentagon." The Commerce Committee dutifully voted for contempt, but the full House, under pressure from the liberals and the usually conservative broadcasting lobby, voted Staggers down. It was the first time in recent memory that a committee chairman had been so repudiated.

The incident represents another mark in the slow decline of committee chairmen in general, and also indicates Stagger's lack of influence in particular. Among the Congressman's constituents, however, the CBS affair was not an important one. Their electoral judgment of Staggers was more affected when one of the two high-speed Turbo Trains was taken off the Boston-to-Washington run and placed on the one between Washington and Parkersburg, West Virginia. The Turbo Train is operated by Amtrak, over which the Commerce Committee has jurisdiction. It now stops in Keyser, West Virginia (pop. 6,500), Harley Stagger's home town.

Census Data Pop. 436,140. Central city, 0%; suburban, 0%. Median family income, $6,437; families above $15,000: 7%; families below $3,000: 20%. Median years education, 9.9.

1972 Share of Federal Outlays $344,613,025

DOD	$26,937,000	HEW	$178,847,386
AEC	–	HUD	$902,036
NASA	$50,782	DOI	$10,834,529
DOT	$33,626,805	USDA	$37,340,209
		Other	$56,074,278

Federal Military-Industrial Commitments

DOD Contractors Hercules (Ridgely), $11.714m: propellant for Sprint missile of ABM.

Economic Base Agriculture, notably cattle, dairy products and poultry; bituminous coal mining; finance, insurance and real estate; pressed or blown glass not otherwise classified, and other stone, clay and glass products; and lumber and wood products especially sawmill and planing mill products. Also higher education (West Virginia Univ.).

The Voters

Registration 266,493 total. 167,274 D (63%); 94,297 R (35%); 4,922 Ind. (2%).
Median voting age 45.6
Employment profile White collar, 37%. Blue collar, 45%. Service, 14%. Farm, 4%.
Ethnic groups Black, 4%. Total foreign stock, 3%.

Presidential vote

1972	Nixon (R)	124,917	(65%)
	McGovern (D)	66,597	(35%)
1968	Nixon (R)	80,122	(43%)
	Humphrey (D)	86,730	(47%)
	Wallace (AI)	17,904	(10%)

Representative

Harley O. **Staggers** (D) Elected 1949; b. Aug. 3, 1907, Keyser; home, Keyser; Emory and Henry Col., B.A., 1931; USN, WWII; married, six children; Methodist.

Career High school, col. coach; Sheriff, Mineral County, 1937–41; Right-of-Way Agent, W.Va. Road Commission, 1941–42; Dir., W.Va. Office of Govt. Reports, 1942.

Offices 2366 RHOB, 202-225-4331. Also P.O. Box 906, Keyser 26726, 304-788-1298.

Administrative Assistant Marguerite Furfari

Committees

Interstate and Foreign Commerce (Chm.); Sub: Sp. Sub. on Investigations.

Group Ratings

	ADA	COPE	LWV	RIPON	NFU	LCV	CFA	NAB	NSI	ACA
1972	31	90	55	62	86	16	50	18	89	33
1971	32	100	100	38	79	–	71	–	–	33
1970	52	92	–	50	83	80	88	0	88	26

Key Votes

1) Busing	AGN	6) Cmbodia Bmbg	FOR	11) Chkg Acct Intrst	FOR
2) Strip Mines	AGN	7) Bust Hwy Trust	AGN	12) End HISC (HUAC)	AGN
3) Cut Mil $	AGN	8) Farm Sub Lmt	AGN	13) Nixon Sewer Veto	AGN
4) Rev Shrg	AGN	9) School Prayr	FOR	14) Corp Cmpaign $	FOR
5) Pub TV $	ABS	10) Cnsumr Prot	FOR	15) Pol $ Disclosr	AGN

Election Results

1972 general:	Harley O. Staggers (D)	128,286	(70%)
	David Dix (R)	54,949	(30%)
1972 primary:	Harley O. Staggers (D)	68,092	(77%)
	Tom Bell (D)	16,201	(18%)
	Richard Baylor (D)	4,427	(5%)
1970 general:	Harley O. Staggers (D)	56,263	(63%)
	Richard M. Reddecliff (R)	33,509	(37%)

THIRD DISTRICT Political Background

Charleston is West Virginia's capital, the center of its largest metropolitan area, and, until the 1970 census, the state's largest city (that title now belongs to Huntington). Along the banks of the Kanawha River (pronounced kan-AW) stands the state capitol building, one of the largest and most beautiful in the country; but a little more typical of Charleston are the large Union Carbide plants a little farther downriver. Like most West Virginia cities, Charleston is situated in a narrow river valley hemmed in by mountains; so situated, the city lies victim to a smog which sometimes rivals that in Los Angeles.

Charleston and surrounding Kanawha County is the population center and political pivot of West Virginia's 3rd congressional district. Upriver in the mountains is coal mining country, containing the kind of destitute hollows where Jay Rockefeller lived when he first came to the state as an antipoverty worker. Later, Rockefeller was West Virginia Secretary of State and an unsuccessful Democratic candidate for Governor in 1972. The territory below Charleston, down to the Ohio River, is less mountainous and also less densely populated. The coal counties are usually heavily Democratic; the Ohio River counties, however, seem to retain a Republicanism that goes back to the days when West Virginia first became a state during the Civil War. Charleston itself, perhaps surprisingly for an industrial city, leans a little more to the Republicans than to the Democrats. One factor behind this inclination may be the large number of patronage jobs in the capital, all of which lie firmly in the hands of Republican Gov. Arch Moore.

Just as Jay Rockefeller is a younger, more idealistic type of West Virginia politician—a breed that met with mixed results in the 1972 election—Congressman John Slack of the 3rd district is typical of the older, more patronage-oriented, go-along-to-get-along breed of West Virginia Democrat. Slack, an old real estate man, made his way to Congress via the Kanawha County Assessor's office, and is one of the two former assessors in the House. (The other is Andrew Hinshaw of California's Orange County.) Slack's politics are fairly conservative; he votes liberal often enough to please organized labor, but not often enough to satisfy other liberal groups. His presence, and that of other, similarly inclined Democrats from non-Southern states, is one of the reasons why the House Appropriations Committee is much more conservative on most major issues than the House as a whole. And Appropriations, of course, is the unit that must put up the money to run the programs the rest of the Congress votes to establish. Slack attracts little publicity in Washington, but back home manages to win reelection easily.

Census Data Pop. 434,165. Central city, 16%; suburban, 36%. Median family income, $7,574; families above $15,000: 11%; families below $3,000: 18%. Median years education, 10.8.

1972 Share of Federal Outlays $446,235,998

DOD	$18,320,000	HEW	$179,868,785
AEC	–	HUD	$4,215,166
NASA	–	DOI	$1,545,353
DOT	$121,025,075	USDA	$27,331,999
		Other	$93,929,620

Federal Military-Industrial Commitments

No installations or contractors receiving prime awards greater than $5,000,000.

Economic Base Industrial chemicals and other chemicals and allied products; oil and gas extraction; finance, insurance and real estate; and bituminous coal mining.

The Voters

Registration 263,606 total. 162,117 D (61%); 97,449 R (37%); 4,040 Ind. (2%).
Median voting age 44.8
Employment profile White collar, 44%. Blue collar, 43%. Service, 12%. Farm, 1%.
Ethnic groups Black, 3%. Total foreign stock, 2%.

Presidential vote

1972	Nixon (R)	122,907	(62%)
	McGovern (D)	74,219	(38%)
1968	Nixon (R)	82,591	(43%)
	Humphrey (D)	88,493	(47%)
	Wallace (AI)	19,110	(10%)

Representative

John Slack (D) Elected 1958; b. Mar. 18, 1915, Charleston; home, Charleston; Virginia Mil. Institute; married, one child; Presbyterian.

Career Businessman; mbr. Kanawha County Ct., 1948–52; assessor, Kanawha County, 1952–58.

Offices 2230 RHOB, 202-225-2711. Also 500 Quartier St., Charleston 25301, 304-343-8923.

Administrative Assistant Paul H. Becker

Committees

Appropriations (12th); Subs: Public Works, AEC; State, Justice, Commerce, and Judiciary; Treasury, Postal Service, General Government.

Group Ratings

	ADA	COPE	LWV	RIPON	NFU	LCV	CFA	NAB	NSI	ACA
1972	25	70	42	29	83	11	50	27	100	62
1971	24	73	67	38	75	–	67	–	–	44
1970	24	75	–	27	69	60	65	18	90	39

Key Votes

1) Busing	AGN	6) Cmbodia Bmbg	AGN	11) Chkg Acct Intrst	AGN
2) Strip Mines	FOR	7) Bust Hwy Trust	AGN	12) End HISC (HUAC)	AGN
3) Cut Mil $	AGN	8) Farm Sub Lmt	ABS	13) Nixon Sewer Veto	AGN
4) Rev Shrg	AGN	9) School Prayr	FOR	14) Corp Cmpaign $	FOR
5) Pub TV $	ABS	10) Cnsumr Prot	ABS	15) Pol $ Disclosr	AGN

Election Results

1972 general:	John Slack (D)	118,346	(64%)
	T. David Higgins	67,441	(36%)
1972 primary:	John Slack (D), unopposed		
1970 general:	John Slack (D)	57,630	(65%)
	Neal A. Kinsolving (R)	30,525	(35%)

FOURTH DISTRICT Political Background

The 4th district of West Virginia is the southern part of the state—most of it coal country. In fact, the eight counties of the 4th have probably produced more bituminous coal over the years than any other single congressional district in the United States. Not all the district is coal country, however; it also contains the state's largest city, Huntington (pop. 74,000), a manufacturing and railroad-junction town on the Ohio River. But from the banks of the Ohio, the mountains rise steeply, and the heart of the 4th lies in the small coal towns sitting between the mountainsides. These last 25 years, the coal counties have been hard hit by the decline of employment in the mines. As a result, the district lost much of its population—some 13% in the 1960s alone; moreover, some 25% of the people here live below the poverty level as defined by the Census Bureau.

The politics of this poverty-stricken area has not developed along the lines of notions held by liberal reformers. In a place like southern West Virginia, there is no way for a bright young man to make money except by owning a coal company, or by winning public or union office. The latter are often more lucrative than official salaries suggest; moreover, in such surroundings, little room exists for concern about problems like unsafe mine conditions, black lung disease, and air and water pollution. People say that you can still buy votes in some of the counties here, and in others, local officials provide, shall we say, creative vote totals on election night—or a few days later. All in all, it seems that altruism in politics—an undiluted devotion to public good rather than personal gain—is a luxury most easily afforded by the rich.

But this view is perhaps too cynical, at least to judge by the results of the 1972 elections here. The current 4th district is an amalgam of the old 4th and the old 5th; with its population declining, West Virginia lost a congressional seat in the 1970 census. The redistricting plan in the new 4th was to throw two Democratic incumbents, Ken Hechler of Huntington and James Kee of Bluefield, into the same district. The plan also gave Kee a definite edge.

On paper, Kee most certainly got the advantage. Counties from his old district contained 56% of the new 4th district's population and 60% of its Democratic primary voters. Kee's father was first elected in 1932 to represent the coal counties in the House, and served until his death in 1951. He was succeeded by his widow Elizabeth, who was in turn succeeded, on her retirement in 1964, by her son James. For years, none of the Kees encountered a major challenge. Moreover, Congressman Kee had the support of the Boyle leadership in the United Mine Workers and of the major coal companies as well. All of which would seem to add up to an easy James Kee victory.

But such an assessment fails to reckon with Kee's lackluster record and high absenteeism, from both the House and the campaign trail. It also leaves out Ken Hechler. Hechler is an unlikely West Virginia politician: a professor, an assistant in the Truman White House, and a speechwriter for Adlai Stevenson. After the 1956 presidential campaign, Hechler moved to Huntington, where he got a job teaching at Marshall University; he also became a commentator on a local TV station. Huntington was then represented in the House by a 83-year-old Republican, who, in 1958, a Democratic year, was challenged by Hechler.

Hechler won that year, and he has been running and winning ever since. Hechler has shown himself to be an untiring and resourceful campaigner, with a taste for the kind of highjinks that many of his former academic colleagues find distasteful. But Hechler does more than campaign hard and provide good constituency service. He took on the coal companies and the Boyle leadership of the UMW over black lung legislation, and won. He is also the principal sponsor of legislation that would ban the strip mining of coal in the United States. And in 1969 and 1971, he campaigned hard for UMW insurgent candidates Joseph Yablonski and Arnold Miller.

These things take political—and physical—courage. Many West Virginia politicians felt that opposition to strip mining would bring little but political suicide, even if fewer men are actually employed in strip operations than coal-company propaganda suggests. And in light of what happened to Yablonski, it took raw guts for Hechler to campaign in the coal counties for Miller. But Hechler's courage has paid off. In the 1972 primary, he finished first among 64 candidates to become West Virginia's Delegate-at-Large to the Democratic National Convention. And on the same day, he won his primary against Kee by more than 25,000 votes. Hechler took 52% of the votes, Kee 26%, and a third candidate, Dr. Hawey Wells, 19%. (Wells is the son-in-law of 2nd-district Rep. Harley Staggers.) Hechler won a whopping 77% of the votes in the three counties that were in his old 4th district; and in the five coal counties formerly represented by Kee, Hechler ran just 1,500 votes behind the incumbent.

In 1972, Jay Rockefeller, whose positions on the issues were similar to those of Hechler, ran for Governor and lost to incumbent Republican Arch Moore. Why did Hechler triumph and other candidates like him lose? For one thing, Hechler has been at it longer. For another, his commitment to West Virginia and to the poor people of the hollows is clear; in an age of distrust of politicians, Hechler has established real credibility. He has taken real risks in behalf of what he believes are the interests of ordinary West Virginians. That is rare enough anywhere, and against the cynical backdrop of West Virginia politics, people seem to appreciate it.

Census Data Pop. 437,595. Central city, 17%; suburban, 16%. Median family income, $7,039; families above $15,000: 9%; families below $3,000: 19%. Median years education, 10.1.

1972 Share of Federal Outlays $388,383,926

DOD	$36,754,000	HEW	$221,604,075
AEC	–	HUD	$3,976,113
NASA	–	DOI	$1,770,846
DOT	$17,881,867	USDA	$22,596,377
		Other	$83,800,648

Federal Military-Industrial Commitments

No installations or contractors receiving prime awards greater than $5,000,000.

Economic Base Bituminous coal mining; finance, insurance and real estate; pressed or blown glass and glassware, and other stone, clay and glass products; food and kindred products; and agriculture, notably poultry and cattle. Also higher education (Marshall Univ.).

The Voters

Registration 260,939 total. 189,710 D (73%); 68,193 R (26%); 3,036 Ind. (1%).
Median voting age 45.3
Employment profile White collar, 42%. Blue collar, 46%. Service, 12%. Farm, –%.
Ethnic groups Black, 7%. Total foreign stock, 2%.

Presidential vote

1972	Nixon (R)	110,238	(63%)
	McGovern (D)	65,884	(37%)
1968	Nixon (R)	60,891	(34%)
	Humphrey (D)	99,574	(55%)
	Wallace (AI)	19,180	(11%)

Representative

Ken Hechler (D) Elected 1958; b. Sept. 20, 1914, Roslyn, Long Island; home, Huntington; Swarthmore Col., B.A., 1935; Columbia U., M.A., 1936, Ph.D., 1940; Army, WWII; unmarried; Episcopalian.

Career Section Chief, Census, 1940; Office of Emergency Mgmt., 1941; Analyst, Bureau of the Budget, 1941–42, 1946–47; Asst. Prof., Princeton, 1947–49; Sp. Asst. to Pres. Truman, 1949–53; Research Dir., Stevenson-Kefauver campaign; radio-TV commentator, Huntington, 1957–58; Assoc. Prof. Pol. Science, Marshall University, 1957.

Offices 242 CHOB, 202-225-3452. Also Rm. 219, P.O. Bldg., Huntington 25701, 304-529-3350, and Rm. B-006, Fed. Bldg., Neville St., Beckley 25801, 304-252-5000, and 1005 Fed. Bldg., Bluefield 24701, 304-325-6222.

Administrative Assistant Dick Leonard

Committees

Science and Astronautics (2nd); Sub: Aeronautics and Space Technology (Chm.)

Group Ratings

	ADA	COPE	LWV	RIPON	NFU	LCV	CFA	NAB	NSI	ACA
1972	100	100	92	81	86	93	100	17	0	13
1971	95	75	100	78	80	–	100	–	–	17
1970	88	83	–	71	77	80	95	8	10	37

Key Votes

1) Busing	FOR	6) Cmbodia Bmbg	AGN	11) Chkg Acct Intrst	FOR
2) Strip Mines	AGN	7) Bust Hwy Trust	FOR	12) End HISC (HUAC)	FOR
3) Cut Mil $	FOR	8) Farm Sub Lmt	FOR	13) Nixon Sewer Veto	AGN
4) Rev Shrg	AGN	9) School Prayr	FOR	14) Corp Cmpaign $	AGN
5) Pub TV $	FOR	10) Cnsumr Prot	FOR	15) Pol $ Disclosr	FOR

Election Results

1972 general:	Ken Hechler (D)	100,600	(61%)
	Joe Neal (R)	64,242	(39%)
1972 primary:	Ken Hechler (D)	50,872	(52%)
	James Kee (D)	25,004	(26%)
	Hawey Wells (D)	18,311	(19%)
	Homer Heck (D)	3,474	(4%)
1970 general:	Ken Hechler (D)	62,531	(67%)
	Ralph Shannon (R)	30,255	(33%)

WISCONSIN

Political Background

Wisconsin is a state of political anomalies. It spawned Bob La Follette and the Progressive movement, and Joe McCarthy and his campaign against Communists in high places. Richard Nixon has carried Wisconsin, the state where the Republican party was founded, three times, and yet the same state appears now to have become one of the nation's most Democratic at all levels. Wisconsin is heavily industrial, though it is also the nation's leading producer of dairy products; a heavily urban state, yet filled with lakes and forests.

Wisconsin probably owes its unusual politics to the German and Scandinavian immigrants who first settled it. Here, as in Minnesota and North Dakota, the immigrants left a distinctive kind of political stamp. In all three states there developed—against the background of an overwhelming dominance by the Republican party—a politics of almost radical economic reform and an isolationist foreign policy. The term "progressive" was coined in Wisconsin, and it was personified by Robert "Fighting Bob" La Follette. Elected Governor in 1900, he completely revamped the state government before going on to the Senate in 1906. There La Follette supported other insurgent reformers and voted against American entry into World War I. In 1924, he ran for President under the banner of the Progressive party, and won 17% of the nation's votes—the best third-party showing in the last 60 years. La Follette's sons sustained the tradition of Wisconsin progressivism. Robert La Follette, Jr., served in the Senate from 1925 to 1947, and Philip La Follette was Governor of the state from 1935 to 1942. During the 1930s, the La Follettes ran on the Progressive party line in Wisconsin, and dreamed of forming a national third party. But the onset of World War II destroyed the plans of the isolationist reformers. And in 1946, Sen. La Follette, busy with the congressional reorganization act in Washington, was upset in the 1946 Republican party by one Joseph R. McCarthy.

How did the same state produce politicians as different as La Follette and McCarthy at roughly the same time? Part of the answer lies in the leanings of Wisconsin's ethnic groups, especially those of the largest—the German-Americans. These people supported both La Follette isolationism and McCarthy anticommunism. As Samuel Lubell has pointed out, much of the impetus behind postwar hard-line anticommunism came from those who never believed we should have fought World War II—a conflict which the United States, allied with Communists, waged against Germany. In any case, McCarthy was far less typical of Wisconsin than were the La Follettes. "Tail-gunner Joe" won his first primary in an upset; moreover, his two victories in the general elections of 1946 and 1952 occurred in heavily Republican years, and only the first did he win by a large margin. If McCarthy had not died a broken man in 1957, after his censure by the Senate in 1954, he would probably have been defeated in the 1958 elections.

During the McCarthy years, conservative Republicans dominated Wisconsin elections more or less by default. The party's Progressive faction was dormant, and the Democrats had never been a factor in state politics. But in the early 1950s, a group of liberal Democrats—none of whom had ever held public office—assumed control over the hulk of the party, and they laid plans to make it a majority force. A simple recitation of some of their names gives evidence of their success: Sen.

William Proxmire, Sen. Gaylord Nelson, Gov. Patrick Lucey, Congressmen Henry Reuss and Robert Kastenmeier. The group's first victory occurred in the 1957 special election to fill McCarthy's Senate vacancy. The Republican nominee was ex-Gov. (1951–56) Walter Kohler; the Democratic choice was Proxmire, fresh from three electoral defeats in three consecutive gubernatoral campaigns. But by 1957, the booming economy of the mid-Eisenhower years had begun to turn sour: factories were laying off workers and the farm belt, burdened by surpluses, was beginning to revolt. Proxmire's previous campaigning finally paid off; he beat Kohler by a whopping 56–41 margin. Since then, the Democrats have won every Wisconsin Senate election, and they seem almost certain to continue to do so for at least the next ten years.

Proxmire was an unorthodox Senator from the start. He is the only Senator who runs four miles from his home to Capitol Hill every morning, the only one to stand, not sit, at his desk, and the only one who has had hair transplants. Almost as soon as he walked into the Senate chambers, he managed to irritate then all-powerful Senate Majority Leader Lyndon Johnson; so sage insiders quickly decided to write Proxmire off as an unreliable maverick and a political accident. During the 1960s, the Senator appeared to specialize in hopeless causes; in 1964, for example, he began an attack on Boeing's supersonic transport (SST). All along, however, the Senate was undergoing more change than the aficionados of its once arcane ways noticed. In 1971, Proxmire finished off the SST once and for all.

But Proxmire did not stop with the SST. He has also proved mettlesome to big defense contractors, the Pentagon, and their assorted friends in other ways. Proxmire was the Senator who brought A. Ernest Fitzgerald before a congressional hearing; the cost analyst then revealed the huge cost overruns accumulated by Lockheed in its production of the C-5A aircraft. In fact, Proxmire has become an expert in Pentagon peccadilloes. Lately, he has taken on the Grumman Corporation, which he says is getting soft treatment and improper loans from the Navy while bungling a naval aircraft contract. The Senator has also led moves to cut down on the number of government limousines in service, and the number of enlisted men working as servants to generals and admirals.

Meanwhile, Proxmire has risen slowly on the seniority ladder. He is now the Chairman of the Appropriations subcommittee that passes on the budgets of HUD, NASA, and VA. And he is the second-ranking Democrat on the Banking, Housing, and Urban Affairs Committee. Contributions from large bankers were a big factor in the 1972 reelection of Alabama's John Sparkman, the committee's 75-year-old Chairman. The big bankers dread the day when Proxmire assumes control of the committee.

Proxmire, however, does not accept all of the standard liberal agenda. In 1972, when he appeared to have entertained some thoughts about a presidential candidacy, the Senator came out against busing. And he has criticized some aspects of the way the press handled the Watergate scandal. Moreover, his penchant for economy goes beyond Pentagon largesse. He has freely criticized many domestic programs, and has voted to cut their budgets as well. In a book, Proxmire has called Uncle Sam "the last of the big-time spenders," saying that waste never fed a single hungry child.

In 1964, Proxmire won reelection by a margin smaller than expected. He had apparently been taking Wisconsin voters for granted. But in 1970, Proxmire conclusively demonstrated his popularity. His opponent, a former general manager of the Milwaukee Bucks basketball team, attacked Proxmire for attacking the Pentagon. As it turned out, the strategy was not good politics in Wisconsin, which ranks 46th in per capita Defense Department outlays—only Michigan, Oregon, Iowa, and West Virginia rank lower. Proxmire won 71% of the votes, and carried all 72 of the state's counties. It is said that the Senator still harbors some national ambitions. And it is true that his ideology—an opposition to bloated federal bureaucracies of all sorts—could catch on. But no matter how effective Proxmire has become in the Senate, he is probably still too much of a maverick to assemble a wide national following.

Before Proxmire's 1970 victory, the state's top Democratic vote-getter was Sen. Gaylord Nelson. And Nelson may once again assume the role after the 1974 Senate elections. When Nelson became Governor of Wisconsin in 1959, he launched an attack against industrial polluters and sponsored programs to protect the environment. In so doing, he anticipated the current ecology crazd by more than a decade. Nelson was reelected Governor in 1960, and two years later unseated four-term, 78-year-old Republican Sen. Alexander Wiley.

Nelson has not attracted as much publicity in the Senate as Proxmire, nor has he emerged the maverick quite as often. Nevertheless, Nelson was one of the very first Senators to speak and vote against the Vietnam war, just after Wayne Morse and Ernest Gruening said no to the Gulf of Tonkin Resolution. Recently, Nelson has devoted most of his efforts to cutting drug prices. He charges that a prescription drug under a brand name often costs far more than the identical generic drug, and that American companies sell the same drug abroad at much lower prices. Though its chances of immediate passage are dim, the Senator has introduced a comprehensive drug reform law. Nevertheless, in this field—as the efforts of the late Estes Kefauver show—plugging away constantly can eventually produce a major piece of legislation, one of Washington's shrewdest lobbies notwithstanding. Nelson has also been the Senate's main battler against scheduled postal-rate increases that threaten to bankrupt many magazines, especially those of heterodox political complexion, both left and right. Nelson serves as a member of the Labor and Public Welfare and Finance committees; over the years, he has compiled a 100% COPE voting record.

One mystery about Nelson is why his name has not been entered, even tentatively, in the presidential sweepstakes speculation that is always with us. George McGovern, or so he told reporter Joe McGinniss, did consider Nelson for the Vice-Presidential nomination in 1972. But Nelson didn't especially want it, and McGovern succumbed to more conventional considerations —the nominee had to be Catholic, from the "center" of the party, and so on. Accordingly, McGovern picked Tom Eagleton instead. At any rate, Nelson's electoral position in Wisconsin seems secure. After receiving 62% of the votes in 1968, everyone expects him to do even better in 1974.

One person who apparently thinks so is Melvin Laird, former Secretary of Defense and Congressman (1953–69) from Wisconsin's 7th district. In early 1973, Laird returned to Wisconsin to take some political soundings. He reportedly discovered that Nelson would clobber him, and that he had little chance against Gov. Pat Lucey. That intelligence was presumably one reason why he decided to become Richard Nixon's chief domestic counselor after the departure of John Ehrlichman. Laird found that since he had last run for office here in 1968, Wisconsin had moved solidly to the left. In fact, Wisconsin was one of four non-Southern states to give McGovern a higher percentage of its votes than it had Humphrey in 1968. And, of course, it was the state that provided McGovern the momentum needed to win the 1972 Democratic presidential nomination. Against the advice and prediction of all the pundits, the South Dakotan won a smashing primary victory here over George Wallace, Hubert Humphrey, Edmund Muskie, and John Lindsay. McGovern's triumph resulted from the efforts of an impressive organization, which Gene Pokorny had strived to assemble for over a year.

But the results of the 1970 Wisconsin elections presaged McGovern's 1972 showing. Not only was Sen. Proxmire reelected by an overwhelming margin, but the Democrats, in the person of Patrick Lucey, took the Governor's office with a solid 55% of the votes, captured control of the state House and nearly won the state Senate, knocked off one Republican Congressman, easily held on to another seat (Laird's old one) picked up in a 1969 special election, and came close to unseating three other Republican Congressmen. None of these victories, or near victories, was achieved by catering to the "center" of the electorate. They were won by liberal Democrats whose positions on the issues are similar to those of McGovern, Proxmire, and Nelson. Wisconsin was the only state where the Governor and both Senators endorsed McGovern well before the convention.

In 1972, the Democrats nearly captured another congressional district and easily won a race where two incumbents had been forced into the same district. So for the first time in history, Wisconsin Democrats enjoy an edge (5–4) in the House delegation; as recently as 1968, the delegation was 7–3 Republican. And the Democrats have a real chance to pick up more seats in 1974, when Lucey will probably win reelection by a comfortable amrgin.

Census Data Pop. 4,417,933; 2.18% of U.S. total, 16th largest; change 1960–70, 11.8%. Central city, 27%; suburban, 30%. Median family income, $10,065; 15th highest; families above $15,000: 20%; families below $3,000: 8%. Median years education, 12.1.

1972 Share of Federal Tax Burden $4,180,370,000; 2.00% of U.S. total, 16th largest.

1972 Share of Federal Outlays $3,226,016,269; 1.49% of U.S. total, 22nd largest. Per capita federal spending, $730.

DOD	$488,931,000	32nd (0.78%)	HEW	$1,527,687,413	13th	(2.14%)
AEC	$4,320,973	23rd (0.16%)	HUD	$29,407,213	30th	(0.96%)
NASA	$6,958,797	22nd (0.23%)	VA	$235,698,539	17th	(2.06%)
DOT	$74,259,797	35th (0.94%)	USDA	$302,582,350	19th	(1.97%)
DOC	$5,426,165	37th (0.42%)	CSC	$39,292,579	27th	(0.95%)
DOI	$10,226,611	37th (0.48%)	TD	$248,862,562	12th	(1.51%)
DOJ	$15,098,545	22nd (1.54%)	Other	$237,263,725		

Economic Base Agriculture, notably dairy products, cattle, hogs and corn; machinery, especially engines and turbines; finance, insurance and real estate; food and kindred products, especially dairy products, and beverages; electrical equipment and supplies, especially electrical industrial apparatus; fabricated metal products; paper and allied products, especially paper mills, other than building paper.

Political Line-up Governor, Patrick J. Lucey (D); seat up, 1974. Senators, William Proxmire (D) and Gaylord Nelson (D). Representatives, 9 (5 D and 4 R). State Senate (18 R and 15 D); State Assembly (63 D and 36 R).

The Voters

Registration No statewide registration.
Median voting age 43.7
Employment profile White collar, 43%. Blue collar, 37%. Service, 14%. Farm, 6%.
Ethnic groups Black, 3%. Total foreign stock, 17%. Germany, 5%; Poland, 2%; Norway, 1%.

Presidential vote

1972	Nixon (R)	989,430	(55%)
	McGovern (D)	810,174	(45%)
1968	Nixon (R)	809,997	(48%)
	Humphrey (D)	748,804	(44%)
	Wallace (AI)	127,835	(8%)
1964	Johnson (D)	1,050,424	(62%)
	Goldwater (R)	638,495	(38%)

Senator

William Proxmire (D) Elected Aug. 1957, seat up 1976; b. Nov. 11, 1915, Lake Forest, Ill.; home, Madison; Yale, B.A., 1938; Harvard, M.B.A., 1940, M.P.A., 1948; married; Episcopalian.

Career Pres., Artcraft Press, 1953–57; Wis. Legislature, 1951; Dem. nominee for Gov., 1952, 1954, 1956.

Offices 5241 NSOB, 202-225-5653. Also Rm. 235, Fed. Bldg., Madison 53701, 608-257-4654.

Administrative Assistant Howard E. Shuman

Committees

Appropriations (9th); Subs: Agriculture, Environmental and Consumer Protection; Labor, and Health, Education, and Welfare, and Related Agencies; Military Construction; Housing and Urban Development, Space, Science, and Veterans (Chm.); Foreign Operations.

Banking, Housing and Urban Affairs (2nd); Subs: Financial Institutions; Housing and Urban Affairs; Securities, Consumer Credit (Chm.).

Joint Com. on Defense Production (2nd).

Joint Economic Com. (Vice-Chm.); Subs: Economic Progress; Priorities and Economy in Government (Chm.); Fiscal Policy; Consumer Economics.

Joint Study Com. on Budget Control.

Group Ratings

	ADA	COPE	LWV	RIPON	NFU	LCV	CFA	NAB	NSI	ACA
1972	75	70	82	72	80	90	100	67	0	18
1971	96	75	92	72	100	–	100	–	–	21
1970	78	92	–	69	93	94	–	33	0	25

Key Votes

1) Busing	AGN	8) Sea Life Prot	FOR	15) Tax Singls Less	FOR
2) Alas P-line	AGN	9) Campaign Subs	FOR	16) Min Tax for Rich	FOR
3) Gun Cntrl	FOR	10) Cmbodia Bmbg	AGN	17) Euro Troop Rdctn	FOR
4) Rehnquist	FOR	11) Legal Srvices	FOR	18) Bust Hwy Trust	FOR
5) Pub TV $	FOR	12) Rev Sharing	AGN	19) Maid Min Wage	FOR
6) EZ Votr Reg	FOR	13) Cnsumr Prot	FOR	20) Farm Sub Limit	FOR
7) No-Fault	FOR	14) Eq Rts Amend	FOR	21) Highr Credt Chgs	AGN

Election Results

1970 general:	William Proxmire (D)	948,445	(71%)
	John E. Erickson (R)	381,297	(29%)
1970 primary:	William Proxmire (D), unopposed		
1964 general:	William Proxmire (D)	892,013	(53%)
	Wilbur N. Renk (R)	780,116	(47%)

Senator

Gaylord Nelson (D) Elected 1962, seat up 1974; b. June 4, 1916, Clear Lake; home, Madison; San Jose State Col., B.A., 1939; U. of Wis., LL.B., 1942; Army, WWII; married; Methodist.

Career Practicing atty., 1946–58; Wis. Legislature, 1949–58; Gov. of Wis., 1959–62.

Offices 221 OSOB, 202-225-5323. Also Rm. 570, Fe.d Bldg., 517 E. Wisconsin Ave., Milwaukee 53202, 414-272-8600.

Administrative Assistant William B. Cherkasky

Committees

Finance (7th); Subs: International Trade; Private Pension Plans (Chm.); State Taxation of Interstate Commerce.

Labor and Public Welfare (5th); Subs: Children and Youth; Employment, Poverty, and Migratory Labor (Chm.); Health; Labor; Railroad Retirement; Sp. Sub. on Arts and Humanities; Human Resources.

Sel. Com. on Small Business (3rd); Subs: Government Regulation; Monopoly (Chm.); Retailing, Distribution, and Marketing Practices.

Sel. Com. on Nutrition and Human Needs (6th).

Group Ratings

	ADA	COPE	LWV	RIPON	NFU	LCV	CFA	NAB	NSI	ACA
1972	95	90	100	72	90	100	100	18	0	9
1971	96	83	85	65	100	–	100	–	–	5
1970	97	100	–	72	100	83	–	10	0	6

Key Votes

1) Busing	FOR	8) Sea Life Prot	FOR	15) Tax Singls Less	FOR
2) Alas P-line	AGN	9) Campaign Subs	FOR	16) Min Tax for Rich	FOR
3) Gun Cntrl	FOR	10) Cmbodia Bmbg	AGN	17) Euro Troop Rdctn	FOR
4) Rehnquist	AGN	11) Legal Srvices	FOR	18) Bust Hwy Trust	FOR
5) Pub TV $	FOR	12) Rev Sharing	AGN	19) Maid Min Wage	FOR
6) EZ Votr Reg	FOR	13) Cnsumr Prot	FOR	20) Farm Sub Limit	FOR
7) No-Fault	FOR	14) Eq Rts Amend	FOR	21) Highr Credt Chgs	AGN

Election Results

1968 general:	Gaylord Nelson (D)	1,020,931	(62%)
	Jerris Leonard (R)	633,910	(38%)
1968 primary:	Gaylord Nelson (D), unopposed		
1962 general:	Gaylord Nelson (D)	662,342	(53%)
	Alexander Wylie (R)	594,846	(47%)

FIRST DISTRICT Political Background

There is little question these days what member of the House consistently churns out the most headlines and solid news stories. He is not Speaker Carl Albert, or Minority Leader Gerald Ford, or even Chairman Wayne Hays of the House Administration Committee. He is, instead, a 34-year-old, second-term Democrat from Wisconsin named Les Aspin. This member is not the chairman of any committee or subcommittee, far from it; nor can he command a majority on the one committee on which he serves, Armed Services. But press releases from his office keep coming out day after day, and day after day they get printed because young Aspin generates solid copy. Examples from the first six months of 1973:

*Aspin hit Air Force Chief of Staff John Ryan for paying himself and other desk-bound generals flight-pay bonuses, which violate a law prohibiting such lagniappe.

*Aspin charged the Pentagon with a "bail out of a lousy contractor" in connection with Grumman's contract to build the Navy's F-14.

*Aspin charged that the cost of 50 small Navy patrol frigates rose $500 million even before a single ship was built.

*Aspin attacked Roy Ash, Director of the Office of Management and Budget, for not disposing of all of his Litton Industries stock, and for so violating his explicit promise.

Aspin has not confined himself to targets in the Pentagon. He was a critic of the Alaska pipeline and a leader of House efforts to promote the construction of a pipeline through Canada to the Midwest. He has also spoken out on school bus safety, industrial polluters, and food and drug contamination. Nevertheless, Aspin has made the biggest splashes and scored the greatest successes in the area of defense. For the Congressman is not simply a publicity hound; he also gets results.

Take the flight pay issue. On the floor of the House in June 1973, Aspin and Congressman Otis Pike of New York defeated a move to extend flight pay to desk-bound officers. The margin was 238–175—a stunning defeat for the traditionally pro-military Armed Services Committee leadership. Even more stunning was the success in July 1973 of Aspin's amendment to cut the fiscal 1974 defense budget to the 1973 level, plus an allowance for inflation. This, in effect, cut $950 million out of the bill reported by the Armed Services Committee. Aspin's move was a classic David and Goliath confrontation. On one side was Committee Chairman Edward Hébert, a member of Congress for 33 years; behind him was the tradition—inviolate since World War II—that no Armed Services Chairman was ever defeated on a military authorization bill on the floor. On the other side was Aspin, just beginning his second term in the House. But Aspin mobilized a coalition of antiwar liberals and fiscal conservatives to carry the day by an amazing 242–163 vote.

How does Aspin do it? For one thing, the Congressman knows his technical stuff. Before he turned 30, Aspin served as a staff aid to Chairman Walter Heller of the Council of Economic Advisers and to Defense Secretary Robert McNamara. So in Congress, he has demonstrated a capacity to ferret out information about defense contracts and beat everybody else to the punch. Among the small band of liberals on the Armed Services Committee, Aspin probably has the best developed notions of what the capabilities of the defense budget actually are.

For another thing, Aspin came to Congress at age 32 with a wide background in Wisconsin politics. He once served as an aide to Sen. William Proxmire and, in 1968, while employed at the Pentagon, Aspin worked on the Wisconsin primary campaign for Lyndon Johnson. Aspin reportedly told the Administration that the situation was hopeless—an analysis that was probably as unwelcomed as it was accurate.

Aspin's constituency is Wisconsin's 1st district, the southeast corner of the state. The district contains a fairly good microcosm of Wisconsin as a whole. In the eastern part of the 1st, along Lake Michigan, are the industrial cities of Racine and Kenosha; during the 1970 campaign, both had unemployment rates around 8%. Farther inland is the Republican stronghold of Walworth County, an area of small farms around the posh resort of Lake Geneva. To the west are the cities of Janesville and Beloit; like Racine and Kenosha, these are predominantly industrial, but they are smaller and have much smaller ethnic communities. Here the blue-collar workers are usually Yankees or German-Americans from the farm countries of southern Wisconsin. Janesville and Beloit ordinarily produce Republican majorities.

When Aspin first ran in 1970, the 1st was the state's most marginal congressional district. During the 1960s, no one won an election here with more than 53% of the votes. For most of the decade, aside from the two years after 1964, the district was represented by Republican Henry Schadeberg, a Congregationalist minister of conservative bent. Schadeberg voted against measures like the Civil Rights Act of 1968, higher minimum wages, and the Peace Corps. In 1970, with rising employment, Schadeberg attracted formidable opposition; in the Democratic primary, Aspin just barely defeated Douglas La Follette by 20 votes.

The general election was another story. Aspin attacked Schadeberg's record on the Vietnam war and pollution issues. But the challenger spent the most time talking about his academic speciality, economics, with heavy emphasis on unemployment. Schadeberg's response was weak: "I haven't noticed many people out of work." But the statistics and the unemployment lines belied the Congressman's assessment. Aspin won with an astounding 61% of the votes—a figure that made Schadeberg the most soundly defeated House incumbent in recent years.

Some felt that Aspin might face a tough fight for reelection in 1972. As it turned out, McGovern did rather poorly in the district; moreover, Aspin's opponent, Merrill Stalbaum, came down hard on the incumbent's anti-defense-spending record. Stalbaum also criticized the incumbent for supporting the Environmental Protection Agency's emission-control guidelines for automobiles. The latter issue appeared to have more direct impact in the 1st district, which has virtually no defense industry. In fiscal 1972, the district received a miniscule $20 million from the Pentagon; a figure in that range indicates that the district has no major contractor or installations, but only former military personnel getting retirement checks. But autos are something else. Kenosha has American Motors' main assembly plant, and auto workers and their families cast a sizeable percentage of the district's votes. Nevertheless, Stalbaum's strategy failed to work. Aspin won with 64% of the votes this time, and appears on his way toward bigger margins in future elections.

So far Aspin's brief career has comprised a series of superlatives. And the future appears to hold few limits. But he is barred, at least temporarily, from higher office, since both Wisconsin seats and the governorship are now occupied by well-entrenched Democrats. There are, however, other avenues. It may have crossed Aspin's mind that at least one President has appointed a Wisconsin Congressman Secretary of Defense.

Census Data Pop. 490,817. Central city, 35%; suburban, 23%. Median family income, $10,478; families above $15,000: 20%; families below $3,000: 6%. Median years education, 12.1.

1972 Share of Federal Outlays $271,787,084

DOD	$20,352,268	HEW	$150,714,785
AEC	–	HUD	$1,041,956
NASA	$41,970	DOI	$578,565
DOT	$2,249,490	USDA	$17,427,840
		Other	$79,380,210

Federal Military-Industrial Commitments

No installations or contractors receiving prime awards greater than $5,000,000.

Economic Base Machinery; agriculture, notably dairy products, grains and cattle; transportation equipment; fabricated metal products; and electrical equipment and supplies. Also higher education (Wisconsin State Univ., Whitewater).

The Voters

Registration No party and no district-wide registration.
Median voting age 42.4
Employment profile White collar, 41%. Blue collar, 42%. Service, 14%. Farm, 3%.
Ethnic groups Black, 3%. Spanish, 2%. Total foreign stock, 18%. Germany, 4%; Italy, 2%; Poland, 1%.

Presidential vote

1972	Nixon (R)	111,281	(59%)
	McGovern (D)	77,321	(41%)
1968	Nixon (R)	86,577	(48%)
	Humphrey (D)	77,191	(43%)
	Wallace (AI)	16,550	(9%)

Representative

Les Aspin (D) Elected 1970; b. Jul. 21, 1938, Milwaukee; home, Racine; Yale, B.A., 1960; Oxford U., M.A., 1962; M.I.T., Ph.D., 1965; Army, Vietnam, 1966–68; married; United Church of Christ.

Career Asst. Sen. Proximire, 1960, Campaign Mgr., 1964; Asst. Walter Heller, Chm., Council of Economic Advisors, 1963; Econ. Advisor to Sec. of Def. Robert McNamara; prof. economics, Marquette.

Offices 515 CHOB, 202-225-3031. Also Rm. 200, 603 Main St., Racine 53403, 414-632-8194, and 210 Dodge St., Janesville 53545, 608-752-9074.

Administrative Assistant Gretchen Koitz

Committees

Armed Services (20th); Sub: No. 4.

District of Columbia (11th); Subs: Business, Commerce, and Taxation; Revenue and Financial Affairs.

Group Ratings

	ADA	COPE	LWV	RIPON	NFU	LCV	CFA	NAB	NSI	ACA
1972	94	82	100	80	86	86	50	8	0	0
1971	86	83	100	88	93	–	100	–	–	11

Key Votes

1) Busing	FOR	6) Cmbodia Bmbg	AGN	11) Chkg Acct Intrst	FOR
2) Strip Mines	AGN	7) Bust Hwy Trust	FOR	12) End HISC (HUAC)	FOR
3) Cut Mil $	FOR	8) Farm Sub Lmt	FOR	13) Nixon Sewer Veto	AGN
4) Rev Shrg	FOR	9) School Prayr	AGN	14) Corp Cmpaign $	AGN
5) Pub TV $	FOR	10) Cnsumr Prot	FOR	15) Pol $ Disclsr	FOR

Election Results

1972 general:	Les Aspin (D)	122,973	(64%)
	Merrill E. Stalbaum (R)	66,665	(35%)
	Charles J. Fortner (American)	1,299	(1%)

1972 primary:	Les Aspin (D)	28,211	(91%)
	Gerald H. Janca (D)	2,943	(9%)
1970 general:	Les Aspin (D)	87,428	(61%)
	Henry C. Schadeberg (R)	56,067	(39%)

SECOND DISTRICT Political Background

Madison (pop. 173,000) is Wisconsin's second-largest city, and the state capital. Of more significance politically, Madison is one of the nation's most important university communities —home of the University of Wisconsin and its 30,000 students. The University was a factor in Wisconsin politics long before the current craze for student votes. Back in 1900, Robert La Follette, a Madison native, was elected Governor; once in office, he called on professors from the University to set up the Wisconsin Tax Commission and to draft a state workmen's compensation law—both firsts in the nation. Wisconsin's progressive movement, including *The Progressive* magazine, which is published in Madison, has always relied heavily on the University community. Consequently, Madison has always been the major center of Wisconsin progressivism.

But by the 1950s, after Joe McCarthy had defeated Sen. Robert La Follette, Jr., the original Progressive movement had almost petered out completely. Though Madison stayed with the La Follettes' odyssey into the Progressive party and back again into Republican ranks, the Wisconsin GOP by the 1950s was firmly in the hands of conservatives. So Madison became the center of the rising liberal movement that resuscitated the Democratic party. Today, the city remains the home base of Sens. William Proxmire and Gaylord Nelson and Gov. Patrick Lucey. And in the spring of 1973, Madison elected as Mayor 28-year-old Paul Soglin, who calls himself a "mellowed radical." Finally, the *Madison Capital Times*, one of two local newspapers, is one of the most liberal in the country.

Madison is the center of Wisconsin's 2nd congressional district, with Madison and surrounding Dane County casting 62% of the district's votes. The history of Madison's representation in the House runs a rough parallel to the politics of the state as a whole. During the 1950s, its Congressman was Glenn Davis, at the time a strong supporter of Joe McCarthy and now Congressman from the 9th district. Davis' strength, however, did not lie in Madison, but in Waukesha County, which contains some of Milwaukee's most affluent and Republican suburbs.

The Republicans failed to hold the seat in 1958 when a Democratic tide saw Sen. William Proxmire elected to a full term and Gaylord Nelson win his first gubernatorial race. In the same year, liberal Democrat Robert Kastenmeier captured the House seat by a narrow margin. In Washington, Kastenmeier did not behave like a normal freshman willing to pay any price for reelection. Instead, he quickly established himself as one of the most liberal members of the House. His original staff included such people as Marcus Raskin—later an aide of President Kennedy, head of the leftish Institute for Policy Studies, and a co-defendant in the Spock-Coffin trial.

In 1960 and 1962, Kastenmeier won reelection with only thin majorities. He was unable to carry Waukesha, and the dairy country around Madison was always less liberal (or progressive) than the capital city. But after the 1963 redistricting removed Waukesha from the 2nd, Kastenmeier won his first big majority in the 1964 Democratic landslide. Since then, the Congressman's margins have grown; in 1970 and 1972, for example, he was reelected with 68% of the votes.

The student vote here has of course helped Kastenmeier, who was one of the very first congressional opponents of the Vietnam war. But another factor in the Congressman's growing strength is the slow leftward trend in both Madison and the surrounding agricultural countryside—a movement that is perceptible throughout the entire upper Midwest. In 1972, George McGovern carried the 2nd district in both the primary and the general election; in fact, McGovern took a larger percentage of the votes than Hubert Humphrey did in 1968.

Kastenmeier has slowly climbed the seniority ladder on the Judiciary and Interior committees. He is now Chairman of a Judiciary subcommittee whose name was changed in 1973 from the antique Patents, Trademarks, Copyrights to the more descriptive Courts, Civil Liberties, and the Administration of Criminal Justice. Kastenmeier has presided at hearings over the thorny issue of a newsman's privilege to keep sources confidential; the work of the Congressman's unit will eventually have to be reconciled with what comes out of Sam Ervin's Senate Subcommittee on Constitutional Rights.

Census Data　Pop. 490,941. Central city, 35%; suburban, 24%. Median family income, $10,397; families above $15,000: 23%; families below $3,000: 7%. Median years education, 12.4.

1972 Share of Federal Outlays　$500,816,133

DOD	$104,614,243	HEW	$213,232,453
AEC	$2,725,007	HUD	$2,908,919
NASA	$2,436,974	DOI	$3,831,238
DOT	$6,073,042	USDA	$45,970,283
		Other	$119,023,974

Federal Military-Industrial Commitments

DOD Contractors Olin Corp. (Baraboo), $52.755m: operation of Badger Army Ammunition plant. Oscar Mayer Co. (Madison), $12.525m: foodstuffs. Chemical Construction Corp. (Baraboo), $9.714m: unspecified.

Economic Base　Agriculture, notably dairy products, hogs and sheep, and cattle; finance, insurance and real estate; food and kindred products; machinery; and fabricated metal products, especially fabricated structural metal products. Also higher education (Univ. of Wisconsin).

The Voters

Registration　No party and no district-wide registration.
Median voting age　40.2
Employment profile　White collar, 49%. Blue collar, 28%. Service, 14%. Farm, 9%.
Ethnic groups　Total foreign stock, 13%. Germany, 4%; Norway, 2%.

Presidential vote

1972	Nixon (R)	108,506	(49%)
	McGovern (D)	111,508	(51%)
1968	Nixon (R)	84,220	(46%)
	Humphrey (D)	89,620	(49%)
	Wallace (AI)	9,170	(5%)

Representative

Robert W. Kastenmeier (D)　Elected 1958; b. Jan. 24, 1924, Beaver Dam; home, Watertown; U. of Wis., LL.B., 1952; Army, WWII; married, three children.

Career　Practicing atty., 1952–58.

Offices　2232 RHOB, 202-225-2906. Also 119 Monona Ave., Madison 53703, 608-252-5206.

Administrative Assistant　Kaz Oshiki

Committees

Interior and Insular Affairs (7th); Subs: Environment; Mines and Mining; National Parks and Recreation; Territorial and Insular Affairs.

Judiciary (4th); Subs: Courts, Civil Liberties, and Administration of Justice (Chm.); Criminal Justice.

Group Ratings

	ADA	COPE	LWV	RIPON	NFU	LCV	CFA	NAB	NSI	ACA
1972	100	91	92	75	86	93	50	8	0	9
1971	95	82	89	88	93	–	100	–	–	11
1970	92	100	–	76	85	90	100	0	0	11

Key Votes

1) Busing	FOR	6) Cmbodia Bmbg	AGN	11) Chkg Acct Intrst	FOR
2) Strip Mines	AGN	7) Bust Hwy Trust	FOR	12) End HISC (HUAC)	FOR
3) Cut Mil $	FOR	8) Farm Sub Lmt	FOR	13) Nixon Sewer Veto	AGN
4) Rev Shrg	FOR	9) School Prayr	AGN	14) Corp Cmpaign $	AGN
5) Pub TV $	FOR	10) Cnsumr Prot	FOR	15) Pol $ Disclosr	FOR

Election Results

1972 general:	Robert W. Kastenmeier (D)	148,136	(69%)
	J. Michael Kelly (R)	68,167	(31%)
1972 primary:	Robert W. Kastenmeier (D), unopposed		
1970 general:	Robert W. Kastenmeier (D)	102,879	(69%)
	Norman Anderson (R)	46,620	(31%)

THIRD DISTRICT Political Background

The 3rd district of Wisconsin occupies the western and southwestern parts of the state. This is rolling farmland, stretching some 200 miles along the Mississippi and St. Croix rivers. The countryside here probably looks little different from when it first took white settlers during the 1840s and 1850s—in the south is gentle, hilly dairy land, in the north, more forests. The district has only two significant urban centers, La Crosse (pop. 51,000) and Eau Claire (pop. 44,000). Both are names that recall the French chevaliers who came paddling down the Mississippi and St. Croix in the seventeenth century. The 3rd of Wisconsin is one of the nation's premier dairy districts; accordingly, its Congressman finds himself concerned with the arcane details of milk marketing regulations and import restrictions on Dutch and Swiss cheese.

The current incumbent is Republican Vernon W. Thomson, who was Governor of the state in 1957 and 1958 until he was beaten by now-Sen. Gaylord Nelson. Thomson is a quiet, usually reliable Midwestern conservative Republican—the kind of politician who contributes noiselessly to the House votes at Gerald Ford's command. But surprisingly—for this is historically one of the most Republican parts of historically Republican Wisconsin—Thomson has encountered stiff opposition in the last two elections.

One factor, certainly, is age. Thomson turns 69 in 1974, while his Democratic opponents have been much younger and much more vigorous campaigners. Another factor—less noticed here than in Madison, but nearly as important—is the vast number of college students in the district. The Wisconsin State University system has no less than four campuses here, with 23,000 students—a full 8% of the eligible voters. Little did the Republican legislators who located the campuses in the Wisconsin boondocks realize that in so doing thousands of Democratic votes were being planted in the fertile political soil of the upper Midwest. The third factor is simply the shift toward the Democrats in the upper Midwest generally. Unemployment is a serious problem here. In 1970, some 10% of the work force was out of a job in La Crosse; so in November of that year, Thomson failed to carry the usually Republican county. And while the Nixon Administration, supported with votes from Thomson, pours money into Sun Belt defense contractors like Lockheed and Litton, the 3rd district receives precious little from the federal treasury. Finally, Wisconsin is a state where traditional moral fervor becomes disgusted less at hair length than at public officials breaking the law and telling falsehoods. Accustomed to clean government, Wisconsin natives were quite upset about Watergate—particularly, one might guess, with the scandal's fetid Caribbean ambiance produced by the Cuban burglars and money laundered through Mexican banks.

So it appears that the Democrats will have a chance to win the 3rd district in 1974. Their problem will be finding the best possible candidate. At present, a divisive primary seems to be shaping up, one that could deliver the district to Thomson for another term. But all indications point to a good Democratic year in 1974, with the 3rd being one of the top priorities for Wisconsin Democrats.

Census Data Pop. 491,034. Central city, 10%; suburban, 6%. Median family income, $8,485; families above $15,000: 14%; families below $3,000: 12%. Median years education, 12.1.

1972 Share of Federal Outlays $519,484,371

DOD	$177,199,938	HEW	$181,731,418
AEC	$1,173,756	HUD	$1,019,755
NASA	–	DOI	$1,745,675
DOT	$17,239,313	USDA	$69,007,968
		Other	$70,366,548

Federal Military-Industrial Commitments

DOD Contractors National Presto Industries (Eau Claire), $146.896m: components for 105mm and 15mm projectiles.
DOD Installations Osceola AF Station (Osceola).

Economic Base Agriculture, notably dairy products, hogs and sheep, and dairy cattle; food and kindred products; finance, insurance and real estate; and machinery. Also higher education (Wisconsin State Univ., Eau Claire).

The Voters

Registration No party and no district-wide registration.
Median voting age 45.4
Employment profile White collar, 37%. Blue collar, 33%. Service, 15%. Farm, 15%.
Ethnic groups Total foreign stock, 13%. Norway, Germany, 4% each; Sweden, 1%.

Presidential vote

1972	Nixon (R)	122,445	(59%)
	McGovern (D)	85,348	(41%)
1968	Nixon (R)	102,105	(53%)
	Humphrey (D)	77,099	(40%)
	Wallace (AI)	12,656	(7%)

Representative

Vernon W. Thomson (R) Elected 1960; b. Nov. 5, 1905, Richland Center; home, Richland Center; U. of Wis., B.A., 1928, LL.B., 1932; married, three children; Presbyterian.

Career Asst. Dist. Atty., Richland County, 1933–35; city atty., 1933–37; Wis. Legislature, 1935–49; Mayor, Richland Center, 1944–50; Sec., Wis. Legislative Council, 1949–51; Wis. Atty. Gen., 1951–56; Wis. Gov., 1956–58; practicing atty., 1958-60.

Offices 2305 RHOB, 202-225-5506. Also Farmers & Mechanics Bank Bldg., Richland Center 53581, and 421 Main St., LaCrosse 54601.

Administrative Assistant Jean Gilligan

Committees

Foreign Affairs (6th); Subs: Asian and Pacific Affairs; National Security Policy and Scientific Developments; State Department Organization and Foreign Operations (Ranking Mbr.).

Sel. Com. on the House Restaurant (Ranking Mbr.).

Sel. Com. on Small Business (5th); Subs: Environmental Problems Affecting Small Business (Ranking Mbr.); Minority Small Business Enterprise and Franchising; Small Business Problems in Smaller Towns and Urban Areas.

Group Ratings

	ADA	COPE	LWV	RIPON	NFU	LCV	CFA	NAB	NSI	ACA
1972	13	36	55	64	86	26	0	58	100	57
1971	11	33	56	50	40	–	38	–	–	68
1970	24	17	–	63	46	22	45	100	100	79

Key Votes

1) Busing	AGN	6) Cmbodia Bmbg	FOR	11) Chkg Acct Intrst	AGN
2) Strip Mines	AGN	7) Bust Hwy Trust	AGN	12) End HISC (HUAC)	AGN
3) Cut Mil $	AGN	8) Farm Sub Lmt	FOR	13) Nixon Sewer Veto	FOR
4) Rev Shrg	FOR	9) School Prayr	FOR	14) Corp Cmpaign $	AGN
5) Pub TV $	AGN	10) Cnsumr Prot	AGN	15) Pol $ Disclosr	AGN

Election Results

1972 general:	Vernon W. Thomson (R)	112,905	(55%)
	Walter Thoresen (D)	91,953	(45%)
	Keith Ellison (American)	1,482	(1%)
1972 primary:	Vernon W. Thompson (R)	34,720	(79%)
	Peter E. Berg (R)	9,073	(21%)
1970 general:	Vernon W. Thompson (R)	64,891	(55%)
	Ray Short (D)	52,085	(45%)

FOURTH DISTRICT Political Background

The 4th district of Wisconsin is the south side of Milwaukee and the Milwaukee County suburbs to the south and west. The Milwaukee River splits the city into two distinct sections. Traditionally, the north side has been German; today, it also includes practically all of Milwaukee's medium-sized black community. Like all of Wisconsin, the south side has large numbers of German-Americans, but since the days of industrial growth at the turn of the century, south side Milwaukee has been the Polish part of town. Today, the south side remains all white and heavily Polish, while the suburbs to the south are filled mainly with the newly prosperous blue- and white-collar descendants of the original Polish immigrants. The western suburbs, Wauwatosa and West Allis, are more German and more white-collar.

Numerous magazine articles have characterized the south side as the home of the white backlash and a stronghold of George Wallace. It is true that Wallace nearly carried the district in the 1964 presidential primary, but the Alabaman's showing was as much a revolt against the unpopular tax program of the Democratic Governor, President Johnson's stand-in, as anything else. In 1968, the 4th district actually cast just under 10% of its votes for Wallace—far less than he got in many other northern districts or the nation as a whole. In the 1972 presidential primary, Wallace failed to carry the 4th; instead, George McGovern surprised virtually everybody and won here. Much of the credit for his triumph goes to 27-year-old Carl Wagner, described by writer Hunter Thompson as "one of the best field organizers in the business." McGovern's performance in the 4th marked a crucial point in the primary. The South Dakotan demonstrated that he could carry even solid blue-collar areas; meanwhile, the fact that Edmund Muskie lost one of the nation's most heavily Polish-American districts pretty well finished his campaign.

The south side had a Democratic tradition long before the rest of Wisconsin developed one. In fact, its current Congressman, Clement Zablocki, was first elected over 25 years ago, in 1948. Most of Zablocki's attitudes seem closer to those held by machine Democrats from cities like Chicago and Philadelphia than to those belonging to the ideological liberals in the rest of the Wisconsin delegation. For example, he is the only Wisconsin Democrat to have supported the Vietnam policies of the Johnson and Nixon administrations. And his approach to social problems, one that he presumably shares with his constituency, has been considerably more conservative.

Thanks to his abundant seniority, Zablocki is the number-two Democrat on the House Foreign Relations Committee. He first joined the committee when many of his Polish-American constituents felt convinced, understandably but unrealistically, that the United States should liberate Poland and the other countries of Eastern Europe from Soviet domination. Lately, Zablocki has spent much of his time working on the war powers issue. He sponsored the bill passed by the House in 1972, which was criticized for imposing too few limits on the President's power to wage war. Zablocki's 1973 bill, not yet passed at this writing, is considered much tougher; in fact, some observers believe it is much more stringent than the bill that has already gone through the Senate. Problems lie ahead. A conference committee will have to iron out the differences, a task that proved impossible in 1972; moreover, President Nixon will probably veto any war powers measure that reaches his desk. Nonetheless, Zablocki has been the work horse in the House on a major issue, one that could some day be of monumental importance.

As predicted in the 1972 *Almanac*, the legislature added the middle-class suburb of Wauwatosa to the 4th to bring it up to the state population average. And, as predicted, the addition reduced Zablocki's margin only slightly, cutting it to a still very safe 76% of the votes in 1972.

Census Data   Pop. 490,690. Central city, 46%; suburban, 54%. Median family income, $11,285; families above $15,000: 24%; families below $3,000: 5%. Median years education, 12.1.

1972 Share of Federal Outlays $337,027,299

DOD	$40,299,097	HEW	$159,352,462
AEC	$40,399	HUD	$7,320,577
NASA	$1,565,708	DOI	$423,782
DOT	$10,591,925	USDA	$14,819,974
		Other	$102,613,375

Federal Military-Industrial Commitments

DOD Contractors General Motors (Oak Creek), $17.069m: warheads for MK 48 torpedo.
NASA Contractors Astronautics Corp. (Milwaukee), $5.037m: various engineering services.

Economic Base Machinery, especially construction and related machinery; electrical equipment and supplies; food and kindred products, especially malt liquors; primary metal industries; and fabricated metal products. Also higher education (Marquette Univ.).

The Voters

Registration No party and no district-wide registration.
Median voting age 44.2
Employment profile White collar, 47%. Blue collar, 40%. Service, 13%. Farm, –%.
Ethnic groups Spanish, 2%. Total foreign stock, 24%. Germany, Poland, 6% each; Austria, 1%.

Presidential vote

1972	Nixon (R)	96,755	(49%)
	McGovern (D)	99,537	(51%)
1968	Nixon (R)	74,783	(39%)
	Humphrey (D)	100,446	(51%)
	Wallace (AI)	18,968	(10%)

Representative

Clement J. Zablocki (D) Elected 1948; b. Nov. 18, 1912, Milwaukee; home, Milwaukee; Marquette U., Ph.B., 1936; married, two children; Catholic.

Career High school teacher, 1938–40; organist, choir dir., 1932–48; Wis. Senate, 1942–48.

Offices 2184 RHOB, 202-225-4572. Also 1401 W. Lincoln Ave., Milwaukee 53215, 414-383-4000.

Administrative Assistant Ivo Spalatin

Committees

Foreign Affairs (2nd); Subs: Foreign Economic Policy; National Security Policy and Scientific Developments (Chm.); State Department Organization and Foreign Operations; Sp. Sub. for Review of Foreign Aid Programs.

Group Ratings

	ADA	COPE	LWV	RIPON	NFU	LCV	CFA	NAB	NSI	ACA
1972	44	91	75	63	83	33	50	17	100	26
1971	38	100	67	33	57	–	75	–	–	38
1970	44	100	–	59	100	80	85	0	90	26

Key Votes

1) Busing	AGN	6) Cmbodia Bmbg	FOR	11) Chkg Acct Intrst	AGN
2) Strip Mines	AGN	7) Bust Hwy Trust	AGN	12) End HISC (HUAC)	AGN
3) Cut Mil $	AGN	8) Farm Sub Lmt	FOR	13) Nixon Sewer Veto	AGN
4) Rev Shrg	FOR	9) School Prayr	FOR	14) Corp Cmpaign $	FOR
5) Pub TV $	FOR	10) Cnsumr Prot	FOR	15) Pol $ Disclosr	AGN

Election Results

1972 general:	Clement J. Zablocki (D)	149,078	(76%)
	Phillip D. Mrozinski (R)	45,003	(23%)
	Eugene Annell (American)	2,946	(2%)
1972 primary:	Clement J. Zablocki (D)	32,087	(88%)
	Therese M. Heiman (D)	4,337	(12%)
1970 general:	Clement J. Zablocki (D)	102,464	(80%)
	Phillip D. Mrozinski (R)	23,081	(18%)
	John A. Zierhut (American)	1,985	(2%)

FIFTH DISTRICT Political Background

The 5th congressional district of Wisconsin is made up of the north side of Milwaukee. As predicted in the 1972 *Almanac*, the district was expanded to the city limits and includes no suburbs. The north side is traditionally the German half of Milwaukee, with the gemütlichkeit atmosphere of old Milwaukee now part of the nation's legacy. For years, Milwaukee has been famous for beer—the brewing of which is an art practiced by Germans for centuries. Today, Milwaukee is the home of Schlitz, Miller's, Pabst, Blatz, and others. Not as well-known is that for years Milwaukee supported its own, unique kind of politics, which had roots deep in the German tradition. During the years when Robert La Follette and his progressive Republicans were ascendent in the rest of Wisconsin, Milwaukee elected a series of Socialist party Mayors and Congressmen. The most notable among them was Victor Berger, who served in the House from 1911 to 1913 and again from 1923 to 1929.

After the 1918 and 1920 elections, Berger was denied his seat because of his opposition to American entry into World War I. For those who think that prosecution of antiwar dissenters is only a recent phenomenon in the United States, it should be remembered that in 1919 Berger was sentenced to 20 years in prison for having written antiwar articles. The prosecution was brought under the Wilson Administration and, after the conviction was reversed by the Supreme Court, all charges were dropped by the "return to normalcy" Harding Administration. It is a measure of the strength of German Milwaukee's opposition to World War I that Berger was reelected to Congress while his case was on appeal and after he had been denied his seat.

Today, many descendants of the first German immigrants have left the north side for the suburbs, with some of them having been replaced by blacks from the rural south. In 1970, some 21% of the 5th's population were black, which may not appear an especially high figure, though it does represent 82% of the black population of the entire state. In recent years, Milwaukee has been the scene of some racial turbulence. The most notable demonstrations were led several years ago by Father James Groppi, protesting the City Council's refusal to enact an open-housing ordinance.

Since the 1954 election, the 5th has been represented in the House by Henry Reuss, whose last name recalls the German origin of so many of the district's residents. Reuss is one of the most liberal members of the House, and one of the very few in that category who at the same time possesses great seniority. For some years, Reuss was Chairman of the Banking Committee's Subcommittee on International Finance. He remains perhaps the leading congressional expert on such mysterious matters as the balance of payments, the gold market, and the ups and downs of various European and Asian currencies and the American dollar.

Reuss gave up the chair of International Finance to head the Government Operations' Subcommittee on Conservation and Natural Resources. Here Reuss occupies an excellent position from which to exercise oversight into the government's diverse activities in environmental regulation. His record in the field has made him one of the congressional heroes of ecology activists. It was Reuss, for example, who unearthed the 1899 Refuse Act, which baldly prohibits the dumping of pollutants into interstate waterways. Though the ancient statute had been completely forgotten, Reuss persuaded the government to revive it. The law is now a major weapon against industrial polluters.

In 1973, Reuss emerged as one of the leading House critics of the Nixon Administration involvement in the Watergate scandal. Reuss attended a monetary conference in Europe during the summer of 1973, and found confidence in the Nixon Administration battered by Watergate. The Congressman then called on the President and the Vice-President to resign, thus making way for a truly bipartisan Administration to run the federal government for the next three years. That such a proposal could come from a respected and intellectually distinguished Congressman like Reuss was yet another indication of the deep trouble in which the Nixon Administration found itself.

Reuss has had no difficulty whatever winning reelection in the 5th. The increasing number of black voters here has made this safe Democratic district even safer; besides, Reuss usually runs ahead of his party anyway. In 1972, George McGovern got 58% of the votes in the 5th, with Milwaukee being the only million-plus metropolitan area where the South Dakotan ran ahead of Hubert Humphrey's 1968 percentage. In the same year, Reuss was reelected with 77% of the votes, one of the largest margins of any opposed Democrat in the House.

Census Data Pop. 490,708. Central city, 100%; suburban, 0%. Median family income, $10,067; families above $15,000: 19%; families below $3,000: 9%. Median years education, 12.0.

1972 Share of Federal Outlays $337,123,730

DOD	$40,310,628	HEW	$159,398,057
AEC	$40,411	HUD	$7,322,672
NASA	$1,566,156	DOI	$423,908
DOT	$10,594,955	USDA	$14,824,214
		Other	$102,642,729

Federal Military-Industrial Commitments

DOD Contractors General Motors (Milwaukee), $6.941m: design of XM803 combat tank. Kearney Trecker Corp. (Milwaukee), $5.739m: milling machines.

Economic Base Machinery, especially construction and related machinery; electrical equipment and supplies; food and kindred products; primary metal industries; and fabricated metal products. Also higher education (Univ. of Wisconsin, Milwaukee).

The Voters

Registration No party and no district-wide registration.
Median voting age 42.9
Employment profile White collar, 47%. Blue collar, 38%. Service, 15%. Farm, –%.
Ethnic groups Black, 21%. Spanish, 2%. Total foreign stock, 21%. Germany, 7%; Poland, 2%; Italy, Austria, 1% each.

Presidential vote

1972	Nixon (R)	71,196	(42%)
	McGovern (D)	97,596	(58%)

1968	Nixon (R)	63,698	(37%)
	Humphrey (D)	92,352	(54%)
	Wallace (AI)	14,581	(9%)

Representative

Henry S. Reuss (D) Elected 1954; b. Feb. 22, 1912, Milwaukee; home, Milwaukee; Cornell U., A.B., 1933; Harvard, LL.B., 1936; Army, WWII; married, four children; Episcopalian.

Career Practicing atty., 1936–55; lecturer, Wis. State Col., 1950–51; Asst. Counsel, Milwaukee County, 1939–40; Asst. Gen. Counsel, OPA, 1941–42; Chief, Price Control Branch, Mil. Govt. for Germany, 1945; Dep. Counsel, Marshall Plan, 1949; Milwaukee County Grand Jury Sp. Prosecutor, 1950.

Offices 2186 RHOB, 202-225-3571. Also 211 W. Wisconsin, 8th floor, Milwaukee 53203, 414-272-1226.

Administrative Assistant Donald Robinson

Committees

Banking and Currency (4th); Subs: Housing; International Finance.

Government Operations (7th); Subs: Conservation and Natural Resources (Chm.); Special Studies.

Joint Economic Com. (3rd); Subs: International Economics (Chm.); Economic Progress; Consumer Economics.

Joint Study Com. on Budget Control.

Group Ratings

	ADA	COPE	LWV	RIPON	NFU	LCV	CFA	NAB	NSI	ACA
1972	100	82	100	81	71	83	100	8	0	4
1971	97	82	100	94	73	–	100	–	–	14
1970	88	100	–	76	92	95	100	0	0	17

Key Votes

1) Busing	FOR	6) Cmbodia Bmbg	AGN	11) Chkg Acct Intrst	ABS
2) Strip Mines	AGN	7) Bust Hwy Trust	FOR	12) End HISC (HUAC)	FOR
3) Cut Mil $	FOR	8) Farm Sub Lmt	FOR	13) Nixon Sewer Veto	AGN
4) Rev Shrg	FOR	9) School Prayr	AGN	14) Corp Cmpaign $	AGN
5) Pub TV $	FOR	10) Cnsumr Prot	FOR	15) Pol $ Disclosr	FOR

Election Results

1972 general:	Henry S. Reuss (D)	127,273	(77%)
	Frederick Van Hecke (R)	33,627	(20%)
	George Sprague (American)	2,802	(2%)
	R. Julian Chapman (Ind.)	937	(1%)
1972 primary:	Henry S. Reuss (D), unopposed		
1970 general:	Henry S. Reuss (D)	60,630	(76%)
	Robert J. Dwyer (R)	18,360	(23%)
	Earl R. Denny (American)	640	(1%)

SIXTH DISTRICT Political Background

The 6th district of Wisconsin is an almost perfectly rectangular slice of central Wisconsin, which extends from Lake Michigan to a point near the Mississippi River. On the lake are the cities of Manitowoc (pop. 33,000) and Sheboygan (pop. 48,000), both of which lean Democratic. During the 1950s, Sheboygan was the scene of a bitter, eight-year-long UAW strike against the Kohler

Company. To the west are the quiet, more Republican cities of Oshkosh (pop. 53,000) and Fond du Lac (pop. 35,000); both of them lie along Lake Winnebago, the state's largest inland lake. The rest of the district is rural dairy country, with small paper-mill towns here and there.

The 6th district also includes the small town of Ripon (pop. 7,053), where the Republican party is said to have been founded in 1854. (Jackson, Michigan, also claims the distinction.) It is therefore appropriate that the 6th sends to Congress one of the few congressional favorites of the Ripon Society, Republican William Steiger. When first elected in 1966, Steiger was the youngest member of Congress, at 28; so youthful was his appearance that he was sometimes mistaken for a page. But he had already spent six years in the Wisconsin legislature, and won a seat in the House after scoring a relatively easy upset of a Democrat elected in the LBJ landslide.

Steiger's record on substantive issues is really not as liberal as the Ripon group would like. In the Education and Labor Committee and on the floor, Steiger has often supported the position taken by the Nixon Administration on both domestic and foreign-policy issues. The Congressman has saved his major initiatives for areas where Administration and Ripon goals coincide. For example, he was one of the important congressional backers of the abolition of the draft, though not a member of the Armed Services Committee. Steiger remains today one of the most vocal defenders of the all-volunteer Army.

Steiger also has a major political assignment outside the halls of the Capitol. He heads the Republican party's Rule 29 Committee, which was mandated by the 1972 convention to come up with a set of delegate-selection procedures to broaden the base of the GOP. Southerners and conservatives attacked his appointment, since Steiger was part of the unsuccessful move at the '72 Convention to increase the share of delegates allotted to the most populous states. Steiger is against any kind of quotas like those the Democrats used in 1972 requiring a reasonable representation of certain age and ethnic groups in each delegation. So at this writing, the Congressman's efforts appear to have met with wider approval in the Republican party than some had anticipated.

Reelection is no problem for Steiger. His speaking skills overcome whatever detriment his youthful appearance might have been to him. Moreover, like so many other Congressmen, Steiger augments his reelection chances by providing capable ombudsman-like services to his constituents. Despite the recent Democratic surge in Wisconsin, Steiger was reelected with 68% of the votes in 1970 and 66% in 1972, when he ran 6% ahead of Richard Nixon in the 6th district. He is the only Wisconsin Republican Congressman whom the Democrats have conceded they have no chance to beat.

Census Data Pop. 490,934. Central city, 12%; suburban, 21%. Median family income, $9,727; families above $15,000: 17%; families below $3,000: 8%. Median years education, 12.1.

1972 Share of Federal Outlays $75,618,867

DOD	$26,185,920	HEW	$115,378,517
AEC	–	HUD	$21,303
NASA	–	DOI	$255,610
DOT	$3,732,617	USDA	$22,085,795
		Other	$67,959,105

Federal Military-Industrial Commitments

DOD Contractors Oshkosh Motor Truck, Inc. (Oshkosh), $16.937m: fire-fighting and snow-removal trucks.

Economic Base Agriculture, notably dairy products, dairy cattle, and hogs and sheep; machinery; fabricated metal products; food and kindred products; and paper and allied products. Also higher education (Wisconsin State Univ., Oshkosh).

The Voters

Registration No party and no district-wide registration.
Median voting age 44.8
Employment profile White collar, 38%. Blue collar, 41%. Service, 13%. Farm, 8%.
Ethnic groups Total foreign stock, 14%. Germany, 6%.

Presidential vote

1972	Nixon (R)	114,461	(57%)
	McGovern (D)	85,778	(43%)
1968	Nixon (R)	97,980	(52%)
	Humphrey (D)	79,801	(42%)
	Wallace (AI)	11,810	(6%)

Representative

William A. Steiger (R) Elected 1966; b. May 15, 1938, Oshkosh; home, Oshkosh; U. of Wis., B.A., 1960; married, one child; Episcopalian.

Career Wis. Legislature, 1961–66.

Offices 1025 LHOB, 202-225-2476. Also 201 P.O. Bldg., Oshkosh 54901, 414-231-6333.

Administrative Assistant Maureen Drummy

Committees

Education and Labor (8th); Subs: No. 1 (Gen. Sub. on Education); No. 4 (Sel. Sub. on Labor); No. 7 (Equal Opportunities) (Ranking Mbr.); No. 8 (Agricultural Labor).

Şel. Com. on Committees of the House (4th).

Group Ratings

	ADA	COPE	LWV	RIPON	NFU	LCV	CFA	NAB	NSI	ACA
1972	25	22	82	75	43	63	0	91	100	48
1971	32	17	56	71	33	–	50	–	–	71
1970	24	33	–	71	46	50	53	75	100	58

Key Votes

1) Busing	FOR	6) Cmbodia Bmbg	FOR	11) Chkg Acct Intrst	ABS
2) Strip Mines	AGN	7) Bust Hwy Trust	AGN	12) End HISC (HUAC)	AGN
3) Cut Mil $	AGN	8) Farm Sub Lmt	AGN	13) Nixon Sewer Veto	FOR
4) Rev Shrg	FOR	9) School Prayr	AGN	14) Corp Cmpaign $	AGN
5) Pub TV $	AGN	10) Cnsumr Prot	FOR	15) Pol $ Disclosr	FOR

Election Results

1972 general:	William A. Steiger (R)	130,701	(66%)
	James A. Adams (D)	63,643	(32%)
	Valeria M. Sitter (American)	4,260	(2%)
1972 primary:	William A. Steiger (R), unopposed		
1970 general:	William A. Steiger (R)	98,587	(68%)
	Franklin R. Utech (D)	44,794	(31%)
	Rani V. Davidson (American)	2,150	(1%)

SEVENTH DISTRICT Political Background

Because the state's population failed to grow as fast as the national average during the 1960s, Wisconsin lost one congressional seat after the 1970 census. As predicted in the 1972 *Almanac*, the Wisconsin legislature responded by combining the old 7th district, represented by Democrat David Obey, with the old 10th district, represented by Republican Alvin O'Konski. Neither decided to retire. So one might expect a close race in the new 7th, a contest decided by a few votes as is usually the case in this part of Wisconsin. But the result in the Obey-O'Konski confrontation was a rout. The 34-year-old Obey, after three years in the House, got 63% of the votes to the 37% won by the 65-year-old O'Konski, a 30-year House veteran.

Several factors combined to produce the result, which was, like the redistricting, predicted in the 1972 *Almanac*. First was the composition of the new 7th district. Though O'Konski had represented 11 of the new district's 17 counties, only 43% of its population and 44% of its votes came out of the veteran Republican's old constituency. Most of the 11 counties are forest-covered north woods, with occasional paper- and saw-mill towns. The only major urban center in this part of the district is Superior (pop. 32,000), which lies across an inlet from Duluth, Minnesota. Workers on the Duluth-Superior docks load most of the iron ore from Minnesota's Mesabi Range onto giant Great Lakes freighters; but because the range is being depleted, Superior has been steadily losing population since 1910. In most elections, the territory up here is heavily Democratic; George McGovern came within 3,000 votes of carrying it in 1972, despite doing poorly among Eastern European ethnics in Superior. Nevertheless, O'Konski had won here since the 1942 elections, as he compiled a relatively liberal voting record on economic issues. In 1970, however, O'Konski's share of the votes fell sharply, to 51%. He did not come back to campaign in the district, citing the press of congressional business, but local reporters discovered that he really spent weekends getting treatment at Bethesda Naval Hospital. So O'Konski was in serious trouble in his old home territory in 1972.

The six counties from Obey's old district are somewhat more Republican by tradition. Large Democratic margins usually come out of Portage County (Stevens Point), with its high concentration of Polish-Americans; but the largest county here, Marathon (Wausau) is pretty marginal. In fact, the Congressman before Obey was none other than Melvin Laird, who was Chairman of the House Republican Conference when he resigned to become Secretary of Defense in 1969.

A special election was held in 1969 to fill the vacancy created by Laird's departure. Like several such contests that year, the Democrats captured a seat previously held by a Republican. The winner was David Obey, just 30, who had first won election to the state legislature at age 24. Obey made a liberal record in Madison on issues like education, and during the congressional campaign, attacked his Republican opponent on economic issues. One factor in Obey's 2% victory margin was the unpopularity of Republican Gov. Warren Knowles' state sales tax.

After the narrow win, the Republicans were determined to wage a tough campaign to reclaim the seat in 1970. But Obey, a quiet, workmanlike legislator, did his homework. He concentrated on bread-and-butter issues and constituency service; though he votes with the liberal bloc on most issues, he does not flash the kind of style popular among the radical chic salons of Manhattan. The work paid off. Obey won reelection in 1970 with 67% of the votes—a larger share than Laird managed in recent outings.

Obey's popularity in his old district obviously gave him a great advantage in 1972, and he compounded that advantage by campaigning vigorously all over the new 7th district. But another issue probably played some role in the result: Project Sanguine. This was a Navy program to plant hundreds of electronic sensors in the ground over thousands of acres. Taken together, the sensors would form a gigantic antenna which, through low-frequency impulses, could communicate with submarines the world over while they remained submerged. Presently the subs have to surface to transmit and receive messages.

Northern Wisconsin was picked as the site for Sanquine, presumably because the terrain here possessed the requisite geological formation and O'Konski was the second-ranking Republican on the House Armed Services Committee. For his part, O'Konski enthusiastically endorsed the project; it promised to bring employment, however brief, to job-starved northern Wisconsin. But when experimental electronic sensors were implanted, things started to go wrong. Television reception was disturbed, and electrical appliances appeared to jam. People in the area began to find Sanguine a little scary, and to wonder just what it might do to their environment of dairy fields and north woods. Down in the old 7th district, David Obey refused to support Sanguine until it was proved militarily necessary, scientifically workable, and environmentally harmless —criteria that the Congressman thought the Navy had failed to meet. After Obey's 63% victory, Melvin Laird, in one of his last acts as Defense Secretary, quietly scrubbed Project Sanguine in Wisconsin. He then announced that if it were built anywhere, it would be Texas. Laird, who was then considering a run for something in Wisconsin in 1974, had obviously retained an ability to read the election returns.

But an Obey-Laird contest is unlikely to occur. Obey's seat now seems as safe as a seat can be. The Congressman also serves on the House Appropriations Committee; and though he currently ranks twenty-fourth out of the committee's thirty-three Democrats, he is still its youngest member. Because Obey has exhibited no signs of a desire to run for statewide office, he stands an excellent chance of becoming Chairman of Appropriations some day. Assuming every other Democrat on the committee retires, or is retired, at age 65, Obey will become Chairman in 1988, when he will be 50. So this young, matter-of-fact legislator may be one of the most important people in the federal government in the 1990s and after the turn of the century.

Census Data   Pop. 491,030. Central city, 7%; suburban, 3%. Median family income, $8,424; families above $15,000: 12%; families below $3,000: 12%. Median years education, 11.8.

1972 Share of Federal Outlays $330,427,463

DOD	$10,874,258	HEW	$181,927,032
AEC	$303,949	HUD	$50,000
NASA	–	DOI	$1,345,543
DOT	$9,487,355	USDA	$57,580,496
		Other	$68,858,830

Federal Military-Industrial Commitments

No installations or contractors receiving prime awards greater than $5,000,000.

Economic Base   Agriculture, notably dairy products, dairy cattle, and cattle; paper and allied products; finance, insurance and real estate; lumber and wood products, especially millwork, plywood and related products; and food and kindred products, especially dairy products.

The Voters

Registration   No party and no district-wide registration.
Median voting age   46.4
Employment profile   White collar, 38%. Blue collar, 38%. Service, 14%. Farm, 10%.
Ethnic groups   Total foreign stock, 19%; Germany, 6%; Poland, Sweden, Norway, 2% each; Canada, 1%.

Presidential vote

	1972	Nixon (R)	110,826	(53%)
		McGovern (D)	98,230	(47%)
	1968	Nixon (R)	86,217	(44%)
		Humphrey (D)	95,168	(48%)
		Wallace (AI)	15,369	(8%)

Representative

David R. Obey (D) Elected 1968; b. Oct. 3, 1938, Okmulgee, Okla; home, Wausau; U. of Wis., M.A., 1960; married, one child; religion unspecified.

Career   Wis. Legislature, 1962–68.

Offices   415 CHOB, 202-225-3365. Also Fed. Bldg., 317 First St., Wausau 54401, 715-842-5606.

Administrative Assistant   Lyle Stitt

Committees

Appropriations (24th); Subs: Labor, Health, Education, and Welfare; Military Construction.

Group Ratings

	ADA	COPE	LWV	RIPON	NFU	LCV	CFA	NAB	NSI	ACA
1972	100	100	92	67	86	91	100	0	0	0
1971	86	83	89	83	100	–	100	–	–	14
1970	84	92	–	63	77	100	100	9	55	33

Key Votes

1) Busing	FOR	6) Cmbodia Bmbg	AGN	11) Chkg Acct Intrst		ABS
2) Strip Mines	AGN	7) Bust Hwy Trust	FOR	12) End HISC (HUAC)		FOR
3) Cut Mil $	FOR	8) Farm Sub Lmt	FOR	13) Nixon Sewer Veto		AGN
4) Rev Shrg	FOR	9) School Prayr	AGN	14) Corp Cmpaign $		AGN
5) Pub TV $	FOR	10) Cnsumr Prot	FOR	15) Pol $ Disclosr		FOR

Election Results

1972 general:	David R. Obey (D)	135,385	(63%)
	Alvin E. O'Konski (R)	80,207	(37%)
1972 primary:	David R. Obey (D), unopposed		
1970 general:	David R. Obey (D)	88,746	(67%)
	André E. Le Tendre (R)	41,330	(32%)
	Richard D. Wolfe (American)	1,189	(1%)

EIGHTH DISTRICT Political Background

The 8th of Wisconsin might be called the Packers' district. Centered on the Midwest metropolis of Green Bay (pop. 87,000), it is the home of the Green Bay Packers and the smallest city with any kind of big-time professional athletic franchise. The team here is a remnant of the early days of pro football, when the National Football League included such teams as Jim Thorpe's Canton (Ohio) Bulldogs. During the 1960s, the "Pack" under Vince Lombardi was a stringently disciplined unit that dominated both the NFL and the fantasy life of millions of American males. The Packers are the aspect of the 8th district best known to the outside world, though this 13-county district in northwest Wisconsin has other features of note. It includes the city of Appleton (pop. 57,000), Joe McCarthy's home town. Nathan M. Pusey, later president of Harvard, served in the same office at Lawrence College in Appleton and defied McCarthy's pronunciamentos in the early 1950s. And the 8th district contains the only recently formed county in the United States, Menominee, which was created when the Menominee Indian Reservation was liquidated in accordance with the termination policy of the Eisenhower Administration.

Though the 8th is generally considered a solidly Republican district, the assessment is not quite the case. Green Bay, which usually goes Republican, is a German Catholic town that gave a majority of its votes to John F. Kennedy in 1960 and even gave George McGovern a fair percentage in 1972. There are some heavily Republican counties here (Shawano, Waupaca), but also some that usually go Democratic (Florence, Forest). The balance, and more than half the votes, are cast in Brown and Outagamie counties, which contain Green Bay and Appleton, respectively.

From 1945 to 1973, the 8th district was represented by John Byrnes, a man who shared some of the views, but little of the temperament, of the late Senator from Appleton. When Byrnes' announced a surprising decision to retire in 1972, he was the third-most-senior Republican in the House and the ranking minority member of the Ways and Means Committee. On Ways and Means, the usual partisan strife was avoided largely because Byrnes and Chairman Wilbur Mills had, over the years, developed a close working relationship. The two would usually work out disagreements in executive session, which allowed them to report a bill to the floor with bipartisan support. And these bills usually passed easily, largely because the Rules Committee ordinarily prohibited the House from amending them. The bipartisan cooperation prevented a lot of chaos; without the efforts of Byrnes and Mills, bills on such important matters as tax legislation, Social Security, welfare, and international trade could have been encumbered with all kinds of expedient amendments. But the close cooperation also meant that on many of the major issues, legislative decisions were made by just two men, Wilbur Mills and John Byrnes. It was a concentration of power unequalled anywhere else in the legislative process.

With Byrnes' retirement and Mills' aching back (which put him on the operating table in September 1973 and may force him to retire in 1974), power has become more diffuse. In practice, the diffusion could mean that nothing at all happens in Ways and Means, which is the case at the moment on the 1973 international trade bill.

One thing that may have prompted Byrnes to retire was the uncomfortably close margin—55–44—by which he beat Jesuit priest Robert Cornell in the 1970 general election. In 1972, Cornell tried again. This time his Republican opponent was Harold Froehlich, Minority

Leader of the Wisconsin Assembly, and the outcome was even closer. Cornell won 49%, Froehlich 50%, with the other 1% going to American party candidate Clyde Bunker (no relation to Archie). In the House, Froehlich had compiled a pretty solidly conservative record. In 1974, Wisconsin Democrats hope they can erase Froehlich's less than 4,000-vote margin of victory in 1972. Father Cornell may be the candidate once more.

Census Data Pop. 490,974. Central city, 29%; suburban, 27%. Median family income, $9,190; families above $15,000: 15%; families below $3,000: 9%. Median years education, 12.1.

1972 Share of Federal Outlays $318,407,541

DOD	$33,629,818	HEW	$161,888,248
AEC	$2,667	HUD	$3,419,420
NASA	–	DOI	$1,158,146
DOT	$4,533,598	USDA	$43,132,495
		Other	$70,643,149

Federal Military-Industrial Commitments

DOD Contractors Marinette Marine Corp. (Marinette), $10.175m: harbor tugboats.
DOD Installations Antigo AF Station (Antigo).

Economic Base Agriculture, notably dairy products, dairy cattle, and cattle; paper and allied products, especially paper mill products, except building paper; food and kindred products; finance, insurance and real estate; and machinery.

The Voters

Registration No party and no district-wide registration.
Median voting age 45.0
Employment profile White collar, 39%. Blue collar, 40%. Service, 13%. Farm, 8%.
Ethnic groups Total foreign stock, 14%. Germany, 5%; Poland, Canada, 1% each.

Presidential vote

1972	Nixon (R)	122,672	(61%)
	McGovern (D)	76,912	(39%)
1968	Nixon (R)	106,148	(56%)
	Humphrey (D)	66,437	(35%)
	Wallace (AI)	15,145	(8%)

Representative

Harold V. Froehlich (R) Elected 1972; b. May 12, 1932, Appleton; home, Appleton; U. of Wis., B.A., 1959, LL.B., 1962; married, one child; Lutheran.

Career U.S. Navy, 1951–55; Atty.; C.P.A; Real Estate Broker; partner, law firm of Patterson, Froehlich, Jensen and Wylie; Treas., Black Creek Improvement Corp; Pres., 322 Investment, Ltd.; Wis. Assembly, 1962–72, Speaker, 1967–71.

Offices 503 CHOB, 202-225-5665. Also 325 E. Walnut, Rm. 207, Green Bay 54305, 414-435-6600; and 129 N. Superior, Rm. 208, Appleton 54911, 414-731-2663.

Administrative Assistant David T. Prosser, Jr.

Committees

House Administration (11th); Subs: Electrical and Mechanical Office Equipment; Library and Memorials.

Judiciary (15th); Subs: No. 6 (Revision of the Laws); No. 2 (Claims).

Group Ratings: Newly Elected

Key Votes

1) Busing	NE	6) Cmbodia Bmbg	FOR	11) Chkg Acct Intrst	AGN
2) Strip Mines	NE	7) Bust Hwy Trust	AGN	12) End HISC (HUAC)	AGN
3) Cut Mil $	NE	8) Farm Sub Lmt	NE	13) Nixon Sewer Veto	FOR
4) Rev Shrg	NE	9) School Prayr	NE	14) Corp Cmpaign $	NE
5) Pub TV $	NE	10) Cnsumr Prot	NE	15) Pol $ Disclosr	NE

Election Results

1972 general:	Harold V. Froehlich (R)	101,634	(50%)
	Robert J. Cornell (D)	97,795	(49%)
	Clyde Bunker (American)	2,192	(1%)
1972 primary:	Harold V. Froehlich (R)	20,355	(38%)
	James R. Long (R)	15,095	(28%)
	Myron P. Lotto (R)	14,862	(28%)
	Frederick D. Kile (R)	2,118	(4%)
	Atlee A. Dodge (R)	1,013	(2%)

NINTH DISTRICT Political Background

The 9th is Wisconsin's only predominantly suburban congressional district and also its fastest-growing. It was first created in 1963 when population changes and the Supreme Court's one-man-one-vote decision required the elimination of a rural district and the full recognition of the growth of Milwaukee's suburbs. Today—the district was redrawn in 1971—the 9th forms something of an arc north and west of Milwaukee. The district includes the wealthy, long-established suburbs like Shorewood and Whitefish Bay, just north of downtown Milwaukee on Lake Michigan, and a ring of suburbs around Milwaukee in Ozaukee, Washington, and Waukesha counties: Mequon, Germantown, Menomonee Falls, Brookfield, and New Berlin. The territory combines country clubs, tree-shaded streets, shopping centers, and starkly new suburban housing. Though the 9th also includes some of the rural dairy country between Milwaukee and Madison, most of its residents live in Waukesha County, which grew from 158,000 in 1960 to 231,000 in 1960.

This district was originally designed to remove Republican voters from Robert Kastenmeier's 2nd and Henry Reuss' 5th districts. The job was done so well that the 9th is the state's most heavily Republican district. Its creation also set the stage for the political comeback of Glenn Davis, who had represented the old 2nd district, including Madison, from 1947 to 1957. A strong supporter of Joseph McCarthy and Richard Nixon, Davis relinquished the seat to make an unsuccessful primary bid against moderate Sen. Alexander Wiley in 1956. Davis then made another unsuccessful race for the Senate vacancy created by McCarthy's death in 1957. In 1964, despite the LBJ landslide, Davis was returned to Congress from the 9th. Given the district's Republican leanings, he no doubt expected automatic reelection and greater seniority on the House Appropriations Committee.

Davis has accumulated seniority, but reelection has been more of a problem than he might have preferred. He won easily in 1972, the year of the Nixon landslide, but two years earlier Democrat Fred Tabak came within 4% of upsetting the Republican Congressman. It was Waukesha County that saved him in 1970, and he may need help there again in 1974. Davis' seat is not as high on the list of Wisconsin Democrats' priorities as some others (the 3rd and the 8th), but it is possible that the right Democratic candidate could give the incumbent a real fight in 1974.

Census Data Pop. 490,805. Central city, 0%; suburban, 86%. Median family income, $12,479; families above $15,000: 34%; families below $3,000: 4%. Median years education, 12.4.

1972 Share of Federal Outlays $326,347,769

DOD	$35,422,889	HEW	$158,336,775
AEC	$34,781	HUD	$6,302,608
NASA	$1,347,987	DOI	$459,141
DOT	$9,716,353	USDA	$16,444,153
		Other	$98,283,082

Federal Military-Industrial Commitments

DOD Contractors Gulf and Western Industries (Waukesha), $22.713m: hand grenades and small arms ammunition. Chrysler Outboard Corp. (Hartford), $7.915m: general purpose military engines.

Economic Base Machinery; finance, insurance and real estate; agriculture, notably dairy products, dairy cattle, and hogs and sheep; fabricated metal products; and electrical equipment and supplies.

The Voters

Registration No party and no district-wide registration.
Median voting age 42.5
Employment profile White collar, 51%. Blue collar, 35%. Service, 11%. Farm, 3%.
Ethnic groups Spanish, 1%. Total foreign stock, 16%. Germany, 6%.

Presidential vote

1972	Nixon (R)		131,288	(63%)
	McGovern (D)		77,944	(37%)
1968	Nixon (R)		108,269	(56%)
	Humphrey (D)		70,741	(37%)
	Wallace (AI)		13,602	(7%)

Representative

Glenn R. Davis (R) Elected 1946–56, 1964; b. Oct. 28, 1914, Vernon; home, Waukesha; Platteville State Teachers Col., B.Ed., 1934; U. Wis., J.D., 1940; USNR, WWII; married, five children; United Church of Christ.

Career Wis. Legislature, 1941–42; practicing atty., 1957–64; Pres. New Berlin State Bank, 1959–65.

Offices 2242 RHOB, 202-225-5101. Also 7746 Menomonee River Parkway, Wauwatosa 53213, 414-771-5780.

Administrative Assistant James Bolton

Committees

Appropriations (6th); Subs: Defense; Military Construction (Ranking Mbr.); Public Works, AEC.

Joint Study Com. on Budget Control.

Group Ratings

	ADA	COPE	LWV	RIPON	NFU	LCV	CFA	NAB	NSI	ACA
1972	0	13	20	46	33	25	0	100	100	83
1971	5	8	44	53	27	–	25	–	–	88
1970	20	9	–	71	38	14	38	100	100	79

Key Votes

1) Busing	AGN	6) Cmbodia Bmbg	FOR	11) Chkg Acct Intrst	AGN
2) Strip Mines	FOR	7) Bust Hwy Trust	AGN	12) End HISC (HUAC)	AGN
3) Cut Mil $	AGN	8) Farm Sub Lmt	FOR	13) Nixon Sewer Veto	FOR
4) Rev Shrg	AGN	9) School Prayr	FOR	14) Corp Cmpaign $	FOR
5) Pub TV $	AGN	10) Cnsumr Prot	AGN	15) Pol $ Disclosr	FOR

Election Results

1972 general:	Glenn R. Davis (R)	128,230	(61%)
	Ralph A. Fine (D)	76,585	(37%)
	George Reed (American)	4,024	(2%)
1972 primary:	Glenn R. Davis (R)	32,244	(59%)
	Verne R. Read (R)	20,466	(37%)
	Robert Baggs (R)	2,204	(4%)
1970 general:	Glenn R. Davis (R)	84,732	(52%)
	Fred N. Tabak (D)	78,123	(48%)

WYOMING

Political Background

Until the late 1860s, a coalition of Sioux, Cheyennes, and Arapahoes kept permanent white settlers out of Powder River country, much of which is the present state of Wyoming. During the time of Indian domination, Wyoming was only a geographical expanse to be explored by mountain men or traversed by Yankee farmers on their way to the Willamette Valley via the Oregon Trail. Two developments led to the abrogation of Indian treaty rights and the assertion of white man needs—first, the coming of the transcontinental railroad to Cheyenne in 1867, and second, the appearance of Texas cattle on the Wyoming plains.

Cattlemen had always figured that only the buffalo, deer, and antelope could survive the brutal Wyoming winters. Then, according to one story, a pioneer eager to reach Oregon set out in the fall and was caught in an early-season blizzard. He cut loose his livestock and returned on foot to spend the winter in one of the Territory's settlements. In the spring, the wayfarer returned to collect his abandoned belongings and examine the carcasses of his dead animals. Instead, he found them alive and flourishing. Whereupon it was deduced that livestock could live not only on the summertime tufts of grass amongst the sagebrush, but also survive the wintertime wind, cold and snow of the high plains. The animals simply pawed through the covering of snow to get at the grass stored away below like so much farm-grown hay.

Accordingly, Texas cattlemen and cowboys began to drive herds north, as the "dogies knew that Wyoming would be their new home." Times were flush for a while. Following the "open range" policy, cattlemen let their livestock range over the land, then rounded them up for sale. Expenses ran about a dollar a head per year, with the critters fetching from five to fifteen dollars a head at market. Soon enough, however, sheepmen, along with a few homesteaders, showed up and disrupted the operation. The sheep, the cattlemen said, first, cropped the grass too close to the roots; second, trampled it dead with their tiny hoofs, and third, used up scarce supplies of water. Besides, the cowpunchers figured that they were magnificent men on horseback, while the sheepherder was a forlorn figure, often a Mexican-American, accompanied by only a dog. As a corollary, cattle were glorious creatures, and sheep smelly and generally undignified. The homesteaders, of course, began to fence off the open range. This state of affairs produced some bloody confrontations, the outlines of which are familiar to anyone who has watched a few late-night movies.

During the state's territorial days, the Wyoming Stock Growers' Association pretty much had things its own way. In fact, a Wyoming statute of 1884 specially recognized the "by-laws and rules" of the Association and placed legal control of round-ups into the hands of the organization.

So when cattlemen had trouble with sheepherders, homesteaders, or rustlers, the Association would mete out quick and sometimes severe punishment. Rustlers often came from the ranks of the rancher's own bunch of cowboys, who, from time to time, would cut out a few head in order to start their own herds. Some went up a tree; others were quite successful, and these would of course join the Wyoming Stock Grower's Association. The flush times ended with the winter of 1886–87, when a blizzard wiped out many herds. Cattle froze and starved to death, as the blowing snow reached depths of five, ten, and fifteen feet. Following the catastrophe, Wyoming quieted down. Soon many livestock men began to run both cattle and sheep (sheep are now more important), and to grow a winter's supply of feed on irrigated pastureland.

Nevertheless, Wyoming is still the closest thing we have to the Wild West. It is one of the few states where ranchers, through the Stock Growers' Association, and a railroad, the Union Pacific, remain major wielders of political clout. Next to Uncle Sam, the Union Pacific is Wyoming's largest landowner; the road earned alternate 30-mile sections when it built the transcontinental railroad. Later, the UP holdings yielded large deposits of coal and oil. In the Powder River country, the strip mining of coal has just begun. There are millions upon millions of tons present just below the surface, but if the Wyoming politicians and the federal government give the coal interests what they want, the state's heritage may be destroyed, never to be reclaimed. In the face of coal company greed and the clamor over the "energy crisis," no one has yet even mentioned the fact that the deep mines of the Union Pacific contain more recoverable coal than the strippable stuff in Powder River country. Stripping usually is cheaper.

Politically, the ranchers, the small businessmen, and the farmers working irrigated land to the north always have been heavily Republican. The people who came to build and maintain the UP, along the state's southern edge, remain the state's most solid Democrats. Over the years in Wyoming, the Republicans have won many more elections than Democrats. Cheyenne (pop. 41,000), Casper (pop. 39,000), Laramie (pop. 23,000), Rock Springs (pop. 12,000), and Sheridan (pop. 11,000) are the state's urban concentrations; in fact, they are the only five "cities" in the state having more than 10,000 residents. More common are places like Ten Sleep (pop. 320) or Medicine Bow (pop. 455). Between the Wyoming settlements, for stretches of 50 and 100 miles, lies the high, desolate, and serene plateau country of the Rocky Mountains to the east and south, and the mountains themselves to the west and north.

The wide-open spaces here mean that Wyoming has not experienced the frenetic development that has hit its "Californicated" neighbor to the south, Colorado. In 1960, Wyoming, the ninth-largest state in area, had just 330,000 residents; in 1970, 332,000. In the 1970 census, Wyoming's population was passed by Nevada, and by the next census, Alaska will also have more people. Wyoming will then become the least populous state in the Union. But there are parts of the state that are growing: the Jackson Hole area, near Grand Teton and Yellowstone national parks; Laramie, the home of the University of Wyoming; and Campbell County (Gillette), site of a recent oil and natural gas boom, and the probable site of extensive strip mining operations.

Oil has always figured greatly in Wyoming life. For example, Teapot Dome, a naval oil reserve outside of Casper, was the focus of the biggest scandal in American history until Watergate. And, of course, most Wyoming politicians have adamantly supported the most generous oil-depletion allowance feasible. But such federal largesse points up an irony. As in most Rocky Mountain states, the establishment in Wyoming is a stern, Goldwaterish foe of the federal government in the abstract. Many of the people here like to think of themselves as totally self-reliant, just like their grandfathers. Yet it remains a fact that the state is too sparsely populated to generate any kind of internal market. Consequently, without national parks, national forests, the Bureau of Reclamation, the Bureau of Land Management, federal subsidies to feeder airlines, federal subsidies to agriculture, federal highway construction, federal on and on, there would be little to the economy of Wyoming. Without the federal government, the construction of Interstate 25, some 300 miles of superhighway that connects maybe 100,000 people, would have been impossible. According to government figures, Wyoming paid some $314 million in federal taxes in fiscal 1972, and got back some $404 million in the same year. People outside of Wyoming made up the difference.

Gale McGee, the state's senior Senator, is one politician who has paid the requisite attention to the interests of Wyoming. He has an unlikely background for a Wyoming Senator: a history professor at the University of Wyoming for 12 years before winning his seat in 1958. For the first few years of service, McGee was a little-known member of the class of '58, a term applied to the large number of Democratic Senators first elected in that year. In Wyoming, McGee was regarded a liberal and a friend of organized labor.

Soon after McGee went to Washington, Wyoming began to trend heavily toward candidates of the Goldwater type. So among the class of '58, McGee was one of the most seriously threatened in 1964. But the professor pulled out a 54–46 victory over Republican State Chairman John Wold of Casper that year. The Senator then went on to a considerably more distinctive term. He became Chairman of the Post Office and Civil Service Committee, the first of the '58ers to reach a chairmanship. More notably, however, the Wyomingite established himself as one of the leading defenders of Johnson's and then Nixon's Vietnam war policies. After a while, McGee's stance put him in rather odd political company; most Senate liberals, even those who backed the war initially, were never so vigorous and enthusiastic about whatever it was we tried to do in Vietnam. But McGee was and is. In 1973, he expressed dismay that the Senate voted almost unanimously to cut off funds for the bombing in Cambodia, and earlier, in 1970, he boasted of his "vibrant, ringing defense of our Vietnam policy." To say "vibrant and ringing" is right on the mark, for McGee is one of the Senate's most polished orators; his only competitor, perhaps, is another mountain state Democrat of far more dovish disposition, Frank Church of Idaho. Unfortunately for both men, oratory alone has swung few votes since the time of Sen. Daniel Webster, before the Civil War.

In any case, McGee's politics have gone over well in Wyoming. When the 1970 election rolled around, the Senator had something to please everyone: a liberal domestic record for organized labor, a hawkish stand on the war for admirers of Richard Nixon, and 12 years of seniority to boot. Moreover, McGee can say that he is one of the Senate's staunchest supporters of Israel—something that means little in Wyoming, but makes it easier to raise some political contribution money in New York and California. A little bit of money goes a long way in a small state like Wyoming. In 1970, McGee brushed aside a challenge from a peace candidate in the primary, talked (with the help of John Gardner) a liberal, antiwar Casper lawyer out of an independent candidacy, and then beat the same Republican who opposed him in 1964, John Wold, who in the meantime (1968) had gotten himself elected Congressman-at-Large. This time McGee won by an even larger margin, 56–44; so the Democrat now appears to have a safe seat until some years hence when age catches up with him.

According to some reports, the Nixon Administration, grateful for McGee's support on foreign policy and military spending issues, did not provide Wold much money or other support. However that may be, McGee's victory was a considerable achievement. In 1964, Wold was a political unknown, but by 1970 he had become a champion vote-getter, winning 63% in the congressional race of 1968. Yet McGee bested Wold in the challenger's home county of Natrona (Casper), an oil-dominated conservative bastion.

During the first six months of 1973, McGee concentrated his legislative efforts on a bill, reported out by his Post Office and Civil Service Committee, to allow citizens to register to vote by postcard. A similar measure was defeated in the 92nd Congress, and in the 93rd, McGee's idea was opposed by almost all Republicans, with the notable exception of Tennessee's Bill Brock, and by many conservative Southern Democrats. What the opponents feared was what McGee and the bill's backers wanted; namely, that the legislation would facilitate the registration and ballot casting of far more Democrats and liberals than Republicans and conservatives. McGee fought like a tiger for postcard registration. The Senator threatened to hold up legislative authorization for wage and price controls, which was expiring, and with a big boost from organized labor, he broke an attempted filibuster led by Alabama's James Allen. The bill passed the Senate and, at this writing, is before John Dent's House Education and Labor Subcommittee. Its backers apparently want to attach the measure to some vital piece of legislation; otherwise it faces almost certain veto by President Nixon. But its Senate passage represented a formidable McGee accomplishment.

The state's junior Senator, Clifford Hansen, is more in line with the traditions of Wyoming—a conservative Republican cattle rancher. Hansen was Governor from 1963 to 1966. Back then, he had something of a reputation for liberal Republicanism. He once suggested that the state permit legalized gambling in the Jackson Hole area, a proposal that did not sit well among most Wyomingites; and in 1964, Hansen made some noises of supporting Nelson Rockefeller over Barry Goldwater at the national convention. In 1966, Hansen had the good fortune to be Governor when aging Republican Sen. Milward Simpson of Cody decided to retire. The Governor won the Senate seat by a relatively close margin against then (and now) Congressman-at-Large Teno Roncalio. Hansen won reelection in 1972 over a weak Democratic opponent with 71% of the votes, which was two points better than Richard Nixon's showing in the state.

In Washington, Hansen sits on the Senate Interior Committee. The unit handles many matters vital to Wyoming, since over half of the state's acreage is still owned by the federal government. Hansen received some national attention when *The Progressive* magazine and the *New York Times* charged that the Senator was allowed to graze his cattle within the Grand Teton National Park—a privilege, it was asserted, that few people not members of the Senate Interior Committee enjoy. But both publications failed to recognize that Hansen and several other Teton County ranchers had grazing permits in the area the park was extended to cover in 1950. The permits predated the extension, and their continued validity was part of the deal struck by the Park Service with the ranchers to obtain more land for the national park. Nevertheless, it now seems that the Park Service needs to make an arrangement to get all cattle out of the Grand Tetons; the hoofs of the creatures occasionally destroy the delicate flora. Hansen has also attracted criticism for favoring construction of a jetport in the Jackson Hole area.

Hansen also serves on the Senate Finance Committee, which among other things passes on the oil depletion allowance. In the committee and on the floor, Hansen usually lines up with the Senate's conservative bloc. In a noteworthy exception, however, the Wyoming Senator voted against the SST program, despite a special plea from Nixon himself. A vote against massive federal funding of the Boeing project was not inconsistent with a commitment to the free enterprise system, in which Hansen firmly believes. Moreover, he said that he wanted to prevent the possibility of sonic booms disrupting the silent expanses of his home state.

Wyoming's one and only Congressman is Teno Roncalio. He is an Episcopalian Democrat of Italian descent from the Union Pacific town of Rock Springs. First elected to the House in 1964, Roncalio lost the Senate race to Hansen in 1966. He then sat out the 1968 elections, while supporting Robert Kennedy for President, and ran for Congress again in 1970. This time Roncalio regained his seat by a paper-thin 51–49 margin; in 1972, he increased his edge to 52%. Teno always has a tough race, but he, like McGee and Hansen, is a master of the personal style that is both unique and necessary in Wyoming. In a small state, a politician can get to know just about everybody. So any candidate who wants to win had better be ready to explain his position on the issues, eye-to-eye. To do this, officeholders like Roncalio put plenty of miles on their cars driving from one small town to another meeting the voters.

Contrary to the prediction made in the 1972 *Almanac*, Roncalio did not run for the Senate in 1972. He thus broke something of a precedent. For the last 30 years, the office of Congressman-at-Large has been bandied about between the parties, mostly because of its occupants' habit of running for Senator. The most noteworthy Wyoming Congressman-at-Large of recent years was William Henry Harrison, a conservative Republican from Sheridan and a descendant of two Presidents Harrison. He served in the House from 1953 to 1955, from 1961 to 1965, and again from 1967 to 1969. And Harrison was not the only Wyoming Congressman to run for the Senate. After all, a politician has to run a statewide campaign anyway, and if he wins a Senate seat, he has more power and fewer campaign hassles. Congressman Frank Barrett tried in 1952; Harrison in 1954; Keith Thomson in 1960; Roncalio in 1966; and John Wold in 1970. Only Barrett and Thomson won, and Thomson died of a heart attack a month after the election.

Thomson's widow now serves as Wyoming's Secretary of State, which brings to mind an interesting footnote to Wyoming politics. This is the first state to grant women the right to vote (in 1890). It was a natural move for a frontier state with an undersupply of females, and Wyoming later made history again by electing the first woman Governor, Nellie Taylor Ross, in 1924.

Census Data Pop. 332,416; 0.16% of U.S. total, 49th largest; change 1960–70, 0.7%. Central city, 0%; suburban, 0%. Median family income, $8,944; 27th highest; families above $15,000: 16%; families below $3,000: 9%. Median years education, 12.4.

1972 Share of Federal Tax Burden $313,530,000; 0.15% of U.S. total, 50th largest.

1972 Share of Federal Outlays $403,965,490; 0.19% of U.S. total, 50th largest. Per capita federal spending, $1,215.

DOD	$75,065,000	49th (0.12%)	HEW	$95,446,166	50th (0.13%)
AEC	$71,495	41st (—)	HUD	$3,744,760	49th (0.12%)
NASA	$100,588	43rd (—)	VA	$28,317,304	47th (0.25%)
DOT	$46,176,562	43rd (0.59%)	USDA	$46,167,540	41st (0.30%)
DOC	$1,492,277	47th (0.12%)	CSC	$6,244,174	50th (0.15%)
DOI	$56,113,630	14th (2.65%)	TD	$15,797,935	49th (0.10%)
DOJ	$1,712,253	50th (0.17%)	Other	$27,515,806	

Federal Military-Industrial Commitments

DOD Contractors Boeing Co. (Cheyenne), $10.000m: services at Minuteman missile site.
DOD Installations Warren AFB (Cheyenne).

Economic Base Agriculture, notably cattle, sheep, sugar beets and dairy products; oil and gas extraction, especially oil and gas field services; finance, insurance and real estate; metal mining, especially uranium-radium-vanadium ores; petroleum refining and other petroleum and coal products; food and kindred products. Also tourism (Yellowstone and Grand Tetons), and higher education (Univ. of Wyoming).

Political Line-up Governor, Stanley K. Hathaway (R); seat up, 1974. Senators, Gale W. McGee (D) and Clifford P. Hansen (R). Representatives, 1 D At Large. State Senate (17 R and 13 D); State House (44 R, 17 D, and 1 Ind.).

The Voters

Registration 138,936 total. 55,552 D (40%); 63,099 R (45%); 20,285 other (15%).
Median voting age 42.7
Employment profile White collar, 47%. Blue collar, 30%. Service, 14%. Farm, 9%.
Ethnic groups Total foreign stock, 11%.

Presidential vote

1972	Nixon (R)	100,464	(69%)
	McGovern (D)	44,358	(31%)
1968	Nixon (R)	70,927	(56%)
	Humphrey (D)	45,173	(35%)
	Wallace (AI)	11,105	(9%)
1964	Johnson (D)	80,718	(57%)
	Goldwater (R)	61,998	(43%)

Senator

Gale William McGee (D) Elected 1958, seat up 1976, b. Mar. 17, 1915, Lincoln, Neb.; home, Laramie; Neb. State Teachers Col., B.A., 1936; U. of Colo., M.A., 1939; U. of Chicago, Ph.D., 1947; married, four children; Presbyterian.

Career Teacher, 1936–40; prof., Neb. Wesleyan U., 1940–43, Iowa State, 1943–44, Notre Dame, 1944–45, U. of Chicago, 1945–46, U. of Wyoming, 1945– ; Legislative Asst., Sen. Joseph O' Mahoney, 1955–56.

Offices 344 OSOB, 202-225-6441. Also 150 N. Center, Casper 82601, 301-235-6218.

Administrative Assistant K. Richard Cook

Committees

Appropriations (7th); Subs: Agriculture, Environmental and Consumer Protection (Chm.); Foreign Operations; Interior; Public Works, AEC; Defense.

Foreign Relations (7th); Subs: African Affairs; Arms Control, International Law and Organization; FarEastern Affairs; Western Hemisphere Affairs (Chm.); South Asian Affairs.

Post Office and Civil Service (Chm.).

Group Ratings

	ADA	COPE	LWV	RIPON	NFU	LCV	CFA	NAB	NSI	ACA
1972	35	83	100	50	89	24	100	14	80	40
1971	48	73	100	35	70	–	100	–	–	22
1970	47	83	–	58	100	60	–	25	90	32

Key Votes

1) Busing	FOR	8) Sea Life Prot	AGN	15) Tax Singls Less	FOR
2) Alas P-line	FOR	9) Campaign Subs	FOR	16) Min Tax for Rich	AGN
3) Gun Cntrl	AGN	10) Cmbodia Bmbg	ABS	17) Euro Troop Rdctn	AGN
4) Rehnquist	FOR	11) Legal Srvices	ABS	18) Bust Hwy Trust	AGN
5) Pub TV $	FOR	12) Rev Sharing	ABS	19) Maid Min Wage	FOR
6) EZ Votr Reg	FOR	13) Cnsumr Prot	FOR	20) Farm Sub Limit	AGN
7) No-Fault	FOR	14) Eq Rts Amend	FOR	21) Highr Credt Chgs	AGN

Election Results

1970 general:	Gale W. McGee (D)	67,207	(56%)
	John S. Wold (R)	53,279	(44%)
1970 primary:	Gale W. McGee (D)	32,956	(80%)
	D. P. Svilar (D)	8,448	(20%)
1964 general:	Gale W. McGee (D)	76,485	(54%)
	John S. Wold (R)	65,185	(46%)

Senator

Clifford P. Hansen (R) Elected 1966, seat up 1978; b. Oct. 16, 1912, Zenith; home, Jackson; U. of Wyo., B.S., 1934; married, two children; Episcopalian.

Career Cattle rancher; Gov. of Wyo., 1963–66.

Offices 3107 NSOB, 202-225-3424. Also Box 425, Cheyenne 82001, 307-634-7981.

Administrative Assistant Paul R. Holtz

Committees

Finance (4th); Subs: International Trade; Health (Ranking Mbr.); State Taxation of Interstate Commerce (Ranking Mbr.).

Interior and Insular Affairs (2nd); Subs: Minerals, Materials and Fuels; Parks and Recreation (Ranking Mbr.); Water and Power Resources.

Veterans' Affairs (Ranking Mbr.); Subs: Compensation and Pensions (Ranking Mbr.); Health and Hospitals.

Sp. Com. on Aging (2nd); Subs: Consumer Interests of the Elderly; Federal, State, and Community Services; Employment and Retirement Incomes (Ranking Mbr.); Health of the Elderly.

Sp. Com. on the Termination of the National Emergency (4th).

Group Ratings

	ADA	COPE	LWV	RIPON	NFU	LCV	CFA	NAB	NSI	ACA
1972	0	0	20	25	33	8	0	91	100	95
1971	4	8	25	25	18	–	0	–	–	96
1970	3	0	–	27	27	26	–	100	100	87

Key Votes

1) Busing	AGN	8) Sea Life Prot	AGN	15) Tax Singls Less	AGN
2) Alas P-line	FOR	9) Campaign Subs	AGN	16) Min Tax for Rich	ABS
3) Gun Cntrl	AGN	10) Cmbodia Bmbg	FOR	17) Euro Troop Rdctn	AGN
4) Rehnquist	FOR	11) Legal Srvices	AGN	18) Bust Hwy Trust	AGN
5) Pub TV $	AGN	12) Rev Sharing	FOR	19) Maid Min Wage	AGN
6) EZ Votr Reg	AGN	13) Cnsumr Prot	AGN	20) Farm Sub Limit	AGN
7) No-Fault	AGN	14) Eq Rts Amend	AGN	21) Highr Credt Chgs	FOR

Election Results

1972 general:	Clifford P. Hansen (R)	101,314	(71%)
	Mike M. Vinich (D)	40,753	(29%)
1972 primary:	Clifford P. Hansen (R), unopposed		
1966 general:	Clifford P. Hansen (R)	63,548	(52%)
	Teno Roncalio (D)	59,141	(48%)

Representative

Teno Roncalio (D) Elected 1964–66, 1970; b. Mar. 23, 1916, Rock Springs; home, Cheyenne; U. of Wyo., LL.B., 1947; Army, WWII; married, six children.

Career Asst., Sen. Joseph O'Mahoney, 1941; practicing atty., 1948– ; Dep. County Atty., Laramie County, 1950–56; Founder and Bd. Chm., Cheyenne Natl. Bank, 1960–68; Chm., Wyo. Dem. Com., 1957–61; U.S. Senate candidate, 1966; Wyo. Dem. Natl. Committeeman, 1969–72.

Offices 1314 LHOB, 202-225-2311.

Administrative Assistant Kathy Karpan

Committees

Interior and Insular Affairs (15th); Subs: National Parks and Recreation; Water and Power Resources; Environment.

Public Works (14th); Subs: Public Buildings and Grounds; Economic Development; Energy; Investigations and Review; Transportation.

Joint Com. on Atomic Energy (4th); Subs: Communities; Licensing and Regulation; Military Applications; Raw Materials.

Group Ratings

	ADA	COPE	LWV	RIPON	NFU	LCV	CFA	NAB	NSI	ACA
1972	50	55	60	54	100	79	100	97	25	36
1971	95	82	89	72	92	–	88	–	–	14

Key Votes

1) Busing	FOR	6) Cmbodia Bmbg	AGN	11) Chkg Acct Intrst	ABS
2) Strip Mines	ABS	7) Bust Hwy Trust	AGN	12) End HISC (HUAC)	AGN
3) Cut Mil $	ABS	8) Farm Sub Lmt	FOR	13) Nixon Sewer Veto	AGN
4) Rev Shrg	FOR	9) School Prayr	FOR	14) Corp Cmpaign $	FOR
5) Pub TV $	FOR	10) Cnsumr Prot	FOR	15) Pol $ Disclosr	AGN

Election Results

1972 general:	Teno Roncalio (D)	75,632	(52%)
	Bill Kidd (R)	70,667	(48%)
1972 primary:	Teno Roncalio (D), unopposed		
1970 general:	Teno Roncalio (D)	58,456	(50%)
	Harry Roberts (R)	57,848	(50%)

DISTRICT OF COLUMBIA

Washington, D.C. is a paradoxical city: a place obsessed with politics and government, which has virtually no local politics of its own. In 1874, the District lost the right to elect its local officials, in part because of heavy spending by Gov. Alexander Sheppard and in part because of a fear of the city's already large black electorate. Since then, Washington has remained a ward of the federal government, particularly of the House District of Columbia Committee—a unit dominated by Southerners until 1972. Today, the Commissioner of the District of Columbia—the "Mayor" of Washington—is still appointed by the President, as is the City Council. Moreover, not until 1964 were the residents of the District able to vote for President. And not until 1968 were they entitled to elect their own School Board, and not until 1971 did the District get a Delegate in the House of Representatives. The Delegate has a voice, but no vote, on the floor of the House, though he has both in committee.

The real brake on District self-determination is the Congress' long-standing fear of the city's black majority. Since before the Civil War, Washington has been a haven for blacks; the slave trade was abolished here as part of the Compromise of 1850. Even after Reconstruction, blacks continued to win appointment to high position in the District government. In 1960, the census reported that a majority of the District's citizens were black; by 1970, the black percentage had risen to 71%. That majority, however, is not the only unusual sociological fact about the nation's capital. It is now our only major city without a white working-class. Most of its white residents are relatively well-off and live in a part of the city west of Rock Creek Park. And in recent years, many of its black citizens have moved across the District line to Prince Georges County, Maryland (see Maryland 5). So in the next decade, Washington may be left with a large number of poor blacks, a small number of middle-class and wealthy blacks, plus one of the wealthiest white communities in the nation.

Having limited political power, it is no surprise that the District of Columbia's level of voter participation is one of the lowest in the country. Of course, those who do vote cast overwhelming Democratic margins. In presidential contests, the city's black majority goes about 90% Democratic; the white minority, despite its affluence, splits about 50–50 or gives the Democrats a small majority. In 1972, George McGovern took 78% here—his highest percentage anywhere in the nation save one county. The School Board elections interest very few Washingtonians; most whites are either childless or send their children to private schools, as do many blacks. Many District citizens retain a voting residence in another state and vote there; many of the rest just don't bother.

If home rule finally comes to Washington, city politics will probably assume a pattern exhibited in the January 1971 Democratic primary for the District's delegate seat. The principal candidates were black: Rev. Channing Phillips, leader of the Robert Kennedy slate that swept the District's 1968 presidential primary; Joseph Yeldell, a politician tied to Mayor Washington and the city's business community; and Rev. Walter Fauntroy, a former aide to Martin Luther King, Jr. Fauntroy was minister of a church in the Shaw district, the heart of the 1968 Washington riot. Yeldell and Phillips ran well ahead of Fauntroy in the city's predominantly white precincts, which cast a mere 20% of the Democratic vote. In the black areas, however, Fauntroy won an absolute majority in the divided field. Black churches constituted the winner's political base. In a place like Shaw, the voting bloc with clout is made up of the kind of people who attend church faithfully every Sunday, and not the kind who looted stores in the 1968 riot.

In some of the more sophisticated quarters of Washington, Fauntroy's style is regarded as corny, and his efforts to control the District delegation to the 1972 Democratic Convention blatantly old politics. In 1972, he ran far behind even George McGovern in the city's affluent wards. But the affection which the inner city holds for him was enought for a large, if not overwhelming, majority. The prospect is for the same in future District elections.

To get home rule for the District is Fauntroy's major task in the 93rd Congress. Now that Charles Diggs of Michigan has replaced John McMillan of South Carolina as Chairman of the House D.C. Committee, Fauntroy has a subcommittee chairmanship (Judiciary), a vote, and a substantial voice in Committee decisions. At this writing, it is widely assumed that the Congress will report home-rule legislation to the floor. But sticky problems remain to be solved—the form of the new District government, the amount of money the federal government will commit itself to pay the District in lieu of taxes, and the question of voice-and-vote representation. Some, like Julius Hobson, who opposed Fauntroy in the 1971 general election, favor statehood for Washington. Finally, the climate in Congress grew less favorable toward home rule when Sen. John Stennis was shot by muggers outside his home in northwest Washington in early 1973. So the betting is that if home rule is passed by this Congress, it won't be until 1974.

The liberals sympathetic to home rule have for years struggled to win control of the House D.C. Committee. Ironically, now that the liberals control the committee, they will give up most of their power once home rule is effected. But for Fauntroy, at least, another avenue is open. Once the District is no longer what bumper stickers call "the last colony," Fauntroy is widely expected to run for Mayor of Washington, or, if the position is so styled, Governor, the title used in the nineteenth century.

Census Data   Pop. 756,510; 0.37% of U.S. total; change 1960–70, –1.0%. Central city, 100%; suburban, –%. Median family income, $9,583; families above $15,000: 25%; families below $3,000: 11%. Median years education, 12.2.

1972 Share of Federal Tax Burden $1,024,190,000; 0.49% of U.S. total.

1972 Share of Federal Outlays $8,045,942,428; 3.71% of U.S. total. Per capita federal spending, $10,636.

DOD	$1,696,395,000	(2.71%)	USDA	$224,192,955	(1.46%)
HEW	$919,088,842	(1.29%)	DOC	$187,246,879	(14.46%)
AEC	$2,263,015	(0.09%)	CSC	$1,341,214,410	(32.54%)
HUD	$152,284,172	(4.96%)	DOI	$172,723,397	(8.14%)
NASA	$83,086,456	(2.78%)	TD	$387,711,261	(2.35%)
VA	$212,505,774	(1.86%)	DOJ	$37,615,905	(14.02%)
DOT	$589,544,845	(7.47%)			

Economic Base   Government service; finance, insurance and real estate; printing and publishing, especially newspapers; tourism; food and kindred products.

Federal Military-Industrial Commitments

DOD Contractors   U.S. Atomic Energy Commission, $106.453m: unspecified. Chesapeake and Potomac Telephone, $15.402m: unspecified. Sperry Rand, $14.219m: computer equipment and consultant services. American Telephone and Telegraph, $11.142m: unspecified. IBM, $9.783m: rental of data processing equipment. Steuart Petroleum Company, $8.596m: petroleum products. Airtronics, Inc., $6.313m: electronic warfare equipment. Southern Air Transport, $6.051m: transportations services.
DOD Installations   Army Map Service. Harry Diamond Army Laboratories. Fort McNair AB. Walter Reed Army Medical Center. Naval Observatory. Naval Photographic Center. Naval Reconnaissance & Technical Support Center. Naval Research Laboratory. Naval Security Station. Naval Station. Bolling AFB.

Political Line-up   Delegate, Walter Fauntroy (D).

The Voters

Registration   305,072 total. 233,101 D (76%); 39,598 R (13%); 31,377 Ind. (10%); 504 Statehood (–%); 492 other (–%).
Median voting age 40
Employment profile   White collar, 60%. Blue collar, 17%. Service, 22%. Farm –%.
Ethnic groups.   Black, 71%. Foreign Stock, 10%.

Presidential vote

1972	Nixon (R)	35,226	(22%)
	McGovern (D)	127,627	(78%)
1968	Nixon (R)	32,517	(18%)
	Humphrey (D)	143,570	(82%)
	Wallace (AI)	–	(–)
1964	Johnson (D)	169,796	(85%)
	Goldwater (R)	28,801	(15%)

DELEGATE

Walter Edward Fauntroy (D) *Elected* Mar. 23, 1971; b. Feb. 6, 1933, Wash. D.C.; Virginia Union U., A.B., 1955, Yale Divinity Schl., B.D., 1958; married, one child; Baptist.

CAREER Pastor, New Bethel Baptist Church, 1958– ; founder, former dir., Model Inner City Community Org.; dir., Washington Bureau, Southern Christian Leadership Conf., 1960–71; Vice-Chm., D.C. City Council, 1967–69; coordinator, Selma to Montgomery March, 1965; Chm., Bd. of Dir., Martin Luther King, Jr. Center for Social Change, 1969– ; mbr., Yale Univ. Council.

OFFICES 506 CHOB, 202-225-8050. Also 1121 Vermont Ave., NW 20005, 202-254-6460.

ADMIN. ASST. Clifford A. Brown (S.A.)

COMMITTEES District of Columbia. Sub.: Judiciary (Chm.). Banking and Currency. Sub.: Consumer Affairs (2nd).

ELECTION RESULTS

1972 general	Walter Fauntroy (D)	95,300	(61%)
	William Chin-Lee (R)	39,487	(25%)
	Charles Cassell (Statehood)	18,730	(12%)
	David Dabney (I)	2,514	(2%)
	Herman Fagg (SW)	1,133	(1%)
1972 primary	Walter Fauntroy (D)	unopposed	
1971 general*	Walter Fauntroy (D)	68,166	(59%)
	John A. Nevius (R)	29,249	(25%)
	Julius Hobson (Statehood)	15,427	(13%)
	Franklin E. Kameny (I)	1,888	(2%)
	Douglas Moore (I)	1,301	(1%)

* Special election held March 23, 1971.

SENATE COMMITTEES

Committee on Aeronautical and Space Sciences

Senator Frank E. Moss, Chairman
Democratic Majority (7 D). Senators Moss (Utah), Magnuson (Wash.), Symington (Mo.), Stennis (Miss.), Cannon (Nev.), Abourezk (S. Dak.), Haskell, (Colo.).
Republican Minority (6 R). Senators Goldwater (Ariz.), Curtis (Neb.), Weicker (Conn.), Bartlett (Okla.), Helms (N.C.), Domenici (N. Mex.)

(No Subcommittees)

Committee on Agriculture and Forestry

Senator Herman E. Talmadge, Chairman
The Chairman is an ex-officio member of all subcommittees.
Democratic Majority (7 D). Senators Talmadge (Ga.), Eastland (Miss.), McGovern (S. Dak.), Allen (Ala.), Humphrey (Minn.), Huddleston (Ky.), Clark (Iowa).
Republican Minority (6 R). Senators Curtis (Neb.), Aiken (Vt.), Young (N. Dak.), Dole (Kans.), Bellmon (Okla.), Helms (N.C.).

Subcommittees

ENVIRONMENT, SOIL CONSERVATION AND FORESTRY
James O. Eastland, Chairman
Majority (3 D). Senators Eastland, Allen, Huddleston.
Minority (2 R). Senators Helms, Aiken.
AGRICULTURAL CREDIT AND RURAL ELECTRIFICATION
George McGovern, Chairman
Majority (4 D). Senators McGovern, Allen, Humphrey, Huddleston.
Minority (3 R). Senators Aiken, Dole, Helms.
AGRICULTURAL PRODUCTION, MARKETING AND STABILIZATION OF PRICES
Walter D. Huddleston, Chairman
Majority (5 D). Senators Huddleston, McGovern, Eastland, Humphrey, Clark
Minority (4 R) Senators Young, Bellmon, Dole, Helms.
AGRICULTURAL RESEARCH AND GENERAL LEGISLATION
James B. Allen, Chairman
Majority (4 D). Senators Allen, Eastland, Clark, McGovern.
Minority (3 R). Senators Dole, Young, Bellmon
RURAL DEVELOPMENT
Dick Clark, Chairman
Majority (4 D). Senators Clark, Humphrey, Eastland, Allen.
Minority (3 R). Senators Curtis, Dole, Bellmon.
FOREIGN AGRICULTURAL POLICY
Hubert H. Humphrey, Chairman
Majority (4 D). Senators Humphrey, McGovern, Huddleston, Clark.
Minority (3 R). Senators Bellmon, Helms, Dole.

Committee on Appropriations

Senator John L. McClellan, Chairman
Senator McClellan, as Chairman of the committee, and Senator Young, as ranking minority member, are ex-officio members of all subcommittees of which they are not regular members.
Democratic Majority (15 D). Senators McClellan (Ark.), Magnuson (Wash.), Stennis (Miss.), Pastore (R.I.), Bible (Nev.), Byrd (W. Va.), McGee (Wyo.), Mansfield (Mont.), Proxmire (Wis.), Montoya (N. Mex.), Inouye (Hawaii), Hollings (S.C.), Bayh (Ind.), Eagleton (Mo.), Chiles (Fla.).
Republican Minority (11 R). Young (N. Dak.), Hruska (Neb.), Cotton (N.H.), Case (N.J.), Fong (Hawaii), Brooke (Mass.), Hatfield (Ore.), Stevens (Alaska), Mathias (Md.), Schweiker (Pa.), Bellmon (Okla.).

Subcommittees

AGRICULTURE, ENVIRONMENTAL AND CONSUMER PROTECTION
Gale W. McGee, Chairman

Majority (8 D). Senators McGee, Stennis, Proxmire, Byrd (W. Va.), Inouye, Bayh, Hollings, Eagleton.

Minority (5 R). Senators Fong, Hruska, Young, Hatfield, Bellmon.

DEFENSE
John L. McClellan, Chairman

Majority (7 D). Senators McClellan, Stennis, Pastore, Magnuson, Mansfield, Bible, McGee.

Minority (6 R). Senators Young, Hruska, Cotton, Case, Fong, Brooke.

Intelligence Operations: Senators McClellan, Stennis, Pastore, Young, Hruska.

DISTRICT OF COLUMBIA
Birch Bayh, Chairman

Majority (3 D). Senators Bayh, Inouye, Chiles.

Minority (2 R). Senators Mathias, Bellmon.

FOREIGN OPERATIONS
Daniel K. Inouye, Chairman

Majority (4 D). Senators Inouye, McGee, McClellan, Chiles.

Minority (3 R). Senators Brooke, Hatfield, Mathias.

HOUSING AND URBAN DEVELOPMENT, SPACE, SCIENCE, AND VETERANS
William Proxmire, Chairman

Majority (7 D). Senators Proxmire, Pastore, Stennis, Mansfield, Inouye, Bayh, Chiles.

Minority (5 R). Senators Mathias, Case, Fong, Brooke, Stevens.

INTERIOR
Alan Bible, Chairman

Majority (7 D). Senators Bible, McClellan, Byrd (W. Va.), McGee, Montoya, Inouye, Chiles.

Minority (5 R). Senators Stevens, Young, Hruska, Hatfield, Bellmon.

LABOR, AND HEALTH, EDUCATION, AND WELFARE, AND RELATED AGENCIES
Warren G. Magnuson, Chairman

Majority (8 D). Senators Magnuson, Stennis, Bible, Byrd (W. Va.), Proxmire, Montoya, Hollings, Eagleton.

Minority (6 R). Senators Cotton, Case, Fong, Brooke, Stevens, Schweiker.

LEGISLATIVE
Ernest F. Hollings, Chairman

Majority (3 D). Senators Hollings, Bayh, Eagleton.

Minority (2 R). Senators Cotton, Schweiker.

MILITARY CONSTRUCTION
Mike Mansfield, Chairman

Majority (4 D). Senators Mansfield, Proxmire, Montoya, Hollings.

Minority (3 R). Senators Schweiker, Mathias, Bellmon.

PUBLIC WORKS, AEC
John C. Stennis, Chairman

Majority (8 D). Senators Stennis, McClellan, Magnuson, Bible, Byrd (W. Va.), Pastore, McGee, Montoya.

Minority (7 R). Senators Hatfield, Young, Hruska, Case, Stevens, Schweiker, Bellmon.

STATE, JUSTICE, AND COMMERCE, THE JUDICIARY, AND RELATED AGENCIES
John O. Pastore, Chairman

Majority (6 D). Senators Pastore, McClellan, Mansfield, Hollings, Magnuson, Eagleton.

Minority (4 R). Senators Hruska, Fong, Brooke, Cotton.

TRANSPORTATION
Robert C. Byrd, Chairman

Majority (6 D). Senators Byrd (W. Va.), Stennis, Magnuson, Pastore, Bible, Mansfield.

Minority (5 R). Senators Case, Cotton, Stevens, Mathias, Schweiker.

TREASURY, U.S. POSTAL SERVICE, AND GENERAL GOVERNMENT
Joseph M. Montoya, Chairman

Majority (4 D). Senators Montoya, Bayh, Eagleton, Chiles.

Minority (2 R). Senators Bellmon, Hatfield.

Committee on Armed Services

Senator John C. Stennis, Chairman

Democratic Majority (9 D). Senators Stennis (Miss.), Symington (Mo.), Jackson (Wash.), Ervin (N.C.), Cannon (Nev.), McIntyre (N.H.), Byrd (Va.), Hughes (Iowa), Nunn (Ga.).
Republican Minority (6 R). Senators Thurmond (S.C.), Tower, (Tex.), Dominick (Colo.), Goldwater (Ariz.), Saxbe (Ohio), Scott (Va.).

Subcommittees

CENTRAL INTELLIGENCE
John C. Stennis, Chairman

Majority (3 D). Senators Stennis, Symington, Jackson.
Minority (2 R). Senators Dominick, Thurmond.

PREPAREDNESS INVESTIGATING
John C. Stennis, Chairman

Majority (6 D). Senators Stennis, Symington, Jackson, Cannon, McIntyre, Byrd (Va.).
Minority (5 R). Senators Thurmond, Tower, Dominick, Goldwater, Saxbe.

BOMBER DEFENSE

John C. Stennis, Chairman

Majority (3 D). Senators Stennis, McIntyre, Byrd (Va.).
Minority (2 R). Senators Thurmond, Dominick.

NATIONAL STOCKPILE AND NAVAL PETROLEUM RESERVES
Howard W. Cannon, Chairman

Majority (4 D). Senators Cannon, Symington, Ervin, Nunn.
Minority (3 R). Senators Scott (Va.), Dominick, Goldwater.

STATUS OF FORCES
Sam J. Ervin, Jr., Chairman

Majority (3 D). Senators Ervin, McIntyre, Nunn.
Minority (2 R). Senators Scott (Va.), Saxbe.

MILITARY CONSTRUCTION AUTHORIZATION
Stuart Symington, Chairman

Majority (5 D). Senators Symington, Jackson, Ervin, Cannon, Byrd (Va.).
Minority (3 R). Senators Tower, Thurmond, Dominick.

ARMS CONTROL
Henry M. Jackson, Chairman

Majority (5 D). Senators Jackson, Stennis, Symington, Byrd (Va.), Hughes.
Minority (3 R). Senators Goldwater, Saxbe, Scott (Va.).

NUCLEAR TEST BAN TREATY SAFEGUARDS
Henry M. Jackson, Chairman

Majority (2 D). Senators Jackson, Symington.
Minority

RESEARCH AND DEVELOPMENT
Thomas J. McIntyre, Chairman

Majority (3 D). Senators McIntyre, Byrd (Va.), Hughes.
Minority (2 R). Senators Dominick, Goldwater.

TACTICAL AIR POWER
Howard W. Cannon, Chairman

Majority (4 D). Senators Cannon, Symington, Jackson, Nunn.
Minority (3 R). Senators Goldwater, Tower, Thurmond.

GENERAL LEGISLATION
Harry F. Byrd, Jr., Chairman

Majority (4 D). Senators Byrd (Va.), McIntyre, Hughes, Nunn.
Minority (3 R). Senators Saxbe, Tower, Scott (Va.).

REPROGRAMMING OF FUNDS
John C. Stennis, Chairman

Majority (3 D). Senators Stennis, Ervin, Byrd (Va.).
Minority (2 R). Senators Tower, Thurmond.

DRUG ABUSE IN THE MILITARY
Harold E. Hughes, Chairman
Majority (3 D). Senators Hughes, McIntyre, Nunn.
Minority (2 R). Senators Dominick, Scott (Va.).

Committee on Banking, Housing and Urban Affairs
John Sparkman, Chairman
Democratic Majority (9 D). Senators Sparkman *(Ala.),* Proxmire *(Wis.),* Williams *(N.J.),* McIntyre *(N.H.),* Cranston *(Calif.),* Stevenson *(Ill.),* Johnston *(La.),* Hathaway *(Me.),* Biden *(Del.).*
Republican Minority (7 R). Senators Tower (Tex.), Bennett (Utah), Brooke (Mass.), Packwood (Ore.), Brock (Tenn.), Taft (Ohio), Weicker (Conn.).

Subcommittees

CONSUMER CREDIT
William Proxmire, Chairman
Majority (4 D). Senators Proxmire, Sparkman, Johnston, Hathaway.
Minority (3 R). Senators Brock, Bennett, Brooke.

FINANCIAL INSTITUTIONS
Thomas J. McIntyre, Chairman
Majority (4 D). Senators McIntyre, Sparkman, Proxmire, Williams.
Minority (3 R). Senators Bennett, Tower, Brock.

HOUSING AND URBAN AFFAIRS
John Sparkman, Chairman
Majority (5 D). Senators Sparkman, Proxmire, Williams, Cranston, Stevenson.
Minority (4 R). Senators Tower, Brooke, Packwood, Taft.

INTERNATIONAL FINANCE
Adlai E. Stevenson III, Chairman
Majority (4 D). Senators Stevenson, Cranston, Hathaway, Biden.
Minority (3 R). Senators Packwood, Brock, Taft.

PRODUCTION AND STABILIZATION
J. Bennett Johnston, Jr., Chairman
Majority (4 D). Senators Johnston, Stevenson, Hathaway, Biden.
Minority (3 R). Senators Taft, Tower, Weicker.

SECURITIES
Harrison A. Williams, Jr., Chairman
Majority (4 D). Senators Williams, Proxmire, McIntyre, Biden.
Minority (3 R). Senators Brooke, Bennett, Weicker.

SMALL BUSINESS
Alan Cranston, Chairman
Majority (4 D). Senators Cranston, Sparkman, McIntyre, Johnston.
Minority (3 R). Senators Weicker, Tower, Packwood.

Committee on Commerce
Warren G. Magnuson, Chairman
The chairman and the ranking minority member are members ex officio of all subcommittees.
Democratic Majority (11 D). Senators Magnuson (Wash.), Pastore (R.I.), Hartke (Ind.), Hart (Mich.), Cannon (Nev.), Long (La.), Moss (Utah), Hollings (S.C.), Inouye (Hawaii), Tunney (Calif.), Stevenson (Ill.).
Republican Minority (7 R). Senators Cotton (N.H.), Pearson (Kans.), Griffin (Mich.), Baker (Tenn.), Cook (Ky.), Stevens (Alaska), Beall (Md.).

Subcommittees

AVIATION
Howard W. Cannon, Chairman
Majority (8 D). Senators Magnuson, Hart, Hartke, Hollings, Inouye, Moss, Tunney, Stevenson.
Minority (7 R). Senators Cotton, Pearson, Baker, Griffin, Cook, Stevens, Beall.

COMMUNICATIONS
John O. Pastore, Chairman
Majority (7 D). Senators Hartke, Hart, Long, Moss, Cannon, Hollings, Inouye.
Minority (6 R). Senators Baker, Griffin, Cook, Pearson, Stevens, Beall.

CONSUMER
Frank E. Moss, Chairman
Philip A. Hart, Vice Chairman
Majority (8 D). Senators Moss, Hart, Pastore, Hartke, Inouye, Cannon, Tunney, Stevenson.
Minority (4 R). Senators Cook, Pearson, Stevens, Beall.

ENVIRONMENT
Philip A. Hart, Chairman
Frank E. Moss, Vice Chairman
Majority (6 D). Senators Hart, Moss, Pastore, Long, Tunney, Stevenson.
Minority (3 R). Senators Cook, Baker, Pearson.

FOREIGN COMMERCE AND TOURISM
Daniel K. Inouye, Chairman
Majority (6 D). Senators Inouye, Hartke, Cannon, Long, Moss, Stevenson.
Minority (5 R). Senators Griffin, Cook, Pearson, Baker, Stevens.

MERCHANT MARINE
Russell B. Long, Chariman
Majority (5 D). Senators Long, Pastore, Hollings, Inouye, Tunney.
Minority (3 R). Senators Beall, Griffin, Stevens.

OEANS AND ATMOSPHERE
Ernest F. Hollings, Chairman
Majority (7 D). Senators Hollings, Pastore, Hart, Long, Inouye, Moss, Tunney.
Minority (4 R). Senators Stevens, Griffin, Cook, Beall.

SURFACE TRANSPORTATION
Vance Hartke, Chairman
Majority (5 D). Senators Hartke, Cannon, Hollings, Long, Stevenson.
Minority (3 R). Senators Pearson, Baker, Beall.

Committee on District of Columbia

Thomas F. Eagleton, Chairman
Democratic Majority (4 D). Senators Eagleton (Mo.), Inouye (Hawaii), Stevenson (Ill.), Tunney (Calif.).
Republican Minority (3 R). Senators Mathias (Md.), Bartlett (Okla.), Domenici (No. Mex.).

Subcommittees

BUSINESS, COMMERCE, AND JUDICIARY
Adlai E. Stevenson III, Chairman
Majority (2 D). Senators Stevenson, Tunney.
Minority (1 R). Senator Domenici.

FISCAL AFFAIRS
Daniel K. Inouye, Chairman
Majority (2 D). Senators Inouye, Eagleton.
Minority (1 R;. Senator Bartlett.

PUBLIC HEALTH, EDUCATION, AND WELFARE, AND SAFETY
John V. Tunney, Chairman
Majority (2 D). Senators Tunney, Stevenson.
Minority (1 R). Senator Mathias.

Committee on Finance

Russell B. Long, Chairman
Democratic Majority (10 D). Senators Long (La.), Talmadge (Ga.), Hartke (Ind.), Fulbright (Ark.), Ribicoff (Conn.), Byrd (Va.), Nelson (Wis.), Mondale (Minn.), Gravel (Alaska), Bentsen (Tex.).

Republican Minority (7 R). Senators Bennett (Utah), Curtis (Neb.), Finnin (Ariz.), Hansen (Wyo.), Dole (Kans.), Packwood (Ore.), Roth (Del.).

Subcommittees

INTERNATIONAL TRADE
Abraham A. Ribicoff, Chairman
Majority (5 D). Senators Ribicoff, Talmadge, Nelson, Mondale, Bentsen.
Minority (4 R). Senators Fannin, Curtis, Hansen, Packwood.

HEALTH
Herman E. Talmadge, Chairman
Majority (5 D). Senators Talmadge, Hartke, Fulbright, Ribicoff, Mondale.
Minority (4 R). Senators Hansen, Dole, Packwood, Roth.

PRIVATE PENSION PLANS
Gaylord Nelson, Chairman
Majority (4 D). Senators Nelson, Ribicoff, Byrd (Va.), Bentsen.
Minority (3 R). Senators Curtis, Dole, Roth.

STATE TAXATION OF INTERSTATE COMMERCE
Walter F. Mondale, Chairman
Majority (3 D). Senators Mondale, Nelson, Bentsen.
Minority (2 R). Senators Hansen, Packwood.

FOUNDATIONS
Vance Hartke, Chairman
Majority (3 D). Senators Hartke, Fulbright, Gravel.
Minority (2 R). Senators Curtis, Fannin.

INTERNATIONAL FINANCE AND RESOURCES
Harry F. Byrd, Jr., Chairman
Majority (3 D). Senators Byrd (Va.), Hartke, Gravel.
Minority (2 R). Senators Dole, Roth.

Committee on Foreign Relations

The chairman of the full committee is an ex officio member of each subcommittee.
Majority (10 D). Senators Fulbright (Ark.), Sparkman (Ala.), Mansfield (Mont.), Church (Idaho), Symington (Mo.), Pell (R.I.), McGee (Wyo.), Muskie (Me.), McGovern (S. Dak.), Humphrey (Minn.).
Minority (7 R). Senators Aiken (Vt.), Case (N.J.), Javits (N.Y.), Scott (Pa.), Pearson (Kans.), Percy (Ill.), Griffin (Mich.).

Subcommittees

NEAR EASTERN AFFAIRS
J. W. Fulbright, Chairman
Democratic Majority (5 D). Senators Fulbright, Mansfield, Symington, Pell, Humphrey.
Republican Minority (3 R). Senators Aiken, Scott (Pa.), Percy.

EUROPEAN AFFAIRS
John Sparkman, Chairman
Majority (4 D). Senators Sparkman, Symington, Pell, Humphrey.
Majority (6 R). Senators Case, Javits, Scott (Pa.), Pearson, Percy, Griffin.

FAR EASTERN AFFAIRS
Mike Mansfield, Chairman
Majority (4 D). Senators Mansfield, Sparkman, McGee, McGovern.
Minority (4 R). Senators Aiken, Scott (Pa.), Pearson, Percy.

OCEANS AND INTERNATIONAL ENVIRONMENT
Claiborne Pell, Chairman
Majority (3 D). Senators Pell, Church, Muskie.
Minority (2 R). Senators Case, Griffin.

WESTERN HEMISPHERE AFFAIRS
Gale W. McGee, Chairman

Majority (6 D). Senators McGee, Sparkman, Mansfield, Church, Muskie, Humphrey.
Minority (5 R). Senators Aiken, Case, Javits, Scott (Pa.), Griffin.

ARMS CONTROL, INTERNATIONAL LAW AND ORGANIZATION
Edmund S. Muskie, Chairman

Majority (5 D). Senators Muskie, Church, Pell, McGee, Humphrey.
Minority (3 R). Senators Case, Javits, Pearson.

SOUTH ASIAN AFFAIRS
George McGovern, Chairman

Majority (2 D). Senators McGovern, McGee.
Minority (2 R). Senators Percy, Griffin.

AFRICAN AFFAIRS
Hubert H. Humphrey, Chairman

Majority (2 D). Senators Humphrey, McGee.
Minority (1 R). Senator Pearson.

U.S. SECURITIES AGREEMENTS AND COMMITMENTS ABROAD
Stuart Symington, Chairman

Majority (5 D). Senators Symington, Fulbright, Sparkman, Mansfield, McGovern.
Minority (3 R). Senators Aiken, Case, Javits.

MULTINATIONAL CORPORATIONS
Frank Church, Chairman

Majority (3 D). Senators Church, Symington, Muskie.
Minority (2 R). Senators Case, Percy.

Committee on Government Operations

Sam J. Ervin, Jr., Chairman

Democratic Majority (10 D). Senators Ervin (N.C.), McClellan (Ark.), Jackson (Wash.), Muskie (Me.), Ribicoff (Conn.), Metcalf (Mont.), Allen (Ala.), Chiles (Fla.), Nunn (Ga.), Huddleston (Ky.).
Republican Minority (6 R). Senators Percy (Ill.), Javits (N.Y.), Gurney (Fla.), Saxbe (Ohio), Roth (Del.), Brock (Tenn.).

Subcommittees

PERMANENT INVESTIGATIONS
Henry M. Jackson, Chairman

Majority (6 D). Senators Jackson, McClellan, Ervin, Ribicoff, Allen, Huddleston.
Minority (4 R). Senators Percy, Javits, Gurney, Saxbe

INTERGOVERNMENTAL RELATIONS
Edmund S. Muskie, Chairman

Majority (5 D). Senators Muskie, Ervin, Metcalf, McClellan, Chiles.
Minority (3 R). Senators Gurney, Roth, Brock.

REORGANIZATION, RESEARCH, AND INTERNATIONAL ORGANIZATIONS
Abraham A. Ribicoff, Chairman

Majority (5 D). Senators Ribicoff, Allen, Jackson, Chiles, Nunn.
Minority (3 R). Senators Javits, Percy, Roth.

BUDGETING, MANAGEMENT, AND EXPENDITURES
Lee Metcalf, Chairman

Majority (5 D). Senators Metcalf, McClellan, Muskie, Nunn, Huddleston.
Minority (4 R). Senators Saxbe, Brock, Percy, Roth.

Committee on Interior and Insular Affairs

Henry M. Jackson, Chairman

Democratic Majority (7 D). Senators Jackson (Wash.), Bible (Nev.), Church (Idaho), Metcalf (Mont.), Johnston (La.), Abourezk (S. Dak.), Haskell (Colo.).
Republican Minority (6 R). Senators Fannin (Ariz.), Hansen (Wyo.), Hatfield (Ore.), Buckley (N.Y.), McClure (Idaho), Bartlett (Okla).

Subcommittees

INDIAN AFFAIRS
James Abourezk, Chairman
Majority (4 D). Senators Abourezk, Jackson, Metcalf, Haskell.
Minority (3 R). Senators Bartlett, McClure, Fannin.

MINERALS, MATERIALS, AND FUELS
Lee Metcalf, Chairman
Majority (4 D).Senators Metcalf, Jackson, Bible, Johnston.
Minority (3 R). Senators Buckley, Hansen, Bartlett.

PARKS AND RECREATION
Alan Bible, Chairman
Majority (4 D). Senators Bible, Jackson, Church, Johnston.
Minority (3 R). Senators Hansen, Hatfield, McClure.

PUBLIC LANDS
Floyd K. Haskell, Chairman
Majority (4 D). Senators Haskell, Jackson, Church, Abourezk.
Minority (3 R). Senators McClure, Hatfield, Buckley.

TERRITORIES AND INSULAR AFFAIRS
J. Bennett Johnston, Jr., Chairman
Majority (4 D). Senators Johnston, Jackson, Metcalf, Abourezk
Minority (3 R). Senators Fannin, Buckley, Bartlett.

WATER AND POWER RESOURCES
Frank Church, Chairman
Majority (4 D). Senators Church, Jackson, Metcalf, Haskell.
Minority (3 R). Senators Hatfield, Hansen, Fannin.

SPECIAL SUBCOMMITTEE ON LEGISLATIVE OVERSIGHT
Henry M. Jackson, Chairman
Majority (2 D). Senators Jackson, Bible.
Minority (1 R). Senator Fannin.

Committee on the Judiciary

James O. Eastland, Chairman
Democratic Majority (9 D), Senators Eastland (Miss.), McClellan (Ark.), Ervin (N.C.), Hart (Mich.), Kennedy (Mass.), Bayh (Ind.), Burdick (N. Dak.), Byrd (W. Va.), Tunney (Calif.).
Republican Minority (7 R). Senators Hruska (Neb.), Fong (Hawaii), Scott (Pa.), Thurmond (S.C.), Cook (Ky.), Mathias (Md.), Gurney (Fla.).

Subcommittees

ADMINISTRATIVE PRACTICE AND PROCEDURE
Edward M. Kennedy, Chairman
Majority (5 D). Senators Kennedy, Hart, Bayh, Burdick, Tunney.
Minority (3 R). Senators Thurmond, Mathias, Gurney.

ANTITRUST AND MONOPOLY
Philip A. Hart, Chairman
Majority (5 D). Senators Hart, McClellan, Ervin, Kennedy, Tunney.
Minority (4 R). Senators Hruska, Fong, Thurmond, Gurney.

CONSTITUTIONAL AMENDMENTS
Birch Bayh, Chairman
Majority (6 D). Senators Bayh, Eastland, Ervin, Byrd (W. Va.), Burdick, Tunney.
Minority (5 R). Senators Fong, Hruska, Thurmond, Cook, Scott (Pa.).

CONSTITUTIONAL RIGHTS
Sam J. Ervin, Jr., Chairman
Majority (6 D). Senators Ervin, McClellan, Kennedy, Bayh, Byrd (W. Va.), Tunney.
Minority (5 R). Senators Gurney, Hruska, Fong, Thurmond, Scott (Pa.).

CRIMINAL LAWS AND PROCEDURES
John L. McClellan, Chairman

Majority (6 D). Senators McClellan, Ervin, Hart, Eastland, Kennedy, Byrd (W. Va.).
Minority (4 R). Senators Hruska, Scott (Pa.), Thurmond, Cook.

FEDERAL CHARTERS, HOLIDAYS, AND CELEBRATIONS
Roman L. Hruska, Chairman

Majority (1 D). Senator McClellan.
Minority (1 R). Senator Hruska.

IMMIGRATION AND NATURALIZATION
James O. Eastland, Chairman

Majority (5 D). Senators Eastland, McClellan, Ervin, Kennedy, Hart.
Minority (3 R). Senators Fong, Thurmond, Cook.

IMPROVEMENTS IN JUDICIAL MACHINERY
Quention N. Burdick, Chairman

Majority (4 D). Senators Burdick, McClellan, Hart, Ervin.
Minority (3 R). Senators Hruska, Scott (Pa.), Gurney.

INTERNAL SECURITY
James O. Eastland, Chairman

Majority (4 D). Senators Eastland, McClellan, Ervin, Bayh.
Minority (4 R). Senators Scott (Pa.), Thurmond, Cook, Gurney.

JUVENILE DELIQUENCY
Birch Bayh, Chairman

Majority (4 D). Senators Bayh, Hart, Burdick, Kennedy.
Minority (4 R). Senators Cook, Hruska, Fong, Mathias.

PATENTS, TRADEMARKS, AND COPYRIGHTS
John L. McClellan, Chairman

Majority (3 D). Senators McClellan, Hart, Burdick.
Minority (2 R). Senators Scott (Pa.), Fong.

PENITENTIARIES
Quentin N. Burdick, Chairman

Majority (3 D). Senators Burdick, Hart, Bayh.
Minority (2 R). Senators Cook, Mathias.

REFUGEES AND ESCAPEES
Edward M. Kennedy, Chairman

Majority (3 D). Senators Kennedy, McClellan, Hart.
Minority (2 R). Senators Fong, Mathias.

REVISION AND CODIFICATION
Sam J. Ervin, Jr., Chairman

Majority (2 D). Senators Ervin, Hart.
Minority (1 R). Senator Scott (Pa.).

SEPARATION OF POWERS
Sam J. Ervin, Jr., Chairman

Majority (4 D). Senators Ervin, McClellan, Burdick, Byrd (W. Va.).
Minority (2 R). Senators Mathias, Gurney.

Committee on Labor and Public Welfare

Harrison A. Williams, Jr., Chairman
Democratic Majority (10 D). Senators Williams (N.J.), Randolph (W. Va.), Pell (R.I.), Kennedy (Mass.), Nelson (Wis.), Mondale (Minn.), Eagleton (Mo.), Cranston (Calif.), Hughes (Iowa), Hathaway (Me.).
Republican Minority (6 R). Senators Javits (N.Y.), Dominick (Colo.), Schweiker (Pa.,), Taft (Ohio), Beall (Md.), Stafford (Vt.).

Subcommittees

LABOR
Harrison A. Williams, Jr., Chairman

Majority (7 D). Senators Williams, Randolph, Pell, Nelson, Eagleton, Hughes, Hathaway.
Minority (4 R). Senators Javits, Schweiker, Taft, Stafford.

HANDICAPPED
Jennings Randolph, Chairman

Majority (7 D). Senators Randolph, Cranston, Williams, Pell, Kennedy, Mondale, Hathaway.
Minority (4 R). Senators Stafford, Taft, Schweiker, Beall.

EDUCATION
Claiborne Pell, Chairman

Majority (8 D). Senators Pell, Randolph, Williams, Kennedy, Mondale, Eagleton, Cranston, Hathaway.
Minority (5 R). Senators Dominick, Javits, Schweiker, Beall, Stafford.

HEALTH
Edward M. Kennedy, Chairman

Majority (8 D). Senators Kennedy, Williams, Nelson, Eagleton, Cranston, Hughes, Pell, Mondale.
Minority (5 R). Senators Schweiker, Javits, Dominick, Beall, Taft.

EMPLOYMENT, POVERTY AND MIGRATORY LABOR
Gaylord Nelson, Chairman

Majority (7 D). Senators Nelson, Kennedy, Mondale, Cranston, Hughes, Randolph, Hathaway.
Minority (5 R). Senators Taft, Javits, Schweiker, Dominick, Beall.

CHILDREN AND YOUTH
Walter F. Mondale, Chairman

Majority (7 D). Senators Mondale, Williams, Randolph, Kennedy, Nelson, Cranston, Hathaway.
Minority (3 R). Senators Taft, Beall, Stafford.

AGING
Thomas F. Eagleton, Chairman

Majority (7 D). Senators Eagleton, Cranston, Kennedy, Randolph, Williams, Hughes, Pell.
Minority (4 R). Senators Beall, Schweiker, Taft, Stafford.

RAILROAD RETIREMENT
William D. Hathaway, Chairman

Majority (5 D). Senators Hathaway, Pell, Nelson, Hughes, Mondale.
Minority (3 R). Senators Schweiker, Taft, Beall.

ALCOHOLISM AND NARCOTICS
Harold E. Hughes, Chairman

Majority (6 D). Senators Hughes, Randolph, Williams, Kennedy, Mondale, Cranston.
Minority (4 R). Senators Schweiker, Javits, Dominick, Beall.

SPECIAL SUBCOMMITTEE ON ARTS AND HUMANITIES
Claiborne Pell, Chairman

Majority (4 D). Senators Pell, Nelson, Eagleton, Mondale.
Minority (2 R). Senates Javits, Taft.

SPECIAL COMMITTEE ON NATIONAL SCIENCE FOUNDATION
Edward M. Kennedy, Chairman

Majority (5 D). Senators Kennedy, Pell, Eagleton, Cranston, Mondale.
Minority (2 R). Senators Dominick, Stafford.

SPECIAL COMMITTEE ON HUMAN RESOURCES
Alan Cranston, Chairman

Majority (3 D). Senators Cranston, Randolph, Nelson.
Minority (2 R). Senators Beall, Stafford.

Committee on Post Office and Civil Service
Gale W. McGee, Chairman

Democratic Majority (5 D). Senators McGee (Wyo.), Randolph (W. Va.), Burdick (N. Dak.), Hollings (S.C.), Moss (Utah).
Republican Minority (4 R). Senators Fong (Hawaii), Stevens (Alaska), Bellmon (Okla.), Saxbe (Ohio).

Subcommttees

CIVIL SERVICE POLICIES AND PRACTICES
Jennings Randolph, Chairman

Majority (3 D). Senators Randolph, Burdick, Moss.
Minority (2 R). Senators Bellmon, Saxbe.

COMPENSATION AND EMPLOYMENT BENEFITS
Quentin N. Burdick, Chairman
Majority (3 D). Senators Burdick, Hollings, Moss.
Minority (2 R). Senators Stevens, Bellmon.

POSTAL OPERATIONS
Ernest F. Hollings, Chairman
Majority (3 D). Senators Hollings, Moss, Randolph.
Minority (2 R). Senators Saxbe, Stevens.

Committee on Public Works

Jennings Randolph, Chairman
Democratic Majority (8 D). Senators Randolph (W. Va.), Muskie (Me.), Montoya (N. Mex.), Gravel (Alaska), Bentsen (Tex.), Burdick (N. Dak.), Clark (Iowa), Biden (Del.).
Republican Minority (6 R). Senators Baker (Tenn.), Buckley (N.Y.), Stafford (Vt.), Scott (Va.,), McClure (Idaho), Domenici (N. Mex.).

Subcommittees

WATER RESOURCES
Mike Gravel, Chairman
Majority (5 D). Senators Gravel, Bentsen, Burdick, Clark, Biden.
Minority (4 R). Senators Scott (Va.), Buckley, Stafford, McClure.

AIR AND WATER POLLUTION
Edmund S. Muskie, Chairman
Majority (7 D). Senators Muskie, Randolph, Montoya, Bentsen, Clark, Biden.
Minority (5 R). Senators Buckley, Baker, Stafford, McClure, Domenici.

PANEL ON ENVIRONMENTAL SCIENCE AND TECHNOLOGY
Joseph R. Biden, Jr., Chairman
Majority (3 D). Senators Biden, Bentsen, Clark.
Minority (2 R). Senators Buckley, Stafford.

ROADS
Lloyd Bentsen, Chairman
Majority (5 D). Senators Bentsen, Montoya, Gravel, Muskie, Burdick.
Minority (4 R). Senators Stafford, Buckley, Scott (Va.), Domenici.

ECONOMIC DEVELOPMENT
Joseph M. Montoya, Chairman.
Majority (5 D). Senators Montoya, Muskie, Gravel, Bentsen, Burdick.
Minority (4 R). Senators McClure, Stafford, Scott (Va.), Domenici.

PUBLIC BUILDINGS AND GROUNDS
Dick Clark, Chairman
Majority (3 D). Senators Clark, Gravel, Biden.
Minority (1 R). Senator Scott (Va.).

DISASTER RELIEF
Quentin N. Burdick, Chairman
Majority (3 D). Senators Burdick, Clark, Biden.
Minority (2 R). Senators Domenici, Buckley.

Committee on Rules and Administration

Howard W. Cannon, Chairman
Democratic Majority (5 D). Senators Cannon (Nev.), Pell (R.I.), Byrd (W. Va.), Allen (Ala.), Williams (N.J.).
Republican Minority (4 R). Senators Cook (Ky.), Scott (Pa.), Griffin (Mich.), Hatfield (Ore.).

Subcommittees

STANDING RULES OF THE SENATE
Robert C. Byrd, Chairman
Majority (2 D). Senators Byrd (W. Va.), Cannon.
Minority (1 R). Senator Griffin.

PRIVILEGES AND ELECTIONS
Clairborne Pell, Chairman
Majority (2 D). Senators Pell, Byrd (W. Va.).
Minority (1 R). Senator Griffin.

PRINTING
Howard W. Cannon, Chairman
Majority (2 D). Senators Cannon, Allen.
Minority (1 R). Senator Scott (Pa.).

LIBRARY
Howard W. Cannon, Chairman
Majority (2 D). Senators Cannon, Pell.
Minority (1 R). Senator Hatfield.

SMITHSONIAN INSTITUTION
Claiborne Pell, Chairman
Majority (2 D). Senators Pell, Williams.
Minority (1 R). Senator Cook.

RESTAURANT
James B. Allen, Chairman
Majority (2 D). Senators Allen, Williams.
Minority (1 R). Senator Cook.

COMPUTER SERVICES
Howard W. Cannon, Chairman
Majority (2 D). Senators Cannon, Williams.
Minority (1 R), Senator Hatfield.

Committees on Veterans' Affairs

Vance Hartke, Chairman
Senators Hartke and Hansen are ex officio members of all subcommittees.
Democratic Majority (5 D). Senators Hartke (Ind.), Talmadge (Ga.), Randolph (W. Va.), Hughes (Iowa), Cranston (Calif.).
Republican Minority (4 R). Senators Hansen (Wyo.), Thurmond (S.C.), Stafford (Vt.), McClure (Idaho).

Subcommittees

COMPENSATION AND PENSIONS
Herman E. Talmadge, Chairman
Majority (3 D). Senators Talmadge, Randolph, Hughes.
Minority (2 R). Senators Hansen, Thurmond.

HEALTH AND HOSPITALS
Alan Cranston, Chairman
Majority (3 D). Senators Cranston, Randolph, Hughes.
Minority (2 R). Senators Thurmond, Hansen.

HOUSING AND INSURANCE
Harold E. Hughes, Chairman
Majority (3 D). Senators Hughes, Talmadge, Cranston.
Minority (2 R). Senators McClure, Stafford.

READJUSTMENT, EDUCATION AND EMPLOYMENT
Vance Hartke, Chairman
Majority (3 D). Senators Hartke, Talmadge, Cranston.
Minority (2 R). Senators Stafford, McClure.

SELECT COMMITTEES

Select Committee on Nutrition and Human Needs

George McGovern, Chairman

Democratic Majority (8 D). Senators McGovern, (S. Dak.), Talmadge (Ga.), Hart (Mich.), Mondale (Minn.), Kennedy (Mass.), Nelson (Wis.), Cranston (Calif.), Humphrey (Minn.).
Republican Minority (6 R). Senators Percy (Ill.), Cook (Ky.), Dole (Kans.), Bellmon (Okla.), Schweiker (Pa.), Taft (Ohio).

Select Committee on Presidential Campaign Activities

Sam J. Ervin, Jr., Chairman

Democratic Majority (4 D). Senators Ervin (N.C.), Talmadge (Ga.,), Inouye (Hawaii), Montoya (N. Mex.).
Republican Minority (3 R). Senators Baker (Tenn.,), Gurney (Fla.), Weicker (Conn.).

Select Committee on Small Business

Alan Bible, Chairman

Democratic Majority (9 D). Senators Bible (Nev.), Sparkman (Ala.), McIntyre (N.H.), Nunn (Ga.), Johnston (La.), Hathaway (Me.), Abourezk (S. Dak.), Haskell (Colo.).
Republican Minority (7 R). Senators Javits (N.Y.), Dominick (Colo.), Dole (Kans.), Gurney (Fla.), Beal (Md.), Buckley (N.Y.), Scott (Va.).

Select Committee on Standards and Conduct

John Stennis, Chairman
Wallace F. Bennett, Vice Chairman

Democratic Majority (3 D). Senators Stennis (Miss.), Talmadge (Ga.), and one vacancy.
Republican Minority (3 R). Senators Bennett (Utah), Curtis (Nebr.), Brooke (Mass.).

Special Committee on Aging

Frank Church, Chairman

Democratic Majority (13 D). Senators Church (Idaho), Williams (N.J.), Bible (Nev.), Randolph (W. Va.), Muskie (Me.), Moss (Utah), Kennedy (Mass.), Mondale (Minn.), Hartke (Ind.), Pell (R.I.), Eagleton (Mo.), Tunney (Calif.), Chiles (Fla.).
Republican Minority (7 R). Senators Fong (Hawaii), Hansen (Wyo.), Gurney (Fla.), Saxbe (Ohio), Brooke (Mass.), Percy (Ill.), Stafford (Vt.), Beall (Md.), Domenici (N. Mex.).

Special Committee to Study Questions Related to Secret and Confidental Government Documents

Mike Mansfield, Co-Chairman
Hugh Scott, Co-Chairman

Democratic Majority (5 D). Senators Mansfield (Mont.), Pastore (R.I.), Hughes (Iowa), Cranston (Calif.), Gravel (Alaska).
Republican Minority (5 R). Senators Scott (Pa.), Javits, (N.Y.), Hatfield (Ore.), Gurney (Fla.), Cook (Ky.).

Special Committee on the Termination of the National Emergency

Frank Church, Co-Chairman
Charles McC. Mathias, Co-Chairman

Democratic Majority (4 D). Senators Church (Idaho), Hart (Mich.), Pell (R.I.), Stevenson (Ill.).
Republican Minority (4 R). Senators Mathias (Md.), Case (N.J.), Pearson (Kans.), Hansen (Wyo.).

HOUSE COMMITTEES

Committee on Agriculture

W. R. Poage, Chairman

The chairman and ranking minority member are ex officio members of all subcommittees.
Democratic Majority (20 D). Congressmen Poage (Tex. 11), Stubblefield (Ky. 1), Foley (Wash. 5), de la Garza (Tex. 15), Vigorito (Pa. 24), Jones (N.C. 1), Sisk (Calif. 16), Alexander (Ark. 1), Rarick (La. 6), Jones (Tenn. 7), Melcher (Mont. 2), Mathis (Ga. 2), Bergland (Minn. 7), Denholm (S. Dak. 1), Matsunaga (Hawaii 1), Brown (Calif. 38), Bowen (Miss. 2), Rose (N.C. 7), Litton (Mo. 6), Gunter (Fla. 5).
Republican Minority (16 R). Congressmen Teague (Calif. 13), Wampler (Va. 9), Goodling (Pa. 19), Mathias (Calif. 18), Mayne (Iowa 6), Zwach (Minn. 6), Price (Tex. 13), Sebelius (Kans. 1), Mizell (N.C. 5), Findley (Ill. 20), Baker (Tenn. 3), Thone (Neb. 1), Symms (Idaho 1), Young (S.C. 6), Johnson (Colo. 4), Madigan (Ill. 21).

Subcommittees

COTTON
B. F. Sisk, Chairman
Majority (5 D). Congressmen Sisk, de la Garza, Jones (Tenn.), Bowen, Rose.
Minority (4 R). Congressmen Mathias, Price, Mizel, Young.

DAIRY AND POULTRY
Ed Jones, Chairman
Majority (5 D). Congressmen Jones (Tenn.), Stubblefield, Bergland, Brown, Bowen.
Minority (4 R). Congressmen Wampler, Zwach, Findley, Thone.

FORESTS
John R. Rarick, Chairman
Majority (5 D). Congressmen Rarick, Foley, Vigorito, Melcher, Gunter.
Minority (4 D). Congressmen Goodling, Baker, Thone, Symms.

LIVESTOCK AND GRAINS
Thomas S. Foley, Chairman
Majority (10 D). Congressmen Foley, Rarick, Jones (N.C.), Sisk, Melcher, Bergland, Denholm, Matsunaga, Litton, Gunter.
Minority (8 R). Congressmen Mayne, Zwach, Price, Sebelius, Findley, Thone, Johnson, Symms.

OILSEEDS AND RICE
Walter B. Jones, Chairman
Majority (5 D). Congressmen Jones (N.C.), Rarick, Alexander, Mathis, Rose.
Minority (4 R). Congressmen Wampler, Baker, Johnson, Madigan.

TOBACCO
Frank A. Stubblefield, Chairman
Majority (5 D). Congressmen Stubblefield, Jones (N.C.), Mathis, Rose, Litton.
Minority (4 R). Congressmen Mizell, Wampler, Madigan, Young.

CONSERVATION AND CREDIT
W. R. Poage, Chairman
Majority (5 D). Congressmen Poage, Stubblefield, de la Garza, Alexander, Bergland.
Minority (4 R). Congressmen Goodling, Findley, Johnson, Symms.

DOMESTIC MARKETING AND CONSUMER RELATIONS
Joseph P. Vigorito, Chairman
Majority (5 D). Congressmen Vigorito, Foley, Sisk, Denholm, Matsunaga.
Minority (4 R). Congressmen Goodling, Findley, Johnson, Symms.

DEPARTMENT OPERATIONA
Eligio de la Garza, Chairman
Majority (5 D). Congressmen de la Garza, Jones (Tenn.), Matsunage, Denholm, Litton.
Minority (4 R). Congressmen Price, Mathias, Sebelius, Mayne.

FAMILY FARMS AND RURAL DEVELOPMENT
Bill Alexander, Chairman
Majority (5 D). Congressmen Alexander, Vigorito, Melcher, Mathis, Brown.
Minority (4 D). Congressmen Sebelius, Mizell, Baker, Young.

Committee on Appropriations
George H. Mahon, Chairman

Democratic Majority (33 D). Congressmen Mahon (Tex. 19), Whitten (Miss. 1), Rooney (N.Y. 14), Sikes (Fla. 1), Passman (La. 5), Evins (Tenn. 4), Boland (Mass. 2), Natcher (Kent. 2), Flood (Pa. 11), Steed (Okla. 4), Shipley (Ill. 22), Slack (W. Va. 3), Flynt (Ga. 6), Smith (Iowa 4), Giaimo (Conn. 3), Hansen (Wash. 3), Addabbo (N.Y. 7), McFall (Calif. 15), Patten (N.J. 15), Long (Md. 2), Yates (Ill. 9), Casey (Tex. 22), Evans (Colo. 3), Obey (Wis. 7), Roybal (Calif. 30), Stokes (Ohio 21), Roush (Ind. 4), McKay (Utah 1), Bevill (Ala. 4), Green (Ore. 3), Tiernan (R.I. 2), Chappell (Fla. 4), Burlison (Mo. 10).

Republican Minority (22 R). Congressmen Cederberg (Mich. 10), Rhodes (Ariz. 1), Minshall (Ohio 23), Michel (Ill. 18), Conte (Mass. 1), Davis (Wis. 9), Robison (N.Y. 27), Shriver (Kans. 4), McDade (Pa. 10), Andrews (N. Dak. AL), Wyman (N.H. 1), Talcott (Calif. 12), Wyatt (Ore. 1), Edwards (Ala. 1), Scherle (Iowa 5), McEwen (N.Y. 30), Myers (Ind. 7), Robinson (Va. 7), Miller (Ohio 10), Ruth (N.C. 8), Veysey (Calif. 43), Coughlin (Pa. 13).

Subcommittees

AGRICULTURAL, ENVIRONMENTAL AND CONSUMER PROTECTION
Jamie L. Whitten, Chairman

Majority (7 D). Congressmen Whitten, Shipley, Evans, Burlison, Natcher, Smith, Casey.
Minority (4 R). Congressmen Andrews, Michel, Scherle, Robinson.

DEFENSE
George H. Mahon, Chairman

Majority (8 D). Congressmen Mahon, Sikes, Flood, Addabbo, McFall, Flynt, Giaimo, Whitten
Minority (4 R). Congressmen Minshall, Rhodes, Davis, Wyman.

DISTRICT OF COLUMBIA
William N. Natcher, Chairman

Majority (7 D). Congressmen Natcher, Stokes, Tiernan, Chappell, Burlison, McKay, Roush.
Minority (4 R). Congressmen McEwen, Myers, Veysey, Coughlin.

FOREIGN OPERATIONS
Otto E. Passman, Chairman

Majority (7 D). Congressmen Passman, Rooney, Long, Roybal, Bevill, Roush, Yates.
Minority (4 R). Congressmen Shriver, Miller, Conte, Coughlin.

HUD, SPACE, SCIENCE AND VETERANS
Edward P. Boland, Chairman

Majority (7 D). Congressmen Boland, Evins, Shipley, Roush, Tiernan, Chappell, Giaimo.
Minority (4 R). Congressmen Talcott, McDade, Scherle, Ruth.

INTERIOR
Julia Butler Hansen, Chairwoman

Majority (5 D). Congressmen Hansen, Yates, McKay, Long, Evans.
Minority (3 R). Congressmen McDade, Wyatt, Veysey.

LABOR, HEALTH, EDUCATION AND WELFARE
Daniel J. Flood, Chairman

Majority (7 D). Congressmen Flood, Natcher, Smith, Casey, Patten, Obey, Green.
Minority (4 R). Congressmen Michel, Shriver, Conte, Robinson.

LEGISLATIVE
Bob Casey, Chairman

Majority (7 D). Congressmen Casey, Evans, Giaimo, Green, Flynt, Roybal, Stokes.
Minority (4 R). Congressmen Wyman, Cederberg, Rhodes, Ruth.

MILITARY CONTRSTRUCTION
Robert L. F. Sikes, Chairman

Majority (5 D). Congressmen Sikes, Patten, Long, Obey, McKay.
Minority (3 R). Congressmen Davis, Talcott, McEwen.

PUBLIC WORKS AND AEC
Joe L. Evins, Chairman

Majority (5 D). Congressmen Evins, Boland, Whitten, Slack, Passman.
Minority (3 R). Congressmen Rhodes, Davis, Robison.

STATE, JUSTICE, COMMERCE AND JUDICIARY
John J. Rooney, Chairman
Majority (5 D). Congressmen Rooney, Slack, Smith, Flynt, Sikes.
Minority (3 R). Congressmen Cederberg, Andrews, Wyatt.

TRANSPORTATION
John J. McFall, Chairman
Majority (5 D). Congressmen McFall, Yates, Steed, Hansen, Boland.
Minority (3 R). Congressmen Conte, Minshall, Edwards.

TREASURY, POSTAL SERVICE AND GENERAL GOVERNMENT
Tom Steed, Chairman
Majority (7 D). Congressmen Steed, Addabbo, Roybal, Stokes, Bevill, Shipley, Slack.
Minority (4 R). Congressmen Robison, Edwards, Myers, Miller.

Committee on Armed Services

F. Edward Hebert, Chairman
The chairman and ranking minority member are ex officio members of all subcommittees.
Democratic Majority (24 D). Congressmen Hébert (La. 1), Price (Ill. 23), Fisher (Tex. 21), Bennett (Fla. 3), Stratton (N.Y. 28), Pike (N.Y. 1), Ichord (Mo. 8), Nedzi (Mich. 14), Randall (Mo. 4), Wilson (Calif. 31), Leggett (Calif. 4), Hicks (Wash. 6), White (Tex. 16), Nichols (Ala. 3), Brinkley (Ga. 3), Mollohan (W. Va. 1), Daniel (Va. 5), Montgomery (Miss. 3), Runnels (N. Mex. 2), Aspin (Wis. 1), Dellums (Calif. 7), Davis (S.C. 1), Jones (Okla. 1), Schroeder (Colo. 1).
Republican Minority (19 R). Congressmen Bray (Ind. 6), Arends (Ill. 15), Wilson (Calif. 40), Gubser (Calif. 10), King (N.Y. 29), Dickinson (Ala. 2), Hunt (N.J. 1), Whitehurst (Va. 2), Young (Fla. 6), Spence (S.C. 2), Powell (Ohio 8), Price (Tex. 3), Treen (La. 3), Armstrong (Colo. 5), O'Brien (Ill. 17), Beard (Tenn. 6), Mitchell (N.Y. 31), Holt (Md. 4), Daniel (Va. 4).

Subcommittees

SUBCOMMITTEE NO. 1
Melvin Price, Chairman
Majority (6 D). Congressmen Price (Ill.), Pike, Ichord, Leggett, Hicks, Runnels.
Minority (5 R). Congressmen Gubser, Dickinson, Young, Spence, Price (Tex.).

SUBCOMMITTEE NO. 2
O. C. Fisher, Chairman
Majority (6 D). Congressmen Fisher, Nedzi, Randall, Charles Wilson, Dan Daniel, Montgomery.
Minority (4 R). Congressmen Dickinson, Powell, Treen, Holt.

SUBCOMMITTEE NO. 3
Charles E. Bennett, Chairman
Majority (6 D). Congressmen Bennett, Randall, White, Mollohan, Jones, Schroeder.
Minority (4 R). Congressmen Bob Wilson, Spence, Armstrong, Robert Daniel.

SUBCOMMITTEE NO. 4
Samuel S. Stratton, Chairman
Majority (6 D). Congressmen Stratton, Leggett, Nichols, Aspin, Dellums, Davis.
Minority (4 R). Congressmen Hunt, Young, Powell, Mitchell.

SUBCOMMITTEE NO. 5
Otis G. Pike, Chairman
Majority (6 D). Congressmen Pike, Bennett, Stratton, Charles Wilson, White, Brinkley.
Minority (4 R). Congressmen King, Whitehurst, O'Brien, Beard.

ARMED SERVICES INVESTIGATING
F. Edward Hebert, Chairman
Majority (6 D). Congressmen Hébert, Stratton, Pike, Randall, Mollohan, Dan Daniel.
Minority (4 R). Congressmen Arends, Gubser, Dickinson, Hunt.

HUMAN RELATIONS
Floyd V. Hicks, Chairman
Majority (6 D). Congressmen Hicks, Ichord, Mollohan, Dan Daniel, Runnels, Dellums.
Minority (4 R). Congressmen Hunt, Young, O'Brien, Holt.

INTELLIGENCE
Lucien N. Nedzi, Chairman
Majority (4 D). Congressmen Nedzi, Hebert, Melvin Price, Fisher.
Minority (3 R). Bray, Arends, Bob Wilson.

Committee on Banking and Currency
Wright Patman, Chairman
Democratic Majority (24 D). Congressmen Patman (Tex. 1), Barrett (Pa. 1), Sullivan (Mo. 3), Reuss (Wis. 5), Ashley (Ohio 9), Moorhead (Pa. 14), Stephens (Ga. 10), St. Germain (R.I. 1), Gonzalez (Tex. 20), Minish (N.J. 11), Hanna (Calif. 34), Gettys (S.C. 5), Annunzio (Ill. 11), Rees (Calif. 26), Hanlet (N.Y. 32), Brasco (N.Y. 11), Koch (N.Y. 18), Cotter (Conn. 1), Mitchell (Md. 7), Fauntroy (Delegate, D.C.), Young (Ga. 5), Moakley (Mass. 9), Stark (Calif. 8), Boggs (La. 2).
Republican Minority (16 R). Congressmen Widnall (N.J. 7), Johnson (Pa. 23), Stanton (Ohio 11), Blackburn (Ga. 4), Borwn (Mich. 3), Williams (Pa. 7), Wylie (Ohio 15), Heckler (Mass. 10), Crane (Ill. 12), Rousselot (Calif. 24), McKinney (Conn. 4), Frenzel (Minn. 3), Roncallo (N.Y. 3), Conlan (Ariz. 4), Burgener (Calif. 42), Rinaldo (N.J. 12).

Subcommittees

BANK SUPERVISION AND INSURANCE
Fernand J. St. Germain, Chairman
Majority (9 D). Congressmen St. Germain, Annunzio, Barrett, Hanley, Brasco, Cotter, Moakley, Ashley, Moorhead.
Minority (6 R). Congressmen Rousselot, Johnson, Wylie, Williams, Roncallo, Rinaldo.

CONSUMER AFFAIRS
Leonor K. Sullivan, Chairwomen
Majority (9 D). Congressmen Sullivan, Fauntroy (Delegate, D.C.), Mitchell, Barrett, Gonzalez, Young, Stark, Moakley, Koch.
Minority (6 R). Congressmen, Wylie, Heckler, McKinney, Rinaldo, Roncallo, Burgener.

DOMESTIC FINANCE
Wright Patman, Chairman.
Majority (9 D). Congressmen Patman, Annunzio, Minish, Gettys, Rees, Fauntroy (Delegate, D.C.), Stark, Ashley, Stephens.
Minority (6 R). Congressmen Crane, Widnall, Blackburn, Frenzel, Conlan, Rinaldo.

HOUSING
William A. Barrett, Chairman
Majority (9 D). Congressmen Barrett, Sullivan, Ashley, Moorhead, Stephens, St. Germain, Gonzalez, Reuss, Hanna.
Minority (6 R). Congressmen Windall, Brown, Stanton, Blackburn, Heckler, Rousselot.

INTERNATIONAL FINANCE
Henry B. Gonzalez, Chairman
Majority (9 D). Congressmen Gonzalez, Reuss, Moorhead, Rees, Hanna, Fauntroy (Delegate, D.C.), Young, Stark, Stephens.
Minority (6 R). Congressmen Johnson, Stanton, Crane, Frenzel, Conlan, Burgener.

INTERNATIONAL TRADE
Thomas L. Ashley, Chairman
Majority (9 D). Congressmen Ashley, Rees, Mitchell, St. Germain, Hanna, Koch, Young, Moakley, Sullivan.
Minority (6 R). Congressmen Blackburn, Brown, Johnson, McKinney, Frenzel, Conlan.

SMALL BUSINESS
Robert G. Stephens, Jr., Chairman
Majority (9 D). Congressmen Stephens, Mitchell, Koch, Gonzalez, Gettys, Annunzio, Hanley, Brasco, Cotter.
Minority (6 R). Congressmen Stanton, Williams, Heckler, Rousselot, Burgener, Roncallo.

URBAN MASS TRANSPORTATION
Joseph G. Minish, Chairman

Majority (9 D). Congressmen Minish, Gettys, Hanley, Brasco, Koch, Cotter, Young, Moakley, Stark.

Minority (6 R). Congressmen Brown, Widnall, Williams, Wylie, Crane, McKinney.

Committee on District of Columbia

Charles C. Diggs, Chairman

Democratic Majority (14 D). Congressmen Diggs (Mich. 13), Fraser (Minn. 5), Stuckey (Ga. 8), Dellums (Calif. 7), Rees (Calif. 26), Adams (Wash. 7), Fauntroy (Delegate, D.C.), Howard (N.J. 3), Mann (S.C. 4), Mazzoli (Ky. 3), Aspin (Wis. 1), Rangel (N.Y. 19), Breckinridge (Ky. 6), Stark (Calif. 8).

Republican Minority (11 R). Congressmen Nelsen (Minn. 2), Harsha (Ohio 6), Broyhill (Va. 10), Gude (Md. 8), Smith (N.Y. 36), Landgrebe (Ind. 2), McKinney (Conn. 4), Symms (Idaho 1), Ketchum (Calif. 26), Taylor (Mo. 7), Shuster (Pa. 9).

Subcommittees

BUSINESS, COMMERCE AND TAXATION
W. S. (Bill) Stuckey, Jr., Chairman

Majority (5 D). Congressmen Stuckey, Mann, Aspin, Rangel, Stark.
Minority (4 R). Congressmen Harsha, Broyhill, Gude, Taylor.

EDUCATION
Ronald V. Dellums, Chairman

Majority (4 D). Congressmen Dellums, Howard, Breckinridge, Stark.
Minority (3 R). Congressmen McKinney, Landgrebe, Taylor.

GOVERNMENT OPERATIONS
Brock Adams, Chairman

Majority (5 D). Congressmen Adams, Fraser, Fauntroy (Delegate, D.C.), Howard, Breckinridge.
Minority (3 R). Congressmen Landgrebe, Broyhill, Symms.

JUDICIARY
Walter E. Fauntroy, Chairman

Majority (5 D). Congressmen Fauntroy (Delegate, D.C.), Rees, Mann, Rangel, Breckinridge.
Minority (4 R). Congressmen Smith, Harsha, Ketchum, Shuster.

LABOR, SOCIAL SERVICES AND THE INTERNATIONAL COMMUNITY
Romano L. Mazzoli, Chairman

Majority (5 D). Congressmen Mazzoli, Fraser, Stuckey, Rangle, Stark.
Minority (3 R). Congressmen Gude, Smith, Symms.

REVENUE AND FINANCIAL AFFAIRS
Thomas M. Rees, Chairman

Majority (6 D). Congressmen Rees, Adams, Dellums, Fauntroy (Delegate, D.C.), Mazzoli, Aspin.
Minority (4 R). Congressmen Broyhill, McKinney, Ketchum, Shuster.

Committee on Education and Labor

Carl D. Perkins, Chairman

Democratic Majority (22 D). Congressmen Perkins (Ky. 7), Thompson (N.J. 4), Dent (Pa. 21), Daniels (N.J. 14), Brademas (Ind. 3), O'Hara (Mich. 12), Hawkins (Calif. 21), Ford (Mich. 15), Mink (Hawaii 2), Meeds (Wash. 2), Burton (Calif. 5), Gaydos (Pa. 20), Clay (Mo. 1), Chisholm (N.Y. 12), Biaggi (N.Y. 10), Grasso (Conn. 6), Mazzoli (Ky. 3), Badillo (N.Y. 21), Andrews (N.C. 4), Lehman (Fla. 13), Benitez (Delegate, P.R.), one vacancy.

Republican Minority (16 R). Congressmen Quie (Minn. 1), Ashbrook (Ohio 17), Bell (Calif. 28), Erlenborn (Ill. 14), Dellenback (Ore. 4), Esch (Mich. 2), Eshleman (Pa. 16), Steiger (Wis. 6), Landgrebe (Ind. 2), Hansen (Idaho 2), Forsythe (N.J. 6), Kemp (N.Y. 38), Peyser (N.Y. 23), Towell (Nev. AL), Sarasin (Conn. 5), Huber (Mich. 18).

Subcommittees

SUBCOMMITTEE NO. 1 (GENERAL SUBCOMMITTEE ON EDUCATION)
Carl D. Perkins, Chairman

Majority (11 D). Congressmen Perkins, Meeds, Ford, Hawkins, Mink, Chisholm, Biaggi, Mazzoli, Badillo, Lehman, Andrews.
Minority (6 R). Congressmen Bell, Ashbrook, Forsythe, Peyser, Steiger, Towell.
SUBCOMMITTEE NO. 2 (SPECIAL SUBCOMMITTEE ON LABOR)
Frank Thompson, Jr., Chairman
Majority (5 D). Congressmen Thompson, Clay, Brademas, O'Hara, Ford.
Minority (3 R). Congressmen Ashbrook, Dellenback, Esch.
SUBCOMMITTEE NO. 3 (GENERAL SUBCOMMITTEE ON LABOR)
John H. Dent, Chairman
Majority (8 D). Congressmen Dent, Burton, Clay, Gaydos, Biaggi, Mazzoli, Daniels, Benitez (Delegate, P.R.).
Minority (5 R). Congressmen Erlenborn, Hansen, Kemp, Sarasin, Huber.
SUBCOMMITTEE NO. 4 (Select Subcommittee on Labor)
Dominick V. Daniels, Chairman
Majority (8 D). Congressmen Daniels, Gaydos, Meeds, Burton, Grasso, Dent, O'Hara, Badillo.
Minority (5 R). Congressmen Esch, Steiger, Forsythe, Peyser, Sarasin.
SUBCOMMITTEE NO. 5 (SELECT COMMITTEE ON EDUCATION)
John Brademas, Chairman
Majority (8 D). Congressmen Brademas, Mink, Meeds, Chisholm, Grasso, Mazzoli, Badillo, Lehman.
Minority (5 R). Congressmen Eshleman, Landgrebe, Hansen, Peyser, Sarasin.
SUBCOMMITTEE NO. 6 (SPECIAL SUBCOMMITTEE ON EDUCATION)
James G. O'Hara, Chairman
Majority (8 D). Congressmen O'Hara, Biaggi, Burton, Brademas, Gaydos, Andrews, Lehman, Benitez (Delegate, P.R.).
Minority (5 R). Congressmen Dellenback, Erlenborn, Esch, Kemp, Huber.
SUBCOMMITTEE NO. 7 (SUBCOMMITTEE ON EQUAL OPPORTUNITIES)
Augustus F. Hawkins, Chairman
Majority (5 D). Congressmen Hawkins, Chisholm, Mink, Clay, Benitez (Delegate, P.R.).
Minority (3 R). Congressmen Steiger, Bell, Eshleman.
SUBCOMMITTEE NO. 8 (SUBCOMMITTEE ON AGRICULTURAL LABOR)
William D. Ford, Chairman
Majority (5 D). Congressmen Ford, Grasso, Thompson, Hawkins, Lehman.
Minority (3 R). Congressmen Landgrebe, Towell, Steiger.

Committee on Foreign Affairs

Thomas E. Morgan, Chairman

The chairman and ranking minority member are ex officio members of all standing subcommittees.
Democratic Majority (22 D). Congressmen Morgan (Pa. 22), Zablocki (Wis. 4), Hays (Ohio 18), Fountain (N.C. 2), Fascell (Fla. 15), Diggs (Mich. 13), Nix (Pa. 2), Fraser (Minn. 5), Rosenthal (N.Y. 8), Culver (Iowa 2), Hamilton (Ind. 9), Kazen (Tex. 23), Wolff (N.Y. 6), Bingham (N.Y. 22), Yatron (Pa. 6), Taylor (N.C. 11), Davis (Ga. 7), Reid (N.Y. 24), Harrington (Mass. 6), Ryan (Calif. 11), Wilson (Tex. 2), Riegle (Mich. 7).
Republican Minority (18 R). Congressmen Mailliard (Calif. 6), Frelinghuysen (N.J. 5), Broomfield (Mich. 19), Gross (Iowa 3), Derwinski (Ill. 4), Thomson (Wis. 3), Findley (Ill. 20), Buchanan (Ala. 6), Burke (Fla. 12), Vander Jagt (Mich. 9), Steele (Conn. 2), du Pont (Del. AL), Whalen (Ohio 3), Mathias (Calif. 18), Biester (Pa. 8), Winn (Kans. 3), Gilman, (N.Y. 26), Guyer (Ohio 3).

Subcommittees

AFRICA

Charles C. Diggs, Jr., Chairman
Majority (5 D). Congressmen Diggs, Nix, Culver, Yatron, Harrington.
Minority (4 R). Congressmen Derwinski, Vander Jagt, Biester, Winn.

ASIAN AND PACIFIC AFFAIRS

Robert N. C. Nix, Chairman

Majority (7 D). Congressmen Nix, Hamilton, Wolff, Davis, Taylor, Ryan, Riegle.
Minority (5 R). Congressmen Broomfield, Thomson, Burke, du Pont, Guyer.

EUROPE
Benjamin S. Rosenthal, Chairman
Majority (7 D). Congressmen Rosenthal, Hays, Hamilton, Yatron, Taylor, Reid, Riegle.
Minority (5 R). Congressmen Frelinghuysen, Findley, Burke, Buchanan, Vander Jagt.

FOREIGN ECONOMIC POLICY
John C. Culver, Chairman
Majority (7 D). Congressmen Culver, Zablocki, Yatron, Wolff, Davis, Harrington, Ryan.
Minority (5 R). Congressmen Burke, Steele, Whalen, Vander Jagt, Gilman.

INTER-AMERICAN AFFAIRS
Dante B. Fascell, Chairman
Majority (5 D), Congressmen Fascell, Kazen, Rosenthal, Taylor, Harrington.
Minority (4 R). Congressmen Steele, Gross, Frelinghuysen, Whalen.

INTERNAL ORGANIZATIONS AND MOVEMENTS
Donald M. Fraser, Chairman
Majority (6 D). Congressmen Fraser, Fascell, Fountain, Rosenthal, Taylor, Harrington.
Minority (5 R). Congressmen Gross, Derwinski, Findley, Mathias, Winn.

NATIONAL SECURITY POLICY AND SCIENTIFIC DEVELOPMENTS
Clement J. Zablocki, Chairman
Majority (7 D). Congressmen Zablocki, Hays, Fountain, Fraser, Bingham, Davis, Wilson.
Minority (5 R). Congressmen Findley, Broomfield, Thomson, du Pont, Biester.

NEAR EAST AND SOUTH ASIA
Lee H. Hamilton, Chairman
Majority (7 D). Congressmen Hamilton, Fountain, Wolff, Bingham, Reid, Kazen, Wilson.
Minority (5 R). Congressmen Buchanan, Gross, Broomfield, Mathias, Gilman.

STATE DEPARTMENT ORGANIZATION AND FOREIGN OPERATIONS
Wayne L. Hays, Chairman
Majority (7 D). Congressmen Hays, Zablocki, Fraser, Fascell, Kazen, Culver, Diggs.
Minority (5 R). Congressmen Thomson, Buchanan, Frelinghuysen, Derwinski, Guyer.

SPECIAL SUBCOMMITTEE FOR REVIEW OF FOREIGN AID PROGRAMS
Thomas E. Morgan, Chairman
Majority (5 D). Congressmen Morgan, Zablocki, Hays, Fountain, Fascell.
Minority (4 R). Congressmen Mailliard, Frelinghuysen, Broomfield, Gross.

Committee on Government Operations

Chet Holifield, Chairman
The Chairman and ranking minority member are ex officio members of all subcommittees on which they do not hold a regular assignment.
Democratic Majority (23 D). Congressmen Holifield (Calif. 19), Brooks (Tex. 9), Fountain (N.C. 2), Jones (Ala. 5), Moss (Calif. 3), Fascell (Fla. 15), Reuss (Wis. 5), Macdonald (Mass. 7), Moorhead (Pa. 14), Randall (Mo. 4), Rosenthal (N.Y. 8), Wright (Tex. 12), St. Germain (R.I. 1), Culver (Iowa 2), Hicks (Wash. 6), Fuqua (Fla. 2), Conyers (Mich. 1), Alexander (Ark. 1), Abzug (N.Y. 20), Donohue (Mass. 3), Stanton (Ohio 20), Ryan (Calif. 11), Collins (Ill. 7).
Republican Minority (18 R). Congressmen Horton (N.Y. 34), Erlenborn (Ill. 14), Wydler (N.Y. 5), Brown (Ohio 7), Vander Jagt (Mich. 9), Gude (Md. 8), McCloskey (Calif. 17), Buchanan (Ala. 6), Steiger (Ariz. 3), Brown (Mich. 3), Thone (Neb. 1), Mallary (Vt. AL), Parris (Va. 8), Regula (Ohio 16), Hinshaw (Calif. 39), Steelman (Tex. 5), Pritchard (Wash. 1), Hanrahan (Ill. 3).

Subcommittees

CONSERVATION AND NATURAL RESOURCES
Henry S. Reuss, Chairman
Majority (7 D). Congressmen Reuss, Moss, Fascell, Hicks, Ryan, Fountain, Brooks.
Minority (5 R). Congressmen Vander Jagt, Gude, McCloskey, Steelman, Pritchard.

FOREIGN OPERATIONS AND GOVERNMENT INFORMATION
William S. Moorhead, Chairman

Majority (7 D). Congressmen Moorhead, Moss, Macdonald, Wright, Alexander, Abzug, Stanton.
Minority (5 R). Congressmen Erlenborn, McCloskey, Gude, Thone, Regula.

GOVERNMENT ACTIVITIES
Jack Brooks, Chairman

Majority (6 D). Congressmen Brooks, Jones, Culver, Donohue, Stanton, Collins.
Minority (4 R). Congressmen Buchanan, Hanrahan, Parris, Hinshaw.

INTERGOVERNMENTAL RELATIONS
L. H. Fountain, Chairman

Majority (7 D). Congressmen Fountain, Rosenthal, Culver, Fuqua, Alexander, Macdonald, Stanton.
Minority (5 R). Congressmen Brown (Ohio), Vander Jagt, Buchanan, Brown (Mich.), Steelman.

LEGAL AND MONETARY AFFAIRS
William J. Randall, Chairman

Majority (6 D). Congressmen Randall, Fascell, St. Germain, Conyers, Ryan, Collins.
Minority (4 R). Congressmen Steiger, Brown (Mich.), Parris, Hinshaw.

LEGISLATION AND MILITARY OPERATIONS
Chet Holifield, Chairman

Majority (7 D), Congressmen Holifield, Rosenthal, Wright, St. Germain, Fuqua, Moorhead, Jones.
Minority (5 R). Congressmen Horton, Erlenborn, Wydler, Brown (Ohio), Mallary.

SPECIAL STUDIES
Floyd V. Hicks, Chairman

Majority (6 D). Congressmen Hicks, Randall, Abzug, Reuss, Conyers, Donohue.
Minority (4 R). Congressmen Wydler, Regula, Pritchard.

Committee on House Administration

Wayne L. Hays, Chairman

Domocratic Majority (15 D). Congressmen Hays (Ohio 18), Thompson (N.J. 4), Dent (Pa. 21), Nedzi (Mich. 14), Brademas (Ind. 3), Gray (Ill. 24), Hawkins (Calif. 21), Gettys (S.C. 5), Podell (N.Y. 13), Annunzio (Ill. 11), Gaydos (Pa. 20), Jones (Tenn. 7), Mollohan (W. Va. 1), Koch (N.Y. 18), Mathis (Ga. 2).
Republican Minority (11 R). Congressmen Dickinson (Ala. 2), Devine (Ohio 12), Cleveland (N.H. 2), Harvey (Mich 8), Hansen (Idaho 2), Crane (Ill. 12), Ware (Pa. 5), Frenzel (Minn. 3), Wiggins (Calif. 25), Hastings (N.Y. 39), Froehlich (Wis. 8).

Subcommittees

ACCOUNTS
Frank Thompson, Chairman

Majority (7 D). Congressmen Thompson, Dent, Hawkins, Gettys, Podell, Annunzio, Gaydos.
Minority (4 R). Congressmen Devine, Cleveland, Crane, Hastings.

CONTRACTS
Tom S. Gettys, Chairman

Majority (2 D). Congressmen Gettys, Koch.
Minority (1 R). Congressmen Cleveland.

ELECTIONS
John H. Dent, Chairman

Majority (5 D). Congressmen Dent, Gray, Jones, Mollohan, Mathis.
Minority (3 R). Congressmen Harvey, Ware, Frenzel.

ELECTRICAL AND MECHANICAL OFFICE EQUIPMENT
Augustus F. Hawkins, Chairman

Majority (7 D). Congressmen Hawkins, Nedzi, Podell, Brademas, Gray, Gaydos, Mollohan.
Minority (4 R). Congressmen Harvey, Crane, Hastings, Froehlich.

LIBRARY AND MEMORIALS
Lucien N. Nedzi, Chairman

Majority (6 D). Congressmen Nedzi, Gray, Brademas, Gaydos, Thompson, Gettys.
Minority (3 R). Congressmen Harvey, Frenzel, Froehlich.

PERSONNEL
Frank Annunzio, Chairman
Majority (2 D). Congressmen Annunzio, Gettys.
Minority (1 R). Congressman Crane.

POLICE
Kenneth J. Gray, Chairman
Majority (5 D). Congressmen Gray, Hawkins, Gettys, Annunzio, Mathis.
Minority (3 R). Congressmen Devine, Ware, Wiggins.

PRINTING
John Brademas, Chairman
Majority (5 D). Congressmen Brademas, Gettys, Gaydos, Jones, Koch.
Minority (3 R). Cleveland, Hansen, Wiggins.

Committee on Interior and Insular Affairs

James A. Haley, Chairman
The chairman and ranking minority member are ex officio members of all subcommittees
Democratic Majority (23 D). Congressmen Haley (Fla. 8), Taylor (N.C. 11), Johnson (Calif. 2), Udall (Ariz. 2), Burton (Calif. 5), Foley (Wash. 5), Kastenmeier (Wis. 2), O'Hara (Mich. 12), Mink (Hawaii 2), Meeds (Wash. 2), Kazen (Tex. 23), Stephens (Ga. 10), Vigorito (Pa. 24), Melcher (Mont. 2), Roncalio (Wyo. AL), Bingham (N.Y. 22), Seiberling (Ohio 14), Runnels (N. Mex. 2), Burke (Calif. 37), Antonio Borja Won Pat (Delegate, Guam), Owens (Utah 2), de Lugo (Delegate, V.I.), Jones (Okla. 1).
Republican Minority (19 R), Congressmen Saylor (Pa. 12), Hosmer (Calif. 32), Skubitz (Kans. 5), Steiger (Ariz. 3), Clausen (Calif. 1), Ruppe (Mich. 11), Camp (Okla. 6), Lujan (N. Mex. 1), Dellenback (Ore. 4), Sebelius (Kans. 1), Regula (Ohio 16), Steelman (Tex. 5), Maraziti (N.J. 13), Towell (Nev. AL), Martin (N.C. 9), Ketchum (Calif. 36), Cronin (Mass. 5), Young (Alas.), Bauman (Md. 1).

Subcommittees

SUBCOMMITTEE NO. 1 (NATIONAL PARKS AND RECREATION)
Roy A. Taylor, Chairman
Majority (12 D). Congressmen Taylor, Johnson, Kastenmeier, O'Hara, Mink, Meeds, Kazen, Stephens, Roncalio, Bingham, Seberling, Antonio Borja Won Pat (Delegate, Guam), Owens, de Lugo (Delegate, V.I.).
Minority (11 R). Congressmen Skubitz, Saylor, Clausen, Ruppe, Camp, Sebelius, Regula, Steelman, Maraziti, Martin, Ketchum, Cronin, Bauman.

SUBCOMMITTEE NO. 2 (WATER AND POWER RESOURCES)
Harold T. Johnson, Chairman
Majority (10 D). Congressmen Johnson, Udall, Foley, Meeds, Kazen, Stephens, Roncalio, Runnels, Burke, Jones.
Minority (9 R). Congressmen Hosmer, Saylor, Clausen, Camp, Lujan, Dellenback, Steelman, Towell, Ketchum.

SUBCOMMITTEE NO. 3 (ENVIRONMENT)
Morris K. Udall, Chairman
Majority (13 D). Congressmen Udall, Foley, Kastenmeier, O'Hara, Vigorito, Melcher, Roncalio, Bingham, Seiberling, Burke, Owens, de Lugo (Delegate, V.I.), Jones.
Minority (12 R). Congressmen Ruppe, Saylor, Hosmer, Steiger, Dellenback, Sebelius, Steelman, Maraziti, Towell, Martin, Cronin, Bauman.

SUBCOMMITTEE NO. 4 (TERRITORIAL AND INSULAR AFFAIRS)
Phillip Burton, Chairman
Majority (12 D). Congressmen Burton, Taylor, Foley, Kastenmeier, Mink, Meeds, Stephens, Vigorito, Bingham, Burke, Antonio Borja Won Pat (Delegate, Guam), de Lugo (Delegate, V.I.).
Minority (11 R). Congressmen Clausen, Saylor, Hosmer, Skubitz, Ruppe, Lujan, Sebelius, Regula, Maraxiti, Martin, Bauman.

SUBCOMMITTEE NO. 5 (MINES AND MINING)
Patsy T. Mink, Chairman

Majority (13 D). Congressmen Mink, Udall, Burton, Foley, Kastenmeier, O'Hara, Kazen, Vigorito, Melcher, Seiberling, Runnels, Owens, Jones.
Minority (12 R). Congressmen Camp, Saylor, Hosmer, Skubitz, Steiger, Ruppe, Steelman, Maraziti, Martin, Ketchum, Cronin, Young, Bauman.

Subcommittee No. 6 (Indian Affairs)
Lloyd Meeds, Chairman

Majority (7 D). Congressmen Meeds, Yaylor, Udall, Burton, Runnels, Antonio Borja Won Pat (Delegate, Guam), Jones.
Minority (7 R). Congressmen Lujan, Saylor, Steiger, Camp, Maraziti, Towell, Young.

SUBCOMMITTEE NO. 7 (PUBLIC LANDS)
John Melcher, Chairman

Majority (7 D). Congressmen Melcher, Johnson, Udall, Burton, Runnels, Antonio Borja Won Pat (Delegate, Guam), Owens.
Minority (7 R). Congressmen Steiger, Saylor, Clausen, Dellenback, Regula, Towell, Young.

Committee on Internal Security
Richard H. Ichord, Chairman

Democratic Majority (5 D). Congressmen Ichord (Mo. 6), Pepper (Fla. 14), Preyer (N.C. 6), Drinan (Mass. 4), Davis (S.C. 1).
Republican Minority (4 R). Congressmen Ashbrook (Ohio 17), Zion (Ind. 8), Burke (Fla. 12), Guyer (Ohio 4).

(No Subcommittees)

Committee on Interstate and Foreign Commerce
Harley O. Staggers, Chairman

The Chairman and ranking minority member are ex officio members, with vote, of all subcommittees.
Democratic Majority (24 D). Congressmen Staggers (W. Va. 2), Macdonald (Mass. 7), Jarman (Okla. 5), Moss (Calif. 3), Dingell (Mich. 16), Rogers (Fla. 11), Van Deerling (Calif. 41), Pickle (Tex. 10), Rooney (Pa. 15), Murphy (N.Y. 17), Satterfield (Va. 3), Adams (Wash. 7), Stuckey (Ga. 8), Kyros (Me. 1), Eckhardt (Tex. 8), Preyer (N.C. 6), Podell (N.Y. 13), Helstoski (N.J. 9), Symington (Mo. 2), Carney (Ohio 19), Metcalfe (Ill. 1), Byron (Md. 6), Roy (Kans. 2), Breckinridge (Ky. 6).
Republican Minority (19 R). Congressmen Devine (Ohio 12), Nelsen (Minn. 2), Broyhill (N.C. 10), Harvey (Mich. 8), Carter (Ky. 5), Brown (Ohio 7), Kuykendall Tenn. 8), Skubitz (Kans. 5), Hastings (N.Y. 39), Collins (Tex. 3), Frey (Fla. 9), Ware (Pa. 5), McCollister (Neb. 2), Shoup (Mont. 1), Goldwater (Calif. 27), Lent (N.Y. 4), Heinz (Pa. 18), Hudnut (Ind. 11), Young, (Ill. 10).

Subcommittees
COMMERCE AND FINANCE
John E. Moss, Chairman

Majority (5 D). Congressmen Moss, Stuckey, Eckhardt, Helstoski, Breckinridge.
Minority (4 R). Congressmen Broyhill, Ware, McCollister, Young.

COMMUNICATIONS AND POWER
Torbert H. Macdonald, Chairman

Majority (5 D). Congressmen Macdonald, Van Deerlin, Rooney, Murphy, Byron.
Minority (4 R), Congressmen Brown, Collins, Frey, Goldwater.

PUBLIC HEALTH AND ENVIRONMENT
Paul G. Rogers, Chairman

Majority (6 D), Congressmen Rogers, Satterfield, Kyros, Preyer, Symington, Roy.
Minority (5 R). Congressmen Nelsen, Carter, Hastings, Heinz, Hudnut.

TRANSPORTATION AND AERONAUTICS
John Jarman, Chairman

Majority (5 D). Congressmen Jarman, Dingell, Adams, Podell, Metcalfe.
Minority (4 R). Congressmen Harvey, Kuykendall, Skubitz, Shoup.

SPECIAL SUBCOMMITTEE ON INVESTIGATIONS
Harley O. Staggers, Chairman
Majority (3 D). Congressmen Staggers, Pickle, Carney.
Minority (2 R). Congressmen Devine, Lent.

Committee on the Judiciary

Peter W. Rodino, Jr., Chairman
Democratic Majority (21 D). Congressmen Rodino (N.J. 10), Donohue (Mass. 3), Brooks (Tex. 9), Kastenmeier (Wis. 2), Edwards (Calif. 9), Hungate (Mo. 9), Conyers (Mich. 1), Eilberg (Pa. 4), Waldie (Calif. 14), Flowers (Ala. 7), Mann (S.C. 4), Sarbanes (Md. 3), Seiberling (Ohio 14), Danielson (Calif. 29), Drinan (Mass. 4), Rangel (N.Y. 19), Jordan (Tex. 18), Thornton (Ark. 4), Holtzman (N.Y. 16), Owens (Utah 2), Mazvinsky (Iowa 1).
Republican Minority (17 R). Congressmen Hutchinson (Mich. 4), McClory (Ill. 13), Smith (N.Y. 36), Sandman (N.J. 2), Railsback (Ill. 19), Wiggins (Calif. 25), Dennis (Ind. 10), Fish (N.Y. 25), Mayne (Iowa 6), Hogan (Md. 5), Keating (Ohio 1), Butler (Va. 6), Cohen (Me. 2), Lott (Miss. 5), Moorhead (Calif. 20), one vacancy.

Subcommittees

SUBCOMMITTEE NO. 1 (IMMIGRATION AND NATIONALITY)
Joshua Eilberg, Chairman
Majority (5 D). Congressmen Eilberg, Waldie, Flowers, Seiberling, Holtzman.
Minority (4 R). Congressmen Keating, Railsback, Wiggins, Dennis.
SUBCOMMITTEE NO. 2 (CLAIMS)
Harold D. Donohue, Chairman
Majority (5 D). Congressmen Donohue, Mann, Danielson, Jordan, Thornton.
Minority (4 R). Congressmen Butler, Fish, Moorhead, one vacancy.
SUBCOMMITTEE NO. 3 (PATENTS, TRADEMARKS, COPYRIGHTS)
Robert W. Kastenmeier, Chairman
Majority (5 D). Congressmen Kastenmeier, Danielson, Drinan, Owens, Mezvinsky.
Minority (4 R). Congressmen Railsback, Smith, Sandman, Cohen.
SUBCOMMITTEE NO. 4 (BANKRUPTCY AND CIVIL RIGHTS OVERSIGHT)
Don Edwards, Chairman
Majority (5 D). Congressmen Edwards, Waldie, Sarbanes, Drinan, Rangel.
Minority (4 R). Congressmen Wiggins, McClory, Butler, Lott.
SUBCOMMITTEE NO. 5 (ANTITRUST MATTERS)
Peter W. Rodino, Jr., Chairman
Majority (6 D). Congressmen Rodino, Brooks, Flowers, Seiberling, Jordan, Mezvinsky.
Minority (4 R). Congressmen Hutchinson, McClory, Sandman, Dennis.
SUBCOMMITTEE NO. 6 (REVISION OF THE LAWS)
John Conyers, Jr., Chairman
Majority (5 D). Congressmen Conyers, Sarbanes, Rangel, Thornton, Owens.
Minority (4 R). Congressmen Fish, Keating, Cohen, Froehlich.
SPECIAL SUBCOMMITTEE ON REFORM OF FEDERAL CRIMINAL LAWS
William L. Hungate, Chairman
Majority (5 D). Congressmen Hungate, Kastenmeier, Edwards, Mann, Holtzman.
Minority (4 R). Congressmen Smith, Dennis, Mayne, Hogan.

Committee on Merchant Marine and Fisheries

Leonor K. Sullivan, Chairwoman
The Chairman and ranking minority member are ex officio members of all subcommittees.
Democratic Majority (22 D). Congressmen Sullivan (Mo. 3), Clark (Pa. 25), Ashley (Ohio 9), Dingell (Mich. 16), Downing (Va. 1), Rogers (Fla. 11), Stubblefield (Ky. 1), Murphy (N.Y. 17), Jones (N.C. 1), Leggett (Calif. 4), Biaggi (N.Y. 10), Anderson (Calif. 35), de la Garza (Tex. 15), Kyros (Me. 1), Metcalfe (Ill. 1), Breaux (La. 7), Rooney (Pa. 15), Eckhardt (Tex. 8), Sarbanes (Md. 3), Ginn (Ga. 1), Studds (Mass. 12), Bowen (Miss. 2).

Republican Minority (17 R). Congressmen Grover (N.Y. 2), Mailliard (Calif. 6), Mosher (Ohio 13), Ruppe (Mich. 11), Goodling (Pa. 19), McCloskey (Calif. 17), Snyder (Ky. 4), Steele (Conn. 2), Forsythe (N.J. 6), du Pont (Del. AL), Cohen (Me. 2), Lott (Miss. 5), Treen (La. 3), Pritchard (Wash. 1), Young (S.C. 6), Young (Alaska), Bauman (Md. 1).

Subcommittees

COAST GUARD AND NAVIGATION
John M. Murphy, Chairman

Majority (11 D). Congressmen Murphy, Clark, Jones, Biaggi, Bowen, Breaux, Sarbanes, Rogers, de la Garza, Rooney, one vacancy.
Minority (10 R). Congressmen Ruppe, Grover, Snyder, Steele, Lott, Treen, Young (S.C.), Young (Alaska), Bauman.

FISHERIES AND WILDLIFE CONSERVATION AND THE ENVIRONMENT
John D. Dingell, Chairman

Majority (13 D). Congressmen Dingell, Rogers, Leggett, Biaggi, Anderson, de la Garza, Kyros, Metcalfe, Breaux, Rooney, Eckhardt, Studds, Bowen.
Minority (9 R). Congressmen Goodling, McCloskey, Mailliard, Ruppe, Forsythe, Steele, Mills, du Pont, Cohen, Pritchard.

MERCHANT MARINE
Frank M. Clark, Chairman

Majority (14 D). Congressmen Clark, Ashley, Downing, Stubblefield, Murphy, Dingell, Rooney, Sarbanes, Ginn, Kyros, Eckhardt, Studds, Jones. Anderson.
Minority (11 R). Congressmen Mailliard, Mosher, Ruppe, McCloskey, du Pont, Snyder, Lott, Treen, Cohen, Pritchard.

OCEANOGRAPHY
Thomas N. Downing, Chairman

Majority (14 D). Congressmen Downing, Rogers, Ashley, Jones, Leggett, Anderson, de la Garza, Ginn, Biaggi, Kyros, Metcalfe, Breaux, Eckhardt, Studds.
Minority (10 R). Congressmen Mosher, Mailliard, Steele, Forsythe, du Pont, McCloskey, Lott, Treen, Pritchard, Bauman.

PANAMA CANAL
Robert L. Leggett, Chairman

Majority (9 D). Congressmen Leggett, Murphy, Clark, Stubblefield, Metcalfe, Sarbanes, Ginn, Bowen, one vacancy.
Minority (7 R). Congressmen Snyder, Mosher, Forsythe, Mailliard, Young (S.C.), Young (Alaska), Bauman.

Committee on Post Office and Civil Service

Thaddeus J. Dulski, Chairman

The chairman and ranking minority member are ex officio voting members of all subcommittees on which they do not hold a regular assignment.

Democratic Majority (15 D). Congressmen Dulski (N.Y. 37), Henderson (N.C. 3), Udall (Ariz. 2), Daniels (N.J. 14), Nix (Pa. 2), Hanley (N.Y. 32), Wilson (Calif. 31), Waldie (Calif. 14), White (Tex. 16), Ford (Mich. 15), Brasco (N.Y. 11), Clay (Mo. 1), Schroeder (Colo. 1), Moakley (Mass. 9), Lehman (Fla. 13).
Republican Minority (10 R). Congressmen Gross (Iowa 3), Derwinski (Ill. 4), Johnson (Pa. 23), Hogan (Md. 5), Rousselot (Calif. 24), Hillis (Ind. 5), Powell (Ohio 8), Mallary (Vt. AL), Hinshaw (Calif. 39), Bafalis (Fla. 10).

Subcommittees

CENSUS AND STATISTICS
Richard C. White, Chairman

Majority (5 D). Congressmen White, Hanley, Udall, Lehman, Wilson.
Minority (3 R). Congressmen Rousselot, Hinshaw, Bafalis.

INVESTIGATIONS
Thaddeus J. Dulski, Chairman

Majority (5 D). Congressmen Dulski, Daniels, Schroeder, Moakley, Henderson.
Minority (2 R). Congressmen Powell, Hinshaw.

MANPOWER AND CIVIL SERVICE
David N. Henderson, Chairman
Majority (5 D). Congressmen Henderson, Ford, Clay, Leyman, Brasco.
Minority (2 R). Congressmen Derwinski, Mallary.

POSTAL FACILITIES, MAIL AND LABOR MANAGEMENT
Charles H. Wilson, Chairman
Majority (5 D). Congressmen Wilson, Nix, Waldie, Clay, Schroeder.
Minority (3 R). Congressmen Hillis, Rousselot, Powell.

POSTAL SERVICE
James N. Hanley, Chairman
Majority (5 D). Congressmen Hanley, Udall, Nix, White, Ford.
Minority (3 R). Congressmen Johnson, Derwinski, Mallary.

RETIREMENT AND EMPLOYEE BENEFITS
Jerome R. Waldie, Chairman
Majority (5 D). Congressmen Waldie, Brasco, Daniels, Wilson, Moakley.
Minority (3 R). Congressmen Hogan, Hillis, Bafalis.

Committee on Public Works

John A. Blatnik, Chairman

The chairman and ranking minority member are ex officio members, with vote, of all subcommittees.

Democratic Majority (23 D). Congressmen Blatnik (Minn. 8), Jones (Ala. 5), Kluczynski (Ill. 5), Wright (Tex. 12), Gray (Ill. 24), Clark (Pa. 25), Johnson (Calif. 2), Dorn (S.C. 3), Henderson (N.C. 3), Roberts (Tex. 4), Howard (N.J. 3), Anderson (Calif. 35), Roe (N.J. 8), Roncalio (Wyo. AL), McCormack (Wash. 4), Stanton (Ohio 20), Abzug (N.Y. 20), Breaux (La. 7), Studds (Mass. 12), Burke (Calif. 37), Milford (Tex. 24), one vacancy.

Republican Minority (16 R). Congressmen Harsha (Ohio 6), Grover (N.Y. 2), Cleveland (N.H. 2), Clausen (Calif. 1), Snyder (Ky. 4), Zion (Ind. 8), Hammerschmidt (Ark. 3), Mizell (N.C. 5), Baker (Tenn. 3), Shuster (Pa. 9), Walsh (N.Y. 33), Cochran (Miss. 4), Bafalis (Fla. 10), Abdnor (S. Dak. 2), Hanrahan (Ill. 3), Taylor (Mo. 7).

Subcommittees

ECONOMIC DEVELOPMENT
Robert E. Jones, Chairman
Majority (16 D). Congressmen Jones, Kluczynski, Clark, Johnson, Dorn, Henderson, Howard, Roe, Roncalio, Abzug, Breaux, Studds, Burke, Ginn, Milford, one vacancy.
Minority (11 R). Congressmen Hammerschmidt, Cleveland, Clausen, Mizell, Baker, Shuster, Walsh, Cochran, Bafalis, Abdnor, Taylor.

ENERGY
James J. Howard, Chairman
Majority (16 D). Congressmen Howard, Jones, Clark, Johnson, Dorn, Henderson, Roberts, Anderson, Roncalio, Abzug, Breaux, Studds, Burke, Ginn, Milford.
Minority (11 R). Congressmen Snyder, Grover, Cleveland, Zion, Mizell, Baker, Walsh, Cochran, Abdnor, Hanrahan, Taylor.

INVESTIGATIONS AND REVIEW
Jim Wright, Chairman
Majority (16 D). Congressmen Wright, Jones, Kluczynski, Gray, Clark, Henderson, Howard, Roe, Roncalio, McCormack, Stanton, Breaux, Studds, Ginn, Milford, one vacancy.
Minority (11 R). Congressmen Cleveland, Grover, Clausen, Zion, Hammerschmidt, Mizell, Shuster, Walsh, Cochran, Bafalis, Hanrahan.

PUBLIC BUILDINGS AND GROUNDS
Kenneth J. Gray, Chairman
Majority (16 D). Congressmen Gray, Jones, Kluczynski, Wright, Roberts, Anderson, Roe, Roncalio, McCormack, Stanton, Abzug, Breaux, Studds, Burke, Ginn, Milfrod.

Minority (11 R). Congressmen Grover, Snyder, Mizell, Baker, Shuster, Walsh, Cochran, Bafalis, Abdnor, Hanrahan, Taylor.

TRANSPORTATION
John C. Kluczynski, Chairman

Majority (16 D). Congressmen Kluczynski, Johnson, Wright, Gray, Clark, Dorn, Henderson, Roberts, Anderson, Roe, Roncalio, Stanton Hozug, Burke, Milford, Jones.
Minority (11 R.). Congressmen Harsha, Cleveland, Clausen, Snyder, Zion, Hammerschmidt, Mizell, Baker, Shuster, Bafalis, Hanrahan.

WATER RESOURCES
Ray Roberts, Chairman

Majority (16 D). Congressmen Roberts, Johnson, Wright, Gray, Dorn, Henderson, Howard, Anderson, Roe, McCormack, Stanton, Abzug, Breaux, Studds, Ginn, one vacancy.
Minority (11 R). Congressmen Clausen, Grover, Snyder, Zion, Hammerschmidt, Baker, Shuster, Bafalis, Abdnor, Hanrahan, Taylor.

Committee on Rules
Ray J. Madden, Chairman

Democratic Majority (10 D). Congressmen Madden (Ind. 1), Delaney (N.Y. 9), Bolling (Mo. 5), Sisk (Calif. 16), Young (Tex. 14), Pepper (Fla. 14), Matsunaga (Hawaii 1), Murphy (Ill. 2), Ling (La. 8), McSpadden (Okla. 2).
Republican Minority (5 R). Congressmen Martin (Neb. 3), Anderson (Ill. 16), Wuillen (Tenn. 1), Latta (Ohio 5), Clawson (Calif. 23).

(No Subcommittees)

Committee on Science and Aeronautics
Olin E. Teague, Chairman

The chairman and ranking minority members are ex officio members, with vote, of all subcommittees.
Democratic Majority (17 D). Congressmen Teague (Tex. 6), Hechler (W. Va. 4), Davis (Ga. 7), Downing (Va. 1), Fuqua (Fla. 2), Symington (Mo. 2), Hanna (Calif. 34), Flowers (Ala. 7), Roe (N.J. 8), Cotter (Conn. 1), McCormack (Wash. 4), Bergland (Minn. 7), Pickle (Tex. 10), Brown (Calif. 38), Milford (Tex. 24), Thornton (Ark. 4), Gunter (Fla. 5).
Republican Minority (13 R). Congressmen Mosher (Ohio 13), Bell (Calif. 28), Wydler (N.Y. 5), Winn (Kans. 3), Frey (Fla. 9), Goldwater (Calif. 27), Esch (Mich. 2), Camp (Okla. 6), Conlan (Ariz. 4), Parris (Va. 8), Cronin (Mass. 5), Martin (N.C. 9), one vacancy.

Subcommittees

AERONAUTICS AND SPACE TECHNOLOGY
Ken Hechler, Chairman

Majority (5 D). Congressmen Hechler, Davis, Cotter, Pickle, Thornton.
Minority (4 R). Congressmen Wydler, Goldwater, Conlan, Parris.

ENERGY
Mike McCormack, Chairman

Majority (10 D). Congressmen McCormack, Fuqua, Hanna, Roe, Bergland, Pickle, Brown, Milford, Thornton, Gunter.
Minority (8 R). Congressmen Goldwater, Wydler, Esch, Conlan, Parris, Cronin, Martin, one vacany.

INTERNATIONAL COOPERATION IN SCIENCE AND SPACE
Richard T. Hanna, Chairman

Majority (6 D). Congressmen Hanna, Symington, Davis, Roe, McCormack, Milford.
Minority (5 R). Congressmen Frey, Bell, Winn, Camp, one vacancy.

MANNED SPACE FLIGHT
Don Fuqua, Chairman

Majority (6 D). Congressmen Fuqua, Flowers, Roe, Cotter, Bergland, Gunter.
Minority (5 R). Congressmen Winn, Bell, Wydler, Frey, Camp.

SCIENCE, RESEARCH AND DEVELOPMENT
James W. Symington, Chairman
Majority (5 D). Congressmen Symington, Downing, Bergland, Brown, Milford.
Minority (4 R). Congressmen Esch, Winn, Goldwater, Camp.

Committee on Standards of Official Conduct

Melvin Price, Chairman
Democratic Majority (6 D). Congressmen Price (Ill. 23), Teague (Tex. 6), Hébert (La. 1), Holifield (Calif. 19), Flynt (Ga. 6), Foley (Wash. 5).
Republican Minority (6 R). Congressmen Quillen (Tenn. 1), Williams (Pa. 7), Hutchinson (Mich. 4), King (N.Y. 29), Spence (S.C. 2), Hunt (N.J. 1).

(No Subcommittees)

Committee on Veterans' Affairs

William Jennings Bryan Dorn, Chairman
The chairman and ranking minority member are ex officio members of all subcommittees.
Democratic Majority (15 D). Congressmen Dorn (S.C. 3), Teague (Tex. 6), Haley (Fla. 8), Dulski (N.Y. 37), Roberts (Tex. 4), Satterfield (Va. 3), Helstocki (N.J. 9), Edwards (Calif. 9), Montgomery (Miss. 3), Carney (Ohio 19), Danielson (Calif. 29), Grasso (Conn. 6), Wolff (N.Y. 6), Brinkley (Ga. 3), Wilson (Tex. 2).
Republican Minority (11 R). Congressmen Hammerschmidt (Ark. 3), Saylor (Pa. 12), Teague (Calif. 13), Heckler (Mass. 10), Zwach (Minn. 6), Wylie (Ohio 15), Hillis (Ind. 5), Maraziti (N.J. 13), Abdnor (S. Dak. 2), Huber (Mich. 18), Walsh (N.Y. 33).

Subcommittees

COMPENSATION AND PENSION
Olis E. Teague, Chairman
Majority (4 D). Congressmen Teague (Tex.), Roberts, Montgomery, Brinkley.
Minority (3 R). Congressmen Hammerschmidt, Saylor, Wylie.
EDUCATION AND TRAINING
Henry Helstoski, Chairman
Majority (8 D). Congressmen Helstoski, Teague (Tex.), Edwards, Danielson, Grasso, Wolff, Brinkley, Wilson.
Minority (7 R). Congressmen Heckler, Zwach, Wylie, Maraziti, Abdnor, Huber, Walsh.
HOSPITALS
David E. Satterfield III, Chairman
Majority (14 D). Congressmen Satterfield, Teague (Tex.), Haley, Dulski, Roberts, Montgomery, Edwards, Carney, Danielson, Grasso, Wolff, Helstoski, Wilson.
Minority (11 R). Congressmen Saylor, Hammerschmidt, Teague (Calif.), Heckler, Zwach, Wylie, Hillis, Maraziti, Abdnor, Huber, Walsh.
HOUSING
Charles J. Carney, Chairman
Majority (6 D). Congressmen Carney, Roberts, Satterfield, Helstoski, Edwards, Wilson.
Minority (5 R). Congressmen Hillis, Heckler, Hammerschmidt, Huber, Walsh.
INSURANCE
G. V. (Sonny) Montgomery, Chairman
Majority (6 D). Congressmen Montgomery, Grasso, Dulski, Satterfield, Carney, Danielson.
Minority (5 R). Congressmen Zwach, Saylor, Hillis, Maraziti, Abdnor.

Committee on Ways and Means

Wilbur D. Mills, Chairman
Democratic Majority (15 D). Congressmen Mills (Ark. 2), Ullman (Ore. 2), Burke (Mass. 11), Griffiths (Mich. 17), Rostenkowski (Ill. 8), Landrum (Ga. 9), Vanik (Ohio 22), Fulton (Tenn. 5),

Burleson (Tex. 15), Corman (Calif. 22), Green (Pa. 3), Gibbons (Fla. 7), Carey (N.Y. 15), Waggonner (La. 4), Karth (Minn. 4). *Republican Minority* (10 R). Congressmen Schneebeli (Pa. 17), Collier (Ill. 6), Broyhill (Va. 10), Conable (N.Y. 35), Chamberlain (Mich. 6), Pettis (Calif. 33), Duncan (Tenn. 2), Brotzman (Colo. 2), Clancy (Ohio 2), Archer (Tex. 7).

(No Subcommittees)

SELECT COMMITTEES

Select Committee on Committees

Richard Bolling, Chairman
Dave Martin, Vice-Chairman
Democratic Majority (5 D). Congressmen Bolling (Mo. 5), Stephens (Ga. 10), Culver (Iowa 2), Meeds (Wash. 2), Sarbanes (Md. 3).
Republican Minority (5 D). Congressmen Martin (Neb. 3), Frelinghuysen (N.J. 5), Wiggins (Calif. 25), Steiger (Wis. 6), Young (Fla. 6).

Select Committee on Crime

Claude Pepper, Chairman
Democratic Majority (6 D). Congressmen Pepper (Fla. 14), Waldie (Calif. 14), Brasco (N.Y. 11), Mann (S.C. 4), Murphy (Ill. 2), Rangel (N.Y. 19).
Minority (5 R). Congressmen Wiggins (Calif. 25), Steiger (Ariz. 3), Winn (Kans. 3), Sandman (N.J. 2), Keating (Ohio 1).

Select Committee on the House Beauty Shop

Martha W. Griffiths, Chairwoman
Democratic Majority (2 D). Congresswomen Griffiths (Mich. 17), Green (Ore. 3).
Republican Minority (1 R). Congresswoman Heckler (Mass. 10).

Select Committee on the House Restaurant

John C. Kluczynski, Chairman
Democratic Majority (3 D). Congressmen Kluczynski (Ill. 5), Steed (Okla. 4), Burke (Mass. 11).
Republican Minority (2 R). Congressmen Thomson (Wis. 3), Johnson (Pa. 23).

Select Committee on Parking

B. F. Sisk, Chairman
Democratic Majority (2 D). Congressmen Sisk (Calif. 16), Hays (Ohio 18).
Republican Minority (1 R). Congressman Gross (Iowa 3).

Select Committee on Small Business

Joe L. Evins, Chairman
Democratic Majority (12 D). Congressmen Evins (Tenn. 4), Lluczynski (Ill. 5), Dingell (Mich. 16), Smith (Iowa 4), Corman (Calif. 22), Addabbo (N.Y. 7), Hungate (Mo. 9), St. Germain (R.I. 1), Carney (Ohio 19), Mitchell (Md. 7), Bergland (Minn. 7).
Republican Minority (7 R). Congressmen Conte (Mass. 1), Broyhill (N.C. 10), Stanton (Ohio 11), McDade (Pa. 10), Thomson (Wis. 3), Kemp (N.Y. 38), McCollister (Neb. 2).

JOINT COMMITTEES OF THE CONGRESS

Joint Committee on Atomic Energy

Melvin Price, Chairman
John O. Pastore, Vice-Chairman

Congressmen. Holifield (D-Calif 19), Young (D-Tex. 14), Roncalio (D-Wyo. AL), McCormack (D-Wash. 4), Hosmer (R-Calif. 32), Anderson (R-Ill. 16), Hansen (R-Idaho 2), Lujan (R-N. Mex. 1), Price (D-Ill. 23).
Senators. Jackson (Wash.), Symington (Mo.), Bible (Nev.), Montoya (N. Mex.), Aiken (Vt.), Bennett (Utah), Dominick (Colo.), Baker (Tenn.), Pastore (R.I.).

Joint Committee on Congressional Operations

Lee Metcalf, Chairman
Jack Brooks, Vice-Chairman

Congressmen. Brooks (D-Tex. 9), Giaimo, (D-Conn. 3), O'Hara (D-Mich. 12), Cleveland (R-N.H. 2), Dellenback (R-Ore. 4).
Senators. Metcalf (Mont.), Gravel (Alaska), Chiles (Fla.), Taft (Ohio), Helms (N.C.).

Joint Committee on Defense Production

John Sparkman, Chairman
Wright Patman, Vice-Chairman

Congressmen. Patman (D-Tex. 1), Barrett (D-Pa. 1), Sullivan (D-Mo. 3), Widnall (R-N.J. 7), Brown, (R-Mich. 3).
Senators. Sparkman (Ala.), Proxmire (Wis.), Williams (N.J.), Tower (Tex.), Bennett (Utah).

Joint Economic Committee

Wright Patman, Chairman
William Proxmire, Vice-Chairman

Congressmen. Patman (D-Tex. 1), Bolling (D-Mo. 5), Reuss (D-Wis. 5), Griffiths (D-Mich. 17), Moorhead (D-Pa. 14), Carey (D-N.Y. 15), Widnall (R-N.J. 7), Conable (R-N.Y. 35), Brown (R-Ohio 7), Blackburn (R-Ga. 4).
Senators. Proxmire (Wis.), Sparkman (Ala.), Fulbright (Ark.), Ribicoff (Conn.), Humphrey (Minn.), Bentsen (Tex.), Javits (N.Y.), Percy (Ill.), Pearson (Kans.), Schweiker (Pa.).

Joint Committee on Internal Revenue Taxation

Wilbur D. Mills, Chairman
Russell B. Long, Vice-Chairman

Congressmen. Mills (D-Ark. 2), Ullman (D-Ore. 2), Burke (D-Mass. 11), Schneebeli (R-Pa. 17), Collier (R-Ill. 6).
Senators. Long (La.), Talmadge (Ga.), Hartke (Ind.), Bennett (Utah), Curtis (Neb.).

Joint Committee on the Library

Lucien N. Nedzi, Chairman
Howard W. Cannon, Vice-Chairman

Congressmen. Nedzi (D-Mich. 14), Hays (D-Ohio 18), Brademas (D-Ind. 3), Devine (R-Ohio 12), Hansen (R-Idaho 2).
Senators. Cannon (Nev.), Pell (R.I.), Williams (N.J.), Cook (Ky.), Hatfield (Ore.).

Joint Committee on Printing

Howard W. Cannon, Chairman
Wayne L. Hays, Vice-Chairman

Congressmen. Hays (D-Ohio 18), Brademas (D-Ind. 3), Dickinson (R-Ala. 2).
Senators. Cannon (Nev.), Allen (Ala.), Scott (Pa.).

Joint Committee on Reduction of Federal Expenditures

George H. Mahon, Chairman

Congressmen. Mahon (D-Tex. 19), Mills (D-Ark. 2), Whitten (D-Miss. 1), Ullman (D-Ore. 2), Cederberg (R-Mich. 10), Collier (R-Ill. 6).
Senators. Long (La.), McClellan (Ark.), Stennis (Miss.), Hartke (Ind.), Hruska (Neb.), Bennett (Utah).

Joint Study Committee on Budget Control

Co-Chairmen: Jamie L. Whitten, House Appropriations
Al Ullman, House Ways and Means
Vice-Chairmen: John L. McClellan, Senate Appropriations
Russell B. Long, Senate Finance
Roman L. Hruska, Senate Appropriations
Herman T. Schneebeli, House Ways and Means

Congressmen. Appropriations Committee: Whitten (D-Miss. 1), Mahon (D-Tex. 19), Rooney (D-N.Y. 14), Sikes (D-Fla. 1), Cederberg (R-Mich. 10), Rhodes (R-Ariz. 1), Davis (R-Wis. 9). Ways and Means Committee: Schneebeli (R-Pa. 17), Burke (D-Mass. 11), Griffiths (D-Mich. 17), Rostenkowski (D-Ill. 8), Collier (R-Ill. 6), Broyhill (R-Va. 10), Ullman (D-Ore. 2). At Large: Reuss (D-Wis. 5), Broyhill (R-N.C. 10).
Senators. Appropriations Committee: McClellan (Ark.), Hruska (Neb.), Stennis (Miss.), Pastore (R.I.), Bible (Nev.), Young (N. Dak.), Cotton (N.H.). Finance Committee: Long (La.), Talmadge (Ga.), Hartke (Ind.), Fulbright (Ark.), Bennett (Utah), Curtis (Neb.), Fannin (Ariz.). At Large: Proxmire (Wis.), Roth (Del.).

NATIONAL OUTLAYS

Federal Information Exchange System
National Summary, Outlays

DEPARTMENT OR AGENCY	FISCAL 1970	FISCAL 1971	FISCAL 1972
Department of Agriculture	$12,858,526,390	$13,801,277,226	$15,649,996,173
Department of Commerce	1,160,099,531	1,328,298,442	1,494,318,661
Department of Defense	57,653,475,000	59,368,905,000	64,678,223,000
HEW	52,536,934,491	61,975,877,609	73,122,649,562
Department of Housing and Urban Development	1,950,867,536	1,957,070,090	3,247,582,469
Department of the Interior	2,397,794,908	2,029,755,308	2,368,565,152
Department of Justice	575,998,342	794,240,419	1,131,770,240
Department of Labor	2,407,652,747	2,975,674,693	5,012,216,161
Post Office Department	7,311,471,999	8,225,992,732	–
Department of State	406,585,952	434,292,406	527,293,681
Department of Transportation	7,172,212,141	7,759,852,458	8,536,808,183
Treasury Department	15,972,748,090	16,310,972,089	16,993,783,167
ACTION	–	–	128,455,887
Advisory Comm. on Intergov. Relations	748,884	704,187	862,873
Agency for International Development	1,322,496,969	1,424,292,578	1,368,947,409
American Battle Monuments Comm.	2,418,312	2,509,563	2,972,038
Atomic Energy Commission .	2,603,856,927	2,612,525,705	2,632,753,992
Bureau of the Budget	12,047,601	–	–
Department or Agency	Fiscal 1970	Fiscal 1971	Fiscal 1972
Civil Aeronautics Board	$45,031,418	$74,193,686	$78,908,653
Civil Service Commission	4,049,168,209	4,698,353,081	5,514,521,777
Commission on Civil Rights .	2,393,250	2,979,284	3,327,575
Council of Economic Advisors	1,134,273	1,267,915	2,094,742
Domestic Council	–	1,203,042	1,550,551
Environmental Protection Agency	–	1,162,705,996	1,138,743,764
Equal Employment Opportunity Comm.	11,951,687	14,691,985	20,613,095
Farm Credit Administration .	3,833,970	3,928,922	4,590,324
Federal Communications Comm.	13,035,095	26,788,444	30,523,753
Federal Coal Mine Safety Board	76,396	–	–
Federal Home Loan Bank Board	161,964,317	125,439,843	82,276,824
Federal Maritime Commission	3,767,667	4,344,580	4,980,414
Federal Mediation and Conciliation Service	8,977,092	9,679,994	10,371,469
Federal Power Commission ..	18,175,663	19,943,607	21,862,031
Federal Radiation Council	333,488	38,165	–
Federal Trade Commission ...	18,880,256	20,332,269	21,985,644
General Services Admin.	1,738,775,003	1,972,467,705	2,315,092,728
Interstate Commerce Comm. .	26,574,131	73,191,751	28,362,445

DEPARTMENT OR AGENCY	FISCAL 1970	FISCAL 1971	FISCAL 1972
NASA	$3,681,179,846	$3,176,948,867	$3,075,043,278
NASA Council	491,856	406,977	385,980
Natl. Council, Marine Res. ...	506,915	302,820	–
Natl. Foundation on Arts and Humanities	24,990,965	34,262,345	68,189,598
Natl. Labor Relations Bd.	37,354,422	36,995,865	42,229,929
Natl. Mediation Bd.	2,105,216	2,146,060	2,590,847
Natl. Science Foundation	449,349,237	476,306,698	565,548,174
OEO	759,865,454	885,737,796	699,443,046
Office of Emergency Preparedness	191,445,860	150,568,815	102,601,111
Office of Management and Budget	–	15,043,436	18,943,694
Panama Canal	92,847,215	111,961,792	109,758,272
Peace Corps	77,600,962	74,742,859	–
Public Land Law Review Comm.	1,071,237	382,786	–
Railroad Retirement Bd.	1,710,065,344	2,031,789,231	2,270,105,870
Renegotiation Bd.	3,873,519	4,430,432	4,658,419
Securities and Exchange Commission	21,243,871	22,746,176	25,480,467
Selective Service System	68,816,000	69,759,000	68,427,056
Small Business Administration	71,022,269	578,920,309	626,712,378
Smithsonian Institution	33,108,589	38,581,809	47,616,568
Department or Agency	*Fiscal 1970*	*Fiscal 1971*	*Fiscal 1972*
U.S. Tax Court	$3,020,810	$3,406,002	$3,983,608
Tennessee Valley Auth.	690,697,726	952,363,317	1,086,631,340
U.S. Information Agency	137,824,111	124,355,012	101,705,483
U.S. Soldiers Home	8,324,439	9,233,642	9,728,371
Veterans Administration	9,487,344,990	10,824,195,911	11,901,785,901
Water Resources Council	5,821,098	8,769,356	5,415,789
NATIONAL TOTALS	**$190,009,979,646**	**$208,848,148,087**	**$227,013,989,625**

Department of Defense outlays do not include moneys spent by the military for building and maintaining foreign military installations. Total fiscal 1970 budget: $77.9 billion. Total fiscal 1971 budget: $72.9 billion. Total fiscal 1972 budget: $77.1 billion.

Index of 100 parent companies which with their subsidiaries received the largest dollar volume of military prime contract awards in fiscal year 1972.

Rank Companies	Dollars	Percent of U.S. total	Cumulative percent of U.S. total
1. Lockheed Aircraft Corp.	$1,705,434,000	5.11%	5.11%
2. McDonnell Douglas Corp.	1,700,217,000	5.10	10.21
3. General Dynamics Corp.	1,289,167,000	3.86	14.07
4. General Electric Co.	1,258,673,000	3.77	17.84
5. Boeing Co.	1,170,878,000	3.51	21.35
6. American Telephone and Telegraph Co.	1,121,512,000	3.36	24.71
7. Grumman Corp.	1,119,760,000	3.36	28.07
8. United Aircraft Corp.	995,619,000	2.98	31.05
9. North American Rockwell Corp.	702,862,000	2.11	33.16
10. Hughes Aircraft Co.	688,132,000	2.06	35.22
11. Litton Industries, Inc.	616,299,000	1.85	37.07
12. Raytheon Co.	506,762,000	1.52	38.59
13. Tenneco, Inc.	504,874,000	1.51	40.10
14. LTV Corp.	449,343,000	1.35	41.45
15. Sperry Rand Corp.	414,427,000	1.24	42.69
16. Westinghouse Electric Corp.	387,386,000	1.16	43.85
17. Northrop Corp.	369,562,000	1.11	44.96
18. Honeywell, Inc.	334,382,000	1.00	45.96
19. RCA Corp.	274,554,000	0.82	46.78
20. International Business Machines Co.	259,654,000	0.78	47.56
21. International Telephone and Telegraph Corp.	257,754,000	0.77	48.33
22. Martin Marietta Corp.	255,942,000	0.77	49.10
23. General Motors Corp.	255,714,000	0.77	49.87
24. Textron, Inc.	241,469,000	0.72	50.59
25. Standard Oil Co. (New Jersey)	209,112,000	0.63	51.22
26. Bendix Corp.	200,492,000	0.60	51.82
27. General Tire and Rubber Co.	197,441,000	0.59	52.41
28. Ford Motor Co.	196,524,000	0.59	53.00
29. Texas Instruments, Inc.	190,426,000	0.57	53.57
30. American Motors Corp.	187,137,000	0.56	54.13
31. FMC Corp.	179,651,000	0.54	54.67
32. Teledyne, Inc.	179,650,000	0.54	55.21
33. Gould, Inc.	172,174,000	0.52	55.73
34. Avco Corp.	166,214,000	0.50	56.23
35. Singer Co.	165,371,000	0.50	56.73
36. General Telephone and Electronics Corp.	162,164,000	0.49	57.22
37. Kiewit Morrison Fischbach (JV)	160,928,000	0.48	57.70
38. National Presto Industries, Inc.	146,896,000	0.44	58.14
39. Standard Oil Co. of California	145,665,000	0.44	58.58
40. TRW, Inc.	145,559,000	0.44	59.02
41. Harris-Intertype Corp.	142,511,000	0.43	59.45
42. Sanders Associates, Inc.	134,964,000	0.40	59.85
43. Pan American World Airways, Inc.	131,455,000	0.39	60.24
44. Massachusetts Institute of Technology (N)	127,275,000	0.38	60.62
45. Magnavox Co.	127,143,000	0.38	61.00
46. Day and Zimmerman, Inc.	122,341,000	0.37	61.37
47. Reynolds (RJ) Industries, Inc.	118,269,000	0.35	61.72
48. Texaco, Inc.	114,253,000	0.34	62.06
49. Hercules, Inc.	113,440,000	0.34	62.40

Rank Companies	Dollars	Percent of U.S. total	Cumulative percent of U.S. total
50. Thiokol Chemical Corp.	$110,311,000	0.33%	62.73%
51. Mobil Oil Corp.	110,149,000	0.33	63.06
52. DuPont E.I. De Nemours and Co.	105,147,000	0.32	63.38
53. E Systems, Inc.	103,634,000	0.31	63.69
54. Norris Industries	100,837,000	0.30	63.99
55. ICI America, Inc.	96,348,000	0.29	64.28
56. Collins Radio Co.	94,941,000	0.28	64.56
57. Chrysler Corp.	94,421,000	0.28	64.84
58. Olin Corp.	92,805,000	0.28	65.12
59. Goodyear Tire and Rubber Co.	86,082,000	0.26	65.38
60. Automation Industries, Inc.	83,823,000	0.25	65.63
61. Chamberlain MFG Corp.	82,982,000	0.25	65.88
62. Eastman Kodak Co.	81,809,000	0.25	66.13
63. Uniroyal Inc.	80,745,000	0.24	66.37
64. AMF, Inc.	78,638,000	0.24	66.61
65. Kidde Walter and Co., Inc.	73,460,000	0.22	66.83
66. Signal Companies, Inc.	72,277,000	0.22	67.05
67. Johns Hopkins University (N)	71,717,000	0.21	67.26
68. Aerospace Corp. (N)	70,538,000	0.21	67.47
69. Lear Siegler, Inc.	70,434,000	0.21	67.68
70. Standard Oil of Indiana	68,170,000	0.20	67.88
71. Asiatic Petroleum Corp.	67,932,000	0.20	68.08
72. Pacific Architects and Engineers, Inc.	61,848,000	0.19	68.27
73. Control Data Corp.	61,739,000	0.19	68.46
74. Motorola Inc.	56,054,000	0.17	68.63
75. Western Union Corp.	56,022,000	0.17	68.80
76. Mason and Hanger Silas Mason Co.	55,950,000	0.17	68.97
77. Federal Cartridge Corp.	55,804,000	0.17	69.14
78. Fairchild Industries, Inc.	54,586,000	0.16	69.30
79 City Investing Co.	52,324,000	0.16	69.46
80. Diamond Red Trucks, Inc.	52,195,000	0.16	69.62
81. System Development Corp.	52,042,000	0.16	69.78
82. Gulf Oil Corp.	50,125,000	0.15	69.93
83. Curtiss-Wright Corp.	49,993,000	0.15	70.08
84. Itek Corp.	48,554,000	0.15	70.23
85. Sverdrup and Parcell and Associates, Inc.	48,476,000	0.15	70.38
86. Ogden Corp.	47,078,000	0.14	70.52
87. Amerada Hess Corp.	43,402,000	0.13	70.65
88. Transamerica Corp.	42,440,000	0.13	70.78
89. Seatrain Lines, Inc.	41,704,000	0.13	70.91
90. Flying Tiger Corp.	40,782,000	0.12	71.03
91. Gulf and Western Industries	40,164,000	0.12	71.15
92. Xerox Corp.	39,127,000	0.12	71.27
93. Kaman Corp.	38,095,000	0.11	71.38
94. Colt Industries, Inc.	38,030,000	0.11	71.49
95. Raymond Morrison Knudsen (JV)	38,000,000	0.11	71.60
96. Fairchild Camera and Instrument Corp.	37,511,000	0.11	71.71
97. International Harvester Co.	36,590,000	0.11	71.82
98. Shell Oil Co.	35,979,000	0.11	71.93
99. Mitre Corp. (N)	35,555,000	0.11	72.04
100. Marathon MFG Co.	35,380,000	0.11	72.15

ALABAMA

(7 districts)

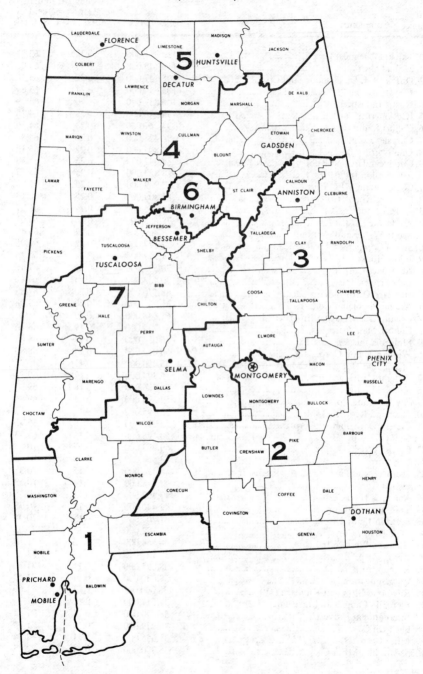

ALASKA

(1 at large)

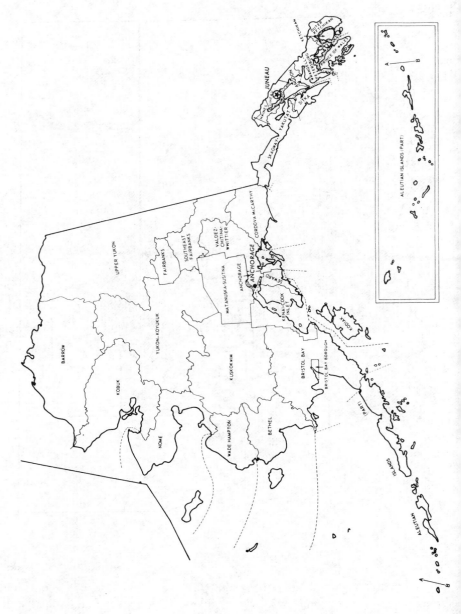

ARIZONA

(4 districts)

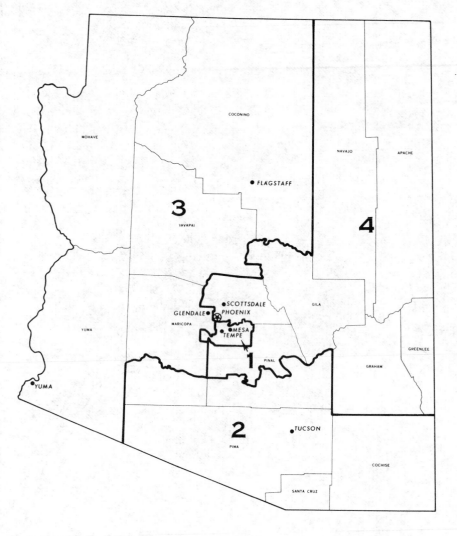

ARKANSAS

(4 districts)

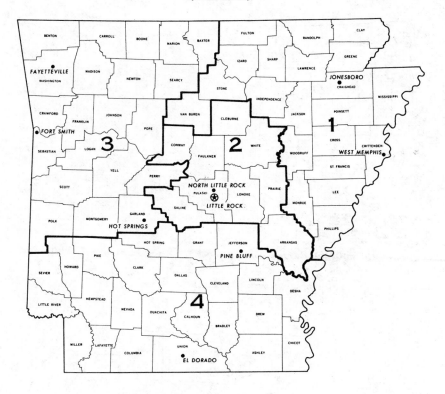

CALIFORNIA

(43 districts)

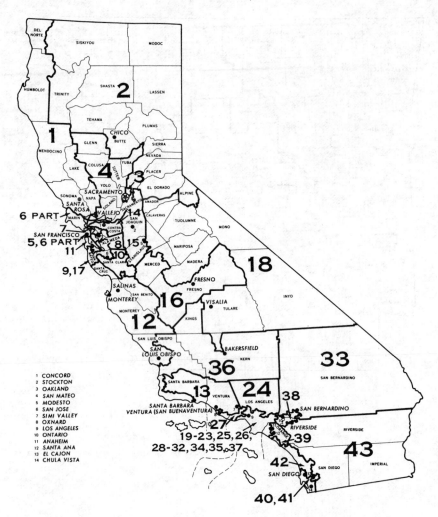

1 CONCORD
2 STOCKTON
3 OAKLAND
4 SAN MATEO
5 MODESTO
6 SAN JOSE
7 SIMI VALLEY
8 OXNARD
9 LOS ANGELES
10 ONTARIO
11 ANAHEIM
12 SANTA ANA
13 EL CAJON
14 CHULA VISTA

CALIFORNIA
Districts Established February 15, 1972

ORANGE COUNTY

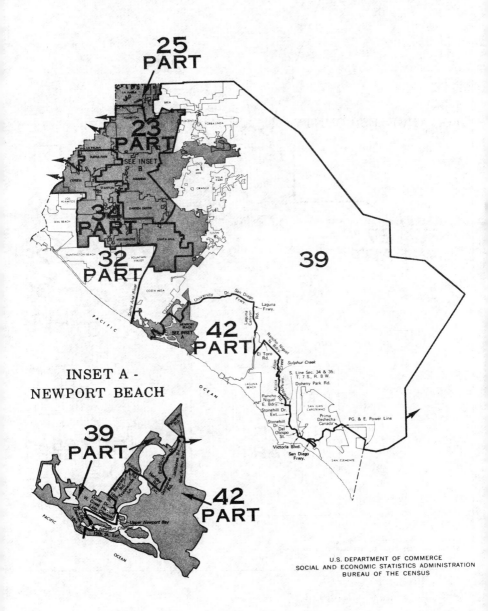

INSET A -
NEWPORT BEACH

U.S. DEPARTMENT OF COMMERCE
SOCIAL AND ECONOMIC STATISTICS ADMINISTRATION
BUREAU OF THE CENSUS

CALIFORNIA
Districts Established February 15, 1972

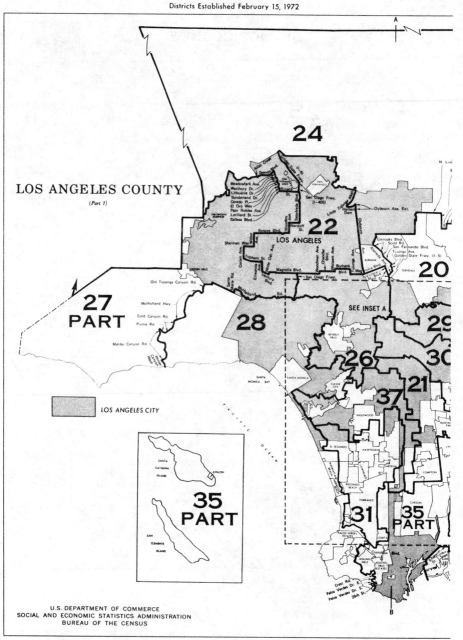

LOS ANGELES COUNTY
(Part 1)

24

22

LOS ANGELES

Meadowlark Ave.
Westbury Dr.
Lithuania Dr.
Sunderland Dr.
Caredo Pl.
El Oro Way
Paso Robles Ave.
Lorillard St.
Balboa Blvd.

San Diego Frwy. (I-405)

Clybourn Ave. Ext.

Glenoaks Blvd.
Scott Rd.
San Fernando Blvd.
Tujunga Ave.
Golden State Frwy. (I-5)

20

GLENDALE

27 PART

Old Topanga Canyon Rd.

Mulholland Hwy.
Cold Canyon Rd.
Piuma Rd.

Malibu Canyon Rd.

28

Mulholland Rd.

San Diego Frwy.

SEE INSET A

29

30

BEVERLY HILLS

26

21

SANTA MONICA BAY

37

SANTA MONICA

CULVER CITY

INGLEWOOD

LOS ANGELES CITY

P A C I F I C   O C E A N

EL SEGUNDO

HAWTHORNE

GARDENA

COMPTON

REDONDO BEACH

TORRANCE

CARSON

SANTA CATALINA ISLAND

AVALON

35 PART

SAN CLEMENTE ISLAND

31

PALOS VERDES ESTATES

35 PART

ROLLING HILLS ESTATES

Crenshaw Blvd.

Crest Rd.
Palos Verdes Dr.
Palos Verdes Dr. S.
25th St.

ROLLING HILLS

B

U.S. DEPARTMENT OF COMMERCE
SOCIAL AND ECONOMIC STATISTICS ADMINISTRATION
BUREAU OF THE CENSUS

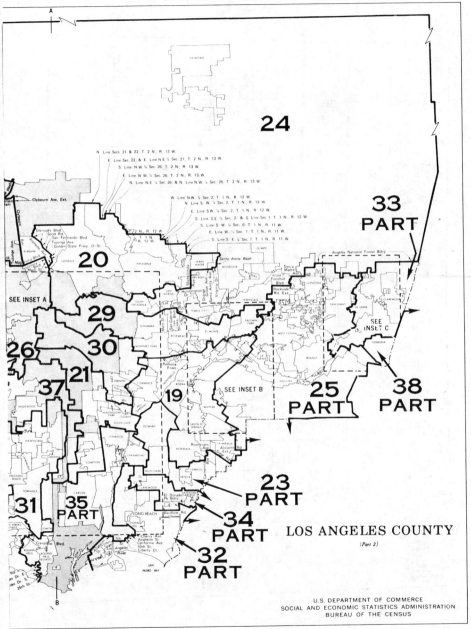

LOS ANGELES COUNTY
(Part 2)

U.S. DEPARTMENT OF COMMERCE
SOCIAL AND ECONOMIC STATISTICS ADMINISTRATION
BUREAU OF THE CENSUS

COLORADO

(5 districts)

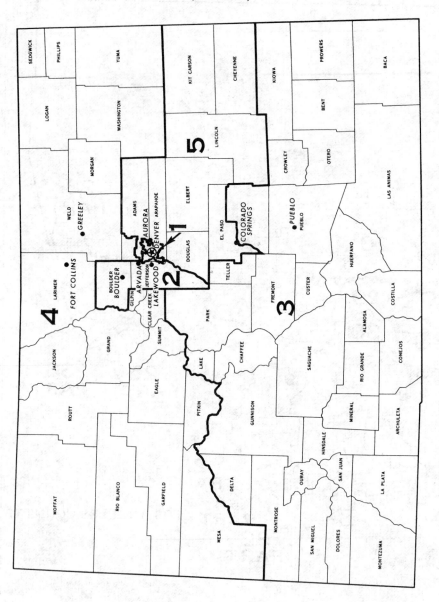

CONNECTICUT

(6 districts)

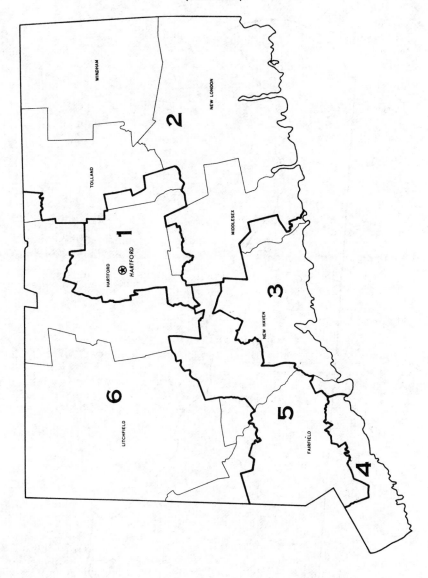

DELAWARE

(1 at large)

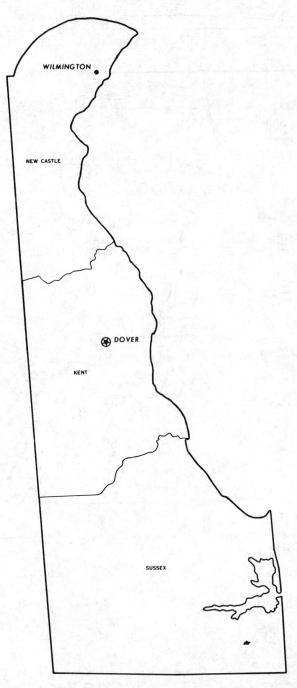

FLORIDA

(15 districts)

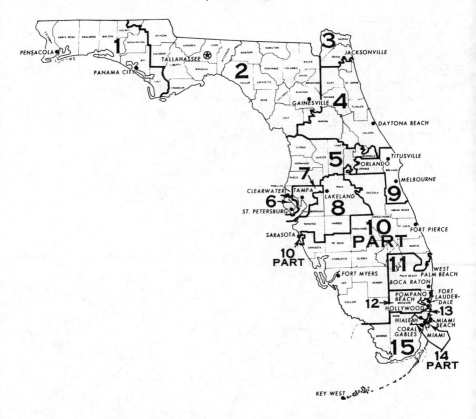

GEORGIA

(10 districts)

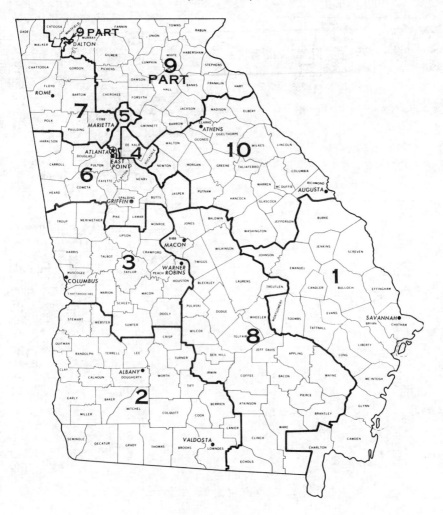

HAWAII

(2 districts)

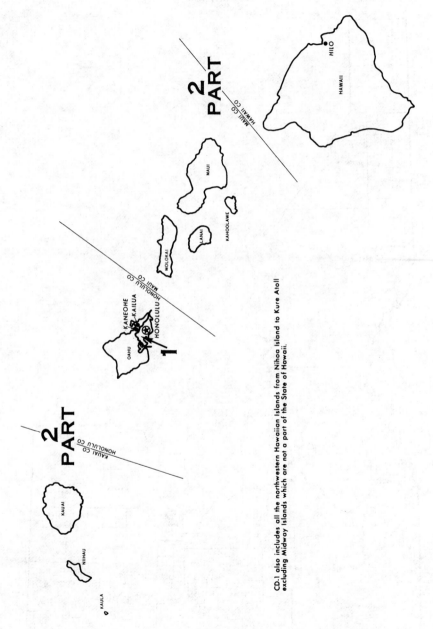

CD-1 also includes all the northwestern Hawaiian Islands from Nihoa Island to Kure Atoll excluding Midway Islands which are not a part of the State of Hawaii.

IDAHO

(2 districts)

ILLINOIS

(24 districts)

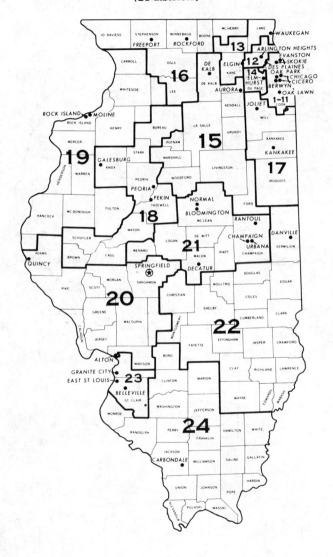

ILLINOIS
Districts Established September 20, 1971

COOK AND DU PAGE COUNTIES

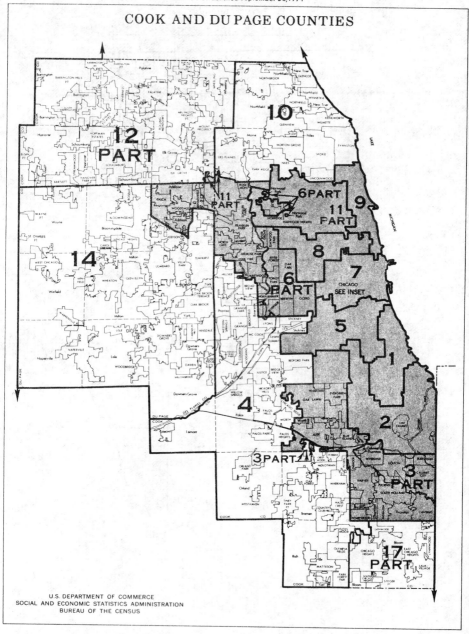

U.S. DEPARTMENT OF COMMERCE
SOCIAL AND ECONOMIC STATISTICS ADMINISTRATION
BUREAU OF THE CENSUS

INDIANA

(11 districts)

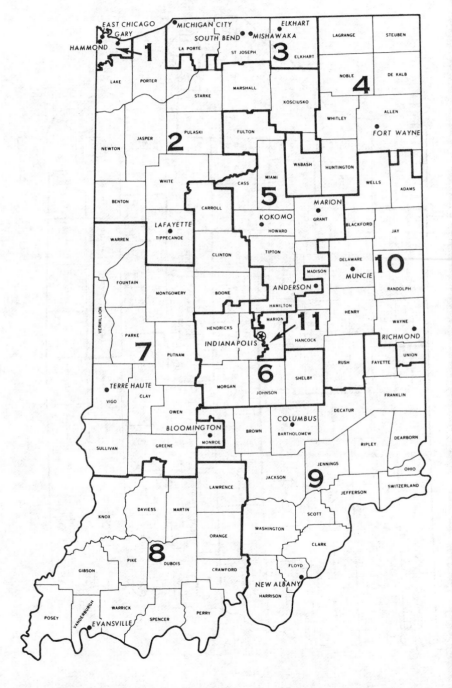

IOWA

(6 districts)

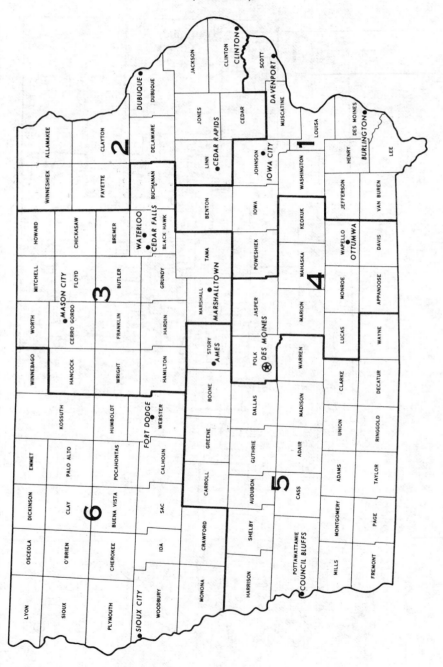

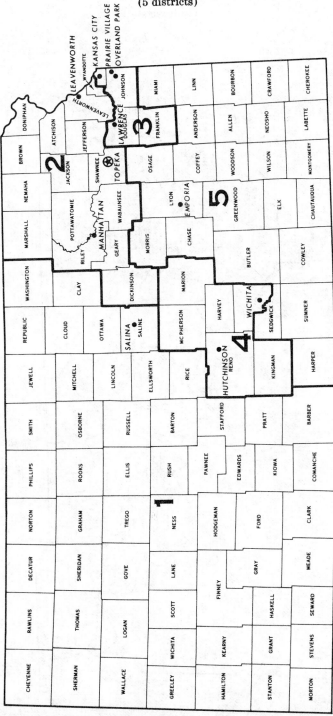

KANSAS

(5 districts)

KENTUCKY

(7 districts)

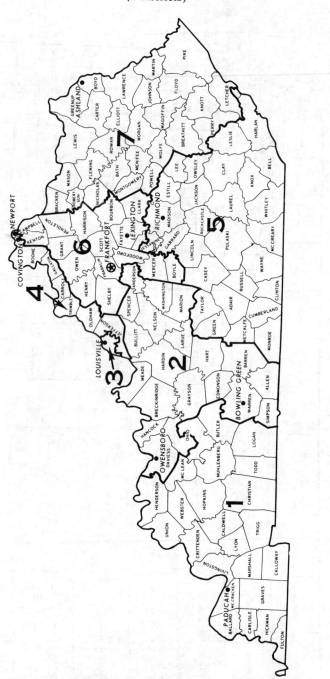

LOUISIANA

(8 districts)

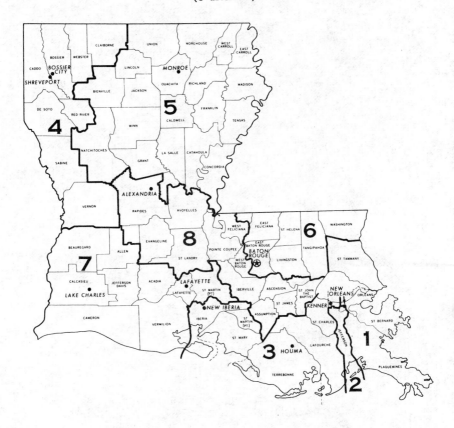

MAINE

(2 districts)

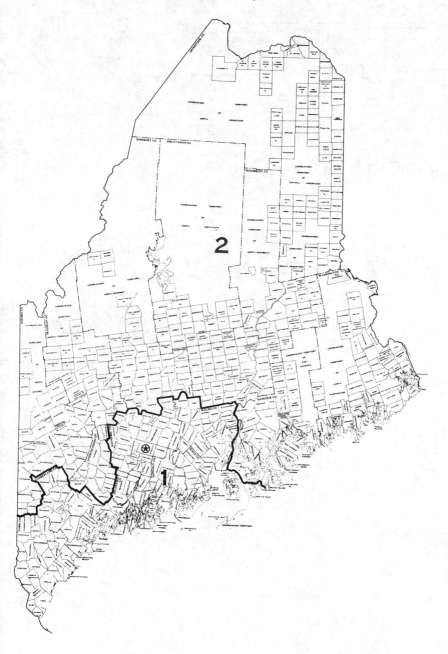

MARYLAND

(8 districts)

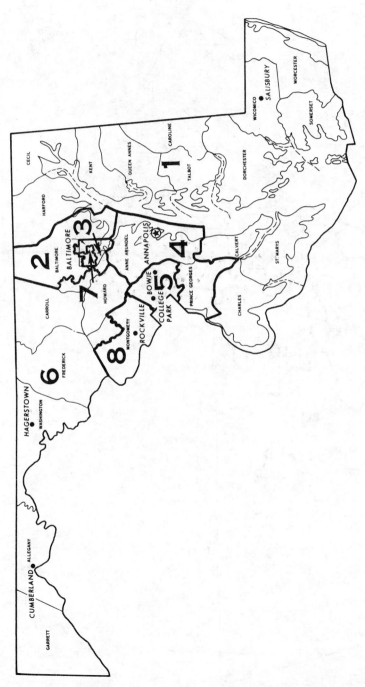

MASSACHUSETTS

(12 districts)

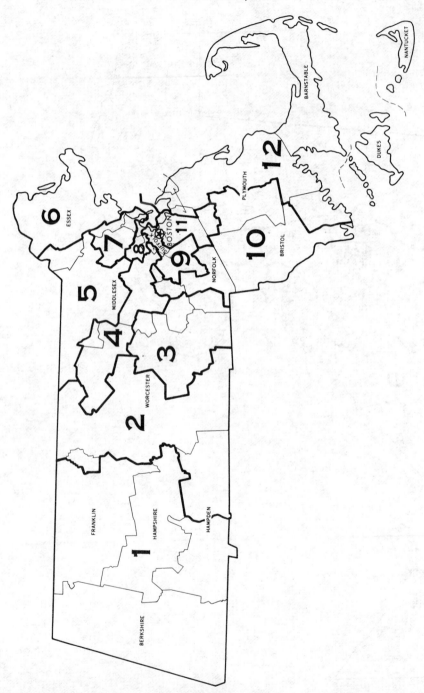

MICHIGAN

(19 districts)

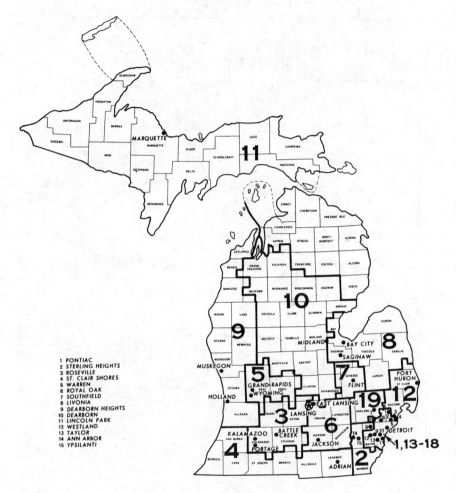

1 PONTIAC
2 STERLING HEIGHTS
3 ROSEVILLE
4 ST. CLAIR SHORES
5 WARREN
6 ROYAL OAK
7 SOUTHFIELD
8 LIVONIA
9 DEARBORN HEIGHTS
10 DEARBORN
11 LINCOLN PARK
12 WESTLAND
13 TAYLOR
14 ANN ARBOR
15 YPSILANTI

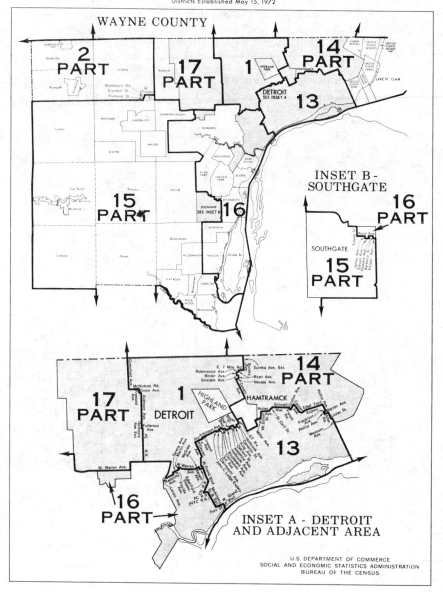

MICHIGAN
Districts Established May 15, 1972

INSET A - DETROIT AND ADJACENT AREA

INSET B - SOUTHGATE

U.S. DEPARTMENT OF COMMERCE
SOCIAL AND ECONOMIC STATISTICS ADMINISTRATION
BUREAU OF THE CENSUS

MINNESOTA

(8 districts)

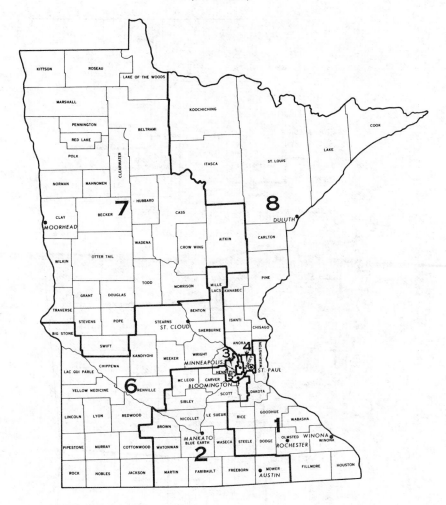

MISSISSIPPI

(5 districts)

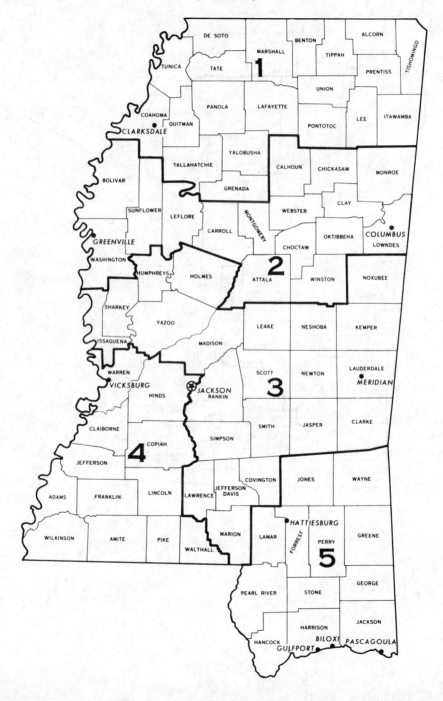

MISSOURI

(10 districts)

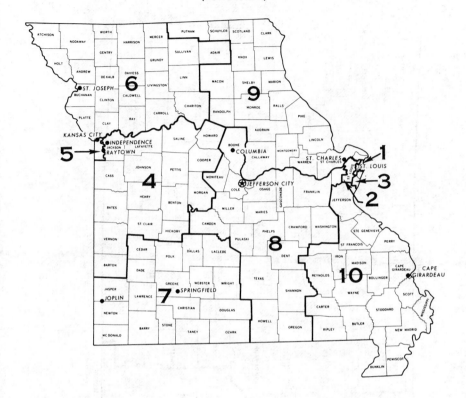

MONTANA

(2 districts)

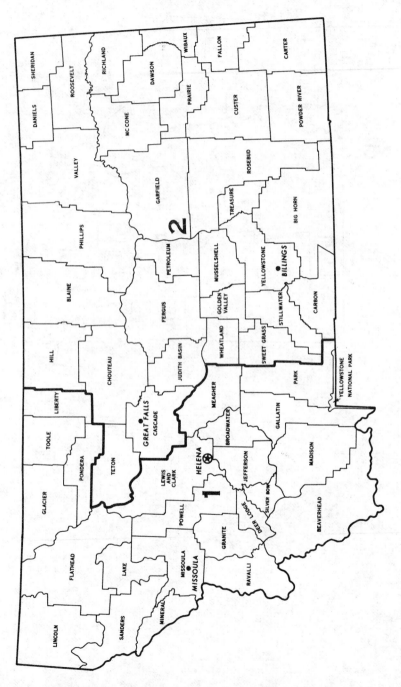

NEBRASKA

(3 districts)

Map of Nebraska showing 3 congressional districts and county boundaries. Labeled counties include: RICHARDSON, NEMAHA, PAWNEE, JOHNSON, OTOE, GAGE, JEFFERSON, THAYER, NUCKOLLS, WEBSTER, FRANKLIN, HARLAN, FURNAS, RED WILLOW, HITCHCOCK, DUNDY, CHASE, HAYES, FRONTIER, GOSPER, PHELPS, KEARNEY, ADAMS, CLAY, FILLMORE, SALINE, SEWARD, YORK, HAMILTON, MERRICK, NANCE, POLK, BUTLER, LANCASTER, LINCOLN, SAUNDERS, CASS, SARPY, DOUGLAS, OMAHA, WASHINGTON, DODGE, COLFAX, PLATTE, BOONE, ANTELOPE, MADISON, STANTON, CUMING, BURT, THURSTON, WAYNE, PIERCE, KNOX, CEDAR, DIXON, DAKOTA, BOYD, HOLT, WHEELER, GREELEY, HOWARD, SHERMAN, HALL, GRAND ISLAND, BUFFALO, DAWSON, CUSTER, VALLEY, GARFIELD, LOUP, BLAINE, THOMAS, HOOKER, MCPHERSON, LOGAN, KEITH, LINCOLN, PERKINS, ROCK, BROWN, KEYA PAHA, CHERRY, GRANT, ARTHUR, SHERIDAN, GARDEN, DEUEL, CHEYENNE, MORRILL, DAWES, BOX BUTTE, SIOUX, SCOTTS BLUFF, BANNER, KIMBALL. Districts numbered 2 and 3.

NEVADA

(1 at large)

NEW HAMPSHIRE

(2 districts)

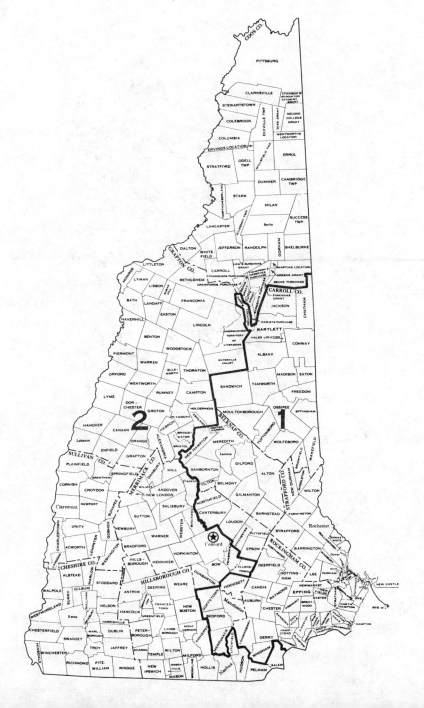

NEW JERSEY

(15 districts)

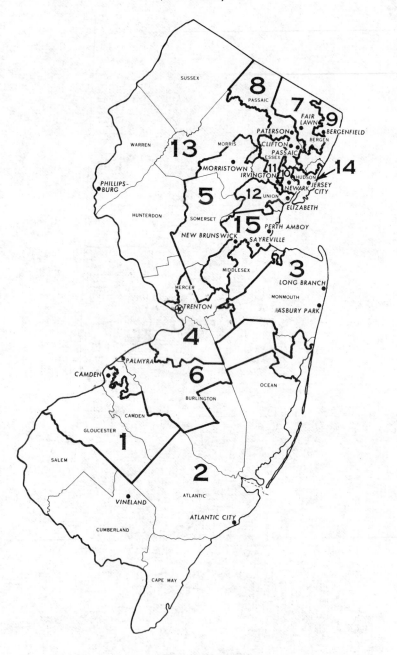

NEW JERSEY
Districts Established April 12, 1972

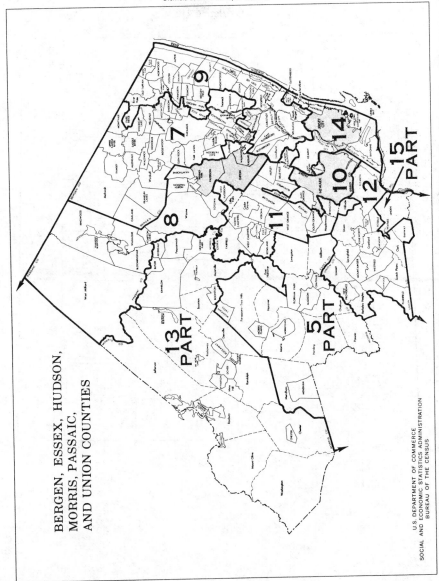

BERGEN, ESSEX, HUDSON, MORRIS, PASSAIC, AND UNION COUNTIES

U.S. DEPARTMENT OF COMMERCE
SOCIAL AND ECONOMIC STATISTICS ADMINISTRATION
BUREAU OF THE CENSUS

NEW MEXICO

(2 districts)

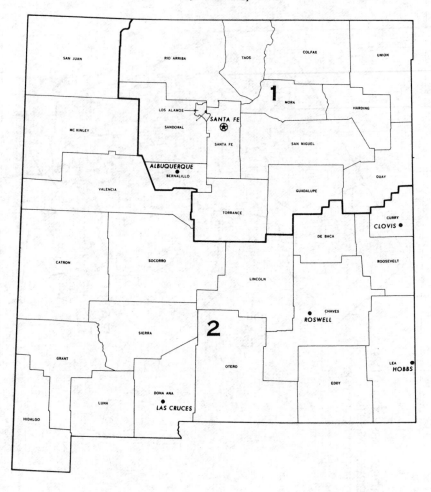

NEW YORK

(39 districts)

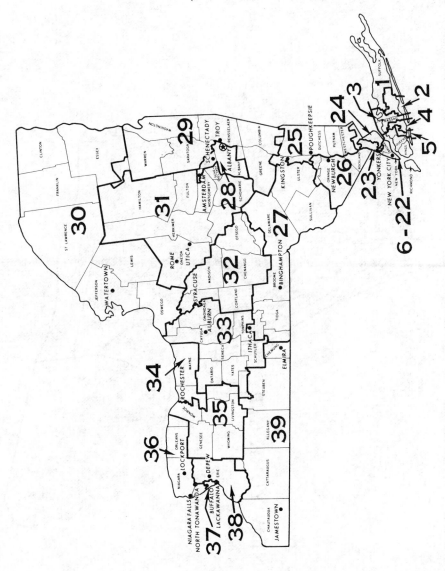

NEW YORK CITY

NORTH CAROLINA

(11 districts)

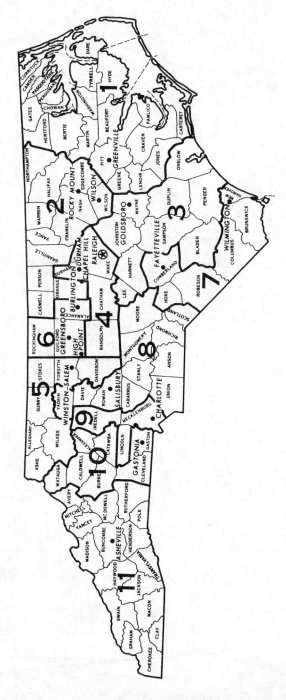

NORTH DAKOTA

(1 at large)

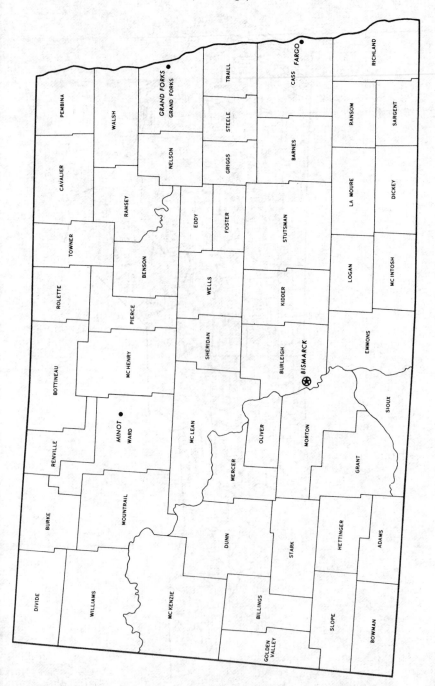

OHIO

(23 districts)

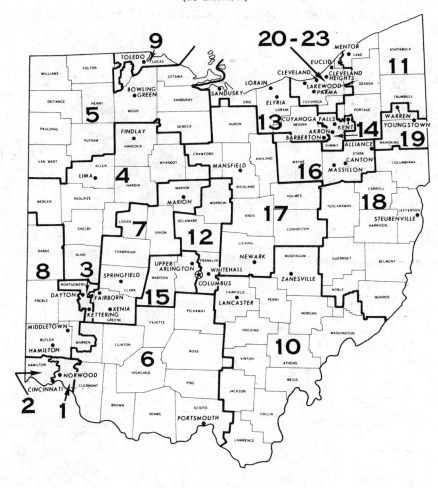

OHIO
Districts Established January 20, 1972

CUYAHOGA, MEDINA, AND SUMMIT COUNTIES

U.S. DEPARTMENT OF COMMERCE
SOCIAL AND ECONOMIC STATISTICS ADMINISTRATION
BUREAU OF THE CENSUS

OKLAHOMA

(6 districts)

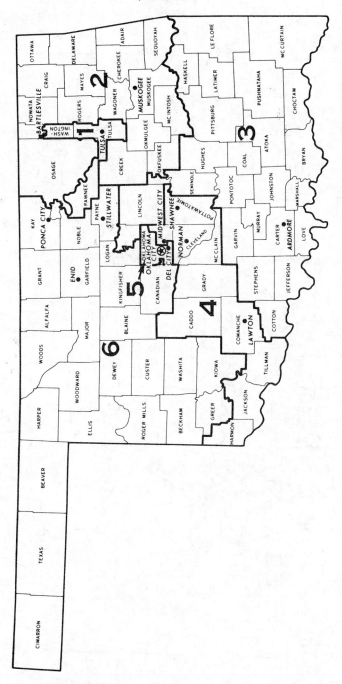

OREGON

(4 districts)

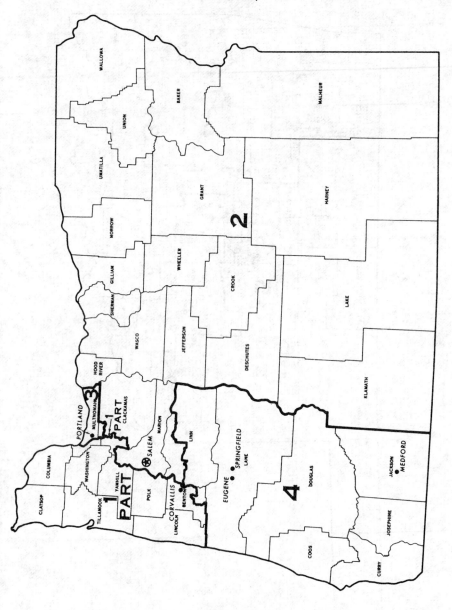

PENNSYLVANIA

(25 districts)

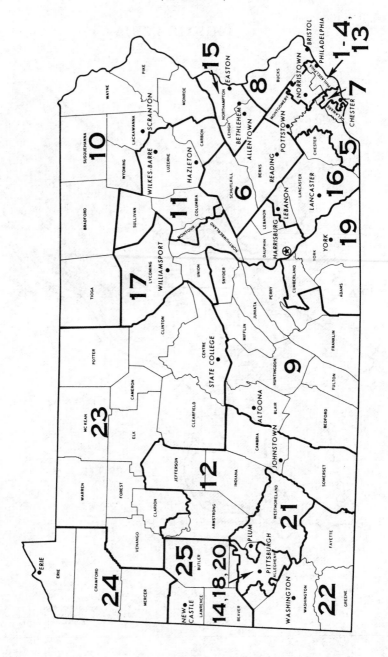

PENNSYLVANIA
Districts Established January 25, 1972

PHILADELPHIA

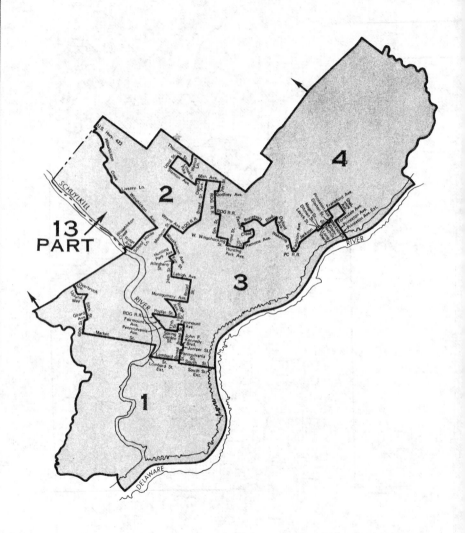

U.S. DEPARTMENT OF COMMERCE
SOCIAL AND ECONOMIC STATISTICS ADMINISTRATION
BUREAU OF THE CENSUS

Representative

W. Jack Edwards (R) Elected 1964; b. Sept. 20, 1928, Birmingham; home, Mobile; U. of Ala., B.S., 1952, LL.B., 1954; USMC, 1946–48, 1950–51; married, two children; Presbyterian.

Career Practicing atty., 1954–64.

Offices 2439 RHOB, 202-225-4931. Also Suite 806, First Federal Tower, Mobile 36606, 205-471-1851.

Administrative Assistant David C. Pruitt III

Committees

Appropriations (14th); Subs: Transportation; Treasury-Postal Service-General Government.

Group Ratings

	ADA	COPE	LWV	RIPON	NFU	LCV	CFA	NAB	NSI	ACA
1972	0	10	11	54	50	18	50	88	100	78
1971	8	17	38	35	27	–	0	–	–	81
1970	4	0	–	41	31	0	44	90	100	83

Key Votes

1) Busing	AGN	6) Cmbodia Bmbg	FOR	11) Chkg Acct Intrst	ABS
2) Strip Mines	AGN	7) Bust Hwy Trust	FOR	12) End HISC (HUAC)	AGN
3) Cut Mil $	AGN	8) Farm Sub Lmt	AGN	13) Nixon Sewer Veto	FOR
4) Rev Shrg	FOR	9) School Prayr	FOR	14) Corp Cmpaign $	FOR
5) Pub TV $	AGN	10) Cnsumr Prot	AGN	15) Pol $ Disclosr	AGN

Election Results

1972 general:	Jack Edwards (R)	104,606	(77%)
	D. W. McCrory (D)	24,357	(18%)
	Thomas McAboy, Jr. (NDPA)	7,747	(6%)
1972 primary:	Jack Edwards (R), unopposed		
1970 general:	Jack Edwards (R)	63,457	(61%)
	John Tyson (D)	27,457	(26%)
	Noble Beasley (NDPA)	13,789	(13%)

SECOND DISTRICT Political Background

Alabama's Black Belt was first named for the fertility and color of the region's topsoil. For all of the nineteenth and most of the twentieth century, the economics of cotton-making required abundant, cheap labor. For many years after the Civil War the majority of the Black Belt's citizens were descendants of the slaves brought here to chop and pick cotton. But black migration to the North so reduced the black percentage in this part of Alabama that when the 1965 Voting Rights Act finally gave blacks the ballot, only a handful of small, predominantly rural counties were left with black majorities.

On a map, Alabama's congressional-district lines look perfectly regular. Closer inspection, however, shows them to have been carefully crafted to divide the black-majority counties among several districts; this, of course, was intended to prevent blacks from exerting a major influence in any congressional election. The 2nd district, for example, contains only one black-majority county (Bullock), but just outside district lines are three others (Macon, Lowndes, and Wilcox).

So the blacks in the 2nd are heavily outnumbered by the whites in Montgomery, the state's capital, and by those in the "piney woods" counties to the south of the Black Belt. The whites here are no doubt pleased to remind visitors that Montgomery was the Cradle of the Confederacy, the rebels' capital before Richmond. Local boosters are less likely to talk about the 1956 Montgomery bus boycott, which gave national prominence to a young black minister, Martin Luther King, Jr.

The 2nd is basically an amalgam of the old 2nd and 3rd districts, a conjunction rendered necessary by the results of the 1970 census, which cost Alabama a congressional seat. The state's Democratic legislature drew the lines of the new 2nd with the probable hope that Democratic Congressman George W. Andrews, a 28-year House veteran and third ranking member of the Appropriations Committee, would knock off the old 2nd's Republican Congressman William L. Dickinson. But Andrews died in the winter of 1971, after which it was decided more or less by common consent that his widow serve out the term and retire.

At that, the 2nd was still the most hotly-contested Alabama congressional race in 1972. Five Democrats wanted the seat; the winner, after the first primary and the runoff, was Ben C. Reeves, a young state legislator. About 44% of the districts population is in the old 3rd, an area where Dickinson was an unknown, and as a Montgomery Republican, perhaps even a citified alien. In the general election, Reeves carried the old 3rd part of the district by 6,000, certainly an achievement against an incumbent. But Dickinson won just as big in the rural counties of the old 2nd, and swept Montgomery County better than two-to-one. As in many other parts of the South, the urban area of the 2nd provided the Republican with his most commanding margins.

Dickinson's win leaves him in good shape for the rest of the seventies. Because he can now cover with franked mail parts of the district he lost, the Congressman will probably have little trouble winning in the foreseeable future. To the national press, Dickinson is still best known for his charge in 1965 that the Selma marchers—who passed through part of his district—engaged in obscenities; though he promised to document the accusation, he never did.

In the House Dickinson is the second ranking Republican on the House Administration Committee and also sits on Armed Services—a position that enables him to look after Montgomery's two Air Force bases and the Army's giant Fort Rucker near Dothan. On Armed Services, he is known to pepper military officials with critical questions, but in the end the Congressman usually votes with the committee's pro-Pentagon majority.

Census Data Pop. 491,676. Central city, 27%; suburban, 7%. Median family income, $6,749; families above $15,000: 10%; families below $3,000: 21%. Median years education, 11.0.

1972 Share of Federal Outlays $700,875,788

DOD	$300,133,000	HEW	$183,270,275
AEC	–	HUD	$7,238,397
NASA	$78,748	DOI	$1,812,170
DOT	$19,180,371	USDA	$74,416,034
		Other	$114,746,793

Federal Military-Industrial Commitments

DOD Contractors Worthrop Worldwide ADCT Services (Fort Rucker), $21.041m: aircraft maintenance. Hayes International Corp. (Dothan), $9.825m: aircraft maintenance.
DOD Installations Fort Rucker AB (Ozark). Gunter AFB (Montgomery). Maxwell AFB (Montgomery).

Economic Base Agriculture, notably poultry, cattle, dairy products, and hogs and sheep; apparel and other textile products, especially men's and boy's furnishings; finance, insurance and real estate; lumber and wood products, especially sawmill and planing mill products; and food and kindred products.

The Voters

Registration No party registration; no accurate total registration figures available.
Median voting age 42.5
Employment profile White collar, 42%. Blue collar, 39%. Service, 14%. Farm, 5%.
Ethnic groups Black, 30%. Total foreign stock, 2%.

Presidential vote

1972	Nixon (R)	107,702	(78%)
	McGovern (D)	31,190	(22%)

1968	Nixon (R)	12,337	(8%)
	Humphrey (D)	26,179	(18%)
	Wallace (AI)	109,223	(73%)

Representative

William L. Dickinson (R) Elected 1964; b. June 5, 1925, Opelika; home, Montgomery; U. of Ala., B.A., 1948, LL.B., 1950; Navy WWII; married, four children; Methodist.

Career Practicing atty., 1950–; Judge, Opelika City Ct., 2 yrs., Lee County Ct. of Common Pleas and Juv. Ct., 4 yrs., Fifth Jud. Circuit of Ala., 4 yrs.; Asst. V.P. Southern Railway System, 18 mos.

Offices 339 CHOB, 202-225-2901. Also 401 P.O. Bldg., Montgomery 36104, 205-265-5611, ext. 453, and 111 Hoyle Ave., Bay Minette 36507, 205-937-8818.

Administrative Assistant J. C. Steen

Committees

Armed Services (6th); Subs: No. 1; No. 2 (Ranking Mbr.).

Sp. Sub. on Armed Services Investigation.

House Administration (Ranking Mbr.).

Joint Com. on Printing (Ranking House Mbr.).

Group Ratings

	ADA	COPE	LWV	RIPON	NFU	LCV	CFA	NAB	NSI	ACA
1972	0	0	20	46	40	2	0	92	100	95
1971	3	17	22	31	20	–	0	–	–	86
1970	4	0	–	35	62	0	44	90	100	79

Key Votes

1) Busing	AGN	6) Cmbodia Bmbg	FOR	11) Chkg Acct Intrst	ABS
2) Strip Mines	AGN	7) Bust Hwy Trust	AGN	12) End HISC (HUAC)	AGN
3) Cut Mil $	AGN	8) Farm Sub Lmt	AGN	13) Nixon Sewer Veto	FOR
4) Rev Shrg	FOR	9) School Prayr	FOR	14) Corp Cmpaign $	FOR
5) Pub TV $	AGN	10) Cnsumr Prot	AGN	15) Pol $ Disclosr	AGN

Election Results

1972 general:	William L. Dickinson (R)	80,362	(55%)
	Ben C. Reeves (D)	60,769	(42%)
	Richard Boone (NDPA)	4,991	(3%)
1972 primary:	William L. Dickinson (R), unopposed		
1970 general:	William L. Dickinson (R)	62,316	(61%)
	Jack Winfield (D)	25,966	(26%)
	Percy Smith, Jr. (NDPA)	13,281	(13%)

THIRD DISTRICT Political Background

The 3rd district extends from the cotton-growing Black Belt of southern Alabama to the red clay hills of the north. To the south is Tuskegee, a black-majority town in a black-majority county and the home of Booker T. Washington's Tuskegee Institute; also to the south is Phenix City, a one-time Alabama "sin city" across the Chattahoochee River from Georgia's huge Fort Benning. A mid-fifties clean-up of Phenix City propelled a young prosecutor, John Patterson, into the Governor's chair; he beat George Wallace to do it, and was the last man to beat Wallace in Alabama. To the north is the small industrial city of Anniston (pop. 31,000) and, adjacent to the city, Fort McClellan. This area is one of the few in the state to show a significant population growth during the sixties; in fact, virtually all Deep South counties with substantial population increases are those blessed with military installations.

Outside of the Black Belt counties in the south, the 3rd district is mostly white, and the whites living in the 3rd's small towns and hilly farm country comprise George Wallace's kind of people. The current Congressman, Bill Nichols, was a Wallace floor leader in the Alabama Senate, and his House voting record is what one might expect from that affiliation. In 1966, Nichols was the only Democrat who managed to unseat a Republican elected in the 1964 Alabama Goldwater landslide. Since then he has each time been sent back to Washington with more than 75% of the votes. With a junior position on the Armed Services Committee, Nichols has made little impression on Capitol Hill, except perhaps to contribute yet another vote to the already lopsided margins enjoyed by the committee's Southern Democrat-Republican majority.

Census Data Pop. 493,588. Central city, 0%; suburban, 16%. Median family income, $6,817; families above $15,000: 8%; families below $3,000: 19%. Median years education, 10.2.

1972 Share of Federal Outlays $430,832,295

DOD	$144,411,000	HEW	$160,794,654
AEC	$41,072	HUD	$3,001,957
NASA	$627,070	DOI	$841,491
DOT	$15,902,752	USDA	$26,046,234
		Other	$79,136,065

Federal Military-Industrial Commitments

DOD Contractors Golden Industries (Sylacauga), $23.063m: 155mm projectiles.
DOD Installations Anniston Army Depot (Anniston). Fort McClellan AB (Anniston).

Economic Base Textile mill products, especially cotton weaving mill products; apparel and other textile products; agriculture, notably poultry and cattle; primary metal industries, especially iron and steel foundries; and finance, insurance and real estate. Also higher education (Auburn Univ.).

The Voters

Registration No party registration; no accurate total registration figures available.
Median voting age 42.0
Employment profile White collar, 34%. Blue collar, 50%. Service, 14%. Farm, 2%.
Ethnic groups Black, 31%. Total foreign stock, 1%.

Presidential vote

1972	Nixon (R)	98,640	(75%)
	McGovern (D)	33,480	(25%)
1968	Nixon (R)	14,611	(11%)
	Humphrey (D)	26,024	(19%)
	Wallace (AI)	98,246	(71%)

Representative

William Nichols (D) Elected 1966; b. Oct. 16, 1918, near Becker, Miss.; home, Sylacauga; Auburn U., B.S., 1939, M.S., 1941; Army, WWII; married, three children; Methodist.

Career Ala. House of Reps., 1959; Ala. State Senate, 1963; V.P. Parker Fertilizer Co., Pres. Parker Gin Co., 1947–66.

Offices 1037 LHOB, 202-225-3261. Also Fed. Bldg. P.O. Box 2042, Anniston 36201, 205-236-5655.

Administrative Assistant Thomas L. Foster